The Pan English Dictionary

The Pan English Dictionary

Pan Books London and Sydney
in association with Heinemann Educational Books

Note Words in this Dictionary which we believe to be trademarks have been acknowledged as such. The presence or absence of such acknowledgement should not be regarded as affecting the legal status of any trade mark or proprietary name.

First published 1979 by
Heinemann Educational Books Limited
This edition published 1980 by Pan Books Limited,
Cavaye Place, London SW10 9PG

ISBN 0 330 25918 0
Printed in Great Britain by
Richard Clay (The Chaucer Press) Ltd, Bungay, Suffolk

CONTENTS

PREFACE

This dictionary has been designed as a clear, convenient, and immediately accessible reference book. Every aspect of its conception and layout has been planned to help the reader to find the information he needs with the minimum of difficulty.

Research has shown that most schoolchildren and many adults are deterred from making full use of the range of information which the majority of dictionaries provide. They are often confused by the density of the text and by the extensive use of symbols and abbreviations characteristic of traditional dictionaries.

For this reason our overriding concern has been to ensure that the user can immediately and easily grasp *all* the information contained in an entry. Entries are well spaced; sub-sections of entries start new lines; compounds (whether hyphenated or not) are treated as headwords; words are never broken (since the breaking of words can lead to confusion over hyphenation); and abbreviations and symbols are almost totally avoided. This last point involved the greatest sacrifice for the editors and publishers since there is obvious space-saving appeal in the use of abbreviations and symbols. Our research showed, however, that their avoidance was the feature which readers most appreciated when comparing this dictionary with others.

Even the pronunciation guides provided for all irregular words are immediately self-explanatory in the majority of cases. We have used a simple re-spelling system, backed up occasionally by rhyming comparisons, which users of this dictionary should be able to follow clearly without reference to tables or explanations. The only exceptions are three or four sounds (e.g. the distinction between *th* in 'this' and *th* in 'think') for which simple conventions are used; these are explained on pages xi–xii.

The section 'How to Use the Dictionary', which follows this preface, outlines fully the principles upon which each aspect of the dictionary has been planned, while the labelled specimen entries provide a quick guide to layout and content.

This dictionary has a number of innovative features which the editors hope will make it a helpful reference tool for all its users, particularly students and secondary-school pupils. As to its general content, we have concentrated on modern English as it is actually used in education, science and technology, literature, the media, sports, and everyday written and spoken communication. Definitions are frequently reinforced by usage examples, and new words are included where they seem likely to have more than an ephemeral presence in the language. In so far as any concise dictionary can do so, we hope that this dictionary accurately reflects and illuminates the living, changing face of English in all its variety and richness.

HOW TO USE THE DICTIONARY 1

headword

colloquial or slang word

clout *noun*
(*informal*) a blow or knock, especially with the hand: 'he received a heavy *clout* on the head'

common prefix as separate entry

co-
a prefix meaning together or associated, as in *cooperate.*

part of speech

consecutive (*say* **k'n-sek-yootiv**)
adjective
following without interruption: 'she missed school on 4 *consecutive* days'
Word Family: **consecutively,** *adverb.*
[CON- + Latin *secutus* followed]

Common Error: CONSECUTIVE, SUCCESSIVE both refer to things following one another, but *consecutive* refers to following in an arranged or logical order, whereas *successive* refers to any sequence: 'these two paragraphs are not *consecutive*'; 'we were pestered by *successive* visitors over the weekend'

common error

numbered headwords of different meaning and/or derivation

converse (1) (*say* **k'n-verse**) *verb*
to talk informally.
[Latin *conversari* to associate with]

converse (2) (*say* **kon**-verse) *noun*
something which is the opposite of another.
Word Family: **converse,** *adjective*; **conversely,** *adverb.*
[Latin *conversus* turned round]

self-evident guide to pronunciation and stress

convert (*say* **k'n-vert**) *verb*
1. to change into a different form, etc.: '*convert* 1 kilometre into metres'
2. to cause to change to another way of life, belief, etc.
3. (*Law*) to take another's property unlawfully.
Word Family: **convert** (*say* **kon**-vert), *noun*, a person who has been converted; **conversion** (*say* **k'n-ver-*zh*'n**), *noun.*

clearly separated definitions

word used in special field

creep *verb*
(**crept, creeping**)
1. to move or crawl close to the ground: 'a *creeping* plant'
2. to move slowly, quietly or secretly.
3. to be or feel as if covered with creeping things: 'the sight of the snake made her flesh *creep*'

irregular conjugation

earthenware *noun*
any glazed or unglazed low-fired (under 1100°C) pottery with a porous body. Compare STONEWARE and PORCELAIN.

cross-reference to related entries

emphasis (*say* **emfa-sis**) *noun*
a stress on or importance attached to something: 'we must put more *emphasis* on taxes in this election campaign'.
emphasize, emphasise *verb*
to put emphasis upon: 'that blue dress *emphasizes* the colour of her eyes'
emphatic (*say* **em-fattik**) *adjective*
full of force and emphasis: 'his *emphatic* answer startled the reporter'
Word Family: **emphatically**, *adverb*.
[Greek]

alternative spellings

directly related words

evidence (*say* **evvi-d'nce**) *noun*
1. anything which provides a basis for belief.
Usage: 'there was little *evidence* of suffering in her face' (= sign, indication).
2. *Law:* the statements, documents or objects presented in a court to prove disputed facts.
in evidence, 'her talent was very much *in evidence* during the play' (= plainly seen).
Word Family: **evidence**, *verb*, to show clearly; **evidential** (*say* **evvi-den-sh'l**), *adjective*, serving as or based on evidence; **evidentially**, *adverb*.
[Latin *evidens* plain to see]

usage example with 'translation' of particular sense

common phrase in which word appears with example and 'translation'

etymology

evil (*say* **eevil**) *adjective*
1. morally bad: '*evil* deeds'
2. causing injury, damage, etc.: 'smoking is an *evil* habit'
3. full of suffering, misfortune or bad luck: 'the war caused *evil* times'
evil *noun*
anything which is evil or causes harm, suffering, etc.: 'the *evils* of the war would never be forgotten'
Word Family: **evilly**, *adverb*; **evilness**, *noun*.

same word as different part of speech

evil eye
a stare believed to have the power to cause bad luck, injury, etc.
evil-minded *adjective*
full of malice or evil intentions.

compounds or near-compounds as separate entries

HOW TO USE THE DICTIONARY 2

Headword Most entries are for a single headword which is printed in bold and followed by its part of speech.

Headwords which have identical spellings but different meanings and/or derivations are inserted separately and numbered, usually in the order of frequency of use.
Example: **mare** (1), **mare** (2).

If a word has an irregular plural (i.e. not formed by the simple addition of -s, -es, or -ies) this is given on the line below the headword.

If a word has two common and equally accepted spellings, they are placed side by side, separated by a comma.
Example: **encyclopaedia, encyclopedia** *noun.*

If two words represent slightly varied forms of the same root, with similar or identical meanings, they may also be placed together as a dual headword, separated by a comma.

A headword which consists of two or more words which are not joined by hyphens is not given a part of speech.

A word formed directly from a headword is usually entered as a subheadword followed by its part of speech and definition. Thus, **adhesion** is a subheadword under **adhere.** Where such a word has a distinct or specialized meaning, it may be entered as a separate headword. For example, **exhibition** is not defined under the headword **exhibit** (verb); it is defined as a separate headword.

Related forms which are separated alphabetically from the headword are included in the headword list with a cross-reference to the headword under which they are treated.

Pronunciation Any word which might present difficulties of stress or pronunciation is followed by a simple guide in brackets, which is as far as possible self-explanatory.
Example: **nomad** (*say* **no**-mad).

The bold type used for **no** shows that this is where the stress falls in this word, and the hyphen separates the syllables and helps to show the pronunciation.

Words are respelled if this helps to avoid pronunciation problems.
Example: **photosynthesis** (*say* foto-**sin**tha-sis).

Occasionally a familiar rhyming word may be supplied if this is the clearest way of indicating the pronunciation.
Example: **ochre** (*rhymes with* poker).

There are a few sounds which cannot be unambiguously indicated by the methods indicated above. For these sounds the following conventions are used:

An apostrophe (') indicates the common unstressed vowel known technically as the schwa:
Example: **oxidation** (*say* oksi-**day**-sh'n).

When 'th' is pronounced as in 'think' it is printed in ordinary type; when it is pronounced as in 'this' it is in italic type (*th*):
Examples: **thief** (say theef) **thine** (*say* *th*ine).

When 'u' is pronounced as in 'cup' it is printed in ordinary type; when it is pronounced as in 'bull' it is printed in italics (*u*):
Examples: **muscle** (*say* **muss**'l);
ombudsman (*say* **om**-b*u*dz-man).

The letters *zh* in italics are used to indicate the sound common to 'measure', 'adhesion', and certain words of French origin:
Examples: **bourgeois** (*say* **boor**-*zh*wa);
treasure (*say* **tre*zh*a**).

Definitions

Definitions of nouns generally begin with 'a', 'any', or 'the' and definitions of verbs begin with 'to'. Certain very common prepositions, conjunctions and adverbs are explained in terms of their function.

A short example of the word in context has been provided in cases where this helps to clarify meaning.

Extended meanings or usages are treated under the label *Usage*. The word is used in a simple idiomatic sentence followed by a translation of its sense in brackets.

Where the headword occurs in a commonly used phrase, this phrase is listed under the appropriate part of speech, after the definitions and usages. It is followed by

a) an explanation; or
b) an example in context, followed by a translation of its sense in brackets.

Cross-references to important related or opposite concepts are given, where relevant, at the end of definitions, introduced by the word 'Compare'.

In certain cases, the definitions of a particular headword may not be found in its alphabetical position. In such cases the reader is referred to the headword under which the definition is provided.

Tenses of irregular verbs which are separated alphabetically from the infinitive are included in the text with an explanation of the tense and verb they relate to.

Archaic words included have been defined as 'an old word for', with their current equivalent meaning.

Where appropriate, labels are provided before definitions to indicate subject areas, national usage, etc.

Explanation of how the headword is normally used is indicated by the following labels:

1 (*plural*) where a word is more commonly used in its plural form.
2 (*used with singular verb*) where a plural noun is to be used with a singular verb.
3 (*informal*) where the meaning or use of a word is considered to be colloquial or slang.
4 (*capital*), (*not capital*) where a word is used with or without an initial capital.
5 (*formerly*) where a former meaning of the word is given.

Word Family Words directly related to the headword, or words formed directly from it, are not usually given separate definitions. They are grouped under the label *Word Family*.

Example: **stammer** *noun*
a) a stutter. b) any hesitation in speech.
Word Family: **stammer,** *verb;* **stammerer,** *noun;* **stammeringly,** *adverb.*

Where necessary, a pronunciation guide is provided in the *Word Family* list, together with irregular plurals or conjugations, or extensions in meaning.

Etymologies Etymologies are supplied (within square brackets at the end of the entry) wherever they throw light on the origin, evolution, or modern meaning of the word. This applies particularly to words deriving from Greek, Latin, and modern foreign languages. Etymologies are not generally given for words of Old English origin, where the word and meaning have not significantly changed; nor are they provided in cases where the etymology is so complex that a brief summary would cause confusion. Where no English equivalent is given for a classical or foreign word cited in the etymology, it may be assumed that the word has essentially the same meaning as the headword. Where the headword is a foreign word adopted in English, only the language of origin is given.

Common Error In cases where one headword is likely to be confused with another of similar spelling, function, usage, or pronunciation, a brief note labelled *Common Error* distinguishes the two words.

Aa

a *article*
Grammar: an indefinite article. See ARTICLE.

a–
a prefix meaning not or without, as in *asymmetrical.* A variant is **an–**, as in *anarchy.*

aardvark *noun*
a large, burrowing, African mammal with a long snout and ears, feeding on termites and ants.
[Afrikaans *aarde* earth + *vark* pig]

aardwolf *noun*
a hyena-like, African mammal feeding on carrion, termites and insect larvae.

ab–
a prefix meaning off, from or away from, as in *abnormal.*

aback *adverb*
Nautical: backwards.
taken aback, 'she was *taken aback* by his rudeness' (= startled).

abacus (*say* **abba**–kus) *noun*
1. a device used for counting by sliding beads along thin rods set in a frame.
2. *Architecture:* a flat slab forming part of the top of a column.
[Greek *abakos* of a tablet]

abaft *adverb, preposition*
Nautical: at or towards the stern.

abandon *verb*
1. to leave something without intending to return for it: 'we had to *abandon* all our possessions and flee'.
2. to stop going on with: 'we *abandoned* the search after 4 days with no results'.
Usage: 'the child *abandoned* himself to grief' (= surrendered).

abandon *noun*
a freedom from restraint: 'the class cheered with great *abandon*'.
Word Family: **abandonment,** *noun.*

abase *verb*
to humble or degrade: 'the prisoner *abased* himself before the judge'.
Word Family: **abasement,** *noun.*

abashed *adjective*
ashamed or embarrassed.
Word Family: **abash,** *verb.*

abate (*say* a–**bate**) *verb*
to lessen in amount or intensity.
Word Family: **abatement,** *noun.*

abattoir (*say* **abba**–twar) *noun*
(*often plural*) a place where cattle, sheep, etc. are killed for food.
[French]

abbé (*say* **ab**bay) *noun*
a French clergyman.

abbey (*say* **abbee**) *noun*
a) a monastery or convent. b) a church or house that was once part of an abbey, such as Westminster Abbey.
Word Family: **abbot,** *noun,* the male head of an abbey; **abbess,** *noun,* a female abbot.

abbreviate (*say* a–**breevi**–ate) *verb*
to shorten or contract, especially a word or phrase.
abbreviation *noun*
1. the act of abbreviating.
2. a shortened form of a word, especially one using only the first letter or letters. Compare CONTRACTION.
[AB– + Latin *brevis* short]

abdicate *verb*
1. to renounce the throne.
2. to give up a claim, position, privilege, etc.
Word Family: **abdication,** *noun.*

abdomen (*say* **abda**–m'n) *noun*
also called the **belly**
Anatomy: the region below the chest at the front of the trunk, containing the intestines.
Word Family: **abdominal** (*say* ab–**dommi**–n'l), *adjective.*
[Latin]

abduct *verb*
to take away a person, illegally or by force. Compare KIDNAP.
Word Family: **abduction,** *noun;* **abductor,** *noun,* a person who abducts someone.
[Latin *abductus* led away]

abeam (*say* a–**beem**) *adverb*
Nautical: opposite to the middle of a ship.

aberration (*say* abba–**ray**–sh'n) *noun*
1. a deviation from the normal course: 'he destroyed his own work in a moment of *aberration*'.
2. *Physics:* the distortion of an image produced by a lens or mirror. **Spherical aberration** is a lack of clear focus caused by the use of a spherical rather than a parabolic surface and **chromatic aberration** is the presence of coloured fringes in the image cast by a simple lens.
Word Family: **aberrant** (*say* a–**berr**ent), *adjective.*
[Latin *aberrare* to wander away]

abet (*say* a–**bet**) *verb*
(abetted, abetting)
to encourage or assist someone to commit a crime.
Word Family: **abetter, abettor** (Law), *noun.*

abeyance (*say* a–**bay**'nce) *noun*
a state of temporary inactivity: 'the project is in *abeyance* because of a lack of support'.

abhor (*say* ab–**hor**) *verb*
(abhorred, abhorring)
to regard with hatred or disgust.
abhorrent (*say* ab–**horr**unt) *adjective*
causing disgust or horror.
Word Family: **abhorrently,** *adverb*; **abhorrence,** *noun.*
[Latin *abhorrere* to shrink back]

abide *verb*
(abided or **abode, abiding)**
1. to continue or remain.
2. an old word meaning to dwell.
3. (*informal*) to tolerate: 'I can't *abide* fools'.
abide by, 'he *abided by* his decision' (= kept to).
Word Family: **abidance,** *noun*; **abode,** *noun,* the place where one lives.

ability *noun*
the quality of being able to do something.
[Latin *habilitas* aptitude]

abiogenesis (*say* ay–by–o–**jenni**–sis) *noun*
see SPONTANEOUS GENERATION.
[A– + Greek *bios* life + *genesis* creation]

abject (*say* **ab**–jekt) *adjective*
1. contemptible: 'an *abject* coward'.
2. humble: 'an *abject* apology'.
3. wretched: 'he lived in *abject* poverty'.
Word Family: **abjectly,** *adverb*; **abjection,** *noun.*
[AB– + Latin *jactus* thrown]

abjure *verb*
to renounce publicly a belief, opinion, etc.
Word Family: **abjuration,** *noun.*
[Latin *abjurare* to deny on oath]

ablative case (*say* **abla**–tiv case)
Grammar: see CASE (1).

ablaze *adverb, adjective*
on fire or lit up: 'the town was *ablaze* with lights'.

able *adjective*
1. clever: 'he is an *able* man'.
2. having the skill to do something: 'are you *able* to drive a car?'.
3. having the opportunity or permission to do something: 'will you be *able* to start work tomorrow?'.
Word Family: **ably,** *adverb.*
[Latin *habilis* fit, apt]

–able
a suffix indicating: a) ability or tendency, as in *obtainable*; b) worthiness, as in *likable.* A variant is **–ible**, as in *visible.*

able–bodied *adjective*
healthy or strong.

abluent (*say* a–**bloo**'nt) *noun*
a substance which cleans or purifies, such as a detergent.

ablution (*say* a–**bloo**–sh'n) *noun*
(*usually plural*) the act of washing oneself.

abnegate (*say* **abni**–gate) *verb*
to renounce.
Usage: 'I will not *abnegate* my rights in this matter' (= give up).
Word Family: **abnegation,** *noun.*
[Latin *abnegare* to deny]

abnormal *adjective*
different from what is normal or expected.
Word Family: **abnormally,** *adverb*; **abnormality,** *noun.*

aboard *adverb, preposition*
on a ship, aircraft, etc.

abode (*say* a–**bode**) *noun*
Word Family: see ABIDE.
abode *verb*
a past tense of the verb **abide**.

abolish (*say* a–**bol**–ish) *verb*
to put an end to: 'it took many years to *abolish* the slave trade'.
Word Family: **abolition** (*say* abba–**lish**'n), **abolishment,** *nouns.*
[Latin *abolere*]

abomasum (*say* abba–**may**–z'm) *noun*
the true stomach of ruminant mammals, e.g. cows.
[AB– + Latin *omasum* a paunch]

A–bomb *noun*
short form of **atomic bomb**
see NUCLEAR WEAPON.

abominable (*say* a–**bommina**–b'l) *adjective*
dreadful or shocking.
Word Family: **abominably**, *adverb*; **abomination**, *noun*, a person or thing that is abominable; **abominate**, *verb*, to detest.

aborigines (*say* abba–**riji**–neez) *plural noun*
the original inhabitants of a country.
Aborigine *noun*
an original inhabitant of Australia.
Aboriginal (*say* abba–**rija**–n'l) *noun*
a) any of the original inhabitants of Australia. b) any of their languages.
Word Family: **aboriginal**, **Aboriginal**, *adjective*.
[Latin *ab origine* from the beginning]

abortifacient (*say* a–borti–**fay**–sh'nt) *adjective*
of or relating to any substance inducing an abortion.
Word Family: **abortifacient**, *noun*.

abortion (*say* a–**bore**–sh'n) *noun*
1. the expulsion or removal of a human foetus from the uterus before the foetus is capable of independent survival, usually about the 28th week.
2. anything which is a failure.
3. a monstrous creature or thing.
Word Family: **abort**, *verb*; **abortive**, *adjective*, unsuccessful; **abortionist**, *noun*.
[Latin *abortus* a miscarriage]

abound *verb*
to be plentiful.

about *preposition, adverb*
1. around: 'he looked *about* as he walked'.
2. on the subject of: 'what is the book *about*?'.
3. approximately: 'she ate *about* 14 cakes'.
4. engaged in doing: 'what are you *about*?'.
Phrases:
about to, 'he is *about to* jump' (= just going to).
up and about, 'she won't be *up and about* for at least a week' (= out of bed, active).

about–face, about–turn *verb*
to turn so as to face the opposite direction.
Word Family: **about–face**, **about–turn**, *nouns*, a sudden reversal.

above *adverb, preposition*
in a higher position: 'the sun rose *above* the horizon'.
Usage: 'there were *above* 400 people at the meeting' (= more than).
Word Family: **above**, *adjective*.

aboveboard *adverb, adjective*
open and honest.

abracadabra (*say* abra–ka–**dabra**) *interjection*
an exclamation used as a magic spell.

abrade *verb*
to scrape off or wear away by rubbing.
abrasion *noun*
1. the act or process of abrading.
2. a place where something has been rubbed away.
Word Family: **abrasive**, *adjective*, a) serving to abrade, b) (of a personality, etc.) harsh, irritating or annoying; **abrasive**, *noun*, something which abrades.
[Latin *abradere* to scrape off]

abreast *adverb*
side by side.

abridge *verb*
to shorten: 'the book was *abridged* for publication in serial form'.
Word Family: **abridgement**, **abridgment**, *noun*.

abroad *adverb*
1. in or to another country: 'we went *abroad* for our holidays'.
2. outside: 'he did not venture *abroad* all day'.
Usage: 'vicious rumours are *abroad*' (= circulating).

abrogate (*say* **abra**–gate) *verb*
to repeal or annul.
Word Family: **abrogation**, *noun*.
[Latin *abrogare* to repeal]

abrupt *adjective*
1. sudden or unexpected.
2. discourteous or brief, especially in manner.
Word Family: **abruptly**, *adverb*; **abruptness**, *noun*.
[Latin *abruptus* broken off]

abscess (*say* **ab**sis) *noun*
an acute, local, bacterial infection containing pus, such as a boil.
Word Family: **abscessed**, *adjective*.
[Latin *abscessus* a going away]

abscissa (*say* ab–**sissa**) *noun*
Maths: the horizontal distance of a point from the origin of a graph; the *x* coordinate. Compare ORDINATE.
[Latin *abscissus* cut away]

abscission (*say* ab–**sizh**'n) *noun*
the act of cutting off.
Word Family: **abscind** (*say* ab–**sind**), *verb*.

abscond (*say* ab–**skond**) *verb*
to leave suddenly or secretly, especially after doing wrong: 'she *absconded* with the money'.
[Latin *abscondere* to hide away]

absent (*say* **ab**–s'nt) *adjective*
1. away: 'she was *absent* from school'.
2. inattentive or preoccupied: 'he had an *absent* look about him'.
Word Family: **absent** (*say* ab–**sent**), *verb*, to take or keep (oneself) away; **absently**, *adverb*; **absence**, *noun*; **absentee** (*say* abs'n–**tee**), *noun*, a person who is absent.
[Latin *absens* being away]

absenteeism (*say* abs'n–**tee**–izm) *noun*
the practice of staying away from one's place of work, study, property, etc., habitually or without good excuse or permission.

absent-minded *adjective*
vague or forgetful.
Word Family: **absent-mindedly**, *adverb*; **absent-mindedness**, *noun*.

absinth, absinthe *noun*
a strong drink made with wormwood.

absolute (*say* absa–loot) *adjective*
complete, perfect or unlimited: a) 'the day was an *absolute* success'; b) 'the dictator had *absolute* power'.
Word Family: **absolutely**, *adverb*.
[Latin *absolutus* freed]

absolute alcohol
Chemistry: ethyl alcohol, at least 99 per cent pure by mass.

absolute humidity
see HUMIDITY.

absolute majority
a winning number of votes which is more than the combined votes received by all other candidates or parties in an election.

absolute temperature
Physics: the temperature measured from absolute zero.

absolute zero
Physics: the lowest temperature possible, which is equal to 0 kelvin (−273·15°C).

absolutism (*say* absa–loo–tizm) *noun*
the principle or practice of absolute power and control, especially in government.
Word Family: **absolutist**, *noun*, a supporter of absolutism; **absolutist**, *adjective*.

absolve *verb*
to pardon or release from guilt, blame, obligation, etc.
Word Family: **absolution** (*say* absa–**loo**–sh'n), *noun*.
[Latin *absolvere* to acquit]

absorb *verb*
to take in or soak up: 'the sponge *absorbed* the water'. Compare ADSORB.
Usages:
a) 'she was completely *absorbed* by the book' (= engrossed).
b) 'the international corporation *absorbed* its competitors' (= took over).
c) 'a black surface tends to *absorb* heat, whereas a white surface tends to reflect it' (= retain).
Word Family: **absorbent**, *adjective*; **absorption**, *noun*.
[AB– + Latin *sorbere* to suck in]

abstain *verb*
to refrain voluntarily from doing something: a) 'some people *abstain* from drinking alcohol'; b) 'he *abstained* from voting'.
Word Family: **abstinence** (*say* **absti**–nence), *noun*, self-restraint; **abstention**, *noun*, the act of abstaining; **abstainer**, *noun*, a person who abstains.
[Latin *abstinere* to keep away from]

abstemious (*say* ab–**steemius**) *adjective*
tending to eat and drink sparingly.
[Latin *abstemius*]

abstract (*say* **ab**–strakt) *adjective*
1. concerning things which have no real or physical existence, such as ideas.
2. based on theory: '*abstract* arguments'.
3. *Art:* not representing people or things, but relying on colour, form, etc.

abstract *noun*
1. the state of being abstract.
2. a summary.

abstract (*say* ab–**strakt**) *verb*
to remove or take away.
Usage: 'she had a vague, *abstracted* look' (= preoccupied, withdrawn).
Word Family: **abstractly**, *adverb*; **abstraction**, *noun*.
[Latin *abstractus* drawn away]

abstract noun
Grammar: see NOUN.

abstruse (*say* ab–strewce) *adjective*
obscure or difficult to understand: 'I couldn't follow the lawyer's *abstruse* argument'.
Word Family: **abstrusely**, *adverb*; **abstruseness**, *noun*.
[Latin *abstrusus* hidden]
Common Error: see OBTUSE.

absurd *adjective*
foolish or illogical.
Word Family: **absurdly**, *adverb*; **absurdity**, *noun*, a) the quality of being absurd, b) something which is absurd.
[Latin *absurdus* out of tune]

abundance (*say* a–bun–d'nce) *noun*
a full or ample supply or amount.
Word Family: **abundant**, *adjective*; **abundantly**, *adverb*.
[Latin *abundare* to overflow]

abuse (*say* a–bewz) *verb*
1. to use wrongly or maltreat: 'never *abuse* a chisel by using it as a screwdriver'.
2. to speak insultingly: 'the drunk *abused* the barman'.
Word Family: **abuse** (*say* a–bewce), *noun*; **abusive**, *adjective*; **abusively**, *adverb*; **abusiveness**, *noun*.
[AB– + USE]

abut (*say* a–but) *verb*
(abutted, abutting)
to border on or be next to: 'his farm *abuts* on the park'.

abutment *noun*
Architecture: a supporting structure extending from the ends or piers of a bridge.

abuzz *adverb, adjective*
buzzing.

abyss (*say* a–biss) *noun*
1. an immeasurable depth or chasm.
2. anything very profound or deep: 'she wept in an *abyss* of grief'.
abysmal (*say* a–biz–m'l) *adjective*
1. of, like or as deep as an abyss: 'your *abysmal* ignorance appals me'.
2. (*informal*) very bad: 'I thought the performance was *abysmal*'.
Word Family: **abysmally**, *adverb*.
[Greek *abyssos* bottomless]

ac–
a variant of the prefix **ad–**.

acacia (*say* a–kay–sha) *noun*
any of a large group of trees or shrubs, mostly tropical or sub-tropical, usually thorny, some yielding gum arabic.
[Greek *akakia* a thorny tree]

academic (*say* akka–demmik) *adjective*
1. of or relating to learning or studies, especially in a university or similar institution.
2. theoretical rather than practical: 'that is just an *academic* quibble'.
academic *noun*
a person who teaches or does research in a university or other advanced institution.
Word Family: **academically**, *adverb*.

academy (*say* a–kadda–mee) *noun*
1. a scientific or artistic association: 'the Royal *Academy*'.
2. a specialized college: 'the Royal Military *Academy*'.
3. *Scottish:* a secondary school.
[Greek *Akademeia* the garden where Plato taught]

acanthus (*say* a–kanthus) *noun*
1. any of a group of plants with spiny leaves.
2. *Architecture:* a conventional design of deeply notched leaves, used on Greek columns.

accede (*say* ak–seed) *verb*
1. to agree: 'I *accede* to your request'.
2. to attain a position, office, etc.: 'the prince *acceded* to the throne'.
[Latin *accedere* to go towards]

accelerate (*say* ak–sella–rate) *verb*
1. to move or cause to move faster: 'the car *accelerated* and passed the van'.
2. *Physics:* to change velocity.
acceleration *noun*
1. an increase in swiftness of movement.
2. *Physics:* the vector quantity describing the rate of change in velocity of an object, including linear acceleration, expressed in metres per second per second, and angular acceleration, expressed in radians per second per second.
[AC– + Latin *celer* swift]

accelerator (*say* ak–sella–rayta) *noun*
1. a device to increase or control speed, especially the device in a motor vehicle which controls the throttle.
2. *Physics:* a device to alter the velocity of subatomic particles: 'a nuclear *accelerator*'. See CYCLOTRON.

accent (*say* ak–s'nt) *noun*
1. a particular way of pronouncing a language: 'she speaks French with an American *accent*'.
2. *Language:* any of the marks used with letters, to change their sound or to indicate stress:

a) an **acute** may indicate stress or pronunciation: **attaché** (*say* a–**tash**ay).
b) a **grave** (*say* grahv) generally flattens the vowel sound, as in French: **père** (*say* pair).
c) a **circumflex** indicates a dropped s, as in French: **arrêter** (= to arrest or stop).
d) a **tilde** (*say* **til**da) introduces the sound of a y, as in Spanish: **señor** (*say* sen–**yor**).
e) a **cedilla** (*say* si–**dil**la) softens a hard c(k) to a soft c(s) as in French: **façade** (*say* fa–**sahd**).
f) a **diaeresis** (*say* die–**err**i–sis), placed over the second of two adjacent vowels, indicates that both vowel sounds should be pronounced: **noël** (*say* no–**el**).
g) an **umlaut** (*say* **um**–lout), indicates a change from the normal vowel sound, as in German: **Köln** (*say* kerln).
3. any stress or emphasis.
Word Family: **accent** (*say* ak–**sent**), *verb*; **accentual**, *adjective*.
[AD– + Latin *cantus* tone]

accentuate (*say* ak–**sen**choo–ate) *verb*
to emphasize.
Word Family: **accentuation**, *noun*.

accept (*say* ak–**sept**) *verb*
to receive, especially with approval: 'please *accept* my apologies'.
Word Family: **acceptable**, *adjective*, welcome or worthy of being accepted.
[Latin *acceptus* received]

acceptance *noun*
1. the act of taking or receiving something offered.
2. *Commerce:* an agreement to pay a draft, order or bill of exchange.

access (*say* **ak**–sess) *noun*
1. a means of entry or approach: 'the only *access* to the island is by boat'.
2. the right or opportunity of reaching, approaching, etc., such as the right of a divorced parent to visit the children.
Word Family: **accessible** (*say* ak–**sessi**–b'l), *adjective*, able to be reached or obtained; **accessibility**, *noun*.
[Latin *accessus* an approach]

accession *noun*
1. the act of acceding: 'the king's *accession* to the throne'.
2. an addition or increase: 'numbers rose with the *accession* of new members'.

accessory (*say* ak–**sessa**–ree) *noun*
1. a) any extra non–essential item: 'most cars today have a radio as an *accessory*'. b) (*plural*) any additional items of clothing, such as shoes, handbags, etc. to complement one's dress.
2. *Law:* any person who helps a criminal before or after a crime.
[Latin *accessio* an addition]

accident (*say* **ak**si–d'nt) *noun*
1. anything which is unexpected or unintentional: 'I met him by *accident*'.
2. any unfortunate event, especially one involving injury: 'a car *accident*'.
[Latin *accidere* to happen suddenly]

accidental *adjective*
occurring by chance.
accidental *noun*
Music: a sign used before a note to indicate change to a sharp, flat or natural.
Word Family: **accidentally**, *adverb*.
Common Error: ACCIDENTAL, INCIDENTAL have related but distinct meanings: *accidental* describes something which occurs unexpectedly or unintentionally, while *incidental* refers to something which accompanies an event or is of secondary importance.

acclaim (*say* a–**claim**) *verb*
to applaud or express loud approval.
Word Family: **acclaim**, **acclamation**, *nouns*.
[Latin *acclamare* to shout approval]

acclimatize (*say* a–**klime**–a–tize)
acclimatise *verb*
to make or become used to something new: 'it took a month to become *acclimatized* to the tropical heat'.
Word Family: **acclimatization**, *noun*.

acclivity *noun*
any upward slope.
[Latin *acclivis* steep]

accolade (*say* **akka**–lade) *noun*
1. a ceremonial touching of the shoulder with a sword, a symbol of the award of knighthood.
2. a special recognition of, or praise for, merit.
[AC– + Latin *collum* neck]

accommodate (*say* a–**komma**–date) *verb*
1. to do a favour for, especially by providing something: 'can you *accommodate* me with a loan?'.
2. to adapt: 'it takes a few minutes for my eyes to *accommodate* to the dark'.
3. to have rooms or beds for: 'the hotel *accommodates* 14 guests'.

accommodation *noun*
1. the act of accommodating.
2. any rooms provided for visitors or paying guests, such as in a hotel.
[AC– + Latin *commodus* convenient]

accommodation ladder
any steps over the side or stern of a ship by which to climb aboard from boats alongside.

accompaniment (*say* a–kumpni–m'nt) *noun*
anything which goes with or adds to another: 'there was no piano *accompaniment* for the singer'.
Word Family: **accompanist** (*say* a–kumpa–nist), *noun*, a person who plays a musical accompaniment.

accompany (*say* a–kumpa–nee) *verb*
(accompanied, accompanying)
1. to exist, or go, with: 'we will *accompany* you to the airport'.
2. to be or provide an accompaniment to.

accomplice (*say* a–kumpliss) *noun*
a partner in crime or wrongdoing.

accomplish (*say* a–kumplish) *verb*
to bring about or complete successfully: 'he *accomplished* his task ahead of time'.
accomplished *adjective*
1. already done: 'my task is *accomplished*'.
2. skilled: 'an *accomplished* singer'.
accomplishment *noun*
1. something achieved.
2. an acquired skill: 'his many *accomplishments* include horseriding and operatic singing'.
[AC– + Latin *complere* to complete]

accord (*say* a–kord) *verb*
1. to agree or be in harmony: 'what he said today doesn't *accord* with what he said yesterday'.
2. to give or grant: 'he was *accorded* a warm welcome'.
accord *noun*
an agreement or harmony.
Phrases:
of one's own accord, 'she did it quite *of her own accord*' (= voluntarily).
with one accord, 'the whole crowd cheered *with one accord*' (= spontaneously together).
according *adverb*
according to, a) 'we sorted the fruit *according to* size' (= in relation to); b) '*according to* all reports she's quite mad' (= as stated by).
Word Family: **accordance,** *noun*; **accordant,** *adjective*; **accordingly,** *adverb*, therefore or for that reason.
[AC– + Latin *cordis* of the heart]

accordion *noun*
a portable, keyed musical instrument with bellows and two sets of metal reeds.
Word Family: **accordionist,** *noun*.

accost (*say* a–kost) *verb*
to greet or approach, often offensively: 'the beggar *accosted* me in the street'.
[AC– + Latin *costa* side]

account *noun*
1. any statement which lists, describes or explains: a) 'the radio gave a full *account* of the match'; b) 'the clerk kept the financial *accounts*'.
2. an agreement allowing one to buy goods on credit, of which a record is kept.
3. see BANK ACCOUNT.
Usage: 'he's a man of no *account*' (= importance).
Word Family: **account,** *verb*.

accountable *adjective*
1. able to be explained.
2. responsible: 'I'm not *accountable* for your debts'.
Word Family: **accountably,** *adverb*; **accountability,** *noun*.

accountant *noun*
a person who keeps the accounts and draws up the balance sheets for a business.
Word Family: **accounting, accountancy,** *nouns*.

accoutrements (*say* a–kootra–m'nts) *plural noun*
1. a soldier's equipment, apart from clothes and weapons.
2. any equipment.
Word Family: **accoutre** (*say* a–koota), *verb*, to equip.
[French]

accredit *verb*
1. to give credit for: 'he is *accredited* with several inventions'.
2. to authorize or recognize officially: 'an ambassador is the *accredited* representative of his country'.

accretion (*say* a–kree–sh'n) *noun*
any growth or increase by addition.
Word Family: **accrete,** *verb*.
[Latin *accretio* an increasing]

accrue (*say* a–kroo) *verb*
(accrued, accruing)

to occur as a natural increase or addition: 'interest *accrues* at 8 per cent a year'.
accrual *noun*
1. the act of accruing.
2. an entry in an account representing a debt which is due but which has not yet been paid.

accrued interest
Commerce: see INTEREST.

acculturation (*say* a–kulcha–**ray**–sh'n) *noun*
Anthropology: the process in which a person or group adopts the customs of a society by social or economic necessity.

accumulate (*say* a–**kew**–mew–late) *verb*
to gather or pile up.
Word Family: **accumulation,** *noun,* a) the act of accumulating, b) a number of things collected together; **accumulative,** *adjective.*
[Latin *accumulare* to heap up]

accumulator *noun*
1. a person or thing that accumulates.
2. *Electricity:* any rechargeable battery, such as a car battery.

accurate (*say* **ak**–yoorit) *adjective*
free from error or deviation: a) 'my new watch is more *accurate* than my old one'; b) 'she made an *accurate* guess'.
Word Family: **accurately,** *adverb*; **accuracy, accurateness,** *nouns.*
[Latin *accuratus* prepared with care]

accursed (*say* a–**kerst** *or* a–**kersed**) *adjective*
1. under a curse.
2. (*informal*) hateful or irritating: 'this *accursed* knife is blunt'.

accusative case (*say* a–**kewza**–tiv case)
Grammar: see CASE (1).

accuse (*say* a–**kewz**) *verb*
to blame with having done wrong: 'I *accuse* you of stealing the money'.
accused *noun*
Law: the defendant in a criminal court case.
Word Family: **accusation** (*say* ak–yoo–**zay**–sh'n), *noun*; **accusatory,** *adjective.*
[Latin *accusare*]

accustom *verb*
to become familiar with through use or habit: 'you'll have to *accustom* yourself to our strange ways'.
Word Family: **accustomed,** *adjective,* a) familiar with, b) usual or customary.

ace *noun*
1. a playing card with a single pip, the highest or lowest card in its suit.
2. a person who excels in a particular field, such as a fighter pilot.
Usage: 'the tennis player served an *ace*' (= a service which the opponent could not even touch).
Word Family: **ace,** *verb,* to play an ace.
[Latin *as* a unit]

acerbic (*say* a–**ser**–bik) *adjective*
sharp or bitter.
Word Family: **acerbity,** *noun*; **acerbate** (*say* **assa**–bate), *verb.*
[Latin *acerbus* bitter]

acetabulum (*say* assi–**tab**–yoo–l'm) *noun*
Anatomy: the socket in the hipbone, into which fits the head of the femur.
[Latin, a vessel for vinegar]

acetate (*say* **assi**–tate) *noun*
Chemistry: a salt or ester of acetic acid.

acetic acid (*say* a–**seetik** assid)
Chemistry: a colourless liquid (formula $CH_3.COOH$), the principal part of vinegar and producing its characteristic smell.

acetone (*say* **assi**–tone) *noun*
Chemistry: a colourless, highly inflammable liquid (formula CH_3COCH_3), used as an industrial solvent, in making rayon, and as nail polish remover.

acetylene (*say* a–**setti**–leen) *noun*
1. *Chemistry:* a colourless, poisonous inflammable gas (formula C_2H_2) used in making organic compounds and in welding.
2. (*plural*) a related series of aliphatic hydrocarbons forming a homologous series, general formula C_nH_{2n-2}. Also called the **acetylene series** or **alkyne series.**

acetylsalicylic acid
(*say* a–settil–salla–**sillik** assid)
see ASPIRIN.

ache (*rhymes with* take) *noun*
any dull, continuous pain.
Word Family: **ache,** *verb.*

achieve (*say* a–**cheev**) *verb*
to attain or accomplish something.
Word Family: **achiever,** *noun,* a person who achieves; **achievement,** *noun.*

Achilles' heel (*say* a–**killeez** heel)
a fatal weakness.

[after *Achilles,* a hero in Greek mythology, who was vulnerable only in the heel]

achromatic (*say* ay–kro–**mattik**) *adjective*
1. being colourless, and therefore composed of black, white and grey tones only.
2. *Physics:* (of a lens or mirror) having been corrected for chromatic aberration.
3. *Music:* without accidentals or changes in key.
[A– + Greek ***khroma*** colour]

acid (*say* **assid**) *noun*
1. *Chemistry:* a substance which liberates hydrogen ions when dissolved in water. *Example*: hydrochloric acid (formula HCl) dissociates in water to form one hydrogen ion (H^+) and one chloride ion (Cl^-). Compare BASE (1).
2. (*informal*) lysergic acid diethylamide (LSD).
acid *adjective*
sharp or bitter: a) 'an *acid* taste'; b) 'an *acid* comment'.
Word Family: **acidly,** *adverb*; **acidity,** *noun*; **acidify (acidified, acidifying),** *verb*; **acidic,** *adjective.*
[Latin *acidus* sour]

acid test
any decisive or crucial test.

acidulous (*say* a–**sid**–yoolus) *adjective*
slightly sour or caustic.
Word Family: **acidulate,** *verb,* to make or become sour.

ack–ack *noun*
anti–aircraft fire or guns.

acknowledge (*say* ak–**nollij**) *verb*
1. to confess or accept responsibility for: 'will you *acknowledge* your mistake?'.
2. to mention having received something, etc.: 'I'd like to *acknowledge* your letter'.
Word Family: **acknowledgement, acknowledgment,** *noun.*

acme (*say* **ak**–mee) *noun*
the peak or highest point: 'the *acme* of perfection'.
[Greek *akmé*]

acne (*say* **ak**–nee) *noun*
an inflammation of the skin, common in adolescence, causing pimples.

acolyte (*say* **akka**–lite) *noun*
1. *Christian:* a person who assists the priest at religious services, especially at the Eucharist. Also called a **server.**
2. any assistant or helper.
[Greek *akolouthos* follower]

acorn (*say* **ay**–korn) *noun*
the fruit of an oak tree, consisting of a nut with a cup–shaped base.

acoustic (*say* a–**koo**stik) **acoustical** *adjective*
a) of or relating to hearing. b) of or relating to the study of sound.
acoustics *plural noun*
1. (*used with singular verb*) a branch of physics which studies sound.
2. the properties of a particular space which determine the quality of sound.
Word Family: **acoustically,** *adverb.*
[Greek *akouein* to hear]

acoustic tile
a tile made of a soft substance such as cork, etc., used to absorb sound in buildings.

acquaint (*say* a–**kwaint**) *verb*
to make familiar: 'who will *acquaint* him with the facts?'.
acquaintance *noun*
1. familiarity: 'I have no *acquaintance* with the French language'.
2. a person known slightly, as distinct from a friend.

acquiesce (*say* ak–wee–**ess**) *verb*
to agree or submit passively: 'although I disagree with you, I will *acquiesce* to avoid argument'.
Word Family: **acquiescent,** *adjective*; **acquiescence,** *noun.*
[AC– + Latin *quiescere* to keep quiet]

acquire (*say* a–**kwire**) *verb*
to get or obtain.
Word Family: **acquisition** (*say* akwi–**zish**'n), **acquirement,** *nouns,* a) the act of acquiring, b) something which is acquired.

acquired taste
a liking for something gained through experience: 'a preference for blue cheeses is an *acquired taste*'.

acquisitive (*say* a–**kwizzi**–tiv) *adjective*
having a liking for or habit of acquiring or collecting things.
Word Family: **acquisitively,** *adverb.*

acquit (*say* a–**kwit**) *verb*
(acquitted, acquitting)
to declare a person free of guilt, especially in a court of law.
to acquit oneself, 'she *acquitted herself* well in the exam' (= performed).
Word Family: **acquittal,** *noun.*
[AC– + QUIT]

acre (*say* **ay**–ka) *noun*
a unit of area equal to about 0·4 hectare. See UNITS in grey pages.
acre–foot *noun*
a unit of volume for water, equal to an area of one acre to the depth of one foot, or approximately $1{\cdot}23\times10^3$ m^3. See UNITS in grey pages.
Word Family: **acreage**, *noun*, an area expressed in acres.

acrid *adjective*
sharp or biting: 'an *acrid* smell of burning rubber'.
[Latin *acer, acris* pungent]

Acrilan *noun*
an acrylic fibre used in textiles.
[a trademark]

acrimonious (*say* akra–**mo**–nee–us) *adjective*
bitter or resentful.
Word Family: **acrimony** (*say* **ak**rima–nee), *noun*.
[Latin *acrimonia* pungency]

acrobat (*say* **ak**ra–bat) *noun*
a skilled entertainer who performs tricks on a tightrope or trapeze.
acrobatics *plural noun*
1. the feats of an acrobat.
2. any elaborate or agile behaviour.
[Greek *akrobatos* walking on tiptoe]

acronym (*say* **ak**ra–nim) *noun*
a word formed from the first letter or letters of several words, such as ANZAC from *Australian and New Zealand Army Corps.*
[Greek *akros* top + *onyma* name]

acropolis (*say* a–**krop**pa–lis) *noun*
Ancient history: any citadel of a Greek city, especially the Acropolis in Athens.
[Greek *akros* top + *polis* city]

across *preposition, adverb*
1. from one side to the other:
(as a preposition) 'a track *across* the desert'.
(as an adverb) 'the river is 1 km *across*'.
2. on the opposite side of:
(as a preposition) 'the house *across* the street'.
(as an adverb) 'are you *across* yet?'.

acrostic (*say* a–**kross**–tik) *noun*
a poem in which the first or last letters of each line form a word.
[Greek *akron* end + *stikhos* row]

acrylic (*say* a–**krill**ik) *adjective*
being made from acrylic acid (formula $CH_2.CH.COOH$).

acrylic *noun*
a quick–drying paint based on acrylic resins and soluble in water.

acrylic resin
any of a group of colourless, transparent plastics which soften when heated, made by polymerizing derivatives of acrylic acid. It is often used to make substitutes for glass, such as Perspex.

act *noun*
1. a) anything done: 'an *act* of great bravery'. b) the process of doing: 'she was caught in the *act*'.
2. a law or decree, especially one passed by a parliament.
3. *Theatre:* a) a main division in a play or opera. b) a single item in a programme: 'the next *act* will be a juggler'.
act *verb*
1. to do or perform: 'he *acted* wisely'.
2. to take part in a play or film, especially imitating or representing a particular character.
act up, 'without its teacher, this class always *acts up*' (= misbehaves).
acting *adjective*
being a substitute for: 'he is the *acting* Prime Minister'.
Word Family: **acting**, *noun*, the profession of being an actor.
[Latin *actus*]

actinide *noun*
Chemistry: any of a group of rare metal elements, numbers 89–103 inclusive, similar to the lanthanides.

actinium *noun*
element number 89, a dense, radioactive metal found in combination with uranium. See ACTINIDE.
See CHEMICAL ELEMENTS in grey pages.
[Greek *aktinos* of a ray]

action (*say* **ak**–sh'n) *noun*
1. the process of acting or doing: 'is the machine in *action* yet?'.
Usage: 'the soldiers saw no *action* abroad' (= fighting, combat).
2. the manner of acting or operating: 'that racehorse has a very graceful *action*'.
3. any legal proceedings: 'they started an *action* against the company'.
4. (*informal*) lively or exciting occurrences: 'where's the *action* in this town?'.

action stations
the positions taken up in preparation for combat, activity, etc.

activate *verb*
1. to put into action or operation: 'press this button to *activate* the alarm'.
2. *Chemistry:* to treat a substance, such as charcoal, to increase its chemical activity.
Word Family: **activation** (*say* akti-vay-sh'n), *noun.*

active *adjective*
1. a) being in action: 'only one engine is *active*'. b) busy or lively: 'she leads an *active* life'.
2. *Grammar:* see VOICE.
Word Family: **actively**, *adverb.*

activist *noun*
a person who encourages and practises direct action, especially in politics.
Word Family: **activism**, *noun.*

activity *noun*
1. the state of being active: 'her life was one of constant *activity*'.
2. a pastime or occupation: 'swimming is usually a summer *activity*'.

act of God
Law: an event for which no person was responsible, such as a flood, earthquake, etc.

actor *noun*
a person who performs a role in a play, film, etc.
Word Family: **actress**, *noun*, a female actor.

actual (*say* **ak**-tew'l) *adjective*
real or existing.
Word Family: **actually**, *adverb*; **actuality**, *noun*; **actualize**, **actualise**, *verb*, to make actual; **actualization**, *noun.*

actuary (*say* **ak**-tew-a-ree) *noun*
Insurance: a person who calculates risks, rates, etc., based on recorded facts.
Word Family: **actuarial**, *adjective.*
[Latin *actuarius* a bookkeeper]

actuate (*say* **ak**-tew-ate) *verb*
to cause to act or move: 'this button *actuates* the engine'.
Word Family: **actuation**, *noun.*

acuity (*say* a-**kew**-it-ee) *noun*
sharpness: 'he has great *acuity* of vision'.
[Latin *acuere* to sharpen]

acumen (*say* **ak**-yoo-men) *noun*
a quickness of mind or perception.
[Latin, acuteness]

acupuncture (*say* **ak**-yoo-punkcher) *noun*
the Chinese technique of puncturing the skin with needles to reach the nerve areas, used as an anaesthetic or to treat and cure illness.
[Latin *acus* needle + PUNCTURE]

acute *adjective*
1. sharp or keen.
2. *Maths:* (of an angle) being less than 90°.
3. intense, severe and usually short-term: a) 'a boil is an *acute* local infection'; b) 'since the floods there has been an *acute* shortage of tomatoes'.
acute *noun*
Language: see ACCENT.
Word Family: **acutely**, *adverb*; **acuteness**, *noun.*
[Latin *acutus* sharp]

ad *noun*
(*informal*) an advertisement.
Word Family: **adman**, *noun*, a person involved in advertising; **admass**, *noun*, the general public, seen as an audience for advertising.

ad-
a prefix meaning in the direction of, towards, or in addition, as in *advent.* Variants of ad- are: **ac-** (*access*), **af-** (*affinity*), **ag-** (*aggression*), **al-** (*allegiance*), **an-** (*announce*), **ap-** (*approach*), **ar-** (*arrange*), **as-** (*assault*), **at-** (*attract*).

adage (*say* **addij**) *noun*
a proverb.

adagio (*say* a-**dah**-jee-o) *adverb*
Music: slowly or in a leisurely manner.
[Italian]

Adam *noun*
Biblical: the first man.
Phrases:
know someone from Adam, 'I wouldn't *know him from Adam*' (= know what he looks like).
the old Adam, 'drink brought out *the old Adam* in him' (= natural wickedness).

adamant (*say* **adda**-m'nt) *adjective*
stubborn or inflexible: 'she was *adamant* in her opinion'.
Word Family: **adamantine** (*say* adda-**man**-tine), *adjective*, very hard or impenetrable as, for example, a diamond.
[Greek *adamantinos* invincible]

Adam's apple
(*informal*) the larynx.

adapt (*say* a-**dapt**) *verb*
to alter or adjust: 'one must *adapt* to change'.

adaptation (*say* addap–**tay**–sh'n) *noun*
a) the act of adapting. b) anything which has been adapted: 'this film is an *adaptation* of a novel'.
Word Family: **adaptable** (*say* a–**dap**ta–b'l), *adjective,* easily or able to be adapted; **adaptability,** *noun.*
[AD– + Latin *aptus* suited]

adaptor *noun*
1. a person or thing that adapts.
2. a) any device which fits together parts of different sizes, etc. b) any device which modifies a machine or tool.

add *verb*
1. to find the sum of two or more numbers.
2. to join one thing to another: a) '*add* an extension to the house'; b) 'I'd like to *add* some advice'.
add up, 'your explanation does not *add up*' (= make sense).
Word Family: **addition,** *noun,* a) the act of adding, b) something which is added; **additional,** *adjective;* **additionally,** *adverb.*

addendum *noun*
plural is **addenda**
anything added, such as an appendix to a book.
[Latin]

adder *noun*
any of various kinds of snake, mostly poisonous, including the common European viper.

addict (*say* **add**ikt) *noun*
a person who cannot free himself from a particular habit, such as smoking.
Word Family: **addict** (*say* a–**dikt**), *verb;* **addiction,** *noun;* **addictive,** *adjective,* causing addiction.
[Latin *addictus* surrendered]

addition *noun*
Word Family: see ADD.

additive *noun*
anything which is added, such as preservatives in tinned foods.
Word Family: **additive,** *adjective.*

addled *adjective*
(of eggs) rotten.
Usage: 'he has an *addled* mind' (= confused, muddled).
Word Family: **addle,** *verb.*

address *noun*
1. a) the destination of a letter, parcel, etc., written on it. b) the place where someone lives or may be contacted.
2. a formal talk made to an audience.
3. any adroit or skilful behaviour: 'she handled the matter with great *address*'.
address *verb*
1. to speak to: 'in a debate speakers must *address* the chair'.
2. to write an address on: '*address* this letter'.
3. to direct attention or energy: 'he *addressed* himself to the task'.
Word Family: **addresser, addressor,** *noun,* a person who addresses; **addressee,** *noun,* one to whom something is addressed.

adduce (*say* a–**dewce**) *verb*
to offer or present in argument: 'he *adduced* several reasons for his behaviour'.
[Latin *adducere* to lead to]

adenine *noun*
Biology: see PURINE.

adenoids (*say* **adda**–noyds) *plural noun*
Anatomy: the lymphatic tissue, similar to the tonsils, in the cavity at the back of the nose, which may affect breathing and speech.
Word Family: **adenoidal,** *adjective.*
[Greek *aden* a gland]

adept (*say* **add**ept) *adjective*
highly skilled or clever.
Word Family: **adeptly,** *adverb;* **adeptness,** *noun;* **adept,** *noun,* a person who is skilled.
[Latin *adeptus* having attained]

adequate (*say* **addi**–kwit) *adjective*
sufficient or enough.
Word Family: **adequately,** *adverb;* **adequacy** (*say* **addi**–kwa–see), *noun.*
[AD– + Latin *aequus* equal]

adhere *verb*
to stick: a) 'the label must *adhere* to the bottle'; b) 'we must *adhere* to our plans'.
adhesion (*say* ad–**hee**–*zh*'n) *noun*
1. a) the act of adhering, such as the growing together of living tissues which are not usually joined. b) the state of being adhered.
2. *Physics:* the force holding molecules of different substances together. Compare COHESION.
adhesive *noun*
any substance, such as cement, etc., used for sticking two surfaces together.
Word Family: **adhesive,** *adjective;* **adhesiveness,** *noun;* **adherent,** *noun,* a person who follows or supports a cause, etc.; **adherent,** *adjective;* **adherence,** *noun.*
[Latin *adhaerere* to stick to]

ad hoc
for a special purpose: 'we will set up an *ad hoc* committee to deal with the matter'.
[AD– + Latin *hoc* this]

adiabatic (*say* addia–**battik**) *adjective*
Chemistry: (of a reaction or a system) taking place without absorbing or giving off energy.

adieu (*say* ad–**yer** *or* a–**dew**) *interjection*
goodbye.
[French *à Dieu* to God]

ad infinitum (*say* ad infi–**nite**–um)
without end.
[AD– + Latin *infinitum* infinity]

adios (*say* addi–**oss**) *interjection*
goodbye.
[Spanish]

adipose *adjective*
fatty.
[Latin *adipis* of fat]

adit *noun*
an entrance or corridor, especially a nearly horizontal, tunnel-like passage leading into a mine.
[Latin *aditus* an entrance]

adjacent (*say* a–**jay**–s'nt) *adjective*
next to or near: 'they occupied *adjacent* seats'.
[Latin *adjectus* something added]

adjective (*say* **ajjik**–tiv) *noun*
Grammar: any word which describes or adds to the meaning of a noun. *Example*: the *young* boy bought a *big* book.
Word Family: **adjectival** (*say* ajjik–**tie**–v'l), *adjective*; **adjectivally,** *adverb.*
[Latin *adjicere* to add]

adjoin *verb*
to be connected or next to: 'the bedroom *adjoins* the balcony'.
[AD– + Latin *jungere* to join]

adjourn (*say* a–**jern**) *verb*
to break off or postpone: 'the meeting was *adjourned* until the next day'.
Word Family: **adjournment,** *noun,* a) the act of adjourning, b) the state or time of being adjourned.
[AD– + Latin *diurnus* daily]

adjudge (*say* a–**juj**) *verb*
to pronounce a decision, as in a court of law: 'the prisoner was *adjudged* guilty'.

adjudicate (*say* a–**joodi**–kate) *verb*
to judge or settle a dispute, etc.
Word Family: **adjudication,** *noun*; **adjudicator,** *noun,* a person who adjudicates.

adjunct (*say* **ajjunkt**) *noun*
something added or attached.
[Latin *adjunctum* something connected]

adjure (*say* a–**joor**) *verb*
to solemnly command or request: 'he *adjured* me to silence'.
Word Family: **adjuration,** *noun.*
[AD– + Latin *jurare* to swear]

adjust (*say* a–**just**) *verb*
1. to change the shape, form or position of something, so that it fits: 'please *adjust* these brakes'.
2. to change oneself to match the circumstances: 'it is hard to *adjust* to a new way of life'.
Word Family: **adjustment,** *noun*; **adjustable,** *adjective.*

adjutant (*say* **ajjoo**–t'nt) *noun*
an officer acting as an administrative assistant to a commanding officer.
Word Family: **adjutancy,** *noun.*
[Latin *adjutare* to help]

ad lib
freely, or as one pleases.
Word Family: **ad–lib** (**ad–libbed, ad–libbing**), *verb,* to improvise.
[Latin *ad libitum* at pleasure]

administer, administrate *verb*
1. to manage or have charge of: 'the park is *administered* by the local council'.
2. to give or apply: 'the doctor *administered* first aid to the patient'.
Usage: 'the nurses *administered* to the wounded' (= gave help, etc.)
[Latin *administrare*]

administration
(*say* ad–minni–**stray**–sh'n) *noun*
1. the act of administering: 'the treasurer was gaoled for dishonest financial *administration*'.
2. a group of people appointed to govern, manage or have charge.
Word Family: **administrator,** *noun*; **administrative** (*say* ad–**minni**–stra–tiv), *adjective.*

admiral (*say* **adma**–r'l) *noun*
a commissioned officer of the highest or second highest rank in the navy.
Word Family: **Admiralty,** *noun,* the department that administers the navy.
[Arabic *amir al–* commander of the]

admire *verb*
to have a high regard or respect for: 'I *admire* the way she makes friends easily'.
Word Family: **admirable** (*say* **ad**mera-b'l), *adjective*, worthy or deserving to be admired; **admirably**, *adverb*; **admiration**, *noun*; **admiringly**, *adverb*; **admirer**, *noun*.
[Latin *admirari* to wonder at]

admissible *adjective*
capable or worthy of being allowed or considered: 'a letter is *admissible* evidence in a court of law'.
Word Family: **admissibility**, *noun*.

admission *noun*
1. a) the act of entering. b) the state of being allowed to enter.
2. the act of admitting something: 'he made an *admission* of guilt to his lawyer'.

admit *verb*
(admitted, admitting)
1. to give entrance to: 'dogs not *admitted*'.
2. to say that one is responsible for something: 'will you *admit* to eating all the ice-cream?'.
3. to agree that something is true or valid: 'will you *admit* that the ice-cream has disappeared?'.
Usage: 'the problem *admits* of no easy solution' (= has).
Word Family: **admittance**, *noun*, the right to enter; **admittedly**, *adverb*, without denial.
[Latin *admittere*]

admixture *noun*
1. the act of mixing.
2. a mixture or its ingredients.

admonish *verb*
to advise or warn in a firm but gentle manner.
Word Family: **admonition** (*say* adma-**nish**'n), *noun*; **admonitory**, *adjective*.
[Latin *admonere* to warn]

ad nauseam (*say* ad **nawzi**-am)
to a sickening length or extent.
[Latin]

ado (*say* a-**doo**) *noun*
any bustle, excitement or fuss.

adobe (*say* a-**doe**-bee) *noun*
a sun-dried, mud brick.
[Spanish *adobar* plaster]

adolescence (*say* adda-**less**'nce) *noun*
the period between puberty and adulthood.
Word Family: **adolescent**, *noun*, *adjective*.
[Latin *adolescere* to grow up]

adopt *verb*
1. to make a member of one's family by legal means: 'to *adopt* a child'.
2. to make one's own: 'to *adopt* the customs of a new country'.
3. to accept by vote: 'the committee *adopted* both suggestions'.
Word Family: **adoption**, *noun*; **adoptive**, *adjective*, related by adoption.
[Latin *adoptare*]

adore *verb*
1. to worship or love devotedly.
2. (*informal*) to like very much: 'I *adore* ice-cream'.
adorable *adjective*
enchanting or lovable: 'what an *adorable* puppy!'.
Word Family: **adoration**, *noun*; **adoringly**, *adverb*.
[Latin *adorare*]

adorn *verb*
to decorate or make beautiful: a) 'the crown was *adorned* with jewels'; b) 'his speech was *adorned* with elaborate phrases'.
Word Family: **adornment**, *noun*, a) the act of adorning, b) something which adorns.

adrenal (*say* a-**dreen**'l) *adjective*
being near the kidneys.
adrenal gland
Anatomy: either of two small glands forming a cap over each kidney and secreting hormones, including adrenalin, which control a wide range of body functions.
[AD- + Latin *renes* the kidneys]

adrenalin (*say* a-**drenna**-lin)
adrenaline *noun*
a hormone which is secreted by the adrenal gland and stimulates the heart at times of emotional stress.

adrift *adverb*
loose or drifting.

adroit (*say* a-**droyt**) *adjective*
skilful or clever: 'she is very *adroit* in weaving'.
Word Family: **adroitly**, *adverb*; **adroitness**, *noun*.
[French *à droit* rightly]

adsorb *verb*
(of a substance) to cling to the surface of another material, e.g. water to skin. Compare ABSORB.

Word Family: **adsorbent,** *adjective*; **adsorption,** *noun.*
[AD– + Latin *sorbere* to suck]

adulation (*say* ad–yoo–lay–sh'n) *noun*
any excessive praise or flattery.
Word Family: **adulate,** *verb*; **adulatory,** *adjective.*
[Latin *adulare* to fawn like a dog]

adult *noun*
a fully grown, mature animal or plant.
Word Family: **adulthood,** *noun.*
[Latin *adultus*]

adulterate (*say* a–**dulta**–rate) *verb*
to lower the quality or make impure, especially by adding inferior substances: 'this milk is *adulterated* with water'.
adulteration *noun*
a) the act of adulterating. b) an adulterated substance or condition: 'this fruit drink is an *adulteration*'.
Word Family: **adulterate,** *adjective*; **adulterant,** *noun,* a substance which adulterates.
[Latin *adulterare* to defile or alter]

adultery (*say* a–**dulta**–ree) *noun*
the act of a married person having sexual intercourse with a person other than his or her spouse.
Word Family: **adulterer, adulteress,** *nouns*; **adulterous,** *adjective.*
[Latin *adulterare*]

adumbrate (*say* **addam**–brate) *verb*
to give only a faint or shadowy outline, especially of something in the future: 'the scheme is complex, but I will *adumbrate* its main points'.
Word Family: **adumbration,** *noun.*
[Latin *adumbrare* to sketch in outline]

ad valorem (*say* ad val–**or**–em)
Commerce: (of a tax) proportional to the value of the thing taxed.
[Latin, according to value]

advance *verb*
to move forward: a) 'the troops *advanced* towards the enemy'; b) 'how far have you *advanced* with your music lessons?'.
Usages:
a) 'the bank *advanced* me £100' (= lent).
b) 'being rude will not *advance* your cause' (= assist).
c) 'the shares *advanced* on the stock exchange' (= rose in price).
advance *noun*
1. a forward movement or progress: 'have you made any *advance* in your inquiries?'.
2. something done or given before it is actually due, such as a loan or an early payment of a wage.
Usage: 'the boy encouraged her *advances*' (= attempts to establish friendly relations).
in advance, 'rent must be paid one month *in advance*' (= ahead).
Word Family: **advancement,** *noun.*

advantage (*say* ad–**vahntij**) *noun*
1. anything which is favourable or profitable: 'you will not gain any *advantage* by shouting'.
2. *Tennis:* the first point after a score of deuce. Short form is **vantage** or **van.**
take advantage of, a) 'we *took advantage of* the shelter' (= made use of); b) 'she always *takes advantage of* his weakness' (= exploits).
Word Family: **advantage,** *verb,* to help; **advantageous,** *adjective*; **advantageously,** *adverb.*

advection *noun*
Physics: the transfer of heat or particles by the horizontal motion of gases, especially air. Compare CONVECTION.
[AD– + Latin *vectus* carried]

advent *noun*
1. a coming or arrival: 'we'll have to buy warm clothes with the *advent* of winter'.
2. *Christian:* (*capital*) the festival which includes the four Sundays immediately preceding Christmas.
[Latin *adventus* coming]

adventitious (*say* adven–**tishus**) *adjective*
1. occurring by chance or accident.
2. *Biology:* occurring in an unusual place, e.g. roots which may grow from branches.
[Latin *adventicius* not normally pertaining to]

adventure *noun*
a dangerous or exciting activity or experience.
adventurous *adjective*
1. exciting: 'an *adventurous* expedition through the jungle'.
2. willing to seek or risk danger: 'an *adventurous* young explorer'.
Word Family: **adventure,** *verb*; **adventurer,** *noun*; **adventurously,** *adverb.*

adverb *noun*
Grammar: any word which adds to the meaning of a verb, adjective or other adverb, by telling how, why,

when or where an action takes place. *Example*: the boy walked *slowly* home. *Word Family:* **adverbial,** *adjective.*

adverse *adjective*
unfavourable or opposing one's interests: '*adverse* weather prevented the picnic'.
Word Family: **adversary,** *noun,* an opponent.
[Latin *adversus* opposite]
Common Error: ADVERSE, AVERSE both describe opposition, but *adverse* refers to something which is different from what is expected or desired and suggests misfortune, whereas *averse* means unwilling or reluctant to do something.

adversity *noun*
any hardship or misfortune: 'in times of *adversity* we seek help'.

advert (*say* ad-**vert**) *verb*
to refer to something: 'the lecturer *adverted* to the approaching exams'.
[Latin *advertere* to turn towards]

advertise *verb*
to promote or make known to the public, especially through the media: 'the job was *advertised* in several newspapers'.
advertisement (*say* ad-**vertis**-m'nt) *noun*
short form is **ad** or **advert** (*say* **ad**-vert)
a public notice or announcement offering service, goods for sale, etc.
advertising *noun*
1. the use of advertisements.
2. the business of creating, producing and circulating advertisements.
Word Family: **advertiser,** *noun.*

advice *noun*
1. an opinion or suggestion: 'we need an expert's *advice* to solve this problem'.
2. a piece of information: 'we received *advice* from the bank that the money had arrived from France'.

advisable (*say* ad-**vize**-a-b'l) *adjective*
being the sensible or recommended thing to do: 'it is *advisable* to wear a life-jacket when sailing in a small boat'.
Word Family: **advisably,** *adverb*; **advisability,** *noun.*

advise (*say* ad-**vize**) *verb*
to give advice to: 'she *advised* me to get a haircut'.
advisory *adjective*
1. of or giving advice: 'she said a few *advisory* words'.
2. having the duty or power to advise: 'we will appoint an *advisory* committee'.
Word Family: **advisedly,** *adverb,* after careful thought; **adviser,** *noun.*
[AD- + Latin *visum* according to what seems best]

advocate (*say* **adva**-kit) *noun*
1. a person who recommends or supports a particular cause: 'she is an *advocate* of abortion reform'.
2. a person, especially a barrister, who presents a case for, or speaks on behalf of, another.
advocate (*say* **adva**-kate) *verb*
to urge or support, especially by argument.
Word Family: **advocacy,** *noun.*
[Latin *advocare* to call in as legal adviser]

adze *noun*
in America spelt **adz**
a tool with a broad steel blade set at right angles to the handle, used for shaving or shaping wood.

aegis (*say* **ee**-jis) *noun*
any protection or patronage: 'under the *aegis* of the King the subjects grew prosperous'.
[after *aigis*, the shield of Zeus in Greek mythology]

aegrotat (*say* **eye**-gro-tat) *noun*
a) a certificate that a student is too ill to sit an exam. b) a pass granted for that reason.
[Latin, he is sick]

aeolian (*say* ee-**ole**-ee-an) *adjective*
a) windswept. b) transported or deposited by wind, e.g. desert sands.
[after *Aeolus*, the lord of the winds in Greek mythology]

aeon (*say* **ee**-on) **eon** *noun*
an immensely long period of time.
[Greek *aion* an age]

aerate (*say* **air**-rate) *verb*
to add air or gas to a liquid under pressure, as in making lemonade.
Word Family: **aeration** (*say* air-**ray**-sh'n), *noun*; **aerator,** *noun,* a device used to aerate liquids.

aerial (*say* **airiul**) *noun*
also called an **antenna**
a device which receives or sends out radio waves.
aerial *adjective*
a) of or existing in the air: 'this tree has *aerial* roots'. b) from the air: '*aerial* bombardment'.
[Greek *aër* air]

aerobatics (*say* aira-**battiks**) *plural noun*

any acrobatics carried out by an aeroplane, such as loops or dives.
Word Family: **aerobatic**, *adjective.*
[AERO(plane) + (acro)BATICS]

aerobe (*say* **air**–robe) *noun*
any organism which requires oxygen to live. Compare ANAEROBE.
Word Family: **aerobic** (*say* air–**ro**–bik), *adjective.*
[Greek *aër* air + *bios* life]

aerodrome (*say* **aira**–drome) *noun*
an airport, especially a small one.
[AERO(plane) + Greek *dromos* a running track]

aerodynamics (*say* airo–die–**nammiks**) *plural noun*
(*used with singular verb*) the study of the motion of gases, especially in relation to moving or flying objects.

aerofoil (*say* **airo**–foil) *noun*
any surface on an aircraft, such as a wing or tail, which deflects the passing airstream to provide lift or control.

aerogramme *noun*
see AIRLETTER.

aeronautics (*say* aira–**nawtiks**) *plural noun*
(*used with singular verb*) the study of flight, especially of aircraft.
Word Family: **aeronaut**, *noun*, a person who travels in an aircraft, such as a balloon; **aeronautical**, *adjective.*
[AERO(plane) + NAUTIC(al)]

aeroplane (*say* **aira**–plane) *noun*
an aircraft which is heavier than air and is driven by jet engines or propellers.
[Greek *aër* air + *planos* wandering]

aerosol (*say* **aira**–sol) *noun*
1. *Physics:* a state where a solid or liquid is dispersed as fine particles in a gas.
2. a can or container with a substance, such as perfume, stored under pressure and released as an aerosol.
[Greek *aër* air + SOL(ution)]

aerospace *adjective*
of or relating to the earth's atmosphere and the space outside it, in which spacecraft travel.

aesthetic (*say* ees–**thettik**) *adjective*
in America spelt **esthetic**
relating to the appreciation of beauty: 'the old building was saved for *aesthetic* rather than practical reasons'.

aesthetics *plural noun*
(*used with singular verb*) a branch of philosophy dealing with the principles and judgements of art and beauty.

aesthete (*say* **ees**–theet) *noun*
a) a person who cultivates sensitivity and a love of beauty. b) a person whose sensitivity is considered to be affected or excessive.
Word Family: **aesthetically**, *adverb.*
[Greek *aisthetikos* concerning the senses]
Common Error: do not confuse with ASCETIC.

aether (*say* **eetha**) *noun*
see ETHER.

aethereal (*say* ee–**theeriul**) *adjective*
see ETHEREAL.

aetiology (*say* eeti–**olla**–jee) *noun*
also spelt **etiology**
the study of causes, especially the causes of disease.
Word Family: **aetiologist**, *noun.*

af–
a variant of the prefix **ad–**.

afar *adverb*
far away: 'we could see the city lights from *afar*'.

affable (*say* **affa**–b'l) *adjective*
friendly or pleasant.
Word Family: **affably**, *adverb*; **affability**, *noun.*
[Latin *affabilis* that can be easily spoken to]

affair *noun*
1. (*usually plural*) any particular interests: 'the *affairs* of state must be dealt with first'.
2. a particular event or matter: 'have you heard any details of that kidnapping *affair*?'.
3. a sexual relationship between two people who are not married to each other. Short form of **love affair.**

affect (1) *verb*
to act on or influence: 'the sight of the accident did not *affect* me at all'.
Word Family: **affect**, *noun*, (Psychology) emotion; **affecting**, *adjective*, moving; **affective**, *adjective*, emotional.
[Latin *afficere* to do something to]
Common Error: do not confuse with EFFECT.

affect (2) *verb*
1. to pretend or imitate: a) 'he *affected* complete innocence about the trick'; b) 'Sally *affects* the manners of a princess'.
2. to inhabit: 'tree ferns *affect* the mossy banks of the creek'.

Word Family: **affectation** (*say* affek–**tay**–sh'n), *noun*, a pretended or artificial manner, etc.

affection *noun*
any liking or warm feeling: 'she greeted her daughter with *affection*'.
Word Family: **affectionate,** *adjective,* showing affection; **affectionately,** *adverb.*
[Latin *affectio* goodwill]

afferent (*say* **affa**–r'nt) *adjective*
Medicine: leading towards a central organ. Compare EFFERENT.
[Latin *afferre* to bring to]

affiance (*say* a–**fie**'nce) *verb*
an old word meaning to betroth.

affidavit (*say* affi–**day**vit) *noun*
Law: a written statement made under oath.
[Latin, he has sworn]

affiliate (*say* a–**filli**–ate) *verb*
to join or unite, especially as part of something larger: 'the local associations are now *affiliated* with the national body'.
Word Family: **affiliation,** *noun.*
[Latin *affiliare* to adopt as a son]

affinity *noun*
1. a mutual attraction or resemblance.
2. any relationship through marriage. Compare CONSANGUINITY.
3. *Chemistry:* the force holding atoms together, especially atoms of the same element.
Word Family: **affinitive,** *adjective.*
[Latin *affinitas*]

affirm *verb*
1. to firmly declare or confirm: 'I *affirm* my right to decide for myself'.
2. *Law:* to solemnly promise to tell the truth, as distinct from making a formal oath.
affirmative *adjective*
being in agreement: 'he gave an *affirmative* answer'.
Word Family: **affirmatively,** *adverb*; **affirmation** (*say* affa–**may**–sh'n), *noun.*
[Latin *affirmare* to make firm]

affix (*say* a–**fix**) *verb*
to attach or fasten: 'he *affixed* two stamps to the envelope'.
affix (*say* **affix**) *noun*
1. *Grammar:* any of various forms which can be added to a word to change its meaning. A **prefix** is added at the beginning of a word, as *de–* in *devalue,* whereas a **suffix** is added at the end of a word, as *–ness* in *kindness.*
2. something which is added or attached.
[Latin *affixus* fastened]

afflatus (*say* a–**flay**–tus) *noun*
a creative inspiration.
[Latin, a breathing upon]

afflict *verb*
to trouble or cause distress: 'he is *afflicted* with gout'.
Word Family: **affliction,** *noun.*
[Latin *afflictus* distressed]

affluence (*say* **aff**–loo'nce) *noun*
any wealth or abundance, especially of possessions: 'the size of their house is one indication of their *affluence*'.
Word Family: **affluent,** *adjective.*
[Latin *affluens* abounding in]
Common Error: do not confuse with EFFLUENCE.

afford *verb*
1. to have enough of something for a particular purpose: a) 'I cannot *afford* a new coat this winter'; b) 'no–one can *afford* to miss the next lecture'.
2. to give: 'it *affords* me great pleasure'.

afforestation (*say* afforris–**tay**–sh'n) *noun*
the planting of trees to form forests.
Word Family: **afforest,** *verb.*

affray *noun*
a noisy quarrel or brawl.

affright *verb*
an old word meaning to frighten or terrify.
Word Family: **affright,** *noun.*

affront (*say* a–**frunt**) *verb*
to upset or offend: 'I was *affronted* by his rudeness'.
Word Family: **affront,** *noun.*

Afghan (*say* **af**–gan) *noun*
1. a native of Afghanistan. Also called an **Afghani** (*say* af–**gah**–nee).
2. any of a breed of large, long–haired hounds, originally from Afghanistan.

aficionado (*say* a–fish–ya–**nah**doe) *noun*
an enthusiastic follower.
[Spanish]

afield (*say* a–**feeld**) *adverb*
away, especially from home: 'do not go too far *afield*'.

afire *adverb, adjective*
on fire.

aflame *adverb, adjective*
flaming or glowing: 'her face was *aflame* with delight'.

afloat *adverb, adjective*
floating or carried on water: 'the lifeboat stayed *afloat* for several days'.
Usage: 'the government has provided loans to keep the corporation *afloat*' (= in business).

afoot *adverb, adjective*
in progress: 'there is trouble *afoot*'.

afore *adverb, preposition*
an old word meaning before, now found only in compound words such as *aforethought.*

aforesaid *adjective*
also called **aforementioned**
Law: said or mentioned earlier.

aforethought (*say* a-**for**-thawt) *adjective*
Law: premeditated: 'the crime was committed with malice *aforethought*'.

afoul *adverb*
entangled: 'the nets are *afoul* under the water'.
run afoul of, 'she has *run afoul of* the police' (= become entangled with).

afraid *adjective*
feeling fear or apprehension: 'I'm *afraid* of the dark'.
Usage: 'I'm *afraid* we cannot come tonight' (= regretful).

afresh *adverb*
again: 'you must start *afresh*'.

Afrikaans (*say* afri-**kahns**) *noun*
one of the official languages of the republic of South Africa, derived from 17th-century Dutch.

Afrikaner (*say* afri-**kahna**) *noun*
a) a person born in South Africa of European, usually Dutch, descent. b) a person who speaks Afrikaans.

Afro *noun*
a bushy hairstyle with frizzy curls, based on an African style.

aft *adverb, adjective*
Nautical: towards the stern of a boat. Compare FORE (1).

after *preposition, adverb, conjunction, adjective*
later or behind:
(as a preposition) 'he came *after* me'.
(as an adverb) 'the dog trotted *after*'.
(as a conjunction) '*after* we left'.
(as an adjective) 'the *after* parts of a boat'.
Usages:
a) 'they asked *after* you' (= about).
b) 'a man *after* my own heart' (= in agreement with).
c) 'he paints *after* Nolan's style' (= in imitation of).
d) 'who are you named *after*?' (= in honour of).
after all, 'we are able to come *after all*' (= in spite of everything).

afterbirth *noun*
the placenta expelled from the uterus after birth.

after-effect *noun*
the delayed result of something: 'the operation has had no *after-effects*'.

afterlife *noun*
life after death.

aftermath *noun*
the time or conditions after something: 'they discovered much damage in the *aftermath* of the storm'.

afternoon *noun*
the time of day between noon and sunset.

aftertaste *noun*
a taste or sensation which lingers.

afterthought *noun*
an idea or reflection which comes to mind after an event: 'that outhouse was added as an *afterthought*'.

afterwards *adverb*
later: 'I'm too busy now, but I'll speak to you *afterwards*'.

ag-
a variant of the prefix **ad-**.

aga (*say* **ah**-ga) **agha** *noun*
a title of honour in Moslem countries. [Turkish, master]

again *adverb*
1. once more or another time: 'let us try *again*'.
2. besides or on the other hand: 'we may come, but then *again* we may not'.

against *preposition*
not in favour of: 'I'm *against* the idea of Saturday morning school'.
Usages:
a) 'he fell heavily *against* the chair' (= in collision with).
b) 'we must save *against* the possibility of no work' (= in preparation for).
c) 'the trees stood out *against* the sky' (= in contrast with).

agapanthus *noun*
a blue and white South African flower related to the lily.
[Greek *agapé* love + *anthos* flower]

agape (*say* a-**gape**) *adverb*
with the mouth wide open: 'he stood *agape* in horror at the sight'.

agar (*say* **ay**-gar) *noun*
short form of **agar-agar**

a substance obtained from seaweed, used in cooking and to make jellies of liquid nutrient material on which micro-organisms are grown.
[Malay]

agate (*say* **aggit**) ***noun***
1. *Geology:* see CHALCEDONY.
2. a playing marble, usually made of glass in imitation of chalcedony.
[Greek *Akhates*, a river in Sicily where first found]

age ***noun***
1. the length of time during which something has existed: 'she is 12 years of *age*'.
2. a particular period of time in history: a) 'the Ice *Age*'; b) 'the Middle *Ages*'.
Usage: 'I've been waiting here for *ages*' (= a long time).
age *verb*
1. to become or appear older: 'he has *aged* a lot since we last saw him'.
2. to allow wine, etc. to stand so that it matures or becomes mellow.
aged *adjective*
1. (*say* **ayjd**) having the age of: 'a boy *aged* 13'.
2. (*say* **ay**-jid) old: 'an *aged* grandparent'.
Word Family: **ageless**, *adjective*, a) not growing or seeming to grow old, b) without definable age.

agency (*say* **ay**-j'n-see) ***noun***
1. a business organization which provides a particular service: 'an employment *agency*'.
2. anything which acts or produces a result: 'it was achieved through the *agency* of his friends'.

agenda (*say* a-**jen**da) ***plural noun***
singular is **agendum**
(***used with singular verb***) any matters to be dealt with or introduced, usually in the form of a list: 'an *agenda* has been prepared for the meeting'.

agent (*say* **ay**-j'nt) ***noun***
1. anything which produces an effect or result: 'storms can be *agents* of destruction'.
2. a person who has authority to act for another person, company or a government.
3. *Chemistry:* any substance causing a reaction.
[Latin *agens* acting]

agent provocateur (*say* **ar***zh***on** pro-vokka-**ter**)
plural is **agents provocateurs**
a person paid, especially by a government, to foment illegal acts in order to unmask possible trouble-makers.
[French *agent* agent + *provocateur* provoking]

agglomerate (*say* a-**glomm**a-rate) ***verb***
to collect into a mass or cluster.
agglomerate (*say* a-**glomm**a-rit) ***noun***
Geology: a rock composed of large volcanic fragments.
Word Family: **agglomeration**, ***noun***.
[AG- + Latin *glomeris* of a ball]

agglutination (*say* a-glooti-**nay**-sh'n) ***noun***
the process of fusing or massing together, e.g. cells or particles into larger clumps.
Word Family: **agglutinate**, *verb*; **agglutinate**, *adjective*.
[AG- + Latin *glutinis* of glue]

aggradation (*say* agra-**day**-sh'n) ***noun***
Geography: the process of a river depositing sediment on its bed, thereby raising its level.
Word Family: **aggrade**, *verb*.
[AG- + Latin *gradus* a step]

aggrandizement (*say* a-**grand**iz-m'nt)
aggrandisement ***noun***
an increase in size, strength, wealth, importance, etc.: 'he is ambitious and seeks personal *aggrandizement*'.
Word Family: **aggrandize**, *verb*.

aggravate (*say* **agra**-vate) ***verb***
to irritate or make more intense: a) 'eating onions will only *aggravate* your indigestion'; b) 'don't *aggravate* the dog by teasing him'.
Word Family: **aggravation**, ***noun***.
[AG- + Latin *gravis* heavy]

aggregate (*say* **agri**-git) ***noun***
1. a) a number of separate things brought together in a group. b) a total.
2. a mixture of different minerals used in making concrete, etc.
aggregation (*say* agri-**gay**-sh'n) ***noun***
1. any collection or total forming a unified whole.
2. *Biology:* a group of organisms living close together.
Word Family: **aggregate** (*say* **agri**-gate), *verb*.
[AG- + Latin *gregis* of a flock]

aggression (*say* aggre**sh**'n) ***noun***
1. a hostile act, especially if unprovoked.
2. the tendency to attack or be hostile.
Word Family: **aggressive**, *adjective*, feeling or showing aggression; **aggressor**, ***noun***, a person or thing that

is aggressive; **aggressiveness**, *noun*; **aggressively**, *adverb*.
[Latin *aggressio*]

aggrieve (*say* a–**greev**) *verb*
to pain or make resentful: 'mother was *aggrieved* by the rareness of our visits home'.

aggro *noun*
(*informal*) any aggressiveness, especially if deliberate or for perverse excitement.

aghast (*say* a–**gahst**) *adjective*
amazed and horrified: 'I'm *aghast* at your suggestion'.

agile (*say* **aj**–ile) *adjective*
quick or nimble.
Word Family: **agility**, *noun*; **agilely**, *adverb*.
[Latin *agilis* nimble]

agistment (*say* a–**jist**–m'nt) *noun*
the renting of pasture to another person for use by his horses or cattle.
Word Family: **agist**, *verb*.

agitate (*say* **aj**ji–tate) *verb*
1. to shake or move rapidly from side to side: 'the clothes in the washing machine were *agitated* in the soapy water'.
2. to disturb or excite: 'she became *agitated* after the accident'.
3. to arouse public feelings about something, such as a political or social reform.
agitator *noun*
1. a machine or device for stirring or shaking.
2. a person who agitates: 'the student was well-known as a political *agitator*'.
Word Family: **agitation**, *noun*; **agitatedly**, *adverb*.
[Latin *agitare* to shake]

aglow (*say* a–**glo**) *adverb*
glowing: 'her cheeks were *aglow* with health'.

agnostic (*say* ag–**noss**–tik) *noun*
a person who believes that one cannot know whether God exists. Compare ATHEIST.
Word Family: **agnosticism** (*say* ag–**noss**ti–sizm), *noun*.
[A– + Greek *gnostikos* knowing]

ago *adverb*
in the past: 'it happened long *ago*'.

agog *adverb*
eager or excited: 'we are all *agog* for news'.

agony (*say* **agga**–nee) *noun*
a state of extreme pain or anguish: 'the injury caused him great *agony*'.
agonize, agonise *verb*
to suffer agony or intense worry: 'do not *agonize* over your mistake'.
Word Family: **agonizingly**, *adverb*.
[Greek *agonia* a struggle, anguish]

agora (*say* **agga**–ra) *noun*
an open marketplace or place of assembly in ancient Greece.
[Greek]

agoraphobia (*say* agra–**fo**–bea) *noun*
an abnormal fear of open spaces.
[AGORA + PHOBIA]

agouti (*say* a–**goo**–tee) *noun*
a short-haired, short-eared rodent found in South America and the West Indies.

agrarian (*say* a–**grair**iun) *adjective*
relating to farming land or agriculture.
[Latin *ager* field]

agree *verb*
1. to decide in favour of a request, suggestion, etc.: 'I *agreed* to help'.
2. to hold or come to the same idea, etc.: 'we all *agreed* that the film was good'.
3. to exist without difference or friction: a) 'the children rarely *agree*'; b) 'your story *agrees* with what your sister said'.
agree with, 'spicy foods don't *agree with* me' (= suit).
agreement *noun*
1. the fact of thinking the same things or in the same way: 'everyone was in *agreement* about the quality of the film'.
2. an arrangement: 'we came to an *agreement* with the landlord about the repairs'.
3. a contract.

agreeable *adjective*
1. to one's liking: a) 'she has an *agreeable* smile'; b) 'do you find your new job *agreeable*?'.
2. willing or ready to agree: 'I'm *agreeable* to either plan'.
Word Family: **agreeably**, *adverb*; **agreeableness, agreeability**, *nouns*.

agriculture (*say* **agri**–kulcher) *noun*
the use of land for planting and growing crops, and raising animals.
Word Family: **agricultural**, *adjective*; **agriculturally**, *adverb*; **agriculturist, agriculturalist**, *nouns*.
[Latin *ager* field + *cultura* a tilling]

agronomy (*say* a-**gronn**a-mee) *noun*
the application of scientific principles to the growing of crops.
Word Family: **agronomist,** *noun.*
[Greek *agros* land + *nomos* an arrangement]

aground *adverb*
(of a boat) touching the ground in shallow water, so that it is stranded.

ague (*say* **ay**-gew) *noun*
a) malaria. b) a fever accompanied by chills and shivering.
[for ACUTE (fever)]

ahead *adverb*
in front or forward: 'walk *ahead* of us'.
go ahead, 'please *go ahead* with your argument' (= continue).

ahoy *interjection*
Nautical: a call to attract attention.

aid *noun*
1. any help or assistance: 'we must have the *aid* of a doctor'.
2. something which helps: 'films, maps, and other teaching *aids*'.
in aid of, 'what is all this noise *in aid of*?' (= for).
Word Family: **aid,** *verb.*

aide *noun*
an assistant.
[French]

aide-de-camp (*say* ay-der-**kom**) *noun*
plural is **aides-de-camp**
an officer acting as personal assistant and secretary to a general, governor, etc.
[AIDE + French *de camp* at camp]

aigrette *noun*
a) a tuft of feathers worn to decorate a hat. b) a spray of jewels imitating this.
[French]

ail *verb*
to trouble or feel pain, discomfort, etc.: a) 'what *ails* you?'; b) 'my children *ail* without proper food'.

aileron (*say* ayla-ron) *noun*
a movable, hinged section mounted near the trailing edge of an aeroplane wing and used to control balance.
[French, small wing]

ailment *noun*
any mild illness: 'a cold is a common *ailment*'.

aim *verb*
1. to point or direct towards something: 'he carefully *aimed* his gun at the target'.
2. to have a purpose or intention: 'where do you *aim* to go first?'.
Word Family: **aim,** *noun*; **aimless,** *adjective,* without purpose; **aimlessness,** *noun*; **aimlessly,** *adverb.*

air *noun*
1. the gases surrounding the earth.
2. a simple tune or melody.
3. a particular manner or appearance: 'she has the *air* of a kind, gentle person'.
Phrases:
off the air, (of a radio station) no longer broadcasting.
on the air, (of a radio station) broadcasting.
put on airs, put on airs and graces, 'he *put on airs* to impress us' (= behaved affectedly).
up in the air, 'the decision is still *up in the air*' (= uncertain).
air *verb*
to expose to the air: 'we must *air* the spare room to get rid of the smell'.
Usage: 'he *airs* his new ideas at parties' (= circulates, tests).
Word Family: **airless,** *adjective,* a) having no air, b) having no fresh air.
[Greek *aër*]

air-base *noun*
an airfield used as a base for military aircraft.

air-bed *noun*
an inflatable mattress.

airborne *adjective*
being in the air.

air-brake *noun*
1. a brake operated by air-pressure.
2. a hinged panel set in the wing or body of an aeroplane, used to reduce its speed. Also called a **flap.**

air-brush *noun*
an atomizer capable of producing a fine spray of ink or paint.

air chief marshal
a commissioned officer in the airforce, equal in rank to a general.

air commodore
a commissioned officer in the airforce, above the rank of group captain.

air-conditioning *noun*
the process of controlling temperature, moisture and dust content of air in a building.
Word Family: **air-condition,** *verb*; **air-conditioner,** *noun.*

air-cool *verb*
to remove heat by means of a stream of air.

air-corridor *noun*
a route along which aircraft are permitted to fly in an otherwise prohibited area.

aircraft *noun*
plural is **aircraft**
any vehicle which is capable of flight, such as an aeroplane or helicopter.

aircraft-carrier *noun*
a warship with a very large upper deck (the **flight deck**), for carrying, launching or receiving aircraft.

aircraftman *noun*
a) the lowest rank in the airforce. b) a person with this rank.

aircrew *noun*
the personnel in an aircraft.

air-cushion *noun*
the layer of high-pressure air, produced by fans, which lifts and supports a Hovercraft, etc.

airdrop *noun*
the dropping of troops or supplies by parachute from an aircraft.

Airedale *noun*
any of a breed of large, wire-haired terriers.
[first bred in Yorkshire]

airfield *noun*
a large, open, level area with runways, buildings, etc. for the operation and maintenance of aircraft.

airforce *noun*
the armed forces of a country concerned with fighting in the air.

airfreight (*say* **air-frate**) *noun*
a) any cargo carried by aircraft. b) its cost: 'what is the *airfreight* to Sydney?'

airgun *noun*
a gun using compressed air to fire pellets or darts.

air-hostess *noun*
a female who attends to the needs of passengers on an aeroplane.

airily *adverb*
Word Family: see AIRY.

airlane *noun*
any route specified for regular use by commercial aircraft.

airless *adjective*
Word Family: see AIR.

airletter *noun*
also called an **aerogramme**
a letter consisting of a single sheet of paper which is folded and sent by air mail without an envelope.

airlift *noun*
the transporting of large numbers of people or goods by aircraft, often in an emergency.

airline *noun*
any organization which provides scheduled air transport between specified points.
airliner *noun*
any large passenger or cargo-carrying aircraft.

airlock *noun*
1. an airtight compartment at the entrance of a pressure chamber, to prevent loss of pressure or gases when the chamber is entered.
2. a stoppage of the flow of liquid in a pipe, caused by an air bubble.

air mail
the carrying of post in aircraft. Compare SURFACE MAIL.
Word Family: **airmail**, *adjective.*

airman *noun*
a member of an aircrew, especially in the airforce.

air marshal
a commissioned officer in the airforce, equal in rank to a lieutenant-general.

air-pocket *noun*
a downward current of air causing an aircraft to drop suddenly.

airport *noun*
a large airfield with runways, hangars, workshops and one or more passenger terminals.

air-raid *noun*
an attack by enemy aircraft, especially bombers.

air-sac *noun*
any of the millions of small cavities in the lungs, where oxygen is absorbed into the blood and carbon dioxide is released.

airscrew *noun*
an aeroplane propeller.

airship *noun*
any aircraft lighter than air, with a rigid structure containing hydrogen or helium gas, driven by propellers and able to be steered.

airspace *noun*
the space above an area or country.

air speed
the speed of an aircraft relative to the air around it. Compare GROUND SPEED.

airstream *noun*
1. a flow of air, especially past a flying aeroplane.
2. a wind, especially at high altitude.

airstrip *noun*
a) a runway. b) an airfield for small aircraft, especially if in a remote area or privately owned.

air-terminal *noun*
a building, including offices, where aircraft passengers assemble.

airtight *adjective*
not allowing the passage of air.

air vice-marshal
a commissioned officer in the airforce, equal in rank to a major-general.

airworthy *adjective*
(of an aircraft) meeting certain safety requirements for flight.
Word Family: **airworthiness,** *noun.*

airy *adjective*
1. open to the passage of air: 'this is a very *airy* room'.
2. light or carefree: 'she apologized in an *airy* manner'.
Word Family: **airiness,** *noun*; **airily,** *adverb.*

airy-fairy *adjective*
(*informal*) light or fanciful: 'he is full of *airy-fairy* ideas'.

aisle (*say* ile) *noun*
any passage between blocks of seats, as in a theatre.

aitchbone *noun*
the pelvic bone of an animal, or a cut of meat containing this bone.

ajar (*say* a-**jar**) *adverb, adjective*
(of a door) partly open.

akimbo *adverb*
having the hands on the hips, with the elbows pointed outwards.

akin (*say* a-**kin**) *adjective*
similar or related: 'your fears are *akin* to superstition'.

al-
a variant of the prefix **ad-**.

alabaster *noun*
a white or tinted, fine-grained gypsum or a banded variety of calcite, used for ornaments and statues.
Word Family: **alabaster,** *adjective,* a) made of alabaster, b) smooth, white or cold like alabaster.
[Greek *alabastos*]

à la carte (*say* ah la kart)
(of a menu) giving a choice for each course of a meal. Compare TABLE D'HÔTE.
[French]

alack *interjection*
an old word used as a cry of dismay.

alacrity (*say* a-**lak**ra-tee) *noun*
a prompt and cheerful willingness: 'she accepted the invitation with *alacrity*'.
[Latin *alacritas* briskness]

à la mode (*say* ah la **mod**)
fashionable: 'that new suit is very *à la mode*'.
[French]

alar (*say* **ay**-lah) *adjective*
a) of or having wings. b) wing-shaped.
[Latin *ala* wing]

alarm *noun*
1. any noise or signal used as a warning.
2. a sudden fear or apprehension caused by an awareness of danger: 'she felt great *alarm* at the sight of the huge dog'.
Word Family: **alarm,** *verb,* to cause or feel alarm.
[Italian *all' arme!* to arms!]

alarm clock
a clock with a bell which can be set to ring at a certain time.

alarmist *noun*
a person with a habit of causing alarm, especially with little reason.

alarum *noun*
an old word for an alarm.

alas (*say* a-**lass**) *interjection*
a cry of sorrow, grief or pity.

alb *noun*
a full-length white robe worn by Christian priests during celebration of the Eucharist.
[Latin *albus* white]

albatross *noun*
a large, long-winged seabird related to the petrel, found especially in the Pacific regions.
[Portuguese]

albeit (*say* awl-**bee**-it) *conjunction*
although: 'it was a brave, *albeit* foolish, act'.

albinism *noun*
Biology: the failure, usually inherited, to develop pigment in the skin, hair, eyes, etc.

albino (*say* al–beeno) *noun*
a person or animal suffering from albinism.
[Latin *albus* white]

album *noun*
1. a book or similar container for storing stamps, photographs, etc.
2. a long–playing record.
[Latin, a blank (white) tablet]

albumen (*say* al–bew–min) *noun*
see EGG WHITE.
[Latin, the white of egg]

albumin (*say* al–bew–min) *noun*
Chemistry: any of a group of water–soluble proteins found in animals and plants.

alchemy (*say* alka–mee) *noun*
1. a medieval science which attempted to change ordinary metals into gold.
2. any strange or magical process, change, etc.
Word Family: **alchemist**, *noun*, a person who practises alchemy.
[Arabic *al–* the + CHEM(istr)Y]

alcohol (*say* alka–hol) *noun*
1. *Chemistry:* any of a class of organic compounds (general formula ROH where R is any alkyl radical).
2. a liquid containing this substance, especially any intoxicating drink made by the fermentation of sugar with fruits, etc.
[Arabic]

alcoholic (*say* alka–hollik) *noun*
also called a **dipsomaniac**
a person who compulsively drinks alcohol.
alcoholic *adjective*
1. of or containing alcohol.
2. of or relating to an alcoholic.
Word Family: **alcoholism** (*say* alka–hol–izm), *noun*.

alcove *noun*
a section of a room or other space which is set back from the main part.
[Arabic, the vault]

aldehyde (*say* aldi–hide) *noun*
Chemistry: any of a class of organic compounds (general formula RCHO where R is any alkyl or aryl radical), such as acetaldehyde (formula CH_3CHO).
[for DEHYD(rogenated) AL(cohol)]

alder (*say* awlda) *noun*
a small, deciduous tree related to the birch, found especially by river–sides.

alderman (*say* awlda–m'n) *noun*
1. *History:* a high–ranking official.
2. a senior, co–opted member of a county, borough or city council.
[from Old English for elder man]

ale *noun*
any of various types of beer, as pale ale, brown ale, etc.
real ale
(*informal*) non–pressurized draught beer.

alembic (*say* a–lembik) *noun*
1. an apparatus or vessel formerly used in distilling.
2. anything which refines or purifies.
[Arabic]

alert *adjective*
wide–awake or attentive: 'he fought to stay *alert* despite his tiredness'.
alert *noun*
1. a state of readiness or caution: 'you must be on the *alert* for trouble'.
2. a warning or alarm, as before an air–raid or attack.
Word Family: **alert**, *verb*; **alertness**, *noun*.
[Italian *all' erta*! to the watch–tower]

alexandrine *noun*
Poetry: see FOOT.
[from the title of an old French romance concerning *Alexander the Great*, written in this metre]

alexia (*say* ay–leksia) *noun*
an inability to read, often caused by brain damage.
[A– + Greek *lexis* speech]

alfalfa *noun*
see LUCERNE.
[Arabic *al–fasfasah* the best sort of fodder]

alfresco *adjective, adverb*
outside or in the open air: 'lunch will be served *alfresco*'.
[Italian *al fresco* in the cool]

alga *noun*
plural is **algae** (*say* al–jee)
Biology: any of a group of simple plants with single–celled reproductive structures, growing in fresh water, seawater or damp places and varying in size from microscopic to several metres long.
Word Family: **algal**, *adjective*.
[Latin, seaweed]

algebra (*say* alji–bra) *noun*
the branch of maths which studies the properties and relationships of quantities by the use of symbols such as letters of the alphabet.

Word Family: **algebraic** (*say* alji–**bray**–ik), *adjective*; **algebraically**, *adverb.*
[Arabic *al-jabr* bone-setting, the reunion of broken parts]

algorithm (*say* alga–ri*th*'m) *noun*
Maths: a clearly-defined sequence of operations for solving a particular mathematical problem.
[from the name of a Persian mathematician]

alias (*say* **ay**–lee–ass) *noun*
an assumed or false name: 'the criminal travelled under an *alias*'.
alias *adverb*
also called: 'Dawson *alias* Bass'.
[Latin, at another time or place]

alibi (*say* **ali**–by) *noun*
plural is **alibis**
1. *Law:* a defence by an accused person that he was elsewhere at the time the crime was committed.
2. (*informal*) any excuse: 'I hope you have a good *alibi* for being away from work'.
[Latin, elsewhere]

alien (*say* **ay**–lian) *noun*
a) a foreigner or non-naturalized citizen. b) any person or thing that is strange or unfamiliar.
alien *adjective*
foreign or strange: 'his ideas are *alien* to our standards'.
Word Family: **alienable**, *adjective.*
[Latin *alienus* belonging to another]

alienate (*say* **ay**–lee–a–nate) *verb*
to turn away or make hostile: 'that attitude will *alienate* many of your friends'.
Word Family: **alienation** (*say* ay–lee–a–**nay**–sh'n), *noun.*

alight (1) (*say* a–**lite**) *verb*
to get out of or down from a vehicle: 'a ramp was provided for us to *alight* from the train'.

alight (2) (say a–**lite**) *adverb, adjective*
lit up or burning: 'is your pipe *alight*?'.

align (*say* a–**line**) *verb*
also spelt **aline**
to arrange in a line: 'these posts are not quite *aligned*'.
Usage: 'his ambitions do not *align* with his family's hopes' (= match, agree).
Word Family: **alignment**, *noun.*

alike *adverb, adjective*
similar or in the same way: 'I think all politicians are *alike*'.

alimentary (*say* ali–**menta**–ree) *adjective*
relating to food, nutrition and digestion.
alimentary canal
Anatomy: the system within the body, including the mouth, oesophagus, stomach, intestines and anus, which receives food, digests it and expels the remains.
[Latin *alimentum* food]

alimony (*say* alimma–nee) *noun*
Law: any regular payment of money due to a separated or divorced person from his or her spouse.
[Latin *alimonia* sustenance]

aline *verb*
see ALIGN.

aliphatic (*say* ali–**fattik**) *adjective*
Chemistry: relating to any of a major class of organic compounds whose molecules are open chains of carbon atoms, including the paraffins, olefines and acetylenes. See AROMATIC COMPOUND.
[Greek *aleiphatos* of fat]

aliquot (*say* **ali**–kwot) *noun*
Maths: a quantity which is an exact divisor of another: '3 is an *aliquot* of 27'.

alive (*rhymes with* arrive) *adjective*
living or active.
Usage: 'his eyes were *alive* with excitement' (= lively, full).
alive to, 'she is not *alive to* the danger' (= aware of).

alkali (*say* **alka**–lie) *noun*
Chemistry: the soluble hydroxide of a metal, all of which are strong bases, that is, they release hydroxyl ions when dissolved in water, such as sodium hydroxide (formula NaOH).
Word Family: **alkaline**, *adjective*; **alkalinity** (*say* alka–**linni**–tee), *noun.*
[Arabic, ashes]

alkali metal
Chemistry: any of the strongly reactive univalent metals, group I of the periodic table, whose hydroxides are all strong alkalis.

alkaline earth metal
Chemistry: any of the reactive bivalent metals, group II of the periodic table, whose oxides are called **alkaline earths**.

alkaloid (*say* **alka**–loyd) *noun*
Chemistry: any of a group of complex organic bases derived from plants and containing nitrogen, such as morphine, codeine and quinine.

alkane series
see PARAFFIN SERIES.

alkene series
see OLEFINE SERIES.

alkyl (*say* alkil) *adjective*
of or relating to univalent radicals derived from aliphatic compounds, such as the methyl group (formula CH_3-) or the ethyl group (formula C_2H_5-).

alkyne series
see ACETYLENE.

all (*say* awl) *adjective, adverb, pronoun*
being the whole quantity or number of anything:
(as an adjective) '*all* men are equal'.
(as an adverb) 'he sat *all* alone'.
(as a pronoun) 'we *all* laughed'.
Usage: 'come with *all* speed' (= the greatest possible).
Phrases:
above all, '*above all*, remember my advice' (= most importantly).
all in, 'we were *all in* after the game' (= exhausted).
all in all, '*all in all* it was a great success' (= altogether).
at all, 'I cannot agree *at all*' (= in any way).

Allah *noun*
the Moslem name for God, the supreme ruler and creator of the universe.
[Arabic *al-ilah* the God]

allay (*say* a-**lay**) *verb*
to relieve or reduce: 'the pilot tried to *allay* their fears'.

allege (*say* a-**lej**) *verb*
to declare or assert, often without actual proof: 'he still *alleges* his innocence'.
Word Family: **allegation** (*say* ali-**gay**-sh'n), *noun*; **allegedly**, *adverb*.

allegiance (*say* a-**lee**-j'nce) *noun*
a loyalty or duty, especially to a government or ruler of a country.

allegory (*say* **ali**-gree) *noun*
a literary form which presents, through its characters, events or qualities, other corresponding but unstated characters, events or qualities.
Word Family: **allegorical**, **allegoric**, *adjective*.
[Greek *allegoria* another speaking]

allegro (*say* a-**lay**-gro) *adverb*
Music: fast and lively.
[Italian]

allele (*say* a-**leel**) *noun*
short form of **allelomorph**
Biology: one of two or more genes occupying a specified position on a chromosome.
[Greek *allelé* another + *morphé* shape]

alleluia (*say* ali-**loo**-ya) *noun*
see HALLELUJAH.

allergy (*say* **al**-a-jee) *noun*
an abnormal physical sensitivity to any substance, such as to certain fruits, plants, etc.
allergic (*say* a-**ler**jik) *adjective*
having an allergy: 'I am *allergic* to pollen'.
Word Family: **allergen** (*say* **ala**-j'n), *noun*, any substance which can cause an allergy.
[Greek *allos* other + *ergon* work]

alleviate (*say* a-**leevi**-ate) *verb*
to lessen or make easier to bear: 'nothing could *alleviate* her misery'.
Word Family: **alleviation**, *noun*.
[AL- + Latin *levare* to relieve]

alley (1) (*say* **al**-ee) *noun*
1. a narrow path or street, usually between buildings. Short form of **alleyway**.
2. a long, narrow, enclosed lane with a polished wooden floor, used for bowling.

alley (2) (*say* **al**-ee) *noun*
a large marble.
[from ALABASTER, of which marbles were originally made]

alliance (*say* a-**lie**'nce) *noun*
an association or union, usually made by formal agreement.
[AL- + Latin *ligare* to bind]

allied (*say* **al**-ide) *verb*
the past tense and past participle of the verb **ally**.

alligator (*say* **ali**-gayta) *noun*
any of various large amphibian freshwater reptiles with a broad rounded snout and growing up to about 5 m long.
[Spanish *el lagarto* the lizard]

alliteration (*say* a-litta-**ray**-sh'n) *noun*
the commencement of two or more closely connected words with the same letter or sound, especially a consonant.
Example: 'five *m*iles *m*eandering with a *m*azy *m*otion' (S. T. Coleridge).
Word Family: **alliterate**, *verb*; **alliterative**, *adjective*.
[AL- + Latin *littera* letter]

allocate (*say* **al**-a-kate) *verb*
to set aside for a particular purpose: 'the city council has *allocated* money for public transport'.

Word Family: **allocation**, *noun.*
[AL– + Latin *locus* a place]

allopathy (*say* a-**loppa**-thee) *noun*
the usual method of treating diseases using substances which produce effects different from those of the disease being treated.
Compare HOMOEOPATHY.
[Greek *allos* other + *pathos* suffering]

allot (*say* a-**lot**) *verb*
(**allotted, allotting**)
to share out or distribute: 'you have been *allotted* several tickets'.
allotment *noun*
1. a) the act of allotting: 'there will be an *allotment* of shares'. b) a person's share of anything: 'what was the teacher's *allotment* of classes last term?'.
2. a plot of land: 'a vacant *allotment*'.
[AL– + LOT]

allotropy (*say* a-**lotra**-pee) *noun*
Chemistry: the existence of an element in more than one physical form (called an **allotrope**) but producing identical chemical compounds. *Example:* charcoal, graphite, diamond and soot are all allotropes of the one element, carbon, and all form carbon dioxide when heated with oxygen.
Word Family: **allotropic** (*say* al-a-**tropp**ik), *adjective.*
[Greek *allos* other + *tropos* manner]

allow (*rhymes with* a cow) *verb*
to permit or agree to: 'you are not going out tonight. I won't *allow* it'.
Usages:
a) 'my dogs are *allowed* in the house' (= given the right to enter).
b) 'I *allow* I was wrong' (= admit).
c) 'she is *allowed* £15 a week for clothes' (= given).
allow for, 'you have not *allowed for* his forgetfulness' (= taken into consideration).
allowance *noun*
1. the act of allowing: 'the *allowance* of a claim'.
2. a sum of money, etc. given for particular needs: 'many salesmen receive a travelling *allowance*'.
make allowance for, a) to make provision for; b) to make concession or excuse for.

alloy (*say* **al**oy) *noun*
any substance consisting of a metal mixed with one or more other elements.

alloy (*say* a-**loy**) *verb*
to mix metals to form an alloy.
Usage: 'nothing could *alloy* her happiness' (= spoil, impair).
[AL– + Latin *ligare* to bind]

all right
satisfactory or in good order: 'are you *all right*?'.

all-rounder *noun*
a person with equal ability in many different things, especially in sport.

allspice *noun*
also called **pimento**
a sweet-smelling, sharp spice made from a dried berry.
[ALL + SPICE]

allude (*say* a-**lood**) *verb*
to refer to something indirectly: 'several times he *alluded* to his past, but he told us nothing'.
Word Family: **allusion** (*say* a-**loo**-*zh*'n), *noun*; **allusive**, *adjective*; **allusively**, *adverb.*
[Latin *alludere* to play with]

allure (*say* al-**yoor**) *verb*
to attract or entice: 'many gimmicks were used to *allure* customers'.
Word Family: **allurement**, *noun.*

alluvial (*say* a-**loo**viul) *adjective*
made of soil, sand, etc. deposited by flowing water.
alluvial plain
an area of flat land where a river has deposited silt.

alluvium (*say* a-**loo**vi-um) *noun*
the silt carried by a river and deposited in its valley or delta.
[Latin *alluvio* an overflowing]

ally (*say* **al**-eye) *noun*
1. a person or group united with another, especially by formal agreement: 'Australia's trade *allies*'.
2. any close friend or supporter.
Word Family: **ally** (**allied, allying**), *verb*, a) to unite by formal agreement, etc., b) to connect or associate.
[AL– + Latin *ligare* to bind]

alma mater (*say* alma **may**ta)
a person's former school, college or university.
[Latin *alma* bounteous + *mater* mother]

almanac (*say* **awl**ma-nak) *noun*
a yearly calendar giving information about the sun, moon, tides, etc.

almighty (*say* awl-**my**-tee) *adjective*
1. having absolute power.
2. (*informal*) very great: 'what an *almighty* noise!'.

the Almighty
Christian: God.

almond (*say* **ah**–m'nd) *noun*
1. an edible, oval nut with a mild taste.
2. a pale creamish-brown colour.
Word Family: **almond,** *adjective.*

almoner (*say* **ahm**'na *or* **alm**'na) *noun*
a medically trained social worker attached to a hospital.

almost (*say* **awl**–most) *adverb*
very nearly: 'we are *almost* there'.

alms (*say* ahms) *plural noun*
(*sometimes used with singular verb*)
any money or gifts given to the poor.

aloe (*say* **al**–o) *noun*
plural is **aloes**
1. a large African plant with long, cactus-like leaves.
2. (*plural*) a bitter drug extracted from this plant, used as a laxative.
[Greek]

aloft *adverb*
high up or in the air: 'the glider stayed *aloft* for several hours'.

alone *adjective, adverb*
by oneself: 'do not leave me penniless and *alone*'.
Phrases:
let alone, 'he can hardly walk, *let alone* run' (= not to mention).
let well alone, 'he won't change his mind, so *let well alone*' (= be satisfied).
Word Family: **aloneness,** *noun.*

along *preposition, adverb*
1. following the length of: 'the guide asked us to move *along* the path'.
2. on or onwards: 'they went *along* together'.
Usage: 'I thought I'd bring my dog *along*' (= with me).
Phrases:
all along, 'I knew that *all along*' (= all the time).
get along, a) 'they *get along* well' (= manage, like each other); b) 'I must be *getting along* now' (= leaving).

alongside *adverb*
beside or at the side of anything: 'the car drew up *alongside*'.

aloof *adverb, adjective*
apart or at a distance, especially from people:
(as an adverb) 'he stands *aloof* from family quarrels'.
(as an adjective) 'she seems *aloof* but I know she is only shy'.
Word Family: **aloofness,** *noun.*

aloud *adverb*
a) in a voice to be heard: 'recite the poem *aloud*'. b) loudly: 'she cried *aloud* for joy'.

alp *noun*
a high mountain.
Word Family: **alpine,** *adjective,* of or growing on the alps.

alpaca (*say* al–**pakka**) *noun*
see GUANACO.

alpha (*say* **alfa**) *noun*
1. the first letter of the Greek alphabet.
2. the beginning of anything. Compare OMEGA.

alphabet (*say* **alfa**–bet) *noun*
1. the letters or signs of a particular language, set in an established order.
2. the basic principles of anything: 'the *alphabet* of survival'.
alphabetical (*say* alfa–**betti**–k'l) *adjective*
being in the order of the alphabet, as in a dictionary.
Word Family: **alphabetically,** *adverb;* **alphabetize, alphabetise,** *verb,* to make alphabetical.
[Greek *alpha* A + *beta* B]

alpha particle
Physics: a heavy, positively charged particle, containing two protons and two neutrons, released during some types of radioactive decay.

alpha ray
Physics: a stream of alpha particles.

alpine *adjective*
Word Family: see ALP.

already (*say* awl–**reddi**) *adverb*
by or before a particular time: 'when we arrived he was *already* there'.

Alsatian (*say* al–**say**–sh'n) *noun*
any of a breed of large, strong, smooth-haired dogs used as police-dogs, etc.
[from *Alsace,* a region of France]

also (*say* **awl**–so) *adverb*
as well or in addition: 'we *also* bought you a present'.

also-ran *noun*
the loser of a race, competition, etc.

altar (*say* **awl**–ta) *noun*
a raised structure where sacrifices are offered or religious rites are performed.

altarpiece *noun*
a painting or other work of art behind the altar of a church.

alter (*say* **awlta**) *verb*
to make or become different: 'we must *alter* our plans'.

alteration *noun*
a) the act of altering: 'the house needs much *alteration* to make it comfortable'. b) a change or modification: 'the *alterations* to the law have been accepted'.
Word Family: **alterable,** *adjective*; **alterably,** *adverb.*
[Latin, other]

altercation (*say* awlta-**kay**-sh'n) *noun*
an angry or noisy quarrel: 'there was a long *altercation* between the two drivers'.
Word Family: **altercate,** *verb.*
[Latin *altercatio* a dispute]

alter ego
a) a very close or faithful friend: 'she has always been my *alter ego*'. b) another part of oneself: 'my *alter ego* warned me not to do it'.
[Latin *alter* another + *ego* I]

alternate (*say* **awl**ta-nate) *verb*
to replace each other by turns: 'her moods *alternate* between joy and depression'.
alternate (*say* awl-**ter**nit) *adjective*
(of two things) first one and then the other.
Usage: 'we play squash on *alternate* Saturdays' (= every second).
Word Family: **alternation,** *noun.*
[Latin *alternare* to do one thing and then a second thing]
Common Error: ALTERNATE, ALTERNATIVE have related but distinct meanings; *alternate* means in turn, or every second part of a series, whereas *alternative* refers to choosing between two possibilities.

alternating current
Electricity: see ELECTRIC CURRENT.

alternating voltage
Electricity: a time-varying voltage which regularly changes direction.

alternative (*say* awl-**ter**na-tiv) *noun*
1. a choice between two possibilities: 'is there no *alternative* to your method?'.
2. any choice: 'are there no other *alternatives*?'.
3. something other than what is generally accepted.
Word Family: **alternative,** *adjective*; **alternatively,** *adverb.*
Common Error: see ALTERNATE.

alternator (*say* **awl**ta-nayta) *noun*
Electricity: a generator for producing alternating current. Compare DYNAMO.

although (*say* awl-***tho***) *conjunction*
even though: 'I will go *although* I would prefer not to'.

altimeter (*say* **al**ti-meeta) *noun*
an instrument similar to a barometer, used to measure altitude by the decrease of atmospheric pressure.

altitude *noun*
1. the height of anything, especially above sea-level.
2. *Astronomy:* see ELEVATION.
Word Family: **altitudinal** (*say* alti-**tew**di-n'l), *adjective.*
[Latin *altitudo* height]

alto (*say* **al**-toe) *noun*
Music: a) the range between tenor and soprano. b) a contralto, the lowest female singing voice. c) a countertenor, a high, adult male singing voice. d) any instrument having this range.
[Italian, high]

altogether (*say* awlta-**ge*th***a) *adverb*
a) entirely or completely: 'he is *altogether* unpleasant'. b) in total: '*altogether* it adds up to £400'.
in the altogether, 'the children swam *in the altogether*' (= nude).

altruism (*say* **al**troo-izm) *noun*
an unselfish generosity to, or concern for, other people.
Word Family: **altruist,** *noun*; **altruistic** (*say* altroo-**is**tik), *adjective*; **altruistically,** *adverb.*
[Italian *altrui* somebody else]

alum (*say* **al**um) *noun*
Chemistry: a) potassium aluminium sulphate, a white crystalline solid used in chemical processes, dyeing and medicine.
b) any of a class of related compounds which act as two separate compounds in solution, but crystallize as one.

alumina (*say* a-**loo**mina) *noun*
Chemistry: aluminium oxide (formula Al_2O_3), occurring naturally as corundum and bauxite.

aluminium (*say* al-yoo-**min**-y'm) *noun*
in America spelt **aluminum** (*say* a-**loo**minum)
element number 13, a light, soft, very abundant metal which is ductile, malleable and a good conductor of electricity. It is used extensively in alloys, lightweight utensils, etc.
See CHEMICAL ELEMENTS in grey pages.
[Latin *aluminis* of alum]

aluminium foil
also called **silver foil** or **tinfoil**
a thin sheet of aluminium or similar substance, used for wrapping, etc.

alumnus (*say* a–**lumnus**) *noun*
plural is **alumni**
American: a former male student of a college or university.
Word Family: **alumna** (plural is **alumnae**), *noun*, a female alumnus.
[Latin, a foster–son]

alveolus (*say* alvi–**o**–lus *or* al–**vee**–a–lus) *noun*
plural is **alveoli**
Anatomy: a) a small air–sac in the lungs. b) the socket or cavity of a tooth.
Word Family: **alveolar**, *adjective*.
[Latin *alveus* a hollow]

always (*say* **awl**–ways) *adverb*
at all times or continually: a) 'has the earth *always* been round?'; b) 'the bus is *always* late'.

alyssum (*say* a–**liss**'m) *noun*
a low garden plant with small white or yellow flowers.

am *verb*
the first person singular, present tense of the verb **be**.

amalgam (*say* a–**mal**–g'm) *noun*
1. *Chemistry:* any alloy of mercury and another metal, particularly gold.
2. a mixture or combination.
[Greek *malagma* an ointment]

amalgamate (*say* a–**malga**–mate) *verb*
to combine or mix: 'the three companies *amalgamated* last month'.
Word Family: **amalgamation**, *noun*.

amanuensis (*say* a–man–yoo–**ensis**) *noun*
plural is **amanuenses**
a secretary or person employed to take dictation, especially for a writer.
[Latin, a secretary]

amaranth (*say* **amma**–ranth) *noun*
any of a group of plants with spikes of long–lasting brightly coloured flowers.
[Greek *amarantos* unfading]

amass *verb*
to collect or heap together, especially for oneself: 'the Duke had *amassed* a great fortune'.

amateur (*say* **amma**–ter) *noun*
1. a person who engages in any activity for enjoyment as distinct from making money.
2. a person who lacks skill or ability.
Word Family: **amateurish**, *adjective*, unskilled; **amateurishly**, *adverb*.
[Latin *amator* lover]

amatol (*say* **amma**–tol) *noun*
an explosive mixture of ammonium nitrate and trinitrotoluene (TNT).
[AM(monium nitrate) + (trinitro)TOL(uene)]

amatory (*say* **amma**–tree) *adjective*
relating to love or love–making: 'his intentions were obviously *amatory*'.

amaze *verb*
to surprise or astonish: 'his wide knowledge *amazed* us'.
Word Family: **amazement**, *noun*; **amazing**, *adjective*; **amazingly**, *adverb*.

amazon (*say* **amma**–zon) *noun*
1. *Ancient mythology:* (*capital*) a member of a race of female warriors and hunters who excluded men from their country.
2. a physically strong or powerful woman.
[a Greek name]

ambassador *noun*
Politics: the chief representative of a government, sent to a foreign country. A **chargé d'affaires** is an official taking his place in his absence. Compare CONSUL.
Word Family: **ambassadorial**, *adjective*.
[from French]

amber *noun*
1. *Geology:* the yellow, reddish or brown fossilized resin of coniferous trees, used in jewellery.
2. an orange to yellowish–brown colour.
[Arabic *anbar* ambergris]

ambergris (*say* **amba**–griss) *noun*
a grey waxy substance obtained from the intestine of the sperm whale and used in making perfume.
[Arabic *anbar* + French *gris* grey]

ambi–
a prefix meaning both, as in *ambidextrous*.
[Latin *ambo*]

ambidextrous *adjective*
able to use both hands equally well.
Word Family: **ambidexterity**, *noun*.
[AMBI– + Latin *dextera* the right hand]

ambience *noun*
an environment or atmosphere: 'the country has a peaceful *ambience*'.
Word Family: **ambient**, *adjective*.
[Latin *ambire* to go round]

ambient temperature
Physics: the temperature of the area surrounding a body.

ambiguous (*say* am–**big**–yewus) *adjective*
having two or more possible meanings.

Word Family: **ambiguity** (*say* ambi–**gewi**–tee), *noun*; **ambiguously,** *adverb.*
[Latin *ambiguus* changing sides]

ambit *noun*
the boundary or range of anything: 'ancient history was not within the *ambit* of his knowledge'.
[Latin *ambire* to go round]

ambition *noun*
a strong desire for success, fame, etc.
Word Family: **ambitious,** *adjective*; **ambitiously,** *adverb.*
[Latin *ambitio* striving for honour]

ambivalent (*say* am–**bivva**–l'nt) *adjective*
having opposite and conflicting feelings about something: 'she loves him but is *ambivalent* about marriage'.
Word Family: **ambivalence,** *noun*; **ambivalently,** *adverb.*
[AMBI– + Latin *valens* strong]

amble *verb*
to walk at a relaxed or easy pace: 'the cattle *ambled* across the field'.
Word Family: **amble,** *noun.*
[Latin *ambulare* to walk]

ambrosia (*say* am–**bro**–zee–a) *noun*
1. *Greek mythology:* the food of the gods.
2. anything delightfully pleasing or delicious to taste or smell.
Word Family: **ambrosial,** *adjective.*
[Greek *ambrotos* immortal]

ambulance (*say* **am**–bew–l'nce) *noun*
a vehicle equipped to carry sick or injured people.
[Latin *ambulare* to walk]

ambulant (*say* **am**–bew–l'nt) *adjective*
moving from place to place.

ambulatory (*say* ambew–**layta**–ree) *adjective*
related to or capable of walking.
Word Family: **ambulate,** *verb*; **ambulation,** *noun*; **ambulatory,** *noun,* an area for walking, such as a cloister.

ambush (*say* **am**–bush) *verb*
also called to **ambuscade**
to lie in wait in order to make a surprise attack.
Word Family: **ambush,** *noun.*

ameba *noun*
see AMOEBA.

ameliorate (*say* a–**meelia**–rate) *verb*
to make or become better: 'prison conditions may be *ameliorated* by the new law'.
Word Family: **amelioration** (*say* a–meelia–**ray**–sh'n), *noun.*
[Latin *melior* better]

amen (*say* **ahmen** *or* **aymen**) *interjection*
a word meaning 'so be it', usually said at the end of a prayer.
[Hebrew, certainly or true]

amenable (*say* a–**meena**–b'l) *adjective*
1. willing or agreeable: 'he was not *amenable* to the suggestion'.
2. responsible or answerable: 'all members are *amenable* to club rules'.
Word Family: **amenability, amenableness,** *nouns*; **amenably,** *adverb.*
[French *amener* to lead to]

amend *verb*
1. to make changes in a law, etc.: 'the committee has *amended* the rule'.
2. to correct or improve: 'here is an *amended* version of the original script'.
amendment *noun*
a) the act of amending: 'the *amendment* of the Bill took several hours'. b) the change or correction made: 'the *amendments* to the script are marvellous!'.
amends *noun*
make amends, 'how can I *make amends* for my carelessness?' (= make up).
Word Family: **amendable,** *adjective.*
[Latin *emendare* to remove faults from]
Common Error: do not confuse with EMEND.

amenity (*say* a–**menni**–tee *or* a–**meeni**–tee) *noun*
1. (*usually plural*) anything which adds to comfort, ease or pleasure: 'the cooking *amenities* in this flat are excellent'.
2. any pleasantness: 'the *amenity* of the holiday resort made them want to stay longer'.
[Latin *amoenitas* a pleasing sight]

American *noun*
a) an inhabitant of the continents of North or South America. b) an inhabitant of the United States of America. c) the English language as spoken in the United States of America.
[after *Amerigo Vespucci,* 1451–1512, an Italian explorer and adventurer]

americium (*say* amma–**rissium**) *noun*
element number 95, a man-made radioactive metal. See TRANSURANIC ELEMENT and ACTINIDE.
See CHEMICAL ELEMENTS in grey pages.

Amerindian (*say* ammer-indian) *noun*
a) one of the race of people who were the original inhabitants of North or South America. b) any of their languages.
Word Family: **Amerindian,** *adjective.*

amethyst (*say* **amma**-thist) *noun*
a purple or violet quartz, used as a gem.
[Greek *amethystos* not drunk, because the stone was believed to remedy the effects of drink]

amiable (*say* **aymia**-b'l) *adjective*
friendly or kind.
Word Family: **amiably,** *adverb*; **amiability,** *noun.*

amicable (*say* **ammika**-b'l) *adjective*
peaceful and friendly: 'it was an *amicable* agreement'.
Word Family: **amicably,** *adverb*; **amicability,** *noun.*
[Latin *amicabilis* friendly]

amid, amidst *preposition*
among or in the middle of: 'she disappeared *amid* the crowd'.

amidships *adverb*
being in, or referring to, the middle part of a ship.

amigo (*say* a-**meego**) *noun*
a friend.
[Spanish]

amino group (*say* a-**meen**-o group)
Chemistry: an ammonia molecule (formula NH_3) from which one hydrogen atom is missing, forming the univalent radical $-NH_2$.
Word Family: **amino acid,** an acid containing an amino group; **amine** (*say* ay-mine *or* **ammine**), *noun,* a compound formed from an amino group and an organic radical, general formula $R-NH_2$; **amide** (*say* **ay**-mide), *noun,* a compound formed from an amino group and an organic acid radical, general formula $R-CO-NH_2$.
[from AMMONIA]

amir (*say* a-**meer**) **ameer** *noun*
1. a title given to certain Turkish officials.
2. an emir.
[Arabic, a commander]

amiss *adverb, adjective*
wrong or faulty: 'something must have gone *amiss* with their plans'.
take amiss, 'do not *take* his comments *amiss*' (= resent).

amity (*say* **amma**-tee) *noun*
a state of friendship and harmony: 'the peace treaty led to greater *amity* between the nations'.
[Latin *amicus* friend]

ammeter (*say* **ammita**) *noun*
an instrument used to measure the strength of electric current in ampere.
[AM(pere) + METER]

ammonia (*say* a-**mo**-nee-a) *noun*
a colourless, strong-smelling gas (formula NH_3), which is very soluble in water where it produces an alkaline solution. It is used in refrigerators, cleaning mixtures, explosives and fertilizers.
[from the Temple of *Ammon* in Libya, where first found]

ammunition (*say* am-yoo-**nish**'n) *noun*
any of the materials, e.g. shot, shells, etc. used in firing guns.
[from MUNITION]

amnesia (*say* am-**neezia**) *noun*
a loss of memory.
[A- + Greek *mnestis* recollection]

amnesty (*say* **amna**-stee) *noun*
a general pardon, especially for crimes against a government.
[Greek *amnestia* forgetting a wrong]

amnion *noun*
the sac containing the unborn offspring of a reptile, bird or mammal.
Amniotic fluid is the watery fluid which surrounds the embryo in this sac and is expelled before birth.
Word Family: **amniotic** (*say* amni-**ottik**), *adjective.*
[Greek]

amoeba (*say* a-**meeba**) *noun*
plural is **amoebae** or **amoebas**
in America spelt **ameba**
a microscopic, unicellular animal which moves by changing its shape and reproduces by simple division into two parts.
Word Family: **amoebic,** *adjective.*
[Greek *amoibé* change]

amok (*say* a-**mok** *or* a-**muk**) *adverb*
also spelt **amuck**
run amok, to rush about wildly or violently.
[Malay]

among (*say* a-**mung**) **amongst** *preposition*
a word used to indicate the following:
a) 'he stood *among* the crowd' (= surrounded by).

b) 'the chocolates were divided *among* the children' (= to each of).
c) 'the family dispute must be settled *among* themselves' (= between).
d) 'I number him *among* my friends' (= within the group of).
e) 'she is *among* the best known singers' (= one of).
[Old English *on* in + *gemang* the crowd]

amoral (*say* ay-**morr**'l) *adjective*
of or relating to behaviour which is not based on any moral standards.
Word Family: **amorally**, *adverb*; **amorality** (*say* ay-mo-**ralla**-tee), *noun*.
[A- + MORAL]
Common Error: AMORAL, IMMORAL have related but distinct meanings: *amoral* describes behaviour which is not based on any moral standards and may therefore not be judged by such standards, whereas *immoral* refers to actions which offend against an accepted moral law or standard.

amorous (*say* **amma**-rus) *adjective*
a) of or showing love: 'an *amorous* glance'. b) inclined or disposed to love: 'his intentions were clearly *amorous*'.
Word Family: **amorously**, *adverb*; **amorousness**, *noun*.
[Latin *amor* love]

amorphous (*say* a-**morfus**) *adjective*
having no definite form or shape.
Word Family: **amorphously**, *adverb*; **amorphousness**, *noun*.
[A- + Greek *morphé* a shape]

amortize (*say* **am**-or-tize) **amortise** *verb*
Commerce: to write off or recover the cost of a capital investment.
[AD- + Latin *mortis* of death]

amount *noun*
the extent or total of anything: 'the *amount* of effort required is minimal'.
amount *verb*
to add up or be equal to: 'her debts *amounted* to £1500'.
[Old French *amont* upward or to the mountain]

amour (*say* a-**moor**) *noun*
a love affair.
[French, love]

amour-propre (*say* **ammoor-propra**) *noun*
self-esteem.
[French]

ampere (*say* **am**-pair) *noun*
short form is **amp**
the base SI unit of electric current. See SI UNIT.

amperage (*say* **ampa**-rij) *noun*
the electric current expressed in ampere.
[after *A. M. Ampère*, 1775–1836, a French physicist]

ampersand *noun*
the sign (&), meaning *and*.

amphetamine (*say* am-**fetta-meen**) *noun*
a drug used to relieve congestion or stimulate the nervous system.

amphi- (*say* **am**fi)
a prefix meaning on both or all sides, as in *amphitheatre*.

amphibian (*say* am-**fibbi**-an) *noun*
1. any of a group of animals, with a backbone, able to live in water and on land, usually developing in water but spending most of its adult life on land.
2. an aircraft which can take off and land on land or water.
3. a vehicle which can travel on land or water.
Word Family: **amphibian**, **amphibious**, *adjectives*.
[Greek *amphibios* living a double life]

amphitheatre (*say* **am**fi-theerta) *noun*
a circular or oval area with sloping sides rising around it, such as a theatre gallery, sports arena, etc.

amphora (*say* **am**fora) *noun*
plural is **amphorae** (*say* **am**fo-ree)
a two-handled vessel with a narrow neck, used by ancient Greeks and Romans.
[AMPHI- + Greek *phoreus* carried]

amphoteric (*say* amfa-**terrik**) *adjective*
Chemistry: acting as an acid or a base.
[Greek *amphoteros* both]

ample *adjective*
large or plentiful: 'the house has *ample* room for all of us'.
Word Family: **amply**, *adverb*; **ampleness**, *noun*.
[Latin *amplus* spacious]

amplifier (*say* **am**pli-fire) *noun*
Electricity: any device which uses power from another source to increase the strength of a signal fed into it, such as that used in a hi-fi system to increase volume.

amplify (*say* **am**pli-fie) *verb*
(**amplified**, **amplifying**)
1. to enlarge, extend or increase: 'could you *amplify* that statement?'.
2. *Physics:* to increase the amplitude.
Word Family: **amplification**, *noun*.
[Latin *amplificare* to widen]

amplitude (*say* ampli-tewd) *noun*
1. the extent, breadth or fullness of anything.
2. *Physics:* the amount of movement away from the middle position, such as the swing of a pendulum from its resting place or the maximum variation of a light-wave.

amplitude modulation
short form is **AM**
a method of radio broadcasting, in which the amplitude of the transmitted wave is varied, producing long-range but low-fidelity reception. Compare FREQUENCY MODULATION.

ampoule (*say* am-pool) *noun*
a small, sealed, glass container for sterile liquids or solids.
[Latin *ampulla* a bottle]

amputate (*say* am-pew-tate) *verb*
to cut off a diseased or injured limb, etc. by surgical operation.
Word Family: **amputation,** *noun*; **amputee,** *noun*, a person who has had a limb amputated.
[AMBI- + Latin *putare* to prune]

amuck *adverb*
see AMOK.

amulet (*say* am-yoo-let) *noun*
an ornament or charm believed to protect the wearer from misfortune.

amuse (*say* a-mewz) *verb*
1. to cause to smile or laugh.
2. to make time pass pleasantly: 'can you *amuse* yourself until we return?'.
Word Family: **amusement,** *noun*, a) the state of being amused, b) anything which amuses; **amusingly,** *adverb*; **amusedly,** *adverb*.
[Old French *amuser* to waste time]

amyl (*say* ammil) *adjective*
Chemistry: of or relating to organic compounds containing the univalent pentyl group ($C_5H_{11}-$).
[Latin *amylum* starch]

amylase (*say* ammi-laze) *noun*
an enzyme found in animals and plants, which changes starch into sugar.
[AMYL + -ASE]

amytal (*say* ammi-tal) *noun*
Medicine: a drug used as a sedative.

an *article*
Grammar: an indefinite article. See ARTICLE.

an- (1)
a variant of the prefix **a-**.

an- (2)
a variant of the prefix **ad-**.

-an
a suffix meaning belonging to, often used of a person who is associated with a particular country, group, etc., as in *American*.

-ana
a suffix meaning a collection of material related to a particular subject, as in *Australiana*.

anabolism (*say* a-nabba-lizm) *noun*
the process, in living organisms, of building up complex substances from more simple ones. Compare CATABOLISM.
Word Family: **anabolic** (*say* anna-bollik), *adjective*.
[Greek *anabolé* a heaping up]

anachronism (*say* a-nakra-nizm) *noun*
the assigning of something to a wrong, especially an earlier, date.
Usage: 'horse-drawn transport is an *anachronism* in large modern cities' (= something chronologically out of place).
Word Family: **anachronistic, anachronous,** *adjectives*.
[Greek *ana-* against + *khronos* time]

anaconda (*say* anna-konda) *noun*
a very large South American snake related to the boa, reaching at least 10 m in length.

anaemia (*say* a-neemia) *noun*
in America spelt **anemia**
a shortage of red blood cells due to loss of blood or reduced production of cells, causing weakness and a pale colouring of the skin.
anaemic *adjective*
1. suffering from anaemia.
2. colourless or weak: 'an *anaemic* complexion'.
[Greek *an-* without + *haima* blood]

anaerobe (*say* anna-robe) *noun*
an organism that does not require oxygen to live. Compare AEROBE.
Word Family: **anaerobic** (*say* anna-ro-bik), *adjective*.
[Greek *an-* without + AEROBE]

anaesthesia (*say* annis-theez-ya) *noun*
in America spelt **anesthesia**
a general loss of feeling, especially of pain.
anaesthetic (*say* annis-thettik) *noun*
any substance, such as ether or chloroform, producing a general or local loss of feeling, pain, etc.
Word Family: **anaesthetize** (*say* a-neestha-tize), **anaesthetise,** *verb*;

anaesthetist (*say* a–**neestha**–tist), *noun*, a person trained to give anaesthetics. [Greek *an–* without + AESTHETIC]

anagram (*say* **anna**–gram) *noun*
a word formed by rearranging the letters of another word. *Example*: *march* is an anagram of *charm*.
[Greek *ana* again + *gramma* a letter]

anal (*say* ayn'l) *adjective*
Word Family: see ANUS.

analgesia (*say* annal–**jeez**–ya) *noun*
an inability to feel pain.
analgesic (*say* annal–**jeezik**) *noun*
any substance which relieves pain.
[Greek *an–* without + *algos* pain]

analogy (*say* a–**nalla**–jee) *noun*
an agreement or partial correspondence in things between which a comparison may be made: 'there is an *analogy* between the heart and a pump'.
analogous (*say* a–**nalla**–gus) *adjective*
comparable in several respects.
Word Family: **analogical** (*say* anna–**loji**–k'l), *adjective*; **analogically,** *adverb*; **analogize, analogise,** *verb,* to use or explain by analogy; **analogously,** *adverb*; **analogue** (*say* **anna**–log), *noun,* anything which has an analogy to something else.
[Greek *analogos* proportionate]

analyse (*say* **anna**–lize) *verb*
1. to examine critically or establish the essential features of: 'we all tried to *analyse* his motives'.
2. to divide into the constituent parts and examine each element: 'to *analyse* a chemical compound'.

analysis (*say* a–**nalla**–sis) *noun*
1. the process of separating something into its constituent parts, so as to examine or describe it. Compare SYNTHESIS.
2. *Maths:* a) the branch of maths which uses algebraic and calculus methods. b) the exposition of the principles involved in solving a problem.
3. *Psychology:* see PSYCHOANALYSIS.
Word Family: **analyst,** *noun,* a person skilled in analysis; **analytic** (*say* anna–**littik**), **analytical,** *adjective*; **analytically,** *adverb.*
[Greek, a breaking up]

analytical geometry
also called **coordinate geometry**
a branch of geometry using algebraic and analytical methods to solve problems.

anapaest (*say* **anna**–peest) *noun*
Poetry: see FOOT.

anarchy (*say* **anna**–kee) *noun*
1. a lack of established government or control, usually leading to disorder.
2. a general state of disorder or uproar: '*anarchy* reigned in the school during the teachers' strike'.
anarchist (*say* **anna**–kist) *noun*
a person who believes that all organized authority should be abolished in the interest of individual freedom.
Word Family: **anarchism,** *noun*; **anarchic** (*say* a–**narkik**), **anarchical,** *adjective.*
[Greek *an–* without + *arkhos* a ruler]

anathema (*say* a–**nathema**) *noun*
1. *Christian:* a curse by God or the Church.
2. anything which is detested or loathed: 'wedding receptions are *anathema* to him'.
Word Family: **anathematize, anathematise,** *verb.*
[Greek, a curse]

anatomy (*say* a–**natta**–mee) *noun*
1. the internal structure of anything.
2. the study of the structure of an organism. Compare PHYSIOLOGY.
Word Family: **anatomist,** *noun*; **anatomical,** *adjective*; **anatomically,** *adverb.*
[Greek *anatomé* a cutting up]

ancestor (*say* **ansesta**) *noun*
a person from whom descent can be traced through either of one's parents.
Word Family: **ancestral** (*say* an–**sess**–tr'l), *adjective*; **ancestrally,** *adverb.*
[ANTE– + Latin *cedere* to go]

ancestry (*say* **an**–sess–tree) *noun*
a) a line of descent. b) all one's ancestors.

anchor (*say* **anka**) *noun*
Nautical: a heavy object attached to a ship by a rope or chain and lowered into the seabed to prevent the ship drifting.
anchor-man, a) the man at the end of a tug of war rope; b) the final runner in a relay; c) a compère.
anchor *verb*
a) to lower an anchor. b) to hold or be held fast by an anchor.
Usage: 'fear *anchored* her to the spot' (= firmly fixed).
Word Family: **anchorage,** *noun,* a) an area where ships may anchor, b) the fee paid for this.

anchorite (*say* **anka**–rite) *noun*
a religious hermit.
[Greek *anakhoreein* to retire or retreat]

anchovy (*say* ancha–vee) *noun*
any of a group of small, edible, oily fish, related to the herring.
[Spanish]

ancient (*say* **ane**–sh'nt) *adjective*
1. existing or occurring in times long past, especially before the fall of the Western Roman Empire in A.D. 476.
2. very old: 'an *ancient* pensioner knitting socks on the verandah'.
Word Family: **ancient,** *noun,* a) a person who lived in ancient times, b) a very old person.

ancillary (*say* an–**silla**–ree) *adjective*
auxiliary.
[Latin *ancilla* a servant]

and *conjunction*
1. a word used to indicate the following:
a) (connection or joining of ideas, etc.) 'we ate dinner *and* then we left'.
b) (continuation) 'we talked *and* talked for hours'.
c) (addition) 'seven *and* eight equals fifteen'.
2. as well as: 'the house was dark *and* cold'.
3. (*informal*) to: 'please try *and* find it'.

andante (*say* an–**dan**–tee) *adverb*
Music: slowly.
[Italian]

andiron *noun*
see FIREDOG.

androgen (*say* **andra**–j'n) *noun*
any of various hormones which control the appearance and development of masculine characteristics.
[Greek *andros* of a man + GEN(esis)]

androgynous (*say* an–**droji**–nus) *adjective*
having both male and female characteristics.
[Greek *andros* of a man + *gyne* woman]

anecdote (*say* **annek**–dote) *noun*
a short, interesting or amusing story about a particular person or event.
Word Family: **anecdotal** (*say* **annek–doe**–t'l), *adjective.*
[Greek *anekdotos* unpublished]

anemia (*say* a–**nee**mia) *noun*
see ANAEMIA.

anemone (*say* a–**nemma**–nee) *noun*
1. a small garden flower growing from a corm and resembling a poppy.
2. a sea–anemone.
[Greek *anemos* wind]

aneroid barometer (*say* anna–royd ba–**rommi**ta)
an instrument for measuring air–pressure by the movement of the elastic top of a box which has been emptied of air.
[A– + Greek *neros* wet + –OID]

anesthesia (*say* annis–**theez**–ya) *noun*
see ANAESTHESIA.

aneurysm (*say* **an**–yoo–rizm) *noun*
also spelt **aneurism**
a disorder of the heart or arteries in which the wall bulges outwards at an area of weakness.
[Greek *aneurysma* a widening]

anew *adverb*
once more or again: 'we will start *anew*'.

angel (*say* **ane**–j'l) *noun*
1. *Jewish, Christian:* a divine or spiritual being, usually pictured as having wings, who is an attendant or messenger of God.
2. (*informal*) any beautiful or kind person: 'you're an *angel* for doing my shopping'.
Word Family: **angelic** (*say* an–**jellik**), *adjective*; **angelically,** *adverb.*
[Greek *aggelos* messenger]

angelica (*say* an–**jellika**) *noun*
a fragrant plant, the crystallized stalks of which are used in cooking as a decoration.

angelus (*say* **anja**–lus) *noun*
Roman Catholic: a prayer to the Virgin Mary in remembrance of the Annunciation, said daily at 6 a.m., noon and 6 p.m.
angelus bell, the bell tolled at these times.

anger *noun*
a strong feeling of displeasure and often hostility: 'her clumsy apology only made his *anger* greater'.
Word Family: **anger,** *verb.*

angina pectoris (*say* an–**jie**–na pekta–ris)
short form is **angina**
brief severe pain in the heart due to the blockage of a coronary artery and a lack of oxygen reaching the heart muscle.
[Latin *angina* spasm + *pectoris* of the chest]

angiosperm (*say* **anjio**–sperm) *noun*
any of a large group of flowering plants in which the seeds are enclosed by

an ovary, which becomes a fruit after fertilization.
Compare GYMNOSPERM.
[Greek *aggeion* vessel + *sperma* seed]

angle (1) *noun*
1. the space between two lines or planes which diverge from a point.
2. the inclination to each other of such lines or planes, measured in degrees (360 making a revolution) or in radians (2π making a revolution).
3. an aspect or point of view: 'we must consider all *angles* of the matter'.
angle *verb*
to move or direct at an angle: 'the roof was *angled* steeply to allow snow to slide off'.
Usage: 'the question was *angled* so that only one answer was possible' (= biased, slanted).
[Latin *angulus*]

angle (2) *verb*
to fish.
Usage: 'she *angled* for an invitation to the party' (= schemed, tried).
Word Family: **angler,** *noun,* a fisherman.

angle iron
a steel bar with an L-shaped cross-section.

Anglican Church
Christian: see CHURCH OF ENGLAND.
Word Family: **Anglican,** *noun.*

Anglicism (*say* **angli**-sizm) *noun*
an English expression or idiom.
[Late Latin *Anglice* in English]

anglicize (*say* **angli**-size) **anglicise** *verb*
to make or become English in character, habits, etc.: 'the *anglicized* pronunciation of a foreign word'.

Anglo-Indian *noun*
a) a person with mixed Indian and British parentage. b) (*formerly*) a person of British descent who has lived in India for a long time.

Anglophile (*say* anglo-file) *noun*
a person who has an admiration for Britain and British things.
Word Family: **Anglophilia** (*say* anglo-**fillia**), *noun.*

Anglo-Saxon *noun*
1. a person of English descent, particularly in Great Britain or North America.
2. *History:* an inhabitant of England during the six centuries before the Norman Conquest (A.D. 1066).
3. *Language:* see ENGLISH.
[from *Angul,* a district in Schleswig, northern Germany, and *Saxony,* formerly the north-west coast of Germany]

angora (*say* an-**gawra**) *noun*
a) a cat, goat or rabbit having long, silky hair. b) the yarn or fabric made from the coat of such an animal.
[from *Angora* Ankara, the capital of Turkey]

angry *adjective*
full of anger: 'he was unabashed by her *angry* glare'.
Word Family: **angrily,** *adverb.*

angst *noun*
(*use is often ironical*) a morbid anxiety, especially about the state of the modern world.
[German, anguish]

angstrom *noun*
a unit of length equal to 10^{-10} m. See UNITS in grey pages.
[after *A. J. Angstrom,* 1814-74, a Swedish physicist]

anguish (*say* **ang**-wish) *noun*
an extreme pain or suffering: 'she was in *anguish* over his death'.
Word Family: **anguish,** *verb.*

angular (*say* **ang**-yoo-la) *adjective*
1. a) having, consisting of or forming an angle. b) measured by an angle: 'the *angular* distance'.
2. (of a person) bony or awkward.
Word Family: **angularity,** *noun.*

angular distance
the distance between two bodies, measured as an angle from the observer.

angular momentum
the product of the angular velocity of an object, its mass and the square of its distance from the centre.

angular velocity
Physics: the rate of movement through an angle around a centre, measured in degrees, radians or revolutions per unit of time.

anhydride (*say* an-**high**-dride) *noun*
Chemistry: a compound which is formed from another compound, such as an acid or a base, by the removal of one or more molecules of water. The process is usually reversible.
Word Family: **anhydrous,** *adjective,* of or relating to a substance which contains no water.
[Greek *an-* without + *hydor* water]

aniline (*say* **anni**–leen) *noun*
Chemistry: an oily liquid (formula $C_6H_5NH_2$), prepared from benzene. It is the basis of many dyes, plastics and resins.
[from Arabic, indigo]

animadvert (*say* annim–ad**vert**) *verb*
to criticize.
Word Family: **animadversion** (*say* annim–ad–**ver**–*zh*'n), *noun*.
[Latin *animus* mind + *vertere* to turn]

animal *noun*
1. any living organism which is able to move about for at least part of its life, but cannot make its own food from chemical elements or simple compounds. Compare PLANT.
2. any beast-like or uncivilized person.
animal *adjective*
1. of or relating to animals.
2. of the physical rather than intellectual nature of man: 'food is an *animal* need'.
[Latin, a living being]

animal spirits
a vigorous state of good health.

animate *verb*
to make alive or lively: 'her face was *animated* by her smile'.
Word Family: **animate**, *adjective*, alive or possessing life; **animately**, *adverb*; **animation**, *noun*.

animated cartoon
see CARTOON.

animism (*say* **anni**–mizm) *noun*
the belief that all beings and objects have a soul.
Word Family: **animist**, *noun*; **animistic**, *adjective*.
[Latin *anima* the soul]

animosity (*say* anni–**mossi**–tee) *noun*
a feeling of hostility or aggression.
[Latin *animosus* spirited]

animus *noun*
1. animosity.
2. a moving or animating force.

anion (*say* **an**–eye–on) *noun*
Chemistry: a negatively charged ion which is attracted to the anode during electrolysis. Compare CATION.
[Greek *ana* up + ION]

aniseed *noun*
the strong-smelling seed of a plant called **anise**, used in medicine and cooking.
[Greek *anison* anise + SEED]

ankle *noun*
1. the joint connecting the lower leg to the foot, made up of seven bones called **tarsal bones**.
2. the slender part of the leg immediately above the foot.

anklet *noun*
1. *American:* a short sock covering the ankle.
2. an ornamental band or chain worn around the ankle.

annals *plural noun*
a) a history of events recorded year by year. b) the books containing such records.
Word Family: **annalist**, *noun*.
[Latin *annales* chronicles]

anneal (*say* a–**neel**) *verb*
to heat and then carefully cool a material, such as glass, to remove any structural weaknesses and hence toughen it.

annelid (*say* **an**–ellid) *noun*
any of a group of segmented (ringed) worms, e.g. the earthworm.
[Latin *anulus* a ring]

annex (*say* a–**neks**) *verb*
1. to attach or join to something larger: 'the farm was *annexed* to the neighbouring estate'.
2. to take over or attach land to one's own: 'the empire *annexed* several small territories during the short war'.
Word Family: **annexation**, *noun*.
[AN- (2) + Latin *nexus* tied to]

annexe (*say* **an**–eks) **annex** *noun*
1. a building or structure added to or situated near a larger one.
2. anything which has been added or joined.

annihilate (*say* a–**nigh**–a–late) *verb*
to completely destroy or defeat.
Word Family: **annihilation**, *noun*.
[AD- + Latin *nihil* nothing]

anniversary (*say* anni–**versa**–ree) *noun*
a) the annual return of the date of an event: 'a wedding *anniversary*'. b) the celebration of this.
[Latin *annus* year + *versus* turning]

anno domini (*say* anno **dommin**–eye)
(*informal*) advancing age: 'his main worry is *anno domini*'.
[Latin, in the year of the Lord; normally abbreviated to A.D., as in A.D. 1066]

annotate *verb*
to supply or add notes, e.g. in explanation, criticism, etc.: 'this book is *annotated* in the margins'.

Word Family: **annotation**, *noun*; **annotator**, *noun.*
[AN– (2) + Latin *notare* to record]

announce *verb*
to state or make known publicly: 'the Prime Minister *announced* the new policies'.
Usage: 'snow *announced* the beginning of winter' (= introduced).
Word Family: **announcement**, *noun*; **announcer**, *noun*, a person who announces or narrates, especially on radio or television.
[AN– (2) + Latin *nuntius* a messenger]

annoy (*say* a–**noy**) *verb*
to displease or irritate: 'she was *annoyed* by the delay'.
Word Family: **annoyance**, *noun*, a) something which annoys, b) the act of annoying, c) the feeling of being annoyed.

annual *adjective*
1. occurring once a year: 'an *annual* race meeting'.
2. happening over the course of a year: 'the *annual* journey of the planets'.
annual *noun*
1. a book published once a year.
2. *Biology:* any plant which completes its life cycle within one season or one year.
[Latin *annus* a year]

annuity (*say* a–**new**–it–ee) *noun*
Insurance: a sum of money paid as a regular yearly income from an insurance policy.

annul (*say* a–**nul**) *verb*
(**annulled, annulling**)
to abolish or make void, e.g. a law or marriage.
Word Family: **annulment**, *noun.*
[AN– (2) + Latin *nullus* none]

annular (*say* **an**–yewla) *adjective*
ring-shaped.
annular eclipse, an eclipse of the sun when a narrow ring of light is visible round the dark body of the moon.
[Latin *anulus* a ring]

Annunciation
(*say* a–**nun**–see–ay–sh'n) *noun*
Christian: a) the angel Gabriel's announcement to the Virgin Mary that she would give birth to Christ. b) the festival celebrating this.
[Latin, announcement]

anode (*say* **an**–ode) *noun*
a positive electrode. Compare CATHODE.
[Greek *ana* up + *hodos* a way]

anodize (*say* **anna**–dize) **anodise** *verb*
to coat metal with a protective layer by electrolysis.

anodyne (*say* **anna**–dine) *noun*
1. any drug which relieves pain.
2. anything which relieves distress.
[Greek *an–* without + *odyné* pain]

anoint *verb*
to put oil on as a sign of consecration, especially in a religious ceremony.
Word Family: **anointment**, *noun.*

anomaly (*say* a–**nomma**–lee) *noun*
anything which is irregular or different from what is normal: 'a flightless bird is an *anomaly*'.
Word Family: **anomalous**, *adjective.*
[Greek *anomalos* uneven]

anon *adverb*
an old word meaning soon.
ever and anon, now and then.

anonymous (*say* a–**nonni**–mus) *adjective*
having no known or acknowledged name or authorship: 'an *anonymous* poem'.
Usage: 'an *anonymous* face which she could not recall' (= lacking individuality).
Word Family: **anonymously**, *adverb*; **anonymity** (*say* anna–**nimmi**–tee), *noun.*
[Greek *an–* without + *onyma* name]

anorak (*say* **anna**–rak) *noun*
also called a **parka**
a waterproof jacket, usually with a hood; originally a fur jacket worn by Eskimos.
[Eskimo]

anorexia (*say* anna–**reksia**) *noun*
an illness causing complete loss of appetite.
[Greek *an–* without + *orexis* appetite]

another (*say* a–**nutha**) *adjective*
1. an additional: 'pass me *another* cake'.
2. a different: 'come *another* day'.
another *pronoun*
1. an additional one: 'choose *another*'.
2. a different one: 'going from one place to *another*'.
3. a similar or identical one.
one another, 'you must look after *one another*' (= each other).

answer (*say* **ahnsa**) *noun*
1. a reply or response: 'please give me an *answer* to my request'.
2. a solution to a problem: 'what *answer* did you get for that maths problem?'.

answer *verb*
to respond.
Usages:
a) 'this should *answer* our purpose' (= suit, serve).
b) 'this man *answers* to your description' (= corresponds).
answer for, a) 'who will *answer for* the damage?' (= accept responsibility for); b) 'he must *answer for* such cruel violence' (= pay for, suffer the consequences of).
answerable *adjective*
1. responsible or accountable: 'who is *answerable* for this child's behaviour?'.
2. able to be answered.

ant *noun*
any of a group of very small insects which form, and live in, communities.

antacid (*say* an-**tassid**) *noun*
any substance which neutralizes or counteracts acids, e.g. in the stomach.

antagonism (*say* an**tagga**-nizm) *noun*
any active opposition or hostility: 'he feels great *antagonism* towards his wife'.
antagonist *noun*
a person actively opposed to, or in competition with, another.
Word Family: **antagonize, antagonise,** *verb*, to make hostile; **antagonistic** (*say* an-tagga-**nistik**), *adjective.*
[ANTI- + Greek *agon* a contest]

antarctic *adjective*
at or near the South Pole.
[Greek *antarktikos* opposite the north]

Antarctica *noun*
the continent around the South Pole, almost entirely covered by a vast icesheet.

Antarctic Circle
a line drawn on a map showing the most northerly point at which the sun does not set on one day a year, at about 66°30′ south.

ante (*say* **anti**) *noun*
Cards: a minimum bet placed before the first card is dealt, e.g. in poker.
[from ANTE-]

ante- (*say* **anti**)
a prefix meaning before, as in *antecedent.*

anteater *noun*
any of various animals which live on ants, such as the echidna.

antecedent (*say* anti-**see**-d'nt) *noun*
1. (*plural*) one's ancestors or past history.
2. *Grammar:* the word or phrase in a sentence to which a pronoun refers. *Example*: in the sentence 'have you seen the book that I bought yesterday?' *book* is the antecedent of *that.*
antecedent *adjective*
occurring before or earlier.
[ANTE- + Latin *cedere* to go]

antechamber *noun*
see ANTEROOM.

antedate (*say* **anti**-date) *verb*
to predate.

antediluvian (*say* anti-de-**loo**vian) *adjective*
before the Biblical Flood.
Usage: 'that is a very *antediluvian* belief' (= primitive, outdated).
[ANTE- + Latin *diluvium* deluge]

antelope (*say* **anti**-lope) *noun*
any of various horned, ruminant mammals similar to deer, such as the chamois, gazelle and gnu.

ante meridiem (*say* anti mer-**riddi**-em)
short form is **a.m.**
the time before midday. Compare POST MERIDIEM.
[ANTE- + Latin *meridiem* midday]

antenatal (*say* anti-**nay**-t'l) *adjective*
during pregancy but before birth: 'an *antenatal* clinic'.
[ANTE- + Latin *natus* born]

antenna (*say* an-**tenna**) *noun*
1. *Biology:* either of the pair of jointed outgrowths occurring on the heads of insects and some other animals. Plural is **antennae** (*say* an-**tennee**).
2. *Electronics:* an aerial. Plural is **antennas.**
[Latin, sail-yard]

anterior (*say* an-**teeria**) *adjective*
1. situated before or to the front: 'an *anterior* room'.
2. preceding in time.
[Latin, earlier, before]

anteroom *noun*
also called an **antechamber**
a waiting room outside a larger room.

anthem *noun*
a short, solemn song of praise. A **national anthem** is one adopted by a country to express patriotism and loyalty.

anther *noun*
Biology: the end of a stamen containing the pollen.
[Greek *anthos* a flower]

anthology (*say* an–**tholl**a–jee) *noun*
a collection of poems or literary extracts.
Word Family: **anthologist**, *noun.*
[Greek *anthos* a flower + *legein* to collect]

anthracite (*say* anthra–site) *noun*
also called **hard coal**
a coal which is almost pure carbon.
[Greek *anthrakos* of coal]

anthrax *noun*
an often fatal, bacterial infection of cattle and man, often causing severe carbuncles.
[Greek, coal, carbuncle]

anthropo–
a prefix meaning man, or relating to man, as in *anthropology.*

anthropocentric
(*say* an–thropp a–**sen**trik) *adjective*
interpreting the universe exclusively in terms of human values and experience.

anthropoid *adjective*
of or resembling man.
anthropoid *noun*
an ape which resembles man, such as a gorilla.
[ANTHROPO– + –OID]

anthropology (*say* anthra–**poll**a–jee) *noun*
the study of man and the customs, characteristics, etc. of human societies.
Word Family: **anthropological** (*say* an–thropp a–**lo**ji–k'l), *adjective*; **anthropologist**, *noun.*
[ANTHROPO– + –LOGY]

anthropomorphic
(*say* an-throppa-**mor**fik) *adjective*
attributing human characteristics to something which is non-human, such as a god.
[ANTHROPO– + Greek *morphé* a shape]

anti–
a prefix meaning against, opposite or opposed to, as in *antibiotic.*

anti–aircraft *adjective*
relating to weapons and equipment used against enemy aircraft.

antibiotic (*say* anti–by–**ott**ik) *noun*
a substance, such as penicillin, produced by living organisms, which will kill or prevent the growth of other organisms, and is widely used to treat disease.

antibody (*say* **anti**–body) *noun*
Medicine: a protein produced when any foreign substance, called an **antigen**, enters the body. By combining with and neutralizing antigens, antibodies provide immunity to disease.

antic *noun*
(*often plural*) any ludicrous or absurd behaviour: 'journalists love the *antics* of politicians'.

anticipate (*say* an**tissi**–pate) *verb*
to expect or realize beforehand: 'I *anticipated* a better response'.
Usages:
a) 'the general successfully *anticipated* the enemy's strategy' (= forestalled).
b) 'Jules Verne *anticipated* modern technology by 50 years' (= foresaw).
Word Family: **anticipation**, *noun*; **anticipatory**, *adjective.*
[Latin *anticipare* to take before]

anticlerical (*say* anti–**klerri**–k'l) *adjective*
opposed to the exercise of political influence by the clergy.
Word Family: **anticlericalism**, *noun.*

anticlimax (*say* **anti**–klie–maks) *noun*
a) the weakening of an effect, especially in a literary work. b) a disappointing outcome or conclusion.
Word Family: **anticlimactic** (*say* anti–klie–**mak**tik), *adjective.*

anticline (*say* **anti**–kline) *noun*
Geology: an upward curve in layers of folded rock. Compare SYNCLINE.
Word Family: **anticlinal** (*say* anti–**kline**'l), *adjective.*
[ANTI– + Greek *kleinein* to lean]

anticlockwise *adjective, adverb*
in a direction opposite to the movement of the hands of a clock.

anticyclone (*say* anti–**sigh**–klone) *noun*
Weather: see HIGH.

antidepressant (*say* anti–de–**press**'nt) *noun*
any of a group of drugs used to prevent or relieve mental depression.

antidote *noun*
1. *Medicine:* any substance that will counteract the effects of a poison, disease, etc.
2. any remedy: 'time is the only *antidote* for a broken heart'.
Word Family: **antidotal**, *adjective.*
[ANTI– + Greek *dotos* given]

antifouling *noun*
Nautical: a protective coating painted on the bottom of boats to discourage marine growths.

antifreeze *noun*
a substance added to the water in car radiators, etc. to prevent freezing.

antigen (*say* **anti**–j'n) *noun*
Medicine: see ANTIBODY.

anti–hero *noun*
a character cast as the hero of a modern novel or play, but devoid of heroic qualities.

antihistamine (*say* anti–**hista**–meen) *noun*
any of a group of drugs which neutralize histamines, used to treat allergies.

antiknock (*say* **anti**–nok) *noun*
a substance which prevents pre–ignition in an internal combustion engine.

antilogarithm (*say* anti–**logga**–ri*th*'m) *noun*
see LOGARITHM.

antimacassar (*say* anti–ma–**kassa**) *noun*
a decorative cover for the back and arms of a chair.
[ANTI– + *Macassar* oil, a hair oil]

antimatter (*say* **anti**–matter) *noun*
Physics: a) a phenomenon, possible in theory but as yet undetected, formed from antiparticles in the same way that matter is formed from particles. b) any antiparticles.

antimony (*say* an–**timma**–nee) *noun*
element number 51, a brittle metal which expands on solidifying, used in alloys, such as type metal, and in medicine.
See CHEMICAL ELEMENTS in grey pages.

antinode *noun*
Physics: a point of greatest amplitude in a standing wave. Compare NODE.

antinomy (*say* an–**tinna**–mee) *noun*
an opposition or contradiction.
[ANTI– + Greek *nomos* a law]

anti–oxidant *noun*
Chemistry: a chemical added to a substance or product to prevent it deteriorating by oxidation.

antiparticle (*say* **anti**–parti–k'l) *noun*
Physics: a particle identical to a corresponding elementary particle except for opposite charge and opposite magnetism: 'the positron is the *antiparticle* of the electron'.

antipasto (*say* anti–**pasto**) *noun*
an appetizer.
[Italian *anti* before + *pasto* a meal]

antipathy (*say* an–**tippa**–thee) *noun*
a strong, fixed dislike or aversion: 'my *antipathy* towards him is entirely instinctive'.
Word Family: **antipathetic** (*say* anti–pa–**thettik**), *adjective.*
[ANTI– + Greek *pathos* feeling]

antipersonnel (*say* anti–persa–**nel**) *adjective*
(of weapons) designed to destroy people rather than buildings, etc.

antiperspirant (*say* anti–**perspi**–r'nt) *noun*
any substance which is used to prevent or decrease sweating.

antipodes (*say* an–**tippa**–deez) *plural noun*
1. any two points directly opposite each other on a globe, such as the North and South Poles.
2. (*often capital*) Australia and New Zealand.
Word Family: **antipodean** (*say* an–tippa–**dee**–an), *adjective, noun.*
[ANTI– + Greek *podos* of a foot]

antiquarian (*say* anti–**kwair**–ian) *adjective*
of or relating to the study of antiquities.
Word Family: **antiquarian, antiquary** (*say* **anti**–kwerri), *nouns,* an expert on, or dealer in, antiquities.

antiquated (*say* anti–**kwaytid**) *adjective*
old–fashioned, quaint or obsolete: '*antiquated* machinery is often valued as a collector's item'.

antique (*say* an–**teek**) *noun*
any rare or valued object from the past, especially one more than 100 years old.
antique *adjective*
a) of or relating to antiques. b) of or relating to the distant past: 'the fountain gave the courtyard an *antique* charm'.
antiquity (*say* an–**tikwi**–tee) *noun*
1. a) any ancient time or remote period: 'the origins of the legend are lost in *antiquity*'. b) the quality of being ancient: 'it is a city of great *antiquity*'.
2. (*usually plural*) any works of art or ruins from the distant past: 'we studied the Greek *antiquities* in the museum'.
[Latin *antiquus* ancient]

anti–Semitism *noun*
a dislike or ill–treatment of Jews.
Word Family: **anti–Semitic**, *adjective;* **anti–Semite**, *noun.*

antiseptic (*say* anti–**sep**tik) *adjective*
of or relating to the killing of micro–organisms.
Word Family: **antiseptic,** *noun,* a substance which kills micro–organisms.

antiserum (*say* anti–seer'm) *noun*
a serum containing antibodies.

antisocial (*say* anti–**so**–sh'l) *adjective*
withdrawn from or actively hostile to others or social institutions.

antithesis (*say* an–**tith**a–sis) *noun*
the direct opposite of something: 'certainty is the *antithesis* of doubt'.
Word Family: **antithetical, antithetic,** *adjective.*
[ANTI– + THESIS]

antitoxin *noun*
an antibody produced by the body in order to counteract a poison.
Word Family: **antitoxic,** *adjective.*

antler *noun*
either of the bony growths on the skull of deer, covered by soft, velvety skin during growth and shed and renewed annually. Compare HORN.

antonym (*say* **an**ta–nim) *noun*
a word with opposite meaning to another: 'good is an *antonym* of bad'. Compare SYNONYM.
[ANTI– + Greek *onyma* name]

antrum *noun*
plural is **antra**
either of two large sinuses within the bones of the upper jaw.
[Greek *antron* a cave]

anus (*say* **ay**–nus) *noun*
Anatomy: the ring of muscle at the lower end of the alimentary canal, connecting the rectum to the exterior, through which solid waste matter is excreted.
Word Family: **anal** (*say* ayn'l), *adjective.*
[Latin]

anvil *noun*
a heavy iron block, often with a horn–like projection on one end, on which metals are hammered into shape.

anxiety (*say* ang–**zie**–a–tee) *noun*
a state of worry or apprehension: 'his *anxiety* about public speaking is hard to understand'.

anxious (*say* **ang**–shus) *adjective*
1. suffering from or causing anxiety: a) 'I can't help being *anxious* about the examination'; b) 'his illness was an *anxious* time for all of us'.
2. eager: 'she was *anxious* to please'.
Word Family: **anxiously,** *adverb.*
[Latin *anxius*]

any (*say* **en**nee) *adjective*
1. one or some: 'do you have *any* friends?'.
2. every: '*any* fool knows that'.
3. a great or unlimited amount: '*any* number of things could still go wrong'.
any *pronoun*
any person: 'do *any* of you know him?'.
any *adverb*
at all: 'are you feeling *any* better?'.
anybody *pronoun*
any person: 'didn't *anybody* help you?'.
anyhow *adverb*
1. in any case: '*anyhow,* the contract was already signed'.
2. in a careless manner: 'the table was put together *anyhow*'.
anyone *pronoun*
anybody.
anything *pronoun*
any thing whatever: 'did *anything* strange happen last night?'.
anyway *adverb*
however or in any case: '*anyway,* I'll see you tomorrow'.
anywhere *adverb*
in, at or to any place: 'we can't find it *anywhere*'.

Anzac *noun*
a soldier from Australia or New Zealand in World War I.
[from A(*ustralia*) *and* N(*ew*) Z(*ealand*) A(*rmy*) C(*orps*)]

aorta (*say* ay–**or**ta) *noun*
Anatomy: the largest artery in the body, arching out of the heart and down through the diaphragm into the abdomen.
Word Family: **aortic, aortal,** *adjectives.*

ap–
a variant of the prefix **ad–**.

apace *adverb*
quickly or rapidly.

apart *adverb*
separated or at a distance: a) 'let's take the engine *apart*'; b) 'joking *apart,* what did you think of my speech?'.
Word Family: **apart,** *adjective,* separate or independent.

apartheid (*say* a–**par**tite *or* a–**par**tate) *noun*
a policy or law segregating racial groups in South Africa.
[Afrikaans *apart* apart + *heid* –hood]

apartment *noun*
1. a) a single room. b) a suite of furnished rooms.
2. *American:* a flat.

apathy (*say* **appa**–thee) *noun*
a lack of interest or energy: 'the appeal for funds met with general *apathy*'.
Word Family: **apathetic** (*say* appa–**thet**tik), *adjective*; **apathetically**, *adverb*.
[Greek *apatheia* insensibility]

apatite (*say* **appa**–tite) *noun*
a calcium phosphate mineral containing some fluorine and water, present in the enamel of teeth and used in making superphosphate.
[Greek *apatein* to deceive]

ape *noun*
any of the tail-less primates closest to man in evolutionary development, such as the chimpanzee, gibbon, gorilla and orang-outang. Compare MONKEY.
ape *verb*
to imitate or mimic: 'children frequently *ape* their teachers'.

aperient (*say* a–**peer**i–ent) *adjective*
of or relating to a substance acting as a mild laxative
Word Family: **aperient**, *noun*.
[Latin *aperire* to open]

apéritif (*say* a–perri–**teef**) **aperitif** *noun*
also called an **aperitive** (*say* a–**perri**–tiv)
an alcoholic drink taken before a meal to stimulate the appetite.
[French]

aperture (*say* **appa**–cher) *noun*
1. a gap or opening.
2. *Photography:* the size of the adjustable diaphragm in a camera.
[Latin *apertura* an opening]

apex (*say* **ay**–peks) *noun*
plural is **apexes** or **apices** (*say* **aypi**–seez)
the highest point or summit: 'the *apex* of a triangle is opposite its base'.
[Latin, point or summit]

aphasia (*say* a–**faze**–ya) *noun*
the loss of the ability to use language, caused by lesions in the brain.
Word Family: **aphasiac**, *noun*, a person suffering from aphasia; **aphasic**, *adjective*.
[A– + Greek *phasis* speech]

aphelion (*say* af**feel**–y'n) *noun*
plural is **aphelia**
Astronomy: the point in the orbit of a planet or comet when it is furthest from the sun. Compare PERIHELION.
[Greek *apo* from + *helios* sun]

aphid (*say* **ay**fid) **aphis** *noun*
any of a group of small insects which suck plant juices.

aphonia (*say* af**fone**–ya) *noun*
a loss of voice, arising from physical or psychological causes.
[A– + Greek *phoné* a voice]

aphorism (*say* **affa**–rizm) *noun*
a short, pithy saying which expresses a truth, such as a proverb.
[Greek *aphorismos* a definition]

aphrodisiac (*say* afra–**dizzi**–ak) *noun*
any food, drink or drug arousing sexual desire.
[from APHRODITE]

Aphrodite (*say* afra–**die**–tee) *noun*
Greek mythology: the goddess of beauty, fertility and sexual love, identified with the Roman goddess Venus.

apiary (*say* **ape**–y'ree) *noun*
an area, usually containing beehives, in which bees are kept.
Word Family: **apiarian**, *adjective*, relating to the breeding and care of bees; **apiarist**, *noun*, a person who keeps bees.
[Latin *apis* a bee]

apical (*say* **appi**–k'l) *adjective*
of, at or forming the apex.

apices *plural noun*
see APEX.

apiculture (*say* **ay**–pikkulcher) *noun*
the breeding and care of bees.

apiece (*say* a–**peece**) *adverb*
each, or for each one: 'the chairs at the sale were £10 *apiece*'.

apish (*say* **ay**–pish) *adjective*
imitative, especially in a silly manner.
Word Family: **apishly**, *adverb*.

aplomb (*say* a–**plom**) *noun*
poise or self-possession.
[French]

apocalypse (*say* a–**pokka**–lips) *noun*
1. any revelation or remarkable disclosure.
2. *Christian:* the revelation described in the Bible in the Book of Revelation.
Word Family: **apocalyptic** (*say* a–pokka–**lip**tik), **apocalyptical**, *adjective*; **apocalyptically**, *adverb*.
[Greek *apokalypsis* a revelation]

apocrypha (*say* a–**pokri**–fa) *plural noun*

any writings or works considered not to be genuine or authentic.
Word Family: **apocryphal,** *adjective,* doubtful or false.
[Greek *apokryphos* hidden]

apogee (*say* **appa**–jee) *noun*
1. *Astronomy:* the point in the orbit of the moon, a planet or an artificial satellite when it is furthest from the earth. Compare PERIGEE.
2. the highest point or climax.
[Greek *apogaion* from the earth]

Apollo *noun*
Greek mythology: the god of youth, light, archery, healing, prophecy and music.

apology (*say* a–**poll**a–jee) *noun*
an expression of regret for some wrong or injury: a) 'please accept my *apologies* for being so late'; b) 'I expect an *apology* from that rude child'.
Usage: 'do you call that *apology* for a horse a thoroughbred?' (= poor substitute).
Word Family: **apologize, apologise,** *verb;* **apologetic,** *adjective;* **apologetically,** *adverb;* **apologia** (*say* appa–**lo**–ja), *noun,* a formal justification or defence.
[Greek *apologia* a speech in defence]

apoplexy *noun*
1. *Medicine:* a sudden loss of a bodily function, such as speech, due to a brain haemorrhage.
2. (*informal*) a fit of rage: 'merely mentioning the subject gives him *apoplexy*'.
Word Family: **apoplectic,** *adjective;* **apoplectically,** *adverb.*
[Greek *apoplexia* a stroke]

apostasy (*say* a–**pos**ta–see) *noun*
the desertion of a religious faith, political principle, cause, etc.
Word Family: **apostate,** *noun.*
[Greek *apostasis* a standing away from]

a posteriori (*say* ay posterri–**aw**–rye)
based on experience and observation rather than theory; by induction. Compare A PRIORI.
[Latin, from what comes after]

apostle (*say* a–**poss**'l) *noun*
1. a) any of the early Christian disciples, missionaries and teachers. b) the founder of the Christian faith in any region or country.
2. any reformer, pioneer or leader of a cause: 'he was respected as an *apostle* of freedom'.

apostolic (*say* appa–**stoll**ik) *adjective*
1. *Christian:* of or relating to an apostle or apostles.
2. *Roman Catholic:* of or relating to the Pope, as successor to St. Peter.
[Greek *apostolos* one sent forth]

apostrophe (1) (*say* a–**pos**tra–fee) *noun*
a punctuation mark ('), used to indicate the following:
(the possessive case) 'that is *John's* book'.
(the omission of letters or numbers) a) '*I'll* tell him'; b) 'in the *'20s*'.
(the formation of certain plurals) 'three *9's* are 27'.
[Greek *apo–* away + *strephein* to turn]

apostrophe (2) (*say* a–**pos**tra–fee) *noun*
a passage in a speech or discourse addressing an absent person as if he were present.

apothecaries' weight
a system of units of mass for drugs. The units are grain, scruple, drachm, ounce and pound. See UNITS in grey pages.

apothecary (*say* a–**poth**a–ka–ree) *noun*
an old word for a chemist or pharmacist.
[Greek *apotheké* a storehouse]

apotheosis (*say* a–pothi–**o**–sis) *noun*
plural is **apotheoses**
1. the act of raising a person to the status of a god or saint.
2. the essence or perfect example of something: 'she thinks table manners are the *apotheosis* of good breeding'.
[Greek *apo* from + *theos* a god]

appal (*say* a–**pawl**) *verb*
(appalled, appalling)
in America spelt **appall**
to shock or fill with horror: 'I was *appalled* at the news of her death'.
[Old French *apallir* to make or become pale]

apparatus (*say* appa–**ray**tus) *noun*
plural is **apparatuses**
a set of instruments, machinery or appliances for a particular task.
Usage: 'the *apparatus* of government is both costly and unwieldy' (= organization, administration).
[Latin, instruments]

apparel (*say* a–**parr**'l) *noun*
any clothing or dress.

apparent (*say* a–**parr**'nt) *adjective*
a) clearly seen or understood: 'it is quite *apparent* that you don't want to come'. b) seeming: 'her confidence is *apparent* rather than real'.

Word Family: **apparently**, *adverb.*
[Latin *apparens* becoming visible]

apparent horizon
see HORIZON.

apparition (*say* appa-**rish**'n) *noun*
a sudden or frightening vision, especially of a ghost.

appeal (*say* a-**peel**) *verb*
1. to call upon or make an earnest or desperate plea: 'he *appealed* for understanding'.
2. to offer interest or attraction: 'does that book *appeal* to you?'.
3. *Law:* to apply for a case to be heard again by a higher court.
Word Family: **appeal**, *noun.*
[Latin *appellare* to address, call by name]

appear (*say* a-**peer**) *verb*
1. to become clear or visible: 'the sun *appeared* at last'.
2. to look like: 'try not to *appear* frightened'.
3. to come or perform before the public: 'the orchestra has *appeared* in several countries'.
appearance *noun*
1. the act of appearing.
2. (*plural*) any outward signs or indications: 'you shouldn't judge by *appearances*'.
Phrases:
keep up appearances, to maintain an acceptable outward show.
to all appearances, 'he was *to all appearances* a wealthy man' (= as far as could be seen).
[Latin *apparere* to become visible]

appease (*say* a-**peez**) *verb*
to quiet or calm, especially to placate someone who is hostile: 'the employers tried to *appease* the workers by offering a bonus'.
Word Family: **appeasement**, *noun.*
[Old French *à pais* to peace]

appellation (*say* appa-**lay**-sh'n) *noun*
1. a name or title: 'the official *appellation* is Your Excellency'.
2. the act of naming.
[Latin *appellare* to address, call by name]

append *verb*
to add, join or attach: 'I hereby *append* my signature'.
appendage *noun*
a subordinate or subsidiary part: a) 'only a biologist would refer to an arm as an *appendage*'; b) 'he regarded his secretary as a mere *appendage*'.
[AP- + Latin *pendere* to hang]

appendicectomy
(*say* a-pendi-**sekta**-mee) *noun*
also called an **appendectomy** (*say* appen-**dekta**-mee)
an operation to remove the appendix.
[APPENDIX + Greek *ektomé* a cutting out]

appendicitis (*say* a-pendi-**sigh**-tis) *noun*
an inflammation of the appendix causing severe abdominal pain, which may require the removal of the appendix.
[APPENDIX + -ITIS]

appendix *noun*
plural is **appendices** (*say* a-pendi-seez) or **appendixes**
1. any material added at the end of a book, such as lists, tables, etc.
2. *Anatomy:* a small tube which is closed at one end and opens into the caecum.
[Latin, something added on]

appertain (*say* appa-**tane**) *verb*
to pertain, belong or relate to: 'the facts *appertaining* to his dismissal were not mentioned'.
[AP- + PERTAIN]

appetite (*say* appi-tite) *noun*
a desire or craving, especially for food.
[Latin *appetitio* a desire]

appetizer, appetiser *noun*
any food or drink served before a meal to stimulate the appetite.

appetizing *adjective*
stimulating or appealing to the appetite: 'an *appetizing* smell from the kitchen'.

applaud (*say* a-**plawd**) *verb*
to express approval or praise, especially by clapping.
Word Family: **applause**, *noun.*
[AP- + Latin *plaudere* to clap hands]

apple *noun*
a round fruit with crisp, firm flesh and a green, yellow or red skin.
Phrases:
in apple-pie order, neatly arranged.
the apple of one's eye, 'John's youngest daughter is *the apple of his eye*' (= specially loved by him).
upset the applecart, 'be careful not to *upset the applecart*' (= spoil the plans).

applejack *noun*
a brandy made from cider.

appliance (*say* a-**ply**-ance) *noun*
a device designed for a special use, especially a domestic device such as an iron.

applicable (*say* a-**plikka**-b'l) *adjective*
suitable or relevant: 'community standards are not *applicable* in this case'.
Word Family: **applicability,** *noun.*

applicant (*say* **apli**-k'nt) *noun*
a candidate or person who applies: '*applicants* for the position must supply references'.

application *noun*
1. a request: a) 'further information will be supplied on *application* to the organizers'; b) 'we regret to inform you that your *application* has been unsuccessful'.
2. the use or relevance of something for a particular purpose: 'past grievances have no *application* now'.
3. a thing applied, especially a preparation: 'this *application* will soothe your sunburn'.
4. the act of applying: 'an *application* of this cream will soothe your sunburn'.
5. any sustained effort or concentration: 'she shows little *application* in science subjects'.

applicator (*say* apli-kayta) *noun*
an instrument for applying something, such as a brush used to apply make-up.

appliqué (*say* **ap**-lee-kay) *adjective*
ornamented by applying pieces of material, etc. to a surface.
[French, put on]

apply (*say* a-**ply**) *verb*
(applied, applying)
1. to put on or into use: a) '*apply* the glue sparingly'; b) 'I solved it by *applying* common sense'.
2. to request or ask to be given: '20 people have *applied* for the job'.
3. to have reference to: 'the pay rise *applies* to all employees'.
to apply oneself, 'he *applied himself* to the task with gusto' (= devoted himself).
applied *adjective*
put into or designed for practical use: '*applied* maths'. Compare PURE.
[Latin *applicare*]

appoint *verb*
1. to select for a post.
2. to equip: 'a *well-appointed* study'.

appointment *noun*
1. an arrangement to meet or visit: 'I have an *appointment* with the dentist at 2.30 p.m.'.
2. an office or position to which a person is appointed: 'his new *appointment* is with the Department of Trade'.
Word Family: **appointee,** *noun,* a person who is appointed.

apportion (*say* a-**por**-sh'n) *verb*
to divide or distribute evenly.
Word Family: **apportionment,** *noun.*

apposite (*say* **appa**-zit) *adjective*
particularly relevant or pertinent.
Word Family: **appositely,** *adverb*; **appositeness,** *noun.*
[Latin *appositus* appropriate]

apposition (*say* appa-**zish**'n) *noun*
the act of adding to or placing together.
Word Family: **appose,** *verb.*

appraise (*say* a-**praze**) *verb*
to estimate the value, quality or price of something.
Word Family: **appraisal,** *noun.*

appreciate (*say* a-**preeshi**-ate) *verb*
1. to value something highly: 'I *appreciate* your help more than I can say'.
2. to understand: 'we *appreciate* your reluctance to supply names'.
3. to rise in value: 'this property has *appreciated* greatly in the past year'. Compare DEPRECIATE.
Word Family: **appreciation,** *noun*; **appreciative, appreciatory,** *adjectives*; **appreciable,** *adjective,* a) noticeable, b) fairly large.
[AP- + Latin *pretium* price]

apprehend (*say* ap-ree-**hend**) *verb*
1. to arrest or seize a person: 'he was *apprehended* a week after the robbery'.
2. to grasp the meaning of something: 'she was quick to *apprehend* my statement'.
3. to anticipate with fear or anxiety: 'I *apprehend* bloodshed before this day is out'.
Word Family: **apprehension,** *noun.*
[Latin *apprehendere* to seize]

apprehensive (*say* ap-ree-**hen**siv) *adjective*
fearful about something which may happen.
Word Family: **apprehensively,** *adverb*; **apprehensiveness,** *noun.*

apprentice (*say* a-**pren**tis) *noun*
a) a person who undertakes to work in a trade for a specified period, in

return for instruction. b) any learner or beginner.
Word Family: **apprenticeship,** *noun*; **apprentice,** *verb.*
[French *apprendre* to learn]

apprise (*say* a–**prize**) *verb*
to inform: 'he *apprised* me of the fact that legal action would be taken'.
[French *appris* taught]

approach *verb*
1. to move nearer or draw near: a) '*approach* the house cautiously'; b) 'as dawn *approached* we made ready to leave'.
2. to make a request: 'you should *approach* your local Member of Parliament about this problem'.
3. to begin or set about something: 'I wouldn't *approach* the problem like that'.
approach *noun*
1. the act of approaching: 'the *approach* of winter'.
2. (*often plural*) an advance made to a person to gain interest or attention: 'he has made *approaches* about buying the house'.
3. any way or means of access: a) 'the *approach* to the camp site was densely overgrown'; b) 'a practical *approach* is usually best'.
Word Family: **approachable,** *adjective*; **approachability,** *noun.*
[French *approcher*]

approbation (*say* apro–**bay**–sh'n) *noun*
approval: 'he gave the scheme his *approbation* upon certain conditions'.
[AP– + Latin *probare* to approve]

appropriate (*say* a–**pro**–pree–it) *adjective*
suitable or fitting: 'an *appropriate* dress for the occasion'.
appropriate (*say* a–**pro**–pree–ate) *verb*
1. to set aside for a special purpose: 'funds for the new project have already been *appropriated*'.
2. to take, especially without permission: 'his book, far from being original, merely *appropriates* my ideas'.
Word Family: **appropriately,** *adverb*; **appropriateness,** *noun*; **appropriation,** *noun,* a) the act of appropriating, b) something which has been appropriated.
[Latin *appropriatus* made one's own]

approval (*say* a–**proo**–v'l) *noun*
a) any agreement or confirmation. b) the act of approving.
on approval, 'she took the chair home *on approval* before deciding to buy it' (= without obligation to buy).

approve (*say* a–**proov**) *verb*
to agree to or consider as worthy, correct, etc.: a) 'I do not *approve* of such behaviour'; b) 'the committee has officially *approved* the minutes'.
[AP– + Latin *probare* to approve]

approximate (*say* a–**proksi**–mit) *adjective*
nearly correct or accurate: 'just tell me the *approximate* price'.
approximate (*say* a–**proksi**–mate) *verb*
to approach or be nearly equal to.
Word Family: **approximation,** *noun*; **approximately,** *adverb.*
[AP– + Latin *proximus* nearest]

appurtenance (*say* a–**pertin**–ance) *noun*
something attached or belonging to another, more important, thing.

apricot (*say* **ay**–prikkot) *noun*
1. a small, round fruit with orange flesh and a hard stone.
2. a yellowish–orange colour.
Word Family: **apricot,** *adjective.*

April *noun*
the fourth month of the year in the Gregorian calendar.
[Latin *Aprilis* the month of opening buds, from *aperire* to open]

a priori (*say* ay pry–**aw**–rye)
not based on fact, observation or study; deduced or presumed. Compare A POSTERIORI.
[Latin, from something prior]

apron (*say* **ay**–pr'n) *noun*
1. a loose piece of clothing worn over clothes to protect them, usually tied at the back.
2. a paved area, especially on an airfield.
tied to the apron–strings, emotionally dependent.
[for *à napron,* from Old French *nape* a tablecloth]

apropos (*say* apra–**po**) *adverb*
to the purpose: 'that's hardly *apropos* to this discussion'.
apropos of, '*apropos of* Judy Garland, who was her last husband?' (= with reference to).
Word Family: **apropos,** *adjective.*
[French *à propos* to the purpose]

apse *noun*
Architecture: a recess in a church, usually vaulted and semicircular.
[Greek *hapsis* an arch]

apt *adjective*
1. relevant or appropriate: 'I think his criticism of the novel is very *apt*'.
2. having a tendency to: 'she is *apt* to talk too much'.
3. intelligent or quick to learn: 'an *apt* student in all subjects'.
Word Family: **aptly**, *adverb*; **aptness**, *noun*.
[Latin *aptus* fitting]

aptitude *noun*
a natural ability or skill: 'he has a great *aptitude* for maths'.

aqua *noun*
Colour: see AQUAMARINE.
[Latin, water]

aqualung (*say* **akwa**–lung) *noun*
also called a **scuba**
an apparatus of one or more cylinders of compressed air, used by a diver to breathe underwater by means of a tube attached to a mouthpiece.

aquamarine (*say* akwa–ma–**reen**) *noun*
1. *Colour:* a light bluish-green colour. Short form is **aqua**.
2. *Geology:* a translucent, pale blue or green variety of beryl, used as a gem.
Word Family: **aquamarine**, *adjective*.
[Latin *aqua marina* seawater]

aquanaut (*say* **akwa**–nawt) *noun*
a skin-diver.
[AQUA + Latin *nauta* a sailor]

aquaplane (*say* **akwa**–plane) *noun*
a single, wide board used as a water-ski.
Word Family: **aquaplane**, *verb*.

aquarium (*say* a–**kwairi**–um) *noun*
plural is **aquariums** or **aquaria**
a pond, tank or building in which living aquatic animals and plants are kept and displayed.

Aquarius (*say* a–**kwairi**–us) *noun*
also called the **Water-bearer**
Astrology: a group of stars, the eleventh sign of the zodiac.
[Latin, water-carrier]

aquatic *adjective*
living or growing in or near water: 'seaweed is an *aquatic* plant'.
[Latin *aquaticus* watery]

aquatint (*say* **akwa**–tint) *noun*
a) an etching process which gives an effect like a watercolour. b) a print made by this process.
[AQUA + TINT]

aqueduct (*say* **akwi**–dukt) *noun*
a man-made channel for carrying water, e.g. on a bridge across a valley.
[AQUA + Latin *ductus* led]

aqueous (*say* **ay**–kwee–us) *adjective*
relating to or containing water.
aqueous humour
Anatomy: the thin clear fluid which fills the space at the front of the eye between the lens and the cornea. Compare VITREOUS HUMOUR under VITREOUS.

aquifer *noun*
a layer of rock which holds or may be permeated by water.
[AQUA + Latin *ferre* to carry]

aquiline *adjective*
(of a nose) curved or hooked like the beak of an eagle.
[Latin *aquila* eagle]

ar–
a variant of the prefix **ad–**.

Arab *noun*
1. any of a people inhabiting parts of North Africa and the Middle East.
2. any of a breed of horses, originally from Arabia, noted for their speed and intelligence.
Word Family: **Arab**, **Arabic**, **Arabian** (*say* a–**ray**bee–an), *adjectives*.

arabesque (*say* arra–**besk**) *noun*
1. *Ballet:* a position with one leg raised backwards in the air and held straight.
2. an ornamental design of leaves, flowers and geometric figures, used in some Eastern architecture.

Arabic numerals
also called **Arabic figures**
the numerical symbols, 1, 2, 3, 4, 5, 6, 7, 8, 9, and 0.

arable (*say* **arra**–b'l) *adjective*
(of land) suitable for cultivation.
[Latin *arare* to plough]

arachnid (*say* a–**rak**nid) *noun*
any of various arthropods, such as spiders, mites, etc., with the body divided into two parts and having four pairs of walking legs.
Word Family: **arachnoid**, *adjective*.
[Greek *arachné* spider]

arbiter (*say* **ar**–bitta) *noun*
1. a person who leads, decides or establishes: 'French designers are the *arbiters* of fashion'.
2. an arbitrator.
[Latin]

arbitrary (*say* **ar**–bitra–ree) *adjective*
1. based on personal opinion or whim rather than reason, etc.: 'an *arbitrary* choice'.
2. despotic or tyrannical: 'the *arbitrary* rule of a dictator'.
Word Family: **arbitrarily**, *adverb*; **arbitrariness**, *noun.*

arbitrate *verb*
to judge or decide, especially in order to settle a dispute.
arbitrator *noun*
also called an **arbiter**
a person appointed to settle disputes.
Word Family: **arbitration**, *noun.*
[Latin *arbitrari*]

arboreal (*say* ar–**bawri**–ul) *adjective*
of, like or adapted to living in trees: 'a squirrel is an *arboreal* rodent'.

arbour (*say* **arba**) *noun*
in America spelt **arbor**
a shady place among trees, especially in a garden.
[Latin *arbor* a tree]

arc (*say* ark) *noun*
1. any part of the circumference of a circle or other curved line.
2. anything shaped like an arc.
3. *Electricity:* a continuous electric discharge across a gap, producing an intense light, as in an arc lamp.
Word Family: **arc**, *verb*, to form an electric arc.
[Latin *arcus* a bow or arch]

arcade *noun*
a) a series of arches. b) a covered hall or passage, often with shops on one or both sides.

arcadian (*say* ar–**kay**–dian) *adjective*
simple, peaceful or innocent.
[after *Arcadia*, a region in ancient Greece considered to be the ideal of rural contentment]

arcane *adjective*
secret or mysterious.
[Latin *arcanus* hidden]

arch (1) *noun*
1. a curved, supporting structure over an opening.
2. something with the shape or function of an arch, such as the curved lower part of the human foot.
Word Family: **arch**, *verb*, a) to form an arch or curve, b) to supply with an arch.
[Latin *arcus* an arch]

arch (2) *adjective*
1. chief or most important: 'an *arch* enemy'.
2. mischievous or cunning in a playful way: 'he gave her an *arch* glance'.
Word Family: **archly**, *adverb*, slyly or roguishly; **archness**, *noun.*
[Greek *arkhos* chief]

arch–
a prefix meaning first or chief, as in *archbishop.*

archaeology (*say* arki–**olla**–jee) *noun*
in America spelt **archeology**
the study of history, especially ancient cultures, by digging up and describing remains, such as buildings, coins, etc.
Word Family: **archaeologist**, *noun*; **archaeological** (*say* arkia–**loji**–k'l), *adjective.*
[Greek *arkhaios* ancient + –LOGY]

archaic (*say* ar–**kay**–ik) *adjective*
being from long ago and therefore not in modern use: 'alarum is an *archaic* word'.
Word Family: **archaism**, *noun.*
[Greek *arkhaios* ancient]

archangel (*say* **ark**–ane–j'l) *noun*
an angel of the highest rank.
[ARCH (2) + ANGEL]

archbishop *noun*
Christian: a bishop of the highest rank.
archbishopric *noun*
the position of an archbishop.
archdiocese (*say* arch–**die**–a–sis) *noun*
the area under the control of an archbishop.

archdeacon *noun*
Christian: a church administrative official next below a bishop.
archdeaconry *noun*
the position of an archdeacon.

archduke *noun*
History: a supreme prince in Austria.
Word Family: **archducal** (*say* arch–**dew**–k'l), *adjective*; **archduchess**, *noun*, a) a female archduke, b) the wife of an archduke.

archer *noun*
1. a person who shoots with a bow and arrow, especially for sport. Also called a **bowman**.
2. *Astrology:* (*capital*) see SAGITTARIUS.
[Latin *arcus* a bow]

archery *noun*
the sport of shooting with bows and arrows.

archetype (*say* **arki**–tipe) *noun*
a first, perfect type or form from which copies, usually inferior, may be made.
Word Family: **archetypal**, *adjective.*
[ARCH (2) + TYPE]

archipelago (*say* arki-**pelli**-go) *noun*
a) a large group of islands. b) a sea which contains a large group of islands.
[ARCH (2) + Greek *pelagos* sea]

architecture (*say* **arki**-tekcher) *noun*
a) the art or science of designing buildings, etc. b) a particular style of building: 'Gothic *architecture*'.
Word Family: **architect**, *noun*, a) a person trained in architecture, b) a person who plans, designs or constructs; **architectural**, *adjective*.
[ARCH (2) + Greek *tekton* a builder]

architrave (*say* **arki**-trave) *noun*
a decorative moulding around an opening, such as a doorway.
[ARCH (2) + Latin *trabs* a beam]

archives (*say* **ar**-kives) *plural noun*
a) any public documents or historical records relating to a particular organization or country. b) the place where such records are kept.
Word Family: **archivist** (*say* **arki**-vist), *noun*.
[Greek *arkheion* a law court]

archway *noun*
a) the passage beneath an arch. b) an arch forming an entrance, etc.

arc lamp
a lamp which uses an electric arc as its source of light.

arctic *adjective*
at or near the North Pole.
Word Family: **arctic**, *noun*, the arctic regions.
[Greek *arktos* the (Great) Bear]

Arctic Circle
a line drawn on a map showing the most southerly point at which the sun does not set on one day of the year, at about 66° 30′ North.

ardent (*say* **ar**-d'nt) *adjective*
full of ardour or enthusiasm.
Word Family: **ardently**, *adverb*; **ardency**, *noun*.

ardour (*say* **arda**) *noun*
in America spelt **ardor**
an eagerness or passion: 'she has a great *ardour* for work'.
[Latin *ardor* fire]

arduous (*say* **ard**-yewus) *adjective*
requiring great effort or energy.
Word Family: **arduously**, *adverb*; **arduousness**, *noun*.
[Latin *arduus* steep, laborious]

are (1) (*say* ar) *verb*
a) the second person singular, present tense of the verb **be**. b) the plural, present tense of the verb **be**.

are (2) (*say* ar) *noun*
a metric unit of area, equal to 100 m^2.

area (*say* **airi**-a) *noun*
1. the surface measurement: 'what is the *area* of the paddock?'.
2. a particular extent or piece of land: 'this is a rural *area*'.
3. the scope of an activity, operation or concept: 'his skills cover a wide *area* of human accomplishments'.
[Latin]

arena (*say* a-**reena**) *noun*
1. a field or space set aside for sports, contests, etc.
2. any area of activity, conflict, etc.: 'he entered the *arena* of politics'.
[Latin, sand, arena]

areola (*say* a-**ree**-a-la) *noun*
plural is **areolae** (*say* a-**ree**-a-lee) or **areolas**
1. *Anatomy:* a darkened circle around a centre, such as around the human nipple.
2. a very small area.
[Latin, a small area]

arête (*say* a-**rate**) *noun*
a sharp mountain ridge.
[French, a fish-bone or ridge]

argent (*say* **arj**'nt) *adjective*
silver.
[Latin *argentum*]

argon *noun*
element number 18, a colourless, odourless, inert gas found in the earth's atmosphere and used in electric light bulbs, fluorescent tubes, etc. See CHEMICAL ELEMENTS in grey pages.
[Greek *argos* idle]

argosy (*say* **arga**-see) *noun*
a) a large merchant ship. b) a fleet of such ships.

argot (*say* **argo**) *noun*
the particular language or vocabulary of a group, especially of thieves, vagabonds, etc.
[French]

arguable (*say* ar-**gewa**-b'l) *adjective*
a) capable of being maintained or asserted. b) open to dispute or argument.
Word Family: **arguably**, *adverb*.

argue (*say* **ar**-gew) *verb*
(argued, arguing)

1. to give reasons for or against something: 'they *argued* about the method they should use'.
2. to exchange angry words: 'they *argued* about the money'.
[Latin *argutari* to prattle]

argument (*say* **argew**–m'nt) *noun*
1. the act of arguing.
2. a series of reasons given to explain or prove.
3. a theme or subject: 'the introduction sets out the book's *argument*'.
Word Family: **argumentative** (*say* argew–**men**ta–tiv), *adjective*, fond of arguing; **argumentatively**, *adverb*.

aria (*say* **ari**–a) *noun*
an opera song for one person.
[Italian]

arid (*say* **arrid**) *adjective*
very dry: 'the *arid* Sahara desert'.
Usage: 'what an *arid* and unrewarding task!' (= dull, uninteresting).
Word Family: **aridity** (*say* a–**riddi**–tee), **aridness**, *nouns*.
[Latin *aridus* parched]

Aries (*say* **air**–eez) *noun*
also called the **Ram**
Astrology: a group of stars, the first sign of the zodiac.
[Latin, ram]

aright *adverb*
an old word meaning properly or correctly.

arise *verb*
(**arose, arisen, arising**)
1. to appear or come into existence, especially as a result of something: 'new problems may *arise* during your investigations'.
2. to get up or move upwards.

aristocracy (*say* arriss–**tokra**–see) *noun*
1. the upper or privileged classes, usually hereditary.
2. the governing of a state or country by the aristocracy.
3. any superior group or class.
aristocrat (*say* **arrista**–krat) *noun*
1. a member of the aristocracy.
2. a person who has the tastes, manners, etc. considered characteristic of the aristocracy.
Word Family: **aristocratic** (*say* arrista–**krattik**), *adjective*; **aristocratically**, *adverb*.
[Greek *aristos* best + *kratia* rule]

arithmetic (*say* a–**rithma**–tik) *noun*
the branch of maths which studies numbers and their combination, using addition, subtraction, multiplication and division.
Word Family: **arithmetic** (*say* arrith–**mettik**), **arithmetical**, *adjective*; **arithmetician** (*say* arrith–ma–**tish**'n), *noun*.
[Greek *arithmos* number]

arithmetic mean
Maths: the average. Compare GEOMETRIC MEAN.

arithmetic progression, arithmetical progression
Maths: a sequence of numbers which increases or decreases by a constant quantity, as in the series 6, 8, 10, 12. Compare GEOMETRIC PROGRESSION.

ark *noun*
(*often capital*) the boat built by Noah in order to survive the Biblical Flood.
[Latin *arca* cupboard]

arm (1) *noun*
1. *Anatomy:* a) the part of the body between the elbow and the shoulder. b) the entire limb from the wrist to the shoulder.
2. the part of a garment covering the arm.
3. something which has the shape or function of an arm: 'the *arm* of a chair'.
Usage: 'an *arm* of the sea flows inland' (= branch, division).

arm (2) *noun*
(*usually plural*) any weapons.
arm *verb*
to equip with weapons.
Usage: 'you must *arm* yourself against boredom' (= prepare, equip).

armada (*say* ar–**mah**da) *noun*
a large fleet of warships.
[Spanish *armata* navy]

armadillo (*say* arma–**dillo**) *noun*
a burrowing, South American mammal, which is covered with bony plates like armour.
[Spanish, the little armoured thing]

Armageddon (*say* arma–**ged**'n) *noun*
1. *Christian:* the site of the final battle between good and evil which will mark the end of the world.
2. any large-scale international war.

armament (*say* **arma**–m'nt) *noun*
(*often plural*) the weapons with which a military unit, vehicle, etc. is equipped.

armature (*say* **arma**–cher) *noun*
1. *Electricity:* a) a piece of metal connecting the poles of a magnet. b) the movable part of a dynamo or electric motor, consisting essentially

of coils of wire wound around an iron core.
2. *Sculpture:* a framework used as a support for wet clay.
[Latin *armatura* equipment]

armchair *noun*
a comfortable chair with supports for the arms.
armchair *adjective*
lacking direct or active involvement: 'an *armchair* critic'.

armistice (*say* **armi**–stis) *noun*
a temporary peace agreement between countries.
[Latin *arma* arms + *sistere* to stop]

armorial *adjective*
of or relating to heraldry.
[Latin *arma* arms]

armorial bearings
the individual symbols and designs on a coat of arms.

armour (*say* **ar**–ma) *noun*
in America spelt **armor**
1. any protective covering, such as chain mail for the body, steel plating on battleships, etc.
2. anything which protects or keeps something safe.
Word Family: **armour,** *verb,* to fit with armour; **armourer,** *noun,* a person who makes or sells armour or weapons.
[Latin *arma* arms]

armour-plate *noun*
a sheet of hardened steel used on vehicles for protection.

armoury (*say* **arma**–ree) *noun*
in America spelt **armory**
a place where weapons and military equipment are stored.

armpit *noun*
also called an **axilla**
Anatomy: the hollow beneath the shoulder, where the arm joins the trunk.

army *noun*
1. an organized group trained and equipped to fight on land.
2. any large, organized group: 'we need an *army* of cleaners'.

aroma (*say* a–**ro**–ma) *noun*
1. a sweet or pleasant smell.
2. a characteristic quality: 'he has an *aroma* of wealth'.
Word Family: **aromatic** (*say* arra–**mattik**), *adjective,* having a sweet or pleasant smell.
[Greek, spice]

aromatic compound
Chemistry: any of a major class of organic compounds with a benzene ring forming part of the molecule.

arose (*say* a–roze) *verb*
the past tense of the verb **arise.**

around *adverb, preposition*
1. on all sides of: 'there were people all *around* us'.
2. from one place to another of: 'we walked *around* the city'.
Usages:
a) 'I'll meet you *around* one o'clock' (= at approximately).
b) 'we had to stay *around* the camp site' (= near).

arouse (*say* a–**rowze**) *verb*
to wake or stir up: 'his behaviour *aroused* her suspicions'.
Word Family: **arousal,** *noun.*

arpeggio (*say* ar–**pej**io) *noun*
Music: the playing of the notes of a chord in quick succession instead of simultaneously.
[Italian]

arraign (*say* a–**rane**) *verb*
to accuse or put on trial.
Word Family: **arraignment,** *noun.*
[French *arraigner*]

arrange (*say* a–**range**) *verb*
1. to set in a certain or proper order: '*arrange* those chairs around the table'.
Usages:
a) 'who will *arrange* the details of the trip?' (= prepare, organize).
b) 'he *arranged* this composition for an orchestra' (= adapted).
2. to agree or settle: 'we *arranged* to meet later'.
arrangement *noun*
1. the act of arranging.
2. something which has been arranged: a) 'a flower *arrangement*'; b) 'party *arrangements*'.

arrant (*say* **arr**'nt) *adjective*
complete or thorough: 'that man is an *arrant* liar'.

arras *noun*
a tapestry, often used as a wall-hanging.
[after *Arras,* France, where first made]

array (*say* a–**ray**) *verb*
1. to place in order or position: 'the tribes *arrayed* themselves against the army'.
2. to clothe or adorn: 'the bride was *arrayed* in white'.
Word Family: **array,** *noun.*

arrears (*say* a–**reerz**) *plural noun*
1. something which still remains to be paid, fulfilled, etc.
2. the state of being behind with something which is owing or due: 'our rent is three months **in** *arrears*'.

arrest (*say* a–**rest**) *verb*
1. to stop or catch: 'her words *arrested* our attention'.
2. to take a person into legal charge or keeping.
Word Family: **arrest,** *noun.*

arrive (*say* a–**rive**) *verb*
to reach or be reached: a) 'the hour of reckoning *arrived*'; b) 'at last we *arrived* at a decision'.
Word Family: **arrival,** *noun,* a) the act of arriving or reaching, b) something which has arrived.

arrogant (*say* **arra**–g'nt) *adjective*
overbearingly proud: 'his *arrogant* manner made him unpopular'.
Word Family: **arrogantly,** *adverb*; **arrogance,** *noun.*

arrogate (*say* **arra**–gate) *verb*
to assume or claim without right: 'he *arrogated* to himself the position of leader'.
[Latin *arrogare* to claim by right]

arrow *noun*
1. a long, slender shaft with a point at one end and often feathers at the other, shot from a bow as a missile.
2. something with the shape of an arrow, especially a sign used to indicate direction.

arrowroot *noun*
a starch derived from the roots of an American plant, used in cooking.

arse *noun*
(*informal*) the buttocks.
[Old English *assa* donkey]

arsenal (*say* **arsa**–n'l) *noun*
a place where weapons and ammunition are manufactured or stored.
[from Arabic, factory]

arsenic (*say* **arse**–nik) *noun*
element number 33, a brittle, highly poisonous metal whose compounds are used in insecticides and weedkillers.
See CHEMICAL ELEMENTS in grey pages.
[Arabic]

arson (*say* **arse**'n) *noun*
Law: the act of deliberately burning or setting fire to something, especially a building.
Word Family: **arsonist,** *noun.*

art (1) *noun*
1. any objects or activities in which man expresses feelings and ideas about life by giving them some imaginative form.
2. a particular skill or ability: 'the *art* of diplomacy'.
3. (*plural*) see HUMANITIES.
[Latin *ars* skilled work]

art (2) *verb*
the old form of the second person singular, present tense of the verb **be.**

artefact (*say* **arti**–fakt) **artifact** *noun*
anything made by man for his own use.
[Latin *arte* by skill + *factus* made]

arteriole (*say* ar–**teeri**–ole) *noun*
Anatomy: a small artery.

arteriosclerosis
(*say* ar–teerio–skla–**ro**–sis) *noun*
a disease of the arteries causing a reduced flow of blood due to a thickening of vessel walls.
[ARTERY + SCLEROSIS]

artery (*say* **arta**–ree) *noun*
1. *Anatomy:* any of the thick-walled tubes carrying oxygenated blood away from the heart to other parts of the body. Compare VEIN and CAPILLARY.
2. a major road or similar part in a system of communication or transport.
Word Family: **arterial** (*say* ar–**teer**–ial), *adjective.*
[Greek *arteria* the windpipe]

artesian well (*say* ar–**tee**–*zh*'n well)
a well in which water rises, under pressure, above the level of the water-bearing rock to the earth's surface.
[Latin *Artesium* Artois, the region of France where the Romans sank wells]

artful *adjective*
sly or crafty.
Word Family: **artfully,** *adverb*; **artfulness,** *noun.*

arthritis (*say* ar–**thry**–tis) *noun*
an inflammation of the joints causing pain and difficulty in movement.
Word Family: **arthritic** (*say* ar–**thrit**tik), *adjective, noun.*
[Greek *arthron* joint + –ITIS]

arthropod (*say* **arthra**–pod) *noun*
any of a large group of segmented invertebrate animals, such as insects, spiders, etc., with jointed legs and sometimes a hard, external skeleton.
[Greek *arthron* joint + *podos* of a foot]

artichoke *noun*
either of two species of plants used as vegetables.
a **globe artichoke** is a thistle-like plant with an edible flower head consisting of many small, fleshy, tightly folded leaves.
a **Jerusalem artichoke** is a type of sunflower with edible underground stems.
[Arabic]

article *noun*
1. an individual thing or object: 'they stole several valuable *articles*'.
2. *Grammar:* any of three words (*a*, *an* or *the*) used before a noun.
the **definite article** (*the*) indicates a particular person or thing: '*the* boy was happy'.
the **indefinite article** (*a*, *an*) does not specify which particular thing: 'I would like *a* new car'.
3. a piece of writing which gives information or an opinion and forms part of a magazine, newspaper, etc.: 'an *article* on gardening'.
4. *Law:* a) a section of a document. b) (*plural*) a document, especially a contract: 'the *articles* of apprenticeship'.
Word Family: **article,** *verb,* to put down in or bind by articles.

articled clerk
a person training in a solicitor's office.

articulate (*say* artik-yoo-lit) *adjective*
1. clear in one's speech or expression.
2. able to speak.
articulate (*say* artik-yoo-late) *verb*
1. to pronounce words distinctly.
2. to unite by a joint or joints.
Word Family: **articulateness,** *noun,* the quality of being articulate; **articulately,** *adverb*; **articulation,** *noun,* the act of articulating.
[Latin *articulare* to divide into joints]

articulated vehicle
a jointed vehicle, such as a semi-trailer.

artifact *noun*
see ARTEFACT.

artifice (*say* arti-fis) *noun*
a) a clever trick or device. b) any skilful trickery.
Word Family: **artificer,** *noun.*
[Latin *arte* by skill + *facere* to make]

artificial (*say* arti-**fish**'l) *adjective*
made as an imitation, as distinct from being natural: 'they only sell *artificial* flowers'.
Usage: 'her *artificial* smile did not fool any of us' (= false, affected).
Word Family: **artificially,** *adverb*; **artificiality** (*say* arti-fishi-**alli**-tee), *noun.*

artificial insemination
the placing of sperm in a female to make her pregnant without direct sexual contact.

artillery (*say* ar-**tilla**-ree) *noun*
a) any large-calibre guns, such as cannons, howitzers, etc. b) the branch of an army which uses such guns.
Word Family: **artillery,** *adjective.*
[from Old French, equipment]

artisan (*say* arti-zan) *noun*
a trained or skilled manual worker.

artist *noun*
1. a painter, sculptor or other person who creates works of art.
2. an entertainer, especially a singer or dancer. Also called an **artiste.**
Word Family: **artistic** (*say* ar-**tistik**), *adjective,* of or characteristic of art or artists; **artistically,** *adverb.*

artistry *noun*
the degree of skill in practising an art.

artless *adjective*
free from deceit or cunning.
Word Family: **artlessly,** *adverb*; **artlessness,** *noun.*

art nouveau
a decorative art style used from about 1890 to 1910.

artwork *noun*
Printing: any illustrations or typing from which a block or plate will be made.

aryl (*say* **arril**) *adjective*
(of a radical) derived from an aromatic compound, such as phenyl (formula C_6H_5-).
[from AROMATIC]

as *adverb*
1. to the amount or degree that: 'hard *as* he tries, he never wins'.
2. for example: 'cities such *as* London and Sydney'.
as *conjunction*
1. when or while: '*as* we approached, the door opened'.
2. because: '*as* he was late, we could not start'.
3. like or in the manner of: 'quick *as* lightning'.
as *pronoun*
in the function or position of: 'let this serve *as* a warning'.

Phrases:
as for, as to, '*as for* his work, nothing more can be said' (= with regard to).
as it were, in some way.

as–
a variant of the prefix **ad–**.

asbestos (*say* az–**bestos**) *noun*
a heat-resistant, fibrous mineral containing complex silicates of calcium and magnesium and used to make fireproof and heatproof articles.
[from Greek]

ascend (*say* a–**send**) *verb*
to rise or climb: 'he carefully *ascended* the ladder'.
Word Family: **ascent,** *noun,* a) the act of ascending, b) an upward slope or gradient; **ascension,** *noun.*
[Latin *ascendere* to climb]

ascendant (*say* a–**sen**–d'nt) **ascendent** *noun*
1. a position of influence, control, etc.: 'in the *ascendant*'.
2. *Astrology:* the sign of the zodiac which is above the horizon at the time of a person's birth.
ascendant *adjective*
1. having influence, power or control: 'prosperity is *ascendant* in our society'.
2. rising: 'an *ascendant* star'.
Word Family: **ascendance, ascendancy,** *noun,* a governing or controlling influence.

ascertain (*say* assa–**tane**) *verb*
to find out: 'we must *ascertain* the true facts'.
Word Family: **ascertainable,** *adjective;* **ascertainment,** *noun.*

ascetic (*say* a–**settik**) *adjective*
severely strict and self-denying.
ascetic *noun*
a person who practises strict self-denial.
Word Family: **ascetically,** *adverb;* **asceticism** (*say* a–**setti**–sizm), *noun.*
[Greek *asketes* a hermit]
Common Error: do not confuse with AESTHETIC.

ascorbic acid (*say* a–**skawbik** assid)
see VITAMIN C under VITAMIN.
[A– + medieval Latin *scorbutus* scurvy]

ascribe (*say* a–**scribe**) *verb*
to attribute: 'that discovery is *ascribed* to a German scientist'.
Word Family: **ascribable,** *adjective;* **ascription** (*say* a–**skrip**–sh'n), *noun.*
[Latin *ascribere*]

asdic (*say* **az**–dik) *noun*
an echo sounder used to detect underwater objects, especially submarines.
[from A(nti) S(ubmarine) D(etection) I(nvestigation) C(ommittee)]

–ase
Chemistry: a suffix indicating an enzyme, as in *amylase.*

aseptic (*say* ay–**septik**) *adjective*
free from living germs, etc.
Word Family: **asepsis,** *noun;* **aseptically,** *adverb.*
[A– + SEPTIC]

asexual (*say* ay–**seksual**) *adjective*
a) having no sex or sexual organs. b) unrelated to sex or sexual processes.
Word Family: **asexually,** *adverb;* **asexuality,** *noun.*
[A– + SEXUAL]

ash (1) *noun*
1. the powdery remains of anything which has been burnt: 'cigarette *ash*'.
2. *Geology:* the fine particles sent up by an erupting volcano.
3. (*plural*) any ruins or remains, especially of a human body after cremation.
Word Family: **ashy,** *adjective.*

ash (2) *noun*
any of a group of trees with grey bark and hard, tough wood used for timber.

ashamed *adjective*
feeling shame or guilt.
Usage: 'don't be *ashamed* to confess your mistakes' (= unwilling through fear of shame).
Word Family: **ashamedly,** *adverb.*

ashen (*say* **ash**'n) *adjective*
grey or pale: 'her face was *ashen* with fear'.

ashore (*say* a–**shore**) *adverb*
on or to land: 'they went *ashore* from the boat'.

ashtray *noun*
a small dish or bowl for tobacco ash.

ashy (*say* **ashee**) *adjective*
Word Family: see ASH (1).

aside *adverb*
on or to one side: 'put *aside* some money for the holiday'.
aside *noun*
a word or words spoken so that only certain people will hear.

asinine (*say* **assi**–nine) *adjective*
silly or stupid.

Word Family: **asininity** (*say* assi–**ninni**–tee), *noun*; **asininely**, *adverb*.
[Latin *asinus* ass]

ask *verb*
1. to seek a reply or response from or concerning: a) 'don't *ask* me!'; b) 'may I *ask* how old you are?'.
Usages:
a) 'we *asked* them to come tomorrow' (= invited).
b) 'this job will *ask* for all your concentration' (= require).
2. to act in such a way as to bring: 'he is *asking* for trouble'.

askance (*say* a–**skance**) *adverb*
with a sideways glance.
Usage: 'mother looked *askance* at our plan' (= with disapproval or mistrust).

askew (*say* a–**skew**) *adverb*
crooked or out of position: 'your hat is quite *askew*'.

aslant (*say* a–**slahnt**) *adverb, preposition*
at a slanting angle.

asleep (*say* a–**sleep**) *adverb, adjective*
in or into a state of sleep.
Usage: 'my foot is *asleep*' (= numb).

asp *noun*
any of various small poisonous snakes, such as the Egyptian viper.
[Greek *aspis*]

asparagus (*say* a–**sparra**–gus) *noun*
the long, edible, soft-tipped shoots of a plant related to the lily.
[Greek *aspharagos*]

aspect (*say* **ass**–pekt) *noun*
1. the look or appearance of anything: 'he has a serious *aspect*'.
Usage: 'we must consider all *aspects* of the matter' (= views, sides).
2. the view or direction to which something faces: 'the front rooms have a northerly *aspect*'.
3. *Astrology:* the position of a star or group of stars in relation to others, which affects its influence on events. Also called a **configuration.**
[Latin *aspectus* a view]

aspen *noun*
a kind of poplar whose leaves quiver even in a light breeze.

asperity (*say* a–**sperri**–tee) *noun*
a harshness or severity: 'she spoke with *asperity*'.
[Latin *asper* rough, biting]

aspersion (*say* a–**sper**–sh'n) *noun*
(*often plural*) any unkind or damaging criticism: 'do not cast *aspersions* on his character'.
[Latin *aspersus* bespattered]

asphalt (*say* **ass**–falt) *noun*
1. a black, sticky substance composed mainly of bitumen and oils mixed with mineral matter.
2. a mixture of bitumen and small stones used for road surfaces, etc. Also called **tarmac.**
Word Family: **asphalt,** *verb.*
[Greek *asphaltos* bitumen]

asphyxiate (*say* ass–**fiksi**–ate) *verb*
to produce difficulty in breathing, unconsciousness or death through a lack of oxygen.
Word Family: **asphyxia,** *noun,* the severe condition caused by a lack of oxygen; **asphyxiation,** *noun.*
[Greek *asphyxia* a stopping of the pulse]

aspic *noun*
a clear, savoury jelly made of meat, fish or vegetable stock, and often gelatine.
[French]

aspidistra (*say* aspi–**distra**) *noun*
an evergreen Chinese plant with broad, pointed leaves, usually grown indoors.

aspirate (*say* **aspa**–rate) *verb*
1. *Medicine:* to remove fluids from the body through a needle and syringe.
2. *Language:* to begin a word or syllable with an *h* sound, as in *hiss* or *hit.*
Word Family: **aspirate** (*say* **aspa**–rit), *noun,* the sound of the letter *h.*

aspiration (*say* aspa–**ray**–sh'n) *noun*
1. an eager desire or ambition: 'his greatest *aspiration* is to become a politician'.
2. the act of aspirating.

aspire (*say* a–**spire**) *verb*
to seek or desire ambitiously: 'she *aspires* after wealth'.
Word Family: **aspirant,** *noun,* a person who aspires to or seeks a position.
[Latin *aspirare* to pant after]

aspirin (*say* **ass**–prin) *noun*
a white crystalline drug, **acetylsalicylic acid,** used to relieve pain, fever, etc.

ass *noun*
1. a donkey.
2. a stupid person.

assail (*say* a–**sail**) *verb*
to attack or overcome: 'she was *assailed* by doubts'.

assailant *noun*
an attacker: 'the victim of the attack could not identify her *assailant*'.
Word Family: **assailable**, *adjective*.
[Latin *assilire* to leap upon]

assassin (*say* a-sassin) *noun*
a person who murders another, especially for political reasons.
assassinate *verb*
to kill deliberately and violently, especially for political reasons.
Usage: 'the young artist's reputation was *assassinated* by the critics' (= maliciously attacked).
Word Family: **assassination** (*say* a-sassi-**nay**-sh'n), *noun*.
[from Arabic, *hashshashin*, hashish eaters, radical Moslems who took hashish before killing their victims]

assault (*say* a-**sawlt**) *verb*
1. to attack violently
2. *Law:* to threaten or attempt to injure another person.
Word Family: **assault**, *noun*, the act of assaulting.

assay (*say* a-**say**) *verb*
1. to analyse a mixture, especially to estimate the metal content in ores.
2. to test: 'he *assayed* his strength'.
Word Family: **assay**, *noun*.
[French *essai* a trial or sample]

assegai (*say* **assi**-guy) *noun*
a light spear or javelin used by the Bantu peoples of southern Africa.
[from Arabic, spear]

assemblage (*say* a-**sem**blij) *noun*
a collection of people or things.

assemble (*say* a-**sem**-b'l) *verb*
1. to meet or gather: 'let's *assemble* outside the hall'.
2. to put together: 'to *assemble* a model aeroplane'.

assembly (*say* a-**sem**-blee) *noun*
1. a group of people gathered together for a particular purpose: 'a Legislative *Assembly*'.
2. the putting together of something, especially parts of machines, etc.

assembly line
a line of workers, machines, etc. in a factory, along which a product passes to be assembled in stages.

assent (*say* a-**sent**) *verb*
to agree.
Word Family: **assent**, *noun*.
[Latin *assentiri* to agree with]

assert (*say* a-**sert**) *verb*
to claim positively: 'he still *asserts* his innocence'.
assert oneself, 'you must *assert yourself* in business matters' (= insist on your rights, put yourself forward).
Word Family: **assertion**, *noun*; **assertive**, *adjective*, dogmatic; **assertively**, *adverb*; **assertiveness**, *noun*.
[Latin *assertus* claimed]

assess (*say* a-**sess**) *verb*
1. to estimate or judge: 'let's *assess* the situation'.
2. to work out or estimate an amount to be paid, a value, etc.
Word Family: **assessor**, *noun*, a person appointed to assess or advise; **assessment**, *noun*.
[Latin *assessor* one who sits by, an assessor]

asset (*say* **ass**-et) *noun*
1. anything which is useful or valuable: 'an alert mind is a great *asset*'.
2. (*usually plural*) any property with money value.
[AD- + Latin *satis* enough]

assiduous (*say* a-**sid**-yewus) *adjective*
diligent or hard-working.
Word Family: **assiduity** (*say* assi-**dewi**-tee), **assiduousness**, *nouns*; **assiduously**, *adverb*.
[Latin *assiduus* continually present]

assign (*say* a-**sine**) *verb*
1. to appoint or allocate: 'we must *assign* a day for the next meeting'.
2. *Law:* to transfer property, or property rights.

assignation (*say* assig-**nay**-sh'n) *noun*
an appointment to meet, especially between lovers.
[Latin *assignare* to allot]

assignment (*say* a-**sine**-m'nt) *noun*
1. the act of assigning.
2. a particular task or duty: 'a homework *assignment*'.

assimilate (*say* a-**simmi**-late) *verb*
to absorb, especially into a system: 'the immigrants were *assimilated* into their new society'.
Word Family: **assimilation**, *noun*; **assimilable**, *adjective*.
[AD- + Latin *similis* similar]

assist *verb*
to help or support.
assistant *noun*
a helper.
Word Family: **assistance**, *noun*, help; **assistant**, *adjective*.
[Latin *assidere* to sit by]

assize (*say* a–**size**) *noun*
Law: (*usually plural*) a court in session.
[Latin *assidere* to sit by]

associate (*say* a–**so**–she–ate) *verb*
1. to connect, as in the mind: 'I *associate* swimming with summer'.
2. to spend one's time: 'he *associates* with some odd people'.
associate (*say* a–**so**–she–it) *noun*
1. a partner or colleague.
2. a person who is granted partial membership of an organization.
[AD– + Latin *socius* an ally]

association *noun*
1. a group of people joined or organized together for a common purpose.
2. a) the act of associating: 'the *association* of ideas'. b) the state of being associated: 'working in close *association* with my publisher'.

assonance (*say* **assa**–n'nce) *noun*
a similarity between sounds, especially the repeating of vowel sounds in the words of a line of poetry, etc.
[AD– + Latin *sonus* sound]

assort (*say* a–**sort**) *verb*
to arrange or classify according to size, kind, etc.
assorted *adjective*
of different sorts or kinds: '*assorted* chocolates'.
Usage: 'they are a badly *assorted* couple' (= matched).
Word Family: **assortment**, *noun*, a) the act of assorting, b) a mixed collection.

assuage (*say* a–**swayj**) *verb*
to satisfy or make less severe: 'what will *assuage* my thirst?'.
Word Family: **assuagement**, *noun.*
[AD– + Latin *suavis* pleasant]

assume *verb*
1. to suppose to be a fact, especially without proof: 'let us *assume* you are right'.
2. to take on: 'he *assumed* command of the group'.
assumption *noun*
a) the act of assuming. b) something which is assumed: 'that is an *assumption*, not a fact'.

assurance (*say* a–**sure**'nce) *noun*
1. a positive declaration that something will be done, etc.: 'he has given his *assurance* of payment'.
2. a confidence or courage, especially in oneself.
3. life assurance.

assure (*say* a–**sure**) *verb*
1. to convince or tell earnestly: 'he *assured* us that he would return'.
2. to make sure or secure: 'our victory is *assured*'.
Word Family: **assuredly**, *adverb.*

astatine (*say* **asta**–teen) *noun*
element number 85, a man-made, radioactive non-metal. See HALOGEN. See CHEMICAL ELEMENTS in grey pages.
[Greek *astatos* unstable]

aster *noun*
any of a large group of flowering plants, of which the best known is the Michaelmas Daisy.
[Greek, star]

asterisk (*say* **asta**–risk) *noun*
a mark (*) used beside a word in writing or printing, to refer the reader to a footnote, etc.
[Greek *asteriskos* small star]

astern (*say* a–**stern**) *adverb, adjective*
Nautical: behind or at the back.

asteroid (*say* **asta**–royd) *noun*
1. any of a vast number of small planetary bodies all less than 500 km in diameter, between the orbits of Mars and Jupiter. Also called a **planetoid.**
2. any organism with a body shaped like a star, such as a starfish.
asteroid *adjective*
of or relating to a star.
[Greek *aster* a star + –OID]

asthma (*say* **ass**ma) *noun*
a disorder due to narrowing of air passages, causing shortness of breath and wheezing.
Word Family: **asthmatic**, *adjective*, of or suffering from asthma; **asthmatic**, *noun*; **asthmatically**, *adverb.*
[Greek, panting]

astigmatism (*say* a–**stigma**–tizm) *noun*
a faulty deflection of light rays producing poor focusing or vision in an eye, lens, etc.
Word Family: **astigmatic** (*say* astig–**mattik**), *adjective.*
[A– + Greek *stigmatos* of a point]

astir (*say* a–**ster**) *adjective, adverb*
moving or in motion: 'the village was *astir* with excitement'.
Usage: 'he was *astir* very early' (= out of bed).

astonish *verb*
to surprise greatly: 'we were *astonished* at the news'.
Word Family: **astonishment**, *noun*; **astonishingly**, *adverb.*

astound *verb*
to overcome with amazement.
Word Family: **astoundingly,** *adverb.*

astrakhan (*say* **astra–kan**) *noun*
the fur–like woolly skin of the young lamb of a Central Asian breed of sheep.
[a region and city in Russia]

astral *adjective*
of or relating to the stars.

astray (*say* **a–stray**) *adverb, adjective*
away from the right path: 'he was led *astray* by criminals'.

astride (*say* **a–stride**) *preposition*
with one leg on each side of: 'he sat *astride* the chair'.
Word Family: **astride,** *adverb.*

astringent (*say* **a–strin–j'nt**) *adjective*
causing skin or tissue to contract.
Usage: 'his *astringent* comments made us flinch' (= harsh, severe).
astringent *noun*
any of various substances which cause skin or tissue to contract, used in medicine, cosmetics, etc.
Word Family: **astringently,** *adverb*; **astringency,** *noun.*
[Latin *adstringere* to compress]

astrology (*say* **a–strolla–jee**) *noun*
the study of the possible influence of the stars on human events. Compare ASTRONOMY.
Word Family: **astrologer,** *noun*; **astrological** (*say* astra–**loji**–k'l), *adjective*; **astrologically,** *adverb.*
[Greek *aster* a star + –LOGY]

astronaut (*say* **astra–nawt**) *noun*
also called a **cosmonaut**
a person trained to operate and travel in spacecraft.
astronautics *plural noun*
(*used with singular verb*) the study of flight outside the earth's atmosphere.
[Greek *aster* a star + *nautes* a sailor]

astronomical unit
the average distance between the sun and the earth, about 149 600 000 km, used as the unit of distance within the solar system.

astronomy (*say* **a–stronna–mee**) *noun*
the study of planets and stars, their movements, relative positions and composition. Compare ASTROLOGY.
astronomical, astronomic
1. of or relating to astronomy.
2. immensely large or numerous: 'an *astronomical* rise in prices'.
Word Family: **astronomer,** *noun*; **astronomically,** *adverb.*
[Greek *aster* a star + *nomos* an arrangement, law]

astrophysics (*say* **astro–fizziks**) *noun*
the study of the physical properties of the planets and stars, a branch of astronomy.

astute (*say* **a–stewt**) *adjective*
shrewd or mentally alert: 'her comments are always *astute*'.
Word Family: **astutely,** *adverb*; **astuteness,** *noun.*

asunder (*say* **a–sunda**) *adverb*
apart or into separate pieces: 'the roof was torn *asunder* in the storm'.

asylum (*say* **a–sigh–l'm**) *noun*
1. a hospital or home for people with mental disorders, etc.
2. a) the protection given by one country to a political refugee from another. b) any place of shelter or refuge.
[Greek *asylos* inviolable]

asymmetrical (*say* ay–**sim–metri–k'l**)
asymmetric *adjective*
not symmetrical.
Word Family: **asymmetry** (*say* ay–**simma**–tree), *noun.*

asymptote (*say* **assim–tote**) *noun*
Maths: a straight line which is approached, but never reached, by an infinitely long curve.
[Greek *asymptotos* not close]

at *preposition*
1. used to indicate place: 'we will meet *at* home'.
2. used to indicate time: 'be there *at* noon'.
Usages:
a) 'the car started *at* the second push' (= on).
b) 'dogs bark *at* night' (= during).
3. used to indicate action, state or manner: a) 'set your mind *at* rest'; b) 'he came *at* a run'.
Usage: 'I was horrified *at* the news' (= because of).

at–
a variant of the prefix **ad–**.

atavism (*say* **atta–vizm**) *noun*
1. *Biology:* the reappearance of a feature or character after it has not been evident for several generations.
2. a reversion to primitive instincts.
Word Family: **atavistic,** *adjective.*
[Latin *atavus* a forefather]

ataxia (*say* **a–taksia**) *noun*
Medicine: any of a group of disorders of the nervous system causing

difficulty in maintaining balance or normal movements.
[A– + Greek *taxis* order]

atheist (*say* **ay**–thee–ist) *noun*
a person who does not believe in the existence of a god or gods. Compare AGNOSTIC.
Word Family: **atheism**, *noun*; **atheistic** (*say* ay–thee–**is**tik), *adjective*; **atheistically**, *adverb*.
[A– + Greek *theos* a god]

athirst (*say* a–**ther**st) *adjective*
eager or having a great desire: '*athirst* for knowledge'.

athlete (*say* **ath**–leet) *noun*
a person trained to take part in competitive sports, especially athletics.
[Greek *athletes* a contender for a prize]

athlete's foot
also called **tinea**
a fungal infection of the skin between the toes.

athletic *adjective*
1. of or relating to physical sports or activities.
2. physically strong and active: 'he is quite *athletic* despite his age'.
athletics *plural noun*
1. physical sports or activities such as running, jumping, etc.
2. (*used with singular verb*) the system or principles of training for such activities.

athwart (*say* a–**thwawt**) *preposition*
1. across or from side to side.
2. *Nautical:* at right angles to the keel of a boat.
Word Family: **athwart**, *adverb*.

atlas *noun*
plural is **atlases**
1. a book of maps.
2. *Anatomy:* the first bone of the vertebral column, supporting the head.
[after *Atlas*, a giant in Greek mythology who was condemned to support the heavens on his shoulders as a punishment for rebellion against Zeus]

atmosphere (*say* **at**mos–feer) *noun*
1. the mixture of gases surrounding the earth, a star or a planet.
2. a unit of pressure equal to the average atmospheric pressure at sea–level (equal to $1{\cdot}01 \times 10^5$ pascal). See UNITS in grey pages.
3. the dominant feeling or mood of a situation, etc.: 'the *atmosphere* at the meeting was hostile'.
Word Family: **atmospheric**, **atmospherical**, *adjective*.
[Greek *atmos* smoke, vapour + SPHERE]

atmospheric pressure
the pressure at a particular place, caused by the weight of the earth's atmosphere. The atmospheric pressure on top of a mountain is less than at sea–level.

atoll (*say* **at**tol) *noun*
a circular coral reef, usually forming one or more islands around a lagoon.

atom (*say* **at**'m) *noun*
1. *Physics:* the smallest unit of a chemical element which, by containing equal numbers of protons and electrons, has no net electric charge. Removal or addition of an electron ionizes the atom. See ION.
2. anything which is extremely small.
Word Family: **atomic**, *adjective*.
[Greek *atomos* indivisible]

atomic bomb
short form is **A–bomb**
see NUCLEAR WEAPON.

atomic energy
see NUCLEAR ENERGY.

atomic mass unit
Physics: the unit for the mass of an atom, being one–twelfth part of the mass of one atom of the carbon 12 isotope ($^{12}_{6}C$) and equal to about $1{\cdot}66 \times 10^{-27}$ kg.

atomic number
Physics: the number used to classify an element, equal to the number of protons in its nucleus. Compare MASS NUMBER.

atomic pile
see NUCLEAR REACTOR.

atomizer, atomiser *noun*
a device for converting a liquid, such as perfume, into a fine spray under pressure.

atone (*say* a–**tone**) *verb*
to make amends, especially for a sin or offence: 'you must *atone* for your mistake'.
Word Family: **atonement**, *noun*.
[AT + ONE]

atop *preposition*
on or at the top of: '*atop* the mountain'.

atrium (*say* **at**–ree–um) *noun*
plural is **atria**
1. a courtyard, usually at the centre of a building, common in ancient Rome.

2. *Anatomy:* either of the two chambers in the heart which receive blood from the veins.
[Latin, central court]

atrocious (*say* a–**tro**–shus) *adjective*
1. extremely cruel or wicked: 'an *atrocious* act'.
2. (*informal*) very bad.
Word Family: **atrocity** (*say* a–**trossi**–tee), *noun,* a) the quality of being atrocious, b) an atrocious act; **atrociously**, *adverb.*
[Latin *atrox, atrocis* cruel]

atrophy (*say* atra–fee) *noun*
a wasting away or diminishing, especially of all or part of an organism.
Word Family: **atrophy** (**atrophied, atrophying**), *verb.*
[A– + Greek *trophé* nourishment]

atropine *noun*
a poisonous drug obtained from belladonna.

attach *verb*
to connect or fasten: 'the cupboards are *attached* to the wall'.
Usages:
a) 'she is very *attached* to her cat' (= bound by affection).
b) 'I *attach* little importance to it' (= give).
attachment *noun*
1. the act of attaching.
2. a bond of affection between people.
3. a) something which is attached, such as an extra part or device. b) something which attaches, such as a strap, fastener, etc

attaché (*say* a–**tash**ay) *noun*
Politics: a member of an embassy or legation: 'a press *attaché*'.
[French]

attaché case
a small rectangular case for carrying documents or papers.

attack *verb*
to set upon with force: 'the enemy *attacked* the fort at nightfall'.
Usages:
a) 'the newspaper was *attacked* for its biased editorial' (= strongly criticized).
b) 'we all hungrily *attacked* our meal' (= began energetically).
attack *noun*
the act of attacking.
Usages:
a) 'an *attack* of measles' (= occurrence).
b) 'we must make an *attack* on the dishes' (= start).
c) 'their performance was full of *attack*' (= vigour).
Word Family: **attacker**, *noun.*

attain *verb*
to reach or accomplish by one's efforts: 'he finally *attained* his ambition'.
Word Family: **attainment**, *noun,* a) the act of attaining, b) something attained; **attainable**, *adjective.*
[AT– + Latin *tangere* to touch]

attar *noun*
a sweet-smelling oil obtained from petals, especially rose petals.
[Arabic, the perfume]

attempt *noun*
1. an effort to achieve something: 'she made several *attempts* before she succeeded'.
2. an attack: 'an *attempt* was made on the princess's life'.
Word Family: **attempt**, *verb.*
[AT– + Latin *temptare* to attempt]

attend *verb*
1. to be present at: 'did you *attend* the meeting?'.
2. to accompany: a) 'the President was *attended* by his bodyguards'; b) 'her cold was *attended* by fever'.
Usages:
a) 'a doctor *attended* the victims' (= helped, looked after).
b) 'please *attend* to your work' (= pay attention).
Word Family: **attendance**, *noun,* a) the act of attending, b) the number of people present; **attendant**, *adjective,* accompanying; **attendant**, *noun,* a person or thing that attends.
[Latin *attendere* to turn the mind to]

attention *noun*
1. the act of concentrating or directing one's thoughts: 'one must pay *attention* when driving'.
Usage: 'your letter will receive early *attention*' (= consideration).
2. (*often plural*) any courtesy or helpfulness.
at attention, standing with one's heels together and arms at one's sides.
Word Family: **attentive**, *adjective,* helpful or giving attention; **attentively**, *adverb*; **attentiveness**, *noun.*

attenuate (*say* a–**ten**–yew–ate) *verb*
to weaken or reduce in size or intensity.
Word Family: **attenuation**, *noun.*
[AT– + Latin *tenuis* slender]

attest (*say* a–**test**) *verb*
to declare to be true or genuine: 'will you *attest* to the truth of this statement?'.

Word Family: **attestation** (*say* attes–**tay**–sh'n), *noun.*
[AT– + Latin *testari* to attest]

attic *noun*
also called a **garret**
the room or space immediately under the roof of a house.

attire (*say* a–**tire**) *noun*
any clothes.
Word Family: **attire**, *verb.*

attitude *noun*
a physical or mental position: a) 'he stood in a menacing *attitude*'; b) 'what is your *attitude* to gambling?'.
Word Family: **attitudinize** (*say* atti–**tewdi**–nize), **attitudinise**, *verb*, to assume affected attitudes.

atto–
a prefix used for SI units, meaning one million million millionth (10^{-18}).

attorney (*say* a–**terni**) *noun*
any person, such as a lawyer, appointed by another to act on his behalf.
power of attorney
a legal authority given by one person to another, to act on his behalf.
[Old French *atorner* to assign]

attract (*say* a–**trakt**) *verb*
1. to pull or cause to move towards.
2. to arouse interest or attention: 'the speech *attracted* a large audience'.
attraction *noun*
1. the act or power of attracting: 'magnetic *attraction*'.
2. something which attracts, such as a public event.
Word Family: **attractive**, *adjective*, having the power to attract or please; **attractively**, *adverb*; **attractiveness**, *noun.*
[AT– + Latin *tractus* drawn towards]

attribute (*say* a–**trib**–yewt) *verb*
to consider as belonging to or created by: 'although unsigned this painting is *attributed* to Raphael'.
attribute (*say* **attrib**–yewt) *noun*
a quality or characteristic: 'she has the *attributes* of intelligence and beauty'.
Word Family: **attribution** (*say* attri–**bew**–sh'n), *noun*; **attributable**, *adjective*, able to be attributed to; **attributive** (*say* a–**trib**–yewtiv), *adjective*, of or expressing an attribute.
[Latin *attribuere*]

attrition (*say* a–**trish**'n) *noun*
a wearing away, as by friction or rubbing.
war of attrition, a war in which the victor is the side that can hold out the longest.
[AT– + Latin *tritus* worn out]

attune *verb*
to bring into tune or harmony: 'his ideas are not *attuned* to ours'.

atypical (*say* ay–**tippi**–k'l) *adjective*
not typical or normal.
Word Family: **atypically**, *adverb.*
[A– + TYPICAL]

aubergine (*say* **o**–ber–*zheen*) *noun*
also called an **eggplant**
a pear-shaped fruit with a dark purple skin and pale firm flesh, used as a vegetable.
[Arabic]

auburn (*say* **awb**'n) *noun*
a rich, reddish-brown colour.
Word Family: **auburn**, *adjective.*
[Late Latin *alburnus* whitish]

auction (*say* **awk**–sh'n) *noun*
a public sale at which goods are sold to the highest bidder.
Word Family: **auction**, *verb*; **auctioneer**, *noun*, a person who conducts an auction.
[Latin *auctio*]

audacious (*say* aw–**day**shus) *adjective*
daring or recklessly bold.
Word Family: **audacity** (*say* aw–**dassi**–tee), *noun*; **audaciously**, *adverb.*
[Latin *audax, audacis* daring]

audible (*say* **aw**–dibb'l) *adjective*
loud enough to be heard.
Word Family: **audibly**, *adverb*; **audibility**, *noun.*

audience (*say* **awdi**'nce) *noun*
1. the people attending or listening to something, especially a play, concert, lecture, etc.
2. a formal meeting held by a high official or ruler: 'an *audience* with the Pope'.

audio *adjective*
of or relating to sound, especially the devices, etc. used to transmit, receive or reproduce soundwaves, such as tape-recorders or gramophones.
audio frequency
any frequency at which vibrations can be heard by man.
[Latin *audire* to hear]

audiovisual *adjective*
involving the use of both sight and hearing, as in television, etc.: '*audiovisual* teaching aids'.

audit *noun*
an official examination of financial records and statements.
Word Family: **audit,** *verb*; **auditor,** *noun*, a) a person appointed to make an audit, b) a listener.

audition (*say* aw-**dish**'n) *noun*
1. *Theatre:* a trial performance to test a person's suitability for a part in a play, orchestra, etc.
2. the act or power of hearing.
Word Family: **audition,** *verb.*

auditorium (*say* awdi-**tawrium**) *noun*
a) a large theatre, concert hall, etc. b) the area in such a building where the audience sits.

auditory (*say* **or**da-tree) *adjective*
relating to hearing: 'the *auditory* nerve'.

au fait (*say* o fay)
well informed about something: '*au fait* with the latest gossip'.
[French, to the fact]

Augean (*say* **aw**-jee-an) *adjective*
filthy dirty.
[In Greek mythology one labour of Hercules was to clean out the stables of *King Augeas*]

auger (*say* **aw**ga) *noun*
a tool, such as a small gimlet, for drilling holes.

aught (*say* awt) *noun*
an old word meaning anything whatever: 'for *aught* I know'.

augment (*say* awg-**ment**) *verb*
to increase or add to.
Word Family: **augmentation,** *noun.*
[Latin *augmen* an increase]

augur (*say* **aw**ga) *noun*
any prophet or soothsayer.
augur *verb*
to foretell or be a sign of: 'the weather *augurs* well for our holiday'.
Word Family: **augury,** *noun.*
[Latin]

august (1) (*say* aw-**gust**) *adjective*
imposing or majestic: 'the king had an *august* manner'.
Word Family: **augustly,** *adverb.*
[Latin *augustus* majestic]

August (2) (*say* **aw**-gust) *noun*
the eighth month of the year in the Gregorian calendar.
[after the Roman Emperor *Augustus*]

auk (*rhymes with* hawk) *noun*
any of various short-winged, black and white, salt-water, diving birds, e.g. the **guillemot** and **puffin.**

aunt (*say* ahnt) *noun*
a) a sister of one's parent. b) the wife of one's uncle.
[Latin *amita*]

au pair (*say* **o** pair)
a young foreigner, usually female, who lives with a family, minds the children, etc., and often studies the language.
[French, board and lodging without pay]

aura (*say* **or**-a) *noun*
plural is **auras** or **aurae** (*say* **or**-ee)
a distinct air or atmosphere surrounding something: 'an *aura* of wisdom'.
[Greek, breath]

aural (*say* **owr**'l) *adjective*
of or perceived by the ear.
Word Family: **aurally,** *adverb.*
[Latin *auris* ear]

aureole *noun*
also spelt **aureola**
a halo.
[Latin *aureolus* golden]

au revoir (*say* orri-**vwa**)
goodbye for now.
[French, until we see each other again]

auric (*say* **aw**-rik) *adjective*
Chemistry: of or relating to compounds of gold in which gold has a valency of three.
[Latin *aurum* gold]

auricle (*say* **awri**-k'l) *noun*
1. the outer part of the ear.
2. either of the two upper chambers of the heart which receives blood from the veins.
Word Family: **auricular** (*say* aw-**rik**-yewla), *adjective.*

auriferous (*say* aw-**rifferus**) *adjective*
yielding or containing gold.
[Latin *aurum* gold + *ferre* to carry]

aurora (*say* aw-**rawra**) *noun*
a glowing display in the upper layers of the atmosphere near the poles, caused by fast, charged particles from the sun. The **aurora borealis** occurs near the North Pole and the **aurora australis** occurs near the South Pole.

aurous (*say* **aw**-rus) *adjective*
Chemistry: of or relating to compounds of gold in which gold has a valency of one.

auspice (*say* **aw**spis) *noun*
plural is **auspices** (*say* **aw**spi-seez)
1. (*usually plural*) any help or patronage: 'the research was carried out under the *auspices* of the government'.

2. a favourable omen.
[Latin *auspicium* divination]

auspicious (*say* aw–**spish**us) *adjective*
fortunate or favourable.
Word Family: **auspiciously,** *adverb.*

Aussie (*say* ozzee) *noun*
(*informal*) an Australian.

austere (*say* aw–**steer**) *adjective*
1. morally strict or self–restrained: 'the *austere* life of a monk'.
2. lacking comfort or ornament: 'an *austere* building'.
Word Family: **austerely,** *adverb*; **austerity** (*say* os–**terri**–tee), *noun*, the quality of being austere.
[Greek *austeros* severe]

Australasian (*say* ostra–**lay**–*zh*'n) *adjective*
of or relating to Australia, New Zealand and the nearby South Pacific islands.

autarchy (*say* **aw**–tar–kee) *noun*
despotism; absolute rule.
[AUTO– + Greek *arkhos* a leader]
Common Error: do not confuse with AUTARKY.

autarky (*say* **aw**–tar–kee) *adjective*
self–sufficiency, especially of a country's economy.
[AUTO– + Greek *arkios* sufficient]
Common Error: do not confuse with AUTARCHY.

authentic (*say* aw–**then**tik) *adjective*
genuine or believable: 'her French accent sounds quite *authentic*'.
Word Family: **authentically,** *adverb*; **authenticity** (*say* awthen–**tissi**–tee), *noun*, the quality of being authentic.
[Greek *authentikos* genuine]

authenticate (*say* aw–**thenti**–kate) *verb*
to make or prove to be authentic.
Word Family: **authentication,** *noun.*

author (*say* **aw**tha) *noun*
1. a person who writes a book, essay, etc.
2. any person who originates something: 'who was the *author* of this scheme?'.
Word Family: **authoress,** *noun*, a female author; **authorship,** *noun*; **authorial,** *adjective.*
[Latin *auctor* originator]

authoritarian (*say* aw–thorri–**tair**ian) *adjective*
in favour of obedience to authority, rather than the exercise of individual freedom.
Word Family: **authoritarian,** *noun*, a person who has an authoritarian manner; **authoritarianism,** *noun.*

authority (*say* aw–**thorri**–tee) *noun*
1. the power or right to give orders and make others obey.
Usage: 'who gave you *authority* to act?' (= permission).
2. an expert or reliable source: 'he is an *authority* on road safety'.
3. an organization or group having control over public affairs.
Word Family: **authoritative,** *adjective*, having or using authority; **authoritatively,** *adverb.*
[Latin *auctoritas* responsibility]

authorize (*say* **aw**tha–rize) **authorise** *verb*
to give authority to or for: 'you must *authorize* your solicitor to act for you'.
Word Family: **authorization,** *noun.*

autism (*say* **aw**–tizm) *noun*
an abnormal tendency to withdraw into a private world to such an extent that normal human communication is impossible.
Word Family: **autistic** (*say* aw–**tis**tik), *adjective.*
[Greek *autos* self + –ISM]

auto–
a prefix meaning self, as in *autobiography.*

autobiography (*say* auto–by–**ogra**–fee) *noun*
the life story of a person written by himself. Compare BIOGRAPHY.
Word Family: **autobiographical** (*say* auto–by–a–**graffi**–k'l), **autobiographic,** *adjective*; **autobiographically,** *adverb*; **autobiographer,** *noun.*

autoclave *noun*
a closed vessel for sterilizing equipment by using steam under pressure.
[AUTO– + Latin *clavis* a key]

autocracy (*say* aw**tokra**–see) *noun*
despotism.
Word Family: **autocrat** (*say* awta–krat), *noun*, a person having or using absolute power; **autocratic,** *adjective*; **autocratically,** *adverb.*
[AUTO– + Greek *kratia* rule]

auto–da–fé (*say* auto–dah–**fay**) *noun*
plural is **autos–da–fé**
the burning of a heretic after sentence by the Inquistion.
[Portuguese, act of the Faith]

autograph (*say* awta-graf) *noun*
a) a person's signature or handwriting.
b) an original manuscript in a person's own handwriting.
Word Family: **autographic, autographical**, *adjective*.
[AUTO- + Greek *graphein* to write]

automat *noun*
a coin-operated machine which supplies a variety of goods, usually food.

automatic *adjective*
1. done without thought or conscious effort: 'breathing is an *automatic* process'.
2. (of a machine) operating without direct human control.
3. (of a gun) using the pressure of the exploding cartridge to operate a mechanism which reloads the chamber for repeated firing.
Word Family: **automatically**, *adverb*; **automatic**, *noun*.
[Greek *automatos* self-moving]

automatic pilot
an automatic steering device in an aeroplane.

automation (*say* awta-**may**-sh'n) *noun*
the process of replacing manpower by machinery, especially in industry.
Word Family: **automate**, *verb*, to apply the principles of automation.

automaton (*say* aw-**tomma**-t'n) *noun*
plural is **automatons** or **automata**
1. a person who acts in an automatic or unthinking way.
2. an automatic device or machine, such as a robot.

automobile (*say* awta-mo-beel) *noun*
a motor car.
[AUTO- + Latin *mobilis* movable]

automotive (*say* awta-**mo**-tiv) *adjective*
1. self-propelled.
2. of or relating to motor vehicles: 'the *automotive* industry'.

autonomy (*say* aw-**tonna**-mee) *noun*
1. the ruling of a country by its own people.
2. any independence or freedom.
Word Family: **autonomous**, *adjective*, independent.
[AUTO- + Greek *nomos* law]

autopsy (*say* **aw**-topsee) *noun*
see POST-MORTEM.

autosome (*say* **awto**-some) *noun*
any chromosome which is not a sex chromosome.
[AUTO- + (chromo)SOME]

autosuggestion
(*say* auto-sujjess-ch'n) *noun*
Psychology: a change in a person's outlook or attitude, caused by his own thoughts or belief.

autotrophic (*say* auto-**troffik**) *adjective*
(of an organism) being able to make its own food by photosynthesis. Compare HETEROTROPHIC.
Word Family: **autotroph**, *noun*.
[AUTO- + Greek *trophé* nourishment]

autumn (*say* **aw**-t'm) *noun*
in America called the **Fall**
the season of the year between summer and winter.
Word Family: **autumnal** (*say* aw-**tum**-n'l), *adjective*; **autumnally**, *adverb*.
[Latin *autumnus*]

auxiliary (*say* awg-**zillia**-ree) *adjective*
giving support or aid: '*auxiliary* troops'.
Word Family: **auxiliary**, *noun*, a person or thing that gives aid of any kind.
[Latin *auxilium* assistance]

auxin (*say* **oksin** *or* **awksin**) *noun*
a group of plant hormones produced by dividing cells, promoting growth in certain parts of a plant and often inhibiting it in others.
[Greek *auxé* growth]

avail (*say* a-**vale**) *noun*
usefulness or advantage: 'it is of little *avail* to shout'.
avail *verb*
to be of use or value.
avail oneself of, 'you should *avail yourself of* this chance' (= make use of).

available (*say* a-vayla-b'l) *adjective*
suitable or ready for use: 'no more seats *available* for the concert'.
Word Family: **availability** (*say* a-vayla-**billi**-tee), *noun*; **availably**, *adverb*.

avalanche (*say* **avva**-lahnch) *noun*
1. a sudden fall or movement of a mass of snow, rock or mud down a slope.
2. something which has the force or movement of an avalanche: 'an *avalanche* of angry questions'.
[French]

avant-garde (*say* **avvon**-gard) *adjective*
in the forefront of modern trends, in arts, etc.
Word Family: **avant-garde**, *noun*.
[French, vanguard]

avarice (*say* **avva**–ris) *noun*
an extreme greed for wealth, possessions, etc.
Word Family: **avaricious** (*say* avva–**rish**us), *adjective*; **avariciously,** *adverb*; **avariciousness,** *noun.*
[Latin *avarus* greedy]

avast (*say* a–**vahst**) *interjection*
Nautical: a call to stop.

avaunt (*say* a–**vawnt**) *interjection*
an old word meaning go or away.

avenge (*say* a–**venj**) *verb*
to take revenge for.
Word Family: **avenger,** *noun.*

avenue (*say* **avva**–new) *noun*
1. a street or road, originally a wide, tree–lined street.
2. a means: 'to search for *avenues* of escape'.

aver (*say* a–**ver**) *verb*
(**averred, averring**)
to declare in a positive way.

average (*say* **av**–rij) *noun*
1. the result obtained by dividing the sum of several quantities by the number of quantities added.
2. the most common or usual amount, quality, kind, etc.
Word Family: **average,** *adjective*; **averagely,** *adverb*; **average,** *verb,* a) to calculate the average of, b) to be or obtain an average.
[from Arabic]

averse (*say* a–**verse**) *adjective*
opposed or reluctant: 'I'm not *averse* to hard work'.
[Latin *aversus* turned round]
Common Error: **see** ADVERSE.

aversion (*say* a–**ver**–sh'n) *noun*
a) an extreme dislike: 'I have an *aversion* to spiders'. b) a person or thing that is disliked.

avert (*say* a–**vert**) *verb*
to turn away: 'she *averted* her eyes'.
Usage: 'it was too late to *avert* the disaster' (= avoid).

aviary (*say* **ave**–y'ree) *noun*
a large cage or enclosure in which birds are kept.
[Latin *avis* a bird]

aviation (*say* ay–vee–**ay**–sh'n) *noun*
the science or skill of flying aircraft.
Word Family: **aviator,** *noun,* a pilot.
[Latin *avis* a bird]

avid (*say* **avvid**) *adjective*
1. greedy: '*avid* for power'.
2. very enthusiastic or keen: 'he is an *avid* collector of old guns'.
Word Family: **avidly,** *adverb*; **avidity** (*say* a–**viddi**–tee), *noun.*
[Latin *avidus* desirous]

avocado (*say* avva–**kah**do) *noun*
1. an edible, tropical fruit with a dark green or black skin, creamy yellowish flesh and a large seed. Short form of **avocado pear.**
2. a pale yellowish–green colour.
Word Family: **avocado,** *adjective.*
[an Aztec name]

avocet (*say* **avva**–set) *noun*
a large wading bird with a long, up–curved beak and blue legs.

avoid (*say* a–**voyd**) *verb*
to keep away from: 'most people try to *avoid* danger'.
Word Family: **avoidable,** *adjective*; **avoidance,** *noun*; **avoidably,** *adverb.*

avoirdupois weight
(*say* av–wa–doo–**pwa** wate)
a system of units of mass for goods other than precious metals, gems and drugs. The units are the grain, dram, ounce, pound, stone, quarter, hundredweight and ton. See UNITS in grey pages.
[French, goods of weight]

avow (*say* a–**vow**) *verb*
to acknowledge or confess.
Word Family: **avowal,** *noun.*

avuncular (*say* a–**vunk**–yewla) *adjective*
of or like an uncle: 'children love his kindly, *avuncular* manner'.
[Latin *avunculus* uncle]

await *verb*
to wait for or expect: 'we will *await* your decision'.

awake *adjective*
not asleep.
Usage: 'I think he is *awake* to the danger' (= alert).
awake, awaken *verbs*
(**awoke, awoken** or **awaked, awaking**)
to wake from sleep.
Word Family: **awakening,** *noun,* a) the act of waking from sleep, b) an arousing of interest, etc.

award *verb*
to officially give or grant: 'he was *awarded* several prizes'.
award *noun*
1. any prize or token which is awarded.
2. the minimum legal rate of pay for a particular type of work.
3. *Law:* a decision, e.g. of an arbitrator.

aware *adjective*
having knowledge or understanding of: 'he was *aware* of the danger'.
Word Family: **awareness**, *noun.*

awash *adjective, adverb*
covered by water.

away *adverb, adjective*
towards or at a different place, etc.: 'please go *away*!'.
Usages:
a) 'they worked *away* all morning' (= continuously).
b) 'the water has boiled *away*' (= out of existence).
c) 'please do it straight *away*' (= immediately).
d) 'the team plays *away* next week' (= not at the club's ground).

awe (*rhymes with* paw) *noun*
respect mixed with fear.
Word Family: **awe**, *verb*; **awesome**, *adjective*, inspiring awe.

aweigh (*say* away) *adverb*
Nautical: (of an anchor) raised just clear of the bottom of the sea.

awful (*say* aw–f'l) *adjective*
1. (*informal*) a) extremely bad or unpleasant: 'what an *awful* day'. b) very great: 'he has an *awful* lot of money'.
2. inspiring fear or dread.
Word Family: **awfully**, *adverb*; **awfulness**, *noun.*

awhile (*say* a–wile) *adverb*
for a short time: 'let us rest *awhile*'.

awkward *adjective*
1. lacking grace or skill: 'he is very *awkward* with his hands'.
2. causing problems or embarrassment: '10.00 a.m. is an *awkward* time for me to come'.
3. difficult or dangerous: 'he is an *awkward* person to deal with'.
Word Family: **awkwardly**, *adverb*; **awkwardness**, *noun.*

awl *noun*
a small pointed tool for piercing holes in wood or leather.

awning *noun*
a roof–like cover, usually canvas, for protecting doorways or windows.

awoke *verb*
the past tense of the verb **awake**.

awry (*say* a–rye) *adverb, adjective*
1. crooked or turned to one side.
2. wrong or off the right course: 'our plans went *awry*'.

axe *noun*
plural is **axes**
a tool with a long, wooden handle and a sharp, wedge-shaped metal head, used for chopping wood, etc.
have an axe to grind, to have a private grievance.
Word Family: **axe**, *verb*, (informal) to reduce or abolish.

axes (*say* ak–seez) *plural noun*
see AXIS.

axial *adjective*
relating to or situated at an axis.

axilla *noun*
plural is **axillae**
see ARMPIT.
Word Family: **axillary**, *adjective.*
[Latin]

axiom (*say* aks–ee–um) *noun*
an established or accepted truth, such as a general statement which is used as a basis for reasoning or argument.
Word Family: **axiomatic** (*say* aksi–amattik), *adjective.*
[Greek *axioma* a self-evident principle]

axis *noun*
plural is **axes** (*say* ak–seez)
1. the line around which a rotating body turns.
2. a line which divides something in half.
3. *Maths:* a fixed line chosen as a reference, e.g. for a graph.
[Latin, axle]

axle (*say* ak–s'l) *noun*
a supporting shaft on which a wheel or wheels turn.

ay (*say* eye) **aye** *noun*
plural is **ayes**
a vote in favour of something.

azalea (*say* a–zaylia) *noun*
any of a group of garden shrubs which are smaller, often scented, forms of rhododendron and have bright decorative flowers.
[Greek *azaleos* dry (soil)]

azimuth (*say* azzi–m'th) *noun*
Astronomy: the angle made between a vertical circle through a planet or star and the observer's meridian.
[Arabic, the directions]

azure (*say* azher) *noun*
a clear, sky–blue colour.
Word Family: **azure**, *adjective.*
[from Persian, lapis lazuli]

Bb

babble *verb*
1. to utter incoherent or meaningless sounds: 'the baby *babbled* happily in its cot'.
2. to talk continuously or thoughtlessly: 'knowing him, he'll *babble* on for hours'.
3. (of flowing water) to make a continuous murmuring or rippling sound.
Word Family: **babble**, *noun*, a babbling sound; **babbler**, *noun*.

babe *noun*
a baby.

babel (*rhymes with* table) *noun*
a confused mixture of many different sounds.
[from the *Tower of Babel* in the Bible]

baboon (*say* ba-**boon**) *noun*
a large monkey of Africa and Arabia with a muzzle rather like a dog's.
[Old French *babuin* a stupid person]

baby *noun*
1. a very young child or animal.
2. the youngest member of a group: 'she is the *baby* of her class'.
3. an inexperienced or naïve person: 'he's only a *baby* when it comes to business matters'.
4. (*informal*) a) an affectionate term for a girl or man. b) an invention or creation: 'as the plan is your *baby*, you present it at the meeting'.
Word Family: **baby** (**babied, babying**), *verb*, to pamper or coddle; **babyhood**, *noun*.

baby-sit *verb*
(**baby-sat, baby-sitting**)
to mind children when their parents are out.
Word Family: **baby-sitter**, *noun*.

baccalaureate (*say* bakka-**lorri**-at) *noun*
(in France) the first stage of university examinations taken by high-school students.

baccarat (*say* **bakka**-rah) *noun*
Cards: a game played against a banker in which the aim is to collect nine points, or the closest below that number for each round.
[French]

Bacchus *noun*
Roman mythology: the god of wine and fertility.
bacchanalian (*say* bakka-**naylian**) *adjective*
drunken, wild and unrestrained, like the festivals in honour of Bacchus.

bachelor (*say* **batcha**-la) *noun*
1. an unmarried man.
2. a person who holds the first degree awarded by a university: 'a *Bachelor* of Arts'.
[Old French *bacheler* a young man aspiring to knighthood]

bacillus (*say* ba-**sillus**) *noun*
plural is **bacilli** (*say* ba-**sil**-eye)
Biology: any of a group of rod-shaped bacteria, especially one causing disease.
[Latin *baculus* rod]

back *noun*
1. a) the rear part of the human body between the shoulders and the buttocks. b) the corresponding part of any animal's body.
Usage: 'he's broken his *back*' (= spine).
2. the rear side or part of anything: 'at the *back* of the shop'.
3. the keel of a boat: 'the ship broke its *back* on the reef'.
4. *Sport:* a player in a defensive position.
Phrases:
break the back of, 'another 2 hours' work should *break the back of* it' (= deal with the hardest part of).
get off one's back, '*get off my back!*' (= stop criticizing or pestering).
get, put one's back up, 'she always *gets his back up*' (= annoys him).
turn one's back on, 'you can't *turn your back on* family responsibilities' (= ignore, neglect).

back *verb*
1. to move or cause to move backwards: 'he *backed* the truck skilfully'.
2. to support or bet on: 'we should *back* that horse in today's race'.
3. to be placed at the rear or to form a background: a) 'the workshop *backs* onto a lane'; b) 'the view is *backed* by rising foothills'.
Phrases:
back down, to retreat.
back out, to withdraw or refuse.
back up, a) 'do you have any witnesses who can *back up* your story?' (= corroborate); b) to assist or support.
Word Family: **backup**, *noun.*
back *adjective*
1. placed behind or in the rear: 'enter by the *back* door'.
2. of or for a date earlier than the present: '*back* issues of a periodical'.
back *adverb*
1. at, to or towards the rear: 'move *back*, please, and let the doctor near'.
2. in, to or towards a former place, time or condition: a) 'to go *back* home'; b) 'my cold has come *back*'; c) 'she remembers *back* 50 years'.
Usages:
a) 'I take *back* everything I said' (= in withdrawal).
b) 'sit *back* and be comfortable' (= in a reclining position).
c) 'in spite of his fury prudence held him *back*' (= in restraint).
d) 'she was punished because she answered *back*' (= cheekily in reply).
Word Family: **backer**, *noun*, a person who supports an enterprise, especially with money; **backless**, *adjective.*

backbencher *noun*
Parliament: a member of the House of Commons who is not entitled to occupy the front benches which are reserved for ministers and shadow ministers. Compare FRONTBENCHER.

backbite *verb*
to gossip about or slander a person in his absence.
Word Family: **backbiter**, *noun.*

backbone *noun*
the vertebral column.
Usages:
a) 'the *backbone* of the Establishment' (= main support).
b) 'he didn't have the *backbone* to admit he was wrong' (= strength of character).

backchat *noun*
any impertinent answering back: 'I won't put up with any more *backchat*'.
Word Family: **backchat (backchatted, backchatting)**, *verb.*

backdate *verb*
to date or apply at an earlier date than the present: 'your pay rise will be *backdated* two months'.

backdrop *noun*
also called a **backcloth**
Theatre: a painted curtain or hanging at the back of a stage, forming part of the set.

backer *noun*
Word Family: see BACK.

backfire *verb*
(of an internal combustion engine) to explode through the exhaust pipe, owing to the accumulation of unburnt fuel.
Usage: 'our plans *backfired* at the last moment' (= went wrong).
Word Family: **backfire**, *noun.*

backgammon *noun*
a board game for two people, each with fifteen pieces which move according to the throw of dice.
[BACK + Middle English *gamen* a game, because sometimes the pieces must return to the start]

background *noun*
the remoter part of a scene or setting, against which things are seen or represented: 'the view overlooks the lake with the mountains in the *background*'.
Usages:
a) 'my essay is on the *background* of the French Revolution' (= events surrounding or causing).
b) 'Smith's *background* in science makes him ideal for the job' (= experience, training).
c) 'a politician's advisers usually remain in the *background*' (= relative obscurity).

backhand *noun*
1. *Tennis:* a stroke made across the body with the back of the hand facing forwards. Compare FOREHAND.
2. any handwriting which slopes to the left.
backhanded *adjective*
1. (of a stroke or blow) delivered or made with the back of the hand, or the back of the hand facing forward.
2. (of handwriting) sloping to the left.
backhanded compliment, an ambiguous, double-edged compliment.

Word Family: **backhandedly**, *adverb*; **backhander**, *noun*, a backhanded blow or stroke.

backing *noun*
1. any support, promotion or assistance: 'the enterprise will never succeed without proper *backing*'.
2. a supporting or strengthening back part: 'the *backing* on this furniture isn't very strong'.

backlash *noun*
1. a backward whipping or jarring motion in worn machine parts.
2. a hostile reaction to something considered to be a threat.

backless *adjective*
Word Family: see BACK.

backlog *noun*
an accumulation of work, etc.: 'there is a huge *backlog* of mail to answer'.

back-pedal *verb*
(**back-pedalled, back-pedalling**)
1. to pedal backwards.
2. to retreat or abandon one's position in an argument, commitment, etc. Also called to **backtrack**.

backroom boys
any people engaged in work behind the scenes, especially researchers, scientists, etc.

back seat
a seat at or towards the back.
take a back seat, 'she *took a back seat* in the discussion' (= played an inconspicuous part).
back-seat driver
(*informal*) anyone who interferes or gives unwanted advice, such as a car passenger who constantly corrects the driver.

backside *noun*
1. a back part.
2. (*informal*) the buttocks.

backslide *verb*
(**backslid, backsliding**)
to fall back into error or wrongdoing.
Word Family: **backslider**, *noun.*

backstage *noun*
Theatre: the area behind or at the sides of the stage, containing the dressing-rooms, props and other equipment.
Word Family: **backstage**, *adjective*, private or behind the scenes.

backstreet *noun*
a small out-of-the-way street in a city or town.

backstreet *adjective*
illegal or underhand: 'a *backstreet* enterprise'.

backstroke *noun*
a swimming style in which the swimmer lies on his back, reaching back and pulling alternately with each arm.

backtrack *verb*
to back-pedal.

backward *adjective*
1. towards the back or in reverse: 'she left without a *backward* glance'.
2. a) retarded or showing no progress: 'a *backward* child'. b) shy or retiring: 'he isn't *backward* in making his opinions known'.
backwards, backward *adverb*
towards the back or in reverse: 'he leant *backwards* in his chair'.
bend, fall or **lean over backwards**, 'they *bent over backwards* to help her' (= went to great trouble).
Word Family: **backwardly**, *adverb*; **backwardness**, *noun.*

backwash *noun*
Nautical: the wave or broken water left by a boat or oars.
Usage: 'the *backwash* of the revolution left them penniless' (= aftermath).

backwater *noun*
a stagnant stretch of a river or a still pool fed by a river.
Usage: 'she was bored living in such a *backwater*' (= backward or unprogressive place).

backwoods *plural noun*
1. uncleared land away from settled areas.
2. any obscure or remote area.

bacon (*say* **bay**-k'n) *noun*
a cut of pork from the back or sides of a pig, usually salted or smoked.
Phrases:
bring home the bacon, to succeed in an enterprise.
save one's bacon, 'a good alibi might *save his bacon*' (= get him out of trouble).

bacteria (*say* bak-**teer**ia) *plural noun*
singular is **bacterium**
a large group of unicellular micro-organisms which display both plant and animal characteristics. Bacteria are important in the decay of plant and animal tissue, providing food, such as nitrates, for higher plants, and assisting in processes such as the fermentation of wines and the maturing of cheese. Some bacteria

cause severe diseases, such as typhoid, diphtheria, etc.
Word Family: **bacterial**, *adjective.*
[Greek *bakterion* a small stick]

bacteriology (*say* bak–teeri–**olla**–jee) *noun*
the study of bacteria.
Word Family: **bacteriologist,** *noun.*

bad (1) *adjective*
(worse, worst)
having unpleasant or disagreeable qualities: 'a *bad* dream'.
Usages:
a) 'this car has *bad* brakes' (= faulty).
b) 'she is selfish, but she's not a *bad* person' (= malicious).
c) 'the milk will go *bad* if you leave it out' (= sour, spoiled).
d) 'he is a *bad* tennis player' (= incompetent).
e) 'he has a *bad* toothache' (= severe, serious).
f) 'a *bad* debt' (= not able to be recovered or made good).
g) 'reading by a poor light is *bad* for the eyes' (= harmful).
h) 'I feel very *bad* about having lost my temper' (= sorry, regretful).
not bad, rather good.
Word Family: **bad**, *noun*; **badly,** *adverb*, a) poorly or inadequately, b) very much; **badness**, *noun.*

bad (2) *verb*
a past tense of the verb **bid.**

bade (*say* bad) *verb*
an old past tense of the verb **bid.**

badge (*say* baj) *noun*
an emblem signifying rank or membership in an organization: 'a Boy Scout *badge*'.

badger (*say* **baja**) *noun*
a small, burrowing, flesh–eating mammal which hunts at night.
badger *verb*
to pester or harass: 'stop *badgering* me with questions'.

badinage (*say* **baddi**–nah*zh*) *noun*
any playful or witty exchange in conversation.
[French *badiner* to jest]

badly *adverb*
Word Family: see BAD (1).

badminton *noun*
a game similar to tennis but using a high net and a light shuttlecock which does not bounce.
[invented at the Duke of Beaufort's home at *Badminton*, Gloucestershire]

badness *noun*
Word Family: see BAD (1).

baffle *verb*
to confuse or puzzle: 'why does my remark *baffle* you?'.
baffle *noun*
any of various devices used to control flow or movement, as in a car silencer (to control hot gases) or in a loudspeaker (to control soundwaves).
Word Family: **bafflingly,** *adverb*; **bafflement,** *noun.*

bag *noun*
1. any of various containers made from paper, cloth, leather, etc., such as a mailbag or a travelling bag.
2. (*informal, plural*) a large quantity: 'he has *bags* of money'.
3. (*informal*) an unattractive woman.
in the bag, 'a business deal which is *in the bag*' (= assured, secured).
bag *verb*
(bagged, bagging)
1. to put into a bag: 'to *bag* wheat'.
2. to sag or hang loosely: 'his trousers *bagged* at the knees'.
3. to catch or kill, especially game: 'we *bagged* an elephant first day out'.
bags *interjection*
(*informal*) a claim for first use of, right to, etc.: '*bags* I have the top bunk!'.
Word Family: **bagging,** *noun,* any material, especially jute or hemp, from which bags are made.

bagatelle (*say* bagga–**tel**) *noun*
1. anything of little importance: 'a mere *bagatelle*'.
2. see PINBALL.
[French]

baggage (*say* **baggij**) *noun*
1. any luggage.
2. (*informal*) a saucy or lively young woman: 'she is a brazen *baggage*'.

baggy *adjective*
bulging or hanging in folds: '*baggy* trousers'.

bagpipe *noun*
Music: (*often plural*) any of several reed instruments for which wind from the mouth or bellows is stored in a bag, and expelled through a number of pipes.

bail (1) *noun*
Law: the sum of money given to a court as a guarantee that an accused person, who is freed until his trial, will return to court for the trial.
go bail for, to provide bail for.
Word Family: **bail,** *verb.*
[Old French, power or custody]

bail (2) *verb*
see BALE (2).

bailiff *noun*
1. *Law:* a person employed by a sheriff to serve writs and carry out court orders.
2. *Medieval history:* a) a chief magistrate or administrative official representing the king in a town or district. b) the agent for a feudal lord. Also called a **reeve**.
[Latin *bajulus* a porter or manager]

bairn *noun*
a Scottish word for a child.

bait *noun*
a lure in the form of food, used to attract fish, game, etc.
Usage: 'they offered him a salary rise as a *bait* to stop him resigning' (= enticement).
bait *verb*
1. to prepare a fishhook, trap, etc. by attaching bait.
2. to anger or torment deliberately.

baize (*say* baze) *noun*
a woollen felt-like fabric, usually green, used as a cover for billiard tables, etc.

bake *verb*
1. to cook or heat in an oven.
2. to harden by heating.

bakehouse *noun*
a bakery.

Bakelite (*say* **bay**ka-lite) *noun*
any of various synthetic resins made from phenols and formaldehyde, formerly used for making electrical insulators, telephone receivers, etc.
[a trademark, after its inventor, *L.H. Baekeland*, 1863–1944, an American chemist]

baker *noun*
a person who bakes and sells bread, cakes, etc.

baker's dozen
thirteen.
[after the former practice among bakers of adding an extra loaf to each dozen to ensure full weight]

bakery *noun*
also called a **bakehouse**
a place where bread, cakes, buns, etc. are baked or sold.

baking powder
a raising agent used in making cakes and biscuits.

baking soda
see BICARBONATE OF SODA.

balaclava (*say* balla-**klah**va) *noun*
a woollen hood which covers the head, ears and neck.
[as worn at the battle of *Balaclava* in the Crimean War]

balalaika (*say* balla-**lie**-ka) *noun*
Music: a triangular, Russian instrument related to the guitar, with three strings.

balance *noun*
1. an equal distribution of weight, amount, etc.: 'the *balance* of the load must be carefully arranged'.
2. a condition of steadiness, especially when two opposing forces, influences, etc. are equal: 'don't lose your *balance* on that bike'.
3. an instrument for measuring mass, especially one with two pans on an arm which pivots about a central point.
4. something which is used to produce a state of balance.
5. (in bookkeeping) a) an equality between the debit and credit sides of an account. b) the difference between such totals.
6. the remainder: a) 'the *balance* of my report can wait'; b) 'the *balance* of a bill'.
7. *Astrology:* (*capital*) see LIBRA.
Phrases:
balance of payments, the difference between the amount a country spends abroad on imports, etc. and the amount it earns through its exports, etc., called the **trade gap** when the first exceeds the second.
balance of power, a) the condition in which no single nation or group of nations is stronger than any other; b) 'which party holds the *balance of power* in parliament?' (= power to decide or determine).
hang in the balance, to be or remain undecided.
strike a balance, to find a solution that is considered to be fair to all.
balance *verb*
1. to weigh on a balance.
2. to bring into or keep in a steady condition or position: a) 'can you *balance* a book on your head?'; b) 'the acrobat *balanced* on one hand'.
3. to make or be equal in weight, amount, force, etc.: 'his good points probably *balance* his bad'.
Usage: 'he was left *balancing* one alternative against the other' (= comparing).
4. (in bookkeeping) a) to estimate the difference between the debit and credit

sides of an account. b) to make the necessary adjustments so that the debit and credit sides of an account are equal.
[Latin *bilanx* having two scales]

balance sheet
a statement of the assets and liabilities of a business at a certain date.

balcony (*say* **balka-nee**) *noun*
1. a platform projecting from a building, usually with a railing or balustrade.
2. a raised gallery with seats, in a theatre or public building.

bald (*say* bawld) *adjective*
1. lacking hair on the scalp.
Usage: 'a *bald* mountain' (= lacking vegetation).
2. blunt or plain: a) 'a *bald* lie'; b) 'he gave a *bald* statement of the facts'.
Word Family: **baldly,** *adverb*; **baldness,** *noun.*

balderdash (*say* **bawlda-dash**) *noun*
nonsense or words jumbled illogically together.

bale (1) *noun*
a large, compact package or bundle held together by wires, cord or cloth: 'a *bale* of hay'.
Word Family: **bale,** *verb*; **baler,** *noun.*

bale (2) *verb*
also spelt **bail**
to dip out water from the bottom of a boat.
bale out, (*informal*) a) to parachute from an aircraft; b) to abandon any dangerous situation.
[Old French *baille* a bucket]

baleful *adjective*
menacing or evil: 'he replied with a *baleful* stare'.
Word Family: **balefully,** *adverb*; **balefulness,** *noun.*

balk (*rhymes with* walk) *verb*
also spelt **baulk**
1. to stop and refuse to continue: a) 'my horse *balked* at the gate'; b) 'she *balked* at the idea of marriage'.
2. to prevent or thwart: 'a publicity campaign *balked* by a newspaper strike'.
balk *noun*
1. any obstacle or hindrance.
2. an unploughed strip of land between furrows.

ball (1) (*say* bawl) *noun*
1. a) a spherical object, either hollow or solid, such as that used in cricket, tennis, etc. b) a rounded protuberance or part of something: 'he balanced on the *balls* of his feet'.
2. (*informal, plural*) the testicles.
Phrases:
on the ball, (*informal*) alert or in touch.
play ball, to cooperate.
Word Family: **ball,** *verb,* to shape into a ball.

ball (2) (*say* bawl) *noun*
a large social gathering, usually formal, with dancing, eating and drinking.
have a ball, (*informal*) to enjoy oneself thoroughly.
[Old French *baler* to dance]

ballad *noun*
1. a simple narrative poem, often adapted for singing.
2. a light, popular song.
Word Family: **balladry,** *noun,* any or all ballads.

ballast (*say* **bal**-ast) *noun*
1. any heavy material, such as lead or bags of sand, placed in the hold of a ship, etc. to ensure stability.
2. gravel or broken rock used as a bed for railway sleepers, drainage, etc.
Word Family: **ballast,** *verb.*

ball-bearing *noun*
a) a bearing which moves on small steel balls placed in a ring-shaped groove. b) one of the small steel balls.

ballet (*say* **bal**-ay) *noun*
a) an artistic dance form characterized by stylized steps, movements and gestures. b) a performance of such a dance, usually with a musical accompaniment, scenery and theatrical effects, acting out a story or theme. c) a company of dancers which performs ballets.
Word Family: **ballet-dancer,** *noun*; **ballerina** (*say* balla-**reena**), *noun,* a female ballet-dancer.

ballistic missile
a missile which is propelled and guided only in the first stages of its flight. Compare GUIDED MISSILE.

ballistics (*say* ba-**listiks**) *plural noun*
(*used with singular verb*) the study of the motion of projectiles, such as bullets or missiles.
Word Family: **ballistic,** *adjective,* having to do with projectiles and their movement.
[Greek *ballein* to throw]

balloon (*say* ba-**loon**) *noun*
1. an aircraft which is lighter than air and consists of a large bag filled

with hydrogen, helium or hot air, and a basket or harness to carry the crew. **2.** an inflatable rubber bag, usually coloured, used as a toy or for decoration.
when the balloon goes up, when trouble starts.
Word Family: **balloon**, *verb*, a) to swell up like a balloon, b) to go aloft in a balloon; **balloonist**, *noun.*
[French *ballon*]

ballot *noun*
a) a system of secret voting in an election, in which the voter is given a paper printed with the names of candidates, on which he indicates the candidate he has chosen, before placing it in the ballot-box. b) the piece of paper used. c) the total number of votes cast.
ballot *verb*
(balloted, balloting)
a) to vote by ballot. b) to draw lots.
[Italian *ballotta* a little ball, because originally votes were cast by dropping a ball into a box]

ballpoint pen
a pen containing a supply of ink and a point consisting of a metal ball which turns on contact with paper and releases a small amount of ink onto the paper.

ballroom *noun*
a large room or hall in which balls are held.

balls-up *noun*
(*informal*) a mistake causing confusion.

ballyhoo *noun*
(*informal*) a) sensational or misleading publicity or advertising. b) an uproar or outcry.

balm (*rhymes with* calm) *noun*
1. any of various ointments made from the resin of certain trees.
2. anything which heals or soothes: 'sleep, the *balm* of troubled minds'.
balmy *adjective*
1. (of weather) mild or warm.
2. fragrant or healing.
Word Family: **balmily**, *adverb*; **balminess**, *noun.*
[Latin *balsamum* balsam]

baloney (*say* ba-**lo**-nee) *noun*
also spelt **boloney**
(*informal*) any nonsense or stupid assertion.

balsa (*say* **bawl**sa) *noun*
a tropical, South American tree with extremely light soft wood, used for timber in rafts, life-preservers, model aircraft, etc.
[Spanish]

balsam (*say* **bawls**'m) *noun*
any of various secretions from plants, used as a balm.
[Latin *balsamum*]

balustrade (*say* **bal**la-strade) *noun*
a series of upright supports (called **balusters**), joined at the top by a rail, as in a stone balcony, etc.
[Greek *balaustion* the pomegranate flower, because a baluster supposedly resembles it in shape]

bamboo *noun*
plural is **bamboos**
any of a group of tropical, woody grasses with long, hollow, jointed stems up to 10 m or more in height.
[Malay]

bamboozle *verb*
a) to trick or deceive: 'the cardsharp *bamboozled* the other players out of £100'. b) to puzzle or mystify: 'I was completely *bamboozled* by the time he'd finished explaining it to me'.

ban *verb*
(banned, banning)
to prohibit: 'I can't see why that book was *banned*'.
ban *noun*
an official order or prohibition: 'there is a *ban* on fires in the open today'.
[Old English *bannan* to summon]

banal (*say* ba-**nahl**) *adjective*
hackneyed, ordinary or trivial: 'a *banal* conversation about the weather'.
Word Family: **banally**, *adverb*; **banality** (*say* ba-**nalli**-tee), *noun*, a) the quality of being banal, b) something which is banal.
[French]

banana (*say* ba-**nah**na) *noun*
a finger-shaped, tropical fruit with a yellow skin, growing in bunches called hands.
[Spanish]

banana republic
(*informal*) a small tropical country almost wholly dependent on fruit exports and thus regarded as economically and politically unstable.

band (1) *noun*
1. a group of people acting together: 'a small *band* of soldiers led the expedition'.
2. a) a group of musicians playing brass and percussion instruments: 'a Salvation Army *Band*'. b) a pop group.

Word Family: **band,** *verb,* to unite or join together; **bandsman,** *noun,* a musician who plays in a brass band.

band (2) *noun*
1. a flat strip of any material for binding, trimming, etc.: 'the box was strengthened with metal *bands*'.
2. a broad stripe crossing any surface: 'the fish had *bands* of red and silver'.
3. *Radio:* see WAVEBAND.
Word Family: **band,** *verb,* to stripe or mark with bands.

bandage (*say* **bandij**) *noun*
a strip of fabric, etc. used to bind a wound.
Word Family: **bandage,** *verb.*

bandanna *noun*
also spelt **bandana**
a large, coloured handkerchief or cotton scarf.

bandbox *noun*
a light box, often circular, for storing or carrying women's hats.

bandicoot *noun*
1. any of a group of rat-like Australian marsupials with long pointed snouts.
2. any of various large rats found in south-east Asia.
[Hindi]

bandit *noun*
a robber or outlaw.
[Italian *bandito* outlawed or banished]

bandoleer (*say* banda-**leer**) *noun*
also spelt **bandolier**
Military: a belt worn over one shoulder and fitted with small loops for carrying cartridges.

bandsaw *noun*
a saw consisting of an endless metal band with one cutting edge, usually turned by a motor.

bandsman *noun*
Word Family: see BAND (1).

bandwagon *noun*
a wagon carrying a musical band at the head of a procession.
climb, jump on the bandwagon, (*informal*) to follow or join a popular movement, fashion, etc. because it appears likely to succeed.

bandy *verb*
(bandied, bandying)
to pass back and forth: a) 'don't *bandy* words with me'; b) 'the story was *bandied* about but she didn't believe it'.
bandy *adjective*
bandy-legged.

bandy-legged *adjective*
having the legs curved outwards at the knees.

bane *noun*
1. an old word for poison.
2. anything which causes ruin or death: 'gambling is the *bane* of my life'.
Word Family: **baneful,** *adjective*; **banefully,** *adverb*; **banefulness,** *noun.*

bang (1) *noun*
1. a sudden loud noise.
2. any violent blow or knock: 'a nasty *bang* on the head'.
bang-on, absolutely accurate.
Word Family: **bang,** *verb*; **bang,** *adverb,* with a bang.

bang (2) *noun*
a fringe of hair cut straight across the forehead.

banger *noun*
(*informal*) a sausage.

bangle *noun*
an ornamental band or chain without a clasp, worn around the arm or ankle.
[Hindi *bangri* a glass bracelet]

banish *verb*
1. to send a person into exile.
2. to put or drive something away: 'to *banish* fear'.
Word Family: **banishment,** *noun.*

banister, bannister *noun*
1. one of the supports of a stair rail.
2. (*plural*) a stair rail with its supports.

banjo *noun*
plural is **banjos or banjoes**
Music: a fretted, stringed instrument plucked with fingers or a plectrum.
[Greek *pandoura* a three-stringed lute]

bank (1) *noun*
1. any slope or piled mass: a) 'the river has steep *banks*'; b) 'a *bank* of clouds hid the sun'.
2. a raised portion of the sea-floor, a riverbed, etc.
bank *verb*
1. to form into a bank: 'the earth is *banked* up near the construction site'.
2. to tilt an aircraft laterally in flight.

bank (2) *noun*
1. *Commerce:* an organization whose business is the safekeeping of money and valuables, lending and borrowing money, and in some cases issuing and exchanging foreign money.
2. any storage place, such as a blood bank.

3. any reserve or fund to or from which money may be paid, as in various card or gambling games.
bank *verb*
to deposit in a bank: 'I *banked* the cheque'.
bank on, 'we are *banking on* you to do a good job' (= relying on).
Word Family: **banker**, *noun*, a) a person who directs the business of a bank, b) a person in charge of the bank in card games, etc.

bank (3) *noun*
a set of objects arranged in a line: 'a *bank* of spotlights'.

bank account
short form is **account**
the money kept by a customer at a bank, from which withdrawals may be made in cash or by cheque (called a **current account**), and in which deposits may be added to obtain interest (called a **deposit account**).

bank-draft *noun*
Commerce: a) a bill of exchange for use in international trade. b) a written order for the payment of a sum of money.

bank holiday
any of several public holidays, originally days when the banks were closed by law.

banknote *noun*
a piece of paper money.

bank rate
the basic rate of interest announced from time to time by the Bank of England; now replaced by the similar Minimum Lending Rate (MLR).

bankrupt *noun*
Law: a person who cannot pay his debts and whose possessions are given to a trustee to be distributed among the people to whom he owes money.
bankrupt *adjective*
1. a) being subject to legal proceedings because of an inability to pay one's debts. b) legally declared a bankrupt.
2. destitute: 'he is morally *bankrupt*'.
Word Family: **bankrupt**, *verb*, to make bankrupt; **bankruptcy** (*say* **bank**rup-see), *noun*, the state of being bankrupt.
[BANK (2) + Latin *ruptus* broken]

banner *noun*
1. a flag, especially of a country, army, etc.: 'the star-spangled *banner*'.
2. a piece of cloth, etc. held up on a pole in a procession.
3. a headline in a newspaper which extends the full width of the page.

bannister *noun*
see BANISTER.

banns *plural noun*
an announcement made in a church on three successive Sundays, declaring that two people intend to be married, so that any legal objection to the marriage may be made known.
[the old plural of *ban*]

banquet (*say* **bang**-kwit) *noun*
a feast or ceremonial public dinner.
Word Family: **banquet**, *verb*.

banshee *noun*
(in Scottish and Irish mythology) a supernatural being, believed to wail around a house if someone is about to die.
[Irish *bean sidhe* a woman of the fairies]

bantam (*say* **ban**-t'm) *noun*
a small domestic fowl, the male having brightly coloured feathers.
[probably from *Bantam*, Indonesia]

bantamweight *noun*
a weight division in boxing, equal to about 54 kg.

banter *noun*
any playfully teasing or mocking talk.
Word Family: **banter**, *verb*; **banteringly**, *adverb*.

Bantu (*say* **ban**too) *noun*
a) a widespread group of languages in southern Africa. b) the large group of Negroid tribes speaking these languages.
[Bantu, people]

banyan, banian *noun*
an Indian fig tree whose branches send down roots which develop into new trunks.
[Sanskrit, a trader]

baobab (*say* **bay**-o-bab) *noun*
a large African tree with a very thick trunk.

baptism *noun*
Religion: a ritual washing or bath, especially as a sign of spiritual rebirth, purification or initiation.
baptism of fire, a) a soldier's first experience of battle; b) any severe or crucial test.
baptize, baptise *verb*
also called to **christen**
to perform the ritual of baptism.

Word Family: **baptismal** (*say* bap–**tizm**'l), *adjective*; **baptismally**, *adverb*.
[Greek *baptizein* to dip]

Baptist *noun*
Christian: a member of any Protestant sect teaching that only adult believers should be baptized

bar *noun*
1. a piece of some solid material, usually longer than it is wide: a) 'the *bars* of a railing'; b) 'a *bar* of chocolate'.
2. any barrier or obstruction: a) 'conservative attitudes are a *bar* to reform'; b) 'the trawler ran aground on a *sandbar*'.
3. a stripe or band: 'a *bar* of colour'.
4. *Music:* a) a group of beats, of which the first usually has an accent, marked off from similar groups of beats. b) the line dividing such groups. Short form of **bar line**.
5. a) a counter where drinks, food or other goods are served. b) a room or small establishment where alcohol is served.
6. *Law:* a) the railing in a courtroom separating the general public from the judge, jury, lawyers, etc. b) the place in a courtroom where prisoners stand to plead or hear sentence. c) all practising barristers.
Usage: 'he has been called to the *bar*' (= admitted as a barrister).
7. any forum or tribunal: 'you must put your case before the *bar* of public opinion'.
8. *Weather:* a metric unit of pressure, equal to 10^5 pascal.
bar *verb*
(barred, barring)
1. to fasten or shut with or as if with a bar: 'don't forget to *bar* the gate'.
2. to block, prohibit or obstruct: a) 'police *barred* access to the building'; b) 'he *barred* any discussion of politics'.
3. to exclude: 'he must be the biggest idiot in the place, *barring* none'.
4. to mark with stripes or bands: 'the sunset *barred* the clouds with colour'.
Word Family: **bar**, *preposition*, except or omitting.

barb *noun*
1. a sharp backward point at the end of a fishhook, harpoon, etc.
2. a sharp or cutting remark: '*barbs* or taunts rarely anger her'.
Word Family: **barb**, *verb*.
[Latin *barba* a beard]

barbarian (*say* bar–**bair**ian) *noun*
a person who is crude, coarse, brutal or uncivilized.
barbarism (*say* **barba**–rizm) *noun*
a primitive or early stage of civilization: 'living in a state of *barbarism*'.
barbarity (*say* bar–**barri**–tee) *noun*
any brutal or cruel behaviour: 'the development of modern weapons is sheer *barbarity*'.
Word Family: **barbarian, barbaric, barbarous**, *adjectives*; **barbarianism**, *noun*; **barbarically, barbarously**, *adverbs*; **barbarize, barbarise**, *verb*.
[Greek *barbaros* foreign, having unintelligible speech]
Common Error: BARBARIC, BARBAROUS and BARBARIAN all mean uncivilized but *barbaric* suggests crudeness or wildness, especially in taste or manner, 'the symphony had a *barbaric* grandeur'; *barbarous* stresses cruelty or brutality, 'the *barbarous* practice of torturing prisoners'; *barbarian* is more neutral in tone '*barbarian* tribes which were led by Genghis Khan'.

barbecue (*say* **barbi**–kew) *noun*
a) an outdoor meal at which meat is grilled. b) the structure or device on which the meat is grilled.
Word Family: **barbecue**, *verb*.
[Haitian]

barbed wire
a type of wire with barbs at intervals, used for fences.

barbell *noun*
a steel bar about 2 m long, with weighted discs attached to each end, and used in weight-lifting.

barber *noun*
a person who cuts, shaves or dresses hair as a trade.
Word Family: **barber**, *verb*.
[Latin *barba* a beard]

barbican *noun*
a watch-tower guarding a town or castle gate.

barbiturate (*say* bar–**bit**–yoorit) *noun*
any of a group of drugs used as sedatives.

barcarolle (*say* bar–ka–**roll**) **barcarole** *noun*
a) a gondolier's song. b) any music in a similar style.

bard *noun*
an old word for a poet or singer.

bare *adjective*
1. plain, empty or without covering; a) 'you shouldn't drive with *bare* feet'; b) 'the room was *bare* except for the table'.

2. just sufficient: 'as a writer he earned a *bare* living'.
Usage: 'the *bare* facts' (= unadorned).
Word Family: **bare,** *verb,* to make bare; **barely,** *adverb,* only, just or not quite; **bareness,** *noun.*

bareback *adjective, adverb*
(of riding horses, etc.) without a saddle.

barefaced *adjective*
shameless or insolent: 'he told a *barefaced* lie'.

bargain (*say* **bar**gin) *noun*
1. an agreement between two parties about how a transaction is to be conducted, especially with regard to buying and selling.
2. an item bought or offered for sale at a low price: 'there are always good *bargains* in the shops after Christmas'.
into the bargain, 'she tripped and broke her watch *into the bargain*' (= in addition).
bargain *verb*
to arrive at an agreement, especially by haggling: 'she enjoys *bargaining* with the greengrocer'.
Phrases:
bargain for, 'the strong competition was more than he *bargained for*' (= expected).
bargain on, 'can I *bargain on* you getting there on time?' (= rely on).

barge (*rhymes with* large) *noun*
1. a flat-bottomed boat, sometimes without an engine, used for loading and unloading ships, or for transporting goods.
2. a boat set aside for the use of high-ranking naval officers, such as admirals.
barge *verb*
1. to move clumsily or heavily.
2. (*informal*) to rush in or intrude: 'don't *barge* into the room without knocking'.
[Greek *baris* an Egyptian boat]

baritone (*say* **barri**-tone) *noun*
Music: a) the male singing voice between tenor and bass. b) any instrument having this range.
[Greek *barys* deep + *tonos* tone]

barium (*say* **bairi**-um) *noun*
element number 56, a soft, poisonous metal. Its compounds are used in making glass and fireworks, and in medicine. See ALKALINE EARTH METAL. See CHEMICAL ELEMENTS in grey pages.
[Greek *baros* weight]

barium meal
barium sulphate fed to a patient so that any obstruction in the intestines will show up on an X-ray photograph.

bark (1) *noun*
the harsh, abrupt sound made by a dog or other animal.
bark *verb*
1. to make the harsh, abrupt sound of a dog or other animal.
2. to speak sharply or gruffly: 'the general *barked* out his orders'.
3. (*informal*) to attract customers at the entrance of a cheap show by proclaiming its attractions.
Word Family: **barker,** *noun.*

bark (2) *noun*
the outer covering of the trunk and branches of a tree.
bark *verb*
to remove the bark from a tree.
Usage: 'he *barked* his shins on that chair' (= scraped, skinned).

bark (3) *noun*
see BARQUE.

barley (*say* **bar**-lee) *noun*
a cereal plant used as food and in making malt and beer.

barley sugar
a sweet made from sugar boiled until it is hard and brittle.

barman *noun*
a man who serves drinks in a bar.
Word Family: **barmaid,** *noun,* a female barman.

barmitzvah (*say* bar-**mits**-vah) *noun*
a) a Jewish boy of thirteen who assumes adult status by taking on moral and religious responsibilities. b) the service and celebration associated with this. Compare BATMITZVAH.
[Hebrew *bar mitzvah* son of the commandment]

barmy *adjective*
(*informal*) silly, stupid or mad.
[from *barm,* a froth which forms on the top of fermenting malt liquors]

barn *noun*
a simple farm building used to store hay, etc.
[Old English *bere* barley + *aern* house]

barnacle (*say* **bar**na-k'l) *noun*
a small marine shellfish which clings firmly to rocks, floating timber and the bottoms of ships.

barnacle goose
a medium-sized black and white goose which breeds in the Arctic and visits Europe in winter.

barney *noun*
(*informal*) an argument.

barn owl
a pale-coloured owl with a monkey-like face which haunts buildings and parks, identifiable by its hissing and snoring noises.

barnstorm *verb*
(*informal*) to travel in country areas making speeches in a political campaign, etc.
Word Family: **barnstormer**, *noun.*

barnyard *noun*
the central yard of farm buildings, partly surrounded by barns.

barometer (*say* ba-**rommita**) *noun*
1. an instrument for measuring atmospheric pressure.
2. anything which indicates change: 'opinion polls are not true *barometers* of public opinion'.
Word Family: **barometric** (*say* barra-**metrik**), **barometrical**, *adjective.*
[Greek *baros* weight + METER]

baron *noun*
1. a feudal lord who held power and lands under the authority of the King.
2. a nobleman ranking below a viscount, occupying the lowest rank of the peerage.
3. a magnate or powerful man in industry or big business.
Word Family: **baroness**, *noun*, a) a female baron, b) the wife of a baron; **baronial** (*say* ba-**ro**-nee-al), *adjective.*

baronet (*say* **barra**-net) *noun*
a member of the lowest hereditary titled British order.
Word Family: **baronetcy** (*say* **barra**-net-see), *noun*, the rank of a baronet.

Baroque (*say* ba-**rok**) *noun*
a) a style of art and architecture developed in Europe during the 17th century, characterized by bold and contorted forms, exaggeration and theatrical effects. b) the ornate style characteristic of some 17th century music.
Word Family: **baroque**, *adjective*, overwrought, florid or extravagantly ornamental in style.
[Portuguese *barroco* an irregular pearl]

barouche (*say* ba-**roosh**) *noun*
an open, four-wheeled carriage, with two seats facing each other and a hood over the back seat.
[Latin *birotus* two-wheeled]

barque (*say* bark) *noun*
also spelt **bark**
1. *Nautical:* a sailing vessel with three or more masts, having square sails on all but the mast furthest to the stern.
2. an old word for any boat or sailing vessel.
[Latin *barca* a boat]

barrack (1) (*say* **barruk**) *noun*
(*usually plural*) a large building or group of buildings, used as living quarters for soldiers.
Word Family: **barrack**, *verb.*
[Italian *baracca* a soldier's tent]

barrack (2) (*say* **barruk**) *verb*
to shout against or jeer at, especially a sporting team.
[Aboriginal *borak* banter]

barracouta (*say* barra-**koota**) *noun*
a fish similar, but unrelated, to the barracuda, found in the Southern Hemisphere, usually with long needle-like teeth.
[from Spanish *barracuda*]

barracuda (*say* barra-**kooda**) *noun*
any of a group of savage fast-swimming fish, found in the West Indies, and usually with one sharp tooth near the tip of the lower jaw.
[Spanish]

barrage (*say* **barrahzh**) *noun*
1. *Military:* a concentration of artillery fire.
Usage: 'the Prime Minister faced a *barrage* of questions at the news conference' (= overwhelming number).
2. an artificial barrier in a river, etc. to regulate the flow of water.

barrel *noun*
1. a large cylindrical container with flat ends, made of curved wooden strips bound together with hoops.
2. the tube-like part of a gun through which a projectile is discharged.
3. any of various units of volume for liquids, such as an oil barrel, in America equal to about 159 litre.
4. the part of a lock into which a key is inserted.
Phrases:
over a barrel, 'we've got him *over a barrel*' (= at our mercy).

scrape the barrel, 'they must have *scraped the barrel* before they made him chairman' (= tried everyone else first).
barrel *verb*
(**barrelled, barrelling**)
1. to put in a barrel.
2. (*informal*) to move fast.

barrel organ
a hand-turned musical instrument in which pins projecting from a rotating barrel work a small row of organ pipes to produce a tune.

barren *adjective*
sterile or unfruitful: a) 'a *barren* woman'; b) 'the country is dry and *barren*'.

barricade *noun*
a temporary barrier or obstruction, usually across a street.
Word Family: **barricade,** *verb,* to obstruct, enclose or defend with or as if with a barricade.
[Spanish *barrica* a cask]

barrier *noun*
1. anything which obstructs or restrains: a) 'police installed *barriers* to control the crowd'; b) 'the Canadian Rockies were the *barrier* which delayed exploration'.
2. anything which separates: 'a language *barrier*'.

barrister *noun*
Law: a lawyer who is permitted to practise as advocate in the higher courts, such as the High Court. Compare SOLICITOR.

barrow (1) *noun*
any of various handcarts, such as a wheelbarrow, or a street cart where vegetables, fruit, etc. are sold.

barrow (2) *noun*
a mound of earth or stones built over a grave, usually dating from prehistoric times.

bar sinister
Heraldry: a band running from the top left to the bottom right of a shield (instead of from right to left), a sign of bastardy.

barter *verb*
to trade goods in return for other goods rather than for money: 'the farmer *bartered* his best horse for 10 cattle'.
Word Family: **barter,** *noun.*

basalt (*say* **bass**-awlt) *noun*
a basic, dark-coloured igneous rock with small, even grains, formed by the rapid cooling of lava on the earth's surface, and used mainly for buildings and road metal.
Word Family: **basaltic** (*say* ba-**sawl**tik), *adjective.*
[Latin *basaltes* a touchstone]

base (1) *noun*
1. the bottom part of something, especially the part which provides physical support: 'a vase with a narrow *base*'.
2. the fundamental part: 'the *base* of this soup is meat'.
3. *Baseball:* any of the four fixed stations around which the player must run.
4. any place from which work, operations, etc. proceed and where equipment, etc. is located: 'a military *base*'.
5. *Maths:* a) the line or surface on which a figure stands. b) see LOGARITHM. c) the number which, when raised to various powers, forms the main counting units of a system. See BINARY NUMBER SYSTEM.
6. *Chemistry:* any substance which liberates hydroxyl ions when dissolved in water.
Example: calcium hydroxide dissociates in aqueous solution to form one calcium ion (Ca^{2+}) and two hydroxyl ions ($(OH)^-$). Compare ACID.
base *verb*
to establish or build upon: 'his theory is *based* on careful research'.
Word Family: **baseless,** *adjective,* having no base or support.
[Greek *basis* a step or pedestal]

base (2) *adjective*
low or contemptible: 'a *base* crime'.
Word Family: **basely,** *adverb*; **baseness,** *noun.*

baseball *noun*
a) a ball game played between two teams of nine on a diamond formed by four bases. Having hit the ball, the striker tries to score by running round the four bases before the ball is thrown home. b) the ball used.

baseline *noun*
also called a **service line**
Tennis: the boundary line at each end of the court, behind which a player must stand when serving.

basement *noun*
the lowest level of a building, usually below ground level: 'many large stores have a bargain *basement*'.

bases (*say* **bay**-seez) *plural noun*
the plural of **basis.**

bash *verb*
to strike violently.
bash *noun*
1. a crushing blow.
2. (*informal*) a try: 'Tim will have a *bash* at anything'.

bashful *adjective*
timid or easily embarrassed.
Word Family: **bashfully,** *adverb*; **bashfulness,** *noun*.
[same origin as *abash*]

basic (*say* **bay**-sik) *adjective*
1. essential: 'the *basic* principles of chess are easy to learn'.
2. *Chemistry:* of, relating to or having the properties of a base.
Word Family: **basically,** *adverb*, essentially.

basil (*say* **bazzil**) *noun*
an aromatic herb used in cooking.
[Greek *basilikos* royal]

basilica (*say* ba-**zillika**) *noun*
Christian: an oblong church with colonnades, a wide nave, side aisles, and an apse at one end.
[Greek *basilikē* royal (palace)]

basilisk *adjective*
Mythology: of a reptile whose look and breath were fatal.
Usage: 'she responded with a *basilisk* stare' (= cold and hostile).
basilisk *noun*
a small American lizard.
[Greek *basileus* king (of reptiles)]

basin (*say* **bay**sin) *noun*
1. a) a deep, round container with sloping sides, used to hold liquids. b) any similar vessel for mixing, cooking, etc.
2. *Geography:* an area in which the strata dip from all directions towards a common central point.
a **river basin** is the area drained by a river and its tributaries.
a **tidal basin** is a basin in which the water-level rises and falls with the tide.

basis (*say* **bay**sis) *noun*
plural is **bases** (*say* **bay**-seez)
the foundation or fundamental principle, constituent, etc. of something: 'the *basis* of my argument is this'.
[Greek, a step or pedestal]

bask (*rhymes with* ask) *verb*
to enjoy a pleasant warmth: a) 'to *bask* in the sun'; b) 'she has always *basked* in his approval'.

basket *noun*
a) a container, usually with handles, made of woven reeds, straw, twigs, etc. b) anything which has the shape or function of a basket, such as the net in basketball.
Word Family: **basketry, basketwork,** *nouns*.

basketball *noun*
a) a game played on a rectangular court between two teams of five, six or seven players. The aim is to throw an inflated leather ball through the basket suspended from an iron ring at either end of the court. b) the ball used in this game. Compare NETBALL.

Basque (*say* bassk) *noun*
a) any of a people living in the Pyrenees between Spain and France. b) their language, which is not related to any other European language.

bas-relief (*say* bass-re-**leef**) *noun*
any sculpture in low relief.
[Italian *basso relievo* low relief]

bass (1) (*say* base) *adjective*
Music: deep-sounding or low in pitch: a) 'a rich *bass* voice'; b) 'a *bass* guitar'.
bass *noun*
a) the lowest, male singing voice. b) any instrument having this range.
[Italian *basso*]

bass (2) (*say* bass) *noun*
plural is **bass** or **basses**
any of a group of marine or freshwater fish, related to the perch.

bass clef
Music: see CLEF.

basset hound
one of a breed of medium-sized hounds with short legs, originally used to hunt small animals.
[French *bas* low]

bassinet *noun*
a basket, sometimes with a hood, used as a baby's cradle.
[French *bassin* a basin]

bassoon (*say* ba-**soon**) *noun*
Music: a double-reed wind instrument with a deep rich tone, made from a long wooden tube which doubles back on itself.
Word Family: **bassoonist,** *noun*.
[Italian]

bast *noun*
a fibrous plant material used in making matting.

bastard (*say* **basst'd** *or* **bahst'd**) *noun*
1. a child whose parents were not married at the time of his birth.

2. something which is inferior or spurious.
3. (*informal*) a) a person who is selfish or unscrupulous. b) any person: 'the poor *bastard* lost his job'.
bastardize, bastardise *verb*
1. an old word meaning to declare or prove someone a bastard.
2. to debase or corrupt.
bastard *adjective*
1. non-standard.
2. (of a file) having coarse teeth for cutting metal.
Word Family: **bastardization**, *noun*; **bastardy**, *noun*, the state of being a bastard; **bastardly**, *adverb*.

baste (1) *verb*
Cooking: to pour liquid, especially melted fat, over meat which is being roasted.

baste (2) *verb*
Needlework: see TACK.

baste (3) *verb*
a) to thrash or beat. b) to denounce or berate: 'the press *basted* the Foreign Minister for his policies'.

bastinado (*say* basti-**nay**do) *verb*
to torture by beating the soles of the feet.
Word Family: **bastinado**, *noun*.
[Spanish *baston* stick]

bastion (*say* **basti**-on) *noun*
1. a protecting part of a rampart in a fortification.
2. a person or thing that provides strong defence or support: 'they consider themselves *bastions* of democracy'.
[Italian *bastione* bulwark]

bat (1) *noun*
1. any of various implements, usually wooden, used to hit the ball in games such as cricket, baseball, etc.
2. *Cricket:* a batsman.
Phrases:
at a bat, 'the get-away car roared off *at a bat*' (= very fast).
off one's own bat, independently or without assistance.
bat *verb*
(**batted, batting**)
to hit the ball with a bat, as in table tennis or cricket.

bat (2) *noun*
any of various flying mammals with membranes joining the front and hind legs to form wings.
bats in the belfry, 'he has *bats in the belfry*' (= mad or crazy ideas).
Word Family: **bats, batty**, *adjectives*, (informal) mad.

bat (3) *verb*
(**batted, batting**)
to blink: 'she admitted lying without *batting* an eye'.

batch *noun*
a number of things together: 'a *batch* of scones'.
[Old English *bacan* to bake]

bate *verb*
to lessen.
with bated breath, 'she waited for the decision *with bated breath*' (= breathlessly).
[from ABATE]

bath (*rhymes with* path) *noun*
1. any washing of the body, especially by putting it in water.
2. any large vessel containing water in which one sits to wash.
3. (*plural*) a public swimming pool.
4. a preparation in which something is immersed: 'the printing plates were placed in an acid *bath*'.
Word Family: **bath**, *verb*.

bathe (*say* **bay***th*) *verb*
1. to immerse or wash in liquid: a) '*bathe* the wound with antiseptic'; b) 'her eyes were *bathed* with tears'.
Usage: 'the street was *bathed* in sunlight' (= covered, enveloped).
2. to swim in the sea, a river, lake, etc.
Word Family: **bathe**, *noun*.

bathos (*say* **bay**thos) *noun*
a sudden change of mood or tone from dignity or intensity to an absurd anticlimax, especially in literature. Compare PATHOS.
Word Family: **bathetic** (*say* ba-**thet**tik), *adjective*.
[Greek, depth]

bathroom *noun*
a room for washing in, usually having a basin, shower, bath, etc.

bathysphere (*say* **batha**-sfeer) *noun*
a spherical device from which marine life, etc. may be observed in deep-sea diving.
[Greek *bathys* deep + SPHERE]

batik (*say* **bar**tik *or* **bat**tik) **battik** *noun*
a) a method of printing on fabric using wax and dyes to make a pattern. b) a fabric printed in this way.
[Malay]

batiste (*say* ba-**teest**) *noun*
a delicate cotton fabric with a plain weave.

[after Jean *Baptiste* of Cambrai, France, who first made it]

batman *noun*
a soldier acting as an officer's servant.
[from *bat*, an old word for a pack-saddle + MAN]

batmitzvah (*say* bat-**mits**-vah) *noun*
a barmitzvah for a girl.

baton (*say* **batton**) *noun*
a short stick or rod: 'the conductor raised his *baton* and the orchestra began to play'.
[French *bâton*]

bats *adjective*
Word Family: see BAT (2).

batsman *noun*
Cricket: the player using the bat.

battalion (*say* ba-**tal**-y'n) *noun*
1. *Military:* a basic infantry unit consisting of several companies.
2. any large group.
[Italian *battaglia* a battle]

batten (1) *verb*
to prosper or grow fat, especially at the expense of others: 'the landlord *battened* on his unfortunate tenants'.

batten (2) *noun*
1. *Nautical:* a thin strip of wood or plastic slipped into a sail to keep it flat.
2. a light strip of wood for fastening or joining items such as fence wires.
batten *verb*
batten down, to fasten a ship's hatches with battens.

batter (1) *verb*
to damage by repeatedly striking or beating: 'the ship was *battered* against the rocks'.

batter (2) *noun*
Cooking: a beaten mixture of water or milk with flour, eggs, etc. used to coat foods for frying, make pancakes, etc.

batter (3) *noun*
Sport: the player using the bat in a game of baseball, softball, etc.

battering ram
a long, heavy beam, formerly used as a weapon for breaking down walls or gates.

battery *noun*
1. *Electricity:* a group of cells connected together in order to produce a higher electric current or voltage.
2. *Engineering:* a set of similar machines or parts: 'a *battery* of printing presses'.
3. a group of guns on a warship.
4. *Military:* a) a tactical unit of artillery, equivalent to an infantry company. b) a platform or other structure supporting guns.
5. *Law:* an attack on a person by striking or wounding 'he was charged with assault and *battery*'.

battery hen
a hen kept with its fellows in a battery of cages and mechanically fed throughout its life, to promote high egg production. Compare FREE-RANGE HEN.

batting *noun*
any cotton or wool fibre padded together and used to fill bed covers, etc.

battle *noun*
1. a fight, especially between organized forces.
2. any struggle: 'the *battle* against poverty'.
Word Family: **battle**, *verb*; **battler**, *noun*, a person who battles or struggles, often unsuccessfully.
[Latin *battuere* to strike]

battleaxe *noun*
1. a large, broad-headed axe, formerly used as a weapon.
2. (*informal*) a domineering woman.

battledore *noun*
a light racket used in **battledore and shuttlecock**, which was an early form of badminton.

battledress *noun*
the uniform worn by soldiers in battle.

battle fatigue
see COMBAT FATIGUE.

battlefield *noun*
also called a **battleground**
the place where a battle is or was fought.

battlement *noun*
(*often plural*) the upper edge of a wall containing a series of openings and used for defence.

battle royal
a hard, determined battle or argument.

battleship *noun*
any of a class of the most powerful and heavily armoured warships.

batty *adjective*
Word Family: see BAT (2).

bauble (*say* **bawb**'l) *noun*
a pretty but worthless object.

baulk (*rhymes with* walk) *verb*
to balk.

baulk *noun*
1. the area of a billiard table at and behind the place from which opening shots are made.
2. a balk.

bauxite (*say* **bawk**–site) *noun*
the main ore of aluminium, being a rock composed mainly of aluminium oxide or hydroxide.
[from *Les Baux*, France, where first found]

bawbee *noun*
Scottish: a halfpenny.

bawdy *adjective*
crudely or coarsely humorous: 'a *bawdy* joke'.
Word Family: **bawdily,** *adverb*; **bawdiness,** *noun*; **bawd,** *noun*, a female pimp; **bawdry,** *noun*, obscene language or behaviour.

bawl *verb*
1. to shout or yell out loudly: 'he *bawled* out my name from across the street'.
2. (*informal*) to cry or sob noisily: 'she broke down on the spot and just *bawled*'.
bawl out, 'she was *bawled out* for cheating' (= scolded severely).
Word Family: **bawl,** *noun*.
[Latin *baulare* to bark]

bay (1) *noun*
a body of water almost enclosed by land but opening to the sea.

bay (2) *noun*
1. *Architecture:* the part of a wall between two columns or arches.
2. a recess or area set back or apart from another: 'a parking *bay*'.

bay (3) *noun*
1. a deep, drawn–out bark, such as that made by hounds when hunting.
2. the defiant stand made by a hunted animal, person, etc. when cornered.
Phrases:
bring to bay, 'the criminal was finally *brought to bay*' (= forced into a last stand).
hold, keep at bay, 'this medicine will *hold* the pain *at bay*' (= keep at a distance).
Word Family: **bay,** *verb*, (of a hound) to utter a bay.

bay (4) *noun*
any of various European or West Indian trees related to the laurel.
bay leaf
the dried leaf of a bay tree, used as a herb in cooking.

bay (5) *noun*
a dark brown horse, usually with a black mane and tail.

bayonet (*say* **bay**–o–net) *noun*
a sharp blade attached to the end of a rifle, used to stab or slash.
Word Family: **bayonet,** *verb*.
[French, from *Bayonne* where first made]

bayou (*say* **by**–yoo) *noun*
American: a small, marshy tributary of a lake or river.
[Amerindian *bayuk* a small stream]

bay window
also called a **bow window**
a window projecting from a building.

bazaar (*say* ba–**zar**) *noun*
1. an Eastern marketplace or street of shops.
2. a) any place or shop where miscellaneous objects are sold, often to aid a charity. b) any sale of such goods.
[Persian]

bazooka (*say* ba–**zoo**ka) *noun*
a portable rocket–launcher firing a small, armour–piercing rocket, used by infantry against tanks.
[American slang *bazoo* mouth]

be *verb*
(**I am**; he, she, it **is**; we, you, they **are**; I, he, she, it **was**; we, you, they **were**; **been, being**; *old forms:* thou **art**; thou **wast** or **wert**)
1. to exist or live.
2. to take place or occur: 'when *is* your birthday?'.
3. to become: 'what will you *be* when you grow up?'.
4. special use joining subject and predicate:
a) 'you *are* late'.
b) 'today *is* Wednesday'.
5. special use with other verbs to form present continuous, past and future tenses and the passive voice:
a) 'he *is* playing outside'.
b) 'you *were* walking too fast'.
c) 'she *is* coming later'.
d) 'we *were* left alone'.
Phrases:
be–all and end–all, 'to win the championship was the *be–all and end–all* of his hopes' (= the highest aim).
for the time being, 'let us finish here *for the time being*' (= for the present).
to–be, 'her husband *to–be*' (= future).

be–
a prefix meaning about or all over, as in *bedraggled.*

beach *noun*
1. the gently sloping land at the water's edge, composed of sand, pebbles, etc. formed by the waves
2. this area as a place for an outing, etc.
beach *verb*
to bring a boat, etc. up onto a beach from the water.

beachcomber (*say* **beech**–koma) *noun*
a person who collects articles washed up onto beaches, often as a living.

beachhead *noun*
an area on an enemy shore occupied by an advance force, before support troops and supplies are landed.

beacon (*say* **beek'n**) *noun*
1. any signal used as a guide or warning, such as a fire on a hilltop, a flashing light from a lighthouse or a radio signal.
2. anything which serves as or shines like a beacon.
[Old English *beacn* a sign]

bead *noun*
1. a small ball of glass, wood or similar material, pierced so that it may be put on a string.
2. a drop or bubble: '*beads* of sweat'.
3. (*plural*) a rosary.
draw a bead on, 'he *drew a bead on* the rabbit' (= aimed at).
Word Family: **bead,** *verb,* to decorate or form with beads.
[Middle English *bede* a prayer or rosary bead]

beading *noun*
1. a narrow strip of rounded wood used to trim joints or corners.
2. the threading of beads into patterns or designs for decoration, etc. Also called **beadwork.**

beadle *noun*
a mace-bearer or other leader of a ceremonial procession at a university, official function, etc.

beady *adjective*
small and bright like a bead: '*beady* eyes'.
Word Family: **beadily,** *adverb.*

beagle *noun*
any of a breed of small, smooth-haired hounds used for hunting hares, etc.
[Old French *beegueule* a noisy person]

beak *noun*
1. the horny mouthparts of a bird. Also called a **bill.**
2. any beak-like projection, such as the lip of a jug.
3. (*informal*) a) a nose. b) a magistrate. c) a headmaster.

beaker *noun*
1. a flat-bottomed cylindrical vessel, usually with a beak for pouring liquids, used in laboratories.
2. a wide-mouthed drinking vessel, usually made of plastic or glass.

beam *noun*
1. a long, thick piece of wood, steel or concrete, used as a horizontal support, such as a joist.
2. a bundle of parallel light rays or other radiation.
Usage: 'a *beam* of hope' (= faint suggestion).
3. *Nautical:* a) the widest part of a ship. b) the side of a ship.
4. the crossbar of a balance, supporting the pans.
5. a radiant smile.
Phrases:
broad in the beam, 'too much eating has made her *broad in the beam*' (= large, overweight).
off the beam, 'that answer was quite *off the beam*' (= wrong).
on one's beam-ends, almost penniless.
on the beam, 'she is always *on the beam*' (= right, in touch).

bean *noun*
a long, thin, green or yellow vegetable which grows on a vine and contains small seeds.
Phrases:
full of beans, energetic, cheerful.
not have a bean, 'I *haven't a bean* to spend this week' (= have no money at all).
spill the beans, (*informal*) 'you must try not to *spill the beans*' (= let out the information).

beanbag *noun*
1. a small cloth bag filled with beans and used as a toy.
2. a large bag made of leather, cloth, etc., filled with small soft objects and able to be formed into a comfortable seat.

beanpole *noun*
1. a tall pole for a bean plant to climb on.
2. (*informal*) a tall, thin person.

beanshoots *plural noun*
also called **beansprouts**

the germinated seeds of millet, used as a vegetable and especially popular in Asian cookery.

bear (1) (*say* bair) *verb*
(bore, borne or **born, bearing)**
1. to support: a) 'will that branch *bear* my weight?'; b) 'I am willing to *bear* the blame for my mistakes'.
2. to carry or give birth to an offspring: 'she *bore* him three sons'.
3. to convey: a) 'the carriage *bore* us to our destination'; b) 'I loathe people who *bear* tales'.
4. to put up with or suffer: a) 'I cannot *bear* pain'; b) '*bear* with me until I've finished'.
5. to move or lie in a certain direction: 'we must *bear* hard right at the next intersection'.
Usages:
a) 'the responsibility *bears* heavily upon him' (= weighs).
b) 'he *bore* himself well during that difficult time' (= conducted).
c) 'his story will not *bear* close inspection' (= survive).
d) 'do not *bear* grudges' (= harbour).
e) 'this tree *bears* lots of lemons every year' (= produces).
f) 'the two accounts of the accident *bear* almost no relation to each other' (= have, contain).
g) 'he *bears* the unlikely name of Blake Fox' (= possesses).
Phrases:
bear down on, a) to press hard upon; b) 'the ship *bore down on* the raft' (= approached).
bear out, 'his story *bears out* what you said' (= confirms).
bear up, to keep up one's spirits or strength when under a strain.
bear witness, see WITNESS.
bring to bear, 'pressure was *brought to bear* on her by her family' (= applied).
Word Family: **bearable,** *adjective,* endurable; **bearably,** *adverb,* **bearableness,** *noun.*

bear (2) (*say* bair) *noun*
1. any of various large mammals with a shaggy coat and a short tail, such as the brown **grizzly bear** of America or the white **polar bear** of the arctic regions.
2. an uncouth or bad-tempered person.
3. *Stock Exchange:* a person who sells, for future delivery, shares he does not possess, hoping to buy at a lower price before he has to deliver. Compare BULL (1).
Word Family: **bearish,** *adjective.*

bear-baiting *noun*
History: a cruel sport in which dogs attacked a captive bear.

beard (*say* beerd) *noun*
the coarse hair on the face of adult males, especially on or below the chin.
beard *verb*
to oppose or defy: 'to *beard* the lion in his den'.
Word Family: **bearded,** *adjective,* having a beard.

bearer (*say* **bair**a) *noun*
1. a person who brings or carries something: 'please pay the *bearer* of this letter'.
2. *Commerce:* a person who presents a cheque, money order, etc. at a bank.

bearing (*say* **bair**-ing) *noun*
1. a person's posture, manner, etc: 'he has a friendly *bearing*'.
2. the act, capacity or period of producing: 'a tree past *bearing*'.
3. a relevance or relation: 'that evidence has little *bearing* on the case'.
4. (*often plural*) the direction or relative position of anything: 'I cannot find my *bearings*'.
5. *Engineering:* any part which supports a rotating part in a machine.
6. a direction measured as an angle from one position to another: 'a compass *bearing*'.
7. *Architecture:* a) a supporting part in a structure. b) the contact area between a load-carrying structure and its support.

beast *noun*
1. any four-footed animal.
2. a wild, cruel or inhuman person.
3. a coarse or cruel nature.
beastly *adjective*
1. like a beast.
2. (*informal*) nasty or unpleasant: 'what *beastly* weather!'.
Word Family: **beastliness,** *noun.*
[Latin *bestia*]

beat (1) *verb*
(beat, beaten, beating)
1. to hit or strike repeatedly: 'the rain *beat* against the windows'.
2. to stir or mix thoroughly: '*beat* 6 eggs'.
3. to defeat: a) 'the team was *beaten* by two points'; b) 'it *beats* me!'.
Usages:
a) 'the trapped bird was frantically *beating* its wings' (= flapping).

b) 'the animals had *beaten* a broad track to the water-hole' (= made by trampling).
c) 'the conductor was *beating* time with his baton' (= marking, measuring).
Phrases:
beat about the bush, beat around the bush, see BUSH (1).
beat down, 'we *beat* him *down* to £6' (= bargained with to lower the price).
beat it, (*informal*) 'we had better *beat it* before someone comes' (= leave).
beat out, a) 'this copper ashtray has been *beaten out* by hand' (= hammered out); b) 'we got together to *beat out* a joint proposal' (= produce).
beat up, 'she was *beaten up* and robbed' (= assaulted violently).
beat *noun*
1. a regular, repeated stroke or sound.
2. *Music:* a pulse or rhythm.
3. a regular route or area: 'the policeman's *beat* covered most of the suburb'.
4. *Hunting:* the flushing out of game by moving noisily through scrub, etc.
Word Family: **beat,** *adjective,* (informal) worn-out or defeated: **beater,** *noun,* a person or thing that beats.

beat (2) *adjective*
of or relating to beatniks.

beatific (*say* bee-a-**tiffik**) *adjective*
a) making blessed. b) blissful: 'a *beatific* smile'.
Word Family: **beatifically,** *adverb.*

beatification
(*say* bee-atti-fik-**ay**-sh'n) *noun*
Roman Catholic: the Pope's official statement that a dead person is in heavenly bliss, as a step towards declaring that person a saint.
Word Family: **beatify** (*say* bee-**atti**-fie), (**beatified, beatifying**), *verb.*
[Latin *beatus* blessed + *facere* to make]

beatitude (*say* bee-atti-tewd) *noun*
a state of bliss or blessedness.

beatnik *noun*
a person who avoids or rejects conventional standards of behaviour, dress, etc.
[probably from BEAT (rhythm) + Yiddish suffix *-nik* person]

beau (*say* bo) *noun*
plural is **beaux** or **beaus**
a boyfriend or lover.
[French, handsome]

Beaufort scale (*say* **bo**-fort skale)
Weather: a scale and description of wind in which 0 is calm and force 12 is a hurricane.
[after its inventor, *Sir Francis Beaufort,* 1774-1857, a British admiral]

beauteous (*say* **bew**ti-us) *adjective*
a poetic word for beautiful.

beautician (*say* bew-**tish**'n) *noun*
a person whose work is to care for the body, chiefly with massage, manicure and facials.

beautiful (*say* **bew**ti-full) *adjective*
giving pleasure or delight to the senses: 'a *beautiful* face'.
Word Family: **beautifully,** *adverb,* **beautify** (**beautified, beautifying**), *verb,* to adorn or make beautiful.

beauty (*say* **bew**-tee) *noun*
1. the quality of being pleasing and exciting to the senses.
2. anything which is beautiful or particularly pleasing.

beauty salon
also called a **beauty parlour**
a shop which provides services such as hairdressing, manicures, massage or skin care.

beaux (*say* boze) *noun*
a plural of **beau.**

beaver *noun*
1. a small, amphibious North American, dam-building mammal with webbed hind feet, thick fur and a paddle-like tail.
2. a) the fur of this animal. b) a hat made from this or similar material.
eager beaver, see EAGER.

becalmed (*say* be-**kahmd**) *adjective*
(of a sailing ship) being unable to move because there is no wind.
Word Family: **becalm,** *verb.*

became *verb*
the past tense of the verb **become.**

because (*say* be-**koz**) *conjunction, adverb*
for the reason that: 'we could not see *because* it was dark'.

beck (1) *noun*
at the beck and call of, 'he is *at the beck and call of* his mother' (= obedient to the slightest wish of).

beck (2) *noun*
a small mountain stream or brook.

beckon *verb*
to signal or summon by a gesture: 'he *beckoned* us to follow'.

become (*say* be-**kum**) *verb*
(**became, become, becoming**)
1. to come to be: a) 'it has *become* a habit'; b) 'what will *become* of you?'.
2. to suit well: 'that hat *becomes* you'.
becoming *adjective*
a) proper or suitable: 'such behaviour is not *becoming* to your position'. b) attractive: 'what a *becoming* dress'.
Word Family: **becomingly**, *adverb*.

bed *noun*
1. a) any fixture or surface for sleeping on, usually with a frame, mattress, pillow and coverings. b) a place to sleep for the night.
2. any flat base on which something rests: 'the benches in the park were set into a *bed* of concrete'.
3. the ground or surface beneath something: 'the sunken ship rested on the *seabed*'.
4. *Geology:* a layer of sedimentary rock of varying thickness.
5. an area of soil in a garden in which plants are grown.
bed *verb*
(**bedded, bedding**)
1. to provide with or put into a bed.
2. to go to bed with for the purpose of sexual intercourse: 'to *bed* a wench'.

bedbug *noun*
a flat, blood-sucking insect sometimes found in houses, especially beds.

bedclothes *plural noun*
the blankets and sheets for a bed.

bedding *noun*
any materials used to form a bed, such as straw for animals.

bedeck (*say* be-**dek**) *verb*
to decorate or adorn: 'the hall was *bedecked* with flowers'.

bedevil (*say* be-**devvil**) *verb*
(**bedevilled, bedevilling**)
to confuse or torment: 'he was *bedevilled* by all their questions'.

bedfellow *noun*
a person who shares one's bed.
make strange bedfellows, to have close relationships between unlikely people.

bedlam *noun*
1. a scene of noisy uproar and confusion: 'there was *bedlam* in the school after the fire'.
2. an old word for a lunatic asylum.
[corrupt abbreviation of Hospital of St Mary of *Bethlehem*, a notorious 15th-century asylum at Bishopsgate, London]

bed linen
the sheets and pillowcases for a bed.

Bedouin (*say* **bed**oo-in) *noun*
any nomadic Arab of the deserts of North Africa and Arabia.
[Arabic *badawin* desert dwellers]

bedpan *noun*
1. a pan used as a toilet by people confined to bed.
2. a warming pan.

bedraggled (*say* be-**dragg**'ld) *adjective*
limp, wet and dirty: 'she was *bedraggled* after her fall in the river'.
Word Family: **bedraggle**, *verb*.

bedridden *adjective*
forced to remain in bed because of illness, old age, etc.

bedrock *noun*
1. *Geology:* the solid rock under the soil and subsoil.
2. the bottom or lowest level of anything: 'our morale has really hit *bedrock*'.
3. any firm or solid base.

bedroom *noun*
a room for sleeping in.

bed-sitting room
also called a **bed-sitter**
a flat consisting of one room for living and sleeping in, often without a separate kitchen.

bedsore *noun*
a sore caused by a prolonged stay in bed.

bedspread *noun*
a decorative, cloth cover for a bed.

bedstead (*say* **bed**-sted) *noun*
a framework of wood or metal, supporting the springs and mattress of a bed.

bee *noun*
1. any of a group of stinging insects with licking mouthparts for gathering nectar and often forming communities.
2. a meeting for work, entertainment, etc: 'a spelling *bee*'.
have a bee in one's bonnet, 'she *has a bee in her bonnet* about health foods' (= is obsessed).

beech *noun*
any of a group of deciduous trees found in the Northern Hemisphere, with shiny leaves, small triangular nuts and smooth bark, whose timber is used for furniture.

beef *noun*
1. the flesh of a cow, bull, ox, etc.

2. (*informal*) a complaint: 'do not tell us your *beefs*'.
beef up, (*informal*) to strengthen or reinforce.
Word Family: **beef**, *verb*, (informal) to complain.
[Latin *bovis* of an ox]

beefburger *noun*
a hamburger.

Beefeater *noun*
a Yeoman of the Guard.

beehive *noun*
see HIVE.

beeline *noun*
make a beeline for, 'we all *made a beeline for* the birthday cake' (= went directly to).

Beelzebub (*say* bee-**elzi**-bub) *noun*
the devil.
[Hebrew *ba'alzebub* lord of the flies]

been *verb*
the past participle of the verb **be**.

beer *noun*
1. an alcoholic drink brewed and fermented from malt and flavoured with hops.
2. a non-alcoholic drink made from roots, sugar and yeast, such as ginger beer.
small beer, a person or thing of no importance.

beeswax *noun*
a wax secreted by bees and often used for polishing wood.

beet *noun*
any of various biennial plants with an edible root and leaves. **Beet sugar** is made from the roots of the sugar beet.

beetle (1) *noun*
any of a very large group of flying insects with biting mouthparts and in which the forewings have become hard and protect the hind wings.
[Old English *bitula* a biting thing]

beetle (2) *verb*
to project or overhang: 'his dark eyebrows *beetled* over and almost covered his eyes'.

beetroot *noun*
a round, dark red root of a variety of beet, used as food.
beetroot *adjective*
crimson like beetroot: 'her face was *beetroot* with embarrassment'.

befall (*say* be-**fall**) *verb*
(**befell, befallen, befalling**)
to happen or occur: 'whatever *befalls*, let us remain friends'.

befit (*say* be-**fit**) *verb*
(**befitted, befitting**)
to be suitable or appropriate for: 'it does not *befit* your position to talk like that'.
Word Family: **befittingly**, *adverb*.

before *adverb*
1. ahead: 'he rode *before* to show us the way'.
2. previously or earlier: a) 'has that man been here *before*?'; b) 'start when I say, and not *before*'.
before *preposition*
1. ahead of or in advance of: 'we stood *before* the door'.
2. earlier or sooner than: '*before* the war'.
3. in the presence of: 'I get tongue-tied *before* an audience'.
4. under consideration by: 'the issue *before* us is this'.
before *conjunction*
1. previously to the time when: '*before* we leave'.
2. rather than: 'death *before* dishonour'.

beforehand *adverb*
earlier or in advance: 'I knew about it *beforehand*'.

befriend (*say* be-**frend**) *verb*
to become a friend of: 'she *befriended* her new neighbours'.

befuddle *verb*
to make stupid or confused: 'his mind was *befuddled* with alcohol'.

beg *verb*
(**begged, begging**)
1. a) to ask for charity: 'he had to *beg* for his meals'. b) to ask for earnestly: 'to *beg* forgiveness'.
2. to take the liberty of: 'I *beg* to differ with you there'.
Phrases:
beg the question, to take for granted the very matter which is in question.
go begging, 'if these clothes are *going begging*, I will take them' (= unwanted).

began *verb*
the past tense of the verb **begin**.

begat *verb*
the old past tense of the verb **beget**.

beget *verb*
(**begot, begotten** or **begot, begetting**)
to generate or produce: a) 'he has *begotten* four sons'; b) 'poverty *begets* hardship'.

beggar *noun*
1. a) a person who lives by begging. b) any poor person.
2. a wretched or roguish person: 'what a naughty little *beggar*'.
beggar *verb*
to reduce to poverty.
Usage: 'the beautiful landscape *beggared* description' (= made inadequate).
Word Family: **beggary,** *noun,* the state of being a beggar; **beggarly,** *adjective.*

begin *verb*
(**began, begun, beginning**)
1. to start: 'we will *begin* work after lunch'.
2. (of an action or state) to come into existence: 'it *began* to rain'.
Word Family: **beginner,** *noun,* a person who is learning or has little experience.

beginning *noun*
the start or first part of anything: 'have you read the *beginning* of that story?'.

begone (*say* be–**gon**) *interjection*
an old exclamation meaning go away!

begonia (*say* be–**go**–nia) *noun*
a garden plant with brightly coloured flowers and leaves.
[after *M.Bégon,* 1638–1710, a French patron of botany]

begot *verb*
the past tense and a past participle of the verb **beget.**

begotten *verb*
a past participle of the verb **beget.**

begrudge (*say* be–**gruj**) *verb*
to be envious of: 'do not *begrudge* him his wealth'.
Word Family: **begrudgingly,** *adverb.*

beguile (*say* be–**gile**) *verb*
1. to get or take by dishonesty or tricks: 'she was *beguiled* out of her savings'.
2. to charm or amuse: 'we *beguiled* the child with fairy stories'.
Usage: 'we *beguiled* the time by telling stories in turn' (= whiled away).
Word Family: **beguilement,** *noun.*

begun *verb*
the past participle of the verb **begin.**

behalf *noun*
interest or part: 'on whose *behalf* are you acting?'.

behave (*say* be–**hayv**) *verb*
to act, especially in relation to what is accepted or expected: 'how did she *behave* today?'.
Usages:
a) 'you must promise to *behave* while your grandparents are here' (= behave well).
b) 'the car will *behave* perfectly in any conditions' (= respond).

behaviour (*say* be–**hayv**–y'r) *noun*
in America spelt **behavior**
any actions or manner of acting: 'his *behaviour* at home is dreadful'.

behaviourism (*say* be–**hayv**–y'r–izm) *noun*
in America spelt **behaviorism**
the belief that psychology, sociology, etc. should study only actual behaviour as distinct from unobservable qualities like the mind, and that behaviour is mainly determined by emotions of fear, anger or content.

behead (*say* be–**hed**) *verb*
to cut off the head.

beheld *verb*
the past tense and past participle of the verb **behold.**

behest *noun*
a command or bidding: 'you must do it at the law's *behest*'.

behind *preposition, adverb*
at the back of:
(as a preposition) a) '*behind* the house'; b) 'what is *behind* his friendliness?'.
(as an adverb) 'you must walk *behind*'.
Usages:
a) 'we're all *behind* you in this matter' (= supporting).
b) 'he's *behind* his class in maths' (= less advanced than).
c) 'she left her car *behind* and walked' (= at a place already passed).
d) 'you're a month *behind* with the rent' (= late, in arrears).
behind *noun*
the hindquarters of a person or animal.

behindhand *adverb, adjective*
late or behind in progress: 'she's *behindhand* in her studies'.

behold *verb*
(**beheld, beholding**)
an old word meaning to see or look at.
Word Family: **beholder,** *noun.*

beholden *adjective*
bound by gratitude or in debt: 'we are *beholden* to the government for the wage increase'.

behove *verb*
to be right and fitting: 'it *behoves* you to make a speech'.

beige (*say* bay*zh*) *noun*
a light, brownish-yellow colour.
Word Family: **beige,** *adjective.*
[French]

being *noun*
1. the state of existence or life: 'a new leader has come into *being*'.
2. anything which exists or lives: 'a human *being*'.

belabour (*say* be-**layb**'r) *verb*
in America spelt **belabor**
to beat or strike hard: 'he was *belaboured* with clubs'.

belated (*say* be-**lay**tid) *adjective*
late: 'a *belated* happy birthday for last week'.
Word Family: **belatedly,** *adverb*; **belatedness,** *noun.*

belay *verb*
(belayed, belaying)
1. to fasten a rope around an object without using a knot.
2. *Nautical:* (*informal*) to stop: '*belay* there!'.

bel canto
a style of opera singing showing a brilliant, flowing technique.
[Italian *bel* beautiful + *canto* song]

belch *verb*
1. to eject gas or wind noisily from the stomach through the mouth.
2. to gush or burst out: 'the volcano *belched* out lava and smoke'.
Word Family: **belch,** *noun.*

beleaguer (*say* be-**leeg**'r) *verb*
to besiege or surround: 'the lecturer was *beleaguered* with questions'.

belfry (*say* **bel**-free) *noun*
a belltower.
bats in the belfry, see BAT (2).

belie (*say* be-**lie**) *verb*
(belied, belying)
1. to give a false or wrong idea of: 'his words *belied* his actual feelings'.
2. to fail to justify or fulfil: 'you have *belied* our faith in you'.

belief (*say* be-**leef**) *noun*
1. the feeling or confidence that something is real, true or worthwhile: a) 'your claim is beyond *belief*'; b) 'he has lost his *belief* in life'.
2. something which is taught or accepted as true: 'a religious *belief*'.

believe (*say* be-**leev**) *verb*
a) to accept as real or true: 'do you *believe* in ghosts?'. b) to have faith or trust in: 'you must *believe* in me'.
make believe, 'let's *make believe* we are pirates' (= imagine).
Word Family: **believable,** *adjective*; **believably,** *adverb*; **believer,** *noun,* a person who believes, especially one belonging to a particular religious faith.

Belisha beacon (*say* ba-**leesha** **beek**'n)
a pole with an amber flashing light, indicating a street crossing.
[after *Leslie Hore-Belisha,* Minister of Transport when they were introduced in 1934]

belittle *verb*
to make something seem unimportant or less valuable: 'do not *belittle* his efforts'.
Word Family: **belittlement,** *noun.*

bell (1) *noun*
1. a) a hollow metal cup, usually with a tongue or hammer inside, which makes a ringing sound when hit. b) the sound made by a bell.
2. any device which produces a ringing sound: 'an electric *doorbell*'.
3. something which has the shape of a bell, such as the flared end of a brass musical instrument.
4. *Nautical:* the stroke of the bell that marks off each half-hour of the watch, so that a four-hour watch ends at eight bells.
rings a bell, see RING (2).
bell *verb*
to bell the cat, to volunteer for a risky venture decided on jointly with others. (From a fable in which mice wanted to tie a warning bell round the cat's neck, but none dared do it.)

bell (2) *noun*
the cry of the male deer in the mating season.

belladonna (*say* bella-**donna**) *noun*
also called **deadly nightshade**
a poisonous plant with red flowers and black berries from which a drug (atropine) is made.
[Italian *bella* beautiful + *donna* woman]

bell-bottomed *adjective*
(of trousers) widening into a bell-shape at the bottom.

bellboy *noun*
a boy servant in a hotel, etc.

belle (*say* bel) *noun*
a beautiful girl or woman.
[French, beautiful]

bellhop *noun*
American: a bellboy.

bellicose (*say* **belli**–kose) *adjective*
warlike or eager to fight: 'the ill–treated inhabitants became *bellicose*'.
Word Family: **bellicosity** (*say* belli–**kossi**–tee), *noun.*
[Latin *bellum* war]

belligerent (*say* billija–r'nt) *adjective*
1. aggressive or hostile: 'we were shocked at her *belligerent* reply'.
2. engaged in war: 'a *belligerent* nation'.
Word Family: **belligerently,** *adverb*; **belligerence, belligerency,** *noun*; **belligerent,** *noun,* a person or group engaged in a war.
[Latin *belligerare* to wage war]

bell jar
a bell–shaped glass vessel, used for protecting delicate instruments, holding gases, etc. in laboratory experiments.

bellow (*say* **bell**–o) *verb*
to make a loud animal cry or roar: 'he *bellowed* with rage and pain'.
Word Family: **bellow,** *noun.*

bellows (*say* **bell**–oze) *plural noun*
a device for pumping a stream of air, e.g. to kindle a fire or to produce sound from the pipes of an organ or similar musical instrument.

belltower *noun*
a tower containing a bell.

belly *noun*
1. the lower part of the body containing the stomach and intestines.
2. the lower or inner part of anything: 'the *belly* of a ship'.
3. any bulging or rounded part or surface: 'the *belly* of a guitar'.

belly–ache *verb*
(*informal*) to grumble or complain.
Word Family: **belly–ache,** *noun,* a) a pain in the stomach, b) a complaint.

belly–button *noun*
(*informal*) the navel.

belly dance
a solo dance consisting of movements of the stomach muscles.

belly–flop *noun*
Swimming: an awkward dive in which one lands forwards flat on the water.

bellyful *noun*
(*informal*) far more than enough: 'that's enough of your complaining – I've had a *bellyful* of it already'.

belly landing
the landing of an aeroplane on its fuselage when its landing gear fails to operate.

belly laugh
a deep, loud laugh.

belong *verb*
to have a correct, proper or usual place: 'where do these books *belong*?'.
belong to, a) 'that house *belongs to* my aunt' (= is owned by); b) 'she *belongs to* the golf club' (= is a member of).

belongings *plural noun*
any possessions, especially personal ones.

beloved (*say* be–**luvd** *or* be–**luvv**id) *adjective*
much loved.
Word Family: **beloved,** *noun.*

below *preposition, adverb*
in or to a lower place or position: (as a preposition) 'the sun sank *below* the horizon'.
(as an adverb) 'the lift descended to the floor *below*'.
Usages:
a) 'see the footnote *below*' (= at a later point).
b) 'all the ship's passengers stayed *below* during the storm' (= not on the deck).
c) 'the tree just *below* the bridge' (= downstream from).
d) 'she thought it *below* her to travel second–class' (= below (her) dignity).

belt *noun*
1. a band worn around the waist, hips, etc. to attach objects or keep clothes in place.
2. a large strip of land with common features or characteristics: 'the wheat *belt*'.
3. a flexible band passing around two or more pulleys: 'a conveyor *belt*'.
below the belt, 'that remark was a bit *below the belt*' (= unfair).
belt *verb*
1. to fasten with a belt: 'a loosely *belted* jacket'.
2. (*informal*) a) to thrash or hit. b) to go very quickly: 'the sports car *belted* around the corner'.
belt up, (*informal*) '*belt up* before mother hears' (= be quiet).

belvedere (*say* **bell**va–deer) *noun*
an ornamental tower on an estate, commanding a view.
[Italian *bel* beautiful + *vedere* to see]

bemoan *verb*
to mourn or show sorrow for: 'they *bemoaned* the loss of their leader'.

bemused (*say* be–**mewzd**) *adjective*
1. confused or perplexed: 'a *bemused* frown'.
2. lost in thought
Word Family: **bemuse**, *verb.*

ben *noun*
Scottish: a mountain.

bench *noun*
1. a long seat for several people.
2. a long, heavy work–table: 'a carpenter's *bench*'.
3. *Geography:* a raised strip of relatively level earth or rock.
4. *Parliament:* the seat occupied by certain ranks of members: 'the Opposition *bench*'.
5. *Law:* a) the judge or judges of a court: 'the *bench* will now pass sentence'. b) the seat or position of a judge: 'the prisoner will stand before the *bench*'.

bend *verb*
(bent, bending)
to turn or force into a particular shape or direction: a) 'he *bent* the wire into a loop'; b) 'the road *bends* sharply here'; c) 'we *bent* our steps towards home'.
Usage: 'the prisoner still didn't *bend* after weeks of torture' (= yield, submit).
Phrases:
bend over backwards, see BACKWARDS.
round the bend, (*informal*) mad.
bend *noun*
a turn or change in direction.

bender *noun*
(*informal*) a drinking spree.

bends *noun*
also called **caisson disease**
the appearance of nitrogen bubbles in the blood when external pressure changes too quickly, as when a diver ascends to the surface too rapidly. See DECOMPRESSION CHAMBER.

bene– (*say* **benni**)
a prefix meaning well, as in *beneficial.* [Latin]

beneath *adverb, preposition*
under or below: a) 'they sat *beneath* the oak tree'; b) 'it is *beneath* my dignity to comment'.

benediction (*say* benni–**dik**–sh'n) *noun*
a grace or blessing: 'don't leave on your journey without receiving my *benediction*'.
[BENE– + Latin *dictio* a declaration]

benefactor (*say* **benni**–fakt'r) *noun*
a person giving kindly help or support, especially financial aid.
Word Family: **benefactress**, *noun*, a female benefactor; **benefaction** (*say* benni–**fak**–sh'n), *noun*, a good deed or charitable gift.
[BENE– + Latin *factor* a doer]

benefice (*say* **benni**–fis) *noun*
the church property from which a clergyman earns a living.

beneficence (*say* be–**neffi**–s'nce) *noun*
any act of goodness or kindness.
Word Family: **beneficent**, *adjective.*

beneficial (*say* benni–**fish**'l) *adjective*
having a good or helpful effect: 'a balanced diet is *beneficial* to one's health'.
Word Family: **beneficially**, *adverb.*

beneficiary (*say* benni–**fisha**–ree) *noun*
1. a person who receives a benefit or advantage, such as an inheritance.
2. the holder of a church benefice.

benefit *noun*
1. anything which is helpful or favourable: 'I hope the money will be of *benefit* to you'.
2. any payment or assistance given by an institution, government, etc.: 'unemployment *benefits*'.
3. any entertainment held to raise money for charity, etc.
Word Family: **benefit**, *verb.*

benevolent (*say* be–**nevva**–l'nt) *adjective*
1. kind or wishing well to others: 'a *benevolent* attitude'.
2. formed for charitable purposes rather than profit: 'a *benevolent* society'.
Word Family: **benevolence**, *noun*; **benevolently**, *adverb.*
[BENE– + Latin *volens* wishing]

benighted (*say* be–**nigh**–tid) *adjective*
ignorant.

benign (*say* be–**nine**) *adjective*
1. gentle and kind: 'a *benign* smile'.
2. (of diseases, etc.) not threatening life. Compare MALIGNANT.
3. favourable: 'the climate has a *benign* effect on the vegetation'.
Word Family: **benignly**, *adverb*; **benignity** (*say* be–**nigni**–tee), *noun.*
[Latin *benignus* kind–hearted]

benison (*say* **benni**–s'n) *noun*
an old word for blessing.
[same origin as *benediction*]

bent *noun*
a natural liking or bias: 'he has always had a *bent* for writing'.
bent *adjective*
1. out of the true shape or course.
2. (*informal*) dishonest: 'the accountant is *bent*'.
bent on, being determined to or set on.
bent *verb*
the past tense of the verb **bend.**

benumb (*say* be–**num**) *verb*
to stupefy or make numb: 'her fingers were *benumbed* with cold'.

Benzedrine (*say* **ben**zi–dreen) *noun*
a stimulant drug causing wakefulness and loss of appetite.
[a trademark]

benzene (*say* **ben**–zeen) *noun*
also called **benzol**
a colourless, liquid hydrocarbon (formula C_6H_6), with its carbon atoms arranged in a hexagonal ring, and used as a solvent, in motor fuel, and in making a wide variety of organic compounds.
[from *benzoin* an aromatic gum]

benzine (*say* **ben**–zeen) *noun*
Chemistry: a colourless liquid mixture of hydrocarbons of the paraffin series, with a boiling–point range of 50–60°C, and used for dry–cleaning and as a solvent.

bequeath (*say* be–**kweeth**) *verb*
to hand down or leave to those who come after, as in a will: 'this knowledge was *bequeathed* to us by the ancient Greeks'.

bequest (*say* be–**kwest**) *noun*
a legacy.

berate (*say* be–**rate**) *verb*
to scold: 'she was *berated* for losing her coat'.

bereave (*say* be–**reev**) *verb*
(bereft or **bereaved, bereaving)**
1. to take away or deprive: 'anger *bereft* her of words'.
2. to make sad through loss or death.
Word Family: **bereavement,** *noun,* a loss, especially by death.

beret (*say* **ber**ray) *noun*
a soft round cap, such as worn by some soldiers.
[French]

beri–beri *noun*
a disease due to lack of vitamin B in the diet, causing weakness and loss of function of the nerves and the heart muscles.
[Sinhalese, weakness]

berkelium (*say* ber–**keel**i–um) *noun*
element number 97, a man–made, radioactive metal. See TRANSURANIC ELEMENT and ACTINIDE.
See CHEMICAL ELEMENTS in grey pages.
[after *Bishop Berkeley,* 1685–1753, an Irish philosopher]

berry *noun*
any of various small, juicy, stoneless fruits, such as the strawberry, blackberry, etc.

berserk (*say* ber–**zerk**) *adverb, adjective*
go berserk, to become uncontrollable.
[Icelandic *berserkr* wild warrior]

berth *noun*
1. a bunk or sleeping–place in a ship, train, etc.
2. a place where a ship may be moored.
3. any place or position: 'he has a cosy *berth* in his father's business'.
give a wide berth to, to avoid.
Word Family: **berth,** *verb,* to come to a mooring.

beryl (*say* **berr**il) *noun*
Geology: a hard crystalline silicate mineral, used as a gem and as a source of beryllium. See EMERALD and AQUAMARINE.
[Greek *beryllos* a sea–green gem]

beryllium (*say* **berr**il–ium) *noun*
element number 4, a hard, light metal used in copper alloys. See ALKALINE EARTH METAL.
See CHEMICAL ELEMENTS in grey pages.

beseech *verb*
(beseeched or **besought, beseeching)**
to implore or ask earnestly and urgently: 'we *beseech* you not to be angry'.
Word Family: **beseechingly,** *adverb.*

beset *verb*
(beset, besetting)
to attack or harass: 'the family is *beset* by financial worries'.
besetting *adjective*
continually attacking or tempting: 'overeating is one of my *besetting* sins'.

beside *preposition*
at the side of or close to: 'sit *beside* me'.
Usage: '*beside* our house, yours is quite large' (= compared with).
Phrases:
beside oneself, 'he is still *beside himself* with grief' (= greatly affected).

beside the point, 'that argument is quite *beside the point*' (= unconnected with the issue).

besides *adverb, preposition*
1. in addition to: a) 'who else came *besides* you?'; b) 'the dress cost too much, *besides* which it was the wrong colour'.
2. other than: 'she has no other possessions *besides* her motorbike'.

besiege (*say* be-**seej**) *verb*
to surround or crowd in upon, especially with troops: a) 'the enemy *besieged* the city for 4 months'; b) 'the stranger was *besieged* with questions'.

besmirch *verb*
to make dirty: a) 'a face *besmirched* with chocolate'; b) 'the family's name was *besmirched* by the scandal'.

besot *verb*
(besotted, besotting)
to make or become stupid or muddled: 'he is *besotted* by love'.

besought *verb*
a past tense and past participle of the verb **beseech**.

bespatter *verb*
to soil by spattering: 'his trousers were all *bespattered* with mud'.

bespeak *verb*
(bespoke, bespoken or **bespoke, bespeaking)**
an old word meaning to reserve or order something in advance.
bespoke suit, a specially made, not ready-made, suit.

best *adjective*
the superlative form of **good**.
best *adverb*
the superlative form of **well (1)**.
had best, 'we *had best* not answer' (= would be wiser to).
best *noun*
the best quality, thing or part: 'nothing but the *best*'.
Phrases:
at best, on the most hopeful view.
get, **have the best of**, to defeat.
make the best of, to do as well as possible in circumstances which are unfavourable.
Word Family: **best**, *verb*, to outdo or defeat.

bestial *adjective*
of or like a beast: 'murder is a *bestial* crime'.
Word Family: **bestiality** (*say* besti-**alli**-tee), *noun*, brutal or beastly behaviour.

bestir *verb*
(bestirred, bestirring)
to rouse up or exert: '*bestir* yourselves, for there is much work to be done'.

best man
the chief attendant to the groom at a wedding.

bestow (*say* be-**sto**) *verb*
to give or present: 'many gifts were *bestowed* on him'.
Word Family: **bestowal, bestowment**, *nouns*.

bestride *verb*
(bestrode, bestriding)
to have one leg on each side of: 'the rider *bestrode* the horse'.
Usage: 'the city *bestrides* the river' (= is on both sides of).

best-seller *noun*
a book of which many copies are sold, especially in a short time.

bet *noun*
also called a **wager**
a) a promise made between two or more people on the probable outcome of an uncertain fact or event, usually in the form of money. b) the thing or event on which one makes a bet: 'that horse is not a good *bet* at all'.
bet *verb*
(bet or **betted, betting)**
1. to make a bet.
2. (*informal*) to be certain: 'I *bet* I'm right'.
Word Family: **better, bettor**, *noun*.

beta (*say* **beeta**) *noun*
the second letter of the Greek alphabet.

betake *verb*
(betook, betaken, betaking)
to go: 'she *betook* herself to London'.

beta particle
Physics: an electron or a positron released during radioactive decay.
beta ray
a stream of beta particles.

betel (*say* **beet**'l) *noun*
an Asian climbing plant, the leaves of which are chewed as a stimulant.

betel nut
the seed of the orange or scarlet fruit of an Asian palm tree, chewed with lime or betel leaves as a stimulant.

bête noire (*say* bate **nwah**)
a person or thing that one particularly dreads or dislikes.
[French *bête* beast + *noire* black]

betide *verb*
woe betide, '*woe betide* you if you fail!' (= trouble will come to).

betoken *verb*
to indicate or be a sign of: 'these gems *betoken* great wealth'.

betook *verb*
the past tense of the verb **betake.**

betray *verb*
1. to act disloyally or treacherously towards: 'he has *betrayed* our trust'.
2. to reveal unintentionally: 'extreme nervousness *betrayed* his guilt'.
Word Family: **betrayal,** *noun*; **betrayer,** *noun*, a person who betrays.

betrothed (*say* be–tro*th*ed) *adjective*
engaged to be married.
Word Family: **betroth,** *verb*; **betrothal,** *noun.*

better *adjective, adverb*
1. the comparative form of **good**: 'your car is good, but mine is *better*'.
2. the comparative form of **well (1)**: 'my car is *better* built than yours'.
Usage: 'I hope you are *better*' (= no longer sick).
Phrases:
better off, 'you would be *better off* not to come' (= in a better position).
had better, 'you *had better* obey' (= would be wiser to).
think better of, 'we *thought better of* playing the joke' (= decided against).
better *verb*
1. to surpass: 'his record in long–distance races has never been *bettered*'.
2. to make better: 'the government finally *bettered* the economic situation'.
better oneself, to improve one's circumstances.
Word Family: **better,** *noun*, a) that which is better, b) (plural) one's superiors, c) superiority; **betterment,** *noun.*

between *preposition, adverb*
a word used to indicate the following:
1. (within the given limits) a) 'come *between* 1 and 2 o'clock'; b) 'a mountain range *between* here and the sea'.
2. (connection) a) 'love *between* two people'; b) 'a similarity *between* two things'.
3. (sharing) 'we own the house *between* us'.
4. (distinction) 'there is little difference *between* onions and shallots'.
Phrases:
between ourselves, between you and me, in confidence.
few and far between, being sparse or rare.

betwixt *preposition, adverb*
an old word for between.

bevel (*say* **bevv**'l) *noun*
a) the sloping angle which one line or surface makes with another, when not at right angles. b) a tool for cutting such an angle.
Word Family: **bevel (bevelled, bevelling),** *verb.*

beverage (*say* **bevva**–rij) *noun*
any drink.
[Latin *bibere* to drink]

bevy (*say* **bev**–ee) *noun*
a gathering or group: 'a *bevy* of girls turned the corner'.

bewail *verb*
to express great sorrow or grief: 'she *bewailed* the loss of her husband'.

beware *verb*
be cautious or careful of: '*beware* the Ides of March!'.

bewigged *adjective*
wearing a wig: 'the *bewigged* barrister'.

bewilder *verb*
to puzzle or make uncertain: 'the strange language *bewildered* her'.
Word Family: **bewilderment,** *noun.*

bewitch *verb*
to put a charm or magic spell on: 'the sorceress *bewitched* the animals'.
Usage: 'the children were *bewitched* by the puppets' (= fascinated).
Word Family: **bewitchingly,** *adverb.*

bey (*say* bay) *noun*
(*formerly*) a title of respect, used in Turkey.

beyond *preposition, adverb*
further on than: a) '*beyond* us lay the desert'; b) 'don't stay *beyond* midday'.
Usages:
a) 'it is *beyond* understanding' (= outside the limits of).
b) 'the police found nothing *beyond* some fingerprints' (= except).

bi– (*say* by)
a prefix meaning two or twice, as in *biennial.*

biannual (*say* by–**an**–yew'l) *adjective*
occurring twice a year.
Word Family: **biannually,** *adverb.*

bias (*say* **by**–us) *noun*
1. a movement or prejudice in a particular direction: a) 'he has a *bias*

against foreigners'; b) 'the ball spun with a *bias* towards the left'.
2. a slanting or diagonal cut.
bias *verb*
to prejudice or influence unfairly.
Word Family: **biased, biassed,** *adjective,* prejudiced.

bib *noun*
1. a piece of cloth tied around the neck of a child to protect clothes while eating.
2. the upper part of an apron.
bib and tucker, (*informal*) clothes, especially one's best.

bible *noun*
1. *Christian:* (*capital*) the sacred writings, consisting of the Old and New Testaments.
2. (*informal*) any text or book considered as an authority: 'that encyclopaedia is his *bible*'.
Word Family: **biblical** (*say* **bibli**–k'l), *adjective.*
[Greek *biblos* book]

bibliography (*say* bibli–**ogra**–fee) *noun*
1. a list of books or sources for a particular topic, sometimes printed at the end of a book.
2. the description, history or classification of books, etc.
Word Family: **bibliographical** (*say* biblio–**graffi**–k'l), **bibliographic,** *adjective.*
[Greek *biblion* book + *graphein* to write]

bibliophile (*say* **bi**blio–file) *noun*
also called a **bibliophil** (*say* biblio–fill)
a lover of books.
[Greek *biblion* book – *philos* loving]

bibulous (*say* **bib**–yoolus) *adjective*
addicted to drinking alcohol.
[Latin *bibulus*]

bicameral (*say* by–**kamma**–r'l) *adjective*
Parliament: having two chambers, e.g. the House of Commons and the House of Lords. Compare UNICAMERAL.
[BI– + Latin *camera* chamber]

bicarbonate (*say* by–**karba**–nit) *noun*
Chemistry: a salt containing the univalent $(HCO_3)^-$ ion.

bicarbonate of soda
also called **baking soda**
sodium bicarbonate (formula $NaHCO_3$), a white crystalline solid used as a medicine, and in cooking as a raising agent.

bicentenary (*say* by–sen**teena**–ree) *noun*
a 200th anniversary.
Word Family: **bicentennial,** *adjective.*

biceps (*say* **by**–seps) *noun*
Anatomy: a large muscle in two parts, controlling movement of the elbow and forearm.
[Latin, two–headed]

bicker *verb*
to quarrel over petty things.

bicuspid (*say* by–**kuspid**) *noun*
also called a **premolar**
any of eight two–pointed teeth in the mouth, four on each jaw.
Word Family: **bicuspid, bicuspidate,** *adjectives,* (of teeth) having two points.

bicycle (*say* **by**–sik'l) *noun*
a two–wheeled vehicle with one wheel in front of the other, for one person and propelled by the feet turning pedals. A **tricycle** has three wheels. A **tandem** is a lengthened bicycle for two or more people, having two or more sets of pedals.

bid *verb*
(**bid, bidding;** *old forms:* **bade, bidden, bidding**)
1. to make an offer to buy, especially at an auction: 'no–one *bid* for that chair'.
2. to command or tell: 'we *bid* the travellers farewell'.
3. *Cards:* to declare the number of tricks a player thinks he will win.
Word Family: **bid,** *noun;* **bidding,** *noun,* an order or command.

biddy *noun*
(*informal*) an old woman.
[diminutive of *Bridget*]

bide *verb*
bide one's time, to wait for a favourable opportunity.

bidet (*say* **bee**–day) *noun*
a low basin on which one sits to wash one's genitals and posterior.
[French, a small horse]

biennial (*say* by–**ennial**) *adjective*
relating to or occurring every two years, especially a plant which takes two years to complete its life cycle.
Word Family: **biennial,** *noun;* **biennially,** *adverb.*

bier (*say* beer) *noun*
a stand on which a corpse, or the coffin containing it, is placed before burial.

bifocals (*say* by–**fo**–k'ls) *plural noun*
a pair of spectacles in which the lenses are in two sections, the upper half

for seeing distant objects, the lower half for reading.

bifurcate (*say* **by**–fir–kate) *verb*
to divide into two branches.
Word Family: **bifurcate,** *adjective*; **bifurcation,** *noun.*
[BI– + Latin *furca* a fork]

big *adjective, adverb*
large in size, importance, etc.:
(as an adjective) 'she has *big* ambitions but no drive'.
(as an adverb) 'she thinks *big* but does little'.
Usages:
a) 'a mare *big* with young' (= pregnant).
b) 'it was *big* of you to pay for us' (= generous).
c) 'that's all just *big* talk' (= boastful, exaggerated).
Word Family: **bigness,** *noun.*

bigamy (*say* **bigga**–mee) *noun*
Law: the crime of going through a marriage ceremony with one person when already married to another.
Word Family: **bigamist,** *noun*; **bigamous,** *adjective.*
[BI– + Greek *gamos* marriage]

big business
any powerful large–scale financial or business interests.

big dipper
see ROLLER–COASTER.

big end
short form of **big end bearing**
the end of a connecting rod attached to the crankshaft of a piston engine.

big game
1. any large animals hunted for sport.
2. any important or valuable objectives.

big–headed *adjective*
(*informal*) conceited.

big–hearted *adjective*
generous or kind.

bight (*say* bite) *noun*
1. a) a bend in the coastline. b) a body of water bounded by such a bend: 'the Great Australian *Bight*'.
2. the part of a rope between the ends.

bigot (*say* **big**–ut) *noun*
a person who is intolerant or prejudiced in matters of religion, race, etc.
Word Family: **bigoted,** *adjective*; **bigotry,** *noun.*

big–time *adjective*
(*informal*) at the top or most important level: 'a *big–time* gangster'.
Word Family: **big–time,** *noun,* the top.

big toe
Anatomy: see GREAT TOE.

big top
a) the main tent used in a circus. b) the circus itself.

bigwig *noun*
(*informal*) an important person.

bike *noun*
(*informal*) a bicycle.

bikini (*say* be–**keenee**) *noun*
a very small two–piece swim–suit, consisting of a bra and pants.
[name of the Pacific atoll laid bare by atomic bomb tests]

bilateral (*say* by–**latta**–r'l) *adjective*
of or affecting two sides or parties: 'Britain and Australia made a *bilateral* trade agreement'.
Word Family: **bilaterally,** *adverb.*

bilberry *noun*
also called a **whortleberry**
a small, round, edible, dark purple berry with a firm skin.

bile *noun*
1. *Biology:* the bitter yellow secretion of the liver, which is stored in the gall bladder and is essential for fat digestion.
2. bad temper or irritability.
[Latin *bilis* gall, bile, anger]

bilge (*say* bilj) *noun*
1. *Nautical:* a) the lowest parts of the inside of a boat. b) the water which collects in these parts.
2. (*informal*) nonsense.

bilingual (*say* by–**ling**–w'l) *adjective*
able to speak two languages with equal ease.
Word Family: **bilingually,** *adverb*; **bilingualism,** *noun.*

bilious (*say* **bil**–yus) *adjective*
1. of or relating to bile.
2. feeling nauseous.
3. bad–tempered.
Word Family: **biliousness,** *noun.*

bilk *verb*
to cheat or defraud.

bill (1) *noun*
1. a statement of money owed for goods supplied or services rendered.
2. (*capital*) a suggested or proposed law which has not yet been passed by parliament.
3. a notice, advertisement or poster.
4. *American:* a banknote.
bill of fare, a menu.
bill *verb*
1. to send a bill to: '*bill* me for the goods'.

2. to advertise or proclaim: 'he is *billed* as a top star'.

bill (2) *noun*
a bird's beak.

billabong *noun*
also called an **oxbow**
Australian: a branch of a river which flows away from the main stream and forms a separate curve or bend.

billboard *noun*
see HOARDING.

billet (1) *verb*
to assign to a lodging: 'the soldiers were *billeted* at private homes in the town'.
Word Family: **billet,** *noun.*

billet (2) *noun*
1. a stick of firewood.
2. a solid block of metal suitable for rolling or extrusion.

billet-doux (*say* billay-**doo**) *noun*
a love-letter.
[French *billet* note + *doux* sweet]

billfold *noun*
American: a wallet.

billhook *noun*
a long-handled tool with a hooked blade for trimming or pruning trees.

billiards *noun*
a game for two played on a rectangular table using a long rod and three balls. The aim is to hit balls into pockets at the side, or to hit two other balls in succession.
[French *billard*]

billion *noun*
a cardinal number, the symbol 1 000 000 000 000 or 10^{12} (a million million) in most countries, as distinct from 1 000 000 000 or 10^9 in America and France. Compare TRILLION.
Word Family: **billionaire,** *noun,* a person who has a billion dollars, pounds, etc.
[BI- + (mi)LLION]

bill of exchange
a written order for the payment of a specific sum of money to a particular person. Compare PROMISSORY NOTE.

bill of rights
Politics: an official statement of the rights of citizens in a country.

bill of sale
a document transferring property from one person to another.

billow *noun*
a large wave or surge: 'the smoke rose in great *billows*'.
Word Family: **billow,** *verb*; **billowy,** *adjective.*

billy *noun*
short form of **billycan**
Australian, New Zealand: a tin-plated pot with a lid and a handle, used over open fires to boil water, etc.
[Aboriginal *billa* water]

billy-goat *noun*
a male goat. Compare NANNY-GOAT.

biltong *noun*
strips of sun-dried meat used as iron rations on trek.
[Afrikaans]

bimonthly (*say* by-**munthlee**) *adjective*
a) occurring once every two months.
b) occurring twice every month.

bin *noun*
a container, usually with a lid, for holding foods, rubbish, etc.

binary (*say* **by**-na-ree) *adjective*
of or relating to two.
[Latin *bini* a pair]

binary number system
also called the **binary code, binary notation** or **binary scale**
a number system to the base 2, using only 0 and 1 and often used in computers. *Examples:* 10 means 2, 11 means 3, 100 means 4, 101 means 5, etc.

binary star
also called a **double star**
any pair of stars which revolve around each other.

bind (*rhymes with* kind) *verb*
(bound, binding)
to tie or secure.
Usages:
a) 'he is *bound* to pay' (= almost certain).
b) '*bind* the cake mixture with eggs' (= cause to stick together).
c) 'the old manuscript was *bound* in leather' (= covered).
Word Family: **bind,** *noun,* a) something that binds, b) (informal) a bore or nuisance; **binding,** *noun,* a book cover.

binder *noun*
anything which binds, such as a substance used to join bricks or a machine which ties cut grain.

bindweed *noun*
convolvulus.

binge (*say* binj) *noun*
(*informal*) a wild or prolonged bout of drinking, eating, etc.
[Lincolnshire dialect *binge* to soak]

bingo *noun*
also called **lotto**
a game in which contestants match numbers on a card with those drawn at random.

binnacle (*say* **bin**ni–k'l) *noun*
the case which contains a ship's compass.

binoculars (*say* bin–**nok**–yoolarz) *plural noun*
an instrument with lenses for both eyes, used for making distant objects appear closer.
Word Family: **binocular**, *adjective*, involving the use of both eyes.
[Latin *bini* a pair + *oculus* an eye]

binomial (*say* by–**no**–mee–ul) *adjective*
Maths: of or relating to an expression containing two terms, e.g. $x+y$.
binomial theorem, a method for calculating the nth power of a binomial without lengthy multiplication.
Word Family: **binomial,** *noun.*
[BI– + Greek *nomos* a part]

bio–
a prefix meaning life or living things, as in *biology.*

biochemistry (*say* by–o–**kem**mis–tree) *noun*
the study of the chemical substances and processes in living things.
Word Family: **biochemical**, *adjective*; **biochemically**, *adverb*; **biochemist**, *noun.*

biodegradable
(*say* by–o–de**grade**–a–b'l) *adjective*
able to be broken down into natural substances by organisms, especially bacteria, in the environment.

biodynamics (*say* by–o–die–**nam**miks) *plural noun*
(*used with singular verb*) the study of energy and activity in living things.

biogenesis (*say* by–o–**jen**ni–sis) *noun*
Biology: the principle that living matter is produced only from other living matter. Compare SPONTANEOUS GENERATION.

biography (*say* by–**og**ra–fee) *noun*
the life story of a person written by another. Compare AUTOBIOGRAPHY.
Word Family: **biographical** (*say* by–o–**graf**fik'l), *adjective*; **biographer**, *noun.*
[BIO– + Greek *graphein* to write]

biological control
the use of living things to control pests and parasites, e.g. by using a viral disease to kill rabbits.

biological warfare
any warfare using poisons, bacteria, etc. to destroy human, animal or plant life.

biology (*say* by–**ol**la–jee) *noun*
the study of living things.
Word Family: **biological** (*say* by–o–**loj**i–k'l), *adjective*; **biologist**, *noun.*
[BIO– + –LOGY]

bionic *adjective*
(*informal*) showing superhuman strength.

biophysics (*say* by–o–**fiz**ziks) *noun*
the application of the science of physics to the study of biological processes.

biopsy (*say* **by**–opsee) *noun*
Medicine: the removal and study of a sample of body tissue, usually to aid in diagnosis.
[BIO– + Greek *opsis* sight]

biosphere (*say* **by**–o–sfeer) *noun*
the part of the earth where living organisms are found.

biotic *adjective*
pertaining to life.

biotite (*say* **by**–o–tite) *noun*
Geology: a dark brown, green or black mineral of the mica group, widely found in igneous rocks such as granite.
[after *J. B. Biot*, 1774–1862, a French physicist]

bipartisan (*say* by–**par**tizan) *adjective*
involving the agreement of two parties, especially political parties.

bipartite (*say* by–**par**tite) *adjective*
divided into or involving two parts.

biped (*say* **by**–ped) *adjective*
having two feet.
Word Family: **biped**, *noun.*
[BI– + Latin *pedis* of a foot]

biplane (*say* **by**–plane) *noun*
an old type of aeroplane with two pairs of wings, one above the other.

birch *noun*
1. any of a group of deciduous, Northern Hemisphere trees with slender branches and smooth bark, used for timber.
2. a rod or bundle of birch twigs, used as a whip.
Word Family: **birch,** *verb*, to punish with a birch.

bird (1) *noun*
1. any of a large group of warm-blooded, feathered, vertebrate animals with wings by which most are able to fly.
2. (*informal*) a person, especially one with some peculiarity.

bird (2) *noun*
(*informal*) a girl.
[Middle English *burde* lady]

birdie *noun*
Golf: a score of one stroke less than par for a hole. Compare EAGLE.

birdlime *noun*
a sticky substance which is smeared on branches, to catch small birds.

bird of paradise
a tropical bird with brilliantly coloured feathers, found especially in New Guinea.

bird's-eye *adjective*
1. seen from above.
2. general: 'a *bird's-eye* view of history'.

biretta *noun*
a square cap worn by certain members of the Roman Catholic and Anglican clergy.
[Spanish *birreta*]

Biro *noun*
a ballpoint pen.
[a trademark]

birth *noun*
1. the act, time or process of being born: 'the baby weighed 4 kg at *birth*'.
Usage: 'this book examines the *birth* of Islam' (= beginning).
2. one's descent or origin: 'he is German by *birth*'.

birth control
any method of contraception.

birthday *noun*
the day or date of one's birth.

birthday suit
(*informal*) the state of being naked.

birthmark *noun*
a congenital mark on the body.

birth rate
the number of births in proportion to the total population at a given time, expressed per 1000 people. Compare DEATH RATE.

birthright *noun*
something to which one is entitled by birth.

biscuit (*say* **bis**kit) *noun*
1. a small baked food made from flour, fat and flavourings.
2. any unglazed low-fired pottery.

bisect (*say* by-**sekt**) *verb*
to divide into two, usually equal, parts.
Word Family: **bisection**, *noun*; **bisector**, *noun*, something which bisects.
[BI- + Latin *sectus* cut]

bisexual *adjective*
1. of or relating to both sexes, male and female.
2. *Biology:* containing both male and female reproductive organs.
Word Family: **bisexually**, *adverb*; **bisexual**, *noun*.

bishop *noun*
1. *Christian:* a clergyman of high rank in charge of a diocese.
2. *Chess:* a piece that may move any number of squares diagonally.
Word Family: **bishopric**, *noun*, the office or diocese of a bishop.
[Greek *episkopos* overseer]

bismuth (*say* **biz**-muth) *noun*
element number 83, a brittle metal used in alloys with a low melting point. Its compounds are used in medicine. See CHEMICAL ELEMENTS in grey pages.

bison (*say* **by**-s'n) *noun*
plural is **bison**
in America called a **buffalo**
a large-hoofed American mammal with a shaggy mane and short, curved horns.

bisque (*say* bisk) *noun*
a) a handicap stroke in golf, which can be claimed when desired, at any stage of the game. b) a similar concession at croquet and tennis.

bistro (*say* **bee**-stro) *noun*
a small casual restaurant with a bar.
[French]

bit (1) *noun*
1. a bar of metal or rubber passing through a horse's mouth and attached to the reins to help control the horse.
2. the cutting part of certain tools, especially drills.
take the bit between one's teeth, to act boldly and independently.

bit (2) *noun*
a small piece or amount.
Usages:
a) 'wait a *bit*' (= short time).
b) 'a threepenny *bit*' (= coin).

Phrases:
bit by bit, 'he built his home *bit by bit*' (= slowly, in stages).
do one's bit, 'we felt obliged to *do our bit*' (= make a contribution).
not a bit of it, not at all, by no means.

bit (3) *noun*
Computers: a unit of information fed into a computer.
[B(inary) + (dig)IT]

bitch *noun*
1. a female dog.
2. (*informal*) a) a malicious or unpleasant woman. b) a complaint.
bitch *verb*
(*informal*) a) to complain. b) to talk maliciously about someone.

bite *verb*
(bit, bitten, biting)
to cut or cut into with or as if with the teeth.
Usages:
a) 'the acid *bit* into the metal' (= ate, corroded).
b) 'what's *biting* him?' (= annoying).
c) 'the fish are *biting* well tonight' (= taking the lure).
d) 'the dentist asked him to *bite* on the X-ray film' (= close the teeth).
bite off more than one can chew, to take on more than one can cope with.
bite *noun*
1. the act of biting.
2. an injury resulting from biting.
3. a mouthful.
4. a small meal or snack.

biting (*say* **by**-ting) *adjective*
1. keen or piercing: 'a *biting* wind'.
2. sarcastic or cutting: 'a *biting* comment'.

bit part
a small or unimportant role in a play, film or opera.

bitter *adjective*
being harsh or disagreeable in taste.
Usages:
a) 'don't go out in that *bitter* cold without your scarf' (= piercing).
b) 'she suffered *bitter* sorrow after his death' (= distressing, hard to bear).
c) 'he had only *bitter* words for his ex-girlfriend' (= sarcastic, cutting).
d) 'he cherished *bitter* hatred in his heart' (= intense).
bitter *noun*
a strong draught beer with a sharp taste. Compare MILD.
Word Family: **bitterly**, *adverb*; **bitterness**, *noun*.

bittern *noun*
a long-legged tawny marsh-bird which emits a unique booming call.

bitters *plural noun*
a liquid obtained from herbs, used in small amounts to flavour drinks.

bitumen (*say* **bit**-yoomin) *noun*
a black sticky mixture of hydrocarbons obtained from natural deposits or by distilling petroleum.
Word Family: **bituminous** (*say* bit-**yoomi**-nus), *adjective*.
[Latin, asphalt]

bivalent (*say* by-**vay**-l'nt) *adjective*
also called **divalent**
Chemistry: having a valency or combining power of two.
[BI- + Latin *valens* strong]

bivalve (*say* **by**-valv) *noun*
Biology: a mollusc having a shell with two hinged parts, such as an oyster. Compare UNIVALVE.

bivouac (*say* **bivvoo**-ak) *verb*
(bivouacked, bivouacking)
to camp in the open.
Word Family: **bivouac**, *noun*.

biweekly *adjective*
a) occurring every two weeks. b) occurring twice a week.

bizarre (*say* biz-**ar**) *adjective*
very strange or odd.
Word Family: **bizarrely**, *adverb*; **bizarreness**, *noun*.

blab *verb*
(blabbed, blabbing)
a) to reveal a secret. b) to tell tales.
Word Family: **blabbermouth**, *noun*, a person who blabs.

black *noun*
1. the darkest achromatic colour, reflecting virtually no light.
2. something which has this colour: 'dressed in *black*'.
3. any member of a dark-skinned race of people.
in the black, a) being on the credit side of an account, entered in black ink; b) having money or capital. Compare IN THE RED under RED.
black *adjective*
having the colour black.
Usages:
a) 'it was a *black* day for all concerned' (= unlucky, calamitous).
b) 'a *black* look' (= sullen, nasty).
c) 'we ordered two *black* coffees' (= without milk or cream).
d) 'he committed many *black* deeds' (= evil, wicked).

e) 'the film is an example of *black* comedy' (= pessimistic, bitter or gruesome).

black *verb*
to impose a ban on a firm, product or country, in a trade union dispute.
Word Family: **blackish,** *adjective*; **blackly,** *adverb*; **blackness,** *noun.*

blackball *verb*
to deny a person membership of something, usually by voting against him.

blackbeetle *noun*
the common house cockroach, which is neither black nor a beetle.

black belt
a sign of rank awarded to a grade of mastership in judo, etc.

blackberry *noun*
an edible, dark purple berry which grows on a thorny bush.

blackbird *noun*
a songbird related to the thrush, the male being black and the female brown.

blackbirding *noun*
Australian history: the kidnapping of natives from the Pacific islands in the 19th century, to provide labour for the sugar industry in Queensland.
Word Family: **blackbirder,** *noun.*

blackboard *noun*
a board painted black, suitable for writing on with chalk.

black box
a specially protected electronic device installed in an aircraft to record any information about its flight which may be useful if there is a crash.

blackcock *noun*
also called a **black grouse** or **black game**
a black and white grouse of northern Europe; the female is called a **greyhen.**

blackcurrant *noun*
a small, black, edible fruit growing on a shrub.

Black Death
History: the bubonic plague which spread from Asia to Europe in the 14th century.

blacken *verb*
to make or become black.
Usage: 'the gossip began as an attempt to *blacken* his character' (= defame, malign).

blackguard (*say* blaggard) *noun*
a scoundrel.
Word Family: **blackguardly,** *adverb, adjective.*

blackhead *noun*
a blocked skin pore having a dark, greasy head.

black hole
Astrophysics: a theoretically possible region of space where matter is so condensed by gravitation that no radiation can escape from it and anything approaching it will disappear.

blacking *noun*
a preparation, such as polish, for blackening shoes, stoves, etc.

blackjack *noun*
1. (*formerly*) a large cup or jug, usually made of leather.
2. the flag of a pirate ship.
3. *Cards:* see PONTOON (2).
Word Family: **blackjack,** *verb,* to strike with a club.

blacklead (*say* blak-led) *noun*
graphite.

blackleg *noun*
1. a worker who refuses to join a trade union or take part in a strike. Also called a **scab.**
2. an infectious disease of cattle and sheep which causes swellings in the legs and is usually fatal.

black list
a list of people who are suspected or disapproved of.
Word Family: **black-list,** *verb.*

black magic
magic which is used for evil purposes.

blackmail *noun*
the crime of demanding payment in return for not revealing damaging information.
Word Family: **blackmail,** *verb*; **blackmailer,** *noun.*

Black Maria
(*informal*) a police patrol wagon for carrying prisoners.

black market
the illegal buying and selling of commodities, ignoring price controls, rationing, etc.
Word Family: **black marketeer,** a person who operates on the black market.

blackout *noun*
1. the extinguishing or concealment of lights in a city or district, as a result of power failure or during enemy air attacks at night.

Usage: 'the government ordered a *blackout* of news on the scandal' (= concealment).
2. (*informal*) a sudden, temporary loss of consciousness.
Word Family: **black out,** to lose consciousness for a short period.

black pudding
also called **blood pudding**
a dark sausage made from blood, fat, flour and seasonings packed into a skin and boiled.

black sheep
a person regarded as worthless or inferior by his family, group, etc.

blacksmith *noun*
a craftsman who forges iron objects, such as horseshoes, with a hammer and anvil.

blackthorn *noun*
a thorny deciduous shrub with white blossoms and purple, plum-like fruit (sloes).

black tie
see BOW TIE.

black widow
a very poisonous American spider, the female of which eats its mate.

bladder *noun*
1. *Biology:* any elastic sac for storing fluids, such as urine, in an organism.
2. any inflatable bag: 'a football *bladder*'.

bladderwrack (*say* **bladda**-rak) *noun*
a large, branched, brown seaweed with many air-bladders, usually found attached to rocks in shallow water.

blade *noun*
1. a) the flat, cutting part of a sword, knife, etc. b) a sword.
2. a thin, broad, flat part of anything: a) 'the *blade* of an oar'; b) 'a *blade* of grass'.
3. a smart, dashing young fellow.

bladebone *noun*
a cut of beef from the shoulder of the animal.

blame *verb*
to find fault with or hold responsible for a wrong or error.
to blame, 'who's *to blame* for this awful mess?' (= responsible).
Word Family: **blame,** *noun*; **blameworthy,** *adjective,* deserving blame; **blameless,** *adjective,* innocent or free from blame.

blanch (*rhymes with* branch) *verb*
1. to make or become pale or white: 'to *blanch* with fear'.
2. to immerse in water, often boiling, in order to remove skins, separate grains, etc.
[French *blanc* white]

blancmange (*say* bla-**monj**) *noun*
a flavoured, jelly-like dessert.
[French *blanc* white + *manger* to eat]

bland *adjective*
mild, smooth or non-stimulating: a) 'a *bland* diet'; b) 'a *bland* smile'.
Word Family: **blandly,** *adverb*; **blandness,** *noun.*
[Latin *blandus* smooth-tongued]

blandishment *noun*
(*usually plural*) flattering or coaxing words.
Word Family: **blandish,** *verb.*

blank *adjective*
1. unmarked: 'put your name in the *blank* space'.
2. empty: 'a *blank* cartridge'.
Usages:
a) 'a *blank* look' (= expressionless).
b) 'her behaviour was *blank* stupidity' (= utter).
c) 'a *blank* wall' (= with no openings, exits, etc.).

blank *noun*
1. an empty space: a) '*blanks* in a document'; b) 'the accident is a *blank* in her memory'.
2. an empty or unmarked object, such as a form to be filled in, or a sheet of metal to be stamped into a finished article.
3. a cartridge containing powder but no bullet and therefore harmless.
draw a blank, to fail.
Word Family: **blankly,** *adverb,* a) without expression or understanding, b) directly; **blankness,** *noun.*

blanket *noun*
a piece of soft woollen or other material, especially used as a bed covering.
Usage: 'there was a *blanket* of smog above the city' (= layer).
Word Family: **blanket,** *verb,* to cover with or as if with a blanket; **blanket,** *adjective,* being general or covering a whole group.

blank verse
see VERSE.

blare *verb*
to make a prolonged, harsh, loud noise: 'the hi-fi next door was *blaring* all night'.
Word Family: **blare,** *noun.*

blarney (*say* **blar–nee**) *noun*
smooth, flattering but obviously deceptive talk.
[after a stone in *Blarney Castle*, Ireland, said to give the gift of persuasive speech]

blasé (*say* **blahzay**) *adjective*
indifferent or bored.
[French *blaser* to exhaust]

blaspheme (*say* blas–**feem**) *verb*
to speak disrespectfully about a deity or sacred things.
Word Family: **blasphemer**, *noun*, a person who blasphemes; **blasphemy**, *noun*; **blasphemous** (*say* **blas**fa–mus), *adjective*.
[Greek *blasphemia* slander]

blast (*say* blahst) *noun*
1. a strong gust of wind, jet of air, etc.: a) 'the furnace gave out a *blast* of hot air'; b) 'a *blast* of sound'.
2. a) an explosive charge. b) the ignition of an explosive charge. c) the shockwave caused by an explosion.
full blast, 'the car was going *full blast*' (= at top speed).
blast *verb*
1. to blow a trumpet, car horn, etc.
2. to explode or blow up: 'the bomb *blasted* three city blocks'.
3. to wither, shrivel or destroy: 'a late spring frost *blasted* the tomato plants'.
4. (*informal*) to damn.

blast furnace
a vertical, cylindrical furnace heated from the bottom by a blast of hot air, and used to extract iron from its ores.

blast–off *noun*
the launching or lift–off of a space vehicle.

blatant (*say* **blay–t'nt**) *adjective*
extremely obvious or conspicuous: a) '*blatant* advertisements insult the intelligence'; b) 'a *blatant* lie'.
Word Family: **blatantly**, *adverb*.

blather (*say* **bla*tha***) *noun*
any stupid or babbling talk.
Word Family: **blather**, *verb*; **blatherskite**, *noun*, a babbling or foolish person.

blaze (1) *noun*
1. a bright flame or fire: 'firemen rushed to the *blaze*'.
Usages:
a) 'the flowers were a *blaze* of colour' (= glow).
b) 'she threw the plate at him in a *blaze* of fury' (= sudden outburst).
2. (*plural*, *informal*) hell.
like blazes, (*informal*) very energetically.
blaze *verb*
to burn or shine brightly.
Usage: 'the battleship's guns *blazed* away' (= fired).

blaze (2) *noun*
1. a mark made on a tree by removing a patch of bark, to indicate a path, boundary, etc.
2. a white mark on the face of a horse, cow, etc.
blaze *verb*
to mark a tree with blazes.
blaze a trail, a) to mark a trail with blazes; b) to pioneer or be the first.

blaze (3) *verb*
to proclaim or make known.

blazer *noun*
a coloured, often blue, lightweight jacket, usually with a school or club badge on the breast pocket.

blazon (*say* **blayz'n**) *verb*
to proclaim publicly or in a conspicuous manner: 'headlines *blazoned* the outbreak of war'.

bleach *verb*
to make or become white, pale or colourless: 'his hair was *bleached* by the sun'.
Word Family: **bleach**, *noun*, a chemical agent used to bleach clothes, etc.

bleak *adjective*
a) cold or windswept: 'a *bleak* hillside'.
b) cheerless, dismal or dreary: 'the future seemed *bleak* to her'.

bleary (*say* **bleer–ee**) **blear** *adjective*
(of the eyes) blurred and watery.
Word Family: **blear**, *verb*, to make bleary; **blearily**, *adverb*; **bleariness**, *noun*.

bleat *verb*
to cry like a sheep or goat.
Usage: 'I wish you'd stop *bleating* about being misunderstood' (= complaining).
Word Family: **bleat**, *noun*.

bleed *verb*
(bled, bleeding)
to lose blood from an artery or vein.
Usages:
a) 'the sap *bled* from the tree' (= oozed).
b) 'the new shirt *bled* in the wash' (= ran).
c) 'I *bleed* for the families of the drowned men' (= feel deep sympathy).

d) (*informal*) 'the blackmailer *bled* him for years' (= got money from).
Word Family: **bleeder**, *noun*; **bleeding**, *adjective*, (informal) bloody.

bleep *noun*
a short, high-pitched sound, especially that made by electronic or radio equipment.
Word Family: **bleep**, *verb*.

blemish *noun*
a stain, mark or defect: a) 'there were no *blemishes* on her skin'; b) 'a parking fine is not a *blemish* on one's driving record'.
Word Family: **blemish**, *verb*.

blench *verb*
to shrink back or draw away: 'she *blenched* at the idea'.

blend *verb*
to join different things together so that they can no longer be separately distinguished: a) 'this wine was *blended* from local and imported wines'; b) 'the rabbit's colouring *blended* with that of the dry grass'.
Word Family: **blend**, *noun*, a mixture of several things; **blender**, *noun*, an electrical device in which foods can be finely chopped to an even texture.

bless *verb*
(**blessed** or **blest**, **blessing**)
1. to make or pronounce holy: 'the archbishop *blessed* the new church'.
2. to ask divine favour for: a) '*bless* this house'; b) '*bless* you for being so kind'.
3. *Christian:* to make the sign of the cross: 'to *bless* oneself on entering a church'.
Usage: 'she is *blessed* with a good brain' (= favoured, endowed).
blessed (*say* **bless**id *or* blest) *adjective*
1. a) holy or sacred. b) divinely favoured or fortunate.
2. (*informal*) a) damned: 'this *blessed* machine won't work'. b) a word used for emphasis: 'he spent every *blessed* cent on gambling'.
Word Family: **blessedly**, *adverb*; **blessedness**, *noun*, the state of being blessed.

blessing *noun*
1. the words or ceremony used to bless.
2. anything which leads to happiness, favour, etc.: 'the legacy was a *blessing* to the impoverished family'.

blew (1) *verb*
the past tense of the verb **blow (2)**.

blew (2) *verb*
the past tense of the verb **blow (3)**.

blight *noun*
1. any of various plant diseases, usually caused by fungi.
2. any destructive influence.
Word Family: **blight**, *verb*, to destroy, ruin or cause to decay.

blighter *noun*
(*informal*) a fellow, often one who is disliked or pitied.

blind *adjective*
lacking the sense of sight.
Usages:
a) 'he has *blind* faith in doctors' (= unquestioning).
b) 'there's a *blind* corner at the bottom of the hill' (= hidden from view).
c) 'she murdered him in a fit of *blind* passion' (= uncontrolled).
d) (*informal*) 'your brother became *blind* at the party' (= very drunk).
Phrases:
blind to, 'he is *blind to* his own faults' (= unable or unwilling to see).
turn a blind eye to, to pretend not to notice.
blind *verb*
to make blind or as if blind: a) 'he was *blinded* by the explosion'; b) 'the headlights *blinded* her for a moment'.
Usage: 'he was *blinded* by success' (= deprived of common sense).
blind *noun*
1. a strip of cloth or other material pulled down over a window to keep light out.
2. a cover which hides or conceals: a) 'we could observe the wild animals from a *blind*'; b) 'the import business was a *blind* for a smuggling racket'.
Word Family: **blindly**, *adverb*, in a blind manner; **blindness**, *noun*; **blindingly**, *adverb*.

blind alley
1. an alley closed at one end.
2. a place from where it is not possible to proceed: 'the false clue was just another *blind alley* in the investigation'.

blind date
a date with a person of the opposite sex whom one has not met before.

blindfold *verb*
to cover the eyes with a cloth or bandage to prevent sight.
Word Family: **blindfold**, *noun*.

blind man's buff
a children's game in which a blindfolded player tries to catch and identify other players.

blind spot
1. *Anatomy:* the small spot on the eye which has no light-sensitive cells, where the optic nerve attaches to the retina.
2. a subject about which a person cannot think or judge clearly.

blindworm *noun*
see SLOW-WORM.

blink *verb*
1. to open and shut the eyes rapidly.
2. (of lights) to shine intermittently.
Usage: 'he would not *blink* at using violence to get his way' (= hesitate).
blink *noun*
the act of blinking.
on the blink, (*informal*) not working, out of order.
Word Family: **blinking,** *adjective,* (informal) confounded.

blinker *noun*
either of two stiff leather flaps attached to a bridle on either side of a horse's head to stop it seeing sideways.

blip *noun*
a spot of light on a radar screen, representing a particular object.

bliss *noun*
a state of ecstatic happiness and contentment.
Word Family: **blissful,** *adjective*; **blissfully,** *adverb.*

blister *noun*
1. a thin-walled swelling on the skin containing a watery liquid, usually due to rubbing or a burn.
2. any similar swelling, as in old paint.
Word Family: **blister,** *verb,* to raise or cause to raise blisters; **blistering,** *adjective,* severely critical or scathing.

blithe (*say* bli*the*) *adjective*
cheerful, gay or carefree.
Word Family: **blithely,** *adverb.*

blithering *adjective*
(*informal*) stupid, foolish or talkative.

blitz *noun*
1. a sudden attack in a military offensive, especially using aircraft.
2. any intense attack or campaign: 'a *blitz* against untidiness'.
Word Family: **blitz,** *verb.*
[short form of German *Blitzkrieg* lightning war]

blizzard *noun*
a fierce storm of wind and snow.

bloat *verb*
to swell out or puff up, especially with a gas or liquid.

bloat, bloating *noun*
a condition in cattle, horses, sheep, etc., caused by eating excessive amounts of green fodder which ferments and distends the stomach.

bloater *noun*
a salted smoke-cured herring.

blob *noun*
1. a small, round mass, drop or spot.
2. a shapeless mass.

bloc (*say* blok) *noun*
a group of parties or countries joining together for a particular purpose.

block *noun*
1. a solid mass or piece, especially of wood, stone, etc. and usually flat-sided or cube-like.
2. a) an area in a city or town bounded by four roads: 'the chemist is in the next *block*'. b) a building lot: 'a *block* of land'. c) a row of houses. d) a large building containing flats, offices, etc.
3. anything which obstructs: 'police have set up a *roadblock*'.
4. *Printing:* a metal plate with a raised image from which an illustration is printed.
5. a writing pad: 'do you sell scribbling *blocks*?'.
6. a quantity, number or section taken as a whole: 'a *block* of cinema tickets'.
7. *Athletics:* a starting block.
block *verb*
to hinder or prevent the movement of: a) 'a large dog *blocked* the way'; b) 'the Opposition *blocked* the Bill in Parliament'.
Usage: 'the batsman *blocked* the ball with his bat' (= stopped).
Phrases:
block in, 'I'll *block in* the details later' (= fill in).
block out, 'I'll *block out* the plan so you'll have a general idea' (= sketch, outline).
Word Family: **blockish,** *adjective,* a) like a block, b) stupid; **blockishly,** *adverb*; **blockishness,** *noun.*

blockade *noun*
1. the blocking of sea or land communications by an armed force.
2. any blocking or obstruction of progress, movement, etc.
Word Family: **blockade,** *verb.*

blockage (*say* **blokkij**) *noun*
an obstruction or blocking.

block and tackle
a set of ropes and pulleys with a hook, used for lifting.

blockbuster *noun*
a very heavy, World War 2 bomb, designed to penetrate concrete blockhouses, etc.
Usage: 'the famous author's new novel was hailed as a *blockbuster*' (= startling or astonishing work).

blockhead *noun*
a person who is stupid.

blockhouse *noun*
a fortified building with small openings for shooting through.

blockish *adjective*
Word Family: see BLOCK.

bloke *noun*
(*informal*) a man.

blond, blonde *adjective*
(of hair, etc.) light in colour.
Word Family: **blonde,** *noun,* a woman with blond hair; **blondness,** *noun.*

blood (*say* blud) *noun*
1. *Biology:* the red fluid, a mixture of cells and liquid plasma, pumped by the heart throughout the body.
2. a person's descent or ancestry: 'they are related by *blood*'.
Usages:
a) 'the defeated team are really out for *blood*' (= revenge, violence).
b) 'we need a bit of new *blood* in the office' (= life).
c) 'don't tease her when her *blood* is up' (= temper).
Phrases:
bad blood, hostility or ill feeling.
in cold blood, deliberately.
blood *verb*
1. to cause to bleed.
2. to give hunting dogs their first taste of blood.
Word Family: **bloodless,** *adjective,* a) without bloodshed, b) cold or unfeeling.

blood bank
a store of blood plasma of different types, kept for use in blood transfusions.

bloodbath *noun*
a massacre or slaughter.

blood brother
a person who has sworn brotherhood, especially by the ceremonial mingling of blood.

blood count
a count of the number of red or white cells in a specific volume of blood.

bloodcurdling *adjective*
terrifying or horrible.

blood feud
a murderous feud between families or clans.

blood group
any of several classes into which blood is grouped depending on its reactions with specific antibodies.

bloodhound *noun*
one of a breed of large, strong, smooth-haired, keen-scented hounds, used for tracking and hunting.

bloodless *adjective*
Word Family: see BLOOD.

blood money
any money gained at the cost of another's life.

blood-poisoning *noun*
see SEPTICAEMIA.

blood pressure
1. the pressure exerted by the blood on the inner walls of blood vessels, arteries, etc. which varies in different parts of the body.
2. (*informal*) high blood pressure.

blood pudding
black pudding.

blood relation
a person related by birth, not marriage.

bloodshed *noun*
any slaughter or shedding of blood.

bloodshot *adjective*
(of eyes) being red because of dilated blood vessels.

blood sport
any sport where blood is shed, such as hunting.

bloodstock *noun*
any thoroughbred horses.

bloodstone *noun*
also called **heliotrope**
a greenish variety of chalcedony with small, scattered red spots.

bloodstream *noun*
Anatomy: the blood flowing through the body.

bloodthirsty *adjective*
violent or murderous.
Word Family: **bloodthirstily,** *adverb*; **bloodthirstiness,** *noun.*

blood vessel
Anatomy: any tube or vessel which contains or transports blood within the body.

bloody (*say* **bluddee**) *adjective*
1. marked or stained with blood: 'a *bloody* handkerchief'.

2. violent or accompanied by bloodshed: 'a *bloody* battle'.
3. (*informal*) a) damned: 'you *bloody* fool'. b) very: 'a *bloody* big piece of timber just missed him'.
bloody *verb*
(bloodied, bloodying)
to mark or stain with blood.
Word Family: **bloody,** *adverb,* (informal) very; **bloodily,** *adverb*; **bloodiness,** *noun.*

bloody-minded *adjective*
(*informal*) deliberately obstructive or unhelpful.
Word Family: **bloody-mindedness,** *noun.*

bloom *noun*
1. a flower.
2. the time or state of flowering: 'the roses are in *bloom* early this year'.
3. a white, powdery coating on a surface, as on certain fruits, metals, etc.
Usages:
a) 'her daughters are in the *bloom* of youth' (= peak, prime)
b) 'she looked thin and there was no *bloom* on her cheeks' (= healthy glow).
bloom *verb*
1. to flower.
2. to flourish or grow vigorous and healthy.
Word Family: **blooming,** *adjective,* (informal) damned.

bloomer *noun*
a silly or embarrassing blunder.

bloomers *plural noun*
1. a pair of soft, loose underpants.
2. a loose pair of women's trousers, formerly used for cycling, etc.
[after *Mrs Amelia Bloomer*, 1818–94, an American feminist]

blossom (*say* **bloss**'m) *noun*
1. a flower, especially the flower of a fruit tree.
2. the time or state of flowering: 'the apple trees are in *blossom*'.
blossom *verb*
1. to flower.
2. to flourish or develop fully.
Word Family: **blossomy,** *adjective.*

blot *noun*
a spot or stain, especially of ink.
Usage: 'the newspaper's allegations are a *blot* on his character' (= blemish).
blot *verb*
(blotted, blotting)
1. to spot or stain.
2. to dry or soak up.
blot out, a) 'the sun was *blotted out* by the clouds' (= hidden); b) 'she tried to *blot out* the memory' (= destroy, wipe out).

blotch *noun*
a large irregular spot.
Word Family: **blotchy,** *adjective.*

blotting paper
also called **blotter**
any thick, absorbent paper used to dry ink.

blotto *adjective*
(*informal*) drunk.

blouse (*rhymes with* cows) *noun*
a shirt, especially a loose or decorative one.

blow (1) (*rhymes with* slow) *noun*
1. a hard, sudden stroke with the hand, a weapon, etc.: 'a painful *blow* on the head'.
2. a shock or setback: 'her death was a great *blow* to the family'.

blow (2) (*rhymes with* slow) *verb*
(blew, blown, blowing)
1. (of air) to be in motion: 'the winter wind *blows* hard in this climate'.
2. a) to produce or emit a current of air: 'she *blew* on her cold hands'. b) to move something by a current of air: 'the wind *blew* the tree down'. c) to produce sound by a current of air: '*blow* your trumpet'.
3. (*informal*) to squander: 'he *blew* the whole inheritance at the races'.
Usage: 'the fuse *blew*' (= burnt out).
Phrases:
blow in, (*informal*) to arrive unexpectedly.
blow one's own trumpet, to praise oneself.
blow out, to extinguish.
blow over, 'the scandal will soon *blow over*' (= subside, be forgotten).
blow up, a) to explode; b) to enlarge a photograph, etc.; c) to inflate.

blow (3) *verb*
(blew, blown, blowing)
to flower, especially of a bud opening into a flower.

blower (*say* **blo**-er) *noun*
1. a device which forces air through a fire, etc.
2. (*informal*) a telephone.

blowfly *noun*
any of a group of flies which usually deposit their eggs or larvae in flesh, etc. on which the larvae feed.

blowgun *noun*
see BLOWPIPE.

blowhole *noun*
a hole worn through the roof of a coastal cave by wave action and through which air and water are forced by the rising tide.

blowlamp *noun*
also called a **blowtorch**
a torch which burns paraffin under pressure to produce a very hot flame, used for burning off old paint, etc.

blow-out *noun*
1. a sudden bursting of a tyre on a motor vehicle.
2. an escape of oil or gas from a well, due to a sudden surge of high pressure below ground which forces the oil through the safety devices which normally contain it.

blowpipe *noun*
1. a weapon consisting of a tube through which a dart or pellet is blown. Also called a **blowgun**.
2. a pipe through which a stream of gas is directed at a flame to increase its heat.

blow-up *noun*
1. an explosion.
2. a large copy of a print or negative.

blow-wave *noun*
any hairstyle created using a hand-held drier and shaping the hair as it dries.
Word Family: **blow-wave,** *verb.*

blowy (*say* **blo-ee**) *adjective*
windy: 'a *blowy* winter's day'.

blowzy (*rhymes with* lousy) *adjective*
1. untidy or dishevelled.
2. having a ruddy complexion.

blub *verb*
(blubbed, blubbing)
(*informal*) to weep or sob noisily.

blubber *noun*
Biology: a thick layer of fat under the skin of aquatic mammals, such as whales and seals, which provides insulation and is a source of oil.
blubber *verb*
to weep noisily.

bludgeon (*say* **bluj**'n) *noun*
a short, heavy club.
Word Family: **bludgeon,** *verb.*

blue (*say* bloo) *noun*
1. a) a primary colour like that of a clear sky. b) the colour between green and indigo in the spectrum.
2. something which has this colour: 'dressed in *blue*'.
3. a blue powder used to whiten laundry.
4. a person who has played for his university in certain sports.
out of the blue, suddenly or unexpectedly.
blue *adjective*
of or having the colour blue.
Usages:
a) 'a *blue* mood' (= depressed, unhappy).
b) '*blue* movies' (= obscene, pornographic).
blue *verb*
(*informal*) to squander: 'he *blued* all his money on drink'.
Word Family: **blueness,** *noun*; **bluish,** *adjective.*

bluebell *noun*
1. a small European plant with spikes of blue, bell-shaped flowers, growing from a bulb.
2. *Scottish:* the harebell.

blueberry *noun*
a small, smooth, edible, bluish berry which grows on a shrub.

blue blood
aristocratic descent.
Word Family: **blue-blooded,** *adjective.*

bluebottle *noun*
any of a group of large blue and green flies.

blue cheese
also called **blue vein**
any cheese with a greenish-blue mould through it.

blue chip
Stock Exchange: a share regarded as almost as safe an investment as gilt-edged securities.

blue-collar worker
any person employed in a trade or manual work, and receiving a wage. Compare WHITE-COLLAR WORKER.

blue-eyed boy
a favourite who can do no wrong: 'Jim is his boss's *blue-eyed boy*'.

bluegrass *noun*
1. any of various grasses, used as fodder, etc.
2. traditional country music, especially from the southern states of America.

bluejacket *noun*
a seaman of the British or American Navy.

blue-pencil *verb*
to make deletions in a script, etc., with or as if with a blue pencil, especially to remove indecencies.

Blue Peter
a blue flag with a white square, flown by a ship about to sail.

blueprint *noun*
1. a photographic copy printed in white on blue paper.
2. a detailed outline or plan.

Blue Ribbon
also called **Blue Riband**
1. the ribbon of the Order of the Garter.
2. a title formerly given to the liner making the fastest Atlantic crossing, and later extended to other fields.

blues *plural noun*
1. a state of depression or melancholy.
2. *Music:* a style of jazz which developed from the slow, sad songs of the early American Negroes.
[from *blue devils*, an old phrase for melancholia]

bluetongue lizard
any of a group of Australian lizards growing up to 0·5 m long, with a greyish-brown body and a vivid blue tongue.

blue vein
see BLUE CHEESE.

blue whale
also called a **sulphur-bottom**
a whale found in arctic and antarctic waters. It is the largest mammal which has ever lived, growing from 21–30 m in length and weighing up to 100 tonne.

bluff (1) *noun*
a prominent, steep headland or cliff.
Word Family: **bluff,** *adjective,* abrupt; **bluffly,** *adverb*; **bluffness,** *noun.*
[German *blaf* flat]

bluff (2) *verb*
to mislead or deceive by a display of confidence.
Word Family: **bluff,** *noun.*

bluish *adjective*
Word Family: see BLUE.

blunder *noun*
a stupid mistake.
Word Family: **blunder,** *verb,* a) to make a stupid mistake, b) to move or act awkwardly.

blunderbuss *noun*
a large musket having a short barrel with a wide muzzle which scatters shot at close range.
[Dutch *donder* thunder + *buss* gun]

blunt *adjective*
1. having a dull, rounded edge or tip: 'a *blunt* knife'.
2. abrupt and straightforward in manner.
Word Family: **blunt,** *verb*; **bluntly,** *adverb*; **bluntness,** *noun.*

blur *verb*
(blurred, blurring)
to make or become indistinct: 'the tears in her eyes *blurred* her vision'.
Word Family: **blurry,** *adjective*; **blur,** *noun.*

blurb *noun*
an advertisement or description of a product, especially one printed on the jacket of a book.

blurt *verb*
to speak impulsively: 'he *blurted* out the secret'.

blush *verb*
1. to become red in the face, from embarrassment or shame.
2. to be ashamed: 'she *blushed* to admit her mistake'.
Word Family: **blush,** *noun.*

bluster *verb*
to blow in loud, violent gusts, as wind.
Usage: 'he *blustered* confusedly throughout the argument' (= spoke noisily).
Word Family: **bluster,** *noun*; **blustering, blustery,** *adjectives.*

boa (*say* bo-a) *noun*
1. any of various large, non-poisonous snakes, such as the South American **boa constrictor**, noted for coiling around its prey and crushing it to death.
2. a long wrap made of feathers, fur, etc. worn around the neck.

boar (*say* bore) *noun*
a male pig.

board (*say* bawd) *noun*
1. a long, flat piece of timber, used in building.
2. a thin, flat slab of wood, card, etc. used for a special purpose: a) 'an *ironing-board*'; b) 'a chess *board*'.
3. the daily meals, especially when paid for: 'bed and *board*'.
4. a group of people appointed to manage the affairs of a company, etc.
5. (*plural*) the theatre.
Phrases:
go by the board, to be discarded or neglected.
on board, on or in a ship, aeroplane, etc.

board *verb*
1. to fit or close with boards.
2. to enter a ship, aeroplane, etc.

3. to be supplied with meals, and usually accommodation, in exchange for payment.
Word Family: **boarder**, *noun*, a person who pays for food and lodgings.

boarding house
a building with accommodation for paying guests.

boarding school
a school which provides some or all students with board and lodgings.

boast (*rhymes with* post) *verb*
1. to speak with excessive pride, especially about oneself.
2. to possess something which one is proud of: 'this city *boasts* the oldest church in the country'.
Word Family: **boast**, *noun*; **boaster**, *noun*, a person who boasts.

boastful *adjective*
tending to boast.
Word Family: **boastfully**, *adverb*; **boastfulness**, *noun*.

boat *noun*
1. a vessel built to float and travel on water.
2. something with the shape or function of a boat: 'a gravy *boat*'.
Phrases:
burn one's boats, to commit oneself to a course of action from which there is no turning back.
in the same boat, all in the same situation, especially an unfortunate one.
Word Family: **boat**, *verb*.

boater *noun*
a light straw hat with a flat, round crown and brim.

boathouse *noun*
a shed built near or over the water for storing small boats.

boatswain (*say* **bo**–s'n) *noun*
also spelt **bo's'n** or **bosun**
a seaman in charge of a ship's rigging, boats and anchors.

bob (1) *verb*
(bobbed, bobbing)
1. to move up and down: 'we could see the ball *bobbing* in the water'.
2. to curtsy.
bob up, to appear or come into view suddenly.
Word Family: **bob**, *noun*.

bob (2) *noun*
1. a short haircut.
2. a small dangling object, such as the weight on a pendulum.
3. a short chorus.
Word Family: **bob (bobbed, bobbing)**, *verb*, to cut short, as a horse's tail.

bob (3) *noun*
(*informal*) a shilling.

bobbin *noun*
an object around which thread or yarn is wound for use in weaving, sewing, etc.

bobble *noun*
a small ball which dangles, as on a hat.

bobby *noun*
(*informal*) a policeman.
[after *Sir Robert Peel*, who was Home Secretary in Britain when the Police Force was created]

bobby socks
a pair of short socks.

bobcat *noun*
a wildcat common in America.

bobsleigh (*say* **bob**–slay) *noun*
a racing sledge carrying two or more people and having two sets of runners, the front set of which is used to steer the vehicle.

bobtail *noun*
a short or docked tail.

bod *noun*
(*informal*) a person: 'an odd *bod*'.
[short form of BODY]

bode *verb*
to be an omen of: 'these results do not *bode* well for his future'.

bodice (*say* **boddis**) *noun*
a woman's fitted garment covering the upper part of the body, often forming part of a dress, etc.

bodkin *noun*
1. a blunt needle for sewing with tape, cord, etc.
2. a small, pointed instrument for making holes in cloth, etc.

body *noun*
1. a) the structure of bones, flesh, etc. of an animal. b) the trunk of an animal: 'he was wounded in the leg and *body*'.
Usages:
a) 'a *body* was found in the boot of the car' (= corpse).
b) 'this wine has a good *body*' (= strength, consistency).
c) 'it is in the *body* of the poem' (= main part).
2. a distinct object or piece of matter: 'the stars and planets are celestial *bodies*'.

3. a group or quantity of things or matter: a) 'a *body* of troops'; b) 'a *body* of water'.
Word Family: **bodily,** *adjective.*

bodyguard *noun*
a personal or private guard, e.g. for an important person.

body politic
a nation or society forming a single unit under its government.

bodywork *noun*
the outer shell of a motor vehicle.

Boer (*say* **bo**–a *or* bore) *noun*
also called an **Afrikaner**
a descendant of the early Dutch settlers in South Africa.
Word Family: **Boer,** *adjective.*
[Dutch, farmer]

boffin *noun*
(*informal*) a) an inventor, originally of airforce equipment. b) a backroom boy.

bog *noun*
an area of permanently wet, spongy ground, formed especially by decaying plants.
bog *verb*
(bogged, bogging)
to sink in or as if in a bog: 'the car got *bogged* in the mud'
Word Family: **boggy,** *adjective.*
[Irish, soft]

bogey (*say* **bo**–gee) *noun*
Golf: the estimated hole or course score for a good player, sometimes one more than par.

boggle *verb*
to be startled or hesitate in fear: a) 'the mind *boggles* at the idea'; b) 'the horse *boggled* at the high jump'.
Usage: 'her eyes *boggled* and her jaw dropped' (= became wide in surprise).

bogie (*say* **bo**–gee) *noun*
a trolley or truck, e.g. one supporting a railway locomotive.

bogus *adjective*
counterfeit or sham.

bogy (*say* **bo**–gee) *noun*
an evil spirit, or something which causes fear.

bohemian *noun*
(*often capital*) an artistic or intellectual person who disregards conventional standards of behaviour.
Word Family: **bohemian,** *adjective.*
[French *Bohémien* a gipsy from Bohemia (now in Czechoslovakia)]

boil (1) *verb*
1. to change a liquid to a vapour by applying heat.
2. to cook in boiling water, etc.: '*boil* the chicken for 3 hours'.
Usages:
a) 'she *boiled* with fury at the insult' (= was very agitated).
b) (*informal*) 'it's *boiling* outside in that sun' (= very hot).
boil down, a) to reduce by boiling; b) 'it all *boils down* to this' (= shortens, adds up).
Word Family: **boil,** *noun,* the condition of boiling.

boil (2) *noun*
an infection of the skin, causing a swelling with a small pus-filled centre.

boiler *noun*
1. a vessel in which water is stored, heated and circulated, to be used for heating or power.
2. a chicken suitable for boiling rather than roasting, etc.

boilersuit *noun*
a piece of clothing consisting of trousers and a long-sleeved shirt in one piece.

boiling point
1. *Physics:* the temperature at which the vapour pressure of a liquid is equal to the external pressure, and bubbles of vapour freely form within the liquid.
2. the peak of anger or vexation.

boisterous (*say* **boy**–sta–rus) *adjective*
noisy, rough or unrestrained.
Word Family: **boisterously,** *adverb;* **boisterousness,** *noun.*

bolas *plural noun*
a throwing weapon consisting of balls attached to cords, used in South America to catch cattle, etc.

bold *adjective*
1. fearless and courageous.
2. impudent: 'her *bold* reply shocked us all'.
3. clear and distinct: 'he has *bold* handwriting'.
4. *Printing:* having thick, dark lines, as in **bold** typeface.
Word Family: **boldly,** *adverb;* **boldness,** *noun.*

bole *noun*
Biology: the trunk of a tree.

bolero *noun*
1. (*say* **bol**–airo) a very short jacket, usually sleeveless.
2. (*say* ba–**lairo**) a) a lively dance from Spain, usually accompanied by singing

and castanets. b) the music for such a dance.
[Spanish]

boll (*say* bole) *noun*
Biology: a rounded seed-pod of some plants, such as cotton.

bollard *noun*
a short, strong post, e.g. one to which a ship may be tied at a dock.

boloney *adjective*
see BALONEY.

Bolshevik (*say* **bol**sha-vik) *noun*
1. a Russian communist in the early 20th century.
2. a revolutionary person.
Word Family: **Bolshevik,** *adjective*; **bolshie,** *adjective,* (informal) rebellious or having left-wing views.

bolster (*say* **bole**-sta) *noun*
a long, narrow pillow or cushion.
bolster *verb*
to reinforce or support: 'to *bolster* up one's courage'.

bolt *noun*
1. a) a sliding device for fastening a door, etc. b) the part of a lock moved forward or withdrawn when the key is turned.
2. a heavy metal pin with a thread at one end, used with a nut for holding things together.
3. the length of fabric in a roll, usually about 37 m.
4. a sliding, metal bar which closes the breech of a rifle or artillery piece.
5. a short, heavy arrow used with a crossbow.
Usage: 'they made a desperate *bolt* for the door' (= sudden swift dash).
bolt from the blue, 'the news came as a *bolt from the blue*' (= complete surprise, like a thunderbolt from a blue sky).
bolt *verb*
1. to fasten with a bolt.
2. to move or escape hurriedly or without control: 'the horse *bolted* after its jockey fell'.
Usage: 'please don't *bolt* your food' (= eat hurriedly).
Word Family: **bolt upright,** stiffly erect.

bolt-hole *noun*
any place or means of escape.

bomb (*say* bom) *noun*
any destructive device containing an explosive or incendiary charge.
go like a bomb, (*informal*) 'the party *went like a bomb*' (= was a great success).
bomb *verb*
to attack or destroy with bombs.
bomb out, (*informal*) to fail.
[Latin *bombus* a booming sound]

bombard *verb*
1. to attack with bombs or other artillery weapons.
Usage: 'to *bombard* with questions' (= attack vigorously).
2. *Physics:* to send a stream of particles towards something.
Word Family: **bombardment,** *noun.*

bombardier (*say* bomba-**deer**) *noun*
a non-commissioned officer in an artillery regiment, equal in rank to a corporal.

bombastic *adjective*
pompous in speech or writing.
Word Family: **bombastically,** *adverb*; **bombast,** *noun.*

bomber (*say* **bomma**) *noun*
a type of aircraft designed to carry and drop bombs.

bombshell *noun*
1. a bomb.
2. a sudden or shocking surprise: 'the news came as a *bombshell*'.

bona fide (*say* **bo**-na **fie**-dee)
sincere or without fraud: 'he is a *bona fide* representative of that company'.
[Latin, in good faith]

bonanza *noun*
any source of good luck or wealth: 'that mineral strike was a *bonanza*'.
[Spanish, fair weather, prosperity]

bonbon *noun*
a small sweet.
[French]

bond *noun*
1. something which binds or holds things together: a) 'a prisoner in *bonds*'; b) 'a *bond* of affection'.
2. a formal promise to perform or not to perform certain actions, etc.: 'a good behaviour *bond*'.
3. a sum of money paid as a security: 'the tenants must pay a *bond* in case of damage'.
4. *Commerce:* a certificate of debt from a government, etc. and offering repayment with interest by a fixed date.
5. *Chemistry:* see COVALENT BOND, IONIC BOND, and DATIVE BOND.
6. the state of having goods stored until the taxes or duties due are paid: 'the shipment was held in *bond*'.
7. *Building:* the arrangement of bricks or stones in a wall in overlapping layers to make the structure stronger.

8. a high-quality paper used for writing, typing, etc.
Word Family: **bond**, *verb*, a) to join or hold together firmly, b) to place under a bond, c) to provide with a bond; **bondage** (*say* **bond**ij), *noun*, the state of being subjected or enslaved to some force, power or control.

bondsman *noun*
1. a serf.
2. a person who gives a bond.

bone *noun*
1. a) any of the separate pieces forming the rigid framework of the body of a vertebrate. b) the hard substance of which this framework is composed, consisting of strands of protein in a bed of calcium phosphate.
2. a piece of this substance with meat attached: 'a juicy *bone* for the dog'.
3. any substance or object which resembles or is made of bone.
4. a point of dispute: 'he made no *bones* about leaving the moment the project was over'.
Phrases:
bare bones, the essentials.
feel in one's bones, to know instinctively.
pick a bone, 'I have a *bone to pick* with you' (= reprimand, complaint).
bone *verb*
to remove the bones from.
bone up, bone up on, (*informal*) to study in a hurry.
Word Family: **boneless**, *adjective*.

bone china
see CHINA.

bone-dry *adjective*
(*informal*) very dry.

bone-idle *adjective*
also called **bone-lazy**
extremely lazy.

bonemeal *noun*
a coarse powder of ground bones, used as fertilizer.

bone-setter *noun*
a person who treats dislocations and broken bones, especially one not professionally qualified.

boneshaker *noun*
(*informal*) any decrepit old bike.
[from the nickname of an 1870 bicycle with steel tyres]

bonfire *noun*
a large fire built in the open.

bongos, bongoes *plural noun*
a pair of small drums struck with the hands.
[Spanish-American]

bonhomie (*say* bonna-**mee**) *noun*
a pleasant, good-natured manner.
[French *bonhomme* a good sort]

bonkers *adjective*
(*informal*) crazy.

bon mot (*say* bon **mo**)
plural is **bons mots** (*say* bon **mo**)
a witty remark.
[French *bon* good + *mot* word]

bonnet *noun*
1. a woman's soft hat, with its sides pulled down over the ears and tied under the chin.
2. any of various covers or protective devices, such as the hinged or detachable cover for the engine of a motor vehicle.

bonny *adjective*
looking healthy and pretty: 'a *bonny* girl'.

bonsai (*say* **bon**-zigh) *noun*
a) the art of growing miniature, decoratively shaped trees. b) a tree grown in this way.
[Japanese *bon* pot + *sai* plant]

bonus *noun*
something which is given in addition to what is usual or expected, such as extra money given to an employee as well as his salary.
[Latin, good]

bon voyage (*say* bon voy-**ahzh**)
a wish for a pleasant trip.
[French]

bony *adjective*
1. of or like bones.
2. containing many bones: 'this is a *bony* piece of fish'.
3. very thin: 'that girl is *bony*'.

boo *interjection*
a shout expressing disapproval or contempt, or used to frighten someone.
Word Family: **boo** (**booed, booing**), *verb*.

boob *noun*
(*informal*) a) a fool. b) a foolish mistake. c) (*usually plural*) breasts.
Word Family: **boob**, *verb*, (informal) to make a foolish mistake; **booboo**, *noun*, (informal) a mistake.

booby *noun*
a fool.

booby prize
a prize given in consolation or as a joke to the worst competitor.

booby trap
a device or situation which catches a person off guard.

boogie–woogie *noun*
an early style of blues piano music dominated by a continuous bass accompaniment.

book (*say* buk) *noun*
1. a group of sheets of paper bound or fastened together between covers for a particular purpose: a) '*a storybook*'; b) '*a chequebook*'.
2. a written or printed work in this form, especially a literary composition.
3. a division of a larger written or printed work.
4. a record of bets, accounts or similar transactions.
Usage: 'to be in somebody's good *books*' (= favour, opinion).
Phrases:
bring to book, to demand an account of.
by the book, 'he does everything *by the book*' (= formally, absolutely correctly).
take a leaf out of one's book, to copy or follow the example of.
throw the book at, to make every possible charge against.
book *verb*
1. to write or enter in a book or other record.
Usage: 'the police *booked* her for speeding' (= recorded a charge against).
2. to reserve in advance: 'to *book* tickets for a play'.
Word Family: **booking**, *noun*, an advance reservation.

bookcase *noun*
a series of shelves, usually in a frame, for storing books.

book end
a support for keeping books upright on a shelf.

bookie *noun*
(*informal*) a bookmaker.

bookish *adjective*
fond of reading and study, especially to an extreme degree.

book–keeping *noun*
the art or process of recording financial transactions, accounts, etc.

booklet *noun*
a small book or pamphlet.

bookmaker *noun*
a person who takes bets on races, competitions, etc.

bookmark, bookmarker *noun*
a slip of paper or material inserted between the pages of a book to mark one's place.

bookworm *noun*
a person who reads or studies a lot.

boom (1) *verb*
1. to make a loud, hollow sound, such as the echo of an explosion.
2. to flourish or progress vigorously: 'business *boomed* in the big city'.
boom *noun*
1. a loud, hollow sound.
2. a sudden increase or growth, as of business, popularity, etc.

boom (2) *noun*
1. a long pole attached to the bottom of the sail and often by one end to the mast.
2. a long pole, chain, etc. which can be held across an area of land or water to prevent movement of traffic, etc.
3. a device with a movable arm from which a microphone, etc. can be hung during filming.

boomerang *noun*
Australian: a curved, wooden Aboriginal throwing device which returns to the thrower.
boomerang *verb*
to rebound with harmful effects upon the originator.

boon (1) *noun*
a benefit or thing to be enjoyed.

boon (2) *adjective*
jolly or jovial: 'a *boon* companion'.

boondocks *noun*
American: (*informal*) an uninhabited or remote area.
[from Philippines word for mountain]

boor *noun*
a person who is rude, surly and ill–mannered.
Word Family: **boorish**, *adjective*; **boorishly**, *adverb*.
[Dutch *boer* peasant]

boost *verb*
1. to raise by pushing from behind or below.
Usage: 'the advertising campaign *boosted* sales' (= increased, promoted).
2. *Engineering:* to supercharge.
Word Family: **boost**, *noun*, a) an upwards lift, b) an increase; **booster**, *noun*, something which boosts or increases, such as an extra injection

which prolongs immunity to a disease, or a device which increases power.

boot (1) *noun*
1. a heavy shoe, usually reaching above the ankle.
2. a compartment in the front or rear of a motor car for carrying luggage, etc. In America called a **trunk**.
3. a kick.
Usage: (*informal*) 'he was given the *boot* for stealing' (= dismissal).
Phrases:
boot's on the other foot, the situation is reversed.
put the boot in, to kick a prostrate victim mercilessly.

boot (2) *noun*
to boot, in addition.

booth (*say* boo*th*) *noun*
a small, enclosed structure or stall: 'a telephone *booth*'.

bootleg *noun*
any illegally traded or smuggled alcohol.
Word Family: **bootleg (bootlegged, bootlegging)**, *verb*; **bootlegger**, *noun*.

bootless *adjective*
an old word for unprofitable: 'a *bootless* errand'.

booty *noun*
anything stolen or captured in war or by robbery, etc.

booze *noun*
(*informal*) alcohol.
Word Family: **booze**, *verb*, to drink heavily; **boozy**, *adjective*; **boozer**, *noun*.

boracic acid (*say* **borassik assid**)
see BORIC ACID.

borax (*say* **baw-raks**) *noun*
sodium borate, a white crystalline solid used as a flux and in making glass.
[Arabic *burak*]

border *noun*
1. a part or line which forms the end or furthest sides of something.
2. the line or area which separates one country, state or place from another.
border *verb*
1. to form or provide with a border.
2. to lie on the border of: 'Italy *borders* France and Austria'.
border on, border upon, a) 'Spain *borders on* France' (= adjoins); b) 'his fits of temper *border on* madness' (= are close to).

borderline *adjective*
close to a given limit, margin or condition: 'a *borderline* pass in the exam'.

bore (1) *verb*
to make a hole by digging, drilling, etc.
Usage: 'lights *bored* through the darkness' (= penetrated, forced their way).
bore *noun*
1. a hole made by drilling.
2. the internal diameter of a cylinder, especially that of a gun barrel.

bore (2) *verb*
to tire by being dull and tedious: 'he *bored* us with his long tales'.
Word Family: **bore**, *noun*, a person or thing that bores; **boredom**, *noun*, the state of being bored.

bore (3) *noun*
a tidal wave in a river or estuary.

bore (4) *verb*
the past tense of the verb **bear (1)**.

borer *noun*
a person or thing that bores holes, especially an insect which burrows into trees, wood, etc.

boric acid
also called **boracic acid**
a white crystalline solid used in medicine, tanning and for glazing pottery.

born *verb*
a past participle of the verb **bear (1)**.
be born, to be brought into the world.
born *adjective*
having an innate quality or talent: 'a *born* writer'.

borne *verb*
a past participle of the verb **bear (1)**.

boron *noun*
element number 5, a brown, brittle metal used for hardening steel and in enamels and glass.
See CHEMICAL ELEMENTS in grey pages.
[BOR(ax) + (carb)ON]

borough (*say* **burra**) *noun*
1. a town, especially one founded on a charter from a monarch.
2. a town or district with its own local government.
[Middle English *burgh* town]

borrow *verb*
to obtain on loan with a promise to return: 'may I *borrow* £5 until tomorrow?'.
Usage: 'he has *borrowed* my idea' (= adopted for his own use).
Word Family: **borrower**, *noun*.

borsch (*say* borsh) *noun*
also spelt **bortsch**

a Russian soup made from beetroot and served hot or cold.

Borstal *noun*
a reformatory where young offenders are disciplined, educated and trained for industry.
[after the first, instituted in 1902 at *Borstal* Kent]

borzoi (*say* **bor**zoy) *noun*
one of a breed of large, long-legged hounds with a pointed head and a soft coat, formerly used to hunt wolves.
[Russian, swift]

bosh *noun*
(*informal*) nonsense.

bo's'n, bosun *noun*
see BOATSWAIN.

bosom (*say* **b*uz***'m) *noun*
1. the breasts of a woman.
2. the part of a garment covering the bosom.
Usage: 'in the *bosom* of the family' (= affectionate centre).
Word Family: **bosom**, *adjective*, close or intimate; **bosomy**, *adjective*, having large breasts.

boss (1) *noun*
a person who has charge or control, especially over workers.
boss *verb*
to act in a domineering manner.
Word Family: **bossy**, *adjective*, domineering.
[Dutch *baas* master]

boss (2) *noun*
a knob-like projection.

bossa nova
a) a rhythmic, jazz-style dance originally from Brazil. b) the music for such a dance.
[Portuguese, new movement]

botanical gardens
a public park displaying a wide variety of plants.

botany (*say* **botta**-nee) *noun*
the study of plants.
Word Family: **botanist**, *noun*; **botanic** (*say* ba-**tannik**), **botanical**, *adjective*.
[Greek *botané* plant]

botch *verb*
to spoil through poor work or clumsiness.
Word Family: **botch**, *noun*.

botfly *noun*
any of a group of flies with parasitic larvae which feed beneath the skin of mammals.

both *adjective, pronoun*
the two together:
(used as an adjective) 'use *both* hands!'.
(used as a pronoun) '*both* of us will go'.
both *conjunction*
equally: 'there is pollution in *both* Auckland and New York'.

bother (*say* **bo*th***-a) *verb*
to cause trouble or annoyance: 'stop *bothering* me while I'm reading'.
Usage: 'don't *bother* to reply' (= concern yourself).
bother *noun*
1. something which bothers or troubles: 'is it a *bother* to do those tasks now?'.
2. a worried or agitated state: 'she got into a real *bother* over it'.
Word Family: **bothersome**, *adjective*, giving or causing bother.

bottle *noun*
a glass or plastic container for liquid, usually with a narrow neck and an opening which may be sealed.
bottle *verb*
to put into a bottle.
bottle up, 'she *bottled up* her emotions' (= confined or restrained).

bottle-brush *noun*
1. a brush for cleaning bottles.
2. an Australian shrub with dense, coloured flower heads consisting of stamens all around the stem, resembling a bottle-brush.

bottle green
a deep green colour.
Word Family: **bottle-green**, *adjective*.

bottleneck *noun*
any narrow, congested area: 'the street is a *bottleneck* for traffic'.

bottom *noun*
the lowest part of anything, as compared with the top: 'the *bottom* of the cupboard'.
Usages:
a) 'the *bottom* of the sea' (= ground under).
b) 'we must get to the *bottom* of this' (= fundamental aspect).
c) 'he slapped her on the *bottom*' (= buttocks).
Word Family: **bottom**, *adjective*; **bottom**, *verb*, to reach or touch the bottom; **bottomless**, *adjective*.

botulism (*say* **bot**-yoolizm) *noun*
a disease of the nervous system due to eating contaminated food, and causing double vision and paralysis.

Word Family: **botulinus** (*say* bot–yoo–**lie**–nus), *noun*, the bacterium which causes botulism.
[Latin *botulus* a sausage]

bouclé (*say* **boo**–klay) *noun*
a yarn with loops which produces a fabric with a rough appearance.
[French, curled]

boudoir (*say* **boo**–dwar) *noun*
a lady's bedroom.
[French *bouder* to pout or sulk]

bouffant (*say* **boo**–fon) *adjective*
puffed out, e.g. sleeves or a hairstyle.
[French]

bougainvillaea (*say* boo–gan–**villia**) *noun*
a climbing, tropical American plant, now common in Australia, New Zealand and other warm countries.
[after *Admiral de Bougainville*, 1729–1811, a French navigator]

bough (*rhymes with* cow) *noun*
a large branch of a tree, usually starting at the trunk.

bought (*say* bawt) *verb*
the past tense and past participle of the verb **buy**.

boulder (*say* **bole**–da) *noun*
a large stone.

boulevard (*say* **boola**–vard) *noun*
a wide, usually tree-lined street.
[French]

bounce *verb*
1. to spring or cause to spring back after hitting something: 'the ball *bounced* on the concrete'.
2. to move in a lively manner: 'she *bounced* into the room'.
3. (*informal*) (of a cheque) to be returned unpaid from a bank.
bounce *noun*
a bound or spring.

bouncer *noun*
1. a person or thing that bounces, such as a fast ball bowled in cricket which bounces up dangerously at the batsman.
2. (*informal*) a person hired to remove disorderly persons from a dance, etc.

bouncing *adjective*
strong and healthy: 'a *bouncing* baby'.

bound (1) *adjective*
1. certain or determined: 'their plan is *bound* to fail'.
2. (used in compound words) unable to operate, progress, etc. due to: '*snowbound*'.

bound *verb*
the past tense and past participle of the verb **bind**.

bound (2) *verb*
to move in leaps: 'he *bounded* energetically into the room'.
Word Family: **bound,** *noun.*

bound (3) *noun*
(*usually plural*) any limit or boundary: 'there are no *bounds* to his ambition'.
out of bounds, an area where access is forbidden.
Word Family: **bound,** *verb,* to limit or form the limit of; **boundless,** *adjective,* unlimited.

bound (4) *adjective*
on the way or intending to go: 'homeward *bound*'.

boundary *noun*
1. anything which indicates the edge: 'this is the *boundary* of our property'.
2. *Cricket:* a four.

bounteous *adjective*
bountiful: 'a *bounteous* harvest'.
Word Family: **bounteously,** *adverb*; **bounteousness,** *noun.*

bountiful *adjective*
a) generous: 'a *bountiful* giver'. b) plentiful: 'a *bountiful* supply'.
Word Family: **bountifully,** *adverb*; **bountifulness,** *noun.*

bounty *noun*
1. generosity.
2. a bonus or reward, especially one given by a government.
[Latin *bonitas* goodness]

bouquet (*say* bo–**kay** *or* boo–**kay**) *noun*
1. a bunch of flowers.
2. the characteristic smell of wines or liqueurs.
[Old French *bosquet* little wood]

bourbon (*say* **berb**'n) *noun*
a whisky made from maize.
[first made in *Bourbon County*, America]

bourgeois (*say* **boor**–*zhwa*) *adjective*
of or thought to be characteristic of the middle class.
Word Family: **bourgeois** (plural is **bourgeois**), *noun,* a member of the middle class; **bourgeoisie** (*say* boor–*zhwa*–**zee**), *noun,* the middle class, often with hostile implications that it is stuffily conventional, anti-socialist or anti-communist.
[French, townsman]

bout *noun*
a period of time in some activity, work, etc.: 'a *bout* of flu'.
Usage: 'a boxing *bout*' (= contest).

boutique (*say* boo–**teek**) *noun*
a small, fashionable shop usually selling women's clothing or gifts.
[French]

bovine (*say* **bo**–vine) *adjective*
1. of or belonging to a group of four–legged, cloven–hoofed mammals, usually with horns, such as cows, oxen, etc.
2. stolid or dull.
[Latin *bovis* of a bull]

bow (1) (*rhymes with* cow) *verb*
to bend down or sideways: a) 'the branches *bowed* in the wind'; b) 'he *bowed* courteously to the princess'.
Usage: 'you must *bow* to their wishes' (= yield, submit).
Word Family: **bow**, *noun.*

bow (2) (*rhymes with* go) *noun*
1. a weapon made from a length of wood or other flexible material with a string tightly stretched between the two ends, used to shoot arrows.
2. a bend or curve.
3. a decorative looped knot.
4. *Music:* a stick with horsehairs stretched along it, used to sound the strings of a violin or similar instrument.
Word Family: **bow**, *verb.*

bow (3) (*rhymes with* cow) *noun*
Nautical: (*often plural*) the front end of a boat. Compare STERN (2).

bowdlerize (*say* **bow**dla–rize)
bowdlerise *verb*
to censor words in a book which are believed to be unsuitable for certain readers.
Word Family: **bowdlerization**, *noun.*
[after *Dr. T. Bowdler*, who published a censored version of Shakespeare's plays in the 19th century]

bowel (*rhymes with* towel) *noun*
1. *Anatomy:* (*usually plural*) the intestine.
2. (*plural*) the innermost part: 'in the *bowels* of the earth'.

bower (*rhymes with* flower) *noun*
a shady, leafy shelter.

bowerbird *noun*
any of various Australian birds which live in scrub and build an elaborate, walled enclosure (a **bower**), to attract the females.

bowie knife (*say* **bo–ee** nife)
a sheath–knife which has a long blade and one cutting edge.
[after *James Bowie*, 1796–1836, an American pioneer]

bowl (1) (*say* bole) *noun*
1. a deep, round dish.
2. any rounded, hollow object or area: 'the *bowl* of a pipe'.

bowl (2) (*say* bole) *noun*
1. a ball made of wood, rubber or a synthetic material, used in the game of bowls, tenpin bowling, etc.
2. a roll or delivery of the bowl.
bowl *verb*
1. to throw or roll a ball.
2. to move along smoothly and rapidly.
3. *Cricket:* to pitch the ball towards the batsman, with the arm held straight using a circular, overarm motion.
Word Family: **bowler**, *noun*; **bowling alley**, a long, indoor wooden alley for tenpin bowling or skittles.

bow–legged (*say* bo–**leggid**) *adjective*
having legs which bend outwards so that the knees are separated when the ankles are close together.

bowler hat (*say* **bole**–a hat)
short form is **bowler**
a man's hat with a rounded crown and narrow brim, usually made of felt.

bowline *noun*
a non–slipping knot which forms a loop.

bowls (*say* boles) *noun*
a game played on a green by two to eight players who aim to place their bowls which are biased (weighted on one side), as close as possible to a small white ball, called the **jack**.

bowman (*say* **bo**–man) *noun*
an archer.

bowsprit (*say* **bo**–sprit) *noun*
Nautical: a spar projecting from the bow of a boat and holding the forestay.

bow tie
a tie made into a bow at the neck. A **black tie** is a black bow tie worn on formal occasions with a dinner jacket; a **white tie** is for the most formal occasions, worn with tails.

bow window
a curved bay window.

box (1) *noun*
1. a container, usually rectangular, and with a lid, made of cardboard, wood, etc.

2. a separate compartment, container or enclosure: a) 'the glove *box* of a car'; b) 'witness *box*'.
3. something with the shape of a box: a) 'a *box* kite'; b) 'a *box* camera'.
4. a collection of money for a charitable purpose or the container in which the money is collected: 'the judge ordered him to put £20 in the poor *box*'.
5. *Baseball:* the place where the batter stands to face the pitcher.
6. a small, raised seat in a horse-drawn vehicle, for the driver.
7. (*informal*) television.
Word Family: **box**, *verb*, to enclose in or as if in a box.

box (2) *verb*
to fight with the fists.
Usage: 'he *boxed* her ears' (= struck, slapped).
Word Family: **boxing**, *noun*, the art or sport of a person who boxes.

box (3) *noun*
a small evergreen tree, often used for ornamental hedging and having hard, fine-grained timber.
[Latin *buxus*]

boxcar *noun*
American: a large, enclosed and covered railway freight van.

boxer *noun*
1. a person who boxes, especially in competitions.
2. any of a breed of large, short-haired dogs of the bulldog type, usually tan or brindled.

Boxing Day
the day after Christmas Day.
[when *money-boxes* were brought around by tradesmen, etc.]

box number
a number given in a newspaper advertisement to which replies are sent.

box office
1. the organization selling tickets in or for a theatre.
2. the likely popularity or financial success of an entertainment.

box seat
the best or most favourable position.

boy *noun*
1. a male child.
2. a male servant in certain African and Asian countries.
Word Family: **boyish**, *adjective*; **boyishly**, *adverb*; **boyhood**, *noun*.

boycott *verb*
to refuse to use or deal with, as a method of protest or threat: 'to *boycott* imported goods'.
Word Family: **boycott**, *noun*.
[after *Captain Boycott*, 1832–97, an English land agent who was boycotted by Irish workers]

boyfriend *noun*
the current chosen companion and escort of a girl or woman.

bra *noun*
short form of **brassière**
a close-fitting support for the breasts.

brace *noun*
1. something which holds parts together or acts as a support, such as the arrangement of wires and bands fitted against teeth to straighten them.
2. (*plural*) the straps worn over the shoulders to hold up trousers.
3. *Grammar:* a mark similar to a single bracket, used to connect a series of lines or words.
4. a pair: 'a *brace* of rabbits'.
brace *verb*
to support, fix or strengthen with or as if with a brace.
Usage: 'she *braced* herself to hear the news' (= prepared, summoned up courage).
Word Family: **bracing**, *adjective*, invigorating.

brace and bit
a drill with a U-shaped crank handle (the **brace**) which turns the bit.

bracelet (*say* **brace-lit**) *noun*
1. a decorative band, chain, etc. worn on the arm.
2. (*informal*, *plural*) handcuffs.

bracer *noun*
1. something which braces.
2. a stimulating drink.

bracken *noun*
a large, coarse fern or clump of ferns.

bracket *noun*
1. a frame-like support for a shelf, rack, etc.
2. either of the marks, [or], used to indicate that the enclosed word, words or figures are to be treated as a separate unit, as in a sentence or a mathematical formula.
3. a grouping or category: 'people in the high income *bracket*'.
Word Family: **bracket**, *verb*, a) to support with a bracket, b) to enclose in or as if in brackets.

brackish *adjective*
slightly salty: '*brackish* water'.

bract *noun*
a leaf-like part at the base of a flower.

brad *noun*
a small, fine nail with little or no head. A **bradawl** is an awl for making small holes to hold nails in wood, etc.

brag *verb*
(**bragged, bragging**)
to boast.
Word Family: **braggart,** *noun,* a person who boasts or brags.

brahmin *noun*
1. any of a breed of cattle with a humped back, bred from Indian zebus.
2. (*capital*) a member of the highest Hindu caste, originally priests.
3. (*informal*) an aloof intellectual.
[Sanskrit *brahman* priest]

braid *noun*
1. a decorative band of fabric made of various woven threads and used for trimming, decoration, etc.
2. a plait.
Word Family: **braid,** *verb,* to weave or plait.

braille (*say* brale) *noun*
(*often capital*) a system of printing for blind people, using raised symbols which are identified by touch.
[invented by *Louis Braille,* 1809–52]

brain *noun*
1. the mass of nerve tissue which controls the functions of the body in most forms of animal life.
2. (*usually plural*) intelligence.
3. (*informal*) an intelligent person.
Phrases:
have something on the brain, to be obsessed or concerned about something.
pick someone's brains, to use someone else's ideas.
brain *verb*
(*informal*) to hit on the head.

brainchild *noun*
plural is **brainchildren**
an original plan or thought.

brain drain
the alleged departure abroad of large numbers of highly qualified professional people in search of higher pay and lower taxation.

brainless *adjective*
stupid or unintelligent.

brains trust
a panel of speakers who answer questions put by the audience, as in the original BBC radio programme of this name.
[nickname given to President Franklin Roosevelt's team of experts]

brainwashing *noun*
a systematic indoctrination to change a person's beliefs or attitudes.
Word Family: **brainwash,** *verb.*

brainwave *noun*
(*informal*) a sudden inspiration.

brainy *adjective*
clever.

braise *verb*
to cook by browning in fat and then stewing with little moisture.

brake (1) *noun*
1. any device for slowing the motion of a wheel, motor or vehicle.
2. (*plural*) the parts which make up such a device or system.
Word Family: **brake,** *verb,* to slow down or stop by or as if by a brake.

brake (2) *noun*
a small area or thicket of dense undergrowth.

brake horsepower
the horsepower developed by an engine measured by the resistance offered by a brake.

bramble *noun*
any coarse prickly shrub, especially the blackberry bush.

bran *noun*
the husks of corn after the flour has been removed.

branch *noun*
1. a division or offshoot of the stem of a tree or other plant.
2. any smaller division or section: a) 'the suburban *branch* of a bank'; b) 'botany is a *branch* of biology'.
Word Family: **branch,** *verb.*

branchiae (*say* **brangki-ee**) *plural noun*
the gills of fish.
[Latin]

brand *noun*
1. a trademark or name used to identify a product: 'which *brand* of soap is best?'.
2. a) something which indicates type, quality, etc., such as a mark burnt onto cattle as a sign of ownership. b) a tool or iron used for branding.
3. a piece of burning wood.
Word Family: **brand,** *verb,* to label accusingly.

brandish *verb*
to wave about: 'to *brandish* a sword'.

brand–new *adjective*
completely new.

brandy *noun*
an alcoholic drink made by distilling wine or fermented fruit juice.
Word Family: **brandy** (**brandied, brandying**), *verb*, to flavour or preserve with brandy.

brash *adjective*
impertinent, rash or bold.

brass (*rhymes with* grass) *noun*
1. any of a large group of malleable, ductile alloys composed of zinc and over 50 per cent copper.
2. something which is made of brass.
3. *Music:* a) any metal instruments, such as trumpets, horns, etc., in which sound is produced by blowing through a mouthpiece. b) the section of an orchestra having these instruments. Compare WOODWIND.
4. (*informal*) a) any important officials, especially military officers. Short form of **top brass**. b) money. c) impudence.
Word Family: **brass,** *adjective.*

brassière (*say* **brassi–air**) *noun*
see BRA.

brass tacks
(*informal*) the basic facts or realities. [slang rhyme with *fax* = facts]

brassy (*say* **bra**–see) *adjective*
1. harsh or metallic: 'a *brassy* noise'.
2. bold or vulgar: 'a *brassy* woman'.

brat *noun*
a child, especially an irritating one.

bravado (*say* bra–**vah**do) *noun*
a display of bravery or courage, especially false bravery.
[Spanish *bravata*]

brave *adjective*
having or displaying courage: 'a *brave* deed'.
brave *noun*
a warrior, especially an American Indian.
brave *verb*
to meet or face courageously.
Word Family: **bravely,** *adverb*; **bravery,** *noun*, a brave spirit or conduct.

bravo (*say* brah–vo) *interjection*
well done! good!

bravura (*say* bra–vewra) *noun*
any daring or brilliant performance. [Italian, bravery]

brawl *noun*
a noisy quarrel or fight.
Word Family: **brawl,** *verb.*

brawn (1) *noun*
muscles, or muscular strength.
Word Family: **brawny,** *adjective*, muscular or strong.

brawn (2) *noun*
boiled and moulded meat made from pig's head chopped up with beef.

bray *noun*
a) the harsh, noisy cry of a donkey.
b) any similar sound.
Word Family: **bray,** *verb.*

braze *verb*
to join metals by drawing a molten metal, usually a brass alloy, between them.

brazen *adjective*
1. bold or shameless.
2. like or made of brass.

brazier (1) *noun*
a person who works with brass.
Word Family: **braze**, *verb*, to make or cover with brass.

brazier (2) *noun*
a metal container for holding burning fuels such as coal.

brazil nut
a large, oily, edible nut.
[originally from *Brazil*, South America]

breach *noun*
1. a break, rupture or gap.
2. the act of breaking: 'a *breach* of promise'.
Word Family: **breach,** *verb.*

bread (*say* bred) *noun*
1. a shaped, baked food made of flour, liquid and yeast or another raising agent.
2. any food or sustenance: 'to earn one's *bread*'.
3. (*informal*) money
bread and butter letter, a letter of thanks for hospitality.
Word Family: **bread**, *verb*, to coat with breadcrumbs.

breadbasket *noun*
(*informal*) the stomach.

breadfruit *noun*
a large, round, tropical fruit commonly used in the Pacific Islands.

breadline *noun*
a subsistence level of living.

breadth (*say* bredth) *noun*
width.
Usage: 'he showed great *breadth* of feeling' (= extent).

breadwinner *noun*
a person who earns the money for a family or household.

break (*rhymes with* cake) *verb*
(broke, broken, breaking)
1. to divide into parts, usually by force: 'the vase *broke* when it fell to the floor'.
2. to interrupt or discontinue: 'to *break* a habit'.
Usages:
a) 'to *break* out of gaol' (= force one's way).
b) 'you *broke* your promise' (= failed to keep).
c) 'his gambling losses finally *broke* him' (= ruined).
d) 'to *break* a world record' (= outdo).
e) 'the ball *broke* as it bounced' (= changed direction).
f) 'to *break* a young horse' (= train).
3. (of a voice, etc.) to change in range or tone.
Phrases:
break down, a) to analyse; b) to cease to function; c) to be overcome physically or emotionally.
break up, a) 'school *breaks up* next week' (= ends, separates); b) 'we *broke up* at the mad sight' (= laughed uncontrollably).
break *noun*
1. the act of breaking.
2. an opening, etc. made by breaking: 'a *break* in the wall'.
Usages:
a) 'the *break* of day' (= beginning).
b) 'a gaol *break*' (= attempt to escape).
c) (*informal*) 'what a lucky *break*!' (= chance).
d) 'morning tea *break*' (= rest).
3. *Billiards:* a series of successful shots.
Word Family: **breakage,** *noun,* a) the act of breaking, b) the amount which is broken.

breakdown *noun*
1. a collapse or failure to function: 'a mental *breakdown*'.
2. an analysis or summary of important points.
3. *Science:* the act of separating into constituent parts.

breaker *noun*
1. a person or thing that breaks.
2. a wave which breaks into foam when it reaches shallow water.

breakfast (*say* **brek**–f'st) *noun*
the first meal of the day.
Word Family: **breakfast,** *verb.*
[Middle English *brek* break + *faste* a fast]

breakneck (*say* **brake**–nek) *adjective*
dangerous.

breakthrough (*say* **brake**–throo) *noun*
any new discovery, development or success which increases progress.

breakwater *noun*
a jetty built out from a beach or river bank, to prevent movement or erosion of the beach.

bream *noun*
plural is **bream**
an edible fish with a compressed body and silvery scales.

breast (*say* brest) *noun*
1. *Anatomy:* a human mammary gland.
2. the chest.
Usage: 'music charmed his savage *breast*' (= mind, mood).
make a clean breast of, to confess.
breast *verb*
to meet or face.

breastbone *noun*
Anatomy: see STERNUM.

breastfeed *verb*
(breastfed, breastfeeding)
to feed a baby by allowing it to suck milk from the nipple of a woman's breast.

breastplate *noun*
1. a piece of armour covering the chest.
2. the part of a harness which crosses the horse's chest.

breast stroke
Swimming: a style in which the swimmer lies face–down in the water with both arms extended forward and pulls them out sideways in horizontal arcs.

breath (*say* breth) *noun*
1. the air that is taken in and given out during respiration.
2. the act of taking in and giving out such air: 'take a deep *breath*'.
3. the smallest amount of something: 'there was not a *breath* of wind'.
Phrases:
below, under one's breath, in a whisper.
in the same breath, at the same time.
out of breath, unable to breathe freely.
take one's breath away, to astonish.
Word Family: **breathless,** *adjective,* a) out of breath, b) holding the breath, as in fear, excitement, etc.

breathalyser (*say* **bretha**–lize–a) *noun*
an instrument which measures the amount of alcohol in exhaled breath.

breathe (*say* bree*th*) *verb*
to take in and give out air.

Usages:
a) 'now we can *breathe* freely again' (= relax).
b) 'don't *breathe* a word about what I've said' (= disclose).
Word Family: **breather,** *noun,* a) a person who breathes; b) (informal) a pause or rest.

breathtaking *adjective*
inspiring awe and admiration: 'the view was *breathtaking*'.

bred *verb*
the past tense and past participle of the verb **breed.**

breech *noun*
the lower or rear part of something, such as the part of a gun behind the barrel.

breech birth
a birth in which the baby's buttocks appear first.

breeches (*say* **britchiz**) *plural noun*
a pair of trousers, especially ones reaching to or just below the knee.

breed *verb*
(bred, breeding)
1. to produce offspring: 'many animals *breed* in the spring'.
2. to produce and raise crops, livestock, etc.: 'to *breed* bantams'.
Usages:
a) 'he was born and *bred* in England' (= brought up, educated).
b) 'hatred *breeds* violence' (= causes).
breed *noun*
a group of animals within a species, which has a common origin: 'a *breed* of dog'.
Usage: 'a rare *breed* of courage' (= kind, sort).
Word Family: **breeder,** *noun.*

breeder reactor
short form is **breeder**
a nuclear reactor which produces more fissile material than it consumes in converting uranium to plutonium.

breeze *noun*
a light, steady wind.
breeze *verb*
to move lightly and easily: 'he *breezed* gaily into the party'.
Word Family: **breezily,** *adverb*; **breezy,** *adjective*; **breeziness,** *noun.*

bren gun
a light machine-gun.
[from BR(no) in Czechoslovakia where originally made + EN(field) where made in England]

brethren (*say* **bre*th*-rin**) *noun*
an old plural of **brother.**

breve (*say* breev) *noun*
Music: the longest note, equal to two whole notes.

brevet rank (*say* **brevvit** rank)
a one-step higher rank without higher pay: 'he was promoted *brevet* colonel for outstanding service in Korea'.
[French, a commission]

breviary (*say* **breev**-ya-ree) *noun*
Roman Catholic: a book containing the services for each day.
[Latin *breviarium* a summary]

brevity *noun*
the fact of being short or brief.
[Latin *brevis* short]

brew (*say* broo) *verb*
to make a drink by soaking, boiling or fermenting: 'to *brew* beer'.
Usage: 'there is trouble *brewing* between the unions' (= forming).
brew *noun*
a drink made by brewing.
Usage: 'he is a strange *brew* of kindness and egotism' (= mixture).
Word Family: **brewer,** *noun,* a person who brews; **brewery,** *noun,* a place where beer and similar drinks are brewed.

briar *noun*
see BRIER.

bribe *noun*
anything offered or given to persuade a person to do something, usually dishonest: 'the judge was offered several *bribes* to acquit the politician'.
Word Family: **bribe,** *verb*; **bribery,** *noun.*

bric-a-brac, bric-à-brac *noun*
any odd items of furniture, jewellery or ornaments of decorative or antique interest.
[Old French *à bric et à brac* at random]

brick *noun*
1. a block made of baked clay or a similar substance, used to build walls, etc.
2. any shaped block of a substance: 'a *brick* of vanilla ice-cream'.
3. (*informal*) a kind or generous person.
drop a brick, to make a clumsy or indiscreet mistake.
Word Family: **brick,** *verb,* to fit, enclose or build with bricks.

bricklayer *noun*
a person whose work is to build structures with bricks.

bride *noun*
a woman who is about to be or is newly married.
Word Family: **bridal**, *adjective*, relating to a bride or wedding.

bridegroom *noun*
see GROOM.

bridesmaid *noun*
an unmarried woman who attends the bride at a wedding.

bridge (1) *noun*
1. any structure built over and across something, usually to provide passage: 'a wooden *bridge* across the river'.
2. something which has the shape or function of a bridge, such as a thin support for the strings of a musical instrument.
3. *Anatomy:* the bony, upper line of the nose.
4. an artificial tooth or teeth, usually supported on either side by the natural teeth.
5. a raised platform over the deck of a ship, used by the captain or officers.
Word Family: **bridge**, *verb*, to cross or extend across.

bridge (2) *noun*
a card game for four players in which one pair attempts to win the number of rounds specified by bids. In **auction bridge** all tricks won count towards the score but in **contract bridge** only the winning tricks which were bid for count towards the game.

bridgehead *noun*
a fortified area established in enemy territory, especially on the enemy side of a river, etc.

bridle *noun*
1. an arrangement of leather strips, with a bit and reins, fitted around the head of a horse to guide or control it.
2. any device used to restrain or control, such as a cable used to limit movement of machine parts.
bridle *verb*
to put a bridle on.
Usages:
a) 'you must *bridle* your resentment' (= control).
b) 'she *bridled* with indignation at the remarks' (= drew back in pride and scorn).

bridlepath *noun*
a path or track for horses.

brief (*say* breef) *adjective*
short: a) 'a *brief* weather forecast'; b) 'a *brief* skirt'.
brief *noun*
1. any outline or instructions given concerning a project, duty, etc., e.g. to a barrister concerning a case.
2. (*plural*) short underpants.
in brief, 'here is today's news *in brief*' (= in a few words).
Word Family: **brief**, *verb*, to give a briefing to; **briefly**, *adverb*; **briefness**, *noun*.
[Latin *brevis* short]

briefcase *noun*
a case, often leather, for carrying books, papers, etc.

briefing *noun*
any instructions, especially those given to a military unit before an operation.

brier, briar *noun*
1. a European shrub with a hard, woody root used in making tobacco pipes.
2. any prickly bush, especially a rosebush.

brigade *noun*
1. an organized group of people, usually in uniform, who perform special duties: 'a fire *brigade*'.
2. *Military:* a tactical army unit consisting of three battalions or armoured units.
[Italian *brigata* a troop]

brigadier (*say* brigga-**deer**) *noun*
a commissioned officer in the army ranking between a colonel and a major general.

brigand (*say* **brigg**and) *noun*
a bandit or robber.
Word Family: **brigandage**, *noun*.

bright *adjective*
shining or giving out much light: 'a *bright* star'.
Usages:
a) 'a *bright* smile' (= cheerful).
b) '*bright* red' (= vivid).
c) 'a *bright* pupil' (= clever).
brighten *verb*
to make more bright or cheerful: 'sunlight *brightened* the room'.
Word Family: **brightly**, *adverb*; **brightness**, *noun*.

brill *noun*
an edible European flatfish resembling and related to the turbot.

brilliant *adjective*
very bright or sparkling: '*brilliant* sunshine'.
Usages:
a) 'it was a *brilliant* victory' (= distinguished, admirable).

b) 'he is *brilliant* at maths' (=very clever).
brilliant *noun*
a cut diamond or other gem which sparkles.
Word Family: **brilliance,** *noun*; **brilliantly,** *adverb.*

brim *noun*
the upper or outer edge of anything: 'the *brim* of a hat'.
brim *verb*
(brimmed, brimming)
to be full to overflowing: 'her eyes *brimmed* with tears'.
Word Family: **brimfull,** *adjective,* completely full.

brimstone *noun*
an old word for sulphur.

brindle *noun*
a) a brownish-grey colour with darker streaks or spots. b) an animal of this colour.
Word Family: **brindled, brindle,** *adjectives.*

brine *noun*
1. water which contains or is saturated with salt, used for preserving meat, etc.
2. the sea.
Word Family: **briny,** *adjective*; **briny,** *noun,* (informal) the sea; **brine,** *verb,* to treat or pickle in brine.

bring *verb*
(brought, bringing)
a) to cause to come with oneself: 'do *bring* a friend to the party'. b) to cause to come: 'what *brought* that to mind?'.
Usages:
a) 'I could not *bring* myself to do it' (= persuade, make).
b) 'the house *brought* a good price' (= sold for).
Phrases:
bring about, 'what *brought about* the accident?' (= caused).
bring off, 'how on earth did you *bring* it *off*?' (= do successfully).
bring on, 'the drinking spree *brought on* a gout attack' (= caused).
bring round, bring to, a) to restore to consciousness; b) to convince.
bring up, a) to raise or educate; b) 'do not *bring up* that subject' (= mention); c) to vomit.

brink *noun*
the very edge: 'the *brink* of a cliff'.

brinkmanship *noun*
the practice of tempting disaster or danger to achieve one's aims.

briquette (*say* briket) **briquet** *noun*
a small block of compressed coal dust, used for fuel.
[French, a small brick]

brisk *adjective*
quick or lively: 'a *brisk* walk'.
Word Family: **briskly,** *adverb*; **briskness,** *noun.*

brisket *noun*
the breast of an animal, especially a cut of meat containing this part.

bristle (*say* **briss'l**) *noun*
any short, coarse, stiff hair.
bristle *verb*
to stand on end like a bristle: 'her hair *bristled*'.
Usages:
a) 'mother *bristled* at the suggestion' (= reacted in horror and anger).
b) 'the house *bristled* with police' (= was full of).
Word Family: **bristly** (*say* **briss-lee**), *adjective,* like or covered with bristles.

British thermal unit
a unit of energy, equal to about 1060 joule. See UNITS in grey pages.

Briton *noun*
an inhabitant of Britain, especially ancient Britain.

brittle *adjective*
hard but fragile and easily broken: 'a *brittle* glass'.
Usages:
a) 'a *brittle* temper' (= difficult to deal with).
b) 'a *brittle* smile' (= false).
brittle *noun*
a sweet made of burnt sugar, nuts, etc.: 'peanut *brittle*'
Word Family: **brittleness,** *noun.*

broach (*rhymes with* coach) *verb*
1. to begin to talk about: 'please do not *broach* the subject again'.
2. to pierce, especially to draw liquid out of a cask.
broach *noun*
a long, tapered tool, e.g. for making holes larger.

broad (*say* brawd) *adjective*
wide or large: a) 'a *broad* smile'; b) 'a person of *broad* experience'.
Usages:
a) 'in *broad* daylight' (= full, complete).
b) 'a *broad* outline' (= general).
c) 'a *broad* hint' (= obvious).
d) 'a *broad* Australian accent' (= strong).
e) '*broad* jokes' (= crude).

broad *noun*
American: (*informal*) a girl or woman.
Word Family: **broadly,** *adverb*; **broaden,** *verb.*

broad bean
a variety of bean with large, flat edible seeds and a thick pod.

broadcast *verb*
(**broadcast** or **broadcasted, broadcasting**)
to send out by television or radio: 'all stations *broadcast* the news at 7 o'clock'.
Usage: 'please do not *broadcast* the secret' (= spread).
broadcast *noun*
any programme which is sent out by television or radio.

broad-minded *adjective*
having an open or tolerant mind: 'in spite of her strict upbringing she is *broad-minded* about most things'.
Word Family: **broad-mindedly,** *adverb*; **broad-mindedness,** *noun.*

broadsheet *noun*
a large, single sheet of paper, originally having a ballad or song printed on one side.

broadside *noun*
1. a) the whole side of a ship which is above the waterline. b) all the guns on one side of a ship. c) the simultaneous firing of all these guns. **2.** a strong verbal attack.

brocade (*say* bro-**kade**) *noun*
a woven cloth, originally of silk, but now of cotton or fibre, patterned with areas of different weaves, giving raised or shiny effects.
Word Family: **brocade,** *verb.*

broccoli (*say* **brokka**-lee) *noun*
a vegetable with tightly bunched green heads, resembling a cauliflower.
[Italian, cabbage-tops]

brochure (*say* **bro**-sher) *noun*
a booklet or commercial pamphlet.

brogue (*rhymes with* rogue) *noun*
1. a strong leather shoe with small decorative holes on the upper surface.
2. a soft accent, especially Irish.
[Irish *brog* shoe]

broil (1) *verb*
to grill.
[Old French *bruler* to burn]

broil (2) *noun*
an old word for a loud quarrel or brawl.
[Old French *brouiller* disorder]

broiler chicken
a three-month old chicken prepared for sautéing or broiling.

broke *verb*
the past tense of the verb **break.**
broke *adjective*
(*informal*) having no money.

broken *verb*
the past participle of the verb **break.**

broker *noun*
a person who buys and sells goods or securities, on behalf of others, for a commission.
brokerage *noun*
the commission charged by a broker.

brolly *noun*
(*informal*) an umbrella.

bromide (*say* **bro**-mide) *noun*
1. *Chemistry:* a salt containing the univalent Br^- ion, sometimes used as a sedative.
2. *Photography:* a print made on paper containing light-sensitive silver bromide.
3. (*informal*) a boring observation.

bromine (*say* **bro**-meen) *noun*
element number 35, a dark red, fuming, poisonous, non-metal liquid with a choking, irritating smell, used in making organic chemicals. Its compounds are used in photography and medicine. See HALOGEN.
See CHEMICAL ELEMENTS in grey pages.
[Greek *bromos* stench]

bronchi (*say* **bron**-kee) *plural noun*
see BRONCHUS.

bronchial (*say* **bron**kiul) *adjective*
Word Family: see BRONCHUS.

bronchial tube
a bronchus or any of its branches.

bronchiole (*say* **bron**ki-ole) *noun*
Anatomy: any of the numerous, fine, tube-like extensions of a bronchus.

bronchitis (*say* bron-**kie**-tis) *noun*
an inflammation of the membranes lining the bronchial tubes.
[BRONCH(us) + -ITIS]

bronchus (*say* **bron**kus) *noun*
plural is **bronchi**
Anatomy: either of the two branched tubes of the trachea leading to the lungs.
Word Family: **bronchial,** *adjective.*
[Latin]

bronco (*say* bronko) *noun*
also spelt **broncho**

a horse which has not been broken in.
[Spanish, rough or wild]

brontosaurus (*say* bronta–**sawrus**)
noun
a long–extinct, plant–eating reptile, one of the largest animals ever known.
[Greek *bronté* thunder + *sauros* lizard]

bronze *noun*
1. any of a group of alloys of copper (more than 80 per cent) and other metals such as tin or aluminium.
2. any object, such as a statue, made from bronze.
3. a lustrous, yellowish or reddish–brown colour.
bronze *verb*
to provide with a bronze or bronze–like surface.
Usage: 'her skin was *bronzed* during her summer holiday' (= deeply suntanned).

Bronze Age
a period in man's history between the Stone Age and the Iron Age, when tools and weapons were first made of bronze.

brooch (*rhymes with* coach) *noun*
a decorative clasp which fastens by a pin at the back.

brood *noun*
a group of young animals, especially birds, hatched at the same time.
brood *verb*
1. (of birds) to sit over eggs or young offspring.
2. to dwell moodily on something: 'the prisoner *brooded* on his fate'.
Word Family: **broody**, **brooding**, *adjectives*; **broodily**, *adverb*.

brook (1) (*rhymes with* book) *noun*
a small stream.

brook (2) (*rhymes with* book) *verb*
to put up with: 'he is a stern man who will *brook* no opposition'.

broom *noun*
1. a long–handled brush for sweeping floors.
2. a European shrub with small leaves and yellow flowers.

broomstick *noun*
the handle of a broom.

broth *noun*
a thin soup made with meat, fish or vegetable juices.

brothel *noun*
a place where prostitutes work.

brother (*say* **bru***tha*) *noun*
plural is **brothers** or **brethren**
1. a son of the same parents as another child (a **full brother**), or having only one parent the same as another child (a **half–brother**).
2. any person who has a close bond with another: 'he is a *brother* to them'.
3. a man belonging to a religious order, who has not taken vows or who is not a priest.
Word Family: **brotherly**, *adjective*; **brotherhood**, **brotherliness**, *nouns*.

brother–in–law *noun*
plural is **brothers–in–law**
1. the brother of one's husband or wife.
2. the husband of one's sister.
3. the husband of a husband's or wife's sister.

brougham (*say* **broo**–um) *noun*
an enclosed, four–wheeled, box–like carriage for two or four passengers and with the driver's seat outside.
[after *Lord Brougham*, 1778–1868, a British statesman]

brought (*say* brawt) *verb*
the past tense and past participle of the verb **bring**.

brouhaha (*say* **broo**–ha–ha) *noun*
a hubbub or uproar.
[French, imitating the confused noise of a marketplace]

brow (*rhymes with* cow) *noun*
a) the ridge above the eye. b) the eyebrow. c) the forehead.
Usage: 'we rowed the boat under the *brow* of a cliff' (= overhanging edge).

browbeat *verb*
to bully or domineer: 'they tried to *browbeat* him into signing the contract'.

brown *noun*
a dark colour formed by mixing such colours as red, black and yellow.
Word Family: **brown**, *adjective*; **brown**, *verb*; **brownness**, *noun*.

brown ale
a bottled beer which is milder and sweeter than pale ale, having fewer hops, but may be as strong.

brown coal
also called **lignite**
a brownish–black natural deposit consisting of carbon and various carbon compounds, formed by the decomposition of vegetable matter over millions of years, but of more recent origin than black coal, and used in fuel such as briquettes.

browned–off *adjective*
(*informal*) bored or fed–up.

brownie *noun*
1. *Folklore:* a small, friendly elf or goblin.
2. (*capital*) an early, inexpensive box camera.
3. *American:* a small flat chocolate cake with nuts.

brown study
a deep absorption in thought.

browse (*rhymes with* cows) *verb*
1. (of animals) to graze or nibble on grass.
2. to glance or look at random: '*browsing* in a bookshop'.
Word Family: **browse**, *noun.*

brucellosis (*say* broosa–**lo**–sis) *noun*
also called **Malta fever** or **undulant fever**
a bacterial disease of cattle, pigs and goats, occasionally transmitted to man.
[after *Sir David Bruce*, 1855–1931, a Scottish physician]

bruise (*say* brooz) *noun*
also called a **contusion**
a discoloured area on skin, due to an injury which did not break the skin but damaged the underlying blood vessels.
bruise *verb*
to cause or develop a bruise: 'the fall *bruised* her leg'.
Usage: 'his feelings are easily *bruised*' (= hurt).
Word Family: **bruiser**, *noun*, (informal) a strong or tough person.

brunch *noun*
(*informal*) a midmorning meal which replaces breakfast and lunch.
[BR(eakfast) + (l)UNCH]

brunette (*say* broo–**net**) *adjective*
(of hair or eyes) dark, especially dark brown.
Word Family: **brunette**, *noun*, a woman with dark hair or eyes.

brunt *noun*
the main strength or force of something: 'the *brunt* of his argument occurs in the last chapter'.

brush (1) *noun*
1. an object used for painting, smoothing the hair, sweeping, etc. usually made of hair or bristles set into a solid base.
2. the bushy tail of an animal, especially a fox.
3. a short fight or hostile encounter: 'the demonstrators had a *brush* with the police'.
4. *Electricity:* a block, usually of carbon or copper, allowing electricity to flow between the moving and stationary parts of an electric motor or generator.
brush *verb*
1. a) to use a brush on: 'she vigorously *brushed* her hair'. b) to sweep or touch as if with a brush: 'his objections were *brushed* aside'.
2. to touch lightly in passing: 'he *brushed* past the staring children'.
Phrases:
brush off, 'she tried to *brush* him *off*' (= dismiss). *Word Family*: **brush–off,** *noun.*
brush up, a) 'I must *brush up* before we go' (= smarten up); b) 'you should *brush up* your French before going to Paris' (= revise).

brush (2) *noun*
a dense growth of bushes or shrubs.

brusque (*say* broosk) *adjective*
blunt or abrupt in speech or manner: 'his *brusque* reply provided little information'.
Word Family: **brusquely**, *adverb*; **brusqueness**, *noun.*
[Italian *brusco* sour]

brussels sprout
(*sometimes capital*) a small, green vegetable like a tiny cabbage–head, growing in clusters on the stalk of a variety of cabbage.

brut (*rhymes with* hoot) *adjective*
(of wine or champagne) very dry.
[French]

brutal (*say* **broo**t'l) *adjective*
savage or cruel: 'it was a *brutal* attack'.
brutality (*say* broo–**talli**–tee) *noun*
a) the act of being brutal: 'it was an act of great *brutality*'. b) a brutal act: 'whipping is an old–fashioned *brutality*'.
Word Family: **brutally**, *adverb*; **brutalize, brutalise**, *verb*, to make or become brutal.

brute *noun*
1. any four–legged animal or beast.
2. a strong or cruel person.
Word Family: **brute**, **brutish**, *adjectives*, a) animal–like, b) very strong.
[Latin *brutus* dull, stupid]

bubble *noun*
1. a small ball of gas in or rising through a liquid.
2. a light, transparent ball of liquid containing gas.
3. anything which is fragile or temporary: 'the *bubble* of his hopes was violently shattered'.

bubble *verb*
to rise in or make the sound of bubbles: 'the stew *bubbled* on the stove'.
Usage: 'the children were *bubbling* with excitement' (= active, vigorous).

bubble-and-squeak *noun*
any left-over vegetables or meat fried together, especially cabbage and potato.

bubblegum *noun*
a chewing gum which can be blown into bubbles.

bubbly *adjective*
like or containing bubbles.
bubbly *noun*
(*informal*) champagne.

bubonic plague (*say* **bew-bonnik** plague)
an often fatal infectious, bacterial disease causing swelling of the lymph glands, chills and fevers.
[Greek *boubon* groin]

buccal (*say* **bukk**'l) *adjective*
of or relating to the cheeks or mouth.
[Latin *bucca* cheek]

buccaneer (*say* bukka-**neer**) *noun*
1. any pirate or bold adventurer.
2. *History:* a pirate of Spanish and American ships, especially in the 17th and 18th centuries.
Word Family: **buccaneer**, *verb.*
[French *boucanier* to barbecue]

buck (1) *noun*
1. a male deer, rabbit, etc. Compare DOE.
2. a young man: 'a *buck's* party'.
3. (*informal*) a dollar.

buck (2) *verb*
short form of **buckjump**
(of an animal) to leap in the air with its head down, back arched and all four feet off the ground.
buck up, a) '*buck up* or we'll be late' (= hurry); b) 'she *bucked up* greatly after we gave her an ice-cream' (= cheered up).

buck (3) *noun*
pass the buck, to shift responsibility or blame on to another person.

buckboard *noun*
American: a light, four-wheeled, horse-drawn carriage with a thin board instead of springs.

bucket *noun*
a flat-bottomed container, usually round, for holding or carrying liquids.
kick the bucket, (*informal*) to die.

bucket seat
a seat for one person in a motor vehicle, etc., slightly curved to give support at the sides.

buckle *noun*
1. a clasp with a movable pin set in a frame through which a strap is passed and held in place by the pin, e.g. on a belt.
2. a bend or kink in anything.
buckle *verb*
1. to fasten with a buckle.
2. to bend or give way suddenly owing to pressure, heat, etc.
buckle down, 'we must *buckle down* to work now' (= set to).

buckler *noun*
a small round shield.

buckram (*say* **buk**-r'm) *noun*
a stiff, cotton fabric used for interlining, binding books, etc.

buckshot *noun*
a large size of lead shot used for hunting big game.

buckskin *noun*
1. a soft, pale leather formerly made from deerskin but now made from sheepskin.
2. *American:* see DUN (2).

buckteeth *plural noun*
any projecting teeth.

bucolic (*say* bew-**kollik**) *adjective*
of rural life or the country.

bud (1) *noun*
1. *Biology:* a) a tightly folded undeveloped shoot of a plant. b) a subsidiary growth from a simple animal, such as a hydra or yeast cell, which forms another individual.
2. any small or undeveloped thing.
nip in the bud, to stop something before it has really started or developed.
bud *verb*
(**budded, budding**)
1. to produce buds.
Usage: 'his talent is just beginning to *bud*' (= develop).
2. to graft a single bud onto a plant.

bud (2) *noun*
(*informal*) a brother or man.

Buddhism (*say* **bud**-izm) *noun*
a religion stressing that human existence is pain, caused by desire, which may be overcome by contemplation and a right way of life. See NIRVANA.
Word Family: **Buddhist**, *adjective, noun.*

[Sanskrit *Buddha* the enlightened one, the title given to a 6th–century B.C. Indian teacher on whose ideas Buddhism is based]

buddleia (*say* **bud**–lee–a) ***noun***
any of a small group of shrubs, typically with spikes of scented mauve or yellow flowers.
[after *Adam Buddle*, died 1715, an English botanist]

buddy ***noun***
(*informal*) a friend.

budge ***verb***
to move or give way slightly.

budgerigar (*say* **buj**–a–re–gar) ***noun***
also called a **love–bird**
a) a small, green Australian parrot living in open country. b) a bird of this species kept as a pet, with specially bred colours, usually blue, yellow or white.
[Aboriginal *budgeri* good + *gar* or *kaar* cockatoo]

budget (*say* **buj**–it) ***noun***
1. a plan or summary giving details of expected income and expenditure.
2. the sum of money allotted for a particular purpose: 'the film was made on a very small *budget*'.
Word Family: **budget**, *verb*, to plan the use of money in advance.

budgie ***noun***
(*informal*) a budgerigar.

buff ***noun***
1. a pale brownish–yellow colour.
2. a thick, light, brownish–yellow leather, first made from buffalo skins, used for belts, etc.
3. (*informal*) a) the bare skin. b) an enthusiast: 'a film *buff*'.
buff ***verb***
to polish or shine.
Word Family: **buff**, *adjective*.

buffalo (*say* **buff**a–lo) ***noun***
plural is **buffaloes** or **buffalo**
1. any of various large–hoofed, African and Asian mammals, like oxen, with broad, flat horns which curve downwards.
2. *American:* a bison.

buffer (1) ***noun***
1. anything which absorbs or neutralizes shock, especially between opposing forces, such as a projecting bumper bar on the end of a railway vehicle.
2. *Chemistry:* a solution whose acidity or alkalinity tends to remain unchanged on dilution or on the addition of acid or alkali.
Word Family: **buffer**, *verb*.

buffer (2) ***noun***
1. any object or device used for polishing.
2. a silly old man.

buffet (1) (*say* **buff**et) ***verb***
to strike or knock.
Usage: 'the plane was *buffeted* about by strong winds' (= tossed, shaken).
Word Family: **buffet**, *noun*.

buffet (2) (*say* b**uff**ay *or* **buff**ay) ***noun***
1. a sideboard.
2. an informal meal at which guests stand and serve themselves.
3. a refreshment bar at a railway station or on a train.
[Old French *bufet* a stool]

buffoon ***noun***
a person who stupidly acts the fool.
Word Family: **buffoonery**, *noun*.
[Italian *buffone* jester]

bug ***noun***
1. any insect.
2. (*informal*) a) an infection. b) a defect or difficulty. c) something, especially an idea, with which one is obsessed.
3. a hidden microphone used to record other peoples' conversations secretly.
Word Family: **bug** (**bugged, bugging**), *verb*, a) (informal) to irritate, b) to install or use a hidden microphone.

bugbear ***noun***
anything which causes needless fear, irritation, etc.

bugger ***noun***
1. a person who has anal intercourse with people or sexual intercourse with animals.
2. (*informal, use is often derogatory*) a person: 'you silly *bugger*, why did you break that glass?'.
Word Family: **bugger**, *verb*; **buggery**, *noun*.

buggy ***noun***
a light, four–wheeled passenger vehicle pulled by one or two horses.

bugle (*say* **bewg**'l) ***noun***
Music: a simple brass, wind instrument used by armies to signal movements, etc.
Word Family: **bugler**, *noun*.

build (*say* bild) ***verb***
(**built, building**)
to join or assemble parts to make a whole structure.

Usages:
a) 'he has *built* his business from nothing' (= established, developed).
b) 'do not *build* any hopes on his promises' (= base, form).
Word Family: **build,** *noun,* the form in which something is made; **builder,** *noun,* a person who builds or makes things.

building *noun*
anything which is built or constructed, especially for a particular use, such as a house, office, etc.

building society
a business organization which lends money to people buying or building houses, etc. and offers interest to those investing in the company.

build-up *noun*
1. any progressive increase, e.g. of military troops for a particular battle.
2. a flattering description or campaign on behalf of a person.

built (*say* bilt) *verb*
the past tense and past participle of the verb **build**.

built-up area
any length of road with street lights, dense housing, etc. along which speed restrictions are enforced.

bulb *noun*
1. *Biology:* a) a modified bud of a plant, usually underground, which is an organ of vegetative reproduction. b) a plant which is grown from a bulb, such as an onion.
2. a rounded or pear-shaped object: 'an electric light *bulb*'.
Word Family: **bulbous,** *adjective,* having the bulging or rounded shape of a bulb.
[Greek *bolbos* onion]

bulge (*say* bulj) *noun*
a rounded swelling or part.
Word Family: **bulge,** *verb.*
[Latin *bulga* bag]

bulk *noun*
the size or volume of anything.
Usage: 'the *bulk* of his work is in country districts' (= main amount).
in bulk, a) in large quantities; b) not packaged.
Word Family: **bulky,** *adjective,* very large or awkward; **bulkiness,** *noun.*

bulkhead *noun*
a) a partition or wall in a boat. b) any partition designed to withstand pressure.

bull (1) (*say* bull) *noun*
1. a) any uncastrated, male, bovine mammal, especially of beef or dairy cattle. b) the male of various other mammals, especially the elephant. Compare cow (1).
2. *Astrology:* (*capital*) see TAURUS.
3. (*informal*) anything considered to be nonsense.
4. *Stock Exchange:* a person who buys, for future delivery, shares he hopes to sell at a profit before he has to take delivery. Compare BEAR (2).

bull (2) (*say* bull) *noun*
a formal letter or instruction from the Pope, containing his official seal.

bulldog *noun*
any of a breed of low, sturdy, short-haired dogs, originally bred in England for baiting bulls.

bulldog clip
a large clip operated by a spring.

bulldozer *noun*
a powerful tractor with a vertical blade at the front for moving earth, etc.
Word Family: **bulldoze,** *verb,* a) to use a bulldozer, b) to bully or intimidate.

bullet (*say* **bull**-it) *noun*
a small cylindrical projectile fired from a rifle, pistol, etc.

bulletin (*say* **bull**-a-tin) *noun*
1. a public statement giving news or a report.
2. a magazine, especially of a society or organization.
[French, a daily or official report]

bullfight *noun*
a ritual, fighting sport between a man and a bull, held in an arena.
Word Family: **bullfighter,** *noun,* a person trained to bullfight; **bullfighting,** *noun.*

bullfinch *noun*
a vividly coloured finch, beautiful but a garden pest.

bullfrog *noun*
a large frog with a very deep voice.

bull-headed *adjective*
very obstinate or determined.

bullion (*say* **bull**-y'n) *noun*
1. any mass or large quantity of gold or silver, especially in bars, etc.
2. a twisted cord fringe, especially one of fine gold or silver wire.

bullock *noun*
also called a **steer**
a castrated bull reared for beef.

bullring *noun*
an arena for bullfights.

bullroarer *noun*
a piece of wood on a string which makes a loud noise when whirled around, used in religious rites by pre-literate tribes and as a toy by children.

bull's-eye *noun*
a) the centre of a target. b) a shot which hits it.

bullshit *noun*
(*informal*) any meaningless nonsense.

bull terrier
a crossbreed of bulldog and terrier, thickset and short-haired.

bully (1) (*rhymes with* woolly) *noun*
a person who takes pleasure in hurting or intimidating weaker people.
bully *interjection*
(*informal*) very good or excellent: '*bully* for you!'.
Word Family: **bully (bullied, bullying)**, *verb.*

bully (2) (*rhymes with* woolly) *noun*
short form of **bully-off**
Hockey: the start or restart of a game, where two players, with the ball between them, must alternately tap the ground and each other's stick three times before trying to hit the ball.
Word Family: **bully (bullied, bullying)**, *verb.*

bully beef
any pressed tinned beef.

bulrush (*say* **bull**-rush) *noun*
any of a group of large reeds found in swampy areas. The leaves are used to make mats, etc.

bulwark (*say* **bull**-work) *noun*
1. a mound or wall of earth used as protection.
2. anything used for defence or protection: 'the police force is a *bulwark* of society'.
3. (*usually plural*) the part of a ship's side which extends above the deck.

bum *noun*
(*informal*) a) the buttocks. b) a lazy or worthless person.
Word Family: **bum**, *adjective,* of poor quality; **bum (bummed, bumming)**, *verb,* a) to lead a lazy or worthless life, b) to cadge.

bumble *verb*
to act or speak in a clumsy way: 'she *bumbled* nervously through the speech'.
Word Family: **bumble**, *noun.*

bumblebee *noun*
any of a group of large bees with a loud buzz.

bump *verb*
1. to strike or collide with: 'the car *bumped* into the fence'.
2. to move with jolts or jerks: 'the motorcycle *bumped* over the paddock'.
Phrases:
bump off, (*informal*) to kill.
bump up, 'they've *bumped* the prices *up* again' (= increased).
bump *noun*
a) the act or sound of bumping: 'there was a loud *bump* as she fell off the chair'. b) the raised mark left by a collision or blow: 'a large *bump* on her forehead'.
Word Family: **bumpy**, *adjective.*

bumper (1) *adjective*
unusually large or full: 'a *bumper* crop of tomatoes'.

bumper (2) *noun*
a horizontal rounded bar at the front of a motor vehicle, to protect the body in collisions.

bumpkin *noun*
an awkward, rustic or unsophisticated person.

bumptious (*say* **bump**shus) *adjective*
unpleasantly conceited: 'an annoyingly *bumptious* young man'.
Word Family: **bumptiously**, *adverb*; **bumptiousness**, *noun.*

bun *noun*
1. a type of sweet, bread roll, usually round and containing spices or fruit.
2. a long bunch of hair wound into a bun shape on the head.

bunch *noun*
a group of things attached or collected together: a) 'a *bunch* of grapes'; b) 'a nice *bunch* of people'.
Word Family: **bunch**, *verb,* to form into bunches or folds; **bunchy**, *adjective.*

bundle *noun*
1. a number of things fastened or carried together: 'a *bundle* of firewood'.
2. *Biology:* a group of longitudinal strands of cells which carry material in a plant, or give it support.
bundle *verb*
to carry or tie in a bundle: '*bundle* these parcels together'.
Usage: 'the money was *bundled* into a sack' (= put hastily).
Phrases:
bundle away, bundle off, to send or go away in a hurry.

bundle up, a) to gather up hastily; b) to dress warmly.

bung *noun*
a stopper for closing a hole in a barrel, etc.
Word Family: **bung**, *verb*, to block or close with or as if with a bung.

bungalow (*say* **bunga**–lo) *noun*
a single-storey dwelling.
[Hindi *bangla* of Bengal]

bungle *verb*
to do something clumsily or without success: 'you have *bungled* the job'.
Word Family: **bungle**, *noun*, a bungled attempt; **bungler**, *noun*; **bunglingly**, *adverb*.

bunion (*say* **bun**–y'n) *noun*
a swelling at the base of the big toe due to an inflammation of a bursa.

bunk (1) *noun*
a) a simple bed, often built-in and having another bed set above it. b) any bed.

bunk (2) *noun*
bunkum.

bunk (3) *noun*
do a bunk, (*informal*) 'the culprits had *done a bunk* and could not be found' (= run away).

bunker (1) *noun*
1. a large container, such as a coal compartment on a ship.
2. *Golf:* an obstacle consisting of a pit filled with sand, backed by a grassy ridge.

bunker (2) *noun*
an underground shelter for protection against fires, air-raids, etc.

bunkum *noun*
any meaningless talk or nonsense.
[from a long-winded Congressman, in the 1820s, from *Buncombe County*, America]

bunny *noun*
(*informal*) a rabbit.

Bunsen burner
a gas burner, commonly used in scientific laboratories.
[after *R.W. Bunsen* 1811–99, a German chemist]

bunt *verb*
to push or butt with the horns or head: 'the cow gently *bunted* its calf aside'.
Word Family: **bunt**, *noun*.

bunting *noun*
1. a coarse, open fabric used for flags.
2. a collection of flags.

buoy (*say* boy) *noun*
Nautical: a fixed floating object marking a channel or obstruction in the water, or used as a mark in yacht racing.
buoy *verb*
1. to support or mark with a buoy.
2. to sustain or support: 'she was *buoyed* up by the hope of victory'.

buoyant (*say* **boy**ant) *adjective*
1. able to float: 'the boat remained *buoyant* despite its damage'.
2. lively or cheerful: 'her spirits were *buoyant* when she passed her exams'.
Word Family: **buoyancy**, **buoyance**, *noun*; **buoyantly**, *adverb*.

bur *noun*
see BURR (1).

burble *verb*
to make a gurgling or bubbling sound: 'she *burbled* with excitement at the news'.
Word Family: **burble**, *noun*.

burden *noun*
a heavy or difficult load to carry: 'the *burden* of responsibility is on your shoulders'.
burden of proof, 'the *burden of proof* remains with us' (= duty to prove a claim).
Word Family: **burden**, *verb*; **burdensome**, *adjective*.

burdock *noun*
a roadside wildflower with prickly flower heads and foliage resembling dock leaves.
[BUR(r (1)) + DOCK (4)]

bureau (*say* **bew**–ro) *noun*
plural is **bureaux** or **bureaus**
1. an office or department with particular duties: 'the weather *bureau*'.
2. a writing desk with drawers.
3. *American:* a chest of drawers.
[French, desk or office]

bureaucracy (*say* bew–**rok**ra–see) *noun*
1. any rule by departmental civil servants rather than by elected politicians.
2. any official organization with too much power or having too many rules.
Word Family: **bureaucrat** (*say* **bew**ra–krat), *noun*, a member of the bureaucracy; **bureaucratic** (*say* bewra–**krat**tik), *adjective*, too official or attached to rules; **bureaucratically**, *adverb*.
[BUREAU + Greek *kratia* rule]

burette (*say* bew–ret) *noun*
a graduated glass tube with a tap at the bottom, used for accurate measurement of small amounts of liquid.
[French]

burgeon (*say* berj'n) *verb*
to begin to grow or blossom: 'she *burgeoned* into a beautiful woman'.

burgess (*say* berjiss) *noun*
a citizen, especially one living in a borough.

burgher (*say* berga) *noun*
a person who lives in a town.

burglar *noun*
a person who breaks into a house at night in order to steal.
cat–burglar *noun*
a burglar who enters a house by climbing.
Word Family: **burgle**, *verb*; **burglary**, *noun*, a) the crime of breaking into a house at night in order to steal, b) an instance of this.

burgomaster (*say* burga–mahsta) *noun*
History: the chief magistrate or mayor of a borough or town in certain European countries, such as Holland.
[Dutch *burge* town + *meester* master]

burgundy (*say* berg'n–dee) *noun*
1. any of various rich red or dry white French wines made from grapes grown in Burgundy.
2. a deep bluish–red colour.
[after *Burgundy*, France, where the wine was first made]

burial (*say* **berri**–ul) *noun*
the act or ceremony of burying.

buried (*say* berrid) *verb*
the past tense and past participle of the verb **bury**.

burl *noun*
a small knot or lump in wool or fabric.

burlap *noun*
see HESSIAN.

burlesque (*say* ber–**lesk**) *noun*
any ridiculous parody or caricature.
Word Family: **burlesque**, *verb*.
[Italian *burla* mockery]

burly *adjective*
big and strong: 'a *burly* policeman grabbed his arm'.

burn (1) *verb*
(**burnt** or **burned**, **burning**)
1. to produce, or be on, fire: 'these wet matches will not *burn*'.
2. to injure or mark with extreme heat, cold, chemicals, etc.
Usages:
a) 'this stove *burns* wood' (= uses as fuel).
b) 'he *burnt* with furious indignation at the insult' (= felt strongly, was filled).
c) 'her face *burnt* with embarrassment' (= was hot).
d) 'the lights *burnt* all night in the house' (= were alight).
Phrases:
burn off, to clear land by burning.
burn one's bridges, to commit oneself to a course of action from which there is no turning back.
burn *noun*
any injury produced by extreme heat, cold, chemicals, etc.: 'the victims received bad *burns* in the accident'.

burn (2) *noun*
Scottish: a small stream.

burner reactor
a nuclear reactor which consumes more fissile nuclei than it produces.

burnish *verb*
to polish or make smooth by rubbing, etc.
Word Family: **burnish**, *noun*, a shine or gloss.

burnt sienna
see SIENNA.

burnt umber
see UMBER.

burp *verb*
(*informal*) a) to belch. b) to cause a baby to belch after feeding in order to reduce flatulence.
Word Family: **burp**, *noun*.

burr (1) *noun*
also spelt **bur**
1. *Biology:* a round, prickly case covering the seeds of some plants.
2. a rough edge left on a metal surface caused by cutting or drilling.
Word Family: **burr**, *verb*, to form a rough edge on.

burr (2) *noun*
1. a rough or indistinct pronunciation, especially of the letter *r*.
2. a low or muffled buzzing or whirring sound.
Word Family: **burr**, *verb*.

burrow *noun*
1. a hole made in the ground by a rabbit or similar animal.
2. any snug shelter or place.

burrow *verb*
to dig into.
Usages:
a) 'he *burrowed* into his mother's lap' (= snuggled).
b) 'I *burrowed* into my handbag for some money' (= searched).

bursa *noun*
Anatomy: a sac or pouch, especially near a joint.
Word Family: **bursal**, *adjective*; **bursitis**, *noun*, an inflammation of a bursa.
[Latin, bag, purse]

bursar *noun*
a person who manages the finances in a school or college.
Word Family: **bursarship**, *noun.*

bursary (*say* **bersa-ree**) *noun*
a scholarship given by a school or college.

burst *verb*
(**burst, bursting**)
1. to explode or break open suddenly: 'the balloon *burst* loudly'.
2. to be full to overflowing: a) 'their pockets were *bursting* with chestnuts'; b) 'the children are *bursting* with excitement'.
Usage: 'the children *burst* into the room' (= entered loudly or suddenly).
burst *noun*
1. a sudden or violent explosion: 'there was a *burst* of gunfire and then silence'.
2. a sudden display of energy or activity: 'he cleaned the car in a *burst* of enthusiasm'.

bury (*say* **berree**) *verb*
(**buried, burying**)
1. to place a dead body in a grave, in the sea, etc.
2. to put underground or cover from view: 'the dog has *buried* his bone in the garden'.
Usage: 'she *buried* her face in her hands' (= hid).
bury oneself in, 'the children *buried themselves in* their books' (= gave their attention to).

bus *noun*
1. a public motor vehicle with a long body, containing seats for many passengers. Short form of **omnibus**.
2. (*informal*) any motor vehicle, especially a car or aeroplane.
to miss the bus, to miss an opportunity.
Word Family: **bus** (**bussed, bussing**), *verb*, to transport by bus, especially schoolchildren being educated some distance from their homes for social or racial reasons.

busbar *noun*
Electricity: the group of conductors in a power station, through which power is fed to the distribution network.
[(omni)BUS + BAR]

busby (*say* **buz-bee**) *noun*
a high, fur hat worn by Hussar regiments.

bush (1) (*say* bush) *noun*
1. a small woody shrub with branches which begin near the ground.
2. *Australian, New Zealand, African:* the natural countryside, especially where it is uncleared or uncultivated.
3. any thick clump or growth: 'a *bush* of hair around his head'.
beat about the bush, beat around the bush, to avoid or take too long coming to the point or issue.
Word Family: **bushy**, *adjective.*

bush (2) (*say* bush) *noun*
a cylindrical metal lining, placed in a hole to reduce wear.

bushbaby *noun*
also called a **galago**
a small African and Asian lemur which lives in trees and feeds at night.

bushel (*say* **bush'l**) *noun*
a) a unit of volume for grain, fruit, etc. equal to about 1·28 ft,^{3} or $3{\cdot}64\times10^{-2}$ m^3. A bushel is equal to 4 pecks, 8 gallons or 64 pints. Short form of **imperial bushel**. See UNITS in grey pages. b) (in America) a unit of volume for grain, fruit, etc. equal to about $3{\cdot}53\times10^{-2}$ m^3.
c) a unit of mass equal to the mass of a bushel of a particular substance, which varies depending on the substance being measured.
hide one's light under a bushel, to be modest about one's good qualities or talents.

bushfire *noun*
a fire in uncleared or forest land.

bushman *noun*
1. a person experienced in living in the bush.
2. (*capital*) a) any of a nomadic people inhabiting the extreme south-west of Africa. b) their language.

bushranger *noun*
Australian history: a bandit who hid in the bush, robbing people who passed on the roads.

bush telegraph
1. a system of communication between tribal villages using drumbeats, fires, etc.
2. (*informal*) any line of communication along which rumour spreads.

bushwhacker *noun*
a person used to living in uncleared or remote country.
Word Family: **bushwhack,** *verb,* to live as a bushwhacker.

busily *adverb*
Word Family: see BUSY.

business (*say* **bizniss**) *noun*
1. a person's occupation or work: 'his *business* is selling cars'.
2. any moneymaking organization or institution, such as a shop, factory, etc.: 'he is in the advertising *business*'.
Usages:
a) 'what she does is no longer your *business*' (= affair).
b) 'that robbery was a mysterious *business*' (= event, matter).
c) 'the merchant did good *business* in camels' (= trade).
mean business, 'those boxers look as if they *mean business*' (= are in earnest).
businesslike *adjective*
methodical, efficient and practical: 'for a doctor a *businesslike* approach to death is essential'.

busker *noun*
a street entertainer, especially one who performs for cinema queues, etc.

busman's holiday
a holiday during which one does one's regular work or similar activities, e.g. a housepainter painting his own house.

buss *noun*
an old word for a kiss.

bust (1) *noun*
1. a sculpture of the head and shoulders.
2. the bosom, especially of a female.

bust (2) *verb*
(*informal*) a) to break. b) to arrest: 'they were *busted* for possessing heroin'.
Phrases:
busted flush, a) a useless hand at poker; b) a useless person.
go bust, to become bankrupt.
Word Family: **bust,** *noun,* a) a failure, b) an arrest.

bustard (*rhymes with* custard) *noun*
a large, shy, fast-running brown and white bird living in open country in Australia, Europe and Africa.

bustle (1) (*say* **buss**'l) *verb*
to move or act with energy or fuss: 'the waiters *bustled* about amongst the guests'.
Word Family: **bustle,** *noun.*

bustle (2) (*say* **buss**'l) *noun*
a frame set under the back of an old-fashioned skirt to support or shape it.

bust-up *noun*
(*informal*) a serious fight or quarrel: 'they have had a huge *bust-up* and will not speak to one another'.

busy (*say* **biz**-ee) *adjective*
fully or continuously engaged in work, etc.: 'she is kept *busy* with 13 children to look after'.
Usages:
a) 'a *busy* city' (= full of activity).
b) 'the phone is *busy* at the moment' (= being used).
c) 'he is *busy* this morning so come back tonight' (= has things to do).
d) 'he produces rather *busy* paintings' (= cluttered).
Word Family: **busily,** *adverb*; **busyness,** *noun.*

busybody *noun*
a person who interferes or meddles in the affairs of others.

but *conjunction*
except or on the contrary: a) 'they laughed *but* we didn't'; b) 'I will take all *but* the last two'.
Usage: 'it never rains *but* it pours' (= unless).
but for, 'he would not be here *but for* you' (= without).
but *adverb*
only: 'we have *but* one choice left'.
all but, 'the game is *all but* over' (= almost).
but *noun*
an objection or restriction: 'there were many ifs and *buts* to the suggestion'.
Word Family: **but,** *preposition, pronoun.*

butane (*say* **bew**-tane) *noun*
Chemistry: a colourless, inflammable gas (formula C_4H_{10}), the fourth member of the paraffin series of hydrocarbons. It is used as a fuel and in making synthetic rubber.
[from BUTYL]

butch (*say* butch) *adjective*
(*informal*) (of a woman) a) lesbian. b) having aggressive or masculine characteristics.

butcher *noun*
1. a) a person who cuts up and sells animal flesh for food. b) a person who slaughters animals and prepares the flesh to be sold.
2. a person who causes cruel or needless death: 'some of the guerrillas were robbers and *butchers*'.
butcher *verb*
1. to kill and prepare animal flesh for food.
2. to kill cruelly or needlessly.
3. to spoil or bungle: 'you have *butchered* the meal'.
Word Family: **butchery,** *noun.*

butcher-bird *noun*
a black and grey shrike, with a white breast and brown wings, living in forests and woodland areas.
[so called because it hangs its prey on thorns or small branches before eating it]

butler *noun*
the head male servant of a household.
[Old French *bouteillier* a bottler]

butt (1) *noun*
the end of anything, especially the thicker end: 'the *butt* of a rifle'.
Usage: 'the *butt* of a cigarette' (= unused end).

butt (2) *noun*
1. a person who is an object of ridicule: 'she is the *butt* of all their jokes'.
2. either of two banks of earth beneath and behind the targets on a rifle range, used to stop bullets safely.
butt *verb*
to join or be joined at the ends: 'this property *butts* on to a lane'.
butt joint
a joint made by putting the ends of two things together, as distinct from overlapping them.

butt (3) *verb*
to hit with the head or horns: 'the goat *butted* the boy in the back'.
butt in, to interrupt or interfere.
Word Family: **butt,** *noun.*

butt (4) *noun*
a large cask or barrel.

butte (*say* bewt) *noun*
American: a flat-topped, steep-sided hill, similar to, but smaller than, a mesa.

butter *noun*
a) the fatty part of milk which separates when cream is churned. b) this substance solidified for use as a food or spread and used in cooking. c) any of various similar spreads: 'peanut *butter*'.
butter *verb*
to spread with butter: '*butter* a baking dish'.
butter up, to flatter.
[Greek *boutyron*]

butterbean *noun*
a type of small, edible, yellow bean.

buttercup *noun*
a wild plant with yellow, cup-shaped flowers.

butter-fingers *noun*
a clumsy person who drops things.

butterfly *noun*
1. any of a group of insects with short antennae and large, often brightly coloured wings covered with scales.
2. any frivolous or gay person.
3. *Swimming:* a style in which the swimmer lifts both arms simultaneously out of the water, bringing them strongly forwards and down.

butterfly fish
any of a group of brightly coloured, carnivorous fish living among coral reefs.

buttermilk *noun*
the liquid which remains when butter is separated from cream or milk.

butterscotch *noun*
Cooking: a flavouring, sauce or toffee made with brown sugar, vanilla essence and butter.

buttery (*say* **butta-ree**) *adjective*
like or containing butter: 'a *buttery* mixture'.

buttock *noun*
1. *Anatomy:* either of the two rounded fleshy areas at the base of the trunk.
2. (*plural*) the rump.

button *noun*
1. a small disc or knob attached to clothing as a decoration or passed through a hole as a fastener.
2. something which has the shape or function of a button, especially a knob or switch for an electrical appliance.
Word Family: **button,** *verb,* to fasten with a button or buttons.

buttonhole *noun*
1. a slit in clothing, etc. through which a button is passed.

2. a single flower worn as a decoration on the lapel.
buttonhole *verb*
(*informal*) to stop and detain a person: 'she *buttonholed* me and lectured me for an hour'.

buttress *noun*
1. a structure built into or against a wall to support or strengthen it. Compare FLYING BUTTRESS.
2. anything used as a support or reinforcement: 'he quoted many scholars as a *buttress* for his argument'.
Word Family: **buttress**, *verb.*

butyl (*say* **bew**til) *adjective*
Chemistry: of or relating to organic compounds containing the univalent (C_4H_9-) radical.
[Latin *butyron* butter, as butyl is found in butter]

buxom (*say* **buks**'m) *adjective*
a) large and healthy. b) large-breasted.

buy (*say* by) *verb*
(**bought, buying**)
1. to get in exchange for payment, especially money: 'we are *buying* a new car'.
2. (*informal*) to accept the truth of: 'I can't *buy* that story'.
Phrases:
buy off, to bribe in order to get rid of opposition, etc.
buy out, to obtain ownership by buying all other shares, etc.
Word Family: **buy**, *noun.*

buyer *noun*
1. any person who buys.
2. a person who selects, orders and buys stock for a department store, etc.

buzz *verb*
1. to make a low humming sound: 'flies *buzzed* noisily in the kitchen'.
2. to move rapidly or busily: 'people *buzzed* around the scene of the accident'.
3. to communicate by telephone or an intercom system: 'I will *buzz* his office'.
4. (*informal*) to fly an aircraft very low to attract attention.
buzz off, (*informal*) to leave.
Word Family: **buzz**, *noun.*

buzzard *noun*
any of various large, heavy birds of the falcon family.

buzzer *noun*
an electrical device, such as a doorbell, which produces a buzzing sound.

buzz saw
see CIRCULAR SAW.

bwana (*say* **bwah**–na) *noun*
a form of address meaning sir or master.
[Swahili]

by *preposition, adverb*
1. used to indicate direction:
a) 'sit *by* me' (= near).
b) 'he walked *by* without a word' (= past).
c) 'north *by* north–west' (= towards).
d) 'let's walk *by* the beach' (= along, through).
2. used to indicate time:
a) 'we will travel *by* day' (= during).
b) 'come *by* 5 o'clock' (= not later than).
3. used to indicate manner or method:
a) 'it only missed us *by* a small amount' (= to the extent of).
b) 'don't judge *by* appearances' (= according to).
c) 'they were paid *by* the hour' (= per).
Phrases:
by and by, 'it will rain *by and by*' (= before long).
by and large, on the whole; more or less.
by the way, by the by, by the bye, incidentally.

by–
a prefix meaning secondary or incidental, as in *bypass.*

bye *noun*
1. *Sport:* the state of having no opponent for a particular round in a contest and therefore entering automatically into the next.
2. *Cricket:* a run scored when a ball passes the batsman and the wicket without touching either of them.
3. *Golf:* any holes which remain unplayed at the end of a match.

bye–bye *interjection*
goodbye.

by–election *noun*
see ELECTION.

bygone (*say* **by**–gon) *adjective*
being in the past: 'in *bygone* days people believed the world was flat'.
bygone *noun*
let bygones be bygones, to forgive and forget a past disagreement, offence, etc.

by–law *noun*
also spelt **bye–law**

a law or rule having effect in a local area only, and generally made by a local council.

by-line *noun*
an author's name printed above or below an article he has written for a newspaper or magazine.

bypass, by-pass *noun*
a road which passes around or avoids a busy area such as a city centre.
bypass *verb*
to avoid or ignore: 'the officials *bypassed* normal procedures'.

byplay *noun*
any action or speech carried on apart from the main action: 'the *byplay* at the back of the stage brought much laughter from the audience'.

by-product *noun*
any thing or effect which is produced during another process or by an event: 'canite is a common *by-product* of the manufacture of sugar'.

bystander *noun*
a person who is present at, or sees, but does not take part in, an event.

byway *noun*
a minor road or path.

byword *noun*
1. something which represents or characterizes a quality, type, etc.: 'in our office Keith is a *byword* for efficiency'.
2. a common saying.

Cc

cab *noun*
1. a taxi.
2. any of various horse-drawn carriages formerly for public hire.
3. see CABIN.
[short form of CABRIOLET]

cabal (*say* ka-**bahl**) *noun*
a faction or group of people working towards a common aim, especially by secret methods.

caballero (*say* kabbal-**yairo**) *noun*
a Spanish gentleman.
[Spanish, horseman]

cabaret (*say* **kabba**-ray) *noun*
a form of entertainment consisting of songs and dances, usually performed in a restaurant or nightclub.
[French, a tavern]

cabbage *noun*
a large, broad-leafed vegetable, with the leaves arranged in a tight head.

cabby *noun*
(*informal*) a taxi driver.

caber (*say* **kay**-ber) *noun*
a long, heavy pole which is lifted at one end and tossed in Scottish Highland games.

cabin *noun*
1. a small, simple house, often in the country.
2. a) a room for the accommodation of passengers on a ship. b) the space available for passengers or crew on an aircraft.
3. the covered part of a vehicle where the driver sits. Short form is **cab.**

cabinet *noun*
1. a piece of furniture with shelves and drawers for storage or display.
2. *Parliament:* (*capital*) a group of ministers from the ruling political party, which advises the Prime Minister on policy and each of whom leads a government department.

cabinet-maker *noun*
a person who builds household equipment such as cupboards, shelves, etc.

cable *noun*
1. a thick, strong rope or chain.
2. a bundle of insulated wires for carrying electricity.
3. an overseas telegram. Short form of **cablegram.**
cable *verb*
1. to send a telegram overseas.
2. to secure with a cable.

cable car
a vehicle suspended from an overhead cable and forming part of a transport system.

caboodle *noun*
(*informal*) the whole lot.

cabriole *noun*
a curved and tapering furniture leg, often ending in the form of an animal's paw.

cabriolet (*say* **kabrio**-lay) *noun*
an open, horse-drawn, two-wheeled carriage with a hood.

cacao (*say* ka-**kayo**) *noun*
the seeds from a small, evergreen, tropical tree, from which cocoa, chocolate, etc. are made.

cache (*say* kash) *noun*
a) a hiding-place. b) a supply of things hidden or stored.
[French *cacher* to hide]

cachet (*say* **kash**ay) *noun*
an indication, usually of distinction.
Usage: 'his music has the *cachet* of genius' (= all the signs of).
[French, a seal]

cachou (*say* **kash**oo *or* ka-**shoo**) *noun*
a tablet for sweetening the breath.

cackle *verb*
1. to make a shrill, broken sound similar to that of a hen after it lays an egg.
2. to laugh or chatter noisily.
Word Family: **cackle,** *noun.*

cacophonous (*say* ka-**koffa**-nus) *adjective*
having a harsh, discordant sound.
Word Family: **cacophony** (*say* ka-**koffa**-nee), *noun.*
[Greek *kakos* bad + *phoné* sound]

cactus *noun*
plural is **cacti** or **cactuses**
any of various desert plants which store water in their fleshy, spike-covered stems.
[Greek *kaktos*]

cad *noun*
(*informal*) a person who disregards accepted standards of decent behaviour.
Word Family: **caddish**, *adjective.*
[(Army) CAD(et)]

cadastral map
a map showing boundaries and ownership of land.

cadaver (*say* **ka-dahva** *or* **ka-davva**) *noun*
a human corpse, especially one used for dissection.
cadaverous (*say* **ka-davverus**) *adjective*
pale and haggard: 'the long illness made her face quite *cadaverous*'.
[Latin]

caddie, caddy (1) *noun*
Golf: a person assisting a player by carrying his golf bag or selecting his clubs.
Word Family: **caddie (caddied, caddying)**, *verb.*

caddy (2) *noun*
a small, airtight tin or box for holding food, especially tea.

cadence (*say* **kay-d'nce**) *noun*
1. the rise and fall of sounds in the pitch of a voice, a line of poetry, etc.
2. *Music:* a group of chords which ends a composition, phrase, etc. Also called a **close.**
[Latin *cadens* falling]

cadenza (*say* **ka-denza**) *noun*
Music: an elaborate passage for a solo instrument towards the end of a concerto, etc.
[Italian]

cadet *noun*
a young person being trained to serve in an organization, especially the armed forces, police, etc.

cadge *verb*
to beg or borrow without intending to repay.
Word Family: **cadger**, *noun.*

cadmium *noun*
element number 48, a ductile metal used as a pigment, for protective plating and in alloys. See TRANSITION ELEMENT.
See CHEMICAL ELEMENTS in grey pages.

cadre (*say* **kahda** *or* **kahdra**) *noun*
a group of trained men appointed to organize or establish another group, operation, etc.
[French]

caecum (*say* **see-k'm**) *noun*
plural is **caeca**
in America spelt **cecum**
Anatomy: any pouch, especially the one from which the appendix hangs at the junction of the small intestine and the colon.
[Latin *caecus* blind]

Caesarian section, Caesarean section
short form is **Caesarian**
an operation to deliver a developed foetus by cutting the wall of the uterus.
[after *Julius Caesar*, a Roman statesman, at whose birth such an operation was supposedly performed]

caesium (*say* **seezium**) *noun*
in America spelt **cesium**
element number 55, a rare, strongly reactive metal used in photoelectric cells. See ALKALI METAL.
See CHEMICAL ELEMENTS in grey pages.

caesura (*say* **siz-yoora**) *noun*
a pause within a line of poetry.
[Latin *caesus* cut]

café (*say* **kaffay**) *noun*
a restaurant where coffee and light meals are served.
[French *café* coffee]

cafeteria (*say* **kaffa-teeria**) *noun*
a self-service restaurant, especially in an office building, department store, etc.
[Spanish, a coffee shop]

caffeine (*say* **kaffeen**) *noun*
a bitter, crystalline drug found in tea, coffee, etc. and used in medicine as a stimulant and diuretic.

caftan *noun*
also spelt **kaftan**
a loose garment with long, wide sleeves.

cage *noun*
1. a box-like enclosure with wires or bars in which birds, animals, etc. are kept.
Usage: 'to the bored patient the hospital was a *cage*' (= prison).
2. a structure resembling a cage, such as an enclosed lift in a coalmine.
Word Family: **cage**, *verb*, to enclose in or as if in a cage.

cagey (*say* **kay**–jee) **cagy** *adjective*
(*informal*) indirect, secretive or cautious: 'his *cagey* replies gave the police little information'.
Word Family: **cagily**, *adverb*; **caginess**, *noun*.

cagoule (*say* k'**gool**) *noun*
a lightweight, loose-fitting outer garment with hood attached, made of waterproofed nylon and worn by walkers and mountain climbers.

cahoots (*say* ka–**hoots**) *plural noun*
in cahoots, (*informal*) 'the two boys were *in cahoots* to trick their friend' (= in partnership).

Cain *noun*
Biblical: the son of Adam who murdered his brother Abel.
raise Cain, 'when he hears that his car has been wrecked he will *raise Cain*' (= make a violent fuss).

Cainozoic (*say* kie–no–**zo**–ik *or* kayno–**zo**–ik) *noun*
Geology: the most recent geological era, which began about 65 million years ago and contains the Tertiary and Quaternary periods.
Word Family: **Cainozoic**, *adjective*.
[Greek *kainos* new, modern + *zoion* animal (as mammals first appeared then)]

cairn *noun*
a pile of stones erected as a landmark, monument, etc.

cairn terrier
short form is **cairn**
a shaggy, short-legged Scotch terrier, originally bred to flush foxes from among cairns.

caisson (*say* ka–**soon**) *noun*
a watertight tank used in the under-water construction of bridge foundations, etc.
caisson disease, the bends.

cajole (*say* ka–**jole**) *verb*
to coax or persuade by flattery, promises, etc.
Word Family: **cajolery**, *noun*, persuasion by flattery.

cake *noun*
1. a sweet, baked food usually made of flour, eggs, liquid and a raising agent.
2. a compressed block of any substance, such as soap.
Phrases:
a piece of cake, (*informal*) anything which is easily gained or accomplished.
take the cake, (*informal*) to be the best or most outstanding.
Word Family: **cake**, *verb*, to form into or cover with a compact mass.

calabash *noun*
any of various gourds, used when dried to hold liquids and as musical instruments, etc.

calamine lotion
a soothing liquid made from zinc oxide (formula ZnO), used on the skin for sunburn, rashes, etc.

calamity (*say* ka–**lamm**a–tee) *noun*
a disaster or unfortunate event.
Word Family: **calamitous**, *adjective*; **calamitously**, *adverb*.
[Latin *calamitas* a blight, damage]

calcareous (*say* kal–**kair**ius) *adjective*
of or relating to a substance which contains calcium, usually in the form of calcium carbonate (formula $CaCO_3$).
[Latin *calcarius* of lime]

calcify (*say* **kal**si–fie) *verb*
(**calcified**, **calcifying**)
to deposit calcium salts which harden tissue.
Word Family: **calcification**, *noun*.

calcine *verb*
to heat an ore in order to obtain the oxide or drive off volatile constituents such as sulphur.
[Latin *calcis* of a stone, of lime]

calcium (*say* **kal**sium) *noun*
element number 20, a soft metal whose compounds are found in limestone, chalk, teeth and bones. See ALKALINE EARTH METAL.
See CHEMICAL ELEMENTS in grey pages.
[Latin *calcis* of limestone]

calculate (*say* **kal**–kew–late) *verb*
to solve a problem using mathematical methods: 'we *calculated* how long our trip would take'.
Usages:
a) 'her indifference was *calculated* to irritate me' (= deliberately intended).
b) 'don't *calculate* on his being there' (= count, rely).
Word Family: **calculation**, *noun*, a) the act of calculating, b) the result of calculating; **calculator**, *noun*, a person or machine that calculates; **calculating**, *adjective*, a) shrewd or slyly clever, b) able to perform calculations.
[Latin *calculus* a pebble (used in reckoning)]

calculus (*say* **kalkew–lus**) *noun*
1. *Maths:* a branch of analysis which studies the properties of functions using derivatives and integrals. Plural is **calculuses.**
differential calculus is used to find the rates of change of functions, maxima and minima, and the slopes of tangents to curves.
integral calculus is used to find areas, volumes and lengths of arcs.
2. *Medicine:* see STONE. Plural is **calculi.**

caldera (*say* kal–**daira**) *noun*
a deep, often lake–filled, cavity at the summit of a volcano, formed by the top of the volcano subsiding or being blown off by an eruption.
[Spanish, cauldron]

calendar (*say* **kallen**–da) *noun*
1. a) a list of the days, weeks and months of a particular year. b) a list of important dates: 'a *calendar* of social events'.
2. any system of dividing time into fixed periods and marking the beginning and end of a year. See GREGORIAN CALENDAR and YEAR.
[Latin *Kalendae* (first day of) a month]

calender *noun*
a machine with rollers, used to smooth cloth, paper, etc.
Word Family: **calender,** *verb.*

calf (1) *noun*
plural is **calves**
the offspring of a cow, whale, seal, etc.

calf (2) *noun*
plural is **calves**
the fleshy, muscular area at the back of the leg below the knee.

calibrate (*say* **kalli**–brate) *verb*
to determine or mark the scale on an instrument.
Word Family: **calibration,** *noun.*

calibre (*say* **kalliba**) *noun*
in America spelt **caliber**
1. the diameter of a circular part, especially the bore of a rifle, etc.
2. the quality or worth of a person: 'he is a man of great *calibre*'.
[Arabic *kalib* mould]

calico *noun*
a coarse, cotton fabric, usually off–white in colour.
[first made in *Calicut,* India]

californium *noun*
element number 98, a man–made, radioactive metal. See TRANSURANIC ELEMENT and ACTINIDE.
See CHEMICAL ELEMENTS in grey pages.

caliph (*say* **kallif**) *noun*
also spelt **calif**
a Moslem religious and civil leader believed to be a successor to Mohammed.
Word Family: **caliphate** (*say* **kallif**–it), *noun,* the leadership or rank of a caliph.
[Arabic *khalifah* successor]

call (*say* cawl) *verb*
1. a) to utter loudly or clearly: 'she *called* for help'. b) to read out: 'the teacher *called* the roll'.
Usage: '*call* the office before 5 o'clock' (= telephone).
2. a) to demand the presence of: 'the barrister *called* her next witness'. b) to bring together the members of: 'to *call* a meeting'.
Usage: 'try not to *call* attention to the mistake' (= attract, bring).
3. to pay a visit: 'may I *call* tomorrow?'.
4. a) to give a name to. b) to consider: 'it was hardly what you would *call* a success'.
5. *Cards:* to bid.
Phrases:
call for, a) to collect; b) 'the good news *calls for* a celebration' (= needs, demands).
call off, to cancel.
call on, to visit.
call up, a) to summon for military service; b) to telephone.
call *noun*
1. the act of calling: a) 'her *calls* for help went unheeded'; b) 'I think I'll pay her a *call* soon'.
2. the sound of calling: 'listen to the bird *calls*'.
Usages:
a) 'no telephone *calls* should be made during work hours' (= conversations).
b) 'you had no *call* to do such a thing' (= need, occasion).
c) 'your *call* was six hearts, wasn't it?' (= bid).
d) 'I realize there are lots of *calls* on your time' (= claims, demands).
on call, available at short notice.
Word Family: **caller,** *noun,* a person who calls.

callbox *noun*
a telephone box.

callgirl *noun*
a prostitute, formerly one who made appointments by telephone.

calligraphy (*say* ka–**ligra**–fee) *noun*
the art of fine handwriting.
[Greek *kallos* beauty + *graphein* to write]

calling *noun*
1. a vocation or career.
2. an inner urge or impulse: 'he felt a strong *calling* to help the poor'.

calliper, caliper *noun*
1. a brace or support, such as one worn to straighten a deformed limb.
2. (*usually plural*) an instrument with two arms hinged at one end, used to measure curved surfaces.

callisthenics (*say* kallis–**thenniks**) *plural noun*
(*used with singular verb*) a series of exercises performed to improve gracefulness, suppleness and control of the muscles.
Word Family: **callisthenic**, *adjective.*
[Greek *kallos* beauty + *sthenos* strength]

callous *adjective*
being hardened or having calluses.
Usage: 'his *callous* treatment of animals shocked us' (= insensitive, unfeeling).
Word Family: **callously**, *adverb*; **callousness**, *noun.*
[Latin *callosus* thick-skinned]

callow *adjective*
inexperienced or immature.

callus *noun*
plural is **calluses**
Medicine: a) a hard, thickened area of skin, due to continual pressure. b) the tissue formed by bones during the healing of a fracture.

calm *adjective*
quiet or undisturbed: 'she remains *calm* in any crisis'.
Usage: 'today is predicted to be *calm* and sunny' (= without wind).
Word Family: **calm**, *verb*, to make or become calm; **calmly**, *adverb*; **calm, calmness**, *nouns.*

calomel *noun*
a compound of mercury and chlorine used in medicine.

Calor gas
bottled, liquefied butane used for light and heat, especially in caravans, boats, etc.
[a trademark]

calorie (*say* **kalla**–ree) *noun*
1. the quantity of heat required to raise the temperature of one gram of water one degree Celsius, equal to about 4·19 joule. See UNITS in grey pages.
2. a) (*capital*) a unit of energy equal to 1000 calorie (4190 joule). Also called a **kilocalorie.**
b) the quantity of food capable of producing this amount of energy.
Word Family: **caloric** (*say* ka–**lorrik**), *adjective*, relating to heat; **calorific** (*say* kalla–**riffik**), *adjective*, relating to calories or conversion into heat.
[Latin *calor* heat]

calorimeter (*say* kallo–**rimmi**–ta) *noun*
an instrument used to measure quantities of heat.
Word Family: **calorimetry**, *noun.*

calumniate (*say* ka–**lumni**–ate) *verb*
to speak falsely or maliciously of.
Word Family: **calumniation** (*say* ka–lumni–**ay**–sh'n), *noun*; **calumnious,** *adjective*; **calumny**, *noun*, a false or malicious statement.
[Latin *calumnia* trickery]

calvary (*say* **kalva**–ree) *noun*
Christian: a model of the Crucifixion.
[after *Calvary*, the place where Christ was crucified]

calve *verb*
to give birth to a calf.

calves *plural noun*
the plural of **calf (1)** and **calf (2).**

Calvinist *noun*
a follower of a religious movement which emphasizes strict church discipline, the theory of predestination and the sinfulness of man.
Word Family: **Calvinism**, *noun*, the beliefs or practices of Calvinists; **Calvinistic, Calvinistical**, *adjective.*
[after *John Calvin*, 1509–64, on whose system of theology the movement is based]

calypso (*say* ka–**lipso**) *noun*
plural is **calypsos**
a type of music from the West Indies having topical words and a strong rhythm.

calyx (*say* **kay**–lix *or* **kal**lix) *noun*
plural is **calyces** (*say* **kay**–la–seez) or **calyxes**
Biology: the sepals or outermost group of floral parts.
[Greek *kalyx* husk]

cam *noun*
a device in a machine for changing circular motion into movement back and forth.

camaraderie (*say* kamma–**rahda**–ree) *noun*

comradeship.
[French]

camber *noun*
a slight upward curve or arch in the middle, e.g. on a road to allow drainage.
Word Family: **camber**, *verb*, to curve upwards slightly in the middle.

cambium *noun*
Biology: a layer of tissue in a root or stem which produces new cells on either side of itself and thus increases thickness.

Cambrian *noun*
Geology: see PALAEOZOIC.
Word Family: **Cambrian**, *adjective*.

cambric *noun*
a finely woven cotton or linen fabric.

came *verb*
the past tense of the verb **come**.

camel *noun*
a large mammal with long legs and a hump on its back for storing food. It is found in the desert regions of Africa and Asia and is valued for its milk, wool, meat and as a pack animal.
the **dromedary** (also called an **Arabian camel**) has one hump.
the **Bactrian camel** (also called a **Mongolian camel**) has two humps.

camellia (*say* ka-**meelia**) *noun*
an evergreen, winter-flowering garden shrub with shiny leaves and white, pink or red rose-like flowers.

cameo (*say* **kammio**) *noun*
plural is **cameos**
a raised engraving, usually on a brooch and showing a head in profile, in which the coloured layers of the material are used to distinguish the design from its background.

camera (*say* **kamra**) *noun*
a lightproof device which records a photographic image by allowing a focused beam of light to fall on a sensitized surface, such as a film.
in camera, (*Law*) in private.
[Greek *kamara* a (vaulted) room]

camisole (*say* **kammi**-sole) *noun*
a light, decorative under-bodice.

camomile (*say* **kammo**-mile) *noun*
a fragrant plant with daisy-like flowers which are used in medicine and cooking.

camouflage (*say* **kamma**-flah*zh*) *noun*
a method of disguise in which an object or organism assumes the colour, texture, etc., of its surroundings and thus appears to be a part of it.
Word Family: **camouflage**, *verb*, to disguise or deceive by means of a camouflage.

camp (1) *noun*
1. a) a group of tents, caravans or other kinds of temporary shelter in one place. b) the place where such shelters are situated. c) a similar military establishment.
2. a group of people with the same ideals, etc.: 'which political *camp* are you in?'.
Word Family: **camp**, *verb*, to pitch or live temporarily in tents, etc.; **camper**, *noun*.

camp (2) *adjective*
1. exaggerated or artificial in style.
2. homosexual.
[possibly from American police abbreviation *KAMP* Known As Male Prostitute]

campaign (*say* kam-**pane**) *noun*
1. *Military:* the active operations of an army, especially during one season or period.
2. any organized operations for a particular purpose: 'a political *campaign*'.
Word Family: **campaign**, *verb*; **campaigner**, *noun*.

campanile (*say* kampa-**neeli**) *noun*
plural is **campaniles** or **campanili**
the belltower of an Italian church, usually a completely separate building.
[Italian *campana* a bell]

campanula *noun*
any of numerous kinds of plants with bell-shaped flowers, usually blue or white, e.g. the Canterbury Bell.
[Italian *campana* a bell]

camp follower
a hanger-on.

camphor (*say* **kamfir**) *noun*
a white crystalline solid with a characteristic, pleasant smell and used in mothballs, medicine and making celluloid.
Word Family: **camphorate**, *verb*, to impregnate with camphor.

campion *noun*
also called **lychnis**
any of various wild or cultivated plants, typically with scarlet flowers.

campus *noun*
the grounds of a tertiary institution, e.g. a university.
[Latin, a level space]

camshaft *noun*
a shaft with cams on it, such as the camshaft used to operate the valves on an internal combustion engine.

can (1) *verb*
(could)
an auxiliary verb indicating power or ability to do something: '*can* you lift the suitcase?'.
Usages:
a) 'you *can* only enter if you have a pass' (= are allowed to).
b) 'she *can* be very nasty' (= has a tendency or ability to).
c) '*can* I go now please?' (= may).
Word Family: **cannot** (short form is **can't**), can not.

can (2) *noun*
any metal container, such as one in which items such as food are sealed by the manufacturer.
carry the can, 'he was left to *carry the can*' (= take the blame).
can *verb*
(canned, canning)
to put into cans.
canned *adjective*
1. packed in cans.
2. *Radio, Television:* pre-recorded: '*canned* laughter'. Compare LIVE (2).

Canada goose
a large North American wild goose with brown back, black head and neck and white cheek-patches.

canal (*say* ka-**nal**) *noun*
1. a man-made waterway.
2. *Biology:* a long tubular passage in an animal or plant, e.g. for carrying food.
Word Family: **canalize, canalise,** *verb*, to give a direction to or provide an outlet for.
[Latin *canalis* a channel]

canapé (*say* **kanna**-pee *or* **kanna**-pay) *noun*
a thin piece of bread or toast spread with cheese, caviar, etc.
[French, a couch]

canary (*say* ka-**nair**-ee) *noun*
a small, yellow finch, often kept in a cage as a pet.
[originally from the *Canary Islands*]

canary yellow
a light yellow colour.

canasta (*say* ka-**nasta**) *noun*
a card game played by two to six people, in which the aim is to collect seven or more similar cards, each set of which is called a **canasta**. See MELD (1).
[Spanish, basket]

cancan *noun*
a lively French stage dance featuring fast high kicks.
[French]

cancel (*say* **kan**-s'l) *verb*
(cancelled, cancelling)
1. to make void: a) 'the match was *cancelled* because of rain'; b) 'he *cancelled* the order'.
2. to cross out or mark: 'to *cancel* a postage stamp'.
3. to balance or compensate for.
4. *Maths:* a) to divide integers out of the numerator and denominator of a fraction. b) to remove two quantities which equal zero in an algebraic equation. *Example*: $2x + 3y - 2x$ is equal to $3y$.
Word Family: **cancellation** (*say* kansel-**ay**-sh'n), *noun.*

cancer (*say* **kan**-sa) *noun*
1. any of various diseases in which a group of cells grows and multiplies rapidly, destroying nearby tissue. Pieces of the growth may break off and spread throughout the body. *Word Family*: **cancerous,** *adjective.*
2. *Geography:* see TROPIC OF CANCER under TROPIC.
3. *Astrology:* (*capital*) a group of stars, the fourth sign of the zodiac. Also called the **Crab**.

candela (*say* kan-**dayla**) *noun*
the base SI unit of luminous intensity.
[Latin, a candle]

candelabrum, candelabra *noun*
plural is **candelabra** or **candelabras**
an ornamental holder with branches in which candles are supported.

candid *adjective*
frank or honest: 'a *candid* opinion'.
Word Family: **candidly,** *adverb*; **candidness,** *noun.*
[Latin *candidus* dazzling white]

candidate (*say* **kandi**-date) *noun*
a person who seeks or is nominated for a certain position, prize, honour, etc.: a) 'he is the new parliamentary *candidate*'; b) '100 *candidates* sat for the exam'.
Word Family: **candidacy, candidature,** *nouns.*

candied *adjective*
Word Family: see CANDY.

candle *noun*
a stick of wax or fat containing a length of thread which provides light when burned.
Phrases:
burn the candle at both ends, to attempt to do more than one's energy allows.
cannot hold a candle to, (*informal*) is totally inferior to.
[Latin *candela*]

candlepower *noun*
Physics: the luminous intensity, expressed in candela.

candour (*say* **kanda**) *noun*
the quality of being candid or honest.

candy *noun*
1. a hard sweet made by boiling sugar.
2. *American:* any sweet or sweets.
Word Family: **candied,** *adjective,* covered or impregnated with sugar; **candy** (**candied, candying**) *verb,* a) to cook in heavy syrup, b) to boil down to a crystalline form.
[Persian *kand* sugar]

cane *noun*
1. the long, hollow, jointed stems of certain grass-like plants such as bamboo, used to make furniture, etc.
2. a) a stick used to beat someone with. b) a walking stick.
cane *verb*
to hit with a stick, especially as a punishment.
[Greek *kanna* a reed]

cane sugar
sucrose.

canine (*say* **kay-nine**) *adjective*
of or relating to dogs.
canine *noun*
1. any animal in the dog family.
2. a canine tooth.
[Latin *canis* dog]

canine tooth
Dentistry: any of the four single-pointed teeth, one on each side of each jaw next to the incisors, which are very prominent in dogs.

canister (*say* **kannista**) *noun*
an airtight tin or jar for storing tea, flour, etc.

canker *noun*
an ulcerous sore.

cannabis *noun*
see MARIJUANA.
[Greek *kannabis* hemp]

cannery *noun*
a factory where food is put into tins or cans.

cannibal *noun*
any animal, especially a human being, which eats its own species.
cannibalism *noun*
the practice of eating the flesh of one's own species.
cannibalize, cannibalise *verb*
to take serviceable parts from damaged machinery for use in the repair of other equipment.
Word Family: **cannibalistic,** *adjective.*
[Spanish *Canibales* peoples of the Caribbean]

cannily *adverb*
Word Family: see CANNY.

cannon *noun*
1. any of various large mounted guns; the old type fired a solid, metal ball, called a **cannonball.**
2. *Billiards:* a shot in which a ball hits two other balls in succession.
cannon *verb*
1. to collide heavily.
2. *Billiards:* to make a cannon.
3. to discharge a cannon.

cannonade *noun*
a continuous firing of guns, especially in a battle.

canny *adjective*
cautiously shrewd and wary: 'he is very *canny* when it comes to money matters'.
Word Family: **cannily,** *adverb;* **canniness,** *noun.*

canoe (*say* **ka-noo**) *noun*
any light, narrow boat which is propelled by paddles.
paddle one's own canoe, to be independent and manage on one's own.
Word Family: **canoe,** *verb;* **canoeist,** *noun.*
[Haitian]

canon (1) (*say* **kan'n**) *noun*
1. any law or rule, especially a religious one.
2. a basic standard by which something is judged.
3. *Music:* any music in which one or more melodies are repeated by different instruments or voices, each repeat overlapping its predecessor in counterpoint.
4. a list of works considered to be genuine.
Word Family: **canonical** (*say* **ka-nonni-k'l**), *adjective;* **canonize, canonise,** *verb,* to declare to be a saint; **canonization** (*say* **kanna-nize-ay-sh'n**), *noun.*

canon (2) (*say* **kan**'n) *noun*
Religion: a clergyman attached to a cathedral.

canopy (*say* **kanna**–pee) *noun*
1. a) a hanging, roof–like cover, e.g. for a bed. b) any similar outdoor shelter.
2. the transparent covering of the cockpit of an aircraft.
[Greek *konopeion* a mosquito net]

cant (1) *noun*
1. any hypocritically pious language.
2. the jargon used by a particular group of people.
Word Family: **cant**, *verb*.

cant (2) *noun*
1. any angular deviation from the horizontal or vertical plane.
2. a slanted or tilted position or edge.
Word Family: **cant**, *verb*, to cause to slant or tilt.

cantabile (*say* kan–**tah**bi–lay) *adjective*
Music: in a singing manner.
[Italian]

cantaloup (*say* **kanta**–loop *or* **kanta**–lope) **cantaloupe** *noun*
also called a **rock melon**
a round melon with sweet, orange flesh and a tough, wrinkled skin.
[first grown in Europe at *Cantalupo*, Italy]

cantankerous (*say* kan–**tank**erus) *adjective*
bad–tempered or quarrelsome.
Word Family: **cantankerously**, *adverb*; **cantankerousness**, *noun*.

cantata (*say* kan–**tah**ta) *noun*
a long, musical composition for soloists, chorus and often an orchestra.
[Italian, sung]

canteen (*say* kan–**teen**) *noun*
1. a cafeteria or place of entertainment for the personnel of a military base, institution, etc.
2. a box containing a set of cutlery, etc.
3. the eating and drinking utensils of a soldier, especially his water–bottle.

canter *noun*
a gait of a horse between a trot and a gallop, in which groups of three distinct hoof–beats may be heard.
Word Family: **canter**, *verb*.
[from CANTER(bury gallop), the pace at which pilgrims supposedly travelled to Canterbury]

canticle (*say* **kan**ti–k'l) *noun*
Christian: a short hymn or chant with words taken from the Bible and used in church services, e.g. the Te Deum.

cantilever (*say* **kan**ti–leeva) *noun*
a projecting part, such as the bracket supporting a balcony or a horizontal beam anchored at one end only.
Word Family: **cantilever bridge**, a bridge resting on cantilevers projecting from either side of each of two piers.

canto *noun*
one of the divisions of a long poem.

canton *noun*
a small district, especially in Switzerland.

cantonment *noun*
a large camp for soldiers, usually with permanent quarters.

cantor *noun*
Religion: the main singer or person who leads the singing in a service.
[Latin, singer]

canvas (*say* **kan**–vus) *noun*
1. a heavy fabric made from flax or cotton and used for tents, sails, etc.
2. anything made of canvas, such as a piece of canvas used by an artist as a painting surface.
3. any or all of the sails on a boat.
4. *Boxing:* the covering, usually padded, over the floor of the ring.
[same root as *cannabis*]

canvass (*say* **kan**–vus) *verb*
1. to campaign for support, donations, etc., e.g. for a charity or a political candidate.
2. to try to find out the views of electors in a forthcoming election.
3. to put forward a proposal for discussion.
Word Family: **canvass**, *noun*, the act of canvassing; **canvasser**, *noun*, a person who canvasses.

canyon *noun*
a narrow, steep–sided river valley.
[Spanish, *cañon*]

caoutchouc (*say* **kow**–chook) *noun*
untreated rubber.
[Carib]

cap *noun*
1. a soft, round hat with no brim, usually with a peak at the front.
2. the removable top of a pen, jar, etc.
3. something resembling a cap, such as the top, curved part of a mushroom.
4. a small explosive used to make a noise in a toy gun.

Phrases:
cap in hand, humbly.
set one's cap at, 'she *set her cap at* the handsome office boy' (= tried to capture the affections of).
cap *verb*
(**capped, capping**)
to cover with or as if with a cap.
Usage: 'he *capped* her story with an even funnier one' (= surpassed, outdid).

capable (*say* **kaypa**-b'l) *adjective*
able, competent or efficient: 'a *capable* student'.
be capable of, a) 'he *is capable of* murder' (= might); b) 'this situation *is capable of* improvement' (= is susceptible to).
Word Family: **capability** (*say* kaypa-**billi**-tee), *noun*; **capably**, *adverb*.

capacious (*say* ka-**pay**shus) *adjective*
able to hold a large amount: 'a *capacious* memory'.
Word Family: **capaciously**, *adverb*; **capaciousness**, *noun*.
[Latin *capax*, *capacis* spacious]

capacitance (*say* ka-**passi**-t'nce) *noun*
Electricity: the ability of a system to store electric charge when a potential difference is applied across it.

capacitor (*say* ka-**passi**-ta) *noun*
also called a **condenser**
Electricity: any device for storing electric charge, consisting in its simplest form of two conducting surfaces with an insulator between them.

capacity (*say* ka-**passi**-tee) *noun*
1. a) the power of receiving, holding or absorbing. b) a measure of this: 'the *capacity* of this bottle is one litre'.
Usage: 'she has a great *capacity* for learning' (= ability, power).
2. the maximum amount: 'the theatre was filled to *capacity*'.
3. the quality of being susceptible to certain treatment: 'the *capacity* of elastic to be stretched'.
4. a position or function: 'in his *capacity* as leader'.

cape (1) *noun*
also called a **mantle**
a short, sleeveless cloak fastened at the neck and hanging around the shoulders, often attached to a coat.

cape (2) *noun*
Geography: a piece of land jutting out into the sea.

caper (1) *noun*
the flower bud of a prickly, Mediterranean shrub, usually pickled and used in sauces, etc.

caper (2) *noun*
1. a playful leap or skip.
2. a prank.
Word Family: **caper**, *verb*.
[Latin *caper* a goat]

capercaillie (*say* kaypa-**kayl**-yee) *noun*
also called a **capercailzie** (*say* kaypa-**kayl**-zee)
a very large grouse of the pine-woods, with black and brown plumage.
[Gaelic, great cock of the woods]

capillarity (*say* kappi-**larri**-tee) *noun*
Physics: the tendency of a liquid in a narrow tube to move either up or down depending on the relative attraction of the liquid molecules to each other and to the walls of the container.

capillary (*say* ka-**pilla**-ree) *noun*
Anatomy: any of the smallest blood vessels in the body which connect the arteries to the veins.
Word Family: **capillary**, *adjective*, relating to or occurring in a narrow tube.
[Latin *capillus* a hair]

capital (1) *noun*
1. the city or town which is the official seat of government in a country, state, etc.
2. a capital letter.
3. the total amount of money or property owned, used or invested by an individual or group.
capital *adjective*
1. of or relating to capital.
2. involving the loss of life: '*capital* punishment'.
3. (*informal*) splendid or excellent.

capital (2) *noun*
Architecture: the top of a column, often decorated.
[Latin *capitalis* chief]

capital gains
any profits from the sale of fixed assets.

capital intensive
(of an industry) requiring large amounts of money in comparison to labour. Compare LABOUR INTENSIVE.

capitalism *noun*
an economic and political system where industry, trade, etc. are owned and controlled by private individuals or groups. Compare COMMUNISM.

Word Family: **capitalist,** *noun*; **capitalistic,** *adjective.*

capitalize, capitalise *verb*
1. to write or print in capital letters.
2. *Commerce:* to use as or change into capital.
Usage: 'you must *capitalize* on this marvellous piece of luck' (= make the most of).
Word Family: **capitalization,** *noun.*

capital letter
an enlarged letter such as is used at the beginning of a sentence or name: 'the **A** in **Adelaide** is a *capital letter*'.

Capitol *noun*
1. *Ancient history:* the temple of Jupiter on the Capitoline hill, Rome.
2. *American:* the building in which Congress or a State legislature meets.
[Latin *Capitolium* citadel on a hill, from *caput* head]

capitulate (*say* ka-**pit**-yoo-late) *verb*
to surrender, usually on stated conditions.
Word Family: **capitulation,** *noun.*

capon (*say* **kay**-pon) *noun*
a domestic cock which has been castrated to improve its flesh for eating.

cappuccino (*say* kappa-**cheeno**) *noun*
an espresso coffee made with frothy milk.
[Italian]

caprice (*say* ka-**preece**) *noun*
a) the tendency to change one's mind on a whim. b) such a change.
Word Family: **capricious** (*say* ka-**prishus**), *adjective*; **capriciousness,** *noun.*

Capricorn *noun*
1. *Geography:* see TROPIC OF CAPRICORN under TROPIC.
2. *Astrology:* a group of stars, the tenth sign of the zodiac. Also called the **Goat.**
[Latin *caper* goat + *cornus* horned]

capsicum (*say* **kapsi**-k'm) *noun*
also called a **pepper**
a long or bell-shaped, green to red fruit, varying in taste from mild to hot.

capsize *verb*
to overturn anything floating, especially a boat.

capstan (*say* **kap**-st'n) *noun*
Nautical: an upright post on a dock or ship which may be turned to pull in a rope.

capsule (*say* **kaps**-yool) *noun*
1. a small soluble container for a dose of medicine.
2. *Biology:* a) a sheath or envelope of fibrous tissue. b) a membrane covering an organ or joint. c) a dry, dehiscent fruit on a plant.
3. the part of a spacecraft containing the instruments and crew.
[Latin *capsula* little box]

captain *noun*
1. a person appointed to have leadership or authority over others: 'he is the *captain* of the team'.
2. *Military:* a commissioned officer in the army ranking between a lieutenant and a major.
3. *Nautical:* a commissioned officer in the navy ranking between a commander and a rear admiral.
Word Family: **captain,** *verb.*
[Latin *caput* head]

caption (*say* **kap**-sh'n) *noun*
a heading, description or short explanation, e.g. one accompanying a cartoon or illustration.

captious (*say* **kap**shus) *adjective*
apt to find trivial faults and defects.
Word Family: **captiously,** *adverb*; **captiousness,** *noun.*
[Latin *captiosus* fallacious]

captivate (*say* **kapti**-vate) *verb*
to enthral: 'he was *captivated* by her beauty'.
Word Family: **captivation,** *noun.*

captive (*say* **kap**-tiv) *noun*
a person who is captured or captivated.
Word Family: **captivity** (*say* kap-**tivvi**-tee), *noun*, the state of being a captive; **captive,** *adjective.*
[Latin *captivus* caught]

capture (*say* **kap**-cher) *verb*
to seize as a prisoner.
Usage: 'his description *captured* our imaginations' (= inspired, took control of).
Word Family: **capture,** *noun*, the act of capturing; **captor,** *noun*, a person who captures another.

capuchin (*say* **kap**-yoo-chin) *noun*
a long-tailed, South American monkey, with tufts of hair on its head resembling a hood.
Roman Catholic: (*capital*) one of the Franciscan orders of monks.
[Italian *cappuccino* hooded one]

car *noun*
1. a motor car.

2. any of various specific, wheeled vehicles, e.g. a railway dining-car.
[Latin *carrus* a four-wheeled wagon]

carafe (*say* ka-**rahf** *or* ka-raff) ***noun***
a stopperless decanter.
[Arabic *gharraf* a drinking vessel]

caramel (*say* **karra**-mel) ***noun***
1. a) sugar cooked to a dark brown colour, used as a flavouring in desserts, etc. b) a sweet with this taste.
2. a pale, golden-brown colour.
Word Family: **caramelize, caramelise,** *verb,* to turn or be turned into caramel.

carapace (*say* **karra**-pace) ***noun***
Biology: a shell or hard covering on the back of some animals, such as a crab, tortoise, etc.

carat (*say* **karr**et) ***noun***
1. a metric unit of mass for gems, equal to 200 mg. Also called a **metric carat.**
2. a twenty-fourth part by weight used in expressing the pureness of gold. *Example*: 9 *carat* gold has $\frac{9}{24}$ gold by weight.

caravan (*say* **karra**-van) ***noun***
1. a vehicle in which people may live, designed to be drawn by a motor vehicle or horses. Also called a **trailer.**
2. a group of people travelling together, usually across a desert.
[Persian *karwan*]

caravanserai (*say* karra-**vansa**-rye) ***noun***
an inn built for the accommodation of caravans in Eastern countries.
[Persian *karwan* caravan + *serai* inn]

caraway (*say* **karra**-way) ***noun***
a herb whose strong-smelling, seed-like fruits are used in cooking and medicine.

carbide ***noun***
Chemistry: a compound of carbon and one other element, especially a metal.

carbine ***noun***
a) a light, short rifle, formerly used by cavalry. b) a light, automatic or semiautomatic rifle.

carbohydrate (*say* karbo-**high**-drate) ***noun***
any of a group of complex organic compounds, such as sugars, starches, cellulose, etc., which contain carbon, hydrogen and oxygen and are present in all living things.

carbolic acid (*say* kar-**bollik** assid)
see PHENOL.

carbon ***noun***
element number 6, a non-metal found in the pure state in graphite and diamond. It forms the large molecules which are the basis of living tissue and is also found in petroleum, coal, etc. See CHEMICAL ELEMENTS in grey pages.
[Latin *carbonis* of charcoal]

carbonate (*say* **karb**'n-it) ***noun***
Chemistry: a salt containing the bivalent $(CO_3)^{2-}$ ion.
carbonate (*say* **karb**'n-ate) *verb*
1. to form into a carbonate.
2. to add carbon dioxide: 'to *carbonate* a drink'.
Word Family: **carbonation,** ***noun,*** the state of being saturated with carbon dioxide.

carbon black
also called **lampblack**
a pure, finely divided form of carbon used in making inks, rubber products and certain plastics.

carbon copy
1. a copy made by using carbon paper.
2. any exact copy.

carbon dating
see RADIOCARBON DATING.

carbon dioxide
also called **carbonic acid gas**
a colourless, odourless, incombustible gas (formula CO_2), formed during respiration and widely used in industry as dry ice, in aerated drinks, etc.

carbonic acid
Chemistry: the weak acid (formula H_2CO_3), formed when carbon dioxide dissolves in water.

Carboniferous (*say* karba-**niffa**-rus) ***noun***
Geology: see PALAEOZOIC.

carbonize, carbonise *verb*
to reduce to or form carbon.
Word Family: **carbonization,** ***noun,*** the formation of carbon from organic matter.

carbon monoxide
a colourless, odourless, poisonous gas (formula CO), which forms when carbon burns in an insufficient supply of oxygen.

carbon paper
a chemically treated paper placed between pages so that anything marked on the top sheet will be reproduced on the others.

carbon tetrachloride (*say* **karb**'n tetra-**klaw**-ride)
a colourless liquid (formula CCl_4), used in medicine and as a cleaning fluid, solvent, etc.

carborundum (*say* karba–**run**–d'm) *noun*
Metallurgy: silicon carbide (formula SiC), a dark, crystalline solid which is nearly as hard as diamond and is used as an abrasive.

carbuncle *noun*
1. a large area of infection in the skin, producing pus.
2. a bright red gem.
Word Family: **carbuncled,** *adjective,* having carbuncles; **carbuncular,** *adjective,* of or like a carbuncle.
[Latin *carbunculus* a live coal]

carburettor (*say* karb–ya–**retta**) *noun*
in America spelt **carburetor**
a device in an internal combustion engine for mixing fuel and air in the correct proportions.

carcass (*say* **kar**kus) *noun*
also spelt **carcase**
the dead body of an animal.

carcinogen (*say* kar–**sinna**–j'n) *noun*
any substance producing a cancer in an organism.
Word Family: **carcinogenesis,** *noun*; **carcinogenic** (*say* kar–sinna–**jen**nik), *adjective.*

carcinoma (*say* karsi–**no**–ma) *noun*
plural is **carcinomata** or **carcinomas**
Medicine: a form of cancer.
[Greek *karkinos* crab + *–oma* a tumour]

card (1) *noun*
1. a piece of stiff paper or thin cardboard, often printed for a particular purpose: a) 'a Christmas *card*'; b) 'a pack of playing *cards*'.
2. (*plural*) any of a number of games played with playing cards.
Usages:
a) 'I wonder what other *cards* he has to use' (= methods, tricks).
b) 'what is on the *card* for this afternoon?' (= programme).
c) (*informal*) 'he's a *card*!' (= amusing person).
on the cards, 'it's *on the cards* that he will be elected' (= likely).
[Greek *khartes* a papyrus leaf]

card (2) *noun*
an instrument used to disentangle fibres of wool, etc. before spinning.
Word Family: **card,** *verb.*

cardamom (*say* **kar**da–mum) *noun*
also spelt **cardamon**
the seed of an Asian plant, used in cooking and medicine.
[Greek]

cardboard *noun*
a sheet of thick, stiff pasteboard.
Word Family: **cardboard,** *adjective,* a) of or relating to cardboard, b) being insubstantial and precarious.

cardiac *adjective*
of or relating to the heart.
[Greek *kardia* the heart]

cardigan *noun*
a knitted jacket which fastens down the front.
[after the 7th Earl of *Cardigan* (who led the Charge of the Light Brigade)]

cardinal (*say* **kar**di–n'l) *noun*
1. *Roman Catholic:* (*capital*) a member of the council called the **Sacred College** which elects and advises the Pope.
2. a deep, rich red colour, like a Cardinal's cassock.
cardinal *adjective*
1. very important: 'this evidence is of *cardinal* value to the case'.
2. of or relating to a deep, rich red colour.
[Latin *cardo, cardinis* that on which all depends]

cardinal number
Maths: any whole number. Compare ORDINAL NUMBER.

cardinal points
the four main directions of the compass: north, south, east and west.

cardiograph (*say* **kar**dio–graf) *noun*
an electrocardiograph.

cardiology (*say* kardi–**olla**–jee) *noun*
the study of the heart and its functions.
Word Family: **cardiologist,** *noun.*

cardsharp, cardsharper *noun*
a person, especially a professional gambler, who cheats at cards.

care (*rhymes with* hair) *noun*
1. any worry or mental distress: 'she hasn't a *care* in the world'.
2. any serious attention: 'he takes great *care* in everything he does'.
3. any supervision: 'she left the children in the *care* of an aunt'.
care of, 'we wrote to her *care of* the Post Office' (= at the address of).
care *verb*
to be concerned or interested.
Usage: 'I don't *care* to go out today' (= wish).
care for, a) 'the government should *care for* the poor' (= look after); b) 'I don't *care for* chocolates' (= like).

careen (*say* ka–**reen**) *verb*
1. to tip or sway to one side.

2. an old word meaning to turn a ship on her side for cleaning and repair. [Latin *carina* a keel]

career (*say* ka–**reer**) *noun*
a chosen pursuit or occupation: 'a *career* in medicine'.
career *verb*
to move rapidly: 'the car *careered* down the hill'.
Word Family: **careerist,** *noun,* a person devoted to advancing himself in his career.

carefree *adjective*
free of worry or anxiety.

careful *adjective*
1. cautious: 'he's very *careful* about what he says in public'.
2. thorough: 'a *careful* study of the situation'.
Word Family: **carefully,** *adverb*; **carefulness,** *noun.*

careless *adjective*
resulting from or showing a lack of care, attention, thought, etc.: a) 'a *careless* remark'; b) '*careless* work'.
Word Family: **carelessly,** *adverb*; **carelessness,** *noun.*

caress (*say* ka–**ress**) *verb*
to touch or embrace in an affectionate manner.
Word Family: **caress,** *noun.*
[Latin *carus* dear]

caretaker *noun*
a person employed to look after a building, goods, etc.
caretaker *adjective*
holding office temporarily until a new appointment is made: 'a *caretaker* Prime Minister'.

careworn *adjective*
tired and troubled with worries: 'a *careworn* businessman'.

cargo *noun*
plural is **cargoes**
the goods carried on a ship, aircraft, etc.
[Spanish]

caribou (*say* **karri**–boo) *noun*
plural is **caribou**
a North American reindeer with large antlers.

caricature (*say* **karri**–k'chaw) *noun*
a sketch or description of a person which exaggerates a predominant or peculiar feature, as in a cartoon.
Word Family: **caricature,** *verb.*
[Italian *caricare* to exaggerate]

caries (*rhymes with* fairies) *noun*
any decay in a tooth, bone, etc.
Word Family: **carious,** *adjective.*
[Latin]

carillon (*say* ka–**ril**–y'n) *noun*
a) a set of bells in a tower on which tunes are played by hand or machinery.
b) a tune played on such bells.
[French]

carmine *noun*
a deep, purplish-red colour.
Word Family: **carmine,** *adjective.*

carnage (*say* **karnij**) *noun*
a massive slaughter or massacre.

carnal *adjective*
1. sensual or sexual.
2. not spiritual.
carnal knowledge, (*Law*) sexual intercourse.
Word Family: **carnally,** *adverb*; **carnality** (*say* kar–**nalli**–tee), *noun.*
[Latin *carnis* of flesh]

carnation (*say* kar–**nay**–sh'n) *noun*
1. a garden plant with sweet-smelling, rose-like flowers growing on long stems.
2. a strong, pink colour.
Word Family: **carnation,** *adjective.*
[Latin *carnatio* fleshiness]

carnival *noun*
1. a festive occasion with noisy revelry and merrymaking.
2. a fair or amusement show, especially a temporary one.

carnivorous (*say* kar–**nivv**'rus) *adjective*
of or relating to an organism which eats flesh.
Word Family: **carnivore,** *noun*; **carnivorously,** *adverb.*
[Latin *carnis* of flesh + *vorare* to swallow]

carol (*say* **karr**'l) *noun*
a song for Christmas or other religious festivals.
Word Family: **carol** (**carolled, carolling**), *verb,* to sing joyously.

carotene (*say* **karra**–teen) *noun*
Biology: a yellow pigment found in plants and changed into vitamin A in the liver.
[same origin as CARROT]

carotid (*say* ka–**rotid**) *noun*
Anatomy: either of two main arteries, one on each side of the neck, which carry blood to the head.

carousal (*say* ka–**rowz**'l) *noun*
a noisy or drunken gathering, celebration, etc.
Word Family: **carouse,** *verb.*

carousel (*say* karra–**sel**) *noun*
also spelt **carrousel**
a merry–go–round.

carp (1) *verb*
to find fault or complain unreasonably.
Word Family: **carpingly**, *adverb.*

carp (2) *noun*
plural is **carp**
any of a group of freshwater fish used as food and often bred in ponds.

carpal bone
see WRIST.

carpel *noun*
also called the **pistil**
Biology: the seed–bearing part of a flower, comprising the ovary, style and stigma.
[Greek *karpos* fruit]

carpenter *noun*
a person who builds or fixes wooden parts or structures.
Word Family: **carpentry**, *noun*; **carpenter**, *verb.*
[Latin *carpentarius*]

carpet (*say* **kar**–pit) *noun*
a thick covering for the floor, made of various fabrics, and often patterned.
on the carpet, being reprimanded by a person in authority.
Word Family: **carpet**, *verb*, a) to cover with carpet, b) (informal) to reprimand; **carpeting**, *noun*, the material used for carpets.

carpetbag *noun*
an oblong travelling bag made of carpeting.

carpetbagger *noun*
1. *American history:* a Northerner who went to the South after the Civil War to seek political or other advantages.
2. anyone who moves into an area seeking gain.

carport *noun*
an open–sided shelter for cars, with a roof supported by posts.

carriage (*say* **karr**ij) *noun*
1. a wheeled vehicle, usually horse–drawn, for carrying passengers.
2. a part, e.g. of a machine, designed to hold or carry something: 'a gun *carriage*'.
3. the manner of holding the head and body.
4. a) the act of transporting: 'you will have to bear the cost of *carriage*'. b) the cost of transporting.

carriageway *noun*
the part of a road for use by vehicles.

carrier *noun*
1. a person or thing that carries or conveys: 'a furniture *carrier*'.
2. *Medicine:* a person who transmits a disease without contracting it himself.
3. *Radio:* a wave which has its amplitude or frequency modulated so that it can carry a signal.

carrion *noun*
any dead or decaying flesh.

carrot *noun*
a plant with a cone–shaped, orange root which is used as a vegetable.
Word Family: **carroty**, *adjective*, resembling a carrot in colour.
[Greek *karoton*]

carry *verb*
(carried, carrying)
to bear or take, especially from one place to another.
Usages:
a) 'his voice *carries* well' (= travels, transmits).
b) 'this shop *carries* a wide range of goods' (= has, offers).
c) 'the motion was *carried* unanimously' (= accepted, adopted).
d) '5 into 31 goes 6 and *carry* 1' (= transfer to the next column).
e) 'will that branch *carry* your weight?' (= support).
f) '*carry* your head high' (= hold).
g) 'reinforcements enabled the fire–fighters to *carry* the day' (= win).
Phrases:
carry away, 'she was *carried away* by all the excitement' (= strongly affected).
carry off, a) 'she *carried off* all the prizes' (= won); b) 'he *carried off* the deception' (= performed successfully).
carry on, a) to manage or continue; b) to behave in an excited or foolish manner.
carry out, to put into practice.
carry over, to postpone.
carry through, to complete.

cart *noun*
1. a wheeled vehicle used to carry goods or passengers.
2. any small vehicle pulled by hand.
put the cart before the horse, to reverse the natural order.
Word Family: **cart**, *verb*, to carry, especially in a cart; **cart away, cart off**, to remove forcefully or unceremoniously; **cartage** (*say* **kar**tij), *noun*, a) the act of transporting, b) the cost of transporting; **carter**, *noun.*

carte blanche (*say* kart blonsh)
a full or unconditional power, authority, etc.: 'the assistant was given *carte blanche* while his boss was away'.
[French *carte* card + *blanche* white]

cartel (*say* kar–**tel**) *noun*
a) an agreement between the manufacturers or distributors of a commodity to control output or prices.
b) a group making such an agreement.

Cartesian coordinates
Maths: the coordinates which locate a point in a plane or in space by giving the perpendicular distance from two or three axes which intersect at the origin at right angles.
[from Latinized name of *René Descartes,* 1596–1650, a French philosopher]

cartilage (*say* **kar**ta–lij) *noun*
Anatomy: the tough, elastic tissue forming the ends of the bones and also found in the ears and nose.
Word Family: **cartilaginous** (*say* karta–**la**jinus), *adjective.*

cartography (*say* kar–**to**gra–fee) *noun*
the drawing and study of maps and charts.
Word Family: **cartographer,** *noun.*

carton (*say* **kart**'n) *noun*
a cardboard box or container.
[French]

cartoon *noun*
1. a) a drawing or series of drawings which comment in an amusing and often exaggerated way on a person or event. b) a comic strip.
2. a film consisting of a series of drawings which form continuous movement when shown through a projector. Short form of **animated cartoon.**
3. *Art:* a preliminary sketch for a painting, decorative pattern, etc.
Word Family: **cartoonist,** *noun.*

cartridge (*say* **kar**–trij) *noun*
1. a cylindrical case containing the charge of powder, primer and bullet or shot for a gun.
2. any similar object, such as a disposable ink container for a fountain pen.
3. *Audio:* the device which changes mechanical vibrations, received through the stylus from the groove of a record, into electronic signals for amplification.

cartridge paper
a rough paper used for drawing or printing.

cartwheel *noun*
1. the wheel of a cart.
2. a somersault performed sideways with hands and legs extended.

carve *verb*
to cut into a shape: 'a statue *carved* from stone'.
Usages:
a) 'who will *carve* the roast?' (= slice).
b) 'he has *carved* a career in medicine' (= made, established).
Word Family: **carver,** *noun,* a person or thing that carves; **carving,** *noun,* a carved object or sculpture.

caryatid (*say* karri–**attid**) *noun*
plural is **caryatids** or **caryatides** (*say* karri–**atta**–deez)
a sculpture of a female figure used as a supporting column, e.g. in ancient Greek architecture.

casbah *noun*
also spelt **kasbah**
(in North Africa) a citadel or palace, or the quarter adjoining it.
[Arabic, citadel]

cascade (*say* kass–**kade**) *noun*
a) a waterfall or series of waterfalls.
b) something resembling a waterfall.
Word Family: **cascade,** *verb.*
[Italian *cascare* to fall]

cascara (*say* kass–**kar**–a) *noun*
short form of **cascara sagrada**
the bark of a Californian tree, used as a laxative.
[Spanish *cascara* bark + *sagrada* sacred]

case (1) *noun*
1. an instance, event or example: 'in that *case* I will not come'.
Usages:
a) 'this is a *case* requiring some thought' (= matter, problem).
b) 'there is a strong *case* for reform' (= argument).
c) 'however it may appear to you, that is not the *case*' (= actual state of affairs).
2. a) an occurrence of disease or disorder. b) a patient or client, as of a doctor, social worker, etc.
3. a law suit.
4. *Grammar:* a) the relationship of a word or pronoun to another word in a sentence. b) the change of the word's form indicating this.
the noun or pronoun which rules the action of the verb is in the **nominative case.** *Example*: *he* hit the ball.
a noun or pronoun which is ruled by a verb or preposition is in the **objective**

case, (in certain inflected languages called the **accusative case**). *Example*: the ball hit *him*.
the **possessive case**, (in certain inflected languages called the **genitive case**), expresses ownership. *Example:* the *boy's* football.
the **dative case** is used in certain inflected languages to indicate the indirect object.
the **ablative case** in Latin adds the sense *by*, *with* or *from* to the word. *Example: bona fide*, ablative of *bona fides* (= *with* good faith).
Phrases:
in any case, a) in any circumstances; b) moreover or besides.
in case of, '*in case of* fire, break the glass' (= in the event of).

case (2) *noun*
1. a container, box or covering.
2. a suitcase.
3. *Printing:* a tray containing type, usually arranged in a set of two, the upper case containing capital letters and the lower case containing the small letters.
Word Family: **case**, *verb*, a) to put in a container, b) (informal) to watch or examine a house, etc. when planning a crime.

case history
all relevant information about a person, including background and previous illnesses, used to help doctors, social workers, etc. diagnose or solve problems.

casein (*say* **kay**–sin *or* **kay**–seen) *noun*
the main protein in milk, forming the basis of cheese, and used in paints, adhesives, plastics and artificial textile fibres.
[Latin *caseus* cheese]

casement *noun*
a window which opens outwards on hinges which are attached at one side of it.

cash *noun*
a) any money in the form of banknotes or coins as distinct from cheques, etc. b) immediate payment rather than hire-purchase or other credit.
cash *verb*
to give or get cash in exchange for: 'the gambler *cashed* his chips'.
cash in on, (*informal*) to gain a profit or advantage from.

cashew (*say* **kashoo**) *noun*
a small, kidney-shaped, edible nut, originally from South America.

cash flow
Economics: the regulating of incoming and outgoing cash.

cashier (1) (*say* kash–**eer**) *noun*
a person who receives and pays out money, as in a bank.

cashier (2) (*say* kash–**eer**) *verb*
Military: to dismiss in disgrace, especially from a position of responsibility.

cashmere (*say* **kash**–meer) *noun*
a soft, woollen fabric of twill weave.
[first made from the hair of goats from *Kashmir*, India]

cash register
a machine used to record cash sales, equipped with a drawer to keep banknotes and coins.

casing *noun*
a) any outer case or covering. b) the material from which it is made.

casino (*say* ka–**seeno**) *noun*
a place where gambling and other amusements are provided.

cask (*rhymes with* ask) *noun*
a barrel.

casket (*rhymes with* basket) *noun*
1. a small, often ornamental, box for storing jewels, letters, etc.
2. a coffin.

cassava (*say* ka–**sahva**) *noun*
a fleshy root grown in the tropics and made into flour or tapioca.

casserole (*say* **kassa**–role) *noun*
1. an ovenproof dish, usually of glass or pottery and often with a lid, used for baking.
2. any food cooked in such a dish, usually a mixture of meats and vegetables.

cassette (*say* ka–**set**) *noun*
a small plastic box containing a recording tape on two spools which do not need rethreading.

cassock *noun*
a long close-fitting robe, usually black, worn by Christian priests.

cassowary (*say* **kassa**–wairee) *noun*
a large, blue-black, flightless bird of Australia and New Guinea, with a large, horny crest on the head and brightly coloured skin on the face and neck.
[Malay]

cast (*rhymes with* fast) *verb*
1. to throw: 'the fisherman *cast* his line into the water'.

2. to pour liquid into a mould and allow it to set: 'to *cast* a statue in bronze'.
3. to calculate: 'the astrologer *cast* my horoscope'.
4. to choose actors for the roles in a play, film, etc.
Usages:
a) 'she *cast* a nervous glance at the others' (= directed, turned).
b) '*cast* your votes here' (= deposit, give).
c) 'the horse *cast* a shoe' (= shed, dropped).
Phrases:
cast about, 'he *cast about* for a good excuse' (= searched).
cast back, to refer to the past.
cast off, a) to reject or discard; b) to let go, e.g. as a ship from its mooring; c) to remove the last row of stitches from the needle in knitting.
cast on, to place the first row of stitches on the needle in knitting.
cast *noun*
1. the act of casting.
2. *Theatre:* all the actors in a play, film, etc.
3. something shaped into a mould while in a fluid state, such as plaster for a broken limb.
4. a sort or kind: 'he is a different *cast* of person'.
5. a squint: 'he has a *cast* in one eye'.

castanets (*say* **kasta**–nets) *plural noun*
Music: a percussion instrument used in Spanish dances, etc. and made from two hollowed, round pieces of wood which are clicked together by the fingers.
[Spanish *castañetas* little chestnuts]

castaway (*say* **kahsta**–way) *noun*
a person who has been shipwrecked.

caste (*say* kahst) *noun*
a hereditary social group defined by occupation or trade, wealth, religion and marriage laws, such as the Hindu castes in India.
[Spanish *casta* lineage]

caster *noun*
see CASTOR (2).

castigate (*say* **kasti**–gate) *verb*
to punish or criticize severely.
Word Family: **castigation**, *noun*; **castigator**, *noun*, a person who castigates.
[Latin *castigare* to chastise]

cast iron
any hard, brittle alloy of iron and carbon (2–4 per cent), which may be cast into shape.
cast–iron *adjective*
made of cast iron.
Usage: 'the witness had a *cast–iron* excuse' (= unquestionable).

castle (*say* **kahs**'l) *noun*
1. a large fortified building.
2. *Chess:* a rook.
castle *verb*
Chess: to move the king two squares towards a rook, then place the rock on the first square passed by the king.
[Latin *castellum* fort]

castle in the air
a daydream.

cast–off *noun*
a person or thing that has been rejected or discarded, especially an item of clothing.

castor (1) (*say* **kah**sta) *noun*
a bitter, strong–smelling cream obtained from glands in the beaver and used in perfume and medicine.
[Greek *kastor* beaver]

castor (2) (*say* **kah**sta) *noun*
also spelt **caster**
1. a small wheel or roller made to swivel in any direction, such as that used on furniture legs.
2. a container with holes in the top for sprinkling sugar, salt or flour.

castor oil
a thick oil obtained from the seeds of a tall Indian plant and used as a laxative.

castor sugar
a finely ground sugar.

castrate (*say* **kass**–trate) *verb*
to remove the testicles to make sterile or prevent fertilization. Compare SPAY.
Word Family: **castration** (*say* kass–**tray**–sh'n), *noun*.
[Latin]

casual (*say* ka*zh*–yew'l) *adjective*
1. happening by chance: 'a *casual* meeting'.
2. careless or unconcerned: 'her *casual* attitude towards work made her parents angry'.
3. informal: '*casual* dress'.
4. irregular or occasional: '*casual* employment'.
Word Family: **casual**, *noun*, a person who is in casual employment; **casually**, *adverb*; **casualness**, *noun*.
[Latin *casus* a chance]

casualty (*say* **kazh**–yew'l–tee) *noun*
1. a person injured or killed.
2. an unfortunate accident, especially one involving injury.

casuarina (*say* kaz–yoo–**reena**) *noun*
any of a group of Australian and Indian trees, often found in swampy areas and having needle-like leaves, flat-topped cones and slender, wiry branches.

casuistry (*say* **kaz**–yewis–tree) *noun*
any false but clever arguments, especially those used to settle questions of conscience.
Word Family: **casuistic** (*say* kaz–yoo–**istik**), **casuistical**, *adjective*; **casuistically**, *adverb*; **casuist**, *noun*, a person who practises casuistry.

cat *noun*
1. a small domesticated mammal kept as a pet.
2. any of a family of flesh-eating mammals including lions, tigers, etc.
3. a gossipy, spiteful woman.
4. (*informal*) a cat–o'–nine–tails.
5. *Nautical:* see CATAMARAN.
Phrases:
let the cat out of the bag, to reveal information, usually unintentionally.
rain cats and dogs, to rain very heavily.

catabolism (*say* ka–**tabba**–lizm) *noun*
also spelt **katabolism**
the process in a living organism of breaking down complex substances into simpler ones. Compare ANABOLISM.
[Greek *katabolé* a throwing down]

cataclysm (*say* **katta**–klizm) *noun*
any sudden upheaval or change.
Word Family: **cataclysmic** (*say* katta–**klizmik**), **cataclysmal**, *adjective.*
[Greek *kataklysmos* deluge]

catacomb (*say* **katta**–koom *or* **katta**–kome) *noun*
(*usually plural*) an underground cemetery consisting of tunnels with recesses for graves.

catafalque (*say* **katta**–falk) *noun*
a temporary stand on which a corpse lies in state.

catalepsy (*say* **katta**–lepsee) *noun*
a form of epilepsy marked by paralysis instead of fits.
Word Family: **cataleptic** (*say* katta–**leptik**), *adjective, noun.*
[Greek *katalepsis* a seizure]

catalogue (*say* **katta**–log) *noun*
in America spelt **catalog**
a list of items, names, goods, etc., often in alphabetical order: 'a *catalogue* of paintings in an exhibition'.
Word Family: **catalogue** (**catalogued**, **cataloguing**), *verb*; **cataloguer**, **cataloguist**, *nouns.*
[Greek *katalogos* list]

catalyst (*say* **katta**–list) *noun*
1. *Chemistry:* a substance which causes or increases the rate of a chemical reaction, remaining unchanged at the end of the reaction.
2. any person or thing that causes or accelerates change, etc.
Word Family: **catalyze**, **catalyse**, *verb*; **catalysis** (*say* ka–**talla**–sis), *noun*; **catalytic** (*say* katta–**littik**), *adjective.*
[Greek *katalysis* dissolution]

catamaran (*say* **katta**–m'ran) *noun*
short form is **cat**
a boat or raft with two parallel hulls which are joined above the water. Compare TRIMARAN.
[Tamil]

catapult (*say* **katta**–pult) *noun*
a device for throwing objects, such as a Y-shaped device for shooting stones, a device for launching aircraft from ships, etc.
Word Family: **catapult**, *verb*, to hurl from or as if from a catapult.
[Greek *katapeltes*]

cataract *noun*
1. a waterfall or series of waterfalls.
2. a condition in which the lens of the eye becomes increasingly opaque.
[Greek *katarrhaktes* rushing down]

catarrh (*say* ka–**tar**) *noun*
an inflammation of the mucous membranes, which produces excess mucus, especially in the respiratory tract.
Word Family: **catarrhal**, *adjective.*
[Greek *katarrhein* to run down]

catastrophe (*say* ka–**tastra**–fee) *noun*
a sudden, widespread disaster.
Word Family: **catastrophic** (*say* katta–**stroffik**), *adjective*; **catastrophically**, *adverb.*
[Greek *katastrophé* the turning point of a play]

catatonia (*say* katta–**toe**–nee–a) *noun*
Psychology: a form of schizophrenia in which the body remains rigid for long periods of time, sometimes alternating with periods of excessive activity.
Word Family: **catatonic** (*say* katta–**tonnik**), *adjective, noun.*
[Greek *kata* down + *tonos* tension]

cat-burglar *noun*
see BURGLAR.

catcall (*say* **kat**-kawl) *noun*
a cry or sound used to express disapproval, disgust, etc

catch *verb*
(caught, catching)
1. to stop and hold a moving object: 'throw the ball and I'll *catch* it'.
Usages:
a) 'she has *caught* the flu' (= become infected with).
b) 'mother *caught* him stealing' (= detected in the act of).
c) 'he *caught* my eye and winked' (= got the attention of).
d) 'I *caught* my foot on the carpet' (= entangled).
e) 'the stick *caught* him on the shoulder' (= hit).
f) 'I don't *catch* your meaning' (= understand).
g) 'the briquettes *caught* instantly' (= began to burn).
2. *Sport:* to catch a hit ball before it lands or bounces, causing the batter to be dismissed.
Phrases:
catch it, (*informal*) 'you'll *catch it* when Dad finds out!' (= get into trouble).
catch on, a) 'long skirts have certainly *caught on* this year' (= become popular or fashionable); b) 'do you think he *caught on* to the joke?' (= understood).
catch out, 'I was *caught out* by their trick' (= trapped).
catch up, to become level with or overtake.
catch *noun*
1. the act of catching.
2. a) anything which catches or holds: 'a safety *catch*'. b) anything which is caught: 'a good *catch* of fish'.
Usages:
a) 'there must be a *catch* to the plan' (= trick, complication).
b) 'he is considered quite a *catch*' (= eligible partner for marriage).
catch-22, (*informal*) a regulation or procedure which offers the person subject to it no hope of meeting its stipulations. (From *Catch-22* a novel by Joseph Heller).

catchment area
the drainage area of a river and its tributaries.

catchword, catchphrase *noun*
a word or phrase repeated to achieve effect, such as a slogan in an election.

catchy *adjective*
1. easily remembered: 'a *catchy* tune'.
2. tricky: 'that's a *catchy* question'.

catechism (*say* **katta**-kizm) *noun*
1. *Christian:* a book of instruction containing a summary of beliefs in the form of questions and answers.
2. any similar book of simple questions and answers.
Word Family: **catechize, catechise,** *verb,* to teach or test by question and answer; **catechist,** *noun,* an instructor in catechism; **catechistic** (*say* katta-**kis**tik), **catechistical,** *adjective.*

categorical (*say* katta-**gorri**-k'l) *adjective*
direct or unconditional: 'his reply was a *categorical* "no!" '.
Word Family: **categorically,** *adverb.*

category (*say* **katta**-gree) *noun*
a division or class within a complete field: 'he puts gardening into the *category* of hard work'.
Word Family: **categorize, categorise,** *verb,* to put into a category or categories.
[Greek *kategoria* a statement]

cater (*say* **kay**ter) *verb*
to provide for or supply with, especially food, entertainment, etc.: 'that firm only *caters* for formal parties'.
caterer *noun*
a person or business that provides food and other services for parties, etc.

caterpillar (*say* **katta**-pilla) *noun*
1. the herbivorous larva of a butterfly or moth.
2. a tractor or other device which moves on an endless ribbed belt passing around its wheels.
[Old French *chatepelose* hairy cat]

caterwaul (*say* **katta**-wawl) *verb*
to cry or howl like a cat.
Word Family: **caterwaul,** *noun.*

catfish *noun*
any of a large group of fish, usually freshwater, with whiskers near the mouth and a ridged spine which can inflict painful wounds.

catgut *noun*
the dried, twisted intestines of sheep or other animals, used to make strings for musical instruments, tennis rackets, etc.

catharsis (*say* ka-**thar**sis) *noun*
plural is **catharses**
the release or relief of strong feelings, e.g. by acting out an impulse in drama, art, etc.

Word Family: **cathartic**, *adjective.*
[Greek *katharsis* cleansing]

cathedral (*say* ka-**thee**-dr'l) *noun*
Christian: the principal church in a diocese, containing the bishop's throne.
[Greek *kathedra* chair]

catherine-wheel *noun*
a firework which spins as it burns.

catheter (*say* **kath**ita) *noun*
Medicine: a hollow tube inserted to drain fluids, especially urine, from the body.
[Greek *katheter* anything let down into]

cathode *noun*
a negative electrode. Compare ANODE.
[Greek *kata* down + *hodos* a way]

cathode ray
a beam of electrons produced at the cathode, such as is used in a television picture tube.

cathode-ray oscilloscope
an instrument in which electronic impulses, waves, etc. are displayed and measured on a cathode-ray tube.

cathode-ray tube
a vacuum tube in which a beam of electrons produces a bright spot on a luminescent screen at the front of the tube. A television picture tube is a special type of cathode-ray tube.

catholic (*say* **katha**-lik) *adjective*
1. universal: 'a matter of *catholic* interest'.
2. liberal or wide-ranging: 'his taste in music is *catholic*'.
3. *Christian:* (*capital*) a) of or relating to the whole Church. b) of the Western or Roman Church as distinct from the Eastern or Greek Church.

catholic *noun*
(*capital*) a member of the Roman Catholic Church.
Word Family: **Catholicism** (*say* ka-**tholla**-sizm), *noun*, the beliefs and practices of the Roman Catholic Church; **catholicity** (*say* katha-**lissa**-tee), *noun*, the quality of being catholic.
[Greek *katholikos* universal]

cation (*say* **kat**-eye-on) *noun*
Chemistry: a positively charged ion which is attracted to the cathode during electrolysis. Compare ANION.
[Greek *kata* down + ION]

catkin *noun*
a spike of soft, down-like flowers hanging from twigs, as on a willow or birch.

catnap *noun*
a brief sleep.
Word Family: **catnap** (**catnapped, catnapping**), *verb.*

catnip *noun*
a variety of mint with strongly scented leaves.

cat-o'-nine-tails *noun*
plural is **cat-o'-nine-tails**
a whip for flogging a person, usually consisting of nine knotted cords attached to the handle.

cat's-eye *noun*
1. a gem of the quartz group which reflects a single ray of light when cut in a rounded form.
2. a reflector marking the centre or boundaries of a road.

cattle *noun*
any bovine mammals, such as cows, bulls, etc.

catty, cattish *adjective*
of or like a cat.
Usage: 'I dislike his *catty* remarks' (= spiteful).

catwalk *noun*
a narrow path or platform, e.g. on the sides of a bridge, etc.

Caucasian (*say* kaw-**kay**-*zh*'n) *noun*
also called a **Caucasoid** (*say* **kaw**ka-zoyd)
any of a major race of people, including those of Europe, south-west Asia and northern Africa, with light to brown skin and fine, straight or wavy hair.
Word Family: **Caucasian**, *adjective.*
[after *Caucasia*, Russia, where the race supposedly originated]

caucus (*say* **kaw**-kus) *noun*
(*sometimes derogatory*) a small group within a political party, formed to influence policy.

caudal (*say* **kaw**-d'l) *adjective*
Biology: of or near the tail of an organism: 'a *caudal* fin'.
[Latin *cauda* tail]

caught *verb*
the past tense and past participle of the verb **catch**.

caul (*rhymes with* ball) *noun*
a thin covering membrane, such as that surrounding a foetus, covering the lower intestines of pigs, etc.

cauldron (*say* **kawl**–dr'n) *noun*
a large pot for cooking.
[Latin *calidarium* a hot bath]

cauliflower (*say* **kolli**–flower) *noun*
a large, white vegetable with a compact head of many sections, each with a broad stalk.

cauliflower ear
a flattened or deformed ear, especially one caused by blows in boxing.

caulk (*rhymes with* walk) *verb*
to fill seams or joints, such as gaps between planks in a boat, to make them watertight, etc.

causal (*say* **kaw**–z'l) *adjective*
of or expressing cause.
causality (*say* kaw–**zalli**–tee) *noun*
the relationship between cause and effect.
Word Family: **causally**, *adverb.*

cause *noun*
anything which produces an effect, action or result: 'a virus was the *cause* of his illness'.
Usages:
a) 'they are working for a noble *cause*' (= purpose, aim).
b) 'which barrister is pleading the defendant's *cause*?' (= case).
c) 'you have no *cause* to complain' (= reason).
cause *verb*
to bring about: 'what *caused* the explosion?'.
Word Family: **causation**, *noun.*
[Latin *causa*]

cause célèbre (*say* koze say–**lebra**)
a law suit which causes much debate or interest.

causeway *noun*
a raised road or path, e.g. across wet or swampy ground.

caustic (*say* **kos**–tik *or* **kaw**–stik) *adjective*
Chemistry: (of an alkali) able to corrode organic matter.
Usage: 'she embarrassed me with her *caustic* wit' (= sarcastic, biting).
Word Family: **caustically**, *adverb.*
[Greek *kaustikos* capable of burning]

caustic potash
Chemistry: potassium hydroxide (formula KOH), a very strong alkali used for making soap, etc.

caustic soda
Chemistry: sodium hydroxide (formula NaOH), a very strong alkali.

cauterize (*say* **kawta**–rize) **cauterise** *verb*
to seal or destroy tissue by burning.

caution (*say* **kaw**–sh'n) *noun*
1. the act of taking care, especially to avoid danger: 'drive with *caution*'.
2. a warning: 'the prisoner was released from gaol with a *caution* not to repeat his crime'.
Word Family: **caution**, *verb*, to warn or advise; **cautionary**, *adjective.*
[Latin *cautio* wariness]

cautious (*say* **kaw**–shus) *adjective*
very careful or wary: 'he is *cautious* about investing money'.
Word Family: **cautiously**, *adverb*; **cautiousness**, *noun.*

cavalcade (*say* **kavv**'l–kade) *noun*
a procession, originally of horsemen: 'a *cavalcade* of official cars followed the President's vehicle'.

cavalier (*say* kavva–**leer**) *noun*
1. an old word for a horseman or knight.
2. a courteous or gallant man.
Word Family: **cavalier**, *adjective*, arrogant or offhand.
[French, a horserider]

cavalry (*say* **kavv**'l–ree) *noun*
the branch of the army which originally fought on horseback. Compare INFANTRY.
[French]

cave *noun*
an underground space in the earth's surface.
cave *verb*
to fall in or collapse.
cave in, a) to collapse, b) to submit or yield.
[Latin *cavum* a hollow]

caveat (*say* **kay**–vi–at) *noun*
1. *Law:* a request to postpone a case, transaction, etc. until further evidence is found or heard.
2. a warning.
[Latin, let him beware]

caveman *noun*
a cave–dweller, especially a person from prehistoric times.

cavern (*say* **kavv**'n) *noun*
a large cave.
cavernous *adjective*
deep or hollow: 'a *cavernous* yawn'.
Word Family: **cavernously**, *adverb.*

caviare (*say* **kavvi**–ah) **caviar** *noun*
the tiny, salted eggs of the sturgeon or other fish, considered a delicacy.

cavil (*say* **kavvil**) *verb*
(**cavilled, cavilling**)
to quibble or make petty objections.
Word Family: **cavil,** *noun.*
[Italian *cavilla* mockery]

cavity (*say* **kavvi**–tee) *noun*
a hole or hollow in a solid object: 'a *cavity* in a tooth'.

cavort (*say* ka–**vort**) *verb*
to jump or dance around.

caw *noun*
the harsh cry of a crow, magpie, etc.
Word Family: **caw,** *verb.*

cay (*say* kay *or* kee) *noun*
also called a **key**
a small island.

cayenne *noun*
a hot, red pepper made from the ground pods and seeds of certain varieties of capsicum.

cayman *noun*
any of a group of South American freshwater reptiles, related to the alligator.

cease *verb*
to stop or come to an end: 'the old mill has *ceased* to function'.
Word Family: **cease,** *noun*; **ceaseless,** *adjective,* without end; **ceaselessly,** *adverb.*
[Latin *cessare* to give way, to rest]

cease–fire *noun*
an end of hostilities, especially a truce.

cecum *noun*
see CAECUM.

cedar (*say* **seed**a) *noun*
any of a group of evergreen trees with short needle–like leaves, seeds in cones and hard, fragrant, red wood used for timber.
[Greek *kedros*]

cede (*say* seed) *verb*
to give up or surrender something to another: 'the property was *ceded* to the government'.
[Latin *cedere* to yield]

cedilla (*say* si–**dill**a) *noun*
Language: see ACCENT.
[Spanish, a little *z*]

ceilidh (*say* **kay**–lee) *noun*
an informal evening of song, dance and story–telling.
[Gaelic, a visit]

ceiling (*say* **seel**ing) *noun*
the underside lining of a roof.
Usage: 'you'll have to put a *ceiling* on your spending' (= top limit).

celandine (*say* **sel**'n–dine) *noun*
greater celandine, a plant of the poppy family with yellow flowers in summer.
lesser celandine, a plant of the buttercup family with yellow flowers in spring.
[Greek *khelidon* a swallow, as the greater celandine flower appears and departs with the swallows]

celebrate (*say* **sell**a–brate) *verb*
1. to hold a ceremony or other festivity: 'we *celebrated* Christmas at home'.
2. to praise: 'her beauty was *celebrated* in poetry'.
celebrated *adjective*
famous: 'a *celebrated* singer'.
Word Family: **celebration,** *noun,* a) the act of celebrating, b) anything that celebrates something; **celebrant** (*say* **sell**a–brunt), *noun,* a person leading or taking part in a ceremony or celebration.
[Latin *celebrare* to make widely known]

celebrity (*say* se–**lebra**–tee) *noun*
a) fame. b) a famous person.
[Latin *celeber* famous]

celeriac *noun*
a variety of celery with swollen, turnip–like roots, used in cooking.

celerity (*say* se–**lerra**–tee) *noun*
a swiftness or speed: 'he did the job with great *celerity*'.
[Latin *celer* swift]

celery (*say* **sell**a–ree) *noun*
a vegetable with long pale green edible stalks.

celesta (*say* se–**lesta**) *noun*
Music: an instrument like a small piano in which hammers strike metal bars to give a bell–like sound.
[French *céleste* heavenly]

celestial (*say* se–**lest**iul) *adjective*
heavenly or divine.
[Latin *caelestis* of the sky]

celestial sphere
Astronomy: an imaginary sphere around the observer, in which the planets and stars appear to be fixed.

celibacy (*say* **selli**–b'see) *noun*
the state of remaining chaste or unmarried, especially because of religious vows.
Word Family: **celibate,** *adjective, noun.*
[Latin *caelebs* bachelor]

cell (*say* sell) *noun*
1. a small room, usually for one person, as in a prison or monastery.

2. a unit of protoplasm, usually containing a nucleus. It is enclosed by a membrane in animals and by a cell wall in plants.
3. *Electricity:* a single device for producing electricity by chemical action. A **wet cell**, e.g. in a motor car battery, has a liquid electrolyte. A **dry cell**, e.g. in a torch battery, has the electrolyte in a jelly or absorbed in some porous material so that it will not spill.
4. a small group or unit dependent on a larger organization: 'a communist *cell* was established in every small town'.
Word Family: **cellular** (*say* **sel**–yew–la), *adjective*, relating to or composed of cells.
[Latin *cella* storeroom]

cellar (*say* **sella**) *noun*
an underground room, usually beneath a building and used to store wine, etc.
Usage: 'she has an extensive *cellar* to draw upon' (= supply of wine).
cellarage (*say* **sella**–rij) *noun*
a) the capacity of a cellar. b) the cost of storage in a cellar.
Word Family: **cellar,** *verb*, to store in a cellar.

cell–division *noun*
Biology: the division of a cell in growth or reproduction.

cello (*say* **chello**) **'cello** *noun*
short form of **violoncello**
Music: a large, low-pitched, stringed instrument, usually played with a bow by a seated player.
Word Family: **cellist** (*say* **chellist**), *noun*, a person who plays the cello.

cellophane (*say* **sello**–fane) *noun*
a transparent, waterproof paper obtained from wood cellulose and used for wrapping food, etc.
[a trademark]

cellular (*say* **sel**–yew–la) *adjective*
Word Family: see CELL.

celluloid (*say* **sel**–yoo–loyd) *noun*
a hard, elastic, inflammable plastic which softens when heated.
[a trademark]

cellulose (*say* **sel**–yoo–lose) *noun*
Chemistry: a complex substance consisting of long chains of glucose units forming strong fibres, found in cell walls of plants. It is used in making paper, rayon, plastics and explosives.

cellulose acetate
Chemistry: any of a range of substances made from cellulose and acetic acid, used in rayon and plastics.

cellulose nitrate
also called **nitrocellulose**
Chemistry: any of a range of substances produced by the action of nitric acid on cellulose, used in plastics, lacquers and explosives.

Celsius (*say* **selsi**–us) *adjective*
of or relating to a scale of temperature with 0°C set at the melting point of ice, and 100°C set at the boiling point of water. Compare KELVIN and FAHRENHEIT.
See UNITS in grey pages.
[after *Anders Celsius*, 1701–44, a Swedish astronomer]

Celtic (*say* **kel**–tik *or* **sel**–tik) *adjective*
of or pertaining to the languages or inhabitants of ancient Gaul and ancient Britain, or their descendants today.
Celtic fringe, the western parts of the British Isles and northern France where these languages are still, or were until recently, spoken, inhabited by the Highland Scots, Welsh, Irish, Cornishmen, Manxmen and the Bretons of Brittany.
[Latin *Celtae* the Celts]

cement (*say* **simment**) *noun*
1. any substance which, after mixing with a solvent such as water, sets to a hard mass. **Portland cement** is made by heating clay and lime.
2. any substance which joins or fills, such as the natural material which binds rock particles together, or the adhesive, plastic substance used to fill teeth.
Word Family: **cement,** *verb*, a) to cover with cement, b) to join firmly with or as if with cement; **cementation** (*say* seemen–**tay**–sh'n), *noun.*
[Latin *caementum* rubble]

cemetery (*say* **semma**–tree) *noun*
also called a **graveyard**
an area of land reserved for the burial of the dead.
[Greek *koimeterion* dormitory]

cenotaph (*say* **senna**–taf *or* **senna**–tahf) *noun*
a monument, especially as a war memorial, in memory of a person or people whose bodies are buried elsewhere.
[Greek *kenos* empty + *taphos* tomb]

Cenozoic (*say* **senno**–zo–ik) *noun*
Geology: see CAINOZOIC.

censer (*say* **sen**sa) *noun*
a container in which incense is burned for religious ceremonies.

censor (*say* **sen**sa) *noun*
an official appointed to examine books, newspapers, films, etc. and cut out any parts believed to be undesirable.
censorship *noun*
the act or process of censoring.
Word Family: **censor**, *verb*, to perform the work of a censor; **censorial** (*say* sen–**sawri**–al), *adjective.*
[Latin, a magistrate]
Common Error: do not confuse with CENSURE.

censorious (*say* sen–**sawri**–us) *adjective*
being apt to find fault or criticize.
Word Family: **censoriously**, *adverb*; **censoriousness**, *noun.*

censure (*say* **sen**sha) *noun*
a formal expression of blame or disapproval: 'your *censure* of his bad behaviour was appropriate'.
Word Family: **censure**, *verb.*
Common Error: do not confuse with CENSOR.

census (*say* **sen**sus) *noun*
an official count of the inhabitants of a country.
[Latin]

cent (*say* sent) *noun*
a coin worth one hundredth of a dollar.
[Latin *centum* hundred]

centaur (*say* **sen**taw) *noun*
Greek mythology: a creature with the head and upper body of a man, and the lower body and legs of a horse.

centenary (*say* sen–**teena**–ree *or* sen–**tenna**–ree) *noun*
a 100th anniversary.
Word Family: **centennial,** *adjective,* a) lasting 100 years, b) occurring every 100 years; **centennial,** *noun.*

center *noun*
see CENTRE.

centi–
a prefix used for SI units, meaning one hundredth (10^{-2}). See UNITS in grey pages.

centigrade (*say* **senti**–grade) *adjective*
Celsius.

centipede (*say* **senti**–peed) *noun*
any of a group of arthropods with firm, flattened, segmented bodies, each segment having a pair of legs, the first pair being modified into poisonous fangs.
[Latin *centum* hundred + *pedis* of a foot]

central (*say* **sent**–r'l) *adjective*
1. at or near the centre: 'the rooms in the house opened onto the *central* passage'.
2. principal or chief: 'the *central* issue, according to the article, is inflation'.
Word Family: **centrally**, *adverb.*

central heating
a system of heating a building from one source by circulating steam, hot water or air through pipes.

centralize (*say* **sen**tra–lize) **centralise** *verb*
1. to bring to a centre or make central.
2. (of governments, institutions, etc.) to bring administration, the making of decisions, etc. under central control.
Word Family: **centralization,** *noun*; **centralism**, *noun*, a process or policy of centralizing; **centralist,** *adjective, noun.*

central nervous system
see NERVOUS SYSTEM.

centre (*say* **sen**ta) *noun*
in America spelt **center**
1. a middle point, especially the point within a circle or sphere which is equidistant from the circumference.
Usages:
a) 'she is always the *centre* of attention' (= main object).
b) 'a shopping *centre*' (= principal place for).
2. (*capital*) those politicians and their supporters of any political party who hold moderate views on most issues. Compare LEFT WING and RIGHT WING.
3. *Sport:* a player in one of various positions across or down the centre of a field.
Word Family: **centre,** *verb,* to place in, at or towards the centre.
[Greek *kentron* a sharp point]

centre of gravity
the point in an object about which the weight is evenly balanced in any position.

centrepiece *noun*
1. a decorative object or arrangement, especially one placed at the centre of a dining table.
2. a chief feature.

centrifugal (*say* sentri–**few**–g'l *or* sen–**triff**–yew–g'l) *adjective*
moving or tending to move away from the centre.

centrifugal force
Physics: the tendency of a rotating body to move away from its circular path at a tangent.
[CENTRE + Latin *fugere* to flee]

centrifuge (*say* **sentri**–fewj) *noun*
any machine with a compartment which spins around a central axis, used to separate substances of different densities, etc.

centripetal (*say* sen–**trippi**–t'l) *adjective*
towards or moving towards the centre.
centripetal force
Physics: the force applied to a body which causes it to rotate in a circle.
[CENTRE + Latin *petere* to seek]

centurion (*say* sen–**tewri**–on) *noun*
Ancient history: an officer in the Roman army commanding a company of 100 foot soldiers.

century (*say* **sencha**–ree) *noun*
1. a period of one hundred years.
2. any group or collection of one hundred, e.g. of runs in cricket.
[Latin *centum* hundred]

cephalopod (*say* **seffala**–pod) *noun*
any of a group of molluscs, including the squid, octopus and cuttlefish, which have tentacles attached to their heads.
[Greek *kephalé* head + *podos* of a foot]

ceramics (*say* se–**rammiks**) *plural noun*
a) (*used with singular verb*) the art of making pottery, etc. from moist clays which are shaped, then fired to dry and harden. b) any articles made in this way.
[Greek *keramikos* of pottery]

cere (*say* seer) *noun*
a bare patch, in birds such as the parrot, at the base of the upper beak, where the nostrils are situated.
[Latin *cera* wax]

cereal (*say* **seerial**) *noun*
a) any cultivated plant belonging to the grass family, producing an edible, starchy seed. b) a food made from such seed.
[after *Ceres*, the goddess of agriculture in Roman mythology]

cerebellum (*say* serri–**bellum**) *noun*
plural is **cerebella**
Anatomy: the rear part of the brain, which coordinates muscle movement.
[Latin, the smaller brain]

cerebral (*say* **serri**–br'l) *adjective*
of or relating to the brain.
Usage: 'modern composers are too *cerebral* for her taste' (= intellectual, analytic).
cerebral palsy
a form of paralysis usually due to brain injury at or during birth, causing difficulty in developing controlled movements.

cerebrum (*say* **serri**–br'm) *noun*
Anatomy: the large front part of the brain, controlling conscious thought and muscular action.
[Latin, brain]

ceremonial (*say* serri–**mo**–nee–ul) *adjective*
relating to formal or ritual occasions, etc.: 'the tribal chieftain wore a *ceremonial* cloak'.
ceremonial *noun*
formalities: 'he was installed as mayor with due *ceremonial*'.
Word Family: **ceremonially**, *adverb*.

ceremonious (*say* serri–**mo**–nee–us) *adjective*
elaborately formal or polite.
Word Family: **ceremoniously**, *adverb*; **ceremoniousness**, *noun*.

ceremony (*say* **serra**–mo–nee) *noun*
the formal behaviour or set of acts performed on certain sacred or important occasions: a) 'an initiation *ceremony*'; b) 'a wedding *ceremony*'.
Usage: 'we were greeted with *ceremony* rather than friendship' (= formal politeness).
stand on ceremony, 'our host urged us not to *stand on ceremony*' (= insist on formality).
[Latin *caerimonia* reverence]

cerise (*say* s'**reez**) *noun*
a bright, cherry-red colour.
Word Family: **cerise**, *adjective*.
[French, cherry]

cerium (*say* **seerium**) *noun*
element number 58, a rare metal. Its alloys are used in cigarette-lighter flints, and its compounds are used for making gas mantles and in glass-polishing. See LANTHANIDE.
See CHEMICAL ELEMENTS in grey pages.

certain (*say* **sir**–t'n) *adjective*
sure or free from doubt: 'I am *certain* he won't forget a second time'.
Usages:
a) 'she promised to meet me at a *certain* time' (= specific).
b) 'there's a *certain* arrogance about him' (= undefined).
c) 'I agree with you to a *certain* extent' (= limited).

d) 'everyone knows a *certain* person is responsible for the theft' (= not named but assumed to be known).
Word Family: **certainly**, *adverb*, without doubt; **certainly!**, *interjection*, of course!; **certainty**, *noun*, a) the state of being certain, b) a person or thing about which it is possible to be certain.
[Latin *certus* settled]

certificate (*say* sir–**tiffa**–kit) *noun*
a document or printed statement, often used as evidence for something: 'a birth *certificate*'.
Word Family: **certificate** (*say* sir–**tiffa**–kate), *verb*, to provide with or attest by a certificate; **certification**, *noun*.

certify (*say* **sirti**–fie) *verb*
(certified, certifying)
1. to confirm that something is true or genuine.
2. to officially declare a person insane.
3. *Commerce:* to guarantee that there is enough money in a bank account for a cheque to be paid.
Word Family: **certifier**, *noun*; **certifiable**, *adjective*.

certitude (*say* **sirti**–tewd) *noun*
a sense of absolute conviction.

cerulean (*say* sir–**roolian**) *adjective*
sky–blue.
[Latin *caeruleus*]

cervical (*say* **sirvi**–k'l) *adjective*
a) of or relating to the neck. b) of or relating to the cervix.

cervix (*say* **sir**–viks) *noun*
Anatomy: the cylindrical opening of the uterus of mammals which leads into the vagina.
[Latin, neck]

cesium *noun*
see CAESIUM.

cessation (*say* sess–**ay**–sh'n) *noun*
a ceasing or stopping: 'discussion of peace terms began after the *cessation* of hostilities'.

cession (*say* **sesh**'n) *noun*
the transfer of land by one country to another, usually under the threat of war or after military defeat.

cesspool (*say* sess–pool) *noun*
also called a **cesspit**
a hole or pit into which drains empty.

chafe *verb*
1. to make warm by rubbing.
2. to wear or make sore by rubbing: 'the new shoes *chafed* his feet'.
Usage: 'she *chafed* at the idea of waiting so long' (= became irritated or impatient).
[French *chauffer* to warm]

chaff (1) (*say* chahf) *noun*
1. the husks of grains and grasses separated from the seeds.
2. a finely chopped hay used as fodder.

chaff (2) (*say* chahf) *verb*
to tease or make fun of.

chaffinch *noun*
a small European finch with a reddish–brown breast.

chagrin (*say* **shagrin** *or* sha–**green**) *noun*
a feeling of vexation or disappointment.
[French]

chain *noun*
1. a series of interlocked rings or links, usually of metal.
Usage: 'the convicts were held in *chains*' (= shackles).
2. any connected series: a) 'the mountain *chain* extended the length of the country'; b) 'he owns a *chain* of motels'.
3. *Chemistry:* a number of similar atoms joined together, particularly carbon, whose chains form the basis of all organic compounds.
4. a measuring instrument used in surveying.
5. a unit of length equal to about 20 m.
6. (*plural*) an apparatus put on vehicle wheels to give traction in snow and ice.
Word Family: **chain**, *verb*, to bind or fasten with a chain.

chain–gang *noun*
a group of convicts chained together for work outdoors.

chain mail
see MAIL (2).

chain–reaction *noun*
1. *Chemistry:* a reaction which produces substances that take a further part in the reaction, the rate of which rapidly increases. Most gaseous explosions are chain reactions.
2. any series of reactions caused by a single event.

chainsaw *noun*
a portable saw consisting of a continuous, turning loop of chain with teeth set on it, powered by a small motor.

chain-smoke *verb*
to smoke continually, as by lighting one cigarette from another.
Word Family: **chain-smoker**, *noun.*

chain-store *noun*
any of a group of shops owned and controlled by one company.

chair *noun*
1. a movable seat for one person, usually having four legs and a support for the back.
2. a person who presides over business at a meeting: 'please direct your questions to the *chair*'.
3. the position of a professor in a university, especially as the head of a department.
chair *verb*
also called to **take the chair**
to preside over a meeting.

chair-lift *noun*
a series of seats hanging from a moving overhead cable, used to take people up and down a mountain, etc.

chairman *noun*
1. a person who presides over business at a meeting.
2. the chief executive of a company.
Word Family: **chairmanship**, *noun*; **chairwoman**, *noun*, a female chairman.

chaise (*say* shaze) *noun*
an open, two-wheeled carriage with a hood, pulled by a horse.
[French]

chaise longue (*say* shaze long)
a chair with a long seat which serves as a full-length leg rest.
[French]

chalcedony (*say* kal-**sedda**-nee) *noun*
Geology: any of a group of minerals composed of very fine quartz crystals, showing a wide range of colours and patterns.
agate is usually made up of concentric coloured bands forming a nodule, and is used as a pivot for beam balances, and in jewellery.
onyx has coloured bands, and is used in ornaments.
jasper is reddish and opaque, and is used in ornaments.
[Greek *khalkedon*]

chalet (*say* **shallay**) *noun*
a building, often with a wide, gently sloped, overhanging roof, common in Switzerland and other alpine regions.
[Swiss-French]

chalice (*say* **challis**) *noun*
1. *Christian:* a sacred vessel like a large goblet, used in religious services to hold Communion wine.
2. a poetic word for a drinking cup.
[Latin *calix* cup]

chalk (*rhymes with* walk) *noun*
1. *Geology:* a soft, white, fine-grained limestone, composed of minute fossils.
2. a prepared stick made from this substance, for drawing, marking, etc.
chalk *verb*
to mark or write with chalk.
chalk up, a) 'by lunch the visiting team had *chalked up* 300 runs' (= scored); b) 'losing money in the stock market is something you can *chalk up* to experience' (= attribute).
Word Family: **chalky**, *adjective*, having the colour or texture of chalk; **chalkiness**, *noun.*
[Latin *calx* lime]

challenge *noun*
1. a call to engage in a contest: 'he issued a *challenge* to fight after school'.
2. a call or demand to explain, identify oneself, etc.: 'the sentry shouted a *challenge* to the approaching group'.
Usages:
a) 'this work presents a real *challenge*' (= demand on one's abilities, etc.).
b) 'his integrity was proved to be beyond *challenge*' (= doubt, objection).
Word Family: **challenge**, *verb.*

challenger *noun*
a person or team playing against an official champion, hoping to win the title.

chamber (*say* **chame**-ber) *noun*
1. an old word for a room, especially a bedroom.
2. (*plural*) the rooms attached to a courthouse where judges carry out legal business which need not be done in court.
3. a legislative, judicial or administrative body: 'the lower *chamber* of the House is sitting now'.
4. a compartment or enclosed space: 'the *chambers* of the heart'.
5. the part of the breech of a rifle or a cylinder of a revolver, which receives the cartridge.
[Greek *kamara* a (vaulted) room]

chamberlain (*say* **chame**-ber-lin) *noun*
a high official in the court of a monarch.

chambermaid *noun*
a woman employed to clean bedrooms in hotels, etc.

chamber music
any music composed for a small group of instruments, originally for performance in a private home or small concert hall.

chamber of commerce
an association of businessmen for the protection and promotion of commerce.

chamber-pot *noun*
a portable bowl used in bedrooms instead of a toilet.

chameleon (*say* ka-**meel**ian) *noun*
1. any of various slow-moving, tree-dwelling lizards which are able to change colour to blend with their surroundings.
2. a person who is changeable or fickle.
[Greek *khamai* ground + *leon* lion]

chamfer *verb*
to bevel the sharp edges or corners of a piece of woodwork, etc.
Word Family: **chamfer,** *noun,* a surface made by chamfering.

chamois *noun*
1. (*say* **sham**wah) an antelope found in the mountains of Europe and Asia, noted for the soft leather made from its hide.
2. (*say* **shammi**) a soft, pliable leather treated with oil and used for cleaning, etc. Also spelt **shammy.**

champ *verb*
to bite on or munch.
champ at the bit, to show restless impatience.

champagne (*say* sham-**pane**) *noun*
a sparkling, white wine which is fermented in the bottle.
[made in *Champagne,* France]

champignon (*say* **sham**pin-yon) *noun*
a mushroom.
[French]

champion *noun*
a person or thing that wins first prize or takes first place in a competition.
Usage: 'he is well known as a *champion* of free speech' (= supporter, defender).
Word Family: **champion,** *verb,* to support or defend; **champion,** *adjective,* a) being first or best of all competitors, b) (informal) first-rate or excellent.
[Latin *campio* a fighter on a battlefield]

championship *noun*
1. a) the position or honour of being a champion. b) a competition to decide who shall be champion.
2. any defence or support: 'her *championship* of the new ideas encouraged others to accept them'.

chance (*rhymes with* dance) *noun*
the random or unexpected nature of events: 'their careful preparations left nothing to *chance*'.
Usages:
a) 'is there no *chance* of recovery?' (= possibility).
b) 'I met her purely by *chance*' (= accident).
c) 'this is your *chance* to prove yourself' (= opportunity).
d) 'take no *chances* with him' (= risks).
e) 'he considers roulette a game of *chance*' (= fate).
chance *verb*
1. to happen by chance: 'she *chanced* upon a really superb flat close to the city'.
2. to attempt or risk: 'in spite of my warning he said he would *chance* it'.
Word Family: **chancy,** *adjective,* risky or uncertain.

chancel (*say* **chahn**-s'l *or* **chan**-s'l) *noun*
the part of a church near the altar, set aside for the clergy and choir.

chancellor (*say* **chahn**-s'la *or* **chan**-s'la) *noun*
1. a title for various high officials, such as the elected leader in West Germany.
2. the honorary head of a university who has few official duties.
Word Family: **chancellery** (*say* **chahn**sel-ree), *noun,* a) the position of chancellor, b) the office or building used by a chancellor.

Chancery (*say* **chahn**sa-ree) *noun*
a division of the High Court that deals with estates, partnerships, the wardship of infants, etc.

chancre (*say* **shang**ka) *noun*
Medicine: a small ulcer with a hard base, as in the early stages of syphilis.
[French, a canker]

chandelier (*say* **shanda**-leer) *noun*
an ornamental support for two or more lights, which hangs from a ceiling.
[French *chandelle* candle]

chandler *noun*
a) an old word for a person who makes or sells candles, soap, etc. b) a dealer in special types of goods, such as the rope, tackle, etc. for a ship.

change *verb*
to make or become different.

Usages:
a) 'will you *change* places with me?' (= exchange, substitute).
b) 'don't expect a bus conductor to *change* a £10 note' (=exchange for smaller money).
c) 'shouldn't you *change* before you go out?' (= put on different clothes).

change *noun*
1. a) the act of changing. b) anything which is changed or different.
2. a) any money returned when the amount given is greater than necessary. b) any money in the form of coins as distinct from banknotes. Short form of **small change**.
Word Family: **changeable**, *adjective*; **changeably**, *adverb*; **changeability**, *noun*; **changeless**, *adjective*.

changeling *noun*
a child who is exchanged or substituted secretly for another, traditionally by fairies.

change of life
see MENOPAUSE.

changeover *noun*
the changing or exchanging of one system, position, etc. for another.

channel *noun*
1. a) the bed of a stream. b) the deeper part of a waterway such as a river or harbour. c) a passage or stretch of water.
2. any passage through which something is carried or directed: 'he dug a *channel* along the fence'.
Usage: 'you must make your request through the proper *channels*' (= means).
3. the waveband used by a particular transmitter, television or radio station. Short form of **frequency channel**.

channel *verb*
(channelled, channelling)
to form or cut a channel in: 'the river *channelled* its way through the rocks to the sea'.
Usage: 'he *channelled* his energies into pig farming' (= directed).
[Latin *canalis* canal]

chant *noun*
1. the music to accompany the singing of psalms: 'a Gregorian *chant*'.
2. a monotonous, singsong speaking voice.

chant *verb*
1. to sing.
2. to speak in a singsong manner: 'the crowd *chanted* "we want jobs" for about an hour'.
[Latin *cantare* to sing]

chantry (*say* **chahn**–tree) *noun*
a chapel used for the saying of Masses or prayers for the soul of the person who endowed it.

chaos (*say* **kay**–os) *noun*
total confusion or disorder: 'the prolonged strikes reduced the transport system to *chaos*'.
Word Family: **chaotic** (*say* kay–**ottik**), *adjective*; **chaotically**, *adverb*.
[Greek *khaos* a void or chasm]

chap (1) *verb*
(chapped, chapping)
(of skin, hands, etc.) to become cracked, split or roughened as a result of cold or exposure.

chap (2) *noun*
(*informal*) any man: 'he's a very pleasant *chap*'.
[from CHAP(man), an old word for a hawker or pedlar]

chapel *noun*
a) a room or building, other than a church, used for worship. b) a section of a large church or cathedral having its own altar.

chaperon (*say* **shappa**–rone)
chaperone *noun*
an older person in charge of a young, unmarried woman or unmarried couples.
Word Family: **chaperon**, *verb*.

chaplain (*say* **chaplin**) *noun*
Christian: a clergyman looking after the religious needs of an institution, such as a school, hospital or regiment.
Word Family: **chaplaincy**, *noun*.

chaplet *noun*
a wreath of flowers, leaves, etc., for the head.

chaps *plural noun*
American: strong leather protective trousers with no seat, worn by cowboys, etc. when horseriding.

chapter *noun*
1. a division or section of a book.
2. a branch of a society or fraternity: 'the local *chapter* of the Association'.
3. *Religion:* a) a meeting of monks from a particular order or place. b) a meeting of the canons of a cathedral.
chapter and verse, 'he couldn't give me *chapter and verse*, but he seemed sure of his facts' (= exact reference or source).

char (1) *verb*
(charred, charring)

1. to burn and reduce to carbon because of incomplete combustion.
2. to scorch.

char (2) *noun*
any of various fish related to the trout.

char (3) *noun*
a charwoman.
Word Family: **char** (**charred, charring**), *verb,* to be employed to do housework.

charabanc (*say* **sharra**–bang) *noun*
an open, four–wheeled, horse–drawn or motorized carriage with bench seats.
[French *char* carriage + *à bancs* with chairs]

character (*say* **karr**ikta) *noun*
1. the combination of qualities which distinguishes an individual, thing, or group: a) 'it is not in his *character* to be dishonest'; b) 'their house is luxurious but lacks *character*'.
2. the quality of moral strength or integrity: 'some schools place great emphasis on building *character*'.
3. (*informal*) a person, especially an odd person: 'our old postman is a real *character*'.
4. a person portrayed in a novel, play, film, etc.
5. *Biology:* any observable trait in an organism which is due to the interaction of one or more genes with the environment.
6. a symbol or letter, as in an alphabet.
Word Family: **characterless**, *adjective.*
[Greek *kharakter* a seal or its impression]

characteristic (*say* karrikta–**ristik**) *noun*
1. any distinguishing feature: 'aggressiveness seems to be a *characteristic* of drunken drivers'.
2. *Maths:* the integer in a logarithm. *Example*: in the log 2000=3·3010, the **characteristic** is 3 and the **mantissa** is 0·3010.
Word Family: **characteristic,** *adjective*; **characteristically**, *adverb.*

characterize (*say* **karr**ikta–rize)
characterise *verb*
a) to distinguish or mark: 'his work is *characterized* by attention to detail'. b) to describe the qualities or characteristics of.
characterization *noun*
the dramatizing of character: 'her last novel had an ingenious plot but poor *characterization*'.

charade (*say* sha–**rahd**) *noun*
1. (*plural*) any of various games in which certain players mime a word or phrase which others try to guess.
2. anything which is pointless or deceptive.

charcoal *noun*
1. any of various forms of impure carbon which remains after the incomplete burning of plant or animal tissue. Being porous, it is often used for filters, etc.
2. a stick of charred willow used for drawing.

charge (*rhymes with* large) *verb*
1. to accuse formally: 'he was *charged* with assault and battery'.
2. a) to ask as payment: 'they *charge* very high prices for all their meat'. b) to record as a debt to be paid: 'please *charge* it to my account'.
3. to attack by rushing forward: 'the bull *charged* him before he could reach the tree'.
4. to command or instruct: 'he *charged* me to stay here until help arrived'.
5. to fill or supply: a) 'his words were *charged* with meaning'; b) 'please *charge* your glasses and we will drink a toast'.
charge *noun*
1. a) the act of charging: 'the cavalry's *charge* took the enemy by surprise'. b) anything which is charged: 'what is the *charge* for delivering goods to my home?'.
2. a) a care or responsibility. b) any person or thing in the care of another: 'the teacher and her *charges* crowded into the museum'.
3. *Electricity:* see ELECTRIC CHARGE.
4. an explosive.
in charge, 'who is *in charge* of this meeting?' (= in command).
Word Family: **chargeable**, *adjective.*
[Latin *carricare* load]

chargé d'affaires (*say* shar*zh*ay da–**fair**)
plural is **chargés d'affaires**
Politics: see AMBASSADOR.
[French *chargé* entrusted + *d'affaires* with affairs]

charger (*say* **char**ja) *noun*
1. a cavalry horse.
2. an apparatus used for charging storage batteries.

charily *adverb*
Word Family: see CHARY.

chariot *noun*
an open, two-wheeled carriage pulled by horses and formerly used in wars, racing, etc.
Word Family: **charioteer**, *noun*, the driver of a chariot.

charisma (*say* ka-**riz**-ma) *noun*
a special quality or power to attract people and inspire their devotion.
Word Family: **charismatic**, *adjective*.
[Greek, a divine gift]

charity (*say* **charri**-tee) *noun*
1. a) the helping of poor or underprivileged people. b) an organization or fund set up for this purpose.
2. a loving kindness towards others.
Word Family: **charitable**, *adjective*, concerned with or showing charity; **charitably**, *adverb*; **charitableness**, *noun*.
[Latin *caritas* dearness]

charlatan (*say* **sharla**-tin) *noun*
an impostor or fake.
Word Family: **charlatanism**, **charlatanry**, *nouns*.

charleston (*say* **charl**-st'n) *noun*
a dance like a lively foxtrot, popular in America and Europe in the 1920's.
[from *Charleston*, an American city where the dance first began]

charm *noun*
1. a) a magic formula or spell. b) any object worn or carried because it is believed to have magic powers.
2. a trinket worn on a bracelet.
3. the power or quality of attracting or pleasing: 'she has *charm*, wit and poise'.
work like a charm, to work successfully or perfectly.
Word Family: **charm**, *verb*, a) to act on with or as if with magic, b) to please or attract greatly; **charming**, *adjective*, delightful; **charmingly**, *adverb*; **charmer**, *noun*, a person or thing that charms.

charnel-house *noun*
short form is **charnel**
an old word for a place where the bodies or bones of the dead are kept.

chart *noun*
1. a sheet or record showing special information, variations, etc. in a methodical form: 'a weather *chart*'.
2. *Geography:* a map showing sea-depth and coastal outlines.
chart *verb*
to make a map or chart of: 'to *chart* Australia's coastline'.
Usage: '*chart* your course of action carefully' (= plan).
[Latin *charta* a writing]

charter *noun*
1. any written or printed statement of rights, permission, etc. granted by a ruler or government.
2. the leasing or hiring of a vehicle, especially an aeroplane or boat.
Word Family: **charter**, *verb*, a) to establish by a charter, b) to hire or lease.

chartreuse (*say* shah-**trerz**) *noun*
1. a pale green or yellow liqueur.
2. a clear, light, yellowish-green colour.
[first made at *la Grande Chartreuse*, a French monastery]

charwoman *noun*
short form is **char**
also called a **charlady**
a woman employed to do scrubbing and cleaning.

chary (*say* **chair**-ee) *adjective*
1. cautious or wary: 'Miss Smith is *chary* of strangers'.
2. sparing or stingy: 'she is *chary* of her praise of others'.
Word Family: **charily**, *adverb*; **chariness**, *noun*.

chase (1) *verb*
to pursue, especially in order to hunt or overtake: 'the police *chased* the suspect's car'.
Usage: 'she *chased* Fido away from the cat's dish' (= drove).
chase *noun*
1. the act of chasing or hunting.
2. any private land on which animals to be hunted are kept.
give chase, to set out in pursuit.

chase (2) *verb*
to decorate metal or some hard surface by cutting grooves, engraving, etc.
Word Family: **chasing**, *noun*.

chaser *noun*
1. a person or thing that chases.
2. (*informal*) a drink of water, beer or other mild liquid taken after strong liquor.

chasm (*say* kazm) *noun*
a gorge or any deep cleft in the earth's surface.
Usage: 'the disagreement between the two nations became an unbreachable *chasm*' (= difference, gap).
[Greek *khasma*]

chassis (*say* **shassee**) *noun*
the frame of a motor vehicle on which the body, wheels and other fittings are mounted.
[French]

chaste (*say* chayst) *adjective*
1. refraining from sexual intercourse outside marriage.
2. restrained, simple or spare in style: 'the building was *chaste* and elegant'.
Word Family: **chastity** (*say* **chas**ti-tee), *noun*, the quality of being chaste; **chastely**, *adverb*.
[Latin *castus* pure]

chasten (*say* **chay**-s'n) *verb*
to correct by imposing punishment or suffering.
Usage: 'she was *chastened* by her failure' (= abashed, softened).

chastise (*say* chast-**ize**) *verb*
1. to criticize severely or reproach.
2. to punish, usually by beating.
Word Family: **chastisement**, *noun*.

chastity belt
a belt with a lock or device to prevent sexual intercourse, which women in the Middle Ages were sometimes forced to wear while their husbands were away.

chat *verb*
(chatted, chatting)
to talk casually or lightly.
chat up, (*informal*) to talk flirtingly or persuasively with.
chat *noun*
1. any informal conversation.
2. any of a range of European birds related to the thrush, e.g. whinchats, stonechats, etc.

château (*say* **sha**-toe) *noun*
plural is **châteaux**
a French castle or large country house.
[French]

chatelaine (*say* **shatta**-lane) *noun*
1. *History:* an ornamental bunch of chains carrying keys, scissors, etc. worn at the waist by the mistress of the house.
2. the mistress of a large house.
[French *château* castle]

chattel *noun*
(*usually plural*) a personal possession, usually movable, as distinct from land and buildings.
[Old French *chatel* cattle]

chatter *verb*
1. a) to talk rapidly, especially in a very casual or silly manner. b) to utter short, inarticulate sounds: 'squirrels *chattered* in the trees'.
2. to click together rapidly: 'his teeth *chattered* with cold'.
Word Family: **chatter**, *noun*; **chatterbox, chatterer**, *nouns*, a person who is very talkative; **chatty**, *adjective*, informal or conversational; **chattily**, *adverb*.

chauffeur (*say* **sho**-fa) *noun*
a person employed to drive a car.
Word Family: **chauffeur**, *verb*, to act as a chauffeur for.
[French, stoker]

chauvinism (*say* **sho**-va-nizm) *noun*
1. an extreme or unthinking enthusiasm for the military glory of one's country.
2. an excessive loyalty to or belief in the superiority of a cause: 'male *chauvinism*'.
Word Family: **chauvinist**, *noun*; **chauvinistic** (*say* sho-va-**nis**tik), *adjective*; **chauvinistically**, *adverb*.
[after *Nicholas Chauvin*, an extreme admirer of Napoleon 1]

cheap *adjective*
costing a relatively low amount.
Usages:
a) 'if you want the dress to hang properly, don't use *cheap* material' (= inferior).
b) 'spreading the rumour behind her back was a *cheap* trick' (= mean).
Word Family: **cheaply**, *adverb*; **cheapness**, *noun*; **cheapskate**, *noun*, (informal) a person who is mean or stingy.
[Old English *ceap* barter]

cheapen *verb*
1. to make cheap or cheaper.
2. to belittle or bring into contempt.

cheat *verb*
to act deceitfully or dishonestly to gain something.
cheat *noun*
1. an act of cheating.
2. a person who cheats.
Word Family: **cheatingly**, *adverb*; **cheater**, *noun*.

check *verb*
1. to stop or restrain: 'the legislation will *check* inflation'.
2. to investigate or establish the correctness of: 'add these figures and then *check* the total'.
Usage: 'her story *checks* with the facts' (= matches, corresponds).
3. *Chess:* to directly threaten an opponent's king.

Phrases:
check in, (at a hotel, etc.) to arrive and register.
check off, 'he *checked off* the listed items one by one' (= marked as correct).
check out, (at a hotel, etc.) to pay the bill and leave.
check *noun*
1. anything which hinders, controls or restrains: 'you must keep your temper in *check*'.
2. any method or device for examining accuracy, correctness, etc.: 'we use a pocket calculator as a *check* on our sums'.
3. a pattern consisting of squares, as those on a chessboard.
4. *Chess:* a situation in which a king is directly threatened by an opposing piece.
5. *American:* a cheque.
Word Family: **checker,** *noun,* a person or thing that checks.

checkers *plural noun*
American: draughts.

checkmate *noun*
1. *Chess:* the winning move, in which the opponent's king is prevented from making any move to escape a check. Short form is **mate.**
2. any complete or total defeat.
Word Family: **checkmate,** *verb.*
[Persian *shah* the king + *mat* is dead]

checkout *noun*
the exit desk of a large store, usually a supermarket, where a customer's purchases are examined and paid for.

checkpoint *noun*
a point where traffic or competitors are stopped for inspection, etc.

checkup *noun*
(*informal*) a thorough examination, especially a periodic medical examination.

cheek *noun*
1. *Anatomy:* a) the side of the face below the eye. b) a buttock.
2. insolent or impudent behaviour.
Phrases:
cheek by jowl, 'we stood *cheek by jowl* with many famous people at the charity function' (= side by side).
tongue in cheek, see TONGUE.
Word Family: **cheeky,** *adjective,* impudent; **cheekily,** *adverb*; **cheekiness,** *noun.*

cheep *verb*
to make a faint chirping like young birds.
Word Family: **cheep,** *noun.*

cheer *verb*
1. to shout out encouragement or applause.
2. to gladden or fill with hope: 'she was greatly *cheered* by the good news'.
cheerful *adjective*
in good spirits.
Word Family: **cheer,** *noun,* a) encouragement or gladness, b) a shout of approval, etc.; **cheerfully,** *adverb*; **cheerfulness,** *noun*; **cheerless,** *adjective,* miserable or mournful.

cheerio *noun, interjection*
goodbye.

cheers *interjection*
(as a toast) to your health! all the best!

cheery *adjective*
openly bright or giving cheer: 'they had a *cheery* fire going when we arrived'.
Word Family: **cheerily,** *adverb*; **cheeriness,** *noun.*

cheese (*say* cheez) *noun*
1. any of various solid foods made from the curd of milk.
2. a conserve of fruit with a similar texture: 'apple *cheese*'.
[Latin *caseus*]

cheesecloth *noun*
a loosely woven fabric, formerly used in cheese-making.

cheesed-off *adjective*
also spelt **cheesed off**
(*informal*) a) bored. b) angry or disgusted.

cheeseparing (*say* **cheez**-pair-ing) *adjective*
mean or very cautious, especially with money.

cheetah *noun*
a long-legged mammal of the cat family, living in Africa and Asia, and sometimes trained to hunt. It is the fastest land animal.
[Sanskrit *chitra* spot]

chef (*say* shef) *noun*
a cook, especially the head cook in a restaurant.
[French, chief]

chef d'oeuvre (*say* shay **dervr**)
the best example of the work of a writer, composer or artist.
[French, chief work]

chemical (*say* **kemmi**–k'l) *adjective*
of or relating to the science or processes of chemistry.
chemical *noun*
any substance used or produced in a chemical process.
Word Family: **chemically**, *adverb.*

chemical engineering
the study and development of the applications of chemistry to industrial processes.

chemical warfare
any warfare using chemical weapons other than explosives, especially poisonous gases, irritants, etc.

chemise (*say* sha–**meez**) *noun*
a woman's loose undergarment or shift.

chemist (*say* **kemmist**) *noun*
1. a scientist who specializes in chemistry.
2. a) a pharmacist. b) a pharmacy.

chemistry (*say* **kemmi**–stree) *noun*
the study of the composition of substances and their effect upon each other.
[Greek *khemia* the (Egyptian) art of transmuting metals (alchemy)]

chemotherapy
(*say* kemmo–**therra**–pee) *noun*
the treatment of disease using chemicals such as antibiotics to treat an infection.

chenille (*say* sha–**neel**) *noun*
a fabric with a cut pile on both sides and velvety or woolly lines or ridges.
[French, hairy caterpillar]

cheque (*say* chek) *noun*
in America spelt **check**
a written order, usually on a printed form, directing a bank to pay a specific amount from the drawer's account.
Word Family: **chequebook**, *noun*, a booklet containing a series of cheques.

chequer (*say* chekker) *verb*
to mark in checks or an alternating pattern: 'sunlight shining through the leaves *chequered* the lawn'.
chequer *noun*
1. a pattern of squares or checks.
2. one of the pegs or marbles used in Chinese chequers.
Word Family: **chequered**, *adjective*, varied or eventful.

chequers *noun*
see DRAUGHTS.

cherish *verb*
to hold dear or care for tenderly: 'the widow *cherished* her few possessions'.
Usage: 'we do not *cherish* any hope that it will be a short war' (= hold, cling to).
[French *cher* dear]

cheroot (sha–**root**) *noun*
a thin cigar with open ends.
[Tamil]

cherry *noun*
1. a) a small, round, juicy red fruit with a small stone. b) the wood of the tree on which it grows.
2. a bright purplish–red colour.
Word Family: **cherry**, *adjective.*

cherub (*say* **cherr**ub) *noun*
1. an angel, often pictured as a child with wings. Plural is **cherubim**.
2. a) a chubby–faced child. b) a well–behaved child. Plural is **cherubs**.
Word Family: **cherubic** (*say* cher–**rubik**), *adjective.*

chess *noun*
a game played by two players on a square **chessboard** with 64 alternately light and dark squares. Each player has 16 **chessmen**: a king and queen, 2 bishops, 2 knights, 2 rooks and 8 pawns; they are moved according to specific rules with the aim of checkmating the opponent's king.

chest *noun*
1. *Anatomy:* the upper front part of the trunk, between the neck and the abdomen.
2. a box with a hinged or detachable lid, used for storing things.
get something off one's chest (*informal*), to confess or tell of a worry.

chesterfield *noun*
a large late Victorian sofa with thickly padded back and arms.
[after an Earl of *Chesterfield*]

chestnut *noun*
1. a) a large, edible nut growing on trees, often roasted on coals. b) the wood from such a tree.
2. a coppery–brown horse, with a slightly darker mane and tail.
[Greek *kastanea*]

chest of drawers
a piece of furniture with drawers, for storing clothes, etc.

chevalier (*say* shevva–**leer**) *noun*
History: a) a horseman or knight. b) the lowest rank in the French nobility.
[French, horseman]

chevron (*say* **shev**–r'n) *noun*
a V–shaped stripe worn on the sleeve of a uniform to indicate non–commissioned rank.

chew *verb*
1. to crush or grind with or as if with the teeth.
2. to consider or ponder: 'I'll *chew* over the problem and decide later'.
Word Family: **chew**, *noun*, a) the act of chewing, b) anything which is chewed or for chewing, such as a lump of tobacco.

chiaroscuro (*say* kee-a-ro-**skew**ro) *noun*
a) the balance of light and dark in a painting or drawing. b) the technique of creating effects by this means.
[Italian *chiaro* bright + *oscuro* dark]

chic (*say* sheek *or* shik) *adjective*
elegant and stylish, especially in dress.
[French]

chicanery (*say* shi-**kay**-n'ree) *noun*
any deception or trickery, especially by legal means.
[French *chicaner* to quibble]

chick *noun*
1. a young bird, especially a young chicken.
2. (*informal*) a young woman.

chicken *noun*
1. a) the common domestic fowl. b) one of its young.
2. (*informal*) a coward.
chicken *verb*
chicken out, (*informal*) to lose one's nerve.

chickenfeed *noun*
(*informal*) an insignificant amount, especially of money.

chickenpox *noun*
a highly contagious viral disease causing small blisters, most common among children.

chickpea *noun*
an edible, pea-like seed of a bushy plant found in Mediterranean countries, Asia and the Middle East.

chickweed *noun*
a common weed with small, white, star-shaped flowers.

chicory (*say* **chick**a-ree) *noun*
a herb, the leaves of which are used in salads. Its root is dried, roasted and ground and used for mixing with coffee or as a coffee substitute.
[Greek *kikhorion*]

chide *verb*
(**chided** or **chid**, **chided** or **chidden**, **chiding**)
to scold or rebuke: 'her last letter *chided* me for not writing'.
Word Family: **chidingly**, *adverb*.

chief (*say* cheef) *noun*
the head or ruler of a group.
chief *adjective*
highest in rank or importance: a) 'our *chief* complaint concerns wages'; b) 'who is the new *Chief* Justice?'
Word Family: **chiefly**, *adverb*, to the greatest degree or extent.

chieftain (*say* **cheef**-t'n) *noun*
the leader of a clan or tribe.

chiffon (*say* **shiff**on) *noun*
a thin, sheer fabric made from silk, nylon or rayon.
[French]

chiffonier (*say* shiffon-**eer**) *noun*
a low cupboard or chest of drawers, usually with a flat top which may be used as a shelf or table.
[French]

chignon (*say* **sheen**-yon) *noun*
a hairstyle in which long hair is arranged in a roll at the back of the head.
[French, nape]

chihuahua (*say* chi-**wah**-wah) *noun*
any of a breed of very small dogs with large pointed ears.
[originally from *Chihuahua*, Mexico]

chilblain *noun*
an inflamed swelling of the fingers, toes, etc. caused by poor blood circulation in cold weather.

child *noun*
plural is **children**
1. any young person.
2. an offspring.
with child, pregnant.
childhood *noun*
the state or time of being a child.
second childhood, a state of foolishness in old age.
Word Family: **childless**, *adjective*.

childbirth *noun*
the act of giving birth to a child.

childish *adjective*
petulant or immature: 'his outburst was quite *childish*'.
Word Family: **childishly**, *adverb*; **childishness**, *noun*.

childlike *adjective*
having the innocence, openness or freshness of a child.

children *plural noun*
see CHILD.

child's play
a very easy task.

chill *noun*
1. a sensation of cold.

Usage: 'news of the crash cast a *chill* over the meeting' (= a feeling of depression or uneasines).
2. a fever preceded by shivering, as an early symptom of a cold, etc.
chill *verb*
to make or become cold: '*chill* the wine before serving'.
Usage: 'her obvious indifference to the outing *chilled* our enthusiasm' (= dampened, discouraged).
chilly, chill *adjective*
cold, especially cold enough to produce shivering.
Usage: 'the uninvited guest met with a *chilly* reception' (= hostile, aloof).
Word Family: **chilling,** *adjective,* frightening; **chillingly,** *adverb*; **chillness, chilliness,** *nouns.*

chilli *noun*
a hot spice made from the pod of a variety of capsicum.

chime *noun*
1. a bell or device which creates a ringing, musical sound: 'a door *chime*'.
2. a tuned set of bells.
chime *verb*
to ring bells or to make the sound of bells.
Usage: 'his opinion on the matter *chimed* with my own ideas' (= harmonized, agreed).
chime in, to break into a conversation.

chimera (*say* kie-**meera**) *noun*
also spelt **chimaera**
an unreal or fanciful idea or image: 'his hope of becoming a millionaire is a *chimera*'.
Word Family: **chimerical** (*say* kie-merri-k'l), *adjective*; **chimerically,** *adverb.*
[after *Chimaera,* a monster in Greek mythology]

chimney (*say* **chim**-nee) *noun*
plural is **chimneys**
1. an upright, hollow structure which carries away smoke from a fire by creating a draught.
2. a glass tube for enclosing the flame of a lamp.
[Greek *kaminos* furnace]

chimneypiece *noun*
see MANTELPIECE.

chimneystack *noun*
a group of chimneys built as one unit on a roof.

chimneysweep *noun*
a person employed to clean out chimneys.

chimpanzee *noun*
short form is **chimp**
an African ape, found in tropical forests and noted for its intelligence.
[Bantu]

chin *noun*
Anatomy: the lower part of the face, below the mouth.
keep one's chin up, to remain cheerful, especially under stress.

china *noun*
any low-fired, porcelain ceramics, such as cups, plates, etc. **Bone china** is fine, translucent china made with calcium phosphate from bone ash. **Eggshell china** is a very fine, thin china.

china clay
also called **kaolin**
a very fine clay, a natural form of hydrated aluminium silicate, used in glazes and for making porcelain.

chinchilla *noun*
1. a small squirrel-like mammal found in the mountains of South America and bred for its hide and fur.
2. a fabric with a tufted surface.

Chinese chequers
(*used with singular verb*) a game for two or more people, played with pegs or marbles on a board with holes.

chink (1) *noun*
a small crack or opening.

chink (2) *verb*
to make a short, sharp ringing or metallic sound.
Word Family: **chink,** *noun.*

chintz *noun*
plural is **chintzes**
a glazed cotton, sometimes linen, fabric with printed flowery designs, used for curtains and loose covers.
[Hindi *chint* spotted cloth]

chip *noun*
1. a small piece or slice, usually broken or cut from something larger: a) 'a potato *chip*'; b) 'a wood *chip*'.
2. a mark or dent caused by breaking off a small piece: 'this cup has a *chip* in it'.
3. a small disc or counter used in certain card or gambling games.
Phrases:
a chip off the old block, a person who is very like one or both parents.
a chip on the shoulder, a grudge or resentment.

chip *verb*
(**chipped, chipping**)
1. to remove a chip or chips from: 'be careful not to *chip* that plate'.
2. to hit or cut with short strokes: a) 'the sculptor *chipped* at the marble'; b) 'the golfer *chipped* the ball onto the green'.
chip in, a) 'we all *chipped in* to buy the present' (= contributed); b) 'don't *chip in* while your father is speaking' (= interrupt).
Word Family: **chipper**, *noun*.

chipboard *noun*
a material made of sawdust, wood scraps or similar material pressed into sheets and used for boxes, furniture, etc.

chipmunk *noun*
a small squirrel-like mammal with a striped back, found in forests in northern America.

chipolata *noun*
a thin sausage.
[Italian *cipollata* a dish of onions]

chiropody (*say* kiroppa-dee) *noun*
the treatment of minor foot complaints, such as corns.
Word Family: **chiropodist**, *noun*.
[Greek *kheir* hand + *podos* of a foot]

chiropractic (*say* **kie**-ro-praktik) *noun*
a method of treating disease by manipulating segments of the spinal column, based on the idea that all disease is caused by interfering with the function of the nerves as they pass out of the spinal column.
Word Family: **chiropractor**, *noun*.
[Greek *kheir* hand + *praktikos* practical]

chirp *verb*
also called to **chirrup**
to make a short, high-pitched sound like a bird.
Word Family: **chirp**, *noun*; **chirpy**, *adjective*, lively or chatty; **chirpily**, *adverb*.

chisel (*say* **chizz**'l) *noun*
a tool with a finely sharpened edge at one end, used for cutting and shaping. A **cold chisel** is a steel chisel which is hard enough to cut cold metal.
chisel *verb*
(**chiselled, chiselling**)
to use or work with a chisel.
Usage: 'he *chiselled* the old lady out of her money' (= cheated).
Word Family: **chiselled**, *adjective*, a) cut with a chisel, b) clear-cut or well-shaped; **chiseller**, *noun*, (informal) a cheat or swindler.

chit (1) *noun*
a note, especially a bill or account.

chit (2) *noun*
(*use is often derogatory*) a young girl or woman.

chitchat *noun*
any casual or light-hearted conversation.

chitin (*say* **kie**-tin) *noun*
a horny substance which is a component of the outer layer of certain insects, shellfish, etc.
[Greek *khiton* a coat of mail]

chiton (*say* **kie**-t'n) *noun*
a small, oval mollusc with ridges on its outer surface, usually found attached to rocks.

chivalry (*say* **shivv**'l-ree) *noun*
1. any polite or courteous behaviour.
2. *Medieval history:* the knightly system of virtue, honour, courage, duty, etc.
Word Family: **chivalrous**, *adjective*; **chivalrously**, *adverb*; **chivalrousness**, *noun*.
[Old French *chevalerie*, from *cheval* horse]

chive *noun*
a small grass-like plant related to the onion, used to add flavour in cooking.

chivvy, chivy *verb*
to nag, harass or make to hurry.

chloral (*say* **klorr**'l) *noun*
a colourless liquid used in medicine as a sedative.
[first made from CHLOR(ine) + AL(cohol)]

chloride (*say* **klaw**-ride) *noun*
Chemistry: a salt containing the univalent Cl^- ion.

chlorinate (*say* **klorri**-nate) *verb*
to combine or treat with chlorine, especially to disinfect water.
Word Family: **chlorination**, *noun*.

chlorine (*say* **klaw**-reen) *noun*
element number 17, a poisonous greenish-yellow gas with a choking, irritating smell, used as a bleach and to purify water. See HALOGEN.
See CHEMICAL ELEMENTS in grey pages.
[Greek *khloros* green]

chloroform (*say* **klorra**-form) *noun*
a colourless, heavy liquid with a strong, sweet smell, used as an anaesthetic and a solvent.

Word Family: **chloroform,** *verb,* to apply chloroform to.

chlorophyll (*say* **klorra**–fil) *noun*
Biology: the green pigment, found in most plants, which traps energy from sunlight and makes photosynthesis possible.
[Greek *khloros* green + *phyllon* leaf]

chloroplast (*say* **klorra**–plast) *noun*
Biology: a plastid containing chlorophyll.

chlorosis (*say* kla–**ro**–sis) *noun*
a deficiency of iron, causing a yellowish–green colour, especially in plants.
[Greek *khloros* green + -OSIS]

chock *noun*
1. a block of wood or other material used as a wedge to prevent movement of a door, furniture, etc.
2. *Nautical:* a heavy metal or wooden fitting through which a rope, etc. may be passed.
Word Family: **chock,** *verb.*

chock–a–block *adverb*
tightly packed or filled.

chock–full *adjective*
tightly packed or filled.

chocolate (*say* **chok**–lit) *noun*
1. a sweet or flavouring made from cacao.
2. a dark brown colour.
Word Family: **chocolate,** *adjective.*
[Aztec *chocolatl*]

choice (*rhymes with* voice) *noun*
1. a) the act of choosing: 'the *choice* between the two candidates was very difficult'. b) anything which is chosen: 'what is your *choice* for dinner?'.
2. the power or right to choose: 'she likes to exercise her *choice* when buying for the family'.
3. a number or variety of things from which to choose: 'there is a wide *choice* of subjects to study'.
Word Family: **choice,** *adjective,* a) excellent or fine, b) carefully selected.

choir (*say* kwire) *noun*
1. a group of singers, as in a church.
2. a part of a church between the nave and the altar, set aside for the choir.

choke *verb*
to stop or cause to stop breathing by pressing or blocking the trachea.
Usages:
a) 'he *choked* back a sob' (= stopped, stifled).
b) 'the garden is *choked* with weeds' (= clogged, overgrown).

choke *noun*
1. a device which increases the proportion of fuel to air entering the combustion chamber of an internal combustion engine.
2. the act or sound of choking.
3. *Electricity:* a device which allows direct electric current to flow, but greatly weakens alternating current.

choler (*say* **kolla**) *noun*
an old word meaning anger or irritability.
Word Family: **choleric,** *adjective.*
[Greek *khole* bile]

cholera (*say* **koll**'ra) *noun*
an often fatal bacterial disease causing severe vomiting and diarrhoea, spread by contaminated water.
[Greek *kholera*]

cholesterol (*say* ka–**lesta**–rol) *noun*
Biology: a fatty alcohol found in some animal tissues.
[Greek *kholé* bile + *stereos* solid]

choose (*say* chooz) *verb*
(chose, chosen, choosing)
to decide on or take from a number of things: '*choose* whichever career you wish'.
Word Family: **choosy,** *adjective,* fussy or difficult to please.

chop (1) *verb*
(chopped, chopping)
1. to cut with heavy strokes.
Usage: '*chop* the onions finely' (= cut into pieces).
2. *Sport:* to hit the ball with a short, downward stroke.

chop *noun*
1. a cutting stroke or movement: 'he made a wild *chop* at his opponent's neck'.
2. a small cut of lamb or pork containing a bone, taken from the loin and including a rib of the animal.
3. dismissal from a job or position: 'he was given the *chop* for continually arriving late'.

chop (2) *verb*
(chopped, chopping)
chop and change, to change repeatedly.

chopper *noun*
1. a person or thing that chops, such as a cleaver for chopping meat.
2. (*informal*) a helicopter.

choppy *adjective*
(of water, wind, etc.) forming short, irregular waves or movements.

chops *plural noun*
the jaws.

chopsticks *plural noun*
a pair of fine sticks made of ivory, bamboo, etc. used by Asians to raise food to the mouth.
[Pidgin *chop* quick + STICKS]

chop suey (*say* chop **soo**–ee)
a Chinese dish of chopped meat, rice and vegetables, fried or stewed with soya sauce.
[Chinese, mixed bits]

choral (*say* **kor**–al) *adjective*
of or sung by a choir or chorus.

chorale (*say* kor**rahl**) *noun*
also spelt **choral**
Music: a) a simple, slow tune or hymn sung or played in harmony. b) a choir or musical society.

chord (1) (*say* kord) *noun*
1. *Maths:* a straight line segment joining two points on a curve.
2. a string on a musical instrument.
[from CORD]

chord (2) (*say* kord) *noun*
Music: a group of three or more notes played together in harmony.
[from ACCORD]

chordate (*say* **kor**date) *adjective*
Biology: of or belonging to the large group of animals which includes vertebrates and animals with a primitive backbone.
Word Family: **chordate,** *noun.*
[Latin *chorda* chord (1)]

chore *noun*
a small job considered to be boring, unpleasant, etc.

chorea (*say* ko–**ree**–a) *noun*
also called **St Vitus's dance**
a disease in which there is uncontrolled, involuntary movement of the limbs.
[Greek *khoreia* dance]

choreography (*say* korri–**og**ra–fee) *noun*
the art of composing, arranging or directing ballets and dance routines.
Word Family: **choreographer,** *noun.*
[Greek *khoreia* dance + *graphein* to write]

chorister (*say* **korr**ista) *noun*
a singer in a choir.

chortle (*say* **chaw**–t'l) *verb*
to chuckle and snort with glee.
[from CH(uck)LE + (sn)ORT, coined by Lewis Carroll in 1871]

chorus (*say* **kaw**–rus) *noun*
1. *Theatre:* a) a group of singers or dancers who perform together. b) a performer or group of performers who speak the prologue, epilogue, etc. or comment on the action of a play.
2. a) a song or part of a song which is sung by a number of singers. b) a part of a song which is repeated at intervals.
Usage: 'the students replied in *chorus*' (= together).
chorus *verb*
to sing or speak in a chorus.
[Greek *khoros*]

chose *verb*
the past tense of the verb **choose.**

chosen *verb*
the past participle of the verb **choose.**

chow (*rhymes with* cow) *noun*
1. one of a breed of medium–sized, long–haired dogs, originally bred in China.
2. (*informal*) food.

chowder (*rhymes with* powder) *noun*
American: a soup or stew made from sea–foods, such as clams, or vegetables, with many other ingredients.

chow mein (*say* chow **mane**)
a Chinese dish of fried noodles, shredded chicken and vegetables.
[Chinese, fried flower]

Christ *noun*
also called **Jesus**
a religious teacher, living in Israel about 2000 years ago, who preached universal love; the founder of Christianity.
[Greek *khristos* anointed]

christen (*say* **kriss**'n) *verb*
a) to baptize. b) to give a name to, especially at baptism.
Usage: 'have you *christened* that new tablecloth yet?' (= used for the first time).
Word Family: **christening,** *noun.*
[Old English *cristnian* to make Christian]

Christendom (*say* **kriss**'n–dom) *noun*
all Christian people, churches or countries.

Christian (*say* **kris**–ch'n) *adjective*
1. of or relating to Christ and the religion based on his teachings.
2. kind or humane: 'helping the old couple was a *Christian* act'.
Word Family: **Christian,** *noun*; **Christianity** (*say* kristi–**anni**–tee), *noun*, the Christian religion or beliefs.

Christian name
a) the name a person receives at baptism. b) a person's first name or names, as distinct from his surname.

Christian Scientist
a member of a religious sect founded in America in the 19th century by Mary Baker Eddy, emphasizing the need for pure goodness and believing that disease may be cured by spiritual methods, especially by the mental effect of the patient's Christian faith.

Christmas (*say* **krismus**) ***noun***
Christian: the annual festival celebrating the birth of Christ.
Christmas Day is the day of Christmas celebrations, December 25th.
Christmas Eve is the day and night before Christmas Day.

chroma (*say* **kro**–ma) ***noun***
the purity or intensity of a colour or its freedom from white or grey.
[Greek *khroma* colour]

chromatic (*say* kro–**mattik**) ***adjective***
1. of or relating to colour or colours.
2. *Music:* relating to a chromatic scale.
Word Family: **chromatically,** ***adverb.***

chromatic aberration
Physics: see ABERRATION.

chromatic scale
Music: a scale which ascends or descends by semitones. Compare DIATONIC SCALE.

chromatography
(*say* kro–ma–**togra**–fee) ***noun***
Chemistry: a method of chemical analysis of a liquid mixture by passing the mixture along an absorbent material such as paper or chalk, the parts of the mixture separating into different layers as they seep along.

chrome (*say* krome) ***noun***
something which is coated with chromium.

chrome red
a strong, reddish-orange colour.

chromium (*say* **kro**–mee–um) ***noun***
element number 24, a hard metal used to make stainless steel and for protective electroplating. See TRANSITION ELEMENT. See CHEMICAL ELEMENTS in grey pages.
[Greek *khroma* colour, as lead chromates are used in paint]

chromosome (*say* **kro**–ma–zome) ***noun***
Biology: a thread-like body carrying the hereditary material and usually occurring in pairs in the nuclei of most cells.
[Greek *khroma* colour + *soma* body]

chronic (*say* **kronnik**) ***adjective***
continuing or firmly established: 'he has *chronic* bronchitis and must live in a warm climate'.
Word Family: **chronically,** ***adverb.***
[Greek *khronos* time]

chronicle (*say* **kronni**–k'l) ***noun***
a history or record of events in the order in which they happened.
Word Family: **chronicle,** ***verb*; chronicler,** ***noun.***
[Greek *khronika* annals]

chronological (*say* kronna–**loji**–k'l) ***adjective***
arranged in the order of time.
Word Family: **chronologically,** ***adverb.***

chronology (*say* kr'**nolla**–jee) ***noun***
1. a record of the particular order of events in time.
2. the science of establishing and fixing historical dates.

chronometer (*say* kr'**nomma**–ta) ***noun***
a specially designed clock used in navigation and other fields where precise measurement of time is required.
Word Family: **chronometric** (*say* kronno–**mettrik**), **chronometrical,** *adjective*; **chronometry** (*say* kr'**nomma**–tree), ***noun.***

chrysalis (*say* **krissa**–lis) ***noun***
plural is **chrysalises** or **chrysalides** (*say* krisalla–deez)
also called a **chrysalid**
the hard-shelled pupa of a butterfly or moth.
[Greek *khrysallis* from *khrysos* gold]

chrysanthemum
(*say* kriz–**antha**–mum) ***noun***
any of a large group of plants with large, showy and often brightly coloured flowers.
[Greek *khrysos* gold + *anthos* flower]

chub ***noun***
any of a group of common, thick-bodied freshwater fish related to the carp.

chubby ***adjective***
plump and tubby.

chuck (1) ***verb***
1. to throw.
2. to pat or tap lightly: 'the old lady *chucked* the baby under the chin'.

chuck (2) *noun*
1. a cut of beef between the neck and the shoulder-blade.
2. a) the part of a drill used to hold the bit. b) a similar part of a lathe used to hold the object being turned.

chuck (3) *verb*
to cluck like a hen.

chuckle *verb*
to laugh softly or to oneself.
Word Family: **chuckle,** *noun.*

chuffed *adjective*
(*informal*) pleased or delighted.

chug *verb*
(**chugged, chugging**)
a) to make a dull, short repeated sound: 'the engine *chugged* as it climbed the hill'. b) to move while making this sound: 'a boat *chugged* into sight'.
Word Family: **chug,** *noun.*

chukker, chukka *noun*
any of the periods into which a polo match is divided.

chum *noun*
a close friend or companion.
Word Family: **chummy,** *adjective,* very friendly.

chump *noun*
a silly or stupid person.

chump chop
a chop, usually lamb or pork, cut from the tail end of the loin.

chunk *noun*
a thick or large uneven piece.
chunky *adjective*
1. in a chunk or chunks.
2. thickset or stocky.

church *noun*
Christian: a) a building for public worship and services. b) (*capital*) the whole community of believers or any branch or denomination within it: 'the Presbyterian *Church*'.
church *adjective*
relating to religious or ecclesiastical matters: 'a *church* fund'.
[Greek *kyriakon* (house) of the Lord (*kyrios*)]

Church of England
also called the **Anglican Church**
the national religion of England, with branches in other countries, which separated from the Roman Catholic Church in the 16th century, and which has both Catholic and Protestant characteristics.

churchyard *noun*
the area next to a church, often used as a cemetery.

churlish *adjective*
1. bad-tempered.
2. rustic.
Word Family: **churl,** *noun,* a) a bad-tempered person, b) a peasant; **churlishly,** *adverb;* **churlishness,** *noun.*

churn *noun*
1. a machine for agitating cream until butter is produced.
2. a large metal milk-can.
churn *verb*
to stir or agitate violently, as when making butter.
churn out, 'the young writer has *churned out* a vast number of novels in his short career' (= produced in a routine way).

chute (*say* shoot) *noun*
1. a sloping passage or channel for carrying things to a lower level.
2. a waterfall.
3. (*informal*) a parachute.

chutney (*say* **chut**-nee) **chutnee** *noun*
a highly seasoned, thick sauce made from mangoes and other fruit or vegetables.
[Hindi *chutni*]

chyle (*say* kile) *noun*
Biology: a milky fluid containing emulsified fat and found in lymphatic vessels which drain the small intestine.
Word Family: **chylous,** *adjective.*
[Greek *khylos* juice]

chyme (*say* kime *or* chime) *noun*
the pulpy mass of partly digested food which passes from the stomach to the duodenum.
Word Family: **chymous,** *adjective.*
[Greek *khymos* juice]

cicada (*say* se-**kay**da *or* se-**kah**da) *noun*
an insect with four wings and long piercing mouthparts. The males produce a very long, shrill noise by means of a pair of drum-like membranes on the sides of the body.
[Latin]

cicatrice (*say* **sik**ka-treece) *noun*
also spelt **cicatrix** (*say* **sik**ka-triks)
the tissue forming over a wound and later becoming a scar.
[Latin *cicatrix*]

cider (*say* **sigh**-da) *noun*
an alcoholic drink made from fermented apple juice.

cigar *noun*
a cylinder of rolled up tobacco leaves for smoking.
[Spanish *cigarro*]

cigarette *noun*
a narrow cylinder of cut tobacco, rolled in thin paper for smoking.
[French, little cigar]

cilia (*say* **sill**ia) *plural noun*
singular is **cilium**
Biology: the fine hair-like projections on the surface of certain cells.
Word Family: **ciliary**, *adjective*, relating to cilia; **ciliate, ciliated,** *adjectives*, having cilia.
[Latin *cilium* eyelash]

cinch (*say* sinch) *noun*
1. *American:* a girth for a saddle.
2. (*informal*) anything which is easy or certain.

cincture (*say* **sink**-cher) *noun*
a belt.
[Latin *cinctus* girded]

cinder (*say* **sin**da) *noun*
any burnt or partly burnt piece or particle.

cine- (*say* **sinnee**)
a prefix meaning motion, as in *cinematography.*

cinema (*say* **sin**nima) *noun*
1. a public theatre in which films are shown on a screen.
2. the film industry.
Word Family: **cinematic**, *adjective.*
[Greek *kinema* motion]

cinematography
(*say* sinnima-**togra**-fee) *noun*
the art or process of making films.
Word Family: **cinematographic** (*say* sinni-matto-**graff**ik), *adjective.*

cineraria (*say* sinna-**rair**ia) *noun*
a garden plant with nearly circular leaves and clusters of brightly coloured, daisy-like flowers.

cinnamon (*say* **sinna**-m'n) *noun*
1. a sweet spice made from the inner bark of some tropical trees, used in cooking and medicine.
2. a yellowish or reddish-brown colour.
Word Family: **cinnamon**, *adjective.*
[Greek *kinnamon*]

cipher (*say* **sigh**-fir) **cypher** *noun*
1. a) the figure 0, representing nought.
b) any Arabic numeral.
2. any method of secret writing, especially using codes or symbols.
3. any person or thing having no importance or influence.
Word Family: **cipher**, *verb*, to calculate or use figures.
[Arabic *sifr* empty]

circa (*say* **sir**ka) *preposition, adverb*
about or approximately: 'he is believed to have died *circa* 1874'.
[Latin]

circle (*say* **sir**-k'l) *noun*
1. a closed, round plane figure formed by a moving point which is always the same distance from its centre.
2. any object, arrangement, path, etc. in the shape of a circle or part of a circle: 'we sat in the dress *circle* to watch the play'.
Usage: 'he has a strange *circle* of friends' (= group, range).
3. *Geography:* a line of latitude.
come full circle, to return to the original or first position.
circle *verb*
to move in or form a circle: 'the plane *circled* above the airport before landing'.
[Latin *circulus*]

circlet (*say* **sir**klet) *noun*
1. a small circle or ring.
2. a decorative band worn on the head, neck or arm.

circuit (*say* **sir**kit) *noun*
1. a circular line or path: 'he ran five *circuits* of the track'.
Usage: 'the play will be presented by all theatres in the *circuit*' (= group, association).
2. *Electricity:* any electrical network having at least one closed path for the flow of current. A **printed circuit** is formed by printing or soldering the circuit onto a surface instead of using wires. Compare INTEGRATED CIRCUIT.
closed-circuit television, transmitted by wire to authorized receivers, e.g. as used to keep watch on shoplifting.
Word Family: **circuitry**, *noun*, any system of electrical circuits.

circuitous (*say* sir-**kew**a-tus) *adjective*
indirect or roundabout: 'the *circuitous* reasoning made the argument difficult to follow'.
Word Family: **circuitously,** *adverb*; **circuitousness, circuity,** *nouns.*
[Latin *circuitus* a roundabout way]

circular (*say* **sirk**-yoola) *adjective*
1. of, forming or moving in a circle.
Usage: 'his *circular* arguments made it difficult to reason with him' (= indirect, roundabout).
2. intended for large numbers of people: 'a *circular* letter'.
circular *noun*
a notice or letter which is sent to several people.

Word Family: **circularity** (*say* sirk–yoo–**larri**–tee), *noun*; **circularly,** *adverb*; **circularize, circularise,** *verb.*

circular saw
a saw with a flat, rotating disc which has a toothed edge, usually powered by electricity. A **buzz saw** is a small circular saw.

circulate (*say* **sir**kew–late) *verb*
1. to move in a circle or circuit.
2. to pass from place to place: 'the rumour *circulated* rapidly in the small town'.
Word Family: **circulatory,** *adjective.*

circulation *noun*
1. a) the act of circulating: 'the *circulation* of the news was banned by the government'. b) a circuit or circular movement: 'blood *circulation*'.
2. the number of copies of an issue of a newspaper or magazine which are distributed or sold.

circum– (*say* **sirk**'m)
a prefix meaning movement around or on all sides, as in *circumnavigate.*
[Latin]

circumambient (*say* sirk'm–**am**bi–ent) *adjective*
all around or surrounding.

circumambulate
(*say* sirk'm–**am**–bewlate) *verb*
to walk around.

circumcise (*say* **sirk**'m–size) *verb*
to remove the foreskin of the penis, often a religious rite, as in Islam and Judaism.
Word Family: **circumcision** (*say* sirk'm–**si***zh*'n), *noun,* the act or ceremony of circumcising.
[CIRCUM– + Latin *caedere* to cut]

circumference (*say* sir–**kum**–fr'nce) *noun*
a) the outer line of a circle. b) the length of this line.

circumflex (*say* **sirk**'m–fleks) *noun*
Language: see ACCENT.

circumlocution
(*say* sirk'm–la–**kew**–sh'n) *noun*
a) a roundabout or too lengthy way of speaking. b) anything said or written in this way.
Word Family: **circumlocutory** (*say* sirk'm–lok–**yoo**ta–ree), *adjective.*
[CIRCUM– + LOCUTION]

circumnavigate
(*say* sirk'm–**navvi**–gate) *verb*
Nautical: to sail around something, especially the world.
Word Family: **circumnavigation,** *noun*; **circumnavigator,** *noun,* a person who circumnavigates.

circumscribe (*say* **sirk**'m–skribe) *verb*
to draw or form a line around, especially a circle.
Usage: 'his powers are *circumscribed* by the many rules and regulations' (= limited, defined).
Word Family: **circumscription,** *noun,* a) the act of circumscribing, b) anything which circumscribes, especially the circular inscription on a coin.
[CIRCUM– + Latin *scribere* to write]

circumspect *adjective*
cautious and watchful.
Word Family: **circumspectly,** *adverb*; **circumspection** *noun.*
[Latin *circumspectus* a looking around]

circumstance (*say* **sirk**'m–stance) *noun*
a condition which accompanies or affects a particular event.
Usages:
a) 'the doctor's early arrival was a lucky *circumstance*' (= event, occurrence).
b) 'his financial *circumstances* do not concern us' (= position, status).

circumstantial (*say* sirk'm–**stan**–sh'l) *adjective*
1. dealing with particular details or circumstances: 'a *circumstantial* report'.
2. secondary or not essential: 'the new law had many *circumstantial* effects'.
circumstantial evidence, (*Law*) any evidence which supplies reasonable but not definite grounds for believing in a fact.
Word Family: **circumstantiality** (*say* sirk'm–stanshi–**alli**–tee), *noun*; **circumstantially,** *adverb.*
[CIRCUM– + Latin *stans, stantis* standing]

circumstantiate
(*say* sirk'm–**stanshi**–ate) *verb*
to support or describe fully with details.

circumvent (*say* sirk'm–**vent**) *verb*
to avoid or find a way round: 'it was impossible to *circumvent* the carefully worded rules'.
Word Family: **circumvention,** *noun.*
[CIRCUM– + Latin *ventus* come]

circus (*say* **sir**'kus) *noun*
1. a form of entertainment consisting of acrobats, clowns and trained animals, usually performed by a travelling group.

2. a place, formerly circular, where several streets converge: 'Piccadilly *Circus*'.
3. *Ancient history:* a circular place with seats on all sides, used for public sports, etc. in Rome.
[Latin, ring or circle]

cirque (*say* sirk) *noun*
a corrie.

cirrhosis (*say* sirro–sis) *noun*
a group of diseases of the liver, sometimes due to drinking large amounts of alcohol, in which fibrous tissue replaces normal liver cells resulting in a progressive loss of normal liver function.
[Greek *kirros* tawny + –OSIS]

cirrus (*say* **sirrus**) *noun*
a high feathery cloud.
[Latin, ringlet]

cissy (*say* **sissi**) *noun*
also spelt **sissy**
an effeminate or cowardly man or boy.
[from SISTER]

cistern (*say* **sist'n**) *noun*
a vessel or place where liquid is stored, such as a raised tank which supplies the liquid to a lower level.

citadel (*say* **sitta–del**) *noun*
a fortress protecting or overlooking a city.
[Italian *citadella* little city]

cite (*say* site) *verb*
1. to quote or refer to: 'the lecturer *cited* several authorities to demonstrate his theory'.
Usage: 'the young soldier was *cited* in several despatches' (= commended for bravery).
2. to summon or call, especially to appear in a court of law.
Word Family: **citation** (*say* sigh–tay–sh'n), *noun*; **citatory**, *adjective.*
[Latin *citare* to call to witness]

citizen (*say* **sitti–z'n**) *noun*
a person belonging to or living in a city or country, usually with certain rights and duties.
Word Family: **citizenship**, *noun*, the status or rights of a citizen; **citizenry**, *noun*, any or all citizens.

citric acid (*say* **sitrik** assid)
an organic acid present in large quantities in lemons but found in most living cells.

citron (*say* **sit–r'n**) *noun*
a pale yellow, citrus fruit resembling a lemon but with a thicker skin.

citrus (*say* **sit–rus**) *noun*
any of a group of evergreen trees including the lemon, orange, etc.
Word Family: **citrus**, **citrous**, *adjectives.*
[Latin, a citron tree]

city (*say* **sittee**) *noun*
a) any large or important, often cathedral, town, usually the centre of a region. b) its inhabitants.
the City, a) the City of London, the square mile which contains the chief financial institutions of the UK; b) these institutions collectively.

city hall
American: a town hall.

civet (*say* **sivvit**) *noun*
a musk–smelling substance obtained from glands of the civet cat and used in perfume.

civet cat
any of various small, spotted African or Asian mammals of the cat family, having a strong musky smell.

civic (*say* **siv–ik**) *adjective*
of or relating to a city or citizens.
civics *plural noun*
(*used with singular verb*) the study of cities, their government and people.
[Latin *civis* citizen]

civil (*say* **sivv'l**) *adjective*
1. of or relating to citizens or citizenship: '*civil* law'.
2. of or relating to private citizens and community life as distinct from military or religious matters: 'a *civil* marriage'.
3. polite: 'although she was extremely angry she gave a *civil* reply'.
Word Family: **civilly**, *adverb*; **civility**, *noun*, a politeness or polite expression.

civil engineering
the design and construction of public works such as bridges, large buildings, roads, etc.
[*engineer* originally meant a military engineer]

civilian (*say* **sivil–yen**) *noun*
a person who is not a member of the armed forces.

civilization (*say* sivvi–lie–**zay**–sh'n)
civilisation *noun*
1. a) a society of any period or place, unified by language and having distinctive legal systems, customs, art styles and governing powers. b) the process in a society which brings about such a unity.

2. an advanced stage of society and culture, embodied in a high level of art, science and government: 'China achieved *civilization* thousands of years ago'.
Word Family: **civilize, civilise,** *verb,* to refine or educate.

civil liberty
the complete liberty of any individual in a society, in relation to free speech and opinion.

civil rights
the natural rights of a citizen or individual in society, often established in the country's constitution.

civil service
(*usually capitals*) the staff employed by the central government in the various departments of state, excluding political, judicial and military personnel.
Word Family: **civil servant,** a person who works in the civil service.

civil war
any war between people of the same country.

clack *verb*
to make a sharp, harsh, metallic sound: 'the typists *clacked* away on their machines'.
Word Family: **clack,** *noun.*

clad *verb*
a past tense and past participle of the verb **clothe.**

cladding *noun*
a protective layer of one material over another.

claim *verb*
to demand or state as a right.
Usages:
a) 'he *claims* that he saw a ghost' (= says).
b) 'have you *claimed* on your car accident?' (= demanded insurance payment).
c) 'new problems are continually *claiming* his attention' (= requiring).
claim *noun*
1. a) the assertion of a right. b) a right or fact which is asserted: 'he has no *claim* to fame'.
2. anything which is claimed, such as a piece of land for mining rights.
Word Family: **claimer, claimant** (Law), *nouns,* a person who makes a claim.

clairvoyance (*say* klair-voy-ence) *noun*
also called **second sight**
the apparent ability to perceive objects or events which are outside the range of the senses.
Word Family: **clairvoyant,** *adjective, noun.*
[French *clair* clear + *voyant* seeing]

clam *noun*
any of a group of bivalve molluscs, most of which are edible.
clam up, (*informal*) a) to remain silent; b) to stop talking.

clamber *verb*
to climb with effort or difficulty, especially using both hands and feet.
Word Family: **clamber,** *noun.*

clammy *adjective*
cold and damp.

clamour *noun*
in America spelt **clamor**
a loud noise or outcry, especially of dissatisfaction or protest: 'there is a general *clamour* for improved education'.
Word Family: **clamour,** *verb;* **clamorous,** *adjective.*
[Latin *clamor* a shout]

clamp *noun*
any of various devices for pressing, holding or fastening things together, usually with adjustable ends connected by a screw.
clamp *verb*
to fasten with or fix in a clamp.
Usage: 'a hand was *clamped* over his mouth' (= pressed firmly).
clamp down, 'the government is *clamping down* on the use of drugs' (= restricting, becoming more strict).

clan *noun*
1. *Anthropology:* a social group descended in either the male or female line from a real or supposed common ancestor.
2. a large family or group of related families.
Usage: 'the whole *clan* from school came to the airport' (= clique, set).
Word Family: **clansman,** *noun,* a member of a clan, especially of Scottish Highlanders; **clannish,** *adjective,* a) of or characteristic of a clan, b) tending to be exclusive or secretive; **clannishly,** *adverb;* **clannishness,** *noun.*

clandestine (*say* klan-**destin** *or* **klanda**-stine) *adjective*
surreptitious or secretive, especially to deceive or conceal.
Word Family: **clandestinely,** *adverb.*
[Latin *clandestinus* secret]

clang *verb*
to make a loud, resonant, metallic sound: 'the cell door *clanged* shut'.
Word Family: **clang,** *noun.*

clanger *noun*
(*informal*) a stupid or embarrassing remark, mistake, etc.

clank *verb*
to make a hard, dull, metallic sound: 'the chains *clanked* as the drawbridge fell open'.
Word Family: **clank,** *noun.*

clap (1) *verb*
(clapped, clapping)
to strike the hands together with a sharp, sudden sound.
Usages:
a) 'a large hand *clapped* him on the shoulder' (= slapped, grasped).
b) 'he was *clapped* into gaol without a trial' (= put promptly).
clap eyes on, (*informal*) to catch sight of.
clap *noun*
the act or sound of clapping, especially as an expression of approval, etc.
Usage: 'a *clap* of thunder frightened the horse' (= loud, sudden noise).
Word Family: **clapper,** *noun,* a person or thing that claps, such as the tongue of a bell.

clap (2) *noun*
(*informal*) any venereal disease, especially gonorrhoea.

clapped-out *adjective*
(*informal*) completely worn out.

clapper-board *noun*
Films: a jointed board bearing a number, clapped and photographed at the beginning of each shot to aid in identification and in synchronizing sound with vision.

claptrap *noun*
any pretentious or insincere language.

claret (*say* **klarret**) *noun*
1. a dry red wine, especially of Bordeaux.
2. a deep purplish-red colour.
Word Family: **claret,** *adjective.*
[Old French, light-coloured]

clarify (*say* **klarri-fie**) *verb*
(clarified, clarifying)
1. to make clear: 'can you *clarify* the problem for me?'.
2. to remove impurities by heating, straining and allowing to cool: 'to *clarify* fat'.
Word Family: **clarification,** *noun.*
[Latin *clarus* clear + *facere* to make]

clarinet *noun*
Music: a wind instrument with a straight tube and a single-reed mouthpiece, played by means of fingerholes and keys.
Word Family: **clarinettist,** *noun,* a person who plays the clarinet.

clarion (*say* **klarrion**) *noun*
1. a medieval trumpet with a shrill, clear tone.
2. any clear or rousing call.

clarity (*say* **klarri-tee**) *noun*
clearness.

clash *verb*
to collide or hit with a loud, harsh sound: 'the cymbals *clashed* dramatically'.
Usages:
a) 'our tastes in most things *clash* dreadfully' (= disagree, conflict).
b) 'my French and Biology classes *clash* on Monday mornings' (= coincide).
Word Family: **clash,** *noun,* the act or sound of clashing.

clasp (*say* klahsp) *noun*
1. any of various devices with a catch, used to fasten or join two things together.
2. a hold or grasp: 'a firm *clasp* of the hand'.
clasp *verb*
1. to fasten with a clasp.
2. to hold or grasp tightly.

claspknife *noun*
see POCKET-KNIFE.

class *noun*
1. any number of people or things seen as a division or group, based on type, quality, etc.
2. *Sociology:* see SOCIAL CLASS.
3. *Education:* a) a group of students taught together. b) the meeting of students for a lesson: 'I'm late for my history *class*'.
4. *Biology:* the group below phylum used in the classification of animals and plants.
5. (*informal*) a high quality in manner, dress, etc.: 'that girl certainly has *class*'.
Word Family: **class,** *verb,* to arrange or rate according to type, quality, etc.
[Latin *classis* a social class]

classic *adjective*
1. of the highest class or quality: 'a *classic* novel'.
2. serving as a model or guide: 'here is a *classic* example of bad architecture'.

3. classical.

classic *noun*
1. a person or thing considered to be of the highest standard or quality: 'this novel is a *classic* of the 18th century'.
2. (*plural*) a) the literature of ancient Greece and Rome. b) the study of this literature.

classical *adjective*
1. of or characteristic of the art, literature or civilization of ancient Greece and Rome.
2. (of music) having a serious artistic intent and usually taking the form of a symphony, concerto, etc.
Word Family: **classically**, *adverb.*

Classicism (*say* **klassi**-sizm) *noun*
1. *Art:* an emphasis on the purity of form and a control of emotion derived from the art and literature of ancient Greece and Rome.
2. (*not capital*) a scholarly knowledge of classical culture, especially literature.
Word Family: **classicist**, *noun.*

classification (*say* klassifi-**kay**-sh'n) *noun*
1. a) the act of classifying. b) a class or division.
2. *Biology:* the ordering of animals and plants, based on similarities, into a series of groups which indicate evolutionary relationships.
Word Family: **classificatory**, *adjective.*

classified advertisement
a small advertisement printed in a magazine or newspaper under particular headings.

classify (*say* **klassi**-fie) *verb*
(**classified, classifying**)
1. to arrange or organize in classes.
2. to declare that a government or military document must be kept secret.

classy (*say* **klah**-see) *adjective*
(*informal*) elegant or stylish.

clatter *verb*
to make harsh, rapid rattling sounds: 'the plates *clattered* against each other'.
Word Family: **clatter**, *noun.*

clause (*say* klawz) *noun*
1. *Grammar:* a group of words containing a verb, forming part of a complex sentence and usually having the function of a noun, adjective or adverb. *Example*: the boy, *who was called Claude*, was born in France.
2. a separate article or section of a document, etc.

claustrophobia (*say* klostra-**fo**-bia) *noun*
an abnormal fear of being enclosed or shut in.
Word Family: **claustrophobic**, *adjective.*
[Latin *claustrum* enclosure + PHOBIA]

clavichord (*say* **klavvi**-kawd) *noun*
Music: the earliest type of keyboard instrument with a soft tone in which the strings are hit by metal blades attached to the keys.
[Latin *clavis* key + *chorda* chord]

clavicle (*say* **klavvi**-k'l) *noun*
also called the **collarbone**
Anatomy: either of two long, slender bones joining the chest to the shoulder.
Word Family: **clavicular** (*say* kla-**vik**-yoola), *adjective.*

claw *noun*
1. a hard, sharp, usually curved nail on the end of the limb of an animal.
2. the jointed grasping part of a crab, etc.
3. any similar part or object, such as the divided head of a hammer.
Word Family: **claw**, *verb*, to scratch, tear or pull with or as if with the claws.

claw hammer
see HAMMER.

clay *noun*
any of a group of common, earthy minerals, mainly hydrated aluminium silicates, which are plastic when wet and hard when baked, used for making bricks, pottery, etc.
feet of clay, 'so your hero has *feet of clay*' (= faults you were unaware of).

claymore *noun*
a large broadsword formerly used by Scottish Highlanders.

clay pigeon
1. a disc, usually made of baked clay, which is hurled into the air as a target for shot-gun practice.
2. (*informal*) a person who is set up by another or others as a target.

clean *adjective*
1. free from dirt, foreign matter or defects: 'are your hands quite *clean*?'.
Usages:
a) 'give me a *clean* sheet of paper' (= new).
b) 'this new car has a *clean*, streamlined body' (= neat, simple).
c) 'a *clean* joke' (= not obscene).
d) 'the athlete made a *clean* leap over the bar' (= skilful, clear).
2. *Physics:* free of radioactivity.

clean *verb*
to make clean.
clean up, a) 'please *clean up* your room' (= tidy); b) (*informal*) 'he *cleaned up* at the casino' (= made a lot of money).
clean *adverb*
cleanly or completely.
come clean, to make a full confession.
Word Family: **cleanness,** *noun*; **cleaner,** *noun,* a person or thing that cleans; **cleanly,** *adverb.*

clean-bowl *verb*
Cricket: to dismiss a batsman by bowling a ball which passes him, hits the stumps and dislodges the bails.

cleanliness (*say* **klenn**li–ness) *noun*
the state of being clean and neat.
Word Family: **cleanly,** *adjective.*

cleanse (*say* klenz) *verb*
to make thoroughly clean or pure.

clear (*rhymes with* here) *adjective*
1. transparent or free from darkness, cloudiness, etc.: '*clear* water'.
2. distinct or plain: 'he left *clear* instructions on how to work the machine'.
Usages:
a) 'is the alpine road *clear* yet?' (= open, free of obstruction).
b) 'he was declared *clear* of all blame' (= free).
c) 'are you quite *clear* about what you have to do?' (= certain).
d) 'it was a *clear* victory for the champion' (= unqualified, absolute).
e) 'he now earns a *clear* £9000' (= net).
clear *verb*
to make or become clear or clearer: 'the sky *cleared* and the sun shone brightly'.
Usages:
a) 'the athlete *cleared* the high jump bar' (= passed over without touching).
b) 'you'll have to be *cleared* through customs' (= checked and allowed to pass).
c) 'he used the inheritance to *clear* his debts' (= pay off).
Phrases:
clear out, to go away.
clear the air, to remove emotional differences or tension.
clear up, a) 'it *cleared up* after lunch so play continued' (= became fine and sunny again); b) 'can you *clear up* this mystery?' (= solve, make clear); c) 'let's *clear up* this mess before dad gets back' (= tidy up).
clear *noun*
in the clear, free from guilt or blame.
Word Family: **clear,** *adverb,* distinctly or completely; **clearly,** *adverb,* without doubt; **clearness,** *noun.*
[Latin *clarus* clear]

clearance *noun*
1. a clear space or distance, especially for movement within, beneath, etc.
2. a clearing away: 'slum *clearance*'.

clear-cut *adjective*
distinctly defined.

clearing *noun*
a piece of land cleared of trees, within a forest area.

clearing house
an institution which settles debts and other transactions, e.g. between banks.

clearly *adverb*
Word Family: see CLEAR.

clearway *noun*
a road along which vehicles are not allowed to park.

cleat (*say* kleet) *noun*
a) a piece of metal or wood, with horn-shaped projections, around which a rope may be tied. b) a piece of metal or wood fixed across a surface to give it strength. c) a metal or rubber fitting for boot soles, to prevent slipping.

cleavage (*say* **klee**vij) *noun*
1. a) the act of cleaving or dividing, such as the splitting of a crystal along planes within it. b) a division or split made by cleaving. Also called a **cleft.**
2. (*informal*) the separation between a woman's breasts.

cleave (1) *verb*
(cleaved, cleaving)
an old word meaning to hold fast or cling to.

cleave (2) *verb*
(cleft, cleaved or **clove; cleft, cleaved** or **cloven; cleaving)**
to split or separate, especially by cutting.
cleaver *noun*
a heavy chopper used to divide large sections of meat, etc.

clef *noun*
Music: a sign on the staff which indicates the name and pitch of the notes which follow it. The **treble clef** is on the second line and indicates that the note G is on this line. The **bass clef** is on the fourth line and

indicates that the note F is on this line.
[French, key]

cleft (1) *noun*
see CLEAVAGE.

cleft (2) *adjective*
split or divided.
cleft *verb*
a past tense and past participle of the verb **cleave (2)**.

cleft palate
a defect in which a child is born with a longitudinal slit along the roof of the mouth.

cleg *noun*
a horsefly with a vicious bite; sometimes confused with the non-biting gadfly.

clematis (*say* **klemma**–tis *or* klem–**ay**tis) *noun*
any of a group of climbing plants.
[Greek *klematis* of a vine-branch]

clemency (*say* **klemm**'n–see) *noun*
a mercy or kindness: 'the judge showed great *clemency* towards the thief'.
Usage: 'the *clemency* of the weather made their holiday very enjoyable' (= pleasantness, mildness).
Word Family: **clement,** *adjective*; **clemently,** *adverb.*
[Latin *clemens* gentle]

clementine *noun*
a small orange bred from the tangerine and a sour orange.

clench *verb*
to close or clasp tightly: 'he *clenched* his teeth in pain'.
Word Family: **clench,** *noun.*

clerestory (*say* **kleer**–story) *noun*
Architecture: the part of the wall of a church nave which is above the aisle roof and is furnished with windows.
[CLEAR + STOREY]

clergy (*say* **klerjee**) *noun*
Christian: all those who are trained and ordained as priests or ministers.
Word Family: **clergyman, cleric,** *nouns,* a member of the clergy.

clerical (*say* **klerri**–k'l) *adjective*
1. relating to clerks or office workers: 'where are the advertisements for *clerical* jobs?'.
2. relating to the clergy.
Word Family: **clerically,** *adverb.*

clerk (*say* klark) *noun*
a person employed to keep records of accounts or to deal with correspondence.

clever *adjective*
a) quick or intelligent: 'a *clever* solution to the problem'. b) skilful: 'his *clever* hands repaired the clock'.
Word Family: **cleverly,** *adverb*; **cleverness,** *noun.*

clew *noun*
1. *Sailing:* the outer, lower corner of a sail.
2. a ball of thread.
3. (*plural*) the cords by which a hammock is hung.

cliché (*say* **klee**–shay) *noun*
an idea or saying which is considered to be overused or trite.
[French *clicher* to stereotype]

click *noun*
a short, sharp, snapping sound: 'the *click* of a key in the lock'.
click *verb*
1. to make a click or clicks: 'the door *clicked* shut behind them'.
2. (*informal*) to be a success: 'his play really *clicked* with the public'.
Usage: 'the message finally *clicked* and we knew what to do' (= was understood).

client (*say* **klie**'nt) *noun*
a person who employs the help or services of a professional person or institution: 'most of the solicitor's *clients* are sent by an advisory service'.
[Latin *cliens*]

clientele (*say* klee–on–**tel**) *noun*
all the clients of a particular person or institution.

cliff *noun*
a very steep, almost vertical slope, usually of rock.
cliff–hanger *noun*
anything which is full of suspense or uncertainty, often melodramatic: 'his first novel was a *cliff–hanger*'.

climacteric (*say* klie–**makta**–rik) *noun*
any very important or crucial time, especially in a person's life.
[Greek *klimakter* a dangerous period in life]

climactic (*say* klie–**mak**tik)
climactical *adjective*
of or being a climax: 'there have been some *climactic* changes'.

climate (*say* **klie**–mit) *noun*
1. the weather conditions of a place or region during a year.
2. the general attitudes or feelings of a group of people: 'the *climate* of opinion is against the government'.

Word Family: **climatic** (*say* klie–**mattik**), *adjective*; **climatically**, *adverb*.
[Greek *klimatos* of a region]

climax (*say* **klie**–maks) *noun*
1. the highest or most exciting point of anything: 'the play reached its *climax* in the second act'.
2. *Biology:* a stable plant community which is in balance with everything around it and can reproduce itself.
Word Family: **climax**, *verb*.
[Greek *klimax* a ladder or staircase]

climb (*say* klime) *verb*
to move or go upwards: 'the plane *climbed* above the clouds'.
climb down, a) to go down or descend, especially with effort; b) 'the government has *climbed down* over its new taxation measures' (= withdrawn, retracted).
Word Family: **climb**, *noun*, a) the act of climbing, b) a place or height to be climbed; **climber**, *noun*, a) a person who climbs or attempts to climb, b) a plant which grows by attaching itself to a support.

clime *noun*
an old word for a region.

clinch *verb*
1. to make something secure: 'the signing of this document will *clinch* the deal'.
2. *Boxing:* to hug an opponent in order to prevent blows being struck.
3. to fasten with a knot similar to a half–hitch.
Word Family: **clinch**, *noun*, a) anything which clinches or is clinched, b) (informal) an embrace; **clincher**, *noun*, something which is decisive.

cling *verb*
(clung, clinging)
to be attached or remain close to: 'the child *clung* to its mother'.

clinic *noun*
1. a) a specialized section of a hospital, usually treating out–patients. b) any medical centre, especially one giving special treatment, such as X–rays, etc.
2. a class of students, especially medical students, taught through actual observation of treatments, etc.
[Greek *klinikos* of a bed]

clinical *adjective*
1. of or relating to a clinic.
2. of or relating to the treatment or management of disease in a patient. A **clinical diagnosis** is based on observed symptoms.
Usage: 'he has developed a *clinical* attitude towards death' (= scientific, unemotional).
Word Family: **clinically**, *adverb*.

clinical psychology
see PSYCHOLOGY.

clink (1) *verb*
to make a light, ringing or metallic sound: 'his fork *clinked* against the glass dish'.
Word Family: **clink**, *noun*.

clink (2) *noun*
(*informal*) a gaol.
[from a prison in *Clink Street*, London]

clinker *noun*
slag or the incombustible residue in coke ovens, etc.

clinker–built *adjective*
(of a boat) built with overlapping planks, in contrast to carvel–built boats with flush planks.

clip (1) *verb*
(clipped, clipping)
1. to cut or trim with or as if with scissors, etc.: 'the hedge was *clipped* in the shape of a pheasant'.
2. to hit sharply or quickly: 'the car *clipped* the edge of the fence'.
clip *noun*
1. a) the act of clipping. b) something which is clipped or cut, especially all the wool shorn from sheep at one time or the total wool shorn in a season.
2. a short, sharp blow: 'a *clip* over the ear'.
3. (*informal*) rate: 'he completed the lap at a fast *clip*'.

clip (2) *noun*
a) any device for holding or gripping: 'a *paperclip*'. b) a metal container for the cartridges of a gun.
Word Family: **clip (clipped, clipping)**, *verb*, to fasten with a clip.

clipper *noun*
1. (*usually plural*) any of various devices for clipping or cutting: 'nail *clippers*'.
2. a fast, square–rigged sailing ship of the 19th century with tall masts and overhanging bows.

clipping *noun*
anything which is clipped off or cut out: 'a newspaper *clipping*'.

clique (*say* kleek) *noun*
a small group of people which snobbishly excludes others.
Word Family: **cliquy**, **cliquey**, **cliquish**, *adjectives*.

clitoris (*say* **klitta-ris**) ***noun***
Anatomy: a small organ in the upper part of the female vulva, containing erectile tissue and corresponding to the penis in males.

cloaca (*say* klo-ayka) ***noun***
plural is **cloacae** (*say* klo-ay-kee)
Biology: a cavity in an animal into which the rectum and urogenital ducts open.
Word Family: **cloacal,** *adjective.*
[Latin, a sewer]

cloak ***noun***
a long, loose piece of clothing without sleeves, usually fastened at the neck and worn over clothes.
Usage: 'the soldiers marched under the *cloak* of darkness' (= cover, disguise).
cloakroom ***noun***
a room for leaving coats, etc., sometimes with a basin or toilet.
Word Family: **cloak,** ***verb,*** to cover with or as if with a cloak.

cloak-and-dagger *adjective*
melodramatic and full of espionage, intrigue, secrecy, etc.

clobber *verb*
(*informal*) to hit or strike heavily.
Usage: 'that last question really *clobbered* him!' (= defeated utterly).
clobber ***noun***
(*informal*) clothing.

cloche (*say* klosh) ***noun***
1. a woman's small, close-fitting, round hat.
2. a glass or plastic, sometimes bell-shaped, covering to protect garden plants.
[French, bell]

clock ***noun***
any of various mechanical or electrical instruments, with moving hands for measuring and showing time, which are designed to stand or hang in a room.
Phrases:
against the clock, in a race to finish before a certain time.
around the clock, all day and all night.
clock *verb*
to test or measure the time of: 'his run was *clocked* at 13·56 seconds'.
Phrases:
clock in, to register one's time of arrival.
clock out, to register one's time of departure.

clockwise *adverb, adjective*
in the same direction as the moving hands of a clock.

clockwork ***noun***
like clockwork, 'the plan went *like clockwork*' (= smoothly, perfectly).

clod ***noun***
1. a lump or mass, especially of earth or clay.
2. (*informal*) a stupid person.

clodhopper ***noun***
a country bumpkin.

clog ***noun***
a backless shoe with a thick sole which is usually made of wood or cork.
clog *verb*
(clogged, clogging)
to block or become blocked: 'the sink is *clogged* with dirt'.

cloister (*say* **kloysta**) ***noun***
1. a monastery or convent.
2. a roofed path joined to a church or other building and usually situated around an open courtyard.
cloistered *adjective*
1. secluded or sheltered: 'a *cloistered* life'.
2. having a cloister or covered path, as a church.
Word Family: **cloister,** ***verb.***
[Latin *claustrum* an enclosure]

clone ***noun***
Biology: a) the descendants of a single cell which has divided asexually. b) a group of plants grown from parts of a single plant.
Word Family: **clone,** ***verb.***
[Greek ***klon*** a twig]

clop ***noun***
the light drumming sound made by a horse's hoofs on a hard surface.
Word Family: **clop (clopped, clopping),** ***verb.***

close (*say* kloze) ***verb***
to shut or stop: a) 'please *close* the door'; b) 'we will *close* the meeting now'.
close in, 'the police *closed in* on the demonstrators' (= approached and surrounded).
close (*say* klose) *adjective, adverb*
1. near: 'don't go too *close* to the edge'.
2. detailed or precise: 'pay *close* attention to this advice'.
3. strongly united: 'a *close* group of friends'.
4. restricted: 'the *close* season for duck shooting'.

Usages:
a) 'the air in here is very *close*' (= limited, oppressive).
b) 'please keep the story *close* as I have not told my parents yet' (= secret).
c) 'it was a very *close* competition' (= nearly equal).
close call, close shave, a narrow escape.
close *noun*
1. (*say* kloze) an end or conclusion: 'at the *close* of day'.
2. *Music:* (*say* kloze) a cadence.
3. (*say* klose) a road closed at one end.
4. (*say* klose) the land around a cathedral or other building.
Word Family: **closely,** *adverb*; **closeness,** *noun.*
[Latin *clausus* shut]

closed book
(*informal*) a) a matter about which one knows very little. b) a matter which is completely finished.

closed shop
a factory or industry whose workers must belong to a trade union.

close-fisted (*say* **klose**-fistid) *adjective*
mean or miserly.

closet (*say* **klozz**it) *noun*
a room or cupboard for storing clothing, etc.
closet *verb*
to be shut up in a private room for discussion, etc.: 'the girls have been *closeted* away since lunch'.

close-up (*say* **klose**-up) *noun*
a close view of anything, especially a photograph taken at close range.

closure (*say* **klo**-*zh*er) *noun*
1. the act of closing: 'the *closure* of the mines was due to falling rock'.
2. *Parliament:* the stopping of a debate, after which a vote is taken to decide the issue.
Word Family: **closure** (Parliament), *verb.*

clot *noun*
1. a mass or lump.
a **blood clot** is a half-solid lump of altered elements of blood.
2. (*informal*) a stupid person: 'what a *clot* you are to believe that story'.
clot *verb*
(clotted, clotting)
to form into clots: '*clotted* cream'.

cloth *noun*
1. any fabric, usually made by weaving wool, cotton or other yarn and used to make clothes, curtains, etc.
2. a piece of cloth used for a particular purpose: 'a *tablecloth*'.
3. the profession of the clergy.

clothe (*say* klo*the*) *verb*
(clothed or **clad, clothing)**
to dress or provide with clothes.
Usage: 'the city streets were *clothed* in mist' (= covered, surrounded).

clothes *plural noun*
all the items worn to cover the body.

clothing (*say* **klo**-*th*ing) *noun*
clothes.
Usage: 'a *clothing* of darkness' (= covering).

cloud *noun*
1. a dense mass of suspended water drops or ice crystals formed in the air by the condensation of water-vapour.
2. any similar dark or moving mass: 'a *cloud* of smoke'.
Phrases:
cloud-nine, (*informal*) an exalted state.
in the clouds, dream-like or not paying attention.
under a cloud, under suspicion.
cloud *verb*
to make or become covered or shadowed with, or as if with clouds: 'her eyes *clouded* with tears'.
Usage: 'the illness *clouded* the house' (= made gloomy).
Word Family: **cloudy,** *adjective,* a) full of clouds, b) opaque or indistinct.

cloudburst *noun*
a sudden fall of very heavy rain.

cloud chamber
Physics: an apparatus consisting of a closed chamber containing saturated water-vapour, which indicates the presence of fast, charged particles, e.g. electrons, by producing rows of water droplets.

clout *noun*
(*informal*) a blow or knock, especially with the hand: 'he received a heavy *clout* on the head'.
Word Family: **clout,** *verb.*

clout nail
a short nail with a large head, used to fasten pliable or brittle materials, such as galvanized iron.

clove (1) *noun*
a sweet, hot spice made from the dried flower bud of a tropical tree and used in cooking.

clove (2) *noun*
any of the small, rounded, separate sections of a bulb: 'a *clove* of garlic'.

clove (3) *verb*
a past tense of the verb **cleave (2)**.

cloven *verb*
a past participle of the verb **cleave (2)**.

cloven–hoofed, cloven–footed *adjective*
1. having divided hoofs, as a cow.
2. devilish or evil: 'a *cloven–hoofed* nature'.

clover *noun*
a fodder plant, usually with three leaves on each stalk, grown as food for cattle and sheep and also to add nitrogen to the soil.
in clover, in great comfort or luxury.

cloverleaf *noun*
1. the leaf of a clover.
2. a major road junction with a pattern of ramps, underpasses, etc. resembling a four–leaved clover.

clown *noun*
1. a comic actor in a circus or pantomime.
2. any funny or clumsy person.
Word Family: **clown,** *verb,* to perform as or like a clown; **clownery,** *noun;* **clownish,** *adjective.*

cloy *verb*
to make or become sick or weary with too much of something: 'her enjoyment of films was *cloyed* after four weeks at the film festival'.

club *noun*
1. a heavy stick, usually thicker at one end.
2. a stick with a shaped wooden or metal head, used in golf.
3. an organized group of people, sharing similar beliefs or interests and having regular meetings: 'a chess *club*'.
4. a social meeting–place for its members, often with a bar, restaurant, sleeping accommodation and facilities for sports or games.
5. *Cards:* a) a black figure like a cloverleaf on a playing card. b) a playing card with this figure. c) (*plural*) the suit with this figure.
club *verb*
(clubbed, clubbing)
1. to hit with, or as if with, a club.
2. to join together for a particular purpose: 'we all *clubbed* together to buy a boat'.
Word Family: **clubhouse,** *noun,* the buildings used by members of a club or association.

club foot
a deformed foot, usually with the sole turning inwards and the heel raised.
Word Family: **club–footed,** *adjective.*

cluck *verb*
to make a short cry like a brooding hen: 'mother *clucked* her disapproval'.
Word Family: **cluck,** *noun.*

clue (*say* kloo) *noun*
anything which gives a guide to the solution of a problem, mystery, question, etc.: 'the police have found no *clue* to the identity of the thief'.
clueless *adjective*
(*informal*) stupid.

clump *noun*
1. a cluster or mass of things together: 'a *clump* of rose bushes'.
2. a heavy, dull noise or tread.
Word Family: **clump,** *verb.*

clumsy (*say* **klum**–zee) *adjective*
ungraceful, heavy or awkward: a) 'the *clumsy* workman dropped a load of cement'; b) 'his apology was rather *clumsy*'.

clung *verb*
the past tense and past participle of the verb **cling**.

cluster *noun*
a number of things growing, grouped or moving together: 'the guests stood in *clusters* at the gate'.
Word Family: **cluster,** *verb.*

clutch (1) *verb*
to seize and hold tightly: 'the rider *clutched* the saddle for support'.
clutch *noun*
1. the act of clutching.
2. (*usually plural*) any control or power: 'in the *clutches* of a fever'.
3. a device by which working parts of a machine may be easily engaged or disengaged while the machine is operating.

clutch (2) *noun*
a number of things produced at one time, especially a hatch of eggs or chickens.

clutter *verb*
to make untidy or confused: 'the room was *cluttered* with old newspapers'.
Word Family: **clutter,** *noun.*

co–
a prefix meaning together or associated, as in *cooperate.*

coach *noun*
1. a large, enclosed vehicle, such as a bus or railway carriage.
2. a person employed to teach, train or prepare people for a particular purpose.
Word Family: **coach,** *verb,* to train or prepare.

coagulate (*say* ko–**ag**–yoolate) *verb*
to change from a liquid into a solid, thickened state, such as a clot.
coagulant *noun*
a substance which causes a liquid to coagulate.
Word Family: **coagulation,** *noun.*
[Latin *coagulum* rennet]

coal *noun*
1. a black or dark brown burnable substance composed of layered deposits of carbon–bearing material derived from vegetable matter.
2. a glowing or charred fragment of wood or other fuel: 'rake over the *coals* to stir up the fire'.
Phrases:
coals of fire, 'she heaped *coals of fire* on him by returning good for evil' (= filled him with remorse).
coals to Newcastle, a superfluous act, like sending coal to where coal comes from.
haul over the coals, to scold.

coalesce (*say* ko–a–**less**) *verb*
to join, grow or come together.
Word Family: **coalescence,** *noun.*
[Latin *coalescere* to grow together]

coalition (*say* ko–a–**lish**'n) *noun*
1. a union or joining together of several things.
2. a joining together of political parties with each retaining its own principles.

coalscuttle *noun*
a bucket in which coal for a fire is carried or stored.

coarse (*rhymes with* horse) *adjective*
composed of large particles: '*coarse* sand'.
Usages:
a) 'the sailors shouted with *coarse* laughter' (= crude, vulgar).
b) 'the *coarse* cloth scratched her skin' (= rough, harsh).
Word Family: **coarsely,** *adverb*; **coarseness,** *noun*; **coarsen,** *verb.*

coarse fishing
freshwater fishing with a hook and bait and not a fly. Compare FLY FISHING.

coast *noun*
1. the area of land which borders the sea or any large area of water.
2. the seaside.
the coast is clear, there is no danger.
coast *verb*
to move without effort: 'the bicycle *coasted* down the hill'.
Word Family: **coastal,** *adjective,* of or at a coast.
[Latin *costa* rib or flank]

coaster *noun*
a small mat or tray placed under a drinking glass to protect the table surface.

coastguard *noun*
an officer or group of officers appointed to patrol a coast for smugglers, ships in trouble, etc.

coastline *noun*
the outline of a coast.

coat *noun*
1. a piece of clothing, with sleeves, a collar or lapels, which fastens down the front, worn over other clothes.
2. any outer covering: a) 'a dog's wiry *coat*'; b) 'a *coat* of paint'.
trail one's coat, to act in a provoking manner.
Word Family: **coat,** *verb,* to provide with a coat or cover; **coating,** *noun,* a layer.

coat of arms
plural is **coats of arms**
Heraldry: a shield decorated with pictorial designs and used by noble families, etc.

coax (*say* cokes) *verb*
to get something by flattery or patient persuasion: 'the dog had to be *coaxed* into having a bath'.
Word Family: **coaxingly,** *adverb*; **coaxer,** *noun.*

coaxial (*say* ko–**aksial**) *adjective*
having the same axis.
coaxial cable
Radio: a cable with a pair of electrical conductors, one inside the other, used to carry high–frequency signals such as television programmes.

cob *noun*
1. a male swan.
2. a sturdy, short–legged horse for riding.

cobalt (*say* **ko**–bawlt) *noun*
element number 27, a hard, magnetic metal, similar to iron, used in alloys. Its compounds are used in glass and as dyes. See TRANSITION ELEMENT.

See CHEMICAL ELEMENTS in grey pages.
Word Family: **cobaltic,** *adjective.*

cobble *verb*
1. to make or mend shoes.
2. to make or put together clumsily.
3. to pave with cobblestones.
Word Family: **cobbler,** *noun,* a person who mends shoes.

cobblestone *noun*
a rounded stone used for paving.

cobra *noun*
any of a group of very poisonous, front-fanged snakes of Africa and Asia noted for spreading their neck-ribs to form a hood of skin when disturbed.
[Latin *colubra* snake]

cobweb *noun*
1. a thin thread or threaded structure spun by spiders to catch prey, usually insects.
2. any flimsy or intricate structure or thing.
3. (*plural*) fustiness: 'to blow away the *cobwebs* in the mind'.
[Middle English *coppe* spider + WEB]

cocaine (*say* ko-**kane**) *noun*
a bitter, crystalline drug made from the dried leaves of a tropical plant and used as an anaesthetic.

coccus (*say* **kokkus**) *noun*
plural is **cocci** (*say* **kok**-eye)
Biology: any round bacterium.
[Greek *kokkos* berry]

coccyx (*say* **kok**-siks) *noun*
Anatomy: the small, rough, triangular bone at the base of the spine, formed by four fused vertebrae.
[Greek *kokkyx* cuckoo, because the bone was thought to resemble its bill]

cochineal (*say* kochi-**neel**) *noun*
1. a red dye obtained from an insect and used as a food-colouring.
2. a strong, light red colour.
[Spanish *cochinilla* woodlouse]

cock (1) *noun*
1. a male adult bird, especially a domestic fowl.
2. any of various devices, such as a valve, used to control the flow of a liquid or gas.
3. a) the hammer of a gun. b) the position to which it is pulled before firing.
4. a weathervane shaped like a rooster.
5. (*informal*) penis.
cock *verb*
to pull back and set the hammer of a gun before firing.

cock (2) *verb*
to turn upwards or to the side in a jaunty or defiant manner: 'he *cocked* an eyebrow at the impudent question'.
Word Family: **cock,** *noun.*

cockade *noun*
a knot of ribbons worn on a hat, usually as part of a uniform.

cockatoo (*say* kokka-**too**) *noun*
a large, crested parrot, found in Australia and New Guinea.

cockatrice (*say* **kokka**-trice) *noun*
1. *Biblical:* a poisonous snake.
2. *Ancient mythology, Heraldry:* a fabulous monster, often confused with the basilisk.

cockchafer *noun*
a large brown European beetle which flies with a loud whirring noise.

cockerel *noun*
a young domestic cock.

cocker spaniel
one of a breed of small, long-haired dogs with long drooping ears.
[as used to flush *woodcock*]

cockeyed *adjective*
1. crooked or twisted to one side.
2. (*informal*) absurd or foolish: 'a *cockeyed* story'.
3. having a squint.

cockle *noun*
any of a group of edible, bivalve molluscs with ribbed shells.
cockles of the heart, 'his words warmed the *cockles of my heart*' (= deepest or innermost feelings).

cockney (*say* **kok**-**nee**) *noun*
(*often capital*) a native of inner London, especially one having a characteristic accent.

cockpit *noun*
the space for the pilot or crew controlling an aircraft.

cockroach *noun*
any of a group of large, usually nocturnal, insects with dark, oval, flattened bodies, long legs and antennae.

cockscomb *noun*
1. *Biology:* see COMB.
2. a pointed cap worn by a clown or jester.

cocksure (*say* **cok**-shaw) *adjective*
overly confident: 'a *cocksure* young man'.
Word Family: **cocksureness,** *noun.*

cocktail *noun*
1. a strong, alcoholic drink made of one or more spirits and often sweetened.
2. a dish of seafood served as an appetizer.
3. a mixture of fruit.

cocky *adjective*
(*informal*) arrogant or conceited: 'his *cocky* reply made his mother furious'.
Word Family: **cockily,** *adverb*; **cockiness,** *noun.*

cocoa (*say* **ko**–ko) *noun*
a) the ground seeds of the cacao tree.
b) a drink made from this.

cocoa bean
the seed of the cacao tree.

cocoa butter
a mixture of semisolid oils derived from cocoa, used in the manufacture of chocolate.

coconut (*say* **ko**–k'nut) **cocoanut** *noun*
a) the large seed of a palm tree, with a hard shell, a white, fleshy, edible lining and containing a milky liquid.
b) the white lining, often grated and used in cooking.
[Spanish *coco* grinning face, which the base of the shell resembles]

coconut ice
a sweet made from sugar and coconut.

coconut oil
a mixture of oils obtained from coconuts, and used in making soaps, cosmetics, etc.

coconut–shy *noun*
an entertainment at fairs, etc. in which coconuts are set up as targets to be thrown at, and awarded as prizes.

cocoon (*say* k'**koon**) *noun*
Biology: a protective covering made by an animal for its eggs or by an insect for the pupa.

cod *noun*
any of a group of large, soft–finned, edible fish, sometimes brightly coloured.

coda (*say* **ko**–da) *noun*
Music: the section of music at the end of a movement.
[Italian, from Latin *cauda* tail]

coddle *verb*
1. to boil gently.
2. to pamper or indulge.

code *noun*
1. a systematic collection of rules relating to a particular subject: 'a *code* of behaviour'.
2. any system of communication which is based on randomly chosen symbols: a) 'a computer *code*'; b) 'most communications during wartime are transmitted in *code*'.
Word Family: **code,** *verb.*

codeine (*say* **ko**–deen) *noun*
a white, slightly bitter chemical made from opium and used in medicine to relieve pain.
[Greek *kodeia* poppyhead]

codger *noun*
(*informal*) an odd, usually old, person.

codicil (*say* **koddi**–sil) *noun*
a supplement or added part, especially to a will.
[Latin *codicilli* a note]

codify (*say* **koddi**–fie *or* **ko**–diff–eye) *verb*
(**codified, codifying**)
1. to arrange systematically.
2. to put into a code.
Word Family: **codification,** *noun.*

codling moth
also spelt **codlin moth**
a small moth, the larvae of which feed on the flesh of apples.

cod–liver oil
an oil which is obtained from the liver of cod or sharks, and is used as a source of vitamins A and D.

codpiece *noun*
a pouch attached to the crotch of tight–fitting breeches, worn by men in the Middle Ages.

codswallop (*say* **kodz**–wollop) *noun*
(*informal*) any nonsense or rubbish.
[originally ginger beer, invented by *Hiram Codd* of London in 1871; *wallop* meaning poor beer]

co–ed *adjective*
(*informal*) coeducational.
Word Family: **co–ed,** *noun,* a female student at a coeducational institution.

coeducation (*say* ko–eddu–**kay**–sh'n) *noun*
the teaching of males and females together.
Word Family: **coeducational,** *adjective.*

coefficient (*say* ko–a–**fish**'nt) *noun*
1. *Maths:* a number or symbol placed in front of, and multiplying, another quantity. *Example*: in $3a^2y$, $3a^2$ is the coefficient of y.
2. *Physics:* a factor which is constant for a specified system.

coelacanth (*say* **seela**–kanth) *noun*
any of a group of fish thought, until 1938, when a living specimen was found, to have been extinct for 70 million years.
[Greek *koilos* hollow + *akantha* spine]

coelenterate (*say* see–**lenta**–rate) *noun*
any of a large group of aquatic animals, such as the hydra, which have only one internal cavity.
[Greek *koilos* hollow + *enteron* intestine]

coerce (*say* ko–**erse**) *verb*
to force or compel: 'rebellious children must be *coerced* into obedience'.
Word Family: **coercion** (*say* ko–**er**–sh'n), *noun*; **coercive** (*say* ko–**ersiv**), *adjective*.
[Latin *coercere* to restrain]

coeval (*say* ko–**ee**–v'l) *adjective*
a) of the same age. b) existing at or lasting for the same period of time.
Word Family: **coeval,** *noun*, a contemporary; **coevally,** *adverb*.
[co- + Latin *aevum* a lifetime]

coexist (*say* ko–**egzist**) *verb*
to exist together.
Word Family: **coexistence,** *noun*; **coexistent,** *adjective*.

coffee *noun*
a) a substance made by grinding the bean-like seeds of a tropical, evergreen shrub. b) a drink made from this.

coffer *noun*
1. a large, strong box, especially for storing money or valuables.
2. (*plural*) the treasury or funds: 'the *coffers* of the Church were badly depleted'.
3. an ornamental, sunken panel in a ceiling, etc.

coffin *noun*
a box into which a dead body is placed for burial.
[Greek *kophinos* basket]

cog *noun*
1. a tooth or projection on a wheel or bar which fits into and pushes against a matching tooth or projection on another wheel or bar.
2. an insignificant person in a large organization: 'he is only a *cog* in that company'.

cogent (*say* **ko**–j'nt) *adjective*
having the power to convince or prove: 'we could not disagree with his *cogent* arguments'.
Word Family: **cogently,** *adverb*; **cogency,** *noun*.
[Latin *cogens* compelling]

cogitate (*say* **koji**–tate) *verb*
to think hard or ponder.
Word Family: **cogitation,** *noun*; **cogitative,** *adjective*.
[Latin *cogitare* to consider thoroughly]

cognac (*say* **kon**–yak) *noun*
a fine brandy.
[first made in *Cognac*, France]

cognate (*say* **kog**–nate) *adjective*
having the same source, descent or origin: 'English and German are *cognate* languages'.
Word Family: **cognate,** *noun*.
[Latin *cognatus* related by birth]

cognition (*say* kog–**nish**'n) *noun*
the mental process by which knowledge is acquired.
Word Family: **cognitive** (*say* **kogni**–tiv), *adjective*.
[Latin *cognitio* a learning]

cognizance (*say* **kogni**–z'nce)
cognisance *noun*
knowledge or notice: 'did you have any *cognizance* of the fact?'.
Word Family: **cognizant,** *adjective*.

cognomen (*say* kog–**no**–men) *noun*
a) a surname. b) a nickname.
[Latin, a surname]

cogwheel *noun*
a wheel with cogs, used to transmit or receive motion.

cohabitation (*say* ko–habbi–**tay**–sh'n) *noun*
the act of living together, especially as man and wife.
Word Family: **cohabit,** *verb*; **cohabiter,** *noun*.

cohere (*say* ko–**heer**) *verb*
(**cohered, cohering**)
1. to stick together.
2. to agree or be consistent.
Word Family: **coherence,** *noun*; **coherent,** *adjective*, a) sticking together, b) logically connected; **coherently,** *adverb*.
[Latin *cohaerere* to stick together]

cohesion (*say* ko–**hee**–*zh*'n) *noun*
1. the state of cohering.
2. *Physics:* the force that holds molecules or groups of atoms together. Compare ADHESION.
Word Family: **cohesive,** *adjective*.

cohort *noun*
1. *Ancient history:* a tenth part of a Roman legion.

2. a group or band, especially of warriors.

coif *noun*
a close-fitting cap or hood.
Word Family: **coif,** *verb,* to cover the head with or as if with a coif.

coiffeur (*say* kwa-**fir**) *noun*
a hairdresser.

coiffure (*say* kwa-**fewer**) *noun*
a hairstyle.

coign (*say* koin) *noun*
see QUOIN.

coil *noun*
1. a) a length of rope, wire, etc., wound into a continuous series of rings or spirals. b) a single ring in such a series.
2. *Electronics:* an induction coil.
Word Family: **coil,** *verb.*

coin *noun*
a) a metal disc stamped to show its value as money. b) any or all coins.
coin *verb*
to make coins.
Usage: 'to *coin* a phrase' (= make, invent).
Word Family: **coinage,** *noun.*

coincide (*say* ko-**inside**) *verb*
to occur at the same time or place: 'my holidays *coincide* with Easter'.
Usage: 'her opinions usually *coincide* with mine' (= agree, correspond).

coincidence (*say* ko-**insi**-d'nce) *noun*
1. the act of coinciding.
2. something which occurs at the same time as, or corresponds with, another by chance: 'it was a complete *coincidence* that he should arrive just as we were talking about him'.
Word Family: **coincidental** (*say* ko-insi-**dent**'l), *adjective,* of or involving coincidence; **coincident,** *adjective,* a) coinciding, b) in exact agreement; **coincidentally,** *adverb.*
[co- + Latin *incidere* to happen]

coitus, coition (*say* **koy**-it-us *and* ko-**ish**'n) *noun*
the act of sexual intercourse.
[Latin *coire* to go together]

coke *noun*
a hard, dark grey, brittle, porous solid containing about 80 per cent carbon. It is prepared by heating coal in the absence of air, and is used as fuel or in the production of iron and steel.

col *noun*
Geography: a saddle between two higher parts of a mountain range, etc.
[French, neck]

colander (*say* **kull**'nda) *noun*
also spelt **cullender**
a bowl-shaped vessel with many small holes, used for draining off liquids from food.
[Latin *colare* to strain]

cola nut
a nut containing caffeine, grown in Africa and the West Indies and used in some non-alcoholic drinks.

cold *adjective*
lacking heat or having a low temperature: a) '*cold* toes'; b) 'a *cold* morning'.
Usages:
a) 'a *cold* and indignant stare' (= unfriendly).
b) 'the boxer was knocked *cold*' (= unconscious).
c) 'the dogs can't follow a *cold* scent' (= faint, no longer fresh).
Phrases:
get, have cold feet, 'at the last moment he *got cold feet* and didn't propose' (= lost courage).
leave cold, 'his attempts to impress people *leave* me *cold*' (= fail to affect).
cold *noun*
1. an absence of heat or warmth: 'I dislike the *cold* of winter'.
2. *Medicine:* an infectious disease causing fever, a sore throat and a blocked nose.
in the cold, 'I always feel *in the cold* at strange parties' (= neglected, left out).
Word Family: **coldly,** *adverb*; **coldness,** *noun.*

cold-blooded *adjective*
1. coolly deliberate or cruel: 'a *cold-blooded* act'.
2. *Biology:* having a body temperature which changes with the temperature of the environment, e.g. a fish. Also called **poikilothermic.** Compare WARM-BLOODED.
Word Family: **cold-bloodedly,** *adverb*; **cold-bloodedness,** *noun.*

cold chisel
see CHISEL.

cold comfort
little or no comfort or consolation.

cold cream
a thick cream-like substance used to clean or soften the skin.

cold front
Weather: see FRONT.

cold-hearted *adjective*
indifferent or unsympathetic: 'the *cold-hearted* landlord did not care about the plight of his tenants'.
Word Family: **cold-heartedly**, *adverb*; **cold-heartedness**, *noun*.

cold snap
a sudden, short period of very cold weather.

cold sore
a viral skin infection causing sores on or near the lips, especially during a cold. See HERPES.

cold storage
the storage of perishable foods, etc. in a refrigerated place.
Usage: (*informal*) 'they put the suggestion in *cold storage*' (= a state of indefinite postponement).

cold war
a state of aggression or rivalry between countries, which stops short of actual fighting.

cold wave
1. *Beauty:* see PERMANENT WAVE.
2. *Weather:* a burst of cold air, usually from polar areas, often felt after a low has passed.

coleopterous (*say* kolli-**opterus**) *adjective*
of or relating to beetles.
[Greek *koleos* sheath + *pteron* wing]

coleoptile (*say* kolli-**optile**) *noun*
Biology: the first leaf above the ground in grasses.
[Greek *koleos* sheath + *ptilon* feather]

coleslaw *noun*
a salad made from raw, shredded cabbage with a creamy dressing.
[Dutch *kool* cabbage + *sla* salad]

colic (*say* **kollik**) *noun*
the severe recurring spasms of pain in the abdomen due to partial or complete blockage of a hollow organ, such as the bowel or ureter.
Word Family: **colicky**, *adjective*.

colitis (*say* k'**lie**-tis) *noun*
an inflammation of the colon.
[Greek *kolon* + -ITIS]

collaborate (*say* k'**labba**-rate) *verb*
to work together: 'the two departments *collaborated* on the project'.
Word Family: **collaboration**, *noun*; **collaborator**, *noun*, a person who collaborates.
[CO- + Latin *laborare* to labour]

collage (*say* k'l-**ahzh**) *noun*
an art form in which various materials such as paper, cloth, string, etc. are stuck onto a surface.
[French, gluing]

collagen (*say* **kolla**-jen) *noun*
a protein found in connective tissue and bones, which forms gelatine on boiling.
[Greek *kolla* glue + -GEN]

collapse *verb*
1. to fall down suddenly: 'the wall *collapsed*'.
Usages:
a) 'the scheme *collapsed* owing to a lack of finance' (= stopped).
b) 'she *collapsed* in tears at the terrible news' (= broke down).
2. to fold compactly: 'this bed *collapses*'.
Word Family: **collapsible**, *adjective*; **collapse**, *noun*.
[CO- + Latin *lapsus* a fall]

collar *noun*
1. anything worn or tied around the neck: 'a dog's *collar*'.
2. the part of a shirt, coat, dress, etc. which surrounds the neck and is usually folded over.
3. a part of a harness, around the horse's shoulders, which enables a load to be pulled.
4. any of various devices encircling a pipe, shaft, rod, etc.
collar *verb*
to seize by the collar or neck.
Usages:
a) (*informal*) 'he *collared* me on the way to work and asked me for a loan' (= captured, waylaid).
b) (*informal*) 'who *collared* my exercise book?' (= took, stole).
collar the market, to gain a monopoly.
[Latin *collum* neck]

collarbone *noun*
see CLAVICLE.

collate (*say* k'l-**ate**) *verb*
to compare copies, accounts, etc. carefully in order to note agreements and disagreements.
[CO- + Latin *latus* brought]

collateral (*say* ko-**latta**-r'l) *adjective*
1. secondary or subordinate to the main subject, action, etc.
2. being descended from the same ancestors, but through different lines.
collateral *noun*
an asset, such as a car, given as a guarantee for the repayment of a loan.
[CO- + Latin *lateris* of a side]

collation (*say* k'l–**ay**–sh'n) *noun*
1. the act of collating.
2. a light meal.

colleague (*say* **koll**–eeg) *noun*
a fellow member of a profession, official body, etc.
[Latin *conlega*]

collect (1) (*say* k'**lekt**) *verb*
1. to gather together or accumulate: 'to *collect* money for charity'.
Usage: 'she tried to *collect* her thoughts before answering his unexpected question' (= regain control over).
2. to fetch: 'when will the mail be *collected*?'.
collect *adjective, adverb*
American: to be paid for on delivery: 'to send a parcel *collect*'.
collection (*say* k'**lek**–sh'n) *noun*
1. the act of collecting: 'mail *collection* stopped during the strike'.
2. anything which is collected, such as the money collected during a church service.
Word Family: **collected**, *adjective*, self-possessed; **collectedly**, *adverb*; **collectedness**, *noun*; **collector**, *noun*, a person or thing that collects.
[Latin *collectus* gathered together]

collect (2) (*say* **koll**ekt) *noun*
Christian: a short, set prayer in a traditional form, usually for a particular season of the year.

collective *adjective*
1. combined or united: 'a *collective* effort will have the job done much more quickly'.
2. forming a collection: 'his publishers have produced a *collective* edition of his works'.
collective *noun*
see COMMUNE (2).
Word Family: **collectively**, *adverb.*

collective noun
Grammar: see NOUN.

collectivism *noun*
any social or political system based on equal sharing of work, products, etc., such as socialism.
Word Family: **collectivize**, **collectivise**, *verb*, to organize according to the principles of collectivism; **collectivist**, *noun, adjective.*

collector *noun*
Word Family: see COLLECT (1).

college (*say* **koll**ij) *noun*
1. *Education:* a) a self-governing residential component of a university. b) a name adopted by some secondary schools. c) an institution for professional or technical education, e.g. the Royal College of Music. d) college buildings.
2. *American education:* a tertiary institution giving a general education.
3. an organized group of people with a common profession, interest or pursuit: 'the Royal *College* of Surgeons'.
Word Family: **collegian** (*say* ka–**lee**jun), *noun*, a member of a college; **collegiate** (*say* ka–**lee**jit), *adjective*, of or relating to a college.
[Latin *collegium*]

collet (*say* **koll**it) *noun*
1. *Dress:* an encircling band or collar.
2. *Jewellery:* the rim within which a gem is set.
3. a device, like a collar, fitting into a groove in a rod to hold it in place, such as those used on poppet valves in some internal combustion engines.

collide (*say* k'**lide**) *verb*
to crash together or come into violent contact.
Word Family: **collision** (*say* ka–**lizh**'n), *noun.*
[co– + Latin *laedere* to injure]

collie *noun*
any of several breeds of large, wavy-haired, Scottish sheep-dogs.

collier (*say* **koll**ia) *noun*
1. a ship which carries coal.
2. a coal-miner.
Word Family: **colliery** (*say* **koll**ia–ree), *noun*, a coalmine with its buildings and equipment.

collimator (*say* **koll**i–mayter) *noun*
1. an optical system for obtaining a parallel beam of light.
2. a small, fixed telescope attached to a more powerful one for accurately adjusting it.

collinear (*say* ko–**linn**ia) *adjective*
being in the same straight line.

collision *noun*
Word Family: see COLLIDE.

collocation (*say* kolla–**kay**–sh'n) *noun*
the placing of things together or in their correct order.
Word Family: **collocate**, *verb.*
[co– + Latin *locus* a place]

colloid (*say* **koll**–oyd) *noun*
Chemistry: a suspension of very fine particles in a liquid. The particles are finer than a simple suspension, but larger than particles in a solution.

Word Family: **colloidal** (*say* k'**loy**-d'l), *adjective.*
[Greek *kolla* glue + -OID]

collop *noun*
a small slice of anything, especially of meat.

colloquial (*say* kol-**o**-kwee-al) *adjective*
of or relating to casual conversation, as distinct from written or formal speech. *Example*: they *ain't* here, for they *are not* here. Compare SLANG.
Word Family: **colloquially,** *adverb*; **colloquialism,** *noun,* a colloquial expression.

colloquy (*say* **kolla**-kwee) *noun*
1. a conversation or conference.
2. a piece of writing in the form of a dialogue.
[CO- + Latin *loqui* to speak]

collusion (*say* k'**loo**-*zh*'n) *noun*
a secret agreement between two or more people to defraud another.
Word Family: **collusive** (*say* k'**loo**-siv), *adjective*; **collude,** *verb.*
[CO- + Latin *ludere* to play]

collywobbles *plural noun*
(*informal*) a) a stomach-ache. b) diarrhoea.

cologne (*say* ka-**lone**) *noun*
see EAU DE COLOGNE.

colon (1) (*say* **ko**-lon) *noun*
Grammar: a punctuation mark (:), used before a quotation, list, statement, etc. which was introduced by the previous words. *Example*: Susan sent invitations to the following people: Margaret, Peter, Alice, David, Ian and Kate.

colon (2) (*say* **ko**-lon) *noun*
also called the **large intestine**
Anatomy: the large, thin-walled tube forming the lower part of the alimentary canal, which connects the small intestine and the caecum to the anus.
[Greek *kolon*]

colonel (*say* **kern**'l) *noun*
a commissioned officer in the army ranking between a lieutenant colonel and a brigadier.
[Latin *columna* a column]

colonial (*say* k'**lo**-nee'l) *noun*
a person who lives in a colony.
Word Family: **colonial,** *adjective,* of or relating to a colony or a colonist; **colonially,** *adverb.*

colonialism *noun*
see IMPERIALISM.

colonize (*say* **kolla**-nize) **colonise** *verb*
to make into a colony: 'Australia was *colonized* by Great Britain'.
Word Family: **colonization,** *noun.*

colonnade (*say* **kolla**-nade) *noun*
a) a series of columns supporting a roof, a series of arches, etc. b) a long row of trees.

colony (*say* **kolla**-nee) *noun*
1. a) a country settled in and developed by another and remaining under its control. Compare PROTECTORATE.
b) the group of people living in such a settlement.
2. any group of people with similar interests, background, etc. who live together: a) 'a nudist *colony*'; b) 'a *colony* of Australians in London'.
3. *Biology:* a) a visible growth of micro-organisms on the surface of a solid medium. b) a group of similar organisms living close together. Compare AGGREGATION.
Word Family: **colonist,** *noun,* a person who lives in or first establishes a colony.
[Latin *colonus* a farmer, a colonist]

colophon (*say* **kolla**-fon) *noun*
any decorative initial or small drawing identifying a publishing firm and printed on its books.
[Greek *kolophon* the end]

color *noun*
see COLOUR.

coloratura (*say* kollera-**tewra**) *noun*
Music: an elaborate style of singing, usually soprano.
[Italian, colouring]

colossal (*say* k'**loss**'l) *adjective*
1. enormous.
2. (*informal*) marvellous: 'we had a *colossal* time at the party'.
Word Family: **colossally,** *adverb.*
[Greek *kolossos* a giant statue]

colossus (*say* k'**loss**us) *noun*
anything of enormous size or importance.
[from the bronze statue of Apollo at Rhodes, called the *Colossus,* whose legs straddled the entrance to the harbour]

colostomy (*say* k'**losta**-mee) *noun*
an operation to produce an opening in the colon.
[Greek *kolon* colon + *stoma* mouth]

colour (*say* **kulla**) *noun*
in America spelt **color**
1. the sensation produced in the eye by light of different wavelengths.

2. any paint, pigment or dye.
3. a person's complexion or skin pigmentation: 'without distinction of race, *colour* or creed'.
Usage: 'the commentator's descriptions added much *colour* to the events' (= interest, brightness).
4. (*plural*) a) an award, such as that given to leading sportsmen in a team. b) any distinctive colour, symbol, flag, etc. of identification: 'a jockey's *colours*'.
Phrases:
flying colours, 'she passed her exams with *flying colours*' (= great success).
give, lend colour to, 'if we add some circumstantial details it will *give colour to* our excuse' (= make probable or realistic).
off colour, 'he seemed *off colour*' (= unwell).
colour *verb*
to add colour.
Usages:
a) 'she *coloured* at the coarse suggestion' (= blushed).
b) 'her story was *coloured* by emotion' (= influenced).
coloured *adjective*
1. having colour.
Usage: 'he used *coloured* language to sway his audience' (= not impartial or neutral).
2. of or relating to a member of any non-white race of people.
Word Family: **coloration,** *noun,* a) the arrangement of colours, b) the colouring; **colourful,** *adjective,* a) full of colour, b) interesting or picturesque; **colourfully,** *adverb*; **colourfulness,** *noun.*
[Latin *color*]

colour-bar *noun*
any discrimination against members of a non-white race.

colt (1) *noun*
a young, male horse, especially one up to three years old.
Word Family: **coltish,** *adjective,* young or inexperienced.

Colt (2) *noun*
a type of revolver.
[a trademark, after *Samuel Colt,* 1814–62, an American inventor]

columbine *noun*
1. (*capital*) Harlequin's sweetheart.
2. a garden plant whose flowers have five petals resembling a cluster of doves.
[Latin *columba* a dove]

column (*say* **kol**lum) *noun*
1. an upright support, usually made of brick or stone. Also called a **pillar**.
2. anything with a similar shape, such as the vertical blocks of lines of type on a page: a) 'this page has two *columns*'; b) 'a thin *column* of smoke'.
3. a short magazine or newspaper article which appears regularly, usually written by the same person.
4. *Military:* a formation of troops or vehicles following one after another.
Word Family: **columnar** (*say* k'**lum**na), *adjective.*
[Latin *columna*]

columnist (*say* **kol**lum-nist) *noun*
a person who writes a newspaper or magazine column.

com–
a prefix meaning with or jointly, as in *compare.* Variants of com– are: **con–** (*connect*) and **cor–** (*corrupt*).

coma (1) (*say* **ko**–ma) *noun*
plural is **comas**
a state of deep unconsciousness, usually due to injury or disease.
Word Family: **comatose,** *adjective,* affected with or as if with coma.
[Greek *koma* deep sleep]

coma (2) (*say* **ko**–ma) *noun*
plural is **comae** (*say* **ko**–mee)
Astronomy: the hazy cloud surrounding the nucleus of a comet.
[Greek *komé* the hair of the head]

comb (*say* kome) *noun*
1. an object of bone, plastic, etc., with teeth for smoothing or untangling hair, wool, etc.
2. any part or device with the shape or function of a comb.
3. *Biology:* the fleshy growth on the head of a domestic fowl. Short form of **cockscomb.**
comb *verb*
to arrange or untangle with a comb.
Usage: 'police *combed* the district for the missing child' (= searched thoroughly).

combat (*say* **kom**–bat) *noun*
1. a fight or battle.
2. any vigorous opposition or struggle.
combatant (*say* **kom**ba–t'nt) *noun*
a person taking part in a fight or combat: 'the two determined *combatants* were separated by the onlookers'.
Word Family: **combat** (*say* kom–**bat**), *verb,* to oppose or fight against; **combatant,** *adjective.*
[COM– + Latin *battuere* to strike]

combat fatigue
also called **battle fatigue** or **shell shock** a mental disorder caused by extreme stress, especially among soldiers at war.

combative (*say* **komba**–tiv) *adjective*
eager to fight.

comber (*say* **ko**–ma) *noun*
a long curling wave in the surf.

combination (*say* kombi–**nay**–sh'n) *noun*
1. a) the act of combining. b) anything formed by a number of things joining or combining: 'the soup was a *combination* of meat and vegetables'.
2. a sequence or series of things, such as the numbers or letters used to operate a combination lock.
3. *Maths:* a set of elements selected from a given larger set, regardless of their arrangement. Compare PERMUTATION.
combination lock
a lock which can only be opened if its dial is turned through a certain sequence of positions which are shown by numbers or letters.
Common Error: mathematical **combinations** and **permutations** are often confused. For example, a combination lock is really a permutation lock, and a football pool 'perm' is really a combination.

combine (*say* kom–**bine**) *verb*
to join several things into one: 'metal and timber workers have *combined* to form a union'.
combine (*say* **kom**–bine) *noun*
a combination, especially of people or businesses joining together for commercial or political reasons, e.g. to fix prices.
[COM– + Latin *bini* a pair]

combine harvester
a machine which reaps, threshes and winnows grain in one process.

combo *noun*
a small group of jazz musicians.

combustible (*say* kom–**busta**–b'l) *adjective*
able to burn.
Word Family: **combustibility** (*say* kom–busti–**billi**–tee), *noun.*

combustion (*say* kom–**bus**–ch'n) *noun*
1. the act or process of burning.
2. *Chemistry:* a chemical reaction in which a substance combines with oxygen to produce heat.
[Latin *combustus* burnt up]

come (*say* kum) *verb*
(came, coming)
1. to approach or move towards: '*come* and sit beside me'.
2. to arrive or reach: 'they *came* to a small, deserted house'.
3. to occur or happen: 'my birthday *comes* after yours'.
Usage: 'some cheeses *come* in tins' (= are packed).
4. to be derived from: 'he *comes* from a very wealthy family'.
5. to undergo or change into a particular state: 'the parcel *came* undone'.
6. (*informal*) to have an orgasm.
Phrases:
come about, to happen.
come across, a) to find or meet with, especially by chance; b) to be understood.
come along, to hurry.
come by, 'how did you *come by* that chair?' (= acquire).
come in, a) 'this money will *come in* handy' (= be); b) to finish in a race, etc.
come into, to inherit.
come of, a) 'see what *comes of* carelessness' (= results from); b) 'whatever *came of* him in the end?' (= happened to).
come off, a) to take place; b) to succeed; c) to become unfastened.
come on, a) to progress; b) to appear onstage.
come out, a) to be published; b) to become evident.
come out with, 'he *came out with* the whole story' (= told, revealed).
come over, 'what has *come over* him?' (= changed, affected).
come round, a) to regain consciousness; b) to change an opinion, etc.
come through, 'she *came through* two bouts of pneumonia' (= survived).
come to, a) to total; b) to regain consciousness.
come up, 'a new problem has *come up*' (= arisen).
come upon, 'we *came upon* a pile of old coins' (= found, discovered).
come up with, to produce or propose.

comedian (*say* k'**meedian**) *noun*
1. a performer in a comedy or comic act.
2. any person who is or attempts to be funny.
Word Family: **comedienne** (*say* k'meedi–**en**), *noun,* a female comedian.

comedy (*say* **komma**–dee) ***noun***
1. any form of entertainment which causes amusement or light-hearted enjoyment. Compare TRAGEDY.
2. any funny event or series of events: 'a *comedy* of errors'.
black comedy
a comedy with a tragic or pessimistic theme.
[Greek *komoidia*]

comely (*say* **kum**–lee) *adjective*
pleasing or attractive.
Word Family: **comeliness,** ***noun.***

comestible (*say* kom–**estib**'l) ***noun***
(*usually plural*) food.
[Latin *comestus* eaten up]

comet ***noun***
a celestial body moving around the sun and containing a bright nucleus surrounded by a hazy cloud which extends into a tail.
[Greek *kometes* long-haired]

comfort (*say* **kum**–fut) *verb*
to cheer: 'we were *comforted* in our grief by her kindness'.
comfort ***noun***
1. a state of pleasant freedom from suffering: 'they live in great *comfort*'.
2. a) any relief or consolation. b) anything which causes comfort: 'visits from old friends are a *comfort* to her'.
Word Family: **comforting,** *adjective*; **comfortingly,** *adverb*; **comfortless,** *adjective*, without cheer.
[COM- + Latin *fortis* strong]

comfortable (*say* **kumf**ta–b'l) *adjective*
1. having or giving comfort: 'a *comfortable* old armchair'.
2. being in a state of comfort: 'I'm *comfortable* here, thanks'.
Word Family: **comfortably,** *adverb.*

comforter (*say* **kum**–fut'r) ***noun***
1. a thick woollen scarf or wrapper.
2. a person or thing that comforts.

comfy (*say* **kumfee**) *adjective*
(*informal*) comfortable.

comic *adjective*
of or relating to comedy: 'a *comic* actor'.
comic ***noun***
1. a magazine of stories, etc. told in comic strips.
2. a funny person or actor: 'that man is a natural *comic*'.

comical *adjective*
amusing or funny: 'his *comical* expression made all of us laugh'.

comic relief
see LIGHT RELIEF.

comic strip
also called a **cartoon**
a series of drawings which tell a story or joke.

comity (*say* **kommi**–tee) ***noun***
a friendly politeness or recognition, especially between countries.
[Latin *comitas* courteous]

comma ***noun***
Grammar: a punctuation mark (,) used between words, phrases or clauses to introduce a short pause.
[Greek *komma* a short clause]

command *verb*
to order, demand or have control over: 'he *commands* a battalion'.
Usages:
a) 'he *commands* as much money as he needs' (= has the use of).
b) 'his age *commands* great respect' (= deserves).
c) 'the farmhouse *commands* a view of the whole valley' (= overlooks).
command ***noun***
1. an order given: 'he ignored the *commands* to stop'.
2. the possession of control or authority: a) 'who is in *command* here?'. b) 'she has great *command* over her feelings'.
3. *Military:* a force or clearly defined region under the authority of an officer.
[COM- + Latin *mandare* to entrust]

commandant (*say* **komm**'n–dant) ***noun***
the commanding officer of a military establishment, such as a fortress or school.

commandeer (*say* komm'n–**deer**) ***verb***
to take or seize something, especially for official use: 'the police *commandeered* a private launch to continue the chase'.

commander (*say* k'm–**ahnda**) ***noun***
1. any person who leads or has command, such as the chief commissioned officer of a military unit.
2. *Nautical:* a commissioned officer in the navy ranking below a captain.

commandment (*say* k'**mahnd**–m'nt) ***noun***
1. a command.
2. *Religion:* a divine law, such as the Ten Commandments in the Bible.

commando (*say* k'**mahndo**) ***noun***
plural is **commandos**
a member of a special combined military and naval force trained for swift, destructive raids or attacks.

command performance
the performance of a play or other entertainment at the request of a monarch or other high official.

commemorate (*say* k'**memma**-rate) *verb*
to honour the memory of something, especially by a ceremony or celebration.
Word Family: **commemoration,** *noun*; **commemorative,** *adjective.*
[COM- + Latin *memorare* to mention]

commence *verb*
to start or begin: 'the game will *commence* after lunch'.
Word Family: **commencement,** *noun.*

commend *verb*
1. to praise or speak of as worthy, suitable, etc.: 'the young soldier was *commended* for his bravery in action'.
2. to give to the care of.
commendation *noun*
any praise or approval: 'his new novel received great *commendation* from the critics'.
Word Family: **commendable,** *adjective,* being worthy of praise; **commendatory,** *adjective,* giving praise or approval.
[COM- + Latin *mandare* to entrust]

commensurate (*say* k'**men**sha-rit) *adjective*
being of the same or equal value: 'pay will be *commensurate* to the standard of work'.
[COM- + Latin *mensura* measurement]

comment *noun*
a note or remark made to explain, criticize, etc.: 'the doctor refused to make any *comment* on the matter'.
Word Family: **comment,** *verb.*

commentary (*say* **komm**'n-tree) *noun*
a continuous sequence of comments or notes, especially on one particular subject: 'a news *commentary*'.
[Latin *commentari* to think over]

commentator (*say* **komm**'n-tayta) *noun*
a person who gives a commentary: 'a racing *commentator*'.

commerce *noun*
1. any trade or business activity, especially on a large scale.
2. any exchange, especially between people.
[COM- + Latin *mercis* of merchandise]

commercial (*say* k'**mer**-sh'l) *adjective*
1. of or relating to commerce.
2. made for sale or profit: 'a *commercial* product'.
3. financed or sponsored by advertisers: '*commercial* radio'.
commercial *noun*
an advertisement on radio or television.
Word Family: **commercialize, commercialise,** *verb,* to turn something into a business or moneymaking project; **commercialization,** *noun.*

commercial art
the use of certain forms of art or design to promote products, etc.
Word Family: **commercial artist,** a person skilled or trained in commercial art.

commercial traveller
a travelling salesman.

commiserate (*say* k'**mizza**-rate) *verb*
to express sorrow or pity: 'we *commiserate* with you about the accident'.
Word Family: **commiseration,** *noun.*
[COM- + Latin *misereri* to pity]

commissar (*say* **kommi**-sar) *noun*
the head of a government department in certain countries, especially Russia.

commission (*say* k'**mish**'n) *noun*
1. an order or authority given for a particular task, duty or appointment: 'he received his *commission* as a second lieutenant'.
2. a group of people officially appointed for a particular duty: 'a government *commission* on women's rights'.
3. any fee paid to an agent for services such as buying or selling goods.
4. the act of committing: 'the *commission* of such a crime is unthinkable'.
out of commission, 'both engines are *out of commission*' (= not working).
commission *verb*
1. to give a commission to.
2. to give authority to: 'he was *commissioned* to paint a mural for the museum'.

commissionaire (*say* k'**mish**'n-air) *noun*
a doorkeeper or porter in uniform, at a cinema, large hotel, etc.

commissioner (*say* k'**mish**'n-er) *noun*
an appointed official, especially one in charge of a department: 'a police *commissioner*'.

commit (*say* kommit) *verb* **(committed, committing)**
1. to do or perform: 'he is charged with *committing* murder'.
2. to give or put into the trust or charge of: 'she *committed* the whole poem to memory'.

commit oneself, 'don't *commit yourself* to anything dangerous' (= pledge, bind yourself).
Word Family: **commitment,** *noun,* a) the act of committing, b) the state of being committed, c) a promise to do something; **committal,** *noun,* the act of committing.
[Latin *committere* to entrust]

committee *noun*
a small group of people appointed to represent a larger group.

commode *noun*
a low, box-like stand into which a chamber-pot is fitted.

commodious (*say* k'**mo**-dee-us) *adjective*
spacious: 'it's a *commodious* house for such a small family'.
[Latin *commodus* convenient]

commodity (*say* k'**moddi**-tee) *noun*
anything useful, especially an article of trade: 'a household *commodity*'.

commodore (*say* **komma**-dor) *noun*
1. a commissioned officer in the navy, ranking below a rear admiral.
2. the president of a yacht or boat club.

common *adjective*
1. being shared by two or more people: 'the story is *common* knowledge'.
2. usual or frequent: 'a *common* event'.
3. inferior or ordinary: 'she has very *common* table manners'.
4. *Grammar:* see GENDER.
common *noun*
a piece of land used by a community for grazing animals, etc.
in common, 'they have very little *in common*' (= shared, that is alike).
Word Family: **commonly,** *adverb.*
[Latin *communis*]

commonalty (*say* **kommen**-al-tee) *noun*
the common people; ordinary citizens.

common denominator
Maths: see DENOMINATOR.

commoner *noun*
a person who is not a peer.

common fraction
Maths: see FRACTION.

common law
Law: the system of law based on old customs or court decisions, as distinct from laws made by an Act of Parliament.

common logarithm
Maths: a logarithm to the base 10.

common noun
Grammar: see NOUN.

common-or-garden *adjective*
ordinary or uninteresting.

commonplace *adjective*
ordinary or dull.
Word Family: **commonplace,** *noun.*

common room
a sitting room for students or staff in a school or college.

commons *plural noun*
1. commoners, as a group.
2. (*capital*) the House of Commons, to which representatives of the commons are elected.
3. shared provisions, especially food: 'we shall be on short *commons* today'.

common sense
a practical sense or judgement: 'she is very intelligent but lacks *common sense*'.

commonweal *noun*
1. the welfare of the public.
2. an old word for a Commonwealth or a whole nation of people.

Commonwealth *noun*
1. an association of sovereign countries: 'the British *Commonwealth* of Nations'.
2. a federation of states: 'the *Commonwealth* of Australia'.
3. *History:* a republic, especially England under Cromwell.

commotion (*say* k'**mo**-sh'n) *noun*
a noisy or violent disturbance.

communal (*say* k'**mewn**'l) *adjective*
being shared or for common use: 'a *communal* bathroom'.
Word Family: **communally,** *adverb.*

commune (1) (*say* k'**mewn**) *verb*
to talk together.

commune (2) (*say* **kom**-yoon) *noun*
1. a local community having a degree of self-government, but subject to central control.
2. a group of people who share property and tasks, living together by their own rules and standards. Also called a **collective.**
[Latin *communis* shared]

communicate (*say* k'**mewni**-kate) *verb*
1. to pass on or share: 'who *communicated* the news to you?'.
Usage: 'he finds it difficult to *communicate* with young people' (= share, exchange ideas).
2. *Christian:* to administer or receive Communion.

Word Family: **communicant,** *noun,* a) a person who communicates, b) a person who receives or is entitled to receive Communion; **communicative,** *adjective,* willing to communicate.
[Latin *communicare* to confer with]

communication *noun*
1. the act of communicating: 'there is little *communication* between the two families'.
2. something which is communicated.
3. (*plural*) the means of sending messages, etc. between places, e.g. by telephone or radio.

communion (*say* **k'mewn**–y'n) *noun*
1. a sharing or exchange of thoughts or feelings.
2. (*capital*) the Eucharist. Short form of **Holy Communion.**

communiqué (*say* **k'mewni**–kay) *noun*
an official statement, especially one made by a government concerning special events.

communism (*say* **kom**–yoo–nizm) *noun*
the belief in or practice of a social system based on the sharing of all work and property by the whole community. Compare CAPITALISM.
Word Family: **communist,** *noun, adjective.*

community (*say* **k'mewni**–tee) *noun*
any group living in one place or having common interests.
Usages:
a) 'environment protection is the responsibility of the *community*' (= general public).
b) 'we must allow for a *community* of interests' (= sharing, similarity).

commutable (*say* **k'mewta**–b'l) *adjective*
able to be changed or exchanged.

commute (*say* **k'mewt**) *verb*
1. to alter or make less severe: 'the prisoner's death sentence was *commuted* to life imprisonment'.
2. to travel regularly between home and work, especially over a considerable distance.
Word Family: **commuter,** *noun,* a person who commutes.
[Latin *commutare* to alter]

compact (1) (*say* kom–**pakt**) *adjective*
closely packed or fitted together: 'a *compact* motor car'.
compact *noun*
a container for face powder.
Word Family: **compact** (*say* kom–**pakt**), *verb,* to join or pack firmly together; **compactly,** *adverb;* **compactness,** *noun.*

compact (2) (*say* **kom**–pakt) *noun*
an agreement or contract.
[Latin *compactus* joined together]

companion (*say* k'm–**pan**–y'n) *noun*
1. a person who accompanies or associates with another: 'a travelling *companion*'.
2. a book used as a guide or reference.
Usage: 'do you have the *companion* to the first volume?' (= matching pair).
Word Family: **companionship,** *noun.*
[COM- + Latin *panis* bread, originally a person who ate bread with another]

companionable (*say* k'm–**pan**–y'na–b'l) *adjective*
friendly: 'a *companionable* chat'.

companionway *noun*
Nautical: the steps leading from the deck of a boat to a cabin.

company (*say* **kum**pa–nee) *noun*
1. a group of people together.
Usages:
a) 'we have *company* for tea' (= guests).
b) 'she doesn't like the *company* I keep' (= friends, associates).
c) 'a ship's *company*' (= crew).
2. a business organization owned by shareholders: 'a manufacturing *company*'.
3. an army unit consisting of three platoons.
Phrases:
keep company, to spend time with.
part company, to separate or leave.

comparative (*say* kom–**parra**–tiv) *adjective*
1. based on or involving comparison: a) 'a matter of *comparative* importance'; b) 'the *comparative* study of Eastern and Western religions'.
2. *Grammar:* see DEGREE.
Word Family: **comparatively,** *adverb.*

compare (*say* kom**pair**) *verb*
1. to judge or note the similarities or differences of: 'let us *compare* our answers'.
2. to represent as similar or like: 'you could *compare* me to Einstein'.
Phrases:
cannot compare with, 'the film *cannot compare with* the book' (= is not as good as).
compare notes, 'they *compared notes* on the party' (= exchanged ideas, feelings).
Word Family: **compare,** *noun,* comparison or equal; **comparable** (*say*

kompra–b'l), *adjective*, able or suitable to be compared.
[Latin *comparare* to match together]

comparison (*say* k'm–**parri**–s'n) *noun*
1. a) the act of comparing. b) the state of being compared.
2. likeness or similarity: 'there is no *comparison* between them'.

compartment *noun*
a) any of several separate parts or divisions of a structure: 'he keeps everything in separate *compartments* in his brain'. b) any separate space or area: 'a luggage *compartment*'.
[COM– + Latin *partiri* to share]

compass (*say* **kum**pus) *noun*
1. an instrument used to find direction, having a magnetized needle which points to magnetic north.
2. an instrument for drawing circles, consisting of two rods, one pointed and the other holding a marker, hinged together at one end. Also called a **pair of compasses**.
3. the range or limits of anything: 'the wide *compass* of her voice made her a unique singer'.
Word Family: **compass**, *verb*, to surround.

compassion (*say* k'm–**pash**'n) *noun*
a strong feeling of understanding, pity or sympathy for the sufferings of another.
Word Family: **compassionate**, *adjective*; **compassionately**, *adverb*.
[COM– + Latin *passus* suffered]

compatible (*say* k'm–**patti**–b'l) *adjective*
well suited or able to exist together in harmony: 'our political ideas are not *compatible*'.
Word Family: **compatibly**, *adverb*; **compatibility**, *noun*.

compatriot (*say* k'm–**pattri**–ut) *noun*
a person from the same country as oneself.

compel (*say* k'm–**pell**) *verb*
(**compelled**, **compelling**)
to force: 'heavy rain *compelled* us to cancel the picnic'.
Word Family: **compelling**, *adjective*, forceful.
[Latin *compellere*]

compendium *noun*
plural is **compendiums** or **compendia**
a detailed or comprehensive summary.
Word Family: **compendious**, *adjective*.
[Latin, an abbreviating]

compensate (*say* **kom**pen–sate) *verb*
to make up for something: 'payment could not *compensate* for the damage'.
Word Family: **compensatory** (*say* kompen–**say**ta–ree *or* kom–**pen**sa–tree), *adjective*.
[Latin *compensare* to counterbalance]

compensation (*say* kompen–**say**–sh'n) *noun*
1. a) the act of compensating. b) something which compensates: 'the injured worker was given *compensation*'.
2. *Psychology:* any behaviour which attempts to make up for a weakness or sense of inferiority.

compère (*say* **kom**pair) *noun*
a person who introduces each item in a radio or television programme, variety show, etc.
Word Family: **compère**, *verb*.

compete (*say* kompeet) *verb*
to take part in a competition or contest: 'small shops cannot *compete* with the low prices of supermarkets'.
Word Family: **competitor** (*say* kom–**pett**ita), *noun*.
[COM– + Latin *petere* to seek]

competent (*say* **kom**pa–t'nt) *adjective*
having the ability, power or qualifications to do something: 'are you *competent* to drive such a powerful car?'.
Word Family: **competence**, **competency**, *noun*.

competition (*say* kompa–**tish**'n) *noun*
1. any activity in which people try to outdo or defeat each other: a) 'a wrestling *competition*'; b) 'there was fierce *competition* between countries for the trade contract'.
2. the person or group that one opposes in a competition: 'your *competition* in this race is very weak'.
Word Family: **competitive** (*say* kom–**petta**–tiv), *adjective*, of or involving competition; **competitively**, *adverb*.

compile *verb*
to collect and put together a number of things, especially to form a book, etc: 'the index was *compiled* and arranged by a computer'.
Word Family: **compilation** (*say* kompa–**lay**–sh'n), *noun*.
[Latin *compilare* to cram together hastily]

complacent (*say* k'm–**play**–s'nt) *adjective*

self-satisfied or smug: 'the *complacent* speech did not please the angry audience'.
Word Family: **complacently**, *adverb*; **complacence, complacency**, *noun*.
[COM- + Latin *placere* to please]

complain *verb*
to talk of or express dissatisfaction, pain, etc: 'they have *complained* to the police about the threats'.
Word Family: **complainingly**, *adverb*; **complainer**, *noun*.
[COM- + Latin *plangere* to bewail]

complainant *noun*
Law: a plaintiff.

complaint *noun*
1. an expression or statement of discontent, pain, etc: 'have you any *complaints* about the meal, Sir?'.
2. an illness: 'measles is usually quite a mild *complaint*'.

complement (*say* **kom**pli-m'nt) *noun*
1. anything which completes or makes something else whole: 'this volume is the *complement* to the set'.
2. the full or total number or amount: 'the ship's *complement*'.
3. *Maths:* a) the number of degrees that must be added to an acute angle to make it a right angle. **Complementary angles** add up to a right angle and each is the complement of the other. b) all the elements in the universal set except those in the given set.
4. *Grammar:* a word or words which complete the meaning of a phrase or sentence. *Example*: the present made him *happy*.
Word Family: **complement**, *verb*; **complementary**, *adjective*.
Common Error: do not confuse with COMPLIMENT.

complete (*say* k'm-**pleet**) *adjective*
having all its parts: 'a *complete* replica of the house'.
Usages:
a) 'the story is now *complete*' (= finished).
b) 'he is a *complete* fool' (= in every way).
c) 'the *complete* play had to be rewritten' (= whole).
Word Family: **complete**, *verb*, a) to make whole or perfect, b) to finish or bring to an end; **completely**, *adverb*; **completeness**, *noun*.
[COM- + Latin *pletus* filled up]

completion (*say* k'm-**plee**-sh'n) *noun*
1. the act of making complete: 'the *completion* of the bridge took five years'.
2. the state of being complete: 'when the project reaches *completion* all employees will be dismissed'.

complex *adjective*
intricate or complicated: 'a *complex* design'.
complex *noun*
1. anything made up of different, connected parts: 'a shopping *complex*'.
2. *Psychology:* any mental state resulting from past and sometimes repressed experiences.
Usage: 'she has a *complex* about her weight' (= obsession).
Word Family: **complexity**, *noun*.
[Latin *complexus* an embrace]

complexion (*say* kom-**plek**-sh'n) *noun*
the natural appearance or colour, especially of the skin: 'she has a pale, unhealthy *complexion*'.
Usages:
a) 'the quarrel changed the *complexion* of their relationship' (= appearance, nature).
b) 'his illness put a new *complexion* on the affair' (= appearance).

compliant *adjective*
Word Family: see COMPLY.

complicate (*say* **kom**pli-kate) *verb*
to make something difficult to do, understand, etc: 'do not *complicate* the argument with new ideas'.
complicated *adjective*
a) difficult. b) made up of many parts: 'a *complicated* legal document'.
Word Family: **complication**, *noun*, a) a difficulty, b) something which complicates.
[COM- + Latin *plicare* to fold]

complicity (*say* k'm-**plissi**-tee) *noun*
the state of being a partner in wrongdoing: 'the driver of the get-away van was charged with *complicity* in the robbery'.
[Late Latin *complicis* of a confederate]

compliment (*say* **kom**pli-m'nt) *noun*
1. an expression of praise or respect: 'the chef received many *compliments* for the delightful meal'.
2. (*plural*) greetings or kind wishes: 'give my *compliments* to your mother'.
Word Family: **compliment**, *verb*; **complimentary**, *adjective*, a) expressing a compliment, b) free of charge.

Common Error: do not confuse with COMPLEMENT.

compline (*say* **komp**–lin) *noun*
Christian: evening service.
[Latin (*hora*) *completa* the final hour]

comply (*say* kom–**ply**) *verb*
(**complied, complying**)
to do what is asked or demanded: 'all competitors will *comply* with the rules'.
Word Family: **compliant**, *adjective*, willing to comply; **compliantly**, *adverb*; **compliance, compliancy**; *noun*.

component (*say* k'm–**po**–nent) *noun*
anything which forms part of a whole system or thing: 'an engine has many *components*'.
[COM– + Latin *ponere* to put]

comport (*say* k'm–**port**) *verb*
to conduct or behave: 'the duchess *comported* herself with her usual dignity'.
comport with, 'such frivolity does not *comport with* your age' (= suit).
Word Family: **comportment**, *noun*.
[COM– + Latin *portare* to carry]

compose (*say* k'm–**poze**) *verb*
1. to make up or form: 'the class is *composed* of 24 students'.
2. to put words, ideas, notes, etc. together in literary or musical form.
3. *Printing:* to typeset.
4. to control or make calm: 'you must *compose* your thoughts before answering the question'.
Usage: 'you must *compose* your differences' (= settle, reconcile).
Word Family: **composer**, *noun*, a person who composes music, etc.; **composedly**, *adverb*; **composure** (*say* kom–**po**–*zh*er), *noun*, calmness or self-control.

composite (*say* **kom**pa–zit) *adjective*
made up of different parts.
composite *noun*
something made up of different parts, such as the heads of some flowers which are made up of many small flowers.
Word Family: **compositely**, *adverb*; **compositeness**, *noun*.
[COM– + Latin *positus* placed]

composition (*say* kompa–**zish**'n) *noun*
1. a) the act of composing: 'the *composition* of the symphony took 3 years'. b) something which is composed: 'it was his last but greatest *composition*'.
2. the way something is composed: 'she studies the *composition* of the earth's atmosphere'.
3. an essay.
4. an agreement or settlement, especially by compromise.

compositor (*say* kom–**pozzita**) *noun*
a person who typesets.

compost (*say* **kom**–posst) *noun*
a mixture of decaying plant matter put in the soil to fertilize it.

composure *noun*
Word Family: see COMPOSE.

compote (*say* **kompot**) *noun*
a dish of stewed fruit.

compound (1) (*say* **kom**pound) *adjective*
made up of two or more parts, actions, etc.: 'blackberry is a *compound* word'.
compound *noun*
anything made up of combined parts, such as a chemical substance consisting of two or more elements.
compound (*say* kom**pound**) *verb*
1. to put parts together to form a whole.
Usage: 'he *compounded* his crime by lying about it' (= made greater).
2. to settle a quarrel, etc. by mutual agreement.
3. *Law:* to agree not to prosecute or punish, in return for payment: 'to *compound* a felony'.

compound (2) (*say* **kom**pound) *noun*
an enclosed area with buildings, used as a residence for workers, a prison during war, etc.

compound interest
Commerce: see INTEREST.

comprehend (*say* **kompri**–hend) *verb*
1. to understand or know fully: 'can you *comprehend* the importance of what has happened?'.
2. to include: 'the book *comprehends* many new ideas'.
Word Family: **comprehendingly**, *adverb*.
[COM– + Latin *prehendere* to take hold of]

comprehensible
(*say* kompri–**hensa**–b'l) *adjective*
able to be comprehended.
Word Family: **comprehensibly**, *adverb*; **comprehensibility** (*say* kompri–hensa–**billi**–tee), *noun*.

comprehension
(*say* kompri–**hen**–sh'n) *noun*
the act or power of understanding: 'for you to make such an obvious mistake is beyond my *comprehension*'.

comprehensive *adjective*
inclusive or detailed in content: 'this newspaper gives *comprehensive* reports on sporting events'.
Word Family: **comprehensively,** *adverb*; **comprehensiveness,** *noun.*

comprehensive school
a school replacing and combining the formerly separate grammar, secondary modern and technical schools of a district.

compress (*say* kompress) *verb*
to press closely together or force into a smaller space: 'the sardines were *compressed* into tins'.
compress (*say* **kom**press) *noun*
Medicine: a soft pad of material held against the body or a wound, especially to apply pressure.
Word Family: **compressor,** *noun,* anything which compresses, such as a machine for compressing gases; **compression** (*say* kom-**presh**'n), *noun.*
[COM- + Latin *pressus* pressed]

compression ratio
the ratio of the volume of a cylinder in an internal combustion engine, when the piston is at the bottom of its stroke to the volume when the piston is at the top of its stroke.

comprise (*say* k'm-**prize**) *verb*
to consist or be composed of: 'the book *comprises* essays on eight famous historians'.

compromise (*say* **kom**pra-mize) *verb*
1. to settle differences by each side giving up something and receiving less than it asked for: 'the strike was settled when both the government and the unions *compromised* on the matter of wage increases'.
2. to expose to danger, suspicion, etc: 'do not *compromise* your position by acting foolishly'.
compromise *noun*
1. a settlement by compromising.
2. anything which is halfway between, or combines different things: 'the new job represented a *compromise* between her abilities and her expectations'.
[COM- + Latin *promissus* promised]

comptometer (*say* kom-**tomma**-ta) *noun*
a high-speed calculating machine.
[a trademark]

comptroller (*say* k'n-**tro**-la) *noun*
see CONTROLLER.

compulsion (*say* k'm-**pul**-sh'n) *noun*
1. the act of compelling or forcing: 'there is no *compulsion* for you to come with us'.
2. the state of being compelled or forced: 'she felt a great *compulsion* to sneeze'.
[Latin *compulsus* forced]

compulsive (*say* k'm-**pul**siv) *adjective*
having an uncontrollable urge or desire: 'a *compulsive* gambler'.
Word Family: **compulsively,** *adverb.*

compulsory (*say* k'm-**pul**sa-ree) *adjective*
forced or required: 'English lessons are *compulsory* for all pupils'.
Word Family: **compulsorily,** *adverb*; **compulsoriness,** *noun.*

compunction (*say* k'm-**punk**-sh'n) *noun*
a feeling of regret or uneasiness caused by guilt or shame: 'she felt no *compunction* in hitting the burglar'.
[COM- + Latin *punctus* stung, troubled]

compute (*say* k'm-**pewt**) *verb*
to find an answer by calculating mathematically.
Word Family: **computation,** *noun,* a) the act of computing, b) the amount computed.
[Latin *computare* to reckon up]

computer (*say* k'm-**pewta**) *noun*
1. a person or thing that computes.
2. an electronic machine performing complicated calculations. A **digital computer** expresses information as digits.

comrade (*say* **kom**rad *or* **kom**-rade) *noun*
1. a close or loyal friend.
2. a fellow member of a trade union or political party, especially a communist party.
Word Family: **comradeship,** *noun*
[Spanish *camarada* room-mate]

con (1) *noun*
short form of **contra-**
an argument or person against something. See PRO (1).
Word Family: **con,** *adverb,* against or in opposition to.

con (2) *verb*
(conned, conning)
(*informal*) to trick or swindle.
Word Family: **con,** *noun.*
[short form of CONFIDENCE TRICK]

con (3) *verb*
(conned, conning)

to study or learn thoroughly: 'have you *conned* your part in the play yet?'.

con (4) *noun*
(*informal*) a convict.

con–
a variant of the prefix **com–**.

concatenate (*say* kon–**katti**–nate) *verb*
to link together in a series or chain.
Word Family: **concatenation,** *noun.*
[CON– + Latin *catena* chain]

concave *adjective*
curved inwards like the inner surface of a hollow sphere. Compare CONVEX.
[CON– + Latin *cavus* hollow]

conceal (*say* k'n–**seel**) *verb*
to keep from view or discovery: 'the cupboard *concealed* a hole in the wall'.
Word Family: **concealment,** *noun.*
[CON– + Latin *celare* to hide]

concede (*say* k'n–**seed**) *verb*
to admit or allow an argument, claim, etc.: '*concede* defeat or die'.
[CON– + Latin *cedere* to yield]

conceit (*say* k'n–**seet**) *noun*
1. a very high opinion of oneself or one's abilities: 'he is too full of *conceit* to be likable'.
2. *Literature:* an exaggerated or elaborate metaphor, simile, etc.
Word Family: **conceited,** *adjective*; **conceitedly,** *adverb*; **conceitedness,** *noun.*

conceive (*say* k'n–**seev**) *verb*
1. to form, hold or imagine an idea, opinion, etc.: 'it is difficult to *conceive* of such wealth'.
2. to become pregnant.
Word Family: **conceivable,** *adjective,* able to be conceived or believed; **conceivably,** *adverb.*

concentrate (*say* **kon**sen–trate) *verb*
1. to direct one's thoughts or actions towards something: 'how can I *concentrate* with all this noise?'.
2. to bring or come towards a central point: '*concentrate* the troops in the mountainous areas'.
3. to make or become more intense, stronger, purer, etc.
concentration *noun*
a) the act of concentrating: 'this puzzle needs close *concentration*'. b) the state of being concentrated: 'the *concentration* of alcohol in beer varies between countries'.
Word Family: **concentrate,** *noun,* a concentrated form of something.

concentration camp
a place where political prisoners, refugees, etc. are held, especially the Nazi camps of World War 2.

concentric (*say* k'n–**sen**trik) *adjective*
having a common centre, such as circles or spheres.

concept (*say* **kon**–sept) *noun*
an idea, especially one generalized from various instances: '*concepts* of right or wrong'.
Word Family: **conceptual** (*say* k'n–**sep**–tew'l), *adjective*; **conceptually,** *adverb*; **conceptualize, conceptualise,** *verb.*
[Latin *conceptus* perceived]

conception (*say* k'n–**sep**–sh'n) *noun*
1. the act of conceiving.
2. an idea or thought: 'they had little *conception* of the importance of their act'.

concern (*say* k'n–**sern**) *verb*
1. a) to be of interest or importance to: 'it is a problem which *concerns* only the family'. b) to interest or involve: 'you should not *concern* yourself'.
2. a) to cause worry or unhappiness: 'her illness has *concerned* us gravely over the months'. b) to be worried or unhappy about: 'we were *concerned* about her illness'.
concern *noun*
1. anything which is of interest or importance: 'his private actions are no *concern* of mine'.
2. an anxiety or worry: 'her reply was full of pity and *concern*'.
3. any business or enterprise: 'the farm is a small, fruit-growing *concern*'.
concerning *preposition*
about: 'have you heard any more *concerning* the accident'.
[CON– + Latin *cernere* to discern]

concert (*say* **kon**sert) *noun*
1. a public performance by musicians, singers, etc.
2. an agreement or harmony: 'residents were in *concert* against the new airport'.
concert (*say* k'n–**sert**) *verb*
to do together or in agreement: 'let's *concert* our efforts'.
Word Family: **concerted,** *adjective,* planned or decided in union.

concertina (*say* konsa–**teena**) *noun*
Music: a small accordion, played by pressing buttons at each end.

concertmaster *noun*
American: the leader of an orchestra, especially the first violinist.

concerto (*say* k'n–**cher**toe) *noun*
Music: a composition, usually in three movements, having one or more parts for solo instruments.

concession (*say* k'n–**sesh**'n) *noun*
1. the act of conceding or yielding.
2. anything conceded or granted: 'the government made no *concession* to the trade unions'.
3. a right or privilege granted by a government, institution, etc.: 'student *concessions* for cheap travel'.

conch (*say* konch) *noun*
the spiral shell of a marine mollusc.

concierge (*say* kon–see–air*zh*) *noun*
the doorkeeper or porter of a hotel, block of flats, etc.
[French]

conciliate (*say* k'n–**silli**–ate) *verb*
1. to gain goodwill, support or favour by friendly acts: 'he tried to *conciliate* his wife by buying her flowers'.
2. to reconcile or bring into harmony: 'an arbitrator should try to *conciliate* opposing factions in a dispute'.
Word Family: **conciliator,** *noun*; **conciliatory** (*say* k'n–**sillia**–tree), *adjective*; **conciliation,** *noun.*

concise (*say* k'n–**sise**) *adjective*
giving much clear information in few words: 'a detailed but *concise* speech'.
Word Family: **concisely,** *adverb*; **conciseness,** *noun.*
[Latin *concisus* cut short]

conclave *noun*
1. a private or secret meeting.
2. *Roman Catholic:* a meeting of cardinals.
[CON– + Latin *clavis* a key]

conclude *verb*
1. to bring or come to an end: 'the meeting *concluded* with a short speech'.
2. to come or bring to a final decision or settlement: a) 'the treaty was *concluded* with the formal signing by all parties'; b) 'the judge *concluded* that the prisoner was guilty'.
3. to deduce: 'he *concluded* that he was not going to get his way'.
conclusion (*say* k'n–**kloo**–*zh*'n) *noun*
a) the end or last part of something.
b) a final result, decision or opinion.
c) a deduction.
[Latin *concludere*]

conclusive (*say* k'n–**kloo**siv) *adjective*
final and leaving no doubt: 'the fingerprints in the house were *conclusive* proof of his guilt'.
Word Family: **conclusively,** *adverb.*

concoct (*say* k'n–**kokt**) *verb*
to make or create by preparing and mixing: 'to *concoct* a home-made soup'.
Usage: 'she *concocted* an excuse for being late' (= invented).
Word Family: **concoction,** *noun,* something which has been concocted.
[Latin *concoctus* thoroughly cooked]

concomitant (*say* k'n–**kommi**–t'nt) *adjective*
being together or in accompaniment with: 'pain and weakness are *concomitant* with that illness'.
Word Family: **concomitant,** *noun,* anything which accompanies; **concomitantly,** *adverb*; **concomitance,** *noun.*
[CON– + Latin *comitis* of a companion]

concord (*say* **kon**–kord) *noun*
any agreement or harmony between persons or things.
Word Family: **concordant** (*say* k'n–**kord**'nt), *adjective*; **concordance,** *noun,* a) harmony or agreement, b) an index of important words in a book.
[CON– + Latin *cordis* of the heart]

concordat (*say* kon–**kor**dat) *noun*
a formal pact or agreement, especially one between the Pope and a government concerning control of church affairs.

concourse *noun*
1. a crowd or throng of people.
2. an open area where people meet or assemble: 'the airport *concourse*'.
3. a moving or coming together: 'the island was situated at the *concourse* of the two rivers'.
[CON– + Latin *cursus* a running]

concrete (*say* **kon**–kreet) *noun*
a mixture of cement, sand, water and minerals which sets very hard and is used for building, etc. Compare MORTAR.
concrete *adjective*
1. having physical existence: 'trees are *concrete* objects but ideas are not'.
2. specific or particular: 'give me a *concrete* example'.
concrete *verb*
1. (*say* **kon**kreet) to lay concrete.
2. (*say* kon**kreet**) to form or grow into a solid mass.

Word Family: **concretion** (*say* k'n-**kree**-sh'n), *noun,* a) the act of concreting, b) a solid mass formed by concreting; **concretely,** *adverb.*
[Latin *concretus* condensed]

concubine (*say* **kon**-kew-bine) *noun*
a mistress or secondary wife, as in some Eastern societies.
Word Family: **concubinage** (*say* kon-**kew**bi-nij), *noun.*
[CON- + Latin *cumbere* to lie]

concupiscence
(*say* k'n-**kew**-piss'nce) *noun*
any abnormally strong desire, usually sexual.
Word Family: **concupiscent,** *adjective.*
[Latin *concupiscere* to covet]

concur (*say* k'n-**ker**) *verb*
(**concurred, concurring**)
1. to agree: 'our political opinions usually *concur*'.
2. to occur at the same time: 'several things *concurred* to stop me coming'.
concurrent (*say* k'n-**kurr**'nt) *adjective*
1. in agreement.
2. existing or occurring together.
3. *Maths:* intersecting at one point.
Word Family: **concurrently,** *adverb*; **concurrence,** *noun.*
[CON- + Latin *currere* to run]

concussion (*say* k'n-**kush**'n) *noun*
1. a temporary injury to the brain due to a sudden shock, such as a fall or blow, and causing headache, dizziness, blurred vision, etc.
2. any violent shock caused by a blow, explosion, etc.: 'the *concussion* of the bomb blast stunned the city'.
Word Family: **concuss,** *verb.*
[Latin *concussus* shaken violently]

condemn (*say* k'n-**dem**) *verb*
to make a judgement against: 'the murderer was *condemned* to life imprisonment'.
Usages:
a) 'the old houses were *condemned* by the council' (= declared unfit for use).
b) 'the accident *condemned* him to a wheelchair for many years' (= forced).
Word Family: **condemnation** (*say* kondem-**nay**-sh'n), *noun*; **condemnatory** (*say* k'n-**dem**na-tree), *adjective.*
[CON- + Latin *damnare* to condemn]

condense (*say* k'n-**dense**) *verb*
1. to reduce in volume or make more dense: 'the newspaper gave a *condensed* account of the election speech'.
2. (of a gas or vapour) to change or be changed into a liquid.
3. (of light) to focus upon an object.
Word Family: **condensation** (*say* konden-**say**-sh'n), *noun,* a) the act or process of condensing, b) something which is condensed.
[CON- + Latin *densus* crowded]

condenser *noun*
1. any device or apparatus which condenses.
2. a lens system used to gather and concentrate light upon an object, as in a microscope.
3. *Electricity:* a capacitor.

condescend (*say* kondi-**send**) *verb*
1. to voluntarily or graciously accept a lower position, duty, etc.: 'the Queen *condescended* to visit our exhibition'.
2. to do something in an ungracious or patronizing manner: 'they actually *condescended* to wash the dishes!'
Word Family: **condescension** (*say* kondi-**sen**-sh'n), *noun*; **condescendingly,** *adverb.*
[CON- + Latin *descendere* to come down]

condiment *noun*
anything used to flavour or season foods, such as spices, pickles, etc.
[Latin *condire* to pickle]

condition (*say* k'n-**dish**'n) *noun*
1. the particular state or circumstances of a person or thing: 'the house is in a very neglected *condition*'.
Usage: 'my father has a slight heart *condition*' (= ailment).
2. something which another thing depends on or is limited by: 'there are no *conditions* attached to the free offer'.
on condition that, 'you may stay up late *on condition that* you don't make any noise' (= only if).
condition *verb*
1. to limit or regulate: 'book publishing is *conditioned* by paper supplies'.
2. to make fit, healthy, etc: 'dry hair should be *conditioned* with this herbal oil'.
3. *Psychology:* to create responses to stimuli which would not normally produce such responses.
Word Family: **conditioner,** *noun,* a person or thing that conditions.
[Latin *condicio* an agreement]

conditional (*say* k'n-**disha**-n'l) *adjective*
1. containing or depending on conditions: 'the sale is *conditional* on getting a bank loan'.

2. not absolutely definite or certain: 'let us make a *conditional* date for the meeting and confirm it later'.

conditioning *noun*
Psychology: a method of learning in which a response (called a **conditioned reflex**) comes to be associated with a stimulus which would normally not produce that response. This result may be achieved through a system of reward and punishment.
conditioned *adjective*
(of an action) being learned as a result of conditioning.

condolence (*say* k'n-**doe**-l'nce) *noun*
(*usually plural*) a declaration of sympathy: 'please accept our *condolences* for your father's death'.
Word Family: **condole,** *verb*; **condolent,** *adjective.*
[CON- + Latin *dolens* grieving]

condominium (*say* konda-**minnium**) *noun*
a) joint sovereignty. b) a country under joint sovereignty.

condone *verb*
1. to pardon or forgive: 'we cannot *condone* violence in any society'.
2. to make up for: 'being charming and friendly cannot *condone* his selfishness'.
Word Family: **condonation** (*say* konda-**nay**-sh'n), *noun.*
[Latin *condonare* to forgive]

condor *noun*
a very large American vulture.

conducive (*say* k'n-**dew**siv) *adjective*
helpful in producing: 'hot weather is *conducive* to laziness'.
Word Family: **conduce,** *verb.*

conduct (*say* **kon**dukt) *noun*
1. a person's behaviour or way of acting: 'his drunken *conduct* at the party was disgraceful'.
2. management or guidance: 'the *conduct* of a large business is very tiring'.
conduct (*say* k'n-**dukt**) *verb*
1. to behave: 'he *conducted* himself very badly at the party'.
2. to control, direct or manage: a) 'to *conduct* a business'; b) 'to *conduct* an orchestra'.
3. to lead or direct: 'latecomers were *conducted* to the back seats'.
4. to carry or transmit: 'electricity is *conducted* along wires to each house'.
[CON- + Latin *ductus* led]

conduction (*say* k'n-**duk**-sh'n) *noun*
the carrying or transmitting of something along or through a body, especially energy such as heat and electricity. Compare CONVECTION.

conductivity (*say* konduk-**tivva**-tee) *noun*
Physics: the ability of a substance to conduct energy such as light, sound or electric current.
Word Family: **conductive,** *adjective.*

conductor *noun*
1. a person who conducts, directs or leads: 'the *conductor* of an orchestra'.
2. a person in charge of passengers, collecting fares, etc., on public transport: 'a bus *conductor*'.
3. *Physics:* a body which will allow a particular type of energy to flow through it: 'a lightning *conductor*'.
Word Family: **conductress,** *noun,* a female conductor.

conduit (*say* **kon**-dit) *noun*
a) a pipe or channel, such as a drain. b) a protective tube covering electrical wires.

cone *noun*
1. a solid or hollow body with a curved or circular base which narrows to a point.
2. any object or device with this shape: 'an ice-cream *cone*'.
3. *Biology:* a reproductive structure of seed-bearing parts arranged spirally around the centre, as in pine cones.
4. *Geography:* a hill composed of volcanic ash or lava.
5. *Anatomy:* any of the light-sensitive cells in the retina of higher animals, used for seeing colour and very fine detail. Compare ROD.
Word Family: **conic** (*say* **kon**nik), **conical,** *adjective*; **conically,** *adverb.*
[Greek *konos* a pine cone]

confab *noun*
short form of **confabulation**
a friendly conversation or chat.
Word Family: **confabulate,** *verb.*

confection (*say* k'n-**fek**-sh'n) *noun*
a sweet.
[CON- + Latin *factus* made]

confectioner (*say* k'n-**fek**-sh'na) *noun*
a person who makes or sells sweets, cakes, ice-creams, etc.
confectionery, confectionary *noun*
a) any or all sweets. b) a shop where sweets are sold or made. c) the act of making sweets.

confederacy (*say* k'n-**feddera**-see) *noun*

a group of people or nations joined for a common cause: 'all building trade unions have formed a *confederacy*'.

confederate *adjective*
united or joined by agreement.
confederate (*say* k'n–**fedda**–rit) *noun*
1. an ally or accomplice: 'a *confederate* in crime'.
2. *American history:* a soldier fighting for the independence of the eleven southern States which seceded from the Union during the Civil War (1861–65).
Word Family: **confederate,** *verb*; **confederation,** *noun.*

confer (*say* k'n–**fir**) *verb*
(**conferred, conferring**)
1. to give or award: 'a medal was *conferred* upon him for bravery'.
2. to discuss or exchange opinions: 'the lawyers *conferred* for several minutes before answering'.
Word Family: **conferment,** *noun.*
[CON– + Latin *ferre* to bring]

conference *noun*
a meeting for discussion or exchange of opinions: 'will we attend the dental *conference* in London?'.

confess *verb*
to say or admit something: 'he *confessed* to having stolen four bicycles in one week'.
confession (*say* k'n–**fesh**'n) *noun*
a) the act of confessing. b) something which is confessed.
Word Family: **confessor,** *noun,* a person who makes or receives a confession; **confessional,** *noun,* a small stall in a church where priests hear confessions.
[Latin *confessus* declared]

confetti *plural noun*
the small pieces of coloured paper thrown into the air at weddings, celebrations, etc.
[Italian *confetto* a sweet or candy]

confidant (*say* konfi–**dant**) *noun*
a person with whom secret or private matters are discussed.
Word Family: **confidante,** *noun,* a female confidant.

confide (*say* k'n–**fide**) *verb*
1. to trust with a secret: 'she *confided* to me that her husband has a criminal record'.
2. to place in somebody's keeping: 'the youngest pupils were *confided* to the care of the most experienced teacher'.
Word Family: **confidingly,** *adverb.*
[CON– + Latin *fides* trust]

confidence (*say* **konfi**–d'nce) *noun*
1. a firm trust: 'he has full *confidence* in the surgeon who will perform the operation'.
2. a sureness or trust in oneself: 'the *confidence* of her violin playing was remarkable for a 10-year-old'.
3. a secret: 'he isn't the sort of person who exchanges *confidences*'.
in confidence, 'he mentioned it *in* strict *confidence*' (= as a secret or private matter).
Word Family: **confident,** *adjective,* sure or certain; **confidently,** *adverb.*

confidence man
a person who tricks or defrauds by gaining other peoples' confidence.

confidence trick
a fraud carried out by first gaining a person's confidence.

confidential (*say* konfi–**den**–sh'l) *adjective*
1. secret or private: '*confidential* documents must be kept in the safe'.
2. entrusted with secret or private matters: 'a *confidential* secretary'.
Word Family: **confidentially,** *adverb*; **confidentiality** (*say* konfi–denshi–**alli**–tee), *noun.*

configuration
(*say* k'n–fig–yoo–**ray**–sh'n) *noun*
1. the arrangement of all the elements and details within a form: 'the painting was a *configuration* of circles, squares and triangles'.
2. *Chemistry:* the relative positions of the atoms of a molecule in space.
3. *Geology:* the height and shape of a section of the earth's surface.
4. *Astrology:* see ASPECT.
Word Family: **configurative** (*say* k'n–**fig**–yoora–tiv), *adjective.*

confine (*say* k'n–**fine**) *verb*
to restrict or limit: 'please *confine* your remarks to the subject being discussed'.
Usage: 'difficult prisoners are *confined* in a separate part of the prison' (= shut away, enclosed).
confine (*say* **kon**–fine) *noun*
(*usually plural*) a limit or boundary: 'the child was forbidden to leave the *confines* of the garden'.
confinement *noun*
1. the act of confining.
2. the state of being imprisoned: 'he was sentenced to solitary *confinement*'.
3. the period when a woman is in bed during childbirth.
[CON– + Latin *finis* boundary]

confirm (*say* k'n–**firm**) *verb*
1. to show something to be true or correct: 'there were no facts to *confirm* his theory'.
2. to approve formally or make valid: 'the Director's letter *confirmed* her appointment as supervisor'.
3. to strengthen or make firm: 'the reprimand merely *confirmed* his negative attitude'.
Word Family: **confirmation,** *noun,* a) the act of confirming, b) something which confirms, such as proof or evidence; **confirmable,** *adjective;* **confirmatory,** *adjective,* serving to confirm.
[CON– + Latin *firmare* to make firm]

confiscate (*say* **konfi**–skate) *verb*
to take or seize by authority: 'the drugs discovered on the ship were *confiscated* by Customs officers'.
Word Family: **confiscation,** *noun.*
[Latin *confiscare* to seize for the public treasury (*fiscus*)]

conflagration (*say* konfla–**gray**–sh'n) *noun*
a huge, destructive fire.
[CON– + Latin *flagrare* to blaze]

conflict (*say* **konflikt**) *noun*
1. a battle or struggle: 'two hundred soldiers died in the *conflict*'.
2. the opposition of two forces or things: 'the *conflict* of ideas in the debate was very stimulating'.
conflict (*say* k'n–**flikt**) *verb*
to be or come into opposition: 'his modern ideas *conflict* with the old–fashioned policies of the school'.
[Latin *conflictus* dashed together]

confluence (*say* **konfloo**–ence) *noun*
1. a) the flowing together of two streams. b) the place where they meet.
2. a large gathering of people or things.
Word Family: **confluent,** *noun,* a stream which joins another; **confluent,** *adjective.*
[CON– + Latin *fluens* flowing]

conform (*say* k'n–**form**) *verb*
to be or act in agreement or accordance, especially with rules, customs, etc.: 'the architect's plan must *conform* to building regulations'.
conformity *noun*
1. an agreement, similarity or correspondence: 'the findings of the two scientists were in *conformity*'.
2. any action or behaviour which follows the attitudes, customs or rules of others: 'this school teaches *conformity* to old–fashioned values'.
Word Family: **conformist,** *noun,* a person who conforms.
[Latin *conformare* to shape]

conformation (*say* konfa–**may**–sh'n) *noun*
1. the structure, shape or form of a thing.
2. the act of conforming or adapting.

confound *verb*
1. to confuse or bewilder completely: 'she was *confounded* by the unexpected news'.
2. to fail to distinguish between: 'don't *confound* economy with stinginess'.
3. (*formerly*) to defeat or overthrow: 'the strategy *confounded* the enemy'.
4. (used to express annoyance): '*confound* this screwdriver!'.
confounded *adjective*
(*informal*) damned: 'you're a *confounded* nuisance'.
Word Family: **confoundedly,** *adverb.*
[CON– + Latin *fundere* to mix up, bewilder]

confrère (*say* **kon**–frair) *noun*
a colleague or fellow member.
[CON– + French *frère* brother]

confront (*say* k'n–**frunt**) *verb*
to be, come or bring face to face with: 'the detective *confronted* the suspect with the stolen goods'.
Word Family: **confrontation** (*say* kon–frun–**tay**–sh'n), *noun,* the act of confronting or opposing, especially in a hostile manner.
[CON– + Latin *frontis* of a face]

confuse (*say* k'n–**fewz**) *verb*
1. to puzzle or bewilder: 'her complicated road directions always *confuse* me'.
2. to mistake one thing for another: 'he *confused* question 6 with question 7 in the exam'.
Word Family: **confusedly,** *adverb,* in a confused manner; **confusingly,** *adverb,* in a manner which is likely to cause confusion; **confusion** (*say* k'n–**few**–*zh*'n), *noun,* a) the act of confusing, b) the state of being confused, c) disorder.
[Latin *confusus* mixed, jumbled]

confute *verb*
to prove to be wrong or incorrect: 'the prosecutor *confuted* the defence argument'.
Word Family: **confutation,** *noun.*
[Latin *confutare* to check]

congeal (*say* k'n–**jeel**) *verb*
to change from a liquid to a jelly–like solid state, especially as a result of cooling.
[CON– + Latin *gelare* to freeze]

congenial (*say* k'n–**jeeni**'l) *adjective*
pleasant or agreeable.
Word Family: **congenially**, *adverb*; **congeniality** (*say* k'n–jeeni–**alli**–tee), *noun.*
[CON– + GENIAL]

congenital (*say* k'n–**jenni**–t'l) *adjective*
of or relating to any condition acquired at or before birth but not through heredity.
Usage: 'he has a *congenital* dislike of insurance salesmen' (= deep–rooted).
Word Family: **congenitally**, *adverb.*
[CON– + Latin *genitus* born]

conger (*say* **kon**–ga) *noun*
short form of **conger eel**
a large eel, found especially along rocky coastlines.
[Latin]

congest (*say* k'n–**jest**) *verb*
1. to make or become overcrowded or too full: 'traffic *congested* the main city streets during peak hour'.
2. *Medicine:* to accumulate too much fluid in an organ, especially blood in the blood vessels or mucus in the lungs.
Word Family: **congestion**, *noun.*
[Latin *congestus* heaped up]

conglomerate (*say* k'n–**glomma**–rit) *noun*
1. something composed of different or random things, such as a large company which incorporates many different sorts of businesses.
2. *Geology:* a sedimentary rock formed of rounded pebbles deposited in or by water and cemented together.
Word Family: **conglomerate** (*say* k'n–**glomm**a–rate), *verb*; **conglomeration**, *noun*, a) the act of conglomerating, b) any conglomerate collection.
[CON– + Latin *glomeris* of a ball]

congratulate (*say* k'n–**grat**–yoo–late) *verb*
to express pleasure at another's success or good fortune: 'he *congratulated* her on her exam results'.
Word Family: **congratulation**, *noun*; **congratulatory** (*say* k'n–**grat**–yoola–tree), *adjective.*
[CON– + Latin *gratulari* to wish joy]

congregate (*say* **kon**gri–gate) *verb*
to come together in a group: 'a small crowd *congregated* at the scene of the accident'.
Word Family: **congregation**, *noun*, a) the act of congregating, b) a gathering or assembly, as of people in a church.
[CON– + Latin *gregis* of a flock]

congress *noun*
1. a formal meeting of people with similar interests, for discussion of problems, etc.: 'a world *congress* of political scientists'.
2. *Politics:* (*capital*) the body of elected representatives in America, consisting of the Senate and the House of Representatives.
Word Family: **congressional** (*say* k'n–**greshe**n'l), *adjective.*
[Latin *congressus* a coming together]

congruent (*say* **kon**–groo–ent) *adjective*
1. agreeing in nature or qualities.
2. identical in every aspect: '*congruent* triangles coincide exactly if they are superimposed'.
Word Family: **congruently**, *adverb*; **congruence**, *noun.*
[Latin *congruens* running together]

congruous (*say* **kon**–groo–us) *adjective*
agreeing or harmonious.
Word Family: **congruously**, *adverb*; **congruity** (*say* kon–**grewi**–tee), *noun.*

conic, conical *adjective*
Word Family: see CONE.

conic section
Maths: a curve formed by the intersection of a plane with a cone, being an **ellipse**, **parabola** or **hyperbola** according to the inclination of the intersecting plane to the axis of the cone.

conifer (*say* **ko**–niffa) *noun*
any of a group of trees with naked seeds, often in cones, such as the pine or fir.
Word Family: **coniferous** (*say* k'**niff**erus), *adjective.*
[Latin, cone–bearing]

conjecture (*say* k'n–**jek**cher) *verb*
to guess or make a judgement without sufficient evidence.
Word Family: **conjecture**, *noun*; **conjectural**, *adjective.*
[Latin *conjectus* deduced]

conjoin *verb*
to join together or unite.
Word Family: **conjoint**, *adjective*; **conjointly**, *adverb.*

conjugal (*say* **kon**–joo–g'l) *adjective*
relating to marriage.
Word Family: **conjugally,** *adverb*; **conjugality** (*say* kon–joo–**galli**–tee), *noun.*
[Latin *conjugis* of a wife]

conjugate (*say* **kon**–joo–gate *or* **kon**–joo–git) *adjective*
1. joined in pairs.
2. *Maths:* reciprocally related or interchangeable with respect to certain properties.
Word Family: **conjugate,** *noun,* either of a pair of conjugate qualities.
[Latin *conjungere* to yoke together]

conjugation (*say* kon–joo–**gay**–sh'n) *noun*
Grammar: the inflections of a verb which express its tense, number, person, etc., especially in a language such as Latin.
Example: I have (= first person) becomes *he has* (= third person), *I had* (= past tense), *having* (= participle), etc.
Compare DECLENSION.
Word Family: **conjugate** (*say* **kon**joo–gate), *verb,* to list the inflections of a verb.

conjunction (*say* k'n–**junk**–ch'n) *noun*
1. a) the act of joining or combining. b) the state of being joined: 'the police worked in *conjunction* with the health department to fight the plague'.
Usage: 'a strange *conjunction* of events' (= simultaneous occurrence).
2. *Grammar:* a joining or linking word, such as *and* or *but.* Also called a **conjunctive.**
Word Family: **conjunctive,** *adjective,* joined or joining.
[Latin *conjunctus* yoked together]

conjunctivitis (*say* k'n–junkti–**vie**–tis) *noun*
an infection of the membrane (called the **conjunctiva**) which lines the eyelids and covers the front of the eyeball.

conjure *verb*
1. (*say* **kun**ja) to summon or produce by or as if by magic: 'the magician *conjured* a rabbit from his hat'.
2. (*say* k'n–**joor**) to appeal solemnly or earnestly to: 'whatever happens, I *conjure* you to keep silent'.
conjure up, 'the music *conjured up* a vision of the sea' (= evoked, brought to mind).
Word Family: **conjurer, conjuror,** *noun,* a magician.

conk *noun*
(*informal*) a) the nose. b) a sharp blow.
conk *verb*
(*informal*) to strike or hit: 'she *conked* me on the head'.
conk out, 'my car *conked out* halfway up the hill' (= stopped).

conker *noun*
1. a horse–chestnut.
2. (*plural*) a children's knock–out competition with conkers threaded on string.

con–man *noun*
a confidence man.

connect (*say* k'**nekt**) *verb*
to join or be joined: '*connect* the batteries to the wires and switch the radio on'.
Usages:
a) 'is your telephone *connected* yet?' (= in operation).
b) 'I never thought you would be *connected* with the crime' (= involved).
c) 'this train *connects* with an express to the city' (= meets).
d) 'I did not *connect* the two names' (= bring together mentally).
connection, connexion *noun*
1. a) the act of connecting. b) the state of being connected.
2. anything that connects: 'the *connection* between the two gas pipes broke'.
3. an international carrier service for illicit goods.
Usages:
a) 'he says he has *connections* in high places' (= influential friends).
b) 'in what *connection* did he mention me?' (= context).
Word Family: **connectedly,** *adverb.*
[CON– + Latin *nectere* to bind]

conning tower
the superstructure of a submarine, which serves as an observation tower as well as an entrance.

connive (*say* k'**nive**) *verb*
1. to plot or conspire: 'the trainer and the jockey *connived* to lose the race'.
2. to encourage or allow wrongdoing by pretending not to notice it.
Word Family: **connivance, connivence,** *noun.*
[Latin *connivere* to shut the eyes]

connoisseur (*say* konna–**sir**) *noun*
a person who is experienced and discriminating in a particular field, especially the arts.
[Old French, one who knows]

connote (*say* k'**note**) *verb*
to suggest or imply.
Word Family: **connotation,** *noun.*
Common Error: see DENOTE.

connubial (*say* k'n-**yoo**-biul) *adjective*
of or relating to marriage.
[CON- + Latin *nubere* to marry]

conquer (*say* **kon**ka) *verb*
to defeat or overcome, e.g. to gain control of territory, etc.
Word Family: **conqueror,** *noun.*

conquest (*say* **kon**kwest) *noun*
1. the act of conquering: 'the *conquest* of the mountain region cost many lives'.
2. anything which is conquered: 'Gaul was one of Caesar's *conquests*'.

conquistador (*say* kon-**kwista**-dor) *noun*
plural is **conquistadores**
History: a title given to Spanish conquerors of Mexico and Peru in the 16th century.

consanguinity
(*say* konsan-**gwinna**-tee) *noun*
a relationship by descent from a common ancestor.
[CON- + Latin *sanguis* blood]

conscience (*say* **kon**-sh'nce) *noun*
a person's sense of right and wrong, especially in relation to his own actions and motives.
on one's conscience, 'his failure to save the child was always *on his conscience*' (= in his mind causing guilty feelings).
Word Family: **conscionable** (*say* **kon**shena-b'l), *adjective,* according to conscience.
[CON- + Latin *sciens* knowing]
Common Error: do not confuse with CONSCIOUS.

conscientious (*say* konshi-**en**shus) *adjective*
scrupulous or painstakingly careful: 'she is a *conscientious* worker'.
Word Family: **conscientiously,** *adverb*; **conscientiousness,** *noun.*

conscientious objector
a person who refuses to do military service because of his religious or moral beliefs.

conscious (*say* **kon**-shus) *adjective*
awake: 'the mother wanted to stay *conscious* during her baby's birth'.
Usages:
a) 'she was *conscious* of a faint smell of burning' (= aware).
b) 'his action was a *conscious* attempt to conceal the truth' (= deliberate).
Word Family: **consciously,** *adverb*; **consciousness,** *noun.*
Common Error: do not confuse with CONSCIENCE.

conscript (*say* k'n-**skript**) *verb*
to call up or enlist recruits for compulsory military service.
Usage: 'she has *conscripted* me for yet another of her tasks' (= forced to work).
Word Family: **conscript** (*say* **kon**-skript), *noun,* a person who is conscripted; **conscription,** *noun.*
[CON- + Latin *scriptus* written on a list, enlisted]

consecrate (*say* **kon**si-krate) *verb*
to dedicate to a special or sacred purpose: 'she *consecrated* her life to music'.
Word Family: **consecration,** *noun.*
[CON- + Latin *sacer* sacred]

consecutive (*say* k'n-**sek**-yootiv) *adjective*
following without interruption: 'she missed school on 4 *consecutive* days'.
Word Family: **consecutively,** *adverb.*
[CON- + Latin *secutus* followed]
Common Error: CONSECUTIVE, SUCCESSIVE both refer to things following one another, but *consecutive* refers to following in an arranged or logical order, whereas *successive* refers to any sequence: 'these two paragraphs are not *consecutive*'; 'we were pestered by *successive* visitors over the weekend'.

consensus *noun*
a general agreement: 'there was a *consensus* of opinion at the meeting that the treasurer should resign'.
[CON- + Latin *sensus* a sentiment]

consent (*say* k'n-**sent**) *verb*
to agree, accept or give permission.
consent *noun*
any permission or agreement.
age of consent
Law: the age at which it is legal for a person to marry, or for a girl to have sexual intercourse.
Word Family: **consentingly,** *adverb.*
[CON- + Latin *sentire* to feel]

consequence (*say* **kon**si-kw'nce) *noun*
1. an effect or result: 'lung cancer is a possible *consequence* of smoking'.
2. importance or distinction: 'he was a man of some *consequence* in the business world'.
Word Family: **consequent,** *adjective,* following as a result; **consequential**

(*say* konsi-**kwen**-sh'l), *adjective*, a) consequent, b) self-important.
[CON- + Latin *sequens* following]

consequently *adverb*
as a result or therefore.
Common Error: CONSEQUENTLY, SUBSEQUENTLY both mean afterwards, but *consequently* means caused by or resulting from, whereas *subsequently* means merely following in time or order: 'his car broke down and *consequently* he missed the appointment' (= therefore); 'in the novel the hero *subsequently* dies' (= later).

conservation (*say* konsa-**vay**-sh'n)
noun
1. the act of conserving.
2. the preservation of natural environments, especially by the wise use of resources.
conservation of energy, the law that within a given system the total quantity of energy is constant.
Word Family: **conservationist**, *noun*.
[CON- + Latin *servare* to keep]

conservative (*say* k'n-**serva**-tiv)
adjective
1. *British politics:* (*capital*) connected with the **Conservative Party**, one of the two major parties: 'the *Conservative* candidate made a speech'.
2. opposed to any great or sudden change: 'in the newly independent state the *conservative* elements in the army forestalled a revolt'.
Usages:
a) 'a *conservative* estimate' (= moderate).
b) 'a *conservative* style of dress' (= sober and traditional).
Word Family: **conservative**, *noun*, a) a supporter of conservative ideas, b) (capital) a member of the Conservative Party; **conservatively**, *adverb*; **conservatism**, *noun*, a cautious approach to new ideas or changes.

conservatory (*say* k'n-**serva**-tree)
noun
a greenhouse attached to a house, where exotic plants can be grown.

conserve (*say* k'n-**serve**) *verb*
to keep something valuable, especially to prevent it being wasted or used up: 'during the drought the public was urged to *conserve* water'.
conserve (*say* **kon**-serve) *noun*
a jam-like preserve made from fruits and sugar.

consider (*say* k'n-**sidda**) *verb*
to think or deliberate in order to decide: 'the committee will *consider* all applications for the new post'.
Usages:
a) 'John *considers* himself to be a genius' (= believes).
b) '*consider* the cheapness of the meal before you complain about it' (= take into account).
Word Family: **considerable**, *adjective*, great; **considerably**, *adverb*.
[Latin *considerare* to look at carefully]

considerate (*say* k'n-**sidda**-rit)
adjective
thoughtful of other people's feelings and needs: 'she is very *considerate* of older people'.
Word Family: **considerately**, *adverb*.

consideration
(*say* k'n-sidda-**ray**-sh'n) *noun*
1. the act of considering: 'after careful *consideration* we signed the lease'.
Usages:
a) 'she shows no *consideration* for her parents' (= respect).
b) 'the main *consideration* in his decision was the pay' (= factor).
2. any payment or compensation for a service, etc.: 'he will do the job for a small *consideration*'.

consign (*say* k'n-**sine**) *verb*
1. to hand over formally: 'the orphan was *consigned* to the care of a foster-mother'.
2. to forward and deliver goods.
Word Family: **consignment**, *noun*, a) the act of consigning, b) anything which is consigned.
[Latin *consignare* to seal up]

consist (*say* k'n-**sist**) *verb*
to be made up of: 'the mixture *consists* of 3 eggs, 2 cups of milk and a tablespoon of sugar'.
Usage: 'the main idea of the film *consists* in trying to shock the audience' (= exists, lies).

consistency, consistence *noun*
1. any agreement or correspondence between things: 'your statement shows no *consistency* with what you said yesterday'.
2. the density or texture of something: 'whip the eggs until they have a fluffy *consistency*'.
Word Family: **consistent**, *adjective*; **consistently**, *adverb*.

consolation prize
a prize given to the runner-up in a competition.

console (1) (*say* k'n–**sole**) *verb*
to lessen grief or distress: 'her husband *consoled* her after she lost her job'.
Word Family: **consolation,** *noun,* a) the act of consoling, b) something which consoles; **consolatory** (*say* k'n–**solla**–tree), *adjective.*
[CON– + Latin *solari* to comfort]

console (2) (*say* **kon**–sole) *noun*
1. the case which encloses the keyboard, stops, etc. of an organ.
2. a radio, radiogram or television cabinet designed to rest on the floor.

consolidate (*say* k'n–**solli**–date) *verb*
to strengthen or make solid: 'you must *consolidate* the gains you have already made'.
Usage: 'the two companies decided to *consolidate* rather than compete' (= unite, merge).
Word Family: **consolidation,** *noun.*

Consols (*say* **kon**–s'ls) *plural noun*
short form of **Consolidated annuities** government stocks which provide a perpetual fixed–interest income for as long as they are held.

consommé (*say* k'n–**somm**ay) *noun*
a clear, thin soup made from meat juices.

consonant (*say* **kon**sa–nant) *noun*
Language: a) a sound pronounced with partial or complete blockage of the breath. b) any of the letters of the alphabet expressing these sounds, being all those except a,e,i,o,u, and sometimes y. Compare VOWEL.
consonant *adjective*
in agreement or accord: 'his behaviour is not *consonant* with his beliefs'.
Word Family: **consonantly,** *adverb;* **consonance,** *noun.*
[CON– + Latin *sonus* sound]

consort (1) (*say* **kon**–sort) *noun*
a husband or wife, especially of a reigning monarch.
consort (*say* k'n–**sort**) *verb*
to keep company: 'the police encouraged the informer to *consort* with criminals'.
[Latin *consors, consortis* sharing a common lot]

consort (2) (*say* **kon**–sort) *noun*
Music: a harmonious group of instruments or voices.

consortium (*say* k'n–**sorti**–um) *noun*
1. a temporary combination of banks or corporations to carry out some large–scale financial operation.
2. any partnership.
[Latin, partnership]

conspicuous (*say* k'n–**spik**–yewus) *adjective*
easily seen or standing out very clearly: 'the brightly coloured dress made her *conspicuous* in the crowd'.
[Latin *conspicuus* in sight]

conspire (*say* k'n–**spire**) *verb*
1. to plan secretly to do something unlawful: 'they *conspired* to defraud their business partner'.
2. to combine or act together: 'everything *conspired* to make the wedding a happy event'.
Word Family: **conspiracy** (*say* k'n–**spirra**–see), *noun,* a plot; **conspirator** (*say* k'n–**spirri**–ta), *noun,* a person who conspires; **conspiratorial** (*say* k'n–spirra–**taw**–riul), *adjective.*
[Latin *conspirare* to breathe together]

constable (*say* **kun**sta–b'l) *noun*
a police officer below the rank of sergeant.
constabulary
(*say* k'n–**stab**–yoola–ree) *noun*
the police force of a city or district.
[Late Latin for count of the stable]

constant (*say* **kon**–st'nt) *adjective*
1. persistent or not changing: 'the *constant* din of pneumatic drills at the construction site'.
2. loyal or faithful: 'a *constant* wife'.
constant *noun*
a number, quantity or factor which does not change.
Word Family: **constantly,** *adverb;* **constancy,** *noun.*
[CON– + Latin *stans, stantis* standing]

constellation (*say* konsta–**lay**–sh'n) *noun*
1. *Astronomy:* any pattern into which stars are grouped and according to which they are named, such as the Southern Cross.
2. *Astrology:* the position of the stars at the time of one's birth, which is said to influence one's character.
Usage: 'the *constellation* of ideas in a novel' (= grouping).
[CON– + Latin *stella* star]

consternation (*say* konsta–**nay**–sh'n) *noun*
sudden dismay or confusion: 'to his great *consternation* he saw a policeman on the doorstep'.
Word Family: **consternate,** *verb,* to dismay or terrify.
[Latin *consternare* to stampede]

constipation (*say* konsti-**pay**-sh'n) *noun*
a difficulty in emptying the bowels.
Word Family: **constipate,** *verb*; **constipated,** *adjective.*
[CON- + Latin *stipare* to press together]

constituent (*say* k'n-**stit**-yew'nt) *adjective*
forming a necessary part of a whole: 'oxygen and hydrogen are the *constituent* elements of water'.
constituent *noun*
1. a necessary part of a whole.
2. a person living in a constituency, who is entitled to vote in an election.
Word Family: **constituency,** *noun,* a) a body of electors, b) the area in which they live.
[CON- + Latin *statuere* to set up]

constitute (*say* **kon**sti-tewt) *verb*
to make up or form: a) 'seven days *constitute* a week'; b) 'we'll *constitute* a complaints committee'.

constitution (*say* konsti-**tew**-sh'n) *noun*
1. the act or process of constituting.
2. the way something is constituted: 'the *constitution* of a molecule usually includes two or more atoms'.
Usage: 'he has the *constitution* of an ox' (= strength or health).
3. *Politics:* the group of laws or principles on which the government of a country is based.
constitutional *noun*
a walk for the sake of one's health.
Word Family: **constitutional,** *adjective*; **constitutionally,** *adverb.*

constrain *verb*
1. to compel by physical or moral force: 'he was *constrained* by conscience to confess his crime'.
2. to confine in bonds: 'she *constrained* the vicious dog by chaining it to a tree'.
Word Family: **constraint,** *noun,* a) compulsion, b) restriction.

constrict *verb*
to draw together or compress: 'she tied a handkerchief round his arm to *constrict* the artery'.
Word Family: **constriction,** *noun*; **constrictive,** *adjective,* tending to constrict.
[CON- + Latin *strictus* bound]

construct *verb*
to make or put together in a careful or intricate way: 'the new bridge was *constructed* under the supervision of an engineer'.

construction *noun*
1. a) the act of constructing. b) something which has been constructed, such as a building.
Usage: 'what *construction* do you put on her statement?' (= meaning, explanation).
2. *Grammar:* the arrangement of words into phrases or sentences.
[CON- + Latin *structus* built]

constructive *adjective*
tending to construct or be helpful: 'he usually gives *constructive* criticism'.

construe (*say* k'n-**stroo**) *verb* (**construed, construing**)
to interpret or explain: 'how would you *construe* his meaning?'.

consul (*say* **kon**-s'l) *noun*
a government official sent to a foreign country to look after people from his own country. Compare AMBASSADOR and LEGATION.
Word Family: **consular,** *adjective*; **consulate,** *noun,* the offices and official home of a consul.
[Latin, one of the two highest magistrates in the Republic]

consult *verb*
1. to seek advice from: 'she *consulted* a doctor about her sore leg'.
2. to discuss or exchange views: 'we *consulted* for several hours before reaching a decision'.
Word Family: **consultation,** *noun,* a meeting in order to consult.

consultant *noun*
a person who gives expert or professional advice, such as a surgeon, engineer, etc.

consume (*say* k'n-**sume**) *verb*
to use or absorb all of something: 'the job *consumed* all his strength'.
Usages:
a) 'the fire *consumed* the house' (= destroyed).
b) 'we *consumed* a huge meal' (= ate).

consumer (*say* k'ns-**yoo**ma) *noun*
any person who buys goods or services.
consumer goods goods bought for personal or domestic use.

consummate (*say* **kon**sa-mate) *verb*
to make complete or perfect.
Word Family: **consummation,** *noun*; **consummate** (*say* kon-**summ**it), *adjective*; **consummately,** *adverb.*
[CON- + Latin *summus* highest]

consumption (*say* k'n-**sump**-sh'n) *noun*

1. the act of consuming. b) the amount that is consumed: 'this car has a very high petrol *consumption*'.
2. *Medicine:* any wasting disease, especially tuberculosis of the lungs.
Word Family: **consumptive,** *adjective.*

contact *noun*
1. a touching or communication.
2. a person or thing that provides communication with or between others.
3. *Electricity:* any device which completes or breaks a circuit.
contact *verb*
to put or bring into contact.
[CON– + Latin *tactus* touched]

contact lens
a small, thin, curved disc of glass or plastic with a central lens, which is worn directly on the eyeball instead of spectacles.

contact print
Photography: a print made by placing a negative directly on to sensitized paper and exposing it to light, so that the print is the same size as the negative.

contagious (*say* k'n–**tay**jus) *adjective*
able to be spread or passed on easily: 'a *contagious* disease'.
Word Family: **contagiously,** *adverb*; **contagiousness,** *noun*, the fact of being contagious; **contagion** (*say* k'n–**tay**jen), *noun*, the passing on of a disease, bad influence, undesirable idea, etc. from one person or thing to another.
[Latin *contagio* a contact]

contain (*say* k'n–**tain**) *verb*
1. to have inside: 'this book *contains* 10 pages'.
2. to check or restrain: 'she *contained* her emotions'.
containment *noun*
1. the act or policy of preventing the expansion of hostile powers, etc.
2. the prevention, in uranium processing, of release, even under conditions of a reactor accident, of unacceptable quantities of radioactive material beyond a controlled zone.
[Latin *continere* to hold together]

container *noun*
any object, such as a tin, etc., in which objects are carried or stored.

containerize, containerise *verb*
to equip ships, etc. to carry goods in large containers of a standard size.
Word Family: **containerization,** *noun.*

contaminate (*say* k'n–**tammi**–nate) *verb*
to pollute or make impure.
Word Family: **contamination,** *noun*; **contaminant,** *noun*, anything which contaminates.
[Latin *contaminare* to bring into contact]

contemplate (*say* **kon**tem–plate) *verb*
to look at or think about: a) 'she *contemplated* the painting'; b) 'I am *contemplating* leaving my job'.
Word Family: **contemplation,** *noun*, a) the act of contemplating, b) religious or spiritual meditation; **contemplative** (*say* k'n–**tem**pla–tiv), *noun*, a person who practises religious meditation; **contemplative,** *adjective.*
[Latin *contemplari* to gaze on]

contemporaneous
(*say* k'n–tempa–**ray**nius) *adjective*
occurring at the same time.

contemporary (*say* k'n–**tem**pa–raree) *adjective*
1. living, existing or occurring in the same period.
2. of the present time: 'this shop sells *contemporary* furniture'.
contemporary *noun*
a person living at the same time or having the same age as another.
[CON– + Latin *temporis* of time]

contempt *noun*
a feeling of scorn or utter dislike.
contempt of court, (*Law*) the act of showing disrespect to a court, often by disobeying its commands.

contemptible *adjective*
deserving contempt: '*contemptible* behaviour'.
Word Family: **contemptibly,** *adverb.*

contemptuous (*say* k'n–**temp**–tewus) *adjective*
showing contempt: 'he is *contemptuous* of all authority'.
Word Family: **contemptuously,** *adverb.*

contend *verb*
to struggle or strive for: 'which teams will *contend* for the cup?'.
Usage: 'I still *contend* that I was right' (= argue).
Word Family: **contender,** *noun.*

content (1) (*say* **kon**–tent) *noun*
1. (*usually plural*) anything which is contained in something: 'the *contents* of a parcel'.
Usage: 'what is the *content* of butterfat in milk?' (= amount).

2. (*plural*) a list of topics or chapters in a book.
[CON– + Latin *tentus* held fast]

content (2) (*say* k'n–**tent**) *adjective*
satisfied or willing: 'I am *content* to wait'.
Word Family: **content,** *verb,* to make content; **contentedly,** *adverb*; **contentment,** *noun.*
[Latin *contentus* satisfied]

contention (*say* k'n–**ten**–sh'n) *noun*
1. a dispute: 'it is a matter of *contention* whether motor cars are dangerous or not'.
2. a point of view: 'it is my *contention* that motor cars are dangerous'.
3. the act of contending.
Word Family: **contentious,** *adjective,* causing contention; **contentiously,** *adverb.*

contest (*say* **kon**–test) *noun*
a competition: 'a *contest* of strength'.
contest (*say* k'n–**test**) *verb*
to take part in a contest or argument.
Word Family: **contestant** (*say* k'n–**test**'nt), *noun,* a person who takes part in a contest; **contestable,** *adjective.*
[CON– + Latin *testari* to testify]

context (*say* **kon**–tekst) *noun*
1. the circumstances, facts, etc. which surround something.
2. the words or phrases which are connected with and accompany a particular word or passage.
Word Family: **contextual** (*say* kon–**tekst**–yew'l), *adjective.*
[CON– + Latin *textus* woven]

contiguous (*say* k'n–**tig**–yewus) *adjective*
very close or connected.
Word Family: **contiguity** (*say* kontig–yewa–tee), *noun.*
[Latin *contiguus* touching]

continent (*say* **konti**–nent) *noun*
a large, unbroken land mass, such as Europe, Asia, etc.
continent *adjective*
having self-control, especially over one's body.
Word Family: **continental** (*say* konti–**nen**–t'l), *adjective,* relating to a continent; **continence,** *noun.*
[Latin (*terra*) *continens* continuous land]

continental drift
the theory that the continents of the world are fractured parts of a single land mass, and are moving very slowly over the earth's surface.

continental shelf
the gently sloping, shallow area around the coast of a continent.

contingency (*say* k'n–**tin**–j'n–see) *noun*
1. the fact of being uncertain or dependent on chance.
2. an event which is uncertain or subject to chance: 'we must be prepared for all *contingencies* of the weather'.
[Latin *contingens* touching closely]

contingent (*say* kon–**tin**–j'nt) *adjective*
1. dependent: 'the result is *contingent* on each player's fitness'.
2. uncertain or happening by chance.
contingent *noun*
a group representing a larger one: 'a *contingent* of troops'.

continual (*say* k'n–**tin**–yew'l) *adjective*
occurring without stopping or only with short breaks.
Word Family: **continually,** *adverb.*
Common Error: CONTINUAL, CONTINUOUS have related but distinct meanings: *continual* describes something which happens all or most of the time, whereas *continuous* refers to something which has no break between its beginning and end.

continue (*say* k'n–**tin**–yoo) *verb*
1. to go onwards or further in a particular activity or state: 'it *continued* to rain all day'.
2. to start again after a break: 'we will *continue* the meeting after lunch'.
Word Family: **continuation,** *noun.*

continuity (*say* konti–**newi**–tee) *noun*
1. the state of being continuous or in a logical sequence.
2. *Film:* the process of making sure that all parts of a movie are consistent, such as costumes or scenery.

continuo (*say* k'n–**tin**–yoo–o) *noun*
Music: a bass accompaniment, usually played by a keyboard instrument.

continuous (*say* k'n–**tin**–yewus) *adjective*
occurring without a break: 'a *continuous* roll of drums'.
Word Family: **continuously,** *adverb*; **continuousness,** *noun.*
[Latin *continuus* holding together]
Common Error: see CONTINUAL.

continuum (*say* k'n–**tin**–yoo–um) *noun*
1. a continuous range between two extremes: 'in society the rich and the poor are at opposite ends of a *continuum*'.
2. *Maths:* all rational and irrational numbers.

contort *verb*
to twist or bend out of the normal shape: 'father's face was *contorted* with rage'.
Word Family: **contortion,** *noun.*
[CON– + Latin *tortus* twisted]

contortionist (*say* k'n–**tor**–sh'nist) *noun*
an acrobat who bends his body into unusual or difficult shapes.

contour (*say* **kon**–toor) *noun*
1. the outline of a figure or body.
2. *Geography:* a line on a map joining points which are an equal height above sea-level. Also called a **contour line.**

contour map
Geography: a map on which land forms are shown by a pattern of contours.

contra–
a prefix meaning against or opposite, as in *contraception.*
[Latin]

contraband *noun*
any articles forbidden to be brought into or taken out of a country.
[CONTRA– + Italian *bando* ban]

contraception (*say* kontra–**sep**–sh'n) *noun*
the methods or process of preventing a woman becoming pregnant.
Word Family: **contraceptive,** *noun,* any device or drug used for contraception; **contraceptive,** *adjective.*
[CONTRA– + (con)CEPTION]

contract (*say* k'n–**trakt**) *verb*
1. to draw together or make smaller.
2. to get or incur: 'she *contracted* many debts'.
3. to settle by agreement.
contract (*say* **kon**–trakt) *noun*
1. a legal or formal agreement made between two or more people.
2. *Cards:* a) the highest bid in a game of bridge. b) the number of tricks in that bid.
contraction (*say* k'n–**trak**–sh'n) *noun*
1. the act of contracting.
2. a shortened form of a word which ends in the same letter as the word itself, as in *Mr* for *Mister.* Compare ABBREVIATION.
[CON– + Latin *tractus* drawn, dragged]

contractile (*say* k'n–**trak**–tile) *adjective*
capable of contracting.

contractor (*say* kon–**trakta**) *noun*
a person who agrees to supply goods or services for a named price.

contradict (*say* **kon**tra–dikt) *verb*
to assert the opposite or deny.
Word Family: **contradiction,** *noun;* **contradictory,** *adjective.*
[CONTRA– + Latin *dicere* to say]

contralto (*say* k'n–**trahl**–toe) *noun*
Music: see ALTO.
[Italian]

contraption (*say* k'n–**trap**–sh'n) *noun*
an elaborate device or gadget.

contrapuntal (*say* kontra–**pun**–t'l) *adjective*
Music: of or relating to counterpoint.

contrary *adjective*
1. (*say* **kon**tra–ree) opposite or opposed: '*contrary* to all advice she sold the house'.
2. (*say* k'n–**trair**–ree) perverse or wilful: 'she is very *contrary* and refuses to do what she is told'.
contrary (*say* **kon**tra–ree) *noun*
the opposite of something.
Phrases:
on the contrary, in opposition to what has been stated.
to the contrary, with the opposite effect.
Word Family: **contrarily,** *adverb.*
[Latin *contrarius* opposite]

contrast (*say* k'n–**trahst**) *verb*
to compare by showing differences: 'to *contrast* good with bad'.
contrast (*say* **kon**–trahst) *noun*
1. the act of contrasting.
2. an obvious difference, such as between colours in a photograph, etc.
[CONTRA– + Latin *stare* to stand]

contravene (*say* kontra–**veen**) *verb*
to come into conflict with: 'his behaviour often *contravenes* the law'.
Word Family: **contravention** (*say* kontra–**ven**–sh'n), *noun.*
[CONTRA– + Latin *venire* to come]

contretemps (*say* **kon**tra–tom) *noun*
an annoying, embarrassing or unfortunately timed mishap.
[French, out of time (in music)]

contribute (*say* k'n–**trib**–yoot) *verb*
to give, especially with others: 'have you *contributed* money to the appeal?'.
Usage: 'the mistake *contributed* to his embarrassment' (= added).
Word Family: **contribution,** *noun,* a) the act of contributing, b) something which is contributed or given; **contributor,** *noun,* a person or thing that contributes; **contributory** (*say* k'n–**trib**–yoo–tree), *adjective.*
[CON– + *tribuere* to allot]

contrite (*say* **kon**–trite) *adjective*
sorry or repentant.
Word Family: **contritely,** *adverb*; **contrition** (*say* k'n–**trish**'n), *noun.*
[Latin *contritus* bruised]

contrivance (*say* k'n–**try**–v'nce) *noun*
1. a mechanical device.
2. the act or manner of contriving.

contrive *verb*
to plan, plot or find a way of doing something: 'let's *contrive* not to argue any more'.
Word Family: **contrivance,** *noun.*

control (*say* k'n–**trole**) *verb*
(controlled, controlling)
1. to have power over, especially to restrain: 'I cannot *control* my temper'.
2. *Science:* to test the validity of an experiment by conducting similar experiments.
control *noun*
1. the act of controlling.
2. (*plural*) the device used to operate a machine, vehicle, etc.
Word Family: **controllable,** *adjective.*

controller *noun*
1. a person appointed to check spending in a business or organization. Also spelt **comptroller**.
2. anyone who controls something.

controversy (*say* k'n–**trovva**–see *or* **kon**tra–ver–see) *noun*
a prolonged argument or difference of opinion.
Word Family: **controversial** (*say* kontra–**ver**–sh'l), *adjective,* causing controversy.
[CONTRA– + Latin *versus* turned]

contumacy (*say* **kon**–tewma–see) *noun*
a stubborn or wilful disobedience of authority.
Word Family: **contumacious** (*say* kon–tew–**may**–shus), *adjective.*

contumely (*say* **kon**–tewm–lee) *noun*
any insulting treatment.
Word Family: **contumelious** (*say* kontew–**meelius**), *adjective.*
[CON– + Latin *tumere* to swell]

contusion (*say* k'n–**tew**–*zh*'n) *noun*
a bruise.
[CON– + Latin *tusus* beaten]

conundrum (*say* k'**nun**–dr'm) *noun*
a puzzle, especially a riddle whose answer is a pun.

conurbation (*say* konna–**bay**–sh'n) *noun*
a large urban area formed by a group of towns growing towards and meeting each other.
[CON– + Latin *urbs* city]

convalescence (*say* konva–**less**'nce) *noun*
a) the gradual recovery after an accident, illness, operation, etc. b) the time this takes.
Word Family: **convalesce,** *verb*; **convalescent,** *adjective, noun.*
[CON– + Latin *valescere* to grow strong]

convection (*say* k'n–**vek**–sh'n) *noun*
Physics: the transferring of heat in a liquid or gas, due to the lighter parts rising and the denser parts sinking. Compare ADVECTION and CONDUCTION.
Word Family: **convectional,** *adjective.*
[CON– + Latin *vectus* carried]

convene *verb*
to meet or assemble, e.g. for a public meeting: 'the committee will *convene* on Friday'.
Word Family: **convener,** *noun,* a person who summons people together for a meeting.
[CON– + Latin *venire* to come]

convenient (*say* k'n–**veeni**–ent) *adjective*
useful or suitable for a purpose, especially in aiding comfort or ease: 'a *convenient* bus–stop outside the house'.
convenience *noun*
1. a) the state of being convenient or suitable. b) a convenient time: 'please call in at your own *convenience*'.
2. an appliance or useful device, such as a toilet.
Word Family: **conveniently,** *adverb.*

convent (*say* **kon**–v'nt) *noun*
a) a community of nuns. b) the buildings in which they live.
[Latin *conventus* assembly]

convention (*say* k'n–**ven**–sh'n) *noun*
1. a formal meeting, especially one of representatives brought together to make decisions.
2. any generally accepted rule or practice, especially for social behaviour.

conventional (*say* k'n–**vensha**–n'l) *adjective*
based on tradition or convention.
Word Family: **conventionally,** *adverb*; **conventionalism,** *noun,* a) a tendency to be conventional, b) something which is a convention; **conventionalize, conventionalise,**

verb, to make or represent as conventional.

converge (*say* k'n-**verj**) *verb*
to meet at a common point: 'we *converged* on the picnic area'.
Word Family: **convergence,** *noun*; **convergent,** *adjective.*
[CON- + Latin *vergere* to turn]

conversant (*say* k'n-**ver**-s'nt) *adjective*
having knowledge of: 'are you *conversant* with all the rules of the game?'.

conversation (*say* konva-**say**-sh'n) *noun*
an informal exchange of words.
Word Family: **conversational,** *adjective*; **conversationalist,** *noun.*

converse (1) (*say* k'n-**verse**) *verb*
to talk informally.
[Latin *conversari* to associate with]

converse (2) (*say* **kon**-verse) *noun*
something which is the opposite of another.
Word Family: **converse,** *adjective*; **conversely,** *adverb.*
[Latin *conversus* turned round]

convert (*say* k'n-**vert**) *verb*
1. to change into a different form, etc.: '*convert* 1 kilometre into metres'.
2. to cause to change to another way of life, belief, etc.
3. *Law:* to take another's property unlawfully.
Word Family: **convert** (*say* **kon**-vert), *noun*, a person who has been converted; **conversion** (*say* k'n-**ver**-*zh*'n), *noun.*

convertible *adjective*
capable of being converted.
convertible *noun*
a motor car with a roof that can be folded back.

convex *adjective*
curved outwards like the outer surface of a sphere. Compare CONCAVE.
[Latin *convexus* an arch]

convey (*say* k'n-**vay**) *verb*
to carry or communicate: 'can you *convey* this message for me?'.
Word Family: **conveyor, conveyer,** *noun*, a mechanical device for moving objects.

conveyance (*say* k'n-**vay**-ence) *noun*
1. a) the act or means of conveying: 'pamphlets are for the *conveyance* of ideas'. b) anything which carries or conveys, such as a vehicle.
2. *Law:* the transfer of land from one owner to another.

convict (*say* k'n-**vikt**) *verb*
Law: to declare a person guilty of a crime, especially after a trial.
Word Family: **convict** (*say* **kon**-vikt), *noun*, a person declared guilty of a crime, especially if in prison.
[CON- + Latin *victus* conquered]

conviction (*say* k'n-**vik**-sh'n) *noun*
1. a strong belief or opinion: 'it is my *conviction* that the report is not true'.
2. a) the act of convicting. b) the state of being convicted: 'he has had eight *convictions* for burglary'.

convince *verb*
to persuade by argument or evidence.
Word Family: **convincing,** *adjective*; **convincingly,** *adverb.*
[CON- + Latin *vincere* to conquer]

convivial (*say* k'n-**vivvi**-ul) *adjective*
friendly and sociable.
Word Family: **conviviality** (*say* k'n-vivvi-**alli**-tee), *noun.*
[Latin *convivium* a banquet]

convocation (*say* konva-**kay**-sh'n) *noun*
a meeting or assembly, especially one of Anglican clergymen.
Word Family: **convoke** (*say* k'n-**voke**), *verb.*
[CON- + Latin *vocare* to summon]

convoluted (*say* konva-**lootid**) *adjective*
coiled or twisted.
Word Family: **convolute** (*say* **konva**-loot), *verb*; **convolution,** *noun.*
[CON- + Latin *volutare* to roll about]

convolvulus (*say* k'n-**volvew**-lus) *noun*
also called **bindweed**
any of a group of climbing plants, with bell-shaped flowers.

convoy *noun*
a formation of ships, vehicles, etc., often travelling with a protecting escort.
Word Family: **convoy,** *verb.*

convulsion (*say* k'n-**vul**-sh'n) *noun*
1. *Medicine:* a fit.
2. any violent agitation, such as excessive laughter.
Word Family: **convulse,** *verb*, to shake or contort violently; **convulsive,** *adjective*, like or produced by a convulsion.

coo *verb*
(cooed, cooing)
to make a soft, murmuring sound like a pigeon.

cooee *interjection*
a call used as a signal.
[originally used by Australian Aboriginals and later adopted by settlers]

cook (*rhymes with* book) *verb*
to prepare by heating, especially food.
cook up, 'he has *cooked up* a new scheme' (= invented).
cook *noun*
a person who cooks, especially one employed to do so.
Word Family: **cookery**, *noun*, the art or practice of cooking; **cooker**, *noun*, an apparatus for heating or cooking.

cookie *noun*
American: a sweet biscuit.

cool *adjective*
1. moderately cold.
Usage: 'we received a *cool* welcome' (= restrained, unenthusiastic).
2. (*informal*) acceptable or pleasing.
3. (of colour) towards bluish tones.
Word Family: **cool**, *verb*, to make or become cool; **coolly**, *adverb*; **coolness**, *noun*, the state of being cool; **cooler**, *noun*, a) something which makes or keeps cool, b) (informal) a gaol; **cool**, *noun*, (informal) a calm or relaxed self-control.

coolant *noun*
a substance used to remove heat from a primary source such as a reactor core.
Word Family: **coolant**, *adjective*.

coolie *noun*
a hired Asian labourer.

coon *noun*
(*informal*) a raccoon.

coop *noun*
a cage or pen for fowls, etc.
coop *verb*
to confine or shut in.

co-op *noun*
(*informal*) a cooperative.

cooper (*say* koopa) *noun*
a person who makes or repairs barrels, tubs, etc.
Word Family: **cooperage**, *noun*.
[Latin *cupa* cask]

cooperate (*say* ko-oppa-rate)
co-operate *verb*
to work together.
Word Family: **cooperation**, *noun*.
[co- + Latin *operari* to work]

cooperative (*say* ko-opra-tiv)
co-operative *adjective*
helpful or willing to cooperate.

cooperative *noun*
a group of people who cooperate in an activity or business by sharing work, goods, services, etc.

co-opt (*say* ko-opt) *verb*
to elect or appoint to a group by the vote of existing members.

coordinate (*say* ko-ordi-nate)
co-ordinate *verb*
to bring or place parts in proper relation to each other.
Usage: 'the new foreman tried to *coordinate* the various sections of the factory' (= combine harmoniously).
coordinate (*say* ko-ordi-nit) *noun*
Maths: a number that can be used to determine the position of a point, by reference to a set of axes, etc.
coordinate *adjective*
of equal rank or importance.
Word Family: **coordination**, *noun*; **coordinator**, *noun*.
[co- + Latin *ordinis* of an order]

coordinate bond
see DATIVE BOND.

coordinate geometry
see ANALYTICAL GEOMETRY.

coot (*rhymes with* hoot) *noun*
1. any of various swimming birds with short wings and tail.
2. (*informal*) a fool.

cop *noun*
(*informal*) a policeman.
cop *verb*
(copped, copping)
(*informal*) to receive: 'he *copped* a terrible blow on the head'.

cope (1) *verb*
to manage: 'the young mother *coped* very well'.

cope (2) *noun*
a long loose sleeveless cloak worn by Christian priests during processions, etc.

copier (*say* **koppia**) *noun*
Word Family: see COPY.

coping (*say* **ko**-ping) *noun*
the protective top layer of a wall, designed to carry away water.

copious (*say* **ko**-pee-us) *adjective*
plentiful or abundant.
Word Family: **copiously**, *adverb*; **copiousness**, *noun*.
[Latin *copia* plenty]

copper (1) *noun*
1. element number 29, a ductile, malleable metal. It is a good conductor of heat and electricity and is used in alloys. See TRANSITION ELEMENT.

See CHEMICAL ELEMENTS in grey pages.
2. a coin made from or containing copper.
3. a large old-fashioned vessel for boiling clothes.
4. a lustrous, reddish-brown colour.
Word Family: **copper**, *adjective.*
[Latin (*aes*) *Cyprium* Cyprus ore = copper]

copper (2) *noun*
(*informal*) a policeman.

copperplate *noun*
1. a) an etching or engraving done on a flat copper surface. b) a print made from this.
2. an elaborate, precise style of handwriting.

coppersmith *noun*
a person who makes copper articles.

copra *noun*
the dried, white flesh of a coconut, used to make coconut oil.

copse *noun*
also called a **coppice**
a small group or plantation of trees or bushes.

copulation (*say* kop-yoo-**lay**-sh'n) *noun*
1. sexual intercourse.
2. the connecting of things.
Word Family: **copulate**, *verb.*
[Latin *copula* a rope, link]

copy *noun*
1. reproduction: 'please make a *copy* of this letter'.
2. any specimen of a particular book, newspaper, etc.
3. any material to be printed: 'we supplied the *copy* to the printer'.
copy *verb*
(copied, copying)
1. to make a copy of.
2. to imitate.
Word Family: **copier**, *noun*, a person or machine that makes copies.
[Latin *copia* plenty]

copybook *noun*
a book with printed examples of handwriting for learners to copy.
blot one's copybook, to ruin one's reputation or past record.
copybook *adjective*
exactly according to the rules.

copycat *noun*
(*informal*) a person who copies the actions or words of another.

copyright *noun*
the exclusive right to distribute or control something original, such as the publication of a book, the performance of a play, etc.
Word Family: **copyright**, *verb*, to acquire a copyright for.

copywriter *noun*
a person who writes copy for advertisements, etc.

coquette (*say* kokk-**et**) *noun*
a woman who flirts.
Word Family: **coquetry** (*say* **kokki**-tree), *noun*; **coquettish**, *adjective*; **coquettishly**, *adverb.*
[French]

cor-
a variant of the prefix **com-**.

coracle (*say* **korra**-k'l) *noun*
a small oval rowing boat made of animal skins or canvas stretched over a light wooden frame and formerly used in Wales and Ireland.

coral *noun*
1. a coloured, porous substance formed from the skeletons of polyps in tropical waters and often forming reefs. It is used in jewellery, ornaments, etc.
2. a pale, reddish-yellow colour.

cor anglais (*say* kor **on**glay)
also called an **English horn**
Music: a long, thin double-reed wind instrument with a lower pitch than an oboe.
[French *cor* horn + *anglais* English]

corbel *noun*
Architecture: a projection from a wall, especially one to support a beam.

cord *noun*
1. a strong, thick string made by weaving or twisting several strands together.
2. a ribbed fabric, especially corduroy.
3. (*plural*) a pair of corduroy trousers.
[Latin *corda* string]

cordage (*say* **kor**dij) *noun*
Nautical: any ropes and cords.

cordial *adjective*
polite or friendly.
cordial *noun*
an essence made into a drink by adding water.
Word Family: **cordially**, *adverb*, in a cordial manner; **cordiality** (*say* kordi-**alli**-tee), *noun*, a friendly politeness.
[Latin *cordialis* from the heart]

cordillera (*say* kordil-**yaira**) *noun*
a series of almost parallel mountain ranges.
[Spanish]

cordite *noun*
a smokeless explosive prepared from cellulose nitrate and nitroglycerine, used as a propellant for bullets, artillery, etc.

cordon *noun*
1. a line of troops, police, etc. guarding or enclosing an area.
2. a cord, ribbon or sash worn as a badge of honour.
[French, cord]

cordon bleu (*say* kordon **bler**)
of the highest degree of excellence: '*cordon bleu* cookery'.
[French, blue ribbon, being the ribbon formerly worn by the highest order of French knighthood]

corduroy (*say* **kor**da-roy *or* **kord**-y'roy) *noun*
a coarse, thick-ribbed, cotton fabric.

core *noun*
1. the central or essential part: a) 'an apple *core*'; b) 'we must get to the *core* of the problem'.
2. *Geology:* the dense, partly molten, central portion of the earth, beneath the mantle.
3. *Mining:* a cylinder of rock cut out by a drill and used for assays, etc.
Word Family: **core**, *verb*, to remove the core from; **corer**, *noun*, a cylindrical knife used for removing cores from fruit, etc.

co-respondent *noun*
Law: the person with whom the respondent in a divorce case is said to have committed adultery.

corgi *noun*
short form of **Welsh corgi**
either of two breeds of small, short-legged dogs with erect ears, bred as cattle-dogs and watch-dogs.
[Welsh *cor-ci* dwarf dog]

coriander (*say* korri-**an**da) *noun*
a herb, the aromatic leaves and seeds of which are used in cooking and medicine.
[Greek *koriannon*]

coriolis force (*say* korri-**ole**-iss force)
Weather: a force due to the earth's rotation which causes tides and the winds generated by cyclones and lows to circulate anticlockwise in the Northern and clockwise in the Southern Hemisphere.
[after *G. G. Coriolis*, 1792-1843, a French mathematician]

cork *noun*
1. the tough, light bark of a variety of oak found in Mediterranean countries.
2. a piece of this material used as a stopper for a bottle, etc.
Word Family: **cork**, *verb*, to fit with a cork.

corkage (*say* **kor**kij) *noun*
a charge made by a restaurant for opening and serving bottles of wine supplied by the customers.

corkscrew *noun*
a pointed, spiral-shaped piece of metal for extracting the cork from a bottle.

corm *noun*
Biology: the fleshy, enlarged, underground base of a plant's stem, which acts as an organ of vegetative reproduction.

cormorant (*say* **kor**ma-r'nt) *noun*
also called a **shag**
any of various large diving sea-birds with a long neck and a pouch under the beak in which fish are held.
[Old French *corp* raven + *marenc* of the sea]

corn (1) *noun*
1. a general name for the seed of cereal plants, especially wheat (or, in America, maize).
2. a round, hard grain or particle.
3. (*informal*) a) a sentimental style of writing, etc. b) dated, old-fashioned humour.
corn *verb*
to preserve meat in brine: '*corned* beef'.

corn (2) *noun*
a hard area of skin, usually on the foot, caused by continual pressure or rubbing.

corncob *noun*
the middle, woody stem on which the kernels of maize grow.

corncrake *noun*
a bird of skulking, solitary habit, with a loud rasping call; once common in cornfields.

cornea (*say* **kaw**-nee-a) *noun*
the horny membrane which covers the front of the eyeball.
[Latin *cornu* horn]

cornelian, carnelian *noun*
a semi-transparent reddish chalcedony, used in jewellery, etc.

corner *noun*
1. the point at which two edges, surfaces, etc. meet: 'a street *corner*'.

Usages:
a) 'his lies got him into a *corner*' (= difficult situation or position).
b) 'a quiet *corner* of the world' (= region).
2. *Sport:* a free shot taken from a corner of the field in hockey or soccer.
Phrases:
cut corners, to take short cuts, especially in official procedure.
round the corner, very close.
corner *verb*
1. to turn a corner, especially in a vehicle.
2. to get into a difficult or trapped situation: 'the cat finally *cornered* the mouse'.
corner the market, to have enough power or control to regulate price, production, etc.

cornerstone *noun*
a stone built into the corner of walls or foundations.
Usage: 'they claimed democracy to be the *cornerstone* of their society' (= basis, foundation).

cornet *noun*
Music: a brass, wind instrument similar to a small trumpet.

cornflour *noun*
a flour made from finely ground corn, used to thicken sauces, etc.

cornflower *noun*
a small, blue, European flower.
[a wild variety grows among *corn*]

cornice (*say* **korniss**) *noun*
Architecture: a) a moulding between a wall and the ceiling. b) a part of the structure just above a column.

Cornish pasty
pastry containing baked meat, onion, potato and seasoning.

corn plaster
a medicated bandage used to remove the thick skin from a corn.

cornucopia (*say* kornew-**ko**-pee-a) *noun*
any unlimited supply.
[Latin *cornu* horn + *copiae* of plenty, after a magical horn in Greek mythology providing unlimited supplies of food, etc.]

corny *adjective*
(*informal*) a) sickly sentimental. b) dated, old-fashioned. c) weakly humorous.

corolla (*say* ka-**rolla**) *noun*
Biology: all the petals of a flower.
[Latin, garland]

corollary (*say* ka-**rolla**-ree) *noun*
1. a natural consequence or result.
2. *Maths:* an additional theorem, which can be deduced from the theorem just proved.

corona (*say* ka-**ro**-na) *noun*
Astronomy: the white halo around the sun, which is only seen during a total eclipse.
[Latin, crown]

coronary (*say* **korr**en-ree) *adjective*
relating to the heart or the arteries which supply blood to it.

coronary occlusion
see HEART ATTACK.

coronation (*say* korra-**nay**-sh'n) *noun*
the ceremony of crowning a king or queen.

coroner (*say* **korr**a-na) *noun*
an official appointed by the government to make enquiries into any death that was not clearly due to natural causes.
[Middle English *corouner* officer of the crown]

coronet (*say* korra-**net**) *noun*
a) a small crown worn by a peer or peeress. b) a garland or ribbon of precious materials worn by women as part of a headdress.

corporal (1) *adjective*
of or relating to the body.
Word Family: **corporally,** *adverb*; **corporality** (*say* korpa-**ralli**-tee), *noun.*
[Latin *corporis* of the body]

corporal (2) *noun*
a non-commissioned officer in the armed forces, ranking below a sergeant.

corporal punishment
any physical punishment, especially whipping or flogging.

corporate (*say* **korpa**-rit) *adjective*
united.
Word Family: **corporately,** *adverb.*

corporation (*say* korpa-**ray**-sh'n) *noun*
an association of persons regarded in law as a single person, and formed to administer a city, public service, etc.

corporeal (*say* kor-**paw**riul) *adjective*
of or relating to physical matter, especially the body.

corps (*say* kor) *noun*
plural is **corps** (*say* korz)
1. *Military:* a wartime army unit consisting of several divisions.

2. any organized group: 'the diplomatic *corps*'.
[French, body]

corpse *noun*
a dead body, usually of a human being.

corpulent (*say* **kor**–pew–l'nt) *adjective*
fat or stout.
Word Family: **corpulence,** *noun.*

corpus (*say* **korpus**) *noun*
a large collection of something, especially all the writings of one author.
[Latin, body]

corpuscle (*say* **kor**–puss'l) *noun*
1. *Biology:* a blood cell.
2. any small particle.
Word Family: **corpuscular** (*say* kor–**puss**–kew–la), *adjective.*
[Latin *corpusculum* little body]

corral (*say* ka–**rahl**) *noun*
an enclosed area for horses, cattle, etc.
Word Family: **corral** (**corralled, corralling**), *verb,* to enclose in a corral.
[Spanish]

correct *adjective*
1. free from error.
2. in accordance with accepted standards: 'his behaviour is very *correct*'.
correct *verb*
to make right or free of error.
Usages:
a) 'please *correct* my essay' (= point out the errors in).
b) 'I shall *correct* him if it happens again' (= rebuke).
c) 'he *corrected* the number to three decimal places' (= adjusted, altered).
Word Family: **correctly,** *adverb*; **correctness,** *noun,* the state of being correct; **correction,** *noun,* a) the act of correcting, b) an indication or alteration marked when correcting; **correctional, corrective,** *adjectives*; **corrective,** *noun,* something intended to correct.
[Latin *correctus* put straight]

correlate (*say* **korra**–late) *verb*
to have or bring into relation.
Word Family: **correlation,** *noun,* correct relation; **correlative** (*say* ka–**rella**–tiv) *adjective.*

correspond (*say* korri–**spond**) *verb*
1. to be in agreement: 'his actions do not *correspond* with his ideas'.
2. to communicate by writing letters.
3. to be similar to: 'the British House of Commons *corresponds* to the Australian House of Representatives'.
Word Family: **correspondent,** *noun,* a) a person who communicates by letters, b) a person employed by a newspaper, etc. to report regularly from another place or on a particular subject; **correspondingly,** *adverb,* in agreement.

correspondence
(*say* korri–**spon**–d'nce) *noun*
1. the fact of corresponding or agreeing.
2. a) the act of communicating by exchanging letters. b) letters exchanged between people.

corridor *noun*
1. a passage linking several rooms on one floor of a building.
2. any similar passage or narrow strip: 'an air *corridor*'.

corrie *noun*
also called a **cirque**
a hollow in the side of a hill or mountain, often containing a lake.
[Gaelic *coire* cauldron]

corrigenda (*say* korri–**jenda**) *plural noun*
singular is **corrigendum**
see ERRATA.

corroborate (*say* ka–**robba**–rate) *verb*
to confirm or support evidence, stories, etc.
Word Family: **corroboration,** *noun*; **corroborative** (*say* ka–**robbera**–tiv), *adjective,* providing confirmation.
[COR– + Latin *roboris* of strength]

corroboree (*say* ka–**robba**–ree) *noun*
a) a festive gathering of Aboriginals, often held at night. b) the tribal dance or dances performed at such a gathering.
[Aboriginal]

corrode (*say* ka–**rode**) *verb*
to eat away gradually, especially the surface of a metal by chemical action.
Usage: 'fears and guilt *corroded* his self-confidence' (= lessened).
Word Family: **corrosive,** *adjective,* capable of corroding; **corrosion** (*say* ka–**ro**–*zh*'n), *noun.*
[COR– + Latin *rodere* to gnaw]

corrugated iron
a sheet of iron or steel, usually galvanized, strengthened by parallel ridges or ripples and used on roofs, etc.

corrugation (*say* korra–**gay**–sh'n) *noun*
a ridge or furrow, e.g. on the surface of a road.

Word Family: **corrugate** (*say* **korra**–gate), *verb*, to bend or form into furrows.
[Latin *corrugatus* wrinkled]

corrupt (*say* ka–**rupt**) *adjective*
dishonest, evil or no longer innocent.
Word Family: **corrupt**, *verb*, to destroy the innocence or integrity of; **corruptly**, *adverb*; **corruption**, *noun*.
[Latin *corruptus* broken in pieces]

corsage (*say* kor–**sah*zh***) *noun*
a very small bouquet of flowers to be pinned to a dress.
[French]

corsair *noun*
a) a North African pirate. b) a fast ship used by such pirates.

corset *noun*
also called a **girdle**
a stiffened, but elastic, piece of underwear, worn to shape or support the waist, abdomen or upper legs, especially by women.
Word Family: **corsetry** (*say* **kor**sa–tree), *noun*, a) any or all corsets, b) the process of making corsets.
[Old French, little body]

cortège (*say* kor–**tay*zh***) *noun*
1. a procession, especially at a funeral.
2. any attendants: 'the king and his *cortège* arrived'.

cortex *noun*
plural is **cortices**
an outer layer, such as the bark of a tree.
Word Family: **cortical**, *adjective*, of or like a cortex.
[Latin, bark]

corticosteroid (*say* kortiko–**sterroid**) *noun*
Biology: any of the fat-soluble hormones made by the cortex of the adrenal glands.

cortisone (*say* **korti**–zone) *noun*
a hormone secreted by the adrenal glands and having many functions, including the reduction of local inflammation.

corundum (*say* k'**run**–dum) *noun*
Geology: a very hard mineral (formula Al_2O_3), used as a gem and as an abrasive. See RUBY and SAPPHIRE.
[Tamil, ruby]

corvette *noun*
Nautical: a small, fast vessel used to escort convoys, etc.

cos (1) *noun*
a type of lettuce with oblong, crisp leaves.
[first grown on *Cos*, a Greek island]

cos (2) *noun*
see COSINE.

cosecant (*say* ko–**see**–k'nt) *noun*
short form is **cosec**
Maths: the reciprocal of sine. See TRIGONOMETRIC FUNCTIONS.

cosh *noun*
a heavy, usually flexible, weapon.
Word Family: **cosh**, *verb*, to hit with a cosh, especially on the head.

cosine (*say* **ko**–sine) *noun*
short form is **cos**
Maths: the ratio of the length of the adjacent side of an angle to the length of the hypotenuse of a right-angled triangle. See TRIGONOMETRIC FUNCTIONS.

cosmetic (*say* koz–**mettik**) *noun*
any product used to beautify or clean a part of the body, especially the face.
Word Family: **cosmetician** (*say* kozma–**tish**un), *noun*, an expert in the preparation or use of cosmetics.

cosmic *adjective*
relating to the cosmos: '*cosmic* travel'.
cosmic rays
Astronomy: the high-energy radiation, consisting mainly of protons, electrons and alpha particles, which falls on the earth.

cosmogony (*say* koz–**moja**–nee) *noun*
any theory of the origins of the universe.

cosmology (*say* koz–**molla**–jee) *noun*
the study of the nature, composition, origin and history of the universe.
Word Family: **cosmological** (*say* kozma–**loji**–k'l), **cosmologic**, *adjective*; **cosmologist**, *noun*.

cosmonaut (*say* **kozma**–nawt) *noun*
an astronaut.
[COSMOS + Greek *nautes* sailor]

cosmopolitan (*say* kozma–**pollitan**) *adjective*
1. of or relating to all parts of the world: 'the World Trade Fair was a *cosmopolitan* event'.
2. being at home in all parts of the world and free from regional or national prejudices: 'much international travelling has given him a *cosmopolitan* outlook'.
Word Family: **cosmopolite** (*say* koz–**moppa**–lite), **cosmopolitan**, *nouns*,

a person who is cosmopolitan; **cosmopolitanism**, *noun.*
[COSMOS + Greek *polites* citizen]

cosmos *noun*
the whole universe, seen as an organized system.
[Greek *kosmos* order, the world]

Cossack *noun*
any of a people of southern Russia, famous as horsemen and dancers.

cosset *verb*
to pamper or treat as a pet.

cost *noun*
1. any amount which is given or required as payment: 'the *cost* of building a house has increased greatly'.
Usage: 'the battle was won at the *cost* of many lives' (= loss).
2. *Law:* (*plural*) the sum of money awarded by a court to pay lawyers' fees and other expenses.
cost *verb*
1. to require the payment of: a) 'it *cost* £4'; b) 'his foolishness *cost* him his life'.
2. to estimate the price of.

costal *adjective*
of the ribs or the side of the body: 'the *costal* vertebrae are joined to the ribs'.
[Latin *costa* rib]

co-star *verb*
(co-starred, co-starring)
(of one actor or performer) to share equal status with another in a play, film, etc.
Word Family: **co-star**, *noun.*

costermonger *noun*
short form is **coster**
a Cockney street vendor, especially one selling fruit and vegetables from a stall or barrow.
[from old words *costard* a kind of apple + *monger* a trader]

costive *adjective*
suffering from constipation.

costly *adjective*
having a high cost or price: 'avocados are very *costly* out of season'.
Word Family: **costliness**, *noun.*

cost of living
the cost of the necessities of life for a person or family, based on average prices of food, shelter, clothing, etc.

cost price
the amount paid by a manufacturer or merchant for something he intends to sell.

costume *noun*
the style of dress, etc. which is characteristic of or suitable for a particular time or place: a) 'the actors all wore peasant *costumes* for the play'; b) 'she had her swimming *costume* in her bag'.
costume *verb*
to provide a costume or costumes for: 'the local historical society will *costume* the play'.

costume jewellery
any decorative but inexpensive jewellery, such as paste or imitation gems.

cosy (*say* **ko**-zee) *adjective*
warm and comfortable: 'it's a *cosy* room in winter'.
cosy *noun*
a padded cover for a teapot, etc. to keep it warm.
Word Family: **cosily**, *adverb*; **cosiness**, *noun.*

cot *noun*
a small bed with enclosed sides, especially for a child.

cotangent (*say* ko-**tan**-j'nt) *noun*
short form is **cot**
Maths: the reciprocal of tangent. See TRIGONOMETRIC FUNCTIONS.

cote *noun*
a cage or shelter for birds or animals: 'a *dovecote*'.

coterie (*say* **kote**-a-ree) *noun*
a close, exclusive group of people: 'the local boys formed a *coterie* within the school'.
[French]

cottage (*say* **kottij**) *noun*
a small simple rural house, usually old.
cottage industry
any industry which can be done at home, such as pottery, weaving, etc.

cottage cheese
a soft, white crumbly cheese made of milk curd.

cottager (*say* **kotti**-ja) *noun*
1. *History:* a peasant holding a cottage and small piece of land belonging to a larger farm, in exchange for labour.
2. *American:* a person who owns a house at a holiday resort.

cotter pin
a device, such as a wedge or pin, which is fitted into a hole to fasten parts together.

cotton *noun*
1. the soft, white fibres around the seeds of an annual plant, used for making cloth, etc.
2. a fine thread spun from cotton yarn: 'a reel of white *cotton*'. In America called **thread**.
3. a yarn or fabric made from cotton.
cotton *verb*
cotton on, 'nobody has *cottoned on* to the mistake yet' (= noticed, realized, understood).
[from Arabic *kutn*]

cotton gin
a machine which separates the cotton fibres from the seeds.

cottonwool *noun*
in America called **cotton**
the raw cotton with its wax removed, used for surgical dressings, etc.

cotyledon (*say* kotta-**lee**-d'n) *noun*
also called a **seed leaf**
Biology: the first leaf of an embryo of a plant.
[Greek *kotyledon* a cup-shaped hollow]

couch (*say* kowch) *noun*
a) a sofa. b) a flat bed with a headrest, used by doctors for patients.
couch *verb*
to express or put into words: 'can you *couch* your question more simply?'.

couch-grass (*say* **kooch** grass) *noun*
a tough, coarse grass with long, creeping roots.

cough (*say* koff) *verb*
to eject air forcibly from the lungs with a loud, harsh sound.
cough up, (*informal*) 'the bank has not *coughed up* the loan' (=given).
Word Family: **cough**, *noun*, the act or sound of coughing.

could (*rhymes with* good) *verb*
1. the past tense of the auxiliary verb **can (1)**.
2. used instead of **can** as a polite form: '*could* you help me?'.
Usage: 'it *could* be true' (= might).

coulomb (*say* **koo**lom) *noun*
the SI unit of electric charge, equal to the quantity of electricity moved in one second by an electric current of one ampere. See UNITS in grey pages.
[after *C.A. Coulomb*, 1736–1806, a French physicist]

coulter (*say* **kole**-ter) *noun*
a sharp blade attached to a plough, to cut the earth in front of the share.

council (*say* **kown**-s'l) *noun*
a group of people appointed or elected to meet regularly for discussion, making decisions, etc.: 'the city *council*'.
Word Family: **councillor,** *noun*, a member of a council.
[Latin *concilium* an assembly]

counsel (*say* **kown**-s'l) *noun*
1. any advice, opinion or exchange of views.
2. *Law:* a barrister or barristers, representing a client in court.
keep one's own counsel, 'you must *keep your own counsel* about family matters' (=keep your views, etc. secret).
Word Family: **counsel (counselled, counselling)**, *verb*.
[Latin *consilium* a consultation]

counsellor (*say* **kown**-s'la) *noun*
1. an adviser.
2. *American:* a lawyer, especially a barrister.

count (1) *verb*
1. to list or name numbers, things, etc., usually in order: 'can you *count* to 100?'.
Usages:
a) 'they are *counting* the votes now' (= finding the total number of).
b) 'there are 300 people in the town, not *counting* babies' (= including).
c) '*count* yourself lucky that you weren't hurt' (= consider).
d) 'you can *count* on Peter to eat all the cakes' (= expect, rely).
e) 'every effort will *count* in this game' (= be important).
2. *Boxing:* to count out ten seconds to a knocked down boxer who must rise before the last number or lose the contest.
count for, 'his opinion *counts for* little in this house' (= is worth).
count *noun*
1. the act of counting: 'who will take a *count* of hands?'.
2. the number arrived at by counting: 'what was the final *count*?'.
3. *Law:* any of the separate charges in an accusation: 'you are charged with two *counts* of robbery'.
take count, 'he *takes* little *count* of what people look like' (= notices).

count (2) *noun*
a nobleman in certain European countries, such as France.
Word Family: **countess,** *noun*, a) a female count, b) the wife of a count.
[Latin *comitis* of a companion]

countdown *noun*
the final preparation for an event, especially firing a missile, launching a rocket, etc. The time of firing is taken as zero and the time (days, hours, minutes and seconds) is counted backwards to it.

countenance (*say* **kown**ti–nance) *noun*
the face, especially its appearance or expression: 'his fierce *countenance* hides a gentle nature'.
out of countenance, 'he was put *out of countenance* by her bitter attack' (= disconcerted, embarrassed).
countenance *verb*
to support or approve: 'the committee will not *countenance* the plan'.

counter (1) *noun*
1. a table or similar structure at which business is done or goods are displayed and served in a shop, etc.
2. a small piece of wood, plastic or metal, often an imitation coin, used to keep count or scores in games.
under the counter, 'much of his business was carried on *under the counter*' (= secretly, dishonestly).

counter (2) *adverb*
in opposition or the opposite direction: 'the result went *counter* to his hopes'.
counter *verb*
to meet or oppose in response: 'the boxer *countered* his opponent's blow with a strong punch'.

counter–
a prefix meaning opposite or in reply to, as in *counteract.*
[Latin *contra*]

counteract *verb*
also called to **countervail**
to act against something and reduce its effectiveness: 'antibodies are developed in the body to *counteract* bacteria'.

counterattack *noun*
an attack made in reply to another.
Word Family: **counterattack,** *verb.*

counterbalance *verb*
to weigh or act against with equal strength: 'the company's lowered prices were *counterbalanced* by a general increase in sales'.
Word Family: **counterbalance,** *noun.*

countercharge *noun*
also called a **counterclaim**
a claim or charge made by an accused person in reply to another: 'the demonstrator made a *countercharge* of brutality by the police'.

counterclockwise *adjective, adverb*
anticlockwise.

counterespionage *noun*
the spying by one government or institution on the spies of another.

counterfeit (*say* **kown**ta–fit *or* **kown**ta–feet) *adjective*
1. made in imitation or as a forgery: '*counterfeit* money'.
2. false or insincere.
Word Family: **counterfeit,** *verb*; **counterfeiter,** *noun.*
[CONTRA + French *fait* made]

counterfoil *noun*
Commerce: see STUB.

counterintelligence *noun*
a government organization which works to prevent the discovery of valuable information by the enemy, collects political information, etc.

countermand (*say* kownta–**mahnd**) *verb*
to cancel a command or instruction already given: 'the captain's order was later *countermanded* by one from headquarters'.

countermine *verb*
to plot against or frustrate: 'the bankrobbers had a second plan which would *countermine* any police attempts to capture them'.

counterpane *noun*
a bedspread or quilt.

counterpart *noun*
something which resembles or is the matching pair of another: 'his job is unique and has no *counterpart* in any other profession'.

counterpoint *noun*
Music: the playing of two or more melodies together, in harmony.

counterpoise *noun*
also called a **counterweight**
1. a weight used to balance another weight, as on a scale or steelyard.
2. a) anything which balances equally with another. b) the state of being equally balanced.
Word Family: **counterpoise,** *verb.*
[COUNTER– + French *poids* weight]

countersign *verb*
to add another signature to a document so that it is accepted as authentic.
countersign *noun*
a sign, especially a password given in reply to another.
Word Family: **countersignature,** *noun.*

countertenor *noun*
Music: a) the highest adult male singing voice. b) any instrument having this range.

countervail *verb*
to counteract.

counterweight (*say* **kow**nta-wate) *noun*
a counterpoise.
Word Family: **counterweigh**, *verb.*

countess *noun*
Word Family: see COUNT (2).

countless *adjective*
being too many or unable to be counted.

countrified (*say* **kun**tri-fide) *adjective*
characteristic of country life.

country (*say* **kun**-tree) *noun*
1. a) the defined area of land occupied by a particular nation and under one government: 'the *countries* of Europe'. b) all the people of a particular country: 'the *country* has voted against the government'.
2. any land outside cities or towns.
3. any particular district or area: 'this is certainly very desolate *country*'.

country-and-western *noun*
a form of music consisting of popularized rural ballads, etc.

country cousin
an unsophisticated person who is unused to city life.

country house, country seat
a large house in spacious grounds and rural surroundings (originally in distinction from the owner's town house in London).

countryside *noun*
a particular area in the country: 'the farm is set amongst densely wooded *countryside*'.

county *noun*
also called a **shire**
a geographical division of the kingdom for administrative and judicial purposes, but often having a historic basis, with a two-tier administrative structure of county council and district or borough councils.

county court
Law: a local court which sits at intervals to deal with civil cases.

coup (*say* koo) *noun*
plural is **coups** (*say* koo *or* kooz)
1. an unexpected or clever victory: 'the wage rise was a *coup* for the unions'.
2. *Politics:* a coup d'état.
[French, blow]

coup de grâce (*say* koo de **grahs**)
a deciding or finishing stroke: 'that last quotation was the *coup de grâce* of the whole argument'.
[French, blow of grace]

coup d'état (*say* koo day **tah**)
plural is **coups d'état**
Politics: a sudden, often violent action or revolt, usually to overthrow a government.
[French, blow of state]

coupé (*say* **koo**pay *or* koop) **coupe** *noun*
an enclosed motor car with two doors.

couple (*say* **kupp**'l) *noun*
1. two things or people together: 'a married *couple*'.
2. *Physics:* the effect of two forces which pull in opposite directions, tending to cause a rotation. Compare TORQUE.

couple *verb*
to join: 'the train carriages were *coupled* by heavy metal links'.
[Latin *copula* a link]

couplet (*say* **kup**lit) *noun*
Poetry: a pair of rhyming lines.

coupling (*say* **kup**ling) *noun*
also called a **coupler**
any of various devices which connects parts or things, such as a connection between two electrical circuits which transfers current from one to the other.

coupon (*say* **koo**pon) *noun*
a detachable form or ticket used for entering competitions, entitling the holder to receive something in exchange, etc.
[French, a piece cut off]

courage (*say* **kurr**ij) *noun*
the ability to control fear when facing danger, pain or the unknown: 'his family's support gave him *courage* to face his long illness'.
have the courage of one's convictions, to act according to one's beliefs.
Word Family: **courageous** (*say* ka-**ray**jus), *adjective,* having courage; **courageously**, *adverb.*

courgette (*say* koor-**zhet**) *noun*
also called a **zucchini**
a small edible marrow with a dark green skin and pale flesh.

courier (*say* **koo**ria) *noun*
a person appointed to carry messages or do other jobs.
[Latin *currere* to run]

course (*rhymes with* horse) *noun*
1. the path or direction taken by anything: a) 'the ship changed its *course* to avoid the storm'; b) 'what will be your next *course* of action?'.
2. the particular area on which a game, etc. is played: 'a golf *course*'.
3. the normal order of movement or progress: 'during the *course* of the discussion the truth became obvious'.
4. any of the separate parts of a meal: 'I'll have soup for my first *course*'.
5. an organized series, especially of lessons: 'we are taking a *course* of Italian lessons'.
6. *Building:* a complete layer of bricks or stones in a wall.
Phrases:
as a matter of course, 'he will inherit the money *as a matter of course*' (= as a natural right).
in due course, 'dinner will be ready *in due course*' (= at the appropriate time).
of course, '*of course* we will help you!' (= naturally, certainly).
course *verb*
1. to run: 'tears of rage *coursed* down her face'.
2. to hunt or pursue, especially game.
[Latin *cursus* running, direction, flow]

court (*say* kort) *noun*
1. an open area surrounded by walls or buildings.
2. *Sport:* a level area marked with lines, for playing certain sports: 'a tennis *court*'.
3. a short street or alley.
4. *Law:* a) a place where cases are heard. b) the judges or magistrates who sit in that place: 'the *court* will retire to consider its verdict'.
5. a) the official residence of a monarch. b) the people who live or work there.
Phrases:
out of court, 'his suggestion was ruled *out of court*' (= unworthy of being considered).
pay court, to seek the favour of.
court *verb*
1. to pursue or seek the affections of: 'she *courted* him for 3 years'.
2. to provoke: 'don't *court* trouble by answering back'.
[Latin *cohors* a courtyard, an escort]

court card
a jack, queen or king in a pack of playing cards.

courteous (*say* **ker**tius) *adjective*
polite and well-mannered: 'he is always *courteous* to old ladies'.
Word Family: **courteously**, *adverb.*

courtesan (*say* **kor**ti-zan) *noun*
a prostitute, especially one to men of wealth or high rank.

courtesy (*say* **ker**ti-see) *noun*
any courteous behaviour or act: 'the guards saluted in *courtesy* to the Queen'.

courtier (*say* **kor**tia) *noun*
an attendant in a royal court.

courtly (*say* **kort**-lee) *adjective*
1. gracious or elegant: 'he gave a *courtly* bow'.
2. of or relating to the court of a monarch or ruler.
Word Family: **courtliness**, *noun.*

court martial (*say* kort **marsh**'l)
plural is **court martials** or **courts martial**
a) the trial of a member of the armed forces by his officers, for an offence against military law. b) the tribunal of officers brought together for such a trial.
Word Family: **court-martial** (**court-martialled, court-martialling**), *verb.*

courtship *noun*
the act or time of courting.

courtyard *noun*
an open area enclosed by buildings or walls and usually paved, often at the front of a large house or the back of an inn.

cousin (*say* **kuzz**'n) *noun*
the child of one's aunt or uncle. Also called a **first cousin.**
a **first cousin once removed** is the child of one's first cousin.
the children of two first cousins are **second cousins** to each other.

couture (*say* koo-**tewer**) *noun*
the business of designing and making clothes.
[French *coudre* to sew]

couturier (*say* koo-**too**ria) *noun*
a person who designs, makes or sells fashionable clothes.

covalency, covalence
(*say* ko-**vay**len-see *and* ko-**vay**-l'nce) *noun*
Chemistry: a) the phenomenon by which two or more atoms share electrons, this sharing process holding the component atoms together in a single molecule. b) the number of

electrons available for sharing in this way. *Example*: carbon has a covalency of four.

covalent bond
Chemistry: a bond between atoms formed by the sharing of a pair of electrons, usually occurring in organic compounds. Compare IONIC BOND and DATIVE BOND.

cove (1) *noun*
Geography: a small bay or inlet.

cove (2) *noun*
(*informal*) a fellow: 'he's a strange-looking *cove*'.

coven (*say* **kuvv**'n) *noun*
a group or meeting of witches.

covenant (*say* **kuvva**-nant) *noun*
a formal agreement or contract.

cover (*say* **kuvva**) *verb*
1. to place something over or around another: '*cover* the cake with chopped nuts'.
2. to report an event for a newspaper, radio or television programme, etc.: 'the American election will be *covered* by our New York political correspondent'.
Usages:
a) 'are you *covered* against fire damage?' (= insured).
b) 'the law does not *cover* that offence' (= deal with).
c) 'will £30 *cover* the cost of the trip?' (= be enough for, provide for).
d) '*cover* the front gate while we go round the back' (= protect, guard).
e) 'the farm *covers* the entire hill' (= occupies).
f) 'she was *covered* with confusion' (= overcome).
g) 'we *covered* nearly 30 km today' (= travelled).
cover *noun*
1. anything which covers or provides protection: 'this book has a hard *cover*'.
Usages:
a) 'the players ran for *cover* as the rain started' (= shelter).
b) 'have they any *cover* for the loss of the car?' (= insurance).
2. an envelope on which postage stamps are stuck: 'a first-day *cover* contains a newly issued stamp'.
Word Family: **covering,** *noun*, something which covers.

coverage (*say* **kuvva**-rij) *noun*
the extent to which something is covered.
Usage: 'there will be extensive radio *coverage* of the event' (= reporting, descriptions).

cover charge
a fixed, additional charge made by a restaurant, etc. for certain services.

covering letter
a letter which accompanies something and explains or recommends it.

coverlet *noun*
a bedspread.

covert (*say* **kuvvert**) *adjective*
disguised or secretive: 'the guilty pair exchanged *covert* glances'.
covert *noun*
an area of thick undergrowth which gives shelter to animals, etc.

covet (*say* **kuvvit**) *verb*
to want something enviously or eagerly, especially something belonging to someone else.
covetous *adjective*
being full of eager or envious desire: 'his *covetous* concern for possessions was disliked by many people'.
Word Family: **covetously,** *adverb*; **covetousness,** *noun.*

covey (*say* **kuvvi**) *noun*
1. a hatch or flock of game-birds, especially partridge.
2. a group of people.

cow (1) *noun*
a) any female bovine mammal that has calved, especially of beef or dairy cattle. b) the female of various mammals, especially the elephant, whale, etc. Compare BULL (1).

cow (2) *verb*
to frighten or threaten into doing something: 'the child was *cowed* into obedience by his father's violence'.

coward *noun*
a person who lacks courage: 'I'm a complete *coward* about having injections'.
Word Family: **cowardly,** *adjective, adverb*; **cowardice,** *noun.*
[Latin *cauda* tail, referring to a dog with its tail between its legs]

cowboy *noun*
American: a man who works on a cattle ranch.

cowcatcher *noun*
American: a fender across the front of a locomotive, to clear obstacles from the track.

cower *verb*
to shrink or move away in fear: 'the dog *cowered* when he saw his master's stick'.

cowl *noun*
1. a) a long loose robe with a hood, worn by monks. b) the hood of a monk's robe.
2. any hood-shaped covering, such as those used on a chimney to increase the draught.
cowling *noun*
the streamlined covering for an aircraft engine.

cowlick *noun*
a tuft of hair which stands up, especially from the head.

cowpox *noun*
a disease which is transmitted to man by cows and is similar to, but milder than, smallpox.

cowrie (*say* **kow**-ree) *noun*
the shiny shell of a marine mollusc, used as ornaments and formerly as money in Asia and Africa.

cowslip *noun*
a small plant with pale yellow scented flowers.

cox *noun*
short form of **coxswain** (*say* **koks**-wane *or* **koks**'n)
the person who steers a boat, especially in rowing.
Word Family: **cox**, *verb*, to act as a cox.

coxcomb (*say* **koks**-kome) *noun*
a person who is excessively concerned about his appearance.

coy *adjective*
shy or modest, often in an affected way.
Word Family: **coyly**, *adverb*; **coyness**, *noun*.

coyote (*say* **koy**-ote *or* koy-**o**-tee) *noun*
the prairie wolf of western North America.

coypu (*say* **koy**-poo) *noun*
a beaver-like South America mammal, valued for its fur which is called **nutria**. It is now common in the Norfolk Broads, where it does great damage.

cozen (*say* **kuzz**'n) *verb*
to cheat or deceive.

crab (1) *noun*
1. any of a group of crustaceans with a short, flattened body and ten legs, the first two being pincers which can cause painful wounds.
2. *Astrology:* (*capital*) see CANCER.
crab *verb* (**crabbed, crabbing**)
to fish for crabs.

crab (2) *verb* (**crabbed, crabbing**)
to find fault with.

crab-apple *noun*
a small, bitter variety of apple.

crabbed (*say* **krabb**id) *adjective*
1. (of handwriting) bad.
2. bad-tempered.

crabby *adjective*
ill-natured or irritable.

crack *verb*
1. to make a sharp sound: 'to *crack* a whip'.
2. to break without falling into pieces: 'the cup *cracked* when I dropped it'.
Usages:
a) 'he *cracked* the mystery' (= solved).
b) 'let's *crack* a bottle of wine' (= open).
c) 'the speaker *cracked* some terrible jokes' (= told).
d) 'her voice *cracked* with emotion' (= changed sharply in pitch).
Phrases:
crack down, 'the boss *cracked down* on latecomers' (= took severe measures).
crack up, a) (*informal*) to have a mental collapse, b) to collapse or crash.
Word Family: **crack-up**, *noun*.
get cracking, (*informal*) to start an activity.
crack *noun*
1. the act or result of cracking.
2. a slight opening: 'he opened the door a *crack*'.
Usages:
a) 'she rises each day at the *crack* of dawn' (= first light).
b) (*informal*) 'let's have a *crack* at it' (= attempt).

cracker *noun*
1. any firework which explodes.
2. a roll of paper, often containing a gift or motto, which explodes harmlessly when the ends are pulled.
3. a dry or savoury biscuit.

crackers *adjective* (*informal*) crazy.

cracking *adjective*
energetic or quick: 'he walks at a *cracking* pace'.

crackle *verb*
to make a series of small, cracking sounds.

Word Family: **crackle,** *noun.*

crackling *noun*
1. a series of small, cracking sounds.
2. the crisp, browned rind on roast pork.

crackpot *noun*
(*informal*) an eccentric or insane person.

cradle (*say* **kray–d'l**) *noun*
1. a small bed for a baby, usually set on rockers.
2. the place where anything originates or is nurtured: 'the *cradle* of freedom'.
3. any of various structures used as a support, such as the wooden framework supporting a ship in dry dock.
Word Family: **cradle,** *verb,* to hold or protect as if in a cradle.

craft *noun*
1. a trade or art, especially one requiring manual skill.
2. cunning, skill or deceit.
3. a) a boat or aircraft. b) (*used with plural verb*) any or all boats or aircraft.
Word Family: **craftsman,** *noun*; **craftsmanship,** *noun.*

crafty *adjective*
cunning or slyly deceitful.
Word Family: **craftily,** *adverb*; **craftiness,** *noun.*

crag *noun*
a steep, rugged rock.
Word Family: **craggy,** *adjective,* rugged or rough.

cram *verb*
(**crammed, cramming**)
to overfill or squeeze into a space which is too small: 'he *crammed* everything into a suitcase'.
Usage: 'the students were all *cramming* for the exam' (= hastily learning facts).

cramp (1) *noun*
a sudden, uncontrollable contraction of the muscles, especially in the limbs, usually accompanied by severe pain.

cramp (2) *noun*
anything which confines or holds things together, such as a metal bar which holds together bricks, etc.
cramp *verb*
1. to fasten with a cramp.
2. to confine or restrain.
cramp one's style, to hinder or restrict one's efforts.

crampon *noun*
1. a grappling iron.
2. a spiked metal plate worn on the shoe to prevent slipping when mountaineering.

cranberry *noun*
a small, red, acid berry used in jams and sauces.

crane *noun*
1. a large wading bird with long legs.
2. any of various mechanical structures with a long arm for lifting heavy objects.
crane *verb*
to stretch out one's neck.

cranefly *noun*
any of a group of slender insects with long, fragile legs and two long wings.

cranesbill *noun*
any of various kinds of wild geranium, named after their long beak-like carpels.

cranium (*say* **krayni–um**) *noun*
Anatomy: the bony box of the skull enclosing the brain.
Word Family: **cranial,** *adjective,* relating to the skull. [Greek *kranion*]

crank *noun*
1. any of various devices for changing circular motion into motion up and down or backwards and forwards, etc. The simplest form consists of a bar projecting from, or at right angles to, a small wheel.
2. (*informal*) an eccentric person.
crank *verb*
to cause a shaft to move by using a crank.

crankcase *noun*
the heavy metal casing which encloses an engine crankshaft and allied parts.

crankshaft *noun*
the main shaft in an internal combustion engine, which is made to turn by the up-and-down motion of the pistons.

cranky *adjective*
a) bad-tempered. b) eccentric.

cranny *noun*
a small crevice or opening.

crap *noun*
1. (*informal*) faeces.
2. (*informal*) nonsense.
Word Family: crap, *verb,* to defecate.

craps *noun*
American: a gambling game played with two dice.
Word Family: **crapshooter,** *noun,* a person who plays craps.

crash *verb*
1. to come together, break or collapse noisily: 'the cars *crashed* into each other'.
Usage: 'the old firm *crashed* during the slump' (= went bankrupt).
2. (of aircraft) to fall on to land or into the sea.
3. (*informal*) to come uninvited to: 'he *crashed* our party'.
Word Family: **crash,** *noun,* the act or sound of crashing; **crash,** *adjective,* (informal) intensive.

crash-helmet *noun*
a fibreglass or metal cap worn by horseriders, racing drivers, etc., to protect the head in case of accident.

crash-landing *noun*
an emergency landing of an aircraft.
Word Family: **crash-land,** *verb.*

crass *adjective*
gross or stupid: '*crass* ignorance'.
[Latin *crassus* thick]

crate *noun*
a wooden box in which goods are packed for transport, storage, etc.

crater *noun*
a large hole or depression, e.g. in the top of a volcano or resulting from an explosion.
[Greek *krater* mixing-bowl]

cravat (*say* kra-vat) *noun*
a man's scarf worn loosely folded round the neck.

crave *verb*
to desire intensely: 'the reformed smoker still *craved* a cigarette after dinner'.

craven *adjective*
cowardly.
Word Family: **craven,** *noun,* a coward.

crawl *verb*
1. to move the body slowly along the ground, especially on one's hands and knees.
Usages:
a) 'the time *crawled* by' (= moved slowly).
b) 'he *crawls* to the boss in the hope of promotion' (= behaves servilely).
2. to be or feel as if covered with crawling things: 'her flesh *crawled* in horror'.
crawl *noun*
1. the act of crawling.
2. the fastest swimming style, in which there is an alternate overarm movement while the legs scissor-kick.
Word Family: **crawler,** *noun.*

crayfish *noun*
short form is **cray**
in America called a **crawfish**
a freshwater lobster.

crayon *noun*
a stick of coloured wax, chalk, etc. for writing or drawing.

craze *noun*
1. a popular fashion: 'long skirts are the *craze* this year'.
2. a fine crack, especially in a pottery glaze.
craze *verb*
1. to make or become insane.
2. to produce a network of fine cracks, as in glaze on pottery, etc.

crazy (*say* **kray-zee**) *adjective*
insane.
be crazy about, 'he's *crazy about* me' (= madly in love with).
Word Family: **crazily,** *adverb;* **craziness,** *noun.*

crazy paving
ornamental paving composed of irregularly shaped slabs of various colours.

creak *verb*
to make or move with a squeaking or grating sound: 'the door *creaked* as it was opened'.
Word Family: **creak,** *noun;* **creaky,** *adjective.*

cream *noun*
1. the fatty part of milk which rises to the top when the milk is left to stand.
2. any substance with the texture of cream, such as cosmetics, certain desserts, etc.
3. the best part of anything: 'the snob thought he belonged to the *cream* of society'.
4. a yellowish-white colour.
Word Family: **cream,** *verb;* **cream, creamy,** *adjectives.*

creamery *noun*
a place where butter and cheese are made.

cream of tartar
the main ingredient of baking powder and sometimes used with bicarbonate of soda as a raising agent.

crease *noun*
1. a line or mark produced in anything by folding or wrinkling.
2. *Cricket:* a) any of three parallel lines drawn on the pitch near the stumps.
b) the space between these lines,

within which the batsman stands. Also called the **wicket**.
Word Family: **crease,** *verb.*

create (*say* kree-**ate**) *verb*
1. to produce or bring into existence: 'according to the Bible, God *created* the world in seven days'.
2. to make a fuss: 'my father's going to *create* when he hears I've failed my exams'.
creation *noun*
1. a) the act of creating. b) something which is created: 'this dress is one of his latest *creations*'.
2. a) (*capital*) the world or universe, as created by God. b) the original act by which the world or universe came into being: '*creation* myths'.
Word Family: **creative,** *adjective,* having a talent for imaginative creation; **creatively,** *adverb*; **creator,** *noun,* a person or thing that creates; **creativity** (*say* kree-ay-**tivvi**-tee), *noun.*

creature (*say* **kree**cha) *noun*
1. any living thing, especially an animal other than man.
2. (*informal*) a contemptible person: 'what a vicious *creature* he is'.
[Latin *creatura* something created]

creche (*say* kraysh) **crèche** *noun*
a public nursery for young children.

credence (*say* **kree**-d'nce) *noun*
a belief or acceptance: 'I cannot give *credence* to statements like that'.

credentials (*say* kre-**den**-sh'ls) *plural noun*
any letters or documents which prove or affirm the identity, honesty, etc. of a person.

credibility gap
the difference between what is said and what is actually done, especially in politics.

credible *adjective*
able to be believed: 'his story is scarcely *credible*'.
Word Family: **credibility** (*say* kreddi-**billi**-tee), *noun.*

credit *noun*
1. any belief or trust: 'you should not give *credit* to everything you hear'.
2. a confidence in the financial position of a person or group, which entitles them to a loan, etc.
3. a) the amount of money in one's favour in an account. b) a record of this amount entered in an account. Compare DEBIT.
4. (*plural*) the printed acknowledgement of the people who took part in making a film.
5. *Education:* a high pass in an examination. b) an official acceptance of work completed in a particular course.
Phrases:
do one credit, 'your children *do you credit*' (= are a source of honour to you).
to one's credit, a) 'it was *to her credit* that she did not retaliate' (= admirable of her); b) 'the team has six victories *to its credit*' (= acknowledged or recorded to it).
Word Family: **credit,** *verb,* a) to believe, b) to acknowledge or ascribe, c) to give financial credit to; **creditable** (*say* **kredd**ita-b'l), *adjective,* bringing honour or credit; **creditably,** *adverb.*

credit card
a card entitling the holder to goods and services which are charged to his account.

creditor *noun*
a person to whom money is owed. Compare DEBTOR under DEBT.

credo (*say* **kree**-doe *or* **kray**-doe) *noun*
a creed.
[Latin, I believe]

credulous (*say* **kred**-yoo-lus) *adjective*
liable to believe anything, often without sufficient proof.
Word Family: **credulity** (*say* kred-**yooli**-tee), *noun.*

creed *noun*
1. *Christian:* a statement of the main beliefs, usually in a set form.
2. any system of beliefs, opinions, etc.

creek *noun*
a) a short arm of a river. b) a narrow coastal inlet.
up the creek, (*informal*) confused or in a difficult situation.

creel *noun*
a wicker basket, especially one used by anglers for carrying fish.

creep *verb*
(**crept, creeping**)
1. to move or crawl close to the ground: 'a *creeping* plant'.
2. to move slowly, quietly or secretly.
3. to be or feel as if covered with creeping things: 'the sight of the snake made her flesh *creep*'.

creep *noun*
1. the act of creeping.
2. (*plural*) a feeling of something creeping over the skin, as in horror, etc.
3. (*informal*) an unpleasant person.
Word Family: **creeper,** *noun,* a person or thing that creeps, especially a plant which grows on or along a wall or other surface; **creepy,** *adjective,* horrible or frightening.

cremate (*say* kre-**mate**) *verb*
to burn and reduce to ashes, especially a dead body.
Word Family: **cremation,** *noun,* the act of cremating; **crematorium** (*say* kremma-**taw**-rium), *noun,* a place where dead bodies are cremated.

crenellated (*say* **krenni**-lay-tid) *adjective*
having slits or openings, e.g. the battlement on a castle.

Creole (*say* **kree**-ole) *noun*
1. any person of European descent in the West Indies and South America.
2. any person descended from the original French or Spanish settlers of Louisiana in America.
3. a person with mixed blood who is native to these regions.
4. the languages spoken by these people.

creosote (*say* **kree**-a-sote) *noun*
a dark oily liquid containing phenol and cresol, obtained by distilling tar and used for preserving wood.
[Greek *kreas* flesh + *sotor* saviour, because of its antiseptic properties]

crêpe (*say* krape) *noun*
a thin gauzy fabric made from cotton or silk and having a crinkled surface.

crêpe paper
a thin, wrinkled paper.

crept *verb*
the past tense and past participle of the verb **creep.**

crescendo (*say* kre-**shen**-doe) *noun*
a gradual increase in strength or loudness.
[Italian]

crescent (*say* **kress**'nt) *noun*
1. a curved shape or figure whose two ends each taper to a point.
2. something with this shape.
3. a curved street.
[Latin *crescens* increasing]

cresol (*say* **kree**-sol) *noun*
an aromatic, oily liquid obtained from coal tar and used in making plastics, explosives, dyes and as a disinfectant.
[CRE(O)S(OTE) + O(I)L]

cress *noun*
any of various plants related to mustard, with sharp-tasting leaves.

crest *noun*
1. the highest part of something: 'the *crest* of a hill'.
2. *Biology:* a) a growth of hair or feathers on the top of an animal's head. b) a longitudinal ridge in a bone or on an animal's back.
3. a distinguishing design, as on a coat of arms, notepaper, etc.: 'a family *crest*'.
Word Family: **crest,** *verb,* a) to reach the top or highest part of, b) to form into a crest, such as a wave; **crested,** *adjective.*

crestfallen *adjective*
dejected or disheartened.

cretaceous (*say* kre-**tay**-shus) *noun*
1. *Geology:* (*capital*) see MESOZOIC.
2. of or resembling chalk.
[Latin *creta* chalk]

cretinism (*say* **kretti**-nizm) *noun*
a disease due to a lack of hormones produced by the thyroid gland, causing physical and mental changes, especially dwarfism and idiocy.
Word Family: **cretin,** *noun,* a) a person suffering from cretinism, b) (informal) a fool or stupid person; **cretinous,** *adjective.*

cretonne (*say* kre-**tonn**) *noun*
a printed cotton fabric similar to chintz, but heavier and not glazed, used for curtains and loose covers.
[named after *Creton* a Normandy village]

crevasse (*say* kre-**vass**) *noun*
a deep crack, especially in a glacier.
[French, crevice]

crevice (*say* **krevvis**) *noun*
a narrow crack or fissure, e.g. in a wall, rock, etc.

crew (1) *noun*
1. all the people doing a particular job.
2. the personnel of a ship or aircraft: 'the captain and *crew* wish to welcome you aboard'.
3. (*informal*) a group or mob.

crew (2) *verb*
a past tense of the verb **crow (2).**

crew cut
a very short haircut.

crewel *noun*
1. a sewing needle with a large eye.
2. a worsted yarn used for embroidery.

crew-neck *adjective*
(of a jumper or shirt) having a round neck without a collar. Compare POLO-NECK.
Word Family: **crew-neck**, *noun*, a) a crew-neck collar, b) a garment having such a collar.

crib *noun*
1. a baby's cradle.
2. a rack or container in a stable, holding food for horses, cattle, etc.
Word Family: **crib** (**cribbed, cribbing**), *verb*, to copy or cheat.

cribbage (*say* **kribb**ij) *noun*
a card game played by two to four people, in which the aim is to collect pairs, runs, etc.

crick *noun*
a sudden stiffness of the muscles of the neck and back, causing a sharp pain and difficulty in moving.
Word Family: **crick**, *verb*, to develop a crick in.

cricket (1) *noun*
an insect similar to a grasshopper, but usually brown with long filaments at the end of the abdomen.

cricket (2) *noun*
a field game played between two teams of eleven using bats and a ball.
Word Family: **cricketer**, *noun.*

cried *verb*
the past tense and past participle of the verb **cry**.

crier *noun*
History: a town official making public announcements in the streets or a courthouse.

crime *noun*
1. *Law:* any act which is forbidden by law.
2. any foolish or wicked act: 'it would be a *crime* to make this bright child leave school'.
Word Family: **criminal** (*say* **krimmi**-n'l), *noun*, a person who is guilty or convicted of a crime; **criminal**, *adjective*, of, involving or guilty of a crime; **criminally**, *adverb*.
[Latin *crimens* accusation, guilt]

criminology (*say* krimmi-**nolla**-jee) *noun*
the study of crime and criminals.
Word Family: **criminologist**, *noun.*

crimp *verb*
to make wavy or curly.
Word Family: **crimp**, *noun.*

crimson (*say* **krim**-z'n) *noun*
a deep purplish-red colour.
Word Family: **crimson**, *verb*, to become crimson, as when blushing; **crimson**, *adjective.*

cringe (*say* krinj) *verb*
to shrink back or act servilely.
[Old English *cringan* to fall in battle]

crinkle *verb*
to wrinkle.
Word Family: **crinkly**, *adjective*; **crinkle**, *noun.*

crinoline (*say* **krinna**-leen *or* **krinna**-lin) *noun*
1. a coarse stiff horsehair fabric.
2. any of various types of skirt flounced out with hoops or a bustle.
[Latin *crinis* hair + *linum* linen]

cripple *noun*
a person who cannot use one or more limbs, especially the legs.
Word Family: **cripple**, *verb*, to disable.

crisis (*say* **kry**-sis) *noun*
plural is **crises** (*say* **kry**-seez)
a crucial time or turning point in any series of events: 'a political *crisis*'.
[Greek *krisis* decision]

crisp *adjective*
1. firm but easily broken: 'a *crisp* wafer'.
2. brisk, fresh or sharp: a) '*crisp* air'; b) 'a *crisp* manner'.
crisp *noun*
any crisp food, especially a potato crisp.
Word Family: **crisp**, *verb*, to make or become crisp.
[Latin *crispus* curled]

crisscross *adjective*
crossed or having crossed markings.

criterion (*say* kry-**teer**ion) *noun*
plural is **criteria**
a standard on which judgement can be based: 'what is your *criterion* for a good restaurant?'.
[Greek *kriterion* a standard or test]

critic *noun*
1. a person skilled in judging the merits of something: 'an art *critic*'.
2. anyone who points out faults or mistakes: 'he has always been a *critic* of young people's attitudes'.
[Greek *kritikos* capable of judging]

critical *adjective*
1. tending to find fault: 'a *critical* attitude'.

2. of serious or decisive importance: 'it was a *critical* period in his life'.
3. relating to or involving criticism: 'a *critical* analysis'.
4. *Science:* denoting a constant value at which a substance undergoes an abrupt change: 'what is the *critical* temperature at which water changes to ice?'.
Word Family: **critically,** *adverb.*

critical mass
Physics: the minimum amount of fissile material necessary for a chain reaction to take place.

criticize (*say* **kritti**-size) **criticise** *verb*
1. to find faults: 'she's always *criticizing* the way I dress'.
2. to make judgements as to merits and faults.
criticism (*say* **kritti**-sizm) *noun*
1. a) the act of criticizing. b) a judgement: 'that is a valid *criticism*'.
2. the detailed investigation or examination of literary works, etc.: 'historical *criticism*'.

critique (*say* kriteek) *noun*
a critical essay or review: 'the magazine contains a *critique* of the film'.
[French]

croak *verb*
1. to make a low, hoarse sound like a frog.
2. (*informal*) to die.
Word Family: **croaky,** *adjective.*

crochet (*say* **kro**-shay) *noun*
a form of needlework using a needle with a hook at one end which is used to draw successive loops of yarn through preceding ones.
Word Family: **crochet** (**crocheted** (*say* **kro**-shade), **crocheting** (*say* **kro**-shay-ing)), *verb.*
[French, a small hook]

crock (1) *noun*
an earthenware container or jar.

crock (2) *noun*
(*informal*) anything which is old or useless.

crockery *noun*
any earthenware or china objects such as dishes, etc.

crocodile (*say* **krokka**-dile) *noun*
1. any of a group of large, amphibious reptiles with tough, armoured skin, found in tropical regions of Australia, Central America, Africa and elsewhere and growing up to 5·4 m long.
2. a line of people walking in pairs.
[Greek *krokodeilos* a lizard]

crocodile tears
any false tears or sorrow.

crocus (*say* **kro**-kus) *noun*
plural is **crocuses**
1. a small plant with yellow, purple or white flowers growing from a bulb.
2. a deep yellow colour.
[Greek *krokos*]

croft *noun*
Scottish: the smallholding of a tenant farmer.
Word Family: **crofter,** *noun,* such tenant.

croissant (*say* **krwa**-son) *noun*
a flaky bread roll baked in a crescent shape.
[French, crescent]

cromlech (*say* **krom**-lek) *noun*
an old word for a dolmen.
[Welsh, a crooked stone]

crone *noun*
an old woman.

crony (*say* **kro**-nee) *noun*
a close friend.

crook (*rhymes with* book) *noun*
1. any of various curved or hook-shaped sticks: 'a shepherd's *crook*'.
2. (*informal*) a criminal or dishonest person.

crooked (*say* **krook**id) *adjective*
1. bent or twisted: 'they followed a *crooked* path through the forest'.
2. dishonest: 'he runs a *crooked* business'.

croon *verb*
to sing or hum softly: 'she *crooned* the baby to sleep'.
crooner *noun*
(*informal*) a popular singer of sentimental songs.
[Old German *kronen* to groan]

crop *noun*
1. any produce of the soil which is used as food: 'a *crop* of wheat'.
2. any group of things together: 'the loud noise produced a *crop* of protests'.
3. a short haircut.
4. a short riding whip.
5. a) a pouch-like enlargement of the gullet in many birds, through which food passes and where digestion begins. b) a similar organ in some other animals.
crop *verb*
(**cropped, cropping**)
1. to cut off or cut short: 'he *cropped* the dead leaves from the tree'.
2. to yield or produce a crop.

crop up, 'a new problem has just *cropped up*' (= appeared unexpectedly).

crop-dusting *noun*
the spraying of crops with insecticides or fertilizers from low-flying aircraft.
Word Family: **crop-dust**, *verb.*

cropper *noun*
to come a cropper, (*informal*) a) 'his foot slipped and he *came a cropper*' (= fell heavily); b) 'the bad season caused the business to *come a cropper*' (= fail, collapse).

croquet (*say* **kro**-kay *or* **kro**-kee) *noun*
a game played on a lawn between teams of two or four players using mallets to hit balls through small hoops set in the ground.

croquette (*say* kro-**ket**) *noun*
a ball of ground meat or vegetables, usually coated in breadcrumbs and fried.
[French *croquer* to crunch]

crosier (*say* **kro**-zee-a) *noun*
also spelt **crozier**
Christian: the staff carried by a bishop or abbot, shaped like a shepherd's crook.

cross *noun*
plural is **crosses**
1. a mark or sign made by one line intersecting another.
2. a post with another piece of wood across it, on which people were executed in ancient times.
3. (*capital*) a) the cross used to execute Christ. b) the symbol of Christianity.
4. anything which is a combination of the qualities of two or more things: 'the colour is a *cross* between purple and maroon'.
Usage: 'during his short life he had many *crosses* to bear' (= misfortunes).
cross *verb*
1. to go from one side to the other: 'do not *cross* the road at that dangerous corner'.
2. to put a line or cross through: 'we have *crossed* your name off the list'.
3. to meet and pass: 'our letters must have *crossed* in the post'.
4. to crossbreed.
5. to oppose or go against: 'do not *cross* him for he has a terrible temper'.
Phrases:
cross oneself, (*Christian*) to make the sign of the cross over one's breast.
cross one's mind, 'it *crossed my mind* not to tell you' (= came to me as an idea).

cross *adjective*
angry or annoyed: 'don't be *cross* with Ann for breaking the window'.
Word Family: **crossly**, *adverb*; **crossness**, *noun.*

cross-
a prefix meaning: a) going across, as in *crossroad*; b) opposition, as in *cross-purpose*; c) in the shape of a cross, as in *cross-legged.*

crossbow *noun*
a medieval weapon consisting of a short, strong bow mounted at right angles to a stock with a groove, along which a short arrow was fired by a trigger mechanism.

crossbreed *verb*
to produce a hybrid by mating two similar but different types of organisms.
Word Family: **crossbred, crossbreed,** *nouns.*

crosscheck *verb*
to check the accuracy of something by referring to another or other sources.

cross-country *adjective*
not following the main roads: 'a *cross-country* run'.

crosse (*say* kross) *noun*
a long-handled, hooked racket with a net across the hook, used in lacrosse.

cross-examine *verb*
to question a person in detail in order to test the truth of answers already given, especially in a court of law.
Word Family: **cross-examination,** *noun*; **cross-examiner,** *noun,* a person who cross-examines.

cross-eyed *adjective*
having a squint in which one eye turns away from its normal position.

cross-fertilization,
cross-fertilisation *noun*
Biology: the fusion of the female gamete of one individual with the male gamete of another individual of the same species, as in the cross-pollination of flowers. Compare SELF-FERTILIZATION.
Word Family: **cross-fertilize,** *verb.*

cross-fire *noun*
1. *Military:* the meeting of lines of fire from two or more positions.
2. any violent meeting or exchange: 'she got caught in the *cross-fire* of their argument'.

crosshatch (*say* kross-hatch) *verb*
to shade with intersecting parallel lines.

crossing *noun*
a place at which a road, etc. crosses another or may be travelled across: 'the cars lined up at the railway *crossing*'.

cross-legged *adjective*
having one leg placed across the other when sitting.

crossly *adverb*
Word Family: see CROSS.

crosspatch *noun*
(*informal*) a cross or bad-tempered person.

cross-purpose *noun*
be at cross-purposes, 'it's obvious that we *are at cross-purposes*' (= misunderstand each other).

cross-question *verb*
to cross-examine.

cross-reference *noun*
a reference from one part of a book, etc. to another, for extra information.

crossroad *noun*
a road which crosses another.
at the crossroads, at a critical turning point.

cross-section *noun*
1. a) a line or piece made by cutting crosswise through something. b) a drawing, etc. of what something would look like if it had been cut through in this way.
2. a sample taken as a typical example: 'the poll was taken from a *cross-section* of secondary students'.

cross-stitch *noun*
an embroidery stitch resembling a small 'x'.
Word Family: **cross-stitch,** *verb.*

crossword puzzle
a puzzle consisting of a rectangle divided into squares, into which the answers to numbered clues must be fitted horizontally and vertically.

crotch *noun*
any part or place which is forked, as between the legs of the human body.

crotchet *noun*
1. a hook or hook-like part.
2. *Music:* a note with a quarter of the time value of a semibreve. In America called a **quarter-note.**
[French, a small hook]

crotchety (*say* **krotcha**-tee) *adjective*
(*informal*) cross or irritable.

crouch (*rhymes with* ouch) *verb*
to lower the body with the legs bent, as when starting a race.
Word Family: **crouch,** *noun.*

croup (*say* kroop) *noun*
an inflammation and swelling of the larynx, especially in young children, causing breathlessness and a high-pitched cough.
Word Family: **croupy,** *adjective.*

croupier (*say* **kroo**pia) *noun*
a person who collects and pays out money at a gambling table

crouton (*say* **kroo**ton) *noun*
a small cube of fried bread, used in soups.
[French *croûte* crust]

crow (1) (*say* kro) *noun*
any of a family of birds with shiny black feathers and a harsh voice.
as the crow flies, 'the distance is 11 km *as the crow flies*, but 15 km by road' (= in a straight line).

crow (2) (*say* kro) *verb*
(**crowed** or **crew, crowed, crowing**)
1. to make the harsh, loud cry of a crow or rooster.
2. to boast or express glee.

crowbar *noun*
a long metal bar, used as a lever, with one end shaped like a crow's beak.

crowd (*rhymes with* loud) *noun*
1. a large, unorganized group of people: 'a *crowd* gathered around the speaker'.
2. (*informal*) a clique or close set of friends: 'he doesn't see that *crowd* any more'.
crowd *verb*
to come or pack together in a crowd: 'the spectators *crowded* around the players'.

crown *noun*
1. a) an ornamental headdress, especially that worn by a monarch as a symbol of royal power. b) the office or power of a monarch.
2. (*capital*) the central government in a monarchy.
3. a) anything in the shape of a crown. b) the top or highest part of anything: 'the *crown* of his hat was dented'.
4. *Dentistry:* a) the top of a tooth. b) an artificial replacement for it, usually made of gold or porcelain.
5. an old coin equal to 5 shillings.
crown *verb*
1. to give royal authority officially by providing a crown.

2. to reward: 'his efforts were *crowned* by victory'.
3. to complete: 'to *crown* our misery, it started raining'.
4. (*informal*) to hit on the head.
[Latin *corona* a garland]

Crown Court
any of the courts which replaced Assize Courts and Quarter Sessions, presided over by visiting judges or recorders with varying powers in civil or criminal cases.

crown land
any land belonging to the monarch or government of a country.

crown of thorns
a type of starfish covered with long spines. It eats coral polyps, causing the slow destruction of coral reefs.

crown prince
the heir of a monarch.

crow's-foot *noun*
plural is **crow's-feet**
(*plural*) the wrinkles in the skin at the outer corner of the eye.

crow's-nest *noun*
a box or other structure formerly used as a lookout at the top of a mast of a sailing ship.

crozier (*say* **kro**-zee-a) *noun*
Christian: see CROSIER.

crucial (*say* **kroo**-sh'l) *adjective*
being the decisive or most important: 'the *crucial* moments of the game were just after half-time'.
[CRUX]

crucible (*say* **kroo**si-b'l) *noun*
a vessel in which substances are heated or melted, usually made from a hard substance such as porcelain.

crucifix (*say* **kroo**si-fiks) *noun*
1. *Christian:* a model of a cross carrying a figure of Christ.
2. any cross.
[Latin *crucifixus* fixed to a cross]

crucifixion (*say* kroosi-**fik**-sh'n) *noun*
1. the act of crucifying.
2. *Christian:* the putting to death of Christ on the Cross.

cruciform (*say* **kroo**si-form) *adjective*
having the shape of a cross.

crucify (*say* **kroo**si-fie) *verb*
(**crucified, crucifying**)
1. to execute by fastening the body to a cross.
2. to treat severely or cruelly: 'the art exhibition was *crucified* by the critics'.

crude *adjective*
1. natural, as distinct from refined or manufactured: '*crude* sugar'.
Usage: 'the introduction gave a *crude* summary of his theories' (= undeveloped).
2. lacking refinement or elegance: 'his *crude* behaviour at parties shocks many people'.
Word Family: **crudely**, *adverb*; **crudity** (*say* **kroo**di-tee), **crudeness**, *nouns*.
[Latin *crudus* raw, harsh]

crude oil
see PETROLEUM.

cruel (*say* kroo'l) *adjective*
deliberately causing pain or suffering to others.
Usage: 'his *cruel* remarks hurt her deeply' (= distressing, upsetting).
cruelty *noun*
1. the state of being cruel: 'the *cruelty* of their remarks caused her much unhappiness'.
2. a cruel act.
Word Family: **cruelly**, *adverb.*

cruet (*say* **kroo**-it) *noun*
a set of small containers for salt, pepper, vinegar, oil, etc.

cruise (*say* krooz) *verb*
1. to sail or travel from place to place, usually for pleasure.
2. to travel at a moderate speed for efficiency or economy: 'the jet *cruised* above the clouds'.
Word Family: **cruise**, *noun*, a pleasure trip by boat; **cruiser**, *noun*, a) a motor boat, b) a medium-sized warship.

crumb (*say* krum) *noun*
a tiny piece or flake of anything: 'she left only a few *crumbs* of cake on her plate'.
crumb *verb*
1. to coat with crumbs, especially breadcrumbs.
2. to break or separate into crumbs.

crumble (*say* **krum**-b'l) *verb*
to break or fall into pieces: 'she *crumbled* the biscuit between her fingers'.
Usage: 'her hopes *crumbled* as the car drove away' (= collapsed).
crumble *noun*
1. anything which is crumbled.
2. a baked dessert consisting of fruit topped with a mixture of flour, fat and sugar.
Word Family: **crumbly**, *adjective*, easily crumbled.

crummy *adjective*
(*informal*) of very poor quality.

crumpet *noun*
1. a spongy bread-like food usually eaten toasted with butter, etc.
2. (*informal*) a pretty girl.

crumple *verb*
to crush into, or become full of, folds or wrinkles: 'be careful not to *crumple* your dress before we go out'.
crumple up, 'as soon as he left her she *crumpled up*' (= collapsed).
Word Family: **crumple**, *noun*, an uneven fold or wrinkle.

crunch *verb*
to crush or grind noisily: 'their heavy boots *crunched* over the gravel'.
crunch *noun*
1. the act or sound of crunching.
2. (*informal*) a crisis: 'the financial *crunch* will come with the new Budget'.

crusade (*say* kroo-**sade**) *noun*
1. *Medieval history:* (*plural*) any of the military expeditions by Christians between the 11th and the 13th century to recapture the Holy Land (Palestine) from the Moslems.
2. any organized struggle or movement: 'doctors have begun a *crusade* against cigarette smoking'.
Word Family: **crusade**, *verb*; **crusader**, *noun*.
[Spanish *Cruz* the Cross]

crush *verb*
1. to press or squeeze out of shape or into fine fragments: 'he was *crushed* by a falling tree'.
2. to overpower or subdue: 'her pride was *crushed* by the continual criticisms'.
crush *noun*
1. the act of crushing or pressing.
2. a large crowd: 'the *crush* of excited spectators was held back by police'.
3. (*informal*) an infatuation: 'she has a *crush* on her new teacher'.
4. a drink made of crushed fruits.

crust *noun*
1. a hard, outer layer or surface: 'cut the *crusts* off the bread'.
2. *Geology:* the outer layer of the earth, about 35 km thick in continental land masses, but much thinner under the oceans.
Word Family: **crust**, *verb*, to form a crust; **crusty**, *adjective*, a) of or having a crust, b) harsh or irritable.
[Latin *crusta* rind]

crustacean (*say* krus-**tay**-sh'n) *noun*
any of a group of arthropods, including shrimps, crabs, etc., with two pairs of antennae.

crutch *noun*
1. a stick, usually fitted under the armpit and used as an aid in walking.
2. something which supports.
3. the crotch.

crux *noun*
plural is **cruxes**
the most basic or important point: 'the *crux* of the problem'.
[Latin, cross]

cry *verb*
(**cried, crying**)
1. to utter a loud sound or call: 'she *cried* out but I didn't hear'.
2. to shed tears: 'the baby began to *cry* as soon as its mother left'.
cry off, 'you promised to do it and you can't *cry off* now' (= break the promise).
cry *noun*
1. a loud utterance or call: 'nobody heard her *cry* for help'.
2. a general or public demand: 'there is a *cry* for social reform'.
Phrases:
a far cry, 'their house is *a far cry* from what we expected' (= a long way, very different).
in full cry, 'they ran *in full cry* after the ice-cream man' (= in eager pursuit).

crying shame
(*informal*) a great pity.

cryogenics *noun*
a branch of physics which studies phenomena at very low temperatures.
[Greek *kryos* frost + -GEN]

crypt (*say* kript) *noun*
a cellar, especially one under a church and used as a burial place.

cryptic (*say* **krip**tik) *adjective*
having a double meaning, mysterious or secret: 'someone has left a *cryptic* message on my desk'.
Word Family: **cryptically**, *adverb*.
[Greek *kryptos* hidden]

cryptogram *noun*
anything written in cipher.
Word Family: **cryptographer**, *noun*; **cryptographic**, *adjective*; **cryptography**, *noun*.
[Greek *kryptos* hidden + *gramma* letter]

crystal (*say* **kriss**–t'l) *noun*
1. a) a clear mineral or glass similar to quartz. b) an object or objects made from high–quality glass, such as drinking glasses, etc.
2. a substance which has a regular, geometrical form: 'a sugar *crystal*'.
Word Family: **crystalline,** *adjective*, like or containing crystals; **crystalloid,** *adjective*, having the shape or qualities of a crystal.
[Greek *krystallos* ice]

crystal–gazing *noun*
the practice of looking into a crystal ball to try and see events, predict the future, etc.

crystallize (*say* **krista**–lize) **crystallise** *verb*
1. to form into crystals: 'the solution will *crystallize* as it cools'.
2. *Cooking:* to cover with sugar.
3. to become clear and definite: 'a new and better plan *crystallized* in his mind'.
Word Family: **crystallization,** *noun.*

crystal set
the earliest form of radio in which the electric current is controlled by a crystal in contact with a fine wire.

csárdás (*say* **chah**–dash) **czárdás** *noun*
plural is **csárdás**
a) a Hungarian national dance which begins slowly and works up to a frenzied finish. b) the music for such a dance.
[Hungarian *csarda* a tavern]

cub *noun*
1. the young of a wild mammal, especially a lion, wolf, etc.
2. a learner or apprentice: 'a *cub* newspaper reporter'.
3. a member of the junior section of the Scout Association.

cubbyhole *noun*
a small enclosed space or hiding place.

cube (*say* kewb) *noun*
1. a solid or hollow body with six square faces.
2. *Maths:* the third power of a number. *Example*: the **cube** of 2, written 2^3, is $2 \times 2 \times 2 = 8$.
cube *verb*
1. to cut or make into cubes: '*cube* the meat and vegetables before cooking'.
2. *Maths:* to find the cube of.
Word Family: **cuboid** (*say* **kew**–boyd), *adjective*, having the shape of a cube; **cubic,** *adjective*; a) solid or of three dimensions, b) having the shape of a cube, c) (Maths) of the third power or degree.
[Greek *kybos*]

cubicle (*say* **kew**bi–k'l) *noun*
a small, separate compartment.
[Latin *cubiculum* bedchamber]

cubism (*say* **kew**–bizm) *noun*
an art style originating in the early 20th century, aiming to analyse the structure or form of objects by expressing them in geometrical shapes.
Word Family: **cubist,** *noun, adjective.*

cubit *noun*
an old measure equal to the length of the forearm, about 50 cm.
[Latin *cubitum* elbow]

cuckold (*say* **kukk**old) *noun*
the husband of an unfaithful wife.
Word Family: **cuckold,** *verb*, to make a cuckold of.
[Old French *cucu* cuckoo]

cuckoo (*say* **ku**–koo) *noun*
any of various migrating birds which lay their eggs in nests of other birds.

cuckoo–spit *noun*
the protective layer of froth exuded by the larvae of various kinds of plant–sucking insects called froghoppers.

cucumber (*say* **kew**–kumba) *noun*
a long, green–skinned fleshy fruit, used in salads, etc.
[Latin *cucumeris* of a cucumber]

cud *noun*
the partially digested food which a ruminant animal returns to the mouth to chew again.
chew one's cud, 'leave him to *chew his cud* on the problem' (= meditate).

cuddle *verb*
to hold close affectionately: 'the proud father *cuddled* the new baby'.
Word Family: **cuddle,** *noun*; **cuddlesome, cuddly,** *adjectives.*

cudgel (*say* **kud**–j'l) *noun*
a short club used as a weapon.
cudgel *verb*
(cudgelled, cudgelling)
to beat or hit with a cudgel.
cudgel one's brains, 'he *cudgelled his brains* for an answer' (= thought hard).

cue (1) (*say* kew) *noun*
1. *Theatre:* a word or action which is the signal for another actor to present a particular line or action.
2. a hint or guiding suggestion: 'if you're unsure of what to do, take your *cue* from me'.

cue (2) (*say* kew) *noun*
Billiards: a long rod used to hit a ball.

cuff (1) *noun*
a fold or band at the bottom of trousers or a sleeve.
off the cuff, spontaneously or without preparation.
cufflink *noun*
either of a pair of decorative fastenings for shirt cuffs, used in place of a button.

cuff (2) *verb*
to strike with the hand or fist.
Word Family: **cuff**, *noun*.

cuirass (*say* kwi-**rass**) *noun*
a piece of protective armour, especially for the breast and back.

cuisine (*say* kwi**zeen**) *noun*
a particular type of cooking: 'this restaurant specializes in Italian *cuisine*'. [French, kitchen]

cul-de-sac (*say* **kul**-de-sak) *noun*
a road closed at one end and giving access to a group of houses.
[French *cul* bottom + *de sac* of the sack]

culinary (*say* **kullin**-ree) *adjective*
relating to the kitchen, food or cooking. [Latin *culina* kitchen]

cull *verb*
to pick or select.
Word Family: **cull**, *noun*.

cullender *noun* see COLANDER.

culminate (*say* **kul**mi-nate) *verb*
to reach the highest point or climax: 'the argument *culminated* in a fight'.
Word Family: **culmination**, *noun*.
[Latin *culminis* of the top]

culpable (*say* **kul**pa-b'l) *adjective*
deserving blame or punishment: 'the man was accused of *culpable* negligence after the accident'.
Word Family: **culpably**, *adverb*; **culpability** (*say* kulpa-**billi**-tee), *noun*.
[Latin *culpa* blame]

culprit *noun*
a person guilty of a fault or crime.
[CUL(pable) + Old French *prit* ready, meaning the prosecution is ready to prove guilt]

cult *noun*
1. a specific system of beliefs and ceremonies, usually directed towards an object or person believed to have magical or religious significance. Compare SECT.
2. (*informal*) any group of people who hold strong beliefs.
[Latin *cultus* worship]

cultivate (*say* **kul**ti-vate) *verb*
1. to prepare, improve and work land in order to raise crops, cattle, etc.
2. to promote the growth or development of anything: 'he *cultivates* friends that he feels may be useful to him'.
cultivated *adjective*
refined or well-educated: 'a *cultivated* woman'.
Word Family: **cultivation**, *noun*; **cultivator**, *noun*, a) a person who cultivates, b) an implement for loosening soil, etc.
[Latin *cultus* tilled]

cultural (*say* **kul**cher'l) *adjective*
relating to culture or cultivation: 'he has many *cultural* interests'.

culture (*say* kulcher) *noun*
1. the distinctive practices and beliefs of a society.
2. the act or process of cultivating land, animals, etc.
3. a development or improvement of the intellect or behaviour due to education, training or experience.
4. *Biology:* the growing of micro-organisms in or on a medium. A **subculture** is a culture of micro-organisms started from another culture. A **tissue culture** is a culture of animal cells grown in a laboratory.
culture *verb*
1. to cultivate.
2. *Biology:* to grow micro-organisms in or on a medium in a laboratory.
[Latin *cultura* a cultivating]

culvert *noun*
a drain to allow water to pass under a road.

cum *preposition*
combined with: 'this is my bedroom *cum* studio'. [Latin, with]

cumbersome (*say* **kum**ba-sum) *adjective*
also called **cumbrous** (*say* **kum**brus) clumsy or difficult to manage.
Word Family: **cumber**, *verb*, to burden or trouble.

cumin (*say* **kum**min) *noun*
also spelt **cummin**
a small plant, the seeds of which are used in cooking and medicine.

cum laude (*say* kum **law**day)
(of a degree, diploma, etc.) with honour.
[Latin]

cummerbund *noun*
a broad sash worn around the waist, especially on formal occasions.
[Hindi, waist-band]

cumquat (*say* **kum**kwot) *noun*
also spelt **kumquat**
a small orange citrus fruit with a sweet skin and acid flesh.
[Chinese]

cumulative (*say* **kew**-mewla-tiv) *adjective*
increasing by continuous additions.
Word Family: **cumulate**, *verb*, to accumulate.

cumulus (*say* **kew**-mew-lus) *noun*
plural is **cumuli**
a cloud which extends upwards with a rounded top and a flat base.
[Latin, a heap]

cuneiform (*say* **kew**ni-form) *noun*
an early form of writing, consisting of wedge-shaped symbols inscribed on clay or stone.
[Latin *cuneus* wedge + FORM]

cunning *adjective*
cleverly shrewd in getting what one wants, often by deceit.
Word Family: **cunning**, *noun*; **cunningly**, *adverb*.

cunt *noun*
1. (*informal*) the vagina.
2. (*informal*) a stupid, treacherous or otherwise contemptible male.

cup *noun*
1. a small, open container with a handle, usually for drinking.
2. anything shaped like a cup, such as the round tin set into each hole on the golf links.
3. a) an ornamental cup used as a prize. b) a competition with a cup for its prize: 'the America's *Cup* is a famous yacht race'.
4. any of various drinks, usually a mixture of wine, spirits or juices: 'fruit *cup*'.
one's cup of tea, 'those colours are not *my cup of tea*' (= to my taste or liking).
cup *verb*
(cupped, cupping)
to form into the shape of a cup: 'he *cupped* his hand over the match to keep it alight'.

cupboard (*say* **kubb**'d) *noun*
an enclosed series of shelves or drawers for storage, often built into a wall.

Cupid (*say* **kew**pid) *noun*
Roman mythology: the god of love, the son of Venus.
[Latin *cupido* desire, passion]

cupidity (*say* kew-**piddi**-tee) *noun*
a greed for possessions or wealth.

cupola (*say* **kew**pa-la) *noun*
a small dome-shaped roof.
[Italian]

cupric (*say* **kew**prik) *adjective*
Chemistry: of or relating to compounds of copper in which copper has a valency of two.
[Latin (*aes*) *Cyprium* Cyprus ore = copper]

cupronickel (*say* **kew**pro-nikk'l) *noun*
an alloy of copper and nickel used for making silver-coloured coins, such as the 10p piece.

cuprous (*say* **kew**prus) *adjective*
Chemistry: of or relating to compounds of copper in which copper has a valency of one.

cur *noun*
1. a worthless, growling dog.
2. a despicable person.

curable (*say* **kew**ra-b'l) *adjective*
able to be cured.
Word Family: **curability**, *noun*.

curare (*say* kew-**rah**-ree) *noun*
a powerful poison obtained from a South American tree.

curate (*say* **kew**-rit) *noun*
Christian: a newly ordained priest who assists a parish priest.
Word Family: **curacy** (*say* **kew**ra-see), *noun*, the office or position of a curate.

curative (*say* **kew**ra-tiv) *adjective*
of or causing a cure.

curator (*say* kew-**ray**tor) *noun*
a guardian or director: 'the *curator* of a museum'.

curb *noun*
1. anything which restrains or controls: 'increased taxation is intended as a *curb* on inflation'.
2. a strap or chain attached to the ends of a bit and passing under the chin to help control the horse.
3. *American:* a kerb.
curb *verb*
to control or restrain with or as if with a curb.
[Latin *curvare* to bend]

curd *noun*
a) a soft, solid substance obtained by allowing milk to coagulate, used as

a food or in cheese. b) any similar substance: 'bean *curd*'.

curdle *verb*
to coagulate or change into curd.

cure *verb*
1. to restore to health.
Usage: 'has she been *cured* of biting her nails yet?' (= made free of, remedied).
2. to preserve meat or fish by drying, smoking or salting.
cure *noun*
1. anything which cures.
2. the responsibility for the spiritual welfare of others, such as of a parish priest towards his parishioners.
[Latin *cura* care]

curé (*say* **kew**-ray) *noun*
French: a parish priest.

curette (*say* kew-**ret**) *noun*
Medicine: a scoop-shaped instrument used to remove diseased tissue, etc. from a cavity, especially the uterus.
[French, a clearing or cleansing]

curfew *noun*
1. an official instruction that people shall remain indoors after a certain time at night, usually during a war or emergency.
2. *History:* a) the ringing of a bell at a fixed time, especially in medieval Europe, as a signal to cover fires or to regulate the movement of citizens. b) the time at which this bell was rung.
[Old French *cuevrefeu* cover fire]

curia (*say* **kew**ria) *noun*
Roman Catholic: a) the court of the Pope. b) the departments in charge of administration at the palace of the Pope.
[Latin, the senate house]

curie (*say* **kew**-ree) *noun*
the metric unit of radioactivity.
[after *Marie Curie,* 1867–1934, a Polish-French physicist and chemist]

curio (*say* **kew**rio) *noun*
any collectable object considered to be interesting or unusual.
[short form of CURIOSITY]

curious (*say* **kew**ri-us) *adjective*
1. eager or interested to know and learn.
2. unusual, strange or interesting: 'what a *curious* bracelet'.
Word Family: **curiously,** *adverb*; **curiosity,** *noun,* a) the state of being curious, b) something unusual or strange.
[Latin *curius* inquisitive]

curium (*say* **kew**-ree-um) *noun*
element number 96, a man-made, radioactive metal. See TRANSURANIC ELEMENT and ACTINIDE.
See CHEMICAL ELEMENTS in grey pages.

curl *verb*
1. to form into a curve, ring or spiral.
2. to play at curling.
curl one's lip, to sneer.
curl *noun*
anything in the shape of a curve, spiral or coil.
Word Family: **curly,** *adjective.*

curler *noun*
Beauty: a roller.

curlew *noun*
any of various birds with a down-curved beak, living on estuaries and moorland.

curling *noun*
a game played on ice between two teams of four players who slide heavy, round stones to a target.

curmudgeon (*say* ker-**mud**-j'n) *noun*
an irritable or miserly old man.

currant *noun*
1. a small, dark seedless raisin.
2. a small, round, acid berry growing on a shrub.

currency (*say* **kurren**-see) *noun*
1. any banknotes or coins accepted as a medium of exchange in financial transactions.
2. the state of being commonly accepted or used: 'strict moral beliefs have less *currency* now than in the past'.

current *adjective*
belonging to or existing in the present time: 'a programme on *current* affairs'.
Usage: 'what is the *current* attitude towards divorce reform?' (= generally accepted).
current *noun*
1. a flow or stream: 'a *current* of cold air rushed in as the door opened'.
Usage: 'the *current* of feeling ran against the proposal' (= general tendency).
2. a portion of a large body of water, air, etc. moving in a particular direction.
3. *Electricity:* see ELECTRIC CURRENT.
[Latin *currens, currentis* running]

curriculum (*say* ka-**rik**-yoo-lum) *noun*

plural is **curricula**
a) the subjects or courses usually taught in a school, university, etc. b) any organized course of study.
curriculum vitae (*say* ka–**rik**–yoo–lum **vee**–tie)
a summary of one's career up to the present time.

curry (1) *noun*
a) a combination of hot spices made into a powder, sauce or paste. b) a dish of meat or vegetables flavoured with this mixture.
Word Family: **curry (curried, currying),** *verb.* [Tamil]

curry (2) *verb*
1. to groom a horse with a currycomb.
2. to treat tanned leather by beating, scraping, colouring, etc.
curry favour, to seek or gain approval by flattery, etc.

currycomb *noun*
an object made of rubber or metal with serrated ridges for cleaning brushes or removing dried mud from a horse.
Word Family: **currycomb,** *verb.*

curse (*say* kerse) *noun*
1. a) a call or appeal to supernatural powers to bring harm or evil to another person. b) anything which produces harm or evil.
2. an obscene oath or blasphemy.
3. (*informal*) menstruation.
Word Family: **curse,** *verb;* **cursed** (*say* **kersid** *or* kerst), *adjective;* **cursedness,** *noun.*

cursive (*say* **kersiv**) *adjective*
(of writing or print) flowing and joined.

cursor (*say* **kersa**) *noun*
a transparent slide marked with reference lines to assist in the reading of instruments.

cursory (*say* **kersa**–ree) *adjective*
hasty or superficial: 'he gave the letter only a *cursory* glance'.
Word Family: **cursorily,** *adverb;* **cursoriness,** *noun.*

curt *adjective*
brief or abrupt, especially in a rude manner.
Word Family: **curtly,** *adverb;* **curtness,** *noun.*
[Latin *curtus* shortened]

curtail (*say* ker–**tale**) *verb*
to reduce or cut short: 'we must try to *curtail* our spending this month'.
Word Family: **curtailment,** *noun.*

curtain (*say* **kertin**) *noun*
1. a length of cloth hung at a window or door to shut out light or for decoration.
2. anything which screens or covers: 'a *curtain* of mist'.
3. *Theatre:* the screen separating the audience from the stage, usually opened at the beginning of each act and closed at the end.
4. (*informal, plural*) the end, especially death.

curtain call
Theatre: the applause or calls by an audience, demanding that an actor should return to the stage after a performance. Compare ENCORE.

curtain–raiser *noun*
1. *Theatre:* a short play preceding the principal play.
2. any preliminary or introductory event.

curtsy (*say* **kert**–**see**) **curtsey** *noun*
(of a female) a gesture of respect made by bending one knee behind the other and lowering the body slightly.
Word Family: **curtsy (curtsied, curtsying), curtsey,** *verb.*
[from COURTESY]

curvaceous (*say* ker–**vay**–shus) *adjective*
having a full or shapely figure.

curvature (*say* **kerva**–cher) *noun*
a) the state of being curved: 'he suffers from *curvature* of the spine'. b) the amount or degree to which something is curved.

curve *noun*
1. a line or form which bends continuously and has no angles or straight parts.
2. *Maths:* the line, which may be a straight line, connecting all the points on a graph.
Word Family: **curve,** *verb;* **curvy,** *adjective,* having curves.
[Latin *curvus* curved]

cushion (*say* **kush**'n) *noun*
1. a bag with a soft filling such as feathers or rubber, used for comfort when sitting, etc.
2. anything which provides soft support or absorbs shock: 'a hovercraft travels on a *cushion* of air'.
3. *Billiards:* the raised, padded edge around the table.
Word Family: **cushion,** *verb,* to protect against or lessen the shock of something.

cushy (*say* **ku**–shee) *adjective*
(*informal*) easy or comfortable: 'he has a *cushy* job in the civil service'. [Hindi *khush* pleasant]

cusp *noun*
a pointed end especially where two curved lines meet, such as the point of a crescent moon, the ridge on a tooth, etc.

cuspid *noun*
Anatomy: a tooth with a single point. [Latin *cuspis* point]

cuss *verb*
(*informal*) to swear or curse.
cuss *noun*
(*informal*) a) a curse. b) an odd person.
cussed (*say* **kussid**) *adjective*
a) cursed. b) obstinate or difficult.
Word Family: **cussedness**, *noun*, obstinacy.

custard (*say* **kustid**) *noun*
a sweet dish made from a thickened mixture of eggs, sugar and milk.

custody (*say* **kusta**–dee) *noun*
the care or authorized keeping of a person or thing: 'the child remained in her mother's *custody*'.
Word Family: **custodian** (*say* kustoe–dee–an), *noun*, a person who has custody or keeping of something. [Latin *custodis* of a guardian]

custom *noun*
1. a usual or generally accepted action, practice or form of behaviour: 'it is the *custom* in our home to have a late dinner'.
2. (*plural*) a) the government organization collecting taxes on objects brought into or out of a country. b) the tax paid on such goods.
3. the regular customers of a shop or particular business.

customary (*say* **kust**'m–ree) *adjective*
based on custom or accepted practice: 'it is *customary* for all workers to wear a uniform'.
Word Family: **customarily**, *adverb*.

custom-built (*say* kust'm–**billt**) *adjective*
also called **custom-made**
American: made to the specific order of the customer.
[from German *gebraucht* custom, purpose]

customer *noun*
a person who buys goods or services from another.

customs duty
any duties imposed by law on imported goods.

cut *verb*
(cut, cutting)
1. to penetrate or separate with something sharp: 'he *cut* the apple into four pieces'.
2. to stop: '*cut* the engine'.
3. to reduce or shorten: 'manufacturers must *cut* their prices'.
4. to go directly: 'she *cut* through the paddocks to save time'.
5. (of teeth) to appear above the gums.
6. *Sport:* to hit the ball so that it spins or changes direction in its flight.
Usages:
a) 'she *cut* him deeply with her insults' (= hurt, upset).
b) 'this track *cuts* the highway 3 km further on' (= crosses).
c) 'the dealer shuffled and *cut* the pack of cards' (= divided into parts).
d) 'he *cut* three biology lessons last week' (= did not attend).
Phrases:
cut and dried, clear or settled.
cut dead, 'she *cut* him *dead*' (= refused to acknowledge acquaintance).
cut in, to interrupt.
cut off, a) 'try to *cut* him *off* at the gate' (= intercept); b) 'our phone has been *cut off*' (= disconnected); c) 'he was *cut off* without a penny' (= disinherited).
cut out, a) 'he *cuts* me *out* of all his activities' (= excludes); b) 'the engine *cut out* and the boat drifted' (= stopped); c) 'you are not *cut out* for this work' (= suited).
cut *noun*
1. a) a blow or stroke, especially one which cuts. b) a piece cut off: 'a *cut* of meat'. c) the result of cutting, such as a mark, wound, etc.
2. the manner or style in which something is cut: 'I do not like the *cut* of that suit'.
3. a direct path: 'we took a short *cut* through the school grounds'.
4. *Sport:* a stroke at the ball which causes it to spin or change direction in its flight.
Usages:
a) 'a *cut* in the price of petrol' (= reduction).
b) 'what is your *cut* of the profits?' (= share).
c) 'she felt his remarks were a personal *cut*' (= insult).
a cut above, superior to.

cutaneous (*say* kew–**tay**nius) *adjective*
of or relating to the skin.

cute *adjective*
1. pert and attractive or pleasing.
2. clever or too clever: 'don't try to be *cute* with me, young man!'.

cuticle (*say* **kew**ti–k'l) *noun*
Anatomy: the skin that covers the base of the fingernails and toenails.

cutlass (*say* **kut**lus) *noun*
a short, heavy sword with a curved blade, having one cutting edge.

cutlery (*say* **kut**la–ree) *noun*
the instruments used for eating, such as knives, forks and spoons.

cutlet *noun*
a cut of meat containing a rib, usually eaten grilled or fried.

cut–off *noun*
1. the limit or point at which something ends or is completed.
2. a device in some engines for switching them off by stopping the flow of air, fuel, steam, etc.

cutpurse *noun*
an old word for a pickpocket.

cutter *noun*
Nautical: a warship's small boat fitted with sails and oars.

cutthroat *adjective*
ruthless or merciless: 'the *cutthroat* competition between the large companies forced smaller businesses to close'.
cutthroat *noun*
1. a razor with a large, slightly curved, open blade.
2. a ruthlessly violent person, especially one considered capable of murder.

cutting *noun*
1. anything which is cut off or out: 'a newspaper *cutting*'.
2. anything which is produced by cutting, such as an excavation through a hill, etc. when building a road or railway.

cuttlebone *noun*
the light, white, solid, internal skeleton of a cuttlefish, used to make powder for polishing, poultry food, etc.

cuttlefish *noun*
a flat, squid–like, marine mollusc, having tentacles with suckers and producing an inky substance when attacked.

cyanide (*say* **sigh**–a–nide) *noun*
any compound of hydrocyanic acid (formula HCN), such as potassium cyanide, (formula KCN). All cyanides are extremely poisonous.

cyanosis (*say* sigh–a–**no**–sis) *noun*
a blueness of the skin due to a lack of oxygen in the blood.

cybernetics (*say* sigh–ber–**net**tiks) *plural noun*
(*used with singular verb*) the study of methods of communication and control common to living things and machines.
[Greek *kybernetes* helmsman]

cyclamate (*say* **sigh**–kla–mate) *noun*
any of a group of artificial chemicals used as low–calorie substitutes for sugar.

cyclamen (*say* **sik**–la–m'n) *noun*
a small plant growing from a tuber with white, red or pink flowers, often grown indoors.

cycle (*say* **sigh**–k'l) *noun*
1. a series of events which are repeated in a regular order: 'the *cycle* of the seasons'.
2. any complete period or course: 'a life *cycle*'.
3. a series of poems or songs.
4. a bicycle.
cycle *verb*
1. to ride a bicycle.
2. to move in cycles.
[Greek *kyklos* a circle]

cyclic (*say* **sigh**–klik) *adjective*
1. of or recurring in cycles.
2. *Maths:* (of a figure) able to be drawn within a circle: 'a *cyclic* quadrilateral'.
3. *Chemistry:* of or relating to organic compounds, such as benzene, where some or all of the carbon atoms of the molecule are joined in a closed ring structure.

cyclist (*say* **sigh**–klist) *noun*
a person who rides a bicycle or motorcycle.

cyclone (*say* **sigh**–klone) *noun*
Weather: a) see TROPICAL CYCLONE. b) see LOW (1).
Word Family: **cyclonic** (*say* sigh–**klon**nik), *adjective.*

Cyclops (*say* **sigh**–klops) *noun*
Greek mythology: any of a race of giants with one eye in the centre of the forehead.

cyclotron (*say* **sigh**–klo–tron) ***noun***
a device which accelerates charged particles, used in nuclear research work.

cygnet (*say* **sig**–nit) ***noun***
the young of a swan.
[Greek ***kyknos*** a swan]

cylinder (*say* **sill**inda) ***noun***
1. a solid or hollow body having circular, equal ends and parallel sides.
2. something which has the shape of a cylinder.
3. the rotating part of a revolver containing the cartridge chambers.
4. a chamber in an internal combustion engine within which a mixture of petrol and air is compressed by the piston and exploded by a spark from a spark plug.
Word Family: **cylindrical,** ***adjective.***
[Greek ***kylindein*** to roll]

cylinder block
the metal casing which contains the cylinders of an internal combustion engine.

cylinder head
a heavy metal cover over the cylinders of an internal combustion engine, usually forming part of the combustion space.

cymbals (*say* **sim**–b'ls) ***plural noun***
Music: a percussion instrument consisting of two slightly concave, brass plates either clashed against each other, or hit separately with a stick.
[Greek ***kymbalon***]

cynical (*say* **sinni**–k'l) ***adjective***
having no belief or trust in goodness, honesty, sincerity, etc.
Word Family: **cynic,** ***noun***; **cynically,** ***adverb***; **cynicism** (*say* **sinni**–sizm), ***noun.***
[Greek ***kynikos*** dog–like, churlish]

cypher (*say* **sigh**–fer) ***noun***
see CIPHER.

cypress (*say* **sigh**–pris) ***noun***
a type of evergreen tree with dark, small, needle–like leaves and hard wood.
[Greek ***kyparissos***]

cyst (*say* sist) ***noun***
1. *Medicine:* an abnormal, closed sac containing fluid.
2. *Biology:* a) a spore or reproductive cell with a thick, outer covering. b) a hollow organ in an animal or plant containing a liquid. c) a thick, protective membrane enclosing diseased tissue.
Word Family: **cystic,** ***adjective.***
[Greek ***kystis*** bladder]

cytology (*say* sigh–**toll**a–jee) ***noun***
the study of the processes within the cells of living things.

cytoplasm (*say* **sigh**–ta–plazm) ***noun***
Biology: the contents of a cell except the nucleus.
[Greek ***kytos*** a vessel + ***plasma*** a shape]

cytosine (*say* **sigh**–ta–zine) ***noun***
Biology: see PYRIMIDINE.

czar (*say* zar) ***noun***
see TSAR.

Dd

dab (1) *verb*
(dabbed, dabbing)
to touch or apply lightly: 'the girl *dabbed* make-up on her cheeks'.
Word Family: **dab**, *noun*, a) the act of dabbing, b) a small amount.

dab (2) *noun*
(*informal*) an expert.
dab hand, 'he is a *dab hand* at photography' (= expert).

dab (3) *noun*
an edible marine flatfish related to the plaice.

dabble *verb*
1. to splash in a liquid, especially with the hands or feet.
2. to do as a hobby or casual interest: 'she *dabbles* in pottery during her spare time'.
Word Family: **dabbler**, *noun.*

dabchick *noun*
see GREBE.

dace *noun*
a small freshwater fish related to the chub.

dacha *noun*
a Russian country villa provided by the State for those approved of by the authorities.
[Russian, payment]

dachshund (*say* **daks**-hûnd) *noun*
one of a breed of small, short-legged, dogs with long bodies.
[German *Dachs* badger + *Hund* dog]

dactyl (*say* **dak**til) *noun*
1. *Biology:* a digit.
2. *Poetry:* see FOOT.
Word Family: **dactylic** (*say* dak-**till**ik), *adjective.*
[Greek *daklylos* finger, which has three bones]

dad, daddy *noun*
(*informal*) father.

daddy-long-legs *noun*
also called a **cranefly**
any of a group of insects with a tiny, round body and very long, slender legs. The larvae, called **leather-jackets**, are a garden pest.

dado (*say* day-doe) *noun*
1. any panelling or other decoration at the base of the wall of a room.
2. a decorative border at picture-rail level on the wall of a room.

daffodil *noun*
an early spring plant of the narcissus family with reed-like leaves and bright yellow or creamy white trumpet-shaped flowers, growing from a bulb.
[from Greek *asphodelos* asphodel]

daft (*say* dahft) *adjective*
foolish or mildly insane.
Word Family: **daftly**, *adverb*; **daftness**, *noun.*

dagger *noun*
a short-bladed weapon, like a small sword.
look daggers, to cast angry or threatening glances.

daguerreotype (*say* da-**gerro**-type) *noun*
an early image fixing process, related to photography, where a positive image becomes etched upon a sensitive metal plate.
[invented by *L. J. M. Daguerre*, 1789-1851]

dahlia (*say* **dale**-ya) *noun*
an autumn garden plant with brightly coloured flowers, growing from a tuber.
[after *A. Dahl*, died 1789, a Swedish botanist]

Dáil Eireann (*say* dile **air**-an)
short form is the **Dáil**
Irish Republic: the lower house of parliament.
[Irish *dáil* assembly + *Eireann* Irish]

daily *adjective*
of or occurring every day.
daily *noun*
1. a newspaper published every day.
2. a cleaning woman who comes every day.
Word Family: **daily**, *adverb.*

dainty *adjective*
very delicate or neat.

Word Family: **daintiness**, *noun*; **daintily**, *adverb*; **dainty**, *noun.*

dairy *noun*
a place where milk is stored, processed or sold.
dairy farm
a farm producing milk or milk products.
dairy cattle
any cattle bred or kept to produce milk rather than meat.

dais (*say* day-iss) *noun*
a raised platform, e.g. for a speaker, etc.

daisy (*say* **day**-zee) *noun*
any of a group of plants with composite flowers, usually with a yellow centre.
[Middle English *dayseye* day's eye, because it opens at morning]

dale *noun*
a valley, especially in northern England.

dally *verb*
(dallied, dallying)
1. to trifle with, as in a love affair.
2. to waste time.
Word Family: **dalliance**, *noun.*

Dalmatian *noun*
any of a breed of large, short-haired, white dogs with black spots.
[after *Dalmatia*, a region of Yugoslavia]

dam (1) *noun*
a wall or other structure built to keep water back, e.g. across a river. Compare DYKE.
Word Family: **dam (dammed, damming)**, *verb.*

dam (2) *noun*
a female parent, especially of a horse.
[short form of DAME]

damage (*say* **dammij**) *noun*
1. any injury which causes loss of usefulness or value.
2. *Law:* (*plural*) a sum of money claimed because of a loss, e.g. when a contract has been broken.
3. (*informal*) the cost.
Word Family: **damage**, *verb*, to cause damage to; **damageable**, *adjective*; **damagingly**, *adverb.*
[Latin *damnum* damage]

damascene (*say* **damma**-seen) *verb*
to ornament metalwork with inlaid designs or by etching.
[from *Damascus* in Syria]

damask (*say* **dam**'sk) *noun*
1. a twilled cotton, fibre or linen fabric, used for tablecloths, curtains, etc.
2. a deep pink colour, as of the damask rose.
Word Family: **damask**, *adjective.*

dame *noun*
1. (*capital*) a form of address for a woman of rank.
2. (*informal*) a woman.

damn (*say* dam) *verb*
to curse or condemn.
damnable *adjective*
1. deserving to be damned: 'a *damnable* offence'.
2. (*informal*) detestable or annoying: 'this *damnable* heat is very tiring'.
damned *adjective*
1. condemned to hell: 'a *damned* soul'.
2. (*informal*) detestable: 'what a *damned* cheek'.
Word Family: **damnation**, *noun*, the state of being damned, especially to hell; **damn! damnation!**, *interjections*; **damnably**, *adverb*; **damned**, *adverb*, extremely, very; **damning**, *adjective*, proving guilt.
[Latin *damnare* to condemn]

damp *adjective*
moist or slightly wet.
damp *verb*
1. to make damp.
2. to discourage or dull: 'the disappointment *damped* our enthusiasm a bit'.
3. *Physics, Music:* to reduce the amplitude of a vibrating string, wave, etc.
4. to retard the energy of.
damp *noun*
1. any moisture or moistness.
2. a poisonous or suffocating vapour or gas, especially in a mine.
Word Family: **damply**, *adverb*; **dampness**, *noun.*

dampcourse *noun*
Building: a layer of moisture-proof material such as slate or bitumen, laid in a wall to stop moisture rising.

dampen *verb*
1. to make damp.
2. to dull or depress: 'the sight of the leaden sky *dampened* our enthusiasm for a picnic'.
Word Family: **dampener**, *noun* something which depresses.

damper *noun*
1. a movable metal plate for regulating the flow of air into a fire in a stove or furnace.
2. *Music:* a device in a keyboard instrument which deadens the vibration of the strings.

damsel (*say* **damz'l**) *noun*
an old word for a young unmarried woman.

damson *noun*
a small purple plum.
[from *Damascene*, of Damascus]

dance *noun*
1. a) a series of steps and movements, usually in time to music. b) a piece of music for this.
2. a social function at which one dances.
dance attendance on, to be excessively polite or obliging to.
Word Family: **dance**, *verb*, a) to perform a dance, b) to move quickly or nimbly; **dancer**, *noun*.

dandelion (*say* **dandi**-lion) *noun*
a small weed with deeply notched leaves and bright yellow flowers which form a ball of downy seeds.
[French *dent* tooth + *de lion* of lion, because of the shape of the leaves]

dandle *verb*
to move a child up and down on the knees or in the arms.

dandruff *noun*
also called **scurf**
any small scales of dead skin on the scalp.

dandy *noun*
a man who is excessively concerned with his clothes and appearance.
dandy *adjective*
American: fine or very good.
Word Family: **dandify** (**dandified**, **dandifying**), *verb*.

danger (*say* **dane**-ja) *noun*
1. a likelihood of harm or injury: 'the mountaineer enjoyed the element of *danger* in the sport'.
2. something which may cause danger: 'that hidden reef is a *danger* to shipping'.
Word Family: **dangerous**, *adjective*; **dangerously**, *adverb*; **dangerousness**, *noun*.

dangle *verb*
to swing or hang loosely.

dank *adjective*
unpleasantly damp: 'a *dank* cellar'.
Word Family: **dankly**, *adverb*; **dankness**, *noun*.

daphne (*say* **daf**-nee) *noun*
a garden shrub with pink, fragrant flowers.
[Greek, laurel]

dapper *adjective*
neat and smart.

dappled *adjective*
having spots of different colours.
Word Family: **dapple**, *verb*; **dapple**, *noun*, a spot or marking.

dare *verb*
1. to be bold enough: 'he *dared* to contradict his father'.
2. to challenge: 'I *dare* you to do it'.
dare say, 'I *dare say* we will win' (= suppose).
Word Family: **dare** *noun*, a challenge; **daringly**, *adverb*; **daring**, **daringness**, *nouns*.

daredevil *noun*
a reckless person.

dark *adjective*
1. with little or no light: 'a *dark*, cloudy night'.
2. (of colours, surfaces, etc.) reflecting or radiating little or no light.
Usages:
a) 'he has a *dark* complexion' (= not pale).
b) 'she gave him a *dark* look' (= angry).
c) 'he brooded over *dark* thoughts' (= sad or evil).
d) 'Sue tried to keep the news *dark*' (= secret).
a dark horse, a person of unknown capabilities.
dark *noun*
a) an absence of light: 'children afraid of the *dark*'. b) nightfall: 'be home before *dark*'.
in the dark, in ignorance or without knowledge.
Word Family: **darkly**, *adverb*; **darkness**, *noun*, a) absence of light, b) the state or quality of being dark; **darken**, *verb*, to make or become dark or darker.

Dark Ages
a name given to the period from about A.D. 450–1000, especially the early Middle Ages.

darkroom *noun*
Photography: a lightproof room for developing and printing films.

darling *noun*
a person or thing very much loved.
Usage: 'he is the latest *darling* of the social world' (= favourite).
[from *dearling*, dear little thing]

darn (1) *verb*
to repair a hole in a garment by using interlacing stitches.
Word Family: **darn**, *noun*; **darning**, *noun*, anything which has been or needs to be darned.

darn (2) *interjection*
(*informal*) a mild exclamation of irritation, etc.
darn *noun*
not give a darn, (*informal*) to be completely indifferent.
Word Family: **darned,** *adjective, adverb,* damned.

dart *noun*
1. a small, sharp, metal arrow with feathers at one end.
2. (*plural*) a game in which each player throws a series of darts at a numbered target.
3. a tapering tuck sewn in a garment to alter its shape.
4. a sudden swift movement: 'he made a *dart* for the door'.
dart *verb*
to move swiftly.
Word Family: **dartingly,** *adverb,* with swift movements.

Darwinism *noun*
Biology: the theory of evolution of separate species from a common origin. See NATURAL SELECTION.
[suggested by *Charles Darwin,* 1809–82, a British naturalist]

dash (1) *verb*
to throw or strike violently: 'the boat was *dashed* against the rocks during the storm'.
Usages:
a) 'he *dashed* across the road' (= rushed).
b) 'his hopes were *dashed* when she left him' (= ruined, frustrated).
dash off, 'he *dashed off* an article for the school newspaper' (= wrote hurriedly).
dash *noun*
1. a sudden rush or violent movement: 'the ambulance made a mercy *dash* to the hospital'.
2. a small quantity added to something: 'he always has Scotch with a *dash* of water'.
3. vigour: 'an exciting performance which was full of *dash*'.
4. *Grammar:* a punctuation mark (–), used to introduce a break in a sentence or dialogue. *Example*: 'if the report is true – and I believe it is – we must act immediately'.
cut a dash, to be very impressive in appearance, behaviour, etc.

dash (2) *interjection*
a mild exclamation expressing irritation, etc.

dashboard *noun*
also called the **fascia**
the instrument panel of a motor vehicle or aeroplane.

dashing *adjective*
showy, stylish or spirited.
Word Family: **dashingly,** *adverb.*

dastardly (*say* **dasst**'d–lee) *adjective, adverb*
mean and cowardly.

data (*say* **dayta** *or* **dahta**) *plural noun*
singular is **datum**
the facts or information on a particular subject.
[Latin, the given things]

date (1) *noun*
1. a particular point or period of time.
Usages:
a) 'please state your *date* of birth' (= day, month and year).
b) 'what is the *date* on that coin?' (= year inscribed).
2. a) an appointment to meet. b) the person with whom an appointment is made.
Phrases:
out of date, old-fashioned or obsolete.
to date, 'I have collected over 1000 stamps *to date*' (= until the present time).
date *verb*
1. a) to assign a date to: 'to *date* an ancient manuscript'. b) to put or have a date on: 'all letters should be *dated* correctly'.
Usage: 'most 19th-century scientific textbooks are badly *dated* by now' (= out of date).
2. (*informal*) to go out with.
date from, date back to, 'this church *dates from* Norman times' (= has existed since).

date (2) *noun*
a small, oblong, brown fruit of a palm, widely grown in Africa and the Middle East.

date line
1. a line at the start of a letter, newspaper article, etc. giving the date and place of origin.
2. the international date line.

dative bond
also called a **coordinate bond**
Chemistry: a covalent bond, where both of the shared pair of electrons are donated by the one atom. Compare COVALENT BOND and IONIC BOND.

dative case
Grammar: see CASE (1).

datum (*say* **day**–t'm *or* **dah**–t'm) *noun*
the singular of **data**.

daub (*say* dawb) *verb*
to cover a surface with paint, mud, etc.
daub *noun*
a covering of sticky material, such as clay: 'a hut made of wattle and *daub*'.
Word Family: **dauber,** *noun,* an unskilful painter.

daughter (*say* **daw**ta) *noun*
1. a female child in relation to her parents.
2. a female person strongly influenced by or involved with something: 'the *daughters* of the revolution'.
Word Family: **daughterly,** *adjective.*

daughter-in-law *noun*
plural is **daughters-in-law**
the wife of one's son.

daunt (*say* dawnt) *verb*
to discourage or lessen the enthusiasm of.
Word Family: **dauntless,** *adjective*; **dauntlessly,** *adverb.*

dauphin (*say* **daw**-fin *or* **doe**-fan) *noun*
History: the title given to the eldest son of the king of France, from the 14th century to the 19th century.
Word Family: **dauphine** (*say* **daw**-feen *or* **doe**-feen), **dauphiness,** *nouns,* the wife of a dauphin.

davenport *noun*
1. *American:* a large sofa.
2. a small, ornamental writing desk.

davit *noun*
Nautical: either of a pair of curved arms at the side of a ship by which small boats, etc. may be raised from or lowered into the water by means of tackle.

Davy lamp
a safety lamp used by coal-miners.
[invented by *Sir Humphry Davy*, 1778–1829, a British chemist]

dawdle *verb*
to waste time or fall behind, e.g. when walking.
Word Family: **dawdler,** *noun.*

dawn *noun*
the first appearance of daylight.
Usage: 'the *dawn* of time' (= beginning).
Word Family: **dawn,** *verb,* a) to begin to grow light, b) to begin to develop or be perceived.

day *noun*
1. a) the period of light from dawn to dusk. b) the 24-hour period from one midnight to the next. c) the period one is awake or active: 'I've had a hard *day*'.
2. *Astronomy:* the time taken for the earth or another planet to rotate once on its axis.
a **sidereal day** is measured relative to a star.
a **solar day** is measured relative to the sun.
3. (*often plural*) a particular period: 'in *days* gone by'.
Phrases:
call it a day, to finish or stop.
day in, day out, every day or indefinitely.
win the day, 'our team *won the day* in all sections' (= was most successful).

daybreak *noun*
the dawn.

daydream *noun*
an imaginative fantasy indulged in while awake.
Word Family: **daydream** (**daydreamed** or **daydreamt, daydreaming**), *verb*; **daydreamer,** *noun.*

daylight-saving *noun*
summer time.

daze *verb*
to stun or bewilder.
Word Family: **daze,** *noun*; **dazedly,** *adverb.*

dazzle *verb*
to overpower with or as if with intense light.
Usage: 'her beautiful face *dazzled* the stranger' (= excited admiration in).

D-day *noun*
6 June 1944, when Allied forces landed in Europe.
[*D* is the military symbol for the *day* on which an operation is planned to begin]

de-
a prefix meaning: a) the opposite of, as in *decode*; b) down, as in *depress*; c) away or off, as in *deport*; d) completely, as in *despoil.*

deacon *noun*
Christian: a) a member of the third order of clergy beneath bishops and priests, and assisting them in their duties. b) a lay person who assists in worship and takes care of other lay matters, in some Protestant churches.
[Greek *diakonos* servant]

deaconess *noun*
Christian: a woman minister in certain churches, especially concerned with work for charity.

deactivate (*say* dee-**akti**-vate) *verb*
to make inactive or reduce the activity of.
Word Family: **deactivation,** *noun.*

dead (*say* ded) *adjective*
without life or no longer living: 'the *dead* leaves fell from the tree'.
Usages:
a) 'Latin is a *dead* language' (= no longer spoken).
b) 'there was a *dead* silence' (= complete, absolute).
c) 'she fell down in a *dead* faint' (= resembling death).
d) 'he is known to be a *dead* shot' (= accurate, perfect).
e) (*informal*) 'I'm really *dead* by the end of the week' (= exhausted).
f) 'the sleeping child was a *dead* weight in my arms' (= unrelieved).
dead *noun*
any person or people who are dead: 'a memorial was erected to the *dead* of World War 2'.
Usage: 'in the *dead* of night' (= middle, quiet part).
dead *adverb*
1. completely: 'you are *dead* wrong'.
2. abruptly: 'he stopped *dead* in his tracks'.
3. directly: 'the reef lay *dead* ahead'.
deaden *verb*
to reduce or make dull: 'he was given medicine to *deaden* the pain'.

dead-beat *adjective*
(*informal*) exhausted: 'I'm *dead-beat* by Friday'.

dead-end *adjective*
1. (of a street) having one end closed.
2. leading nowhere or having no future.
Word Family: **dead end,** a) a dead-end street, b) a point or condition from which no progress can be made.

dead heat
a competition or race in which two or more competitors have an equal score or finish together.

dead letter
1. a law which has not been abolished formally but is no longer observed.
2. a letter which is not claimed and cannot be delivered because it is wrongly addressed.

deadline *noun*
the time by which something must be done: 'the *deadline* for entries is next Friday'.

deadlock *noun*
a situation from which further progress is impossible.
Word Family: **deadlock,** *verb.*

deadly *adjective*
1. causing or tending to cause death: 'a *deadly* poison'.
2. aiming to destroy or kill: '*deadly* enemies'.
3. like death: 'a *deadly* paleness'.
Word Family: **deadly,** *adverb,* a) in a manner suggesting death, b) excessively; **deadliness,** *noun.*

deadly nightshade
belladonna.

deadpan *adjective*
(of a face) lacking expression or reaction.

deaf (*say* def) *adjective*
1. unable to hear or to hear well.
2. refusing to listen: 'he turned a *deaf* ear to her pleas'.
Word Family: **deafness,** *noun.*

deafen (*say* **deff**'n) *verb*
1. to make deaf.
2. to overwhelm with noise.
Word Family: **deafeningly,** *adverb.*

deaf-mute *noun*
a person who is deaf and dumb.

deal (1) *verb*
(dealt, dealing)
to be occupied with or manage: 'let us *deal* with this problem first'.
Usages:
a) 'I always *deal* with that company' (= do business with).
b) 'we *dealt* a hand of cards' (= distributed).
c) 'the boxer *dealt* his opponent a heavy blow' (= delivered).
deal *noun*
1. an agreement or arrangement: 'we made a *deal* not to say anything'.
2. the act or an instance of dealing.
Phrases:
a good deal of, a large amount or quantity of.
a great deal of, much or most.
a raw deal, any unfair treatment.
Word Family: **dealer,** *noun,* a trader or merchant.

deal (2) *noun*
a board or plank of softwood, usually pine.

dean *noun*
1. a teacher or official in charge of students and the internal running of a college or a faculty of a university.
2. *Christian:* the chief clergyman of a cathedral, college church or part of a diocese.
Word Family: **deanery,** *noun,* a) the residence of a dean, b) the office of a dean.

dear *adjective*
1. beloved or highly regarded: 'a *dear* friend'.
2. a greeting in letters, etc.: '*Dear* John'.
3. expensive.
Word Family: **dear,** *noun, adverb*; **dearly,** *adverb.*

dearth (*say* derth) *noun*
a lack or scarcity.

death (*say* deth) *noun*
a) the act of dying: 'his *death* occurred last week'. b) the state of being dead: 'he drank himself to *death*'.
Usages:
a) 'it was the *death* of all hope' (= extinction).
b) 'a hero's *death*' (= manner of dying).
Phrases:
do to death, a) to kill; b) to repeat until stale.
put to death, to execute.
sick to death, (*informal*) extremely annoyed or irritated.
Word Family: **deathly,** *adjective,* like death; **deathly,** *adverb,* a) in a manner resembling death, b) extremely or utterly.

death duty
also called an **estate duty**
(*usually plural*) a tax paid upon the inheriting of property.

death rate
also called the **mortality rate**
the number of deaths in proportion to the total population at a given time, expressed per 1000 people. Compare BIRTH RATE.

deathtrap *noun*
a situation involving risk of death: 'this intersection is a *deathtrap*'.

death-watch beetle
a small furniture beetle, the larvae of which seriously damage ancient timber.
[from its mating call, like a ticking watch and made by knocking its head against the wood, once thought to herald death in the household]

deb *noun*
(*informal*) a débutante.

débâcle (*say* day-**bah**-k'l) *noun*
a sudden or overwhelming collapse or disaster.
[French *débâcler* to unfasten]

debar *verb*
(**debarred, debarring**)
a) to exclude: 'he was *debarred* from the club'. b) to prevent or prohibit: 'he was *debarred* from driving after the accident'.
Word Family: **debarment,** *noun.*

debase *verb*
to lower in quality, rank or dignity.
Word Family: **debasement,** *noun*; **debaser,** *noun,* a person who debases.

debate *noun*
1. a discussion, especially of a public question.
2. an organized contest in which opposing points of view are argued.
debate *verb*
to discuss.
Usage: 'I'm *debating* whether to sell my car or not' (= considering, deliberating upon).
Word Family: **debater,** *noun*; **debatable,** *adjective,* open to question.

debauchery (*say* de-bawcha-ree) *noun*
an excessive indulgence in sensual pleasures.
Word Family: **debauch,** *verb*; **debauched,** *adjective,* corrupt; **debauchee** (*say* de-baw-**chee**), *noun,* a person who makes a habit of debauchery; **debaucher,** *noun,* a person who corrupts others.

debenture (*say* de-bencher) *noun*
an interest-bearing loan or mortgage on the assets of a company, often traded on stock exchanges.
[Latin *debens* owing]

debility (*say* de-billi-tee) *noun*
a general weakness or feebleness.
Word Family: **debilitate,** *verb*; **debilitation,** *noun.*
[Latin *debilis* weak]

debit *noun*
a record of a debt entered in an account. Compare CREDIT.
Word Family: **debit,** *verb.*

debonair (*say* debba-nair) **debonaire** *adjective*
1. urbane or pleasantly gracious.
2. cheerful or lively.
[French *de bon* of good + *aire* disposition]

debouch (*say* de-**bowch** *or* de-**boosh**) *verb*
1. to emerge: 'the troops left the ravine and *debouched* on to the main road'.
2. to issue: 'there the river *debouches* into the sea'.

debriefing (*say* dee-**bree**-fing) *noun*
the questioning of soldiers, astronauts, etc. who have returned from a mission, in order to assess the success of the mission.
Word Family: **debrief**, *verb.*

débris (*say* **deb**-ree *or* **day** bree) *noun*
the remains of anything broken or destroyed: 'the road was covered with *débris* after the accident'.
[French *débriser* to break down]

debt (*say* det) *noun*
anything which one person owes to another.
bad debt, a debt which is unlikely to be paid.
debtor (*say* **dett**or) *noun*
a person who owes money to another. Compare CREDITOR.
[Latin *debitum*]

debug *verb*
(**debugged, debugging**)
1. to discover and remove faults in a computer program, electronic device, etc.
2. (*informal*) to remove electronic listening devices from.

debunk *verb*
(*informal*) to expose exaggeration or falseness.

début (*say* **day**-boo) *noun*
a first public appearance on the stage, television, etc.
Usage: 'the President's daughter made her *début* last night' (= introduction and entry into society).
Word Family: **débutante** (*say* **deb**-yoo tant), *noun,* a girl who makes her social début.
[French *débuter* to make the first stroke in a game]

deca-
a prefix meaning ten, as in *decahedron.* Compare DEKA-.
[Greek *deka* ten]

decade (*say* **dek**-ade) *noun*
a period of ten years.

decadence (*say* **dekka**-d'nce) *noun*
a process or condition of deterioration, especially in a moral or artistic sense: 'the *decadence* of the 1890's showed itself in a taste for exotic and perverse pleasures'.
Word Family: **decadent**, *adjective,* involved in or practising decadence; **decadently**, *adverb.*
[DE- + Latin *cadere* to fall]

decagon (*say* **dekka**-g'n) *noun*
any closed, plane figure with ten straight sides.
Word Family: **decagonal** (*say* dek-**agga**-n'l), *adjective.*
[DECA- + Greek *gonia* corner]

decahedron (*say* dekka-**hee**-dr'n) *noun*
a solid or hollow body with ten plane faces.
Word Family: **decahedral**, *adjective.*
[DECA- + Greek *hedra* base]

decamp *verb*
to leave suddenly or secretly: 'the accountant *decamped* with the company funds'.
Word Family: **decampment**, *noun.*

decant (*say* de-**kant**) *verb*
to pour a liquid, especially wine, from one container to another.

decanter *noun*
an ornamental flask or bottle for serving wines.

decapitate (*say* de-**kappi**-tate) *verb*
to behead.
Word Family: **decapitation**, *noun.*
[DE- + Latin *caput* head]

decarbonize, decarbonise *verb*
to remove accumulated deposits of carbon from the combustion chamber of an internal combustion engine.

decasyllable (*say* dekka-**silla**-b'l) *noun*
Poetry. a line with ten syllables.
Word Family: **decasyllabic** (*say* dekka-sil-**abbik**), *adjective.*

decathlon (*say* de-**kath**lon) *noun*
a contest in which athletes compete for the highest total score in ten separate events.
[DECA- + Greek *athlon* contest]

decay *verb*
1. to rot away or deteriorate: a) 'the previous owners allowed the house to *decay* around them'; b) 'the leaves slowly *decayed* on the lawn'.
2. *Physics:* (of a nucleus) to disintegrate owing to the effect of radioactivity.
Word Family: **decay**, *noun.*
[Latin *de-* down + *cadere* to fall]

decease (*say* de-**seece**) *noun*
death: 'on his uncle's *decease* he expects to become a wealthy man'.

Word Family: **decease,** *verb.*
[DE- + Latin *cessus* gone]

deceit (*say* de-**seet**) *noun*
1. the act or practice of misleading someone by concealing or distorting the truth.
2. a trick or stratagem.
Word Family: **deceitful,** *adjective*; **deceitfully,** *adverb*; **deceitfulness,** *noun.*
[Latin *decipere* to cheat]

deceive (*say* de-**seev**) *verb*
to mislead by concealing or distorting the truth.
Word Family: **deceivingly,** *adverb*; **deceiver,** *noun.*

decelerate (*say* dee-**sella**-rate) *verb*
to decrease in velocity.
deceleration *noun*
Physics: see RETARDATION.
Word Family: **decelerator,** *noun,* something which causes deceleration.

December (*say* de-**semba**) *noun*
the twelfth month of the year in the Gregorian calendar.
[Latin *decem* ten, because December was the tenth month of the Roman calendar]

decent (*say* **dee**-s'nt) *adjective*
conforming to accepted social standards in matters of taste or conduct.
Usages:
a) 'they come from a very *decent* family' (= respectable).
b) 'the workers demanded a *decent* living wage' (= fair, tolerable).
c) 'it was *decent* of you to lend me your car' (= kind).
d) 'are you *decent* yet?' (= properly dressed).
decency *noun*
1. the state or quality of being decent.
2. (*plural*) the requirements of a decent way of life: 'the corpse was buried so hastily that none of the *decencies* could be observed'.
Word Family: **decently,** *adverb.*
[Latin *decens* seemly or proper]

decentralization, decentralisation (*say* dee-sentra-lie-zay-sh'n) *noun*
the distribution of administrative powers among local or regional authorities.
Word Family: **decentralize,** *verb.*

deception (*say* de-**sep**-sh'n) *noun*
1. the act of deceiving: 'the impostor practised *deception* on his victims'.
2. the state of being deceived.
3. a trick or artifice: 'his mean *deceptions* were finally exposed'.
Word Family: **deceptive,** *adjective,* deceiving or misleading; **deceptively,** *adverb.*

deci- (*say* dessi)
a prefix used for SI units, meaning one tenth (10^{-1}). See UNITS in grey pages.

decibel (*say* **dessi**-bel) *noun*
a unit of sound intensity.

decide (*say* de-**side**) *verb*
1. to make a choice: 'she *decided* to continue despite her lawyer's advice'.
2. to settle a question or conflict: 'the election will not be *decided* until all votes are counted'.
decided *adjective*
definite or unquestionable: 'there is a *decided* difference between them'.
Word Family: **decidedly,** *adverb*; **decider,** *noun.*
[Latin *decidere* to cut short, to settle]

deciduous (*say* dee-**sid**-yewus) *adjective*
Biology: of or relating to an animal or plant which regularly sheds part of itself, such as skin, antlers, leaves, etc.
[Latin *decidere* to fall down]

decimal (*say* **dessi**-m'l) *noun*
a fraction in which the denominator is a power of ten, usually written with a point, called the **decimal point.**
Example: 0·03 is $\frac{3}{100}$.
decimal *adjective*
a) relating to or based on tens: '*decimal* currency'. b) expressed or expressible as a decimal: 'a *decimal* fraction'.
Word Family: **decimally,** *adverb*; **decimalize, decimalise,** *verb,* to express in decimals.
[Latin *decimus* tenth]

decimate (*say* **dessi**-mate) *verb*
to kill or destroy a large part of: 'the massive air-raids *decimated* the civilian population'.
Word Family: **decimation,** *noun.*
[Latin *decimare* to kill every tenth man, as punishment in a disgraced army]

decipher (*say* de-**sigh**-fir) *verb*
1. to find the meaning of something indistinct or hard to understand: 'the lawyer tried to *decipher* the faded writing of the will'.
2. to decode something written in cipher.
Word Family: **decipherable,** *adjective.*

decision (*say* de-**sizh**'n) *noun*
1. the act of deciding: 'he was faced with a difficult *decision*'.
2. a judgement reached or given: 'the government's *decision* on wage rises will be announced soon'.
3. a firmness or lack of hesitation: 'act with *decision*'.

decisive (*say* de-**sigh**-siv) *adjective*
1. giving a definite result or determining the course of something: 'it was the *decisive* battle of the war'.
2. determined or resolute: 'the sergeant gave his orders in a *decisive* tone of voice'.
Word Family: **decisively,** *adverb*; **decisiveness,** *noun.*

deck *noun*
1. a) a horizontal floor or platform extending from one side of a ship to the other. b) any similar platform or level: 'the top *deck* of the bus'.
2. *American:* a pack of cards.
3. *Audio:* see TAPE DECK.
deck *verb*
to decorate or adorn: 'they *decked* the streets with flags'.
deck out, to clothe or attire.
decking *noun*
any material, especially timber, used to make the deck of a ship.

deckchair *noun*
a light, folding chair, used outdoors, with the back and seat usually made of canvas.

declaim *verb*
to speak formally or rhetorically, especially in public: 'the Church council *declaimed* against the decay of public morals'.
Word Family: **declamation** (*say* dekla-**may**-sh'n), *noun*; **declamatory** (*say* de-**klamma**-tree), *adjective.*
[Latin *declamare* to shout down]

declaration (*say* dekla-**ray**-sh'n) *noun*
a) the act of declaring. b) that which is declared: 'the American *Declaration* of Independence was written in 1776'.
declaratory (*say* de-**klarra**-tree)
declarative *adjective*
serving to explain or make clear: 'a *declaratory* statement'.

declare (*say* de-**klair**) *verb*
1. to announce formally or officially: 'the authorities *declared* a ban on all fires in the open'.
2. to assert forcefully: 'she *declared* that she would never darken his door again'.
3. to make a statement of goods on which customs duties must be paid.
4. *Cricket:* to close an innings voluntarily, before all ten wickets have fallen.
Word Family: **declarable,** *adjective*; **declared,** *adjective,* openly avowed; **declaredly,** *adverb.*
[Latin *declarare* to announce with authority]

declassify *verb*
(**declassified, declassifying**)
to remove a document from a security classification.

declension (*say* de-**klen**-sh'n) *noun*
1. *Grammar:* the inflection of a noun, pronoun or adjective, to express its case, number, or gender, especially in a language such as Latin. *Example: who,* in the nominative case, becomes *whose* in the possessive case and *whom* in the objective case.
2. a) a group of such words which have similar endings for each case: 'Latin nouns are usually divided into five *declensions*'. b) the complete set of the inflected forms of such a word: 'I was asked to recite the *declension* of a Latin noun'.
3. a downward slope or movement: 'the steep *declension* of the land near the sea'.

declination (*say* dekli-**nay**-sh'n) *noun*
1. *Astronomy:* the angle between the direction of a planet or star and the plane of the celestial equator.
2. a downward bend or slope.
3. the deviation of the needle of a compass from true north or south.

decline *verb*
1. to refuse politely: 'he *declined* our offer of a loan'.
2. to slope or cause to slope downward: 'this road *declines* steeply for the next two miles'.
3. *Grammar:* to list the inflections of a noun, pronoun or adjective.
Usages:
a) 'as he grew older his health began to *decline*' (= weaken).
b) 'profits *declined* in the first 6 months of the year' (= decreased).
decline *noun*
1. a falling or sinking: 'a *decline* in prices'.
2. a downward slope or incline.
Usage: 'a *decline* in health' (= gradual weakening).
[Latin *declinare* to deviate]

declivity (*say* de-**klivvi**-tee) *noun*
a steep downward slope.
[Latin *declivis* steep]

declutch *verb*
to disengage the clutch of a motor vehicle when changing gears.

decoct (*say* de-**kokt**) *verb*
a) to extract an essence or part of a substance by boiling in water. b) to reduce or concentrate by boiling down.
Word Family: **decoction,** *noun.*
[DE- + Latin *coctus* boiled]

decode (*say* dee-**kode**) *verb*
to convert a code into the original message or form.

decoke *verb*
(*informal*) to decarbonize.

décolleté (*say* day-**koltay**) *adjective*
(of a dress) having a low neckline.
Word Family: **décolletage** (*say* day-kolt-**ahzh**), *noun*, the neckline of a dress cut low in front.
[DE- + Latin *collum* neck]

decompose (*say* dee-k'm-**poze**) *verb*
1. to break down or separate into component parts or elements: 'some bacteria *decompose* nitrates to nitrogen and oxygen'.
2. to decay: 'the corpse had begun to *decompose* by the time the police found it'.
decomposer *noun*
Biology: any organism, such as a fungus, which obtains energy by breaking down complex substances into simpler ones.
Word Family: **decomposition** (*say* dee-kompa-**zish**'n), *noun*; **decomposable,** *adjective.*

decompress (*say* deek'm-**press**) *verb*
to relieve pressure.
Word Family: **decompression,** *noun.*

decompression chamber
a chamber in which divers, or pilots of unpressurized aircraft, are treated for the bends. The air-pressure is increased until nitrogen bubbles in the blood and tissues redissolve, after which the pressure is reduced slowly.

decontaminate
(*say* dee-k'n-**tammi**-nate) *verb*
to neutralize or destroy the harmful effects of poisonous chemicals or radioactive substances.
Word Family: **decontamination,** *noun.*

décor (*say* **day**-kor) *noun*
1. the style or scheme of decoration in a room, home, restaurant, etc.
2. *Theatre:* the scenery or scenic decoration.
[French, from Latin *decor* grace, beauty]

decorate (*say* **dekka**-rate) *verb*
1. to add to something to make it look more beautiful or pleasing: a) 'they *decorated* the kitchen in vivid colours'; b) 'a Christmas tree *decorated* with coloured lights'.
2. to confer honour on a person by awarding a medal, badge, etc.: 'his father was *decorated* for bravery during World War 2'.
decoration *noun*
1. the act of decorating.
2. something which decorates or makes more beautiful.
Word Family: **decorator,** *noun*, a person who decorates houses, offices, etc. as a profession; **decorative** (*say* **dekra**-tiv), *adjective*; **decoratively,** *adverb*; **decorativeness,** *noun.*
[Latin *decorare* to adorn]

decorous (*say* **dekka**-rus) *adjective*
conforming to accepted social standards of propriety or good taste: 'her *decorous* behaviour made her a welcome guest'.
Word Family: **decorously,** *adverb*; **decorousness,** *noun.*

decorum (*say* de-**kaw**-r'm) *noun*
propriety and good taste in conduct, dress, speech, etc.
[Latin, propriety, grace]

decoy (*say* **dee**-koy) *noun*
1. a bird or model of a bird, used to lure game.
2. a person used to lure or entice another into a trap.
decoy *verb*
to lure or trap by using a decoy.
[Dutch *de kooi* the cage]

decrease (*say* dee-**kreece**) *verb*
to make or become less in size, quantity, intensity, etc.
decrease (*say* **dee**-kreece) *noun*
a) the process of decreasing: 'industrial accidents are on the *decrease*'. b) the amount by which something is decreased: 'a large *decrease* in industrial accidents'.
Word Family: **decreasingly,** *adverb.*
[Latin *decrescere* to grow less]

decree (*say* de-**kree**) *noun*
1. an official pronouncement or edict: 'the government *decree* announced an amnesty for all political prisoners'.
2. *Law:* a court order or judgement.

decree *verb*
(decreed, decreeing)
to issue a decree.
Usage: 'fate *decreed* that she would never have children' (= ordained).
Word Family: **decretal** (*say* de-**kree**-t'l), *adjective.*
[Latin *decretus* a decision]

decree nisi (*say* de-kree **nigh**-sigh)
Law: a decree of divorce which will be made final after three months, unless cause is shown why it should not be made final.
[Latin *decretus* a decision + *nisi* unless]

decrement (*say* **dek**ri-m'nt) *noun*
a) a decrease. b) the amount by which something decreases.

decrepit (*say* de-**kreppit**) *adjective*
broken down by old age or ill health.
Word Family: **decrepitly,** *adverb*; **decrepitude,** *noun,* the state of being decrepit.
[DE- + Latin *crepare* to creak]

decrepitate (*say* de-**kreppi**-tate) *verb*
a) to heat or roast a substance, especially a salt, until it makes a crackling sound or until this sound ceases. b) to make a crackling sound.
Word Family: **decrepitation,** *noun.*

decretal *adjective*
Word Family: see DECREE.

decry *verb*
(decried, decrying)
to condemn or speak disparagingly of.

dedicate *verb*
(of an author) to inscribe a book, poem, etc., with a person's name as a sign of affection, gratitude, respect, etc.
Usage: 'he *dedicated* himself to work' (= devoted).
Word Family: **dedication,** *noun*; **dedicated,** *adjective,* wholly devoted to something; **dedicatory,** *adjective.*
[Latin *dedicare* to devote to a purpose]

deduce (*say* de-**dewce**) *verb*
to reach a conclusion by reasoning from something known: 'the detective *deduced* from the size of the footprints that the intruder was a child'.
Word Family: **deducible,** *adjective.*
[DE- + Latin *ducere* to lead]

deduct *verb*
to take away from a total amount: 'he *deducted* the running costs of his car from his taxable income'.
Word Family: **deductable, deductible,** *adjective.*

deduction *noun*
1. a) the act or process of deducting. b) something which is deducted: 'a tax *deduction*'.
2. a) a process of reasoning from a general law to a particular instance. b) a conclusion reached by this process. Compare INDUCTION.
Word Family: **deductive,** *adjective,* arguing or reasoning by deduction; **deductively,** *adverb.*

deed *noun*
1. a) an act or something done. b) an exploit or feat: 'the *deeds* of Richard the Lion-Heart were celebrated in song and legend'.
2. *Law:* a formal document which is proof of an agreement between two or more people, especially in the transfer of land.

deed poll
Law: a deed declaring formally and publicly a person's act or intentions, especially in the case of changing one's name.

deem *verb*
1. *Law:* to assume as a fact.
2. to think or to have an opinion: 'the lawyer *deemed* it against his client's interests to call the witness'.

deep *adjective*
1. far down or going far down: a) 'take a *deep* breath'; b) 'the water is only a few metres *deep* at this point'.
2. extending far in width: 'I pushed it to the back of that *deep* shelf'.
Usages:
a) 'the Lord Mayor spoke in a *deep,* commanding voice' (= low in pitch).
b) 'she has a *deep* mistrust of politicians' (= intense).
c) 'the radio telescope receives signals from *deep* space' (= far distant).
d) (*informal*) 'he appears to be very open, but I was told he's a *deep* one' (= shrewd, cunning).
e) 'we discovered him *deep* in thought' (= engrossed, occupied).
f) (*informal*) 'nuclear physics is too *deep* for me' (= difficult, involved).
go off the deep end, to become enraged.

deep *noun*
any deep place, especially in the ocean: 'our ancestors believed in monsters of the *deep*'.
Word Family: **deep, deeply,** *adverbs*; **deepness,** *noun*; **deepen,** *verb,* to make or become deep or deeper.

deep-freeze *noun*
a freezer.
Word Family: **deep-freeze,** *verb.*

deep-fry *verb*
(deep-fried, deep-frying)
to cook something by immersing it in hot oil.
Word Family: **deep-frier, deep-fryer,** *noun.*

deer *noun*
plural is **deer**
any of various hoofed mammals, the males of which have antlers, e.g. the red deer and fallow deer.

deerstalker *noun*
a helmet-shaped, cloth cap with earflaps and a peak at the back and the front.

deface (*say* de-**face**) *verb*
to damage or spoil something deliberately: 'vandals had *defaced* the railway carriage by slashing the seats'.
Word Family: **defacement,** *noun.*

de facto (*say* day **fak**-toe)
occurring or existing in fact, even if not by right: 'the rebels formed a *de facto* government'. Compare DE JURE.
[Latin, from the fact]

defame (*say* de-**fame**) *verb*
to destroy or attempt to destroy a person's good name and reputation.
defamation (*say* deffa-**may**-sh'n) *noun*
the wrong of injuring a person's good name without cause: 'to sue for *defamation* of character'.
Word Family: **defamatory** (*say* de-**famma**-tree), *adjective.*

default (*say* de-**folt**) *noun*
a failure to perform a required act: 'the defendant's *default* in not appearing for trial cost him the case'.
Phrases:
by default, 'they won the game *by default* when the opposing team didn't turn up' (= without having to compete).
in default of, in the absence of.
Word Family: **default,** *verb*; **defaulter,** *noun,* a person who defaults.

defeat (*say* de-**feet**) *verb*
1. to win a victory over: 'the enemy forces were *defeated* by superior numbers'.
2. to frustrate or thwart: 'repeated strikes *defeated* his hopes of expanding production'.
defeat *noun*
a) the act of defeating: 'his *defeat* of the World Champion earned him renown in the boxing world'. b) a loss: 'the football team suffered four successive *defeats*'.

defeatist *noun*
a person who expects defeat or failure and therefore considers that effort is useless.
Word Family: **defeatist,** *adjective*; **defeatism,** *noun.*

defecate (*say* **deffa**-kate) *verb*
to expel faeces from the bowels.
Word Family: **defecation,** *noun.*
[DE- + Latin *faeces* dregs]

defect (*say* **dee**-fekt) *noun*
a fault or flaw: 'the spluttering noise in the stereo was caused by a *defect* in the amplifier'.
defect (*say* de-**fekt**) *verb*
to abandon a cause or desert one's country, especially for political reasons: 'the spy attempted to *defect* to the East'.
Word Family: **defection,** *noun.*
[Latin *defectus* failed, deserted]

defective (*say* de-**fek**tiv) *adjective*
1. having a defect: 'the police officer pointed out that the car's brakes were *defective*'.
2. *Psychology:* having less than normal intelligence.
Word Family: **defectively,** *adverb*; **defectiveness,** *noun.*

defence (*say* de-**fence**) *noun*
in America spelt **defense**
1. the act or process of defending: 'the *defence* of the outpost cost many lives'.
2. something that defends: 'the city's *defences* were weakened by continual artillery fire'.
3. an argument or speech in justification of something: 'he put up an able *defence* of the re-zoning proposals'.
4. *Law:* a) the pleading of a defendant in answer to the charge against him. b) the defendant together with his legal counsel: 'the *defence* rests its case, Your Honour'.
Word Family: **defenceless,** *adjective*; **defencelessness,** *noun.*

defence mechanism
Psychology: a process by which a person, often unconsciously, protects himself from threatening or unpleasant ideas or emotions.

defend *verb*
1. to protect from danger or attack: 'to *defend* one's honour'.
2. to uphold or support, especially a belief or opinion: 'the Minister

defended the Government's housing scheme'.
3. *Law:* (of a barrister) to represent a defendant in a court case.
Word Family: **defendable,** *adjective;* **defender,** *noun.*
[Latin *defendere* to protect]

defendant (*say* de-**fend**'nt) *noun*
Law: a person against whom a charge or suit is brought in a court. Compare PLAINTIFF.

defense *noun*
American: defence.

defensible (*say* de-**fensi**-b'l) *adjective*
capable of being defended: 'a *defensible* argument'.
Word Family: **defensibly,** *adverb;* **defensibility, defensibleness,** *nouns.*

defensive *adjective*
serving to defend: a) 'a *defensive* manoeuvre by the army'; b) 'her attitude was *defensive*'.
Word Family: **defensively,** *adverb;* **defensiveness,** *noun.*

defer (1) (*say* de-**fir**) *verb*
(deferred, deferring)
to delay or postpone intentionally: 'the surgeon *deferred* the operation until the results of tests were checked'.
Word Family: **deferment,** *noun.*
[Latin *differre* to delay]

defer (2) (*say* de-**fir**) *verb*
(deferred, deferring)
to give way or yield to the opinion or authority of another: 'he refused to *defer* to his father when it came to politics'.
deference (*say* **deffa**-r'nce) *noun*
any courteous and polite respect: 'he treats his parents with *deference* even when he disagrees with them'.
Word Family: **deferential** (*say* deffa-**ren**-sh'l), *adjective;* **deferent,** *adjective;* **deferentially,** *adverb.*
[Latin *deferre* to grant]

defiance (*say* de-**fie**'nce) *noun*
the state of defying or refusing to recognize authority: 'he expressed his *defiance* in wild behaviour'.
Word Family: **defiant,** *adjective;* **defiantly,** *adverb.*

deficiency (*say* de-**fish**'n-see) *noun*
a lack or insufficiency: 'a *deficiency* of iron in the body may cause anaemia'.
Word Family: **deficient,** *adjective;* **deficiently,** *adverb.*
[Latin *deficiens*]

deficiency disease
an illness caused by an insufficiency of one or more essential constituents of the diet.

deficit (*say* **deffi**-sit) *noun*
Commerce: the amount by which expenditure exceeds receipts.
[Latin, it fails]

defile (1) (*say* de-**file**) *verb*
1. to make filthy or unclean: 'toxic chemicals had *defiled* the river'.
2. to corrupt or desecrate.
Word Family. **defilement,** *noun.*
[Middle English *defoul*]

defile (2) (*say* **dee**-file) *noun*
a narrow pass or gorge between mountains.
[French *défiler* to go in file]

define (*say* de-**fine**) *verb*
1. a) to state the exact meaning of: '*define* that word'. b) to describe the nature or properties of: '*define* an elementary particle for me'.
2. to determine or state the limits or boundary of: 'please *define* the area you are describing'.
3. to make the outline or form show clearly: 'the artist *defined* the shape by drawing a black line around it'.
[DE- + Latin *finis* a limit]

definite (*say* **deffa**-nit) *adjective*
clear or unambiguous: 'she didn't give me a *definite* answer either way'.
Usage: 'she was *definite* that she had seen that face before' (= sure, certain).
Word Family: **definitely,** *adverb;* **definiteness,** *noun.*

definite article
Grammar: see ARTICLE.

definition (*say* deffi-**nish**'n) *noun*
1. the act of defining.
2. the statement of the precise meaning of a word, phrase, term, etc.
3. *Physics:* a) the clarity of an image formed by a mirror, lens or cathode-ray tube. b) the clarity of reproduction of sound.

definitive (*say* de-**finni**-tiv) *adjective*
1. final or conclusive: 'the Battle of Britain was a *definitive* victory in World War 2'.
2. being the most authoritative or comprehensive: 'a *definitive* history of the Middle Ages'.
Word Family: **definitively,** *adverb;* **definitiveness,** *noun.*
[Latin *definitus* brought to a finish]

deflate *verb*
1. to release air or gas from a container, such as a balloon, tyre, etc.
Usage: 'the scandal *deflated* his good name' (= reduced).
2. *Economics:* to produce deflation.
deflation (*say* de–**flay**–sh'n) *noun*
1. the act of deflating.
2. *Economics:* a) any measures taken to lower the prices of goods and services, such as the reduction of the amount of currency in circulation. b) the effects of such measures. Compare INFLATION.
Word Family: **deflationary,** *adjective.*
[DE– + (in)FLATION]

deflect (*say* de–**flekt**) *verb*
to turn aside: a) 'the golf ball hit a tree and was *deflected* from its course'; b) 'Jimmy is easily distracted or *deflected* from his purpose'.
Word Family: **deflection, deflexion,** *noun*; **deflective,** *adjective,* causing deflection; **deflectable,** *adjective,* capable of being deflected.
[DE– + Latin *flectere* to bend]

deflower (*say* dee–**flower**) *verb*
to deprive of virginity.

defoliate (*say* de–**fole**–ee–ate) *verb*
to strip plants of their leaves, especially by using a chemical spray.
Word Family: **defoliant,** *noun,* a chemical used to strip plants of their leaves; **defoliation,** *noun.*
[DE– + Latin *folium* leaf]

deforestation
(*say* dee–forri–**stay**–sh'n) *noun*
the removal of trees or forests.
Word Family: **deforest,** *verb.*

deform (*say* de–**form**) *verb*
to spoil or disfigure the natural shape or appearance of: 'his leg was *deformed* by a large tumour'.
Word Family: **deformation,** *noun*; **deformity,** *noun,* a) the state of being deformed, b) something which is deformed.

defraud (*say* de–**frawd**) *verb*
to cheat or swindle a person out of property or a right.

defray (*say* de–**fray**) *verb*
to pay: 'the expenses of the motorway are to be *defrayed* out of taxation'.
Word Family: **defrayal, defrayment,** *nouns,* a payment of costs or expenses; **defrayable,** *adjective.*

defrock (*say* de–**frok**) *verb*
also called to **unfrock**
Religion: to expel a priest from the priesthood for an offence.

defrost (*say* de–**frost**) *verb*
a) to remove ice and frost from a refrigerator. b) to thaw out frozen food.

deft *adjective*
skilful or adroit: 'her *deft* hands swiftly bandaged the wound'.
Word Family: **deftly,** *adverb*; **deftness,** *noun.*

defunct (*say* de–**funkt**) *adjective*
having ceased to exist or function: 'all London's trolleybuses are now *defunct*'.
Word Family: **defunctness,** *noun.*
[Latin *defunctus* having done with, dead]

defuse (*say* dee–**fewz**) *verb*
to remove the fuse of: 'experts were called in to *defuse* the unexploded bomb'.
Usage: 'the diplomat tried to *defuse* the tense political situation' (= render safe or calm).

defy (*say* de–**fie**) *verb*
(defied, defying)
to oppose actively or boldly, often in the sense of a challenge: 'the cornered man *defied* the police to come and get him'.
Usage: 'the speed and ferocity of the bushfire *defied* belief' (= went beyond).

dégagé (*say* day–gah–***zhay***) *adjective*
free and easy in manner.
[French *dégager* to disengage]

degenerate (*say* de–**jenna**–rate) *verb*
1. to lose or decline in good qualities: a) 'he *degenerated* into a selfish playboy'; b) 'his health *degenerated* rapidly'.
2. *Biology:* to change to a less complex, specialized or active form: 'in man, the appendix has *degenerated* to the stage where it serves no useful purpose'.
degenerate (*say* de–**jenna**–rit) *adjective*
degraded or corrupt: 'a weak and *degenerate* ruler who ignored the people's needs'.
degenerate (*say* de–**jenna**–rit) *noun*
a person who has degenerated: 'he has become a moral *degenerate*'.
Word Family: **degenerately,** *adverb*; **degeneracy,** *noun*; **degeneration,** *noun,* a) the process of degenerating, b) the state of being degenerate; **degenerative,** *adjective.*
[DE– + Latin *genus* a breed, a kind]

degrade (*say* de-**grade**) *verb*
1. to lower in rank, status, quality or degree.
2. to deprave, corrupt or disgrace: 'I felt *degraded* by my disgusting actions'.
3. *Geography:* to wear down by erosion.
4. *Chemistry:* (of complex compounds) to break down into simpler compounds.
Word Family: **degradation** (*say* degra-**day**-sh'n), *noun,* a) the act of degrading, b) the state of being degraded.
[DE- + Latin *gradus* a step]

degree (*say* de-**gree**) *noun*
1. a step or level in a scale or process: a) 'the *degree* of proficiency reached by a student'; b) 'Aunt Emily came from a family of high *degree*'.
2. *Maths:* a unit of angular measurement, one 360th of a full circle, equal to $1{\cdot}75\times10^{-2}$ radian. See UNITS in grey pages.
3. *Geography, Astronomy:* a unit of latitude or longitude.
4. *Physics, Chemistry:* a unit in a temperature scale.
5. *Education:* a certificate given in recognition of a student's completion of all the requirements in a course of study.
6. *Grammar:* any of three forms taken by an adjective or adverb to express comparison, being **positive** (she is *pretty*), **comparative** (she is *prettier* than her sister), **superlative** (she is the *prettiest* in her class).
the third degree, the use of extreme methods, often torture, to obtain information or a confession from a person.

dehisce (*say* dee-**hiss**) *verb*
(of the pods of plants) to burst open.
Word Family: **dehiscence,** *noun;* **dehiscent,** *adjective.*
[DE- + Latin *hiscere* to open]

dehumanize (*say* dee-**hew**ma-nize) **dehumanise** *verb*
to brutalize or take away the human qualities of.
Word Family: **dehumanization,** *noun.*

dehydrate (*say* dee-**high**drate) *verb*
to lose or remove water.
Word Family: **dehydration,** *noun.*
[Greek *de-* away + *hydor* water]

deify (*say* **dee**-iff-eye) *verb*
(**deified, deifying**)
to make or worship as a god.
Word Family: **deification** (*say* dee-iffi-**kay**-sh'n), *noun.*

deign (*say* dane) *verb*
to condescend: 'she would not *deign* to answer such a rude question'.

deism (*say* **dee**-izm) *noun*
a belief in the existence of a god, based only upon reason or logic and denying all supernatural revelation. Compare THEISM.
Word Family: **deist,** *noun;* **deistic** (*say* dee-**istik**), *adjective.*
[Latin *deus* god]

deity (*say* **dee**-a-tee) *noun*
a) a god or goddess. b) the divine nature of a god.
the **Deity,** God.

déjà vu (*say* day-*zha* **voo**)
a feeling of familiarity when encountering a completely new scene or experience.
[French]

dejected (*say* de-**jek**tid) *adjective*
sad and depressed.
Word Family: **dejectedly,** *adverb;* **dejectedness, dejection,** *nouns;* **deject,** *verb.*
[DE- + Latin *jactus* thrown]

de jure (*say* day **joo**-ray)
occurring or existing by right, even if not in fact: 'though in exile, he was still the *de jure* president'.
[Latin, by right]

deka-
a prefix used for SI units, meaning ten (10^1). See UNITS in grey pages.
[Greek, ten]

dekko *noun*
(*informal*) a look: 'let's have a *dekko* at the bike'.
[Hindi]

delay (*say* de-**lay**) *verb*
1. to put off until later: 'we must *delay* our departure until next week'.
2. to make late: 'the flat tyre *delayed* us for several hours'.
Word Family: **delay,** *noun.*

delectable (*say* de-**lek**ta-b'l) *adjective*
delightful or pleasing.
Word Family: **delectably,** *adverb;* **delectation,** *noun,* delight or enjoyment.
[Latin *delectare* to attract]

delegate (*say* **delli**-gate) *verb*
1. to appoint or send someone as a representative: 'when he could not go to the meeting he *delegated* Smith to go'.
2. to give powers, duties, etc. to someone else: 'she *delegated* work to her assistant'.

Word Family: **delegate** (*say* **delli**–git), *noun*, a person who acts for or represents another; **delegation,** *noun*, a) the act of delegating, b) a group of delegates.
[DE– + Latin *legare* to depute]

delete (*say* de–**leet**) *verb*
to strike out or erase: 'several scenes have been *deleted* from the film'.
Word Family: **deletion**, *noun*, a) the act of deleting, b) something deleted.
[Latin *deletus* wiped out]

deleterious (*say* delli–**teeri**–us) *adjective*
harmful, especially to health.
Word Family: **deleteriousness,** *noun*.
[Greek *deleterios* poisonous]

deliberate (*say* de–**libba**–rit) *adjective*
1. carefully considered and intended: 'a *deliberate* act of cruelty'.
2. slow and cautious in action, etc.: 'the politician has a *deliberate* manner'.
deliberate (*say* de–**libba**–rate) *verb*
to think or talk about carefully: 'the jury *deliberated* before giving a verdict'.
Word Family: **deliberately,** *adverb*; **deliberateness,** *noun*; **deliberation,** *noun*, a) careful consideration, b) slowness or caution in action, etc.; **deliberative,** *adjective*, involved in deliberation.
[DE– + Latin *libra* scales]

delicacy (*say* **dellika**–see) *noun*
1. a fineness of texture, quality, manner, etc.
Usage: 'the *delicacy* of the child's health leaves him prone to sickness' (= weakness).
2. the state of requiring careful or tactful treatment: 'a matter of some *delicacy*'.
3. anything fine or pleasing, especially to the palate: 'many people think caviar is a *delicacy*'.

delicate (*say* **delli**–kit) *adjective*
fine in texture, quality, manner, etc.
Usages:
a) 'a *delicate* vase' (= fragile).
b) 'a *delicate* situation' (= requiring tact).
Word Family: **delicately,** *adverb*; **delicateness,** *noun*.
[Latin *delicatus* dainty]

delicatessen (*say* dellika–**tess**'n) *noun*
a shop selling cooked meats, cheeses and other foods, especially ones which have been imported.
[German *Delikatesse* delicacy]

delicious (*say* de–**lishus**) *adjective*
highly pleasing, especially in taste or smell: 'a *delicious* meal'.
Word Family: **deliciously,** *adverb*; **deliciousness,** *noun*.
[Latin *deliciae* enticements]

delight (*say* de–**lite**) *noun*
a) any great pleasure or joy. b) anything which gives pleasure.
Word Family: **delight,** *verb*; **delightedly,** *adverb*; **delightful,** *adjective*, highly pleasing; **delightfully,** *adverb*; **delightfulness,** *noun*.

delimit (*say* dee–**limm**it) *verb*
to fix or mark the limits of.
Word Family: **delimitation,** *noun*.
[DE– + Latin *limitis* of a boundary]

delineate (*say* de–**linni**–ate) *verb*
to describe or give an outline of: 'he *delineated* the plan'.
Word Family: **delineation,** *noun*.
[DE– + Latin *linea* a line]

delinquent (*say* de–**link**–w'nt) *noun*
a person who fails in his duty or is guilty of misdeeds: 'a juvenile *delinquent*'.
delinquent *adjective*
failing in a duty or obligation.
Word Family: **delinquently,** *adverb*; **delinquency,** *noun*.
[Latin *delinquens* being at fault]

deliquescent (*say* delli–**kwess**'nt) *adjective*
Chemistry: (of a crystal) absorbing water from the atmosphere in such quantities that the substance becomes a liquid. Compare EFFLORESCENT.
Word Family: **deliquesce,** *verb*; **deliquescence,** *noun*.
[Latin *deliquescere* to melt away]

delirious (*say* de–**leerius**) *adjective*
1. affected with delirium.
2. wildly excited or enthusiastic.
Word Family: **deliriously,** *adverb*; **deliriousness,** *noun*.
[Latin *delirus* demented]

delirium (*say* de–**leerium**) *noun*
1. a disorder of the mind, usually temporary, causing visions, delusions and irrational behaviour.
2. any wild emotion or excitement.

delirium tremens
short form is **DTs**
a state of delirium and shaking as a symptom of prolonged alcoholism.
[Latin *tremens* trembling]

deliver (*say* de–livva) *verb*
1. to give into the possession of someone else: 'to *deliver* a letter'.
2. to give birth to, or assist at a birth.
Usages:
a) 'the bowler *delivered* the ball to the batsman' (= directed, cast).
b) 'they were *delivered* from the peril' (= saved).
c) 'the jury *delivered* its verdict' (= pronounced).
delivery *noun*
1. the act of delivering: 'there will be no mail *delivery* on Saturdays'.
2. the act or manner of giving or sending forth: a) 'the actor had very poor *delivery*'; b) 'another good *delivery* from the bowler'.
Word Family: **deliverance,** *noun,* release or rescue.
[DE– + Latin *liberare* to set free]

dell *noun*
a small valley.

delphinium (*say* del–**finn**ium) *noun*
a garden plant with spikes of blue flowers.

delta *noun*
a deposit, usually fan–shaped, of large amounts of silt at the mouth of a river, which divides it into branches.
[from *delta,* a triangular letter of the Greek alphabet]

delude (*say* de–**lood**) *verb*
to mislead or deceive.
[DE– + Latin *ludere* to mock]

deluge (*say* **del**–yooj) *noun*
a flood or downpour.
Usage: 'at the press conference he faced a *deluge* of questions' (= overwhelming number).
Word Family: **deluge,** *verb.*

delusion (*say* de–**loo**–*zh*'n) *noun*
1. a) the act of deluding. b) the fact of being deluded.
2. a) a false opinion: 'he has *delusions* about his own importance'. b) a belief which is held despite contradictory evidence, etc.
Word Family: **delusive** (*say* de–loosiv), **delusory,** *adjectives.*
Common Error: see ILLUSION.

de luxe (*say* de **luks** *or* de **luks**)
luxurious or of a high quality: 'a *de luxe* hotel'.
[French, of luxury]

delve *verb*
to search deeply: 'in the investigation you must *delve* into all the evidence'.

demagogue (*say* **demma**–gog) *noun*
a leader who uses people's emotions and prejudices for his own interests.
Word Family: **demagoguery** (*say* demma–**gogga**–ree), **demagogy,** *nouns*; **demagogic** (*say* demma–**goggik**), **demagogical,** *adjective.*
[Greek *demos* people + *agogos* leader]

demand (*say* de–**mahnd**) *verb*
1. to ask for, leaving no chance of refusal.
2. to require: 'this job *demands* skill'.
demand *noun*
1. a) the act of demanding. b) something which is demanded.
2. a) a requirement: 'all the *demands* on my time'. b) the state of being required: 'articles in great *demand*'.
3. *Commerce:* any specific need for goods or services.
[DE– + Latin *mandare* to order]

demarcation *noun*
a) the division of anything into separate parts. b) the fixing or marking of boundaries or limits.
demarcate (*say* **dee**–mar–kate) *verb*
to fix or mark the boundaries of.

demean (*say* de–**meen**) *verb*
to lower in dignity: 'do not *demean* yourself by falling for their tricks'.

demeanour (*say* de–**meena**) *noun*
a person's behaviour or manner.

demented (*say* de–**men**tid) *adjective*
1. insane.
2. suffering from dementia.
Word Family: **dement,** *verb*; **dementedly,** *adverb.*
[DE– + Latin *mentis* of the mind]

dementia (*say* de–**mensha**) *noun*
Psychology: a decrease of mental powers characteristic of some mental disorders, and often only temporary.

demerara (*say* demma–**raira**) *noun*
unrefined brown sugar.
[after a town in Guyana]

demerit (*say* dee–**merrit**) *noun*
a fault.

demesne (*say* da–**mane** *or* da–**meen**) *noun*
a) the possession of land as one's own.
b) the land and buildings possessed.

demi–
a prefix meaning half.
[Greek]

demigod *noun*
a) a being who is part god and part man. b) a person worshipped as if a god.

demijohn *noun*
a large, narrow-necked bottle, usually covered in cane.

demilitarize (*say* dee-**mill**ita-rize) **demilitarise** *verb*
to remove military forces, usually to restore civil control.

demise (*say* dim**mize**) *noun*
death.

demo *noun*
(*informal*) a demonstration.

demobilize (*say* dee-**mo**-billize) **demobilise** *verb*
short form is **demob**
to disband armed forces.
Word Family: **demobilization**, *noun.*

democracy (*say* de-**mok**ra-see) *noun*
the government of a country by its people, usually through a parliament of representatives elected by them.
Word Family: **democratic** (*say* demma-**krat**tik), *adjective*; **democrat** (*say* **demm**a-krat), *noun*; **democratically**, *adverb.*
[Greek *demos* people + *kratia* rule]

democratize (*say* de-**mok**ra-tize) **democratise** *verb*
to make or become democratic.
Word Family: **democratization**, *noun.*

demography (*say* de-**mog**ra-fee) *noun*
the study of the statistics of birth, illness and death in communities.
Word Family: **demographer**, *noun*; **demographic** (*say* demma-**graff**ik), *adjective.*
[Greek *demos* people + *graphein* to write]

demolish (*say* de-**moll**ish) *verb*
to pull down or destroy: a) 'the house was *demolished* and flats erected'; b) 'he *demolished* the weak argument'.
Word Family: **demolition** (*say* demma-**lish**'n), *noun.*
[DE- + Latin *moliri* to construct]

demon (*say* **deem**'n) *noun*
1. an evil spirit or devil.
2. a person of great energy: 'he is a *demon* for work'.
Word Family: **demoniacal** (*say* deema-**nigh**i-k'l), **demonic** (*say* de-**monn**ik), **demoniac** (*say* de-**mo**-nee-ak), *adjectives.*
[Greek *daimon* a god]

demonstrate (*say* **demm**'n-strate) *verb*
1. to prove by arguments, evidence, etc.
2. to exhibit or show: 'she *demonstrates* great ability'.
Usages:
a) 'he *demonstrated* the new machine' (= showed and explained).
b) 'over 1000 people *demonstrated* in support of higher wages' (= held a public meeting or march).
demonstration *noun*
1. a) a clear proof: 'a *demonstration* that the earth is round'. b) an exhibition or explanation by means of examples, experiments, etc.: 'a *demonstration* of a new car'.
2. a show or expression: 'a *demonstration* of love'.
3. a display of public feeling, e.g. a mass meeting or march.
Word Family: **demonstrable** (*say* **demm**'n-str'b'l), *adjective*, able to be demonstrated; **demonstrably**, *adverb*; **demonstrator**, *noun.*
[DE- + Latin *monstrare* to show]

demonstrative (*say* de-**mon**stra-tiv) *adjective*
1. showing one's feelings or affections openly.
2. serving to explain or prove.

demoralize (*say* de-**morr**a-lize) **demoralise** *verb*
to reduce the confidence or morale of: 'she was *demoralized* when she failed her driving test'.
Word Family: **demoralization**, *noun.*

demote *verb*
to lower in rank.
Word Family: **demotion**, *noun.*

demur (*say* dim**mur**) *verb*
(**demurred, demurring**)
to make objections or disagree.
Word Family: **demur**, *noun*; **demurral**, *noun.*

demure (*say* de-**mewer**) *adjective*
1. affectedly modest.
2. quiet and serious.
Word Family: **demurely**, *adverb*; **demureness**, *noun.*

demurrage *noun*
any compensation paid for delay in loading or unloading a ship or railway goods wagon.

den *noun*
1. a place, such as a cave, where wild animals live.
Usage: 'a *den* of iniquity' (= place, abode).
2. a quiet, cosy room for personal use.

dendrite *noun*
Geology: a) a branchlike figure or marking found on or in certain rocks, due to the presence of a foreign

material. b) any branchlike crystalline form.
Word Family: **dendritic** (*say* den-**drit**tik), *adjective.*
[Greek *dendron* a tree]

denial *noun*
Word Family: see DENY.

denied *verb*
the past tense and past participle of the verb **deny**.

denier (*say* **denn**ia) *noun*
a unit of weight used to measure the fineness of silk, cotton, etc. and equal to the weight in grams of 9000 m of yarn.
[French, a standard weight]

denigrate (*say* **denni**-grate) *verb*
to attack the reputation of.
Word Family: **denigration,** *noun.*
[DE- + Latin *niger* black]

denim *noun*
a strong, cotton fabric of twill weave, used for trousers, etc.
[French *denîmes* from Nîmes, France, where it was first made]

denizen (*say* **denn**iz'n) *noun*
a resident or inhabitant.

denominate *verb*
to give a specific name to.

denomination *noun*
1. a religious movement or group sharing common beliefs and identified by a particular name.
2. a unit of a specified value in a system of weights or currency: 'in Australia the coin of the lowest *denomination* is the cent'.
Word Family: **denominational,** *adjective,* relating to a religious group.

denominator (*say* de-**nommi**-nayta) *noun*
Maths: the part of the fraction below the line, showing how many equal parts a quantity is divided into, such as the 4 in $\frac{1}{4}$. Two fractions with the same denominator, such as $\frac{1}{4}$ and $\frac{3}{4}$ are said to have a **common denominator**. Compare NUMERATOR.

denote *verb*
1. to indicate or be a sign of: 'an asterisk often *denotes* a footnote'.
2. to mean or designate: 'what does this word *denote*?'.
Word Family: **denotation,** *noun.*
Common Error: DENOTE, CONNOTE have related but distinct meanings: *denote* refers to what a word means in its strict sense, whereas *connote* refers to all of the meanings connected with a word.

dénouement (*say* day-**noo**-mon) *noun*
the final unravelling of a plot or story.
[French *dénouer* to untie]

denounce *verb*
1. to speak or inform against: 'he was *denounced* as a traitor'.
2. to express strong disapproval: 'all banks *denounced* the government's policy on home loans'.
Word Family: **denunciation** (*say* de-nunsi-**ay**-sh'n), *noun.*
[Latin *denuntiare* to announce, to warn]

dense *adjective*
1. thickly or closely packed together: 'the airport was closed owing to *dense* fog'.
2. (*informal*) stupid.
Word Family: **densely,** *adverb*; **denseness,** *noun.*
[Latin *densus* crowded]

density (*say* **den**sa-tee) *noun*
1. the state or quality of being dense.
2. *Physics:* the amount of a particular property, such as mass, possessed by a substance per unit of volume.

dent *noun*
a hollow in a surface, usually due to a blow.
Word Family: **dent,** *verb.*

dental *adjective*
of or relating to the teeth.

dentine (*say* den-**teen**) *noun*
a hard tissue found underneath the enamel of teeth.

dentist *noun*
a person medically qualified to care for people's teeth, including surgical operations and fitting false teeth.
Word Family: **dentistry** (*say* **den**tis-tree), *noun.*
[Latin *dens* tooth]

dentition *noun*
the type, number and arrangement of teeth in the mouth.

denture (*say* **den**cher) *noun*
a plate with one or more artificial teeth.

denude (*say* de-**newd**) *verb*
to make bare or naked.
Word Family: **denudation** (*say* dee-new-**day**-sh'n), *noun.*
[DE- + Latin *nudus* naked]

denunciation *noun*
Word Family: see DENOUNCE.

deny (*say* de-**nigh**) *verb*
(**denied, denying**)
1. to declare as untrue: 'he *denied* their charges of assault'.

2. to refuse to believe or acknowledge: 'she *denies* the existence of a god'.
3. to refuse to grant: 'they *denied* him the right to see a lawyer'.
Word Family: **denial,** *noun.*

deodorant (*say* dee-**o**-da-r'nt) ***noun***
any substance for masking smells.

deodorize (*say* dee-**o**-da-rize)
deodorise ***verb***
to remove smells.
Word Family: **deodorizer,** *noun.*

deoxyribonucleic acid
(*say* dee-oksi-**rye**-bo-new-klee-**ik** assid)
short form is **DNA**
Biology: an organic compound found in chromosomes as a double spiral and controlling and transmitting genetic characters.

depart ***verb***
1. to leave.
2. to vary from the normal course: 'he *departed* from the topic to talk about the coming exams'.
Word Family: **departed,** *adjective,* dead.

department ***noun***
any of the various sections into which something is divided: a) 'the shoe *department* is on the first floor'; b) 'which government *department* is in charge of social welfare?'.
Word Family: **departmental** (*say* deepart-**men**-t'l), *adjective;* **departmentally,** *adverb.*
[Latin *dispertire* to separate into parts]

department store
a large shop in which many kinds of goods are sold in different departments.

departure (*say* de-**parcher**) ***noun***
the act of departing: a) 'time of *departure* is 7 p.m.'; b) 'this is a *departure* from the normal routine'.

depend ***verb***
1. to rely: 'you may *depend* on him for support'.
2. to be determined by: 'it all *depends* on the weather'.
dependable ***adjective***
able to be depended on.
dependant ***noun***
a person who depends on another for aid or support.
Word Family: **dependent,** *adjective,* depending on something else; **dependably,** *adverb;* **dependability,** *noun,* the state of being dependable; **dependence,** *noun,* the state of being dependent.
[DE- + Latin *pendere* to hang]

dependency ***noun***
1. the state of being dependent.
2. a small country ruled by another.

dependent variable
Maths: see FUNCTION.

depersonalize (*say* dee-**pers**'na-lize)
depersonalise ***verb***
1. to make less personal: 'the introduction of computers *depersonalized* the company'.
2. *Psychology:* to lose the feeling of the reality of one's own personality or body.
Word Family: **depersonalization,** *noun.*

depict ***verb***
to represent in words or a picture.
Word Family: **depiction,** *noun.*
[DE- + Latin *pictus* painted]

depilatory (*say* de-**pilla**-tree) ***adjective***
(of cosmetics) able to remove hair from the body.
Word Family: **depilatory,** ***noun;*** **depilate** (*say* **deppi**-late), *verb.*
[DE- + Latin *pilus* hair]

deplete (*say* de-**pleet**) ***verb***
to reduce or lessen until little remains: 'the stock was *depleted* by the increased demand'.
Word Family: **depletion,** *noun.*
[Latin *depletus* emptied out]

deplorable (*say* de-**plawra**-b'l)
adjective
worthy of regret or reproach: 'the wretched state of their house is *deplorable*'.
Word Family: **deplorably,** *adverb;* **deplore,** *verb,* to feel or express pity or disapproval.
[Latin *deplorare* to weep bitterly]

deploy (*say* de-**ploy**) ***verb***
to spread out troops, etc., especially in strategic positions.
Word Family: **deployment,** *noun.*

depolarize, depolarise ***verb***
to deprive of polarity or polarization.

deport (*say* de-**port**) ***verb***
1. to expel from a country.
2. to conduct or behave: 'he *deported* himself with dignity in a trying situation'.
Word Family: **deportation,** *noun;* **deportee,** *noun,* a person who is deported.
[DE- + Latin *portare* to carry]

deportment *noun*
the manner of conducting oneself.

depose (*say* de-**poze**) *verb*
to remove from office or a position of power: 'the President was *deposed* by a military coup'.

deposit (*say* de-**pozz**it) *verb*
1. to put or lay down: 'silt was *deposited* at the mouth of the river'.
2. to put for safekeeping: 'she *deposited* her jewels in the bank's safe'.
3. to make a part payment.
Word Family: **deposit**, *noun*, something which is deposited; **depositor**, *noun.*
[DE- + Latin *positus* placed]

deposition (*say* deppa-**zish**'n) *noun*
1. the act of deposing.
2. the act of depositing.
3. *Law:* the written record of evidence given under oath.

depository (*say* de-**pozzi**-tree) *noun*
a storehouse.

depot (*say* **deppo**) *noun*
1. a place where things are kept or stored: 'a bus *depot*'.
2. *American:* a railway station or bus terminal.

deprave (*say* de-**prave**) *verb*
to corrupt or make bad.
Word Family: **depravity** (*say* dee-**pravvi**-tee), *noun.*
[Latin *depravare* to make crooked]

deprecate (*say* depri-kate) *verb*
to express disapproval of.
deprecatory (*say* depra-**kayta**-ree) *adjective*
1. expressing disapproval.
2. apologetic.
Word Family: **deprecatingly**, *adverb*; **deprecation**, *noun.*
[DE- + Latin *precari* to pray]

depreciate (*say* de-**preeshi**-ate) *verb*
1. to lessen in value. Compare APPRECIATE.
2. to disparage or belittle.
Word Family: **depreciation**, *noun*; **depreciatory**, *adjective.*
[DE- + Latin *pretium* price]

depredation (*say* depri-**day**-sh'n) *noun*
the act of preying upon or plundering.
Word Family: **depredate**, *verb*; **depredator**, *noun.*
[DE- + Latin *praedari* to plunder]

depress (*say* de-**press**) *verb*
1. to sadden or lower the spirits of: 'she seemed *depressed* after his departure'.
2. to lower or press down on: 'to operate the machine *depress* this lever'.
3. to lower or lessen in value, price, etc.
Word Family: **depressive**, *adjective*; **depressively**, *adverb.*
[Latin *depressus* weighed down]

depressant (*say* de-**press**'nt) *adjective*
1. serving to lower the rate of bodily processes.
2. tending to sadden or lower the spirits of.
depressant *noun*
a sedative.

depressed area
an area where there is widespread unemployment, low incomes and poor housing.

depression *noun*
1. the state of being depressed.
2. a sunken part or place.
3. *Weather:* see LOW (1).
4. *Economics:* a decline in business activity, usually accompanied by an increase in unemployment and a lowering of income.

deprive (*say* de-**prive**) *verb*
a) to take away from. b) to withhold.
Word Family: **deprivation** (*say* depri-**vay**-sh'n), *noun.*
[DE- + Latin *privare* to rob]

depth *noun*
1. the state of being deep.
2. the distance downwards, inwards or backwards: a) 'the *depth* of the pool is 3 m'; b) 'what is the *depth* of this shelf?'.
3. (*usually plural*) a) a deep or distant part: 'to plumb the *depths* of the sea'. b) an intense state or feeling: 'we found him in the *depths* of despair'.
Usages:
a) 'the ship struck the reef in the *depth* of night' (= most intense part).
b) 'the picture has great *depth* of colour' (= richness).
c) 'politics is definitely out of my *depth*' (= understanding, comprehension).

depth charge
a type of bomb designed to explode underwater and used to destroy submarines.

deputation (*say* dep-yoo-**tay**-sh'n) *noun*
a group appointed to represent others: 'the employer talked with the *deputation* from a trade union'.

depute (*say* de-**pute**) *verb*
1. to appoint as one's agent or deputy.

2. to assign a responsibility, task, etc. to a deputy.

deputize (*say* **dep**–yoo–tize) **deputise** *verb*
a) to appoint as a deputy. b) to act as a deputy: 'can you *deputize* for the boss while he is away?'.

deputy (*say* **dep**–yoo–tee) *noun*
1. an appointed or elected assistant: 'a *deputy* prime minister'.
2. a person appointed to act for another.

deracinate (*say* de–**rassi**–nate) *verb*
to uproot.
[DE– + Latin *radicis* of a root]

derail *verb*
to cause a railway vehicle to leave the track.
Word Family: **derailment,** *noun.*

derange *verb*
to throw into disorder or confusion: 'his mind was *deranged* by his bereavement'.
Word Family: **deranged**, *adjective,* a) disturbed, b) insane; **derangement,** *noun.*

derby (*say* **dar**–bee) *noun*
1. *American:* a bowler hat.
2. an important race: 'the Greyhound *Derby*'.
local derby, a match, especially soccer, between local teams.
[after *The Derby,* the premier flat race for horses]

derelict (*say* **derri**–likt) *adjective*
abandoned or neglected: 'a *derelict* old house'.
Word Family: **derelict,** *noun,* a neglected person, especially a vagrant; **dereliction,** *noun.*
[Latin *derelictus* forsaken]

deride (*say* de–**ride**) *verb*
to mock or jeer in contempt: 'the others *derided* his ignorant questions'.
Word Family: **deridingly**, *adverb.*
[Latin *deridere* to laugh to scorn]

de rigueur (*say* der re–**ger**)
necessary or required by tradition or social custom.
[French]

derision (*say* de–**rizh**'n) *noun*
the act of deriding or mocking: 'his speech was greeted with *derision* by the crowd'.
Word Family: **derisive** (*say* de–**rye**–siv), *adjective,* mocking; **derisory** (*say* de–**rye**–za–ree), *adjective,* mocking or inviting derision; **derisively,** *adverb.*

derivation (*say* derri–**vay**–sh'n) *noun*
1. a) the act or process of deriving. b) the source or origin of anything: 'that word has a Latin *derivation*'.
2. *Maths:* the proof of a theorem.
3. *Grammar:* the process by which new words are formed from existing root words by adding affixes. *Example:* understand*ing*, *mis*understand are formed from *understand.*
[Latin *derivare* to draw off]

derive (*say* de–**rive**) *verb*
to come or obtain from a source or origin: 'many English words *derive* from ancient Greek'.
Usage: 'he *derives* much pleasure from gardening' (= gets, obtains).
derivative (*say* de–**rivva**–tiv) *adjective*
being derived from another source.
Usage: 'this essay is obviously *derivative*' (= copied, not original).
derivative *noun*
1. anything which is derived, such as one chemical compound prepared from another: 'petrol is a *derivative* of crude oil'.
2. *Maths:* the instantaneous rate of change of a function, with respect to the independent variable.

dermatitis (*say* derma–**tie**–tis) *noun*
Medicine: an inflammation or allergy of the skin.
[Greek *dermatos* of the skin + –ITIS]

dermatology (*say* derma–**tolla**–jee) *noun*
the study of the skin and its diseases.
Word Family: **dermatologist,** *noun.*

derogatory (*say* da–**rogga**–tree) *adjective*
tending or intended to damage or discredit: 'a *derogatory* name'.
Word Family: **derogatorily,** *adverb*; **derogatoriness,** *noun*; **derogate** (*say* **derra**–gate), *verb,* to damage or take away a good quality, etc.; **derogation,** *noun.*

derrick *noun*
a stationary device for supporting or lifting, such as a ship's crane or the framed tower erected over oilwells.
[after *Derrick,* a famous hangman in London in the early 17th century]

derring–do *noun*
an old word meaning great courage or daring.
[from *daring to do*]

derris *noun*
a tropical plant, the roots of which are used to make an insecticide.

derv *noun*
a diesel oil for large road vehicles.
[from D(iesel) E(ngined) R(oad) V(ehicle)]

dervish *noun*
a member of any of various Moslem mendicant orders devoted to poverty and chastity, some of whom achieve religious ecstasy through religious chants, whirling dances, etc.
[Persian *darvesh* poor]

desalination (*say* dee-salli-**nay**-sh'n) *noun*
the process of removing salt from seawater, usually by distillation, to make it suitable for drinking or use in farm irrigation.
Word Family: **desalinate, desalinize, desalinise,** *verbs.*
[DE- + Latin *salis* of salt]

descant (*say* **dess**-kant) *noun*
Music: an extra part in a song or melody, played or sung at a higher pitch.

descend (*say* de-**send**) *verb*
to come or go down: a) 'he *descended* the ladder carefully'; b) 'the road *descends* steeply to the lake'.
Usages:
a) 'he is *descended* from French ancestors' (= derived by birth).
b) 'she would not *descend* to such nastiness' (= lower herself).
descend on, descend upon, 'the whole family *descended on* us last weekend' (= visited unexpectedly).
Word Family: **descendant,** *noun,* a person who is descended from another; **descendent,** *adjective.*

descent (*say* de-**sent**) *noun*
1. the act of descending: 'their *descent* from the snow-covered peak was dangerous'.
2. a slope: 'the road follows a steep *descent* into the valley'.
3. the relationship or link between a person and his ancestors.

describe (*say* de-**skribe**) *verb*
1. to give a picture or account of something in words: 'can you *describe* the man who attacked you?'.
2. *Maths:* to draw: '*describe* a line between points A and B'.
[DE- + Latin *scribere* to write]

description (*say* de-**skrip**-sh'n) *noun*
a picture in words: 'she was able to give a detailed *description* of the thief'.
Usage: 'the vintage car rally was attended by old cars of every *description*' (= sort, variety).

descriptive *adjective*
relating to or using description: '*descriptive* poetry'.

descry *verb*
(**descried, descrying**)
to catch sight of something distant or difficult to see: 'the lookout *descried* three enemy ships on the horizon'.

desecrate (*say* **dessi**-krate) *verb*
to misuse something sacred by treating it with disrespect.
Word Family: **desecration,** *noun*; **desecrator,** *noun,* a person who desecrates.
[DE- + Latin *sacer* sacred]

desegregate (*say* dee-**segri**-gate) *verb*
to end segregation of different races, sexes, etc.
Word Family: **desegregation,** *noun.*

desensitize (*say* dee-**sensi**-tize) **desensitise** *verb*
1. *Biology:* to limit or eliminate the sensitivity of the whole or a part of an organism to an external stimulus.
2. to make less sensitive.
Word Family: **desensitization,** *noun.*

desert (1) (*say* **dezz**ert) *noun*
a barren, often sandy, area of land having low rainfall.
[Latin *desertus* forsaken]

desert (2) (*say* de-**zert**) *verb*
to leave or abandon, especially without intending to return: 'to *desert* the army'.
Word Family: **deserted,** *adjective*; **deserter,** *noun*; **desertion,** *noun,* the act of deserting.

desert (3) (*say* de-**zert**) *noun*
(*usually plural*) a deserved reward or punishment: 'I hope that bad driver gets his *deserts*'.

deserve (*say* de-**zerv**) *verb*
to earn or have a right to: 'he *deserves* to win because he tries so hard'.
deserving *adjective*
worthy of help, reward, etc.: 'please give generously to this *deserving* charity'.
Word Family: **deservedly,** *adverb,* justly; **deservingly,** *adverb.*
[Latin *deservire* to serve with devotion]

déshabillé (*say* dayza-**bee**-yay) *adjective*
carelessly or only partly dressed.
[French *déshabiller* to undress]

desiccate *verb*
to dry thoroughly, especially in order to preserve.

desiccator *noun*
any of various devices used for drying foodstuffs or chemical substances.
Word Family: **desiccation,** *noun.*
[DE– + Latin *siccus* dry]

desiderate (*say* de–**zidda**–rate) *verb*
to desire or long for something felt to be missing.
Word Family: **desideration,** *noun.*

desideratum (*say* de–zidder–**ah**–t'm) *noun*
plural is **desiderata**
something which is lacking but desired.
[Latin]

design (*say* de–**zine**) *verb*
to invent or plan, especially by preparing outlines or drawings: 'their house was *designed* by a young architect'.
Usage: 'we *design* to go overseas next year' (= intend).
design *noun*
1. a) an outline or drawing from which something is made. b) the art of designing: 'a school of graphic *design*'.
2. the arrangement of lines, shapes and details which gives unity to a painting, structure, etc.
3. a plan or scheme.
Phrases:
by design, 'police feel that the huge fire was lit *by design*' (= deliberately, on purpose).
have designs on, 'I think the dog *has designs on* your meal' (= wants, intends to take).
Word Family: **designing,** *adjective,* cunning or crafty; **designedly,** *adverb,* on purpose.

designate (*say* **dezzig**–nate) *verb*
1. to mark or point out clearly: 'voters should *designate* their preferences by ticks in the margin'.
2. to nominate or appoint to a position.
Word Family: **designation,** *noun,* a) the act of designating or appointing, b) a name; **designate** (*say* **dezzig**–nit), *adjective,* appointed but not yet installed.
[Latin *designatus*]

designer *noun*
a person who creates and produces designs: 'a fashion *designer*'.

desirable (*say* de–**zire**–a–b'l) *adjective*
worthy to be desired: 'it is not a very *desirable* area to live in'.
Usages:
a) 'I don't think that is a *desirable* idea' (= advisable).
b) 'she's a very *desirable* woman' (= sexually attractive).

desire (*say* de–**zire**) *verb*
1. to hope strongly to have or obtain: 'he *desires* success more than anything'.
2. to ask for or request: 'the manager *desires* that all the staff should come to his office'.
Word Family: **desire,** *noun,* a strong hope or longing; **desirous,** *adjective,* desiring.
[Latin *desiderare*]

desist (*say* de–**zist**) *verb*
to cease or stop: 'please *desist* from making that dreadful noise!'.
[DE– + Latin *sistere* to stop]

desk *noun*
a table designed for use when reading or writing.

desolate (*say* **dessa**–lit) *adjective*
lonely, bare or dismal: a) 'it's a bleak and *desolate* part of the country'; b) 'she lived a *desolate,* friendless life'.
desolate (*say* **dessa**–late) *verb*
to make desolate: 'the troops *desolated* much farmland in their raids'.
Word Family: **desolately,** *adverb;* **desolation,** *noun,* a) the act of making desolate, b) the state of being wretched or lonely; **desolateness,** *noun,* the state of being desolate.
[DE– + Latin *solus* alone]

despair (*say* dis–**pair**) *noun*
a) a complete loss of hope: 'to weep in *despair*'. b) something which causes a loss of hope: 'she is the *despair* of her family'.
Word Family: **despair,** *verb,* to be filled with despair.

despatch *noun, verb*
see DISPATCH.

desperado (*say* despa–**rah**–doe) *noun*
plural is **desperadoes** or **desperados**
a reckless or dangerous criminal.

desperate (*say* **despa**–rit) *adjective*
being full of despair and ready to take any risk: 'the bank clerk made a *desperate* attempt to tackle the thieves'.
Usages:
a) 'the police have issued a warning that three *desperate* criminals are in the area' (= dangerous, violent).
b) 'the drought has caused a *desperate* shortage of staple foods' (= extremely serious).
Word Family: **desperately,** *adverb;* **desperateness,** *noun,* the state of being

desperate; **desperation,** *noun,* extreme despair.
[DE– + Latin *sperare* to hope]

despicable (*say* de–**spikka**–b'l) *adjective*
deserving contempt or scorn: 'his cruel treatment of that dog is quite *despicable*'.
Word Family: **despicably,** *adverb*; **despicableness,** *noun.*
[DE– + Latin *spicere* to look]

despise (*say* de–**spize**) *verb*
to feel scorn or contempt for: 'I *despise* fools'.

despite (*say* de–**spite**) *preposition*
in spite of: 'she continued *despite* our warning'.

despoil (*say* de–**spoil**) *verb*
to rob or plunder.
Word Family: **despoliation** (*say* de–spole–ee–**ay**–sh'n), *noun,* the act of despoiling.

despondent *adjective*
unhappy or melancholy due to disappointment, etc.: 'the players were *despondent* at losing the game'.
Word Family: **despondently,** *adverb*; **despondency,** *noun.*
[Latin *despondere* to lose courage]

despot (*say* **dess**pot) *noun*
a ruler with complete and oppressive power.
Word Family: **despotic** (*say* dess–**pottik**), *adjective,* of or like a despot; **despotically,** *adverb.*
[Greek *despotes* master]

despotism *noun*
also called **autocracy**
a) a government with complete power, authority and control. b) any unlimited power.

dessert (*say* de–**zert**) *noun*
any sweet food served as the last course of a meal.
dessertspoon *noun*
an oval spoon between a teaspoon and a tablespoon in size.
[French *desservir* to clear the table]

destination *noun*
the place or point to which something is going: 'their *destination* was London but they went via Asia'.

destine (*say* **destin**) *verb*
to set apart for a particular use, future, etc.: 'she was *destined* to die young'.

destiny (*say* **desti**–nee) *noun*
a) the inevitable fate or course of events which affect a person, considered to be beyond human control: 'his final *destiny* was a lonely death'. b) the power believed to determine these events: '*destiny* has played us a cruel trick'.
[Latin *destinare* to determine beforehand]

destitute (*say* **desti**–tewt) *adjective*
completely deprived of or without something.
Word Family: **destitution,** *noun.*

destroy (*say* de–**stroy**) *verb*
1. to ruin or make useless: 'the fire completely *destroyed* the building'.
2. to put an end to.
[DE– + Latin *struere* to build]

destroyer *noun*
1. a person or thing that destroys.
2. a small, fast warship.

destructible *adjective*
able to be destroyed.

destruction *noun*
1. a) the act of destroying: 'the insects' *destruction* of the crops was complete'. b) the state of being destroyed: 'the *destruction* throughout the countryside was terrible'.
2. a cause or means of destroying: 'drinking was his final *destruction*'.

destructive *adjective*
tending or intended to destroy or hurt.
Word Family: **destructively,** *adverb*; **destructiveness,** *noun.*

destructive distillation
Chemistry: the strong heating of a complex substance, such as coal, so that it decomposes into a number of simpler substances which are distilled off.

desuetude (*say* **dess**–yewi–tewd) *noun*
the state of being no longer used: 'many of the country's laws had fallen into *desuetude* under the new government'.
[DE– + Latin *suetus* accustomed]

desultory (*say* **dezzul**–tree) *adjective*
disconnected or random: 'the *desultory* chatter faded away as the teacher entered the room'.
Word Family: **desultorily,** *adverb*; **desultoriness,** *noun.*

detach (*say* de–**tach**) *verb*
to separate or take apart: a) '*detach* this coupon from the page by cutting along the dotted line'; b) 'a small troop was *detached* to guard the town'.

detached *adjective*
separate or unattached.
Usages:
a) 'this is the only *detached* house in the street' (= not joined to another).
b) 'he takes a surprisingly *detached* view of his own life' (= objective, unconcerned).
Word Family: **detachable**, *adjective*, able to be detached.

detachment *noun*
1. the state of being detached or unconcerned: 'his air of *detachment* makes it difficult to talk to him'.
2. the act of detaching or separating.
3. something which is detached from a larger group, etc., such as a number of troops sent out for a particular task.

detail (*say* **dee**–tale) *noun*
1. all the small, particular parts which make up a whole: a) 'the elaborate *detail* in the painting received close examination'; b) 'tell us all the *details* of the party'.
2. a small group chosen for a special task: 'the young constable joined the traffic *detail*'.
detail *verb*
1. to describe fully: 'let me *detail* my plans for tomorrow'.
2. to choose or appoint for a special task: 'he was *detailed* to supervise the clean–up'.

detain (*say* de–**tane**) *verb*
to keep back or confine: 'police *detained* three men for questioning'.
Word Family: **detainment,** *noun*; **detainee,** *noun*, a person confined or imprisoned, especially by police.
[DE- + Latin *tenere* to hold]

detect *verb*
to discover or notice: 'I *detect* a smell of burning in the kitchen'.
detection *noun*
the act of detecting: 'he has always been fascinated by methods of crime *detection*'.
Word Family: **detectable, detectible,** *adjective*, able to be detected.
[DE– + Latin *tectus* covered]

detective *noun*
a member of the police force or a private organization who obtains information or evidence about crimes, criminals, etc.

detector *noun*
1. a person or thing that detects.
2. *Radio:* a device which registers or records signals, currents, etc.

détente (*say* day–**tont**) *noun*
an easing or relaxing of strained relationships between countries.
[French, a relaxation]

detention *noun*
1. the act of detaining.
2. the confining or keeping back of a person, often as a form of punishment.

deter (*say* de–**ter**) *verb*
(deterred, deterring)
to discourage by creating fear, doubt, etc.: 'don't be *deterred* by his haughty mānner'.
Word Family: **determent,** *noun.*
[DE– + Latin *terrere* to frighten]

detergent (*say* de–**ter**–j'nt) *noun*
any cleaning agent, especially a synthetic substance made from petroleum products.
Word Family: **detergent,** *adjective*, having the power to clean or purify.
[Latin *detergere* to wipe off]

deteriorate (*say* de–**teeria**–rate) *verb*
to become worse or of less value: 'the standard of living *deteriorated* rapidly during the national strike'.
Word Family: **deterioration,** *noun.*
[Latin *deterior* worse]

determinant (*say* de–**termi**–nant) *noun*
also called a **determinative**
anything which decides or determines: 'cost was the main *determinant* in their decision to drop the plan'.

determinate (*say* dee–**terminit**) *adjective*
definite or fixed: 'there is no *determinate* time limit for repaying our loan'.
Word Family: **determinately,** *adverb*; **determinateness,** *noun.*

determine (*say* de–**termin**) *verb*
1. to decide or establish: 'society *determines* a large part of our attitudes'.
2. to settle conclusively: 'three judges were appointed to *determine* the dispute'.
determined *adjective*
firmly decided or resolved: 'we could see that she was *determined* to come'.
determination *noun*
1. the quality of being firmly decided or determined: '*determination* to win'.
2. the act of determining or deciding.
Word Family: **determinedly,** *adverb*; **determinable,** *adjective.*
[DE– + Latin *terminare* to set a boundary to]

determinism (*say* dee–**termi**–nizm) *noun*

Philosophy: the belief that we are not free to act otherwise than we do since all our actions are determined by past events and our environment.
Word Family: **determinist,** *noun;* **determinist, deterministic,** *adjectives.*

deterrent (*say* de–**terr**'nt) *noun*
anything which deters or restrains: 'the sight of the sharks was a *deterrent* even to enthusiastic swimmers'.
Word Family: **deterrence,** *noun;* **deterrent,** *adjective.*

detest (*say* de–**test**) *verb*
to hate or dislike strongly: 'she *detests* being called a baby'.
detestable *adjective*
deserving to be detested: 'what a *detestable* liar!'.
Word Family: **detestably,** *adverb;* **detestation,** *noun.*

dethrone *verb*
to remove a monarch from the throne.
Word Family: **dethronement,** *noun.*

detonate (*say* **detta**–nate) *verb*
to explode or cause to explode violently.
detonator *noun*
a small explosive device used to make another substance or object explode.
[DE– + Latin *tonare* to thunder]

detonation (*say* detta–**nay**–sh'n) *noun*
1. an explosion.
2. *Chemistry:* a violent, rapid combustion which forms a shockwave.

detour (*say* **dee**–toor) *noun*
an alternative route, especially one used temporarily to avoid an obstruction on the main route.
Word Family: **detour,** *verb,* to make a detour.
[French, a way round]

detract (*say* de–**trakt**) *verb*
to take away from the value or quality of something: 'his baldness rather *detracts* from his good looks'.
detraction *noun*
1. belittlement or slander: 'his criticism of the artist's work seems to be based on personal *detraction*'.
2. the act of detracting.
Word Family: **detractive, detractory,** *adjectives;* **detractor,** *noun.*
[Latin *detractus* dragged off]

detrimental (*say* detri–**men**–t'l) *adjective*
harmful or damaging: 'smoking is *detrimental* to your health'.
Word Family: **detrimentally,** *adverb;* **detriment,** *noun,* any harm or damage.
[Latin *detrimentum* a rubbing off]

detritus (*say* de–**try**–tus) *noun*
Geology: any particles of rock or other material which are worn or broken away by weathering, erosion, etc.
[Latin, rubbed away]

de trop (*say* der **tro**)
unwelcome or in the way: 'he felt himself to be *de trop* at the party'.
[French, (one) too many]

deuce (1) (*say* **dewce**) *noun*
1. the number two on playing cards or dice.
2. *Tennis:* a stage in the game where scores are equal and one player must win two consecutive points to win the game.
[Old French *deus* two]

deuce (2) (*say* **dewce**) *noun*
(*informal*) bad luck or the devil.
deuced *adjective*
(*informal*) annoying.
[from DEUCE (1), the throw of the dice which is the least wanted]

deuterium (*say* dew–**teerium**) *noun*
an isotope of hydrogen, having a neutron as well as a proton in the nucleus. Deuterium oxide (also called **heavy water**) is present in natural water at about one part in 5000 and is used in some nuclear reactors as a moderator.
[Greek *deuteros* second]

devalue (*say* dee–**val**–yoo) *verb*
also called to **devaluate**
1. *Economics:* to lower the value of the currency of one country in relation to the currencies of other countries or to gold, thus making imports dearer and exports cheaper.
2. to lower or reduce the value of anything.
Word Family: **devaluation,** *noun.*

devastate (*say* **devva**–state) *verb*
to make desolate: 'we were *devastated* by the loss of the two cats'.
Word Family: **devastation,** *noun.*
[DE– + Latin *vastare* to lay waste]

devastating *adjective*
tending to devastate: 'a *devastating* storm has hit the coast'.
Usage: 'she wore a *devastating* green dress' (= very effective).

develop (*say* de–**vellup**) *verb*
1. to grow or cause to grow more fully or completely: 'girls *develop* breasts at puberty'.
Usages:
a) 'you must *develop* your knowledge' (= expand).

b) 'the council has *developed* a plan to block off traffic from the city' (= created and advanced).
2. *Photography:* to treat exposed film, etc. with chemicals to produce a visible image.
3. to build on or increase the value of land, e.g. by providing electricity, sewerage, etc.
development *noun*
1. the act of developing: 'land *development* in the outer suburbs has caused a rise in prices'.
2. a new stage or event during growth or evolution: 'are there any *developments* in the industrial dispute?'.
developer *noun*
1. *Photography:* the chemical used to develop film.
2. a person or organization that develops land.
[French *développer* to unwrap]

deviate (*say* **deevi–ate**) *verb*
1. to differ or turn aside from what is usual or accepted: 'let us *deviate* from the lecture for a moment and talk about exams'.
2. to differ from an established average.
deviant *adjective*
different from what is usual or accepted.
Word Family: **deviant,** *noun,* a person or thing that is deviant.
[Latin *de–* off + *via* the way]

deviation (*say* deevi–**ay**–sh'n) *noun*
1. the act of deviating.
2. a movement away from the established path, average, etc.
3. *Maths:* the difference between any element in a set of observations and some standard value, often the mean. The **standard deviation** is a quantity that measures the spread of a set of values around the average.

device (*say* de–**vice**) *noun*
anything which is invented or used for a particular purpose, especially a mechanical tool.
Usages:
a) 'a metaphor is a literary *device*' (= tool).
b) 'I have a *device* to make sure we are not seen' (= plan, scheme).
c) 'the kangaroo and the emu are *devices* on the Australian coat of arms' (= emblems, figures).
leave to one's own devices, 'let's see how he does it if he is *left to his own devices*' (= allowed to do as he wishes).

devil (*say* **devv**'l) *noun*
1. *Religion:* (*sometimes capital*) a) the chief spirit of evil opposed to God. b) any subordinate evil spirit opposed to God.
2. a very evil person.
3. an unlucky or unfortunate person: 'poor *devil*!'.
4. a person of great energy, cleverness, etc.: 'she's a *devil* at tennis'.
Phrases:
give the devil his due, to be fair or just, even to the wicked.
play the devil with, to ruin or upset badly.
speak, talk of the devil, here comes the person we were just speaking about.
devil *verb*
(devilled, devilling)
1. *Cooking:* to grill or prepare food with hot spices, such as mustard, etc.
2. to work, often without payment, in order to gain experience, especially of a young barrister.

devilish (*say* **devv**'l–ish) *adjective*
1. evil or like a devil.
2. (*informal*) great: '*devilish* skill'.
Word Family: **devilish, devilishly,** *adverbs.*

devil–may–care *adjective*
careless or reckless: 'he had a *devil–may–care* attitude to his work, which worried his parents'.

devilry, devilment *noun*
mischievous or wicked behaviour.

devil's advocate
a person who tests an argument or policy by putting forward the criticisms likely to be made by its opponents.

devious (*say* **deevius**) *adjective*
not straight or direct: 'we came by a *devious* route to avoid the traffic'.
Usage: 'I think he makes his money in *devious* ways' (= tricky, dishonest).
Word Family: **deviousness,** *noun;* **deviously,** *adverb.*

devise (*say* de–**vize**) *verb*
1. to make or think out: 'we have *devised* a perfect scheme for dividing the work'.
2. *Law:* to bequeath.

devitalize (*say* dee–**vie**–ta–lize)
devitalise *verb*
to make weak or lifeless.

devoid (*say* de–**void**) *adjective*
empty or lacking.

devolve *verb*
1. to pass on or transfer: 'during his absence the ambassador's duties *devolved* on his assistant'.
2. *Biology:* to degenerate.
Word Family: **devolution** (*say* deeva–**loo**–sh'n), *noun*, the transfer of power.
[Latin *devolvere* to roll down]

Devonian (*say* de–**vo**–nee–an) *noun*
Geology: see PALAEOZOIC.

devote (*say* de–**vote**) *verb*
to give all one's time or attention to something: 'he *devotes* his days to reading'.
devoted *adjective*
very loving or affectionately attached: 'she is *devoted* to her horses'.
devotee (*say* **devvo**–tee) *noun*
a fanatical or enthusiastic follower: 'he is a *devotee* of football'.
[DE– + Latin *votus* vowed]

devotion *noun*
1. a strong love or affection.
2. (*usually plural*) prayers or worship: 'the priest spent two hours at his *devotions*'.
devotional *adjective*
used in devotions: 'the church's library was filled with *devotional* literature'.

devour (*say* de–**vowr**) *verb*
to eat or swallow greedily: 'the lion *devoured* its kill'.
Usages:
a) 'the fire *devoured* many acres of crops' (= destroyed).
b) 'she *devoured* every detail of the story' (= took in, absorbed).
c) 'an overwhelming fear *devoured* her' (= filled).
Word Family: **devouringly**, *adverb*.
[DE– + Latin *vorare* to swallow]

devout (*say* de–**vowt**) *adjective*
devoted to one's religion: 'the *devout* old man went to church daily'.
Usage: 'a *devout* tennis fan' (= keen, devoted).
Word Family: **devoutly**, *adverb*; **devoutness**, *noun*.

dew *noun*
drops of moisture accumulated on the ground during calm weather when the night air near the ground cools below the dewpoint.

Dewar flask
a thermos flask.
[invented by *Sir James Dewar*, 1842–1923, a Scottish physicist]

dewclaw *noun*
an inner claw on the foot of a dog, which has no function and does not touch the ground in walking.

dewlap *noun*
the loose fold of skin under the throat of cattle or other animals, including man.

dewpoint *noun*
Weather: the temperature at which air becomes saturated with water–vapour.

dewy *adjective*
being moist with or as if with dew.

dewy–eyed *adjective*
naive or trusting.

Dexadrine (*say* **deksa**–dreen) *noun*
a white, water–soluble, stimulant drug used for reducing weight.
[a trademark]

dexterity (*say* dex–**terri**–tee) *noun*
a manual or mental adroitness.
Word Family: **dextrous** (*say* **dex**trus), **dexterous**, *adjectives*; **dextrousness**, *noun*.
[Latin *dexter* on the right]

dextrose *noun*
a sugar, found in animal and plant tissues, which can be produced artificially from starch.

dhoti (*say* **doe**–tee) *noun*
a garment worn by Hindu men.

dhow (*rhymes with* cow) *noun*
a small Arab trading vessel with one lateen sail, regularly crossing the Indian Ocean.

di– (*say* die)
a prefix meaning two or double, as in *dicotyledon*.

dia–
a prefix meaning: a) through, as in *diarrhoea*; b) across, as in *diagonal*; c) apart, as in *diagnosis*.
[Greek]

diabetes (*say* die–a–**beeteez**) *noun*
a disease caused by a build–up of sugar in the blood, due to a lack of insulin to metabolize it.
Word Family: **diabetic** (*say* die–a–**bettik**), *adjective*, *noun*.
[Greek *diabainein* to go through]

diabolical (*say* die–a–**bolli**–k'l)
diabolic *adjective*
devilish or extremely wicked.
[Greek *diabolos* a slanderer]

diacritic (*say* die–a–**krittik**) **diacritical** *adjective*

serving to distinguish: 'a circumflex is a *diacritic* symbol'.
[Greek *diakritikos* distinguishing]

diadem (*say* **die**–a–dem) *noun*
a crown or headband, worn usually by royalty.
[Greek *diadema* a headband]

diaeresis (*say* die–**erra**–sis) *noun*
Language: see ACCENT.
[Greek *diairesis* separation]

diagnosis (*say* die–ag–**no**–sis) *noun*
plural is **diagnoses**
1. *Medicine:* the determination of the cause of a disease by studying the symptoms, signs and results of tests.
2. *Biology:* a description which enables an organism to be identified.
Word Family: **diagnose** (*say* **die**–agnoze), *verb*, to make a diagnosis; **diagnostic** (*say* die–ag**nostik**), *adjective*; **diagnostician** (*say* die–agnos–**tish**'n), *noun*.
[Greek, a distinguishing]

diagonal (*say* die–**agga**–n'l) *adjective*
1. having an oblique or slanted direction.
2. *Maths:* connecting two non-adjacent vertices or edges.
Word Family: **diagonally**, *adverb*; **diagonal**, *noun*, a diagonal line or plane.
[DIA- + Greek *gonia* a corner]

diagram (*say* **die**–a–gram) *noun*
a simplified drawing which explains, represents or describes.
Word Family: **diagrammatic** (*say* die–a–gra–**mattik**), *adjective*; **diagrammatically**, *adverb*.
[DIA- + Greek *gramma* something written]

dial (*rhymes with* pile) *noun*
the front part or face of a clock, telephone, gauge, or other instrument.
dial *verb*
(dialled, dialling)
to use a telephone dial to ring a number.

dialect *noun*
the language of a certain class or place, as a variant form of the established language of the whole country, etc.
Word Family: **dialectal**, *adjective*.

dialectic *noun*
(*often plural*) the art or process of logical argument to establish or discover a truth, etc.
Word Family: **dialectical**, *adjective*.
[Greek *dialektos* conversation]

dialogue (*say* **die**–a–log) *noun*
1. a conversation between two or more people.
2. any exchange of thoughts or ideas.
3. the spoken text of a play or film.
[Greek *dialogos* conversation]

dialysis (*say* die–**alli**–sis) *noun*
Physics: the separation of colloidal particles from dissolved substances in a solution by diffusion through a membrane.
Word Family: **dialyse** (*say* **die**–a–lize), *verb*.
[Greek, a separating]

diamanté (*say* die–a–**mon**–tay) *noun*
a fabric made to glitter by covering it with shiny particles.
[French *diamant* diamond]

diameter (*say* die–**ammi**–ter) *noun*
Maths: a) a chord passing through the centre of a circle. b) the length of this line.
[DIA- + Greek *metron* a measure]

diametric (*say* die–a–**metrik**)
diametrical *adjective*
1. relating to a diameter.
2. absolute or direct: 'good and bad are *diametric* opposites'.
Word Family: **diametrically**, *adverb*.

diamond (*say* **die**–a–m'nd) *noun*
1. a natural crystalline form of carbon which is colourless when pure. It is the hardest known substance and is used for cutting-tools, drill tips and as a gem.
2. a plane figure having four equal sides, with diagonals which are vertical and horizontal.
3. *Cards:* a) a red figure like a diamond on a playing card. b) a playing card with this figure. c) (*plural*) the suit with this figure.
4. *Baseball:* the distance or area between the four bases.
diamond *adjective*
1. of, made of or shaped like a diamond.
2. indicating the 60th (sometimes the 75th) anniversary of an event, e.g. a wedding anniversary.
[Greek *adamantis* of adamant]

diaper (*say* **die**–per) *noun*
American: a nappy.
[Greek *diaspros* pure white]

diaphanous (*say* die–**affa**–nus) *adjective*
transparent: 'chiffon is a *diaphanous* fabric'.
[DIA- + Greek *phainein* to show]

diaphragm (*say* **die**–a–fram) *noun*
1. *Anatomy:* any membrane which separates and divides, particularly the muscular wall separating the chest from the abdomen in mammals.
2. *Photography:* an adjustable hole in a camera, controlling the amount of light which passes through the lens on to the film.
[DIA– + Greek *phragma* a fence]

diarrhoea (*say* die–a–**ree**–a) *noun*
Medicine: an intestinal disorder which causes the faeces to be fluid and their passage frequent.
[Greek *diarrhoia* a flowing through]

diary (*say* **die**–a–ree) *noun*
1. a book in which one records experiences, feelings, thoughts, etc. day by day.
2. a book in which a record of appointments, etc. is kept.
Word Family: **diarist**, *noun*, a person who keeps a diary.
[Latin *diarius* daily]

diastole (*say* die–**asta**–lee) *noun*
Biology: the rhythmical relaxation phase of the heartbeat. Compare SYSTOLE.
Word Family: **diastolic** (*say* die–a–**stoll**ik), *adjective.*
[Greek *diastolé* expansion]

diathermy (*say* **die**–a–thermee) *noun*
Medicine: the use of electric currents to apply heat to tissues, e.g. to relieve muscular pain.
Word Family: **diathermic** (*say* die–a–**ther**mik), *adjective.*
[DIA– + Greek *thermé* heat]

diatom (*say* **die**–a–tom) *noun*
Biology: any of a group of microscopic algae having one cell which has silica in the cell walls.
Word Family: **diatomaceous** (*say* die–atta–**may**shus), *adjective*, relating to diatoms or their fossil remains.
[Greek *diatomos* cut through]

diatomaceous earth
(*say* die–a–ta–**may**–shus erth)
also called **kieselguhr**
a siliceous sediment, almost entirely composed of the remains of diatoms, and used for filtering and absorbing liquids.

diatomic (*say* die–a–**tom**mik) *adjective*
Chemistry: having two atoms in a molecule, such as oxygen gas (formula O_2).
[DI– + ATOM]

diatonic scale (*say* die–a–**tonn**ik skale)
Music: a scale which includes five whole tones and two semitones. Compare CHROMATIC SCALE.
[DIA– + Greek *tonos* tone]

diatribe (*say* **die**–a–tribe) *noun*
a bitter attack or criticism.
[DIA– + Greek *tribein* to rub]

dibble *noun*
also called a **dibber**
a short, pointed tool used to make holes in the ground for planting seeds, etc.

dice *plural noun*
singular is **die**
1. a) the small cubes of plastic, bone, etc. having each side marked with dots representing the numbers 1–6, and used in some games. b) any game, especially a gambling game, in which these objects are thrown on to a flat surface.
2. any small cubes: 'cut the meat into *dice*'.
dice *verb*
1. to cut into small pieces.
2. to play with dice.

dicey (*say* **die**–see) *adjective*
(*informal*) risky or dangerous.

dichlorodiphenyl–trichloroethane
(*say* die–klaw–ro–die–fennel try–klaw–ro–**ee**thane) *noun*
short form is **DDT**
a white powder used as an insecticide.

dichotomy (*say* die–**kotta**–mee) *noun*
a division into two, usually contradictory, parts.
[Greek *dikho–* apart + *tomé* division]

dicky (1) *noun*
a false shirt–front.

dicky (2) *adjective*
(*informal*) shaky or unsound: 'a *dicky* heart'.

dicotyledon (*say* die–kotta–**lee**–d'n) *noun*
Biology: a plant having two seed leaves in the embryo, with the flower parts occurring in groups of four or five, or multiples of these. Compare MONOCOTYLEDON.
Word Family: **dicotyledonous**, *adjective.*
[DI– + COTYLEDON]

Dictaphone *noun*
a machine similar to a tape–recorder, used to record and replay dictation.
[a trademark]

dictate (*say* dik–**tate**) *verb*
1. to say or speak something to be written or recorded by another.
2. to command or order.
dictate (*say* **dik**–tate) *noun*
an authoritative order.
Word Family: **dictation,** *noun.*
[Latin *dictare*]

dictator *noun*
a ruler with unlimited power, especially one who has taken control by force.
Word Family: **dictatorship,** *noun.*
[Latin]

dictatorial (*say* dikta–**tawr**iul) *adjective*
1. of or relating to a dictator.
2. domineering: 'the manager's *dictatorial* behaviour made him unpopular'.
Word Family: **dictatorially,** *adverb.*

diction (*say* **dik**–sh'n) *noun*
1. a style of speaking or writing.
2. the degree of distinctness or clarity in speech.
[Latin *dictio* speaking]

dictionary (*say* **dik**–sh'n–ree) *noun*
a book listing words of a language in alphabetical order with their meanings, pronunciation, use and derivation.

dictum *noun*
a) a formal statement of opinion. b) a popular saying.
[Latin]

did *verb*
the past tense of the verb **do.**

didactic (*say* die–**dak**tik) *adjective*
intended to teach or instruct.
Word Family: **didacticism** (*say* die–**dak**ta–sizm), *noun*; **didactically,** *adverb.*
[Greek *didaskein* to teach]

diddle *verb*
(*informal*) to cheat or swindle.

die (1) *verb*
(**died, dying**)
1. to stop living, when all vital functions cease.
2. to cease to exist: 'that law *died* in the 19th century!'.
Usages:
a) 'the engine *died* and the car drew to a standstill' (= stopped).
b) 'the chatter *died* away as the door was thrown open' (= faded).
3. (*informal*) to desire greatly: 'I am *dying* for an ice-cream'.
Phrases:
die down, 'the noise *died down* gradually' (= subsided).
die out, to disappear.

die (2) *noun*
1. a tool used to shape a material, e.g. by forging or extrusion.
2. *Metallurgy:* a) a hole in a block through which wire can be drawn.
b) a hole lined with teeth for cutting a thread on bolts, screws, etc.
3. see DICE.
the die is cast, the decision or situation cannot be changed.

diehard *noun*
a person who stubbornly resists change.

dieldrin (*say* **deel**drin) *noun*
a white crystalline solid which is a powerful insecticide.

diesel (*say* **dee**–z'l) *noun*
any vehicle powered by a diesel engine.

diesel engine
an internal combustion engine in which the mixture of fuel and air is ignited by the heat produced when it is compressed in the cylinders.
[invented by *R. Diesel,* 1858–1913, a German engineer]

diesel oil
an oily liquid extracted after petrol and kerosene have been distilled from crude oil, used as fuel in diesel engines.

diet (1) (*say* **die**–ut) *noun*
1. the usual food which one eats.
2. a restricted selection of food to cure disease, regulate weight, etc.
diet *verb*
to eat restricted foods, especially to regulate weight.
Word Family: **dietary** (*say* **die**–a–tree), *adjective*; **dietitian** (say die–a–**tish**'n), **dietician,** *noun,* a person trained to plan balanced diets.
[Greek *diaita* a way of life]

diet (2) (*say* **die**–et) *noun*
a formal congress of the states of an empire, etc. to discuss or carry out its business.

dietetics (*say* die–a–**tet**tiks) *plural noun*
(*used with singular verb*) the study of the composition of foods and the control of the diet.
Word Family: **dietetic,** *adjective.*

differ *verb*
1. to be unlike.

2. to have different or opposing opinions, beliefs, etc.: 'we *differ* on politics and religion'.

difference *noun*
1. the state of being different.
2. a point which differs: 'I can see no *difference* between the two'.
3. an argument.
4. *Maths:* a) the amount by which one number is greater or less than another. b) the amount remaining when one quantity is subtracted from another.
[Latin *differens*]

different *adjective*
not alike.
Usages:
a) 'we rang on three *different* occasions' (= separate).
b) 'let's do something *different* today' (= unusual).
Word Family: **differently,** *adverb.*

differential (*say* diffa-**ren**-sh'l) *noun*
1. *Maths:* an equation which contains the derivatives of the function to be determined.
2. *Engineering:* a gear mechanism which drives two shafts, such as the axles in a motor vehicle, allowing them to rotate at different speeds.
Word Family: **differential,** *adjective,* of or expressing a difference.

differential calculus
Maths: see CALCULUS.

differentiate (*say* diffa-**ren**shi-ate) *verb*
1. to notice or indicate differences between.
2. *Maths:* to find the derivatives of a function.
3. *Biology:* (of cells, tissues or organs) to change from a simple, uniform structure into several specialized types during development.
Word Family: **differentiation,** *noun.*

difficult *adjective*
1. hard to do or accomplish.
2. (*informal*) being hard to please or get along with.
difficulty *noun*
1. the fact of being difficult.
2. trouble or hardship: a) 'I had great *difficulty* understanding his mumbled words'; b) 'financial *difficulties*'.
3. anything which is difficult: 'learning their new language is a *difficulty* for many immigrants'.
[Latin *difficultas*]

diffidence (*say* **diffi**-d'nce) *noun*
a lack of self-confidence.
Word Family: **diffident,** *adjective;* **diffidently,** *adverb.*
[Latin *diffidens* mistrusting]

diffraction (*say* de-**frak**-sh'n) *noun*
Physics: the scattering of a wave, such as light, by an obstacle or aperture.
Word Family: **diffract,** *verb;* **diffractive,** *adjective.*
[Latin *diffractus* broken in pieces]

diffuse (*say* dif-**yooz**) *verb*
to spread out or scatter.
diffuse (*say* dif-**yooce**) *adjective*
spread out or scattered.
Usage: 'the *diffuse* prose was difficult to read' (= very long).
Word Family: **diffuser,** *noun,* something which diffuses or causes diffusion, such as glass placed over the lens of a camera to soften or enlarge the picture; **diffusible,** *adjective,* capable of being diffused; **diffusibility** (*say* dif-yooza-**billa**-tee), *noun.*
[Latin *diffusus* spread out]

diffusion (*say* dif-**yoo**-*zh*'n) *noun*
1. the act of diffusing.
2. *Physics:* a) the mixing of molecules of different gases. b) the scattering and crisscrossing of light rays produced by reflection from a rough surface or passage through frosted glass, fog, etc.

dig *verb*
(**dug, digging**)
1. to break up, remove or turn over soil, etc. with a spade or similar tool.
2. to make a hole with or as if with a spade.
Usages:
a) 'he *dug* his hands into his pockets and walked off' (= thrust, pushed).
b) 'she *dug* around for a suitable answer' (= searched).
3. (*informal*) to understand or appreciate.
4. to poke.
Phrases:
dig one's heels in, see HEEL.
dig up, dig out, 'where did you *dig up* that old hat?' (= find, discover).
dig *noun*
1. a poke: 'a *dig* in the ribs'.
2. (*plural*) any rented accommodation for students, etc.
3. an archaeological excavation

digest (*say* die-**jest**) *verb*
to break up food in the alimentary canal so that it can be absorbed into the body.

Usage: 'the judge had to *digest* many facts before making a decision' (= take in, absorb).
digest (*say* **die**–jest) *noun*
a) a shortened version of a book, report, etc. b) a collection of such works.
Word Family: **digestion**, *noun*, the function or process of digesting food; **digestible**, *adjective*, able to be digested; **digestive**, *adjective*.
[Latin *digestus* distributed]

digger *noun*
1. a person or thing that digs, especially a gold-digger.
2. (*informal*, *capital*) a soldier from Australia or New Zealand.

diggings *plural noun*
a place where digging is carried out, such as a mine.

digit (*say* **dij**–it) *noun*
1. a finger or toe.
2. any of the figures, 0–9, in the Arabic system.
Word Family: **digital** (*say* **diji**–t'l), *adjective*, having or resembling a digit or digits.
[Latin *digitus* finger or toe]

digital computer
see COMPUTER.

dignify *verb*
(**dignified, dignifying**)
to confer honour or dignity upon.
Word Family: **dignified**, *adjective*, full of dignity.

dignitary (*say* **digna**–tree) *noun*
a person of high rank.

dignity *noun*
1. a bearing or character which commands respect: 'it would be beneath her *dignity* to do that'.
2. a high rank or office.
stand on one's dignity, to be touchy about slights.
[Latin *dignitas* worthiness]

digress (*say* die–**gress**) *verb*
to deviate from the main line or purpose.
Word Family: **digression** (*say* die–**gresh**'n), *noun*; **digressive**, *adjective*, tending to digress.
[Latin *digressus* having moved away]

dihedral (*say* die–**hee**–dr'l) *noun*
the angle between the wings of an aeroplane when viewed head on.
[DI– + Greek *hedra* base]

dike *noun*
see DYKE.

dilapidated (*say* de–**lappi**–day–tid) *adjective*
fallen into ruin or disrepair: 'it would be expensive to restore such a *dilapidated* old house'.
Word Family: **dilapidation**, *noun*; **dilapidate**, *verb*.
[DI– + Latin *lapides* stones]

dilate (*say* die–**late**) *verb*
to make or become larger or wider.
Word Family: **dilation, dilatation** (*say* dilla–**tay**–sh'n) *nouns*, a) the act of dilating, b) a dilated part; **dilator**, *noun*, something which dilates, e.g. a muscle, drug, etc.
[DI– + Latin *latus* wide]

dilatory (*say* **dilla**–tree) *adjective*
1. slow to act, decide, etc.
2. intended to delay.
Word Family: **dilatorily**, *adverb*; **dilatoriness**, *noun*.
[Latin *dilatus* postponed]

dilemma *noun*
a situation requiring a choice between difficult or undesirable alternatives.
[DI– + Greek *lemma* an assumption]

dilettante (*say* dilli–**tan**–tee) *noun*
plural is **dilettanti**
a person who concerns or amuses himself with culture and the arts in a casual or amateur manner.
Word Family: **dilettantism**, *noun*.
[Italian]

diligent (*say* **dilli**–j'nt) *adjective*
careful and earnest in one's work.
Word Family: **diligence**, *noun*.
[Latin *diligens* conscientious]

dill *noun*
a small plant, the seeds and leaves of which are used in medicine, cooking and pickling foods.

dillydally *verb*
(**dillydallied, dillydallying**)
to waste time, especially by being undecided.

dilute (*say* die–**loot**) *verb*
to make weaker or thinner, by adding water, etc.
Word Family: **dilute**, *adjective*, reduced or weakened; **diluent**, *adjective*, serving to dilute.
[Latin *dilutus* washed apart]

dilution (*say* die–**loo**–sh'n) *noun*
1. the act of diluting.
2. *Chemistry:* the amount of solvent in which a unit quantity of solute is dissolved.

diluvial (*say* die–**looviul**) *adjective*
of or relating to a flood.
[Latin *diluvium* a flood]

dim *adjective*
(dimmer, dimmest)
faint or unclear, due to a lack of light, colour, etc.
Usages:
a) 'her eyes were *dim* with tears' (= clouded).
b) 'mother takes a *dim* view of our jokes' (= adverse).
c) 'he is quite *dim* when it comes to physics' (= stupid).
dim *verb*
(dimmed, dimming)
to make dim: 'we *dimmed* the lights'.
Word Family: **dimly**, *adverb*; **dimness**, *noun*; **dimmer**, *noun*, a person or thing that dims, such as a rheostat.

dime *noun*
American: a ten-cent coin.

dimension (*say* de-**men**-sh'n) *noun*
(*usually plural*) the size of anything, especially the length, width or height.
Word Family: **dimensional**, *adjective*, having the specified number of dimensions; **dimensionally**, *adverb*.
[Latin *dimensio* a measuring]

diminish *verb*
to make or become smaller: 'drought *diminished* the country's food supplies'.
diminishing returns
Economics: a theory stating that there comes a point where further increases in tax, investment, effort, etc. become less and less profitable or effective.
Word Family: **diminishingly**, *adverb*; **diminution** (*say* dimmi-**new**-sh'n), *noun*, the process of diminishing.

diminutive (*say* di**min**-yootiv) *adjective*
1. very small.
2. *Grammar:* (of a suffix) indicating smallness, affection, etc., as in *piglet.*
Word Family: **diminutive**, *noun*, something which is diminutive; **diminutively**, *adverb*; **diminutiveness**, *noun*.
[Latin *diminutus* diminished]

dimity (*say* **dimmi**-tee) *noun*
a thin, cotton fabric woven with a stripe or check in a heavier yarn.
[DI- + Greek *mitos* a thread]

dimmer *noun*
Word Family: see DIM.

dimorphism (*say* die-**morfizm**) *noun*
Biology: the appearance of two distinct forms among organisms of the same species.
Word Family: **dimorphous**, **dimorphic**, *adjectives.*
[DI- + Greek *morphé* a shape]

dimple *noun*
a small hollow or fold, especially on the cheek.
dimple *verb*
to make or produce dimples: 'her face *dimpled* as she laughed'.

din *noun*
a loud noise.

dine *verb*
to eat a meal, especially the main meal of the day.
diner *noun*
1. a person who dines.
2. *Railways:* a dining car.
3. *American:* a roadside snack-bar.

dinette (*say* die-**net**) *noun*
a small room or part of a room set aside for eating.

ding-dong *adjective*
(*informal*) vigorous: 'the argument turned into a *ding-dong* fight'.

dinghy (*say* **ding**-gee) *noun*
a small boat which may be rowed or sailed.
[Hindi]

dingle *noun*
an old word for a small, deep, wooded valley.

dingo *noun*
plural is **dingoes**
a wild dog of Australia, about 50 cm high and usually sandy-coloured.
[Aboriginal]

dingy (*say* **din**-jee) *adjective*
dark, dull or shabby: 'a *dingy* room lit only by candles'.
Word Family: **dinginess**, *noun*.

dining car
also called a **diner**
Railways: a carriage in which meals or snacks are served.

dinner *noun*
1. the main meal of the day, eaten at midday or in the evening.
2. a formal meal.

dinner jacket
a jacket, usually black, worn with a bow tie on formal occasions, especially at night.

dinosaur (*say* **die**-na-sor) *noun*
a long-extinct reptile of the Mesozoic era, the largest land animal ever known.
[Greek *deinos* terrible + *sauros* lizard]

dint *noun*
a dent.
by dint of, 'she won *by dint of* her great enthusiasm' (= by the force or power of).
dint *verb*
to make a dent in.

diocese (*say* **die**–a–sis) *noun*
also called a **see**
Christian: a district under the religious control of one bishop or archbishop.
Word Family: **diocesan** (*say* die–**ossi**san), *adjective, noun.*
[Latin *diocesis* district]

diode (*say* **die**–ode) *noun*
Electricity: a valve with two electrodes, used for converting alternating current into direct current.
[DI– + Greek *hodos* a way]

Dionysus (*say* die–a–**nice**–us) *noun*
Greek mythology: the god of wine and fertility.
Word Family: **Dionysiac, Dionysian,** *adjectives.*

diorama *noun*
a miniature, three-dimensional scene with modelled, painted figures and a painted background.
Word Family: **dioramic,** *adjective.*
[DIA– + Greek *horama* a sight]

diorite (*say* **die**–a–rite) *noun*
a coarse-grained igneous rock, consisting mainly of feldspar and ferromagnesian minerals.
[Greek *diorizein* to distinguish]

dioxide (*say* die–**ok**side) *noun*
Chemistry: an oxide with two atoms of oxygen per molecule.

dip *verb*
(dipped, dipping)
1. to put or lower briefly into something, especially a liquid: '*dip* the fish in batter before cooking'.
Usages:
a) 'they *dipped* water out of the boat with a bucket' (= scooped, lifted).
b) 'I have only *dipped* into the subject' (= become slightly involved).
2. to immerse sheep, etc. in a solution to destroy bacteria, parasites, etc.
3. to drop or direct downwards: 'he *dipped* his car's lights as he approached the hill'.
dip *noun*
1. anything into which something is dipped: a) 'a sheep *dip*'; b) 'a savoury *dip* for biscuits'.
2. a plunge or brief immersion: 'let's have a *dip* in the sea before lunch'.
3. a downward slope or movement: 'there is a slight *dip* in the road ahead'.
4. *Geology:* the angle which a stratum makes with a horizontal plane.

diphtheria (*say* dip–**theer**ia *or* diff–**theer**ia) *noun*
an infectious, bacterial disease causing inflammation or blockage of the throat, usually in children.
[Greek *diphthera* a membrane]

diphthong (*say* **dip**–thong *or* **diff**–thong) *noun*
Language: one sound made up of two vowel sounds, as *u* in *duke* (dee–uke).
[DI– + Greek *phthongos* sound]

diploid *adjective*
Biology: (of a cell) having a double set of chromosomes. Compare HAPLOID.
Word Family: **diploid,** *noun,* a diploid cell or organism.
[Greek *diplous* double + –OID]

diploma (*say* de–**plo**–ma) *noun*
Education: a certificate awarded when a student has satisfactorily completed a particular course of study: 'a *diploma* of physical education'.
Word Family: **diplomate** (*say* **dip**la–mate), *noun,* a person who has received a diploma.
[Greek *diploma* folded letter (of recommendation)]

diplomacy (*say* de–**plo**–ma–see) *noun*
1. the art of maintaining relationships and agreements between countries, e.g. through an ambassador.
2. any tact or skill in dealing with people: 'it will take some *diplomacy* to break the news gently'.
Word Family: **diplomat** (*say* **dip**la–mat), **diplomatist** (*say* dip–**lo**–ma–tist), *nouns,* a person employed or skilled in diplomacy.
[Greek *diploma* folded letter (of introduction)]

diplomatic (*say* dipla–**mat**tik) *adjective*
1. of or engaged in diplomacy: 'a member of the *diplomatic* service'.
2. tactful.
Word Family: **diplomatically,** *adverb.*

diplomatic immunity
the immunity of diplomatic officials from the laws of the country in which they are working.

dipole (*say* **die**–pole) *noun*
1. *Physics:* any pair of electric charges or magnetic poles, separated by a small distance, such as a bar magnet

2. an aerial consisting of two rods each equal to half the wavelength to be received.
Word Family: **dipolar,** *adjective.*

dipper (1) *noun*
anything used for dipping, such as a ladle.

dipper (2) *noun*
a bird resembling a large wren, which haunts mountain streams and can swim or walk under water.

dipsomaniac (*say* dipso-**may**-nee-ak) *noun*
an alcoholic.
Word Family: **dipsomania,** *noun.*
[Greek *dipsa* thirst + MANIAC]

dip stick
a rod used for measuring the amount of liquid in a container, such as the oil in the sump of a motor car engine.

diptych (*say* **dip**-tik) *noun*
a pair of paintings on two panels, which are often hinged together. Compare TRIPTYCH.
[Greek *diptykos* double-folded]

dire *adjective*
disastrous or terrible: 'the snow had a *dire* effect on their crops'.

direct *verb*
1. to guide or control: 'who *directed* the company while the chairman was away?'.
Usages:
a) 'can you *direct* me to the Post Office?' (= show the way).
b) 'who *directed* you to say that?' (= ordered).
c) 'try to *direct* your efforts towards something useful' (= turn).
2. to organize and supervise the actors and actual performance of a play or film.
direct *adjective*
1. straight or uninterrupted: 'a *direct* line'.
Usages:
a) 'a *direct* question' (= frank, straightforward).
b) 'a *direct* descendant of Queen Victoria' (= immediate, in an unbroken line).
2. exact or absolute: 'that is the *direct* opposite of what you said earlier'.
Word Family: **directness,** *noun*; **directly,** *adverb.*
[Latin *directus* arranged]

direct current
Electronics: see ELECTRIC CURRENT.

direction *noun*
1. the act of directing: 'he acted under the *direction* of his boss'.
2. the point or position towards which something faces or moves: 'he drove off in the *direction* of the city'.
3. (*often plural*) guidance: 'can you give me *directions* to the zoo?'.
Word Family: **directional,** *adjective,* relating to direction in space.

direction-finder *noun*
Radio: a device similar to an aerial, attached to a receiver, used to establish the direction from which radiowaves are sent.

directive *noun*
any detailed instruction or command: 'the staff received *directives* on what to wear'.

direct object
Grammar: see OBJECT.

director *noun*
1. a person who controls the affairs of a business company.
2. the person who directs actors and the artistic performance of a play or film. Compare PRODUCER.
Word Family: **directorship,** *noun*; **directorial** (*say* dirrek-**tawr**iul), *adjective.*

directorate *noun*
a) the position or office of a director.
b) a board of directors.

directory *noun*
a book with an alphabetical list of names or subjects: 'a street *directory*'.

direct speech
the exact words used by a person.

dirge (*say* derj) *noun*
a sad, slow song of lament for someone who has died.

dirigible (*say* **dirr**ija-b'l) *adjective*
able to be controlled or steered.
dirigible *noun*
an airship which may be controlled, directed or steered.

dirk *noun*
a dagger, especially one formerly used by Scottish Highlanders.

dirndl (*say* **dern**-d'l) *noun*
a colourful dress with a close-fitting top and a full skirt worn by girls in the Austrian mountains.
[Austro-German, little girl]

dirt *noun*
1. any unclean matter or substance: 'please clean that *dirt* off your clothes before dinner'.
2. any earth or soil.

Word Family: **dirt,** *adjective,* made of earth.

dirt–cheap *adjective*
(*informal*) very inexpensive.

dirty *adjective*
covered with dirt: 'I must clean these *dirty* windows'.
Usages:
a) 'the footballer was suspended for *dirty* play' (= unfair).
b) 'the book was banned because of its *dirty* language' (= indecent).
c) '*dirty* weather' (= rough, stormy).
Word Family: **dirtily,** *adverb*; **dirtiness,** *noun*; **dirty** (**dirtied, dirtying**), *verb,* to make dirty.

dis–
a prefix meaning: a) not or without, as in *distrust*; b) reversal or removal, as in *discard*; c) apart, as in *disintegrate.*

disability (*say* dissa–**billi**–tee) *noun*
a lack or loss of faculty or power: 'she obviously has a serious reading *disability*'.

disable (*say* dis–**ay**–b'l) *verb*
to take away or destroy the ability or power of: 'the yacht was *disabled* during the storm'.
Usage: 'a *disabled* soldier' (= crippled).
Word Family: **disablement,** *noun.*

disabuse (*say* dissa–**bewz**) *verb*
to free from error or misunderstanding.

disadvantage (*say* dissad–**vahn**–tij) *noun*
an unfavourable or harmful condition, circumstance, etc.: 'the lecturer's soft voice put him at a *disadvantage* in the large hall'.
Word Family: **disadvantageous** (*say* dis–advan–**tay**–jus), *adjective,* unfavourable; **disadvantage,** *verb.*

disaffected *adjective*
having become discontented or disloyal.
Word Family: **disaffect,** *verb,* to make disaffected; **disaffection,** *noun.*

disagree (*say* dissa–**gree**) *verb*
(**disagreed, disagreeing**)
to have a different opinion or view: 'I must *disagree* with what you said'.
disagree with, 'rich food *disagrees with* my stomach' (= upsets).
Word Family: **disagreement,** *noun,* a) the act of disagreeing, b) an argument.

disagreeable *adjective*
unpleasant or offensive.
Word Family: **disagreeably,** *adverb.*

disallow *verb*
to refuse to allow or accept: 'the judge *disallowed* the prisoner's claim of insanity'.
Word Family: **disallowance,** *noun*; **disallowable,** *adjective.*

disappear *verb*
to go out of sight: 'my gloves have *disappeared* from the sideboard'.
Word Family: **disappearance,** *noun.*

disappoint *verb*
to fail to be equal to what is expected or hoped for: 'the film *disappointed* me'.
Usage: 'we were *disappointed* that you couldn't come' (= made unhappy).
disappointment *noun*
1. the state of being disappointed: 'our *disappointment* at the result was enormous'.
2. anything which disappoints: 'the Prime Minister was a great *disappointment* to those who elected him'.

disapprobation
(*say* dis–apro–**bay**–sh'n) *noun*
disapproval.

disapprove (*say* dissa–**proov**) *verb*
to have or show an unfavourable opinion: 'the family *disapproves* of his new group of friends'.
disapproval *noun*
the act or a feeling of disapproving.
Word Family: **disapprovingly,** *adverb.*

disarm *verb*
1. to take away weapons or the means of attack: 'police *disarmed* the two men'.
2. to overcome the suspicions, hostility, etc. of: 'her frankness *disarmed* the reporters'.
Word Family: **disarming,** *adjective,* tending to charm or win over; **disarmingly,** *adverb.*

disarmament *noun*
the limiting of the number of military forces and equipment.

disarrange *verb*
to disturb the order or arrangement of: 'the strong wind had *disarranged* her hair'.
Word Family: **disarrangement,** *noun.*

disarray *noun*
a confusion or lack of order.
Word Family: **disarray,** *verb.*

disassociate (*say* dissa–**so**–see–ate) *verb*
to dissociate.

disaster (*say* de–**zah**sta) *noun*
a greatly unfortunate accident or event.
Word Family: **disastrous**, *adjective*, causing ruin or disaster.
[DIS– + Italian *astro* a lucky star]

disavow *verb*
to deny or reject responsibility, etc. for.
Word Family: **disavowal**, *noun*.

disband *verb*
(of a group) to break up or separate: 'the gang *disbanded* as soon as they had the money'.

disbar *verb*
(disbarred, disbarring)
Law: to expel a barrister from membership of the profession.
Word Family: **disbarment**, *noun*.

disbelief (*say* dis–**beleef**) *noun*
a refusal or inability to believe.
Word Family: **disbelieve**, *verb*.

disburden *verb*
to relieve of or remove a burden.

disburse *verb*
to pay out.
disbursement *noun*
a) the act of paying out: 'the *disbursement* of committee funds must be controlled'. b) the money paid: 'this month's miscellaneous *disbursements* total £247'.
[DIS– + Medieval Latin *bursa* purse]

disc *noun*
also spelt **disk**
1. any flat, round object or part, such as a coin or the rings of cartilage in the vertebral column.
2. a gramophone record.
Word Family: **discal**, *adjective*.
[Greek *diskos*]

discard *verb*
to put or throw away: '*discard* all bruised or damaged fruit before cooking'.
discard *noun*
a) the act of discarding. b) anything which is discarded.

disc brake
a type of brake consisting of a flat metal disc which is gripped by pads, used in motor vehicles and the undercarriages of aircraft.

discern (*say* di**ssern**) *verb*
1. to see or recognize clearly: 'mother *discerned* from our silence that we were angry'.
2. to discriminate or judge between.

discerning *adjective*
perceptive or discriminating: 'a *discerning* knowledge of wine'.
Word Family: **discerningly**, *adverb*; **discernment**, *noun*; **discernible**, *adjective*, able to be seen or recognized; **discernibly**, *adverb*.
[DIS– + Latin *cernere* to separate]

discharge (*say* dis–**charj**) *verb*
1. to relieve of a load, duty, etc.: 'the injured soldier was *discharged* from all combat duties'.
2. to send out or away: 'to be *discharged* from hospital'.
Usages:
a) 'the company has now *discharged* all its debts' (= paid).
b) 'the factory *discharges* its waste into the sea' (= releases).
c) 'the driver was *discharged* for stealing' (= dismissed).
3. *Electronics:* to remove or reduce an electric charge.
Word Family: **discharge** (*say* **dis**–charj), *noun*, a) the act of discharging, b) a person or thing that is discharged.

disciple (*say* de–**sigh**–p'l) *noun*
a follower, companion or student: 'the *disciples* of Christ'.
Word Family: **discipleship**, *noun*.
[Latin *discipulus* a learner]

discipline (*say* **dissa**–plin) *noun*
1. a) the establishing of correct order and behaviour with rules, training, etc.: 'there is not enough *discipline* in this class'. b) the methods used, such as rules, instruction, punishment, etc.: 'more *discipline* will be used in future'.
2. a branch or subject of learning, etc.: 'the science *disciplines* are not taught at this college'.
Word Family: **discipline**, *verb*, to use discipline; **disciplinary** (*say* **dissa**–plin–ree), *adjective*, of or promoting discipline; **disciplinarian** (*say* dissa–plin–**airian**), *noun*, a person who uses or encourages discipline.
[Latin *disciplina* training]

disc jockey
a person who introduces and plays popular records on radio programmes.

disclaim *verb*
to deny connection or a claim to: 'he has *disclaimed* the inheritance for personal reasons'.
disclaimer *noun*
a statement which disclaims.

disclose (*say* dis-**kloze**) *verb*
to allow to be seen or known: 'the solicitor *disclosed* the contents of the will after the funeral'.
Word Family: **disclosure,** *noun.*

disco *noun*
(*informal*) a discothèque.

discolour *verb*
in America spelt **discolor**
to change or spoil the colour of: 'her dress was *discoloured* by stains'.
Word Family: **discoloration, discolourment,** *nouns.*

discomfit (*say* dis-**kum**fit) *verb*
to frustrate, defeat or humiliate.
Word Family: **discomfiture** (*say* dis-**kum**fi-cher), *noun.*

discomfort (*say* dis-**kum**-fut) *noun*
a lack of comfort or peace: 'the crowded bus caused them great *discomfort*'.

discompose *verb*
to disturb the calmness of: 'the shouting audience *discomposed* the actors'.
Word Family: **discomposure** (*say* dis-kom-**po**-*zher*) *noun,* the state of being discomposed.

disconcert (*say* diskon-**sert**) *verb*
to upset or perturb: 'she was *disconcerted* by the family's silent stares'.
Word Family: **disconcertingly,** *adverb*; **disconcertment, disconcertion,** *nouns.*

disconnect *verb*
to take apart or detach: 'the electricity was *disconnected* because we did not pay the bill'.
disconnected *adjective*
1. not connected.
2. having unrelated parts: 'the *disconnected* film was very difficult to follow'.
Word Family: **disconnection,** *noun.*

disconsolate (*say* dis-**konsa**-lit) *adjective*
unhappy and unable to be comforted.
Word Family: **disconsolation** (*say* dis-konsa-**lay**-sh'n), *noun*; **disconsolately,** *adverb.*

discontent *noun*
also called **discontentment**
a lack of contentment or satisfaction.
Word Family: **discontented,** *adjective*; **discontentedly,** *adverb.*

discontinue (*say* diskon-**tin**-yoo) *verb*
to end or cause to end.
Word Family: **discontinuation,** *noun.*

discontinuous (*say* diskon-**tin**-yewus) *adjective*
interrupted or not continuous.
Word Family: **discontinuously,** *adverb*; **discontinuity** (*say* dis-konti-**newa**-tee), *noun.*

discord *noun*
a) a disagreement or difference of opinion, etc. b) any arguments or fighting caused by this.
Usage: 'the audience flinched at the *discord* in the symphony' (= lack of harmony).
discordant *adjective*
lacking agreement or harmony: 'their *discordant* political opinions lead to many arguments'.
Word Family: **discordance,** *noun*; **discordantly,** *adverb.*
[DIS- + Latin *cordis* of the heart]

discothèque (*say* **disko**-tek) *noun*
a place for dancing, usually with records or taped music.
[French, record library]

discount (*say* **dis**-count) *noun*
a reduction in price: 'a *discount* is available for cash purchases'.
discount (*say* dis-**count**) *verb*
1. to reduce the price of something, often by a set amount or percentage.
2. to ignore or refuse to believe: 'you should not *discount* all the rumours that you hear'.

discourage (*say* dis-**kurr**ij) *verb*
to take away the hope or confidence of: 'don't be *discouraged* by their criticisms'.
Word Family: **discouragingly,** *adverb*; **discouragement,** *noun.*

discourse (*say* **dis**-korse) *noun*
a lecture, speech or discussion, especially a formal one.
Word Family: **discourse** (*say* dis-**korse**), *verb,* to talk or discuss.
[Latin *discursus* a running to and fro]

discourteous (*say* dis-**ker**tius) *adjective*
not polite.
Word Family: **discourtesy,** *noun.*

discover *verb*
1. to find out or realize something not known before.
2. to find: 'I have *discovered* a new cake-shop'.
discovery *noun*
1. the act of discovering.
2. anything which is discovered.
Word Family: **discoverer,** *noun,* a person who has discovered something.

discredit *verb*
to destroy confidence in: 'the author's theory was *discredited* by leading economists'.
discreditable *adjective*
causing discredit or disgrace: 'his *discreditable* behaviour angered his family'.
Word Family: **discredit,** *noun*; **discreditably,** *adverb.*

discreet *adjective*
tactful and careful to avoid mistakes, embarrassment, etc.
Word Family: **discreetly,** *adverb*; **discreetness,** *noun.*
[Latin *discretus* discerned]
Common Error: do not confuse with DISCRETE.

discrepancy (*say* dis-**krepp**'n-see) *noun*
a lack of consistency or agreement.
Word Family: **discrepant,** *adjective*; **discrepantly,** *adverb.*
[Latin *discrepans* out of tune]

discrete *adjective*
1. separate.
2. having many or separate parts.
Word Family: **discretely,** *adverb*; **discreteness,** *noun.*
[Latin *discretus* separated]
Common Error: do not confuse with DISCREET.

discretion (*say* dis-**kresh**'n) *noun*
1. the quality of being discreet: 'we would appreciate your *discretion* in this matter'.
2. the freedom to act or decide for oneself.
at one's discretion, 'you may decide the price *at your discretion*' (= as you wish).
Word Family: **discretionary, discretional,** *adjectives*; **discretionally,** *adverb.*

discriminate (*say* dis-**krimmi**-nate) *verb*
to notice, indicate or treat with a difference: 'that company *discriminates* against its female employees'.
Word Family: **discriminating,** *adjective,* showing good taste or judgement; **discrimination,** *noun,* a) the act of discriminating, b) good or perceptive judgement; **discriminatory, discriminative,** *adjectives,* indicating differences.
[Latin *discriminis* of a dividing line]

discursive (*say* dis-**kersiv**) *adjective*
1. passing irregularly from one point or subject to another.
2. based on reasoning: 'a *discursive* argument'.
[Latin *discursus* a running to and fro]

discus (*say* **dis**kus) *noun*
plural is **discuses**
Athletics: a) a disc-shaped wooden plate thrown in competitions. b) the contest in which it is thrown.
[Greek]

discuss (*say* dis-**kuss**) *verb*
to speak about together and exchange opinions: 'we must *discuss* the idea in detail'.
Usage: '*discuss* this question in an essay' (= argue for and against).
Word Family: **discussion** (*say* dis-**kush**'n), *noun,* a talk to exchange opinions or views.

disdain *verb*
to regard or treat with scorn: 'he *disdained* their offer of help'.
Word Family: **disdain,** *noun*; **disdainful,** *adjective*; **disdainfully,** *adverb.*
[DIS- + Latin *dignus* worthy]

disease (*say* diz-**eez**) *noun*
an unhealthy state of all or part of a body.
Word Family: **diseased,** *adjective,* affected by disease.
[DIS- + French *aise* ease]

disembark (*say* dissem-**bark**) *verb*
to go or put ashore from a ship.
Word Family: **disembarkation,** *noun.*

disembowel *verb*
(**disembowelled, disembowelling**)
to remove the bowels or intestines.

disenchant (*say* dissen-**chahnt**) *verb*
to cause to lose illusions or beliefs: 'the country family soon became *disenchanted* with city life'.
Word Family: **disenchantment,** *noun.*

disencumber *verb*
to free from a burden or hindrance.

disenfranchise (*say* dissen-**franchize**) *verb*
also called to **disfranchise**
to take away a person's rights of citizenship, especially the right to vote.
Word Family: **disenfranchisement,** *noun.*

disengage *verb*
to release or unfasten.
Usage: 'the troops *disengaged* and returned to camp' (= stopped fighting).
Word Family: **disengagement,** *noun.*

disentangle *verb*
to clear or make free of tangles: 'it was difficult to *disentangle* sense from nonsense in the poem'.
Word Family: **disentanglement,** *noun.*

disentwine *verb*
to free from being entwined: 'he *disentwined* himself from the ropes and jumped from the tree'.

disfavour *noun*
in America spelt **disfavor**
disapproval.

disfigure (*say* dis–**figga**) *verb*
to spoil the appearance, shape or effect of.
Word Family: **disfigurement,** *noun.*

disfranchise *verb*
to disenfranchise.

disgorge (*say* dis–**gorj**) *verb*
to emit or eject, as if from the throat: 'the train *disgorged* its passengers on to the platform'.

disgrace *noun*
1. a loss of favour, approval or respect: 'you are in *disgrace* with the whole family for telling such a lie'.
2. anything which causes disgrace or reproach: 'this untidy room is an absolute *disgrace*!'.
Word Family: **disgrace,** *verb*; **disgraceful,** *adjective,* bringing disgrace; **disgracefully,** *adverb.*

disgruntled *adjective*
displeased or in a bad mood.

disguise (*say* dis–**gize**) *verb*
to change the appearance of something in order to conceal its identity, true nature, etc.
Word Family: **disguise,** *noun*; **disguisedly,** *adverb.*

disgust *noun*
a strong feeling of dislike.
Word Family: **disgust,** *verb,* to cause disgust in; **disgusting,** *adjective,* causing disgust; **disgustingly,** *adverb,* to a disgusting degree; **disgustedly,** *adverb,* in a disgusted manner.
[DIS– + Latin *gustare* to taste]

dish *noun*
1. a) a shallow, flat–bottomed vessel from which food may be served or eaten. b) anything shaped like this.
2. a particular kind or preparation of food: 'my favourite *dish* is roast chicken with vegetables'.
3. (*informal*) an attractive person, especially a girl.

dish *verb*
dish out, dish up, to serve or distribute.
Word Family: **dished,** *adjective,* concave.

disharmony (*say* dis–**harma**–nee) *noun*
a lack of harmony.
Word Family: **disharmonious** (*say* dis–har–**mo**–nee–us), *adjective.*

dishearten (*say* dis–**har**–t'n) *verb*
to discourage: 'he was *disheartened* by the slow progress of his work'.
Word Family: **dishearteningly,** *adverb.*

dishevelled (*say* di–**shev**'ld) *adjective*
(of the clothes or hair) untidy, unkempt or disarranged.
Word Family: **dishevel (dishevelled, dishevelling),** *verb.*
[DIS– + Old French *chevel* hair]

dishonest (*say* dis–**onnist**) *adjective*
not honest.
Word Family: **dishonestly,** *adverb*; **dishonesty,** *noun,* a) a lack of honesty, b) a dishonest act.

dishonour (*say* dis–**onna**) *noun*
in America spelt **dishonor**
1. a loss of honour or reputation: 'his actions brought *dishonour* upon his family'.
2. a person or thing that causes dishonour: 'he was a *dishonour* to his battalion'.
dishonour *verb*
1. to bring dishonour on or to.
2. *Commerce:* to refuse to honour a cheque, bank–draft, etc.
Word Family: **dishonourable,** *adjective*; **dishonourably,** *adverb.*

disillusion (*say* dissa–**loo***zh*en) *verb*
to disenchant or make aware of unpleasant realities.
Word Family: **disillusionment,** *noun.*

disincentive (*say* dissin–**sentiv**) *noun*
something which discourages effort, such as low wages.

disincline (*say* dis–in**kline**) *verb*
to make or be reluctant: 'I felt *disinclined* to argue with him over such a small matter'.
Word Family: **disinclination** (*say* dis–inkla–**nay**–sh'n), *noun.*

disinfect *verb*
to destroy all the bacteria in or on something.
disinfectant *noun*
any chemical which destroys bacteria.
Word Family: **disinfection,** *noun.*

disingenuous (*say* dissin–**jen**–yewus) *adjective*

pretending to be less artful, or more candid, than one is.

disinherit (*say* dissin-**herr**it) *verb*
to exclude an heir from an inheritance.

disintegrate (*say* dis-**in**ti-grate) *verb*
1. to break into fragments.
2. to lose unity or cohesion.
disintegration *noun*
1. the act or process of disintegrating: 'beneath the glacier the rocks underwent a slow *disintegration*'.
2. the state of being disintegrated.

disinter (*say* dissin-**ter**) *verb*
(**disinterred, disinterring**)
to dig up something buried, especially a corpse: 'the body was *disinterred* for examination by the coroner'.
Word Family: **disinterment,** *noun.*

disinterested *adjective*
unaffected by personal interest, involvement or advantage: 'a *disinterested* judge'.
Word Family: **disinterestedly,** *adverb*; **disinterestedness,** *noun*; **disinterest,** *noun*, a lack of interest or concern.
Common Error: DISINTERESTED, UNINTERESTED both refer to a lack of interest, however *disinterested* describes impartiality or absence of selfishness, whereas *uninterested* suggests merely indifference or lack of sympathy.

disjointed *adjective*
disconnected or incoherent.
Word Family: **disjointedly,** *adverb*; **disjointedness,** *noun.*

disjunctive *adjective*
serving to disconnect or separate.
Word Family: **disjunctive,** *noun*, a word, such as *but*, which indicates separation or contrast; **disjunction,** *noun.*
[DIS- + Latin *junctus* joined]

disk *noun*
see DISC.

dislike *verb*
to have no liking for.
Word Family: **dislike,** *noun*; **dislikable,** *adjective.*

dislocate (*say* **dis**la-kate) *verb*
to put out of the proper place or position, e.g. two bones forming a joint.
dislocation *noun*
1. a) the act of dislocating. b) the state of being dislocated: 'the bad news threw our plans into *dislocation*'. c) a dislocated joint or part.
2. *Geography:* a fault.

dislodge *verb*
to move or force out of place or position.
Word Family: **dislodgement,** *noun.*

disloyal *adjective*
not loyal.
Word Family: **disloyally,** *adverb*; **disloyalty,** *noun.*

dismal (*say* **diz**-m'l) *adjective*
gloomy or melancholy: 'what *dismal* weather!'.
Word Family: **dismally,** *adverb.*
[Latin *dies mali* unlucky days]

dismantle *verb*
1. to take to pieces: 'we had to *dismantle* the engine to inspect the crankshaft bearings'.
2. to strip of fittings, apparatus, etc.: 'the old warship was *dismantled* as part of its conversion to a transport vessel'.
[from DIS- + MANTLE]

dismay *noun*
a feeling of fear or hopeless discouragement.
Word Family: **dismay,** *verb*, to fill with dismay.

dismember *verb*
to tear or cut the limbs from.
Usage: 'the conquering powers *dismembered* the defeated country' (= divided into parts).
Word Family: **dismemberment,** *noun.*

dismiss *verb*
to send away or allow to leave: 'to *dismiss* a class'.
Usages:
a) 'he was *dismissed* from the police force for taking bribes' (= removed).
b) 'he *dismissed* the idea as a complete waste of time' (= rejected).
c) 'the fast bowler *dismissed* the batsman for five runs' (= got out).
Word Family: **dismissal,** *noun*, a) the act of dismissing, b) the state of being dismissed, c) a spoken or written order of discharge; **dismissive,** *adjective*, expressing contempt or dismissal.
[DIS- + Latin *missus* sent]

dismount *verb*
to get down or off, e.g. from a horse, bicycle, etc.
Usages:
a) 'the gun was *dismounted* from the guncarriage' (= removed).
b) 'the knight was *dismounted* by a powerful blow of the lance' (= knocked off his mount).

disobey (*say* disso-**bay**) *verb*
to fail or refuse to obey.

Word Family: **disobedient** (*say* dissa-beedient), *adjective*; **disobediently**, *adverb*; **disobedience**, *noun*.

disoblige *verb*
to fail or refuse to oblige.
Word Family: **disobliging**, *adjective*; **disobligingly**, *adverb*.

disorder *noun*
a lack of order or arrangement.
Usages:
a) 'he suffered for years from a variety of stomach *disorders*' (= ailments).
b) 'troops were finally called in to put down the *disorders* in the capital' (= riots).
Word Family: **disorder**, *verb*; **disorderly**, *adverb*; **disorderliness**, *noun*.

disorganize, disorganise *verb*
a) to upset the organization of: 'the heavy snowfall *disorganized* public transport services'. b) to lack organization: 'his work is completely *disorganized*'.
Word Family: **disorganization**, *noun*.

disorientate (*say* dis-**awri**-en-tate) **disorient** *verb*
to confuse, especially about direction.
Word Family: **disorientation**, *noun*.

disown *verb*
to refuse to acknowledge as one's own: 'after his wild pranks at college the family *disowned* him completely'.

disparage (*say* dis-**parr**ij) *verb*
to belittle or treat slightingly: 'the modest girl *disparaged* her own abilities'.
Word Family: **disparagingly**, *adverb*; **disparagement**, *noun*.

disparate (*say* **dispa**-rit) *adjective*
basically unlike or different.
Word Family: **disparity** (*say* dis-**parra**-tee), *noun*, a lack of equality or similarity.
[Latin *dispar* unequal]

dispassionate (*say* dis-**pasha**-nit) *adjective*
free from emotion or bias.
Word Family: **dispassionately**, *adverb*.

dispatch, despatch *verb*
to send off: '*dispatch* this urgent telegram immediately'.
Usages:
a) 'the gladiator *dispatched* his opponent' (= killed).
b) 'their business was quickly *dispatched* and the two executives went out for a drink' (= transacted, finished).
dispatch *noun*
1. the act of dispatching: 'please speed up the mail *dispatch*'.
2. efficiency or promptness: 'he completed the task with *dispatch*, and was back for more work'.
3. a service or a means by which messages or goods are sent speedily: 'he sent the urgent message by special *dispatch*'.
4. a) a story sent in by a media reporter. b) an official communication carried by special messenger, e.g. between officers of an army.
[Italian *dispacciare* to hasten]

dispel (*say* dis-**pel**) *verb*
(dispelled, dispelling)
to drive off or scatter: 'the clear sky *dispelled* all fears of rain'.
[Latin *dispellere* to drive apart]

dispense *verb*
1. to deal out or distribute: 'he *dispensed* money to the poor'.
2. to mix, prepare and give out medicines, etc., e.g. on prescription.
dispense with, to do without or do away with.
dispensation *noun*
1. a) the act of dispensing: 'law courts supervise the *dispensation* of justice'. b) something dispensed: 'money and other charitable *dispensations*'.
2. a management or system.
3. *Roman Catholic:* the removal or relaxation of a law, penalty, etc.
Word Family: **dispensable**, *adjective*, able to be done without; **dispensary**, *noun*, a place where something, such as medicine, is dispensed.
[Latin *dispensare* to pay out]

disperse *verb*
to scatter: 'the demonstrators *dispersed* when the police charged the crowd'.
Usages:
a) 'the sun *dispersed* the morning mists' (= drove away).
b) 'knowledge of how to use iron took a long time to *disperse* throughout Europe' (= spread).
[DI- + Latin *spargere* to scatter]

dispersion (*say* dis-**per**-sh'n) *noun*
1. a) the act of dispersing. b) the state of being dispersed. Also called **dispersal**.
2. *Physics:* the splitting of ordinary white light into the colours of the spectrum.

3. *Maths:* the spread of values around the average value, usually measured by the standard deviation.
4. *Chemistry:* a suspension of particles in a solid, liquid or gas.

dispirited *adjective*
depressed or disheartened.
Word Family: **dispiritedly,** *adverb*; **dispiritedness,** *noun*; **dispiriting,** *adjective*; **dispiritingly,** *adverb*; **dispirit,** *verb.*

displace *verb*
1. to put out of its usual place: 'he had *displaced* his shoulder bone'.
Usage: 'after the scandal about police corruption several senior police officers were *displaced* from positions of high authority' (= removed).
2. to take the place of: 'Bob has *displaced* Rick in Ellen's affections'.

displaced person
a person forced to leave his own country, such as a refugee.

displacement *noun*
1. a) the act of displacing. b) the state of being displaced.
2. *Physics:* the fundamental quantity describing the change in position of a body, including linear displacement, expressed in metres, and angular displacement, expressed in radians.
3. *Geology:* the movement of rocks along a fault.
4. the weight of water displaced by a ship: 'a liner of 25 000 tonnes *displacement*'.

display *verb*
to show: a) 'to *display* fear'; b) 'to *display* goods in a shop window'.
Word Family: **display,** *noun.*
[DIS- + Latin *plicare* to fold]

displease *verb*
to offend or cause dissatisfaction.
Word Family: **displeasing,** *adjective*; **displeasingly,** *adverb*; **displeasure,** *noun.*

disport *verb*
to divert or amuse oneself.

dispose (*say* dis-**poze**) *verb*
1. to make willing: 'the high pay *disposed* her to accept the job'.
Usage: 'his weak constitution *disposes* him to illness' (= makes susceptible).
2. to put in a certain order or arrangement: 'the troops were *disposed* in ranks'.
dispose of, to get rid of or part with.

disposal *noun*
the act of disposing: 'rubbish *disposal*'.
at one's disposal, under one's control or direction.
Word Family: **disposable,** *adjective,* able to be disposed of.
[Latin *dispositum* distributed]

disposition (*say* dispa-**zish**'n) *noun*
1. a person's natural way of acting or thinking: 'he has a cheerful *disposition*'.
2. a tendency or inclination: 'he has a *disposition* to argue when drunk'.
3. the act of putting in order or position: 'the general supervised the *disposition* of his troops on the battlefield'.

dispossess (*say* dispa-**zess**) *verb*
to deprive of possession: a) 'the Europeans *dispossessed* the Aboriginals of their land'; b) 'rage *dispossessed* him of his senses'.
Word Family: **dispossession,** *noun.*

disproportionate
(*say* dispra-**por**-sh'n) *adjective*
also called **disproportional**
lacking in proportion.
Word Family: **disproportion,** *noun*; **disproportionately,** *adverb.*

disprove (*say* dis-**proov**) *verb*
to prove to be false or wrong.

dispute *verb*
1. to argue, quarrel or debate.
2. to question the truth or validity of: 'he *disputed* her account of the incident'.
Word Family: **dispute,** *noun*; **disputable,** *adjective*; **disputant,** *noun,* a person who disputes; **disputation** (*say* dis-pew-**tay**-sh'n), *noun,* the act of disputing.
[Latin *disputare* to discuss]

disqualify (*say* dis-**kwolli**-fie) *verb*
(**disqualified, disqualifying**)
1. to make unsuitable for or unable to do something: 'his club foot *disqualified* him from military service'.
2. to deprive of the right to compete in a contest.
Word Family: **disqualification** (*say* dis-kwollifi-**kay**-sh'n), *noun.*

disquiet *verb*
to make anxious or uneasy.
Word Family: **disquiet, disquietude,** *nouns*; **disquieting,** *adjective,* causing disquiet.

disquisition (*say* diskwi-**zish**'n) *noun*
a formal speech or treatise examining and discussing a subject.
[Latin *disquisitio* an inquiry]

disregard *verb*
to pay no attention to.
Word Family: **disregard**, *noun*, a lack of attention or regard.

disrepair *noun*
the state of needing repair.

disreputable (*say* dis–**rep**–yewta–b'l) *adjective*
a) having a bad reputation: 'he haunts *disreputable* nightclubs'. b) not respectable in appearance: 'she wore a *disreputable* old coat'.
Word Family: **disreputably**, *adverb*; **disrepute** (*say* dis–re–**pewt**), *noun*, the condition of being disreputable.

disrespect *noun*
a lack of respect.
Word Family: **disrespectful**, *adjective*; **disrespectfully**, *adverb*.

disrobe *verb*
to undress: 'the bishop *disrobed* after the coronation ceremony'.

disrupt *verb*
to break up or throw into confusion: 'the hecklers succeeded in *disrupting* the meeting'.
Word Family: **disruptive**, *adjective*, tending to disrupt; **disruption** (*say* dis–**rup**–sh'n), *noun*.
[DIS– + Latin *ruptus* broken]

dissatisfy *verb*
(**dissatisfied**, **dissatisfying**)
to make discontented or fail to satisfy: 'he was *dissatisfied* with his salary'.
Word Family: **dissatisfaction**, *noun*; **dissatisfactory**, *adjective*.

dissect (*say* die–**sekt**) *verb*
to cut an organism apart to examine its structure.
Usage: 'the barrister *dissected* the evidence' (= examined carefully).
Word Family: **dissection**, *noun*, a) the act of dissecting, b) the state of being dissected, c) something which has been dissected.
[Latin *dissectus* cut up]

dissemble *verb*
a) to disguise or hide one's real feelings, thoughts, etc.: 'she *dissembled* her rage with a sweet smile'. b) to feign or pretend: 'the bored party guest *dissembled* gaiety'.
Word Family: **dissembler**, *noun*.
[DIS– + Latin *simulare* to imitate]

disseminate *verb*
to scatter or spread widely: 'the news was quickly *disseminated* by radio'.
Word Family: **dissemination**, *noun*.
[DIS– + Latin *seminare* to sow]

dissension (*say* dissen–sh'n) *noun*
angry quarrelling or disagreement.

dissent *verb*
1. to differ in opinion: 'one juryman *dissented* from the opinion of his fellow jurors'.
2. *Religion:* to refuse to conform to the rules or beliefs of an established church.
Word Family: **dissent**, *noun*; **dissentient** (*say* dissen–sh'nt), *adjective*, differing from the general opinion; **dissenter**, *noun*, a person who dissents.
[DIS– + Latin *sentiri* to feel]

dissertation (*say* dissa–**tay**–sh'n) *noun*
a) a long essay or thesis. b) a formal speech.

disservice *noun*
any harmful or unhelpful action: 'to do someone a *disservice*'.

dissidence (*say* **dissi**–d'nce) *noun*
any disagreement.
Word Family: **dissident**, *adjective*, differing; **dissident**, *noun*, a person who disagrees.
[Latin *dissidere* to sit apart]

dissimilar *adjective*
unlike or different.
Word Family: **dissimilarity** (*say* dis–simmi–**larri**–tee), *noun*; **dissimilarly**, *adverb*.

dissimulate (*say* dissim–yoolate) *verb*
to disguise or hide under a pretence.
Word Family: **dissimulation**, *noun*, the act of dissimulating; **dissimulator**, *noun*, a person who dissimulates.

dissipate (*say* **dissi**–pate) *verb*
to disperse: 'I tried to *dissipate* the child's fear of the dark'.
Usage: 'he *dissipated* his energies in a frantic attempt to do everything at once' (= wasted foolishly, frittered away).
Word Family: **dissipation**, *noun*, a) the act of dissipating, b) a dissolute way of life.
[Latin *dissipare* to scatter]

dissociate (*say* dis–**so**–see–ate) *verb*
also called to **disassociate**
to separate or not associate with: 'we don't agree with you and *dissociate* ourselves from your comments'.
dissociation *noun*
a) the act of dissociating. b) the state of being dissociated.

dissoluble (*say* dis–**sol**–yew–b'l) *adjective*

capable of being dissolved.
Word Family: **dissolubility**, *noun.*

dissolute (*say* **dissa**–loot) *adjective*
debauched or sexually unrestrained.
Word Family: **dissoluteness**, *noun*; **dissolutely**, *adverb.*
[Latin *dissolutus* lax]

dissolve (*say* di**zolv**) *verb*
1. *Chemistry:* to enter into solution.
2. to bring to or come to an end: a) 'to *dissolve* a marriage'; b) 'to *dissolve* parliament'.
Usage: 'the figure *dissolved* into the mist' (= disappeared gradually).
3. *Film:* to make two scenes overlap by darkening one picture slowly as another is lightened and becomes visible. *Word Family:* **dissolve**, *noun*, a scene made by dissolving.
dissolve into tears, to be overcome by emotion and begin to cry.
dissolution (*say* dissa–**loo**–sh'n) *noun*
a) the act of dissolving: 'the election defeat caused the *dissolution* of parliament'. b) the state of being dissolved: 'parliament was soon in *dissolution*'.
[Latin *dissolvere* to unloose]

dissonance (*say* **dissa**–nance) *noun*
a discord or disagreement, especially of sounds.
Word Family: **dissonant**, *adjective*; **dissonantly**, *adverb.*
[DIS– + Latin *sonus* sound]

dissuade (*say* dis–**wade**) *verb*
to persuade against doing something: 'the policeman finally *dissuaded* the young man from jumping off the roof'.
Word Family: **dissuasion** (*say* **dis–way–zh'n**), *noun.*
[DIS– + Latin *suadere* to persuade]

distaff (*say* **dis**–tahf) *noun*
a part of a spinning wheel which holds the cotton or other raw material to be spun.
distaff side, the female branch of a family.

distal *adjective*
being situated away from the point of origin or attachment: 'toenails are at the *distal* ends of toes'. Compare PROXIMAL.

distance *noun*
the extent of space or time between two points or things: a) 'the *distance* from here to Perth is about 500 km'; b) 'a *distance* of 50 years'.
Usage: 'the dirty city looked quite pleasant from a *distance*' (= long way away).
keep one's distance, to avoid familiarity.
distance *verb*
to put at a distance: 'try to *distance* yourself from your present troubles and look at them objectively'.

distant *adjective*
situated at a considerable distance: 'the sun is *distant* from the earth'.
Usages:
a) 'we were headed for a village 3 km *distant*' (= away).
b) 'a second cousin is a *distant* relative' (= not close).
c) 'my ex-girlfriend greeted me with a *distant* nod' (= reserved, not friendly).
Word Family: **distantly**, *adverb.*
[Latin *distans, distantis* standing apart]

distaste *noun*
a dislike or aversion.
Word Family: **distasteful**, *adjective*; **distastefully**, *adverb*; **distastefulness**, *noun.*

distemper (1) *noun*
an often fatal, infectious, viral disease in young dogs, which causes catarrh and may lead to convulsions by affecting the central nervous system.

distemper (2) *noun*
a type of paint in which powdered colours are mixed with gluey or starchy substances, used in interior decoration, etc.

distend (*say* dis–**tend**) *verb*
to expand or swell: 'their bellies were *distended* by overeating'.
Word Family: **distension**, *noun.*
[DIS– + Latin *tendere* to stretch]

distil (*say* dis–**til**) *verb*
(distilled, distilling)
a) to subject to distillation: 'to *distil* water'. b) to extract by means of distillation: 'petrol is *distilled* from crude oil'.
Usage: 'the jury must *distil* the truth from this mass of conflicting evidence' (= extract).
[Latin *destillare* to drip down]

distillation (*say* disti–**lay**–sh'n) *noun*
Chemistry: a process for purifying liquids, by which solid impurities are separated by boiling off the liquid and then cooling it in a separate condensing chamber. Mixtures of liquids can be separated by **fractional distillation**, where the temperature of the mixture is progressively raised, and the liquid with the lowest boiling point (the first fraction) boils off and

is collected first, followed by the others.
Word Family: **distillate,** *noun,* a) a distilled liquid, b) diesel fuel, one of the fractions distilled from crude oil.

distillery *noun*
a place where alcoholic spirits are made.
Word Family: **distiller,** *noun,* a person or thing that distils.

distinct *adjective*
1. plain: 'outlines become more *distinct* when I wear my spectacles'.
Usage: 'she showed a *distinct* improvement in her work' (= definite).
2. different or separate: a) 'bats and birds belong to two *distinct* species'; b) 'you must keep the two ideas *distinct* in your mind'.
Word Family: **distinctly,** *adverb*; **distinctness,** *noun.*
[Latin *distinctus* separated]

distinction *noun*
1. a) the act of distinguishing: 'he makes no *distinction* between rich and poor'. b) a difference: 'what is the *distinction* between the two words?'.
Usages:
a) 'the prince treated me with *distinction* all evening' (= special favour or attention).
b) 'Charles Dickens is a writer of *distinction*' (= renown).
2. the highest honour awarded in an examination at a university, etc.: 'she got a *distinction* in History'.
Word Family: **distinctive,** *adjective,* characteristic; **distinctively,** *adverb*; **distinctiveness,** *noun.*

distinguish (*say* dis–**ting**–wish) *verb*
1. to recognize as being distinct or different: 'fool's gold, which is really iron pyrites, is difficult to *distinguish* from real gold'.
2. to see or hear plainly: 'from our seats at the back of the theatre it was hard to *distinguish* what the actors were saying'.
3. to make different or set apart: 'the ability to use language symbols *distinguishes* man from the other animals'.
4. to make famous: 'he *distinguished* himself in the field of medical research'.
Word Family: **distinguishable,** *adjective.*
[Latin *distinguere* to separate]

distinguished *adjective*
a) famous or eminent. b) having the appearance of an important person: 'her *distinguished* air caused people to treat her with great respect'.

distort *verb*
to pull or twist out of its usual shape: 'her face was *distorted* with pain'.
Usage: 'to *distort* the truth' (= misrepresent).
Word Family: **distortion,** *noun,* a) the act of distorting, b) the state of being distorted, c) something which is distorted.
[DIS– + Latin *tortus* twisted]

distract *verb*
to divert the attention of: 'the radio *distracts* me from my work'.
distracted *adjective*
confused or greatly troubled in mind: 'the tragedy left her quite *distracted*'.
distraction *noun*
a) the act of distracting. b) the state of being distracted: 'you'll drive her to *distraction* with your behaviour'. c) something which distracts: 'the radio is a constant *distraction*'.
Word Family: **distractedly,** *adverb.*
[DIS– + Latin *tractus* dragged]

distrain *verb*
to seize goods in payment of a debt.

distraught (*say* dis–**trawt**) *adjective*
deeply upset or troubled in mind: 'the *distraught* woman kept tearing at her hair and weeping for her dead children'.

distress *noun*
any acute or extreme suffering or trouble: 'his mother's death had caused him great *distress*'.
Usage: 'we picked up the radio signals of a ship in *distress*' (= serious difficulties or danger).
Word Family: **distress,** *verb,* to cause distress to; **distressing,** *adjective*; **distressingly,** *adverb*; **distressful,** *adjective,* a) causing distress, b) full of distress.

distribute (*say* dis–**trib**–yoot) *verb*
1. to divide and share out: 'the dying man *distributed* all his goods among his friends'.
2. to spread out: 'the explosion *distributed* wreckage over a wide area'.
3. to sort out or classify: 'the results were *distributed* into three main categories'.
distribution *noun*
1. a) the act of distributing: 'the *distribution* of presents took a long time'. b) the manner of being distributed: 'we studied the *distribution* of plants in the area'.

2. *Maths:* the frequency of sets of values in observations.

distributor *noun*

1. a person or thing that distributes.
2. a device in a petrol engine which directs the surge of electricity from the coil to each spark plug in the correct sequence.

[DIS– + Latin *tribuere* to allot]

district *noun*

a region, especially one marked off for administrative purposes, etc.

distrust *noun*

a lack of trust or confidence.

Word Family: **distrust,** *verb*; **distrusting, distrustful,** *adjectives*; **distrustfully,** *adverb*; **distrustfulness,** *noun.*

disturb *verb*

to break or destroy the peace, quiet or rest of: 'the noise of fighting dogs *disturbed* the night'.

Usages:

a) 'who has *disturbed* the papers on my desk?' (= put out of order, interfered with).

b) 'he was deeply *disturbed* by news of his father's illness' (= troubled).

c) 'they came home early and *disturbed* an intruder in the house' (= interrupted).

Word Family: **disturbance,** *noun,* a) the act of disturbing, b) the state of being disturbed, c) anything which disturbs; **disturbing,** *adjective*; **disturbingly,** *adverb.*

[DIS– + Latin *turba* an uproar]

disunity (*say* dis–**yew**ni–tee) *noun*

a lack of unity: 'if there is *disunity* in the ranks, we shall fail'.

Word Family: **disunion,** *noun*; **disunite** (*say* dis–yoo–**nite**), *verb.*

disuse (*say* dis–**yooce**) *noun*

a lack of use or the state of not being used: 'the door latch was rusted from *disuse*'.

Word Family: **disuse** (*say* dis–**yooz**), *verb.*

ditch *noun*

a long narrow trench dug in the earth. **last ditch,** 'a *last ditch* attempt' (= last, extreme).

ditch *verb*

to land an aircraft in the sea in an emergency.

Usage: (*informal*) 'the criminal *ditched* the stolen car' (= got rid of).

dither (*say* di*th*–a) *verb*

to fuss about in a confused or indecisive way.

Word Family: **dither,** *noun.*

ditto *noun*

a word or mark used in lists, etc. to indicate repetition of the same word or words.

Word Family: **ditto,** *adverb,* likewise.

ditty *noun*

a short song.

diuretic (*say* die–ya–**rettik**) *noun*

a drug which increases the amount of liquid urinated.

[DI– + Greek *ouresis* urination]

diurnal (*say* die–**er**–n'l) *adjective*

1. lasting one day.
2. of or belonging to the daytime: 'a *diurnal* animal is awake during the day and sleeps at night'. Compare NOCTURNAL.

[Latin *diurnus* by day]

diva (*say* **dee**va) *noun*

see PRIMA DONNA.

[Italian, goddess]

divalent *noun*

see BIVALENT.

divan (*say* de–**van**) *noun*

a low, bed-like seat with no back or sides.

[Arabic *diwan* a bench, a court]

dive *verb*

1. to plunge headfirst, often from a height, into the water.
2. to go deeply under water: 'she *dives* for pearls'.

Usages:

a) 'share prices *dived* on the Stock Exchange' (= dropped sharply).

b) 'he *dived* into the bushes to avoid the car' (= leapt).

c) 'he *dived* into his pocket and pulled out some money' (= reached quickly).

dive *noun*

1. the act of diving.
2. (*informal*) a cheap, disreputable place.

diving *noun*

the sport in which a person dives into the water from a board, set at various heights, often performing prescribed movements while in the air.

Word Family: **diver,** *noun,* a) a person or thing that dives, e.g. a naval frogman, b) any of a family of large birds that can swim under water.

dive–bomber *noun*
a military aeroplane which drops bombs while diving steeply towards its target.
Word Family: **dive–bomb**, *verb.*

diverge (*say* die–**verj** *or* de–**verj**) *verb*
to branch off in different directions: 'the road and railway line *diverge* at the foot of the hill'.
Usages:
a) 'my brother–in–law and I *diverge* on many issues' (= disagree).
b) 'let me *diverge* for a moment from my theme to tell a little story' (= digress).
Word Family: **divergent**, *adjective*; **divergence**, *noun.*
[DI– + Latin *vergere* to turn]

divers (*say* **die**–verz) *adjective*
an old word meaning several or various.

diverse (*say* die–**vers** *or* **die**–vers) *adjective*
of different kinds, forms, etc.: 'the people at the meeting had very *diverse* backgrounds'.
Word Family: **diversity**, *noun*; **diversely**, *adverb.*
[Latin *diversus* different, separate]

diversify (*say* die–**versi**–fie) *verb* (**diversified, diversifying**)
to give variety or diversity to: a) 'during her medical course she had little time to *diversify* her interests'; b) 'the company chairman urged the board to *diversify* investments'.
Word Family: **diversification**, *noun.*

diversion (*say* die–**ver**–*zh*'n) *noun*
1. a) the act of turning aside. b) a detour.
2. an amusement or hobby: 'for most people chess is a *diversion* rather than a serious study'.
3. *Military:* a manoeuvre to draw the enemy's attention away from the main point of an attack.
Word Family: **diversionary**, *adjective.*

divert (*say* die–**vert**) *verb*
1. to turn or cause to turn in another direction: 'to *divert* traffic'.
2. to turn from serious thought or activity, especially by amusement.

divertimento (*say* dee–verti–**mentoe**) *noun*
plural is **divertimenti**
Music: a light composition in several movements for a small group of instruments.
[Italian]

divest (*say* die–**vest**) *verb*
to strip or deprive of: 'the new law *divests* landowners of some of their privileges'.
[DI– + Latin *vestire* to clothe]

divide *verb*
1. to separate into parts: 'we *divided* the loot into equal shares'.
Usage: 'opinions *divided* over the issue' (= went different ways, were no longer united).
2. *Maths:* to calculate how many times one number contains another: '12 *divided* by 4 equals 3'.
3. *Parliament:* to vote on a question by separating into two groups, for and against the issue.
divide *noun*
Geography: a) a range of mountains separating rivers flowing towards opposite sides of a continent. b) a watershed.

dividend (*say* **divvi**–dend) *noun*
1. *Maths:* the number to be divided. Compare DIVISOR.
2. a share of something which has been divided, such as money paid to shareholders from a company's profits.

divider *noun*
1. anything which divides.
2. (*plural*) a pair of compasses used for measuring.

divine (*say* div**vine**) *adjective*
1. of or relating to God or a god.
2. sacred.
3. (*informal*) heavenly or excellent: 'she said my dress was *divine*'.
divine *noun*
Christian: a theologian.
divine *verb*
to learn or discover by intuition, inspiration or magic.
Word Family: **divinely**, *adverb*; **divination** (*say* divvi–**nay**–sh'n), *noun*, the foretelling of events; **diviner**, *noun.*

diving *noun*
see DIVE.

divining rod
see WATER DIVINER.

divinity (*say* div**vinni**–tee) *noun*
1. the quality of being divine.
2. a divine being; a god.
3. the formal study of religion or scriptures.

divisible (*say* div**vizzi**–b'l) *adjective*
able to be divided: '21 is exactly *divisible* by 3'.
Word Family: **divisibility**, *noun.*

division *noun*
1. a) the act of dividing. b) the state of being divided: 'the *division* of opinions became obvious during the debate'.
2. any of the parts into which something is divided: 'he was sent to the spare parts *division* of the factory'.
3. *Biology:* one of the large groups used in the classification of plants.
4. *Military:* a tactical army unit consisting of three or more brigades.
Word Family: **divisional**, *adjective*.

divisive (*say* **dee-vie-**siv) *adjective*
creating division or dissension.
Word Family: **divisively**, *adverb*; **divisiveness**, *noun*.

divisor (*say* **divvie-**zor) *noun*
Maths: a) the number by which another number is to be divided. Compare DIVIDEND. b) see FACTOR.

divorce (*say* div**vorse**) *noun*
1. *Law:* the ending of a marriage by a court decree.
2. any complete separation.
Word Family: **divorce**, *verb*; **divorcee** (*say* de-vor-**see**), *noun*, a divorced person.
[Latin *divortium* separation]

divot (*say* **divv**'t) *noun*
Sport: a piece of turf cut out by the edge of a club or bat as the player hits the ball.

divulge (*say* die-**vulj**) *verb*
to disclose or reveal a secret, etc.: 'the official refused to *divulge* the information to the press'.
Word Family: **divulgence**, *noun*.
[Latin *divulgare* to make publicly known]

dixie *noun*
a small tin pot used by troops or campers to make tea or stew.

dizzy *adjective*
having or causing a sensation of spinning.
Usage: 'he felt *dizzy* with success' (= overcome).
Word Family: **dizziness**, *noun*; **dizzily**, *adverb*.

djinn *noun*
a jinn or genie.

do (*say* doo) *verb*
(I **do**, you **do**, he **does**; **did**, **done**, **doing**; *old forms*: thou **doest** or **dost**, he **doeth** or **doth**)
1. to perform an action: 'she still hasn't *done* her work'.
2. to attend to: a) 'who'll *do* the dishes?'; b) 'have you *done* your teeth?'; c) 'Mrs Jones is *doing* the flowers for the wedding'.
3. special uses:
a) (in questions) '*did* you kill her?'.
b) (in negatives) 'I *did* not know her'.
c) (to emphasize a verb) '*do* stop talking nonsense'.
d) (as a substitute for a verb that has already been used) 'she looks even younger now than she *did*' (= looked before).
Usages:
a) 'his attitude can *do* harm' (= cause).
b) 'the critics *did* justice to the play' (= rendered).
c) 'the car will *do* 100 miles per hour' (= travel at).
d) 'we *did* half the journey today' (= covered).
e) 'we are *doing* a film on camels' (= making).
f) 'my sister *does* French at school' (= studies).
g) 'the roast will be *done* soon' (= cooked).
h) 'can you *do* this crossword?' (= solve).
i) 'will two sugars *do*?' (= be enough).
j) 'what will you *do* when you leave school?' (= work at).
k) 'how are you *doing*?' (= managing).
l) (*informal*) 'you've really *done* it this time' (= spoiled, ruined).
Phrases:
could do with, 'the house *could do with* a coat of paint' (= needs, would benefit from).
done for, dead or doomed.
do or die, to make a great effort.
do out of, (*informal*) 'she was *done out of* the job' (= cheated out of).
do up, 'this house needs *doing up*' (= renovating, decorating).
do *noun*
plural is **do's** or **dos**
1. something which should be done: 'the *do's* and don'ts of social behaviour'.
2. (*informal*) a party or celebration.

dobbin *noun*
a horse, especially a patient, plodding farm horse.

docile (*say* **doe-**sile) *adjective*
easily managed or led: 'the wild colt was broken and made *docile*'.
Word Family: **docilely**, *adverb*; **docility** (*say* doe-**silli-**tee), *noun*.
[Latin *docilis* easily taught]

dock (1) *noun*
a) a wharf. b) a harbour with equipment for loading, unloading or repairing ships.
dock *verb*
1. to come or bring into a dock.
2. to lock spacecraft together while in orbit.
Word Family: **dockage,** *noun,* the charge for using a dock; **docker,** *noun,* a person employed to work on the docks loading and unloading ships, etc.

dock (2) *noun*
the solid part of an animal's tail, as distinct from the hair.
dock *verb*
1. to cut off part of an animal's tail.
2. to deduct from: 'to *dock* one's allowance'.

dock (3) *noun*
Law: the enclosure in a courtroom where the accused person stands.
[Flemish *dok* a cage]

dock (4) *noun*
a weed with green flowers and a long taproot.

docket *noun*
1. a label on a package listing contents, etc.
2. a receipt, especially for customs duties.

dockyard *noun*
a harbour where ships are built and repaired.

doctor *noun*
1. a person allowed by law to practise medicine, or some branch of it.
2. a person who has received the highest university degree, usually after several years of research or study beyond a bachelor's degree.
3. (*capital*) a title of respect for such persons.
doctor *verb*
1. to treat with medicines.
2. (*informal*) to tamper with or alter.
Word Family: **doctoral,** *adjective;* **doctorate,** *noun,* the degree received by a doctor.
[Latin, teacher]

doctrinaire *noun*
a person who tries to apply a theory without considering the practical side.
doctrinaire *adjective*
1. dogmatic: 'he shouts his views in a *doctrinaire* manner'.
2. theoretical: '*doctrinaire* socialism'.

doctrine (*say* **dok**trin) *noun*
a particular principle, belief or theory: 'a religious *doctrine*'.
Word Family: **doctrinal** (*say* dok-**try**-n'l), *adjective;* **doctrinally,** *adverb.*

document (*say* **dok**-yoo-m'nt) *noun*
a written piece of information, evidence, etc.: 'when you apply for a passport you must supply certain *documents,* such as a birth certificate'.
document *verb*
to supply with or support by documents.
documentary (*say* dok-yoo-**men**-tree) *noun*
a non-fiction film.
Word Family: **documentation,** *noun;* **documentary,** *adjective.*
[Latin *documentum* a lesson or example]

dodder *verb*
to shake or totter.
Word Family: **doddery, doddering,** *adjectives;* **dodderer,** *noun.*

dodge (*say* doj) *verb*
to move aside or change position suddenly, especially so as to avoid something: 'Paul *dodged* when he saw the car coming towards him'.
Usage: 'the Mayor had no trouble in *dodging* the reporters' questions' (= evading).
dodge *noun*
1. the act of dodging.
2. (*informal*) a trick.
Word Family: **dodger,** *noun,* (informal) a sly or tricky person.

dodgem (*say* **doj**'m) *noun*
a small low-powered electric car driven in special rinks at amusement parks, etc.

dodo (*say* doe-doe) *noun*
a large, extinct, flightless bird of Mauritius.
[Portuguese *doudo* silly]

doe *noun*
a female deer, rabbit, etc. Compare BUCK (1).

doer (*say* **doo**-a) *noun*
a person of action.

does (*say* duz) *verb*
the third person singular, present tense of the verb **do.**

doeskin (*say* **doe**-skin) *noun*
1. a leather made from the skin of a doe.
2. a woollen fabric in a twill weave.

doest *verb*
an old form of the second person singular, present tense of the verb **do**.

doeth *verb*
an old form of the third person singular, present tense of the verb **do**.

doff *verb*
to take off: 'he *doffed* his hat'.
[from *do off*]

dog *noun*
1. a) any of various breeds of four-legged, flesh-eating mammals, either wild, such as the dingo, or domesticated, such as the poodle. b) the male of this animal.
2. (*informal*) a fellow: 'a gay *dog*'.
3. (*plural*) greyhound racing: 'have a bet on the *dogs*'.
Phrases:
dog in the manger, a person who keeps something of no particular use to himself so that others cannot use it.
go to the dogs, (*informal*) to go to ruin.
lead a dog's life, to have a harassed or unhappy existence.
let sleeping dogs lie, to leave a situation as it is.
dog *verb*
(**dogged, dogging**)
to chase relentlessly.
Word Family: **doggish**, *adjective*; **doggishly**, *adverb*.

dog-collar *noun*
(*informal*) the reversed collar worn by clergymen.

dog days
the hottest days of the year, particularly from early July to mid-August in the Northern Hemisphere.
[thought by the Romans to coincide with the period when the Dog Star rose with the sun]

dog-ear *noun*
a creased corner of a page which has been folded over like a dog's ear.
Word Family: **dog-ear**, *verb*; **dog-eared**, *adjective*.

dogfight *noun*
a fierce fight between aircraft at close range.

dogged (*say* **doggid**) *adjective*
obstinate.
Word Family: **doggedly**, *adverb*; **doggedness**, *noun*.

doggerel *noun*
any poorly written verse with faulty rhyme and rhythm.

doggish *adjective*
Word Family: see DOG.

doggo *adverb*
lie doggo, to hide or remain in concealment.

doggy *adjective*
Word Family: see DOG.

dogma *noun*
plural is **dogmas**
any established opinion or system of principles or beliefs, such as those laid down by a church.
dogmatic (*say* **dog-mattik**) *adjective*
stating opinions in a positive or overbearing manner.
Word Family: **dogmatically**, *adverb*; **dogmatist**, *noun*, a dogmatic person; **dogmatism**, *noun*; **dogmatize**, **dogmatise**, *verb*.

dog paddle
a simple swimming stroke in which the swimmer paddles his arms and legs below the surface of the water.

dogsbody *noun*
(*informal*) a drudge.

dog's breakfast
(*informal*) a mess.

dog-tired *adjective*
extremely tired.

dog-watch *noun*
Nautical: either of the two short, 2-hour watches (4–6 p.m. and 6–8 p.m.).

doh *noun*
Music: the spoken name for the first note in the scale. The notes in ascending order are: **doh, ray, me, fah, soh, lah, te, doh**.

doily *noun*
also spelt **doyly**
a small, decorative napkin made of paper, lace, etc. placed under objects on a shelf, table, etc.

doing (*say* **doo-ing**) *noun*
an action for which one is responsible: 'it is your *doing* that we're late'.
doing *verb*
the present participle of the verb **do**.

doldrums *plural noun*
1. *Geography:* the equatorial region where both calm and very turbulent weather is common.
2. a time of inactivity, low spirits, etc.

dole *noun*
the money paid by a government to unemployed people who cannot find a suitable job.

on the dole, receiving unemployment payment.
dole *verb*
dole out, to distribute, especially in small portions.

doleful *adjective*
sad or full of grief: 'the funeral was a *doleful* affair'.
Word Family: **dolefully**, *adverb*; **dolefulness**, *noun*.
[from *dole*, an old word for grief]

dolerite (*say* **dolla**-rite) *noun*
a medium-grained igneous rock.

doll *noun*
1. a toy which resembles a person.
2. (*informal*) an attractive female.
doll *verb*
doll up, to dress smartly or showily.

dollar *noun*
a) the basic unit of money in America, Australia and certain other countries, equal to 100 cents. b) a coin or banknote worth one dollar.
[German *thaler* a silver coin]

dollop *noun*
(*informal*) a lump or mass, especially of food: 'a large *dollop* of mashed potato'.

dolly *noun*
1. a child's name for a doll.
2. a low platform on wheels which is used to move heavy equipment, such as cameras around a studio, etc. *Word Family*: **dolly**, *verb*.
3. a shaped block of wood or metal used to form a sheet of metal when panel beating.

dolmen *noun*
Archaeology: a structure consisting of two or more large upright stones capped by a horizontal stone.

dolomite *noun*
a) a very common mineral, calcium magnesium carbonate. b) any rock consisting mainly of this mineral.
[after *D.G. de Dolomieu*, 1750–1801, a French geologist]

dolorous *adjective*
sad or mournful.
Word Family: **dolour**, *noun*, an old word for grief or sorrow; **dolorously**, *adverb*.
[Latin *dolor* grief]

dolphin (*say* **dolfin**) *noun*
any of a group of large, highly intelligent marine mammals with a long snout, similar to whales and porpoises.

dolt *noun*
a stupid person.
Word Family: **doltish**, *adjective*, **doltishly**, *adverb*; **doltishness**, *noun*.

dom *noun*
Christian: (*often capital*) a title for a monk in certain religious orders.

–dom
a suffix meaning: a) a domain, as in *kingdom*; b) a collection of people, as in *officialdom*; c) a general condition, as in *boredom*.

domain *noun*
1. a territory under rule or control.
2. an area of action or interest: 'the book belongs to the *domain* of philosophy rather than that of practical politics'.
3. *Maths:* the set of possible values for the independent variable of a function.

dome *noun*
a hemispherical roof.
Word Family: **domed**, *adjective*.

domestic *adjective*
1. of or relating to the home or family: 'the quarrel was purely a *domestic* affair'.
2. tame: '*domestic* animals'.
3. relating to business within a country: '*domestic* air transport'.
domestic *noun*
a person employed to do household chores.
Word Family: **domestically**, *adverb*; **domesticate**, *verb*; **domestication**, *noun*, the act of domesticating; **domesticity** (*say* dommess-**tissi**-tee), *noun*, the state of being domesticated.
[Latin *domus* a home]

domicile (*say* **dommi**-sile) *noun*
a home or established place of residence.
Word Family: **domicile**, *verb*; **domiciliary** (*say* dommi-**sillia**-ree), *adjective*.

dominant *adjective*
1. having the most influence, power or control: 'in our house my father is the *dominant* person'.
Usage: 'the *dominant* peak in the range is Mont Blanc' (= main, major).
2. *Biology:* of or relating to a hereditary character which shows itself whether one allele or two are present in a cell. Compare RECESSIVE.
Word Family: **dominance**, *noun*, the state of being dominant.
[Latin *dominus* lord]

dominate *verb*
1. to rule over or control.
2. to tower over: 'the mountain *dominates* the village'.
Word Family: **domination,** *noun.*

domineering *adjective*
tyrannical or arrogant.
Word Family: **domineeringly,** *adverb*; **domineer,** *verb.*

dominie (*say* **dommin–ee**) *noun*
Scottish: a schoolmaster.
[Latin *domine* O sir!]

dominion (*say* d'**min**–y'n) *noun*
1. a) the power or right to govern or control. b) the area so governed.
2. a self–governing country of the British Commonwealth.

domino *noun*
plural is **dominoes**
a) (*plural, used with singular verb*) a game played with small, flat, oblong pieces whose faces are divided into two, each half being blank or marked with one to six spots. b) one of these pieces.

domino theory
a theory which suggests that political change in one country tends to precipitate similar change in neighbouring countries, resulting in a chain–reaction like a falling row of dominoes.

don (1) *noun*
1. a Spanish nobleman.
2. a college tutor or fellow, especially at Oxford or Cambridge.
Word Family: **donnish,** *adjective,* (informal) stuffy or pedantic.
[Spanish]

don (2) *verb*
(donned, donning)
to put on clothes, etc.
[from *do on*]

donate (*say* doe **nate**) *verb*
to give as a gift: 'he *donated* £50 to the appeal'.
Word Family: **donation,** *noun,* a) the act of donating, b) something which is donated; **donator,** *noun.*
[Latin *donare* to give]

done (*say* dun) *verb*
the past participle of the verb **do.**

Don Juan (*say* don **jew**'n)
a womanizer.
[after such a character in an old Spanish legend]

donkey *noun*
1. a long–eared mammal related to the horse and valued as a pack animal because of its sure–footedness and endurance.
2. (*informal*) a silly person.

donkey's years
a long time.

donnish *adjective*
Word Family: see DON (1).

donor (*say* **doe**–nor) *noun*
a person who donates something: 'a blood *donor*'.

doodle *verb*
to draw or scribble idly.
Word Family: **doodle,** *noun*; **doodler,** *noun,* a person who doodles.

doodlebug *noun*
also called the **flying bomb**
a nickname for Hitler's pilotless bomber, launched against the London area in 1944.

doom *noun*
an unhappy or terrible fate: 'the general sent the soldiers to their *doom*'.
doom *verb*
to condemn to ruin or destruction: 'because of lack of finance the project was *doomed* from the start'.

doomsday *noun*
Religion: the day of Judgement, at the end of the world.

door *noun*
1. a) a movable barrier which opens or closes the entrance to a room, etc. b) the entrance itself.
2. any means of access: 'the *door* to success'.
Phrases:
next door to, in the next house, room, etc.
out of doors, in the open air.

dope *noun*
1. (*informal*) a) any illegal drug. b) a stimulating drug given illegally to racehorses, etc. so as to improve their performance. c) a stupid person. d) information: 'give us the *dope* on the secret meeting'.
2. any of various varnish–like preparations used for treating cloth, and formerly on aeroplane wings, etc. to waterproof or strengthen.
Word Family: **dope,** *verb,* to administer drugs to; **dopey,** *noun,* (informal) stupid.
[Dutch *doop* a sauce]

Doppler effect
Physics: the apparent change in frequency of sound, light or other waves caused by the movement or

movements of the source relative to the observer.
Example: the whistle of a train appears to the stationary observer to change in pitch as the train approaches, passes and continues.
[noted by *C. Doppler*, 1803–53, an Austrian physicist]

dormant *adjective*
1. a) in a state resembling sleep. b) non-active, e.g. during hibernation.
2. (of a volcano) not erupting. Compare EXTINCT.
Word Family: **dormancy,** *noun,* the state of being dormant.
[Latin *dormire* to sleep]

dormer *noun*
an upright window built out from a sloping roof.

dormitory (*say* **dorma-tree**) *noun*
a large room in an institution, such as a boarding school, where several people sleep.

dormouse *noun*
plural is **dormice**
a mouse-like mammal, living in trees and feeding on acorns and nuts; it sleeps for 6 months of the year.

dorsal *adjective*
Biology: relating to the back of an organ or organism.
[Latin *dorsum* back]

dory *noun*
also called a **John Dory**
an edible, yellow, marine fish.
[French *doré* gilded]

dose *noun*
1. the amount of medicine to be taken at one time: 'the *dose* is written on the bottle'.
2. any portion or quantity.
Word Family: **dose,** *verb*; **dosage,** *noun,* a) the giving of medicine in doses, b) the amount given.
[Greek *dosis* a gift]

doss *verb*
(*informal*) to sleep, especially in a cheap lodging house or temporary place.
Word Family: **doss,** *noun,* a) a temporary sleeping place, b) sleep.

dosshouse *noun*
a place providing cheap lodging.

dossier (*say* **dossia**) *noun*
a collection of documents containing special information on some person or subject.

dost (*say* dust) *verb*
an old form of the second person singular, present tense of the verb **do.**

dot (1) *noun*
a small spot or point, such as a full stop.
Phrases:
in the year dot, (*informal*) long ago.
on the dot, (*informal*) punctually.
Word Family: **dot (dotted, dotting),** *verb,* a) to mark with or as if with dots, b) to place like dots.

dot (2) *noun*
a dowry.

dotage (*say* **doe-tij**) *noun*
1. a feebleness of mind, especially resulting from old age: 'he has been in his *dotage* since he was sixty'.
2. an excessive fondness or affection.

dotard (*say* **dote-ard**) *noun*
an old, feeble-minded person.

dote *verb*
1. to lavish excessive love or affection on: 'she really *dotes* on that child'.
2. to be senile.
Word Family: **dotingly,** *adverb.*

doth (*say* duth) *verb*
an old form of the third person singular, present tense of the verb **do.**

dotterel *noun*
see PLOVER.

dotty *adjective*
(*informal*) crazy or eccentric.

double (*say* **dubb'l**) *adjective*
1. twice as big: 'a *double* whisky'.
2. having two parts, etc.: 'the word has a *double* meaning'.
3. *Music:* (of an instrument) producing tones one octave lower than the notes indicated on a score: 'a *double* bassoon'.
double *noun*
1. a twofold size or amount: '12 is the *double* of 6'.
2. a) a substitute: 'the actor used a *double* for the dangerous stunts'. b) a duplicate: 'he is the *double* of his twin'.
3. a sudden backward turn or bend: 'he made a quick *double* to escape his pursuer'.
4. a bet in which the winners of two races must be chosen.
5. (*plural*) a game in which there are two players on each side.
at the double, quickly.

double *verb*
1. to make or become twice as great: a) 'to *double* a bet'; b) 'they *doubled* their money by investing in stocks'.
2. to bend or fold with one part on another.
Usage: 'she *doubled* her fists with rage' (= clenched).
3. to serve in two capacities, e.g. a person who plays two instruments in a band.
4. to act as a double in a film, etc.
Phrases:
double back, to turn back on a course.
double up, a) to duplicate an item, etc., especially inadvertently. b) to curl up the body in pain or laughter.
[Latin *duplus*]

double bass
Music: a very large, low-pitched, stringed instrument played with a bow.

double-breasted *adjective*
(of a coat) having overlapping flaps at the front and two rows of buttons. Compare SINGLE-BREASTED.

double-cross *verb*
(*informal*) to betray.
Word Family: **double-cross,** *noun*; **double-crosser,** *noun,* a person who betrays another.

double-dealing *noun*
deceitfulness.
Word Family: **double-dealing,** *adjective*; **double-dealer,** *noun.*

double-decker *adjective*
having two tiers or layers: 'a *double decker* bus'.

double-declutch *verb*
(in a motor vehicle) to move from one gear into neutral and then into another gear, operating the clutch separately for each movement.

double decomposition
also called **metathesis**
Chemistry: a reaction between two compounds in which both decompose and form two new compounds.

double-edged *adjective*
1. having two cutting edges.
2. having two effects or meanings: 'her praise was *double-edged*'.

double entendre (*say* dubb'l on-tondra)
a word or phrase with a second or hidden meaning.
[French *double* double + *entendre* to hear]

double-jointed *adjective*
having very flexible joints which allow free or unusual movement.

double standard
a moral or social principle which one person or group expects another to follow, without doing so themselves.

double star
see BINARY STAR.

doublet (*say* **dub**lit) *noun*
1. a close-fitting upper garment worn by men from the 15th to the 17th century.
2. a) a pair of similar things. b) one of a pair of similar things.

double take
a surprised second look at something not understood or seen clearly at first.

doubletalk *noun*
any ambiguous talk.

double time
the payment of double wages to employees who work extra hours, e.g. on a public holiday.

doubloon (*say* dub**loon**) *noun*
an obsolete Spanish gold coin.

doubly (*say* **dub**-lee) *adverb*
a) twice as much or many. b) in two ways.

doubt (*rhymes with* out) *noun*
a feeling of uncertainty, disbelief or distrust: 'there is no *doubt* that you were wrong'.
doubt *verb*
to feel uncertain or hesitant about: 'I *doubt* whether we will get there before 7 o'clock'.
Word Family: **doubtingly,** *adverb*; **doubtless,** *adverb, adjective,* without a doubt; **doubtlessly,** *adverb.*
[Latin *dubitare* to hesitate]

doubtful *adjective*
1. having doubts: 'she seemed *doubtful* about being able to come'.
2. causing doubt.
Word Family: **doubtfully,** *adverb*; **doubtfulness,** *noun.*

douche (*say* doosh) *noun*
a) a jet of liquid applied to the body, especially to the vagina for hygiene or as a means of contraception. b) an instrument used to apply it.
Word Family: **douche,** *verb.*
[French *douche* shower]

dough (*say* doe) *noun*
1. a thick paste of flour and milk or water, used to make bread, cakes, etc.
2. (*informal*) money.

Word Family: **doughy**, *adjective*, of or like dough.

doughnut *noun*
a round or ring-shaped sweet cake, usually deep-fried.

doughty (*say* **dow-tee**) *adjective*
an old word meaning brave or bold.

dour (*say* **doo-er**) *adjective*
being sullen or gloomy.
[Latin *durus* hard]

douse (*rhymes with* house) **dowse** *verb*
to throw water on, such as on a fire to extinguish it.
Usage: 'last one to bed *douses* the lights' (= puts out, extinguishes).

dove (*say* duv) *noun*
1. a pigeon.
2. a person favouring mild action, such as peace or friendship with another country. Compare HAWK (1).

dovetail *noun*
a joint made by cutting one or more wedge-shaped holes in the end of one piece of timber, etc., into which the matching end of another piece is interlocked.
Word Family: **dovetail**, *verb.*

dowager (*say* **dow-a-ja**) *noun*
1. a woman who has inherited a title or property from her deceased husband.
2. any dignified elderly lady.

dowdy *adjective*
shabbily or unfashionably dressed.
Word Family: **dowdiness**, *noun*; **dowdily**, *adverb.*

dowel (*rhymes with* towel) *noun*
a narrow cylindrical piece of wood or metal fitted into matching holes in two surfaces, to join them.

dower (*rhymes with* flower) *noun*
1. *Law:* a widow's share of her dead husband's property, for use during her lifetime.
2. an old word for a dowry.
Word Family: **dower**, *verb*, to provide with a dower or dowry.

down (1) *adverb, preposition, adjective*
from a higher to a lower position, level, degree, etc.: a) 'she came *down* the stairs very slowly'; b) 'slow *down* at intersections'; c) 'calm *down*'.
Usages:
a) 'the back tyre was *down*' (= flat).
b) 'she was knocked *down* by the galloping horse' (= to the ground).
c) 'boil the syrup *down* until it thickens' (= to a smaller volume).
d) 'the house was passed *down* from their ancestors' (= by way of inheritance).
e) 'she is kept *down* by her husband' (= in submission).
f) 'I felt rather *down* the day after the accident' (= unhappy, depressed).
g) 'I will put *down* £5 and pay the rest next week' (= as a deposit).
h) 'New Zealand is *down* by 42 runs this innings' (= losing by).
i) 'take *down* my address' (= in writing).
j) 'it was hard to settle *down* to study' (= in place, in preparation).
Phrases:
be down to earth, see EARTH.
down and out, 'the street was full of *down and out* derelicts' (= penniless, jobless).
down on, 'this town is *down on* tourists' (= severe or critical towards).
down with, a) '*down with* homework' (= let's get rid of); b) 'he is *down with* measles' (= sick in bed with).
send down, see SEND.

down *noun*
1. a reversal or descent: 'the ups and *downs* of life'.
2. a feeling of dislike or hostility: 'she has a *down* on us at the moment'.

down *verb*
to put or throw down: 'the workers *downed* tools and went on strike'.
Usage: '*down* your coffee and let's go' (= drink).
Word Family: **downward**, *adjective*, moving or pointing down; **downwards**, **downward**, *adverb*, to a lower place, position, etc.

down (2) *noun*
1. the first, soft, fluffy feathers on some birds.
2. any soft, furry growth.
Word Family: **downy**, *adjective.*

down (3) *noun*
(*usually plural*) any open, rolling country.

downbeat *adjective*
(*informal*) casual, unemphatic or gloomy.

downcast *adjective*
1. looking downwards: 'her *downcast* eyes avoided the dreadful sight'.
2. sad or depressed.

downer *noun*
(*informal*) something, especially a drug, which counteracts stimulation.

downfall *noun*
a) a destruction or ruin: 'his love of adventure caused his *downfall*'. b) anything which causes destruction or ruin: 'gambling was his *downfall*'.

downgrade *verb*
to reduce in status, salary, etc.
downgrade *noun*
a descending slope, e.g. of a road, hill, etc.
on the downgrade, declining in health, prosperity, reputation, etc.

downhearted *adjective*
discouraged or dejected.

downhill *adverb, adjective*
in a downward direction.
go downhill, 'he *went downhill* very rapidly after the second heart attack' (= got worse).

down payment
the first payment of a series, usually made before delivery of the goods.

downpipe *noun*
a pipe down the side of a building which carries water away from the guttering.

downpour *noun*
a heavy shower of rain.

downright *adjective*
1. complete: 'a *downright* fool'.
2. honest or candid: '*downright* sincerity'.
Word Family: **downright**, *adverb*, completely.

Down's syndrome
see MONGOLISM.

downstage *adverb, adjective*
Theatre: at or towards the front of the stage: 'the actors stood *downstage* from the chorus'.
Word Family: **downstage**, *noun.*

downstairs *adverb*
to, at or on a lower floor: 'I told them to wait *downstairs*'.
Word Family: **downstairs, downstair**, *adjective*; **downstairs**, *noun.*

downstream *adverb, adjective*
in the direction of the moving stream or current: 'the canoe was carried rapidly *downstream*'.

downswing *noun*
a swinging downwards.
Usage: 'how can we stop a *downswing* in the economy?' (= decline).

downtown *adverb, adjective*
American: in or to the main business section of a city: 'we went *downtown* for dinner'.

downtrodden *adjective*
oppressed or badly treated.

down-under *noun*
(*informal*) Australia and New Zealand.
Word Family: **down-under**, *adverb.*

downward *adjective*
Word Family: see DOWN (1).

downwind *adverb*
1. with or in the direction of the wind.
2. on or towards the leeward side: 'the tug is approaching *downwind* of us'.
Word Family: **downwind**, *adjective.*

downy *adjective*
Word Family: see DOWN (2).

dowry *noun*
any property or money a bride brings to her husband at marriage, usually provided by her father.

dowse (1) *verb*
see DOUSE.

dowse (2) (*rhymes with* house) *verb*
to search for water, etc. with a divining rod.
Word Family: **dowser**, *noun*, a water diviner.

doyen *noun*
the eldest or leading member of a group.
Word Family: **doyenne**, *noun*, a female doyen.
[French, dean]

doyly *noun*
see DOILY.

doze *verb*
to sleep lightly or briefly: 'he *dozed* by the fire for a few minutes'.
Word Family: **doze**, *noun*; **dozy**, *adjective*, a) drowsy, b) slow or stupid.

dozen (*say* **duzzen**) *noun*
any group of twelve things.
[French *douze* twelve]

drab *adjective*
having a dull, usually brown or greyish colour: 'the *drab* uniforms of the soldiers blended with the colourless buildings'.
Usage: 'what a *drab*, humourless discussion' (= dull, boring).

drachm (*say* dram) *noun*
a unit of mass equal to about 3·89 g.

drachma (*say* **drakma**) *noun*
plural is **drachmas** or **drachmae** (*say* **drakmi**)
the basic unit of money in modern and ancient Greece.

draconian *adjective*
(*usually capital*) harsh or severe: '*Draconian* punishment'.

[after *Draco*, an ancient Athenian statesman noted for his harsh laws]

draft *noun*
1. a first or preliminary version of a speech or document.
2. a written order for payment of money, especially from a bank.
3. a detachment or contingent selected for a particular purpose.
the draft, (*informal*) conscription.
draft *verb*
1. to make a draft or outline of: 'his advisers *drafted* the main points of his speech'.
2. to conscript.

drag *verb*
(dragged, dragging)
1. to pull along with effort or difficulty: 'they *dragged* the table over to the window'.
Usages:
a) 'her first week in hospital *dragged*' (= passed slowly).
b) 'he *dragged* thoughtfully on his pipe' (= puffed heavily).
c) 'your skirt is *dragging* along behind you' (= trailing).
2. to search with nets, etc.: 'police *dragged* the river for the stolen car'.
3. (*informal*) a puff of a cigarette, etc.
drag one's feet, to move or act slowly.
drag *noun*
1. anything which is dragged, such as a fishing net.
2. anything which slows down progress or movement, especially the force of a current of water or air against a moving body.
3. (*informal*) a) a very boring person or thing. b) female clothing when worn by a male. c) a car acceleration race.

draggle *verb*
1. to make wet or dirty, especially by dragging on the ground.
2. to follow in a slow, disorderly way.

dragnet *noun*
1. a net dragged through water to catch fish, etc.
2. any intricate system for catching or trapping, such as is used by the police force.

dragoman *noun*
plural is **dragomans** or **dragomen**
an interpreter or guide in Middle Eastern countries such as Turkey.
[Arabic *targuman* interpreter]

dragon (*say* **drag'n**) *noun*
1. *Mythology:* a monster, usually pictured as a huge, winged, fire-breathing reptile with claws and scaly skin.
2. (*informal*) a strict or overbearing person, especially a woman.
3. any of various tree-dwelling or running lizards. The Asian species, called the **flying dragon,** can glide by stretching the skin on the sides of its body over elongated ribs.
[Greek *drakon* serpent]

dragonfly *noun*
any of a group of large, harmless insects often with slender, brightly coloured bodies and wings.

dragoon (*say* dra-**goon**) *noun*
1. (*formerly*) a cavalry soldier trained to fight on foot.
2. a member of certain former cavalry regiments, now part of the Royal Armoured Corps.
dragoon *verb*
to force, often by violent or oppressive means: 'the whole town was *dragooned* into feeding and serving the invading army'.
[after their carbines, once called *dragons*]

dragster *noun*
a low car built to race at full speed over very short distances.

drain *verb*
to remove or empty slowly, especially liquids: 'the swamp areas were *drained* to reduce the risk of malaria'.
Usages:
a) 'the country's fuel reserves were *drained* during the petrol strike' (= used up).
b) 'he *drained* his glass and stood up to leave' (= emptied).
drain *noun*
1. any pipe, channel or other device which carries water, etc., especially away from a building.
2. anything which causes loss or expense: 'his long stay in the nursing-home was a *drain* on the family's savings'.
down the drain, 'buying all those clothes is just money *down the drain*' (= wasted).
Word Family: **drainage,** *noun,* a) the act of draining, b) a system of drains, c) anything which is drained or carried away, such as sewage.

drake *noun*
a male duck.

dram *noun*
1. an obsolete unit of mass equal to about 1·77 g.

2. a small quantity of anything, especially alcohol.

drama (*say* **drah**–ma) *noun*
1. a play or other literary composition, especially one in which there is conflict or tragedy.
2. the art of composing and presenting such works, especially for the theatre.
3. an event which is exciting or interesting: 'the *drama* of the election held everybody's attention'.
[Greek, a deed, a (tragic) play]

dramatic (*say* dra–**mattik**) *adjective*
1. of or relating to drama or the theatre: 'he is doing a course in *dramatic* production'.
2. lively, forceful or exciting: 'the commentator gave a *dramatic* description of the match'.
dramatics *plural noun*
1. any dramatic productions: 'amateur *dramatics*'.
2. any exaggerated behaviour.
Word Family: **dramatically,** *adverb.*

dramatis personae (*say* dramma–tis per–**so**–nigh)
Theatre: a list of the characters in a play.
[Latin]

dramatist (*say* **dramma**–tist) *noun*
a playwright.

dramatize, dramatise *verb*
1. to put a story, etc. into the form of a play.
2. to express in a dramatic way: 'he *dramatized* his account of the meeting'.
Word Family: **dramatization,** *noun.*

drank *verb*
the past tense of the verb **drink**.

drape *verb*
to hang or adjust loosely in folds: 'she *draped* a blanket around her shoulders to keep warm'.
Usage: 'he *draped* his legs over the arm of the chair' (= placed casually).

draper *noun*
a person who sells textiles and clothes to the public.
drapery *noun*
1. any textiles or fabric, especially when used as curtains or covers.
2. a draper's shop.

drastic *adjective*
extremely strong or violent: 'the rain had a *drastic* effect on the crops'.
Word Family: **drastically,** *adverb.*

drat *interjection*
curse or damn: '*drat* this terrible weather'.

draught (*rhymes with* raft) *noun*
1. a flow of air through an enclosed space: 'close the door to keep out the *draught*'.
2. a haul of fish.
3. the drawing of liquid, such as beer, from a cask or other container.
4. a drink: 'he drank a long *draught* of water'.
5. *Nautical:* the depth of water a vessel needs in order to float.
draught *adjective*
1. (of animals) used for pulling loads: 'a *draught* horse'.
2. (of drinking liquids) being drawn straight from the container without being bottled: '*draught* beer'.
draughty *adjective*
having draughts: 'what a *draughty* old house!'.

draughts (*rhymes with* rafts) *plural noun*
also called **chequers**
a game for two players, each with 12 pieces which are moved diagonally on a board of 64 alternately coloured squares.

draughtsman *noun*
1. a person who draws architectural plans, etc.
2. any of the 24 pieces or discs used in draughts.

draw *verb*
(**drew, drawn, drawing**)
1. a) to make a picture or outline with pen, pencils, etc.: 'she *drew* a quick map of the area'. b) to describe in words: 'the characters in the play are not well *drawn*'.
2. to pull: '*draw* your chair closer to the fire'.
Usages:
a) 'she *drew* a deep breath before diving under the water' (= took in).
b) 'as Christmas *draws* nearer the city becomes crowded' (= moves, comes).
c) 'the visiting ballet company *drew* large audiences' (= attracted).
d) 'I can only *draw* one conclusion from your behaviour' (= make, arrive at).
3. to pick or choose at random: 'let us *draw* lots to decide who goes first'.
4. to end a competition or game with no outright winner.
5. *Commerce:* to prepare a cheque or bill of exchange, etc. The person ordering payment is called the **drawer**

and the person from whom payment is required is called the **drawee.** The person to whom the payment is made is called the payee, who may or may not be the drawer.
Phrases:
draw on, draw upon, 'the stranded hikers had to *draw on* their emergency food supplies' (= make use of).
draw out, a) 'let's not *draw out* this boring discussion any longer' (= extend, lengthen); b) 'the shy guest was *drawn out* by their friendliness' (= encouraged to talk).
draw the line at, see LINE (1).
draw up, a) 'the car *drew up* at the kerb' (= stopped); b) 'the battalion was *drawn up* for battle' (= arranged in formation); c) 'the two governments will *draw up* a trade agreement' (= prepare).
draw *noun*
1. a) the act of drawing: 'a lottery *draw*'. b) the state of being drawn: 'the game ended in a *draw*'.
2. anything which draws or attracts: 'this new actress is bound to be a great *draw*'.

drawback *noun*
a disadvantage.

drawbridge *noun*
a bridge which may be raised or lowered.

drawer *noun*
1. (*say* dror) a sliding, storage compartment in a piece of furniture.
2. *Dress:* (*plural*) underpants.
3. (*say* **draw**-er) a person who draws anything, e.g. a person who draws a cheque.

drawing *noun*
any picture or composition made up of lines and shades, usually of a single colour, using a pen, pencil, brush, etc.

drawing-pin *noun*
a short tack with a broad head designed to be pushed in with the thumb.

drawing room
a room in a house used for receiving guests, etc.
[from *withdrawing room*]

drawl *verb*
to speak so that the vowel sounds are much longer and slower than usual.
Word Family: **drawl,** *noun.*

drawn *adjective*
1. haggard or lined: 'her face was *drawn* with anxiety'.
2. pulled together: '*drawn* curtains'.

drawn *verb*
the past participle of the verb **draw.**

drawstring *noun*
a cord or string, the end or ends of which are pulled to close a bag, etc.

dray *noun*
a cart pulled by horses and used to carry heavy loads.

dread (*say* dred) *verb*
to have great fear or apprehension of: 'he *dreads* driving in heavy traffic'.
Word Family: **dread,** *noun, adjective.*

dreadful *adjective*
1. causing dread or horror: 'the details of the *dreadful* accident were withheld'.
2. unpleasant or bad.: 'what a *dreadful* day!'.
Word Family: **dreadfully,** *adverb;* **dreadfulness,** *noun.*

dreadnought (*say* **dred**-nawt) *noun*
an old type of battleship built before World War I.

dream *noun*
1. a sequence of images, etc. occurring in the mind during sleep.
2. any imagined vision, hope or fancy: 'a *dream* of future peace'.
3. anything which is beautiful or pleasing.
dream *verb*
(**dreamt** or **dreamed, dreaming**)
to have a dream.
Usages:
a) 'stop *dreaming* and concentrate on your work' (= daydreaming).
b) 'I never *dreamt* we would win' (= imagined).
dream up 'what mad idea will you *dream up* next?' (= invent).
Word Family: **dreamer,** *noun;* **dreamless,** *adjective;* **dreamy,** *adjective,* vague, unreal or dream-like.

dreary *adjective*
dull or gloomy: 'miles of *dreary* suburbs'.
Word Family: **dreariness,** *noun;* **drearily,** *adverb;* **drear,** *adjective.*

dredge (1) *noun*
any of various machines using scoops or suction pumps to draw up silt or other materials from the bed of a river, etc.
Word Family: **dredge,** *verb,* a) to use a dredge, b) to explore or remove with or as if with a dredge; **dredger,** *noun,* a boat equipped with a dredge.

dredge (2) *verb*
to sprinkle or scatter: '*dredge* the cutlets with flour before frying'.
Word Family: **dredger**, *noun*, an implement used for sprinkling.

dregs *plural noun*
1. the sediment of wine or other liquids.
2. the most worthless or inferior parts of anything: 'he treats us like the *dregs* of humanity'.

drench *verb*
1. to soak or wet completely: 'we were *drenched* in the storm'.
2. to give medicine to an animal.
Word Family: **drench**, *noun*.

dress *noun*
1. a piece of female clothing consisting of a skirt and a top in one piece.
2. a) any clothing. b) formal clothing.
dress *verb*
a) to put on clothes. b) to put on formal clothes.
Usages:
a) 'the nurse *dressed* and bandaged his cuts' (= treated).
b) 'the shop windows were *dressed* for the Christmas sale' (= decorated).
Phrases:
dress down, 'he was severely *dressed down* for cheating' (= scolded).
dress up, a) 'let's *dress up* as pirates' (= put on the costume of); b) 'do I need to *dress up* for dinner?' (= wear formal clothes).

dressage (*say* **dress**-ahj) *noun*
a) the art of training a horse in obedience, etc. b) a competition based on these skills.

dress circle
the curving section of seats upstairs in a theatre.

dresser *noun*
1. a piece of kitchen furniture with open shelves at the top, drawers for cutlery, and cupboards at the bottom.
2. *American:* a dressing-table.
3. a person who looks after and arranges the clothes of an actor or actress in a theatre's dressing-room.

dressing *noun*
1. a sauce for food: 'salad *dressing*'.
2. a medicated cloth for covering and protecting a wound.
3. anything used to treat or prepare soil, such as fertilizer, compost, etc.

dressing-gown *noun*
a loose coat, usually tied with a sash and worn over nightclothes.

dressing-room *noun*
a room set aside for a person to dress in, e.g. one backstage in a theatre.

dressing-table *noun*
a bedroom table with drawers and usually a mirror on top, used when dressing.

dress rehearsal
see REHEARSAL.

drew *verb*
the past tense of the verb **draw**.

dribble *verb*
1. to flow or allow to flow in slow, small drops: 'blood *dribbled* from the cut on her knee'.
2. *Sport:* to propel the ball with a series of short kicks, pushes or bounces.
Word Family: **dribble**, *noun*.

driblet *noun*
a very small amount of anything.

dribs and drabs
any small, irregular amounts: 'he paid his rent in *dribs and drabs*'.

dried (*say* dride) *verb*
the past tense and past participle of the verb **dry**.

drier *noun*
also spelt **dryer**
1. anything which dries: 'a clothes *drier*'.
2. a substance added to paints, varnishes, etc., to make them dry more quickly.

drift *verb*
to be carried or moved along without particular direction: 'the boat *drifted* on the calm sea after the engine broke down'.
Usage: 'he has *drifted* about the country all his life' (= wandered aimlessly).
drift *noun*
1. a drifting or carrying movement: 'the *drift* of the tides'.
Usages:
a) 'the *drift* of world events seemed to be towards peace' (= trend, movement).
b) 'what was the main *drift* of his argument?' (=aim, meaning).
2. *Geography:* a) any deposit on the earth transported by wind, a glacier or water. b) a broad, shallow current in the sea or a lake.
3. *South African:* a ford.

drifter *noun*
a person who drifts without aim or purpose.

driftwood *noun*
any wood found floating in the sea or deposited on the beach.

drill (1) *noun*
1. any of various tools for boring holes.
2. any strict method of exercise and training, e.g. for soldiers.
Usage: 'what is the *drill* for insuring my car?' (= procedure).
drill *verb*
1. to make holes with a drill.
2. to train and instruct by strict methods.

drill (2) *noun*
a) a small furrow in the soil, in which seeds are planted. b) a machine which plants seeds in rows and covers them with soil.
Word Family: **drill**, *verb.*

drill (3) *noun*
a strong cotton fabric used to make uniforms, sails, etc.

drill (4) *noun*
a small baboon found in western Africa.

drily *adverb*
Word Family: see DRY.

drink *verb*
(drank, drunk, drinking)
to take in or swallow liquid: '*drink* your tea while it's still hot'.
Usages:
a) 'I don't think that they *drink* at all' (= consume alcohol).
b) 'we eagerly *drank* in every word of his story' (= took, absorbed).
drink *noun*
1. a) any liquid for drinking: 'I need a *drink* to quench my thirst'. b) an alcoholic drink: 'let's have a *drink* before dinner'.
2. (*informal*) the sea.
Word Family: **drinkable**, *adjective*, fit for drinking; **drinker**, *noun.*

drip *verb*
(dripped, dripping)
to fall or allow to fall in drops: 'water was *dripping* noisily from the leaking tap'.
drip *noun*
1. a) the act of dripping. b) the liquid which drips or the noise it makes.
2. *Surgery:* a device for intravenous feeding.
3. (*informal*) an insipid or foolish person.

dripdry *adjective*
(of fabric) drying without creases.

dripping *noun*
the fat obtained while cooking meat, which can be re-used.

drive *verb*
(drove, driven, driving)
1. to guide or cause to move: a) '*drive* the cows into the next paddock'; b) 'the engine was *driven* by steam'.
Usages:
a) 'she *drives* me mad with her chatter' (= sends, makes).
b) 'the snow *drove* against the house' (= dashed).
c) 'what are your questions *driving* at?' (= aiming).
2. to operate, control or guide a motor vehicle, machine, etc: 'can you *drive* a car yet?'.
drive *noun*
1. the act of driving or being driven: 'let's go for a *drive* to the country'.
2. a private road or path leading to a house, etc. Also called a **driveway**.
3. a) a source of motivation: 'the sex *drive*'. b) energy or vigour: 'she shows ambitious *drive* at work'.
4. an organized attempt or effort: 'we are planning a *drive* to raise money for a new library'.
5. a) a means of mechanical power: 'chain *drive*'. b) a means of applying power: 'four-wheel *drive*'.
Word Family: **driver**, *noun*, a person or thing that drives.

drive-in *adjective*
relating to an establishment designed for customers to be served or attended in their cars: 'a *drive-in* bank'.

drivel (*say* **drivv'l**) *verb*
(drivelled, drivelling)
1. to dribble or drool.
2. to talk or act foolishly.
Word Family: **drivel**, *noun.*

driveway *noun*
a private road or path leading to a house, etc.

drizzle *verb*
to rain in light, small drops.
Word Family: **drizzle**, *noun*; **drizzly**, *adjective.*

droll *adjective*
strangely comical or amusing: 'what a *droll* remark!'.
drollery *noun*
a) the quality of being droll. b) a strangely amusing joke or trick.
Word Family: **drollness**, *noun*; **drolly**, *adverb.*

drome *noun*
(*informal*) an aerodrome.

dromedary (*say* **dromma**–dree) *noun*
see CAMEL.

drone (1) *noun*
1. a male bee which develops from an unfertilized egg, does not produce honey, and dies or is killed soon after mating.
2. a lazy person.
3. an aircraft or other vehicle guided by remote control.

drone (2) *verb*
to make a dull, continuous sound: 'the voice of the lecturer *droned* on in the half–filled hall'.
drone *noun*
1. a dull continuous sound or voice.
2. a boring person or dull speaker.

drool *verb*
to dribble saliva.
drool over, (*informal*) to regard with greedy desire.

droop *verb*
to hang or bend down loosely: 'her head *drooped* wearily over her books'.
Usage: 'his spirits *drooped* after several hours of waiting for rescue' (= fell, sank).
Word Family: **droopy,** *adjective.*

drop *verb*
(dropped, dropping)
1. to fall: a) 'beads of water were still *dropping* from the branches'; b) 'he has *dropped* into the habit of arriving late'.
2. to cause or allow to fall: '*drop* that gun or you're a dead man!'.
3. to make or become lower: 'I've *dropped* the hem another couple of inches'.
Usages:
a) 'please *drop* me at the corner' (= let out).
b) 'she was *dropped* from the team because of injury' (= left out).
c) 'I *dropped* maths at the beginning of the year' (= stopped studying).
d) '*drop* me a note to say you arrived safely' (= send).
e) 'stop arguing and we'll *drop* the whole subject' (= end).
Phrases:
drop in, to make a visit.
drop off, a) 'don't *drop off* in front of the fire' (= fall asleep); b) 'sales *dropped off* after Christmas' (= decreased).
drop out, to withdraw or disappear.
drop *noun*
1. a) the act of dropping: 'a *drop* in prices'. b) the amount by which something drops: 'a cliff with a 500 m *drop*'.
2. a very small quantity or amount, especially a small sphere of liquid.
Usage: 'have one of my cough *drops*' (= lozenges).

drop forging
a forging made by the dropping of a heavy weight (called a **drop hammer**) on to the metal which is usually placed between the dies.
Word Family: **drop–forge,** *verb.*

drop kick
Football: a kick, in Rugby, in which the ball is dropped at an angle and kicked as it leaves the ground.
Word Family: **drop–kick,** *verb.*

droplet *noun*
a small drop.

drop–out *noun*
a person who rejects or withdraws from an established institution or normal society.

dropper *noun*
a device consisting of a tube with a rubber bulb at one end, for releasing a liquid in drops.

droppings *plural noun*
the dung of animals.

drop scone
a pikelet.

dropsy *noun*
see OEDEMA.

dross *noun*
1. a scum of oxide and other impurities on the surface of molten metal.
2. any waste matter.

drought (*rhymes with* out) *noun*
a long period of weather without rain.
Word Family: **droughty**, *adjective*, dry or lacking rain.

drove (1) *verb*
the past tense of the verb **drive.**

drove (2) *noun*
1. a group of sheep, cattle, etc. in one herd.
2. a large crowd of people.
Word Family: **drover,** *noun.*

drown *verb*
to die or cause to die by suffocating in water or other liquid.
Usage: 'the roars of the crowd *drowned* his voice' (= overwhelmed, muffled).

drowse (*rhymes with* cows) *verb*
to be half–asleep: 'he spent the afternoon *drowsing* by the fire'.

Word Family: **drowsy,** *adjective,* tired or half-asleep; **drowse,** *noun;* **drowsily,** *adverb;* **drowsiness,** *noun.*

drub *verb*
(drubbed, drubbing)
to beat severely.
Word Family: **drubbing,** *noun.*

drudge *noun*
a person who works at a dreary or uninteresting task.
Word Family: **drudgery,** *noun,* any hard or uninteresting work; **drudge,** *verb.*

drug *noun*
1. any chemical substance used to treat disease.
2. any addictive substance, such as certain narcotics.
drug *verb*
(drugged, drugging)
to administer a drug to.
Usage: 'she was still *drugged* with sleep as she stumbled to the shower' (= stupefied).

druggist *noun*
American: a pharmacist.

drugstore *noun*
American: a shop selling general merchandise and sometimes prescription medicines.

drum *noun*
1. *Music:* any of various percussion instruments consisting of a tightly stretched skin or membrane on a round frame, which is struck with sticks or the hands.
2. a large spool wound with cable, wire or heavy rope.
3. a cylindrical container: 'a petrol *drum*'.
beat the drum for, to proclaim or praise.
drum *verb*
(drummed, drumming)
to thump or tap rhythmically on, or as if on, a drum.
Usage: 'the army certainly *drums* discipline into its recruits' (= forces by repetition).
Phrases:
drum out, to expel or dismiss in disgrace.
drum up, 'he's trying to *drum up* support for his ideas' (= obtain).
Word Family: **drummer,** *noun,* a person who plays a drum.

drumstick *noun*
1. a stick used for beating a drum.
2. the lower part of the leg of a chicken, duck or turkey.

drunk *adjective*
intoxicated or overcome with, or as if with, alcohol.
drunk *noun*
short form of **drunkard**
a person who is often drunk.
drunk *verb*
the past participle of the verb **drink.**

drunken *adjective*
of or showing the effects of drinking alcohol: 'his *drunken* behaviour embarrassed all the guests'.
Word Family: **drunkenly,** *adverb;* **drunkenness,** *noun,* the state of being drunk.

drupe *noun*
also called a **stone fruit**
Biology: a juicy fruit with an outer fleshy layer around a covered seed, such as a plum.
[Latin *druppa* an overripe olive]

dry *adjective*
1. not wet or producing liquid: 'wood must be *dry* or it will not burn properly'.
Usages:
a) 'a boiled egg and a piece of *dry* toast' (= unbuttered).
b) 'they found the speech rather *dry* and boring' (= uninteresting).
c) 'his short talk gave only the *dry* facts' (= plain).
d) 'we found that the party was *dry*' (= without alcohol).
e) 'a *dry* sense of humour' (= tersely expressed, ironically matter-of-fact).
2. (of wines, biscuits, etc.) not sweet.
dry *verb*
(dried, drying)
to make or become free of moisture: 'please *dry* the plates thoroughly before you put them away'.
dry up, a) 'the stream *dries up* in summer' (= becomes completely dry); b) 'she *dried up* as she stood nervously on the stage' (= forgot her lines); c) (*informal*) 'please *dry up,* I can't concentrate with all that chatter' (= be quiet).
Word Family: **drily, dryly,** *adverb;* **dryness,** *noun.*

dryad *noun*
Greek mythology: a nymph of the woods.
[Greek *dryados* of a tree]

dry battery
Electricity: a dry cell or a battery containing dry cells.

dry cell
Electricity: see CELL.

dry-cleaning *noun*
the process of cleaning clothes with chemical solvents, etc.
Word Family: **dry-clean,** *verb*; **dry-cleaner,** *noun.*

dry dock
a dock from which the water may be removed to allow a ship to be painted and repaired.

dry ginger
ginger ale.

dry goods
1. any non-liquid goods, such as corn.
2. *American:* textiles, as opposed to groceries and hardware.

dry ice
frozen carbon dioxide, which is useful as a refrigerant because it evaporates directly from solid ice into a gas. See SUBLIME.

dry point
a print made from a copper plate, engraved directly by a needle, without using acid. Compare ETCH.

dry rot
a decay caused by fungi in dry seasoned timber which has not been kept properly ventilated.

dry run
also called a **dummy run**
a try-out or rehearsal.
[formerly it referred to American army manoeuvres in which blank cartridges were fired]

dual (*say* **dew**'l) *adjective*
a) having two parts: 'this car has *dual* controls'. b) relating to two.
[Latin *duo* two]
Common Error: do not confuse with DUEL.

dual carriageway
a main road divided into two separate one-way roads, but not qualifying as a motorway.

dualism (*say* **dew**a-lizm) *noun*
1. the state of having two parts. Also called **duality** (*say* dew-**alli**-tee).
2. *Philosophy:* the belief that there are two opposing, independent basic principles in the world, such as mind and body or good and evil. Compare MONISM.
Word Family: **dualistic,** *adjective*; **dualist,** *noun.*

dub (1) *verb*
(dubbed, dubbing)
1. to strike lightly on the head or shoulder when conferring a knighthood.
2. to dress the surface of wood or leather.
Word Family: **dubbing,** *noun.*

dub (2) *verb*
(dubbed, dubbing)
Film: to change or add to the soundtrack of a film, e.g. by replacing the original dialogue with one in a different language.
Word Family: **dubbing,** *noun.*

dubbin *noun*
a mixture of oil and tallow used to soften and waterproof leather.

dubious (*say* **dew**bi-us) *adjective*
doubtful or uncertain.
Usage: 'the motives for his generosity are rather *dubious*' (= open to question or suspicion).
Word Family: **dubiousness, dubiety** (*say* dew-**by**-a-tee), *nouns*; **dubiously,** *adverb.*
[Latin *dubium* doubt]

ducal (*say* **dew**k'l) *adjective*
of or relating to a duke.

ducat (*say* **dukk**'t) *noun*
an obsolete European gold coin.

duchess (*say* **dutch**-ess) *noun*
Word Family: see DUKE.

duchy (*say* **dutch**-ee) *noun*
the land ruled by a duke or duchess.

duck (1) *noun*
any of various wild or domesticated waterbirds with a broad, flat bill, short legs and webbed feet.

duck (2) *verb*
1. to stoop or move aside quickly: 'he *ducked* his head as the ball hurtled past'.
2. to avoid: 'she tries to *duck* responsibility'.
3. to plunge or be plunged quickly under water.
Word Family: **duck,** *noun.*

duck (3) *noun*
a heavy, plain fabric used for tents, bags, etc.

duck (4) *noun*
Cricket: a batsman's score of zero.

duck-billed platypus
see PLATYPUS.

duckboard *noun*
one section of a wooden pathway laid over a swamp or heavy mud.

duckling *noun*
a young duck.

ducky *adjective*
(*informal*) dear or darling.

Duco (*say* **dew**–ko) *noun*
a paint used on motor vehicles.
[a trademark]

duct *noun*
any tube through which gases or liquids are conveyed, such as the tubes through which the secretions of certain glands flow in the bodies of animals.
Word Family: **ducting**, *noun.*
[Latin *ductus* conveyed]

ductile *adjective*
1. able to be drawn out into thin wires. Compare MALLEABLE.
2. able to be shaped or moulded.
Usage: 'it was easy to persuade such a *ductile* audience' (= easily influenced).
Word Family: **ductility** (*say* duk–**tilla**–tee), *noun.*

dud *noun*
1. a person or thing that is a failure, such as a bomb which fails to explode.
2. anything which is fake or useless, such as a counterfeit coin.

dude (*say* dewd) *noun*
American: a) a city–dweller. b) a fop.
a **dude ranch** is a farm operated as a holiday resort for tourists.

dudgeon (*say* **dud**jen) *noun*
a feeling of anger or hurt pride.

duds *plural noun*
(*informal*) clothes or belongings: **'I'll** just pack my *duds*'.

due (*say* dew) *adjective*
1. owing or expected: 'the rent is *due* next Wednesday'.
2. proper or adequate: 'you must take *due* care when driving on wet roads'.
due to, 'his stutter is *due to* extreme shyness' (= caused by).
due *noun*
1. anything which is owed or deserved: 'success is his *due* for so much hard work'.
2. (*plural*) a membership fee or payment.
due *adverb*
(of direction) directly or exactly: 'we sailed *due* east towards the islands'.
Word Family: **duly**, *adverb*, a) at the appropriate time, b) in the appropriate manner.
Common Error: **due to** must refer back to a noun, not a clause. Thus 'the match was cancelled *due to* rain' is incorrect, but 'the cancellation of the match was *due to* rain' is correct.

duel (*say* **dew**el) *noun*
1. a prearranged combat between two people, fought under fixed conditions with deadly weapons, to avenge an insult, etc.
2. any contest between two people, groups, etc.
Word Family: **duel** (**duelled, duelling**), *verb*; **dueller, duellist,** *nouns.*
Common Error: do not confuse with DUAL.

duenna (*say* dew–**enna**) *noun*
a woman acting as an escort or chaperon to a young woman, especially in Spain and Portugal.
[Spanish *dueña*]

duet (*say* dew–**et**) *noun*
a piece of music to be sung or played by two people.

duffel *noun*
also spelt **duffle**
a coarse, woollen fabric with a thick nap on both sides.
[after *Duffel*, a Dutch town]

duffel bag
a cylindrical canvas bag for carrying light, personal articles.

duffel coat
a heavy woollen coat with a hood, usually knee–length and fastened with toggles.

duffer *noun*
(*informal*) a person who is slow to learn.

dug (1) *verb*
the past tense and past participle of the verb **dig.**

dug (2) *noun*
the udder or nipple of a female animal.

dugong (*say* **doo**gong) *noun*
also called a **sea–cow**
a large, herbivorous, aquatic mammal which lives in tropical waters and has a whale–like body, flipper–like limbs and a flat, rounded tail.
[Malay]

dugout *noun*
1. a canoe made by hollowing out a log.
2. a shelter dug in the ground for protection.

duke *noun*
1. the ruling prince of a small state.
2. a nobleman of the highest rank after a prince.
Word Family: **dukedom,** *noun,* a) a duchy, b) the rank or office of a duke; **duchess,** *noun,* a) a female duke, b) the wife of a duke.
[Latin *dux* leader]

dulcet (*say* **duls**'t) *adjective*
(of sounds) pleasing or soothing.

dulcimer (*say* **dul**sima) *noun*
Music: an old instrument, still used in traditional music, in which strings stretched over a sounding-board are struck with hammers.

dull *adjective*
not bright, sharp or clear: 'the *dull* light made it difficult to read'.
Usages:
a) 'he was a *dull* student and could not understand maths' (= unintelligent, slow).
b) 'she put aside the *dull* book and went to play outside' (= uninteresting).
Word Family: **dull**, *verb*, to make or become dull; **dully**, *adverb*; **dullness**, *noun*.

dullard *noun*
a dull or stupid person.

duly (*say* **dew**-lee) *adverb*
Word Family: see DUE.

dumb (*say* dum) *adjective*
1. not able to speak.
2. lacking intelligence.
Word Family: **dumbness**, *noun*; **dumbly**, *adverb*.

dumbbell *noun*
an apparatus similar to a barbell, but smaller and used in one hand.

dumbfound *verb*
to amaze or surprise greatly.

dumb waiter
1. *American:* a small box-like lift used to carry food or other goods between the floors of a building.
2. a stand, often on wheels, with shelves for serving food at table.

dumdum *noun*
a hollow-nosed bullet which flattens out on impact, inflicting a severe wound.
[after *Dum Dum*, India, a former military and ammunitions centre]

dummy *noun*
1. a model or imitation of something used for display, etc., such as a sample of a book to be printed.
2. a rubber teat given to a baby to suck.
3. (*informal*) a stupid person.
dummy *adjective*
imitation or substitute.

dummy run
a dry run.

dump (1) *verb*
1. to throw down or unload heavily.
Usages:
a) 'the campers *dumped* their rubbish at the tip' (= left, disposed of).
b) 'the bankrupt man was *dumped* by his former friends' (= rejected).
2. *Commerce:* to sell some commodity in large quantities at a low price, often in a foreign country.
dump *noun*
1. any place where things are dumped or discarded: 'a rubbish *dump*'.
2. a pile of discarded or dumped things.
3. a storage place or depot, especially for military supplies.
4. (*informal*) any place which is unattractive or uncared for.

dump (2) *noun*
in the dumps, 'he's been *in the dumps* all day for no apparent reason' (= depressed, gloomy).

dumpling *noun*
a small ball of savoury or sweet dough, cooked in soups, stews, etc.

dumpy *adjective*
short and plump.

dun (1) *verb*
to make constant or repeated demands, especially for the payment of debts, etc.
Word Family: **dun**, *noun*, a) a person who duns, b) a demand for payment.

dun (2) *noun*
1. a muddy, greyish-brown colour.
2. a horse of this colour.

dunce *noun*
an unintelligent person.

dune (*rhymes with* tune) *noun*
short form of **sand-dune**
a mound or ridge of sand built up by the wind.

dung *noun*
any animal manure.

dungaree *noun*
(*plural*) trousers or overalls made from a coarse cotton fabric.
[Hindi]

dungeon (*say* **dun**jen) *noun*
a dark cell or room, especially one which is underground.

dunghill *noun*
1. a pile of dung.
2. a foul or wretched place.

dunk *verb*
to dip something briefly into a liquid, e.g. biscuits into tea.

dunnage (*say* **dunn**ij) *noun*
any loose material packed around goods to prevent damage.

duo *noun*
any group of two people or things.
[Greek and Latin, two]

duo–
a prefix meaning two, as in *duologue.*

duodenum (*say* dewo–**deen**'m) *noun*
Anatomy: the C–shaped first part of the small intestine between the stomach and the jejunum, receiving bile from the gall bladder and digestive juices from the pancreas.
Word Family: **duodenal,** *adjective.*
[Latin *duodecim* twelve, because it was considered to be twelve finger breadths long]

duologue (*say* **dewo**–log) *noun*
a conversation between two people.
[Greek *duo* two + *logos* word]

dupe *verb*
to deceive or trick.
Word Family: **dupe,** *noun,* a person who has been deceived or tricked.

duplex (*say* **dew**–pleks) *adjective*
1. double.
2. having two identical parts which are used together: 'a *duplex* chain'.

duplicate (*say* **dewpli**–kit) *adjective*
1. being exactly like or copied from another thing: 'carbon paper is used to produce *duplicate* copies'.
2. having two identical parts.
duplicate *noun*
anything which is identical to something else, especially an exact copy or imitation.
Word Family: **duplicate** (*say* **dewpli**–kate), *verb;* **duplication,** *noun.*
[Latin *duplex, duplicis* double]

duplicator (*say* **dewpli**–kayta) *noun*
a machine which makes copies of printed matter, e.g. from a stencil.

duplicity (*say* dew–**plissi**–tee) *noun*
a deceitfulness or hypocrisy.

durable (*say* **dewra**–b'l) *adjective*
not easily worn out.
Word Family: **durability,** *noun;* **durably,** *adverb.*
[Latin *durus* hard]

dura mater (*say* **dewra mayta**)
Anatomy: the fibrous outer covering of the brain and spinal cord.

duration (*say* **dew–ray**–sh'n) *noun*
the length of time for which something exists or continues.

duress (*say* dew–**ress**) *noun*
the use of force to achieve something, especially illegally: 'the witness claimed his evidence was given under *duress*'.

during (*say* **dew**–ring) *preposition*
within the time of: 'he was very unhappy *during* his childhood'.

durst *verb*
an old word meaning dared.

dusk *noun*
the period of half–light in the early part of the evening.

dusky *adjective*
dark, especially in a shadowy or dim way.
Word Family: **duskiness,** *noun;* **duskily,** *adverb.*

dust *noun*
a fine powder, such as of earth.
Phrases:
bite the dust, to be killed or wounded.
throw dust in one's eyes, to mislead.
dust *verb*
1. to remove dust from something.
2. to sprinkle with a powdered substance.
Word Family: **dusty,** *adjective.*

dustbin *noun*
a container for domestic refuse.

dust bowl
a man–made desert created by overcropping, causing impoverished topsoil to be blown away in dust storms after drought.

dustcoat *noun*
a light, loose–fitting coat worn over clothes for protection, e.g. in a laboratory.

duster *noun*
a cloth for removing dust.

dust jacket
a printed paper cover or wrapper put around a hardback book.

dustman *noun*
a refuse collector.

dust–up *noun*
(*informal*) a fight or commotion.

duty (*say* **dew**–tee) *noun*
1. what a person is obliged, or feels obliged, to do: 'what are my *duties* as host of the party?'.
Usage: 'you have a *duty* to look after your parents' (= moral obligation).
2. any of various government taxes: 'a customs *duty*'.
Phrases:
off duty, not at work.
on duty, at work.
Word Family: **dutiful, duteous** (*say* **dew**–tee–us), *adjectives,* performing the necessary duties; **dutifully,** *adverb;* **dutiable,** *adjective,* subject to a tax or duty.

duty–free *adjective*
free of customs duty.

duvet (*say* **doo**-vay) *noun*
a thick, downy quilt used on a bed as a substitute for blankets.
[French, down]

dwarf (*say* dwawf) *noun*
1. *Folklore:* a very small man-like being often having magical powers.
2. anything, such as a plant, which is much smaller or shorter than the average.
dwarf *verb*
to cause to appear very small: 'the factory was *dwarfed* by the multistorey buildings on either side of it'.
Word Family: **dwarfish,** *adjective,* very small like a dwarf.

dwell *verb*
(**dwelt** or **dwelled, dwelling**)
1. to live as a resident.
2. to continue or remain: 'let's not *dwell* on such an unpleasant topic'.

dwelling *noun*
a house or home.

dwindle *verb*
to make or become smaller and smaller.

dyad (*say* **die**-ad) *noun*
a pair or group of two.

dye *noun*
any substance used to colour material.
dyed-in-the-wool, complete, through and through.
Word Family: **dye** (**dyed, dyeing**), *verb,* to colour with or as if with a dye; **dyer,** *noun;* **dyestuff,** *noun,* any substance producing, or used as, a dye.

dying *verb*
the present participle of the verb **die (1).**

dyke (*say* dike) *noun*
also spelt **dike**
1. a ridge or wall built along a river or the sea to stop the water rising on to the land. Compare DAM (1).
2. *Geology:* the solidified rock found in vertical cracks between other rocks.
Word Family: **dyke,** *verb,* to enclose or protect with a dyke.

dynamic (*say* die-**nammik**) *adjective*
relating to motion, force or energy.
Usage: 'she succeeds because of her *dynamic* personality' (= forceful, vigorous).
dynamics *plural noun*
Physics: (*used with singular verb*) the study of the motion of bodies or particles.
Usage: 'the *dynamics* of mental illness' (= forces at work in).
Word Family: **dynamically,** *adverb;* **dynamism** (*say* **die**-na-mizm), *noun.*
[Greek *dynamis* power]

dynamite (*say* **die**-na-mite) *noun*
1. a high explosive made by absorbing nitroglycerine in some suitable substance.
2. (*informal*) a person or thing seen as dangerous or troublesome.

dynamo (*say* **die**-na-mo) *noun*
1. *Electricity:* a generator used to produce direct current. Compare ALTERNATOR.
2. a very energetic person.

dynamometer (*say* die-na-**mommita**) *noun*
a device which measures power, especially of an engine.

dynasty (*say* **dinna**-stee) *noun*
a series of monarchs belonging to the same family: 'the Habsburg *dynasty* in Austria ruled from the 13th to the early 20th century'.
Word Family: **dynastic** (*say* die-**nastik**), *adjective;* **dynast,** *noun,* a ruler, especially a hereditary one.
[Greek *dynastes* a ruler]

dyne (*say* dine) *noun*
an obsolete metric unit of force.

dysentery (*say* **diss**'n-tree) *noun*
an infection of the bowel causing fever, abdominal pain and diarrhoea, usually spread by contaminated food and water.
[Greek DYS- bad + *entera* bowels]

dysfunction (*say* dis-**funk**-sh'n) *noun*
Medicine: the poor functioning of an organ.

dyslexia (*say* dis-**leksia**) *noun*
an extreme difficulty in learning to read.
Word Family: **dyslexic, dyslectic,** *adjectives.*
[Greek DYS- bad + *lexis* speech]

dyspepsia (*say* dis-**pepsia**) *noun*
indigestion.
Word Family: **dyspeptic,** *adjective,* a) suffering from indigestion, b) gloomy or pessimistic.
[Greek DYS- bad + *peptikos* able to digest]

dysprosium (*say* dis-**pro**-zee-um) *noun*
element number 66, a very rare metal forming magnetic compounds. See LANTHANIDE.
See CHEMICAL ELEMENTS in grey pages.

Ee

each *adjective, pronoun, adverb*
every one taken individually:
(as an adjective) '*each* story had an interesting plot'.
(as a pronoun) '*each* went his own way'.
(as an adverb) 'apples cost 10 pence *each*'.

each way
(of a bet) paying whether the racehorse or greyhound finishes first, second or third.
Usage: 'there's an *each way* chance that it will rain' (= good, likely).

eager *adjective*
keen or showing desire: 'he is *eager* to win the race'.
eager beaver, (*informal*) a very zealous person.
Word Family: **eagerly,** *adverb*; **eagerness,** *noun.*

eagle *noun*
1. a large, strong bird of prey with a huge hooked beak.
2. *Golf:* a score of two strokes less than par for a hole. Compare BIRDIE.
Word Family: **eaglet,** *noun,* a young eagle.

ear (1) *noun*
1. *Anatomy:* the external organ of hearing.
2. a perception of the difference between sounds: 'an *ear* for music'.
Phrases:
be all ears, to listen eagerly.
have, keep an ear to the ground, to be well-informed.
up to one's ears, being deeply involved or very busy.
wet behind the ears, immature or naive.

ear (2) *noun*
the part of a cereal plant containing the seeds or flowers.

eardrum *noun*
Anatomy: a taut membrane in the ear which vibrates as soundwaves strike it, passing these vibrations to the inner ear.

earl (*say* erl) *noun*
a nobleman ranking between a marquis and a viscount.
Word Family: **earldom,** *noun,* the rank or title of an earl.

early (*say* **er**-lee) *adverb, adjective*
1. in the first part of some division of time: '*early* in the morning'.
2. prior to the usual or arranged time: 'an *early* lunch'.
3. far back in time: '*early* New Zealand history'.
4. in the near future: 'at your *earliest* convenience'.

earmark *verb*
1. to set aside for a special purpose: 'we *earmarked* the money for our holiday'.
2. to mark the ear of an animal for identification.
Word Family: **earmark,** *noun.*

earn (*say* ern) *verb*
to gain as a result of one's labour, etc.: a) 'he *earns* £150 a week'; b) 'she *earned* a reputation as a good doctor'.
Usage: 'my investment *earns* 10 per cent interest' (= yields, produces).

earned income
salary or wages. Compare UNEARNED INCOME.

earnest (1) (*say* **er**-nest) *adjective*
1. serious or zealous: 'an *earnest* student'.
2. sincere: 'he made an *earnest* plea for mercy'.
earnest *noun*
seriousness.
in earnest, 'I think he is *in earnest*' (= serious about what he says).
Word Family: **earnestness,** *noun*; **earnestly,** *adverb.*

earnest (2) (*say* **er**-nest) *noun*
a part of something, such as money, given in advance as a pledge of full, later payment.

earning (*say* erning) *noun*
(*plural*) any money earned.

earphones *plural noun*
see HEADPHONES.

earring *noun*
any ring or ornament for the ear.

earshot *noun*
the reach or range of hearing: 'the man across the road was within *earshot* of our screams'.

earth (*say* erth) *noun*
1. *Astronomy:* (*often capital*) the planet in the solar system on which we live.
2. the dry land, especially the soil.
3. the hole or shelter of a burrowing animal.
Phrases:
be down to earth, to be practical.
come down to earth, to return to reality.
run to earth, to track down.
earth *verb*
also called to **ground**
Electricity: to connect electric devices to the ground.

earthen (*say* **er–th**en) *adjective*
made of earth or baked clay.

earthenware *noun*
any glazed or unglazed low-fired (under 1100°C) pottery with a porous body. Compare STONEWARE and PORCELAIN.

earthly (*say* **erth**–lee) *adjective*
of or inhabiting the earth.
no earthly, 'this machine is of *no earthly* use' (= no possible).

earthquake (*say* **erth**–kwake) *noun*
a movement in the earth's crust or mantle, caused by a build-up of pressure which sends out a series of three distinct sets of shockwaves.

earthworm *noun*
any of various kinds of annelid worms whose activity helps to fertilize and drain the soil.

earthy (*say* **erth–ee**) *adjective*
1. of or relating to the earth.
2. hearty, coarse or lacking refinement.

earwig *noun*
any of a group of insects having pincers on the end of the abdomen and forewings modified as small scales which cover the folded hind legs.

ease (*say* eez) *noun*
a freedom from pain, worry, constraint or difficulty: a) 'she accomplished her goal with *ease*'; b) 'his wealth allowed him to live a life of *ease*'.
ease *verb*
1. to free from pain, worry, constraint or difficulty.
2. to move slowly and carefully: 'the robber *eased* himself over the balcony'.

easel (*say* **eez**'l) *noun*
any of various upright, frame-like structures or supports used to hold a painter's canvas, a blackboard, etc.

easement (*say* **eez**–m'nt) *noun*
1. the act of easing.
2. *Law:* a right held over another person's property, such as a right of way.

easily *adverb*
1. with ease: 'this can be done *easily*'.
2. without question: 'this is *easily* the best method'.
Word Family: **easiness,** *noun.*

east *noun*
a) the direction of the sun at sunrise.
b) the cardinal point of the compass at 90° to the right of north and opposite west.
the East
1. the countries of Asia.
2. (*informal*) the countries with communist governments, such as Russia and China. Compare WEST.
Word Family: **east,** *adjective, adverb.*

Easter *noun*
Christian: a festival to commemorate the resurrection of Christ.

easterly *adjective*
(of a direction, course, etc.) being from or towards the east: 'we set off on an *easterly* course'.
easterly *noun*
a wind coming from the east.
Word Family: **easterly,** *adverb.*

eastern *adjective*
(of a place) being situated in the east: 'the *eastern* states of America'.

eastward (*say* **eest**–w'd) *adjective*
being towards the east.
Word Family: **eastwards, eastward,** *adverb.*

easy (*say* **ee**–zee) *adjective*
1. not difficult: 'an *easy* exam'.
2. free from pain, worry, constraint or difficulty: 'she had her first *easy* sleep after many nights of disturbing dreams'.
Usages:
a) 'an *easy* manner' (= relaxed).
b) 'she is too *easy* with those naughty children' (= lenient).

easy chair
a comfortable chair, usually an armchair.

easygoing *adjective*
relaxed or unconcerned.

easy street
living on easy street, having everything one's own way.

eat *verb*
(ate, eaten, eating)
1. to chew and swallow food: 'all I *ate* for lunch was an apple'.
2. to have a meal: 'we will *eat* at 8 p.m.'.
Usages:
a) 'the acid *ate* into the surface of the metal' (= wore away).
b) (*informal*) 'what's *eating* you?' (= worrying).
Phrases:
eat humble pie, see HUMBLE (2).
eat one's words, to take back what one has said.

eau de cologne (*say* o de ka-**lone**)
short form is **cologne**
also called **toilet water**
a perfume diluted with alcohol which dries and cools the skin.
[French, water of Cologne, where it was first made]

eaves *plural noun*
the lower edge of a roof which overhangs the walls.

eavesdrop *verb*
(eavesdropped, eavesdropping)
to listen secretly to a conversation.
[from to be on the *eavesdrop*, the place on which water dropped from the eaves]

ebb *noun*
1. the return of the tide towards the sea.
2. a point of decline: 'his business was at a low *ebb*'.
Word Family: **ebb,** *verb.*

ebony (*say* **ebba**-nee) *noun*
a very hard black wood obtained from a tropical tree.
[Greek *ebenos*]

ebullient (*say* ib**bull**-y'nt) *adjective*
1. full of excitement or enthusiasm.
2. boiling.
Word Family: **ebullience, ebullition** (*say* ebba-**lish**'n), *nouns*; **ebulliently,** *adverb.*
[Latin *ebulliens* bubbling]

eccentric (*say* ek-**sen**trik) *adjective*
1. different, peculiar or irregular: 'an *eccentric* person who collects old shoes'.
2. *Maths:* a) not having the same centre. b) being off-centre.
3. deviating from a circular form, such as a planet's orbit, etc.
Word Family: **eccentrically,** *adverb*; **eccentricity** (*say* eksen-**trissa**-tee), *noun*; **eccentric,** *noun,* a person who is different or peculiar.
[Greek *ek* out + *kentron* centre]

ecclesiastic (*say* ik**klee**zi-astik) *noun*
a clergyman.
ecclesiastical, ecclesiastic *adjective*
of or relating to the Church.
[Greek *ekklesia* assembly, church]

ecdysis (*say* **ek**di-sis) *noun*
moulting.
[Greek *ekdysis* shedding (clothes)]

echelon (*say* **esh**a-lon) *noun*
1. an arrowhead formation of infantry, aircraft or warships to give maximum fire-power in all directions.
2. a particular group or grade of persons: 'the higher *echelons* of industry'.
[French *échelon* rung of a ladder]

echinoderm (*say* e**kinna**-derm) *noun*
any of a group of marine animals, such as the starfish, with radially symmetrical bodies and some calcareous skeletal plates in the skin.
[Greek *ekhinos* a sea-urchin + *derma* skin]

echo (*say* **ek**ko) *noun*
plural is **echoes**
1. a repetition of sound produced by soundwaves reflecting off a surface.
2. any repetition or imitation.
Word Family: **echo (echoed, echoing),** *verb.*
[Greek *ekho*]

echo sounder
an instrument using soundwaves to measure the depth of water or the depth of an object below the surface.

éclair (*say* **ay**-klair)
a light, finger-shaped cake with a cream or custard filling and coated with icing.
[French *éclair* lightning, because it is eaten in a flash]

éclat (*say* **ay**-klah) *noun*
1. a brilliant success, effect, distinction, etc.
2. any acclaim or applause.
[French, a burst (of sound, light, etc.)]

eclectic (*say* ik**klek**-tik) *adjective*
using or derived from many different sources.
Word Family: **eclectic,** *noun*; **eclectically,** *adverb*; **eclecticism,** *noun.*
[Greek *eklektikos* picking out]

eclipse (*say* **ikklips**) *noun*
1. *Astronomy:* the passing of one planet or satellite, especially the sun, moon or earth, in front of another.
2. any overshadowing or loss of brilliance.
eclipse *verb*
1. to cause an eclipse.
2. to surpass or overshadow.
[Greek *ekleipsis* a failing to appear]

ecliptic (*say* **ikklip**–tik) *noun*
Astronomy: the apparent yearly path of the sun among the stars.
ecliptic *adjective*
of or relating to an eclipse.

eclogue (*say* **eklog**) *noun*
a short poem in dialogue form, especially one dealing with rural life.
[Greek *eklogé* a selection]

ecology (*say* eekolla–jee *or* ekolla–jee) *noun*
the study of the interactions of animals and plants with each other and their environment, a branch of biology.
Word Family: **ecologist**, *noun*; **ecological** (*say* eeka–**loji**–k'l), *adjective*; **ecologically**, *adverb*.
[Greek *oikos* household + –LOGY]

economic (*say* eeka–**nommik** *or* ekka–**nommik**) *adjective*
1. of or relating to the economy or economics.
2. economical.

economical (*say* eeka–**nommi**–k'l *or* ekka–**nommi**–k'l) *adjective*
thrifty and avoiding unnecessary expense or waste.
Word Family: **economically**, *adverb*.

economics (*say* eeka–nommiks *or* **ekka**–nommiks) *plural noun*
1. (*used with singular verb*) the study of the production and distribution of goods, services and wealth.
2. the financial aspects: 'the *economics* of this project are not sound'.
Word Family: **economist** (*say* ee–**konna**–mist *or* **ekkonna**–mist), *noun*.
[Greek *oikonomia* household management]

economize (*say* ee–**konna**–mize *or* ek–**onna**–mize) **economise** *verb*
to practise economical management of one's resources.

economy (*say* ee–**konna**–mee *or* ek–**onna**–mee) *noun*
1. any efficient or economical use of resources.
2. a) the management of the money, property and goods of a country, community or household. b) a system for such management.

ecosystem (*say* **eeko**–sist'm *or* **ekko**–sist'm) *noun*
a system of ecological relationships. In a stable ecosystem the relationship between the different organisms is such that each member mutually supports the continued existence of the other members and of the system itself.

ecstasy (*say* **eksta**–see) *noun*
1. an extreme state of emotion, especially delight.
2. a mystical, spiritual trance or frenzy.
Word Family: **ecstatic** (*say* ek–**stattik**), *adjective*; **ecstatically**, *adverb*.
[Greek *ekstasis* standing aside, a trance]

ecumenical (*say* ek–yoo–**menni**–k'l) *adjective*
1. universal.
2. *Religion:* a) of or relating to the whole Church. b) of the movement to reunite all Christian Churches.

eczema (*say* **eksma**) *noun*
an inflammation of the skin causing an itchy, flaky or ulcerated surface.

eddy *noun*
a circular or whirling current, e.g. of liquid, smoke or air.
Word Family: **eddy** (**eddied**, **eddying**), *verb*.

edelweiss (*say* **aidel**–vice) *noun*
an Alpine plant with white woolly star-shaped flowers.
[German *edel* noble + *weiss* white]

edema (*say* ee–**deema**) *noun*
see OEDEMA.

Eden *noun*
1. *Biblical:* the garden which was the first home of Adam and Eve.
2. a) any delightful place. b) a state of innocence and purity.
[Hebrew *eden* delight]

edge (*say* **ej**) *noun*
1. a border or line where one thing ends or meets another: a) 'the *edge* of a cliff'; b) 'the *edge* of a box'.
2. the thin, sharp side of a blade, etc.
Usages:
a) 'because of his experience he has an *edge* over the other applicants' (= advantage).
b) 'that snack took the *edge* off my appetite' (= keenness, sharpness).

Phrases:
on edge, 'she felt *on edge* because the aeroplane was late' (= nervous, uncomfortable).
set one's teeth on edge, 'his continual chatter *set her teeth on edge*' (= annoyed, irritated her).
edge *verb*
1. to provide with an edge.
2. to move gradually or cautiously: 'he *edged* his way up the face of the cliff'.

edgeways, edgewise *adverb*
with an edge forwards.
not get a word in edgeways, to be unable to break into a long or animated conversation.

edgy (*say* **ej**–ee) *adjective*
irritable or nervous.

edible (*say* **eddi**–b'l) *adjective*
fit to be eaten.
[Latin *edere* to eat]

edict (*say* **ee**dikt) *noun*
an official command.

edifice (*say* **eddi**–fiss) *noun*
a large or imposing building.
[Latin *aedis* a house + *facere* to make]

edify (*say* **eddi**–fie) *verb*
(**edified, edifying**)
to instruct, especially for personal or moral improvement.
Word Family: **edification,** *noun.*

edit *verb*
a) to collate a book to which other writers have contributed. b) to act as an editor. c) to correct and prepare a manuscript for printing. d) to complete a film or recording by altering, rearranging or selecting from its parts.
[Latin *editus* put forth]

edition (*say* **iddish**'n) *noun*
any of the copies of a book, newspaper, etc. printed at one time.
a **second edition** is a later, completely revised printing of a book in which many alterations have been made.

editor *noun*
1. a person who edits books, papers, films, etc.
2. a person responsible for the content of all or a part of a newspaper, magazine, etc.: 'she is the fashion *editor* of our magazine'.

editorial *noun*
also called a **leader** or a **leading article** an article in a newspaper, etc., expressing the opinion of the newspaper or its editor on current issues.
editorial *adjective*
of or relating to editing or an editor.

educate (*say* **ed**–yoo–kate) *verb*
to instruct or develop, especially through formal teaching or training.
Word Family: **educated,** *adjective,* a) having undergone education, b) showing culture and learning; **educable,** *adjective,* able to be educated.

education (*say* ed–yoo–**kay**–sh'n) *noun*
a) the act or process of educating: '*education* is free in some countries'. b) the result of educating: 'she has a good *education* in science'.
Word Family: **educational,** *adjective;* **educationist, educationalist,** *noun,* an expert in the theory or method of education; **educator,** *noun,* a teacher.
[Latin *educare* to train]

educe (*say* iddewce) *verb*
to draw out or elicit.
[Latin *educere*]

-ee
a suffix of nouns indicating a person who undergoes or receives something, as in *employee.*

eel *noun*
any of a large group of snake-like edible fish which migrate from rivers to the Sargasso Sea to breed.

eerie (*say* **eer**–ee) *adjective*
strange or weird.

efface (*say* ifface) *verb*
to wipe out or destroy.
Word Family: **effacement,** *noun.*

effect (*say* iffekt) *noun*
1. a) a direct result: 'what is the *effect* of sunlight on this fabric?'. b) the power to produce results: 'our arguments were of no *effect* as he did not change his mind'.
Usage: 'yes, he said something to that *effect*' (= meaning, idea).
2. the state of being in operation: 'his plan was put into *effect*'.
3. a technique or device used to create an impression: 'elaborate stage *effects* were needed'.
4. (*plural*) any goods or movable objects: 'he has only a few personal *effects*'.
Phrases:
for effect, in order to create a particular impression.
in effect, a) in reality; b) in operation.
take effect, to begin to operate.

effect *verb*
to bring about, achieve or cause to happen: 'he *effected* his escape by digging a tunnel'.
[Latin *effectus* made or brought about]
Common Error: do not confuse with AFFECT (1). *Examples:* 'he *effected* his escape without difficulty' (= achieved), but 'this *affects* my plan to escape' (= has an effect on, making it easier or more difficult).

effective (*say* iffektiv) *adjective*
1. producing the intended effect: 'advertising is an *effective* way of increasing sales'.
2. being in effect: 'the pay rise is *effective* from last month'.
Word Family: **effectively,** *adverb*; **effectiveness,** *noun.*
Common Error: do not confuse with EFFICIENT. *Example:* 'this method of keeping your accounts may be *effective* but it is not *efficient*' (= it may produce the results you want, but it is not the best or quickest way).

effectual (*say* iffek-tew'l) *adjective*
1. producing the required effect.
2. legally binding.
Word Family: **effectually,** *adverb.*

effeminate (*say* iffemmi-nit) *adjective*
(of a man) having excessively feminine qualities.
Word Family: **effeminacy,** *noun.*

efferent *adjective*
Medicine: leading away from a central organ. Compare AFFERENT.
[Latin *efferens* carrying away]

effervesce (*say* effa-vess) *verb*
1. to give off small bubbles of gas.
2. to be lively or vivacious.
Word Family: **effervescence,** *noun*; **effervescent,** *adjective.*
[Latin *effervescere* to begin to boil over]

effete (*say* effeet) *adjective*
exhausted, feeble or lacking energy.
[Latin *effetus* worn out by child-bearing]

efficacious (*say* effi-kay-shus) *adjective*
effective, especially as a method or remedy.
Word Family: **efficacy** (*say* effika-see), *noun.*

efficient (*say* iffish'nt) *adjective*
1. competent or able to obtain the desired results: 'an *efficient* secretary'.
2. *Physics:* (of machinery, etc.) producing the desired result with minimum waste or expenditure of energy.
Word Family: **efficiency,** *noun*; **efficiently,** *adverb.*
Common Error: do not confuse with EFFECTIVE.

effigy (*say* effi-jee) *noun*
an image or sculptured likeness of a person.
[Latin *effigies* a copy]

efflorescent (*say* eflor-ess'nt) *adjective*
1. (of a flower) blossoming.
2. *Chemistry:* (of a crystal) losing water to the atmosphere in such quantities that the substance becomes dry and powdery. Compare DELIQUESCENT.
Word Family: **efflorescence,** *noun*; **effloresce,** *verb.*
[Latin *e* out + *florescens* beginning to flower]

effluence (*say* efloo-ence) *noun*
1. an outward flow.
2. anything which flows out.
Common Error: do not confuse with AFFLUENCE.

effluent (*say* efloo-ent) *adjective*
flowing out.
effluent *noun*
1. a stream flowing out of a lake, etc.
2. any waste liquid flowing out of a sewage farm, chemical works, etc.
[Latin *effluens*]

effluvium (*say* efloovium) *noun*
plural is **effluvia**
a noxious or foul-smelling vapour.

effort *noun*
1. a) a use of physical or mental energy. b) the result of this.
2. a struggle or attempt.
3. a force acting on something.
Word Family: **effortless,** *adjective,* done without, or as if without, effort.

effrontery (*say* iffrunta-ree) *noun*
a shameless or impudent boldness.

effusion (*say* iffew-*zh*'n) *noun*
1. an unreserved expression of feelings, etc.
2. the act of pouring forth.
3. *Physics:* the passage of gases through small holes under pressure.

effusive *adjective*
unreserved or freely showing one's feelings: 'an *effusive* woman rushed up and hugged the diplomat'.
Word Family: **effusively,** *adverb*; **effusiveness,** *noun*; **effuse,** *verb.*
[Latin *effusus* poured out]

eft *noun*
a newt.

egalitarian (*say* igalli-tairian) *adjective*
of or favouring equality for all people.

Word Family: **egalitarian,** *noun,* a person who favours equality; **egalitarianism,** *noun.*
[French *égalité* equality]

egg (1) *noun*
1. the roundish body formed during the development of a bird or reptile and consisting of a shell which contains a yolk surrounded by a clear fluid substance. If fertilized the egg may develop into a new individual.
2. the egg of the domestic hen, eaten raw or cooked.
3. a female reproductive cell. Short form of **egg cell.**
Phrases:
as sure as eggs, safely predictable.
put all one's eggs in one basket, to risk everything in one attempt.

egg (2) *verb*
egg on, to urge or encourage.

egger, eggar *noun*
a large reddish-brown moth with a shell-like cocoon which gives it its name.

eggnog *noun*
also called an **egg-flip**
a drink made from milk, eggs and spices, usually with wine or spirits.

eggplant *noun*
see AUBERGINE.

eggshell china
see CHINA.

egg white
also called the **albumen**
the clear, outer fluid substance in an egg, which becomes firm and white when cooked.

ego (*say* **eego** *or* **eggo**) *noun*
1. the part of a person which is able to think, feel, act and distinguish itself from all other people or objects.
2. self-esteem: 'their criticisms bruised her *ego*'.
3. *Psychology:* the conscious part of the personality which is in touch with the outside world. Compare ID.
[Latin, I]

egocentric (*say* **eego**-sentrik *or* **eggo**-sentrik) *adjective*
being most concerned with one's own interests and considering everything in relation to oneself.
Word Family: **egocentricity,** *noun.*

egoist (*say* **eego**-ist *or* **eggo**-ist) *noun*
1. a self-interested or self-conceited person.
2. *Philosophy:* a person believing in or practising solipsism.
Word Family: **egoistic,** *adjective;* **egoism,** *noun.*

egotist (*say* **eega**-tist *or* **egga**-tist) *noun*
1. an egoist; an offensively selfish person.
2. a person unduly given to talking about himself.
Word Family: **egotistic, egotistical,** *adjective;* **egotism,** *noun.*

egregious (*say* ig-**ree**j's) *adjective*
(*use is derogatory*) outstanding or notorious: 'what an *egregious* liar!'.
[Latin *e grege* out of the flock]

egress (*say* **ee**gres) *noun*
a) the act of going out. b) an exit.
[Latin *egressus* come out]

egret (*say* **ee**gret) *noun*
a type of small heron noted for its long, fine feathers.
[from AIGRETTE]

eiderdown (*say* **eye**-der-down) *noun*
a quilt or bedspread.
[from *eider,* a species of duck, the soft breast feathers of which were originally used to fill bedspreads]

eight (*say* ate) *noun*
1. a cardinal number, the symbol 8 in Arabic numerals, VIII in Roman numerals.
2. *Rowing:* the crew of a light, narrow racing boat, consisting of a cox and eight rowers.
Word Family: **eight,** *adjective;* **eighth,** *noun, adjective.*

eighteen (*say* ay-**teen**) *noun*
a cardinal number, the symbol 18 in Arabic numerals, XVIII in Roman numerals.
Word Family: **eighteen,** *adjective;* **eighteenth,** *noun, adjective.*

eighth note
Music: see QUAVER.

eightsome reel
Scottish: an energetic Highland dance for eight people.

eighty (*say* **ay**-tee) *noun*
1. a cardinal number, the symbol 80 in Arabic numerals, LXXX in Roman numerals.
2. (*plural*) the numbers 80–89 in a series, such as the years in a century.
Word Family: **eighty,** *adjective;* **eightieth,** *noun, adjective.*

einsteinium (*say* ine-**sty**nium) *noun*
element number 99, a man-made, radioactive metal. See TRANSURANIC ELEMENT and ACTINIDE.
See CHEMICAL ELEMENTS in grey pages.

[after *Albert Einstein*, 1879–1955, a German physicist]

eisteddfod (*say* eye-**sted**-f'd) *noun*
plural is **eisteddfods** or **eisteddfodau**
a festival for musical competitions.
[Welsh, session]

either (*say* **eye**-tha *or* **ee**-tha)
adjective, pronoun, conjunction, adverb
1. one or the other of two things:
(as an adjective) 'I do not like *either* colour very much'.
(as a pronoun) 'I have two pens, so take *either*'.
(as a conjunction) '*either* ring me up or write a letter'.
(as an adverb) 'he must be *either* blind or stupid'.
2. both one and the other: 'there were guards on *either* side of the President'.
Common Error: see NEITHER.

ejaculation (*say* ijjak-yoo-**lay**-sh'n) *noun*
1. a sudden exclamation.
2. the discharge of seminal fluid from the penis.
Word Family: **ejaculate**, *verb*; **ejaculatory**, *adjective*.
[Latin *ejaculari* to shoot forth]

eject (*say* ij**jekt**) *verb*
to force out or cause to be removed: 'police were called to *eject* the demonstrators from the building'.
Word Family: **ejection**, *noun*; **ejector**, *noun*, a person or device that ejects, such as the mechanism in a gun which throws away the empty shell.
[Latin *ejectus* cast out]

eke (1) *verb*
(**eked, eking**)
eke out, a) 'we must *eke out* a living somehow' (= try to make); b) 'can we *eke out* our supplies till winter?' (= stretch).

eke (2) *adverb, conjunction*
an old word meaning also.

elaborate (*say* e**labba**-rit) *adjective*
carefully detailed and exact: 'the architect presented an *elaborate* design for the house'.
elaborate (*say* e**labba**-rate) *verb*
to work out or describe in detail: 'please *elaborate* your plans for the job'.
Word Family: **elaborately**, *adverb*; **elaborateness**, *noun*, the quality of being elaborate; **elaboration**, *noun*.
[Latin *elaborare* to use every effort]

élan (*say* ay-**lan**) *noun*
an enthusiasm or liveliness: 'he approaches life with great *élan*'.
[French *élancer* to hurl or rush forward]

eland (*say* **ee**land) *noun*
an ox-like African antelope with short twisted horns.
[Dutch, elk]

elapse *verb*
(of time) to pass.
Word Family: **elapse**, *noun*.
[Latin *elapsus* slipped away]

elastic (*say* ill**ass**-tik) *adjective*
able to recover its shape after being pulled, pressed, etc.: 'an *elastic* band'.
Usages:
a) 'our schedule for the trip is quite *elastic*' (= flexible, able to be adapted).
b) 'his *elastic* step expressed his happiness' (= springy).
elastic *noun*
any material which is made elastic by inserting rubber.
Word Family: **elasticize** (*say* ill**ass**sta-size), **elasticise**, *verb*; **elasticity** (*say* illass-**tissi**-tee), *noun*.

elated (*say* il**lay**-t'd) *adjective*
in high spirits: 'the sculptor was *elated* by the success of her exhibition'.
elation *noun*
a state of high spirits and great pleasure.
Word Family: **elate**, *verb*; **elatedly**, *adverb*; **elatedness**, *noun*.
[Latin *elatus* raised, carried away]

elbow (*say* **el**-bo) *noun*
1. *Anatomy:* the joint in the middle of the arm.
2. anything which is bent or shaped like an elbow, such as a joint in a pipe.
at one's elbow, 'he's always *at my elbow* with some silly question' (= nearby).
elbow *verb*
to push or nudge with the elbow: 'we *elbowed* our way through the crowd'.

elbow grease
any hard work or effort.

elbow-room *noun*
enough room to move freely.

elder (1) *adjective*
(of a relation) older: 'his *elder* brother is 19 now'.
elder *noun*
1. a person with influence or authority in a group: 'the tribal *elders* held a council'.
2. a person who is older: 'she is my *elder* by four years'.

3. *Christian:* a) a member of the early Church with spiritual authority. b) a lay official in some Protestant sects.

elder (2) *noun*
any of a group of deciduous shrubs and trees with white scented flowers and black or red berries.

elderly *adjective*
being rather old.

eldest *adjective*
(of a relation) oldest: 'my *eldest* sister is overseas'.
Word Family: **eldest**, *noun.*

eldorado (*say* eldor-**ah**-doe) *noun*
any place where fortunes can be made quickly.
[Spanish *El Dorado* the Gilded One, the name given by the Conquistadores to the ruler of the legendary golden city they hoped to find north of the Amazon]

elect *verb*
to choose, especially by voting.
elect *adjective*
1. chosen or selected: 'an *elect* group of businessmen attended the conference'.
2. chosen for an office or position but not yet installed: 'he is the *ambassador-elect*'.
[Latin *electus* picked out]

election *noun*
the selection by voting of one or more people for position or office.
a **by-election** is a political election held in one electorate to choose its representative for parliament.
a **general election** is the election of the whole of the House of Commons.
Word Family: **electoral**, *adjective*, relating to electors or political elections.

electioneer (*say* illek-sh'**neer**) *verb*
to promote or work for the election of a particular candidate or party.

elective *adjective*
1. relating to election or an election.
2. a) appointed by election. b) having the power to elect or appoint.
3. open to choice or election.

elector *noun*
1. a person who may vote.
2. *History:* (*capital*) a prince entitled to participate in the choice of a Holy Roman Emperor.

electoral college
American: a group of representatives who vote to elect the President and Vice-President.

electorate (*say* illekta-rit) *noun*
a) an area with a representative in a council or parliament. b) the people living in an electorate who are qualified to vote.
Word Family: **electoral**, *adjective.*

Electra complex
Psychology: the complex of emotions which may motivate a daughter who loves her father and is jealous of her mother.
[in Greek legend, *Electra* conspired with her brother to kill her mother]

electric *adjective*
1. involving or producing electricity: 'an *electric* current'.
2. thrilling or exciting: 'there was an *electric* atmosphere during the competition'.
electrical *adjective*
1. involving or producing electricity.
2. relating to the practical use of electricity: 'an *electrical* engineer'.
Word Family: **electrically**, *adverb.*

electrical engineering
the branch of applied science which is concerned with electric power, especially with the design and construction of electrical machinery, power lines and electronic equipment.

electric chair
a device which uses electricity to execute a convicted criminal.

electric charge
short form is **charge**
Electricity: a quantity of energy. Two types of charge, called positive and negative, are known. Bodies with the same electric charge repel each other and bodies with the opposite electric charge attract each other.

electric current
short form is **current**
Electricity: the rate of transfer of an electric charge.
alternating current is an electric current which regularly changes direction, so that the average flow over a period is zero.
direct current is an electric current flowing in one direction only.

electric eye
(*informal*) a photoelectric cell.

electric guitar
a guitar with a device which transmits the sounds through an amplifier to a loudspeaker.

electrician (*say* illek-**trish**'n) *noun*
a person with theoretical and practical knowledge of the installation, repair and maintenance of various types of electrical equipment.

electricity (*say* illek-**trissi**-tee) *noun*
a) all the effects associated with electric charge at rest or moving. b) the energy released by the movement of charged particles, such as electrons.

electric storm
a thunderstorm with lightning.

electrify (*say* ill-**ektri**-fie) *verb*
(**electrified, electrifying**)
1. to apply electric charge or current to electrical equipment.
2. to thrill, shock or excite: 'the audience was *electrified* by the music'.
Word Family: **electrification**, *noun*.

electro-
a prefix meaning of or caused by electricity, as in *electromotive*.
[Greek *elektron* amber, which produces electrostatic effects when it is rubbed]

electrocardiogram
(*say* illektro-**kardio**-gram) *noun*
short form is **cardiogram** or **ECG**
a representation of the heartbeat, made by recording the flow of electric currents in the heart muscle.
[ELECTRO- + Greek *kardia* heart + *gramma* something written]

electroconvulsive therapy
the application of electric shocks to the brain as a method of treating psychological depression, etc.

electrocute (*say* illektra-kewt) *verb*
to kill with an electric shock.
Word Family: **electrocution**, *noun*.

electrode *noun*
Electricity: a conductor by which electrons enter, leave, or are controlled within an electrical device.
[ELECTRO- + Greek *hodos* a way]

electroencephalogram
(*say* illektro-enseffila-gram) *noun*
short form is **EEG**
the recording of the electrical activity of the brain, detected by placing leads on the scalp.
[ELECTRO- + Greek *egkephalos* brain + *gramma* something written]

electrolysis (*say* illek-**trolla**-sis) *noun*
Chemistry: the decomposition of a substance by passing electricity through it.
[ELECTRO- + Greek *lysis* a loosening]

electrolyte (*say* illektra-lite) *noun*
Chemistry: a compound which, in solution or when molten, forms ions which conduct electricity.

electromagnet *noun*
a device consisting of a coil of wire around a soft iron core which becomes a magnet when electricity flows through the coil.
electromagnetic *adjective*
see MAGNETIC.
Word Family: **electromagnetism**, *noun*, the magnetism caused by a moving electric charge.

electromagnetic radiation
also called a **hertzian wave**
Physics: a form of radiation consisting of **electromagnetic waves** which consist of an electric field and a magnetic field at right angles to each other. *Examples*: heat, light, X-rays and radiowaves are all forms of electromagnetic radiation.

electromotive *adjective*
of or producing a flow of electricity.

electromotive force
short form is **emf**
Electricity: the amount of energy, measured in volts, required to produce a flow of electricity.

electron *noun*
Physics: the stable, negatively charged elementary particle which orbits atomic nuclei and forms the basis of electricity.
[from ELECTR(ic) + (i)ON]

electronic (*say* illek-**tronnik**) *adjective*
of or relating to electrons or electronics.

electronics (*say* illek-**tronniks**) *plural noun*
a) (*used with singular verb*) the study of the flow of electricity in a gas, vacuum, semiconductor, etc., and of devices and systems to control and utilize it. b) the techniques of manufacturing such devices, e.g. the semiconductors in transistors, and the photoelectric cells, printed and integrated circuits used in aerospace equipment, pocket-size computers, etc. The more minute devices are classed as microelectronic.

electron-volt *noun*
a unit of energy equal to about $1{\cdot}60 \times 10^{-19}$ joule. See UNITS in grey pages.

electrophoresis
(*say* illektro-fa-**reesis**) *noun*

Chemistry: the attraction and movement of colloidal particles towards electrodes in a fluid.
[ELECTRO- + Greek *phoresis* a being carried]

electroplate *verb*
to coat with a thin film of metal by electrolysis.
Word Family: **electroplate,** *noun,* any objects which have been electroplated; **electroplating,** *noun.*

electrostatic (*say* illektro-**stattik**) *adjective*
of or relating to stationary electric charges.

electrovalence *noun*
electrovalency.

electrovalency
(*say* illektro-**vayl**'n-see) *noun*
see VALENCY.

electrovalent bond
see IONIC BOND.

elegant *adjective*
tasteful and refined, especially in dress or manner: 'she wore a simple but *elegant* dress'.
Word Family: **elegantly,** *adverb;* **elegance,** *noun.*
[Latin *elegans* discriminating]

elegiac (*say* ella-**jigh**-ac) **elegiacal** *adjective*
1. of or suited to an elegy.
2. mournful or sad.

elegy (*say* **ella**-jee) *noun*
a sad song or funeral poem in memory of the dead.
Word Family: **elegist,** *noun,* the writer of an elegy.
[Greek *elegos* a song of mourning]

element (*say* **ella**-m'nt) *noun*
1. a basic and necessary part or feature of a whole: 'good health is one of the *elements* of happiness'.
2. (*plural*) a) the basic principles or beginnings of a subject: 'the *elements* of grammar'. b) the forces of nature, weather, etc.: 'the abandoned house had been exposed to the *elements* for years'.
3. *Chemistry:* a substance made up of atoms, all of which have the same number of protons.
4. a preferred or more suitable environment: 'she is in her *element* at parties'.
5. *Electricity:* a wire conductor in an electrical appliance, etc. which opposes the electric current and changes it into heat.
6. any of the four substances, air, earth, water and fire, which ancient philosophers believed combined to form the universe.
7. *Maths:* a) a number forming part of an array, e.g. in a matrix. b) a single figure or symbol in a set. Also called a **member.**
Word Family: **elemental,** *adjective;* **elementally,** *adverb.*
[Latin *elementum*]

elementary (*say* ella-**men**-tree) *adjective*
basic, simple or undeveloped: 'an *elementary* description of a subject'.

elementary particle
also called a **fundamental particle**
Physics: any of the basic units from which all matter is composed, e.g. the electron, proton, neutron, meson, positron.

elementary school
American: a primary school.

element number
the number equal to the number of protons in the nucleus of an element.

elephant *noun*
a member of either of two species of very large mammals of Africa and Asia, with thick leathery skins, long prehensile trunks and curved tusks, the African elephant having larger, fan-shaped ears.
white elephant, a useless or annoying possession.
Word Family: **elephantine** (*say* ella-**fan**tine), *adjective,* of or like an elephant.
[Greek *elephantos* of an elephant]

elephantiasis (*say* ella-fan-**tie**-a-sis) *noun*
a blocking of the lymph vessels due to parasitic worms, which causes swelling in the legs or scrotum.

elevate (*say* **ella**-vate) *verb*
to lift up or raise: 'he was *elevated* to a managerial job'.
Usages:
a) 'we were *elevated* by the beautiful weather' (= put in high spirits).
b) 'the teacher's presence in the room *elevated* the discussions' (= raised the tone of).
[Latin *elevare* to lift up]

elevation *noun*
1. the height of anything, especially above the ground or sea-level.
2. the act of elevating: 'his *elevation* to the position of manager came as a surprise'.

3. *Architecture:* a drawing of one side of a building.
4. *Astronomy:* an angle made above the horizon or horizontal plane, e.g. by a star or planet. Also called the **altitude**.

elevator (*say* **ell**a–vayta) *noun*
1. a lift.
2. a person or thing that lifts.

eleven *noun*
1. a cardinal number, the symbol 11 in Arabic numerals, XI in Roman numerals.
2. the 11 players in a cricket, soccer, etc. team.
Word Family: **eleven,** *adjective*; **eleventh,** *noun, adjective.*

eleven–plus *noun*
the examination taken at age 11–12 to decide the type of state secondary school best suited to the pupil; the development of the comprehensive school led to its progressive abolition.

elevenses *noun*
a morning tea or snack eaten at about 11 o'clock.

eleventh hour
the very last moment for doing something: 'the criminal's death sentence was commuted at the *eleventh hour*'.

elf *noun*
plural is **elves**
also called an **imp** or a **pixie**
Folklore: a small, often mischievous, fairy.
Word Family: **elfin, elfish, elvish,** *adjectives,* of or like an elf.

elicit (*say* **illiss**it) *verb*
to bring or cause to come out: 'the book fails to *elicit* the truth about his death'.
[Latin *elicitus* enticed out]

elide *verb*
to leave out a sound, such as a vowel or syllable, when pronouncing a word, as the *a* in *we're* (we are).
Word Family: **elision** (*say* ee–**lizh**'n), *noun.*
[Latin *elidere* to knock out]

eligible (*say* **ell**ij'b'l) *adjective*
suitable or having the right qualifications: 'we do not feel that such a young person is *eligible* for this job'.
Usage: 'an *eligible* bachelor' (= worthwhile, desirable).
Word Family: **eligibly,** *adverb*, **eligibility** (*say* ellija–**billa**–tee), *noun.*
[Latin *eligere* to pick out]

eliminate (*say* ill**immi**–nate) *verb*
1. to remove or get rid of: 'we have *eliminated* several more names from the list'.
2. *Maths:* to solve simultaneous equations by systematically removing variables and reducing the number of independent equations.
Word Family: **elimination,** *noun.*
[Latin *eliminare* to throw outside]

élite (*say* ay–**leet**)
a) a superior or select few within a group or society. b) a clique: 'they have formed a social *élite* which excludes many of their old friends.
[French *élit* chosen]

elixir (*say* ee–**lik**sa) *noun*
1. a potion or remedy believed to prolong life or cure anything: 'the *elixir* of eternal youth'.
2. *Medicine:* a solution of a drug in alcohol.
[Arabic *al–iksir* the philosopher's stone of alchemy]

elk *noun*
also called **wapiti**
in America called a **moose**
the largest existing deer of Europe, Asia and North America.

ell *noun*
an old measure equal to about 45 inches (about 1·1 m).
Usage: 'give him an inch and he'll take an *ell*' (= undue advantage of the slightest concession).

ellipse *noun*
a plane, regular, closed curve formed when a cone is cut by a plane which is not parallel to, and does not pass through, the base of the cone. See CONIC SECTION.

ellipsis *noun*
plural is **ellipses** (*say* el–**lip**seez)
Grammar: a) the leaving out of a word or words in a sentence, which would make it more complete or correct. *Example*: 'while (*I was*) crossing the road I held mother's hand'.
b) a mark, such as – or ...., used to indicate this.
[Greek *elleipsis* a falling short]

ellipsoid *noun*
a solid ellipse.
Word Family: **ellipsoidal,** *adjective.*

elliptical, elliptic *adjective*
1. having the shape of an ellipse.
2. of or relating to ellipses.
Word Family: **elliptically,** *adverb.*

elm *noun*
any of a group of very tall, deciduous trees used for timber.

elocution (*say* ello–**kew**sh'n) *noun*
the art or study of speaking clearly or well in public.
Word Family: **elocutionary**, *adjective*; **elocutionist**, *noun*, a person skilled in elocution.
[Latin *elocutio* oratorical delivery]

elongate (*say* **ee**longate) *verb*
to make or become longer.
Word Family: **elongation**, *noun*.

elope *verb*
to run away with a lover, especially in order to get married without parents' permission.
Word Family: **elopement**, *noun*.

eloquent (*say* **ell**a–kw'nt) *adjective*
skilful, fluent and expressive in speech: 'his *eloquent* praise of the film inspired many people to see it'.
Word Family: **eloquently**, *adverb*; **eloquence**, *noun*.
[Latin *eloquens* speaking out]

else *adverb*
1. other than or as well: 'do you want anything *else* to eat?'.
2. otherwise: 'we must leave now *else* we'll be late'.
Usage: 'do as Kate says or *else*!' (= otherwise there will be trouble).
3. used with pronouns to indicate a person or thing other than the one mentioned: 'that is someone *else's* hat'.

elsewhere *adverb*
in or to another place: 'let's go *elsewhere* if this restaurant is full'.

elucidate (*say* ill**oo**si–date) *verb*
to make clear or distinct: 'will you *elucidate* the main points of the plan?'.
Word Family: **elucidation**, *noun*.
[Latin *e–* perfectly + *lucidus* clear, from *lucis* of light]

elude *verb*
to escape or avoid cleverly: 'the robbers had *eluded* police for three weeks'.
Word Family: **elusion**, *noun*.
[Latin *eludere* to outmanoeuvre]

elusive *adjective*
also called **elusory** (*say* ill**oo**za–ree)
difficult to catch, recall, etc.
Word Family: **elusiveness**, *noun*.

elves *plural noun*
see ELF.

elvish *adjective*
Word Family: see ELF.

Elysian Fields (*say* ell**iz**–ee–an feelds)
short form is **Elysium**
also called **Isles of the Blessed**
1. *Greek mythology:* the abode of heroes after death, placed somewhere in the far west.
2. a Utopia or Paradise.

em *noun*
Printing: a) the square of the body of any size of type. b) a pica, equal to about 4 mm.
[an *em* was originally equal to the space occupied by the letter *m* in a line]

em–
a variant of the prefix **en–**.

emaciate (*say* imm**ay**–see–ate) *verb*
to make or become thin: 'she was *emaciated* by her long illness'.
Word Family: **emaciation**, *noun*.
[Latin *e–* very + *macies* thinness]

emanate (*say* **emm**a–nate) *verb*
to come or be produced from: 'his fear of water *emanated* from an accident in the bath when he was young'.
Word Family: **emanation**, *noun*.
[Latin *emanare* to flow out]

emancipate (*say* imm**an**si–pate) *verb*
to set free from any restraint, especially slavery: 'her attitudes were *emancipated* by several years at university'.
Word Family: **emancipator**, **emancipationist**, *nouns*, a person who believes in, or practises, emancipation; **emancipatory**, *adjective*.
[Latin *emancipatus* declared free]

emancipation (*say* immansi–**pay**sh'n) *noun*
the act of setting free: 'the *emancipation* of women has been a popular cause throughout the 20th century'.

emasculate (*say* imm**ass**–kew–late) *verb*
1. to take away the masculinity or strength of: 'he was *emasculated* by 40 years spent with his overbearing mother'.
2. to castrate.
Word Family: **emasculation**, *noun*; **emasculatory**, **emasculative**, *adjectives*.
[Latin *e* ex + *masculus* male]

embalm (*say* em–**bahm**) *verb*
to preserve a dead body by treating it with chemicals.
Usage: 'the happiness of those years was *embalmed* in her memory' (= kept, cherished).

Word Family: **embalmer**, *noun*; **embalmment**, *noun*.

embankment *noun*
any raised wall or mound, such as a dyke, used to support a road, hold back water, etc.
Word Family: **embank**, *verb*.

embargo *noun*
plural is **embargos**
1. a government order which stops or restricts trade, movement of ships, etc.: 'an oil *embargo*'.
2. any restriction on commerce, etc.
Word Family: **embargo**, *verb*.
[Spanish *embargar* to restrain]

embark *verb*
to get on a ship: 'the family *embarked* at Southampton for the journey to Auckland'.
embark on, embark upon, 'the college will *embark on* a new language course this year' (= start).
Word Family: **embarkation**, *noun*.

embarrass *verb*
1. to cause to feel uncomfortable or self-conscious: 'she was *embarrassed* by the ugly scars on her face'.
2. to obstruct or hinder: 'the company was financially *embarrassed* by many unpaid debts'.
embarrassment *noun*
1. the state of being embarrassed: 'there was much *embarrassment* when the forgotten guest arrived'.
2. anything which causes one to be embarrassed: 'his lack of tact has always been an *embarrassment* to us'.

embassy (*say* **emba**–see) *noun*
a) the offices and official home of an ambassador. b) an ambassador and his staff.

embattle *verb*
to get ready for battle, especially by taking up arranged positions.

embed *verb*
(**embedded, embedding**)
to sink or fix firmly into a substance: 'the boulders were completely *embedded* in the soil'.

embellish *verb*
to add details or decoration to: 'tell the story simply without *embellishing* the facts'.
embellishment *noun*
1. the act of embellishing: 'his careful *embellishment* of the cake took hours'.
2. any added details or decoration: 'new *embellishments* to a house'.
[EM- + Latin *bellus* handsome]

ember *noun*
(*often plural*) a burning piece of wood, ash, etc., especially in the remains of a fire.

embezzle *verb*
to steal money placed in one's care: 'the bank teller had *embezzled* £10 000'.
Word Family: **embezzlement**, *noun*; **embezzler**, *noun*, a person who embezzles.

embitter *verb*
to make a person feel bitter.
Word Family: **embitterment**, *noun*.

emblazon (*say* em-**blay**–z'n) *verb*
to decòrate richly, especially with heraldic inscriptions and devices.

emblem (*say* **embl**'m) *noun*
a distinctive object or design which represents or symbolizes something: 'a dove is the *emblem* of peace'.
Word Family: **emblematic** (*say* embla-**mattik**), *adjective*, of or like an emblem; **emblematically**, *adverb*.

embody *verb*
(**embodied, embodying**)
to represent or give a form to: a) 'his new theory was *embodied* in the title of the book'; b) 'she *embodies* both beauty and sense'.
Word Family: **embodiment**, *noun*, anything which embodies something.

embolden *verb*
to encourage or make bold: 'your past kindness *emboldens* me to ask you a favour'.

embolism (*say* **emba**–lizm) *noun*
Medicine: the blocking of a blood vessel by an embolus.

embolus (*say* **emba**–lus) *noun*
plural is **emboli**
any material, such as tissue fragments, which is carried in the blood and lodges in a vein or artery. Compare THROMBUS.
Word Family: **embolic** (*say* em-**bollik**), *adjective*.
[Greek *embolos* a stopper]

embonpoint (*say* on–bon–**pwahn**) *noun*
a plumpness or stoutness.
[French *en bon point* in good condition]

emboss *verb*
to carve, mould or stamp a design so that it stands out on a surface.

embouchure (*say* om–boosh–**oor**) *noun*
Music: a) the mouthpiece of a wind instrument. b) the technique of using

the lips and face muscles on such an instrument.
[French, mouthpiece]

embrace *verb*
1. to hug or take closely in one's arms.
Usages:
a) 'the speech *embraced* many interesting topics' (= included).
b) 'the ocean *embraces* the tiny island' (= surrounds).
2. to accept or receive willingly: 'I *embrace* this opportunity of speaking to you all'.
Word Family: **embrace,** *noun.*
[EM- + Latin *bracchium* arm]

embrasure (*say* embray-*zh*er) *noun*
a slit or opening in a wall or parapet through which guns, arrows, etc. may be fired.

embrocation (*say* embra-**kay**sh'n) *noun*
a) the act of rubbing with ointment, etc., especially to relieve pain or stiffness. b) the ointment or lotion used.
Word Family: **embrocate,** *verb.*
[Greek *embrokhé* lotion]

embroider *verb*
to sew with decorative stitches.
Usage: 'he *embroidered* the story with many colourful details' (= embellished).
embroidery *noun*
1. the art of embroidering.
2. anything which is embroidered: 'the cuffs on her shirts were edged with red, blue and yellow *embroidery*'.

embroil *verb*
1. to involve in argument or hostility: 'the two teams became *embroiled* during the rugby match'.
2. to make confused or complicated: 'let's not get *embroiled* in details'.

embryo (*say* **embri**-o) *noun*
plural is **embryos**
Biology: an organism in the early stages of development from a fertilized egg.
in embryo, 'our plans for the farm are still *in embryo*' (= in the early stages).
Word Family: **embryonic** (*say* embri-**onn**ik), *adjective,* of or undeveloped like an embryo; **embryology** (*say* embri-**olla**-jee), *noun,* the study of embryos and their development; **embryologist,** *noun.*
[Greek *embryon*]

emend (*say* im**mend**) *verb*
to correct or remove errors from a manuscript or text.
Word Family: **emendation,** *noun.*
Common Error: do not confuse with AMEND.

emerald *noun*
1. *Geology:* a rare, bright green variety of beryl, used as a gem.
2. a strong bright green colour.
Word Family: **emerald,** *adjective.*
[Greek *smaragdos*]

emerge (*say* im**merj**) *verb*
to appear or come into sight, especially from concealment: 'the sun *emerged* again from behind the clouds'.
Usages:
a) 'some new facts have *emerged* about the crime' (= become known).
b) 'several new powerful nations have *emerged*' (= developed, become strong).
Word Family: **emergence,** *noun.*
[Latin *emergere* to rise from the waters]

emergency (*say* im**merj**'n-see) *noun*
a sudden, serious event for which immediate action is necessary: 'ring this doctor if there is an *emergency*'.
emergency *adjective*
designed or useful as a stand-by or substitute in case of need: 'the railway guard applied the *emergency* brakes'.

emergent (*say* im**merj**'nt) *adjective*
coming into view or independent existence, often unexpectedly: 'this country must now be seen as an *emergent* nuclear power'.

emeritus (*say* ee-**merri**-t's) *adjective*
(of a professor, etc.) retired but keeping an honorary title because of outstanding service.
[Latin, having served his time (in the army)]

emersion (*say* ee-**mer**sh'n) *noun*
1. the act of emerging.
2. *Astronomy:* the reappearance of a planet after an eclipse, etc. Compare IMMERSION.

emery (*say* **emma**-ree) *noun*
a fine-grained, very hard mineral substance used for grinding and polishing.
an **emery board** is a strip of card or wood coated with emery and used to file fingernails.
emery paper is a sheet of paper coated with emery and used as an abrasive.
wet and dry is fine emery paper treated with a lubricant to give a smoother finish.

emetic (*say* immettik) *noun*
a substance used to cause vomiting.
[Greek *emetikē*]

emigrate (*say* **emmi**-grate) *verb*
to go from one's own country to live in another: 'the family *emigrated* from Yugoslavia in 1967'. Compare IMMIGRATE.
Word Family: **emigration**, *noun*, the act of emigrating; **emigrant**, *noun*, a person who emigrates.
[Latin *emigrare* to move out]

émigré (*say* **emmi**-gray) *noun*
a person who emigrates to escape political persecution.
[French]

eminent *adjective*
1. having high rank, distinction or reputation: 'an *eminent* professor gave a lecture to the school'.
2. remarkable or conspicuous: 'his *eminent* politeness makes him a welcome guest'.
eminence *noun*
1. a position of high rank or distinction: 'his *eminence* in the legal profession is due to many years of hard work'.
2. *Roman Catholic:* (*capital*) a title of respect for a cardinal.
Word Family: **eminently**, *adverb*.
[Latin *eminens* standing out, lofty]

emir (*say* em-**eer**) *noun*
also spelt **amir**
a governor, prince, nobleman, chief or high official of a Moslem state.
[from Arabic, *amir*, ruler]

emissary (*say* **emmi**-sa-ree) *noun*
an envoy.

emit (*say* immit *or* ee-mit) *verb*
(**emitted, emitting**)
to give out or utter: 'the girl *emitted* a shriek as the bull approached'
emission (*say* immish'n *or* ee-**mish**'n) *noun*
a) the act of emitting, such as the discharge of fluid or semen from the body. b) anything which is emitted or discharged.
[Latin *emittere* to send forth]

emollient *adjective*
having the power to soothe or soften: 'an *emollient* face lotion'.
Word Family: **emollient**, *noun*, any emollient substance.
[Latin *emolliens* making soft]

emolument (*say* immol-yoo-m'nt) *noun*
any profit from employment, such as a fee, salary, wage, etc.
[Latin *emolumentum* gain, profit]

emote *verb*
to show or act out emotion, especially in a dramatic way.

emotion (*say* immo-sh'n) *noun*
any strong sensation, such as fear, joy, sorrow, etc.: 'her voice expressed her intense *emotion*'.
emotional *adjective*
1. of or caused by emotion: 'it was an *emotional* rather than a reasoned decision'.
2. easily affected by emotion: 'she gets very *emotional* about animals'.
emotive *adjective*
relating to or exciting emotion: 'his *emotive* speech stirred the audience'.
Word Family: **emotionally**, *adverb*; **emotively**, *adverb*; **emotionalism**, *noun*, the tendency to display excessive emotion.

empanel *verb*
(**empanelled, empanelling**)
Law: to enrol on a jury.
Word Family: **empanelment**, *noun*.

empathy (*say* **empa**-thee) *noun*
an ability to see into another's mind and heart and so reach a full and sympathetic understanding of his thought, feeling or experience.
Word Family: **empathize, empathise**, *verb*; **empathic** (*say* em-pathik), **empathetic** (*say* empa-**thettik**), *adjectives*.
[a translation into Greek form of German *Einfühlung* in-feeling]

emperor *noun*
the male ruler of an empire.
[Latin *imperator*]

emphasis (*say* **em**fa-sis) *noun*
a stress on or importance attached to something: 'we must put more *emphasis* on taxes in this election campaign'.
emphasize, emphasise *verb*
to put emphasis upon: 'that blue dress *emphasizes* the colour of her eyes'.
emphatic (*say* em-**fattik**) *adjective*
full of force and emphasis: 'his *emphatic* answer startled the reporter'.
Word Family: **emphatically**, *adverb*.
[Greek]

emphysema (*say* emfi-**seema**) *noun*
Medicine: an abnormal inflation of an organ or other part due to air or gas, causing difficult breathing and increased susceptibility to infection.
[Greek, a stomach inflation]

empire *noun*
1. a group of countries ruled by a single person or government.
2. any supreme government or control.
[Latin *imperium*]

empirical (*say* em-**pirri**-k'l) **empiric** *adjective*
based on or guided by experience, experiment or observation, as distinct from theory.
Word Family: **empirically**, *adverb.*
[Greek *empeirikos* experienced]

empirical formula
Chemistry: see FORMULA.

empiricism (*say* em-**pirra**-sizm) *noun*
1. any empirical process or method.
2. *Philosophy:* the belief that experience is the basis of all knowledge. Compare RATIONALISM.
Word Family: **empiricist**, *noun, adjective.*

emplacement *noun*
1. the act of placing.
2. a prepared position or place, especially for a heavy gun.

employ *verb*
to give work to or use the services of: 'this company *employs* 1300 workers'.
Usage: 'you must try to *employ* your spare time' (= make use of).
employment *noun*
a) the act of employing: 'this company encourages the *employment* of school-leavers'. b) the state of being employed: 'are you in *employment* at the moment?'. c) the work or business in which one is employed: 'I am looking for part-time *employment*'.
Word Family: **employer**, *noun*; **employee**, *noun*, a person in paid employment.

emporium (*say* em-**pawri**-um) *noun*
a large shop or market selling a variety of goods.
[Greek *emporion* a trading place]

empower *verb*
to give power or authority to: 'the police are *empowered* to arrest any violent demonstrators'.
Word Family: **empowerment**, *noun.*

empress *noun*
a) a female emperor. b) the wife of an emperor.

empty *adjective*
having nothing inside: 'he drank until the glass was *empty*'.
Usages:
a) 'his life was *empty* of interest or happiness' (= lacking).
b) 'the *empty* praise of the critics did not encourage the author' (= meaningless).
empty *verb*
(emptied, emptying)
1. to make or become empty: 'he *emptied* the bucket of water out the window'.
2. to discharge: 'this river *empties* into the sea'.
Word Family: **emptily**, *adverb*; **emptiness**, *noun*; **empty**, *noun*, something which is empty.

emu (*say* **ee**-mew) *noun*
a large, flightless, Australian bird, which is long-legged, greyish-brown and lives in grassland and scrub.

emulate (*say* **em**-yoo-late) *verb*
to try to equal or do better than: 'the class tried to *emulate* the teacher's French accent'.
Word Family: **emulation**, *noun*; **emulative**, *adjective*; **emulator**, *noun*, a person who emulates.
[Latin *aemulari*]

emulous (*say* **em**-yoo-lus) *adjective*
eager to equal or do better than another.

emulsify (*say* im**mulsi**-fie) *verb*
(emulsified, emulsifying)
to make into an emulsion.
Word Family: **emulsification** (*say* immulsiffi-**kay**-sh'n), *noun*; **emulsifier**, *noun*, anything which emulsifies.

emulsion (*say* im**mul**-sh'n) *noun*
1. a fine milky suspension of one liquid in another, such as oil in water.
2. *Photography:* a fine, light-sensitive coating on a film, etc.

en *noun*
Printing: one half of an em.

en-
a prefix meaning: a) in or into, as in *engulf*; b) to make or cause to be, as in *enable.*

-en (1)
a suffix indicating appearance, as in *golden.*

-en (2)
a suffix forming the plural of certain nouns, as in *children.*

enable (*say* en-**ay**-b'l) *verb*
to make able or possible: 'the fine weather *enabled* us to spend a lot of time outside'.

enact *verb*
1. to act out or play: 'the murder method was *enacted* for police by the confessed criminal'.
2. to make into a law or act: 'a new traffic code has been *enacted* for all drivers'.
Word Family: **enactment,** *noun.*

enamel *noun*
1. any of various mineral substances, similar in composition to glass, used to decorate metal, ceramic and glass surfaces.
2. any enamel-like substance, such as certain paints or varnishes.
3. the very hard, creamy-white, shiny coating on the outside of teeth.
4. an artistic work using enamel substances: 'an exhibition of pottery and *enamels*'.
Word Family: **enamel (enamelled, enamelling),** *verb,* to coat or decorate with enamel.

enamour (*say* en-**am**ma) *verb*
be enamoured of, to be delighted, charmed or in love with.
[EN- + French *amour* love]

en bloc (*say* on blok)
as a whole.
[French]

encamp *verb*
to settle in a camp: 'the troops were *encamped* by a creek'.
Word Family: **encampment,** *noun.*

encapsulate (*say* en-**kaps**-yoolate) *verb*
to enclose in a capsule or similar small space: 'he *encapsulated* his advice in a short statement'.
Word Family: **encapsulation,** *noun.*

encase *verb*
to cover or surround with or as if with a case: 'the knife was *encased* in an ornate sheath'.
Word Family: **encasement,** *noun.*

encephalitis (*say* en-keffa-**lie**-tis *or* en-seffa-**lie**-tis) *noun*
an inflammation of the brain.
[Greek *egkephalos* brain + -ITIS]

enchant *verb*
1. to charm or delight: 'we were all *enchanted* by the tiny puppets'.
2. to use magic or spells on: 'the witch *enchanted* the prince and turned him into a toad'.
enchantment *noun*
a) the state of being enchanted: 'our *enchantment* with the puppets was great'. b) anything which enchants: 'the *enchantment* of moonlight'.
Word Family: **enchanting,** *adjective*; **enchantingly,** *adverb*; **enchanter,** *noun,* a person who enchants.

encircle (*say* en-**sirk**'l) *verb*
to surround or form a circle round: 'the field was *encircled* with oak trees'.

enclave (*say* **en**-klave) *noun*
1. a territory or district completely surrounded by foreign land.
2. a district, e.g. in a city, inhabited by a minority group.
[French *enclaver* to shut in]

enclose *verb*
to put or shut in completely: 'the garden was *enclosed* by a high brick wall'.
Usage: 'he *enclosed* two tickets with the letter' (= sent in the envelope).

enclosure (*say* en-**klo**-*zh*er) *noun*
1. a) the act of enclosing b) something which is enclosed: 'the horses were kept in an *enclosure* during the sale'. c) something, such as a fence, which encloses.
2. *History:* the act of fencing common land in order to make it private property, widely practised in Britain in the 18th and 19th centuries.

encomium (*say* en-**ko**-mee-um) *noun*
plural is **encomiums** or **encomia**
a formal expression of praise.

encompass (*say* en-**kum**pis) *verb*
to surround.
Usage: 'the essay *encompassed* many historical facts' (= contained).

encore (*say* **on**-kor) *noun*
Theatre: a) any applause or calls by an audience, demanding that a particular part of a performance be repeated. b) the performance given in response to such a call. Compare CURTAIN CALL.
Word Family: **encore,** *interjection*; **encore,** *verb,* to give or call for an encore.
[French, again]

encounter *verb*
to meet or be faced with: 'we *encountered* some language difficulties in Germany'.
Word Family: **encounter,** *noun,* a meeting, especially with something difficult or unexpected.

encourage (*say* en-**kurr**ij) *verb*
to give hope or confidence to: 'the team was *encouraged* by the shouts and applause'.

encouragement *noun*
a) the act of encouraging: 'I hope that our *encouragement* of her ambition was not wrong'. b) anything which encourages: 'your interest in the project is a great *encouragement* to us'.
Word Family: **encouragingly**, *adverb.*

encroach *verb*
to intrude or go beyond the set limits: 'I hope that we are not *encroaching* on your hospitality by staying so long'.
Word Family: **encroachment**, *noun.*

encrust *verb*
to cover with or form a crust: 'the purse was *encrusted* with beads'.
Word Family: **encrustation**, *noun.*

encumber *verb*
1. to burden or overcome with: 'the bankrupt company is *encumbered* with many debts'.
2. to block or fill up: 'the room was *encumbered* with old furniture'.
encumbrance *noun*
anything which burdens or hinders: 'grandmother began to feel she was an *encumbrance* to the family'.

encyclical (*say* en–**sigh**–klik'l) *noun*
Roman Catholic: a letter written by the Pope for wide distribution.

encyclopaedia
(*say* en–sigh–kla–**peedia**)
encyclopedia *noun*
a book or set of books giving information about every branch of a subject or all subjects, usually arranged in alphabetical order.
Word Family: **encyclopaedic**, *adjective*, knowing about or dealing with a wide variety of subjects; **encyclopaedist**, *noun.*
[Greek *egkyklios* general + *paideia* education]

end *noun*
1. the farthest part: 'you hold the other *end* of the rope'.
2. the last or concluding part: 'what happened at the *end* of the film?'.
3. an aim or purpose: 'does the *end* justify the means?'.
Usages:
a) 'he met an unfortunate *end* in a boating accident' (= death).
b) 'really, that's the *end*!' (= limit).
Phrases:
at a loose end, 'if you're *at a loose end* tonight, come out with us' (= without anything to do).
make ends meet, 'after losing his job he found it difficult to *make ends meet*' (= have enough money to live).
on end, a) 'his hair stood *on end* in horror' (= upright); b) 'she chattered for hours *on end*' (= continuously).
end *verb*
to come or bring to an end: 'the film *ended* without telling us why he disappeared'.
Usage: 'your gambling will *end* in disaster' (= result).
Word Family: **ending**, *noun*, the last or concluding part.

endanger (*say* en–**dane**–jer) *verb*
to expose to danger: 'you will *endanger* your health if you work so hard'.

endear *verb*
to make dear or beloved: 'her simple happiness *endeared* her to all of us'.
endearment *noun*
a gesture or expression of affection, such as fond words.
Word Family: **endearingly**, *adverb.*

endeavour (*say* en–**devva**) *verb*
in America spelt **endeavor**
to strive or make an effort: 'we must *endeavour* to work harder'.
endeavour *noun*
an effort or attempt: 'their continual *endeavours* for world peace were frustrated'.
[French *se mettre en devoir* to do one's utmost]

endemic (*say* en–**demm**ik) *adjective*
(of a disease, etc.) characteristic of or widespread among a particular group of people. Compare EPIDEMIC.

ending *noun*
Word Family: see END.

endive *noun*
a herb with small, pale, crinkly leaves, used in salads.

endless *adjective*
continuous or without an end: 'an *endless* round of parties preceded the wedding'.
Word Family: **endlessly**, *adverb*; **endlessness**, *noun.*

endo–
a prefix meaning internal, as in *endocrine gland.*
[Greek, within]

endocrine gland
Anatomy: any gland, such as an adrenal gland, which passes its secretions directly into the bloodstream or lymph vessels.
Word Family: **endocrine**, *adjective.*
[ENDO– + Greek *krinein* to separate]

endocrinology
(*say* en–doe–krin–**olla**–jee) *noun*

the study of the endocrine glands and their relation to the rest of the body. *Word Family:* **endocrinologist**, *noun.*

endorse *verb*
1. to write something on a document, such as comments or a signature: 'the court *endorsed* her driving licence with the speeding offence'.
2. to give approval or support: 'the candidate's nomination was *endorsed* by the party'.
endorsee *noun*
a person authorized by an endorsement to receive payment.
[EN- + Latin *dorsum* back]

endorsement *noun*
1. the act of endorsing: 'the people's *endorsement* of the government was seen in the election results'.
2. anything endorsed on a document, such as a change written into an existing insurance policy.

endothermic (*say* en-doe-**ther**mik) *adjective*
Chemistry: of or relating to a chemical reaction in which heat is absorbed. Compare EXOTHERMIC.
[ENDO- + Greek *thermé* heat]

endow *verb*
to give or provide a fund or income.
be endowed with, 'she *is endowed with* great musical talent' (= possesses, is gifted with).

endowment *noun*
1. the act of endowing.
2. any endowed payment or income: 'child *endowment*'.
3. (*usually plural*) a natural gift or talent.

end point
1. *Chemistry:* the point which marks the end of a reaction during a titration, usually marked by a change in colour of the indicator.
2. *Maths:* see RAY (1).

end product
the final product or result of anything: 'the severe food shortage was an *end product* of the drought'.

endurance (*say* end-yoor'nce) *noun*
the ability or power to endure: 'the cross-country hike was a test of their *endurance*'.

endure (*say* end-**yoor**) *verb*
1. to suffer, bear or put up with: 'it is difficult to *endure* this pain'.
2. to continue: 'his fame *endured* long after his death'.
Word Family: **endurable**, *adjective*, able to be endured or tolerated; **enduring**, *adjective*, a) long-lasting or continual, b) patient.

endways, endwise *adverb*
1. a) with the end forwards. b) standing on end.
2. lengthwise.

enema (*say* **enn**ema) *noun*
Medicine: the placing of a fluid in the rectum to encourage the expulsion of faeces.
[Greek, an injection]

enemy (*say* **enna**-mee) *noun*
a person, group or thing that is hostile, aggressive or violently opposed to another: 'the revolutionary guerrilla force was declared an *enemy* of the nation'.
Word Family: **enemy**, *adjective*, hostile or representing the enemy.

energetic (*say* enna-**jett**ik) *adjective*
active or full of energy: 'the old man was still an *energetic* walker'.
Word Family: **energetically**, *adverb.*

energy (*say* **enna**-jee) *noun*
1. the physical ability, force or power to act, work, etc.: 'do not waste your *energy* trying to lift that box by yourself'.
2. *Physics:* a conserved quantity equal to the mass of a body multiplied by its velocity squared.
Word Family: **energize, energise**, *verb*, to fill with energy.
[EN- + Greek *ergon* work]

energy crisis
a crisis caused by a world shortage of easily obtainable energy sources.

enervate (*say* **enna**-vate) *verb*
to take away the strength or force of: 'a tropical climate is very *enervating*'.
Word Family: **enervation**, *noun*; **enervative**, *adjective.*
[Latin *e-* without + *nervus* sinew, vigour]

enfant terrible (*say* on-fon ter**reeb**'l)
a young person who is known for unconventional, indiscreet or embarrassing behaviour.
[French *enfant* child + *terrible* terrible]

enfeeble *verb*
to make weak or feeble.
Word Family: **enfeeblement**, *noun.*

enfilade (*say* enfil–**ade**) *verb*
Military: to fire or be in a position to fire from a flank along a whole length of trench or line of troops.
[French *enfiler* to pass right through]

enfold *verb*
to wrap around or embrace: 'she *enfolded* the child in her arms'.

enforce *verb*
to compel obedience to: 'policemen *enforce* the law'.
Word Family: **enforcement**, *noun*, the act of enforcing; **enforceable**, *adjective*.

enfranchise (*say* en–**fran**–chize) *verb*
to give political or civil rights to, such as the right to vote.
Word Family: **enfranchisement**, *noun*.

engage (*say* en–**gay**j) *verb*
1. to obtain the attention, aid, services, etc. of: 'they *engaged* a guide to lead them over the mountains'.
2. to undertake or promise: 'they became *engaged* to be married'.
3. to keep busy or occupied: 'he will be *engaged* in a meeting all afternoon'.
4. to make two pieces of machinery lock or move together: 'he *engaged* first gear and the car moved forward'.
engage in, 'employees of this firm must not *engage in* any other work' (= take part in).

engagement (*say* en–**gay**j–m'nt) *noun*
1. the act of engaging.
2. a promise or agreement, especially to marry.
3. an appointment or arrangement: 'a business *engagement*'.

engaging (*say* en–**gay**–jing) *adjective*
charming, attractive or interesting: 'an *engaging* smile'.
Word Family: **engagingly**, *adverb*; **engagingness**, *noun*.

engender (*say* en–**jen**da) *verb*
to cause or produce: 'racial prejudice *engenders* bitterness and often violence'.

engine (*say* **en**jin) *noun*
1. any device which produces mechanical energy from other forms of energy: 'an internal combustion *engine*'.
2. a railway locomotive.
[Latin *ingenium* genius, an invention]

engineer (*say* **en**ja–neer) *noun*
a person trained or skilled in designing, constructing or maintaining machinery, bridges, chemical plants, etc.

engineer *verb*
to work as an engineer.
Usage: 'he skilfully *engineered* his own election to the council' (= contrived, manoeuvred).
Word Family: **engineering**, *noun*.

engine–turned *adjective*
(of silver, etc.) ornamented with machine–engraved symmetrical lines.

English *noun*
the language of the British Isles and many other countries, such as America and Australia. **Old English** (also called **Anglo–Saxon**) was the form of the language until the 12th century, and **Middle English** was the form between the 12th and the 16th century.
Word Family: **English**, *adjective*, a) of England, b) of the United Kingdom (especially used outside the United Kingdom).
[from *Angul*, see ANGLO–SAXON]

English horn
see COR ANGLAIS.

engorge (*say* en–**gorj**) *verb*
Medicine: to become filled with blood.

engrave *verb*
to cut marks, such as letters or designs, into a hard surface.
Usage: 'the beautiful countryside was *engraved* upon his memory' (= impressed or fixed deeply).
Word Family: **engraving**, *noun*, a work or design produced by cutting into a hard surface.

engross *verb*
to take and hold all the attention or time of: 'the new novel *engrossed* him for many hours'.
[French *en gros* wholesale]

engulf *verb*
to swallow or surround completely: 'the timber house was soon *engulfed* by the fire'.

enhance *verb*
to make more valuable or attractive: 'the meal was greatly *enhanced* by the delicious wines'.
Word Family: **enhancement**, *noun*.

enigma (*say* in**nig**ma) *noun*
anything which puzzles or is difficult to explain: 'her many different moods were an *enigma* to us'.
Word Family: **enigmatic**, *adjective*; **enigmatically**, *adverb*.
[Greek *ainigma* riddle]

enjoin *verb*
to urge or command.
Word Family: **enjoinment**, *noun*.

enjoy *verb*
to find delight in: 'we *enjoyed* the party so much'.
Usage: 'the children all *enjoy* good health' (= have, experience).
enjoyable *adjective*
giving pleasure or joy: 'what an *enjoyable* holiday!'.
Word Family: **enjoyment,** *noun.*

enlarge *verb*
to make larger: 'ask the photographer to *enlarge* these four prints'.
Usage: 'we asked the speaker to *enlarge* on several of the points mentioned' (= give more detail).
enlargement *noun*
a) the act of enlarging: 'the *enlargement* of their house was directed by an architect'. b) something, especially a photograph, which has been enlarged.
Word Family: **enlarger,** *noun,* a device which enlarges.

enlighten *verb*
to give knowledge or understanding to: 'can you *enlighten* me on the meaning of this proverb?'.
enlightened *adjective*
well-informed and free from prejudice, ignorance, etc.: 'do we live in an *enlightened* age?'.
Word Family: **enlightenment,** *noun,* a) the act of enlightening, b) the state of being enlightened.

enlist *verb*
1. to request and obtain: 'they *enlisted* our help in moving the furniture'.
2. to join one of the armed services.
Word Family: **enlistment,** *noun.*

enliven (*say* en-**lie**-v'n) *verb*
to make more lively: 'the party was greatly *enlivened* when the music started'.

en masse (*say* on **mass**)
all together: 'the family arrived *en masse* for the barbecue'.
[French]

enmesh *verb*
to catch or tangle up, as if in a net.

enmity (*say* **enma**-tee) *noun*
a hatred, hostility or violent opposition: 'the country's trade policies aroused the *enmity* of its neighbours'.

ennoble (*say* **inno**-b'l) *verb*
to make noble or dignified: 'his tragic death was *ennobled* by his courage'.
Word Family: **ennoblement,** *noun.*

ennui (*say* on-**wee**) *noun*
a listless boredom or lack of interest.
[French]

enormity *noun*
1. hugeness: 'the *enormity* of the task overwhelmed us'.
2. a) the quality of being outrageous. b) something which is outrageous, such as an offence, crime, etc.

enormous (*say* innor-mus) *adjective*
1. very large: 'the *enormous* elephant terrified the children'.
2. (*informal*) outrageous: 'he had *enormous* cheek to say that!'.
Word Family: **enormously,** *adverb;* **enormousness,** *noun.*

enough (*say* **innuf**) *adjective, adverb*
as much or as many as is needed: (as an adjective) 'is there *enough* pie left for me to have some more?'. (as an adverb) 'this meat is not cooked *enough*'.
Usage: 'oddly *enough*, we did not see them at all' (= quite, rather).
enough *noun*
a sufficient or necessary amount: 'have you got *enough* to pay for the tickets?'.

enquire (*say* en-**kwire**) *verb*
to inquire.
Word Family: **enquiry,** *noun.*

enrage *verb*
to make very angry: 'the bull was *enraged* by the toreador's taunts'.

enrapture (*say* en-**rap**-cher) *verb*
to fill with great delight or rapture: 'we were all *enraptured* by the haunting symphony'.

enrich *verb*
1. a) to improve: 'the soil was *enriched* with compost'. b) to make richer.
2. *Chemistry:* to increase the abundance of a particular isotope in a mixture of the isotopes of an element.
Word Family: **enrichment,** *noun.*

enrol (*say* en-**role**) *verb*
(**enrolled, enrolling**)
to enter one's name or have it entered on a list or register for membership, etc.
Word Family: **enrolment,** *noun.*

en route (*say* on **root**)
on the way: 'we will stop and buy food *en route* to the city'.
[French]

ensconce (*say* en-**skonce**) *verb*
to settle or establish oneself in comfort: 'she is *ensconced* by the fire with a book'.

ensemble (*say* on–**som**–b'l) *noun*
1. all the parts of a whole, seen or considered together.
2. any small group of musicians.
3. a matching outfit.
[French, together]

enshrine *verb*
to cherish or keep as if in a shrine: 'the fond memories were *enshrined* in her heart'.

enshroud *verb*
to shroud or cover.

ensign (*say* **ensine**) *noun*
1. a flag, especially of a country or particular group.
2. (*formerly*) the lowest commissioned officer in the British infantry.
3. the lowest ranking commissioned officer in the American navy.
blue ensign, of Customs and other government departments.
red ensign, of the Merchant Navy.
white ensign, of the Royal Navy and Royal Yacht squadron.

enslave *verb*
to dominate or make a slave of: 'she was *enslaved* by an overbearing husband'.
Word Family: **enslavement**, *noun*.

ensnare *verb*
to catch in or as if in a snare or trap.

ensue *verb*
to happen afterwards, especially as a result: 'a strike *ensued* from the employer's refusal to pay the workers overtime'.

en suite (*say* on **sweet**)
in a series or succession.
[French]

ensure (*say* en–**shor**) *verb*
to make sure or certain: 'we must *ensure* that the dogs do not escape'.

entablature (*say* en–**tab**la–cher) *noun*
Architecture: the part of a building which rests on columns.

entail *verb*
1. to involve as a necessary part of a process: 'this project will *entail* much extra reading'.
2. *Law:* to limit an inheritance to a fixed line of heirs who may neither sell nor give it away.

entangle *verb*
to make or become caught up or tangled.
Word Family: **entanglement**, *noun*.

entente (*say* **ontont**) *noun*
a friendly understanding or agreement, especially between governments.
[French]

enter *verb*
to come or go in: 'we *entered* the theatre by the side door'.
Usages:
a) 'he *entered* the army when he was 18' (= joined).
b) 'they *entered* and won all four events' (= competed in).
c) '*enter* your name and age at the top' (= put, record).
enter into, to become involved with.
[Latin *intrare* to go in]

enteritis (*say* enta–**rye**–tis) *noun*
an inflammation of the intestines.
[Greek *enteron* intestine + –ITIS]

enterprise *noun*
1. any attempted project, task, etc.: 'he is involved in a new business *enterprise*'.
2. an organized business or company: 'they manage a small hardware *enterprise*'.
3. energetic resourcefulness and spirit.

enterprising *adjective*
bold, resourceful and energetic: 'such an *enterprising* plan must succeed'.
Word Family: **enterprisingly**, *adverb*.

entertain *verb*
1. to keep amused, interested or attentive: 'a magician *entertained* the children before the concert'.
2. to admit or receive as guests: 'we *entertained* 12 people for dinner last night'.
Usage: 'I cannot *entertain* such an outrageous idea' (= accept, consider).
entertainer *noun*
a person who entertains, especially a public or professional performer.
Word Family: **entertainment** *noun*, a) the act of entertaining, b) anything which entertains, such as a public performance.

enthral (*say* en**thrawl**) *verb*
(enthralled, enthralling)
to hold the fascinated attention of: 'grandfather *enthralled* us with his ghost stories'.
Word Family: **enthralment**, *noun*.

enthrone *verb*
to place on or as if on a throne.
Word Family: **enthronement**, *noun*.

enthusiasm (*say* en–**thewz**i–azm) *noun*
a strong interest, eagerness or delight: 'the audience showed their *enthusiasm* by thunderous applause and cries'.

enthusiast *noun*
a person who has great enthusiasm for some activity, etc.: 'a skiing *enthusiast*'.
Word Family: **enthusiastic**, *adjective*, full of enthusiasm; **enthusiastically**, *adverb*; **enthuse**, *verb*, to show enthusiasm.
[Greek *enthousiasmos* inspiration from *theos* a god]

entice *verb*
to attract or tempt with promises, bait, etc.: 'we tried to *entice* the cat down from the tree with a saucer of milk'.
enticement *noun*
a) the act of enticing. b) something used to entice: 'a generous salary was the main *enticement* of the job'.
Word Family: **enticingly**, *adverb*.

entire *adjective*
being whole and undivided: 'his *entire* wealth was donated to a Lost Dogs' Home'.
Usage: 'she is an *entire* stranger to me' (= thorough).
entirety (*say* en-**tie**-ra-tee) *noun*
the wholeness or completeness of anything: 'the evidence must be presented in its *entirety*'.
Word Family: **entirely**, *adverb*, completely or exclusively.

entitle *verb*
1. to give a name or title to, e.g. a book.
2. to allow or give a right to: 'you are *entitled* to the prize money if you are over 21'.

entity (*say* **enta**-tee) *noun*
anything which has a real, independent existence.

entomb (*say* en**toom**) *verb*
to bury in or as if in a tomb.
Word Family: **entombment**, *noun*.

entomology (*say* enta-**molla**-jee) *noun*
the study of insects.
Word Family: **entomologist**, *noun*; **entomological** (*say* enta-m'**loji**-k'l), *adjective*.
[Greek *entoma* insects + -LOGY]

entourage (*say* **on**too-rah*zh*) *noun*
a group of attendants or followers: 'the President arrived with his usual *entourage* of bodyguards'.
[French *entourer* to surround]

entr'acte (*say* on-trakt) *noun*
a) the interval between the acts of a play. b) a performance, especially of music, given in this interval.

entrails (*say* **en**-trales) *plural noun*
the intestines or inner parts.

entrance (1) (*say* **en**-tr'nce) *noun*
1. a) the act of entering: 'his *entrance* was greeted with wild applause'. b) the right or permission to enter: 'he has *entrance* into the highest business circles'.
2. any place by or through which one enters.

entrance (2) (*say* in-**trance**) *verb*
to fill with wonder and delight: 'we were *entranced* by the delicate music'.
Word Family: **entrancement**, *noun*; **entrancingly**, *adverb*.

entrant (*say* **entr**'nt) *noun*
a person who officially enters a competition or organization: 'this year the poetry competition had only 70 *entrants*'.

entrap *verb*
to trick or catch in, or as if in, a trap.
Word Family: **entrapment**, *noun*.

entreat *verb*
to ask or request earnestly: 'they *entreated* her not to go out after dark'.
entreaty *noun*
an earnest request: 'the driver ignored my *entreaties* to slow down'.

entrecôte (*say* **on**tra-kote) *noun*
a steak cut from the upper part of the sirloin.
[French, between the rib]

entrée (*say* **on**tray) *noun*
1. a dish served before the main course of a meal.
2. the right or privilege to enter.
[French *entrer* to enter]

entrench *verb*
1. to establish or settle firmly: 'he is completely *entrenched* in his beliefs and will not change'.
2. *Military:* to defend or consolidate a position by digging trenches.
entrenchment *noun*
1. *Military:* any defensive fortification consisting of trenches.
2. a) the act of entrenching. b) the state of being entrenched: 'his *entrenchment* in his beliefs is so complete it's frightening'.

entrepreneur (*say* ontra-pren-**er**) *noun*
a person who undertakes and controls an enterprise or business venture, especially one in which risk is involved.
[French *entre* between + *preneur* taker]

entropy (*say* **en**tra–pee) *noun*
1. *Physics:* a measure of the molecular disorder of a system: 'the *entropy* of a solid increases as it melts'. Because all changes from order to disorder absorb energy, entropy is also a measure of the free energy in a system.
2. the tendency of a system towards increasing disorder and inertness: 'many modern authors portray the world as being in the throes of *entropy*'.
[EN– + Greek *tropé* a change]

entrust *verb*
to give in trust: 'I have *entrusted* my will to a solicitor'.
Word Family: **entrustment,** *noun.*

entry *noun*
1. the act of entering: 'their *entry* into the house was not noticed'.
2. any place by which one enters: 'the *entry* to the stables was in the yard'.
3. anything which is entered or recorded: 'postal *entries* in this competition will not be accepted after Monday'.

entwine *verb*
to twine or curl around, together, etc.

enumerate (*say* in**new**ma–rate) *verb*
to name or list one by one: 'you must clearly *enumerate* your reasons'.
Word Family: **enumeration,** *noun,* the act of enumerating.

enunciate (*say* in**nun**si–ate) *verb*
1. to pronounce: 'he *enunciates* all his words with great care'.
2. to state or declare: 'he first *enunciated* his theories in 1942'.
Word Family: **enunciation,** *noun.*

envelop (*say* in–**vell**up) *verb*
to wrap up or cover completely: 'the taller city buildings were *enveloped* in cloud'.
Word Family: **envelopment,** *noun.*

envelope (*say* **en**va–lope *or* **on**va–lope) *noun*
a cover, especially the flat, folded sheet of paper used to enclose letters, etc.
[French *envelopper* to wrap up]

enviable (*say* **en**via–b'l) *adjective*
desirable or worthy to be envied: 'the President's job is not an *enviable* one'.

envious (*say* **en**vi–us) *adjective*
full of envy: 'he felt proud when he saw the *envious* glances at his car'.
Word Family: **enviously,** *adverb*; **enviousness,** *noun.*

environment (*say* en–**vie**–ron–m'nt) *noun*
the surrounding influences, physical conditions or circumstances of anything: 'the home *environment* of a child has an important effect on its attitudes in later life'.
Word Family: **environmental** (*say* en–vie–ron–**men**–t'l), *adjective*; **environmentalist,** *noun,* a person concerned with the problems of the environment, especially the effects of pollution.

environs (*say* en–**vie**–r'nz) *plural noun*
the surrounding districts or suburbs of a city, town, etc.
[French, surroundings]

envisage (*say* en–**vizz**ij) *verb*
to see or picture in the mind: 'I didn't *envisage* that there would be such a crowd here'.

envoy (*say* **en**–voy) *noun*
an official representative, especially a diplomat sent to another country.
[French *envoyé* sent]

envy (*say* **en**–vee) *noun*
1. a feeling of discontent or resentment aroused by seeing another person's good fortune, superiority, etc., usually accompanied by a desire to possess the advantages of the other person.
2. anything which causes envy: 'their swimming pool is the *envy* of the neighbourhood'.
envy *verb*
(envied, envying)
to regard with envy: 'it is difficult not to *envy* his success'.
Word Family: **envyingly,** *adverb.*

enzyme (*say* **en**–zime) *noun*
a substance, usually a protein, which is a biological catalyst.
[EN– + Greek *zymé* yeast]

Eocene (*say* **ee**–o–seen) *noun*
Geology: see TERTIARY.
[Greek *eos* dawn + *kainos* modern (= the dawn of modern forms of life)]

eon *noun*
see AEON.

epaulette (*say* **eppa**–let) **epaulet** *noun*
a buttoned shoulder flap on military uniforms.
[French *épaule* shoulder]

épée (*say* **epp**ay) *noun*
a stiff, steel, fencing sword, having a blade with a triangular cross-section and a rounded button on the point to prevent injuring the opponent.
[French]

ephemeral (*say* ef**femma**–r'l) *adjective*
lasting only a short time.

Word Family: **ephemera** (plural is **ephemeras** or **ephemerae**), *noun*, anything which lasts only a short time; **ephemerally**, *adjective.*
[EPI- + Greek *hemera* day]

epi-
a prefix meaning on, to or against, as in *epicentre.*
[Greek]

epic *noun*
1. a long story of heroic events and actions, often in a noble style.
2. any great or dramatic event likened to an epic.
epic *adjective*
1. of or characteristic of an epic.
2. grand or heroic.
[Greek *epikos*]

epicentre (*say* **eppi**-senta) *noun*
in America spelt **epicenter**
also called an **epicentrum**
a point on the surface of the earth directly above the point of origin of an earthquake or impact of a bomb.
Word Family: **epicentral**, *adjective.*

epicure (*say* **eppi**-kewer) *noun*
a person who appreciates or cultivates fine taste in wine, food, the arts, etc.
epicurean (*say* eppi-**kew**rian) *adjective*
1. of or fit for an epicure: 'it was an *epicurean* meal'.
2. devoted to luxury and sensuous pleasures.
Word Family: **epicurean**, *noun.*
[after *Epicurus*, a Greek philosopher in the 4th century B.C. who taught that the highest good in life is happiness]

epidemic (*say* eppi-**dem**mik) *noun*
the occurrence of a disease in one area and for a short time affecting many individuals in that area. Compare ENDEMIC.
Word Family: **epidemic, epidemical**, *adjective.*
[EPI- + Greek *demos* people]

epidermis (*say* eppi-**der**mis) *noun*
Biology: the skin or outside layer of cells in animals or plants.
Word Family: **epidermic, epidermal**, *adjectives*, of or relating to epidermis; **epidermoid**, *adjective*, resembling epidermis.
[Greek, the outer skin]

epigastrium (*say* eppi-**gas**tri-um) *noun*
the upper middle region of the abdomen.
Word Family: **epigastric**, *adjective.*
[Greek *epigastrios* over the belly]

epiglottis (*say* eppi-**glot**tis) *noun*
Anatomy: a movable ridge of cartilage at the back of the throat, which prevents food entering the windpipe during swallowing.
Word Family: **epiglottal, epiglottic**, *adjectives.*
[EPI- + Greek *glotta* tongue]

epigram *noun*
1. a short poem with one theme and usually a witty or satirical ending.
2. any concise, witty statement.
Word Family: **epigrammatic** (*say* eppi-gra-**mat**tik), *adjective*; **epigrammatically**, *adverb.*
[Greek *epigramma* an inscription]

epigraph (*say* **eppi**-graf *or* **eppi**-grahf) *noun*
a brief inscription or quotation, as on a statue or at the beginning of a book, poem, etc.

epilepsy (*say* **eppi**-lep-see) *noun*
a nervous disease, sometimes due to brain damage and causing fits.
Word Family: **epileptic**, *noun*, a person who suffers from epilepsy; **epileptic**, *adjective.*
[Greek *epilepsia* an attack]

epilogue (*say* **eppi**-log) *noun*
the closing part or speech of a play, book, etc. Compare PROLOGUE.
[Greek *epilogos* conclusion]

Epiphany (*say* ip**piff**a-nee) *noun*
Christian: a festival celebrated on January 6th, to commemorate the showing of the infant Christ to the Magi.
[Greek *epiphaneia* manifestation]

episcopal (*say* ip**pis**ka-p'l) *adjective*
1. of or relating to a bishop.
2. (*usually capital*) of or relating to bishops or any church governed by bishops: 'the Protestant *Episcopal* Church in America'.
episcopacy (*say* ip**pis**ka-p'see) *noun*
Religion: a) the administration of a church by bishops. b) the office or rank of a bishop.
Word Family: **episcopalian** (*say* ippiska-**pay**lian), *noun*, a person who supports episcopal church government; **episcopalian**, *adjective.*
[Greek *episkopos* overseer]

episode (*say* **eppi**-sode) *noun*
1. an incident or event in a larger series or course of events.
2. one complete section of a serial.

Word Family: **episodic** (*say* eppi-**soddik**), **episodical**, *adjective*; **episodically**, *adverb.*
[Greek *epeisodios* an interlude]

epistemology (*say* ippista-**molla**-jee) *noun*
Philosophy: the study, investigation or theory of human knowledge.
Word Family: **epistemological** (*say* ippista-m'**loji**-k'l), *adjective*; **epistemologist**, *noun.*
[Greek *episteme* knowledge + -LOGY]

epistle (*say* ippiss'l) *noun*
a letter, especially any of the apostles' letters in the New Testament.
Word Family: **epistolary** (*say* ippista-l'ree), **epistolatory**, *adjectives.*
[Greek *epistolé* letter]

epitaph (*say* **eppi**-tahf) *noun*
a short inscription on a tomb.
[Greek *epitaphios* over the grave, a funeral oration]

epithalamium
(*say* eppitha-**lay**-mee-um) *noun*
also spelt **epithalamion**
a poem in honour of a marriage, dedicated to the bride and groom.
[Greek *epithalamios* at the bridal chamber, a bridal song]

epithelium (*say* eppi-**thee**lium) *noun*
Anatomy: any tissue consisting of one or more layers of cells and covering the body, its internal surfaces and cavities.
Word Family: **epithelial**, *adjective.*
[EPI- + Greek *thelé* nipple]

epithet (*say* **eppi**-thet) *noun*
a word or name, especially one used to describe some characteristic of a person, as in Ethelred *the Unready.*
Word Family: **epithetical** (*say* eppi-**thet**tik'l), *adjective.*
[Greek *epithetos* added]

epitome (*say* ippitta-mee) *noun*
1. any person or thing that is typical or characteristic of some quality, etc.
2. a summary.
Word Family: **epitomize, epitomise,** *verb,* to be typical or characteristic of.
[Greek, incision, abridgement]

epoch (*say* eepok) *noun*
1. a particular period of time, especially one seen as a new or significant beginning.
2. *Geology:* the main division of a geological period, being the amount of time taken for a rock series to form.

epoch-making *adjective*
opening a new era of time or progress: 'it was an *epoch-making* discovery for medical science'.
Word Family: **epochal** (*say* **eppo**-k'l), *adjective.*

eponymous (*say* ippo-nimmus) *adjective*
a) giving the name to a place, work, invention, etc.: 'David Copperfield, the *eponymous* hero of Dickens's novel'. b) taking its name from a person.
[EPI- + Greek *onyma* name]

epoxy resin (*say* ee-pok-see **rezzin**)
short form is **epoxy**
Chemistry: any of a wide variety of synthetic organic compounds which contain oxygen and are used in plastics, surface coatings and adhesives.

epsilon (*say* ep-**sigh**-lon) *noun*
the fifth letter of the Greek alphabet, representing short *e.*

Epsom salts
magnesium sulphate, a white, water-soluble, crystalline solid, used in leather processing and medicine.
[first made from mineral spring waters of *Epsom,* Surrey]

equable (*say* **ekwa**-b'l) *adjective*
(of temperament, climate, etc.) steady, even or regular.
Word Family: **equably**, *adverb*; **equability** (*say* ekwa-**billi**-tee), *noun.*

equal (*say* **eekw**'l) *adjective*
having the same size, amount, degree, value, etc.: 'we received *equal* shares of the pie'.
equal to, 'I do not feel *equal to* the occasion' (= adequate for, able to cope with).
equal *verb*
(**equalled, equalling**)
to be or do something equal to: 'I doubt if you will *equal* the record'.
equal *noun*
a person or thing which is equal to another: 'we are *equals* in age but not in size'.
Word Family: **equally**, *adverb*; **equality** (*say* ik**kwolli**-tee), *noun.*
[Latin *aequus* even]

equalize (*say* **eekwa**-lize) **equalise** *verb*
to make equal: 'the government has *equalized* the tax burden for all sections of the community'.

Word Family: **equalization,** *noun*; **equalizer,** *noun*, something which equalizes.

equanimity (*say* ekwa-**nimmi**-tee) *noun*
a calmness of mood or temper.
[EQUI- + Latin *animus* mind]

equate (*say* ik**kwate**) *verb*
to see or represent one thing as equal to another.

equation (*say* ik**kway**-*zh*'n) *noun*
1. the act of making or representing as equal.
2. *Maths:* a formula expressing the equality of two quantities.

equator (*say* ik**kway**ta) *noun*
a great circle on the earth's surface lying midway between the North and South Poles.
Word Family: **equatorial** (*say* ikkwa-**taw**riul), *adjective*, of, near or characteristic of the equator.
[Latin *circulus aequator diei et noctis* circle equalizing day and night]

equerry (*say* **ek**wa-ree) *noun*
1. an officer who attends a member of the British royal family or their representatives in other countries.
2. a person who looks after the horses of a royal household, etc.

equestrian (*say* ik**kwes**trian) *noun*
a horserider.
equestrian *adjective*
of or relating to horseriding: 'an *equestrian* event'.
Word Family: **equestrianism,** *noun.*
[Latin *equester* from *equus* horse]

equi- (*say* ee-kwee *or* **ek**-wee)
a prefix meaning equal, as in *equilibrium.*
[Latin]

equiangular (*say* ee-kwee-**ang**-gewla) *adjective*
having equal angles.

equidistant (*say* eekwi-**dis**tant) *adjective*
being at an equal distance.
Word Family: **equidistance,** *noun.*

equilateral (*say* eekwi-**lat**ta-r'l) *adjective*
having sides equal in length.

equilibrium (*say* eekwi-**lib**rium) *noun*
plural is **equilibria**
1. a state of equal balance or rest between opposing forces.
2. *Chemistry:* a state of balance in a chemical reaction, where the substances produced decompose at the same rate as they are being formed.
[EQUI- + Latin *libra* balance]

equine (*say* **ek**wine) *adjective*
of or resembling a horse.

equinox (*say* **ee**kwi-noks) *noun*
the time when the sun crosses the equator, making day and night all over the earth of equal length, occurring on about March 21st (the vernal equinox) and September 22nd (the autumnal equinox).
Word Family: **equinoctial,** *adjective.*
[EQUI- + Latin *nox* night]

equip (*say* ik**kwip**) *verb*
(**equipped, equipping**)
to provide or fit with what is needed for a particular purpose.

equipment (*say* ik**kwip**m'nt) *noun*
1. the act of equipping: 'the *equipment* of the ship is in progress'.
2. the things which are needed or used for a particular purpose or task: 'this shop sells all kinds of sporting *equipment*'.

equipoise (*say* **ek**wi-poyz) *noun*
an even balance or distribution.

equitable (*say* **ek**witta-b'l) *adjective*
fair and just.
Word Family: **equitably,** *adverb.*

equitation (*say* ekwi-**taysh**'n) *noun*
horsemanship.
[Latin *equus* horse]

equity (*say* **ek**wi-tee) *noun*
1. the quality of being fair or impartial.
2. *Law:* an old system of civil law in which abstract justice overrode the letter of the law; now merged into Common Law.
3. *Commerce:* a) the value of a company's shares. b) (*often plural*) ordinary shares in a public company, as distinct from fixed-interest shares.
[Latin *aequitas* fairness, justice]

equivalent (*say* ik**kwiv**va-l'nt) *adjective*
equal or nearly equal in value, effect, amount, etc.
Word Family: **equivalently,** *adverb*; **equivalence, equivalency,** *noun.*
[EQUI- + Latin *valens* strong]

equivocal (*say* ik**kwiv**vi-k'l) *adjective*
ambiguous or unclear.

equivocate (*say* ik**kwiv**va-kate) *verb*
to mislead or evade by using equivocal language.
Word Family: **equivocation,** *noun.*
[EQUI- + Latin *vocis* of a voice]

–er (1)
a suffix which indicates: a) a person or thing that performs the action or function related to the root word, as in *photographer*; b) a person coming from a particular region or area, as in *Southerner.*

–er (2)
a suffix indicating the comparative degree of: a) adjectives, as in *brighter*; b) adverbs, as in *later.*

era (*say* **eera**) *noun*
a) a period of time counted from some fixed point in the past: 'the Christian *era*'. b) a period of time marked by distinctive events or features: 'an *era* of progress'.

eradicate (*say* **irraddi**–kate) *verb*
to uproot or get rid of completely: 'the doctors have succeeded in *eradicating* smallpox from this district'.
Word Family: **eradication,** *noun*; **eradicable,** *adjective,* able to be eradicated; **eradicator,** *noun,* a person or thing that eradicates.
[Latin *e–* away + *radicis* of a root]

erase (*say* **irraze**) *verb*
to rub or clean off.
eraser *noun*
anything which erases, especially a rubber.
Word Family: **erasure,** *noun*; **erasable,** *adjective.*
[Latin *erasus* scratched out]

erbium *noun*
element number 68, a rare metal. See LANTHANIDE.
See CHEMICAL ELEMENTS in grey pages.

ere (*say* air)
preposition, conjunction
an old word meaning before.

erect (*say* **irrekt**) *adjective*
upright or on end.
erect *verb*
1. to build, construct or establish: 'a monument was *erected* in his honour'.
2. to raise into an upright position.
Word Family: **erectly,** *adverb*; **erectness,** *noun.*

erectile tissue
Anatomy: any spongy tissue which becomes firm and rigid when it is filled with blood, such as in the penis and nipples in males and the clitoris and nipples in females.

erection *noun*
1. a) the act of erecting. b) anything which has been erected, such as a building.
2. the expanding and hardening of the penis or clitoris when it fills with blood due to sexual stimulation.

erector *noun*
anything which erects, such as a muscle in the body.

erg *noun*
an obsolete metric unit of work or energy, equal to 10^{-7} joule. See UNITS in grey pages.
[Greek *ergon* work]

ergo *conjunction, adverb*
an old word meaning therefore.
[Latin]

ermine (*say* **ermin**) *noun*
a) a weasel with a black-tipped tail and brown fur which turns white in winter. It is called a **stoat** while it has its brown coat. b) the valuable white fur of this animal.

erode (*say* **irrode**) *verb*
to wear or eat away: a) 'the soil was *eroded* by wind'; b) 'support for the government was *eroded* by inflation'.
Word Family: **erosive,** *adjective,* causing erosion.
[Latin *e–* away + *rodere* to gnaw]

erogenous (*say* **irroji**–n's) *adjective*
arousing or tending to arouse sexual excitement.
[Greek *eros* love + –GEN]

erosion (*say* irro–*zh*'n) *noun*
the act or process of eroding, especially the wearing away of the land surface by sun, wind, water, frost or ice.

erotic (*say* **irrottik**) *adjective*
a) of or relating to sexual love: '*erotic* poems'. b) arousing sexual desire: 'a very *erotic* performance by the striptease dancer'.
erotica (*say* **irrottika**) *noun*
any art or literature based on, or attempting to stimulate, sexual love or desire.
Word Family: **erotically,** *adverb*; **eroticism** (*say* irrotti–sizm), *noun.*
[after *Eros,* the god of love in Greek mythology]

err *verb*
to make mistakes or go astray.
Word Family: **errancy,** *noun*; **erringly,** *adverb.*
[Latin *errare* to stray]

errand *noun*
a) a short trip for a particular task or purpose: 'I must send you on another shopping *errand*'. b) the purpose of such a trip: 'our *errand* is to invite you to dinner tonight'.

errant *adjective*
1. wandering or roving: 'a medieval *knight-errant*'.
2. erring: 'you'll come to regret your *errant* ways'.
Word Family: **errantly,** *adverb*; **errantry,** *noun*, the conduct or career of a knight-errant.

errata (*say* err**ah**ta) *plural noun*
singular is **erratum**
also called **corrigenda**
any printing or writing errors, often noted in a list added to a book after it has been printed.

erratic (*say* ir**rat**tik) *adjective*
lacking a fixed or certain course, etc: a) '*erratic* winds'; b) '*erratic* behaviour'.
Word Family: **erratically,** *adverb.*

erroneous (*say* irro-**nee**-us) *adjective*
1. containing errors or mistakes: 'his *erroneous* solution of the problem was based on faulty reasoning'.
2. *Geology:* (of large rocks, etc.) moved from their original site, e.g. by a glacier.
Word Family: **erroneously,** *adverb.*
[Latin *erroneus* straying]

error *noun*
a mistake.
in error, 'you are *in error* about the date of that tomb' (= mistaken).
[Latin, a wandering about]

ersatz (*say* **air**-zahtz) *adjective*
being an imitation, usually inferior: '*ersatz* jewellery can always be recognized when next to real gems'.
[German *Ersatz* replacement]

Erse *noun*
an old name for the Gaelic language.
Word Family: **Erse,** *adjective.*

erstwhile *adjective*
former: 'her *erstwhile* friends do not come to see her any more'.
[from *erst*, an old word for earliest + WHILE]

erudite (*say* **erroo**-dite) *adjective*
having or showing great learning.
Word Family: **eruditely,** *adverb*; **erudition,** *noun.*

erupt *verb*
to burst or force out violently: 'the volcano *erupted* rocks and molten lava'.
Usage: 'her skin *erupted* into a rash' (= broke out).
Word Family: **eruption,** *noun*; **eruptive,** *adjective.*

erythrocyte (*say* er**rith**ro-site) *noun*
see RED BLOOD CELL.
[Greek *erythros* red + *kytos* vessel]

erythromycin (*say* errithro-**my**-sin) *noun*
Medicine: an antibiotic, useful against bacteria which are resistant to penicillin.

escalate (*say* **eska**-late) *verb*
to increase, intensify or enlarge by stages: 'the war was *escalated* on several fronts'.
Word Family: **escalation,** *noun.*

escalator (*say* **eska**-layter) *noun*
a moving, mechanical stairway which consists of an endless belt.

escalope (*say* **eska**-lop) *noun*
a very thin slice of meat, especially veal.
[French]

escapade (*say* **eska**-pade) *noun*
a reckless or wild adventure.

escape *verb*
to get free from capture, confinement, pursuit, etc.: 'the rabbit *escaped* from his hutch'.
Usages:
a) 'they were lucky to *escape* injury in that accident' (= avoid).
b) 'the mistake had *escaped* his attention' (= failed to attract).
escape *noun*
1. the act of escaping: 'his *escape* from prison was organized by the rest of the gang'.
2. any means of escaping: a) 'a *fire-escape*'; b) 'he sees films as an *escape* from everyday life'.
escapee (*say* eska-**pee**) *noun*
a person who has escaped from captivity: 'a prison *escapee*'.

escapism (*say* es**kay**-pizm) *noun*
the tendency to avoid unpleasant reality by entertaining or absorbing the mind in other matters.
Word Family: **escapist,** *noun, adjective.*

escarpment *noun*
a long, steep ridge of rock.

eschatology (*say* eska–**tolla**–jee) *noun*
Christian: any teachings concerned with final things, such as death, judgement, heaven and hell.
Word Family: **eschatological** (*say* eskatta–**lo**ji–k'l), *adjective*.
[Greek *eskhatos* last + -LOGY]

eschew (*say* es–**choo**) *verb*
to avoid or keep away from.

escort (*say* **es**kort) *noun*
a person or group that travels with or accompanies another.
escort (*say* es**kort**) *verb*
to go with as an escort or to offer protection.

escritoire (*say* eskri–**twa**) *noun*
a writing desk with drawers.
[French *écrire* to write]

escutcheon (*say* es–**kutch**'n) *noun*
Heraldry: the shield in a coat of arms, usually divided into segments.

Eskimo *noun*
plural is **Eskimo** or **Eskimos**
a) any of a Mongoloid people inhabiting the arctic coasts of America, Greenland and north–east Siberia. b) their language.
[Amerindian *askimow* eater of raw flesh]

esophagus *noun*
see OESOPHAGUS.

esoteric (*say* esso–**terr**ik) *adjective*
1. (of mystical doctrine, etc.) taught only to the initiated.
2. made for or understood by only a small select group.
Word Family: **esoterically**, *adverb*.
[Greek *esoterikos* inner]

espalier (*say* es–**pal**lia) *noun*
a) a trellis or other framework on which trees, etc. are trained. b) a tree or shrub trained in this way.
Word Family: **espalier**, *verb*.
[Italian *spalliera* a support]

especial (*say* es**pesh**'l) *adjective*
special or particular: 'do you have an *especial* friend?'.
Word Family: **especially**, *adverb*.

Esperanto (*say* espa–**ranto**) *noun*
a language invented in 1877 by Dr. L. Zamenhof, a Polish scholar, using common words from the major European languages and intended for international use.
[Spanish *esperanza* hope, Zamenhof's pen–name]

espionage (*say* **es**pia–nah*zh*) *noun*
the act of spying, especially on foreign governments.
[French]

esplanade (*say* **es**pla–nahd *or* **es**pla–nade) *noun*
a public path or road, usually by the sea.
[from Spanish]

espouse (*say* es–**powz**) *verb*
to marry.
Usage: 'the Government has *espoused* the conservation movement' (= adopted, supported).
Word Family: **espousal**, *noun*, support or advocacy.

espresso *noun*
a strong coffee made by forcing steam under pressure through ground coffee beans.
[Italian, pressed out]

esprit de corps (*say* ess–pree de **kor**)
a feeling of loyalty and enthusiasm uniting members of a group.
[French, the corps spirit]

espy *verb*
(**espied**, **espying**)
to catch sight of.
Word Family: **espial**, *noun*.

esquire (*say* es–**kwire**) *noun*
1. a polite title for a man, used when addressing a letter, etc.
2. *Medieval history:* see SQUIRE.
[Latin *scutarius* shield–bearer]

–ess
a suffix used to form feminine nouns, as in *actress*.

essay *noun*
1. a short piece of writing about a particular subject.
2. an attempt.
Word Family: **essay**, *verb*, to attempt or put to the test; **essayist**, *noun*, a person who writes essays.
[French *essai* attempt]

essence *noun*
1. the property of a thing which gives it its identity: 'the *essence* of his character is kindness'.
2. a concentrated form of any substance: 'vanilla *essence*'. Also called an **extract**.
3. *Medicine:* a solution of an oil in alcohol.

essential (*say* is**sen**–sh'l) *adjective*
1. absolutely necessary: 'it is *essential* that you post this letter'.
2. relating to the essence or most fundamental part.

Word Family: **essentially**, *adverb*; **essential**, *noun*, something which is fundamental or extremely important.

-est
a suffix indicating the superlative degree of: a) adjectives, as in *brightest*; b) adverbs, as in *latest*.

establish *verb*
to set up or bring about on a firm basis: 'the group *established* a new progressive school in the area'.
Usages:
a) 'we have not *established* why you were so angry' (= found out, proved).
b) 'that fact has been *established* for years' (= settled, accepted).
[Latin *stabilis* stable]

established church
a religious denomination which is officially recognized and often supported by a country's government.

establishment *noun*
1. the act of establishing.
2. a household or any place of residence.
3. any established and organized group, business or institution.
the Establishment
an established group having power and status in a community, often considered to be conservative or reactionary.

estate *noun*
1. a large piece of private land, especially in the country.
2. an area of land developed for housing.
3. *Law:* a person's possessions, especially those left by a dead person.
4. a person's circumstances or condition in life or society: 'the holy *estate* of matrimony'.

estate agent
short form of **real estate agent**
a person who buys and sells houses or land on behalf of other people.

estate car
a motor car with a long body, having space behind the rear seats for luggage or goods and a door or tailgate at the back.

estate duty
see DEATH DUTY.

esteem *verb*
to regard with great respect or favour: 'his work is highly *esteemed* by the company'.
esteem *noun*
a respect or favourable opinion.

ester *noun*
Chemistry: the organic equivalent of an inorganic salt, formed by replacing the hydrogen of an organic acid with an organic radical. Many esters are pleasant-smelling liquids, and are used in artificial flavourings.

esthetic *adjective*
see AESTHETIC.

estimable (*say* **estimma-b'l**) *adjective*
1. worthy of esteem or respect.
2. able to be estimated.
Word Family: **estimably**, *adverb*.

estimate (*say* **esti-mate**) *verb*
to judge or calculate approximately: 'we *estimate* the cost to be about £200'.
estimate (*say* **esti-m't**) *noun*
an approximate opinion, judgement or calculation: 'what is your *estimate* of his abilities?'.
estimation *noun*
1. the act of estimating.
2. a judgement or opinion: 'in your *estimation*, what are the chances of success?'.
[Latin *aestimare* to judge the price or worth of]

estrange *verb*
to turn away or lose the affections, loyalty, etc. of: 'his selfish behaviour *estranged* his friends'.
Word Family: **estrangement**, *noun*.

estuary (*say* **estew-erree**) *noun*
the wide mouth of a river, where its current meets, and is affected by, the sea's tides.
[Latin *aestus* tide]

et cetera (*say* **et settera**)
short form is **etc**.
and other similar things as well.
[Latin *et* and + *cetera* the rest]

etch *verb*
to engrave a picture on a metal plate, by scratching the design through a layer of wax, and then letting acid eat into the exposed metal. Compare DRY POINT.
Usage: 'his face was *etched* in her memory' (= impressed clearly).
Word Family: **etching**, *noun*, a design or picture etched on a metal plate.

eternal (*say* **ittern'l**) *adjective*
lasting for ever, with no beginning or end.
Usage: 'please stop your *eternal* quarrelling' (= seemingly endless).
Word Family: **eternally**, *adverb*.

eternal triangle
the situation which occurs when one party in a relationship takes a second lover, seen as an ageless or continual event.

eternity (*say* ee-**ter**na-tee) *noun*
an endless time without beginning or end, especially as distinct from mortal life.
Usage: 'it took an *eternity* for the doctor to arrive' (= seemingly endless time).

ethane (*say* **ee**thane) *noun*
Chemistry: a colourless, odourless gas (formula C_2H_6), the second member of the paraffin series of hydrocarbons. It is used in making organic compounds.

ethene (*say* **eth**-een) *noun*
see ETHYLENE.

ether (*say* **ee**tha) *noun*
1. *Chemistry:* a) any class of organic compounds with the general formula ROR′, where R and R′ are any aryl or alkyl radicals.
b) diethyl ether, a highly inflammable volatile liquid, used as an anaesthetic and solvent.
2. a) the heavens or upper regions of space. b) a substance which was believed by 19th-century scientists to fill all space and transmit light, heat, etc. Also spelt **aether**.
[Greek *aither* upper air]

ethereal (*say* ee-**theer**ial) *adjective*
1. of the heavens or pure upper regions of space.
2. light and delicate.
Word Family: **ethereally**, *adverb*; **etherealize, etherealise**, *verb*.

ethic *noun*
a principle or rule of right conduct.
ethics *plural noun*
1. a system of rules or principles for behaviour within a group or society, according to which actions are judged.
2. (*used with singular verb*) any science or study of morals and moral standards, especially as a branch of philosophy or law.
3. the rightness or moral quality of an action, etc.
ethical *adjective*
1. in agreement with accepted principles or rules for right conduct.
2. of or relating to ethics.

ethnic *adjective*
1. of or relating to a particular population having a common language or common racial or cultural origins.
2. relating to or characteristic of any racial or cultural group.
Word Family: **ethnically**, *adverb*.
[Greek *ethnos* nation]

ethno-
a prefix meaning race or nation, as in *ethnography*.

ethnocentric (*say* ethno-**sen**trik) *adjective*
tending to believe in the absolute superiority of one's own group or culture and thus despising other groups, etc.
Word Family: **ethnocentrism**, *noun*.

ethnography (*say* eth-**nog**ra-fee) *noun*
a) the collecting and recording of information about a society or culture.
b) a published description based on this field work.
Word Family: **ethnographic** (*say* ethna-**graff**ik), **ethnographical**, *adjective*; **ethnographer**, *noun*.

ethnology *noun*
Anthropology: the analytic study of ethnographic information.
Word Family: **ethnologic, ethnological**, *adjective*; **ethnologist**, *noun*.

ethology (*say* ee-**tholl**a-jee) *noun*
the scientific study of the behaviour of animals in relation to their environment.

ethos (*say* **ee**thos) *noun*
the fundamental and distinctive character or spirit of a social group, culture, community, etc.
[Greek, nature, habits]

ethyl (*say* **eth**il) *adjective*
Chemistry: of or relating to organic compounds or radicals containing the univalent C_2H_5- group.
Word Family: **ethanol**, *noun*, (also called **ethyl alcohol**) the alcohol based on the ethyl group, a constituent of alcoholic drinks.

ethylene (*say* **eth**il-een) *noun*
also called **ethene**
a colourless inflammable gas (formula C_2H_4), with a sweetish smell. It is the first member of the olefine series and is used as an anaesthetic and in making polythene.

etiolate (*say* **ee**ti-o-late) *verb*
to turn, or cause to turn, white or pale through lack of light.
Word Family: **etiolation**, *noun*.

etiology *noun*
see AETIOLOGY.

etiquette (*say* **etti**–ket) *noun*
the rules of conduct for a particular group or social situation.
[French]

–ette
a suffix indicating: a) something small, as in *cigarette*; b) the feminine form of certain nouns, as in *usherette*.

etymology (*say* etti–**molla**–jee) *noun*
a) the study of the origin, history and changes of form in a word or words. b) an account of the history of a particular word.
Word Family: **etymologist**, *noun*; **etymological** (*say* ettima–**loji**–k'l), *adjective*; **etymologically**, *adverb*.
[Greek *etymon* the true meaning + –LOGY]

eucalyptus (*say* yooka–**liptus**) *noun*
1. any of a large group of native Australian trees, many of which have brightly coloured flowers.
2. a thin, inflammable oil obtained from the leaves of the eucalyptus, having a strong distinctive smell and used in medicine. Short form of **eucalyptus oil**.
[Greek *eu* well + *kalyptos* covered (of the bud)]

Eucharist (*say* **yooka**–rist) *noun*
Christian: a) any of various services which celebrate the Last Supper. b) the consecrated bread and wine used in this sacrament.
Word Family: **Eucharistic**, *adjective*.
[Greek *eukharistos* grateful]

euchre (*say* **yooker**) *noun*
Cards: a simplified form of bridge played by two to four players with 32 cards.

Euclidean geometry
(*say* yoo–kliddian jee–**omma**–tree)
the classical geometry of points, lines, planes and a variety of curves and solids, used to represent physical space.
[first studied by *Euclid*, a Greek mathematician in about 300 B.C.]

eugenics (*say* yoo–**jenniks**) *noun*
the science of improving the qualities of offspring, e.g. by careful selection of parents, control of genes, etc.
Word Family: **eugenic**, *adjective*; **eugenicist** (*say* yoo–**jenna**–sist), *noun*, a person who advocates eugenics.
[Greek *eu* good + –GEN]

eulogy (*say* **yoola**–jee) *noun*
also called a **panegyric**
a) a speech or piece of writing in praise of a person. b) any praise.
Word Family: **eulogistic** (*say* yoola–**jistik**), *adjective*; **eulogistically**, *adverb*; **eulogize**, **eulogise**, *verb*, to praise highly; **eulogist**, *noun*.
[Greek *eu* good + –LOGY]

eunuch (*say* **yoo**–nuk) *noun*
a castrated man, especially one formerly used as a harem attendant by oriental rulers.
[Greek *eunouchos* chamber attendant]

euphemism (*say* **yoofa**–mizm) *noun*
a) the use of a mild or indirect expression instead of one considered likely to offend or upset. b) any expression substituted in this way.
Example: *to pass away* is a euphemism for *to die*.
Word Family: **euphemistic** (*say* yoofa–**mistik**), *adjective*; **euphemistically**, *adverb*.
[Greek *eu* good + *phemé* speaking]

euphonious (*say* yoo–**foe**–nee–us) *adjective*
pleasant–sounding.
Word Family: **euphoniously**, *adverb*; **euphony** (*say* **yoofa**–nee), *noun*.
[Greek *eu* good + *phoné* sound]

euphonium (*say* yoo–**foe**–nee–um) *noun*
Music: a brass wind instrument similar to the tuba.

euphoria (*say* yoo–**fawria**) *noun*
a feeling of elation or happiness, especially if based on illusion.
Word Family: **euphoric** (*say* yoo–**forrik**), *adjective*.
[Greek *eu* good + *phoros* bearing]

Eurasian (*say* yoo–**ray** zh'n) *adjective*
a) of Eurasia, the combined land mass of Europe and Asia. b) (of a person) having one European and one Asian parent.
Word Family: **Eurasian**, *noun*, a person with one European and one Asian parent.

eureka (*say* yoo–**reeka**) *interjection*
an exclamation of triumph at a discovery.
[Greek *heureka* I have found it, attributed to Archimedes when he conceived his Principle, about 260 B.C.]

eurhythmics *plural noun*
(*used with singular verb*) a system of developing grace and rhythm through movements of the body made in response to music.
[Greek *eu* good + *rhythmos* rhythm]

Eurodollar (*say* **yoo**ro dollar) *noun*
any currency deposited in banks outside its country of origin and forming a freely convertible currency not subject to national legal restrictions.
[originally used of American dollars deposited in Europe]

europium (*say* yoo–**ro**–pee–um) *noun*
element number 63, a rare metal. See LANTHANIDE.
See CHEMICAL ELEMENTS in grey pages.

Eustachian tube (*say* yoo–**stay**–sh'n tube)
Anatomy: either of two fine tubes connecting the inner ears to the back of the nose and throat, balancing the air-pressure inside and outside the eardrum.
[after *B. Eustachio,* an Italian anatomist]

euthanasia (*say* yootha–**nay**zia) *noun*
the causing of death painlessly, or by withholding treatment, especially when a person is suffering from an incurable disease.
[Greek *eu* good + *thanatos* death]

eutrophy (*say* **yoo**–tr'fee) *noun*
healthy nutrition.
Word Family: **eutrophic** (*say* yoo-**troff**ik), *adjective.*

evacuate (*say* ivvak–yoo–ate) *verb*
to make empty or remove the contents of.
Usages:
a) 'the families were *evacuated* from the flooded town' (= removed to a safe place).
b) 'the troops *evacuated* the garrison' (= left, withdrew from).
Word Family: **evacuation,** *noun*; **evacuee** (*say* ivvak–yoo–**ee**), *noun,* a person who is evacuated.

evade *verb*
to escape or avoid cleverly: 'the prison escapee *evaded* capture for many days'.

evaluate (*say* ivval–yoo–ate) *verb*
to estimate the amount, quantity or value of.
Word Family: **evaluation,** *noun.*

evanescent (*say* evva–**ness**'nt) *adjective*
passing away or vanishing.
Word Family: **evanescently,** *adverb*; **evanescence,** *noun*; **evanesce,** *verb,* to disappear gradually.
[Latin *evanescere* to vanish]

evangelical (*say* eevan–**jell**ik'l) *adjective*
1. *Christian:* of or relating to the Gospel.
2. Low Church.

evangelist (*say* ivvanja–list) *noun*
1. *Christian:* (*capital*) any of the authors of the four Gospels in the New Testament.
2. any preacher who stresses the necessity for conversion before salvation.
Word Family: **evangelism,** *noun*; **evangelize, evangelise,** *verb.*
[Greek *eu* good + *angelia* news]

evaporate (*say* ivvappa–rate) *verb*
1. to become or convert into vapour.
2. to remove moisture or liquid from so as to dry or concentrate: 'powdered milk has been *evaporated*'.
Word Family: **evaporation,** *noun.*

evasion (*say* ivvay–*zh*'n) *noun*
1. the act of evading: '*evasion* of income tax'.
2. any method used to evade: 'her supposed ignorance was just an *evasion*'.
Word Family: **evasive** (*say* ivvay–siv), *adjective,* characterized by evasion; **evasively,** *adverb*; **evasiveness,** *noun.*

eve *noun*
the day or evening before an important day or event: 'Christmas *Eve*'.

even (*say* **eev**'n) *adjective*
1. having no change in level, quality, amount, etc.: 'the cricket pitch is not as *even* as it should be'.
Usages:
a) 'the picture is *even* with the top of the door' (= level, parallel).
b) 'the scores were *even* at half-time' (= equal).
c) 'you could hardly say he has an *even* temper' (= calm, steady).
2. *Maths:* (of a number) having no remainder when divided by two, such as 2, 4, 6, etc.
even *adverb*
a word used to indicate the following:
a) 'their car is *even* bigger than ours' (= still).
b) 'she was pleased, *even* grateful, that we did not come' (= indeed).
c) '*even* if it rains we will still have our picnic' (= notwithstanding).
d) '*even* as they watched, the sun sank below the horizon' (= at the same time).
e) 'he forgave *even* his enemies' (= unlikely as it may seem).

Phrases:
break even, 'this financial year the company *broke even* for the first time' (= had credits equal to its losses).
even so, nevertheless.
get even with, 'how can I *get even with* him for that nasty trick?' (= take revenge on).
even *verb*
to make or become even.
Word Family: **evenly**, *adverb*; **evenness**, *noun*.

even-handed *adjective*
just and fair: 'her *even-handed* treatment of all the children was highly praised'.

evening (*say* **eev-ning**) *noun*
the part of the day between sunset and nightfall.

evening dress
the clothes worn on formal occasions in the evening.

evening star
see VENUS.

even-minded *adjective*
not easily disturbed or upset.
Word Family: **even-mindedness**, *noun*.

even money
a winning payment which is the same amount as the money placed on the bet.

evensong *noun*
Christian: (*often capital*) an Anglican service held in the evening.

event (*say* **ivvent**) *noun*
anything which happens or takes place, especially something important.
Sport: any of the separate competitions in a tournament or programme: 'the long jump is the third *event* after lunch'.
Phrases:
at all events, in any event, '*at all events*, do not show that you are scared' (= whatever happens).
in the event of, '*in the event of* you missing the train, I will drive you to the city' (= if it happens that).
Word Family: **eventful**, *adjective*, a) full of events or incidents, especially exciting ones, b) having important consequences; **eventfully**, *adverb*; **eventfulness**, *noun*.
[Latin *eventus* consequence, event]

eventide *noun*
an old word for evening.

eventual (*say* **ivven-tew'l**) *adjective*
happening finally or in the end: 'what was the *eventual* outcome of their argument?'.
Word Family: **eventually**, *adverb*; **eventuality**, *noun*.

eventuate (*say* **ivven-tew-ate**) *verb*
1. to happen or take place: 'we sat waiting for the ghost, but nothing *eventuated*'.
2. to result: 'if we do that, war may *eventuate*'.
Word Family: **eventuation**, *noun*.

ever *adverb*
1. always: 'she is *ever* ready to help other people'.
2. at any time: 'have you *ever* seen such a violent storm?'.
3. at all or in any way: 'how *ever* did you get away with it?'.
4. continuously: '*ever* since then they have hated each other'.
ever so, (*informal*) 'I'm *ever so* glad you like it' (= greatly, extremely).

evergreen *noun*
a tree or plant which has leaves throughout the year.
Word Family: **evergreen**, *adjective*.

everlasting *adjective*
continuing for ever.
Usage: 'her *everlasting* grumbles make us all angry' (= often repeated).
everlasting *noun*
1. any of a group of plants with paper-like flowers which keep their colour and shape for a long time when dried. Also called an **immortelle**.
2. a time which continues for ever.
Word Family: **everlastingly**, *adverb*; **everlastingness**, *noun*.

evermore *adverb*
for ever.

every (*say* **ev-ree**) *adjective*
1. referring one by one to all separate members of a group: '*every* girl in that family has red hair'.
2. the greatest possible degree of: 'we wish you *every* happiness in your new home'.
Phrases:
every bit, 'it's *every bit* as cold as they predicted' (= equally).
every other, 'she comes to clean the house *every other* week' (= every second).
every so often, from time to time.

everybody *pronoun*
every person.

everyday *adjective*
1. suitable for ordinary occasions: '*everyday* clothes'.
2. usual or routine: 'his *everyday* business worries vanished during the holiday'.

everyone *pronoun*
every person.

everything *pronoun*
all.
Usage: 'her family is *everything* to her' (= most important).

everywhere *adverb*
in or to all places.

evict (*say* ivv**ikt**) *verb*
to expel a tenant.
Word Family: **eviction,** *noun.*

evidence (*say* **evvi**–d'nce) *noun*
1. anything which provides a basis for belief.
Usage: 'there was little *evidence* of suffering in her face' (= sign, indication).
2. *Law:* the statements, documents or objects presented in a court to prove disputed facts.
in evidence, 'her talent was very much *in evidence* during the play' (= plainly seen).
Word Family: **evidence,** *verb,* to show clearly; **evidential** (*say* evvi–**den**–sh'l), *adjective,* serving as or based on evidence; **evidentially,** *adverb.*
[Latin *evidens* plain to see]

evident *adjective*
being clearly seen or understood: 'it was *evident* that she was not amused'.
Word Family: **evidently,** *adverb.*

evil (*say* **ee**vil) *adjective*
1. morally bad: '*evil* deeds'.
2. causing injury, damage, etc.: 'smoking is an *evil* habit'.
3. full of suffering, misfortune or bad luck: 'the war caused *evil* times'.
evil *noun*
anything which is evil or causes harm, suffering, etc.: 'the *evils* of the war would never be forgotten'.
Word Family: **evilly,** *adverb*; **evilness,** *noun.*

evil eye
a stare believed to have the power to cause bad luck, injury, etc.

evil–minded *adjective*
full of malice or evil intentions.

evince *verb*
to indicate or show clearly: 'her slow reply *evinced* a lack of interest in the discussion'

eviscerate (*say* ivv**iss**a–rate) *verb*
a) to remove the intestines or bowels of. b) to remove the important or essential parts of.
Word Family: **evisceration,** *noun.*
[Latin *e*– out + *viscera* the internal organs]

evocative (*say* ivv**okk**a–tiv) *adjective*
having the power to evoke a response.
Word Family: **evocation,** *noun,* the act of evoking or summoning; **evocatively,** *adverb*; **evocativeness,** *noun.*
[Latin *e*– out + *vocare* to call]

evoke (*say* ivv**oke**) *verb*
to call up or produce: 'the song *evoked* memories of her childhood'.

evolution (*say* **ee**va–loo–sh'n *or* **ev**va–loo–sh'n) *noun*
1. any gradual process of growth or development: 'the *evolution* of her political ideas was based on her own experiences'.
2. *Biology:* the slow, continuous process of change in the characteristics of organisms from one generation to the next.
See DARWINISM and NATURAL SELECTION.
Word Family: **evolutionary,** *adjective*; **evolutionally,** *adverb*; **evolutionist,** *noun,* a person who believes in biological evolution.
[Latin *evolutus* unrolled]

evolve *verb*
1. to grow or develop gradually.
2. *Biology:* to develop by the processes of evolution.

ewe (*say* yoo) *noun*
a female sheep.

ewer (*say* **yoo**–a) *noun*
a large jug with a wide spout, especially one holding water for washing.

ex–
a prefix meaning: a) out of or away from, as in *expel*; b) thoroughly, as in *exasperate*; c) former, as in *ex–husband.*
[Latin and Greek]

exacerbate (*say* eg–**zass**a–bate) *verb*
to intensify or make worse: 'tension between the countries was *exacerbated* by a broken agreement'.
Word Family: **exacerbation,** *noun.*
[EX– + Latin *acerbus* bitter]

exact (*say* eg–**zakt**) *adjective*
being precisely correct or accurate: 'what is the *exact* time?'.

exact *verb*
1. to demand or require: 'this job *exacts* the utmost attention to detail'.
2. to force or compel the payment, performance, etc., of: a) 'to *exact* tribute'; b) 'to *exact* obedience'.
exacting *adjective*
having strict demands or requirements: 'an *exacting* taskmaster'.
exactly *adverb*
1. in an exact manner: 'it is important to measure the ingredients *exactly*'.
2. completely: 'you may do *exactly* as you please'.
Word Family: **exactness**, **exactitude** (*say* eg–**zak**ti–tewd), *nouns*, the quality of being exact; **exactingly**, *adverb*; **exactingness**, *noun*.
[Latin *exactus* exacted, exact]

exaggerate (*say* eg–**zaj**a–rate) *verb*
to represent something beyond its true limits, value or size.
exaggeration *noun*
a) the act of exaggerating. b) a statement which exaggerates: 'I think her description of the argument was an *exaggeration*'.
Word Family: **exaggerator**, *noun*.
[EX– + Latin *aggerare* to heap up]

exalt (*say* eg–**zawlt**) *verb*
1. to lift or raise in rank, quality, honour, etc.
2. to praise highly.
3. to elate or excite.
Word Family: **exaltation**, *noun*, a) the act of exalting, b) a rapture or excitement, often unnatural.
[EX– + Latin *altus* high]

exam *noun*
(*informal*) an examination.

examine (*say* eg–**zam**min) *verb*
1. to inspect or test carefully.
2. to test the knowledge, qualifications, etc. of a person by questions or exercises.
examination *noun*
1. the act of examining.
2. a written or oral test of a person's understanding and knowledge of a subject.
Word Family: **examinee**, *noun*, a person who is examined; **examiner**, *noun*, a person who examines.
[Latin *examinare* to weigh, test]

example (*say* eg–**zahm**–p'l) *noun*
1. something which is seen to represent the qualities of other things in its group or kind: 'this house is a good *example* of Victorian architecture'.
2. something to be learnt from: 'let her silly mistake be an *example* to you'.
3. a problem or exercise used to illustrate a general principle or set of rules.
[Latin *exemplum* a sample]

exasperate (*say* eg–**zah**spa–rate) *verb*
to irritate or provoke intensely: 'we were *exasperated* at missing the second bus in a row'.
Word Family: **exasperatedly**, *adverb*; **exasperatingly**, *adverb*, in a manner which exasperates; **exasperation**, *noun*.
[EX– + Latin *asper* rough]

excavate (*say* **eks**–k'vate) *verb*
a) to make a hole in. b) to uncover by digging: 'several ancient, glazed bowls were *excavated* at the building site'.
excavation *noun*
1. the act of excavating
2. a hole or site being excavated: 'an archaeological *excavation*'.
Word Family: **excavator**, *noun*, a person or thing that excavates.
[EX– + Latin *cavus* hollow]

exceed (*say* ek–**seed**) *verb*
to go beyond the fixed or expected limits of: 'the success of the party far *exceeded* our hopes'.
Word Family: **exceeding**, *adjective*, great or extreme; **exceeding**, **exceedingly**, *adverbs*, extremely.
[Latin *excedere* to go beyond]

excel (*say* ek–**sel**) *verb*
(**excelled**, **excelling**)
to be unusually talented or better than others: 'she *excels* in all the science subjects'.

excellence (*say* **eks**a–l'nce) *noun*
1. a) the quality of excelling. b) a superior or excellent quality: 'the *excellence* of the local hotel surprised many international tourists'.
2. (*capital*) Excellency.
[Latin *excellens* surpassing]

Excellency *noun*
also called **Excellence**
a form of address used to certain officials, such as governors, ambassadors, etc.

excellent (*say* **eks**a–l'nt) *adjective*
having unusual and superior merit: 'the restaurant's *excellent* wines compensate for its mediocre food'.
Word Family: **excellently**, *adverb*.

except (*say* ek–**sept**) *preposition*
with the exception of: 'I like all card games *except* bridge'.

except *conjunction*
with the exception: 'they look alike, *except* that he is taller than she is'.
except *verb*
to leave out.
[Latin *exceptus* removed]

exception (*say* ek–**sep**–sh'n) *noun*
1. the act of leaving out or excluding.
2. something which is left out of or does not conform to a general rule, etc.
3. an opposition or objection: 'we all took *exception* to her unfair criticism'.
Word Family: **exceptionable,** *adjective,* open to exception or objection; **exceptional,** *adjective,* unusual or extraordinary; **exceptionally,** *adverb.*

excerpt (*say* **ek**–serpt) *noun*
an extract from a book, speech, etc.
Word Family: **excerpt** (*say* ek–**serpt**), *verb.*
[Latin *excerptus* picked out]

excess (*say* ek–**sess**) *noun*
1. the condition or fact of exceeding what is usual, necessary or approved: 'avoid *excess* in all things'.
2. an extreme or unrestrained quantity, degree, extent, etc.: 'an *excess* of enthusiasm'.
3. a) the amount by which one thing exceeds another: 'an *excess* of credits over debits'. b) an amount which is left over or greater than is necessary or wanted: 'an *excess* of dairy products'.
4. *Insurance:* a stated amount of money which must be paid by an insured person before a claim may be made on a policy.
Word Family: **excess,** *adjective,* more than is usual, necessary or approved.

excessive *adjective*
extreme or beyond the usual limit: 'her plumpness is due to *excessive* eating'.
Word Family: **excessively,** *adverb;* **excessiveness,** *noun.*

exchange *verb*
to give or receive something in return for another: 'the family *exchanged* gifts on Christmas Day'.
exchange *noun*
1. the act of exchanging: 'their *exchange* of angry words was heard by all the neighbours'.
2. anything which is exchanged for something else.
3. a central office or building which connects and controls: 'a telephone *exchange*'.
4. a place for buying, selling or exchanging goods, especially securities, shares, etc.: 'a stock *exchange*'.
5. the changing of money from the currency of one country to the currency of another, e.g. changing pounds sterling to dollars.
Word Family: **exchangeable,** *adjective,* able to be exchanged or returned.

exchange rate
see RATE OF EXCHANGE.

exchequer (*say* eks–**chekka**) *noun*
(*sometimes capital*) the treasury of a country, state or organization.

excise (1) (*say* **ek**–size) *noun*
a) a tax on the production, sale, etc. of certain goods, such as tobacco. b) (*capital*) a public service department which organizes and collects such taxes.

excise (2) (*say* ek–**size**) *verb*
to cut out or off: 'the censor *excised* several passages from the book'.
Word Family: **excision** (*say* ek–**sizh**'n), *noun.*

excitable (*say* ek–**site**–a–b'l) *adjective*
easily excited.
Word Family: **excitably,** *adverb;* **excitableness, excitability,** *nouns.*

excitation (*say* eksi–**tay**–sh'n) *noun*
1. a) the act of exciting. b) anything which excites.
2. *Physics:* the addition of energy to a nucleus, atom or molecule.

excite (*say* ek–**site**) *verb*
1. to arouse, stir or stimulate, especially to interest or action: 'she was *excited* about her recent holiday in Asia'.
2. *Physics:* to add energy to a nucleus, atom or molecule.
excitement *noun*
1. the state of being excited.
2. anything which excites: 'their first visit to the airport was a great *excitement* for the children'.
Word Family: **excitingly,** *adverb.*
[Latin *excitare* to rouse]

exclaim (*say* eks–**klame**) *verb*
to speak out suddenly and loudly, as from surprise or pain.
Word Family: **exclamation,** *noun,* a cry or other loud expression; **exclamatory** (*say* eks–**klamma**–tree), *adjective,* using or expressing an exclamation.

exclamation mark
a punctuation mark (!), used to indicate strong emphasis. *Example*: 'stop thief!'.

exclude (*say* eks-**klood**) *verb*
1. to leave out: 'I haven't *excluded* that possibility entirely'.
2. to prevent: 'she was *excluded* from membership'.
Word Family: **exclusion** (*say* eks-**kloo**-*zh*'n), *noun*, the act of excluding.

exclusive (*say* eks-**kloo**siv) *adjective*
1. belonging to a single individual, group, source, etc.: a) 'we have *exclusive* rights to the book'; b) 'an *exclusive* interview with Mae West'.
Usages:
a) 'he belongs to an *exclusive* golf club' (= fashionable, select).
b) 'I must ask for your *exclusive* attention during the lecture' (= whole, undivided).
2. incompatible: 'mutually *exclusive* ideas'.
3. not including: 'this is the estimated price, *exclusive* of delivery costs'.
Word Family: **exclusively**, *adverb*; **exclusiveness**, *noun*.

excommunicate
(*say* eks-k'**mewni**-kate) *verb*
Religion: to cut off from membership of a church.
Word Family: **excommunication**, *noun*; **excommunicate**, *adjective*, *noun*.

excrement (*say* **eks**kra-m'nt) *noun*
any waste matter expelled by an organism, especially faeces.
Word Family: **excremental**, *adjective*.

excrescence (*say* eks-**kress**'nce) *noun*
any additional growth or outgrowth, especially an abnormal one.

excrete (*say* eks-**kreet**) *verb*
to discharge or expel from a body, especially harmful or waste matter.
excreta *plural noun*
any matter, such as sweat, which is excreted from a body.
Word Family: **excretion**, *noun*, a) the act of excreting, b) anything which is excreted; **excretory**, *adjective*.
[Latin *excretus* sifted out]

excruciating
(*say* ek-**skroo**-shee-ayting) *adjective*
causing intense pain or suffering: 'the doctors could provide no relief for his *excruciating* pain'.
Word Family: **excruciatingly**, *adverb*.
[Latin *excruciare* to torture]

exculpate (*say* **eks**-kul-pate) *verb*
to free from blame or guilt.
Word Family: **exculpation**, *noun*; **exculpatory** (*say* eks-**kul**pa-tree), *adjective*.
[EX- + Latin *culpa* blame]

excursion (*say* eks-**kersh**'n) *noun*
1. a short trip or outing.
2. a deviation or digression.
Word Family: **excursive**, *adjective*, tending to ramble or wander.
[Latin *excursio* a running out]

excuse (*say* eks-**kewz**) *verb*
1. to forgive or overlook a fault, etc.: 'please *excuse* me for being so late'.
Usage: 'his unhappiness does not *excuse* his rudeness' (= justify).
2. to seek pardon or forgiveness: 'she *excused* herself for being so late'.
excuse from, a) 'she was *excused from* the room' (= allowed to leave); b) 'we were *excused from* the meeting' (= given permission not to attend).
excuse (*say* ex-**kewce**) *noun*
a reason given to explain or defend a fault, etc.
Usage: 'that is a poor *excuse* for a coat' (= example).
Word Family: **excusable**, *adjective*, worthy of being excused.

exeat (*say* **eksi**-at) *noun*
permission to leave, especially for a brief absence from school.
[Latin, let him go out]

execrable (*say* **eksikra**-b'l) *adjective*
very bad or detestable: 'his dirty jokes are in *execrable* taste'.
Word Family: **execrably**, *adverb*.

execrate (*say* **eksi**-krate) *verb*
1. to denounce violently or curse: 'the bishop *execrated* all such abominable practices'.
2. to detest.
Word Family: **execration**, *noun*, a) the act of denouncing or cursing, b) a curse, c) extreme loathing.
[EX- + Latin *sacra* the sacred rites]

execute (*say* **eksi**-kewt) *verb*
1. to do, accomplish or perform: 'the diver *executed* a perfect somersault in midair'.
2. to put to death as legal punishment.
3. *Law:* to carry out the terms of a will, etc.
execution *noun*
1. the carrying out of a task: 'he was praised for his prompt *execution* of the command'.
2. the putting to death of a convicted criminal.

Word Family: **executioner**, *noun*, a public official appointed to perform the punishment of execution.
[Latin *exsecutio* a following up]

executive (*say* eg-**zek**-yoo-tiv) *adjective*
having authority or power to decide, direct or administer: 'the company has promoted him to an *executive* position'.
executive *noun*
1. a person with administrative power, e.g. in a company.
2. the part of an organization which puts policies into effect, such as the Cabinet in a government.

executor (*say* eg-**zek**-yoota) *noun*
Law: a person appointed to carry out the instructions in a will.
Word Family: **executorial** (*say* egzek-yoo-**tawr**iul), *adjective*; **executorship**, *noun*; **executrix** (*say* eg-**zek**-yoo-triks), *noun*, a female executor.

exegesis (*say* eksi-**jee**sis) *noun*
plural is **exegeses** (*say* eksi-**jee**-seez)
a detailed or critical interpretation.
Word Family: **exegetic** (*say* eksi-**jet**tik), **exegetical**, *adjective*.
[Greek]

exemplar (*say* eg-**zem**pla) *noun*
a typical example or model, especially an original form.

exemplary (*say* eg-**zem**pla-ree) *adjective*
1. serving as a model or example worthy of imitation: 'the policeman won a medal for *exemplary* bravery'.
2. serving as a warning: 'an *exemplary* punishment'.

exemplify (*say* eg-**zem**pli-fie) *verb*
(**exemplified, exemplifying**)
a) to illustrate by using examples. b) to be an example of: 'Buddhism *exemplifies* the Eastern belief that life is full of suffering'.
Word Family: **exemplification**, *noun*.

exempt (*say* eg-**zempt**) *verb*
to free or release from a duty, obligation, etc.: 'he was *exempted* from military service because of his religious beliefs'.
Word Family: **exempt**, *adjective*; **exemption**, *noun*.
[Latin *exemptus* removed]

exercise (*say* **ek**sa-size) *noun*
1. (*usually plural*) any activity performed as a means of training, physical conditioning, etc.
2. any lesson, problem, etc. designed to train some particular function or skill: 'maths *exercises*'.
3. a putting into action or effect: 'in the *exercise* of his duties the judge was always impartial'.
exercise *verb*
to put through practice or exercises in order to train, improve, etc.: 'she *exercised* the horse for several hours before the competition'.
Usages:
a) 'I must *exercise* my powers as chairman and close the meeting' (= put into effect or use).
b) 'those boys *exercise* too much influence over the class' (= exert).
c) 'he *exercised* all his duties most successfully' (= performed).
[Latin *exercere* to train or practise]

exert (*say* eg-**zert**) *verb*
to apply or put into force: 'the community *exerted* pressure on the local council'.
Word Family: **exertion**, *noun*, any vigorous effort or action.
[Latin *exsertus* put forth]

ex gratia (*say* eks **gray**-shee-a)
as an act of grace although there is no legal obligation: 'he received an *ex gratia* lump sum on his early retirement'.
[Latin, from favour]

exhale (*say* eks-**hale**) *verb*
to breathe out or give off.
Word Family: **exhalation** (*say* eksa-**lay**-sh'n), *noun*, a) the act of exhaling, b) something which is exhaled.

exhaust (*say* eg-**zawst**) *verb*
to use up or drain completely: 'they *exhausted* the supply of drink'.
Usages:
a) 'the athlete was *exhausted* by the race' (= drained of strength).
b) 'we had *exhausted* the topic of our holiday and began to talk of other things' (= discussed thoroughly).
exhaust *noun*
a) the hot gases which are discharged from an internal combustion engine.
b) the pipe or other outlet through which the hot gases are discharged.
exhaustion *noun*
1. the act of exhausting: 'the *exhaustion* of our supplies did not take long'.
2. the state of being exhausted: 'to suffer from *exhaustion*'.

exhaustive *adjective*
extremely thorough: 'an *exhaustive* inquiry into the murder will take many months'.
Word Family: **exhaustively,** *adverb*; **exhaustiveness,** *noun*; **exhaustible,** *adjective*, able to be exhausted.
[Latin *exhaustus* drained dry]

exhibit (*say* eg–**zibbit**) *verb*
to show or display: 'the artist has *exhibited* his works throughout Europe as well as Australia'.
exhibit *noun*
any object or collection of objects which are exhibited.
Word Family: **exhibitor, exhibiter,** *noun*, a person who exhibits.

exhibition (*say* eksi–**bish**'n) *noun*
1. a public show or display: 'an art *exhibition*'.
2. a scholarship.
make an exhibition of oneself, to act in a foolish or ridiculous way.
[Latin *exhibitus* produced in public]

exhibitionist (*say* eksi–**bish**'n–ist) *noun*
a person who behaves and acts so as to attract attention.
Word Family: **exhibitionism,** *noun.*

exhilarate (*say* eg–**zilla**–rate) *verb*
to make lively or cheerful: 'we were all *exhilarated* by the sea air'.
Word Family: **exhilaratingly,** *adverb*; **exhilaration,** *noun.*
[EX– + Latin *hilaris* cheerful]

exhort (*say* eg–**zort**) *verb*
to urge or request earnestly.
exhortation *noun*
a) the act of exhorting. b) any sincere request or persuasion.
Word Family: **exhortatory** (*say* egzor–tayta–ree), **exhortative,** *adjectives.*

exhume (*say* eks–**yoom**) *verb*
to disinter a dead body for examination.
Word Family: **exhumation,** *noun.*
[EX– + Latin *humus* ground]

exigency (*say* eks–**ij**'n–see) *noun*
1. a) urgency. b) an emergency or urgent situation.
2. (*usually plural*) the demands or requirements of a particular occasion or situation.
[Latin *exigens* exacting (payment)]

exile *noun*
a) a long absence from one's home or country, often imposed as a punishment. b) a person separated from his home or country in this way.
Word Family: **exile,** *verb.*
[EX– + Latin *solum* soil, country]

exist (*say* eg–**zist**) *verb*
to have life or reality: 'does God *exist*?'.
Usage: 'this species *exists* only in the mountainous regions of South America' (= occurs).
[Latin *exsistere* to come forth]

existence (*say* eg–**zist**'nce) *noun*
1. the state or fact of existing or being: 'I don't believe in the *existence* of ghosts'.
2. a way of being or living: 'he lives the lonely *existence* of a friendless old man'.
Word Family: **existent,** *adjective*, having existence or reality.

existentialism (*say* egzi–**stensha**–lizm) *noun*
Philosophy: any of various systems of thought emphasizing the loneliness of the individual, and his freedom and sole responsibility in making personal choices.
Word Family: **existentialist,** *noun*; **existential, existentialist,** *adjectives.*

exit *noun*
1. a way out.
2. a departure or going out, such as an actor's departure from the stage.
exit *verb*
to go out.
[Latin, he goes out]

exodus (*say* **eksa**–dus) *noun*
the departure of a large number of people.
[Greek, a going out]

ex-officio (*say* eks–o–**fishio**) *adjective*
because of one's office or position.
[Latin]

exonerate (*say* eg–**zonna**–rate) *verb*
to set free from blame or responsibility.
Word Family: **exoneration,** *noun.*
[EX– + Latin *onere* from a burden]

exorbitant (*say* eg–**zorbi**–t'nt) *adjective*
too great or extreme: 'the *exorbitant* price of meat'.
Word Family: **exorbitantly,** *adverb.*
[EX– + Latin *orbita* a rut]

exorcize (*say* **eksor**–size) **exorcise** *verb*
to drive out an evil spirit by religious ceremonies.
exorcism (*say* **eksor**–sizm) *noun*
a) the act of exorcizing. b) the words or ceremony used.
Word Family: **exorcist,** *noun*, a person who exorcizes.

[EX- + Greek *orkizein* to give the oath to]

exoskeleton (*say* ekso-**skelli**-t'n) *noun*
Biology: a protective, usually hard, outer covering, such as the shell of a tortoise, etc.
[Greek *exo* outside + SKELETON]

exothermic (*say* ekso-**thermik**) *adjective*
Chemistry: of or relating to a chemical reaction in which heat is produced: 'burning is an *exothermic* reaction'. Compare ENDOTHERMIC.
[Greek *exo* outside + *thermé* heat]

exotic (*say* eg-**zottik**) *adjective*
1. foreign or introduced from another country.
2. strikingly different or fascinating.
Word Family: **exotically**, *adverb.*
[Greek *exotikos* foreign]

expand *verb*
to make or become larger: 'the company *expanded* its staff to cope with all the work'.
Usages:
a) 'please *expand* your story so that it makes sense' (= express in more detail).
b) 'his face *expanded* into a broad, welcoming smile' (= spread).
[Latin *expandere* to spread out]

expanse *noun*
a large or widespread area.

expansion (*say* eks-**pan**-sh'n) *noun*
a) the act of expanding or enlarging. b) the amount by which something is expanded. c) any expanded or enlarged part.

expansive *adjective*
1. having a wide range or extent: 'the *expansive* deserts of Africa'.
2. free or open: 'her *expansive* manner makes all guests feel welcome'.

expatiate (*say* eks-**payshi**-ate) *verb*
to speak or write more fully: 'he *expatiated* on that theme for several hours'.
[EX- + Latin *spatiari* to walk]

expatriate (*say* eks-**patri**-it) *noun*
a person living outside his native country.
Word Family: **expatriate** (*say* eks-**patri**-ate), *verb*, to leave or be forced to leave one's native country; **expatriation**, *noun.*
[EX- + Latin *patria* native land]

expect *verb*
1. to believe that a particular thing will take place: 'we *expect* him to come before lunch'.
2. to suppose or presume: 'I *expect* that you are right'.
expectant *adjective*
full of anticipation: 'an *expectant* silence filled the theatre'.
Usage: 'an *expectant* mother' (= pregnant).
Word Family: **expectantly**, *adverb.*
[Latin *exspectare* to wait]

expectation *noun*
also called **expectancy**
1. the act or state of expecting: 'we waited eagerly in *expectation* of a delicious dinner'.
2. anything which is expected: 'the concert did not live up to our *expectations*'.

expectorate (*say* eks-**pek**ta-rate) *verb*
to cough or spit in order to remove matter from the lungs or throat.
Word Family: **expectoration**, *noun*; **expectorant**, *noun*, a medicine which causes a person to expectorate.
[Latin *ex pectore* from the chest]

expedient (*say* eks-**peedi**'nt) *adjective*
1. suitable or advisable under the circumstances: 'it is *expedient* to work near home'.
2. serving one's interest or advantage, rather than what is right: 'though he knew his client was guilty, it was *expedient* for the lawyer to win the case'.
Word Family: **expedient**, *noun*, anything which is expedient; **expediently**, *adverb*; **expediency**, **expedience**, *noun*, the quality of being expedient.
[Latin *expediens* being advantageous]

expedite (*say* **eks**pa-dite) *verb*
to hasten the progress of.
Word Family: **expeditious** (*say* ekspa-**dish**us), *adjective*, quick or prompt; **expeditiously**, *adverb.*
[Latin *expedire* to extricate]

expedition (*say* ekspa-**dish**'n) *noun*
1. a) a trip made for a special purpose, such as to explore. b) the people on such a trip.
2. a promptness in accomplishing something.
Word Family: **expeditionary**, *adjective*, relating to an expedition.

expel *verb*
(expelled, expelling)
to force or drive out.

Usage: 'John was *expelled* from school for smoking in class' (= forced to leave permanently).
Word Family: **expulsion** (*say* eks-**pul**-sh'n), *noun*; **expulsive,** *adjective,* tending to expel.

expend *verb*
to use up or spend.
[Latin *expendere* to weigh out]

expendable *adjective*
1. capable of being expended.
2. able to be sacrificed to achieve an aim.

expenditure (*say* eks-**pen**di-cher) *noun*
a) the act of expending. b) the amount which is expended.

expense *noun*
1. the expenditure.
2. (*often plural*) the money spent, needed or provided for a particular purpose: 'travelling *expenses*'.
Usage: 'running a car is a great *expense*' (= cause of expenditure).
at the expense of, at the cost of.

expense account
a list of expenses incurred by an employee, such as hotel bills when travelling, paid by an employer as well as the usual salary or claimed as a tax deduction.

expensive *adjective*
very costly.
Word Family: **expensively**, *adverb*; **expensiveness**, *noun.*

experience (*say* eks-**peer**i'nce) *noun*
a) any event or circumstance which one has lived through, encountered or observed. b) any skill or knowledge gained in such circumstances.
Word Family: **experience**, *verb*; **experiential** (*say* eks-peeri-**en**-sh'l), *adjective,* of or derived from experience.

experiment (*say* eks-**perri**-m'nt) *noun*
a test to show a known truth, examine a hypothesis or discover something unknown.
Word Family: **experiment**, *verb*; **experimental**, *adjective*; **experimentally**, *adverb*; **experimentation**, *noun*, the process of making experiments; **experimenter**, *noun*, a person who experiments.
[Latin *experimentum* proof from experience]

expert *noun*
a person who has special knowledge or training.
Word Family: **expert**, *adjective*; **expertly**, *adverb*; **expertise** (*say* eksper-**teez**), *noun*, the skill or knowledge of an expert.

expiate (*say* **ek**spi-ate) *verb*
to make amends for.
Word Family: **expiation**, *noun*; **expiatory**, *adjective,* able or intended to make amends.
[Latin *expiare* to purify]

expire *verb*
1. to come to an end: 'the contract *expired* last week'.
Usage: 'the old man *expired* in his home' (= died).
2. to breathe out.
Word Family: **expiry** (*say* eks-**pie**-ree), **expiration** (*say* ekspi-**ray**-sh'n), *nouns.*
[EX- + Latin *spirare* to breathe]

explain *verb*
to make clear and understandable: 'he *explained* the meaning of the poem'.
Word Family: **explanation** (*say* ekspla-**nay**-sh'n), *noun*; **explanatory** (*say* eks-**planna**-tree), *adjective,* serving to explain; **explicable,** *adjective,* able to be explained.
[Latin *explanare* to make level or plain]

expletive (*say* eks-**plee**tiv) *noun*
an exclamation, usually an oath.

explication (*say* ekspli-**kay**-sh'n) *noun*
an explanation or interpretation of a piece of writing.
Word Family: **explicate**, *verb.*
[Latin *explicatus* unfolded]

explicit (*say* eks-**pliss**it) *adjective*
being clearly and precisely expressed.
Word Family: **explicitly**, *adverb.*

explode *verb*
Word Family: see EXPLOSION.

exploit (1) (*say* **eks**-ployt) *noun*
a notable act.

exploit (2) (*say* eks-**ployt**) *verb*
to use for profit or personal gain.
Word Family: **exploitation**, *noun*, the act of exploiting; **exploiter**, *noun*; **exploitative** (*say* eks-**ployta**-tiv), *adjective,* serving to exploit; **exploitable**, *adjective.*

explore *verb*
1. to travel for the purpose of discovery.
2. to examine closely: 'we *explored* all possibilities before reaching a decision'.
Word Family: **explorer**, *noun*, a person who explores; **exploration** (*say*

ekspla-**ray**-sh'n), *noun*; **exploratory** (*say* eks-**plorra**-tree), *adjective*.
[Latin *explorare* to investigate]

explosion (*say* eks-**plo**-*zh*'n) *noun*
1. a) a violent and rapid release of energy. b) the loud sound accompanying this.
2. a sudden outburst, increase, etc.: 'a population *explosion*'.
Word Family: **explode**, *verb*.

explosive (*say* eks-**plo**-siv) *adjective*
a) of or relating to an explosion. b) tending to explode.
explosive *noun*
a substance capable of undergoing rapid chemical change, producing enormous quantities of gas relative to the volume of substance.
Word Family: **explosively**, *adverb*.

exponent *noun*
1. a person who expounds, explains or interprets.
2. a person who represents or symbolizes something: 'I am an *exponent* of the free enterprise system'.
3. *Maths:* a symbol placed above and to the right of a number, indicating the power to which it is to be raised, as the 2 in x^2. Also called an **index** or a **power**.
[Latin *exponens* displaying]

exponential (*say* ekspa-**nen**-sh'l) *adjective*
1. *Maths:* relating to an exponent, especially of the constant *e* (2.71828 . . .).
2. increasing more and more rapidly.

export *verb*
to send goods to another country.
export *noun*
a) the act of exporting. b) anything which is exported.
Word Family: **exporter**, *noun*, a person who exports; **exportation**, *noun*; **exportable**, *adjective*, able to be exported.
[Latin *exportare* to convey out]

expose *verb*
1. to uncover, lay open or reveal.
2. *Photography:* to subject a film, etc. to the action of light.

exposé (*say* eks-**po**-zay) *noun*
a public exposure, expecially of something discreditable.
[French]

exposition (*say* ekspa-**zish**'n) *noun*
1. a detailed explanation.
2. a public exhibition.
Word Family: **expository** (*say* eks-**pozzi**-tree), *adjective*, serving to explain.
[French, exhibition]

expostulate (*say* eks-**poss**-tew-late) *verb*
to remonstrate or protest.
Word Family: **expostulation**, *noun*; **expostulatory**, *adjective*.

exposure (*say* ex-**po***zh*er) *noun*
1. the act of exposing: 'we delighted in the *exposure* of the plot'.
2. the effects of being exposed, especially to the weather: 'the lost child was found alive but suffering from *exposure*'.
3. a position in relation to direction or weather: 'the house has a northern *exposure*'.
4. *Photography:* the length of time the film, etc. is exposed to light.
exposure meter
also called a **light meter**
Photography: an instrument in or for a camera which indicates the setting of the diaphragm and shutter, to allow the film to be correctly exposed to the light.

expound *verb*
1. to state in detail.
2. to explain.
Word Family: **expounder**, *noun*.

express *verb*
1. to show or reveal, usually by putting into words: 'he has difficulty in *expressing* his feelings'.
Usage: '*express* this fraction as a decimal' (= represent).
2. to send fast or by special delivery.
3. to press: 'to make wine one must *express* the juice from grapes'.
express *adjective*
1. definite or explicit: 'the money is set aside for an *express* purpose, so we must not spend it'.
2. fast: 'an *express* train'.
express *noun*
1. a fast train.
2. a speedy system of sending money, parcels, etc.
Word Family: **express**, *adverb*, fast; **expressly**, *adverb*, explicitly; **expressible**, *adjective*, able to be put into words.
[Latin *expressus* pressed out]

expression (*say* eks-**presh**'n) *noun*
1. the act of expressing: 'an *expression* of opinion'.
2. an indication of feeling, as on the face, in the voice, etc.: 'even before

he spoke his sad *expression* told us something was wrong'.

3. *Maths:* a symbol, or collection of symbols, used to represent a quantity.

expressionism (*say* eks-**presh**'n-izm) *noun*
a style of painting using simple exaggeration and distortions of line and colour to achieve emotional impact.
Word Family: **expressionist**, *adjective, noun.*

expressive *adjective*
1. serving to express.
2. full of expression or feeling: 'an *expressive* face'.
Word Family: **expressively**, *adverb*; **expressiveness**, *noun.*

expropriate (*say* eks-**pro**-priate) *verb*
to take or acquire from another, e.g. for public use: 'the police *expropriated* his house during the flood and used it as a soup kitchen'.
Word Family: **expropriation**, *noun*; **expropriator**, *noun*, a person who expropriates.
[EX- + Latin *proprium* property]

expulsion *noun*
Word Family: see EXPEL.

expunge (*say* eks-**punj**) *verb*
to rub out or erase.

expurgate (*say* **eks**pa-gate) *verb*
to amend by removing offensive parts, such as obscene passages in a book.
Word Family: **expurgation**, *noun.*
[EX- + Latin *purgare* to cleanse]

exquisite (*say* eks-**kwizz**it *or* **eks**-kwizzit) *adjective*
1. having great beauty or excellence.
2. intense or keen: '*exquisite* pleasure'.
Word Family: **exquisitely**, *adverb*; **exquisiteness**, *noun.*
[Latin *exquisitus* sought out]

extant *adjective*
still existing.

extemporaneous
(*say* eks-tempa-**ray**-nee-us) *adjective*
impromptu or without preparation: 'an *extemporaneous* speech'.
Word Family: **extempore** (*say* eks-**tempa**-ree), *adjective, adverb*; **extemporize, extemporise**, *verb*, to do something impromptu; **extemporaneously**, *adverb.*
[Latin *ex tempore* on the spur of the moment]

extend *verb*
to spread or stretch out: 'the hills seemed to *extend* for ever'.
Usages:
a) 'she had to *extend* herself to finish the race' (= exert).
b) 'they *extended* their hospitality to the wounded soldier' (= offered).

extended play
short form is **E.P.**
a 45 r.p.m. 7 inch (17·46 cm) record with extra grooves to extend its playing time. Compare SINGLE and LONG PLAY.

extension (*say* eks-**ten**-sh'n) *noun*
1. a) the act of extending. b) the state of being extended.
2. an additional part or facility: a) 'we built an *extension* to the house'; b) 'our telephone has an *extension* upstairs'.
[EX- + Latin *tensus* stretched]

extensive *adjective*
large or widespread: 'an *extensive* search was made for the missing child'.
Word Family: **extensively**, *adverb.*

extent *noun*
1. the range or scope of anything: 'the *extent* of his power is limited by the government'.
2. a length, area or volume of something: 'an *extent* of land by the river'.

extenuate (*say* eks-**ten**-yoo-ate) *verb*
to make a fault, crime, etc. appear less serious: 'nothing can *extenuate* his terrible behaviour'.
Word Family: **extenuation**, *noun.*
[Latin *extenuatus* made thin]

exterior (*say* eks-**teer**ia) *adjective*
outside: a) '*exterior* decoration'; b) '*exterior* influences'.
exterior *noun*
the outer surface or view: 'the *exterior* of the house is in bad repair'.
[Latin, outer]

exterminate (*say* eks-**termi**-nate) *verb*
to destroy completely: 'poison has *exterminated* thousands of rabbits'.
Word Family: **extermination**, *noun*, the act of exterminating; **exterminator**, *noun.*
[Latin *exterminare* to expel outside the boundaries]

external *adjective*
of or relating to the outside or outer part: a) 'the *external* appearance is good'; b) 'he has been subject to *external* pressures'; c) '*external* students study by correspondence'.
Usage: 'who is in charge of *external* affairs?' (= foreign).

Word Family: **externals**, *plural noun*, any non-essential or superficial aspects, circumstances, etc.; **externally**, *adverb*; **externalize**, **externalise**, *verb*, to make or treat as external.

extinct *adjective*
1. no longer in existence: 'dinosaurs are now *extinct*'.
2. (of a volcano) no longer capable of erupting. Compare DORMANT.
Word Family: **extinction**, *noun*.

extinguish (*say* eks-**ting**-wish) *verb*
to put out or bring to an end: a) 'we *extinguished* the fire'; b) 'all hope was *extinguished* when the crashed plane was found'.

extinguisher *noun*
short form of **fire-extinguisher**
any of various portable appliances which spray liquid or foam under pressure, used to put out fires.

extirpate (*say* **eks**ta-pate) *verb*
to destroy completely: 'he hoped to *extirpate* social injustices'.
Word Family: **extirpation**, *noun*.
[Latin *ex stirpe* by the root]

extol (*say* eks-**tole**) *verb*
(**extolled**, **extolling**)
to praise highly: 'he *extolled* the virtues of hard work'.
[Latin *extollere* to lift up]

extort *verb*
to obtain money, information, etc. by the use of threats or violence.
extortion *noun*
1. the act of extorting.
2. *Law:* the crime of using one's official position to obtain money, etc. to which one is not entitled
Word Family: **extortionist**, *noun*; **extortionate**, *adjective*.
[Latin *extortus* twisted out]

extra *adjective*
more than is usual or necessary: 'the employees asked for an *extra* £15 a week'.
extra *noun*
1. anything which is additional.
Usage: 'the newspaper put out an *extra* to cover the murder story' (= special edition).
2. *Films:* a person hired for a very small part, such as a member of a large crowd.
3. *Cricket:* any run gained by the batting side other than by hitting the ball, e.g. by a wide, bye, etc.
Word Family: **extra**, *adverb*.

extra-
a prefix meaning outside or beyond, as in *extraordinary*.

extract (*say* eks-**trakt**) *verb*
1. to get out with difficulty or by force: a) 'the dentist *extracted* his tooth'; b) 'the police *extracted* information from the suspect'.
2. to obtain or derive: 'he *extracts* great pleasure from reading'.
extract (*say* **eks**-trakt) *noun*
1. anything which is extracted.
2. a passage taken from a book, etc.
3. an essence.
Word Family: **extractor**, *noun*, a person or thing that extracts.
[Latin *extractus* pulled out]

extraction (*say* eks-**trak**-sh'n) *noun*
1. a) the act of extracting. b) the state of being extracted.
2. descent or lineage: 'he is of Russian *extraction*'.
3. *Chemistry:* the separation of a part from a mixture usually by using a solvent which selectively dissolves the required part.

extracurricular
(*say* ekstra-kur**rik**-yoola) *adjective*
outside the usual curriculum.

extradite (*say* **ek**stra-dite) *verb*
to hand over a criminal to another country or authority.
Word Family: **extradition** (*say* ekstra-**dish**'n), *noun*.

extramural (*say* ekstra-**mew**-r'l) *adjective*
(of university studies) for non-resident students.
[Latin *extra muros* outside the walls]

extraneous (*say* **ex-traynee**-us) *adjective*
not relevant or essential.
Word Family: **extraneously**, *adverb*; **extraneousness**, *noun*.

extraordinary (*say* eks-**trord**'n-ree) *adjective*
unusual or remarkable.
Word Family: **extraordinarily**, *adverb*.

extrapolate (*say* eks-**trappa**-late) *verb*
to estimate an unknown quantity by projecting from the basis of what is already known. Compare INTERPOLATE.
Word Family: **extrapolation**, *noun*.
[EXTRA- + (inter)POLATE]

extrasensory *adjective*
beyond the range of normal senses.

extrasensory perception
any knowledge or experience gained without the use of normal senses, e.g. by clairvoyance.

extravagant (*say* eks–**travva**–g'nt) *adjective*
1. wasteful, especially with money.
2. exceeding reasonable limits: a) '*extravagant* praise'; b) '*extravagant* prices'.
Word Family: **extravagantly**, *adverb*; **extravagance**, *noun.*
[EXTRA– + Latin *vagans* straying]

extravaganza (*say* eks–travva–**ganza**) *noun*
an elaborate, spectacular entertainment.
[Italian]

extravert *noun*
see EXTROVERT.

extreme *adjective*
1. of the highest degree: 'we did not realize we were in *extreme* danger'.
2. going beyond the usual limits: 'an *extreme* fashion'.
Usage: 'the *extreme* edge of the paddock' (= outermost).
Word Family: **extreme**, *noun*, a) the highest degree, b) the utmost length; **extremely**, *adverb*, very.
[Latin *extremus* outermost]

extreme unction
Religion: see UNCTION.

extremist (*say* eks–**treem**ist) *noun*
a person who goes to extremes, especially in politics.
Word Family: **extremism**, *noun.*

extremity (*say* eks–**tremm**i–tee) *noun*
1. the extreme part or end of anything.
2. (*plural*) the ends of the limbs.
3. an extreme degree: 'the *extremity* of joy'.

extricate (*say* ekstri–kate) *verb*
to free from difficulty or entanglement: 'he *extricated* the animal from the trap'.
Word Family: **extrication**, *noun*; **extricable**, *adjective.*
[EX– + Latin *tricae* hindrances]

extrinsic (*say* eks–**trin**zik) *adjective*
1. not essential or inherent. Compare INTRINSIC.
2. external.
Word Family: **extrinsically**, *adverb.*
[Latin *extrinsecus* from outside]

extrovert, extravert *noun*
Psychology: a person interested chiefly in other people and the world around him rather than his own thoughts and feelings. Compare INTROVERT.
Word Family: **extroversion** (*say* ekstra–**ver**–*zh*'n), *noun.*
[EXTRA– + Latin *vertere* to turn]

extrude *verb*
1. to force or push out.
2. to shape metal, plastic, etc. by forcing it through a die.
Word Family: **extrusion** (*say* eks–**troo**–*zh*'n), *noun.*
[EX– + Latin *trudere* to push]

exuberant (*say* eg–**zoo**ba–r'nt) *adjective*
unrestrained and vigorous.
Word Family: **exuberance**, *noun*; **exuberantly**, *adverb.*
[EX– + Latin *uberans* fruitful]

exude (*say* egz–**yood**) *verb*
to ooze: 'gum *exuded* from the cut branch of the tree'.
Usage: 'he *exudes* confidence' (= has an air of).
Word Family: **exudation**, *noun*, a) the act of exuding, b) something which is exuded.
[Latin *exudare* to sweat out]

exult *verb*
to rejoice greatly: 'the prince *exulted* in his army's victory'.
Word Family: **exultant**, *adjective*; **exultation**, *noun.*
[EX– + Latin *saltare* to leap]

eye *noun*
1. *Anatomy:* the organ of sight.
2. something which has the shape, function, etc. of an eye: a) 'the *eye* of a needle', b) 'an electronic *eye*'.
Usages:
a) 'he has an *eye* for detail' (= ability to notice or discern).
b) 'I'm keeping my *eye* on you' (= attention).
3. *Weather:* the small central area of a tropical cyclone where the wind is calm.
Phrases:
an eye for an eye, retaliation in kind.
in the eyes of, '*in the eyes of* the law he is guilty' (= in the opinion of).
see eye to eye, to agree.
turn a blind eye to, see BLIND.
with an eye to, 'it is all done *with an eye to* his own advantage' (= looking to, with a view to).
with one's eyes open, 'she went into marriage *with her eyes open*' (= aware of the possible risks).

eye *verb*
(**eyed, eyeing** or **eying**)
to observe or watch closely: 'he *eyed* the growling dog nervously'.

eyebrow *noun*
Anatomy: a crest of hair on the forehead just above the eye.

eyeglasses *plural noun*
spectacles.

eyelash *noun*
any or all of the hairs forming a fringe at the edge of each eyelid.

eyelet *noun*
a) a small hole with a trimmed edge, e.g. in a shoe for the lace. b) a small metal ring used to reinforce such a hole.

eyelid *noun*
Anatomy: a fold of skin which may be closed to protect the eye and spread lubricating fluid over it.

eyepiece *noun*
the lens or group of lenses in an optical instrument, such as a telescope, closest to the viewer's eye. Compare OBJECTIVE.

eyesight *noun*
1. the power to see.
2. the range of seeing.

eye socket
Anatomy: see ORBIT.

eyesore *noun*
something which is offensive to look at: 'the old house was an *eyesore* in the newly developed area'.

eyetooth *noun*
plural is **eyeteeth**
an upper, canine tooth.
give one's eyeteeth for, to be willing to give up a great deal for.

eyewitness *noun*
a person who has seen an event and can give evidence about it.

eyrie (*say* eeri) **noun**
an eagle's nest, usually built on a mountain or cliff.

Ff

fa, fah *noun*
Music: see DOH.

Fabian *adjective*
1. (of tactics) cautious or avoiding pitched battles.
2. (of socialism) achieving socialist aims by gradual evolution, not revolution.
[after *Fabius Cunctator*, a Roman general who checked Hannibal by avoiding pitched battles]

fable *noun*
a) a short story with a moral, often about supernatural people or animals. b) any legend or myth. c) an improbable story.
[Latin *fabula* a story]

fabric *noun*
1. a thin, solid substance made by weaving, knitting or felting fibres and used to make clothes, curtains, etc.
2. a framework or structure: 'apathy is undermining the *fabric* of our society'.
[Latin *fabrica* skilled work]

fabricate *verb*
1. to make up or invent: 'the gang had carefully *fabricated* their alibi'.
2. to assemble ready-made sections of something.
Word Family: **fabrication,** *noun,* a) the act of fabricating, b) something which is fabricated, such as a lie; **fabricator,** *noun.*

fabulous (*say* **fab**-yoolus) *adjective*
1. of or occurring in fable: 'dragons are *fabulous* beasts'.
2. (*informal*) wonderful or very good: 'what a *fabulous* dress!'.
Word Family: **fabulous,** *interjection,* excellent or marvellous; **fabulously,** *adverb*; **fabulousness,** *noun.*

façade (*say* fa-**sahd**) *noun*
1. the outside front of a building.
2. a false or deceptive exterior: 'behind her tough *façade* hides a frightened little girl'.
[French]

face *noun*
1. the front part of the head from the forehead to the chin.
Usages:
a) 'the young man had a sad *face*' (= expression).
b) 'you strike the ball with the *face* of a cricket bat' (= the front part).
2. the surface of anything: 'they disappeared off the *face* of the earth'.
3. standing or reputation: 'if I back down now I'll lose *face*'.
Phrases:
in the face of, a) 'what could he do *in the face of* all these difficulties?' (= when confronted with); b) 'he succeeded *in the face of* continual opposition' (= in spite of).
make faces, 'he *made faces* behind the teacher's back' (= grimaced).
on the face of it, judging by the appearance.

face *verb*
1. to look or turn the face towards: a) '*face* me when you are speaking to me'; b) 'the windows *face* the sea'.
Usage: 'the illustration *faces* page 3' (= is opposite to).
2. to meet or confront: 'he strode out of the house to *face* the waiting reporters'.
3. to cover with a layer of another material: 'the stonemason spent a day *facing* the brick wall with stone blocks'.
Phrases:
face it out, 'no-one can really help you in a crisis; you have to *face it out* alone' (= see it through).
face up to, 'we have to *face up to* the fact that the economy is in a bad way' (= acknowledge, meet).
[Latin *facies*]

facelift *noun*
the use of plastic surgery to remove wrinkles, scars, etc. from the face.
Usage: 'the old building got a *facelift* when the painters moved in' (= improved appearance).
Word Family: **facelift,** *verb.*

face-pack *noun*
Beauty: a liquid or paste for cleaning the skin, left to set on the face and then washed off.

facet (*say* **fassit**) *noun*
1. an aspect: 'there are many *facets* to a business like publishing'.
2. one of the sides of a cut gem.
3. *Biology:* the cornea of one element of a compound eye, as found in some insects.
Word Family: **facet,** *verb,* to cut facets on.

facetious (*say* fa-**see**-shus) *adjective*
of an ill-timed or silly attempt to be amusing: 'no-one appreciates *facetious* remarks during a serious discussion'.

face value
Commerce: the value stated on a document, a company's shares, etc.
Usage: 'I took what you said at *face value*' (= its direct or apparent meaning).

facial (*say* **fay**-sh'l) *noun*
a treatment of the face involving careful cleaning, toning, massage and applying new make-up.
facial *adjective*
of or for the face: a) '*facial* acne'; b) '*facial* cream'.
Word Family: **facially,** *adverb.*

facile (*say* **fassile**) *adjective*
done or produced with ease or too little thought or care.
Word Family: **facilely,** *adverb;* **facileness,** *noun.*
[Latin *facilis* easy]

facilitate (*say* fa-**silli**-tate) *verb*
to make easier or assist: 'we hired a computer to *facilitate* the examining process'.
Word Family: **facilitation,** *noun.*

facility (*say* fa-**silli**-tee) *noun*
1. an ease or readiness in doing something: 'his *facility* at knitting surprised his mates'.
2. (*usually plural*) something that makes it easier to do things: 'transport *facilities* will be suspended during the drivers' strike'.

facing (*say* **fay**-sing) *noun*
any material applied to an outer edge or layer of something.

facsimile (*say* fak-**simmi**-lee) *noun*
an exact reproduction.
[Latin *fac* make + *simile* like]

fact *noun*
1. something that has really occurred or actually exists.
2. something known to be true or accepted as true: 'no-one can deny the *fact* that fire burns'.
as a matter of fact, in fact, in point of fact, really or indeed.
Word Family: **factual,** *adjective;* **factually,** *adverb;* **factualness,** *noun.*
[Latin *factus* done]

faction (*say* **fak**-sh'n) *noun*
1. a small discontented group within a larger one. Compare IN-GROUP and CLIQUE.
2. any party strife or intrigue.
Word Family: **factional,** *adjective,* of or relating to a faction; **factionalism,** *noun;* **factious,** *adjective,* promoting faction.
[Latin *factionis* of a (political) party]

factitious (*say* fak-**tish**us) *adjective*
artificial or false: 'advertising often creates a *factitious* demand for one particular brand of goods'.
Word Family: **factitiously,** *adverb;* **factitiousness,** *noun.*
[Latin *facticius* artificial]

factor *noun*
1. anything that helps to bring about a result: 'hard work was one *factor* in his success'.
2. *Maths:* an integer that divides exactly into another integer: '3 is a *factor* of 6'. Also called a **divisor.**
3. *Biology:* a gene or a genetic unit of heredity.
4. a person who buys, sells or acts as an agent for another.
Word Family: **factorize, factorise,** *verb,* to break up into factors; **factorization,** *noun.*

factorial (*say* fak-**taw**riul) *noun*
Maths: the product of all whole numbers less than and including the given whole number. *Example:* factorial 4 = $4 \times 3 \times 2 \times 1 = 24$.
Word Family: **factorial,** *adjective,* relating to a factor or factorial.

factory (*say* **fak**ta-ree) *noun*
a building or group of buildings where something is manufactured or assembled.

factory ship
a fishing ship which processes and freezes its catch while still at sea.

factotum (*say* fak-**toe**-t'm) *noun*
a person who does all kinds of work.
[Latin *fac* do + *totum* all]

factual *adjective*
Word Family: see FACT.

faculty (*say* **fakk**'l–tee) *noun*
1. an ability or aptitude for something: 'small boys have an uncanny *faculty* for getting into trouble'.
2. any of the powers of the mind or body: a) 'the *faculty* of reason'; b) 'the *faculties* of sight and hearing'.
3. a) a section of a university or college studying related subjects. b) the teaching staff of such a section.
[Latin *facultas* ability]

fad *noun*
a temporary enthusiasm.
Word Family: **faddish, faddy,** *adjectives.*

fade *verb*
1. to lose or cause to lose brightness or colour: a) 'this material has *faded* with the years'; b) 'sunlight has *faded* this material'.
Usages:
a) 'the flowers *faded* and died in the heat' (= withered).
b) 'his smile *faded*' (= disappeared gradually).
2. *Film:* to change the clarity of a picture slowly by increasing it (**fade in**) or decreasing it (**fade out**).

faeces (*say* **fee**–seez) *plural noun*
in America spelt **feces**
Biology: the solid waste material remaining after digestion, expelled from the lower end of the alimentary canal.
Word Family: **faecal** (*say* **feek**'l), *adjective.* [Latin, dregs]

fag *noun*
1. (*informal*) a) a cigarette. b) anything causing weariness: 'going to parties is a real *fag*'.
2. (in certain public schools) a junior pupil required to perform certain services for a senior.
3. (*informal*) a male homosexual.
Word Family: **fag (fagged, fagging),** *verb,* a) to tire, b) to act as a school fag.

faggot *noun*
1. a bundle of sticks, twigs, etc. bound together and used for fuel.
2. (*informal*) a homosexual.

Fahrenheit (*say* **farren**–hite) *adjective*
of or relating to a scale of temperature with the melting point of ice (0°C) set at 32°F and the boiling point of water (100°C) set at 212°F. Compare CELSIUS.
See UNITS in grey pages.
[devised by Gabriel *Fahrenheit*, 1686–1736, a German physicist]

fail *verb*
1. to be unsuccessful: 'he *failed* to make his meaning clear'.
Usages:
a) 'the examiners *failed* half the candidates' (= did not give a passing mark to).
b) 'the bank *failed*' (= went bankrupt).
c) 'words *failed* him' (= did not come to).
2. to lose strength or cease to function: a) 'his health has been *failing* for years'; b) 'he ran into the back of a van when his brakes *failed*'.
3. to omit or neglect: 'he *failed* to keep his promise'.
fail *noun*
any mark awarded to an examinee which is below the pass mark.
without fail, for certain.
Word Family: **failure,** *noun.*

failing *noun*
a weakness or shortcoming: 'we all have our little *failings*'.
failing *preposition*
in the absence of: '*failing* payment, we will be forced to sue'.

fail–safe *adjective*
1. relating to any supplementary device which automatically comes into action if the main mechanism fails, e.g. in a lift.
2. *Military:* of a system of checks and controls which automatically prevents aircraft, ballistic missiles, etc. being put into operation.

fain *adverb*
an old word meaning gladly or willingly.

faint *adjective*
1. weak or indistinct: a) 'a *faint* light glimmering in the distance'; b) 'a *faint* hope'.
2. liable to lose consciousness: 'for days after the accident she felt *faint* and weak'.
faint *noun*
a sudden loss of consciousness.
faint *verb*
to lose consciousness temporarily.
Word Family: **faintly,** *adverb*; **faintness,** *noun.*

faint–hearted *adjective*
lacking courage or conviction: 'there's no use being *faint–hearted* in the middle of a fight'.
Word Family: **faint–heartedly,** *adverb*; **faint–heartedness,** *noun.*

fair (1) *adjective*
1. honest or in accordance with the rules: a) 'a *fair* trial'; b) 'a *fair* fight'.
2. average or moderately good: 'she has a *fair* knowledge of Latin'.
3. light in complexion or colouring.
4. (of weather) without rain.
5. an old word meaning beautiful: 'a *fair* maiden'.
fair and square, 'I hit him *fair and square* on the jaw' (= directly, straight).
Word Family: **fairly, fair**, *adverbs*, a) in a fair manner, b) (informal) completely; **fairness**, *noun*.

fair (2) *noun*
1. an amusement show.
2. a place at which goods are exhibited, bought and sold.

Fair Isle
a complex, multicoloured pattern knitted into a garment.
[first made on *Fair Isle*, Scotland]

fairway *noun*
Golf: the cleared ground on a golf links, between the tee and the green.

fairy *noun*
1. *Folklore:* a small supernatural being with magical powers.
2. (*informal*) an effeminate male, especially a homosexual.

fairy light
a small, coloured light bulb used for decoration.

fairytale *noun*
1. a story about fairies or magical events.
2. (*informal*) any exaggerated or unlikely story.

fait accompli (*say* fate a-kom-**plee**)
a thing which is already done and cannot be reversed.
[French, fact accomplished]

faith *noun*
1. any trust or confidence.
2. a religion or religious movement: 'the Christian *faith*'.
in good faith, 'he made the offer *in good faith*' (= sincerely, honestly).

faithful *adjective*
1. loyal: 'a *faithful* servant'.
2. accurate or truthful: 'a *faithful* description'.
Word Family: **faithfully**, *adverb*; **faithfulness**, *noun*; **faithless**, *adjective*, a) not faithful, b) not trustworthy.

faith-healer *noun*
a person attempting to cure illness, etc. through religious faith.
Word Family: **faith-healing**, *noun*.

fake *verb*
to reproduce or imitate something, in order to deceive: 'he *faked* an illness in order to get out of work'.
Word Family: **fake**, *adjective*, not genuine; **fake**, *noun*, a) something faked, b) a person who deceives; **faker**, *noun*; **fakery**, *noun*, false or deceptive actions.

fakir (*say* **fay**-keer) **fakeer** *noun*
1. a Moslem mendicant devoted to poverty and chastity.
2. the title for a very holy man.
[Arabic *faqir* poor man]

falcon *noun*
any of various birds of prey, such as the hawk or kestrel, often used to hunt other birds or game.
falconry *noun*
the breeding and training of falcons.
Word Family: **falconer**, *noun*, a person who hunts with or trains falcons.

fall (*say* fawl) *verb*
(**fell, fallen, falling**)
to move downwards: a) 'a leaf *fell* from the tree'; b) 'prices *fell*'.
Usages:
a) 'he *fell* in battle' (= was killed).
b) 'the government *fell* at the last election' (= was defeated).
c) 'the bombs *fell* on target' (= landed).
d) 'her hair *fell* softly about her shoulders' (= hung).
e) 'the wind has *fallen*' (= become less).
f) 'he *fell* asleep quickly' (= became).
g) 'at the bad news, his face *fell*' (= showed dejection).
h) 'the subject *falls* into four divisions' (= divides naturally).
i) 'Christmas *falls* on a Wednesday next year' (= occurs).
j) 'Eve *fell* in the Garden of Eden' (= was disgraced).
Phrases:
fall back, to retreat.
fall back on, to have recourse to.
fall down on the job, to do the work badly or improperly.
fall for, a) to be deceived by; b) to fall in love with.
fall foul of, to come into conflict with.
fall in, to take one's proper place in a formation or group.
fall on, fall upon, to rush suddenly at or attack.

fall out, a) to leave the ranks or a formation; b) to quarrel; c) to happen or result.
fall over backwards, see BACKWARDS.
fall through, to come to nothing.
fall to, a) to begin, b) 'it *falls to* me to introduce the guests' (= is the lot or duty of).
fall *noun*
1. a) the act or an instance of falling: 'she had a bad *fall*'. b) something which has fallen: 'a light *fall* of snow'. c) the distance through which anything falls: 'a long *fall* to the bottom'.
2. the way something hangs: 'the *fall* of a dress'.
3. (*usually plural*) a waterfall.
4. *American:* the autumn.

fallacy (*say* fal-a-see) *noun*
1. any mistaken or false belief or opinion.
2. *Logic:* any error in reasoning.
Word Family: **fallacious** (*say* fa-lay-shus), *adjective*, **fallaciously**, *adverb*; **fallaciousness**, *noun*.
[Latin *fallax, fallacis* deceiving]

fall guy
American: (*informal*) a person who is left to take the blame or punishment.

fallible (*say* fal-a-b'l) *adjective*
liable to be mistaken.
Word Family: **fallibility**, *noun*; **fallibly**, *adverb*.

falling star see METEOR.

Fallopian tube (*say* fal-o-pee-an tube)
Anatomy: the tube through which the ovum moves from an ovary to the uterus. Also called a **uterine tube**.

fall-out *noun*
1. *Physics:* any radioactive substance on the earth's surface or in the atmosphere, resulting from nuclear explosions.
2. the incidental results or by-products of an experiment or event.

fallow (1) (*say* fallo) *adjective*
(of land) left uncultivated for one or more seasons.

fallow (2) (*say* fallo) *adjective*
light yellow or brown: 'a *fallow* deer'.

false (*say* fawls) *adjective*
1. not true or correct: 'a *false* statement'.
2. not genuine: '*false* teeth'.
3. not faithful or loyal: 'a *false* friend'.
Word Family: **falsely, false**, *adverbs*; **falseness**, *noun*, the quality of being false; **falsity**, *noun*, a) falseness, b) something which is false.
[Latin *falsus* mistaken, untrue]

falsehood *noun* a lie.

false pretences
any misrepresentation of one's circumstances, identity, etc.

false rib
Anatomy: see FLOATING RIB.

falsetto (*say* fawl-setto) *noun*
an unusually high-pitched man's voice.

falsies (*say* fawl-seez) *plural noun*
(*informal*) a) imitation breasts. b) false teeth.

falsify (*say* fawlsi-fie) *verb*
(falsified, falsifying)
to make false: 'he managed to *falsify* the evidence by lying'.
Word Family: **falsification**, *noun*.

falsity (*say* fawlsi-tee) *noun*
Word Family: see FALSE.

falter (*say* fawl-ter) *verb*
to hesitate or waver: 'the line of troops *faltered*'.
Word Family: **falter**, *noun*; **falteringly**, *adverb*.

fame *noun*
the condition of being widely known or esteemed. [Latin *fama* reputation]

familiar (*say* fa-millia) *adjective*
1. a) well-known: 'a *familiar* face'. b) having a thorough knowledge of: 'are you *familiar* with radio technology?'.
2. a) intimate or close: 'they are on *familiar* terms'. b) too intimate or presumptuous: 'don't be so *familiar* with your teacher'.
familiar *noun*
1. an intimate friend.
2. a demon supposed to attend a witch at her call.
Word Family: **familiarly**, *adverb*; **familiarity** (*say* fa-milli-arri-tee), *noun*; **familiarize** (*say* fa-millia-rize), **familiarise**, *verb*, to make or become familiar with; **familiarization**, *noun*.
[Latin *familiaris* of the household]

family *noun*
1. any parents and their children.
2. *Biology:* the group below order in the classification of animals and plants.
3. all persons descended from the same ancestors, such as parents, children, aunts, uncles, cousins, etc.
Word Family: **familial** (*say* fa-millial), *adjective*.

family planning
the regulating of the number of children born into a family.

family tree
a chart showing the descent and relationship of members of a family.

famine (*say* **fammin**) *noun*
a widespread and serious shortage, especially of food.
[French *faim* hunger]

famished *adjective*
extremely hungry.

famous (*say* **faymus**) *adjective*
being celebrated or well-known: 'the Battle of Waterloo is a *famous* event'.
Word Family: **famously**, *adverb*, (informal) excellently.

fan (1) *noun*
any of various devices, operated by hand or mechanically, for creating a current of air.
fan *verb*
(fanned, fanning)
1. to send a current of air on to.
Usage: 'to *fan* the flames of discontent' (= increase).
2. to spread out like a fan: 'the searchers *fanned* out across the countryside'.

fan (2) *noun*
(*informal*) an enthusiastic follower or devotee: 'he's a mad-keen football *fan*'. [short form of *fanatic*]

fanatic (*say* fa-**nattik**) *noun*
a person with an excessive enthusiasm for something: 'he's a fresh-air *fanatic*'.
Word Family: **fanatic, fanatical,** *adjective*; **fanatically,** *adverb*; **fanaticism** (*say* fa-**natti**-sizm), *noun*.
[Latin *fanaticus* inspired by a god, frenzied]

fancy *verb*
1. to imagine: '*fancy* living with him all your life'.
2. to have a liking or preference for: 'what do you *fancy* for dinner tonight?'.
fancy *noun*
1. a) a playful imagination: 'your story is the product of *fancy*'. b) something which is imagined: 'he thought he heard a siren but it was only a *fancy*'.
2. a fondness or liking.
fancy *adjective*
not plain or ordinary: 'she went to the parade all done up in a *fancy* hat'.
Word Family: **fancier**, *noun*, a person with a special interest or enthusiasm; **fanciful**, *adjective*; **fancifully**, *adverb*; **fancy-free**, *adjective*, not in love.
[short form of FANTASY]

fancy dress
any clothes worn by a person to represent a costume of another time, a famous character, animal, etc.

fanfare *noun*
a loud, elaborate musical introduction, played on trumpets, etc.

fang *noun*
a long, pointed tooth.

fanlight *noun*
a window above a door.

fantail *noun*
1. any of various small birds with fan-like tails, especially a domestic pigeon.
2. a goldfish with a double tail fin.

fantasia (*say* fan-**tayzia**) *noun*
a piece of music, literature, etc. that follows no set rules.

fantastic (*say* fan-**tastik**) *adjective*
1. (*informal*) wonderful: 'what a *fantastic* party!'.
2. impossible to carry out: 'world government is an attractive but wholly *fantastic* idea'.
3. having the characteristics of fantasy.
Word Family: **fantastically**, *adverb*.

fantasy (*say* **fanta**-see) *noun*
1. a) a wild or extravagant imagination. b) any product of this, such as a daydream.
2. a fantasia.
Word Family: **fantasize, fantasise,** *verb*.

fan vaulting
Architecture: a decorated style of arched ceiling, supported by ribs which spread like a fan.

far *adverb*
(further or **farther, furthest** or **farthest)**
1. to, from, or at a considerable distance: a) 'how *far* did you go?'; b) 'she can see *far* into the future'.
2. to a considerable degree: 'he's *far* better now that he has moved to another school'.
Phrases:
as far as, so far as, in so far as, '*as far as* I know, he's honest' (= to the extent that).
by far, far and away, 'he's *by far* the best batsman on the team' (= very much, clearly).
far be it from me, '*far be it from me* to criticize your paintings!' (= I would not hope or dare).

so far, a) '*so far* the escaped prisoners have eluded the police search' (= up till now); b) 'the surgeon only went *so far* in his exploration and then closed the incision' (= to a limited extent).
far *adjective*
(**further** or **farther, furthest** or **farthest**)
a) distant: 'a *far* country'. b) more distant: 'the *far* corner of the room'.

farad (*say* farrad) *noun*
the SI unit of electrical capacitance. See UNITS in grey pages.
[after *Michael Faraday*, 1791–1867, a British physicist]

farce *noun*
1. any absurd or futile situation or set of events: 'the Peace Conference was a *farce* because it solved nothing'.
2. a play intended merely to amuse, usually emphasizing situation rather than character, and often containing an improbable plot and slapstick humour.
Word Family: **farcical** (*say* farsi–k'l), *adjective*; **farcically**, *adverb*.

fare (*say* fair) *noun*
1. any fee a passenger is charged for the use of transport.
2. any passenger on a hired vehicle.
3. any food provided at table.
fare *verb*
1. to manage: 'how did you *fare* in your interview?'.
2. an old word meaning to go.

Far East
the countries of eastern and south–eastern Asia, such as China and Japan.

farewell (*say* fair–**well**) *interjection*
goodbye.
Word Family: **farewell**, *noun*, a leave–taking.

far–fetched *adjective*
improbable or only remotely connected: 'he has a habit of making *far–fetched* comparisons'.

farinaceous (*say* farrin–**ay**–shus) *adjective*
containing flour, meal or starch.
[Latin *farina* flour]

farm *noun*
an area of land used to raise crops or animals.
farm *verb*
to use land for growing crops, raising animals, etc.
farm out, to give or send out to others.
Word Family: **farmer**, *noun*; **farming**, *noun*.

far–out *adjective*
(*informal*) unconventional.

farrago (*say* fa–**rah**–go) *noun*
a confused mixture.
[Latin, mixed fodder]

farrier *noun*
a blacksmith who shoes horses.
[Latin *ferrum* iron]

farrow *noun*
a litter of pigs.

fart *verb*
(*informal*) to emit wind from the anus.
fart *noun*
(*informal*) an emission of wind from the anus.

farther (*say* **far***ther*) *adjective*
(used especially of distances) a comparative form of **far**.

farthest (*say* **far***thest*) *adjective*
(used especially of distances) a superlative form of **far**.

farthing (*say* **far**–*th*ing) *noun*
an old coin equal to one quarter of the former penny, or about one–tenth of the current penny.
[Old English *feortha* fourth]

fascia (*say* **fay**sha *or* **fash**i–a) *noun*
1. the layers of fibrous connective tissue beneath the skin, enclosing or connecting muscles or internal organs.
2. a dashboard.
Word Family: **fascial**, *adjective*.

fascinate (*say* **fass**i–nate) *verb*
to attract irresistibly or hold spellbound: 'the audience was *fascinated* by the eloquence of the speaker'.
Word Family: **fascination**, *noun*; **fascinating**, *adjective*; **fascinatingly**, *adverb*.
[Latin *fascinare* to cast a spell on]

fascism (*say* **fash**izm) *noun*
1. (*often capital*) a form of extreme right–wing dictatorship in which the government controls all the affairs of a country, including industry and finance, and restricts individual liberties. It is characterized by an aggressive nationalism, and is anti–communist.
2. (*informal*) any set of extremely right–wing political beliefs, especially those involving racism.
Word Family: **fascist**, *noun*, *adjective*.

[from *fasces*, the ancient Roman symbol of state power, first adopted by the Italian dictatorship as its emblem, in 1922]

fashion (*say* **fash**'n) *noun*
1. a style or custom, e.g. of dress, manners, etc. which is considered the most admirable or worthy of imitation at a certain time.
2. a way or manner of doing something: 'he settled down to the job in a businesslike *fashion*'.
after a fashion, in a fashion: 'because of his rush he only finished the job *after a fashion*' (= in a way, but not well).
Word Family: **fashion**, *verb*, to form or mould; **fashionable**, *adjective*, conforming to fashion; **fashionably**, *adverb*.

fast (1) *adjective*
1. swift or quick: 'a *fast* horse'.
2. ahead of the correct time: 'that clock is *fast*'.
3. promoting quick motion: 'a *fast* cricket pitch'.
4. firmly fixed: a) 'the post is *fast* in the ground'; b) '*fast* colours will not run when the garment is washed'.
Usage: 'we were always *fast* friends' (= close).
fast *adverb*
1. firmly, securely or tightly: a) 'hold *fast* to the rail'; b) 'she was *fast* asleep'.
2. quickly: 'don't speak so *fast*'.
play fast and loose, to act in an irresponsible or fickle manner.
fastness *noun*
1. a) the state of being fixed or firm. b) the state of being rapid.
2. a remote hide-out: 'the bandits fled to their mountain *fastness*'.

fast (2) *noun*
a time of eating little or no food, e.g. as a religious duty or in protest.
Word Family: **fast**, *verb*.

fasten (*say* **fah**-s'n) *verb*
1. to fix safely or join together: a) 'have you *fastened* all the windows?'; b) 'he *fastened* his seat belt before starting the car'.
2. to direct attention, looks, etc. at someone or something: 'the murderer's eyes were *fastened* on the girl's back'.
fasten on, fasten upon, to seize or lay hold of.
Word Family: **fastening**, *noun*; **fastener**, *noun*.

fastidious (*say* fass-**tiddius**) *adjective*
fussy or difficult to please.
Word Family: **fastidiously**, *adverb*; **fastidiousness**, *noun*.
[Latin *fastidium* distaste]

fat *noun*
the greasy white or yellow substance in animal bodies, forming a store of food and providing insulation.
fat *adjective*
1. plump.
2. large or abundant: 'a *fat* profit'.
Word Family: **fatness**, *noun*; **fatten**, *verb*; **fatty**, *adjective*; **fattiness**, *noun*; **fatted**, *adjective*, an old word for fattened.

fatal (*say* **fay**-t'l) *adjective*
1. causing death or disaster: 'a *fatal* blow to the head'.
2. decisive or fateful: 'the *fatal* day finally arrived'.
Word Family: **fatally**, *adverb*.
[Latin *fatalis* preordained, deadly]

fatalism (*say* **fay**ta-lizm) *noun*
a tendency to accept everything as inevitable or unchangeable.
Word Family: **fatalist**, *noun*; **fatalistic**, *adjective*; **fatalistically**, *adverb*.

fatality (*say* fa-**talli**-tee) *noun*
1. a) a disaster resulting in death. b) a person killed in a disaster or accident.
2. deadliness: 'the *fatality* of cancer'.
3. the condition of being subject to fate: 'he believed in the *fatality* of human life'.

fate *noun*
1. the power that predetermines events: 'the Greeks believed *fate* ruled men's lives'.
2. the final condition of a person or thing: 'concern for the *fate* of the missing yachtsman'.
Usage: 'he met his *fate* before a firing squad' (= death).
Word Family: **fate**, *verb*, to be destined; **fateful**, *adjective*.

father (*say* **fah**-*th*er) *noun*
1. a male parent.
2. a male who starts or establishes something: 'the *father* of science'.
3. *Christian:* (*capital*) a) a name for God. b) a title for a priest or abbot.
Word Family: **fatherhood**, *noun*; **father**, *verb*; **fatherly**, *adjective*.

father-in-law *noun*
plural is **fathers-in-law**
one's husband's or wife's father.

fatherland *noun*
a) the land of one's birth. b) the native land of one's ancestors.

Father Superior
the head of a monastery.

fathom (*say* **fa*th*'m**) *noun*
a unit used for measuring the depth of water, equal to 6 ft (about 1.83 m).
fathom *verb*
1. to find the depth of.
2. to understand or work out.
Word Family: **fathomable**, *adjective*; **fathomless**, *adjective.*

fatigue (*say* fa–**teeg**) *noun*
1. the state of being very tired, especially owing to vigorous activity
2. *Metallurgy:* the weaknesses caused in a material by repeated stresses, vibrations, etc.
3. a non-military task, such as digging ditches, assigned to soldiers in training, sometimes as a punishment.
4. (*plural*) the work clothes worn by soldiers doing manual labour.
Word Family: **fatigue** (**fatigued, fatiguing**), *verb.*
[Latin *fatigare* to weary]

fatness *noun*
Word Family: see FAT.

fatty acid
Chemistry: any of a large group of organic acids, such as acetic acid (formula CH_3COOH). Fatty acids with large molecules form essential parts of soaps, fats and oils.

fatuous (*say* **fat**–yewus) *adjective*
stupid or foolish.
Word Family: **fatuously**, *adverb*; **fatuity** (*say* fat–**yew**a–tee), *noun.*
[Latin *fatuus* gaping]

faucet (*say* **faw**–set) *noun*
any of various devices, such as a tap, used to control the flow of a liquid from a pipe.

fault (*say* fawlt) *noun*
1. anything which makes a person or thing imperfect: 'despite her *faults* she's a good worker'.
2. the responsibility or cause of blame for wrongdoing: 'whose *fault* is it that you missed the train?'.
3. *Tennis:* a breaking of the rules when serving. A **foot–fault** is when a player steps over the baseline while serving.
4. *Geography:* a break in a rock formation caused by movement of the earth's crust.
Phrases:
at fault, guilty.
to a fault, 'she is kind *to a fault*' (= excessively).
Word Family: **fault**, *verb*; **faulty**, *adjective*; **faultily**, *adverb*; **faultiness**, *noun.*

fauna (*say* **fawna**) *noun*
Biology: all the animals of a certain area or period. Compare FLORA.
[after *Fauna*, Roman goddess of the earth]

faux pas (*say* foe pah)
plural is **faux pas** (*say* foe pah *or* foe pahz)
an indiscreet remark or action, especially a social blunder.
[French, false step]

favour *noun*
in America spelt **favor**
1. a helpful or considerate act: 'would you do me a *favour* and lend me some money?'.
2. a friendly attitude or condition: a) 'it did not take him long to win her *favour*'; b) 'his superiors viewed his request with *favour*'.
3. partiality: 'without fear or *favour*'.
Phrases:
find favour, to gain acceptance or approval.
in favour, having approval.
in favour of, a) 'I'm *in favour of* accepting the offer' (= in support of); b) 'the plan worked *in favour of* everyone' (= to the advantage of).
out of favour, not viewed with favour.
favour *verb*
1. to like or support: 'fortune *favours* the brave'.
2. to oblige: 'she *favoured* me with a sweet smile'.
3. to treat gently or spare: 'the dog *favoured* his sore paw'.
Word Family: **favourable**, *adjective*, helpful or approving; **favourably**, *adverb.*
[Latin *favor*]

favourite (*say* **fayva**–rit) *noun*
1. a) a person or thing liked above all others. b) a person granted special privileges: 'a *favourite* of the president'.
2. *Sport:* a competitor expected to win, such as a horse in a race.
Word Family: **favouritism**, *noun*, an unfair partiality to one person or group, to the disadvantage of others; **favourite**, *adjective.*

fawn (1) *noun*
1. a young deer.
2. a light, yellowish-brown colour.
Word Family: **fawn**, *adjective.*

fawn (2) *verb*
1. (of dogs) to show pleasure and affection by tail-wagging, licking, etc.
2. (of people) to try to win someone's favour by flattery, etc.
Word Family: **fawning,** *adjective*; **fawningly,** *adverb.*

fay *noun*
Folklore: a fairy.

faze *verb*
(*informal*) to disconcert.

fealty (*say* **feel**-tee) *noun*
loyalty, especially the sworn loyalty of a medieval vassal to his master.

fear *noun*
1. a troubled feeling caused by awareness or expectation of danger or some frightening event.
2. an awe and reverence: 'the *fear* of God'.
no fear!, (*informal*) certainly not!
fear *verb*
to feel fear.
Usage: 'I *fear* that she misunderstood me' (= suspect).
Word Family: **fearful,** *adjective,* a) having or causing fear, b) (informal) of a great measure; **fearfully,** *adverb*; **fearsome,** *adjective,* fearful.
[Old English *faer* danger, sudden calamity]

feasible (*say* feezi-b'l) *adjective*
capable of being done or put into effect: 'this is a *feasible* plan'.
Word Family: **feasibly,** *adverb*; **feasibility** (*say* feeza-**billi**-tee), *noun.*

feast *noun*
1. a large, elaborate meal.
2. anything that gives pleasure: 'the concert was a musical *feast*'.
3. a religious festival.
Word Family: **feast,** *verb.*
[Latin *festus* full of rejoicing]

feat *noun*
a remarkable achievement.

feather *noun*
1. any of the light, hollow-shafted, fluffy structures that grow from a bird's skin.
2. any similar synthetic object, e.g. on a dart, arrow, etc.
Phrases:
a feather in one's cap, an achievement to be proud of.
birds of a feather, people of the same type.
in fine feather, in good feather, in good spirits or health.

feather *verb*
to fit with a feather, e.g. on an arrow.
feather one's nest, to make things comfortable for oneself.
Word Family: **feathery,** *adjective.*

featherweight (*say* **fe***tha*-wate) *noun*
a weight division in boxing, under 9 stone (about 57 kg).

feature (*say* **fee**cher) *noun*
1. a distinguishing aspect or part: 'her eyes are her best *feature*'.
2. (*usually plural*) the face.
3. a special descriptive article or interview in a newspaper, magazine, etc.
Word Family: **feature,** *verb,* a) to make a feature of, b) to present.

feature film
the chief film shown in a cinema programme.

febrile *adjective*
having a fever.

February *noun*
the second month of the year in the Gregorian calendar.
[named after *Februa,* the Roman festival of purification]

feces *plural noun*
Biology: see FAECES.

feckless *adjective*
1. feeble or ineffective.
2. worthless or irresponsible.
Word Family: **fecklessly,** *adverb*; **fecklessness,** *noun.*
[Scots *feck* worth + -LESS]

fecundity (*say* fe-**kun**di-tee) *noun*
the capacity to produce or create in abundance.
Word Family: **fecund** (*say* **fek**kund *or* **fee**kund), *adjective,* fertile or prolific; **fecundate,** *verb,* to make fecund; **fecundation,** *noun.*
[Latin *fecundus* fruitful]

fed *verb*
the past tense and past participle of the verb **feed.**

federal *adjective*
of the joining of states or countries under one central government, as distinct from each state's separate government: 'the *Federal* Government of Australia'.
Word Family: **federate,** *verb*; **federation,** *noun*; **federalist,** *noun,* a supporter of federal government; **federalism,** *noun.*
[Latin *foederis* of a league]

fee *noun*
1. a charge or payment, e.g. for a professional service.
2. *Medieval history:* a fief.

feeble *adjective*
weak or ineffective.
Word Family: **feebleness,** *noun*; **feebly,** *adverb.*

feeble-minded *adjective*
mentally deficient.
Word Family: **feeble-mindedness,** *noun.*

feed *verb*
(fed, feeding)
1. to give food to.
2. to keep supplied: 'we *fed* the material into the machine'.
fed up, (*informal*) 'I am *fed up* with work!' (= out of patience, disgusted).
feed *noun*
any food, especially for livestock.

feedback *noun*
1. any information that helps to calculate the results or success of something.
2. the return of part of the output of a system into the input, such as the intense howling sometimes heard in public address systems.

feeder *noun*
1. anything that feeds or provides food.
2. a baby's bib.
3. a branch or connecting part of a larger system, such as a tributary stream, secondary road, etc.

feel *verb*
(felt, feeling)
1. to perceive through the sense of touch.
2. to examine by touching: 'in the dark we *felt* our way down the stairs'.
3. to be conscious of or affected by: a) 'he *felt* ashamed'; b) 'we *feel* it is time to leave'.
Phrases:
feel for, to have sympathy for.
feel like, 'I *feel like* a bath' (= want, would like).
feel like oneself, to be in one's normal state of health, spirits, etc.
feel out, to try to discover people's opinions, etc. indirectly.
feel up to, to seem to oneself to be capable of or ready to do something.

feeler *noun*
1. an organ of touch in insects, such as an antenna.
2. any action or remark intended to discover another's thoughts or intentions.

feeling *noun*
1. the sense of touch.
2. an awareness or sensation: a) 'I have a *feeling* this plan will not work'; b) 'a *feeling* of joy'.
3. (*plural*) the emotional part of a person, as distinct from the intellect: 'his *feelings* were hurt'.
4. sympathy or sensitivity: 'she has no *feeling* for her husband'.

feet *plural noun*
see FOOT.

feign (*say* fane) *verb*
to pretend or invent in order to deceive: 'she *feigned* a headache so as to miss the party'.

feint (*say* faint) *verb*
to make a pretended attack to deceive an opponent, as in swordfighting, etc.
Word Family: **feint,** *noun.*

feldspar *noun*
also spelt **felspar**
any of a group of alkaline aluminium silicate minerals; an important part of igneous rocks such as granite.
[German *Feld* field + SPAR (3)]

felicitation (*say* fe-lissi-**tay**-sh'n) *noun*
(*usually plural*) congratulations.
Word Family: **felicitate,** *verb.*

felicity (*say* fe-**lissi**-tee) *noun*
1. a) a great happiness. b) something causing this.
2. a) an aptness of manner or style. b) an instance of this.
Word Family: **felicitous,** *adjective,* apt.

feline (*say* **fee**-line) *adjective*
of or like a cat.
[Latin *feles* a cat]

fell (1) *verb*
the past tense of the verb **fall.**

fell (2) *verb*
to cut or knock down, especially trees.

fell (3) *adjective*
an old word meaning dreadful or deadly.

fell (4) *noun*
an area of high moorland.

fellah *noun*
plural is **fellahin** (*say* fella-**heen**)
Egyptian: a peasant.

fellow *noun*
1. a person, especially a male.
2. a comrade, associate or peer.
3. a member of an academic or professional society.

4. *Education:* a postgraduate research student in a university who receives money from an established fund.
5. (at older universities) a member of the governing body of a college.
Word Family: **fellowship**, *noun.*

felony (*say* **fell**a–nee) *noun*
Law: any serious crime, such as murder.
Word Family: **felon**, *noun*, a person who has committed a felony; **felonious** (*say* fe–**lo**–nee–us), *adjective.*

felspar *noun*
see FELDSPAR.

felt (1) *verb*
the past tense and past participle of the verb **feel**.

felt (2) *noun*
a matted fabric of wool, fur or hair.

female *noun*
1. a) a person of the sex conceiving and having children; a woman or girl. b) any animal of this sex.
2. *Biology:* a flower which has only fruiting organs (the style and ovary).
Word Family: **female**, *adjective*, a) of or characteristic of a female, b) (of a machine part, etc.) designed for a corresponding part to fit into it.

feminine (*say* **femm**a–nin) *adjective*
1. of or relating to the female sex.
2. having the qualities said to be appropriate to females.
3. *Grammar:* see GENDER.
Word Family: **femininity** (*say* femma–**ninn**a–tee), *noun.*

feminism (*say* **femm**a–nizm) *noun*
the principle or practice of social and political advancement or liberation for women.
Word Family: **feminist**, *noun, adjective.*

femme fatale (*say* fem fa–**tahl**)
a dangerously attractive woman.
[French, fatal woman]

femoral (*say* **femm**a–r'l) *adjective*
of or relating to the thigh or groin.

femto–
a prefix used for SI units, meaning one thousand million millionth (10^{-15}). See UNITS in grey pages.

femur (*say* **fee**–ma) *noun*
plural is **femurs** or **femora** (*say* **femm**a–ra)
Anatomy: the long bone of the thigh or upper hindlimb in animals, joining the hip to the knee.
[Latin, the thigh]

fen *noun*
an area of low, marshy land.

fence *noun*
1. a barrier or boundary of wire, wood etc. around a house, garden, etc.
2. a hedge or other obstacle to be jumped in a steeplechase or showjumping competition.
3. a person who receives and disposes of stolen goods.
sit on the fence, to remain neutral.
fence *verb*
1. to build or put a fence around.
2. to take part in the sport of fencing.
3. to avoid direct questions, arguments, etc.
Word Family: **fencer**, *noun.*
[short form of *defence*]

fencing *noun*
1. any material used for fences.
2. the sport of fighting with long, slender swords.

fend *verb*
to repel or resist: 'he *fended* off the blows with his arms'.
fend for oneself, to protect or provide for oneself.

fender *noun*
1. a metal surround to prevent fuel rolling out of a fire.
2. any device which protects against impact, e.g. the bumper bar on a car.
3. the roping or other material hung over a ship's side when docking.

fennel *noun*
a tall herb with yellow flowers, used in cooking and medicine.

feral *adjective*
wild.
[Latin *ferus* wild]

ferment (*say* fer–**ment**) *verb*
1. to convert sugar to carbon dioxide and alcohol, usually with yeast or bacteria carrying out the necessary chemical reactions.
2. to excite or agitate.
ferment (*say* **fer**–ment) *noun*
1. something that causes fermenting, such as yeast or an enzyme.
2. a state of excitement or agitation.
Word Family: **fermentation**, *noun.*
[Latin *fermentum* yeast]

fermium *noun*
element number 100, a man-made radioactive metal. See TRANSURANIC ELEMENT and ACTINIDE.
See CHEMICAL ELEMENTS in grey pages.
[after *E. Fermi*, 1901–54, an Italian-American physicist]

fern *noun*
any of a group of plants with large, feather-like leaves and no flowers, usually growing in damp areas and reproducing by spores.
Word Family: **ferny**, *adjective*; **fernery**, *noun*, a place where ferns are grown.

ferocious (*say* fe-ro-shus) *adjective*
being extremely savage or cruel.
Word Family: **ferociously**, *adverb*; **ferocity** (*say* fe-rossi-tee), **ferociousness**, *nouns*.
[Latin *ferox, ferocis* untameable]

ferret *noun*
the domesticated form of the polecat trained to drive rabbits and rats from their holes.
ferret *verb*
1. to hunt with a ferret.
2. to search out criminals, facts, etc.
[Latin *fur* thief]

ferric *adjective*
Chemistry: of or relating to compounds of iron in which iron has a valency of three.
[Latin *ferrum* iron]

ferroconcrete (*say* **ferro-kon**-kreet) *noun*
concrete which is strengthened with metal bars or wire.

ferromagnesian
(*say* ferro-mag-**nee**-*zh*'n) *adjective*
(of minerals and rocks) containing iron and magnesium.

ferromagnetic *adjective*
see MAGNETIC.

ferrous *adjective*
Chemistry: of or relating to compounds of iron in which iron has a valency of two.

ferrule (*say* **ferrul**) *noun*
a ring or cap fitted over the end of something, e.g. on the end of an umbrella.

ferry *noun*
a boat used to carry passengers, vehicles, etc. across a short stretch of water.
ferry *verb*
(**ferried, ferrying**)
to transport from one place to another, especially on a ferry.

fertile *adjective*
1. *Biology:* a) capable of sexual reproduction. b) (of eggs or seeds) capable of developing.
2. highly productive: a) '*fertile* soil'; b) 'a *fertile* imagination'.
Word Family: **fertility** (*say* fir-**tilli**-tee), *noun*.
[Latin *fertilis* able to bear]

fertilize, fertilise *verb*
1. *Biology:* to unite male and female reproductive cells.
2. to add substances to the soil to increase growth.
Word Family: **fertilizer**, *noun*, any substance used to fertilize soil; **fertilization**, *noun*.

fervent *adjective*
warm or enthusiastic: 'a *fervent* admirer'.
Word Family: **fervently**, *adverb*; **ferventness, fervency**, *nouns*.
[Latin *fervens* boiling]

fervid *adjective*
spirited or passionate: 'a *fervid* defence of his actions'.
Word Family: **fervidly**, *adverb*.

fervour *noun*
in America spelt **fervor**
an enthusiasm or passion.

festal *adjective*
relating to or characteristic of a festival.
[Latin *festus* full of rejoicing]

fester *verb*
1. to produce pus, as in a wound.
2. to irritate or rankle.

festival *noun*
a day or period of celebration.

festive *adjective*
1. of or relating to a feast or festival.
2. joyous.

festivity (*say* fess-**tivvi**-tee) *noun*
1. a) a festival. b) the gaiety characteristic of a festival.
2. (*plural*) joyous celebrations: 'there was much preparation for the wedding *festivities*'.

festoon *noun*
a) a chain of ribbons, flowers, etc. hung decoratively between two points.
b) a sculptured form of this.
Word Family: **festoon**, *verb*.

fetch *verb*
to go for and bring back: 'she went to *fetch* a policeman'.
Usages:
a) 'this old chair should *fetch* a good price at the auction' (= sell for).
b) 'your rude letter should *fetch* a reply from him' (= draw).

fetching *adjective*
attractive or charming.
Word Family: **fetchingly**, *adverb*.

fête (*say* fate) ***noun***
a small fair, usually held to raise money for an institution or charity.
fête *verb*
(fêted, fêting)
to honour or celebrate by entertaining.
[French, feast]

fetid (*say* **fee**tid) *adjective*
having a foul smell.
[Latin *fetidus*]

fetish (*say* **fet**tish) ***noun***
1. an excessive devotion to or obsession with anything.
2. an object worshipped because it is believed that powerful spirits live in it.
Word Family: **fetishistic**, *adjective*; **fetishism**, *noun.*

fetlock *noun*
Anatomy: the part of a horse's leg just above the hoof, often with a tuft of hair on it.

fetter *noun*
1. a chain placed around the ankles to prevent movement or escape.
2. (*usually plural*) anything that restricts or hinders.
Word Family: **fetter,** *verb.*

fettle *noun*
good health or spirits: 'only a week after the accident he seemed in fine *fettle*'.

fetus (*say* **fee**tus) ***noun***
see FOETUS.
Word Family: **fetal,** *adjective.*

feud (*say* fewd) ***noun***
a long-standing, bitter quarrel, especially between families.
Word Family: **feud**, *verb.*

feudalism (*say* **few**-da-lizm) ***noun***
Medieval history: the system of social and political organization common from the 9th to the 15th century, in which land was held by a vassal in return for homage and service to the lord.
Word Family: **feudal**, *adjective.*

fever (*say* **fee**va) ***noun***
a) an increased body temperature due to disease. b) any of various diseases causing this.
Usage: 'the fans were in a *fever* of excitement' (= high state).
Word Family: **feverish**, *adjective*, of, like or having a fever; **fevered,** *adjective*, affected by fever; **feverishly,** *adverb*; **feverishness,** *noun.*
[Latin *febris*]

few *adjective*
not many: '*few* people have true qualities of leadership'.
few *noun*
a small number: 'his books are read by the *few* who share his ideas'.
a good few, quite a few, a fairly large number.

fey (*say* fay) *adjective*
(of a person) strange or otherworldly.

fez *noun*
a conical, stiff cap with a flat top and a long tassel, formerly the national headdress of Turkey.
[after *Fez*, a town in Morocco]

fiancé (*say* fee-**on**say) ***noun***
a man who is engaged to be married.
Word Family: **fiancée**, *noun*, a female who is engaged to be married.
[French]

fiasco (*say* fee-**ass**-ko) ***noun***
plural is **fiascos**
a complete or disastrous failure.
[Italian]

fiat (*say* **fee**-at) ***noun***
an official authority for action.
[Latin, let it be done]

fib *noun*
a harmless or trivial lie: 'it was obvious that her excuse was a *fib*'.
Word Family: **fib (fibbed, fibbing),** *verb*, to tell a fib; **fibber,** *noun*, a person who tells a fib.

fibre (*say* **fie**-ber) ***noun***
a) a thread or thread-like piece. b) a material made from such pieces.
Usage: 'she's a person of great moral *fibre*' (= strength, character).
Word Family: **fibrous**, *adjective.*
[Latin *fibra*]

fibreglass *noun*
a material made from fine glass fibres which are woven and saturated with resins, used for the bodies of cars, small boats, etc.

fibrin (*say* **fie**-brin) ***noun***
Biology: a white, insoluble, fibrous protein formed when blood clots.

fibrinogen (*say* fie-**brinna**-j'n) ***noun***
a complex protein present in blood which yields fibrin when blood clots.

fibroid (*say* **fie**-broyd) *adjective*
resembling or composed of fibre or fibrous tissue.
Word Family: **fibroid,** *noun*, a fibroid tumour of the womb.
[FIBR(e) + -OID]

fibrosis (*say* fie–**bro**–sis) *noun*
the production of fibrous tissues, as in the healing of a wound.
[FIBR(e) + –OSIS]

fibrositis (*say* fie–bro–**sigh**–tis) *noun*
a mild inflammation in fibrous or muscular tissue, causing pain and difficulty in movement.
[Latin *fibrosus* fibrous + –ITIS]

fibrous (*say* **fie**–brus) *adjective*
Word Family: see FIBRE.

fibula (*say* **fib**–yoo–la) *noun*
plural is **fibulas** or **fibulae** (*say* **fib**–yoo–lee)
Anatomy: the thinner of the two long bones of the lower leg or hind limb.
Word Family: **fibular**, *adjective.*
[Latin, a fastener]

fickle *adjective*
inconstant in feelings or intentions.
Word Family: **fickleness**, *noun.*

fiction (*say* **fik**–sh'n) *noun*
1. any novels, short stories or other imaginative prose writings.
2. something imagined or invented: 'the judge said the whole case was *fiction*'.
Word Family: **fictional**, *adjective*, belonging to or having the nature of fiction; **fictionally**, *adverb*; **fictive**, *adjective*, a) fictitious, b) relating to the creation of fiction.
[Latin *fictio*, *fictionis* a forming, feigning]

fictitious (*say* fik–**tishus**) *adjective*
1. imaginatively created or invented: 'the novelist claimed that all his characters were *fictitious*'.
2. false or untrue: 'the newspaper story was distorted and perhaps even *fictitious*'.
Word Family: **fictitiously**, *adverb.*

fiddle *noun*
1. *Music:* a violin.
2. (*informal*) an underhand or illegal enterprise.
Phrases:
fit as a fiddle, very healthy.
play second fiddle, 'she dislikes *playing second fiddle* to her husband' (= taking second place).
fiddle *verb*
1. to play a violin.
2. to move the hands restlessly or aimlessly.
3. (*informal*) to distort or falsify dishonestly: 'the clerk *fiddled* the accounts'.
fiddle about, to waste time.
Word Family: **fiddly**, *adverb*, intricate and difficult; **fiddler**, *noun.*

fiddlesticks *interjection*
nonsense.

fidelity (*say* fid**delli**–tee) *noun*
1. loyalty: 'the king rewarded his old servant for his *fidelity*'.
2. exactness or accuracy: 'the *fidelity* of sound produced by a radio'.
[Latin *fides* trust]

fidget (*say* **fij**–it) *verb*
to move restlessly or impatiently: 'the children began to *fidget* during the long church service'.
Word Family: **fidget**, *noun*, a person who fidgets; **fidgety**, *adjective.*

fiduciary (*say* fee–**dew**sha–ree) *noun*
Law: a person appointed to manage or look after property, such as a trustee.
[from Latin, *fiducia*, trust]

fie (*rhymes with* die) *interjection*
an old word used as an exclamation of shock or disgust.

fief (*say* feef) *noun*
Medieval history: the land rented by a nobleman to a vassal in return for personal and military service.

field (*say* feeld) *noun*
1. a) an open, cleared area of land used for farming, etc. b) an area of land containing natural resources: 'a *goldfield*'. c) a large expanse: 'a *field* of ice'.
2. a place where a particular event or activity takes place: a) 'a *field* of battle'; b) 'a hockey *field*'.
3. an area: a) 'it lay outside my *field* of vision'; b) 'he works in the *field* of science'.
4. *Sport:* the arrangement of players in a side: 'a defensive *field*'.
5. *Horseracing:* all the horses in a race.
6. any place away from the office or laboratory, where data and other research material are collected.
7. *Physics:* the space in which a force exerts its influence.
field *verb*
1. *Sport:* a) to stop or catch the ball, and return it to the wicket-keeper, pitcher, etc. from a position on the field. b) to put a team into the field.
2. to fend off by verbal agility: 'the politician *fielded* the reporter's probing questions'.
Word Family: **fielder**, *noun.*

field artillery
artillery which can be moved easily from one position to another.

field day
1. *Military:* a day for training exercises, manoeuvres, etc.
2. an enjoyable or successful time.

field-glasses *plural noun*
binoculars.

field-gun *noun*
an artillery gun mounted on wheels.

field marshal
the highest-ranking commissioned officer in the army.

field rank
Military: any rank above captain and below general in the army.

field sports
any open-air sports, especially hunting, shooting and fishing.

fiend (*say* feend) *noun*
1. a devil or evil spirit.
2. a cruel or wicked person.
3. (*informal*) an addict: 'a golf *fiend*'.
Word Family: **fiendish**, *adjective*; **fiendishly**, *adverb.*

fierce *adjective*
hostile, threatening or aggressive: 'their dog is *fierce* towards strangers'.
Usage: 'she stayed in bed with a *fierce* cold' (= intense, severe).
Word Family: **fiercely**, *adverb*; **fierceness**, *noun.*

fiery (*say* **fire**-ee) *adjective*
1. of or like fire: a) 'a *fiery* glow'; b) 'a *fiery* desert wind'.
2. passionate or intense: 'a *fiery* temper'.

fiesta (*say* fee-**esta**) *noun*
a festival.
[Spanish]

fife *noun*
Music: a high-pitched flute used in military bands.
Word Family: **fifer**, *noun.*

fifteen *noun*
a cardinal number, the symbol 15 in Arabic numerals, XV in Roman numerals.
Word Family: **fifteen**, *adjective*; **fifteenth**, *adjective, noun.*

fifth *adjective, noun*
Word Family: see FIVE.

fifth column
a group of traitors.
[in the Spanish Civil War, 1936, Madrid was attacked by four columns of fascist troops, while a *fifth column* of fascists within the city assisted them]

fifty *noun*
1. a cardinal number, the symbol 50 in Arabic numerals, L in Roman numerals.
2. (*plural*) the numbers 50 to 59 in a series, such as the years within a century.
Word Family: **fifty**, *adjective*; **fiftieth**, *adjective, noun.*

fifty-fifty *adjective, adverb*
(*informal*) in two equal portions.

fig *noun*
a soft, medium-sized, dark-skinned fruit containing many seeds, eaten fresh, preserved or dried.

fight *noun*
a struggle, quarrel or contest.
Usage: 'after ten years in prison there was no *fight* left in him' (= ability or desire to fight).
Phrases:
fighting chance, a fair chance.
fighting fit, very fit or healthy.
Word Family: **fight (fought, fighting)**, *verb*; **fighter**, *noun*, a person or thing that fights.

figment *noun*
something imagined or invented.

figurative (*say* **fig**-yoora-tiv) *adjective*
1. involving a metaphor or figure of speech.
2. (of a painting, sculpture, etc.) representing a figure.
Word Family: **figuratively**, *adverb*; **figurativeness**, *noun.*

figure (*say* **figger**) *noun*
1. a symbol for a number.
2. a form or shape: a) 'geometrical *figures*'; b) 'a girl's slim *figure*'.
Usages:
a) 'the house was sold for a very high *figure*' (= amount, sum).
b) 'John is a wizard at *figures*' (= calculations, arithmetic).
c) 'a literary *figure*' (= person, character).
d) 'the couples danced elaborate *figures*' (= movements).
e) 'the children saw the clown as a *figure* of fun' (= emblem, object).
f) 'the *figures* in the instruction manual explain the parts' (= diagrams).
cut a fine figure, 'he *cuts a fine figure* in his velvet dinner jacket' (= creates a fine appearance).

figure *verb*
1. to appear conspicuously: 'his name *figures* quite often in historical documents of that time'.

2. (*informal*) to be as one expected: 'it *figures* that an unhappy girl would act as she has'.
figure out, (*informal*) 'it was very difficult to *figure out* what he meant' (= understand, work out).
[Latin *figura* shape]

figurehead *noun*
1. a person in a high position but having no real power.
2. *Nautical:* a carved model of a woman or mermaid which decorated the bow of sailing ships.

figure of speech
an expression, such as a simile or metaphor, in which words are not used in their usual sense.

figurine (*say* fig-yoo-**reen**) *noun*
a small, sculptured or carved figure.

filament (*say* **fill**a-m'nt) *noun*
1. any very fine thread or thread-like part, such as the wire in a light globe which heats as electricity passes through it.
2. *Biology:* the stalk of a stamen, supporting the anther.
[Latin *filum* a thread]

filch *verb*
to pilfer.

file (1) *noun*
1. a) a group of papers or records kept in order. b) the container in which they are kept.
2. a row or line of persons or things placed one behind the other.
on file, on record in a file.
file *verb*
1. to put papers, documents, records, etc. in order, for easy access.
2. *Law:* to begin a lawsuit by bringing it before a court.
3. to send in copy to a newspaper.
4. to march or walk in file.

file (2) *noun*
a flat or rounded steel tool, covered with fine ridges or teeth, for smoothing metal or wood.
Word Family: **file,** *verb.*

filial (*say* **fill**i-ul) *adjective*
1. relating to or expected of a son or daughter: '*filial* obedience'.
2. *Biology:* relating to the sequence of generations from the original parents: F_1 is the first filial generation, F_2 is the second, etc.; used of controlled fertilization between selected plants to improve a particular characteristic.
Word Family: **filially,** *adverb.*
[Latin *filius* son]

filibuster (*say* **fill**i-busta) *verb*
to obstruct business in parliament by making long speeches or using other delaying tactics.
Word Family: **filibuster,** *noun*; **filibusterer,** *noun.*
[Spanish *filibustero* a pirate]

filigree (*say* **fill**i-gree) *noun*
a delicate ornamental work of metallic thread, especially of gold or silver, woven into a lace-like design.
Word Family: **filigree,** *verb.*

filings *plural noun*
the small particles removed by a file.

fill *verb*
to make or become full: a) 'let me *fill* your glass'; b) 'the dam *filled* during the wet season'.
Usages:
a) 'her room was *filled* with books' (= plentifully supplied).
b) 'I was told that the position of secretary had been *filled*' (= occupied).
c) 'the author said he wrote the book to *fill* a need' (= satisfy).
Phrases:
fill in, a) 'it took an hour to *fill in* the forms' (= complete); b) 'what's the best way to *fill in* time?' (= occupy); c) 'she *filled in* for me when I was sick' (= stood in).
fill out, 'he didn't begin to *fill out* till he was over forty' (= put on weight).
fill the bill, 'the doctor said that 2 weeks rest should *fill the bill*' (= be adequate).
fill *noun*
1. a full supply or quantity: 'we let the thirsty horses drink their *fill*'.
2. any material used to fill a hole, cavity, etc.: 'broken bricks make good *fill* on building sites'.
Word Family: **filler,** *noun,* a person or thing that fills, such as putty used to fill cracks; **filling,** *noun,* anything that fills, such as amalgam used to fill a tooth; **filling,** *adjective,* causing a feeling of being full.

fillet *noun*
1. a) any boneless section of meat or fish. b) a cut of tender meat, usually from the loin.
2. a narrow hair band or ribbon.
3. *Architecture:* a squared timber or moulding used to cover joins, etc.
Word Family: **fillet,** *verb.*

filling station
a service station.

fillip *noun*
a flick of the finger.
Usage: 'the newspaper article gave the fund drive a *fillip*' (= boost).
Word Family: **fillip**, *verb.*

filly *noun*
a female horse or pony up to 4 years old.

film *noun*
1. *Photography:* a strip of cellulose ester, coated with a light-sensitive emulsion which will record a series of separate images when exposed in a camera.
2. a) a positive print of such a film, the images of which create the impression of movement when projected consecutively at high speed. b) the story or events so presented.
3. a very thin skin, membrane or coating: 'a *film* of oil on the water'.
film *verb*
1. to cover with or as if with a film: 'his eyes *filmed* with tears'.
2. a) to photograph with a cine camera. b) to produce or create a film.
Word Family: **filmy**, *adjective*, of or like a film.

filter *noun*
any substance or device which prevents certain materials passing through it while allowing the passage of others, such as porous paper to separate sand from water, or a screen on a camera lens to control the colours reaching the film.
filter *verb*
1. to remove or separate by a filter.
2. to pass through or as if through a filter: 'the new ideas finally *filtered* through into people's minds'.
Word Family: **filtration**, *noun*, the act or process of filtering; **filtrate**, *noun*, any liquid that has passed through a filter.

filth *noun*
something that is foul, putrid or repulsive: 'prisoners were forced to eat and sleep in *filth*'.
Word Family: **filthy**, *adjective*; **filthily**, *adverb*; **filthiness**, *noun.*

fin *noun*
1. an external, thin structure on an aquatic animal, used to guide or propel it.
2. a fin-shaped structure on an aircraft, submarine, etc. which has a stabilizing or guiding function.
3. any fin-like projection on a radiator, the cylinders of an air-cooled internal combustion engine, etc., used to dissipate heat.

final (*say* **fie**-n'l) *adjective*
coming at the end: 'the *final* preparations have been completed'.
Usage: 'my answer is *final*' (= decisive).
final *noun*
1. (*often plural*) any contest, examination, etc. coming at the end of a series.
2. *Newspapers:* the last edition for that day.
finalize, finalise *verb*
to put into final form: 'have you *finalized* the arrangements yet?'.
Word Family: **finally**, *adverb*; **finality** (*say* fie-**nalli**-tee), *noun*, the state of being final; **finalist**, *noun*, a person qualified to take part in a final; **finalization**, *noun.*
[Latin *finis* limit, end]

finale (*say* fin-**ah**-lay) *noun*
the last or concluding part of anything, such as the last movement of a piece of music or the last act of a play, ballet, opera, etc.

finance (*say* **fie**-nance *or* fie-**nance**) *noun*
a) money or funds: 'the *finances* of the club are running low'. b) the management of money: 'she is an expert in *finance*'.
financial (*say* fie-**nan**-sh'l *or* fi-**nan**-sh'l) *adjective*
of or relating to finance: 'a special adviser on *financial* matters'.
Word Family: **finance**, *verb*, to provide money for; **financially**, *adverb.*

financial year
a specified period of twelve months, used by governments and businesses when accounting for money received and paid.

financier (*say* fie-**nansia**) *noun*
a person skilled or engaged in borrowing and lending money, especially on a large scale.

finch *noun*
any of a group of small birds such as sparrows, many having strong beaks for crushing seeds.

find *verb*
(**found, finding**)
1. to meet with by chance: 'the campers *found* a cave filled with prehistoric rock drawings'.
2. to obtain by search or effort: 'I finally *found* the answer to the problem'.

Usages:
a) 'the arrow *found* its mark' (= reached).
b) 'she was so surprised by the news that she couldn't *find* her tongue' (= get the use of).
c) 'lately I haven't *found* time to read' (= managed to arrange).
d) 'she *found* that she worked better at night' (= discovered by experience).
e) 'the jury *found* the accused man innocent' (= determined, pronounced).
Phrases:
find fault, 'he *finds fault* with everything she does' (= criticizes).
find oneself, to discover one's true vocation, abilities, etc.
find one's feet, see FOOT.
find out, 'most criminals assume they won't be *found out*' (= detected).
find *noun*
a) the act of finding: 'the oil company made a big *find*'. b) something found, especially something valuable: 'the table we bought was a real *find*'.
Word Family: **finder**, *noun*, a) a person who finds, b) something which finds, such as a viewfinder in a camera.

finding *noun*
Law: the decision of a court on a question of fact at the end of a court case.

fine (1) *adjective*
1. of very high quality: a) 'a *fine* building'; b) '*fine* gold'.
2. thin or slender: 'a *fine* thread'.
Usages:
a) '*fine* weather is forecast for the weekend' (= sunny, without rain).
b) 'she has a gift for *fine* needlework' (= delicate).
c) 'the lawyers quibbled over a *fine* distinction' (= subtle, difficult to grasp).
d) 'the pencil had a *fine* point' (= sharp).
e) 'the furniture was coated with *fine* dust' (= composed of minute particles).
f) 'the fisherman used a *fine* net' (= small-holed).
fine *verb*
1. to make or become fine.
2. to clarify wine, beer, etc. by filtering.
Word Family: **fine**, *adverb*, well; **finely**, *adverb*; **fineness**, *noun*.

fine (2) *noun*
a sum of money paid as punishment for breaking a law or rule.
Word Family: **fine**, *verb*.

fine arts
any forms of art which are considered the highest expression of beauty, such as painting, music, architecture, poetry, etc.

finery *noun*
any richly elegant clothes.

finesse (*say* fin-**ess**) *noun*
1. any skill or delicacy in doing something: 'the ambassador conducted negotiations with great *finesse*'.
2. *Cards:* an attempt to take a trick by playing a low card in the hope that a higher card is not in the hand of an opponent who is yet to play.
Word Family: **finesse**, *verb*, to make a finesse at cards.
[French, fineness]

finger *noun*
1. *Anatomy:* any of the five members of the hand, especially one other than the thumb.
2. a finger-like piece, part or measure: a) 'the *finger* of a glove'; b) a *finger* of toast'; c) a *finger* of gin'.
Phrases:
burn one's fingers, 'he *burnt his fingers* in a business deal' (= suffered a loss).
have a finger in the pie, to be involved in or have a part in an enterprise or scheme.
keep one's fingers crossed, to hope for good luck.
lay a finger on, 'the police said they didn't *lay a finger on* the suspect' (= harm in any way).
lift a finger, see LIFT.
put one's finger on, 'I can't quite *put my finger on* the problem' (= identify, locate).
twist round one's little finger, 'it's quite obvious that his mother-in-law *twists him round her little finger*' (= manipulates or dominates him).
Word Family: **finger**, *verb*, to touch or handle with the fingers.

fingerboard *noun*
Music: the wooden part of a stringed instrument, against which the strings are pressed to vary the pitch of a note.

fingerbowl *noun*
a small bowl to hold water for rinsing the fingers at a meal.

fingernail *noun*
the horny growth at the end of a finger.

fingerprint *noun*
the pattern formed by the tiny ridges on the tips of the fingers.

fingerprint *verb*
to record a person's fingerprints with ink, for purposes of identification.

finicky (*say* **finni-kee**) *adjective*
also called **finicking** or **finical**
fussy or too particular.
Word Family: **finically**, *adverb.*

finis (say **finnis**) *noun*
the end.
[Latin]

finish *verb*
1. to bring or come to an end: 'I shall *finish* the job by 2 o'clock'.
Usage: 'the horse *finished* well but didn't win' (= completed the last stage).
2. to put a final coating or surface on.
finish off, a) to consume completely; b) (*informal*) to kill.
finish *noun*
the end or conclusion: 'most of the characters in the novel are dead at the *finish*'.
Usages:
a) 'she is a person of considerable poise and *finish*' (= sophistication).
b) 'the furniture had a very shiny *finish*' (= surface or coating).
c) 'the cabinet-maker used his own brand of *finish*' (= material for finishing wood).

finite (*say* **fie** nite) *adjective*
1. having limits or bounds: 'some scientists think the universe is *finite*'.
2. *Maths:* a) capable of being completely counted. b) neither infinite nor infinitesimal.
Word Family: **finitely**, *adverb*; **finiteness**, *noun.*
[Latin *finitus* bounded]

finnan haddock
a large split haddock smoked over a peat fire.
[after *Findon*, a Kincardineshire fishing village]

fiord (*say* **fee-ord**) **fjord** *noun*
a long, deep, narrow inlet of the sea with steep, often mountainous sides, originally deepened by the action of glaciers.
[Norwegian]

fir *noun*
any of a group of evergreen, Northern Hemisphere trees with erect cones and short, needle-like leaves.

fire *noun*
1. a) the flame, heat and light produced by burning. b) a body of burning material.
2. something resembling this in intensity of heat or light: 'the *fire* of a diamond'.
Usage: 'the speech lacked any *fire*' (= energy, intensity).
3. the discharge of firearms or artillery.
Phrases:
catch fire, to burst into flames.
hang fire, 'until plans were approved the company had to *hang fire* on the new building project' (= delay).
on fire, burning.
open fire, to start shooting.
play with fire, to take chances with something dangerous.
under fire, a) being shot at; b) 'a government minister *under fire* for his policies' (= under criticism or verbal attack).
fire *verb*
1. to set on fire.
2. to discharge firearms, artillery, etc.
3. (*informal*) to dismiss from a job.
4. to harden pottery, etc. in a kiln by heating it slowly to a high temperature.
Usages:
a) 'she was *fired* with the promise of success' (= inspired).
b) 'the engine finally *fired*' (= started).
fire away, (*informal*) to begin speaking or go ahead.

firearm *noun*
any of various small arms, such as rifles, revolvers or light machine-guns.

fireball *noun*
any brightly burning sphere, such as a meteor.

firebrand *noun*
1. a piece of wood lit at one end from a fire, used as a torch or to light other fires.
2. a person who excites or inspires passions, trouble, etc.

firebreak *noun*
a strip of land which is cleared to stop the spread of a fire.

firebrick *noun*
a brick made of a special heat-resistant clay, used in chimneys, etc.

fire brigade
an organized group of firemen, usually belonging to a particular district and wearing a uniform.

firebug *noun*
a person who deliberately sets fire to things, especially buildings.

firecracker *noun*
any firework which explodes.

firedamp *noun*
the methane gas found in coal mines, potentially explosive in air.

firedog *noun*
also called an **andiron**
either of a pair of iron supports holding logs in a fireplace.

fire drill
a practice in the use of fire–fighting equipment or methods of escape in case of fire.

fire–engine *noun*
a motor vehicle equipped for fighting fires with high–pressure hoses, pumps, etc.

fire–escape *noun*
any exit from a building for use in case of fire, such as an outside staircase.

fire–extinguisher *noun*
see EXTINGUISHER.

fire–fighter *noun*
a person who fights fires.

firefly *noun*
any of two groups of soft–bodied, nocturnal beetles which can produce light. The females of some species are called **glow–worms.**

fireguard *noun*
also called a **firescreen**
a metal screen placed in front of a fire for protection.

fire hydrant
see HYDRANT.

fire irons
any tools for arranging a fire, especially tongs, a poker, etc.

firelighter *noun*
a block of highly inflammable substance used to start fires.

fireman *noun*
1. a person skilled or trained in preventing or fighting fires.
2. a) a person who tends the fire in a steam–engine. Also called a **stoker.**
b) the assistant driver of a railway locomotive.

fireplace *noun*
the part of a chimney opening into a room, in which fires are lit.

fire power
the amount of fire delivered by a weapon or military unit.

fireproof *adjective*
designed or constructed so as to resist fire.
Word Family: **fireproof,** *verb*; **fireproofing,** *noun*, any material used to make something fireproof.

firescreen *noun*
a fireguard.

fire station
a building used by a fire brigade for storing equipment, etc.

fire tower
a watchtower, usually in a wooded area, in which a person is posted to watch for and report fires.

firetrap *noun*
a building, etc. which is especially dangerous in the event of fire.

firewall *noun*
a wall designed to resist fire and stop it spreading, e.g. between the engine compartment and the rest of an aircraft.

firework *noun*
1. (*usually plural*) any explosive device used to produce a bright light or a loud noise, often for a display or as a signal at night.
2. (*plural*) an outburst of bad temper, violence, etc.

firing line
the point at which troops are close enough to the enemy positions to fire on them.
in the firing line, subjected by one's position or situation to blame, verbal attack, etc.

firing pin
a pin in the mechanism of a gun which, when released, strikes the primer of a cartridge to fire the gun.

firing squad
a detachment of soldiers appointed to shoot a condemned person.

firm (1) *adjective*
solid or secure: 'he climbed out of the water on to *firm* dry ground'.
Usages:
a) 'the nurse's *firm* hands tied the bandages' (= steady).
b) 'my decision to leave is quite *firm*' (= definite, fixed).
Word Family: **firm,** *verb*, to make or become firm; **firmly, firm,** *adverbs*; **firmness,** *noun.*

firm (2) *noun*
a business organization, such as a company or partnership.
[Italian *firma* a signature]

firmament *noun*
an old word for the sky, seen as a vault or arch.
[Latin *firmamentum* a support]

first *adjective, adverb*
1. being number one in a series.
2. before all others in time, importance, etc.
first *noun*
1. (*informal*) anything which is first in time, importance, etc.: 'this model is an exciting *first* in car design'.
2. first-class honours in a university exam.
Word Family: **firstly**, *adverb.*

first aid
any emergency assistance given to a sick or injured person after an accident, etc.

firstborn *noun*
the eldest.

first class
the most expensive and comfortable passenger accommodation on a train, aeroplane, etc.
first-class *adjective*
1. being the highest grade possible in passing an examination.
2. of the highest or best quality: 'even by world standards this is a *first-class* restaurant'.
3. of or relating to the first class: 'a *first-class* carriage'.

first cousin
see COUSIN.

first floor
American: the ground floor.

first-generation *adjective*
(of a country's citizen) having been born in a foreign country or having foreign parents.

first-hand *adjective*
direct from the original source: 'we receive *first-hand* racing information from the jockeys'.

First Lady
American: the wife of the President or a State Governor.

firstly *adverb*
Word Family: see FIRST.

first night
the first performance of a play, opera, etc.

first person
Grammar: see PERSON.

first principle
(*usually plural*) the fundamental basis or principles from which a law, concept, etc. is derived.

first-rate *adjective*
excellent.

first water
the highest degree of quality or excellence: 'a diamond of the *first water*'.

firth *noun*
Scottish: a long, narrow inlet in the seacoast.

fiscal (*say* **fis** -k'l) *adjective*
of or relating to finance.
[Latin *fiscus* a money-box]

fish *noun*
plural is **fish** or **fishes**
1. a cold-blooded, aquatic animal having a spine and gills and usually with fins and scales on its body.
2. *Astrology:* (*capital, plural*) see PISCES.
Phrases:
a fine kettle of fish, **a pretty kettle of fish**, a difficult or perplexing situation.
a fish out of water, a person who is ill at ease or uncomfortable in new or strange surroundings.
other fish to fry, other more important matters or business to be dealt with.
fish *verb*
1. to catch or attempt to catch fish.
2. to search for or remove: 'he *fished* a handkerchief out of his back pocket'.
3. to seek by indirect methods: 'to *fish* for compliments'.
Word Family: **fishing**, *noun*, the art or practice of catching fish; **fisherman**, **fisher**, *nouns*, a person who fishes.

fishcake *noun*
a patty made from fish, deep-fried in breadcrumbs or batter.

fishery *noun*
a) the occupation or industry of catching fish. b) a place where fish are bred, hatched and reared.

fisheye lens
Photography: an extremely curved lens with a viewing angle of up to 180°.

fishhook *noun*
any of various barbed hooks used to catch fish.

fishmonger (*say* fish-**munga**) *noun*
a person who sells fish.

fishplate *noun*
a thin, rectangular plate, usually steel, for joining railway lines, stanchions, etc.

fishwife *noun*
plural is **fishwives**
1. a coarse or abusive woman.
2. a woman who sells fish.

fishy *adjective*
1. of or like fish.
2. causing doubt or suspicion: 'there is something *fishy* about the way he answered our questions'.

fissile *adjective*
1. able to be split or divided.
2. *Physics:* capable of undergoing nuclear fission by any process.
[Latin *fissilis* easily split]

fission (*say* **fish**'n) *noun*
1. the act of splitting or dividing into parts, such as the biological reproduction of an organism by dividing into several parts, each of which forms a new organism.
2. *Physics:* see NUCLEAR FISSION.

fissure (*say* **fish**er) *noun*
a narrow opening formed by cleavage or the separation of parts.
Word Family: **fissure,** *verb.*

fist *noun*
1. a tightly closed hand.
2. (*informal*) the hand.
Word Family: **fistful,** *noun,* a handful.

fisticuffs *plural noun*
any fighting with the fists.

fistula (*say* **fist**-yoola) *noun*
a body passage formed by disease or injury, linking a hollow space or abscess to the surface of the skin.
Word Family: **fistular,** *adjective.*
[Latin, a tube]

fit (1) *verb*
(fitted, fitting)
1. to be or make the right shape or size for: a) 'these shoes do not *fit* properly'; b) 'the salesman *fitted* the jacket'.
2. to put carefully into place: 'the mechanic *fitted* new wheels on to the car'.
3. to be or make suitable or appropriate to: a) 'the punishment must be made to *fit* the crime'; b) 'he has few qualities which *fit* him for leadership'.
Phrases:
fit in, a) to have room for; b) to adapt to.
fit out, fit up, to equip.

fit *adjective*
1. suitable or right: 'that burnt toast is not *fit* to be eaten'.
2. being in good health or physical condition: 'she is still not quite *fit* after the long illness'.
fit *noun*
the manner in which something fits: 'the *fit* of that coat is perfect'.
Word Family: **fitness,** *noun*; **fitly,** *adverb,* in a suitable manner.

fit (2) *noun*
1. a sudden, violent burst or outburst: 'in a *fit* of rage she threw the plate against the wall.
2. *Medicine:* an uncontrollable, repeated contraction of the muscles, leading to a loss of consciousness. Also called a **convulsion.**
by fits and starts, by fits, 'he's only capable of working *by fits and starts*' (= in intermittent bursts).
fitful *adjective*
irregular or intermittent.
Word Family: **fitfully,** *adverb*; **fitfulness,** *noun.*
[Old English *fytt* a struggle]

fitter *noun*
a person whose work is to fit things, especially in the assembly of mechanical parts or machines.

fitting *noun*
1. the act of fitting, especially the trying on and adjusting of clothes for size.
2. (of clothes) a size.
3. any device or equipment provided for something, such as furnishings or fixtures in a house.
Word Family: **fitting,** *adjective,* appropriate or suitable; **fittingly,** *adverb*; **fittingness,** *noun.*

five *noun*
a cardinal number, the symbol 5 in Arabic numerals, V in Roman numerals.
Word Family: **five,** *adjective*; **fifth,** *noun, adjective.*

fiver *noun*
(*informal*) a five pound note.

fives *plural noun*
a game similar to squash but in which a hard ball is played with the gloved hand. The Rugby fives court has four walls; the Eton version has three walls and a buttress.
[possibly from *bunch of fives,* the fingers of the hand]

fix *verb*
1. to make or hold secure: 'the post was *fixed* into the ground'.
2. to repair or put in good condition: 'can you *fix* this broken light?'.
3. to make permanent and unchanging: 'he *fixed* the colour with a chemical spray'.
Usages:
a) 'we all *fixed* our attention on the speaker' (= directed).
b) 'the teacher *fixed* her with an angry glare' (= singled out).
c) 'the rent is *fixed* at £35 a month' (= settled).
d) (*informal*) 'the result of the fight was *fixed* by an organized syndicate' (= arranged dishonestly).
e) 'the insect was *fixed* for study under the microscope' (= killed and preserved).
fix on, fix upon, 'we have not yet *fixed on* a place to go for our holiday' (= decided on, chosen).
fix *noun*
1. a difficult or awkward situation.
2. the finding of one's position or bearings by observation, calculation, etc.
3. (*informal*) an injection of a hard drug such as heroin.
Word Family: **fixedly,** *adverb.*

fixation *noun*
Psychology: a persistent attachment to a person, object or type of behaviour, usually formed at an early stage in psychological development and leading to an inability to form normal relationships, etc.
Word Family: **fixate,** *verb.*

fixative (*say* **fiksa**–tiv) *noun*
any substance which fixes, hardens or preserves.

fixed assets
Commerce: any assets, such as machinery, which are kept for use rather than resale.

fixed star
Astronomy: a star in a constellation which, being so remote, appears not to move in relation to its companion stars. Compare PLANET.

fixer *noun*
Photography: a chemical used on developed film to stop further action of light changing the image.

fixity (*say* **fiksi**–tee) *noun*
the state of being fixed or permanent.

fixture (*say* **fiks**–cher) *noun*
1. an object which is fixed into position, such as the lights in a house.
Usage: 'the cleaner has been a *fixture* in the firm for 57 years' (= permanent or long–established figure).
2. the fixing or prearrangement of the date of a sporting event.

fizz *verb*
to hiss or bubble vigorously, as an aerated drink.
Word Family: **fizz,** *noun*; **fizzy,** *adjective.*

fizzle *verb*
to splutter weakly.
fizzle out, 'the party *fizzled out* after the music stopped' (= ended feebly or in failure).
Word Family: **fizzle,** *noun.*

fjord (*say* fee–**ord**) *noun*
see FIORD.

flabbergast (*say* **flabba**–gahst) *verb*
to shock or astonish extremely.

flabby *adjective*
hanging loosely and limply.
Usage: 'his *flabby* excuses only irritated us' (= weak).
Word Family: **flabbily,** *adverb*; **flabbiness,** *noun.*

flaccid (*say* **flak**–sid *or* **flass**id) *adjective*
flabby or drooping: 'his *flaccid* muscles indicated a lack of exercise'.
Word Family: **flaccidness, flaccidity** (*say* flak–**siddi**–tee), *nouns*; **flaccidly,** *adverb.*
[Latin *flaccidus* flabby]

flag (1) *noun*
a square or oblong cloth with a distinctive pattern, usually coloured, indicating nationality, ownership, a club or a signal; usually attached by one edge to a cord, stick or post.
flag *verb*
(flagged, flagging)
to wave or signal a person to stop: 'we *flagged* down a passing truck to ask for help'.

flag (2) *verb*
(flagged, flagging)
to weaken or lose strength: 'our enthusiasm *flagged* as we realized the hard work ahead'.

flag (3) *noun*
a flagstone.
Word Family: **flag (flagged, flagging),** *verb,* to pave with flagstones.

flagellate (*say* **flaja**–late) *verb*
to whip or flog.

flagellant (*say* **flaja**–lant) ***noun***
a person who whips or punishes himself, especially as a religious discipline.
Word Family: **flagellation**, ***noun.***

flagellum (*say* fla–**jell**'m) ***noun***
plural is **flagella**
Biology: a long hair-like appendage serving as an organ of locomotion on bacteria, etc.
Word Family: **flagellate**, *adjective*, having flagella.
[Latin, a whip]

flagitious (*say* fla–**jish**us) *adjective*
extremely wicked or criminal.
[Latin *flagitium* a vicious act]

flag officer
any naval officer having the rank of rear admiral, vice-admiral or admiral and therefore entitled to fly a flag showing his rank.

flagon (*say* **flagg**'n) ***noun***
a large bottle or container for wine or liquor.

flagrant (*say* **flay**–gr'nt) *adjective*
being shamefully or deliberately obvious: 'his *flagrant* disobedience made the teachers very angry'.
Word Family: **flagrantly**, *adverb*; **flagrancy**, *noun.*
[Latin *flagrans* blazing]

flagstone ***noun***
short form is **flag**
a flat heavy piece of stone used for making paths, roads, etc.

flail ***noun***
a tool with a long handle and a freely moving bar at the end, used to thresh grain.
flail *verb*
to thresh with or as if with a flail.
Usage: 'the swimmer's arms *flailed* wildly as the wave swept over him' (= thrashed about).

flair ***noun***
a natural ability or talent.
[Old French *flairer* to smell out]

flak ***noun***
any anti-aircraft fire.
[from German, FL(ieger) A(bwehr) K(anone), anti-aircraft gun]

flake ***noun***
a small light piece of anything, especially one detached from a larger mass: 'a *flake* of skin peeled off her sunburnt nose'.
flake *verb*
to peel, separate or fall in flakes.
flake out, (*informal*) 'the athlete *flaked out* after completing the race' (= collapsed, fainted).
Word Family: **flaky**, *adjective*; **flakily**, *adverb*; **flakiness**, *noun.*

flamboyant (*say* flam–**boy**'nt) *adjective*
bold, elaborate or showy, especially in an exaggerated way.
Word Family: **flamboyantly**, *adverb*; **flamboyance**, **flamboyancy**, *noun.*
[French, flaming]

flame ***noun***
1. a sheet or tongue of fire.
2. a reddish-orange colour.
Usages:
a) 'the *flame* of the neon lights made the city look like a fairyland' (= brilliant colour or light).
b) 'she finally married an old *flame* from her youth' (= sweetheart).
flame *verb*
to burn or glow with flames.
Usage: 'her face *flamed* with embarrassment' (= became red).

flamenco (*say* fla–**menko**) ***noun***
a lively style of guitar music and dancing characteristic of the gipsies of southern Spain.

flamingo (*say* fla–**mingo**) ***noun***
plural is **flamingoes**
a long-legged, tropical, wading bird with a long neck and pink or red feathers.
[Latin *flamma* a flame]

flammable (*say* **flamma**–b'l) *adjective*
inflammable.

flan ***noun***
a round, open pastry shell, filled with fruit, custard or cream.

flange (*say* flanj) ***noun***
a projecting rim by which objects are joined or kept in place.
Word Family: **flange**, *verb*, a) to project like a flange, b) to form as a flange.

flank ***noun***
1. the fleshy part of the side of animals, including man.
2. a cut of meat from the flank of an animal.
3. the side of anything: 'the left *flank* of the army opened fire first'.
flank *verb*
to be situated at the flank or side of, especially to provide protection.

flannel *noun*
1. a warm, soft woollen fabric.
2. (*usually plural*) any clothes made of flannel, especially cricket trousers.
3. a facecloth.

flannelette (*say* flanna-**let**) *noun*
a soft, cotton fabric made to imitate flannel.

flap *noun*
1. a loose, partly joined piece: 'he sealed down the *flap* of the envelope'.
2. a) a loose, swinging or waving movement. b) the sound it makes.
3. (*informal*) a fuss or panic.
4. *Aeronautics:* see AIR-BRAKE.
flap *verb*
(flapped, flapping)
1. a) (of wings, arms, etc.) to move vigorously up and down. b) to swing or wave loosely: 'the flag *flapped* in the breeze'.
2. to make a muffled slapping sound.
3. (*informal*) to panic or make a fuss.

flapjack *noun*
1. a compact and puff for face-powder.
2. a thick pancake.

flapper *noun*
a defiantly unconventional young woman in the 1920's.

flare *verb*
1. to burst into a bright, strong flame: 'the match *flared* in the darkness'.
Usage: 'tempers *flared* during the long and exhausting debate' (= erupted, burst fiercely).
2. to burn with an unsteady flame: 'the candle *flared* in the breeze'.
3. to spread or curve outwards: 'her skirt *flared* from the waist'.
flare *noun*
1. a flaring or blazing flame.
2. any of various devices which give a brilliant white or coloured light, used as distress signals at sea, etc.
3. a spreading or curving outwards.

flare-up *noun*
a sudden flaring or outburst of anger, excitement or fighting.

flash *noun*
1. a sudden burst of light, fire, colour, etc.: 'a *flash* of lightning'.
Usage: 'in a *flash* of inspiration, he wrote two more chapters of his novel' (= brief burst).
2. a short item of urgent news or information.
3. *Photography:* any device, such as a flashbulb, attached to a camera to provide a brief source of artificial light for a photograph. An **electronic flash** provides continuous single flashes from a store of electricity.
4. an emblem of a military unit, usually worn on the sleeve.
Phrases:
flash in the pan, 'his clever solution to the problem was a *flash in the pan*' (= brilliant but short-lived effort).
in a flash, 'this detergent will clean your windows *in a flash*' (= instantly, at once).
flash *verb*
to give off or send a flash.
Usages:
a) 'the idea *flashed* through his mind' (= went suddenly and quickly).
b) 'her eyes *flashed* with rage' (= shone brightly).
c) (*informal*) 'he *flashes* his money to try and impress people' (= displays ostentatiously).
flash, flashy *adjective*
brilliant or smart, especially in a showy or vulgar way.

flashback *noun*
a return to events or actions which occurred in the past, such as the showing of parts of a story out of sequence in a film, novel, etc.

flash flood
a sudden flood, such as water rushing down a mountain valley after heavy rain.

flashing *noun*
Building: a protective strip of metal used to cover corners or joints, e.g. where a roof meets a wall.

flashlight *noun*
a torch or other light with a very bright, strong beam.

flashpoint *noun*
the lowest temperature at which a substance gives off sufficient inflammable vapour to produce a flash in the presence of a small flame.
Usage: 'tempers reached a *flashpoint* after he was sacked' (= uncontrollable level).

flashy *adjective*
see FLASH.

flask *noun*
a small, flat bottle for liquids.

flat (1) *adjective*
1. level and smooth: 'the *flat* desert country stretched unendingly to the horizon'.
2. not deep or high: '*flat* shoes'.
3. fixed or absolute: a) 'there is a *flat* rate for the hire of all cars'; b) his *flat* refusal did not surprise us'.

4. *Music:* being lowered in pitch by a semitone. Compare SHARP.
Usages:
a) 'he fell *flat* on his face in the mud' (= at full length).
b) 'my bicycle has a *flat* front tyre' (= deflated).
c) 'his low, *flat* voice was difficult to hear' (= monotonous, uninteresting).
d) 'this lemonade is quite *flat*' (= without bubbles).
e) 'the unsuccessful comedian made several *flat* jokes' (= pointless).
f) 'the walls were painted in a *flat* yellow' (= not shiny).
flat *noun*
1. any flat surface or part.
Usage: 'the car has another *flat*' (= flat tyre).
2. (*usually plural*) any low-lying land, especially near water: 'river *flats*'.
3. *Theatre:* any flat piece of scenery, usually of canvas or wood and joined with others to make up the set.
4. *Music:* a) a flat note. b) the sign indicating this.
flat *adverb*
1. in a flat position: 'he laid the paper *flat* on the table'.
2. exactly or absolutely.
Phrases:
fall flat, to fail.
flat out, 'he ran *flat out* to catch the bus' (= as fast as possible).
Word Family: **flatness**, *noun*; **flatly**, *adverb.*

flat (2) *noun*
in America called an **apartment**
one or more rooms rented to live in, usually with kitchen and bathroom.
flat *verb*
(**flatted, flatting**)
to live with other people, usually peers, as a domestic unit.
Word Family: **flatmate**, *noun*, someone who shares a flat.

flatfish *noun*
any of a group of side-swimming fish, such as the flounder, having a flattened body and both eyes on one side of its head.

flat-footed *adjective*
1. having the arch of the foot flattened so that most of the sole rests on the ground when standing.
2. (*informal*) clumsy or awkward.

flatiron (*say* **flat**-cye on) *noun*
an iron, especially one that is heated on a stove, etc.

flat race
a race run on a level course with no obstacles.

flat spin
(*informal*) a state of great confusion or panic.

flatten *verb*
to make or become flat.
Usage: 'he *flattened* her with his stinging rebuke' (= disconcerted, crushed).

flatter *verb*
1. to praise extremely, especially in order to please or win favour.
2. to please or make grateful: 'the young mother was *flattered* by our attention to her baby'.
3. to show or portray favourably: 'this photo really *flatters* you'.
flatter oneself, 'do not *flatter yourself* that you will win the prize' (= wrongly believe).
Word Family: **flatterer**, *noun*, a person who flatters; **flattery** *noun.*

flatulence (*say* **flat**-yoo-l'nce)
flatulency *noun*
the state of having excess gas in the stomach or intestines which causes belching or a bloated feeling.
Word Family: **flatulent**, *adjective*, a) suffering from flatulence, b) pretentious; **flatulently**, *adverb.*
[Latin *flatus* blowing]

flatworm *noun*
any platyhelminth.

flaunt (*say* flawnt) *verb*
to display boldly or ostentatiously.

flautist (*say* **flaw**-tist) *noun*
a person who plays the flute.

flavour (*say* **flay**-va) *noun*
in America spelt **flavor**
1. a distinctive taste.
2. a characteristic quality: 'there is a *flavour* of dishonesty about this transaction'.
flavour *verb*
to give flavour to: 'the stew was *flavoured* with fresh herbs'.
Usage: 'he *flavoured* his story with many romantic details' (= added colour to).
Word Family: **flavoursome**, *adjective*, full of flavour.

flavouring *noun*
in America spelt **flavoring**
any substance used to add flavour.

flaw *noun*
1. anything which lessens the value or beauty of another: 'laziness is the only *flaw* in her character'.
2. a crack or break: 'the antique cup had a small *flaw* in the handle'.
Word Family: **flaw**, *verb*, to spoil or mar; **flawlessly**, *adverb*; **flawlessness**, *noun.*

flax *noun*
1. any of various annual plants with narrow leaves and blue flowers, cultivated for their oil-bearing seeds (linseed) and fine fibre.
2. a fibre made from this plant and used to make linen yarn.

flaxen *adjective*
1. of or made of flax.
2. having the pale yellowish colour of treated flax.

flay *verb*
to strip the skin off.
Usage: 'the theatre company's latest performance was *flayed* by the critics' (= criticized harshly).

flea *noun*
any of a group of small, wingless leaping insects which suck blood and are parasitic on mammals and birds.
a flea in one's ear, a sharp rebuke.

flea-bitten *adjective*
1. covered with fleas.
2. (of a horse, etc.) having a spotted or flecked coat.

flea market
a market, especially one in the open air, where second-hand articles are sold.

fleck *noun*
a small spot or mark of colour or light.
Word Family: **fleck**, *verb*, to mark with flecks or spots.

fledge *verb*
see FLETCH.
fledged *adjective*
(of birds) having feathers and able to fly.
Usage: 'the scheme is now fully *fledged* and ready for trial' (= prepared).

fledgling (*say* **flej**-ling) **fledgeling** *noun*
1. a young bird just able to fly.
2. a young or inexperienced person.

flee *verb*
(fled, fleeing)
to run away from danger, pursuers, etc.: 'the villagers *fled* as the troops invaded'.

fleece *noun*
1. the wool of a sheep, especially the wool shorn at one time.
2. a fabric with a soft pile, used for lining garments to give them extra warmth.
fleece *verb*
to remove the fleece from a sheep.
Usage: 'investors were *fleeced* by the dishonest company' (= swindled).
Word Family: **fleecy**, *adjective*, being lined with or made of fleece.

fleet (1) *noun*
1. a large group of ships or other vehicles travelling together or organized by one company.
2. *Navy:* the largest organized unit of ships or warships under one officer.

fleet (2) *adjective*
swift or fast.
Word Family: **fleetness**, *noun*; **fleetly**, *adverb.*

fleeting *adjective*
passing or moving swiftly: 'a *fleeting* glance'.
Word Family: **fleetingly**, *adverb.*

flense *verb*
also called to **flench**
to strip the blubber from a whale or seal.

flesh *noun*
1. the soft part of an animal body, fruit or vegetable, excluding the skin, etc.
2. the physical body or nature of man, as distinct from the soul or spirit.
3. the surface of the body: 'his *flesh* was pale'.
Phrases:
flesh and blood, a) 'do not be afraid of him, he is only *flesh and blood*' (= human); b) 'we are of the same *flesh and blood*' (= family).
in the flesh, 'you will soon be able to see this famous international star *in the flesh*' (= in person).
flesh *verb*
to remove flesh from hides for the processing of leather.

flesh colour
a pinkish-cream colour.

fleshly *adjective*
of or relating to flesh or the body, especially as distinct from the spirit.

fleshpots *plural noun*
(*informal*) a place or condition of luxury or good living.

fleshy *adjective*
of or having much flesh: 'this climate produces large, *fleshy* fruit'.
Word Family: **fleshiness**, *noun.*

fletch *verb*
also called to **fledge**
Archery: to fit feathers or plastic vanes to an arrow.

fleur-de-lis (*say* fler-de-**lee**) *noun*
plural is **fleurs-de-lis**
an emblem with three petals or leaves gathered at the base, which was used as the armorial bearings of the French monarchy.
[French *fleur* flower + *de lys* of lily]

flew *verb*
the past tense of the verb **fly (1)**.

flex *verb*
to bend or stretch something springy, such as a muscle.
flex *noun*
a length of insulated electric cable.

flexible (*say* **fleksi**-b'l) *adjective*
able to be bent easily.
Usage: 'his political beliefs are very *flexible*' (= adaptable).
Word Family: **flexibly**, *adverb*; **flexibility** (*say* fleksi-**billi**-tee), *noun.*
[Latin *flexibilis* pliant, tractable]

flexitime, flextime *noun*
the policy of allowing employees to vary their time of arrival and departure as long as they work for the usual number of hours in a week.

flibbertigibbet (*say* **flibba**-tee-jibbet) *noun*
a silly or flighty person.

flick *verb*
to strike or touch quickly and lightly: 'he impatiently *flicked* the dust off his coat'.
flick *noun*
1. a) a quick, light blow or the noise it makes: 'with a *flick* of the switch the lights sprang on'. b) anything flicked or thrown: 'a *flick* of paint landed on her chin'.
2. (*informal, usually plural*) a) a film at the cinema. b) the cinema.

flicker *verb*
to burn, shine or move briefly and unsteadily: 'the dying fire *flickered* gently'.
flicker *noun*
a brief, unsteady movement or light: a) 'there was a *flicker* of light from the globe before it burnt out'; b) 'a *flicker* of hope sprang into her eyes'.
[Old English *flicorian* to move the wings]

flick-knife *noun*
also called a **switchblade**
a knife with a spring-loaded, retractable blade which is released when a switch is pressed.

flier *noun*
see FLYER.

flies *plural noun*
the plural of **fly (1)** and **fly (2)**.

flight (1) *noun*
1. a) the act or manner of flying. b) a journey made by air: 'their *flight* across the Atlantic was long and tiring'.
Usages:
a) 'the *flight* of time amazed us all' (= swift movement).
b) 'in a *flight* of fancy he believed he was the King' (= extraordinary soaring).
2. a number of things flying together: 'a *flight* of seagulls swooped down to the water'.
3. the distance covered by a flying object, such as a missile, aircraft, etc.
4. any unbroken row of stairs.
5. the smallest tactical unit of an airforce, consisting of two or more aircraft.
Word Family: **flight**, *verb*, to attach feathers to an arrow, dart, etc. to make it fly straight.

flight (2) *noun*
take flight, to flee or run away.

flight deck
1. the part of an aeroplane where the controls are situated.
2. *Navy:* see AIRCRAFT-CARRIER.

flightless *adjective*
not able to fly.

flight lieutenant
a commissioned officer in the airforce, ranking between a flying officer and a squadron leader.

flight sergeant
a non-commissioned officer in the airforce.

flighty *adjective*
silly, frivolous or fickle.

flimsy (*say* **flim**-zee) *adjective*
weak and easily damaged or destroyed.
Word Family: **flimsiness**, *noun.*

flinch *verb*
to move back or away from, as in fear, repulsion, etc.
Word Family: **flinch**, *noun.*

fling *verb*
(**flung, flinging**)
to throw violently: 'he *flung* the door open'.
Usage: 'she *flung* off with an angry exclamation' (= rushed).
fling *noun*
1. the act of flinging or throwing.
2. a spree: 'have a *fling* and buy yourself some new clothes'.
3. a lively Scottish dance in which the arms and legs are flung about.

flint *noun*
a) a very hard and brittle form of silica which produces a spark when struck with steel. b) the alloy which produces a spark in cigarette lighters.

flintlock *noun*
a musket fired by lighting the gunpowder with a spark from a flint.

flinty *adjective*
of or resembling flint.
Usage: 'the *flinty* eyes of the bandit terrified the hostages' (= hard, cruel).
Word Family: **flintily,** *adverb*; **flintiness,** *noun.*

flip (1) *verb*
(**flipped, flipping**)
1. to move or throw with a snapping or jerking movement: 'to *flip* a coin into the air'.
2. to strike lightly and quickly: 'he *flipped* the page with his finger'.
3. (*informal*) to become angry or upset.
flip *noun*
1. a quick, abrupt movement: 'a *flip* of the wrist'.
2. a somersault: 'a back *flip*'.

flip (2) *noun*
a drink made with alcohol, eggs, sugar and often spices.

flip–flop *noun*
1. a light, repeated flapping movement or noise.
2. an electronic device which has alternate states, such as on or off.

flippant *adjective*
not suitably or sufficiently serious.
Word Family: **flippancy, flippantness,** *nouns*; **flippantly,** *adverb.*

flipper *noun*
1. *Anatomy:* a broad, flat limb on certain aquatic animals, such as whales and seals, used for swimming, guidance, etc.
2. either of two rubber objects shaped like animal flippers and attached to the feet to aid swimming.

flip side
the side of a gramophone record carrying a less popular song, etc.

flirt *verb*
1. to behave in a light–hearted amorous manner.
2. to treat or consider light–heartedly: 'we have been *flirting* with the idea of buying a new car'.
Word Family: **flirt,** *noun,* a person who flirts; **flirtation,** *noun,* a) the act of flirting, b) a light–hearted love affair; **flirtatious,** *adjective,* given to flirtation; **flirtatiously,** *adverb*; **flirtatiousness,** *noun.*

flit *verb*
(**flitted, flitting**)
to move lightly and quickly: 'all she saw was a shadow *flit* behind the tree'.
Word Family: **flit,** *noun.*

flitch *noun*
a side of bacon.

flitter *verb*
to flutter.

float *verb*
1. to rest on, move or be held up in air, liquid, etc.: a) 'she *floated* on her back in the pool'; b) 'the memory continued to *float* in his mind'.
Usage: 'she *floated* through the day in happy contentment' (= moved easily).
2. *Commerce:* a) to sell shares to the public so that a company may gain listing on a stock exchange. b) to remove restrictions on the value of a currency in the world market so that it may find its own natural level.
float *noun*
1. anything which floats or provides support for floating, such as the quill and cork device on a fishing line, or the floating device in a cistern or carburettor which regulates the level or supply of liquid.
2. a large trailer used to transport horses.
3. a low cart or platform on wheels, drawn in processions.
4. a small reserve of cash to provide a till with the means of giving change on the first sales.

floating rib
also called a **false rib**
Anatomy: any of the lower two pairs of ribs, so called because they are not joined to the sternum.

flocculation (*say* flok–yoo–**lay**–sh'n) *noun*

the clotting of fine particles into larger lumps.
Word Family: **flocculate,** *verb*; **flocculant,** *noun,* a substance added to solutions to produce flocculation; **flocculent,** *adjective,* having loose, woolly masses.

flock (1) *noun*
a) a group of birds, sheep or goats. b) a crowd of people.
Word Family: **flock,** *verb,* to go or gather in a flock.

flock (2) *noun*
1. a tuft of wool, hair or other substance.
2. wool refuse, rags, etc. cut in small pieces and used to stuff furniture, mattresses, etc.
flock *verb*
to cover or fill with flock, as a mattress.
[Latin *floccus*]

floe *noun*
a small mass of floating ice.
[Norwegian *flo* a layer]

flog *verb*
(flogged, flogging)
1. to strike or beat with a whip, stick, etc.
2. (*informal*) to sell.
flog a dead horse, to persist in a useless argument or effort.
flogging *noun*
a punishment by whipping or beating.

flood (*say* flud) *noun*
1. an overflowing of water, especially on to land which is usually dry.
2. any large flow or stream: 'a *flood* of congratulations greeted the winners'.
3. a floodlight.
flood *verb*
1. to rise or overflow in a flood.
2. to occur in great quantities: 'entries *flooded* in for the competition'.

floodlight *noun*
short form is **flood**
a light with a strong, broad beam, used in a theatre or outdoors.
Word Family: **floodlight (floodlit** or **floodlighted, floodlighting),** *verb.*

floor (*say* flor) *noun*
1. the lower, horizontal surface of a room or other structure.
Usage: 'the sunken ship rested on the *floor* of the sea' (= bottom).
2. the main part of a hall, etc.: 'the *floor* of the stock exchange'.
3. a storey.
Phrases:
have, take the floor, 'when he *has the floor* nobody is allowed to interrupt' (= is speaking).
wipe the floor with, 'the champion *wiped the floor with* his opponent' (= defeated completely).
floor *verb*
1. to cover or provide with a floor.
2. (*informal*) a) to defeat. b) to stun or confound: 'I was quite *floored* by her sudden change of mood'.
Word Family: **flooring,** *noun,* a) a floor or floors, b) the materials used to make a floor.

floor show
a form of entertainment consisting of songs, dances or a comedy act, usually in a nightclub.

floozy (*say* **floo**-zee) *noun*
also spelt **floozie**
a flashy or vulgar woman.

flop *verb*
(flopped, flopping)
1. to fall, drop or collapse suddenly.
2. to fail.
Word Family: **flop,** *noun*; **floppy,** *adjective,* tending to droop or flop; **floppiness,** *noun*; **floppily,** *adverb.*

flora *noun*
Biology: all the plants of a certain area or period. Compare FAUNA.
[Latin *Flora* goddess of Flowers]

floral (*say* **florr**'l) *adjective*
of or relating to flowers.
[Latin *floris* of a flower]

floret (*say* **florr**it) *noun*
also called a **floweret**
a small, individual flower of a composite flower head.

floribunda rose
a vigorous hybrid producing dense clusters of roses.

floriculture (*say* florri-**kul**cher) *noun*
the production and cultivation of flowers and other decorative plants.
Word Family: **floricultural,** *adjective*; **floriculturist,** *noun.*

florid (*say* **florr**id) *adjective*
1. flushed or highly coloured: 'a healthy *florid* complexion'.
2. highly decorated or elaborate: 'his *florid* prose was difficult to read and understand'.
[Latin *floridus* flower]

florin (*say* **florr**in) *noun*
an old coin equal to 2 shillings.

florist (*say* **florrist**) ***noun***
a person who sells flowers, indoor plants, etc.

floss ***noun***
1. a fine, silk fibre used for decoration in embroidery.
2. any silky thread–like substance.

flotation (*say* flo–**tay**–sh'n) **floatation** ***noun***
1. the act of floating or causing to float.
2. *Geology:* a process for separating different materials in an ore by suspending them in a liquid.

flotilla (*say* flo–**tilla**) ***noun***
a small fleet, or division of a fleet. [Spanish]

flotsam ***noun***
any wreckage or rubbish floating on the sea. Compare JETSAM.

flounce (1) (*rhymes with* bounce) ***verb***
to move or go with quick, impatient movements: 'she *flounced* furiously out of the room slamming the door behind her'.
Word Family: **flounce,** ***noun.***

flounce (2) (*rhymes with* bounce) ***noun***
a strip of gathered material attached by one edge to a skirt, etc. for decoration.
Word Family: **flounce,** ***verb,*** to decorate with one or more flounces.

flounder (1) ***verb***
to struggle helplessly or clumsily: 'he *floundered* through his speech and sat down with relief'.
Word Family: **flounder,** ***noun.***

flounder (2) ***noun***
any of various flatfish with a large mouth and both eyes usually occurring on the left side of the head.

flour (*say* flower) ***noun***
1. the finely ground substance made from wheat, used in cooking.
2. the finely ground substance made from other specified grain, e.g. cornflour, rye–flour, etc.
flour ***verb***
to cover or sprinkle with flour.
Word Family: **floury,** ***adjective,*** like or covered with flour.

flourish (*say* **flurrish**) ***verb***
1. to grow or be well, healthy, active, etc.: 'business *flourished* under the new management'.
2. to wave or display enthusiastically: 'she rushed in *flourishing* her first pay cheque'.
flourish ***noun***
1. an enthusiastic wave or display.
2. a decorative curve in handwriting.
3. *Music:* a fanfare.
[Latin *florere* to bloom]

flout (*rhymes with* out) ***verb***
to oppose or treat with contempt: 'despite the school's stern warnings he continues to *flout* the rules'.

flow (*say* flo) ***verb***
(of liquid) to move smoothly: 'water *flowed* from the roof down the walls'.
Usages:
a) 'her hair *flowed* down her back' (= hung loosely).
b) 'the meeting *flowed* very smoothly except for a few interruptions' (= proceeded).
c) 'has anything *flowed* from your inquiries?' (= resulted).
flow ***noun***
1. any continuous flowing or pouring movement.
2. the quantity or volume which flows.

flow chart
also called a **flow diagram**
a diagram showing a logical step–by–step sequence of events.

flower ***noun***
1. *Biology:* the part of a seed plant containing the reproductive organs.
2. a plant grown or considered for its decorative flowers.
3. the best or finest part or example of anything: 'he died tragically in the *flower* of his youth'.
flower ***verb***
to produce flowers.
Usage: 'his talent *flowered* under the encouragement of his teacher' (= developed fully).

floweret ***noun***
a floret.

flower head
a flower consisting of a dense cluster of small individual flowers.

flowery ***adjective***
(of language) highly decorative or elaborate.
Word Family: **floweriness,** ***noun.***

flown (*say* flone) ***verb***
the past participle of the verb **fly (1)**.

flu ***noun***
(*informal*) influenza.

fluctuate (*say* **flukt**–yoo–ate) ***verb***
to vary in a wave–like or irregular way: 'her moods *fluctuate* between extreme happiness and deep depression'.
Word Family: **fluctuation,** ***noun.***

[Latin *fluctuare* to move like the waves]

flue (*say* floo) *noun*
a) a passage for smoke in a chimney. b) a pipe or tube, e.g. on an oven or furnace, through which smoke and hot gases are drawn off.

fluent (*say* **floo**–ent) *adjective*
1. able to express oneself clearly and easily: 'her *fluent* Italian surprised the other tourists'.
2. flowing smoothly and gracefully: 'the *fluent* curves of the dome–shaped building blended with the undulating land'.
Word Family: **fluency**, *noun*; **fluently**, *adverb*.
[Latin *fluens* flowing]

fluff *noun*
1. any light, downy substance.
2. (*informal*) a failed or mismanaged attempt.
fluff *verb*
1. to make or become puffed out.
2. (*informal*) to do clumsily or unsuccessfully.
Word Family: **fluffy**, *adjective*, like or covered with fluff.

fluid (*say* **floo**–id) *noun*
a substance, a liquid or gas, which flows.
fluid *adjective*
1. of or consisting of fluid.
2. able to flow.
Usage: 'the *fluid* voice of the speaker soothed the audience' (= flowing, smooth).
Word Family: **fluidity** (*say* floo–**idda**–tee), **fluidness**, *nouns*; **fluidly**, *adverb*.

fluid ounce
a unit of volume for liquids, equal to a twentieth of a pint (about 28·4 ml). See UNITS in grey pages.

fluke (1) *noun*
1. the flat triangular blade at either end of the arm of an anchor.
2. either triangular half of the tail of a whale.

fluke (2) *noun*
a stroke of good luck.
Word Family: **fluke**, *verb*, to win or gain by a fluke; **fluky**, **flukey**, *adjective*, obtained by chance or a fluke.

fluke (3) *noun*
also called a **trematode**
a parasitic flatworm with one or more suckers.

flume *noun*
an artificial water channel for industrial use or for carrying logs.
[Latin *flumen* a river]

flummery (*say* **flumma**–ree) *noun*
a light, fluffy dessert made of milk eggs, sugar, flour, etc
[Welsh]

flummox *verb*
to bewilder or confuse.

flung *verb*
the past tense and past participle of the verb **fling**.

flunkey *noun*
(*use is often derogatory*) a male servant or obsequious person.

fluorescence (*say* flor–**ess**'nce) *noun*
the property, possessed by certain substances, of absorbing radiation of a particular wavelength and giving it off as light. b) the light produced.
Word Family: **fluorescent**, *adjective*, having the property of fluorescence, as certain electric lights; **fluoresce**, *verb*.

fluoridation (*say* floo–a–rye–**day**–sh'n) *noun*
the addition of small traces of a fluoride (usually sodium fluoride, formula NaF) to the water supply to strengthen tooth enamel.
Word Family: **fluoridate**, *verb*.

fluoride (*say* **floo**–a–ride) *noun*
Chemistry: any compound containing the univalent F^- ion.

fluorine (*say* **floo**–a–reen) *noun*
element number 9, a yellow, highly reactive gas. Its organic compounds are widely used in industry, especially in plastics and as refrigerants. See HALOGEN.
See CHEMICAL ELEMENTS in grey pages.

fluorocarbon (*say* **floo**–a–ro–karb'n) *noun*
Chemistry: any of a group of man–made organic compounds in which some or all of the hydrogen atoms have been replaced by fluorine.

flurry *noun*
a sudden whirling movement: 'a *flurry* of snow'.
Usage: 'we were all in a *flurry* of excitement on Christmas morning' (= confused hurry).
Word Family: **flurry** (**flurried**, **flurrying**), *verb*, to cause to be in a flurry.

flush (1) *verb*
1. to make or become red: 'the child's face was *flushed* with joy and excitement'.
Usage: 'the team was *flushed* with their first success' (= elated, excited).
2. to flood with water for cleaning purposes, etc.
flush *noun*
a red or rosy glow of colour.
Usages:
a) 'he was quite bewildered in the first *flush* of his success' (= excitement).
b) 'the *flush* of youth was still on the old man's cheeks' (= freshness).

flush (2) *adjective*
1. even or level: 'this picture is not quite *flush* with the top of the door'.
2. (*informal*) having plenty of money.
Word Family: **flush,** *adverb.*

flush (3) *verb*
Hunting: to cause game to burst from hiding.

flush (4) *noun*
Cards: a hand all of one suit.

fluster *verb*
to make confused, excited or nervous.
Word Family: **fluster,** *noun,* a nervous or confused state.

flute *noun*
1. *Music:* a wind instrument consisting of a long silver tube with keys or fingerholes, held by the player who blows air across the mouthpiece.
2. a flautist.
3. *Architecture:* a long, rounded furrow or channel, e.g. on a column.
flute *verb*
1. to play or make sounds like a flute.
2. to form flutes or furrows in a surface.

fluting (*say* **floo**–ting) *noun*
Architecture: a collection of flutes or furrows on a surface.

flutter *verb*
to wave or move quickly and lightly: 'the flag *fluttered* in the warm breeze'.
Usage: 'the children *fluttered* around the Christmas tree' (= moved excitedly).
flutter *noun*
1. a) a light, quick movement. b) a short, high-pitched sound.
2. a nervous or excited state.
3. (*informal*) a bet.

fluvial (*say* **floo**vial) *adjective*
of or produced by a river: '*fluvial* deposits'.
[Latin *fluvius* a river]

flux *noun*
1. a flowing or continuous movement or change.
2. *Physics:* a) a flow of matter or energy. b) the rate of such a flow.
3. *Metallurgy:* a substance used to assist the joining or fusion of two metals.
Word Family: **flux,** *verb,* to melt or flow.
[Latin *fluxus* flowing]

fly (1) *verb*
(**flew, flown, flying**)
to move or cause to move through the air: 'the seagull *flew* high above the water'.
Usages:
a) 'the door *flew* open' (= moved quickly).
b) 'the gang will probably try to *fly* the country' (= flee).
Phrases:
fly in the face of, 'his behaviour *flies in the face of* all we have taught him' (= openly defies).
fly off the handle, see HANDLE.
fly *noun*
1. the front fastener of a pair of trousers, usually consisting of buttons or a zip covered with a flap of cloth.
2. a flap of cloth forming the door of a tent.
3. *Theatre:* (*plural*) the space above the stage, used for storing scenery, etc.
4. a one-horse carriage.

fly (2) *noun*
1. any of a group of two-winged insects (**true flies**), in which the hind legs are modified to aid balance.
2. any of various similar but unrelated winged insects, such as the firefly.
Phrases:
a fly in the ointment, 'his bad temper was rather *a fly in the ointment*' (= spoiling element).
be no flies on, 'there *are no flies on* that shrewd young man' (= is nothing naïve or incautious about).

flyblown *adjective*
1. (of meat) maggoty.
2. a) dirty: 'a *flyblown* restaurant'. b) tarnished: 'a *flyblown* reputation'.

fly-by-night *noun*
an untrustworthy person, especially one who leaves in secret to avoid responsibilities, debts, etc.

flycatcher *noun*
any of numerous kinds of small birds which perch upright on vantage points and swoop on passing insects.

flyer *noun*
also spelt **flier**
a person or thing that flies, such as a pilot.

fly fishing
fishing with artificial flies as bait. Compare COARSE FISHING.

flying boat
an aeroplane designed to take off and land on water.

flying bomb
a doodlebug.

flying buttress
an arched support for a wall which stands separately but is attached by one or more bars or structures. Compare BUTTRESS.

flying doctor
Australian: a doctor using air transport to reach patients in otherwise inaccessible bush or inland areas.

flying fish
any of a group of fish with an enlarged, wing-like pectoral fin enabling it to fly through the air.

flying fox
a large, tropical fruit-eating bat with a head resembling that of a fox.

flying officer
a commissioned officer in the airforce, ranking between a pilot officer and a flight lieutenant.

flying saucer
also called an **unidentified flying object (UFO)**
a disc-shaped object which some claim to have seen in the sky.

flying squad
a motorized police squad available for special assignments in any part of the country.

flyleaf *noun*
plural is **flyleaves**
a blank page at the beginning or end of a book.

flyover *noun*
a bridge which carries one road over another at an intersection.

flypaper *noun*
a paper treated with sticky poison for catching flies.

flyweight *noun*
a weight division in boxing, not exceeding 8 stone (51 kg).

flywheel *noun*
a heavy wheel which, because of its momentum, tends to smooth out rapid variations in speed, as in motor vehicle engines, machinery, etc.

foal *noun*
the young of a horse or ass.
Word Family: **foal,** *verb*, to produce a foal.

foam *noun*
1. a collection of tiny bubbles of gas or liquid formed on a surface.
2. any of various light, spongy materials used for insulation in packaging, etc.
Word Family: **foam,** *verb*; **foamy,** *adjective*; **foaminess,** *noun.*

fob (1) *noun*
a) a small pocket in trousers or a waistcoat to hold a watch, etc. b) a chain, ribbon, etc. attached to the watch and worn hanging from the pocket.

fob (2) *verb*
(fobbed, fobbing)
fob off, (*informal*) to get rid of, especially in a cunning way.

focal length
Physics: the distance from the centre of a lens or mirror to the focus.

focal plane
Physics: the plane through the focus of a lens or mirror, which is perpendicular to a line through the focus and the centre.

focal point
1. the main point of interest, activity, etc.
2. *Physics:* a focus.

fo'c'sle (*say* **foke-s'l**) *noun*
also spelt **forecastle**
a) the part of a ship, near the bow, where the seamen live. b) the compartment nearest the bow of a yacht.

focus (*say* **fo-kus**) *noun*
plural is **foci** (*say* **fo-kee** *or* **fo-sigh**)
1. the position or adjustment of an object or optical device needed to produce a clearly defined image: 'my camera is not in *focus*'.
2. *Physics:* a) the point at which converging rays, such as light, meet. b) the point from which diverging rays, such as light, appear to come.
3. a central point of attention, attraction, etc.
4. *Maths:* a fixed point.
5. *Geology:* the point where an earthquake starts.

focus *verb*
(**focused** or **focussed, focusing**)
to bring into focus.
Word Family: **focal**, *adjective*, relating to a focus; **focalize, focalise**, *verb*, to focus.
[Latin, fireplace, hearth]

fodder *noun*
1. any food given to livestock, such as hay, etc.
2. people considered as being consumed or used up in a particular process or activity: 'factory *fodder*'.

foe *noun*
an enemy or opponent.

foetus (*say* **fee**–tus) *noun*
in America spelt **fetus**
Biology: the unborn offspring of an animal.
Word Family: **foetal**, *adjective*.
[Latin, a bringing forth, breeding]

fog *noun*
1. a dense mass of water droplets suspended in the air.
2. *Photography:* the darkening of a negative or print due to light or chemicals.
in a fog, puzzled or confused.
Word Family: **fog** (**fogged, fogging**), *verb*; **foggy**, *adjective*; **fogginess**, *noun*.

foghorn *noun*
Nautical: a horn used by a ship in fog to warn other ships that it is nearby.

fogy (*say* **fo**–gee) **fogey** *noun*
plural is **fogies** or **fogeys**
a person with extremely old-fashioned ideas.

foible *noun*
a slight peculiarity or defect of character.

foie gras (*say* fwah **grah**)
a pâté made with the livers of specially fattened geese.
[French, fat liver]

foil (1) *verb*
to prevent from being successful: 'the attempted robbery was *foiled* by the quick action of the clerk'.

foil (2) *noun*
1. a fine paper-like sheet of metal: 'aluminium *foil*'.
2. something which improves or distinguishes the characteristics of something else by contrast.
3. *Architecture:* a leaf-shaped decorative division, especially around church windows.

foil (3) *noun*
a steel sword used in fencing, having a blade with a square cross-section and a rounded button on its point.

foist *verb*
to impose something on to a person by deceit or trickery.

fold (1) *verb*
1. to bend or cause to bend over on itself: a) 'he *folded* up the newspaper'; b) 'to *fold* one's arms'.
Usage: 'he *folded* his arms around her' (= put, wrapped).
2. *Cooking:* to mix ingredients by slowly and gently turning one part over another.
fold up, to collapse or fail.
fold *noun*
1. the act or an instance of folding.
2. the junction of two folded parts.
3. *Geology:* a bend in layers of rock caused by movement in the earth's crust.

fold (2) *noun*
a) an enclosed area for sheep. b) a flock of sheep.
return to the fold, to return to one's family or other group that one has deserted.

-fold
a suffix meaning multiplied by a specified number, as in *twofold*.

folder *noun*
1. a person or thing that folds.
2. a folded piece of cardboard, plastic, etc. to hold loose papers.
3. a folded sheet with advertisements, etc. printed on it.

foliage *noun*
any leaves, especially all the leaves on a tree or plant.
[Latin *folium* leaf]

foliation (*say* fole–ee–**ay**–sh'n) *noun*
1. the act of putting forth leaves.
2. the state of having leaves.
3. an arrangement of leaves in a bud.
Word Family: **foliate**, *adjective*, having leaves; **foliate**, *verb*, to put forth leaves.

folic acid
one of the substances in the vitamin B group, used in treating some types of anaemia.

folio (*say* **fo**–lee–o) *noun*
plural is **folios**
1. a large cover or case for loose papers: 'an art *folio*'.
2. a book with large pages.

3. *Printing:* a) a page number. b) a sheet of paper folded once.

folk (*say* foke) *noun*
plural is **folk** or **folks**
1. people: 'old *folk*'.
2. (*informal, plural*) parents.
folk *adjective*
originating among the people.

folk dance
a traditional dance of a particular country or region.

folklore *noun*
the traditional customs, legends and beliefs of the people of a particular country or region.

folk song
a) a traditional song handed down through many generations of people in a particular country or region. b) any song with a similar style of music.

folkways *plural noun*
the traditional ways of living or behaving, which influence people without their being aware of it.

follicle (*say* **folli**–k'l) *noun*
Biology: a very small sac or gland.

follow *verb*
to come or go behind.
Usages:
a) '*follow* this path to the river' (= go along).
b) 'they *followed* the teacher's instructions' (= obeyed).
c) 'this conclusion *follows* from the evidence' (= comes as a result of).
d) 'can you *follow* my reasoning?' (= understand).
e) 'we *followed* her career with interest' (= watched the progress of).
f) '*follow* my example' (= imitate).
Phrases:
follow on, (*Cricket*) to be obliged to bat again immediately, having failed to obtain half of the other team's score in the first innings. *Word Family:* **follow–on,** *noun.*
follow suit, see SUIT.
follow through, (*Sport*) to continue the swing of a racket or bat after the ball has been hit.
follow up, to pursue to a conclusion.
Word Family: **following,** *noun,* a group of followers or supporters; *adjective,* about to be mentioned. **follower,** *noun,* a person who follows, especially one who imitates or admires another.

folly *noun*
a foolish or senseless act, idea, etc.
[French *folie* madness]

foment (*say* foe–**ment**) *verb*
1. to promote the development of trouble, rebellion, etc.
2. to apply or bathe in warm or medicated lotions.
Word Family: **fomentation,** *noun;* **foment,** *noun.*

fond *adjective*
liking or loving: 'she has always been *fond* of children'.
Usage: 'we had *fond* hopes of us all spending Christmas together' (= cherished, great).
Word Family: **fondly,** *adverb;* **fondness,** *noun.*

fondant (*say* **fon**–d'nt) *noun*
a thick, sugary paste used in icing, sweets, etc.

fondle *verb*
to handle or stroke with affection.

fondue (*say* **fon**doo) *noun*
any of various dishes cooked in a special pot at the table, such as a mixture of cheese, wine and spices into which cubes of bread are dipped.
[French *fondre* to melt]

font (1) *noun*
Christian: a basin, usually stone, which holds water for baptism in a church.

font (2) *noun*
also spelt **fount**
Printing: a complete range of type characters in one size and face.

food *noun*
1. any material, especially solid material, taken into the body and assimilated for growth, etc.
2. anything providing nourishment, ideas, etc.: '*food* for thought'.

food chain
Biology: a chain of organisms in which energy is passed from one organism to the one that eats it. *Example:* grass is eaten by a cow which, in turn, is eaten by man.

foodstuff *noun*
any substance suitable for use as food.

fool *noun*
1. a person who lacks sense and judgement: 'he was a *fool* to be talked into buying that old car'.
2. a person who is an object of ridicule, disrespect, etc.: 'they made a *fool* of you'.
3. a jester, formerly kept by kings, etc. to entertain at court.

fool *verb*
1. to trick or deceive.
2. to joke or play: 'stop *fooling* about and do some work'.
Word Family: **foolish,** *adjective,* lacking sense or wisdom; **foolishly,** *adverb*; **foolishness, foolery,** *nouns.*

foolhardy *adjective*
unwisely bold or rash.
Word Family: **foolhardiness,** *noun*; **foolhardily,** *adverb.*

foolproof *adjective*
of a kind that no-one can mistake or misuse: 'a *foolproof* plan'.

foolscap *noun*
a traditional size of typing paper about 330 mm × 210 mm.

fool's gold
see PYRITES.

foot (*say* fut) *noun*
plural is **feet**
1. *Anatomy:* the lower end of the leg below the ankle.
2. something which has the position or function of a foot.
Usages:
a) 'she dances with a light *foot*' (= step).
b) 'it stands at the *foot* of the hill' (= lower end, bottom).
3. a unit of length equal to 12 inches or about 30·48 cm. See UNITS in grey pages.
4. *Poetry:* the basic unit of division in scansion, each with two or three syllables:
a) an **anapaest** has two short or unstressed syllables followed by one long or stressed syllable.
b) an **iambic** has one short or unstressed syllable followed by one long or stressed syllable. An **alexandrine** is a verse or line containing six iambic feet.
c) a **dactyl** has one long or stressed syllable followed by two short or unstressed syllables.
d) a **spondee** has two long or stressed syllables.
e) a **trochee** has one long or stressed syllable followed by a short or unstressed syllable.
Phrases:
fall on one's feet, land on one's feet, to be lucky or successful.
find one's feet, to become independent of the help of others.
my foot!, nonsense!
put one's foot down, to be strict or firm.
put one's foot in it, to make an embarrassing blunder.
stand on one's own feet, to be self-sufficient.
sweep off one's feet, a) 'the wave *swept* her *off her feet*' (= knocked over); b) 'he tried to *sweep* her *off her feet*' (= impress, overwhelm).

foot *verb*
1. to walk: 'we *footed* it to the shop'.
2. (*informal*) to pay: 'he *footed* the bill'.

footage (*say* fut-ij) *noun*
1. the length in feet.
2. *Film:* a length of film.

foot-and-mouth disease
an infectious, viral disease of cattle and similar animals, causing puffy growths around the feet and mouth.

football *noun*
1. a leather ball inflated by means of a rubber bladder.
2. any of various field games played with a football, such as Rugby, soccer or Rugby League.
Word Family: **footballer,** *noun.*

football pools
short form is the **pools**
an organized form of gambling based on the results of football matches.

footfall *noun*
a footstep.

foot-fault *noun*
Tennis: see FAULT.

foothill *noun*
a hill at the base of a mountain range.

foothold *noun*
1. a place giving support for the foot in climbing, etc.
2. a secure position from which one may advance, succeed or make progress.

footing *noun*
a secure position of or for the feet.
Usage: 'let's put the interview on a more relaxed *footing*' (= basis).

footlights *plural noun*
Theatre: a row of lights set at the edge of the stage.

footloose *adjective*
free of responsibilities and able to travel about.

footman *noun*
a male servant employed to wait at table, attend the door, etc.

footnote *noun*
an explanation or note printed in smaller type at the bottom of a page in a book.

footpad *noun*
an old word for a highwayman who went on foot.

footpath *noun*
1. a pedestrian path, usually raised, beside a road. In Britain called a **pavement** and in America called a **sidewalk.**
2. any path for people to walk on.

footrot *noun*
an infection of the feet of sheep due to constantly wet ground and causing inflammation and decay of the toes which leads to lameness.

footstep *noun*
a tread of a foot or the sound it produces.
follow in someone's footsteps, to continue or imitate the progress of another.

footwork *noun*
1. the manner in which the feet are moved, e.g. in boxing, etc.
2. any skilful manoeuvring.

fop *noun*
a man who is excessively concerned with his clothes and appearance.
Word Family: **foppery,** *noun;* **foppish,** *adjective.*

for *preposition*
a word used to indicate the following:
1. (purpose, intention) a) 'that chair was made *for* decoration only'; b) 'we are fighting *for* justice'.
2. (destination) 'she left *for* the city'.
3. (suitability) 'you are perfect *for* the job'.
4. (equality, proportion) 'she is very strong *for* her size'.
5. (preparation, progress) 'hurry and get ready *for* school'.
6. (extent) 'we hiked *for* miles'.
7. (attention, interest) a) 'now *for* a cup of tea'; b) 'she has an eye *for* detail'.
8. (time, duration) 'not *for* long'.
9. (result, effect) 'he was gaoled *for* his part in the robbery'.
10. used to introduce an infinitive, equivalent to clauses such as *that he might,* etc.: 'our wish is *for* you to stay'.
Usages:
a) 'three apples *for* 20 pence' (= cost).
b) 'will you do it *for* me?' (= on behalf of).
c) 'I know you don't want to, but please do it *for* me' (= as a favour to).
d) 'the party is *for* her birthday' (= in honour of, to celebrate).
e) '*for* all her talking she is very shy' (= despite).
f) 'the newspaper was sued *for* libel' (= on account of).
g) 'who's *for* a game of tennis?' (= in favour of).
h) 'she cried *for* joy' (= because of).
i) 'everyone took him *for* a fool' (= as being).
j) '*for* my part, I'd never do it' (= as regards).
k) 'a man of limited education, *for* a lawyer' (= considering the nature of).
for *conjunction*
since or because: 'I cannot go, *for* I am ill'.

forage (*say* **forr**ij) *verb*
1. to hunt or search, especially for military supplies.
2. to rummage about.
3. to raid or plunder.
Word Family: **forage,** *noun,* a) fodder, especially for horses and cattle, b) an act of foraging.

forasmuch as
since; seeing that.

foray (*say* **forr**ay) *noun*
a plundering raid.
Usage: 'he made a brief *foray* into another sort of work' (= entry, attempt).
Word Family: **foray (forayed, foraying),** *verb.*

forbear *verb*
(forbore, forborne, forbearing)
1. to refrain from
2. to be patient or tolerant.
Word Family: **forbearance,** *noun.*

forbid *verb*
(forbade or **forbad, forbidden** or **forbid, forbidding)**
to command not to do: 'I *forbid* you to go out'.
Usage: 'smoking is *forbidden* in this theatre' (= not allowed).

forbidding *adjective*
disagreeable, frightening or off-putting: 'a *forbidding* task'.

force *noun*
1. the strength of something: 'the *force* of the wind'.
Usage: 'they used *force* to enter the building' (= violence).
2. an organized body of people: 'a police *force*'.
3. *Physics:* the vector quantity equal to the mass of a body multiplied by its acceleration.

in force, a) 'they attacked *in force*' (= in full strength); b) 'the new law is *in force* from today' (= operative, effective).
force *verb*
1. to make or cause to do something, often using effort or strength.
2. to produce or do with effort: 'she felt like crying but *forced* a smile'.
Usage: 'we had to *force* the lock because the key was lost' (= break open).
Word Family: **forced**, *adjective*, not genuine; **forceful**, *adjective*, powerful or vigorous; **forcefully**, *adverb*; **forcefulness**, *noun*.
[Latin *fortis* strong]

forcemeat *noun*
a stuffing for meat, etc., usually consisting of minced meat, breadcrumbs, etc.

forceps *noun*
plural is **forceps**
Medicine: a pair of tongs for holding tissues or objects, e.g. during an operation, etc.

forcible (*say* **forsi**-b'l) *adjective*
1. forceful or convincing: 'a *forcible* argument'.
2. using force.
Word Family: **forcibly**, *adverb*.

ford *noun*
a shallow part of a river where people may cross on foot or in vehicles.
Word Family: **ford**, *verb*.

fore (1) *adjective*
located at or towards the front.
fore *adverb*
Nautical: at or towards the bow. Compare AFT.
fore *noun*
to the fore, in or to a conspicuous position.

fore (2) *interjection*
Golf: a cry used to warn other players that a ball has been hit nearby.

fore-
a prefix meaning before in time or position, as in *foresee*.

fore-and-aft-rigged *adjective*
Nautical: having the sails (usually triangular) set on gaffs and booms along the line of the keel. Compare SQUARE-RIGGED.

forearm *noun*
Anatomy: the lower part of the arm.

forebear, forbear *noun*
(*usually plural*) an ancestor.

forebode *verb*
to predict, especially something ominous.
Word Family: **foreboding**, *noun*, a premonition; **forebodingly**, *adverb*.

forebrain *noun*
Anatomy: the front part of the brain, considered to be the region controlling thought.

forecast *verb*
(**forecast** or **forecasted, forecasting**) to predict.
Word Family: **forecast**, *noun*; **forecaster**, *noun*, a person who forecasts.

forecastle *noun*
see FO'C'SLE.

foreclosure (*say* for-**klo**-*zh*er) *noun*
Law: the taking over or removing of property on which mortgage payments have not been paid regularly.
Word Family: **foreclose**, *verb*; **foreclosable**, *adjective*.

forecourt *noun*
1. an enclosed court in front of a large building.
2. the front part of a garage, where petrol is sold.

forefather *noun*
an ancestor.

forefinger *noun*
Anatomy: the first finger, next to the thumb.

forefront (*say* **for**-frunt) *noun*
the front place or position.

forego *verb*
see FORGO.

foregone conclusion
an inevitable result or conclusion.

forehand *noun*
Tennis: a stroke made with the palm of the hand facing forward. Compare BACKHAND.

forehead (*say* **forrid** *or* **for**-hed) *noun*
also called the **brow**
Anatomy: the area at the top and front of the face, above the eyes and below the hairline.

foreign (*say* **forrin**) *adjective*
1. relating to or from a country other than one's own: 'a *foreign* language'.
2. involving other countries: '*foreign* trade agreements'.
3. not belonging to the place where it is found: '*foreign* matter in the eye'.
4. unfamiliar or strange.

Word Family: **foreigner**, *noun*, a person from another country.
[Latin *foras* out of doors, abroad]

foreign correspondent
a person who sends news from abroad to a newspaper, broadcasting organization, etc.

Foreign Secretary
also called a **Foreign Minister**
the senior government minister in charge of foreign affairs.

foreknowledge (*say* **for**–nollij) *noun*
a knowledge of something before it happens or exists.

foreland *noun*
a cape or headland.

forelock *noun*
Anatomy: the part of the hair that grows or hangs from the top of the forehead.

foreman *noun*
1. a person in charge of a group of workers.
2. the spokesman for a jury.

foremost *adjective*
first in position, rank, etc.

forename *noun*
a Christian or other first name.

forenoon *noun*
an old word for the late morning.

forensic (*say* fo–**renzik**) *adjective*
of or employed in legal proceedings: '*forensic* science'.
[Latin *forensis* of the forum]

forequarter *noun*
a carcass, including the front end of the leg and shoulder.

forerunner *noun*
a person who or situation which introduces or does something first: 'medieval guilds were the *forerunners* of the modern trade unions'.
Word Family: **forerun** (**foreran, forerunning**), *verb*, to come or exist before.

foresail *noun*
Nautical: the principal sail hoisted in front of the main mast.

foresee *verb*
(**foresaw, foreseen, foreseeing**)
to see or know beforehand.
Word Family: **foreseeable**, *adjective*.

foreshadow *verb*
to suggest or indicate beforehand.

foreshore *noun*
the beach or section of the shore between the high and low watermarks.

foreshorten *verb*
1. to reduce the length of part or all of a represented object, so that it appears to the viewer to be in correct perspective.
2. to cut short or reduce.

foresight *noun*
1. a perceptiveness or prudence about the future.
2. the act or ability of foreseeing.

foreskin *noun*
also called the **prepuce**
Anatomy: a fold of skin which covers the tip of the penis and may be removed by circumcision.

forest (*say* **for**rist) *noun*
1. a large area of land covered with trees.
2. the trees themselves.
Usage: 'a *forest* of sails covered the harbour' (= thick cluster).

forestall (*say* for–**stawl**) *verb*
to prevent or deal with beforehand.

forestay (*say* **for**–stay) *noun*
Nautical: a strong rope or wire which runs from the top of the foremast to the stem of a ship.

forestry (*say* **forra**–stree) *noun*
the study of planting and maintaining forests.
Word Family: **forester**, *noun*, a person skilled or trained in forestry.

foretell *verb*
(**foretold, foretelling**)
to predict or prophesy.

forethought (*say* **for**–thawt) *noun*
a prudent and careful planning beforehand.

foreword (*say* **for**–werd) *noun*
an introduction in a book, usually written by someone other than the author. Compare PREFACE.

forfeit (*say* **for**fit) *noun*
a penalty or fine, especially something given up or lost as punishment.
Word Family: **forfeit**, *verb*, to lose as a forfeit; **forfeiture**, *noun*, the act of forfeiting.

forgather, foregather *verb*
to gather together.

forgave *verb*
the past tense of the verb **forgive**.

forge (1) (*say* forj) *noun*
1. a furnace, etc. in which metal is heated before shaping.
2. the place in which a smith, especially a blacksmith, works. Also called a **smithy**.

forge *verb*
1. to work heated metal by hammering or pressing it into shape.
Usage: 'the countries *forged* a new friendship' (= formed).
2. to make or reproduce for fraudulent purposes.
Word Family: **forger,** *noun.*

forge (2) (*say* forj) *verb*
to advance, especially with an abrupt increase of speed.

forgery (*say* **for**ja-ree) *noun*
a) the producing of an imitation in order to deceive or pass it off as genuine. b) anything made in this way.

forget *verb*
(forgot, forgotten, forgetting)
to fail to remember.
Usage: 'she tried to *forget* her troubles' (= stop thinking about).
forget oneself, to lose one's reserve or self-restraint.
Word Family: **forgetful,** *adjective,* tending to forget; **forgetfully,** *adverb;* **forgetfulness,** *noun;* **forgettable,** *adjective,* able to be forgotten.

forget-me-not *noun*
a small plant with blue flowers, considered to be a symbol of friendship and constancy.

forgive *verb*
(forgave, forgiven, forgiving)
1. to give pardon for a fault, etc.
2. to cease to resent: 'to *forgive* one's enemies'.
Word Family: **forgiveness,** *noun;* **forgivable,** *adjective,* able to be forgiven; **forgivably,** *adverb;* **forgiving,** *adjective,* tending to forgive; **forgivingly,** *adverb.*

forgo, forego *verb*
(forwent, forgone, forgoing)
to abstain from or do without: 'students usually *forgo* many social activities during their exams'.

forgot *verb*
the past tense of the verb **forget.**

forgotten *verb*
the past participle of the verb **forget.**

fork *noun*
1. an instrument with two or more prongs, for eating, gardening, etc.
2. a) a part or place where something divides into branches: 'a *fork* in the road'. b) either of the branches into which something divides: 'proceed for 1 km and then take the left *fork*'.

fork *verb*
1. to lift, toss, pierce, etc. with a fork: 'to *fork* hay into a truck'.
2. to divide into branches.
fork out, (*informal*) 'he had to *fork out* the whole £50' (= give, hand over).

fork-lift truck
a vehicle with two movable, horizontal arms at the front for lifting and carrying goods in factories, warehouses, etc.

forlorn *adjective*
1. sad or pitiful: 'her *forlorn* face told of her suffering'.
2. forsaken.
forlorn hope, a hope with little or no expectation of getting what is desired.
Word Family: **forlornly,** *adverb;* **forlornness,** *noun.*

form *noun*
1. the shape or structure: 'the human *form*'.
2. the particular state, character, appearance, etc. of something: 'water in the *form* of steam'.
3. any procedure or manners based on accepted social etiquette, etc.: 'it is not considered good *form* to shout'.
4. *Education:* the name given to a class, especially in a secondary school.
5. a) a printed piece of paper with spaces which are to be filled in with appropriate information. b) a printed piece of paper used as a guide for writing other documents.
6. a long bench or seat.
Usages:
a) 'bacteria are generally thought to be a *form* of plant life' (= kind, variety).
b) 'we poured the concrete into the *form* and waited for it to set' (= mould).
c) 'all the players will be in top *form* for the match' (= condition, fitness).

form *verb*
1. to shape.
2. a) to be an element of: 'hunches and guesswork *form* the larger part of his theory'. b) to have as its parts: 'the class is *formed* of 24 students'.
Usages:
a) 'I have *formed* a plan for our escape' (= devised).
b) 'you've *formed* a lot of bad habits lately' (= developed).
c) 'we should *form* a committee to look into this' (= arrange, organize).

formal *adjective*
1. following accepted conventions, forms, etc.: 'please make a *formal* application in writing'.
Usage: 'she greeted them in a *formal* manner' (= stiff).
2. relating to form rather than content: 'he made a *formal* analysis of the piece of music'.
Word Family: **formally,** *adverb*; **formality** (*say* for-**malli**-tee), *noun*, a) the quality of following accepted conventions, b) (usually plural) any established procedure or order.

formaldehyde (*say* for-**malda**-hide) *noun*
a gas (formula HCHO) which has a very irritating smell. It is soluble in water and is used in making plastics, dyes, and in the textile industry. Compare FORMALIN.

formalin (*say* **forma**-lin) *noun*
a 40 per cent solution of formaldehyde in water, used as a disinfectant and for preserving scientific specimens.

formalize, formalise *verb*
to give a legal or official form to.
Word Family: **formalization,** *noun.*

format *noun*
the plan, style or layout of something: 'the *format* of a new television series'.

formation *noun*
1. a) the process of forming. b) the manner in which something is formed or arranged: 'the aircraft flew in close *formation* over the city'.
2. something which is formed: 'a rock *formation*'.
[Latin *formare* to mould]

formative *adjective*
1. having the power to form or shape: 'he was a *formative* influence on my life'.
2. of or relating to formation or development: 'the *formative* years'.

former *adjective*
1. coming before in time, place or order: 'a *former* president'.
2. being the first mentioned of two: 'of Purcell and Handel, I prefer the *former* (Purcell)'. Compare LATTER.

formerly *adverb*
in time past: 'a convent was *formerly* called a nunnery'.

Formica (*say* for-**myka**) *noun*
a hard, usually heat-resistant plastic used to cover tables, etc.
[a trademark]

formic acid
a colourless irritant fluid found in ants and nettles, and synthesized for use in the textiles and other industries.
[Latin *formica* ant]

formidable (*say* **form**idda-b'l *or* for-**midda**-b'l) *adjective*
1. difficult or requiring great effort to overcome: 'cleaning up the city was a *formidable* task'.
2. causing fear and apprehension: 'the headmaster had a *formidable* appearance, but in fact he was a very gentle man'.
Word Family: **formidably,** *adverb.*
[Latin *formido* a fear]

formula (*say* **form**-yoo-la) *noun*
plural is **formulae** (*say* **form**-yoo-lee) or **formulas**
1. an established procedure for doing something, such as a set wording for a ceremony, etc.
2. *Maths:* a general statement of the relationship between two or more quantities. *Example*: $d=2r$ is a formula stating that the diameter of a circle, d, is always twice the radius, r.
3. *Chemistry:* the representation of atoms in a radical or molecule by the use of symbols for each atom. *Example*: the formula for water, H_2O shows that a molecule of water is composed of two atoms of hydrogen (H) and one atom of oxygen (O).
an **empirical formula** indicates the proportion of each kind of atom without giving the total number or arrangement of atoms in the molecule. *Example*: the empirical formula of glucose (formula $C_6H_{12}O_6$) is CH_2O.
a **structural formula** shows the arrangement and linkage of atoms of a molecule in a diagram.
4. a liquid food or preparation, e.g. for a baby.
5. *Car Racing:* any of the classes into which competing cars are divided.
[Latin]

formulate (*say* **for**-mew-late) *verb*
1. to express in a systematic or precise way.
2. to state as a formula.
Word Family: **formulation,** *noun.*

fornication (*say* forni-**kay**-sh'n) *noun*
sexual intercourse between a man and woman who are not married to each other.
Word Family: **fornicate,** *verb.*
[Latin *fornicis* of a brothel]

forsake *verb*
(forsook, forsaken, forsaking)

to desert, abandon or give up.
Word Family: **forsakenly,** *adverb.*

forsooth (*say* for–**sooth**) *adverb*
an old word meaning indeed or in truth.

forswear (*say* for–**swair**) *verb*
(forswore, forsworn, forswearing)
to swear to give up completely: 'after the accident she *forswore* driving'.

fort *noun*
short form of **fortress** and **fortification**
a strengthened building for defence, such as a castle.
hold the fort, to manage or look after affairs during someone's absence.
[Latin *fortis* strong]

forte (1) (*say* **for**tay) *noun*
something in which a person excels.
[French, strong]

forte (2) (*say* **for**tay) *adverb*
Music: loudly.
[Italian]

forth *adverb*
forward in time, place or order: a) 'from that day *forth*'; b) 'he set *forth* on the journey'.
Usage: 'the sun came *forth* from the clouds' (= out into view).
and so forth, see SO.

forthcoming *adjective*
1. approaching in time: 'arrangements are being made for the *forthcoming* royal visit'.
2. available when required: 'we were ready to start building, but finance was not *forthcoming*'.
3. (*informal*) helpful with information, etc.: 'the secretary was quite rude and not at all *forthcoming*'.

forthright *adjective*
outspoken or straightforward.
Word Family: **forthright,** *adverb*; **forthrightness,** *noun.*

forthwith *adverb*
immediately.

fortieth *noun, adjective*
Word Family: see FORTY.

fortification *noun*
1. the act of fortifying.
2. see FORT.

fortify (*say* **forti**–fie) *verb*
(fortified, fortifying)
1. to strengthen: a) 'we *fortified* the dugout with sandbags'; b) 'she *fortified* herself against the cold with a stiff brandy'.
2. (of wine, etc.) to strengthen by adding alcohol: 'port is a *fortified* wine'.

fortissimo (*say* for–**tissi**–mo) *adverb*
Music: very loudly.
[Italian]

fortitude (*say* **forti**–tewd) *noun*
a patient courage or strength.

fortnight *noun*
a period of two weeks.
Word Family: **fortnightly,** *adjective, adverb,* once every fortnight.
[from FOURT(een) + NIGHT(s)]

fortress *noun*
see FORT.

fortuitous (*say* for–**tewi**–tus) *adjective*
happening by accident or chance.
Word Family: **fortuitously,** *adverb*; **fortuitousness,** *noun.*
[Latin *forte* by chance]

fortune *noun*
1. chance or luck regarded as a cause of events and changes in one's life.
2. wealth or riches: 'the farmer made a *fortune* when oil was discovered on his property'.
tell someone's fortune, to predict future events in a person's life.
fortunate (*say* **for**–tew–nit) *adjective*
1. lucky: 'a *fortunate* coincidence'.
2. successful: 'people less *fortunate* than ourselves'
Word Family: **fortunately,** *adverb.*

fortune–hunter *noun*
a person who seeks a fortune, especially through marriage.

fortune–teller *noun*
a person who professes to see future events related to another person, e.g. by palmistry.

forty *noun*
1. a cardinal number, the symbol 40 in Arabic numerals, XL in Roman numerals.
2. (*plural*) the numbers 40–49 in a series, such as the years within a century.
forty winks, see WINK.
Word Family: **forty,** *adjective*; **fortieth,** *noun, adjective.*

forum *noun*
plural is **forums**
1. an assembly for discussion, usually public.
2. *Ancient history:* the public square in a Roman town, used for business and meetings.

forward (*say* **for**–w'd) *adjective*
1. near or moving towards the front: 'we took up a *forward* position on the battlefield'.

2. bold or presumptuous: 'a *forward* young lady'.
3. of or for the future: '*forward* planning'.
Usage: 'a *forward* nation' (= progressive, developed).
forward, forwards *adverb*
1. toward the front: '*forward* march!'
2. toward the future: 'looking *forward* to meeting you'.
Usage: 'he's never reluctant to bring *forward* an opinion' (= into prominence).
forward *noun*
Sport: a player in an attacking position.
forward *verb*
to send on: 'he *forwarded* the mail to my new address'.
Usage: 'this type of behaviour will not *forward* your plan' (= promote).
Word Family: **forwardly,** *adverb*; **forwardness,** *noun.*

forwent *verb*
the past tense of the verb **forgo**.

fossick *verb*
1. to search or hunt.
2. *Australian, New Zealand:* to search for gold in abandoned mines, etc.
Word Family: **fossicker,** *noun.*

fossil *noun*
1. *Geology:* the remains, impression or trace of any living thing preserved in or as a rock.
2. (*informal*) an old-fashioned person or thing.
Word Family: **fossilize, fossilise,** *verb*; **fossilization,** *noun.*
[Latin *fossilis* dug up]

foster *verb*
1. to encourage or promote the growth or development of: 'to *foster* good relations with one's neighbours'.
2. to bring up a child who is not one's own son or daughter without legal adoption.

foster-child *noun*
plural is **foster-children**
a child brought up by someone other than its own parents.
Word Family: **foster home,** the family home where a foster-child is brought up; **foster-parent,** *noun,* the person who takes the place of a parent in bringing up a child.

fought (*say* fawt) *verb*
the past tense and past participle of the verb **fight**.

foul (*say* fowl) *adjective*
1. offensive to the senses, such as a bad taste or smell.
2. wicked or obscene: '*foul* language'.
3. stormy or disagreeable: '*foul* weather'.
4. *Sport:* relating to a foul.
foul play, 'the police suspect *foul play*' (= violent crime or murder).
foul *noun*
Sport: a breaking of the rules in a sport or game.
foul *adverb*
in a foul manner.
fall foul of, see FALL.
foul *verb*
1. to make or become foul or dirty.
2. to entangle or become entangled: 'the rope has *fouled* in the pulley'.
3. *Sport:* to commit a foul against.
Word Family: **foully,** *adverb*; **foulness,** *noun,* the state or quality of being foul.

found (1) *verb*
the past tense and past participle of the verb **find**.

found (2) *verb*
to set up or establish: 'to *found* a kingdom in a new land'.
Usage: 'a story *founded* on fiction' (= based).
Word Family: **founder,** *noun.*

found (3) *verb*
to melt metal or glass for moulding and casting.

foundation *noun*
1. the act of founding: 'after the *foundation* of the colony'.
2. anything on which something rests or is based: a) 'the *foundations* of a building'; b) 'the *foundation* of democracy is the free vote'.
3. an institution supported by donations or a legacy: 'a *foundation* for cancer research'.
4. *Beauty:* a skin-coloured cream or liquid, often in the form of a cake or stick and used as a base for face powder.

foundation garment
any piece of women's underwear worn to shape or support the body, such as a bra or a corset.

founder (1) *noun*
Word Family: see FOUND (2).

founder (2) *verb*
1. (of ships, etc.) to fill with water and sink.
2. (of horses) to go lame.
Word Family: **founder,** *noun,* a condition causing lameness in horses.

foundling *noun*
a child abandoned by its parents.

foundry *noun*
a factory where metal is moulded and cast.

fount (1) *noun*
an old word for a fountain or spring.

fount (2) *noun*
Printing: see FONT (2).

fountain (*say* **fown**–t'n) *noun*
1. a spring of water, especially an artificially constructed jet of water.
2. a structure for discharging a jet or jets of water.
[Latin *fontis* of a spring]

fountainhead *noun*
a primary source.

fountain pen
a pen containing a reservoir of ink which flows down the nib on contact with paper.

four (*say* for) *noun*
1. a cardinal number, the symbol 4 in Arabic numerals, IV in Roman numerals.
2. *Cricket:* a score of four runs, obtained when a batsman hits the ball to the boundary. Also called a **boundary**.
3. *Rowing:* a) a racing boat for a cox and four rowers each with one oar. b) the crew of such a boat.
on all fours, on hands and knees.
Word Family: **four**, *adjective*; **fourth**, *adjective, noun*; **fourthly**, *adverb.*

four–poster *noun*
a bed with a post at each corner to support a canopy or curtain above it.

fourscore *adjective*
four times twenty; eighty.

four–stroke *adjective*
of or relating to an internal combustion engine in which the fuel is taken into the cylinder, compressed, burnt and released into the exhaust in four successive strokes of the piston. Compare TWO–STROKE.

fourteen *noun*
a cardinal number, the symbol 14 in Arabic numerals, XIV in Roman numerals.
Word Family: **fourteen**, *adjective*; **fourteenth**, *noun, adjective.*

fourth *adjective, noun*
Word Family: see FOUR.

fourth dimension
Physics: time.

fowl *noun*
a bird, especially one bred or kept for its flesh and eggs, such as the common domestic cock or hen.
Word Family: **fowler**, *noun*, a person who shoots birds; **fowling–piece**, *noun*, a shotgun for shooting birds.

fox *noun*
plural is **foxes**
1. a small, dog–like mammal, with reddish–brown fur, a pointed muzzle, upright ears and a bushy tail.
2. the fur of this animal.
3. a crafty person.
fox *verb*
(*informal*) to deceive or trick.
Word Family: **foxy**, *adjective*; **foxily**, *adverb*; **foxiness**, *noun.*

foxglove *noun*
a plant with many trumpet–shaped, white or purple flowers on one long stem, the leaves of which are used to produce a heart stimulant.

foxhole *noun*
a small trench for one or two men, used for protection in a battle area.

foxhound *noun*
a hound bred for foxhunting from the old keen–scented sleuth–hound and the swift greyhound.

fox terrier
a small wire–haired or smooth–haired dog, once used to dig out foxes and now kept to catch rats and as a pet.

foxtrot *noun*
a ballroom dance for two people consisting of varied groups of quick or slow, short steps.
Word Family: **foxtrot** (**foxtrotted**, **foxtrotting**), *verb.*

foyer (*say* **foy**–yay) *noun*
an entrance hall, especially in a theatre, hotel or large building.
[French, hearth, home]

fracas (*say* **frak**–ah) *noun*
a noisy disturbance or fight.
[French]

fraction (*say* **frak**–sh'n) *noun*
1. *Maths:* a) a part of a whole number. b) a ratio of algebraic symbols above and below a line.
in a **common fraction** (also called a **simple fraction** or a **vulgar fraction**) both the numerator and denominator are integers.
in a **proper fraction** the numerator is less than the denominator, as in $\frac{1}{2}$, $\frac{1}{4}$, etc.

in an **improper fraction** the numerator is greater than the denominator, as in $\frac{3}{2}$.
2. a part, especially a small part, of something: 'only a *fraction* of the members attended the meeting'.
3. *Chemistry:* a product of fractional distillation.
Word Family: **fractional**, *adjective*; **fractionally**, *adverb.*
[Latin *fractus* broken]

fractious (*say* **frak**–shus) *adjective*
irritable or bad–tempered.
Word Family: **fractiously**, *adverb*; **fractiousness**, *noun.*

fracture (*say* **frak**–cher) *noun*
a break or crack, especially in a bone.
Word Family: **fracture**, *verb.*

fragile (*say* **fraj**–ile) *adjective*
easily broken or damaged.
Word Family: **fragilely**, *adverb*; **fragility** (*say* fra–**jilli**–tee), *noun.*

fragment (*say* **frag**–m'nt) *noun*
a part broken off.
Usage: 'we overheard *fragments* of the conversation' (= incomplete parts).
Word Family: **fragment** (*say* frag–**ment**), *verb,* to break into fragments; **fragmentary**, *adjective*; **fragmentation**, *noun,* the act or process of fragmenting.

fragrant (*say* **fray**–gr'nt) *adjective*
having a pleasant smell.
Word Family: **fragrantly**, *adverb*; **fragrance, fragrancy**, *nouns.*

frail *adjective*
1. delicate in health: 'a *frail* child'.
2. easily broken: 'a *frail* china vase'.
Usage: 'she proved *frail* in the face of temptation' (= weak).
frailty *noun*
1. the condition or quality of being frail.
2. (*often plural*) a fault or moral weakness.
Word Family: **frailly**, *adverb*; **frailness**, *noun.*
[Latin *fragilis* fragile]

frame *noun*
1. an enclosing border for a picture, etc.
2. a) a structure composed of parts joined together: 'a bicycle *frame*'. b) any structure or system: 'the *frame* of government'.
3. a particular state of mind.
4. any of the successive small pictures on a strip of film.
5. *Snooker:* a) the triangular frame in which the balls are set at the start of a game. b) the time it takes to play all the balls into the pockets.
frame *verb*
1. to provide with a frame.
2. to arrange or give shape to: 'he *framed* the question carefully'.
Usage: 'he was *framed* by the gangster' (= incriminated with falsely arranged evidence).

frame–up *noun*
(*informal*) a conspiracy to incriminate a person falsely, or to bring about a fraudulent outcome to a contest, etc.

framework *noun*
a structure composed of parts joined together.

franc (*say* frank) *noun*
the basic unit of money in Belgium, France, Switzerland and certain other countries.

franchise (*say* **fran**–chize) *noun*
a right or privilege, such as the right to vote or the permission given by a manufacturer for a retailer to sell his goods.

francium (*say* **fran**–see–um) *noun*
element number 87, a man–made, radioactive metal. See ALKALI METAL. See CHEMICAL ELEMENTS in grey pages.

frangipani (*say* franji–**panni**) *noun*
a tree with fragrant, slightly waxy flowers from which perfume is made.

frank *adjective*
open in thought or speech: 'a *frank* answer'.
frank *verb*
to mark a letter with an official stamp showing that the postage has been paid.
Word Family: **frankly**, *adverb*; **frankness**, *noun*; **frank**, *noun,* a mark put on a letter to show that the postage has been paid.

frankfurter *noun*
a small smoked beef or beef and pork sausage.
[from *Frankfurt-am-Main,* West Germany]

frankincense (*say* **frank**in–sense) *noun*
a pleasant–smelling gum resin used as incense.

frantic *adjective*
nearly mad, as with grief, excitement, pain, etc.
Word Family: **frantically**, **franticly**, *adverbs.*
[Greek *phrenetikos* having inflammation of the brain]

fraternal (*say* fra–**tern**'l) *adjective*
of or like a brother or brothers: 'I have a *fraternal* feeling towards him'.
Word Family: **fraternally,** *adverb.*
[Latin *frater* brother]

fraternity (*say* fra–**terni**–tee) *noun*
1. a feeling of brotherhood.
2. a group of people who share an interest or purpose: 'the medical *fraternity*'.
3. *American:* a society of male students. Compare SORORITY.

fraternize (*say* **frattern**–ize) *verb*
to associate with others in a friendly way.
Word Family: **fraternization,** *noun.*

fratricide (*say* **fratri**–side) *noun*
Law: a) the crime of killing one's brother or sister. b) a person who does this.
Word Family: **fratricidal** (*say* fratri–**sigh**–d'l), *adjective.*
[Latin *frater* brother + *caedere* to kill]

Frau (*rhymes with* cow) *noun*
the title for a married German woman.

fraud (*say* frawd) *noun*
1. the act of deliberately deceiving another person, especially for unlawful or unfair gain.
2. a person who is not what he pretends to be.
Word Family: **fraudulent** (*say* fraw–**dew**–l'nt), *adjective;* **fraudulently,** *adverb;* **fraudulence,** *noun.*
[Latin *fraudis* of deception]

fraught (*say* frawt) *adjective*
involving or accompanied by: 'an undertaking *fraught* with danger'.

Fräulein (*say* **fraw**–line) *noun*
the title for an unmarried German woman.

fray (1) *noun*
a noisy dispute or fight.

fray (2) *verb*
1. (of cloth) to become worn, so that there are loose threads.
2. (of a person's temper) to exasperate: 'tempers became *frayed* at the meeting'.

frazzle *noun*
(*informal*) exhaustion: 'worn to a *frazzle*'.

freak (*say* freek) *noun*
a very unusual person, animal or event: a) 'by some *freak* the car stayed on the road after it skidded'; b) 'the calf with five legs was a *freak*'.
freak *verb*
freak out, (*informal*) a) to suffer hallucinations from drugs; b) to opt out of society; c) to react extremely.
Word Family: **freak, freakish, freaky,** *adjectives;* **freakishly,** *adverb;* **freakishness,** *noun.*

freckle *noun*
a small brown mark or spot on the skin.
Word Family: **freckle,** *verb.*

free *adjective*
(freer, freest)
1. not restrained by authority or external forces: a) 'a *free* citizen'; b) '*free* choice'.
2. without payment or charge: 'a *free* ride'.
Usages:
a) 'the *free* end of a rope' (= not attached).
b) 'is the room *free* yet?' (= unoccupied).
c) 'he is very *free* with his advice' (= ready, liberal).
d) 'your teeth are *free* of decay' (= devoid, without).
e) 'she walks with a *free* step' (= swinging).
f) 'a *free* translation' (= not exact).
Phrases:
free and easy, casual or relaxed.
free hand, 'the police were given a *free hand* in their investigations' (= complete authority).
free *verb*
(freed, freeing)
to set or make free.
Word Family: **free, freely,** *adverbs.*

freebooter *noun*
a buccaneer or pirate.

freedom *noun*
the state or condition of being free: a) 'to fight for *freedom*'; b) '*freedom* of speech'; c) 'the tight clothes allowed her little *freedom* of movement'.

free enterprise
commerce or private business in which competition may occur with a minimum of government control.

free–for–all *noun*
a dispute or contest which is open to everyone.

freehand *adjective*
done by hand without the aid of instruments or measurement: 'a *freehand* sketch'.

freehold *noun*
Law: any house or land held in absolute possession, not rented.

Word Family: **freeholder**, *noun*, an owner of freehold land.

free house
a public house free to sell any brand of beer. Compare TIED HOUSE.

freelance (*say* **free**–lahnce) *noun*
1. a person, such as a journalist, artist, etc., who sells work to employers rather than working on a full-time basis for a salary.
2. *Medieval history:* a wandering knight who gave military service in exchange for money.
Word Family: **freelance**, *verb*, to work as a freelance; **freelance**, *adjective*.

freely *adverb*
Word Family: see FREE.

Freemason *noun*
a member of a secret order which promotes mutual assistance and brotherly love among its members.

free port
a port without taxes, open to all traders.

free-range hen
a hen free to range for food. Compare BATTERY HEN.

freesia (*say* **free***zh*a) *noun*
a plant with fragrant white or yellow flowers growing from a corm.
[after *E. M. Fries*, 1794–1878, a Swedish botanist]

freestyle *noun*
Swimming: a race in which competitors may use any style of swimming, usually the crawl.

freethinker *noun*
a person who remains independent of or unaffected by tradition, authority, etc. in matters such as religion.

free trade
international trade unrestricted by taxes, quotas or other forms of protection by government regulations. Compare PROTECTION.

free verse
see VERSE.

freeway *noun*
American: a motorway.

freewheel *verb*
to coast on a bicycle, etc. without pedalling.

free will
1. the power to choose or decide freely.
2. *Philosophy:* the doctrine that man is free to work out his own destiny. Compare DETERMINISM and PREDESTINATION.

freeze *verb*
(**froze, frozen, freezing**)
1. to change into ice or a solid.
2. to become blocked or ineffective due to frost, ice, etc.: 'the pipes *froze*'.
Usages:
a) 'you will *freeze* without a coat' (= be very cold).
b) 'she *froze* with horror at the sight' (= was unable to move).
c) 'the government *froze* wages for six weeks' (= fixed at a particular level).
freeze *noun*
1. the act of freezing
2. a period of intensely cold weather when the temperature is below 0°C.

freeze-dry *verb*
(**freeze-dried, freeze-drying**)
to dry food or chemicals while frozen to prepare them for longer periods of storage.

freezer *noun*
also called a **deep-freeze**
a refrigerator or part of a refrigerator, usually with a temperature below −10°C in which food may be frozen quickly and stored for long periods.

freezing point
the constant temperature, at a given pressure, at which a liquid freezes.

freight (*say* frate) *noun*
a) goods which are transported as cargo. b) the carrying of goods or cargo by land, sea or air. c) the charge for this.
Word Family: **freight**, *verb*, to carry or send by freight; **freighter**, *noun*, a ship or aircraft which carries freight.

freight train
American: a train which carries freight.

French chalk
powdered talc used in dry-cleaning, soap manufacture, toilet products, etc.

French horn
Music: a brass, wind instrument consisting of a long coiled tube ending in a flared bell.

French seam
Needlework: a seam sewn on both sides of the material so that no raw edges are showing.

French windows
a pair of glass doors which open outwards.

frenetic (*say* fra–**nettik**) *adjective*
frantic or highly excited.
Word Family: **frenetically**, *adverb*.

frenzy *noun*
an extreme excitement, agitation or activity.
Word Family: **frenzied**, *adjective*, highly excited or maddened.
[Greek *phrenitis* inflammation of the brain]

Freon (*say* **free**-on) *noun*
Chemistry: any of a group of fluorocarbon monomers used as refrigerants and solvents.
[a trademark]

frequency (*say* **free**-kw'n-see) *noun*
1. the number of times something occurs, especially in a particular interval of time, space, etc.: 'what is the *frequency* of earthquakes in this area?'.
2. the state or fact of being frequent: 'the *frequency* of her visits became tedious'.
3. *Music, Physics:* the number of oscillations per second of a wave or wave-like phenomenon, including sound, light, etc.
[Latin *frequens* crowded, repeated]

frequency channel
see CHANNEL.

frequency distribution
Maths: a set of equal categories for which the number of observed values in each are recorded.
Example: a graph showing the proportions of the population falling into various income-tax groups.

frequency modulation
short form is **FM**
a method, used and usable only in very high frequency (VHF) broadcasting in which the frequency of the transmitted wave is varied, producing short-range but high-fidelity reception. Compare AMPLITUDE MODULATION.

frequency response
Audio: the range of frequencies to which an amplifier or loudspeaker can respond.

frequent (*say* **free**-kw'nt) *adjective*
occurring often or at short intervals: 'she has *frequent* attacks of asthma'.
Usage: 'he is a *frequent* visitor at their house' (= regular, constant).
frequent (*say* free-**kwent**) *verb*
to go often to a place: 'as a collector he *frequents* second-hand bookshops'.
Word Family: **frequently**, *adverb*; **frequenter**, *noun*, a constant or regular visitor.

fresco (*say* **fres**ko) *noun*
plural is **frescos** or **frescoes**
a painting done with water-based paint on a plastered wall, usually when it is still damp.
[Italian, fresh]

fresh *adjective*
1. recently made, obtained, arrived, etc.: a) 'they get *fresh* milk and eggs from the farm'; b) 'a young doctor *fresh* from medical school'.
2. full of energy or brightness: 'I feel quite *fresh* after that sleep'.
Usages:
a) 'these fish are not found in *fresh* water' (= not salt).
b) 'she has a very *fresh* complexion' (= rosy, healthy).
c) 'the room was painted in *fresh* colours' (= bright).
d) 'don't get *fresh* with me, young lady' (= cheeky).
e) 'in autumn the nights are *fresh*' (= cool).
Word Family: **freshly**, *adverb*; **freshness**, *noun*.

freshen *verb*
1. to make or become fresh: 'to *freshen* a room by opening the window'.
2. (of a wind) to increase in strength or become cold.
freshen up, 'our guests decided to *freshen up* after the long trip' (= wash and refresh themselves).

fresher *noun*
also called a **freshman**
a first year student at a college or university.

freshwater *adjective*
of, consisting of or living in fresh water: 'a *freshwater* fish'.

fret (1) *verb*
(fretted, fretting)
1. to worry or be anxious, unhappy or irritable: a) 'she has done nothing but *fret* since her husband died'; b) 'he's *fretting* about the money he lost at the races today'.
2. to rub, wear or eat away: 'the rope broke because it had *fretted*'.
Word Family: **fret**, *noun*, a state of fretting; **fretful**, *adjective*, irritable or given to fretting; **fretfully**, *adverb*; **fretfulness**, *noun*.

fret (2) *noun*
an ornamental band or design consisting of repeated, geometrical lines or figures.
Word Family: **fretwork**, *noun*; **fretted**, *adjective*, decorated with frets.

fret (3) *noun*
Music: any of the wooden or metal ridges set across the fingerboard of a stringed instrument.
Word Family: **fretted**, *adjective*, having frets.

fretsaw *noun*
a saw with a long, fine blade set in a frame, used for cutting ornamental work in wood.

Freudian slip (*say* **froy**dian slip)
a slip of the tongue which may reveal a person's unconscious feelings.
[after *Sigmund Freud*, 1856–1939, an Austrian psychoanalyst]

friable (*say* **frya**–b'l) *adjective*
crumbly or easily crumbled: 'sandstone is often *friable*'.
Word Family: **friableness, friability** (*say* frya–**billi**–tee), *nouns.*

friar (*say* frya) *noun*
Roman Catholic: a brother of certain religious orders, especially the orders which work among the people and not in a monastery, and which formerly lived by begging. Compare MONK.
Word Family: **friary**, *noun*, a community of friars.
[Latin *frater* brother]

fricassee *noun*
a dish of veal or chicken cut up and cooked in a sauce.
[French]

friction (*say* **frik**–sh'n) *noun*
1. the rubbing of one object or surface against another.
Usage: 'her actions caused much *friction* in the family' (= conflict).
2. *Physics:* the forces which tend to prevent the movement of one surface over another, resulting from the nature of the two surfaces.
Word Family: **frictional**, *adjective*, relating to or produced by friction; **frictionally**, *adverb*; **frictionless**, *adjective.*
[Latin *frictus* rubbed]

Friday *noun*
the sixth day of the week.
girl Friday, man Friday, an assistant or helper.

fridge *noun*
(*informal*) a refrigerator.

fried *verb*
the past tense and past participle of the verb **fry (1)**.

friend (*say* frend) *noun*
any person whom one knows and likes well.
Usages:
a) 'the wealthy man was a *friend* to the poor' (= helpful or kind person).
b) 'in a difficult situation, discretion is my best *friend*' (= asset).
Word Family: **friendly**, *adjective*, a) like a friend, b) pleasant; **friendliness**, *noun*; **friendship**, *noun*, a friendly relationship; **friendless**, *adjective*, without friends.

friendly society
a society in which voluntary subscriptions from the members are used to provide them with assistance in case of illness, etc.

frieze (*say* freeze) *noun*
a decorative strip or band on a wall.

frigate (*say* **frigg**it) *noun*
a) a small destroyer used to escort other ships. b) a medium–sized warship used from the 17th to the 19th century.

frigate–bird *noun*
either of two types of large, tropical seabirds with long wings, able to fly long distances.

fright *noun*
sudden, intense fear, usually as a reaction to something threatening: 'the huge shadow on the wall gave him an awful *fright*'.
Usage: 'you look a *fright* in that old coat' (= strange or grotesque sight).
frightful *adjective*
1. shocking, revolting or causing fright: 'the battle scene was a *frightful* sight'.
2. (*informal*) bad or unpleasant: '*frightful* weather'.
Word Family: **fright**, *verb*, to frighten; **frightfully**, *adverb*; **frightfulness**, *noun.*

frighten *verb*
to terrify or fill with fear.
Word Family: **frighteningly**, *adverb.*

frigid (*say* **frij**id) *adjective*
intensely cold: 'we had a week of *frigid* weather'.
Usages:
a) 'her *frigid* stare was not encouraging' (= unfriendly).
b) 'a *frigid* wife' (= sexually unresponsive).
Word Family: **frigidly**, *adverb*; **frigidity** (*say* frij–**iddi**–tee), **frigidness**, *nouns.*
[Latin *frigus* cold]

frill *noun*
1. an ornamental strip or border, usually gathered, used for trimming, etc.: 'a hem with *frills*'.
2. something unnecessary or merely ornamental: 'the tune is simple and free of *frills*'.
Word Family: **frilly,** *adjective.*

fringe (*say* frinj) *noun*
1. an ornamental border with hanging threads, especially on a carpet, tablecloth, etc.
2. any hair falling over the forehead.
Usage: 'their house is situated on the *fringe* of the forest' (= edge).
Word Family: **fringe,** *verb,* a) to put a fringe on, b) to grow or exist along the edge of.

fringe benefit
anything received by an employee in addition to wages or salary, such as a pension, the use of a car, etc.

frippery *noun*
any unnecessary decoration or display, as in one's manner of dress.

frisk *verb*
1. to move about with quick, eager, playful movements: 'the dogs *frisked* all over the picnic area'.
2. (*informal*) to search a person for concealed weapons by running the hands rapidly over his clothes.
Word Family: **frisk,** *noun*; **frisky,** *adjective,* lively or playful; **friskily,** *adverb*; **friskiness,** *noun.*

fritter (1) *verb*
to waste or squander little by little: 'he *frittered* away his money on gambling'.

fritter (2) *noun*
a piece of food, such as a slice of meat or fruit, coated in a batter and deep-fried.
[Latin *frictus* fried]

frivolous (*say* **frivva**-lus) *adjective*
1. of little importance: 'the chairman dismissed the motion as *frivolous*'.
2. silly or flippant: 'I disapprove of *frivolous* behaviour'.
Word Family: **frivolously,** *adverb*; **frivolousness,** *noun*; **frivolity** (*say* fri-**volli**-tee), *noun,* a) the state or quality of being frivolous, b) a frivolous act or remark.
[Latin *frivolus* trifling]

frizz *verb*
to form into small, tight waves or curls: 'to *frizz* one's hair'.
Word Family: **frizz,** *noun,* tightly curled hair; **frizzy,** *adjective,* consisting of tight curls.

frizzle *verb*
to make a spluttering, sizzling noise, as in frying.

fro *adverb*
see TO AND FRO under TO.

frock *noun*
a woman's dress: 'a cotton *frock*'.

frockcoat *noun*
a coat formerly worn by men, close-fitting to the waist and flaring out to the knees.

frog (1) *noun*
any of a group of tail-less, web-footed, amphibious animals which move by jumping.
Usage: 'she has a *frog* in the throat' (= hoarseness).

frog (2) *noun*
a decorative fastener, consisting of a button passed through a long, narrow loop.

frog (3) *noun*
a horny growth in the underside of a horse's hoof.

frogman *noun*
a person trained and equipped for underwater work, such as reconnaissance, demolition, etc.

frogmarch *verb*
to carry a resisting person face-down with four people each holding a limb.

frolic (*say* **frol**lik) *verb*
(**frolicked, frolicking**)
to play merrily and joyfully.
Word Family: **frolic,** *noun,* playful fun or merriment; **frolicsome,** *adjective,* playful or full of fun.

from *preposition*
a word used to indicate the following:
1. (a starting point in space, time or order) a) '*from* Melbourne to Sydney'; b) 'he improved his position *from* 8th to 2nd'.
2. (removal or absence) 'she is away *from* school today'.
3. (release) 'freedom *from* hunger'.
4. (difference) 'I can't tell one twin *from* the other'.
5. (source or origin) 'a letter *from* his uncle'.
6. (reason or cause) 'his mother suffered *from* bad eyesight'.

frond *noun*
Biology: the large, feather-like leaf of a fern.

front (*say* frunt) *noun*
1. the foremost or most important side, surface or part: a) 'the entrance is at the *front* of the building'; b) 'the title is at the *front* of the book'.
2. a place or position directly before anything.
Usages:
a) (*informal*) 'the import business was only a *front* for the spy ring' (= cover).
b) 'he put on a bold *front* in the face of his critics' (= appearance, bearing).
3. *Military.* the line or area between opposing armies when fighting is taking place.
4. a group of people joined together for a particular purpose, usually political.
5. *Weather:* a boundary between two air masses of different density. In a **cold front** advancing cold air near the ground wedges under and displaces warmer air. In a **warm front** advancing warm air near the ground rises over colder air. An **occluded front** occurs when a cold overtakes a warm front, forcing the warm air up to a higher level.
front *verb*
1. to face in the direction of: 'their house *fronts* the ocean'.
2. to confront: 'they are prepared to *front* any danger'.
3. to provide with or serve as a front.
Word Family: **front**, *adjective*, of or situated at the front; **frontal**, *adjective*, a) of or to the front, b) relating to the forehead.
[Latin *frontis* of the forehead]

frontage (*say* **frun**tij) *noun*
1. a) the front of a building or block of land. b) the length of such a front: 'the land has a *frontage* of 20 m'.
2. the land or position adjacent to: 'the house has a river *frontage*'.

frontal bone
Anatomy: the saucer-shaped bone at the front of the skull, forming the forehead.

frontbencher (*say* frunt-**bencher**) *noun*
Parliament: a member who is a minister or an Opposition spokesman, and who sits at the front of the chamber. Compare BACKBENCHER.

frontier (*say* **frunt**-eer) *noun*
a border or region which forms a dividing line, as between settled and unsettled areas.
Usage: 'cancer research is one of the *frontiers* of medical science' (= an area that has not been fully explored).
Word Family: **frontiersman**, *noun*, (American) a man who lives on the frontier.

frontispiece (*say* **frun**tis-peece) *noun*
an illustration facing the titlepage of a book.

frost *noun*
minute particles of frozen moisture formed when the air in contact with the ground is below freezing point. Compare HOARFROST and RIME (2)
frosty *adjective*
a) cold enough for frost to form: 'a *frosty* morning'. b) covered with frost: '*frosty* grass'.
Usage: 'there was a *frosty* silence between them' (= hostile, unfriendly).
frosting *noun*
1. a fluffy icing for cakes, etc.
2. a roughened or speckled surface on glass or metal.
Word Family: **frost**, *verb*, a) to freeze, b) to cover with frost or frosting; **frostily**, *adverb*; **frostiness**, *noun*.

frostbite *noun*
Medicine: a freezing of tissues due to extreme cold, causing pale, firm skin, usually on the toes, fingers or face, and in extreme cases resulting in gangrene.
Word Family: **frostbitten**, *adjective*.

froth *noun*
a mass of small bubbles or foam.
froth *verb*
1. to give out froth: 'to *froth* at the mouth'.
2. to cover with froth or foam.
Word Family: **frothy**, *adjective*; **frothily**, *adverb*; **frothiness**, *noun*.

frown *verb*
to draw the brows together expressing displeasure, thoughtfulness, etc.
frown on, frown upon, 'the temperance society *frowns on* the drinking of alcohol' (= disapproves of).
Word Family: **frown**, *noun*; **frowningly**, *adverb*.

frowzy (*say* **frow**-zee) *adjective*
untidy and dirty.
Word Family: **frowzily**, *adverb*; **frowziness**, *noun*.

froze *verb*
the past tense of the verb **freeze**.

frozen *adjective*
1. made into or covered with ice: 'a *frozen* lake'.

2. *Commerce:* not able to be changed, removed, etc.
Usages:
a) '*frozen* peas' (= preserved by freezing).
b) 'I'm *frozen* without a coat' (= very cold).
c) 'his *frozen* stare made me nervous' (= cold, unemotional).
frozen *verb*
the past participle of the verb **freeze**.

fructify (*say* **frukti**–fie) *verb*
(**fructified, fructifying**)
to bear fruit.
Word Family: **fructification,** *noun.*

fructose (*say* **fruk**–tose) *noun*
also called **fruit sugar**
the sugar (formula $C_6H_{12}O_6$), found in overripe fruit, flower nectar and honey.

frugal (*say* **froo**–g'l) *adjective*
careful or economical: 'the *frugal* use of petrol was essential during the fuel shortage'.
Word Family: **frugally,** *adverb*; **frugality** (*say* froo–**galli**–tee), **frugalness,** *nouns.*

fruit (*rhymes with* hoot) *noun*
1. the edible part of a plant developed from a flower, such as an apple, etc.
2. *Biology:* the fertilized and developed ovary of a plant.
Usage: 'his wealth is the *fruit* of many years of hard work' (= product, result).
Word Family: **fruit,** *verb,* to bear fruit; **fruitful,** *adjective,* a) bearing fruit abundantly, b) useful or productive; **fruitfully,** *adverb*; **fruitfulness,** *noun*; **fruitless,** *adjective*; **fruitlessly,** *adverb*; **fruitlessness,** *noun.*
[Latin *fructus* the produce, profit]

fruiterer *noun*
a greengrocer.

fruit–fly *noun*
any of a group of small flies, the larvae of which cause damage to fruit.

fruition (*say* froo–**ish**'n) *noun*
the final achievement of a desired result: 'it will still be some time before the plan comes to *fruition*'.
[Latin *frui* to enjoy]

fruit machine
also called a **one–armed bandit**
a coin–operated gambling machine in which a lever spins drums bearing symbols, such as fruit, and dividends are paid for certain combinations of these when they come to rest.

fruit sugar
see FRUCTOSE.

fruity *adjective*
1. having the taste or smell of fruit: 'a *fruity* claret'.
2. rich: 'his *fruity* voice filled the auditorium'.

frump *noun*
a badly dressed or unattractive woman.
Word Family: **frumpish, frumpy,** *adjectives*; **frumpishly, frumpily,** *adverbs*; **frumpishness, frumpiness,** *nouns.*

frustrate *verb*
to disappoint or thwart one's hopes, plans, etc.: 'the continuous rain *frustrated* his attempts to wash the car'.
frustration *noun*
1. the state of being frustrated, especially in relation to personal desires.
2. a) anything which frustrates: 'it's been a day full of *frustrations*'. b) the act of frustrating: 'the *frustration* of the criminal's plan was easily achieved'.
[Latin *frusta* in vain]

fry (1) *verb*
(**fried, frying**)
to cook in hot fat or oil.

fry (2) *noun*
plural is **fry**
a) any newly hatched fishes. b) any young or small animals.

fuchsia (*say* **few**sha) *noun*
a garden shrub with drooping, trumpet–shaped, usually red or purple flowers.
[after *L. Fuchs,* 1501–66, a German botanist]

fuck *verb*
(*informal*) to have sexual intercourse (with).
fuck *noun*
(*informal*) sexual intercourse.
Usage: 'he doesn't give a *fuck*'. (=damn)
fuck off! go away!
fucking *adjective*
(*informal*) damned, bloody: a) 'you *fucking* idiot!', b) 'it's no *fucking* use'.
fucking *adverb*
(*informal*) very, extremely, emphatically: 'a *fucking* great lorry just missed me'.
Word Family: **fuck!,** *interjection*;

fucker, *noun,* a person: 'some silly *fucker* has pinched my pen'.

fuddle *verb*
to confuse or muddle.
Word Family: **fuddle,** *noun.*

fuddy-duddy *noun*
a prim, old-fashioned or boring person.
Word Family: **fuddy-duddy,** *adjective.*

fudge *noun*
a soft, chewy sweet made by boiling milk, sugar and butter, usually flavoured with chocolate or caramel.

fuel (*say* **few**'l) *noun*
any substance used for producing heat and energy.
Word Family: **fuel (fuelled, fuelling),** *verb,* to provide with fuel.

fuel-injection *noun*
a method of spraying fuel directly into the manifold of an engine instead of using a carburettor.

fug *noun*
a smoke-filled or stifling atmosphere.

fugitive (*say* **few**ji-tiv) *noun*
a person who flees or runs away.
fugitive *adjective*
1. having run away.
2. not fixed or lasting: 'I glimpsed a *fugitive* resentment in her eyes'.
[Latin *fugere* to flee]

fugue (*say* **fewg**) *noun*
Music: a contrapuntal composition for several parts, each of which imitates the previous one.
Word Family: **fugal** (*say* **few**-g'l), *adjective.*
[Latin *fuga* flight]

fulcrum (*say* **ful**-krum) *noun*
plural is **fulcrums** or **fulcra**
see LEVER. [Latin, bedpost]

fulfil (*say* full-**fill**) *verb*
(fulfilled, fulfilling)
1. to satisfy: 'his desire for fame was *fulfilled* by the success of his first novel'.
2. to carry out: 'to *fulfil* a promise'.
Word Family: **fulfilment,** *noun.*

full *adjective*
having or containing as much as possible.
Usages:
a) 'it took a *full* day for the climbers to reach the first peak' (= complete).
b) 'his *full* voice drowned out the piano' (= rich, strong).
c) 'that's a very *full* skirt you're wearing' (= having wide, loose folds).
Phrases:
full of, 'she's so *full of* the wedding plans she hardly knows what's going on around her' (= absorbed in).
full of oneself, 'she is rather bossy and *full of herself*' (= conceited).
in full force, 'the family was there *in full force*' (= with nobody missing).
full *adverb*
1. completely.
2. directly: 'the ball hit him *full* in the face'.
full *noun*
in full, completely or to the full amount.
Word Family: **fully,** *adverb,* to a complete or full degree; **fullness,** *noun.*

full-back *noun*
Football: the player who defends his team's goal.

full-blooded *adjective*
1. of pure and unmixed breeding.
2. vigorous and healthy.

full-blown *adjective*
completely developed: 'there were many buds and one *full-blown* rose on the bush'.

full-bodied *adjective*
having all possible strength, flavour, etc.

full brother
see BROTHER.

full house
1. a theatre with all the seats sold for a performance.
2. *Cards:* a hand in poker consisting of three of a kind and a pair, such as three kings and two tens.

fullness *noun*
Word Family: see FULL.

full sister
see SISTER.

full stop
in America called a **period**
the point or character (.) used to mark the end of a sentence, indicate an abbreviation, etc.

full tilt
(*informal*) at top speed.

full-time *adjective*
taking all of one's time or normal working hours.

full toss
Cricket: a ball bowled so that it does not touch the ground between the two wickets.

fully *adverb*
Word Family: see FULL.

fulmar *noun*
a bull-necked gull-like bird, often seen following trawlers in northern waters.

fulminate (*say* **full**-minate) *verb*
to make loud or violent denunciations: 'to *fulminate* against the new taxes'.
Word Family: **fulmination,** *noun.*
[Latin *fulminare* to hurl thunderbolts]

fulsome (*say* **ful**-s'm) *adjective*
excessive in an insincere way: '*fulsome* praise'.
Word Family: **fulsomely,** *adverb*; **fulsomeness,** *noun.*

fumble *verb*
to feel, grope about or handle clumsily: a) 'he *fumbled* at his shirt button'; b) 'Jones *fumbled* that big deal with Fuller Brothers'.
Word Family: **fumble,** *noun*; **fumbler,** *noun,* a person who fumbles.

fume *noun*
(*usually plural*) any strong-smelling smoke, gas, etc.
fume *verb*
to give off fumes.
Usage: 'he *fumed* with indignation' (= burnt, raged). [Latin *fumus* smoke]

fumigate (*say* **fewmi**-gate) *verb*
to use smoke and fumes to disinfect.
Word Family: **fumigation,** *noun.*

fun *noun*
any playfulness or amusing enjoyment.
make fun of, poke fun at, 'you should not *make fun of* that poor old man' (= ridicule).
Word Family: **fun (funned, funning),** *verb,* (informal) to joke or play.

function (*say* **funk**-sh'n) *noun*
1. the special purpose or working use of anything: 'your *function* as captain is to lead and inspire the team'.
2. a formal ceremony or gathering.
3. *Maths:* a quantity f which relates two variables x and y such that $y = f(x)$. Since the values of y depend on the values of x, y is called the **dependent variable** and x the **independent variable.**
function *verb*
to perform or carry out one's normal work or function.
Word Family: **functional,** *adjective,* a) of or designed for a particular function, b) in working order; **functionally,** *adverb.*
[Latin *functio* a performance (of duty, etc.)]

functionary *noun*
an official.

fund *noun*
1. a supply or stock of something, especially money: 'he has an unlimited *fund* of jokes'.
2. (*plural*) any available money: 'what *funds* do you have for the holiday?'.
fund *verb*
1. to put into a store or fund.
2. to find money or funds for: 'how was the school hall *funded*?'.
[Latin *fundus* a piece of land]

fundamental (*say* funda-**men**-t'l) *adjective*
1. being a basis or starting point of something complex: 'this course will give you a *fundamental* knowledge of the language'.
2. affecting or having to do with the basis: 'we need *fundamental* changes before the organization will make a profit'.
fundamental *noun*
(*usually plural*) a first or essential part or principle.
Word Family: **fundamentally,** *adverb.*
[Latin *fundamentum* a foundation]

fundamental particle
an elementary particle.

funeral (*say* **few**na-r'l) *noun*
a) a ceremony for the burial or cremation of a dead person. b) a funeral procession.
Word Family: **funereal** (*say* few-**neer**ial), *adjective,* a) of or relating to a funeral, b) gloomy or mournful.
[Latin *funeris* of a burial]

fungicide (*say* **fungi**-side) *noun*
any substance that kills fungi.

fungus *noun*
plural is **fungi** or **funguses**
any of a group of simple plants, such as a mould, mushroom or toadstool, which lacks chlorophyll.
Word Family: **fungal, fungous,** *adjectives,* of or relating to a fungus; **fungoid,** *adjective,* of or growing like a fungus.
[Latin, mushroom]

funicular railway
a short-distance railway system of cable-linked trains for steep slopes.
[Latin *funiculus* a cord]

funk *noun*
(*informal*) a state of terror or extreme nervousness.

funnel *noun*
1. a tube with a wide mouth narrowing to a thin outlet, often used to pour liquid into bottles.
2. the metal chimney on ships and steam-engines.
funnel *verb*
(funnelled, funnelling)
to converge to or into a particular place, etc.: 'the police cordon *funnelled* the angry crowd into a blind alley'.

funny *adjective*
1. causing laughter and amusement.
2. strange or peculiar.
funny *noun*
(*informal*) a joke.
Word Family: **funnily,** *adverb*; **funniness,** *noun.*

funny bone
Anatomy: a ridge on the humerus near the elbow over which a nerve passes.

funny business
(*informal*) any foolish or underhand behaviour.

fur *noun*
1. the soft, thick hair of some animals, such as the beaver or rabbit.
2. (*often plural*) any clothing made of treated animal fur.
3. any soft coating on a surface, especially on the tongue.
Word Family: **furry,** *adjective,* covered with or resembling fur; **furriness,** *noun.*

furbish *verb*
to polish or make as if new.

furious (*say* **few**ri-us) *adjective*
extremely or violently angry.
Usage: 'the *furious* strength of the storm lashed the tiny houses' (= intense, uncontrolled).
Word Family: **furiously,** *adverb.*
[Latin *furiosus* frantic]

furl *verb*
to roll up tightly.

furlong *noun*
a unit of length equal to one-eighth of a mile (about 201 m).
[Old English *furh* furrow + *long* long, the length of a furrow in a common field]

furlough (*say* **fur**lo) *noun*
Military: a holiday or leave of absence.

furnace (*say* **fir**-niss) *noun*
any of various structures containing a fire of intense heat, used for generating steam, melting ore, etc.

furnish *verb*
to supply or equip, especially with appliances, furniture, etc.
furnishing *noun*
(*plural*) the fittings, furniture, covers, etc. in a house, office, etc.

furniture (*say* **fir**ni-cher) *noun*
any movable objects for use in buildings, such as chairs or tables.

furore (*say* **few**-ror *or* **few**-rori) *noun*
1. a general uproar or disorder.
2. an outburst of enthusiasm, anger or excitement. [Italian, raging]

furrier (*say* **furr**ia) *noun*
a person who treats, prepares, buys or sells furs.

furriness *noun*
Word Family: see FUR.

furrow *noun*
1. a narrow trench made in the ground, especially by a plough.
2. anything which resembles a furrow: 'he contracted his brow into *furrows*'.
Word Family: **furrow,** *verb.*

furry *adjective*
Word Family: see FUR.

further (*say* **fir**-*th*er) *adverb, adjective*
1. a comparative form of **far.**
2. in addition or more: 'this theatre will be closed until *further* notice'.
3. furthermore.
further *verb*
to promote or help move forward: 'he *furthered* the cause of social reform with progressive legislation'.
Word Family: **furtherance,** *noun,* the act of furthering.

furthermore (*say* fir-*th*'**mor**) *adverb*
also called **further**
also or besides: 'it's too cold to go out, and *furthermore,* it's going to rain'.

furthest (*say* **fir**-*th*'st) *adverb, adjective*
a superlative form of **far.**

furtive (*say* **fir**-tiv) *adjective*
secretive or sly.
Word Family: **furtively,** *adverb*; **furtiveness,** *noun.*
[Latin *furtivus* stolen]

fury (*say* **few**-ree) *noun*
1. a state of violent excitement or anger.
2. a violent or fierce person.
[Latin *Furia* a spirit of madness]

furze *noun*
gorse.

fuse (1) (*say* **fewz**) *noun*
1. a device which protects electric

circuits by melting when the current exceeds a specified limit.
2. any of various devices, such as a cord soaked in a combustible substance, used to ignite explosives.
fuse *verb*
(of an electric circuit) to burn out.

fuse (2) (*say* **fewz**) *verb*
a) to combine or join by melting together. b) to melt or become liquid.
Word Family: **fusible**, *adjective*, able to be melted. [Latin *fusus* poured]

fuselage (*say* **fewza**-lahj) *noun*
the body of an aircraft.
[French *fuselé* spindle-shaped]

fusel oil
a smelly mixture of amyl and other alcohols, the by-product of distillation which collects at the top of a bottle of whisky, etc.
[German *Fusel* bad brandy]

fusilier (*say* fewza-**leer**) *noun*
(*formerly*) a soldier armed with a musket or flintlock.
[French *fusil* gun]

fusillade (*say* **fewzi**-lade) *noun*
a simultaneous or continuous discharge of firearms.

fusion (*say* **few**-*zh*'n) *noun*
1. a) the act of fusing, melting or joining. b) the state of being fused or melted.
2. *Physics:* see NUCLEAR FUSION.

fuss *noun*
an unnecessary display of excitement or anxiety.
fussy *adjective*
1. too concerned or particular about details, etc.
2. full of elaborate or unnecessary detail: 'she wore a *fussy* dress with flowers, ribbons and false buttons'.
fusspot *noun*
(*informal*) a person who is always making a fuss.
Word Family: **fuss**, *verb*; **fussily**, *adverb*; **fussiness**, *noun.*

fustian *noun*
1. a coarse, strong cotton fabric.
2. any pompous, meaningless talk.

fusty *adjective*
1. mouldy or stale.
2. old-fashioned or extremely conservative.
Word Family: **fustiness**, *noun.*

futile (*say* **few**-tile) *adjective*
having no use, effect or result: 'her efforts to clean the house were made *futile* by the children running in and out'.
Word Family: **futilely**, *adverb*; **futility** (*say* few-**tilli**-tee), *noun.*
[Latin *futilis* leaky]

future (*say* **few**-cher) *noun*
the time or events still to come.
Usage: 'there is little *future* for an outdoor restaurant in this climate' (= chance of success).
future *adjective*
1. of or occurring at a later time than the present: 'what are your *future* plans for the business?'.
2. *Grammar:* see TENSE (2).
Word Family: **futureless**, *adjective*, having no prospect of future success.
[Latin *futurus* about to be]

futurity (*say* few-**tewri**-tee) *noun*
a) future time: 'in *futurity* such a society may come about'. b) a future event. c) the quality of being future.

fuzz *noun*
1. any fluffy, frizzy substance, especially hair.
2. (*informal*) the police.
fuzzy *adjective*
1. covered with or resembling fuzz.
2. unclear or blurred.
Word Family: **fuzzily**, *adverb*; **fuzziness**, *noun.*

Gg

gab *verb*
(gabbed, gabbing)
(*informal*) to talk idly or too much.
gift of the gab, a talent for talking easily or well.

gabble *verb*
to speak so rapidly that one cannot be understood.
Word Family: **gabble**, *noun*; **gabbler**, *noun*, a person who gabbles.

gaberdine (*say* gabba-**deen**)
gabardine *noun*
a twill-woven fabric usually made from wool, cotton or viscose, often used for raincoats.
[Old French *gallevardine* pilgrim's robe]

gable (*rhymes with* table) *noun*
any triangular section of an outside wall between sloping roofs.
Word Family: **gabled**, *adjective*.

gad *verb*
(gadded, gadding)
to move about restlessly or excitedly: 'young people *gadding* about all over the place'.
gadabout *noun*
(*informal*) a person who flits about restlessly or frivolously.

gadfly *noun*
1. any of various kinds of fly which bite cattle and horses.
2. (*informal*) a person who provokes or irritates another person.

gadget (*say* **gajet**) *noun*
any small device or tool, usually a mechanical one.
Word Family: **gadgetry**, *noun*, any or all gadgets.

gadolinium (*say* gadda-**linnium**) *noun*
element number 64, a rare magnetic metal. See LANTHANIDE.
See CHEMICAL ELEMENTS in grey pages.

Gaelic (*say* **gaylik**) *adjective*
of or relating to the inhabitants of Scotland and Ireland, and their languages.

gaff *noun*
1. a strong hook with a long handle, used for landing large fish.
2. *Sailing:* a spar on the top of a sail forming an extension of the mast.

gaffe (*say* gaf) *noun*
a blunder, such as an indiscreet act or remark.

gaffer *noun*
(*informal*) a) an elderly villager. b) a foreman.
[short form of *godfather*]

gag *noun*
1. anything placed in or over the mouth to prevent speech, sound, etc.
2. *Parliament:* a closure.
3. a joke, especially an impromptu joke made on stage.
gag *verb*
(gagged, gagging)
to apply or introduce a gag.

gaga (*say* **gah**-gah) *adjective*
(*informal*) senile or childishly foolish.
[French, mad]

gaggle *noun*
1. a flock of geese.
2. any noisy group.
gaggle *verb*
to cackle, like a goose.

gaiety (*say* **gaya**-tee) *noun*
the state of being gay.

gaily *adverb*
Word Family: see GAY.

gain *verb*
1. to obtain something wanted or needed: 'to *gain* one's living'.
2. to increase: 'I have *gained* 2 kg in weight'.
Usage: 'my watch has *gained* five minutes' (= got ahead of the correct time).
3. to reach or arrive at: 'we *gained* the summit of the mountain after a hard climb'.
gain on, gain upon, a) to get closer to something being pursued; b) to get further in front of one's pursuer.
gain *noun*
1. an increase, especially of money, possessions, etc.

2. *Electronics:* an increase in signal power, usually expressed in decibel.

gainful *adjective*
profitable.
Word Family: **gainfully**, *adverb*; **gainfulness**, *noun*.

gainsay *verb*
(**gainsaid**, **gainsaying**)
to deny: 'there's no *gainsaying* his integrity'.

gait *noun*
a manner of moving, especially walking: 'a shuffling *gait*'.

gaiter (*say* **gay**ta) *noun*
a covering for the lower leg or ankle, made of cloth, leather, etc.

gala (*say* **gah**la) *adjective*
festive or marked by celebration: 'a *gala* occasion'.
Word Family: **gala**, *noun*, a festival or a celebration.
[Old French *gale* pleasure]

galactose (*say* ga-**lak**toze) *noun*
a simple sugar (formula $C_6H_{12}O_6$), commonly occurring in lactose.
[Greek *galaktos* of milk]

galantine *noun*
white meat cooked with sausage meat, ham, etc. pressed and served cold in aspic.

galaxy (*say* **gal**lak-see) *noun*
Astronomy: a) the Milky Way. b) any of the millions of enormous, regularly shaped collections of stars, dust and gas.
Usage: 'a *galaxy* of famous film stars attended the concert' (= glittering collection).
Word Family: **galactic** (*say* ga-**lak**tik), *adjective*.
[Greek *galaktos* of milk]

gale *noun*
1. a strong wind of at least 39 miles (63 km) per hour.
2. (*informal*) a noisy outburst: 'a *gale* of laughter swept through the audience'.

gall (1) (*say* gawl) *noun*
1. a bitterness or severity.
2. bile.
Usage: 'he had the *gall* to ask for another loan' (= impudence, nerve).

gall (2) (*say* gawl) *noun*
a sore spot on the skin, especially of horses, caused by rubbing, etc.
gall *verb*
to rub or chafe.
Usage: 'I was *galled* by his stupid interjections' (= irritated, vexed).

gall (3) (*say* gawl) *noun*
an abnormal external growth on plants.

gallant (*say* **gal**-ant *or* ga-**lant**) *adjective*
1. brave or courageous: 'he was decorated for his *gallant* deeds'.
2. courteous and attentive to women: 'he was very *gallant* at the ball'.
gallant *noun*
a fashionable or dashing man, especially one who is very attentive to women.
Word Family: **gallantry**, *noun*, chivalrous or heroic behaviour; **gallantly**, *adverb*; **gallantness**, *noun*, the quality of being courteous or gallant.

gall bladder (*say* **gawl** bladda)
Anatomy: a small bag underneath the liver, which stores bile and releases it into the duodenum to aid fat digestion.

galleon (*say* **gal**lion) *noun*
a large, three-masted sailing ship used during the 15th and 16th centuries, especially by Spain.

gallery (*say* **gal**la-ree) *noun*
1. a raised, enclosed passage.
2. a room for displaying works of art.
3. a structure projecting from the inside walls of a building, as in a theatre, and containing seats. Also called a **balcony**.
4. a long narrow room: 'a shooting *gallery*'.

galley *noun*
1. a ship's kitchen.
2. *Printing:* a) the metal tray in which a column of type is placed before being made into pages. b) a proof printed on a long piece of paper from a column of type in the tray.
3. an early seagoing vessel propelled by oars, or oars and sails.

galleyslave *noun*
a) a person condemned to row in a galley. b) any overworked person.

Gallic *adjective*
of France or its inhabitants.

gallium *noun*
element number 31, a rare metal, used in high-temperature thermometers and semiconductors.
See CHEMICAL ELEMENTS in grey pages.

gallivant (*say* **gal**li-vant) *verb*
also spelt **galavant**
to move or go about in a frivolous manner or in search of pleasure.

gallon *noun*
a unit of volume for liquids, equal to about 4·55 litre. A gallon contains 4 quart, 8 pint or 32 gill. In America it is equal to about 3·79 litre. See UNITS in grey pages.

gallop *noun*
the fastest gait of a horse, in which groups of four distinct hoof-beats may be heard.
Word Family: **gallop** (**galloped, galloping**), *verb*, a) to ride or run at a gallop, b) to rush.

gallows (*say* **gal**-oze) *noun*
a wooden frame with two upright posts and a crosspiece, used to hang a person. A **gibbet** has one upright post and a projecting crosspiece.

gallstone (*say* **gawl**-stone) *noun*
Medicine: a small stony mass often formed in the gall bladder or the bile passages.

Gallup Poll
a public opinion poll, often used to predict election results.
[a trademark, after *G. H. Gallup*, born 1901, an American statistician]

galore (*say* gal-**or**) *adverb*
in abundance.

galoshes *plural noun*
also spelt **goloshes**
a pair of waterproof covers worn over ordinary shoes for protection.

galumph (*say* gal-**umf**) *verb*
to prance or leap triumphantly.
[from GAL(lop) + (tri)UMPH, coined by Lewis Carroll in 1871]

galvanic (*say* gal-**vannik**) *adjective*
a) of or relating to electricity from a chemical battery. b) relating to or affected by or as if by an electric shock.
Word Family: **galvanism,** *noun.*

galvanic cell
also called a **voltaic cell**
Electronics: a cell containing a liquid electrolyte capable of producing electrical energy by chemical action.
[after *Luigi Galvani*, 1737–98, an Italian physiologist]

galvanize (*say* **galva**-nize) **galvanise** *verb*
1. *Metallurgy:* to coat a material, especially iron, by dipping it into molten zinc.
2. to stimulate by an electric current.
Usage: 'the workers were *galvanized* into action by the whistle' (= startled).
Word Family: **galvanization,** *noun.*

galvanometer (*say* galva-**nommi**ta) *noun*
an instrument used for detecting and measuring electric current.

gambit *noun*
any action by which one hopes to gain an advantage.
[Italian *gambetto* a tripping-up]

gamble *verb*
to take a risk, usually involving the loss of something valuable on the outcome of a chance.
Word Family: **gamble,** *noun*; **gambler,** *noun*, a person who gambles.
[Middle English *gamen* to play]

gambol *verb*
(**gambolled, gambolling**)
to skip or spring about in play.

game (1) *noun*
1. a form of sport or amusement, especially one with rules.
Usages:
a) 'national sports are played at the Highland *Games*' (= athletic contests).
b) 'we won four *games* in the first set' (= single rounds).
c) 'he was badly off his *game* today' (= usual style of playing).
d) 'he's in the teaching *game*' (= profession, business).
e) 'so that's your *game*!' (= scheme, plan).
2. a) any wild animals hunted for sport or food. b) the flesh of such animals.
Phrases:
fair game, any target thought fit for attack, criticism, etc.
play the game, to act fairly.
game *verb*
to gamble.
game *adjective*
1. of or relating to animals hunted for game: 'shooting *game* birds'.
2. plucky or courageous: 'he's a *game* little sportsman'.
3. (*informal*) willing or having the spirit for: 'young Jack is *game* for anything'.
Word Family: **gamely,** *adverb*, bravely; **gameness,** *noun*, a) braveness, b) willingness; **gamester,** *noun*, a person taking part in a game, especially a gambler.

game (2) *adjective*
lame: 'a *game* leg'.
Word Family: **gamely,** *adverb*; **gameness,** *noun*; **gammy,** *adjective*, (informal) lame.

gamecock *noun*
a cock trained for fighting.

gamekeeper *noun*
a person employed on an estate to look after game, prevent poaching, etc.

gamete (*say* **gam**–eet) *noun*
Biology: a cell which fuses with another during reproduction to form a zygote that will develop into a new organism.
Word Family: **gametic** (*say* ga–**mettik**), *adjective.*

game theory
the principal method of operational research, in which mathematical analysis and computers are used to work out the possible results of various combinations of moves and countermoves in war, business rivalry, etc.
[the name refers to the bluff and counterbluff in the *game* of poker]

gamin *noun*
a mischievous child.
Word Family: **gamine**, *noun,* a girl or woman with an elfish or boy–like look; **gamin, gamine,** *adjective.*

gamma globulin
a protein present in blood plasma, containing antibodies effective against certain micro–organisms, such as those causing measles, infectious hepatitis and polio.

gamma ray
Physics: a form of electromagnetic radiation similar to, but of shorter wavelength than, X–rays.

gammon *noun*
the quick–cured hind leg of a bacon pig, bought boned and uncooked and then boiled or grilled as rashers. Compare HAM.

gammy *adjective*
(*informal*) lame.

gamp *noun*
(*informal*) a baggy umbrella.
[after *Sairey Gamp* in Dickens's 'Martin Chuzzlewit']

gamut (*say* **gamm**ut) *noun*
the entire range: 'her face expressed the full *gamut* of emotions'.

gamy *adjective*
(of meat) having the strong flavour characteristic of game.

gander *noun*
1. a male goose.
2. (*informal*) a look or glance.

gang *noun*
a group of people working together or associating for a particular purpose: a) 'a road *gang*'; b) 'a *gang* of criminals'.
gang *verb*
to form or act as a gang: 'groups of residents *ganged* together to fight the developers'.
gang up on, to join together against.
ganger *noun*
the foreman of a group of labourers.

gangling, gangly *adjective*
awkwardly tall and spindly: 'a *gangling* adolescent'.

ganglion (*say* **gangli**–on) *noun*
plural is **ganglia**
Anatomy: a bundle of nerve cells outside the brain or spinal cord.

gangplank *noun*
a plank used as a temporary bridge between a ship and the shore or another ship.

gangrene (*say* **gang**–green) *noun*
the death of tissue, usually the limbs, due to a lack of blood.
Word Family: **gangrene**, *verb*; **gangrenous** (*say* **gangrin**–us), *adjective.*
[Greek *gaggraina* an eating sore]

gangster *noun*
a member of a gang of criminals.

gangway *noun*
1. a passage between seats, as in a theatre or the House of Commons.
2. *Nautical:* a) a railed bridge temporarily linking ship and dockside. b) a gangplank.
gangway *interjection*
clear the way!

gannet *noun*
a white goose–sized seabird with black–tipped wings, which plunges on fish from a height.

gantry *noun*
an overhead framework which supports a load, such as a mobile crane or railway signals.

gaol (*say* jale) *noun*
also spelt **jail**
a building where convicted criminals are kept.
Word Family: **gaoler**, *noun,* a person in charge of prisoners or a gaol; **gaol,** *verb,* to put into gaol.

gaolbird (*say* **jale**–bird) *noun*
a person who is or has been in gaol.

gap *noun*
1. an unfilled space: 'a *gap* in the hedge'.

Usage: 'a wide *gap* between their views' (= difference, divergence).
2. a break in a mountain range.

gape *verb*
1. to open the mouth widely.
2. to stare in amazement.
Usage: 'holes *gaped* in the road after the earthquake' (= opened widely).
Word Family: **gape**, *noun*; **gapingly**, *adverb*.

garage (*say* **garr**ahj) *noun*
a) a building where motor vehicles are housed or repaired. b) a service station.
[French *garer* to put in shelter]

garb *noun*
clothes: 'clerical *garb*'.
Word Family: **garb**, *verb*, to clothe or dress.

garbage (*say* **gar**-bij) *noun*
any rubbish, especially household refuse.

garble *verb*
to distort something so that it cannot be understood.

garden *noun*
1. any piece of ground used for growing flowers, fruit or vegetables.
2. (*usually plural*) ornamental grounds used as a public park.
lead up the garden path, to mislead purposely.
Word Family: **garden**, *verb*; **gardener**, *noun*, a person who tends a garden.

gardenia (*say* gar-**dee**nya) *noun*
an evergreen hot-house plant with large, fragrant, white or yellow, waxy flowers.
[after *A. Garden*, 1730–91, an American botanist]

garfish *noun*
any of a group of small, plant-eating fish with an extended lower jaw forming a beak.
[Old English *gar* spear + FISH]

gargantuan (*say* gar-**gan**-tewan) *adjective*
gigantic.
[after *Gargantua*, a greedy, giant king in a 16th-century satire by Rabelais]

gargle *verb*
to keep a liquid in the back of the mouth while blowing a stream of air through it from the lungs.
Word Family: **gargle**, *noun*.
[Latin *gurgulio* gullet]

gargoyle (*say* **gar**-goil) *noun*
a decorative rainwater spout on the side of a building, often in the shape of a grotesque animal or human.

garish (say **gair**-ish) *adjective*
excessively coloured or ornamented.
Word Family: **garishly**, *adverb*; **garishness**, *noun*.

garland *noun*
a wreath or ring of flowers used for decoration or as a token of honour.
Word Family: **garland**, *verb*, to decorate with garlands.

garlic *noun*
the strong-flavoured bulb of a lily-like plant used in salads and cooking.

garment *noun*
any article of clothing.

garner *verb*
to gather in or store up, such as grain in a granary.
garner *noun*
an old word for a granary.

garnet *noun*
Geology: a hard, crystalline mineral of many colours, used as a gem (in its dark red form) and as an abrasive.

garnish *verb*
to decorate.
Word Family: **garnish**, *noun*, anything added for decoration; **garnishment**, *noun*.

garnishee *noun*
Law: a person ordered by a court to pay money owned by or owed to a judgement debtor or bankrupt direct to the creditors.

garret *noun*
an attic.

garrison *noun*
a) a group of soldiers stationed in a building or town. b) the fort or building where the soldiers are based.
Word Family: **garrison**, *verb*.

garrotte (*say* ga-**rot**) **garotte** *noun*
a) a strangling or throttling, especially with wire. b) the instrument used.
Word Family: **garrotte**, *verb*.
[Spanish *garrote* a stick used for twisting a cord tight]

garrulous (*say* **garra**-lus) *adjective*
very talkative, especially about unimportant matters.
Word Family: **garrulously**, *adverb*; **garrulousness**, *noun*.

garter *noun*
a band of elastic worn around the leg to keep a sock or stocking in place.

gas *noun*
plural is **gases**
1. *Physics:* a substance which has no definite volume and completely fills any container in which it may be kept. Compare LIQUID and SOLID.
2. any of various gases or mixtures of gases used as fuel, etc.: 'natural *gas*'.
3. *Medicine:* a mixture of such substances used as an anaesthetic.
4. *American:* petrol.
5. (*informal*) something which gives great pleasure or delight.
gas *verb*
(**gassed, gassing**)
1. to overcome or suffocate with gas.
2. to treat with gas: 'bananas are *gassed* to help them ripen'.
3. (*informal*) to talk idly or boastfully.
Word Family: **gaseous** (*say* **gassi**–us), *adjective*, of or like gas; **gassy**, *adjective*, full of gas.

gasbag *noun*
(*informal*) a talkative person.

gash *noun*
a long, deep wound, especially in the flesh.
Word Family: **gash**, *verb*.

gasket *noun*
any substance used to seal joints and prevent gas escaping.

gas mantle
a fine, net–like hood giving light from the glow of burning gas.

gasmask *noun*
also called a **respirator**
a facemask which filters air through charcoal and certain chemicals before it is inhaled, in order to prevent poisoning or irritation by gases.

gasoline (*say* gassa–**leen**) **gasolene** *noun*
American: petrol.

gasometer (*say* gas–**ommita**) *noun*
a large cylindrical tank for storing gas.

gasp (*say* gahsp) *verb*
to catch or struggle for breath with the mouth open.
Word Family: **gasp**, *noun*.

gas ring
a metal ring pierced with holes, through which gas is supplied for cooking.

gassy *adjective*
Word Family: see GAS.

gastric *adjective*
Anatomy: of or relating to the stomach.

gastro–
a prefix meaning stomach, as in *gastroenteritis*.
[Greek *gastros* of a belly]

gastroenteritis
(*say* gastro–enter–**eye**–tis) *noun*
an inflammation of the stomach and intestines, dangerous in young children.

gastronomy (*say* gas–**tronna**–mee) *noun*
the art and knowledge of food and eating.
Word Family: **gastronomist**, *noun*; **gastronomic** (*say* gastra–**nommik**), *adjective*; **gastronomically**, *adverb*.
[GASTRO– + Greek *nomos* an arrangement]

gastropod *noun*
any of a group of molluscs, including snails, having an external, coiled shell and a ventral muscular foot on which it slides about.
[GASTRO– + Greek *podos* of a foot]

gate *noun*
1. a movable barrier, usually on hinges, which opens and closes an entrance in a fence, etc.
2. any device or structure which regulates passage, etc. or provides entrance.
3. the total amount of money paid by spectators for admission to a public exhibition, sporting match, etc.
4. the series of slots controlling the movement of the gear lever in a motor vehicle.

gatecrash *verb*
to attend a party or other gathering without having been invited.
Word Family: **gatecrasher**, *noun*.

gatepost *noun*
either of the two fence posts between which a gate is hung.

gateway *noun*
1. a space or structure within which a gate is situated.
2. (*informal*) an entrance: 'Hawaii – the *gateway* to the Pacific'.

gather *verb*
1. to pick up or bring together: a) '*gather* the fallen fruit'; b) 'to *gather* one's thoughts'.
Usages:
a) 'her skirt was *gathered* at the waist' (= drawn together in folds).
b) 'the car *gathered* speed as it approached the corner' (= increased).
2. to conclude or understand: 'I *gather* you are not very enthusiastic'.

3. (of a sore) to form a head of pus.
gather *noun*
a drawing together, especially of folds in fabric.
gathering *noun*
1. a group of people assembled together.
2. a series of gathers in fabric.

gauche (*say* **goash**) *adjective*
awkward or tactless.
Word Family: **gaucherie**, *noun*, awkwardness.
[French, left, left hand]

gaucho (*say* **gow**-cho) *noun*
1. a South American cowboy of mixed Spanish and Indian parentage.
2. (*plural*) a pair of knee-length culottes.

gaudy (*say* **gaw**dee) *adjective*
vulgarly bright or showy.
Word Family: **gaudiness**, *noun*; **gaudily**, *adverb*.

gauge (*say* gayj) *noun*
1. a scale or standard of measure: 'there is no real *gauge* of a person's character'.
2. any instrument for measuring something, such as pressure, temperature, etc.
3. the thickness or diameter of something, such as wire.
4. *Railways:* the distance between the rails.
gauge *verb*
to measure or estimate: 'it was not difficult to *gauge* his motives'.

gaunt (*say* gawnt) *adjective*
thin or haggard.
Word Family: **gauntness**, *noun*.

gauntlet (1) (*say* **gawnt**-let) *noun*
1. a mailed or armoured glove formerly used in battle.
2. a strong glove with a wide cuff reaching to the elbow.
Phrases:
pick, take up the gauntlet, to accept a challenge.
throw down the gauntlet, to issue a challenge.
[Old French *gant* glove]

gauntlet (2) (*say* **gawnt**-let) *noun*
run the gauntlet, a) to be forced to run between two rows of men who strike the passing victim, formerly used as a military punishment; b) to expose oneself to extreme danger, criticism, etc.
[Swedish *gata* lane + *lopp* a running course]

gauss (*rhymes with* house) *noun*
a unit of magnetic induction.
[after *K. F. Gauss*, 1777–1855, a German mathematician]

gauze (*say* gawz) *noun*
a) any thin, transparent woven fabric.
b) any similar open material consisting of crossed lines, such as wire.

gave *verb*
the past tense of the verb **give**.

gavel (*say* **gavv**'l) *noun*
a small hammer used to signal for silence, in court, at a meeting, etc.

gawk *verb*
to stare stupidly or rudely.

gawky *adjective*
awkward or clumsy.
Word Family: **gawkily**, *adverb*; **gawkiness**, *noun*.

gay *adjective*
1. happy, and full of joy.
2. (*informal*) homosexual.
Word Family: **gaily**, *adverb*, in a gay manner; **gayness**, *noun*.

gaze *verb*
to look with fixed attention, curiosity, etc.
Word Family: **gaze**, *noun*.

gazebo (*say* ga-**zee**bo) *noun*
a structure, such as a glass pavilion, with a wide view.

gazelle (*say* ga-**zel**) *noun*
a small African or Asian antelope.
[Arabic]

gazette (*say* ga-**zet**) *noun*
1. an official or government publication.
2. a title for certain newspapers.
Word Family: **gazette**, *verb*, to publish in a gazette.
[Italian *gazeta* a Venetian coin, the price of a gazette]

gazetteer (*say* gazza-**teer**) *noun*
a geographical dictionary

gazump *verb*
(*informal*) to outbid the original buyer of a property after his offer has been accepted by the vendor: 'we thought we had a lovely house, but we were *gazumped* before the contract could be signed'.

gear *noun*
1. a mechanism for transmitting or changing movement, e.g. by cogwheels.
2. any tools or apparatus for a particular purpose: 'he packed his fishing *gear* into the car'.

3. (*informal*) any clothes.
gear *verb*
1. to provide with gears.
2. to adjust or adapt: 'the nation's economy is *geared* to support primary industry'.

gearbox *noun*
the case within which the gears of a motor vehicle are enclosed.

gecko *noun*
any of various small flat house lizards, usually with pads on their toes which stick to surfaces for climbing.
[Malay]

geese *plural noun*
the plural of **goose**.

geezer *noun*
(*informal*) an odd person, especially an old man.
[from *guiser*, an old word for a person who wears a disguise]

Geiger counter (*say* **gie**–ga counter)
a portable instrument used for detecting and measuring radioactivity.
[after *H. Geiger*, 1882–1945, a German physicist]

geisha (*say* **gee**sha *or* **gay**sha) *noun*
a Japanese girl trained to entertain with dancing, conversation, etc.
[Japanese]

gel (*say* jel) *noun*
a colloidal solution which has set to a jelly.
Word Family: **gel** (**gelled**, **gelling**), *verb*, to form or become a gel.
[short form of *gelatine*]

gelatine (*say* **jell**a–teen) *noun*
also spelt **gelatin** (*say* **jell**a–tin)
1. a complex protein derived from animal tissue, soluble in water and setting into a jelly. It is used in foods, photography and medicine.
2. any of various similar jelly-like substances.
Word Family: **gelatinous** (*say* jel–**attin**–us), *adjective*, of or like jelly.
[Latin *gelatus* frozen]

geld *verb*
to castrate an animal, especially a horse.
gelding *noun*
a castrated animal, especially a horse.

gelignite (*say* **jell**ig–nite) *noun*
an explosive containing nitroglycerine, used for blasting.
[GEL(atine) + Latin *ignis* fire]

gem (*say* jem) *noun*
also called a **jewel**
1. a precious or semi-precious stone, cut and polished in order to show off its beauty.
2. anything which is highly valued for its worth or beauty: 'this poem is a literary *gem*'.

Gemini (*say* **jemm**in–eye) *noun*
also called the **Twins**
Astrology: a group of stars, the third sign of the zodiac.

gen (*say* jen) *noun*
(*informal*) the general or correct information about something.
[from GEN(eral information)]

-gen
a suffix meaning producing, as in *hydrogen.*
[Greek]

gendarme (*say* **zhon**–darm) *noun*
a member of the armed military police force in certain European countries, such as France.
Word Family: **gendarmerie** (*say* zhon–**darma**–ree), *noun*, a force of gendarmes.
[French *gens* men + *d'armes* bearing arms]

gender (*say* **jen**da) *noun*
1. *Grammar:* any of the classifications given to nouns or pronouns according to the sex of the person or thing described, as **masculine** (he); **feminine** (she); **neuter** (it) or **common** (child).
2. (*informal*) the sex of any animal.

gene (*say* jeen) *noun*
Biology: the unit of heredity associated with deoxyribonucleic acid (DNA), and found on a chromosome, transmitting characteristics (e.g. eye colour).

genealogy (*say* jeeni–**alla**–jee) *noun*
a family tree or the record of a person's ancestors and relatives.
Word Family: **genealogical** (*say* jenni–a–**lo**ji–k'l), *adjective*; **genealogist** (*say* jeeni–**alla**–jist), *noun.*
[Greek *genea* race + -LOGY]

genera (*say* **jenn**era) *plural noun*
see GENUS.

general (*say* **jenn**a–r'l) *adjective*
1. of, affecting or including all or the whole: a) 'a *general* election'; b) 'a *general* strike'.
Usages:
a) 'the *general* opinion' (= most common, majority).
b) 'as a *general* rule' (= not rigid, limited or restricted).

c) 'she only gave very *general* directions' (= vague, not exact).
2. having superior or chief rank: 'the director *general*'.
general *noun*
a commissioned officer in the armed forces next below a field marshal.
in general, a) 'we spoke about things *in general*' (= as a whole, not particular); b) '*in general* summer is a warm season' (= as a general rule).

general election
see ELECTION.

generalissimo (*say* jenna-r'l-**issi**-mo) *noun*
a title for the supreme commander of the armed forces in certain countries.

generality (*say* jenna-**ralli**-tee) *noun*
1. a vague or general statement.
2. a general principle.

generalize (*say* **jenn**era-lize)
generalise *verb*
1. to draw a general conclusion from one or more particular cases.
2. to make a vague or sweeping statement.
Word Family: **generalization**, *noun.*

generally *adverb*
1. usually: 'I am *generally* home by 7 o'clock'.
2. in a general or vague way: '*generally* speaking I don't like small dogs'.
3. for the most or larger part: 'his plan was *generally* approved'.

general practitioner
short form is **G.P.**
a doctor whose practice deals with the general health of a community, as distinct from specialized areas of medicine.

generalship *noun*
a) skill as a commander of troops.
b) the rank of a general.

general staff
a group of officers assisting a commander in planning military operations.

generate (*say* **jenn**a-rate) *verb*
to produce or cause: 'the strikes *generated* much hostility towards the unions'.

generation (*say* jenna-**ray**-sh'n) *noun*
1. a) each successive stage in a family descent: 'three *generations* of the family were present – father, son, and grandson'. b) the average time between any two such stages, usually considered as being about 30 years among human beings.
2. any group of people born at about the same time: 'they had become known as the pop *generation*'.
3. the act of generating or producing: 'the *generation* of electricity'.

generative (*say* **jenn**a-ra-tiv) *adjective*
relating to or capable of producing offspring or new forms.

generator (*say* **jenn**a-rayter) *noun*
a device which converts one form of energy into another, especially a machine which produces electrical energy from mechanical energy.

generic (*say* jen**err**ik) *adjective*
of or common to a whole genus or group: 'Hoover has become a *generic* name for vacuum cleaners'.
Word Family: **generically**, *adverb.*
[Latin *generis* of a kind]

generous (*say* **jenn**a-rus) *adjective*
1. ready to give freely.
2. plentiful or large: '*generous* slices of cake'.
generosity (*say* jenna-**rossi**-tee) *noun*
the quality of being generous or unselfish.
Word Family: **generously**, *adverb.*
[Latin *generosus* of noble birth]

genesis (*say* **jenn**a-sis) *noun*
plural is **geneses** (*say* **jenn**a-seez)
a beginning or creation.
[Greek]

genetic (*say* jen**ett**ik) *adjective*
1. of or relating to genes or genetics.
2. of or relating to genesis or creation.
Word Family: **genetically**, *adverb.*

genetics (*say* jen**ett**iks) *plural noun*
(*used with singular verb*) the study of heredity and the differences between living things due to inheriting certain characteristics.
Word Family: **geneticist** (*say* jen**ett**a-sist), *noun.*
[Greek *gennetikos* productive]

genial (*say* **jee**ni-ul) *adjective*
mildly pleasant, kind or favourable.
Word Family: **genially**, *adverb*; **geniality** (*say* jeeni-**alli**-tee), *noun.*
[Latin]

genie (*say* **jee**ni) *noun*
plural is **genii**
Folklore: a spirit or demon, especially one capable of changing into many different forms.
[Arabic *jinni*]

genitals (*say* **jenni**–t'ls) *plural noun*
also called the **genitalia** (*say* jenni–**tay**–lee–a)
Anatomy: the organs of reproduction, being the penis, testes and associated parts in the male and the ovaries, uterus, vagina and associated parts in the female.
Word Family: **genital,** *adjective.*

genitive case
Grammar: see CASE (1).

genius (*say* **jeeni**–us) *noun*
plural is **geniuses**
1. a) an exceptionally high intelligence or creative ability. b) a person with this talent or ability.
2. any natural ability or talent: 'he has a *genius* for getting into trouble'.
3. *Folklore:* a genie. Plural is **genii.**
[Latin, a natural taste]

genocide (*say* **jenno**–side) *noun*
a systematic attempt to destroy a racial group or nation.
Word Family: **genocidal** (*say* jenno–**side**–al), *adjective.*
[Greek *genos* race + Latin *caedere* to kill]

genotype (*say* **jenno**–tipe) *noun*
Biology: the genetic constitution of an organism. Compare PHENOTYPE.

genre (*say* **zhon**ra) *noun*
a style, variety or category, especially in art, film, literature, etc.
genre painting, paintings of rustic or other scenes of local everyday life familiar to the artist.
[French]

gent (*say* jent) *noun*
(*informal*) a gentleman.

genteel (*say* jen–**teel**) *adjective*
over–refined in manners, speech or outlook.
genteelism *noun*
an over–refined word substituted for plain English, as 'unpleasant odour' for 'nasty smell'.
Word Family: **genteelly,** *adverb;* **gentility** (*say* jen–**tilli**–tee), *noun.*

gentian (*say* **jen**–sh'n) *noun*
a) a small alpine plant, with deep blue, trumpet–shaped flowers. b) any of various similar but unrelated flowers.

gentile (*say* **jen**–tile) *noun*
(*often capital*) any person who is not Jewish, especially a Christian.
[Late Latin *gentilis* foreign]

gentle *adjective*
1. soft or kind: a) '*gentle* words soothed his anger'; b) 'a *gentle* breeze'.
Usage: 'the *gentle* slopes did not take long to climb' (= moderate, not severe).
2. being born of a respected family.
Word Family: **gently,** *adverb;* **gentleness,** *noun.*

gentleman *noun*
plural is **gentlemen**
1. a) a well–bred, educated man with socially correct manners. b) a polite form of address for any man.
2. *History:* a personal servant at court.
Word Family: **gentlemanly,** *adjective.*

gentlemen's agreement
an agreement guaranteed by trust and honour rather than by legal means.

gentlewoman *noun*
plural is **gentlewomen**
1. an old word for a woman of gentle breeding.
2. *History:* a personal servant at court.

gentry (*say* **jen**–tree) *plural noun*
the well–born or privileged people in a society.

genuflect (*say* **jen**–yoo–flekt) *verb*
to kneel or bend the knee or knees, especially as an act of worship.
Word Family: **genuflection, genuflexion,** *noun.*
[Latin *genu* knee + *flectere* bend]

genuine (*say* **jen**–yoo–in) *adjective*
real or true: a) '*genuine* fear'; b) 'a *genuine* antique'.
Usage: 'I like a person to be honest and *genuine*' (= sincere).
Word Family: **genuinely,** *adverb;* **genuineness,** *noun.*

genus (*say* **jeenus**) *noun*
plural is **genera** (*say* **jennera**)
Biology: the group below family, used in the classification of animals or plants.
[Latin, a stock, category]

geo– (*say* **jee**–o)
a prefix meaning the earth, as in *geology.*
[Greek *ge*]

geocentric (*say* jee–o–**sen**trik) *adjective*
having the earth as the centre.

geochemistry
(*say* jee–o–**kemmi**–stree) *noun*
the study of the chemical composition of the earth's crust, and the changes taking place within it.
Word Family: **geochemist,** *noun;* **geochemically,** *adverb.*

geodesic (*say* jee–o–**deesik** *or* jee–o–**dessik**) *adjective*

also called **geodetik** (*say* jee-o-**dettik**) relating to the geometry of curved surfaces.
geodesic dome
a hemispherical dome formed of interlocking polygons.

geodesy (*say* jee-**odda**-see) *noun*
also called **geodetiks** (*say* jee-o-**dettiks**)
the science of surveying large areas of the earth, allowing for its curvature.
[GEO- + Greek *daisia* division]

geography (*say* jee-**ogra**-fee) *noun*
1. the study of the earth's surface, including its physical features, climates, vegetations, soils, population distribution, etc.
2. the physical features of a particular area.
Word Family: **geographer**, *noun*, a person who studies geography; **geographic** (*say* jee-o-**graffik**), **geographical**, *adjective*; **geographically**, *adverb*.
[GEO- + Greek *graphein* to write]

geology (*say* jee-**olla**-jee) *noun*
1. the study of the earth, its origin, structure, composition and history.
2. the features of a region in relation to geology: 'the *geology* of Queensland'.
Word Family: **geological** (*say* jee-o-**loji**-k'l), *adjective*; **geologically**, *adverb*; **geologist** (*say* jee-**olla**-jist), *noun*.
[GEO- + -LOGY]

geometric (*say* jee-o-**mett**-rik)
geometrical *adjective*
1. of or relating to geometry.
2. using or resembling the lines and shapes characteristic of geometry: 'the chocolates were arranged in *geometric* patterns in the box'.
Word Family: **geometrically**, *adverb*.

geometric mean
Maths: a mean of *n* numbers found by taking the *n*th root of the product of the numbers. *Example*: the geometric mean of 2 and 8 is 4 because $2 \times 8 = 16$ and the square root of 16 is 4. Compare ARITHMETIC MEAN.

geometric progression, geometrical progression
Maths: a sequence of numbers which increases or decreases at an increasing rate, as in the series 2, 4, 8, 16, in which each term bears a constant ratio to its predecessor. Compare ARITHMETIC PROGRESSION.

geometry (*say* jee-**omma**-tree) *noun*
a branch of maths studying the properties of figures in space.
Word Family: **geometrician** (*say* jee-omma-**trish**'n), *noun*.
[GEO- + Greek *metron* a measure]

geomorphology
(*say* jee-o-mor**folla**-jee) *noun*
the study of landforms on the earth and their relationship to the underlying rocks.
Word Family: **geomorphologist**, *noun*; **geomorphic**, *adjective*.
[GEO- + MORPHOLOGY]

geophysics (*say* jee-o-**fizziks**) *plural noun*
(*used with singular verb*) the study of the physical processes related to the earth's structure, e.g. gravitation, tides, earthquakes and the earth's magnetism.
Word Family: **geophysicist** (*say* jee-o-**fizza**-sist), *noun*; **geophysical**, *adjective*.

Geordie *noun*
a native of Tyneside.
[for *Georgie*]

geothermal (*say* jee-o-**therm**'l) *adjective*
of or relating to the internal heat of the earth.

geranium (*say* jer-**ray**-nee-um) *noun*
1. the cranesbill or true geranium.
2. the pelargonium, a garden or greenhouse plant with red, pink or white flowers, the scented leaves of which often have a zone of lighter or darker colour.
[Greek *geranos* a crane, because the fruit of the plant was thought to resemble a crane's bill]

geriatrics (*say* jerri-**atriks**) *plural noun*
(*used with singular verb*) the medical, hygienic and related care of aged people.
Word Family: **geriatric**, *adjective*, of or relating to the care of aged people; **geriatric**, *noun*, an aged person; **geriatrician** (*say* jerri-a**trish**'n), *noun*.
[Greek *geras* old age + *iatros* physician]

germ (*say* jerm) *noun*
1. any micro-organism which may cause disease.
2. anything which serves as a basis or beginning of growth, development, etc.: 'the *germ* of an escape plan formed in the prisoner's mind'.
[Latin *germen* a bud]

germane (*say* jer**mane**) *adjective*
significantly related or relevant.
[Latin *germanus* of the same parents]

Germanic (*say* jer–**mannik**) *adjective*
1. of or relating to Germany or the Germans.
2. of or relating to a northern European race which includes Germans, Scandinavians, Dutch, etc. or their languages. Also called **Teutonic**.

germanium (*say* jer–**may**–nee–um) *noun*
element number 32, a rare metal used as a semiconductor.
See CHEMICAL ELEMENTS in grey pages.

German measles
also called **rubella**
a mild infectious, viral disease, usually in children, causing red spots. If contracted in early pregnancy it may damage the unborn child.

germ cell
Biology: a reproductive cell at any stage of its development into a gamete.

germicide (*say* **jermi**–side) *noun*
any substance which kills germs or micro–organisms.
Word Family: **germicidal**, *adjective.*
[GERM + Latin *caedere* to kill]

germinal (*say* **jermi**–n'l) *adjective*
relating to a germ or germ cell.
Usage: 'the plan is still in its *germinal* stages' (= early, beginning).

germinate (*say* **jermi**–nate) *verb*
to develop and grow, as a plant from a seed.
Word Family: **germination**, *noun.*

germ theory
the doctrine of biogenesis.

germ warfare
a form of biological warfare using bacteria, viruses, etc. to destroy life.

gerontology (*say* jeron–**tolla**–jee) *noun*
the study of the ageing process and of the disabilities of old age.
[Greek *gerontos* of an old man + –LOGY]

gerrymander (*say* **jerri**–manda) *verb*
Politics: to arrange the boundaries of electorates to the advantage of a particular party or candidate.
Word Family: **gerrymander**, *noun.*
[from *E. Gerry*, a governor of Massachusetts who created new boundaries there in 1812 + (sala)MANDER, which animal the rearranged map was considered to resemble]

gerund (*say* **jerr**und) *noun*
Grammar: a noun formed from a verb.
Example: he does not like *reading.*

gesso (*say* **jesso**) *noun*
a mixture of chalk, glue, etc. carved or moulded into decoration on ceilings, picture–frames and furniture, and usually painted or gilded.
[Italian]

Gestapo (*say* ges–**tah**po) *noun*
the secret police in Germany from 1933–45, working to ensure obedience to the Nazi Government.
[German GE(heime) STA(ats) PO(lizei) secret state police]

gestation (*say* jes–**tay**–sh'n) *noun*
Biology: the act or period of carrying a developing embryo in the uterus.
Word Family: **gestate** (*say* jes–**tate**), *verb.*
[Latin *gestatus* carried]

gesticulate (*say* jes**tik**–yoolate) *verb*
to make gestures, especially for emphasis or explanation.
Word Family: **gesticulation**, *noun.*

gesture (*say* **jes**–cher) *noun*
a movement of the body or limbs, made to express or emphasize an idea, emotion, etc.
Usage: 'she did it as a *gesture* of her friendship' (= indication).

get *verb*
(got, getting)
1. to obtain: 'he *got* a good mark in the exam.'
Usages:
a) 'the bullet *got* him in the back' (= hit).
b) 'I will go and *get* the book' (= fetch, bring).
c) (*informal*) 'I do not *get* your meaning' (= understand).
d) 'he *got* 10 years in prison for rape' (= was sentenced to).
e) 'you must put petrol in the car to *get* it to start' (= cause).
f) 'I shall *get* dinner now' (= make ready).
g) 'can you *get* him to visit me?' (= persuade).
h) (*informal*) 'he has *got* to be there' (= an obligation or duty).
i) (*informal*) 'let's *get* the informer' (= punish, kill).
j) 'she *gets* tired very easily' (= becomes).
k) 'some bricklayers *get* more than doctors' (= earn).

2. used to indicate movement away, in, out, over, through, etc.: 'we all *got* out of the car'.
Phrases:
get across, to make understood.
get around, get about, a) 'she *gets around* a lot' (= travels, moves about); b) 'the rumour *got around*' (= circulated).
get at, a) 'that shelf is difficult to *get at*' (= reach); b) 'I cannot see what you are *getting at*' (= hinting, suggesting); c) 'vandals *got at* our house' (= tampered with).
get away, to escape. *Word Family*: **get–away**, *noun.*
get away with, 'the robbers thought they would *get away with* their crime' (= escape punishment for).
get by, 'how will we *get by* without a car?' (= manage).
get down to, 'we must *get down to* work' (= concentrate on).
get off, to evade or escape the consequences of one's actions.
get on, get along, a) to advance or make progress; b) to manage or succeed; c) to be friendly with.
get over, 'it took her many months to *get over* the accident' (= recover from).
get round, a) to outwit or overcome; b) to humour someone into being nice, lenient, etc.
get round to, 'we finally *got round to* discussing tactics' (= came to).
get through to, (*informal*) to make understand.
get up, to rise, especially from bed.

get–together *noun*
an informal gathering or party.

get–up *noun*
an outfit or costume.

gew–gaw *noun*
a trinket.

geyser *noun*
1. (*say* **gie**–za *or* **gee**za) a spring which sends up jets of hot water and steam.
2. (*say* **gee**za) a gas device which heats but does not store water.
[Icelandic *geysir* a hot spring]

ghastly (*say* **gahst**–lee) *adjective*
1. dreadful or terrifying.
Usage: 'what a *ghastly* smell!' (= very unpleasant).
2. extremely pale.

ghee (*say* gee) *noun*
a kind of clarified butter.

gherkin (*say* **ger**kin) *noun*
a small cucumber, usually pickled.

ghetto (*say* **get**to) *noun*
an area in a city where a minority group lives separately from other groups in the community.
[Italian]

ghost *noun*
also called a **shade**
the spirit or semblance of a dead person, believed to visit or haunt living people.
give up the ghost, (*informal*) to die.
Word Family: **ghostly**, *adverb*; **ghostliness**, *noun.*

ghost writer
a person who writes a work which will be attributed to another person, who commissioned it.

ghoul (*say* gool) *noun*
1. an evil spirit believed, by Moslems, to eat human bodies or rob graves.
2. a person who enjoys revolting or horrible things.
Word Family: **ghoulish**, *adjective*; **ghoulishly**, *adverb.*
[Arabic]

giant (*say* **jie**–ant) *noun*
a person or thing of unusually large size, importance, etc.
Word Family: **giant**, *adjective.*

gibberish (*say* **jibb**a–rish) *noun*
any rapid or unintelligible talk.

gibbet (*say* **jibb**it) *noun*
see GALLOWS.

gibbon (*say* **gibb**en) *noun*
a small, long–armed ape, living in the forests of tropical Asia.

gibe (*say* jibe) *verb*
also spelt **jibe**
to mock or jeer.
Word Family: **gibe**, *noun.*

giblets (*say* **jib**lets) *plural noun*
the heart, neck and gizzard of a fowl, usually removed from the bird and cooked separately.

giddy (*say* **gidd**ee) *adjective*
1. having a light–headed spinning sensation.
2. frivolous or flighty: 'a *giddy* girl'.
Word Family: **giddily**, *adverb*; **giddiness**, *noun.*

gift *noun*
1. a present.
2. a special ability: 'she has a *gift* for languages'.
Word Family: **gifted**, *adjective*, having a special ability or talent.

gift–horse *noun*
look a gift–horse in the mouth, to accept a gift or favour ungraciously.

gift–wrap *verb*
(**gift–wrapped, gift–wrapping**)
to wrap something in decorative paper and ribbon.

gig *noun*
also called a **sulky**
an open, two–wheeled carriage pulled by one horse.

giga–
a prefix used for SI units, meaning one thousand million (10^9). See UNITS in grey pages.
[Greek *gigas* giant]

gigantic (*say* jie–gantik) *adjective*
extremely large.
Word Family: **gigantically**, *adverb.*

giggle *verb*
to laugh in a silly or nervous manner.
Word Family: **giggle**, *noun*; **giggly**, *adjective.*

gigolo (*say* **jigg**a–lo) *noun*
a young man who is employed as a dancing–partner or escort, or is kept as a lover, by an older woman.
[French]

Gilbertian *adjective*
ludicrously topsy–turvy: 'a *Gilbertian* situation'.
[from the *Gilbert* and Sullivan comic operas, 1875–96]

gild *verb*
(**gilded** or **gilt, gilding**)
to cover with a fine layer of gold or golden colour.
gild the lily, to spoil beauty by overdecorating.
Word Family: **gilding**, *noun*, a) a golden surface or coating, b) any fine but deceptive appearance.

gill (1) *noun*
1. *Biology:* an external organ in aquatic animals, used for gas exchange in respiration.
2. one of the thin, radial plates on the underside of the cap of a mushroom, etc.
green about the gills, sickly in appearance.

gill (2) (*say* jill) *noun*
see GALLON.

gill (3), ghyll *noun*
a deep wooded glen or a mountain torrent, especially in the Lake District.

gillie (*say* **gill**ee) *noun*
Scottish: a guide and attendant employed by anglers and deerstalkers.
[Gaelic *gille* lad]

gilt *noun*
a thin layer of gold or similar material.

gilt *verb*
a past tense and past participle of the verb **gild**.
Word Family: **gilt**, *adjective*, golden.

gilt–edged *adjective*
1. having the edges gilded.
2. of the highest quality, especially of stock which is issued by the Government or is extremely safe as an investment: '*gilt–edged* securities'.

gimbals (*say* **jim**–belz) *plural noun*
Nautical: the rings and pivots in which an object, such as a compass, sits and swings to remain level as the boat moves.

gimcrack (*say* **jim**–crack) *adjective*
ill–made, tawdry or worthless.

gimlet *noun*
a small tool with a pointed spiral end for drilling holes.
gimlet eyes, eyes which look piercingly or penetratingly.
Word Family: **gimlet**, *verb*, to pierce with or as if with a gimlet.

gimmick *noun*
a novel or tricky means or device, especially one intended to boost sales.
Word Family: **gimmicky**, *adjective.*

gimp *noun*
a trimming on a garment.

gin (1) (*say* jin) *noun*
a strong liquor made from rye or other grain and flavoured with juniper berries.

gin (2) (*say* jin) *noun*
1. a machine for separating the seeds from a cotton plant.
2. a trap or snare for animals.
[Old French *engin* engine]

ginger (*say* **jin**ja) *noun*
1. the strong–smelling root of a tropical plant, used in cooking and medicine.
2. a sandy–red colour.
Word Family: **gingery**, *adjective*; **ginger**, *adjective*, (of hair) sandy–red.

ginger ale
also called **dry ginger**
a soft drink with a ginger flavour, often mixed with spirits.

ginger beer
a soft drink with a ginger flavour, consisting of water brewed with sugar and yeast.

gingerbread *noun*
a treacle or honey cake flavoured with ginger.
gilt off the gingerbread, 'that takes some of the *gilt off the gingerbread*'

(= deprives the project of some of its attractions).

ginger group
a group of people working within a larger group or association to introduce changes or a modern outlook.

gingerly (*say* **jin**ja–lee) *adverb, adjective*
with extreme caution or care.

ginger wine
a fermented drink of sugar, lemon and raisins, flavoured with ginger and other spices.

gingery *adjective*
Word Family: see GINGER.

gingham (*say* **ging**um) *noun*
a cotton fabric with a coloured check pattern.

gingivitis (*say* jinji–**vie**–tis) *noun*
an infection of the gums.
[Latin *gingiva* gum + -ITIS]

gin rummy
a card game similar to rummy in which a player may finish when he has ten or less unmatched points.

gipsy (*say* **jip**–see) **gypsy** *noun*
1. (*often capital*) a) a member of a nomadic people, of Hindu origin, now found mainly in Europe. Also called a **Romany**. b) their language.
2. any person who lives in gipsy style.
[a short form of *Egyptian*, because they were believed to come from Egypt]

giraffe (*say* je**rahf**) *noun*
a spotted mammal which has a long neck, long legs and feeds on leaves in open forests in Africa. It is the tallest known mammal.

gird (1) *verb*
(**girt** or **girded**, **girding**)
1. to encircle with or as if with a belt, band, etc.
2. to prepare for action.
gird one's loins, see LOIN.

gird (2) *verb*
to jeer.

girder *noun*
a large, usually horizontal, beam supporting a structure.

girdle *noun*
1. a belt or cord worn around the waist.
2. any belt or band, such as a ring of bark cut from a tree trunk.
3. a corset.
4. *Anatomy:* a connected ring of bones, such as the shoulder girdle or the pelvic girdle.

girdle *verb*
1. to encircle or enclose.
2. to cut away the bark of a tree in a ring.

girl *noun*
a female child.
Word Family: **girlish**, *adjective*; **girlishly**, *adverb*; **girlhood**, *noun.*

girlfriend *noun*
a female friend, especially one being courted by a man.

Giro (*say* **jie**–ro) *noun*
a cheap method of transferring money directly from one account to another through the Post Office or banks.
[Italian, circulation]

girt *verb*
a past tense and past participle of the verb **gird (1)**.

girth *noun*
1. the measurement around something.
2. a band passed under a horse's belly to hold a saddle or pack in place.

gist (*say* jist) *noun*
the essential part of something: 'what exactly is the *gist* of your argument?'.

give *verb*
(**gave**, **given**, **giving**)
1. to provide or hand over, especially without expecting payment, etc. in return: 'she *gave* the beggar some coins'.
2. to cause: 'does your leg *give* you pain?'.
3. to pronounce: 'the jury *gave* a verdict of guilty'.
4. to result in: 'the latest trade figures *give* a gloomy picture of our prospects'.
5. to submit: 'he was stubborn at first, but then he began to *give*'.
6. to make suddenly: 'she *gave* a start when she saw him'.
Usages:
a) 'how much will you *give* me for my car?' (= pay).
b) 'the newspaper *gave* the true facts' (= presented).
c) 'she *gave* the rest of her life to nursing him' (= dedicated).
d) 'I don't *give* a damn what you think' (= care).
e) 'he *gave* a marvellous party' (= was host at).
Phrases:
give and take, 'life is a matter of *give and take*' (= compromise).

give away, a) to give as a present; b) 'let's *give* the work *away* for a while' (= stop); c) 'her smile *gave* her *away*' (= betrayed).
give in, 'I *give in*, what's the answer?' (= acknowledge defeat).
given to, 'he is *given to* lying' (= in the habit of).
give or take, 'he must be 70, *give or take* a year' (= approximately).
give out, a) 'let's *give out* the presents now' (= distribute); b) 'she *gave out* a terrible cry' (= made, let out); c) 'his voice *gave out* during the speech' (= became exhausted).
give over, 'the day was *given over* to celebrating' (= devoted).
give up, a) 'you must *give* yourself *up*' (= surrender); b) 'try to *give up* smoking' (= stop).
give way, to yield or submit, especially in traffic.

gizzard *noun*
a muscular organ in certain animals, such as birds, which grinds and digests food.

glacé (*say* **gla**–say) *adjective*
1. coated with sugar.
2. having a smooth glossy surface, as on kid leather.
[French, iced]

glacier (*say* **glay**–see–a *or* **gla**–see–a) *noun*
a large mass of moving ice, formed from compacted snow.
Word Family: **glacial**, *adjective*, a) relating to or associated with the action of ice or glaciers, b) extremely cold; **glaciate**, *verb*, to cover with or affect by ice.
[French *glace* ice]

glaciology (*say* glay–see–**olla**–jee *or* gla–see–**olla**–jee) *noun*
the study of ice and its effects on landscapes.

glacis (*say* **glassis**) *noun*
a gentle slope, originally as a defence round a fort.
[French *glace* ice]

glad *adjective*
(gladder, gladdest)
pleased or happy: 'I'm *glad* you could visit me'.
Word Family: **gladly**, *adverb*; **gladness**, *noun*; **gladden**, *verb*, to make or become glad.

glade *noun*
an open space in a forest.

gladiator (*say* **gladdi**–ayta) *noun*
Ancient history: a person trained to perform public fights in Roman arenas.
Word Family: **gladiatorial** (*say* gladdia–**tawriul**), *adjective*.
[Latin *gladius* sword]

gladiolus (*say* gladdi–**ole**–us) *noun*
plural is **gladioli** (*say* gladdi–**ole**–eye)
a garden plant growing from a corm with reed-like leaves and brightly coloured flowers on a long stem.
[Latin *gladius* sword]

gladsome (*say* **glad**–sum) *adjective*
an old word for glad.

Gladstone bag
a light travelling case consisting of two compartments hinged together at the centre.
[after *W. E. Gladstone*, 1809–98, a British statesman]

glamour (*say* **glamma**) *noun*
in America spelt **glamor**
an alluring charm or fascination.
Word Family: **glamorous**, *adjective*; **glamorously**, *adverb*; **glamorize**, **glamorise**, *verb*, to make glamorous or attractive.

glance *verb*
1. to look briefly.
2. to be deflected off an object: 'the bullet *glanced* off the tree and struck the wall'.
Word Family: **glance**, *noun*.

gland *noun*
Anatomy: a group of cells which produce a substance necessary for the body to function, such as the salivary glands. See ENDOCRINE GLAND.
Word Family: **glandular** (*say* **glan**–dew–la), *adjective*.
[Latin *glandis* of an acorn]

glanders *noun*
a rare but sometimes fatal infectious, bacterial disease of horses, of which the first symptoms are swelling below the jaw and discharge of mucus from the nostrils.

glandular fever
also called **mononucleosis**
an infectious, viral disease causing fever and swollen lymph glands.

glare *noun*
1. an angry or fixed look.
2. a bright, intense light.
Word Family: **glare**, *verb*; **glaring**, *adjective*, a) dazzlingly bright, b) very conspicuous; **glaringly**, *adverb*; **glary**, *adjective*.

glass *noun*
plural is **glasses**
1. a hard, brittle, usually transparent substance with no crystalline form, composed of silicates of various metals, especially sodium and calcium.
2. any object made of glass, such as a container for drinking, a mirror, etc.
3. (*plural*) spectacles.

glass-blowing *noun*
the art of shaping glass by heating it and then blowing into it while it is liquid.
Word Family: **glass-blower**, *noun.*

glass fibre
a flame-resistant fabric made from very thin fibres of glass, used mainly for curtains.

glasshouse *noun*
a greenhouse.

glasspaper *noun*
a strong paper coated with glass particles, used for smoothing, polishing, etc.

glass wool
glass spun into very fine threads resembling cotton wool, used as insulation, to filter corrosive liquids, etc.

glassy *adjective*
1. of or having the texture, appearance, etc. of glass.
2. expressionless: 'a *glassy* stare'.
Word Family: **glassily**, *adverb*; **glassiness**, *noun.*

glaucoma (*say* glaw-**ko**-ma) *noun*
an increased pressure by the fluid in the eyeball, which may lead to blindness if not treated.
[Greek *glaukos* bluish-green + *-oma* a tumour]

glaze *noun*
a) a smooth, glossy surface or coating: 'the *glaze* on an iced bun'. b) any substance which produces such a surface: 'a pottery *glaze*'.
glaze *verb*
1. to fit or cover with glass.
2. to cover with glaze.
Word Family: **glazier** (*say* **glay**-zee-a), *noun*, a person who fits windows, etc. with glass.

gleam *noun*
a) a brief flash of light. b) a subdued glow of light.
Word Family: **gleam**, *verb.*

glean *verb*
to gather or collect.
Usage: 'can you *glean* any sense from his story' (= discover).
Word Family: **gleaner**, *noun.*

glee *noun*
1. lively joy or amusement.
2. an unaccompanied part-song for three or more voices.
Word Family: **gleeful**, *adjective*, merry or joyful; **gleefully**, *adverb.*

glen *noun*
Scottish: a small, narrow valley.

glengarry *noun*
a Scottish Highlander's boat-shaped bonnet with ribbons at the back.
[from *Glengarry*, Inverness-shire]

glib *adjective*
easy and fluent, but often superficial or insincere.
Word Family: **glibly**, *adverb*; **glibness**, *noun.*
[Dutch *glibberig* slippery]

glide *verb*
1. to move smoothly or effortlessly: 'the ghost *glided* out of the room'.
2. (of a bird, aeroplane, etc.) to fly in the air by using air currents or already acquired momentum.
glider *noun*
1. a person or thing that glides.
2. an aeroplane without an engine which is kept aloft by the action of air currents.
Word Family: **glide**, *noun*, a gliding movement, as in a dance; **glidingly**, *adverb.*

glimmer *noun*
a faint, wavering light: 'a *glimmer* of moonlight through the trees'.
Usage: 'the news brought no *glimmer* of hope' (= suggestion).
Word Family: **glimmer**, *verb*; **glimmeringly**, *adverb.*

glimpse *noun*
a fleeting view or look: 'people waited for hours to catch a *glimpse* of the film star'.
Word Family: **glimpse**, *verb.*
[Middle English *glimsen* to shine faintly]

glint *noun*
a quick, bright flash of light, especially off a reflecting surface such as metal.
Word Family: **glint**, *verb.*

glisten (*say* **gliss**'n) *verb*
to shine or sparkle, as a wet or highly polished surface.
Word Family: **glisten**, *noun.*

glitter *verb*
to sparkle with reflected light.
Word Family: **glitter**, *noun.*

gloaming *noun*
an old word for twilight.

gloat (*rhymes with* boat) *verb*
to think about or gaze on with pleasure or malicious delight: 'the chess player *gloated* over his opponent's hopeless position'.
Word Family: **gloatingly**, *adverb*; **gloater**, *noun.*

globe *noun*
1. a sphere or spherical object.
2. a sphere with a map of the earth on it.
3. an electric light bulb.
the globe, 'the Bible is translated into all the languages of *the globe*' (= the earth).
Word Family: **global** (*say* **glo**–b'l), *adjective*, a) of or relating to a globe; b) relating to the whole world; **globally**, *adverb.*
[Latin *globus*]

globe artichoke
see ARTICHOKE.

globetrotter *noun*
(*informal*) a person who travels widely.

globule (*say* **glob**–yool) *noun*
a very small globe, especially a drop of liquid.
Word Family: **globular**, *adjective*, a) composed of globules, b) globe-shaped.

glockenspiel (*say* **glokken**–shpeel) *noun*
Music: a) a percussion instrument of tuned, metal bars played with small hammers. b) a set of hanging bells played from a keyboard.
[German *Glocke* bell + *spielen* to play]

gloom *noun*
1. darkness, dimness or deep shadow.
2. a state of depression or hopelessness.
Word Family: **gloomy**, *adjective*; **gloomily**, *adverb*; **gloominess**, *noun.*

glorify (*say* **glawri**–fie) *verb*
(**glorified**, **glorifying**)
to praise, honour or make glorious.
Word Family: **glorified**, *adjective*, a) made glorious, b) (informal) given more importance than is due; **glorification**, *noun.*

glory *noun*
1. high praise, honour or renown: 'the *glory* of winning the big match'.
2. an object of pride: 'a stately home which is one of the *glories* of colonial architecture'.
3. magnificence, or radiant beauty: 'a painting by an old master showing Christ in all his *glory*'.
glory *verb*
1. to rejoice triumphantly.
2. to exult arrogantly or boastfully: 'students *glory* in their ability to embarrass a teacher'.
Word Family: **glorious**, *adjective*, a) having or bringing glory, b) magnificent; **gloriously**, *adverb*; **gloriousness**, *noun.*
[Latin *gloria*]

gloss (1) *noun*
a surface shine or lustre.
Usage: 'don't be taken in by his *gloss* of respectability' (= deceptive appearance).
gloss *verb*
to put a gloss on.
gloss over, 'at the interview he tried to *gloss over* his lack of qualifications' (= cover up, disguise).
Word Family: **glossy**, *adjective*; **glossy**, *noun*, an expensive magazine printed on glossy paper; **glossily**, *adverb*; **glossiness**, *noun.*

gloss (2) *noun*
a note, written in the margin or between the lines of a text, explaining a difficult passage.
Word Family: **gloss**, *verb*, to annotate or insert glosses in a text.

glossary (*say* **glossa**–ree) *noun*
a list of technical terms or dialect words, usually at the end of a book, with explanations or definitions.
[Greek *glossa* a tongue, a foreign word]

glottis *noun*
Anatomy: the space between the vocal cords at the top of the larynx.
Word Family: **glottal**, *adjective.*
[Greek *glotta* a tongue]

glove (*say* gluv) *noun*
a fitted covering for the hand, with a separate sheath for each finger.
glove box
also called a **glove compartment**
a small compartment in the dashboard of a car in which small articles, maps, etc. are kept.
Word Family: **glove**, *verb*, to put on or provide with gloves; **glover**, *noun*, a person who makes or sells gloves.

glow (*rhymes with* slow) *verb*
to give off light and heat without flame: 'the embers *glowed* in the hearth'.

Usage: 'the cold wind makes your cheeks *glow*' (= be red and shining).
glowing *adjective*
a) incandescent. b) intense and brilliant: '*glowing* colours'.
Usage: 'he came home with a *glowing* report from his teacher' (= enthusiastic).
Word Family: **glow**, *noun*; **glowingly**, *adverb.*

glower (*rhymes with* flower) *verb*
to stare sullenly or angrily.
Word Family: **glower**, *noun*; **gloweringly**, *adverb.*

glow-worm *noun*
see FIREFLY.

glucagon (*say* **gloo**ka-gon) *noun*
Biology: a hormone secreted by the pancreas, which increases the amount of sugar in the blood.

glucose (*say* **gloo**koze) *noun*
a simple sugar (formula $C_6H_{12}O_6$), found in animals and plants and used as a source of energy in respiration.
[Greek *glykys* sweet]

glue (*say* gloo) *noun*
an adhesive, especially one made from animal tissue and soluble in water.
glue *verb*
to stick or adhere firmly.
Usage: 'they were *glued* to the television all evening' (= unable to move from).
Word Family: **gluey**, *adjective*, like or covered with glue.

glum *adjective*
(**glummer, glummest**)
downcast or dejected.
Word Family: **glumly**, *adverb*; **glumness**, *noun.*

glut *verb*
(**glutted, glutting**)
to fill or supply to excess: 'he *glutted* himself at the dinner party'.
glut *noun*
an excess or full supply: 'a *glut* of tomatoes brought the price down sharply'.

glutinous (*say* **gloo**tin-us) *adjective*
thick, gluey or sticky.
[Latin *glutinis* of glue]

glutton *noun*
1. a person who eats to excess.
2. a person with a great capacity or tendency to take, etc.: 'a *glutton* for punishment'.
Word Family: **gluttonous**, *adjective*; **gluttonously**, *adverb*; **gluttony**, *noun*, the habit or practice of eating to excess.
[from Latin]

glycerol (*say* **glissa**-rol) **glycerine** *noun*
also called **glycerin**
a thick, syrupy liquid alcohol with a sweet taste, obtained from the fat in soap manufacture and used in the manufacture of explosives (nitroglycerine), plastics and antifreeze.
[Greek *glykeros* sweet]

glycogen (*say* **glike**-o-jen) *noun*
Biology: a carbohydrate which is stored in plant and animal cells and may be easily converted into glucose.

glyph (*say* glif) *noun*
a hieroglyph.

gnarled (*say* narld) *adjective*
knotty, twisted and rough: 'a *gnarled* old tree'.
Word Family: **gnarl**, *noun*, a knot or knob on a tree trunk; **gnarl**, *verb*, to make knotty or twisted.

gnash (*say* nash) *verb*
to grind the teeth together, especially in pain or rage.
Word Family: **gnash**, *noun.*

gnat (*say* nat) *noun*
also called a **midge**
any of a group of small biting flies related to the mosquito.

gnaw (*say* naw) *verb*
(**gnawed, gnawing**)
to chew or bite on something persistently.
Usage: 'the crime *gnawed* his conscience' (= troubled).
Word Family: **gnawingly**, *adverb*, persistently.

gneiss (*say* nice) *noun*
metamorphic rock with irregular alternate light and dark bands of quartz, feldspar and mica.
[German, sparkling]

gnome (*say* nome) *noun*
1. *Folklore:* a small dwarf-like old man, believed to live in underground caves in order to guard the precious metals.
2. any replica of this kind.
Word Family: **gnomish**, *adjective.*

gnomic (*say* **no**-mik) *adjective*
pithy and sententious: 'he replied with some such *gnomic* utterance as "time will tell" '.
[Greek *gnomikos* dealing in maxims]

Gnostic (*say* **noss**–tik) *noun*
Religion: a member of any of various pre-Christian or Christian sects which claimed secret knowledge of religious mysteries.
Word Family: **Gnosticism,** *noun.*
[Greek *gnosis* knowledge]

gnu (*say* noo *or* new) *noun*
plural is **gnus** or **gnu**
also called a **wildebeest**
a large, South African antelope with a head like an ox.

go *verb*
(I, you, we, they **go**; he, she, it **goes**; **went, gone, going**)
1. to move: 'the car is *going* too fast'.
2. to become: a) 'her aunt *went* mad'; b) 'she has *gone* very brown this summer'.
Usages:
a) 'the intruders were told to *go* at once' (= depart).
b) 'he is *going* to jump' (= intending).
c) 'on the map this road *goes* north' (= runs).
d) 'she *goes* by the latest fashions' (= is guided).
e) 'my watch has stopped *going*' (= working).
f) 'the bell has *gone*' (= been rung).
g) 'the story *goes* that she has a rich uncle' (= relates).
h) 'he *goes* by the name of Standish' (= is known).
i) 'as small flats *go,* it's very comfortable' (= are usually).
j) 'how did everything *go*?' (= turn out).
k) 'these dishes *go* in the bottom cupboard' (= belong).
l) 'in the flood the fence *went* in three places' (= gave way).
m) 'all his sons *go* to university' (= attend).
n) 'your skirt does not *go* with your shoes' (= harmonize).
o) 'let's *go* halves in the cake' (= share).
p) 'all the facts *go* to show she is innocent' (= serve).
q) 'what I say *goes*' (= has final authority).
r) '8 *goes* into 24 three times' (= divides).
Phrases:
go along, 'he refused to *go along* with my advice' (= agree).
go back on, 'you can't *go back on* your promise' (= break, fail to keep).
go down, a) 'the team *went down* in the finals' (= was beaten); b) 'the battle *went down* in history' (= was remembered); c) 'she has *gone down* with tonsillitis' (= fallen ill); d) 'that explanation will never *go down*' (= be believed).
go for, 'he *goes for* girls with dark hair' (= likes, is attracted to).
go in for, 'do you *go in for* old movies?' (= have a keen interest in).
go into, 'I didn't *go into* the details' (= examine, study).
go off, a) 'the fireworks *went off* suddenly' (= exploded); b) 'the milk has *gone off*' (= turned sour); c) 'I've *gone off* coffee lately' (= stopped liking).
go on, 'he *went on* about his inconsiderate children' (= talked continually).
go out, 'the union *went out* for two weeks' (= went on strike).
go over, a) 'we *went over* the fine print in the contract' (= checked thoroughly); b) 'her speech *went over* very well' (= was received).
go steady, see STEADY.
go through, a) 'he will *go through* any trials for his beliefs' (= endure); b) 'he *goes through* money as if it was nothing' (= uses up, consumes).
go through with, 'he failed to *go through with* it' (= complete, finish).
let oneself go, 'the rock music made everyone *let themselves go*' (= become uninhibited).

go *noun*
plural is **goes**
1. energy or vitality: 'as an organizer he is full of *go*'.
2. a try or attempt: 'she wants to have a *go* at learning German'.
3. a turn in a game or series: 'it's your *go*'.
4. a success: 'let's see if we can make a *go* of it'.
5. approval: 'the pilot was given the *go* for take-off'.
Phrases:
from the word go, from the beginning.
on the go, 'he's tired because he's always *on the go*' (= very busy, active).
Word Family: **goer,** *noun.*

goad *noun*
a pointed stick used to drive cattle, etc.
Usage: 'his insults were a *goad* to me' (= stimulus).
goad *verb*
to prod or drive with a goad.
Usage: 'his wife's complaints about money *goaded* him to a fury' (= drove).

goal *noun*
1. an aim or purpose towards which effort is directed: a) 'the *goal* of the campaign was to capture votes'; b) 'my *goal* in life is to have 10 children'.
2. *Sport:* a) any of various structures or areas in field games through or over which a ball must be directed for a player to score. b) the score itself.

goalkeeper *noun*
Sport: a player whose task is to stop the ball from entering the goal area.
Word Family: **goalie,** *noun,* (informal) a goalkeeper.

goat *noun*
1. any of a group of wild or domesticated mammals with horns, shaggy hair and a beard, which eat shrubs, etc. and are valued for their meat and milk.
2. *Astrology:* (*capital*) see CAPRICORN.
3. (*informal*) a man who is lecherous.
Phrases:
act the goat, to play around in a silly way.
get one's goat, to annoy or irritate.
Word Family: **goatherd,** *noun,* a person who looks after goats.

goatee (*say* go–tee) *noun*
a small beard trimmed to a point below the chin, like a goat's beard.

gob (1) *noun*
a lump or mass.
[Old French *gobe* a mouthful]

gob (2) *noun*
(*informal*) the mouth.

gobbet *noun*
a piece or hunk: 'a *gobbet* of food'.

gobble (1) *verb*
to eat and swallow rapidly.

gobble (2) *verb*
to make the throaty sound of a turkey.
gobbler *noun*
a male turkey.

gobbledegook (*say* **gobb**'l–dee–gook) *noun*
confusing, pompous and roundabout language.

go–between *noun*
a person who carries messages, proposals, etc. between two persons or parties.

goblet *noun*
a large–bowled drinking vessel with a stem and a base but no handles.

goblin *noun*
a mischievous, ugly elf.

gobstopper *noun*
a large round sweet for sucking.

go–cart *noun*
a low, flat vehicle with wheels, for children to ride.

god *noun*
1. *Jewish, Christian, Moslem:* (*capital*) the one Supreme Being, Creator and Ruler of the universe.
2. a worshipped being who is thought to have power over human affairs: 'in Greek mythology Eros is the *god* of love'.
3. the image of a god or an idol.
4. a person viewed as or worshipped like a god.
the gods, the highest gallery seats in a theatre.
Word Family: **goddess,** *noun,* a) a female god, b) an extremely beautiful woman; **godless,** *adjective,* not believing in God, b) evil or wicked; **godly,** *adjective,* pious; **godliness,** *noun.*

godchild *noun*
Christian: a child for whom an adult takes spiritual responsibility at baptism.
Word Family: **godparent,** *noun,* a person who takes spiritual responsibility for a child at its baptism.

godhead *noun*
Religion: (*often capital*) a god or the actual nature of a god.

godsend *noun*
an unexpected piece of good fortune.

godspeed *interjection*
have a safe and successful journey!

goer (*say* **go**–er) *noun*
Word Family: see GO.

goes *verb*
the third person singular, present tense of the verb **go.**

go–getter *noun*
(*informal*) a forceful and energetic person who is successful in getting what he wants.

goggle *verb*
to stare with widely opened eyes: 'she *goggled* at the news'.
goggle *noun*
(*plural*) spectacles, especially those with special protective rims, as worn by skin–divers, etc.

going (*say* **go**–ing) *noun*
the condition of something: 'that field path is rough *going*'.

Phrases:
goings-on, actions or events, especially ones disapproved of.
going-over, a) 'he gave the car a thorough *going-over*' (= examination); b) (*informal*) 'the informer got a *going-over* from the gangsters' (= beating).
going *adjective*
moving or working: 'the car is in *going* condition'.
Usages:
a) 'the business was a *going* concern' (= flourishing, prosperous).
b) 'I bought it for less than the *going* price' (= current).
going *verb*
the present participle of the verb **go**.

goitre (*say* **goy**-ter) *noun*
an enlarged thyroid gland, usually due to insufficient iodine in the diet and causing swelling of the neck.
[Latin *guttur* the throat]

gold *noun*
1. element number 79, a ductile, malleable metal, used in alloys with copper and silver to make coins and jewellery. See TRANSITION ELEMENT. See CHEMICAL ELEMENTS in grey pages.
2. a lustrous, yellowish-ochre colour.
3. money or wealth.
4. something which is very precious or rare: 'she has a heart of *gold*'.
golden *adjective*
1. gold in colour or lustre: '*golden* hair'.
2. made of gold: 'a *golden* chalice'.
Usage: 'the advertisement says the offer is a *golden* opportunity' (= ideal, excellent).
Word Family: **gold**, *adjective.*

gold-digger *noun*
1. a person who digs or prospects for gold.
2. (*informal*) a person, especially a woman, who has an ambitious greed to acquire money or profit.

golden rule
any basic or important rule.

golden syrup
a thick, sweet liquid made from sugar cane.

golden wedding
the fiftieth anniversary of a wedding.

goldfish *noun*
any of several small varieties of carp, usually golden in colour, and kept in an aquarium.

gold plate
1. tableware, etc. of gold.
2. articles thinly veneered with gold.
Word Family: **gold-plate**, *verb*, to plate with gold by immersion (with copper articles) or electrolysis (with other metals).

gold reserve
the gold held by a central authority to maintain the value of paper money.

gold rush
a mass movement of people to an area where gold has been discovered.

goldsmith *noun*
a person who makes articles of gold.

gold standard
a monetary system in which the currency unit is based on gold of a fixed weight.

golf *noun*
an outdoor game in which a player attempts to hit a small ball into a series of holes with special clubs, using as few strokes as possible.
Word Family: **golf**, *verb*; **golfer**, *noun.*

golf course
the ground or course over which golf is played. A sandy seaside course is also called a **golf links.**

golliwog *noun*
also spelt **gollywog**
a soft, floppy doll with a black face.

goloshes (*say* ga-**loshes**) *plural noun*
see GALOSHES.

gonad (*say* **go**-nad) *noun*
Anatomy: a sex gland, such as the testis in the male or the ovary in the female.
[Greek *goné* seed]

gondola (*say* **gonda**-la) *noun*
1. a narrow boat, with high pointed ends, which is propelled from the stern with an oar, used on canals in Venice.
2. the passenger compartment hanging from an airship or balloon.
Word Family: **gondolier** (*say* gonda-**leer**), *noun*, a person who propels a gondola with an oar.
[Italian]

gone (*say* gon) *adjective*
far gone, dying or almost exhausted.
gone *verb*
the past participle of the verb **go**.
Word Family: **goner**, *noun*, (informal) a person or thing that is dead, ruined or past help.

gong *noun*
a bronze disc which is sounded with a hammer, used to summon people to a meal, etc.
[Malay]

gonorrhoea (*say* gonna-ree-a) *noun*
a venereal disease causing a thick, creamy discharge from the sexual organs and pain on passing urine.
[Greek *gonos* semen + *rhoia* a flow]

goo *noun*
(*informal*) a thick sticky substance.
Word Family: **gooey,** *adjective.*

good *adjective*
(**better, best**)
favourable or desirable: 'the sunny morning seemed a *good* omen for the trip'.
Usages:
a) 'he is a *good* man' (= upright, responsible).
b) 'the bank says my credit rating is *good*' (= reliable).
c) 'my nephew is a *good* little boy' (= well-behaved).
d) 'it will take a *good* week's work' (= full).
e) 'she is a *good* teacher' (= competent).
f) 'he loves *good* food' (= of a high standard).
g) 'I don't feel so *good*' (= healthy).
Phrases:
as good as, 'it's *as good as* done' (= virtually, in effect).
good for, a) 'the tyres are *good for* another 5000 km' (= able to last); b) 'the ticket is only *good for* tonight' (= valid).
make good, a) 'since she went into films she has *made good*' (= been prosperous, succeeded); b) 'the court ordered that he *make good* his debts' (= pay).
good *noun*
1. something which is good, beneficial, profitable, etc.: a) 'that attitude will do more harm than *good*'; b) 'you should have a holiday for your own *good*'.
2. (*plural*) a) personal property or possessions, etc.: '*goods* and chattels'. b) articles of trade, especially those which are transportable: 'imported *goods*'.
Usages:
a) 'it's no *good* complaining' (= use).
b) (*informal*) 'the electorate has every right to demand that a government deliver the *goods*' (= what was promised).
for good, for good and all, 'I heard that she'd given up teaching *for good*' (= permanently, for ever).
Word Family: **goodness,** *noun*; **good!,** *interjection,* an expression of satisfaction or approval; **goodly,** *adjective,* a) handsome or fine, b) of considerable size or amount.

goodbye *interjection*
an expression used when parting.
Word Family: **goodbye,** *noun.*
[short form of *God be with ye*]

good faith
a) honesty or sincerity: 'I am telling you this information in *good faith*'.
b) the expecting of these qualities in others: 'I am accepting your application in *good faith*'.

good-for-nothing *adjective*
worthless.
Word Family: **good-for-nothing,** *noun.*

Good Friday
Christian: the Friday before Easter, a holiday in memory of the crucifixion of Christ.

good nature
a pleasant disposition: 'he has a *good nature* and gets along well with everyone'.
Word Family: **good-natured,** *adjective*; **good-naturedly,** *adverb*; **good-naturedness,** *noun.*

goodness *noun*
Word Family: see GOOD.

good-oh *interjection*
(*informal*) an exclamation of approval or satisfaction.

goodwill *noun*
1. a friendly disposition or cheerful acquiescence: 'he consented to the change in plans with *goodwill*'.
2. the good reputation and friendly relations with customers of a well-established business: 'the *goodwill* will be sold with the business'.

goody *noun*
1. (*usually plural*) any nice things, especially food.
2. any person who is primly or pretentiously virtuous. Also called a **goody-goody.**
goody *interjection*
an exclamation of delight.

gooey *adjective*
Word Family: see GOO.

goof *noun*
(*informal*) any foolish or stupid person.
goof *verb*
(*informal*) to blunder or bungle.
goof off, (*informal*) to try to avoid work.

Word Family: **goofy**, *adjective*; **goofily**, *adverb*; **goofiness**, *noun.*

googly *noun*
Cricket: a ball spun with a wrist action which turns it in the opposite direction to that expected by the batsman.

goon *noun*
1. (*informal*) a) any stupid or awkward person. b) a comic.
2. *American:* a hired thug.
[after the hairy monster on a desert island where Popeye the Sailor was stranded]

goose *noun*
plural is **geese**
1. any of various wild or domesticated web-footed birds, larger than ducks, and kept on farms to be fattened for eating.
2. (*informal*) a silly or foolish person.
Phrases:
cook one's goose, to spoil or ruin one's chances, plans, etc.
wild goose chase, any pointless pursuit.

gooseberry (*say* **guz**-berry) *noun*
a round, green, acid, edible berry, growing on a prickly bush.

goose pimples
also called **gooseflesh**
a rough, bumpy skin due to cold or fear, when the muscle fibres at the base of a hair contract.

goosestep *noun*
a way of marching without bending the knees, kicking each leg forward stiffly and sharply.

gopher (*say* **go**-fer) *noun*
any of various North American burrowing animals, including ground squirrels, rodents and a land tortoise.
[French *gaufre* a honeycomb (of burrows)]

Gordian knot
cut the Gordian knot, to solve a difficulty in an unorthodox or forceful way.
[in Greek mythology *Gordius* severed a knot with his sword instead of trying to untie it]

gore (1) *noun*
any clotted blood from a cut or wound.
gory *adjective*
1. bloody.
2. (*informal*) unpleasant: 'let's not go into all the *gory* details'.

gore (2) *verb*
to wound or pierce, as with a horn: 'the matador was *gored* to death by the bull'.

gorge (*say* gorj) *noun*
1. a narrow, steep-sided river valley.
2. the contents of the stomach.
Usage: 'his *gorge* rose at the sight of the accident' (= feeling of disgust or repulsion).
Word Family: **gorge**, *verb*, to stuff with food or eat greedily; **gorger**, *noun.*

gorgeous (*say* **gor**jus) *adjective*
1. splendid in appearance or colouring.
2. (*informal*) very good or enjoyable: 'I had a *gorgeous* time in the country last weekend'.
Word Family: **gorgeously**, *adverb*; **gorgeousness**, *noun.*

gorgon *noun*
a terrifying or ugly woman.
[after the *Gorgons*, three sisters in Greek mythology who had snakes instead of hair, and who turned those who looked at them to stone]

gorilla *noun*
a very large ape found in the tropical forests of Africa.

gormandize, gormandise *verb*
to eat too much. Compare GOURMAND.
Word Family: **gormandizer**, *noun.*

gormless *adjective*
(*informal*) stupid or senseless: 'you *gormless* man'.

gorse *noun*
also called **furze**
a wild, prickly, evergreen shrub with yellow flowers during most of the year.

gory *adjective*
see GORE (1).

goshawk (*say* **goss**-hawk) *noun*
a powerful, short-winged hawk, sometimes trained for hunting.
[*gos*- for *goose*]

gosling *noun*
a young goose.

go-slow *noun*
also called a **work-to-rule**
the deliberate slowing down of work or production by workers, as a threat or protest to employers.

gospel *noun*
1. (*usually capital*) a) the first four books of the New Testament considered as a unit. b) any one of these books. c) a portion of one of these books.
Usage: 'he preaches the *gospel* of hard work' (= doctrine).

2. something which is accepted as unquestionably true: 'you can take what he says as *gospel*'.
[Old English *god* good + *spell* news]

gossamer (*say* **goss**ama) *noun*
1. a thread or web of the fine, silky substance made by spiders.
2. an extremely delicate variety of gauze.
Word Family: **gossamer**, *adjective*, light and fine as gossamer.

gossip *noun*
1. idle talk, especially about the affairs of others.
2. a person who talks idly or lets out secrets.
Word Family: **gossip**, *verb*; **gossipy**, *adjective.*

got *verb*
the past tense and past participle of the verb **get**.
Phrases:
have got, 'I *have got* a cold' (= have).
have got to, 'I *have got to* be home by lunchtime' (= am obliged to).

Gothic *adjective*
1. relating to the style of art and architecture of medieval Europe, in which pointed arches, etc. expressed a strong sense of upward movement.
2. (of literature, etc.) concerned with horror or grotesque mystery.
Gothic *noun*
1. *Printing:* a thick, heavy style of lettering, much used in old manuscripts. Also called **Old English**.
2. Gothic architecture or art: 'today we will study English *Gothic*'.

gouache (*say* goo-**ahsh**) *noun*
a) an opaque watercolour paint thickened with gum and honey. b) a painting in which it is used.
[Italian *guazzo* puddle]

gouge (*say* gowj) *noun*
a chisel with a curved blade for cutting grooves.
gouge *verb*
to scoop out with or as if with a gouge: 'they *gouged* his eyes out with their thumbs'.

goulash (*say* **goo**-lash) *noun*
a stew of meat and onions flavoured with paprika.
[Hungarian *gulyás* shepherd('s food)]

gourd (*say* goord) *noun*
a) a climbing plant which produces large, hard-skinned, fleshy fruit. b) a dried shell of such fruit, used as a bowl, cup, etc.

gourmand (*say* **goor**mand) *noun*
1. a greedy eater.
2. a person who is too fond of good food.
[Middle English from Old French]

gourmet (*say* **goor**may) *noun*
a person who displays a fine knowledge and discrimination in relation to food and drink.
[French, wine-taster]

gout (*rhymes with* out) *noun*
1. a disease due to an excess of uric acid in the blood, causing painful inflammation of the joints, especially in the big toe.
2. a drop or clot, especially of blood: 'the murder weapon was covered with *gouts* of blood'.
Word Family: **gouty**, *adjective.*

govern (*say* **guvv**'n) *verb*
1. to rule with authority: 'to *govern* a country'.
Usages:
a) 'you must learn to *govern* your temper' (= keep in check).
b) 'be *governed* in this matter by the opinion of others' (= influenced, directed).
2. *Grammar:* to require a noun or pronoun to be in a particular case, or a verb to be in a certain mood. *Example*: in the sentence *we left them*, the verb left governs the objective case of the pronoun, so *them* is used instead of *they.*
Word Family: **governance**, *noun.*
[Latin *gubernare* to steer]

governess (*say* **guvv**a-ness) *noun*
a female teacher employed in a private household.

government (*say* **guvv**'n-m'nt) *noun*
1. a) the control or organization of a country and its people. b) the group of officials elected or appointed to govern a country.
2. any control or direction: 'the *government* of their conduct was placed in his hands'.
Word Family: **governmental** (*say* guvv'n-**men**tal), *adjective*; **governmentally**, *adverb.*

governor (*say* **guvv**'na) *noun*
1. any person who governs or controls, such as the official in charge of a country, state, prison, etc.
2. the representative of a monarch in a dependent territory.
3. (*informal*) a form of respectful address: 'excuse me, *governor*'.

4. anything which controls or regulates, such as a device which limits engine speeds.
Word Family: **governorship,** *noun.*

governor-general *noun*
plural is **governor-generals** or **governors-general**
Politics: an appointed official representing a country's leader in a distant territory.

gown *noun*
a) a dress, especially a long or formal one. b) a long, loose cloak with wide sleeves, worn as a sign of rank in some professions: 'an academic *gown*'. Also called a **robe.**

grab *verb*
(**grabbed, grabbing**)
1. to seize, especially roughly or hastily: 'the child *grabbed* a handful of chocolates'.
2. (*informal*) to affect: 'how does the good news *grab* you?'.
Word Family: **grab,** *noun.*

graben (*say* **grah**ben) *noun*
see RIFT VALLEY.
[German, a ditch]

grace *noun*
1. an elegance or beauty of form, movement, expression, etc.
Usage: 'at least he had the *grace* to apologize' (= good manners).
2. any favour or mercy: 'the traitor begged the King to show *grace* towards him and spare his life'.
3. a short prayer said before or after a meal.
4. (*capital*) a form of address, as in your Grace, used to a duke or archbishop.
Phrases:
put on airs and graces, to behave in an affected way intended to impress other people.
with bad grace, grudgingly.
with good grace, willingly.
grace *verb*
to adorn or confer honour upon: 'I *graced* the occasion with my presence'.
Word Family: **graceful,** *adjective*; **gracefully,** *adverb*; **gracefulness,** *noun*; **graceless,** *adjective.*
[Latin *gratia* a pleasingness]

gracious (*say* **gray**-shus) *adjective*
kind or courteous: 'she greeted us with a *gracious* smile'.
gracious *interjection*
an exclamation of surprise.
Word Family: **graciously,** *adverb*; **graciousness,** *noun.*

gradation (*say* gra-**day**-sh'n) *noun*
the state or process of change taking place by degrees or stages: 'the almost imperceptible *gradation* of colours in a rainbow'.
Word Family: **gradate** (*say* gra-**date**), *verb.*

grade *noun*
1. a step or stage in rank, quality, value or skill: 'this job calls for a high *grade* of intelligence'.
2. a group of people of the same level of skill.
Usage: 'all *grades* of railway employees will receive the rise' (= classes).
make the grade, to achieve a desired standard.
grade *verb*
1. to arrange in grades or classes: 'eggs are *graded* by size'.
2. to give a gradient to.
3. to level off an unsurfaced road, etc. with a grader.
[Latin *gradus* a step]

grader *noun*
a motor vehicle with a vertical blade set between the front and back wheels for levelling earth, making roads, etc.

grade school
American: a primary school.

gradient (*say* **gray**d-y'nt) *noun*
1. the steepness of a slope expressed as height risen per unit of horizontal distance covered. *Example*: a road which rises 100 m while covering 1000 m on the map has a gradient of 1 in 10. Also called a **grade.**
2. the slope of the tangent to a curve at a particular point.

gradual (*say* **grad**-yew'l) *adjective*
taking place by degrees: 'over the years there has been a *gradual* change in moral attitudes'.
Word Family: **gradually,** *adverb*; **gradualness,** *noun.*

graduate (*say* **grad**-yoo-it) *noun*
a person who has received a diploma or degree, at the end of a course of study, from a college or university.
graduate (*say* **grad**-yoo-ate) *verb*
1. to receive an academic degree: 'he *graduated* in law'.
2. to mark with degrees for measuring: 'a ruler *graduated* in centimetres'.
3. to change gradually.
Word Family: **graduation,** *noun.*

graffiti (*say* gra-**feeti**) *plural noun*
singular is **graffito**

any drawings or inscriptions on a wall, etc., often obscene.
[Italian *graffio* a scratch]

graft (1) (*say* grahft) *noun*
1. any shoot or bud united with a living plant to form a new growth.
2. a) the replacing of diseased or damaged tissue with tissue from another part of the body, or by artificial material. b) the tissue used in replacement.
Word Family: **graft,** *verb*; **grafter,** *noun.*

graft (2) (*say* grahft) *noun*
1. a) the unscrupulous use of one's position to gain profit or advantage. b) anything gained by such means.
2. (*informal*) hard work.
Word Family: **graft,** *verb*, to work hard.

grail *noun*
an old word for a dish.
Holy Grail (*Medieval mythology*) a) the chalice used by Christ at the Last Supper; b) this as a symbol of spiritual regeneration, sought by King Arthur's knights.

grain *noun*
1. a) any or all cereal plants: 'the farmer had 40 hectare under *grain*'. b) the seeds of these plants: 'the silo was full of *grain*'. c) a single seed of these plants: 'a *grain* of wheat'.
2. a) any small, hard particle: 'a *grain* of sand'. b) the smallest amount of something: 'he hasn't a *grain* of sense in his head'.
3. a unit of mass equal to about 63·8 mg.
4. the lines made by fibres in wood, fabric, etc., or by strata in a mineral substance.
5. texture: 'the rock had a coarse *grain*'.
go against the grain, to be contrary to one's natural inclinations.
Word Family: **grainy,** *adjective*, a) of, like or composed of grains, b) having a marked grain.

gram *noun*
also spelt **gramme**
a metric unit of mass equal to 1×10^{-3} kg.

graminivorous
(*say* grammi-**nivva**-rus) *adjective*
of or relating to an organism which eats grass. Compare CARNIVOROUS.
[Latin *graminis* of grass + *vorare* to devour]

grammar (*say* **gramma**) *noun*
the science or study of words and their relationships in a language.
grammatical (*say* gra-**matti**-k'l) *adjective*
1. of or relating to grammar.
2. following the rules of grammar: 'she speaks *grammatical* English'.
Word Family: **grammatically,** *adverb*; **grammarian** (*say* gra-**mair**iun), *noun*, an expert in grammar.

grammar school
1. a secondary school, usually with selective entry.
2. *History:* an old-established school founded primarily to teach Latin.

gramme (*say* gram) *noun*
see GRAM.

gramophone (*say* **gramma**-fone) *noun*
a record-player.

grampus *noun*
1. a large, dolphin-like marine mammal.
2. a blustering, snorting person.

granary (*say* **granna**-ree) *noun*
a building for storing grain.

grand *adjective*
1. magnificent or splendid: 'the troops made a *grand* display'.
Usage: 'she has the *grand* manner of a queen' (= stately, dignified).
2. being the main or most important: a) 'the *grand* staircase'; b) 'the *Grand* Canal in Venice'.
3. complete: 'the *grand* total'.
4. (*informal*) excellent or first-rate: 'we had a *grand* time at the zoo'.
5. (of family relationships) being one generation removed from the relationship named: 'a *grandmother*'.
grand *noun*
American: (*informal*) one thousand dollars.
Word Family: **grandly,** *adverb*; **grandness,** *noun.*
[Latin *grandis* full-grown]

grandchild *noun*
plural is **grandchildren**
a child of one's son or daughter.
Word Family: **granddaughter, grandson,** *nouns.*

grandee *noun*
a Spanish nobleman.
[from Spanish]

grandeur (*say* **gran**-dewer) *noun*
greatness or magnificence: 'the *grandeur* of the alps'.
[French]

grandfather *noun*
Word Family: see GRANDPARENT.

grandfather clock
a large clock operated by a pendulum, in a tall wooden case.

grandiloquence
(*say* gran-**dilla**-kw'nce) *noun*
any pompous or bombastic eloquence.
Word Family: **grandiloquent**, *adjective*; **grandiloquently**, *adverb*.
[Latin *grandis* grand + *loquens* speaking]

grandiose (*say* **grandi**-oze) *adjective*
1. on a large or impressive scale: 'a *grandiose* old mansion'.
2. being too grand or pompous: 'a *grandiose* idea of his own importance'.

grand jury
History: a jury called to decide whether there is sufficient evidence for an indictment.

grandly *adverb*
Word Family: see GRAND.

Grand Master
a highly expert player and winner of international competitions in games such as chess or bridge.

grand opera
any opera, usually serious, in which all parts are sung and there is no spoken dialogue.

grandparent *noun*
a parent of one's parent, each person having four grandparents, one's mother's parents and one's father's parents.
Word Family: **grandmother**, **grandfather**, *nouns*.

grand piano
see PIANO (1).

Grand Prix (*say* gron **pree**)
any of various major races for motor vehicles.
[French *grand* big + *prix* prize]

grand slam
Cards: see SLAM (2).

grandson *noun*
Word Family: see GRANDCHILD.

grandstand *noun*
a raised, often sloping, structure with seats for watching sporting events, etc.

grange (*rhymes with* strange) *noun*
1. a country house with its various farm buildings.
2. *Medieval history:* a building on a feudal estate, for storing crops, etc.

granite (*say* **grann**it) *noun*
Geology: a hard, coarse-grained, igneous rock, composed of quartz, feldspar and mica, and used as a building material.
[Italian *granito* grained]

granny *noun*
(*informal*) a grandmother.

granny knot
a knot similar to a reef knot, but capable of slipping.

grant *verb*
1. to give as a favour, privilege or in response to a request: 'the King *granted* him his wish'.
2. to admit or acknowledge: 'I *grant* that point'.
take for granted, a) 'I *take* it *for granted* you'll be home on time' (= assume); b) 'he *takes* his wife's hard work *for granted*' (= accepts without appreciating).
grant *noun*
something which is granted, especially money or land: 'he went through school on a government *grant*'.

granulate (*say* **gran**-yoo-late) *verb*
1. to form into granules or grains.
2. to make rough on the surface.
3. to form the new tissue characteristic of healing wounds, ulcers, etc.
Word Family: **granulator**, *noun*, a machine for forming substances into granules; **granulation**, *noun*.

granule (*say* **gran**-yew'l) *noun*
any small grain.
Word Family: **granular**, *adjective*.

grape *noun*
1. a small, round green or purple fruit, growing in clusters on vines. They may be eaten fresh, dried (as currants or raisins), or made into wine.
2. a dark, purplish-red colour.
Word Family: **grape**, *adjective*.

grapefruit *noun*
a large, round, yellow citrus fruit with a thick skin and a juicy, acid centre.

grapeshot *noun*
a cluster of small iron balls, formerly used as ammunition in cannons.

grapevine *noun*
1. any vine which bears grapes.
2. (*informal*) any means by which rumours or secrets are passed on, e.g. by word of mouth.

graph (*say* graf *or* grahf) *noun*
a diagram produced by plotting, often on squared paper, the relationship between two variables along a

horizontal and vertical line (axis) respectively.

graphic (*say* **graffik**) *adjective*
1. of or relating to writing, drawing or painting.
2. vivid or life-like: 'a *graphic* account of the battle'.
3. of or using lines, diagrams or graphs: 'tabulate your results in *graphic* form'.
graphics *plural noun*
(*used with singular verb*) the art of drawing, especially of making geometrical drawings as aids to calculating quantities, stresses, etc., particularly in engineering and architecture.
Word Family: **graphically**, *adverb.*

graphite (*say* **graf**-ite) *noun*
also called **plumbago** or **black lead**
a soft, black, greasy-feeling form of carbon, used in pencils and as a lubricant. See ALLOTROPY.

graphology (*say* **grafolla**-jee) *noun*
the study of handwriting, usually to analyse the writer's personality, etc.

graph paper
a piece of paper printed with small, regular squares, used for drawing graphs and diagrams.

grapple *verb*
a) to seize or hold firmly: 'he *grappled* his opponent to his chest'. b) to struggle or wrestle: 'she *grappled* with the problem'.
Word Family: **grapple**, *noun*, something which grapples, such as a grappling iron.

grappling iron
also called a **grapnel**
any of various implements for hooking, grasping or holding, especially a small anchor with several hooks at the end.

grasp *verb*
to seize firmly, especially with the hands or arms: 'he *grasped* the shovel by its handle'.
Usage: 'he tried hard to *grasp* the argument' (= understand).
grasp at, a) 'he *grasped at* the rope as it swung near' (= tried to seize); b) 'he *grasped at* the opportunity' (= eagerly accepted).
grasp *noun*
a firm hold or grip.
Usage: 'he has a thorough *grasp* of the problem' (= understanding).

grass *noun*
1. any of a large group of plants, including cereals, with narrow leaves, jointed stems and spikes or clusters of inconspicuous flowers.
2. the plants eaten by cattle, sheep, etc.
3. any ground, especially lawn or pasture, covered with such plants.
4. (*informal*) marijuana.
put out to grass, to be retired from active service.
grass *verb*
to cover or feed with grass.
Word Family: **grassy**, *adjective.*

grasshopper *noun*
any of a group of herbivorous insects, including locusts, with hind legs adapted for jumping.

grassland *noun*
an area where only grass grows, usually because of low rainfall.

grassroots *adjective*
(*informal*) emerging spontaneously from the people: 'there was a great deal of *grassroots* opposition to the government's proposals'.
grassroots *plural noun*
(*informal*) the basics or essentials: 'let's get down to the *grassroots* of this problem from the outset'.

grass snake
a harmless, brown, ringed snake with two spots behind the head and without the adder's zigzag marking.

grass widow
a woman whose husband is away temporarily, e.g. on a business trip.

grate (1) *noun*
also called a **grating**
any of various metal frameworks of crossed or parallel bars, used to cover drains or to hold logs in a fireplace.

grate (2) *verb*
1. to shred or to reduce to small particles, usually by rubbing against a rough surface: '*grate* the cheese into the pan'.
2. to make or cause to make a harsh rasping sound: 'the knife *grated* on the stone'.
Usage: 'his bad manners *grated* on the company' (= had an irritating effect).
Word Family: **gratingly**, *adverb.*

grateful *adjective*
1. feeling or expressing thanks: 'I'm *grateful* for the help you gave'.
2. welcome or acceptable: 'a *grateful* breeze cooled their brows'.

Word Family: **gratefully,** *adverb*; **gratefulness,** *noun.*

grater *noun*
a kitchen utensil for shredding vegetables, cheese, etc.

graticule (*say* **gratti**–kewl) *noun*
a scale or grid of fine lines, used in the eyepiece of a telescope or microscope for accurate sighting, or on a map to show latitude and longitude, etc.

gratify (*say* **gratti**–fie) *verb*
(gratified, gratifying)
to give pleasure to or satisfy: a) 'I was *gratified* by his kindness'; b) 'to *gratify* desires or appetites'.
Word Family: **gratifyingly,** *adverb*; **gratification,** *noun.*

grating *noun*
see GRATE (1).

gratis (*say* **grah**tis *or* **gray**tis) *adverb, adjective*
for nothing; free.
[Latin, out of kindness]

gratitude (*say* **gratti**–tewd) *noun*
the state of being grateful: 'to express one's *gratitude* with flowers'.
[Latin *gratus* pleasing]

gratuitous (*say* gra–**tewi**–tus) *adjective*
1. free: 'a *gratuitous* health service'.
2. unnecessary: 'the film was full of *gratuitous* violence'.
Word Family: **gratuitously,** *adverb*; **gratuitousness,** *noun.*
[Latin *gratuitus* done as a favour]

gratuity (*say* gra–**tewi**–tee) *noun*
something given freely, especially a gift of money, such as a tip or a payment to an employee on retirement.

grave (1) *noun*
the burial place of a corpse, especially a hole dug in the ground.
Phrases:
have one foot in the grave, to be infirm, old or near to death.
turn in one's grave, 'modern dances would make grandpa *turn in his grave*' (= be shocked or horrified).

grave (2) *adjective*
serious or requiring careful consideration: a) 'a *grave* situation has developed in the Middle East'; b) 'a *grave* illness'.
grave (*say* grarv) *noun*
Language: see ACCENT.
Word Family: **gravely,** *adverb.*
[Latin *gravis* heavy]

grave (3) *verb*
(graven, graving)
an old word meaning to carve: 'the image of his face is *graven* permanently on my mind'.
graven image, an idol.

grave (4) (*say* grarv *or* **grar**vay) *adverb*
Music: very slowly.
[Italian]

gravel (*say* **gravv**'l) *noun*
Geology: any grains larger than coarse sand and finer than pebbles.
Word Family: **gravel (gravelled, gravelling),** *verb,* a) to cover with gravel, b) to baffle or confuse; **gravelly,** *adjective,* a) of, like or containing gravel, b) (of a voice) harsh or hoarse.

gravestone *noun*
a stone, usually engraved or ornamental, placed at the head of a grave.

graveyard *noun*
a cemetery, often surrounding a church.

gravitate (*say* **gravvi**–tate) *verb*
to move or have a natural attraction towards: 'the flies *gravitated* towards the open wound'.

gravitation (*say* gravvi–**tay**–sh'n) *noun*
1. *Physics:* a) the force of attraction between all particles or bodies or the acceleration of one towards another. b) the process caused by this force.
2. a natural tendency or attraction towards something.
Word Family: **gravitational,** *adjective.*

gravity (*say* **gravvi**–tee) *noun*
1. *Physics:* the force existing between any two bodies because of their mass, such as the force between the earth and a body on its surface. Compare WEIGHT.
2. seriousness: 'the *gravity* of this crime demands severe punishment'.
[Latin *gravitas* weight, dignity]

gravy (*say* **gray**–vee) *noun*
a sauce, usually seasoned and thickened, made from the juices produced while cooking meat.

gravy train
a source of easy profit.

graze (1) *verb*
1. (of cattle, sheep, etc.) to eat grass.
2. to keep cattle or sheep.
grazier (*say* **gray**–zee–a) *noun*
a person who raises cattle or sheep.

graze (2) *verb*
to touch or scrape lightly in passing.
Word Family: **graze,** *noun,* a slight scrape or abrasion.

grease (*say* greece) *noun*
1. animal fat, especially when melted.
2. any soft, oily or fatty substance, such as a lubricant made from oil thickened with soap.
grease (*say* greece *or* greez) *verb*
to put grease on or in.
Word Family: **greasy**, *adjective*; **greasily**, *adverb*; **greasiness**, *noun.*

grease gun
any of various devices for forcing grease into mechanical parts.

greasepaint *noun*
any make-up used by actors or performers, formerly a mixture of lard or fat with colouring.

great (*say* grate) *adjective*
1. large: 'the accident left a *great* scar on her leg'.
Usage: 'she was in *great* pain' (= considerable, more than ordinary).
2. important or remarkable: 'he is one of the *great* jazz musicians of this century'.
Usage: 'it was a *great* slogan during the depression years' (= popular, much in use).
3. (*informal*) very good: 'it was a *great* party'.
4. (of family relationships) being one generation removed from the named relationship: 'a *great-grandmother*'.
Word Family: **great**, *noun*, (informal) a significant or important person; **greatly**, *adverb*; **greatness**, *noun.*

great circle
any calculated circle on the earth's surface, such as the equator, whose plane bisects the earth into two hemispheres. A line along a great circle is the shortest distance between two points on the earth's surface.

greatcoat *noun*
a heavy overcoat.

Great Dane
any of a breed of tall, strong smooth-haired dogs, originally used to hunt wild boar.

greatness *noun*
Word Family: see GREAT.

great toe
also called a **big toe**
the largest of the toes, corresponding to the thumb on the hand.

grebe (*say* greeb) *noun*
any of various short-winged, almost tail-less diving birds.

greed *noun*
an extreme desire for more than is needed or deserved, especially of food or wealth.
greedy *adjective*
very eager for large quantities of anything.
Word Family: **greedily**, *adverb*; **greediness**, *noun.*

green *noun*
1. a) a primary colour like that of growing grass. b) the colour between yellow and blue in the spectrum.
2. a grassy lawn or area, such as a **putting green** which surrounds each hole on the golf links.
3. (*plural*) any green or leafy vegetable.
green *adjective*
1. having the colour green.
2. covered with grass or foliage: '*green* fields'.
3. consisting of green or leafy vegetables: 'a *green* salad'.
Usages:
a) 'use *green* tomatoes to make chutney' (= not ripe).
b) '*green* timber does not burn well' (= not dry, untreated).
c) 'the apprentices are too *green* to work on such a difficult job' (= inexperienced).
d) 'she was *green* with envy' (= pale).
e) 'I had a devil of a time trying to buy *green* prawns' (= uncooked, fresh).
Word Family: **green**, *verb*, to make or become green; **greenness**, *noun.*

green belt
an area around a city, including parks, playing fields and gardens, where building is not allowed.

greenery *noun*
any green foliage or plants.

green-eyed *adjective*
jealous.

green fingers
also called a **green thumb**
a skill in gardening and growing plants.

greenfly *noun*
the green aphid.

greengrocer *noun*
also called a **fruiterer**
a person selling fresh fruit and vegetables.

greenhorn *noun*
an inexperienced person.

greenhouse *noun*
also called a **glasshouse**

a sheltered glass building for growing plants.

green light
(*informal*) permission or opportunity to proceed with a project.
[from the railway signal light]

greenness *noun*
Word Family: see GREEN.

green-room *noun*
an old name for the backstage room where the chief actors and, in a separate room, actresses awaited their cues and received friends.
[possibly because the walls were coloured a restful *green*]

greenstone *noun*
any of various basaltic rocks having a dark green colour.

green thumb
see GREEN FINGERS.

Greenwich Mean Time (*say* **grenn**ich meen time)
the time at Greenwich, used internationally as a standard reference.
[former London site of the Royal Observatory]

Greenwich meridian (*say* **grenn**ich ma-**ridd**ian)
see PRIME MERIDIAN.

greet *verb*
to meet and welcome.
greeting *noun*
(*often plural*) any words or gestures of goodwill or welcome.

gregarious (*say* gri-**gairi**-us) *adjective*
tending to live or form in groups: 'ants are *gregarious* insects'.
Usage: 'his *gregarious* nature helped him to collect many friends' (= sociable, friendly).
Word Family: **gregariously**, *adverb*; **gregariousness**, *noun*.
[Latin *gregis* of a flock]

Gregorian calendar
the calendar in everyday use, having 365 days per year and 366 days in a leap year.
[established by *Pope Gregory XIII*, 1582]

gremlin *noun*
an imaginary gnome-like creature to which airmen, etc. like to attribute engine and other mechanical troubles.

grenade (*say* gren-**ade**) *noun*
a small bomb thrown by hand or fired from a rifle.
[Spanish *granada* a pomegranate]

grenadier (*say* grenna-**deer**) *noun*
a) a member of the Grenadier Guards. b) (*formerly*) a soldier who used grenades.

grew *verb*
the past tense of the verb **grow**.

grey (*say* gray) *noun*
1. a colour between black and white or composed of a mixture of black and white.
2. anything of this colour, especially a horse.
Word Family: **grey**, *adjective*; **grey**, *verb*, to make or become grey.

greyhound *noun*
any of a breed of slender, long-legged, smooth-haired dogs, noted for their speed.

grey matter
1. *Anatomy:* the parts of the central nervous system composed of nerve cells. Compare WHITE MATTER.
2. (*informal*) brain or intelligence.

grid *noun*
1. a framework of parallel or crossed bars, such as in a fire grate.
2. a network of regular vertical and horizontal lines on a map, used for reference.
3. *Car racing:* the starting place where cars line up before a race.

griddle *noun*
a flat, iron plate for baking or toasting cakes, biscuits, etc.

gridiron (*say* grid-**eye**-on) *noun*
1. a) a grill. b) any structure resembling a grill or grid.
2. *American:* a) a form of football played between two teams of 11 players who try to score by running with or passing the ball to the opponent's goal line. b) the field, which is marked with white parallel lines at equal intervals, on which this is played.

grief (*say* greef) *noun*
a) a deep or intense sorrow. b) anything which causes sorrow or distress.
come to grief, to fail or meet with disaster.
grieve *verb*
to cause or feel grief.
[Latin *gravis* heavy]

grievance (*say* **gree**-v'nce) *noun*
a real or imaginary cause for complaint or resentment.

grievous (*say* **gree**vus) *adjective*
1. severe or terrible: 'he was charged with *grievous* bodily harm'.

2. causing or expressing grief.
Word Family: **grievously**, *adverb.*

griffin *noun*
also spelt **griffon** or **gryphon**
Greek mythology: a creature with the head and wings of an eagle and the body of a lion.
[Greek *grypos* hook-nosed]

grill *noun*
1. a metal utensil with parallel bars on which meat, etc. is cooked by direct heat.
2. any food cooked in this way: 'a mixed *grill*'.
grill *verb*
1. to cook food on a grill. Also called to **broil**.
2. (*informal*) to interrogate or question persistently.

grille (*say* gril) *noun*
a metal screen or lattice, often decorative, e.g. for a gate or the front of a motor vehicle.

grill-room *noun*
a room in a large restaurant where formal dress is not required or where grills are a speciality.

grim *adjective*
1. severe or merciless: 'he took a *grim* view of the situation'.
2. stern or harsh in appearance: 'he approached the *grim* castle with fear'.
Usage: 'a *grim* joke' (= sinisterly ironic).
Word Family: **grimly**, *adverb*; **grimness**, *noun.*

grimace *verb*
to twist or distort the face, expressing pain, annoyance, etc.
Word Family: **grimace**, *noun.*
[Spanish *grimazo* a caricature]

grime *noun*
any dirt, especially as a thick layer or ingrained into a surface.
Word Family: **grime**, *verb*; **grimy**, *adjective*; **griminess**, *noun.*

grin *verb*
(grinned, grinning)
1. to smile widely, especially in a relaxed, friendly or amused way.
2. to draw back the lips and show the teeth, in anger, pain, etc.
Word Family: **grin**, *noun*; **grinningly**, *adverb.*

grind (*rhymes with* kind) *verb*
(ground, grinding)
1. to rub or crush a substance so as to reduce it to a powder.
2. to rub hard, especially in order to produce a smooth or sharp surface.
3. to work or produce by turning a handle: 'to *grind* out a tune on a barrel organ'.
4. (*informal*) to work or study very hard or with great effort.
grind *noun*
1. the act or noise of grinding.
2. (*informal*) any hard or monotonous work.
Word Family: **grinder**, *noun*, a person or thing that grinds.

grindstone *noun*
a large, coarse stone, shaped like a wheel and turned to grind, polish or sharpen tools.

gringo *noun*
(in Central and South America) a foreigner, especially a North American.
[Spanish, gibberish]

grip *verb*
(gripped, gripping)
to take or hold firmly.
Usage: 'the audience was *gripped* by the dramatic scene' (= fascinated, enthralled).
grip *noun*
1. the act or power of gripping: 'his *grip* on the branch loosened and he fell from the tree'.
Usages:
a) 'she has little *grip* of the problems' (= understanding).
b) 'the fever has lost its *grip* on her' (= hold, control)
2. a light travelling bag.
3. a handle.
come to grips with, to deal with decisively or energetically.
Word Family: **grippingly**, *adverb.*

gripe *noun*
1. (*plural*) any sharp or violent pains in the abdomen.
2. (*informal*) a complaint or grumble.
Word Family: **gripe**, *verb*, (informal) to grumble or complain persistently.

grippe (*say* grip) *noun*
influenza.
[French *gripper* to seize]

grisly (*say* **griz**-lee) *adjective*
causing fear or horror.

grist *noun*
any grain to be ground or already ground.
grist to one's mill, something which may be useful or advantageous.

gristle (*say* **griss**'l) *noun*
any cartilage present in meat.

Word Family: **gristly**, *adjective*, of or containing gristle.

grit *noun*
1. any small, hard particles of stone, etc.
2. strength or courage.
grit *verb*
(**gritted, gritting**)
to clench or grind: 'to *grit* one's teeth'.
Word Family: **gritty**, *adjective*; **grittiness**, *noun*.

grizzle *verb*
to whine or complain.
Word Family: **grizzle**, *noun*; **grizzler**, *noun*, a person who grizzles.

grizzled (*say* **grizz**'ld) *adjective*
(of hair, etc.) grey.
[French *gris* grey]

grizzly *adjective*
grey or greyish.
grizzly *noun*
a grizzly bear.

grizzly bear
see BEAR (2).

groan *verb*
to make a long, low, deep sound: 'we *groaned* in despair at the thought of more work'.
Word Family: **groan**, *noun*.

grocer (*say* **gro**–ser) *noun*
a person selling general foods or such household goods as detergents.
grocery *noun*
1. a grocer's shop.
2. (*plural*) any articles bought from a grocer, such as tea, sugar, cereals, etc.

groggy *adjective*
dazed and unsteady: 'she got out of bed still *groggy* with sleep'.
Word Family: **groggily**, *adverb*; **grogginess**, *noun*.

groin *noun*
Anatomy: the area at the base of the trunk where the thighs join the body and where the genitals are situated.

grommet *noun*
also spelt **grummet**
a rubber or metal ring or eyelet.

groom *noun*
1. a man who is about to be or is newly married. Short form of **bridegroom**.
2. a person who cares for horses.
groom *verb*
1. to brush and clean a horse.
2. to make neat and tidy: 'her hair is always beautifully *groomed*'.
Usage: 'he was *groomed* from childhood to be a politician' (= carefully prepared).

groove *noun*
1. a long narrow channel, such as the track cut in a gramophone record from which the stylus receives the signal to be amplified.
2. (*informal*) something which is very enjoyable: 'it's a *groove*!'.
into, in a groove, 'they have got *into a groove* and rarely see their old friends' (= into a fixed way of life).
groove *verb*
1. to cut or fix in a groove.
2. (*informal*) a) to give or get enjoyment. b) to fit in well with others.
Word Family: **groovy**, *adjective*, (informal) a) very enjoyable or exciting, b) (of a jazz musician) at his best.

grope *verb*
to feel or search uncertainly: a) 'I *groped* for the light switch in the dark'; b) 'I was *groping* for his name all through our conversation'.
Word Family: **gropingly**, *adverb*.

grosgrain (*say* **gro**–grain) *noun*
a heavy, corded fabric made from silk or rayon, used for ribbons.
[French *gros* coarse + *grain* texture]

gross (*say* groce) *adjective*
1. being the total amount without deductions: 'what is your *gross* salary?'. Compare NET (2).
2. large, thick or heavy.
3. coarse or vulgar.
Usage: 'such a *gross* injustice must be remedied' (= extreme, outrageous).
gross *noun*
1. any group of twelve dozen or 144. Plural is **gross**.
2. the total weight, quantity, amount, etc., e.g. of a vehicle and its load or contents. Plural is **grosses**. Compare TARE (1).
gross *verb*
to earn a total of.
Word Family: **grossly**, *adverb*; **grossness**, *noun*.

grotesque (*say* gro–**tesk**) *adjective*
odd or unnatural in shape, appearance, etc.: a) 'the *grotesque* statue frightened the children'; b) 'a *grotesque* sense of humour'.
Word Family: **grotesquely**, *adverb*; **grotesqueness, grotesquerie**, *nouns*.
[Italian *grottesca* like an excavation, because art works dug up by archaeologists were considered bizarre]

grotto *noun*
a cave or cave-like area.
[from Italian]

grotty *adjective*
(*informal*) dirty or unpleasant.
[short form of *grotesque*]

grouch (*rhymes with* crouch) *verb*
to complain or grumble.
Word Family: **grouch**, *noun*, a) a complaint, b) a person who complains or grumbles; **grouchy**, *adjective*; **grouchily**, *adverb*; **grouchiness**, *noun*.

ground (1) *noun*
1. the solid surface of the earth: 'he fell to the *ground* unconscious'.
2. soil or earth: 'the crops could not survive on the stony *ground*'.
3. an area used for a particular purpose: a) 'a cricket *ground*'; b) 'the hospital *grounds*'.
Usage: 'the questions covered a great deal of *ground*' (= material, subject).
4. the position held by a person or group: 'the demonstrators stood their *ground* and refused to move on'.
5. (*often plural*) a basis or reason: 'the court must be told the *grounds* for the divorce'.
ground *verb*
1. to place or fix on the ground.
Usage: 'the pilot was *grounded* for one year' (= forbidden to fly).
2. to base or establish: 'on what facts do you *ground* your argument?'.
3. *Electricity:* see EARTH.
4. to give basic training or instruction: 'all our pupils are well *grounded* in science subjects'.
Word Family: **ground**, *adjective*, being on, near or level with the ground.

ground (2) *adjective*
consisting of fine, dust-like particles as the result of grinding: '*ground* pepper'.
ground *noun*
(*plural*) sediment consisting of something which has been ground: 'coffee *grounds*'.
ground *verb*
the past tense and past participle of the verb **grind**.

ground-bait *noun*
the bait thrown to the bottom of a river, etc. to attract fish to the area being fished.

ground crew
the mechanics and other non-flying people working at an airfield.

ground floor
in America called the **first floor**
the floor at ground level in a building.

grounding *noun*
any basic training or knowledge.

groundless *adjective*
having no basis or reason.
Word Family: **groundlessly**, *adverb*; **groundlessness**, *noun*.

groundnut *noun*
see PEANUT.

ground rent
the rent paid to a landowner for the lease of the land on which a building is sited.

groundsheet *noun*
a waterproof sheet spread on the ground for protection from moisture, etc.

groundsman *noun*
a person in charge of the care and maintenance of a sports field, etc.

ground speed
the speed of an aircraft relative to the ground directly underneath it. Compare AIR SPEED.

ground swell
the smooth, massive waves resulting from a distant or past severe storm.

ground water
any water within about 100 m of the earth's surface, especially rainwater which has seeped down.

groundwork *noun*
the basis or foundation of anything.

group (*say* groop) *noun*
1. a number of persons or things considered together, usually having related or similar characteristics.
2. *Medicine:* a blood group.
3. *Chemistry:* a vertical column in the periodic table containing elements with similar properties.
4. *Military:* a tactical unit of an airforce, consisting of several squadrons, a headquarters, etc.
group *verb*
to form into a group or groups.

group captain
a commissioned officer in the airforce ranking between an air commodore and a wing-commander.

group theory
a branch of maths used especially in atomic physics to produce the equivalent of a periodic table for elementary particles.

group therapy
the formation of groups of people with similar problems, e.g. alcoholism, to exchange ideas on their difficulties and successes.

grouse (1) (*rhymes with* house) *noun*
plural is **grouse**
any of various plump birds with a short, curved bill, short legs and feathered feet, shot for game.

grouse (2) (*rhymes with* house) *verb*
(*informal*) to grumble or complain.
Word Family: **grouse,** *noun,* a) a complaint, b) a person who grumbles or complains.

grout (*rhymes with* out) *verb*
Building: to fill or cover joints between tiles, bricks or stones with a thin mortar, often waterproof.
Word Family: **grout,** *noun.*

grove *noun*
a small group of trees.

grovel (*say* **grovv**'l) *verb*
(grovelled, grovelling)
1. to act in an excessively humble or undignified way.
2. to throw oneself or lie on the ground, especially in fear, humility, etc.

grow (*say* gro) *verb*
(grew, grown, growing)
to become larger in size, amount, etc.: a) 'we *grow* quite rapidly during adolescence'; b) 'our fears *grew* as night fell'.
Usages:
a) 'it's hard to believe this mighty oak *grew* from a tiny seed' (= came, arose).
b) 'everyone is urging me to *grow* a beard' (= cause or allow to grow).
c) 'it *grew* darker as the sun went down' (= became).
Phrases:
grow on, 'the colour of the walls *grows on* you after a while' (= becomes more attractive).
grow out of, a) 'you have *grown out of* that jumper' (= become too big for); b) 'their friendship *grew out of* their mutual loneliness' (= resulted from).
grow up, 'what will you do when you *grow up*?' (= become adult).
grower *noun*
1. a person who grows things: 'a fruit *grower*'.
2. anything which grows in a particular way: 'that rose is a vigorous *grower*'.

growl (*rhymes with* trowel) *verb*
(of a dog, etc.) to make a deep, threatening, rumbling sound.
Usage: 'mother *growled* at us for being late' (= spoke angrily).
Word Family: **growl,** *noun;* **growlingly,** *adverb.*

growth *noun*
1. the act or process of growing: 'we did a survey on population *growth*'.
2. something which has grown: 'a *growth* of weeds'.
3. *Medicine:* a tumour.

groyne *noun*
a stone or timber breakwater built out from the seashore to check erosion and sand-drift.

grub *noun*
1. a worm-like larva of certain insects.
2. (*informal*) food.
grub *verb*
(grubbed grubbing)
to dig up by the roots or clear of roots.

grubby *adjective*
dirty or unkempt.
Word Family: **grubbily,** *adverb;* **grubbiness,** *noun.*

grudge *noun*
a deep feeling of resentment, envy, etc.
Word Family: **grudge,** *verb,* a) to feel a grudge because of another's wealth, good fortune, etc., b) to give or allow unwillingly; **grudgingly,** *adverb.*

gruel (*say* grew'l) *noun*
a thin cereal made by boiling oatmeal in water or milk.
gruelling *adjective*
exhausting or severe.
Word Family: **gruel (gruelled, gruelling),** *verb,* to exhaust or punish severely.

gruesome (*say* **groo**sum) *adjective*
causing horror or disgust.

gruff *adjective*
rough or harsh: 'he complained in a *gruff* voice'.
Word Family: **gruffly,** *adverb;* **gruffness,** *noun.*

grumble *verb*
to complain discontentedly.
Word Family: **grumble,** *noun;* **grumbler,** *noun,* a person who grumbles; **grumblingly,** *adverb.*

grummet *noun*
see GROMMET.

grumpy *adjective*
bad-tempered or surly.

Word Family: **grumpily**, *adverb*; **grumpiness**, *noun*.

grunt *verb*
to make a low, harsh sound characteristic of pigs.
Word Family: **grunt**, *noun*.

gryphon (*say* **griff**in) *noun*
see GRIFFIN.

G–string *noun*
a strip of cloth between the legs secured by a string round the waist.

G–suit *noun*
an inflatable suit worn by fighter pilots to prevent blackouts when manoeuvring at high speed.

guanaco (*say* gwah–**nahk**o) *noun*
either of two wild species of camel–like mammals of South America. The **llama** and **alpaca** are domesticated forms.

guanine (*say* **gwa**–neen) *noun*
Biology: see PURINE.

guano (*say* **gwah**–no) *noun*
the droppings of seabirds, or a synthetic product of similar composition, used as manure and in the production of chemical fertilizers.

guarantee (*say* garren–**tee**) *noun*
1. a formal or official promise that something is made or will be done to specified standards.
2. an assurance: 'money is no *guarantee* of happiness'.
3. *Law:* a) a written promise to be responsible for someone else's debts if the person does not pay them himself. b) a person who makes such a promise.
Word Family: **guarantee**, *verb*.

guarantor (*say* garren–**tor**) *noun*
a person who makes or gives a guarantee.

guaranty (*say* **garren**–tee) *noun*
Law: a guarantee.

guard (*say* gard) *verb*
to keep safe or in control.
Usages:
a) '*guard* against a cold' (= take precautions).
b) 'she *guarded* her words' (= was careful about).
guard *noun*
1. a person who guards: a) 'the *guard* on a train'; b) 'a *guard* of honour'.
2. the act of guarding: 'the prisoner was kept under close *guard*'.
3. a) a piece of equipment designed to give some form of physical protection, e.g. shinguards, fireguards and mudguards. b) anything which offers protection: 'the insurance policy provides a *guard* against loss'.
Word Family: **guardedly**, *adverb*.

guard cell
Biology: a crescent–shaped plant cell, two of which surround each stoma and regulate its opening and closing.

guardian (*say* **gar**dian) *noun*
1. a person who guards or protects: 'he is known as a *guardian* of civil rights'.
2. *Law:* a person who has the right and duty to protect another person.
Word Family: **guardianship**, *noun*.

guardroom *noun*
a building housing military police on duty and their prisoners.

guava (*say* **gwah**–va) *noun*
a subtropical American tree, the fruit of which is used to make jam, jelly, etc.

gudgeon (1) (*say* **gud**–j'n) *noun*
any of a group of small, oblong fish much used for bait.
[Greek *kobios*]

gudgeon (2) (*say* **gud**–j'n) *noun*
the part of a hinge or pivot which turns on a pin.

guernsey (*say* **gern**–zee) *noun*
a heavy woollen jumper such as is worn by sailors, etc.
[originally from *Guernsey*, Channel Islands]

guerrilla (*say* ger–**illa**) **guerilla** *noun*
a member of an independent military force, often revolutionary, which makes surprise attacks on enemy positions, supplies, etc.
[Spanish, little war]

guess (*say* gess) *verb*
1. to give an answer or opinion based on uncertain knowledge.
2. to offer a chance estimate or solution: 'he *guessed* my age to be about 20'.
Word Family: **guess**, **guesswork**, *nouns*, something based on guessing.

guest (*say* gest) *noun*
1. a person who receives hospitality, entertainment, etc. from another.
2. a person who pays for board, lodging, etc.: 'a hotel *guest*'.

guesthouse (*say* **gest**–house) *noun*
a house which gives temporary accommodation to paying guests, e.g. during holidays, etc.

guff *noun*
(*informal*) nonsense.

guffaw *noun*
a noisy, coarse laugh.
Word Family: **guffaw**, *verb.*

guide (*rhymes with* wide) *verb*
1. to show the way to: 'he *guided* the old lady safely across the street'.
2. to direct a person's actions: 'ambition *guided* his every action'.
Usage: 'she *guided* me on the books I should read' (= advised).
guide *noun*
1. a person who guides, especially one employed to guide tourists, etc.
2. a book with useful advice or information.
3. (*capital*) a member of the Guide Association, a youth organization which emphasizes self-reliance and proficiency in a wide range of activities.
Word Family: **guidance**, *noun*, a) the act of guiding, b) advice or instruction; **guideline**, *noun*, any suggestion, rule, etc. which guides.

guided missile
a missile whose direction is controlled throughout its flight. Compare BALLISTIC MISSILE.

guide-dog *noun*
a dog of a suitable bred, such as a Labrador, specially trained to lead a blind person.

guild (*say* gild) *noun*
a group of people, such as weavers, belonging to the same trade and joined together for mutual protection.

guile (*say* gile) *noun*
deceit or cunning.
Word Family: **guileful**, *adjective*; **guileless**, *adjective*, sincere and honest.

guillemot (*say* **gilli**-mot) *noun*
see AUK.
[French]

guillotine (*say* **gillo**-teen) *noun*
1. a machine consisting of a heavy blade which falls between two grooved posts, used to behead a person.
2. a device with a long blade for trimming paper.
3. a timetable imposed to stop filibustering and to hasten a Bill through Parliament.
Word Family: **guillotine**, *verb.*
[after *J. I. Guillotin*, 1738-1814, a French doctor who recommended its use]

guilt (*say* gilt) *noun*
1. the condition of being responsible for a wrongdoing.
2. a feeling of responsibility or shame for a wrongdoing, etc.

guilty (*say* **gil**-tee) *adjective*
1. having done wrong: 'we all knew he was *guilty*, despite his objections'.
2. feeling or showing guilt: 'she had a *guilty* conscience after she lied to her mother'.
Word Family: **guiltily**, *adverb.*

guinea (*say* **ginnee**) *noun*
a sum of money equal to one pound and one shilling, no longer used.

guineafowl (*say* **ginnee**-fowl) *noun*
a dark grey bird with white spots valued for its flesh and eggs. The female is called a **guinea hen**.
[first bred on the *Guinea coast*, Africa]

guineapig (*say* **ginnee**-pig) *noun*
1. a short-eared, short-tailed rodent, kept as a pet and used in laboratory experiments, originally bred by the Indians of the Andes for its flesh.
2. (*informal*) a person used as the subject of an experiment.

guise (*say* gize) *noun*
1. an external appearance, especially an assumed appearance.
2. a manner or style of dress: 'the policeman was in the *guise* of a railway porter'.

guitar (*say* gi-**tar**) *noun*
Music: any of a family of fretted instruments, usually with six strings, which are plucked with the fingers or a plectrum.
Word Family: **guitarist**, *noun.*

gulch *noun*
American: a narrow, deep ravine.

gulf *noun*
1. a large bay which extends far into the land area.
2. a wide gap or distance: a) 'the earthquake left a great *gulf* in the road'; b) 'the *gulf* between them widened over the years'.

gull (1) *noun*
short form of **seagull**
any of a family of long-winged seabirds with webbed feet, often white with grey wings.

gull (2) *verb*
to cheat or deceive.
gull *noun*
a person who is easily cheated or deceived.

gullet *noun*
Anatomy: the oesophagus.

gullible *adjective*
easily cheated or deceived.

Word Family: **gullibly**, *adverb*; **gullibility** (*say* gulli-**billi**-tee), *noun*.

gully *noun*
1. *Geography:* a long, narrow channel cut by water or due to soil erosion.
2. *Cricket:* a) a fielding position between slips and point. b) a player in this position.

gulp *verb*
1. to swallow in large amounts.
2. to gasp or choke.
Word Family: **gulp**, *noun*.

gum (1) *noun*
1. any of a group of water-soluble, complex substances derived from plants and used as glues, in medicine, in food and in industrial substances.
2. a) chewing gum. b) a hard gelatinous sweet.
Word Family: **gummy**, **gummous**, *adjectives*; **gum** (**gummed**, **gumming**), *verb*, to fill, cover or stick together with or as if with gum.

gum (2) *noun*
Anatomy: the firm flesh in which the teeth are set.

gumboot *noun*
also called a **wellington**
a waterproof rubber boot, reaching to the knee.

gumption (*say* **gump**-sh'n) *noun*
(*informal*) initiative and common sense.

gum tree
a eucalyptus.

gun *noun*
any weapon or device having a tube or barrel through which a projectile is discharged.
stick to one's guns, to insist on one's ideas, rights, etc.
gun *verb*
(**gunned**, **gunning**)
to hunt or shoot with a gun.

gunboat *noun*
a boat with light guns, used for patrols, etc.

guncarriage (*say* **gun**-carrij) *noun*
the wheeled structure on which an artillery gun is mounted.

guncotton *noun*
an explosive formed by the action of sulphuric and nitric acids on cellulose.

gun-dog *noun*
a dog, such as a spaniel, pointer or setter, trained to find, flush or fetch game birds.

gunfire *noun*
the firing of a gun or guns.

gunmetal *noun*
a dark grey alloy of copper, tin and zinc, used for belt buckles, etc.

gunnel *noun*
see GUNWALE.

gunner *noun*
1. a private in an artillery unit.
2. (*informal*) any member of an artillery unit.
3. the officer in charge of a ship's guns.

gunny *noun*
1. a coarse fabric, often made from jute, used for sacks, etc.
2. a bag made from this fabric.

gunpowder *noun*
a mixture of potassium nitrate, powdered charcoal and sulphur, used as an explosive.

gun-running *noun*
the smuggling of guns between countries.
Word Family: **gun-runner**, *noun*.

gunshot *noun*
a) the range of a gun. b) the firing or discharge of a gun. c) the bullet fired from a gun.

gunsmith *noun*
a person who makes or repairs firearms.

gunwale (*say* **gunn**'l) *noun*
also spelt **gunnel**
Nautical: the upper edge around the hull of a small boat, or, formerly, a warship.

guppy *noun*
a small West Indian fish, often kept in home aquariums.

gurgle *verb*
to make a bubbling sound, such as is made by flowing water.
Word Family: **gurgle**, *noun*.

gurnard *noun*
any of a group of small, sluggish, usually red fish which have spikes, a bony case around the head and often large, coloured wing-like fins.

guru (*say* **goo**-roo) *noun*
Hinduism: a spiritual teacher.
[Hindi]

gush *verb*
1. to flow suddenly and with force.
2. to display emotion or enthusiasm extravagantly.
Word Family: **gush**, *noun*; **gushy**, **gushing**, *adjectives*, **gusher**, *noun*.

gusset *noun*
a flat insert, usually triangular, to

connect and reinforce the parts of something, such as clothes, steel frameworks, etc.

gust *noun*
a sudden rush or burst.
Word Family: **gust**, *verb*; **gusty**, *adjective*; **gustily**, *adverb*.

gusto *noun*
a vigorous enjoyment.
[Italian, taste, relish]

gut *noun*
1. *Anatomy:* see INTESTINE.
2. (*plural*) the entrails.
3. (*informal*, *plural*) courage or endurance: 'it takes *guts* to sail around the world alone'.
4. a preparation of the intestines of some animals used for violin strings, tennis rackets, etc.
gut *verb*
(**gutted**, **gutting**)
1. to take out the entrails of.
2. to destroy the interior of: 'the house was *gutted* by fire'.

gutta-percha *noun*
a resinous, rubbery but inelastic, substance obtained from certain Malayan trees, used in electrical insulation, golf balls, etc.

gutter *noun*
1. a channel for carrying off fluids.
2. any low-class, wretched or degrading surroundings: 'she rose from the *gutter* to stardom'.

guttersnipe *noun*
a street urchin or neglected slum child.

guttural (*say* **gutta**-r'l) *adjective*
throaty or harsh, as a sound produced at the back of the throat.

guy (1) (*rhymes with* high) *noun*
1. (*informal*) a man.
2. an effigy of Guy Fawkes, burnt on November 5.
Word Family: **guy**, *verb*, (informal) to ridicule.

guy (2) (*rhymes with* high) *noun*
a rope or device used to steady, guide or fix something firmly in place.
Word Family: **guy**, *verb*.

guzzle *verb*
to eat or drink greedily.

gybe (*say* jib) *verb*
also spelt **jibe**
Sailing: to turn a boat, when sailing before the wind, so that the boom swings across from one side to the other.

gym (*say* jim) *noun*
short form of **gymnasium** and **gymnastics**.

gymkhana (*say* jim-**kahna**) *noun*
a horseriding competition consisting of various events.
[from Hindi]

gymnasium (*say* jim-**nay**zium) *noun*
plural is **gymnasiums** or **gymnasia**
a room fitted with equipment for physical training and gymnastics.
[Greek *gymnazein* to exercise]

gymnastics (*say* jim-**nas**tiks) *plural noun*
a) any exercises which develop agility, suppleness and strength. b) (*used with singular verb*) the principles of such exercises.
Word Family: **gymnastic**, *adjective*; **gymnast** (*say* **jim**-nast), *noun*, a person trained or skilled in gymnastics.

gymnosperm (*say* **jim**no-sperm) *noun*
any of a large group of plants, mainly the conifers, whose seeds are not enclosed in an ovary. Compare ANGIOSPERM.

gynaecology (*say* gie-na-**kolla**-jee) *noun*
the study of the female reproductive system and its diseases. Compare OBSTETRICS.
Word Family: **gynaecological** (*say* gie-na-ka-**lo**ji-k'l), *adjective*; **gynaecologist**, *noun*.
[Greek *gynaikos* of a woman + -LOGY]

gynoecium (*say* gie-**nee**sium) *noun*
plural is **gynoecia**
also called a **pistil**
Biology: all the carpels in a flower.

gyp (*say* jip) *verb*
(**gypped**, **gypping**)
to swindle or cheat.

gypsum (*say* **jip**sum) *noun*
a soft mineral (hydrous calcium sulphate), used for plaster of Paris and as a fertilizer.

gypsy *noun*
see GIPSY.

gyrate (*say* jie-**rate**) *verb*
to revolve or move in a circle.
Word Family: **gyration**, *noun*, a turning or circular movement.

gyroscope (*say* **jie**-ra-skope) *noun*
a device consisting of a rotating wheel which resists any movement when spinning, used as the basis of stabilizers in ships, compasses, etc.
[Greek *gyros* ring + *skopein* to look at]

Hh

ha *interjection*
an exclamation of triumph, suspicion, surprise, etc.

habeas corpus (*say* **hay**-bee-ass **kor**pus)
Law: an order that an imprisoned person must be brought before a court for trial, as a protection against illegal imprisonment.
[Latin, you shall produce the body]

haberdasher (*say* **habba**-dasha) *noun*
1. a person who sells items such as ribbons, thread, needles, etc.
2. *American:* a person who sells men's hats, shirts, socks, etc.
Word Family: **haberdashery,** *noun,* a) the goods sold by a haberdasher, b) the shop in which such goods are sold.

habit *noun*
1. a regular practice or usage.
2. a) the dress worn by members of a religious order: 'a monk's *habit*'. b) a woman's riding outfit.
habit *verb*
an old word meaning to clothe.
Word Family: **habitual** (*say* ha-**bit**-yew'l), *adjective,* a) due to or established by habit, b) regularly used; **habitually,** *adverb*; **habitualness,** *noun.*

habitable (*say* **habbita**-b'l) *adjective*
fit to be lived in: 'a house in *habitable* condition'.
Word Family: **habitability** (*say* habbita-**billi**-tee), **habitableness,** *nouns.*

habitat (*say* **habbi**-tat) *noun*
1. the particular environment where a plant or animal is usually found, e.g. in the sea, in alpine areas, etc.
2. any place of abode.

habitation (*say* habbi-**tay**-sh'n) *noun*
1. a place of abode.
2. the act of inhabiting: 'slums unfit for human *habitation*'.

habitual *adjective*
Word Family: see HABIT.

habituate (*say* ha**bit**-yoo-ate) *verb*
1. to accustom to: 'nurses are *habituated* to the sight of blood'.
2. to visit often: 'he *habituates* disreputable nightclubs'.

habitude *noun*
any customary behaviour or manner.

habitué (*say* ha**bit**-yoo-ay) *noun*
a person who regularly goes to a place.
[French *habituer*]

hacienda (*say* hassi-**enda**) *noun*
Spanish-American: a large estate.
[Spanish]

hack (1) *verb*
1. to cut roughly or clumsily: 'he *hacked* away at the tree trunk'.
2. to cough spasmodically with a dry throat.
hack *noun*
1. any cut or gash: 'the axe cut a great *hack* out of his leg'.
2. a short, dry cough.

hack (2) *noun*
1. a) a horse used for general riding. b) any old, worn-out horse.
2. a person employed to do dull and arduous literary work.
Word Family: **hack,** *verb,* to ride a horse for pleasure.
[short form of *hackney*]

hackle *noun*
1. one of the long feathers on the neck of some birds.
2. (*usually plural*) the hairs on the back of a dog's neck.
3. *Fishing:* an artificial fly or part of a fly, made from the hackles of a bird.
have, get one's hackles up, to be or become very angry.

hackney *noun*
1. one of a breed of horses for ordinary riding or for pulling carriages.
2. a horse-drawn cab kept for hire.

hackneyed (*say* **hak**-nid) *adjective*
stale or trite, as a result of too frequent use: 'a *hackneyed* phrase'.
Word Family: **hackney,** *verb.*

hacksaw *noun*
a saw with a narrow blade set in a frame, used for cutting metal, etc.

hackwork *noun*
any dull or uninspiring work.

had *verb*
the past tense and past participle of the verb **have.**

haddock (*say* **hadd**'k) *noun*
any of a group of edible fish related to the cod and found in the North Atlantic, often eaten smoked.

Hades (*say* **hay**-deez) *noun*
the Underworld.
[after *Hades,* the god of the underworld in Greek mythology]

haematite (*say* **heema**-tite) *noun*
in America spelt **hematite**
Geology: a common mineral (formula Fe_2O_3), the principal source of iron.
[Greek *haimatites* blood-like]

haematology (*say* **heema**-tolla-jee) *noun*
in America spelt **hematology**
Medicine: the study of the nature, function and diseases of the blood.
Word Family: **haematologist** (*say* heema-**tolla**-jist), *noun.*
[Greek *haimatos* of blood + -LOGY]

haematosis (*say* heema-**toe**-sis) *noun*
in America spelt **hematosis**
Biology: the oxygenation of the blood in the lungs.

haemoglobin (*say* heema-**glo**-bin) *noun*
in America spelt **hemoglobin**
Biology: a red pigment found in the red blood cells of vertebrates, which transports oxygen around the body.

haemophilia (*say* heema-**fillia**) *noun*
in America spelt **hemophilia**
a hereditary disease in which blood clots poorly, causing small injuries to bleed excessively.
Word Family: **haemophiliac** (*say* heema-**filli**-ak), *noun,* a person with haemophilia.
[Greek *haima* blood + *philein* to love]

haemorrhage (*say* **hemma**-rij) *noun*
in America spelt **hemorrhage**
a loss of blood, especially internally.
[from Greek]

haemorrhoid (*say* **hemma**-roid) *noun*
in America spelt **hemorrhoid**
also called **piles**
(*plural*) a painful, expanded mass of veins in the anus.

hafnium *noun*
element number 72, a metal used in making tungsten filaments and useful in research because it readily emits electrons. See TRANSITION ELEMENT. See CHEMICAL ELEMENTS in grey pages.

haft (*rhymes with* raft) *noun*
the handle of a knife, dagger, or sword.

hag *noun*
a) an ugly old woman. b) a witch.

haggard (*say* **hagg**'rd) *adjective*
looking worn or exhausted.
Word Family: **haggardly,** *adverb*; **haggardness,** *noun.*

haggis *noun*
Scottish: a food like a large sausage, made of the offal of a sheep, minced with oatmeal, suet, flavourings, etc. and boiled in the sheep's stomach.

haggle *verb*
to argue or dispute in a petty way, especially over a price.
Word Family: **haggler,** *noun.*

hagiography (*say* hag-ee-**ogra**-fee) *noun*
the biography of saints.
[Greek *hagios* holy + *graphein* to write]

hag-ridden *adjective*
tormented or distressed.

haha *noun*
a fence sunk out of view from a house.
[French]

haiku (*say* **high**-koo) *noun*
a Japanese verse form in three lines of five, seven and five syllables respectively.

hail (1) *verb*
1. to greet or welcome: 'she *hailed* her friends'.
2. to acclaim enthusiastically: 'the critics *hailed* the author's latest play'.
Usage: 'shall we *hail* a taxi?' (= obtain by calling out to).
3. to come or belong to: 'which part of Australia does she *hail* from?'.
hail *noun*
a shout to attract attention: 'I heard a *hail* from across the street'.
hail *interjection*
an exclamation of greeting or welcome.
hail-fellow-well-met *adjective*
very familiar or effusively friendly: 'I can't abide his *hail-fellow-well-met* heartiness'.

hail (2) *noun*
a) frozen raindrops which fall from the sky in a shower. b) a shower of such pellets.
Usage: 'the gangster died in a *hail* of bullets' (= shower).
hail *verb*
to fall as hail.
Usage: 'they *hailed* blows upon her back' (= delivered plentifully).

Word Family: **hailstone,** *noun,* a pellet of hail; **hailstorm,** *noun.*

hair *noun*
1. *Anatomy:* a) any of the fine thread-like structures which grow from the skin of most animals. b) a growth of such threads, forming the natural covering of the human head, etc.
2. any fabric made from the fur of an animal: 'a *camelhair* coat'.
Phrases:
let one's hair down, (*informal*) to behave in a relaxed or uninhibited way.
split hairs, to make unimportant or petty distinctions.
without turning a hair, (*informal*) remaining calm or untroubled.

haircut *noun*
a) the act of cutting hair. b) the style in which hair is cut.

hairdo *noun*
(*informal*) a hairstyle.

hairdressing *noun*
the art of cutting, styling, colouring and caring for the hair.
Word Family: **hairdresser,** *noun,* a person who is trained or skilled in hairdressing.

hairiness *noun*
Word Family: see HAIRY.

hairline *noun*
1. the junction between the edge of the hair and the skin, especially at the forehead.
2. a very thin line.

hairpiece *noun*
a mass of real or artificial hair attached to a base, worn on the head to cover a bald patch or to add to a hairstyle.

hairpin *noun*
also called a **bobby pin**
a loop of thin metal squeezed together, used to hold the hair in place.

hairpin bend
a U-shaped bend in a road.

hair-raising *adjective*
terrifying.

hair's-breadth *noun*
a very small space or distance: 'he won by a *hair's-breadth*'.

hair shirt
a shirt of haircloth worn as a penance.

hairsplitting *noun*
the act of making petty or unnecessary distinctions.

hairspring *noun*
a fine coiled spring in a watch or clock, which helps to regulate the beats.

hairstyle *noun*
the way in which the hair is arranged.
Word Family: **hairstylist,** *noun.*

hair-trigger *noun*
a trigger which is operated by a very slight pressure.

hairy *adjective*
1. covered with or resembling hair.
2. (*informal*) dangerous or hair-raising: 'what a *hairy* adventure!'.
Word Family: **hairiness,** *noun.*

hajji (*say* **haj-ee**) **hadji** *noun*
a Moslem who has made a pilgrimage (*haj*) to Mecca.

hake *noun*
any of a group of marine fish related to the cod.

halberd *noun*
a medieval spear with an axe-like blade.
Word Family: **halberdier** (*say* halba-**deer**), *noun,* a soldier armed with a halberd.

halcyon (*say* **hal**-see-an) *adjective*
calm or peaceful.
[Greek *halkyon* kingfisher, in mythology a bird believed to have the power to calm the winter seas while hatching its eggs in a floating nest]

hale *adjective*
in good health.

half (*say* hahf) *noun*
plural is **halves**
either of two equal parts into which something is divided.
Phrases:
by half, 'he's too clever *by half*' (= by a great deal too much).
by halves, 'he never does anything *by halves*' (= incompletely).
half *adjective*
1. being either of two equal parts of something: 'I only want a *half* bottle of wine'.
2. incomplete: 'a *half* truth'.
half *adverb*
to the extent of half or approximately half: 'the sink is *half* full of dishes'.

half-back *noun*
Football: a player in a position halfway between the centre players and the backs.

half-baked *adjective*
(*informal*) incomplete or immature: '*half-baked* ideas'.

half-breed *noun*
the offspring of parents of different races, breeds, etc.

half-brother *noun*
see BROTHER.

half-caste *noun*
a person having parents of different races.

half-cock *noun*
a safe position of the firing mechanism of a rifle or revolver, between fired and fully cocked.
go off at half-cock, (*informal*) to act prematurely and unsuccessfully.

half-hardy *adjective*
(of plants) able to withstand fairly low temperatures, but more tender than a hardy plant.

half-hearted *adjective*
having or displaying little enthusiasm or interest.
Word Family: **half-heartedly,** *adverb*; **half-heartedness,** *noun.*

half-hitch *noun*
a simple knot made by passing the end of a rope once around the rope, and then drawing the end through the loop that has been formed, and pulling it tight.

half-life *noun*
Physics: the constant time taken for the radioactivity of a particular substance to decay to half its original value.

half-mast *adverb*
(of a flag) flown halfway down the pole, as a signal of mourning, distress, etc.

half-nelson *noun*
see NELSON.

half-note *noun*
Music: see MINIM.

halfpenny (*say* **hape**-nee) *noun*
plural is **halfpennies**
any coin worth half a penny.
Word Family: **halfpenny,** *adjective,* a) of the price or value of half a penny, b) of little value.

half-sister *noun*
see SISTER.

half-timbered *adjective*
(of a house) having a visible frame of heavy timber filled in with brick and plaster.

half-time *noun*
the interval midway through a game.

halftone *noun*
1. any tone or shade intermediate between intense light and deep shade.
2. a picture, such as a photograph in a newspaper, made up of tiny dots produced by taking the photograph through a fine mesh screen.

half-volley *noun*
Sport: a low stroke in which the ball is hit just after it has bounced from the ground.

halfway *adjective*
1. being midway between two things, places, etc.
2. incomplete: '*halfway* measures aren't good enough in an emergency'.
halfway *adverb*
to or at half the distance.
meet someone halfway, to compromise.

halfwit *noun*
a feeble-minded or foolish person.
Word Family: **half-witted,** *adjective*; **half-wittedly,** *adverb*; **half-wittedness,** *noun.*

halibut *noun*
any of a group of large, edible flatfish resembling the turbot.

halide (*say* **hay**-lide) *noun*
Chemistry: a compound of two ions, one of which is a halogen.

halitosis (*say* halli-**toe**-sis) *noun*
unpleasant-smelling breath.
[Latin *halitus* breath + -OSIS]

hall (*say* hawl) *noun*
1. a) a passage or corridor in a building. b) the entrance room of a building.
2. a large building or room, especially one used for public meetings, entertainment, dining, etc.
3. a large country house, especially one belonging to the chief landowner in the district.

hallelujah (*say* halli-**loo**-ya) *noun*
also called **alleluia**
Jewish, Christian: a song or exclamation of praise to God.
[Hebrew *halleluyah* praise Jehovah]

hallmark (*say* hawl-mark) *noun*
a mark placed on an article to indicate quality, purity, etc.
Usage: 'he has all the *hallmarks* of a real military commander' (= distinguishing signs).

hallo *interjection*
hello.

halloo *interjection*
an exclamation or cry used to incite hounds to the chase, to attract attention, etc.

hallow *verb*
to make or honour as holy.

Halloween (*say* hallo–**een**) *noun*
an annual festival celebrated on October 31st, the eve of All Saints' Day.

hallucination (*say* ha–loosi–**nay**–sh'n) *noun*
the experience of seeing or hearing things that seem to be real, but do not actually exist.
Word Family: **hallucinate** (*say* ha–**loosi**–nate), *verb*, to experience hallucinations; **hallucinatory** (*say* ha–**loosina**–tree), *adjective.*

hallucinogenic
(*say* ha–loosina–**jennik**) *adjective*
producing hallucinations.
Word Family: **hallucinogenic, hallucinogen**, *noun*, a drug which produces hallucinations.

halo (*say* **hay**–lo) *noun*
plural is **haloes**
a brightness or circle of light around the head of a religious image or figure.
[Greek *halos* the sun's disc]

halogen (*say* **halla**–j'n) *noun*
Chemistry: any of the univalent, reactive non–metal elements (fluorine, chlorine, bromine, iodine and astatine), which form group VIII in the periodic table.
[Greek *halos* of salt + –GEN]

halt (*say* hawlt) *verb*
to make a temporary stop.
Word Family: **halt**, *noun.*

halter (*say* **hawlta**) *noun*
a device made of rope or straps, fitted around the head of a horse, cow, etc. for tying or leading it.
halter *verb*
to fit or restrain with a halter.

halter–neck *adjective*
(of a dress, etc.) having the top part fastened or tied behind the neck, leaving the back and shoulders bare.

halting (*say* **hawlting**) *adjective*
hesitating or wavering: 'the *halting* speech of a nervous person'.
Word Family: **haltingly**, *adverb.*

halve (*say* hahv) *verb*
1. to divide into halves: 'we *halved* the cake'.
2. to reduce by half: 'express trains have *halved* the time the journey takes'.

halves (*rhymes with* calves) *plural noun*
the plural of **half**.

halyard (*say* **hal**–y'd) *noun*
Nautical: a wire or rope used to hoist or lower a sail.

ham *noun*
1. the slow–cured hind leg of a bacon pig, bought ready cooked and usually eaten cold. Compare GAMMON.
2. (*often plural*) a) the back of the thighs. b) the thigh and buttocks.
3. (*informal*) a) an actor who exaggerates his role. b) any amateur.
Word Family: **ham** (**hammed, hamming**), *verb*, to exaggerate or overact.

hamadryad (*say* **hamma**–dry–ad) *noun*
also called a **king cobra**
a very poisonous, front–fanged snake of tropical Asia, growing up to 5 m long.
[Greek *hamadryas* a wood nymph]

hamburger *noun*
also called a **beefburger**
a) a patty of seasoned, minced meat.
b) a similar patty served in a round bread roll, often with salad, etc.

ham–fisted *adjective*
clumsy: 'he made a *ham–fisted* attempt at an apology'.

hamlet *noun*
a small village.

hammer *noun*
1. a tool with a handle and a heavy metal head for driving in nails, beating, etc. A **claw hammer** has one end of the head curved and split for pulling out nails.
2. any part or device with the shape or function of a hammer, such as the padded lever which strikes the strings in a piano or the part of a gun which strikes the percussion cap and causes it to explode.
3. *Athletics:* a metal ball attached to a flexible handle, which is thrown in contests.
come, go under the hammer, to be sold by auction.
hammer *verb*
to strike with or as if with a hammer.
Usage: 'he *hammered* away at the essay' (= worked persistently).

hammer and tongs
(*informal*) with great energy, noise or violence.

hammerhead shark
a type of shark with a head that resembles a double-headed hammer.

hammer lock
a wrestling hold in which the opponent's arm is twisted and pushed behind his back.

hammertoe *noun*
a deformed toe which points downwards permanently.

hammock *noun*
a sheet of canvas or netting suspended by cords at each end, serving as a sailor's bed, etc.

hamper (1) *verb*
to obstruct or impede.

hamper (2) *noun*
a large basket, usually having a lid.

hamster *noun*
a small, short-tailed mammal resembling a guineapig.

hamstring *noun*
1. either of the tendons at the rear of the knee in man.
2. the large sinew at the back of the hock in a quadruped.
hamstring *verb*
(hamstrung, hamstringing)
to cripple by cutting the hamstring.
Usage: 'he's doing all he can to *hamstring* our investigations' (= obstruct).

hand *noun*
1. *Anatomy:* the part of the arm beyond the wrist, used for holding, grasping, etc.
2. something with the shape, position or function of a hand: 'the *hands* of a clock'.
3. a worker or helper employed in a particular situation: 'a factory *hand*'.
Usages:
a) 'the matter is out of my *hands*' (= control, responsibility).
b) 'do you think he had a *hand* in the robbery?' (= share, part).
c) 'he's got a nice legible *hand*' (= style of handwriting).
d) 'you can see the *hand* of an expert in this job' (= skill).
e) 'give the actors a big *hand*' (= applause).
f) 'can you give a *hand*?' (= help).
4. *Cards:* a) all the cards held by a player. b) any part of a game in which these cards are played.
hands up!, put your hands up, e.g. in surrender.
5. a unit used to measure the height of horses, equal to 4 inches (about 10·2 cm).
Phrases:
at hand, 'the end of the world is *at hand*' (= near).
change hands, to pass from one owner to another.
force someone's hand, to compel someone to act before they are ready to.
get, have the upper hand, to win or hold an advantage over.
hands down, 'they won the game *hands down*' (= easily).
hands off!, do not touch or interfere.
keep one's hand in, to practise so as to remain skilful.
old hand, 'he's an *old hand* at decorating houses' (= expert, experienced person).
show one's hand, to reveal one's intentions.
throw one's hand in, to give up, especially in defeat.
to hand, 'we have your letter *to hand*' (= in our possession).
wash one's hands of, to disclaim all responsibility for.
hand *verb*
to give or pass with, or as if with, the hands: a) '*hand* me a biscuit, please'; b) 'the story was *handed* down through many generations'.
hand down, 'the court *handed down* its decision' (= gave, announced).

handbag *noun*
a bag for carrying small articles such as a handkerchief, money, keys, etc., mainly used by women.

handbill *noun*
a small printed paper or advertisement given out by hand.

handbook *noun*
a reference book on a subject.

handcuffs *plural noun*
a pair of metal rings joined by a chain to lock around a prisoner's wrists.
Word Family: **handcuff**, *verb.*

handful *noun*
1. as much as can be held in the hand.
Usage: 'only a *handful* of residents attended the meeting' (= small number).
2. (*informal*) a person or thing that is difficult to control.

handicap *noun*
1. any physical or mental disability which prevents or restricts normal achievement.

2. *Sport:* a disadvantage or advantage placed on competitors of different standards in a race or match, to try to equalize their chances of winning.
Word Family: **handicap, (handicapped, handicapping)**, *verb*, a) to be a handicap to, b) to impose a handicap on; **handicapper**, *noun.*

handicraft *noun*
a) the art of making things with the hands. b) any article made with the hands.

handily *adverb*
Word Family: see HANDY.

hand-in-glove *adjective, adverb*
in close collaboration.

handiwork *noun*
any work done with the hands.
Usage: 'this disaster was all your *handiwork*' (= doing, efforts).

handkerchief (*say* **hanka**-cheef) *noun*
plural is **handkerchiefs** or **handkerchieves**
a small, square piece of cloth for wiping the nose or face.

handle *noun*
1. the part of an object or device by which it is held.
2. (*informal*) a name or title.
fly off the handle, (*informal*) to become very angry suddenly.
handle *verb*
to feel or touch with the hands.
Usages:
a) 'she *handled* the difficult situation very well' (= controlled).
b) 'we only *handle* antiques in this shop' (= deal in).
Word Family: **handler**, *noun.*

handlebar *noun*
(*often plural*) a bar at the front of a bicycle, motorcycle, etc., used for steering.

handmaid, handmaiden *noun*
an old word for a female servant.

hand-me-down *noun*
something, especially clothing, which is handed down from one person to another.

hand-out *noun*
a) anything which is given away. b) a prepared statement given to the press for publication.

hand-pick *verb*
to choose carefully: 'to *hand-pick* one's workers'.

handrail *noun*
a light bar along the edge of stairs or steps, used as a support.

handset *noun*
the part of a telephone held in the hand, containing both the transmitter and receiver.
handset *verb*
Printing: to set type by hand.

handshake *noun*
the grasping of hands by two people as a sign of greeting, farewell, agreement, etc.
golden handshake, a large sum of money given to a company's senior executives on retirement or in compensation for dismissal.

handsome (*say* **hans**'m) *adjective*
attractive or pleasing in appearance.
Usages:
a) 'we expect a *handsome* return on our investment' (= considerable).
b) 'she gave them a most *handsome* wedding present' (= generous).
Word Family: **handsomely**, *adverb*; **handsomeness**, *noun.*

handspike *noun*
a metal bar used as a lever to lift heavy objects.

handspring *noun*
a somersault in which the body turns in the air while supported with one or both hands.

handstand *noun*
the balancing of the body upside-down in a vertical position, using the hands as a base.

hand-to-hand *adjective*
at very close quarters: '*hand-to-hand* combat'.

hand-to-mouth *adjective*
having little or no resources: 'the poor live a *hand-to-mouth* existence'.

handwriting *noun*
a) any writing done by hand. b) a particular or individual style of writing: 'she has neat *handwriting*'.

handy *adjective*
nearby or easily reached: 'keep your weapons *handy*'.
Usages:
a) 'he is a very *handy* workman' (= skilful).
b) 'this is a very *handy* screwdriver' (= useful).
Word Family: **handyman**, *noun*, a person who is skilled at doing odd jobs; **handily**, *adverb*; **handiness**, *noun.*

hang *verb*
(hung, hanging)
1. to suspend or support from above: 'to *hang* one's coat'.

Usages:
a) 'it took hours to *hang* the wallpaper' (= attach).
b) '*hang* on to my arm' (= grip, hold).
c) 'the smell *hung* in the air' (= floated).
d) 'the matter *hangs* on your answer' (= depends).
e) 'he *hung* out of the window and shouted' (= leaned).
f) 'we *hung* on her every word' (= concentrated).
2. (past tense and past participle **hanged**) to suspend a person by the neck until dead.
Phrases:
hang about, hang around, to pass time without aim or purpose.
hang back, 'do not *hang back* when asked for your opinion' (= hesitate).
hang on, a) 'the injured man was urged to *hang on* until help arrived' (= not give up, persevere); b) (*informal*) '*hang on*, I'll be there in a minute' (= wait).
hang one's head, to show that one is ashamed, especially by dejectedly drooping one's head.
hang out, (*informal*) 'she *hangs out* in Kensington' (= lives or regularly spends time).
hang up, a) to suspend from a hook, etc.; b) to end a telephone conversation by replacing the receiver.
hang *noun*
1. the way in which something hangs: 'he liked the *hang* of her skirt'.
2. (*informal*) the correct or particular way of doing, using, etc.: 'I can't get the *hang* of this machine'.

hangar (*say* **hang**-a) *noun*
a building in which aircraft are kept.

hangdog *adjective*
ashamed or furtive: 'a *hangdog* expression'.

hanger *noun*
any device on which things may be hung: 'a *coat-hanger*'.

hanger-on *noun*
plural is **hangers-on**
(*informal*) a person who attaches himself to another in a parasitic way.

hang-glider *noun*
a large kite-like apparatus with the aid of which the user is able to glide through the air from a hilltop, etc.
Word Family: **hang-gliding,** *noun.*

hanging *noun*
1. an execution performed by hanging a person by the neck.
2. a wall-hanging.

hangman *noun*
a person appointed to hang those condemned to death.

hangnail *noun*
torn skin at the base of a fingernail.

hangover *noun*
1. the unpleasant after-effects of drinking too much alcohol.
2. something remaining or left over from an earlier time.

hang-up *noun*
(*informal*) an obsession or emotional difficulty, especially one which inhibits.

hank *noun*
a skein, coil or loop: 'a *hank* of hair'.

hanker *verb*
to have a restless desire for something: 'I *hanker* after more travel'.
Word Family: **hankering,** *noun.*

hanky *noun*
(*informal*) a handkerchief.

hanky-panky *noun*
(*informal*) any mischievous or tricky activity.

Hansard *noun*
the official published reports of debates in parliament.
[after *L. Hansard* who printed and published them from 1774]

hansom (*say* **hans**'m) *noun*
a two-wheeled, covered carriage for two passengers, pulled by a horse and with an elevated seat at the rear for the driver.
[after *J. A. Hansom*, 1803-82, a British architect]

hap *verb*
(**happed, happing**)
an old word meaning to happen.

haphazard (*say* hap-**hazz**'rd) *adjective*
random or occurring merely by chance.
Word Family: **haphazardly,** *adverb*; **haphazardness,** *noun.*

hapless *adjective*
unfortunate or unlucky.
Word Family: **haplessly,** *adverb.*

haploid *adjective*
Biology: (of a cell) having a single set of chromosomes. Compare DIPLOID.

haply *adverb*
an old word meaning perhaps or by chance.

happen *verb*
to be or become an event: 'the robbery *happened* while we were on holidays'.
Usage: 'I *happened* to meet her in the street' (= chanced).

happening *noun*
1. an event.
2. (*informal*) an improvised entertainment, usually intended to startle any observers.

happy *adjective*
1. feeling or showing contentment or pleasure: 'she is *happy* in the new job'.
Usage: 'it was a *happy* decision to leave when we did' (= lucky).
2. (*informal*) having an excessive liking for: 'the new sheriff is *trigger–happy*'.
Word Family: **happily,** *adverb*; **happiness,** *noun.*

happy–go–lucky *adjective*
carefree or trusting to luck.

harakiri (*say* harra–**kirree**) *noun*
a traditional form of suicide in Japan by cutting open the abdomen, especially used by the upper class or officials who have been disgraced.
[Japanese, belly cut]

harangue (*say* ha–**rang**) *noun*
a passionate, vehement speech.
Word Family: **harangue (harangued, haranguing),** *verb.*

harass (*say* **harras** *or* ha–**rass**) *verb*
to pester or torment.
Word Family: **harassingly,** *adverb*; **harassment,** *noun.*
[Old French *harer* to set a dog on]

harbinger (*say* **harbinja**) *noun*
a person or thing that announces or comes before a future event.

harbour (*say* **harba**) *noun*
in America spelt **harbor**
a sheltered area of water deep enough for ships to anchor in.
Usage: 'a *harbour* from the storm' (= place of shelter).
harbour *verb*
a) to give shelter to: 'it is illegal to *harbour* an escaped criminal'. b) to take shelter in a harbour.
Usage: 'she is not a person to *harbour* a grudge' (= secretly hold).

hard (*rhymes with* card) *adjective*
1. firm, solid or not easily cut: 'the wood was as *hard* as iron'.
2. a) requiring considerable effort or endurance: '*hard* work'. b) not easy: 'a *hard* problem in physics'.
Usages:
a) 'he's had a *hard* time since he lost his job' (= unhappy, difficult).
b) 'she said she had no *hard* feelings about the argument' (= hostile).
c) 'the newspaper article presented the *hard* facts' (= bare, indisputable).
d) 'he drives a *hard* bargain' (= severe).
e) 'to pay in *hard* cash' (= actual).
f) 'no *hard* liquor is to be drunk at the party' (= strong).
g) 'a *hard* worker' (= energetic).
3. (of water) having mineral salts which prevent the lathering of soap.
4. (of the sounds *c* and *g*) pronounced sharply as in *cattle* and *game.*
Phrases:
hard and fast, 'a *hard and fast* rule' (= firm, fixed).
hard of hearing, partly deaf.
hard up, (*informal*) short of money.
hard *adverb*
solid: 'the concrete had set *hard*'.
Usages:
a) 'don't work too *hard*' (= energetically).
b) 'the policeman stared *hard* at the suspect' (= intently).
c) 'it will go *hard* with you if the job isn't done properly' (= severely, badly).
d) 'his pursuers followed *hard* on his heels' (= immediately, closely).
e) 'it rained *hard* all night' (= heavily).
f) 'the smugglers were given seven years *hard*' (= hard labour).
Phrases:
hard by, 'the Post Office is *hard by* the general store' (= close to).
hard put, 'she was *hard put* to explain the money under her bed' (= in difficulty).
hardness *noun*
1. the state or quality of being hard.
2. (of minerals) the degree to which they may scratch or be scratched by another mineral. See MOHS SCALE.

hardback *noun*
a book bound with a stiff cover. Compare PAPERBACK.

hard–baked *adjective*
callous or toughened by experience, etc.

hard–bitten *adjective*
tough or stubborn: 'that politician is a *hard–bitten* campaigner'.

hardboard *noun*
a building material made of wood fibres pressed into sheets.

hard coal
see ANTHRACITE.

hard core
a resistant central part of something: 'the *hard core* of the movement refused to compromise on any issue'.

Word Family: **hard-core,** *adjective,* deep-rooted or absolute.

hard court
a tennis court of asphalt, clay or any surface but grass.

hard drug
any drug, such as heroin, considered to cause addiction.

harden *verb*
to make or become hard.
hardening *noun*
a) the process of becoming hard. b) an alloy or other material which hardens another.

hard-fisted *adjective*
mean or stingy.

hard-headed *adjective*
shrewd or practical, especially in business matters.
Word Family: **hard-headedness,** *noun.*

hard-hearted *adjective*
unfeeling or unsympathetic.
Word Family: **hard-heartedly,** *adverb*; **hard-heartedness,** *noun.*

hardihood *noun*
Word Family: see HARDY.

hard labour
the heavy manual labour formerly imposed on prisoners sentenced for serious crimes.

hardly *adverb*
1. barely or not quite: a) 'there is *hardly* any water left'; b) 'it is *hardly* true to say that'.
2. severely or harshly: 'she claims that she has been *hardly* done by'.

hardness *noun*
see HARD.

hard pad
a fatal form of distemper among dogs which can be prevented by inoculation, the first symptom being hardening of the paws.

hardship *noun*
a) a state of suffering, trial or severe need. b) something which causes such suffering: 'he said it would be a great *hardship* to ride a bicycle to work'.

hard shoulder
an additional lane provided on the nearside of motorways for parking in the event of a breakdown or other emergency.

hardware *noun*
1. any articles such as cutlery, tools, building and gardening supplies, etc.
2. (*informal*) a weapon or weapons, especially a gun.
3. computer equipment. Compare SOFTWARE.

hardwood *noun*
the compact wood from flowering deciduous trees, such as oak or mahogany. Compare SOFTWOOD.

hardy *adjective*
1. strong, durable or capable of resisting exposure, hardship, etc.: 'a *hardy* breed of cattle developed in the harsh climate'.
2. courageous or willing to face danger.
Word Family: **hardily,** *adverb*; **hardihood,** *noun,* hardy character or boldness; **hardiness,** *noun,* strength, toughness or ability to endure.

hare *noun*
a mammal related to the rabbit but having longer ears and stronger hind legs.
Word Family: **hare** (**hared, haring**), *verb,* to run or move very fast.

hare and hounds
a paperchase.
run with the hare and hunt with the hounds, to give support to both sides in a quarrel.

harebell *noun*
the Scottish bluebell, a wildflower of the campanula family with blue or white bell-shaped flowers.

harebrained *adjective*
reckless or rash.

harelip *noun*
a deformed upper lip which has a vertical slit or slits in it.
Word Family: **hare-lipped,** *adjective.*

harem (*say* **hair**em *or* hah-**reem**) *noun*
a) the women of a Moslem household, including wives, female relatives, concubines, etc. who live in a separate part of the house. b) the part of a house where the women live.
[Arabic *harim* forbidden]

haricot bean (*say* **harri**-ko been)
a kidney bean (haricot blanc) or French bean (haricot vert).
[French]

hark *verb*
to listen.
hark back, to refer back to an earlier subject.

harken *verb*
see HEARKEN.

harlequin (*say* **harli**-kwin) *adjective*
having bright or varied colours.

[after *Harlequin*, a traditional pantomime character who wears a mask and a brightly coloured costume with a diamond pattern]

harlot *noun*
a prostitute.
Word Family: **harlotry**, *noun*, the practice of prostitution.

harm (*rhymes with* arm) *noun*
damage: 'the prisoner was charged with causing grievous bodily *harm*'.
harm *verb*
to damage or hurt.
Word Family: **harmful**, *adjective*, causing or likely to cause harm; **harmfully**, *adverb*; **harmless**, *adjective*, not having the power or tendency to harm; **harmlessly**, *adverb*; **harmlessness**, *noun*.

harmonic (*say* har-**monnik**) *noun*
also called an **overtone**
Music: any of the series of almost inaudible tones above the note played on e.g. a violin string, corresponding to the notes produced by $\frac{1}{2}$, $\frac{1}{3}$, $\frac{1}{4}$.... the length of the string and at the same intervals as the major diatonic scale.
harmonics *plural noun*
(*used with singular verb*) the science or study of musical sounds.
Word Family: **harmonic**, *adjective*, a) full of harmony, b) relating to harmony or harmonics as distinct from rhythm or melody.

harmonica (*say* har-**monnika**) *noun*
Music: the modern name for the **mouth organ**, a small wind instrument with metal reeds.

harmonious (*say* har-**mo**-nee-us) *adjective*
1. full of harmony: 'a *harmonious* orchestra'.
2. showing agreement in ideas, actions, etc.. 'a *harmonious* relationship'.
Usage: 'this building has a very *harmonious* design' (= attractively combined).
Word Family: **harmoniously**, *adverb*; **harmoniousness**, *noun*.

harmonium (*say* har-**mo**-nee-um) *noun*
Music: a small reed organ in which air is pumped out through the reeds.

harmony (*say* **harma**-nee) *noun*
1. a state of agreement or pleasing arrangement: 'they live in perfect *harmony*'.
2. *Music:* a) the blending of different notes to make chords. b) the science of the structure or combination of chords.
harmonize, harmonise *verb*
1. to bring into harmony.
2. *Music:* a) to play or sing in harmony. b) to add notes in harmony with a main melody.
Word Family: **harmonization**, *noun*.
[Greek *harmonia* a fitting together]

harness (*say* **har**-niss) *noun*
1. the straps and fittings by which a horse or other animal pulls a vehicle.
2. any arrangement of straps, etc. by which something is attached or raised.
3. an old word for armour.
in harness, at one's regular work.
harness *verb*
to put on a harness.
Usage: 'he *harnessed* his energy for the task' (= directed, organized).

harp *noun*
Music: a large instrument with strings set in a triangular frame and plucked with the fingers.
harp *verb*
to play on a harp.
harp on, harp upon, to speak about or insist on tediously.
Word Family: **harpist**, **harper**, *nouns*, a person who plays a harp.

harpoon *noun*
a barbed spear attached to a line, thrown by hand or shot from a gun, used for catching whales or fish.
Word Family: **harpoon**, *verb*.

harpsichord (*say* **harpsi**-kord) *noun*
Music: a keyboard instrument in which the strings are sounded by a plucking mechanism.
Word Family: **harpsichordist**, *noun*.

harpy *noun*
a scheming or cruel person.
[after a *Harpy*, a creature in Greek mythology, with the head of a woman and the body of a bird]

harridan (*say* **harri**-d'n) *noun*
a vicious old woman.

harrier (1) (*rhymes with* barrier) *noun*
1. a person who harries.
2. any of various slim, low-flying hawks with long wings and tail.

harrier (2) (*rhymes with* barrier) *noun*
1. any of a breed of small hounds trained to hunt hares.
2. a cross-country runner.

harrow (*rhymes with* barrow) *noun*
a heavy frame set with spikes or discs, used to level soil, cover seed, break clods, etc.

harrowing *adjective*
extremely distressing or disturbing.
Word Family: **harrowingly,** *adverb*; **harrow,** *verb,* to break or level soil with a harrow.

harry (*rhymes with* marry) *verb*
(**harried, harrying**)
to harass or torment by repeated attacks, demands, etc.

harsh *adjective*
disagreeable, rough or jarring to the senses: 'a *harsh* wind'.
Usage: 'the prisoners complained of poor food and *harsh* treatment' (= severe, cruel).
Word Family: **harshly,** *adverb*; **harshness,** *noun.*

hart *noun*
plural is **harts** or **hart**
a stag.

hartebeest (*say* **harti–beest**) *noun*
a large African antelope with a long face and ringed horns.
[Afrikaans]

harum–scarum (*say* **hair'm–skair'm**) *adjective*
reckless or wild.
Word Family: **harum–scarum,** *adverb*; **harum–scarum,** *noun,* a) a reckless person, b) reckless behaviour.

harvest (*say* **har**–vist) *noun*
a) the gathering of a crop or crops. b) the crop, especially grain, which is gathered. c) the season when crops are gathered.
Usages:
a) 'success was the *harvest* of her efforts' (= product, result).
b) 'a *harvest* of gifts' (= store, supply).
harvest *verb*
to gather or collect, especially a crop.
Word Family: **harvester,** *noun,* a person or machine that harvests crops.

harvest bug
a tiny, scarlet, six–legged mite which in hot weather lodges in the skin of man and other animals, causing intense irritation.

harvest festival
a thanksgiving service after the harvest, when churches are decorated with corn, fruit, flowers, etc.

harvest moon
the full moon which occurs nearest to the autumn equinox, when the moon rises at almost the same time for several nights.

has *verb*
the third person singular, present tense of the verb **have.**

has–been *noun*
a person or thing that is no longer successful, popular, useful, etc.

hash (1) *noun*
1. a dish of small pieces of meat cooked or reheated with vegetables.
2. a jumble or muddle.
make a hash of, to ruin or make a mess of something.
Word Family: **hash,** *verb,* to make into a hash.
[French *hache* an axe]

hash (2) *noun*
(*informal*) hashish.

hashish *noun*
also called **pot** or **marijuana**
the compressed flowers and resin of the Indian hemp plant, smoked or eaten as a narcotic.
[Arabic, dried herb]

hasp (*say* hahsp) *noun*
a fastener for a door, etc., consisting of a metal plate which fits over a U–shaped staple and is secured by a padlock or pin.

hassle *verb*
(*informal*) to harass or trouble.
Word Family: **hassle,** *noun.*

hassock (*say* **hass**–uk) *noun*
1. a thick cushion for kneeling.
2. a tuft or clump of thick grass.

hast *verb*
the old form of the second person singular, present tense of the verb **have.**

haste (*rhymes with* paste) *noun*
speed or hurry in actions: 'this letter is written in *haste*'.
hasten (*say* **hay**–s'n) *verb*
to move or act with speed.
hasty (*say* **hay**–stee) *adjective*
1. moving, made or performed with haste: 'this is only a *hasty* visit'.
2. irritable or easily angered.
Word Family: **hastily,** *adverb*; **hastiness,** *noun.*

hat *noun*
any shaped covering for the head, worn for decoration or protection.
Phrases:
at the drop of a hat, without hesitation.
talk through one's hat, to talk nonsense.
under one's hat, 'keep this information *under your hat*' (= secret, confidential).

Word Family: **hat (hatted, hatting)** *verb*, to put on or provide with a hat.

hatch (1) *verb*
a) to produce offspring from eggs. b) to break out of an egg.
Usage: 'she has *hatched* a new scheme' (= produced).
Word Family: **hatch**, *noun*; **hatchery**, *noun*, a place for hatching eggs.

hatch (2) *noun*
a) an opening in a floor, wall, ceiling, etc. b) a cover for such an opening.
Word Family: **hatchway**, *noun*, the opening of a hatch or trapdoor, especially in a ship's deck.

hatch (3) *verb*
Art: to draw a series of close parallel lines, as in shading or etching.
Word Family: **hatch**, *noun*, a line used when drawing shade; **hatching**, *noun*, a series of such lines.

hatchet *noun*
a short-handled axe or tomahawk.
bury the hatchet, to make peace.

hatchet face
a long face with sharp features.
Word Family: **hatchet-faced**, *adjective.*

hate *verb*
to have a passionate or strong dislike for someone or something.
Word Family: **hate**, *noun*, a) a feeling of strong or passionate dislike, b) something which is hated.

hateful *adjective*
detestable or provoking hate.
Word Family: **hatefully**, *adverb*; **hatefulness**, *noun.*

hath *verb*
the old form of the third person singular, present tense of the verb **have**.

hatred (*say* **hay**-trid) *noun*
a hate or passionate dislike.

hatter *noun*
a person who makes or sells hats.
mad as a hatter, mad or eccentric.

hat-trick *noun*
1. *Cricket:* the achievement of a bowler taking three wickets with three successive balls.
2. any similar achievement of three wins or successes in a row.

haughty (*rhymes with* naughty) *adjective*
rudely or excessively proud.
Word Family: **haughtily**, *adverb*; **haughtiness**, *noun.*

haul *verb*
1. to pull or drag, usually with considerable effort: 'the fireman *hauled* the desperate woman to safety'.
2. to transport goods, especially in a road vehicle.
3. *Nautical:* to change course or direction: 'the ship *hauled* about to search for the missing man'.
haul over the coals, see COAL.
haul *noun*
the act of hauling or pulling.
Usages:
a) 'there was a heavy *haul* of fish in the net' (= quantity).
b) 'on the map it's a long *haul* to the next large town' (= distance).
c) 'the robbers divided up their *haul*' (= loot, takings).
haulage *noun*
1. the act of hauling or transporting.
2. the cost of hauling, transport, etc.
Word Family: **haulier**, *noun*, a person or business concerned with haulage.

haunch *noun*
1. the upper thigh and buttock: 'he was squatting on his *haunches* waiting for us'.
2. the hindquarter of an animal.

haunt *verb*
to visit or appear repeatedly as a ghost or spirit: 'the spirit of the murdered prince *haunts* the castle'.
Usages:
a) 'she was *haunted* by her memories' (= disturbed, worried).
b) 'he *haunts* second-hand shops' (= often visits).
haunt *noun*
a place which is frequently visited: 'the *haunts* of his student days'.
Word Family: **haunted**, *adjective*, a) visited or occupied by ghosts, b) deeply worried or disturbed; **haunting**, *adjective*, a) fascinating, b) recurring.

hautboy (*say* **hote**-boy) *noun*
an old word for an oboe.
[French *haut* high + *bois* wood]

haute couture (*say* ote koo-**tewer**)
the most fashionable or elegant clothes, made by the leading fashion designers.
[French, high fashion]

hauteur (*say* o-**ter**) *noun*
haughtiness or arrogance.
[French]

have (*say* hav) *verb*
(I **have**; he, she, it **has**; we, you, they **have**; **had**, **having**; *old forms*: thou **hast**, he **hath**)

1. to possess: 'the family *has* three cars'.
Usages:
a) 'they were *had* by glamorous advertising' (= tricked, taken in).
b) 'will you *have* sugar?' (= take).
c) 'I hope you *have* a good weekend' (= enjoy, experience).
d) 'he is the best surgeon to be *had*' (= obtained).
e) 'have you *had* any news?' (= received).
f) 'please *have* patience!' (= use, exercise).
g) 'she *has* a bad cold' (= is suffering from).
h) 'they *had* a game of chess last night' (= engaged in).
i) '*have* him phone me as soon as possible' (= cause to, urge).
j) 'she said her mother won't *have* it' (= permit).
k) 'when the fingerprints matched, the police knew they *had* him' (= held at a disadvantage).
l) 'rumour *has* it that she drinks secretly' (= asserts).
m) 'the cat *had* three kittens' (= gave birth to).
2. special use with past participles to express completed actions: a) 'he *has finished* his meal'; b) 'he *had finished* his meal when they arrived'; c) 'he will *have finished* by then'.
Phrases:
had better, 'we *had better* post this letter now' (= ought to, should).
have had it, 'we can't use his car because it *has* really *had it*' (= is beyond repair).
have it in for, to hold a grudge against.
have it out, to come to a final settlement or decision.
have on, to tease or deceive.
have to, 'she *has to* be at work by eight' (= must, is required to).
have up, (*informal*) 'he was *had up* for careless driving' (= brought before a court).

haven (*say* **hay-v'n**) *noun*
a place of shelter or safety, such as a harbour for ships.

haver (*say* **hayver**) *verb*
1. to vacillate.
2. *Scottish:* to talk nonsense.

haversack (*say* **havva-sak**) *noun*
any of various light packs carried on the back, especially by hikers or soldiers.
[German *Hafersack* oats-sack]

havoc (*say* **havvik**) *noun*
destruction, damage or chaos.
play havoc with, to destroy or ruin.

hawk (1) *noun*
1. a general term for birds of prey which hunt during the day, including falcons, buzzards, harriers, kites and ospreys, but excluding eagles and vultures.
2. any of various swift low-flying birds with short wings and long tails, such as sparrowhawks and goshawks.
3. a person who is aggressive or militant. Compare DOVE.
hawk *verb*
to hunt with trained hawks.
Word Family: **hawkish,** fierce; **hawker,** *noun,* a person who hunts with hawks.

hawk (2) *verb*
to offer goods for sale by going from house to house.
Word Family: **hawker,** *noun,* a person who hawks goods.

hawk-eyed *adjective*
having keen or sharp eyesight.

hawk-moth *noun*
any of various kinds of large, night-feeding moths which can hover like hawks.

hawser *noun*
Nautical: a thick rope or cable.

hawthorn *noun*
also called **may**
a thorny shrub or tree with white or pink blossom and red berries (called haws), often used to form hedges.

hay *noun*
any cut grass which is dried and used as fodder. Compare STRAW.

haycock *noun*
a small pile of hay left in a field to dry.

hay fever
Medicine: an allergy due to sensitivity to certain pollens, causing frequent sneezing, blocked nasal passages and redness and watering of the eyes.

haystack *noun*
also called a **hayrick**
a large pile of hay stored in the open air, sometimes with a cover.

haywire *adjective*
(*informal*) crazy or out of control: 'the plan went *haywire* from the beginning'.

hazard (*say* **hazz'rd**) *noun*
1. a risk or source of danger: 'poorly marked signs are a road *hazard*'.

2. a game of chance played with two dice.
3. *Golf:* an obstacle such as a bunker, water, rough grass, etc.
4. *Billiards:* pocketing the object ball (winning hazard) or one's own ball off another (losing hazard).
hazard *verb*
to risk or venture, especially when the result is in doubt: 'to *hazard* a guess'.
Word Family: **hazardous**, *adjective*, dangerous or risky; **hazardously**, *adverb*; **hazardousness**, *noun*.
[Arabic *az-zahr* the die]

haze *noun*
a suspension of fine dust, smoke or vapour particles in the air, which reduces visibility.
Usage: 'she's always in a *haze* first thing in the morning' (= vague state of mind).
Word Family: **haze**, *verb*, to become misty or blurred; **hazy**, *adjective*, a) misty, b) dim or vague.

hazel (*say* **hayz'l**) *noun*
1. a small evergreen tree or shrub which produces edible nuts.
2. a light, yellowish-brown colour.
Word Family: **hazel**, *adjective*; **hazelnut**, *noun*.

H-bomb *noun*
short form of **hydrogen bomb**
see NUCLEAR WEAPON.

he *pronoun*
plural is **they**
1. the third person singular nominative pronoun, used to indicate a male: '*he* ate the cake'.
2. (used to represent any person whose sex is not specified) '*he* who hesitates is lost'.
3. (used as a noun) 'is the cat a *he*?'.
4. (used in combination to indicate a male) 'a *he-goat*'.
See HIM, HIS and SHE.

head (*say* hed) *noun*
1. *Anatomy:* the part of the body above the neck, containing the brain, eyes, etc.
2. something which has the shape, position or function of a head: a) 'a *head* of cabbage'; b) 'the *head* of a nail'.
3. a) (*often capital*) the leader, commander or chief executive of a nation, institution, company, etc.: 'the *Head* of State'. b) the headmaster or headmistress of a school.
Usages:
a) 'he is now a *head* taller than his father' (= a head's height).
b) 'the tickets are £10 a *head*' (= person).
c) 'I have no *head* for figures' (= ability).
d) 'I had a terrible *head* all morning' (= headache).
e) 'at last we reached the *head* of the queue' (= front).
4. *Audio:* a small magnetic device across which the tape passes in a tape recorder. The **recording head** transmits on to tape the electronic signal of the sound being recorded. The **playing head** changes the recorded signal on a tape into sounds which are amplified.
5. the foam on a liquid which has just been poured, especially beer.
6. (*informal*) a person who habitually uses or is addicted to drugs.
7. (*usually plural*) the side of a coin bearing the image of a head.
Phrases:
bite, eat, laugh, talk, etc. one's head off, 'she *bit my head off* when I gave her some advice' (= replied angrily).
come to a head, to come to a crisis.
go to one's head, 'success has *gone to his head*' (= made him conceited).
head over heels, a) 'she tumbled *head over heels* into the haystack' (= rolling, somersaulting); b) 'they are *head over heels* in love' (= completely).
heads or tails, a call made before tossing a coin to guess which side up it will fall.
lose one's head, to panic.
make head or tail of, 'I cannot *make head or tail of* this letter' (= understand at all).
off, out of one's head, mad.
off the top of one's head, 'he gave the answer *off the top of his head*' (= without reflection, from memory).
on one's own head, 'the result of your actions must be *on your own head*' (= your own responsibility).
over one's head, a) 'we went *over his head* with our demands' (= to a higher authority); b) 'that book is way *over my head*' (= beyond my understanding).
turn somebody's head, 'don't let their flattery *turn your head*' (= make you vain).
head *verb*
1. to lead or be in front of.
2. to go in the direction of: 'we *headed* home'.

3. *Soccer:* to propel or direct the ball with the head; an attempt at goal in this way is called a **header**.
head off, '*head off* those sheep before they reach the gate' (= intercept).
Word Family: **head**, *adjective*, having a position of leadership or authority.

headache (*say* **hed**-ake) *noun*
a pain in the head.
Usage: 'her continual complaints are a real *headache* to the police' (= problem, trouble).

headdress *noun*
a covering or decoration for the head.

header (*say* **hedda**) *noun*
1. (*informal*) a headfirst dive or fall.
2. *Farming:* see REAPER under REAP.

headfirst *adverb*
with the head first.
Usage: 'she always goes *headfirst* into new adventures' (= rashly, recklessly).

head-hunting *noun*
the practice among some tribes of cutting off the heads of enemies and keeping them as trophies or charms.
Word Family: **head-hunter**, *noun*.

heading *noun*
a group of words printed at the top of an article, page of a book, etc. to indicate what follows.

headland *noun*
also called a **promontory**
a piece of land which juts out into the sea.

headlight *noun*
also called a **headlamp**
any of the large lights at the front of a motor vehicle.

headline *noun*
1. *Newspapers:* the title of an article or a news heading printed in large, bold type.
2. (*plural*) a broadcast summary of news.

headlock *noun*
Wrestling: a hold in which the wrestler curls his arm tightly around his opponent's head and neck.

headlong *adjective, adverb*
headfirst.

headmaster *noun*
the male teacher in charge of a school.
Word Family: **headmistress**, *noun*, a female headmaster.

headmost *adjective*
being the most advanced.

head-on *adjective, adverb*
with the front parts meeting first: 'a *head-on* collision'.

headphones *plural noun*
also called **earphones** or a **headset**
a pair of small speakers, one for each ear, mounted on a band which can be connected to a radio, etc.

headpiece *noun*
any covering for the head, especially a helmet.

headquarters *plural noun*
(*used with plural or singular verb*) the central office or building of an organization.

headroom *noun*
the amount of space above or around a head or the top of something: 'the low ceilings left little *headroom* for those standing up'.

headset *noun*
see HEADPHONES.

head-shrinker *noun*
short form is **shrink**
(*informal*) a psychiatrist.

headstand *noun*
the act of balancing the body upright, using either the head or the arms as a support.

headstone *noun*
a gravestone.

headstrong *adjective*
obstinate or determined, especially about having one's own way.

headteacher *noun*
a headmaster or headmistress.

headwaters *plural noun*
the upper tributaries of a river.

headway *noun*
any progress: 'police have made little *headway* in the difficult investigation'.

headwind *noun*
a wind blowing in the opposite direction to which a vehicle is travelling, thus decreasing its speed. Compare TAILWIND.

headword *noun*
a word which heads or begins a paragraph, chapter, etc.

heady *adjective*
1. having an intoxicating effect.
2. impulsive or rash.

heal *verb*
to make or become healthy, whole or free of disease.
Word Family: **healing**, *adjective*, able to heal; **healer**, *noun*.

health (*say* helth) *noun*
1. a normal functioning of the body and mind.
2. a person's mental or physical state: 'his *health* is no longer good'.
drink a person's health, to drink a toast to.
healthy *adjective*
1. in good health: 'a *healthy* athlete'.
2. good for the health: 'a *healthy* climate'.
3. characteristic of health: 'a *healthy* appearance'.
Word Family: **healthily**, *adverb*; **healthiness**, *noun*; **healthful**, *adjective.*

health food
assorted foods with a high nutritional content which are usually free from artificial preservatives.

heap *noun*
1. a pile.
Usage: 'we have *heaps* of time before the plane leaves' (= plenty).
2. (*informal*) something very old or in bad condition, such as an old car.
heap *verb*
to pile up or put in a heap.
Usages:
a) 'he has *heaped* up many debts' (= accumulated).
b) 'insults were *heaped* on the head of the unfortunate officials' (= cast).

hear *verb*
(**heard** (*say* herd), **hearing**)
to perceive with the ears.
Usages:
a) 'I *hear* that you are going away' (= have been told).
b) 'do you ever *hear* from your brother?' (= get news).
c) 'you must *hear* this new record' (= listen to).
d) 'the judge *heard* several minor cases this morning' (= presided over).
Phrases:
hear out, 'please *hear out* my speech before asking questions' (= listen to the end of).
not hear of, 'she *would not hear of* us paying for dinner' (= refused to allow).

hearing *noun*
1. the power or faculty by which sound is perceived: 'the old man's *hearing* is not good'.
2. the opportunity of being heard: 'please give us a *hearing*'.
Usage: 'a court *hearing*' (= trial).
3. the range within which something can be heard: 'we called for help but no-one was within *hearing*'.

hearken (*say* **hark**'n) *verb*
also spelt **harken**
to listen.

hearsay *noun*
any rumour or gossip.

hearse (*rhymes with* purse) *noun*
any vehicle for carrying a corpse to the place of burial or cremation.

heart (*say* hart) *noun*
1. *Anatomy:* the muscular pump within the chest which circulates the blood.
2. one's emotions, affections or capacity for love, as distinct from the intellect: 'a kind *heart*'.
3. courage or enthusiasm: 'he has no *heart* for fighting'.
4. the centre or most important part of anything: 'the *heart* of the matter is this'.
5. *Cards:* a) a red figure like a heart on a playing card. b) a playing card with this figure. c) (*plural*) the suit with this figure.
Phrases:
after one's own heart, 'when it comes to wines, he is a man *after my own heart*' (= who shares my tastes, etc.).
be close to one's heart, 'social inequality is an issue that is very *close to his heart*' (= deeply affects him).
by heart, 'please learn these rules *by heart*' (= by memory).
have a heart, '*have a heart* and let me get some rest' (= be sympathetic or merciful).
have at heart, 'I am sure they *have* your interests *at heart*' (= are concerned about).
have one's heart in one's mouth, to be afraid.
in one's heart of hearts, '*in my heart of hearts* I knew he was right' (= deep inside me).
lose one's heart to, 'she *lost her heart to* the smallest kitten in the litter' (= fell in love with).
set one's heart at rest, to relax or remove anxiety.
take to heart, 'do not *take* their jokes so much *to heart*' (= think seriously about, grieve over).
wear one's heart on one's sleeve, to display one's feelings too openly.

heartache (*say* **hart**-ake) *noun*
a painful sorrow or unhappiness.

heart attack
also called a **coronary thrombosis**
a deficiency in blood supplied to the heart muscle due to a blockage in an artery, leading to reduced efficiency of blood pumping.

heartbroken *adjective*
overcome with grief, misery, etc.
Word Family: **heartbrokenly,** *adverb*; **heartbreak,** *noun,* an overwhelming sorrow or grief; **heartbreaking,** *adjective.*

heartburn *noun*
a burning sensation in the chest due to excess acid in the stomach.
Word Family: **heartburning,** *noun,* (often plural) jealousy, envy or suppressed discontent.

hearten *verb*
to cheer up or encourage.

heart failure
any failure or faulty functioning of the heart pump.

heartfelt *adjective*
deeply felt or sincere.

hearth (*say* harth) *noun*
the floor of a fireplace and the area around it.

heartily *adverb*
Word Family: see HEARTY.

heartless *adjective*
cruel or without mercy.
Word Family: **heartlessly,** *adverb*; **heartlessness,** *noun.*

heart-lung machine
Medicine: a machine used to take over and perform the functions of a patient's heart and lungs during an operation on the heart or lungs.

heart murmur
a sound caused by an irregular flow of blood in the heart.

heart-rending *adjective*
causing or expressing great grief.

heartsick *adjective*
greatly unhappy or disappointed.

heart-stricken *adjective*
full of grief or anguish.

heartstrings *plural noun*
one's deepest or strongest feelings.

heart-throb *noun*
a person with whom one is infatuated.

heart-to-heart *adjective*
frank or sincere.

hearty (*say* **har-tee**) *adjective*
1. enthusiastic, friendly or sincere.
2. strong and healthy.
Usage: 'a *hearty* meal' (= substantial, satisfying).
Word Family: **heartily,** *adverb*; **heartiness,** *noun.*

heat *noun*
1. the condition or sensation of being hot: 'the *heat* of a tropical summer is very tiring'.
Usage: 'in the *heat* of the argument many insults were exchanged' (= intensity of feeling).
2. *Physics:* a form of energy, causing or caused by the vibrations of the molecules of a substance.
3. *Biology:* a period of sexual urge in animals during the breeding season.
4. a single division in a competition, the winner of which takes part in further or final rounds.
Word Family: **heat,** *verb,* to make or become hot; **heater,** *noun,* any device for heating, such as a radiator; **heatedly,** *adverb,* vehemently.

heat capacity
also called **water equivalent**
Physics: the heat required to raise the temperature of a unit mass of a substance 1°C.

heath *noun*
1. an area of flat land covered with low shrubby vegetation.
2. any of various low, evergreen shrubs, some of which are also called heathers.

heathen (*say* **hee-*th*'n**) *noun*
1. a person who does not worship the God of the established religions.
2. any irreligious or barbaric person.
Word Family: **heathenish,** *adjective*; **heathenism,** *noun.*

heather (*say* **he*th*a**) *noun*
a type of low, evergreen, autumn-flowering shrub, usually growing on moors, especially Scotch heather and ling.

heatstroke *noun*
a fever or collapse due to exposure to excessive heat and dehydration.

heatwave *noun*
a period of unusually hot weather.

heave (*rhymes with* sleeve) *verb*
(**heaved** or **hove** (Nautical), **heaving**)
1. to raise, lift or throw with an effort.
Usages:
a) 'his chest *heaved* with the effort of coughing' (= rose and fell).
b) 'she *heaved* a sigh of relief as the last guest departed' (= uttered).
2. *Nautical:* to cause a ship to move in a certain direction.
Phrases:
heave in sight, 'just at that moment John *hove in sight*' (= appeared).

heave to, to stop the forward movement of a ship, especially by heading into the wind.
Word Family: **heave**, *noun.*

heaven (*rhymes with* seven) *noun*
1. a) the place where gods, angels and other supernatural beings live.
b) (*often capital*) the place of reward for the righteous or faithful. Compare HELL.
2. any place or condition of extreme bliss or happiness.
3. (*plural*) the sky.
seventh heaven, a state of extreme happiness.
heavenly *adjective*
1. of or belonging to heaven or the heavens.
2. excellent, pleasing or beautiful.
Word Family: **heavens**!, *interjection*, an exclamation of surprise.

heaven sent *adjective*
being provided by a miracle or extreme good fortune.

heavy (*say* **hevvee**) *adjective*
1. having great weight, size or force.
Usages:
a) 'a *heavy* heart' (= sad, depressed).
b) 'he is quite a *heavy* smoker' (= habitual).
c) 'the *heavy* movements of an elephant' (= slow, deliberate).
d) 'the *heavy* lettering caught his eye' (= thick, dark).
e) 'they found the climb very *heavy* going' (= difficult).
f) 'we felt the poetry was rather *heavy*' (= dull, uninteresting).
g) 'she was not used to such *heavy* food' (= hard to digest)
h) 'a *heavy* sky indicates rain' (= dark, cloudy).
i) 'the roads were *heavy* after the storm' (= wet, difficult to travel).
2. concerning the manufacture of goods of more than the usual weight: '*heavy* industry'.
heavy *noun*
1. a villainous or tragic role in a play, film, etc.
2. (*informal*) a) a person of great influence or importance. b) a thug or tough person.
Word Family: **heaviness**, *noun*; **heavily**, *adverb.*

heavy-duty *adjective*
designed for strength and durability.

heavy-handed *adjective*
1. oppressive or harsh: 'the *heavy-handed* dictator showed no sympathy to the peasants'.
2. lacking delicacy or subtlety.
Word Family: **heavy-handedness**, *noun.*

heavy water
see DEUTERIUM.

heavyweight (*say* **hevvi**-wate) *noun*
1. the heaviest weight division in boxing, over 12 stone 7 lb. (amateur) or 12 stone 10 lb. (professional), about 79–81 kg.
2. (*informal*) a person of great influence or importance.

Hebrew (*say* **hee**-broo) *noun*
the ancient Jewish language used in the Old Testament and now the official language of Israel.
Word Family: **Hebrew**, **Hebraic** (*say* hee-**bray**-ik), *adjectives.*

heck *interjection*
a euphemism for hell.

heckle *verb*
to disturb or harass with persistent questions, interruptions, etc.
Word Family: **heckler**, *noun*, a person who heckles.

hectare (*say* **hek**-tar) *noun*
a metric unit of area used in land measurement, equal to 10 000 m^2 or about 2·5 acres.

hectic *adjective*
1. full of energetic activity, haste, confusion, etc.
2. feverish.
Word Family: **hectically**, *adverb.*

hecto-
a prefix used for SI units, meaning one hundred (10^2). See UNITS in grey pages.

hector (*say* **hek**ta) *verb*
to treat in a bullying, domineering way.
[after *Hector* of Troy in Homer's 'Iliad']

hedge (*say* hej) *noun*
1. a row of similar shrubs, usually cut evenly and grown close together to form a boundary or barrier.
2. any method of protection against loss: 'he bought mining shares as a *hedge* against inflation'.
hedge *verb*
1. to surround or enclose with a hedge.
2. to avoid direct commitment by evasive answers to questions, etc.
3. to protect oneself against loss.
hedge in, 'he felt *hedged in* by rules and regulations' (= restricted).

hedgehog *noun*
a small, nocturnal, pig-snouted mammal, related to shrews and moles, which has a protective coat of long spines.

hedonism (*say* **heed**'n–izm) *noun*
Philosophy: the belief that happiness or pleasure is the chief or proper aim in life.
Word Family: **hedonistic** (*say* heed'n–istik), *adjective*; **hedonistically**, *adverb*; **hedonist**, *noun*.
[Greek *hedoné* pleasure]

heebie–jeebies *plural noun*
(*informal*) a state of nervousness.

heed *verb*
to listen or pay attention to.
Word Family: **heed**, *noun*, attention; **heedful**, *adjective*, attentive; **heedless**, *adjective*.

heel (1) *noun*
1. *Anatomy:* the rear part of the foot below the ankle.
2. the part of a shoe, sock, etc. covering the heel.
3. something with the shape, position or function of a heel: 'the *heel* of a golf club'.
4. an untrustworthy or contemptible person.
Phrases:
at, on one's heels, behind one.
come to heel, a) (of a dog) to come and stay at heel; b) to submit to authority.
cool, kick one's heels, to wait or be kept waiting.
dig one's heels in, to maintain one's position obstinately.
down at heel, shabby or untidy.
kick up one's heels, 'let's *kick up our heels* and celebrate' (= have fun).
show a clean pair of heels to, 'the winner of the race *showed a clean pair of heels to* all the other competitors' (= far outdistanced).
take to one's heels, to run away.
heel *verb*
1. to put a heel or heels on: 'I must have my shoes *heeled*'.
2. to follow close behind: 'he could not persuade his dog to *heel*'.
Word Family: **heeler**, *noun*, a dog which heels.

heel (2) *verb*
Nautical: to lean or cause to lean to one side.

heeltap *noun*
the dregs or last drops of a drink.
no heeltaps!, an exclamation meaning drink up.

hefty *adjective*
heavy and strong.
Usage: 'a *hefty* tax' (= large).
Word Family: **heftiness**, *noun*.

hegemony (*say* **hegimma**–nee) *noun*
a leadership or powerful influence, especially of one state or country over others.
[Greek]

heifer (*say* **heffa**) *noun*
a cow under three years of age which has not yet had a calf.

height (*say* hite) *noun*
1. the distance from the bottom or a given level to the top of something.
2. a high level, place or part.
3. the highest level or degree: 'she dressed in the *height* of fashion'.
heighten *verb*
to increase in height or intensity: 'his anger was *heightened* by their childish comments'.

heinous (*say* **heenus** *or* **haynus**) *adjective*
hateful or vile: 'a *heinous* crime'.
Word Family: **heinously**, *adverb*; **heinousness**, *noun*.

heir (*say* air) *noun*
1. a person who inherits, or will inherit, money, property, title, etc.
2. a person, group or society to which something such as tradition, ideas, etc. is passed on.
heir apparent
plural is **heirs apparent**
a person who has an unquestionable right to succeed to a throne or title.
heir presumptive
a person who will succeed to a throne or title unless someone with a higher claim is born.
Word Family: **heiress**, *noun*, a female heir.

heirloom (*say* **air**–loom) *noun*
any family possession passed down from generation to generation.

held *verb*
the past tense and past participle of the verb **hold (1)**.

helical (*say* **helli**–k'l) *adjective*
of or shaped like a helix.

helices *plural noun*
a plural of **helix**.

helicopter *noun*
an aircraft which takes off vertically and which is supported and moved forward by a rotor.
[Greek *heliko–* helix + *pteron* wing]

helio–
a prefix meaning sun, as in *heliocentric*.
[Greek *helios*]

heliocentric (*say* heelio–**sentrik**) *adjective*
1. having the sun as a centre.
2. measured or seen from the centre of the sun.

heliograph (*say* **heelio**–graf) *noun*
a device for signalling by using a movable mirror to reflect sunlight in flashes.
Word Family: **heliograph**, *verb*.
[HELIO– + Greek *graphein* to write]

heliotrope (*say* **hell**–ya–trope) *noun*
1. *Biology:* any plant which turns towards the sun.
2. any of various greenhouse and garden plants with small, purplish flowers.
3. a tint of purple.
4. see BLOODSTONE.
[HELIO– + Greek *tropé* a turning]

heliport *noun*
a landing place for helicopters, often on the roof of a building.

helium (*say* **heeli**–um) *noun*
element number 2, a colourless, inert gas much lighter than air, traces of which are found in the earth's atmosphere and in natural gas. See CHEMICAL ELEMENTS in grey pages.
[Greek *helios* sun]

helix (*say* **heelix**) *noun*
plural is **helices** (*say* **helli**–seez) or **helixes**
a spiral or coil, such as a corkscrew.
[Greek]

hell *noun*
1. the place where the dead, evil spirits and devils live. Also called **hades**.
2. (*often capital*) the place of punishment for the wicked. Compare HEAVEN.
3. any place or condition of misery or unpleasantness.
Phrases:
for the hell of it, for fun or no particular reason.
hell for leather, at top speed.
hell to pay, great trouble.
play hell with, 'this cold weather *plays hell with* his rheumatism' (= causes trouble or injury to).

hell–bent *adjective*
recklessly determined.

Hellenic (*say* hel–**lennik**) *adjective*
a) of the modern Greeks. b) of the ancient Greeks, and their language and culture before the time of Alexander the Great, about 330 B.C.
Word Family: **Hellene**, *noun*, a Greek.

hellish *adjective*
(*informal*) extremely unpleasant or difficult.
Word Family: **hellishness**, *noun*; **hellishly**, *adverb*.

hello *interjection*
also spelt **hallo** or **hullo**
a cry of greeting or to attract attention.

helm *noun*
1. the equipment for steering a boat, being a tiller or wheel connected to a rudder.
2. any position of leadership or control
Word Family: **helmsman**, *noun*.

helmet *noun*
any of various protective coverings for the head.

helminth *noun*
an internal parasitic worm.
[from German]

helot (*say* **hell**–ot) *noun*
1. *Ancient history:* a state–owned slave in Sparta.
2. a person treated like such a slave.
[from Greek]

help *verb*
to make something easier, better or less painful for a person or thing: a) 'can I *help* to carry your bags?'; b) 'this medicine *helps* me to sleep'.
Usage: 'she couldn't *help* laughing at the joke' (= stop herself from).
help oneself to, to take.
help *noun*
1. the act of helping or relieving: 'your *help* is needed to reduce car accidents'.
2. any person or thing that helps: 'your suggestions have been a great *help* to us'.
Usage: 'the damage is done, and there is no *help* for it now' (= way of remedying).
Word Family: **helper**, *noun*.

helpful *adjective*
useful or giving help.
Word Family: **helpfully**, *adverb*; **helpfulness**, *noun*.

helping *noun*
a quantity of food served to a person at one time.

helpless *adjective*
1. unable to stop oneself: 'he is a *helpless* liar'.
2. having no help or remedy: 'a *helpless* situation'.
Usages:
a) 'the victim was left *helpless* by the roadside' (= unattended to).
b) 'she is quite *helpless* without her husband' (= unable to cope).
Word Family: **helplessly,** *adverb*; **helplessness,** *noun.*

helpmate *noun*
a helpful friend or companion.

helter-skelter *adverb*
in great haste or disorder.

Helvetian (*say* hel-vee-sh'n) *adjective*
of Switzerland and the Swiss.
Word Family: **Helvetian,** *noun.*
[from Latin]

hem *noun*
the edge of a garment or cloth which has been turned under and sewn down.
hem *verb*
(**hemmed, hemming**)
to fold back and sew down the edge of fabric, etc.
hem in, hem round, 'we were *hemmed in* on all sides by shouting spectators' (= surrounded, enclosed).

he-man *noun*
a strong or aggressively masculine man.

hematite *noun*
see HAEMATITE.

hematology *noun*
see HAEMATOLOGY.

hematosis *noun*
see HAEMATOSIS.

hemi-
a prefix meaning half, as in *hemisphere.*
[Greek]

hemisphere (*say* **hemmi**-sfeer) *noun*
a half of a sphere, such as the Southern Hemisphere which is the half of the earth south of the equator.
Word Family: **hemispherical** (*say* hemmis-**ferri**-k'l), **hemispheric,** *adjective.*

hemlock *noun*
a poisonous plant with finely divided leaves, purple spotted stems and small white flowers, used as a sedative.

hemoglobin *noun*
see HAEMOGLOBIN.

hemophilia *noun*
see HAEMOPHILIA.

hemorrhage *noun*
see HAEMORRHAGE.

hemorrhoid *noun*
see HAEMORRHOID.

hemp *noun*
1. a) a tall, annual herb, originally from Asia, but now widely cultivated.
b) the stem fibres of this plant, used to make rope, etc.
2. Indian hemp. See MARIJUANA.
Word Family: **hempen,** *adjective.*

hen *noun*
a female bird, especially a female adult fowl.

henbane *noun*
a poisonous Mediterranean plant with an unpleasant smell and yellowish flowers.

hence *adverb*
1. for this reason.
2. from this time: 'a week *hence* we shall be in India'.
henceforth, henceforward *adverb*
from now on.

henchman *noun*
a follower or supporter, especially of a criminal, etc.

henna *noun*
1. a shrub from North Africa and Asia, the leaves of which contain a reddish-orange dye, used in cosmetics.
2. a colour varying from reddish-orange to coppery-brown.

henpecked *adjective*
dominated or nagged by a woman.

henry *noun*
the derived SI unit of inductance.
[after *J. Henry,* 1797-1878, an American physicist]

hep *adjective*
(*informal*) being up-to-date with current styles, especially in jazz.

heparin (*say* **heppa**-rin) *noun*
a substance produced by the liver which stops the blood clotting.

hepatic (*say* hep-**attik**) *adjective*
1. of or relating to the liver.
2. *Biology:* of or relating to liverworts.
Word Family: **hepatic,** *noun,* a) any medicine which acts on the liver, b) a liverwort.

hepatitis (*say* heppa-**tie**-tis) *noun*
an infectious, viral inflammation of the liver, causing fever and jaundice, usually in young adults.
[Greek *hepatos* of liver + ITIS]

heptagon (*say* **hepta**–gon) *noun*
any closed, plane figure with seven straight sides.
[Greek *hepta* seven + *gonia* corner]

her *pronoun*
plural is **them**
the objective form of the pronoun **she**: a) 'he hit *her*'; b) 'give the cake to *her*'.
her *possessive adjective*
plural is **their**
belonging to the female referred to: 'it is *her* cake'.

herald *noun*
a messenger.
herald *verb*
to proclaim or usher in: 'the change of government *heralded* many changes'.

heraldry (*say* **herr**'l–dree) *noun*
a) the art or science of tracing and recording the histories of families, their coats of arms, etc. b) any symbols or devices related to this process, such as coats of arms, armorial bearings, etc.
Word Family: **heraldic** (*say* her–**raldik**), *adjective.*

herb *noun*
a) a flowering plant with a non-woody stem above the ground. b) any plant of this type used in medicine, cooking, etc.
Word Family: **herbaceous** (*say* her–**bay**shus), *adjective,* leafy or non-woody; **herbal**, *adjective,* of or consisting of herbs; **herbalist**, *noun,* a person who uses herbs to treat diseases.
[Latin *herba* grass]

herbage (*say* **herb**ij) *noun*
1. any non-woody vegetation, especially that used for grazing.
2. the fleshy, often edible parts of plants.

herbarium (*say* her–**bair**ium) *noun*
plural is **herbaria** or **herbariums**
a) a collection of dried plants used for scientific study. b) the place in which such a collection is kept.

herbivorous (*say* her–**biv**verus) *adjective*
of or relating to an organism which eats plants.
Word Family: **herbivore** (*say* **herb**i–vor), *noun,* a herbivorous animal.
[Latin *herba* grass + *vorare* to devour]

herculean (*say* herkew–**lee**–an) *adjective*
having or requiring great strength.
[after *Hercules,* a hero in Greek and Roman mythology who was celebrated for his strength]

herd (1) *noun*
1. a group of animals, especially cattle.
2. a large group of people.
herd *verb*
to unite or assemble as a group.

herd (2) *verb*
to look after, drive or lead a group of cattle, sheep, etc.
Word Family: **herdsman, herd**, *nouns,* the keeper of a herd of cattle, sheep, etc.

herd testing
the testing of dairy herds to estimate milk production.
Word Family: **herd tester**, a person who tests dairy herds.

here (*say* heer) *adverb*
1. at, to or in this place: a) 'put it *here*'; b) 'come *here*'.
2. at this point: '*here* I would like to expand my argument'.
Phrases:
here and there, in or to various places.
neither here nor there, irrelevant or unimportant.
here *noun*
the here and now, this world or life.
hereabouts, hereabout *adverb*
in this general area.
hereafter *adverb*
1. after this in time, order, etc.
2. in the afterlife. *Word Family:* **hereafter**, *noun.*
hereby *adverb*
by this means.
herein *adverb*
in or into this place.
hereinafter *adverb*
afterwards in this document, etc.
hereinbefore *adverb*
before in this document, etc.
hereof *adverb*
of or about this.
hereto *adverb*
to this place, thing, etc.
heretofore *adverb*
before this time.
hereunder *adverb*
1. under this.
2. under authority of this.
hereupon *adverb*
upon this.
herewith *adverb*
1. together with this.
2. by means of this.

hereditary (*say* h'**reddi**–tree) *adjective*
derived or inherited from one's parents or ancestors: a) 'a *hereditary* disease'; b) 'a *hereditary* title'.
heredity (*say* h'**reddi**–tee) *noun*
a) the transmitting of characteristics from parents to offspring through the genes. b) the characteristics transmitted.
[Latin *heredis* of an heir]

heresy (*say* **herra**–see) *noun*
a) any belief or teaching which opposes an established doctrine, especially that of a church or religion. b) the holding of such opinions.
Word Family: **heretic**, *noun*, a person who holds such opinions; **heretical** (*say* h'**retti**–k'l), *adjective*, expressing heresy; **heretically**, *adverb*.
[Greek *hairesis* choice, a sect]

heritage (*say* **herri**–tij) *noun*
a position, possession or privilege which is inherited.

hermaphrodite (*say* her–**mafra**–dite) *noun*
Biology: an animal or plant with both male and female reproductive organs.
Word Family: **hermaphroditic** (*say* her–mafra–**dittik**), *adjective*.
[after *Hermaphrodites*, the son of Hermes and Aphrodite in Greek mythology, who became united in one body with a nymph]

hermetic (*say* her–**mettik**) *adjective*
airtight.
Word Family: **hermetically**, *adverb*.

hermit *noun*
a person who lives in seclusion, often for religious reasons.
Word Family: **hermitage** (*say* **her**–mit–ij), *noun*, a place of retreat or seclusion.
[Greek *eremites* of the desert]

hermit crab
any of various small organisms which protect themselves by living inside the cast–off shell of a mollusc.

hernia (*say* **her**–nee–a) *noun*
also called a **rupture**
Medicine: the protruding of an organ, such as the intestine, through the wall of its surrounding tissue.

hero (*say* **heero**) *noun*
plural is **heroes**
1. a man who displays courage or noble qualities.
2. the main male character in a story, play, film, etc.

heroic (*say* hee–**ro**–ik) *adjective*
1. brave, courageous or noble: 'a *heroic* rescue'.
2. adapted from or characteristic of classical epic poetry: '*heroic* couplets'.
Word Family: **heroically**, *adverb*; **heroics**, *plural noun*, melodramatic behaviour or language.
[Greek *heros*]

heroin (*say* **herro**–in) *noun*
a drug made from morphine, originally used as a sedative but now also used as a highly addictive hallucinatory drug.

heroine (*say* **herro**–in) *noun*
a female hero.

heroism (*say* **herro**–izm) *noun*
a) noble or heroic actions. b) the qualities of a hero or heroine.

heron *noun*
a wading bird with long legs, neck and beak.

hero–worship *noun*
an extreme admiration for another person.
Word Family: **hero–worship**, *verb*; **hero–worshipper**, *noun*.

herpes (*say* **her**–peez) *noun*
a viral disease which produces cold sores around the nose, mouth or genitals.
[Greek, a creeping infection]

Herr (*say* hair) *noun*
plural is **Herren**
the title for a German man.

herring *noun*
a coldwater fish which occurs in enormous shoals off Atlantic shores.

herringbone *noun*
a pattern consisting of rows of slanted parallel lines, with the direction of the slant alternating from row to row, used in textiles, embroidery, etc.

hers *possessive pronoun*
plural is **theirs**
belonging to her: 'the cake is *hers*'.

herself *pronoun*
1. the reflexive form of **she**: 'she washed *herself*'.
2. the emphatic form of **she**: 'she did it *herself*'.
3. her normal or usual self: 'for many weeks after the accident she was not *herself*'.

hertz (*say* hurts) *noun*
the SI unit of frequency, equal to one cycle per second.
[after *Heinrich Hertz*, 1857–94, a German physicist]

hertzian wave
see ELECTROMAGNETIC RADIATION.

hesitate (*say* **hezzi**–tate) *verb*
to show uncertainty or unwillingness.
Word Family: **hesitation**, *noun*; **hesitant**, *adjective*, slow due to uncertainty; **hesitantly**, *adverb*; **hesitance, hesitancy**, *noun*.
[Latin *haesitare* to stick fast, stammer]

hessian (*say* **hess**–ee–an) *noun*
also called **burlap**
a strong, coarse fabric made from jute, used for sacks, etc.

hetero– (*say* **hetta**–ro)
a prefix meaning other or different, as in *heterosexual*. Compare HOMO–.
[Greek]

heterodox (*say* **hetta**–ro–doks)
adjective
1. not agreeing with established or accepted beliefs, especially religious doctrine.
2. holding unorthodox opinions.
Word Family: **heterodoxy**, *noun*.
[HETERO– + Greek *doxa* opinion]

heterogeneous (*say* hetta–ro–**jeeni**–us)
adjective
composed of unlike parts.
Word Family: **heterogeneity** (*say* hetta–ro–je**nnee**–a–tee), *noun*.
[HETERO– + –GEN]

heterosexual
(*say* hetta–ro–**seks**–yew'l) *adjective*
being sexually attracted to members of the opposite sex.
Word Family: **heterosexual**, *noun*, a heterosexual person; **heterosexuality** (*say* hetta–ro–seks–yoo–**alli**–tee), *noun*.

heterotrophic (*say* hetta–ro–**troffik**)
adjective
(of an organism) unable to make proteins and carbohydrates from simple substances. Compare AUTOTROPHIC.
Word Family: **heterotroph**, *noun*.
[HETERO– + Greek *trophé* nourishment]

het–up *adjective*
(*informal*) anxious or worried.
[from *heated*]

heuristic (*say* hew–**ristik**) *adjective*
serving to find out or encourage investigation.
[Greek *heuriskein* to find]

hew *verb*
(**hewed, hewed** or **hewn, hewing**)
to cut or chop.
Word Family: **hewer**, *noun*.

hex *verb*
to bewitch or cast a spell on.
Word Family: **hex**, *noun*, a spell.

hexa–
a prefix meaning six, as in *hexagon*.
[from Greek]

hexagon *noun*
any closed, plane figure with six straight sides.
Word Family: **hexagonal** (*say* heks–**agga**–n'l), *adjective*.
[HEXA– + Greek *gonia* corner]

hexagram *noun*
a six-pointed star formed by two intersecting equilateral triangles, such as the Star of David.

hexahedron (*say* heksa–**hee**–dr'n)
noun
a solid or hollow body with six plane faces.
Word Family: **hexahedral**, *adjective*.
[HEXA– + Greek *hedra* a base]

hexameter (*say* heks–**ammita**) *noun*
Poetry: a line with six metrical feet.
Example: 'dowń in a deép dark hóle sat an óld cow múnching a beánstalk'.

hexane *noun*
Chemistry: a colourless, inflammable liquid (formula C_6H_{14}), the sixth member of the paraffin series and used as a fuel, especially in petrol.

hexose *noun*
any of a class of sugars containing six carbon atoms, such as glucose.

hey *interjection*
an exclamation of surprise, pleasure, etc., or used to attract attention.

heyday *noun*
the period of greatest prosperity, power, etc.

hey–presto *interjection*
an exclamation used at the end of some feat, trick or accomplishment.

hi *interjection*
an exclamation used as a greeting.

hiatus (*say* high–aytus) *noun*
a gap or interruption.
[Latin]

hibernal (*say* high–**bern**'l) *adjective*
of or relating to winter.
[from Latin]

hibernate (*say* **high**–ber–nate) *verb*
Biology: to spend winter in a resting or inactive state.
Usage: 'after her death he *hibernated* for many months' (= remained in seclusion).
Word Family: **hibernation**, *noun*.

Hibernian (*say* high–**bernian**) *adjective*
of Ireland, its people or their language.

hibiscus (*say* hibb–**iskus**) *noun*
a tropical shrub with brightly coloured flowers.
[Greek *hibiskos* marshmallow]

hiccup (*say* **hik**–up) **hiccough** *noun*
the short characteristic sound produced when the larynx closes involuntarily after a contraction of the diaphragm.
Word Family: **hiccup** (**hiccupped, hiccupping**), *verb.*

hick *noun*
(*informal*) an unsophisticated person, especially one from the country.

hickory (*say* **hikk**a–ree) *noun*
any of a group of deciduous American trees with feather–like leaves, some varieties of which bear nuts such as the pecan, and others produce a high–quality wood.

hide (1) *verb*
(**hid, hidden** or **hid, hiding**)
to prevent from being seen or discovered: 'he *hid* his true feelings'.
hide one's head, (*informal*) to be ashamed.

hide (2) *noun*
the skin of an animal, such as a calf.
neither hide nor hair, no sign or clue.

hide–and–seek *noun*
a children's game in which one person looks for all the other players, who hide.

hidebound *adjective*
being rigidly conventional in one's ideas.

hideous (*say* **hiddi**–us) *adjective*
ugly or repulsive.
Word Family: **hideously**, *adverb*; **hideousness**, *noun.*

hideout *noun*
a hiding place.

hiding *noun*
(*informal*) a flogging or thrashing.

hie (*say* high) *verb*
(**hied, hieing**)
an old word meaning to hasten.

hierarch (*say* **hire**–rark) *noun*
a person who has a high position of authority.
hierarchy *noun*
a body of persons or things arranged or organized according to rank, authority or importance: 'the Prime Minister is at the top of the government *hierarchy*'.
Word Family: **hierarchical** (*say* hire–**rar**ki–k'l), *adjective*, of or belonging to a hierarchy.
[Greek *hieros* sacred + *arkhos* leader]

hieratic (*say* hire–**rat**tik) *adjective*
of or relating to priests or the priesthood.

hieroglyph (*say* **high**–ra–glif) **hieroglyphic** *noun*
a picture, symbol, etc. used to represent a word or sound, as in the ancient Egyptian system of writing.
Word Family: **hieroglyphic**, *adjective.*
[Greek *hieros* sacred + *glyphé* a carving]

hi–fi *noun*
short form of **high fidelity**
a) a degree of fidelity in which the sounds reproduced by mechanical and electronic means are acceptably close to reality. b) a record–player and its equipment.

higgledy–piggledy *adverb*
(*informal*) in a disorganized or confused manner.
Word Family: **higgledy–piggledy**, *adjective.*

high (*rhymes with* my) *adjective*
1. tall or elevated: 'a *high* building'.
2. of great size, quantity or degree: 'the fever gave her a *high* temperature'.
3. shrill or sharp in tone, sound, etc.: 'a *high* voice'.
4. having a relatively complex structure: 'the primates are the *highest* order of mammals'.
5. (*informal*) being stimulated by a drug such as marijuana.
Usages:
a) 'he was promoted to a *high* rank' (= important).
b) 'the *high* priest offered a sacrifice' (= leading).
c) 'this meat is *high*' (= beginning to go bad).
d) 'a *high* standard of living' (= advanced, luxurious).
e) 'he has *high* political ideals' (= lofty).
high and mighty, arrogant or haughty.
high *adverb*
in or to a high position, degree, etc.: a) 'the plane flew *high* overhead'; b) 'aim *high* and you will succeed'.
Phrases:
high and dry, stranded or abandoned.
high and low, 'we searched *high and low* but could not find it' (= everywhere).

high *noun*
1. a high level: 'prices have reached a new *high*'.
2. *Weather:* an area of calm winds and high pressure from which winds blow anticlockwise in the Southern Hemisphere and clockwise in the Northern Hemisphere. Also called an **anticyclone**. Compare LOW (1).
Word Family: **highly**, *adverb.*

highbrow *adjective*
(*informal*) intellectual, especially in a pretentious way.
Word Family: **highbrow**, *noun.*

High Church
also called **Anglo-Catholic**
belonging to a section of the Church of England which stresses the importance of Catholic ritual, sacraments and the confessional. Compare LOW CHURCH.

high commissioner
the chief representative of a British Commonwealth country in the country of another member.

higher education
post-secondary and especially university education.

high explosive
a powerful, fast-acting explosive, such as trinitrotoluene (TNT).

high fidelity
see HI-FI.

high-flown *adjective*
extravagant or pretentious: '*high-flown* ideas'.

high frequency
a radio frequency in the range $3\text{–}30 \times 10^6$ hertz.
Word Family: **high-frequency**, *adjective.*

high-handed *adjective*
arrogant or overbearing.
Word Family: **high-handedly**, *adverb*; **high-handedness**, *noun.*

high jump
Athletics: jumping over a high bar.
for the high jump, 'you're *for the high jump*, my lad' (= going to be in severe trouble).

highland *noun*
1. any high land.
2. (*plural*) an area of hills or mountains.
Word Family: **highlander**, *noun*, a person from the highlands.

Highland fling
a Scottish Highland dance to the bagpipes.

Highland Games
the annual meetings of Scottish Highlanders for sports contests, e.g. tossing the caber, and also for Highland dancing and music.

high-level *adjective*
involving or carried out by persons of high position or rank: '*high-level* talks'.

high life, high living
luxurious living, as practised e.g. by the jet set.

highlight *noun*
1. an outstanding event, detail, etc.
2. *Art:* any of the most intensely lit details in a painting or photograph.
highlight *verb*
to emphasize or make prominent.

highly *adverb*
Word Family: see HIGH.

highly strung
acutely tense, nervous or sensitive.

high-minded *adjective*
characterized by morally lofty ideals or conduct.

highness *noun*
1. the state of being high.
2. (*capital*) a form of address used to members of royalty.

high-octane *adjective*
(of petrol) very efficient through having a high octane number.

high-pitched *adjective*
1. having a high pitch, such as a voice.
2. (of a discussion, etc.) intensely emotional.
3. (of a roof) having a steep slope.

high-rise *adjective*
multistorey.

highroad *noun*
1. a highway.
2. a direct or easy way: 'the *highroad* to success'.

high school
a secondary school, particularly in America.

high seas
the area of sea outside the boundary claimed by any country as territorial waters.

high-spirited *adjective*
bold, excitable or vivacious.

high spot
an outstanding feature in a programme, etc.

high tea
a late tea or early supper, often including a cooked dish.

high-tension *adjective*
Electronics: of or relating to electric cables, etc. carrying a high voltage.

high time
the time just before it is too late: 'it's *high time* that you finished that task'.

high treason
treason against the monarch or state.

high-water mark
the level along the shore reached by the sea at high tide.

highway *noun*
1. an old word and legal or official term for any public road: 'the *Highway* Code'.
2. a route or way: 'hard work is the *highway* to success'.

highwayman *noun*
(*formerly*) a robber on a highway, especially one on horseback.

hijack (*say* **high**-jak) *verb*
to steal or take over a travelling vehicle by force, for political or other reasons.
Word Family: **hijack, hijacking,** *nouns*; **hijacker,** *noun*, a person who hijacks.

hike *verb*
to walk long distances through the country.
Word Family: **hike,** *noun*; **hiker,** *noun*, a person who hikes.

hilarious (*say* hill-**airi**-us) *adjective*
1. extremely funny.
2. very merry.
Word Family: **hilariously,** *adverb*; **hilarity** (*say* hill-**arri**-tee), *noun*.
[Greek *hilaros* cheerful]

hill *noun*
1. a raised, rounded area of land, especially one less than 300 m high.
2. a pile or mound: 'an *anthill*'.
Word Family: **hilly,** *adjective*, a) steep, b) having many hills.

hillbilly *noun*
an unsophisticated person from the country, especially one from mountainous areas.

hillock *noun*
a small hill.
Word Family: **hillocky,** *adjective*.

hilt *noun*
the handle of a sword, dagger, etc.
to the hilt, 'he was armed *to the hilt*' (= fully, completely).

him *pronoun*
plural is **them**
the objective form of the pronoun **he**: a) 'I hit *him*'; b) 'give the cake to *him*'.

himself *pronoun*
1. the reflexive form of **he**: 'he washed *himself*'.
2. the emphatic form of **he**: 'he did it *himself*'.
3. his normal or usual self: 'for many weeks after the accident he was not *himself*'.

hind (1) (*rhymes with* find) *adjective*
(**hinder, hindmost** or **hindermost**)
being at the back: 'the *hind* legs'.

hind (2) (*rhymes with* find) *noun*
a female deer, especially a red deer more than three years old.

hinder (1) (*say* **hin**da) *verb*
to prevent or hamper.

hinder (2) (*say* **hine**-da) *adjective*
at the back: 'the *hinder* part of the boat'.

Hindi (*say* **hin**-dee) *noun*
a group of languages spoken by northern Indians.

hindmost, hindermost *adjective*
the superlative forms of **hind (1)**.

hindquarter (*say* hined-kworta) *noun*
either of the two back quarters of a carcass of beef, lamb, etc.

hindrance (*say* **hin**-dr'nce) *noun*
a) something which obstructs or hinders. b) the act of hindering.

hindsight *noun*
any insight into an event after it has occurred.

Hinduism (*say* **hin**doo-izm) *noun*
a religious, philosophical and cultural system widespread in India, having many gods and goddesses but regarding them as different forms of one supreme source of life.
Word Family: **Hindu,** *noun, adjective*.

hinge (*say* hinj) *noun*
a) the movable joint on which a door or gate swings. b) any similar device or part.
hinge *verb*
to attach by or fit with a hinge.
Usage: 'it all *hinges* on your decision' (= depends).

hinny *noun*
the offspring of a female ass and a stallion. Compare MULE.

hint *noun*
1. a subtle or slight suggestion.

2. a helpful suggestion: 'this book contains many gardening *hints*'.
Usage: 'there was a *hint* of envy in her voice' (= small amount).
Word Family: **hint**, *verb.*

hinterland *noun*
1. the remote areas of a country.
2. the land surrounding and served by a port or city.
[German]

hip (1) *noun*
Anatomy: the projecting part on each side of the body between the waist and thighs, formed by the side of the pelvic girdle and the upper part of the femur.

hip (2) *noun*
the ripe fruit of a rose.

hip (3) *interjection*
an exclamation used as a cheer or signal for cheers: '*hip, hip,* hurrah!'.

hippie, hippy *noun*
a person who rejects conventional social standards in favour of universal love and fellowship.
[from *hep*]

hippo *noun*
(*informal*) a hippopotamus.

hippodrome (*say* **hippa**-drome) *noun*
Ancient history: an arena for horseraces, etc.
[Greek *hippos* horse + *dromos* racecourse]

hippopotamus (*say* hippa-**potta**-mus) *noun*
plural is **hippopotamuses** or **hippopotami**
a heavy, thick-skinned, semi-aquatic African mammal with a broad head and muzzle.
[Greek *hippopotamos* a river-horse]

hipster *adjective*
(of trousers, skirts, etc.) hanging from the hips rather than the waist.

hire *verb*
1. to obtain the services of someone, or the temporary use of something, in return for payment.
2. to permit the temporary use or services of, for payment.
hire *noun*
a) the price asked or paid in exchange for hiring. b) the act of hiring.

hireling *noun*
(*use is often derogatory*) a person whose services may be hired.

hire-purchase *noun*
a system of buying by which a person pays a specified number of instalments and has the use of the object after the first payment.

hirsute (*say* **her**-suit) *adjective*
hairy.
[from Latin]

his *possessive adjective*
plural is **their**
belonging to him: 'it is *his* cake'.
his *possessive pronoun*
plural is **theirs**
belonging to him: 'the cake is *his*'.

hiss *verb*
1. to make a sharp, prolonged *s* sound.
2. to express disapproval or dislike by making this sound.
Word Family: **hiss**, *noun.*

hist *interjection*
a hissing sound used to attract attention, etc.

histamine (*say* **hista**-meen) *noun*
a crystalline substance found in animal and plant tissues and released in allergic reactions.
[Greek *histos* web + AMINE]

histogram *noun*
Maths: a graph using rectangles with different areas to show frequency distribution.
[Greek *histos* web + *gramma* something written]

histology (*say* hiss-**tolla**-jee) *noun*
the study of the tissues of living things.
Word Family: **histologist**, *noun.*
[Greek *histos* web + -LOGY]

historian (*say* hiss-**tawri**-un) *noun*
a person who writes or is expert in history.
[Greek *historia* a finding out]

historic (*say* hiss-**torrik**) *adjective*
memorable or sure of a place in history: 'the victory celebration was a *historic* occasion'.

historical (*say* hiss-**torri**-k'l) *adjective*
1. relating to history, especially as distinct from legend.
2. concerned or dealing with history.
Word Family: **historically**, *adverb.*

historicity (*say* hista-**rissa**-tee) *noun*
the proven historical truth of facts or events.

historiography
(*say* hiss-torri-**ogra**-fee) *noun*
the writing of the history of a particular subject.
Word Family: **historiographer**, *noun.*

history (*say* **hiss**-tree) *noun*
1. the study of the past.

2. a systematic and chronological record of past events relating to a particular period, country, etc.
3. a recorded or connected series of facts, especially concerning a particular group or subject.
Usages:
a) '*history* has repeated itself' (= the past).
b) 'she is a woman with a *history*' (= scandalous or extraordinary past).

histrionic (*say* hiss-tree-**onn**ik) *adjective*
1. relating to the theatre or acting.
2. theatrical or overdone.
histrionics *plural noun*
any exaggerated or dramatic behaviour.
Word Family: **histrionically**, *adverb.*
[Latin *histrionis* of an actor]

hit *verb*
(**hit, hitting**)
1. to strike: a) 'he *hit* the ball over the fence'; b) 'the car *hit* the pole'.
2. to move or drive by hitting: 'he *hit* the ball at least 100 metres'.
Usages:
a) 'those shares have *hit* an all-time low' (= reached).
b) 'every farmer in the district was *hit* by the drought' (= severely affected).
3. (*informal*) a) to begin to travel: 'let's *hit* the road'. b) to drink excessively: 'you can tell he's been *hitting* the bottle'.
Phrases:
hit it off, 'the children *hit it off* immediately' (= got on well together).
hit off, 'he *hit off* her gestures perfectly' (= imitated, reproduced).
hit on, hit upon, 'I have just *hit on* the perfect answer' (= discovered, thought of).
hit *noun*
1. an impact or blow.
2. anything which is very successful or popular: 'this song is sure to be a *hit*'.
3. (*informal*) an injection of a hard drug.
Word Family: **hitter,** *noun.*

hit-and-run *adjective*
(of a motorist) failing to stop after having an accident.

hitch *verb*
1. to fasten or tie, e.g. with a rope: 'he *hitched* the horse-box to the car'.
2. to become hooked or fastened: 'her jumper *hitched* on a nail as she went past'.
Usage: 'they were *hitched* in a registry office' (= married).
3. to pull up quickly or jerkily: 'she *hitched* up her loose stocking'.
4. to hitchhike.
hitch *noun*
1. a sudden lifting or pulling.
2. *Nautical:* any of various ways of fastening one rope to another or round a bollard, etc.
3. any difficulty or obstruction: 'there has been a *hitch* in our plans'.
4. (*informal*) a ride obtained by hitchhiking.

hitchhike *verb*
to travel by getting free rides in passing vehicles.
Word Family: **hitchhike,** *noun,* a ride obtained by hitchhiking; **hitchhiker,** *noun.*

hither (*say* hi*tha*) *adverb*
an old word meaning to or towards this place.
hither and thither, in different directions.

hitherto *adverb*
until now.

hit parade
also called the **charts**
a weekly list of the highest selling gramophone records of popular music.

hive (*rhymes with* five) *noun*
short form of **beehive**
1. a) a natural or artificial structure housing bees. b) a colony of bees living in this structure.
2. any busy or active place: 'the sewing room was a *hive* of activity'.
Word Family: **hive,** *verb,* to put or store in a hive.

hives *plural noun*
a skin condition, usually a form of allergy, which causes small red itchy spots.

hoar (*say* hor) *noun*
1. a hoarfrost.
2. a grey or white colour, as of the hair of an elderly person.
Word Family: **hoary,** *adjective.*

hoard (*say* hord) *noun*
a hidden store or fund.
Word Family: **hoard,** *verb,* to save and store up; **hoarder,** *noun.*
[Middle English *hord* treasure]

hoarding (*say* **hord**ing) *noun*
1. a temporary fence, such as one enclosing a construction site.
2. a board for advertisements or posters. Also called a **billboard.**

hoarfrost *noun*
the ice crystals which form on the ground instead of dew when the dewpoint is below freezing.

hoarse (*say* horse) *adjective*
having a rough or croaking sound: 'a *hoarse* cry'.
Word Family: **hoarseness**, *noun*; **hoarsely**, *adverb*.

hoary *adjective*
Word Family: see HOAR.

hoax (*rhymes with* cokes) *noun*
a mischievous trick or something intended to deceive.
Word Family: **hoax**, *verb*; **hoaxer**, *noun*.

hob *noun*
a shelf close to a fire for heating kettles, etc. or keeping them hot.

hobble *verb*
1. to walk with pain or difficulty.
2. to tie the legs of a horse to restrict its movement.
Word Family: **hobble**, *noun*, a) a limping walk, b) a rope used to hobble a horse.

hobbledehoy *noun*
an awkward or clumsy youth.

hobby *noun*
any activity which is done in one's spare time for personal enjoyment.

hobbyhorse *noun*
1. a stick with a horse's head and sometimes with wheels on the other end, for children to ride.
2. a favourite or obsessive interest: 'he was riding his *hobbyhorse* about the power of the trade unions'.

hobgoblin *noun*
Folklore: a mischievous goblin.

hobnail *noun*
a large nail with a wide head, used in the base of heavy shoes.

hobnob *verb*
(**hobnobbed, hobnobbing**)
to meet or associate in a friendly way, especially with one's social superiors.

hobo *noun*
a tramp.

Hobson's choice
an apparent choice which in fact does not exist, since there are no true alternatives.
[*Thomas Hobson* was a 17th-century hirer of horses who allocated them in strict rotation]

hock (1) *noun*
the joint above the fetlock in the lower part of the leg of a horse or other animal.

hock (2) *noun*
a light white wine from the Rhine valley.
[after *Hockheim* in the Rhineland]

hock (3) *verb*
(*informal*) to pawn.
Word Family: **in hock**, (informal) pawned.

hockey *noun*
a game for two teams of eleven using long-handled sticks with curved ends to try to hit the ball into the opponent's goal.

hocus-pocus *noun*
1. a phrase used in conjuring as a spell.
2. any elaboration or mystery intended to conceal the simplicity of something.

hod *noun*
1. a light, trough-shaped container on a long handle, for carrying bricks or mortar.
2. a coalscuttle.

hodgepodge *noun*
a hotchpotch.

hoe *noun*
any of various long-handled tools with prongs or a flat iron blade for loosening soil, etc.
Word Family: **hoe** (**hoed, hoeing**), *verb*.

hog *noun*
1. a) a pig. b) a castrated boar.
2. a greedy or dirty person.
go the whole hog, to do something thoroughly and completely.
hog *verb*
(**hogged, hogging**)
1. to take more than one's share of.
2. to cut a horse's mane short.
Word Family: **hoggish**, *adjective*, greedy or selfish; **hoggishly**, *adverb*.

hogget *noun*
short form is **hogg**
a) a young sheep, especially up to the age of one year. b) the meat from such an animal.

hogmanay (*say* hogma-nay) *noun*
Scottish: New Year's Eve.

hogsback *noun*
Geology: a long, sharply crested ridge.

hogshead *noun*
a) an old unit of volume for alcoholic drinks, usually equal to about 240 l.
b) a large cask of this volume.

hogtie *verb*
(**hogtied, hogtying**)
1. to tie all the feet of an animal, etc. together.
2. to restrict the movement of.

hogwash (*say* **hog**–wosh) *noun*
(*informal*) nonsense.

hoi polloi (*say* hoy pa–**loy**)
(*use is derogatory*) the common people. [Greek, the many]

hoist (*rhymes with* moist) *verb*
to lift or raise, especially by using a mechanical device.
hoist *noun*
any of various lifting devices using a pulley or a hydraulic system.

hoity–toity *adjective*
haughty.

hokey–pokey *noun*
hocus–pocus.

hokum *noun*
(*informal*) nonsense.

hold (1) *verb*
(**held, holding**)
1. to have and keep, especially in the hands.
2. to contain or be filled with: 'how much liquid will that jar *hold*?'.
3. to be valid or have force: 'that rule does not *hold* in the senior school'.
Usages:
a) 'try to *hold* them here until the police arrive' (= detain).
b) 'he has *held* the office of President for 37 years' (= occupied).
c) 'that chair will not *hold* your weight' (= sustain).
d) 'I *hold* you all equally responsible' (= consider).
e) '*hold* still while I brush your hair' (= stay).
f) 'the court *held* that he was guilty' (= decided, ruled).
Phrases:
hold forth, 'he *held forth* for some hours about his experiences' (= talked).
hold good, to be valid.
hold one's hand, to delay action until a better moment.
hold one's head high, to face the world proudly and confidently.
hold one's own, 'I thought our team *held their own* very well' (= kept their position).
hold one's tongue, to refrain from speaking.
hold out, a) 'will our supplies *hold out*?' (= last); b) 'stop *holding out* and tell us the news' (= keeping something back); c) 'he *held out* for a higher price' (= refused to yield without).
hold over, 'the meeting has been *held over* till Christmas' (= postponed).
hold up, a) 'what *held* the train *up*?' (= delayed); b) 'the bank was *held up* by a masked gunman' (= robbed).
Word Family: **hold–up**, *noun*.
hold water, 'your excuses don't *hold water*' (= stand up to examination).
hold with, 'father does not *hold with* loud music' (= approve of).
hold *noun*
1. a) the act of holding or gripping: 'his *hold* on the rope loosened and he fell'. b) something to hold a thing by, such as a handle.
2. a strong influence or power: 'the union has a *hold* on most workers in the trade'.
Word Family: **holder**, *noun*, a person or thing that holds.

hold (2) *noun*
Nautical: the inner part of a ship below the deck, where goods are carried.

holdall (*say* **hold**–awl) *noun*
a light bag or case.

holding *noun*
1. (*plural*) property owned, especially stocks and shares.
2. *Law:* the decision of a court on a question of law.

hole *noun*
1. an opening or hollow in something solid.
Usages:
a) 'your argument is full of *holes*' (= faults).
b) (*informal*) 'this town is a real *hole*' (= dirty or depressing place).
2. an awkward situation: 'his gambling has got him into a financial *hole*'.
3. *Golf:* a) a small tin–lined hole in the ground, into which the ball must be hit. b) the distance between a tee and the green.
hole *verb*
1. to make a hole or holes in.
2. to put in a hole: 'the golfer *holed* his ball in four strokes'.
hole up, 'the guerrillas were *holed up* in the mountains' (= hidden, secluded).

hole–and–corner *adjective*
surreptitious or underhand: 'a *hole–and–corner* conspiracy'.

holiday (*say* **holli**–day) *noun*
1. any day on which work or business ceases, especially in honour of a person or past event.

2. (*plural*) a period of rest from work, school, etc., usually a specified number of weeks in a year. Also called a **vacation**.
Word Family: **holiday**, *verb*.
[HOLY + DAY]

holier-than-thou *adjective*
smug or self-righteous.

holiness (*say* **ho**-lee-ness) *noun*
1. the state of being holy.
2. *Roman Catholic:* (*capital*) a title of respect for the Pope.

hollow (*say* **holl**-o) *adjective*
not solid or filled: 'a *hollow* barrel'.
Usages:
a) 'it was a *hollow* victory' (= worthless, vain).
b) 'his *hollow* thanks were worse than no thanks at all' (= insincere).
c) 'his *hollow* cheeks told me he was ill' (= sunken, indented).
d) 'there was a *hollow* thud on the roof' (= dull, echoing).
hollow *noun*
1. an empty space or gap.
2. a concave or indented area: 'they sat in a leafy *hollow* near the river'.
Word Family: **hollow**, *verb*, to make or become hollow; **hollowness**, *noun*; **hollow**, *adverb*, (informal) thoroughly; **hollowly**, *adverb*.

holly *noun*
an evergreen shrub with red berries and sharp, pointed, shiny leaves used as a Christmas decoration.

hollyhock *noun*
a tall plant with spikes of many large, brightly coloured flowers.

holmium (*say* **holmi**-um) *noun*
element number 67, a rare-earth metal which forms magnetic compounds. See LANTHANIDE.
See CHEMICAL ELEMENTS in grey pages.

holocaust (*say* **holla**-kawst) *noun*
any great destruction or loss of life.
[Greek *holokaustos* burnt whole]

Holocene (*say* **hollo**-seen) *noun*
Geology: see QUATERNARY.
Word Family: **Holocene**, *adjective*.
[Greek *holos* whole + *kainos* modern]

holster *noun*
a leather case for a pistol, attached to a belt or saddle.

holt (*rhymes with* bolt) *noun*
the lair of certain animals, especially the otter and badger.

holus-bolus *adverb*
all at once.

holy *adjective*
1. sacred: 'a *holy* day'.
2. pious: 'a *holy* person'.

Holy Communion
Christian: see COMMUNION.

Holy Spirit
also called the **Holy Ghost**
Christian: the third person in the Trinity.

homage (*say* **hommij**) *noun*
an act or expression of respect or honour.

homburg *noun*
a man's felt hat, with a lengthwise dent in the crown and a narrow, often upturned brim.
[the German spa where it became fashionable]

home *noun*
1. the place where one lives, belongs or was born: a) 'he left *home* at 19 to see the world'; b) 'Australia is the *home* of the kangaroo'.
2. a house, flat, etc.: 'the planners aimed to build 30 000 new *homes*'.
3. an institution which provides care and services: 'a *home* for the aged'.
4. a place or region used as headquarters or a base for activities, etc.
5. *Baseball:* the base at which the batter stands, and the last to be touched when completing a run around the diamond.
at home, a) 'we are not *at home* this weekend' (= receiving visitors); b) 'they always make guests feel *at home*' (= at ease).
home *adjective*
connected with one's home or country: 'the *Home* Secretary'.
Usage: 'the team plays at *home* next week' (= at the club's ground).
home *adverb*
1. in or to one's home or country: 'please come straight *home* after the party'.
2. to the point aimed at: 'he drove the last nail *home* with a sigh of relief'.
Usage: 'his criticism of her work really struck *home*' (= effectively, to the heart).
bring home to, 'we could not *bring home to* him the folly of his plan' (= make realize or understand).
home *verb*
1. to go home.
2. to direct or be directed towards a target or destination.

home body
a person who likes or prefers to be at home.

Home Counties
the English counties which surround London, such as Surrey and Hertfordshire.

home help
a person employed for cleaning one's home, especially a paid employee of a local council who helps the aged or infirm with their housework.

homeland *noun*
one's native land.

homely *adjective*
1. simple and plain: '*homely* food'.
2. *American:* not attractive: 'a *homely* girl'.

home rule
1. the right of internal self-government granted to a region of a state.
2. *History:* (*capitals*) this right for Ireland.

home run
also called a **homer**
Baseball: a non-stop run around all the bases, made by a batter who has hit the ball a long distance.

homesick *adjective*
depressed from a longing for home.
Word Family: **homesickness**, *noun.*

homespun *adjective*
spun or made at home: 'a *homespun* jumper'.
Usage: 'his *homespun* philosophy of life' (= simple, unrefined).

homestead (*say* **home**–sted) *noun*
the house and outbuildings on a farm or property.

home straight
the straight part of a racetrack leading to the finishing line.

home truth
a statement of fact about a person, told in the knowledge that it will be painful or difficult to accept.

homeward *adjective*
towards home.
Word Family: **homewards, homeward,** *adverb.*

homework *noun*
a school task for a student to do at home.
do one's homework, 'the planners produced an impractical transport scheme because they hadn't *done their homework*' (= carried out adequate research).

homicide (*say* **hommi**–side) *noun*
the crime of killing a person.
Word Family: **homicidal** (*say* **hommi**–sigh–d'l), *adjective*, of or having a tendency towards homicide; **homicidally**, *adverb.*
[Latin *homo* man + *caedere* to kill]

homily (*say* **hommi**–lee) *noun*
a) a sermon. b) any moralizing talk.
Word Family: **homiletic** (*say* hommi–**lettik**), **homiletical**, *adjective.*
[Greek *homilia* a communion]

homing pigeon
a pigeon trained to fly home from wherever it is released, especially in competitions.

hominy (*say* **hom**–in–ee) *noun*
American: the hulled and ground kernels of maize, boiled for eating.

Homo (1) *noun*
plural is **Homines** (*say* **hommi**–neez)
any member of the genus which includes extinct and modern man.
Homo sapiens
the scientific name for the species of man which exists at present.
[Latin, wise man]

homo (2) *noun*
(*informal*) a homosexual.

homo–
a prefix meaning the same, as in *homosexual.* Compare HETERO–.
[from Greek]

homoeopathy
(*say* ho–mee–**oppa**–thee) *noun*
the method of treating diseases using minute doses of a substance, often herbal, which normally produces symptoms like those of the disease being treated. Compare ALLOPATHY.
Word Family: **homoeopath** (*say* ho–mee–o–path), **homoeopathist,** *nouns*; **homoeopathic** (*say* ho–mee–o–**path**–ik), *adjective.*
[Greek *homoios* similar + *pathos* suffering]

homoeostasis (*say* ho–mee–o–**stay**sis) *noun*
Biology: the process of maintaining physiological equilibrium in the functions, chemical composition, etc. of an organism.
[Greek *homoios* like + *stasis* standing still]

homogeneous (*say* ho–mo–jeeni–us) *adjective*
composed of like parts.

Word Family: **homogeneously**, *adverb*; **homogeneity** (*say* ho-mo-jinee-a-tee), *noun*.
[HOMO- + -GEN]

homogenize (*say* ha-**mojj**a-nize)
homogenise *verb*
to make homogeneous or uniform in texture, consistency, etc.
Word Family: **homogenization**, *noun*.

homoiothermic
(*say* ha-moyo-**thermik**) *adjective*
see WARM-BLOODED.
[Greek *homoios* like + *thermé* heat]

homologous (*say* ho**molla**-gus) *adjective*
similar in position, shape, etc.
[HOMO- + Greek *logos* proportion]

homologous series
Chemistry: a series of organic compounds showing a regular gradation in physical and chemical properties, and capable of being represented by a general molecular formula.

homologue (*say* **homma**-log) *noun*
in America spelt **homolog**
Chemistry: any member of a homologous series.

homonym (*say* **homma**-nim) *noun*
a word having the same sound, and sometimes spelling, as another but a different meaning, as *sale* and *sail*.
[HOMO- + Greek *onyma* name]

homosexual (*say* ho-mo-**seks**-yew'l) *adjective*
being sexually attracted to members of one's own sex.
Word Family: **homosexual**, *noun*, a homosexual person; **homosexuality** (*say* ho-mo-seks-yoo-**alli**-tee), *noun*.

homunculus (*say* ho**munk**-yoolus) *noun*
plural is **homunculi**
a fully formed miniature human being, such as a dwarf or pygmy.
[Latin]

homy, homey *adjective*
comfortable and friendly.

hone *noun*
a very fine abrasive stone used for sharpening razors, etc.
Word Family: **hone**, *verb*, to smoothe on or as if on a hone.

honest (*say* **onn**est) *adjective*
truthful or free from deceit or pretence.
Word Family: **honesty**, *noun*; **honestly**, *adverb*.
[Latin *honestus* honourable]

honey (*rhymes with* funny) *noun*
1. a thick, sweet liquid produced by bees from nectar for food.
2. any sweet person, thing or quality.

honeycomb (*say* **hunnee**-kome) *noun*
a structure of wax made by honeybees, containing rows of cells in which honey and pollen are stored and eggs and larvae develop.
honeycomb *verb*
to pierce with many holes: 'a hill *honeycombed* with caves'.

honeydew *noun*
1. a sweet, sticky substance excreted by aphids.
2. a sweet musk melon with a smooth pale green rind and slightly darker flesh.

honeyed (*say* **hunn**id) *adjective*
containing or full of honey.

honeymoon *noun*
1. the holiday taken by a newly married couple.
2. any early, harmonious period in a relationship, union, etc.

honeysuckle *noun*
any of various climbing shrubs with small, fragrant, trumpet-shaped, yellow or pink flowers.

honk *noun*
a harsh, deep sound, such as the cry of a goose, the horn of a car, etc.
Word Family: **honk**, *verb*.

honky-tonk *noun*
1. an early form of ragtime piano music, characterized by tinny echoing notes.
2. *American:* a cheap dance hall or nightclub.

honorarium (*say* onna-**rair**ium) *noun*
plural is **honoraria** or **honorariums**
a voluntary payment for professional services where no fee is claimed or claimable.

honorary (*say* **onna**-ra-ree) *adjective*
given or received as an honour, without the usual duties, payment, etc.: 'he remained *honorary* chairman despite his retirement'.

honorific (*say* onna-**riffik**) *noun*
any title or term of respect, such as Sir, Doctor, Your Majesty, etc.

honour (*say* **onna**) *noun*
in America spelt **honor**
1. a respect or esteem.
2. an expression or display of respect: 'the doctor was received with *honour* in his home town'.

3. anything which brings respect or credit: 'this student is an *honour* to the school'.
4. a good or noble character: 'a man of *honour*'.
5. a privilege: 'it is an *honour* to serve you'.
6. *Education:* a) a high grade in passing an examination. b) (*plural*) a course or degree in which such results are necessary to graduate: 'an *honours* degree in Law'.
7. *Cards:* any of the five highest cards in each suit.
8. a title or decoration awarded by a monarch or government: 'he picked up an O.B.E. in the New Year *honours* list'.
Phrases:
do the honours, 'will you *do the honours* and carve the roast?' (= act as the host).
on, upon one's honour, 'you are *on your honour* not to tell anybody' (= bound by a promise or sense of responsibility).
honour *verb*
to show respect or honour for.
Usage: 'the bank refused to *honour* his cheque' (= accept and pay on).
[from Latin]

honourable (*say* **onn**era-b'l) *adjective*
in America spelt **honorable**
1. having high principles: 'an *honourable* man'.
2. based on the principles of honour: 'an *honourable* agreement'.
3. worthy of honour: 'the victory was an *honourable* achievement'.
Word Family: **honourably**, *adverb*; **honourableness**, *noun*.

hood (*say* h**u**d) *noun*
1. a soft, loose covering for the head and neck.
2. something which has the shape, position or function of a hood, such as the canvas roof of a pram.
3. (*informal*) a hoodlum.
Word Family: **hood**, *verb*, to cover with or as if with a hood.

-hood (*say* h**u**d)
a suffix indicating: a) state, condition or character, as in *manhood*; b) a group with a particular character, as in *neighbourhood*.

hoodlum (*say* **hood**-l'm) *noun*
a gangster or violent, destructive youth.

hoodoo (*say* **hoo**-doo) *noun*
1. *American:* bad luck.
2. voodoo.

hoodwink (*say* **hud**-wink) *verb*
to deceive or trick.

hooey (*say* **hoo**-ee) *noun*
(*informal*) nonsense.

hoof *noun*
plural is **hoofs** or **hooves**
the hard covering encasing the foot of some animals, such as the ox and horse.
on the hoof, (of livestock) alive.
hoof *verb*
hoof it, (*informal*) to walk.

hook (*say* h**u**k) *noun*
1. any of various curved or angular devices for pulling or grasping: 'a *fishhook*'.
2. something which has the shape or function of a hook, such as a sharply curved part or angle.
3. *Sport:* a stroke in which the ball curves away behind or to the side of the player. Also called a **pull**. Compare SLICE.
4. *Boxing:* a short, swinging blow made with the arm bent.
Phrases:
by hook or by crook, by any means, however desperate.
hook, line and sinker, completely.
off the hook, (*informal*) freed from blame, a difficulty, etc.
Word Family: **hook**, *verb*, a) to grasp or catch with or as if with a hook, b) (Sport) to hit a hook; **hooked**, *adjective*, a) having or resembling a hook, b) (informal) addicted.

hookah (*say* h**u**k-ah) *noun*
also called a **water-pipe**
an Oriental tobacco pipe with a long tube which passes through a container of water to cool the smoke.
[from Arabic]

hook and eye
a fastener for clothes consisting of a hook which catches onto a loop of thread or wire.

hooker *noun*
1. a person or thing that hooks, such as a rugby player whose task is to hook the ball from the scrum.
2. (*informal*) a prostitute.

hook-up (*say* **huk**-up) *noun*
a connection or joining, e.g. between several radio or television stations to broadcast a special programme.
Usage: 'there is a *hook-up* between businessmen and illegal gambling in this town' (= connection).

hookworm (*say* **huk**–werm) *noun*
a parasitic worm with hooks in its mouth, infesting the intestine of man and other animals.

hooky (*say* **huk**–ee) **hookey** *noun*
play hooky, (*informal*) to stay away from school without permission.

hooligan (*say* **hoo**–lig'n) *noun*
a young ruffian.
Word Family: **hooliganism**, *noun.*

hoop *noun*
a circular band or ring, sometimes used to support or strengthen something.
Word Family: **hoop**, *verb*, to fasten or encircle with a hoop.

hoopla *noun*
a game in which small hoops are thrown in an attempt to encircle objects offered as prizes.

hoopoe (*say* **hoo**–poo) *noun*
a pink bird with black and white wings and tail and a fan–like crest.

hoot *verb*
1. a) to make the hollow cry of an owl. b) to make a similar sound, especially in disapproval or derision.
2. to sound a horn.
hoot *noun*
1. the act or sound of hooting.
2. (*informal*) an amusing or funny thing.
Word Family: **hooter**, *noun*, something which hoots, such as a horn.

Hoover *noun*
a vacuum cleaner.
[a trademark]

hooves *plural noun*
a plural of **hoof**.

hop (1) *verb*
(hopped, hopping)
a) (of a person) to jump on one foot.
b) (of an animal) to jump on all feet.
Usage: 'he *hopped* onto the bus as it set off' (= jumped).
hop *noun*
1. a light springy jump, especially on one foot.
Usage: 'from here it's only a short *hop* to Asia' (= trip, distance).
2. (*informal*) a dance.
on the hop, a) 'he was caught *on the hop*' (= unprepared); b) 'they are always *on the hop*' (= moving, busy).

hop (2) *noun*
1. a twining plant with cone–like flowers.
2. (*plural*) the dried, ripe flowers of this plant, used in brewing, medicine, etc.

hope *verb*
to wish for or look forward to what one anticipates or expects.
hope *noun*
1. a wish that what is anticipated or expected will occur.
2. a reason for confidence, hope or expectation: 'there is little *hope* that the child will be found'.
3. a person or thing in which one places confidence: 'she is the *hope* of the family'.
Word Family: **hopeful**, *adjective*, full of hope or expectation; **hopefully**, *adverb*; **hopefulness**, *noun*; **hopeless**, *adjective*, a) allowing no hope, b) impossible.

hopper *noun*
a funnel–shaped device in which materials, such as grain, are stored and released through the bottom.

hopping mad
very angry.

hopsack *noun*
a fabric woven from various fibres, with yarns running in pairs, used for chair–covers, etc.
[originally of hemp to make *sacks* for *hops*]

hopscotch *noun*
a children's game in which each player tosses an object into a pattern of squares drawn on the ground, then hops along the pattern to retrieve it.

hop, skip and jump
also called the **hop, step and jump** and **triple jump**
Athletics: a contest in which competitors must get as far as possible by making a hop, a step and a jump in a continuous movement.

horde *noun*
a large group of people, animals or insects.

horehound *noun*
a herb with silky leaves and small, white flowers, containing a bitter liquid used in medicine.

horizon (*say* ha–**rye**–z'n) *noun*
1. the apparent boundary of the sea or flat land with the sky. Also called the **apparent horizon** or **visible horizon**.
2. a limit or range, as of knowledge, experience, thinking, etc.

3. *Geology:* any of the layers found in a vertical section of soil, such as a layer of rock containing fossils, etc.
[Greek *horizon* (*kyklos*) limiting circle]

horizontal (*say* horri–**zont**'l) *adjective*
parallel to or in the plane of the horizon.
Word Family: **horizontal**, *noun*, a horizontal line, plane or position; **horizontally**, *adverb*.

horizontal bar
a fixed bar used for various gymnastic exercises, such as swinging.

hormone *noun*
Biology: an organic substance produced in one part of an organism and transported to another part where it controls various metabolic functions.
Word Family: **hormonal** (*say* hor–**mo**–n'l), *adjective*.
[Greek *hormon* setting in motion]

horn *noun*
1. a hollow growth on the head of certain animals, consisting of a tough, fibrous layer over a permanent bony core. Compare ANTLER.
2. an object which is made of horn or similar substance.
3. *Music:* a coiled, brass, wind instrument in which the sound produced is controlled by the player's lips.
4. a warning device such as a foghorn or car–horn.
Word Family: **horn**, *verb*, a) to wound with a horn, b) to provide with a horn or horns; **horny**, *adjective*, a) hard like a horn, b) having or consisting of a horn.

hornbill *noun*
any of various tropical birds with a very large bill surrounded by a hard, often large, projection.

hornet *noun*
a very large wasp with brown markings and an extremely painful sting.
a hornet's nest, 'the politician's tactless speech stirred up ***a hornet's nest***' (= noisy opposition).

hornpipe *noun*
a) a lively dance for one person, originally performed by sailors. b) the music for such a dance.

horny *adjective*
Word Family: see HORN.

horology (*say* horolla–jee) *noun*
the science of measuring time, making clocks, etc.
[Greek *hora* hour + –LOGY]

horoscope (*say* **horra**–skope) *noun*
Astrology: a) an analysis of the position of the stars at a particular place and time, e.g. at a person's birth, for predicting future events or analysing character. b) a diagram of this.
[Greek *horoskopos* one who observes the hour of a birth]

horrendous (*say* ha–**rendus**) *adjective*
dreadful or horrible.
[from Latin]

horrible (*say* **horri**–b'l) *adjective*
1. causing horror: 'the ***horrible*** scene in the film gave me nightmares'.
2. extremely unpleasant or offensive.
Word Family: **horribly**, *adverb*.

horrid *adjective*
extremely unpleasant.
Word Family: **horridly**, *adverb*.
[Latin *horridus* shaggy, uncouth]

horror (*say* horra) *noun*
1. an intense feeling of repugnance and fear.
Usage: 'she has a ***horror*** of most insects' (= extreme dislike).
2. something which causes dislike or horror.
Word Family: **horrify** (*say* **horri**–fie), (**horrified, horrifying**), *verb*; **horrific** (*say* ho–**riffik**), *adjective*, horrible.
[Latin]

hors d'oeuvre (*say* or **derv**)
any of a variety of appetizers such as olives, curried eggs, etc., served before the main meal.
[French, apart from the main work]

horse *noun*
1. a four–legged, solid–hoofed mammal with a long mane and tail.
2. a male horse as distinct from the female (called a mare).
3. a device or frame on which one sits, exercises, etc. or on which something is supported: a) 'a vaulting ***horse***'; b) 'a clothes ***horse***'.
Phrases:
a dark horse, a person whose abilities are not clearly seen or known.
back the wrong horse, to support what turns out to be an unsuccessful cause, especially in politics.
from the horse's mouth, from an authoritative source.
get on one's high horse, to act haughtily.
hold one's horses, to restrain oneself.
look a gift–horse in the mouth, see GIFT–HORSE.

horse *verb*
an old word meaning to provide with, or to mount or go on, a horse.
horse about, horse around, to act or play roughly or boisterously.
Word Family: **horsy, horsey,** *adjective,* a) horse-like in appearance or manner, b) concerned with or devoted to horses; **horsemanship,** *noun,* the art or skill of caring for and riding horses.

horseback *adverb*
on a horse: 'I like riding on *horseback*'.

horse-box *noun*
a closed van which can be hitched on to a motor vehicle for transporting a horse to a hunt, racecourse, etc.

horse chestnut
1. a large shade-tree, unrelated to the sweet chestnut, with white flowers in May.
2. the bitter nut from this tree, eaten by cattle, etc. (but not by horses), and used as a conker.
3. a smaller tree with red flowers.

horsehair *noun*
the coarse hair taken from a horse's tail or mane, used to stuff mattresses, etc.

horse latitudes
the areas of calm or light winds between the trade winds and the westerly winds in subtropical regions.

horseplay *noun*
any noisy or rough play.

horsepower *noun*
a unit of power, equal to about 746 watt.

horseradish *noun*
a white root with an extremely strong smell and taste, usually finely chopped and used in sauces, etc.

horse sense
(*informal*) good or practical sense.

horseshoe *noun*
1. a U-shaped piece of iron, nailed to the bottom of a horse's hoof to protect it.
2. something of this shape, often regarded as a symbol of good luck.

horsewhip *noun*
a long whip used in driving horsed vehicles.
horsewhip *verb*
(horsewhipped, horsewhipping)
to lash a person with a horsewhip.

horst *noun*
also called a **block mountain**
a block of the earth's crust raised between two faults.

horsy *adjective*
Word Family: see HORSE.

horticulture (*say* **horti**-kulcher) *noun*
the science or study of cultivating and maintaining garden plants.
Word Family: **horticultural** (*say* horti-**kulcha**-r'l), *adjective*; **horticulturist,** *noun.*
[Latin *hortus* garden + CULTURE]

hosanna (*say* ho-**zanna**) *noun*
a cry of praise to God.
[Hebrew *hoshi'ahnna* save, pray]

hose (*say* hoze) *noun*
1. a flexible tube for carrying or spraying water, etc.
2. a trade term for hosiery.
Word Family: **hose,** *verb,* to spray or wet with water, etc. from a hose.

hosiery (*say* **ho**-zha ree) *noun*
clothing, such as socks, stockings, etc. for the feet or legs.
Word Family: **hosier,** *noun,* a person who makes or sells hosiery.

hospice (*say* **hoss**-piss) *noun*
1. a house for travellers, etc. especially one kept by a religious order.
2. a nursing home for patients in the later stages of terminal illnesses such as cancer.

hospitable (*say* hoss-**pitta**-b'l) *adjective*
giving a warm welcome to guests or strangers.
Usage: 'she is quite *hospitable* to new ideas' (= open, receptive).
Word Family: **hospitably,** *adverb*; **hospitality** (*say* hospi-**talli**-tee), *noun.*
[Latin *hospes* a host, a guest]

hospital (*say* **hoss**-pitt'l) *noun*
a place where sick or injured people are given medical treatment.
Usage: 'a dolls' *hospital*' (= repair shop).
Word Family: **hospitalize, hospitalise,** *verb,* to place in a hospital for treatment; **hospitalization,** *noun.*
[Latin *hospitalis* relating to guests]

host (1) (*rhymes with* most) *noun*
1. a person who entertains guests.
2. *Biology:* an organism on or in which a parasite lives.
Word Family: **host,** *verb,* to entertain; **hostess,** *noun,* a female host.

host (2) (*rhymes with* most) *noun*
1. a large group of people or things: 'a *host* of angels'.
2. an old word meaning an army.

host (3) (*rhymes with* most) *noun*
Christian: (*capital*) the consecrated bread used in the Eucharist.
[Latin *hostia* a victim]

hostage (*say* **host**ij) *noun*
a person held or given as a pledge that certain actions will be performed.
[Latin *obses*]

hostel (*say* **hoss**–t'l) *noun*
a supervised house which gives accommodation at low rents, e.g. for students, nurses, etc.
[Old French]

hostile (*say* **hoss**–tile) *adjective*
1. unfriendly or showing a desire to fight.
2. of or relating to an enemy: '*hostile* territory'.
hostility (*say* hoss–**tilli**–tee) *noun*
1. the state of being hostile.
2. (*plural*) open warfare: '*hostilities* started along the border'.
Word Family: **hostilely**, *adverb.*
[from Latin]

hot *adjective*
1. having or producing a high temperature.
Usages:
a) 'beware of her *hot* temper' (= passionate, violent).
b) 'a *hot* curry' (= very spicy).
c) 'they were *hot* on our trail' (= very close).
d) 'this town is *hot* for criminals' (= dangerous).
e) '*hot* pink' (= bright).
2. (*informal*) a) skilled or clever: 'not too *hot* at maths'. b) fresh: '*hot* off the press'. c) stolen: 'a *hot* car'.
3. radioactive, especially to a degree injurious to health.
Phrases:
hot under the collar, angry.
in hot water, in trouble.
not so hot, (*informal*) disappointing.
Word Family: **hotly**, *adverb*; **hotness**, *noun.*

hot air
(*informal*) any empty or pretentious talk or writing.

hotbed *noun*
a place favouring rapid growth, especially of something bad: 'a *hotbed* of vice'.

hot–blooded *adjective*
passionate or excitable.

hotchpotch *noun*
a jumble.

hot dog
a hot frankfurter usually served in a long bread roll.

hotel *noun*
a building providing accommodation for paying guests.

hotfoot *adverb*
in great haste: 'she arrived *hotfoot* from the scene of the accident'.
hotfoot *verb*
hotfoot it, to hurry.

hot–headed *adjective*
impetuous or rash.
Word Family: **hothead**, *noun*; **hot–headedness**, *noun.*

hothouse *noun*
a greenhouse maintained at a high temperature.

hot line
a direct telephone link open for instant contact between the heads of major governments in case of an emergency.

hotness *noun*
Word Family: see HOT.

hotplate *noun*
a heated metal plate, usually on a stove, on which food is cooked or heated.

hot–pot *noun*
a lamb and vegetable stew cooked in a casserole, e.g. Lancashire hot–pot.

hot rod
an old car which has been modified to increase its speed.

hot seat
(*informal*) a position involving difficulties or danger.

hound (*rhymes with* round) *noun*
1. a dog, especially one trained to hunt by following a scent.
2. (*informal*) an addict or enthusiast.
hound *verb*
to pursue or harass relentlessly: 'the landlord has been *hounding* us for the rent'.

hound's–tooth *noun*
a pattern of contrasting jagged checks.

hour (*say* our) *noun*
1. a unit of time equal to 60 minutes, one 24th part of a day.
2. (*plural*) the usual or specific time for: 'office *hours*'.
Usages:
a) 'what is the *hour*?' (= time of day).
b) 'the *hour* of his glory' (= moment).
Word Family: **hourly**, *adjective*, of, relating to or occurring every hour.
[Greek and Latin]

hourglass *noun*
an instrument for measuring time, consisting of two glass bulbs joined by a narrow passage through which sand or mercury runs from one bulb to the other in a set time.

house *noun*
1. a) a building or part of a building where people live. b) a household.
2. a building or establishment for a particular purpose: a) 'a *house* of worship'; b) 'a gambling *house*'; c) 'a publishing *house*'.
3. a family considered as a line of descent: 'the *house* of Stuart'.
4. a) a theatre. b) the audience in a theatre.
5. a legislative or advisory group: 'the *House* of Commons'.
6. *Astrology:* see ZODIAC.
7. *Education:* a section of a school having some students from every age-group, for sport, debates, etc.
Phrases:
bring the house down, 'his act *brought the house down*' (= was enthusiastically received).
keep house, 'his daughter *keeps house* for him' (= manages the household affairs).
on the house, 'the landlord offered everyone a drink *on the house*' (= free).
house *adjective*
(of hospital staff) resident: 'a *house* surgeon'.
Word Family: **house** (*rhymes with* cows), *verb*, a) to put in a house, b) to contain or shelter.

house agent
an estate agent.

house arrest
the keeping of an arrested person in his own home.

houseboat *noun*
a boat permanently moored in a river or lake and fitted with living accommodation.

housebreaker *noun*
1. a person who breaks into and enters a hóuse for a criminal purpose.
2. a person employed to demolish old houses.
Word Family: **housebreaking**, *noun*.

housefly *noun*
a common fly which breeds in dung and refuse and is able to transmit diseases such as typhoid.

household *noun*
all the people of a house or home.

household word
a well-known phrase or name.
Word Family: **householder**, *noun*, the owner or tenant of a house.

housekeeper *noun*
a person employed to direct and manage a household.
Word Family: **housekeeping**, *noun*, a) the duties of a housekeeper, b) the money used for managing a household.

housemaid *noun*
a junior household servant.
housemaid's knee, a form of bursitis, inflammation of the kneecap caused by too much kneeling.

house-martin *noun*
short form is **martin**
a member of the swallow family which builds nests in the eaves of houses and has a white rump patch.

housemother *noun*
a woman who looks after a group of children who live in an institution.
Word Family: **housefather**, *noun*.

House of Commons
the lower house of parliament, consisting wholly of elected members.

House of Lords
the upper house of parliament, consisting of hereditary and life peers and senior bishops.

house-trained *adjective*
(of a pet) trained not to excrete inside the house.

house-warming *noun*
a party to celebrate one's moving into a new home.

housewife *noun*
plural is **housewives**
a woman, especially a married woman, who is in charge of a household.

housework *noun*
the work of cleaning, cooking, etc. for a household.

housey-housey *noun*
the old army name for bingo.

housing (*say* **how-zing**) *noun*
1. houses or accommodation.
2. the providing of houses: 'student *housing*'.
3. a framework or covering which supports or protects parts of a machine.

hove *verb*
a past participle and past tense of the verb **heave**.

hovel (*say* **hovv'l**) *noun*
a small house in poor condition.

hover (*say* **hovva**) *verb*
1. to fly or remain in the air as if suspended.
2. to linger or wait close by.
3. to pause or waver: 'he *hovered* between life and death'.

Hovercraft *noun*
a vehicle designed to travel over a surface, usually water, supported on a cushion of air.
[a trademark]

how *adverb*
1. by what means or in what manner?: '*how* did you do it?'.
2. in what state or condition?: '*how* are you?'.
3. to what extent, amount, etc.?: '*how* often do you see her?'.
4. at what rate or price?: '*how* much is it?'.
5. for what reason?: '*how* is it that you are late?'.
Phrases:
how about?, what is your opinion concerning?
how come?, (*informal*) why?
how *conjunction*
1. in what way or manner: 'tell us *how* you do it'.
2. of the state or condition in which: 'I wonder *how* this hat looks'.
3. concerning degree or amount: 'does it matter *how* late we are?'.
however *adverb*
1. no matter how: 'buy the dress *however* much it costs'.
2. by whatever manner: 'do it *however* you can'.
however *conjunction*
nevertheless.

howdah (*rhymes with* powder) *noun*
a seat, usually with a railing and canopy, placed on the back of an elephant.
[Arabic *haudaj* a litter carried by a camel or elephant]

howitzer *noun*
a cannon which fires shells, high into the air, to hit targets which cannot be reached directly.

howl *verb*
a) to utter a loud, long, mournful cry, such as that of a dog or wolf. b) to make a similar sound.
Word Family: **howl**, *noun*; **howling**, *adjective*, a) producing a howl, b) (informal) enormous.

howler *noun*
1. a person or thing that howls.
2. (*informal*) a ridiculous mistake.

hoyden, hoiden *noun*
a girl who behaves boisterously; a tomboy.
Word Family: **hoydenish**, *adjective*.

hub *noun*
the central part of a wheel, fan, etc.
Usage: 'the film star was the *hub* of attention' (= centre, focus).

hubbub *noun*
a confused noise or uproar.

hubby *noun*
(*informal*) a husband.

hubris (*say* **hew-**bris) *noun*
arrogant pride inviting nemesis.
[Greek]

huckaback *noun*
rough towelling.

huckleberry *noun*
an American shrub with small, dark blue, edible berries.

huckster *noun*
1. a hawker or pedlar.
2. (*informal*) a mean, mercenary person.

huddle *verb*
a) to crowd together. b) to curl or hunch oneself up.
Word Family: **huddle**, *noun*, a) a confused jumble, b) a private conference.

hue (1) *noun*
a) any distinct colour in the range from red to yellow to green through to blue and back to red. b) a particular tint or shade of one colour.

hue (2) *noun*
hue and cry, a loud outcry, as of protest or pursuit.

huff *noun*
a fit of petulance.
huff *verb*
to offend.
Usage: 'I'll *huff* and I'll puff' (= blow).
Word Family: **huffy**, *adjective*, easily angered or offended; **huffily**, *adverb*.

hug *verb*
(hugged, hugging)
to clasp tightly in the arms, especially in affection.
Usage: 'the small boat *hugged* the shore for shelter' (= kept close to).
Word Family: **hug**, *noun*.

huge (*say* hewj) *adjective*
extremely large.
Word Family: **hugely**, *adverb*; **hugeness**, *noun*.

hugger-mugger *noun*
1. a muddle or confusion.
2. an old word meaning secrecy.

hula (*say* **hoo**la) *noun*
short form of **hula-hula**
a) a Hawaiian dance in which intricate hand and arm movements tell a story. b) the music for such a dance.
Word Family: **hula skirt**, a skirt made of grass blades attached to a waistband, as worn by hula dancers.
[Hawaiian]

hulk *noun*
1. the body or wreck of an old boat, originally used as a prison, etc.
2. a person or thing that is bulky or unwieldy.
Word Family: **hulking**, *adjective*, heavy and clumsy.

hull (1) *noun*
1. the shell or outer covering of a seed or fruit.
2. the group of floral parts of a strawberry or similar fruit, usually easily detached.
Word Family: **hull**, *verb*, to shell peas, peanuts, etc.

hull (2) *noun*
1. the body of a boat.
2. the fuselage of a flying boat, rocket, etc.

hullabaloo (*say* hulla-ba-**loo**) *noun*
an uproar.

hullo *interjection*
hello.

hum *verb*
(**hummed, humming**)
1. to make a continuous droning sound.
2. to sing with the lips closed.
3. (*informal*) to be full of activity.
Word Family: **hum**, *noun.*

human (*say* **hew**-m'n) *adjective*
relating to or characteristic of man or mankind.
Word Family: **human**, *noun*, a human being; **humanly**, *adverb.*
[from Latin]

humane (*say* hew-**mane**) *adjective*
feeling or showing tenderness or kindness for those suffering or in distress.
Word Family: **humanely**, *adverb*; **humaneness**, *noun.*
[from Latin]

humanism (*say* **hew**-ma-nizm) *noun*
a concern with human ideals or interests rather than abstract or theoretical subjects.
Word Family: **humanist**, *noun*, a freethinker, pragmatist or humanitarian.

humanitarian
(*say* hew-manni-**tair**ian) *adjective*
concerned with the needs and welfare of mankind in general.
Word Family: **humanitarian**, *noun*, a humanitarian person; **humanitarianism**, *noun.*

humanity (*say* hew-**manni**-tee) *noun*
1. the human race.
2. a) the quality of being humane: 'show *humanity* to others'. b) the state of being human.
3. (*plural*) the study of subjects such as classical literature, history or philosophy, as distinct from the sciences. Also called the **arts**.

humanize (*say* **hew**ma-nize)
humanise *verb*
to make or become human or humane.
Word Family: **humanization**, *noun.*

human nature
the qualities or characteristics inherent in all human beings.

humble (1) *adjective*
1. modest and aware of one's failings, etc.
2. low in rank or importance: '*humble* birth'.
Word Family: **humbleness**, *noun*; **humbly**, *adverb*; **humble**, *verb*, a) to humiliate, b) to lower in rank or importance; **humility** (*say* hew-**milli**-tee), *noun*, the quality of being humble.

humble (2) *adjective*
eat humble pie, to be humiliated or made to apologize humbly.
[Middle English *umbles* the edible organs of an animal]

humbug *noun*
1. a trick or hoax.
2. a hard, boiled peppermint sweet, usually striped.
3. nonsense.
Word Family: **humbug** (**humbugged, humbugging**), *verb*, to trick.

humdinger *noun*
(*informal*) something which is remarkable or extraordinary.

humdrum *adjective*
dull and unexciting.

humerus (*say* **hew**ma-rus) *noun*
plural is **humeri** (*say* **hew**ma-rye)
Anatomy: the long bone of the upper arm or forelimb.

humid (*say* **hew**mid) *adjective*
containing a large amount of vapour or water.
Word Family: **humidly,** *adverb*; **humidness,** *noun.*
[from Latin]

humidicrib (*say* hew-**middi**-krib) *noun*
a chamber in which the humidity and oxygen content are controlled, and in which very small infants are kept to help them breathe.

humidity (*say* hew-**middi**-tee) *noun*
the state of being humid.
relative humidity is the ratio between the amount of water-vapour present and the amount which would be present if the air contained all the water-vapour it could hold.
absolute humidity is the amount of water-vapour present.

humidor (*say* **hew**mi-dor) *noun*
a container for tobacco and tobacco products, designed to keep in moisture.

humiliate (*say* hew-**milli**-ate) *verb*
to lower the pride, position or dignity of.
Word Family: **humiliation,** *noun,* a) the act of humiliating, b) anything which humiliates.

humility *noun*
Word Family: see HUMBLE (1).

hummingbird *noun*
a very small, brightly coloured, quick-moving bird, whose narrow wings hum during flight.

hummock *noun*
a small hill or area slightly above the general height of the surrounding area.

humorist (*say* **hew**ma-rist) *noun*
a person who uses humour, especially a performer or writer of comedy.

humorous (*say* **hew**ma-rus) *adjective*
causing laughter or amusement.
Word Family: **humorously,** *adverb.*

humour (*say* **hew**-ma) *noun*
in America spelt **humor**
1. the quality of being funny: 'we could not see the *humour* in his joke'.
2. a mood or state of mind: 'he is not in good *humour* today'.
3. *Biology:* any plant or animal fluid, whether natural or caused by disease.
humour *verb*
to indulge or satisfy the wishes, mood, etc. of another.

hump *noun*
1. a rounded mass or bump, e.g. that on the back of a camel.
2. a hummock.
hump *verb*
Australian, New Zealand: (*informal*) to carry, especially on the back or shoulders.

humpbacked *adjective*
hunchbacked.

humus (*say* **hew**-mus) *noun*
the dark, organic substance in soil, consisting of decaying vegetable matter which makes the soil more fertile.

hunch *verb*
to bend or draw up in a hump: 'she sat *hunched* over the heater to get warm'.
hunch *noun*
1. a hump.
2. a feeling or suspicion about something.

hunchbacked *adjective*
having severe curvature of the spine which causes a hump on the back.
Word Family: **hunchback,** *noun,* a hunchbacked person.

hundred *noun*
a cardinal number, the symbol 100 in Arabic numerals, C in Roman numerals.
Word Family: **hundred,** *adjective*; **hundredth,** *noun, adjective.*

hundredweight *noun*
a unit of mass equal to 112 lbs. (about 50·8 kg).

hung *verb*
a past tense and past participle of the verb **hang**.

hunger *noun*
1. the need or desire for food.
2. any strong need or desire: 'she has a *hunger* for attention'.
Word Family: **hungry,** *adjective,* feeling or showing hunger; **hungrily,** *adverb*; **hunger,** *verb.*

hunger-strike *noun*
a persistent refusal to eat, usually as a protest against imprisonment, etc.

hunk *noun*
(*informal*) a large piece.

hunky-dory *adjective*
(*informal*) very good or satisfactory.

hunt *verb*
1. to chase wild animals in order to catch or kill them, often as a sport.
2. to search or look for.
hunter *noun*
1. a person who hunts or searches.
2. a horse used or bred for hunting.

Word Family: **hunting**, *noun*, the act of a person or thing that hunts; **hunt**, *noun*, a) the act of searching or hunting, b) an organized group of people meeting to hunt together; **huntsman**, *noun*, a) a person who supervises the hounds at a hunt, b) a person who hunts game.

hunter's moon
the full moon after the harvest moon, with similar characteristics.

hurdle *noun*
1. a) any of a series of barriers set across a racetrack to be jumped by competitors. b) (*often plural*) a race in which these barriers must be jumped.
2. any obstacle or difficult problem to be overcome.
Word Family: **hurdle**, *verb*; **hurdler**, *noun*.

hurdy-gurdy *noun*
a barrel organ or similar musical instrument played by turning a handle.

hurl *verb*
to throw with great force or violence.
Word Family: **hurl**, *noun*.

hurley *noun*
also called **hurling**
Irish hockey, in which teams of fifteen play with wide-bladed sticks.

hurly-burly *noun*
a noisy commotion or uproar.

hurrah, hoorah *interjection*
also spelt **hurray** or **hooray**
a cry of approval, joy, encouragement, etc.

hurricane (*say* **hurri**-k'n) *noun*
Weather: a) a strong wind of at least 120 km per hour. b) a cyclone in the West Indies. See TROPICAL CYCLONE. [from Spanish from Carib]

hurricane lamp
a paraffin lamp with a wick which is protected by glass.

hurry *verb*
(**hurried, hurrying**)
to do or cause to do quickly: a) 'we *hurried* to the station but still missed the train'; b) 'his nagging wife *hurried* him into a decision'.
Word Family: **hurry**, *noun*; **hurriedly**, *adverb*.

hurt *verb*
to cause bodily injury or pain.
Usages:
a) 'it will not *hurt* you to rest for a week' (= have a bad effect on).
b) 'I was very *hurt* by his coldness' (= upset, grieved).
Word Family: **hurt**, *noun*; **hurtful**, *adjective*, causing hurt or harm; **hurtfully**, *adverb*.

hurtle *verb*
to move or rush noisily or violently.

husband *noun*
the male partner in a marriage.
husband *verb*
to manage or use, especially in an economical way: 'the nation must *husband* its mineral resources'.

husbandry (*say* **huz**-b'n-dree) *noun*
1. the business of farming and agriculture.
2. any careful or economical management.

hush *verb*
to make or become silent.
hush up, 'we must *hush up* this scandal' (= keep secret).
Word Family: **hush**, *noun*, a silence or stillness; **hush!**, *interjection*.

hush-hush *adjective*
(*informal*) strictly confidential.

hush money
a bribe to keep silent about something.

husk *noun*
the dry, outer covering of a fruit or seed, especially of an ear of wheat.
Word Family: **husk**, *verb*, to remove the husk from.

husky (1) *adjective*
1. strongly or heavily built.
2. having a dry, hoarse or whispering sound.
Word Family: **huskily**, *adverb*; **huskiness**, *noun*.

husky (2) *noun*
any of a breed of large, sturdy dogs with a thick coat, used by Eskimos to pull sledges.

hussar (*say* h**uzah**) *noun*
a soldier in one of the light cavalry regiments of some European countries, originally Hungary, noted for their colourful uniforms.

hussy (*rhymes with* fussy) *noun*
a badly behaved or worthless female. [Middle English *huswif* housewife]

hustings *plural noun*
the campaigns, speeches, etc. which take place before a political election. [from *hustings*, an old word for the platforms from which candidates spoke]

hustle (*say* **huss**'l) *verb*
1. a) to push or jostle roughly. b) to move or work energetically.
2. (*informal*) to earn money in questionable or illegal ways.
Word Family: **hustle**, *noun*; **hustler**, *noun*, a person who hustles.

hut *noun*
a simple house, usually having only one room.

hutch *noun*
a box or cage, with wire mesh on one side, in which rabbits, etc. are kept.

hyacinth (*say* **high**a-sinth) *noun*
a small garden plant growing from a bulb, with fleshy, reed-like leaves and spikes of perfumed, bell-shaped flowers.
[Greek *Hyakinthos* a boy loved by Apollo]

hybrid (*say* **high**-brid) *noun*
1. *Biology:* any organism, such as a mule, resulting from unlike parents.
2. anything which has mixed origins or is composed of mixed parts.
Word Family: **hybridize**, **hybridise**, *verb*.
[from Latin]

hybrid tea rose
short form is **HT rose**
the rose most commonly seen in gardens, bred from Chinese Tea roses and old-fashioned long-flowering French roses.
[*tea*, from the scent once thought to resemble that of the tea imported in the same ships]

hydatid (*say* high-**dat**tid) *noun*
a cyst in the lungs or liver, produced by a tapeworm and transmitted to man by dogs.

hydra (*say* **high**-dra) *noun*
Biology: a microscopic, freshwater animal.
[Greek, water-snake]

hydrangea (*say* high-**drane**-ja) *noun*
a garden shrub with large, showy clusters of flowers.

hydrant *noun*
also called a **fire hydrant**
an upright pipe connected to a water main and to which a hose can be attached.

hydrate (*say* **high**-drate) *noun*
Chemistry: a compound combined with water, especially a salt containing water of crystallization.
Word Family: **hydrate**, *verb*, to combine chemically with water.

hydraulic (*say* high-**drol**lik) *adjective*
being operated by or using a liquid.
hydraulics *plural noun*
(*used with singular verb*) the study of the motion of liquids and its application in engineering.
Word Family: **hydraulically**, *adverb*.
[HYDRO- (1) + Greek *aulos* pipe]

hydride (*say* **high**-dride) *noun*
Chemistry: a compound of hydrogen and one other element.

hydro (*say* **high**-dro) *noun*
a spa hotel providing medical treatment with mineral waters (hydropathy).

hydro- (1) (*say* **high**-dro)
a prefix meaning water, as in *hydro-electric*.
[Greek *hydros* of water]

hydro- (2) (*say* **high**-dro)
a prefix used in chemical terms, indicating combination of hydrogen, as in *hydrocarbon*.

hydrocarbon *noun*
Chemistry: any of a large class of organic compounds which contain only carbon and hydrogen.

hydrochloric acid
(*say* high-dra-**klor**rik assid)
Chemistry: a colourless, corrosive acid (formula HCl), used in many chemical and industrial processes.

hydro-electric *adjective*
of or relating to electricity produced by the energy of flowing water, e.g. from a dam.
Word Family: **hydro-electricity**, *noun*.

hydrofoil (*say* **high**-dra-foil) *noun*
a boat with ski-like fixtures which support the hull above the water when the boat has reached sufficient speed.

hydrogen (*say* **high**-dra-j'n) *noun*
element number 1, a colourless, odourless, inflammable gas which is the lightest and simplest of all known elements.
See CHEMICAL ELEMENTS in grey pages.
Word Family: **hydrogenate** (*say* high-**dro**ja-nate), **hydrogenize**, **hydrogenise**, *verbs*, to combine or treat with hydrogen.
[HYDRO- (2) + -GEN]

hydrogen bomb
short form is **H-bomb**
see NUCLEAR WEAPON and NUCLEAR FUSION.

hydrology (*say* high-**drol**la-jee) *noun*
the study of water on, or under, land.
[HYDRO- (1) + -LOGY]

hydrolysis (*say* high-**drolla**-sis) *noun*
Chemistry: the decomposition of a compound by water, each new compound containing part of the water.
Word Family: **hydrolytic** (*say* high-dra-**littik**), *adjective*; **hydrolyse**, *verb*.
[HYDRO- (1) + Greek *lysis* a loosening]

hydrometer (*say* high-**drommita**) *noun*
a device for finding the specific gravity of liquids, usually consisting of a sealed tube which is immersed in the liquid.

hydrophobia (*say* high-dra-**fo**-bee-a) *noun*
an abnormal fear of water, as in rabies.
Word Family: **hydrophobic**, *adjective*.
[HYDRO- (1) + Greek *phobia* fear]

hydroplane (*say* **high**-dra plane) *noun*
1. a seaplane.
2. a light, fast boat designed to skim along the surface of the water.

hydroponics *noun*
the growing of plants without soil, on wet sand, peat, water, etc.
[HYDRO- (1) + Greek *ponos* work]

hydroscope (*say* **high**-dra-skope) *noun*
a device used for viewing objects below the surface of the sea.
[HYDRO- (1) + Greek *skopein* to look at]

hydrous (*say* **high**-drus) *adjective*
containing water.

hydroxide (*say* high-**drokside**) *noun*
Chemistry: any inorganic compound containing the hydroxyl radical, such as sodium hydroxide (formula NaOH).

hydroxyl radical (*say* high-**droksil** raddi-k'l)
short form is **hydroxyl**
also called a **hydroxyl ion**
Chemistry: the univalent ion $(OH)^-$.

hyena (*say* high-**eena**) **hyaena** *noun*
an African and Asian mammal of the dog family with powerful jaws and short hind legs.

hygiene (*say* **high**-jeen) *noun*
also called **hygienics** (*say* high-jeeniks *or* high-jenniks)
the study of ways to preserve health.
Word Family: **hygienist**, *noun*.
[Greek *hygieiné* of health]

hygienic (*say* high-**jeenik** *or* high-**jennik**) *adjective*
clean and healthy.
Word Family: **hygienically**, *adverb*.

hygrometer (*say* high-**grommita**) *noun*
an instrument used to measure the humidity of the atmosphere.
[Greek *hygros* wet + METER]

hymen (*say* **high**-men) *noun*
also called the **maidenhead**
Anatomy: a fold of membrane which partly covers the entrance to the vagina in virgins.
[Greek, thin skin]

hymn (*say* him) *noun*
a song of praise, especially one dedicated to a god.
hymnal (*say* **him**-n'l) *noun*
a book containing hymns.
[from Greek]

hyper-
a prefix meaning in great amount or excessive, as in *hypercritical*.
[Greek *hyper* over or above]

hyperbola (*say* high-**perba**-la) *noun*
Maths: a plane regular curve formed when a cone is cut by a plane which makes a greater angle with the base than the side does. See CONIC SECTION.

hyperbole (*say* high-**perba**-lee) *noun*
a deliberate exaggeration used for effect only.
[HYPER- + Greek *bolé* a throw]

hyperbolic (*say* high-per-**bollik**)
hyperbolical *adjective*
1. of or relating to a hyperbola.
2. of or relating to a hyperbole.

hypercritical (*say* high-per-**kritti**-k'l) *adjective*
excessively critical.
Word Family: **hypercritically**, *adverb*.

hypersensitive
(*say* high-per-**sensa**-tiv) *adjective*
excessively sensitive.
Word Family: **hypersensitivity** (*say* high-per-sensa-**tivva**-tee), *noun*.

hypertension (*say* high-per-**ten**-sh'n) *noun*
an abnormally high blood pressure.

hypertonic (*say* high-per-**tonnik**) *adjective*
Biology: (of a solution) having a higher osmotic pressure than normal protoplasm. Compare HYPOTONIC and ISOTONIC.
[HYPER- + Greek *tonos* tension]

hyphen (*say* **high**-f'n) *noun*
Grammar: a punctuation mark (-), used to join words or parts of words, as in *old-fashioned*.

Word Family: **hyphenate,** *verb,* to join words with a hyphen; **hyphenation,** *noun.*
[Greek, together]

hypnosis (*say* hip-**no**-sis) *noun*
plural is **hypnoses** (*say* hip-**no**-seez)
1. an artificially produced sleep-like state, in which sensations like pain are reduced and the patient becomes more relaxed, with increased susceptibility to suggestion.
2. any sleep-like or entranced condition.
Word Family: **hypnotism** (*say* **hip**na-tizm), *noun,* the act or practice of causing hypnosis; **hypnotist,** *noun;* **hypnotize, hypnotise,** *verb;* **hypnotic** (*say* hip-**nott**ik), *adjective;* **hypnotic,** *noun,* a substance which induces sleep.
[Greek *hypnos* sleep]

hypo (*say* **high**-po) *noun*
Chemistry: sodium thiosulphate, a white crystalline solid used in photography.

hypochondriac
(*say* high-po-**kon**-dree-ak) *noun*
a person who is abnormally concerned about his health, especially one who exaggerates minor symptoms, etc.
Word Family: **hypochondria,** *noun.*
[Greek *hypokhondria* the part of the belly where melancholia was thought to originate]

hypocrisy (*say* hip-**okra**-see) *noun*
the pretence of having certain qualities, beliefs or feelings, especially admirable or virtuous ones.
hypocrite (*say* **hippa**-krit) *noun*
a person who practises hypocrisy, especially one pretending to be virtuous.
Word Family: **hypocritical,** *adjective.*
[Greek *hypokrisis* pretence]

hypodermic (*say* high-pa-**der**-mik) *adjective*
a) relating to the introduction of liquid medicines under the skin: 'a *hypodermic* injection'. b) relating to the tissues under the skin.
[Greek *hypo* under + *derma* skin]

hypostyle (*say* **high**-po-stile) *adjective*
Architecture: having the roof supported by many columns.
[Greek *hypo* under + *stylos* column]

hypotenuse (*say* high-**pott**in-yooz) *noun*
the longest side, opposite the right angle, of a right-angled triangle.
[Greek *hypoteinein* to stretch under]

hypothermia
(*say* high-pa-**therm**-ee-a) *noun*
the state of having body temperature well below normal, either deliberately induced as a form of anaesthesia, or the result of prolonged exposure to very low temperatures.
[Greek *hypo* under + *thermé* heat]

hypothesis (*say* high-**pothi**-sis) *noun*
plural is **hypotheses** (*say* high-**pothi**-seez)
1. a suggestion or statement offered as an explanation or starting point for reasoning, etc.
2. an idea or theory, especially one which is assumed as a basis for some action.
Word Family: **hypothesize, hypothesise,** *verb,* to form a hypothesis.
[Greek *hypo* under + *thesis* a placing]

hypothetical (*say* high-pa-**thetti**-k'l) *adjective*
assumed or supposed.
Word Family: **hypothetically,** *adverb.*

hypotonic (*say* high-pa-**tonn**ik) *adjective*
Biology: (of a solution) having a lower osmotic pressure than normal protoplasm. Compare HYPERTONIC and ISOTONIC.
[Greek *hypo* under + *tonos* tension]

hysterectomy (*say* hista-**rekta**-mee) *noun*
Medicine: an operation to remove the uterus.
[Greek *hystera* womb + *ektomé* a cutting out]

hysteria (*say* hiss-**teeria**) *noun*
1. an uncontrollable outburst of extreme emotion, excitement, etc.
2. *Psychology:* a form of neurosis, often unconscious, marked by the exhibiting or experiencing of symptoms of illness to obtain relief from stress.
hysterical (*say* hiss-**terri**-k'l) *adjective*
1. *Psychology:* suffering from hysteria.
2. exhibiting extreme excitement, emotion, impulsiveness, etc.
3. (*informal*) very funny: 'his jokes are always *hysterical*'.
Word Family: **hysterics** (*say* hiss-**terr**iks), *plural noun,* a hysterical outburst.
[Greek *hystera* womb, where hysterics were thought to originate]

Ii

I *pronoun*
plural is **we**
the first person singular nominative pronoun: '*I* have a new book'.
See ME (1), MY and MINE (1).
Common Error: I, ME are both first person singular pronouns, but *I* should only be used in the nominative case: 'between you and *I* and the gatepost' is wrong because a preposition (*between*) should take the objective case (*me*).

iambic (*say* eye–**am**bik) *noun*
also called an **iamb**
Poetry: see FOOT.
[from Greek]

ibex (*say* **eye**–beks) *noun*
plural is **ibexes** or **ibex**
a wild goat with long, curved horns, found in the mountains of Europe and Asia.
[Latin]

ibis (*say* **eye**–bis) *noun*
a large wading bird with a long curved bill, related to the spoonbill and found in Egypt and parts of southern Europe.
[Greek]

-ible
a variant of the suffix **-able**.

ice *noun*
1. *Physics:* a form of water in its solid state, below 0°C.
2. any substance resembling ice, such as ice-cream.
Phrases:
break the ice, 'it took some time to *break the ice* at the party' (= relax the atmosphere).
cut no ice, 'flattering speech *cuts no ice* with him' (= has no effect or influence).
on ice, waiting or in reserve.
on thin ice, in a risky or uncertain position.
ice *verb*
1. a) to freeze or make very cold. b) to cover or become covered with ice.
2. to coat a cake, etc. with icing.

Ice Age
Geology: any of several periods of time during which icesheets covered large areas of the earth.

iceberg *noun*
a large mass of ice floating at sea having broken from a glacier or an icecap, and of which only one-ninth is visible.
[Old Dutch *ijs* ice + *berg* mountain]

icebox *noun*
1. *American:* a refrigerator.
2. a box or compartment holding ice to keep food cool.

icebreaker *noun*
1. a ship with a reinforced hull used for clearing or channelling through ice.
2. a person or thing that helps to relax the atmosphere.

icecap *noun*
a covering of ice over an area, sometimes vast, and sloping in all directions from the centre.

ice-cream *noun*
a sweet, frozen food, made from cream, flavouring, eggs, sugar, etc.

icefloe *noun*
a sheet of floating ice. A large icefloe is called an **icefield**.

ice hockey
a strenuous form of hockey played on ice by teams of six skaters (with ten reserves) who try to strike a rubber disc (puck) into the goal.

ichneumon-fly (*say* ik–**new**–m'n–fly) *noun*
a small parasitic insect which lays its eggs in caterpillars; the larvae feed on their host but take care not to kill it.
[Greek, a hunter]

ichthyology (*say* ikthi–**olla**–jee) *noun*
the study of fish.
[Greek *ikhthys* fish + -LOGY]

-ician (*say* **ish**'n)
a suffix indicating an expert in a particular subject, as in *electrician.*

icicle (*rhymes with* bicycle) *noun*
a pointed, hanging stick of ice formed by the freezing of dripping water.

iciness *noun*
Word Family: see ICY.

icing *noun*
a soft, sugary coating used to decorate cakes.

icon (*say* **eye**–kon) *noun*
also spelt **ikon**
an image, symbol or picture, usually of a sacred or religious subject.
[Greek *eikon* an image]

iconoclast (*say* eye–**konna**–klast) *noun*
1. a person who destroys sacred or religious images.
2. a person attacking established or popular beliefs.
Word Family: **iconoclasm,** *noun*; **iconoclastic** (*say* eye–konna–**klastik**), *adjective.*
[Greek *eikon* image + *klastos* shattered]

iconography (*say* eye–kon–**ogra**–fee) *noun*
the historical study of the meanings or subject matter in paintings.
Word Family: **iconographic** (*say* eye–konno–**graffik**), **iconographical,** *adjective.*
[Greek *eikon* image + *graphein* to write]

icy *adjective*
1. of, like or covered with ice.
2. very cold: a) 'an *icy* wind'; b) 'an *icy* welcome for being late'.
Word Family: **icily,** *adverb*; **iciness,** *noun.*

id *noun*
Psychology: the unconscious part of the personality, which is the source of instinctive energy and has no contact with the outside world. Compare EGO.
[Latin, it]

idea (*say* eye–**deer**) *noun*
something conceived as a part or result of thought: 'have you any *idea* of how to do the job?'.
Usages:
a) 'he has some very unusual political *ideas*' (= beliefs, opinions).
b) 'do you have any particular *ideas* for redecorating the house?' (= plans).
c) 'what's the *idea* of bursting in without knocking?' (= meaning, significance).
[Greek, ideal form (in Plato's philosophy)]

ideal (*say* eye–**deel**) *adjective*
1. best, perfect or most suitable: a) 'an *ideal* place for a picnic'; b) '*ideal* beauty'.
2. existing only in the mind or imagination.
ideal *noun*
1. an example, idea, aim, etc. of the highest or most perfect standard: a) 'she is my *ideal* of womanhood'; b) 'his *ideals* do not allow him to lie'.
2. something which exists only in the mind or imagination.
Word Family: **ideally,** *adverb,* a) perfectly, b) in theory.

idealism (*say* eye–**deel**–izm) *noun*
a) the seeing of things as ideals. b) the pursuit of what one considers to be ideal.
Word Family: **idealist,** *noun,* a) a person who holds or pursues ideals, b) a person whose ideas are unrealistic or impractical; **idealistic,** *adjective*; **idealistically,** *adverb.*

idealize (*say* eye–**dee**lize) **idealise** *verb*
to imagine or exalt as an ideal: 'she *idealizes* her clever brother'.
Word Family: **idealization,** *noun.*

idée fixe (*say* **ee–day** feex)
an obsession.
[French, fixed idea]

identical (*say* eye–**denti**–k'l) *adjective*
exactly equal or the same.
Word Family: **identically,** *adverb.*

identify (*say* eye–**denti**–fie) *verb*
(**identified, identifying**)
1. to establish as being a particular person, thing or quality: 'he *identified* the ring as his mother's'.
2. to represent or treat as the same: 'he *identifies* his aims with those of the party'.
Word Family: **identification,** *noun,* a) the act of identifying, b) something which proves the identity of a person; **identifiable,** *adjective,* able to be recognized or identified.

Identikit (*say* eye–**denti**–kit) *noun*
a system of drawings used by the police for identifying criminals, made by sorting through drawings of parts of the face until a likeness is made.
[a trademark]

identity (*say* eye–**denti**–tee) *noun*
1. the fact of being what or who one is: 'show us your passport to prove your *identity*'.
2. exact sameness or likeness.
3. *Maths:* an equation which is true for all values of its variables.
identity parade, a presentation at which witnesses are asked by the police, army, etc. to identify a suspect

from among a group of people of similar appearance.
[Latin *idem* the same]

ideology (*say* eye-dee-**olla**-jee) *noun*
the organized system of beliefs or way of thinking of a person or group: 'fascist, communist and democratic *ideologies*'.
Word Family: **ideologist**, *noun*; **ideological** (*say* eye-dee-a-**loji**-k'l), *adjective.*

Ides (*rhymes with* rides) *plural noun*
Ancient history: the Roman name given to the 15th days of March, May, July and October, and to the 13th days of the other months.

idiocy (*say* **iddia**-see) *noun*
a) the fact or state of being an idiot. b) any stupid or senseless behaviour.

idiom (*say* **iddi**-um) *noun*
1. a phrase or expression whose meaning is not logically suggested by the words, as in *how do you do?*.
2. the language or form of expression peculiar to one individual or group.
Word Family: **idiomatic** (*say* iddia-**mattik**), **idiomatical**, *adjective*, a) of or expressing an idiom, b) (of language) informal; **idiomatically**, *adverb.*
[Greek *idioma* a peculiarity]

idiosyncrasy (say iddio-**sinkra**-see) *noun*
any behaviour or character which is peculiar to one individual or group.
Word Family: **idiosyncratic** (*say* iddio-sin-**krattik**), *adjective*; **idiosyncratically**, *adverb.*
[Greek *idios* own personal + *syghrasia* mixture]

idiot *noun*
1. a hopelessly foolish or senseless person.
2. a person with subnormal intellectual development who is considered unable to be educated.
Word Family: **idiotic**, (*say* iddi-**ottik**), *adjective*; **idiotically**, *adverb.*
[Greek *idiotes* a private person, non-official, ignoramus]

idle (*say* **eye**-d'l) *adjective*
not busy, working or in use: a) 'the machine had been *idle* since the workers went on strike'; b) 'the *idle* youth sleeps in until midday'.
Usages:
a) 'ignore their *idle* gossip' (= useless, worthless).
b) 'this isn't an *idle* threat you can ignore' (= weak, groundless).

idle *verb*
1. to move or pass time in an idle manner.
2. (of machinery, engines, etc.) to move or turn at minimum speed.
Word Family: **idleness**, *noun*; **idly**, *adverb*; **idler**, *noun*, a lazy person.

idol (*say* **eye**-d'l) *noun*
1. a statue, picture, or image representing a deity and used as an object of worship.
2. any person who is blindly adored: 'a singing *idol*'.
[Greek *eidolon* an image]

idolater (*say* eye-**dolla**-ter) *noun*
a person worshipping an idol or idols.

idolatry (*say* eye-**dolla**-tree) *noun*
a) the worship of idols. b) any blind devotion or adoration.
Word Family: **idolatrous**, *adjective.*
[Greek *eidolon* an image + *latreia* worship]

idolize (*say* **eye**-da-lize) **idolise** *verb*
to worship or admire blindly.
Word Family: **idolization**, *noun.*

idyll (*say* **eye**-dil *or* **iddil**) **idyl** *noun*
a short poem or piece of descriptive music concerned with romanticized rural life.
Word Family: **idyllic**, *adjective*, a) relating to an idyll, b) naturally simple or charming.
[Greek *eidyllion*]

if *conjunction*
1. (used to express a condition) 'you may stay up late *if* you are good'.
2. (used to ask an indirect question) 'tell me *if* you are tired'.
3. (used instead of *when*) '*if* you add 2 and 2, you get 4'.
Phrases:
as if, (used to suggest that the opposite is true) 'it isn't *as if* you are very busy'.
if only, (used to introduce an unfulfilled wish) '*if only* it would stop raining!'.
ifs and buts, 'give me a straight answer, not a lot of *ifs and buts*' (= doubts and qualifications).
if you ask me, '*if you ask me* Bill is crazy' (= I think).

igloo *noun*
a small dome-shaped house of snow blocks, built by Eskimos.

igneous (*say* **igni**-us) *adjective*
1. of or resembling fire.
2. *Geology:* relating to rocks formed from molten material which cooled either deep below the earth's surface,

such as granite, or on the surface, such as basalt.
[Latin *igneus* fiery or burning]

ignite *verb*
to catch or set on fire.

ignition (*say* ig-**nish**'n) *noun*
1. the act of igniting.
2. a) the system for producing the correctly timed sequence of electric sparks which ignite the fuel in an engine.
b) the burning of the fuel.
[Latin *ignis* fire]

ignition coil
a type of induction coil producing the very high voltage which produces a spark in an internal combustion engine.

ignoble *adjective*
below the commonly accepted standards of worthiness, honour or excellence: 'betraying our agreement was an *ignoble* act'.
Word Family: **ignobly**, *adverb*; **ignobility** (*say* igno-**billi**-tee), *noun*.
[Latin *ignobilis* insignificant]

ignominious (*say* igna-**minni**-us) *adjective*
marked by or deserving humiliation and disgrace: 'an *ignominious* defeat'.
Word Family: **ignominiously**, *adverb*; **ignominy** (*say* **igna**-minnee), *noun*, disgrace or humiliation.
[Latin *ignominia* disgrace]

ignoramus (*say* igna-**raymus**) *noun*
plural is **ignoramuses**
an ignorant person.
[Latin, we do not know]

ignorant (*say* **igna**-r'nt) *adjective*
having little or no knowledge: 'I'm quite *ignorant* about art'.
Usage: 'what an *ignorant* question' (= uninformed).
Word Family: **ignorantly**, *adverb*; **ignorance**, *noun*.

ignore *verb*
to fail or refuse to notice, pay attention, etc.

iguana (*say* ee-**gwah**-na) *noun*
any of a group of tropical lizards growing up to about 1·8 m long and found mainly in South America.
[Spanish from Carib]

ikebana (*say* ikki-**bahna**) *noun*
the Japanese art of flower arrangement.
[Japanese, living plant]

ikon (*say* **eye**-kon) *noun*
see ICON.

il–
a variant of the prefix **in–** (2).

ileum (*say* **illi**-um) *noun*
Anatomy: the third portion of the small intestine, merging with the jejunum above and joined to the caecum below and absorbing digested food.
Word Family: **ileac**, *adjective*.

ilk *noun*
a type or kind: 'people of his *ilk* are never happy'.

ill *adjective*
1. not well or healthy.
2. not good or favourable: 'the family has suffered much *ill* luck'.
Phrases:
ill at ease, uncomfortable or uneasy.
ill fame, a bad or immoral reputation.
ill feeling, hostility or resentment.
ill humour, 'his *ill humour* spoilt the dinner party' (= unpleasant mood).
ill will, unfriendliness or hostility.
ill *noun*
1. any evil or immorality.
2. any harm or disaster.
ill *adverb*
1. in an ill way.
2. scarcely: 'we can *ill* afford to lose another member'.

ill-advised *adjective*
not sensible or prudent.

ill-bred *adjective*
not polite or well-mannered.
Word Family: **ill-breeding**, *noun*.

illegal (*say* il-**lee**-g'l) *adjective*
not allowed by law.
Word Family: **illegally**, *adverb*; **illegality** (*say* illi-**galli**-tee), *noun*.

illegible (*say* il-**leji**-b'l) *adjective*
not able to be read or deciphered clearly.
Word Family: **illegibly**, *adverb*; **illegibility** (*say* il-leji-**billi**-tee), *noun*.

illegitimate (*say* illi-**jitti**-mit) *adjective*
1. not legal.
Usage: 'we declared that his argument was *illegitimate*' (= not valid or logical).
2. born of parents who were not married.
Word Family: **illegitimately**, *adverb*; **illegitimacy**, *noun*.

ill-fated *adjective*
doomed or destined for disaster.

ill-favoured *adjective*
not attractive or pleasing in appearance.

ill-founded *adjective*
based on false facts or reasoning: 'an *ill-founded* rumour'.

ill-gotten *adjective*
obtained dishonestly: '*ill-gotten* gains'.

illiberal *adjective*
narrow-minded or intolerant.

illicit (*say* il-**lis**sit) *adjective*
not legal or permitted.

illiterate (*say* il-**lit**ta-rit) *adjective*
not able to read and write.
Usage: 'an *illiterate* belief' (= ignorant, uncultured).
Word Family: **illiterate,** *noun,* a person who is illiterate; **illiteracy,** *noun.*

ill-mannered *adjective*
bad-mannered or rude.

illness *noun*
a) the state or time of being in bad health. b) an ailment or disease.

illogical (*say* il-**loj**i-k'l) *adjective*
not logical or reasonable.
Word Family: **illogically,** *adverb*; **illogicality** (*say* il-loji-**kal**li-tee), *noun.*

ill-starred *adjective*
unlucky or ill-fated.

ill-timed *adjective*
done or occurring at a bad or inappropriate time.

ill-treat *verb*
to treat badly.
Word Family: **ill-treatment,** *noun.*

illuminate (*say* il-**yoo**mi-nate *or* ill-**oo**ma-nate) *verb*
1. to give light to. Also called to **illumine** (*say* il-**yoo**min *or* ill-**oo**min).
Usage: 'can you *illuminate* this discussion for me?' (= make clear).
2. to decorate a book, page, etc., especially with flourishes on the letters, bright colours, etc.
Word Family: **illumination,** *noun*; **illuminator,** *noun,* a person or thing that illuminates.
[IL- + Latin *luminis* of light]

illusion (*say* il-**yoo**-*zh*'n *or* ill-**oo**-*zh*'n) *noun*
1. a false or deceptive appearance, belief, etc.
2. the perceiving of something wrongly or in a way which does not actually exist: 'heavy fog created the *illusion* that it was night-time'.
Word Family: **illusionary, illusional,** *adjectives.*
[Latin *illudere* to mock]
Common Error: ILLUSION, DELUSION both describe false or deceptive mental experiences. An *illusion* is a relatively common experience in which an object is incorrectly perceived, whereas a *delusion* is an extreme belief which is persistently held despite all evidence to the contrary.

illusionist (*say* il-**yoo**-*zh*'n-ist *or* ill-**oo**-*zh*'n-ist) *noun*
a conjurer using mirrors or other devices to produce special effects.

illusory (*say* il-**yoo**za-ree *or* ill-**oo**za-ree) **illusive** *adjective*
1. causing deception or illusion.
2. unreal.
Word Family: **illusorily,** *adverb*; **illusoriness,** *noun.*

illustrate (*say* **il**la-strate) *verb*
1. to provide a book or other publication with drawings, diagrams, etc. related to the text.
2. to make clear or explain, as with examples, etc.
Word Family: **illustrative,** *adjective,* serving to illustrate or explain; **illustrator,** *noun,* an artist who illustrates books, etc.
[IL- + Latin *lustrare* to light]

illustration (*say* illa-**stray**-sh'n) *noun*
1. the act of illustrating or explaining.
2. a reproduction of a drawing, photograph, etc. in a book or other publication.
3. anything which explains or demonstrates: 'she quoted the words of several modern scientists as an *illustration* of her argument'.

illustrious (*say* il-**lus**tri-us) *adjective*
famous or celebrated.
Word Family: **illustriousness,** *noun*; **illustriously,** *adverb.*

im-
a variant of the prefix **in-** (2).

image (*say* **im**mij) *noun*
1. a representation or likeness of something: 'despite her long absence her *image* remains in my memory'.
Usage: 'she is the *image* of her mother' (= exact copy or likeness).
2. the way a person appears to himself or others: 'the Prime Minister's public *image* has improved'.
3. *Physics:* an optical reproduction or duplicate of something, especially one formed by a lens or mirror.
4. a description of something in speech or writing to suggest a certain picture or idea of that thing: 'in describing him she used the *image* of a dog in the manger'.
Word Family: **image,** *verb,* to imagine, reproduce or represent.
[from Latin]

imagery (*say* **immij**–ree) *noun*
1. any mental pictures or images.
2. a) the creation or use of images in speech or writing. b) a pattern of images used.

imaginary (*say* **immaj**–in–ree) *adjective*
1. having existence only in the imagination: 'your fears are purely *imaginary*'.
2. *Maths:* relating to the square root of a negative number, such as $\sqrt{-2}$. Compare REAL.

imagination (*say* immaj–in–**ay**–sh'n) *noun*
the ability to form an image or concept of something not present or in one's experience.

imaginative (*say* **immaj**–in–a–tiv) *adjective*
of or coming from the imagination, especially in a creative or unusual way.
Word Family: **imaginatively,** *adverb*; **imaginativeness,** *noun.*

imagine (*say* **immaj**–in) *verb*
to use one's imagination.
Usages:
a) 'I *imagine* that you're right' (= suppose).
b) 'it was hard to *imagine* what would happen' (= guess).
Word Family: **imaginable,** *adjective,* able to be imagined.

imago (*say* im–**ah**–go) *noun*
plural is **imagines** or **imagos**
Biology: an adult insect.
[Latin]

imbecile (*say* **imbi**–seel *or* **imbi**–sile) *noun*
a) a person who is mentally deficient. b) any stupid person.
Word Family: **imbecile, imbecilic,** *adjectives*; **imbecility** (*say* imbi–**silli**–tee), *noun.*
[Latin *imbecillus* feeble]

imbibe *verb*
to drink.
Usage: 'the students *imbibed* a devotion to literature from their favourite lecturer' (= absorbed, took in).
[IM– + Latin *bibere* to drink]

imbroglio (*say* im–**brole**–ee–o) *noun*
a complicated disagreement.
[Italian *imbrogliare* to confuse]

imbrue (*say* im–**broo**) *verb*
(**imbrued, imbruing**)
an old word meaning: a) to wet or stain; b) to soak or permeate.
Word Family: **imbruement,** *noun.*

imbue (*say* im–**bew**) *verb*
(**imbued, imbuing**)
to saturate or make thoroughly wet.
Usage: 'his poems are *imbued* with a spirit of joy' (= filled).

imitate (*say* **immi**–tate) *verb*
to follow the style or pattern set by another.
Word Family: **imitator,** *noun,* a person, especially an actor, who imitates; **imitative** (*say* **immita**–tiv), *adjective*; **imitatively,** *adverb.*

imitation (*say* immi–**tay**–sh'n) *noun*
a) the act of imitating: 'his *imitation* of her gestures was perfect'. b) a copy or reproduction: 'these jewels are *imitations*'.
[from Latin]

immaculate (*say* immak–yoolit) *adjective*
a) having no blemish, fault or impurity. b) perfectly clean or spotless.
Word Family: **immaculately,** *adverb*; **immaculateness,** *noun.*
[IM– + Latin *macula* a spot]

immanent (*say* **imma**–nint) *adjective*
inherent or remaining within.
Word Family: **immanence,** *noun*; **immanently,** *adverb.*
[IM– + Latin *manens* remaining]

immaterial (*say* imma–**teeriul**) *adjective*
1. unimportant or irrelevant: 'cost is *immaterial* if you want good quality'.
2. having no physical form: 'angels are *immaterial* beings'.
Word Family: **immaterially,** *adverb*; **immateriality** (*say* imma–teeri–**alli**–tee), *noun.*

immature (*say* imma–**tewer**) *adjective*
not mature or developed.
Word Family: **immaturity,** *noun.*

immediate (*say* im–**meedi**–it) *adjective*
1. done or occurring without delay.
2. nearest or closest: 'my *immediate* circle of friends'.
3. relating to the present time: 'we have no *immediate* plans for the house'.
Word Family: **immediately,** *adverb,* a) at once, b) closely or directly; **immediacy,** *noun,* the state of being immediate.

immemorial (*say* imma–**mawriul**) *adjective*
not within human memory or recorded knowledge: 'this temple dates from time *immemorial*'.
Word Family: **immemorially,** *adverb.*
[IM– + Latin *memoria* memory]

immense *adjective*
very large or great: a) 'an *immense* dog'; b) 'a stroke of *immense* good luck'; c) '*immense* pleasure'.
Word Family: **immensely**, *adverb*; **immensity**, *noun.*
[IM– + Latin *mensus* measured]

immerse (*say* im–**merse**) *verb*
to put in or under a liquid.
Usage: 'he is completely *immersed* in writing his new book' (= involved, absorbed).
[IM– + Latin *mersus* dipped]

immersion (*say* im–**mer**–sh'n) *noun*
1. the act of immersing.
2. *Astronomy:* the disappearance of a planet or star during an eclipse, etc. Compare EMERSION.

immersion heater
a hot–water system with an electric element inside the tank.

immigrate (*say* **immi**–grate) *verb*
to enter and settle in a country or region in which one was not born. Compare EMIGRATE.
Word Family: **immigration**, *noun*; **immigrant**, *noun*, a person who immigrates.

imminent (*say* **immi**–nint) *adjective*
about to occur at any moment.
Word Family: **imminence**, *noun*; **imminently**, *adverb.*
[Latin *imminere* to threaten]

immiscible (*say* immissi–b'l) *adjective*
not able to be mixed or combined.

immobile (*say* immo–bile) *adjective*
not moving or mobile.
Word Family: **immobility** (*say* imma–**billi**–tee), *noun.*

immobilize (*say* im–**mo**–bil–ize) **immobilise** *verb*
1. to make incapable of movement.
2. *Commerce:* to withdraw capital from circulation, in order to create reserves.

immoderate (*say* im–**modda**–rit) *adjective*
extreme or unreasonable: 'his *immoderate* love of praise irritated the other performers'.
Word Family: **immoderately**, *adverb*; **immoderateness**, *noun.*

immodest *adjective*
without shame or modesty.
Word Family: **immodestly**, *adverb*; **immodesty**, *noun.*

immolate (*say* **imma**–late) *verb*
to kill as a sacrifice or offering.
Word Family: **immolation**, *noun.*
[from Latin]

immoral (*say* immorr'l) *adjective*
not moral or in accord with accepted moral standards.
Word Family: **immorally**, *adverb*; **immorality** (*say* imma–**ralli**–tee), *noun.*
Common Error: see AMORAL.

immortal (*say* immor–t'l) *adjective*
a) not subject to death or destruction: '*immortal* gods'. b) everlasting: '*immortal* fame'.
Word Family: **immortal**, *noun*, an immortal person or thing; **immortally**, *adverb*; **immortality** (*say* immor–**talli**–tee), *noun.*

immortelle *noun*
see EVERLASTING.

immovable (*say* immoova–b'l) *adjective*
not able to be moved or changed.
Word Family: **immovably**, *adverb.*

immune (*say* im–**yoon**) *adjective*
protected or safe, e.g. from a disease.
immunize, immunise *verb*
to make immune, especially by inoculation or vaccination.
Word Family: **immunity**, *noun*, a) the state of being immune, b) special exemption; **immunization**, *noun.*
[Latin *immunis* exempt from public service]

immunology (*say* im–yoo–**nolla**–jee) *noun*
the study of immunity from disease and methods of producing it.
Word Family: **immunologist**, *noun.*

immure (*say* immewer) *verb*
to enclose or shut in, usually within walls.
[IM– + Latin *murus* a wall]

immutable (*say* immewta–b'l) *adjective*
not changing or able to be changed.
Word Family: **immutably**, *adverb*; **immutability** (*say* im–mewta–**billi**–tee), *noun.*

imp *noun*
1. an elf.
2. a mischievous or naughty child.
Word Family: **impish**, *adjective*, mischievous; **impishly**, *adverb*; **impishness**, *noun.*

impact *noun*
the striking or contact of one thing against another: 'the *impact* of the blow knocked him over'.
Usage: 'the news had little *impact* on us' (= effect).

impacted *adjective*
1. pressed or forced closely together.
2. (of a tooth) not able to grow out naturally.
[Latin *impactus* thrust against]

impair *verb*
to spoil or make worse.
Word Family: **impairment**, *noun.*

impala (*say* im-**pah**-la) *noun*
a large African antelope.

impale *verb*
to pierce through or fix on a sharp pointed object.

impalpable (*say* im-**pal**pa-b'l) *adjective*
not able to be touched or felt.
Usage: 'the painting had an *impalpable* beauty' (= not easy to understand or explain).
Word Family: **impalpably**, *adverb*; **impalpability** (*say* impalpa-**billi**-tee), *noun.*

impart *verb*
1. to tell: 'Helen *imparted* the latest news to Bob'.
2. to give to: 'candlelight *imparted* a cosy glow to the room'.

impartial (*say* im-**par**-sh'l) *adjective*
free from bias, prejudice or favouritism.
Word Family: **impartiality** (*say* im-parshi-**alli**-tee), *noun*; **impartially**, *adverb.*

impassable (*say* im-**pah**sa-b'l) *adjective*
not able to be travelled or passed along.
Word Family: **impassability** (*say* impahsa-**billi**-tee), *noun.*

impasse (*say* **am**-pass) *noun*
a situation which allows no escape or solution.
[French]

impassioned (*say* im-**pash**'nd) *adjective*
full of feeling or passion.
Word Family: **impassion**, *verb.*

impassive *adjective*
not feeling or expressing emotion: 'her *impassive* reaction to the news was very surprising'.
Word Family: **impassivity** (*say* impa-**sivvi**-tee), *noun*; **impassively**, *adverb.*

impatient (*say* im-**pay**-sh'nt) *adjective*
eager for relief, change or progress: '*impatient* because of the delay'.
Word Family: **impatiently**, *adverb*; **impatience**, *noun.*

impeach *verb*
1. *Law:* to accuse a government official of a crime against the public.
2. to attack or bring a charge against.
Word Family: **impeachment**, *noun*; **impeachable**, *adjective*, making one likely to be impeached.

impeccable (*say* im-**pekk**a-b'l) *adjective*
faultless.
Word Family: **impeccably**, *adverb*; **impeccability** (*say* impekka-**billi**-tee), *noun.*
[IM- + Latin *peccare* to sin]

impecunious (*say* impi-**kew**nius) *adjective*
having little or no money.
Word Family: **impecuniousness**, *noun.*
[IM- + Latin *pecunia* money]

impedance (*say* im-**pee**-d'nce) *noun*
Electricity: the total resistance presented by a circuit to an alternating current.

impede (*say* im-**peed**) *verb*
to obstruct.
[Latin *impedire* from *pes, pedis* a foot]

impediment (*say* im-**peddi**-m'nt) *noun*
1. an obstacle or obstruction.
2. a defect, especially of speech.

impel (*say* im-**pel**) *verb*
(**impelled**, **impelling**)
1. to urge to action.
2. to cause to move.
[Latin *impellere* to push against]

impending *adjective*
about to happen or come: 'the town prepared for the *impending* flood'.
[Latin *impendere* to hang over]

impenetrable (*say* im-**penn**itra-b'l) *adjective*
not able to be penetrated or entered.
Usage: 'the crime remained an *impenetrable* mystery' (= incomprehensible).
Word Family: **impenetrability** (*say* im-pennitra-**billi**-tee), *noun.*

impenitent (*say* im-**penni**-t'nt) *adjective*
not repenting.

imperative (*say* im-**perra**-tiv) *adjective*
1. essential or compulsory: 'it is *imperative* that we get there on time'.
2. commanding or requiring obedience: 'his *imperative* gesture made us leave without further ado'.
3. *Grammar:* see MOOD (2).

Word Family: **imperative,** *noun,* a) a command, b) (Grammar) the imperative mood.
[Latin *imperare* to command]

imperceptible (*say* impa-**septi**-b'l) *adjective*
almost unable to be seen or perceived: 'through the heavy beard his smile was *imperceptible*'.
Word Family: **imperceptibly,** *adverb.*

imperfect (*say* im-**per**-fikt) *adjective*
not perfect or complete.
imperfect *noun*
Grammar: the tense of a verb which expresses an event not completed at the time referred to. *Example:* it happened as I *was walking* across the road.
Word Family: **imperfectly,** *adverb;* **imperfection** (*say* impa-**fek**-sh'n), *noun,* a) the state of being imperfect, b) a fault or flaw.

imperial (*say* im-**peer**iul) *adjective*
1. of or characteristic of an empire or its ruler.
2. (of weights and measures) standardized by (British) law: '*imperial* gallon'.

imperialism (*say* im-**peer**ia-lizm) *noun*
also called **colonialism**
the dominance of one country over another, either by direct rule or by economic or military influence.
Word Family: **imperialist,** *noun;* **imperialist, imperialistic,** *adjective.*
[Latin *imperium* command, sovereignty]

imperil (*say* im-**perr**il) *verb*
(imperilled, imperilling)
to put in danger.
Word Family: **imperilment,** *noun.*

imperious (*say* im-**peer**i-us) *adjective*
1. arrogant or domineering.
2. urgent.
Word Family: **imperiously,** *adverb;* **imperiousness,** *noun.*

imperishable *adjective*
not able to perish or be destroyed.

impermeable (*say* im-**per**mia-b'l) *adjective*
not able to be passed through.
Word Family: **impermeability** (*say* im-permia-**billi**-tee), *noun;* **impermeably,** *adverb.*

impersonal (*say* im-**per**sa-n'l) *adjective*
1. not influenced by or expressing personal feelings: 'doctors cultivate an *impersonal* attitude towards patients'.
2. *Grammar:* not referring to a particular person or thing. *Example:* *it* seems you are right.
Word Family: **impersonally,** *adverb.*

impersonate (*say* im-**per**sa-nate) *verb*
to imitate or act the part of.
Word Family: **impersonator,** *noun,* a person, especially an actor, who impersonates others; **impersonation,** *noun.*

impertinent (*say* im-**per**ti-nant) *adjective*
1. rude or presumptuous.
2. not relevant or appropriate.
Word Family: **impertinence,** *noun,* a) the state of being impertinent, b) any cheeky or impudent behaviour; **impertinently,** *adverb.*

imperturbable (*say* impa-**terba**-b'l) *adjective*
not easily agitated or excited.
Word Family: **imperturbability** (*say* impa-terba-**billi**-tee), *noun;* **imperturbably,** *adverb.*

impervious (*say* im-**per**vi-us) **imperviable** *adjective*
not allowing the passage of fluids, etc.: '*impervious* rock'.
impervious to, 'she is *impervious to* criticism from anybody' (= unaffected by).
Word Family: **imperviousness,** *noun;* **imperviously,** *adverb.*

impetigo (*say* impi-**tie**-go) *noun*
an infectious condition of the skin which causes ulcers, usually on the face, especially in children.
[Latin *impetere* to attack]

impetuous (*say* im-**pet**-yewus) *adjective*
hasty or rash.
Word Family: **impetuosity** (*say* im-pet-yoo-**ossi**-tee), **impetuousness,** *nouns;* **impetuously,** *adverb.*

impetus (*say* **impi**-tus) *noun*
a) the energy or force of something which is moving. b) a stimulus or impulse: 'success provided a new *impetus* to work harder'.
[Latin, an attack]

impiety (*say* im-**pie**-a-tee) *noun*
a lack of respect or reverence.

impinge (*say* im-**pinj**) *verb*
to have an effect or impact on.

Usage: 'the harsh voice *impinged* on the restful silence' (= broke in, interrupted).
[Latin *impingere* to thrust against]

impious (*say* **impi**–us) *adjective*
without respect or reverence.
Word Family: **impiously**, *adverb*; **impiousness**, *noun.*

impish *adjective*
Word Family: see IMP.

implacable (*say* im–**plakk**a–b'l) *adjective*
not able to be appeased or pacified: 'the *implacable* enemy ignored all attempts to negotiate'.
Word Family: **implacability** (*say* im–plakka–**billi**–tee), *noun*; **implacably**, *adverb.*

implant (*say* im–**plahnt**) *verb*
to plant or fix in: 'the image was firmly *implanted* in her mind'.
implant (*say* **im**–plahnt) *noun*
any substance put into a body, such as a grafted tissue, a drug, radioactive substances, etc.
Word Family: **implantation**, *noun.*

implausible (*say* im–**plawza**–b'l) *adjective*
not appearing likely to be true.
Word Family: **implausibly**, *adverb*; **implausibility** (*say* im–plawza–**billi**–tee), *noun.*

implement (*say* **impli**–m'nt) *noun*
any tool.
implement *verb*
to put into use or effect: 'the new road rules will be strictly *implemented*'.
Word Family: **implementation**, *noun.*
[Latin *implere* to fill up]

implicate (*say* **impli**–kate) *verb*
to involve in or with something: a) 'he is *implicated* in the crime because he knew of it beforehand'; b) 'the evidence *implicates* him'.
[from Latin]

implication *noun*
1. the state of being implicated: 'her *implication* in the crime was proved beyond doubt'.
2. anything which is implied or suggested: 'the serious *implications* of his words only struck us later'.

implicit (*say* im–**pliss**it) *adjective*
1. being implied or suggested but not actually expressed: 'mother's *implicit* disapproval'.
2. absolute or unquestioning: 'an *implicit* belief in all she was taught'.
Word Family: **implicitly**, *adverb*; **implicitness**, *noun.*
[Latin *implicitus* involved]

implore *verb*
to ask earnestly or urgently.
Word Family: **imploringly**, *adverb.*
[IM– + Latin *plorare* to weep]

implosion (*say* im–**plo**–*zh*'n) *noun*
a bursting inwards.
Word Family: **implode**, *verb.*
[IM– + (ex)PLOSION]

imply (*say* im–**ply**) *verb*
(**implied**, **implying**)
1. to suggest in a subtle or indirect way: 'your terseness *implies* that you are very busy'.
2. to require or involve logically or necessarily: 'movement *implies* energy'.
Common Error: do not confuse with INFER.

impolite *adjective*
not polite.
Word Family: **impolitely**, *adverb.*

imponderable (*say* im–**pondera**–b'l) *adjective*
not able to be weighed or estimated.
Word Family: **imponderably**, *adverb*; **imponderable**, *noun*, something which cannot be weighed or estimated, such as an emotion.
[IM– + Latin *ponderis* of a weight]

import (*say* im**port**) *verb*
1. to bring in from an outside source, especially a foreign country.
2. to mean or signify.
import (*say* **im**port) *noun*
1. anything which is imported or brought from outside.
2. the meaning: 'what was the *import* of his visit?'.
3. importance: 'it was a message of some *import* for all of us'.
Word Family: **importation**, *noun*, a) the act of importing, especially foreign goods, b) something that is imported; **importer**, *noun*, a person or company that imports goods.
[IM– + Latin *portare* to carry]

important (*say* im–**port**'nt) *adjective*
1. of great meaning, significance, value, etc.: 'an *important* role in the play'.
2. having great power or influence: 'an *important* person'.
Word Family: **importance**, *noun*; **importantly**, *adverb.*

importunate (*say* im–**port**–yoonit) *adjective*
urgent or persistent.

Word Family: **importunately**, *adverb*; **importunity** (*say* impor–**tewni**–tee), *noun.*

importune (*say* im–**port**–yoon) *verb*
to beg or press for urgently.
[Latin *importunus* inconvenient]

impose (*say* im–**poze**) *verb*
to establish or place from, or as if from, a position of authority: 'the judge *imposed* a heavy fine on the convicted vandals'.
Usage: 'do not let that lazy man *impose* on you' (= make demands, take advantage of).
[Latin *impositus* placed upon]

imposing *adjective*
impressive.

imposition (*say* impa–**zish**'n) *noun*
1. a) the act of laying or placing on. b) anything which is imposed, such as a burden, punishment, etc.
2. a deceiving or taking advantage of.

impossible *adjective*
1. not possible.
2. not able to be tolerated: 'what an *impossible* person!'.
Word Family: **impossibly**, *adverb*; **impossibility** (*say* impossi–**billi**–tee), *noun.*

impost (*say* **im**–post) *noun*
a tax or duty, especially customs duty.

impostor (*say* im–**posta**) *noun*
a person who deceives or commits a fraud, especially under an assumed name.
Word Family: **imposture**, *noun*, a) the act or practice of deceiving, b) a deception

impotent (*say* **im**pa–t'nt) *adjective*
1. having no strength, power or effect.
2. (of a man) unable to develop an erection in response to sexual stimuli.
Word Family: **impotence**, **impotency**, *noun*, **impotently**, *adverb.*

impound (*say* im–**pound**) *verb*
1. to shut in or as if in a pound: 'the lost dog was *impounded* until its owner could be found'.
2. to seize legally: 'the stolen goods were *impounded* by the police'.

impoverish (*say* im–**povva**–rish) *verb*
to make poor: 'the family was *impoverished* by years of medical costs'.
Usage: 'language is *impoverished* by misuse' (= made poor in quality).
Word Family: **impoverishment**, *noun.*

impracticable (*say* im–**prak**tika–b'l) *adjective*
not practicable.
Word Family: **impracticability** (*say* im–praktika–**billi**–tee), *noun.*

imprecation (*say* impri–**kay**–sh'n) *noun*
a curse.
Word Family: **imprecate**, *verb*; **imprecatory**, *adjective.*
[Latin *imprecari* to invoke a curse]

impregnable (*say* im–**preg**na–b'l) *adjective*
not able to be taken or overcome: 'the strong walls of the fort made it *impregnable*'.
Word Family: **impregnability** (*say* im–pregna–**billi**–tee), *noun*; **impregnably**, *adverb.*
[from Old French]

impregnate (*say* **im**preg–nate) *verb*
1. to fertilize or make pregnant.
2. to fill throughout: 'the water was *impregnated* with salt'.
Word Family: **impregnation**, *noun.*
[from Latin]

impresario (*say* impra–**sah**–rio) *noun*
a producer or manager of theatrical or musical entertainments.
[Italian *impresa* enterprise]

impress (1) (*say* im–**press**) *verb*
1. to affect or influence the opinion of, especially favourably: 'we were all *impressed* by the excellent food at the hotel'.
Usage: 'you must *impress* her with the seriousness of the matter' (= make see).
2. to press or stamp.
Word Family: **impress** (*say* **im**–press), *noun*, a mark made by pressing or stamping.

impress (2) (*say* im–**press**) *verb*
to take forcibly for public use or service: 'civilians were *impressed* into the armed forces when war broke out'.

impression (*say* im–**presh**'n) *noun*
1. a mark or shape made by pressing, stamping, etc.: 'the dentist made a wax *impression* of her front teeth'.
2. an effect or influence on the mind or feelings: a) 'his rudeness creates a bad *impression*'; b) 'I get the *impression* you don't like him'.
3. an imitation: 'he does *impressions* of famous people as a stage act'.

impressionable (*say* im–**presh**'na–b'l) *adjective*
easily impressed or influenced.

impressionism (*say* im–**presh**'n–izm) *noun*

a style of painting, music or literature aimed at suggesting mood or immediate feelings about a subject, rather than close surface detail or analysis.
Word Family: **impressionist,** *noun,* a) a person using the style of impressionism, b) a person who imitates people; **impressionist, impressionistic,** *adjectives.*

impressive *adjective*
having a strong or awesome effect or impression.
Word Family: **impressively,** *adverb;* **impressiveness,** *noun.*

imprimatur (*say* imprim-**ahta**) *noun*
official permission or approval to do something, such as to publish a book.
[Latin, let it be printed]

imprint (*say* **im**-print) *noun*
a mark made by pressing or stamping.
Usage: 'his unhappy childhood left a powerful *imprint* on his character' (= effect, impression).
Word Family: **imprint** (*say* im-**print**), *verb,* to print, stamp or impress.

imprison *verb*
to put in prison.
Word Family: **imprisonment,** *noun.*

improbable (*say* im-**probba**-b'l) *adjective*
not probable or likely.

impromptu (*say* im-**promp**-tew) *adjective, adverb*
done or made without any preparation, practice, etc.
Word Family: **impromptu,** *noun,* an impromptu performance.
[Latin *in promptu* in readiness]

improper (*say* im-**proppa**) *adjective*
not suitable or correct, especially according to moral conventions.

improper fraction
see FRACTION.

impropriety (*say* impra-**prya**-tee) *noun*
a) the state of being improper or unsuitable. b) any improper action, etc.

improve (*say* im-**proov**) *verb*
1. to make or become better.
2. to clear, cultivate or increase the value of land.
improvement *noun*
a) the act of improving. b) anything which improves or adds to the beauty, value, etc. of another: 'bright colours made a great *improvement* to the old house'.

improvident (*say* im-**provvi**-d'nt) *adjective*
1. not cautious or prudent.
2. not providing for the future.
Word Family: **improvidence,** *noun;* **improvidently,** *adverb.*

improvise (*say* **im**pra-vize) *verb*
to do or create something without preparation, practice, sufficient materials, etc.
Word Family: **improvisation,** *noun,* a) the act of improvising, b) anything which is improvised; **improviser, improvisator** (*say* im-**provvi**-zayta), *nouns,* a person who improvises.
[Latin *improvisus* unexpected]

imprudent (*say* im-**proo**-d'nt) *adjective*
not prudent or discreet.
Word Family: **imprudence,** *noun;* **imprudently,** *noun.*

impudent (*say* **im**-pew-d'nt) *adjective*
boldly rude or disrespectful.
Word Family: **impudence,** *noun;* **impudently,** *adverb.*
[from Latin]

impugn (*say* im-**pewn**) *verb*
to challenge or call into doubt or question.
[IM- + Latin *pugnare* to fight]

impulse (*say* **im**-pulse) *noun*
1. a sudden urge or desire: 'he felt a great *impulse* to dance on the sand'.
2. a stimulating force or effect.
3. *Biology:* a nerve impulse.
4. *Physics:* the product of a force and the time for which it acts on a body.
[Latin *impulsus* pressure, incitement]

impulsion (*say* im-**pul**-sh'n) *noun*
a) the act of impelling or driving forward. b) a force or impulse.

impulsive (*say* im-**pulsiv**) *adjective*
1. rash or hasty: 'an *impulsive* spender'.
2. done on an impulse: 'she gave an *impulsive* smile'.
Word Family: **impulsively,** *adverb;* **impulsiveness,** *noun.*

impunity (*say* im-**pewni**-tee) *noun*
a freedom from punishment or the consequences of one's actions.

impure (*say* im-**pure**) *adjective*
not pure.
Word Family: **impurity,** *noun.*

impute (*say* im-**pewt**) *verb*
to attribute to or blame with.
Word Family: **imputation,** *noun.*
[Latin *imputare* to debit or credit]

in *preposition*
a word used to indicate the following:

1. (place) 'a house *in* the country'.
2. (time) '6 o'clock *in* the morning'.
3. (direction) 'walk *in* a straight line'.
4. (situation, condition) a) 'they're *in* love'; b) 'she is *in* a rage'.
5. (inclusion) '6 children *in* the family'.
6. (manner, method) a) 'she talks *in* a posh way'; b) 'he paints *in* oil colours'.
7. (form, shape) a) 'stand *in* a line'; b) 'her hair hung *in* pigtails'.
8. (activity) 'she's *in* advertising'.
Phrases:
in for, 'we are *in for* rain' (= about to experience).
in on, 'who else is *in on* the joke?' (= aware of, involved in).
in that, because.
in *adjective, adverb*
1. special uses with many common verbs to produce specific meanings: a) '*come in*' (= to enter); b) '*fill in*' (= to complete, to substitute); c) '*give in*' (= to surrender); d) '*step in*' (= to intervene).
2. special uses with the verb to be:
a) 'she'll be *in* late' (= back, at home).
b) 'she's *in* with the boss' (= in a favoured position).
c) 'when are artichokes *in*?' (= in season, available).
d) 'which team is *in* at the moment?' (= batting).
3. most fashionable or up-to-date: a) 'are fur hats *in* this winter?'; b) 'she uses the latest *in-words*'.
4. (*informal*) a large or public gathering for a specific activity: 'the strikers staged a *sit-in*'.
in *noun*
ins and **outs**, the details or intricacies.
[Latin]

in- (1)
a prefix meaning in or into, as in *include.*

in- (2)
a prefix meaning not, lacking or without, as in *invariable.* Variants of in- are: **il-** (*illegal*), **im-** (*impossible*) and **ir-** (*irregular*).

inability (*say* inna-**billi**-tee) *noun*
a lack of power or capacity.

in absentia (*say* in ab-**sen**sha)
in or during one's absence.
[Latin]

inaccessible (*say* in-ak**sessi**-b'l) *adjective*
not accessible.
Word Family: **inaccessibly**, *adverb*; **inaccessibility** (*say* in-aksessi-**billi**-tee), *noun.*

inaccurate (*say* in-**ak**-yoorit) *adjective*
not accurate.
Word Family: **inaccurately**, *adverb*; **inaccuracy, inaccurateness**, *nouns.*

inactive (*say* in-**ak**-tiv) *adjective*
not active.
Word Family: **inactivity** (*say* in-aktivvi-tee), **inaction**, *nouns*; **inactively**, *adverb.*

inadequate (*say* in-**addi**-kwit) *adjective*
not adequate.
Word Family: **inadequacy**, *noun*; **inadequately**, *adverb.*

inadmissible (*say* in-ad-**missi**-b'l) *adjective*
not admissible.
Word Family: **inadmissibility** (*say* in-admissi-**billi**-tee), *noun*; **inadmissibly**, *adverb.*

inadvertent (*say* in-ad-**ver**-t'nt) *adjective*
not intended or deliberate: 'her hurtful remark had been quite *inadvertent*'.
Word Family: **inadvertently**, *adverb*; **inadvertency, inadvertence**, *noun.*
[IN- (2) + Latin *advertens* paying attention]

inalienable (*say* in-ayli-enna-b'l) *adjective*
not able to be taken away: 'every citizen has an *inalienable* right to life'.

inane *adjective*
silly or senseless.
Word Family: **inanely**, *adverb*; **inanity** (*say* in-**anni**-tee), *noun.*
[Latin *inanis* empty, vain]

inanimate (*say* in-**anni**-mit) *adjective*
not having life: 'chairs are *inanimate* objects'.

inanition (*say* inna-**nish**'n) *noun*
exhaustion from lack of food.
[Latin *inanis* empty]

inapplicable (*say* inna-**plikka**-b'l) *adjective*
not applicable: 'your theory is *inapplicable* to the present situation'.

inappropriate (*say* inna-**pro**-pree-it) *adjective*
not appropriate or suitable.
Word Family: **inappropriately**, *adverb*; **inappropriateness**, *noun.*

inapt *adjective*
1. unskilful.
2. not apt or appropriate.

Word Family: **inaptly**, *adverb*; **inaptness**, *noun*; **inaptitude**, *noun*, a lack of skill or talent.

inarticulate (*say* innar-**tik**-yoolit) *adjective*
1. not able to speak or express oneself clearly: 'she was made *inarticulate* by indignation'.
2. not using human speech: 'the *inarticulate* cries of animals'.
Word Family: **inarticulateness**, *noun*; **inarticulately**, *adverb*.

inasmuch *adverb*
inasmuch as, since or because.

inattentive *adjective*
not attentive.
Word Family: **inattention**, **inattentiveness**, *nouns*.

inaudible (*say* in-**awdi**-b'l) *adjective*
not able to be heard.
Word Family: **inaudibly**, *adverb*.

inauguration
(*say* in-aw-gew-**ray**-sh'n) *noun*
1. a formal or official introduction, opening, etc., such as the installing of an official in office.
2. any important beginning.
Word Family: **inaugurate** (*say* in-**aw**-gew-rate), *verb*; **inaugural**, *adjective*, of or for an inauguration.
[from Latin]

inauspicious (*say* innaw-**spish**us) *adjective*
not favourable or auspicious.
Word Family: **inauspiciously**, *adverb*.

inboard *adjective, adverb*
being within the hull of a boat: 'an *inboard* motor'.

inborn *adjective*
natural or possessed from birth: 'he has an *inborn* artistic ability'.

inbred *adjective*
1. inborn.
2. relating to or resulting from inbreeding.

inbreeding *noun*
Biology: the mating of closely related individuals which often discloses genetic weaknesses.

Inca *noun*
a) any member of the major tribe of South American Indians in Peru, at the time of the Spanish invasion in 1519. b) the ruler of these people.

incalculable (*say* in-**kalkew**-la-b'l) *adjective*
1. not able to be calculated.
2. uncertain or unpredictable: 'the weather is quite *incalculable* this autumn'.
Word Family: **incalculably**, *adverb*.

incandescent (*say* in-kan-**dess**'nt) *adjective*
giving out light as a result of being heated.
Word Family: **incandescence**, *noun*; **incandesce**, *verb*.
[Latin *incandescens* becoming white]

incantation (*say* in-kan-**tay**-sh'n) *noun*
a) a spell. b) the chanting of a spell.
Word Family: **incantatory** (*say* in-**kan**-tayta-ree), *adjective*.
[from Latin]

incapable (*say* in-**kay**pa-b'l) *adjective*
not capable: 'he is *incapable* of talking quietly'.
Word Family: **incapability** (*say* in-kaypa-**billi**-tee), *noun*.

incapacitate (*say* inka-**passi**-tate) *verb*
to take away the strength, power or ability of: 'the car accident *incapacitated* him for many weeks'.

incapacity (*say* inka-**passi**-tee) *noun*
a lack of ability or capability.

incarcerate (*say* in-**kar**sa-rate) *verb*
to shut in or confine.
Word Family: **incarceration**, *noun*.
[IN- (1) + Latin *carcer* prison]

incarnate (*say* in-**kar**nit) *adjective*
1. having a body or human form: 'a goddess *incarnate*'.
2. being the personification of: 'that man is wisdom *incarnate*'.
Word Family: **incarnation** (*say* in-kar-**nay**-sh'n), *noun*, a) the act of becoming incarnate, b) a person or thing seen as representing a special quality, etc.; **incarnate** (*say* in-**kar**nate), *verb*.
[IN- (1) + Latin *carnis* of flesh]

incautious (*say* in-**kaw**shus) *adjective*
not cautious or careful.

incendiary (*say* in-**send**-ya-ree) *adjective*
relating to the starting of fires.
Usage: 'the union leader's *incendiary* speech inspired the workers' (= provocative).
incendiary *noun*
a person or thing, such as a bomb or shell containing phosphorus, which starts fires.
[from Latin]

incense (1) (*say* **in**–sense) *noun*
a gum or other substance which gives a pleasant smell when burnt, often used in religious ceremonies.

incense (2) (*say* in–**sense**) *verb*
to enrage.
[Latin *incensus* kindled]

incentive (*say* in–**sen**tiv) *noun*
something which encourages a person to do something: 'the promise of a holiday was an *incentive* for her to pass her exams'.
[Latin *incentivus* striking up a tune]

inception (*say* in–**sep**–sh'n) *noun*
a beginning.
[from Latin]

incessant (*say* in–**sess**'nt) *adjective*
unceasing.
Word Family: **incessantly**, *adverb.*

incest (*say* **in**–sest) *noun*
the act of sexual intercourse between a male and a female who are so closely related that marriage between them is forbidden by law.
Word Family: **incestuous**, *adjective*; **incestuously**, *adverb*; **incestuousness**, *noun.*
[Latin *incestus* unchaste]

inch *noun*
1. a unit of length equal to one–twelfth of a foot, about 2·54 cm.
2. a very small distance or margin: 'he escaped death by *inches*'.
every inch, 'the young ruler looked *every inch* a king in his ceremonial robes' (= in every respect).
Word Family: **inch**, *verb*, to move by inches or very small degrees.

inchoate (*say* in–**ko**–ate) *adjective*
just begun, half–formed or undeveloped: 'a vague, *inchoate* idea'.
[from Latin]

incidence (*say* **in**si–d'nce) *noun*
1. the extent or frequency with which something occurs: 'the *incidence* of road accidents'.
2. the act or the manner of falling upon a surface: 'notice the angle of *incidence* of the light falling on this screen'.
3. *Maths:* the partial overlapping of two figures, or a figure and a line.
[Latin *incidens* falling upon, happening]

incident (*say* **in**si–d'nt) *noun*
1. an event, especially one of less importance than others.
2. a serious or unpleasant event, such as a fight.
Word Family: **incident**, *adjective*, incidental to.

incidental (*say* insi–**den**–t'l) *adjective*
1. accompanying but not forming a necessary or important part of: a) '*incidental* music'; b) '*incidental* expenses'.
2. occurring with or as a natural result of: 'scratches and bruises *incidental* to the profession of a lady wrestler'.
Word Family: **incidentally**, *adverb*, in an incidental manner; **incidentals**, *plural noun*, any minor expenses.

incinerate (*say* in–**sinna**–rate) *verb*
to consume by burning.
Word Family: **incineration**, *noun*; **incinerator**, *noun*, an enclosed chamber for burning rubbish.
[IN– (1) + Latin *cineris* of ashes]

incipient (*say* insippi–ent) *adjective*
in an early stage.
[Latin *incipiens* beginning]

incision (*say* in–**sizh**'n) *noun*
a) a cut or gash made with a sharp instrument. b) the act of making such a cut.
Word Family: **incise** (*say* in–**size**), *verb.*
[from Latin]

incisive (*say* in–**sigh**–siv) *adjective*
penetrating or keen: 'her *incisive* comments on the play summed it up in a nutshell'.
Word Family: **incisively**, *adverb*; **incisiveness**, *noun.*

incisor (*say* in–**sigh**–zor) *noun*
Anatomy: any of the sharp flat teeth at the front of the jaw, for cutting and biting food.

incite (*say* in–**site**) *verb*
to stir up or provoke to action.
incitement *noun*
1. the act of inciting: 'you're charged with the *incitement* of a riot'.
2. something which incites: 'your words acted as an *incitement* to the mob'.
Word Family: **inciter**, *noun*; **incitingly**, *adverb.*
[Latin *incitare* to urge on]

inclement (*say* in–**klemm**'nt) *adjective*
(of the weather) stormy or harsh.
Word Family: **inclemently**, *adverb*; **inclemency**, *noun.*

incline (*say* in–**kline**) *verb*
1. to deviate from the vertical or horizontal.
Usage: 'he *inclined* his head in silent agreement' (= bent or bowed).

2. to have or cause a tendency: a) 'I'm *inclined* to be lazy'; b) 'your letter *inclined* her to think you were in trouble'.
inclination (*say* inkli–**nay**–sh'n) *noun*
1. a) a slope or slant. b) the degree of this.
2. a tendency or liking: 'an *inclination* to talk too much'.
3. *Maths:* the angle between two intersecting lines or planes.
Word Family: **incline** (*say* **in**–kline), *noun*, a slope.
[IN– (1) + Latin *clinare* to bend]

include *verb*
to contain or consider as part of a group or whole: 'don't forget to *include* her on the invitation list'.
inclusive *adjective*
1. taking everything into account: 'our charges are *inclusive* of tips'.
2. including the limits specified: 'from 16 to 22 *inclusive*'.
Word Family: **inclusion** (*say* in–**kloo**–*zh*'n), *noun*; **inclusively**, *adverb*; **inclusiveness**, *noun*, the fact of being inclusive.
[IN– (1) + Latin *claudere* to shut]

incognito (*say* in–kog–**nee**to) *adverb, adjective*
with one's name, identity, etc. concealed.
Word Family: **incognito** (*say* in–**kog**nito), *noun*, the false identity assumed by a person who is incognito.
[Italian, unknown]

incoherent (*say* inko–**heer**'nt) *adjective*
1. not connected or ordered: 'rewrite this *incoherent* sentence'.
2. unable to express oneself clearly: 'he was *incoherent* with fury'.
Word Family: **incoherently**, *adverb*; **incoherence**, *noun*.

incombustible *adjective*
unable to be set on fire.
Word Family: **incombustible**, *noun*.

income (*say* **in**kum) *noun*
the total of payments received, usually in a year, from salary or wages, investments, rents, business operations, etc.

incoming *adjective*
a) coming in: 'the *incoming* tide'. b) about to take office: 'the *incoming* President'.

incommensurate
(*say* inka–**men**sha–rit) *adjective*
also called **incommensurable**
disproportionate or not comparable: 'his notions of his own importance are *incommensurate* with his abilities'.
Word Family: **incommensurability** (*say* inka–menshera–**billi**–tee), *noun*.

incommunicado
(*say* inka–mewni–**kah**do) *adjective*
without the means or right of communicating with others, especially as a prisoner.
[from Spanish]

incomparable (*say* in–**kom**pera–b'l) *adjective*
1. not able to be equalled: '*incomparable* beauty'.
2. not capable of comparison: 'they are as *incomparable* as cheese and chalk'.
Word Family: **incomparably**, *adverb*; **incomparability** (*say* in–kompera–**billi**–tee), *noun*.

incompatible (*say* in–kom–**patti**–b'l) *adjective*
1. unable to exist in harmony.
2. not consistent with; logically opposed to.
Word Family: **incompatibly**, *adverb*; **incompatibility** (*say* in–kom–patti–**billi**–tee), *noun*.

incompetent (*say* in–**kom**pi–t'nt) *adjective*
not competent.
Word Family: **incompetent**, *noun*, a person who is incompetent; **incompetently**, *adverb*; **incompetence**, *noun*.

incomplete *adjective*
not complete.

incomprehensible
(*say* in–kompra–**hen**si–b'l) *adjective*
not able to be understood.

inconceivable (*say* inkon–**seeva**–b'l) *adjective*
not able to be imagined.
Word Family: **inconceivably**, *adverb*.

inconclusive (*say* in–kon–**kloo**siv) *adjective*
a) not decisive or convincing: 'an *inconclusive* argument'. b) not bringing a definite result: '*inconclusive* experiments'.
Word Family: **inconclusively**, *adverb*; **inconclusiveness**, *noun*.

incongruent (*say* in–**kon**–grew'nt) *adjective*
not congruent.
Word Family: **incongruence**, *noun*; **incongruently**, *adverb*.

incongruous (*say* in–**kon**–grew–us) *adjective*
out of place or inappropriate: 'the bathroom seemed an *incongruous* place for a writing desk'.
Word Family: **incongruously**, *adverb*; **incongruousness**, *noun*; **incongruity** (*say* in–kon–**grew**i–tee), *noun*, a) the quality of being incongruous, b) something incongruous.

inconsequent (*say* in–**konsi**–kw'nt) *adjective*
not consistent with or following logically from what has gone before: 'an *inconsequent* remark'.
Word Family: **inconsequence**, *noun*; **inconsequently**, *adverb*.

inconsequential (*say* in–konsi–**kwen**–sh'l) *adjective*
1. not consistent or logical.
2. of little or no importance.
Word Family: **inconsequentially**, *adverb*.

inconsiderable (*say* inkon–**sidd**era–b'l) *adjective*
1. small in value, amount, size, etc.
2. unworthy of notice.

inconsiderate (*say* inkon–**sidd**a–rit) *adjective*
lacking regard for the feelings of others.
Word Family: **inconsiderately**, *adverb*; **inconsiderateness**, *noun*.

inconsistent (*say* inkon–**sist**'nt) *adjective*
self-contradictory or lacking agreement between the parts: 'his account of the accident was *inconsistent*'.
Usages:
a) 'what he practises is *inconsistent* with what he preaches' (= not in harmony).
b) 'he's so *inconsistent* you never know what he'll do next' (= changeable).
Word Family: **inconsistently**, *adverb*; **inconsistency**, *noun*, a) the quality of being inconsistent, b) something inconsistent.

inconsolable (*say* inkon–**sole**–a–b'l) *adjective*
not capable of being consoled.

inconsonant (*say* in–**kon**sa–nent) *adjective*
not in accord or agreement: 'her account was *inconsonant* with the facts'.

inconspicuous (*say* inkon–**spik**–yewus) *adjective*
not conspicuous.
Word Family: **inconspicuously**, *adverb*; **inconspicuousness**, *noun*.

inconstant (*say* in–**kon**–st'nt) *adjective*
not constant: '*inconstant* winds'.
Usage: 'her *inconstant* affection for him caused him endless worry' (= fickle).
Word Family: **inconstancy**, *noun*; **inconstantly**, *adverb*.

incontestable (*say* inkon–**testa**–b'l) *adjective*
beyond dispute.
Word Family: **incontestably**, *adverb*.

incontinent (*say* in–**kon**–tinnent) *adjective*
lacking self-control or self-restraint, such as being unable to control one's urination.
Word Family: **incontinence**, *noun*; **incontinently**, *adverb*.

incontrovertible (*say* in kontra–**verta**–b'l) *adjective*
not able to be disputed
Word Family: **incontrovertibly**, *adverb*.

inconvenient (*say* inkon–veeni–ent) *adjective*
not convenient.
Word Family: **inconveniently**, *adverb*; **inconvenience**, *noun*; **inconvenience**, *verb*, to cause trouble, difficulty, etc. to.

inconvertible *adjective*
not able to be converted or exchanged.

incorporate (*say* in–**kor**pa–rate) *verb*
1. to take in or include as part of a whole: 'he *incorporated* my suggestion into his final draft'.
2. to register a business as a company.
Word Family: **incorporation**, *noun*.

incorporeal (*say* inkor–pawriul) *adjective*
having no physical or bodily form.

incorrect (*say* inka–**rekt**) *adjective*
not correct: a) 'an *incorrect* answer'; b) '*incorrect* behaviour'.
Word Family: **incorrectly**, *adverb*; **incorrectness**, *noun*.

incorrigible (*say* in–**korr**ija–b'l) *adjective*
incapable of reform or change: a) 'an *incorrigible* criminal'; b) '*incorrigible* habits'.
Word Family: **incorrigibly**, *adverb*.
[IN– (2) + Latin *corrigere* to put straight]

incorruptible (*say* inko–**rup**ti–b'l) *adjective*
1. not capable of physical decay.
2. not capable of being corrupted.

Word Family: **incorruptibility** (*say* inko-rupta-**billi**-tee), *noun*; **incorruptibly**, *adverb*.

increase (*say* in-**kreece**) *verb*
to make or become greater or larger.
increase (*say* **in**-kreece) *noun*
a) a growing or becoming greater. b) the amount of growth or addition.
Word Family: **increasingly**, *adverb*, more and more.
[IN- (1) + Latin *crescere* to grow]

incredible (*say* in-**kreddi**-b'l) *adjective*
unbelievable: 'an *incredible* act of rudeness'.
Word Family: **incredibly**, *adverb*; **incredibility** (*say* in-kredda-**billi**-tee), *noun*.
Common Error: do not confuse with INCREDULOUS.

incredulous (*say* in-**kred**-yoolus) *adjective*
disbelieving: 'she dismissed my excuse with an *incredulous* sneer'.
Word Family: **incredulously**, *adverb*; **incredulity** (*say* inkred-**yoola**-tee), *noun*.
Common Error: do not confuse with INCREDIBLE.

increment (*say* **in**kri-m'nt) *noun*
1. an increase or gain: 'his salary is subject to annual *increments*'.
2. *Maths:* a small change in a variable.
[from Latin]

incriminate (*say* in-**krimmi**-nate) *verb*
to involve or implicate in an accusation of wrongdoing.
Word Family: **incrimination**, *noun*.
[IN- (1) + Latin *criminis* of an accusation]

incrustation *noun*
1. the act of encrusting.
2. an outer layer, deposit or coat: 'the wind from the sea left an *incrustation* of salt on the car's windscreen'.

incubate (*say* **in**-kewbate) *verb*
to keep something at an even and favourable temperature, as when hatching eggs, keeping premature babies warm, growing bacterial cultures, etc.
Word Family: **incubator**, *noun*, an apparatus which regulates temperature in an enclosed space; **incubatory**, *adjective*; **incubation**, *noun*.
[IN- (1) + Latin *cubare* to lie]

inculcate (*say* **in**-kulkate) *verb*
to instil in the mind, especially by repetition or persistent urging.
Word Family: **inculcation**, *noun*.
[Latin *inculcare* to tread in]

inculpate (*say* **in**-kul-pate) *verb*
1. to accuse.
2. to involve in a charge: 'the evidence *inculpated* his brother as a partner in the crime'.
[IN- (1) + Latin *culpa* fault]

incumbent (*say* in-**kum**-b'nt) *adjective*
resting upon one as a duty: 'it is *incumbent* upon you to warn the children of the dangers of smoking'.
Word Family: **incumbent**, *noun*, a person holding a church or other office; **incumbency**, *noun*, the office held by an incumbent.
[IN- (1) + Latin *cumbens* lying]

incur (*say* in-**ker**) *verb*
(**incurred, incurring**)
1. to become subject to: 'to *incur* a fine'.
2. to bring upon oneself: 'to *incur* great expense'.
[Latin *incurrere* to run into]

incurable (*say* in-**kew**ra-b'l) *adjective*
not capable of being cured: 'an *incurable* disease'.
Word Family: **incurably**, *adverb*; **incurability** (*say* in-kewra-**billi**-tee), *noun*.

incursion (*say* in-**ker**-sh'n) *noun*
a sudden attack or invasion.
Usage: 'buying a car made a considerable *incursion* into my savings' (= inroad).
[from Latin]

indebted (*say* in-**det**tid) *adjective*
1. owing money.
2. under an obligation.
Word Family: **indebtedness**, *noun*.

indecent (*say* in-**dee**-s'nt) *adjective*
1. offensive to good taste.
2. (*informal*) unseemly: 'he left the room in *indecent* haste'.
Word Family: **indecently**, *adverb*; **indecency**, *noun*.

indecipherable
(*say* indi-**sigh**fera-b'l) *adjective*
not capable of being deciphered.

indecision (*say* indi-**si*zh***'n) *noun*
the state of being unable to decide.
Word Family: **indecisive** (*say* indi-**sigh**-siv), *adjective*; **indecisively**, *adverb*.

indecorous (*say* in-**dek**kerus) *adjective*
not decorous.

Word Family: **indecorously**, *adverb*; **indecorum** (*say* indi–**kawrum**), *noun*, indecorous behaviour.

indeed *adverb*
truly or in fact: 'were you pleased with your rise?' 'I was *indeed*!'.

indefatigable (*say* indi–**fattiga**–b'l) *adjective*
untiring or incapable of being tired out.
Word Family: **indefatigably**, *adverb*.
[IN– (2) + Latin *defatigare* to wear out]

indefeasible (*say* indi–**feeza**–b'l) *adjective*
not to be annulled or made void: 'an *indefeasible* right'.

indefensible (*say* indi–**fensi**–b'l) *adjective*
not capable of being defended: a) 'an *indefensible* error'; b) 'an *indefensible* island'.

indefinable (*say* indi–**fine**–a–b'l) *adjective*
not capable of being defined: 'an *indefinable* longing'.
Word Family: **indefinably**, *adverb*.

indefinite (*say* in–**deffi**–nit) *adjective*
1. not definite.
2. unlimited: 'an *indefinite* amount of time'.
indefinite article
Grammar: see ARTICLE.
Word Family: **indefinitely**, *adverb*, without limits.

indelible (*say* in–**delli**–b'l) *adjective*
incapable of being rubbed out or removed.
Word Family: **indelibly**, *adverb*.
[IN– (2) + Latin *delere* to erase]

indelicate (*say* in–**delli**–kit) *adjective*
lacking refinement or good taste: a) 'an *indelicate* remark'; b) '*indelicate* inquiries'.

indemnify (*say* in–**demni**–fie) *verb*
(indemnified, indemnifying)
1. to insure or protect against possible loss or damage.
2. to compensate for damage incurred.
Word Family: **indemnification** (*say* in–demnifi–**kay**–sh'n), *noun*, a) the process of indemnifying, b) compensation.

indemnity (*say* in–**demni**–tee) *noun*
1. a) a protection or security against damage or loss. b) compensation for damage or loss incurred.
2. a legal exemption from penalties incurred.
[Latin *indemnis* unharmed]

indent (*say* in–**dent**) *verb*
1. to set a line or group of lines in from the margin when writing or printing.
2. to form deep notches or recesses in an edge or surface: 'a coastline *indented* by the sea'.
3. to order goods by indent: 'the company's Asian subsidiary *indented* on London for new stock'.
indent (*say* **in**–dent) *noun*
a) an official requisition for stores. b) an order for goods, usually from abroad.
Word Family: **indentation** (*say* inden–**tay**–sh'n), *noun*.
[IN– (1) + Latin *dentatus* toothed]

indenture (*say* in–**dencher**) *noun*
(*usually plural*) an agreement made between two or more persons, especially one between an apprentice and his employer.
Word Family: **indenture**, *verb*.

independent (*say* indi–**pen**–d'nt) *adjective*
not dependent on, influenced or controlled by others: a) 'the colony fought to become *independent* of foreign control'; b) 'let me make an *independent* choice'.
Usage: 'everyone made *independent* transport arrangements' (= separate).
independent means, an income derived by means other than earning a salary, etc.
Word Family: **independent**, *noun*, a person or thing that is independent, especially a person who does not belong to any political party; **independently**, *adverb*; **independence**, *noun*.

independent variable
Maths: see FUNCTION.

indescribable (*say* indi–**skribe**–a–b'l) *adjective*
not able to be described.
Word Family: **indescribably**, *adverb*.

indestructible (*say* indi–**strukta**–b'l) *adjective*
not capable of being destroyed.
Word Family: **indestructibly**, *adverb*; **indestructibility** (*say* indi–strukta–**billi**–tee), *noun*.

indeterminable
(*say* indi–**termina**–b'l) *adjective*

1. not able to be ascertained: 'with no clues, the killer's identity is *indeterminable*'.
2. not able to be decided or settled: 'it's only her word against his, so the argument is *indeterminable*'.

indeterminate (*say* indi-**termi**-nit) *adjective*
not fixed or definite.

index *noun*
plural is **indexes**
1. a list of names, subjects, references etc. in alphabetical order, e.g. at the end of a book, on cards in a library, etc.
2. anything that serves to indicate: 'alertness is an *index* of intelligence'.
3. *Maths:* see EXPONENT. Plural is **indices** (*say* **indi**-seez).
4. a chart or table of relative levels of wages, prices, etc.
index *verb*
1. to provide with or enter into an alphabetical list.
2. to adjust wages, etc. to increases in the cost of living.
Word Family: **indexation** (*say* indek-**say**-sh'n), *noun.*
[Latin, forefinger, sign]

index finger
the forefinger.

Indian *noun*
1. a member of one of the races which inhabit India.
2. an Amerindian.
West Indian, a member of one of the races which inhabit the West Indies.
Word Family: **Indian,** *adjective.*

Indian file
single file.

Indian hemp
see MARIJUANA.

Indian ink
a black ink, originally from China and Japan.

Indian summer
1. (originally of America) a period of fine, warm, summery weather occurring in autumn.
2. a renewal of youthful spirits or health in later life.

indiarubber *noun*
see RUBBER (1).

indicate (*say* **indi**-kate) *verb*
to show or point out: 'the signpost *indicates* the way to town'.
Usage: 'he *indicated* his intention of resigning' (= expressed in a general way).
Word Family: **indication,** *noun,* a) the act of indicating, b) something which indicates.
[INDEX]

indicative (*say* in-**dikk**a-tiv) *adjective*
1. giving indications of: 'that remark is *indicative* of his whole attitude'.
2. *Grammar:* see MOOD (2).
Word Family: **indicatively,** *adverb.*

indicator (*say* **indi**-kayta) *noun*
1. a person or thing that shows or gives information, such as a flashing light used to indicate that a motor vehicle is turning.
2. *Chemistry:* a substance which, by a distinct colour change, shows that a chemical reaction is complete, or shows the acidity or alkalinity (pH) of a solution.

indices (*say* **indi**-seez) *plural noun*
see INDEX.

indict (*say* in-**dite**) *verb*
to accuse, as a means of bringing a person to trial before a jury.
Word Family: **indictable,** *adjective,* making one liable to be indicted; **indictment,** *noun,* an accusation.
[IN- (1) + Latin *dictare* to put in writing]

indifferent *adjective*
1. having no interest in or care for: 'she's coldly *indifferent* to my suffering'.
2. mediocre or commonplace: 'an *indifferent* performance of the opera'.
Word Family: **indifferently,** *adverb;* **indifference,** *noun,* a) lack of interest or concern, b) unimportance, c) mediocre quality.

indigenous (*say* in-**diji**-nus) *adjective*
originating in or being native to a particular place: 'wallabies are *indigenous* to Australia'.
Word Family: **indigenously,** *adverb;* **indigene** (*say* **indi**-jeen), *noun,* a person or thing that is indigenous.
[from Latin]

indigent (*say* **indi**-j'nt) *adjective*
poor.
Word Family: **indigence,** *noun,* poverty.
[from Latin]

indigestion (*say* indi-**jes**-ch'n) *noun*
also called **dyspepsia**
a) difficulty in digesting food properly.
b) any pain or discomfort resulting from this.
Word Family: **indigestible,** *adjective,* not able to be digested.

indignant (*say* in–**dig**nant) *adjective*
angry at something unjust, unworthy or ungrateful.
Word Family: **indignantly**, *adverb*; **indignation**, *noun.*

indignity (*say* in–digni–tee) *noun*
an act which humiliates or injures self–respect: 'the *indignities* suffered by prisoners of war'.

indigo (*say* **in**–dig–o) *noun*
1. a) a dark blue to purplish–blue colour. b) the colour between blue and violet in the spectrum.
2. an important blue dye formerly extracted from plants, but now made artificially.
Word Family: **indigo**, *adjective.*

indirect *noun*
not direct: a) 'her *indirect* reply suggested she was hiding something'; b) 'taxes on goods and services are *indirect* taxes'.
Word Family: **indirectly**, *adverb*; **indirectness**, *noun.*

indirect object
Grammar: see OBJECT.

indiscernible (*say* indi–**ser**–na–b'l) *adjective*
not discernible.
Word Family: **indiscernibly**, *adverb.*

indiscreet *adjective*
not discreet.
Word Family: **indiscreetly**, *adverb*; **indiscretion** (*say* indi–**skresh**'n), *noun*, a) the quality of being indiscreet, b) an indiscreet act or remark.

indiscriminate (*say* in–diskr**imm**i–nit) *adjective*
making no distinctions: a) 'he's an *indiscriminate* admirer of all music'; b) 'the troops dealt out *indiscriminate* slaughter'.
Word Family: **indiscriminately**, *adverb.*

indispensable *adjective*
absolutely essential: 'oxygen is *indispensable* to human life'.
Word Family: **indispensably**, *adverb.*

indisposed *adjective*
1. sick or ill, usually only to a slight degree.
2. disinclined or unwilling.
Word Family: **indisposition** (*say* in–dispa–**zish**'n), *noun.*

indisputable (*say* in–dis–**pew**ta–b'l) *adjective*
beyond doubt or question.
Word Family: **indisputably**, *adverb.*

indissoluble (*say* indi–**sol**–yoo–b'l) *adjective*
1. not able to be broken or undone: 'an *indissoluble* bond of friendship'.
2. not capable of being dissolved.

indistinct *adjective*
not distinct.
Word Family: **indistinctly**, *adverb*; **indistinctness**, *noun.*

indistinguishable
(*say* indis–**ting**wisha–b'l) *adjective*
not capable of being distinguished or discerned.
Word Family: **indistinguishably**, *adverb.*

indium *noun*
element number 49, a rare metal used in protective plating and dental alloys. See CHEMICAL ELEMENTS in grey pages.

individual (*say* indi–**vid**–yew'l) *adjective*
1. of, for or existing as a single or separate person or thing: a) 'an *individual* portion'; b) '*individual* members of a group'.
2. distinctive: 'the author has a very *individual* style'.
individual *noun*
1. a single person or thing.
2. *Biology:* a) a living thing capable of independent existence. b) a single member of a colony.
Word Family: **individually**, *adverb*; **individualize, individualise**, *verb*, a) to make or become individual, b) to select for special attention; **individualization** (*say* indi–vid–yewa–lie–**zay**–sh'n), *noun.*
[Latin *individuus* indivisible]

individualist (*say* indi–**vid**–yewa–list) *noun*
1. a person of independent thought and action.
2. a person who believes that personal interests are more important than those of society as a whole.
Word Family: **individualism**, *noun*; **individualistic** (*say* indi–vid–yewa–**lis**tik), *adjective.*

individuality
(*say* indi–vid–yoo–**alli**–tee) *noun*
1. the particular characteristics which distinguish a person from others and mark him out as an individual.
2. the state of having separate, independent existence.

indivisible (*say* indi–**vizz**i–b'l) *adjective*
not able to be divided.

Word Family: **indivisibility** (*say* indi-vizzi-**billi**-tee), *noun*; **indivisibly,** *adverb.*

indoctrinate *verb*

1. to make someone accept a system of thought uncritically.

2. to instruct in a body of doctrine.

Word Family: **indoctrination,** *noun.*

Indo-European

(*say* indo-yoora-**pee**-an) *noun*

a prehistoric language or group of languages from which most European and some Asian languages developed.

Word Family: **Indo-European,** *adjective,* relating to the languages so developed, including those spoken today.

indolent (*say* **in**da-l'nt) *adjective*

lazy or idle.

Word Family: **indolently,** *adverb*; **indolence,** *noun.*

indomitable (*say* in-**domm**ita-b'l) *adjective*

not capable of being subdued or conquered.

Word Family: **indomitably,** *adverb.*

[IN- (2) + Latin *domitare* to tame]

indoor *adjective*

occurring, used, etc. inside a house or building: '*indoor* plants'.

Word Family: **indoors,** *adverb.*

indubitable (*say* in-**dew**bita-b'l) *adjective*

certain or beyond doubt.

Word Family: **indubitably,** *adverb.*

[IN- (2) + Latin *dubium* doubt]

induce (*say* in-**dewce**) *verb*

1. to persuade or influence: 'she *induced* me to stay another hour'.

2. to produce or cause: 'alcohol at lunchtime *induces* afternoon drowsiness'.

3. to produce or establish by induction.

Word Family: **inducement,** *noun,* a) the act of inducing, b) an incentive.

[IN- (2) + Latin *ducere* to lead]

induct *verb*

1. to install formally in office.

2. *American:* to conscript into military service.

induction (*say* in-**duk**-sh'n) *noun*

1. *Physics:* the process by which a body, having electrical or magnetic properties, can produce similar properties on a nearby body without direct contact.

2. a) a process of inferring or aiming at a general law from observation of particular instances. b) a conclusion reached by this process. Compare DEDUCTION.

3. the act or ceremony of installing a person into an office.

Word Family: **inductance,** *noun,* the ability of a circuit to produce induction; **inductive,** *adjective.*

induction coil

Electricity: a device, basically one coil of a few turns inside another coil of many turns, for producing a very high electromotive force from a very small electromotive force.

indulge (*say* in-**dulj**) *verb*

1. to satisfy or yield to simple desires: a) 'she likes to *indulge* her taste for cigars'; b) 'he always *indulges* his children's wishes'.

2. (*informal*) to drink alcohol.

indulgence *noun*

1. a) the habit or process of indulging: 'too much *indulgence* in wine gave her gout'. b) something indulged in: 'wine wasn't her only *indulgence*!'.

2. any favourable treatment or privilege: 'we'll grant you an *indulgence* of 10 days to pay the debt'.

3. *Religion:* a statement from the Roman Catholic Church releasing a person from a penalty imposed for having sinned.

Word Family: **indulgent,** *adjective,* inclined to indulge the wishes of others; **indulgently,** *adverb.*

[from Latin]

industrial action

a strike, go-slow or sit-in.

industry (*say* **in**dus-tree) *noun*

1. a) any production or manufacturing business. b) a branch of such a business: 'the coal *industry*'.

2. hard work or diligence: 'his quick success was due to his *industry*'.

primary industry

any industry, such as mining or farming, which does not actually manufacture the goods it produces.

secondary industry

any industry, such as the steel industry, etc., which produces manufactured goods.

Word Family: **industrial** (*say* in-**dus**tri-al), *adjective*; **industrially,** *adverb*; **industrialize, industrialise,** *verb,* to introduce industries on a large scale; **industrialization** (*say* in-dustri-a-lie-**zay**-sh'n), *noun*; **industrialist,** *noun,* a person who owns or runs an industry; **industrious,**

adjective, being conscientious or hard-working; **industriously**, *adverb*.
[Latin *industria* diligence]

inebriate (*say* in-**ee**bri-ate) *verb*
to intoxicate or make drunk.
Word Family: **inebriate** (*say* in-**ee**bri-it), *adjective*, drunk or intoxicated; **inebriate**, *noun*, a drunkard; **inebriation** (*say* in-eebri-**ay**-sh'n), *noun*.
[from Latin]

inedible (in-**eddi**-b'l) *adjective*
not fit to be eaten.
Word Family: **inedibility** (*say* in-eddi-**billi**-tee), *noun*.

ineffable (*say* in-**effa**-b'l) *adjective*
1. beyond expression: 'I have an *ineffable* contempt for laziness'.
2. that must not be spoken: 'the *ineffable* name of the Lord'.
Word Family: **ineffably**, *adverb*.
[IN- (2) + Latin *effari* to speak out]

ineffective (*say* inni-**fek**tiv) *adjective*
not effective.
Word Family: **ineffectively**, *adverb*; **ineffectiveness**, *noun*.

ineffectual (*say* inni-**fek**-tew'l) *adjective*
1. vain or futile: '*ineffectual* attempts'.
2. not producing the intended result.
Word Family: **ineffectually**, *adverb*.

inefficient (*say* inni-**fish**'nt) *adjective*
not efficient.
Word Family: **inefficiently**, *adverb*; **inefficiency**, *noun*.

inelastic (*say* inni-**las**tik) *adjective*
not elastic.

inelegant (*say* in-**elli**-g'nt) *adjective*
not elegant.
Word Family: **inelegantly**, *adverb*.

ineligible (*say* in-**ell**ija-b'l) *adjective*
not eligible.
Word Family: **ineligibility** (*say* in-ellija-**billi**-tee), *noun*; **ineligibly**, *adverb*.

inept (*say* in-**ept**) *adjective*
1. not suitable or appropriate.
2. awkward or foolish.
Word Family: **ineptly**, *adverb*; **ineptitude**, *noun*, a) the quality of being inept, b) an inept remark, act, etc.; **ineptness**, *noun*.
[IN- (2) + Latin *aptus* fitting]

inequality (*say* inni-**kwolla**-tee) *noun*
a) the state of being unequal: 'social *inequality*'. b) an instance of this.

inequitable (*say* in-**ekwitta**-b'l) *adjective*
not equitable.
Word Family: **inequitably**, *adverb*; **inequity**, *noun*.

ineradicable (*say* inni-**raddika**-b'l) *adjective*
not eradicable.
Word Family: **ineradicably**, *adverb*.

inert (*say* in-**ert**) *adjective*
1. sluggish or inactive.
2. *Chemistry:* being very difficult to change by chemical reaction.
Word Family: **inertly**, *adverb*; **inertness**, *noun*.
[Latin *iners* unskilled, idle]

inertia (*say* in-**ersha**) *noun*
1. *Physics:* the tendency for the velocity of a body to remain constant unless acted on by a force.
Example: the forward movement of people in a car when it stops suddenly is due to inertia.
2. a state of inactivity or sluggishness.

inertia selling
delivering goods which have not been ordered or are not up to advertised quality in the hope that a householder will be too inert to protest or return them.

inescapable (*say* innis-**kape**-a-b'l) *adjective*
not able to be escaped or avoided.
Word Family: **inescapably**, *adverb*.

inessential (*say* inni-**sen**-sh'l) *adjective*
not essential.

inestimable (*say* in-**estima**-b'l) *adjective*
not able to be estimated, especially something of value.
Word Family: **inestimably**, *adverb*.

inevitable (*say* in-**evvita**-b'l) *adjective*
not able to be avoided or prevented.
Word Family: **inevitably**, *adverb*; **inevitability** (*say* in-evvita-**billi**-tee), **inevitableness**, *nouns*.
[IN- (2) + Latin *evitare* to escape]

inexact *adjective*
not exact.
Word Family: **inexactly**, *adverb*.

inexcusable (*say* inneks-**kewza**-b'l) *adjective*
not excusable.
Word Family: **inexcusably**, *adverb*.

inexhaustible (*say* inneg-**zawsti**-b'l) *adjective*
not exhaustible.
Word Family: **inexhaustibly**, *adverb*.

inexorable (*say* in-**eksera**-b'l) *adjective*

not able to be changed or made to yield.
Word Family: **inexorably**, *adverb.*
[IN– (2) + Latin *exorare* to gain by entreaty]

inexpedient (*say* inneks–**peedi**–ent) *adjective*
not expedient.
Word Family: **inexpediently**, *adverb*; **inexpediency**, *noun.*

inexpensive (*say* inneks–**pensiv**) *adjective*
not expensive.
Word Family: **inexpensively**, *adverb.*

inexperienced (*say* inneks–**peeri**–enced) *adjective*
lacking experience.
Word Family: **inexperience**, *noun.*

inexpert *adjective*
unskilled.
Word Family: **inexpertly**, *adverb.*

inexplicable (*say* inneks–**plikka**–b'l) *adjective*
not able to be explained.
Word Family: **inexplicably**, *adverb.*

inexpressible (*say* inneks–**pressi**–b'l) *adjective*
not able to be expressed or represented in words.
Word Family: **inexpressibly**, *adverb.*

inexpressive (*say* inneks–**pressiv**) *adjective*
not expressive.
Word Family: **inexpressively**, *adverb*; **inexpressiveness**, *noun.*

in extremis (*say* in eks–**tree**–mis)
in great distress or near to death.
[Latin]

inextricable (*say* inneks–**trikka**–b'l) *adjective*
1. impossible to extricate oneself from: 'an *inextricable* maze'.
2. too intricate or complicated to untangle: 'an *inextricable* problem'.
Word Family: **inextricably**, *adverb.*

infallible *adjective*
a) not liable to be wrong, as in judgement: 'I am not *infallible*'. b) not liable to fail: 'is there an *infallible* remedy for a cold?'.

infamous (*say* **infa**–mus) *adjective*
1. having an extremely bad reputation.
2. shocking or detestable: '*infamous* behaviour'.
Word Family: **infamously**, *adverb*; **infamy** (*say* **infa**–mee), *noun,* a) the state or quality of being infamous, b) an infamous act.
[IN– (2) + Latin *fama* good repute]

infant (*say* **in**–f'nt) *noun*
1. a baby.
2. *Law:* any person who is too young to have legal rights.
3. anything in the early stages of development or progress.
Word Family: **infant**, *adjective*; **infantile**, *adjective,* a) of or relating to infants, b) babyish; **infancy**, *noun.*
[Latin *infans* not speaking]

infanticide (*say* in–**fanti**–side) *noun*
a) the crime of killing a newly born child. b) a person who does this.
[INFANT + Latin *caedere* to kill]

infantile paralysis
see POLIO.

infantry (*say* **in**–f'n–tree) *noun*
the branch of an army consisting of soldiers on foot. Compare CAVALRY.
Word Family: **infantryman**, *noun.*
[Italian *infante* a page or foot soldier]

infatuate (*say* in–**fat**–yoo–ate) *verb*
to inspire with foolish or unreasoning passion.
Word Family: **infatuation**, *noun.*
[Latin *infatuatus* made foolish]

infect (*say* in–**fekt**) *verb*
a) to contaminate with disease organisms. b) to transmit a disease to another.
Usage: 'his unhappy mood *infected* us' (= was transferred to).
[Latin *infectus* stained, tainted]

infection (*say* in–**fek**–sh'n) *noun*
a) the act of infecting. b) the state of being infected. c) something, such as a germ, which infects.
infectious *adjective*
1. a) communicated by infection: 'the *infectious* diseases'. b) liable to produce infection.
2. tending to produce similar responses in others: '*infectious* laughter'.

infer (*say* in–**fer**) *verb*
(inferred, inferring)
to conclude by reasoning: 'from his sceptical remarks I *infer* he does not believe the report'.
[from Latin]
Common Error: do not confuse with IMPLY.

inference (*say* **infa**–r'nce) *noun*
a) the process of inferring. b) something which is inferred.
Word Family: **inferential** (*say* infa–**ren**–sh'l), *adjective.*

inferior (*say* in–**feer**ia) *adjective*
1. poor in quality: 'an *inferior* product'.

2. low or lower in order, degree, rank, etc.: 'among the primates the baboon is *inferior* to the orang-outang'.
3. situated under or beneath: 'the 2 in CO_2 is an *inferior* number'.
Word Family: **inferior**, *noun*, a person or thing that is inferior; **inferiority** (*say* in-feeri-**orri**-tee), *noun*.
[Latin, lower]

inferiority complex
1. *Psychology:* a group of suppressed emotions arising from intense feelings of inferiority, and sometimes leading to aggressive behaviour which is intended to conceal such feelings.
2. (*informal*) diffidence.

infernal (*say* in-**fer**-n'l) *adjective*
1. of or relating to hell.
2. (*informal*) abominable: 'an *infernal* commotion'.
Word Family: **infernally**, *adverb*.
[Latin *infernus* that which lies beneath]

inferno (*say* in-**firno**) *noun*
a) hell. b) a place resembling hell: 'the building was a raging *inferno* minutes after the fire started'.
[Italian]

infertile (*say* in-**fir**-tile) *adjective*
not fertile.
Word Family: **infertility** (*say* infir-**tilli**-tee), *noun*.

infest *verb*
to overrun in large numbers to a harmful or unpleasant degree: 'locusts *infested* the area'.
Word Family: **infestation** (*say* in-fes-**tay**-sh'n), *noun*, a) the act of infesting, b) the state of being infested.
[Latin *infestus* hostile]

infidel (*say* **infi**-del) *noun*
1. *History:* a person who does not believe in the religion of the speaker, used especially by Christians of Moslems.
2. a person who does not believe in any religion.
[IN- (2) + Latin *fidelis* faithful]

infidelity (*say* infi-**delli**-tee) *noun*
unfaithfulness, especially adultery.

infield *noun*
Sport: an inner part of the field, such as the area near the wickets in cricket.
Word Family: **infielder**, *noun*, a player in the infield.

infighting *noun*
a struggle between members of the same group or organization, e.g. for leadership of a political party or other institution.
Word Family: **infighter**, *noun*.

infiltrate (*say* **in**-fill-trate) *verb*
to filter into or through.
Usage: 'the spy *infiltrated* the enemy's headquarters' (= entered secretly).
Word Family: **infiltrator**, *noun*, a person who infiltrates; **infiltration**, *noun*, a) the act of infiltrating, b) something which has infiltrated.

infinite (*say* **infi**-nit) *adjective*
1. having no boundaries or limits in time, space, etc.
2. *Maths:* not finite.
Word Family: **infinitely**, *adverb*; **infinity** (*say* in-**finni**-tee), *noun*, the state or quality of being infinite.
[IN- (2) + Latin *finitus* defined]

infinitesimal (*say* in-finni-**tessi**-m'l) *adjective*
immeasurably small.

infinitive (*say* in-**finni**-tiv) *noun*
Grammar: the form of a verb which has no tense, number or person. *Examples*: to buy, to look, to go.

infirm (*say* in-**firm**) *adjective*
1. feeble in body or mind, especially from old age.
2. insecure or irresolute: '*infirm* of purpose'.
Word Family: **infirmity**, *noun*, a physical or moral weakness.
[from Latin]

infirmary (*say* in-**firma**-ree) *noun*
a hospital or place where sick people are cared for.

inflame (*say* in-**flame**) *verb*
1. to set on fire.
2. to arouse strong feelings in: 'his speech was meant to *inflame* the people against their leader'.
3. to produce heat, redness or swelling in.
Word Family: **inflammable**, *adjective*, a) easily burnt, b) capable of inflaming; **inflammatory**, *adjective*, tending to inflame.

inflammation (*say* infla-**may**-sh'n) *noun*
1. a) the act of inflaming. b) the state of being inflamed.
2. a response by living tissue to injury or infection, characterized by swelling, redness, heat and pain.

inflate (*say* in-**flate**) *verb*
1. to fill or expand with a gas.
2. to puff up with pride, satisfaction, etc.

3. *Economics:* to produce inflation.
Word Family: **inflatable**, *adjective.*

inflation (*say* in–**flay**–sh'n) *noun*
1. *Economics:* a general rise in prices and fall in the value of money which may have various causes, e.g. increases in the cost of imported raw materials, higher wages unmatched by higher productivity or an increase in the amount of currency in circulation. Compare DEFLATION.
2. a) the act of inflating: 'the *inflation* of the balloons was aided by a bicycle pump'. b) the state of being inflated.
Word Family: **inflationary**, *adjective,* causing inflation in the economy.
[Latin *inflatus* blown into]

inflexible (*say* in–**flek**si–b'l) *adjective*
not flexible: 'an *inflexible* attitude'.
Word Family: **inflexibly**, *adverb.*

inflexion (*say* in–**flek**–sh'n) *noun*
also spelt **inflection**
1. *Grammar:* a) the change made in the form of a word to alter its meaning, grammatical relations, etc. b) the set of such forms for a single word. c) the suffix added to change the form of a word. *Examples: ran, nicer, cows* are inflexions of *run, nice, cow.* See CONJUGATION and DECLENSION.
2. a bend or angle.
Usage: 'an *inflexion* of the voice, or a raised eyebrow, can convey a great deal' (= modulation).
Word Family: **inflect**, *verb*; **inflexional**, *adjective.*
[Latin *inflexio* a bending]

inflict (*say* in–**flikt**) *verb*
to impose anything unwelcome, such as punishment.
Word Family: **infliction**, *noun,* a) the act of inflicting, b) something inflicted.
[Latin *inflictus* struck against]

inflorescence (*say* infla–**ress**'nce) *noun*
Biology: a) the arrangement of flowers on a stem. b) the flowering parts of a plant.
[Latin *inflorescens* coming into flower]

inflow (*say* **in**–flo) *noun*
a flowing in or arriving.

influence (*say* **in**–floo–ence) *noun*
1. a) the power of persons or things to produce effects on others, especially by invisible or indirect means. b) a person or thing possessing such power.
2. power, etc. resulting from social position, wealth, etc.
Word Family: **influence**, *verb*; **influential** (*say* in–floo–**en**–sh'l), *adjective.*
[Latin *influens* flowing in]

influenza (*say* in–floo–**enza**) *noun*
short form is **flu**
an infectious, viral disease causing symptoms such as aching muscles, fever, sneezing and sore eyes.
[Italian]

influx (*say* **in**–fluks) *noun*
a flowing in: 'this year there has been a large *influx* of tourists'.

inform (*say* in–**form**) *verb*
1. to tell or give information.
2. to pervade: 'the discussions were *informed* by a spirit of cooperation'.
inform oneself of, to supply oneself with knowledge of.
Word Family: **informed** *adjective,* having or showing a high degree of knowledge; **informant**, *noun,* an informer.
[Latin *informare* to shape]

informal (*say* in–**for**–m'l) *adjective*
1. without ceremony or formality.
2. (of speech or writing) characteristic of ordinary conversation, as distinct from formal grammar or construction.
Word Family: **informally**, *adverb*; **informality** (*say* infor–**malli**–tee), *noun.*

information (*say* infa–**may**–sh'n) *noun*
1. a) knowledge communicated or received. b) knowledge on various subjects.
2. a) the act of informing. b) the state of being informed.
3. *Law:* a formal charge made in a court.
Word Family: **informative** (*say* in–**forma**–tiv), *adjective,* giving information.

informer *noun*
1. a person who gives incriminating information.
2. a person who gives information. Also called an **informant**.

infraction (*say* in–**frak**–sh'n) *noun*
a breach or violation: 'an *infraction* of the rules'.
[Latin *infractus* broken into]

infra dig
(*informal*) beneath one's dignity.
[short form of Latin *infra dignitatem*]

infrangible (*say* in–**fran**ji–b'l) *adjective*
1. unbreakable.

2. inviolable.
[IN- (2) + Latin *frangere* to break]

infra-red *noun*
Physics: see LIGHT (1).
[Latin *infra* below + RED]

infrastructure (*say* **infra**-strukcher) *noun*
the basic or supporting organization, facilities, etc. of an institution.
Usage: 'the local council provided electricity, a bus service and other *infra structure* for the new housing estate' (= community services).
[Latin *infra* below + STRUCTURE]

infrequent *adjective*
not often.
Word Family: **infrequently,** *adverb*; **infrequency,** *noun.*

infringe (*say* in-**frinj**) *verb*
1. to break or ignore a rule, etc.
2. to trespass or encroach: 'the children *infringed* on our privacy'.
Word Family: **infringement,** *noun.*
[from Latin]

infuriate (*say* in-**few**-ree-ate) *verb*
to make furious.
Word Family: **infuriatingly,** *adverb.*

infuse (*say* in-**fewz**) *verb*
1. to fill or inspire with: 'his speech *infused* the pilots with courage'.
2. to steep or soak a substance in a liquid to extract its soluble parts.
[Latin *infusus* poured in]

infusion (*say* in-**few**-*zh*'n) *noun*
1. a) the act of infusing. b) something which is infused.
2. a liquid extract, obtained by soaking a substance in a liquid: 'tea is an *infusion* of tea-leaves in hot water'.

ingenious (*say* in-**jeeni**-us) *adjective*
1. (of things, actions, etc.) cleverly or skilfully made.
2. (of a person) inventive.
Word Family: **ingeniously,** *adverb*; **ingeniousness,** *noun.*
[Latin *ingenium* genius]
Common Error: do not confuse with INGENUOUS.

ingénue (*say* an-*zhay*-**new**) *noun*
a simple, innocent girl, especially as represented on the stage.
[French]

ingenuity (*say* inji-**newi**-tee) *noun*
the quality of being ingenious.

ingenuous (*say* in-**jen**-yewus) *adjective*
innocent and without reserve or sophistication.
Word Family: **ingenuously,** *adverb*; **ingenuousness,** *noun.*
[Latin *ingenuus* free-born, frank]
Common Error: do not confuse with INGENIOUS.

ingest (*say* in-**jest**) *verb*
Biology: to take food into an organism.
Word Family: **ingestion** (*say* in-**jes**-ch'n), *noun.*
[Latin *ingestus* carried in]

ingle-nook *noun*
a chimney-corner or fireside-corner.

inglorious *adjective*
dishonourable or shameful: 'the beaten troops made an *inglorious* retreat'.
Word Family: **ingloriously,** *adverb.*

ingot *noun*
a mass of cast metal, especially gold or silver, prepared for later working.
[IN- (1) + Old English *goten* poured]

ingrain *verb*
to fix firmly.

ingrate (*say* **in**-grate) *noun*
an old word for an ungrateful person.
[IN- (2) + Latin *gratus* pleasant]

ingratiate (*say* in-**gray**-shee-ate) *verb*
to establish oneself deliberately in the favour or good graces of another: 'he *ingratiated* himself with his boss by always agreeing with him'.
Word Family: **ingratiatingly,** *adverb.*
[IN- (1) + Latin *gratia* favour]

ingratitude *noun*
the state of being ungrateful.

ingredient (*say* in-**greedi**-ent) *noun*
one of the parts of a mixture: 'the *ingredients* of a cake'.
[Latin *ingrediens* entering]

ingress (*say* **in**-gress) *noun*
a) a right to enter. b) a going in.

in-group *noun*
a group of people with a strong feeling of belonging together and a tendency to exclude others.

inhabit (*say* in-**habbit**) *verb*
to live or dwell in.
Word Family: **inhabitable,** *adjective,* capable of being inhabited; **inhabitant,** *noun,* a permanent resident.
[from Latin]

inhale (*say* in-**hale**) *verb*
to draw in by breathing.
inhalation (*say* inha-**lay**-sh'n) *noun*
the act of inhaling.
Word Family: **inhalant,** *noun,* a substance inhaled for medicinal effect; **inhaler** (*say* in-**hay**-la), a device to

supply medication into the breathing passages.
[from Latin]

inherent (*say* in–**herr**'nt) *adjective*
existing in something as a permanent and inseparable element, quality or attribute.
Word Family: **inhere**, *verb.*
[Latin *inhaerere* to stick to]
Common Error: do not confuse with INNATE.

inherit (*say* in–**herr**it) *verb*
1. to receive property, a title, etc. upon the death of another person.
2. to receive genetic characters from one's ancestors.
Word Family: **inheritor**, *noun.*
[Latin *inhereditare* to appoint an heir]

inheritance (*say* in–**herr**i–t'nse) *noun*
1. a) the act of inheriting. b) anything which is inherited.
2. *Law:* the property which is received by an heir from a person who has died. Compare LEGACY.

inhibit (*say* in–**hibb**it) *verb*
1. to restrain, hinder or repress.
2. *Chemistry:* to reduce the rate of a chemical reaction or stop it completely.
Word Family: **inhibition** (*say* inhi–**bish**'n), *noun*; **inhibitor**, *noun*, a substance which inhibits a chemical reaction; **inhibitory**, *adjective*, tending to inhibit.
[from Latin]
Common Error: do not confuse with PROHIBIT.

inhospitable (*say* inhos–**pitti**–b'l) *adjective*
not hospitable.
Word Family: **inhospitably**, *adverb.*

inhuman *adjective*
1. lacking in natural human feeling or sympathy for others.
2. not human.
Word Family: **inhumanly**, *adverb.*

inhumane *adjective*
not humane.
Word Family: **inhumanely**, *adverb.*

inhumanity (*say* in–hew–**manni**–tee) *noun*
1. the state or quality of being inhuman or inhumane.
2. an inhuman or inhumane act.

inimical (*say* in–**immi**–k'l) *adjective*
1. adverse in tendency or effect.
2. unfriendly or hostile.
Word Family: **inimically**, *adverb.*
[IN– (2) + Latin *amicus* a friend]

inimitable (*say* in–**immi**ta–b'l) *adjective*
not able to be imitated.
Word Family: **inimitably**, *adverb.*

iniquity (*say* in–**ikwa**–tee) *noun*
a) a wicked or unjust act. b) wickedness.
Word Family: **iniquitous**, *adjective.*
[from Latin]

initial (*say* in–**ish**'l) *adjective*
occurring at the beginning.
initial *noun*
the first letter of a name, word, etc.
Word Family: **initial** (**initialled**, **initialling**), *verb*, to mark or sign with one's own initials; **initially**, *adverb.*

initiate (*say* in–**ishi**–ate) *verb*
1. to begin or originate.
2. to introduce a person to a new field, interest, etc.
3. to admit to membership, etc. with formal rituals or ordeals.
Word Family: **initiation**, *noun*; **initiator**, *noun*, a person who initiates something; **initiate** (*say* in–**ishi**–it), *noun*, a person who has been initiated.
[Latin *initium* a going in]

initiative (*say* in–**isha**–tiv) *noun*
1. a ready ability or boldness in beginning or taking on new projects, etc.
2. an introductory act or step: 'he took the *initiative* and began the conversation'.

inject (*say* in–**jekt**) *verb*
1. to introduce fluid into the body, a cavity, etc.
2. to introduce something new: 'he tried to *inject* humour into the dull meeting'.
Word Family: **injection**, *noun.*
[Latin *injectus* thrown in]

injudicious (*say* injoo–**dishus**) *adjective*
not sensible or discreet.
Word Family: **injudiciously**, *adverb.*

injunction (*say* in–**junk**–sh'n) *noun*
Law: a court order requiring or restricting a particular action.
[Latin *injunctus* enjoined]

injure (*say* **in**jer) *verb*
1. to do or cause harm to.
2. to do wrong or injustice to.
Word Family: **injury**, *noun*; **injurious** (*say* in–**joo**rius), *adjective*; **injuriously**, *adverb.*
[Latin *injuria* a wrong]

injustice (*say* in–**justis**) *noun*
a) a lack of justice. b) an instance of this: 'such a severe fine was an *injustice*'.

ink *noun*
1. any of various strongly coloured liquids used for writing and printing.
2. a dark, protective fluid ejected by the squid and related molluscs.

inkling *noun*
1. a hint or suggestion: 'the faint bark gave me an *inkling* of the puppy's whereabouts'.
2. a vague idea or notion: 'I had no *inkling* that she was so ill'.
[Middle English *inkle* to speak in an undertone]

inkwell *noun*
a container for ink, usually set into a desk.

inky *adjective*
1. dark or murky: '*inky* shadows'.
2. resembling or stained with ink: '*inky* fingers'.

inland *adjective*
1. situated in the middle parts of a land mass.
2. occurring or confined within the borders of a country: '*inland* revenue'.
Word Family: **inland**, *adverb, noun.*

inland revenue
1. government revenue from personal and corporation taxes, etc., but excluding customs and excise dues.
2. (*capitals*) the department which collects these taxes.

in-law *noun*
a relative by marriage.

inlay (*say* in-lay) *verb*
(**inlaid**, **inlaying**)
to set something into a surface to form a design.
inlay (*say* **in**-lay) *noun*
1. a layer of material set into a surface.
2. *Dentistry:* a filling which is fitted and fastened as one large piece.

inlet *noun*
1. a small narrow bay.
2. an entrance.
3. something put in or inserted.
Word Family: **inlet** (**inlet, inletting**), *verb,* to insert.

inmate *noun*
a person confined to a hospital, prison, etc.

inmost *adjective*
innermost.

inn *noun*
an old word meaning a small hotel or a public house.
Word Family: **innkeeper**, *noun.*
[Old English, a dwelling]

innards (*say* **inn**uds) *plural noun*
(*informal*) the internal parts of anything, especially the body.
[for *inwards*]

innate (*say* in-**ate**) *adjective*
1. inborn in one's nature: 'an *innate* love of painting'.
2. *Philosophy:* of or coming from the mind, as distinct from experience.
Word Family: **innately**, *adverb.*
[Latin *innatus* born]
Common Error: do not confuse with INHERENT.

inner *adjective*
located or occurring further in: 'an *inner* room'.
Usage: 'he never revealed his *inner* life to others' (= private, secret).

innermost *adjective*
farthest within.
Usage: 'one's *innermost* secrets' (= most intimate).

innings *plural noun*
1. *Cricket:* (*used with singular verb*) the period in which a player or team is batting.
2. (*used with singular verb*) a turn or period at some activity.

innocent (*say* **inna**-s'nt) *adjective*
pure or free from evil and sin: 'an *innocent* child'.
Usages:
a) 'the jury recommended that the prisoner be found *innocent*' (= not guilty).
b) 'she was *innocent* enough to believe the story' (= simple, guileless).
Word Family: **innocently**, *adverb*; **innocence**, *noun,* the state or quality of being innocent; **innocent**, *noun,* any naïve or pure person.
[Latin *innocens* harmless]

innocuous (*say* in-**ok**-yewus) *adjective*
harmless.
Word Family: **innocuously**, *adverb*; **innocuousness**, *noun.*

innovation (*say* inna-**vay**-sh'n) *noun*
a) the introduction of new things or methods. b) something new or different which is introduced.
Word Family: **innovator**, *noun,* a person who brings or makes changes; **innovate**, *verb*; **innovative, innovatory,** *adjectives.*
[Latin *innovare* to renew, start again]

innuendo (*say* in-yoo-**endo**) *noun*
an indirect comment, such as a hint or implication, usually unfavourable.
[Latin, by nodding at, hinting]

innumerable (*say* in–**new**mera–b'l) *adjective*
very numerous.
Word Family: **innumerably**, *adverb.*

inoculate (*say* in–**ok**–yoolate) *verb*
to induce a mild form of a disease so as to produce immunity, as by introducing a virus or bacteria into the body. Compare VACCINATE under VACCINE.
Word Family: **inoculation**, *noun*, a) the act of inoculating, b) the substance inoculated.
[Latin *inoculatus* grafted, implanted]

inoffensive (*say* inni–**fen**siv) *adjective*
not offensive.

inoperable (*say* in–**op**pera–b'l) *adjective*
Medicine: incapable of being cured or removed by surgical operation: 'an *inoperable* brain tumour'.

inoperative (*say* in–**op**ra–tiv) *adjective*
not in operation: 'this regulation proved impossible to enforce and is now *inoperative*'.

inopportune (*say* in–**op**pa–tewn) *adjective*
ill-timed: 'you have chosen an *inopportune* moment for your request'.
Word Family: **inopportunely**, *adverb.*

inordinate (*say* in–**or**di–nit) *adjective*
excessive or unrestrained.
Word Family: **inordinately**, *adverb.*
[Latin *inordinatus* disordered]

inorganic (*say* in–or**gan**nik) *adjective*
1. not forming part of the substance of living bodies.
2. *Chemistry:* of or relating to compounds which do not contain chains of carbon atoms. Compare ORGANIC.

inorganic chemistry
the study of elements and their compounds, except compounds containing chains of carbon atoms.

in-patient (*say* **in**–pay–sh'nt) *noun*
see PATIENT.

input (*say* **in**–put) *noun*
something which is put in or inserted, such as the voltage or power fed into an electrical circuit or device or the information fed into a computer.

inquest (*say* **in**–kwest) *noun*
Law: an official inquiry, especially one to determine how a person died.
[Old French]

inquire (*say* in–**kwire**) *verb*
also spelt **enquire**
to ask: 'she *inquired* about my health'.
Usage: 'to *inquire* into the mystery of someone's disappearance' (= investigate).
Word Family: **inquirer**, *noun*, a person who inquires; **inquiringly**, *adverb.*
[IN– (1) + Latin *quaerere* to seek]

inquiry (*say* in–**kwire**–ree) *noun*
1. an official investigation: 'a court of *inquiry*'.
2. an old spelling of **enquiry**.

inquisition (*say* inkwi–**zish**'n) *noun*
1. an investigation especially a legal or official one.
2. any severe or harsh interrogation of a person.
3. *History:* (*capital*) a Roman Catholic tribunal which imposed severe penalties for heresy, especially the Spanish Inquisition.
Word Family: **inquisitor** (*say* in–**kwiz**zitor), *noun*, a person who conducts or makes an inquisition; **inquisitorial** (*say* in–kwizzi–**taw**riul), *adjective.*

inquisitive (*say* in–**kwiz**za–tiv) *adjective*
1. fond of inquiring into other people's affairs.
2. eager to learn: 'he has an *inquisitive* mind'.
Word Family: **inquisitively**, *adverb*; **inquisitiveness**, *noun.*

inroad (*say* **in**–rode) *noun*
an intrusion: 'his continual questions are making *inroads* on my patience'.

inrush (*say* **in**–rush) *noun*
a rushing in of something: 'a sudden *inrush* of the tide'.

insane (*say* in–**sane**) *adjective*
1. having a severe mental illness, especially one making special custody necessary.
2. of or for mentally ill people: 'an *insane* asylum'.
3. extremely senseless or foolish: '*insane* schemes'.
Word Family: **insanely**, *adverb*; **insanity** (*say* in–**san**ni–tee), *noun.*
[IN– (2) + Latin *sanus* healthy]

insanitary (*say* in–**san**ni–tree) *adjective*
not sanitary.

insatiable (*say* in–**say**sha–b'l) *adjective*
incapable of being satisfied: 'an *insatiable* thirst'.
Word Family: **insatiably**, *adverb.*

inscribe (*say* in–**skribe**) *verb*
1. to write a dedication in a book.

2. to engrave.
3. *Maths:* to draw a figure within another so that the inner figure touches the boundary of the outer at as many points as possible.
Word Family: **inscription** (*say* in–**skrip**–sh'n), *noun.*
[IN– (1) + Latin *scribere* to write]

inscrutable (*say* in–**skroo**ta–b'l) *adjective*
not able to be penetrated or understood.
Word Family: **inscrutability** (*say* in–skroota–**billi**–tee), *noun*; **inscrutably**, *adverb.*
[IN– (2) + Latin *scrutari* to search into]

insect (*say* **in**–sekt) *noun*
an arthropod, the adult having six legs, sometimes wings, and a body divided into three parts (a head, a thorax and an abdomen), such as an ant, a beetle, etc.
[IN– (1) + Latin *sectus* cut]

insecticide (*say* in–**sek**ti–side) *noun*
any substance which is used to kill insects.

insectivorous (*say* insek–**tivva**–rus) *adjective*
of or relating to an organism which eats insects.
Word Family: **insectivore** (*say* in–**sek**ti–vor), *noun*, an animal or plant which is insectivorous.
[IN– (1) + Latin *vorare* to devour]

insecure (*say* insi–**kewer**) *adjective*
1. unsafe or liable to give way, fall, etc.
2. anxious, uncertain, or lacking self–confidence.
Word Family: **insecurely**, *adverb*; **insecurity** (*say* insi–**kewra**–tee), *noun.*

inseminate (*say* in–**semmi**–nate) *verb*
to introduce semen into the uterus of a female to cause fertilization.
Word Family: **insemination**, *noun.*
[Latin *inseminatus* sown, planted in]

insensate (*say* in–**sensate**) *adjective*
not capable of feeling or sensation: '*insensate* rocks and stones'.
Usage: 'he thrashed the boy in an *insensate* rage' (= blind).
Word Family: **insensately**, *adverb.*
[IN– (2) + Latin *sensus* sense]

insensible (*say* in–**sensi**–b'l) *adjective*
1. deprived of consciousness: 'he was *insensible* for hours after the blow on the head'.
2. incapable of feeling or perceiving: 'he is *insensible* of ridicule'.
3. imperceptible: 'the colour changed by *insensible* degrees'.
Word Family: **insensibly**, *adverb*; **insensibility** (*say* in–sensi–**billi**–tee), *noun.*

insensitive (*say* in–**sen**si–tiv) *adjective*
not sensitive.
Word Family: **insensitively**, *adverb*; **insensitivity** (*say* in–sensi–**tivvi**–tee), **insensitiveness**, *nouns.*

insentient (*say* in–**sen**shi–ent) *adjective*
lacking the capacity for feeling or sensation: 'a stone is an *insentient* object'.
Word Family: **insentience**, *noun.*

inseparable (*say* in–**seppera**–b'l) *adjective*
not able to be separated or kept apart.
inseparable *noun*
(*usually plural*) any person or thing that cannot be separated.
Word Family: **inseparably**, *adverb.*

insert (*say* in**sert**) *verb*
to put in: a) 'to *insert* a bolt in a latch'; b) 'to *insert* a notice in the paper'.
Word Family: **insert** (*say* **in**sert), *noun*, something inserted or to be inserted; **insertion**, *noun*, a) the act of inserting, b) something inserted.
[from Latin]

inset (*say* **in**set) *noun*
something set in or inserted: 'a tabletop with a marble *inset*'.
Word Family: **inset** (*say* in**set**), (**inset, insetting**), *verb.*

inshore *adjective, adverb*
(at sea) close to or towards the land.

inside *noun*
1. the inner part: 'the *inside* of a suitcase'.
2. an inner side or surface: 'the *inside* of the hand'.
3. (*informal, usually plural*) the inner parts of a body or machine.
Phrases:
inside out, a) with the inner side reversed to become the outer side; b) thoroughly.
on the inside, being in a position of confidence, influence or special knowledge.
inside *adjective*
1. inner or on the inside: 'the story was continued on the *inside* pages of the newspaper'.
2. (*informal*) acting or originating from within a company, etc.: a) 'the robbery was an *inside* job'; b) '*inside* information'.
inside *preposition*
within: 'she stood *inside* the fence'.

inside *adverb*
1. in or into the inner part: 'please come *inside*'.
2. on the inner side: 'do I wear this coat with the lining *inside* or outside?'.
inside of, (*informal*) 'we can't supply the goods *inside of* a week' (= in less than).
Word Family: **insider**, *noun*, a) a member of a particular group, club, etc., b) a person close to a source of knowledge or information.

insidious (*say* in-**siddi**-us) *adjective*
1. sly or treacherous.
2. doing harm subtly or secretly: 'cancer is an *insidious* disease because it is often extremely advanced before it can be diagnosed'.
Word Family: **insidiously**, *adverb*; **insidiousness**, *noun*.
[Latin *insidiosus* cunning, artful]

insight (*say* **in**-site) *noun*
a) an understanding gained or given: 'the film gave us an *insight* into the lives of primitive peoples'. b) the power of having such understanding: 'he was a man of great *insight*'.

insignia (*say* in-**signi**-a) *plural noun*
the distinguishing marks or badges of office or honour.
[Latin *insignis* distinguished or marked]

insignificant (*say* in-sig-**niffi**-k'nt) *adjective*
unimportant or not significant.
Word Family: **insignificantly**, *adverb*; **insignificance**, *noun*.

insincere (*say* insin-**seer**) *adjective*
not sincere.
Word Family: **insincerely**, *adverb*; **insincerity** (*say* insin-**serri**-tee), *noun*.

insinuate (*say* in-**sin**-yoo-ate) *verb*
1. to suggest indirectly, usually something which is unpleasant.
2. to introduce slyly and gradually: 'he *insinuated* his way into his employer's confidence'.
Word Family: **insinuatingly**, *adverb*; **insinuation**, *noun*.
[Latin *insinuare* to wind one's way into]

insipid (*say* in-**sippid**) *adjective*
flavourless or uninteresting.
Word Family: **insipidly**, *adverb*; **insipidity** (*say* insi-**piddi**-tee), *noun*.
[Latin *insipidus* tasteless]

insist *verb*
to maintain firmly a demand, statement, course of action, position, etc.
Word Family: **insistent**, *adjective*, a) persistent, b) compelling attention; **insistently**, *adverb*; **insistence**, *noun*, a) the act of insisting, b) the quality of being insistent; **insistency**, *noun*, the quality of being insistent.
[Latin *insistere* to stand one's ground]

insole *noun*
the inner sole of a shoe or boot, sometimes detachable.

insolent (*say* **insa**-l'nt) *adjective*
insulting or disrespectful.
Word Family: **insolently**, *adverb*; **insolence**, *noun*.
[Latin *insolens* arrogant]

insoluble (*say* in-**sol**-yoo-b'l) *adjective*
1. incapable of being solved or explained.
2. unable to be dissolved in a particular solvent, usually water.
Word Family: **insolubly**, *adverb*; **insolubility** (*say* insol-yoo-**billi**-tee), *noun*.

insolvent (*say* in-**sol**-v'nt) *adjective*
unable to pay one's debts.
Word Family: **insolvency**, *noun*; **insolvent**, *noun*, a person who is insolvent.

insomnia (*say* in-**somni**-a) *noun*
an inability to sleep, often due to anxiety or depression.
Word Family: **insomniac** (*say* insom-nee-ak), *noun*, a person suffering from insomnia.
[IN- (2) + Latin *somnus* sleep]

insouciant (*say* in-soo-sy'nt) *adjective*
indifferent or unconcerned about consequences, public opinion, etc.
Word Family: **insouciance**, *noun*.
[French, from *souci* care]

inspect (*say* in-**spekt**) *verb*
to look at carefully or officially: 'to *inspect* the troops'.
inspector *noun*
1. an official appointed to inspect.
2. a police officer ranking between a sergeant and a chief inspector.
Word Family: **inspection**, *noun*, the act of inspecting; **inspectorate**, *noun*, a) the office of an inspector, b) a group of inspectors, c) the district under an inspector.
[Latin *inspectus* looked into]

inspiration (*say* inspa-**ray**-sh'n) *noun*
1. the arousing of feelings, ideas, impulses, etc., especially those that lead to creative activity.

2. anything which arouses such activity: 'my wife has been my *inspiration* in all I have done'.
Usage: 'your idea of leaving before the weekend rush was an *inspiration*' (= very good idea).
3. the act of inhaling.
Word Family: **inspirational,** *adjective*; **inspirationally,** *adverb.*
[Latin *inspirare* to breathe into]

inspire (*say* in–**spire**) *verb*
1. to uplift the mind or spirit: 'the beauty of nature *inspired* Wordsworth to write many poems'.
2. to excite a particular emotion: 'his calm manner *inspired* me with confidence'.
3. to inhale.

instability (*say* insta–**billi**–tee) *noun*
a lack of stability, especially of character.

install (*say* in–**stawl**) *verb*
1. to place or fix in position for use.
2. to establish in office.
Usage: 'he *installed* himself in the comfortable armchair by the fire' (= settled).
installation (*say* insta–**lay**–sh'n) *noun*
1. the act of installing
2. something which is installed or established, such as a permanent military base, a group of machines, etc.

instalment (*say* in–**stawl**–m'nt) *noun*
in America spelt **installment**
1. one of a series of cash payments paid, by a buyer to a seller, for goods or services.
2. a single part of something which is supplied or issued over a period of time: 'listen to the next *instalment* of our serial'.

instance (*say* **in**stance) *noun*
1. a particular case: 'in this *instance* he was right'.
2. an example intended to prove or illustrate a point, argument or general truth: 'give us an *instance* of his cruelty'.
at the instance of, at the request of.
Word Family: **instance,** *verb,* to give as an example.

instant (*say* **in**–st'nt) *adjective*
immediate: 'the troops are in a state of *instant* readiness for battle'.
Usage: 'do you like *instant* coffee?' (= quickly prepared, as by simply adding water).

instant *noun*
1. a specific point of time: 'come home this *instant*!'.
2. a short space of time: 'the bystanders had gathered within an *instant* of the crash occurring'.
Word Family: **instantly,** *adverb.*

instantaneous (*say* instan–**tay**–nee–us) *adjective*
happening or done immediately.
Word Family: **instantaneously,** *adverb*; **instantaneousness,** *noun.*

instead (*say* in–**sted**) *adverb*
in place of something: 'there was no fish, so we are having meat *instead*'.

instep *noun*
1. *Anatomy:* the arched upper surface of the human foot, between the ankle and the toes.
2. the part of a shoe or stocking covering the instep.

instigate *verb*
to bring about, especially by provoking.
Word Family: **instigator,** *noun,* a person who instigates; **instigation,** *noun,* the act of instigating.
[Latin *instigare* to goad on]

instil (*say* in–**stil**) *verb*
(instilled, instilling)
in America spelt **instill**
to introduce gradually or by degrees: 'parents must *instil* good behaviour into their children from the start'.
Word Family: **instillation** (*say* insti–**lay**–sh'n), *noun,* the act of instilling.
[Latin *instillare* to pour in drop by drop]

instinct (1) (*say* **in**–stinkt) *noun*
1. *Psychology, Sociology:* the unlearned responses or tendencies of people and animals.
2. a natural aptitude or talent.
Word Family: **instinctive, instinctual** (*say* in–**stinkt**–yew'l), *adjectives,* of or resulting from an instinct; **instinctively,** *adverb.*
[Latin *instinctus* instigated]

instinct (2) (*say* in–**stinkt**) *adjective*
being filled with or animated by: 'a poem *instinct* with feeling'.

institute (*say* **insti**–tewt) *verb*
1. to establish or set up: 'to *institute* a new law'.
2. to start: 'to *institute* legal proceedings'.
institute *noun*
a) an organization founded to promote some cause, such as education. b) the

buildings used by such an organization.
[Latin *institutus* set up or established]

institution (*say* insti–**tew**–sh'n) *noun*
1. a) an organization such as a hospital or university, established for a particular purpose. b) the building or buildings used.
2. any person who has become well-known because of long service: 'our postman had been doing the same round for so long he had become a local *institution*'.
3. something, such as a law or pattern of behaviour, which has become a recognized and accepted part of a culture, etc.
4. the act of instituting.
Word Family: **institutional**, *adjective*, a) of or relating to an institution, b) being characterized by uniformity and dullness; **institutionally**, *adverb*; **institutionalize, institutionalise**, *verb*, a) to make into an institution, b) to confine a person in an institution.

instruct (*say* in–**strukt**) *verb*
1. to give orders or directions to: 'the doctor has *instructed* me to stay in bed'.
2. to teach.
Word Family: **instructor**, *noun*, a person who instructs; **instructive**, *adjective*, informative or serving to instruct; **instructively**, *adverb*; **instructiveness**, *noun*.
[Latin *instructus* built on, equipped]

instruction (*say* in–**struk**–sh'n) *noun*
1. a) the act or practice of instructing. b) any knowledge imparted.
2. (*usually plural*) any orders or directions.

instrument (*say* instra–m'nt) *noun*
1. a device or object for a particular purpose: 'surgical *instruments*'.
2. a device for producing musical sounds: 'the bassoon is a woodwind *instrument*'.
3. any person or thing used for a purpose.
4. a formal, legal document.
instrument *verb*
to arrange a piece of music for instruments, especially for an orchestra.
[Latin *instrumentum* equipment]

instrumental (*say* instra–**men**–t'l) *adjective*
1. serving as a means: 'my friend was *instrumental* in getting me this job'.
2. of or for musical instruments: '*instrumental* music'.
3. of or relating to an instrument: 'the surveyor's inaccuracy was due to an *instrumental* error'.
instrumental *noun*
a piece of music, usually popular, performed without vocal accompaniment.
Word Family: **instrumentalist**, *noun*, a person who plays a musical instrument, especially for popular music; **instrumentally**, *adverb*.

instrumentality
(*say* instra–men–**talli**–tee) *noun*
the agency or means by which something is done: 'he got the job through the *instrumentality* of his father-in-law'.

insubordinate (*say* insa–**bordi**–nit) *adjective*
disobedient or rebellious.
Word Family: **insubordination**, *noun*; **insubordinately**, *adverb*.

insubstantial (*say* insub–**stan**–sh'l) *adjective*
1. not strong or substantial: 'his brief explanation was very *insubstantial*'.
2. imaginary or not real: 'he is full of *insubstantial* fears about being alone'.

insufferable (*say* in–**suffera**–b'l) *adjective*
intolerable or unbearable.
Word Family: **insufferably**, *adverb*; **insufferableness**, *noun*.

insufficient (*say* insa–**fish**'nt) *adjective*
not sufficient or enough: 'his earnings were *insufficient* to keep pace with his wife's extravagant tastes'.
Word Family: **insufficiently**, *adverb*; **insufficiency**, *noun*, a lack.

insular (*say* **in**–sew–la) *adjective*
1. of or relating to an island.
2. narrow-minded: 'absurdly *insular* prejudices'.
Word Family: **insularity** (*say* in–sew–**larri**–tee), *noun*.
[Latin *insula* an island]

insulate (*say* **in**–syoo–late) *verb*
1. to cover with non-conducting material.
2. to isolate: 'the astronauts were *insulated* for several days after returning from the moon'.
Word Family: **insulation** (*say* in–syoo–**lay**–sh'n), *noun*, a) any material used for insulating, b) the act of insulating; **insulator**, *noun*, anything which insulates, especially against electricity.

insulin (*say* **in**–syoo–lin) *noun*
Biology: a hormone secreted in the pancreas, controlling the amount of glucose in the blood, used to treat diabetes.

insult (*say* **in**sult) *noun*
an offensive remark or act.
insult (*say* in**sult**) *verb*
to speak to or treat in a contemptuous or insolent way.
Word Family: **insultingly**, *adverb.*
[Latin *insultare* leap on or at]

insuperable (*say* in–**syoo**–p'ra–b'l) *adjective*
not capable of being overcome or surmounted.
Word Family: **insuperably**, *adverb.*

insupportable (*say* insa–**por**ti–b'l) *adjective*
unendurable or insufferable.

insurance (*say* in–**shore**–ence) *noun*
1. a contract under which a person or company agrees to pay for any loss or damage to certain property provided the owner makes regular payments, called **premiums**. Compare LIFE ASSURANCE.
2. a) the payment made to or by a company issuing an insurance. b) the amount for which anything is insured.
3. any safeguard against risk or harm: 'most people keep their money in a bank as an *insurance* against burglary'.
Word Family: **insured**, *noun*, a person protected by an insurance; **insurer**, *noun*, a person or company issuing an insurance.

insure (*say* in–**shor**) *verb*
to guarantee against risk or harm, as with insurance.
Word Family: **insurable**, *adjective*, capable of being insured.

insurgency (*say* in–**sir**–j'n–see) *noun*
a revolt against a government.
Word Family: **insurgent**, *noun*, a member of an insurgency; **insurgent**, *adjective*, a) rebellious, b) (of the sea) rising or surging up.
[Latin *insurgens* rising]

insurmountable
(*say* in–sir–**mounta**–b'l) *adjective*
not able to be overcome or surmounted.
Word Family: **insurmountably**, *adverb.*

insurrection (*say* insa–**rek**–sh'n) *noun*
a revolt against an established government, especially an organized effort to seize political power.
Word Family: **insurrectionary**, *noun*, *adjective.*
[Latin *insurrectus* risen]

insusceptible (*say* insa–**sep**ti–b'l) *adjective*
not liable to be influenced or affected by: 'he is *insusceptible* to argument'.
Word Family: **insusceptibility** (*say* insa–septa–**billi**–tee), *noun.*

intact (*say* in**takt**) *adjective*
remaining whole, unchanged or undamaged.
Word Family: **intactness**, *noun.*
[Latin *intactus* untouched]

intaglio (*say* in–**tah**li–o) *noun*
1. the art of engraving designs into a surface, especially on gems.
2. a method of printing from plates or cylinders on which the image has been etched below the surface.
[Italian *intagliare* to engrave]

intake *noun*
1. a) the act of taking in. b) anything which is taken in: 'a huge *intake* of students'.
2. the opening through which a fluid is taken into a container, pipe, etc.

intangible (*say* in–**tan**ji–b'l) *adjective*
1. incapable of being touched.
2. vague or indefinable: 'he has *intangible* fears about his future'.
Word Family: **intangibly**, *adverb*; **intangibility** (*say* in–tanji–**billi**–tee), *noun.*

intangible asset
an asset of a business, such as goodwill or a trademark, the value of which is difficult to assess. Compare TANGIBLE ASSET.

integer (*say* **in**ti–jer) *noun*
Maths: any number without a fraction.
[Latin, intact]

integral (*say* **in**ti–grul) *adjective*
1. being an indispensable part of a whole: 'arms and legs are *integral* parts of the human body'.
2. of or relating to integers.
Word Family: **integrally**, *adverb.*

integral calculus
Maths: see CALCULUS.

integrate (*say* **in**ti–grate) *verb*
1. to combine parts into a whole: 'the welfare plan *integrated* all the existing agencies into one comprehensive service'.
2. to absorb into a culture or society: 'some of the newcomers were more quickly *integrated* into the community than others'.

integrated circuit
Electronics: a complete circuit of many components etched on a minute silicon chip, and much smaller than a printed circuit.

integration (*say* inti-**gray**-sh'n) *noun*
1. the bringing or fitting together of parts into a whole.
2. *Maths:* the inverse process of differentiation.
3. the policy or process of making public facilities, such as schools and transport, available to people of all races.
Word Family: **integrationist,** *noun,* a person who favours racial integration.

integrity (*say* in-**tegri**-tee) *noun*
1. the quality of being honest and upright in character.
2. the state or condition of being complete: 'the scholar had restored the text of the manuscript to its original *integrity*'.

integument (*say* in-**teg**-yoo-m'nt) *noun*
any outer covering, such as skin, rind or a shell.
[from Latin]

intellect (*say* **inta**-lekt) *noun*
1. the capacity of the mind to reason and grasp ideas, as distinct from feeling and will.
2. a person of good understanding or reasoning powers.
[from Latin]
Common Error: see INTELLIGENCE.

intellectual (*say* inta-**lek**-tyoo-al) *adjective*
a) of or relating to the intellect: 'the *intellectual* powers'. b) possessing or showing intellect: 'he's a very *intellectual* author'.
intellectual *noun*
any person who enjoys intellectual pursuits or whose work requires a developed intellect.
Word Family: **intellectually,** *adverb;* **intellectualize, intellectualise,** *verb,* to treat in intellectual terms.

intelligence (*say* in-**telli**-j'nce) *noun*
1. the ability to understand, reason and learn to adapt to new situations.
2. news or information, especially about important events.
3. *Military:* the branch of an army which collects and analyses information about foreign armed forces and their equipment, etc.
Word Family: **intelligent,** *adjective,* having or showing intelligence; **intelligently,** *adverb.*
[from Latin]
Common Error: INTELLIGENCE, INTELLECT both refer to the capacity to know, reason and understand: *intelligence* is the more general term, suggesting a natural ability to think and adapt, whereas *intellect* refers to a developed capacity to reason and test ideas.

intelligence quotient
(*say* in-**telli**-j'nce kwo-sh'nt)
short form is **IQ**
an indicator of a person's intelligence as measured by an intelligence test, and in relation to others of the same age. The IQ is mental age divided by real age, multiplied by 100. For the purpose of intelligence testing a person's 'real age' is frozen at 15. Thus the average IQ at any age up to 15 is 100, and the IQ of an 8-year-old with a mental age of 10 is 125.

intelligence test
a method of measuring intelligence by using tasks and problems.

intelligentsia (*say* in-telli-**jen**sia) *noun*
the intellectual class of society.
[Russian]

intelligible (*say* in-**tell**ija-b'l) *adjective*
capable of being understood.
Word Family: **intelligibly,** *adverb;* **intelligibility** (*say* in-tellija-**billi**-tee), *noun.*

intemperate (*say* in-**tem**pa-rit) *adjective*
lacking moderation, e.g. in speech or the consumption of alcohol.
Word Family: **intemperately,** *adverb;* **intemperance,** *noun,* the state or quality of being intemperate.

intend *verb*
to plan or have as a purpose: a) 'he *intends* to quit'; b) 'a room *intended* for study'.
Word Family: **intended,** *noun,* (informal) one's prospective husband or wife.
[Latin *intendere* to stretch (e.g. a bow), to aim]

intense (*say* in-**tense**) *adjective*
1. very great or strong: a) '*intense* light'; b) '*intense* happiness'.
Usage: 'he has devoted years of *intense* study to the problem' (= hard).
2. characterized by strong feelings: 'an *intense* young man'.

intensity (*say* in–**tensi**–tee) *noun*
the quality of being intense.
Word Family: **intensely**, *adverb*; **intensify** (**intensified**, **intensifying**), *verb*, to make or become intense or more intense; **intensification**, *noun*.

intensive (*say* in–**tensiv**) *adjective*
1. concentrated: 'an *intensive* course in economics'.
2. designed to produce maximum results: '*intensive* farming'.
3. *Grammar:* indicating emphasis. *Example*: 'certainly' is an *intensive* adverb.
Word Family: **intensively**, *adverb*; **intensiveness**, *noun*.

intent (1) (*say* in–**tent**) *noun*
any purpose or intention.
to all intents and purposes, in almost every way.

intent (2) (*say* in–**tent**) *adjective*
firmly fixed or concentrated: 'an *intent* gaze'.
Word Family: **intently**, *adverb*; **intentness**, *noun*.
[Latin *intentus* stretched, aimed]

intention (*say* in–**ten**–sh'n) *noun*
1. any plan of action, design, or purpose.
2. any goal or objective which guides some action.
Word Family: **intentional**, *adjective*, intended or deliberate; **intentionally**, *adverb*.

inter (*say* in–**ter**) *verb*
(**interred**, **interring**)
to place a corpse in a grave or tomb.
Word Family: **interment**, *noun*, a burial.
[IN– (1) + Latin *terra* earth]

inter– (*say* **in**–ter)
a prefix meaning: a) between or among, as in *interbreed*; b) reciprocally or mutually, as in *interact*.

interaction (*say* inta–**rak**–sh'n) *noun*
the process of two things acting on each other.
Word Family: **interact**, *verb*; **interactive**, *adjective*.

inter alia (*say* inter **ay**–lee–a)
among other things.
[Latin]

interbreed *verb*
(**interbred**, **interbreeding**)
to crossbreed.

intercede (*say* inta–**seed**) *verb*
to intervene on behalf of another.
[Latin *intercedere* to come between]

intercept (*say* inta–**sept**) *verb*
1. to stop or interrupt the progress of.
2. *Maths:* to cut off by intersecting at two points.
Word Family: **interception**, *noun*, the act of intercepting; **intercept** (Maths), *noun*; **interceptor**, *noun*, a person or thing that intercepts.
[INTER– + Latin *captus* seized]

intercession (*say* inta–**sesh**'n) *noun*
1. the act of interceding.
2. *Christian:* a prayer on behalf of someone else.
Word Family: **intercessory**, *adjective*, making intercession.

interchange *verb*
1. to change places or put in the place of each other.
2. to exchange.
3. to alternate: 'tears *interchanged* with smiles'.
Word Family: **interchange**, *noun*, the act of interchanging; **interchangeable**, *adjective*; **interchangeably**, *adverb*.

intercom *noun*
short form of **intercommunication**
a system of communication between rooms in a building, aircraft, etc., using telephones, microphones, etc.

interconnect *verb*
to connect or be connected one with the other.
Word Family: **interconnection**, *noun*.

intercontinental
(*say* inta–konti–**nen**–t'l) *adjective*
1. between continents: '*intercontinental* shipping'.
2. able to reach from one continent to another: 'an *intercontinental* ballistic missile'.

intercostal *adjective*
of or relating to the muscles or spaces between the ribs.
[INTER– + Latin *costa* rib]

intercourse *noun*
1. a communication or exchange of ideas, feelings, etc.: 'social *intercourse*'.
2. sexual intercourse.

interdenominational
(*say* inta–dinommi–**nay**–sh'n–al) *adjective*
of or common to two or more religious movements.

interdependent (*say* inta–dip–**end**'nt) *adjective*
being dependent on each other.

Word Family: **interdependently**, *adverb*; **interdependence**, **interdependency**, *noun.*

interdict (*say* inta–dikt) *noun*
Roman Catholic: a punishment by which a person remains a member of the Church, but is prohibited from taking part in certain religious acts.
Word Family: **interdict** (*say* inta–**dikt**), *verb*, to forbid or prohibit; **interdiction**, *noun.*
[Latin *interdictus* forbidden]

interest (*say* inta–rest) *noun*
1. a) a feeling of curiosity, fascination, etc.: 'he has an *interest* in pottery'. b) the cause of such a feeling.
2. a share or involvement, especially in property, business, etc.: 'he has a controlling *interest* in the company'.
3. importance: 'material possessions are of little *interest* to her'.
4. (*often plural*) well-being, profit or advantage: 'your father has your *interests* at heart when he sends you to school'.
5. *Commerce:* a payment for the use of money or credit, usually calculated as a percentage of the amount used or owed.
simple interest is calculated on the original amount only.
compound interest is calculated on the original amount together with the interest accumulated over a period.
accrued interest is the interest calculated up to a certain date within the period of the loan.
Usage: 'she returned their criticisms with *interest*' (= more than was originally received).
interest *verb*
1. to arouse the curiosity of: 'the old house *interested* the architect'.
2. to concern or involve: 'we tried to *interest* him in buying a farm'.
Word Family: **interested**, *adjective*, showing interest; **interestedly**, *adverb*; **interesting**, *adjective*, arousing interest; **interestingly**, *adverb.*
[Latin, it is of importance to]

interface *noun*
a surface forming a common boundary between two bodies.

interfere (*say* inta–**feer**) *verb*
(interfered, interfering)
1. to intrude in the affairs of others.
2. to hinder or impede: 'he allowed his personal life to *interfere* with his work'.
3. *Physics, Radio:* to cause interference.
Word Family: **interferingly**, *adverb*; **interferer**, *noun.*
[Old French *s'entreferir* to strike each other]

interference (*say* inta–**feer**'nce) *noun*
1. the act or fact of interfering.
2. *Physics:* the meeting and combination of waves, the effect varying with the phase, amplitude and frequency of the waves.
3. *Radio:* the receiving of radio signals with similar frequencies from more than one source.

intergalactic (*say* inta–ga–**laktik**) *adjective*
Astronomy: of or between galaxies.

interglacial (*say* inta–**glay**–see–ul) *adjective*
Geology: occurring or formed between times of glacial action.

interim (*say* **inta**–rim) *adjective*
1. of or relating to an intervening period of time.
2. temporary: 'an *interim* treaty was made while peace negotiations continued'.
Word Family: **interim**, *noun*, an intervening period of time.
[Latin, meanwhile]

interior (*say* in–**teeria**) *adjective*
1. being inside.
2. inland.
3. relating to the internal affairs of a country.
Word Family: **interior**, *noun.*
[Latin, inner]

interior decorator
a person who plans and supervises the decoration and furnishing of the inside of a building.

interior designer
a person trained to design and coordinate the inside form and appearance of a building.

interject (*say* inta–**jekt**) *verb*
to break in with a comment while someone else is speaking.
Word Family: **interjector**, *noun.*

interjection (*say* inta–**jek**–sh'n) *noun*
1. the act of interjecting.
2. a word or phrase used as an exclamation.
[INTER– + Latin *jactus* thrown]

interlace *verb*
to cross each other as if woven together.

interlard *verb*
to insert at intervals: 'his speech was *interlarded* with swear words'.

interleave *verb*
also called to **interleaf**
to insert or provide blank pages in a book, e.g. for protecting illustrations, making notes, etc.

interlock *verb*
to unite or join closely.
interlock *noun*
a smooth, knitted fabric, usually made from cotton and used for underwear.

interlocutor (*say* inta-**lok**-yoo-ter) *noun*
a person taking part in a conversation or dialogue.
Word Family: **interlocutory**, *adjective*; **interlocution** (*say* inta-lo-**kew**-sh'n), *noun*, a conversation.
[INTER- + Latin *locutus* spoken]

interloper *noun*
a person who intrudes or interferes.
Word Family: **interlope**, *verb*.

interlude (*say* **inta**-lood) *noun*
1. an intervening episode, period, space, etc.
2. a short comedy placed between two plays, developed during the Renaissance.
[INTER- + Latin *ludus* a game]

intermarry *verb*
(intermarried, intermarrying)
1. to marry someone not a member of one's own group or race.
2. (of families) to become connected by marriage.
3. to marry within one's family, tribe or clan.
Word Family: **intermarriage**, *noun*.

intermediary (*say* inta-**meedia**-ree) *noun*
a mediator or agent.
Word Family: **intermediary**, *adjective*, a) being between, b) acting as a mediator.

intermediate (*say* inta-**meedi**-it) *adjective*
situated or occurring between things in time, space, etc.: 'several *intermediate* products were formed during the chemical reaction'.

interment (*say* in-**ter**-m'nt) *noun*
Word Family: see INTER.

intermezzo (*say* inta-**metso**) *noun*
1. *Music:* a) a short piece for the piano. b) an instrumental piece inserted in an opera.
2. (*formerly*) a short comic opera inserted between the acts of a serious opera.
[Italian, interlude]

interminable (*say* in-**ter**-minna-b'l) *adjective*
having no apparent end.
Word Family: **interminably**, *adverb*.

intermingle *verb*
to mingle, one with another.

intermission (*say* inta-**mish**'n) *noun*
1. a pause: 'the rain poured down all day without *intermission*'.
2. *Theatre:* an interval.

intermittent (*say* inta-**mittent**) *adjective*
stopping and starting at intervals.
Word Family: **intermittently**, *adverb*.
[Latin *intermittens* leaving gaps]

intern (*say* in-**tern**) *verb*
to confine to a country or place, especially during wartime.
Word Family: **internment**, *noun*; **internee** (*say* in-ter-**nee**), *noun*, a person who is interned.

internal (*say* in-**tern**'l) *adjective*
1. of or relating to the inside or inner part of something.
2. of or relating to the domestic affairs of a country.
Word Family: **internally**, *adverb*.
[from Latin]

internal combustion engine
an engine with one or more cylinders in which the process of combustion takes place within the cylinder.

internal evidence
evidence which can be gleaned from a book, document, etc. itself.

international (*say* inta-**nash**'n'l) *adjective*
1. of or relating to more than one nation or nationality.
2. between or among nations: 'an *international* trade agreement'.
Word Family: **internationally**, *adverb*; **internationalize**, **internationalise**, *verb*, to make international.

international date line
a calculated line at or near 180° longitude where the date changes by one day when it is crossed.

internationalism *noun*
the policy of countries working together for their common good. Compare NATIONALISM.
Word Family: **internationalist**, *noun*.

international nautical mile
see MILE.

internecine (*say* inta–**nee**–sine) *adjective*
1. mutually destructive.
2. characterized by great slaughter: 'an *internecine* war'.
[Latin *internecio* a massacre]

internee *noun*
Word Family: see INTERN.

interpenetrate (*say* inta–**penni**–trate) *verb*
1. to penetrate thoroughly.
2. to penetrate each other.
Word Family: **interpenetration,** *noun.*

interplay *noun*
the effect of two or more things on each other.

Interpol *noun*
the International Criminal Police Commission through which the police of member states help each other in dealing with crime.

interpolate (*say* in–**terpa**–late) *verb*
1. to insert or introduce something between parts already there.
2. to estimate an unknown quantity within the limits of what is known. Compare EXTRAPOLATE.
Word Family: **interpolation,** *noun.*

interpose *verb*
1. to place between.
2. to interject a question or remark during a speech or conversation.
Usage: 'I *interposed* in their quarrel' (= mediated).
Word Family: **interposition** (*say* inta–po–**zish**'n), *noun,* a) the act of interposing, b) something which is interposed.

interpret (*say* in–**terprit**) *verb*
1. to show, clarify or explain the meaning of: 'we *interpreted* his reply as an apology'.
2. to translate: 'as she did not understand English I had to *interpret* for her'.
Word Family: **interpretation** (*say* in–terpri–**tay**–sh'n), *noun*; **interpreter,** *noun,* a person who interprets.
[Latin *interpretari* to act as broker, to explain]

interracial (*say* inta–**ray**–sh'l) *adjective*
a) existing between races or members of different races. b) of or for people of different races.

interregnum (*say* inta–**regnum**) *noun*
plural is **interregnums** or **interregna**
a time when a country has no official leader or government, such as the time between the death of a monarch and the beginning of his successor's rule.
[INTER– + Latin *regnum* reign]

interrelate (*say* inta–**rillate**) *verb*
to bring into reciprocal relation.
Word Family: **interrelationship,** *noun.*

interrogate (*say* in–**terra**–gate) *verb*
to examine by close questioning, especially in a formal way.
Word Family: **interrogation,** *noun*; **interrogator,** *noun,* a person who interrogates.
[INTER– + Latin *rogare* to ask]

interrogation mark
see QUESTION MARK.

interrogative (*say* inta–**rogga**–tiv) *adjective*
1. of the nature of a question.
2. *Grammar:* (of a word, etc.) forming a question.
Word Family: **interrogative** (Grammar), *noun*; **interrogatively,** *adverb*; **interrogatory,** *adjective,* relating to, expressing or implying a question.

interrupt (*say* inta–**rupt**) *verb*
1. to break the continuity of: 'they *interrupted* their journey for a week to stay with relatives'.
2. to hinder or stop by breaking in on: 'his speech was *interrupted* by many shouts'.
Word Family: **interruption,** *noun.*
[INTER– + Latin *ruptus* broken]

intersect (*say* inta–**sekt**) *verb*
1. to cut across or pass through: 'the roads *intersect* at the bottom of a hill'.
2. *Maths:* to have one or more points in common.
Word Family: **intersection,** *noun,* a) the place where two or more things intersect, b) the act of intersecting.
[INTER– + Latin *sectus* cut]

intersperse (*say* inta–**sperse**) *verb*
to scatter or distribute irregularly among other things.
Word Family: **interspersion** (*say* inta–**sper**–sh'n), *noun.*
[INTER– + Latin *sparsus* scattered]

interstellar *adjective*
between the stars.

interstice (*say* in–**terstis**) *noun*
plural is **interstices** (*say* in–**tersta**–seez)
a small space between things or parts.
Word Family: **interstitial** (*say* inta–**stish**'l), *adjective,* pertaining to, situated in, or forming an interstice; **interstitially,** *adverb.*
[INTER– + Latin *status* put]

intertwine *verb*
to twine together.

interval *noun*
1. an intervening space or period of time.
2. *Music:* the difference in pitch between two notes.
3. *Theatre:* the time between two acts of a play, two films, etc., when the audience leave their seats for refreshments. Also called an **intermission**.
[Latin *intervallum* the space between the ramparts]

intervene (*say* inta–**veen**) *verb*
1. to step in, in order to solve, settle, correct, etc.: 'he *intervened* in the dispute'.
2. to come between in time, place, etc.: 'nothing *intervened* and we were able to take our holiday as planned'.
Word Family: **intervention** (*say* inta–**ven**–sh'n), *noun.*
[INTER– + Latin *venire* to come]

interview *noun*
a) a personal meeting for questioning.
b) a report of such a meeting.
Word Family: **interviewer**, *noun*, a person who asks the questions at an interview; **interview**, *verb.*

interweave *verb*
(**interwove** or **interweaved**, **interwoven** or **interwove**, **interweaving**)
to weave together.

intestate (*say* in–**testate**) *adjective*
Law: having left no valid will. Compare TESTATE.

intestine (*say* in–**testin**) *noun*
also called the **bowel** or the **gut**
Anatomy: the lower part of the food canal below the stomach, part of the alimentary canal. The **small intestine** consists of the duodenum, jejunum and ileum and the **large intestine** consists of the caecum, colon and rectum.
Word Family: **intestinal** (*say* in–testin–al), *adjective.*
[Latin *intestinus* internal]

intimate (1) (*say* **inti**–mit) *adjective*
closely acquainted: 'an *intimate* friend'.
Usages:
a) 'an *intimate* dinner party' (= small and private).
b) 'she refused to tell all the *intimate* details' (= personal).
c) 'he has an *intimate* knowledge of Dutch' (= thorough).
Word Family: **intimately**, *adverb*; **intimacy**, **intimateness**, *nouns.*
[Latin *intimus* innermost]

intimate (2) (*say* **inti**–mate) *verb*
to imply subtly.
Word Family: **intimation** (*say* inti–**may**–sh'n), *noun.*

intimidate (*say* in–**timmi**–date) *verb*
to frighten, especially in order to force someone to do something.
Word Family: **intimidation** (*say* in–timmi–**day**–sh'n), *noun.*
[Latin *in* very + *timidus* afraid]

into *preposition*
a word used to indicate the following:
1. (motion or direction towards the inside) a) 'we went *into* the shop'; b) 'we helped him *into* the car'.
2. (change of condition or result) a) 'the rain changed *into* snow'; b) 'she burst *into* tears'.
3. (entry or introduction) a) 'they entered *into* an agreement'; b) 'to go *into* politics'.
4. (extent in time, space, etc.) 'it rained well *into* the night'.
5. (division) 'two *into* six goes three'.
be into, (*informal*) a) to be deeply involved or interested in; b) to be in debt to.

intolerable (*say* in–**tollera**–b'l) *adjective*
unbearable.
Word Family: **intolerably**, *adverb.*

intolerant (*say* in–**tolla**–r'nt) *adjective*
not tolerant.
Word Family: **intolerance**, *noun*; **intolerantly**, *adverb.*

intonation (*say* inta–**nay**–sh'n) *noun*
1. the rise and fall of the voice in speaking.
2. *Music:* the manner of producing notes, especially in relation to accuracy of pitch.

intone *verb*
to speak with drawn–out vowel sounds and in a monotone, as when or as if reciting a prayer or chanting a psalm.

in toto
wholly or absolutely.
[Latin]

intoxicate (*say* in–**toksi**–kate) *verb*
to cause to lose self–control, especially as the result of taking alcohol, drugs, etc.
Usage: 'the team was *intoxicated* by success' (= wildly excited, elated).

Word Family: **intoxicant,** *noun*; **intoxication** (*say* in-toksi-**kay**-sh'n), *noun*, drunkenness.
[IN- (1) + Latin *toxicum* poison]

intra-
a prefix meaning within, as in *intravenous.*

intractable (*say* in-**trak**ti-b'l) *adjective*
stubborn or difficult to manage.
Word Family: **intractability** (*say* in-trakti-**billi**-tee), **intractableness,** *nouns*; **intractably,** *adverb.*
[IN- (2) + Latin *tractare* to handle]

intramural (*say* intra-**mew**-r'l) *adjective*
existing within the bounds of an institution, especially a university or school.
[INTRA- + Latin *murus* a wall]

intransigent (*say* in-**transi**-j'nt) *adjective*
uncompromising.
Word Family: **intransigent,** *noun*, a person who is uncompromising; **intransigence, intransigency,** *noun*; **intransigently,** *adverb.*
[IN- (2) + Latin *transigens* transacting]

intransitive (*say* in-**tranzi**-tiv) *adjective*
Grammar: (of a verb) not needing a direct object to complete its meaning.
Example: the boy *walked* slowly to buy a book.
Compare TRANSITIVE.
Word Family: **intransitive,** *noun*; **intransitively,** *adverb.*

intravenous (*say* intra-**veenus**) *adjective*
within a vein, such as an injection given into a vein.
[INTRA- + Latin *vena* a vein]

intrepid (*say* in-**trep**-id) *adjective*
fearless or bold.
Word Family: **intrepidly,** *adverb*; **intrepidity** (*say* intrepiddi-tee), *noun.*
[IN- (2) + Latin *trepidus* alarmed]

intricate (*say* **intra**-kit) *adjective*
1. having many interrelating parts or elements: 'an *intricate* machine'.
2. difficult to untangle: 'an *intricate* knot'.
Word Family: **intricately,** *adverb*; **intricacy** (*say* **intrika**-see), *noun.*
[Latin *intricatus* entangled]

intrigue (*say* in-**treeg**) *verb*
(intrigued, intriguing)
1. to arouse the interest or curiosity of, especially by puzzling.
2. to make and carry out secret plans: 'the anarchists *intrigued* to overthrow the government'.
Word Family: **intrigue** (*say* **in**-treeg *or* in-**treeg**), *noun*, a) an underhand plot, b) the use of such plots.
[Latin *intricare* to entangle]

intrinsic (*say* in-**trinzik**) *adjective*
belonging to a thing by its very nature.
Compare EXTRINSIC.
Word Family: **intrinsically,** *adverb.*
[Latin *intrinsecus* inwardly]

introduce *verb*
1. to make acquainted: 'I would like to *introduce* you to a friend of mine'.
2. to use or bring to notice first: 'who *introduced* the fashion of mini skirts?'.
Usages:
a) 'he *introduced* a bill in Parliament' (= presented).
b) 'this term the class will be *introduced* to calculus' (= given first knowledge of).
c) 'the Prime Minister *introduced* sweeping changes' (= instituted).
d) 'an amendment was *introduced* into the bill' (= inserted, put).
e) 'he *introduced* his remarks with a brief summary' (= prefaced).
Word Family: **introduction,** *noun*, a) the act of introducing, b) something which introduces or is introduced; **introductory,** *adjective*, forming an introduction.
[Latin *intro-* inwards + *ducere* to lead]

introspection (*say* intra-**spek**-sh'n) *noun*
the examination of one's own thoughts, sensations, etc.
Word Family: **introspective,** *adjective*; **introspectively,** *adverb*; **introspect,** *verb.*
[Latin *intro-* inwards + *specere* to look]

introvert (*say* **intra**-vert) *noun*
a person interested chiefly in his own thoughts and feelings rather than in the world around him. Compare EXTROVERT.

introvert (*say* intra-**vert**) *verb*
to turn inwards.
Word Family: **introversion** (*say* intra-**ver**-*zh*'n), *noun.*
[Latin *intro-* inwards + *vertere* to turn]

intrude *verb*
to thrust or force in, especially where one is unwelcome.
Word Family: **intruder,** *noun*, a person or thing that intrudes; **intrusive,** *adjective*, tending to intrude.
[IN- (1) + Latin *trudere* to thrust]

intrusion (*say* in-**troo**-*zh*'n) *noun*
1. the act of intruding.
2. something which intrudes, such as a body of igneous rock which forces itself, while molten, into cracks in pre-existing rocks.

intuition (*say* int-yoo-**ish**'n) *noun*
a) an understanding or insight arrived at without conscious reasoning. b) the ability to perceive in this way.
Word Family: **intuitive** (*say* in-**tewa**-tiv), *adjective*; **intuitively**, *adverb.*
[Latin *intueri* to inspect]

inundate (*say* **in**nun-date) *verb*
to overwhelm or cover with or as if with a flood: 'we were *inundated* with applications for the new job'.
Word Family: **inundation** (*say* innun-**day**-sh'n), *noun.*
[IN- (1) + Latin *unda* a wave]

inure (*say* in-**yoor**) *verb*
to accustom to something unpleasant.

invade *verb*
1. to enter as an enemy, or in attack.
Usage: 'the dampness from the cellar *invaded* the living room' (= moved into).
2. to violate or interfere with: 'do not *invade* his privacy'.
Word Family: **invader**, *noun*, a person who invades; **invasion** (*say* in-**vay**-*zh*'n), *noun.*
[Latin *invadere* to come in]

invalid (1) (*say* **in**va-lid) *noun*
a person who is sick or disabled for a long period of time.
Word Family: **invalid**, *verb*; **invalidism**, *noun*, prolonged ill health.
[Latin *invalidus* weak]

invalid (2) (*say* in-**val**lid) *adjective*
not valid.
Word Family: **invalidate**, *verb*, to make invalid; **invalidation**, *noun*; **invalidly**, *adverb.*

invaluable *adjective*
beyond valuing or estimation.
Word Family: **invaluably**, *adverb*; **invaluableness**, *noun.*

invariable (*say* in-**vair**ia-b'l) *adjective*
not subject to variation.
Word Family: **invariably**, *adverb*; **invariable**, *noun*, a constant.

invasion (*say* in-**vay**-*zh*'n) *noun*
Word Family: see INVADE.

invective (*say* in-**vek**tiv) *noun*
violent accusation or abuse.
[Latin *invectus* attacked]

inveigh (*say* in-**vay**) *verb*
to protest or attack vehemently in words.
[Latin *invehere* to attack]

inveigle (*say* in-**vay**-g'l) *verb*
to deceive by flattery, trickery, etc.
[Old French *aveugler* to blind]

invent *verb*
to conceive of or devise first: 'who *invented* the telephone?'.
Usage: 'he *invented* a clever excuse' (= made up, thought of).
invention (*say* in-**ven**-sh'n) *noun*
1. the act or process of inventing: 'when was the *invention* of the telephone?'.
2. something which has been invented or made: 'his machine was hailed as the best *invention* of its type'.
Usage: 'we could tell that the story was just another of his *inventions*' (= falsehoods, lies).
Word Family: **inventor**, *noun*; **inventive**, *adjective*, a) skilful at inventing, b) of or relating to invention; **inventively**, *adverb*; **inventiveness**, *noun.*
[Latin *inventus* discovered]

inventory (*say* **in**ven-tree) *noun*
a list of articles with the description and quantity of each, especially of the stock in a factory, shop, etc.
Word Family: **inventory (inventoried, inventorying)**, *verb.*

inverse (*say* **in**-verse) *adjective*
being reversed in order, opposite in nature, etc.: '4321 is the *inverse* order of 1234'.
inverse ratio
a ratio in which one quantity increases in proportion as the other decreases: 'his charm varied in *inverse ratio* to the amount he had had to drink'.
Word Family: **inverse**, *noun*, the reverse; **inversely**, *adverb.*

inverse-square law
Physics: the law that the intensity of light, electrical, magnetic or gravitational effects varies in inverse ratio to the square of the distance from the source.

invert *verb*
1. to turn upside down or inside out.
2. to reverse the position, order or condition of.
Word Family: **inversion** (*say* in-**ver**-*zh*'n), *noun*, a) the act of inverting, b) the state of being inverted.
[IN- (1) + Latin *vertere* to turn]

invertebrate (*say* in–verti–brit) ***noun***
any animal without a backbone.

inverted commas
see QUOTATION MARKS.

invest ***verb***
1. to use something, especially money, in order to gain profit, e.g. by interest, share dividends, etc.
Usage: 'mother has *invested* large sums on furniture for the new house' (= spent).
2. to provide or endow: 'a president is *invested* with great power'.
3. to besiege.
Word Family: **investor,** ***noun,*** a person or group who invests.
[Old French *investir* to clothe]

investigate (*say* in–vesti–gate) ***verb***
to examine or search into thoroughly, especially to discover facts, causes, etc.
Word Family: **investigation,** ***noun***; **investigatory,** *adjective*; **investigator,** ***noun,*** a person who investigates crimes, etc.
[Latin *investigare* to follow the trail]

investiture (*say* in–vesti–cher) ***noun***
the act or ceremony of bestowing official authority or position on a person.

investment ***noun***
a) the act of investing. b) anything, especially money, which is invested: 'they felt that buying the house was an *investment* for the future'.

inveterate (*say* in–vetta–rit) ***adjective***
being firmly established in a habit or practice, especially a bad one: 'an *inveterate* smoker'.
[Latin *inveteratus* made old, long–established]

invidious (*say* in–viddi–us) ***adjective***
likely to cause offence, dislike or resentment: 'she tends to make *invidious* comparisons between the students'.
[Latin *invidiosus* envious]

invigilate (*say* in–vija–late) ***verb***
to keep watch, especially over students in an exam.
Word Family: **invigilator,** ***noun.***

invigorate (*say* in–vigga–rate) ***verb***
to fill with vigour or energy.
Word Family: **invigoratingly,** ***adverb***; **invigoration,** ***noun.***

invincible (*say* in–vinsa–b'l) ***adjective***
not able to be defeated or conquered.
Word Family: **invincibility** (*say* in–vinsa–**billi**–tee), ***noun***; **invincibly,** ***adverb.***
[IN– (2) + Latin *vincere* to conquer]

inviolable (*say* **in–vie**–a–lab'l) ***adjective***
not to be violated or harmed, as a sacred object.
Word Family: **inviolability** (*say* in–vie–a–la**billi**–tee), **inviolableness,** ***nouns***; **inviolably,** ***adverb.***

inviolate (*say* in–**vie**–alit) ***adjective***
kept sacred or unharmed: 'the ancient temple remained *inviolate* for many years'.

invisible (*say* in–**vizzi**–b'l) ***adjective***
not visible.
invisible exports, services to customers abroad, such as banking, insurance, shipping, which earn foreign currency in the same way as exported goods.
invisible imports, services provided from abroad, such as banking, insurance and shipping.
Word Family: **invisibly,** ***adverb***; **invisibility** (*say* in–vizzi–**billi**–tee), ***noun.***

invisible ink
an ink which remains invisible until the surface is treated in a particular way.

invitation (*say* invi–**tay**–sh'n) ***noun***
a written or spoken request for a person to come, take part, etc.
Usage: 'the deserted house was an open *invitation* to vandals' (= attraction, encouragement).
[from Latin]

invite (*say* **invite**) ***verb***
to request, especially in a formal way.
Usages:
a) 'carelessness *invites* accidents' (= provokes, encourages).
b) 'the prospect of a swim seems *inviting* on a sweltering day' (= tempting).
Word Family: **invite** (*say* **invite**), ***noun,*** an invitation; **invitingly,** ***adverb.***

invoice (*say* **in**–voice) ***noun***
a list of goods or a detailed bill sent to a purchaser.
Word Family: **invoice,** ***verb.***

invoke (*say* in–**voke**) ***verb***
to appeal or call for earnestly, especially to a god.
Word Family: **invocation** (*say* invo–**kay**–sh'n), ***noun.***
[IN– (1) + Latin *vocare* to call]

involuntary (*say* in-**voll**un-tree) *adjective*
being done or occurring without conscious control or choice: 'her *involuntary* sneeze startled all of us'.

involuted (*say* inva-**loo**tid) *adjective*
also called **involute** (*say* **in**va-loot)
1. intricate or complex.
2. (of a leaf) rolled inwards from the edge.
Word Family: **involutedly,** *adverb.*
[IN- (1) + Latin *volutus* rolled]

involution (*say* inva-**loo**-sh'n) *noun*
1. the state of being involuted.
2. *Medicine:* any bodily changes involving a decrease in size or activity, such as when a person grows old.

involve (*say* in-**volv**) *verb*
1. to have or include as a part or element: 'this job will *involve* much travelling'.
2. to draw or get into a complicated or difficult situation: 'she became *involved* in the argument without meaning to'.
3. to make more complicated or difficult: 'please do not *involve* the issue with other matters'.
Usages:
a) 'she is very *involved* in social work' (= engrossed, absorbed).
b) 'he is *involved* with a French girl' (= having a relationship).
Word Family: **involvement,** *noun.*
[IN- (1) + Latin *volvere* to roll]

invulnerable (*say* in-**vul**nera-b'l) *adjective*
not able to be hurt or damaged: 'the soldiers' barricades made their position *invulnerable*'.
Word Family: **invulnerability** (*say* in-vulnera-**billi**-tee), *noun.*

inward (*say* **in**-wud) *adjective*
relating to or situated inside: 'the plane began its *inward* curve from the sea towards the airport'.
Usage: 'he found an *inward* peace from Yoga' (= mental, spiritual).
inwards, inward *adverb*
towards the inside or centre: 'the bedroom windows face *inwards* to the courtyard'.
Usage: 'you must look *inwards* for the cause of your unhappiness' (= into the mind or self).
Word Family: **inwardly,** *adverb;* **inwardness,** *noun,* a) the state of being internal, b) the real nature or essential meaning of something.

iodine (*say* **eye**-o-deen) *noun*
element number 53, a greyish-black, solid non-metal which forms a thick violet vapour when heated and is widely used as an antiseptic and in photography. It is essential in the diet and deficiency causes goitre. See HALOGEN.
See CHEMICAL ELEMENTS in grey pages.
Word Family: **iodize, iodise,** *verb,* to treat or combine with iodine.
[Greek *iodes* like a violet]

ion (*rhymes with* lion) *noun*
Chemistry: an atom or group of atoms which has become electrically charged by losing (positive ion) or gaining (negative ion) one or more electrons.
Word Family: **ionic,** *adjective;* **ionization** (*say* eye-on-eye-**zay**-sh'n), *noun,* the formation of ions; **ionize, ionise,** *verb.*
[Greek, going]

ionic bond (*say* eye-**on**-ik bond)
also called an **electrovalent bond**
Chemistry: a bond between atoms formed by the transfer of one or more electrons from one atom to another. The resulting ions are held together by electrostatic attraction. Compare COVALENT BOND and DATIVE BOND.

ionosphere (*say* eye-**onna**-sfeer) *noun*
the outer layers of the earth's atmosphere where the density is so reduced that electrically charged particles can exist.

iota (*say* eye-**o**-ta) *noun*
a very small quantity.
[from *iota,* the ninth and smallest letter of the Greek alphabet, equal to the English letter i]

ipecacuanha (*say* ippik-ak-yoo-**anna**) *noun*
a substance extracted from the roots of various South American plants, used in medicines, especially as an emetic.

ipso facto
by that very fact: 'he is leader of the ruling political party and, *ipso facto,* Prime Minister'.
[Latin]

ir-
a variant of the prefix **in- (1)** and **in- (2)**.

irascible (*say* irrassi-b'l) *adjective*
irritable or easily angered.
Word Family: **irascibly,** *adverb;* **irascibility** (*say* irrassi-**billi**-tee), *noun.*
[Latin *irasci* to grow angry]

irate (*say* **eye**-rate) *adjective*
full of rage or a sense of outrage.

ire *noun*
anger or rage.
[Latin *ira*]

iridescent (*say* irri-**dess**'nt) *adjective*
having or showing rainbow colours.
Word Family: **iridescence,** *noun*; **iridescently,** *adverb.*
[Greek *iridos* of a rainbow]

iridium (*say* iriddi-um) *noun*
element number 77, a brittle metal similar to platinum, used in pen-nibs, and in alloys requiring extreme hardness and a high melting point. See TRANSITION ELEMENT.
See CHEMICAL ELEMENTS in grey pages.

iris (*say* **eye**-ris) *noun*
1. *Anatomy:* the coloured circular part at the front of the eye, capable of contracting or expanding.
2. any of a group of mainly tuberous plants with sword-shaped leaves and flowers of striking and varied hues.
[Greek, rainbow]

Irish moss
a thickening agent made from seaweed.

irk *verb*
to annoy or weary: 'it *irked* him to wait for so long at the airport'.
Word Family: **irksome,** *adjective.*

iron (*say* **eye**-on) *noun*
1. element number 26, a magnetic metal which rusts readily in moist air. It is widely used in tools and machines and is essential to form blood. See TRANSITION ELEMENT.
See CHEMICAL ELEMENTS in grey pages.
2. a metal appliance with a smooth flat bottom, usually heated by an electric element and used for pressing clothes, etc.
3. something made of or as if of iron: a) 'a fire *iron*'; b) 'hearts of *iron*'.
4. *Golf:* any iron-headed club, used mainly for short or high strokes and each numbered according to the angle of the head to the handle. Compare WOOD.
5. (*plural*) the shackles of a prisoner.
Phrases:
have an iron in the fire, to have a part in some business or undertaking.
strike while the iron is hot, to seize or make the most of a good opportunity.

iron *verb*
to press or smooth with an iron.
iron out, 'let us try to *iron out* our differences' (= settle, work out).
Word Family: **ironing,** *noun,* a) the process of using an iron to press clothes, etc., b) any clothes, linen, etc. which need to be ironed.

Iron Age
a period in man's history following the Bronze Age, during which weapons and tools were first made of iron.

Iron Curtain
Politics: the imaginary barrier formed by the borders of Russia and the communist countries supporting it, separating them from the rest of Europe.

ironic (*say* eye-**ronnik**) **ironical** *adjective*
1. of or containing irony: 'an *ironic* smile'.
2. tending to use irony: 'an *ironic* person'.
Word Family: **ironically,** *adverb.*

ironing *noun*
see IRON.

iron lung
a chamber for paralysed patients, which encloses the chest and, by changing the pressure inside the chamber, causes movement of the chest wall, so breathing for the patient.

ironmonger *noun*
a person who sells domestic metal goods, such as saucepans and nails.
Word Family: **ironmongery,** *noun.*

iron rations
any food or other rations kept for an emergency.

ironwork *noun*
any objects or parts made of iron, such as decorative railings, etc.

irony (*say* **eye**-ra-nee) *noun*
1. a mockingly humorous use of words in which the intended meaning is the opposite of what is actually said.
2. a situation which seems to mock reasonable hopes: 'by an *irony* of fate he died just before he was going to alter his will in my favour'.
[Greek *eironeia* understatement or pretended ignorance]

irradiate (*say* irray-dee-ate) *verb*
1. to brighten or illuminate.
2. *Physics:* to expose to radiation or particles of any kind.
Word Family: **irradiation** (*say* irray-dee-**ay**-sh'n), *noun.*

irrational (*say* irra**sha**–n'l) *adjective*
1. not having the ability to reason.
2. not based on logic or reason: 'an *irrational* argument'.
3. *Maths:* relating to a number which cannot be expressed as a ratio of two integers. Compare RATIONAL.
Word Family: **irrationally**, *adverb*; **irrationality** (*say* irrasha–**nalli**–tee), *noun.*

irreconcilable
(*say* irrek–on–**sile**–a–b'l) *adjective*
not able to be reconciled.
Word Family: **irreconcilably**, *adverb.*

irredeemable (*say* irri–**deema**–b'l) *adjective*
1. not able to be restored or redeemed.
2. (of banknotes) not convertible into coins.
Word Family: **irredeemably**, *adverb.*

irreducible (*say* irri–**dew**sa–b'l) *adjective*
not able to be reduced or made smaller.
Word Family: **irreducibly**, *adverb.*

irrefrangible (*say* irri–**fran**ji–b'l) *adjective*
not to be broken or violated.
Word Family: **irrefrangibly**, *adverb.*

irrefutable (*say* irri–**few**ta–b'l) *adjective*
not able to be proved false.
Word Family: **irrefutably**, *adverb.*

irregular (*say* **irreg**–yoola) *adjective*
1. not regular: a) 'an *irregular* road surface'; b) 'the night-watchman keeps very *irregular* hours'.
2. *Grammar:* of or relating to a verb whose changes of form for each tense do not follow general rules. *Example*: 'bring' is an *irregular* verb.
Usage: '*irregular* troops were called in to join the offensive' (= not permanent).
Word Family: **irregularity** (*say* irreg–yoo–**larri**–tee), *noun.*

irrelevant (*say* **irrella**–v'nt) *adjective*
not relevant.
Word Family: **irrelevance**, *noun*; **irrelevantly**, *adverb.*

irreligious (*say* irri–**lijus**) *adjective*
not religious.

irremediable (*say* irri–**meedia**–b'l) *adjective*
not able to be remedied or repaired.
Word Family: **irremediably**, *adverb.*

irreparable (*say* **irrep**'ra–b'l) *adjective*
not able to be repaired or made better.
Word Family: **irreparably**, *adverb.*

irreplaceable (*say* irri–**place**–a–b'l) *adjective*
not able to be replaced.

irrepressible (*say* irri–**pressa**–b'l) *adjective*
not able to be controlled or held back: 'an *irrepressible* giggle'.
Word Family: **irrepressibly**, *adverb.*

irreproachable (*say* irri–**proacha**–b'l) *adjective*
free from blame or fault.
Word Family: **irreproachably**, *adverb.*

irresistible (*say* irri–**zista**–b'l) *adjective*
not able to be resisted: '*irresistible* charm'.
Word Family: **irresistibly**, *adverb.*

irresolute (*say* **irrezza**–loot) *adjective*
hesitant or lacking in resolve.
Word Family: **irresolutely**, *adverb*; **irresolution** (*say* irrezza–**loo**–sh'n), *noun.*

irrespective (*say* irri–**spek**tiv) *adjective*
not considering or taking into account: '*irrespective* of our parents' wishes we stayed up very late'.

irresponsible (*say* irri–**spon**sa–b'l) *adjective*
not responsible.
Word Family: **irresponsibility**, **irresponsibleness**, *nouns*; **irresponsibly**, *adverb.*

irretrievable (*say* irri–**treeva**–b'l) *adjective*
not able to be retrieved or recovered.
Word Family: **irretrievably**, *adverb.*

irreverent (*say* **irrevva**–r'nt) *adjective*
not reverent or respectful.
Word Family: **irreverently**, *adverb*; **irreverence**, *noun.*

irreversible (*say* irri–**versa**–b'l) *adjective*
not able to be reversed.
Word Family: **irreversibly**, *adverb.*

irrevocable (*say* **irrevva**–ka–b'l) *adjective*
not able to be revoked or changed.
Word Family: **irrevocably**, *adverb.*

irrigate *verb*
1. to supply land with water by means of artificial channels through the fields, etc.
2. *Medicine:* to rinse or wash with a flow of liquid over a wound, etc.
Word Family: **irrigation** (*say* irri–**gay**–sh'n), *noun.*
[IR– + Latin *rigare* to wet]

irritable (*say* **irr**ita–b'l) *adjective*
1. being easily made impatient, angry or irritated.
2. *Biology:* (of an organism) able to react to a stimulus.
Word Family: **irritably**, *adverb*; **irritability** (*say* irrita–**billi**–tee), *noun.*

irritant (*say* **irri**–t'nt) *noun*
anything which irritates: 'her methodical tidiness was a great *irritant* to him'.

irritate (*say* **irri**–tate) *verb*
1. to cause impatience or anger.
2. to cause discomfort such as itching or rubbing: 'the sore was *irritated* by the harsh material of her coat'.
3. *Biology:* to stimulate an organism to some action or function.
Word Family: **irritatingly**, *adverb*; **irritation** (*say* irri–**tay**–sh'n), *noun.*
[from Latin]

irruption (*say* irr–**up**–sh'n) *noun*
a sudden bursting in or invasion.
Word Family: **irrupt**, *verb*; **irruptive**, *adjective.*
[IR– + Latin *ruptus* burst apart]

is *verb*
the third person singular, present tense of the verb **be**.

–ish
1. a suffix used to form adjectives from nouns and meaning: a) belonging to, as in *British*; b) (*use is often derogatory*) like or resembling, as in *childish.*
2. a suffix used to form adjectives from other adjectives and meaning somewhat or about, as in *oldish.*
3. a suffix used to form adjectives from nouns or other adjectives and meaning to have a tendency towards, as in *bookish.*

Islam (*say* **iz**–lahm) *noun*
1. the Moslem religion, based on belief in one supreme God, and the teachings of Mohammed as his prophet. Also called **Mohammedanism**.
2. all Moslem believers or their civilization.
Word Family: **Islamic** (*say* iz–**lah**mik), *adjective*; **Islamite** (*say* **iz**la–mite), *noun.*
[Arabic *islam* resignation or submission to the will of God]

island (*say* **eye**–land) *noun*
1. a smallish piece of land completely surrounded by water.
2. something which has the shape, etc. of an island: 'a traffic *island*'.
Word Family: **islander**, *noun*, a native or inhabitant of an island.

isle (*say* ile) *noun*
an island, especially a small one.

islet (*say* **eye**let) *noun*
a small island.

ism (*say* izm) *noun*
a distinctive theory or doctrine.

–ism (*say* izm)
a suffix indicating: a) an action or process, as in *terrorism*; b) a state, as in *barbarism*; c) a characteristic, as in *Anglicism*; d) a doctrine or theory, as in *communism.*

iso–
a prefix meaning equal, as in *isobar.*
[from Greek]

isobar (*say* **eye**–so–bar) *noun*
a line on a map joining places of equal air–pressure.
[ISO– + Greek *baros* weight]

isohyet (*say* eye–so–**high**–et) *noun*
a line on a map joining places of equal rainfall.
[ISO– + Greek *hyetos* rain]

isolate (*say* **eye**–so–late) *verb*
to separate or put apart from others.
Word Family: **isolation**, *noun.*
[from Italian from Latin *insula* island]

isolationism
(*say* eye–so–**lay**–sh'n–izm) *noun*
Politics: the policy of one country isolating itself from other countries by abstaining from alliances and other international political relations.
Word Family: **isolationist**, *noun, adjective.*

isomerism (*say* eye–**somma**–rizm) *noun*
Chemistry: the existence of two or more compounds, called isomers, with the same atoms in the molecule but having different properties because the atoms in the molecule are arranged differently.
[ISO– + Greek *meros* a share]

isometric (*say* eye–so–**metrik**) *adjective*
of or having equal measurements.
isometrics *plural noun*
(*used with singular verb*) any physical exercises for strengthening muscles by tensing one set of muscles at a time.
Word Family: **isometrical**, *adjective*; **isometrically**, *adverb*; **isometry** (*say* eye–**somma**–tree), *noun*, an equality of measurement.
[ISO– + Greek *metron* measure]

isomorphic (*say* eye-so-**mor**fik) *adjective*
of or having the same shape.
[ISO- + Greek *morphé* a shape]

isosceles (*say* eye-**sossa**-leez) *adjective*
(of a triangle) having two sides equal.
[ISO- + Greek *skelos* a leg]

isotherm (*say* **eye**-so-therm) *noun*
a line on a map joining places of equal temperature.
Word Family: **isothermal**, *adjective*; **isothermally**, *adverb*.
[ISO- + Greek *therme* heat]

isotonic (*say* eye-so-**tonn**ik) *adjective*
Biology: (of a solution) having the same osmotic pressure as normal protoplasm. Compare HYPERTONIC and HYPOTONIC.
[ISO- + Greek *tonos* tension]

isotope (*say* **eye**-so-tope) *noun*
an atom which has a different number of neutrons from other atoms of the same element. The isotopes of an element have identical chemical properties, and vary only in those physical properties which are affected by the mass of the atom, such as density.
[ISO- + Greek *topos* place (in the periodic table)]

issue (*say* **ish**oo *or* **iss**-yoo) *noun*
1. a matter to be discussed, decided or given attention: 'let's consider the political *issues*'.
2. the act of giving out, delivering or distributing: 'the *issue* of new banknotes will begin in two weeks'.
3. anything produced, given out or distributed, especially at one time: 'this is the first *issue* of the evening paper'.
4. a) the act of going or flowing out: 'the *issue* of blood from a wound'. b) anything which comes or flows out.
Usages:
a) 'what was the final *issue* of the debate?' (= result, product).
b) 'the old man died without *issue*' (= offspring).
take issue, 'I must *take issue* with you on that point' (= disagree, dispute).
issue *verb*
(issued, issuing)
1. to put out, deliver or distribute: 'a gale warning has been *issued*'.
2. to discharge or cause to flow out.
3. to proceed or come as a result: 'a deep friendship *issued* from their first meeting'.

-ist
a suffix indicating a person who practises or is concerned with something, as in *dentist*.

isthmus (*say* **iss**-muss) *noun*
plural is **isthmuses**
a narrow strip of land joining two larger areas of land.
[Greek *isthmos* narrow passage, neck]

it *pronoun*
1. a) the third person singular nominative pronoun, used when gender is not indicated: 'has *it* got icing?'. Plural is **they**. b) the third person singular objective pronoun used when gender is not indicated: 'I ate *it* all'. Plural is **them**.
See ITS.
2. used to refer to a group of words which follows: '*it* is easier if you read the instructions first'.
3. used to indicate the general situation or something which will be understood from the context: a) 'how was *it* in Queensland?'; b) '*it* is 7 o'clock'.

italic (*say* it-**all**ik) *noun*
(*usually plural*) a style of printing with sloping characters, used for emphasis, etc.: '*this is italic*'. Compare ROMAN.
Word Family: **italicize, italicise**, *verb*, to print in italics.
[as first used in *Italy*]

itch *noun*
a feeling of irritation on the skin causing a desire or need to scratch.
Usage: 'she has an *itch* to travel' (= restless or persistent desire).
have an itching palm, see PALM.
Word Family: **itch**, *verb*; **itchy**, *adjective*, having an itch.

-ite
a suffix indicating a person associated with a particular place, doctrine, etc., as in *Israelite*.

item (*say* **eye**-t'm) *noun*
a single or separate thing in a list or series: a) 'there are several valuable *items* for sale'; b) 'here is an important news *item*'.
Word Family: **itemize, itemise**, *verb*, to give or state every item of.
[Latin, also]

iterate (*say* **itta**-rate) *verb*
to repeat.
[Latin *iterum* a second time]

itinerant (*say* it-**inna**-r'nt) *adjective*
travelling from place to place.
Word Family: **itinerant**, *noun*, a person who travels from place to place;

itinerancy, itineracy, *nouns*; **itinerantly,** *adverb.*
[Latin *itineris* of a journey]

itinerary (*say* eye–**tinn**a–ree) *noun*
the route or plan of a journey.

–itis (*say* **eye**–tis)
a suffix used in medical terms to indicate inflammation of a particular part, as in *tonsillitis.*

its *possessive adjective*
belonging to it: 'has the house got *its* own garden?'.
its *possessive pronoun*
plural is **theirs**
belonging to it.
Common Error: do not confuse with *it's*, which is the short form of *it is.*

itself *pronoun*
1. the reflexive form of **it**: 'this machine switches *itself* off'.
2. the emphatic form of **it**: 'the distance *itself* is not very great'.
3. its normal or usual self: 'the dog was not *itself* while its owners were away'.

–ive (*say* iv)
a suffix indicating: a) tendency or disposition, as in *active*; b) function, as in *preservative.*

ivory (*say* **eye**–va–ree) *noun*
1. a) the hard, whitish dentine obtained from the tusks of elephants. b) any similar substance.
2. a creamy–white colour.
Word Family: **ivory,** *adjective.*
[Latin *eboris* of ivory]

ivory black
a deep black colour or pigment made from charred ivory.

ivory tower
an attitude of remoteness, withdrawal or aloofness, especially in relation to everyday life.

ivy (*say* **eye**–vee) *noun*
1. an evergreen, climbing plant with dark, shiny leaves, often used as an ornamental covering for walls, etc., to which it attaches itself by means of aerial roots.
2. any of various climbing plants.

–ize, –ise
a suffix forming verbs, indicating: a) following some action, policy, etc., as in *apologize*; b) acting on or affecting in a particular way, as in *legalize.*

Jj

jab *verb*
(**jabbed**, **jabbing**)
to push sharply, as with the end or point of something.
Word Family: **jab**, *noun.*

jabber *verb*
to chatter or talk nonsense.
Word Family: **jabber**, *noun*, nonsensical talk; **jabberer**, *noun.*

jacaranda (*say* jakka-**randa**) *noun*
any of a group of tall, tropical trees with bluish-purple flowers.

jack *noun*
1. any of various mechanical devices for raising heavy objects, as that used to support a car while changing a tyre.
2. *Cards:* a playing card with a picture of a prince, usually having value just below a queen. Also called a **knave.**
3. *Games:(plural)* a) a children's game in which each player tosses and catches five small objects shaped like bones. b) the objects used in this game. Also called **knucklebones**.
4. *Bowls:* a round white ball at which the players aim their bowls.
5. *Electricity:* a socket which accepts a plug at one end and attaches to circuitry at the other.
every man jack, everyone.
Word Family: **jack**, *verb*, a) to lift or move with a jack, b) (informal) to raise.

jackal *noun*
a wild dog of Africa and Asia, hunting in packs and feeding on carrion.

jackanapes *noun*
a) a conceited man. b) a mischievous child.

jackass *noun*
1. a male ass.
2. a very stupid person.
3. a kookaburra.

jackboot *noun*
1. *History:* a long cavalry boot coming up to the thigh.
2. this as a symbol of oppression, dictatorship and especially military government.

jackdaw *noun*
a shiny, black bird related to the crow, with a reputation for stealing bright objects.

jackeroo, jackaroo *noun*
Australian: a young person working on a sheep or cattle station.

jacket *noun*
1. a short coat reaching to the waist or hips.
2. any outer coat or covering around something, as for protection, etc.: a) 'a book *jacket*'; b) 'potatoes cooked in their *jackets*'.

jack-in-the-box *noun*
a toy with a figure on a spring which jumps out of a box when the lid is opened.

jackknife (*say* **jak**-nife) *noun*
plural is **jackknives**
a large claspknife.
jackknife *verb*
to fold or bend double like a jackknife.

jack-of-all-trades *noun*
a person who is able to do many different kinds of work.

jackpot *noun*
1. the largest prize in a competition.
2. any accumulated sum or fund, e.g. the stakes in a gambling game.
hit the jackpot, to be very successful or lucky.

Jacobean (*say* jak-a-**bee**-an) *adjective*
(of architecture, furniture, etc.) in the styles favoured during the reigns of James I and Charles I (1603–42).
[after *Jacobus* the Latin form of *James*]

Jacobin (*say* **jak**-a-bin) *noun*
History: a member of the extreme left wing in the French Revolution, responsible for the Terror.
[after the *Jacobin* convent in Paris where they used to meet]

Jacobite (*say* **jak**-a-bite) *noun*
History: a Tory who, after the Revolution of 1688, still campaigned for the restoration of the exiled Stuarts.

[after *Jacobus* the Latin form of *James* i.e. James 2 and James the Old Pretender]

jade *noun*
1. either of two types of hard, usually green, fine-grained minerals, used as an ornamental stone or in jewellery. **2.** any of various bluish to yellowish-green colours.

jaded *adjective*
tired or worn-out.

jag *noun*
(*informal*) a spree, especially a drinking spree.

jagged (*say* **jagg**id) *adjective*
sharp and ragged: 'the *jagged* edges of broken glass'.
Word Family: **jag (jagged, jagging),** *verb*, to cut or slash.

jaguar (*say* **jag**-yoo-a) *noun*
a large, flesh-eating mammal of the cat family, having a tawny coat with black patches and found in the forests of tropical America.

jail *noun*
a gaol.

jalopy (*say* ja-**loppi**) *noun*
(*informal*) a decrepit old motor car.

jam (1) *verb*
(jammed, jamming)
1. to squeeze into a very tight position.
Usages:
a) 'to *jam* on the brakes' (= apply suddenly or violently).
b) 'the window is *jammed* and I cannot open it' (= stuck).
c) 'a street *jammed* with traffic' (= filled to excess, blocked).
2. *Radio:* to send out signals intended to interfere with other signals of the same frequency.
jam *noun*
1. the state of being jammed or blocked: 'a traffic *jam*'.
2. (*informal*) a difficult situation.

jam (2) *noun*
a spread made by boiling fruit with sugar until it thickens and sets.
Word Family: **jammy,** *adjective,* a) thick or sticky like jam, b) covered with jam.

jamb (*say* jam) *noun*
the upright frame of a door or window.
[French *jambe* leg]

jamboree *noun*
a large rally or gathering.

jam session
an informal gathering of musicians for an impromptu performance.

jangle *verb*
to make or cause to make a harsh or discordant sound.
Word Family: **jangle,** *noun.*

janitor *noun*
a caretaker.

January *noun*
the first month of the year in the Gregorian calendar.
[after the ancient Roman god *Janus,* guardian of doors and gates]

japan *verb*
(japanned, japanning)
to varnish with a hard, glossy, black lacquer.
[originally imported from *Japan*]

jape *noun*
a jest or a practical joke.

japonica (*say* ja-**ponn**ika) *noun*
the common name for the cydonia or Japanese ornamental quince, typically with scarlet flowers in early spring.

jar (1) *noun*
a wide-mouthed, usually cylindrical, container, often with an airtight lid.

jar (2) *verb*
(jarred, jarring)
to cause a jolt, shock or sudden movement to: 'he was *jarred* by the fall'.
Usages:
a) 'her mocking laughter *jarred* on my nerves' (= had an unpleasant or irritating effect).
b) 'those two bright colours *jar* with each other' (= clash).
Word Family: **jar,** *noun,* a shock or jolt.

jardinière (*say* jardin-**yair**) *noun*
an ornamental pot or container for plants, etc.
[French *jardinier* gardener]

jargon *noun*
a) the language of a certain class or profession, usually little understood by others. b) any meaningless talk.

jasmine (*say* **jaz**min) *noun*
a small shrub or climbing plant with fragrant, white, yellow or pink flowers.
[from Persian]

jasper *noun*
Geology: see CHALCEDONY.

jaundice (*say* **jawn**-dis) *noun*
Medicine: a yellow discoloration of the skin due to a build-up of bile in the blood and tissues.

jaundiced *adjective*
1. having jaundice.
2. having embittered or distorted views, ideas, etc.
Word Family: **jaundice**, *verb.*
[French *jaune* yellow]

jaunt (*say* jawnt) *noun*
a short journey, especially one taken for pleasure.
Word Family: **jaunt**, *verb.*

jaunty (*say* **jawn**–tee) *adjective*
having a sprightly or self–assured air.
Word Family: **jauntily**, *adverb*; **jauntiness**, *noun.*

javelin (*say* **javva**–lin) *noun*
a) a light spear, especially one thrown in competitions. b) the athletics competition in which it is thrown.

jaw *noun*
1. *Anatomy:* either of two bones of the head in which the teeth are set.
2. (*usually plural*) something which has the shape or function of the jaws, such as parts in a machine which grasp or hold things.
jaw *verb*
(*informal*) to talk or gossip.

jay *noun*
any of various colourful, noisy, European or American birds related to the crow.

jaywalk *verb*
to cross a road carelessly, ignoring traffic lights or pedestrian crossings.

jazz *noun*
a style of music developed by the American Negroes, with much improvising and syncopated rhythms.
Word Family: **jazz around**, (informal) to act or proceed in a lively or energetic manner; **jazz up**, (informal) to make bright or lively; **jazzy**, *adjective*, (informal) very bright or showy.

jealous (*say* **jellus**) *adjective*
1. resentful or suspicious of a rival or another's success, advantage, etc.: 'her *jealous* husband watches every move she makes'.
2. careful to protect or guard: 'the dog was *jealous* of its huge bone'.
Word Family: **jealously**, *adverb*; **jealousy**, *noun.*
[Greek *zelos* zeal]

jeans *plural noun*
a pair of denim trousers.

jeep *noun*
a small military vehicle used for communication and liaison purposes.
[from G(eneral) P(urpose vehicle)]

jeer *verb*
to mock.
Word Family: **jeeringly**, *adverb*; **jeer**, *noun.*

Jehovah (*say* j'**ho**–va) *noun*
Jewish, Christian: a name for God used in the Old Testament.

jejune (*say* ji–**joon**) *adjective*
uninteresting or unsatisfying to the mind.
[Latin *jejunus* fasting, empty]

jejunum (*say* ja–**joon**um) *noun*
Anatomy: the second part of the small intestine, where the major part of digestion takes place.

Jekyll and Hyde
1. a person who lives a double life, outwardly respectable, secretly criminal.
2. (used as a symbol of) the good and bad in everyone.
[after a character in R. L. Stevenson's *The Strange Case of Dr Jekyll and Mr Hyde*, 1886]

jell *verb*
to set or form a jelly.
Usage: 'after much discussion their plan began to *jell*' (= take shape, become definite).

jelly *noun*
1. a soft but firm food made with gelatine or by boiling a liquid containing sugar until it sets.
2. anything with the consistency of jelly.
Word Family: **jelly (jellied, jellying)**, *verb.*

jellyfish *noun*
also called a **medusa**
any soft, jelly–like, marine organism, usually having an umbrella–like body and long tentacles.

jemmy *noun*
a short crowbar.
Word Family: **jemmy (jemmied, jemmying)**, *verb*, to force open with a jemmy.

jenny *noun*
1. the female of certain animals, such as the donkey.
2. a spinning jenny.

jeopardize (*say* **jeppa**–dize)
jeopardise *verb*
to risk or endanger.
Word Family: **jeopardy** (*say* **jeppa**–dee), *noun*, danger or peril.

jerboa (*say* jer–**bo**–a) *noun*
a small, rat–like, desert mammal with long hind legs for hopping.

jeremiad (*say* jerri–**my**–ad) *noun*
a long–drawn–out complaint or lament. [after the Lamentations of *Jeremiah* in the Old Testament]

jerk *noun*
1. a quick, sharp or violent movement.
2. (*informal*) an ignorant or disagreeable person.
Word Family: **jerk**, *verb*, to give, perform or utter with a jerk or jerks; **jerky**, *adjective*, consisting of jerks; **jerkily**, *adverb*; **jerkiness**, *noun*.

jerkin *noun*
a short, sleeveless jacket.

jeroboam (*say* jerra–**bo**–im) *noun*
a large wine bottle holding 8 or more standard bottles.

jerry *noun*
(*informal*) a chamber–pot.

jerry–built *adjective*
badly or cheaply built.
Word Family: **jerry–builder**, *noun*; **jerry–build** (**jerry–built**, **jerry–building**), *verb*.

jerry can
a flat–sided, closed container for carrying liquids, such as water or petrol.

jersey (*say* **jer**–zee) *noun*
1. a general term for knitted fabrics.
2. a knitted woollen pullover.
[after *Jersey* in the Channel Islands, where knitting was an important industry]

Jerusalem artichoke
see ARTICHOKE.

jess *noun*
a short strap fastened around the leg of a hawk and attached to a leash.

jest *verb*
to speak jokingly or playfully.
Word Family: **jest**, *noun*, a joke; **jester**, *noun*, a person who jokes, especially a professional clown; **jesting**, *adjective*; **jestingly**, *adverb*.

Jesuit (*say* **jez**–yoo–it) *noun*
Roman Catholic: a member of the religious order called the Society of Jesus, founded by Ignatius Loyola in the 16th century.

Jesus (*say* **jee**zez) *noun*
Christ.

jet (1) *noun*
1. a strong, continuous stream of liquid or gas forced out under pressure.
2. something which flows in or as if in such a stream.
3. a spout or device which emits such a stream: 'a gas *jet*'.
4. any vehicle, especially an aeroplane, which is operated by jet propulsion.
Word Family: **jet** (**jetted**, **jetting**), *verb*, to emit a jet.

jet (2) *noun*
Geology: a hard black coal which can be highly polished for use in jewellery, carving, etc.
jet black, a deep black.

jet–lag *noun*
also called **jet–fatigue**
the symptoms experienced by a person travelling quickly through several time zones.

jetliner *noun*
a commercial aeroplane operated by jet propulsion.

jet propulsion
propulsion by means of an engine whose combustion chamber is open at the rear end, resulting in a net forward thrust.

jetsam *noun*
any articles thrown from a ship to lighten it, found afloat or on the beach. Compare FLOTSAM.

jet set
a rich social group, especially one which meets in fashionable parts of the world.

jettison *verb*
to discharge or throw overboard: 'to *jettison* fuel'.

jetty *noun*
a pier.

Jew *noun*
a person of Judaic race or religion.
Word Family: **Jewish**, *adjective*; **Jewess**, *noun*, a female Jew; **Jewry** (*say* **joo**–ree), *noun*, any or all Jews.

jewel *noun*
1. a) a gem. b) an ornament containing gems.
2. (*informal*) a valued person or possession.
jewel *verb*
(**jewelled**, **jewelling**)
to adorn with jewels.
Word Family: **jeweller**, *noun*, a person who makes or deals in jewels or jewellery.

jewelfish *noun*
a very brightly coloured fish, often kept in home aquariums.

jewellery, jewelry *noun*
any or all jewels.

Jewry *noun*
Word Family: see JEW.

jew's–harp *noun*
a simple musical instrument, one end of which is held in the mouth while the fingers pluck the flexible metal tongue.

jib (1) *noun*
Nautical: a small foresail.

jib (2) *verb*
(jibbed, jibbing)
to show reluctance or unwillingness.

jib (3) *noun*
the projecting arm of a crane.

jibe (1) *verb*
see GYBE.

jibe (2) *verb*
see GIBE.

jiffy *noun*
(*informal*) a very short time: 'I'll do that in a *jiffy*'.

jig (1) *noun*
a) a fast, bouncing or irregular dance.
b) the music for such a dance.
the jig is up, the game is up.
Word Family: **jig (jigged, jigging)**, *verb*, a) to dance a jig, b) to move in a quick or jerky manner, especially up and down.

jig (2) *noun*
1. any of various mechanical devices for holding an object in position or guiding a tool.
2. a wire mesh for separating ore by shaking it in water.
Word Family: **jig (jigged, jigging)**, *verb*.

jigger *noun*
1. a person or thing that jigs.
2. any of various mechanical devices for jolting or shaking.
3. a unit of volume for alcoholic drinks, equal to about 42·6 ml.

jiggle *verb*
to move up and down or to and fro with quick, short jerks.
Word Family: **jiggle**, *noun*.

jigsaw *noun*
1. a puzzle in which flat, irregularly shaped pieces are fitted together to form a picture.
2. a saw with a narrow vertical blade, used for cutting curves, etc.

jihad (*say* jee–had) *noun*
1. a crusade for a cause.
2. *History:* a Moslem holy war against infidels (e.g. the Christians).
[Arabic]

jilt *verb*
to reject or cast aside a lover one has encouraged.

jingle *noun*
1. a tinkling sound, such as that made by a bunch of keys.
2. a short poem with a simple rhyme or rhythm, often set to music, e.g. for television advertisements.
Word Family: **jingle**, *verb*, to make or cause to make a tinkling or clinking sound.

jingoism (*say* **jingo–izm**) *noun*
an aggressive nationalism.
Word Family: **jingoist**, *noun*.

jinks *plural noun*
high jinks, (*informal*) any pranks or boisterous merrymaking.

jinn *noun*
also called a **djinn** or **jinnee**
plural is **jinn**
a genie.
[Arabic]

jinx *noun*
a person or thing believed to bring bad luck.
Word Family: **jinxed**, *adjective*, pursued by bad luck.

jitter *verb*
to behave nervously.
jitters *plural noun*
(*informal*) nervousness.
Word Family: **jittery**, *adjective*, full of the jitters.

jitterbug *noun*
1. an energetic dance popular in the 1940's.
2. a person who is nervous or easily flustered.

jive *noun*
a dance to jazz or other lively music.
Word Family: **jive**, *verb*.

job *noun*
1. any work or task, especially when done for a fee or wage.
Usage: 'you'll have to make the most of a bad *job*' (= situation, affair).
2. a particular sort of employment: 'a part–time *job*'.
3. the result of a person's work: 'he did a good *job* in fixing the car'.
4. (*informal*) a robbery or other criminal act.
Phrases:
a good job, 'the banks were closed so it's *a good job* you lent me some cash' (= fortunate).

jobs for the boys, positions granted to one's friends, political supporters, etc.
Word Family: **job** (**jobbed, jobbing**), *verb*, to do piecework.

jobber *noun*
a dealer in stocks and shares who transacts business only with stockbrokers and not with the public.

jobbery *noun*
the practice of making improper private gains from public or official business: 'political *jobbery*'.

job lot
a miscellaneous collection of goods sold together.

jockey *noun*
a person who rides racehorses, especially as a profession.
jockey *verb*
1. to ride a racehorse.
2. to manoeuvre or trick: 'to *jockey* for a promotion'.

jockstrap *noun*
a close-fitting support for the male genitals.

jocose (*say* jo-**kose**) *adjective*
playfully humorous.
Word Family: **jocosely**, *adverb*; **jocosity** (*say* ja-**kossi**-tee), *noun*.
[Latin *jocosus* full of jest]

jocular (*say* **jok**-yoo-la) *adjective*
joking or humorous.
Word Family: **jocularly**, *adverb*; **jocularity** (*say* jok-yoo-**larri**-tee), *noun*.
[Latin *jocularis* laughable]

jocund (*say* **jok**-und) *adjective*
cheerful or merry.
Word Family: **jocundly**, *adverb*; **jocundity** (*say* jok-**unda**-tee), *noun*.
[Latin *jucundus* pleasing]

jodhpurs (*say* **jod**-perz) *plural noun*
a pair of trousers which are loose to the knees and then close-fitting to the ankle, worn when riding horses.
[after *Jodhpur*, India]

jog *verb*
(**jogged, jogging**)
1. to run at a slow, steady pace: 'the athlete *jogged* around the field'.
2. to shake with a push or nudge.
Usage: 'this should *jog* your memory' (= stimulate).
Word Family: **jog**, *noun*; **jogger**, *noun*, a person who jogs.

joggle *verb*
to shake slightly.

John Bull
a person who is typically English.
[probably from *The History of John Bull*, a satire by John Arbuthnot in 1712]

John Dory
see DORY.
[French *doré* gilded]

join *verb*
1. to bring, come or put together.
2. to become a member of: 'he decided to *join* the club'.
Usages:
a) 'we all *joined* in the celebration' (= took part).
b) '*join* us after the meal' (= meet).
join up, to enlist in the armed forces.
Word Family: **join**, *noun*, a place where something joins.

joiner *noun*
a cabinet-maker or one who specializes in jointing timber together, as in doors and window frames.
Word Family: **joinery**, *noun*, the work done or produced by a joiner.

joint *noun*
1. a place where two or more parts or objects join: 'the knee is a *joint* in the leg'.
2. a cut of meat, especially one for roasting.
3. (*informal*) a) a cigarette containing a drug such as hashish, usually mixed with tobacco. Also called a **reefer**. b) a, usually disreputable, club, bistro, etc.
joint *adjective*
shared by or common to two or more: 'the politicians issued a *joint* statement'.
Word Family: **joint**, *verb*, a) to unite with a joint or joints, b) to divide into separate pieces, especially by cutting at the joints; **jointly**, *adverb*.

jointure (*say* **join**-cher) *noun*
Law: a provision made by a husband for the support of his wife after his death.

joist *noun*
a horizontal wooden or metal beam, used as a support for a floor or ceiling.

joke *noun*
1. something which is said or done to cause laughter or amusement.
2. a person or thing that is amusing or ridiculous.
practical joke, an amusing trick played on a person.

Word Family: **joke**, *verb*; **jokingly**, *adverb.*
[Latin]

joker *noun*
1. a person who plays jokes.
2. *Cards:* an extra playing card in a pack, used as the highest card or with its value chosen by the player.
3. (*informal*) any person.

jolly *adjective*
cheerful, amusing or pleasant: 'it was a *jolly* party'.
jolly *verb*
(**jollied**, **jollying**)
to flatter, especially in order to gain an advantage: 'he always *jollies* his boss along'.
jolly *adverb*
(*informal*) very: '*jolly* good!'.
Word Family: **jolliness**, **jollity** (*say* **jolla**–tee), *nouns*; **jollily**, *adverb*; **jollify** (*say* **jolla**–fie), (**jollified**, **jollifying**), *verb.*

jolly-boat *noun*
a small boat carried on the stern of a larger ship.

jolt *verb*
to move or shake jerkily or roughly: 'the car *jolted* over the bumpy track'.
Word Family: **jolt**, *noun*; **jolty**, *adjective.*

jonquil (*say* **jon**–kwil) *noun*
a plant with reed-like leaves and small sweet-scented yellow or white flowers in a cluster, similar to, but smaller than, a daffodil.

joss house
a Chinese temple.
[Latin *deus* god]

joss stick
a stick of incense used in worship by the Chinese.

jostle (*say* **joss**'l) *verb*
to push or knock against roughly: 'he *jostled* his way through the crowd'.

jot *verb*
(**jotted**, **jotting**)
to write down briefly or quickly.
Word Family: **jotting**, *noun*, a brief note; **jotter**, *noun*, a small paper pad for making notes; **jot**, *noun*, a small amount.

joule (*say* jool) *noun*
the SI unit of work and energy.
[after *J. P. Joule*, 1818–89, a British physicist]

journal (*say* **jern**'l) *noun*
1. a daily record or diary, e.g. of financial transactions.
2. any periodical or magazine.
[Latin *diurnus* by day]

journalese (*say* jerna–**leez**) *noun*
the tired and hackneyed English characteristic of some newspapers. *Example:* 'at week's end balding Secretary of State John Smith, 58, will exit from the political arena, hopefully for good, predicted informed sources yesterday'.

journalism (*say* **jer**na–lizm) *noun*
the work of writing, editing or publishing newspapers, magazines, etc.
Word Family: **journalist**, *noun*; **journalistic**, *adjective*; **journalistically**, *adverb.*

journey (*say* **jer**–nee) *noun*
1. a trip, especially by land.
2. the distance travelled in a certain time: 'it's a day's *journey*'.
Word Family: **journey** (**journeyed**, **journeying**), *verb.*

joust (*say* **jow**st) *noun*
also called a **tilt**
Medieval history: a competition between knights on horseback and armed with lances.
Word Family: **joust**, *verb.*

jovial *adjective*
merry and friendly or pleasant: 'he is a *jovial* chap'.
Word Family: **jovially**, *adverb*; **joviality** (*say* jo–vee–**alli**–tee), *noun.*

jowl (*rhymes with* foul) *noun*
1. a) the jaw. b) the cheek.
2. (*usually plural*) fat, sagging cheeks and chin.

joy *noun*
a) a feeling or state of happiness or great pleasure. b) anything which causes such a feeling.
Word Family: **joyful**, **joyous**, *adjectives*, full of joy or pleasure; **joyfully**, **joyously**, *adverbs*; **joyless**, *adjective*, dismal; **joy**, *verb*, to feel joy.

joy-ride *noun*
(*informal*) a pleasure ride, e.g. in a motor car, especially without the owner's permission.

joystick *noun*
(*informal*) the pilot's control stick in an aircraft.

jube *noun*
also called a **jujube**
a small, flavoured lozenge: 'a cough *jube*'.

jubilant (*say* **joo**bi–l'nt) *adjective*
expressing joy or exultation.

Word Family: **jubilation** (*say* joobi–lay–sh'n), **jubilance**, *nouns*; **jubilantly**, *adverb*; **jubilate**, *verb*.
[Latin *jubilans* shouting for joy]

jubilee (*say* joobi–**lee**) *noun*
an anniversary or celebration.
[Hebrew *yobal* ram's horn (blown in a jubilee year)]

Judaism (*say* **joo**–day–izm) *noun*
the religion of the Jews deriving its authority and principles from the Old Testament, based on a belief in one supreme God.
Word Family: **Judaic** (*say* joo–**day**–ik), *adjective*.

judge (*say* juj) *noun*
1. a public officer appointed to settle disputes and administer legal justice.
2. a person appointed to decide in a competition or dispute.
3. a person qualified to give an opinion: 'he is a good *judge* of horses'.
judge *verb*
1. to hear and decide a case in a court of law.
2. to decide or examine critically: 'to *judge* wines'.
3. to form or hold an opinion: 'I *judge* this house to be a good buy'.
[Latin]

judgement, judgment (*say* **juj**–m'nt) *noun*
1. the ability to judge wisely.
2. an opinion or estimation.
3. the decision of a judge concerning the matter in dispute.

judicature (*say* **joo**dika–cher) *noun*
Law: a) the administration of justice. b) the system of courts and their judges.

judicial (*say* joo–**dish**'l) *adjective*
relating to a judge or justice.
judiciary (*say* joo–**disha**–ree) *noun*
a) the branch of government dealing with justice. b) the system of courts and judges in a country.
Word Family: **judicially**, *adverb*; **judiciary**, *adjective*.

judicious (*say* joo–**dishus**) *adjective*
sensible or discreet.
Word Family: **judiciously**, *adverb*.

judo (*say* **joo**–doe) *noun*
a method of self–defence based on jujitsu, often used as a form of physical training.
[Japanese *ju* gentle + *do* way of life]

jug *noun*
1. a container with a spout and a handle, for holding or serving liquids.
2. (*informal*) a prison.
jug *verb*
(**jugged**, **jugging**)
to stew meat, especially hare or rabbit, in a jug or casserole.

juggernaut (*say* **jugga**–nawt) *noun*
1. any large destructive force, especially one which attracts blind worship.
2. a huge and menacing object, especially a huge lorry.
[after *Jagannath*, lord of the world, an enormous idol of the Hindu deity Krishna]

juggle *verb*
to toss and catch several objects in the air in a sequence, in order to keep them in continuous motion.
Usages:
a) 'to *juggle* accounts' (= alter dishonestly).
b) 'she *juggled* the slippery dishes' (= tried to balance).
Word Family: **juggler**, *noun*, a person who juggles, especially an entertainer; **juggle**, *noun*, a dishonest or deceptive trick.

jugular (*say* **jug**–yoo–la) *adjective*
relating to or situated in the throat or neck: 'the *jugular* veins'.
Word Family: **jugular**, *noun*, the main vein of the neck.
[Latin *jugulum* the throat]

juice (*rhymes with* loose) *noun*
1. the liquid part of vegetables, fruit or meat.
2. the fluid in the organs of the body: 'the gastric *juices* aid digestion'.
3. (*informal*) petrol, fuel or electric power.
Word Family: **juicy**, *adjective*, a) full of juice, b) interesting; **juicily**, *adverb*; **juiciness**, *noun*.

jujitsu (*say* joo–**jitsoo**) *noun*
a Japanese method of self–defence without weapons, in which set techniques of balancing and leverage are used to overcome the opponent's strength, and from which karate, aikido and judo are derived.

jujube (*say* **joo**–joob) *noun*
1. the edible plum–like fruit of certain plants.
2. a jube.

jukebox *noun*
a coin–operated record–player offering a selection of records.
[Negro dialect *juke* bawdy or wicked]

julep (*say* **joo**–lep) *noun*
a sweet drink, especially one in which medicine is taken.

July (*say* joo–**lie**) *noun*
the seventh month of the year in the Gregorian calendar.
[after the Roman statesman *Julius Caesar*, who was born in this month]

jumble *noun*
1. a state of confusion.
2. a confused mess.
Word Family: **jumble,** *verb,* to confuse.

jumble sale
a sale of cheap, assorted articles, often to aid charity.

jumbo *adjective*
large or outsize: 'a *jumbo* jet'.
Word Family: **jumbo,** *noun,* the affectionate name for an elephant.

jump *verb*
to move off the ground or some other surface by a sudden muscular effort of the legs.
Usages:
a) 'I *jumped* when the doorbell rang' (= gave a start).
b) 'she *jumped* into a taxi' (= got quickly).
c) 'my rent *jumped* £10 last month' (= increased).
d) 'to *jump* from one subject to another' (= change rapidly).
e) 'he *jumped* a line while reading aloud' (= missed).
f) 'he *jumped* the traffic lights' (= anticipated).
g) 'the train *jumped* the tracks' (= left).
Phrases:
jump bail, to abscond while on bail.
jump on, (*informal*) to scold or reprimand.
jump the gun, (*informal*) to start prematurely.
jump the queue, to get something out of turn.
jump to conclusions, to reach opinions or conclusions hastily or haphazardly.
Word Family: **jump,** *noun*; **jumpy,** *adjective,* nervous; **jumpily,** *adverb*; **jumpiness,** *noun.*

jumped–up *adjective*
(*informal*) conceited or upstart.

jumper (1) *noun*
1. a person or thing that jumps.
2. a temporary connection made in an electric circuit, e.g. across the battery of a car. Short form of **jumper lead.**

jumper (2) *noun*
also called a **pullover** or **sweater**
a garment, usually knitted, worn on the upper part of the body for warmth.

jumpsuit *noun*
a piece of clothing consisting of trousers and a top in one piece, usually with long sleeves.

jumpy *adjective*
Word Family: see JUMP.

junction (*say* **junk**sh'n) *noun*
1. a) the act of joining. b) the state of being joined.
2. a place where several things, such as roads, join or meet.
[Latin *junctus* yoked]

junction box
a box in which several electric circuits are connected.

juncture (*say* **junk**cher) *noun*
1. a point of time, especially a turning point or crisis.
2. a joint.

June *noun*
the sixth month of the year in the Gregorian calendar.
[after the Roman goddess *Juno*]

jungle *noun*
1. a dense tropical rainforest.
2. any wild or overgrown land.

junior *adjective*
1. younger.
2. lower in rank, etc.: 'a *junior* member of staff'.
3. (*capital*) used by the son when father and son have the same name: 'Sammy Davis *Junior*'.
junior *noun*
1. a person who is younger than another.
2. a person of lower rank.
[Latin, younger]

junior school
a primary school, especially one forming part of a larger school.

juniper (*say* **joo**–nipper) *noun*
an evergreen shrub producing purple berries which are used in cooking, medicine and making gin.

junk (1) *noun*
1. any discarded or worthless objects.
2. (*informal*) any narcotic drug.

junk (2) *noun*
a Chinese flat–bottomed ship having a high stern and sails with battens.

junket *noun*
a sweet, thick food made by curdling milk with rennet.

junkie (*say* **jun**-kee) *noun*
(*informal*) a drug addict.

junta (*say* **jun**ta) *noun*
a political group, usually of military officers, which has gained its power by force, as after a revolution.

Jupiter (*say* **joo**-pitter) *noun*
Astronomy: the largest planet in the solar system and fifth from the sun.
[after the chief Roman god *Jupiter*]

Jurassic (*say* joo-**rassik**) *noun*
Geology: see MESOZOIC.
Word Family: **Jurassic**, *adjective.*
[after the *Jura* mountains on the French-Swiss border]

juridical (*say* joo-**riddik**'l) *adjective*
of or relating to the administration of justice.

jurisdiction (*say* jooris-**dik**-sh'n) *noun*
1. power or authority: 'your boss has no *jurisdiction* over your personal life'.
2. the range or area of control or authority: 'such matters are not in our *jurisdiction*'.

jurisprudence
(*say* jooris-**proo**-d'nce) *noun*
the theory or philosophy of law.
[Latin *juris* of law + *prudentia* knowledge]

jurist (*say* **joo**rist) *noun*
a person who practises or is skilled in law.
Word Family: **juristic**, *adjective.*

jury (*say* **joo**-ree) *noun*
1. a group of people summoned to hear a legal case in court and give a verdict.
2. a group of people chosen to judge a competition, etc.
Word Family: **juror** (*say* **joo**ra), *noun,* a member of a jury.
[Latin *juratus* having taken an oath]

just *adjective*
1. fair, even-handed or impartial: 'a negotiator must be *just* to all parties concerned'.
2. honest: 'a *just* man'.
3. morally proper or reasonable: 'I do not want vengeance, only what is *just*'.
Usages:
a) 'the villain got his *just* reward' (= deserved).
b) 'he has a *just* claim to the title' (= lawful).
c) 'it is hard to form a *just* picture of the situation' (= accurate, correct).

just *adverb*
1. not long ago: 'they have *just* left'.
2. by a small amount: 'we *just* won'.
3. only: 'she is *just* a child'.
4. exactly: 'that is *just* the point'.
Word Family: **justly**, *adverb,* a) honestly or fairly, b) accurately; **justness**, *noun.*
[Latin]

justice (*say* **just**iss) *noun*
1. the quality of being just or fair.
2. the principle of fair treatment or conduct.
Usage: 'you can object with *justice* to such unfair treatment' (= good cause).
3. the administration of the law.
4. a judge or magistrate.

justice of the peace
short form is **J.P.**
1. an unpaid lay magistrate appointed by the Lord Chancellor.
2. *History:* a member of the local gentry appointed by the monarch to keep the peace in his district.

justify (*say* **justi**-fie) *verb*
(**justified, justifying**)
1. to show or prove something to be just or right: 'can you *justify* your accusation?'.
Usage: 'you cannot *justify* such rudeness' (= defend).
2. *Printing:* (of lines of type) to be or cause to be of the correct length and spacing.
Word Family: **justification** (*say* justifa-**kaysh**'n), *noun;* **justifiable** (*say* justi-**fie**-a-b'l), *adjective,* able to be justified or defended; **justifiably**, *adverb.*

jut *verb*
(**jutted, jutting**)
to stick out or protrude.

jute *noun*
a strong fibre made from an Asian plant, used to make rope, sacks, etc.
[Sanskrit *juta* braid of hair]

juvenile (*say* **joo**va-nile) *adjective*
1. of or for young people: 'a *juvenile* court'.
2. childish or immature: '*juvenile* behaviour'.
Word Family: **juvenile**, *noun,* a child or young person; **juvenilely**, *adverb.*
[Latin]

juxtapose (*say* juksta-**poze**) *verb*
to place next to or side by side.
Word Family: **juxtaposition**, *noun.*
[Latin *juxta* nearby + *positus* placed]

Kk

kaftan *noun*
see CAFTAN.

Kaiser (*rhymes with* wiser) *noun*
History: an emperor in Austria (1804–1918) or Germany (1871–1918).
[after *Caesar* Octavianus Augustus, first Roman Emperor]

kale *noun*
a variety of cabbage the leaves of which do not form a head.

kaleidoscope (*say* ka–**lie**–da–skope) *noun*
a tube lined with mirrors, containing loose pieces of coloured glass which are reflected as changing symmetrical patterns when the tube is rotated.
Word Family: **kaleidoscopic** (*say* ka–lie–da–**skop**pik), *adjective*, a) relating to a kaleidoscope, b) very intricate or complex.
[Greek *kalos* beautiful + *eidos* image + *skopein* to look at]

kamikaze (*say* kammi–**kah**zi) *noun*
1. any member of a Japanese airforce corps in World War 2 who crashed their aircraft into enemy targets.
2. a suicidal attack.
[Japanese, divine wind]

Kanaka (*say* ka–**nakka**) *noun*
1. a native Hawaiian.
2. a South Sea Islander taken as a labourer to Australia in the 19th century.
[Hawaiian, man]

kangaroo *noun*
any of a large group of Australian grazing marsupials growing up to about 2 m high, with powerful hind legs for leaping and a heavy tail.
[Aboriginal]

kangaroo court
(*informal*) a court or trial conducted without regard for legal procedure.

kaolin (*say* **kay**a–lin) *noun*
see CHINA CLAY.
[after a Chinese mountain, where found]

kapok (*say* **kay**–pok) *noun*
the soft, silky fibre surrounding the seeds of a tropical tree, used for stuffing pillows and for insulation against sound.
[Malay]

karate (*say* ka–**rah**–tee) *noun*
a method of self-defence developed in Japan, in which the hands, elbows, feet and knees are the only weapons used.
[Japanese, empty hand]

karma *noun*
Buddhism: the effect of a person's deeds during life on his status or position in a later incarnation.
[Sanskrit, action, fate]

kart *noun*
a wheeled frame fitted with a small engine, in which young teenagers compete at high speeds.
Word Family: **karting**, *verb*, racing in karts.

karyotype (*say* **karr**ia–tipe) *noun*
Biology: the appearance of the chromosomes in a cell.
[Greek *karyon* kernel + TYPE]

katabolism (*say* ka–**tabba**–lizm) *noun*
see CATABOLISM.

kauri (*say* **kow**–ree) *noun*
a massive, New Zealand, evergreen tree which grows to about 60 m and has thick, parallel-veined leaves.
[Maori]

kava (*say* **kah**va) *noun*
a Polynesian plant, the root of which is used to make an intoxicating drink.

kayak (*say* **kie**–ak) *noun*
a) an Eskimo hunting boat, usually for one person, made from animal skins stretched over a wooden framework. b) a small, lightweight canoe with a small opening for the occupant.

kebab (*say* ki**bbab**) *noun*
see SHISH KEBAB.

kedgeree (*say* kej–a–**ree**) *noun*
a dish of flaked haddock, egg and rice.
[Hindi]

keel *noun*
a) the lowest supporting structure of a boat, running lengthwise along the bottom. b) a fixed or movable wooden board or metal plate in a sailing-boat's bottom which reduces leeway.
on an even keel, in a steady or balanced manner.
keel *verb*
to overturn or upset.
keel over, (*informal*) to collapse suddenly.

keelhaul *verb*
History: to drag a man by ropes under a ship's keel as a form of punishment.

keen (1) *adjective*
1. sharp: a) 'a *keen* blade'; b) 'a *keen* wind'; c) '*keen* perception'.
2. intense or enthusiastic: 'he is a *keen* football supporter'.
Usage: 'a *keen* sense of taste' (= strongly developed).
Word Family: **keenly,** *adverb*; **keenness,** *noun.*

keen (2) *verb*
to lament for the dead.
Word Family: **keen,** *noun.*
[Irish]

keep *verb*
(kept, keeping)
1. to continue: 'I shall *keep* working'.
2. to have or continue to have in possession: a) 'don't *keep* these clothes any longer'; b) 'she was *kept* in gaol overnight'.
Usages:
a) 'the student is *kept* by his father' (= supported).
b) 'she *keeps* bad company' (= associates with).
c) 'we *kept* her from rushing out' (= stopped).
d) 'will the milk *keep* if it's out of the fridge?' (= continue to be fresh).
e) 'he never *keeps* his promises' (= observes).
f) '*keep* off the grass' (= stay).
Phrases:
keep back, to withhold.
keep in with, to make an effort to remain on friendly terms with.
keep time, to mark or record time or rhythm.
keep to, a) 'she did not *keep to* the rules' (= adhere to); b) 'he was forced to *keep to* his bed' (= remain in).
keep to oneself, to stay alone or aloof from others.
keep up, 'I cannot *keep up* with you' (= remain at the same pace); b) '*keep up* the good work' (= continue).
keep up with the Joneses, to strive to maintain a standard of living at least as high as one's neighbours', often for snobbish reasons.
keep *noun*
1. a person's means of support: 'unfortunately I have to work for my *keep*'.
2. the strongest building or central tower of a castle.
for keeps, (*informal*) a) for ever; b) for keeping as one's own.

keeper *noun*
any person who guards or defends: a) 'a *keeper* at the zoo'; b) 'the *goalkeeper* broke his wrist'.

keeping *noun*
the care of: 'the court ordered the girl into her mother's *keeping*'.
in keeping with, in harmony or agreement with.

keepsake *noun*
anything given or kept in memory of a particular person or event.

keg *noun*
a small barrel.

kelp *noun*
any of a group of very large, brown seaweeds.

kelvin *noun*
the basic SI unit of temperature, equal to one degree Celsius. The kelvin scale starts at absolute zero (–273·15°C), so 0°C = 273·15 K.
See SI UNIT.
[after *Lord Kelvin*, 1824–1907, a British physicist and mathematician]

ken *noun*
one's range of sight, knowledge, etc.
Word Family: **ken,** *verb.*
[Scottish, to know]

kennel *noun*
a) a house for a dog. b) (*usually plural*) a place where dogs are kept or bred.
Word Family: **kennel (kennelled, kennelling),** *verb*, to put or keep in or as if in a kennel.

kept *verb*
the past tense and past participle of the verb **keep.**

keratin (*say* **kerra**–tin) *noun*
a tough, fibrous protein forming the outer layer of hair, nails, horns, etc.
[Greek *keratos* of a horn]

kerb *noun*
the raised stone or concrete edge between a footpath and a road.

kerchief (*say* **ker**–chif) *noun*
a scarf or piece of cloth, worn on the head or around the neck.

kernel (*say* **ker**–n'l) *noun*
1. the softer, usually edible, part contained in the shell of a nut or the stone of a fruit.
2. the entire contents of a seed or grain within its coating.
Usage: 'the *kernel* of the problem is lack of money' (= central or important part).

kerosene (*say* kerra–**seen**) **kerosine** *noun*
paraffin.
[Greek *keros* wax]

kestrel *noun*
a small falcon which hovers in the air over an animal it is about to catch.

ketch *noun*
a two–masted yacht with the mizzen–sail not overlapping the stern. Compare YAWL.

ketchup *noun*
a sauce, usually tomato sauce.
[Malay]

ketone (*say* **kee**–tone) *noun*
Chemistry: any of a class of organic compounds having the general formula R.CO.R′, where R and R′ are any aryl or alkyl radicals, such as acetone (formula $CH_3.CO.CH_3$).

kettle *noun*
a container with a spout and a lid, in which water is boiled.
kettle of fish, 'that is a different *kettle of fish*' (= situation, state of affairs).

kettledrum *noun*
a drum consisting of a basin–shaped brass or copper shell with a skin stretched across it.

key (1) (*say* kee) *noun*
1. a metal device which is cut or shaped to fit into and turn the mechanism of a lock, wind a clock, etc.
2. an explanation of symbols, abbreviations, etc., as is used on a map.
Usage: 'he discovered the *key* to the mystery' (= answer, explanation).
3. a button or lever pressed to work something, such as a piano, typewriter, etc.
4. a scale of notes related to each other and to one basic note (the tonic, keynote or doh).
Usage: 'he wrote in a humorous *key*' (= style).

key *adjective*
a) important: 'he holds a *key* position in the government'. b) most important: 'money is the *key* problem'.
key *verb*
(**keyed, keying**)
to regulate or adjust, as when tuning a musical instrument.
key up, to stimulate or increase the energy, excitement, etc. of a person.
Word Family: **keyed–up**, *adjective*, highly tense or intense.

key (2) (*say* kee) *noun*
see CAY.

keyboard *noun*
a group or line of keys to be pressed, e.g. on a piano or typewriter.

keynote *noun*
the lowest or tonic note, on which a musical scale is based.
Usage: 'the *keynote* of his speech was the soundness of the economy' (= main element or idea).

keystone *noun*
the middle stone of an arch, which holds it together.

khaki (*say* **kah**–kee) *noun*
1. a dull yellowish–brown colour.
2. a strong, cotton or wool fabric of this colour, used for uniforms, etc.
Word Family: **khaki**, *adjective*.
[Urdu, dust–coloured]

khan (*say* kahn) *noun*
a hereditary title for a nobleman, or a title of respect in Iran, etc.

kibbutz (*say* kib**buts**) *noun*
plural is **kibbutzim**
a communal farming settlement in Israel.
Word Family: **kibbutznik**, *noun*, a person living and working on a kibbutz.
[Hebrew, gathering]

kick *verb*
1. to strike with the foot: 'the footballer *kicked* the ball'.
2. to score by or as if by kicks: 'the footballer *kicked* a goal'.
3. to recoil, as a gun does after firing.
4. (*informal*) to protest or rebel: 'the students *kicked* against authority'.
Phrases:
kick about, kick around, a) 'we *kicked* the idea *about*' (= discussed and considered); b) to maltreat.
kick out, (*informal*) to get rid of or dismiss.
kick up, (*informal*) 'we really *kicked up* a fuss' (= caused).

kick upstairs, to promote an unsuccessful person to a position where he will do less harm.
kick *noun*
1. the act of kicking.
2. (*informal*) a pleasant or stimulating sensation: a) 'he gets a *kick* out of being mean'; b) 'this home-made wine really has a *kick* in it'.
for kicks, (*informal*) 'he did it *for kicks*' (= for the thrill of it).

kickback *noun*
(*informal*) a) a repercussion. b) any money paid to a person in exchange for a favour, especially as a bribe.

kid (1) *noun*
1. the young of a goat.
2. a leather made from the skin of a kid or goat.
3. (*informal*) a child or young person.

kid (2) *verb*
(kidded, kidding)
to tease.

kid gloves
gloves made of kid.
handle with kid gloves, to treat very gently or tactfully.

kidnap *verb*
(kidnapped, kidnapping)
to take away a person illegally by force, usually with a demand for money in exchange for his release. Compare ABDUCT.
Word Family: **kidnapper**, *noun*.

kidney (*say* **kid**-nee) *noun*
1. *Anatomy:* either of two organs in the abdomen which removes wastes from the blood and excretes urine.
2. temperament: 'he'll come to a sticky end, like others of his *kidney*'.

kidney bean
1. the dwarf French bean or haricot bean.
2. the runner bean.

kieselguhr (*say* **keezel**-goor) *noun*
see DIATOMACEOUS EARTH.
[German]

kilderkin *noun*
a) a cask. b) a liquid measure of about 82 litre.

kill *verb*
a) to deprive of life. b) to deprive of life deliberately.
Usages:
a) 'we had an hour to *kill* before the plane left' (= fill in, pass).
b) 'his jokes really *kill* me' (= affect irresistibly).
c) 'my new shoes are *killing* me' (= causing great discomfort or pain to).
d) 'the editor *killed* the reporter's aggressive story' (= stopped, put an end to).
kill two birds with one stone, in reaching one objective, to gain another satisfactorily.
Word Family: **killer**, *noun*; **kill**, *noun*, a) the act of killing, b) something which is killed.

killer whale
a carnivorous whale, often travelling in groups and attacking other whales, fish, etc.

killing *noun*
the act of deliberately depriving a person, etc. of life.
make a killing, (*informal*) to get or win a very large amount of money.

killjoy *noun*
a person who spoils the enjoyment of others.

kiln *noun*
an oven for drying or baking bricks, lime and pottery.

kilo (*say* **kee**-lo) *noun*
(*informal*) a kilogram.

kilo- (*say* **kee**-lo)
a prefix used for SI units meaning one thousand (10^3). See UNITS in grey pages.
[Greek *khilioi* a thousand]

kilocalorie (*say* killo-**kalla**-ree) *noun*
see CALORIE.

kilogram (*say* **killo**-gram) *noun*
the basic SI unit of mass, equal to about 2·2 lb. See SI UNIT.

kilometre (*say* **killa**-meeta *or* kill-**om**-itta) *noun*
in America spelt **kilometer**
a unit of length in the SI system, equal to 1000 m or about 0.62 mile.

kilotonne (*say* **killo**-tun) *noun*
a unit for measuring the explosive force of nuclear weapons, by comparing it to the mass of trinitrotoluene (TNT) which would produce the same explosion. *Example:* a 20 kilotonne atomic bomb would have the same explosive force as 20 000 tonnes of TNT. Compare MEGATONNE.

kilt *noun*
a short skirt, usually of tartan wool, pleated with broad, vertical folds, worn by Scottish Highlanders.
Word Family: **kilt**, *verb*, to pleat.

kimono (*say* kimo-no) *noun*
a woman's long, loose dress or dressing-gown, with wide sleeves and fastened with a sash, as worn in Japan.

kin *plural noun*
a person's relatives.

kinaesthesia (*say* kie-nis-**theezia**) *noun*
the perception of movement or strain in muscles, tendons or joints.

kind (1) *adjective*
considerate, friendly or generous.
Word Family: **kindly**, *adjective*, kind; **kindly**, *adverb*, a) in a kind way, b) please; **kindness**, *noun*, a) the quality of being kind, b) a kind act, etc.

kind (2) *noun*
a class or category of similar or related things: 'what *kind* of jam is this?'.
Usage: 'they differ in amount but not in *kind*' (= character, nature).
in kind, a) 'we took revenge *in kind*' (= in the same way); b) 'I will pay you *in kind*' (= in goods rather than money).

kindergarten (*say* **kinda**-garten) *noun*
also called a **nursery school**
a school for children under the age of five.
[German *Kinder* children + *Garten* garden]

kind-hearted *adjective*
kind.

kindle (*say* **kin**-d'l) *verb*
1. to start and stimulate a flame in such a manner as to develop larger flames.
2. to excite or rouse: 'the idea *kindled* her enthusiasm'.

kindling (*say* **kin**-dling) *noun*
any material, usually small pieces of wood, used to start a fire.

kindly *adjective, adverb*
Word Family: see KIND (1).

kindred (*say* **kin**-drid) *plural noun*
a person's living relatives.
kindred *adjective*
1. having similar qualities, views, etc.: 'the two boys have *kindred* natures'.
2. related by birth or descent: '*kindred* languages'.

kinetic (*say* kine-**ettik**) *adjective*
of or relating to motion.
[Greek *kinetikos* moving]

kinetic energy
Physics: the energy a body possesses because it is moving. Compare MOMENTUM.

king *noun*
1. a male ruler of a country, usually inheriting his position.
2. a person or thing having great power or control: 'the lion is considered the *king* of beasts'.
3. *Cards:* a playing card with a picture of a king, usually having a value just below an ace.
4. *Chess:* the most important piece, which may move only one square at a time in any direction except when castling.
Word Family: **kingly**, *adjective*.

king cobra
see HAMADRYAD.

kingdom (*say* **king**-dum) *noun*
1. a territory ruled by a king or queen.
2. the province or sphere of a particular thing or activity: a) 'the plant and animal *kingdoms*'; b) 'the mind is the *kingdom* of thought'.

kingfisher *noun*
a brightly coloured, often crested bird with a strong beak which catches fish or insects.

kingpin *noun*
1. the pin placed at the head of the others in skittles, tenpin bowling, etc.
2. (*informal*) the most important person in a group, organization, etc.

King's Bench
(when the reigning monarch is a man) the Queen's Bench.

King's Counsel
(when the reigning monarch is a man) a Queen's Counsel.

King's English
(when the reigning monarch is a man) the Queen's English.

King's evidence
(when the reigning monarch is a man) Queen's evidence.

kingship *noun*
the office or dignity of a king.

king-size, king-sized *adjective*
(*informal*) larger than the usual size: 'a *king-size* double bed'.

kink *noun*
a short twist or curl.
Usage: (*informal*) 'he has a *kink* about flashy cars' (= quirk).
Word Family: **kink**, *verb*, to form twists or curls in.

kinky *adjective*
1. having kinks or twists.

2. (*informal*) eccentric or having bizarre tastes, especially in sexual behaviour.
Word Family: **kinkiness**, *noun.*

kinship *noun*
1. relationship by blood.
2. any relationship or resemblance.
Word Family: **kinsman**, **kinswoman**, *nouns*, a male or female blood relative.

kiosk (*say* **kee**-osk) *noun*
a booth selling cigarettes, newspapers, snacks, etc.
[Turkish *kiushk* a pavilion]

kip *verb*
(kipped, kipping)
(*informal*) to sleep.
Word Family: **kip**, *noun.*

kipper *noun*
a cleaned, salted and smoked herring.

kirk (*rhymes with* work) *noun*
Scottish: a church.

kirtle *noun*
an old word for a skirt or dress.

kismet (*say* **kiz**-met) *noun*
a person's fate or destiny.
[Arabic]

kiss *verb*
to touch or caress with the lips.
Usage: 'the breeze *kissed* the trees' (= touched lightly).
Word Family: **kiss**, *noun.*

kiss-curl *noun*
a small curl of hair, especially on the forehead.

kisser *noun*
1. a person who kisses.
2. (*informal*) the face.

kiss of life
mouth-to-mouth resuscitation.

kit *noun*
a collection of tools, supplies, etc. for a particular purpose: 'a first-aid *kit*'.

kitbag *noun*
a long leather or canvas bag in which kit or other belongings are carried.

kitchen (*say* **kit**-ch'n) *noun*
a room equipped for preparing and cooking food.

kitchenette (*say* kit-ch'n-**et**) *noun*
a small kitchen or part of a room used as a kitchen.

kite *noun*
1. a light frame covered with fabric or paper, which is flown in the wind at the end of a string.
2. a large hawk with long, pointed wings, which kills animals and also eats carrion.

kith and kin
a person's friends and relatives.

kitsch (*say* kitch) *noun*
any art, literature, etc. which is considered to be pretentious or in bad taste.
Word Family: **kitsch**, **kitschy**, *adjectives.*
[German]

kitten *noun*
1. the young of a domestic cat.
2. a playful or lively girl.
Word Family: **kittenish**, *adjective*, playful.

kitty *noun*
a fund or collection of money, especially one shared or contributed to by several people.

kiwi (*say* **kee**-wee) *noun*
1. any of a group of flightless New Zealand birds. It is the national emblem of New Zealand.
2. (*informal*) a person from New Zealand.
[Maori]

klaxon *noun*
a loud funnel-shaped horn or hooter, formerly used on motor cars.

kleptomania (*say* klepta-**may**-nee-a) *noun*
an uncontrollable desire to steal.
Word Family: **kleptomaniac**, *noun.*
[Greek *kleptes* thief + MANIA]

knack (*say* nak) *noun*
the ability to do something well and easily.

knacker (*say* **nakka**) *noun*
a person who buys useless things, such as worn-out horses for slaughter.

knapsack (*say* **nap**-sak) *noun*
a light canvas or leather case, carried on the back for holding provisions, etc. when travelling.

knave (*say* nave) *noun*
1. a dishonest or mischievous person.
2. *Cards:* see JACK.
Word Family: **knavery**, *noun*; **knavish**, *adjective*; **knavishly**, *adverb.*

knead (*say* need) *verb*
to press and mould with the hands, especially dough.

knee (*say* nee) *noun*
1. *Anatomy:* the joint between the thigh and the lower part of the leg.

2. the part of a garment covering a knee. b) something which has the shape of a knee.
knee *verb*
(**kneed, kneeing**)
to strike or touch with the knee.

kneecap *noun*
Anatomy: a movable, curved piece of bone at the front of the knee.

kneel (*say* neel) *verb*
(**knelt** or **kneeled, kneeling**)
to rest on or fall to the knees.

knell (*say* nel) *noun*
the sound of a bell announcing a death or funeral.
Word Family: **knell,** *verb.*

knew (*say* new) *verb*
the past tense of the verb **know**.

knickerbockers (*say* **nikk**a–bokkers) *plural noun*
a pair of short trousers drawn or gathered in at the knee.

knickers *plural noun*
any female underpants.

knick–knack (*say* **nik**–nak) *noun*
any small decorative article.

knife (*say* nife) *noun*
plural is **knives**
a tool with a sharp blade set in a handle, used for cutting.
Word Family: **knife (knifed, knifing),** *verb,* to cut or stab with a knife.

knight (*say* nite) *noun*
1. *Medieval history:* a nobleman given military rank and honour by the king, usually after service as a page and then as a squire.
2. a man honoured by a monarch for merit or service to his country.
3. *Chess:* a piece, usually in the shape of a horse's head, which may make a horizontal or vertical move of one square followed by a diagonal move of one square, and is the only piece that can pass over another.
Word Family: **knight,** *verb,* to dub or create a knight; **knightly,** *adjective;* **knighthood,** *noun,* the rank of a knight.

knight–errant *noun*
plural is **knights–errant**
Medieval history: a knight who travelled in search of fame and adventure.
[Old French *errant* roaming]

knit (*say* nit) *verb*
(**knitted** or **knit, knitting**)
1. to interlock loops of yarn, especially wool, using needles or a machine, to make garments, fabric for clothing, etc.
2. to join or unite: 'the broken bones will soon *knit* together'.
knit the brow, to frown.
Word Family: **knitting,** *noun,* a piece of knitted work.

knob (*say* nob) *noun*
any rounded projection, such as a handle for a door, etc.
Word Family: **knobbly,** *adjective.*

knobkerrie (*say* **nob**–kerree) *noun*
a short club with a thick knobbed head, used by Bantu races in war.

knock (*say* nok) *verb*
1. to strike a blow with the fist or knuckles: '*knock* on the door before entering'.
2. to use a forceful blow or blows to do something: a) 'we *knocked* a hole in the wall'; b) 'she *knocked* over the priceless vase'.
3. (*informal*) to find fault with.
4. (of a car engine, etc.) to make a striking noise as a result of faulty combustion.
Phrases:
knock about, a) to wander or lead an aimless existence; b) to associate; c) to treat roughly.
knock back, 'he felt ill after *knocking back* 6 ice–creams' (= consuming).
knock down, a) to sell at auction; b) to reduce the price of.
knocking copy, (*informal*) an advertisement that implies criticism of a rival's product.
knock off, (*informal*) a) to stop an activity, especially work; b) to steal; c) to kill; d) to compose an article, etc. hurriedly; e) to deduct money, etc.
knock out, to hit or strike someone so that he loses consciousness.
knock up, a) to construct roughly or hastily; b) to score; c) to exhaust or make ill; d) (*informal*) to make pregnant.
Word Family: **knock,** *noun,* the act or sound of knocking.

knockabout *adjective*
(of a garment etc.) suitable for rough use.

knocker *noun*
1. a person or thing that knocks, such as a hinged bar, etc. attached to a door.
2. (*informal*) a critical person.

knock–kneed (*say* **nok**–need) *adjective*
having legs that bend inwards, causing the knees to hit each other in walking.

knockout *noun*
1. the act of knocking a person unconscious.
2. (*informal*) a person or thing that is greatly attractive or successful.
3. a competition in which some competitors are eliminated at each round until only the winner is left.

knoll (1) (*say* nol) *noun*
a small, round hill.

knoll (2) (*say* nol) *noun*
an old word meaning the stroke or sound of a bell.
Word Family: **knoll,** *verb.*

knot (*say* not) *noun*
1. a) a fastening made by passing the free end of a piece of string, rope, etc. through a loop in it and pulling tight. b) a tying together of two pieces of string, rope, etc.
2. a group or cluster: 'a small *knot* of people stood at the gate'.
3. a hard lump, e.g. of wood where a branch joins or once joined the trunk of a tree.
4. a speed of one international nautical mile per hour, used in air and sea navigation, equal to 0·514 m per second, or about 1·12 miles per hour. See UNITS in grey pages.
get in a knot, tie oneself in knots, to become confused.
Word Family: **knot (knotted, knotting),** *verb*; **knotty, knotted,** *adjective.*

knout (*say* nout) *noun*
a knotted whip.
Word Family: **knout,** *verb*, to flog with a knout.
[Russian]

know (*say* no) *verb*
(knew, known, knowing)
to understand: 'I *know* what you mean'.
Usages:
a) 'I *know* her well' (= am acquainted with).
b) 'I would *know* you anywhere' (= recognize).
know *noun*
in the know, having secret or inside information.
Word Family: **knowingly,** *adverb*, a) shrewdly, b) intentionally.

know-all *noun*
(*informal*) a person who claims or appears to know everything.

know-how *noun*
the ability or skill to do something.

knowledge (*say* **noll**ij) *noun*
1. an acquaintance with or understanding of facts, actions, ideas, etc.: a) 'her excellent *knowledge* of music'; b) 'the workers had no *knowledge* of luxury'.
2. that which is known: 'this mystery is beyond human *knowledge*'.
Word Family: **knowledgeable,** *adjective*, possessing knowledge.

known (*rhymes with* bone) *verb*
the past participle of the verb **know**.

knuckle (*say* **nukk'**l) *noun*
1. the joint of a finger, especially the joint where the base of a finger meets the hand.
2. a cut of meat containing the knee of an animal.
3. the joint of a hinge.
knuckle *verb*
Phrases:
knuckle down, 'I must *knuckle down* and finish that history essay' (= work hard).
knuckle under, to yield or submit.

knucklebones *plural noun*
Games: see JACK.

knuckle-duster *noun*
a series of metal rings joined to fit over knuckles of the fist, used as a weapon.

knurl (*say* nerl) *noun*
a small ridge, such as that on the edge of a coin.
Word Family: **knurled,** *adjective.*

koala (*say* ko-**ah**la) *noun*
a tail-less Australian marsupial with grey fur, a flat black nose and strong claws, living in and feeding on eucalyptuses.
[Aboriginal]

kohlrabi (*say* kole-**rah**-bee) *noun*
plural is **kohlrabies**
a vegetable related to the cabbage but with a bulb-like, edible stem similar to a turnip.
[German]

kookaburra (*say* **koo**ka-burra) *noun*
also called a **laughing jackass**
a brown and white, Australian bird with blue markings on its wings, and an unusual, laughing cry.
[Aboriginal]

kopje (*say* **koppie**) *noun*
a small hill.
[Afrikaans, little head]

Koran (*say* **korrahn**) *noun*
the sacred scriptures of Islam, believed by Moslems to be the words of Allah.
[Arabic *qur'an* reading, recitation]

kosher (*say* **ko**–sha) *adjective*
(of food, etc.) prepared according to Jewish rules and rituals.
[Hebrew *kasher* fit, proper, lawful]

kowtow *verb*
to touch the ground with the forehead while kneeling.
Usage: 'he is always *kowtowing* to the boss' (= showing servile respect).
Word Family: **kowtow**, *noun*.
[Chinese *k'o–t'ou* knock the head]

kraal (*say* krahl) *noun*
South African: a) an enclosed area for cattle; a corral. b) a village of huts surrounded by a stockade.
[Afrikaans]

kris (*say* kreece) *noun*
a short sword with a wavy, two–edged blade, used by the Malays.

krypton (*say* **krip**–ton) *noun*
element number 36, a colourless, inert gas found in the earth's atmosphere, used in electric light globes.
See CHEMICAL ELEMENTS in grey pages.
[Greek *kryptos* hidden]

kudos (*say* **kew**–doss) *noun*
personal fame or glory.
[Greek]

kudu (*say* **koo**–doo) *noun*
a large, African antelope, reddish in colour with several thin, white, vertical stripes.
[Bantu]

kukri (*say* **kuk**–ree) *noun*
a short, curved Gurkha knife.
[Hindi]

kumquat (*say* **kum**–kwot) *noun*
a cumquat.

kung fu *noun*
the Chinese form of karate.

Ll

lab *noun*
(*informal*) a laboratory.

label (*rhymes with* table) *noun*
1. a piece of paper or other material attached to an object or person for identification.
2. (*informal*) a word or phrase used to describe a person or group: 'a suitable *label* for mountaineers would be adventurous'.
Usage: 'on what *label* is that record you are playing?'(= brand, trademark).
Word Family: **label** (**labelled, labelling**), *verb,* to mark with a label.

labile (*say* **lay**-bile) *adjective*
changeable or unstable.
[Latin *labi* to slide]

labium (*say* **lay**-bee-um) *noun*
plural is **labia**
Anatomy: a lip or lip-like part.
Word Family: **labial,** *adjective.*
[Latin, lip]

laboratory (*say* la-**borra**-tree) *noun*
1. a room or building fitted with apparatus for scientific experiments.
2. any place where experiments are carried out: 'he tested the ideas in the *laboratory* of his mind'.
[Latin *laboratorium* workshop]

laborious (*say* la-**bawrius**) *adjective*
1. requiring effort or hard work: 'the *laborious* task took 3 weeks'.
Usage: 'the book is written in a *laborious* style' (= ponderous, showing too much evidence of effort).
2. hard-working or conscientious: 'the *laborious* gardener worked for hours'.
Word Family: **laboriously,** *adverb;* **laboriousness,** *noun.*

labour (*say* **lay**ba) *noun*
in America spelt **labor**
1. any work or task involving effort.
2. the work force: 'a meeting was held between *labour* and employers'.
3. *British politics:* (*capital*) one of the two major parties: '*Labour* won the by-election'. Short form of **Labour Party**.
4. a) the effort involved in childbirth. b) the time involved in giving birth: 'she was in *labour* for four hours'.
labour intensive, (of an industry) requiring large amounts of labour in comparison to money. Compare CAPITAL INTENSIVE under CAPITAL.
labour *verb*
1. a) to toil or strive. b) to perform tasks.
2. (of an engine) to overwork.
Usages:
a) 'you are *labouring* under a false impression' (= burdened or hampered by).
b) 'she always *labours* her points when arguing' (= treats at great length).
Word Family: **Labour,** *adjective,* connected with the Labour Party; **labourer,** *noun,* a) a worker whose job requires strength rather than skill, b) anyone who labours; **labouringly,** *adverb.*
[Latin *labor* toil, distress]

Labrador (*say* **labra**-dor) *noun*
one of a breed of large, smooth-haired black or golden retrievers.
[from *Labrador,* an area of Canada]

laburnum (*say* la-**bern'**m) *noun*
a small deciduous tree with drooping, yellow pea-shaped flowers and poisonous seeds.

labyrinth (*say* **labba**-rinth) *noun*
1. a maze.
2. any confusing entanglement of things or events: 'it was impossible to follow the argument through the *labyrinth* of examples'.
Word Family: **labyrinthine,** *adjective.*
[from Greek]

lace *noun*
1. a fine, net-like fabric of interwoven threads.
2. a cord for fastening or tightening shoes, clothing, etc.
lace *verb*
to tie together with lace: '*lace* up your shoes'.
Usages:
a) 'I prefer my coffee *laced* with rum' (= mixed).

b) 'the woman *laced* into the shopkeeper for cheating her' (= attacked).

Word Family: **lacy**, *adjective*; **lacing**, *noun*.

lacerate (*say* **lassa**–rate) *verb*

to tear roughly, especially flesh or tissue: 'he was badly *lacerated* in the car accident'.

Usage: 'he *lacerated* my feelings with his statements' (= hurt).

Word Family: **laceration**, *noun*, a) the act of lacerating, b) the result of lacerating.

[from Latin]

lachrymal gland (*say* **lak**–rim'l gland)

in America spelt **lacrimal gland**

Anatomy: a small gland near the eye, which produces tears.

[Latin *lacrima* tear]

lachrymose (*say* **lakri**–mose) *adjective*

tearful.

lack *noun*

an absence or shortage of something: 'the drought caused a widespread *lack* of food'.

lack *verb*

to be without or in need of: 'he *lacks* the necessary skill for the job'.

[Middle English *lak* deficiency]

lackadaisical (*say* lakka–**dayzi**–k'l) *adjective*

1. careless or slapdash.

2. listless or lacking in energy.

Word Family: **lackadaisically**, *adverb*; **lackadaisicalness**, *noun*.

[from *lackaday* an old word meaning alas the day]

lackey *noun*

also spelt **lacquey**

(*use is often derogatory*) any servant, or a person who is treated as one: 'the King was surrounded by his servile *lackeys*'.

Word Family: **lackey**, *verb*, to act as a servant or in a servile manner.

[from Spanish or Arabic]

lacklustre (*say* **lak**–lusta) *adjective*

dull or lacking in brightness: 'we slept through the actor's *lacklustre* performance'.

laconic (*say* la–**konnik**) *adjective*

brief or concise in speech or style: 'the *laconic* speech gave all the details'.

Word Family: **laconically**, *adverb*.

[Greek *Lakonikos* Spartan (as the Spartans never wasted words)]

lacquer (*say* **lakka**) *noun*

a protective, usually transparent, coating made from a resin or artificial substance and capable of taking a high polish.

Word Family: **lacquer**, *verb*, to coat with lacquer.

lacrosse (*say* la–**kross**) *noun*

a field game for two teams of 12 the object being to force the ball into the goal, using long-handled rackets. See CROSSE.

[French-Canadian, the crosse]

lactate *verb*

Biology: to secrete milk in the mammary glands.

Word Family: **lactation**, *noun*, a) the secreting of milk, b) the period during which milk is secreted, as when a woman is breastfeeding a baby.

[Latin *lactis* of milk]

lacteal (**lakti**–ul) *adjective*

of or like milk.

lactose *noun*

the sugar present in milk, used as a food and in medicine.

lacuna (*say* la–**kewna**) *noun*

plural is **lacunas** or **lacunae**

1. a cavity or space, such as the small space between cells of plants and animals.

2. a missing portion, e.g. in a manuscript.

[Latin, gap]

lacy (*say* **lay**–see) *adjective*

Word Family: see LACE.

lad *noun*

a boy.

Usage: 'in my youth, I was a bit of a *lad*' (= high-spirited or dashing young man).

ladder *noun*

1. a device with steps set into a frame, for climbing up and down.

Usage: 'he is high on the *ladder* for promotion' (= hierarchy).

2. a line of stitches which have come undone, as in a pair of tights or stockings.

Word Family: **ladder**, *verb*, to cause a ladder in stockings, etc.

laddie *noun*

Scottish: a boy.

laden (*say* **lay**–d'n) *adjective*

loaded: 'the trees were *laden* with fruit'.

Usage: 'she was *laden* with cares and sorrows' (= burdened, troubled).

Word Family: **lade**, *verb*, to load.

la-di-da, lah-di-dah *adjective*
(*informal*) pretentious in speech or actions.

lading (*say* **lay**-ding) *noun*
freight or cargo: 'a ship's *lading*'.

ladle (*say* **lay**-d'l) *noun*
a large, deep spoon with a long handle, normally used for serving liquids such as soup.
Word Family: **ladle,** *verb*, to use a ladle.

lady (*say* **lay**-dee) *noun*
1. a) a woman with socially correct manners. b) a term for any woman.
2. (*capital*) a form of address used to a countess, baroness, etc.
[Old English *hlaefdige* loaf-kneader]

ladybird *noun*
in America called a **ladybug**
a type of beetle, often red or orange with black spots, the larvae and adults of which feed on plant lice and other insect pests.

lady-in-waiting *noun*
plural is **ladies-in-waiting**
a female who attends a queen or princess.

lady-killer *noun*
(*informal*) a man who is supposed to be very attractive to women.

ladylike *adjective*
like or befitting a lady.

ladyship *noun*
a form of address for a titled woman: 'her *ladyship* is not at home'.

lag (1) *verb*
(lagged, lagging)
1. to linger or loiter and so fall behind.
2. to insulate pipes to help to retain heat, prevent freezing, etc.
lag *noun*
a lagging behind in time or space in relation to something else: 'there was quite a *time-lag* before he realized that I was joking'.

lag (2) *noun*
(*informal*) a convict.

lager (*say* **lah**ga) *noun*
a beer containing a small amount of hops, made and stored at low temperatures.
[German, a store]

laggard *noun*
a person who lags or falls behind: 'hurry up you old *laggard*'.

lagging *noun*
any material, such as cloth or asbestos, used to insulate pipes, etc.

lagoon (*say* la-**goon**) *noun*
an area of salt water partly or completely separated from the sea by a sandbank, atoll or coral reef.
[Italian *laguna*]

lah *noun*
Music: see DOH.

lah-di-dah *adjective*
see LA-DI-DA.

laid *verb*
the past tense and past participle of the verb **lay (1)**.

lain *verb*
the past participle of the verb **lie (2)**.

lair *noun*
the den or resting place of an animal, especially a wild animal.

laird *noun*
a landowner in Scotland.
[Scottish, lord]

laissez faire (*say* lay-say **fair**) **laisser faire**
the policy of not interfering with others, especially in economic matters.
Word Family: **laissez-faire,** *adjective.*
[French *laissez* leave + *faire* to do]

laity (*say* **lay**-it-ee) *noun*
any people outside a particular profession, especially those outside the clergy.
[Greek *laos* people]

lake (1) *noun*
1. an extensive area of water surrounded by land.
2. any large area of liquid or similar substance.
[Latin *lacus* a basin]

lake (2) *noun*
an insoluble coloured substance obtained by combining a dye and a mordant.

lam *verb*
(lammed, lamming)
(*informal*) to thrash or beat.

lama (*say* **lah**ma) *noun*
Buddhism: a priest or monk.
[Tibetan]

lamb (*say* lam) *noun*
a) a young sheep. b) the flesh of a lamb used as food.
Usage: 'he was led like a *lamb* to the slaughter' (= meek, gentle person).
Word Family: **lamb,** *verb*, to give birth to lambs.

lambaste (*say* lam-**bayst**) **lambast**
verb

(*informal*) to thrash or scold severely: 'during the argument she *lambasted* him with her fists'.

lambent (*say* **lam**–b'nt) *adjective*
a) running lightly over a surface: 'the *lambent* flames licked the side of the house'. b) gently or lightly brilliant: 'his speech showed a *lambent* wit'.
Word Family: **lambently,** *adverb*; **lambency,** *noun.*
[Latin *lambens* licking]

lamb's fry
the offal of a lamb, eaten as a food.

lame *adjective*
crippled in a leg, so as to cause limping.
Usage: 'all I could offer was a *lame* excuse' (= imperfect, weak).
lame duck, 'how could we appoint such a *lame duck* to be principal?' (= ineffective person).
Word Family: **lame,** *verb,* to make lame; **lameness,** *noun*; **lamely,** *adverb.*

lamé (*say* **lah**–may) *noun*
a fabric with silver or gold threads woven into it.
[French]

lamella (*say* la–**mella**) *noun*
plural is **lamellae** (*say* la–**mell**–ee) or **lamellas**
a thin membrane, e.g. in a bone or cell wall.
Word Family: **lamellar,** *adjective.*
[Latin]

lament (*say* la–**ment**) *verb*
to feel or express sorrow or regret for: 'I deeply *lament* the absence of my true love'.
lament *noun*
also called a **lamentation**
a) an expression of grief or regret. b) a formal expression of mourning in verse or song.
Word Family: **lamentable** (*say* **lammen**–ta–b'l), *adjective,* being regrettable; **lamentably,** *adverb.*
[Latin *lamentari* to weep or wail]

lamina (*say* **lammin**–a) *noun*
plural is **laminae** (*say* **lammin**–ee) or **laminas**
1. a thin plate, scale or layer.
2. *Biology:* the blade of a leaf.
[Latin]

laminate (*say* **lammin**–ate) *verb*
a) to cover or overlay with thin layers. b) to split into layers.
laminated plastics, sheets made of layers of plastic and fibrous materials bonded together under pressure, e.g. Formica.
Word Family: **lamination,** *noun.*

lamp *noun*
any of various lights using oil, gas or electricity.

lampblack *noun*
see CARBON BLACK.

lampoon (*say* **lampoon**) *noun*
a satire based on a vicious or critical attack on a person, institution, etc.
Word Family: **lampoon,** *verb,* to attack in a lampoon; **lampoonery,** *noun,* the art or act of lampooning.

lamprey (*say* **lam**–pree) *noun*
any of a group of eel-like, parasitic, aquatic animals.

lance (*rhymes with* dance) *verb*
to cut open with a scalpel or knife: 'the doctor *lanced* the abscess'.
lance *noun*
a long spear formerly used by soldiers on horseback.
Word Family: **lancer,** *noun,* a soldier of a cavalry regiment formerly armed with lances; **lancers,** *noun,* a square dance for four or eight couples.
[Greek *lonkhé*]

lance corporal
the lowest non-commissioned officer in the army.

lanceolate (*say* **lan**si–o–late) *adjective*
shaped like a spearhead: 'the tree had thin, tapering, *lanceolate* leaves'.

lancet (*say* **lahn**–sit) *noun*
Medicine: a small sharp knife for opening abscesses, etc.

land *noun*
1. the part of the earth's surface not covered by water: 'will you travel by *land* or sea?'.
2. an area of ground: a) 'the *land* in this part of the country is very fertile'; b) 'the shed was on the *land* when we bought it'.
Usages:
a) 'the *land* of the living' (= domain).
b) 'she travelled for years in foreign *lands*' (= areas, regions).
see how the land lies, to investigate a situation, etc.
land *verb*
1. a) to come to land or shore: 'the aircraft *landed* safely'. b) to come to rest or arrive in a place or position: 'the space capsule *landed* in the ocean'.
2. to bring a fish out of the water, with a hook, net, etc.

Usages:
a) 'he *landed* a good contract with the firm' (= gained, captured).
b) 'she *landed* him a blow on the head' (= dealt).
land up, 'the way you're going you'll *land up* in gaol' (= find yourself, end).
Word Family: **landed**, *adjective*, owning or consisting of land.

landau (*say* **lan**daw) *noun*
a four-wheeled carriage with two seats facing each other, each covered by a hood, and with a high seat for the driver.
[after the Bavarian town where first made]

landfall *noun*
a sighting of land, especially from a ship: 'we entered the harbour 3 hours after *landfall*'.

landform *noun*
any geographical feature, such as a mountain, valley, etc.

landing *noun*
1. a) the act of landing: 'the aircraft's *landing* was delayed owing to bad weather'. b) the place where people or goods are landed: 'the *landing* was crowded with onlookers when the ship docked'.
2. the open area at the top of a flight of stairs, or between flights.

landing craft
a low, flat-bottomed boat for landing troops, equipment, etc.

landing gear
also called the **undercarriage**
the wheels and supporting struts of an aircraft, lowered just before landing.

landing party
a small group of a ship's crew sent ashore to explore, etc.

landlocked *adjective*
almost or entirely surrounded by land.

landlord *noun*
a person who rents out land, houses or rooms to tenants.
Word Family: **landlady**, *noun*, a female landlord.

landlubber *noun*
Nautical: a person who knows little about boats or the sea.

landmark *noun*
1. an object easily seen and serving as a guide to travellers.
2. an event marking an important stage of development: 'the discovery of gold was a *landmark* in the history of Australia'.

landmine *noun*
any of various explosive devices placed in concealed positions in a minefield on land.

landscape *noun*
1. a view of countryside or inland scenery: 'climb the hill and view the *landscape*'.
2. a painting, etc. of such scenery.
Word Family: **landscape**, *verb*, to do landscape gardening.

landscape gardening
the art of providing gardens with trees, water features, shrubberies, etc. to produce attractive views of seemingly natural landscape.

landslide *noun*
a mass of soil and rocks which slides down a hillside. Also called a **landslip**.
Usage: 'he won the election in a *landslide*' (= overwhelming victory).

lane *noun*
1. a narrow road or alley.
2. a strip marked with lines for a single line of traffic, a runner, etc.

language (*say* **lang**-wij) *noun*
1. the particular form of sounds or words used by a nation or group.
2. the use of sounds or words to express thoughts or feelings to others: 'he always uses very emotional *language*'.
3. any method of communication: 'the *language* of animals'.
4. the science or study of sounds and words.
language laboratory, a place where languages are taught by means of tape-recordings, etc.
[Latin *lingua* tongue]

languid (*say* **lang**-wid) *adjective*
1. having or showing no interest.
2. slow-moving from weakness or tiredness.
Word Family: **languidly**, *adverb*; **languidness**, *noun*.
[from Latin]

languish (*say* **lang**-wish) *verb*
to become weak or feeble.

languor (*say* **lang**-er) *noun*
weakness or lack of energy: 'she lies in bed all day in moody *languor*'.
Usage: 'the *languor* of the heat made us very lazy' (= stillness, heaviness).
Word Family: **languorous**, *adjective*; **languorously**, *adverb*.

lank *adjective*
1. (of a person) tall and lean.

2. (of hair) straight and limp or flat.
lanky *adjective*
(of a person) ungracefully tall and thin.

lanolin (*say* **lanna**–lin) *noun*
a waxy material obtained from wool grease, containing cholesterol and other complex organic substances which are readily absorbed by the skin. It is used in ointments and cosmetics.
[Latin *lana* wool + *oleum* oil]

lantern *noun*
1. a glass case with a metal frame protecting a light. Short form of **storm–lantern.**
2. *Architecture:* a) an open part at the top of a tower or dome. b) a raised part of a roof designed to let in light.

lanthanide (*say* **lan**tha–nide) *noun*
also called a **rare earth element**
Chemistry: any of the rare metal elements, numbers 57–71 inclusive, all of which have chemical properties similar to aluminium.
[Greek *lanthanein* to escape notice]

lanthanum (*say* **lan**tha–num) *noun*
element number 57, a rare metal. See LANTHANIDE.
See CHEMICAL ELEMENTS in grey pages.

lanyard (*say* **lan**–y'd) *noun*
Nautical: a cord worn round the neck or shoulder to carry a whistle or knife.

lap (1) *noun*
the front of the body from the waist to the knees when sitting: 'she held the baby in her *lap*'.
Usage: 'your future is in the *lap* of the gods' (= care, responsibility).
in the lap of luxury, in luxurious circumstances.

lap (2) *verb*
(lapped, lapping)
1. a) to lay something partly over something: 'the roof tiles were closely *lapped*'. b) to wrap or fold about something: 'the Egyptian mummy was *lapped* in a long winding cloth'.
2. to abrade or polish using a rotary motion.
lap *noun*
1. *Sport:* a single circuit around a racetrack.
2. a rotating wheel used for polishing gems, etc.

lap (3) *verb*
(lapped, lapping)
1. to take up liquid with the tongue: 'the cat *lapped* milk from the saucer'.
Usage: 'he really *laps* up the compliments' (= accepts eagerly or greedily).
2. to wash lightly against something: 'we heard the water gently *lapping* the side of the boat'.
Word Family: **lap**, *noun*, the act or sound of lapping.

lap–dog *noun*
any small dog kept as a pet.

lapel (*say* la–**pel**) *noun*
the part of a coat forming an extension of the collar and folded over, reaching down to where the fastening begins.

lapidary (*say* **lapp**i–dree) *noun*
a) a person who cuts, polishes or engraves precious stones. b) the art of cutting and polishing precious stones.
[Latin *lapidis* of a stone]

lapis lazuli (*say* lappis **laz**–yoo–lie)
a rare, deep blue semiprecious stone used mainly in jewellery.
[Latin, stone of azure]

lapse (*say* laps) *noun*
1. a slight slip or failure: 'he suffered a brief *lapse* of memory'.
2. a gradual falling or slipping: 'a *lapse* into bad habits'.
lapse *verb*
to slide or slip slowly: 'he *lapsed* into unconsciousness'.
Usages:
a) 'time *lapses* slowly when you are away' (= passes).
b) 'this insurance policy has *lapsed*' (= become void or ineffective).
[Latin *lapsus* glided]

lapwing *noun*
also called a **pewit**
a gregarious, wading bird related to the plover, with a curved, slender crest and a shrill cry.

larceny (*say* **lar**sa–nee) *noun*
Law: the stealing of another person's possessions.
Word Family: **larcenous,** *adjective*; **larcenously,** *adverb.*

larch *noun*
a deciduous tree with cones, short needle–like leaves and hard, durable wood.
[from Latin]

lard *noun*
the fat from a pig, prepared for use in cooking.

Word Family: **lard**, *verb*, to apply lard or grease to, especially when cooking lean meat.
[from Latin]

larder *noun*
a cool ventilated room for storing foods.

large *adjective*
of more than ordinary size or amount: 'our *large* family has 14 children'.
Usage: 'the chairman has *large* powers of control over policy' (= wide, of great range).
as large as life, 'I turned the corner and saw her, *as large as life*!' (= unexpectedly in person).
large *noun*
at large, a) 'the bandits are still *at large*' (= free); b) 'are travellers *at large* aware of this fact?' (= in general).
Word Family: **largely**, *adverb*, mostly or to a great extent; **largish**, *adjective*, rather large; **largeness**, *noun*.
[Latin *largus* abounding]

large intestine
see COLON (2).

largess (*say* lar-**jess**) **largesse** *noun*
a) the generous giving of gifts. b) gifts which have been given generously.
[French]

lariat (*say* **larri**-ut) *noun*
American: a lasso.
[Spanish *la reata* the rope]

lark (1) *noun*
any of various birds which sing in flight, especially the skylark.

lark (2) *noun*
(*informal*) an amusing prank or frolic: 'we hid his books for a *lark*'.
Word Family: **lark**, *verb*, to have fun or play pranks.

larkspur *noun*
a plant with spur-shaped flowers.

larva *noun*
plural is **larvae** (*say* **larvee**)
Biology: a self-sustaining, preadult stage in the life history of many animals and differing from the mature adult in form.
Word Family: **larval**, *adjective*.
[Latin, a ghost, a mask]

laryngitis (*say* larrin-**jite**-is) *noun*
an inflammation of the larynx causing hoarseness and loss of voice.
[LARYNX + -ITIS]

larynx (*say* **larrinx**) *noun*
plural is **larynges** (*say* la-**rin**-jeez) or **larynxes**
also called the **voice box**
Anatomy: the movable box of cartilage in the neck, through which air passes from the nose to the lungs, and in which the sounds of speech are produced by the vocal cords.
Word Family: **laryngeal** (*say* larrin-**jee**-ul), *adjective*.
[Greek]

lascar *noun*
a seaman from the East Indies.

lascivious (*say* la-**sivvi**-us) *adjective*
a) feeling or expressing lust: 'the boy gave her a *lascivious* leer'. b) tending to cause lustful feelings: 'the principal confiscated the *lascivious* pictures of a nude girl'.
Word Family: **lasciviously**, *adverb*; **lasciviousness**, *noun*.
[Latin *lascivus* playful, impudent]

laser (*say* **layza**) *noun*
an electronic device for producing extremely powerful, almost parallel, beams of light, used in drilling steel, cauterizing tumours, communications, etc.
[from L(ight) A(mplification) by S(timulated) E(mission) of R(adiation)]

lash *verb*
1. a) to strike with a whip. b) to beat or strike violently: 'the rain *lashed* the windows during the storm'.
2. to tie securely with rope, etc.
Usages:
a) 'the horse *lashed* its tail in anger' (= flicked, moved quickly).
b) 'the speaker *lashed* his audience into a frenzy' (= aroused).
c) 'she *lashed* the shopkeeper with angry words' (= attacked).
lash out, a) 'the horse *lashed out* with its hind legs' (= kicked violently); b) 'he *lashed out* at the government in his speech' (= attacked); c) 'tonight we'll really *lash out* and go to the theatre' (= spend money freely).
lash *noun*
1. a) the flexible part of a whip. b) a blow with a whip, etc.: 'the prisoner was sentenced to 16 *lashes*'.
2. an eyelash.

lashing *noun*
1. a whipping or beating.
2. (*informal, plural*) large quantities: 'apple pie with *lashings* of cream'.

lass *noun*
a girl or young woman.

lassie *noun*
Scottish: a girl.

lassitude (*say* **lassi–tewd**) *noun*
tiredness.

lasso (*say* lassoo) *noun*
a long rope with an adjustable noose at one end, used to catch cattle, horses, etc.
Word Family: **lasso** (**lassoed, lassoing**), *verb*, to catch with a lasso.
[Spanish *lazo* noose]

last (1) *adjective, adverb*
1. coming after all the others in time or order: 'my horse ran *last*'.
2. coming immediately before the present: '*last* week she was ill'.
Usages:
a) 'this is the *last* time we shall see each other' (= final).
b) 'that's the *last* thing I thought she would do' (= least expected or likely).
on one's last legs, see LEG.
last *noun*
anything which is at the end: 'we have finished the *last* of the coffee'.
Phrases:
at last, after much delay.
to the last, until the end.
Word Family: **lastly**, *adverb*, finally.

last (2) *verb*
to endure or continue: 'the programme only *lasted* half an hour'.
Usage: 'the food will only *last* another day' (= be enough for).

last (3) *noun*
a model of the human foot used in making shoes.

last–ditch *adjective*
final and desperate.

last post
in America called **taps**
Military: the bugle call signalling soldiers to retire for the night. b) the same call used at military funerals and commemoration services. Compare REVEILLE.

Last Supper
Christian: the supper taken by Christ and his disciples on the eve of his Crucifixion; the basis of the Eucharist.

latch *noun*
a simple fastening on a door, consisting of a bar which falls into a slot.
latch *verb*
to fasten with a latch.
latch on, (*informal*) a) to attach oneself to; b) to understand or comprehend.

latchkey *noun*
the key of the front door, especially as a symbol of freedom from parental control.

late *adjective, adverb*
1. further on than the proper, usual or appointed time: 'everyone was kept waiting as the train was *late*'.
2. being or occurring toward the end: 'the sky had cleared by the *late* afternoon'.
3. recent: 'she came home from Paris with the *latest* fashions'.
Usage: 'her *late* husband was a cheerful man' (= deceased).
of late, 'I have been a bit off–colour *of late*' (= recently).
Word Family: **lately**, *adverb*, recently; **lateness**, *noun*.

latecomer (*say* **late–kumma**) *noun*
a person who arrives late.

latent (*say* **lay–t'nt**) *adjective*
(of a quality) present but not apparent or active: 'a *latent* homosexual'.
Word Family: **latency**, *noun*.
[Latin *latens* lying hidden]

latent heat
Physics: the amount of heat absorbed or given out when a substance changes its state without changing its temperature.

lateral (*say* **latta–r'l**) *adjective*
of or relating to the side: 'prune all the *lateral* branches away from the tree trunk and leave the crown'.
Word Family: **laterally**, *adverb*.
[Latin *lateris* of a side]

laterite (*say* **latta–rite**) *noun*
a) a hard, reddish clay, composed of oxides of iron and aluminium, formed in the tropics by the action of successive wet and dry seasons. b) any soil produced by the decomposition of the rocks beneath it.
[Latin *later* brick]

latex (*say* **lay–teks**) *noun*
Biology: a milky liquid which comes out of cut surfaces of some flowering plants, used in making rubber.
[Latin, liquid]

lath (*say* lahth) *noun*
Building: a narrow strip of wood used to support plaster on a wall or the tiles, etc. on a roof.

lathe (*say* lay*th*) *noun*
a machine which holds and turns pieces of wood, metal or other material,

so that they are rotated against another tool for cutting or shaping.

lather (*rhymes with* father) *noun*
any foam or froth.
lather *verb*
a) to form a lather: 'soap does not *lather* well in hard water'. b) to make a lather on: 'he *lathered* his chin before shaving'.
give someone a lathering, to give someone a beating.

Latin *noun*
1. the language of the ancient Romans.
2. a member of any of the peoples whose languages are derived from Latin: 'the Italians, French and Spanish are all *Latins*'.

Latin America
the countries of Central and South America in which Spanish or Portuguese is spoken.
Word Family: **Latin-American**, *adjective.*

latitude (*say* **latti**-tewd) *noun*
1. any distance north or south of the equator measured in degrees from the centre of the earth.
2. freedom of action, opinion, etc.: 'the conservative churches do not allow much *latitude* in religious belief'.
[Latin *latitudo* breadth]

latrine (*say* la-**treen**) *noun*
(*often plural*) a) a pit or trench used as an outdoor toilet. b) a toilet in a barracks, factory, etc.
[Latin *latrina* a bath]

latter *adjective*
1. being the second mentioned of two: 'of Purcell and Handel, I prefer the *latter* (Handel)'. Compare FORMER.
2. belonging to or coming near the end of something: 'in the *latter* days of his life he became quite senile'.
Word Family: **latterly**, *adverb*, a) lately, b) of the latter part of a period of time.
Common Error: LATTER should only be used for the second of two things. If there are more than two things do not use latter. *Example:* 'of beef and mutton, I prefer the *latter* (mutton)'; 'of beef, mutton and veal, I prefer the *last* (veal)'.

lattice (*say* **lattis**) *noun*
a structure of crossed strips usually in a diamond pattern, used as a screen, etc.

lattice window
a leaded window with diamond-shaped panes.

laud *verb*
an old word meaning to praise.
Word Family: **laudable**, *adjective*, deserving praise; **laudably**, *adverb*; **laudatory**, *adjective*, expressing or showing praise.
[Latin *laudare* to praise]

laudanum (*say* **lawda**-n'm) *noun*
a solution of opium in alcohol, used in medicine.

laugh (*say* lahf) *verb*
to make sounds and facial movements expressing joy, amusement, derision, etc.
laugh at, 'it's unfair to *laugh at* his disability' (= make fun of).
laugh *noun*
a) the sound of laughing. b) the act of laughing: 'we had a good *laugh* over his stories'.
have the last laugh, to triumph or succeed after seeming at a disadvantage.
laughter *noun*
a) the action of laughing: 'he was helpless with *laughter*'. b) the sound of laughing.
Word Family: **laughable**, *adjective*, amusing or causing laughter; **laughingly**, *adverb.*

laughing gas
nitrous oxide (formula N_2O), which may produce an exhilarating effect when inhaled, used as an anaesthetic in dentistry, etc.

laughing jackass
see KOOKABURRA.

laughing-stock *noun*
an object of general ridicule.

launch (1) (*say* lawnch) *noun*
a large, sturdy, open boat, usually with an engine.

launch (2) (*say* lawnch) *verb*
a) to put a boat into the water. b) to propel a rocket, spear, etc., into the air: 'the jet plane was *launched* from the deck of the carrier'.
Usage: 'the publisher *launched* an advertising campaign to promote the new book' (= started, set going).
launch out, 'he is going to *launch out* on a completely new career' (= start out).

launching pad
short form is **launch pad**
the structure from which a rocket is launched.

launder (*say* **lawn**-der) *verb*
to wash and iron clothes.

Word Family: **launderer,** *noun* a person who launders; **laundress,** *noun,* a female who launders.
[Latin *lavanda* things to be washed]

laundrette *noun*
a coin-operated, self-service laundry.

laundry (*say* **lawn**-dree) *noun*
a) a place where articles are washed. b) any articles of clothing, etc. to be washed.
Word Family: **laundryman,** *noun,* a man who collects and delivers laundry.

laurel (*say* **lorrel**) *noun*
an evergreen shrub with shiny leaves, used by the ancient Greeks and Romans to make victory wreaths.
rest on one's laurels, to be content with what one has already achieved.
Word Family: **laureate,** *adjective,* crowned with leaves of laurel or other symbols of honour.
[Latin *laurus*]

lava (*say* **lahva**) *noun*
Geology: the molten rock from inside the earth which flows through an erupting volcano.
[Italian, a stream]

lavatory (*say* **lavva**-tree) *noun*
a toilet.
[Latin *lavare* to wash]

lave *verb*
an old word meaning to wash.

lavender (*say* **lavvin**-da) *noun*
1. a pale, pinkish-violet colour.
2. a) a shrub with spikes of fragrant, pale purple flowers. b) the dried flowers or the perfume made from the oil from this plant.
Word Family: **lavender,** *adjective.*

lavish (*say* **lavvish**) *verb*
to give abundantly or generously: 'the nurse *lavished* attention on the sick child'.
Word Family: **lavish,** *adjective,* abundant or profuse; **lavishly,** *adverb;* **lavishness,** *noun.*
[Old French *lavasse* a downpour of rain]

law *noun*
1. a) the body of official rules of a country which must be obeyed. b) any one of these rules. c) any collection of these rules dealing with a particular subject: 'commercial *law*'. d) a body of knowledge concerned with these rules: 'to study *law*'. e) the profession which deals with these rules and their application: 'to practise *law*'.
2. (*informal*) the police force.
Usages:
a) 'Newton's first *law* of motion' (= rule).
b) 'his word is *law*' (= undisputed authority).
lay down the law, to state one's opinions or wishes authoritatively.
Word Family: **lawful,** *adjective,* allowed by law; **lawfully,** *adverb;* **lawfulness,** *noun;* **lawless,** *adjective,* a) regardless of law, b) unrestrained; **lawlessly,** *adverb;* **lawlessness,** *noun.*

law-abiding *adjective*
obeying the law.

lawcourt *noun*
the room or building in which law cases are heard.

Law Lord
any of several members of the House of Lords who are qualified by high legal office to act as judges when the House sits as a court of appeal.

lawn (1) *noun*
an area of neatly cut grass, e.g. in a private garden.

lawn (2) *noun*
a thin, linen fabric.

lawn tennis
the official name for tennis played on grass or hard courts, as distinct from real tennis.

lawrencium (*say* law-**rensi**-um) *noun*
element number 103, a man-made, radioactive metal. See TRANSURANIC ELEMENT and ACTINIDE.
See CHEMICAL ELEMENTS in grey pages.
[after *E. O. Lawrence,* 1901-58, an American physicist]

lawsuit *noun*
Law: a proceeding in a court of law.

lawyer (*say* **loya**) *noun*
Law: a member of the legal profession. Compare BARRISTER and SOLICITOR.

lax *adjective*
1. not strict or severe: a) '*lax* morals'; b) '*lax* discipline'.
2. (of the bowels) loose.
Word Family: **laxly,** *adverb;* **laxity** (*say* **laksi**-tee), **laxness,** *nouns.*
[Latin *laxus* loose, slack]

laxative *noun*
also called a **purgative**
any substance causing emptying of the bowels.

lay (1) *verb*
(laid, laying)
1. to put, place or set: a) 'he *laid* the book on the table'; b) 'she *lays* great

emphasis on neatness'; c) 'the scene of our story is *laid* in Rome'.
2. to prepare or arrange: 'he *laid* careful plans'.
Usages:
a) 'my prize hen *lays* six eggs a day' (= produces).
b) 'I'll *lay* five to one I can beat you home' (= wager, bet).
c) 'he sprinkled the path with water to *lay* the dust' (= settle).
Phrases:
lay down, a) 'he *laid down* his life' (= sacrificed); b) 'that ship was *laid down* last year' (= begun).
lay in, to build up a store of something.
lay it on thick, (*informal*) to exaggerate a point, especially when flattering someone.
lay low, a) 'he *laid* me *low* with his truncheon' (= knocked unconscious); b) 'flu *laid* him *low* for weeks' (= kept an invalid).
lay off, a) to dismiss an employee temporarily; b) (*informal*) to give up or stop.
lay out, a) to spend money on; b) to prepare a corpse for burial; c) to knock unconscious.
lay up, a) to store up; b) 'he's been *laid up* for a week with back pains' (= kept in bed).
lay *noun*
1. the way or position in which something is laid or lies: 'the *lay* of the land'.
2. an old word for a ballad.
Common Error: do not confuse TO LAY and TO LIE. To *lay* (*laid, laying*) is always transitive (must have an object) and means to put somewhere; to *lie* (*lay, lain, lying*) is always intransitive (cannot have an object) and means to be somewhere. Thus, we say to a dog, '*lie* down' or '*lay* down that stick'. *Examples:* 'he *lay* in the garden all morning' (not laid or layed); 'he could have *lain* there all day' (not laid); 'he was *lying* there' (not laying); 'have you *laid* the table?' (not lain).

lay (2) *verb*
the past tense of the verb **lie (2)**.

lay (3) *adjective*
of or relating to the laity, as distinct from the clergy or the members of a profession.

lay (4) *noun*
a short song or poem.

layabout *noun*
a loafer or idler.

lay-by *noun*
a space at the side of a road, railway, etc. where vehicles can stop temporarily without obstructing traffic.

layer *noun*
1. a single thickness or level.
2. (of hens, etc.) one that lays eggs.
Word Family: **layer**, *verb*, to spread or arrange in layers.

layette (*say* lay-**et**) *noun*
a complete outfit of clothing for a newborn child.
[French, box or drawer]

lay figure
1. a jointed wooden model of the human body used in artists' studios, e.g. to drape clothes over.
2. a nonentity or figurehead.
3. a lifeless fictional character.

laying *verb*
the present participle of the verb **lay (1)**.

layman *noun*
1. a member of the laity.
2. (*informal*) a non-expert.

layout *noun*
an arrangement or plan: 'this map shows the *layout* of the town'.

lazy (*say* **lay**-zee) *adjective*
unwilling to work or be active.
Usage: 'a *lazy* stream gurgling by' (= slowly moving).
Word Family: **lazily**, *adverb*; **laziness**, *noun*; **laze**, *verb*, to be lazy or idle.

lea (*say* lee) *noun*
an old word meaning a meadow.

leach *verb*
Geology: to remove soluble constituents from soil, ashes, etc. by the percolating action of water.

lead (1) (*say* leed) *verb*
(**led, leading**)
1. to take or guide: 'the estate agent *led* us through the house'.
2. to direct or command: 'to *lead* an army'.
3. to begin or open with: 'to *lead* the ace of hearts'.
Usages:
a) 'he *leads* a dull life' (= experiences, spends).
b) 'the marching girls *led* the procession' (= were at the head of).
lead someone on, a) to encourage someone into an undesirable position or action; b) to deceive someone.
lead *noun*
1. a) the first or foremost place: 'the Irishman took the *lead* at the 300 m mark'. b) the extent to which something is ahead: 'he had a *lead* of 100 m on his nearest rival'.

2. something which leads: a) 'the boxer tried to land a sharp left *lead*'; b) 'a *lead* of trumps'.
Usages:
a) 'put the dog on its *lead*' (= leash).
b) 'at present there are no *leads* to the murderer's identity' (= clues, indications).
c) 'I have the *lead* because I won the last trick' (= right of first play).
3. *Theatre:* a) the main role in a play. b) the actor playing it.
4. *Mining:* a) an alluvial deposit containing gold, tin, etc. b) a vein.
5. an insulated piece of wire for conducting electricity.

lead (2) (*say* led) ***noun***
1. element number 82, a soft metal, widely used in alloys, pipes, batteries and paints. See CHEMICAL ELEMENTS in grey pages.
2. a long, thin piece of graphite used in pencils.
3. *Nautical:* a lump of metal attached to a rope and dropped over the side of a boat to measure the depth of the water.
Word Family: **leaden**, *adjective*, a) being made of lead, b) having the colour or appearance of lead, c) being as heavy or dull as lead; **leadenly**, *adverb*.

leader (*say* **lee**–der) ***noun***
1. a person or thing that leads: 'the *leader* of an expedition'.
2. *Newspapers:* see EDITORIAL.
3. the first violin in an orchestra.

leadership ***noun***
a) the position, function, or guidance of a leader. b) the ability to lead.

leading (*say* **lee**–ding) *adjective*
chief or most important: 'she is the *leading* expert in this field'.
leading case, a law case which sets an important precedent for later cases.
leading question, a question so worded that it suggests the desired answer.

leading article
see EDITORIAL.

leaf ***noun***
plural is **leaves**
1. a) a flat organ, usually green, found on the stem of plants. b) a petal: 'rose *leaves*'.
2. a single sheet of paper forming two pages of a book, one on each side.
3. an extra panel to make a table larger, often hinged or sliding.
4. *Metallurgy:* a very thin metal sheet or plate.
Phrases:
take a leaf out of someone's book, to follow someone's example.
turn over a new leaf, to make a new and better start.
leaf *verb*
to put forth leaves.
leaf through, to turn the pages of a book quickly.
Word Family: **leafy**, *adjective*, having or covered with leaves; **leafiness**, *noun*; **leafless**, *adjective*; **leafage**, *noun*, foliage.

leaflet ***noun***
1. a small leaf or leaf-like part.
2. a flat or folded sheet of printed matter.

league (1) (*say* leeg) ***noun***
1. a) an agreement made between persons, groups or nations, for their common good. b) the parties to such an agreement.
Usage: 'our squash team is considered to be in the same *league* as the South African team' (= class, category).
2. a group of sporting clubs which arranges matches between its member teams.
in league with, allied with.
Word Family: **league**, *verb*, to form into or become a league.

league (2) (*say* leeg) ***noun***
an old unit of length varying in different countries and at different times. In England it was equal to about 5·5 km (3 miles).

leak ***verb***
1. to let liquid or gas wrongly enter or escape.
2. to disclose information.
3. (*informal*) to urinate.
leak *noun*
1. any hole, crack, etc., through which liquid or gas may wrongly enter or escape.
2. an act or instance of leaking: 'there's a steady *leak* from the crack in the dam wall'.
Word Family: **leaky**, *adjective*; **leakiness**, *noun*.

leakage (*say* **lee**–kij) ***noun***
a) the act or process of leaking. b) something which leaks in or out. c) the amount which leaks in or out.

lean (1) ***verb***
(**leaned** or **leant, leaning**)
1. to bend from a vertical position or in a particular direction: a) 'the waiter *leaned* over the table'; b) '*lean* out of the window and have a look'.

2. to rest against or on something for support.
Usages:
a) 'he *leans* towards socialism' (= is favourably disposed).
b) 'he *leaned* rather too much on other people's advice' (= relied, depended).
lean over backwards, see BACKWARDS.
Word Family: **lean, leaning**, *nouns*, an inclination.

lean (2) *adjective*
1. having little fat.
Usage: 'the thirties were *lean* years to live through' (= of scarcity).
2. relating to paint containing little oil.
Word Family: **lean**, *noun*, the flesh of an animal containing little fat; **leanness**, *noun*.

lean-to *noun*
a small building which is supported by the wall of a larger building.

leap *verb*
(**leapt** or **leaped, leaping**)
to spring or jump.
Phrases:
by leaps and bounds, with extremely rapid progress.
leap in the dark, an action the consequences of which cannot be foreseen.
Word Family: **leap**, *noun*, a) a spring or bound, b) the space covered in a leap, c) a place leapt from.

leapfrog *noun*
a game where one person jumps across another who is bent over.

leap year
see YEAR.

learn (*say* lern) *verb*
(**learnt** or **learned, learning**)
to gain knowledge or skill from instruction or practice.
Usage: 'I was sorry to *learn* of your illness' (= be told or informed).
Word Family: **learner**, *noun*, a person who is learning.

learned (*say* **lernid**) *adjective*
having or requiring much knowledge.
Word Family: **learnedly**, *adverb*; **learnedness**, *noun*.

learning (*say* **lerning**) *noun*
1. a) the knowledge acquired by scholarly study. b) the act or process of acquiring knowledge or skill.
2. *Psychology:* a relatively permanent change in behaviour as a result of practice or experience.

learnt (*say* lernt) *verb*
a past tense and past participle of the verb **learn**.

lease *noun*
a contract which allows a person to use or occupy property in return for rent.
a new lease of life, a renewed enjoyment of life.
Word Family: **lease**, *verb*, to grant or take possession of by lease.

leasehold (*say* **leese**-hold) *noun*
a right to use, for a specified period, land or property which one does not own.
Word Family: **leaseholder**, *noun*.

leash *noun*
also called a **lead**
a strap or thong for restraining animals.
Word Family: **leash**, *verb*, to hold or secure by a leash.

least *noun*
the smallest amount, quantity, degree, etc.
at least, a) 'he writes *at least* twice as fast as I do' (= at the lowest estimate); b) '*at least* you could say you're sorry' (= at any rate, in any case).
least *adjective, adverb*
a superlative form of **little**.

leastways *adverb*
(*informal*) at least.

leather (*say* **le***tha*) *noun*
the tanned and prepared skin of animals.
hell for leather, see HELL.
Word Family: **leather**, *verb*, (informal) to beat with a leather strap; **leathery**, *adjective*, like leather.

leatherjacket *noun*
see DADDY-LONG-LEGS.

leave (1) *verb*
(**left, leaving**)
1. to go out or away from: 'he *left* the country and returned to the city'.
2. to cause or allow to remain: a) '*leave* your gloves and things on the hall table'; b) 'did you *leave* the radiator turned on?'.
Usages:
a) 'did the postman *leave* a parcel?' (= deliver).
b) 'four from six *leaves* two' (= has, yields as a remainder).
c) 'I *left* all the organizing to him' (= handed over, entrusted).
d) 'my father *left* me a fortune in his will' (= gave).

Phrases:
leave off, to stop or discontinue.
leave out, to omit.
Word Family: **leaver**, *noun*, a person who leaves.

leave (2) *noun*
1. an allowance to do something: 'did I give you *leave* to interrupt?'.
2. a) an allowance to be absent from duty. b) the period of such absence.
3. a departure: 'take *leave* of one's friends'.

leaven (*rhymes with* seven) *noun*
the dough used to start fermentation in new dough.
Word Family: **leaven**, *verb*, a) to add leaven to, b) to act upon like leaven.
[Middle English *levain* that which raises]

leaves *plural noun*
see LEAF.

lechery (*say* **letch**a–ree) *noun*
the unrestrained indulgence of lust.
Word Family: **lecherous**, *adjective*, a) disposed to or characterized by lechery, b) causing lechery; **lecherously**, *adverb*; **lecherousness**, *noun*; **lecher**, *noun*, a man disposed to lechery.

lecithin (*say* **less**a–thin *or* **lekk**a–thin) *noun*
Biology: a nitrogenous fatty substance found in the nerve tissues, the yolk of eggs, etc., and prepared as a health food.
[Greek *lekithos* egg–yolk]

lectern *noun*
a tall, sloping reading desk, from which lessons are read in a church, lecture–hall, etc.

lecture (*say* **lek**cher) *noun*
1. a formal talk given to teach or inform a group.
2. a long, boring warning or scolding: 'dad gave me a *lecture* when I came home late'.
Word Family: **lecture**, *verb*.
[Latin *lector* a reader]

lecturer (*say* **lek**–cha–ra) *noun*
a person who gives lectures, especially at a university or college.
Word Family: **lectureship**, *noun*, the office of a lecturer.

led *verb*
the past tense and the past participle of the verb **lead (1)**.

ledge (*say* lej) *noun*
a narrow shelf: a) 'a window *ledge*'; b) 'a rocky *ledge* halfway down the cliff face'.

ledger (*say* **lej**–a) *noun*
a set of bookkeeping accounts.

lee *noun*
Nautical: a) the sheltered side which is not receiving the wind. b) the direction towards which the wind is blowing.

leech *noun*
1. a small, blood–sucking worm, living in water–holes or very damp places.
2. (*informal*) a parasitic person.

leek *noun*
a vegetable, related to the onion, with a white cylindrical bulb and broad flat leaves.

leer *noun*
a look or roll of the eyes expressing slyness, malice, lust, etc.
Word Family: **leer**, *verb*; **leeringly**, *adverb*.

leery *adjective*
(*informal*) wary or suspicious.

lees *plural noun*
the sediment of wine or other liquids.
Usage: 'to drink life to the *lees*' (= dregs).

leeward (*say* **lee**–wud *or* **loo**–wud) *adjective, adverb*
Nautical: of, on or towards the lee. Compare WINDWARD.
Word Family: **leeward**, *noun*.

leeway *noun*
1. *Nautical:* the drift of a ship or aircraft to leeward.
2. a loss of progress or time: 'we have some *leeway* to make up on this job'.
3. (*informal*) extra time, etc. giving scope for manoeuvre or a margin for error.

left (1) *adjective*
1. of or relating to the side of a person or thing which is towards the west when the subject is facing north.
2. *Politics:* (*often capital*) of or relating to the left wing.
left *noun*
1. anything on or toward the left side.
2. *Politics:* (*often capital*) a collective term for all individuals and groups with a socialist outlook.
Word Family: **left**, *adverb*.

left (2) *verb*
the past tense and the past participle of the verb **leave (1)**.

left–handed *adjective*
a) preferring to use the left hand. b) being done with or adapted to the left hand.

left-handed compliment, an ambiguous or questionable compliment.

leftist *noun*
Politics: (*often capital*) a person who holds or sympathizes with the views of the left wing.
Word Family: **leftist,** *adjective.*

leftover *noun*
(*often plural*) any food remaining after a meal, especially when used for another meal.

left-wing *adjective*
Politics: radical, socialist, etc.: 'despite his conservative background, David adopted *left-wing* views at university'.
left wing
the most radical section of a political party or group, usually meaning (in a parliamentary democracy) extremists in socialist parties and moderates in conservative parties.
Word Family: **left-winger,** *noun.*
[from a European tradition that radical members of a legislative assembly sit on the President's left]

leg *noun*
1. *Anatomy:* the part of the body between the hip and the foot, bearing the weight of the body.
2. a) anything shaped or used like a leg: 'this chair has only 3 *legs*'. b) the part of a garment covering the leg.
3. any of the distinct parts of any course, race, etc.: 'we covered the last *leg* of our trip very quickly'.
4. *Cricket:* the part of the field lying to the left of and behind the batsman. Compare OFF.
Phrases:
give a leg up, to assist in climbing or mounting by giving a boost or providing support.
not have a leg to stand on, not to have a sound or logical basis for an argument, etc.
on one's last legs, on the verge of collapse or death.
pull someone's leg, (*informal*) to tease or make fun of someone.
Word Family: **legless,** *adjective.*

legacy (*say* **legga**-see) *noun*
1. anything handed down from ancestors or predecessors.
2. *Law:* a gift of personal property made by will to any person. Compare INHERITANCE.
Word Family: **legatee,** *noun,* a person who receives a legacy.
[Latin *legare* to bequeath]

legal (*say* **lee**-g'l) *adjective*
a) of or relating to law. b) lawful.
Word Family: **legally,** *adverb*; **legalism,** *noun,* the strict adherence to laws or rules; **legalist,** *noun*; **legalistic,** *adjective.*
[Latin *legis* of law]

legal age
the age at which a person becomes legally competent to deal with his own affairs, or responsible for his own actions.

legal aid
aid towards legal costs, paid from government funds to those who can show need.

legality (*say* lig-**alli**-tee) *noun*
the state of being allowed by law.

legalize, legalise *verb*
to make legal.
Word Family: **legalization,** *noun.*

legal separation
also called a **judicial separation**
an arrangement made by court order whereby a husband and wife, though not divorced, live apart.

legal tender
see TENDER (2).

legate (*say* **legg**et) *noun*
Roman Catholic: an official representative of the Pope.

legatee (*say* legga-**tee**) *noun*
Word Family: see LEGACY.

legation (*say* lig-**ay**-sh'n) *noun*
Politics: a) a group of diplomatic representatives led by an official below the rank of ambassador. b) the offices or official home of a legate or a legation.

leg before wicket
Cricket: a way of getting out in which the batsman's body intercepts a fairly bowled ball which would otherwise have hit the wicket.

legend (*say* **lej**'nd) *noun*
1. a traditional tale about a person or country, often regarded locally as history, but which may or may not be true.
2. a written explanation of the symbols used in a map, diagram, etc.
3. an inscription, as on a coin or monument.
Word Family: **legendary,** *adjective,* a) of or described in legend, b) famous or celebrated.
[Latin *legenda* things to be read]

legerdemain (*say* lej-a-der-**mane**) *noun*

a) a sleight of hand. b) any clever trick or deception.
[French *léger* light + *de main* of hand]

leger line (*say* **le**ja line)
Music: a short line above or below the staff.

leggings *plural noun*
an extra outer covering for the legs, usually extending from the ankles to the knees.

leggy *adjective*
having long legs.

legible (*say* **le**ja–b'l) *adjective*
able to be read easily: 'please make your handwriting *legible*'.
Word Family: **legibility** (*say* leja–**billi**–tee), *noun*; **legibly**, *adverb*.
[Latin *legere* to read]

legion (*say* **lee**–j'n) *noun*
1. any of various military organizations or units: 'the Foreign *Legion*'.
2. a vast multitude: 'they are *legion*'.
3. *Ancient history:* a division of the Roman army, consisting of at least 3000 men.
Word Family: **legionary, legionnaire,** *nouns*, a member of a legion; **legionary,** *adjective.*
[Latin *legere* to choose]

legislate (*say* **le**ji–slate) *verb*
to make or enact laws.
legislative *adjective*
1. having the power or function to make laws: 'a *legislative* assembly'.
2. of or produced by laws.
Word Family: **legislation**, *noun*, a) the act of making laws, b) a law or group of laws; **legislator**, *noun*.

legislature (*say* **le**jis–laycher) *noun*
any organization which makes laws, such as a parliament.

legitimate (*say* lij–**itta**–mit) *adjective*
1. according to the law or established standards, etc.: 'a *legitimate* business'.
Usage: 'that is not a *legitimate* argument' (= logical, valid).
2. born of parents who are legally married.
legitimate drama, theatre, straight plays.
Word Family: **legitimately,** *adverb*; **legitimacy, legitimateness,** *nouns*; **legitimize, legitimise,** *verb*, to make legal or legitimate.
[Latin *legitimare* to make lawful]

leg–pull *noun*
(*informal*) a teasing, light–hearted attempt to mislead.

legume (*say* **leg**–yoom) *noun*
any of a group of plants in which the fruit is a pod, such as the pea.
Word Family: **leguminous,** (*say* le–**gew**mi–nus), *adjective.*
[Latin *legumen* a plant with pods, from *legere* to pick (pods)]

lei (*say* lay) *noun*
a garland of flowers for the neck or head.
[Hawaiian]

leisure (*rhymes with* treasure) *noun*
the time free of work or duties.
Phrases:
at leisure, 'she walked around the town *at leisure*' (= without hurrying).
at one's leisure, 'please come and visit us *at your leisure*' (= when you have some spare time).
Word Family: **leisurely,** *adjective, adverb,* without haste.

leitmotiv (*say* **lite**–mo–teef) **leitmotif** *noun*
a musical theme associated with a particular person or situation, as in Wagner's operas.
[German, leading motive]

lemming *noun*
a small, mouse–like mammal of arctic regions, noted for periodic mass migrations which control the size of the population.

lemon *noun*
1. a medium–sized, yellow, citrus fruit with a bitter taste.
2. a pale yellow colour.
3. (*informal*) something which is disappointing or unsuitable: 'the answer is a *lemon*'.
[Arabic *lima*]

lemonade *noun*
a drink made from lemons, sugar and water, often carbonated.

lemon–curd *noun*
a filling for tarts made of butter and eggs flavoured with the rind and juice of lemons.

lemon grass
a tropical grass from which an oil is obtained, for use in perfumes, cooking, etc.

lemur (*say* **lee**ma) *noun*
a small, nocturnal, tree–dwelling monkey–like mammal with a long furry tail, found in the forests of Madagascar and nearby islands.
[Latin *Lemures* ghosts, from its appearance and nocturnal habits]

lend *verb*
(lent, lending)
1. to give something with the understanding that it will be returned: 'this library *lends* books'.
2. *Commerce:* to permit the temporary use of money, etc. in return for payment: 'the banks *lend* money at high interest rates'.
Usages:
a) 'dark clouds *lent* a threatening appearance to the sky' (= gave).
b) 'this will *lend* itself to my purpose very well indeed' (= adapt).
lend a hand, to help.
Word Family: **lender,** *noun.*

length *noun*
1. the distance from end to end: 'what is the *length* of this room?'.
2. the quality of being long: 'the *length* of the walk made us all rather tired'.
Usages:
a) 'they have lived here for some *length* of time' (= amount).
b) 'the electrician held out a *length* of cable' (= piece).
3. *Sport:* the body-length of a horse, boat, etc., used to judge the distance between competitors in a race.
Phrases:
at arm's length, 'she kept him *at arm's length*' (= at a distance, from undue familiarity).
at length, a) 'she described the accident *at length*' (= in detail, for a long time); b) '*at length* John arrived, apologizing for being so late' (= after some time).
go to any lengths, 'he would *go to any lengths* to get his own way' (= do whatever is necessary).
Word Family: **lengthen,** *verb,* to make or become longer; **lengthwise, lengthways,** *adverbs,* in the direction of the length; **lengthy,** *adjective,* very long.

lenient (*say* **leeni**-ent) *adjective*
mild, merciful or gentle.
Word Family: **leniently,** *adverb*; **leniency, lenience,** *noun.*
[Latin *leniens* softening]

lens (*say* lenz) *noun*
plural is **lenses**
any device, especially a curved piece of glass, which causes a beam of rays, such as light or an electron beam, to converge or diverge on passing through it.
[Latin, a lentil]

lent (1) *verb*
the past tense and past participle of the verb **lend**.

Lent (2) *noun*
Christian: a fast of 40 days in preparation for Easter, in memory of Christ's fast in the wilderness.
Word Family: **Lenten,** *adjective.*

lentil *noun*
the edible bean-like seed of a pod-bearing plant.

lento *adverb*
Music: slowly.
[Italian]

Leo (*say* **lee**-o) *noun*
also called the **Lion**
Astrology: a group of stars, the fifth sign of the zodiac.
[Latin, lion]

leonine *adjective*
of or like a lion.

leopard (*say* **lepp**erd) *noun*
a large, flesh-eating Asian and African mammal of the cat family, usually having a tawny coat, with dark blotches.
Word Family: **leopardess,** *noun,* a female leopard.
[Latin *leo* lion + *pardus* panther]

leotard (*say* **lee**-o-tard) *noun*
a close-fitting garment consisting of a vest, or tights and a vest in one piece, as worn by ballet-dancers.
[after *J. Léotard*, died 1870, a French trapeze artist]

leper (*say* **lepp**a) *noun*
a person who suffers from leprosy.
[Greek *lepros* scaly]

lepidopterous (*say* leppi-**dop**ta-rus) *adjective*
relating to an order of insects, consisting of moths and butterflies, in which the adult form has four scaly, membranous wings.
[Greek *lepidos* of a scale + *pteron* wing]

leprechaun (*say* **lep**ra-kawn) *noun*
an elfin cobbler supposed to possess a crock of gold.
[Irish, small body]

leprosy (*say* **lep**ra-see) *noun*
an infectious, bacterial disease causing changes in the skin and nerves leading, if untreated, to extensive deformities.
Word Family: **leprous,** *adjective.*

lesbian *noun*
a female homosexual.
Word Family: **lesbianism,** *noun.*
[after *Lesbos*, the Greek island home of Sappho, the ancient poet of lesbian love]

lèse-majesté (*say* lays-**majestay**) *noun*
1. *Law:* an offence against a monarch or other ruler.
2. (*informal*) irreverence to someone who is, or thinks he is, important.

lesion (*say* **lee**-*zh*'n) *noun*
an injury or wound, especially a scarring of internal tissue.
[Latin *laesionis* of an injury]

less *adjective*
not as much in size, amount or degree: 'we try to buy *less* expensive meat to save money'.
less *preposition*
minus: 'seven *less* two is five'.
Word Family: **less**, *adverb*, *noun*; **lessen**, *verb*, to make or become less.

-less
a suffix used to form adjectives from nouns and verbs and meaning without, as in *friendless.*

lessee (*say* less-**ee**) *noun*
a person to whom a lease is granted.

lesser *adjective*
smaller.

lesson *noun*
1. a) something to be learnt or studied: 'I have some *lessons* to do tonight'. b) something which is learnt or taught: 'the accident has taught me a *lesson*'. c) something from which one learns or should learn: 'let that be a *lesson* to you'.
2. a period of time in which a pupil or group of pupils is taught one particular subject: 'a maths *lesson*'.
3. *Christian:* a passage from the Bible read aloud during a religious service.
Word Family: **lesson**, *verb*, to reprove.

lessor (*say* less-**or**) *noun*
a person who grants a lease.

lest *conjunction*
1. so that it is impossible that: '*lest* we forget'.
2. that: 'she was frightened *lest* the vandals should return'.

let (1) *verb*
(**let, letting**)
1. to allow or permit: 'please *let* me come with you!'.
2. to rent or hire: 'rooms to *let*'.
3. to make or cause to: 'do *let* us know your decision'.
4. an auxiliary verb indicating intention or suggestion: a) '*let's* go'; b) '*let* us pray'; c) '*let* him get on with it, then'.
Phrases:
let alone, 'I'm too tired to walk, *let alone* run' (= not to mention).
let down, a) 'will you *let down* the blinds?' (= lower); b) 'he *let* us *down*' (= failed).
let off, a) 'I will *let* you *off* without punishment this time' (= excuse); b) 'he *let off* a series of crackers' (= exploded).
let on, (*informal*) 'please don't *let on* to mother about this' (= tell).
let out, a) 'she will *let out* the secret' (= reveal); b) 'he *let out* a cry of rage' (= gave); c) 'can you *let out* this dress at the seams?' (= make larger).
let up, 'the rain didn't *let up* for several days' (= stop).
let well alone, to leave things as they are.

let (2) *noun*
1. *Tennis:* a service which must be repeated because the ball has touched the net in passing.
2. an old word for an obstacle or obstruction: 'without *let* or hindrance'.

letdown *noun*
a disappointment or failure.

lethal (*say* **lee**-th'l) *adjective*
able to cause death.
Word Family: **lethally**, *adverb.*
[Latin *letum* death]

lethargic (*say* leth**ar**-jik) *adjective*
being sluggishly lazy or inactive.
Word Family: **lethargically**, *adverb*; **lethargy** (*say* **letha**-jee), *noun.*
[Greek *lethargos* forgetful]

letter *noun*
1. a written symbol or mark for a speech sound.
2. the actual or exact words, as distinct from the general meaning: 'you must obey these instructions to the *letter*'.
3. a written or printed message to a person or group.
4. (*plural*) literature as a profession or a culture: 'a man of *letters*'.
Word Family: **letter**, *verb*, to write with letters; **lettering**, *noun*, a) the act of writing with letters, b) the letters used; **lettered**, *adjective*, a) marked with letters, b) educated or cultured.
[Latin *littera* a letter of the alphabet]

letterbox *noun*
a) a fixed metal container in which letters are put to be collected and delivered. b) a box or opening at a house where letters are left by the postman.

letterhead *noun*
a) a printed heading on writing paper giving the name, address, etc. of the sender. b) a piece of paper with this heading.

letter of credit
plural is **letters of credit**
a letter from a bank authorizing a person to withdraw up to a specified amount from its branches or agents, or from specified banks overseas.

letter-perfect *adjective*
exactly correct or accurate.

letterpress *noun*
1. a method of printing directly from raised blocks of metal type, etc. It is the oldest and still most widely used method. Also called **relief printing**.
2. the text of a book as distinct from its illustrations.

letting *verb*
the present participle of the verb **let (1)**.

lettuce (*say* **lett**iss) *noun*
a large, green vegetable with many leaves forming a loose head, used in salads.
[Latin *lactuca*]

let-up *noun*
(*informal*) a relieving pause or cessation.

leucocyte (*say* **loo**ka-site) *noun*
see WHITE BLOOD CELL.
[Greek *leukos* white + *kytos* a vessel]

leucotomy (*say* loo-**kott**a-mee) *noun*
see LOBOTOMY.
[Greek *leukos* white + *tomé* a cutting]

leukaemia (*say* loo-**kee**mia) *noun*
in America spelt **leukemia**
an often fatal, cancerous disease causing excess production of white blood cells.
[Greek *leukos* white + *haima* blood]

levee (*say* **lev**vay) *noun*
1. a formal assembly of guests, usually at a palace.
2. *Geography:* a) a river bank formed by a river depositing silt layers when it is in flood. b) a man-made bank which surrounds an irrigated field or protects land from possible floodwaters.
[French *levé* rising, as originally held when the king rose from bed]

level *noun*
1. a position, especially in relation to others: 'he was promoted to the highest *level* of authority'.
Usages:
a) 'his painting is still at an amateur *level*' (= stage).
b) 'she found her *level* among the older members of the class' (= most suitable place).
2. a horizontal line or position: 'tilt that shelf to bring it back to *level*'.
3. an instrument to check or indicate the horizontal.
on the level, 'are you sure that his promise was *on the level*?' (= honest).
level *adjective*
1. having a flat, smooth surface.
2. being at the same height as something else.
3. horizontal.
Usage: 'they're *level* in most subjects' (= equal).
one's level best, one's utmost.
level *verb*
(**levelled**, **levelling**)
1. to make or become level or equal: a) 'the bricklayer *levelled* the ground before starting the wall'; b) 'the scores *levelled* at 10 all'.
2. a) to aim or point: 'the hijacker *levelled* a gun at the hostage'. b) to put forward: 'the police *levelled* a charge against the youth'.
Word Family: **leveller**, *noun*, a person or thing that levels or makes even; **levelly**, *adverb*; **levelness**, *noun*.

level crossing
a place where a road crosses a railway line.

level-headed *adjective*
sensible or calm.

lever (*say* **lee**va) *noun*
1. any device consisting of a rigid bar pivoted on a fixed point, called the **fulcrum** and used to raise or move a weight.
2. a handle used to operate a mechanism: 'a *gearlever*'.
Usage: 'he used his illness as a *lever* to gain sympathy' (= means).
leverage (*say* **lee**va-rij) *noun*
a) the action of a lever. b) the power or movement provided by a lever.
Word Family: **lever**, *verb*, to move with or apply a lever.
[French, to raise]

leveret (*say* **lev**va-rit) *noun*
a young hare.
[Latin *leporis* of a hare]

leviathan (*say* lev-**eye**-a-th'n) *noun*
anything which is very large, especially in the sea.

[after *Leviathan* an unidentifiable sea-monster mentioned in the Old Testament]

levis (*say* **lee**-vize) *plural noun*
heavy-duty jeans, originally reinforced with copper studs.
[after *Levi Strauss* who made them for Californian goldminers in the 1860s]

levitation (*say* levvi-**tay**-sh'n) *noun*
the act of rising into the air without physical support.
Word Family: **levitate**, *verb*.
[Latin *levis* light]

levity (*say* **levvi**-tee) *noun*
a light-heartedness or frivolity.

levy (*say* **lev**-ee) *verb*
(**levied, levying**)
1. to impose or collect, with the use of authority or force: 'a new tax was *levied* on alcohol'.
2. a) to conscript an army. b) to make or declare (war).
Word Family: **levy**, *noun*, a) a raising or collecting, as of taxes, b) something which is raised or collected.
[French *lever* to raise]

lewd *adjective*
obscene or exciting lust.
Word Family: **lewdly**, *adverb*; **lewdness**, *noun*.

lexicography (*say* leksi-**kogra**-fee) *noun*
the art of writing dictionaries.
Word Family: **lexicographer**, *noun*; **lexicographic** (*say* leksi-ka-**graffik**), **lexicographical**, *adjective*.

lexicon *noun*
a) a dictionary, especially of ancient Greek. b) a vocabulary list.
Word Family: **lexical**, *adjective*.
[Greek *lexikon* (*biblion*) a word (-book)]

lexis (*say* **leksis**) *noun*
all the words in a language.

liability (*say* lie-a-**billi**-tee) *noun*
1. an obligation, especially a financial debt: 'the unemployed man could not meet all his *liabilities*'.
2. a handicap or disadvantage: 'long skirts are a *liability* in wet weather'.
3. the state of being liable or under an obligation: 'the company denied *liability* for the accident'.

liable (*say* **lie**-a-b'l) *adjective*
1. legally responsible: 'the company was declared *liable* and had to repay all the money'.
2. exposed or subject to: 'the coast is *liable* to storms in winter'.
Usage: 'we are all *liable* to exaggerate from time to time' (= likely).

liaison (*say* lee-**ay**-z'n) *noun*
a contact, connection or communication between people, groups, etc.: 'continual *liaison* between governments is essential to maintain good relationships'.
Word Family: **liaise**, *verb*, to maintain contact with.
[French]

liana (*say* lee-**ahna**) *noun*
a climbing plant or vine, especially of rain forests.

liar *noun*
a person who tells lies.

libation (*say* lie-**bay**-sh'n) *noun*
the pouring out of wine, etc. as a religious act in honour of a god.
[from Latin]

libel (*say* **lie**-b'l) *noun*
1. *Law:* a false, derogatory written, broadcast or printed statement against another person. Compare SLANDER.
2. any malicious or damaging statement.
Word Family: **libel** (**libelled, libelling**), *verb*; **libellous**, *adjective*; **libellously**, *adverb*; **libeller**, *noun*.

liberal (*say* **libba**-r'l) *adjective*
1. favouring progress, reform and individual freedom in social or political matters.
2. *British politics:* (*capital*) connected with the **Liberal Party**, formerly a large party: 'in the general election the two big parties withstood the *Liberal* challenge'.
3. generous or free in giving: 'she is very *liberal* with her praise of others'.
Usages:
a) 'he took a *liberal* serving of pie' (= large).
b) 'the play is a *liberal* translation of an ancient epic poem' (= broad, general).
c) 'a *liberal* education' (= comprehensive but not technical or scientific).
liberal *noun*
1. a person with liberal or tolerant views, especially in politics.
2. (*capital*) a member of the Liberal Party.
Word Family: **liberally**, *adverb*, freely or generously; **liberality** (*say* libba-**ralli**-tee), **liberalness**, *nouns*; **liberalism**, *noun*, any liberal principles,

especially in a political or religious movement.
[Latin *liberalis* pertaining to a free man]

liberalize (*say* **libba**-r'lize) **liberalise** *verb*
to make or become more liberal or free: 'many people have suggested that drug laws should be *liberalized*'.

liberate (*say* **libba**-rate) *verb*
to set free.
Word Family: **liberation,** *noun*; **liberator,** *noun*, a person who liberates.
[Latin *liber* free]

libertine (*say* **libba**-teen) *noun*
a person considered to be immoral or lacking restraint.
[Latin *libertinus* a freedman]

liberty (*say* **libba**-tee) *noun*
1. the state of being neither confined nor controlled: 'he gained his *liberty* after 37 years in prison'.
2. the power or right to do as one chooses: 'our parents allowed us total *liberty* at an early age'.
Usages:
a) 'officers were granted certain *liberties* denied to the other soldiers' (= privileges).
b) 'would it be a *liberty* to ask for another drink?' (= impertinent act).
at liberty, a) 'you are *at liberty* to do as you wish' (= permitted, privileged); b) 'the prisoners were *at liberty* for several days' (= out of captivity).

libidinous (*say* lib**biddi**-nus) *adjective*
full of lust or desires.
Word Family: **libidinously,** *adverb*; **libidinousness,** *noun.*

libido (*say* lib**bee**-doe) *noun*
1. *Psychology:* the energy resulting from the instincts of the id.
2. the vital impulse in living beings, especially sexual instinct.
[Latin, desire, caprice]

Libra (*say* **lee**-bra) *noun*
also called the **Balance**
Astrology: a group of stars, the seventh sign of the zodiac.
[Latin, a pair of scales]

librarian (*say* lie-**brairian**) *noun*
1. a person in charge of a library.
2. a person whose profession deals with the organization of books and other literary material in a library.
Word Family: **librarianship,** *noun.*

library (*say* **lie**-bra-ree) *noun*
a) a room or building where a collection of books is kept for people to read or borrow. b) any collection of books: 'he has a vast *library* of science fiction'.
[Latin *libraria* bookseller's shop, from *liber* book]

libretto *noun*
plural is **libretti** or **librettos**
the words or text of an opera.
Word Family: **librettist,** *noun,* a person who writes libretti.
[Italian]

lice *plural noun*
see LOUSE.

licence (*say* **lie**-sense) *noun*
in America spelt **license**
1. the permission to do something, especially formal or official permission. b) a document showing this permission: 'a driving *licence*'.
2. a deliberate avoidance of usual rules, etc. to achieve a particular effect: 'poetic *licence*'.
Usages:
a) 'the inexperienced teacher allowed his students too much *licence*' (= unrestrained liberty).
b) 'the King's court was famous for its gambling and *licence*' (= immorality).
Word Family: **license,** *verb,* to give permission or licence to; **licensee,** *noun,* a person to whom a licence is given, especially one to sell alcohol; **licentiate** (*say* lie-**sen**shi-it), *noun,* a person holding a licence to practise a particular profession.
[Latin *licentia* freedom, from *licet* it is permitted]

licentious (*say* lie-**sen**shus) *adjective*
sexually unrestrained.
Word Family: **licentiously,** *adverb*; **licentiousness,** *noun.*
[Latin *licentia* freedom abused, lawlessness]

lichee (*say* **lie**-chee) *noun*
see LYCHEE.

lichen (*say* **lie**-ken) *noun*
Biology: a plant formed by an association of a fungus and alga, often appearing as a light green growth on tree trunks, rocks, etc.
[Greek *leikhen*]

lick *verb*
to pass the tongue over: 'the dog *licked* the plate clean'.
Usages:
a) 'the flames *licked* the side of the house' (= touched lightly).
b) (*informal*) 'we easily *licked* the opposing team' (= defeated).

Phrases:
lick into shape, 'the sergeant swore he would *lick* the new recruits *into shape*' (= put into proper form or condition).
lick one's lips, 'he *licked his lips* at the thought of all that money' (= greedily anticipated).
Word Family: **lick**, *noun*, a) a stroke of the tongue, b) a light touch; **licking**, *noun*, (informal) a thrashing or defeat.

lickety-split *adverb*
(*informal*) at full speed.

licorice (*say* **likka**-riss *or* **likka**-rish) *noun*
see LIQUORICE.

lid *noun*
1. any movable cover for an opening or an open vessel, either detachable or hinged.
2. an eyelid.
flip one's lid, (*informal*) to lose one's temper, sanity, etc.
Word Family: **lidded**, *adjective*.

lie (1) *noun*
a statement known not to be true by the person who makes it.
give the lie to, 'her generosity *gives the lie to* her reputation as a miser' (= shows to be untrue).
Word Family: **lie** (**lied**, **lying**), *verb*, to make untrue statements.

lie (2) *verb*
(**lay**, **lain**, **lying**)
to recline or rest flat on something: a) 'the book *lay* on the table'; b) 'you can't *lie* in bed all day'.
Usages:
a) 'the money *lay* in the bank for 10 years' (= remained).
b) 'your whole future *lies* ahead of you' (= extends).
c) 'the fault *lies* in the steering wheel' (= exists).
Phrases:
lie low, 'the bandits *lay low* until the spring' (= hid).
take lying down, 'he *takes* anything you say to him *lying down*' (= accepts without protest).
lie *noun*
1. the position or direction in which something lies: 'the *lie* of the land'.
2. the place or den where a creature lurks.
Common Error: see LAY (1).

lieder (*say* **lee**-der) *plural noun*
singular is **lied**
songs or ballads.
[German]

lie-detector *noun*
a device to measure pulse and breathing rates, thought to increase when a person is lying.

lief (*say* leef) *adverb*
an old word meaning gladly or willingly: 'I would as *lief* starve as give way to him'.
[Old English *leof* dear]

liege (*say* leej) *noun*
an old word for a person who owes or receives homage or service.
liegeman *noun*
an old word for a person who serves, such as a subject or vassal.

lien (*say* **lee**-en) *noun*
Law: the right to keep someone else's property until a debt due on it is paid.
[French]

lieu (*say* loo) *noun*
in lieu of, 'I gave him my bicycle *in lieu of* actual cash' (= instead of).
[French *au lieu de* in place of]

lieutenant (*say* lef-**tennent**) *noun*
1. a commissioned officer in the army ranking between a second lieutenant and a captain.
2. a commissioned officer in the navy ranking between a sublieutenant and a lieutenant commander.
3. a deputy or substitute: 'when the boss is away I act as his *lieutenant*'.
Word Family: **lieutenancy**, *noun*, the office of a lieutenant.
[French *lieu* place + *tenant* holding]

lieutenant colonel
a commissioned officer in the army ranking between a major and a colonel.

lieutenant commander
a commissioned officer in the navy ranking between a lieutenant and a commander.

lieutenant general
a commissioned officer in the army, ranking between a general and a major general.

life *noun*
plural is **lives**
1. the condition of growth and reproduction that distinguishes plants and animals from earth, stones, etc.
2. an individual's existence: 'many *lives* were lost in the earthquake'.
3. the period of an individual's existence between birth and death: 'in my early *life* I was only interested in football'.

Usages:
a) 'there is no evidence of *life* on Mars' (= living organisms).
b) 'the *life* of a car engine' (= period of effectiveness or usefulness).
c) 'there doesn't seem to be much *life* in this town' (= activity, interest).
d) 'these people have a very hard *life*' (= style or condition of living).
e) 'he wrote a *life* of Rasputin' (= biography).
f) 'he was sentenced to *life* on Devil's Island' (= the maximum term of imprisonment).
Phrases:
for the life of one, 'I can't *for the life of me* remember her name' (= no matter how hard I try).
not on your life, certainly not, never.
take one's life in one's hands, to risk death.

life assurance
an insurance providing payment of a specified sum of money when the person who is insured reaches a certain age or dies. Compare INSURANCE.

lifebelt *noun*
a small buoyant belt worn to keep a person afloat in the water.

lifeblood (*say* **life**-blud) *noun*
something which is necessary to maintain life: 'exports are this country's *lifeblood*'.

lifeboat *noun*
a) a boat based on the coast and equipped to rescue people or vessels in trouble at sea. b) a boat carried on a ship's deck for use in a shipwreck.

lifebuoy (*say* **life**-boy) *noun*
a ring or other object made of buoyant material to assist a person to remain afloat in the water.

life-class *noun*
an art class practising painting or drawing from a living model.

life cycle
Biology: the whole span of life of an organism through its various changes of form, e.g. egg, larva, chrysalis and imago in the butterfly.

life expectancy
the predictable life span according to sex, race, habitat, etc.

life guard
1. see LIFESAVER.
2. (*usually capitals*) a member of a monarch's escort, especially The Life Guards regiment of the Household Cavalry.

life-jacket *noun*
a buoyant garment worn to keep a person afloat in the water.

lifeless *adjective*
a) no longer alive: 'they carried his *lifeless* body away'. b) having no living things: 'the moon is *lifeless*'.
Usage: 'the pop group gave a *lifeless* performance' (= dull, spiritless).
Word Family: **lifelessly**, *adverb*; **lifelessness**, *noun*.

lifelike *adjective*
resembling real life: 'a *lifelike* portrait'.
Word Family: **lifelikeness**, *noun*.

lifeline *noun*
a rope connecting people to each other or to an object, used in a dangerous situation such as mountain climbing or deep-sea diving.
Usage: 'a *lifeline* across the mountains was set up to get supplies to the refugees' (= only means of communication).

lifelong *adjective*
lasting or continuing through the period of a lifetime: 'a *lifelong* friendship'.

life peer
a peer whose title is not hereditary.

life-preserver *noun*
1. a lifebelt or a jacket to keep a person afloat in the water.
2. a stick with a heavy knob, kept by a householder for self-defence.

lifer *noun*
(*informal*) someone serving a life sentence of imprisonment.

lifesaver *noun*
also called a **lifeguard**
a person who rescues and gives first aid to swimmers in danger of drowning.

life span
the usual or expected period between birth and death.

lifetime *noun*
the length of a person's life: 'we had seen nothing like it in our *lifetime*'.

lift *verb*
to raise something to a higher position or level: a) '*lift* this box from the floor onto the table'; b) 'the new manager has *lifted* production by 30 per cent'.
Usages:
a) 'the mist should *lift* soon' (= rise).
b) 'the ban on radios in school has been *lifted*' (= removed).

c) (*informal*) 'he *lifted* a block of chocolate from the shop' (= stole).
d) 'our spirits *lifted* when we saw the sky begin to clear' (= improved).
lift *noun*
1. the act of lifting: 'give me a *lift* onto the table'.
2. a box-like device for moving people or goods vertically between different levels, as in a large store.
3. any upward force, especially that produced by air passing around an aircraft's wings.
Usages:
a) 'give me a *lift* into town in your car' (= ride).
b) 'the drink gave me a well-needed *lift*' (= feeling of well-being).
Word Family: **lifter,** *noun.*

lift-off *noun*
also called **blast-off**
the moment at which a rocket leaves its launching pad.

ligament (*say* **ligga**-m'nt) *noun*
Anatomy: any sheet or band of tough, fibrous tissue connecting parts of the body such as bone joints.
[Latin *ligare* to bind]

ligature (*say* **ligga**-cher) *noun*
1. a) a thread used for tying blood vessels. b) any material used for tying or binding, such as a bandage.
2. a pair of letters cast in one piece of type, such as fl, ff.

light (1) (*say* lite) *noun*
1. a) the medium which makes things visible, such as the radiance from the sun. b) any of various objects or devices for making things visible: 'an electric *light*'.
2. *Physics:* the form of electromagnetic radiation with a frequency of about 10^{12} Hz, to which the human eye is sensitive. Photographic materials may be sensitive to the frequencies immediately above (**ultraviolet**) or below (**infra-red**) the visible range.
Usages:
a) 'the *light* died out of her eyes' (= brightness).
b) 'now I see things in a new *light*' (= aspect).
c) 'this boy is our brightest *light*' (= example, inspiration).
d) 'try to get home while it's still *light*' (= daylight).
e) 'the *lights* changed when I was halfway across' (= traffic lights).
f) 'he gave me a *light* for my cigar' (= match, flame).
Phrases:
come to light, 'new information has *come to light*' (= been revealed).
in the light of, '*in the light of* your previous good behaviour, we shall let you off this time' (= because of).
see the light, 'it was years before I *saw the light*' (= realized the truth).
throw light on, 'perhaps you can *throw light on* this mystery' (= help to solve).
light *adjective*
a) well supplied with light: 'the room is very *light* with the blinds up'. b) pale: 'she wore a *light* green dress'.
light *verb*
(**lit** or **lighted, lighting**)
1. to give light to: a) 'the fire *lit* the whole room'; b) 'the moon will *light* your way'.
2. to kindle or set burning.
light up, 'his face *lit up* in a huge grin' (= brightened).
Word Family: **lightness,** *noun.*

light (2) (*say* lite) *adjective*
1. not heavy or having little weight.
2. not heavy or strong in force or intensity: a) 'a *light* rain fell'; b) 'he has a *light* sleep after lunch'.
Usages:
a) 'he is very *light* on his feet' (= nimble, agile).
b) 'here is some *light* reading for the trip' (= not serious, easy).
c) 'she gave a *light* laugh' (= carefree).
d) 'the grocer has given me 3 oranges *light*' (= short).
e) 'my head feels very *light* this morning' (= dizzy).
3. producing goods relatively easy to manufacture and ready for immediate consumption when finished: '*light* industry'.
make light of, to treat or consider as of little importance.
light *adverb*
travel light, to travel with a minimum of luggage.
Word Family: **lightly,** *adverb*; **lightness,** *noun.*

light (3) (*say* lite) *verb*
(**lighted** or **lit, lighting**)
to come across by chance or accident: 'to *light* upon a clue'.

light ale
a weak beer of low specific gravity.

lighten (1) *verb*
to make or become less dark: 'the dawn *lightened* the sky'.

lighten (2) *verb*
to make or become less heavy.

lighter (1) *noun*
a mechanical device for lighting cigarettes, cigars, etc.

lighter (2) *noun*
a barge.

light-fingered *adjective*
skilful with the fingers, especially at thieving or picking pockets.

light-headed *adjective*
1. not thoughtful or serious: 'only a *light-headed* person laughs at good advice'.
2. dizzy or drunk: 'we felt *light-headed* after the roller-coaster ride'.
Word Family: **light-headedly**, *adverb*; **light-headedness**, *noun.*

light-hearted *adjective*
cheerful or carefree.
Word Family: **light-heartedly**, *adverb*; **light-heartedness**, *noun.*

lighthouse *noun*
a tower, clearly seen from the sea, with a strong light to guide ships, etc.

lighting *noun*
1. the act or process of igniting or illuminating: 'hurry up or you'll miss the *lighting* of the bonfire'.
2. an arrangement of lights: 'the *lighting* of the play produced good effects'.

light meter
Photography: see EXPOSURE METER under EXPOSURE.

lightness (1) *noun*
Word Family: see LIGHT (1).

lightness (2) *noun*
Word Family: see LIGHT (2).

lightning *noun*
a brilliant flash of light in the sky caused by the discharge of natural electricity.
Word Family: **lightning**, *adjective*, extremely fast.

lightning arrester
Electricity: a device protecting electrical equipment, e.g. telephone lines, by reducing the high voltage surges from lightning strikes.

lightning conductor
a metal rod or wire attached to a building, to protect it from lightning damage by earthing it.

light relief
also called **comic relief**
Theatre: an amusing or light-hearted interlude during a serious play, to reduce the tension.

lights *plural noun*
the butcher's name for the lungs of sheep or pigs.

lightship *noun*
a ship with bright lights, anchored in one place to help guide other vessels.

lightweight *adjective*
having little weight.
Usage: 'I only have some *lightweight* objections to your plan' (= minor).
lightweight *noun*
1. a weight division in boxing, equal to about 60 kg.
2. (*informal*) a person of little influence or importance.

light-year *noun*
a unit of length used in astronomy, equal to about $9{\cdot}46 \times 10^{15}$ m, being the distance that light travels in one year.
See UNITS in grey pages.

ligneous (*say* **ligni**-us) *adjective*
woody.
[Latin *lignum* wood]

lignin *noun*
an organic substance which, with cellulose, forms the main part of wood and is usually present in cell walls.

lignite *noun*
see BROWN COAL.

like (1) *preposition*
1. in the same way as or having a close resemblance to: a) 'he acts *like* a baby'; b) 'she is *like* her mother'.
2. used to introduce emphasis, etc: 'it rained *like* anything'.
Usages:
a) 'it would be just *like* her to do that' (= typical of).
b) 'things *like* tables and chairs are needed' (= such as).
c) 'it seems *like* an excellent idea' (= probably).
d) 'right now I feel *like* a good meal' (= as though I need).
like *noun*
a match or equal: 'I've never heard the *like* of such language before'.
the like, 'tables, chairs and *the like*' (= similar things).
like *adjective*
similar in form or character: 'the two machines perform *like* functions'.

like (2) *verb*
to be fond of or find agreeable: 'I should *like* to go now'.
Usage: 'come whenever you *like*' (= wish).

Word Family: **like,** *noun,* a preference or something of which one is fond; **likable** (*say* **like**–a–b'l), **likeable,** *adjective,* easily liked.

–like
a suffix indicating a similarity to, as in *childlike.*

likely *adjective*
1. probable: 'it is *likely* that it will rain this evening'.
2. suitable or reasonable: 'this is a *likely* spot for catching fish'.
Usage: 'she is one of our most *likely* students' (= promising).
a likely story!, a sarcastic expression of disbelief.
likely *adverb*
probably: 'I shall very *likely* be there'.
Word Family: **likelihood, likeliness,** *nouns,* probability.

liken (*say* **lie**–k'n) *verb*
an old word meaning to compare: 'he *likened* his house to a palace'.

likeness *noun*
1. a resemblance: 'there is a close *likeness* between the brothers'.
2. an old word meaning a portrait.

likewise *adverb*
a) also or as well: 'the boys behaved badly and *likewise* the girls'. b) in the same way: 'you've seen how I did it, now go and do *likewise*'.

liking (say **like**–ing) *noun*
a feeling of attraction or a preference.

lilac (*say* **lie**–l'k) *noun*
1. a light purple colour.
2. a deciduous garden shrub with spikes of fragrant purple or white flowers.
Word Family: **lilac,** *adjective.*
[Persian *lilak* bluish]

lilt *noun*
a pleasant, rhythmic change in pitch in a voice, tune, etc.: 'he still speaks with an Irish *lilt*'.
Word Family: **lilt,** *verb,* to sing, speak, etc., with a lilt.

lily (*say* lillee) *noun*
any of a group of plants with trumpet-shaped flowers of various colours, growing from a bulb.
[from Latin]

lily-livered *adjective*
cowardly.

lily-of-the-valley *noun*
plural is **lilies-of-the-valley**
a small stemless plant with many white, bell-shaped, fragrant flowers, growing from a rhizome.

limb (*say* lim) *noun*
a) a leg, arm or wing of an animal. b) any part which projects or extends, such as the branch of a tree.
Usage: 'this office is a *limb* of the parent company' (= extension).
out on a limb, isolated in an awkward predicament from which there is no going back.

limber (*say* **limba**) *adjective*
supple or lithe.
limber *verb*
limber up, 'come into the gym and *limber up*' (= do exercises, etc.)

limbo *noun*
Christian: the place on the edge of hell, formerly designated as suitable for the souls of the just who lived before Christ, and for those of unbaptized infants.
Usage: 'like many another deposed military dictator he now lives in *limbo*' (= oblivion).
[Latin *limbus* border or edge]

lime (1) *noun*
calcium oxide, a white powder (formula CaO), used in cements, mortars, making other calcium compounds and as a fertilizer in soil.
Word Family: **lime,** *verb,* to add lime to soil as a fertilizer.

lime (2) *noun*
a green citrus fruit, similar to a lemon but smaller and more bitter.
[Arabic]

limelight *noun*
1. the glare of publicity: 'the pop group will do anything to stay in the *limelight*'.
2. the brilliant white light used in stage lighting.

limerick (*say* **limma**–rik) *noun*
a five-line nonsense verse with strict rules of metre and rhyme, as in:
There was a young man of Calcutta
Who had a most terrible stutter.
He said p. p. please
Pass the ch. ch. ch. cheese
And the b. b. b. b. b. b. butter.
[from an Irish chorus, 'will you come up to *Limerick*?']

limestone *noun*
Geology: a sedimentary rock composed of calcium carbonate, often formed from the shells and skeletons of tiny organisms.

lime tree
also called a **linden**

a deciduous tree with smooth, heart-shaped leaves and fragrant, yellow flowers, but not bearing fruit.

limewater *noun*
a clear solution of calcium hydroxide (formula $Ca(OH)_2$) in water. It becomes milky on contact with carbon dioxide.

limey (*say* **lie**–mee) *noun*
American: (*informal*) an Englishman. [from the former use of *limes* on British ships to prevent scurvy]

limit *noun*
1. the furthest point that is possible or allowable: a) 'there is a *limit* to what we may spend'; b) 'what is the *speed-limit*?'.
2. a boundary: 'this is the *limit* of my land'.
Phrases:
off limits, forbidden to military personnel except on official business.
the limit, 'that boy down the road is really *the limit*' (= an intolerable person).
limit *verb*
to restrict by imposing a limit: 'I *limit* you to 3 chocolates each'.
Word Family: **limitation**, *noun*, a) the act of limiting, b) a restriction or shortcoming.
[Latin *limitis* of a frontier]

limited (*say* **lim**–it–id) *adjective*
confined or restricted: a) 'the work must be done in a *limited* time'; b) 'I feel very *limited* having to live in a tent'.
limited liability company, limited company, a company in which the liability of the owners (the shareholders) is limited to the face value of their shares.
Word Family: **limitedness**, *noun.*

limousine (*say* **limma**–zeen) *noun*
any large, luxurious car, especially if driven by a chauffeur.

limp (1) *verb*
to walk lamely or unevenly: 'the injured dog *limped* across the road'.
Word Family: **limp**, *noun*, a lame walk; **limpingly**, *adverb.*

limp (2) *adjective*
not stiff or firm: 'this old celery is very *limp*'.
Word Family: **limply**, *adverb*; **limpness**, *noun.*

limpet *noun*
any of a group of marine snails with a flat, conical shell which is open underneath.

limpid *adjective*
clear or transparent.
Word Family: **limpidly**, *adverb*; **limpidity** (*say* limpiddi–tee), *noun.*
[from Latin]

linchpin *noun*
1. a person or thing that is essential to success.
2. a metal peg in an axle which keeps a cart-wheel in its place.

linden *noun*
see LIME TREE.

line (1) *noun*
1. a long narrow mark made on a surface: 'he drew a *line* right across the page'.
2. a) a row: 'a *line* of trees'. b) a single row of words forming a verse in poetry.
3. a length of cord, wire, rope, etc.: a) 'a telephone *line*'; b) 'a clothes *line*'.
Usages:
a) 'her face had deep *lines* of worry' (= wrinkles).
b) 'what *line* is your father in?' (= work, business).
c) 'he supports a conservative *line*' (= policy).
d) 'this old church has splendid *lines*' (= outward shape).
e) 'she forgot her *lines* in the play' (= speech).
f) 'the major inspected the *lines* at dawn' (= camp).
g) 'I was thinking along the same *lines* as you' (= courses of thought).
h) 'he sells groceries and other food *lines*' (= goods).
i) 'the shipping *line* is on strike' (= company).
j) 'drop me a *line* while you are away' (= note, short letter).
k) 'they slipped behind the enemy *line* at nightfall' (= position).
l) 'that car salesman has a good *line* of sales-talk' (= style).
m) 'after that the family *line* died out' (= lineage).
n) 'the work was conceived along heroic *lines*' (= plan of execution, construction, etc.).
Phrases:
bring into line, 'I shall have to *bring* you *into line*' (= make conform).
draw the line at, 'I *draw the line at* washing the dishes as well as cooking' (= refuse).
hard lines!, bad luck!
read between the lines, to discover the real meaning in what a person writes or says.
toe the line, see TOE.

the line
the equator.
line *verb*
a) to mark or trace with lines. b) to form a row.
line up, a) to form or take position in a row; b) 'whom have you *lined up* to take to the party?' (= arranged, organized).
[Latin *linea* a linen thread]

line (2) *verb*
to cover the inner side of something: 'the coat was *lined* with fur'.

lineage (*say* **linnee**–ij) *noun*
a) ancestry or descent: 'he is a man of noble *lineage*'. b) any persons in a line of descent from a common ancestor.
Word Family: **lineal** (*say* **linnee**–ul), *adjective*, in the direct line of descent.

lineament (*say* **linnia**–m'nt) *noun*
a distinctive feature or characteristic.

linear (*say* **linnia**) *adjective*
1. a) pertaining to lines or length: 'a metre is a *linear* measure'. b) arranged in a line: 'a *linear* sequence'.
2. *Maths:* a) of the first degree. b) having the properties of a line.
Word Family: **linearly**, *adverb*; **lineate**, *adjective*, marked with lines.

linen (*say* **linnin**) *noun*
a) a yarn or fabric made from flax. b) clothes or other articles, such as sheets, made from linen.
wash one's dirty linen in public, 'we don't want to *wash our dirty linen in public*' (= let everyone know our discreditable secrets).

liner (*say* **line**–a) *noun*
a large passenger ship.

line–up *noun*
an arrangement of people or things in a line, for inspection, participation in a game, etc.

ling *noun*
1. a rather flavourless fish resembling cod, usually salted.
2. see HEATHER.

linger (*say* **linga**) *verb*
1. to remain or be unwilling to leave: 'you can't *linger* here after hours'.
2. to dawdle: 'to *linger* along the way'.
3. to continue only weakly: 'the old man's hope *lingered* on for a few more days'.
Word Family: **lingering**, *adjective*, long, protracted; **lingeringly**, *adverb*.

lingerie (*say* **lonja**–ree) *noun*
women's underwear.
[French, linen goods]

lingo (*say* **lin**–go) *noun*
(*informal*) a language, especially one which you don't understand: 'I would like to visit France but I can't speak the *lingo*'.
[from LINGUA FRANCA]

lingua franca (*say* ling–wa **franka**)
any language, such as pidgin English, known by and used between people of different nations as a general medium of communication.
[Italian, Frankish language]

lingual (*say* **ling**–wal) *adjective*
a) of or relating to the tongue. b) of or relating to languages.
[Latin *lingua* tongue]

linguist (*say* **ling**–wist) *noun*
a person who studies or speaks foreign languages.
linguistics (*say* ling–**wistiks**) *plural noun*
(*used with singular verb*) the science and study of language.
Word Family: **linguistic**, *adjective*, relating to language.

liniment (*say* **linna**–m'nt) *noun*
any liquid, usually an oil, used to rub into the skin for sprains, etc.
[Latin *linere* to anoint]

lining (*say* **lie**–ning) *noun*
a layer of material on the inside of something: 'the coat's *lining* was made of fur'.

link *noun*
1. a loop or ring forming part of a chain.
2. anything which forms part of a connected series: 'you've discovered the weak *link* in his argument'.
3. any bond or connection: 'the *link* between music and art'.
Word Family: **link**, *verb*, to join; **link–up**, *noun*, a connection.

linkage (*say* **linkij**) *noun*
1. the act of linking.
2. *Biology:* the association of two or more hereditary characters due to the association of their genes on the same chromosome. The nearer the genes are to each other the closer the linkage.

links *plural noun*
see GOLF COURSE.

linnet *noun*
a small finch with a red forehead, partial to linseed.
[Latin *linum* flax]

linocut (*say* **lie**–no–kut) *noun*
a print made by cutting a design into a sheet of linoleum.

linoleum (*say* lin–**o**–lee–um) *noun*
short form is **lino**
a smooth, strong floor covering made of canvas treated with cork, oil and colouring.
[Latin *linum* flax + *oleum* oil]

linotype (*say* **lie**–no–tipe) *noun*
a printing machine which composes type in solid lines (called slugs), used in printing newspapers.
[a trademark, for *line of type*]

linseed (*say* **lin**–seed) *noun*
the seed of flax, from which oil is obtained.

lint *noun*
a) a soft material made from linen, used for covering wounds, etc. b) any bits of thread or fluff.

lintel *noun*
a horizontal support over a door or window.

lion *noun*
1. a large, flesh–eating Asian and African mammal of the cat family, the male having a shaggy mane around its neck and shoulders.
2. *Astrology:* (*capital*) see LEO.
lion's share, 'John always grabs the *lion's share* of the cake' (= largest portion).
Word Family: **lioness,** *noun,* a female lion; **lionize, lionise,** *verb,* to treat as a celebrity.
[Greek *leon*]

lion–hearted *adjective*
brave or fearless.

lip *noun*
1. *Anatomy:* either of the two fleshy parts forming the front of the mouth.
2. something which has the shape or function of a lip: 'the *lip* of a milk jug'.
3. (*informal*) impudence: 'that's enough of your *lip*'.
stiff upper lip, 'keep a *stiff upper lip*' (= show of fortitude).
Word Family: **lip (lipped, lipping),** *verb,* (Golf) to hit the ball around the rim of the hole.

lipid (*say* **lip**–id) *noun*
also spelt **lipide** (*say* **lip**–ide)
any fat, especially one which cannot be dissolved in water.
[Greek *lipos* animal fat]

lip–read (*say* **lip**–reed) *verb*
(lip–read (*say* **lip**–red), **lip–reading)**
to understand speech by watching the lip movements of the speaker.

lip–service *noun*
an insincere expression of affection, loyalty, etc.

lipstick *noun*
a stick of waxy or paste–like lip colouring.

liquefy (*say* **lik**wi–fie) *verb*
(liquefied, liquefying)
to make or become liquid.
Word Family: **liquefaction** (*say* likwi–**fak**–sh'n), *noun;* **liquefier,** *noun.*

liquescent (*say* lik–**wessent**) *adjective*
melting or becoming liquid.
Word Family: **liquescence, liquescency,** *noun.*
[from Latin]

liqueur (*say* lee–**kewer**) *noun*
a strong, sweet, alcoholic drink, usually drunk from a small glass after meals.

liquid (*say* **lik**–wid) *noun*
Physics: a substance with a definite volume but taking the shape of the space in which it is kept. Compare GAS and SOLID.
liquid *adjective*
1. of or in the form of a liquid: '*liquid* food'.
Usages:
a) 'the dancer's movements were *liquid* and graceful' (= flowing).
b) 'her *liquid* voice filled the small room' (= smooth and clear).
c) 'the girl had beautiful skin and large, *liquid* eyes' (= shining, bright).
2. *Commerce:* able to be easily exchanged for cash: '*liquid* assets'.
Word Family: **liquidly,** *adverb;* **liquidness,** *noun;* **liquidize, liquidise,** *verb.*

liquidate (*say* **lik**wi–date) *verb*
a) to pay or settle a debt. b) to conclude the dealings of a business by using the assets to pay the debts.
Usage: 'an assassin was hired to *liquidate* the gang's enemies' (= murder).
Word Family: **liquidation,** *noun;* **liquidator,** *noun,* a person appointed to conclude the dealings of a company.
[Latin *liquidus* fluid]

liquidity (*say* lik–**widdi**–tee) *noun*
the state of having cash or assets which may be easily exchanged for cash.

liquid petroleum gas
a mixture of gaseous products of petroleum refining, mainly propane

and butane, stored under pressure and used as a fuel, e.g. Calor gas.

liquor (*say* **likk**er) *noun*
1. any alcoholic drink, especially one made by distillation rather than fermentation.
2. a solution of a substance in water or alcohol.

liquorice (*say* **likk**a-riss *or* **likk**a-rish) *noun*
also spelt **licorice**
a) a plant found in Europe and Asia, with blue flowers and a sweet, flavoured root. b) the dried root, used to make sweets or flavouring.
[Greek *glykys* sweet + *rhiza* root]

lira (*say* **leer**a) *noun*
plural is **lire** (*say* **leer**i)
the main unit of money in Italy.
[Latin *libra* pound]

lisle (*rhymes with* pile) *noun*
a fine, smooth twisted cotton thread, formerly used to make stockings, etc.
[after *Lille* (formerly *Lisle*) in France]

lisp *noun*
a speech defect in which 's' and 'z' are pronounced as 'th'.
Word Family: **lisp**, *verb*.

lissom *adjective*
also spelt **lissome**
supple or graceful.
Word Family: **lissomness**, *noun*.
[for *lithesome*]

list (1) *noun*
a number of things, such as names or numbers, set down or stated one after the other: 'I must make a *list* of things to buy'.
list price
the price of an article as shown in a catalogue.
Word Family: **list**, *verb*, to make or put on a list.

list (2) *verb*
(of a ship) to lean over to one side.
Word Family: **list**, *noun*.

list (3) *verb*
an old word for listen.

listen (*say* **liss**en) *verb*
to pay attention to sound: 'we *listened* to the speech with great interest'.
listen in, a) to eavesdrop; b) to listen to a broadcast.
Word Family: **listener**, *noun*, a person who listens, especially to radio.

listless *adjective*
having no energy or interest: 'a *listless* reply'.
Word Family: **listlessly**, *adverb*; **listlessness**, *noun*.

lit (1) *verb*
a past tense and past participle of the verb **light (1)**.

lit (2) *verb*
a past tense and past participle of the verb **light (3)**.

litany (*say* **litt**a-nee) *noun*
Christian: a form of prayer consisting of a series of petitions said by the clergy, to which the congregation repeats a set response.
[Greek *litaneia* prayer]

liter (*say* **leet**a) *noun*
American: a litre.

literal (*say* **litt**a-r'l) *adjective*
corresponding exactly to the original: 'this is a *literal* translation of the French play'.
Usages:
a) 'she claims that her story was the *literal* truth' (= accurate, exact).
b) 'he has a very *literal* mind' (= matter-of-fact).
Word Family: **literal**, *noun*, a misprint; **literally**, *adverb*; **literalness**, *noun*.
[Latin *littera* letter of the alphabet]

literary (*say* **litt**era-ree) *adjective*
1. relating to books or literature: 'he has turned from art to *literary* criticism'.
2. having a knowledge of or fondness for literature.

literate (*say* **litt**a-rit) *adjective*
able to read and write.
Word Family: **literacy** (*say* **litt**era-see), *noun*.

literature (*say* **litt**era-cher) *noun*
1. a) any or all written works, especially those exhibiting creative imagination or artistic skill. b) poetry, fiction, essays, etc. as distinct from factual, journalistic or expository writing.
2. any printed material on a particular subject: 'travel *literature*'.

lithe (*say* li*the*) *adjective*
able to move or bend with ease.
Word Family: **lithely**, *adverb*; **litheness**, *noun*.

lithium *noun*
element number 3, a metal, the lightest known solid, used in alloys to make glass and ceramics. See ALKALI METAL. See CHEMICAL ELEMENTS in grey pages.
[Greek *litheios* of stone]

lithograph (*say* **litho**-graf) *noun*
a print, especially a picture, produced by drawing on a flat, specially prepared stone or metal surface from which ink impressions are taken.
Word Family: **lithography**, (*say* lith-**ogra**-fee), *noun*, the art or practice of producing lithographs; **lithographic**, (*say* litho-**graffik**), *adjective*; **lithographer**, *noun*.
[Greek *lithos* stone + *graphein* to write]

litigate (*say* **litti**-gate) *verb*
Law: to conduct a dispute before a court of law.
Word Family: **litigation**, *noun*; **litigant**, *noun*, a person taking part in a law case; **litigious** (*say* lit-**ij**-us), *adjective*, of, relating to or excessively fond of legal disputes.
[Latin *litigare* to go to law]

litmus *noun*
Chemistry: a soluble substance obtained from lichens, which turns red in acids and blue in alkalis, and is used as an indicator, usually in the form of paper.

litre (*say* **lee**ta) *noun*
a metric unit of volume for liquids, approximately a fifth of a gallon.
[Greek *litra* a unit of Sicilian currency]

litter *noun*
1. any rubbish or untidy mess, especially when left in a public place.
2. a number of offspring produced at one birth: 'a *litter* of puppies'.
3. a) a stretcher. b) a vehicle consisting of a couch mounted on a frame, often with a canopy, carried on poles by men or animals.
Word Family: **litter**, *verb*, to scatter objects or rubbish untidily; **litterbug**, *noun*, a person who litters public places, roads, etc.

little *adjective*
(**littler**, **littlest**; **less** or **lesser**, **least**)
small: 'what a cosy *little* room!'.
Usages:
a) 'she should be here in a *little* while' (= short).
b) 'we lived in the country when I was *little*' (= a child).
c) 'she tells you all the *little* details of her day at great length' (= petty, trivial).
little *adverb*
(**less**, **least**)
not much: 'we slept *little* on the exciting journey'.
Usage: '*little* did we know that the train had left early' (= not at all).
little *noun*
a small amount: 'may I have a *little* of your cake?'.
Usage: 'the sun rose a *little* after 5 o'clock' (= short time).
Phrases:
make little of, 'the teacher could *make little of* the essay' (= not understand).
think little of, to treat or regard as unimportant.
Word Family: **littleness**, *noun*.

little end
short form of **little end bearing**
the end of a connecting rod, attached by a gudgeon pin to a piston in internal combustion engines.

littoral *noun*
the coast or seashore.
Word Family: **littoral**, *adjective*.
[Latin *litoris* of the seashore]

liturgy (*say* **litta**-jee) *noun*
Christian: the ritual of public worship.
Word Family: **liturgical** (*say* lee-**terj**i-k'l), *adjective*.
[Greek *leitourgia* public duty, the priesthood]

live (1) (*say* liv) *verb*
to have life: 'how long do dogs usually *live*?'.
Usages:
a) 'that sight will *live* in my memory' (= remain, continue).
b) 'where do you *live* now?' (= have your home).
c) 'the survivors *lived* on berries and grasses' (= fed themselves).
d) 'how can you *live* on such a small income?' (= get by).
e) 'he *lives* according to his own standards' (= acts).
f) 'you haven't *lived* until you have travelled' (= had a full experience).
g) 'he really *lives* his religion' (= puts into practice in his life).
Phrases:
live down, 'how can I *live down* such a terrible failure?' (= cause to be forgotten).
live it up, 'they *lived it up* for three years until the money ran out' (= had an exciting or carefree time).
live up to, 'you must *live up to* your reputation' (= act according to).
Word Family: **livable**, **liveable**, *adjective*, a) suitable for living in, b) able to be endured.

live (2) (*say* live) *adjective*
1. living or having life: '*live* animals'.
Usages:
a) 'be careful not to touch those *live* coals' (= burning).

b) 'the election is no longer a *live* issue' (= interesting, current).
c) 'there are *live* bullets in that rifle' (= unexploded).
d) 'the group will give three *live* concerts' (= personal, not filmed or recorded).
e) 'she got an electric shock from a *live* wire' (= electrically charged).
2. *Radio, Television:* being broadcast at the same time as it is made: 'a *live* interview'.
Word Family: **live**, *adverb*, (of a radio or television programme) at the time of its happening.

livelihood *noun*
the means of maintaining or earning the money to live: 'fishing is not a very good *livelihood*, is it?'.

livelong (*say* **liv**–long) *adjective*
whole or complete: 'she sang and played the *livelong* day'.
[LIEF + LONG]

lively (*say* **live**–lee) *adjective*
full of energy or spirit: 'that's a very *lively* song'.
Word Family: **lively**, *adverb*, vigorously; **liveliness**, *noun*.

liven (*say* **lie**–ven) *verb*
to make or become more lively, cheerful, etc.

liver (*say* **livva**) *noun*
1. *Anatomy:* the large, dark red organ in the abdomen, which produces bile, removes wastes from the blood and controls the use of digested food.
2. a dark, reddish–brown colour.
Word Family: **liver**, *adjective*.

liver fluke
a parasitic tapeworm which lives in the bile ducts of sheep, cows, pigs and sometimes man.

liverish (*say* **livva**–rish) *adjective*
1. having a disorder of the liver.
2. disagreeable or bad–tempered.

liverwort (*say* **livva**–wort) *noun*
Biology: any of a group of small, green, moss–like plants growing in damp areas.

livery (*say* **livva**–ree) *noun*
1. the distinctive clothes, emblems or uniform worn by a particular group, as those formerly worn by the servants of a feudal noble's house.
2. the care and feeding of horses for money.
[Old French *livrée* a gift of clothes from a master to a servant]

livery stable
a place where horses and vehicles are looked after and hired out for money.
Word Family: **liveryman**, *noun*, a person who works in a livery stable.

livestock (*say* **live**–stok) *noun*
short form is **stock**
all the horses, cattle, sheep, etc. kept on a farm.

live wire
an energetic or vivacious person.

livid (*say* **livvid**) *adjective*
1. having a discoloured or bluish area, such as a bruise.
2. (*informal*) very angry.
[Latin *lividus* leaden in colour, spiteful]

living (*say* **liv**–ing) *adjective*
1. having life: 'a *living* being'.
2. of or used for living: 'a *living* allowance was provided for many students'.
Usages:
a) 'he is one of the greatest poets in *living* memory' (= current).
b) 'is Christianity still a *living* faith?' (= active).
c) 'is Latin still a *living* language?' (= in use, existent).
d) 'that picture is the *living* image of him' (= lifelike, real).
living *noun*
1. the manner or condition of life: 'city *living* creates many pressures'.
2. a livelihood: 'how do you earn your *living*?'.

living room
also called a **lounge** or a **sitting room**
a room in a house used by members of a family for relaxing, entertaining, etc.

lizard (*say* **lizzud**) *noun*
any of various small to medium–sized reptiles, usually having four legs, slender bodies and long tails.

llama (*say* **lahma**) *noun*
a camel–like, South American mammal, valued for its thick fleecy wool and its use as a pack animal. See GUANACO.
[Spanish]

lo *interjection*
an old word meaning look.

load (*rhymes with* road) *noun*
1. an object, weight or quantity which is carried or supported.
Usages:
a) 'you have taken a *load* off my mind' (= burden).

b) 'looking after five young children puts a big *load* on you' (= responsibility).
c) 'we all ate *loads* of food at the party' (= a lot, a large amount).
2. the resistance overcome by an engine.
3. *Electricity:* the power demand made upon an electrical device.
get a load of, (*informal*) to listen to or look at.
load *verb*
1. to put a load or weight on: 'they *loaded* the truck with crates of fruit'.
Usages:
a) 'the soldiers all *loaded* their guns at once' (= filled with ammunition).
b) 'grandmother *loaded* us with presents' (= oversupplied).
2. *Insurance:* to add to the normal premium in a case where the risk is considered to be above average.
load the dice, a) to make dice heavier on one side so that they will often land in a certain way; b) to place in a particularly favourable or unfavourable position.
Word Family: **loading**, *noun*, a) the act of a person or thing that loads, b) something which is added on, such as an additional charge on an insurance premium; **loader**, *noun*.

loaded *adjective*
carrying a load.
Usages:
a) (*informal*) 'you can see by their expensive car that they are *loaded*' (= very rich).
b) 'a *loaded* gun lay beside the hunter's tent' (= filled with ammunition).
c) 'you can't expect me to answer such a *loaded* question' (= unfair, biased).

loadstar *noun*
see LODESTAR.

loadstone *noun*
see LODESTONE.

loaf (1) *noun*
plural is **loaves**
1. a shaped, baked mass of bread.
2. any shaped block or mass of food: 'a *loaf* of sugar'.

loaf (2) *verb*
to be lazy or idle.
Word Family: **loafer**, *noun*, a lazy or idle person.

loam (*rhymes with* home) *noun*
a type of soil containing clay, sand and organic matter, usually very fertile.
Word Family: **loamy**, *adjective*.

loan (*say* lone) *noun*
a) the act of lending: 'your *loan* of money was very much appreciated'.
b) anything which is lent, especially a sum of money at a fixed rate of interest.

loath (*rhymes with* oath) *adjective*
also spelt **loth**
unwilling or reluctant.
nothing loath, very willingly.
[Old English *lath* hateful]

loathe (*say* loa*th*) *verb*
to feel intense hatred and disgust for.
Word Family: **loathing**, *noun*, an intense hatred and disgust; **loathingly**, *adverb*; **loathsome**, *adjective*, hateful and disgusting.

loaves *plural noun*
see LOAF (1).

lob *noun*
Sport: the slow, rising, curved flight of a ball hit high in the air.
Word Family: **lob** (**lobbed, lobbing**), *verb*.

lobby *noun*
1. an entrance hall in a building.
2. a group of persons who try to influence or persuade a law-making body: 'the environmentalists' *lobby*'.
Word Family: **lobby** (**lobbied, lobbying**), *verb*, to try to influence or gain advantage from a law-making body; **lobbyist**, *noun*.

lobe *noun*
a rounded part or division, such as the fleshy lower part of the ear.
Word Family: **lobar**, *adjective*, relating to a lobe; **lobate** (*say* **lo**-bate), *adjective*, having or shaped like a lobe or lobes.
[Greek *lobos* a pod]

lobelia (*say* lo-**bee**lia) *noun*
any of various herb-like plants with clusters of coloured flowers.
[after *M. de Lobel*, 1538–1616, a Flemish botanist]

lobotomy (*say* lo-**botta**-mee) *noun*
also called a **leucotomy**
Medicine: an operation cutting into or across a lobe of the brain to alter brain function.
[LOBE + Greek *tomé* a cutting]

lobster *noun*
any of a group of large, edible, marine crustaceans, usually having two large pincers.
[Latin *locusta* a locust, a crustacean]

local (*say* **lo**–k'l) *adjective*
relating to a particular place or part: a) 'he is one of the *local* inhabitants'; b) 'a *local* infection'.
local *noun*
any person who is local.
Usages:
a) (*informal*) 'he has gone to the *local* for a drink' (= pub).
b) (*informal*) 'she was given a *local* before they removed the splinter' (= local anaesthetic).
Word Family: **locally**, *adverb*, in or relating to a particular place; **localize**, **localise**, *verb*, to limit or make local; **localization** (*say* lo-ka-lie-**zay**-sh'n), *noun*.
[Latin *locus* a place]

local anaesthetic
an anaesthetic used so that it affects only a limited area of the body.

local authority
the locally elected council which administers the affairs of a county, district, borough, etc. and collects the rates.

local colour
the distinctive interest or feeling of a place or period of time.

locale (*say* lo-**kahl**) *noun*
a particular place or setting, especially in relation to certain events.

local government
a) the system of using local authorities, partly financed by the rates, to administer such powers as may be delegated to them by the central government. b) a local authority.

locality (*say* lo-**kalli**-tee) *noun*
1. a place or district.
2. the state of being local.

locate (*say* lo-**kate**) *verb*
to find or establish the position of: 'have you *located* any holes in the roof?'.

location (*say* lo-**kay**-sh'n) *noun*
a place, especially one which is or will be settled, used, etc.: 'this is the perfect *location* for a house'.
on location, 'the scenes were filmed *on location* in Hawaii' (= in that actual place).

loch (*say* lok) *noun*
in Ireland spelt **lough**
Scottish: a long stretch of water which may be a lake or an inlet of the sea.

loci *plural noun*
see LOCUS.

lock (1) *noun*
1. any of various mechanical fastening devices which can be operated by a key.
2. any of various devices which prevent or limit movement, etc.: 'a gear *lock*'.
3. any of various holds or grips in wrestling, etc., especially one which limits the movement of the opponent.
4. *Nautical:* an enclosed section of a river or canal with gates at each end, in which boats are raised or lowered from one level to another by altering the depth of the water.
lock, stock and barrel, 'he evicted them, *lock, stock and barrel*' (= completely).
lock *verb*
1. to fasten or become fastened by means of a lock: 'she slammed and *locked* the front door'.
2. to keep, confine, imprison, etc. in or as if in a place fastened by a lock: 'the drunk was *locked* up for the night'.
Usages:
a) 'have you *locked* the cat out for the night?' (= shut).
b) 'the swimmer's arms *locked* around her rescuer's neck' (= clasped).
c) 'the wheels *locked* and the truck went into a spin' (= jammed).

lock (2) *noun*
a) a bunch or curl of hair. b) (*plural*) the hair.

locker *noun*
a small cupboard or compartment with a lock, used for storing possessions or equipment.

locket (*say* **lok**-it) *noun*
a small case to hold a portrait or other keepsake, usually made of gold or silver and worn on a chain around the neck.

lockjaw *noun*
see TETANUS.

locknut *noun*
a nut screwed down on another to stop it becoming loose.

lockout *noun*
the refusal by an employer to let work continue, unless his employees work according to his terms.

locksmith *noun*
a person who makes or mends locks.

lockstitch *noun*
Needlework: a stitch made with two interlocking threads.

lockup *noun*
(*informal*) a gaol.

lock–up shop
a shop without living quarters for the owner, which has to be locked up and made secure at night.

loco (*say* **lo**–ko) *adjective*
(*informal*) mad.
[Spanish]

locomotive (*say* lo–ko–**mo**–tiv) *noun*
a railway engine.
Word Family: **locomotion**, *noun*, the act or power of moving from place to place.
[Latin *loco* in place + *motio* a moving]

locum (*say* **lo**–kum) *noun*
a doctor, clergyman, etc. who temporarily takes over the work of another.
[short form of Latin, *locum tenens*, one holding the place]

locus (*say* **lo**–kus) *noun*
plural is **loci** (*say* **lo**–sigh)
1. a place or position, such as the position of a particular gene on a chromosome.
2. *Maths:* the path traced by a point moving according to a set rule.
[Latin]

locus standi (*say* lo–kus **stan**–die)
Law: a recognized right to intervene in a law case or to be heard on a subject: 'you have no *locus standi* in the matter'.
[Latin, a place to stand]

locust (*say* **lo**–kust) *noun*
any of various large grasshoppers which migrate in vast swarms, eating all the vegetation in their path.
[from Latin]

locution (*say* lo–**kew**–sh'n) *noun*
a verbal expression or phrase.
[Latin *locutus* spoken]

lode *noun*
Geology: see VEIN.

lodestar *noun*
also spelt **loadstar**
1. a star used as a guide or reference point.
2. anything which is a guiding principle or interest.
[Middle English *lode* journey + STAR]

lodestone *noun*
also spelt **loadstone**
a piece of magnetite, which may be used as a magnet.
[Middle English *lode* journey + STONE, because of its former use as a compass]

lodge (*say* loj) *noun*
1. a house used for holidays or temporary accommodation.
2. a small house, especially in a park or the grounds of a larger house: 'the gatekeeper's *lodge*'.
3. a) a branch of certain societies or associations. b) its members.

lodge *verb*
1. to live, especially in a rented room or house.
2. to supply with a room or rooms, especially temporarily: 'the flood victims were *lodged* in the school hall'.
Usages:
a) 'the bullet was *lodged* in his leg' (= stuck).
b) 'the old man refused to *lodge* his savings in the bank' (= deposit).
c) 'we have *lodged* a complaint about the noise' (= placed formally).
Word Family: **lodger**, *noun*, a person who rents a room or rooms in another's house; **lodging**, *noun*, (usually plural) a room or rooms for living, especially if rented.

lodgement *noun*
in America spelt **lodgment**
1. a) the act of lodging. b) anything which is lodged or deposited.
2. *Military:* a position gained in enemy territory.

loess (*say* **lo**–iss) *noun*
a loose, usually yellowish, deposit of wind–blown soil, particularly common in China.
[German]

loft *noun*
1. a) the upper storey of an outbuilding such as a stable. b) a raised gallery in a church or hall.
2. the space between the ceiling of a room and the roof above it.
3. *Sport:* the high curving flight of a ball, especially in golf.
Word Family: **loft**, *verb*, to hit a ball in a high arc.

lofty *adjective*
having great height: '*lofty* mountains towered behind the city'.
Usages:
a) '*lofty* sentiments filled the epic poem' (= noble, dignified).
b) 'her *lofty* manner annoyed us' (= haughty, proud).
Word Family: **loftily**, *adverb*; **loftiness**, *noun*.

log *noun*
1. a length of wood cut from the trunk or branch of a tree.
2. any record of progress, details, etc., especially on a ship. Short form of **logbook**.
3. a logarithm.

log *verb*
(logged, logging)
1. to record in a log.
2. to cut down trees or cut them into logs.
Word Family: **logging,** *noun,* the act or business of cutting down trees for timber; **logger,** *noun.*

loganberry (*say* lo–gan–berree) *noun*
a large, edible, dark red berry.
[first grown in America by *J. H. Logan,* 1841–1928]

logarithm (*say* **lugga–ri*thm*)** *noun*
short form is **log**
Maths: the exponent indicating the power to which it is necessary to raise a given number, called the **base,** to produce another number. *Example:* in $y = b^x$, x is the logarithm of y to the base b and is written $x = \log_b y$; the **antilogarithm** of x is y.
common logarithm
a logarithm to the base 10.
Word Family: **logarithmic** (*say* logga–**ri*th*–**mik), **logarithmical,** *adjective.*
[Greek *logos* ratio + *arithmos* number]

logbook *noun*
see LOG.

loggerhead *noun*
at loggerheads, 'those two children have been *at loggerheads* all afternoon' (= fighting, disagreeing).

logic (*say* **lojik**) *noun*
1. a) the art or science of reasoning. b) the study of the principles of reasoning.
2. a convincing reason or argument: 'I cannot see any *logic* in such a badly timed decision'.
logical *adjective*
1. based on the principles of logic: 'that is not a *logical* argument'.
2. able to reason soundly: 'she has a very *logical* mind'.
Usage: 'the accident was a *logical* result of his carelessness' (= reasonable, to be expected).
Word Family: **logically,** *adverb;* **logicality** (*say* loj–ee–**kalli**–tee), **logicalness,** *nouns;* **logician** (*say* loj–**ish**'n), *noun,* a person skilled in logic.
[Greek *logiké* (*tekhné*) the reasoning (art)]

-logist
a suffix indicating a person who is skilled or trained, as in *genealogist.* A variant is **-ologist,** as in *mythologist.*

logistics (*say* lo–**jis**–tiks) *plural noun* (*used with singular verb*) a) the branch of military science concerned with the transport, quartering and supply of troops. b) the detailed organization of some business or other operation.
Word Family: **logistic,** *adjective.*
[French *logis* lodgings]

log jam
1. a mass of logs blocking a river.
2. a deadlock or impasse.

-logy
a suffix indicating the science or study of, as in *genealogy.* A variant is **-ology,** as in *mythology.*
[from Greek]

loin *noun*
1. (*often plural*) the lower part of the body of a person or four-legged animal, between the ribs and the hips.
2. a cut of meat from this part of an animal.
gird one's loins, to prepare for action.

loincloth *noun*
a strip of cloth worn around the loins.

loiter *verb*
a) to stand about aimlessly. b) to move or proceed slowly.
Word Family: **loiterer,** *noun.*

loll *verb*
to rest or droop loosely or limply: 'his head *lolled* sideways as he fell asleep in the chair'.

lollipop *noun*
a hard, brittle sweet on a stick.

lollop *verb*
to move with heavy, ungainly leaps or bounds.

lolly *noun*
1. a) a lollipop. b) a water-ice on a stick.
2. (*informal*) money.

lone *adjective*
alone or solitary.
lone wolf, see WOLF.
Word Family: **loner,** *noun,* a person who does not seek the company of others.

lonely *adjective*
1. feeling sad or depressed because one is alone: 'were you *lonely* while we were away?'.
2. remote or isolated: 'a *lonely* house in the middle of the moors'.
Word Family: **loneliness,** *noun;* **lonesome,** *adjective,* lonely.

long (1) *adjective*
1. having great or considerable size or distance from end to end: a) 'a *long* walk'; b) 'a *long* time'.
Usages:
a) 'the room is about 10 metres *long*' (= in length).
b) 'her *long* face made me feel rather guilty' (= unhappy).
2. having little likelihood of winning: '*long* odds'.
long in the tooth, see TOOTH.
long *adverb*
1. a) for a long time. b) for a time or period: 'how *long* did he stay?'.
2. for the whole extent of: 'we stood all day *long* in the queue to buy tickets'.
3. at a distant time: 'it happened *long* before I was born'.
Phrases:
as, so long as, 'you may come *as long as* you are very quiet' (= on the condition that).
so long, goodbye.
long *noun*
a long time: 'the job will not take *long* if we work hard'.
Phrases:
before long, 'you'll be a teenager *before long*' (= soon).
the long and the short of, the basic or essential part of.

long (2) *verb*
to wish for strongly: 'I *long* for the end of winter'.
Word Family: **longing**, *noun*, a strong wish or craving; **longingly**, *adverb*.

longboat *noun*
the longest and strongest of the small boats that were carried by a sailing ship.

longbow *noun*
a medieval bow about the height of a man, drawn by hand to fire long feathered arrows.

longevity (*say* lon-**jevvi**-tee) *noun*
long life.
[Latin *longus* long + *aevum* age]

longhand *noun*
usual handwriting in which the words are written out in full. Compare SHORTHAND.

longitude (*say* **longi**-tewd) *noun*
1. any distance east or west of the prime meridian, measured in degrees.
2. any great circle passing through the North and South Poles.
Word Family: **longitudinal** (*say* longi-**tew**da-n'l), *adjective*, a) relating to longitude or length, b) running lengthwise; **longitudinally**, *adverb*.
[Latin *longitudo* length]

long johns
(*informal*) a pair of long underpants.

long play
short form is **LP**
a $33\frac{1}{3}$ r.p.m. record, usually 12 in. (30·16 cm) in diameter. Compare EXTENDED PLAY and SINGLE.

long-range *adjective*
1. extending into the future: 'here is a *long-range* weather forecast'.
2. designed for a great distance.

longshoreman *noun*
American: a person who works on the docks.

long shot
a hopeful attempt considered unlikely to succeed: 'that horse is definitely a *long shot* in this race'.
by a long shot, 'her guess was wrong *by a long shot*' (= by a large amount).

long-sighted *adjective*
able to see distant objects clearly.
Usage: 'the government was praised for its *long-sighted* policies' (= far-seeing, well-planned).
Word Family: **long-sightedness**, *noun*.

longstanding *adjective*
having continued for a long time: 'a *longstanding* disagreement'.

long-suffering *adjective*
patient or uncomplaining in trouble.

long-term *adjective*
involving a long period of time.

long ton
see TON (1).

long-waisted *adjective*
of more than average length from shoulder to waist.

long-wave *adjective*
(of a radiowave) having a wavelength of over 1 km, used for maritime radio, navigation, etc. Compare MEDIUM-WAVE and SHORT-WAVE.

longwinded (*say* long-**win**-did) *adjective*
tediously long: 'a *longwinded* speech'.
Word Family: **longwindedness**, *noun*.

loo *noun*
(*informal*) a toilet.

look (*say* luk) *verb*
1. to use one's sense of sight.
2. to direct one's eyes: '*look* at this beautiful flower!'.

Usages:
a) 'you *look* very happy today' (= give the impression of being).
b) 'she *looked* beautiful in that dress' (= was).
c) 'don't always *look* to win' (= hope, expect).
d) 'the back rooms all *look* onto the river' (= provide a view).
Phrases:
look after, to mind or tend to the needs, wants, etc. of.
look alive, look sharp, hurry up!
look down on, 'she *looks down on* us because we are poor' (= regards with contempt).
look for, 'what are you *looking for* in there?' (= trying to find).
look forward to, to wait for eagerly.
look into, 'the police are *looking into* the complaints' (= investigating).
look out, be careful.
look up, a) 'do *look up* my family if you're going to London' (= visit); b) '*look* it *up* in the dictionary' (= find, refer to); c) 'things have *looked up* since the new manager arrived' (= improved).
look up to, to admire.
look *noun*
1. the act of looking: 'she gave a quick *look* at the paper and then closed it'.
2. the way of looking or appearing: a) 'the *look* of a hunted man'; b) 'I don't like the *look* of the place'.

look-in *noun*
(*informal*) a chance to take part: 'there were so many people waiting that we didn't get a *look-in*'.

looking glass
an old word for a mirror.

lookout *noun*
1. the act of observing or keeping watch.
2. a place, usually elevated, from which one may observe or keep watch.
3. a person who keeps watch.
Usage: (*informal*) 'that's your *lookout*' (= worry, concern).

loom (1) *noun*
a machine for weaving yarn into fabric.

loom (2) *verb*
to appear in a huge, distorted or indistinct form: 'a monstrous shape *loomed* in the shadows'.

loony *adjective*
(*informal*) crazy or foolish.
Word Family: **loony**, *noun.*

loop *noun*
1. a curve doubling over itself so as to leave an opening in the middle.
2. something which has this shape.
Word Family: **loop**, *verb*, a) to make or form into a loop, b) to fasten or encircle with or as if with a loop.

loophole (*say* **loop**-hole) *noun*
1. anything which provides a means of evasion: 'the lawyer found a *loophole* in the law and his client had to be released'.
2. a narrow vertical opening in a wall, especially in a fort or castle.

loopy *adjective*
(*informal*) crazy or foolish.

loose *adjective*
a) free from fastening or restraint.
b) not tight or taut: 'he had a *loose* hold on the rope'.
Usages:
a) 'we bought *loose* potatoes at the farm' (= unpacked).
b) 'the child has a *loose* tooth' (= not firm).
c) 'the company has no *loose* funds' (= uninvested).
d) 'many people think she is a *loose* woman' (= immoral, unchaste).
e) 'her *loose* thinking annoyed the teacher' (= imprecise).
at a loose end, having nothing to do.
loose *adverb*
1. unfastened, loosened: 'my shoelace has come *loose*'.
2. so as to be or become loose: 'he broke *loose* from his captors'.
Word Family: **loose, loosen**, *verbs*, to make or become loose or looser; **loosely**, *adverb*; **looseness**, *noun.*

loosebox *noun*
a stall for a horse, wide enough for it to move about in.

loose-leaf *adjective*
(of a book or folder) having a cover to or from which pages may be easily added or removed.

loot *noun*
goods obtained illegally, such as by thieves, soldiers in time of war, etc.
Word Family: **loot**, *verb*, to pillage or plunder.
[Hindi]

lop *verb*
(**lopped, lopping**)
to cut off, e.g. the branches from a tree, hair from the head, etc.

lope *verb*
to run with long, bounding strides.
[Icelandic *hlaupa* to leap]

lop–eared *adjective*
having long, floppy ears.

lopsided *adjective*
asymmetrical or inclining to one side.
Word Family: **lopsidedly**, *adverb*; **lopsidedness**, *noun*.

loquacious (*say* lo–**kway**–shus) *adjective*
very talkative.
Word Family: **loquaciously**, *adverb*; **loquaciousness**, **loquacity** (*say* lo–**kwassi**–tee), *nouns*.
[Latin *loqui* to speak]

loquat (*say* **lo**–kwot) *noun*
a decorative evergreen tree with large leaves and small orange fruit.
[Chinese *luh kwat* rush orange]

lord *noun*
1. any peer.
2. a person who has authority over others: 'a feudal *lord*'.
3. (*capital*) a form of address: 'the *Lord* Mayor of Perth'.
4. *Religion:* a name for God or Christ.
live like a lord, to live in luxury.
Word Family: **lordly**, *adjective* a) suitable for a lord, b) arrogant or haughty; **lord**, *verb*; **lord it over**, to act in a domineering or arrogant manner towards.
[Old English *hlaford* the keeper of the bread]

Lord Chancellor
the head of the legal profession, ex–officio Leader of the House of Lords and a Cabinet Minister; as a political appointment he loses office on a change of government.

Lord Chief Justice
the senior permanent member of the judiciary, ranking next to the Lord Chancellor.

Lord–Lieutenant
(*say* lord–lef–**tennent**) *noun*
the monarch's representative in a county, a largely honorific appointment.

lordship *noun*
(*capital*) a form of address used to a judge of the High Court or a holder of the title Lord: 'as Your *Lordship* pleases'.

lore *noun*
any accumulated knowledge about a subject, especially of a traditional or popular nature: 'the *lore* of herbalists'.

lorgnette (*say* lorn–**yet**) *noun*
a pair of spectacles held to the eyes by an ornamental handle.
[French *lorgner* to squint]

lorry *noun*
a long motor vehicle used for carrying heavy loads.

lose (*say* looz) *verb*
(**lost, losing**)
to part with, by chance or carelessness, and be unable to find: 'she *lost* her purse'.
Usages:
a) 'she *lost* control and burst into tears' (= failed to keep).
b) 'four people *lost* their lives in the accident' (= were deprived of).
c) 'she *lost* the race' (= was defeated in).
d) 'she was *lost* in thought' (= absorbed).
e) 'you should *lose* weight' (= get rid of).
f) 'you should *lose* no time in doing this' (= waste).
g) 'I was *lost* when he started talking about philosophy' (= unable to understand).
lose sight of, to fail to keep in view.
Word Family: **loser**, *noun*.

loss *noun*
1. the act or an instance of losing: 'the team suffered a decisive *loss*'.
2. a person or thing that is lost: 'the money is a *loss* I cannot afford'.
3. the number or amount lost, such as casualties in a war, etc.: 'our *losses* were very heavy'.
be at a loss, to be puzzled or uncertain.

loss–leader *noun*
a line of goods sold at a loss in a shop to attract custom for other goods.

lost cause
a cause for which defeat is inevitable.

lot *noun*
1. a) one of a set of objects drawn when making a decision by chance.
b) the use of these objects for selection: 'we drew *lots* to decide which of us should do the washing–up'.
2. a number of persons or things considered as a single group or unit.
3. a person's fortune in life: 'his *lot* has been one of severe hardship'.
4. a piece of land: 'we bought the last *lot* on the estate'.
5. *Film:* the site used for making movies.

6. an article or a group of articles for sale at an auction: '*lot* 99 is an antique writing desk'.
7. (*often plural*) a large number.
8. (*informal*) a person of a specified type: 'he's a bad *lot*'.
throw in one's lot with, to support.

loth *adjective*
see LOATH.

lotion (*say* **lo**–sh'n) *noun*
a mixture of an insoluble substance in a liquid, applied to the skin without rubbing.
[Old French, washing]

lottery *noun*
a form of gambling where many numbered tickets are sold, some of which, as determined by lot, entitle their owners to prizes.

lotto *noun*
see BINGO.
[Italian]

lotus (*say* **lo**–tus) *noun*
1. a type of waterlily, common in Egyptian and Hindu decorative art.
2. *Greek mythology:* a plant whose fruit was believed to induce a dreamy state of forgetfulness.
lotus–eater *noun*
1. *Greek mythology:* a person who lost touch with reality by eating the fruit of the lotus.
2. a person who leads an easy, dreamy life and is indifferent to the busy world.
[from Greek]

loud *adjective*
1. having or producing a high volume and intensity of sound.
2. having very bright colours.
Word Family: **loudly**, **loud**, *adverbs*; **loudness**, *noun*.

loud–hailer *noun*
also called a **megaphone**
an electric hand–held device similar to a microphone, which magnifies sounds so they can be heard from a long distance.

loudspeaker *noun*
short form is **speaker**
Audio: any of various devices for converting electronic signals into audible sound, as in a public–address system, radio, etc. Compare MICROPHONE.

lough (*say* lok) *noun*
see LOCH.

lounge *verb*
to stand, sit, lie or move in a lazy, relaxed manner.

lounge *noun*
1. a living room.
2. a room in a hotel, etc. where guests may relax comfortably.

lour (*rhymes with* flower) *verb*
also spelt **lower**
1. (of sky, weather, etc.) to be dark and threatening.
2. to frown or scowl.
Word Family: **lour**, *noun*.

louse (*rhymes with* house) *noun*
plural is **lice**
1. a small, flattened, wingless, usually blood–sucking insect which may be parasitic on man.
2. (*informal*) a despicable person.
Word Family: **louse up**, (*informal*) to bungle or ruin.

lousy *adjective*
1. (*informal*) a) of very poor quality: 'a *lousy* play'; b) unpleasant: 'what *lousy* weather'; c) ill: 'I feel *lousy*'; d) well supplied: 'he's *lousy* with money'.
2. infested with lice.

lout *noun*
a clumsy, stupid, ill–mannered fellow.
Word Family: **loutish**, *adjective*.

louvre (*say* **loo**va *or* **loo**vr) **louver** *noun*
a) a screen of sloping timber slats to shut out light but permit ventilation.
b) any of a series of adjustable panes forming a window.

love (*say* luv) *verb*
1. to have a deep–seated affection for.
2. (*informal*) to having a liking or enthusiasm for: 'I *love* ice–cream'.
love *noun*
1. a strong passion or deep–seated affection.
2. (*informal*) a liking or enthusiasm.
3. a person who is beloved.
4. *Tennis:* a score of nil. A **love game** is a game in which one player does not score.
Phrases:
for love, 'although it was a long and difficult task he did it *for love*' (= without payment).
for the love of, for the sake of.
in love, feeling deep affection.
make love, a) to have sexual intercourse; b) to woo.
no love lost, 'there's *no love lost* between those two' (= mutual dislike).

lovebird *noun*
1. any of various small, South American and African parrots, each

pair keeping very close to each other when perching.
2. (*informal*) a budgerigar.

love child
an illegitimate child.

lovelorn *adjective*
forlorn because of love.

lovely (*say* **luv-lee**) *adjective*
charming, delightful or beautiful.
Word Family: **loveliness,** *noun.*

love-match *noun*
a marriage based on love rather than on social or pecuniary considerations.

lover (*say* **luvva**) *noun*
1. a) a person who is in love with another. b) a person who is having a love affair.
2. a person who likes something: 'a *lover* of modern art'.

lovesick *adjective*
languishing because of love.

loving *adjective*
showing or feeling love: a) '*loving* glances'; b) '*loving* friends'.
Word Family: **lovingly,** *adverb*; **lovingness,** *noun.*

low (1) (*say* lo) *adjective*
1. not tall or high: a) 'a *low* shelf'; b) 'he has a *low* opinion of fools'.
2. not shrill, sharp or loud: 'a *low* murmur'.
3. of small magnitude, quantity, degree, etc.: a) 'a *low* number'; b) 'our stock of food is very *low*'.
4. having a relatively simple structure: 'a fungus is an example of a *lower* plant'.
Usages:
a) 'a person of *low* birth' (= inferior).
b) 'he made a *low* bow to the Queen' (= bending far down).
c) 'what a *low* trick' (= undignified, contemptible).
d) (*informal*) 'I'm *low* on funds this week' (= depleted).
Phrases:
lay low, a) 'the blow to the chin *laid* him *low*' (= knocked down); b) 'an attack of the gout finally *laid* him *low*' (= prostrated, confined to bed).
lie low, see LIE (2).
low spirits, 'she has been in very *low spirits* for several weeks' (= depressed).
low *adverb*
1. in, at or to a low position, point, price, etc.: a) 'aim *low* and you won't overshoot the target'; b) 'buy shares *low* and sell them high'; c) 'I've yet to fall that *low*'.
2. a) at or to a low pitch: 'a tenor cannot get as *low* as a baritone'. b) softly: 'speak *low* and mind your manners'.
low *noun*
a low level: 'morale has reached an all-time *low* among the troops'.
Weather: an area of low pressure into which strong winds blow clockwise in the Southern Hemisphere and anticlockwise in the Northern Hemisphere, bringing unsettled weather and rain. Also called a **depression** or a **cyclone.** Compare HIGH.
Word Family: **lowness,** *noun.*

low (2) (*say* lo) *verb*
to make the hollow, bellowing sound of cattle.
Word Family: **low,** *noun.*

lowbrow (*say* **lo**-brow) *adjective*
(*informal*) of low intellectual taste or standard.
Word Family: **lowbrow,** *noun.*

Low Church
also called **Evangelical**
belonging to a section of the Church of England which frowns on elaborate ritual and believes in salvation by faith (not sacraments). Compare HIGH CHURCH.

low-down (*say* **lo**-down) *noun*
(*informal*) all the facts.
low-down *adjective*
(*informal*) dishonourable or mean.

lower (1) (*say* **lo**-a) *verb*
to let or bring down: a) '*lower* the blinds'; b) '*lower* the rent'; c) '*lower* your voice'.
lower oneself, to stoop or lose one's dignity.

lower (2) (*rhymes with* flower) *verb*
see LOUR.

lower case
Printing: small letters, as these words have. Compare UPPER CASE.

lower deck
Navy: petty officers and men, as distinct from officers.

Lower House
also called **Lower Chamber**
the House of Commons.

lowest common denominator
1. *Maths:* the smallest number which contains all the denominators of a group of fractions an exact number of times.
2. a feature or opinion common to all the members of a group.

lowest common multiple
Maths: the smallest number which contains all of a group of numbers an exact number of times.

low frequency
a radio frequency in the range 30–300 kilohertz.
Word Family: **low-frequency,** *adjective.*

lowlands *plural noun*
an area of low, flat land.

lowly (*say* **lo**–lee) *adjective*
1. humble: 'a *lowly* farmhouse'.
2. low in rank or position: 'he has a *lowly* job in the big firm'.

low profile
a deliberately understated attitude or position: 'to maintain a *low profile* in international affairs'.

low-temperature physics
cryogenics.

low-tension (*say* lo–**ten**–sh'n) *adjective*
Electricity: of or relating to electric cables carrying a low voltage.

loyal *adjective*
showing continued attachment: 'she is very *loyal* to her family'.
Word Family: **loyally,** *adverb*; **loyalty,** *noun,* the state or quality of being loyal.

loyalist *noun*
a person who is loyal, especially a supporter of a monarch, government, etc. in a time of revolt.

lozenge (*say* **lozz**'nj) *noun*
1. a sweet tablet sucked to relieve a sore throat or cold.
2. a diamond-shaped figure.

lubber *noun*
(*informal*) a big, clumsy, stupid person.
Word Family: **lubberly,** *adjective.*

lubricate (*say* **loo**bri–kate) *verb*
to apply oil or an oily substance to, in order to reduce friction, etc.
Word Family: **lubrication,** *noun*; **lubricant,** *noun,* a substance which lubricates.
[Latin *lubricare* to make slippery]

lucerne (*say* **loo**–sern) *noun*
also called **alfalfa**
a cereal plant with bluish-purple flowers, used as fodder.
[French]

lucid (*say* **loo**–sid) *adjective*
1. clear or easily understood: 'a *lucid* explanation of the problem'.
2. rational or mentally sound: 'although he is senile he still has *lucid* moments'.
Word Family: **lucidity** (*say* loo–**siddi**–tee), **lucidness,** *nouns*; **lucidly,** *adverb.*
[Latin *lucidus* shining bright]

Lucifer (*say* **loo**sifa) *noun*
an angel who led the revolt in heaven and was cast into hell; identified with Satan.
[Latin *lucis* of light + *ferre* to bear (= morning star)]

luck *noun*
1. anything which happens by chance: 'what bad *luck* to break a leg'.
2. an advantage or success due to chance: a) 'we wished them *luck* in their travels'; b) 'a stroke of *luck*'.
Phrases:
down on one's luck, going through an unlucky period.
worse luck!, 'I shan't be there, *worse luck!*' (= alas!).

lucky *adjective*
having, bringing or resulting in good luck.
Word Family: **luckily,** *adverb*; **luckiness,** *noun.*

lucky dip
a barrel at fairs, etc. containing articles of varying value, and into which a person dips for a prize.

lucrative (*say* **loo**kra–tiv) *adjective*
profitable: 'it is a small but *lucrative* business'.
[Latin *lucrum* gain]

lucre (*say* **loo**ker) *noun*
money or profit which is sought after greedily.
[Latin *lucrum* gain]

ludicrous (*say* **loo**di–krus) *adjective*
absurdly funny.
[Latin *ludricrum* a stage play]

ludo (*say* **loo**–doe) *noun*
a children's board game for two to four people using counters and dice.
[Latin, I play]

lug (1) *verb*
(lugged, lugging)
to pull or drag with much effort.
Word Family: **lug,** *noun.*

lug (2) *noun*
an ear-like projection for holding or supporting something.

luggage (*say* **lugg**ij) *noun*
any bags or suitcases taken on a journey.

lugger *noun*
an old sailing vessel with obliquely mounted square sails.

lugubrious (*say* loo-**goo**bri-us) *adjective*
mournful or dismal.
Word Family: **lugubriously**, *adverb*; **lugubriousness**, *noun.*
[Latin *lugubris* mourning]

lukewarm *adjective*
moderately warm.
Usage: 'our idea received a *lukewarm* reaction' (= unenthusiastic).

lull *verb*
to soothe or quieten: a) 'mother's singing finally *lulled* the baby off to sleep'; b) 'his explanation *lulled* my suspicions for a few days'.
Word Family: **lull**, *noun*, a brief calm.

lullaby (*say* **lull**a-by) *noun*
a soothing song to put a baby to sleep.

lumbago (*say* lum-**bay**go) *noun*
a severe pain in the lower part of the back.
[Latin *lumbus* the loin]

lumbar (*say* **lum**ba) *adjective*
Anatomy: of or relating to the lower half of the back.

lumber (1) *noun*
1. timber.
2. junk.
lumber *verb*
(*informal*) to burden with something useless or unpleasant: 'he *lumbered* me with the task of firing the old lady'.

lumber (2) *verb*
to move about heavily or clumsily.
Word Family: **lumberingly**, *adverb.*

lumberjack *noun*
also called a **lumberman**
American: a man whose job is cutting down trees and bringing them out of the forest.

lumber-jacket *noun*
a short, heavy, woollen jacket fastening up to the neck, as was formerly worn by lumberjacks.

lumen (*say* **loo**-men) *noun*
the derived SI unit of luminous flux.
[Latin, light]

luminance (*say* **loo**mi-nance) *noun*
Physics: the luminous intensity per unit of area.

luminary (*say* **loo**min-ree) *noun*
something which gives light, such as the sun or moon.
Usage: 'he was one of the *luminaries* of our times' (= eminent persons).

luminescence (*say* loomi-**ness**'nce) *noun*
Physics: the emission of light from some cause other than high temperature, as by chemical action, radioactivity, fluorescence or phosphorescence.
Word Family: **luminesce**, *verb*; **luminescent**, *adjective.*

luminous (*say* **loo**mi-nus) *adjective*
giving off light: 'the sun is a *luminous* body'.
Usages:
a) 'she glanced at me with her *luminous* eyes' (= bright, full of light).
b) 'he gave a *luminous* explanation of the problem' (= clear, enlightening).
Word Family: **luminously**, *adverb*; **luminosity** (*say* loomi-**nossi**-tee), *noun*, the state or quality of being luminous.

luminous flux
the rate of transmission of luminous energy.

luminous intensity
Physics: the amount of light emitted per second in a given direction from a source of radiation which comes from a particular point.

lump (1) *noun*
1. a solid, usually small, mass of no particular shape: a) 'a *lump* of clay'; b) 'a *lump* on the head'.
2. (*informal*) a stupid, clumsy or ungainly person.
lump *verb*
1. to put together in one lump or group without discrimination: 'he *lumped* us all together as idlers'.
2. to form lumps: 'the mixture will *lump* if you don't stir it constantly'.
lump *adjective*
in the form of a lump or lumps.
lump sum, a single, substantial sum of money.
Word Family: **lumpy**, *adjective*, a) full of lumps, b) covered with lumps; **lumpily**, *adverb*; **lumpiness**, *noun*; **lumpish**, *adjective*, a) like a lump, b) stupid or clumsy.

lump (2) *verb*
(*informal*) to endure or put up with: 'you can like it or *lump* it'.

lunacy (*say* **loo**na-see) *noun*
insanity.
[Latin *luna* the moon, formerly believed to cause insanity]

lunar (*say* **loo**na) *adjective*
a) of or relating to the moon. b) measured by the moon's revolutions: 'a *lunar* cycle'.

lunar month
Astronomy: the time from one new moon to the next, equal to 29·53 days.

lunar year
Astronomy: a period of twelve lunar months.

lunatic (*say* **loo**na–tik) *adjective*
of or relating to lunacy: a) '*lunatic* schemes'; b) 'a *lunatic* asylum'.
lunatic fringe
the more extreme or eccentric members of a community or movement.
lunatic *noun*
a person who is insane.

lunch *noun*
the second meal of the day, usually taken about 1 p.m.
Word Family: **lunch**, *verb.*

luncheon (*say* **lun**–ch'n) *noun*
a lunch.
Word Family: **luncheon**, *verb.*

lung *noun*
Anatomy: either of two, large, spongy organs in the chest cavity, which absorb oxygen from the air, and release waste carbon dioxide into it.

lunge (1) (*say* lunj) *noun*
a sudden forward movement, such as a thrust with a bayonet, etc.
Word Family: **lunge**, *verb.*
[French *allonger* to lengthen or extend]

lunge (2) (*say* lunj) *noun*
a long rope used to guide a horse in training or exercise.

lupin (*say* **loo**pin) *noun*
a garden plant bearing brightly coloured flowers in long tapering spikes.
[from Latin]

lurch (1) *noun*
a sudden rolling or swaying to one side: 'the ship gave a terrible *lurch*'.
Word Family: **lurch**, *verb.*

lurch (2) *noun*
leave in the lurch, to leave a person who is helpless or in difficulties.

lure *noun*
anything which attracts or entices, such as a worm used to attract fish.
Word Family: **lure**, *verb*, to attract or entice.

lurid (*say* **loo**rid) *adjective*
1. sensational or shockingly vivid: 'the press delighted in all the *lurid* details of the murder'.
2. lit up by an unnatural reddish glare: 'a *lurid* patch of sky above the burning factory'.
[Latin *luridus* pale yellow, ghastly]

lurk *verb*
to loiter in a secretive or furtive manner: 'a man *lurking* in the shadows'.
Usage: 'a faint doubt still *lurked* in the back of my mind' (= remained).

luscious (*say* **lush**us) *adjective*
delicious.
Word Family: **lusciously**, *adverb*; **lusciousness**, *noun.*

lush (1) *adjective*
luxuriant.
Word Family: **lushly**, *adverb*; **lushness**, *noun.*

lush (2) *noun*
American: (*informal*) a drunkard.

lust *noun*
any strong desire, especially a powerful sexual desire.
Word Family: **lust**, *verb*; **lustful**, *adjective*, **lustfully**, *adverb*; **lustfulness**, *noun.*

lustre (*say* **lus**ter) *noun*
the soft, reflected light playing over a surface: 'the *lustre* of pearls'.
Usage: 'age has dimmed the *lustre* of her beautiful eyes' (= brightness, brilliant quality).
Word Family: **lustrous** (*say* **lus**trus), *adjective*; **lustrously**, *adverb*; **lustrousness**, *noun.*
[Latin *lustrare* to illumine]

lusty *adjective*
vigorous or hearty: a) 'a *lusty* old age'; b) 'a *lusty* appetite'.
Word Family: **lustily**, *adverb*; **lustiness**, *noun.*

lute *noun*
Music: a fretted instrument whose strings are plucked with the fingers, popular in the Middle Ages.
Word Family: **lutenist**, *noun*, a person who plays the lute.

lutetium (*say* loo–**tee**shi–um) *noun*
element number 71, a rare metal. See LANTHANIDE.
See CHEMICAL ELEMENTS in grey pages.
[after *Lutetia Parisiorum*, the Roman name for Paris]

Lutheran (*say* **loo**–tha–r'n) *noun*
a member of the Protestant Church founded on the doctrine of salvation by faith alone, and predominant in Scandinavia and East Germany.
Word Family: **Lutheran,** *adjective*; **Lutheranism,** *noun.*
[after *Martin Luther,* 1483–1546, its German founder]

lux *noun*
the derived SI unit of illumination.
[Latin, light]

luxuriant (*say* lug–*zhoo*ri–ent) *adjective*
growing thickly and abundantly: '*luxuriant* vegetation'.
Word Family: **luxuriantly,** *adverb*; **luxuriance, luxuriancy,** *noun.*

luxury (*say* **luk**sha–ree) *noun*
1. a state of great sumptuousness or comfort, surrounded by things which are rare, expensive, or extremely gratifying.
2. something which is pleasing or elegant, but not really necessary: 'their budget allows few *luxuries*'.
Word Family: **luxurious** (*say* lug–*zhoo*ri–us), *adjective,* being characterized by luxury; **luxuriously,** *adverb*; **luxuriousness,** *noun*; **luxuriate** (*say* lug–*zhoo*ri–ate), *verb,* to indulge oneself in.
[Latin *luxuria* excess, extravagance]

-ly (*say* lee)
a suffix: a) used to form adverbs from adjectives, as in *sadly*; b) meaning like, as in *ghostly*; c) meaning per, as in *monthly.*

lychee (*say* **lie**–chee) *noun*
also spelt **lichee**
a small, Chinese fruit with a firm shell and a soft, jelly–like middle.

lychgate *noun*
also spelt **lichgate**
the roofed gateway of a churchyard where the coffin can rest before a funeral service.
[Old English *lic* corpse]

lying (1) *verb*
the present participle of the verb **lie (1).**

lying (2) *verb*
the present participle of the verb **lie (2).**

lymph (*say* limf) *noun*
Biology: a clear slightly yellow fluid, consisting chiefly of blood plasma and white blood cells, drained from the tissues of the body and collected in the lymphatic vessels.
Word Family: **lymphatic,** *adjective.*
[Latin *lympha* water]

lynch (*say* linch) *verb*
to condemn and kill a person by mob action, without legal authority.
[first employed as a form of rough justice by *Captain William Lynch,* an American magistrate, about 1780]

lynx (*say* links) *noun*
any of various keen–sighted American, African and European wildcats with a short tail and tufted ears.
Word Family: **lynx–eyed,** *adjective,* sharp–sighted.
[Greek]

lyre (*say* lire) *noun*
Music: a stringed instrument of ancient Greece, consisting of two long curved arms meeting in a soundbox at the base.
[from Greek]

lyrebird (*say* **lire**–bird) *noun*
either of two species of brown and grey Australian birds, the male of which spreads his tail feathers into the shape of a lyre to dance and mimic other birds.

lyric (*say* **lirr**ik) *noun*
1. *Poetry:* a short poem, having the form and musical quality of a song, and giving direct expression to the poet's thoughts and feelings.
2. (*plural*) the words of a popular song.
lyric *adjective*
1. of or like a lyric.
2. *Music:* a) having a light, flexible singing voice: 'a *lyric* soprano' b) intended for singing, originally in accompaniment to the lyre: 'a Greek *lyric* chorus'.

lyrical (*say* **lirr**i–k'l) *adjective*
of or relating to a lyric.
Usage: 'the salesman grew quite *lyrical* about his product's merits' (= enthusiastic, poetic).
Word Family: **lyrically,** *adverb*; **lyricist** (*say* **lirr**i–sist), *noun,* a person who writes the words for a song; **lyricism** (*say* **lirr**i–sizm), *noun,* the quality of emotional self–expression in the arts.

lysergic acid diethylamide
short form is **LSD**
a drug producing hallucinations.

Lysol (*say* **lie**–sol) *noun*
a solution of soap mixed with cresol, and used as a disinfectant.
[a trademark]

Mm

ma'am (*say* mam) *noun*
(*informal*) madam.

mac *noun*
(*informal*) a mackintosh.

macabre (*say* ma-**kah**-bra) *adjective*
ghastly, horrible or gruesome.
[Arabic *maqbara* graveyard]

macadam (*say* ma-**kadd**'m) *noun*
the crushed rock or stone used in layers to make roads.
Word Family: **macadamize, macadamise,** *verb.*
[after *J. L. McAdam,* 1756–1836, a Scottish surveyor]

macaroni (*say* makka-**ro**-nee) *noun*
a pasta shaped like short, hollow tubes.
[Italian]

macaroon *noun*
a sweet crisp cake made with coconut or almonds, etc., usually on a rice-paper base.
[Italian]

macaw (*say* ma**kaw**) *noun*
a large, long-tailed, South American parrot, with brightly coloured feathers and a harsh voice.
[Portuguese]

mace (1) *noun*
a) a club-like weapon, usually with a spiked metal head. b) a staff carried by an official as a symbol of office.

mace (2) *noun*
a spice made from the dried outer covering of nutmegs.

macédoine (*say* mass-ay-**dwan**) *noun*
a mixture of sliced fruits in jelly, or of diced vegetables.
[French *Macedonia,* referring to the mixture of nationalities there]

macerate (*say* **massa**-rate) *verb*
1. to soak something in order to soften it.
2. to make or become thin, especially by fasting.
Word Family: **maceration,** *noun.*
[Latin *maceratus* softened]

Mach *noun*
see MACH NUMBER.

machete (*say* ma-**shettee**) *noun*
see MATCHET.
[Spanish]

Machiavellian (*say* makkia-**vell**ian) *adjective*
having no scruples to obtain what one wants, especially in politics.
[after *Niccolo Machiavelli,* 1469–1527, an Italian writer on political theory]

machinate (*say* **makk**in-ate) *verb*
to scheme or plot, usually in an evil way.
Word Family: **machination,** *noun,* a) the act of plotting, b) a plot or scheme.
[Latin *machinari* to contrive]

machine (*say* ma-**sheen**) *noun*
a mechanical device which performs a certain function: 'a sewing *machine*'.
Usage: 'the government *machine* functions smoothly' (= system).
Word Family: **machinery,** *noun,* a) the parts of a machine, b) any or all machines; **machine,** *verb,* to make with a machine; **machinist,** *noun,* a person who operates a machine.
[Greek *mekhané* a contrivance]

machine-gun *noun*
an automatic weapon capable of rapid, continuous fire.

machine tool
a lathe or other power-operated tool for shaping, planing, drilling or milling metal, wood or plastics.

machismo (*say* ma-**chizmo**) *noun*
the male urge to demonstrate virility and intrepidity.
[Spanish]

Mach number (*say* mak number)
Physics: the ratio of the speed of a body to the speed of sound in the medium through which it is travelling. At Mach 1 the body is moving at the speed of sound.
[after *Ernst Mach,* 1836–1916, an Austrian physicist]

mackerel *noun*
any of a large group of edible fish with wavy cross-markings.

mackerel sky, ripples of high cirrus cloud, in patterns resembling a mackerel's back.

mackintosh, macintosh ***noun***
a raincoat made of cotton treated with waterproof rubber.
[after *Charles Macintosh*, 1766–1843, its inventor]

macramé (*say* ma–**krah**–may) ***noun***
a) the knotting of thread or cord in patterns. b) the decorative work made in this way.
[Turkish *magrama* towel]

macrobiotic (*say* makro–by–**ottik**) *adjective*
(of food or a diet) consisting of a high proportion of organically grown fruit, vegetables and grain, and a small amount of meat, eggs, etc., said to make for a long life.
[Greek *makros* long + *bios* life]

macrocosm (*say* **makro**–kozm) ***noun***
the world or universe as a whole.
[Greek *makros* large + *kosmos* world]

mad *adjective*
insane.
Usages:
a) (*informal*) 'I was *mad* with them for teasing me' (= furious).
b) 'there was a *mad* rush for seats' (= excited, chaotic).
Word Family: **madden,** *verb*, to make mad; **madness,** *noun*, a) the state of being mad, b) mad behaviour; **madly,** *adverb*; **madcap,** *noun*, a reckless person.

madam (*say* **mad'**m) ***noun***
a polite form of address to a woman.
[French *ma dame* my lady]

madame (*say* ma–**dahm**) ***noun***
plural is **mesdames** (*say* may–**dahm**)
1. a title for a married woman, especially in non English-speaking countries.
2. the woman in charge of a brothel.
[French *ma dame* my lady]

madder ***noun***
a strong red or reddish-orange colour obtained from the root of a European plant.

made *verb*
the past tense and past participle of the verb **make.**

mademoiselle (*say* mum–**zel**) ***noun***
plural is **mesdemoiselles** (*say* mem–**zel**)
a French title for an unmarried woman.
[French]

madness ***noun***
Word Family: see MAD.

Madonna ***noun***
a) the Virgin Mary. b) a picture or statue of the Virgin Mary.
[Italian *ma donna* my lady]

madrigal ***noun***
an unaccompanied song for several voices singing two or more melodies together.

maelstrom (*say* **male**–strom) ***noun***
a) a great or violent whirlpool. b) a violent force or whirl of events: 'the *maelstrom* of war'.
[Dutch]

maestro (*say* **my**–stro) ***noun***
a master of any art, especially an eminent musician or conductor.
[Italian, master]

Mae West
an inflatable life-jacket.
[after *Mae West*, a film star of ample proportions]

Mafia ***noun***
1. *History:* a secret nationalist society in French-ruled Sicily which by last century had degenerated into a collection of hired thugs specializing in blackmail, 'protection' rackets and murder, and believed to still exist.
2. such thuggery brought to America and other countries by immigrants.
3. (*informal*) a gang of political or other conspirators or suspected conspirators.
Word Family: **Mafioso,** *noun*, a Mafia member.
[from the initials of Italian for 'Death to France is Italy's Cry']

magazine (*say* magga–**zeen**) ***noun***
1. any publication appearing at regular intervals, of more specialized interest than a newspaper. Also called a **periodical.**
2. a place or container where things, such as ammunition, film in a camera, etc., are stored.
[Arabic *makhzan* storehouse]

magenta (*say* ma–**jenta**) ***noun***
a brilliant, reddish-purple colour.
Word Family: **magenta,** *adjective.*
[the dye was discovered in 1859, the year of a battle at *Magenta*, northern Italy]

maggot ***noun***
the larva of a fly, usually living in decaying matter.
Word Family: **maggoty,** *adjective*, infested with maggots.

magi (*say* **may**–jie) *plural noun*
see MAGUS.

magic *noun*
1. the attempted use of supernatural forces and practices to change or influence normal events.
2. conjuring.
Usage: 'we were fascinated by the *magic* of the music' (= mysterious power).
Word Family: **magic, magical,** *adjective,* of or like magic; **magician** (*say* ma–**jish**'n), *noun,* a person who practises magic; **magically,** *adverb.*
[from Greek from old Persian]

magic carpet
a carpet which is supposed to fly through the air, taking one anywhere one wants.
[possessed by King Solomon (according to the Koran) and also featured in the 'Arabian Nights']

magic lantern
an old type of slide projector.

magistrate (*say* **maj**is–trate) *noun*
a person appointed to administer justice in a magistrate's court, either as an unpaid justice of the peace or as a salaried (stipendiary) magistrate.
magisterial (*say* maj–es–**teer**ial) *adjective*
of or like a magistrate.
Usage: 'a *magisterial* manner' (= imperious, domineering).
Word Family: **magistracy** (*say* **maj**–istra–see), *noun,* a) the position of a magistrate, b) magistrates considered as a group.
[Latin *magister* master]

magistrate's court
a local court, with powers to try minor cases (summary jurisdiction), to hold preliminary inquiries into more serious cases which may go to a higher court, and to license publicans, etc.

magma *noun*
Geology: the molten rock layer between the inner solid core of the earth and the mantle.

magnanimous (*say* mag–**nann**imus) *adjective*
generous, forgiving or free from pettiness.
Word Family: **magnanimity** (*say* magna–**nimm**i–tee), *noun,* generosity; **magnanimously,** *adverb.*
[Latin *magnus* great + *animus* spirit]

magnate *noun*
a person who has power, especially due to property, wealth or position.
[Latin *magnus* great]

magnesia (*say* mag–**nee**zia) *noun*
a tasteless white powder used in medicine as an antacid and laxative.

magnesium (*say* mag–**nee**zi–um) *noun*
element number 12, a light metal which burns with a very bright, white flame. It is used in lightweight alloys, many chemical processes and is essential to form chlorophyll. See ALKALINE EARTH METAL.
See CHEMICAL ELEMENTS in grey pages.
[after *Magnesia,* a metal-bearing region in Greece]

magnet *noun*
a piece of metal, usually iron, which attracts other iron objects, and aligns itself north and south when suspended.
Usage: 'this unexplored jungle is a *magnet* to adventurers' (= attracting force).
Word Family: **magnetize, magnetise,** *verb,* to make into a magnet.
[same root as *magnesium*]

magnetic (*say* mag–**nett**ik) *adjective*
1. *Physics:* (of a substance) having a crystal structure such that, if placed in an electric field, it becomes magnetized, either permanently (**ferromagnetic**) or only as long as it remains in the electric field (**electromagnetic**).
2. of or relating to such forces: 'a *magnetic* compass'.
3. attractive: 'a *magnetic* personality'.
Word Family: **magnetism,** *noun,* **magnetically,** *adverb.*

magnetic flux
the total magnetic effect at a particular point through a given cross-section.

magnetic north
see NORTH.

magnetic tape
see TAPE.

magnetite (*say* **magn**i–tite) *noun*
a magnetic, black iron oxide which is an important source of iron.

magneto (*say* mag–**nee**to) *noun*
any of various electrical generators using magnets, especially one used to provide ignition in an internal combustion engine.

magnificent (*say* mag–**niffi**–s'nt) *adjective*
splendid or very fine.

Word Family: **magnificence,** *noun;* **magnificently,** *adverb.*
[Latin *magnificus* grand, on a large scale]

magnify (*say* **magni**–fie) *verb*
(**magnified, magnifying**)
1. to make something appear larger: 'a microscope *magnifies* objects'.
2. (*formerly*) to praise.
Word Family: **magnifier,** *noun,* a person or thing that magnifies; **magnification,** *noun,* a) the act of magnifying, b) the power to magnify, c) a magnified copy or reproduction.

magniloquent (*say* mag–**nilla**–kw'nt) *adjective*
pompous in speech.
Word Family: **magniloquence,** *noun;* **magniloquently,** *adverb.*
[Latin *magnus* great + *loquens* speaking]

magnitude *noun*
1. size or extent.
Usage: 'events of great *magnitude*' (= importance).
2. *Astronomy:* a measure of the apparent brightness of a star.
3. *Maths:* a) the absolute value of a number. b) the length of a vector.
[Latin *magnitudo* greatness]

magnolia *noun*
a shrub or tree with large, pink or white, waxy flowers, widely cultivated for ornament.
[after *P. Magnol*, 1638–1715, a French botanist]

magnum *noun*
a large wine bottle holding 2 quarts (2·27 litre).

magnum opus
a person's greatest achievement, especially a literary work.
[Latin, big work]

magpie *noun*
1. a large, black and white bird related to the crow and noted for its chattering and for stealing miscellaneous objects.
2. (*informal*) a) a chatterbox. b) a random collector of miscellaneous objects.

magus (*say* **may**–jus *or* **may**–gus) *noun*
plural is **magi** (*say* **may**–jie)
an ancient priest, astrologer or wise man; especially used of the Three Wise Men who visited the infant Jesus.
[Persian]

Magyar (*say* **mag**–yar) *noun*
a person from the main ethnic group in Hungary. b) their language.
Word Family: **Magyar,** *adjective.*
[Hungarian]

maharajah (*say* mah–ha–**rah**–ja) **maharaja** *noun*
a title for certain ruling princes in India.
Word Family: **maharani, maharanee,** *nouns,* a) a female maharajah; b) the wife of a maharajah.
[Sanskrit *maha* great + *raja* king]

mah–jong (*say* mah–jong) **mah–jongg** *noun*
a complex Chinese game for four people played with pieces or tiles marked with suits or families.
[Mandarin Chinese]

mahogany (*say* ma–**hogga**–nee) *noun*
1. a tropical tree with a hard, reddish–brown wood, used for furniture.
2. a reddish–brown colour.
Word Family: **mahogany,** *adjective.*

maid *noun*
a) an old word meaning a girl or unmarried woman. b) a female servant.
old maid, a spinster.

maiden *noun*
1. an old word meaning a girl or young woman, especially a virgin.
2. *Cricket:* an over in which no runs are scored. Short form of **maiden over.**
maiden *adjective*
virginal or unmarried.
Usages:
a) 'a *maiden* racehorse' (= having not yet won).
b) 'a *maiden* speech' (= first).
maiden name, a girl's surname before marriage.
Word Family: **maidenly,** *adverb;* **maidenhood,** *noun,* a) the state or time of being a maiden, b) virginity.

maidenhair *noun*
a fern with fine stalks and delicate fronds.

maidenhead *noun*
see HYMEN.

mail (1) *noun*
see POST (2).
mail order, a system of buying goods by post.
Word Family: **mail,** *verb,* to send by post; **mail–order,** *verb.*

mail (2) *noun*
short form of **chain mail**
a flexible armour made of metal rings, chain, or small plates.
Word Family: **mail,** *verb,* to clothe or arm with mail.

maim *verb*
to cripple or injure severely.

main *adjective*
chief or most important: 'the *main* thing to remember'.
main *noun*
1. the principal pipe or cable in a gas or electrical system, etc.
2. strength or force: 'with might and *main*'.
3. a poetic word for the open ocean: 'they sailed the Spanish *main*'.
in the main, mostly.
Word Family: **mainly**, *adverb*, chiefly.

mainland *noun*
the principal land mass, as distinguished from islands.

mainline *verb*
(*informal*) to inject a narcotic drug directly into the vein.
Word Family: **mainliner**, *noun*.

mainsail (*say* main-sail *or* **main**-s'l) *noun*
the principal sail hoisted from the tallest mast on a ship.

mainspring *noun*
1. the chief motivating force.
2. the principal spring of a clock, etc.

mainstay *noun*
1. the chief support.
2. *Nautical:* the rope which secures the mainmast forward.

mainstream *noun*
the main trend in thought, fashion, etc.

maintain *verb*
1. to preserve or continue: 'try and *maintain* good relations with your friends'.
2. to affirm or assert: 'he *maintained* that he was totally innocent'.
Usages:
a) 'my father *maintains* me at boarding school' (= supports financially).
b) 'my job is to *maintain* the house and gardens' (= keep in good order).
Word Family: **maintainer**, *noun*; **maintainable**, *adjective*.
[Latin *manu* in the hand + *tenere* to hold]

maintenance (*say* **mane**-t'n-ance) *noun*
a) the act or process of maintaining.
b) a means of support, such as the money paid by one partner in a marriage to the other after separation.

maisonette (*say* may-z'n-**et**) *noun*
a self-contained flat occupying more than one floor of a house.
[French, small house]

maître d'hôtel (*say* **may**-tra doe-**tel**)
a head waiter.
[French, master of the house]

maize *noun*
1. an American cereal with heads (called **cobs**) thickly packed with large, succulent, usually yellow grain. Also called **Indian corn**.
2. a pale yellow colour.
Word Family: **maize**, *adjective*.
[from Cuban Spanish]

majesty (*say* **maj**-ess-tee) *noun*
1. a) regal grandeur and dignity: 'the procession continued with pomp and *majesty*'. b) supreme or royal authority.
2. (*capital*) a form of address for a monarch.
Word Family: **majestic** (*say* ma-**jes**tik), **majestical**, *adjective*, having great dignity; **majestically**, *adverb*.

majolica (*say* ma-**jol**lika) *noun*
also called **maiolica**
a variety of Italian earthenware with an opaque glaze and rich colours.
[from Italian name of *Majorca*, whence imported]

major (*say* **may**ja) *noun*
1. a commissioned officer in the armed forces ranking between a captain and a lieutenant colonel.
2. a main subject of study at certain universities.
major *adjective*
1. greater or more important: a) 'the *major* part of my money goes on rent'; b) 'he is a *major* artist of our century'.
2. *Music:* relating to the more normal of the two chief arrangements of the semitones in a key or scale. Compare MINOR.
Word Family: **major**, *verb*, to specialize in a subject at certain universities.
[Latin, greater]

major-domo *noun*
a butler or steward, especially one in charge of an important household.
[Spanish *mayor-domo* chief household official]

major general
an officer in the armed forces ranking between a brigadier and a lieutenant general.

majority (*say* ma–**jorri**–tee) *noun*
1. the greater part or number: 'the *majority* of students work hard'.
2. the state or time of being of full legal age: 'I will attain my *majority* next year when I turn 18'.

make *verb*
(made, making)
1. to create, form or bring into existence: a) 'mum *made* an apple pie'; b) 'you *make* too much noise'.
2. to cause something to be done, felt, etc.: a) 'she *made* me clean up the mess'; b) 'what *makes* a car go?'.
3. to cause to be or become: 'the worry is enough to *make* a man old before his time'.
4. to perform or engage in a certain act or activity: a) 'she *made* me an offer'; b) '*make* love, not war'; c) 'the drinkers *made* merry till dawn'.
Usages:
a) 'whom shall we *make* captain of the team?' (= appoint).
b) '*make* the beds!' (= tidy, put into order).
c) 'he *made* a fortune selling horses' (= earned).
d) 'if we include you it *makes* 8 of us' (= totals, adds up to).
e) (*informal*) 'we hope to *make* your place by midnight' (= reach, arrive at).
f) 'you will *make* an excellent doctor' (= become, prove to be).
g) 'he *made* a fine speech' (= delivered).
h) (*informal*) 'that scene *made* the whole film' (= brought success to).
i) (*informal*) 'did you *make* the team?' (= achieve selection for).
j) 'what time do you *make* it?' (= estimate to be).
Phrases:
have it made, (*informal*) to have all one needs for success, prosperity, etc.
make at, 'he *made at* me with an axe' (= lunged at).
make do, 'we'll have to *make do* without electricity' (= manage, get by).
make for, a) 'the thief suddenly *made for* the window' (= moved towards); b) 'a friendly boss *makes for* smooth running of the office' (= helps to create).
make it, to achieve one's goal.
make of, 'what do you *make of* this?' (= reckon it to be, judge of it).
make off with, to steal.
make out, a) 'she *made out* a cheque' (= wrote); b) 'he can't *make out* your writing' (= decipher, understand); c) 'are you *making* me *out* to be stupid?' (= suggesting).
make up, a) to comprise or be comprised of; b) to put together; c) 'he *made up* the whole story' (= invented); d) 'you will have to *make up* the time you have wasted' (= supply, give); e) 'they *made up* after the quarrel' (= became friends again); f) to apply make–up to; g) '*make up* your mind' (= bring to a decision).
make up to, (*informal*) to try to gain favour by fawning, flattery, etc.
make *noun*
the way or style in which something is made: 'this table is of a sturdy *make*'.
Usage: 'what *make* is your car?' (= brand).
on the make, (*informal*) seeking personal gain or advantage.
Word Family: **maker**, *noun*.

makeshift *adjective*
serving as a temporary substitute or alternative: 'we made a *makeshift* shelter for the night'.
Word Family: **makeshift**, *noun*.

make–up *noun*
1. a) any product used on the face to improve its appearance, etc. b) the cosmetics, wigs, etc. used by an actor.
2. the manner of being put together.
3. physical or mental constitution.

makeweight *noun*
1. a small quantity added to make up a deficiency.
2. a person invited, co–opted, etc. merely to fill a gap.

making *noun*
1. the cause of success or advancement: 'she'll be the *making* of him'.
2. (*often plural*) the material from which something can be made: 'he has the *makings* of a fine politician'.

mal–
a prefix meaning bad or wrongful, as in *maltreat*.
[Latin *malé* badly]

malacca (*say* ma–**lakka**) *noun*
a brown, cane walking stick made from the stem of a palm tree.
[after *Malacca*, a district in Malaysia]

malachite (*say* **malla**–kite) *noun*
a green mineral ore of copper, used for decoration.
[Greek *malakhé* mallow (which has leaves of this colour)]

maladjusted (*say* malla–**justid**) *adjective*

badly adjusted, especially of a person who cannot adapt to his surroundings or form relationships.
Word Family: **maladjustment**, *noun*, the condition of being maladjusted.

maladministration *noun*
bad management, especially of public matters.

maladroit (*say* malla-**droyt**) *adjective*
clumsy or awkward.
Word Family: **maladroitly**, *adverb*; **maladroitness**, *noun*.

malady (*say* **malla**-dee) *noun*
a disorder or disease.

malaise (*say* mal-**aze**) *noun*
a general feeling of unexplained discomfort or weakness.
[French *mal* bad + *aise* ease]

malapropism (*say* **malla**-prop-izm) *noun*
a) the inappropriate or unsuitable use of words: 'it is a *malapropism* to say credible when you mean credulous'. b) a word or expression which has been so misused.
[from *Mrs Malaprop*, a character in Sheridan's 'The Rivals' who confused words in this way]

malaria (*say* ma-**lairee**-a) *noun*
a recurrent disease transmitted by mosquitoes and causing fevers and chills.
Word Family: **malarial**, **malarious**, *adjectives*.
[Italian *mala* bad + *aria* air]

malarkey *noun*
(*informal*) humbug, nonsense.

malcontent (*say* **malkon**-tent) *noun*
a person who is discontented and inclined to rebel.
Word Family: **malcontent**, *adjective*.

male *noun*
1. a) a person of the sex which generates, but does not give birth to, children. b) an animal of this sex.
2. the parts of a plant which fertilize the female parts.
Word Family: **male**, *adjective*, of or characteristic of a male, b) (of a machine part, etc.) designed to fit into a corresponding part.

malediction (*say* malla-**dik**-sh'n) *noun*
a curse.
Word Family: **maledictory**, *adjective*.

malefactor (*say* **malli**-fakta) *noun*
a criminal or wrongdoer.

maleficent (*say* ma-**leffi**-s'nt) *adjective*
harmful or doing harm.
Word Family: **maleficence**, *noun*.
[Latin *malé* badly + *faciens* doing]

malevolent (*say* ma-**levva**-l'nt) *adjective*
showing ill will or wishing harm to others.
Word Family: **malevolently**, *adverb*; **malevolence**, *noun*.
[Latin *malé* badly + *volens* willing]

malfeasance (*say* mal-**feezence**) *noun*
Law: an unlawful act.

malformed *adjective*
badly formed or shaped, especially of an animal or plant.
Word Family: **malformation**, *noun*.

malice (*say* **mallis**) *noun*
a desire or intention to hurt or cause suffering.
malicious (*say* ma-**lishus**) *adjective*
full of or showing malice.
Word Family: **maliciously**, *adverb*; **maliciousness**, *noun*.
[Latin *malitia* badness]

malign (*say* ma-**line**) *verb*
to slander or speak ill of someone.
malign *adjective*
causing evil or injury: 'the hardened criminal has a *malign* influence over his son'.
Word Family: **malignly**, *adverb*; **maligner**, *noun*, a person who maligns; **malignity** (*say* ma-**ligni**-tee), *noun*, a) ill will, b) a malign act.
[Latin *malignus* ill-natured]

malignant (*say* ma-**lig**-nant) *adjective*
1. feeling or showing extreme ill will.
2. *Medicine:* (of diseases, etc.) tending to cause death. Compare BENIGN.
Word Family: **malignantly**, *adverb*; **malignance**, **malignancy**, *noun*.

malinger (*say* ma-**linga**) *verb*
to pretend to be ill, especially in order to escape work, etc.
Word Family: **malingerer**, *noun*.

mallard *noun*
the common European wild duck, the female having brown plumage and the male a dark green head.

malleable (*say* **mallia**-b'l) *adjective*
1. able to be hammered into thin sheets or rolled into shape. Compare DUCTILE.
2. easily influenced.
Word Family: **malleability** (*say* mallia-**billi**-tee), *noun*.
[Latin *malleus* a hammer]

mallet *noun*
1 a hammer, especially one with a wooden head.

2. a long-handled, wooden stick used to strike the ball in croquet.

malnutrition (*say* mal-new-**trish**'n) *noun*
poor nutrition due to a lack of the correct foods, especially vitamins or protein.

malodorous (*say* mal-**o**-der-us) *adjective*
having an unpleasant smell.

malpractice (*say* mal-**prak**tis) *noun*
any improper conduct, especially by a professional person.

malt (*say* mawlt) *noun*
a) a germinated grain, often barley, used in brewing and distillation. b) malt extract.
Word Family: **malt**, *verb*, a) to make with malt, b) to convert grain into malt.

Malthusian (*say* mal-**thew**zian) *adjective*
of or based on the theory that population growth must be checked to prevent food shortages.
[after *T. R. Malthus*, 1766–1834, an English political economist who developed the theory]

maltreat *verb*
to treat badly or cruelly.
Word Family: **maltreatment**, *noun.*

mama, mamma *noun*
mother.

mamba *noun*
a deadly poisonous African tree-snake.
[Zulu]

mambo *noun*
a dance of Latin-American origin.
Word Family: **mambo**, *verb*, to dance the mambo.
[West Indian]

mammal *noun*
a member of the group of vertebrates whose young feed on milk from the mother's breast.
Word Family: **mammalian** (*say* mam-**ay**-lian), *adjective.*
[Latin *mamma* breast]

mammary (say **mamma**-ree) *adjective*
of or relating to the breast.
[Latin *mamma* breast]

mammary gland
the milk-producing gland in females. In humans this is called the **breast**, and in other mammals it is called the **udder**.

mammon *noun*
wealth or riches.
[after *Mammon*, wealth and greed personified in the Bible as a false god]

mammoth *noun*
an extinct elephant.
mammoth *adjective*
huge or gigantic.

man *noun*
plural is **men**
1. a) the most highly developed living creature, as distinct from other animals or creatures. b) an adult male of this group.
2. any person, especially an adult: 'give a *man* a chance'.
3. mankind: '*man* dreams of conquering the elements'.
4. a male servant or subordinate.
5. a person who shows the supposed masculine virtues of courage, etc.: 'take it like a *man*'.
6. one of the pieces used in playing certain games, such as chess, etc.
Phrases:
man about town, a person with an active social life.
man of the world, a person of wide experience.
the man in the street, a person supposed to represent the most common point of view.
to a man, to the last man, 'they agreed to stay and fight *to a man*' (= without exception).
man *verb*
(manned, manning)
to supply with men, especially for defence: 'to *man* a fortress'.
Word Family: **manly**, *adjective*, having the qualities considered appropriate to a man; **manliness**, *noun*; **manhood**, *noun*, the state or time of being a man.

manacle (*say* **manni**-k'l) *noun*
a shackle or handcuff.
Word Family: **manacle**, *verb*, to restrain with manacles.
[Latin *manicula* little hand]

manage (*say* **mannij**) *verb*
1. to control or handle something properly or successfully: 'can you *manage* that horse?'.
2. to succeed in doing something: 'she *managed* to sell her car for a good price'.
Usage: 'how are you *managing* without a car?' (= succeeding).
management *noun*
1. a) the act or manner of managing: 'her *management* of the children is excellent'. b) executive skill or ability:

'the young man was trained in *management*'.
2. a person or group in charge of a business.
Word Family: **manager** *noun*, a person who manages, especially a person in charge of a business; **manageress**, *noun*, a female manager; **managerial** (*say* manna-**jeer**ial), *adjective*, of or like a manager; **manageable**, *adjective*.

mañana (*say* man-**yah**-na) *noun*
tomorrow.
[Spanish]

mandala (*say* man-**dah**la) *noun*
a sacred or magical diagram, often a circle representing the universe, used for meditation, etc. in certain Eastern religions.

mandarin *noun*
1. a small, sweet, orange citrus fruit.
2. *History:* a member of any of the nine ranks of public officials during the Chinese Empire.
3. (*capital*) the language of north and west China, including the dialect spoken in Peking, upon which the official language of China is based.

mandate *noun*
1. a command or order.
2. a) the instruction given by an electorate to its representative, expressed by the result of an election: 'the winning party may consider itself to have a *mandate* from the people to carry out its policies'. b) the commission given to one nation to administer the government and affairs of a territory, colony, etc.
Word Family: **mandatory** (*say* **manda**-tree), *adjective*, a) of or like a mandate, b) obliging or permitting no choice.
[Latin *mandatus* commanded]

mandible (*say* **mandi**-b'l) *noun*
1. the bottom part of a bird's beak.
2. *Anatomy:* the lower, movable jawbone.
Word Family: **mandibular** (*say* man-**dib**-yoola), *adjective*.
[Latin *mandere* to chew]

mandolin (*say* manda-**lin**) **mandoline** *noun*
a musical instrument similar to the lute, having four pairs of metal strings plucked with a plectrum.
Word Family: **mandolinist**, *noun*.
[from Italian]

mandrake *noun*
a narcotic herb.
[Greek *mandragoras*]

mandrel, mandril *noun*
a shaft or spindle in a lathe, etc., used to support pieces being worked on.

mandrill *noun*
a large West African baboon with a beard and mane, the male having blue and scarlet markings on its face and buttocks.

mane *noun*
1. the long hair on the neck of animals such as horses, lions, etc.
2. any long or thick hair.

manège (*say* man-**aje**) *noun*
horsemanship.
[French, training]

maneuver *noun*
see MANOEUVRE.

manful *adjective*
brave and determined.
Word Family: **manfully**, *adverb*.

manganese (*say* man-ga-**neez**) *noun*
element number 25, a hard brittle metal element used to strengthen alloys, especially steel. See TRANSITION ELEMENT.
See CHEMICAL ELEMENTS in grey pages.
[corruption of *magnesia*]

mange (*rhymes with* strange) *noun*
any of a group of skin diseases due to parasitic mites, causing scab-like sores and loss of hair, usually in animals.
mangy (say **mane**-jee) *adjective*
1. suffering from mange.
2. (*informal*) shabby or decrepit.

manger (*say* **mane**-ja) *noun*
a box or trough from which cattle or horses feed.

mangle (1) *verb*
to cut or damage something badly.
Usage: 'he *mangled* his speech on television' (= ruined through mistakes).

mangle (2) *noun*
also called a **wringer**
a device which squeezes water out of clothes, etc. by pressing them between rollers.
Word Family: **mangle**, *verb*.

mango *noun*
an oblong tropical fruit having yellow flesh.
[Tamil]

mangold *noun*
also called a **mangel-wurzel**
a large variety of beet, cultivated for cattle food.
[German *mangold* beet + *wurzel* root]

mangrove *noun*
any of a group of low trees with exposed roots, usually found in tropical tidal swamps.

manhandle *verb*
to handle roughly.

manhole *noun*
a hole, usually with a cover, through which a person may enter a boiler, sewer, etc.

manhood *noun*
Word Family: see MAN.

man-hour *noun*
an hour of work done by one person, used as an industrial time unit.

mania (*say* **may**-nia) *noun*
1. a great excitement or enthusiasm.
2. an uncontrollable and often violent form of insanity.
Word Family: **manic** (*say* **mannik**), *adjective*, of or produced by a mania.

-mania
a suffix indicating an extreme enthusiasm or desire for something, as in *megalomania*.
[Greek, madness]

maniac (*say* **may**-nee-ak) *noun*
a mad person.
Word Family: **maniacal** (*say* ma-**nie**-a-k'l), *adjective*, of or characteristic of mania.

manic-depression *noun*
a mental disorder marked by alternate moods of excitement and depression.
Word Family: **manic-depressive,** *noun, adjective.*

manicure *verb*
to treat or care for the hands and fingernails.
Word Family: **manicure,** *noun*; **manicurist,** *noun*, a person who manicures.
[Latin *manus* hand + *cura* care]

manifest (*say* **manni**-fest) *adjective*
plain or obvious: 'he told a *manifest* lie'.
manifest *verb*
to show clearly: 'his guilt was *manifested* in court'.
manifest *noun*
Commerce: a list of cargo.
manifestation
(*say* manni-fes-**tay**-sh'n) *noun*
a) the act of manifesting. b) a sign or indication: 'his house is a *manifestation* of his wealth'.
Word Family: **manifestly,** *adverb.*
[Latin *manifestus* palpable, plain]

manifesto *noun*
plural is **manifestos**
a statement, as by a political party, which explains actions, intentions or policies.

manifold *adjective*
many and various: 'she performs *manifold* duties at work'.
manifold *noun*
a pipe or chamber with a number of inlets or outlets, such as one used for conducting air and fuel into, or exhaust gases out of, an internal combustion engine.

manikin (*say* **manni**-kin) **mannikin** *noun*
1. a dwarf or small man.
2. a tailor's dummy.

manila paper
a strong, light brown paper used to make envelopes, folders, etc.
[made of hemp from *Manila*, Philippines]

manipulate (*say* ma-**nip**-yoo-late) *verb*
to handle or manage something skilfully.
Usage: 'he *manipulates* people for his own ends' (= manages or influences cleverly).
manipulation *noun*
1. the act of manipulating, such as the moving of a body joint beyond its normal range of movement.
2. any skilful or artful management.
Word Family: **manipulator,** *noun*; **manipulative, manipulatory,** *adjectives.*

mankind *noun*
all living people.

manly *adjective*
Word Family: see MAN.

manna *noun*
anything valuable which is received unexpectedly.
[Hebrew, of the bread God rained from heaven upon the famished Israelites in the desert, according to the account in the Bible, Exodus 16]

mannequin (*say* **manni**-kin) *noun*
an old word meaning a fashion model.
[French]

manner *noun*
1. the way in which something happens or is done: a) 'do it in the *manner* I have shown you'; b) 'he kissed her hand in the French *manner*'.

Usages:
a) 'I don't like her *manner* at all' (= way of speaking or behaving).
b) 'what *manner* of person is he?' (= type, sort).
2. (*plural*) ways of behaving, especially in relation to correct, polite or accepted social standards: 'bad *manners*'.
in a manner of speaking, in a way.
Word Family: **mannered**, *adjective*, a) having a particular sort of manners, b) having artificial mannerisms; **mannerly**, *adjective*, polite.

mannerism (*say* **manna**–rizm) *noun*
a distinctive habit or way of behaving, often affected.

mannikin *noun*
see MANIKIN.

mannish *adjective*
like a man.
Word Family: **mannishly**, *adverb*; **mannishness**, *noun*.

manoeuvre (*say* ma–**noova**) *noun*
in America spelt **maneuver**
1. a planned and organized movement, as of troops, warships, etc.
2. any clever or skilful moves or methods.
Word Family: **manoeuvre**, *verb*.
[French]

man of straw
1. a man put up as a surety though having inadequate funds.
2. any unreliable person.

man–of–war *noun*
1. a warship.
2. a Portuguese man–of–war.

manometer (*say* ma–**nommi**ta) *noun*
an instrument used to measure the pressure of a gas or a liquid.
[Greek *manos* thin + METER]

manor *noun*
1. *Medieval history:* the house and lands of a feudal lord.
2. the home of a former or still surviving lord of the manor: 'the old lady up at the *manor* died last week'. Short form of **manor house**.
3. (*informal*) a police district.
Word Family: **manorial** (*say* ma–**naw**riul), *adjective*.

manpower *noun*
1. the physical power of a person or persons, especially in relation to work.
2. power as measured by the number of people available or required.

manqué (*say* **mong**–kay) *adjective*
unsuccessful or unfulfilled: 'the theatre critic was really an actor *manqué*'.
[French, failed]

mansard *noun*
a roof in which the angle of the slope changes halfway, the lower half being steeper than the upper.

manse *noun*
the home of a clergyman, especially in Scotland.

mansion (*say* **man**–sh'n) *noun*
a large, elaborate house usually with extensive grounds around it.
[from Latin]

manslaughter (*say* man–**slaw**ta) *noun*
the unintentional killing of a person. Compare MURDER.

mantelpiece *noun*
also called a **chimneypiece**
a structure above and around a fireplace, usually with a projecting shelf.

mantilla *noun*
a woman's lace headscarf, attached to a comb and falling over the shoulders, worn in Spain.
[Spanish, small mantle]

mantissa *noun*
Maths: the decimal part of a logarithm. See CHARACTERISTIC.
[Latin, makeweight]

mantle *noun*
1. an old word for a woman's cloak.
2. something which covers or conceals: 'a *mantle* of fog'.
3. *Geology:* the layer of solid rock between the earth's crust and the magma.
4. a fine network placed over a gas flame and heated by the flame so that it becomes white hot and produces brilliant light.
Word Family: **mantle**, *verb*, to cover with or as if with a mantle.

manual (*say* **man**–yew'l) *adjective*
1. of or done with the hands: '*manual* labour'.
2. using human rather than mechanical or automatic power: '*manual* gears in a car'.
manual *noun*
1. a book providing information or instruction.
2. the keyboard of an organ, etc., played with the hands.
[Latin *manus* hand]

manufacture (*say* man–yoo–**fak**–cher) *noun*
a) the making or producing of goods by hand or machinery. b) the goods produced: 'their *manufactures* are of good quality'.
manufacture *verb*
to make or produce goods, etc.
Usage: 'I shall have to *manufacture* an excuse to escape doing the work' (= invent).
Word Family: **manufacturer**, *noun.*
[Latin *manu* by hand + *factus* made]

manumit (*say* man–yoo–**mit**) *verb*
(**manumitted, manumitting**)
to release a slave.

manure (*say* ma–**newer**) *noun*
the excrement of animals, or an artificial substance with similar properties, put in the soil to fertilize it.
Word Family: **manure**, *verb*, to add manure to.

manuscript (*say* **man**–yoo–skript) *noun*
a handwritten or typed copy of an article, book, report, etc., before it is printed.
[Latin *manus* hand + *scriptum* writing]

manx cat
one of a breed of short–haired tail–less cats with long hind legs.
[*Manx*, of the Isle of Man]

many *adjective*
(**more, most**)
a large number of: '*many* people have their own homes'.
many *noun*
(*used with plural verb*) a large number: '*many* of them were killed'.
how many?, what number?

Maori (*rhymes with* dowry) *noun*
a) a member of the Polynesian peoples who are native to New Zealand or the Cook Islands. b) their languages.
Word Family: **Maori**, *adjective.*

map *noun*
an illustration of part or all of the surface of the earth, a planet, etc.
put on the map, 'the famous author has *put* Australia *on the map*' (= made well known).
Word Family: **map** (**mapped, mapping**), *verb*, a) to make or put on a map, b) to sketch a plan of something.

maple *noun*
any of a group of trees and shrubs including the sugar maple, ornamental varieties and some which yield timber.

maple syrup
a sweet, thick syrup made from the sap of maple trees.

maquette (*say* ma–**ket**) *noun*
a small, trial model for a sculpture.

mar *verb*
(**marred, marring**)
to spoil or damage.

marabou (*say* **marra**–boo) *noun*
a tall West African, carrion–eating stork with soft feathers under the wings and tail which are used for trimming clothes, etc.

maraca (*say* ma–**rakka**) *noun*
a percussion instrument consisting of a gourd filled with dried seeds, etc.

marathon *noun*
1. a long–distance race, especially a foot race of about 42 km.
2. any long test or competition of endurance.
marathon *adjective*
long and difficult: 'she completed the task after a *marathon* effort'.
[from the running of a messenger to Athens to tell of the Greek victory at the *Battle of Marathon* in 490 B.C.]

maraud (*say* ma–**rawd**) *verb*
to raid in search of plunder.
Word Family: **marauder**, *noun.*
[French, vagabond]

marble *noun*
1. a) a form of hard limestone, usually veined or mottled, which is cut and polished for use in buildings, statues, etc. b) a statue or other object made from this substance.
2. a) a small ball of stone or glass, which is used in a children's game. b) (*plural*) the game itself.
Word Family: **marble**, *verb*, to colour or stain something like marble; **marble**, *adjective*, of or like marble; **marbling**, *noun*, marble–like decoration.

marcasite (*say* **marka**–site) *noun*
Geology: a brass–coloured mineral consisting of iron pyrites, used for jewellery.

march (1) *verb*
a) to walk with measured and regular steps, like soldiers. b) to cause to march: 'the prisoners were *marched* to their cells'.
Usage: 'time *marches* on' (= proceeds).
march *noun*
1. a) the act of marching. b) the distance covered by marching: 'a 10 km *march*'.

Usage: 'the *march* of time' (= advance).
2. a piece of music to accompany marching.
steal a march, to gain or take an advantage.
[French *marcher* to walk]

march (2) *noun*
History: an area of land along the border of a country.

March (3) *noun*
the third month of the year in the Gregorian calendar.
[after the ancient Roman god *Mars*]

marching orders
(*informal*) instructions to leave.

marchioness (*say* marsha-**ness**) *noun*
also called a **marquise** (*say* mar-**keez**)
a) a female marquess. b) the wife of a marquess.

mare (1) (*rhymes with* air) *noun*
a female horse or pony, more than three years old.

mare (2) (*say* **mar**-ray) *noun*
any of several large dark plains on the moon.
[Latin, sea]

mare's nest
the boasted discovery of something which does not and could not exist.

margarine (*say* marja-**reen**) *noun*
a substitute for butter made from vegetable oils or animal fats.

margin (*say* **mar**-jin) *noun*
1. the space between writing and the edge of a page.
2. any edge.
3. *Commerce:* the difference between the cost and the selling price.
Usages:
a) 'she won by a narrow *margin*' (= amount).
b) 'leave yourself a *margin* of 10 minutes' (= extra amount).
marginal *adjective*
of or situated on a margin: '*marginal* notes'.
Usages:
a) 'a *marginal* seat in the election' (= closely contested).
b) 'they only had *marginal* provisions to last the winter' (= barely sufficient).
Word Family: **marginally,** *adverb.*
[from Latin]

margrave *noun*
History: a hereditary title of certain rulers, especially in Germany.
Word Family: **margravine,** *noun,* the wife of a margrave.

marguerite (*say* marga-**reet**) *noun*
any of a group of white, pink or yellow daisies produced on a small, evergreen shrub.
[Latin *margarita* pearl]

marigold (*say* **marri**-gold) *noun*
a garden plant with bright yellow or orange flowers.

marijuana (*say* marri-**wah**-na)
marihuana *noun*
1. the Indian hemp, *Cannabis sativa.*
2. hashish prepared from this.
[Spanish *Maria Juana* Mary Jane]

marimba *noun*
an African musical instrument similar to a large xylophone.

marina (*say* ma-**reena**) *noun*
a harbour for small boats and yachts.
[Italian]

marinate (*say* **marri**-nate) *verb*
also called to **marinade**
to soak meat or game in a seasoned liquid to increase the flavour and make it more tender.
Word Family: **marinade,** *noun.*
[Spanish *marinada* pickle]

marine (*say* ma-**reen**) *adjective*
1. existing in or produced by the sea: '*marine* life'.
2. of or relating to the sea or shipping, etc.: '*marine* navigation'.
marine *noun*
a soldier who serves at sea as well as on land.
[Latin *marinus* of the sea]

mariner (*say* **marrina**) *noun*
an old word for a sailor.

marionette (*say* **marria**-net) *noun*
a puppet moved by strings.

marital (*say* **marri**-t'l) *adjective*
of or relating to marriage.
[Latin *maritus* matrimonial]

maritime (*say* **marri**-time) *adjective*
of or relating to the sea or ships.

marjoram (*say* **mar**ja-r'm) *noun*
a herb with small purplish-white flowers, used in cooking.

mark (1) *noun*
1. a visible impression: a) 'a finger *mark*'; b) 'a dirty *mark*'.
2. *Rugby football:* a clean catch of the ball by a player who, if certain other conditions are met, is then allowed to kick the ball unmolested.
Usages:
a) 'this gift is a *mark* of our esteem' (= token).
b) 'a punctuation *mark*' (= symbol).

c) 'nearly everyone got good *marks* this term' (= ratings).
d) 'his arrow hit the *mark*' (= target).
e) 'what are the *marks* of a good school?' (= distinguishing features).
f) 'her manners are not up to the *mark*' (= established standard).
Phrases:
leave one's mark, 'he *left his mark* on the business world' (= had distinct effect).
make one's mark, to be successful.
on your marks, (*Athletics*) take your starting positions.

mark *verb*
1. to put a mark or sign on: 'the cattle were *marked* with a brand'.
Usages:
a) '*mark* my words, young man' (= pay attention to).
b) 'the day was *marked* by brilliant sunshine' (= distinguished).
c) 'he is a *marked* man' (= chosen as a victim, etc).
2. *Rugby football:* a) to take a mark. b) to stay close to an opponent.
Phrases:
mark down, to reduce the price of.
mark off, to separate by a line, etc.
mark out, 'he was *marked out* for early promotion' (= singled out).
mark time, a) (*Military*) to march on the one spot; b) to wait.
mark up, a) to increase the price of; b) to mark with notations or symbols.
Word Family: **marker,** *noun,* a person or thing that marks; **marked,** *adjective,* very noticeable; **markedly,** *adverb*; **marking,** *noun,* a mark or a series of marks, as on an animal.

mark (2) *noun*
the main unit of money in Germany.

market *noun*
1. an area where people meet to buy and sell goods, especially food.
2. any institution or group of people involved in trade, exchange, etc.: 'the stock *market*'.
Usages:
a) 'the world gold *market*' (= trade).
b) 'there is no *market* for cars here' (= demand).
Phrases:
in the market for, wanting to buy.
market price, the price at which a thing is currently selling.
on the market, for sale.
play the market, to speculate on the stock exchange.

market *verb*
to buy or sell in a market.
Word Family: **marketable,** *adjective,* fit or easy to sell; **marketeer,** *noun.*

market garden
land or a garden on which fruit or vegetables are grown for sale.

market research
Commerce: the systematic investigation of what is the likely market for a product, how well some product is known, etc.

marksman *noun*
a person who shoots firearms accurately.
Word Family: **marksmanship,** the art of accurate shooting.

marl *noun*
a deposit of clay and calcium carbonate, often used as a fertilizer.

marlin *noun*
any of a group of large, strong fish with a spear-like snout.
[from MARLINESPIKE, whose shape it resembles]

marlinespike *noun*
Nautical: a heavy, metal pin used to separate strands of rope in splicing.
[from Dutch]

marmalade *noun*
a jelly-like preserve made from oranges and other citrus fruit.
[Greek *melimelon* honey apple]

marmoset (*say* **marma**-zet) *noun*
a small monkey with soft, woolly fur and a bushy tail, found in tropical America.
[Old French *marmouset* grotesque little figure]

marmot (*say* **mar**-m't) *noun*
a small burrowing rodent which resembles a squirrel, found in the Alps and other mountains of Europe, and recognizable by its piercing scream.

maroon (1) (*say* ma-**roon**) *noun*
a moderate brownish-red colour.
Word Family: **maroon,** *adjective.*
[French *marron* chestnut]

maroon (2) (*say* ma-**roon**) *verb*
to isolate or strand, as after a shipwreck.

marquee (*say* **markee**) *noun*
a large tent or tent-like canopy used for entertaining outdoors.

marquess (*say* **mar**-kwis) *noun*
also called a **marquis**
a person who ranks between a duke and an earl.

marquetry (*say* **marki**–tree) *noun*
also spelt **marqueterie**
any inlaid work of coloured woods or other materials, especially in furniture.

marquis (*say* **mar**–kwis) *noun*
1. a foreign title equivalent to marquess.
2. a title still so spelt by a few British marquesses.

marriage *noun*
1. a formal agreement between a man and a woman to live together according to the customs of their religion or society.
2. any union: 'the *marriage* of true minds'.
Word Family: **marriageable**, *adjective.*

marrow *noun*
1. *Anatomy:* the soft, sometimes liquid, tissue in which blood cells are formed, and which fills the hollow spaces within bones.
2. a large oblong fruit, usually cooked and eaten as a vegetable.
marrow-bone *noun*
a bone containing edible fatty tissue.

marry *verb*
(married, marrying)
1. to join or be joined in marriage.
2. (of a priest or civil official) to join as husband and wife.

Mars *noun*
Astronomy: the planet in the solar system next to the earth and fourth from the sun.
[after the ancient Roman god *Mars*]

Marsala (*say* mar–**sahla**) *noun*
a sweet dark, fortified wine.
[first made in *Marsala,* Sicily]

marsh *noun*
a swamp.
Word Family: **marshy**, *adjective.*

marshal (*say* **marsh**'l) *verb*
(marshalled, marshalling)
1. to arrange in an orderly manner: 'to *marshal* troops for the parade'.
2. to lead or conduct.
marshal *noun*
1. a person who marshals or organizes.
2. the highest ranking officer: 'a field *marshal*'.
3. *American:* an officer appointed to carry out court orders.

marsh gas
methane.

marshmallow *noun*
a soft, spongy sweet made with gelatine, sugar and flavouring.

marsupial (*say* mar–**soopiul**) *noun*
any of a group of primitive mammals which produce living young in a very immature state, the development of the offspring being completed in a pouch on the mother's abdomen.
Word Family: **marsupial**, *adjective.*
[Greek *marsipos* a purse or bag]

mart *noun*
a market.

marten (*say* **mar**–tin) *noun*
a) any of various slender, furry, flesh-eating members of the weasel family, living in conifer woods, they include the pine marten, stone marten, sable and polecat. b) the dark brown fur of such an animal.

martial (*say* **mar**–sh'l) *adjective*
of or relating to war or the armed forces.

martial art
any fighting technique which has developed to the level of an art, e.g. karate and fencing.

martial law
a temporary government of a country by military rule and the superseding of civil law during a serious internal or external crisis.

Martian (*say* **mar**–sh'n) *noun*
1. of or relating to Mars, especially one of an imaginary race of beings inhabiting Mars.
2. a person believed to come from the planet Mars.

martin *noun*
see HOUSE MARTIN.

martinet (*say* martin–**et**) *noun*
a person who enforces strict discipline.
[after *Jean Martinet,* a 17th–century French army officer]

martingale *noun*
a forked strap passing between a horse's forelegs from the girth to the bridle, used to keep its head down.

martyr (*say* **mar**ta) *noun*
a person who chooses death or great suffering rather than give up his religion or beliefs.
make a martyr of oneself, to inconvenience oneself unnecessarily in order to gain pity or praise.
martyrdom *noun*
the suffering or death of a martyr.
Word Family: **martyr**, *verb,* a) to put to death as a martyr, b) to make a martyr of, c) to torment or torture.
[Greek, a witness]

marvel *verb*
(**marvelled, marvelling**)
to wonder or be very suprised.
marvel *noun*
something which is marvellous.

marvellous (*say* **marva**-lus) *adjective*
astonishing or wonderful: 'he's a *marvellous* cook'.
Word Family: **marvellously**, *adverb*; **marvellousness**, *noun.*

Marxism (*say* **mark**-sizm) *noun*
a political and economic theory which states that the struggle between social classes determines historical change, and must lead inevitably to the replacement of capitalism by communism.
Word Family: **Marxist, Marxian,** *adjectives, nouns.*
[after Karl *Marx*, 1818–83, a German political philosopher]

marzipan *noun*
a rich, sugary sweet made from ground almonds, sugar and eggwhites.

mascara (*say* mass-**kar**-a) *noun*
a coloured substance applied to the eyelashes to make them darker or thicker.
[Spanish, mask]

mascot *noun*
a person, animal or object believed to bring good luck.

masculine (*say* **mass**-kewlin) *adjective*
1. of or relating to the male sex.
2. having the qualities said to be appropriate to males.
3. *Grammar:* see GENDER.
Word Family: **masculinity** (*say* mass-kew-**linni**-tee), *noun.*

maser (*say* **may**-zer) *noun*
an electronic device for amplifying microwaves and providing an output of precisely determined frequency, used in improving radar, radio, radio astronomy, satellite communications, etc.
[from M(icrowave) A(mplification) by S(timulated) E(mission) of R(adiation)]

mash *noun*
1. any soft, pulpy mass.
2. a soaked or boiled mixture of grains, such as is fed to livestock, etc.
masher *noun*
an instrument used for mashing: 'a potato *masher*'.
Word Family: **mash**, *verb*, to crush or beat to a mash.

mask *noun*
a covering for the face, worn for protection, disguise, etc.
Usage: 'a *mask* of friendliness' (= disguise, pretence).
Word Family: **mask**, *verb*, a) to wear a mask, b) to hide or disguise.

masochism (*say* **massa**-kizm) *noun*
a pleasure, especially sexual pleasure, in one's own suffering, pain or humiliation.
Word Family: **masochist**, *noun*, a person who indulges in masochism; **masochistic** (*say* massa-**kis**-tik), *adjective*; **masochistically**, *adverb.*
[after *Leopold von Sacher-Masoch*, 1836–1895, an Austrian novelist who described this condition]

mason *noun*
1. a person who works with or builds in stone or brick.
2. (*capital*) a member of a mutual-aid fraternity of Freemasons, which has initiation rites which were originally secret.
Word Family: **masonic** (*say* ma-**sonnik**), *adjective.*

masonry (*say* **may**-s'n-ree) *noun*
a) stonework or brickwork. b) the trade or skill of a mason.

masque (*say* mahsk) *noun*
a form of entertainment popular in England in the 16th and 17th centuries, which consisted of songs, dances, poetry and mime.

masquerade (*say* mass-ka-**rade**) *noun*
1. a social function at which masks and disguises are worn.
2. a pretence or false appearance.
Word Family: **masquerade**, *verb*; **masquerader**, *noun.*
[Spanish *mascara* a mask]

mass (1) *noun*
1. a large body or amount: 'an iceberg is a floating *mass* of ice'.
Usages:
a) 'the *mass* of the spectators sat out in the open' (= main part).
b) 'the sheer *mass* of the mountain overawed us' (= bulk).
2. *Physics:* the fundamental quantity describing the resistance of a body to an accelerating force and expressed in kilograms. Compare WEIGHT.
the masses
the great body of ordinary people.
Word Family: **mass**, *verb*, to form or gather into a mass.

Mass (2) *noun*
1. the celebration of the Eucharist.

2. a musical setting of some of the fixed portions of the Mass.

massacre (*say* **mass**ika) *noun*
the merciless killing of large numbers of people or animals.
Word Family: **massacre**, *verb*.
[French]

massage (*say* mass-ar**zh**) *noun*
the rubbing and kneading of the muscles and joints of the body to relieve stiffness, etc.
Word Family: **massage**, *verb*; **massager**, *noun*, a person who gives massages; **masseur** (*say* mass-**er**), *noun*, a male massager; **masseuse** (*say* mass-**erz**), *noun*, a female massager.

massif (*say* **mass**-eef) *noun*
a compact part of a mountain range, rising into peaks towards the summit.
[French]

massive (*say* **mass**iv) *adjective*
very large, heavy and solid: 'a *massive* oak table'.
Word Family: **massively**, *adverb*; **massiveness**, *noun*.

mass number
Physics: the total number of protons and neutrons in the nucleus of an atom. Compare ATOMIC NUMBER.

mass production
the making of goods in very large amounts by standardized processes.

mass spectrograph
a device which measures the mass of ions from their deflections when they are passed through electric and magnetic fields.

mast (1) (*say* mahst) *noun*
an upright pole, especially one rising from the deck or the keel of a boat for carrying flags, radio aerials, sails, etc.

mast (2) (*say* mahst) *noun*
beech-nuts, acorns, chestnuts, etc., the food of free-range pigs.

mastectomy (*say* mass-**tek**ta-mee) *noun*
a surgical operation to remove the breast.
[Greek *mastos* breast + *ektomé* a cutting out]

master (*rhymes with* faster) *noun*
1. a person or thing that has power, control or authority: a) 'the *master* of a ship', b) 'money should never become your *master*'.
Usage: 'the Geography *master*' (= male teacher).
2. a person who is highly skilled: 'the spy was a *master* of disguise'.
3. a person who holds the second degree awarded by a university, following a bachelor's degree.
4. (*capital*) a title for a boy who is not old enough to be called Mister.
5. an original from which copies are made.
master *verb*
to become master of: a) 'to *master* one's anger'; b) 'he *mastered* French after only 3 months in France'.
master *adjective*
principal or main: a) 'the *master* bedroom'; b) 'a *master* plan'.
[Latin *magister*]

master-at-arms *noun*
Navy: a petty officer appointed as policeman on a ship.

masterful *adjective*
1. domineering: 'he has a *masterful* personality'.
2. highly skilled: 'a *masterful* display of acrobatic grace'.
Word Family: **masterfully**, *adverb*; **masterfulness**, *noun*.

master key
a skeleton key.

masterly (*say* **mah**sta-lee) *adjective*
showing the skill of a master: 'a *masterly* performance'.
Word Family: **masterly**, *adverb*.

mastermind *verb*
to plan and direct some activity at the highest level: 'Mr X *masterminded* the great Postal Robbery'.
Word Family: **mastermind**, *noun*.

master of ceremonies
a person who is in charge of the ceremonial side of a formal occasion, e.g. one who announces speakers at a banquet.

masterpiece *noun*
a very great work of art, or the best work of a given person: 'some people regard 'Hamlet' as Shakespeare's *masterpiece*'.

master stroke
a masterly action or achievement.

mastery *noun*
1. the upper hand: 'at the meeting he showed his complete *mastery* of the situation'.
2. the skill or knowledge of a master: 'his *mastery* of the techniques of violin playing'.

masthead *noun*
1. the top of a mast, especially the tallest mast.
2. the title, etc. at the head of the front page of a newspaper or the formalized headings of a magazine's contents page.

masticate *verb*
to chew.
Word Family: **mastication,** *noun.*
[Greek *mastikhan* to gnash the teeth]

mastiff *noun*
any of a breed of large, heavy, short-haired dogs used as watch-dogs.

mastitis (*say* mass-**tie**-tis) *noun*
a bacterial inflammation in the mammary gland.
[Greek *mastos* breast + -ITIS]

mastodon (*say* **mass**-ta-don) *noun*
a long-extinct elephant-like mammal.

mastoid (*say* **mass**-toyd) *noun*
1. a part of the skull behind the ear.
2. (*informal*) an inflammation of the mastoid. Also called **mastoiditis.**
Word Family: **mastoid,** *adjective.*
[Greek *mastoeides* breast-shaped]

masturbate (*say* **mass**-ta-bate) *verb*
to stimulate the sexual organs, especially one's own, so as to produce orgasm.
Word Family: **masturbation,** *noun;* **masturbatory,** *adjective.*
[from Latin]

mat (1) *noun*
1. a piece of heavy fabric or rug-like material, used as a floor covering.
2. a piece of cork, fabric, etc. placed under ornaments or hot dishes.
Usage: 'the boat's propeller became caught in a *mat* of weeds' (= tangled mass).
Word Family: **mat (matted, matting),** *verb,* to form tangled masses.

mat (2) *adjective*
see MATT.

matador *noun*
a bullfighter on foot who taunts the bull with a cape and tries to kill it with a sword. Compare PICADOR.
[Spanish]

match (1) *noun*
a) a short stick of wood with a head made of phosphorus, etc. which ignites when rubbed on certain surfaces. b) the wick used to fire a cannon, etc.

match (2) *noun*
1. a person or thing that is exactly like or combines well with another: 'the two colours are a good *match*'.
2. a person or thing that is equal to another in strength, skill, etc.: 'to meet one's *match*'.
3. an official competition or game: 'a cricket *match*'.

match *verb*
1. to be a match for: 'his looks *match* his moods'.
2. to make, provide or select a match for: a) 'to *match* colours'; b) '*match* your expenses with your income'.
Usage: 'I would never dare to *match* wits with him' (= oppose).
Word Family: **matchless,** *adjective,* without equal; **matchlessly,** *adverb.*

matchet *noun*
also called a **machete** (*say* ma-**shettee**) a large, heavy, broad-bladed chopping-knife.

matchlock *noun*
a musket fired by lighting the gunpowder with a slow-burning match.

matchmaker *noun*
a person who arranges, or tries to arrange, marriages, etc.
Word Family: **matchmake,** *verb.*

matchwood *noun*
small pieces or splinters of wood: 'the storm reduced the house to *matchwood*'.

mate (1) *noun*
1. one of a pair, especially a partner in marriage.
2. a habitual companion or fellow worker: 'my *mate* and I worked the fields around here for almost 30 years'.
3. *Nautical:* an officer next in rank below the master of a merchant ship.
Word Family: **mate,** *verb,* to join in a pair or match, especially to pair animals for producing offspring.

mate (2) *verb*
Chess: see CHECKMATE.
Word Family: **mate,** *noun.*

material (*say* ma-**teeri**-ul) *adjective*
1. composed of matter: 'the *material* resources of the earth'.
2. a) relating to the body or bodily needs: 'food and shelter are *material* necessities'. b) relating to wealth, etc.: 'his aim is *material* well-being, not spiritual happiness'.
Usage: 'she is a *material* witness in this case' (= important).

material *noun*
1. the substance of which something is made: 'radioactive *material* can be dangerous'.

2. (*usually plural*) a) the substances needed to make something: 'building *materials*'. b) the equipment needed to do something: 'writing *materials*'.
Usages:
a) 'it provided good *material* for his novel' (= information).
b) 'velvet is a heavy *material*' (= fabric).
Word Family: **materially**, *adverb*, a) considerably, b) physically.

materialism *noun*
1. a way of living in which possessions and self-interest are valued more than anything else.
2. *Philosophy:* the belief that all beings and events can be explained by physical laws.
Word Family: **materialist**, *noun*; **materialistic** (*say* ma-teeria-**listik**), *adjective*; **materialistically**, *adverb*.

materialize, materialise *verb*
to give or take on a bodily or visible form: 'three figures *materialized* out of the fog'.
Usage: 'her plan never *materialized*' (= came into effect).
Word Family: **materialization**, *noun*.

maternal *adjective*
a) of or like a mother: '*maternal* love'. b) related through a mother: 'one's *maternal* grandfather'.
Word Family: **maternally**, *adverb*.
[Latin *mater* mother]

maternity (*say* ma-**terni**-tee) *noun*
the state of being a mother.
Word Family: **maternity**, *adjective*, relating to pregnancy or childbirth.

maths *noun*
short form of **mathematics**
the study of logical relationships involving numbers, shapes, functions and sets.
Word Family: **mathematical** (*say* matha-**matti**-k'l), *adjective*, a) of or relating to maths, b) having the precision or exactness of maths; **mathematician** (*say* mathema-**tish**'n), *noun*, a person who is trained or skilled in maths; **mathematically**, *adverb*.

matinée (*say* **mattin**-ay) *noun*
the daytime, usually afternoon, performance of a play, film, ballet, etc.
[French *matin* morning]

matins *plural noun*
Christian: (*used with singular verb*) the service for morning prayer in the Church of England.
[Latin *matutinus* of or in the morning]

matriarch (*say* **may**-tree-ark) *noun*
a female who is the leader or head of a family, group, etc.
Word Family: **matriarchal**, *adjective*; **matriarchy**, *noun*, a social system in which a female is the head of the family.
[Latin *mater* mother + Greek *arkhos* leader]

matrices *plural noun*
see MATRIX.

matricide (*say* **matri**-side) *noun*
Law: a) the crime of killing one's mother. b) the person who does this.
Word Family: **matricidal**, *adjective*.
[Latin *mater* mother + *caedere* to kill]

matriculate (*say* ma**trik**-yoo-late) *verb*
a) to be accepted as qualified to enter a university. b) to pass an examination designed as a university entrance qualification.
matriculation *noun*
short form is **matric**
a) the formal acceptance of a person for entry to a university. b) an examination designed as a university entrance qualification.
[Latin *matrix* a public register or roll]

matrilineal (*say* matri-**linniul**) *adjective*
of or based on descent through the mother's family.
Word Family: **matrilineally**, *adverb*.
[Latin *mater* mother + *linea* a line]

matrimony (*say* **matrima**-nee) *noun*
marriage.
Word Family: **matrimonial** (*say* matri-**mo**-nee-ul), *adjective*.
[from Latin]

matrix (*say* **may**-triks) *noun*
plural is **matrices** (*say* **may**tri-seez) or **matrixes**
1. a mould in which type is cast.
2. an ordered array of numbers or variables, as used for computer programming.
3. rock in which gems, fossils, metals, etc. are embedded.
[Latin, a female animal, a womb]

matron (*say* **may**-tr'n) *noun*
1. a married woman or widow, especially one of middle age or mature dignity: 'a gathering of society *matrons*'.
2. a person in charge of the nursing staff in a hospital.
Word Family: **matronly**, *adjective*, of or like a matron.

matron of honour
a married woman who attends the bride at a wedding.

matt *adjective*
also spelt **mat**
not shiny.
[French *mat*]

matter *noun*
any physical substance, solid, liquid or gas, which exists in time and space and is affected by gravity.
Usages:
a) 'there was little new *matter* in the essay' (= content).
b) 'printed *matter* only' (= objects, articles).
c) 'it is a *matter* of life and death' (= situation concerning).
d) 'it's of no *matter* to me how you lead your life' (= importance).
e) 'the difference in price was a *matter* of pence' (= amount).
Phrases:
as a matter of fact, see FACT.
for that matter, as for that.
matter of course, a natural event or outcome.
no matter, a) '*no matter*, we can always get another one' (= never mind); b) 'you can safely disregard him *no matter* what he says' (= regardless of).
the matter, 'what's *the matter* with you today?' (= wrong).
Word Family: **matter**, *verb*, to be of importance.
[Latin *materia* materials, theme]

matter-of-fact *adjective*
practical or unimaginative.
Word Family: **matter-of-factly**, *adverb.*

matting *noun*
any coarse woven fabric used for floor coverings, packing goods, etc.

mattock *noun*
a tool similar to a pick with a broad blade, used for loosening soil, digging, etc.

mattress *noun*
a long, flat bag filled with a soft substance and used on or as a bed.
[from Arabic]

mature (*say* ma-tewer) *adjective*
fully grown or developed.
Usage: 'he reached his decision after *mature* deliberation' (= careful, fully considered).
Word Family: **mature**, *verb*, a) to come or bring to full development, b) (of a bill, dividends, etc.) to become payable; **maturely**, *adverb*; **maturity** (*say* ma-**tew**ri-tee), *noun*, the state of being mature; **maturation**, *noun*, the process of maturing.
[Latin *maturus* ripe, early]

matzo (*say* matsa) *noun*
plural is **matzoth**
a dry biscuit of unleavened bread eaten by Jews, especially at Passover.

maudlin (*say* **mawd**-lin) *adjective*
sentimental in a melancholy or weak way.
[from *Maudlin*, a popular variation of *(Mary) Magdalene*, who was often depicted in art as weeping]

maul (*say* mawl) *verb*
to handle roughly: 'the bear *mauled* the zoo keeper'.
Word Family: **maul**, *noun*, a heavy mallet for driving piles, etc.; **mauler**, *noun*.
[Latin *malleus* hammer]

maunder (*say* **mawn**da) *verb*
to talk or act in a confused or aimless manner.

mausoleum (*say* mawsa-**lee**-um) *noun*
a magnificent tomb.
[after the tomb of *Mausolus*, a king of Caria who died in 353 B.C.]

mauve (*rhymes with* stove) *noun*
a light pinkish-purple colour.
Word Family: **mauve**, *adjective.*

maverick *noun*
1. *American:* an unbranded or orphaned animal, especially a calf.
2. (*informal*) a person who has unorthodox or dissident views.
[after *S. Maverick*, 1803–70, a Texas lawyer who did not brand his cattle]

mawkish *adjective*
sickly sentimental.
Word Family: **mawkishly**, *adverb*; **mawkishness**, *noun.*

maxi *noun*
a skirt, dress, etc. which reaches to the ankle or just above it.

maxilla (*say* mak-**silla**) *noun*
plural is **maxillae** (*say* mak-**sillee**)
Anatomy: either of the two bones of the skull between the eyes and the teeth, forming the upper jaw.
Word Family: **maxillary**, *adjective.*
[Latin, jaw]

maxim *noun*
a short saying expressing a general rule of conduct, as in *waste not, want not.*

maximum *noun*
plural is **maxima** or **maximums**

the greatest amount that is actual, possible or allowable: 'we can invite a *maximum* of 25 people'. Compare MINIMUM.
Word Family: **maximal**, *adjective*; **maximize, maximise**, *verb*, to increase to the greatest possible amount.
[Latin *maximus* greatest]

may (1) *verb*
(might)
an auxiliary verb indicating:
a) permission: 'you *may* leave now'.
b) possibility: 'that story *may* be totally wrong'.
Usages:
a) '*may* you have a happy journey' (= we hope).
b) 'and who *may* she be, I wonder?' (= could).

May (2) *noun*
the fifth month of the year in the Gregorian calendar.
[named after the Roman goddess *Maia*]

may (3) *noun*
see HAWTHORN.

maybe *adverb*
perhaps.

Mayday *noun*
an international radio distress call used by ships and aeroplanes.
[French *m'aidez* help me]

May Day
a) a spring festival held on May 1st.
b) a workers' international celebration on that day.

mayfly *noun*
any of various waterside flies which, after one to three years as nymphs, emerge to fly for about one day only; many of the angler's artificial flies are imitations of them.
[first appear in *May*]

mayhem (*say* **may-hem**) *noun*
an old word meaning the inflicting of bodily injury.
Usage: 'the *mayhem* at the football match was sickening' (= violence, chaos).
[Old French, maim]

mayonnaise (*say* may-on-aze) *noun*
a thick, creamy sauce made from eggs, vinegar, oil and seasonings and used with salads and vegetables.
[French]

mayor (*say* mare) *noun*
the chief elected official on the council of a city or borough. In a large city the mayor may be called the Lord Mayor.
Word Family: **mayoress**, *noun*, a) a female mayor, b) the wife of a mayor; **mayoralty** (*say* **mare-ul-tee**), *noun*, the office of mayor.
[Latin *major* greater]

maypole *noun*
a pole decorated with ribbons and flowers which is danced around on May Day.

maze *noun*
also called a **labyrinth**
a complicated network of passages, paths, etc. in which it is difficult to find one's way.
Usage: 'I was in a *maze* as I tried to follow his confusing story' (= state of bewilderment).
Word Family: **mazy**, *adjective*.

mazurka (*say* ma-**zerka**) *noun*
a lively Polish dance which was very popular in the 19th century.

me (1) *pronoun*
plural is **us**
the objective or emphatic form of the pronoun **I**: a) 'he hit *me*'; b) 'give the book to *me*'; c) 'open the door, it's *me*'.

me (2) *noun*
Music: see DOH.

mead (1) *noun*
an old word for a meadow.

mead (2) *noun*
an alcoholic drink made by fermenting honey and water.

meadow (*say* **meddo**) *noun*
a clear area of grassy land, especially near a river, used for grazing or hay.
Word Family: **meadowy**, *adjective*, of or like a meadow.

meagre (*say* **meega**) *adjective*
poor in quality or quantity.
[Middle English *megre* lean]

meal (1) *noun*
a) the food eaten at one time. b) any of the usual daily eating times, as breakfast, lunch and dinner.

meal (2) *noun*
an edible grain or pulse which is ground but is less fine than flour.
Word Family: **mealy**, *adjective*, powdery or like meal.

mealie *noun*
(*usually plural*) maize.
[from Afrikaans]

mealy-mouthed *adjective*
avoiding the use of plain or direct words.

mean (1) *verb*
(meant, meaning)
1. to have as an intention or purpose: 'is this *meant* to be a joke?'.
2. to signify: 'what does this word *mean*?'.

mean (2) *adjective*
1. selfish or small-minded: 'it is a *mean* trick to hide your sister's money'.
2. poor or inferior in quality or position: 'they could only afford a small *mean* house'.
Usages:
a) 'although he is wealthy he is very *mean* with money' (= miserly).
b) 'this horse has a *mean* streak' (= vicious).
c) 'that's no *mean* achievement' (= inconsiderable).
Word Family: **meanly,** *adverb*; **meanness,** *noun.*

mean (3) *noun*
1. anything which is halfway between two extremes.
2. *Maths:* the average. Compare GEOMETRIC MEAN.
3. (*plural, used with singular verb*) a method by which something is done or obtained: 'what is your *means* of transport?'.
4. (*plural*) any wealth or resources: 'a person of private *means*'.
Phrases:
by all means, certainly.
by no means, not at all.
mean *adjective*
being in the middle position: 'the *mean* monthly temperature'.

meander (*say* mee-**anda**) *verb*
to wander aimlessly or on a winding course.
meander *noun*
a broad curve in a river.
[from *Meander,* the Greek name for the river Mendereh in Turkey]

meaning *noun*
that which is intended or expressed: 'what is the *meaning* of this word?'.
meaningful, *adjective*
full of meaning: 'she gave me a *meaningful* look'.
Word Family: **meaningfully,** *adverb.*

meanness *noun*
Word Family: see MEAN (2).

meant (*say* ment) *verb*
the past tense and past participle of the verb **mean (1).**

meantime *noun*
the time in between: 'you may leave at noon, but in the *meantime* you will wait here'.

meanwhile *adverb*
a) during the time in between: 'the accident was yesterday; *meanwhile* I have been in bed'. b) at the same time: '*meanwhile,* back at the ranch, our hero was in trouble'.

measles (*say* **mee**zels) *noun*
an infectious viral disease, usually in children, causing small red spots on the skin.
measly (*say* **meez**-lee) *adjective*
1. of, like, or having measles.
2. (*informal*) miserably small: 'after all that work he only gave us a *measly* 20 pence'.

measure (*rhymes with* treasure) *noun*
1. a) the quantity, weight, etc. of something. b) a unit of such quantity: 'a kilometre is a *measure* of length'.
Usages:
a) 'her joy knew no *measure*' (= limit).
b) 'his gift of £100 is a *measure* of his generosity' (= sign).
2. an instrument for taking measures.
3. an action or proposal: 'the council passed a *measure* to ban cars in town'.
4. rhythm or metre in poetry.
for good measure, as an extra act or precaution.
measure *verb*
to find the measurements of.
measure up to, to be adequate for.
measured *adjective*
1. weighed exactly: 'a *measured* gram of gold'.
2. (of language) carefully considered or chosen: '*measured* words'.
3. (of rhythm) slow and regular.
measurement *noun*
a) the act of measuring. b) the dimension of something measured: 'the *measurements* of the table were 1 m by 2 m'. c) a system of measuring: 'the size of the table was found by linear *measurement*'.
[Latin *mensura*]

meat *noun*
1. the edible flesh of an animal.
2. (*formerly*) any food.
meaty *adjective*
1. of or resembling meat.
2. full of ideas or substance: 'this *meaty* book took days to read'.

mechanic (*say* mik-**annik**) *noun*
a person skilled in the maintenance, repair, use or construction of machinery.

[Greek *mekhanikos* ingenious, inventive]

mechanical (*say* mik-**anni**-k'l) *adjective*
of, like or relating to machinery or mechanics: 'trains and buses are forms of *mechanical* transport'.
Usage: 'he was so bored he only made slow *mechanical* movements' (= unthinking, automatic).
Word Family: **mechanically**, *adverb*; **mechanize** (*say* **mekka**-nize), **mechanise**, *verb*, to introduce machinery into an industry which was formerly manual; **mechanization**, *noun*.

mechanics (*say* mik-**anniks**) *plural noun*
(*used with singular verb*) a) the science of machinery. b) the study of the effects of forces on objects.
Usage: 'he gave a talk on the *mechanics* of government' (= system of operating).

mechanism (*say* **mekka**-nizm) *noun*
1. a piece of machinery.
2. a) any structure which operates by various parts working together: 'the human body is a delicate *mechanism*'. b) the internal parts and workings of a structure: 'the *mechanism* of a watch'.

medal *noun*
a small metal disc with a design commemorating a person or event, or given as an award.
Word Family: **medallist**, *noun*, a person who has received a medal.
[Greek *metallon* metal]

medallion (*say* mid-**al**-y'n) *noun*
1. a large medal.
2. a circular ornamental design on furniture, etc.

meddle *verb*
to interfere in other people's affairs without being asked to do so.
Word Family: **meddlesome**, *adjective*; **meddler**, *noun*.
[Old French *medler* to mix]

media (*say* **mee**dia) *plural noun*
1. a plural of **medium**.
2. all the sources by which news, etc. may be relayed, such as radio, television and newspapers.

mediaeval (*say* meddi-**ee**-v'l) *adjective*
see MEDIEVAL.

medial (*say* **mee**di-ul) *adjective*
a) in the middle. b) of average size or amount.

median (*say* **mee**di-an) *noun*
Maths: a) the value above which half the population (that is, cases under consideration) fall and below which the other half fall. b) a straight line from the vertex of a triangle bisecting the opposite side.
Word Family: **median**, *adjective*, in or through the middle.
[Latin *medianus* in the middle]

mediate (*say* **mee**di-ate) *verb*
to bring about an agreement between opposing sides by acting as a go-between.
mediation (*say* meedi-**ay**-sh'n) *noun*
the act of mediating: 'the United Nations makes offers of *mediation* between warring countries'.
Word Family: **mediator**, *noun*, a person who mediates.

medic, medico *noun*
(*informal*) a doctor, medical student or medical orderly.

medical (*say* **meddi**-k'l) *adjective*
of or relating to the science or practice of healing, especially by using drugs rather than surgery.
medical *noun*
(*informal*) a medical examination or checkup.
Word Family: **medically**, *adverb*.

medication (*say* meddi-**kay**-sh'n) *noun*
a substance given to cure, heal or relieve the symptoms of a disease.
Word Family: **medicate**, *verb*.
[Latin *medicare* to cure]

medicine (*say* **med**-s'n) *noun*
1. any substance used to treat a disease, preserve health, etc.
2. the study of diseases and ways of maintaining and restoring health.
3. any unpleasant experience, such as one supposed to build character, etc.: 'his father believes that regular beatings are good *medicine* for growing boys'.
Word Family: **medicinal** (*say* med-**issa**-n'l), *adjective*, of or like medicine.

medicine ball
a heavy ball thrown from one person to another for exercise.

medicine man
a witchdoctor.

medieval (*say* meddi-**ee**-v'l) *adjective*
also spelt **mediaeval**
of or relating to the Middle Ages.
[Latin *medius* middle + *aevum* age]

mediocre (*say* meedi–o–ka) *adjective*
of second–rate or only average quality.
mediocrity (*say* meedi–okra–tee) *noun*
a) the quality of being mediocre. b) a person of mediocre abilities.
[Latin *mediocris* middling, average]

meditate (*say* meddi–tate) *verb*
a) to consider the possibility of: 'he *meditated* murder'. b) to reflect or think deeply and seriously: 'he *meditated* upon the meaning of life'.
Word Family: **meditation,** *noun,* a) the act of meditating, b) deep thought; **meditative,** *adjective,* fond of or characterized by meditation; **meditatively,** *adverb.*
[from Latin]

medium (*say* meedi–um) *noun*
plural is **media** or **mediums**
1. a means by which something is done: 'my favourite *medium* for sculpture is stone, but in painting I prefer oil'.
2. an intermediate thing through which something moves: 'air is the *medium* of sound'.
3. *Biology:* a nutrient material on which micro–organisms may be grown.
4. *Occult:* a person through whom spirits are said to be able to communicate.
medium *adjective*
average in size or quality: 'he was a man of *medium* height'.
[Latin *medius* middle]

medium–wave *adjective*
(of a radiowave) having a wavelength of 200–1000 m, used in medium–range radio broadcasting. Compare SHORT–WAVE, LONG–WAVE and VERY HIGH FREQUENCY.

medley (*say* **med**–lee) *noun*
1. a mixture of things, such as a piece of music combining several different tunes, etc.
2. a race in which the swimmer performs several different strokes in order.

medulla (*say* meddulla) *noun*
plural is **medullae** (*say* meddulli)
Biology: a) the soft inner part of a structure, especially a kidney. b) bone marrow.
[Latin, pith, marrow]

medusa (*say* mi–**dew**sa) *noun*
a jellyfish.
[Greek *Medousa* a Gorgon whose hair consisted of snakes]

meek *adjective*
humble, patient or gentle.
Word Family: **meekly,** *adverb*; **meekness,** *noun.*

meerschaum (*say* **meer**–sh'm) *noun*
a) a white clay mineral (hydrous magnesium silicate) used for carving and especially for pipe bowls. b) a tobacco pipe with the bowl made of meerschaum.
[German, sea–foam]

meet (1) *verb*
(met, meeting)
a) to come face to face with: 'I *met* Mrs Smith at the market'. b) to come into contact with: 'the sounds of music *met* her ears'.
Usages:
a) 'I *met* his swearing with some equally strong cursing' (= matched).
b) 'who will *meet* the cost of the expedition?' (= pay, cover).
c) 'does it *meet* your expectations?' (= live up to).
meet with, 'does it *meet with* your approval?' (= receive).
meet *noun*
Sport: a meeting for competition or enjoyment, such as a hunt.

meet (2) *adjective*
suitable or proper: 'it is only *meet* and right that you pay your debt'.
Word Family: **meetly,** *adverb*; **meetness,** *noun.*

meeting *noun*
a) a contact or coming together: a *meeting* of rivers'. b) an assembly or gathering of people.

mega–
a prefix: a) meaning great, as in *megaphone*; b) used for SI units, meaning one million (10^6). See UNITS in grey pages.
[Greek]

megalithic (*say* megga–**lith**ik) *adjective*
being built of large stones, such as prehistoric monuments.
Word Family: **megalith,** *noun,* a large stone.
[MEGA– + Greek *lithos* stone]

megalomania (*say* meggalo–**may**–nia) *noun*
Psychology: a mental disorder in which the patient thinks he is a person of extreme importance.
megalomaniac *noun*
1. a person suffering from megalomania.
2. (*informal*) a person who constantly seeks power and personal glory.
[Greek *megalé* great + MANIA]

megaphone (*say* **megga**–fone) *noun*
see LOUD–HAILER.
[MEGA– + Greek *phoné* sound]

megatonne (*say* **megga**–ton) *noun*
a unit for measuring the explosive force of nuclear weapons, by comparing them to the mass of trinitrotoluene (TNT) which would produce the same explosion. *Example*: a 10 megatonne hydrogen bomb would have the same explosive force of 10 000 000 tonnes of TNT. Compare KILOTONNE.

meiosis (*say* my–**o**–sis) *noun*
also called **reduction division**
Biology: a type of cell division in sex cells resulting in cells with half the number of chromosomes of the parent cell, each new cell having one of each pair of chromosomes (the haploid number) and forming a gamete. Compare MITOSIS.
[Greek, a lessening]

melancholia (*say* mell'n–**kole**–ee–a) *noun*
Psychology: a mental disorder marked by extreme and continual depression.
Word Family: **melancholic**, *adjective.*
[Greek *melané* black + *kholé* bile]

melancholy (*say* **mell**'n–kollee) *adjective*
sad, gloomy or depressing: 'the funeral was a *melancholy* occasion'.
Word Family: **melancholy**, *noun*, sadness or depression.

mélange (*say* may–**lonj**) *noun*
a mixture.
[French]

meld (1) *verb*
Cards: to lay down a minimum number of cards to start scoring, as in canasta.
[German *melden* to announce]

meld (2) *verb*
to merge or blend.
[from M(elt) + (w)ELD]

mêlée (*say* **mell**ay) *noun*
a confused fight or struggle.
[French]

mellifluous (*say* mel–**if**loo–us) *adjective*
also called **mellifluent**
(of a voice, music, etc.) sweet–sounding.
[Late Latin *mellifluus* flowing with honey]

mellow *adjective*
a) soft and full–flavoured in taste, as ripe fruit or mature wine. b) rich and soft in sound or colour, as music.
Usages:
a) 'last night the wine made me *mellow*' (= pleasantly tipsy).
b) 'my father became *mellow* in his old age' (= genial, easygoing).
Word Family: **mellow**, *verb*, to make or become mellow.

melodrama (*say* **mell**o–drahma) *noun*
a) a play based on an exaggerated or sensational plot and characters. b) any sensational series of events.
melodramatic (*say* mello–dra–**mattik**) *adjective*
of or like a melodrama: 'his *melodramatic* speech was delivered with passionate and exaggerated gestures'.
Word Family: **melodramatics**, *plural noun*, melodramatic behaviour.

melody (*say* **mell**a–dee) *noun*
a) a tune. b) tunefulness: 'the choir sang with fine *melody*'.
Word Family: **melodic** (*say* mel–**oddik**), *adjective*, of or relating to a melody or melodies; **melodious** (*say* mel–**o**–dee–us), *adjective*, tuneful or producing a pleasant sound; **melodiously**, *adverb.*
[Greek *meloidia* singing]

melon *noun*
any of various large, juicy fruits with many seeds, such as a watermelon.
[Greek, apple]

melt *verb*
(**melted, melted** or **molten, melting**)
to make or become liquid through heating.
Usages:
a) 'her heart *melted* when she saw the baby' (= softened).
b) 'the man *melted* into the darkness' (= disappeared, blended).

melting pot
a mixture of various elements, colours, ideas, etc.: 'with all its different languages and races, London is a real *melting pot*'.

member *noun*
1. a person who is included in a group, society, etc.
2. a part of a structural whole, such as a limb of the body, etc.
Usage: 'who is your local *member*?' (= representative in parliament)
3. *Maths:* an element of a set.
membership *noun*
a) the state of being a member: 'I must pay my fees on time to retain my *membership*'. b) the number of

members: 'the club has a total *membership* of 300'.
[Latin *membrum* limb]

membrane *noun*
Biology: any soft, thin sheet of tissue which covers and separates organs and structures in an animal or plant.
Word Family: **membranous** (*say* **mem**bra-nus), *adjective*, of or like a membrane.
[Latin *membrana* skin, parchment]

memento (*say* mim-**en**-toe) *noun*
something to remind one of an event or person.
[Latin, remember!]

memo (*say* **meemo** *or* **memmo**) *noun*
(*informal*) a memorandum.

memoir (*say* **mem**-wah) *noun*
1. (*plural*) an autobiography.
2. a reminder.
[French]

memorable (*say* **memmera**-b'l) *adjective*
notable or worthy of being remembered: 'the solemn procession was a *memorable* occasion'.

memorandum (*say* memma-**randum**) *noun*
plural is **memoranda** or **memorandums**
a) a note made of something to be remembered. b) a record or written statement of a business or other transaction.
[Latin *memorandus* that is to be remembered]

memorial (*say* mim-**awriul**) *noun*
1. something intended to preserve the memory of a person, event, etc., such as a monument.
2. a list of arguments to support a request or petition to parliament, etc.
memorial *adjective*
preserving the memory of a person or thing: 'a *memorial* service was held for the dead soldiers'.
Word Family: **memorialize, memorialise,** *verb.*

memorize (*say* **memma**-rize)
memorise *verb*
to commit to the memory.
Word Family: **memorization,** *noun.*

memory (*say* **memma**-ree) *noun*
1. a) the ability of the mind to recall things. b) something that is remembered: 'my earliest *memory* is of running away from kindergarten'.
2. the part of a computer in which information is stored.
[Latin *memor* remembering]

men *plural noun*
the plural of **man.**

menace (*say* **mennis**) *noun*
a threat or danger: 'famine is a *menace* in underdeveloped countries'.
menace *verb*
to threaten: 'stop *menacing* me with that knife'.

ménage (*say* **may**-nah*zh*) *noun*
a) a husband and wife. b) a family or the household.
ménage à trois, the living together of a husband, wife and a tolerated lover.
[French]

menagerie (*say* min-**aj**-a-ree) *noun*
a) a collection of wild or strange animals, as in a circus. b) the place where they are kept, such as a zoo.
[French]

mend *verb*
to repair or get something back into working condition.
Usages:
a) 'you must try to *mend* your manners' (= reform).
b) 'the patient is *mending* nicely' (= improving).
mend *noun*
a repair.

mendacious (*say* men-**day**-shus) *adjective*
a) untrue: 'a *mendacious* rumour'. b) untruthful: 'a *mendacious* person'.
Word Family: **mendacity** (*say* men-**dassi**-tee), *noun.*
[Latin *mendax* untruthful]

mendelevium (*say* menda-**leevium**) *noun*
element number 101, a man-made, radioactive metal. See TRANSURANIC ELEMENT and ACTINIDE.
See CHEMICAL ELEMENTS in grey pages.

mendicant *noun*
a) a beggar. b) a religious person, such as a monk, who lives by begging.
[Latin *mendicans* begging]

menial (*say* **meeniul**) *adjective*
(of work) done by or suitable for a servant.
Word Family: **menial,** *noun,* a servant.

meninges (*say* **mennin**-jeez) *plural noun*
Anatomy: the membranes that cover the brain and spinal cord.

meningitis (*say* mennin-**jie**-tis) *noun*
a serious illness caused by an inflammation of the meninges,

resulting in headache, vomiting, fever and a stiff neck.
[Greek *meninx* membrane + -ITIS]

meniscus (*say* menniskus) *noun*
plural is **menisci** (*say* menniss-eye)
Physics: the curved, upper surface of a liquid in a container, caused by capillarity.
Word Family: **meniscoid** (*say* menniss-koyd), *adjective,* a) relating to a meniscus, b) crescent-shaped.
[Greek *meniskos* crescent]

menopause (*say* menno-pawz) *noun*
also called the **change of life**
the changes in the glands and organs of middle-aged women when menstruation ends.
[Greek *menos* of a month + *pausis* cessation]

menses (*say* men-seez) *plural noun*
the blood and tissue lining the uterus and discharged during menstruation.

menstruation
(*say* men-stroo-ay-sh'n) *noun*
also called a **period** or (*informal*) the **curse**
the act of discharging the menses, occurring about once every four weeks in any woman who is not pregnant, and has not reached menopause.
Word Family: **menstrual**, *adjective,* **menstruate**, *verb.*
[Latin *menstruus* monthly]

mensuration (*say* mensha-ray-sh'n) *noun*
the study of the procedures for measuring and calculating lengths, areas and volumes.
Word Family: **mensurable** (*say* menshera-b'l), *adjective,* able to be measured; **mensural** (*say* mensha-r'l), *adjective,* relating to measure.
[Latin *mensura* a measure]

mental *adjective*
1. of or relating to the mind: a) 'the psychologist devised a new *mental* test'; b) 'a *mental* illness'.
Usages:
a) 'the teacher gave us a test in *mental* arithmetic' (= done in the head, not written).
b) 'a *mental* hospital' (= for insane people).
2. (*informal*) mad.

mentality (*say* men-talli-tee) *noun*
1. intellectual capacity: 'a child of average *mentality*'.
2. attitude or tendency: 'a warlike *mentality*'.
Word Family: **mentally**, *adverb.*
[Latin *mentis* of a mind]

mental age
a measure of development in intelligence expressed in terms of the age at which an average person reaches such a level. *Example*: a 15 year-old child with a mental age of 10 has the intelligence level of an average 10 year-old child.
Compare INTELLIGENCE QUOTIENT.

mental telepathy
see TELEPATHY.

menthol *noun*
a colourless alcohol found in peppermint oil and used in perfumes, cigarettes, cooking and medicine.
Word Family: **mentholated**, *adjective,* containing menthol.

mention (*say* **men**-sh'n) *verb*
to refer to briefly.
not to mention, in addition to.
Word Family: **mention**, *noun,* a) a reference or allusion, b) a brief notice or recognition.
[Latin *mentio* a calling to mind]

mentor *noun*
a person who advises and helps an inexperienced person.
[after *Mentor,* who advised Ulysses' son during his father's absence]

menu (*say* **men**-yoo) *noun*
a) a list of dishes available at a meal.
b) the dishes served at a meal.
[French, a detailed list]

mercantile (*say* **merk**'n-tile) *adjective*
of or relating to merchants, trade or commerce.
Word Family: **mercantilism**, *noun,* an old economic theory that a state ought to amass gold, by boosting exports, restricting imports and prohibiting the export of gold.
[Latin *mercans* trading]

mercenary (*say* **mers**'n-ree) *adjective*
1. acting merely for gain.
2. hired, especially by a foreign country: 'a *mercenary* soldier'.

mercenary *noun*
a professional soldier serving in a foreign army.
Word Family: **mercenarily**, *adverb;* **mercenariness**, *noun.*
[Latin *mercennarius* hired for pay]

mercer (*say* **mersa**) *noun*
an old word for a person who deals in expensive fabrics.
[Latin *merces* goods]

mercerize (*say* **mer**sa–rize) **mercerise** *verb*
to soak cotton or linen in strong caustic soda in order to give a permanent silky lustre and greater durability.
[after *J. Mercer* who patented this process in 1850]

merchandise (*say* **mer**chen–dice) *noun*
any goods bought and sold for profit
Word Family: **merchandise** (*say* **mer**chen–dize), *verb*, a) to buy and sell, b) to promote through the use of advertising; **merchandiser**, *noun*.

merchant *noun*
1. an old word for a person who buys and sells goods.
2. a wholesale trader, especially in exports and imports.
3. *American:* a shopkeeper.
Word Family: **merchant**, *adjective*, of or relating to trade.
[Latin *mercans* trading]

merchant bank
a bank which specializes in financing international trade, handling bills of exchange and other commercial business.

merchantman *noun*
a trading ship.

Merchant Navy
a) the ships engaged in commerce.
b) their officers and crews.

merciful (*say* **mer**si–f'l) *adjective*
Word Family: see MERCY.

mercurial (*say* mer–**kew**riul) *adjective*
quick and changeable in nature: 'his lively and *mercurial* personality'.
Word Family: **mercurially**, *adverb*.

mercury (*say* **mer**–kew–ree) *noun*
1. element number 80, a metal which is a liquid at normal temperatures and is used in alloys and thermometers. Also called **quicksilver**. See AMALGAM and TRANSITION ELEMENT.
See CHEMICAL ELEMENTS in grey pages.
2. *Roman mythology:* (*capital*) the god of trade, and a messenger of the gods.
3. *Astronomy:* (*capital*) the planet in the solar system closest to the sun.
Word Family: **mercuric** (*say* mer–**kew**rik), *adjective*, of or relating to compounds of mercury in which mercury has a valency of two; **mercurous** (*say* mer–**kew**rus), *adjective*, of or relating to compounds of mercury in which mercury has a valency of one.
[so named because alchemists used the symbol of the planet *Mercury* for the metal]

mercy (*say* **mer**–see) *noun*
kindness or compassion, such as is shown by withholding or reducing a punishment.
Usage: 'we must be thankful for small *mercies*' (= pieces of good fortune).
at the mercy of, 'the rudderless ship was *at the mercy of* every large wave' (= helpless before).
Word Family: **merciful**, *adjective*, having or showing mercy; **mercifully**, *adverb*, a) in a merciful manner, b) thankfully; **mercifulness**, *noun*; **merciless**, *adjective*, showing no mercy.
[Latin *merces* reward (later, pity)]

mercy killing
euthanasia.

mere *adjective*
nothing more than: 'I think your apology is *mere* humbug'.
Word Family: **merely**, *adverb*, only or simply.

meretricious (*say* merri–**trish**us) *adjective*
showily or falsely attractive: 'this novel has attracted attention only because of the *meretricious* gimmicks it employs'.
[Latin *meretricius* pertaining to prostitutes]

merganser *noun*
any of various kinds of fish–eating duck with serrated, spike–like bills.
[Latin *mergus* diver + *anser* goose]

merge (*say* merj) *verb*
to blend with or be absorbed by something larger: 'the twilight *merged* gradually into darkness'.
merger *noun*
the act of merging, such as the combination of two or more business companies into one.

meridian (*say* mer**rid**dian) *noun*
Geography: a line of longitude.
Compare PRIME MERIDIAN.

meringue (*say* mer**rang**) *noun*
a mixture of sugar and beaten egg whites, used to make small cakes, flans or as a covering for pies which are filled with fruit or cream.
[French]

merino (*say* mer**ree**no) *noun*
1. any of a breed of sheep with long fine wool, originally bred in Spain.
2. a soft yarn or fabric, originally one made from the wool of a merino.
[Spanish]

merit *noun*
1. worth, excellence or superior quality: 'there isn't much *merit* in his proposals'.
2. a commendable quality, act, etc.: 'let us discuss the *merits* of the production'.
on its merits, according to the facts rather than a set standard.
meritocracy (*say* merri-**tokra**-see) *noun*
a group of people who have achieved positions of power by working, rather than by reason of birth or social influence.
Word Family: **merit**, *verb*, to be worthy of; **merited**, *adjective*, deserved; **meritorious** (*say* merri-**tawri**-us), *adjective*, worthy of merit or reward.
[Latin *meritum* deserved, earned]

mermaid *noun*
an imaginary creature supposed to live in the sea, having a woman's body and a fish's tail.
[Middle English *mere* lake or pond + MAID]

merry *adjective*
1. cheerful or gay.
2. (*informal*) tipsy: 'he came home from the office party a bit *merry*'.
Word Family: **merriment**, *noun*, any laughter or gaiety; **merrily**, *adverb*.

merry-go-round *noun*
a revolving machine fitted with moving horses, etc. on which children ride at fairs.

mesa (*say* **may**sa) *noun*
a high rocky plateau with steeply sloping sides.
[Latin *mensa* table]

mescaline (*say* **mes**ka-lin) **mescalin** *noun*
a drug made from a Mexican cactus called **mescal** and used to produce hallucinations.

mesembryanthemum
(*say* miz-embri-**anthi**-mum) *noun*
also called a **Livingstone Daisy**
a garden plant of South African origin with fleshy leaves and usually brightly coloured flowers which open only in bright sunlight.
[Greek *mesembria* midday + *anthemon* flower]

mesh *verb*
1. to entangle or fit closely together.
Usage: 'his plans to expand the company *meshed* nicely with ours' (= fitted in).
2. (of gears) to engage.

mesh *noun*
1. the open spaces or threads of a net or sieve.
Usage: 'he was trapped fast in the *meshes* of a political intrigue' (= snares, entanglements).
2. a knitted or woven fabric with open spaces between the threads.

mesmerize (*say* **mez**ma-rize)
mesmerise *verb*
a) to hypnotize. b) to fascinate or spellbind: 'we sat there *mesmerized* by the beauty of the ballet'.
Word Family: **mesmerism**, *noun*, hypnotism; **mesmerist**, *noun*, a hypnotist; **mesmeric** (*say* mez-**merr**ik), *adjective*, a) hypnotic, b) spellbinding or fascinating; **mesmerically**, *adverb*.
[after *F. A. Mesmer*, 1734–1815, an Austrian doctor]

Mesolithic (*say* messo-**lith**ik) *noun*
see STONE AGE.
[Greek *mesos* middle + *lithos* stone]

meson (*say* **mee**-zon) *noun*
Physics: any of a group of unstable elementary particles produced by cosmic rays.
[Greek, middle (as intermediate in mass between proton and electron)]

Mesozoic (*say* messo-**zo**-ik) *noun*
a geological era which extended from about 225 million years ago to about 65 million years ago and contains the **Triassic**, **Jurassic** and **Cretaceous** periods. During this era dinosaurs appeared and gymnosperms and angiosperms were the dominant plants. Towards the end of the era mammals appeared.
[Greek *mesos* middle + *zoion* animal]

mess *noun*
1. a dirty, untidy or confused condition: 'his desk was in a *mess*'.
Usage: 'gambling got her into a financial *mess*' (= difficult or awkward situation).
2. a) a room where officers, etc. in the armed forces eat. b) the meal eaten in such a place.
mess *verb*
to make dirty or untidy.
Phrases:
mess around, mess about, (*informal*) to spend one's time, especially aimlessly.
mess up, a) 'please try not to *mess up* your room again' (= make untidy); b) 'you *messed up* a perfect opportunity by your rudeness' (= spoilt).
Word Family: **messy**, *adjective*; **messily**, *adverb*; **messiness**, *noun*.

message (*say* **mess**ij) *noun*
any information, etc. sent from one person or group to another.
Usage: 'many folk songs have a *message*' (= moral, intended meaning).
Word Family: **messenger**, *noun*, a person who carries a message or goes on an errand.

Messiah (*say* miss-**eye**-ya) *noun*
Jewish, Christian: a) a title for the expected saviour-king of the Jews. b) Christ, viewed as this by his followers.
Word Family: **Messianic** (*say* messi-**ann**ik), *adjective.*
[Hebrew *mashiah* the anointed]

messmate *noun*
a person with whom one takes meals in a mess.

messy *adjective*
Word Family: see MESS.

·**met** *verb*
the past tense and past participle of the verb **meet (1)**.

meta-
a prefix meaning: a) altered, as in *metamorphosis*; b) behind or after, as in *metacarpal*.

metabolism (*say* me**ttab**ba-lizm) *noun*
Biology: the chemical processes occurring in an organism or cell, including the build-up of simple substances into complex substances and the breakdown of complex substances into simple ones.
Word Family: **metabolic** (*say* metta-**boll**ik), *adjective*; **metabolize** (*say* me**ttab**ba-lize), **metabolise**, *verb*, to subject to metabolism.
[Greek *metabolé* change]

metacarpal bone (*say* metta-**karp**'l bone)
Anatomy: any of the five bones in each hand joining the thumb and fingers to the wrist.
[META- + Greek *karpos* wrist]

metal *noun*
1. *Chemistry:* any of those elements which tend to be ductile and malleable, conduct heat and electricity and form positive ions.
2. road metal.
Word Family: **metal**, **metallic** (*say* me**tall**ik), *adjectives*; **metallically**, *adverb.*
[Greek *metallon* a mine]

metalloid (*say* **metta**-loyd) *noun*
Chemistry: any element, such as arsenic, showing some properties of a metal and some properties of a non-metal.

metallurgy (*say* me**ttal**-a-jee) *noun*
the study of metals, their extraction from ores, their properties and uses.
Word Family: **metallurgist**, *noun*, a person skilled or trained in metallurgy; **metallurgic** (*say* metta-**ler**jik), **metallurgical**, *adjective*, relating to metallurgy; **metallurgically**, *adverb.*
[METAL + Greek *ergon* work]

metamorphic (*say* metta-**mor**fik) *adjective*
transformed: '*metamorphic* rocks have had their structure altered by changes in temperature and pressure'.
Word Family: **metamorphism**, *noun.*

metamorphosis (*say* metta-**mor**fa-sis) *noun*
plural is **metamorphoses**
a change or transformation, as that of a caterpillar into a butterfly, a tadpole into a frog, etc.
Word Family: **metamorphose** (*say* metta-**mor**foze), *verb.*
[META- + Greek *morphé* shape + -OSIS]

metaphor (*say* **metta**-for) *noun*
a figure of speech in which one thing is identified with another. *Example:* he *was a tower of strength* during the crisis. Compare SIMILE.
Word Family: **metaphorical** (*say* metta-**forr**i-k'l), **metaphoric**, *adjective*; **metaphorically**, *adverb.*
[Greek *metapherein* to transfer]

metaphysical (*say* metta-**fizz**i-k'l) *adjective*
of or relating to the study of questions which cannot be answered in factual terms: 'science may tell us how the universe works but why it exists at all is a *metaphysical* question'.
Word Family: **metaphysics**, *noun.*
[Greek (*ta*) *meta* (*ta*) *physika* (the works) after (the) Physics, as, in Aristotle's collected works, those on metaphysics happened to be so placed; the word does not mean beyond (the scope of) physics]

metastasis (*say* mit-**asta**-sis) *noun*
plural is **metastases** (*say* mit-**asta**-seez)
Medicine: the transfer of a disease or its manifestations from one part of the body to another, such as can occur in cancer.
Word Family: **metastasize**, **metastasise**, *verb.*
[META- + Greek *stasis* a standing still]

metatarsal bone (*say* metta-**tar**-s'l bone)

Anatomy: any of the five bones in each foot joining the toes to the ankle.
[META- + Greek *tarsos* the flat of the foot]

metathesis (*say* mit-atha-sis) *noun*
plural is **metatheses** (*say* mit-atha-seez)
1. the changing of the order of letters, sounds or syllables in a word. *Example*: Middle English *bridd* became Modern English *bird* by metathesis.
2. *Chemistry:* see DOUBLE DECOMPOSITION.
[META + Greek *thesis* a putting]

mete (*say* meet) *verb*
to deal out or allot: 'the courts are supposed to *mete* out justice'.

metempsychosis
(*say* mett'm-sigh-**ko**-sis) *noun*
see REINCARNATION.
[META- + Greek *empsykhosis* an animating]

meteor (*say* **meeti**-or) *noun*
also called a **falling star** or a **shooting star**
Astronomy: a small solid body from space which usually burns up on entering the earth's atmosphere. One which reaches the earth's surface is called a **meteorite.**
meteoric (*say* meeti-**orrik**) *adjective*
a) of or relating to a meteor. b) of the atmosphere.
Usage: 'a *meteoric* rise to power' (= swift, brilliant).
Word Family: **meteorically,** *adverb.*
[Greek *meteoros* high in the air]

meteorology (*say* meetia-**rolla**-jee) *noun*
the study of the processes of the atmosphere which affect weather.
Word Family: **meteorologist,** *noun,* a person trained in meteorology; **meteorological** (*say* meetia-ra-**loji**-k'l), *adjective*; **meteorologically,** *adverb.*

meter *noun*
any instrument used to measure something: 'a gas *meter*'.
Word Family: **meter,** *verb,* to measure with or register on a meter.
[from METE]

-meter
a suffix indicating an instrument which measures, as in *barometer.*
[Greek *metron* a measure]

methane (*say* **mee**-thane) *noun*
also called **marsh gas**
a colourless, inflammable gas (formula CH_4), the first member of the paraffin series, formed from decaying organic matter and occurring in coal gas and natural gas.
Compare FIREDAMP.

methinks *verb*
(**methought**)
an old word meaning it seems to me.

method *noun*
a way of doing something, especially an orderly or systematic way: 'I have no sympathy with the new teaching *methods*'.
Word Family: **methodical** (*say* meth**oddi**-k'l), *adjective,* done or acting according to an orderly method; **methodically,** *adverb*; **methodicalness,** *noun.*
[Greek *methodos* a pursuit (of knowledge)]

Methodist *noun*
also called a **Wesleyan**
Christian: a member of a revivalist movement based on the ideas of John and Charles Wesley, 18th-century preachers.
Word Family: **Methodist,** *adjective*; **Methodism,** *noun.*
[from their methodical rules of prayer and fasting]

methodology (*say* metha-**dolla**-jee) *noun*
the study of the methods used in a particular subject.
Word Family: **methodological** (*say* metha-da-**loji**-k'l), *adjective.*

methought *verb*
the past tense of the verb **methinks.**

meths *plural noun*
(*informal*) methylated spirits.

methyl (*say* **meth**il) *adjective*
Chemistry: of or relating to organic compounds or radicals containing the univalent (CH_3)- group.
Word Family: **methanol,** *noun,* the alcohol based on a methyl group.
[Greek *methy* wine + *hylé* wood]

methylated spirits
a mixture, mainly methyl alcohol, dyed and rendered poisonous (to avoid duty), used domestically as a fuel and solvent.

meticulous (*say* mittik-yoo-lus) *adjective*
extremely or excessively careful and precise about details.
Word Family: **meticulously,** *adverb*; **meticulousness,** *noun.*
[Latin *meticulosus* fearful]

métier (*say* **metti**–ay) *noun*
a person's trade or line of work, interest, etc., especially the work for which one is particularly suited.
[French]

metonymy (*say* met–**onni**–mee) *noun*
the use of a word to replace or suggest another to which it is in some way related. *Example*: *the pen* (= the power of literature) is mightier than *the sword* (= force).
[META– + Greek *onyma* name]

metre (1) (*say* **meeta**) *noun*
in America spelt **meter**
the base SI unit of length, about 39 inches. See UNITS in grey pages.
See SI UNIT.
Word Family: **metric** (*say* **met**–rik), *adjective*, of or relating to the metre or the system of measurement based on it.
[Greek *metron* measure]

metre (2) (*say* **meeta**) *noun*
a measured rhythm or pattern of stresses, etc. in poetry.
Word Family: **metric** (*say* **met**–rik), **metrical**, *adjective*, a) of or relating to metre, b) composed in verse not prose; **metrically**, *adverb*.

–metre
a suffix indicating a metre, as in *centimetre*.

metrication (*say* metri–**kay**–sh'n) *noun*
the process of changing from British or imperial units to SI units.

metric carat
see CARAT.

metric system
the system of SI units.

metric ton
see TONNE.

metro *noun*
an underground railway system in certain cities, notably Paris.
[French abbreviation of *métropolitaine*]

metronome (*say* **metra**–nome) *noun*
Music: a device for sounding an adjustable number of beats per minute.
[Greek *metron* a measure + *nomos* law]

metropolis (*say* metroppa–lis) *noun*
1. the most important, and usually the largest, city of a country or state.
2. a centre of some specified activity: 'a *metropolis* of learning'.

metropolitan (*say* metra–**polli**–t'n) *noun*
1. a) an inhabitant of a metropolis. b) a person with the manners, customs, etc. of a metropolitan.
2. *Christian:* a) an archbishop. b) (in the Orthodox Church) a dignitary ranking above archbishops.
[Greek, mother state or city]

mettle *noun*
a spirited temperament or courage.
on one's mettle, incited to do one's best.
Word Family: **mettlesome**, *adjective*, spirited or courageous.
[from METAL]

mew (1) *verb*
to make the sound of a cat or seagull.
Word Family: **mew**, *noun*.

mew (2) *noun*
a cage for hawks, especially when they are moulting.

mewl *verb*
to cry feebly like a child.

mews *plural noun*
(*used with singular verb*) a group of stables built around an alley or court, now often converted into private flats.
[originally of the *Royal Mews* which replaced hawks' mews at Charing Cross, London]

mezzanine (*say* **mezza**–neen *or* **metsa**–neen) *noun*
a storey, usually in the form of a balcony or platform, between two main storeys of a building.
[Italian *mezzano* middle]

mezzo-soprano
(*say* metso–so–**prahno**) *noun*
a) the female singing voice between soprano and contralto. b) a woman having such a singing voice.
[Italian]

mezzotint (*say* **metso**–tint) *noun*
Art: a) an engraving process in which the plate is roughened all over with a toothed rocker and the burr partly or wholly scraped away to give halftones and highlights. b) a print produced by this method.
[Italian, half–tint]

miasma (*say* mee–**az**–ma) *noun*
1. the smell of corruption.
2. (*formerly*) swamp mists, once thought to cause malaria.
[Greek, pollution]

mica (*say* **my**–ka) *noun*
a flaky, often transparent mineral, mainly composed of complex silicates

of aluminium and potassium, widely used in electrical apparatus owing to its very high electrical resistance and melting point.
[Latin, a crumb]

mice *plural noun*
the plural of **mouse**.

mickey *noun*
(*capital*) a drink to which a sleeping drug has been added. Short form of *Mickey Finn*.
take the mickey out of (*informal*) to tease or mock.

micro– (*say* **my**–kro)
a prefix meaning: a) very small, as in *microfilm*; b) used for SI units, meaning one millionth (10^{-6}). See UNITS in grey pages.
[Greek *mikros* small]

microanalysis
(*say* my–kro–a–**nalli**–sis) *noun*
Chemistry: a form of analysis using minute quantities of chemicals.

microbe (*say* **my**–krobe) *noun*
see MICRO–ORGANISM.

microbiology
(*say* my–kro–by–**olla**–jee) *noun*
the study of micro–organisms.
Word Family: **microbiologically**, *adverb*; **microbiologist**, *noun*.

microchemical
(*say* my–kro–**kemmi**–k'l) *adjective*
of or relating to chemical processes or techniques using minute amounts of reagents.

microcosm (*say* **my**–kro–kozm) *noun*
a system in which everything is on a small scale.
[MICRO– + Greek *kosmos* universe]

microdot (*say* **my**–kro–dot) *noun*
1. *Photography:* a microfilm which has been further reduced until it is the size of a printed or typed dot, used by spies, etc.
2. (*informal*) a small amount of an hallucinogenic drug.

microelectronics
(*say* my–kro–illek–**tronniks**) *plural noun*
(*used with singular verb*) the design and manufacture of integrated circuits, used in spacecraft, missiles, aircraft, radar, desk–top computers, etc.

microfilm *noun*
Photography: very small pictures taken of documents, etc. to be kept as a record.
Word Family: **microfilm**, *verb*.

microgroove (*say* my–kro–**groov**) *noun*
the narrow groove in a gramophone record along which the stylus travels.

micrometer (*say* my–**krommi**ta) *noun*
an instrument used to measure small lengths, adjusted by a finely threaded screw on which there is a graduated scale.
Word Family: **micrometry**, *noun*, the method or art of measuring with a micrometer.

micron (*say* **my**–kron) *noun*
the millionth part of a metre (10^{-6} m).

micro–organism *noun*
also called a **microbe**
any very small organism which can only be seen with a microscope.

microphone *noun*
a device which changes soundwaves into electrical waves to be transmitted or recorded. Compare LOUDSPEAKER.
[MICRO– + Greek *phonē* sound]

microscope (*say* **my**–kra–skope) *noun*
an optical instrument for viewing objects too small to be seen with the naked eye.
microscopy (*say* my–**kroska**–pee) *noun*
a) the use of a microscope. b) an investigation using a microscope.
Word Family: **microscopic** (*say* my–kra–**skoppik**), *adjective*, a) of or relating to the microscope, b) extremely tiny.
[MICRO– + Greek *skopein* to look at]

microwave (*say* **my**–kro–wave) *noun*
Physics: an electromagnetic wave with a very high frequency, used in television, radar, etc. and including ultra high frequency and super high frequency waves.

microwave oven
an oven which cooks extremely quickly by microwaves rather than by radiant heat.

micturate (*say* **mik**–tew–rate) *verb*
to urinate.
Word Family: **micturition** (*say* miktew–**rish**'n), *noun*.
[from Latin]

mid *adjective*
in the middle of.

mid–
a prefix meaning middle, as in *midway*.

midday (*say* **mid**–day) *noun*
1. 12 noon: 'the train leaves at *midday*'.
2. the middle of the day.

midden *noun*
Archaeology: a mound of kitchen wastes, shells, pots, etc.

middle *noun*
the point or part that is at an equal distance from the edges or extremes: a) 'the chair is in the *middle* of the room'; b) 'ring me in the *middle* of the week'.
Usage: 'can't you see I'm in the *middle* of doing something?' (= process).
middle-of-the-road, moderate.
middle *adjective*
a) at a middle point. b) average or medium: 'a girl of *middle* height'.

Middle Ages
the period from about the 5th to the 15th century, approximately from the end of the Western Roman Empire to the Renaissance.

middle class
the social class generally considered to consist of those in businesses or professions.

Middle East
the countries from the eastern shores of the Aegean and Mediterranean Seas to Iran.

Middle English
see ENGLISH.

middleman *noun*
a) a trader, such as a wholesaler, who buys goods from a manufacturer and sells them to a retailer. b) any person who acts as a go-between or intermediate agent.

middle school
a school for children in the upper primary and lower secondary age-range, in certain areas of Britain, America, etc.

middleweight *noun*
a weight division in boxing, equal to 158 lb (about 75 kg).

middling *adjective*
medium: 'a town of *middling* size'.
Word Family: **middling**, *adverb*, fairly or moderately.

midge (*say* mij) *noun*
a gnat.

midget (*say* **mij**-it) *noun*
a) a very small person. b) any very small object.

midi *noun*
a skirt, dress, etc. between mini and maxi which reaches to the calf.

midland *noun*
the inner or middle part of a country, especially (*the Midlands*) the central counties of England.

midnight *noun*
1. 12 o'clock at night: 'the boat sails at *midnight*'.
2. the middle of the night.
burn the midnight oil, to work late into the night.

midpoint *noun*
a point halfway between the beginning and end of a line, etc.

midriff *noun*
the middle part of the body between the chest and the waist.

midshipman *noun*
a naval officer ranking between naval cadet and sublieutenant.

midst *noun*
the middle.
Usage: 'there is a traitor in our *midst*' (= group, ranks).

midsummer *noun*
the summer solstice, about June 21st, the longest day. **Midsummer Day**, June 24th, is a quarter day.
midsummer madness, the height of foolishness (rabies was once thought to become prevalent at this period).

midway *adjective, adverb*
in or to the middle of the distance.

midwife *noun*
a person trained to assist a mother during childbirth.
Word Family: **midwifery** (*say* mid-wiffa-ree), *noun*, the art or practice of being a midwife.

mien (*say* meen) *noun*
a person's appearance or expression: 'a sorrowful *mien*'.

might (1) *verb*
1. the past tense of the auxiliary verb **may (1)**.
2. used instead of **may**: a) as a polite form: '*might* I speak to you for a moment?'; b) to express a less probable condition: 'we *might* win if we are very lucky'.

might (2) *noun*
a great strength or capacity: 'the army has the *might* to repel the invaders'.
with might and main, with all one's strength and ability.

mighty *adjective*
1. powerful: 'a *mighty* ruler'.
2. great or huge: 'a *mighty* mountain range'.

mighty *adverb*
(*informal*) very: 'you seem *mighty* pleased with yourself'.
Word Family: **mightily**, *adverb*, extremely; **mightiness**, *noun*;

migraine (*say* **mee**-grane) *noun*
1. a periodic, severely painful headache, usually on only one side of the head and often accompanied by nausea or vomiting and blurred vision.
2. (*informal*) any severe headache.
[Greek *hemikrania* a pain on one side of the head]

migrate (*say* my-**grate**) *verb*
1. to move periodically from one area to another, as do certain birds.
2. to move permanently to a new area or country.
migrant (*say* **my**-gr'nt) *noun*
a person, bird, etc. that migrates.
migration (*say* my-**gray**-sh'n) *noun*
the act of migrating.
Word Family: **migratory** (*say* **my**-gra-tree), *adjective*, having the habit of migrating.

mikado (*say* mik-**ahdo**) *noun*
History: (*often capital*) a title for the emperor of Japan.
[Japanese, exalted gate]

mike *noun*
(*informal*) a microphone.

milch *adjective*
(of cows, goats, etc.) kept for the purpose of producing milk.

mild *adjective*
moderate or temperate: '*mild* weather'.
Usage: 'this is a very *mild* cheese' (= one without a sharp flavour).
mildly *adverb*
gently or moderately.
put it mildly, to speak without exaggerating.
mild *noun*
a beer with less hops and a sweeter, milder taste than bitter, though often just as strong.
Word Family: **mildness**, *noun*.

mildew (*say* **mill**-dew) *noun*
a plant disease caused by a fungus producing a powdery growth on a surface.
Word Family: **mildew**, *verb*, to become affected by mildew.

mild steel
any of a range of steels which can be cut or shaped easily.

mile *noun*
1. a unit of length equal to about 1·6 km. An **international nautical mile** is used for navigation and is equal to about 1·85 km. See UNITS in grey pages.
2. (*plural*) a long or great distance.
[Latin *mille* a thousand paces (nearly one mile)]

mileage (*say* **my**-lij) **milage** *noun*
a) the distance in miles: 'what's the *mileage* from here to the next town?'.
b) the total number of miles travelled: 'this car has a low *mileage*'.
Usages:
a) 'I've certainly had good *mileage* out of this coat' (= service, usefulness).
b) 'what is the *mileage* for taxis now?' (= cost per mile).

milepost, milestone *noun*
1. a post or stone at the side of a road showing the distance from a major city.
2. an important stage or event in history or a person's life.

milieu (*say* mil-**yer**) *noun*
environment or surroundings: 'this book is a study of the artist and the *milieu* in which he worked'.
[French]

militant *adjective*
aggressive or eager to fight.
Word Family: **militant**, *noun*, a person who shows militant qualities; **militancy**, *noun*; **militantly**, *adverb*.

militarism (*say* **mill**ita-rizm) *noun*
a belief in the use of military power to solve political problems.
Word Family: **militarist**, *noun*, a supporter of militarism; **militaristic** (*say* millita-**ristik**), *adjective*; **militaristically**, *adverb*.

military (*say* **milli** tree) *adjective*
of or relating to soldiers, the armed forces, war, etc.
Word Family: **military**, *noun*, the armed forces.

militate (*say* **milli**-tate) *verb*
to operate or have effect: 'the weather *militated* against our plans to go away for the weekend'.
[Latin *militare* to soldier]

militia (*say* mil-**isha**) *noun*
a group of citizen-soldiers called to fight in an emergency.
[Latin *militis* of a soldier]

milk *noun*
1. *Biology:* the white liquid produced in the mammary glands of female mammals to feed their young, and, in the case of cows and some other animals, used for food or as a source of dairy products.
2. any liquid resembling this, such as latex from a tree or liquid in a coconut.
milk *verb*
a) to extract milk from a cow, etc. b) to give milk: 'my cows refuse to *milk* at the moment'.
Usage: 'they *milked* him of all his information' (= drew or extracted from).
Word Family: **milky**, *adjective*, a) of or like milk, b) (of liquids) cloudy; **milker**, *noun*, a person or thing that milks; **milkmaid**, *noun*, a girl who milks cows; **milkman**, *noun*, a man who delivers milk.

milk bar
a bar where milk drinks, ice-cream, etc. are sold.

milk of magnesia
magnesium hydroxide (formula $Mg(OH)_2$) in water, used as a laxative or antacid.

milk shake
a sweet drink made by vigorously mixing a syrup flavouring with milk.

milksop *noun*
(*use is derogatory*) a weak, soft person, especially a male.

milk tooth
any of the temporary teeth in young humans and other mammals, later replaced by permanent teeth.

Milky Way
Astronomy: the bright band in the night sky formed by the stars of our galaxy.

mill *noun*
1. a) any of various devices for grinding or crushing. b) a building in which this is done.
2. a building with machinery in which cloth is spun or woven.
go through the mill, to be tested by a difficult experience.
mill *verb*
1. to grind or treat in or as if in a mill.
2. to add fine notches to the edge of a coin when minting.
3. to move around in a confused or aimless way: 'stop *milling* about like cattle'.
[Latin *mola* millstone]

millennium (*say* mil-**ennium**) *noun*
1. a period of a thousand years.
2. *Christian:* a future period of universal happiness based on a Biblical prophecy.
Word Family: **millennial**, *adjective*.
[Latin *mille* thousand + *annus* year]

millepede *noun*
any of a group of slow-moving, plant-eating arthropods with a firm, circular, segmented body, each segment having two pairs of legs.
[Latin *mille* thousand + *pedis* of a foot]

miller *noun*
the owner or operator of a mill, especially a flour mill.

millet *noun*
a cereal plant with small edible grains.

milli-
a prefix used for SI units, meaning one thousandth (10^{-3}). See UNITS in grey pages.

millibar *noun*
a metric unit of pressure used in meteorology, equal to 100 pascal. See UNITS in grey pages.
[MILLI- + Greek *baros* weight]

milliner *noun*
a person who makes or sells hats for women.
[originally a dealer in goods from *Milan*]

million *noun*
a cardinal number, the symbol 1 000 000 or 10^6.

millionaire (*say* **mill-y'n-air**) *noun*
a person who has a million dollars, pounds, etc.
[from French]

millstone *noun*
either of the pair of circular stones between which grain, etc. is ground.
Usage: 'his problems are a *millstone* around his neck' (= heavy burden).

milt *noun*
the spermatozoa from a male fish. Compare ROE (1).

mime *noun*
a) a form of entertainment consisting of scenes performed using only actions or gestures. b) an actor in such entertainment.
Word Family: **mime**, *verb*, a) to act in a mime, b) to imitate a person or action without using words.
[from Greek]

Mimeograph (*say* **mimm**io-graf) *noun*
a) a type of stencil for reproducing letters and drawings. b) a machine using such a stencil.
[a trademark]

mimesis (*say* mim**mee**sis *or* my-**mee**sis) *noun*
imitation.
Word Family: **mimetic** (*say* mim**mett**ik), *adjective.*
[Greek]

mimic *verb*
(mimicked, mimicking)
to imitate a person's speech or manner.
mimic *adjective*
pretended or imitated: 'playing war games, we conducted a *mimic* battle'.
Word Family: **mimic,** *noun,* a person or thing that mimics; **mimicry,** *noun,* the act or an instance of mimicking.

mimosa (*say* mim-**o**-sa) *noun*
a group of tropical herbs, shrubs or trees with pink or red flowers, related to the acacia.

mina (*say* **my**-na) *noun*
a mynah.

minaret (*say* minna-**ret**) *noun*
a tall spire on a mosque, with balconies from which people are called to prayer.
[Arabic *manarat* lighthouse]

minatory (*say* **minna**-tree) *adjective*
threatening or menacing.
[Latin *minari* to threaten]

mince *verb*
1. to cut into small pieces.
2. to make affected, refined or dainty: 'he told the truth and didn't *mince* words'.
3. to walk in an affected way.
mince *noun*
any finely chopped meat.
Word Family: **mincingly,** *adverb,* affectedly.

mincemeat *noun*
a) a mixture of suet, apples, raisins, sultanas, peel, etc. used in mince pies. b) minced meat.
make mincemeat of, to defeat or destroy thoroughly.

mince pie
a small, covered tart made with a filling of mincemeat.

mind (*rhymes with* find) *noun*
1. the faculty which thinks, reasons, remembers, etc.: 'he has a simple *mind*'.
2. a) the soundness of this faculty: 'I think I'm losing my *mind*'. b) a person considered in relation to this faculty: 'the greatest *mind* of our age'.
3. what a person thinks, feels, etc.: a) 'he doesn't know his own *mind*'; b) 'to change one's *mind*'.
Usage: 'we were all of the same *mind*' (= opinion).
Phrases:
a piece of one's mind, a reprimand or scolding.
have a good mind to, 'I *have a good mind to* give you both a thrashing' (= am inclined to).
out of one's mind, 'you must be *out of your mind* to say that' (= mad).
put in mind, 'this joke *puts* me *in mind* of a similar one' (= reminds).
set one's mind on, to determine to do or get.
set one's mind to, 'you won't find it so difficult once you *set your mind to* it' (= concentrate with determination on).
speak one's mind, to say what one really thinks.
mind *verb*
1. to pay attention to or take care of: a) 'will you *mind* the house while I'm away?'; b) '*mind* your manners, young man'.
2. to feel troubled or upset by: 'do you *mind* if I smoke?'.
mind you, '*mind you,* I think it's a wonderful idea' (= please note or understand that).
Word Family: **mindful,** *adjective,* attentive or careful; **mindless,** *adjective,* senseless or careless.

minded *adjective*
used in combination to indicate:
a) having a certain kind of mind, as in *evil-minded.*
b) conscious or aware of a thing, as in *music-minded.*

mind-reading *noun*
telepathy.
Word Family: **mind-reader,** *noun.*

mind's eye
the imagination: 'I can picture the whole scene in my *mind's eye*'.

mine (1) *possessive pronoun*
plural is **ours**
belonging to me: 'that book is *mine*'.
mine *possessive adjective*
an old word for my: '*mine* eyes have seen a wonderful vision'.

mine (2) *noun*
1. any hole dug in the ground to take out minerals, gems, etc.
Usage: 'she is a *mine* of information' (= rich source).

2. any of various explosive devices placed in a concealed position to destroy enemy troops, ships, etc.
mine *verb*
1. a) to extract ore, etc. from the ground. b) to dig.
2. to lay military mines: 'the enemy *mined* the entrance to the harbour'.

minefield *noun*
Military: an area of land or water where mines have been laid.

miner *noun*
a person who works in a mine, especially a coalmine.

mineral (*say* **minna**–r'l) *noun*
a substance, such as quartz, with a definite chemical composition and a constant structure, found in the earth's surface.
Word Family: **mineral**, *adjective*, a) of or relating to minerals, b) containing minerals; **mineralize mineralise**, *verb*, to make into or add minerals to.

mineralogy (*say* minna–**ralla**–jee) *noun*
the study of minerals, a branch of geology.
Word Family: **mineralogist**, *noun*; **mineralogical** (*say* minnera–**loji**–k'l), *adjective.*

mineral spring
a spring that provides mineral water.

mineral water
1. water that contains dissolved minerals or gases.
2. any of various non-alcoholic, effervescent drinks, such as lemonade.

minestrone (*say* mini–**strone**–ee) *noun*
a thick vegetable soup, highly seasoned and served with grated cheese.
[Italian]

minesweeper *noun*
a ship equipped to remove mines from the water.

mingle *verb*
to mix or become mixed or blended: 'the prince *mingled* with the crowd'.

mingy (*say* **min**–jee) *adjective*
(*informal*) mean or stingy.
[M(ean) + (ST)INGY]

mini *noun*
(*informal*) a thing which is small, especially a short skirt or a small car.

mini–
a prefix meaning small, as in *minibus.*

miniature (*say* **minni**–cher) *noun*
any small-scale copy or representation, such as a very small painting.
Word Family: **miniaturize, miniaturise**, *verb*, to make small or on a small scale.

minibus *noun*
a very small bus.

minim *noun*
1. *Music:* a note with a half of the time value of a semibreve. In America called a **half-note.**
2. a unit of volume for liquids equal to about 0·06 ml.
[Latin *minimus* smallest]

minima *plural noun*
see MINIMUM.

minimal *adjective*
being the smallest or least possible: 'he showed *minimal* interest in his work'.

minimize, minimise *verb*
to reduce to the smallest possible amount: 'the rain has *minimized* the chances of a pleasant weekend'.
Usage: 'do not *minimize* your chance of success' (= underestimate).
Word Family: **minimization,** *noun.*

minimum *noun*
plural is **minima**
the least amount: 'the *minimum* I could accept for my car is £100'. Compare MAXIMUM.
[Latin, least]

minion (*say* **min**–y'n) *noun*
1. a favourite, especially a favourite servant.
2. (*use is derogatory*) a person who obeys another like a slave.

minister *noun*
1. *Christian:* a clergyman.
2. *Parliament:* a) a member of either House of Parliament who is the political head of a government department. b) any of various other members of government, e.g. junior ministers, ministers without portfolio, etc.
3. a diplomatic representative.
minister *verb*
to give service or aid.
ministration (*say* minni–**stray**–sh'n) *noun*
the act or an instance of ministering.
[Latin, servant]

ministerial (*say* minni–**steeriul**) *adjective*
of or relating to a minister or ministry.

ministry (*say* **minni**–stree) ***noun***
1. *Parliament:* a) a body of ministers. b) the function or office of a minister. c) the department under the charge of a minister.
2. *Christian:* a) the clergy. b) the profession or duties of a minister.
3. the act of ministering.

mink ***noun***
a) a small, stoat–like mammal with a long, pointed nose, highly prized for its shiny brown fur. b) the fur of this animal.

minnow ***noun***
any of a group of small, silvery, freshwater fish.

minor (*say* **my**–na) *adjective*
1. smaller or less important: a) 'these are only ***minor*** objections, so I shall ignore them'; b) 'he was only a ***minor*** poet'.
2. *Music:* relating to one of two particular arrangements of the semitones in a key or scale.
minor ***noun***
a person who has not reached the legal age of adulthood.
[Latin, less]

minority (*say* my–**norri**–tee) ***noun***
1. the lesser part or number: 'we were only a ***minority***, so our idea was rejected by the meeting'.
2. the state or time of being under full legal age.

minster ***noun***
Christian: a) a church belonging to a monastery. b) a name given to certain large churches.
[Greek ***monasterion*** monastery]

minstrel ***noun***
a) a travelling musician and singer in medieval Europe. b) a singer in a variety show, often with his face painted black.
Word Family: **minstrelsy** (*say* **minstrel**–see), ***noun***, the art or songs, etc. of minstrels.

mint (1) ***noun***
1. a green–leafed herb used in salads and sauces.
2. a sweet flavoured with peppermint.
[Greek ***minthé***]

mint (2) ***noun***
1. a place where coins are made.
2. a vast amount of money: 'he's worth a ***mint***'.
mint ***verb***
a) to issue stamps. b) to make coins.
Usage: 'I have ***minted*** a new phrase' (= invented).
mint *adjective*
unused, or in the condition in which it was issued, e.g. a stamp or coin.
[Latin ***moneta*** money]

minuet (*say* min–yoo–**et**) ***noun***
a) a stately court dance from France. b) the music for such a dance.
[Old French ***menuet*** very small]

minus (*say* **my**–nus) ***preposition***
reduced by: 'two ***minus*** one equals one'.
Usage: 'I was caught in the rain ***minus*** my umbrella' (= without).
minus *adjective*
a) of or denoting subtraction: 'the ***minus*** sign'. b) being in a negative direction: 'the temperature was ***minus*** five degrees this morning'.
minus ***noun***
1. the minus sign (–).
2. a) a negative amount. b) a loss or deficit.
[Latin, less]

minuscule (*say* **minni**–skewl) ***adjective***
very small, especially of print or writing.
[Latin ***minusculus*** rather small]

minute (1) (*say* **minn**it) ***noun***
1. a unit of time equal to 60 seconds or one 60th part of an hour.
Usage: 'I'll only be a ***minute***' (= short time).
2. one 60th part of a degree.
3. (***usually plural***) the official record of the business of a meeting, etc.
Phrases:
this minute, immediately.
up to the minute, most recent or modern.
minute ***verb***
to record the proceedings of a meeting or discussion.
[Latin ***minutus*** little]

minute (2) (*say* my–**newt**) ***adjective***
1. very small: 'some insects are ***minute***'.
2. very precise or exact: '***minute*** detail'.
Word Family: **minutely**, ***adverb***; **minuteness**, ***noun***.

minutiae (*say* my–**new**–tee–eye) ***plural noun***
singular is **minutia**
small or unimportant details.

minx ***noun***
an impudent or flirtatious girl.

Miocene (*say* **my**–o–seen) ***noun***
Geology: see TERTIARY.
[Greek ***meion*** less + ***kainos*** modern (= fewer modern forms of life)]

miracle (*say* **mirri**–k'l) *noun*
a) an event which is believed to have a supernatural or divine cause. b) any wonderful or surprising event.
miraculous (*say* mirr**ak**–yoolus) *adjective*
a) of or like a miracle. b) having the power to work miracles.
Word Family: **miraculously**, *adverb*; **miraculousness**, *noun*.
[Latin *miraculum* a marvel]

mirage (*say* **mir**–ah*zh*) *noun*
1. an optical phenomenon due to atmospheric conditions which creates the illusion of water or the reflected images of distant objects.
2. any delusion or hopeless project.
[French *mirer* to look in a mirror]

mire *noun*
swampy ground or mud.
Usage: 'they dragged him mercilessly through the *mire*' (= disgrace of public exposure).
Word Family: **mire**, *verb*, to dirty with mud; **miry**, *adjective*.

mirror (*say* **mirra**) *noun*
a reflecting surface, usually glass with a metal backing.
Usage: 'this newspaper is a *mirror* of society' (= true reflection).
mirror *verb*
to reflect in or like a mirror: 'the lake *mirrored* the snow-capped mountains'.

mirth *noun*
a) merriment or rejoicing. b) laughter, e.g. at something absurd.
Word Family: **mirthful**, *adjective*, a) full of mirth, b) amusing; **mirthfully**, *adverb*; **mirthfulness**, *noun*; **mirthless**, *adjective*.

mis–
a prefix meaning mistaken or wrongly, as in *misunderstand*.

misadventure *noun*
bad luck.

misadvise *verb*
to advise wrongly.

misalliance *noun*
an unsuitable alliance or marriage.
Word Family: **misally** (*say* missa–**lie**), (**misallied**, **misallying**), *verb*.

misanthrope (*say* **mizz**'n–thrope) *noun*
a person who hates or distrusts mankind.
Word Family: **misanthropic** (*say* mizz'n–**thropp**ik), *adjective*; **misanthropist** (*say* miz–**an**thra–pist), *noun*, a misanthrope; **misanthropy**, *noun*.
[Greek *misos* hatred + *anthropos* man]

misapply *verb*
to use wrongly.

misapprehend (*say* mis–apri–**hend**) *verb*
to misunderstand.
Word Family: **misapprehension** (*say* mis–apri–**hen**–sh'n), *noun*.

misappropriate *verb*
to use in a wrongful way, especially someone else's money.
Word Family: **misappropriation**, *noun*.

misbegotten *adjective*
illegitimate.

misbehave *verb*
to behave badly.
Word Family: **misbehaviour**, *noun*.

miscalculate *verb*
to estimate or calculate wrongly.
Word Family: **miscalculation**, *noun*.

miscall *verb*
1. to call by a wrong name.
2. to give a wrong call, e.g. in tennis.

miscarriage *noun*
1. the premature delivery of a foetus that is too undeveloped to survive.
2. a failure to arrive at a right result or destination: 'a *miscarriage* of justice'.
Word Family: **miscarry** (**miscarried**, **miscarrying**), *verb*.

miscellaneous (*say* missa–**lay**–nee–us) *adjective*
consisting of things of different or various kinds.
miscellany (*say* mis**sell**a–nee) *noun*
a mixed collection, especially of articles in a book.
Word Family: **miscellaneously**, *adverb*; **miscellaneousness**, *noun*.
[Latin *miscellanea* a hash of chopped meat]

mischance *noun*
bad luck or an unlucky event.

mischief (*say* **mis**–chif) *noun*
1. playful conduct which teases or irritates.
2. injury or harm: 'the storm did great *mischief* to the trees'.
mischievous *adjective*
a) fond of mischief. b) causing mischief.
Word Family: **mischievously**, *adverb*; **mischievousness**, *noun*.

miscible (*say* **missi**–b'l) *adjective*
Chemistry: able to be mixed in any proportions to form an even, homogeneous substance.
Word Family: **miscibility** (*say* missi–**billi**–tee), *noun.*
[Latin *miscere* to mix]

misconceive (*say* mis–kon**seev**) *verb*
to misunderstand.
Word Family: **misconception**, *noun.*

misconduct (*say* mis–**kon**–dukt) *noun*
1. wrong or unlawful behaviour.
2. bad or unlawful management, as by an official.
Word Family: **misconduct** (*say* mis–kon–**dukt**), *verb.*

misconstrue *verb*
to misunderstand or misinterpret.
Word Family: **misconstruction**, *noun.*

miscount *noun*
a wrong count, especially of votes.
Word Family: **miscount**, *verb.*

miscreant (*say* **mis**–kree–ant) *noun*
a villainous or criminal person.
Word Family: **miscreant**, *adjective.*
[Old French, unbeliever, heretic]

misdate *verb*
to put the wrong date on something, such as a document, cheque, etc.

misdeal *verb*
(**misdealt, misdealing**)
to deal wrongly, especially playing cards.
Word Family: **misdeal**, *noun.*

misdeed *noun*
a crime or wicked action.

misdemeanour (*say* misdi–**meena**) *noun*
in America spelt **misdemeanor**
1. a minor crime.
2. any misbehaviour.

misdirection *noun*
a wrong indication or instruction.
Word Family: **misdirect**, *verb.*

miser (*say* **my**–za) *noun*
a person who is greedy for or mean with money.
Word Family: **miserly**, *adjective*; **miserliness**, *noun.*
[Latin, wretched]

misère (*say* miz–**air**) *noun*
Cards: a bid indicating an attempt not to win any tricks.
[French, misery]

misery (*say* **mizza**–ree) *noun*
1. extreme unhappiness or distress.
2. something which causes unhappiness or distress.

miserable (*say* **mizz**era–b'l) *adjective*
very unhappy or uncomfortable.
Usage: 'he pays me a *miserable* wage' (= very small).

misfire *verb*
(of a gun) to fail to fire.
Usage: 'the scheme *misfired*' (= was unsuccessful).

misfit *noun*
a person or thing that fits badly, especially a person who cannot adapt to his environment.

misfortune *noun*
bad luck, such as an unlucky accident.

misgiving *noun*
a feeling of doubt, fear or worry.

misgovern *verb*
to govern badly.
Word Family: **misgovernment**, *noun.*

misguided *adjective*
a) foolish. b) misled.
Word Family: **misguide**, *verb*; **misguidance**, *noun.*

mishandle *verb*
to handle or treat badly.

mishap (*say* **mis**–hap) *noun*
an unlucky accident, usually a minor one.

mishmash *noun*
a jumble.

misinform *verb*
to give wrong or misleading information.
Word Family: **misinformation**, *noun.*

misinterpret *verb*
to explain or understand wrongly.
Word Family: **misinterpretation**, *noun.*

misjudge *verb*
to form a wrong or unjust opinion of a person, event, etc.
Word Family: **misjudgement**, *noun.*

mislay *verb*
(**mislaid, mislaying**)
to lose something temporarily by forgetting where it was put.

mislead *verb*
(**misled, misleading**)
to lead astray.
Word Family: **misleadingly**, *adverb.*

mismanagement *noun*
any incompetent or dishonest management.
Word Family: **mismanage**, *verb.*

misnomer (*say* mis–**no**–mer) ***noun***
a) a name wrongly applied to a person or thing. b) the act of naming something wrongly.
[MIS– + Latin *nomen* a name]

misogyny (*say* mis–**oja**–nee) ***noun***
a hatred of women.
Word Family: **misogynist**, ***noun.***
[Greek *misos* hatred + *gyné* woman]

misplace ***verb***
to put something in a wrong place.
Word Family: **misplacement**, ***noun.***

misprint ***noun***
a mistake in printing.
Word Family: **misprint**, ***verb.***

mispronounce ***verb***
to pronounce a word incorrectly.
Word Family: **mispronunciation**, ***noun.***

misquote ***verb***
to quote incorrectly.
Word Family: **misquotation**, ***noun.***

misread ***verb***
(misread, misreading)
to read or interpret something wrongly.

misrepresent ***verb***
to give a false or misleading account, description, etc. of.
Word Family: **misrepresentation**, ***noun.***

misrule ***noun***
bad rule or government.

miss (1) ***verb***
1. to fail to do or perform some action: a) 'I *missed* the ball'; b) 'he *missed* his appointment'.
Usage: 'you just *missed* being killed' (= escaped).
2. to feel regret at the absence of something: 'she's unhappy because she *misses* her teddy bear'.
miss out, to omit or be omitted from something.
miss ***noun***
a failure to perform some action: 'only one of my 5 shots was a *miss*'.
give it a miss, to avoid something.

miss (2) ***noun***
a) (*capital*) a title for an unmarried woman. b) any young unmarried woman.

missal ***noun***
Roman Catholic: a book containing the services of the Eucharist for the year.
[Latin *missa* Mass]

misshapen (*say* mis–**shay**–p'n) *adjective*
deformed or badly shaped.

missile ***noun***
any object, usually a weapon, which is thrown, fired or ejected.
[Latin *missilis* that may be thrown]

missing *adjective*
absent, lacking or lost.

missing link
a hypothetical animal supposed to have formed the link in evolution between apes and man.

mission (*say* **mish**'n) ***noun***
1. a) an assignment for a particular purpose, e.g. military or diplomatic, usually in a foreign country: 'the pilots were briefed for their dangerous *mission*'. b) the person or people sent on such an assignment.
2. an organization or centre for religious and charitable work, especially overseas.
3. a vocation: 'he felt that his *mission* in life was to fight alcoholism'.
Mission hall, a meeting place for Christian worship and community work, particularly in the poorer districts of a city.
[Latin *missio* a sending]

missionary (*say* **mish**'n–ree) ***noun***
a priest or other person sent overseas to spread the teaching of his religion.
Word Family: **missionary**, *adjective*, connected with or engaged on a mission.

missis ***noun***
missus.

missive ***noun***
a letter or written message.

misspell ***verb***
(misspelt, misspelling)
to spell a word incorrectly.

misspend ***verb***
(misspent, misspending)
to waste or squander something, such as money, time, etc.

missus ***noun***
also spelt **missis**
(*informal*) a wife: 'not a word to the *missus!*'.

mist ***noun***
1. a light fog.
2. any fine drops of liquid.
Usage: 'she saw through a *mist* of tears' (= blur).
Word Family: **mist**, *verb*, to become covered with mist; **misty**, *adjective*; **mistily**, *adverb*; **mistiness**, ***noun.***

mistake ***noun***
a wrong idea or action: a) 'it was a *mistake* to leave my umbrella behind';

b) 'I made a *mistake* in my addition and got the wrong answer'.
mistake *verb*
(**mistook, mistaken, mistaking**)
1. to understand wrongly: 'I *mistook* the meaning of her words'.
2. to believe to be someone or something else: 'he always *mistakes* me for my twin brother'.
Word Family: **mistakeable**, *adjective*; **mistakeably**, *adverb*; **mistakenly**, *adverb*, wrongly.

Mister *noun*
a title for a man.

mistime *verb*
to time something wrongly.

mistletoe (*say* **miss**'l-toe) *noun*
any of a group of plants parasitic on trees, with green leaves and white berries.

mistook *verb*
the past tense of the verb **mistake**.

mistreat *verb*
to treat badly or wrongly.
Word Family: **mistreatment**, *noun*.

mistress *noun*
1. (*capital*) a title for a married woman.
2. a female employer or person in authority, especially of a household.
3. a female lover, especially one supported by a married man.

mistrial (*say* miss-**try**'l) *noun*
Law: a trial which is declared invalid due to an error in proceedings.

mistrust *verb*
to doubt or regard with suspicion.
Word Family: **mistrust**, *noun*; **mistrustful**, *adjective*; **mistrustfully**, *adverb*; **mistrustfulness**, *noun*.

misunderstand *verb*
(**misunderstood, misunderstanding**)
to understand wrongly.
misunderstanding *noun*
a) a failure to understand. b) a disagreement: 'the landlord and I had a *misunderstanding* about the rent'.

misuse (*say* mis-**yooz**) *verb*
a) to use something for the wrong purpose or in the wrong way. b) to maltreat.
Word Family: **misuse** (*say* mis-**yoos**), *noun*.

mite *noun*
1. a person or thing that is very small, such as a child.
2. any of a group of small, often parasitic arachnids with sac-like bodies.
a mite, 'this hat is *a mite* too big' (= somewhat).

mitigate (*say* **mitti**-gate) *verb*
to make less intense or severe.
mitigating circumstances
circumstances which make a mistake or crime seem less serious.
Word Family: **mitigatory**, *adjective*; **mitigation**, *noun*.
[Latin *mitigare* to make mild]

mitosis (*say* my-**toe**-sis) *noun*
Biology: the normal type of cell division in growing tissue, resulting in cells with the same number of chromosomes as the parent cell. Compare MEIOSIS.
[Greek *mitos* a thread + -OSIS]

mitre (*say* **my**-ta) *noun*
Christian: the tall headdress worn by a bishop during certain ceremonies.
[Greek *mitra* turban]

mitre-joint *noun*
a joint made by cutting the ends of two pieces at identical angles and fixing the cut faces together.

mitt *noun*
1. a) a type of glove which does not fully cover the fingers. b) a mitten.
2. (*informal*) a hand.

mitten *noun*
a fitted covering for the hand, covering the thumb separately and the other four fingers together.

mix *verb*
1. to put things together so that the various parts are blended or no longer fully distinct: a) 'she *mixed* the ingredients for the cake'; b) 'we *mixed* children of all age-groups for this class'.
Usages:
a) 'to *mix* business with pleasure' (= bring together).
b) 'he does not *mix* well at parties' (= get on with others).
2. to combine various sounds on one soundtrack.
mix up, a) 'he *mixed up* our names' (= confused); b) 'don't get *mixed up* in politics' (= involved).
mix *noun*
a) a mixture. b) a prepared set of ingredients for cooking: 'a cake *mix*'.
[from Latin]

mixed blessing
an event which has disadvantages as well as advantages.

mixed marriage
a marriage between persons of different religions or races.

mixed number
Maths: the sum of an integer and a proper fraction, such as $4\frac{1}{4}$.

mixer *noun*
a person or thing that mixes: a) 'he used the electric *mixer* to make a cake'; b) 'she's a good *mixer* at parties'.

mixture *noun*
any combination of different things, elements, qualities, etc.: 'this stew is a *mixture* of meat and vegetables'.

mix-up *noun*
a confused mistake.

mizzen *noun*
Nautical: a) the mast nearer the stern. b) the sail on this mast.

mnemonic (*say* nim-**onnik**) *noun*
a short verse or phrase which helps one to remember.
Example: 'th*a*t p*e*n *i*s n*o*t m*u*ch g*oo*d' for the short vowels in shorthand.
Word Family: **mnemonic,** *adjective,* assisting the memory.
[Greek *mnemonikos* for the memory]

moa *noun*
a large, extinct, flightless bird of New Zealand, similar to an emu or ostrich.
[Maori]

moan *noun*
1. a) a long, low sound of pain or pleasure. b) any sound similar to this: 'the *moan* of the wind'.
2. (*informal*) a grumble.
Word Family: **moan,** *verb.*

moat *noun*
a pit or ditch, usually filled with water, dug around a building, e.g. a castle, to defend it.

mob *noun*
any large group of people or animals, especially a disorderly or uncontrollable crowd.
mob *verb*
(**mobbed, mobbing**)
to crowd around in great numbers: 'the screaming girls *mobbed* the film star'.
Word Family: **mobster,** *noun,* a criminal.
[Latin *mob*(ile vulgus) fickle crowd]

mob-cap *noun*
a woman's old-fashioned, soft, round cap for indoor wear, drawn in or gathered at the base.

mobile (*say* **mo**-bile) *adjective*
moving or able to be moved easily: 'a *mobile* crane'.
mobile *noun*
a hanging structure or sculpture with freely moving, balanced parts.
mobility (*say* mo-**billi**-tee) *noun*
the quality of being mobile.
[Latin *mobilis* easy to move]

mobilize (*say* **mo**-bilize) **mobilise** *verb*
to prepare armed forces for war.
Word Family: **mobilization,** *noun.*

moccasin (*say* **mokka**-sin) *noun*
a very soft leather shoe, first worn by American Indians.

mocha (*say* mokka) *noun*
1. the flavour of chocolate and coffee combined.
2. a high-quality Arabian coffee.
[exported through the Red Sea port of *Mocha*]

mock *verb*
to ridicule or make fun of a person or thing.
Usage: 'the drought *mocked* his efforts to grow fruit trees' (= made futile).
mock up, to build a model to test or study a proposed device, apparatus, etc. *Word Family:* **mock-up,** *noun,*
mock *adjective*
not real or genuine: 'a *mock* battle'.
Word Family: **mocker,** *noun;* **mockingly,** *adverb.*

mockery *noun*
ridicule.

mockingbird *noun*
a type of American or Mexican songbird which mimics sounds.

mod *adjective*
(*informal*) modern or fashionably up to date.
[short form of MODERN]

mode *noun*
1. a way in which something appears or is done: 'she has a strange *mode* of speech'.
Usage: 'the language she uses is very much the *mode* at the moment' (= fashion).
2. *Music:* a scale: 'the major and minor *modes*'.
3. *Maths:* the category with the highest frequency in a distribution.
Word Family: **modal** (*say* **mo**-dal), *adjective;* **modality** (*say* mo-**dalli**-tee), *noun,* a method of procedure.
[Latin *modus* a measure, manner]

model *noun*
1. a representation of something, usually in miniature, used as a basis or design for copy, construction, etc.: 'a *model* of the proposed urban development'.
Usage: 'she is a *model* of honesty' (= perfect example).
2. a specific design: 'the latest *model* car'.
3. a person who poses for a painter, etc.
4. a) a person employed to wear and display clothes. b) the clothes, etc. displayed: 'the latest Paris *models*'.
model *verb*
(modelled, modelling)
1. to act as a model: 'I *model* hats for a fashion house'.
2. to form or shape: 'she *models* in clay'.
3. to copy: 'he *models* himself on his father'.
Word Family: **model**, *adjective.*
[Latin *modulus* a small measure]

moderate (*say* **modda**-rit) *adjective*
not great or excessive: 'a *moderate* income'.
moderate *noun*
a person who has moderate ideas.
moderate (*say* **modda**-rate) *verb*
to make or become less extreme.
moderation (*say* modda-**ray**-sh'n) *noun*
a) the quality of being moderate: 'she shows *moderation* in her eating'. b) the act of moderating.
moderator *noun*
1. a person or thing that moderates.
2. (*capital*) the chairman of certain religious bodies, e.g. the Presbyterian General Assembly.
3. *Physics:* a material used to moderate neutron energy.
Word Family: **moderately**, *adverb.*
[Latin *moderari* to set bounds to]

modern (*say* **modd**'n) *adjective*
of or characteristic of the present or most recent times: a) '*modern* history'; b) '*modern* jazz'.
modern *noun*
a) a person of modern times. b) a person of modern ideas or opinions.
Word Family: **modernity** (*say* moderni-tee), *noun,* the quality of being modern.
[Latin *modo* lately]

modernism *noun*
sympathy or support for modern methods or ideas.
Word Family: **modernist**, *noun,* a person who supports modern ideas; **modernist, modernistic**, *adjective.*

modernize, modernise *verb*
to make or become modern.
Word Family: **modernization**, *noun.*

modest (*say* **modd**ist) *adjective*
1. not vain or boastful: 'she is a genius but she's very *modest* about it'.
2. moderate in amount, appearance, etc.: '*modest* needs'.
3. bashful or decorous: 'her *modest* demeanour was pleasingly old-fashioned'.
modesty *noun*
the quality of being modest.
Word Family: **modestly**, *adverb.*
[Latin *modestus* restrained, sober]

modicum (*say* **moddi**-k'm) *noun*
a small quantity or portion.
[Latin *modicus* of middling size]

modify (*say* **moddi**-fie) *verb*
(modified, modifying)
1. to make or become somewhat different in form, character, etc.: 'the car was *modified* to suit Australian conditions'.
2. to revise by making less extreme, uncompromising, etc.: 'to *modify* one's views'.
3. *Grammar:* to describe, limit or characterize the meaning of.
Word Family: **modifier**, *noun,* a person or thing that modifies; **modification**, *noun.*

modish (*say* **mo**-dish) *adjective*
fashionable.
Word Family: **modishly**, *adverb*; **modishness**, *noun.*

modulate (*say* **mod**-yoo-late) *verb*
1. to change or regulate, e.g. the tone of voice.
2. *Music:* to move from one key to another.
modulation (*say* mod-yoo-**lay**-sh'n) *noun*
1. a) the act of modulating: 'your voice needs more *modulation*'. b) the state of being modulated.
2. see AMPLITUDE MODULATION and FREQUENCY MODULATION.
Word Family: **modulator**, *noun,* a person or thing that modulates.
[Latin *modulari*]

module (*say* **mod**-yool) *noun*
1. a unit of measure, especially used for building materials.
2. a component made of standardized size so that it can be combined with

others in different ways, used in building, furniture, electronics, etc.
Word Family: **modular** (*say* **mod**-yoola), *adjective.*

modus operandi (*say* mo–dus oppa–**randi**)
a method or plan of operating or working.
[Latin]

modus vivendi (*say* mo–dus **vivendi**)
a) a mode of living. b) a compromise or temporary agreement made between the parties in a dispute.
[Latin]

mogul *noun*
(*informal*) an important or powerful person.
[after Grand *Mogul*, the European name for the Indian Emperors who ruled at Delhi]

mohair *noun*
a) the fleece of an Angora goat. b) a fabric made from this.
[from Arabic]

Mohammedanism
(*say* mo–**hammedan**–izm) *noun*
see ISLAM.

Mohs scale (*say* moze scale)
a scale of hardness used in mineralogy, ranging from soft minerals such as talc and gypsum, to diamond, which is the hardest.
[first devised by *Friedrich Mohs*, 1773–1839, a German mineralogist]

moiety (*say* **moya**–tee) *noun*
a portion, especially a half.

moire (*say* mwah) *noun*
watered silk.
Word Family: **moiré**, *adjective*, having the watered effect of moire; **moiré**, *noun*, the watered or rippled effect given e.g. to ribbed curtain material of cotton or viscose.
[French, mohair]

moist *adjective*
slightly wet.
Word Family: **moisten** (*say* **moy**–sen), *verb*, to make moist; **moistly**, *adverb*; **moistness**, *noun*.

moisture *noun*
any liquid or vapour, especially water–vapour, which makes something moist.
moisturize, moisturise *verb*
to give or restore moisture to: 'to *moisturize* skin'.
Word Family: **moisturizer**, *noun*, something that moisturizes, especially a cream or liquid used on the skin.

moke *noun*
(*informal*) a) a donkey. b) an inferior horse.

molar (1) (*say* **mole**–a) *noun*
Anatomy: any of the 12 square teeth at the back of the mouth.
Word Family: **molar**, *adjective.*
[Latin *mola* millstone]

molar (2) (*say* **mole**–a) *adjective*
Chemistry: of or relating to a mole or measurement in moles.
molarity (*say* mo–**larri**–tee) *noun*
the concentration of a solution, expressed as the number of moles of dissolved substance per litre of solution.

molasses *noun*
1. the syrup obtained from raw sugar.
2. *American:* treacle.
[from Portuguese]

mold *noun*
American: a mould.

mole (1) *noun*
Anatomy: a small, dark, often slightly raised spot on the skin.

mole (2) *noun*
any of various small insect–eating mammals, usually living underground.
molehill *noun*
a small mound of earth raised up by burrowing moles.
make a mountain out of a molehill, to exaggerate, especially a minor difficulty or problem.

mole (3) *noun*
1. the amount of a substance which contains the same number of particles as there are carbon atoms in 12 g of carbon.
2. the SI unit of amount of substance. See SI UNIT.
[German *mol* molecule]

mole (4) *noun*
a pier or breakwater.
[Latin *mola* a mass]

molecular biology
the study of the structure and function of the large molecules found in living cells.

molecule (*say* **molli**–kewl) *noun*
1. *Chemistry:* a stable group of atoms held together by weak attractive forces between electrons in neighbouring atoms; the smallest structural unit into which a chemical substance can be divided and still have the properties of that substance.
2. a small fragment.

molecular (*say* mol**lek**-yoola)
adjective
of, caused by or consisting of molecules.
[Latin *moles* a mass]

molehill *noun*
see MOLE (2).

moleskin *noun*
1. the fur of a mole.
2. a) a strong, cotton fabric. b) (*plural*) trousers made from this fabric.

molest (*say* mol**lest**) *verb*
to interfere with so as to annoy or injure.
Word Family: **molestation,** *noun.*
[Latin *molestus* irksome]

moll *noun*
(*informal*) a) the girlfriend of a gangster. b) a prostitute.
[diminutive of *Mary*]

mollify *verb*
to calm down or appease.
Word Family: **mollification,** *noun.*
[Latin *mollis* soft + *facere* to make]

mollusc *noun*
in America spelt **mollusk**
any of a group of soft, invertebrate organisms, such as oysters, snails, etc., usually with a shell of one or more pieces covering the body.
[Latin *mollis* soft]

mollycoddle *verb*
to pamper or coddle.
Word Family: **mollycoddle,** *noun,* a person who is pampered or weak.

Molotov cocktail
a home-made bomb consisting of a bottle filled with petrol or paraffin, and a wick.
[after *V.M. Molotov,* born 1890, a Russian statesman]

molt *verb*
American: to moult.

molten *verb*
a past participle of the verb **melt.**

molybdenum (*say* mo-**libda**-num)
noun
element number 42, a metal used to strengthen and harden steel in tools. See TRANSITION ELEMENT.
See CHEMICAL ELEMENTS in grey pages.
[Greek *molybdos* lead]

moment *noun*
1. a) a short space of time: 'wait a *moment*'. b) a particular point of time: 'I cannot speak to you at this *moment*'.
2. importance: 'the new discovery is of great *moment*'.
3. *Physics:* a) a tendency to produce motion, especially about an axis. b) the product of a physical quantity and its distance from an axis.
moment of truth, any moment when a person is put to a great test.
momently *adverb*
a) every moment. b) from moment to moment.

momentary (*say* **mo**-men-tree)
adjective
a) lasting only a moment: 'a *momentary* glimpse'. b) at every moment: 'he lives in *momentary* fear of capture by the police'.
Word Family: **momentarily,** *adverb,* for a moment.

momentous (*say* mo-**men**-tus)
adjective
very important or likely to have serious consequences.
Word Family: **momentously,** *adverb*; **momentousness,** *noun.*

momentum (*say* mo-**men**-t'm) *noun*
plural is **momenta**
1. a moving force or energy: 'the rolling car gathered *momentum* as it went down the hill'.
2. *Physics:* a vector quantity equal to the mass of a body multiplied by its velocity.
[Latin, movement]

monad *noun*
1. *Biology:* a single-celled organism.
2. *Chemistry:* an atom, element or radical with a valency of one.
[Greek *monados* of a unit]

monarch (*say* **mon**-ark) *noun*
also called a **sovereign**
a hereditary leader of a country, such as a king or queen, often with powers limited by a constitution or parliament.
monarchic, monarchal *adjective*
of, like or befitting a monarch.
monarchism (*say* **monna**-kizm) *noun*
a) the principles of government by a monarch. b) any support or favour for such principles.
Word Family: **monarchical** (*say* mon-**arki**-k'l), *adjective*; **monarchist,** *noun,* a supporter of monarchism.
[Greek *monos* alone + *arkhein* to rule]

monarchy (*say* **monna**-kee) *noun*
a) government or a country ruled by a monarch. b) the power of a monarch.

monastery (*say* **monna**-stree) *noun*
a) a community of monks. b) the buildings in which they live.

monastic (*say* mo-**nastik**) *adjective*
of or characteristic of monks or a monastery.
Word Family: **monastic,** *noun,* a monk; **monasticism** (*say* mo-**nasti**-sizm), *noun,* the monastic system or way of life.
[Greek *monazein* to live alone]

Monday *noun*
the second day of the week.
[Old English *monen* moon + *daeg* day]

money (*say* **munnee**) *noun*
plural is **monies** or **moneys**
any currency used as a medium of exchange.
Phrases:
for my money, '*for my money* I think the plan won't work' (= in my opinion).
in the money, (*informal*) rich.
money for jam, for old rope, very easily come by.
Word Family: **monetary** (*say* **munna**-tree), *adjective,* of or relating to money, currency or finance; **moneyed,** *adjective,* wealthy.
[Latin *moneta* the mint, a coin]

moneybags *noun*
(*informal*) a very wealthy person.

money-grubber *noun*
(*informal*) a person who is greedy for money.

money order
an order for the equivalent of money deposited at one post office to be paid out at another post office to a person named.

money-spinner *noun*
(*informal*) something which is very profitable.

monger (*say* **mung**-ga) *noun*
a person who sells, deals in or promotes something: a) 'a *fishmonger*'; b) 'a *rumour-monger*'.

mongol (*say* **mon**-g'l) *noun*
(*often capital*) a person suffering from mongolism.

mongolism (*say* **mon**-g'l-izm) *noun*
also called **Down's syndrome**
(*sometimes capital*) a disease caused by abnormal chromosomes, resulting in mental deficiency, slanted eyes and short broad hands.

mongoloid (*say* **mon**-g'loyd) *noun*
1. *Anthropology:* (*capital*) any of a major race of people including those of China and Japan, with yellowish skin, prominent cheekbones and straight black hair.
2. a person suffering from mongolism.
Word Family: **Mongoloid,** *adjective.*

mongoose *noun*
plural is **mongooses**
a small, ferret-like mammal found in Africa and Asia, noted for its ability to kill poisonous snakes.
[Indian *mangus*]

mongrel (*say* **mung**-grel) *noun*
a plant or animal, especially a dog, of mixed breed.
Word Family: **mongrel,** *adjective.*

monism *noun*
Philosophy: the belief that there is only one basic principle or substance in the world. Compare DUALISM.

monitor (*say* **monni**ta) *noun*
1. a pupil appointed to perform certain duties in a class or school: 'a blackboard *monitor*'.
2. any device used to control or check a process, such as a television screen in a studio for checking each stage of a programme being broadcast.
3. any of various large flesh-eating lizards with a slender head and long tail, found in Australia, Africa and Asia.
monitor *verb*
1. to check, observe or supervise.
2. to use a radio or television monitor.
Word Family: **monitorial** (*say* monni-**tawr**iul), *adjective*; **monitress,** *noun,* a female monitor.
[Latin, a reminder, adviser]

monk (*say* munk) *noun*
a male member of a religious order living under vows, often apart from the secular world.
Word Family: **monkish,** *adjective,* of or like a monk; **monkhood,** *noun,* the condition or following of a monk.
[Greek *monakhos* solitary]

monkey (*say* **mung**-kee) *noun*
any of various primates, such as the marmoset, rhesus, etc., found in tropical regions. After the ape, it is the closest to man in evolutionary development.
Phrases:
make a monkey of, to make a fool of.
monkey business, trickery or underhand dealing.
monkey *verb*
to play or fool around.

monkey-nut *noun*
a peanut or groundnut.

monkey-puzzle *noun*
a type of large pine tree originally from Chile.
[so named because it would puzzle a monkey if it tried to climb this tree]

monkey-wrench *noun*
any of various adjustable spanners or wrenches.

mono *adjective*
(*informal*) monophonic.

mono-
a prefix meaning one or single, as in *monochrome.*
[Greek *monos* single, alone]

monochromatic
(*say* monno-kro-**matt**ik) *adjective*
of or relating to waves of one wavelength, such as light of one colour or sound of one frequency.

monochrome (*say* **monn**a-krome) *noun*
1. a) a painting or drawing in tones of one colour. b) the state of being in shades of one colour.
2. a black and white photograph.
[MONO- + Greek *khroma* colour]

monocle (*say* **monn**i-k'l) *noun*
a single lens held in front of the eye by the angle between the nose and the eyebrow.
[MONO- + Latin *oculus* eye]

monocline *noun*
Geology: a single fold in layers of rock.
monoclinal *adjective*
(of strata) dipping in the same direction.

monocotyledon
(*say* monno-kotta-**lee**don) *noun*
Biology: a plant having one seed leaf in the embryo, with the flower parts occurring in groups or multiples of three. Compare DICOTYLEDON.
[MONO- + COTYLEDON]

monoculture *noun*
the growing of only one crop on the land.

monogamy (*say* mon-**ogg**a-mee) *noun*
the custom of having one husband or wife at a time. Compare POLYGAMY.
Word Family: **monogamist**, *noun*; **monogamous**, *adjective.*
[MONO- + Greek *gamos* marriage]

monogram *noun*
a design consisting of several letters combined, such as a person's initials.
[MONO- + Greek *gramma* something written]

monograph *noun*
an account of one particular subject.
Word Family: **monographic**, *adjective.*

monolith *noun*
1. a) a single block of stone or rock of considerable size, such as Cleopatra's Needle. b) something, such as a monument, made from a single block of stone.
2. anything having a massive, uniform or unyielding character or quality: 'the *monolith* of civil service bureaucracy'.
monolithic (*say* monna-**lith**ik) *adjective*
a) of or like a monolith. b) massive and uniform: 'no individual freedom was allowed in the *monolithic* state'.
[MONO- + Greek *lithos* a stone]

monologue (*say* **monn**a-log) *noun*
a speech, especially a long speech, made by one person, e.g. in a play.
[MONO- + Greek *logos* a word]

monomania (*say* monna-**may**-nia) *noun*
an exaggerated obsession with a single thing or subject.
Word Family: **monomaniac,** *noun.*

monomer (*say* **monn**a-ma) *noun*
Chemistry: a chemical compound consisting of single molecules.
[MONO- + Greek *meros* a part]

mononucleosis
(*say* monno-new-klee-**o**-sis) *noun*
glandular fever.

monophonic (*say* monna-**fonn**ik) *adjective*
of or relating to sound reproduction through one sound source. Compare STEREOPHONIC and QUADRAPHONIC.
[MONO- + Greek *phoné* a sound]

monoplane *noun*
an aeroplane with one pair of wings.

monopoly (*say* mon-**opp**a-lee) *noun*
an exclusive control over or right to something.
monopolize, monopolise *verb*
to have or exercise a monopoly: 'she *monopolized* all his attention'.
Word Family: **monopolist**, *noun*, a person who supports or has a monoply; **monopolistic**, *adjective*; **monopolizer,** *noun*, a person who monopolizes; **monopolization**, *noun.*
[MONO- + Greek *polein* to sell]

monorail *noun*
a railway with carriages running on a single rail.

monosodium glutamate
(*say* monno-**so**-dee-um **gloo**ta-mate)

a white crystalline solid, soluble in water, used to intensify the flavour of foods.

monosyllable (*say* **monno**–silla–b'l) *noun*
a word of one syllable.
monosyllabic (*say* monno–sil–**abbik**) *adjective*
using or composed of a monosyllable or monosyllables: 'a *monosyllabic* reply'.

monotheism (*say* **monno**–thee–izm) *noun*
the belief that there is only one god or supreme being. Compare POLYTHEISM.
Word Family: **monotheist,** *noun*; **monotheistic** (*say* monno–thee–**istik**), *adjective.*
[MONO– + Greek *theos* a god]

monotone *noun*
1. a series of sounds in the same tone or pitch.
2. a lack of variety in sound, style, etc.

monotony (*say* mo**notta**–nee) *noun*
a wearisome sameness or a lack of variety: 'he was tired of the *monotony* of his job'.
monotonous *adjective*
lacking variety or interest: 'a flat, *monotonous* landscape'.
Word Family: **monotonously,** *adverb*; **monotonousness,** *noun.*
[MONO– + Greek *tonos* tone]

monotreme (*say* **monna**–treem) *noun*
the most primitive type of mammal, such as the platypus and echidna, found only in Australia and New Guinea. Like birds, they lay eggs and have a common opening at the posterior end for the genital, digestive and urinary tracts.
[MONO– + Greek *trema* hole]

monotropic (*say* monno–**troppik**) *adjective*
Chemistry: existing only in one stable physical form.
[MONO– + Greek *tropos* a manner]

Monotype *noun*
Printing: a typesetting machine which sets single letters.
[a trademark]

monovalent (*say* monno–**vay**–l'nt) *adjective*
see UNIVALENT.
[MONO- + Latin *valens* strong]

monoxide *noun*
Chemistry: an oxide containing one oxygen atom in each molecule.

Monseigneur (*say* mon–**seen**–yer) *noun*
a French title of honour for princes, bishops, etc.
[French *mon* my + *seigneur* lord]

monsieur (*say* m'**syoor**) *noun*
plural is **messieurs**
the French title for a man.

Monsignor (*say* mon–**seen**–yor) *noun*
Roman Catholic: an honorary title for certain officials.
[Italian]

monsoon *noun*
1. a wind of the Indian Ocean and southern Asia, usually blowing from the south–west in summer (the **wet monsoon**), and from the north–east in winter (the **dry monsoon**).
2. the season of the south–west monsoon which brings heavy rain.
[Arabic *mawsim* fixed season]

monster *noun*
1. an imaginary animal.
2. a person or thing of abnormal shape or size.
3. a cruel or wicked person.
Word Family: **monster,** *adjective,* huge.
[Latin *monstrum* a wonder]

monstrous (*say* **mon**strus) *adjective*
1. huge.
2. hideous or shocking: 'a *monstrous* crime'.
monstrosity (*say* mon–**strossi**–tee) *noun*
1. the state of being monstrous.
2. something which is monstrous or like a monster.
Word Family: **monstrously,** *adverb*; **monstrousness,** *noun.*

montage (*say* mon–**tah***zh*) *noun*
the arrangement of several pictures or designs together or on top of each other.
[French, a putting together]

month (*say* munth) *noun*
any of the twelve parts into which the calendar year is divided.
monthly *adjective, adverb*
1. of or occurring once a month. b) of or occurring every month.
2. lasting for a month: 'a *monthly* ticket'.
monthly *noun*
a magazine or publication produced once a month.

monument *noun*
1. a building or structure, such as a statue, built in memory of a person or event.
2. a person or thing that serves as an important example or reminder.
monumental (*say* mon–yoo–**men**–t'l) *adjective*
1. of or like a monument.
Usage: 'he is a *monumental* mason' (= specializing in monuments for the dead).
2. huge, colossal or imposing: 'it was a *monumental* achievement'.
Word Family: **monumentalize, monumentalise,** *verb,* to make a lasting monument of; **monumentally,** *adverb,* hugely.
[Latin *monere* to remind]

mooch *verb*
(*informal*) to loiter or slouch about.

mood (1) *noun*
a state of mind or feeling: 'he was in a good *mood*'.
moody *adjective*
a) changeable in mood. b) gloomy or sulky.
Word Family: **moodily,** *adverb*; **moodiness,** *noun.*

mood (2) *noun*
the change of form in a verb to express the manner in which the statement is made.
the **indicative mood** states a simple fact or asks a question. *Example*: The boy *rode* a bicycle.
the **imperative mood** expresses a command. *Example*: *buy* this book now.
the **subjunctive mood** expresses doubt or supposition. *Example*: if he *should come,* I would be very surprised.

moog synthesizer
short form is **moog**
an electronic musical instrument.

moon *noun*
1. *Astronomy:* a) the natural satellite of the earth. b) any natural satellite of another planet.
2. something with a crescent or rounded shape.
once in a blue moon, very seldom.
moon *verb*
(*informal*) to wander about or gaze dreamily.

moonbeam *noun*
a ray of moonlight.

moonlight *noun*
the light of the moon.
moonlight flit, a secret departure at night to avoid paying the rent.

moonlighter *noun*
1. a person who performs illegal acts at night, such as a poacher or housebreaker.
2. a person who works in a second job at night.
Word Family: **moonlight (moonlit, moonlighting),** *verb.*

moonshine *noun*
1. any nonsensical talk or ideas.
2. (*informal*) any illegally distilled or smuggled liquor.

moonshot *noun*
the launching of a rocket to the moon.

moonstone *noun*
Geology: a translucent, sometimes milky feldspar mineral, used as a gem.

moonstruck *adjective*
dazed or mad, supposedly due to the moon's influence.

moor (1) *noun*
an open, wild area of land covered with coarse grasses and other low vegetation.

moor (2) *verb*
to fix in position by ropes, weights, etc.: 'to *moor* a boat'.
moorage *noun*
a) the state of being moored. b) a place for mooring.

Moor (3) *noun*
a member of the part–Arab nations living in north–west Africa.
Word Family: **Moorish,** *adjective.*
[Greek *Mauros*]

moorhen *noun*
also called a **waterhen**
a small, stout, blackish bird related to the rail.

moose *noun*
plural is **moose**
see ELK.

moot *verb*
to raise a question, etc. for discussion or debate.
moot *noun*
short form of **moot court**
Law: a meeting of law students in order to gain practice by discussing imaginary cases.
Word Family: **moot,** *adjective,* doubtful or open to debate.
[Old English *gemot* a meeting]

mop *noun*
1. a loose bunch of cloth or yarn attached to a long handle and used for cleaning floors, etc.

2. an unruly mass, as of hair.
mop *verb*
(mopped, mopping)
to clean or wipe with or as if with a mop: 'he *mopped* the sweat from his brow'.
mop up, a) to finish off a job, etc.; b) to clear a captured area of any remaining enemy troops. *Word Family:* **mop-up,** *noun.*

mope *verb*
to be listless or dejected.

moped (*say* **mo**-ped) *noun*
a bicycle equipped with a motor.
[MO(tor) PED(als)]

moppet *noun*
an old word for a child or young girl.

moquette (*say* mok-**et**) *noun*
a thick, velvety fabric used for carpets and upholstery.
[French]

moraine (*say* ma-**rane**) *noun*
Geography: the fragments of rock material transported and deposited by a glacier, usually forming a ridge or mound.
[French]

moral (*say* **morr**'l) *noun*
1. (*plural*) principles concerning right and wrong.
2. a lesson taught by the example set in a story or fable.
moral *adjective*
1. relating to principles of right and wrong: 'abortion raises *moral* questions'.
2. based on, expressing or conforming to accepted principles of right and wrong: '*moral* behaviour'.
Usages:
a) 'a *moral* obligation' (= based on a sense of duty).
b) 'I need lots of *moral* support' (= psychological).
moral victory, a result which is not a victory but provides moral satisfaction.
Word Family: **morally,** *adverb*; **moralist,** *noun,* a person who teaches or encourages moral behaviour; **moralistic** (*say* morra-**listik**), *adjective.*
[Latin *mores* customs, morals]

morale (*say* ma-**rahl**) *noun*
the confidence, zeal, cheerfulness, etc. of a person or group of people: 'the troops lost the battle because of low *morale*'.
[from French]

morality (*say* mo-**ralli**-tee *or* morralli-tee) *noun*
1. good or virtuous conduct.
2. a system or code of morals.
3. moral character or quality.

moralize (*say* **morra**-lize) **moralise** *verb*
to speak or write on moral questions, especially in a self-righteous way.
Word Family: **moralizer,** *noun*; **moralizingly,** *adverb*; **moralization,** *noun.*

morass (*say* ma-**rass**) *noun*
a bog or area of soft, wet land.
Usage: 'a *morass* of difficulties' (= complex situation).

moratorium (*say* morra-**tawrium**) *noun*
plural is **moratoria** or **moratoriums**
a temporary halt or delay, such as a legal authorization to delay payment of a debt.
[Latin *morari* to delay]

moray eel
any of various brightly coloured or marked eels found in warm waters.

morbid *adjective*
1. gloomy or mentally unwholesome.
2. of or caused by disease.
Word Family: **morbidly,** *adverb*; **morbidness, morbidity** (*say* mor-**biddi**-tee), *nouns.*
[Latin *morbus* disease]

mordant *noun*
a substance, such as alum, used in dyeing to fix the dye to the surface of the fabric.
mordant *adjective*
1. biting or sarcastic.
2. (of acids) corrosive.
Word Family: **mordantly,** *adverb*; **mordancy,** *noun.*
[Latin *mordere* to bite]

more *adjective*
the comparative form of **much.**
more *adverb*
1. to a greater extent or degree.
2. again.
more or less, approximately.
Word Family: **more,** *noun.*

moreover *adverb*
besides.

mores (*say* **maw**-rayz) *plural noun*
the accepted moral customs of a group or society.
[Latin]

morganatic (*say* morga-**nattik**) *adjective*
relating to a marriage between a man of high rank and a woman of lower rank in which the wife and her

children do not share or inherit the rank or property of the husband.

morgue (*say* morg) *noun*
a place where dead bodies are kept for identification.

moribund *adjective*
close to death or extinction.
[from Latin]

morn *noun*
a poetic word for morning.

morning *noun*
1. the beginning or the early part of the day, before noon.
2. the early part of anything.

morning-glory *noun*
a climbing plant with trumpet-shaped, usually blue, flowers.

morning sickness
nausea, often experienced in the morning during the early months of pregnancy.

morning star
see VENUS.

morocco (*say* ma-**rokko**) *noun*
a fine leather made from goatskins.
[first made in *Morocco*, Africa]

moron (*say* **maw**-ron) *noun*
1. an adult whose mental development corresponds to that of a normal child between the ages of 8 and 12.
2. (*informal*) a stupid person.
Word Family: **moronic** (*say* maw-**ronnik**), *adjective.*
[Greek *moros* foolish]

morose *adjective*
gloomily bad-tempered or unsociable.
Word Family: **morosely**, *adverb*; **moroseness**, *noun.*
[Latin *morosus* peevish]

morphine (*say* **more**-feen) *noun*
also called **morphia**
a bitter substance which is the most important narcotic in opium, used to relieve pain and as a narcotic.
[after *Morpheus*, the ancient Greek god of dreams]

morphology (*say* mor-**folla**-jee) *noun*
the study of the shape, form and structure of anything, such as biological or geographical forms.
Word Family: **morphologist**, *noun*; **morphological** (*say* morfa-**loji**-k'l), *adjective.*
[Greek *morphé* shape + -LOGY]

morris dance
any of various traditional folk dances in fancy dress, sometimes featuring a hobbyhorse or Robin Hood characters, and associated with May Day.
[for *Moorish*, possibly as introduced from Castile by Queen Eleanor]

morrow *noun*
an old word meaning: a) morning; b) the next day.

morse code
a method of signalling, using a combination of short and long pulses (called dots and dashes) for each letter of the alphabet.
[after *Samuel Morse*, 1791-1872, American inventor of the telegraph system]

morsel *noun*
a small piece or amount.
[Latin *morsum* bite]

mortal (*say* **more**-t'l) *adjective*
1. subject to death: 'all men are *mortal*'.
2. causing death: 'the soldier received a *mortal* wound'.
Usage: 'he was my *mortal* enemy' (= extreme, deadly).
mortal *noun*
a human being.
Word Family: **mortally**, *adverb.*
[Latin *mortis* of death]

mortality (*say* more-**talli**-tee) *noun*
1. the condition of being mortal or having to die.
2. any death or loss of life.
3. human beings considered as a group.

mortality rate
see DEATH RATE.

mortar (1) (*say* **more**-ta) *noun*
1. a heavy bowl in which substances may be crushed.
2. a portable cannon with a short barrel, firing shells or bombs at a steep angle.

mortar (2) (*say* **more**-ta) *noun*
a mixture of cement or lime, sand and water which sets hard and is used for joining bricks, etc. Compare CONCRETE.

mortarboard *noun*
also called a **square**
a stiff, square, black cap, often part of formal university clothing.

mortgage (*say* **mor**-gij) *noun*
a) the conditional transferring of property as security for a loan. b) the deed by which such a transfer is made.
Word Family: **mortgage**, *verb*; **mortgagor**, *noun*, a person who mortgages property; **mortgagee**, *noun*,

a person to whom the property is transferred.
[French *mort* dead + *gage* pledge]

mortician (*say* mor–**tish**'n) *noun*
American: an undertaker.

mortify (*say* **mor**ti–fie) *verb*
(mortified, mortifying)
1. to hurt or humiliate the feelings of.
2. to discipline by self–denial, etc.
Word Family: **mortifyingly**, *adverb*; **mortification**, *noun*.

mortise (*say* **mor**tis) *noun*
also spelt **mortice**
a deep rectangular hole or slot in a surface, into which a matching tapered end (a **tenon**), is fitted to form a joint.
Word Family: **mortise**, *verb*, a) to join by, or as if by a mortise, b) to cut a mortise in.
[Arabic *murtazz* fixed in]

mortuary (*say* **mor**–tew–ree) *noun*
a place where bodies are kept before burial.
[Latin *mortuus* dead]

mosaic (*say* mo–**zay**–ik) *noun*
1. a decoration consisting of small pieces of coloured glass, stone, etc. applied to the surface to form a design.
2. any similar form or pattern.
Word Family: **mosaic**, *adjective*.
[Greek *mouseios* of the Muses]

Moslem (*say* **moz**lem) *noun*
also spelt **Muslim**
a follower of Islam.
Word Family: **Moslem**, *adjective*.

mosque (*say* mosk) *noun*
a Moslem house of worship.

mosquito (*say* mosskeeto) *noun*
plural is **mosquitoes**
any of a group of flies with scaly wings and able to transmit diseases such as malaria and yellow fever. The female has a long proboscis for sucking blood.
[Spanish, little fly]

mosquito net
a net for keeping out mosquitoes.

moss *noun*
any of a group of small, green plants with very small leaves and root–like filaments, growing in damp places.
Word Family: **mossy**, *adjective*, like, or overgrown with, moss.

most *adjective*
the superlative form of **much**.

most *noun*
the greatest number, amount, etc.
Phrases:
at the most, 'he can stay until midnight *at the most*' (= as a maximum).
make the most of, to use to the best advantage.

mostly *adverb*
1. almost completely.
2. generally.
Word Family: **most**, *adverb*.

mote *noun*
a particle of dust.

motel (*say* mo–**tel**) *noun*
a hotel which provides accommodation for motorists.

motet (*say* mo–**tet**) *noun*
contrapuntal sacred music, usually for unaccompanied voices.

moth *noun*
any of a group of usually nocturnal insects, similar to butterflies but with longer antennae and often with duller colouring.

mothball *noun*
a small ball made of naphthalene, used in cupboards, etc. to repel moths.

moth–eaten *adjective*
old and shabby, as though eaten by moths.

mother (*say* **mu***th***a**) *noun*
1. a female parent.
2. something which creates, produces or nurtures, like a mother: 'necessity is the *mother* of invention'.
3. the head of a female religious community.

mother *adjective*
being or like a mother: a) 'a *mother* hen'; b) '*mother* church'.
Usage: 'English is my *mother* tongue' (= native).
Word Family: **mother**, *verb*, a) to be the mother of, b) to care for as a mother; **motherly**, *adverb*; **motherliness**, *noun*; **motherhood**, *noun*, a) the state of being a mother, b) the qualities of a mother.

mothercraft *noun*
the knowledge or skill related to the bringing up of children.

mother–in–law *noun*
plural is **mothers–in–law**
the mother of one's husband or wife.

motherland *noun*
a person's native country.

mother–of–pearl *noun*
also called **nacre**

the shiny rainbow-coloured lining of certain shells, especially the pearl oyster, commonly used to make ornaments, ashtrays, etc.

Mother Superior
the head of a convent.

motif (*say* mo-**teef**) ***noun***
a repeated theme, subject or figure, e.g. in a design.
[French]

motion (*say* **mo**-sh'n) ***noun***
1. movement or the process of moving: a) 'the clouds were in constant *motion*'; b) 'watch my *motions* carefully'.
2. a formal proposal at a meeting, etc.
3. *Medicine:* any bowel action or faeces.
go through the motions, to do something in an insincere or incomplete manner.
motion *verb*
to direct or gesture: 'he *motioned* us to be quiet'.
Word Family: **motionless,** *adjective,* still.
[from Latin]

motion picture
a film, such as is shown in a cinema.

motive (*say* **mo**-tiv) ***noun***
something which causes a person to act in a particular way: 'a *motive* for murder'.
motive *adjective*
of or causing motion: 'feet are the *motive* organs of most animals'.
Word Family: **motivate,** *verb,* to provide with a motive or motives; **motivation,** *noun.*

mot juste (*say* mo **zhoost**)
a word which expresses the exact meaning of something.
[French, exact word]

motley *adjective*
1. made up of very different parts: 'a *motley* crowd'.
2. multicoloured.
Word Family: **motley,** *noun.*

motor *noun*
a) a device which receives and converts energy, especially electricity, in order to drive machinery. b) an internal combustion engine, especially as used in a motor vehicle.
motor *adjective*
1. operated by or used in a motor: 'a *motor* vehicle'.
2. causing motion: 'a *motor* nerve excites muscle movement'.
Word Family: **motor,** *verb,* to drive a motor car.
[Latin, a mover]

motorbike *noun*
(*informal*) a motorcycle.

motor boat
a boat propelled by means of an engine.

motorcade *noun*
a procession of motor vehicles.
[MOTOR + (caval)CADE]

motor car
short form is **car**
a vehicle, which is able to carry several people, powered by a motor and usually running on four wheels.
Word Family: **motorist,** *noun,* a person who drives a motor car.

motorcycle *noun*
a motor vehicle similar to a heavy bicycle.
Word Family: **motorcyclist,** *noun.*

motorize, motorise *verb*
1. to provide with a motor.
2. to supply with motor vehicles: 'the police squad has been fully *motorized*'.
Word Family: **motorization,** *noun.*

motor scooter
see SCOOTER.

motorway *noun*
a divided highway with several lanes, no crossroads and limited entry and exit points, designed to speed up the flow of traffic.

mottled *adjective*
marked or covered with spots or blotches of a different colour.
Word Family: **mottle,** *verb.*

motto *noun*
a word or sentence which expresses one's rule or rules of conduct, e.g. 'never say die'.
[Italian, word]

moue (*say* moo) *noun*
a pouting grimace.
[French]

mould (1) (*say* mold) *noun*
in America spelt **mold**
a) a hollow form into which a liquid is poured and left to harden into the required shape. b) something which is formed in this way: 'a *mould* of jelly'.
Usage: 'this boy is of the same *mould* as his father' (= character, nature).
mould *verb*
to model or form into the required shape: 'she *moulded* a head from clay'.
Usage: 'he *moulded* himself after his hero' (= modelled).

mould (2) (*say* mold) *noun*
in America spelt **mold**
a growth of minute fungi forming a furry layer.
mouldy *adjective*
1. covered with mould.
2. musty or stale.

mould (3) (*say* mold) *noun*
in America spelt **mold**
rich, loose earth for growing plants.

moulder (1) *verb*
to decay or rot.

moulder (2) *noun*
a person who moulds.

moulding *noun*
a line of ornamental plaster or woodwork around a wall, window, etc.

moult (*say* molt) *verb*
in America spelt **molt**
to shed feathers, skin, etc. which are replaced by new growth.

mound *noun*
1. a heap of earth, sand, stones, etc.
2. a natural elevation, such as a hillock or knoll.

mount (1) *verb*
1. to ascend or climb on to: 'he *mounted* his horse'.
2. to fix something into a position, setting, etc.: 'to *mount* photographs in an album'.
Usage: 'the musical production was *mounted* by the social club' (= staged, set up).
3. to increase in amount: 'costs were *mounting* rapidly'.
mount *noun*
1. a) the act or manner of mounting. b) a support, etc. on which something is mounted.
2. a horse, etc. for riding.

mount (2) *noun*
a mountain.

mountain *noun*
1. an area of very high land rising to a summit.
2. a large heap or pile.
mountainous *adjective*
1. (of an area) full of mountains.
2. huge or very high: 'a *mountainous* pile of rubbish'.
[Latin *montis* of a mountain]

mountain ash
any of a group of small trees with white flowers and scarlet berries (called rowanberries).

mountaineer *noun*
a mountain climber.
Word Family: **mountaineer,** *verb.*

mountain lion
a puma.

mountebank (*say* **mounti**-bank) *noun*
a quack or trickster.
[Italian *monta in banco* mount on a bench]

mourn (*say* morn) *verb*
to grieve or feel sorrow, especially for a dead person.
Word Family: **mourner,** *noun,* a person who mourns or attends a funeral; **mourning,** *noun,* a) sorrow, b) the outward signs of bereavement or grief.

mournful *adjective*
a) exhibiting, expressing or feeling deep sorrow. b) gloomy.
Word Family: **mournfully,** *adverb*; **mournfulness,** *noun.*

mouse *noun*
plural is **mice**
1. any of various small, very common rodents with a long, hairless tail.
2. (*informal*) a shy or timid person.
Word Family: **mouse,** *verb,* to hunt or catch mice; **mousy,** *adjective,* a) resembling a mouse in colour, etc., b) drab.
[Latin *mus*]

mousetrap *noun*
1. a spring trap to catch mice, often baited with cheese.
2. (*informal*) a cheese which one considers is only fit to be used in such a trap.

mousse (*say* moose) *noun*
a light, fluffy dessert made with cream, eggs, gelatine and flavouring, usually served chilled.
[French, froth]

moustache (*say* mustahsh) *noun*
the hair on the face which grows above the upper lip.
[Greek *mystakos* of the upper lip]

mouth *noun*
1. *Biology:* the opening through which food is taken in.
Usage: 'nine *mouths* to feed' (= people).
2. any opening or entrance: 'the *mouth* of a cave'.
3. something which has the shape, position or function of a mouth: 'the *mouth* of a river'.
Phrases:
down in the mouth, unhappy or depressed.
put words into someone's mouth, to allege that someone said what he did not say.

take the words out of one's mouth, see MOUTH.
mouth (*say* mou*th*) *verb*
1. to form words silently with the mouth.
2. to declaim or speak pompously.

mouth organ
see HARMONICA.

mouthpiece *noun*
the part of something, such as a musical instrument, which is placed near or in the mouth.
Usage: 'this newspaper is a *mouthpiece* for the government' (= spokesman).

mouth-to-mouth resuscitation
a method of artificial respiration in which one person breathes into the mouth of another.

mouth-watering *adjective*
appetizing.

movable (*say* **moova**-b'l) **moveable** *adjective*
1. able to be moved.
2. varying in date: 'Easter is a *movable* feast'.
movables *plural noun*
personal property that can be moved from the house, especially furniture.
Word Family: **movability** (*say* moova-**billi**-tee), *noun.*

move (*say* moov) *verb*
1. to change place or position: a) '*move* this chair into the next room'; b) 'the branches of the tree *moved* gently in the wind'.
Usages:
a) 'to get there by 7 we'll really have to *move*' (= go fast).
b) 'time *moves* slowly when there is nothing to do' (= advances).
c) 'look at the time! it's time we were *moving*' (= leaving).
d) 'they *move* in very arty circles' (= are active in).
2. to arouse, especially feelings of pity, compassion, etc.: 'we were *moved* by her sad story'.
Usage: 'what on earth *moved* you to do such a thing? (= prompted).
3. to make a formal proposal, suggestion, etc.
move *noun*
any movement: 'one *move* and I'll shoot you'.
Phrases:
get a move on, hurry up!
make a move, a) 'it's time we *made a move*' (= began to act); b) (*Games*) to have a turn by moving a piece, etc.
on the move, a) 'the troops are *on the move*' (= moving); b) 'we had to have lunch *on the move*' (= while moving).
Word Family: **movingly,** *adverb.*
[from Latin]

movement *noun*
1. the act, process or result of moving.
Usage: 'I've been following your *movements* closely' (= actions, activities).
2. the organization of a group of people for a special goal: 'the anti-smoking *movement* is very strong'.
3. *Music:* a main division of a symphony, etc.

movie *noun*
(*informal*) a film, especially one shown in a cinema.
[for *moving picture*]

moving staircase
an escalator.

mow (*say* mo) *verb*
(**mowed, mown** or **mowed, mowing**)
to cut down grass, etc. with a scythe or machine.
mow down, to destroy or kill in great numbers.
Word Family: **mower,** *noun,* a person or device that mows.

much *adjective*
(**more, most**)
great in amount, size, etc.: 'I had *much* trouble hiring the camels'.
much *noun*
a great amount or quantity: '*much* of the work was difficult'.
Phrases:
make much of, a) 'I didn't *make much of* the film' (= understand); b) 'you *make* too *much of* such a small thing' (= attach much importance to).
much of a muchness, very similar.
Word Family: **much,** *adverb,* a) greatly, b) approximately.

mucilage (*say* **mewsi**-lij) *noun*
an adhesive or gummy substance, such as glue.
Word Family: **mucilaginous** (*say* mew-see-**lajinus**), *adjective,* sticky.
[Latin *mucus* nasal mucus]

muck *noun*
1. manure or dirt.
2. (*informal*) rubbish.
make a muck of, (*informal*) to spoil.
muck *verb*
1. to fertilize with manure.
2. to make dirty.

Phrases:
muck about, muck around, (*informal*) to loaf or fool around.
muck out, to remove manure or dirt from stables, etc.
muck up, (*informal*) to spoil or ruin.
Word Family: **mucky**, *adjective*, messy or dirty.

muckrake *verb*
(*informal*) to uncover unsavoury facts with undue diligence and hypocritical motives.

mucous membrane (*say* **mewkus** membrane)
Anatomy: a lubricating membrane lining internal surfaces such as the nose and throat.

mucus (*say* **mewkus**) *noun*
a thick secretion of a mucous membrane.
Word Family: **mucous**, *adjective.*
[Latin]

mud *noun*
soft, wet earth.
Phrases:
as clear as mud, not clear at all.
one's name is mud, being in disgrace.
throw mud at, (*informal*) to abuse.

muddle *verb*
to confuse or mix up.
muddle through, to manage to cope, usually without organized planning.
muddle *noun*
a jumbled or confused state: 'my mind is in a *muddle*'.
Word Family: **muddler**, *noun.*

muddle-headed *adjective*
vague or confused.

muddy *adjective*
a) covered with mud. b) not clear or bright.
Word Family: **muddy**, **(muddied, muddying)**, *verb.*

mudguard *noun*
a metal shield preventing mud or water being thrown outwards from the wheels of a vehicle.

mud pack
a cosmetic pack for the face.

mudslinger *noun*
(*informal*) a person who abuses others.

mudstone *noun*
a sedimentary rock formed by the compression of layers of mud.

muesli (*say* **mewz**-lee *or* **mooz**-lee) *noun*
a breakfast food of whole-grain cereals, nuts and dried fruits.
[Swiss-German]

muezzin (*say* moo-**ezzin**) *noun*
a caller who summons Moslems to prayers.
[Arabic *m'adhdhin* to call]

muff *noun*
a cylindrical fur bag with open ends, used to keep the hands warm.
muff *verb*
(*informal*) to bungle or do something clumsily.

muffin *noun*
a flat, round, spongy yeast cake, eaten toasted and buttered.

muffle *verb*
1. to wrap or cover closely, as for warmth, etc.
2. to prevent or deaden sound by covering, wrapping, etc.: 'the robbers crept with *muffled* footsteps'.
Word Family: **muffle**, *noun.*

muffler *noun*
1. a thick scarf.
2. something which muffles, such as a device fitted to the exhaust pipe of an internal combustion engine to reduce noise.

mufti *noun*
any civilian clothes worn by someone who usually wears a uniform.

mug *noun*
1. a simple drinking vessel with a handle, used without a saucer.
2. (*informal*) a) a person who is easily fooled. b) the face.
mug *verb*
(mugged, mugging)
(*informal*) to attack violently, usually in order to rob: 'the old man was *mugged* in the dark alley'.
mug up, (*informal*) to study up.
Word Family: **mugger**, *noun*, a person who mugs.

muggy *adjective*
(of weather) humid and oppressive.

mulatto (*say* mew-**latto**) *noun*
a person who has one white and one Negro parent.

mulberry *noun*
1. a) a tree, the leaves of which are fed to silkworms. b) its purple or white berry similar to a blackberry.
2. a dark reddish-purple colour.
Word Family: **mulberry**, *adjective.*

mulch (*say* mulsh) *noun*
a mixture of peat, leaves, straw, etc. spread on gardens to protect plants, etc.
Word Family: **mulch**, *verb*, to spread or cover with a mulch.

mulct *verb*
to deprive a person of something, either as punishment or by trickery. [Latin *multare* to punish]

mule *noun*
1. the offspring of a male donkey and a female horse. Compare HINNY.
2. (*informal*) a stubborn person.
3. a machine that spins cotton.
mulish *adjective*
as obstinate as a mule.
Word Family: **muleteer**, *noun*, a driver of mules.
[from Latin]

mull (1) *verb*
to ponder or reflect: 'I'll *mull* over what you said'.

mull (2) *verb*
to heat, spice and sweeten for drinking: 'we *mulled* wine'.

mullet *noun*
any of a group of small, edible, oblong fish.

mulligatawny *noun*
a curry soup.
[Tamil, pepper-water]

mullion (*say* **mull**-y'n) *noun*
an upright strip, often of wood or stone, which divides windows or sections of panelling.

multi-
a prefix meaning many, as in *multilingual.*
[Latin *multus*]

multicellular (*say* multi-**sel**-yoola) *adjective*
composed of many cells.

multicoloured *adjective*
having many colours.

multifaceted (*say* multi-**fassi**-tid) *adjective*
1. having many aspects.
2. (of a precious stone) having many cut and polished sides.

multifarious (*say* multi-**fair**ius) *adjective*
having many different parts, forms, etc.

multiform *adjective*
having many shapes.

multigrade *adjective*
(of motor oil) retaining the same thickness over a wide range of temperatures.

multilateral *adjective*
1. having many sides.
2. (of an agreement or treaty) having three or more parties taking part.

multilingual (*say* multi-**ling**-w'l) *adjective*
able to speak three or more languages fluently.

multimillionaire *noun*
a person who has at least two million dollars, pounds, etc.

multipartite (*say* multi-**par**-tite) *adjective*
1. divided into many parts.
2. (of a treaty, etc.) multilateral.

multiple (*say* **multi**-p'l) *adjective*
having many parts, elements, etc.: 'he has a *multiple* fracture of the arm'.
multiple *noun*
Maths: any number formed by multiplying one number by any integer. *Example*: 4, 6 and 8 are multiples of 2.

multiple sclerosis (*say* **multi**-p'l sklerr**o**-sis)
a disease causing progressive deterioration of the nervous system.

multiplex *adjective*
multiple.
[Latin]

multiplicity (*say* multi-**plissi**-tee) *noun*
a large number or variety.

multiply *verb*
(**multiplied, multiplying**)
1. to increase in number, amount, etc.: 'his debts have *multiplied* during the past year'.
Usage: 'rabbits are a pest because they *multiply* so quickly' (= breed).
2. *Maths:* to repeat a number a given number of times in order to find the total. *Example*: 2 repeated 4 times (2×4 or $2+2+2+2$) equals 8.
Word Family: **multiplication**, *noun*; **multiplier**, *noun*, a) a person or thing that multiplies, b) (Maths) the number by which another is multiplied.

multistorey *adjective*
(of a building) having many storeys.

multitude (*say* **multi**-tewd) *noun*
a great number, such as a crowd of people.
Word Family: **multitudinous** (*say* multi-**tewdi**-nus), *adjective.*
[from Latin]

mum (1) *noun*
(*informal*) mother.

mum (2) *adjective*
silent: 'keep *mum* about what we did'.
mum *noun*
mum's the word, say nothing about it!

mumble *verb*
to mutter or speak indistinctly.
Word Family: **mumble,** *noun*; **mumblingly,** *adverb.*

mumbo jumbo
any meaningless speech or ritual.

mummer *noun*
an old word for an actor who wore a mask or disguise, especially in medieval times.
Word Family: **mummery,** *noun.*

mummify (*say* **mummi**–fie) *verb* (**mummified, mummifying**)
1. to make a dead body into a mummy by embalming.
2. to make or become shrivelled or dried up.
Word Family: **mummification,** *noun.*

mummy (1) *noun*
(*informal*) mother.

mummy (2) *noun*
a dead body preserved by embalming or other methods, especially in ancient Egypt.
[Arabic *mum* embalming wax]

mumps *plural noun*
(*used with singular verb*) an infectious viral disease, usually in children and causing swelling of the face due to inflammation of the salivary glands.

munch *verb*
to chew steadily or vigorously, and often noisily.

mundane *adjective*
of or relating to the world or earth.
Usage: 'she leads a very *mundane* life' (= ordinary, unexciting).
[Latin *mundus* world]

municipal (*say* mew–**nissi**–p'l) *adjective*
of or relating to the local government of a town or city: '*municipal* elections'.

municipality (*say* mew–nissi–**palli**–tee) *noun*
any district with its own local government, such as a town or city.
[Latin *municipium*]

munificent (*say* mew–**niffi**–s'nt) *adjective*
extremely generous.
Word Family: **munificently,** *adverb*; **munificence,** *noun.*
[Latin *munus* gift + *faciens* making]

munitions (*say* mew–**nish**'nz) *plural noun*
any military stores, such as ammunition and weapons.
Word Family: **munition,** *verb,* to provide with munitions.
[Latin *munitionis* of a fortification]

mural (*say* **mew**–r'l) *noun*
a painting on a wall or ceiling.
Word Family: **mural,** *adjective,* of or situated on a wall.
[Latin *murus* wall]

murder *noun*
the deliberate killing of a person. Compare MANSLAUGHTER.
be murder, 'it *was murder* trying to park my car near the football ground' (= extremely difficult or unpleasant).
murder *verb*
to kill deliberately.
Usage: 'the inexperienced orchestra *murdered* my favourite symphony' (= ruined, spoilt).
Word Family: **murderer,** *noun,* a person who has murdered someone; **murderess,** *noun,* a female murderer; **murderous,** *adjective,* a) capable of or intending to commit murder, b) deadly.

murex (*say* **mew**–reks) *noun*
plural is **murexes** or **murices** (*say* **mew**ri–seez)
any of a group of marine snails which yield a purple dye.

murky *adjective*
dark or gloomy.
Word Family: **murk,** *noun,* darkness; **murkiness,** *noun.*

murmur *verb*
1. to make a low, continuous sound: 'the leaves *murmured* in the breeze'.
2. to speak very softly: 'he *murmured* gently in her ear'.
murmur *noun*
1. the act or sound of murmuring: 'a *murmur* of disapproval'.
2. a murmuring of the heart revealed by the stethoscope and indicating an abnormality.
[Greek *mormyrein* to roar (of water)]

muscatel (*say* muska–**tel**) *noun*
short form is **muscat**
a) a musk-flavoured grape used as a fruit or to make wine. b) a sweet wine made from this grape.

muscle (*say* **muss**'l) *noun*
Anatomy: a tissue made up of bundles of small fibres that contract to produce body movement.
muscle *verb*
(*informal*) to force one's way by brute strength: 'he *muscled* his way through the crowd'.

[Latin *musculus* little mouse (from the shape of some muscles)]

muscle-bound *adjective*
having enlarged or overdeveloped muscles.

muscular (*say* **mus**-kewla) *adjective*
1. of or affected by a muscle or muscles.
2. strong.
Word Family: **muscularity** (*say* muskew-**larri**-tee), *noun.*

muse (1) (*say* mewz) *verb*
to meditate or think deeply.
Word Family: **musingly**, *adverb.*

Muse (2) (*say* mewz) *noun*
1. *Greek mythology:* any of the nine goddesses of the arts, e.g. of tragedy, song, etc.
2. (*not capital*) the creative power or inspiration of a poet.
[Greek *Mousa*]

museum (*say* mew-**zee**-um) *noun*
a building for storing and exhibiting objects of artistic, scientific or historical interest.
[Greek *Mouseion* the abode of the Muses]

museum piece
(*informal*) a person or thing considered to be out of date.

mush *noun*
1. any thick, soft mass.
2. (*informal*) something which is sickly sentimental.
Word Family: **mushy**, *adjective*; **mushiness**, *noun.*

mushroom *noun*
1. any of various umbrella-shaped fungi, especially any edible variety.
2. a pinkish-brown colour.
mushroom *verb*
1. to gather mushrooms.
2. to have or take on the shape of a mushroom.
Usage: 'new shops *mushroomed* all over the countryside' (= spread quickly).

music *noun*
1. a combination of sounds which express ideas or emotions by the use of rhythm, melody, etc.
Usage: 'the *music* of children's laughter' (= pleasing sound).
2. the printed score of a musical composition.
face the music, to accept the unpleasant consequences of one's actions.
[Greek *mousike (tekhnê)* (art) of the Muses]

musical *adjective*
of or producing music: 'a *musical* instrument'.
Usages:
a) 'a *musical* voice' (= full of harmony or melody).
b) 'she is very *musical*' (= fond of or skilled in music).
musical *noun*
any form of light entertainment in which music is important, as a musical comedy.
Word Family: **musically**, *adverb.*

musical box
a box with a mechanism which produces tunes.

music hall
a theatre for variety entertainment.

musician (*say* mew-**zish**'n) *noun*
a person skilled or trained in music, especially one who plays an instrument professionally.
Word Family: **musicianship**, *noun*, skilful musical performance.

musicology (*say* mewzi-**kolla**-jee) *noun*
the study of the theory and history of music.
Word Family: **musicologist**, *noun.*

musk *noun*
a) a stong-smelling, powdery substance used in perfume and obtained from an Asian deer. b) any similar smell or substance.
Word Family: **musky**, *adjective.*

musket *noun*
an early type of firearm fired from the shoulder.
musketeer (*say* muska-**teer**) *noun*
a soldier armed with a musket.
Word Family: **musketry** (*say* **muski**-tree), *noun*, instruction in the use of rifles, etc.

musk-melon *noun*
the common melon.
[the name is puzzling, as it has no taste or smell of musk]

musk ox
a large ox with a shaggy brownish-black coat, found in northern Canada and Greenland.

muskrat *noun*
also called a **musquash**
a rat-like, aquatic, North American mammal, having a musky smell and valued for its dark brown fur.

Muslim (*say* **muz**-lim) *noun*
see MOSLEM.

muslin (*say* **muz**lin) *noun*
a plain, usually fine, cotton fabric.
[first made in *Mosul*, Iraq]

musquash *noun*
a muskrat.

muss *verb*
(*informal*) to disarrange or rumple.

mussel *noun*
a black, aquatic mollusc with two hinged shells, the edible, marine form of which attaches itself to rocks, etc.

must (1) *verb*
an auxiliary verb indicating obligation or necessity: 'you *must* leave before midnight'.
must *noun*
something which is necessary: 'don't miss that film, it's a *must*!'.

must (2) *noun*
wine before it has fermented.
[Latin *mustus* new (wine)]

must (3) *noun*
mould or staleness.
Word Family: **musty**, *adjective*, stale.

mustang *noun*
a small wild horse of the western plains of North America, descended from Spanish stock.
[Spanish *mestengo* wild]

mustard (*say* **mus**ted) *noun*
the sharp, hot seeds of a herb-like plant, used in medicine and cooking.

mustard gas
an oily liquid causing burns, blindness and death, used in chemical warfare.

muster *verb*
to summon or assemble: a) 'to *muster* troops'; b) 'to *muster* all one's strength'.
muster *noun*
a gathering or assembly.
pass muster, to measure up to a required standard.
[Latin *monstrare* to show]

musty *adjective*
Word Family: see MUST (3).

mutable (*say* **mew**ta-b'l) *adjective*
liable to change.
Word Family: **mutability** (*say* mewta-**billi**-tee), *noun.*

mutation (*say* mew-**tay**-sh'n) *noun*
1. a change or alteration.
2. *Biology:* a sudden change in a gene, chromosome structure or chromosome number, which, if it occurs in a gamete, may result in an individual with different features that can be passed on to the next generation.
Word Family: **mutate** (*say* mew-**tate**), *verb*, to change; **mutant**, *adjective*, changing; **mutant**, *noun.*
[Latin *mutare* to change]

mute *noun*
1. a person who is unable to speak or make sounds.
2. something which is silent, such as a letter which is not pronounced in a word.
3. *Music:* any device used to soften the sound of an instrument.
mute *adjective*
not able to speak or make sounds.
Usage: 'a *mute* appeal in her eyes' (= silent, not spoken).
Word Family: **mutely**, *adverb*; **muteness**, *noun*; **mute**, *verb*, to soften or reduce the sound of.
[from Latin]

mutilate (*say* **mew**ti-late) *verb*
to injure, disfigure or maim severely.
Word Family: **mutilator**, *noun*, something which mutilates; **mutilation**, *noun.*
[from Latin]

mutiny (*say* **mew**ta-nee) *noun*
an open rebellion against authority, especially by soldiers or sailors against their officers.
mutiny *verb*
(mutinied, mutinying)
a) to refuse to obey a command. b) to take part in a mutiny.
Word Family: **mutinous**, *adjective*, rebellious; **mutineer**, *noun.*

mutt *noun*
(*informal*) a) a dog. b) a fool.
[for *mutton-head*]

mutter *verb*
to speak indistinctly or in a low voice.
Word Family: **mutter**, *noun.*

mutton *noun*
the meat of a fully grown sheep.

mutton-chops *plural noun*
a wide, bushy form of sideboards, usually growing over the cheek.

mutual (*say* **mew**-tew-ul) *adjective*
shared or exchanged between two or more people or parties: a) 'she and I have a *mutual* respect'; b) 'the two countries are *mutual* enemies'.
Word Family: **mutually**, *adverb*; **mutuality**, *noun.*
[Latin *mutuus* interchangeable]

muzak (*say* **mew**-zak) *noun*
continuous taped music played in some restaurants, shops, banks, etc.
[a trademark]

muzzle *noun*
1. the open end of a gun from which the bullet is discharged.
2. a) the snout of an animal. b) an arrangement of straps, etc. put on an animal's mouth to prevent it from biting or eating.
muzzle *verb*
to put a muzzle on an animal.

muzzy *adjective*
dazed or confused.
Word Family: **muzzily** *adverb*; **muzziness,** *noun.*

my *possessive adjective*
plural is **our**
belonging to me: 'it is *my* book'.
my *interjection*
(*informal*) an exclamation of surprise.

mycobacteria (*say* my-ko-**bakteeria**) *plural noun*
a group of bacteria causing chronic diseases, such as tuberculosis and leprosy.
[Greek *mykes* mushroom + BACTERIA]

mycology (*say* my-**kolla**-jee) *noun*
the study of fungi, a branch of botany.
Word Family: **mycologist,** *noun.*

mynah (*say* **my**-na) *noun*
also spelt **myna** or **minah**
a bird from Asia which mimics other birds, and is related to the starling.
[Hindi]

myopia (*say* my-**o**-pee-a) *noun*
short-sightedness.
Word Family: **myopic** (*say* my-**oppik**), *adjective.*
[Greek *myein* to shut + *ops* eye]

myriad (*say* **mirri**-ad) *noun*
a very great number.
Word Family: **myriad,** *adjective,* consisting of vast numbers.
[Greek *myrioi* ten thousand]

myrrh (*rhymes with* fur) *noun*
a fragrant resin obtained from a shrub and used for incense and perfume.
[from Greek]

myrtle (*say* **mer**-t'l) *noun*
any of a group of evergreen shrubs with black berries and fragrant, white flowers.

myself *pronoun*
1. the reflexive form of **I**: 'I washed *myself*'.
2. the emphatic form of **I**: 'I did it *myself*'.
3. my normal or usual self: 'I am not *myself* today'.

mysterious (*say* mis-**teeri**-us) *adjective*
puzzling, obscure or full of mystery: 'a *mysterious* murder'.
Word Family: **mysteriously,** *adverb.*

mystery (*say* **mista**-ree) *noun*
1. something that is puzzling, unknown or unexplained: 'his disappearance is a *mystery*'.
Usage: 'its origins are wrapped in *mystery*' (= obscurity).
2. (*plural*) ancient religions to which chosen followers were admitted by secret rites.
[Greek *mysterion* a secret doctrine]

mysticism (*say* **misti**-sizm) *noun*
a belief in or practice of direct spiritual contact with divine things through contemplation or psychic experience.
mystic (*say* **mistik**) *noun*
a person who practises mysticism.
mystic, mystical *adjective*
1. of hidden or mysteriously symbolic meaning: 'ancient *mystic* ceremonies'.
2. of or relating to mysticism or mystics.
[Greek *mystes* an initiate]

mystify (*say* **misti**-fie) *verb*
(**mystified, mystifying**)
to puzzle or bewilder: 'she was *mystified* by his strange behaviour'.
Word Family: **mystification,** *noun.*

mystique (*say* mis**teek**) *noun*
1. a mysterious or fascinating quality or power.
2. the secrets of an art or craft, known only to its practitioners.
[French]

myth (*say* mith) *noun*
1. a traditional tale, usually about supernatural beings or events, sometimes used as an explanation of natural events.
2. a) a fictitious person or thing. b) a baseless popular belief.
Word Family: **mythical,** *adjective,* a) of or relating to myths, b) imaginary or fictitious.
[Greek *mythos* a story].

mythology (*say* mith-**olla**-jee) *noun*
any or all myths.
Word Family: **mythological,** *adjective,* a) of myths or mythology, b) unreal; **mythologist,** *noun.*

myxomatosis (*say* miksa-ma-**toe**-sis) *noun*
an infectious, viral disease in rabbits, artificially introduced to control their numbers.
[Greek *myxa* mucus + *-oma* a tumour + -OSIS]

Nn

nab *verb*
(**nabbed, nabbing**)
(*informal*) to catch or arrest.

nabob (*say* **nay**–bob) *noun*
any wealthy person, originally any Englishman who became rich in India.
[Arabic *na'ib* deputy]

nacre (*say* **nay**ka) *noun*
mother–of–pearl.
Word Family: **nacreous** (*say* **nay**–kree–us), *adjective*, a) of or relating to nacre, b) (of minerals) having a lustre like nacre.

nadir (*say* **nay**–deer) *noun*
Astronomy: the lowest point on the celestial sphere, opposite the zenith.
Usage: 'the *nadir* of the king's fortunes came when he was deposed and humiliated' (= the lowest point).
[Arabic]

nag (1) *verb*
(**nagged, nagging**)
1. to irritate by constant fault–finding, complaints or requests.
2. to cause discomfort or pain: 'financial worries *nagged* at her all day'.
Word Family: **naggingly**, *adverb*; **nagger**, *noun.*

nag (2) *noun*
(*informal*) a horse, especially an old or worthless one.

nail *noun*
1. a metal pin with a flat head, usually used to join two or more objects together.
2. *Anatomy:* a tough horny growth strengthening the upper tip of the fingers and toes.
Phrases:
hit the nail on the head, to say or do the right thing.
on the nail, (*informal*) 'the salesman refused to take a cheque and demanded cash *on the nail*' (= on the spot).
nail *verb*
to fasten something with nails.
Usages:
a) 'terror *nailed* him to the spot' (= fixed firmly).
b) 'the inspector was determined to *nail* the cat–burglar' (= catch, arrest).

nail punch
a short steel rod held against the head of a nail to hammer it level with or below a surface.

naïve (*say* nie–**eev**) **naive** *adjective*
unaffectedly or unsophisticatedly simple and artless.
Word Family: **naïvely**, *adverb*; **naïvety** (*say* nie–**eeva**–tee), **naïveté** (*say* nie–**eeva**–tay), *noun*, the quality of being naïve.
[French]

naked (*say* **nay**–kid) *adjective*
having no clothing or covering: a) '*naked* hills stripped of vegetation'; b) 'the *naked* wound gaped open'.
Usages:
a) 'snowfields lay before us as far as the *naked* eye could see' (= unassisted by optical instruments).
b) 'few people want to hear the *naked* truth about themselves' (= plain, blunt).
Word Family: **nakedly**, *adverb*; **nakedness**, *noun.*

namby–pamby *adjective*
sentimental or insipid: 'a *namby–pamby* mother's boy'.

name *noun*
the word by which a person or thing is known.
Usages:
a) 'she called him all the *names* she could think of' (= insulting terms).
b) 'he has a good *name* in business circles' (= reputation).
c) 'his show was full of big *names*' (= famous people).
Phrases:
in the name of, 'open *in the name of* the law' (= by the authority of).
to one's name, 'not a penny *to my name*' (= belonging to me).
name *verb*
to give a name to: 'I *name* this child John'.

Usages:
a) 'can you *name* all the states in America' (= state the correct name of).
b) 'shall we *name* the day of our wedding?' (= state, specify).

name-dropper *noun*
a person who talks about well-known people as if they were personal friends, in order to impress others.

nameless *adjective*
1. not having a name: 'a *nameless* grave'.
2. not named or specified: 'a certain person, who shall remain *nameless*'.
Word Family: **namelessly**, *adverb*; **namelessness**, *noun.*

namely *adverb*
that is to say: 'Australia's two largest cities, *namely*, Sydney and Melbourne'.

namesake *noun*
a person having the same name as another.

nanny *noun*
a nurse for children.

nanny-goat *noun*
a female goat. Compare BILLY-GOAT.

nano-
a prefix used for SI units, meaning one thousand millionth (10^{-9}). See UNITS in grey pages.
[Latin *nanus* a dwarf]

nap (1) *verb*
(napped, napping)
a) to have a short sleep. b) to be off one's guard: 'that remark caught me *napping*'.
Word Family: **nap**, *noun*, a short sleep.

nap (2) *noun*
a surface on a fabric, made by raising all the short fibres in it and then cutting and smoothing them.
Word Family: **nap (napped, napping)**, *verb*, to raise a nap on.

nap (3) *noun*
short form of **napoleon**
1. *Cards:* a) a game in which players call the number of tricks they hope to make. b) a call of the maximum, five tricks.
2. (*informal*) a tipster's best bet of the day.
to go nap a) (*Cards*) to call five tricks; b) to stake everything one has.

napalm (*say* **nay**-pahm) *noun*
a jelly-like incendiary substance mixed with petrol, used in bombs, flame-throwers, etc.

nape *noun*
Anatomy: the back of the neck.

napery (*say* **naypa**-ree) *noun*
any household linen, especially table linen.

naphtha (*say* **naf**-tha) *noun*
a mixture of liquid hydrocarbons obtained from coal tar, wood, petroleum, etc.

naphthalene (*say* naftha-**leen**) *noun*
a white, crystalline, solid hydrocarbon obtained from coal tar, having a penetrating odour, and used in making organic dyes and mothballs.

Napierian logarithm
see NATURAL LOGARITHM.

napkin *noun*
1. a serviette. Short form of **table napkin**.
2. a nappy.

nappy *noun*
short form of **napkin**
a piece of towel or an absorbent paper pad, worn by a baby underneath or instead of pants.

narcissism (*say* nar-**sis**-izm) *noun*
an extreme self-love.
Word Family: **narcissist**, *noun*; **narcissistic** (*say* narsi-**sis**tik), *adjective.*
[from *Narcissus*, a beautiful youth in Greek mythology who fell in love with his own reflection]

narcissus (*say* nar-**sis**sus) *noun*
plural is **narcissi** or **narcissuses**
any of a group of flowers including jonquils and daffodils.

narcosis (*say* nar-**ko**-sis) *noun*
the state of being sleepy or drowsy due to some external cause, such as gases, drugs, etc.
[Greek *narkosis* a benumbing]

narcotic (*say* nar-**kot**tik) *noun*
a substance which is often habit-forming and dulls the senses, relieves pain or induces sleep. In large amounts it produces complete insensibility.
Word Family: **narcotic**, *adjective*, producing narcosis.

nark *noun*
(*informal*) a person who spies, especially for the police.
nark *verb*
(*informal*) to nag or irritate.
Word Family: **narky**, *adjective*, irritated.
[Romany *nak* a nose]

narrate (*say* na–**rate**) *verb*
to tell the story of an event, experience, etc.
narrative (*say* **narra**–tiv) *noun*
1. a recounting of events, experiences, etc.
2. the subject matter of a narrative.
Word Family: **narrator,** *noun*; **narration,** *noun,* a) a narrative, b) the act or process of narrating.
[Latin *narrare* to make known]

narrow *adjective*
not broad or wide: 'a *narrow* corridor'.
Usages:
a) 'he's really a very *narrow* person' (= limited in views or sympathies).
b) 'a *narrow* escape' (= close).
narrow *verb*
to make or become narrower: 'the path *narrows* near the hedge'.
Usage: 'they *narrowed* down the list of suspects to two or three' (= limited or restricted).
Word Family: **narrowly,** *adverb*; **narrowness,** *noun.*

narrow–minded *adjective*
prejudiced or intolerant.
Word Family: **narrow–mindedly,** *adverb*; **narrow–mindedness,** *noun.*

narwhal (*say* **narwul**) *noun*
an aquatic mammal found in the arctic, the male having a long tusk extending from the upper jaw.

nasal (*say* **nay**–z'l) *adjective*
1. of or relating to the nose.
2. *Language:* of or relating to the making of sounds through the nose, in letters such as **m, n** or **ng.**
Word Family: **nasally,** *adverb*; **nasal,** *noun,* a nasal speech sound.
[Latin *nasus* nose]

nascent (*say* **nassent**) *adjective*
beginning to exist, grow or develop: 'a *nascent* idea'.
[Latin *nascens* being born]

nasturtium (*say* na–**ster**–sh'm) *noun*
any of a group of garden plants with showy, yellow, red or orange flowers and large, edible leaves.
[Latin *nasturcium* cress]

nasty (*say* **nah**–stee) *adjective*
disagreeable or unpleasant: a) 'there is a *nasty* odour in the bathroom'; b) 'he really is a *nasty* little boy'.
Usage: 'he came home from school with a *nasty* cut on his leg' (= rather severe).
Word Family: **nastily,** *adverb*; **nastiness,** *noun.*

natal (*say* **nay**–t'l) *adjective*
of or relating to a person's birth.
[Latin *natus* born]

nation (*say* **nay**–sh'n) *noun*
a large group of people united by some or all factors such as history, government, race, language or geography.
Word Family: **national** (*say* **nasha**–n'l), *adjective*; **national,** *noun,* a citizen of a particular nation; **nationally,** *adverb*; **nationhood,** *noun.*
[Latin *natio* birth, a race]

national anthem
see ANTHEM.

national debt
the total debt of a government, consisting of government stocks, National Savings and all other loans.

nationalism (*say* **nash**–na–lizm) *noun*
1. a sense of national unity.
2. a political movement to assert the right of one's country to full independence. Compare INTERNATIONALISM.
Word Family: **nationalist,** *noun*; **nationalistic,** *adjective.*

nationality (*say* nasha–**nalla**–tee) *noun*
1. the fact of belonging to or being born in a particular country.
2. the status of belonging to a nation by birth or naturalization.
3. a nation or people: 'the various *nationalities* of Africa'.

nationalize (*say* **nashna**–lize)
nationalise *verb*
to make privately owned land, industries, etc. the property of the nation.
Word Family: **nationalization,** *noun.*

nationally *adverb*
Word Family: see NATION.

national park
an area of land set aside by the government to preserve the natural features, wildlife, etc. of the area for public enjoyment.

national service
any compulsory military training or service for young people of a certain age.

native (*say* **nay**–tiv) *adjective*
1. relating to the place where one was born: a) 'this is my *native* country'; b) 'he is a *native* Australian'.
2. a) belonging to a race regarded as the original inhabitants of a country, especially if a non-white race: 'the *native* tribes of Africa'. b) relating

to the members of such races: '*native* customs'.
Usages:
a) 'the plants *native* to these parts' (= occurring naturally).
b) 'English is my *native* tongue' (= belonging by birth).
c) 'her *native* intelligence has never really been tapped' (= natural, inborn).
native *noun*
1. one of the original inhabitants of a country, especially if non-white: 'the *natives* are fighting for independence'.
2. a person who is born in a particular place: 'I am a *native* of Ireland'.
Usage: 'this plant is a *native*' (= one occurring naturally in this region or country).
[Latin *nativus* born, natural, inborn]

nativity (*say* na-tivvi-tee) *noun*
1. *Christian.* (*capital*) a) the birth of Christ. b) the festival commemorating this.
2. an old word for birth.

natter *verb*
(*informal*) to chatter or gossip.
Word Family: **natter,** *noun,* a chat.

natty *adjective*
neat or trim.
Word Family: **nattily,** *adverb.*

natural (*say* **natcha-r'l**) *adjective*
1. existing in or produced by nature: a) 'a *natural* ability'; b) 'he died of *natural* causes'.
2. concerned with nature: '*natural* history'.
3. in accordance with circumstances, etc.: 'an accident was the *natural* result of such carelessness'.
4. based on instinct: 'anger is a *natural* response to provocation'.
5. illegitimate: 'a *natural* son'.
Usage: 'it was a *natural* piece of acting' (= lifelike, unaffected).
6. *Music* a) (of a note) neither sharp nor flat. b) (of a horn, etc.) not having valves or keys and so producing the notes dictated by the length of the tube.
natural *noun*
1. a person or thing that is naturally suited or qualified: 'she's a *natural* for the part'.
2. an idiot.
3. *Music:* a) a note that is not affected by either a sharp or a flat. b) a symbol placed before a note cancelling the effect of a previous sharp or flat. c) (on a keyboard instrument) a white key.
naturally *adverb*
1. in a natural manner: 'even though you will be nervous, try and act *naturally*'.
2. of course: '*naturally,* I would have nothing to do with such an offer'.
3. by nature: 'he is *naturally* obedient and courteous'.
Word Family: **naturalness,** *noun.*
[from Latin.]

natural gas
a mixture of hydrocarbon gases, usually containing methane, found under the earth or seabed near oil deposits and used as fuel and in making organic compounds.

natural history
the study of animal or plant life.

naturalism (*say* **natchera-lizm**) *noun*
1. *Art, Literature:* a form of realism.
2. *Philosophy:* the belief that all things occur naturally and are unrelated to external or divine forces.

naturalist *noun*
a person who studies natural history, especially in the field, e.g. a zoologist or a botanist.

naturalistic *adjective*
1. of or in accordance with nature.
2. of or relating to natural history or naturalists.

naturalized, naturalised *adjective*
having become, by law, a citizen of another country, with all the rights of a person of that nationality.
Word Family: **naturalization,** *noun*; **naturalize,** *verb.*

natural law
Philosophy: any rules or ways of behaving which man knows instinctively to be right and fair.

natural logarithm
also called a **Napierian logarithm**
Maths: a system of logarithms using the base *e* (2·71828.....).

naturally *adverb*
see NATURAL.

natural number
Maths: any positive integer.

natural philosophy
an old term for the physical sciences, especially physics.

natural science
the study of natural or physical objects, e.g. chemistry, as distinct from abstract things such as thought.

natural selection
also called **survival of the fittest**

Biology: Darwin's theory that only those plants and animals which are best adapted to their environment survive to breed, and so, through inheritance, their characteristics become established in future generations. This process is the main agent of evolutionary change. Compare DARWINISM.

nature (*say* **naycher**) *noun*
1. the essential character of something: a) 'the *nature* of a chemical compound'; b) 'he has a forgiving *nature*'.
2. a) (*often capital*) the material world and all things contained in it except those made by man. b) all the forces at work throughout the material world: 'scientists may study the laws of *nature*'.
Usage: 'I didn't intend anything of that *nature* by my remarks' (= sort).
in the nature of, 'a bonus is something *in the nature of* a reward' (= like).
[Latin *natura* blood relationship, quality, disposition, the world]

naught (*say* nawt) *noun*
an old word meaning nothing. Compare NOUGHT.
set at naught, to consider as being of no importance.

naughty (*say* **naw**-tee) *adjective*
1. disobedient or full of mischief: 'they were *naughty* children'.
2. improper: 'a *naughty* word'.
Word Family: **naughtiness,** *noun*; **naughtily,** *adverb.*

nausea (*say* **nawsia**) *noun*
1. a feeling of sickness in the stomach, often followed by vomiting.
2. a feeling of extreme disgust or loathing.
Word Family: **nauseate,** *verb,* to cause nausea in; **nauseous** (*say* **nawsi**-us), *adjective,* causing or feeling nausea.
[Greek *nausia* sea-sickness]

nautical (*say* **nawti**-k'l) *adjective*
of or relating to sailors, ships or navigation.
Word Family: **nautically,** *adverb.*
[Greek *nautes* sailor]

nautical mile
see MILE.

nautilus (*say* **nawti**-lus) *noun*
plural is **nautili** (*say* **nawti**-lie) or **nautiluses**
any of a group of aquatic molluscs related to the cuttlefish, having a spiral, chambered shell with pearly walls.
[Greek *nautilos* sailor]

naval (*say* **nay**-v'l) *adjective*
a) of or relating to a navy: '*naval* affairs'. b) having a navy: 'the great *naval* powers'.
[Latin *navalis* relating to a ship]

nave (1) *noun*
the main body of a church between the aisles, stretching from the entrance to the chancel.

nave (2) *noun*
the hub or central part of a wheel.

navel *noun*
also called the **umbilicus**
Anatomy: the small pit in the centre of the abdomen left by the breaking of the umbilical cord at birth.

navigate (*say* **navvi**-gate) *verb*
1. to guide the direction and speed of a ship, aeroplane, etc.
2. to sail through or over: 'the canal cannot be *navigated* by large ships'.
Word Family: **navigation,** *noun,* the act or art of navigating; **navigational,** *adjective*; **navigable** (*say* **navviga**-b'l), *adjective,* (of waters, vessels, etc.) capable of being navigated; **navigability** (*say* navviga-**billi**-tee), *noun.*
[Latin *navis* ship + *agere* to drive]

navigator *noun*
1. a person who practises, or is skilled in, navigation.
2. a sea explorer.

navvy *noun*
a labourer who makes roads, railways, etc.

navy (*say* **nay**-vee) *noun*
the part of the armed forces of a country that are organized for fighting at sea.
[Latin *navis* a ship]

navy blue
short form is **navy**
a dark, blackish-blue colour.

nawab (*say* na-**wob**) *noun*
a deputy governor in India.
[Arabic *na'ib* deputy]

nay *adverb*
an old word for no.

Nazi (*say* **naht**-see) *noun*
a member of the National Socialist Party in Germany which, led by Adolf Hitler, gained political control of the country in 1933.
Word Family: **Nazism** (*say* **naht**-sizm), *noun.*
[German NA(tionalso)ZI(alist)]

Neanderthal man (*say* nee-**anda**-tahl man)

an extinct species of man.
[the remains were first found at *Neanderthal*, a valley in Germany]

neap tide
short form is **neap**
the tide occurring shortly after the first and third quarters of the moon, when the rise and fall are minimal.

near *adverb, preposition, adjective*
at, within or to a short distance: a) 'they live quite *near*'; b) 'stand *near* me'; c) 'a *near* escape from death'.
Usages:
a) 'he is a very *near* and dear friend' (= intimate).
b) 'it's odd discovering a *near* relative you never knew you had' (= closely related).
near *verb*
to come within a short distance: 'he leapt ashore as the boat *neared* the jetty'.
nearly *adverb*
1. all but: 'he *nearly* perished from hunger'.
2. not distantly, as in space, time, condition, etc.: 'his story approximated very *nearly* to the facts'.
not nearly, 'that's *not nearly* enough money to live on for a week' (= far from).
Word Family: **nearness,** *noun.*

nearby *adjective, adverb*
not far away.

Near East
1. an old term for the Turkish Empire, that is Turkey, the Balkans, Egypt, Palestine, etc.
2. the Middle East.

nearside *adjective*
a) of or relating to the left-hand side of a vehicle where traffic drives on the left. b) the left side of a horse. Compare OFFSIDE.
[originally the side from which one mounts a horse]

near-sighted *adjective*
short-sighted.
Word Family: **near-sightedly,** *adverb*; **near-sightedness,** *noun.*

neat (1) *adjective*
1. tidy or orderly: 'a *neat* desk'.
2. (*informal*) clever: 'a *neat* trick'.
3. undiluted or unadulterated: 'he drinks *neat* gin'.
Word Family: **neatly,** *adverb*; **neatness,** *noun*; **neaten,** *verb,* to make neat.
[Latin *nitidus* shining]

neat (2) *noun*
an old word for cattle.
neat's-foot oil
a pale yellow oil made from the bones of cattle and used as a dressing for leather.

neath *preposition*
an old word for beneath.

neb *noun*
a) the beak of a bird. b) the nose of an animal.

nebula (*say* **neb**-yoo-la) *noun*
plural is **nebulae** (*say* **neb**-yoo-lee)
Astronomy: a cloudy, luminous or dark patch consisting of gas and dust in the night sky.
Word Family: **nebular,** *adjective.*
[Latin]

nebulous (*say* **neb**-yoo-lus) *adjective*
1. vague or unclear.
2. *Astronomy:* cloudy.
Word Family: **nebulously,** *adverb*; **nebulousness,** *noun.*

necessary (*say* **nessis**-ree *or* **nessa**-serri) *adjective*
indispensable or unavoidable: 'food is *necessary* for life'.
necessary *noun*
(*usually plural*) a necessary thing: 'food and clothing are *necessaries* of existence'.
Word Family: **necessarily,** *adverb.*

necessitate (*say* nis-**essa**-tate) *verb*
to make something necessary: 'his sudden collapse *necessitated* calling an ambulance'.
Word Family: **necessitation,** *noun.*

necessitous (*say* nis-**essi**-tus) *adjective*
poor or needing assistance: 'the family was in *necessitous* circumstances'.

necessity (*say* nis-**essi**-tee) *noun*
1. something that is necessary: 'food is a *necessity* for life'.
2. the fact of being necessary: 'we all agree on the *necessity* of eating well-balanced meals'.
3. any circumstances that compel a person to do something: '*necessity* forced him to steal'.
[Latin *necesse* needful]

neck *noun*
1. *Anatomy:* the part of the body that connects the head to the shoulders.
2. the part of a garment covering or extending around the neck.
3. something which has the shape, position or function of a neck: a) 'the

neck of a bottle'; b) 'the *neck* of a violin'.
Phrases:
neck and neck, running even in a race, competition, struggle, etc.
neck of the woods, (*informal*) a particular area or region.
stick one's neck out, to act, express an opinion, etc. in such a way as to expose oneself to danger, criticism or hostility.
neck *verb*
(*informal*) to hug and kiss amorously.

necklace *noun*
an ornament for the neck, often a string of beads, pearls or gems.

necromancy (*say* **nek**ro-man-see) *noun*
1. in ancient times a method of divination by summoning up the dead to ask them about the future.
2. (by confusion of *necro-* with *negro-*) black magic.
Word Family: **necromancer**, *noun*; **necromantic** (*say* nekro-**man**tik), *adjective*.
[Greek *nekros* a corpse + *manteia* divination]

necropolis (*say* nek**kropp**a-lis) *noun*
plural is **necropolises**
an ancient cemetery.
[Greek *nekros* corpse + *polis* city]

necrosis (*say* nek**kro**-sis) *noun*
Biology: the death of a tissue.
Word Family: **necrotic** (*say* nek**krott**ik), *adjective*.
[Greek *nekrosis* a killing]

nectar *noun*
1. *Biology:* the sugary substance that attracts insects and is produced by many flowers.
2. *Ancient mythology:* the drink of the gods.
[Greek]

nectarine (*say* **nek**ta-rin *or* nekta-**reen**) *noun*
a small fruit with a smooth green and red skin, resembling a peach but with a firmer texture.
[from NECTAR]

née (*say* nay) *adjective*
born, used to indicate a married woman's maiden name: 'Mrs Browning, *née* Barrett'.
[French]

need *noun*
1. a want or necessity: a) 'he acted promptly to meet the *needs* of the situation'; b) 'there's no *need* to worry'.
2. a situation or time of difficulty: 'we would all try and help a friend in *need*'.
need *verb*
1. to have or be in need of: a) 'we all *need* love'; b) 'does he *need* any help?'.
2. to be obliged: 'you *need* not go home yet'.
Word Family: **needy**, *adjective*, very poor; **neediness**, *noun*, a state of need or poverty; **needless**, *adjective*, unnecessary; **needlessly**, *adverb*.

needle *noun*
1. a small, slender steel object used for sewing, pointed at one end and with a hole at the other for carrying thread.
2. *Medicine:* a hypodermic needle.
3. something which has the shape of a needle: 'a pine *needle*'.
4. *Audio:* see STYLUS.
needle in a haystack, 'it was like looking for a *needle in a haystack*' (= something unlikely to be found).
Word Family: **needle**, *verb*, a) to tease or annoy, b) to goad.

needle point
an embroidery stitch in which small stitches cover the whole canvas to resemble tapestry.

needle valve
a cone-shaped valve ending in a sharp point, used in motor car carburettors, and in controlling the flow to a waterwheel or turbine.

needlework *noun*
any sewing or embroidery.
Word Family: **needlewoman**, *noun*, a woman skilled in needlework.

needs *adverb*
must needs, of necessity.

needy *adjective*
Word Family: see NEED.

ne'er (*say* nair) *adverb*
a poetic word for never.

ne'er-do-well *noun*
a worthless person.

nefarious (*say* nif-**air**ius) *adjective*
very wicked.
Word Family: **nefariously**, *adverb*; **nefariousness**, *noun*.
[Latin *nefarius* impious]

negate (*say* ni**ggate**) *verb*
1. to make ineffective or futile: 'his efforts to improve their lot were *negated* by their distrust'.
2. to contradict or prove untrue: 'later evidence *negated* my theory'.

negation (*say* niggay–sh'n) *noun*
1. a) the act of negating. b) a denial or negative statement.
2. the absence or opposite of something.

negative (*say* **negg**a–tiv) *adjective*
1. expressing denial or refusal: 'he gave a *negative* answer to my question'.
Usages:
a) 'a *negative* chest X–ray' (= showing no sign of disease).
b) '*negative* criticism is useless' (= not helpful or constructive).
2. *Maths:* relating to a quantity that is less than zero.
3. *Electricity:* having an excess of electrons.
negative *noun*
Photography: an image on a developed film in which the dark parts are light and the light parts dark. Compare POSITIVE.
negativism (*say* **negg**a–tiv–izm) *noun*
the quality of denying or being negative in ideas or behaviour.
Word Family: **negatively**, *adverb*; **negativeness**, **negativity** (*say* negga–**tivv**i–tee), *nouns*; **negativist**, *noun*.
[Latin *negare* to deny]

neglect (*say* ne–**glekt**) *verb*
to ignore, disregard or leave uncared for: 'she *neglected* her duties'.
Word Family: **neglect**, *noun*; **neglectful**, *adjective*; **neglectfully**, *adverb*; **neglectfulness**, *noun*.
[Latin *neglectus* unheeded]

négligé (*say* **negli**–*zh*ay) *noun*
an easy, informal dress worn about the home by a woman.
[French]

negligent (*say* **negli**–j'nt) *adjective*
taking too little care: 'the accident happened because he was *negligent*'.
negligence *noun*
a) the failure to take proper care. b) an instance of this.
Word Family: **negligently**, *adverb*.

negligible (*say* **neg**lija–b'l) *adjective*
unimportant or very little: 'a *negligible* sum of money'.
Word Family: **negligibly**, *adverb*.

negotiate (*say* niggo–shee–ate) *verb*
to bargain or confer with others to reach mutual agreement.
Usage: 'the hurdler successfully *negotiated* all the jumps' (= cleared).

negotiable (*say* niggo–sha–b'l) *adjective*
1. able to be negotiated: 'the salary for the job is *negotiable*'.
2. *Commerce:* (of a cheque) able to be transferred from one person to another.
Word Family: **negotiation**, *noun*, mutual discussion and bargaining; **negotiability**, *noun*.
[Latin *negotium* business]

Negro (*say* **nee**–gro) *noun*
plural is **Negroes**
one of a race of brown–skinned people, originally from Africa.
Word Family: **Negroid**, *adjective*, like or relating to a Negro or the Negro race; **Negress**, *noun*, a female Negro.
[Spanish, black]

neigh (*say* nay) *noun*
the cry of a horse.
Word Family: **neigh**, *verb*.

neighbour (*say* **nay**–ba) **neighbor** *noun*
a) a person who lives next door or close to another. b) any person or thing that is near another: 'France and Spain are *neighbours*'.
neighbourly *adjective*
friendly and helpful: '*neighbourly* advice'.
neighbourhood *noun*
a) a district or locality: 'this is a wealthy *neighbourhood*'. b) the people living in a particular district: 'do you want the whole *neighbourhood* to hear?'.
Word Family: **neighbour**, *verb*, to live or be situated near.

neither (*say* **nigh**–*tha* or **nee** *tha*) *adjective, pronoun, adverb*
not one or the other of two things: '*neither* twin is well–behaved'.
Common Error: neither should be followed by *nor* (not *or*), and by a singular verb unless one of the alternatives referred to is plural. *Examples:* '*neither* smoking *nor* drinking *is* harmful in moderation'; '*neither* drinks *nor* food *are* needed'. Similar rules apply to *either . . . or*.

nelson *noun*
Wrestling: a hold in which one arm (**half–nelson**) or both arms (**full nelson**) are placed under the opponent's armpit from behind, and then up onto the back of his neck.

nematode (*say* **neema**–tode) *noun*
a roundworm.

nemesis (*say* **nemmi**–sis) *noun*
1. retribution by fate for wrongdoing, hubris, etc.

2. *Greek mythology:* (*capital*) the goddess who allotted good and bad fortune and saw to it that great good fortune was offset by subsequent disaster.
[Greek *nemein* to give what is due]

neo–
a prefix meaning new, as in *neologism.*
[Greek *neos* new]

neodymium (*say* nee–o–**dimm**ium) *noun*
element number 60, a rare metal. See LANTHANIDE. See CHEMICAL ELEMENTS in grey pages.

Neolithic *noun*
see STONE AGE.
[NEO– + Greek *lithos* a stone]

neologism (*say* nee–**olla**–jizm) *noun*
a) a new word or phrase. b) the introduction of new words or phrases.
Word Family: **neologize, neologise,** *verb*; **neologist,** *noun.*
[NEO– + Greek *logos* a word]

neon (*say* **nee**–on) *noun*
element number 10, a colourless, odourless, inert gas found in tiny amounts in the earth's atmosphere and used in some electric lights. See CHEMICAL ELEMENTS in grey pages.

neophyte (*say* **nee**–o–fite) *noun*
a person who has newly entered a religious faith or order.
[NEO– + Greek *phytos* planted]

neoplasm *noun*
see TUMOUR.

neoprene *noun*
a synthetic rubber which is stronger and has a greater resistance to heat and ozone than natural rubbers.

nephew (*say* **nef**–yoo) *noun*
1. a son of one's brother or sister.
2. a son of one's husband's or wife's brother or sister.
[Latin *nepos* descendant]

nephritis (*say* nef–**rye**–tis) *noun*
a group of diseases causing the kidneys to function inefficiently.
Word Family: **nephritic** (*say* nef–**rittik**), *adjective.*
[Greek *nephros* kidney + -ITIS]

nepotism (*say* **neppa**–tizm) *noun*
undue favour shown to relatives, e.g. by giving them jobs, etc.
Word Family: **nepotist,** *noun.*
[Latin *nepos* a descendant]

Neptune *noun*
Astronomy: the planet in the solar system eighth from the sun.
[after *Neptune,* the Roman god of the sea]

neptunium (*say* nep–**tew**–nee–um) *noun*
element number 93, a man–made, radioactive metal. See TRANSURANIC ELEMENT and ACTINIDE. See CHEMICAL ELEMENTS in grey pages.

nerve *noun*
1. a cord–like bundle of nerve cells.
Usage: 'she suffers from *nerves*' (= nervousness).
2. courage or self–possession: 'it took *nerve* to climb that mountain'.
3. (*informal*) impudence or impertinence: 'what a *nerve* to insult me like that!'.
Phrases:
get on one's nerves, to irritate.
lose one's nerve, to lose self–confidence.
Word Family: **nerve,** *verb,* to give strength or courage to; **nerveless,** *adjective,* without nerves, especially being weak or afraid; **nervy,** *adjective.*
[Latin *nervus* a sinew]

nerve cell
also called a **neurone**
Anatomy: a type of cell that sends messages from one part of the body to another.

nerve centre
Anatomy: a place where a number of nerves join together, such as a plexus, a ganglion, the brain or the spinal cord.

nerve impulse
Anatomy: a message which travels along a nerve cell and results in a stimulus to a muscle, gland, etc.

nerve–racking *adjective*
extremely trying.

nervous *adjective*
1. a) uneasy or afraid of something: 'I feel *nervous* in the dark'. b) highly excitable: 'that *nervous* girl laughs hysterically at nothing'.
2. *Psychology:* of or relating to the nerves and disorders of the nerves or personality. A **nervous breakdown** is any of various psychiatric disorders resulting in loss of emotional control.
Word Family: **nervously,** *adverb*; **nervousness,** *noun.*

nervous system
the **central nervous system** (the brain and spinal cord) is the body's switchboard for incoming messages and outgoing commands.

the **peripheral nervous system** is the network of nerves all over the body. the **autonomic nervous system** controls the unconscious activities of the heart, intestines, glands, etc.

nescience (*say* **nessi**–ence) *noun*
ignorance.
Word Family: **nescient**, *adjective, noun.*

ness *noun*
an old word for a headland or cape.

–ness
a suffix used to form nouns from adjectives and indicating quality or state, as in *darkness*.

nest *noun*
1. a) a structure made by birds for hatching and rearing their young. b) the breeding place of an animal or insect.
Usage: 'the police searched for the robbers' *nest*' (= hideaway, resting place).
2. a group of articles designed to fit within each other when not in use, such as tables, trays, etc.
nest egg, a sum of money saved for emergencies, etc.
Word Family: **nest**, *verb.*

nestle (*say* **ness**'l) *verb*
a) to settle down comfortably: 'he *nestled* down in the armchair'. b) to cuddle: 'mother *nestled* the baby in her arms'.

nestling (*say* **nest**–ling) *noun*
a bird too young to leave the nest.

net (1) *noun*
1. a lace-like mesh of thread, wire, etc.: 'a fishing *net*'.
2. *Sport:* a) a network barrier stretched across the width of a court over which a ball must be hit or a quoit thrown. b) a net-covered area into which a ball must be hit or kicked.
net *verb*
(netted, netting)
to catch in or cover with a net.
Tennis: to hit the ball into the net.
Word Family: **netting**, *noun*, net fabric.

net (2) *adjective*
also spelt **nett**
remaining after deductions: 'what is your *net* income?'. Compare GROSS.
Usage: 'what was the *net* result of the argument?' (= final).
net weight, the weight of the contents only.
Word Family: **net (netted, netting)**, *verb*, to gain or clear, e.g. a profit.

netball *noun*
a game closely resembling basketball but differing in rules, size of court, etc.

nether *adjective*
lower or under.

nettle *noun*
any of a group of small, wild plants with stinging hairs.
nettle *verb*
to irritate or provoke.

nettle rash
hives.

network *noun*
1. any net-like or interconnected system of lines, passages, filaments, etc.
2. an agency providing ready-made radio or television programmes to certain stations.

neural (*say* **new**–r'l) *adjective*
of or relating to nerve cells, especially their activities or functions.
[Greek *neuron* a nerve]

neuralgia (*say* new–**ral**ja) *noun*
a pain along a nerve.
Word Family: **neuralgic**, *adjective.*
[Greek *neuron* a nerve + *algos* pain]

neurasthenia (*say* new–ras–**thee**nia) *noun*
1. an anxiety neurosis in which extreme fatigue is the chief symptom.
2. a nervous breakdown.
[Greek *neuron* a nerve + *asthenia* weakness]

neuritis (*say* new–**rye**–tis) *noun*
Medicine: an inflammation of a nerve.
[Greek *neuron* a nerve + –ITIS]

neurology (*say* new–**rolla**–jee) *noun*
the study of the nervous systems and their diseases.
Word Family: **neurologist**, *noun*; **neurological** (*say* new–ra–**loji**–k'l), *adjective.*

neurone (*say* **new**–rone) *noun*
see NERVE CELL.

neurosis (*say* new–**ro**–sis) *noun*
plural is **neuroses** (*say* new–**ro**–seez)
Psychology: any of various emotional disorders marked by extreme anxiety, obsessions or hysteria.
[Greek *neuron* a nerve + –OSIS]

neurosurgery (*say* new–ro–**serja**–ree) *noun*
the branch of medicine concerned with surgery of the nerves.
Word Family: **neurosurgeon**, *noun*; **neurosurgical**, *adjective.*

neurotic (*say* new-**rottik**) *adjective*
suffering from a neurosis.
Usage: 'the *neurotic* old man kept 17 cats in his room' (= obsessive, eccentric).
Word Family: **neurotic,** *noun,* a neurotic person; **neurotically,** *adverb.*

neuter (*say* **new**ta) *adjective*
a) having no sexual organs. b) having underdeveloped sexual organs.
neuter *noun*
1. a) a castrated animal. b) a neuter plant or animal.
2. *Grammar:* see GENDER.
[Latin, neither]

neutral (*say* **new**–tr'l) *adjective*
1. not taking part in an argument, dispute, etc.
2. of no definite colour, kind, characteristics, etc.: 'the carpet is a *neutral* colour so that it won't clash with the curtains'.
3. *Electricity:* having no electric charge.
4. *Chemistry:* neither acidic nor alkaline, but containing equal numbers of hydrogen and hydroxyl ions and having a pH of 7.
neutral *noun*
1. a neutral person, country or thing.
2. (of a motor vehicle) the position of disengaged gears.
neutrality (*say* new-**tralli**-tee) *noun*
the state of being neutral: 'her *neutrality* enables her to see both sides of the case clearly'.
Word Family: **neutralize, neutralise,** *verb,* a) to make neutral, b) to make ineffective; **neutralization,** *noun;* **neutrally,** *adverb;* **neutralism,** *noun,* the policy of remaining neutral; **neutralist,** *noun.*

neutrino (*say* new-**treeno**) *noun*
Physics: an elementary particle with no charge and very small mass, observed as a product of certain nuclear reactions.

neutron (*say* **new**–tron) *noun*
Physics: an elementary particle with the same mass as a proton, but no charge. Any variation in the number of neutrons in an atom gives rise to isotopes.

névé (*say* **nev**vay) *noun*
the mixture of compressed snow and ice which forms the beginning of a glacier.
[Swiss French]

never *adverb*
1. not ever or at no time: 'I've *never* seen him before'.
2. not at all: '*never* fear'.

nevermore *adverb*
never again.

never–never *noun*
on the never–never, (*informal*) on hire–purchase.

nevertheless *adverb*
all the same; in spite of that.

new *adjective*
of recent origin, make or existence: 'a *new* style of dress has been created'.
Usages:
a) 'a *new* planet has been discovered' (= previously unknown).
b) 'this shirt is dirty, I must change into a *new* one' (= another).
new to, 'he makes mistakes because he is *new to* the work' (= unfamiliar with).
new *adverb*
lately or recently: '*new–found* vigour'.
newly *adverb*
1. recently or lately: 'the *newly* appointed mayor is an old fogey'.
2. afresh: 'the garage had been *newly* painted'.
Word Family: **newness,** *noun.*

newcomer *noun*
a person who has recently arrived in a place.

newel *noun*
a pillar at the top or bottom of a staircase, supporting the handrail.

newfangled *adjective*
(*use is derogatory*) needlessly or undesirably novel.

newly *adverb*
see NEW.

new moon
Astronomy: the moon when it is between the sun and the earth and only a small crescent is visible.

news *plural noun*
1. (*used with singular verb*) a report of events as given each day by newspapers, radio, etc.
2. (*used with singular verb*) information which was not known before: 'that's *news* to me'.
[Old English *newe* something new]

news agency
an organization that collects news and distributes it to newspapers, radio, etc.

newsagent *noun*
a person who sells newspapers, magazines, stationery, etc.

Word Family: **newsagency**, *noun*, a shop selling these goods.

newscast *noun*
a broadcast of the news on radio or television.
Word Family: **newscaster**, *noun.*

newsletter *noun*
also called a **news–sheet**
a printed letter giving news or details about a group or society.

newspaper *noun*
a) a publication, usually daily or weekly, printed on large sheets of paper, which describes and comments on news and contains features and advertisements. b) the organization publishing this.

newsprint *noun*
the paper on which newspapers are printed.

newsreader *noun*
a person who reads the news bulletin on radio or television.

newsreel *noun*
a short film of the news.

news–sheet *noun*
see NEWSLETTER.

newsy *adjective*
(*informal*) full of news: 'she wrote me a *newsy* letter'.

newt *noun*
any of various small, tailed amphibians related to the salamanders.

New Testament
Religion: the second part of the Bible, produced in the time of the early Christian Church. Compare OLD TESTAMENT.

newton *noun*
the SI unit of force, which is equal to the force required to give a mass of one kilogram an acceleration of one metre per second squared.
[after *Sir Isaac Newton*, 1642–1727, a British scientist]

New World
the American continents.

new year
1. the year approaching or just begun.
2. (*capital*) a new calendar year, beginning on the first day of January in the Gregorian calendar.

next *adjective, adverb*
immediately following:
(as an adjective) 'we shall see you *next* week'
(as an adverb) 'it's my turn *next*'.
Usage: 'the *next* to arrive was Big Louie' (= next person).
Phrases:
next to, a) 'the shop is *next to* the school' (= beside); b) '*next to* vanilla, he likes chocolate flavouring best' (= after).
next to nothing, see NOTHING.

next–door *adverb, adjective*
living in or occupying the adjoining house, building, etc.: 'who lives *next–door* to you?'.

nexus *noun*
plural is **nexuses**
a connecting principle or link: 'the friendship treaty is a *nexus* between the two countries'.
[Latin]

niacin (*say* **nie**–a–sin) *noun*
an acid which is part of the vitamin B complex, found in fresh meat and yeast.

nib *noun*
1. the writing point of a pen.
2. the beak of a bird.

nibble *verb*
to take small bites: 'she *nibbled* the chocolate'.
Usage: 'to *nibble* at an offer' (= show interest).
Word Family: **nibble**, *noun.*

nibs *plural noun*
his nibs, (*informal*) an arrogant or conceited person.

nice *adjective*
1. pleasant, pleasing, agreeable, etc.: a) 'it's a *nice* day'; b) 'it's *nice* of you to say that'.
Usage: 'that is not a *nice* way to behave' (= proper).
2. precise or accurate: 'he made a *nice* distinction between the technical terms'.
Word Family: **nicely**, *adverb*; **niceness**, *noun.*

nicety (*say* **nice**–a–tee) *noun*
1. a refinement or elegance: 'she uses the *niceties* of the language'.
2. accuracy: 'she argued her case with great *nicety*'.
to a nicety, 'she described his character *to a nicety*' (= precisely).

niche (*say* nitch *or* neesh) *noun*
1. a shallow recess in a wall for ornaments, etc.
2. *Biology:* a position or function of an organism in a community of plants and animals.

Usage: 'he found a *niche* in the vast organization' (= suitable and comfortable position).
[Latin *nidus* nest]

nick *verb*
1. to indent or make a notch in something.
2. (*informal*) a) to capture or arrest. b) to steal.
nick off, (*informal*) to go away.
nick *noun*
1. a notch or groove.
2. (*informal*) a prison.
Phrases:
in good nick, (*informal*) in good condition.
in the nick of time, only just in time.

nickel *noun*
1. element number 28, a magnetic metal used in coins, alloys, and for protective plating. See TRANSITION ELEMENT.
See CHEMICAL ELEMENTS in grey pages.
2. *American:* a five-cent coin.

nickelodeon (*say* nikka-**lo**-dee-an) *noun*
a jukebox.

nickel silver
also called **German silver**
an alloy of copper, zinc and nickel, usually electroplated for use in tableware.

nickname *noun*
a name used familiarly in place of or in addition to the proper name of a person, place, etc.
Word Family: **nickname,** *verb.*

nicotine (*say* **nikka**-teen) *noun*
a poisonous alkaloid found in tobacco.
[introduced to France by *Jacques Nicot* in 1560]

niece (*say* neece) *noun*
1. a daughter of one's brother or sister.
2. a daughter of one's husband's or wife's brother or sister.

nifty *adjective*
(*informal*) neat, smart or stylish.

niggardly *adjective*
stingy or miserly.
Word Family: **niggard,** *noun,* a person who is stingy; **niggardliness,** *noun.*

niggle *verb*
to annoy or irritate by constant criticism, etc.
Word Family: **niggle,** *noun,* a trifling complaint; **niggler,** *noun.*

nigh *adverb, adjective*
an old word meaning near or nearly: 'the end of the world is *nigh*'.

night *noun*
the period of dark between two successive days, being between sunset and sunrise.
Word Family: **nightly,** *adjective,* a) of or occurring at night, b) occurring every night; **nightly,** *adverb.*

night-bird *noun*
1. a bird that is awake during the night.
2. (*informal*) a) a night owl. b) a person who prowls at night.

nightcap *noun*
1. a cap that is worn in bed.
2. (*informal*) a drink, usually hot and containing alcohol, taken just before going to bed.

nightclothes *plural noun*
garments that are worn in bed, such as pyjamas.

nightclub *noun*
a place providing food, drink and entertainment between nightfall and morning.

nightfall *noun*
the coming of night.

nightie *noun*
short form of **nightdress**
a woman's loose dress for sleeping in.

nightingale *noun*
a small brown woodland warbler related to the thrush, the male of which sings night and day until the eggs are hatched.
[NIGHT + Old English *galan* to sing]

nightjar *noun*
also called a **goatsucker**
any of various brown, plump birds with a loud churring song at night.

night life
the entertainments provided in towns at night, such as nightclubs, casinos, etc.

nightly *adjective, adverb*
Word Family: see NIGHT.

nightmare *noun*
a frightening dream.
Usage: 'driving through the bush fire was a *nightmare*' (= frightening experience).
Word Family: **nightmarish**, *adjective.*
[NIGHT + Old English *mare* an evil spirit supposed to suffocate people during sleep]

night owl
(*informal*) a person who often stays up late at night.

nightshade *noun*
short form of **deadly nightshade** belladonna.

nightshirt *noun*
a loose garment worn in bed.

night watch
a) a watch or guard kept during the night. b) the person keeping such a watch.

night-watchman *noun*
a person employed to guard property, etc. during the night.

nihilism (*say* **nie**–a–lizm) *noun*
a total rejection of all existing principles, values and institutions.
Word Family: **nihilist**, *noun*; **nihilistic** (*say* nie–a–**lis**tik), *adjective*.
[Latin *nihil* nothing + –ISM]

nil *noun*
nothing.

nimble *adjective*
quick and easy in movement: a) '*nimble* fingers'; b) 'a *nimble* brain'.
Word Family: **nimbly**, *adverb*; **nimbleness**, *noun*.

nimbus *noun*
plural is **nimbi** or **nimbuses**
1. a rain cloud.
2. a halo.
[Latin *nimbus* a thunder cloud]

nincompoop *noun*
a very foolish person.

nine *noun*
a cardinal number, the symbol 9 in Arabic numerals, IX in Roman numerals.
Word Family: **nine**, *adjective*; **ninth**, *adjective*, *noun*.

nine-days wonder
a sensational event which will probably be forgotten in nine days.

ninefold *adjective*
a) being nine times as much. b) having nine parts.

ninepins *plural noun*
the game of skittles.

nineteen *noun*
a cardinal number, the symbol 19 in Arabic numerals, XIX in Roman numerals.
talk nineteen to the dozen, to chatter very quickly or excitedly.
Word Family: **nineteen**, *adjective*; **nineteenth**, *adjective*, *noun*.

nineteenth hole
Golf: (*informal*) the bar in the clubhouse.

ninety *noun*
1. a cardinal number, the symbol 90 in Arabic numerals, XC in Roman numerals.
2. (*plural*) the numbers 90–99 in a series, such as the years within a century.
Word Family: **ninety**, *adjective*; **ninetieth**, *adjective*, *noun*.

ninny *noun*
a very foolish or simple person.

ninth *adjective*, *noun*
Word Family: see NINE.

niobium (*say* nie–**o**–bee–um) *noun*
also called **columbium**
element number 41, a rare metal used to improve the resistance to corrosion of stainless steel at high temperatures. See TRANSITION ELEMENT.
See CHEMICAL ELEMENTS in grey pages.

nip (1) *verb*
(**nipped**, **nipping**)
1. to squeeze.
2. to remove by squeezing: 'he *nipped* off the withered leaves'.
3. to sting or cause pain, as cold does.
Word Family: **nip**, *noun*; **nippy**, *adjective*, sharp and stinging, e.g. cold weather.

nip (2) *noun*
a small quantity of alcoholic spirits: 'a *nip* of brandy put me right'.

nipper *noun*
1. a person or thing that nips, such as a crab's claw.
2. (*informal*) a small child.

nipple *noun*
1. *Anatomy:* a) the small projection on the end of the breast or mammary gland through which a baby mammal sucks its mother's milk. b) a similar, but functionless, projection on male mammals. Also called a **teat**.
2. something which has the shape or function of a nipple, such as the small valve through which grease may be supplied to a bearing.

nippy *adjective*
Word Family: see NIP (1).

Nirvana (*say* neer–**var**na) *noun*
Buddhism: an indescribable state of enlightenment or bliss, where individual identity is lost in complete freedom from concern about oneself or the external world.
[Sanskrit, extinction]

Nissen hut
a prefabricated, semicircular building made of timber and galvanized iron.

[invented by *Colonel P. N. Nissen*, 1871–1930, an army engineer]

nit *noun*
1. the egg or empty eggshell of the louse or other parasitic insect, especially when it remains attached to hair or clothing.
2. (*informal*) a stupid person.

nit-picking *noun*
(*informal*) any fussing over trivial details, especially fault-finding.
Word Family: **nit-picker**, *noun*; **nit-pick**, *verb*.

nitrate (*say* **nigh**–trate) *noun*
1. *Chemistry:* any compound containing the univalent $(NO_3)^-$ ion.
2. a fertilizer containing potassium nitrate and sodium nitrate.
[Greek *nitron* washing-soda]

nitric acid (*say* **nigh**–trik assid)
a strong, colourless, corrosive acid. It attacks most metals and many other substances and is widely used in industry.

nitrify (*say* **nigh**–tri–fie) *verb*
(**nitrified, nitrifying**)
1. to oxidize a substance to nitrates or nitrites, especially by bacterial action.
2. to add nitrates to the soil.
Word Family: **nitrification**, *noun*.

nitrite (*say* **nigh**–trite) *noun*
Chemistry: any compound containing the univalent $(NO_2)^-$ ion.

nitrocellulose *noun*
see CELLULOSE NITRATE.

nitrogen (*say* **nigh**–tra–j'n) *noun*
element number 7, a colourless, odourless, chemically inactive gas forming about 78 per cent of the earth's atmosphere. It is an essential part of protein and is used in fertilizers, explosives and dyes. See CHEMICAL ELEMENTS in grey pages.
Word Family: **nitrogenous** (*say* nigh–**troja**–nus), *adjective*.

nitrogen cycle
a continuous circulation in nature of nitrogen and its compounds between the atmosphere, the soil and organisms.

nitrogen narcosis
an intoxicating and anaesthetic effect of too much nitrogen in the brain, due to the high content of nitrogen in air breathed by divers at depths below about 40 m.

nitroglycerine
(*say* nigh–tro–**glissa**–reen) *noun*
Chemistry: a pale yellow, dense, oily liquid (formula $C_3H_5(NO_3)_3$), used as an explosive.

nitrous oxide (*say* **nigh**–trus oxide)
see LAUGHING GAS.

nitty-gritty *noun*
(*informal*) the basic facts, details, etc.

nitwit *noun*
a slow-witted person.

nix *noun*
(*informal*) nothing.
[for German *nichts*]

no (1) *adverb*
1. used to express dissent or refusal: 'may I go out? *No*, you may not'.
2. used to emphasize a previous negative or qualify a previous statement: '*no*, not even in Paris did I see so many beautiful dresses'.
3. used with a comparative to indicate negation: 'she is *no* prettier than Sue'.

no *noun*
plural is **noes**
1. a denial or refusal: 'she got a definite *no* to her request'.
2. a negative vote or voter.

no (2) *adjective*
1. not any: 'there is *no* food left'.
2. used to imply the opposite: 'he is *no* fool'.

nob *noun*
(*informal*) a) a person of wealth or social distinction. b) the head.

nobble *verb*
(*informal*) a) to tamper with a racehorse, especially by drugging it. b) to catch a criminal, etc.
Word Family: **nobbler**, *noun*.

nobelium (*say* no–**beelium**) *noun*
element number 102, a man-made, radioactive metal. See TRANSURANIC ELEMENT and ACTINIDE.
See CHEMICAL ELEMENTS in grey pages.

nobility (*say* no–**billi**–tee) *noun*
1. a) the peers and their wives. b) the peers, baronets and knights and their wives and children.
2. an excellence of mind or character.

noble *adjective*
1. of high hereditary rank.
2. showing high character or qualities: 'a *noble* sacrifice'.
3. imposing or stately: 'a *noble* monument'.
4. *Chemistry:* unreactive, and not corroded or easily attacked by chemical agents.

noble *noun*
a member of the nobility.
Word Family: **nobly**, *adverb.*
[Latin *nobilis* known, famous]

nobleman *noun*
a male member of the nobility.
Word Family: **noblewoman**, *noun.*

noblesse oblige (*say* no-bless o-**blee***zh*)
the obligations, such as honourable behaviour, associated with high rank or position.
[French *noblesse* nobility + *oblige* obliges]

nobody *pronoun*
no person.
nobody *noun*
a person of no importance.

nocturnal (*say* nok-**ter**-n'l) *adjective*
relating to or active in the night-time: 'a *nocturnal* animal is awake at night'. Compare DIURNAL.
Word Family: **nocturnally**, *adverb.*
[Latin *noctis* of the night]

nocturne (*say* **nok**-tern) *noun*
a short, gentle piece of music, especially for the piano.
[French]

nod *verb*
(**nodded, nodding**)
to bow the head briefly, usually to express agreement, greeting, etc.
Usages:
a) 'he *nodded* off for a few moments by the fire' (= dozed).
b) 'the plants were *nodding* in the breeze' (= swaying, bending).
Word Family: **nod**, *noun.*

node *noun*
1. a knot or knob, such as a joint on a stem from which a leaf grows.
2. a point at which two things intersect.
3. *Physics:* a point where there is no transverse movement in a standing wave. Compare ANTINODE.
4. *Geography:* the area in which some activity occurs.
Word Family: **nodal**, *adjective.*
[Latin *nodus* a knot]

nodule (*say* **nod**-yool) *noun*
a knob or small rounded lump.
Word Family: **nodular**, *adjective.*

Noel (*say* no-**el**) **Noël** *noun*
a name for Christmas.
[Latin *natalis* a birthday]

noggin *noun*
(*informal*) a) the head. b) a glass of beer.

noise (*rhymes with* boys) *noun*
1. any sound, especially when loud or confused: 'deafening *noises*'.
2. *Electronics:* any unwanted electrical disturbance which obscures or reduces the clarity or quality of a signal.
Word Family: **noisy**, *adjective*, making or full of noise; **noisily**, *adverb*; **noisiness**, *noun*; **noiseless**, *adjective*, silent; **noiselessly**, *adverb.*

nolle prosequi (*say* no-lay pross-**ee**-kwie)
Law: a court's record of the fact that a case has been dropped.
[Latin, to be unwilling to pursue]

nomad (*say* **no**-mad) *noun*
1. any of a group of people who move from place to place to find food, etc. according to the seasons.
2. any person who wanders or moves about.
Word Family: **nomadic** (*say* no-**maddik**), *adjective*; **nomadically**, *adverb.*
[Greek *nomas, nomados* roaming about for pasture]

no man's-land *noun*
1. the area between two opposing armies.
2. any unclaimed or disputed area.

nom de plume (*say* **nom** deh ploom)
a pseudonym.
[French *nom* name + *de plume* of pen]

nomenclature (*say* no-**menkla**-cher) *noun*
a system of names used in a particular subject.
[from Latin]

nominal (*say* **nommi**-n'l) *adjective*
1. existing in name only: 'a *nominal* ruler of a country'.
2. small in relation to the real value: 'we only pay a *nominal* rent as the house belongs to my parents'.
3. *Grammar:* of or relating to a noun or name.
Word Family: **nominally**, *adverb.*
[Latin *nominis* of a name]

nominate (*say* **nommi**-nate) *verb*
1. to put forward or suggest a person as suitable for appointment or election.
2. to name: 'which film would you *nominate* as the best?'.
Word Family: **nomination**, *noun*, a) the act of nominating, b) the state of being nominated; **nominator**, *noun*, a person who nominates; **nominee**, *noun*, a person who is nominated.

nominative case
Grammar: see CASE (1).

non–
a prefix meaning not, as in *nonconformist.*
[Latin]

nonagenarian (*say* nonna–j'n–**airian**) *noun*
a person who is over 90 but less than 100 years old.
Word Family: **nonagenarian,** *adjective,* a) being 90 years old, b) being between 90 and 100 years old.
[Latin *nonageni* ninety each]

nonagon (*say* **nonna**–g'n) *noun*
any closed, plane figure with nine straight sides.
[Latin *nonus* ninth + Greek *gonia* a corner]

non–aligned *adjective*
not taking part in an alliance, etc.
Word Family: **non–alignment,** *noun.*

nonce *noun*
for the nonce, for the present.
[Middle English *for then anes* for the one (purpose)]

nonchalant (*say* **non**sha–l'nt) *adjective*
unconcerned, cool or indifferent.
Word Family: **nonchalance,** *noun;* **nonchalantly,** *adverb.*
[French]

non–combatant (*say* non–**kom**ba–t'nt) *noun*
a person who is not involved in fighting, such as a medical officer or chaplain in the armed forces.

non–commissioned officer
a member of the armed forces appointed to a position of authority but subject to the command of officers.

non–committal *adjective*
not committing oneself to a particular view, course of action, etc.

non–compliance *noun*
a failure or refusal to comply.

non compos mentis (*say* non kompus **mentis**)
not sane or responsible for one's actions.
[Latin, not in control of the mind]

nonconformist *noun*
1. a person who does not conform.
2. (*capital*) a member of a Protestant Church which rejects the rule of bishops, e.g. Methodist, Baptist.
Word Family: **nonconformity,** *noun,* a lack of conformity or agreement.

nondescript (*say* **non**da–skript) *adjective*
of no particular type or sort: 'it was such a *nondescript* dress that I don't remember what colour it was'.

none (*say* nun) *pronoun*
1. not any: 'that is *none* of your business'.
2. (*used with singular or plural verb*) not one: '*none* of them would help'.
none *adverb*
not at all; in no way: 'he was *none* the worse for the experience'.

nonentity (*say* non–**en**ta–tee) *noun*
a person or thing of no importance.

nonetheless (*say* **nun**–*the*–less) *adverb*
nevertheless.

non–fiction *noun*
any factual prose writing.
Word Family: **non–fiction, non–fictional,** *adjectives,* not imagined or made-up.

non–intervention *noun*
a failure or refusal to intervene or interfere, especially of one country with the affairs of another.

non–metal *noun*
Chemistry: any element which does not possess the properties of a metal.
Word Family: **non–metallic,** *adjective.*

non–partisan *adjective*
not partisan, especially not supporting any of the established political parties.

nonplus *verb*
(nonplussed, nonplussing)
to puzzle or perplex completely.
[Latin *non plus* no further]

nonproliferation *noun*
the halting of the spread of nuclear weapons among non–nuclear powers by common agreement.

nonsense *noun*
a) something which is absurd or makes no sense. b) senseless or foolish conduct.
Word Family: **nonsensical** (*say* non–**sensi**–k'l), *adjective.*

non sequitur (*say* non **sek**wi–ta)
a conclusion that does not follow from the basic statements or assumptions.
[Latin, it does not follow]

non troppo
Music: not too much.
ma non troppo, but not too much.
[Italian]

noodle (1) *noun*
a pasta in long, flat and narrow pieces used in soup or with a sauce.
[German *nudel*]

noodle (2) *noun*
(*informal*) a) the head. b) a simpleton.

nook (*say* nuk) *noun*
a) a secluded corner. b) a small recess.

noon *noun*
midday.

no-one *pronoun*
nobody.

noontide *noun*
midday.

noose *noun*
a loop, as in a lasso, with a knot which tightens when the rope is pulled.

nor *conjunction*
1. used to connect negative alternatives: 'she is neither brilliant *nor* stupid'.
2. used to emphasize a negative such as *not, never*, etc.: 'never did I meet such an idiot, *nor* do I wish to'.
Common Error: see NEITHER.

norm *noun*
1. a model or standard.
2. the average behaviour or performance for a group of people.
Word Family: **normative,** *adjective*, corresponding with the norm.
[Latin *norma* a carpenter's square]

normal *adjective*
1. conforming to a usual or typical pattern: 'such behaviour is *normal* in young children'.
2. *Maths:* being at right angles.
Word Family: **normal,** *noun*, anything normal; **normally,** *adverb*, usually; **normality** (*say* nor-malli-tee), **normalcy,** *nouns.*

normalize, normalise *verb*
to make normal.
Word Family: **normalization,** *noun.*

north *noun*
1. the direction along the meridian to the left of the position where the sun rises.
2. the cardinal point of the compass at 90° to the left of east and opposite south. Also called **magnetic north.**
Word Family: **north,** *adjective, adverb.*

north-east *noun*
a) the point or direction midway between north and east. b) a region in this direction.
Word Family: **north-east,** *adjective, adverb*, in or towards the north-east; **north-easterly, north-eastern,** *adjectives*, from or towards the north-east; **north-easterly, north-easter,** *nouns*, a wind coming from the north-east.

northerly *adjective, adverb*
(of a direction, course, etc.) from or towards the north: 'we set off on a *northerly* course'.
northerly *noun*
a wind coming from the north.

northern *adjective*
(of a place) situated in the north: 'the *northern* edge of the desert'.

northern lights
the aurora borealis.

North Star
see POLE STAR.

northward *adjective*
towards the north.
Word Family: **northwards, northward,** *adverb.*

north-west *noun*
a) the point or direction midway between north and west. b) a region in this direction.
Word Family: **north-west,** *adjective, adverb*, a) in or towards the north-west, b) coming from the north-west; **north-westerly, north-western,** *adjectives*, from or towards the north-west; **north-westerly, north-wester,** *nouns*, a wind coming from the north-west.

nose (*say* noze) *noun*
1. *Anatomy:* the organ of smell, through which air is taken in.
2. something which has the shape or position of a nose: 'the *nose* of an aeroplane'.
3. the sense of smell.
Usages:
a) 'that reporter has a keen *nose* for a good story' (= ability to detect or discover).
b) 'please keep your *nose* out of our business' (= prying, interference).
Phrases:
by a nose, by a very short distance.
look down one's nose at, to treat or regard with disdain.
pay through the nose, to pay too much.
put someone's nose out of joint, to upset the feelings or pride of a person.
turn up one's nose at, to be ungrateful to or contemptuous of.
nose *verb*
1. to touch or examine with the nose: 'the horse *nosed* the boy's hand'.
2. to sniff or smell.
Usages:
a) 'the car *nosed* forward slowly in the heavy traffic' (= moved).
b) 'don't *nose* into other peoples' affairs' (= pry).

nosebag *noun*
a bag containing dry feed, held near a horse's mouth by straps around its head.

nosedive *noun*
a sudden, downward plunge, especially a dive in which an aircraft is pointed almost straight down.
Word Family: **nosedive**, *verb.*

nosegay *noun*
a small bunch of flowers.

nosey *adjective*
see NOSY.

nosh *verb*
(*informal*) to eat, especially a snack or titbit.
Word Family: **nosh**, *noun*, food.
[Yiddish]

nosology (*say* nos-**olla**-jee) *noun*
the science of diseases.
[Greek *nosos* disease + -LOGY]

nostalgia (*say* nos-**tal**ja) *noun*
a longing for persons, places or things which are past or distant.
Word Family: **nostalgic**, *adjective*; **nostalgically**, *adverb.*
[Greek *nostos* a return home + *algos* pain]

nostril *noun*
either of the two openings in the nose through which air is breathed.

nostrum *noun*
plural is **nostrums**
1. a medicine, especially a false one.
2. a pet scheme or plan for improvement.
[Latin, our own thing]

nosy, nosey *adjective*
inquisitive or meddlesome.
nosy parker, an inquisitive person.
Word Family: **nosily**, *adverb*; **nosiness**, *noun.*

not *adverb*
a word expressing denial, refusal or prohibition: a) 'that is *not* true!'; b) 'you must *not* do that'.

nota bene (*say* **no**-ta **bennay**)
short form is **n.b.**
note well.
[Latin]

notable (*say* **no**-ta-b'l) *adjective*
a) worthy of notice. b) distinguished: 'a *notable* artist'.
Word Family: **notable**, *noun*, an important person; **notably**, *adverb*; **notability** (*say* no-ta-**billi**-tee), *noun.*

notary public
plural is **notaries public**
short form is **notary**
an official authorized to certify contracts, take affidavits, depositions, etc.
[from Latin]

notation (*say* no-**tay**-sh'n) *noun*
1. a system of symbols to represent numbers, quantities, etc., as is used in arithmetic, algebra and music.
2. a note or record of something.
Word Family: **notate**, *verb*; **notational**, *adjective.*

notch *noun*
a V-shaped cut in a surface, sometimes used as a record or to keep count.
Usage: 'her remark cut him down several *notches*' (= degrees, steps).
Word Family: **notch**, *verb*, a) to cut a notch, b) to score.

note *noun*
1. a short written or printed record, used for reference, as a reminder, an informal message, etc.
2. a piece of paper currency: 'a five pound *note*'.
3. *Music:* a) a single sound. b) its written symbol. c) a key on a piano, organ, etc.
4. any musical or expressive sound: 'the *notes* of a magpie's call are very distinctive'.
5. importance or significance: 'did anything of *note* happen while I was away?'.
6. heed or notice: 'please take *note* of the revised timetable'.
7. tone or feeling: 'there was a *note* of warning in the doctor's voice'.
Phrases:
strike a false note, to do or say something inappropriate or which betrays insincerity.
strike the right note, to do or say the appropriate thing.
note *verb*
1. to watch or notice carefully: '*note* the way the batsman is shading his eyes'.
2. to make a note of: '*note* the date on your calendar'.
Word Family: **noted**, *adjective*, famous; **notedly**, *adverb.*
[Latin *nota* a sign, mark, note]

notepaper *noun*
any sheets of paper used for writing letters.

noteworthy *adjective*
worthy of notice or recognition.
Word Family: **noteworthiness**, *noun.*

nothing (*say* **nuthing**) *noun*
1. no thing: 'this carton has *nothing* in it, so throw it away'.
2. nought: 'four minus four equals *nothing*'.
Usages:
a) 'there is *nothing* on television tonight' (= not anything interesting or important).
b) 'she shows *nothing* of her former enjoyment of life' (= no trace or part).
Phrases:
make nothing of, a) 'I could *make nothing of* her hysterical speech' (= not understand); b) 'they all tried kindly to *make nothing of* my clumsiness' (= treat lightly).
next to nothing, very little.
nothing doing!, (*informal*) certainly not!
nothing for it, 'there was *nothing for it* but to jump over the side of the bridge' (= no other possible course of action).
nothing in it, 'there's *nothing in it*' (= no truth, or profit, in it).
Word Family: **nothingness**, *noun*, a) the state of being nothing, b) emptiness or worthlessness; **nothing**, *adverb*, not at all.

notice (*say* **no**–tiss) *noun*
1. attention or awareness: 'it has come to my *notice* that you have been arriving late'.
2. a written or printed announcement.
Usage: 'the new play received very good *notices* after its opening' (= reviews).
3. a formal announcement of intention, especially to leave a job: 'to give *notice*'.
notice *verb*
to be aware of or pay attention to: 'did you *notice* the man wearing pink shoes?'.
Word Family: **noticeable**, *adjective*, a) able to be seen, b) significant; **noticeably**, *adverb*.
[Latin *notitia* a being known]

notifiable disease
a disease which must be reported to the health authorities, e.g. smallpox, diphtheria.

notify (*say* **no**–ti–fie) *verb*
(notified, notifying)
to inform or make known to: 'please *notify* the police if you have seen this car'.
Word Family: **notification**, *noun*, a written notice.

notion (*say* **no**–sh'n) *noun*
1. a general idea or feeling: 'I have a strange *notion* that we have been here before'.
2. an opinion or belief: 'her *notions* about marriage are very old-fashioned'.
[from Latin]

notochord (*say* **no**–ta–kord) *noun*
a rod-like structure found in place of a backbone in many animals.
[Greek *notos* the back + CHORD]

notorious (*say* no–**taw**–ree–us) *adjective*
widely known, especially in an unfavourable way.
Word Family: **notoriously**, *adverb*; **notoriety** (*say* no–ta–**rye**–a–tee), *noun*, the quality of being famous or notorious.
[Latin *notus* known]

notwithstanding *preposition*
in spite of: '*notwithstanding* their warnings, she went out alone'.
notwithstanding *adverb*
nevertheless: 'we continued on our way *notwithstanding*'.

nougat (*say* **noo**–gah) *noun*
a chewy sweet, usually white and containing pieces of nut.
[French]

nought (*say* nawt) *noun*
zero, the symbol **0**.
See NAUGHT.

noughts-and-crosses *noun*
a game for two using noughts and crosses as symbols, in which each player tries to build the first row of three of his symbols within a square consisting of nine compartments.

noun *noun*
Grammar: any word which names something.
a **common noun** expresses the general name for a number of things, such as *boy, dog*, etc.
a **proper noun** expresses the individual name of a person or place and usually begins with a capital letter, such as *John, Newcastle*, etc.
an **abstract noun** expresses a quality rather than an object, such as *beauty, anger*, etc.
a **collective noun** is a singular noun which expresses the name given to certain things when they are in a group, such as *herd, flock*, etc.
[Latin *nomen* a name]

nourish (*say* **nurr**ish) *verb*
1. to feed or sustain with food.

2. to cherish or promote: 'you must *nourish* your natural talent'.
Word Family: **nourishment,** *noun.*

nous (*rhymes with* house) *noun*
(*informal*) common sense.
[Greek, mind]

nouveau riche (*say* **noo**-vo reesh)
plural is **nouveaux riches**
a person who has newly become rich.
[French]

nova *noun*
a faint star which, after an internal explosion, displays a tremendous increase in radiation, but only for a few days or weeks.
[Latin *novus* new (because at first mistaken for a new star)]

novel (1) (*say* **novv**'l) *noun*
a long prose narrative of imaginary people and events. A short novel is sometimes called a **novella.**
Word Family: **novelist,** *noun,* a person who writes novels; **novelistic,** *adjective,* of or like a novel.

novel (2) (*say* **novv**'l) *adjective*
new, unusual or different.
[Latin *novus* new]

novelty *noun*
1. the quality of being novel or new: 'the *novelty* of snow in summer'.
2. anything which is novel: 'eating with chopsticks was a *novelty*'.
3. a small, inexpensive toy or article.

November *noun*
the eleventh month of the year in the Gregorian calendar.
[Latin, the ninth month of the Roman calendar]

novice (*say* **novvis**) *noun*
a person who is new to some activity, religious order, etc.
[Latin *novicius* newly arrived]

novitiate (*say* no-**vishi**-it) *noun*
also spelt **noviciate**
a) a novice or beginner. b) the state or period of being a novice.

novocaine *noun*
a drug similar to cocaine used as a local anaesthetic, especially in dentistry.

now *adverb*
1. at this time or moment: 'what sort of work are you doing *now*?'.
2. at once: 'please stop that noise *now*'.
3. (of events) at that time: 'the rain was *now* falling more heavily than ever'.
4. as a result: '*now* we may never see him again'.
Phrases:
just now, 'it arrived *just now* in the post' (= very recently).
now and again, now and then, occasionally.
now *conjunction*
since: '*now* that you mention it, I do remember that car'.
Word Family: **nowadays,** *adverb,* at the present time.

nowhere *adverb*
not anywhere.
get nowhere, to achieve nothing.
Word Family: **nowhere,** *noun,* an unknown or non-existent place.

noxious (*say* **nok**-shus) *adjective*
harmful.
Word Family: **noxiously,** *adverb;* **noxiousness,** *noun.*
[from Latin]

nozzle *noun*
a projecting spout or end through which something is poured or discharged, such as a fitment on the end of a pipe or hose.

nth (*say* enth) *adjective*
Maths: relating to a general term, the *n*th in a series.
to the nth degree, to the utmost or greatest extent.

nuance (*say* **new**-once) *noun*
a slight or subtle shade or variation, as in colour, meaning, etc.
[French]

nub *noun*
1. a knob or lump.
2. (*informal*) the point or gist of anything: 'let us get to the real *nub* of our discussion'.

nubile (*say* **new**-bile) *adjective*
(of a girl or young woman) physically mature or old enough to marry.
[Latin *nubere* (of a woman) to be married to]

nuclear (*say* **new**-klee-a) *adjective*
1. relating to, involving or powered by nuclear energy.
2. having nuclear weapons: 'is India a *nuclear* power?'.
3. of or forming a nucleus: 'a *nuclear* family'.
4. of or relating to the nucleus of an atom.

nuclear deterrence
the restraint on the use of nuclear weapons imposed by the knowledge that the result would be inconceivably disastrous for aggressor, victim and the world, a knowledge which logically

entails the cessation of nuclear armament.

nuclear energy
also called **atomic energy**
a) the immensely powerful force, the nature of which is unknown, required to keep charged protons and neutrons densely packed in an atom's nucleus.
b) this force released in nuclear fission or nuclear fusion.

nuclear fission
short form is **fission**
the splitting of the nucleus of an atom of a heavy element, e.g. a uranium isotope, producing enormous energy which is controlled in nuclear reactors for peaceful uses or uncontrolled for atomic bombs.

nuclear fuel
the elements used in producing nuclear power, e.g. uranium, plutonium, thorium.

nuclear fusion
short form is **fusion**
the fusion of two nuclei of a light element, e.g. hydrogen, to form one nucleus of a heavier element, e.g. helium, releasing vast amounts of energy (more than that produced by fission), used in the hydrogen bomb but not yet controllable for peaceful use.

nuclear physics
low-energy nuclear physics studies the structure of the nuclei of atoms. **high-energy nuclear physics** studies elementary particles.

nuclear power
1. the product of nuclear fission controlled in a nuclear reactor for peaceful uses.
2. a country which possesses nuclear weapons.

nuclear reactor
also called an **atomic pile**
any of various widely differing systems for damping down the energy released in nuclear fission so that it can be used in generating electricity, propelling ships, etc.

nuclear weapon
1. a tactical or short-range weapon, e.g. an **atomic bomb**, atomic artillery or a ship-launched or vehicle-launched missile with a small warhead in which the explosive force is derived from nuclear fission.
2. a strategic or long-range weapon, e.g. a missile launched from an aircraft, submarine or land-based silo, or a **hydrogen bomb**, in which the explosive force is derived from nuclear fusion triggered off by a nuclear fission detonator, or from nuclear fission alone.

nucleic acid (*say* new-**klee**-ik *or* new-**klay**-ik assid)
Biology: a long-chain molecule found in all living things and forming chromosomes.

nucleon (*say* **new**-klee-on) *noun*
Physics: a proton or neutron.

nucleus (*say* **new**-klee-us) *noun*
plural is **nuclei**
1. a central part around which other things are grouped.
Usage: 'the resigning members formed the *nucleus* of a new progressive party' (= basis, foundation).
2. *Physics:* the heavy, positively charged core of an atom, made up of protons and (except in hydrogen) neutrons.
3. *Biology:* a body within a cell containing the chromosomes and essential for the life of most animal and plant cells.
[Latin, kernel]

nude (*say* newd) *adjective*
naked.
nude *noun*
1. a naked human figure or a drawing, painting or photograph of one.
2. a state of nakedness.
Word Family: **nudity** (*say* **new**di-tee), *noun*; **nudist**, *noun*, a person who believes that dispensing with clothes is healthy and enjoyable.
[from Latin]

nudge *verb*
to push gently, especially with the elbow, in order to attract attention, etc.
Word Family: **nudge,** *noun.*

nugatory (*say* **new**-ga-tree) *adjective*
1. having no value or worth.
2. having no power or effect.
[Latin *nugae* trifles]

nugget *noun*
a small lump or mass, especially of a precious metal such as gold.

nuisance (*say* **new**-sence) *noun*
a person or thing that is annoying, troublesome or inconvenient.

null *adjective*
1. having no effect, force or significance.
2. non-existent.
null and void, having no legal force.

Word Family: **nullify** (**nullified, nullifying**), *verb,* to make or declare null; **nullification**, *noun,* the state of being null or ineffective.
[Latin *nullus* none]

null set
Maths: the set which has no elements.

numb (*say* num) *adjective*
unable to feel or move: a) 'her fingers were *numb* with cold'; b) 'we were *numb* with shock at the news'.
Word Family: **numb**, *verb*; **numbness**, *noun.*

number *noun*
1. any of a series of symbols or figures indicating quantity or position in a series.
2. a particular number given to a person or thing to fix place, establish identity, etc.: 'a telephone *number*'.
3. a quantity, total or amount: 'what is the *number* of children in this class?'.
Usages:
a) '*numbers* of spectators were injured' (= many, a large quantity).
b) 'we lost the vote because we didn't have the *numbers*' (= greater quantity).
4. a single part in a series, such as an item in a programme, an issue of a magazine, etc.
Phrases:
any number of, a large but indefinite quantity of.
make one's number with, to ensure that a person knows who or what one is.
number one, a) 'he always looks after *number one*' (= himself first); b) (*Nautical*) the first lieutenant.
without number, too many to be counted.
number *verb*
1. to add up to: 'his true friends do not *number* very many'.
2. to add, note or give a number to, in turn or one by one.
Usages:
a) 'he was *numbered* among the few survivors' (= included).
b) 'the doctors say that the days of his life are *numbered*' (= limited).
Word Family: **numberless**, *adjective,* a) countless, b) without a number.
[Latin *numerus*]

numberplate *noun*
also called a **registration plate**
a plate with numbers and letters on it to identify the motor vehicle carrying it.

number theory
Maths: the study of integers and their interrelationships.

numbskull, numskull *noun*
(*informal*) a stupid person.

numerable (*say* **new**ma-ra-b'l) *adjective*
able to be counted.

numeral (*say* **new**ma-r'l) *noun*
a letter, figure or word expressing a number: 'the Roman *numeral* for two is II'.
Word Family: **numeral**, *adjective,* of or expressing a number.

numerate (*say* **new**ma-rate) *verb*
to count.
Word Family: **numeration**, *noun,* the act or process of counting; **numerate** (*say* **new**ma-rit), *adjective,* able to do arithmetic or mathematics; **numeracy**, *noun,* the state of being numerate.

numerator *noun*
Maths: the part of a fraction above the line, such as 3 in $\frac{3}{4}$. Compare DENOMINATOR.

numerical (*say* new-**merri**-k'l)
numeric *adjective*
1. relating to a number or series of numbers: 'please put your pages in *numerical* order'.
2. of or expressed in a number or numbers: '7 is a *numerical* symbol'.
Word Family: **numerically**, *adverb.*

numerology (*say* newma-**rolla**-jee) *noun*
the study of numbers, such as a person's birth date, to discover their supposed influence on events.
Word Family: **numerologist**, *noun.*

numerous (*say* **new**ma-rus) *adjective*
forming or having a great number.
Word Family: **numerously**, *adverb.*

numinous (*say* **new**min-us) *adjective*
spiritually or religiously inspired or inspiring.
[Latin *numinis* of divine power]

numismatics (*say* new-miz-**mat**tiks) *plural noun*
(*used with singular verb*) the science or study of coins and medals.
Word Family: **numismatic**, *adjective*; **numismatist** (*say* new-**miz**ma-tist), *noun.*
[Greek *nomismata* currency]

numskull *noun*
see NUMBSKULL.

nun *noun*
Christian: a female member of a religious order living under vows, often apart from the secular world.

nuncio (*say* **nun**shio) *noun*
a diplomatic representative of the Pope.
[Latin *nuntius* messenger]

nunnery *noun*
an old word for a convent.

nuptials (*say* **nup**–sh'ls) *plural noun*
a marriage ceremony or wedding.
Word Family: **nuptial**, *adjective.*
[Latin *nuptiae* a wedding]

nurse *noun*
1. a person trained to care for the sick, young children, etc.
2. any person or thing that encourages growth, development, etc.
nurse *verb*
1. a) to be a nurse. b) to care for or look after.
2. to breastfeed a child.
Usages:
a) 'he *nursed* his sore leg' (= held gently).
b) 'do not *nurse* any grudges' (= carry, cherish).
[Latin *nutricius* that nourishes]

nursemaid *noun*
a woman employed to take care of children.

nursery *noun*
1. a) a place where children are looked after. b) a room in a house for children to sleep and play.
2. a place where plants are grown for sale, experimentation, etc.
Word Family: **nurseryman**, *noun*, a person who owns or works in a plant nursery.

nursery rhyme
a short, traditional poem or song for children.

nursery school
see KINDERGARTEN.

nursing home
a hotel which provides medical care by qualified staff for convalescents and invalids.

nurture (*say* **ner**–cher) *verb*
to feed or nourish.
Usage: 'the new law *nurtured* a feeling of public resentment' (= promoted).
Word Family: **nurture**, *noun*, a) training or upbringing, b) food or nourishment.

nut *noun*
1. a dry fruit enclosed in a hard shell.
2. something which has the shape, size or texture of a nut: 'a *nut* of butter'.
3. (*informal*) a) a person who is eccentric or insane. b) the head.
4. a piece of metal with a hole in the centre for screwing on to the end of a bolt.
a hard nut to crack, a difficult person or problem.
Word Family: **nutty**, *adjective*, a) like a nut, especially in taste, b) (informal) mad or eccentric.

nutcracker *noun*
an implement for breaking the hard, outer shell of a nut.

nuthatch (*say* **nut**–hatch) *noun*
any of a group of small, tree–climbing birds which eats nuts and insects.

nutmeat *noun*
1. a meat substitute made from crushed nuts, grain, etc.
2. the edible kernel of a nut.

nutmeg *noun*
a sweet spice made from the dried berry of an East Indian tree and used in cooking.
[NUT + Latin *muscus* musk]

nutria (*say* **new**tria) *noun*
see COYPU.

nutrient (*say* **new**tri–ent) *noun*
a substance which nourishes, especially as an ingredient in food.

nutriment (*say* **new**tra–m'nt) *noun*
anything which nourishes, sustains or promotes growth.

nutrition (*say* new–**trish**'n) *noun*
1. the act of nourishing, especially the ingestion, digestion and assimilation of food materials by an organism.
2. a) food. b) nutriment.
Word Family: **nutritious**, *adjective*, giving a high degree of nourishment; **nutritive** (*say* **new**tra–tiv), *adjective*, a) providing nourishment, b) relating to nutrition; **nutritional**, *adjective.*

nuts *adjective*
(*informal*) mad.

nutshell *noun*
the hard shell of a nut.
in a nutshell, in brief, concisely.

nutty *adjective*
Word Family: see NUT.

nuzzle *verb*
1. to push against or burrow with the nose.
2. to cuddle or snuggle.

nylon ***noun***
1. any of a large class of polymers that have recurring amide groups along the chain of the molecule. Thread made from nylon is used to make a variety of products, such as yarn, fabric, fishing line, etc.
2. (*plural*) stockings made of nylon.

nymph (*say* nimf) ***noun***
1. *Mythology:* any of various beautiful young goddesses who inhabited the sea, woods, meadows, etc.
2. *Biology:* a young, wingless, sexually immature form in the development of certain insects.
[from Greek]

nymphet ***noun***
a young, sexually attractive girl.

nymphomania
(*say* nimfa-**may**-nee-a) ***noun***
Psychology: an abnormally strong sexual desire in women. Compare SATYRIASIS.
Word Family: **nymphomaniac,** ***noun.***

Oo

oaf *noun*
a stupid or clumsy person.
Word Family: **oafish**, *adjective*; **oafishly**, *adverb*; **oafishness**, *noun.*

oak *noun*
any of a group of large trees which produce acorns and a fine, hard wood, formerly used especially in shipbuilding and furniture.
Word Family: **oaken**, *adjective*, made of oak.

oak-apple *noun*
a rosy apple-shaped gall formed by a gall-wasp on oak tree branches.

oakum (*say* o-kum) *noun*
loose fibre, such as jute or hemp, used for filling joints or seams in ships, etc.

oar (*say* or) *noun*
a long thin piece of wood with a flat blade at one end, fitted into a rowlock and used to row a boat.
put one's oar in, to interfere.
Word Family: **oar**, *verb*; **oarsman**, *noun*, a person who rows a boat.

oasis (*say* o-aysis) *noun*
plural is **oases** (*say* o-ay-seez)
1. an area in a desert made fertile by water from a spring or a stream.
2. a haven of peace amidst turmoil.
[Greek]

oast *noun*
an oven for drying hops and malt.
Word Family: **oast-house**, *noun*, a building containing an oast.

oat *noun*
(*usually plural*) a cereal plant cultivated for its edible seed.
sow one's wild oats, to indulge in dissipation while young, before having to settle down.
Word Family: **oaten**, *adjective*, made of oats or oat straw.

oath *noun*
1. a formal promise made in the name of a god or holy person.
2. an irreverent or blasphemous expression.

oatmeal *noun*
ground oats, used to make porridge, cakes, etc.

obbligato (*say* obbli-**gah**-toe) *noun*
Music: an instrumental accompaniment for a solo voice, as an essential part of a larger composition.
[Italian, obligatory]

obdurate (*say* **ob**dew-rit) *adjective*
1. hard-hearted or stubborn.
2. refusing to repent.
Word Family: **obduracy**, **obdurateness**, *nouns.*
[from Latin]

obedient (*say* a-**bee**di-unt) *adjective*
willing to obey.
Word Family: **obedience**, *noun*, a) the state of being obedient, b) the act of obeying; **obediently**, *adverb.*

obeisance (*say* a-**bay**-s'nce) *noun*
a bow or curtsy expressing respect or reverence.
[French, obedience, allegiance]

obelisk (*say* **obba**-lisk) *noun*
a tapering stone column with four sides and a pyramidal top, common as an ancient Egyptian monument.
[Greek *obeliskos* a pointed instrument]

obese (*say* o-**beece**) *adjective*
excessively fat.
Word Family: **obesity**, *noun*; **obesely**, *adverb.*
[Latin *obesus* having overeaten]

obey (*say* o-**bay**) *verb*
to do as commanded or instructed: 'you must *obey* your parents'.
Usage: 'you must *obey* your intuition' (= act according to).
[Latin *ob* towards + *audire* to hear]

obfuscate (*say* **ob**fa-skate) *verb*
to obscure or confuse: 'his turgid style *obfuscates* the sense of his essay'.
Word Family: **obfuscation**, *noun.*
[Latin *ob* very + *fuscus* murky]

obituary (*say* a-**bit**-yoo-ree) ***noun***
a notice of a death of a person, sometimes accompanied by an article about his or her life.
[Latin *obitus* death]

object (*say* **ob**-jekt) ***noun***
1. anything which can be seen, touched or perceived by any of the senses.
2. a person or thing to which attention, thought, action, etc. is directed: a) 'the unhappy child was an *object* of pity'; b) 'the *object* of the meeting is to elect a president'.
3. *Grammar:* a word or words describing the person or thing to which the activity of a verb is directed. *Example*: the boy ate *a large green apple.*
the **indirect object** represents the person or thing to or for whom the action of the verb is performed. *Example*: the boy gave ***his mother*** a hug.
the **direct object** represents the person or thing upon which the action of the verb is directed. *Example*: the girl bought *a new hat.*
object (*say* ob-**jekt**) ***verb***
to disapprove of, dislike, feel or argue against: 'I *object* to your coming in without knocking first'.
Word Family: **objector**, ***noun***, a person who objects; **objectify** (**objectified**, **objectifying**), *verb*, a) to make objective, b) to present as an object.
[Latin *objectus* thrown in the way]

objection (*say* ob-**jek**-sh'n) ***noun***
1. a) something said or offered in opposition, disagreement or disapproval. b) a reason for such disagreement.
2. dislike.

objectionable (*say* ob-**jek**-sh'n-a-b'l) ***adjective***
unpleasant or offensive: 'an *objectionable* person'.
Word Family: **objectionably**, ***adverb.***

objective (*say* ob-**jek**-tiv) ***adjective***
1. relating to something material, as distinct from thoughts, feelings, etc.: 'the *objective* universe'.
2. not influenced by personal feelings or opinions: 'an *objective* criticism'.
objective ***noun***
1. something which is aimed at or striven for: 'the main *objective* of the war was to recapture lost land'.
2. the lens or lenses in an optical instrument, such as a microscope, closest to the object being viewed. Compare EYEPIECE.
Word Family: **objectivity** (*say* objek-**tivvi**-tee), ***noun***, a) the quality of being objective, b) visible or external reality; **objectively**, ***adverb.***

objective case
Grammar: see CASE (1).

objectivism (*say* ob-**jekti**-vizm) ***noun***
Philosophy: the belief that knowledge should be based on external realities rather than personal feelings. Compare SUBJECTIVISM.

object lesson
an example or illustration of a moral, principle, etc.

objet d'art (*say* **ob**-*zh*ay dar)
an object valued for its artistic worth.
[French *objet* object + *d'art* of art]

objurgate (*say* **ob**ja-gate) ***verb***
to reproach or scold violently.
Word Family: **objurgation**, ***noun.***
[Latin *ob* much + *jurgare* to quarrel]

oblate (1) *adjective*
(of something nearly spherical) flattened at top and bottom, like the earth.

oblate (2) ***noun***
Christian: a person dedicated to religious life or work, without having taken official vows.

oblation (*say* a-**blay**-sh'n) ***noun***
a religious or charitable offering.
Word Family: **oblatory** (*say* **obla**-tree), *adjective.*
[Latin *oblatus* offered]

obligated (*say* **obli**-gatid) ***verb***
morally or legally bound: 'you are *obligated* to pay this fine'.
obligate (*say* **obli**-git) *adjective*
Biology: (of an organism) restricted to a particular type of life, as some parasites that must live with a certain host.

obligation (*say* obli-**gay**-sh'n) ***noun***
1. something which one is or feels obliged, required etc. to do: 'she felt an *obligation* not to smoke in the doctor's waiting room'.
2. a debt, especially of gratitude: 'I am under an *obligation* to you for all your kindness'.
Word Family: **obligatory** (*say* **obligga**-tree), *adjective*, required or compulsory; **obligatorily**, *adverb.*
[Latin *ob* down + *ligare* to bind]

oblige *verb*
1. to be or make compulsory: 'students are *obliged* to attend all lessons'.
2. to place under a debt of gratitude: 'I am *obliged* to you for all your help'.

3. to do a favour for: 'the singer *obliged* the audience with another song'.
Word Family: **obliging**, *adjective*, helpful, polite or kind; **obligingly**, *adverb*; **obligingness**, *noun*.

oblique (*say* a–**bleek**) *adjective*
1. slanting or sloping.
2. not straight or direct.
Usage: 'his *oblique* answers irritated the interviewer and the audience' (= indirect, evasive).
3. *Biology:* having unequal sides, e.g. a leaf.
obliquity (*say* a–**blik**–wit–ee) *noun*
1. a departure from correct conduct or sound judgement.
2. the state of being oblique.
Word Family: **obliqueness**, *noun*; **obliquely**, *adverb*.
[from Latin]

obliterate (*say* a–**blitta**–rate) *verb*
to destroy or remove all traces of something.
Word Family: **obliteration**, *noun*.
[Latin *ob* over + *littera* a letter]

oblivion (*say* a–**blivv**iun) *noun*
1. the state of being forgotten.
2. forgetfulness or disregard.
[from Latin]

oblivious (*say* a–**blivv**ius) *adjective*
1. forgetful.
2. regardless or unaware: 'he seems *oblivious* of her faults'.
Word Family: **obliviousness**, *noun*; **obliviously**, *adverb*.

oblong *adjective*
elongated, especially having a longer length than width.
oblong *noun*
a rectangle, usually having a longer length than width.
[from Latin]

obloquy (*say* **obla**–kwee) *noun*
1. abuse, blame or reproach.
2. disgrace or subjection to abuse.
[Latin *ob* against + *loqui* to speak]

obnoxious (*say* ob–**nok**shus) *adjective*
offensive or unpleasant.
Word Family: **obnoxiously**, *adverb*; **obnoxiousness**, *noun*.
[Latin *ob* exposed to + *noxa* harm]

oboe *noun*
Music: a double-reed, wooden wind instrument consisting of a slender conical tube.
Word Family: **oboist**, *noun*, a person who plays the oboe.
[French *hautbois* high wood]

obscene (*say* ob–**seen**) *adjective*
indecent or morally offensive.
Word Family: **obscenely**, *adverb*; **obscenity** (*say* ob–**senni**–tee), *noun*, a) the quality of being obscene, b) anything which is obscene or offensive.
[from Latin]

obscurantism (*say* ob–skew–**rant**izm) *noun*
an opposition to intellectual achievement, inquiry or knowledge.
Word Family: **obscurantist**, *noun*, *adjective*.

obscure (*say* ob–**skewer**) *adjective*
1. dim or hard to see: 'an *obscure* shape in the shadows'.
2. hard to understand: 'the meaning of the book is too *obscure* for me'.
3. not well known: 'the stranger had an *obscure*, mysterious past'.
Word Family: **obscure**, *verb*, to make dark or unclear; **obscurity**, *noun*, a) the state of being obscure, b) darkness; **obscurely**, *adverb*.
[from Latin]

obsequies (*say* **obsi**–kwiz) *plural noun*
a funeral ceremony.

obsequious (*say* ob–**seekwi**–us) *adjective*
servile or excessively humble.
Word Family: **obsequiously**, *adverb*; **obsequiousness**, *noun*.
[from Latin]

observance (*say* ob–**zer**–v'nce) *noun*
1. the act of obeying or following a law, custom, etc.: '*observance* of the law is enforced by police'.
2. a particular procedure, custom or ceremony: 'a day of religious *observances*'.

observant (*say* ob–**zer**–v'nt) *adjective*
1. alert or quick to notice: 'it was very *observant* of you to notice the button fall'.
2. watchful or attentive: 'if you were more *observant*, you would not make those mistakes'.
Word Family: **observantly**, *adverb*.

observation (*say* obza–**vay**–sh'n) *noun*
1. the act of observing or watching: 'close *observation* of detail'.
2. a remark or comment.
3. any information or record gained by observing or watching: 'weather *observations*'.
Word Family: **observational**, *adjective*.

observatory (*say* ob**zerva**-tree) *noun*
a room or building fitted with apparatus for observing stars, weather, etc., usually equipped with telescopes.

observe (*say* ob-**zerv**) *verb*
1. to watch or look at: a) '*observe* carefully how I do it'; b) 'I only came to *observe* the meeting, not take part'.
Usages:
a) 'do you *observe* Christmas in your country?' (= pay tribute to, celebrate).
b) 'you must *observe* the road laws' (= obey).
2. to comment or remark.
Word Family: **observer**, *noun*, a person who observes, especially as distinct from taking part; **observable**, *adjective*, able to be seen or noticed; **observably**, *adverb*.
[Latin *ob* before + *servare* to keep]

obsess *verb*
to occupy or dominate the thoughts or feelings continually: 'he was *obsessed* by a fear of burglars'.
Word Family: **obsessive**, *adjective*, tending to obsess; **obsession** (*say* ob-**sesh**'n), *noun*, a) something which obsesses or haunts, b) the state of being obsessed or haunted; **obsessional**, *adjective*.
[Latin *obsessus* besieged]

obsidian *noun*
Geology: a black, natural glass produced in small amounts by volcanoes, much used by primitive man for weapons and tools.

obsolete (*say* **obsa**-leet) *adjective*
out-of-date or no longer used.
Word Family: **obsolescent** (*say* obsa-**less**'nt), *adjective*, becoming obsolete; **obsolescence**, *noun*.
[Latin *obsoletus* worn out]

obstacle (*say* **obsti**-k'l) *noun*
something which stands in the way or obstructs.

obstetrics (*say* ob-**stetriks**) *noun*
the study and care of women before, during and after childbirth. Compare GYNAECOLOGY.
Word Family: **obstetric**, *adjective*; **obstetrician** (*say* obsta-**trish**'n), *noun*.
[Latin *obstetrix* one who stands by]

obstinate (*say* **obsti**-nit) *adjective*
a) stubborn: 'she persisted with her *obstinate* refusal'. b) difficult to manage, control, etc.: 'it is impossible to handle such an *obstinate* horse'.
Word Family: **obstinacy** (*say* **ob**-stinna-see), *noun*; **obstinately**, *adverb*.
[Latin *obstinans* persisting in]

obstreperous (*say* ab**streppa**-rus) *adjective*
unruly or noisily resisting control.

obstruct *verb*
to block, close up or make difficult to proceed, pass, etc.: a) 'the fallen rocks *obstructed* our path'; b) 'the Opposition members tried to *obstruct* the legislation'.
Word Family: **obstruction**, *noun*, a) the act of obstructing or hindering, b) anything which obstructs or blocks; **obstructive**, *adjective*; **obstructiveness**, *noun*.
[Latin *ob* in the way + *structus* built]

obstructionist (*say* ab-**struk**-sh'n-ist) *noun*
a person who deliberately obstructs, especially in legislation, etc.
Word Family: **obstructionism**, *noun*.

obtain *verb*
to come to possess, especially as a result of effort or asking: 'did you *obtain* permission to ride the horse?'.
Word Family: **obtainable**, *adjective*.
[Latin *obtinere* to keep firm hold on]

obtrude *verb*
to intrude or push oneself forward.
Word Family: **obtrusion** (*say* ob-**troo**-*zh*'n), *noun*; **obtrusive**, *adjective*; **obtrusively**, *adverb*.
[Latin *ob* in the way + *trudere* to thrust]

obtuse (*say* ob-**tewce**) *adjective*
1. not sharp or acute.
Usage: 'his *obtuse* answers to such simple questions embarrassed us' (= stupid, unintelligent).
2. *Maths:* relating to an angle greater than a right angle but less than two right angles (90–180°).
Word Family: **obtusely**, *adverb*; **obtuseness**, *noun*.
[Latin *ob* towards + *tusus* blunted]
Common Error: OBTUSE, ABSTRUSE should not be confused: *obtuse* means stupid or slow to understand: 'an *obtuse* student', whereas *abstruse* means obscure or difficult to understand: 'an *abstruse* academic debate'.

obverse *adjective*
facing towards the observer.
obverse *noun*
1. a matching or duplicate part, situation, etc.
2. the main face of a coin, medal or postage stamp. Compare REVERSE.
Word Family: **obversely**, *adverb*.

obviate (*say* **ob**–vee–ate) *verb*
to get rid of or prevent difficulties, objections, etc.
Word Family: **obviation,** *noun.*
[Late Latin *obviare* to stand in the way of]

obvious *adjective*
easily seen or understood.
Word Family: **obviously,** *adverb;* **obviousness,** *noun.*
[Latin *obvius* in the way]

ocarina (*say* ocka–**reena**) *noun*
a toy musical instrument with finger–stops and a flute–like tone.
[Italian *oca* goose (as it is the size and shape of a goose's egg)]

occasion (*say* a–**kay**–*zh*'n) *noun*
1. a particular time: 'we have met on several *occasions*'.
2. a special or important event, time, etc.: 'on the *occasion* of your wedding'.
Usage: 'I would like to meet her if the *occasion* arises' (= opportunity).
3. the cause or reason for some action or result: 'what was the *occasion* of his dismissal from the job?'.
rise to the occasion, to show oneself able to deal with matters.
Word Family: **occasion,** *verb,* to cause or bring about.
[Latin *occasio* a happening]

occasional (*say* a–**kay**–*zh*'n–al) *adjective*
1. happening from time to time: '*occasional* rain fell but did not stop the match'.
2. designed for special but not regular use: 'the poet laureate writes *occasional* verse for royal or national events'.
Word Family: **occasionally,** *adverb,* now and then.

occident (*say* **ok**si–d'nt) *noun*
the west or regions in the west.
Word Family: **occidental,** *adjective;* **occidental,** *noun,* (usually capital) an inhabitant of Europe or America.
[Latin *occidens* the west, sunset]

occlude (*say* ok–**lood**) *verb*
1. to close, obstruct or block up.
2. *Chemistry:* (of a solid) to absorb and retain gases.
Word Family: **occlusive,** *adjective.*
[from Latin]

occluded front
also called an **occlusion**
Weather: see FRONT.

occlusion (*say* ok–**loo**–*zh*'n) *noun*
the state of being occluded, e.g. the contact between teeth when the jaws are closed.

occult (*say* **ok**–ult) *adjective*
1. mysterious, supernatural or beyond the scope of human knowledge: 'spiritualism is an *occult* science'.
2. secret or esoteric.
occult *noun*
1. any occult science, study or practice.
2. that which is mysterious or related to magic and the supernatural.
Word Family: **occultism,** *noun,* the study of the occult; **occultist,** *noun.*
[Latin *occultus* hidden]

occupant (*say* **ok**–yoo–p'nt) *noun*
a person who occupies a place, position or building.
Word Family: **occupancy,** *noun,* a) the fact of being an occupant, b) the act or time of occupying.

occupation (*say* ok–yoo–**pay**–sh'n) *noun*
1. a regular activity, especially a person's employment or job.
2. a) the act or time of occupying: 'the people resisted the *occupation* of their country by the enemy'. b) the state of being occupied: '*occupation* with the task took all his attention'.
Word Family: **occupational,** *adjective,* relating to an occupation or activity.

occupational therapy
Medicine: a type of therapy designed to assist recovery from illness or injury by exercising the mind and muscles with handicrafts, painting, etc.

occupy (*say* **ok**–yoo–pie) *verb*
(occupied, occupying)
1. to fill or take up: 'gardening *occupies* much of my spare time'.
2. to live or have an established place in: 'nobody has *occupied* that house for many years'.
Usages:
a) 'the President *occupies* a position of great responsibility' (= has).
b) 'she was so *occupied* with writing that she did not hear the doorbell' (= busy).
3. to take possession or control by invasion, military conquest, etc.
Word Family: **occupier,** *noun.*
[from Latin]

occur (*say* a–**ker**) *verb*
(occurred, occurring)
to happen or take place: 'the accident *occurred* yesterday'.
Usage: 'it did not *occur* to me that the restaurant would be closed' (= suggest itself).

occurrence (*say* a–**kurr**ence) *noun*
1. an event or incident.
2. the act of happening or occurring.
[Latin *occurrere* to run towards]

ocean (*say* **o**–shun) *noun*
1. a) the very large area of salt water which covers about 71 per cent of the earth's surface. b) a major division of this: 'the Pacific *Ocean*'.
2. a very large area or amount: 'an *ocean* of faces in the crowd'.
Word Family: **oceanic** (*say* o–shee–**ann**ik), *adjective,* a) of or relating to the ocean, b) vast or enormous.
[from Latin]

oceanography (*say* o–shun–**og**ra–fee) *noun*
the study of oceans and ocean beds, a branch of geography.
Word Family: **oceanographer**, *noun.*

ocelot (*say* **oss**a–lot) *noun*
a small, leopard–like mammal found in Central and South America.
[Amerindian]

ochre (*rhymes with* poker) **ocher** *noun*
1. any of various types of earth, ranging from pale yellow to reddish–brown, used as pigments.
2. a pale yellowish–brown colour.
Word Family: **ochre**, *adjective.*
[Greek *okhros* pale yellow]

o'clock *adverb*
of or by the clock: 'the time is two *o'clock*'.

octa–
a prefix meaning eight, as in *octagon.* A variant is **octo–**, as in *octopus.*

octagon *noun*
any closed, plane figure with eight straight sides.
Word Family: **octagonal** (*say* ok–**tagg**a–n'l), *adjective.*
[OCTA– + Greek *gonia* a corner]

octahedron (*say* okta–**hee**–dr'n) *noun*
a solid or hollow body with eight plane faces.
Word Family: **octahedral**, *adjective.*
[OCTA– + Greek *hedra* a seat]

octane *noun*
any of a group of 18 isomeric hydrocarbons (formula C_8H_{18}).
octane number
a measure of the antiknock properties of a fuel.

octant *noun*
a sector equal to an eighth of a circle or an eighth of the circumference.

octave (*say* **ok**tiv) *noun*
1. *Music:* an interval of eight steps. The frequency of any note is half that of the same note one octave higher.
2. *Poetry:* a stanza with eight lines.

octavo (*say* ok–**tah**–vo) *noun*
a paper size achieved by folding a sheet into eight.

octet *noun*
1. a) a group of eight musicians. b) a musical composition for eight musicians or instruments.
2. *Poetry:* an octave.
3. any group of eight people or things.

octo–
a variant of the prefix **octa–**.

October *noun*
the tenth month of the year in the Gregorian calendar.
[Latin, the eighth month of the Roman calendar]

octogenarian (*say* okta–j'n–**air**ian) *noun*
a person who is over 80 but less than 90 years old.
Word Family: **octogenarian**, *adjective,* a) being 80 years old, b) being between 80 and 90 years old.
[Latin *octogeni* eighty each]

octopus *noun*
plural is **octopuses** or **octopi** (*say* **ok**ta–pie)
a marine animal having a soft body and eight long tentacles with suckers.
[OCTO– + Greek *pous* foot]

ocular (*say* **ok**–yoo–la) *adjective*
of or relating to the eye.
Word Family: **ocular**, *noun,* the eyepiece of an optical instrument.

oculist (*say* **ok**–yoo–list) *noun*
a doctor who treats diseases of the eye.
[Latin *oculus* eye]

odd *adjective*
1. puzzlingly different from the usual or normal.
2. not matching: '*odd* socks'.
3. *Maths:* having a remainder of one when divided by two, e.g. 3, 5, etc.
4. extra or additional: 'three pounds and a few *odd* pence'.
Usages:
a) 'he does gardening and *odd* jobs around the house' (= not fixed, occasional).
b) 'there were *fifty–odd* people at the lecture' (= about fifty).
Word Family: **oddly**, *adverb,* in an odd or unusual manner; **oddness**,

noun; **oddity,** *noun,* a person or thing that is odd.

oddment *noun*
an object or part which is left over, part of an incomplete set, etc.: '*oddments* of dressmaking fabric'.

odds *plural noun*
1. the difference between the money placed on a bet and the money that would be received as winning payment.
2. chances or possibilities: 'what are the *odds* that the lost child will be found?'.
3. the chances of winning or losing: 'she's fighting against fearful *odds*'.
Phrases:
be at odds, to disagree or quarrel.
odds-on, (*informal*) almost certain.

odds and ends
any remaining or miscellaneous bits.

ode *noun*
a usually dignified, lyric poem, addressed to someone or something.
[Greek]

odious (*say* **o**-dee-us) *adjective*
hateful or repulsive.
Word Family: **odium,** *noun,* a) an intense hatred or disgust, b) reproach or discredit connected with something hateful.
[Latin *odium* dislike]

odontology (*say* odd-on-**tolla**-jee) *noun*
the science or study of the anatomy, growth and diseases of teeth.
Word Family: **odontologist,** *noun*; **odontological** (*say* oddonta-**loji**-k'l), *adjective.*
[Greek *odontos* of a tooth + -LOGY]

odour (*say* **o**-da) *noun*
in America spelt **odor**
a smell or scent.
Word Family: **odorous,** *adjective,* having an odour, especially a pleasant one; **odorously,** *adverb.*
[from Latin]

odyssey (*say* **oddi**-see) *noun*
a long wandering or series of wanderings.
[after *Odysseus,* a hero in Greek mythology who wandered for 10 years]

oedema (*say* ee-**deema**) *noun*
in America spelt **edema**
also called **dropsy**
Anatomy: an excess of fluid in the tissues.
[Greek *oidema* a swelling]

Oedipus complex (*say* **eedipus kompleks**)
Psychology: the complex of emotions said by Freud to occur when a boy adores his mother so much that he becomes jealous of and hostile to his father, often unconsciously. See ELECTRA COMPLEX.
[after *Oedipus,* a king of Thebes in Greek mythology, who unknowingly killed his father and married his mother]

o'er *adverb, preposition*
an old word for over.

oesophagus (*say* ee-**soffa**-gus) *noun*
plural is **oesophagi**
also called the **gullet**
Anatomy: a muscular tube connecting the mouth to the stomach and through which food passes.

oestrogen (*say* **eestra**-jen) *noun*
a female sex hormone secreted in mammals by the ovaries, which controls part of the oestrous cycle.

oestrous cycle (*say* **eestrus sigh**-k'l)
Biology: the reproductive cycle in a mature female mammal, which recurs in the absence of pregnancy and involves ovulation, increased sexual urge and changes in the uterus.

oestrus (*say* **eestrus**) *noun*
also called **heat** or **rut**
the period of increased sexual urge during the oestrous cycle.

of (*say* ov) *preposition*
1. a word used to indicate the following:
a) (material, contents) 'a packet *of* soap'.
b) (distance, separation) 'a few kilometres west *of* here'.
c) (inclusion, possession) 'a cousin *of* ours'.
d) (origin, production, source) 'the sonnets *of* Shakespeare'.
e) (cause) 'the dog died *of* grief'.
f) (identity, name) 'the city *of* Brisbane'.
2. having: 'he is a man *of* fine taste'.
3. about or concerning: 'let's talk *of* a more happy event'.

off *preposition*
1. away from: a) 'the vase fell *off* the desk'; b) 'he is *off* work until he recovers completely'.
Usages:
a) 'the shop is in a lane *off* King Street' (= leading out of).
b) (*informal*) 'I am *off* potatoes until I lose weight' (= abstaining from).
c) 'all goods are selling for £2 *off* the usual price' (= less than).

d) 'the champion seemed to be *off* his game today' (= not up to the usual standard of).
2. from or with what is provided: 'the survivors had lived *off* the island fruits for many months'.
off *adverb*
1. so as to be no longer in place, attached or in contact: a) 'he took *off* his coat'; b) 'please switch *off* the lights before you leave'.
2. away: a) 'he drove *off* quickly'; b) 'Christmas is only a month *off*'.
Usages:
a) 'our employees get five weeks *off* a year' (= free from work).
b) 'this spray will kill *off* all insect pests' (= completely, successfully).
Phrases:
be off, 'we must *be off* before it gets dark' (= leave).
on and off, off and on, see ON.
off *adjective*
1. disconnected: 'is the wireless *off*?'.
Usages:
a) 'the party is *off* because of rain' (= cancelled).
b) 'the menu included mackerel, but the waiter told us it was *off* (= no longer available).
c) 'this milk is *off* (= bad).
2. *Cricket:* being on the same side of the field as the batsman's bat: 'fielding on the *off* side'. Compare LEG.
Word Family: **off**, *noun*, a) the state of being off, b) (Cricket) the off side; **off!**, *interjection*, leave! go away!

offal *noun*
the intestines, heart, kidneys, liver, etc. of an animal, often eaten for their nutritional value.

off-beat *adjective*
unconventional.

off-chance *noun*
a remote possibility.

off-colour *adjective*
1. defective in colour.
2. (*informal*) slightly unwell.

offence (*say* **a-fence**) *noun*
in America spelt **offense**
1. a crime or transgression: 'it is an *offence* to smoke in this theatre'.
2. a) the state of being offended: 'he took *offence* at what I said'. b) something which offends: 'the rubbish tip is an *offence* to the neighbourhood'.
3. the act of attacking: 'weapons of *offence*'.

offend (*say* **a-fend**) *verb*
to hurt or cause resentment: 'her abrupt manner *offends* many people'.
Word Family: **offender**, *noun*, a person who offends, especially one who breaks the law.
[Latin *offendere* to strike against]

offensive (*say* **a-fen-siv**) *adjective*
1. offending the mind or feelings.
2. relating to an attack or aggression.
Word Family: **offensively**, *adverb*; **offensiveness**, *noun*; **offensive**, *noun*, an attacking position or action.

offer *verb*
to put forward for acceptance or rejection: a) 'she *offered* a suggestion'; b) 'how much will you *offer* for the house?'.
Usage: 'the antique shop *offered* old cups and saucers' (= presented for sale).
Word Family: **offer**, *noun*.
[Latin *offerre* to bring before]

offering *noun*
anything offered or given.

offertory (*say* **offa-tree**) *noun*
an offering, such as the collection of money taken during a church service.

offhand *adjective*
1. without previous thought or preparation: 'an *offhand* guess'.
2. disdainful or abrupt in manner: 'her *offhand* refusal irritated me'.

office (*say* **off-iss**) *noun*
1. a) a room or building where administrative work, professional duties, etc. are carried out. b) the staff working in such a place.
2. the duty, function or position of a particular person: 'he holds the *office* of secretary to the football club'.
3. a department or branch of an organization: a) 'a Post *Office*'; b) 'the ticket *office*'.
4. a religious service or set of prayers, etc.
[Latin *opificium* work]

office-bearer *noun*
a person who holds office.

officer (*say* **offi-sa**) *noun*
a person having a position of rank and authority, e.g. in the armed forces, police force, etc.

official (*say* **a-fish'l**) *adjective*
1. of, relating to, or authorized by a recognized authority: a) 'the President has *official* powers'; b) 'this is the first *official* report'.

2. formal or ceremonious: 'an *official* dinner was held for the Prince'.
official *noun*
a person who holds a position, especially in a large organization.
Word Family: **officially**, *adverb.*

officialdom (*say* a-**fish**'l-dum) *noun*
1. all officials.
2. the practices or policies characteristic of officials.

officialese (*say* a-**fish**a-leez) *noun*
a style of writing or speaking said to be characteristic of officials and considered to be too complicated or difficult to understand.

officiate (*say* a-**fish**i-ate) *verb*
to carry out special duties, such as performing the office of a priest or minister, taking charge of a meeting, etc.
Word Family: **officiator**, *noun.*

officious (*say* a-**fish**us) *adjective*
giving unwanted advice or instruction.
Word Family: **officiously**, *adverb*; **officiousness**, *noun.*

offing *noun*
in the offing, likely to occur, appear or be offered.

off-licence *noun*
a shop where alcohol is sold to be drunk elsewhere.

offload *verb*
to unload.

off-peak *adjective*
not at its maximum degree of activity, etc.: '*off-peak* traffic'.

off-putting *adjective*
(*informal*) discouraging or disconcerting.

off-season *noun*
the time of year that is not the most popular for something.

offset *verb*
(**offset, offsetting**)
to compensate for or balance out: 'the company's small profit could not *offset* the losses'.
offset *noun*
1. something that compensates.
2. a method of printing in which the image is transferred from the plate on to paper by a rubber-covered cylinder.

offshoot *noun*
1. something that branches out or originates from a particular source, such as a shoot from the main stem of a plant.
2. a by-product.

offshore *adjective, adverb*
1. off or away from the shore: 'an *offshore* breeze blew the raft out to sea'.
2. at a distance from the shore.

offside *adjective*
1. a) of or relating to the right-hand side of a vehicle where traffic drives on the left. b) the right side of a horse. Compare NEARSIDE.
2. *Sport:* being so placed in front of the opponents' goal that one incurs a penalty if one touches the ball.

offspring *noun*
plural is **offspring**
1. a descendant of an animal or plant.
2. a product or result of something.

off-the-record *adjective*
not intended to be made public.

off-white *noun*
a yellowish or greyish-white colour.

oft *adverb*
an old word for often.

often (*say* **off**'n) *adverb*
occurring repeatedly.

ogle *verb*
to stare at, especially in an amorous or flirtatious way.
Word Family: **ogle**, *noun.*

ogre (*say* o-ga) *noun*
1. a man-eating mythological giant.
2. a person who is cruel, unpleasant or frightening.
Word Family: **ogrish** (*say* **o**-grish), *adjective*; **ogress**, *noun*, a female ogre.

ohm (*say* ome) *noun*
the SI unit of electrical resistance.
[after G. S. *Ohm*, 1787–1854, a German physicist]

-oid
a suffix of nouns and adjectives indicating similarity, as in *asteroid.*
[Greek *eidos* form]

oil *noun*
1. a) any of a large group of substances which are liquid at 20°C, insoluble in water but soluble in organic solvents and used to make a wide variety of products, such as ointments, fuel, lubricants, etc. b) any similar substance.
2. a) an oil paint. b) an oil painting.
pour oil on troubled waters, to calm or pacify.
oil *verb*
to smear or lubricate with oil.

oilcake *noun*
a mass of linseed or cottonseed after the oil has been extracted, used as fodder for cattle or as a fertilizer.

oilcloth *noun*
any fabric made waterproof by using oil.

oilfield *noun*
any area where oil is found.

oil paint
also called **oil colour**
a mixture of pigment and oil for painting.
Word Family: **oil painting**, a work produced with oil paints.

oilskin *noun*
a) a fabric treated with oil to make it waterproof, used for fishermen's clothes, etc. b) any clothes made from this fabric.

oily *adjective*
1. of, like or covered with oil.
2. too smooth or fawning in speech or manner.

ointment *noun*
any substance, such as a paste, cream or liquid, usually medicated, applied to the skin.

OK (*say* o-**kay**) *adjective, adverb*
also spelt **okay** or **oke**
(*informal*) all right; correct.
OK *verb*
(*informal*) to endorse or approve something.
Word Family: **OK,** *noun,* an approval or endorsement.
[possibly from the *OK Club* which supported a presidential candidate from Old Kinderhook, New York State, 1840]

okra *noun*
a tall West African herb, the pods of which are used as a vegetable.

old *adjective*
(**older** or **elder, oldest** or **eldest**)
1. having existed or lived for a relatively long time: 'he was an *old* man of 98 when he died'.
Usages:
a) 'an *old* head on young shoulders' (= mature, sensible).
b) 'I met an *old* school friend yesterday' (= former).
c) 'he always uses the same *old* excuse' (= familiar, worn-out).
2. having a specified age: 'she could read when she was three years *old*'.
3. dear or cherished through long association: a) 'good *old* Tim'; b) 'the *old* country'.
old *noun*
former times: 'we studied the kings of *old*'.

old boy
(*often capital*) a former member of a particular school: 'I am going to an *Old Boys'* reunion'.
old boy network, favouritism, e.g. in filling a vacancy, due to the tendency of old boys of the same school to help each other, possibly to the detriment of others or of efficiency.

olden *adjective*
a poetic word for old.

Old English
1. *Language:* see ENGLISH.
2. *Printing:* see GOTHIC.

old-fashioned (*say* old-**fash**und) *adjective*
out-of-date or no longer fashionable.

old hat
(*informal*) old-fashioned.

old man's beard
wild clematis in its winter form, clothing hedgerows.

Old Master
a) any of the leading or distinguished early European painters, especially from the 15th to the 18th century. b) a painting by such an artist.

old school tie
a) a tie indicating a man's former independent school. b) the alleged traditionalism and clannishness of the wearers of these.

oldster *noun*
(*informal*) an old person.

Old Testament
Religion: the first part of the Bible, containing the Jewish scriptures. Compare NEW TESTAMENT.

old-timer *noun*
(*informal*) a person who has lived, resided, been a member, etc. for a very long time.

old wives' tale
a traditional, superstitious belief.

Old World
the countries in Europe, western Asia and north Africa.
Word Family: **old-world,** *adjective,* a) of or relating to past times, b) of or relating to the Old World.

oleaginous (*say* o-lee-ajinus) *adjective*

oily or greasy.
[Latin *oleum* oil]

oleander (*say* o-lee-**anda**) ***noun***
any of a group of large, poisonous, evergreen shrubs with delicate white or pink flowers.

olefine series (*say* **o**-lee-fin seer-reez)
also called **olefines** or **alkene series**
Chemistry: a homologous series of aliphatic hydrocarbons (general formula C_nH_{2n}), such as ethylene (formula C_2H_4).

olfactory (*say* ol-**fakta**-ree) ***adjective***
of or relating to the sense of smell.
[Latin *olfacere* to smell]

oligarchy (*say* **olli**-gar-kee) ***noun***
a) a government in which a small group of people has power. b) a country with this form of government.
Word Family: **oligarchic** (*say* olli-**garkik**), **oligarchical**, *adjective*; **oligarch**, *noun.*
[Greek *oligos* few + *arkhos* a leader]

Oligocene (*say* olligo-seen *or* olla-ga-seen) ***noun***
Geology: see TERTIARY.
[Greek *oligos* few + *kainos* modern (that is, having few modern forms of life)]

olive (*say* **olliv**) ***noun***
1. a small, green or black, oval fruit with a stone, usually pickled or crushed for its oil.
2. a deep, yellowish or brownish-green colour.
Word Family: **olive**, *adjective.*
[from Latin]

olive branch
something offered as a symbol of peace.

olivine (*say* olliv-**een**) ***noun***
Geology: a dense, common mineral (magnesium silicate), occurring in olive green masses in basic igneous rocks.

-ologist (*say* **olla**-jist)
a variant of the suffix **-logist**.

-ology (*say* **olla**-jee)
a variant of the suffix **-logy**.

olympian (*say* a-**limpian**) ***noun***
1. a person who is calm, aloof and disdainful.
2. *Greek mythology:* (*capital*) one of the gods, believed to live on Mount Olympus.
Word Family: **olympian**, *adjective.*

ombudsman (*say* **om**-budz-man) ***noun***
a government official appointed to investigate complaints by individuals against the government or civil service.
[Swedish, legal representative]

omega (*say* **o**-migga) ***noun***
1. the 24th and last letter of the Greek alphabet.
2. the end of anything. Compare ALPHA.

omelette (*say* **omlet**) ***noun***
also spelt **omelet**
a dish of eggs beaten and lightly fried, often eaten with a sweet or savoury filling.

omen (*say* **o**-men) ***noun***
a sign of a coming event, often regarded as a threat or warning: 'a bad *omen*'.
Word Family: **omen**, *verb.*
[Latin]

ominous (*say* **ommi**-nus) ***adjective***
threatening or suggesting evil.
Word Family: **ominously**, *adverb.*

omit (*say* a-**mit**) ***verb***
(omitted, omitting)
to leave out or fail to do something.
Word Family: **omission** (*say* a-**mish**'n), *noun.*
[from Latin]

omni- (*say* **om**-nee)
a prefix meaning all, as in *omnipresent.*
[Latin *omnis*]

omnibus (*say* **omni**-bus) ***noun***
1. a bus.
2. a single book containing several works on a particular topic or by one author.
Word Family: **omnibus**, *adjective*, covering several items or purposes.
[Latin, for all]

omnipotent (*say* om-**nippa**-t'nt) *adjective*
having great or unlimited power.
Word Family: **omnipotence**, *noun.*

omnipresent (*say* omni-**prezz**'nt) *adjective*
present in all places at the same time.
Word Family: **omnipresence**, *noun.*

omniscient (*say* om-**nissi**-ent) *adjective*
having unlimited knowledge.
Word Family: **omniscience**, *noun*; **omnisciently**, *adverb.*
[OMNI- + Latin *sciens* knowledge]

omnivorous (*say* om-**nivva**-rus) *adjective*

(of an organism) eating all types of food.
[OMNI– + Latin *vorare* to devour]

on *preposition*
a word used to indicate the following:
1. (support, contact) a) 'the book *on* the desk'; b) 'the child scribbled *on* the wall'; c) 'a scar *on* the face'.
2. (time, occasion) a) '*on* Monday'; b) '*on* my arrival home'.
3. (about, concerning) 'a discussion *on* conservation'.
4. (association, activity) a) 'to sit *on* a jury'; b) 'to go *on* holiday'; c) 'she is *on* her best behaviour'.
5. (direction) '*on* the left'.
6. (basis, reason) '*on* good authority'.
7. (proximity) a) 'a town *on* the river'; b) 'just *on* a year ago'.
8. (state, process, etc.) '*on* fire'.
9. (means of conveyance) 'we went *on* foot'.
on *adverb*
1. in place, attached to or in contact with a place or person: a) 'she put her coat *on*'; b) 'he turned *on* the radio'.
2. in continued activity: 'work *on* till midnight'.
Usage: 'we hurried *on*' (= further, onwards).
3. towards: 'we looked *on* while they worked'.
Phrases:
and so on, see SO.
on and off, off and on, intermittently.
on and on, without stopping.
on *adjective*
1. operating: 'the heating is *on*'.
Usages:
a) 'is anything *on* tomorrow?' (= occurring).
b) 'what days are you *on* this week?' (= working).
2. *Cricket:* being on the same side of the field as the batsman's legs.
on to, (*informal*) aware of or informed about.

once (*say* wunce) *adverb*
1. formerly: 'a *once* powerful nation'.
2. at a single time: '*once* a week'.
Phrases:
once and for all, finally and decisively.
once upon a time, long ago.
once *noun*
a single occasion: '*once* is enough'.
Phrases:
all at once, suddenly.
at once, a) immediately; b) at the same time.
Word Family: **once**, *conjunction*, whenever.

once-over *noun*
(*informal*) a quick or superficial inspection.

oncoming (*say* **on**–kumming) *adjective*
approaching: '*oncoming* traffic'.

one (*say* wun) *adjective*
1. being an individual, unit or object.
2. being a particular instance of a number: a) '*one* member of a group'; b) '*one* evening last week'.
Usages:
a) '*one* Fred Brown was chosen' (= a certain).
b) 'we will meet again *one* day' (= some future).
all one, all the same.
one *noun*
1. a cardinal number, the symbol 1 in Arabic numerals, I in Roman numerals.
2. a single person or thing: 'please give me *one* of those'.
Phrases:
one and all, everybody.
one by one, singly and in succession.
one *pronoun*
1. a particular person or thing: 'she's the only musical *one* in the family'.
2. a person: a) 'he is not *one* to be easily frightened'; b) '*one* cannot always find time for reading'.

one-armed bandit
(*informal*) a fruit machine.

one-eyed *adjective*
(*informal*) biased.

one-horse *adjective*
(*informal*) small or unimportant: 'a *one-horse* town'.

oneness (*say* **wun**–ness) *noun*
agreement or unity of thought, purpose, etc.

onerous (*say* **o**–na–rus *or* **onna**–rus) *adjective*
heavy or burdensome: 'the *onerous* task of looking after little brothers and sisters'.
Word Family: **onerously**, *adverb*; **onerousness**, *noun*.
[Latin *oneris* of a burden]

oneself *pronoun*
1. the reflexive form of **one**: 'to wash *oneself*'.
2. the emphatic form of **one**: 'one did it *oneself*'.
3. one's normal or usual self.

one-sided *adjective*
1. considering only one aspect of a matter: 'a *one-sided* view of the situation'.
Usage: 'a *one-sided* fight' (= not equal).
2. having or occurring on only one side.

one-time *adjective*
former: 'a *one-time* friend'.

one-track *adjective*
1. having a single track.
2. (*informal*) restricted to one subject: 'a *one-track* mind'.

one-upmanship *noun*
the art of slyly disconcerting others in order to appear superior, e.g. by competitive name-dropping.
[invented by Stephen Potter, 1952]

onion (*say* **un**-y'n) *noun*
a small to medium-sized, brown or white bulb which has a strong taste or smell and is used as a vegetable.

onlooker *noun*
a spectator.

only (*rhymes with* lonely) *adjective*
being the single one in a class or group: 'he is the *only* millionaire I know'.
Usage: 'she is an *only* child' (= without brothers or sisters).
only *adverb*
1. without anyone or anything else; alone: '*only* Peter was late'.
2. no more than: a) 'the baby can *only* crawl'; b) 'if I could *only* go'; c) 'she is *only* 10 years old'.
only *conjunction*
except: 'I like the car, *only* it is too expensive to buy'.

onomatopoeia
(*say* onna-matta-**pee**-a) *noun*
the formation of a word whose sound suggests its meaning, as in hiss, buzz, etc.
Word Family: **onomatopoeic** (*say* onna-matta-**pee**-ik), **onomatopoetic**, *adjectives.*
[Greek *onoma* name + *poiein* to make]

onrush *noun*
a strong forward rush.

onset *noun*
1. an attack.
2. a beginning: 'at the *onset* of rain the players left the field'.

onslaught (*say* **on**-slawt) *noun*
an attack, especially a fierce or violent one.

ontology (*say* on-**tolla**-jee) *noun*
Philosophy: the study of being or existence.
Word Family: **ontological** (*say* onta-**loji**-k'l), *adjective*; **ontologist**, *noun.*
[Greek *on, ontos* being + -LOGY]

onus (*say* **o**-nus) *noun*
a burden or responsibility.
[Latin]

onward *adjective*
advancing ahead or forwards.
Word Family: **onwards**, **onward**, *adverb.*

onyx (*say* **on**-iks) *noun*
Geology: see CHALCEDONY.
[Greek]

oodles *plural noun*
(*informal*) a large quantity.

ooze (1) *verb*
to flow or leak out slowly.
Word Family: **oozy**, *adjective*, a) oozing moisture, b) damp with moisture.

ooze (2) *noun*
1. *Geography:* the very fine mud found on the bottom of the ocean.
2. any mud or slime.
Word Family: **oozy**, *adjective.*

opal (*say* **o**-pul) *noun*
Geology: a naturally occurring hydrated, amorphous form of silica, often iridescent and used as a gem.

opalescent (*say* opa-**less**'nt) *adjective*
having a shimmer of colours like that of opal.
Word Family: **opalescence**, *noun.*

opaque (*say* o-**pake**) *adjective*
1. a) not able to be seen through. b) not transmitting or reflecting light.
2. obscure or difficult to understand.
Word Family: **opaquely**, *adverb*; **opacity** (*say* o-**passi**-tee), **opaqueness**, *nouns.*
[Latin *opacus* shady, dark]

op art
a style of painting or sculpture which gives the impression of movement due to optical effects. Compare POP ART.
[OP(tical) + ART]

open *adjective*
1. allowing unobstructed entrance and exit: 'the sheep wandered out of the *open* gate'.
2. not closed, covered or enclosed: a) 'an *open* jar'; b) 'the *open* countryside'.
3. not decided or specified: a) 'with no clues, it was an *open* verdict'; b)

'fill this *open* cheque in for any amount you wish'.
4. not limited or restricted: '*open* season'.
Usages:
a) 'is the job you advertised still *open*?' (= available).
b) 'the shop is often *open* on Sundays' (= ready for business).
c) 'I admire his *open* manner' (= candid, unreserved).
d) 'her behaviour leaves her *open* to attack' (= liable, susceptible).
e) 'I have almost decided what to do, but I am still *open* to suggestions' (= receptive).
f) '*open* newspapers lay all over the floor' (= unfolded, spread out).
open *verb*
to become or cause to become open.
Usages:
a) 'she *opened* her birthday present' (= unwrapped).
b) 'the rooms *open* on to the verandah' (= have an outlet).
open *noun*
any unenclosed area: 'we spent the day in the *open*'.
Word Family: **opener**, *noun*, a person or device that opens; **openly**, *adverb*.

open-and-shut *adjective*
obvious or easily decided: 'an *open-and-shut* case of murder'.

opencast mining
mining from the surface by stripping away the overburden.

open cheque
an uncrossed cheque which can be cashed by anyone.

open circuit
Electricity: a circuit with a break in it, so that no electricity can flow.

open day
a day on which visitors are invited to look around a school, hospital, etc.

open-ended *adjective*
being organized so as to allow for various possibilities: 'an *open-ended* agreement'.

opener *noun*
Word Family: see OPEN.

open-eyed *adjective*
a) surprised. b) alert.

open-handed *adjective*
generous.
Word Family: **open-handedness**, *noun*; **open-handedly**, *adverb*.

open-hearted *adjective*
1. frank or unreserved.
2. kind.
Word Family: **open-heartedness**, *noun*; **open-heartedly**, *adverb*.

open house
a) the fact of offering hospitality to all friends or visitors. b) a social event at which such hospitality exists.

opening *noun*
1. a beginning or first movement, such as the first performance of a play, etc.
2. an open space: 'a small, narrow *opening* led into the secret passage'.
3. a vacancy or opportunity: 'we have an *opening* for an ambitious worker'.

openly *adverb*
Word Family: see OPEN.

open-minded *adjective*
unprejudiced and willing to consider new ideas, arguments, etc.
Word Family: **open-mindedness**, *noun*; **open-mindedly**, *adverb*.

open-mouthed *adjective*
gaping with astonishment.

open-plan *adjective*
(of offices, etc.) having few interior walls.

open secret
a matter which is supposed to be secret but is in fact generally known.

open shop
a factory where non-union labour can be employed. Compare CLOSED SHOP.

open verdict
Law: a verdict that an unknown person has committed a crime or that a cause for a violent death is not specified.

opera (1) (*say* **oppera**) *noun*
a) a play which is set to music. b) a performance of such a play.
Word Family: **operatic** (*say* **oppa-rattik**), *adjective*.
[Latin, labour]

opera (2) (*say* **oppera**) *plural noun*
see OPUS.

operable (*say* **oppera-b'l**) *adjective*
1. able to be used or put into practice.
2. *Medicine:* capable of being cured or removed by surgical operation.

opera glasses
a small pair of binoculars for use in a theatre.

operate (*say* **oppa-rate**) *verb*
1. to function: 'this computer *operates* much faster than the human brain'.
2. to use or control the functioning of: 'he *operates* the switchboard'.

3. *Medicine:* to cut a body to remove or repair part of it.
[Latin *operari* to work]

operatic (*say* oppa–**rattik**) *adjective*
Word Family: see OPERA (1).

operation (*say* oppa–**ray**–sh'n) *noun*
1. the act or method of operating: 'your *operation* of the machine shows you are well trained'.
2. the state of being operative: 'the machine is out of *operation*'.
3. a course or process of work, activity, etc., such as a planned military attack.
Word Family: **operational**, *adjective*, a) relating to operations, b) fit for use.

operational research
short form is **OR**
also called **operations research**
the analysis of complex problems, whether military or industrial, which can be set out in quantitative terms, often performed with a computer. Compare GAME THEORY, TIME AND MOTION STUDY, WAR GAMES.

operative (*say* **oppra**–tiv) *adjective*
1. operating or in effect: 'the law became *operative* last week'.
Usages:
a) 'first we must try to formulate an *operative* plan' (= efficient).
b) 'compromise has been the *operative* word during the discussions' (= most significant).
2. of or relating to surgical operations.
operative *noun*
a worker.

operator (*say* **oppa**–rayta) *noun*
1. a person who operates a mechanical device.
2. (*informal*) a shrewd, often unscrupulous, person.

operetta (*say* oppa–**retta**) *noun*
a short and simple form of opera, usually amusing.

ophthalmic (*say* off–**thalmik**) *adjective*
of or relating to the eye.

ophthalmic optician
(*say* off–**thal**–mik op–**tish**'n)
a person qualified to prescribe lenses for spectacles who also makes, sells or dispenses the complete spectacles.

ophthalmologist
(*say* off–thal–**molla**–jist) *noun*
an oculist.
Word Family: **ophthalmology**, *noun*.
[Greek *opthalmos* eye + –LOGY]

opiate (*say* **o**–pee–it) *noun*
1. any substance made from opium.
2. any substance causing dullness or a feeling of inactivity.

opine (*say* a–**pine**) *verb*
to hold or express an opinion.

opinion (*say* a–**pin**–y'n) *noun*
a belief, attitude or viewpoint: a) 'what is your *opinion* of modern art?'; b) 'the lawyer advised me to seek a second *opinion*'.

opinionated *adjective*
dogmatic or obstinately maintaining one's opinions.

opinion poll
a survey of public opinion, particularly voting intentions before an election.

opium (*say* **o**–pee–um) *noun*
the juice of certain poppies, containing morphine and other substances, used in medicine to relieve pain, induce sleep, etc.
[Greek *opos* juice]

opossum *noun*
a small tree-dwelling marsupial, found in North and South America and noted for its habit of feigning death when in danger.

opponent (*say* a–**po**–nent) *noun*
a person who is on the opposite side in a contest, argument, etc.
[Latin *opponere* to place against]

opportune (*say* **oppa**–tewn) *adjective*
favourable or convenient: 'wait for the most *opportune* moment'.
Word Family: **opportunely**, *adverb*.
[from Latin]

opportunism (*say* oppa–**tew**–nizm) *noun*
the policy of taking advantage of situations, often involving the sacrifice of principles.
Word Family: **opportunist**, *noun*.

opportunity (*say* oppa–**tewni**–tee) *noun*
a) a favourable or suitable time. b) a chance.

oppose *verb*
1. to resist or be against: 'some people *opposed* the introduction of daylight-saving'.
2. to set against or put forward as a contrast: 'love is *opposed* to hate'.

opposite (*say* **oppa**–zit) *adjective*
1. placed or situated directly facing a person or object: 'she sat at the *opposite* end of the table to me'.
2. entirely different: 'the *opposite* direction'.

opposite *noun*
something which is opposite: 'north and south are *opposites*'.
[Latin *oppositus* placed against]

opposite number
a person who holds a corresponding position in another situation.

opposition (*say* oppa–**zish**'n) *noun*
the state of being opposed: 'we all voted in *opposition* to the new rule'.
the Opposition
Parliament: the party or parties outside the ruling party who criticize and try to amend government decisions.

oppress *verb*
1. to treat cruelly or unjustly.
2. to weigh down: 'he was *oppressed* with worries'.
Word Family: **oppression**, *noun*; **oppressor**, *noun*, a person or thing that oppresses.
[Latin *oppressus* pressed down]

oppressive *adjective*
1. unjustly cruel.
2. physically or mentally distressing: '*oppressive* heat'.
Word Family: **oppressively**, *adverb*; **oppressiveness**, *noun*.

opprobrium (*say* appro–bree–um) *noun*
a) any disgrace arising from shameful conduct. b) a cause of this.
Word Family: **opprobrious**, *adjective*.
[Latin, a reproach, a scandal]

oppugn (*say* op–**yoon**) *verb*
to argue against or call into question.
[Latin *oppugnare* to fight against]

opt *verb*
to make a choice: 'although I was 15 I *opted* for another year at school'.
opt out, to decide not to participate.
[Latin *optare* to wish for]

optical *adjective*
a) of or relating to the eye or the function of sight. Also called **optic**.
b) designed to assist vision: 'an *optical* lens'.
[Greek *optos* seen]

optician (*say* op–**tish**'n) *noun*
a person who makes or sells optical instruments, especially spectacles.

optic nerve
Anatomy: the nerve that carries visual messages from the eyes to the brain.

optics *plural noun*
(*used with singular verb*) the study of light and vision, a branch of physics.

optimism (*say* **opti**–mizm) *noun*
1. a tendency to look on the favourable or bright side of things.
2. *Philosophy:* the belief that the universe is organized for the good of all, and must certainly improve. Compare PESSIMISM.
Word Family: **optimist**, *noun*; **optimistic** (*say* opti–**mis**tik), *adjective*, tending to take a hopeful or favourable view of things; **optimistically**, *adverb*; **optimize, optimise**, *verb*, to make the best of.
[Latin *optimus* best]

optimum (*say* **opti**–mum) *noun*
the best or most favourable.

option (*say* **op**–sh'n) *noun*
1. the right or power to choose: 'I had no *option* but to accept their offer'.
2. a) the act of choosing. b) anything which is or may be chosen: 'there are only 2 *options* available in this matter'.
3. the right to buy or sell something within a certain time on the stated terms.
Word Family: **optional**, *adjective*, open to choice; **optionally**, *adverb*.
[Latin *optare* to wish for]

optometry (*say* op–**tomma**–tree) *noun*
the practice or profession of testing the eyes for defects in vision, so that suitable spectacles can be prescribed.
Word Family: **optometrist**, *noun*.

opulent (*say* **op**–yoo–l'nt) *adjective*
rich or abundant, especially in wealth.
Word Family: **opulence**, *noun*.
[from Latin]

opus (*say* **o**–pus) *noun*
plural is **opera**
1. a written work, especially a musical composition.
2. one of the compositions of a composer, numbered according to the order of publication.
[Latin]

or *conjunction*
1. used to connect alternatives: a) 'to be *or* not to be'; b) 'either that dog goes, *or* I go'.
2. used to connect synonyms or related words, phrases, etc.: 'a pound *or* 100 pence'.
3. used to suggest uncertainty or approximation: 'there were 20 *or* 30 people at the meeting'.

–or
a suffix indicating a person or thing that performs the action expressed by the verb, as in *governor*. It is often

used in legal terms, etc. as a substitute for **-er (1)**, as in *abettor.*

oracle (*say* **orri**-k'l) *noun*
1. *Ancient religion:* a) a shrine where questions were asked of gods or goddesses. b) the deity's response or the person giving it.
2. any statement or person considered to have infallible authority or wisdom.
Word Family: **oracular** (*say* o-**rak**-yoolar), *adjective.*
[Latin *oraculum* an utterance]

oral (*say* **or**-ul) *adjective*
1. spoken, as distinct from written.
2. of, used in or taken through the mouth: '*oral* medicine'.
oral *noun*
a spoken examination.
Word Family: **orally,** *adverb.*
[Latin *oris* of the mouth]

orange (*say* **orr**inj) *noun*
1. a) a reddish-yellow colour. b) the colour between red and yellow in the spectrum.
2. a round, medium-sized, yellow to red citrus fruit.
Word Family: **orange,** *adjective.*
[Persian *narang*]

orangeade (*say* **orr**inj-ade) *noun*
a) a drink made from orange juice. b) a still or fizzy drink with a flavour of orange.

orange blossom
the white scented flowers of the orange tree, traditionally carried by brides.

orange stick
a small wooden stick, especially of orange-wood, used to clean around the fingernails.

orang-outang (*say* orranga-tang) *noun*
also spelt **orang-utan**
a large, long-armed ape with reddish-brown hair, found in the forests of Borneo and Sumatra.
[Malay *orang-utan* man of the woods]

oration (*say* or-ay-sh'n) *noun*
a) a formal speech. b) a harangue.
Word Family: **orate,** *verb;* **orator** (*say* **orra**-ta), *noun;* **oratorical** (*say* orra-**torri**-k'l), *adjective;* **oratorically,** *adverb.*
[Latin *orare* to speak, to plead a case]

oratorio (*say* orra-**taw**rio) *noun*
a long musical composition written as a drama for singers and orchestra, usually with a religious theme.
[Italian]

oratory (1) (*say* **orra**-tree) *noun*
the art of eloquence or public speaking.

oratory (2) (*say* **orra**-tree) *noun*
Christian: a small chapel or room used for private worship.

orb *noun*
1. a circle or sphere, such as the sun or the moon.
2. an old word for the sun or an eye.
Word Family: **orbicular** (*say* or**bik**-yoolar), *adjective.*

orbit *noun*
1. *Astronomy:* the elliptical path traced around a body by a satellite or planet.
2. any similar curved path of one body around another, such as that of an electron around the nucleus of an atom.
Usage: 'the *orbit* of the country's power extended across the world' (= range of influence).
3. *Anatomy:* either of two holes in the front of the skull in which the eyes are located. Also called an **eye socket.**
4. *Biology:* the part surrounding the eye of an animal.
Word Family: **orbit,** *verb,* to move or travel in an orbit; **orbital,** *adjective.*
[Latin *orbis* a circle]

orchard (*say* **or**-ch'd) *noun*
a) an area of land planted with fruit trees. b) the trees grown in such an area.
Word Family: **orchardist,** *noun.*
[Latin *hortus* a garden + YARD]

orchestra (*say* **or**kistra) *noun*
1. a large group of musicians playing woodwind, brass, percussion and string instruments, etc.
2. the space in a theatre reserved for musicians, usually immediately in front of and below the stage.
Word Family: **orchestrate,** *verb,* to write or arrange music for an orchestra; **orchestration** (*say* orki-**stray**-sh'n), *noun;* **orchestral** (*say* or-**kest**-r'l), *adjective.*
[Greek *orkhestra* the space where the chorus danced during a play]

orchid (*say* **or**kid) *noun*
any of a group of plants with brightly coloured, luxurious flowers.
[Latin *orchis* testicle]

ordain *verb*
1. *Christian:* to appoint as a bishop, priest or deacon.
2. to solemnly order or decide.
Word Family: **ordination** (*say* ordi-**nay**-sh'n), *noun,* a) the act or ceremony of ordaining, b) the fact of being ordained.
[Latin *ordinis* of an order]

ordeal *noun*
1. any severe or distressing experience: 'the interview was an *ordeal* for the nervous applicant'.
2. a primitive form of trial which tested the effect of fire, etc. on the accused person.

order *noun*
1. a direction or command, especially one given officially or with authority.
2. a system or arrangement of things in relation to each other or in a series: a) 'alphabetical *order*'; b) 'a new political and social *order*'.
3. a state or condition: 'the house is in good *order*'.
4. a proper or right condition: a) 'the car is out of *order*'; b) 'the troops couldn't keep *order*'.
5. a) a request to supply or provide: 'he placed an *order* for a car'. b) something requested or acquired in this way: 'your *order* is ready'.
Usage: 'her bravery is of the highest *order*' (= level, degree).
6. *Biology:* the group below class used in the classification of animals and plants.
7. *Religion:* a) a group of people living under a common religious rule, e.g. in a monastery. b) any of the ranks of clergy.
Phrases:
a tall order, (*informal*) a difficult task or request.
in order, 'is it *in order* for the meeting to end earlier?' (= suitable, acceptable).
in order that, in order to, so that.
of the order of, approximately.
on order, having been ordered but not yet delivered.
out of order, broken down; not working.
to order, 'a coat made *to order*' (= to the buyer's instructions).
order *verb*
to give or make an order.
order about, to instruct or direct in a domineering manner.

orderly *adjective*
1. arranged in a tidy or systematic way.
2. obedient or well-behaved: 'an *orderly* crowd watched the finals match'.
orderly *noun*
1. a soldier acting as an officer's messenger.
2. a person who does non-medical work in a hospital.
Word Family: **orderliness,** *noun.*

orderly officer
Military: the officer on duty for the day.

orderly room
Military: a company or regimental office in barracks, used for administrative business.

ordinal (1) *adjective*
relating to an order.
ordinal *noun*
an ordinal number.

ordinal (2) *noun*
Religion: a book of instructions or procedures for certain services or ceremonies.

ordinal number
Maths: a number indicating order, such as first, third, etc. Compare CARDINAL NUMBER.

ordinance *noun*
an official command, law or rule.

ordinary (*say* **ordin-ree**) *adjective*
1. normal or usual: 'this is the *ordinary* way we go to school'.
2. average or not outstanding: 'the meal was quite *ordinary*'.
ordinary *noun*
1. the usual or ordinary condition or situation: 'this talented singer is quite out of the *ordinary*'.
2. *Christian:* a church official, such as a bishop, with authority to oversee.
Word Family: **ordinarily** (*say* **ordinra-lee**), *adverb,* a) usually, b) in the ordinary way; **ordinariness,** *noun.*

ordinary shares
Commerce: the shares in a company on which dividends are paid only after interest has been paid on debentures and preference shares.

ordinate (*say* **orda-nit**) *noun*
Maths: the vertical distance of a point from the origin of a graph; the *y* coordinate. Compare ABSCISSA.

ordination *noun*
Word Family: see ORDAIN.

ordnance *noun*
any military equipment, especially artillery.

ordnance survey
1. (*capitals*) the government civil department which carries out detailed surveys of the whole country.
2. a map published by this department.
[originally carried out by the Army's Board of *Ordnance*]

Ordovician (*say* **ordo-vishian**) *noun*
Geology: see PALAEOZOIC.

[after the Latin name of a tribe in Wales]

ordure (*say* or–**dewer**) *noun*
dung.
[Latin *horridus* uncouth, frightful]

ore *noun*
a mineral or mixture of minerals containing a metal or non–metal in sufficient amounts to be profitable if mined.

oregano (*say* orri–**gah**no) *noun*
also called **origan**
a sweet–smelling herb related to mint, used in cooking.
[Spanish]

organ *noun*
1. *Music:* a keyboard instrument in which notes are sounded by wind blown through pipes by means of bellows or electric power.
2. *Anatomy:* any part of an organism, consisting of one or more kinds of tissue, that forms a structural and functional unit, such as a kidney, a leaf, etc.
3. a means of publicizing (especially political) opinion, e.g. a periodical: 'this quarterly journal is the chief *organ* of the extreme right wing'.
Word Family: **organist**, *noun*, (Music) a person who plays the organ.
[Greek *organon* an instrument, tool]

organdie (*say* **organ**–dee) *noun*
a very fine, stiff muslin, used for dresses, curtains, etc.

organ–grinder *noun*
a street musician who plays a small organ by turning a handle.

organic (*say* or–**gann**ik) *adjective*
1. of or relating to living organisms.
2. a) relating to the organ or organs of an animal or plant. b) (of disease) affecting the structure of an organ.
3. of or produced by the use of natural fertilizers such as compost, etc. as distinct from manufactured ones: '*organic* vegetables'.
4. *Chemistry:* of or relating to an enormous class of substances containing carbon combined with hydrogen and often with oxygen, nitrogen and other elements. The molecules are often very large and complex, containing large numbers of carbon atoms in chains and rings. Compare INORGANIC.
5. organized or arranged systematically: 'an *organic* whole'.
Word Family: **organically**, *adverb.*

organic chemistry
the chemistry of carbon compounds.

organism (*say* **orga**–nizm) *noun*
1. *Biology:* any living thing; an animal or plant.
2. any system or organization with dependent parts.

organist *noun*
Word Family: see ORGAN.

organization (*say* orga–nie–**zay**–sh'n) **organisation** *noun*
1. the act of organizing: 'the *organization* of accommodation should be done before the tour'.
2. the state of being organized: 'there is not enough *organization* in your method'.
3. a number of people or groups joined and organized for some purpose: 'a charitable *organization*'.
Word Family: **organizational**, *adjective*; **organizationally**, *adverb.*

organize (*say* **orga**–nize) **organise** *verb*
to bring or put together as a whole: 'we must *organize* a demonstration'.
Word Family: **organizer**, *noun.*

organza (*say* or–**ganza**) *noun*
a thin, stiff fabric made from silk or nylon mixed with cotton.

orgasm (*say* **or**–gazm) *noun*
the climax of excitement in sexual activity.
Word Family: **orgasmic** (*say* or–**gazmik**), **orgastic**, *adjectives.*
[Greek *organ* to swell or to be excited]

orgy (*say* **or**–jee) *noun*
1. a wild, drunken or immoral festivity or celebration.
2. any excessively indulgent or uncontrolled activity.
[Greek *orgia* secret rites, the mysteries]

oriel (*say* **or**–ee–ul) *noun*
a bay window high in a building.

orient (*say* **or**–ee–ent) *noun*
1. the east or regions in the east.
2. (*capital*) the countries of Asia, especially eastern Asia.
orient *verb*
to orientate.
Word Family: **oriental** (*say* or–ee–**en**–t'l), *adjective*, of or characteristic of the east or the Orient; **oriental**, *noun*, (usually capital) an inhabitant of Asia.
[Latin *oriens* the east, sunrise]

orientate (*say* **or**–ee–entate) *verb*
to place or face in a particular position or direction.

Usage: 'she is not *orientated* to her new life' (= adjusted, adapted).
orientation (*say* or–ee–en–**tay**–sh'n) *noun*
a) the act of orientating. b) the state of being orientated: 'the house's *orientation* is to the north'.

orienteering *noun*
a sport of cross-country running over a set course.

orifice (*say* **orri**–fiss) *noun*
an opening or hole.
[Latin *oris* of the mouth + *facere* to make]

origami (*say* orri–**gah**–mee) *noun*
the art of folding paper into decorative shapes, e.g. animals and flowers.
[Japanese *ori* a folding + *kami* paper]

origin (*say* **orri**–jin) *noun*
1. something from which anything else starts, issues or is derived: 'what is the *origin* of that folk song?'.
2. a beginning or first stage: 'the *origin* of the war dates back several years'.
Usage: 'the politician did not hide the fact of his humble *origin*' (= birth, parentage).
3. *Maths:* the point where two or more axes meet.
[Latin *originis* of the source]

original (*say* a–**riji**–n'l) *adjective*
1. relating or belonging to the origin or beginning of something: 'this Victorian house still has its *original* features'.
2. new, unusual or different: 'she dresses in very *original* clothes'.
3. being the first, from which a copy, translation, etc. is made: 'do you still have the *original* photo?'.
4. creative, individual or inventive in thought or action.
original *noun*
1. something which is original as distinct from a copy or imitation.
2. the person or thing represented in a painting, piece of writing, etc.
3. an eccentric or individual person.
Word Family: **originality**, *noun*, the quality of being original; **originally**, *adverb*, a) at first, b) from the beginning.

original sin
see SIN (1).

originate (*say* a–**riji**–nate) *verb*
1. to bring into being: 'who *originated* the annual reunion?'.
2. to begin or arise: 'their quarrel *originated* from a silly argument'.
Word Family: **origination**, *noun*; **originator**, *noun*, a person who originates something.

oriole (*say* **or**–ee–ole) *noun*
any of a family of bright, yellowish-green and black birds, mostly in America.
[Latin *aureus* golden]

orison (*say* **orri**–z'n) *noun*
an old word for a prayer.

Orlon *noun*
a synthetic, acrylic fibre, similar to nylon, that is lightweight and crease-resistant.
[a trademark]

ormolu (*say* **orma**–loo) *noun*
an alloy of copper, zinc and tin which resembles gold and is used to decorate furniture, clocks, etc.
[French *or moulu* ground gold]

ornament *noun*
an object or detail used to add beauty or decoration.
Word Family: **ornament**, *verb*, a) to provide with ornaments, b) to increase the beauty of; **ornamental**, *adjective*; **ornamentation** *noun*.
[Latin *ornare* to equip, adorn]

ornate (*say* or–**nate**) *adjective*
elaborately decorated.
Word Family: **ornately**, *adverb*; **ornateness**, *noun*.

ornery *adjective*
American: (*informal*) bad-tempered or stubborn.

ornithology (*say* orni–**tholla**–jee) *noun*
the study of birds.
Word Family: **ornithologist**, *noun*.
[Greek *ornithos* of a bird + -LOGY]

ornithorhynchus
(*say* orni–tha–**rinkus**) *noun*
the platypus.
[Greek *ornithos* of a bird + *rhynkos* beak]

orotund (*say* **orra**–tund) *adjective*
1. (of a voice or words) clear and rich in tone.
2. (of speech) pompous.
[Latin *ore rotundo* with round mouth]

orphan (*say* **or**–f'n) *noun*
a child whose parents are dead.
Word Family: **orphan**, *verb*; **orphanage** (*say* **orfa**–nij), *noun*, an institution where orphans are cared for.
[Greek *orphanos* bereaved]

orris *noun*
also spelt **orrice**

a fragrant powder obtained by grinding the root of a variety of iris, used in perfumes, etc.
[from IRIS]

orthochromatic
(*say* ortho-kro-**mattik**) *adjective*
relating to a film, etc. which is sensitive to all colours except red.
[Greek *orthos* straight + *khromatos* of colour]

orthoclase (*say* **ortho**-klas) *noun*
Geology: a potassium feldspar contained in granite.
[Greek *orthos* straight + *klasis* a breaking]

orthodontics (*say* ortho-**dontiks**)
plural noun
(*used with singular verb*) the art of straightening irregular teeth, a branch of dentistry.
Word Family: **orthodontist**, *noun*; **orthodontic**, *adjective*.
[Greek *orthos* straight + *odontos* of a tooth]

orthodox (*say* **ortha**-doks) *adjective*
1. conventional or conforming to accepted standards: 'the barrister's intimidating methods during the trial were not considered *orthodox*'.
2. correct or traditional in religious doctrine or practice.
Word Family: **orthodoxy**, *noun*; **orthodoxly**, *adverb*.
[Greek *orthos* straight + *doxa* an opinion]

orthogonal (*say* or-**thogga**-n'l)
adjective
Maths: relating to right angles or perpendicular lines.
Word Family: **orthogonally**, *adverb*.
[Greek *orthos* straight + *gonia* a corner]

orthographic (*say* ortho-**graffik**)
adjective
relating to a kind of perspective projection, used in maps, elevations of buildings, etc. in which the point of sight is supposed to be at an infinite distance, so that the rays are parallel.

orthography (*say* or-**thogra**-fee) *noun*
the study or use of correct spelling.
[Greek *orthos* straight + *graphein* to write]

orthopaedics (*say* ortha-**peediks**)
plural noun
in America spelt **orthopedics**
(*used with singular verb*) the treatment of deformities of the bones, especially in children, a branch of surgery.
Word Family: **orthopaedist**, *noun*; **orthopaedic**, *adjective*.
[Greek *orthos* straight + *paidos* of a child]

-ory (1)
a suffix of adjectives indicating function or tendency, as in *compulsory*.

-ory (2)
a suffix of nouns indicating a place or thing used for the purpose expressed in the root word, as in *observatory*.

oryx (*say* **orriks**) *noun*
any of various desert antelopes of Africa and Arabia with long, ringed horns.
[Greek]

oscillate (*say* **ossi**-late) *verb*
to move or swing backwards and forwards, as a pendulum.
Usage: 'he *oscillates* between wanting to be a doctor and an architect' (= wavers, fluctuates).
oscillation (*say* ossi-**lay**-sh'n) *noun*
a) the act of oscillating. b) a single swing or movement of a body.
Word Family: **oscillator**, *noun*; **oscillatory**, *adjective*.
[Latin *oscillare* to swing]

oscilloscope (*say* assilla-skope) *noun*
Physics: a device which makes the shape of a wave visible on a cathode-ray tube.
[Latin *oscillare* to swing + Greek *skopein* to look at]

osculate (*say* **oss**-kew-late) *verb*
a) to kiss. b) to bring into close contact.
Word Family: **osculation**, *noun*; **osculatory**, *adjective*.
[from Latin]

osier (*say* **o**-*zh*a) *noun*
a) any of a group of willows, the branches of which are used for wickerwork. b) a willow twig.

-osis
a suffix of nouns indicating action, condition or process, as in *metamorphosis*.
[Greek]

osmium (*say* **ozmi**-um) *noun*
element number 76, a rare, brittle metal, the most dense substance known. It is used in alloys with platinum and iridium. See TRANSITION ELEMENT. See UNITS in grey pages.
[Greek *osmé* smell]

osmosis (*say* oz-**mo**-sis) *noun*
the movement of solvent across a semipermeable membrane in an area where there is a higher concentration

of a substance, e.g. the movement of water from cell to cell.
Word Family: **osmotic** (*say* oz-**mott**ik), *adjective*; **osmotically**, *adverb*; **osmose**, *verb*.
[Greek *osmos* push + -OSIS]

osmotic pressure
Biology: the pressure necessary to prevent movement of water by osmosis.

osprey (*say* **oss**-pree *or* **oss**-pray) *noun*
1. a large eagle-like bird which plunges feet first into the water to catch fish.
2. an egret plume.
[Latin *ossifragus* bone-breaking]

osseous (*say* **oss**i-us) *adjective*
made of or resembling bone.

ossify (*say* **oss**i-fie) *verb*
(**ossified**, **ossifying**)
to change into, or harden like, bone.
Usage: 'the old man's attitudes have *ossified* amid the social changes of today' (= become fixed or set).
Word Family: **ossification**, *noun*.
[Latin *ossis* of a bone + *facere* to make]

ostensible (*say* oss-**ten**si-b'l) *adjective*
professed or supposed: 'few people believed her *ostensible* reason for going overseas'.
Word Family: **ostensibly**, *adverb*.
[Latin *ostendere* to stretch out, exhibit]

ostentation (*say* osten-**tay**-sh'n) *noun*
a showy display intended to impress others.
Word Family: **ostentatious**, *adjective*; **ostentatiously**, *adverb*.

osteoarthritis (*say* ostio-arth-**rye**-tis) *noun*
a degenerative arthritic disease of old age, usually located in the shoulder, knee, hip or spine.
[Greek *osteon* bone + ARTHRITIS]

osteomyelitis (*say* ostio-mya-**lie**-tis) *noun*
a bacterial disease of the bones causing pain and fever, sometimes spreading to other tissues.
[Greek *osteon* bone + *myelos* marrow + -ITIS]

osteopathy (*say* osti-**oppa**-thee) *noun*
the treatment of disease by manipulation of parts of the body, especially the spine, based on the belief that many diseases are chiefly due to misplacement of bones.
Word Family: **osteopath** (*say* **os**tio-path), *noun*, a person who practises osteopathy.
[Greek *osteon* bone + *pathos* suffering]

ostler (*say* **oss**-la) *noun*
an old word for a person who looks after horses at an inn.
[from earlier *hostler*, from HOSTEL(er)]

ostracize (*say* **os**tra-size) **ostracise** *verb*
to exclude or banish from one's company, friendship, country, etc.
Word Family: **ostracism** (*say* **os**tra-sizm), *noun*.
[Greek *ostrakon* a potsherd (citizens voted for a person's exile by writing his name on one)]

ostrich *noun*
a long-legged, two-toed, flightless bird found in Africa and Arabia, the largest bird in existence.
[Greek *strouthion*]

other (*rhymes with* mother) *adjective*
different from the one named or implied: 'her house is at the *other* end of the street'.
Usages:
a) 'where are the *other* members of the team?' (= remaining).
b) 'he needs one *other* person' (= extra, more).
Phrases:
on the other hand, as a contrast to that.
the other day (week, etc.), '*the other day* I saw an old friend' (= a few days ago).
other *pronoun*
the other one: 'I'll have this room and you take the *other*'.
Usage: 'we will get there sometime or *other*' (= another).
Word Family: **other**, *adverb*, otherwise or differently.

otherwise *adverb*
1. under different circumstances: '*otherwise*, I would stay and help'.
2. differently: 'I wanted to come, but John felt *otherwise*'.
3. in other respects: 'he can no longer play football but leads an *otherwise* active life'.

otherworldly *adjective*
1. of or characteristic of another, imaginary or mystical world.
2. impractical or remote from reality.
Word Family: **otherworldliness**, *noun*.

otiose (*say* **o**-shee-ose *or* **o**-tee-ose) *adjective*
a) idle. b) superfluous or useless.
[Latin *otiosus* at leisure, unemployed]

otter *noun*
any of a group of furry, aquatic mammals with webbed feet and a long tail.

ottoman *noun*
1. a silk or rayon fabric with long, parallel ridges.
2. a) an upholstered seat or divan without back or arms. b) a cushioned footstool.
[after *Othman*, the founder of the Turkish Empire]

ouch *interjection*
an exclamation expressing sudden pain.

ought (*say* awt) *verb*
an auxiliary verb indicating:
a) (duty or obligation) 'you *ought* to visit your parents more often'.
b) (probability) 'we *ought* to be there soon at this speed'.
c) (desirability) 'you *ought* to see the splendid camels'.

ouija board (*say* **wee**ja bord)
a board marked with letters, words and symbols, over which rests a planchette which, when touched with the fingers, is believed to move and spell out words, replies, etc. telepathically.
[French *oui* yes + German *ja* yes + BOARD]

ounce (1) *noun*
1. a) a unit of mass in the avoirdupois system, equal to a sixteenth of a pound or $2{\cdot}83 \times 10^{-2}$ kg.
b) a unit of mass in the apothecaries' and troy systems equal to about $3{\cdot}11 \times 10^{-2}$ kg.
See UNITS in grey pages.
2. a very small amount: 'don't you have even an *ounce* of intelligence?'.

ounce (2) *noun*
also called a **snow leopard**
a long-haired leopard found in the mountains of Asia.

our *possessive adjective*
singular is **my**
belonging to us: 'they are *our* books'.

ours *possessive pronoun*
singular is **mine**
belonging to us: 'the books are *ours*'.

ourselves *pronoun*
1. the reflexive form of **we**: 'we washed *ourselves*'.
2. the emphatic form of **we**: 'we did it *ourselves*'.

oust *verb*
to expel or eject.
Word Family: **ouster**, *noun*, (Law) the act of expelling or dispossessing.

out *adverb*
1. away from or not in a particular place, position, state, etc.: a) 'she ran *out* a moment ago'; b) 'this phone is *out* of order'.
Usages:
a) 'may we go *out* and play?' (= into the open).
b) 'stretch *out* your hand' (= away from you).
c) 'they are giving *out* free tickets over there' (= away).
d) 'short skirts went *out* last year!' (= out of fashion).
e) 'the miners are *out* for more pay' (= on strike).
2. to an end, conclusion or extinction: 'my shoes have worn *out*'.
3. a) into view or evidence: 'the sun came *out*'. b) into existence: 'an epidemic broke *out*'.
4. fully or completely: a) 'empty *out* that bucket and bring it here'; b) 'the bride was decked *out* in white'.
Phrases:
all out, 'he has gone *all out* to finish the job in time' (= exerted himself to the utmost).
out of, a) 'six *out of* ten voted for the proposal' (= from amongst); b) 'that chair is made *out of* fibreglass' (= from); c) 'he did it *out of* spite' (= due to, because of).
out to, 'he is *out to* get elected this time' (= trying to, determined to).

out *adjective*
1. a) wrong or inaccurate: 'your guess was *out* by a long way'.
2. torn or worn: 'those trousers are *out* at the knees'.
3. unconscious: 'the boxer was *out* for two minutes'.
4. *Sport:* a) (of a ball) outside the boundary lines of a court, field, etc. b) (of a player or team) removed from play by being caught, etc.
5. finished or over: 'we will be there before the day is *out*'.
out of, 'we are *out of* eggs again' (= without).

out-and-out *adjective*
thorough or complete.

outback *noun*
Australian: the remote, sparsely inhabited inland regions.
Word Family: **outback**, *adverb.*

outbalance *verb*
to outweigh.

outbid *verb*
(**outbid, outbidden** or **outbid, outbidding**)
to bid higher than.

outboard motor
an internal combustion engine with a propeller, clamped to the back of a boat.

outbreak *noun*
a breaking out or eruption, e.g. of a disease, etc.
Usage: 'there were angry *outbreaks* after the new taxes were announced' (= public disturbances, riots).

outbuilding *noun*
any building, such as a barn, close to or adjoining a larger one.

outburst *noun*
a sudden and violent bursting or pouring out: 'her *outburst* of anger stunned us all into silence'.

outcast *noun*
a person who is rejected or homeless.
Word Family: **outcast,** *adjective,* rejected.

outclass *verb*
to be ahead of or do better than: 'the winner of the race easily *outclassed* the other runners'.

outcome *noun*
the result or consequence: 'what was the *outcome* of your argument?'.

outcrop *noun*
something which projects or protrudes: 'a rocky *outcrop*'.
Usage: 'any *outcrops* of violence worried the government' (= sudden occurrences).

outcry *noun*
a loud cry or noise.
Usage: 'there was a public *outcry* at the strictness of the new law' (= protest, expression of indignation).

outdated *adjective*
no longer fashionable.

outdistance *verb*
to leave far behind.

outdo (*say* out-**doo**) *verb*
(**outdid, outdone, outdoing**)
to do better than.

outdoor *adjective*
in the open air.
outdoors *adverb*
outside or in the open air.
Word Family: **outdoors,** *noun.*

outer *adjective*
further out: 'the *outer* circle of spectators found it difficult to see'.
Word Family: **outermost,** *adjective,* furthest out.

outer space
see SPACE.

outface *verb*
to defy or stare at boldly.

outfield *noun*
Sport: an outer part of the field, such as the area beyond the bases in baseball or furthest from the batsman in cricket.
Word Family: **outfielder,** *noun,* a player in the outfield.

outfit *noun*
1. the equipment needed for a particular task: 'an explorer's *outfit*'.
2. (*informal*) the clothes worn by a particular person at one time, usually including shoes and other accessories.
3. a group or organization: 'their company is quite a big *outfit* now'.
Word Family: **outfit** (**outfitted, outfitting**), *verb*; **outfitter,** *noun,* a) a person who supplies equipment, b) a person who sells clothes.

outflank *verb*
to move round and behind the flank of enemy forces.
Usage: 'he *outflanked* his opponent quite easily' (= got the better of).

outgoing *adjective*
1. departing: 'an *outgoing* chairman'.
2. friendly or extroverted.
outgoing *noun*
(*plural*) expenditure.

outgrow *verb*
(**outgrew, outgrown, outgrowing**)
1. to grow too large for something: 'he has *outgrown* all his clothes'.
2. to leave behind due to development or the passing of time: 'she *outgrew* her moodiness'.

outgrowth *noun*
1. a natural result or development.
2. something which grows outwards or protrudes: 'a horn is an *outgrowth* on the head of a bull'.

outhouse (*say* **out**-house) *noun*
an outbuilding.

outing *noun*
a short pleasure trip.

outlandish *adjective*
1. noticeably odd or outrageous: 'her *outlandish* behaviour horrified many people'.
2. remote or strange: 'so he went to some *outlandish* country, I forget where'.
Word Family: **outlandishly,** *adverb*; **outlandishness,** *noun.*

outlast *verb*
to last longer than.

outlaw *noun*
a person, especially a criminal, who defies the law and is deprived of legal rights or protection.
Word Family: **outlaw**, *verb*, a) to exclude from the benefits of the law, b) to forbid or prohibit; **outlawry**, *noun*.

outlay *noun*
a) money spent. b) the spending of money.
Word Family: **outlay** (**outlaid, outlaying**), *verb*.

outlet *noun*
an opening or passage through which something goes out or is released: a) 'a power point is an *outlet* for electricity'; b) 'writing poetry is a useful *outlet* for emotional tension'.
Usage: 'that shop is an *outlet* for home-made goods' (= agency for selling or distributing).

outline *noun*
1. a line representing the outer boundary of something: 'the *outline* of the trees was obscured by the fog'.
2. a drawing consisting only of simple lines.
Usage: 'the introduction gives an *outline* of the plot' (= summary, account).
outline *verb*
to draw or give an outline of.

outlive (*say* out-**liv**) *verb*
to live longer than.

outlook *noun*
a view: 'this room has a beautiful *outlook* on the sea'.
Usages:
a) 'her *outlook* has changed since her overseas trip' (= attitude, point of view).
b) 'the *outlook* was bleak for the impoverished family' (= future).

outlying *adjective*
distant or remote.

outmanoeuvre (*say* out-ma-**noova**) *verb*
to get the better of with superior tactics or manoeuvres.

outmatch *verb*
to outdo: 'he *outmatched* his opponent with his far greater skill'.

outmoded (*say* out-**mo**-ded) *adjective*
obsolete or old-fashioned.

outnumber *verb*
to exceed in number.

out of doors
outside or in the open air.
Word Family: **out-of-doors**, *adjective*.

out of pocket
without, due to spending: 'I was £60 *out of pocket* after I bought those books'.

out of the way
secluded or remote: 'it is very peaceful and *out of the way* here'.

outpace *verb*
to go faster than.

out-patient *noun*
see PATIENT.

outplay *verb*
to play better than.

outpost *noun*
1. a position or station at some distance from the main body of troops.
2. a distant or remote settlement.

outpouring *noun*
a flowing or pouring out.

output *noun*
1. the act of producing.
2. a product or the amount produced: 'our *output* has doubled in the last week'.

outrage *noun*
1. an extreme act of violence or cruelty.
2. something which offends, shocks or insults: 'his frank remarks were an *outrage* to her pride'.
Word Family: **outrage**, *verb*, to shock or offend; **outrageous** (*say* out-**ray**jus), *adjective*, unacceptable, offensive or shocking; **outrageously**, *adverb*; **outrageousness**, *noun*.

outran *verb*
the past tense of the verb **outrun**.

outrank *verb*
to have higher rank than.

outré (*say* **oo**-tray) *adjective*
eccentric or outrageous.
[French *outre* beyond]

outrider *noun*
1. a person, especially a motorcyclist, who rides beside or ahead of a vehicle as an escort, etc.
2. a guide, escort or scout.

outrigger *noun*
a) a framework projecting from the side of a boat or canoe, to which floats are attached to prevent capsizing. b) any projecting frame or support.

outright *adjective*
1. complete or absolute: 'an *outright* criminal'.

2. clear or unqualified: 'the *outright* winner'.
outright *adverb*
1. completely.
2. openly: 'he lied *outright*'.
3. at once: 'the blow killed him *outright*'.

outrun *verb*
(**outran, outrun, outrunning**)
to run faster than.

outset *noun*
the beginning.

outshine *verb*
(**outshone, outshining**)
to be excellent or more splendid than.

outside *noun*
the outer side, edge or part: 'the *outside* of the house needs painting'.
Usage: 'from the *outside* it looked like a very simple matter' (= obvious or superficial aspect).
at the outside, 'there were 50 people *at the outside*' (= at the most).
outside *adjective*
1. from, being or occurring on the outside: 'the *outside* lane of traffic'.
Usages:
a) 'her attitudes were affected by *outside* influences' (= other, not personal).
b) 'there is an *outside* chance that the favourite will be defeated' (= unlikely, remote).
2. extreme or greatest: 'the *outside* price I can pay is £200'.
outside *adverb, preposition*
1. on, to or into the outside: 'he stood in the cell and gazed *outside*'.
2. in, to or into the open air: 'may we go *outside* and play?'.
3. (*informal*) excluding: 'there are four in the family, *outside* myself'.

outsider *noun*
1. a person who does not belong to a particular group, etc.
2. a competitor, especially a horse in a race, considered unlikely to win.

outsize, outsized *adjective*
unusually large.
Word Family: **outsize**, *noun*, an unusual size, especially a larger one.

outskirts *plural noun*
the outer districts.

outsmart *verb*
to be too clever for.

outspoken *adjective*
frank or unreserved: 'she is known for her *outspoken* opinions'.
Word Family: **outspokenly**, *adverb*; **outspokenness**, *noun.*

outstanding *adjective*
1. great or prominent: a) 'the play was an *outstanding* success'; b) 'this medal is for *outstanding* bravery'.
2. still existing, unpaid or unsettled: '*outstanding* debts'.

outstation *noun*
a distant or remote position, station or post.

outstay *verb*
to stay longer than.

outstretched *adjective*
extended or stretched out: 'he welcomed her with *outstretched* arms'.

outstrip *verb*
(**outstripped, outstripping**)
1. to do better than.
2. to go faster than.

outvote *verb*
to defeat in voting.

outward *adjective*
1. of or towards the outside: 'an *outward* voyage'.
2. evident, apparent or visible: 'he gave no *outward* sign of fear although he felt sick with terror'.
outwards, outward *adverb*
out or towards the outside: 'the cyclone moved *outwards* to the sea'.
Word Family: **outwardly**, *adverb*, a) in relation to the outward appearance, b) on or towards the outside.

outwear *verb*
(**outwore, outworn, outwearing**)
to last or wear longer than.
Word Family: **outworn**, *adjective*, a) out-of-date, b) exhausted or worn out.

outweigh (*say* out-way) *verb*
to have greater value or importance than.

outwit *verb*
(**outwitted, outwitting**)
to get the better of someone by superior cleverness or cunning.

ova *plural noun*
see OVUM.

oval (*say* o-vul) *adjective*
egg-shaped.
oval *noun*
1. a closed curve with one axis longer than another.
2. anything which is oval-shaped, especially a field or track for sports, athletics, etc.

ovary (*say* **o**–va–ree) *noun*
1. *Anatomy:* either of the two small solid bodies on each side of the uterus, producing the ova and the sex hormones.
2. *Biology:* the hollow broad part of a carpel containing one or more ovules in a plant.
Word Family: **ovarian** (*say* o–**vair**ian), *adjective.*
[Latin *ovum* egg]

ovation (*say* o–**vay**–sh'n) *noun*
enthusiastic applause.
[Latin *ovatio* rejoicing]

oven (*say* **uvv**'n) *noun*
an enclosed chamber, usually in a stove, in which food or other objects are dried, heated or baked.

ovenware *noun*
any heat–resistant dishes in which food may be baked in the oven.

over *preposition*
1. above: a) 'the sun rose *over* the hill'; b) '*over* 20 people arrived late'; c) 'she prefers mystery stories *over* romances'.
Usage: 'who will rule *over* the country?' (= in control of).
2. on or on top of: a) 'put this rug *over* your legs'; b) 'she has a strange influence *over* you'.
3. through or throughout: a) '*over* the years he has grown grey'; b) 'we'll discuss it *over* dinner'; c) 'show her *over* the house'.
4. on or to the other side of: 'walk *over* the bridge'.
5. about or concerning: 'they argue *over* money all the time'.
over and above, 'we had to pay for accommodation *over and above* the fares' (= as well as).
over *adverb*
1. over the top or edge: 'her hand shook and the coffee spilt *over*'.
2. at or to the place indicated or implied: a) 'she's *over* in France for a month'; b) 'come *over* and see us at home'.
3. to a fallen position: 'don't knock that cup *over*'.
4. to the other side: 'flip the pancake *over*'.
5. remaining: 'I did not have any money left *over*'.
6. all through: 'he has travelled the world *over*'.
7. again: 'I have asked you ten times *over*!'.
Phrases:
all over, a) 'I looked *all over* for him' (= everywhere); b) 'the game is *all over* now' (= finished).
over against, a) 'stand *over against* the wall' (= next to, in front of); b) 'we have democracy, but *over against* that we have a large bureaucracy' (= in contrast to).
over *noun*
Cricket: a group of successive deliveries (six in England, eight in Australia and New Zealand) by one bowler from one end of the pitch.

over–
a prefix meaning: a) too or too much, as in *overweight*; b) position above or across, as in *overhead*; c) movement to a lower or reversed position, as in *overturn.*

overabundance *noun*
an excessive supply.
Word Family: **overabundant,** *adjective*; **overabundantly,** *adverb.*

overact *verb*
to act in an exaggerated manner.

overactive *adjective*
too active or energetic.
Word Family: **overactivity,** *noun.*

over–age *adjective*
beyond the proper or required age.

overall *adjective, adverb*
1. from one end or limit to the other: 'the *overall* dimensions of the land'.
2. including everything: 'the *overall* cost of the renovations'.
overall *noun*
1. (*plural*) a pair of long trousers with a flap covering the chest.
2. a loose–fitting garment, such as a smock, worn to protect ordinary clothes.

overarm *adjective*
(of a stroke or throw) made with the arm raised above the shoulder, moving forward and down. Compare UNDERARM.

overate *verb*
the past tense of the verb **overeat.**

overawe *verb*
to overcome with awe.

overbalance *verb*
to lose one's balance or fall over.

overbearing *adjective*
arrogant or dictatorial in manner.
Word Family: **overbearingly,** *adverb.*

overblown *adjective*
a) too fully open: 'an *overblown* rose'. b) swollen or inflated: '*overblown* pride'.

overboard *adverb*
over the side of a boat into the water.

overburden *verb*
to load too heavily.
overburden *noun*
Mining: the waste material lying above a body of ore.

overcapitalize, overcapitalise *verb*
1. to put an excessively high value on the capital of a company, etc.
2. to provide too much capital.

overcast *adjective*
1. (of the sky) covered by cloud.
2. dark or gloomy.
overcast *verb*
(overcast, overcasting)
1. to sew over the edge of fabric, especially to prevent fraying.
2. to make cloudy or dark.

overcharge *verb*
1. to ask too high a price.
2. to fill or load too much.

overcloud *verb*
1. to spread or fill with clouds.
2. to darken or obscure.

overcoat *noun*
a coat worn over normal clothing.

overcome *verb*
(overcame, overcoming)
to defeat or be too strong for: 'you must *overcome* your silly fears'.
Usage: 'we were *overcome* with helpless laughter' (= made weak).

overcompensate *verb*
to compensate to an exaggerated degree.
Word Family: **overcompensation,** *noun.*

overconfident *adjective*
too confident.
Word Family: **overconfidence,** *noun.*

overcritical *adjective*
too critical.

overcrowd *verb*
to crowd or fill too much.

overdevelop *verb*
to develop too much.

overdo (*say* over-**doo**) *verb*
(overdid, overdone, overdoing)
to do or use to excess.
Usage: 'this steak has been *overdone*' (= cooked too much).

overdose *noun*
an excessive dose, especially of a drug.
Word Family: **overdose,** *verb.*

overdraft *noun*
an amount of money drawn out by a customer beyond the amount in his bank account.

overdraw *verb*
(overdrew, overdrawn, overdrawing)
to draw out money beyond the amount in the bank account.

overdressed *adjective*
dressed in too formal or elaborate a manner.
Word Family: **overdress,** *verb.*

overdrive *noun*
an extra higher gear which can be switched on in a car to give a higher top speed without increased engine revolutions, thus saving petrol consumption and engine wear. Usually a higher-than-top gear, it can also be applied to the lower gears.

overdue *adjective*
1. late: 'your rent is *overdue* by six months'.
2. too long awaited: 'that amendment of the law was *overdue*'.

overeat *verb*
(overate, overeaten, overeating)
to eat too much.

overelaborate (*say* over-ee-**labba**-rit) *adjective*
too elaborate or ornate.
overelaborate
(*say* over-ee-**labba**-rate) *verb*
to describe in too much detail.

overestimate *verb*
1. to estimate too great an amount.
2. to give too high a value to.
Word Family: **overestimation,** *noun.*

overexpose *verb*
to expose too much or for too long.
Word Family: **overexposure,** *noun.*

overflow *verb*
to flow or spill over: 'the bath *overflowed* onto the floor'.
Usage: 'his heart *overflowed* with joy' (= was filled beyond capacity).
Word Family: **overflow,** *noun,* a) the act of overflowing, b) something which is overflowing.

overfold *noun*
Geology: a rock fold so far inclined that both sides dip in the same direction.

overgrow *verb*
(overgrew, overgrown)

to cover with growth.
Word Family: **overgrowth,** *noun.*

overhang *verb*
(overhung, overhanging)
to hang or extend over.
Usage: 'a sense of danger *overhung* their exciting adventure' (= surrounded, threatened).
Word Family: **overhang,** *noun,* something which projects or hangs over, such as part of a balcony.

overhaul *verb*
1. to examine, take apart and repair.
2. to overtake.
Word Family: **overhaul,** *noun.*

overhead *adjective*
situated or moving above the head: 'the *overhead* cables shook in the breeze'.
overhead *adverb*
over one's head or in the air: 'the jet flew silently high *overhead*'.
overhead *noun*
(*plural*) the general costs of running a business, such as rent, electricity, etc.

overhear *verb*
(overheard, overhearing)
to hear something spoken to another.

overhung *verb*
the past tense and past participle of the verb **overhang.**

overindulge (*say* over-in-**dulj**) *verb*
to indulge excessively.
Word Family: **overindulgence,** *noun*; **overindulgent,** *adjective.*

overjoyed *adjective*
highly delighted.

overkill *noun*
the capacity of nuclear armament to destroy infinitely more than is needed to achieve victory.

overladen (*say* over-lay-d'n) *adjective*
overloaded.

overland *adjective*
across or by land: 'an *overland* tour across Europe to Asia'.
Word Family: **overland,** *adverb*; **overland,** *verb,* (Australian) to drive cattle or sheep overland for long distances; **overlander,** *noun.*

overlap *verb*
(overlapped, overlapping)
to fold or lie over part of something else.
Usage: 'many of our interests *overlap*' (= coincide, correspond).

overlay *verb*
(overlaid, overlaying)
to cover with, lay or spread on.
overlay *noun*
a layer on or over something, for decoration, protection, etc.

overleaf *adverb*
on the other side of the page.

overload *verb*
to give too large or heavy a load to.

overlook *verb*
1. to fail to see: 'you have *overlooked* several mistakes'.
2. to ignore or disregard: 'we will *overlook* your rudeness this once'.
3. to have a view of: 'your room *overlooks* the garden'.

overlord *noun*
a person having supreme power or authority.

overly *adverb*
Scottish, American: excessively.

overmaster *verb*
to overpower.

overmuch *adverb*
very much: 'I don't like her *overmuch*'.

overnight *adverb, adjective*
during or throughout the night: 'please stay with us *overnight*'.
Usage: 'she grew up *overnight*' (= very quickly).

overpay *verb*
(overpaid, overpaying)
to pay more than the value or amount due.
Word Family: **overpayment,** *noun.*

overplay *verb*
to act or emphasize too much.
overplay one's hand, 'he *overplayed his hand* when he threatened to resign if they did not agree' (= was oversure of himself).

overpopulate *verb*
to have or cause too large a population.

overpower *verb*
to master or subdue by superior strength: 'police soon *overpowered* the unarmed attacker'.
Usage: 'fear *overpowered* her at the sight of the burglar' (= made helpless or weak).

overprint *verb*
to print on a surface that has already been printed, e.g. to print a new price onto an existing postage stamp.
Word Family: **overprint,** *noun.*

overproduce *verb*
to produce more goods than are needed.
Word Family: **overproduction,** *noun.*

overproof *adjective*
containing more alcohol than proof spirit does.

overran *verb*
the past tense of the verb **overrun.**

overrate *verb*
to value too highly.

overreach *verb*
1. to exert oneself or do too much.
2. to reach beyond the aim or target.

override *verb*
(**overrode, overridden**)
1. to disregard or go against: 'he *overrode* all advice and sold his shares'.
2. to have dominance over: 'the director's decision will *override* all others'.
3. *Medicine:* (of broken bones) to overlap.

overrider *noun*
either of a pair of vertical bars attached to the bumper bar of a motor vehicle to protect it in collisions.

overripe *adjective*
too ripe.

overrule *verb*
to decide against or refuse to allow: 'the judge *overruled* the barrister's objections'.

overrun *verb*
(**overran, overrun, overrunning**)
1. to run beyond: 'the play *overran* the scheduled time'.
2. to defeat or take possession of: 'the country was *overrun* by foreign troops'.
3. to spread or swarm over: 'those weeds will *overrun* the garden soon'.
Word Family: **overrun,** *noun,* a) the act of overrunning, b) its amount.

overseas *adverb*
across or beyond the sea: 'have you ever travelled *overseas?*'.
Word Family: **overseas,** *adjective, noun.*

oversee *verb*
(**oversaw, overseen, overseeing**)
to supervise or watch over, especially over work or workers.
Word Family: **overseer,** *noun,* a person who oversees.

overshadow *verb*
to cast a shadow over.
Usage: 'her quiet personality is *overshadowed* by her brother's boisterousness' (= made insignificant).

overshoes *plural noun*
galoshes.

overshoot *verb*
(**overshot, overshooting**)
to go over or beyond: a) 'the plane *overshot* the runway as it landed and hit trees at the end of the airport'; b) 'the torpedo *overshot* its mark'.

oversight *noun*
a failure to notice or do: 'not locking the door was an *oversight* on my part'.

oversize, oversized *adjective*
abnormally large.

oversleep *verb*
(**overslept, oversleeping**)
to sleep too long or beyond the usual time.

overspend *verb*
(**overspent, overspending**)
to spend more than is necessary or can be afforded.

overspill *noun*
something which spills over or out.
Usage: 'satellite towns were built to provide for the city's *overspill*' (= extra population).
Word Family: **overspill** (**overspilt** or **overspilled, overspilling**), *verb.*

overstate *verb*
to exaggerate when stating.
Word Family: **overstatement,** *noun.*

overstay *verb*
to stay beyond the fixed or expected time of.

oversteer *noun*
the tendency of a motor vehicle to turn in a tighter circle than would be expected from the amount the front wheels have been turned.

overstep *verb*
(**overstepped, overstepping**)
to pass over or beyond.

overstock *verb*
to have or establish too great a stock or supply.

oversupply *verb*
(**oversupplied, oversupplying**)
to supply more than is required.
Word Family: **oversupply,** *noun.*

overt *adjective*
open or unconcealed: 'the review was an *overt* attack on the author'.
Word Family: **overtly,** *adverb.*

overtake *verb*
(**overtook, overtaken, overtaking**)
1. to catch up with or pass.
2. to come upon unexpectedly: 'a storm *overtook* us as we reached the top of the mountain'.

overtax *verb*
to impose too high a tax.
Usage: 'they *overtaxed* themselves by the long walk' (= exhausted).

overthrow *verb*
(overthrew, overthrown)
to defeat or destroy: 'the government was *overthrown* by the revolution'.
Word Family: **overthrow**, *noun.*

overtime *noun*
a) any extra work done by an employee outside the regular working hours. b) the payment received for this work, usually at least one and a half times the normal wage.
Word Family: **overtime**, *adverb.*

overtone *noun*
1. an additional or suggested meaning: 'despite his smile, his voice carried an *overtone* of malice'.
2. *Music:* see HARMONIC.

overtook *verb*
the past tense of the verb **overtake**.

overture (*say* over–**cher**) *noun*
1. an orchestral introduction to an opera or ballet.
2. an opening or introductory part, especially a proposal or offer.

overturn *verb*
1. to turn over or upside down.
2. to defeat or conquer.
Word Family: **overturn**, *noun.*

overweening *adjective*
extreme or exaggerated: 'we were angered by his *overweening* vanity'.
Word Family: **overweeningly**, *adverb.*

overweight (*say* over–**wate**) *adjective*
over the normal or required weight.
Word Family: **overweight**, *noun.*

overwhelm *verb*
1. to overcome completely: 'she was *overwhelmed* with grief at the death of her dog'.
2. to submerge or cover: 'the town was *overwhelmed* by the flood'.
Word Family: **overwhelmingly**, *adverb.*

overwork *verb*
to work or cause to work too hard.
Usage: 'she tends to *overwork* her jokes to a boring degree' (= use too often or too much).

overwrought (*say* over–**rawt**) *adjective*
extremely nervous or excited.

oviduct (*say* **o**–vee–dukt) *noun*
Biology: a tube carrying ova from an ovary to the exterior.

oviparous (*say* o–**vipp**erus) *adjective*
Biology: (of an animal) producing eggs which mature and hatch after leaving the body of the mother, as in birds.
Word Family: **oviparously**, *adverb*; **oviparity** (*say* o–vee–**parri**–tee), *noun.*
[Latin *ovum* egg + *parere* to bring forth]

ovipositor (*say* ovvi–**pozz**ita) *noun*
Biology: an organ at the end of the abdomen in certain insects, through which eggs are deposited.
[Latin *ovum* egg + *positus* placed]

ovulate (*say* **ov** yoolate) *verb*
Biology: to release eggs from an ovary.

ovule (*say* **ov**–yool) *noun*
Biology: the part of a flower containing the egg cell which develops into a seed after fertilization.
Word Family: **ovular**, *adjective.*

ovum (*say* **o**–vum) *noun*
plural is **ova**
Biology: the female reproductive cell.
[Latin, egg]

owe (*say* **o**) *verb*
(owed, owing)
to have a duty to do or provide: a) 'you *owe* me a pound that I lent you last week'; b) 'I *owe* you an apology for my rudeness'.
owing to, (as preposition) on account of: '*owing to* rain the match was postponed'.

owl (*rhymes with* fowl) *noun*
any of a group of nocturnal birds with a broad, flat head, large eyes, and a short, hooked beak.
Word Family: **owlet**, *noun*, a young owl; **owlish**, *adjective*, solemn like an owl.

own (*rhymes with* bone) *verb*
1. to have as one's possession.
2. to acknowledge or admit: 'I *own* that you have proved me wrong'.
own up, 'you must *own up* if you did break the window' (= confess).
own *adjective*
belonging to the person or thing indicated: 'is that your *own* car?'.
own *noun*
Phrases:
come into one's own, to obtain one's rightful position, etc.
get one's own back, to get revenge.
of one's own, 'you should save up for a car *of your own*' (= belonging to yourself).
on one's own, a) 'I went to the cinema *on my own*' (= alone); b) 'you are

on your own in this matter' (= responsible alone, independent).
Word Family: **owner**, *noun*, a person who owns or possesses; **ownership**, *noun*.

ox *noun*
plural is **oxen**
1. an old term meaning a castrated bull used for draught work.
2. (*plural*) male or female draught cattle.

oxbow (*say* **oks**-bo) *noun*
1. a bow-shaped piece of wood placed around the neck of an ox as part of a harness.
2. a billabong.

oxer *noun*
an obstacle in show-jumping comprising a hedge and rail or (in a **double oxer**) a hedge enclosed on either side by rails.
[for *ox fence*, originally a strong cattle fence]

oxidant (*say* **oks**i-d'nt) *noun*
the substance which supplies the oxygen in an oxidation reaction, especially for the burning process in a rocket engine.

oxidation (*say* oksi-**day**-sh'n) *noun*
also called **oxidization** (*say* oksi-die-**zay**-sh'n)
Chemistry: a) the combination of a substance with oxygen. b) the loss of hydrogen from a substance. c) the loss of an electron from an atom or ion.
Word Family: **oxidize**, **oxidise**, **oxidate**, *verbs*; **oxidizer**, *noun*.

oxide *noun*
Chemistry: any simple compound containing oxygen and one other element.

oxtail *noun*
the skinned tail of an ox, used in soups or stews.

oxyacetylene burner
(*say* oksia-**setta**-leen burner)
a device for producing a very high-temperature flame (about 3300°C) by burning a mixture of oxygen and acetylene in a special jet, used for welding and metal cutting.

oxygen (*say* **oks**i-j'n) *noun*
element number 8, a colourless, odourless gas, the most abundant in the earth's crust, forming about 21 per cent of the earth's atmosphere. It is essential for combustion and living tissues and is used in welding and metal cutting.
See CHEMICAL ELEMENTS in grey pages.
Word Family: **oxygenate**, **oxygenize**, **oxygenise**, *verbs*, to treat or combine with oxygen; **oxygenation**, *noun*.

oxygen cycle
a continuous circulation in nature of oxygen and its compounds between the atmosphere, the soil and organisms.

oxygen tent
a small plastic tent with a high oxygen content, used to increase the amount of oxygen in the air breathed by a patient.

oxyhaemoglobin
(*say* oksi-heemo-**glo**-bin) *noun*
Biology: the substance formed when haemoglobin unites with oxygen in the blood.

oyez (*say* o-**yez**) *interjection*
hear! listen! (formerly uttered by town crier or court official).
[Old French]

oyster *noun*
any of a group of edible, bivalve, marine molluscs, often cultivated for food or for the pearls produced by some forms.
[Greek *ostreon*]

oystercatcher *noun*
a large black and white wader of seashores and estuaries, having a long orange bill with which it picks out small molluscs and worms.

ozone (*say* **o**-zone) *noun*
1. *Chemistry:* a poisonous form of oxygen (formula O_3), a bluish gas with a sharp smell produced when oxygen is acted on by an electric discharge such as lightning, and present in the atmosphere. It is a strong oxidizing agent and is used as a bleach.
2. (*informal*) invigorating fresh air.
ozone layer, a restricted region in the outer stratosphere where much of the atmospheric ozone is concentrated.
[Greek *ozein* to smell]

Pp

pabulum (*say* **pab**–yoo–lum) *noun*
food: 'that T.V. documentary was mental *pabulum*'.
[Latin]

pace (1) *noun*
1. the rate or speed of movement: 'our neighbours live life at a hectic *pace*'.
2. a) a single step: 'take one *pace* forward'. b) the distance covered in a step.
3. the manner of stepping, especially the gait of a horse in which groups of two distinct hoof-beats may be heard as the two legs on one side move together.
put through one's paces, to test the abilities, speed, etc. of a person or thing.
pace *verb*
1. a) to cover by paces: 'her anxious husband *paced* the floor of the maternity ward'. b) to measure by paces: 'he *paced* out the distance from the house to the back fence'.
2. to set the pace for.
3. (of a horse) to exercise in pacing.
[from Latin]

pace (2) (*say* **pay**–see) *adverb, preposition*
(used to express polite disagreement) with the permission of: 'and, *pace* Henry Ford, history is not bunk!'
[Latin, with peace (that is, if the person mentioned will not be offended)]

pacemaker *noun*
1. a person, animal or group that sets the pace.
2. *Medicine:* a small electronic machine implanted into a patient and producing an electric current to control the heart rate.

pacer *noun*
1. a pacemaker.
2. a) a horse whose natural gait is a pace. b) a horse bred and trained for pacing.

pachyderm (*say* **pakki**–derm) *noun*
any of a group of large, thick-skinned animals, such as the elephant, hippopotamus or rhinoceros.
[Greek *pakhys* thick + *derma* skin]

pacify (*say* **passi**–fie) *verb*
(**pacified, pacifying**)
to calm or make peaceful: 'it is difficult to *pacify* a crying baby'.
pacifism *noun*
an opposition to all war or violence.
Word Family: **pacifist,** *noun,* a person who believes in pacifism; **pacification,** *noun;* **pacific,** *adjective,* peaceable; **pacifier,** *noun,* a person or thing that pacifies.
[Latin *pacis* of peace + *facere* to make]

pack *noun*
1. a) a bundle or parcel of things tied up for carrying: 'a train of mules carrying *packs*'. b) a light bag, often with a stiffened frame, for carrying on the back.
2. a) any piece of fabric used during a surgical operation to wipe away blood, etc. b) anything placed on the body as a treatment, such as hot or cold cloths, or a cosmetic paste applied to the face.
3. a collection or group: a) 'a *pack* of nonsense'; b) 'a *pack* of thieves'.
4. a mass of floating pieces of ice in the sea.
5. *Cards:* a) a set of 52 playing cards containing 13 cards of different value in each of four suits (called clubs, diamonds, hearts and spades). b) a complete set of cards for any particular game. In America called a **deck.**
6. *Rugby:* all the forwards of a team, especially when acting together.
pack *verb*
1. to put things into a box, bundle, suitcase, etc.: '*pack* your clothes and leave'.
2. to crush or crowd together: 'people *packed* into the store for the sale'.
Usage: 'the chairman only got elected because the meeting was *packed*' (= filled with his supporters).
3. to put soft material around or into something, to prevent damage, loss or leakage: a) 'glassware *packed* in cotton'; b) 'to *pack* an open wound'.

Phrases:
pack it in, (*informal*) 'I'm so sick of this job I feel like *packing it in*' (= giving it up, resigning).
pack someone off, send someone packing, to send someone away unceremoniously or in a hurry.
pack up, (*informal*) 'ten kilometres out of Newcastle the engine *packed up*' (= broke down, failed).
Word Family: **packer,** *noun,* a person or machine that packs things.

package (*say* **pakkij**) *noun*
1. a bundle or parcel.
2. the packing of goods: 'you'll have to pay the cost of *package* as well as freight'.
package deal
a deal which includes a number of matters and has to be accepted as a whole, the less favourable items along with the favourable.
package tour
a holiday which is completely arranged beforehand by the organizer.
Word Family: **package,** *verb.*

pack drill
Army: any extra drill, wearing full kit, imposed as a punishment.

packet *noun*
1. a small parcel or bundle: 'a *packet* of letters'.
2. *Nautical:* a ferry.
3. (*informal*) a large sum of money: 'he lost a *packet* at the races'.

packhorse *noun*
a horse used to carry goods.

packtrain *noun*
a line of animals, especially horses or mules, carrying packs.

pact *noun*
an agreement.
[Latin *pactum* agreed]

pad (1) *noun*
1. a soft, cushion-like mass, used for comfort, protection, stuffing, etc.: 'a batsman wears *pads* to protect himself from injury'.
2. *Biology:* the soft, fleshy underpart of the feet of dogs, foxes, etc.
3. any sheets of paper held together at one edge, especially for writing letters or notes.
4. (*informal*) a) a house or flat. b) a bed.
pad *verb*
(padded, padding)
to fill with something soft: 'he *padded* the seat of the chair with foam rubber'.
Usage: 'when he ran out of things to say in his essay, he *padded* it' (= filled space with unnecessary material).

pad (2) *verb*
(padded, padding)
to walk or move softly: '*padding* round the house at 4 a.m. trying not to disturb the children'.

padded cell
a room in a mental hospital with padded walls and floor, to prevent violent patients injuring themselves.

paddle (1) *noun*
1. a short, thin piece of wood with a flat blade at one end, held in the hand without a rowlock, to propel a boat or canoe.
2. something which has the shape or function of a paddle, such as a broad flat board on a waterwheel.
3. *Engineering:* a wooden panel for controlling a water passage in a lock or sluice.
Word Family: **paddle,** *verb,* to propel a canoe with a paddle.

paddle (2) *verb*
1. to dabble or play in or as if in shallow water.
2. to swim with short, downward strokes, as ducks do.

paddle-steamer *noun*
a boat propelled by a steam-engine, which turns one or more large paddlewheels through the water.

paddlewheel *noun*
a large wheel with paddles on its circumference, used instead of a propeller to propel a boat.

paddock *noun*
1. a small field used as a pasture.
2. *Sport:* an area in which horses or cars are assembled before a race.
Word Family: **paddock,** *verb,* to enclose or confine in a paddock.

paddy *noun*
(*informal*) a rage.

paddy fields
(in Asia) any land which is flooded for growing rice.
[Malay *padi* rice + FIELD]

paddywhack *noun*
(*informal*) a spanking.
Word Family: **paddywhack,** *verb.*

padlock *noun*
a detachable lock, hanging by a curved bar that is hinged at one end and snapped shut at the other.
Word Family: **padlock,** *verb.*

padre (*say* **pah**–dray) *noun*
1. (in Italy, Spain, etc.) a title for a priest.
2. *Military:* a chaplain.
[Latin *pater* father]

paean (*say* **pee**–an) *noun*
a song of praise, joy or triumph.

paediatrics (*say* peedi–**atriks**) *plural noun*
in America spelt **pediatrics**
(*used with singular verb*) the study and treatment of diseases in children.
Word Family: **paediatric,** *adjective*; **paediatrician** (*say* peedi–a–**trish**'n), *noun,* a doctor who specializes in the diseases of children.
[Greek *paidos* of a child + *iatros* healer]

pagan (*say* **pay**–g'n) *noun*
a heathen.
Word Family: **paganism,** *noun,* the beliefs or practices of pagans.
[Latin *paganus* a civilian, because pagans were not considered soldiers of Christ]

page (1) *noun*
a) a sheet of paper in a book, etc.
b) one side of this.
Usage: 'the Battle of Waterloo is a glorious *page* in English history' (= episode).
[from Latin]

page (2) *noun*
1. *Medieval history:* a boy servant or attendant to a person of rank, especially one given education and training in knighthood in exchange for performing household duties.
2. a pageboy.
page *verb*
to seek a person by having his name called, especially in a hotel, club, business, etc.
[Greek *paidion* a small child]

pageant (*say* **paj**'nt) *noun*
an elaborate public spectacle, especially one where there is a procession in costume.
Word Family: **pageantry,** *noun,* a splendid display.

pageboy *noun*
1. a bellboy.
2. a hairstyle in which the hair is long, smooth and turned under at the bottom.
3. a young male attendant at a wedding.

pagination (*say* paji–**nay**–sh'n) *noun*
the numbering of the pages in a book.
Word Family: **paginate,** *verb.*

pagoda (*say* pag–**o**–da) *noun*
an ornate temple in the shape of a pyramid or tower, as in Burma, China, etc.

paid *verb*
the past tense and the past participle of the verb **pay.**

pail *noun*
a bucket.

pain *noun*
1. any physical or mental suffering.
2. (*informal*) an annoying person or task.
on pain of, 'the traitor was banished from his homeland *on pain of* death if he ever returned' (= with the punishment of).
Word Family: **pain,** *verb,* to cause pain to; **painful,** *adjective,* a) causing pain, b) laborious or difficult; **painfully,** *adverb,* **painless,** *adjective*; **painlessly,** *adverb.*
[Latin *poena* penalty]

painstaking *adjective*
extremely careful.

paint *noun*
a liquid containing a pigment in suspension, which hardens to form an opaque coating when applied to a surface.
paint *verb*
1. to cover or decorate with, or as if with, paint.
2. a) to make pictures with paint: 'he *paints* small landscapes'. b) to represent or depict in paint: 'I asked him to *paint* me'.
Usages:
a) 'this novel *paints* a graphic picture of the horrors of civil war' (= gives).
b) 'she's not as awful as she had been *painted*' (= made out to be).
paint the town red, (*informal*) to celebrate wildly.
Word Family: **painting,** *noun,* a) a picture made with paints, b) the act or work of a person who paints.
[Latin *pingere*]

painter (1) *noun*
a) an artist who paints pictures. b) a person whose work is covering or decorating walls, houses, etc. with paint.

painter (2) *noun*
Nautical: a rope used to tie up a small boat.
[from Old French]

pair *noun*
1. a set of two people or things that are the same or go together: a) 'a *pair* of shoes'; b) 'a harmless *pair*'.
2. a single thing consisting of two parts that cannot be used separately: 'a *pair* of trousers'.
3. *Rowing:* a) a racing boat for two people who each use one oar. b) the crew of such a boat.
Word Family: **pair**, *verb*, a) to arrange in pairs, b) to form a pair or pairs.
[Latin *paria* equal things]

paisley (*say* **paze**–lee) *noun*
a soft woollen fabric with a very elaborate and colourful pattern.
[first made in *Paisley*, Scotland]

pal *noun*
(*informal*) a friend or comrade.
Word Family: **pally**, *adjective*, friendly.
[Romany, brother]

palace (*say* **pall**is) *noun*
1. a large elaborate building used as the official home of a monarch or bishop.
2. a large place for exhibitions or entertainment: 'the local picture *palace*'.
Word Family: **palatial** (*say* pa–**lay**–sh'l), *adjective*, of or like a palace; **palatially**, *adverb*.
[Latin *Palatium* the Palatine Hill, Rome, on which the palace of the Emperor Augustus stood]

paladin (*say* **palla**–din) *noun*
Medieval history: a knightly hero or champion.
[Latin *palatinus* of the palace]

palaeo– (*say* **palli**–o)
a prefix meaning old or ancient, as in *Palaeocene*.
[Greek]

Palaeocene (*say* **palli**o–seen) *noun*
Geology: see TERTIARY.
[PALAEO– + CEN(ozoic)]

Palaeolithic (*say* pallio–**lith**ik) *noun*
see STONE AGE.
[PALAEO– + Greek *lithos* stone]

palaeontology (*say* palli–on–**tolla**–jee) *noun*
the study of fossils.
Word Family: **palaeontological** (*say* palli–onta–**loji**–k'l), *adjective*; **palaeontologist**, *noun*.
[PALAEO– + Greek *onta* things + –LOGY]

Palaeozoic (*say* pallio–**zo**–ik) *noun*
a geological era which extended from about 570 million years ago to 225 million years ago and contains the **Cambrian**, **Ordovician**, **Silurian**, **Devonian**, **Carboniferous** and **Permian** periods. During this era green plants became abundant and the first land vertebrates appeared.
Word Family: **Palaeozoic**, *adjective*.
[PALAEO– + Greek *zoion* animal]

palanquin (*say* pall'n–**keen**) *noun*
also spelt **palankeen**
a box-like vehicle, carried by means of poles resting on men's shoulders; used in India and other Eastern countries.
[from Portuguese, from Sanskrit]

palate (*say* **pall**it) *noun*
1. *Anatomy:* the roof of the mouth, hard at the front and soft at the rear.
2. the sense of taste: 'the old wine pleased his *palate*'.
Usage: 'romantic novels just do not suit my *palate*' (= liking, mental taste).
palatable (*say* **pall**ita–b'l) *adjective*
a) agreeable to the sense of taste. b) agreeable or congenial: 'I don't find his ideas very *palatable*'.
Word Family: **palatal**, *adjective*.
[from Latin]

palatial (*say* pa–**lay**–sh'l) *adjective*
Word Family: see PALACE.

palaver (*say* pa–**lah**va) *noun*
1. a) a parley or conference, especially one between traders or explorers and the natives of a country. b) any idle talk, intended to flatter or deceive: 'the smooth *palaver* of a salesman'.
2. (*informal*) any fuss or bother.
Word Family: **palaver**, *verb*.
[Pidgin English from Portuguese *palavra* a word]

palazzo (*say* pa–**lah**tso) *noun*
plural is **palazzi** (*say* pa–**laht**–see)
Italian: a palace or large building.

pale (1) *adjective*
without much colour: a) 'a *pale* complexion'; b) 'a *pale* moon'.
Usage: 'he is only a *pale* resemblance of his former self' (= faint, feeble).
Word Family: **pale**, *verb*, to turn pale; **palely**, *adverb*; **paleness**, *noun*.
[Latin *pallidus*]

pale (2) *noun*
a long narrow board, often pointed at the top, used for fences.
beyond the pale, socially or morally unacceptable.

Word Family: **pale**, *verb*, to enclose with pales.
[Latin *palus*]

pale ale
a trade name for bitter, a strong highly-hopped beer of light colour.

paleface *noun*
Amerindian: a white person.

palette (*say* **pal**lit) *noun*
also spelt **pallet**
Art: a) a board on which a painter mixes colours. b) the range of colours used by a particular painter.
[Latin *pala* a spade]

palette knife
a thin flexible blade used by painters for mixing colours, and applying or removing paint from a surface.

palfrey (*say* **pawl**-free) *noun*
an old word for a gentle riding horse.

palindrome *noun*
a word or words which are spelt the same backwards as they are forwards. *Example*: was it a cat I saw?
[Greek *palindromos* a running back again]

paling (*say* **pay**-ling) *noun*
a fence of pales.

palisade (*say* **pal**li-sade) *noun*
a fence made of upright stakes or pales, used as a defence, etc.

pall (1) (*say* pawl) *noun*
1. a cloth spread over a coffin.
Usage: 'a heavy *pall* of smoke lay over the industrial town' (= covering).
2. *Roman Catholic:* a woollen cloak worn by the Pope as a sign of his office.
[Latin *pallium* covering, cloak]

pall (2) (*say* pawl) *verb*
to have a wearying effect: 'after listening to him for two hours, his monotonous voice began to *pall* on me'.
[from APPAL]

palladium (*say* pa-**lay**-dee-um) *noun*
element number 46, a rare metal, occurring with and similar to platinum, used in alloys and as a catalyst. See TRANSITION ELEMENT.
See CHEMICAL ELEMENTS in grey pages.

pallbearer *noun*
a person helping to carry the coffin at a funeral.

pallet (1) *noun*
a) a bed or mattress of straw. b) a small bed.
[French *paille* straw]

pallet (2) *noun*
1. a flat blade with a handle used by potters for shaping or mixing clay, etc.
2. a movable platform for the storage or transportation of goods, especially one designed to be lifted by a fork-lift truck.
3. *Art:* a palette.
[from PALETTE]

pallet knife
a flat, kitchen utensil with a handle, used to lift cakes.

palliasse (*say* **pal**li-ass) *noun*
also spelt **paillasse**
a mattress filled with straw.
[French *paille* straw]

palliate (*say* **pal**li-ate) *verb*
1. to make something appear less serious: 'in his speech to the jury the lawyer tried to *palliate* his client's offence'.
2. *Medicine:* to ease or relieve the symptoms of a disease without curing it.
Word Family: **palliation**, *noun*; **palliative**, *adjective*, serving to palliate; **palliative**, *noun*, something which palliates.
[Latin *palliatus* covered with a cloak]

pallid *adjective*
pale or wan: 'the *pallid* complexion of a sickly child'.
Word Family: **pallidly**, *adverb*; **pallidness**, *noun*.
[from Latin]

pallor *noun*
an unnatural paleness, such as is caused by illness, fear, death, etc.

pally *adjective*
Word Family: see PAL.

palm (1) (*say* pahm) *noun*
a) the inner surface of the hand between the wrist and the fingers. b) the part of a glove covering the palm.
Phrases:
grease, oil someone's palm, to bribe someone.
have an itching palm, to be greedy for money, especially to be always ready to receive a bribe.
palm *verb*
to conceal in the hand: 'the conjuror *palmed* the coin and the audience thought it had vanished into thin air'.
palm off, to dispose of something unwanted by getting someone else to accept it, especially by fraudulent means.
[from Latin]

palm (2) (*say* pahm) *noun*
1. any of a group of mainly tropical or subtropical trees, usually tall, branchless and with a crown of long leaves.
2. a leaf or branch of a palm as a symbol of victory.
Word Family: **palmy,** *adjective.*
[from Latin]

palmate (*say* **pal**–mate) *adjective*
having the shape of an open palm, e.g. a leaf or antler.

palmistry (*say* **pahmis**–tree) *noun*
also called **palm-reading**
the study of lines on the palm of a hand, allegedly to discover a person's character or destiny.
Word Family: **palmist,** *noun,* a person who practises palmistry.

palomino (*say* palla–**meeno**) *noun*
a breed of golden or tan horses, with a white mane and tail, originally bred in America.
[Spanish, like a dove]

palpable (*say* **palpa**–b'l) *adjective*
1. able to be touched or felt.
2. obvious: 'a *palpable* lie'.
Word Family: **palpably,** *adverb.*
[Latin *palpare* to feel]

palpate *verb*
Medicine: to examine by touching or feeling.

palpitate *verb*
1. to tremble or quiver: 'his body *palpitated* with terror'.
2. (of the heart) to beat unnaturally fast, e.g. from exertion, fear, illness, etc.
Word Family: **palpitation,** *noun.*
[Latin *palpitare* to throb]

palsy (*say* **pawl**–zee) *noun*
paralysis.
Word Family: **palsied,** *adjective.*
[from PARALYSIS]

palter (*say* **pawl**–ta) *verb*
to talk or act insincerely: 'don't *palter* with me, young man; I want the truth'.

paltry (*say* **pawl**–tree) *adjective*
a) trifling or almost worthless: 'a *paltry* sum'. b) mean or petty: 'a *paltry* coward'.
Word Family: **paltrily,** *adverb;* **paltriness,** *noun.*

pampas *noun*
see STEPPE.
[Spanish, plains]

pampas grass
any of a group of large, coarse perennial, South American grasses with large feathery flowers.

pamper *verb*
to treat very indulgently: a) 'to *pamper* an invalid'; b) 'the aristocracy of Europe *pampered* themselves'.

pamphlet (*say* **pam**–flit) *noun*
a) a booklet in paper covers, especially one dealing with a question of current interest: 'a political *pamphlet*'. b) a leaflet.
Word Family: **pamphleteer** (*say* pam–flit**teer**), *verb,* to write and issue pamphlets; **pamphleteer,** *noun,* a person who writes pamphlets.

pan (1) *noun*
1. a) a round metal vessel, usually shallow, used for cooking, etc. b) anything which has the shape of a pan, such as the dishes on a weighing device.
2. (*informal*) the face.
3. *Geography:* a depression in the ground: 'a *saltpan*'.
pan *verb*
(panned, panning)
1. to wash gold-bearing sand, gravel, etc. in a pan to separate the gold.
2. (*informal*) to dismiss as worthless or criticize severely: 'the critic *panned* the new film'.
pan out, 'how did your plans for the trip *pan out*?' (= turn out).

pan (2) *noun*
a) the betel leaf. b) a substance made from this leaf and other ingredients, chewed in India and other parts of Asia.
[Hindi]

pan (3) *verb*
(panned, panning)
short form of **panorama**
Film: to swing a camera around horizontally from a fixed position, so as to cover a wide area, etc.

Pan (4) *noun*
Greek mythology: the god of flocks and herds, with the upper body of a man and the ears, horns and legs of a goat.

pan (5) *adjective*
Photography: see PANCHROMATIC.

pan–
a prefix meaning all, as in *panchromatic.*
[Greek *pas, pantos*]

panacea (*say* panna-**see**-a) *noun*
a universal remedy.
[PAN- + Greek *akes* remedy]

panache (*say* pan-**ash**) *noun*
1. style: 'everything he does, he does with *panache*'.
2. a plume or bunch of feathers, especially one worn as an ornament on a helmet.
[French]

panama hat
a hat made of the plaited leaves of a South American plant.
[after *Panama*, in Central America]

panatella (*say* panna-**tella**) *noun*
a long, thin cigar.
[Spanish, a long, thin biscuit]

pancake *noun*
1. a thin batter made of beaten eggs, milk and flour, lightly fried to form a flat cake-like food.
2. *Beauty:* a solid cake of make-up which combines foundation and powder.

panchromatic (*say* pan-kro-**mattik**) *adjective*
short form is **pan**
Photography: (of a black and white film) sensitive to light of all colours.
[PAN- + Greek *khromatos* of a colour]

pancreas (*say* **pan**-kree-ass) *noun*
Anatomy: a gland lying under the stomach, secreting the hormone insulin and producing digestive juices which pass into the duodenum.
Word Family: **pancreatic** (*say* pan-kree-**attik**), *adjective*.
[PAN- + Greek *kreas* flesh]

panda *noun*
a large, white, bear-like mammal, with black legs and black around the eyes, which feeds on bamboo shoots, fish and small rodents and is found in the mountains of China and Tibet.
[a Nepalese name]

pandemonium
(*say* pandi-**mo**-nee-um) *noun*
1. uproar: 'during the school holidays the home was in *pandemonium*'.
2. *Mythology:* the place where all demons or evil spirits live.
[from PAN- + Greek *daimon* demon]

pander *verb*
1. to indulge or gratify: 'the housekeeper *pandered* to her master's every whim'.
2. to act as a go-between in intrigues of love.
Word Family: **pander**, *noun*.
[after *Pandarus* a character in the old tale of Troilus and Cressida]

Pandora's box
Greek mythology: a box containing all the evils which Pandora (the equivalent of Eve) opened, letting them escape to plague us ever since.

pane *noun*
a single sheet of glass. A **window pane** is set in a frame and used as a window.

panegyric (*say* panni-**jirrik**) *noun*
a eulogy.
[Greek *panegyrikos* a festival oration]

panel (*say* **pann**'l) *noun*
1. a separate part of a door, ceiling, wainscot, etc., usually raised above or sunk below the surrounding area.
2. a broad strip of cloth set into a piece of clothing and usually of a different colour.
3. a thin, flat piece of wood, etc., such as one on which a picture is painted.
4. a group of people gathered together to take part in a discussion, judge a contest, etc.: 'a *panel* of jurors'.
5. the part of a machine on which controls, etc. are mounted.
Word Family: **panel** (**panelled, panelling**) *verb*, to furnish or decorate with panels; **panelling**, *noun*, a) wood or other material made into panels, b) any or all panels; **panellist**, *noun*, a member of a panel.
[Latin *pannus* a piece of cloth]

pang *noun*
a sudden, short, sharp pain or feeling: a) '*pangs* of hunger'; b) 'a *pang* of regret'.

panhandle *verb*
American: (*informal*) to beg.
Word Family: **panhandler**, *noun*.

panic *noun*
1. an extreme and unreasoning fear: a) 'there was a general *panic* when the theatre caught fire'; b) 'I got into a real *panic* when I thought I was drowning'.
2. (*informal*) to worry unnecessarily.
Word Family: **panic** (**panicked, panicking**), *verb*, to affect with or be stricken by panic; **panicky**, *adjective*, a) liable to panic, b) in a state of panic; **panic-stricken, panic-struck**, *adjectives*, full of panic.
[Greek *Panikos* caused by Pan, who was believed to be the cause of sudden or groundless fear]

panjandrum (*say* pan-**jan**-dr'm) *noun*
short form of **grand panjandrum**

a mock name for someone who is, or thinks he is, very important.
[from a piece of meaningless prose invented in 1755 to test an actor's powers of memorizing]

pannier *noun*
a large basket, for carrying on a person's back, or one of a pair slung across the back of an animal, motorcycle, etc.
[Latin *panarium* a basket for bread]

pannikin *noun*
a small metal cup.

panoply (*say* **panna**-plee) *noun*
a brilliant covering or array: 'the native chieftain wore his *panoply* of furs and feathers'.
[Greek *panoplia* full armour]

panorama (*say* panna-**rah**-ma) *noun*
an unbroken view over a wide area.
Usages:
a) 'my novel is a *panorama* of life in Australia' (= comprehensive survey).
b) 'he observed the *panorama* of seething city life' (= continuously changing scene).
panorama *verb*
Film: see PAN (3).
Word Family: **panoramic** (*say* panna-**rammik**), *adjective.*
[PAN- + Greek *horama* a view]

pansy (*say* **pan**-zee) *noun*
1. any of a group of small plants, often cultivated for its brightly coloured flowers.
2. (*informal*) an effeminate man.
[French *pensée* a thought]

pant *verb*
to breathe hard and quickly, as from exertion.
Usages:
a) 'the steam train stood *panting* in the railway yard' (= emitting puffs of steam).
b) 'he had long *panted* for his revenge' (= yearned).
c) 'he climbed the steps to the gallows with his heart *panting* within him' (= violently throbbing).
Word Family: **pant**, *noun*; **pantingly**, *adverb.*

pantaloons *plural noun*
any of various kinds of trousers.
[after *Pantaloon*, a stock character in old Italian comedies]

pantechnichon (*say* pan-**tekni**-k'n) *noun*
a large furniture removal van.
[the name of an old furniture repository in London]

pantheism (*say* **pan**-thee-izm) *noun*
the belief that God and nature, or the universe, are the same.
Word Family: **pantheist**, *noun*, a person who believes in pantheism; **pantheistic** (*say* pan-thee-**istik**), *adjective.*
[PAN- + Greek *theos* god]

pantheon (*say* **pan**-thee-on) *noun*
a) all the gods of a particular mythology. b) a temple dedicated to them.

panther *noun*
the African or Asian leopard during the phase when its coat turns dark although the spots can be detected.
[Greek]

pantihose *noun*
plural is **pantihose**
see TIGHTS.

pantomime *noun*
a form of entertainment, traditionally performed at Christmas, usually based on a fairytale with modern songs or comedy added.
[Greek *pantos* of all + MIME]

pantry *noun*
a larder.
[Old French *panetier* a servant in charge of bread]

pants *plural noun*
(*informal*) a) trousers. b) underpants.

panzer *adjective*
(of troops) using armoured vehicles.
Word Family: **panzer**, *noun*, a tank.
[German, suit of armour]

pap (1) *noun*
any soft food, such as bread soaked in milk, eaten by babies and invalids.

pap (2) *noun*
an old word for a teat or nipple.

papacy (*say* **pay**-pa-see) *noun*
Roman Catholic: a) the rank, office or period of a pope. b) the system of church government in which a pope is supreme leader.
[Medieval Latin *papa* pope]

papal (*say* **pay**-p'l) *adjective*
of or relating to a pope, papacy or the Roman Catholic Church.

papaya (*say* pa-**pie**-ya) *noun*
a pawpaw.

paper *noun*
1. a) a substance, often made from wood pulp, consisting of thin sheets

used for writing on, wrapping, etc. b) a piece or sheet of this substance.
2. a newspaper.
3. (*plural*) documents of identity.
Usages:
a) 'the professor read a *paper* on Egyptian mummies' (= essay, article). b) 'she thinks she has failed the physics *paper*' (= written examination).
on paper, 'your plan sounds fine *on paper*, but will it work in practice?' (= in theory).
paper *verb*
to cover, line or decorate with paper, e.g. a wall or shelf.
paper *adjective*
made or consisting of paper: 'a *paper* bag'.
Usage: 'all this company ever makes is *paper* profits' (= existing only in the accounting books).
Word Family: **papery**, *adjective*, thin or flimsy like paper.
[Latin *papyrus*]

paperback *noun*
a book bound with a flexible paper cover. Compare HARDBACK.

paperchase *noun*
also called **hare and hounds**
a cross–country run following a trail of scraps of paper laid earlier by the 'hare'.

paperclip *noun*
a metal or plastic clasp for holding loose papers together.

paperhanger *noun*
a professional hanger of wallpaper.

paperknife *noun*
a knife–like instrument for opening letters, etc.

paper tape
Computers: a strip of paper punched with holes representing information which can be fed into a computer.

paper tiger
a person or thing that appears strong but is really weak.

paperweight (*say* **pay**pa–wate) *noun*
a small, heavy object placed on top of loose papers to keep them in place.

paperwork *noun*
any written, clerical or administrative work, especially as part of one's normal occupation.

papier–mâché (*say* pappia–**mash**ay) *noun*
a lightweight substance made of any mashed paper, usually newspaper soaked in water, applied in layers with glue and used to make simple models, trays, boxes, etc. and often lacquered, gilded and painted.
[French *mâché* chewed + *papier* paper]

papilla (*say* pa–**pill**a) *noun*
Anatomy: a) a nipple. b) any small nipple–like structure, such as a tastebud or a hair root.
Word Family: **papillary**, *adjective.*
[Latin]

papilloma (*say* pappi–**lo**–ma) *noun*
a small skin tumour, such as a wart or corn.
[Latin *papilla* nipple + *–oma* tumour]

papist (*say* **pay**–pist) *noun*
a supporter of the pope.
Word Family: **papism**, *noun.*

papoose *noun*
a North American Indian baby or young child.

paprika (*say* pa–**pree**ka *or* **pap**rika) *noun*
a red spice made from ground capsicum.
[Hungarian]

papyrus (*say* pa–**pie**–rus) *noun*
plural is **papyri** (*say* pa–**pie**–ree)
1. a tall, aquatic, rush–like plant.
2. a material used for writing on by ancient civilizations, especially the Egyptians, made from soaked, dried and compressed strips of papyrus stem.
[Greek *papyros*]

par *noun*
1. an average or normal amount, degree, condition, etc.: 'the quality of your work is well above *par*'.
2. *Commerce:* the nominal or face value of a stock or share.
3. *Golf:* the average number of strokes that a first–class player, making no mistakes, should take for each hole or a number of holes. Compare BOGEY.
Phrases:
above par, priced above face value.
at par, at face value.
below par, priced below face value.
on a par, 'your work is *on a par* with mine' (= equal in amount, quality, etc.).
[Latin, equal]

para– (*say* parra)
a prefix meaning: a) near or beside, as in *paramilitary*; b) beyond, as in *paranormal.*
[Greek]

parable (*say* **parr**a–b'l) *noun*
a short story which illustrates a moral or lesson.
[Greek *parabolé* comparison]

parabola (*say* pa–**rabb**a–la) *noun*
Maths: a plane, regular curve formed when a cone is intercut by a plane which is parallel to the side of the cone. See CONIC SECTION.
Word Family: **parabolic** (*say* parra–**boll**ik), *adjective,* of, like or having the form of a parabola.
[PARA– + Greek *bolé* a throw]

parachute (*say* **parr**a–shoot) *noun*
an umbrella shaped canopy of lightweight fabric which permits a person or cargo to drop safely to the ground from a height owing to air filling the canopy and retarding its downward fall.
Word Family: **parachute**, *verb,* to descend or land by parachute; **parachutist**, *noun.*
[French *parer* to prevent or avoid + *chute* fall]

parachute brake
a parachute released behind a landing aircraft to slow it down.

Paraclete (*say* **parr**a–kleet) *noun*
1. *Christian:* the Holy Spirit.
2. (*not capital*) a helper or comforter.
[Greek *parakletos* an advocate]

parade (*say* pa–**rade**) *noun*
1. a ceremonial procession, as held on a festive occasion.
2. a) an orderly assembly of troops for inspection or display. b) a parade ground.
Usage: 'he constantly makes a *parade* of his abilities' (= display, exhibition).
3. a promenade.
parade ground
a place where troops assemble for inspection and parade.
Word Family: **parade**, *verb.*
[French, a show]

paradigm (*say* **parr**a–dime) *noun*
a pattern or example, especially of the principal parts of irregular verbs, etc.
[Greek *paradeigma* showing side by side]

paradise (*say* **parr**a–dice) *noun*
1. heaven.
2. a place of extreme beauty or delight.
[ancient Persian, an enclosed garden]

paradox (*say* **parr**a–doks) *noun*
a) a statement which appears to contradict itself, often made intentionally to emphasize a point. b) a person or situation that is puzzling because of contradictory qualities.
Word Family: **paradoxical** (*say* parra–**doks**i–k'l), *adjective,* of or like a paradox; **paradoxically**, *adverb.*
[PARA– + Greek *doxa* opinion]

paraffin (*say* **parr**a–fin) *noun*
also called **kerosene** or **paraffin oil**
1. a mixture of hydrocarbons produced during the distillation of petroleum, used for domestic heating and lighting, as a solvent, and in jet engines.
2. paraffin wax.
[Latin *parum* little + *affinis* related (as being unreactive)]

paraffin series
also called **alkane series** or **paraffins**
Chemistry: a homologous series of hydrocarbons having the general formula C_nH_{2n+2}, such as methane, CH_4. The paraffins are chemically unreactive, stable and inflammable, and range from gases to solids.

paraffin wax
a white translucent solid, melting to a clear liquid and used for candles, waxed paper and polishes.

paragon (*say* **parr**a–g'n) *noun*
a model of excellence: 'my daughter is a *paragon* of good behaviour'.
[Italian *paragone* touchstone]

paragraph (*say* **parr**a–graf) *noun*
a group of sentences placed together because they have a common idea, usually beginning on a new line of the page.
Word Family: **paragraph**, *verb,* to divide into paragraphs.
[PARA– + Greek *graphein* to write]

parakeet (*say* **parr**a–keet) *noun*
also spelt **paroquet**
also called a **lorikeet**
any of various small, slender, Australian parrots such as the budgerigar.

parallax (*say* **parr**a–laks) *noun*
Physics: the apparent change in the position or direction of an object due to the observer changing his position.
Word Family: **parallactic**, *adjective*; **parallactically**, *adverb.*
[Greek *parallaxis* change]

parallel (*say* **parr**a–lel) *adjective*
1. of the same direction or tendency: a) 'the road runs *parallel* to the river'; b) 'my thoughts are *parallel* to yours'.
2. *Maths:* relating to lines or planes that never meet, no matter how far they are extended.

3. *Electricity:* (of two or more conductors) connected between the same two points, so that the electric current is divided between the conductors. Compare SERIES.
parallel *noun*
1. an analogy or comparison: 'he drew a *parallel* between my behaviour and that of a mad dog'.
Usage: 'the brilliance of his last novel is without *parallel*' (= equal, match).
2. *Geography:* a line of latitude.
Word Family: **parallel**, *verb*, a) to be parallel to, b) to compare.
[Greek *parallelos* side by side]

parallelism (*say* **parr**a-lel-izm) *noun*
a) the state of being parallel. b) similarity.

parallelogram (*say* parra-**lell**a-gram) *noun*
a quadrilateral having opposite sides equal and parallel, such as a rhombus or square.

paralyse (*say* **parr**a-lize) *verb*
in America spelt **paralyze**
to affect with paralysis: 'his legs were *paralysed* after the accident'.
Usage: 'she was *paralysed* with terror when she saw the ghost' (= helpless).

paralysis (*say* pa-**ralla**-sis) *noun*
plural is **paralyses** (*say* pa-**ralla**-seez)
Medicine: the loss of voluntary movement of the muscles.
Usage: 'the strikes caused a *paralysis* in shipping trade' (= stoppage, inability to function).
[Greek *para* on one side + *lysis* a loosening]

paralytic (*say* parra-**littik**) *noun*
a person affected with paralysis of the entire body.
paralytic *adjective*
1. of, like or affected with paralysis.
2. (*informal*) extremely drunk.

paramecium (*say* parra-**meesium**) *noun*
plural is **paramecia**
also called **slipper animalcule**
a microscopic freshwater animal with hair-like threads on its outer surface which help it move.
[Greek *paramekes* oval]

paramedical *adjective*
relating to the supplementary work within the medical profession, such as social work, etc.

parameter (*say* pa-**rammi**ta) *noun*
1. *Maths:* a variable in terms of which other interrelated variables are expressed and upon which they may then be regarded as being dependent.
2. a numerical characteristic of a statistical population.
Word Family: **parametric** (*say* parra-**met**rik), *adjective.*

paramilitary *adjective*
having a military structure or organization which is supplementary to the regular armed forces.

paramount (*say* **parr**a-mount) *adjective*
superior or supreme: 'this word is of *paramount* importance'.

paramour (*say* **parr**a-mor) *noun*
a lover, especially one of a married person.

paranoia (*say* parra-**noy**a) *noun*
a mental disorder marked by the unjustified belief that one is being persecuted, usually accompanied by megalomania and insane distrust.
paranoid (*say* **parr**a-noyd) *adjective*
also called **paranoiac** (*say* parra-**noy**-ak)
of, relating to or affected by paranoia.
Word Family: **paranoid**, **paranoiac**, *nouns*, a person affected with paranoia.
[Greek, derangement]

paranormal *adjective*
not able to be explained by normal scientific laws: 'telepathy is a *paranormal* means of communication'.

parapet *noun*
a) a low, defensive wall or bank in front of a trench or other fortification. b) a low wall around the edge of a balcony or the top of a building.

paraphernalia (*say* parra-f'**nay**-lee-a) *plural noun*
miscellaneous belongings or equipment.
[PARA- + Greek *pherné* dowry]

paraphrase (*say* **parr**a-fraze) *noun*
the rewording of a piece of writing to make it shorter or clearer.
Word Family: **paraphrase**, *verb.*

paraplegic (*say* parra-**plee**-jik) *adjective*
having both arms or both legs paralysed.
Word Family: **paraplegia**, *noun*; **paraplegic**, *noun*, a person who is paraplegic.
[PARA- + Greek *plegia* a stroke]

parapsychology (*say* parra-sigh-**kolla**-jee) *noun*
also called **psychical research**

the study of psychological phenomena which cannot be scientifically explained, e.g. clairvoyance, telepathy, seeing ghosts, etc.
Word Family: **parapsychological** (*say* parra-sigh-ka-**loji**-k'l), *adjective.*

parasite (*say* **parra**-site) *noun*
1. a person who lives on others and gives nothing in return.
2. *Biology:* an organism which can obtain food only by living in or on another organism.
parasitic (*say* parra-**sittik**) *adjective*
of, pertaining to or like a parasite.
Word Family: **parasitically,** *adverb*; **parasitism,** *noun.*
[Greek *parasitos* dinner guest]

parasitology (*say* parra-sigh-**tolla**-jee) *noun*
the study of parasites, a branch of biology.
Word Family: **parasitologist,** *noun.*

parasol *noun*
a light umbrella made of cloth or stiffened paper, for protection from sunlight.
[Latin *para* guard against + *sol* sun]

paratrooper *noun*
a soldier trained and equipped to parachute from aircraft, especially in order to fight behind enemy lines.
Word Family: **paratroops,** *plural noun,* any or all paratroopers.

par avion
(of a letter) air mail.
[French, by aeroplane]

parboil *verb*
to boil food until it is partly cooked.
[PART + BOIL, confused with French *parbouillir* to boil thoroughly]

parcel (*say* **par**-s'l) *noun*
a collection or quantity of goods wrapped up together, such as groceries, etc.
Usage: 'he bought a *parcel* of land at the back of the estate' (= piece).
parcel *verb*
(parcelled, parcelling)
1. to make up into a parcel.
2. to divide up or distribute something.
[Latin *particula* a small part]

parch *verb*
to make hot and dry: 'the desert winds *parched* the weary pilgrims'.

parchment *noun*
a) the skin of animals prepared as a surface for writing. b) a paper resembling parchment.

pardon *noun*
1. courteous patience, as in excusing a fault, etc.: 'I beg your *pardon*'.
2. *Law:* the releasing of a convicted person from punishment for his crime.
3. *History:* an indulgence.
pardon *verb*
1. to make allowance for: '*pardon* my interruption, but it's time to go'.
2. *Law:* to release a person from a penalty or liability for a crime.
Word Family: **pardonable,** *adjective,* able or worthy to be pardoned.

pardoner *noun*
History: a person appointed to sell religious pardons for sins.

pare (*rhymes with* air) *verb*
to cut or peel off the outer layer or edge of something: 'she *pared* her fingernails'.
Usage: 'you must *pare* down your expenses' (= reduce).
Word Family: **paring,** *noun,* a) the act of a person or thing that pares, b) a part that is pared off.

paregoric (*say* parra-**gorrik**) *noun*
a soothing medicine, such as one used to check diarrhoea, etc.

parent (*say* **pair**-ent) *noun*
1. a living thing which produces other similar living things; a mother or father.
2. a source or origin of something.
parental (*say* pa-**ren**-t'l) *adjective*
of or like a parent: 'these children need *parental* discipline'.
Word Family: **parentally,** *adverb*; **parenthood,** *noun.*
[Latin *pariens* bringing forth young]

parentage (*say* **pairen**-tij) *noun*
origin or descent: 'he's a man of noble *parentage*'.

parenthesis (*say* pa-**rentha**-sis) *noun*
plural is **parentheses** (*say* pa-**rentha**-seez)
1. a word or words inserted into a sentence or passage as a separate comment.
2. the punctuation marks used to enclose a word or words which may interrupt the flow of a sentence. *Example*: the aeroplane landed in Sydney (Australia) at 9.00 a.m.
Word Family: **parenthesize, parenthesise,** *verb*; **parenthetic** (*say* parren-**thettik**), *adjective.*
[Greek, putting in beside]

par excellence (*say* par eksa-**lonce**)
superior to all others: 'her mother is a cook *par excellence*'.
[French]

parfait (*say* **par**-fay) ***noun***
a rich, frozen, flavoured dessert of egg and ice-cream or whipped cream.
[French, perfect]

pariah (*say* pa-**rye**-a) ***noun***
a person or animal that is despised; an outcast.
[Tamil, a drummer]

parietal (*say* pa-**rye**-t'l) *adjective*
Biology: of or relating to part of the wall of a structure.
parietal bone
Anatomy: either of two bones forming the upper sides and roof of the skull.
[Latin *paries* a partition]

paring ***noun***
Word Family: see PARE.

parish (*say* **parrish**) ***noun***
a) a district with its own church and clergyman. b) a local government area based on this.
[Greek *paroikesis* a neighbourhood]

parishioner (*say* pa-**rishina**) ***noun***
a) a person who lives in a parish. b) a person who attends a parish church.

parity (*say* **parri**-tee) ***noun***
equality: a) 'everyone in this school receives *parity* of treatment'; b) 'the two currencies are at a *parity*'.
[Latin *par* equal]

park ***noun***
1. an area of open land, usually with trees, etc., set aside for public recreational use.
2. the land surrounding a country house.
car park, an area set aside for parking cars.
park *verb*
to leave a vehicle in a particular place.
Usage: (*informal*) '*park* your bags in the hall' (= leave).

parka ***noun***
an anorak.
[Eskimo]

Parkinson's disease
also called **paralysis agitans** or **shaking palsy**
a form of paralysis causing uncontrollable shaking of the limbs and a mask-like face.
[after *J. Parkinson*, 1755–1824, a British doctor]

Parkinson's law
a humorous law stating that 'work expands so as to fill the time available for its completion' and 'subordinates multiply at a fixed rate regardless of the amount of work produced'.
[invented in 1958 by *C. N. Parkinson*, a British historian]

parkland ***noun***
an area of grass with scattered trees.

parlance ***noun***
a way of speaking: 'he has dropped the case or, in legal *parlance*, entered a nolle prosequi'.
[Old French, speaking]

parley (*say* **par**-lee) ***noun***
an informal discussion, especially with an enemy to discuss terms.
Word Family: **parley**, *verb*.

parliament (*say* **parla**-m'nt) ***noun***
1. an assembly of representatives from all parts of a country that meets to make laws, advise the government, control taxation and expenditure, etc.
2. (*capital*) the House of Commons and House of Lords, the two Houses of Parliament.
Word Family: **parliamentary**, *adjective*, of or relating to a parliament.
[Old French *parlement* talking]

parliamentarian
(*say* parla-men-**tairian**) ***noun***
a person who is experienced in parliamentary debate and procedure.
Word Family: **parliamentarianism**, ***noun***, the supporting of a parliamentary system of government.

parlour (*say* **parla**) ***noun***
in America spelt **parlor**
an old word for a living room or room where visitors are entertained.

parlous (*say* **parlus**) *adjective*
an old word meaning dangerous or very bad: 'things are in a *parlous* state'.
[for PERILOUS]

parochial (*say* pa-**ro**-kee-ul) *adjective*
of or relating to a parish: 'the clergyman's *parochial* duties took up much of his time'.
Usage: 'your hatred of everything modern shows a very *parochial* outlook' (= narrow, limited).
Word Family: **parochially**, *adverb*; **parochialism**, ***noun***.

parody (*say* **parra**-dee) ***noun***
a humorous imitation of a serious piece of writing.
Usage: 'he is a mere *parody* of a real gentleman' (= weak imitation).

Word Family: **parody** (**parodied, parodying**), *verb.*
[PARA– + Greek *oidé* an ode]

parole (*say* pa–**role**) *noun*
Law: the early release of a prisoner on a promise of good behaviour. Compare PROBATION.
Word Family: **parole**, *verb*, to release a prisoner on parole.
[French, word (of honour)]

paroquet (*say* **parra**–keet) *noun*
a parakeet.

paroxysm (*say* **parr**ok–sizm) *noun*
a sudden, uncontrolled fit of pain, coughing, laughter, anger, etc.
[Greek *paroxysmos* irritation]

parquet (*say* **par**kay) *noun*
a pattern of inlaid pieces of wood, used to make floors, etc.
parquetry (*say* **par**ka–tree) *noun*
inlaid and patterned woodwork.
Word Family: **parquet**, *verb.*
[French, floor]

parricide (*say* **parri**–side) *noun*
Law: a) the crime of killing either of one's parents or a close relative. b) the person who does this. c) treason.
[Latin *pater* father or *parens* parent + *caedere* to kill]

parrot *noun*
any of a group of brightly coloured birds with hooked bills and fleshy tongues, some of which have a gift for mimicry.
parrot *verb*
to imitate or repeat words like a parrot: 'having no original ideas, he *parrots* what others say'.

parrot fever
psittacosis.

parry *verb*
(**parried, parrying**)
to evade or deflect: a) 'she *parried* the reporter's questions about her elopement'; b) 'he *parried* his opponent's sword thrust'.
Word Family: **parry**, *noun.*

parse (*say* parz) *verb*
Grammar: to give a word its grammatical description.

parsec *noun*
a unit of length used in astronomy and equal to about $3\frac{1}{4}$ light years or $3{\cdot}08 \times 10^{16}$ m.
[PAR(allax) + SEC(ond)]

parsimonious (*say* parsi–**mo**–nee–us) *adjective*
extremely frugal, miserly or stingy.
Word Family: **parsimoniously**, *adverb*; **parsimony** (*say* **par**–simma–nee), *noun.*
[from Latin]

parsley (*say* **par**–slee) *noun*
a garden plant with green, crinkled leaves used for flavouring and to decorate food.

parsnip *noun*
a white, fleshy, cone–shaped root used as a vegetable.

parson *noun*
a clergyman or parish priest.
parsonage (*say* **par**sa–nij) *noun*
the residence of a parson.
[Latin *persona* a person]

parson's nose
the fatty tail of cooked chicken or other poultry.

part *noun*
a piece or portion of a whole: a) 'a *part* of this book is missing'; b) 'I need some new *parts* for my car'.
Usages:
a) 'the actors have learnt their *parts* for the play' (= roles).
b) 'he travelled in foreign *parts* for 25 years' (= areas, lands).
c) 'this choral work is for 8 *parts*' (= types of voices).
d) 'he's a man of many *parts*' (= abilities, skills).
Phrases:
for the most part, mostly.
in part, to some extent.
part and parcel, a necessary part.
take in good part, to take no offence at.
take part, to join in or participate.
take someone's part, 'she always *takes* her sister's *part* in arguments' (= supports, defends).
part *verb*
1. to move things so that they are no longer together: a) 'I'll *part* you two if you don't stop talking!'; b) 'she'll never *part* with her teddy bear'.
2. to make a parting in the hair.
Word Family: **part, partly**, *adverbs*, in part; **part**, *adjective*, being partly composed of.
[from Latin]

partake *verb*
(**partook, partaken, partaking**)
to take part or share in something: a) 'will you *partake* of dinner with us?'; b) 'she *partakes* of her mother's common sense'.

parterre (*say* par–**tair**) *noun*
a formal arrangement of lawns, paths and flower–beds as part of a larger garden.
[French]

parthenogenesis
(*say* partha–no–**jenni**–sis) *noun*
Biology: the development of an ovum without fertilization occurring.
[Greek *parthenos* virgin + GENESIS]

partial (*say* **par**–sh'l) *adjective*
1. not total or complete: 'the meeting was only a *partial* success'.
2. biased or prejudiced: 'it's useless having the dispute decided by a *partial* judge'.
3. fond of: 'he's very *partial* to marmalade sandwiches'.
Word Family: **partially**, *adverb*; **partiality** (*say* parshi–**alli**–tee), *noun*.

participate (*say* par–**tissi**–pate) *verb*
to have a role or share in: a) 'are you *participating* in the football match?'; b) 'after 10 years in the company you may *participate* in the profits'.
Word Family: **participant**, **participator**, *nouns*, a person who participates; **participation**, *noun*, the act of participating.
[Latin *partis* of a part + *capere* to take]

participle (*say* par–**tissi**–p'l) *noun*
Grammar: a word formed from a verb and used as a verb or an adjective.
a **present participle** expresses an action or state which is happening at this moment. *Example*: the *laughing* boy walked home *whistling*.
a **past participle** expresses an action or state which is already completed. *Example*: this car has *travelled* many miles.

particle (*say* **parti**–k'l) *noun*
a very small piece or amount: 'I don't want to see one *particle* of dirt on this floor'.
[from Latin]

particle accelerator
see CYCLOTRON.

particoloured *adjective*
having different colours in different parts.

particular (*say* par**tik**–yoola) *adjective*
1. relating to one person, group or thing rather than to all: 'in this *particular* case I have no sympathy for the accused'.
2. special: 'she is a *particular* friend of mine'.
3. careful or attentive to details: 'she is very *particular* about what she eats'.
particular *noun*
a point: 'you are correct in every *particular*'.
in particular, '*in particular* I think the photography in the film was excellent' (= especially).
Word Family: **particularly**, *adverb*, especially; **particularity** (*say* partik–yoo–**larri**–tee), *noun*; **particularize**, **particularise**, *verb*, to mention or deal with separately or in detail.

particularism *noun*
an exclusive concern for a particular sect, party, etc.
Word Family: **particularist**, *noun*, *adjective*.

parting *noun*
1. a division or separation, such as the dividing line between hair brushed to left and right.
2. a leave–taking or departure.
parting *adjective*
a) said, done, etc. on parting: 'a *parting* word with you, my son'. b) dying or departing: 'the *parting* day'.

partisan (*say* **parti**–zan) *noun*
1. any supporter of a person, party or cause.
2. a member of a military force, but not part of a regular army, fighting for the liberation of his country.
Word Family: **partisan**, *adjective*, biased.
[Italian *partigiano*]

partition (*say* par–**tish**'n) *noun*
a) a separation or division of a whole into parts: 'the *partition* of his farm into building sites made him a wealthy man'. b) something that divides or separates, especially a wall or screen dividing a room. c) a section or part formed by dividing.
Word Family: **partition**, *verb*, to divide or separate into parts.

partly *adverb*
Word Family: see PART.

partner *noun*
1. a person who shares an activity with another: a) 'a dancing *partner*'; b) 'a business *partner*'.
2. a person on the same team as another at tennis, cards, etc.
3. a husband or wife.
partnership *noun*
the state or condition of being a partner: a) 'the brothers own the business in *partnership*'; b) 'the

batsmen had a cricket *partnership* of 120 runs'.
Word Family: **partner**, *verb*, to be or act as someone's partner.

partook *verb*
the past tense of the verb **partake**.

partridge *noun*
any of various plump, brown game-birds with short wings and tail.

part-song *noun*
a song with parts for several voices.

part-time *adjective, adverb*
of work or interest which does not take up the full working hours in a week.
Word Family: **part-timer**, *noun.*

parturition (*say* partew-**rish**'n) *noun*
childbirth.
Word Family: **parturient** (*say* par-**tewri**-ent), *adjective*, giving or about to give birth.
[from Latin]

party *noun*
1. a social gathering, especially a private one.
2. a group of people with the same beliefs and policies, usually in opposition to others: 'a political *party*'.
3. a person who takes part in a proceeding, or enters into a relationship: a) 'I refuse to be a *party* to the plot'; b) 'we have found the guilty *party*'.
Usage: 'the captain sent a *party* ashore' (= group of people).
party *adjective*
1. of or relating to a party.
2. of or relating to something shared: 'the fence between our houses is a *party* fence'.

party line
1. a telephone line shared by more than one household, each having a separate instrument.
2. the official ideas or policies of a political party: 'he was expelled for refusing to follow the *party line*'.

parvenu (*say* **parva**-new) *noun*
a person who has risen above his original status through the sudden attainment of wealth or position.
[French, arrived]

pascal (*say* **pas**-k'l) *noun*
the SI unit of pressure, equal to a force of one newton over an area of one square metre. See UNITS in grey pages.
[after *Blaise Pascal*, 1623–62, a French philosopher and scientist]

paschal (*say* **pas**-k'l) *adjective*
Jewish, Christian: of or relating to the Passover or Easter.

pas de deux (*say* pah deh der)
Ballet: a dance or part of a dance for two people.
[French, step of two]

pasha (*say* **pah**-sha) *noun*
a title added after the names of generals and governors under the old Turkish Empire, and retained in some countries after its collapse.
[Turkish, chief]

pass *verb*
(passed, passed or **past, passing)**
1. to go by: 'the days *pass* quickly during the holidays'.
2. to give or transfer something from one person or position to another: '*pass* me the butter'.
3. to get over or through an obstacle: 'did you *pass* your final exams?'.
Usages:
a) 'how will you *pass* your holidays?' (= spend).
b) 'to *pass* urine' (= excrete).
c) 'boiling water *passes* into steam' (= becomes).
d) 'don't *pass* 100 km an hour' (= exceed).
e) 'he was quick to *pass* judgement' (= utter, pronounce).
f) 'what *passed* at the meeting?' (= took place).
g) 'Parliament has *passed* a new law' (= approved).
h) 'having no high cards, I *passed*' (= did not bid).
i) 'he tries to *pass* for a gentleman' (= be accepted as).
Phrases:
come to pass, to happen.
pass away, to die.
pass off, a) 'the strike *passed off* without violence' (= took place); b) 'he tries to *pass* himself *off* as a genius' (= get people to believe).
pass out, (*informal*) to faint.
pass over, a) to ignore; b) to overlook.
pass up, (*informal*) to refuse or reject.
pass *noun*
1. the act of passing, such as transferring a ball from one footballer to another or not bidding in a game of cards.
2. a narrow route through mountains.
3. a) any written permission to enter or leave a building or area. b) a ticket allowing free entrance to entertainments, public transport, etc.

Usage: 'things have come to a dangerous *pass*' (= stage).
4. the required standard in an examination.
Phrases:
make a pass, to make amorous advances.
pretty pass, 'things have come to a *pretty pass*' (= deplorable state).

passable *adjective*
able to be passed.
Usage: 'he has a *passable* knowledge of mechanics' (= fair, moderate).
Word Family: **passably**, *adverb*, fairly or moderately.

passage (*say* **pass**–ij) *noun*
1. a) the act of passing: 'the *passage* of time'. b) a means of passing, such as a corridor.
2. an extract from any written work or piece of music.
3. a journey across the sea from one port to another.
4. the right to pass through or across someone's land, etc.
[Latin *passus* a pace]

passbook *noun*
a book in which a record of payments is made, as to a bank or building society.

pass degree
the lowest-ranking degree for a university graduate.

passé (*say* **pass**ay) *adjective*
a) old-fashioned or out-of-date. b) aged or stale.
[French, passed]

passenger (*say* **pass**in–ja) *noun*
a person who travels or is carried in a vehicle.
Usage: (*informal*) 'it is obvious that half of the office employees are *passengers*' (= people who do little work).

passer–by *noun*
plural is **passers–by**
a person who passes by.

passerine (*say* **pass**a–rine) *adjective*
of birds that perch.
[Latin *passer* sparrow]

passing *noun*
the act of going by: 'the *passing* of the long summer days'.
Word Family: **passing**, *adjective*, brief or cursory.

passion (*say* **pash**'n) *noun*
1. any emotion or feeling which is very strong and compelling, such as love, hate, anger, hope, grief, etc.
2. a) a strong enthusiasm for someone or something: 'he has a *passion* for poetry'. b) the object of this: 'poetry is his only *passion*'.
3. *Christian:* (*capital*) a) the sufferings of Christ, especially at the crucifixion. b) any of the Gospel accounts of these or a musical setting or enactment of them.

passionate (*say* **pash**a–nit) *adjective*
affected with or characterized by passion: a) 'he is a *passionate* lover'; b) 'she is a *passionate* supporter of women's rights'.
Word Family: **passionately**, *adverb*.
[Latin *passio* suffering]

passionfruit *noun*
a small, round, purple fruit with a tough skin and many small seeds, growing on a vine.

passive (*say* **pass**iv) *adjective*
1. inactive or submissive: 'his dog obeys his every word in *passive* obedience'.
2. *Chemistry:* inactive, especially a metal surface.
3. *Grammar:* see VOICE.
Word Family: **passively**, *adverb*; **passiveness**, **passivity** (*say* pa–**sivvi**–tee), *nouns*.

Passover (*say* **pah**–sover) *noun*
Jewish: a religious feast celebrating the deliverance of the Jews from Egypt.

passport *noun*
an official document which identifies a person wishing to travel in foreign countries. Compare VISA.
Usage: 'this magic lamp is your *passport* to untold riches' (= means of obtaining).
[PASS + PORT]

password *noun*
a secret word or phrase permitting a person using it to pass guards or sentries.

past *adjective*
having occurred at a time before the present: 'I was ill all the *past* month'.
past *noun*
1. a) any time before the present: 'history is a study of the *past*'. b) the events in a person's life or experiences: 'how can I trust you when I know nothing about your *past*?'.
Usage: 'the stranger is a person with a *past*' (= secret, hidden history).
2. *Grammar:* see TENSE (2).
past *preposition*
1. after in time: a) 'it is *past* 6 o'clock'. b) 'the lady is well *past* 70'.

2. beyond or further than: 'the shop is *past* the corner'.
past *verb*
a past participle of the verb **pass.**

pasta *noun*
a mixture of flour and eggs used as a dough in various forms, e.g. for macaroni and spaghetti.
[Italian]

paste *noun*
1. a mixture, usually of flour and water, used for sticking paper, etc.
2. dough for making pastry.
3. any soft smooth preparation: a) '*toothpaste*'; b) 'fish *paste*'.
4. a bright glassy substance used to make artificial gems.
paste *verb*
to fasten or stick something using paste, glue, etc.
[Greek *pasté* barley soup]

pasteboard *noun*
a flat surface made of several sheets of paper and board stuck together.

pastel (*say* **pas**–t'l) *noun*
1. a soft, delicate hue.
2. a) a crayon made of chalk, pigments, etc. b) a picture drawn with pastels.
[from PASTA]

pastern (*say* **pas**–turn) *noun*
the part of a horse's foot between the fetlock and the hoof.

pasteurize (*say* **pah**sta–rize)
pasteurise *verb*
to reduce the number of micro-organisms present in a liquid such as milk, by heating but not boiling.
Word Family: **pasteurization,** *noun.*
[after *Louis Pasteur,* 1822–95, a French chemist]

pastiche (*say* pas–**teesh**) *noun*
a work of art which imitates or borrows from the work or style of other artists.
[Italian *pasta* paste]

pastille (*say* pas–**teel**) *noun*
a small flavoured sweet or lozenge.
[Latin *pastilla* a small loaf]

pastime (*say* **pahs**–time) *noun*
an amusement, hobby or sport that helps time pass pleasantly.

past master
an expert or person with long experience.

pastor *noun*
Christian: a clergyman or minister in charge of a congregation.
Word Family: **pastorate,** *noun,* a) the office or term of office of a pastor, b) any or all pastors.
[Latin, shepherd]

pastoral *adjective*
1. (of land) used as pasture or for grazing, etc.
2. of or characteristic of the country or country life: 'a *pastoral* poem'.
3. of or relating to a clergyman or his duties.
pastoral *noun*
1. a work of art dealing with shepherds or country life.
2. a letter from a bishop to the clergy or congregation.
pastoralist *noun*
a person who uses his land for grazing sheep, cattle, etc.
Word Family: **pastorally,** *adverb*; **pastoralism,** *noun.*

pastorale (*say* pasta–**rahl**) *noun*
Music: a choral or orchestral work depicting or concerning pastoral life.

past participle
see PARTICIPLE.

pastry (*say* **pay**–stree) *noun*
a) dough, especially when used as the base or crust of a pie. b) any foods made with pastry.

pastry–cook *noun*
a person who makes or sells pastries, small cakes, etc.

pasture (*say* **pahs**–cher) *noun*
an area covered with grass used or suitable for grazing cattle, etc.
Word Family: **pasture,** *verb,* a) to put livestock on a pasture, b) to graze.
[from Latin]

pasty (1) (*say* **pay**–stee) *adjective*
1. of or like paste.
2. (of a complexion) pale and sickly.

pasty (2) (*say* **pas**–tee) *noun*
an envelope of pastry filled with meat and vegetables and cooked.

pat (1) *verb*
(patted, patting)
to touch or strike lightly, especially with the open hand or with something flat: a) 'wash your hands if you've been *patting* the dog'; b) 'he *patted* down the earth after planting the seedlings'.
pat on the back, (*informal*) to congratulate.
pat *noun*
1. a) a light strike or touch. b) the sound of this, such as footsteps.

2. a small mass of something, especially butter.

pat (2) *adjective*
1. apt or appropriate: 'that is a *pat* description'.
2. glib or facile: 'your answer was just a little too *pat*'.
pat *adverb*
exactly or aptly.
Phrases:
off pat, 'I had my excuse *off pat*' (= at the ready).
sit, stand pat, to keep or maintain something without changing it.

patch *noun*
a) a piece of fabric used to cover holes in clothing, etc. b) a covering for a wound: 'an *eyepatch*'.
Usages:
a) 'I've bought a small *patch* of land' (= piece).
b) 'she's going through a bad *patch* at the moment' (= time).
not a patch on, not nearly as good as.
patch *verb*
to repair something with a patch.
patch up, a) 'I'll *patch up* this radio so we can hear the news' (= repair simply or quickly); b) 'the girls *patched up* their differences after the fight' (= settled).

patchouli (*say* pa–**choo**–lee) *noun*
the oil of an Asian plant, used as a perfume.
[a Madras name]

patchwork *noun*
1. a form of needlework in which small pieces of fabric are sewn together.
2. anything formed from different pieces: 'his book is a *patchwork* of old and new ideas'.

patchy *adjective*
of uneven quality: 'why can't your work be consistently good rather than *patchy*?'.

pate *noun*
an old word for the head.

pâté (*say* **pa**–tay) *noun*
a savoury paste made from finely chopped meat or fish and herbs.
[French]

patella (*say* pa–**tella**) *noun*
Anatomy: the kneecap.
[Latin, a plate]

patent (*say* **pay**–t'nt *or* **patt**'nt) *noun*
the official right given to an inventor to make or sell his invention for a certain time without it being copied.

patent (*say* **pay**–t'nt) *adjective*
1. plain or obvious: 'I know the truth and what he said was a *patent* lie'.
2. having or protected by a patent.
Word Family: **patent**, *verb*, to obtain a patent for an invention, etc.; **patently**, *adverb*, plainly or obviously.
[Latin *patens* lying open]

patent leather
a leather coated with a hard, glossy surface.

pater (*say* **payta**) *noun*
(*informal*) father.
paterfamilias
(*say* payter–fa–**milli**–ass) *noun*
the head of a family.
[Latin, father]

paternal *adjective*
1. of or like a father: 'he treats us in a *paternal* way'.
2. related on the father's side.
Word Family: **paternally**, *adverb*

paternalism (*say* pa–**terna**–lizm) *noun*
the principle of treating those over whom one has control in the same way that a father treats his children.
Word Family: **paternalistic** (*say* pa–terna–**listik**), *adjective*; **paternalistically**, *adverb.*

paternity (*say* pa–**terni**–tee) *noun*
a) the state of being a father. b) a relationship to or derivation from a father: 'her *paternity* is unknown'.

paternity suit
Law: a case in which a woman tries to prove that a certain man is the father of her child.

path (*say* pahth) *noun*
1. a track or way for walking.
2. the track in which something moves: 'the *path* of the earth around the sun'.
Usage: 'this *path* of action is getting us nowhere' (= line, method).

pathetic (*say* pa–**thettik**) *adjective*
1. causing pity or sympathy: 'the starving child was a *pathetic* sight'.
2. (*informal*) miserably weak or inadequate.
Word Family: **pathetically**, *adverb.*

pathfinder *noun*
1. an explorer or pioneer.
2. an aircraft sent ahead of bombers to mark a target by dropping flares.

patho–
a prefix meaning disease or suffering, as in *pathology.*
[Greek]

pathogen (*say* **patha**–j'n) *noun*
any organism that can cause disease.
[PATHO– + –GEN]

pathogenic (*say* patha–**jennik**) *adjective*
producing disease.
Word Family: **pathogenesis**, *noun.*

pathological (*say* patha–**loji**–k'l) *adjective*
a) of or relating to pathology. b) due to or involving disease.
Usage: 'he's a *pathological* liar so you can't believe anything he tells you' (= compulsive).
Word Family: **pathologically**, *adverb.*

pathology (*say* pa–**tholla**–jee) *noun*
a) the study of diseases and their effects. b) the conditions and progress of a disease.
Word Family: **pathologist**, *noun*, a person who studies diseases.

pathos (*say* **pay**–thos) *noun*
a quality in music, literature, etc. which creates a feeling of sadness or pity. Compare BATHOS.
[Greek]

pathway *noun*
a path.

patience (*say* **pay**–sh'nce) *noun*
1. the ability to endure something or to wait calmly and uncomplainingly: 'I'll see you in a minute, so have *patience*'.
2. *Cards:* any of a large number of games for a single player.

patient (*say* **pay**–sh'nt) *adjective*
having or showing patience: 'I'm only a beginner so you'll have to be *patient* with me'.
patient *noun*
a person being treated by a doctor or in a hospital.
an **in-patient** stays at the hospital during treatment and an **out-patient** goes home between treatments.
Word Family: **patiently**, *adverb*, in a patient manner.
[Latin *patiens* experiencing, suffering]

patina (*say* pa–**teena** *or* **pattina**) *noun*
the greenish surface on old bronze, caused by oxidization.
[Latin, a dish]

patio (*say* **patti**–o) *noun*
a paved area or courtyard adjoining a house.
[Spanish]

patois (*say* **pat**–wah) *noun*
plural is **patois**
a regional dialect of a language.
[French]

patri–
a prefix meaning father, as in *patriarch.*
[Greek *patros*, Latin *patris* of a father]

patriarch (*say* **pay**–tree–ark *or* **pat**–ree–ark) *noun*
1. *Christian:* (in some Eastern sects) a bishop or high dignitary.
2. a male who is the leader or head of a family, group, etc.
Word Family: **patriarchal**, *adjective*; **patriarchy**, *noun*, a social system in which a male is the head of the family.
[PATRI– + Greek *arkhos* a leader]

patrician (*say* pa–**trish'n**) *adjective*
of or characteristic of noble families.
Word Family: **patrician**, *noun*, a nobleman.
[from Latin]

patricide (*say* **patri**–side) *noun*
Law: a) the crime of killing one's father. b) the person who does this.
[PATRI– + Latin *caedere* to kill]

patrimony (*say* **patri**–ma–nee) *noun*
a) property inherited from one's father or ancestors. b) the property of a church, etc.
Word Family: **patrimonial** (*say* patri–**mo**–nee–ul), *adjective.*
[from Latin]

patriot (*say* **pay**–tree–it *or* **pat**–ree–it) *noun*
a person who loves his country.
Word Family: **patriotic** (*say* pay–tree–**ottik**), *adjective*; **patriotically**, *adverb*; **patriotism**, *noun.*
[Greek *patris* fatherland]

patristic (*say* pa–**tristik**) *adjective*
Christian: relating to the early leaders or founders of the Church and their writings.

patrol (*say* pa–**trole**) *verb*
(**patrolled, patrolling**)
to inspect or guard an area.
patrol *noun*
a) the act of patrolling: 'make a quick *patrol* of the grounds'. b) a group of persons sent to patrol.

patrol-car *noun*
a motor car used by police, etc. for making patrols.

patron (*say* **pay**–tr'n) *noun*
a) a person who gives support or protection, especially financial help. b) a client or customer.

Word Family: **patroness**, *noun*, a female patron.
[Latin *patronus* legal defender]

patronage (*say* **patra**–nij) *noun*
1. the support or encouragement given by a patron: 'your shop offers such shoddy service, I am taking my *patronage* elsewhere'.
2. the right or power to grant jobs, offices or privileges.
3. a patronizing manner.

patronize (*say* **patra**–nize) **patronise** *verb*
1. to act as a patron towards: 'we don't *patronize* his shop'.
2. to treat someone as inferior or less intelligent: 'he explained what the word meant but he *patronized* me by using simplified language'.
Word Family: **patronizingly**, *adverb.*

patron saint
a saint who is regarded as giving special protection to a country, profession, etc.: 'St. Andrew is the *patron saint* of Scotland'.

patronymic (*say* patra–**nimm**ik) *noun*
a name formed from the name of a father or ancestor, such as *Johnson* (son of John).
[Greek *pater* father + *onyma* name]

patten *noun*
a shoe or sandal with an elevated sole to protect the feet from mud.

patter (1) *noun*
a series of light tapping sounds, as of rain or footsteps.
Word Family: **patter**, *verb*, to make such sounds.

patter (2) *noun*
1. fast, clever and often meaningless words or speech used to keep one's attention, such as used by a salesman, comedian, etc.
2. the special speech or phrases of a group or class of people.
patter *verb*
to speak or repeat things quickly.

pattern *noun*
1. a) a decorative design, as on carpet or dress material. b) any design or system of markings: 'the *pattern* of footsteps in the snow'.
Usage: 'the world's weather *pattern* seems to be changing' (= system, order).
2. a guide or model: 'cut the cloth according to the paper *pattern*'.
pattern *verb*
a) to decorate something with a pattern. b) to take as a pattern: 'I shall *pattern* my life after the lives of the great artists'.

patty *noun*
a small pie.

paucity (*say* **paw**si–tee) *noun*
scarcity: 'there is a *paucity* of doctors in our town'.
[Latin *paucus* few]

paunch (*say* pawnch) *noun*
a large, protruding belly.
Word Family: **paunchy**, *adjective*; **paunchiness**, *noun.*
[Latin *pantices* the bowels]

pauper (*say* **paw**pa) *noun*
a very poor person.
Word Family: **pauperize**, **pauperise**, *verb*; **pauperism**, *noun.*
[Latin]

pause (*say* pawz) *noun*
1. a short or temporary stop.
2. *Music:* a sign to indicate that a note or rest is to be held for longer than usual.
give pause, 'her dreadful warnings *gave* me *pause*' (= made to hesitate).
pause *verb*
to hesitate or stop briefly: 'I *paused* before knocking because I was afraid of disturbing him'.
Word Family: **pausingly**, *adverb.*
[from Greek]

pavan (*say* pa–**vahn**) **pavane** *noun*
a slow, dignified, court dance from Spain.

pave *verb*
to cover a road, footpath, etc. with stones, bricks, concrete or bitumen.
pave the way, 'if this law is passed it will *pave the way* for many more reforms' (= prepare).
[Latin *pavire* to beat down]

pavement *noun*
a paved footway at the side of a road.

pavement light
a solid glass block used in the roof of an underground room to let in light.

pavilion (*say* pa–**vil**–y'n) *noun*
1. a) a building or other shelter, used for entertainment, exhibitions, etc. b) a large tent for temporary exhibitions, etc. c) a building containing changing rooms, etc. at a sports ground.
2. the lower part of a cut gem.
[Latin *papilio* tent]

paw *noun*
1. the foot of an animal, usually with claws or nails.
2. (*informal*) a hand.

paw *verb*
1. to strike or scrape with, or as if with, the paw.
2. (*informal*) to touch or handle.

pawl *noun*
a pivoted bar or tooth that fits into a ratchet wheel, to move it forwards or to prevent it moving backwards.

pawn (1) *verb*
to deposit personal property with a pawnbroker as security for a loan.
pawn *noun*
the state of being pawned: 'my diamond ring is in *pawn*'.

pawn (2) *noun*
1. *Chess:* a small piece which may move forward two squares on the first move and then one square at a time, but which captures diagonally.
2. a person who is used as the tool of another: 'I was only a *pawn* in his plan'.
[Medieval Latin *pedo* foot soldier]

pawnbroker *noun*
a person who lends money at interest on goods that are left with him.
Word Family: **pawnshop**, *noun.*

pawpaw *noun*
also called a **papaya**
a large, yellow, tropical fruit.

pay *verb*
(paid, paying)
1. to give money or other compensation for goods, labour or services.
2. to return or yield: 'the winning number in the lottery *paid* well'.
Usages:
a) 'it *pays* to be honest' (= is profitable).
b) 'you'll *pay* for that remark' (= suffer).
c) 'let's *pay* him a visit' (= make).
Phrases:
pay back, a) to return a debt; b) to avenge an injury or insult.
pay off, 'I *paid off* the debt' (= paid in full).
put paid to, 'the rain *put paid to* our plans for an enjoyable weekend' (= put an end to).
pay *noun*
a sum of money given for work or services.
Word Family: **payment**, *noun,* a) the act of paying, b) a sum of money paid or to be paid; **payee**, *noun,* a recipient of a payment, especially the person to whom a cheque is made out.
[Latin *pacare* to appease]

payable *adjective*
owed or due: 'the rent is *payable* at the end of the month'.

Pay As You Earn
short form is **PAYE**
a system whereby the Inland Revenue shift responsibility for collecting income tax on to employers, who deduct it from wages and salaries.

paying guest
short form is **PG**
a genteel term for a boarder or lodger.

paymaster *noun*
a person in charge of paying wages or salaries.

pay-off *noun*
a final settlement, especially a financial one.
Usage: (*informal*) 'what *pay-off* did your efforts have?' (= consequences, benefits).

payola (*say* pay-**o**-la) *noun*
a bribe.

payroll (*say* **pay**-role) *noun*
a) a list of employees and the amounts to be paid to each. b) the total amount of wages and salaries to be paid.

pea *noun*
a small, round, green vegetable growing in pods.

peace *noun*
a freedom from war, strife, or disturbance: a) 'we all hope for a lasting *peace* between the nations'; b) 'I am at *peace* with myself'.
hold, keep one's peace, to keep silent.
peaceful *adjective*
1. calm: 'a *peaceful* interlude'.
2. of or relating to a state of peace: '*peaceful* uses of atomic energy'.
Word Family: **peacefully**, *adverb*; **peacefulness**, *noun*; **peaceable**, *adjective*, not quarrelsome; **peaceably**, *adverb*; **peaceableness**, *noun.*
[Latin *pacis* of peace]

peacekeeping *noun*
the maintenance of law and order, especially by the presence of an armed force.

peacemaker *noun*
a person who makes peace between people or groups.

peach (1) *noun*
1. a medium-sized, round, juicy, pink to yellow fruit with a large stone and furry skin.
2. a light pinkish-yellow colour.
3. (*informal*) any admired or beautiful person or thing.

Word Family: **peach**, *adjective*; **peachy**, *adjective*, a) like a peach in colour or appearance, b) (informal) wonderful or excellent.
[Greek *Persikon* Persian apple]

peach (2) *verb*
(*informal*) to inform against a friend or accomplice.
[for IMPEACH]

peacock *noun*
1. a male bird noted for its large and brightly coloured tail. The female is called a **peahen**.
2. a vain person.

peafowl *noun*
a peacock or a peahen.

pea jacket
a heavy woollen jacket, such as worn by sailors.

peak *noun*
1. a pointed part or top.
2. a mountain, especially a pointed one.
3. the highest point of something: 'the *peak* of success'.
peak *verb*
1. to have, reach or project in a point.
2. *Maths:* to reach a highest point: 'a distribution *peaks* around the modal value'.
peak *adjective*
relating to the time when something reaches its maximum degree: '*peak-hour* traffic'.

peaked (*say* **pee**kid) *adjective*
also called **peaky**
thin, pale and sickly.

peak-hour *noun*
the time in the morning and late afternoon when traffic is heaviest.

peal *noun*
1. a prolonged, loud, resonant sound: a) 'a *peal* of bells'; b) 'a *peal* of thunder'.
2. a) a set of bells tuned to one another. b) a tune rung on a set of bells.
Word Family: **peal**, *verb*.

peanut *noun*
also called a **groundnut**
1. a small, oily, edible nut that grows underground.
2. (*informal, plural*) a very small amount of money.

pear (*rhymes with* air) *noun*
a medium-sized, juicy, fruit which is usually round at the base and tapering towards the stem.

pearl (*say* perl) *noun*
1. a) the hard, silver or bluish-white pellet formed as a deposit around any foreign object in an oyster shell and valued as a gem. b) mother-of-pearl.
Usage: 'the flowers had *pearls* of nectar on their petals' (= droplets).
2. a very pale pinkish or bluish grey.
3. any memorable or wise saying, such as a proverb.
cast pearls before swine, to utter words of wisdom above the heads or beyond the comprehension of one's audience.
Word Family: **pearl**, *verb*, to hunt or dive for pearls; **pearl**, **pearly**, *adjectives*; **pearler**, *noun*, a) a diver for pearls, b) a boat engaged in hunting for pearls.

pearl barley
any barley ground into small round grains, for use in soups, etc.

pearlies *plural noun*
clothes covered with mother-of-pearl buttons from top to toe, the traditional costume of Cockney costermongers on festive occasions.

peasant (*say* **pezz**'nt) *noun*
a) a farm labourer, small farmer or rustic. b) an ignorant or unsophisticated person.
Word Family: **peasantry**, *noun*, peasants considered as a group.
[Latin *paganus* a villager]

pease (*say* peez) *noun*
an old word for a pea or peas.

peashooter (*say* pee-shooter) *noun*
a tube through which dried peas are blown at a target.

pea souper (*say* pee **soo**per)
(*informal*) an extremely thick fog.

peat *noun*
a soil composed of accumulated vegetable matter, occurring as the early stage of coal formation, found in swamps and used as fuel when dried.
Word Family: **peaty**, *adjective*.

pebble *noun*
a small rounded stone.
Word Family: **pebbly**, *adjective*; **pebbled**, *adjective*.

pecan (*say* **pee**kan) *noun*
a large, oval, edible nut that grows in North America on the hickory tree.
[Amerindian]

peccadillo (*say* pekka-**dillo**) *noun*
plural is **peccadillos**
a small sin or fault.
[Spanish *pecadillo* little sin]

peccary (*say* **pekka**–ree) *noun*
a South American mammal, like a wild pig.

peck (1) *verb*
a) (of a bird) to strike with the beak, especially repeatedly. b) to make a hole, etc. by pecking.
Usages:
a) 'she only *pecked* at her food' (= ate a little, bit by bit).
b) 'he never stops *pecking* away at me' (= nagging).
peck *noun*
a) a stroke with the beak. b) a hole or mark made by pecking.
Usage: 'he gave her a *peck* on the cheek as he rushed out the door' (= hasty kiss).

peck (2) *noun*
Units: see BUSHEL.

pecker *noun*
a person or thing that pecks.
keep one's pecker up, (*informal*) to stay cheerful.

pecking order
a system of rank or privilege in a group.
[as first noticed among domestic fowls]

peckish *adjective*
(*informal*) hungry.

pectin *noun*
an organic acid found in some ripe fruit, such as apples, used as a setting agent in marmalade, fruit jellies, etc.
Word Family: **pectic**, *adjective.*

pectoral (*say* **pek**ta–r'l) *adjective*
of or relating to the breast or the front of the chest.
Word Family: **pectoral**, *noun*, a cross worn by bishops on the chest.
[Latin *pectoris* of the breast]

peculiar (*say* pik–**yoo**–lee–a) *adjective*
strange, odd or unusual.
Usages:
a) 'this novel has a *peculiar* value for our purposes' (= special, particular).
b) 'each age has certain habits *peculiar* to itself' (= belonging characteristically).
peculiarity (*say* pik–yooli–**arri**–tee) *noun*
a) the quality of being peculiar: 'the *peculiarity* of his behaviour was frightening'. b) something which is strange or odd: 'this work is a *peculiarity* among English novels of that time'.
Word Family: **peculiarly**, *adverb.*
[Latin *peculiaris* one's own (private property)]

pecuniary (*say* pik–yooni–aree) *adjective*
relating to or consisting of money: 'I have a small *pecuniary* interest in the company'.
[Latin *pecunia* property, money]

pedagogue (*say* **pedda**–gog) *noun*
1. a teacher.
2. a pedantic or dogmatic person.
Word Family: **pedagogy** (*say* **pedda**–goji), *noun*, the science or art of teaching; **pedagogic** (*say* pedda–**gojik**), **pedagogical**, *adjective.*
[Greek *paidagogos* a slave who escorted a boy to school]

pedal *noun*
a lever worked by the foot, e.g. on a bicycle, an organ or a sewing machine.
Word Family: **pedal (pedalled, pedalling)**, *verb.*
[Latin *pedis* of the foot]

pedant (*say* **ped**'nt) *noun*
a person who makes an unnecessary or tiresome display of his learning, especially concerning petty details.
Word Family: **pedantic** (*say* ped–**antik**), *adjective*; **pedantically**, *adverb*; **pedantry** (*say* **pedd**'n–tree), *noun*, an unnecessary display of learning.

peddle *verb*
to carry from place to place in order to sell: 'to *peddle* goods from door to door'.
Usage: 'she loves to *peddle* gossip' (= spread, carry about).

peddler *noun*
American: a pedlar.

pederasty (*say* **pedda**–ras–tee) *noun*
a sexual relationship between a man and a boy.
Word Family: **pederast**, *noun.*
[Greek *paidos* of a child + *erastes* lover]

pedestal (*say* **peddi**–st'l) *noun*
a support for a statue, vase, column, etc.
put, set on a pedestal, to idealize or admire extremely.

pedestrian (*say* pid–**estri**–an) *noun*
a person who travels on foot.
pedestrian *adjective*
of or for pedestrians: 'a *pedestrian* crossing'.
Usage: 'he writes in a very *pedestrian* manner' (= dull, unimaginative).
[Latin *pedester* on foot]

pedicel (*say* **peddi**-sel) *noun*
also called a **peduncle**
a small stalk or stalk-like part.

pedicure (*say* **peddi**-kewer) *noun*
the care of the feet and toenails.
[Latin *pedis* of a foot + *cura* cure]

pedigree (*say* **peddi**-gree) *noun*
a) a list of ancestors. b) an ancestry or line of descent, e.g. of a dog.
Word Family: **pedigreed**, *adjective*, having a list of purebred ancestors.

pediment (*say* **peddi**-m'nt) *noun*
a triangular section of a building above a portico in classical architecture.

pedlar *noun*
a person who goes from house to house selling goods.

peduncle (*say* piddun-k'l) *noun*
see PEDICEL.

pee *verb*
(peed, peeing)
(*informal*) to urinate.
Word Family: **pee**, *noun*.

peek *verb*
to peep or peer.
Word Family: **peek**, *noun*.

peel *noun*
the skin of a fruit.
peel *verb*
1. to remove the skin, rind, bark, etc. of: 'to *peel* an orange'.
2. to come off in strips or flakes: 'my face *peeled* after a day in the sun'.
Usage: 'she *peeled* off her clothes and leapt into the pool' (= took).
keep one's eyes peeled, (*informal*) to keep watch carefully.
Word Family: **peeling**, *noun*, anything which is peeled from something; **peeler**, *noun*, a device for removing peel.

peen *noun*
a blunt or rounded end of a hammer head, opposite the face.

peep (1) *noun*
a short, quick look, especially when furtive or prying.
peep *verb*
to take a peep at.
Usage: 'the sun *peeped* out from behind a cloud' (= came partly into view).
Word Family: **peeper**, *noun*, a) a prying or spying person, b) (informal) an eye.

peep (2) *noun*
the weak, shrill cry of young birds, mice, etc.
Usage: 'I don't want to hear a *peep* out of you for at least an hour' (= slightest noise).
peep *verb*
1. to make a peep.
2. to speak in a thin, weak voice.

Peeping Tom
(*informal*) a voyeur.
[after the man who peeped at Lady Godiva riding naked through the streets]

peer (1) *noun*
1. a person of the same rank, ability, age, etc. as another: 'he asked to be tried by a jury of his *peers*'.
2. a duke, marquess, earl, viscount, baron or life peer.
Word Family: **peerage**, *noun*, a) the rank or dignity of a peer, b) the peers of a country collectively, c) a book giving a list of the peers of a country; **peeress**, *noun*, a) a female peer, b) the wife or widow of a peer.
[Latin *par* equal]

peer (2) *verb*
to look closely, in an attempt to see clearly: 'to *peer* through the fog for a landmark'.

peerless *adjective*
having no equal: 'the *peerless* beauty of Italian marble'.

peevish *adjective*
irritable.
Word Family: **peevishly**, *adverb*; **peevishness**, *noun*; **peeve**, *verb*, to make peevish; **peeve**, *noun*, an annoyance.

peewit *noun*
see PEWIT.

peg *noun*
a piece of wood, metal or plastic, used for fastening, hanging, etc.: a) 'a clothes *peg*'; b) 'a surveyor's *peg*'.
Phrases:
a square peg in a round hole, a person who does not fit in well, as in a job, social situation, etc.
off the peg, (*informal*) (of clothes) ready-made to standard sizes.
take down a peg or two, to humiliate or humble.
peg *verb*
(pegged, pegging)
1. to fasten with pegs: 'to *peg* down a tent'.
2. to mark with pegs: 'to *peg* out a mining claim'.
3. *Commerce:* to keep prices or wages at a set level as an official policy.

Phrases:
peg away at, (*informal*) to keep on working at.
peg out, (*informal*) to die.

pegboard *noun*
a board with holes in which pegs, hooks, etc. can be inserted.

peg leg
(*informal*) a wooden leg tapering to a blunt point at the end.

peignoir (*say* **pane**–wah) *noun*
a woman's dressing-gown.
[French]

pejorative (*say* pijjorra–tiv) *adjective*
derogatory or disparaging: ''quack' is a *pejorative* term for a doctor'.
Word Family: **pejoratively**, *adverb.*
[Latin *pejor* worse]

Pekingese (*say* peekin–**eez**) *noun*
also spelt **Pekinese**
short form is **peke**
one of a breed of small, snub-nosed, long-haired dogs.
[originally from *Peking*, China]

pelagic (*say* pel**la**jik) *adjective*
of or relating to the ocean.
[Greek *pelagikos* pertaining to the sea]

pelican *noun*
a large, white seabird, having a long, pouched bill from which the young feed.
[Greek *pelekan*]

pelisse (*say* pel–**eece**) *noun*
a child's or woman's long outdoor cloak with arm openings, originally lined or trimmed with fur.
[Latin *pelliceus* made of skins]

pellagra (*say* pel**lag**gra) *noun*
a disease due to a lack of vitamin B_2 in the diet, causing wasting, a sore mouth, diarrhoea, skin rashes, and mental retardation or insanity.
[Latin *pellis* skin + Greek *agra* seizure]

pellet (*say* **pel**lit) *noun*
a) a small round ball, e.g. of bread, paper, etc. b) a small bullet or piece of shot.

pellicle (*say* **pel**li–k'l) *noun*
a thin skin or membrane.

pell-mell, pellmell *adverb, adjective*
in a disorderly or hasty manner.

pellucid (*say* pel–**yoo**sid) *adjective*
allowing light to pass through.
Usage: 'his *pellucid* explanation helped me really understand' (= clear).
Word Family: **pellucidly**, *adverb*; **pellucidness, pellucidity**, *nouns.*
[Latin *pellucidus* shining through, very bright]

pelmet *noun*
a narrow board or piece of cloth placed along the top of a window to hide the curtain rail.

pelota *noun*
a ball game of Basque origin played in a long walled court by two or four players with wicker baskets attached to their wrists.
[Spanish, ball]

pelt (1) *verb*
1. to throw violently: 'the boys were *pelting* stones at each other'.
Usage: 'the rain was really *pelting* down' (= falling heavily, beating).
2. to hurry: 'the White Rabbit went *pelting* past Alice'.
pelt *noun*
a blow, especially one given by something thrown.
at full pelt, at full speed.

pelt (2) *noun*
the skin of an animal, especially one treated to make garments, etc.

pelvis *noun*
Anatomy: the strong bony framework formed by the two hipbones and the sacrum.
Word Family: **pelvic**, *adjective.*
[Latin, basin]

pen (1) *noun*
an instrument for writing or drawing with ink.
Usage: 'he strove for years to make a living from his *pen*' (= writing).
pen *verb*
(penned, penning)
to write with a pen: 'to *pen* a letter'.
[Latin *penna* feather]

pen (2) *noun*
a) a small enclosure for domestic animals. b) the animals contained in such an enclosure. c) any enclosure: 'a child's *playpen*'.
Word Family: **pen (penned, penning)**, *verb.*

penal (*say* **pee**–n'l) *adjective*
of, relating to or used for punishment: a) '*penal* servitude'; b) 'a *penal* colony'.
[Latin *poena* penalty]

penalize (*say* **peena**–lize) **penalise** *verb*
to subject to a penalty: a) 'a foul is *penalized* in most sports'; b) 'the courts *penalize* those who break the law'.
Word Family: **penalization**, *noun.*

penalty (*say* **penn**'l–tee) *noun*
anything which is imposed to punish an infringement of rules or laws: 'the *penalty* for murder may be death'.
Usage: 'the *penalties* of old age' (= disadvantages, handicaps).
on, under penalty of, 'do not touch this money, *on penalty of* death' (= with (death) as the penalty for disobedience).

penance (*say* **penn**ence) *noun*
a task or punishment accepted by a person as an expression of repentance, especially one given by a priest.

pence *plural noun*
a plural of **penny**.

penchant (*say* **pen**–ch'nt *or* **pon**–shon) *noun*
a taste or liking: 'a *penchant* for good wines'.
[French *pencher* to incline or lean]

pencil (*say* **pen**sil) *noun*
an instrument for writing or drawing, consisting of a wooden cover and a thin, central rod of graphite or other material.
Word Family: **pencil** (**pencilled, pencilling**), *verb*, to write, draw, mark, etc. with a pencil; **penciller**, *noun*.
[Latin *penicillum* paint-brush]

pendant, pendent *noun*
1. a hanging or suspended object, usually worn as an ornament.
2. a chandelier.
Word Family: **pendant**, *adjective*, hanging or overhanging.
[Latin *pendens* hanging]

pending *preposition*
a) while awaiting; until: '*pending* his arrival'. b) during: '*pending* the peace negotiations, all troops will stop fighting'.
Word Family: **pending**, *adjective*, awaiting decision.

pendulous (*say* **pen**–dew–lus) *adjective*
hanging loosely so as to swing freely.

pendulum (*say* **pen**–dew–lum) *noun*
a) any body suspended so that it will move to and fro freely. b) such a device used for controlling the mechanism of a clock.

penetrate (*say* **penni**–trate) *verb*
to get into or through: 'the piece of flying glass *penetrated* the spectator's leg'.
Usages:
a) 'he *penetrated* their feeble disguises immediately' (= saw through).
b) 'the building was *penetrated* by a smell of damp' (= filled, permeated).
c) 'try as we might we could not *penetrate* the mystery of what happened that night' (= understand).
Word Family: **penetratingly**, *adverb*; **penetration**, *noun*, a) the act of penetrating, b) sharpness of intellect; **penetrable** (*say* **penn**itra–b'l), *adjective*, able to be penetrated; **penetrative** (*say* **penn**itra–tiv), *adjective*, tending to penetrate.
[Latin *penitus* in the inside]

penfriend *noun*
a person, usually living in another country, with whom one exchanges letters.

penguin (*say* **peng**win) *noun*
a flightless seabird with webbed feet and flipper-like wings, living in the Southern Hemisphere.
[Old French *pen gwyn* white head]

penicillin (*say* penni–**sill**in) *noun*
an antibiotic produced from penicillium moulds and widely used to treat bacterial infections.

penicillium (*say* penni–**silli**–um) *noun*
any of a group of fungi used in cheese-making and for the production of penicillin.
[Latin *penicillus* small brush]

peninsula (*say* p'**nin**–syoo–la) *noun*
a piece of land almost surrounded by water and joined by a narrow neck to the mainland.
Word Family: **peninsular**, *adjective*.
[Latin *paene* almost + *insula* island]

penis (*say* **pee**nis) *noun*
Anatomy: the organ in males, containing erectile tissue, through which urine and seminal fluid is passed.
Word Family: **penile** (*say* **pee**nile), *adjective*.
[Latin, tail]

penitent (*say* **penni**–t'nt) *adjective*
showing remorse for sin and ready to make amends.
Word Family: **penitent**, *noun*, a person who is penitent; **penitently**, *adverb*; **penitence**, *noun*; **penitential** (*say* penni–**ten**–sh'l), *adjective*.
[Latin *poenitens* being sorry]

penitentiary (*say* penni–**ten**sha–ree) *noun*
an old word meaning a prison.

penknife *noun*
a pocket-knife.

penmanship *noun*
the art of handwriting.
Word Family: **penman,** *noun,* a person with expert handwriting.

pen-name *noun*
see PSEUDONYM.

pennant *noun*
also called a **pennon**
a long triangular flag, used as a signal on naval vessels, a banner, souvenir, etc.

penniless *adjective*
without any money.

penny *noun*
plural is **pence** or **pennies**
1. see POUND (2).
2. *American:* a one-cent coin.
Phrases:
a pretty penny, (*informal*) a lot of money.
spend a penny, (*informal*) to urinate.
the penny has dropped, (*informal*) the explanation or remark has been understood.

penny dreadful
a cheap book or magazine containing popular, especially sensational, fiction.

penny-farthing *noun*
an early type of bicycle with a large front wheel (the penny), and a small rear wheel (the farthing).

penny pincher
a mean, miserly person.
Word Family: **penny-pinching,** *adjective.*

pennyweight (*say* **pennee**-wate) *noun*
a unit of mass in the troy system, equal to about 1·55 g.

penny-wise *adjective*
economical in small matters.
penny-wise and pound-foolish, economical in small matters, but wasteful in large ones.

penology (*say* **pee**-nolla-jee) *noun*
the science that deals with the prevention and punishment of crime, and the management of prisons and reformatories.
Word Family: **penologist,** *noun.*
[Latin *poena* penalty + -LOGY]

pen-pusher *noun*
(*informal*) a person who works with a pen, especially at a boring job.

pensile *adjective*
hanging, e.g. the nests of certain birds.

pension *noun*
1. (*say* **pen**-sh'n) a regular payment of money by a government or firm to retired, aged, sick or needy people.
2. (*say* **ponsi**-on) a Continental boarding house.
full pension, (in hotels, etc.) all meals included.
pension *verb*
to grant a pension to.
pension off, to cause to retire on a pension.
[Latin *pensionis* of a payment]

pensioner *noun*
a person who receives a pension, especially an old age pension.

pensive (*say* **pen**siv) *adjective*
thoughtful in a serious or sad way.
Word Family: **pensively,** *adverb;* **pensiveness,** *noun.*
[Latin *pensare* to ponder]

pent-, penta-
a prefix meaning five, as in *pentagon.*
[Greek]

pentagon *noun*
1. any closed, plane figure with five straight sides.
2. (*capital*) the five-sided building which houses the offices of the American Defence Department.
Word Family: **pentagonal** (*say* pen-**tagga**-n'l), *adjective.*
[PENTA- + Greek *gonia* corner]

pentagram *noun*
a five-pointed star, used as a symbol in magic.
[PENTA- + Greek *gramma* something written]

pentahedron (*say* penta-**hee**-dr'n) *noun*
a solid or hollow figure with five plane faces.
Word Family: **pentahedral,** *adjective.*
[PENTA- + Greek *hedra* a base]

pentameter (*say* pen-**tamm**ita) *noun*
Poetry: a line with five metrical feet.
Example: Shakespeare's verse is written in iambic pentameters: 'once **more** unto the **breach,** dear **friends,** once **more**'.

pentane *noun*
a colourless, volatile liquid (formula C_5H_{12}), the fifth member of the paraffin series, used in petrol and as a solvent and anaesthetic.

pentathlon (*say* pen–**tath**lon) *noun*
Athletics: a contest in which athletes aim for the highest total score in five separate events.
[PENT– + Greek *athlon* contest]

penthouse (*say* **pent**–house) *noun*
a room or flat on the top storey of a building.

pent–up *adjective*
bottled–up or confined: 'his *pent–up* fury exploded in violence'.

penultimate (*say* pen–**ulti**–mit) *adjective*
next to last: 'November is the *penultimate* month of the year'.
[Latin *paene* almost + *ultimus* last]

penumbra (*say* pin–**um**bra) *noun*
Physics: the lighter edge of a shadow. Compare UMBRA.
Word Family: **penumbral**, *adjective.*
[Latin *paene* almost + *umbra* shade or shadow]

penurious (*say* pen–**yoo**rius) *adjective*
a) extremely poor. b) niggardly.
Word Family: **penuriously**, *adverb*; **penuriousness**, *noun.*

penury (*say* **pen**–yoo–ree) *noun*
an extreme poverty.
[Latin *penuria* want or scarcity]

peon (*say* **pee**–on) *noun*
a labourer or servant in South America.
Word Family: **peonage** (*say* **pee**–anij), *noun*, the condition or service of a peon.
[Spanish]

peony (*say* **pee**–a–nee) **paeony** *noun*
any of a group of garden plants with large, showy flowers.

people (*say* **pee**–p'l) *noun*
plural is **people** or **peoples**
1. persons in general.
2. all the persons of a particular area or group: a) 'the *peoples* of Europe'; b) 'a government elected by the *people*'; c) 'medical *people*'.
Usages:
a) 'the *people* fought against the aristocracy' (= lower classes).
b) 'you must come and meet my *people*' (= relatives).
Word Family: **people**, *verb*, to populate.
[Latin *populus*]

pep *noun*
(*informal*) vigour or energy.
pep *verb*
(**pepped, pepping**)
pep up, (*informal*) to give vigour to.

pep *adjective*
intended to inspire or stimulate: a) 'a *pep* talk'; b) 'a *pep* pill'.
[short form of PEPPER]

pepper *noun*
1. a spice made from dried peppercorns, used whole or ground.
2. see CAPSICUM.
pepper *verb*
1. to season or sprinkle with pepper.
Usage: 'John's face is *peppered* with freckles' (= thickly sprinkled).
2. to pelt with small objects.
Word Family: **peppery**, *adjective*, a) like or full of pepper, b) having a hot temper.

pepper–and–salt *adjective*
(of cloth, hair, etc.) consisting of a fine mixture of black and white.

peppercorn *noun*
the berry–like fruit from an East Indian vine.
peppercorn rent, a nominal rent.

peppermint *noun*
a) a type of mint used for its oil. b) a food made from this, such as a small sweet.

pepsin *noun*
Biology: an enzyme, secreted by the stomach, that splits proteins.
[Greek *pepsis* digestion]

peptic *adjective*
of or relating to digestion.

per *preposition*
1. for each: 'we are selling silk for £3 *per* metre'.
2. through: 'to A. Nickson, *per* S. Dawson, with thanks'.
[Latin]

per–
a prefix meaning through or throughout, as in *pervade.*

peradventure *adverb*
an old word meaning perhaps.
[French *par* by + *aventure* chance]

perambulate (*say* per**ram**–bew–late) *verb*
to walk about or stroll.
Word Family: **perambulation**, *noun.*
[PER– + Latin *ambulare* to walk]

perambulator *noun*
see PRAM.

per annum
by the year or yearly.
[Latin]

per capita
per head.

perceive (*say* per-**seev**) *verb*
to become aware of, especially through the sense of sight or the mind: a) 'I was the first to *perceive* the dull red glow of the dawn'; b) 'I *perceive* a change in your attitude'.
Word Family: **perceivable,** *adjective*; **perceivably,** *adverb.*
[Latin *percipere* to grasp]

per cent (*say* per-**sent**)
by, for or in every hundred. *Example:* $\frac{3}{100}$ is 3 **per cent** and is written 3%.
[PER- + Latin *centum* one hundred]

percentage (*say* per-**sentij**) *noun*
a rate per cent.
Usage: 'a large *percentage* of children's books is sheer rubbish' (= part, proportion).

percentile (*say* per-**sentile**) *noun*
Maths: a value which divides a distribution into 100 groups of equal frequency.

percept (*say* **per**-sept) *noun*
that which is perceived.

perceptible (*say* per-**septi**-b'l) *adjective*
able to be perceived.
Word Family: **perceptibly,** *adverb*; **perceptibility,** *noun.*

perception (*say* per-**sep**-sh'n) *noun*
1. the act of perceiving: 'his *perception* of the danger saved us'.
2. the power of perceiving: 'we need someone with the *perception* to show us where we went wrong'.
3. an observation or insight: 'this poem presents us with a series of *perceptions*'.
Word Family: **perceptive,** *adjective,* a) of or relating to perception, b) quick or ready in perceiving; **perceptively,** *adverb*; **perceptiveness,** *noun.*

perceptual (*say* persep-**tew**'l) *adjective*
of or relating to perception.
Word Family: **perceptually,** *adverb.*

perch (1) *noun*
1. anything on which a bird may rest.
Usage: 'from his *perch* up in the treetop he could see a long way' (= high position).
2. a) a unit of length equal to $5\frac{1}{2}$ yards, about 5 m. Also called a **pole** or **rod.** b) a unit of area equal to about 27 m^2.
perch *verb*
to come to rest or alight: 'a canary *perched* on his shoulder'.
Usage: '*perched* on the top of the telephone pole he could see a long way' (= sitting high up).
[Latin *pertica* measuring rod]

perch (2) *noun*
a small, scaly fish, the freshwater varieties of which are used as food.
[Greek *perké*]

perchance (*say* per-**chance**) *adverb*
an old word meaning perhaps.
[French *par* by + *chance* chance]

percipient (*say* per-**sippi**-ent) *adjective*
a) having the power of perception. b) perceiving rapidly or keenly: 'a *percipient* remark'.
Word Family: **percipience,** *noun.*

percolate (*say* **per**ka-late) *verb*
to drip or drain a liquid through a substance, especially when part of the substance dissolves in the liquid: '*percolate* coffee'.
Usage: 'Newton's ideas have *percolated* through to every level of society' (= filtered, circulated).
percolator *noun*
a coffeepot in which boiling water filters through ground coffee.
Word Family: **percolation,** *noun.*
[from Latin]

percussion (*say* per-**kush**'n) *noun*
1. a) the forceful striking of one thing against another. b) the shock produced by this.
2. *Music:* a) any instrument which produces sound by being struck or shaken. b) the section of an orchestra having these instruments.
3. *Medicine:* the striking or tapping of the body in diagnosis.
Word Family: **percussive,** *adjective,* of or relating to percussion; **percussionist,** *noun,* a person who plays a percussion instrument; **percuss** (Medicine), *verb.*
[from Latin]

percussion cap
a small metallic cap or cup containing an explosive substance which sets off the main charge in a gun.

perdition (*say* per-**dish**'n) *noun*
1. hell.
2. a state of eternal damnation.
[Latin *perditio* an act of destroying]

peregrination (*say* perrigri-**nay**-sh'n) *noun*
a) a travelling from one place to another. b) a journey.
Word Family: **peregrinate,** *verb*; **peregrine** (*say* **perri**-grin), *adjective,*

a) coming from foreign regions, b) travelling or wandering.
[Latin *peregrinari* to live or travel abroad]

peregrine (*say* **perri**–grin) *noun*
a large slate-coloured falcon which swoops on its prey in a high-speed vertical dive, much used in hawking.
[Latin *peregrinus* foreign (as caught during migration)]

peremptory (*say* per–**empt**a–ree) *adjective*
a) (of commands) allowing no denial or refusal. b) (of a person, his manner, etc.) commanding, imperious or dictatorial.
Word Family: **peremptorily,** *adverb*; **peremptoriness,** *noun.*
[Latin *peremptus* destroyed, cut off]

perennial (*say* per–**enn**ial) *adjective*
1. continuing throughout the whole year: 'a *perennial* river'.
2. lasting or recurrent: 'an old *perennial* joke'.
3. *Biology:* having a life cycle lasting more than two years.
Word Family: **perennial,** *noun,* something that is perennial, such as a plant.
[PER– + Latin *annus* a year]

perfect (*say* **per**–fikt) *adjective*
1. faultless or without defect: a) 'a *perfect* husband'; b) 'a *perfect* circle'.
Usages:
a) 'we found a house that's just *perfect* for us' (= completely suitable).
b) (*informal*) 'we were *perfect* strangers to each other' (= complete).
2. *Grammar:* denoting the tense of a verb which expresses a completed event. *Example*: I *have seen* that film.
perfect (*say* per–**fekt**) *verb*
a) to make perfect: 'to *perfect* a technique'. b) to bring to completion.
perfection (*say* per–**fek**–sh'n) *noun*
a) the state or quality of being perfect: 'to bring a technique to *perfection*'. b) a perfect embodiment of something: 'as a singer she is just *perfection*'. c) the act or process of perfecting: 'the *perfection* of our technique took a long while'.
Word Family: **perfectly,** *adverb*; **perfectible,** *adjective*; **perfectibility** (*say* per–fekta–**billi**–tee), *noun*; **perfectionist,** *noun,* a person who tries to do everything perfectly; **perfectionism,** *noun.*
[Latin *perfectus* made thoroughly]

perfect number
Maths: a number that is the sum of all its factors except itself. *Example*: 28 is a perfect number because the factors of 28 are 1,2,4,7,14, which add up to 28.

perfidy (*say* **per**fi–dee) *noun*
treachery, especially a deliberate breaking of faith or trust.
Word Family: **perfidious** (*say* per–**fiddi**–us), *adjective*; **perfidiously,** *adverb*; **perfidiousness,** *noun.*
[Latin *perfidia* faithlessness]

perforate (*say* **perfa**–rate) *verb*
to make a hole or holes through, e.g. to make a row of tiny holes in paper so that part may be torn off.
Word Family: **perforation,** *noun,* a) the act of perforating, b) a hole or holes.
[from Latin]

perforce (*say* per–**force**) *adverb*
an old word meaning of necessity.

perform *verb*
1. to carry out or through: a) 'to *perform* an action'; b) 'to *perform* a rite'.
2. to act, sing, dance, etc. in front of an audience.
performance (*say* per–**for**–m'nce) *noun*
a) the act of performing: 'she's lazy in the *performance* of her work'. b) a deed or accomplishment: 'coming top was a splendid *performance*'.
Word Family: **performer,** *noun.*

perfume (*say* **per**–fewm) *noun*
1. any agreeable smell.
2. a liquid obtained from flowers or chemicals which gives a pleasant smell as it evaporates.
perfume (*say* per–**fewm**) *verb*
a) to put on perfume. b) to fill or scent with perfume.
Word Family: **perfumer,** *noun,* a person who makes or sells perfumes; **perfumery,** *noun,* a) the art or business of making perfumes, b) a place where perfumes are made or sold.
[Latin PER– + Latin *fuma* smoke]

perfunctory (*say* per–**funk**ta–ree) *adjective*
performed as a duty, but without interest or care: 'he gave a *perfunctory* greeting, then ignored us'.
Word Family: **perfunctorily,** *adverb*; **perfunctoriness,** *noun.*
[Latin *perfunctorius* done in a superficial way]

pergola (*say* **per**–g'la) *noun*
an arrangement of small columns or posts, supporting a horizontal trellis over which vines or other plants may be grown.
[Latin *pergula* a balcony, arcade]

perhaps *adverb*
possibly.

peri–
a prefix meaning around or about, as in *perimeter.*

perianth *noun*
Biology: the calyx and corolla of a flower.
[PERI– + Greek *anthos* flower]

pericardium (*say* perri–**kar**di–um) *noun*
Anatomy: the membranous sac enclosing the heart.
Word Family: **pericarditis**, *noun*, an inflammation of the pericardium.
[PERI– + Greek *kardia* heart]

pericarp *noun*
Biology: the wall of an ovary after it has matured into a fruit. It may be dry and hard, as in a nut, or soft and fleshy, as in a berry.
[PERI– + Greek *karpos* fruit]

peridotite (*say* perri–**doe**–tite) *noun*
a green or brown rock, composed mainly of olivine.
peridot *noun*
a pale olivine gemstone.

perigee (*say* **perri**–jee) *noun*
Astronomy: the point in the orbit of the moon, a planet or an artificial satellite when it is closest to the earth. Compare APOGEE.
[PERI– + Greek *ge* earth]

perihelion (*say* perri–**heel**–y'n) *noun*
Astronomy: the point in the orbit of a planet or comet when it is closest to the sun. Compare APHELION.
[PERI– + Greek *helios* sun]

peril *noun*
any serious danger: a) 'I felt my life was in *peril*'; b) 'to risk the *perils* of the sea'.
at one's own peril, at one's own risk.
Word Family: **perilous**, *adjective*; **perilously**, *adverb*; **perilousness**, *noun.*
[Latin *periculum* danger]

perimeter (*say* perr**imm**i–ta) *noun*
a) the outside edge of any closed plane figure or area. b) the length of the boundary of any plane figure.
[PERI– + Greek *metron* a measure]

perineum (*say* perri–**nee**–um) *noun*
Anatomy: the region of the body between the anus and the urogenital organs.
Word Family: **perineal**, *adjective.*

period (*say* **peer**iod) *noun*
1. a portion of time: a) 'a *period* of rest'; b) 'geological and historical *periods*'.
2. a specific length or division of time for a single activity, such as the time taken for a school lesson, an orbit by a planet or satellite, etc.
3. *Medicine:* see MENSTRUATION.
4. *Grammar:* a full stop.
Word Family: **period**, *adjective*, of or from a particular historical period; **periodic** (*say* peeri–**odd**ik), *adjective*, appearing or happening at regular intervals; **periodically**, *adverb.*
[Greek *periodos* a going around]

periodical (*say* peeri–**oddi**–k'l) *noun*
a magazine.
periodical *adjective*
1. issued at regularly recurring intervals.
2. periodic.

periodic table
Chemistry: an arrangement of the chemical elements in order of their atomic numbers, demonstrating the law that elements having similar properties occur at regular intervals and fall into groups of related elements.

peripatetic (*say* perripa–**tettik**) *adjective*
wandering from place to place.
[PERI– + Greek *patein* to walk up and down]

peripheral nervous system
see NERVOUS SYSTEM.

periphery (*say* perr**iffa**–ree) *noun*
the outside boundary or surface of something.
Word Family: **peripheral**, *adjective*, a) relating to, situated in, or forming the periphery, b) of minor importance; **peripherally**, *adverb.*
[Greek *periphereia* circumference]

periphrasis (*say* perr**iffra**–sis) *noun*
a roundabout way of saying something.
Example: *the finny denizens of the deep* is a periphrasis for *fish.*
[PERI– + Greek *phrasis* speech]

periscope (*say* **perri**–skope) *noun*
an instrument, consisting of mirrors and a tube, which allows the viewer to see things which are above him

or otherwise out of sight; used in submarines, etc.
Word Family: **periscopic** (*say* perri–**skoppik**), *adjective.*
[PERI– + Greek *skopein* to look]

perish *verb*
1. to die: 'to *perish* in the desert'.
2. to rot or decay: 'many fruits *perish* quickly in summer'.
Usage: 'we were *perished* with cold in the snow' (= numb).
Word Family: **perishable**, *adjective*, liable to spoil or decay; **perishability** (*say* perrisha–**billi** tee), *noun*; **perisher**, *noun*, (informal) an annoying person; **perishing**, *adjective*, (informal) freezing cold; **perishingly**, *adverb.*

peristalsis (*say* perri–**stalsis**) *noun*
plural is **peristalses** (*say* perri–**stalseez**)
Biology: the alternate constriction and dilation of muscular tubes, especially the intestine, which causes the contents of the tube to move in a definite direction.
[PERI– + Greek *stalsis* compression]

peristyle (*say* **perri**–stile) *noun*
a) a row of columns surrounding a temple or court. b) the space or court so enclosed.
[PERI– + Greek *stylos* a column]

peritoneum (*say* perrita–**nee**–um) *noun*
plural is **peritonea**
Anatomy: the membrane lining the abdominal cavity and covering the organs within it.
[PERI– + Greek *tonos* stretched]

peritonitis (*say* perrita–**nie**–tis) *noun*
an inflammation of the lining of the abdomen.

periwig *noun*
an old word for a wig.

periwinkle (1) *noun*
an edible, marine snail.

periwinkle (2) *noun*
a creeping, evergreen plant with blue flowers.

perjury (*say* **per**–ja–ree) *noun*
Law: a statement made under oath which one knows to be untrue.
Word Family: **perjure**, *verb*; **perjurer**, *noun.*
[Latin *perjurare* to break one's oath]

perk (1) *verb*
perk up, a) 'she *perked up* when we told her the good news' (= recovered interest and liveliness); b) 'the robin *perked up* its tail and sang' (= raised quickly or smartly).
Word Family: **perky**, *adjective*, a) pert or sprightly, b) self-assured; **perkily**, *adverb*; **perkiness**, *noun.*

perk (2) *verb*
(*informal*) to percolate coffee.

perk (3) *noun*
(*informal*) a perquisite.

perm *noun*
1. a permanent wave.
2. a permutation.
Word Family: **perm**, *verb.*

permafrost *noun*
any ground which is permanently frozen, often to a great depth.

permanent *adjective*
lasting or intended to last: a) 'a mountain's *permanent* icecap'; b) 'a *permanent* tooth filling'.
Word Family: **permanently**, *adverb*; **permanence**, *noun*, the condition or quality of being permanent; **permanency**, *noun*, a) the condition or quality of being permanent, b) a permanent person, thing, or position.
[Latin *permanens* persisting, enduring]

permanent wave
also called a **cold wave**
a method of treating hair with chemicals to give it a curl which lasts for several months.

permeable (*say* **permia**–b'l) *adjective*
(of one substance) allowing another to pass through it, as water through earth.
Word Family: **permeability** (*say* permia–**billi**–tee), *noun*; **permeate**, *verb*, a) to pass through, b) to pervade; **permeation**, *noun.*
[from Latin]

Permian *noun*
Geology: see PALAEOZOIC.
Word Family: **Permian**, *adjective.*
[after *Perm*, Russia]

permission (*say* per–**mish**'n) *noun*
the act of permitting: 'you have my *permission* to leave the room'.
Word Family: **permissible**, *adjective*, allowable; **permissibly**, *adverb*; **permissibility**, *noun.*

permissive *adjective*
allowing people freedom of choice and expression, especially in sexual matters.
Word Family: **permissively**, *adverb*; **permissiveness**, *noun.*

permit (*say* per–**mit**) *verb*
(permitted, permitting)

to give leave to: a) '*permit* me to introduce myself'; b) 'the council does not *permit* nude sunbathing'.
Usages:
a) 'her parents will not *permit* smoking in their home' (= tolerate).
b) 'the vents *permit* the escape of gases' (= afford opportunity for).
permit (*say* **per**–mit) *noun*
a written order, such as a licence, granting leave to do something.
[Latin *permittere* to allow to go through]

permutation (*say* per–mew–**tay** –sh'n) *noun*
1. the act of rearranging.
2. *Maths:* a) the act of changing the order of sequence of elements in a series, especially the making of all possible changes in a sequence. *Example:* the permutations of the series *xyz*, are *xzy*, *zxy*, *zyx*, *yxz* and *yzx*. b) any of these arrangements by itself, such as *xyz*. Compare COMBINATION.
3. (*informal*) a multiple forecast on a football pool coupon, in the form of a mathematical combination. Short form is **perm**.
Word Family: **permutate**, *verb*.
[Latin *permutare* to change completely]
Common Error: see COMBINATION.

pernicious (*say* per–**nishus**) *adjective*
extremely harmful: 'he has an evil, *pernicious* hold over you'.
Word Family: **perniciously**, *adverb*; **perniciousness**, *noun*.
[Latin *perniciosus* destructive]

pernicious anaemia
a severe type of anaemia due to a lack of hydrochloric acid in the gastric juices.

pernickety (*say* per–**nikka**–tee) *adjective*
(*informal*) fussy.

peroration (*say* perra–**ray**–sh'n) *noun*
1. a lengthy speech.
2. the conclusion of a speech or essay which emphasizes the most important points again.
Word Family: **perorate**, *verb*, a) to make a long speech, b) to sum up at the end.
[from Latin]

peroxide *noun*
a substance used to bleach or lighten the colour of hair.
Word Family: **peroxide**, *verb*; **peroxidize, peroxidise**, *verb*, to convert into a peroxide.

perpendicular (*say* perp'n–**dik**–yoola) *adjective*
1. *Maths:* being at right angles to a line or plane.
2. vertical or upright.
Word Family: **perpendicularity** (*say* perp'n–dik–yoo–**larri**–tee), *noun*; **perpendicular**, *noun*, a perpendicular line, plane, or position; **perpendicularly**, *adverb*.
[Latin *perpendiculum* a plummet]

perpetrate (*say* **per**pa–trate) *verb*
a) (of a crime, etc.) to commit. b) (of a hoax, pun, etc.) to be guilty of.
Word Family: **perpetrator**, *noun*; **perpetration**, *noun*.
[Latin *perpetrare* to accomplish]

perpetual (*say* per–**pet**–yew'l) *adjective*
1. lasting for ever: 'the *perpetual* snows on the mountain peak'.
Usage: 'there's been a *perpetual* stream of phone calls all morning' (= continuous, incessant).
2. (of certain hybrid flowers) blooming all or nearly all the year.
Word Family: **perpetually**, *adverb*; **perpetuate** (*say* per–**pet**–yoo–ate), a) to make perpetual, b) to keep from being forgotten; **perpetuation**, *noun*.
[Latin *perpetuus* uninterrupted]

perpetual motion
the notion of a hypothetical device which would continue in motion for ever without further application of energy.

perpetuity (*say* perpi–**tewi**–tee) *noun*
1. the state of being perpetual.
2. a fixed income paid annually for a lifetime, usually a form of insurance.
in perpetuity, for ever.

perplex (*say* per–**pleks**) *verb*
to bewilder or confuse.
Word Family: **perplexedly**, *adverb*; **perplexity**, *noun*, a) a perplexed condition, b) something which perplexes; **perplexingly**, *adverb*.
[Latin *perplexus* entangled]

perquisite (*say* **per**kwa–zit) *noun*
short form is **perk**
an incidental benefit arising from one's employment, e.g. goods at cost price for a shop assistant, private use of a firm's car, etc.
[Latin *perquisitum* sought for]

perry *noun*
a cider made with pears instead of apples.
[Latin *pirum* pear]

per se (*say* per **say**)
by or in itself: 'there's nothing wrong with socialism, *per se*'.
[Latin]

persecute (*say* **per**sa-kewt) *verb*
to persist in ill-treatment or harassment of someone.
Word Family: **persecution**, *noun*; **persecutor**, *noun*.
[Latin *persequi* to pursue]

persevere (*say* persi-**veer**) *verb*
to keep on doing something despite difficulties or obstacles: 'I will *persevere* in this drudgery'.
Word Family: **perseveringly**, *adverb*; **perseverance**, *noun*, the act or habit of persevering.
[from Latin]

Persian lamb
a fur similar to astrakhan, with tight-curled silky hair obtained from new-born lambs.

persiflage (*say* **per**si-flah*zh*) *noun*
any light-hearted style of speech, as in treating serious matters as trivial and trivial matters as serious.
[French]

persimmon (*say* per-**simm**'n) *noun*
a plum-like, reddish-orange fruit which only becomes sweet when fully ripe.

persist (*say* per-**sist**) *verb*
to continue firmly in some course of action, state, etc. despite opposition or difficulties.
Usage: 'the pain was gone quite quickly, but the bruise *persisted* for weeks' (= lasted).
persistence, persistency *noun*
a) the action or fact of persisting: 'the *persistence* of a head cold'. b) the quality of being persistent: 'he's short on brains but has much *persistence*'.
Word Family: **persistent**, *adjective*; **persistently**, *adverb*.
[from Latin]

person (*say* **per**-s'n) *noun*
1. a human being, whether man, woman, or child.
Usage: 'he's matured to become a *person* in his own right' (= individual personality).
2. the body: 'he received several blows about his *person*'.
3. *Grammar:* either of three forms taken by a pronoun or verb, to indicate either the person speaking (**first person**), the person who is spoken to (**second person**), or the person being spoken about (**third person**). *Example*: yesterday, *I* (first person) came over to see *you* (second person) and your brother. *He* (third person) was at home but you were still at school.
in person, 'he came *in person* to deliver the news' (= himself).

persona (*say* per-**so**-na) *noun*
plural is **personae** (*say* per-**so**-nigh)
1. (*usually plural*) a character in a drama, novel, etc.: 'a list of the characters appearing in a play is called the dramatis *personae*'.
2. the image a person presents, or hopes he presents, to the world.
[Latin, an actor's mask]

personable (*say* **pers**'na-b'l) *adjective*
attractive or pleasing in personal appearance.
Word Family: **personably**, *adverb*.

personage (*say* **per**sa-nij) *noun*
also called a **VIP**
a) an important person: 'the function was attended by several well-known *personages*'. b) any person.

personal *adjective*
1. of or for a particular person: a) 'a *personal* letter'; b) 'a *personal* favour'.
Usages:
a) 'a *personal* interview will be required of all applicants' (= in person).
b) 'she is a woman of considerable *personal* beauty' (= physical).
c) 'there's no point in descending to *personal* remarks' (= attacking or offensive to a person or persons).
2. *Law:* of or relating to all of a person's possessions except land, such as clothing. Compare REAL.
personally *adverb*
1. in person: 'I *personally* interviewed each applicant'.
2. for one's part: '*personally*, I don't care for caviar'.
3. as a person: 'we like him *personally*, we just don't like his style of living'.
4. as though intended for or directed towards oneself: 'don't take his abruptness *personally*, it's just his manner'.

personality (*say* persa-**nalli**-tee) *noun*
the qualities in a person which make him individual and unique.
Usages:
a) 'he's a well-known radio and television *personality*' (= celebrity).

b) 'there's no need to descend to *personalities* in this discussion' (= personal insults).

personalize, personalise *verb*
to make personal: 'he *personalized* his stationery by having his family crest printed on it'.

persona non grata (*say* per-**so**-na non **grah**ta)
an unwelcome or unacceptable person.
[Latin]

personify (*say* per-**sonni**-fie) *verb*
(personified, personifying)
1. to give human characteristics to abstract ideas, animals, objects, etc.
2. to embody: 'she *personifies* grief'.
Word Family: **personification,** *noun.*

personnel (*say* persa-**nel**) *noun*
all the people employed in a particular business or work.

perspective (*say* per-**spek**tiv) *noun*
a) the illusion of space and depth produced on a flat surface, as in a painting or drawing. b) the technique of achieving this.
in perspective, in a true or proper proportion.
[Latin *perspectus* looked through]

Perspex *noun*
Chemistry: a colourless, transparent plastic which softens when heated and is widely used as a substitute for glass. See ACRYLIC RESIN.
[a trademark]

perspicacious (*say* perspi-**kay**-shus) *adjective*
keenly discerning or perceiving.
Word Family: **perspicaciously,** *adverb*; **perspicacity** (*say* perspi-**kassi**-tee), *noun.*
[Latin *perspicax* sharp-sighted]

perspicuous (*say* per-**spik**-yewus) *adjective*
clearly expressed or easily understood.
Word Family: **perspicuously,** *adverb*; **perspicuity** (*say* perspi-**kewi**-tee), **perspicuousness,** *nouns.*
[Latin *perspicuus* transparent]

perspire *verb*
to sweat.
Word Family: **perspiration,** *noun,* a) the act or process of perspiring, b) sweat.
[Latin *perspirare* to breathe through]

persuade (*say* per-**swade**) *verb*
to make willing to do or believe by arguing, urging, etc.: a) 'we couldn't *persuade* him to stay'; b) 'she *persuaded* me I was wrong'.
Usage: 'he's *persuaded* the world will end on Tuesday' (= convinced).

persuasion (*say* per-**sway**-*zh*'n) *noun*
1. a) the act of persuading: 'no *persuasion* could move him from his course'. b) the power of persuading: 'his argument lacks *persuasion*'.
2. a) a firm belief or conviction. b) a religious system or belief.
Word Family: **persuadable, persuasible,** *adjectives*; **persuasive,** *adjective,* able to persuade; **persuasively,** *adverb*; **persuasiveness,** *noun.*
[from Latin]

pert *adjective*
1. bold or impudent.
2. jaunty: 'a *pert* little hat'.
Word Family: **pertly,** *adverb*; **pertness,** *noun.*

pertain (*say* per-**tane**) *verb*
a) to relate: 'where are the files *pertaining* to the investigation?'. b) to belong: 'the house and all the land *pertaining* to it'.
[Latin *pertinere* to reach, relate to]

pertinacious (*say* perti-**nay**-shus) *adjective*
holding firmly or determinedly to a purpose, course of action, idea, etc.
Word Family: **pertinaciously,** *adverb*; **pertinaciousness, pertinacity** (*say* perti-**nassi**-tee), *nouns.*
[Latin *pertinax* very tenacious]

pertinent *adjective*
relevant or to the point: 'a *pertinent* remark'.
Word Family: **pertinently,** *adverb*; **pertinence,** *noun.*

perturb (*say* per-**terb**) *verb*
to disturb greatly: 'the anonymous telephone calls were *perturbing*'.
Word Family: **perturbation,** *noun,* a) the act of perturbing, b) the state of being perturbed, c) anything which perturbs.
[Latin *perturbare* to throw into confusion]

peruke (*say* **perrook**) *noun*
a wig worn by men in Europe in the 17th and 18th centuries.
[from Italian]

peruse (*say* **perrooz**) *verb*
to examine, especially with care or thoroughness: 'I shall *peruse* your application at my leisure'.
Word Family: **perusal,** *noun,* the act of perusing.

pervade (*say* per-**vade**) *verb*
to spread throughout: 'a smell of damp *pervaded* the old house'.
Word Family: **pervasive,** *adjective,* tending to pervade; **pervasively,** *adverb*; **pervasiveness,** *noun.*
[from Latin]

perverse (*say* per-**verse**) *adjective*
1. wilful or wayward: 'a *perverse* refusal to obey'.
2. incorrect: 'to arrive at a conclusion by a process of *perverse* reasoning'.
3. morally wrong.
perversion (*say* per-**ver**-*zh*'n) *noun*
1. a) the act of perverting. b) the state of being perverted. c) a perverse person or thing.
2. unusual or unacceptable behaviour, especially in relation to sex.
Word Family: **perversely,** *adverb*; **perverseness,** *noun*; **perversity** (*say* per-**versi**-tee), *noun,* a) the quality of being perverse, b) an instance of this.
[Latin *perversus* askew, distorted]

pervert (*say* per-**vert**) *verb*
1. to turn from the right course or the truth: a) 'the lawyer tried to *pervert* the course of justice'; b) 'to *pervert* the mind of a child'; c) 'the report *perverts* the true meaning of the speech'.
2. to change to unusual or unacceptable behaviour, especially in relation to sex.
Word Family: **pervert** (*say* **per**-vert), *noun,* a sexually perverted person.

pervious *adjective*
allowing penetration: 'sandy soil is *pervious* to water'.
Word Family: **perviousness,** *noun.*
[PER- + Latin *via* a way]

pesky *adjective*
American: (*informal*) annoying.

peso (*say* **pay**-so) *noun*
the unit of money in various South and Central American countries.
[Spanish, weight]

pessary (*say* **pessa**-ree) *noun*
Medicine: a) an object placed in the vagina to support the uterus after it has been displaced. b) a contraceptive device inserted into the vagina to block the cervix.
[Greek *pessos* an oval stone]

pessimism (*say* **pessi**-mizm) *noun*
1. the tendency to take a gloomy view of things.
2. *Philosophy:* the belief that the universe is evil by nature and that it cannot improve. Compare OPTIMISM.
Word Family: **pessimist,** *noun*; **pessimistic,** *adjective*; **pessimistically,** *adverb.*
[Latin *pessimus* worst]

pest *noun*
any annoying or harmful organism, such as a locust.
Usage: 'this rainy weather is a real *pest*' (= nuisance).
[Latin *pestis* plague or disease]

pester *verb*
to annoy, especially with repeated questions, wants, etc.
[Old French *empestrer* to hobble a horse]

pesticide (*say* **pesti**-side) *noun*
any substance which is used to destroy pests.
[PEST + Latin *caedere* to kill]

pestiferous (*say* pes-**tifferus**) *adjective*
1. (*informal*) troublesome or annoying.
2. morally bad.
Word Family: **pestiferously,** *adverb.*
[PEST + Latin *ferre* to bring]

pestilence (*say* **pesti**-l'nce) *noun*
any deadly epidemic disease.
Word Family: **pestilential** (*say* pesti-**len**-sh'l), *adjective,* a) of or relating to pestilence, b) carrying disease, c) (informal) troublesome or annoying.

pestilent *adjective*
a) harmful to life: 'the *pestilent* disease raged unchecked'. b) harmful to peace, morals, etc.: 'the *pestilent* effects of war'.
[Latin *pestilens* unhealthy]

pestle (*say* **pess**'l) *noun*
a baton-shaped utensil for crushing substances in a mortar.
[Latin *pistillum*]

pet (1) *noun*
1. any animal that is kept and cared for affectionately, as in a home.
2. a favourite person or thing.
pet *verb*
(petted, petting)
to fondle.
pet *adjective*
a) kept as a pet: 'a *pet* dog'. b) favourite: 'a *pet* theory'.
Usages:
a) 'a *pet* name' (= affectionate).
b) 'my *pet* hate is loud noise' (= chief, most important).

pet (2) *noun*
a fit or state of peevishness.

petal (*say* **pett**'l) *noun*
one of the usually brightly coloured outer parts of a flower, forming the corolla.
[Greek *petalon* a leaf]

peter (*say* **pee**ta) *verb*
peter out, to lessen slowly and then disappear altogether.

petiole (*say* **petti**-ole) *noun*
the slender stalk of a leaf.

petite (*say* pet**teet**) *adjective*
(of a female) small and delicate.
[French, little]

petite bourgeoisie (*say* pet**teet** bor*zh*-wa**zzee**)
the lower middle class, such as shopkeepers, etc.

petition (*say* pet**tish**'n) *noun*
a request, especially one presented formally to a person or persons in authority.
petition *verb*
to request by or as if by a petition: 'I shall *petition* the court for damages'.
Word Family: **petitionary**, *adjective*, of or like a petition; **petitioner**, *noun*, a person who petitions.
[from Latin]

petit mal (*say* **pet**tee mal)
a very mild form of epilepsy in which the period of unconsciousness is only a matter of seconds.
[French, small illness]

petit point (*say* **pet**ti point)
a stitch used in tapestry work and fine embroideries.
[French]

petrel *noun*
any of various small, long-winged, usually black and white seabirds.

petri dish
a flat dish used for growing bacterial cultures, etc.
[after *J. R. Petri*, 1852–1921, a German biologist]

petrify (*say* **pet**ri-fie) *verb*
1. to make or become rigid or paralysed: '*petrified* with fear'.
2. to turn into stone: '*petrified* trees'.
Word Family: **petrification**, **petrifaction**, *nouns*.
[Greek *petra* rock]

petrochemical (*say* petro-**kemmi**-k'l) *noun*
any chemical substance derived from petroleum or natural gas.

petrol *noun*
a complex mixture of hydrocarbons and special additives, used as a fuel and a solvent.

petroleum (*say* pet-**ro**-lee-um) *noun*
also called **crude oil**
an oily, naturally occurring liquid which is a source of petrol, oils, waxes and is used as the basis for many man-made compounds.
[Latin *petra* rock + *oleum* oil]

petroleum jelly
a semisolid mixture obtained from petroleum, used as a basis for ointments, protective dressings, etc.

petrology (*say* pet-**roll**a-jee) *noun*
the study of the composition and structure of rocks.
[Greek *petra* rock + -LOGY]

petrol station
a service station.

petticoat *noun*
also called a **slip**
a thin skirt or dress made of cotton, silk or nylon, worn under clothes.

pettifogging *adjective*
petty, mean or dishonest.
Word Family: **pettifogger**, *noun*.

pettish *adjective*
peevish or bad-tempered.
Word Family: **pettishly**, *adverb*; **pettishness**, *noun*.

petty *adjective*
1. unimportant: '*petty* details'.
2. mean or ungenerous: '*petty* criticism'.
Word Family: **pettily**, *adverb*; **pettiness**, *noun*.
[French *petit* small]

petty cash
a sum of money set aside for minor expenses in an office.

petty officer
a non-commissioned officer in the navy.

petty sessions
Law: the sitting of a magistrate's court.

petulant (*say* **pet**-yoo-l'nt) *adjective*
capricious and peevish.
Word Family: **petulantly**, *adverb*; **petulance**, *noun*.
[Latin *petulans* pert, impudent]

petunia (*say* pit-**yoo**-nia) *noun*
any of a group of garden plants with brightly coloured, trumpet-shaped flowers.

pew *noun*
1. a heavy, wooden bench with a back, used in churches and often carved.
2. (*informal*) any seat: 'take a *pew*'.

pewit (*say* **pee**–wit) *noun*
also spelt **peewit**
a lapwing.

pewter *noun*
an alloy of tin and lead with a little antimony and zinc, used for making drinking vessels and utensils.

peyote (*say* pay–o–tee) *noun*
a) mescal, a Mexican cactus from which mescaline is derived. b) a drug made from the root of the plant.

phaeton (*say* **fay**–t'n) *noun*
a light, open, four-wheeled carriage usually drawn by two horses.
[in Greek mythology *Phaeton* drove the chariot of the sun]

phagocyte (*say* **fagga**–site) *noun*
Biology: a type of cell found in the body fluids, which takes in and digests bacteria and other foreign particles.
[Greek *phagein* to eat + *kytos* a cell]

phalange (*say* **fal**–anj) *noun*
also called a **phalanx**
Anatomy: any of the 14 bones in each hand and foot.

phalanx (*say* **fal**–anks) *noun*
plural is **phalanxes** or **phalanges** (*say* fa–**lan**–jeez)
1. a group of soldiers in close formation.
2. *Anatomy:* a phalange.
[Greek]

phallus (*say* **fal**–us) *noun*
plural is **phalluses** or **phalli**
1. the penis.
2. an image of the penis used as a symbol of strength and fertility in some religions.
Word Family: **phallic**, *adjective*.
[from Greek]

phantasm (*say* **fan**–tazm) *noun*
1. a phantom or ghost.
2. a creation of the imagination or fancy.
Word Family: **phantasmal** (*say* fan–**taz**–m'l), **phantasmic**, *adjectives*.
[from Greek]

phantasmagoria
(*say* fan–tazma–**gawria**) *noun*
a changing series of images or appearances, as in a dream.
Word Family: **phantasmagorical** (*say* fantazma–**gorri**–k'l), *adjective*.

phantom (*say* **fan**–t'm) *noun*
a) a ghost or apparition. b) an image in a dream or the mind.
Word Family: **phantom**, *adjective*, ghostly or unreal.
[from Greek]

pharisee (*say* **farri**–see) *noun*
a hypocritical or self-righteous person.
Word Family: **pharisaic**, **pharisaical** (*say* farri–**say**–ik'l), *adjective*.
[after the *Pharisees*, an ancient Jewish sect concerned with strict obedience to tradition and the laws]

pharmacy (*say* **farma**–see) *noun*
1. the study and practice of preparing medicines.
2. a shop where medicines are prepared, dispensed and sold.
pharmacology (*say* farma–**kolla**–jee) *noun*
the study of drugs and their effects.
Word Family: **pharmacist** (*say* **farma**–sist), *noun*, a person trained to prepare and dispense medicines; **pharmaceutical** (*say* farma–**syooti**–k'l), *adjective*, of or relating to medicines; **pharmacologist**, *noun*.
[Greek *pharmakon* a drug]

pharynx (*say* **farrinks**) *noun*
Anatomy: the wide air passage which connects the nose to the throat.
[Greek]

phase (*say* faze) *noun*
1. a stage of development or change: a) 'the adolescent *phase*' b) 'the *phases* of the moon'.
2. *Physics:* any specified point on, or section of, a wave or other periodic phenomenon.
in phase, (of two similar wave patterns) having corresponding phases occurring simultaneously.
phase *verb*
to carry out or do gradually: 'to *phase* in a new method'.
[Greek *phasis* appearance]

pheasant (*say* **fezz**'nt) *noun*
any of various large, long-tailed game-birds related to the fowl, the male of which has brightly coloured feathers.
[Greek *phasianos*]

phenacetin (*say* fee–**nassa**–tin) *noun*
a white, crystalline drug made from coal tar, used to reduce or relieve a fever.

phenol (*say* **fee**–nol *or* **fen**–ol) *noun*
also called **carbolic acid**

a white, crystalline solid (formula C_6H_5OH), which is corrosive and poisonous and is used as a disinfectant and in making plastics, etc.
Word Family: **phenolic** (*say* fee-**noll**ik), *adjective.*

phenomenon (*say* finn**ommi**-non) *noun*
plural is **phenomena**
1. anything which may be seen and observed directly.
2. any remarkable or extraordinary person, object or event.
phenomenal *adjective*
1. remarkable or extraordinary.
2. of or being a phenomenon.
phenomenology
(*say* finnommi-**nolli**-jee) *noun*
the study of the physical appearance of things.
[Greek *phainomenon* appearing]

phenotype (*say* **fee**no-tipe) *noun*
Biology: the characters of an organism due to the genotype and the influence of environment.

phew (*say* few) *interjection*
an exclamation of disgust, relief, surprise, etc.

phial (*say* file) *noun*
also called a **vial**
a small container, usually glass, for storing liquids.
[Greek *phialé* a pan]

philander (*say* fil-**an**da) *verb*
to flirt or have a number of casual affairs.
Word Family: **philanderer**, *noun.*
[Greek *philein* to love + *andros* of a man]

philanthropy (*say* fil-**an**thro-pee) *noun*
a love of humanity, especially as shown by acts of goodness or kindness.
Word Family: **philanthropist**, *noun*; **philanthropic** (*say* fill'n-**thropp**ik), *adjective.*
[Greek *philein* to love + *anthropos* man]

philately (*say* fil-**att**a-lee) *noun*
the study and collection of postage stamps.
Word Family: **philatelist**, *noun*; **philatelic** (*say* filla-**tell**ik), *adjective.*
[Greek *philein* to love + *ateleia* tax exemption (that is, tax has already been paid by buying the stamp)]

philharmonic (*say* fil-har-**monn**ik) *adjective*
fond of music.

philippic (*say* fil-**lipp**ik) *noun*
any bitter or attacking speech.
[from the orations delivered by Demosthenes, an Athenian orator, against *King Philip* of Macedon in the 4th century B.C.]

philistine (*say* **fill**is-tine) *noun*
a person who lacks or dislikes culture and refinement.
Word Family: **philistine**, *adjective*; **philistinism**, *noun.*
[the race which did battle with Saul and David in biblical history, unfairly branded as uncivilized]

philology (*say* fil-**oll**a-jee) *noun*
the study of language, especially of ancient languages and texts.
Word Family: **philologist**, *noun*; **philological** (*say* filla-**loj**i-k'l), *adjective.*
[Greek *philein* to love + *logos* a word]

philosopher's stone
an imaginary substance, long sought by alchemists, which would change baser metals into gold and also produce the elixir of life (that is, confer eternal youth).

philosophy (*say* fil-**oss**a-fee) *noun*
1. the pursuit of wisdom and knowledge about e.g. the purpose of life.
2. the study of the principles of a particular subject, such as science or history.
Usage: 'what is your *philosophy* of life?' (= basic theory or principle).
philosophize, philosophise *verb*
to think or form theories about.
philosophical (*say* filla-**soff**i-k'l)
philosophic *adjective*
1. of or relating to philosophy: 'a *philosophical* theory'.
2. calm and rational: 'we'll have to be *philosophical* about our bad luck'.
Word Family: **philosopher**, *noun*; **philosophically**, *adverb.*
[Greek *philein* to love + *sophia* wisdom]

philtre (*say* **fil**ta) **philter** *noun*
a drink or drug believed to have magic powers, especially to inspire love.
[Greek *philtron* love charm]

phlebitis (*say* flee-**by**-tis) *noun*
an inflammation of the walls of the veins, most commonly in the legs.
[Greek *phlebos* of a vein + -ITIS]

phlegm (*say* flem) *noun*
also called **sputum**

the thick mucus of the throat, brought up by coughing during a cold, etc.
[Greek *phlegma* inflammation]

phlegmatic (*say* fleg–**mattik**) *adjective*
unemotional or not easily excited.

phloem (*say* flome) *noun*
Biology: the cells conducting food in plants.
[Greek *phloos* bark]

phlogiston (*say* flo–**jist'n**) *noun*
a chemical believed, before the discovery of oxygen, to make things burn and to be released during burning.
[Greek *phlogos* of a flame]

phlox (*say* floks) *noun*
plural is **phlox**
any of a group of garden plants cultivated for their bright flowers.
[Greek, flame]

phobia (*say* **fo**–bee–a) *noun*
an abnormal, persistent and morbid fear of some object or situation.
Word Family: **phobic**, *adjective.*
[Greek, fear]

phoenix (*say* **fee**–niks) *noun*
Egyptian mythology: a beautiful bird, the only one of its kind, believed to live for 500 years, then to burn itself on a pyre and to rise again from the ashes as a young bird.

phone (1) (*say* fone) *noun*
(*informal*) a telephone.
Word Family: **phone**, *verb.*

phone (2) (*say* fone) *noun*
a speech sound.
Word Family: **phonal**, *adjective.*
[Greek, sound]

-phone (*say* fone)
a suffix meaning sound, as in *telephone.*

phonetics (*say* fo–**nettiks**) *plural noun*
(*used with singular verb*) the study of sounds in language or speech.
Word Family: **phonetic**, *adjective*; **phonetically**, *adverb.*

phoney (*say* **fo**–nee) *adjective*
(*informal*) false or counterfeit.
Word Family: **phoney**, *noun.*

phonics (*say* **fonniks**) *plural noun*
(*used with singular verb*) a method of teaching reading by using common sounds.
Word Family: **phonic**, *adjective.*

phono- (*say* **fo**–no)
a prefix meaning sound, as in *phonology.*
[Greek]

phonograph (*say* **fo**–no–graf) *noun*
American: a record–player.
[Greek *phoné* sound + *graphein* to write]

phonology (*say* fon–**olla**–jee) *noun*
the science or study of the way in which sounds are made into words.
[Greek *phoné* + -LOGY]

phony (*say* **fo**–nee) *adjective*
phoney.

phosphate (*say* **fos**–fate) *noun*
Chemistry: any compound containing the trivalent $(PO_4)^{3-}$ ion, as in most fertilizers.

phosphor bronze (*say* **fos**fa bronz)
an alloy of copper, tin and phosphorus, used for making instrument springs, gears, turbine blades, etc.

phosphorescence (*say* fosfa–**ress**'nce) *noun*
a) the property of being luminous at temperatures below white heat, e.g. from exposure to light. b) the luminous appearance produced.
Word Family: **phosphorescent**, *adjective*; **phosphoresce**, *verb.*

phosphorus (*say* **fos**fa–rus) *noun*
element number 15, a non–metal forming several allotropes. It is an essential part of protein, and is used in fertilizers, detergents and matches. See CHEMICAL ELEMENTS in grey pages.
Word Family: **phosphoric** (*say* fos–**forr**ik), *adjective.*
[Greek *phosphoros* bringing light]

photo (*say* foto) *noun*
(*informal*) a photograph.

photo- (*say* foto)
a prefix meaning light, as in *photograph.*
[Greek]

photochemical (*say* foto–**kemmi**–k'l) *adjective*
of or relating to chemical reactions that are affected by light.
Word Family: **photochemistry**, *noun.*

photocopy (*say* foto–**koppee**) *noun*
a photostat.
Word Family: **photocopier**, *noun*; **photocopy** (**photocopied**, **photocopying**), *verb.*

photoelectric cell (*say* foto–**illek**trik sel)
Electronics: a cell which produces electricity when exposed to light.

photo finish
a race in which the competitors finish so close together that a photograph is needed to decide the winner.

photogenic (*say* foto–**jennik**) *adjective*
appearing attractive in photographs.
[PHOTO– + –GEN]

photograph (*say* fota–graf) *noun*
an image produced by the chemical effect of light on a light-sensitive surface such as film.
photographic (*say* fota–**graffik**) *adjective*
1. of or relating to photography.
2. having the accuracy or detail of a photograph: 'a *photographic* memory'.
Word Family: **photograph,** *verb.*
[PHOTO– + Greek *graphein* to write]

photography (*say* fo–**togra**–fee) *noun*
the art or process of taking photographs.
Word Family: **photographer,** *noun.*

photogravure (*say* foto–grav–**yoor**) *noun*
a method of printing from an etched metal plate based on a photographic image.

photolithography (*say* foto–lith–**ogra**–fee) *noun*
a method of printing from a flat surface which has been prepared photographically.
Word Family: **photolithograph** (*say* foto–**litha**–graf), *noun, verb.*

photometer (*say* fo–**tommita**) *noun*
an instrument for measuring the intensity of light.

photomicography (*say* foto–my–**kogra**–fee) *noun*
the taking of photographs through a microscope.
Word Family: **photomicrograph,** *noun.*

photon (*say* **fo**–ton) *noun*
Physics: a quantum of electromagnetic radiation.

photo relief
the process of photographing a model of the landforms of an area to make a relief map.

photosensitive (*say* foto–**sensa**–tiv) *adjective*
sensitive to or changed by light.

photostat (*say* **foto**–stat) *noun*
1. a camera which makes copies of documents, letters, etc. directly on sensitized paper.
2. a copy made with such a device. Also called a **photocopy.**
Word Family: **photostat (photostatted, photostatting),** *verb;* **photostat,** *adjective.*
[a trademark]

photosynthesis (*say* foto–**sintha**–sis) *noun*
Biology: the process by which green plants make carbohydrates from water and carbon dioxide using the energy that is absorbed by chlorophyll from sunlight.
Word Family: **photosynthetic** (*say* foto–sin–**thettik**), *adjective.*

phrase (*say* fraze) *noun*
1. a group of words forming a unit within a sentence, usually excluding a verb.
2. any meaningful group of words, such as a short saying.
3. *Music:* a small group of notes forming a unit in a melody.
turn of phrase, a particular manner or style of speaking.
phrase *verb*
1. to express in words: 'if you don't understand, I'll *phrase* it another way'.
2. *Music:* to group or mark off notes in a phrase.
[Greek *phrasis* speech]

phrasebook *noun*
a book of common sentences translated into one or more languages, for use by travellers.

phraseology (*say* fray–zee–**olla**–jee) *noun*
the choice and arrangement of words and phrases in expressing ideas.

phrenology (*say* fren–**olla**–jee) *noun*
the judging of a person's character or intelligence from the shape of the skull.
Word Family: **phrenologist,** *noun.*
[Greek *phren* mind + –LOGY]

phylum (*say* **fie**–lum) *noun*
plural is **phyla**
Biology: the largest group used in the classification of animals or plants.
[Greek *phylon* race]

physic (*say* **fizzik**) *noun*
an old word for a medicine.

physical (*say* **fizzi**–k'l) *adjective*
1. of or relating to the body: '*physical* exercise'.
2. of or relating to natural or material things: '*physical* geography'.
3. relating to physics.
Word Family: **physically,** *adverb.*

physical education
the teaching of sports and gymnastics.

physical science
the study of natural laws and properties other than those restricted to living

things, such as is studied in physics, chemistry, etc.

physician (*say* fiz-**ish**'n) *noun*
a doctor of medicine, especially a specialist or consultant.

physics (*say* **fizz**iks) *noun*
the study of the natural laws and properties of matter and energy which are not restricted to living things.
Word Family: **physicist** (*say* **fizzi**-sist), *noun.*
[Greek *physikos* natural]

physio- (*say* fizzio)
a prefix meaning physical, as in *physiotherapy.*
[Greek *physis* nature]

physiognomy (*say* fizzi-**onna**-mee) *noun*
the type of features of a face, especially when used to assess a person's character.
[Greek *physis* nature + *gnomon* judge]

physiography (*say* fizzi-**ogra**-fee) *noun*
the study of the physical features of the earth.
Word Family: **physiographic** (*say* fizzio-**graff**ik), **physiographical,** *adjective.*
[Greek *physis* nature + *graphein* to write]

physiology (*say* fizzi-**olla**-jee) *noun*
the study of the function of various parts of living things. Compare ANATOMY.
Word Family: **physiologist,** *noun;* **physiological** (*say* fizzia-**loji**-k'l), *adjective;* **physiologically,** *adverb.*
[Greek *physis* nature + -LOGY]

physiotherapy (*say* fizzio-**therra**-pee) *noun*
the treatment of bodily disorders by physical means, such as exercises, massages, etc.
Word Family: **physiotherapist,** *noun.*

physique (*say* fiz-**eek**) *noun*
the physical build of a person.

pi (*say* pie) *noun*
Maths: the symbol π (3·141592....), which is the ratio of the circumference of a circle to its diameter.
[name of the Greek letter used as the symbol]

pianissimo (*say* pee-a-**nissimo**) *adverb*
Music: very softly.
[Italian]

piano (1) (*say* pee-**anno**) *noun*
also called a **pianoforte** (*say* pee-anno-**fortee**)
Music: a large keyboard instrument in which metal strings are struck by felt-covered hammers. A **grand piano** has horizontal strings; an **upright piano** has vertical strings.
Word Family: **pianist** (*say* **pee**-a-nist), *noun,* a person who plays the piano.

piano (2) (*say* pee-**ahno**) *adverb*
Music: softly.
[Italian]

piano accordion
also called a **squeeze-box**
an accordion having a piano-like keyboard for one hand and chord stops for the other.
Word Family: **piano accordionist.**

Pianola (*say* pee-an-**ole**-a) *noun*
also called a **player piano**
a piano with a mechanism which allows it to be played automatically from punched paper rolls.
[a trademark]

piazza (*say* pee-**atsa**) *noun*
a public square or a colonnade.
[Italian]

pica (*say* **pie**-ka) *noun*
Printing: an em of 12 points, about 4 mm.

picador (*say* **pikka**-dor) *noun*
a bullfighter on horseback who uses a lance to taunt the bull. Compare MATADOR.
[Spanish *picar* to pierce]

picaresque (*say* pikka-**resk**) *adjective*
of literature which tells the story of a rogue or knave in a series of episodes.
[Spanish *picaro* rogue]

piccaninny (*say* **pikka**-ninnee) *noun*
a Negro or Aboriginal child.
[Portuguese *pequenino* very little]

piccolo (*say* **pikka**-lo) *noun*
Music: a small, high-pitched flute.
[Italian, small]

pick (1) *verb*
1. to pluck: 'to *pick* flowers'.
2. to choose or select: a) '*pick* the winner of tomorrow's race'; b) 'she *picked* her way through the crowd'.
3. a) to touch, remove or irritate something with or as if with a pointed instrument: 'he's *picked* the scab off that graze on his knee'. b) to make by digging into with a pointed instrument: 'to *pick* a hole in the desk with one's compass'.

Usages:
a) 'the thief *picked* my pocket' (= stole the contents of).
b) 'I lost the key so I *picked* the lock' (= opened with a pointed instrument).
c) 'are you trying to *pick* a fight?' (= seek, start).
d) 'he *picked* my argument to pieces' (= tore, pulled).
Phrases:
pick at, 'the child *picked at* its food' (= only ate a little of).
pick holes in, to find fault with.
pick off, 'the sniper *picked off* his victims one by one' (= shot).
pick on, to blame or criticize continually.
pick out, a) to choose; b) 'can you *pick out* her face in the crowd?' (= distinguish); c) 'he *picked out* the tune on the piano' (= played slowly or hesitantly).
pick up, a) 'we *picked up* a hitchhiker' (= took up into the car); b) 'I *picked up* the language overseas' (= acquired casually); c) 'our radio cannot *pick up* the country stations' (= receive); d) 'the robber was *picked up* at the airport' (= arrested); e) (*informal*) to meet or become acquainted without formal introduction; f) 'the patient's health is *picking up*' (= improving); g) 'the car *picked up* speed' (= gathered).
pick *noun*
1. a choice or selection: 'what's your *pick* for this race?'.
2. something which is picked, gathered or selected.
Usage: 'this horse is the *pick* of the field' (= best one).

pick (2) *noun*
also called a **pickaxe**
a wooden-handled tool with an iron head which is curved and pointed at both ends for breaking hard soil, rock, etc.

pickaback *adverb*
see PIGGYBACK.

picket *noun*
1. a pointed post driven into the ground as part of a fence, etc.
2. a) a detachment of soldiers posted on special duty, such as sentries. b) a group of people stationed at a factory gate, etc. to persuade employees not to report for work during a strike.
Word Family: **picket**, *verb.*

pickings *plural noun*
a) remnants or leftovers selected as worth saving. b) profits, etc. made by dishonest means. c) perquisites.

pickle *noun*
1. a) a vegetable or other food preserved in vinegar and spices. b) the liquid, such as brine, in which food is preserved.
2. (*informal*) a predicament or tricky situation.
pickle *verb*
to store or preserve in a pickle.
pickled *adjective*
1. preserved in a pickle: '*pickled* onions'.
2. (*informal*) drunk.

pick-me-up *noun*
something taken to improve and revive a person's mood, especially an alcoholic drink.

pickpocket *noun*
a person who steals from peoples' pockets, handbags, etc.

pick-up *noun*
1. a device consisting of a movable arm, with a head containing the stylus, which will pick up the sounds recorded on a spinning record when placed in contact with it.
2. a small van.
3. (*informal*) a person of the opposite sex encouraged or taken out without previous acquaintance.

picnic *noun*
1. a) an outing on which one takes food to eat outdoors. b) the meal eaten on such an outing.
2. (*informal*) a) any enjoyable experience. b) an easy task.
Word Family: **picnic** (**picnicked**, **picnicking**), *verb*; **picnicker**, *noun.*
[from French]

pico-
a prefix used for SI units, meaning one million millionth (10^{-12}). See UNITS in grey pages.

pictograph (*say* **pik**to-graf) *noun*
a sign or symbol in the form of a picture, used in some ancient writings.

pictorial (*say* pik-**taw**riul) *adjective*
of, like or illustrated by pictures: 'the photographer made a *pictorial* record of the event'.
pictorial *noun*
a newspaper or magazine in which pictures are the main feature.
Word Family: **pictorially**, *adverb.*

picture (*say* pikt–cher) *noun*
1. a representation of objects, people, scenes, etc. on a flat surface, such as a painting, sketch, photograph, etc.
2. a film, such as is shown in a cinema.
Usages:
a) 'the book gives us a frightening *picture* of war' (= impression).
b) 'she looked a *picture* of health' (= embodiment).
c) 'the twins looked a *picture* in their red caps' (= beautiful sight).
d) 'what is the economic *picture*?' (= situation).
get the picture, be in the picture, to understand fully.
picture *verb*
(pictured, picturing)
1. to portray in a picture.
2. to form a mental impression of: '*picture* the excitement at the big match'.
[Latin *pictura* a painting]

picturesque (*say* pik–cher–esk) *adjective*
1. charming or attractive to look at: 'the countryside was dotted with *picturesque* villages'.
2. (of language) strikingly vivid or graphic.
Word Family: **picturesquely,** *adverb.*

picture tube
the cathode–ray tube in a television set, which changes electric currents into pictures.

picture window
a very large window facing an attractive view.

piddle *verb*
1. (*informal*) to urinate.
2. to do something in an ineffective or trifling way.

pidgin (*say* pij–in) *noun*
a) the basic Chinese English long used in Far Eastern trade. *Example:* 'too much dust table topside' (= there's a lot of dust on the table). b) similar forms of English or other languages used elsewhere, e.g. West African pidgin. *Example:* 'make we go' (= let's go).
one's pidgin, 'that's *my pidgin*' (= my business, affair).
[Chinese pronunciation of *business*]

pie *noun*
a baked dish which contains a sweet or savoury filling, usually covered with a crust of pastry.

piebald *adjective*
having patches of different colours, especially black and white. Compare SKEWBALD.
Word Family: **piebald,** *noun,* a piebald animal, especially a horse.
[(mag)PIE + BALD]

piece (*say* peece) *noun*
1. a portion or fragment: a) 'a *piece* of pie'; b) 'an interesting *piece* of news'.
2. a single example or article: 'how many *pieces* in the chess set?'.
Usages.
a) 'I'll play you a *piece* I learnt today' (= composition).
b) 'do you have a 10p *piece*' (= coin).
c) 'I expect you feel better now that you've said your *piece*' (= view of the matter).
d) 'I refuse to be cast as the villain of the *piece*' (= situation).
Phrases:
a piece of cake, see CAKE.
a piece of one's mind, see MIND.
go to pieces, to lose control.
piece of work, 'he's a selfish *piece of work*' (= person).
piece *verb*
(pieced, piecing)
to make by putting or joining things: a) '*piece* together that broken plate'; b) '*piece* together the picture in your mind'.

pièce de résistance (*say* pee–ess de rayzis–tonce)
the best or most important part in a selection of things, such as a dish at a meal or a work of art at an exhibition.
[French]

piecemeal *adverb*
gradually or piece by piece.
Word Family: **piecemeal,** *adjective.*

piece rate
the wage paid for piece work.

piece work
any work that is paid by the job done rather than by the time it takes.

pied (*say* pide) *adjective*
having patches of two or more colours, like a magpie.

pied–à–terre (*say* pee–ad–ah–tair) *noun*
any lodgings kept for occasional use.
[French *pied* foot + *à terre* on the ground]

pier (*say* peer) *noun*
1. a structure built from the land into water, used as a landing place for boats, etc. Also called a **jetty**.
2. an upright support or pillar of brick or stone, used in building walls, etc.

pierce *verb*
(pierced, piercing)
1. to penetrate or make a hole in: 'a spear *pierced* his arm'.
2. to affect or cut through sharply: a) 'her screams *pierced* the air'; b) 'his story *pierced* her heart'.
Word Family: **piercingly**, *adverb.*

pietà (*say* pee–ay–**ta**) *noun*
a painting or a sculpture of the Virgin Mary mourning over the dead body of Christ.
[Italian, pity]

piety (*say* **pie**–a–tee) *noun*
1. a respect and honour for religious duties, etc.
2. any respect or honour, such as for one's parents, etc.
[Latin *pietas* dutiful conduct]

piezoelectricity
(*say* pie–eezo–il**lek**trissi–tee) *noun*
the property of some crystals, e.g. quartz, of acquiring opposite electrical charges on opposing faces when put under pressure; used in generating ultrasonic waves, etc.
[Greek *piezein* to press + ELECTRICITY]

piffle *noun*
(*informal*) nonsense.
Word Family: **piffling**, *adjective*, petty.

pig *noun*
1. a mammal, usually domesticated, with short legs, bristly hair and a snout.
2. (*informal*) a greedy or dirty person.
3. a block or mould of metal, especially iron or lead.
Word Family: **piggy**, **piggish**, *adjectives*, greedy or dirty; **piggishly**, *adverb*; **piggishness**, *noun.*

pigeon (*say* **pij**–in) *noun*
also called a **dove**
1. any of a family of fast-flying birds with a compact body, small head and short legs.
2. a domesticated variety of the rock-dove trained to home and carry messages.
3. (*informal*) a person who is tricked or deceived.

pigeonhole *noun*
one of a number of small open boxes above a desk, etc., in which papers, etc. are kept.

pigeonhole *verb*
1. to place in a pigeonhole.
2. to put something aside and ignore or forget it: 'the principal *pigeonholed* our suggestions'.

pigeon–toed *adjective*
having the toes or feet turned inwards.

piggery *noun*
a farm where pigs are kept.

piggish *adjective*
Word Family: see PIG.

piggyback *adverb*
also called **pickaback**
on the back or shoulders: 'he carried the child *piggyback*'.

piggy bank
a small moneybox, especially one shaped like a pig.

pig–headed *adjective*
stubborn or obstinate.

pig–iron *noun*
an impure form of iron obtained from blast furnaces.

piglet *noun*
a young pig.

pigment *noun*
any colouring matter, such as that used in paints and inks.
Word Family: **pigmentation**, *noun*, the amount or arrangement of colouring in something.
[from Latin]

Pigmy *noun*
a Pygmy.

pigsticking *noun*
the sport of hunting wild boars with knives, spears and dogs, on horseback.

pigsty *noun*
1. an enclosed area for pigs.
2. (*informal*) any very dirty or untidy place.

pigtail *noun*
a single braid or plait of hair hanging down from the side or back of the head.

pike (1) *noun*
any of a group of large, slender, vicious freshwater fish with long snouts.

pike (2) *noun*
a spear with a pointed metal head.

pikelet *noun*
also called a **drop scone**
1. a small pancake.
2. a crumpet or muffin.
[from Welsh]

piker *noun*
(*informal*) a person who fails or shows weakness, especially in a mean or cowardly way.
Word Family: **pike**, *verb.*

pilaster (*say* pil-**asta**) *noun*
a square strip or column attached to a wall.

pilchard (*say* **pil**-ch'd) *noun*
any of a large group of oily fish related to the herring.

pile (1) *noun*
1. a number of things lying on top of each other.
2. (*informal*) a large quantity or amount, as of money.
pile *verb*
to form into or make a pile.
Usages:
a) 'his debts *piled* up' (= collected, increased).
b) 'we *piled* into the car' (= got in a disorderly way).
c) 'my desk is *piled* with books' (= covered in piles).
pile it on, 'don't believe him – he's always *piling it on*' (= exaggerating).
[Latin *pila* a pillar]

pile (2) *noun*
a large post of wood, concrete or steel, set upright in the ground to support a floor in a house, a bridge, wall, etc.
[Latin *pilum* a javelin]

pile (3) *noun*
a raised surface on fabric, as on a carpet, made of upright loops of yarn or fibre.
[Latin *pilus* a hair]

pile-driver *noun*
a machine for laying piles, usually a tall framework with a weight which forces the pile downwards.

piles *plural noun*
Medicine: haemorrhoids.

pile-up *noun*
1. (*informal*) a collision, especially between cars.
2. a collecting or increasing, as of things to be done.

pilfer *verb*
to steal, especially in small quantities.
Word Family: **pilferage**, *noun*, petty theft; **pilferer**, *noun.*

pilgrim *noun*
1. a person who travels a long distance to a shrine, etc. as an act of devotion.
2. a poetic word for a traveller or wanderer.

pilgrimage *noun*
a journey made by a pilgrim.
[Latin *peregrinus* foreigner]

pill *noun*
1. a small tablet of medicine.
2. any unpleasant thing that has to be endured: 'punishment is a difficult *pill* to swallow'.
3. (*informal*) an insipid or unpleasant person.
the pill
a contraceptive pill.

pillage (*say* **pill**ij) *verb*
to rob or plunder violently, especially in war.
Word Family: **pillage**, *noun*, a) the act of pillaging, b) booty obtained by pillaging; **pillager**, *noun.*

pillar *noun*
1. a column.
2. a person or thing which supports, upholds or preserves: 'he is a *pillar* of society'.
from pillar to post, hither and thither, from one predicament or resource to another.
[Latin *pila*]

pillarbox *noun*
a letterbox.

pillbox *noun*
1. a small box for holding pills.
2. a small, cylindrical, brimless hat.
3. *Military:* a small, low, concrete fortification, usually containing a machine-gun.

pillion *noun*
a seat for an extra passenger, e.g. behind the driver on a motorcycle.

pillory (*say* **pilla**-ree) *noun*
a device forcing a person to stand upright with his head and hands locked through a wooden frame, formerly used for public punishment or ridicule.
Word Family: **pillory** (**pilloried, pillorying**), *verb*, a) to put in a pillory, b) to ridicule publicly.

pillow *noun*
a bag filled with soft material such as feathers, and used as a support for the head, especially in bed.
Word Family: **pillow**, *verb*, a) to rest on a pillow, b) to use something as a pillow.

pillowcase *noun*
also called a **pillowslip**
a cloth bag used to cover a pillow.

pilot *noun*
1. a person who controls an aircraft.

2. *Nautical:* a person who guides a ship through a difficult area of water, e.g. the entrance to a busy port.
3. something used as an experiment or to test a future project, such as a sample film for a television series.
pilot *verb*
to steer, guide or conduct.
Word Family: **pilotage,** *noun,* a) the act of piloting, b) the fee paid to a pilot.

pilot light
a small flame kept burning continuously and used to light a large burner, e.g. in a gas stove.

pilot officer
the lowest commissioned rank in the airforce.

pimento *noun*
1. allspice.
2. a sweet red pepper. Also called **pimiento.**
[Spanish *pimienta* pepper]

pimp *noun*
a person who obtains customers for a prostitute or brothel.
Word Family: **pimp,** *verb.*

pimpernel (*say* **pimpa-nel**) *noun*
a small, wild plant with scarlet flowers.

pimple *noun*
a small swelling on the skin, usually containing pus.
Word Family: **pimply,** *adjective,* having many pimples.

pin *noun*
1. a small, usually pointed, piece of wire or metal for fastening or joining, such as a safety pin or a hatpin.
2. any of various wooden or metal poles or pegs, such as the flagpole marking each hole on a golf links, a rolling pin, etc.
pin *verb*
(pinned, pinning)
1. to fasten or attach with a pin.
Usage: 'the climber was *pinned* under the fallen rocks' (= held fast).
2. *Building:* to underpin.
pin down, to get a definite commitment or decision from.

pinafore *noun*
a smock.

pinball *noun*
1. a game of chance played on a sloping board with a ball which scores points by hitting objects on the board.
2. a form of pinball where the ball is shot into pockets. Also called **bagatelle.**

pince-nez (*say* **pince-nay**) *noun*
plural is **pince-nez**
a pair of spectacles held on the nose by a spring.
[French *pincer* to pinch + *nez* nose]

pincers *plural noun*
1. *Biology:* the prehensile claws of arthropods such as crabs.
2. a tool with a pair of jaws for gripping nails out of wood, etc.

pinch *verb*
to squeeze tightly, especially between the thumb and finger: a) 'she *pinched* his arm'; b) 'I *pinched* my finger in the door'.
Usages:
a) 'I've had to *pinch* and save to buy this' (= be miserly).
b) (*informal*) 'who's *pinched* my ruler?' (= stolen).
c) (*informal*) 'we got *pinched* by the cops' (= arrested).
d) 'her face was *pinched* with hunger' (= made thin and drawn).
e) 'I'm a bit *pinched* for time this week' (= short of).
pinch *noun*
1. a squeeze.
2. a very small amount, such as that held between the finger and thumb: 'a *pinch* of salt'.
3. a painful situation or stress.
at a pinch, if absolutely necessary.
[Latin *punctus* pricked]

pincushion *noun*
a small cushion into which sewing pins are stuck and kept.

pine (1) *noun*
any of a group of evergreen trees with cones and usually long needle-like leaves, used for timber.
[from Latin]

pine (2) *verb*
1. to long greatly: 'the prisoner *pined* for his freedom'.
2. to become weak and waste away: 'he *pined* away from sickness and starvation'.
[Latin *poena* punishment]

pineal body (*say* **pine-eel body**)
also called the **pineal gland**
Anatomy: a gland in the brain, with unknown function but believed to be a sense organ.
[Latin *pinea* pine-cone (in shape)]

pineapple (*say* **pine-app'l**) *noun*
a large fruit with a tough, brown, prickly skin and juicy yellow flesh.

pin-feather *noun*
a young, undeveloped feather.

ping *verb*
to make a short, high-pitched ringing sound.
Word Family: **ping,** *noun,* the sound of pinging.

ping-pong *noun*
the original trade name for table tennis.

pinion (1) *noun*
a small wheel with cogs, which engages a larger similar wheel, bar, etc.

pinion (2) *noun*
the end of a bird's wing.
pinion *verb*
1. to cut or bind a bird's wing to prevent it flying.
2. to tie or fasten a person's arms to prevent movement.

pink (1) *noun*
any of a group of pale red colours.
in the pink, feeling very well.
pink *adjective*
1. having the colour pink.
2. (*informal*) having moderately left-wing political views.

pink (2) *verb*
to cut with a zigzag or notched pattern, such as the raw edge of fabric to prevent fraying.
pinking shears
a pair of scissors with notched blades for giving material a zigzag edge.

pink (3) *verb*
(of a car engine, etc.) to undergo pre-ignition or to 'knock'.

pink elephant (*say* pink **ell**ef-unt)
a hallucination, supposedly seen by alcoholics.

pin money
1. any small sum set aside for incidental expenses.
2. a wife's dress-allowance.
3. a portion of a wife's earnings or savings put aside for the future.

pinnacle (*say* **pinn**a-k'l) *noun*
a high, pointed part or structure, such as a mountain peak.
Usage: 'she reached the *pinnacle* of success' (= highest point or position).

pinnate *adjective*
shaped like a feather.
[Latin *pinna* feather]

pinochle (*say* **pee**-nukkel) *noun*
a card game played by two to four people with a special pack of 48 cards.

pinpoint *verb*
to find or describe exactly: 'can you *pinpoint* precisely where you lost the money?'.

pins and needles
a tingling sensation in a limb, as after numbness.

pinstripe *noun*
a very narrow stripe on a fabric.

pint *noun*
a) see GALLON. b) see BUSHEL.

pin-table *noun*
a table or board on which pinball is played.

pint-size *adjective*
(*informal*) small or unimportant.

pin-tuck *noun*
a very narrow decorative tuck used in dressmaking.

pin-up *noun*
(*informal*) a picture of an attractive or well-known person, such as a filmstar, pinned up on a wall by an admirer.

pinworm *noun*
a small, parasitic worm found in the human intestines, especially in children.

pioneer (*say* pie-a-**neer**) *noun*
a person who first enters, explores or settles a new region.
Usage: 'Picasso was a *pioneer* of modern art' (= innovator, originator).
Word Family: **pioneer,** *verb,* a) to explore or settle for the first time, b) to discover or open the way for.

pious (*say* **pie**-us) *adjective*
1. a) having respect for religion or a god. b) relating to religious or sacred matters: '*pious* literature'.
2. done in the name of religion or a good cause.
3. falsely or excessively moralistic.
Word Family: **piously,** *adverb*; **piousness,** *noun.*
[Latin *pius* dutiful]

pip (1) *noun*
a small seed found in fleshy fruit such as apples or grapes.

pip (2) *noun*
1. any of various marks or spots on dice, playing cards, etc.
2. *Army:* (*informal*) one of the stars indicating rank, worn on the shoulder-strap of an officer's uniform.

pip (3) *noun*
a short high-pitched sound, such as a time signal heard on a radio or telephone.

pip (4) *noun*
a disease of birds, especially poultry, causing a thick discharge which forms a crust in the mouth and throat.
give someone the pip, (*informal*) to irritate or annoy.

pip (5) *verb*
(pipped, pipping)
(*informal*) to defeat in a race or competition, especially by a small margin.

pipe *noun*
1. any hollow tube or cylinder for carrying fluids, etc.
2. any object, part or form which has the shape of a pipe, as in the human body.
3. an object consisting of a hollow tube with a small bowl at one end, used for smoking tobacco, etc.
4. *Music:* a) a hollow cylinder or cone in which air vibrates, as in an organ or wind instrument. b) a simple wind instrument consisting of a tube with holes. c) (*plural*) bagpipes.
5. a high-pitched note, sound or call: 'the *pipe* of a bird'.
pipe *verb*
1. to play on a musical pipe.
2. to carry by means of pipes.
3. to speak, call or sound in a shrill or high-pitched tone.
4. to trim a garment with piping.
Phrases:
pipe down, (*informal*) to keep quiet.
pipe up, (*informal*) to speak up or interrupt shrilly.
[Latin *pipare* to chirp]

pipedream *noun*
a dream or hope which is far-fetched or unlikely to be fulfilled.

pipeline *noun*
1. a length of pipe connecting two places, especially one conveying petroleum or natural gas.
2. a channel or line of communication, supply, etc.
in the pipeline, in the course of being supplied, produced, etc.

piper *noun*
a person who plays a pipe, especially the bagpipes.

pipette (*say* pip-**et**) *noun*
in America spelt **pipet**
a slender, graduated tube, usually open at both ends, used in laboratories for measuring and transferring small volumes of liquids.
[French]

piping (*say* **pie**-ping) *noun*
1. a) a system of pipes, e.g. for plumbing. b) the material used to make pipes.
2. a) the act or sound of playing on pipes. b) a shrill sound.
3. a rolled or rounded strip or part, e.g. of fabric used for trimming garments, etc. or icing on a cake.
piping *adjective*
making a shrill sound.
piping hot, (of food) very hot.

pipit *noun*
any of various small birds similar to the lark.

pippin *noun*
a type of large apple.

pipsqueak *noun*
(*informal*) a small or insignificant person.

piquant (*say* **pee**-k'nt) *adjective*
1. pleasantly sharp or spicy in taste, smell, etc.
2. stimulating or interesting.
Word Family: **piquantly,** *adverb*; **piquancy,** *noun.*
[French, pricking, stinging]

pique (*say* peek) *noun*
a feeling of resentment or irritation due to hurt pride, vanity, etc.
pique *verb*
1. to cause irritation or vexation.
2. to stimulate or arouse: 'our curiosity was *piqued* by their secretive whispering'.
[French *piquer* to prick or sting]

piqué (*say* **pee**-kay) *noun*
a fabric woven with a raised, corded or quilted pattern.

piquet (*say* pee-**ket**) *noun*
a card game for two people, played with a pack of 32 cards.

piranha (*say* pee-**rah**na) *noun*
a small, vicious, South American freshwater fish, which attacks in groups and is dangerous to man and other animals.
[Portuguese *pira* fish + *sainha* tooth]

pirate (*say* **pie**-rit) *noun*
1. a person who plunders, robs or commits illegal acts of violence at sea or along the coast.
2. any person who uses the work of another without permission, especially in breach of copyright or patent.

Word Family: **pirate,** *verb*; **piracy,** *noun*, the practice of being a pirate; **piratical** (*say* pie-**ratti**-k'l), *adjective*. [Greek *peirates*]

pirate radio
a radio station which broadcasts on an unauthorized wavelength.

pirouette (*say* pirroo-**et**) *noun*
a spinning step done on one foot, especially on the tips of the toes, as in dancing.
Word Family: **pirouette,** *verb*.
[French, whirl]

Pisces (*say* **pie-seez**) *noun*
also called the **Fishes**
Astrology: a group of stars, the twelfth sign of the zodiac.
[Latin]

pish *interjection*
an exclamation of contempt.

piss *verb*
(*informal*) to urinate.
piss off, (*informal*) go away.
Word Family: **piss** (informal), *noun*.

pissed *adjective*
(*informal*) drunk.

pistachio (*say* pis-**tah**-shio) *noun*
the nut of a small Mediterranean tree, with a hard shell and an edible green kernel.
[from Persian]

pistil *noun*
Biology: a) a carpel. b) a gynoecium.
Word Family: **pistillate** (*say* **pistil**-it *or* **pistil**-ate), *adjective*.
[Latin *pistillum* a pestle]

pistol *noun*
any of various short-barrelled guns designed to be held and fired with one hand.

pistol-grip *noun*
a handle resembling the stock of a pistol, used on certain tools or devices, such as a saw.

piston *noun*
a cylinder with an attached rod which is driven back and forth by pressure, e.g. in a motor car engine.

piston ring
a ring, usually of metal, which makes a seal between a piston and cylinder.

pit *noun*
1. a) a hole in the ground. b) a hole or hollow filled with a particular substance: 'a *sandpit*'.
2. *Mining:* a) a coalmine. b) the shaft of a mine.
3. a hollow or depression in a surface: 'smallpox had left many *pits* in her skin'.
Usages:
a) 'beware of the many *pits* and snares of greed' (= traps, pitfalls).
b) 'she felt a wave of fear in the *pit* of her stomach' (= depths, base).
4. *Car racing:* an area beside the racetrack where a car may stop for repairs or refuelling during a race.
5. *Theatre:* the part of the auditorium behind the stalls.
pit *verb*
(pitted, pitting)
1. to mark with holes or hollows: 'the accident had *pitted* his face with scars'.
2. to set in opposition or competition: 'they *pitted* all their strength against the raging winds'.

pit-a-pat *noun*
a movement or sound of quick, light taps.

pitch (1) *verb*
1. to throw, fling or toss.
2. to put or set up: 'let's *pitch* the tent by the stream'.
Usage: 'she *pitched* her ambitions very high' (= set, aimed).
3. to fall or plunge: 'he tripped and *pitched* headlong down the slope'.
Usage: 'the ship *pitched* in the rough seas' (= rocked lengthwise).
Phrases:
pitch in, (*informal*) a) 'we all *pitched in* and bought her a gift' (= contributed); b) 'let's *pitch in* and clean up this mess' (= set to work).
pitch into, to attack or assault.
pitch on, pitch upon, to settle or decide upon.
pitch *noun*
1. the highness or lowness of a sound or musical note.
2. the act or movement of pitching.
3. *Sport:* a) the area of play. b) the playing surface in cricket between the wickets, being about 3 × 20 m.
4. the highest point or degree: 'the *pitch* of perfection'.
5. the place where something is pitched.
6. the angle of slope, e.g. of the roof.
queer someone's pitch, to spoil a person's plans.

pitch (2) *noun*
1. a thick, black viscous mixture obtained from the destructive distillation of coal tar, used in road tars, furnace fuels, for waterproofing, caulking, etc.

2. (sometimes used of) bitumen or asphalt.
[from Latin]

pitchblende (*say* **pitch**–blend) *noun*
a brownish–black mineral which is the main ore of uranium.
[PITCH (2) + German *Blende* zinc sulphide]

pitched battle
a fierce or determined battle.

pitcher (1) *noun*
a large jar with a spout and a handle, used for pouring liquids.

pitcher (2) *noun*
a person who pitches, especially the player who throws the ball to the batter in a game of baseball.

pitchfork *noun*
a large heavy garden fork for pitching hay, turning soil, etc.
Word Family: **pitchfork,** *verb.*

pitchpipe *noun*
Music: a small pipe sounded to give a standard pitch or note when tuning an instrument, etc.

piteous (*say* **pitti**–us) *adjective*
inspiring pity or compassion.
Word Family: **piteously,** *adverb*; **piteousness,** *noun.*

pitfall *noun*
a trap or danger.

pith *noun*
1. *Biology:* the central cylinder of tissue in dicotyledons.
Usages:
a) 'the *pith* of his statement was an attack on radicals' (= essence, basic part).
b) 'the *pith* of his attack took us by surprise' (= force, vigour).
2. any soft, spongy substance, such as that between the flesh and rind of an orange.
Word Family: **pith,** *verb,* to remove the pith from; **pithy,** *adjective,* a) of, containing or like pith, b) full of force or vigour; **pithily,** *adverb.*

pithead (*say* **pit**–hed) *noun*
Mining: a) the top of a shaft. b) the offices, plant, etc. necessary for operating a mine.

Pithecanthropus
(*say* pithi–**kan**thra–pus) *noun*
Archaeology: an extinct form of ape–like man who lived half a million years ago and was about 1·5 m tall.
[Greek *pithekos* ape + *anthropos* man]

pith helmet
a light dome–shaped sunhat made from the dried pith of an Indian plant.

pitiable (*say* **pittia**–b'l) *adjective*
1. deserving pity: '*pitiable* sorrow'.
2. wretched or miserable: 'a *pitiable* old man'.
Word Family: **pitiably,** *adverb*; **pitiableness,** *noun.*

pitiful *adjective*
1. inspiring pity.
2. deserving or inspiring contempt: 'a *pitiful* display of cowardice'.
Word Family: **pitifully,** *adverb*; **pitifulness,** *noun.*

pitiless *adjective*
showing no pity or mercy.
Word Family: **pitilessly,** *adverb*; **pitilessness,** *noun.*

piton (*say* **pee–ton**) *noun*
a heavy metal pin with a hole at one end, used by mountaineers for setting into a rock to pass a rope through it.
[French, eye–bolt]

pittance *noun*
a very small or inadequate amount, especially of money or income.

pitter–patter *noun*
a rapid series of light beats or taps.
Word Family: **pitter–patter,** *adverb.*

pituitary gland (*say* p'tewi–tree gland)
Anatomy: a small pea–sized gland at the base of the brain, secreting many hormones which control the other glands of the body.
[Latin *pituita* slime (as formerly thought to secrete nasal mucus)]

pity *noun*
1. a feeling of sympathy or sorrow inspired by the suffering, misfortune, etc. of another.
2. something which causes pity, sorrow or regret: 'what a *pity* that it is raining'.
Word Family: **pity (pitied, pitying),** *verb.*
[Latin *pietas* dutiful conduct]

pivot *noun*
1. a part or point about which something turns.
2. something on which other things depend.
Word Family: **pivot,** *verb,* to turn on or as if on a pivot; **pivotal,** *adjective.*

pixie, pixy *noun*
plural is **pixies**
an elf.

pizza (*say* **peetsa**) *noun*
a pie-like food consisting of a flat dough covered with spiced ingredients such as tomato, cheese, olives, sausage, etc.
[Italian, pie]

pizzicato (*say* pitsi-**kah**to) *adjective*
Music: played by plucking the strings of bowed instruments with the finger.
[Italian *pizzicare* to pinch]

placard (*say* **plak**-ard) *noun*
a poster or notice for public display.
Word Family: **placard**, *verb*, to exhibit or notify by placards.

placate (*say* pla-**kate**) *verb*
to pacify or make calm.
Word Family: **placable** (*say* **plakk**a-b'l), *adjective*, forgiving or able to be placated; **placatory** (*say* pla-**kay**ta-ree), *adjective*, intending to placate.
[from Latin]

place *noun*
1. the particular area of space occupied by or set aside for something: a) 'please put that book back in its right *place*'; b) 'a *place* for relaxing'.
Usages:
a) 'if I were in her *place*, I would do this' (= situation, circumstances).
b) 'come and have dinner at our *place*' (= house, home).
c) 'it is not my *place* to criticize' (= function, duty).
d) 'he's been to *places* I've never even heard of' (= regions).
2. a job or employment: 'he has found a *place* in the civil service'.
3. a) an open court or square in a town or city. b) a name for a street, usually a short street or court.
4. a point in a series: a) 'in the second *place*, I will add this criticism'; b) 'divide the sum to four decimal *places*'; c) 'the horse finished in third *place*'.
Usage: 'I've lost my *place* in the book' (= particular passage).
Phrases:
go places, (*informal*) to be successful in one's career or social circumstances.
in place of, 'may I go *in place of* you?' (= as an alternative to).
out of place, a) out of the correct position; b) 'such a cynical reply was quite *out of place*' (= unsuitable).
put in one's place, 'he needs to be *put in his place*' (= humbled).
take place, 'the accident *took place* on the corner' (= was).

place *verb*
to put or fix in a particular place: a) '*place* your tired feet in these slippers'; b) '*place* your trust in me'; c) 'historians *place* the date in the 4th century'; d) 'her father *placed* her in a law firm'.
Usages:
a) 'I've seen her before but cannot *place* her' (= identify, remember the name of).
b) 'was your horse *placed*?' (= in the first three).
[Greek *plateia* (*hodos*) broad (way)]

placebo (*say* pla-**seebo**) *noun*
a medicine given to a patient for psychological reasons and having no physiological effect.
[Latin, I shall please]

place kick
Football: a kick in which the ball is placed upright on the ground and then kicked.

placement *noun*
a) the act of placing, especially the finding of jobs or positions for people.
b) the state of being placed.

placenta (*say* pla-**sen**ta) *noun*
plural is **placentas** or **placentae** (*say* pla-**sen**-tee)
Anatomy: a spongy organ formed within the uterus during pregnancy so that food and oxygen from the mother's blood supply may reach the foetus and waste products from the foetus may be eliminated.
Word Family: **placental**, *adjective*.
[Greek *plakountos* of a flat cake]

placid (*say* **plass**id) *adjective*
calm or composed.
Word Family: **placidly**, *adverb*; **placidness**, **placidity** (*say* pla-**siddi**-tee), *nouns*.
[from Latin]

placket *noun*
the overlapping piece on the opening in a dress, blouse or skirt.

plagiarist (*say* **play**-ja-rist) *noun*
a person who copies or takes another's work or ideas and pretends they are his own.
Word Family: **plagiarism**, *noun*, a) the act of copying another's work and pretending it is one's own, b) anything which is copied or used in this way; **plagiarize**, **plagiarise**, *verb*, to copy.
[Latin *plagiarius* kidnapper]

plague (*say* playg) *noun*
1. an infectious, epidemic disease, especially bubonic or pneumonic plague.
2. a sudden invasion or arrival of large numbers: 'a *plague* of mosquitoes'.
3. something which is troublesome or a nuisance: 'those headaches of mine are a *plague*'.
plague *verb*
(plagued, plaguing)
to trouble, annoy or bother: 'the police have been *plagued* with complaints about the noise'.
Word Family: **plaguy,** *adjective,* annoying or troublesome.
[Latin *plaga* a blow, a wound]

plaice (*say* place) *noun*
a type of flatfish with bright orange spots, much used as food.
[Greek *platys* broad]

plaid (*say* plad) *noun*
a) a woollen cloak in tartan (Highland) or check (Lowland) patterns. b) any fabric with this design.
[Gaelic]

plain *adjective*
1. easily seen: 'his embarrassment was *plain* to see'.
2. easily heard or understood: 'her meaning was *plain* to all of us'.
3. simple or free from complication, etc.: 'just give us the *plain* facts'.
Usages:
a) 'the poor girl is quite *plain*' (= not attractive).
b) 'they live a *plain* though comfortable life' (= not elaborate).
c) 'her *plain* manner of speaking disconcerts many people' (= frank, candid).
d) 'please write on *plain* paper' (= unlined).
e) 'it is *plain* madness for you to go' (= absolute).
plain *noun*
1. an area of low, generally flat, land.
2. a simple stitch in knitting.
Word Family: **plainly, plain,** *adverbs,* a) in a simple or plain manner, b) clearly or obviously; **plainness,** *noun.*
[Latin *planus* level, clear]

plain clothes
ordinary clothes as distinct from a uniform.
Word Family: **plain-clothes,** *adjective,* wearing plain clothes.

plain sailing
(*informal*) an easy or unobstructed course, progress, etc.

plainsong *noun*
a form of chant used in early church music, using a single melody line with no additional parts or accompaniment.

plain-spoken *adjective*
candid or frank.

plaintiff *noun*
also called a **complainant**
Law: a person who asks for a judgement in court, such as a person demanding payment of a debt. Compare DEFENDANT.
[Latin *plangere* to lament]

plaintive *adjective*
expressing sorrow, sadness or melancholy: 'a *plaintive* smile'.
Word Family: **plaintively,** *adverb*; **plaintiveness,** *noun.*

plait (*say* plat) *noun*
a long bunch of hair, etc. divided into three strands, intertwined and bound at the end.
Word Family: **plait,** *verb.*
[Latin *plicatus* folded]

plan *noun*
1. an action, method or programme worked out beforehand: a) 'do you have a particular *plan* of attack?'; b) 'what are your *plans* for the holidays?'.
2. a drawing or diagram of structure, details, arrangement, etc.: 'may we see a *plan* of the house?'.
plan *verb*
(planned, planning)
1. to form or decide on a plan for: 'the generals met to *plan* the campaign'.
Usage: 'we *plan* to arrive early' (= aim).
2. to draw or devise a plan for: 'the garden was *planned* by a landscape architect'.
Word Family: **planner,** *noun.*

planchette (*say* plon-**shet**) *noun*
a small board on two castors, with a vertical pencil believed to write messages from the spirit world when a person's fingers rest lightly on it. See OUIJA BOARD.
[French, small plank]

Planck's constant
the constant which, multiplied by the frequency of an electromagnetic wave, gives its quantum of energy. See QUANTUM THEORY.
[discovered in 1900 by *Max Planck*, a German physicist]

plane (1) *noun*
1. a flat or level surface.

Usage: 'the preacher's words reached a high *plane* of morality' (= level).
2. (*informal*) an aeroplane.
plane *verb*
1. to glide.
2. to travel on top of the water rather than through it, e.g. as is done by a speedboat, water-skier, etc.
Word Family: **plane**, *adjective*, flat; **planeness**, *noun*.

plane (2) *noun*
a tool with a blade slotted through a smooth surface, for shaping or smoothing the surface of wood, etc.
Word Family: **plane**, *verb*; **planer**, *noun*.
[Latin *planus* level]

plane figure
any figure whose parts all lie on the same plane.

plane geometry
a branch of geometry dealing with plane figures.

planet (*say* **plann**it) *noun*
1. *Astronomy:* any body that does not produce light and revolves around a star, especially the nine planets of our solar system. Compare SATELLITE.
2. *Astrology:* any of the seven heavenly bodies, consisting of Mercury, Venus, the moon, the sun, Mars, Jupiter and Saturn, believed to influence personality and events in conjunction with the stars.
Word Family: **planetary**, *adjective*, a) of or resembling a planet or planets, b) earthly or mundane, c) wandering.
[Greek *planetes* wanderer]

planetarium (*say* planni-**tair**i-um) *noun*
plural is **planetariums** or **planetaria**
a building with a hemispherical ceiling on which the positions and movements of the stars and planets may be displayed by a projector.

planetoid *noun*
see ASTEROID.

plane tree
any of a group of trees with large, broad leaves, spreading branches and flaky bark.
[Greek *platanos*]

plangent (*say* **plan**-j'nt) *adjective*
beating or resounding loudly.
Word Family: **plangency**, *noun*.
[from Latin]

planish (*say* **plann**ish) *verb*
to smooth, flatten or finish metal, etc.

plank *noun*
a long flat piece of cut timber.
walk the plank, to be forced to walk to one's death from a plank extended over the water from a ship's side.
plank *verb*
to cover or fit with planks.
Word Family: **planking**, *noun*, a) any or all planks, b) the process of fitting planks.
[from Latin]

plankton *noun*
Biology: the marine or freshwater, microscopic animals and plants that drift with the surrounding water.
[Greek *plagktos* wandering]

planned obsolescence
the deliberate production of goods which will soon be out of date, in order to make sure of continuing sales.

plant *noun*
1. a living organism that is usually unable to move about but is usually able to make its own food from chemical elements. Compare ANIMAL.
2. a small plant, such as a herb, which has no permanent woody stem, as distinct from a tree, etc.
3. the buildings or equipment for a particular industry or mechanical system: 'an electrical *plant*'.
4. (*informal*) a) a person placed in a certain situation as a spy, decoy, etc. b) something used to trick, swindle or mislead.
plant *verb*
1. to place a seed, cutting, tree, etc. in the ground so it will grow.
Usages:
a) 'he *planted* his suitcase on the platform beside him' (= placed or put firmly).
b) 'new doubts had been *planted* in his mind' (= established, introduced).
2. (*informal*) a) to place a person as a spy, decoy, etc. b) to place or use something in order to trick, mislead, etc.
[Latin *planta* a shoot, sprig]

plantain (1) (*say* **plan**tin) *noun*
a tropical tree with long banana-like fruit.

plantain (2) (*say* **plan**tin) *noun*
a weed with broad leaves and long spikes of small greenish flowers.
[Latin *planta* sole of the foot (from the shape of the leaves)]

plantation (*say* plan-tay-sh'n) *noun*
1. a farm, especially in tropical regions, where tobacco, coffee, sugar, etc. are grown.
2. a group of planted trees.

planter *noun*
1. a person who plants, especially the owner or manager of a plantation.
2. a machine or tool for planting or sowing seeds.

plaque (1) (*say* plak) *noun*
a flat, ornamental disc or tablet used as a wall-hanging.
[French]

plaque (2) (*say* plak) *noun*
a sticky film which forms on teeth and which can cause gum disease.

plasma (*say* **plazma**) *noun*
1. *Anatomy:* the liquid part of unclotted blood in which cells are suspended. Compare SERUM.
2. *Biology:* see PROTOPLASM.
3. *Physics:* an intensely hot gas that has been completely broken up into positive ions and electrons.
Word Family: **plasmatic** (*say* plaz-**mattik**), **plasmic**, *adjectives.*
[Greek, something shaped]

plasma physics
the study of the behaviour of ionized gases, especially at the very high temperatures required for nuclear fusion.

plaster (*say* **plahs**ta) *noun*
1. a mixture of lime and sand or similar substances, used to cover brickwork, etc. inside or outside a house.
2. a solid or partly solid substance, such as plaster of Paris, coated on cloth, etc. as a support for a broken limb.
3. sticking plaster.
plaster *verb*
to apply or cover with plaster.
Usages:
a) 'the train was *plastered* with advertisements' (= spread or covered thickly).
b) 'her wet hair was *plastered* to her head' (= stuck).
c) 'the city was *plastered* by enemy missiles' (= bombed or struck heavily).
Word Family: **plasterer**, *noun*; **plastering**, *noun*; **plastered**, *adjective*, (informal) drunk.
[Greek *emplastos* daubed over]

plaster of Paris
a white powder, calcium sulphate (formula $2CaSO_4.H_2O$) obtained by heating gypsum to 120 - 130°C. It swells and hardens when mixed with water and is used for making moulds, etc.

plastic *noun*
Chemistry: any of a complex group of substances which may be shaped when soft and then hardened. This group includes resins and polymers, and derivatives of casein, protein and cellulose, and has a virtually limitless range of uses.
There are two main types, **thermoplastic** which can be repeatedly softened by heat, and **thermosetting** which, once set, are permanently rigid.
plastic *adjective*
1. made of plastic: 'a *plastic* bag'.
2. able to be moulded or shaped: 'clay is a *plastic* substance'.
3. relating to shaping or modelling: 'the *plastic* arts'.
Word Family: **plasticity** (*say* plas-**tissi**-tee), *noun*; **plasticize** (*say* **plasti**-size), **plasticise**, *verb*, to make or become plastic.
[Greek *plastikos* moulded]

plastic bomb
a bomb consisting of a putty-like explosive and a detonator, often used in guerrilla warfare.

plasticine (*say* **plasti**-seen) *noun*
a plastic modelling compound, obtainable in many colours.

plastic surgery
any surgery which is concerned with remodelling, repairing or restoring normal appearances to external parts of the body.

plastid *noun*
Biology: any of various small bodies found in the cytoplasm of plant cells.

plate *noun*
1. a shallow, usually circular dish, used for eating from, holding articles, etc.
2. a thin, flat, smooth sheet or piece: 'a *plate* of glass'.
3. a) a sheet or surface used in printing, engraving, photography, etc.
b) a print produced from such a surface, especially a full-page illustration in a book.
4. *Geology:* one of the sections of the earth's crust, whose movement relative to that of another, is believed to cause earthquakes, build mountain chains, etc.
5. any metal articles, utensils or objects, especially silver or gold.
6. *Dentistry:* a) a piece of metal or plastic with artificial teeth attached.

b) a piece of metal or plastic with wires to help straighten teeth or to fix a fractured jaw.
7. *Baseball:* any base, especially the base over which the batter stands.
8. *Horseracing:* a) an ornamental metal dish used as a prize. b) a race in which this is awarded. c) a very light horseshoe, often of aluminium.
Phrases:
on a plate, 'the race was handed to the champion *on a plate*' (= like a gift, with no effort required).
on one's plate, 'we don't have much work *on our plate* at the moment' (= to be dealt with).
plate *verb*
1. to coat with a thin layer or film of metal: 'the nickel was *plated* with silver'.
2. to cover with metal plates or armour.
Word Family: **plating**, *noun*, a thin coating or layer, as on metal.
[Greek *platys* flat]

plateau (*say* **platto**) *noun*
plural is **plateaus** or **plateaux** (*say* **plat**–oze)
1. *Geography:* a large, fairly flat area of highland. Also called a **tableland**.
2. any fairly steady or stable period or condition.
[French]

plate glass
a thick, clear glass used for windows, mirrors, etc.

platelayer *noun*
a person who lays or maintains railway lines.

platelet *noun*
Biology: any of the many minute, irregularly shaped bodies in blood, necessary for forming blood clots.

platen (*say* **platt'**n) *noun*
1. the part of a typewriter, printing press, etc., on which the paper is supported during printing.
2. the work-table of a power-operated tool.

platform *noun*
1. any raised floor or horizontal surface, as beside a railway line, in a hall, etc.
2. an open entrance in a bus, etc.
3. *Politics:* the policies or principles of a party, usually declared publicly before an election.

plating (*say* **play**–ting) *noun*
Word Family: see PLATE.

platinum (*say* **platti**–n'm) *noun*
1. element number 78, a ductile, malleable metal resistant to heat and acids. It is used in alloys, electrical contacts, scientific apparatus and jewellery. See TRANSITION ELEMENT. See CHEMICAL ELEMENTS in grey pages.
2. a metallic greyish or bluish-white colour.
[Spanish *plata* silver]

platitude (*say* **platti**–tewd) *noun*
an unoriginal remark or statement, especially one said as if wise or refreshing.
Word Family: **platitudinous** (*say* platti–**tewdin**–us), *adjective*; **platitudinize, platitudinise**, *verb.*

platonic (*say* pla–**tonnik**) *adjective*
(*sometimes capital*) spiritual as distinct from sexual or sensual: '*platonic* love'.
Word Family: **platonically**, *adverb.*
[after *Plato,* an ancient Greek philosopher who advocated ideal love]

platoon (*say* pla–**toon**) *noun*
Military: a part of a company, usually consisting of two or more sections.
[French *peloton* little group]

platter *noun*
a large, shallow dish for serving food, etc.

platyhelminth (*say* platti–**helminth**) *noun*
any of a group of worms with soft, flattened bodies.
[Greek *platys* flat + *helmins* worm]

platypus (*say* **platti**–puss) *noun*
plural is **platypuses**
short form of **duck-billed platypus**
a brown, furry, egg-laying Australian mammal living in rivers and lagoons and growing to about 65 cm long, with webbed feet and a leathery, duck-like snout. See MONOTREME.
[Greek *platys* flat + *pous* foot]

plaudit (*say* **plaw**–dit) *noun*
(*usually plural*) enthusiastic applause or expression of approval.
[Latin *plaudere* to applaud]

plausible (*say* **plawzi**–b'l) *adjective*
1. seeming worthy of belief or acceptance: 'his alibi sounded quite *plausible* to the jury'.
2. glibly lying: 'a *plausible* rogue'.

play *verb*
1. to take part in a game, sport or amusement: a) 'shall we *play* tennis?'; b) 'let's *play* a trick on the others'; c) 'I was only *playing,* not serious'.

Usages:
a) 'you must *play* fair' (= be).
b) 'all the time he was talking he was *playing* with a button on his coat' (= toying).
2. to produce music on an instrument.
3. a) to perform a play. b) to perform a part in a play, film, etc.
Usage: 'don't *play* innocent with me' (= act deceitfully).
4. (in games) to move or lay down: 'he *played* his highest card'.
5. to move in a light, quick, irregular way: 'the sun's rays *played* on the coloured glass'.
6. to direct or operate continuously: 'firemen *played* jets of foam on the fire'.
Usage: 'their constant chatter *played* on my nerves' (= worked irritatingly).
7. *Fishing:* to keep tension on a line so that a hooked fish tires enough to be taken from the water.
Phrases:
play along, (*informal*) to agree or cooperate.
play ball, (*informal*) see BALL (1).
play down, to make little of.
play fair, to act fairly and not cheat.
play for time, to act slowly in order to gain more time for one's own purposes.
play into the hands off, to act in such a way as to give the advantage to.
play it by ear, to see how things go and improvise measures accordingly.
play off, (*Sport*) to play an extra game to decide a draw.
play on, play upon, 'he *played on* her generous nature to gain her sympathy' (= made use of).
play out, to finish or exhaust. *Word Family*: **played-out,** *adjective.*
play to the gallery, to try to win cheap applause.
play up, a) 'please behave and don't *play up*' (= be naughty); b) 'the debating team *played up* its opponent's lack of knowledge' (= emphasized).
play up to, to try and win the favour of.

play *noun*
1. a work written to be acted, especially in a theatre.
2. any activity done for pleasure, recreation, etc.: 'this job is all work and no *play*'.
3. any fun or joking.
4. the act of taking part in a sport or game.
5. a quick, irregular movement: 'the *play* of sunlight on water'.
6. any free movement or activity: a) 'there is too much *play* in the steering wheel'; b) 'she gave her imagination free *play*'.
7. *Sport:* the state of a ball being in use in a game.

play-act *verb*
to pretend.

playback *noun*
Audio: a) the reproducing or replaying of recorded or taped sounds. b) a device in a recording machine for such a process.

playbill *noun*
a programme or announcement for a theatrical performance.

playboy *noun*
a carefree, usually wealthy, man devoted to the pleasures of a social or sophisticated life.

player *noun*
1. a person who plays, especially one taking part in a game, sport or competition.
2. an actor.

player piano
a Pianola.

playfellow *noun*
a friend with whom one plays.

playful *adjective*
1. joking or light-hearted: 'a *playful* fight'.
2. full of fun or high spirits.
Word Family: **playfully,** *adverb*; **playfulness,** *noun.*

playgoer *noun*
a person who attends the theatre.

playground *noun*
an area of land with swings, slides or other facilities for amusement and games for children.
Usage: 'this tropical island is the *playground* of the rich' (= place for amusement and relaxation).

play group
a nursery class which is usually organized privately.

playhouse *noun*
a theatre.

playing card
any of a set of 52 cards divided into 4 suits, used in various games.

playing head
Audio: see HEAD.

playmate *noun*
a person or friend with whom one plays.

play–off *noun*
a game or match played to decide a draw.

playsuit *noun*
rompers.

plaything *noun*
a toy.

playwright (*say* **play**–rite) *noun*
also called a **dramatist**
a person who writes plays.

plaza *noun*
an open area or public square in a city.
[Spanish, place]

plea (*say* plee) *noun*
1. a request or entreaty: 'a *plea* for peace'.
2. *Law:* a statement, especially in answer to a charge.
3. an excuse.

plead (*say* pleed) *verb*
(**pleaded** or **plead** (*say* **pled**), **pleading**)
to make a plea: a) 'the accused man *pleaded* insanity'; b) 'I *pleaded* with him not to go'.
Word Family: **pleadingly**, *adverb.*

pleasant (*say* **plezz**'nt) *adjective*
enjoyable or pleasing.
Word Family: **pleasantly**, *adverb*; **pleasantness**, *noun.*

pleasantry (*say* **plezz**'n–tree) *noun*
a joke or humorous remark.

please *verb*
1. used as a polite form of request: '*please* may I go now?'.
2. to be agreeable or give satisfaction to: 'the king's speech did not *please* the crowd'.
Usage: 'say whatever you *please*' (= like).
please yourself!, do as you please, but do not expect approval.
Word Family: **pleasingly**, *adverb.*
[Latin *placere*]

pleasure (*rhymes with* treasure) *noun*
a satisfying or pleasant experience: a) 'it is a *pleasure* to see you'; b) 'wine is one of the *pleasures* of life'.
Usage: 'what is your *pleasure*?' (= wish, desire).
pleasure *verb*
to give or take pleasure in.
Word Family: **pleasurable**, *adjective*, pleasing; **pleasurably**, *adverb.*

pleat (*say* pleet) *noun*
a fold made by doubling cloth on itself, and sewing or pressing it in place.
Word Family: **pleat**, *verb.*
[for PLAIT]

pleb *noun*
(*informal*) a plebeian.

plebeian (*say* pli–**bee**–an) *adjective*
1. of or characteristic of the common people.
2. common or vulgar.
Word Family: **plebeian**, *noun.*
[Latin *plebeius* belonging to the common people]

plebiscite (*say* **plebbi**–sit) *noun*
a referendum.
[Latin *plebis* of the people + *scitum* a decree]

plectrum *noun*
a small piece of plastic, wood or metal, used to pluck a stringed instrument.
[Greek *plektron*]

pledge *noun*
1. a vow or promise: 'a *pledge* of loyalty'.
2. a) something given as security for a loan or debt. b) the state of being given as security: 'my house is in *pledge*'.
Usage: 'this ring is a *pledge* of my friendship' (= token).
take the pledge, to promise to give up drinking.
Word Family: **pledge**, *verb*, to give or make a pledge.

Pleistocene (*say* **ply**–sta–seen) *noun*
Geology: see QUATERNARY.
Word Family: **Pleistocene**, *adjective.*
[Greek *pleistos* most + *kainos* modern (that is, most modern forms of life)]

plenary (*say* **plee**na–ree) *adjective*
a) (of authority) complete or absolute.
b) (of meetings, etc.) attended by all qualified members.
[Latin *plenus* full]

plenipotentiary
(*say* plennipa–**ten**sha–ree) *noun*
a person who may make decisions on behalf of his government, such as an ambassador.
Word Family: **plenipotentiary**, *adjective*, having full authority.
[Latin *plenus* full + *potentia* power]

plenitude (*say* **plenni**–tewd) *noun*
fullness or abundance.

plenteous (*say* **plenti**–us) *adjective*
plentiful or abundant.
Word Family: **plenteously**, *adverb*; **plenteousness**, *noun.*

plenty *noun*
a) a full or abundant supply: 'we have *plenty* of food'. b) abundance: 'there is food in *plenty*'.

plenty *adverb*
(*informal*) quite or fully: 'this is *plenty* hard enough for my purpose'.
plenty *adjective*
ample or enough: 'no more, this is *plenty*'.
plentiful *adjective*
existing in plenty: 'we have a *plentiful* supply of bread'.
Word Family: **plentifully**, *adverb.*
[Latin *plenitas* fullness]

plethora (*say* **pletha**–ra) *noun*
an overabundance or excess.
[Greek *plethoré* fullness]

pleura (*say* **ploo**–ra) *noun*
plural is **pleurae** (*say* **ploo**–ree)
Anatomy: either of two delicate membranes covering each lung in mammals, folded back to form a lining of the chest wall.
[Greek, ribs]

pleurisy (*say* **ploori**–see) *noun*
an inflammation of the pleura, sometimes accompanying other diseases such as tuberculosis, measles or scarlet fever.

plexus *noun*
plural is **plexuses**
Anatomy: a junction or network of several major nerves or blood vessels.
[Latin, interwoven]

pliable (*say* **plya**–b'l) *adjective*
flexible or easily bent.
Usage: 'she will do what you ask because she's so *pliable*' (= easily influenced).
Word Family: **pliably**, *adverb*; **pliability** (*say* plya–**billi**–tee), *noun.*
[French *plier* to fold or bend]

pliant *adjective*
pliable.
Word Family: **pliantly**, *adverb*; **pliancy**, *noun.*

pliers (*say* **plyerz**) *plural noun*
a small metal tool with long jaws for holding small objects, bending wire, etc.

plight (1) *noun*
a dangerous or difficult situation.

plight (2) *verb*
an old word meaning to pledge or promise, especially in marriage.

plimsoll *noun*
a sandshoe.

Plimsoll line
a mark painted on the outside of the hull of a ship to show how deeply it may sit in the water when loaded.
[after *S. Plimsoll*, 1824–98, an English politician]

plinth *noun*
the lowest part of the base of a column, statue, wall, etc.
[Greek *plinthos* squared stone]

Pliocene (*say* **plyo**–seen) *noun*
Geology: see TERTIARY.
Word Family: **Pliocene**, *adjective.*
[Greek *pleios* more + *kainos* modern (that is, more modern forms of life)]

plod *verb*
(plodded, plodding)
to walk slowly and heavily.
Usage: 'he *plodded* through his boring job' (= worked with dull perseverance).
Word Family: **plodder**, *noun*; **ploddingly**, *adverb.*

plonk (1) *verb*
to drop heavily or suddenly.
Word Family: **plonk**, *noun*, the act or sound of dropping heavily.

plonk (2) *noun*
(*informal*) wine, especially cheap wine.

plop *verb*
(plopped, plopping)
to drop with a dull, quiet sound.
Word Family: **plop**, *noun*, a quiet falling sound.

plot (1) *noun*
1. a secret plan, often with an unlawful purpose.
2. the main story of a novel, play, etc.
plot *verb*
(plotted, plotting)
1. to plan secretly: 'the prisoners *plotted* their escape'.
2. to mark or draw on a map, chart, plan, graph, etc.: 'to *plot* a route on the map'.
Word Family: **plotter**, *noun.*

plot (2) *noun*
a small piece or area of ground: 'a garden *plot*'.

plough (*rhymes with* cow) *noun*
a) a farming implement for cutting or turning soil. b) any similar implement: 'a *snowplough*'.
plough *verb*
to turn soil with a plough.
Usage: 'the ship *ploughed* through the waves' (= moved strongly and steadily).
plough back, 'the profits were *ploughed back* into the company' (= reinvested, put back).
ploughshare *noun*
the broad blade of a plough.

plover (*say* **pluvva**) *noun*
any of various kinds of wading birds found on seashores or moorland, such as the dotterel or the lapwing.
[Latin *pluvia* rain]

plow *noun*
American: a plough.
Word Family: **plow**, *verb.*

ploy *noun*
a ruse or tricky manoeuvre.

pluck *verb*
1. to pull: 'please *pluck* the feathers from this turkey'.
2. *Music:* to sound the strings of an instrument by pulling with the fingers or a plectrum.
pluck up, 'he was unable to *pluck up* enough courage' (= summon).
pluck *noun*
1. a pulling or jerking movement.
2. courage, spirit or resolution: 'she's full of *pluck* and daring'.
Word Family: **plucky**, *adjective*, brave; **pluckily**, *adverb*; **pluckiness**, *noun.*

plug *noun*
1. a piece of metal, rubber, etc. used to stop up a hole, as in a bath.
2. anything which acts as a wedge or stopper, such as the mass of solidified rock in the vent of a volcano.
3. a device which, when inserted in a socket, etc., connects with a supply of electric current.
4. a piece of tobacco, especially one used for chewing.
Usage: (*informal*) 'the disc jockey gave the record a *plug*' (= favourable publicity or mention).
plug *verb*
(plugged, plugging)
to stop up with or insert a plug.
Usages:
a) 'the announcer *plugged* my latest hit' (= mentioned favourably).
b) 'the police *plugged* the hoodlum in the back' (= shot).
plug away, to work hard and consistently.

plum *noun*
a small, round, juicy fruit, usually red, yellow or purple in colour.
a plum in one's mouth, (*informal*) an affected voice.
plum *adjective*
(*informal*) ideal, especially if profitable: 'a *plum* job'.
[Latin *prunum*]

plumage (*say* **ploo**-mij) *noun*
the feathers on a bird.

plumb (*say* plum) *noun*
1. a plummet.
2. a perpendicular angle: 'the wall is out of *plumb*'.
plumb *verb*
to find the depth or test the perpendicularity of something, using a plumbline.
Usage: 'I tried to *plumb* his secretive mind' (= penetrate).
plumb *adverb*
1. exactly or vertically.
2. (*informal*) absolutely: 'he's *plumb* crazy'.
[Latin *plumbum* lead]

plumb-bob *noun*
a plummet.

plumber (*say* **plumma**) *noun*
a person who installs or repairs pipes, etc. for water and drainage systems.
plumbing *noun*
a) the work of a plumber. b) the system of pipes, drains, etc. in a building.

plumbic *adjective*
Chemistry: of or relating to compounds of lead in which lead has a valency of four.
[Latin *plumbum* lead]

plumbline *noun*
a length of cord with a weight (plummet) on the end, used to find the perpendicular or the depth of water.

plumbous (*say* **plumbus**) *adjective*
Chemistry: of or relating to compounds of lead in which lead has a valency of two.

plum duff
a boiled suet pudding with currants or raisins.
[*duff* for DOUGH]

plume (*say* ploom) *noun*
a feather, especially a large one.
plume *verb*
a) (of a bird) to smooth or preen its feathers. b) to provide or cover with plumes.
[from Latin]

plummet *verb*
to drop downwards suddenly and quickly: 'the eagle *plummeted* from the heavens'.
plummet *noun*
also called a **plumb-bob**
the weight on a plumbline.

plummy *adjective*
(*informal*) a) (of jobs, etc.) choice or desirable. b) (of a voice) rich, especially in an affected way.

plump (1) *adjective*
rounded.
Word Family: **plump**, *verb*, to make or become plump; **plumpness**, *noun*.

plump (2) *verb*
1. to drop or fall heavily: 'he *plumped* down his heavy load'.
2. to support or prefer: 'which candidate did you *plump* for?'.
Word Family: **plump**, *noun*.

plum pudding
a rich steamed or boiled pudding made with dried fruits, nuts and spices, eaten especially at Christmas.

plunder *verb*
to steal from or rob, especially violently.
plunder *noun*
any goods which are stolen or gained illegally.

plunge (*say* plunj) *verb*
1. to put or thrust forcibly and suddenly: 'he *plunged* his hand into the water'.
2. to fall quickly and sharply: 'the car *plunged* off the cliff'.
Usage: (*informal*) 'the punters *plunged* on the racehorse' (= bet heavily).
plunge *noun*
a) the act of plunging. b) a leap or dive.
take the plunge, to decide to start a course of action, despite the risks involved.

plunger (*say* **plun**jer) *noun*
1. something which plunges, such as a piston.
2. a device consisting of a rubber suction cup and rod, used to clear drains.

plunk *verb*
to pluck or twang the strings of a musical instrument.
Word Family: **plunk**, *noun*, the act or sound of plunking.

plural (*say* **ploo**–r'l) *adjective*
of, consisting of or expressing more than one.
Word Family: **plural**, *noun*, a plural number, form or word.
[Latin *pluris* of more]

pluralism (*say* **ploo**–r'l–izm) *noun*
1. *Christianity:* the holding of more than one benefice at a time.
2. the retention of their own customs and beliefs by the racial or religious minorities of a country.
Word Family: **pluralist**, *noun*; **pluralistic**, *adjective*.

plurality (*say* ploo–**ralli**–tee) *noun*
1. the state of being plural.
2. *American:* the obtaining of more votes in an election than any other rival candidate.

plus *preposition*
also or in addition to: 'one *plus* one equals two'.
plus *adjective*
Maths: relating to addition.
Usage: 'the *11–plus* exams' (= 11 years and over).
plus *noun*
1. a) the plus sign (+). b) a positive amount.
2. something which is extra or additional.
[Latin]

plus–fours *plural noun*
a pair of short, loose trousers drawn into a band below the knee, worn especially by golfers.
[so called because they overlapped below the knee by four inches]

plush *adjective*
richly luxurious and expensive.
plush *noun*
a thick fabric of silk, wool, etc., with a less dense pile than velvet.

Pluto (*say* **ploo**–toe) *noun*
Astronomy: the planet in the solar system furthest from the sun.
[after *Pluto*, another name for Hades, god of the underworld in Greek mythology]

plutocracy (*say* ploo–**tok**ra–see) *noun*
1. the exercise of power by the rich.
2. the rich viewed as a ruling class.
Word Family: **plutocrat** (*say* **ploo**ta–krat), *noun*, a very rich and influential person; **plutocratic** (*say* ploota–**krat**tik), *adjective*.
[Greek *ploutos* wealth + *kratia* rule]

plutonic (*say* ploo–**ton**nik) *adjective*
Geology: (of igneous rocks such as granite) formed deep below the earth's surface.
Word Family: **pluton**, *noun*, any plutonic rock.
[after PLUTO]

plutonium (*say* ploo–**toe**–nee–um) *noun*
element number 94, a man-made, radioactive metal, discovered while the atomic bomb was being made and later used in nuclear weapons. See TRANSURANIC ELEMENT and ACTINIDE. See CHEMICAL ELEMENTS in grey pages.

[after PLUTO, being next after neptunium as Pluto is next after Neptune]

pluvial (*say* **ploovi–ul**) *adjective*
of or caused by rain.

ply (1) *verb*
(plied, plying)
1. to work with or at: 'she *plied* her needle skilfully'.
2. to go regularly from one place to another, as a ferry does.
Usage: 'I *plied* her with questions' (= repeatedly attacked).

ply (2) *noun*
1. a strand of yarn.
2. a thickness or layer of wood, etc.

plywood *noun*
a building material made of several thin sheets of wood glued together.

pneumatic (*say* **new–mattik**) *adjective*
operated by or filled with compressed air or other gases: 'a *pneumatic* drill'.
[Greek *pneumatos* of a wind]

pneumoconiosis
(*say* newma–koe–nee–**o**–sis) *noun*
the progressive damage to the lungs of miners caused by inhaling coal or metal dust.
[Greek *pneumon* lung + *konia* dust + –OSIS]

pneumonia (*say* new–**mone**–ya) *noun*
any of various types of inflammation of the lungs, caused by bacterial infection.
Word Family: **pneumonic** (*say* new–**monnik**), *adjective*, a) of or relating to the lungs, b) of or suffering from pneumonia.
[Greek *pneumon* a lung]

poach (1) *verb*
to steal game or fish from another's land.
Word Family: **poacher**, *noun*, a person who poaches.

poach (2) *verb*
to cook in simmering water.
Word Family: **poacher**, *noun*, a pan or device for poaching.

pock *noun*
plural is **pox**
a small swelling on the skin, containing pus, as in smallpox.

pocket *noun*
1. a small bag set into clothing for carrying money, etc.
2. a pocket–like or enclosed cavity, area or position.
Usages:
a) 'my *pocket* won't stand another spending spree' (= finances).
b) 'there was still a *pocket* of discontent' (= small, isolated area).
be out of pocket, to be without or to lose money.
pocket *verb*
to put or enclose in a pocket: a) 'I *pocketed* the money'; b) 'the snooker player *pocketed* the ball'.

pocket–book *noun*
1. a wallet.
2. *American:* a purse or handbag.
3. a note–book.

pocket–knife *noun*
plural is **pocket–knives**
also called a **claspknife** or a **penknife**
a knife with one or more blades which fold back into the handle.

pocket–money *noun*
a weekly sum of money for personal expenses, such as is given to a child by a parent.

pockmark *noun*
a mark or scar left by a disease such as smallpox.
Word Family: **pockmark**, *verb.*

pod *noun*
a long, two–sided container of seeds: 'a *pea–pod*'.
Word Family: **pod (podded, podding)**, *verb*, a) to produce pods, b) to shell peas, etc.

podgy (*say* **poj–ee**) *adjective*
short and plump.
Word Family: **podge**, *noun*, a podgy person.

podium (*say* **po**–dee–um) *noun*
plural is **podia**
1. a small platform, used by the conductor of an orchestra, for making speeches, etc.
2. *Biology:* an organ acting as a foot.
[Greek *podis* of a foot]

podzol, podsol *noun*
a poor, acidic forest soil found in cold areas, with a greyish–white upper layer and a brownish lower layer.
Word Family: **podzolize**, *verb*; **podzolization**, *noun.*
[Russian]

poem (*say* **po**–im) *noun*
a composition with a rhythmic form, often in rhyme.

poesy (*say* **po**–a–zee) *noun*
an old word meaning poetry.

poet (*say* **po**–it) *noun*
a person who writes poems.

poetic (*say* po-**ettik**) **poetical**
adjective
1. of or relating to poets or poetry.
2. having the feeling, form or character of a poem.
Word Family: **poetically**, *adverb*; **poetess**, *noun*, a female poet.
[from Greek]

poetaster (*say* po-it-**assta**) *noun*
a person who writes bad or inferior poems.

poetic justice
ideal justice, in which all good is rewarded and all evil punished.

poetic licence
the liberty taken by a poet or writer to ignore normal literary forms, such as rhyme, or to ignore facts and logic, in order to create a better effect.

poet laureate (*say* **po**-it **lorri**-at)
plural is **poets laureate**
a poet appointed to the royal household who writes poems on special royal and national occasions.

poetry *noun*
1. the composing of words in a rhythmic structure and often in rhyme.
2. any or all poems.

pogo stick
a toy consisting of a stick on a spring, with footrests for jumping up and down.

pogrom *noun*
an organized massacre, especially of Jews.
[Russian, destruction]

poignant (*say* **poyn**-y'nt) *adjective*
1. deeply moving or distressing: 'the man's *poignant* tears upset me'.
2. strong or sharp in taste or smell.
Usage: 'this is a topic of *poignant* interest' (= strong).
Word Family: **poignantly**, *adverb*; **poignancy**, *noun*.
[Old French, pricking]

poikilothermic
(*say* poy-killo-**ther**mik) *adjective*
Biology: see COLD-BLOODED.
[Greek *poikilos* changeable + *thermé* heat]

poinsettia (*say* poyn-**settia**) *noun*
a Mexican plant with bright, scarlet bracts which look like flowers.
[after *J. R. Poinsett*, 1799–1851, an American minister to Mexico]

point *noun*
1. a sharp tapering end or part, as of a needle.
2. something which has the shape or position of a point, such as a headland.
3. an exact spot or position: a) 'plot the *points* of your trip on this map'; b) 'at this *point* of time, we can go home'.
Usages:
a) 'what's the *point* of continuing?' (= purpose).
b) 'several *points* are not clear' (= details).
c) 'get to the *point* of the story' (= most important idea).
d) 'what are her good *points*?' (= qualities).
4. a unit of scoring in games such as football, cards, etc.
5. a degree or position on a scale of measurement: a) 'the boiling *point* of water'; b) 'the stock market rose 12 *points*'; c) 'a compass card is divided into 32 equal *points*'.
6. a position directly in front or in the aim of: 'held at the *point* of a gun'.
7. *Maths:* a) a basic element of space which determines position. b) a decimal point.
8. *Grammar:* a full stop.
9. *Cricket:* a fielding position on the offside, near and facing the batsman.
10. any of the contacts controlling the flow of current in a circuit.
11. *Railways:* (*plural*) a device for shifting vehicles from one line to another. Also called a **switch**.
12. *Printing:* a twelfth part of an em.
Phrases:
give points to, a) to be able to give a handicap to (an opponent); b) to be better than.
in point of fact, see FACT.
make a point of, to do or undertake deliberately.
on the point of, at the point of, close or about to.
to the point, apt or relevant.
win on points, (*Boxing*) to win not by a knockout but on general performance.

point *verb*
1. to direct or indicate the direction of: a) 'don't *point* your finger at me'; b) 'the needle *pointed* north'.
2. (of a gun-dog) to stand stiffly with its nose in the direction of the game.
3. to finish off the joints in stone and brickwork with mortar or cement.
point out, to draw attention to.
Word Family: **pointed**, *adjective*, apt or direct; **pointedly**, *adverb*; **pointedness**, *noun*.
[Latin *punctum* a puncture]

point–blank *adjective*
aimed or fired at very close range.
Usage: 'he gave me a *point–blank* refusal' (= blunt, definite).
Word Family: **point–blank**, *adverb.*

point duty
the controlling of traffic at a junction or intersection, by a policeman.

pointer *noun*
1. a person or thing that points.
Usage: 'I'll give you a few *pointers* about the work' (= hints, suggestions).
2. one of a breed of large, long–legged, smooth–haired gun–dogs trained to point when scenting game.

pointillism (*say* **pwanti**–lizm) *noun*
Art: a painting method in which small, closely spaced dots of colour are used, which are blended by the eye to form intermediate colours.
Word Family: **pointillist**, *noun.*
[French *pointiller* to mark with points]

pointless *adjective*
without sense or purpose: 'that was a *pointless* remark'.
Word Family: **pointlessly**, *adverb*; **pointlessness**, *noun.*

point of order
plural is **points of order**
a question as to whether the procedure of a meeting, debate, etc. is according to the rules.

point of view
an attitude or position from which things are considered.

point–to–point *noun*
a meet for steeplechase racing held by a hunt at the end of the hunting season.

poise *noun*
1. balance or steadiness, as in movement: 'she walks with *poise*'.
2. gracious dignity or self–possession.
poise *verb*
to balance evenly: 'the bird *poised* in midair'.
poised *adjective*
dignified and self–assured.

poison *noun*
1. a) any substance which harms or destroys life.
2. any harmful or destructive influence: 'the *poison* of hatred'.
poison *verb*
to give poison to.
Usage: 'jealousy *poisoned* their friendship' (= ruined).

poisonous, poison *adjective*
being, containing or having the effects of a poison.
Word Family: **poisonously**, *adverb.*

poison gas
any of various lethal or disabling gases, first used in large–scale chemical warfare during World War I (1915).

poison–pen *adjective*
(of a letter) anonymous and intended to hurt, e.g. by a revelation.

poke (1) *verb*
to jab or thrust: a) 'he *poked* me in the ribs with his finger; b) '*poke* your head out of the window'.
Word Family: **poke**, *noun,* a jab or thrust.

poke (2) *noun*
a pig in a poke, something which is purchased without prior inspection.
[from *poke*, an old word for a bag or sack]

poker (1) *noun*
a) a person or thing that pokes. b) a metal rod for stirring a fire.

poker (2) *noun*
a card game of each against all, with bets progressively increased by those who stay in. The player who bluffs the others into thinking he has the best hand (or who even actually has it) scoops the jackpot.
[possibly from German *Pochspiel* bragging game]

poker dice
a set of dice which have marks representing the six highest playing cards instead of numbers.

poker face
an expressionless face, such as that of an experienced poker player.
Word Family: **poker–faced**, *adjective.*

poker work
designs burnt on to wood, leather, calabashes, etc. with a hot poker or similar instrument.

poky (*say* **po**–kee) *adjective*
small and confined: 'a *poky* room in a cheap boarding house'.

polar *adjective*
of or relating to a pole, such as the poles of the earth, a magnet, etc.
Usage: 'the twins are *polar* opposites in all their likes and dislikes' (= complete).

polar bear
see BEAR (2).

polar coordinates
Maths: coordinates which define a point by means of a radius vector and the angle it makes with a fixed line through the origin.

polarity (*say* po–**larri**–tee) *noun*
a) the possession of two poles. b) the possession of two directly opposite or contrary tendencies, qualities, etc.

polarization
(*say* pole–a–rye–**zay**–sh'n)
polarisation *noun*
1. *Physics:* the process by which rays of light exhibit different properties in different directions.
2. *Chemistry:* a) the separation of a molecule into positive or negative ions. b) the process by which gases produced during electrolysis are deposited on the electrodes of a cell.
3. the production or acquisition of polarity.
polarize *verb*
to cause or to undergo polarization: 'the meeting, at first undecided, gradually *polarized* into two hostile camps'.
Word Family: **polarizer,** *noun,* anything which polarizes.

Polaroid (*say* **pole**–a–royd) *noun*
a thin film of plastic that produces polarized light; used in cameras, sunglasses, etc.
[a trademark]

polder *noun*
an area of low land reclaimed from the sea and protected by dykes.

pole (1) *noun*
1. a long, rounded piece of wood or metal.
2. *Units:* see PERCH (1).
up the pole, (*informal*) a) in difficulty or error; b) slightly mad.
Word Family: **pole,** *verb,* to propel with a pole, especially a boat or punt.

pole (2) *noun*
1. *Geography:* either of the northernmost or southernmost points of the earth's axis.
2. *Physics:* either of two points where opposite quantities or forces appear to be concentrated: a) 'the *poles* of a battery'; b) 'the *poles* of a magnet'.
poles apart, 'our views on most things are *poles apart*' (= widely different, completely opposite).
[Greek *polos* pivot, axis, sky]

poleaxe *noun*
a) a halberd. b) a combined axe and hammer for felling or stunning animals.
Word Family: **poleaxe,** *verb,* to fell with a poleaxe.

polecat (*say* **pole**–kat) *noun*
a small, flesh-eating mammal with a very unpleasant smell, related to the weasel and found in Europe and Asia.

polemic (*say* pol–**emmik**) *noun*
1. an argument, dispute or controversy.
2. (*plural*) the art or practice of controversial arguing.
Word Family: **polemic, polemical,** *adjective*; **polemically,** *adverb.*
[Greek *polemikos* warlike]

Pole Star
also called the **North Star**
Astronomy: a star situated close to the North Pole of the heavens, formerly used as a guide by sailors.

pole vault
Athletics: a contest in which competitors jump as high as they can over a raised bar, with the help of a long pole.
Word Family: **pole-vault,** *verb*; **pole-vaulter,** *noun.*

police (*say* pol–**eece**) *noun*
a) an organized group of officials appointed to enforce a country's laws and prevent and detect crime. b) the members of such a force.
Word Family: **police,** *verb,* to keep order with or as if with police; **policeman,** *noun,* a member of a police force; **policewoman,** *noun,* a female policeman.

police state
a state in which political dissent is stamped out by secret police.

policy (1) (*say* **polli**–see) *noun*
a plan or course of action or procedure: a) 'a business *policy*'; b) 'a country's foreign *policy*'.
Usage: 'for reasons of *policy* we did not pursue the project at that time' (= prudence, expediency).

policy (2) *noun*
a document stating the conditions of insurance.
Word Family: **policyholder,** *noun,* the person insured by an insurance policy.

polio (*say* **pole**–ee–o) *noun*
also called **infantile paralysis**
an infectious, viral disease of the spinal cord, causing paralysis of muscles.

[short form of *poliomyelitis*, from Greek *polios* grey + *myelos* marrow + -ITIS]

polish (*say* **poll**ish) *verb*
to make or become smooth and shining: a) '*polish* those shoes'; b) 'those shoes *polished* up well'.
Usage: 'he went through his speech again to *polish* it' (= improve, refine).
polish off, (*informal*) to dispose of or finish.
polish *noun*
1. a) the act of polishing. b) a smooth, glossy surface.
2. refinement or elegance.
3. any substance used to make a surface smooth and glossy.
Word Family: **polisher,** *noun.*

Politburo (*say* pollit-bew-ro) *noun*
Politics: the leading committee in a communist party, which decides on policy.

polite *adjective*
displaying good manners or consideration toward others: 'a *polite* request'.
Usage: '*polite* society' (= refined, cultured).
Word Family: **politely,** *adverb*; **politeness,** *noun.*
[Latin *politus* polished]

politic (*say* **polli**-tik) *adjective*
wise or prudent: 'it is *politic* not to anger one's boss'.
Word Family: **politicly,** *adverb.*

political economy
the study of the relationship between political and economic policies and the way they influence social institutions.
Word Family: **political economist,** a person trained or skilled in political economy.

political science
the study of governments, political affairs and principles.
Word Family: **political scientist,** a person trained or skilled in political science.

politics (*say* **polli**-tiks) *plural noun*
(*used with singular verb*) the matters connected with the government or organization of a country or group of countries.
Usages:
a) 'you should never ask a man what his *politics* are' (= opinions or allegiances concerning politics).
b) 'the *politics* of the main office would make life unbearable for me' (= scheming for power or advancement).
politician (*say* polli-**tish**'n) *noun*
a person taking an active part in politics, especially as a party representative in parliament.
Word Family: **political** (*say* po-**litti**-k'l), *adjective*; **politically,** *adverb*; **politick,** *verb,* (informal) to take part in or discuss politics; **politico** (*say* po-**litti**-ko), *noun,* (informal) a politician.
[Greek *politikos* of citizens]

polity (*say* **polli**-tee) *noun*
a) a particular system of government, e.g. a republic, federation or empire. b) a community organized as a State.

polka *noun*
a) a fast dance in which couples move around the room in large circles. b) the music for such a dance.
[from Greek]

polka dot
a dot repeated to make a pattern on a fabric, etc.

poll (*say* pole) *noun*
1. a) the voting in or results of an election. b) the list of voters. c) the number of votes cast.
2. (*plural*) any place where voting is held, usually consisting of small cubicles (called **polling booths**), for people to vote in secret.
3. a survey of opinions on a subject, usually obtained from a sample group.
4. the head, especially the part of it on which the hair grows: 'a bald *poll*'.
poll *verb*
1. to receive votes: 'our candidate *polled* the highest number of votes'.
2. to vote at an election.
3. to take a survey of opinion.

pollard (1) (*say* **poll**-ud) *noun*
partly ground bran and wheat, used in poultry food.

pollard (2) (*say* **poll**-ud) *noun*
a tree with its branches cut back to the trunk so that it will produce denser foliage when it regrows.
Word Family: **pollard,** *verb.*

pollen *noun*
Biology: the fine, yellow powder found in flowers, each grain being a male reproductive cell.
pollinate *verb*
to transfer pollen from an anther of a flower to a stigma.

pollen count
a measure of the pollen in the air.
Word Family: **pollination**, *noun.*
[Latin, fine flour]

polling booth
one of a temporary line of cubicles in which voters can mark their election votes in secrecy.

pollster (*say* **pole**–sta) *noun*
a person who conducts opinion polls.

poll tax
a tax of so much a head (poll) without distinction of wealth.

pollution (*say* pol–**oo**–sh'n) *noun*
1. the act of making dirty or impure.
2. the spoiling of the environment or atmosphere by man–made waste, noise, etc.
Word Family: **pollute**, *verb*; **polluter**, *noun*; **pollutant**, *noun*, any substance causing pollution.
[Latin *pollutus* defiled]

polo (*say* **pole**–o) *noun*
a game, similar to hockey, played on horseback using long–handled mallets and a small wooden ball.
[Tibetan, ball]

polonaise (*say* polla–**naze**) *noun*
a) a slow dance from Poland which includes promenades for couples. b) the music for such a dance.
[French, Polish]

polo–neck *adjective*
also called **roll–neck**
(of a jumper, shirt, etc.) having a raised collar which folds over in one piece. Compare CREW–NECK.
Word Family: **polo–neck**, *noun*, a) a polo–neck collar, b) a garment having such a collar.

polonium (*say* pol–**o**–nee–um) *noun*
element number 84, a radioactive metal produced by the decay of radium. See CHEMICAL ELEMENTS in grey pages.
[discovered by *Polish*–born Marie Curie]

poltergeist (*say* polta–**guyst**) *noun*
a mischievous ghost believed to be the cause of disturbing noises and petty destructiveness in a house.
[German *poltern* to make a noise + *Geist* ghost]

poltroon (*say* pol–**troon**) *noun*
an old word meaning a coward.

poly–
a prefix meaning many, as in *polychromatic.*
[Greek]

polybasic (*say* polli–**bay**–sik) *adjective*
Chemistry: (of an acid) having two or more atoms of hydrogen replaceable by a base or basic radicals.

polychromatic (*say* polli–kro–**mattik**) *adjective*
also called **polychrome**
being of many colours.
Word Family: **polychrome**, *noun*, a work of art executed in many colours.
[POLY– + Greek *khromatos* of colour]

polyester (*say* **polli**–esta) *noun*
Chemistry: any of a class of complex organic compounds used in making synthetic resins, plastics and mixed with other fibres in many crease–resistant fabrics.

polyethylene (*say* polli–**etha**–leen) *noun*
see POLYTHENE.

polygamy (*say* pol–**igga**–mee) *noun*
the custom of having several spouses or mates at one time. Compare MONOGAMY.
Word Family: **polygamist**, *noun*, a person who practises or advocates polygamy; **polygamous**, *adjective*; **polygamously**, *adverb.*
[POLY– + Greek *gamos* marriage]

polyglot (*say* **polli**–glot) *noun*
a person who knows several different languages.
[POLY– + Greek *glotta* tongue]

polygon (*say* **polli**–g'n) *noun*
a closed plane figure with at least five straight sides.
Word Family: **polygonal** (*say* pol–**igga**–n'l), *adjective.*
[POLY– + Greek *gonia* corner]

polyhedron (*say* polli–**hee**–dr'n) *noun*
plural is **polyhedrons** or **polyhedra**
a solid or hollow body bounded by many plane faces.
Word Family: **polyhedral**, *adjective.*
[POLY– + Greek *hedra* a base]

polymerization, polymerisation
(*say* pol–imma–rye–**zay**–sh'n) *noun*
Chemistry: the process of linking together many monomers to produce a substance (called a **polymer**) with a much higher relative molecular mass.
Word Family: **polymerize** (*say* pol–**imma**–rize), *verb.*
[POLY– + Greek *meros* a part]

polymorphism (*say* polli–**mor**–fizm) *noun*
Biology: the existence within a species of several distinct forms of individuals.

Word Family: **polymorphous, polymorphic,** *adjectives*; **polymorph,** *noun*, an organism exhibiting polymorphism.
[POLY- + Greek *morphé* form]

polynomial (*say* polli-**no**-mee-ul) *adjective*
also called **multinomial**
Maths: (of an algebraic expression) consisting of two or more terms.

polyp (*say* **poll**ip) *noun*
1. a form of coelenterate that is fixed to one spot, such as the many small organisms of which coral is composed.
2. a growth on a mucous surface, e.g. in the nose.
[POLY- + Greek *pous* foot]

polyphony (*say* pol-**iffa**-nee) *noun*
Music: music having two or more simultaneous voices or parts, each with an individual melody, but all harmonizing.
Word Family: **polyphonic** (*say* polli-**fonn**ik), *adjective*.
[POLY- + Greek *phoné* sound]

polypropylene
(*say* polli-**pro**-pa-leen) *noun*
a colourless transparent plastic, formed by the polymerization of propylene, with similar properties to polythene but much stronger; used in lightweight upholstery fabrics.

polystyrene (*say* polli-**sty**-reen) *noun*
a colourless solid, softening when heated, made by the polymerization of styrene. It is a good electrical insulator.

polysyllable (*say* **polli**-silla-b'l) *noun*
a word of more than three syllables.
Word Family: **polysyllabic** (*say* polli-sil-**abb**ik), *adjective*.

polytechnic (*say* polli-**tek**nik) *noun*
a college teaching mainly science and technical subjects.
[POLY- + Greek *tekhné* an art]

polytheism (*say* polli-**thee**-izm) *noun*
the belief in more than one god or many gods. Compare MONOTHEISM.
Word Family: **polytheist,** *noun*, a person who believes in more than one god; **polytheistic** (*say* polli-thee-**ist**ik), *adjective*.
[POLY- + Greek *theos* a god]

polythene (*say* **poll**a-theen) *noun*
also called **polyethylene**
Chemistry: a tough, waxy, transparent plastic formed by the polymerization of ethylene, used as insulation and as a protective wrapping in packaging.

polyunsaturated
(*say* polli-un-**satch**a-raytid) *adjective*
(of a fat or oil) lacking hydrogen bonds at several points in its carbon chain, and thus reacting with other compounds.
Word Family: **polyunsaturate,** *noun*, a polyunsaturated fat or oil.

polyvinyl acetate (*say* polli-**vie**-n'l assa-tate)
short form is **PVA**
a colourless solid, softening when heated, used in adhesives, inks, lacquers and fabrics.

polyvinyl chloride (*say* polli-**vie**-n'l klaw-ride)
short form is **PVC**
a colourless solid, softening when heated, having a good resistance to water, alkalis, acids, and alcohol, and used in making many domestic and industrial articles, including upholstery fabrics.

pomade (*say* pom-**ahd**) *noun*
a perfumed ointment formerly applied to the head and scalp.
Word Family: **pomade,** *verb*.

pomander (*say* pom-**anda**) *noun*
a perforated spherical container for potpourri.
[Old French *pomme d'ambre* apple of amber]

pome *noun*
any of various fleshy fruit, such as an apple, pear, etc., which has seeds but no stone.
[Latin *pomum* apple]

pomegranate (*say* **pommi**-grannit) *noun*
a medium-sized, round, red fruit with a tough skin and containing many seeds in the edible, acid flesh.
[Old French *pome granate* many-seeded fruit]

pommel (*say* **pumm**'l) *noun*
a knob-like end to an object, such as that on the front part of a saddle or the hilt of a sword.
pommel *verb*
(pomelled, pomelling)
to pummel.

pommy *noun*
also spelt **pommie**
short form is **pom**
Australian: (*informal*) an Englishman, especially one who has immigrated.
[probably a play on the words *immigrant* and *pomegranate* (referring to red faces)]

pomp *noun*
any stately or ceremonious splendour or display: 'the coronation was conducted with great *pomp*'.
[Greek *pompé* a solemn procession]

pompom *noun*
an automatic multi-barrelled anti-aircraft gun, used by the Navy.

pompon *noun*
also called a **pompom**
a ball of coloured wool used as a trimming on hats, etc.
[French, top-knot]

pompous (*say* **pom**pus) *adjective*
full of self-importance or an exaggerated sense of one's dignity.
Word Family: **pompously,** *adverb*; **pompousness, pomposity** (*say* pom-**possi**-tee), *nouns,* the quality of being pompous.

ponce *noun*
(*informal*) a man who lives off the earnings of a prostitute.
Word Family: **ponce,** *verb.*

poncho *noun*
a blanket-like cloak with a hole in the middle for the head to go through.
[Amerindian]

pond *noun*
a small, often man-made, area of water, surrounded by land.
[from POUND (3)]

ponder *verb*
to consider deeply or carefully.
Word Family: **ponder,** *noun*; **ponderer,** *noun,* a person who ponders.
[Latin *pendere* to weigh]

ponderous *adjective*
heavy and bulky: 'a *ponderous* boulder'.
Usage: 'he writes in a very *ponderous* fashion' (= dull, tedious).
Word Family: **ponderously,** *adverb*; **ponderousness,** *noun.*

pong *noun*
(*informal*) a smell, especially an unpleasant one.
Word Family: **pong,** *verb.*

pontiff *noun*
a high priest or the Pope.
Word Family: **pontifical** (*say* pon-**tiffi**-k'l), *adjective,* a) of or relating to the Pope or papacy, b) pompous; **pontifically,** *adverb.*
[Latin *pontifex* a high priest]

pontificate (*say* pon-**tiffi**-kit) *noun*
the office or jurisdiction of a high priest or the Pope.

pontificate (*say* pon-**tiffi**-kate) *verb*
to speak pompously or with an exaggerated sense of authority.

pontoon (1) (*say* pon-**toon**) *noun*
a boat or floating tank, used to support bridges, piers or other structures on water.
[Latin *pontonis* of a ferry-boat]

pontoon (2) (*say* pon-**toon**) *noun*
also called **vingt-et-un** or **blackjack**
Cards: a game played against the banker where the winner is the player whose points are closest to, but not more than, twenty-one.

pony *noun*
1. a small horse, especially one less than 14 hands in height.
2. (*informal*) twenty-five pounds.

ponytail *noun*
a hairstyle in which a long bunch of hair is pulled back and tied so as to hang like a horse's tail.

poodle *noun*
one of a breed of curly-haired dogs, usually elaborately trimmed and clipped.
[German *Pudelhund*]

pooftah, poofter *noun*
short form is **poof**
(*informal*) a homosexual.

pooh *interjection*
an exclamation of contempt.
pooh-pooh *verb*
to dismiss contemptuously.

pool (1) *noun*
1. a) a small area of still liquid. b) a still, deep part in an area of water.
2. (*informal*) a swimming pool.

pool (2) *noun*
1. a common fund, supply or service: 'all company executives use typists from the typing *pool*'.
2. the stakes played for in certain games.
3. a form of billiards for several players, each having a ball of a different colour.
4. (*plural*) see FOOTBALL POOLS.
pool *verb*
to put things together for common advantage: 'three of us *pooled* our savings to buy an old car'.

poop (1) *noun*
a deck or cabin on the stern of a boat.
poop deck
a short deck built over the main deck at the stern of a ship.
[Latin *puppis* the stern]

poop (2) *verb*
(*informal*) to tire or exhaust: 'I was *pooped* after the long walk'.

poor (*say* por) *adjective*
1. a) having very little money, property or resources. b) showing poverty: 'we alighted outside a *poor* cottage'.
2. lacking something needed: a) '*poor* soil'; b) 'in *poor* health'; c) 'a *poor* excuse'.
Usages:
a) 'he's a *poor* loser' (= ungracious).
b) 'if I may add my *poor* opinion to this discussion' (= humble).
c) 'the *poor* little bird has fallen out of its nest' (= unfortunate).
d) 'a *poor* supply of well-qualified maths teachers' (= small, inadequate).
Word Family: **poorly**, *adjective*, in poor health; **poorly**, *adverb*; **poorness**, *noun*
[Latin *pauper*]

poorbox *noun*
a box in a church, courtroom, etc. in which money may be placed for distribution to the poor.

poorhouse *noun*
History: a workhouse.

pop (1) *verb*
(popped, popping)
1. to make a short, quick, explosive sound: 'the champagne cork *popped* loudly'.
2. (*informal*) to move, come, or go suddenly or unexpectedly: 'a rabbit *popped* up from between my feet'.
Usages:
a) 'he *popped* the book straight into his bag' (= put quickly).
b) 'her eyes *popped* in astonishment at the unusual sight' (= stared, bulged).
Phrases:
pop off, (*informal*) a) to go away; b) to die; c) to fall asleep.
pop the question, (*informal*) to propose marriage.
pop *noun*
1. a short, quick, explosive sound.
2. (*informal*) an effervescent soft drink.
Word Family: **pop**, *adverb*, a) with a pop, b) suddenly or unexpectedly.

pop (2) *adjective*
(*informal*) of or relating to any of the forms of pop culture: '*pop* music'.
Word Family: **pop**, *noun*, a pop tune or song.
[a short form of POPULAR]

pop art
a style of modern art using images of the everyday commercial world, such as advertising slogans, comic strips, etc. Compare OP ART.
[from POP(ular) + ART]

popcorn *noun*
the burst, puffed kernels of maize after they have been heated.

pop culture
an outlook on life characterized by a complete break with past traditions, swift changes in fashion (dress, music, etc.), permissiveness and an absence of race or class consciousness.

pope *noun*
(*usually capital*) the bishop of Rome as the head of the Roman Catholic Church.
popish (*say* **po**–pish) *adjective*
(*use is derogatory*) of or characteristic of the Roman Catholic Church.
Word Family: **popishly**, *adverb*; **popery**, *noun*, the customs and traditions of the Roman Catholic Church.
[Greek *pappas* father]

popeyed (*say* **pop**–ide) *adjective*
having bulging or staring eyes.

popinjay *noun*
a conceited, foppish person.
[Spanish *papagayo* a parrot]

poplar *noun*
any of a group of tall, quick-growing, deciduous trees, used for timber.
[Latin *populus*]

poplin *noun*
a woven fabric of cotton and often polyester with a fine cross-rib.

pop music
commercially produced music for the teenage masses, played and sung with the aid of electronic apparatus.

poppet *noun*
a term of endearment for a girl or child.

poppet valve
a valve which is opened by being lifted totally off its seat; used especially in motor vehicle engines.

poppy *noun*
1. any of a group of plants with showy flowers, one variety of which is the source of opium.
2. a bright reddish-orange colour.
Word Family: **poppy**, *adjective.*
[Latin *papaver*]

poppycock *noun*
(*informal*) nonsense.

populace (*say* **pop**–yoo–lis) *noun*
a) the general public. b) the population.

popular (*say* **pop**–yoola) *adjective*
1. having widespread approval, favour or appreciation: 'she's very *popular*'.
2. of, from or representing the people, especially the general population: 'a *popular* revolutionary government'.
3. general, widespread or common: '*popular* superstitions'.
Word Family: **popularity** (*say* pop–yoo–**larri**–tee), *noun*, the condition of being admired or liked widely; **popularly**, *adverb*; **popularize, popularise**, *verb*, to make or become popular; **popularization**, *noun*; **popularizer**, *noun*, a person who makes something popular.

popular front
Politics: the joining of communist, socialist or other parties in a democratic or revolutionary movement, as against capitalism or fascism.

populate *verb*
a) to supply with inhabitants or a population. b) to inhabit.

population (*say* pop–yoo–**lay**–sh'n) *noun*
1. all the people, organisms or individuals of one biological species, living in a certain area.
2. the act or process of populating.
3. *Maths:* the total group of individuals, scores, etc. from which a sample is taken.
[Latin *populus* people]

populist *noun*
a politician who campaigns for the little man against the élite, Big Business, the Establishment, etc.

populous (*say* **pop**–yoolus) *adjective*
having a large population.
Word Family: **populously**, *adverb*, **populousness**, *noun*.

porcelain (*say* **porsa**–lin) *noun*
a very fine, white, glossy ceramic material, usually translucent and fired at a high temperature. Compare CHINA, EARTHENWARE and STONEWARE.

porch *noun*
a roofed doorway or entrance to a building.
[Latin *porticus* colonnade]

porcupine (*say* **pork**–yoo–pine) *noun*
any of various European, American and Asian rodents covered with long protective spines.
[Old French *porc* pig + *espin* spiny]

pore (1) *verb*
to study or look at closely and carefully.

pore (2) *noun*
a very small opening in a surface, especially the skin, for absorbing or emitting liquid, etc.
[Greek *poros* a passage]

pork *noun*
the flesh of a pig.
[Latin *porcus* pig]

porker *noun*
a young pig fattened for food.

porky *adjective*
(*informal*) fat.

pornography (*say* por–**nogra**–fee) *noun*
grossly obscene literature or art, especially that produced for money.
Word Family: **pornographer**, *noun*; **pornographic** (*say* porno–**graffik**), *adjective*.
[Greek *pornographos* writing about prostitutes]

porous (*say* **pawrus**) *adjective*
1. having pores.
2. allowing the passage of gas or liquid.
Word Family: **porousness, porosity** (*say* paw–**rossi**–tee), *nouns*.

porphyry (*say* **porfi**–ree) *noun*
Geology: any igneous rock which has large crystals scattered in a fine-grained material.
[Latin *porphyrites* purple stone]

porpoise (*say* **porpus**) *noun*
any of a group of large, marine mammals with a short, round snout.
[Latin *porcus* pig + *piscis* fish]

porridge *noun*
a food made by boiling oatmeal and milk or water to a thick paste.

port (1) *noun*
1. a) a town with a harbour where ships load and unload cargo. b) the docks or harbour.
2. any place of shelter.
port of call, a place which is briefly visited.
[Latin *portus*]

port (2) *noun*
the left side of a boat or aeroplane when looking towards the front. Compare STARBOARD.

port (3) *noun*
any of various sweet, fortified red wines.
[first shipped from *Oporto*, a city in Portugal]

port (4) *noun*
1. a porthole.
2. *Engineering:* any of the passages along which gases flow into or out of an internal combustion engine.
[Latin *porta* a passage, gate]

portable *adjective*
able to be carried or moved: 'a *portable* television set'.
Word Family: **portable,** *noun,* something which is portable.
[Latin *portare* to carry]

portage (*say* **por**tij) *noun*
a) the carrying of goods or boats across land from one stretch of water to another. b) the cost of doing this.

portal *noun*
(*often plural*) a doorway or entrance, especially a large or imposing one.

portal vein
Anatomy: the large vein carrying blood rich in digested food from the stomach and intestines to the liver.

portcullis (*say* port–**kull**is) *noun*
a strong grating which may be let down to close a gateway to a castle or other fortified place.
[Old French *porte* door + *coleice* sliding]

portend (*say* por–**tend**) *verb*
to be an omen or warning of.
Word Family: **portent** (*say* **por**–tent), *noun,* an indication or omen, especially of a disaster; **portentous** (*say* por–**ten**–tus), *adjective,* a) having the character of a portent, b) extraordinary.
[Latin *portendere* to predict]

porter (1) *noun*
a person employed to carry luggage, etc., e.g. in a railway station, hotel, etc.
Word Family: **porterage,** *noun,* a) the work of a porter, b) the charge for this service.

porter (2) *noun*
a doorman or gatekeeper.

porter (3) *noun*
a dark brown beer containing malt which has been dried at a high temperature.
[for *porters'* ale]

porterhouse steak
a choice piece of upper cut of beef sirloin.

portfolio *noun*
1. a case, usually leather, for carrying papers, letters or documents.
2. *Politics:* the office or duties of a government minister.
[Italian *portare* to carry + *fogli* sheets or leaves]

porthole (*say* **port**–hole) *noun*
a small circular window in the side of a ship to let in light and air.

portico (*say* **por**–tikko) *noun*
a roof supported by columns, forming an entrance to a building.
[Latin *porticus* colonnade]

portion (*say* **por**–sh'n) *noun*
a) a section of a whole. b) a share or allotment.
Word Family: **portion,** *verb,* to divide.
[from Latin]

Portland cement
see CEMENT.

portly *adjective*
stout and having the gait that goes with it.
Word Family: **portliness,** *noun.*

portmanteau (*say* port–**man**to) *noun*
plural is **portmanteaus** or **portmanteaux**
an oblong piece of luggage which opens into two equal sections.
portmanteau word, a word coined by telescoping two words together, e.g. *chortle* from *chuckle* and *snort.*
[French *porter* to carry + *manteau* a coat]

portrait (*say* **por**trit) *noun*
1. a painting, drawing or photograph of a person, usually showing the face.
2. a description, especially of a person.
Word Family: **portraiture,** *noun,* a) the art of making a portrait or portraits, b) a portrait; **portraitist,** *noun.*
[Latin *protractus* revealed]

portray (*say* por–**tray**) *verb*
to make a picture of or describe.
Word Family: **portrayal,** *noun.*

Portuguese man–of–war
Biology: a marine animal, related to the jellyfish, with a sail–like crest and a very painful sting.

pose (*say* poze) *verb*
1. to take up or hold a position, as in front of a camera, etc.
2. to represent oneself to others: 'he *poses* as a connoisseur of wine'.
3. to act in an affected or pretentious way.
4. to put forward: 'the examiner *posed* several difficult questions'.

Usage: 'lack of seating *posed* quite a problem at the school play' (= caused).
pose *noun*
1. a position or posture of the body: 'please make your *pose* more relaxed'.
Usage: 'he maintained a *pose* of unfriendliness despite our efforts' (= attitude).
2. an affected or pretentious attitude.

Poseidon (*say* poss–**eye**–d'n) *noun*
Greek mythology: the god of the sea, identified with the Roman god Neptune.

poser (1) *noun*
a person who poses.

poser (2) *noun*
a puzzling problem or question.

poseur (*say* po–**zer**) *noun*
a person who behaves in an affected manner.
[French]

posh *adjective*
(*informal*) stylish, high–class or upper–class: a) 'a *posh* hotel'; b) '*posh* clothes'; c) 'a *posh* accent'.
[from P(ort) O(ut) S(tarboard) H(ome), referring to the cooler and therefore more expensive side for accommodation on English ships formerly travelling to India]

posit (*say* **pozzit**) *verb*
to lay down or assume as a fact or a basis for argument.
[Latin *positus* placed]

position (*say* poz**zish**'n) *noun*
1. the place where something is or belongs: 'this car is parked in the wrong *position*'.
2. the way in which something is placed or arranged: 'she had to sit in a cramped *position*'.
Usages:
a) 'the theft put the manager in a difficult *position*' (= situation).
b) 'I have applied for a clerical *position*' (= job).
c) 'what is your personal *position* in this matter?' (= view).
position *verb*
to put in a particular or correct position: 'the general *positioned* his troops along the road'.

positive (*say* **pozzi**–tiv) *adjective*
1. expressing agreement, acceptance or certainty: 'a *positive* reply to the invitation'.
2. allowing no doubt or question: 'the police have found *positive* proof of the murderer's identity'.
Usage: (*informal*) 'that poet is a *positive* genius' (= absolute, complete).
3. optimistic or hopeful: '*positive* thinking'.
4. *Maths:* relating to a number greater than zero.
5. *Grammar:* see DEGREE.
6. *Electronics:* having a deficiency of electrons.
positive *noun*
1. something which is positive.
2. *Photography:* an image on a developed film, in which the light and dark areas appear as photographed. Compare NEGATIVE.
Word Family: **positively**, *adverb*; **positiveness**, *noun.*

positron *noun*
Physics: the antiparticle of an electron.
[POSIT(ive) + (elect)RON]

posse (*say* **possi**) *noun*
American: a force of men called in to help an officer of the law in an emergency.
[abbreviation of Medieval Latin *posse comitatus* county force]

possess (*say* poz**zess**) *verb*
to hold, keep or control as one's own: 'do you *possess* many books?'.
Usage: 'rage *possessed* her at the sight of such cruelty' (= took over, dominated).
Word Family: **possessor**, *noun*; **possessed**, *adjective*, a) obsessed or strongly affected, as by a supernatural force, b) self–assured.
[from Latin]

possession (*say* poz**zesh**'n) *noun*
1. a) the act of possessing. b) the state of being possessed.
2. anything which is possessed: 'that house is my most valuable *possession*'.

possessive (*say* poz**zess**–iv) *adjective*
1. indicating or relating to possession: '**his** is a *possessive* pronoun'.
2. having or showing a desire to possess, control or dominate: 'she is very *possessive* about her lover'.
Word Family: **possessively**, *adverb*; **possessiveness**, *noun.*

possessive case
Grammar: see CASE (1).

posset (*say* **possit**) *noun*
a spiced drink made of hot milk curdled with wine or spirits.

possible *adjective*
1. capable of being, being done or happening: 'is it *possible* to cure such a disease?'.

2. able or likely to be true.
3. likely to be favourable or successful: 'we have found a *possible* place for the picnic'.
Word Family: **possibly**, *adverb*; **possibility** (*say* possi-**billi**-tee), *noun*, a) the fact of being possible, b) something that is possible.

possum *noun*
an opossum.
play possum, to pretend to be unaware, asleep or dead in order to outwit.

post (1) *noun*
1. an upright piece of wood or metal used as a support, etc.
2. the finishing line on a racecourse.
post *verb*
1. to stick or display: '*post* no advertisements on this wall'.
2. to announce, declare or publish: 'five sailors were *posted* as missing after the storm'.
[Latin *postis* a door-post]

post (2) *noun*
a) the system of sending, collecting and delivering letters and parcels, usually organized by a government department or corporation. b) any letters or parcels distributed in this way. Also called the **mail**.
post *verb*
1. to send or place something for delivery by post.
Usage: 'please keep us *posted* of your news' (= informed).
2. to travel quickly.
Word Family: **post**, *adverb*, a) by the post, b) with haste; **postal**, *adjective*.
[Latin *positus* placed]

post (3) *noun*
1. a) the position where a sentry is stationed. b) the buildings and grounds where troops are stationed.
2. a position or appointment.
post *verb*
to appoint or station to a place or position: 'two guards were *posted* behind the bank'.
Usage: 'the young teacher was *posted* to another school' (= transferred).

post-
a prefix meaning behind or after, as in *posthumous*.
[Latin]

postage (*say* **post**-ij) *noun*
the cost of sending letters, etc. by post. A **postage stamp** is a small printed label attached to an envelope or parcel as evidence that postage has been paid.

postal order
a type of money order, in various fixed denominations, bought and cashable at any post office.

postbox *noun*
a letterbox.

postcard *noun*
a card, usually with a picture on one side, which may be sent by post without an envelope.

postcode *noun*
a system by which all districts or towns are given a code number in order to speed the delivery of the post.

postdate *verb*
1. to date with a future date: 'to *postdate* a cheque'.
2. to come after in time.

poster *noun*
a large printed sheet of paper or card, often illustrated, used as an announcement, advertisement or for decoration.

poste restante (*say* post ress-**tont**)
a department in a post office where letters are kept until collected.
[French, post remaining]

posterior (*say* pos-**teer**ia) *adjective*
1. relating to or situated at the rear or behind.
2. coming later in time or position.
posterior *noun*
the buttocks.
[Latin, following after]

posterity (*say* pos-**terri**-tee) *noun*
the future time or generations.

postgraduate (*say* **post**-grad-yew-it) *adjective*
of study beyond the level of a bachelor's degree.
Word Family: **postgraduate**, *noun*, a person engaged in such study.

posthaste *adjective*
as fast as possible.

posthumous (*say* **pos**-tewmus) *adjective*
occurring or continuing after one's death: 'the soldier received a *posthumous* award for bravery'.
Word Family: **posthumously**, *adverb*.
[Latin *postumus* last (confused with *humus* ground, grave)]

postillion (*say* pos-**til**-y'n) **postilion** *noun*
a person who rides one of the horses which is pulling a carriage, to help guide the team.

postman *noun*
also called a **mailman**
a person employed by a post office to carry and deliver the post.

postmark *noun*
a mark stamped on an envelope over the postage stamp, usually showing when and where the letter was posted.
Word Family: **postmark,** *verb.*

postmaster *noun*
the official in charge of a post office.
Word Family: **postmistress,** *noun,* a female postmaster.

post meridiem (*say* post merriddi-em)
short form is **p.m.**
the time after midday. Compare ANTE MERIDIEM.
Word Family: **postmeridian,** *adjective.*
[Latin, after midday]

post-mortem *noun*
also called an **autopsy**
an inspection and dissection of a body after death, often to determine the cause of death.
[Latin, after death]

postnatal (*say* post-**nay**-t'l) *adjective*
of or happening in the period immediately after birth.

post office
1. an office or building in which letters, etc. are received, sorted and sent out, stamps sold, etc.
2. the department of government or corporation responsible for a country's postal and telecommunication services.

post-operative *adjective*
of or relating to the time or events after a surgical operation.

postpaid *adjective*
(of a letter or telegram) having the price of postage already paid.

postpone *verb*
to cause to occur at a date later than planned or expected.
Word Family: **postponement,** *noun.*
[POST- + Latin *ponere* to place]

postscript *noun*
short form is **P.S.**
1. a sentence, note or paragraph added at the end of a letter.
2. any additional part or information.
[POST- + Latin *scriptum* written]

postulant (*say* **pos**-tew-l'nt) *noun*
a person who asks or applies, especially a candidate for admission to a religious order.

postulate (*say* **pos**-tew-late) *verb*
1. to state.
2. to assume without proof, especially as the basis of an argument.
Word Family: **postulate** (*say* **pos**-tew-lit), *noun,* a) something which is postulated, such as a principle, b) a necessary condition; **postulation,** *noun,* the act of postulating.
[Latin *postulatus* claimed]

posture (*say* **pos**-cher) *noun*
1. the arrangement or position of the body: 'an awkward *posture*'.
2. an attitude: 'he maintained a *posture* of defiance despite our threats'.
[from Latin]

posy (*say* **po**-zee) *noun*
a small bunch of flowers.

pot *noun*
1. a round, deep container.
2. any similar round object: 'a *chimneypot*'.
3. (*informal*) a) hashish. b) a potbelly. c) a pot shot.
4. a common fund shared by several people, such as the total amount of money bet by all the players for one hand of cards.
5. a trap or basket for catching fish.
go to pot, to lessen in or lose quality, etc.
pot *verb*
(**potted, potting**)
1. to place or plant in a pot.
2. to cook or preserve food in a pot.
3. (*informal*) to take a wild or random shot.
4. to capture or win: 'they *potted* several prizes between them'.
5. *Billiards:* to hit a ball into a pocket.

potable (*say* **potta**-b'l) *adjective*
suitable for drinking.
[Latin *potare* to drink]

potash *noun*
either potassium carbonate (formula K_2CO_3), or potassium hydroxide (formula KOH), both of which are strongly alkaline.
[as first obtained by evaporating leached *ashes* in a *pot*]

potassium (*say* pot-**assium**) *noun*
element number 19, a soft, strongly reactive metal. Its compounds are essential to life and are used as fertilizers and in liquid soaps. See ALKALI METAL.
See CHEMICAL ELEMENTS in grey pages.
Word Family: **potassic,** *adjective.*
[as first discovered in *potash*]

potato *noun*
plural is **potatoes**
a medium-sized white root growing under the ground and used as a vegetable.
[Haitian *batata* sweet-potato]

potbelly *noun*
a large abdomen.
Word Family: **potbellied,** *adjective.*

potboiler *noun*
(*informal*) a work of literature or art produced quickly for financial gain.
[as done to keep the *pot boiling,* that is, to get food]

potent (*say* **po**–t'nt) *adjective*
1. full of power or strength: 'a *potent* remedy'.
Usage: 'she could not give us any *potent* reason for her behaviour' (= convincing).
2. (of a male) having the ability to perform sexual intercourse.
Word Family: **potency,** *noun,* the quality of being potent or powerful; **potently,** *adverb.*
[Latin *potens* capable]

potentate (*say* **po**–t'n–tate) *noun*
any person with great power, such as a ruler or dictator.

potential (*say* po–**ten**–sh'l) *adjective*
possible: 'come and meet your *potential* classmates'.
potential *noun*
1. a likely ability or capacity: 'she already shows great *potential* as a singer'.
2. *Electricity:* the amount of electric charge on a body with respect to earth, which is considered to have zero potential.
Word Family: **potentially,** *adverb*; **potentiality** (*say* po–tenshi–**alli**–tee), *noun,* a possibility.

potential difference
Electricity: the difference in potential between two bodies. If they are connected together, electric charge will flow between them.

potential energy
Physics: the energy which a body has because of its position, e.g. a coiled spring, a cart at the top of a hill, etc.

potherb (*say* **pot**–herb) *noun*
any herb whose leaves or flowers are used in cooking.

pothole (*say* **pot**–hole) *noun*
1. a hole, e.g. in a road surface.
2. an underground cavern, especially one eroded in limestone by underground streams.
Word Family: **potholing,** *noun,* the exploration of potholes.

pothook (*say* **pot**–hook) *noun*
a hook from which vessels may be suspended over an open fire.

potion (*say* **po**–sh'n) *noun*
a liquid, especially one with medicinal or magical effects.

potluck *noun*
a random or chance choice.

potpourri (*say* po–**poo**–ree) *noun*
1. a mixture of dried petals with herbs or spices kept for its fragrant scent.
2. any mixture of unrelated or miscellaneous things.
[French *pot* pot + *pourri* rotten]

pot roast
a large piece of meat which is cooked slowly in a small amount of water in a covered pot, often with vegetables.
Word Family: **pot-roast,** *verb.*

potsherd (*say* **pot**–sherd) *noun*
a fragment of pottery, such as is found in an archaeological excavation.

pot shot
a wild or random shot.

pottage (*say* **pottij**) *noun*
an old word meaning a soup or stew.

potted *adjective*
1. cooked or preserved in a pot: '*potted* meat'.
2. (*informal*) shortened or condensed: 'a *potted* version of a novel'.

potter (1) *verb*
a) to move or act slowly or aimlessly.
b) to pass time in a relaxed manner.

potter (2) *noun*
a person who makes pottery.

potter's wheel
a rotating metal or wooden disc on which a potter shapes clay.

pottery *noun*
a) any objects made by shaping and baking clay, etc., such as earthenware and stoneware.
b) the art or business of making such objects.

potty (1) *adjective*
(*informal*) mad or foolish.

potty (2) *noun*
(*informal*) a small chamber-pot for young children.

pouch *noun*
1. a small bag to hold tobacco or other miscellaneous small items.
2. a loose or sagging fold of skin under the eye.
3. *Biology:* a pocket–like part of an animal, especially one used to carry the young of a marsupial.

pouffe (*rhymes with* roof) *noun*
1. a large, thick cushion used as a seat.
2. a high, puffed hairstyle.
[French]

poulterer (*say* **pole**–ta–ra) *noun*
a person who sells poultry.

poultice (*say* **pole**–tis) *noun*
a soft, warm, moist dressing, applied to sores or inflamed parts of the body for relief.
Word Family: **poultice**, *verb*, to apply a poultice to.
[Latin *pultis* of pottage]

poultry (*say* **pole**–tree) *noun*
any or all domestic fowls, such as chickens, turkeys, etc.
[Latin *pullus* chicken]

pounce (*rhymes with* bounce) *verb*
to spring at or seize suddenly: 'the cat *pounced* on the trembling mouse'.
Word Family: **pounce**, *noun*, a sudden spring or swoop.

pound (1) *verb*
1. to beat or strike heavily and repeatedly: 'he *pounded* desperately on the door'.
2. to crush: '*pound* the nuts with a hammer'.
Usages:
a) 'they *pounded* grammar into her at an early age' (= forced).
b) 'they *pounded* down the corridor to the front door' (= ran heavily or noisily).
Word Family: **pound**, *noun*, a heavy blow or thump.

pound (2) *noun*
1. a) a unit of mass in the avoirdupois system, equal to about 0·454 kg.
b) a unit of mass in the apothecaries' and troy systems, equal to about 0·373 kg. See UNITS in grey pages.
2. a) the basic unit of money in Britain and Ireland, originally equal to 20 shillings or 240 pence, but now equal to 100 pence.
b) the basic unit of money in various countries in the Middle East, e.g. Egypt, Israel, Lebanon and Syria.
Word Family: **poundage**, *noun*, a rate, cost, etc. calculated per pound.
[Latin *pondo* a pound weight]

pound (3) *noun*
1. a place where stray animals are confined.
2. a place where confiscated goods are kept.

poundal *noun*
a unit of force equal to about 0·138 newton. See UNITS in grey pages.

pour (*rhymes with* door) *verb*
a) to cause to flow or stream: '***pour*** that milk into a cup'. b) to flow strongly: 'the flooding river *poured* over its banks'.
Usage: 'it is *pouring* outside so take your coat' (= raining heavily).
Word Family: **pour**, *noun*.

pout (*rhymes with* out) *verb*
to push out the lips in a disappointed or sullen expression.
Word Family: **pout**, *noun*.

poverty (*say* **povva**–tee) *noun*
a) the state of having little or no money or resources except for the most basic needs. b) the state of voluntarily giving up personal possessions and income, as in certain religious orders.
Usages:
a) 'there has been a *poverty* of statesmen in this century' (= shortage, lack).
b) 'the *poverty* of the parched soil made the land worthless' (= infertility, unproductiveness).
[Latin *paupertas*]

poverty–stricken *adjective*
extremely poor.

powder *noun*
1. a) very fine particles of a substance which has been crushed, ground, etc. b) any of various substances prepared in this form: 'talcum *powder*'.
2. gunpowder.
powder *verb*
a) to crush or reduce to powder. b) to apply or cover with powder: 'the actress *powdered* her cheeks'.
Word Family: **powdery**, *adjective*, of, like or covered with powder.
[Latin *pulvis* dust]

powder blue
a pale, greyish–blue colour.

powder magazine
a place where gunpowder and ammunition are stored.

powder monkey
an old term for a ship's boy who took gunpowder to the guns.

powder puff
a soft pad of cottonwool or fabric for putting powder on the face or body.

powder room
a women's cloakroom and toilet in a restaurant or other public building.

power *noun*
1. the ability to act or do: a) 'most birds have the *power* of flight'; b) 'I'll do all in my *power* to help'.
2. great force, might or superiority: 'he seeks political *power*'.
Usages:
a) 'which political party is in *power*?' (= government).
b) 'the *powers* of the world have made a treaty' (= countries with great power).
c) (*informal*) 'that sleep did me a *power* of good' (= great amount).
3. energy available for doing work, such as that supplied by machinery as distinct from humans or animals.
4. *Physics:* mechanical or electrical energy: '*horsepower*'.
5. *Maths:* see EXPONENT.
the powers that be, those in the positions of power.
power *verb*
to provide with the means of operation or activity: 'the machines are all *powered* by electricity'.
powerful *adjective*
having, producing or exerting power: a) 'a *powerful* man'; b) 'a *powerful* drink'.
Word Family: **powerfully**, *adverb*; **powerfulness**, *noun*.

powerboat *noun*
a fast motor boat which moves on the surface of the water rather than through it.

power of attorney
see ATTORNEY.

power station
also called a **powerhouse**
a place where electrical power is generated.

powwow *noun*
(*informal*) any meeting or conference, originally a ceremony among North American Indians.

pox *noun*
1. see POCK.
2. (*informal*) syphilis.

practicable (*say* **prak**–tikka–b'l) *adjective*
a) able to be done or put into practice: 'think of a *practicable* plan'. b) able to be used: 'the mountain track is not *practicable* in winter'.
Word Family: **practicably**, *adverb*; **practicability** (*say* prak–tikka–**billi**–tee), *noun*.

practical *adjective*
relating to or resulting from practice, action or use: a) 'does your invention have any *practical* value?'; b) 'do you have any *practical* experience in this field?'.
Usages:
a) 'he's a very *practical* man' (= active in a useful manner).
b) 'it's a *practical* certainty he'll win the race' (= virtual).
Word Family: **practically**, *adverb*, a) in a practical manner, b) nearly or almost; **practicality**, *noun*.
[Greek *praktikos* fit for action]

practice (*say* **prak**tis) *noun*
1. action or performance: 'how will your plan turn out in *practice*?'.
2. repeated effort or experience to improve a skill: 'it takes years of *practice* to play golf well'.
3. the usual or customary way in which something is done: 'it is the *practice* in this country to marry young'.
4. the business of a professional person: 'the lawyer opened his *practice* in town'.
out of practice, below one's usual form from lack of recent practice.

practise (*say* **prak**tis) *verb*
1. to make a habit of: 'he tries to *practise* being truthful at all times'.
2. to apply in action: '*practise* what you preach'.
3. to work at repeatedly to improve a skill: '*practise* the piano and you'll quickly improve'.
4. to conduct or exercise a profession, etc.: 'she *practises* medicine at the clinic'.
Word Family: **practised**, *adjective*, experienced or skilful.

practitioner (*say* prak–**tishena**) *noun*
a person who practises a profession: 'a doctor is a medical *practitioner*'.

pragmatic (*say* prag–**mattik**) *adjective*
matter-of-fact, concerned with practical ideas and results: 'she is too *pragmatic* to daydream'.
pragmatism (*say* **pragma**–tizm) *noun*
1. the quality of being pragmatic.
2. *Philosophy:* the belief that the truth or merit of an idea should be judged by its practical results.
Word Family: **pragmatist**, *noun*, a pragmatic person; **pragmatical**,

adjective, meddlesome or opinionated; **pragmatically**, *adverb*.
[Greek *pragmatikos* businesslike]

prairie (*say* **prair**–ee) *noun*
see STEPPE.
[Latin *pratum* meadow]

prairie dog
a short–tailed, short–legged, burrowing squirrel, found in the open plains of North America.

praise (*say* praze) *verb*
1. to express approval or admiration of: 'the critics *praised* the new film for its subtlety'.
2. to worship: '*praise* God'.
praise *noun*
a) admiration or approval which is offered or expressed. b) worship.
Word Family: **praiseworthy**, *adjective*, admirable.
[Latin *pretium* value]

pram *noun*
short form of **perambulator**
a small vehicle, usually with four wheels and pushed from behind, for carrying a baby.

prance *verb*
to walk or move with a springing or bounding movement.
Word Family: **prance**, *noun*; **prancingly**, *adverb*.

prang *noun*
(*informal*) a crash, especially a minor car crash.
Word Family: **prang**, *verb*.

prank *noun*
a playful trick.
Word Family: **prankster**, *noun*, a person who plays pranks.

praseodymium
(*say* pray–zee–o–**dimm**ium) *noun*
element number 59, a metal used to give glass a greenish–yellow colour. See LANTHANIDE.
See CHEMICAL ELEMENTS in grey pages.
[Greek *prasios* green + *didymos* twin]

prate *verb*
to talk long and foolishly.
Word Family: **pratingly**, *adverb*.

prattle *verb*
to talk quickly or chatter childishly.
Word Family: **prattle**, *noun*, childish talk.

prawn *noun*
any of a group of shrimp–like, aquatic animals, some of which are edible.
Word Family: **prawn**, *verb*, to catch or fish for prawns.

pray *verb*
to address a god or saint as an act of worship or entreaty: 'he *prayed* for a miracle'.
Usage: 'I *pray* you to leave me alone' (= earnestly ask).

prayer (*rhymes with* hair) *noun*
a) the act of praying: 'he closed his eyes in *prayer*'. b) an address to a god or saint: 'he said a *prayer* of thanks'. c) a set of words used for praying, such as the Lord's Prayer.
[Latin *precari* to entreat]

praying mantis
any of a group of large, flesh–eating insects which hold their forelegs together as if in prayer.

pre– (*say* pree)
a prefix meaning before, as in *prewar*.
[Latin *prae*]

preach *verb*
a) to deliver a sermon. b) to teach or proclaim in support of an action or idea: 'she *preaches* moderation as a way of life'.
preacher *noun*
a person who preaches, especially a Christian minister.
[Latin *praedicare* to proclaim]

preamble (*say* pree–**am**–b'l) *noun*
any introductory statement, especially at the beginning of a book or document.
[PRE– + Latin *ambulare* to walk]

preamplifier (*say* pree–**ampli**–fire) *noun*
Electronics: an amplifier which strengthens weak signals before they are broadcast.

prearrange (*say* pree–a–**range**) *verb*
to arrange beforehand.
Word Family: **prearrangement**, *noun*.

Pre–Cambrian *noun*
a geological period which ended about 570 million years ago.
Word Family: **Pre–Cambrian**, *adjective*.

precarious (*say* pre–**kairi**–us) *adjective*
uncertain, insecure or unsafe: 'he had a *precarious* balance on top of the ladder'.
Word Family: **precariously**, *adverb*; **precariousness**, *noun*.
[Latin *precarius* uncertain]

precast (*say* pree–**kahst**) *adjective*
Building: (of concrete parts) shaped or constructed before being placed in position.
Word Family: **precast**, *verb*.

precaution (*say* pre-**kaw**-sh'n) *noun*
care taken in advance to guard against something undesirable: 'lock the house as a *precaution* against thieves'.
Word Family: **precautionary**, *adjective.*
[PRE- + Latin *cautus* on guard]

precede (*say* pree-**seed**) *verb*
to come or go before: 'spring *precedes* summer'.

precedence (*say* **pree**si-d'nce *or* **pressi**-d'nce) *noun*
the right to precede or go first: 'you will have to wait because I have *precedence*'.

precedent (*say* **pree**si-d'nt *or* **pressi**-d'nt) *noun*
a case or action which serves as a guide or justification in later cases: 'if I don't punish you it will set a *precedent*, and others will want to be let off too'.
[PRE- + Latin *cedens* going]

precept (*say* **pree**-sept) *noun*
a moral instruction or rule of action: 'the *precept* not to kill is common to most religions'.
Word Family: **preceptive**, *adjective.*

precinct (*say* **pree**-sinkt) *noun*
1. (*plural*) the area immediately around any place, such as the grounds of a church or the environs of a town.
2. an area restricted for a particular group or activity: 'a shopping *precinct*'.
[Latin *praecinctum* an enclosure]

precious (*say* **pre**shus) *adjective*
extremely valuable: 'a diamond is a *precious* stone'.
Usage: 'I don't like his *precious* style of writing' (= overrefined).
precious *adverb*
(*informal*) very: 'you have *precious* little sense'.
Word Family: **preciously**, *adverb*; **preciousness**, *noun*; **preciosity** (*say* preshi-**ossi**-tee), *noun*, overrefinement.
[Latin *pretium* price]

precipice (*say* **pressi**-piss) *noun*
a very steep edge of a cliff.
[Latin *praeceps* headlong]

precipitant (*say* pre-**sippi**-t'nt) *adjective*
precipitate.
precipitant *noun*
Chemistry: anything causing precipitation.
Word Family: **precipitantly**, *adverb.*

precipitate (*say* pre-**sippi**-tate) *verb*
1. to make something happen more quickly: 'swearing at the boss *precipitated* your dismissal'.
Usage: 'the border clash *precipitated* the two countries into war' (= threw, flung).
2. (of water-vapour) to condense and fall as rain, hail, dew, etc.
3. *Chemistry:* to separate a solid from a solution.
precipitate (*say* pre-**sippi**-tit) *adjective*
extremely fast or sudden: 'moving with *precipitate* speed'.
Usage: 'are you sure your decision is not too *precipitate*?' (= rash, overhasty).
precipitate *noun*
Chemistry: an insoluble substance formed from a solution as a result of a chemical reaction.
Word Family: **precipitately**, *adverb.*

precipitation (*say* pre-sippi-**tay**-sh'n) *noun*
1. a) the act of precipitating. b) the state of being precipitated: 'think carefully and act without *precipitation*'.
2. *Weather:* a) any condensed moisture, such as rain or dew. b) the total amount of rain, snow, sleet and hail which falls at a location during a given period.

precipitous (*say* pre-**sip**pitus) *adjective*
extremely steep like a precipice.
Word Family: **precipitously**, *adverb.*

précis (*say* **pray**-see) *noun*
plural is **précis** (*say* **pray**-seez)
a summary.
Word Family: **précis**, *verb.*
[French]

precise (*say* pre-**sice**) *adjective*
accurate: 'give me *precise* directions how to get there'.
Usages:
a) 'I can't stand his *precise* ways' (= finicky).
b) 'just at that *precise* moment, the siren blew' (= very).
Word Family: **precisely**, *adverb.*
[Latin *praecisus* cut short]

precision (*say* pre-**sizh**'n) *noun*
accuracy: 'she remembered the details with *precision*'.

preclude (*say* pre-**klood**) *verb*
(of a previous action, etc.) to exclude or make impossible as a consequence:

'the suicide note *precluded* the possibility of murder'.
Word Family: **preclusive**, *adjective*; **preclusively**, *adverb*; **preclusion**, *noun.*
[PRE- + Latin *claudere* to shut]

precocious (*say* pre-**ko**-shus) *adjective*
developed very early, especially in relation to others of the same age.
Word Family: **precociously**, *adverb*; **precociousness**, **precocity** (*say* pre-**kossi**-tee), *nouns.*
[Latin *praecox* ripe before its time]

preconceive (*say* pree-kon-**seev**) *verb*
to form ideas or opinions about in advance.
Word Family: **preconception** (*say* pree-kon-**sep**-sh'n), *noun*, a preconceived idea or opinion.

precondition *noun*
a condition or requirement that must be fulfilled before a certain result is obtained.

precursor (*say* pre-**kersa**) *noun*
a person or thing that precedes: 'this law is a *precursor* of many more reforms'.
Word Family: **precursory**, *adjective*, preceding or introductory.
[PRE- + Latin *currere* to run]

predate (*say* pree-**date**) *verb*
a) to date with an earlier date: 'to *predate* a cheque'. b) to precede in time: 'this civilization *predates* that one'.

predator (*say* **predda**-ta) *noun*
1. *Biology:* any animal which lives by feeding on other animals.
2. a person or thing that lives by plundering or preying on others.
predatory *adjective*
of or like a predator.
[Latin *praeda* booty, plunder]

predecease (*say* preedi-**seece**) *verb*
to die before: 'most parents *predecease* their children'.

predecessor (*say* preedi-sessa) *noun*
1. a previous holder of a position: 'my *predecessor* retired after 40 years in office'.
2. any person or thing that precedes, such as an ancestor.
[PRE- + Latin *decessor* a retiring official]

predestination
(*say* pree-desti-**nay**-sh'n) *noun*
Christian: the act of God deciding the outcome of all events or actions before they occur, including whether a person is to go to heaven or hell.

predestine (*say* pree-**destin**)
predestinate *verb*
to ordain or decree beforehand: 'the plan was *predestined* to succeed'.

predetermine (*say* pree-**ditter**-min) *verb*
to decide beforehand: 'we followed a *predetermined* plan'.
Word Family: **predetermination,** *noun.*

predicament (*say* pre-**dikka**-m'nt) *noun*
a difficult or unpleasant situation.

predicate (*say* **preddi**-kit) *noun*
Grammar: a group of words in a sentence telling something about the subject. *Example*: the girl *wore a red hat.*
predicate (*say* **preddi**-kate) *verb*
to declare or assert.
Word Family: **predication,** *noun*; **predicative** (*say* pre-**dikka**-tiv), *adjective.*
[Latin *praedicare* to proclaim]

predict (*say* pre-**dikt**) *verb*
to say in advance that something will happen: 'the weather bureau *predicts* rain'.
prediction (*say* pre-**dik**-sh'n) *noun*
a) the act of predicting. b) an instance of this: 'her *prediction* of rain was correct'.
Word Family: **predictable**, *adjective*; **predictability**, *noun.*
[PRE- + Latin *dicere* to say]

predilection (*say* preedi-**lek**-sh'n) *noun*
a preference or liking.
[PRE- + Latin *dilectus* chosen]

predispose (*say* pree-dis-**poze**) *verb*
1. to give a previous tendency to.
2. to render subject or liable: 'old age *predisposed* her to illness'.
Word Family: **predisposition**, *noun.*

predominate (*say* pre-**dommi**-nate) *verb*
to be strongest in power or influence: 'the desire for revenge *predominated* as a motive for murder'.
Usage: 'the old laws have *predominated* for too long' (= prevailed).
predominant *adjective*
having most power or influence: 'what is your *predominant* interest?'.
Word Family: **predominantly**, *adverb*; **predominance, predomination,** *nouns.*

pre-eminent *adjective*
most distinguished or superior: 'the professor is the *pre-eminent* scholar of the decade'.
Word Family: **pre-eminently,** *adverb*; **pre-eminence,** *noun.*
[PRE- + Latin *eminere* to stand out]

pre-empt *verb*
1. to buy or obtain something before others have the chance.
2. *Cards:* to make a bid in bridge high enough to prevent the opposition bidding.
Word Family: **pre-emptive,** *adjective,* intended to pre-empt; **pre-emption,** *noun,* the act or right of pre-empting.
[PRE- + Latin *emptus* bought]

preen *verb*
1. a) (of a bird) to smooth the feathers with a beak. b) (of a person) to arrange the hair or clothes with great care and attention.
2. to pride or congratulate oneself.

pre-exist *verb*
a) to exist beforehand. b) to exist in a previous life or form.
Word Family: **pre-existent,** *adjective*; **pre-existence,** *noun.*

prefab (*say* **pree**-fab) *noun*
(*informal*) one of the bungalows made of standardized, pre-fabricated sections, originally set up on bombed-out sites as temporary replacement for housing destroyed in air-raids.
[short form of *prefabricated building*]

prefabricate (*say* pree-**fabri**-kate) *verb*
to build parts in a factory so that they may be assembled elsewhere.
Word Family: **prefabrication,** *noun.*

preface (*say* **preff**is) *noun*
a) any explanatory notes by the author at the beginning of a book, giving details such as the origin, scope and reason for the book. Compare FOREWORD. b) any introduction, e.g. to a speech.
preface *verb*
to introduce with a preface.
Word Family: **prefatory** (*say* **preff**a-tree), *adjective,* of or like a preface.
[Latin *praefatio* a saying beforehand]

prefect (*say* **pree**-fekt) *noun*
1. a senior pupil with authority to help keep order in a school.
2. any person appointed to supervise or govern, such as a provincial governor in ancient Rome or a district administrator in modern France.
prefecture *noun*
a) the office or term of office of a prefect. b) an administrative area in France, etc.
[Latin *praefectus* overseer]

prefer *verb*
(preferred, preferring)
1. to like better: 'do you *prefer* tea or coffee?'.
2. to put forward or submit: 'to *prefer* a legal charge'.
3. to appoint or promote: 'he has been *preferred* to the position of archbishop'.
preferable (*say* **pref**ra-b'l) *adjective*
better or more desirable: 'I find tea *preferable* to coffee'.
Word Family: **preferably,** *adverb*; **preferability,** *noun.*
[Latin *praeferre* to carry or place before]

preference (*say* **pref**-r'nce) *noun*
1. a) the act of preferring: 'I stated my *preference* for tea'. b) something which is preferred: 'my *preference* was tea'.
2. an advantage or favour, such as granted by one country to another in trade.
preferential (*say* preffa-**ren**-sh'l) *adjective*
showing or giving preference: 'I received *preferential* treatment from the boss after marrying his daughter'.

preference share
Commerce: a share on which a specified rate of interest must be paid before dividends can be paid on ordinary shares.

preferential voting
a system of voting where the voter indicates the order of his preference for each candidate on the ballot-paper.

preferment (*say* pre-**fer**-m'nt) *noun*
appointment or promotion: 'his *preferment* to archbishop took 10 years'.

prefix (*say* **preff**iks) *noun*
see AFFIX.
[Latin *praefixus* fixed in front]

pregnant *adjective*
having a foetus in the womb.
Usages:
a) 'she has a *pregnant* imagination' (= full, abundant).
b) 'a *pregnant* pause' (= significant, full of meaning).

Word Family: **pregnancy,** *noun,* the state of being pregnant.
[PRE– + Latin *gnasci* to be born]

prehensile (*say* pre–**hen**sile) *adjective*
adapted for grasping or holding: 'a possum clings to branches with its *prehensile* tail'.
[PRE– + Latin *hensus* grasped]

prehistoric (*say* pree–his**torr**ik) *adjective*
before recorded history.
prehistory *noun*
the history of man before events were recorded.

pre–ignition *noun*
the igniting of fuel in the combustion chamber of an internal combustion engine before the mixture of fuel and air is completely compressed.

prejudge *verb*
to form an opinion before hearing all the evidence.
Word Family: **prejudgement,** *noun.*

prejudice (*say* **prej**oo–dis) *noun*
1. an opinion formed without reason, knowledge or experience: 'though he has never met one, he has a *prejudice* against Australians'.
2. harm or injury that may result from an action: 'the prisoner was treated without *prejudice* to his rights'.
prejudice *verb*
a) to affect with a prejudice: 'his speech *prejudiced* me in his favour'. b) to affect unfavourably: 'to *prejudice* an issue'.
Word Family: **prejudicial** (*say* prejoo–**dish**'l), *adjective,* causing prejudice or disadvantage.

prelate (*say* **prell**it) *noun*
a high-ranking clergyman, such as a bishop or archbishop.
Word Family: **prelacy,** *noun,* a) the system of church government by prelates, b) prelates considered as a group.
[Latin *praelatus* borne in front]

preliminary (*say* pre–**limm**in–ree) *adjective*
introductory or preparatory: 'first I shall make a *preliminary* statement'.
preliminary *noun*
anything which is preliminary.
[PRE– + Latin *liminis* of a threshold]

preliterate (*say* pree–**litt**a–rit) *adjective*
relating to societies or cultures that have not left written records.

prelude (*say* **prel**–yood) *noun*
1. something which introduces or prepares for a later, more important event.
2. *Music:* a) an introductory piece, such as an overture. b) a short piece of music for a keyboard instrument.
[PRE– + Latin *ludere* to play]

premature (*say* **premm**a–cher) *adjective*
occurring before the proper or usual time: 'a *premature* baby'.
Word Family: **prematurely,** *adverb.*

premeditate (*say* pree–**meddi**–tate) *verb*
to consider or plan beforehand: 'the jury found that the killing was not *premeditated*'.
Word Family: **premeditation,** *noun.*

premier (*say* **premm**ia *or* **pree**mia) *noun*
a leader of government; a prime minister.
premier *adjective*
chief or most important: 'mum holds the *premier* position in our family'.
Word Family: **premiership,** *noun,* the position or term of office of a premier.
[French, first]

première (*say* premmi–**air**) *noun*
the first public performance of a play, film, etc.
[French, first]

premise (*say* **premm**is) *noun*
1. (*plural*) a building and its grounds: 'be off the school *premises* by 6 o'clock'.
2. a proposition or assumption which is used as the basis for an argument or a conclusion.
Word Family: **premise,** *verb,* a) to make an introductory statement, b) to assume.
[Old French *premisse* the aforesaid (buildings, syllogism)]

premium (*say* **pree**mi–um) *noun*
1. the amount of money paid for an insurance policy, loan, etc.
2. a bonus or extra amount, such as the amount by which shares are selling above their established value.
Usage: 'he places a *premium* on careful driving' (= high value).
at a premium, a) at a high price. b) in high demand.
[Latin *praemium* booty, reward]

premolar (*say* pree–**mo**–la) *noun*
see BICUSPID.

premonition (*say* premma–**nish**'n) *noun*

a feeling that something, usually unpleasant, is about to occur.
Word Family: **premonitory** (*say* pree-**monna**-tree), *adjective.*
[PRE- + Latin *monere* to advise]

prenatal (*say* pree-**nay**-t'l) *adjective*
relating to the time before birth.

preoccupy (*say* pree-**ok**-yoo-pie) *verb*
(preoccupied, preoccupying)
to take up all one's attention, etc.: 'thoughts of work *preoccupy* my mind'.
preoccupation
(*say* pree-ok-yoo-**pay**-sh'n) *noun*
a) the state of being preoccupied. b) something which preoccupies: 'work is my greatest *preoccupation*'.

preordain *verb*
to ordain or decree beforehand.

preparatory school
(*say* prep-**arra**-tree skool)
an independent primary school which prepares children for public school.

prepare *verb*
to get or make ready: a) '*prepare* to leave at once'; b) 'mother *prepared* lunch'.
preparation (*say* preppa-**ray**-sh'n) *noun*
a) the act of preparing: '*preparations* were under way'. b) the state of being prepared: 'all was in *preparation*'. c) something which is prepared: 'the chemist mixed a *preparation*'.
preparatory (*say* pre-**parra**-tree) *adjective*
introductory or serving to prepare: '*preparatory* arrangements were made for the visit'.
Word Family: **preparedly**, *adverb*; **preparedness**, *noun*, readiness.
[PRE- + Latin *parare* to make ready]

prepay *verb*
(prepaid, prepaying)
to pay in advance: 'the cost of the telegram has been *prepaid*'.
Word Family: **prepayment**, *noun.*

preponderance (*say* pre-**ponda**-r'nce) *noun*
superiority of size, numbers, power, etc.: 'in our class there is a *preponderance* of girls'.
preponderate *verb*
to be greater in number, power, etc.: 'girls *preponderate* over boys in our class'.
Word Family: **preponderant**, *adjective*; **preponderantly**, *adverb.*
[Latin *praeponderare* to outweigh]

preposition (*say* preppa-**zish**'n) *noun*
a word which indicates the relation of a noun or pronoun to another word, e.g. to indicate position, manner, etc. *Example*: he placed the book *on* the table.
[PRE- + Latin *positus* placed]

prepossess (*say* pree-pozzess) *verb*
1. to preoccupy to the exclusion of other beliefs, etc.
2. to impress or influence beforehand or at once, especially favourably.
Word Family: **prepossession**, *noun*, a) a preconceived opinion, b) a preoccupation with an idea, opinion, etc.

preposterous (*say* pre-**posta**-rus) *adjective*
totally unreasonable or absurd.
Word Family: **preposterously**, *adverb*; **preposterousness**, *noun.*
[Latin *praeposterus* inverted]

prep school
(*informal*) a preparatory school.

prepuce (*say* **pree**-pewce) *noun*
see FORESKIN.
[from Latin]

prerequisite (*say* pree-**rekwi**-zit) *noun*
something that is required as a special qualification or condition.
Word Family: **prerequisite**, *adjective.*

prerogative (*say* prerrogga-tiv) *noun*
a special right or privilege, especially of a ruler or leader.
[Latin *praerogativa* the right of voting first]

presage (*say* **pressij**) *noun*
a) a premonition. b) an omen or warning. c) a prediction.
Word Family: **presage**, *verb*, to have or serve as a presage, b) to predict.

presbyter (*say* **prezbi**-ter) *noun*
a) (in Episcopal Churches) a priest. b) an elected lay official or church elder.
presbytery (*say* **prezba**-tree) *noun*
1. a body of presbyters.
2. *Roman Catholic:* the home of a priest.
3. the part of a church set aside for the clergy and in which the altar stands.
[Greek *presbyteros* elder]

Presbyterianism
(*say* prezbi-**teerian**-izm) *noun*
Christian: a) a form of church government based on representative groups of ministers and elders. b) the

beliefs of Churches which are governed in this way.
Word Family: **Presbyterian,** *noun,* a member of such a Church.

preschool (*say* pree-**skool**) *adjective*
relating to the time before a child starts school.

prescience (*say* **pressi**–ence) *noun*
foresight or a knowledge of something before it occurs.
[PRE– + Latin *sciens* knowing]

prescribe *verb*
to order or recommend: a) 'I don't *prescribe* any particular method'; b) 'he *prescribed* several months rest'.
Word Family: **prescriber,** *noun;* **prescript,** *noun,* a rule or order; **prescriptive,** *adjective,* a) giving orders or directions, b) (Law) based on or acquired by long use.
[PRE– + Latin *scribere* to write]
Common Error: do not confuse with PROSCRIBE.

prescription *noun*
a) the act of prescribing. b) something which is prescribed, such as a written instruction from a doctor or specialist for the preparation of a particular medicine or other remedy.

preselection (*say* pree–sil**lek**–sh'n) *noun*
the act of choosing beforehand, such as choosing a candidate to represent a political party in an election.
Word Family: **preselect,** *verb.*

presence (*say* **prezz**'nce) *noun*
1. the state of being in or at a particular place: 'the *presence* of strangers limited our chatter'.
2. immediate vicinity: 'do not laugh in his *presence*'.
3. a person, especially a dignified one.
Usages:
a) 'her graceful height gives her a distinctive *presence*' (= appearance, air).
b) 'the spiritualists were aware of a *presence* in the room with them' (= supernatural or spiritual being).
presence of mind, the ability to be alert, calm and efficient, especially in a crisis.

present (1) (*say* **prezz**'nt) *adjective*
1. being or occurring here or now: 'the *present* time'.
2. being in the place referred to: 'were you *present* at the meeting?'.
present *noun*
1. the present time.
2. *Grammar:* see TENSE (2).

present (2) (*say* **prezz**'nt) *noun*
something which is given freely, as a token of friendship, affection, etc.
present (*say* pre**zzent**) *verb*
to give or award: 'he was *presented* with first prize'.
Usages:
a) 'may I *present* my parents?' (= make you acquainted with).
b) 'please *present* your tickets at the door' (= show).
c) 'this *presents* a problem' (= establishes, causes).
presentation (*say* prezz'n–**tay**–sh'n) *noun*
a) the act of presenting: 'the *presentation* of prizes is scheduled for tomorrow'. b) something which is given, such as a present or award.
Word Family: **presentable** (*say* pre**zzen**ta–b'l), *adjective,* a) able to be given or displayed, b) fit to be seen or introduced; **presentably,** *adverb.*

present–day *adjective*
occurring or existing now.

presentiment (*say* pre**zzen**ti–m'nt) *noun*
a premonition.
[PRE– + Latin *sentire* to perceive]

presently *adverb*
1. soon.
2. *Scottish:* at the present time.

present participle
see PARTICIPLE.

preservative (*say* pri**zzer**va–tiv) *noun*
a chemical agent added to foods, etc. to make them keep longer.

preserve (*say* pre–**zerv**) *verb*
1. to keep whole, safe or in existence: 'he found it difficult to *preserve* his dignity in such a ridiculous situation'.
2. to prepare food, etc. so that it will not decay or perish.
preserve *noun*
1. something which is preserved, especially fruit cooked with sugar, as in jam.
2. an area or place in which wildlife, etc. is bred or kept for hunting or similar purposes.
Usage: 'lexicography is the *preserve* of eccentrics' (= thing reserved for).

preside (*say* pre–**zide**) *verb*
to control, direct or have authority over: 'the Speaker *presides* over meetings in Parliament'.

president (*say* **prezzi**–d'nt) *noun*
1. a person chosen or elected to preside over a group, meeting, etc.: 'the *president* of a company'.

2. (*usually capital*) the elected leader of a republic, e.g. as in France or North America.
Word Family: **presidential** (*say* prezzi-**den**-sh'l), *adjective*; **presidency**, *noun*, the office or term of a president.

press (1) *verb*
1. to apply or put steady weight or force on: 'he *pressed* the doorbell impatiently'.
2. to produce by pressing: 'to *press* a gramophone record'.
3. to make flat by applying weight: 'to *press* flowers'.
Usages:
a) 'she *pressed* my hand' (= clasped).
b) 'we *pressed* on with the boring task' (= continued).
c) 'they *pressed* for the introduction of new wage rises' (= urged, insisted).
d) 'will you *press* my shirt?' (= iron).
pressed for, 'we cannot stay as we are very *pressed for* time' (= short of).
press *noun*
1. a) newspapers, magazines and other printed publications. b) people who write for such publications.
2. any of various machines or devices which press, squeeze, etc.: 'a garlic *press*'.
3. any of various machines for printing on paper.
4. a) a business engaged in printing and publishing books, etc. b) a place where printing is carried out.
5. the act of pressing: 'he gave her hand a quick *press*'.
6. a pressing or crowding together: 'she became caught in the *press* of tourists'.
7. a cupboard for storing books, clothes, etc.
[Latin *pressus* squeezed]

press (2) *verb*
to force into service, especially in the navy, etc.

press agent
a person employed to organize advertising and publicity for a person, group or business.

press conference
a meeting at which information is given to journalists by a politician or celebrity.

press-cutting *noun*
an item cut out of a newspaper or magazine.

press-gang *noun*
History: a group of men appointed to seize or force other men to join the army, navy, etc.

pressing *adjective*
urgent: 'a *pressing* need to sneeze'.
pressing *noun*
1. the act of applying pressure.
2. a gramophone record.
Word Family: **pressingly**, *adverb.*

press release
a statement or announcement given to the press for publication.

press-stud *noun*
a small metal fastener used on clothing, consisting of two parts pressed together.

press-up *noun*
an exercise in which a person lies face down on the floor and keeps the body rigid while raising it to the full extent of the arms and then lowering it.

pressure (*say* **presh**er) *noun*
1. a) the act of applying weight or force. b) the amount of force acting on a given area.
Usages:
a) 'the *pressures* of work were exhausting' (= demands).
b) '*pressure* was used to have the decision changed' (= influence).
2. *Weather:* see ATMOSPHERIC PRESSURE.
Word Family: **pressure**, *verb*, (informal) to use influence or force on.

pressure cooker
a strong, metal vessel in which food may be rapidly cooked in steam, at above normal boiling temperature.

pressure group
a group or organization which tries to influence others in order to promote its own interests or aims.

pressurize (*say* **presh**a-rize)
pressurise *verb*
1. to maintain the normal air-pressure in an enclosed space, especially in an aeroplane.
2. to compress a gas or liquid to a greater than normal pressure.
Word Family: **pressurization**, *noun.*

prestidigitation
(*say* presti-diji-**tay**-sh'n) *noun*
sleight of hand.
[Latin *praesto* ready + *digitus* finger]

prestige (*say* press–tee*zh*) *noun*
1. importance, influence or good reputation gained through achievement, success or position.
2. an admired status or distinction.
prestigious (*say* press–**tij**us) *adjective* of or producing prestige.
[Latin *praestigiae* an illusion, from *praestringere* to dull the sight, to dazzle]

presto *adverb*
Music: fast.
hey presto! an exclamation used by a conjurer meaning behold! [Italian]

prestress (*say* pree–**stress**) *verb*
to introduce internal stresses in order to counteract stresses resulting from applied loads, e.g. by incorporating cables under tension into concrete.

presumably (*say* priz–**yoo**ma–blee) *adverb*
probably.
Word Family: **presumable**, *adjective.*

presume (*say* priz–**yoom**) *verb*
to assume to be true in the absence of proof to the contrary: 'I *presume* that this is your mother'.
Usage: 'I would not *presume* to contradict you' (= dare, take the liberty) [Latin *praesumere* to forestall]

presumption (*say* pre–**zump**–sh'n) *noun*
1. the act of presuming.
2. supposition or strong probability.
3. a daring or offensive boldness.
Word Family: **presumptive**, *adjective*, based on presumption; **presumptuous**, *adjective*, offensively bold.

presuppose (*say* pree–sup–**oze**) *verb*
to assume or suppose beforehand.
Word Family: **presupposition**, *noun.*

pretence *noun*
in America spelt **pretense**
a) the act of pretending or acting falsely. b) a false or deceptive display or expression: 'his *pretence* of anger was not very convincing'.
Usage: 'I make no *pretence* to cleverness' (= claim).
false pretences, see FALSE.

pretend *verb*
to play a part or act in order to deceive: 'I'm sure she's only *pretending* to be sick'.
Usages:
a) 'I cannot *pretend* to give an estimate' (= dare, undertake).
b) 'she *pretends* to great knowledge of wine' (= claims).
c) 'let's *pretend* we're rich' (= make believe).
pretender *noun*
1. a person who pretends.
2. a person claiming rights to be a monarch.
[Latin *praetendere* to tender (an excuse or pretext)]

pretension (*say* pre–**ten**–sh'n) *noun*
1. a claim.
2. (*usually plural*) a false or exaggerated opinion, assumption or estimate: 'she has no *pretensions* about being beautiful'.

pretentious (*say* pre–**ten**shus) *adjective*
1. showy or ostentatious: 'I'd be embarrassed to ride in such a *pretentious* car'.
2. making claims, especially when false or exaggerated.
Word Family: **pretentiousness**, *noun*; **pretentiously**, *adverb.*

preterite (*say* **pretta**–rit) *noun*
Grammar: a) the tense of a verb that expresses past time. b) a verb in this tense.
[Latin *praeteritus* past and gone]

preternatural (*say* preeta–**natcha**–r'l) *adjective*
1. not normal or usual.
2. supernatural.
[Latin *praeter* beyond, contrary to + NATURE]

pretext (*say* **pree**–tekst) *noun*
a false reason or purpose given: 'they called in to borrow money on the *pretext* of borrowing a book'.
[Latin *praetextus* woven before, alleged as excuse]

pretty (*say* **prit**tee) *adjective*
delicately pleasing: 'a *pretty* face'.
Usage: 'it will cost a *pretty* sum to repair the damage' (= considerable, large).
pretty *adverb*
(*informal*) reasonably or moderately. 'she paints *pretty* well for a beginner'.
sitting pretty, see SIT.
Word Family: **pretty**, *noun*, a pretty person; **prettily**, *adverb*, in a charming or pretty manner; **prettiness**, *noun*; **prettify** (**prettified, prettifying**), *verb.*
[Old English *praetigg* wily or capricious]

pretzel *noun*
a small, crisp, salted biscuit in the

form of a knot or stick.
[German]

prevail (*say* pre-**vale**) *verb*
to triumph or succeed: 'good *prevailed* and the robbers were caught'.
Usages:
a) 'I *prevailed* upon him to change his mind' (= used persuasion or influence successfully).
b) 'with light rains *prevailing* in the afternoon' (= being widespread or predominant).
[PRE- + Latin *valere* to have power]

prevalent (*say* **prevva**-l'nt) *adjective*
widespread or common: 'what is the *prevalent* fashion?'.
Word Family: **prevalence**, *noun*; **prevalently**, *adverb*.

prevaricate (*say* pre-**varri**-kate) *verb*
to speak or act evasively.
Word Family: **prevaricator**, *noun*, a person who prevaricates; **prevarication**, *noun*.
[Latin *praevaricari* to walk crookedly]

prevent (*say* pri**vvent**) *verb*
to stop or keep from taking place: 'it was difficult to *prevent* a fight'.
Word Family: **prevention**, *noun*; **preventive**, **preventative**, *adjectives*, serving to prevent; **preventive**, **preventative**, *nouns*, something which prevents, such as a drug used to prevent disease. [PRE- + Latin *ventus* come]

preview (*say* **pree**-vew) *noun*
a viewing beforehand, especially of a film, etc. before it is released to the public.
Word Family: **preview**, *verb*, to show or be shown beforehand.

previous (*say* **preevi**-us) *adjective*
earlier or former: 'I think we were introduced on a *previous* occasion'.
Usage: 'his judgement was shown to be a bit *previous*' (= too hasty, premature).
Word Family: **previously**, *adverb*.
[Latin *praevius* going before]

prevision (*say* pree-**vizh**'n) *noun*
prescience or foresight.

prewar (*say* **pree**-war) *adjective*
before a war, especially World War 2.

prey (*say* pray) *noun*
1. any animal killed by another animal for food.
2. any victim: 'tourists were the unsuspecting *prey* of local shopkeepers'.
Word Family: **prey**, *verb*, a) to hunt for prey, b) to have a troublesome or destructive effect.
[Latin *praeda* plunder]

price *noun*
1. the amount of money, etc. for which something is bought, sold or acquired.
2. something which occurs as a necessary part of something else: 'misery is the *price* of war'.
Usages:
a) 'what is the *price* for the hijacker's capture?' (= reward offered).
b) 'the bookmakers are offering a high *price* on that horse' (= betting odds).
Phrases:
at a price 'she won his confidence but *at a price*' (= at a high cost to herself).
at any price, 'I will not go *at any price*' (= no matter what).
Word Family: **price**, *verb*, a) to fix the price of, b) to find out the price of; **priceless**, *adjective*, a) beyond value, b) extremely funny or absurd; **pricey**, *adjective*, (informal) expensive.
[Latin *pretium*]

prick *verb*
to make a small hole or mark with a sharp point.
Usages:
a) 'her conscience was *pricked* so she let the wet child come indoors' (= stirred).
b) 'he *pricked* his horse into a gallop' (= urged, by using spurs).
prick up one's ears, a) to raise the ears; b) to listen attentively.
prick *noun*
1. a) the act of pricking. b) the pain or sensation caused by pricking: 'he felt a sharp *prick*'.
2. a hole or mark made by pricking.
3. (*informal*) penis.
4. (*informal*) a contemptible (male) person.

prickle *noun*
1. a small sharp point or thorn.
2. a pricking or sharp tingling sensation.
prickle *verb*
to cause or have a sharp tingling sensation.
Word Family: **prickly**, *adjective*, a) covered with prickles, b) having a pricking sensation, c) easily angered or upset.

prickly pear
a cactus with pear-shaped, usually prickly, edible fruit.

pride *noun*
1. a feeling of pleasure or satisfaction due to something one owns, has done, achieved, etc.: 'she felt great *pride* on receiving the award'.
2. something which causes such a feeling: 'that child is our *pride* and joy'.
3. conceit or an exaggerated opinion of oneself: 'his *pride* and arrogance lost him many friends'.
4. the best or most thriving condition: 'in the *pride* of her youth'.
5. a group of lions.
pride of place, the most important position.
pride *verb*
pride oneself on, to take pride in.

priest (*say* preest) *noun*
1. *Christian:* a clergyman with authority to perform the sacraments.
2. a person trained to perform certain acts or rituals in certain religions.
Word Family: **priestess,** *noun,* a female priest; **priesthood,** *noun,* a) the office or duties of a priest, b) the body of priests in a particular religion; **priestly,** *adjective,* of or like a priest; **priestliness,** *noun.*
[from PRESBYTER]

prig *noun*
a self-righteous person.
Word Family: **priggish,** *adjective*; **priggishly,** *adverb*; **priggishness, priggery,** *nouns.*

prim *adjective*
1. precise, especially in a formal or affected manner.
2. demure or prudish.
Word Family: **primly,** *adverb*; **primness,** *noun.*

primacy (*say* **pry**-ma-see) *noun*
1. the state of being first or most important.
2. *Christian:* the office of primate.

prima donna (*say* **preema** donna)
1. the principal female singer in an opera company. Also called a **diva.**
2. a temperamental or theatrical person.
[Italian, first lady]

primaeval (*say* prime-**eev'l**) *adjective*
see PRIMEVAL.

prima facie (*say* **pry**-ma fay-see)
at first sight.
prima-facie *adjective*
Law: (of evidence) strong enough to establish a fact without further proof.
[Latin *primus* first + *facies* face]

primal (*say* **pry**-m'l) *adjective*
first or original: '*primal* man'.

primarily (*say* **prime**-ra-lee *or* pry-**merri**-lee) *adverb*
a) in the first place. b) mainly.

primary (*say* **pry**-ma-ree) *adjective*
first.
Usages:
a) 'the *primary* causes of war' (= immediate).
b) 'the *primary* meaning of the word' (= original).
c) 'it is of *primary* importance to remember this' (= chief).
primary *noun*
1. something which is first in order or importance.
2. *American:* a preliminary election held in each state to select candidates for the later election of the President.

primary colour
any colour having no trace of another colour: red, yellow, green and blue, plus the achromatic pair black and white. Compare SECONDARY COLOUR and TERTIARY COLOUR.

primary industry
see INDUSTRY.

primary school
a school for children up to about 11 years old.

primate *noun*
1. (*say* **pry**-mate) any mammal of the group which includes man, monkeys, apes, etc.
2. *Christian:* (*say* **pry**-mit) a chief bishop or archbishop in a group of dioceses or a whole country.

prime *adjective*
first in rank or importance: '*prime* minister'.
Usage: 'we serve only *prime* cuts of meat' (= best, excellent).
prime *noun*
the most flourishing or perfect stage or condition: 'in the *prime* of his youth'.
prime *verb*
to prepare or make ready for a particular purpose: 'when you paint the window-frame you must *prime* it with an undercoat'.
Usages:
a) 'she had been well *primed* at the party' (= plied with liquor).
b) 'the judge believed the witness had been *primed* before the case' (= given information).
[Latin *primus* first]

prime meridian
also called the **Greenwich meridian** the line of longitude 0° through Greenwich, London, from which other measures of longitude are taken.

prime minister
(*usually capitals*) the minister leading the government.

prime mover
1. the originator or chief promoter of a scheme of action: 'he was the *prime mover* in the anti-hanging campaign'.
2. the initial source of power, e.g. a windmill or stationary engine.

prime number
Maths: a positive integer that is exactly divisible only by itself and one, such as 5, 7, 11, etc.

primer (1) (*say* **pry**-ma) *noun*
a simple book of instruction or learning.

primer (2) (*say* **pry**-ma) *noun*
1. any first preparation, such as an undercoat of paint on a surface.
2. a part of a cartridge containing a substance which explodes when struck by the firing pin, thus firing the main powder charge.

primeval (*say* prime-**eev**'l) **primaeval** *adjective*
of or relating to prehistoric times.
Word Family: **primevally**, *adverb.*
[Latin *primus* first + *aevum* age]

primitive (*say* **primm**i-tiv) *adjective*
1. being the earliest stage or form of something: '*primitive* man'.
2. having undergone little cultural or technological development: 'a *primitive* tribe'.
Usage: 'we built a *primitive* shelter of bark and foliage' (= simple, crude).
3. *Art:* being in a simple or self-taught style.
Word Family: **primitive**, *noun*, a person or thing that is primitive; **primitively**, *adverb*; **primitiveness**, *noun.*

primogeniture
(*say* prime-o-**jenn**icher) *noun*
1. the fact of being the first-born son.
2. the feudal law that real estate passed to the eldest son unless otherwise bequeathed by will.
[Latin *primo* at first + *genitus* born]

primordial (*say* prime-**ordi**-ul) *adjective*
original or first in time.

primp *verb*
to dress or preen oneself fussily.

primrose *noun*
1. any of a group of small, spring plants with pale yellow flowers.
2. a pale yellow colour.
primrose path, a life of pleasure.
Word Family: **primrose**, *adjective.*
[Late Latin *prima rosa* first rose]

Primus (*say* **pry**mus) *noun*
a portable stove which burns paraffin.
[a trademark]

prince *noun*
1. a male member of a royal family, usually one other than the monarch.
2. the ruler of a small state or territory in a monarchy or empire.
3. any important or leading member of a group: 'merchant *princes*'.
Word Family: **princess**, *noun*, a female prince; **princely**, *adjective*, a) of or worthy of a prince, b) generous; **princedom**, *noun*, a) the rank or status of a prince, b) a principality.
[Latin *princeps* first or principal]

principal (*say* **prin**si-p'l) *adjective*
first in rank or importance.
principal *noun*
1. the head or leading official of a school, college or other organization.
2. a person with the leading part or position, as in one section of an orchestra, a play, etc.
3. a sum of money lent, borrowed or invested, on which interest is paid.
4. *Law:* any person who employs another as his agent.
Word Family: **principally**, *adverb.*
Common Error: do not confuse with PRINCIPLE.

principality (*say* prinsi-**palli**-tee) *noun*
a state or country ruled by a prince.

principle (*say* **prin**si-p'l) *noun*
1. a basic truth, law or policy: a) 'the *principles* of maths'; b) 'he acts according to the *principle* of an eye for an eye'.
2. any standard or rule of right or moral behaviour: 'he is a scoundrel and has no *principles* at all'.
Phrases:
in principle, 'I agree *in principle* but not in practice' (= in theory).
on principle, 'I had to refuse *on principle*' (= as a matter of moral policy).
Common Error: do not confuse with PRINCIPAL.

prink *verb*
to dress up or adorn oneself fussily.

print *noun*
1. a mark made on a surface by pressure: 'a *footprint*'.
2. an engraving or etching produced from a metal plate.
3. a cotton fabric with a design on it.
4. any printed matter.
5. *Photography:* a picture developed when light-sensitive paper is exposed to light through a negative.
Phrases:
in print, (of a book, etc.) available for purchase.
out of print, (of a book, etc.) no longer available for purchase.
print *verb*
1. a) to press a mark, design, picture, etc. on to a surface. b) to produce in inked, typed form, such as a newspaper or book.
Usage: 'the stranger's face was *printed* on her mind' (= fixed, impressed).
2. to write with separated letters similar to those produced by a typewriter, printing press, etc.
3. *Photography:* to produce a print.
Word Family: **printable,** *adjective,* suitable to be printed or published.

printed circuit
Electronics: see CIRCUIT.

printer *noun*
a person or thing that prints, especially a person or company whose business is to produce publications.

printing *noun*
1. the act or process of producing printed matter, especially books, etc.
2. typography.

print-out *noun*
Computers: the information or results delivered in printed form by a computer.

prior (1) (*say* **pry**-or) *adjective*
preceding in time, order, importance, etc.
[Latin]

prior (2) (*say* **pry**-or) *noun*
Christian: a superior of a religious house, ranking below an abbot.
Word Family: **prioress,** *noun,* a female prior; **priory,** *noun,* a religious house in the charge of a prior or prioress.

priority (*say* pry-**orri**-tee) *noun*
a) the state of being first in an established order of importance. b) the right to such a position: 'his age gives him *priority* over us'.

prise (*say* prize) **prize** *verb*
to raise or force with a lever.
[French, a grip]

prism (*say* prizm) *noun*
a solid or hollow body with similar equal and parallel ends, and whose faces are usually parallelograms.
Word Family: **prismatic** (*say* priz-**mat**tik), *adjective.*
[Greek *prisma* something sawn]

prison (*say* **priz**'n) *noun*
a gaol.
prisoner *noun*
1. a person who is kept in captivity, custody or a prison.
2. a person who is restricted or restrained.
[Latin *prensus* caught]

prissy *adjective*
(*informal*) prim or prudish.

pristine (*say* **pris**-tin *or* **pris**-teen) *adjective*
1. original, primitive or belonging to an earlier time: 'he was restored to his *pristine* health'.
2. undamaged or as new: 'in *pristine* condition'.
[Latin *pristinus* former, earlier]

prithee (*say* **pri***th*-ee) *interjection*
an old word meaning I pray you.

private (*say* **pry**-vit) *adjective*
1. not seen, used or shared by others: a) 'a *private* discussion between the leaders'; b) '*private* information'.
2. personal or belonging to oneself: 'the Prime Minister should not express *private* opinions'.
3. used or controlled by individuals, rather than the public or the government: a) 'that young doctor went into *private* practice'; b) 'a *private* detective is not a member of the police force'.
private *noun*
Military: the lowest rank in the army.
Word Family: **privately,** *adverb*; **privacy** (*say* **privva**-see *or* **pry**-va-see), *noun,* a) the state of being private or secluded, b) secrecy.
[from Latin]

private enterprise
any privately owned business or businesses, as distinct from those owned or controlled by the government.

privateer (*say* pry-va-**teer**) *noun*
a) a privately owned ship instructed to attack the ships and cargo of an enemy during war. b) the commander or a crew member of such a ship.

private eye
(*informal*) a private detective.

private hotel
a small, residential hotel, usually unlicensed.

private means
an income not from wages or salary but from property or investments.

private practice
that part of a professional business in which individual clients are charged fees for services rendered, a term used especially of a doctor's work outside the National Health Service.

private school
any school that is run by a private or religious organization which charges a fee for attendance.

privation (*say* pry-**vay**-sh'n) *noun*
a lack of necessities or comforts: 'war led to serious *privation* and poverty'.
[Latin *privatus* deprived]

privative (*say* **privva**-tiv) *adjective*
1. causing lack or loss.
2. *Grammar:* giving a negative meaning to a word, as *a-* in *amoral.*

privet (*say* **privvit**) *noun*
an evergreen shrub with small, white flowers, sometimes used for garden hedges.

privilege (*say* **privvi**-lij) *noun*
1. a right, advantage or opportunity granted to a particular person or group: 'the *privilege* of leading the procession'.
2. the principle of allowing or enjoying such rights or benefits: 'a society with social classes is based on *privilege*'.
Word Family: **privilege,** *verb,* a) to grant a privilege to, b) to exempt.
[Latin *privus* one's own + *legis* of law]

privy (*say* **privvee**) *adjective*
taking part in something private or secret: 'only a few villagers were *privy* to the plot'.
privy *noun*
an outside toilet.
Word Family: **privily,** *adverb,* secretly.
[from PRIVATE]

privy purse
the amount of money allowed by parliament for private use by the monarch.

prize (1) *noun*
1. something offered or given as a reward for success, victory, etc.
2. something captured or seized: 'the pirates' *prize* was a chest of jewellery'.
prize *adjective*
1. offered or given as a prize: '*prize* money'.
2. worthy of or having received a prize: 'our *prize* bull'.
Usage: 'what a *prize* fool you are' (= absolute).

prize (2) *verb*
to value highly: 'I *prize* these books above all my possessions'.

prize (3) *verb*
to prise.

prize ring
a boxing ring.

pro (1) *noun*
an argument, or person, in favour of something.
the pros and cons, facts, arguments, etc. for and against something.
Word Family: **pro,** *adverb,* in favour of.
[Latin, for]

pro (2) *noun*
(*informal*) a professional.

pro (3) *noun*
(*informal*) a prostitute.

pro-
a prefix meaning: a) favour or support, as in *pro-British*; b) forward in space, time, etc., as in *proceed.*
[Latin]

probability (*say* probba-**billi**-tee) *noun*
1. the state of being probable.
2. a probable condition, event, etc.: 'there is a *probability* that the aeroplane will be late'.
3. *Maths:* a measure of chance expressed as the ratio of the number of favourable outcomes to the total number of outcomes.
in all probability, very likely.

probable (*say* **probba**-b'l) *adjective*
1. expected to occur or be true.
2. seemingly true.
Word Family: **probably,** *adverb.*
[Latin *probabilis* commendable, credible]

probate (*say* **pro**-bate) *noun*
Law: a) the formal procedure for establishing the validity of a will. b) the document showing this.
Word Family: **probate,** *verb.*
[Latin *probatus* proved]

probation (*say* pro-**bay**-sh'n) *noun*
1. a trial period, e.g. for a new employee.

2. *Law:* the system of allowing criminals to remain free, instead of being imprisoned, on a promise to behave well in the future. Compare PAROLE.
Word Family: **probationary**, *adjective*; **probationer**, *noun*, a person undergoing probation.

probative (*say* **pro**–ba–tiv) *adjective*
serving to test or prove.

probe *noun*
1. a searching into or close examination.
2. a slender instrument used to explore wounds, etc.
Word Family: **probe**, *verb.*
[Latin *probare* to test]

probity (*say* **pro**–bittee) *noun*
integrity or honesty.
[Latin *probus* good]

problem *noun*
1. a difficult question, situation, person, etc.
2. a question proposed for solution or discussion.
Word Family: **problematic** (*say* probla–**mattik**), **problematical**, *adjective*, uncertain; **problematically**, *adverb.*
[Greek *problema* a defence, excuse, questioning]

proboscis (*say* pro–**bossis**) *noun*
plural is **probosces**
a trunk-like growth from the head, such as on elephants and some insects.
[Greek, a means of providing food]

procedure (*say* pro–**seed**–yer) *noun*
the method or manner of acting or proceeding: 'is there a set *procedure* for this type of job?'.
Word Family: **procedural** (*say* pro–**seed**–yoo–r'l), *adjective.*

proceed (*say* pro–**seed**) *verb*
1. to continue, especially after stopping.
Usage: 'many evils *proceed* from war' (= arise).
2. to take legal action.
proceeds (*say* **pro**–seeds) *plural noun*
the money obtained from a sale or other transaction.
[Latin *procedere* to advance]

proceeding *noun*
1. a course of action.
2. (*usually plural*) a) a particular action. b) legal steps.
3. (*plural*) a record of the activities of a club, society, etc.: 'the *proceedings* of the Royal Society'.

process (*say* **pro**–sess) *noun*
1. a series of actions or changes for a particular purpose: a) 'we studied the *process* of refining sugar'; b) 'the *process* of digestion'; c) 'packing the crockery into boxes was a slow *process*'.
2. *Law:* the proceedings in an action.
3. *Biology:* a natural outgrowth from an organ.
in the process of, 'a building *in the process of* construction' (= in the course of).
process *verb*
1. to treat, adapt or prepare, especially products for sale.
2. to start a legal action against someone.

procession (*say* pros**sesh**'n) *noun*
1. a line or group of people, vehicles, etc. moving along in an orderly way.
2. the act of moving in orderly sequence: 'the *procession* of the seasons'.
Word Family: **processional**, *adjective*, of or for a procession.

proclaim (*say* pro–**klame**) *verb*
to announce or make known, especially publicly or officially.
Word Family: **proclamation** (*say* prokla–**may**–sh'n), *noun.*
[Latin *proclamare* to shout out]

proclivity (*say* prok**klivvi**–tee) *noun*
a natural tendency or disposition: 'a *proclivity* to criticize'.
[Latin *proclivis* steep, inclined]

procrastinate (*say* pro–**krasti**–nate) *verb*
to put off doing something.
Word Family: **procrastination**, *noun*; **procrastinator**, *noun*, a person who procrastinates.
[PRO– + Latin *crastinus* of tomorrow]

procreate (*say* **pro**–kree–ate) *verb*
to produce offspring.
Word Family: **procreation**, *noun*; **procreative**, *adjective.*
[from Latin]

proctor *noun*
(in some universities) an official, especially one responsible for discipline among undergraduates.
[Latin *praecurator* an administrator]

procure (*say* pro–**kewer**) *verb*
1. to obtain, especially by care or effort: 'I managed to *procure* a rare edition of the novel'.
2. to obtain a prostitute for the use of others.

Word Family: **procurement, procuration,** *nouns*; **procurer,** *noun*, a person who procures, especially prostitutes; **procurable,** *adjective.*
[Latin *procurare* to take charge of]

prod *verb*
(prodded, prodding)
to poke or push with a pointed object.
Usage: 'she had to be *prodded* before she accepted the invitation' (= urged).
Word Family: **prod,** *noun*, a) a pointed instrument used for prodding, b) a poke with or as if with a prod, c) a reminder.

prodigal (*say* **proddi**-g'l) *adjective*
1. recklessly wasteful.
2. giving profusely: 'she is *prodigal* of favours'.
prodigal *noun*
a person who is extravagant or wasteful.
Word Family: **prodigally,** *adverb*; **prodigality** (*say* proddi-**galli**-tee), *noun.*
[Latin *prodigus* lavish]

prodigious (*say* pro**ddij**-us) *adjective*
1. enormous: 'he inherited a *prodigious* sum of money from his wealthy father'.
2. wonderful: 'saving those drowning children was a *prodigious* feat'.

prodigy (*say* **proddi**-jee) *noun*
1. a person, especially a child, with extraordinary abilities.
2. something wonderful.
[Latin *prodigium* a marvellous portent]

produce (*say* pro-**dewce**) *verb*
1. to bring forth: a) 'the rabbit *produced* five offspring'; b) 'the novelist *produced* a new book every year'; c) 'the defence lawyer *produced* some new evidence'.
2. to make goods.
Usages:
a) 'one must *produce* one's ticket on demand' (= show, exhibit).
b) 'who *produced* this play?' (= organized and presented).
c) 'her speech *produced* a violent reaction' (= stimulated).
Word Family: **produce** (*say* **prod**-yooce), *noun*, something produced, especially agricultural or natural products.
[Latin *producere* to bring forward]

producer (*say* pro-**dewsa**) *noun*
1. a person or thing that produces.
2. the person who organizes the business side of a play or film. Compare DIRECTOR.

product (*say* **proddukt**) *noun*
1. something which is produced.
2. *Maths:* the result of multiplication. Compare QUOTIENT.

production (*say* pro**dduk**-sh'n) *noun*
1. the act of producing.
2. something which is produced, e.g. a particular play or film.
3. the total amount produced.

productive (*say* pro**dduk**-tiv) *adjective*
producing readily or abundantly: '*productive* soil'.
Usage: 'that was not a very *productive* move' (= profitable).
Word Family: **productively,** *adverb*; **productivity** (*say* prodduk-**tivvi**-tee), **productiveness,** *nouns.*

profane *adjective*
1. having or showing a lack of reverence for God or sacred things.
2. secular.
Usage: 'his *profane* language shocked us' (= blasphemous).
profanity (*say* pro-**fanni**-tee) *noun*
1. any profane conduct or language.
2. the state of being profane: 'the *profanity* of the novel caused it to be banned'.
Word Family: **profane,** *verb*, a) to treat irreverently, b) to put to an unworthy use; **profanely,** *adverb*; **profaner,** *noun.*
[Latin *profanus* outside the temple]

profess *verb*
1. a) to declare: 'he *professed* extreme disappointment'. b) to declare insincerely: 'she *professes* to be a friend'.
Usage: 'I don't *profess* to be an expert' (= claim).
2. to affirm faith in a religion, etc.
Word Family: **professedly,** *adverb.*
[Latin *professus* frankly declared]

profession (*say* pro-**fesh**'n) *noun*
1. an occupation, especially one requiring advanced education and special training: 'he is a dentist by *profession*'.
2. all the people engaged in such an occupation: 'the dental *profession*'.
3. a statement or declaration of belief, feeling, etc.: 'his *professions* of love only made her blush'.

professional (*say* pro**ffesha**-n'l) *adjective*
1. of or relating to a profession: '*professional* salaries'.
2. doing something for payment or as a full-time occupation: 'a *professional* footballer'.

3. maintaining appropriate standards: 'he has a very *professional* manner'.
Usage: 'we sought *professional* advice' (= expert).
Word Family: **professional,** *noun,* a professional person; **professionally,** *adverb*; **professionalism,** *noun,* professional skill or qualities.

professor (*say* proff**essa**) *noun*
the highest-ranking university teacher.
Word Family: **professorial** (*say* proffa-**sawriul**), *adjective,* of or characteristic of a professor.

proffer *verb*
to offer for acceptance.
Word Family: **proffer,** *noun.*

proficient (*say* proff**ish**'nt) *adjective*
skilled or expert in something: 'a *proficient* teacher'.
Word Family: **proficiently,** *adverb*; **proficiency,** *noun.*

profile (*say* **pro**–file) *noun*
1. an outline showing the side view of a person's face.
2. a drawing of a vertical section through something, such as a building, soil, etc.
3. a study or article about a person, published in a newspaper, etc.
Word Family: **profile,** *verb.*

profit (*say* **proff**it) *noun*
1. any gain or benefit: 'his trip overseas was of great *profit* to his studies'.
2. financial gain, especially the amount remaining after expenses, cost of production, etc. have been deducted.
Word Family: **profit,** *verb,* to gain or be of benefit; **profitable,** *adjective,* yielding profit; **profitably,** *adverb.*
[Latin *proficere* to gain advantage]

profiteer (*say* proffi–**teer**) *noun*
a person who seeks or makes excessive profits, especially by taking advantage of a general shortage.
Word Family: **profiteer,** *verb*; **profiteering,** *noun.*

profit sharing
the sharing of profits between employers and employees, in addition to salaries and wages.
Word Family: **profit-sharing,** *adjective.*

profligate (*say* **profl**i–git) *adjective*
1. shamelessly immoral.
2. recklessly extravagant.
Word Family: **profligate,** *noun,* a profligate person; **profligacy,** *noun.*
[Latin *profligatus* debased]

profound *adjective*
very deep: a) '*profound* knowledge'; b) 'a *profound* love of children'.
Usage: 'the *profound* mysteries of science' (= extreme).
Word Family: **profoundly,** *adverb*; **profundity** (*say* proffundi–tee), *noun.*
[Latin *profundus* deep]

profuse (*say* pro–**fewce**) *adjective*
abundant, often to excess: '*profuse* apologies'.
Word Family: **profusely,** *adverb*; **profusion** (*say* pro–**few**–*zh*'n), *noun.*
[Latin *profusus* poured forth]

progenitor (*say* pro–**jenn**ita) *noun*
a direct ancestor.
Usage: 'he is the *progenitor* of modern motor cars' (= originator).

progeny (*say* **proj**a–nee) *noun*
offspring.

progesterone (*say* pro–**jesta**–rone) *noun*
Biology: a hormone secreted by the ovaries of mammals and producing changes before and during pregnancy.

prognosis (*say* prog–**no**–sis) *noun*
plural is **prognoses** (*say* prog–**no**–seez)
a forecast or prediction, especially of the probable course and outcome of a disease.
Word Family: **prognostic,** *adjective.*
[Greek, perceiving beforehand]

prognosticate (*say* prog–**nos**ti–kate) *verb*
to prophesy.
Word Family: **prognosticator,** *noun,* a person who prognosticates; **prognostication,** *noun.*

program (*say* **pro**–gram) *noun*
1. a programme.
2. a series of instructions for a computer.
program *verb*
(programmed, programming)
to provide instructions for a computer.
Word Family: **programmer,** *noun,* a person who prepares computer programs.

programme (*say* **pro**–gram) *noun*
also spelt **program**
1. a list of items, events, etc., e.g. for a concert or theatrical performance.
2. a performance or show: 'my favourite radio *programme*'.
3. any organized list or arrangement of procedures: 'what is the *programme* for today?'.

Word Family: **programme**, *verb*, to organize or include in a programme; **programmer**, *noun.*
[Greek *programma* a public notice]

programme music
any music intended to convey impressions of places, events or actions.

progress (*say* **pro**–gress) *noun*
1. any movement in a desired direction.
2. growth or development.
in progress, 'the meeting is *in progress*' (= under way, taking place).
progression (*say* pro–**gresh**'n) *noun*
1. the act of progressing.
2. *Maths:* a sequence of numbers. See ARITHMETICAL PROGRESSION and GEOMETRICAL PROGRESSION.
Word Family: **progress** (*say* pro–**gress**), *verb*; **progressional**, *adjective.*
[Latin *progressus* advanced]

progressive (*say* proggress–iv) *adjective*
1. favouring improvement, change, etc.: '*progressive* politics'.
2. progressing or advancing by stages: '*progressive* paralysis'.
3. consisting of continuous movement or changes: 'a *progressive* waltz'.
Word Family: **progressively**, *adverb*; **progressiveness**, *noun.*

prohibit (*say* pro–**hibb**it) *verb*
to forbid by authority: 'smoking is *prohibited* in this waiting room'.
Usage: 'the locked door *prohibited* my entry' (= prevented).
prohibitive *adjective*
prohibiting.
Usage: '*prohibitive* food prices' (= extremely high).
[Latin *prohibere* to hinder]
Common Error: do not confuse with INHIBIT.

prohibition (*say* pro–hib**bish**'n) *noun*
1. a) the act of prohibiting. b) a law that prohibits.
2. (*capital*) the period 1920–1933 when it was illegal to manufacture and sell alcoholic drinks in the United States.
Word Family: **prohibitionist**, *noun*, a person who favours prohibition of alcoholic drinks.

project (*say* **proj**–ekt) *noun*
1. a scheme that is contemplated, devised or planned for the future.
2. (in schools) a piece of work, involving research, given to a student or group of students.

project (*say* pro–**jekt**) *verb*
1. to protrude: 'the shelf *projected* from the wall'.
2. to plan or intend: 'is a tunnel under the Channel *projected* for next century?'.
3. to throw: a) 'the ball was *projected* into the air'; b) 'you have to learn to *project* your voice'.
4. *Psychology:* to unknowingly attribute one's own attitudes, etc. to others.
Usages:
a) 'she does not *project* her ideas very well' (= get across, communicate).
b) 'the slides were *projected* onto the wall' (= shown, displayed).
[Latin *projectus* thrown forwards]

projectile *noun*
1. any object fired from a gun by means of an explosive charge, such as a bullet, shell, etc.
2. something thrown.

projection (*say* proj–**ek**–sh'n) *noun*
1. a) the act of projecting: 'her voice *projection* is excellent'. b) something which protrudes: 'a *projection* of rock on the side of a mountain'.
2. a system of lines drawn on a plane surface, as in a map, representing the meridians of longitude and parallels of latitude, upon which the surface of the earth, or some portion of it, may be depicted.

projector (*say* proj–**ek**ta) *noun*
a device throwing still or moving photographic images onto a screen.
Word Family: **projectionist**, *noun*, a person who operates a projector.

prolapse (*say* **pro**–laps) *noun*
Medicine: the downward movement of an organ from its normal position.
Word Family: **prolapse** (*say* pro–**laps**), *verb.*
[Latin *prolapsus* slipped forward]

proleg *noun*
an unjointed, abdominal leg of some larvae, such as a caterpillar.

proletariat (*say* pro–la–**tairi**–at) *noun*
the working class or the people who do not own property.
Word Family: **proletarian**, *adjective, noun.*
[from Latin]

proliferate (*say* pro–**liffa**–rate) *verb*
to increase or reproduce in large quantities.
Word Family: **proliferation**, *noun.*
[Latin *proles* offspring + *ferre* to bear]

prolific (*say* pro–liffik) *adjective*
producing abundantly: 'a *prolific* writer'.
[Latin *proles* offspring + *facere* to make]

prolix (*say* **pro**–liks) *adjective*
lengthy or boring, especially in speaking or writing.
Word Family: **prolixity** (*say* pro–**liksi**–tee), *noun*; **prolixly**, *adverb.*

prologue (*say* **pro**–log) *noun*
1. the introductory part of a play, book, etc. Compare EPILOGUE.
2. any act or event which introduces.
[PRO– + Greek *logos* speech]

prolong (*say* pro–**long**) *verb*
to make longer in time.
Word Family: **prolonged**, *adjective*; **prolongation**, *noun.*

prom *noun*
1. (*informal*) a promenade concert.
2. *American:* a formal dance held for a class at a school or college.

promenade (*say* prommi–**nahd**) *noun*
a) a leisurely walk, sometimes incorporated into a dance. b) a public place for walking such as an esplanade.
Word Family: **promenade**, *verb.*
[French *se promener* to walk]

promenade concert
Music: a concert of classical music at which the audience stands or walks around.

promethium (*say* pro–meethium) *noun*
element number 61, a man-made, radioactive metal. See LANTHANIDE. See CHEMICAL ELEMENTS in grey pages.

prominent (*say* **prommi**–nent) *adjective*
standing out so as to be easily seen: 'the most *prominent* peak in the mountain range'.
Usage: 'he is a *prominent* and respected member of parliament' (= important, well-known).
Word Family: **prominently**, *adverb*; **prominence**, *noun*, a) the state of being prominent, b) something which is prominent.
[from Latin]

promiscuous (*say* prommis–kew–us) *adjective*
1. having an indiscriminate number of casual sexual relationships.
2. lacking order.
Word Family: **promiscuity** (*say* prommis–**kewi**–tee), *noun*; **promiscuously**, *adverb.*
[from Latin]

promise (*say* **prommis**) *noun*
1. an assurance that something will be done, given, etc.
2. an indication or likelihood of future success: 'the child showed little *promise*'.
Word Family: **promise**, *verb*, a) to make an assurance, b) to indicate; **promising**, *adjective*, indicating future success; **promissory** (*say* **prommisa**–ree), *adjective*, of or relating to a promise.

promissory note
a written and signed promise to pay a person a sum of money on a certain date or on demand. Compare BILL OF EXCHANGE.

promontory (*say* **prommen**–tree) *noun*
a headland.

promote *verb*
to raise in position, rank, etc.: 'after two years in the accounts section he was *promoted* to chief accountant'.
Usages:
a) 'who *promoted* the idea of having a bazaar?' (= put forward).
b) 'this tonic will *promote* the growth of new hair' (= encourage, aid).
c) 'he *promotes* detergents' (= publicizes, tries to sell).
Word Family: **promotion** (*say* pro–**mo**–sh'n), *noun*; **promoter**, *noun*, a person who promotes, especially one who provides the capital for an enterprise.
[Latin *promovere* to move forwards]

prompt *adjective*
quick: a) 'a *prompt* reply'; b) 'he is *prompt* to anger'.
prompt *verb*
1. to cause or inspire to action: 'his speech *prompted* me to vote for him'.
2. to give help or suggestions.
3. *Theatre:* to remind an actor of his lines when he forgets them.
prompt side, (*Theatre*) the right side of the stage, viewed from the auditorium, nearer the prompter; the other side is called **o.p.** (opposite the prompter).
Word Family: **promptly**, *adverb*; **promptness**, **promptitude**, *nouns*; **prompt**, *noun*, something which prompts; **prompter**, *noun*, a person who prompts.
[Latin *promptus* brought out]

promulgate (*say* **promm**'l–gate) *verb*
to declare or make known openly, e.g. to the public.

Word Family: **promulgation,** *noun*; **promulgator,** *noun*, a person who promulgates.
[from Latin]

prone *adjective*
1. tending or liable to: 'he is *prone* to accidents'.
2. lying flat or still, especially face downwards.
Word Family: **pronely,** *adverb*; **proneness,** *noun*.
[Latin *pronus* leaning, face-down]

prong *noun*
a sharply pointed part, such as a division of a fork.

pronoun (*say* **pro**-nown) *noun*
Grammar: a word used in place of a noun. *Example*: *they* walked slowly towards *it*.

pronounce *verb*
1. a) to make the sounds of a word or phrase: 'how do you *pronounce* phlegm?'. b) to utter: 'you do not *pronounce* the *t* in *often*'.
2. to state or declare, especially officially or formally: 'the judge *pronounced* the death sentence'.
Word Family: **pronounceable,** *adjective*; **pronouncement,** *noun*, a) a statement, b) the act of pronouncing; **pronouncer,** *noun*; **pronunciation** (*say* pro-nun-see-**ay**-sh'n), *noun*, the manner of pronouncing words.
[Latin *pronuntiare* to announce]

pronounced *adjective*
strongly marked or distinct: 'a *pronounced* limp'.
Word Family: **pronouncedly,** *adverb*.

pronto *adverb*
(*informal*) quickly.
[Spanish]

pronunciation *noun*
Word Family: see PRONOUNCE.

proof *noun*
1. any evidence which establishes that something is true: 'do you have *proof* that a murder was committed?'.
2. the act of proving something claimed or asserted.
3. a trial or test: 'the *proof* of the pudding is in the eating'.
4. *Photography:* a temporary print, often made directly from the film without being enlarged.
5. the strength of an alcoholic liquor.
6. *Printing:* a trial impression of a section of type, engraving, etc. made for the purpose of correction or examination. Also called a **pull**.

proof *adjective*
1. fully resistant: '*proof* against evil'.
2. of standard strength, such as an alcoholic liquor.
[Latin *probare* to test]

-proof
a suffix meaning insulated from or not affected by, as in *fireproof*.

proofread *verb*
to read a manuscript or printer's proof in order to find and mark any mistakes.
Word Family: **proofreader,** *noun*.

proof spirit
a standard mixture of alcohol and water which contains 57·10 per cent alcohol by volume.

prop (1) *verb*
(propped, propping)
to support or rest: '*prop* that chair against the door to keep it open'.
prop *noun*
a) a beam or other rigid support. b) any person or thing serving as a support.

prop (2) *noun*
short form of **property**
Theatre: any object used in a play, opera, etc. apart from the scenery.

prop (3) *noun*
(*informal*) a propeller.

propaganda (*say* proppa-**ganda**) *noun*
any opinions, principles, etc., especially biased or false ones, spread or publicized to persuade, change or reform.
Word Family: **propagandist,** *noun*; **propagandize, propagandise,** *verb*.

propagate (*say* **proppa**-gate) *verb*
1. (of an organism) to multiply or cause to multiply.
2. to send out or spread: a) 'to *propagate* sound'; b) 'to *propagate* a belief'.
Word Family: **propagation,** *noun*; **propagator,** *noun*.
[Latin *propagare* to spread]

propanol (*say* **pro**-pa-nol) *noun*
a colourless liquid alcohol used as a solvent, etc.

propane *noun*
Chemistry: a colourless inflammable gas (formula C_3H_8), the third member of the paraffin series, used as a fuel.

propel (*say* proppel) *verb*
(propelled, propelling)
to drive forward.
Word Family: **propellent,** *adjective*.
[from Latin]

propellant (*say* proppell'nt) *noun*
anything used to provide force or thrust, such as an explosive in a gun, compressed gas in an aerosol container, etc.

propeller *noun*
a device consisting of rotating blades, which propels a ship, aircraft, etc.

propelling pencil
a pencil with a replaceable lead, the length of which is adjusted by moving the outer case.

propensity (*say* proppensi–tee) *noun*
a natural tendency: 'she has a *propensity* to organize everyone'.
[Latin *propensus* inclining towards]

proper (*say* proppa) *adjective*
1. suitable or appropriate: 'is it *proper* to wear jeans to a wedding?'.
Usages:
a) 'he's a very *proper* little man' (= excessively prim or decorous).
b) 'this is the *proper* way to do it' (= correct).
2. strictly so called: 'they travelled through the suburbs to the city *proper*'.
3. (*informal*) thorough: 'we received a *proper* thrashing'.
Word Family: **properly**, *adverb.*
[Latin *proprius* one's own]

proper fraction
see FRACTION.

proper noun
see NOUN.

property (*say* **proppa**–tee) *noun*
1. all of a person's possessions.
2. a particular piece of land owned by a person.
3. an essential quality of something: 'what are the *properties* of a gas?'.
4. *Theatre:* see PROP (2).
[from Latin]

prophecy (*say* **proffa**–see) *noun*
a) a prediction. b) the ability to predict the future: 'the gift of *prophecy*'.
prophesy (*say* **proffa**–sigh) *verb*
(prophesied, prophesying)
to make a prophecy.
[PRO– + Greek *phanai* to speak]

prophet (*say* **proffit**) *noun*
1. a religious teacher claiming divine inspiration and authority.
2. a person who predicts future events. Also called a **seer**.

prophetic (*say* proffet–ik)
prophetical *adjective*
1. of or relating to a prophet.
2. of or having the nature of a prophecy: 'a *prophetic* dream'.
Word Family: **prophetically**, *adverb.*

prophylactic (*say* proffi–**lak**–tik) *noun*
any medicine or device, such as a contraceptive, which protects, prevents, etc.
Word Family: **prophylactic**, *adjective*; **prophylaxis** (*say* proffi–**lak**–sis), *noun*, the prevention of disease, etc.
[Greek *prophylaktikos* guarding against]

propinquity (*say* proppinkwi–tee) *noun*
a nearness, e.g. in place, relationship, etc.: 'her friendship with her neighbour was due to *propinquity* rather than common interests'.
[Latin *propinquus* near]

propitiate (*say* proppishi–ate) *verb*
to pacify or win over: 'he tried to *propitiate* his angry wife with flowers'.
Word Family: **propitiation**, *noun*; **propitiatory**, *adjective.*
[from Latin]

propitious (*say* proppish–us) *adjective*
favourable: 'the accident was hardly a *propitious* start to the day'.

propjet *noun*
see TURBOPROP.

proponent (*say* proppo–nent) *noun*
a person who supports or argues for a particular cause.
[PRO– + Latin *ponere* to put]

proportion (*say* proppor–sh'n) *noun*
1. the comparative relationship of size, quantity, etc. between things or parts: 'what is the *proportion* of yeast to flour in this loaf?'.
2. a correct or balanced relationship: 'the size of the house is not in *proportion* to the garden'.
Usage: 'a large *proportion* of the class failed the exam' (= part).
3. (*plural*) size: 'an inheritance of huge *proportions*'.
4. *Maths:* a statement of equality of two ratios. *Example*: 1 and 2 are in proportion to 5 and 10 because the ratio of the first pair (1:2) equals the ratio of the second (5:10).
Word Family: **proportional**, *adjective*, relative or corresponding; **proportionally**, *adverb*; **proportionate**, *adjective*, in correct proportion; **porportionately**, *adverb.*
[Latin *proportio* symmetry]

proportional representation
Politics: an electoral system where each party receives the same

percentage of seats in parliament as it receives of the total vote.

propose (*say* prop-**oze**) *verb*
to put forward, offer or suggest: 'to *propose* a new law'.
Usages:
a) 'he *proposed* again and was refused' (= proposed marriage).
b) 'what I *propose* to do is this' (= intend).
Word Family: **proposal**, *noun*, a) an offer, especially of marriage, b) something which is proposed, such as a scheme or plan; **proposer**, *noun*.
[from Latin]

proposition (*say* proppa-**zish**'n) *noun*
1. something which is proposed or suggested.
Usage: 'that is a different *proposition* altogether' (= matter).
2. *Logic, Maths:* a statement to be proved or demonstrated.
Word Family: **proposition**, *verb*; **propositional**, *adjective*.

propound *verb*
to propose or suggest.

proprietor (*say* prop-**rye**-a-tor) *noun*
an owner, especially of a business.
proprietary (*say* prop-**rye**-a-tree) *adjective*
1. relating to an owner or ownership.
Usage: 'she treats us in a *proprietary* manner' (= bossy).
2. (of a product) made and sold only by the holder of the trademark, patent, brand name or formula.
Word Family: **proprietorship**, *noun*; **proprietress**, *noun*, a female proprietor.
[Latin *proprius* one's own]

propriety (*say* prop-**rye**-a-tee) *noun*
1. behaviour in accordance with accepted or established standards.
2. the state of being right or appropriate.

propulsion (*say* prop-**ulsh**'n) *noun*
a) the act of propelling or driving forward. b) a propelling force.

propyl (*say* **pro**-pil) *adjective*
Chemistry: of or relating to organic compounds or radicals containing the univalent C_3H_7– group.

propylene (*say* **pro**-pilleen) *noun*
a colourless, inflammable gas (formula CH_2CHCH_3), the second member of the olefine series.

pro rata (*say* pro **rahta**)
in proportion.
[Latin, according to the rate]

prorogue *verb*
to end a session of parliament.
Word Family: **prorogation** (*say* pro-ro-**gay**-sh'n), *noun*.
[Latin *prorogare* to prolong]

prosaic (*say* pro-**zay**-ik) *adjective*
dull or unimaginative.
Word Family: **prosaically**, *adverb*; **prosaicness**, *noun*.
[from PROSE]

proscenium (*say* pro-**seeni**-um) *noun*
Theatre: the front of a stage, especially the curtain and its framework.
[Greek *proskenion* before the stage]

proscribe (*say* pro-**skribe**) *verb*
to condemn or forbid.
Word Family: **proscription** (*say* pro-**skrip**-sh'n), *noun*; **proscriptive**, *adjective*.
[Latin *proscribere* to outlaw]
Common Error: do not confuse with PRESCRIBE.

prose (*say* proze) *noun*
any writing or speech with no formal rhythm or pattern, as distinct from poetry.
Word Family: **prose**, *verb*, to make into or write prose; **prosy**, *adjective*, dull; **prosily**, *adverb*; **prosiness**, *noun*.
[Latin *prosa* straightforward]

prosecute (*say* **prossi**-kewt) *verb*
1. to take legal action against.
2. to perform or carry out, e.g. a task, investigation, etc.
prosecution (*say* prossi-**kew**-sh'n) *noun*
a) the act of prosecuting. b) the lawyer or lawyers appointed to prosecute.
Word Family: **prosecutor**, *noun*, a person who prosecutes, especially a public official appointed to prosecute accused persons.
[Latin *prosecutus* pursued]

proselyte (*say* **prossi** lite) *noun*
a person converted to another belief, opinion or religion.
Word Family: **proselytize** (*say* **pross**-illi-tize), **proselytise**, *verb*, to make a prosylite.
[Greek *proselytos* a newcomer]

prosody (*say* **prossa**-dee) *noun*
the theories or principles of writing or analysing the structure of verse.
[Greek *prosoidia* accentuation]

prospect (*say* **pross**-pekt) *noun*
1. a future possibility or chance: 'there is little *prospect* of the weather improving'.

Usage: 'this job holds many *propects* for a steady worker' (= chances for success, etc.).
2. an extended view or outlook: 'there is a beautiful *prospect* from the upstairs window'.
3. *Mining:* a deposit or indication of a possible deposit.
prospect *verb*
Mining: to search for valuable minerals.
Word Family: **prospector,** *noun,* a person who searches for valuable minerals, etc.

prospective (*say* pross-**pek**tiv) *adjective*
expected or likely in the future: 'this is my *prospective* wife'.
Word Family: **prospectively,** *adverb.*

prospectus *noun*
a printed advertisement for, or description of, a product, business, school, etc., set out as a booklet.
[Latin, a distant view]

prosper *verb*
to flourish or be successful: 'the company *prospered* under the new director'.
Word Family: **prosperity** (*say* pross-**perri**-tee), *noun,* success or wealth; **prosperous,** *adjective,* successful or wealthy; **prosperously,** *adverb*; **prosperousness,** *noun.*
[Latin *prosperus* as one hoped]

prostate gland
short form is **prostate**
Anatomy: a gland surrounding the urethra in male mammals.
[Greek *prostates* standing before]

prosthesis (*say* pross-**thee**sis) *noun*
any artificial device used to build up or replace a damaged or missing part of the body, e.g. an artificial leg.
Word Family: **prosthetic** (*say* pross-**thet**tik), *adjective.*
[Greek, an addition]

prostitute *noun*
a person who engages in sexual activity for payment.
Word Family: **prostitute,** *verb,* to use one's abilities unworthily; **prostitution,** *noun.*
[Latin *prostitutus* exposed for sale]

prostrate (*say* **pross**-trate) *adjective*
lying face down or full-length, as in adoration, etc.: 'the worshippers were *prostrate* before the altar'.
Usage: 'she was *prostrate* with grief' (= overcome).
Word Family: **prostrate** (*say* pross-**trate**), *verb,* to cast oneself down, in adoration or pleading; **prostration,** *noun,* a) the act of prostrating, b) extreme weakness or helplessness.
[Latin *prostratus* thrown to the ground]

prosy (*say* **pro**-zee) *adjective*
Word Family: see PROSE.

protactinium (*say* pro-tak-**tinn**ium) *noun*
element number 91, a radioactive metal. See ACTINIDE.
See CHEMICAL ELEMENTS in grey pages.
[PROTO- + ACTINIUM]

protagonist (*say* pro-**tagg**a-nist) *noun*
1. the main character in a story or play.
2. (*informal*) a person who leads, supports or represents a cause, etc.: 'he is a *protagonist* of women's rights'.
[Greek *protos* first + *agonistes* contestant]

protean (*say* **pro**-tee-an) *adjective*
a) readily changing. b) variable.
[after *Proteus,* a sea-god in Greek mythology who could assume different forms]

protect *verb*
to keep or guard from harm, attack, etc.
Word Family: **protective,** *adjective,* intending or serving to protect; **protectively,** *adverb*; **protector,** *noun,* a person or thing that protects.
[from Latin]

protection (*say* pro**ttek**-sh'n) *noun*
1. a) the act of protecting: 'work for the *protection* of your rights'. b) the state of being protected: 'this coat gives little *protection* from the cold'.
2. an economic system of protecting industry and agriculture from foreign competition by placing a tax on imports.
3. any money paid to criminals in exchange for a promise of safety from their violence.
Word Family: **protectionism,** *noun,* a theory of economic protection; **protectionist,** *noun.*

protective custody
the keeping of a person, such as an important witness for a trial, under guard or in a prison for protection.

protectorate (*say* **prottek**ta-rit) *noun*
a country protected and partly controlled by another.

protégé (*say* **protta**–*zhay*) *noun*
a person given helpful protection, support or favour by another.
Word Family: **protégée**, *noun*, a female protégé.
[French, protected]

protein (*say* **pro**–teen) *noun*
any of a group of complex organic compounds containing carbon, hydrogen, oxygen and nitrogen, composed of amino acid chains and essential for all living things.
[Greek *proteios* primary]

pro tem
for the present.
[short form of Latin *pro tempore*]

protest (*say* pro–**test**) *verb*
1. to express disapproval or objection: 'I must *protest* at such rudeness'.
2. to declare or affirm: 'she continued to *protest* her innocence'.
protest (*say* **pro**–test) *noun*
an expression or display of disapproval, etc.
under protest, 'he agreed *under protest* to play a tune' (= although complaining or objecting).
Word Family: **protester**, *noun*; **protestingly**, *adverb*; **protestation** (*say* pro–tess–**tay**–sh'n), *noun*.
[PRO– + Latin *testari* to assert]

Protestant (*say* **prottis**–t'nt) *noun*
Christian: a member of any of the Churches which separated from the Roman Catholic Church from the 16th century onwards.
Word Family: **Protestantism**, *noun*, a) the religion or principles of a Protestant, b) all Protestant Churches.

proto–
a prefix meaning first, as in *prototype*.
[Greek]

protocol (*say* **prota**–kol) *noun*
the customs and rules relating to ceremonies and other official occasions.
[Greek *protokollon* the summary of the contents of a manuscript]

proton (*say* **pro**–ton) *noun*
Physics: a stable, positively charged elementary particle, equivalent to a hydrogen ion and a part of all atomic nuclei.
[Greek, first thing]

protoplasm (*say* **pro**–toe–plazm) *noun*
also called **plasma**
Biology: the living substance of a cell, consisting of the nucleus and cytoplasm.
[PROTO– + PLASM]

prototype (*say* **pro**–toe–tipe) *noun*
the first example of a type, from which other forms are developed or further refined.

protozoa (*say* pro–toe–**zo**–a) *plural noun*
singular is **protozoon** (*say* pro–toe–**zo**–on)
a large group of microscopic animals with one cell and at least one nucleus.
[PROTO– + Greek *zoion* animal]

protract *verb*
to lengthen or extend in time: 'let's not *protract* this silly argument'.
Word Family: **protraction**, *noun*.
[PRO– + Latin *tractus* dragged]

protractor *noun*
a flat instrument with a graduated scale, used for measuring angles.

protrude *verb*
to push or jut out: 'her lower lip *protruded* sulkily'.
Word Family: **protrusion** (*say* pro–**troo**–*zh*'n) *noun*.
[from Latin]

protuberance (*say* pro–**tew**ba–r'nce) *noun*
1. something which projects or protrudes.
2. the state of protruding.
Word Family: **protuberant**, *adjective*, bulging.
[PRO– + Latin *tuber* a swelling]

proud *adjective*
1. feeling or showing pride or satisfaction, especially in oneself or one's possessions.
2. inspiring pride or self–satisfaction: 'this is a *proud* moment for us'.
Usage: 'a great and *proud* city' (= majestic).
do someone proud, a) to be a source of credit to someone; b) to entertain someone lavishly.
Word Family: **proudly**, *adverb*.
[Latin *prodesse* to do good]

prove (*say* proov) *verb*
(**proved, proved** or **proven, proving**)
1. to show to be true or genuine: 'you must *prove* your accusation'.
Usage: 'it *proved* to be a terrible mistake' (= was shown, turned out).
2. *Cooking:* to cause yeast dough to rise in a warm place before baking.
3. *Law:* to obtain probate of a will.
[Latin *probare* to test]

provenance (*say* **provva**–nence) *noun*
the place where something comes from: 'the *provenance* of an old painting'.
[French]

provender (*say* **provvinda**) *noun*
1. dry food, such as hay or oats, used for livestock.
2. any food.
[Latin *praebenda* food allowance]

proverb (*say* **prov**–erb) *noun*
a short saying, usually containing a useful or well-known belief or truth.
Word Family: **proverbial** (*say* pro–**verb**iul), *adjective*, a) expressed in a proverb or proverbs, b) widely known or referred to; **proverbially**, *adverb.*
[from Latin]

provide *verb*
to supply or make available.
Usages:
a) 'we must *provide* for the possibility of a flood' (= prepare).
b) 'grandfather left the family well *provided*' (= supplied with means of support).
Word Family: **provider**, *noun*, a person who provides, especially one whose income supports a family.
[Latin *providere* to foresee]

provided *conjunction*
on the condition: 'you may come *provided* that you don't talk'.

providence (*say* **provvi**–d'nce) *noun*
1. *Christian:* a) the care or protection provided by God. b) God.
2. any careful or economical management.
Word Family: **providential** (*say* provvi–**den**–sh'l), *adjective*, a) of or due to providence, b) lucky; **providentially**, *adverb.*

provident (*say* **provvi**–d'nt) *adjective*
1. providing for the future.
2. economical or thrifty.
Word Family: **providently**, *adverb.*

providing *conjunction*
provided that: 'we will have a picnic *providing* the weather stays fine'.

province (*say* **provvince**) *noun*
1. an administrative division or unit of a country.
2. (*plural*) the parts of a country outside the capital.
Usage: 'that problem is outside my *province*' (= sphere of knowledge or authority).
[Latin *provincia* sphere of administration]

provincial (*say* prov**vin**–sh'l) *adjective*
of or belonging to a province or provinces: 'a *provincial* newspaper'.
Usage: 'it was difficult to argue against such *provincial* attitudes' (= narrow-minded).
provincial *noun*
1. a) a person who comes from a province. b) an unsophisticated or narrow-minded person.
2. *Christian:* the head of a religious order in a region.

provision (*say* prov**vizh**'n) *noun*
1. the act of supplying or providing: 'let us organize the *provision* of food for the party'.
Usage: 'have you made any *provision* for a change in the weather?' (= preparation, allowance).
2. (*plural*) any supplies, especially of food.
3. a condition inserted into a document or agreement.
provision *verb*
to supply with food.
provisional *adjective*
1. provided for the present only: 'new drivers are given a *provisional* permit for three years'.
2. possible or conditional.
Word Family: **provisionary**, *adjective*, provisional; **provisionally**, *adverb.*

proviso (*say* pro–**vie**–zo) *noun*
a condition or limitation, e.g. in a document or agreement: 'I will pay, with the *proviso* that I may be given a refund if necessary'.
Word Family: **provisory**, *adjective.*
[Latin, it being provided]

provoke *verb*
to stir or stimulate to action, emotion, etc.: 'his taunts *provoked* me to take a swing at him'.
Usage: 'the war *provoked* a severe food shortage' (= caused).
Word Family: **provocation** (*say* provva–**kay**–sh'n), *noun*; **provocative** (*say* pro–**vokka**–tiv), *adjective*, a) stimulating, b) irritating.
[Latin *provocare* to call forth, challenge]

provost (*say* **provvust**) *noun*
1. an old title retained by certain university and church dignitaries.
2. *Scottish:* the chairman of a town council and the town's chief dignitary.
[Latin *praepositus* placed over]

provost marshal (*say* **pro**–vo mar–shal)
an officer commanding military police.

prow (*rhymes with* cow) *noun*
the bow of a boat.
[Greek *proira*]

prowess *noun*
an outstanding skill or courage.

prowl *verb*
to move about furtively or secretively, especially in search of something.
Word Family: **prowler**, *noun*, a person who prowls; **prowl**, *noun*.

proximal (*say* **prok**si-m'l) *adjective*
towards the centre of the body or point of attachment to a limb, etc. Compare DISTAL.

proximity (*say* prok-**simmi**-tee) *noun*
a nearness or closeness.
Word Family: **proximate** (*say* **prok**si-mit), *adjective*, a) close or closely related, b) approximate.
[Latin *proximus* nearest]

proxy (*say* **prok**-see) *noun*
a) the authority to act for another. b) a person authorized to act for another.

prude *noun*
a person who is, or pretends to be, unduly concerned with high standards of propriety in behaviour and speech.
Word Family: **prudish** (*say* **proo**dish), *adjective*; **prudishly**, *adverb*; **prudishness, prudery**, *nouns*.
[French]

prudent (*say* **proo**-d'nt) *adjective*
acting with caution, foresight or discretion; mindful of consequences: 'it was not *prudent* of you to reveal the secret'.
Word Family: **prudently**, *adverb*; **prudence**, *noun*; **prudential** (*say* proo-**den**-sh'l), *adjective*, having or showing good sense.
[from Latin]

prune (1) *noun*
a purplish-black dried plum.
[Greek *prounon* plum]

prune (2) *verb*
to cut branches or parts off plants, especially to promote later growth.
Usage: 'we must try to *prune* our expenses' (= reduce, cut down on).
[PRO- + Latin *rotundus* round]

prunus *noun*
1. any of the numerous forms of ornamental flowering cherry, almond, etc.
2. the genus containing trees which produce stone fruits, e.g. plums, apricots, etc.

prurient (*say* **proo**ri-ent) *adjective*
obsessed by sexual or erotic thoughts, desires, etc.
Word Family: **prurience**, *noun*.
[Latin *pruriens* itching]

Prussian blue
a deep greenish-blue colour or pigment.

prussic acid
hydrocyanic acid, a deadly poison.
[as first obtained from *Prussian* blue]

pry (1) *verb*
(**pried, prying**)
to look or ask with excessive curiosity.
Word Family: **pryingly**, *adverb*.

pry (2) *verb*
(**pried, prying**)
to prise or lever.

psalm (*say* sahm) *noun*
a sacred song or hymn.
Word Family: **psalmist**, *noun*, a person who writes psalms.
[Greek *psalmos* a song sung to the harp]

p's and q's (*say* peez and kewz)
manners.

psephology (*say* seff**olla**-jee) *noun*
the analysis of election results and voting habits.
[Greek *psephos* a pebble (used in voting) + -LOGY]

pseudo- (*say* **syoo**-doe *or* **soo**-doe)
a prefix meaning false or pretended, as in *pseudonym*.
[Greek]

pseudonym (*say* **syoo**-d'nim *or* **soo**-d'nim) *noun*
also called a **pen-name** or a **nom de plume**
a name assumed by an author to protect his anonymity.
[PSEUDO- + Greek *onyma* name]

psittacosis (*say* sitta-**ko**-sis) *noun*
also called **parrot fever**
an infectious viral disease of birds, easily transmitted to man and causing fever and coughing.
[Greek *psittakos* a parrot + -OSIS]

psyche (*say* **sigh**-kee) *noun*
the soul, spirit or mind.
[Greek, breath, life]

psychedelic (*say* sigh-ka-**dellik**) *adjective*
1. a) of greatly increased consciousness, sensitivity or perception. b) relating to any drug or other agent that brings about this state.

2. having vivid or luminous colours and shapes.
[PSYCHE- + Greek *deloein* to reveal]

psychiatry (*say* sigh-**kie**-a-tree) *noun*
the branch of medicine which deals with the diagnosis and treatment of mental disorders.
Word Family: **psychiatrist**, *noun*; **psychiatric** (*say* sigh-kee-**atrik**), *adjective.*
[PSYCHE- + Greek *iatros* healer]

psychic (*say* **sigh**-kik) **psychical** *adjective*
1. a) having supernatural or extrasensory powers. b) relating to or produced by such powers.
2. relating to the mind or self.

psychical research
see PARAPSYCHOLOGY.

psycho- (*say* **sigh**-ko)
a prefix meaning psyche, as in *psychology.*
[PSYCHE]

psychoanalysis
(*say* sigh-ko-**analla**-sis) *noun*
short form is **analysis**
a method of treatment in psychotherapy, concerned with the role of unconscious motives in behaviour.
Word Family: **psychoanalyse**, *verb*; **psychoanalyst**, *noun.*

psychology (*say* sigh-**kolla**-jee) *noun*
1. the branch of science which studies consciousness and behaviour. **Clinical psychology** is concerned with the understanding and treatment of mental disorders.
2. the actual mental processes of a particular person or group.
Word Family: **psychologist**, *noun*, a person trained in psychology; **psychological** (*say* sigh-ko-**loji**-k'l), *adjective*, relating to psychology or the mind; **psychologically**, *adverb.*
[PSYCHO- + -LOGY]

psychopathic (*say* sigh-ko-**pathik**) *adjective*
1. (of a personality) appearing normal, but marked by a lack of social responsibility and an inability to relate closely to other people.
2. of or relating to any mental disorder.
Word Family: **psychopath**, *noun.*

psychopathology
(*say* sigh-ko-pat**holla**-jee) *noun*
the investigation, understanding and treatment of mental disorders.
[PSYCHO- + Greek *pathos* suffering + -LOGY]

psychoprophylaxis
(*say* sigh-ko-proffi-**laksis**) *noun*
the training of pregnant women in the use of breathing control, labour techniques, etc. to prepare for childbirth.
Word Family: **psychoprophylactic**, *adjective.*
[PSYCHO- + PROPYLACTIC]

psychosis (*say* sigh-**ko**-sis) *noun*
plural is **psychoses** (*say* sigh-**ko**-seez)
a term for all mental disorders other than neuroses, including schizophrenia and manic-depression.
Word Family: **psychotic** (*say* sigh-**kottik**), *adjective.*
[PSYCHO- + -OSIS]

psychosomatic
(*say* sigh-ko-so**mattik**) *adjective*
(of a physical illness) caused or affected by the patient's mental or emotional condition, rather than physical factors.
[PSYCHO- + Greek *somatos* of a body]

psychotherapy
(*say* sigh-ko-**therra**-pee) *noun*
the treatment of mental disorders using psychological methods.

ptarmigan (*say* **tar**mee-g'n) *noun*
a grouse of high altitudes, in winter all white except for a black tail, in summer having a grey or brown body and white wings.
[Gaelic]

pterodactyl (*say* terra-**daktil**) *noun*
a large, long-extinct, flying reptile with a bird-like head, and each of whose wings consisted of a flap of skin extending from the body to the long outer finger.
[Greek *pteron* wing + *daktylos* finger]

ptomaine (*say* **toe**-mane) *noun*
any of several, usually poisonous, alkaloids found in putrefying flesh and vegetation.
ptomaine poisoning, food poisoning.
[Greek *ptoma* corpse]

ptyalin (*say* **tie**-a-lin) *noun*
an enzyme found in saliva, converting starch into sugar as the first stage of digestion.
[Greek *ptyalon* spittle]

pub *noun*
(*informal*) a public house.

puberty (*say* **pew**-ba-tee) *noun*
the period of developing sexual maturity, ending when an individual is able to produce an offspring.
[Latin *puber* adult]

pubes (*say* **pew**–beez) *noun*
Anatomy: a) the hair–covered region where the legs join the trunk. b) the hair itself.
[Latin]

pubescent (*say* pew–**bess**'nt) *adjective*
1. approaching or undergoing puberty.
2. *Biology:* being covered with soft, fine hair.
Word Family: **pubescence,** *noun.*

pubic (*say* **pew**–bik) *adjective*
of or relating to the pubis or pubes.

pubis (*say* **pew**–bis) *noun*
Anatomy: the arch of bone in the front of the region where the legs join the trunk.

public *adjective*
1. of or for all the people of a place or country: '*public* transport'.
2. open to any or all people: 'a *public* meeting'.
Usage: 'the matter became a *public* scandal' (= widespread, well–known).
public *noun*
the people belonging to a particular community or country.
Usage: 'the film–going *public*' (= people).
in public, openly, in front of other people.
[Latin *publicus* of the people]

publican *noun*
a person who runs or owns a public house.

publication (*say* publi–**kay**–sh'n) *noun*
a) anything which is published, such as a book or magazine. b) the act of publishing: 'he prepared his novel for *publication*'.

public bar
the cheapest bar in a public house.

public enemy
(*informal*) a criminal at the top of a police list of wanted men: '*Public Enemy* No. 1'.

public house
a house where alcoholic drinks are sold for consumption on the premises; snacks, meals, facilities for playing darts, etc. and sometimes accommodation may also be provided.

publicity (*say* pub–**lissi**–tee) *noun*
a) the bringing of something to the attention of the public by advertising, news items, etc. b) the public notice or attention resulting from this.
Word Family: **publicize** (*say* **publi**–size), **publicise,** *verb,* to advertise or give publicity to.

public prosecutor
the law officer who conducts criminal prosecutions in cases of importance or great difficulty.

public relations
the practice or techniques of establishing a favourable image or relationship for a company, government, etc. with the community.

public school
1. a private secondary, often boarding, school, financed by fees and endowments, a term originally restricted to a few very famous schools.
2. *American:* a school maintained at public expense.

public–spirited *adjective*
eager to act in the interests of the public.

publish *verb*
1. to organize the printing of a book, magazine, newspaper, etc. for distribution to the public.
2. to make known, spread abroad, divulge.
3. to be the author of: 'he has *published* only a couple of books so far'.
publisher *noun*
a person or company that publishes.

puce (*say* **pewce**) *noun*
a dark, purplish–brown colour.
Word Family: **puce,** *adjective.*
[Latin *pulicis* of a flea]

puck *noun*
the flat rubber disc used instead of a ball in ice hockey.

pucker *verb*
to wrinkle.
pucker up, 'she *puckered up* her lips to kiss him' (= pursed).
Word Family: **pucker,** *noun.*

puckish *adjective*
mischievous or impish.
[after *Puck,* a mischievous elf]

pudding (*say* **pudding**) *noun*
a) a dessert made from flour, milk and eggs, usually with added flavouring or fruit. b) any dessert.

puddle *noun*
a small pool of liquid, especially muddy rainwater.
puddle *verb*
to mix clay or sand with water.

pueblo (*say* **pwebb**–lo) *noun*
a communal village or settlement of Amerindians in south–west America and parts of South America.
[Spanish, people]

puerile (*say* **pew**–rile) *adjective*
foolishly childish or trivial.
[Latin *puer* a boy]

puff *noun*
1. a short, quick release of breath, air, smoke, etc.: 'a *puff* of wind'.
2. any soft, rounded mass or part.
3. a powder puff.
puff *verb*
1. to make puffs: a) 'she *puffed* after running uphill'; b) 'he *puffed* smoke into my face'.
2. to inhale a small amount of smoke through a pipe or cigarette.
puff up, to swell or become inflated.
Word Family: **puffed**, *adjective*, (informal) out of breath; **puffed-up**, *adjective*, inflated or swollen.

puffball *noun*
a type of fungus with a ball-like body which releases a cloud of spores when broken.

puffin *noun*
see AUK.

puff pastry
a light and flaky pastry.

puffy *adjective*
1. short of breath.
2. swollen or distended: 'after the bee sting my face became *puffy*'.

pug *noun*
1. any of a breed of dogs with a flat, wrinkled face, short hair and tightly curled tail.
2. *American:* a railway engine.
pug nose
a short, squat nose.
Word Family: **pug-nosed**, *adjective*.

pugilist (*say* **pew**ji–list) *noun*
a boxer.
Word Family: **pugilistic** (*say* pewji–**lis**tik), *adjective*; **pugilism**, *noun*.
[Latin *pugil*]

pugnacious (*say* pug–**nay**–shus) *adjective*
quarrelsome or aggressive.
Word Family: **pugnaciously**, *adverb*; **pugnaciousness**, **pugnacity** (*say* pug–**nass**i–tee), *nouns*.
[Latin *pugna* fight]

puisne judge (*say* **pew**–nee juj)
any of various High Court judges ranking below the Chief Justice, appeal court judges, etc.
[Old French *puis* after + *né* born]

puke *verb*
(*informal*) to vomit

pukka *adjective*
genuine or sound.
[Hindi, cooked, ripe]

pule (*say* pewl) *verb*
an old word meaning to cry or whimper like a child.

pull (*rhymes with* wool) *verb*
to bring towards or after oneself or in a particular direction: 'the horse *pulled* a cart'.
Usages:
a) 'she *pulled* a rude face' (= made).
b) 'I've *pulled* a muscle' (= strained).
c) (*informal*) 'the jockey *pulled* his horse during the race' (= held back).
d) 'he *pulled* on his cigarette' (= inhaled).
e) 'the car *pulled* out into the road' (= moved).
f) 'he *pulled* a knife on me' (= drew out).
Phrases:
pull apart, pull to pieces, a) to divide or separate into pieces; b) to analyse critically and in detail.
pull down, a) to demolish; b) 'the illness *pulled* him *down*' (= weakened).
pull off, (*informal*) to succeed in doing something.
pull oneself together, to recover self-control.
pull over, (of a vehicle or driver) to move to one side of the road and stop.
pull rank, see RANK (1).
pull strings, see STRING.
pull through, to recover from an illness or hardship.
pull up, a) to stop; b) to correct or rebuke.
pull *noun*
1. a) the act of pulling: 'he gave a *pull* on the rope'. b) the act of drawing in, e.g. liquid or smoke into the mouth.
2. *Printing:* see PROOF.
3. *Sport:* see HOOK.

pullet (*say* **pull**–it) *noun*
a young hen.
[Latin *pullus* a chicken]

pulley (*say* **pull**–ee) *noun*
a wheel or system of wheels with grooves in the rim for ropes or chains, used to lift weights, apply force, etc.

Pullman *noun*
a well-appointed railway carriage, especially a sleeping or dining car.
[designed by *George Pullman*, 1831–97, an American industrialist]

pullover *noun*
a knitted outer garment pulled on over the head to cover the upper part of the body.

pulmonary (*say* pul–m'n–ree) *adjective*
of or relating to the lungs.
[Latin *pulmonis* of a lung]

pulp *noun*
1. *Biology:* the fleshy part of a fruit.
2. any soft, moist mass of substance, such as wood which is treated to be made into paper.
pulp *verb*
a) to make into or become pulp: 'old newspapers are often *pulped* and reprocessed'. b) to remove the pulp from fruit, etc.
pulpy *adjective*
of or like pulp.

pulpit (*say* **pull**–pit) *noun*
a stone or timber enclosure with a desk, reached by steps and used for preaching sermons in church.
[Latin *pulpitum* a stage]

pulsar *noun*
Astronomy: a star which emits enormously powerful radio signals in pulses of extreme regularity, having many bizarre features indicative of some final stage in stellar evolution.
[PULS(ating) (st)AR]

pulsate (*say* pulsate) *verb*
to expand and contract regularly, as the heart or an artery does.
Usage: 'the busy town *pulsated* with activity' (= vibrated).
Word Family: **pulsation** *noun*, a) the act of pulsating, b) a single throb or vibration.
[Latin *pulsare* to batter]

pulse (1) *noun*
1. *Biology:* the rhythmic movement in the arteries, caused by the beating of the heart as it pumps the blood through them. b) a single throb.
2. any strong rhythm: 'the *pulse* of city life'.
pulse *verb*
to throb, especially strongly.

pulse (2) *noun*
the edible seeds of plants such as peas, beans and lentils.

pulse–jet *noun*
a jet engine which is thrust forward in periodic bursts as pressure is built up in the combustion chamber.

pulverize, pulverise *verb*
to grind or crush a substance into a powder.
Usage: 'the boxer *pulverized* his opponent' (= utterly defeated).
Word Family: **pulverizer,** *noun*; **pulverization,** *noun.*
[Latin *pulveris* of powder]

puma (*say* **pew**ma) *noun*
also called a **mountain lion**
a flesh–eating American mammal of the cat family, with a tawny coat.

pumice (*say* **pumm**is) *noun*
a light, porous volcanic rock used as an abrasive.
[from Latin]

pummel (*say* **pumm**'l) *verb*
(pummelled, pummelling)
also spelt **pommel**
to hit or beat repeatedly with the fists.

pump (1) *noun*
any of various devices for moving a liquid or a gas through a pipe: 'a petrol *pump*'.
pump *verb*
to transfer or supply with or as if with a pump: a) '*pump* air into the tyres'; b) 'they *pumped* Clyde full of bullets'.
Usages:
a) 'he *pumped* my hand vigorously' (= moved up and down).
b) 'try and *pump* her for information' (= question forcefully).

pump (2) *noun*
a light dancing shoe made of satin or shiny leather.

pumpernickel *noun*
a dark rye–bread.
[German]

pumpkin *noun*
a large vegetable with firm orange flesh.

pun *noun*
a clever or humorous play on the meanings of words which sound or look similar, as in Belloc's suggested epitaph for himself: 'His sins were scarlet but his books were *read*'.
Word Family: **pun (punned, punning),** *verb,* to make a pun or puns.

punch (1) *verb*
to hit hard with the fist.
punch *noun*
a blow with the fist.
Usage: 'the speech had quite a bit of *punch*' (= effect, force).

punch (2) *noun*
a tool or machine for cutting holes, stamping designs, etc.

Word Family: **punch**, *verb*, to pierce or stamp with or as if with a punch.

punch (3) *noun*
any of various spiced drinks made with a combination of fruit juices, wine or spirits.

punch card
a card punched with holes representing information, used in a computer.

punch–drunk *adjective*
1. suffering from a form of brain damage due to repeated blows on the head.
2. (*informal*) dazed.

punching bag
a heavy, suspended, stuffed bag, punched by boxers in training.

punch line
the final line or sentence of a joke on which the whole joke depends.

punch–up *noun*
(*informal*) a fight.

punctilious (*say* punk–**till**ius) *adjective*
very careful about small details.
Word Family: **punctilio**, *noun*, exact detail.
[Latin *puntiglio* a little point]

punctual (*say* **punk**tew–ul) *adjective*
prompt or arriving at the correct time: 'please be *punctual* in your payments'.
punctually *adverb*
on time: 'she arrived *punctually* at 6 o'clock'.
Word Family: **punctuality** (*say* punktew–alli–tee), *noun*.

punctuate (*say* **punk**tew–ate) *verb*
to divide a sentence or paragraph with marks, such as full stops and commas, to make the meaning clearer.
Usage: 'he *punctuated* his speech with short silences' (= interrupted).
punctuation (*say* punktew–ay–sh'n) *noun*
the system or practice of punctuating.
[Latin *punctum* a point]

puncture (*say* **punk**cher) *noun*
a small hole made by a sharp object: 'he mended the *puncture* in his bicycle tyre'.
puncture *verb*
to prick or pierce something with a sharp object: 'the doctor *punctured* the skin with a needle'.

pundit *noun*
(*informal*) an expert.
[Hindi *pandit* learned]

pungent (*say* **pun**–j'nt) *adjective*
sharp or biting in taste or smell: 'a *pungent* curry'.
Usage: '*pungent* criticism' (= severe).
Word Family: **pungently**, *adverb*; **pungency**, *noun*.
[Latin *pungens* pricking]

punish *verb*
to make a person suffer pain or loss as a penalty for wrongdoing.
Usage: 'the fighter *punished* his opponent' (= treated roughly).
punishment *noun*
a) the act of punishing: 'the courts arrange for the *punishment* of crime'. b) a penalty: 'a *punishment* to fit the crime'.
punitive (*say* **pew**ni–tiv) *adjective*
inflicting or serving as punishment: '*punitive* action'.
Word Family: **punishable**, *adjective*, liable to punishment.
[Latin *poena* penalty]

punk (1) *noun*
(*informal*) a) a worthless person. b) a petty criminal.
Word Family: **punk**, *adjective*, worthless or wretched.

punk (2) *noun*
an extreme type of urban pop culture characterized by deliberate ugliness or aggressiveness in appearance, behaviour and language.
punk rock is a type of pop music reflecting punk attitudes. *Word Family:* **punk rocker**.

punnet (*say* **pun**nit) *noun*
a small basket, such as those used to hold strawberries.

punt (1) *noun*
1. a narrow, flat–bottomed boat which is moved along by pushing a long pole against the bottom of the river, etc.
2. *Football:* a kick in Rugby, in which the ball is dropped and kicked before it reaches the ground. Compare DROP KICK.
Word Family: **punt**, *verb*.

punt (2) *verb*
to gamble or bet, especially on horseraces.
Word Family: **punt**, *noun*; **punter**, *noun*, a person who punts.

puny (*say* **pew**–nee) *adjective*
small and weak.

pup *noun*
a puppy.

pupa (*say* **pew**pa) *noun*
plural is **pupae** (*say* **pew**–pee)

the resting stage between larva and adult in some insects, during which great developmental changes occur.
Compare CHRYSALIS.
Word Family: **pupate** (*say* pewpate), *verb*, to become a pupa; **pupation,** *noun.*
[Latin, doll]

pupil (1) (*say* **pewpil**) *noun*
a person who is learning, especially in a school.
[Latin *pupus* boy]

pupil (2) (*say* **pewpil**) *noun*
Anatomy: the clear area in the front of the eye, appearing as a black hole.

puppet (*say* **puppit**) *noun*
1. a hollow doll worn on the hand with its head and arms moved by the operator's fingers.
2. a doll whose legs and arms are moved with strings or sticks. Also called a **marionette.**
3. a person or group controlled or manipulated by another.
Word Family: **puppeteer,** *noun*, a person who manipulates puppets; **puppetry,** *noun.*

puppy *noun*
the young of a dog, shark, etc.
puppy fat
a fatness or plumpness in childhood or adolescence.
puppy love
also called **calf love**
the sentimental love or infatuation of young people.

purblind *adjective*
partially blind.

purchase (*say* **perchis**) *verb*
to buy.
Usage: 'they fought to *purchase* victory' (= achieve).
purchase *noun*
a) the act of buying: 'the *purchase* of goods by post'. b) something which is bought.
Word Family: **purchaser,** *noun.*

purdah *noun*
Hindu, Moslem: a) a curtain or screen hiding women of rank from the sight of men. b) the system of such seclusion.
[Persian]

pure *adjective*
1. unmixed with any other substance: '*pure* orange juice'.
2. abstract or theoretical: '*pure* maths'. Compare APPLIED under APPLY.
Usages:
a) 'you're talking *pure* nonsense' (= utter).
b) 'she writes with a *pure* style' (= clear, simple).
c) 'a *pure* mind' (= clean).
purity (*say* **pewri-tee**) *noun*
the state or quality of being pure.
Word Family: **purely,** *adverb.*
[Latin *purus*]

purée (*say* **pew-ray**) *noun*
Cooking: any fruit or vegetables mashed or sieved to a smooth cream.
[French, strained]

purgative (*say* **perga-tiv**) *adjective*
purging or cleansing, especially of the bowels.
purgative *noun*
something, such as a laxative, which cleanses or purges.

purgatory (*say* **perga-tree**) *noun*
Roman Catholic: a place or condition in which it is believed that the souls of dead people are purified.
Word Family: **purgatorial** (*say* perga-**tawriul**), *adjective*, a) of or like purgatory, b) cleansing.
[Latin *purgare* to cleanse]

purge (*say* **perj**) *verb*
to get rid of unclean or impure elements: a) 'to *purge* the body with medicine'; b) 'they *purged* the group of traitors'.
Usage: 'you will have to *purge* your crime' (= atone for).
purge *noun*
a cleansing or purifying: 'a political *purge* took place after the revolution'.
Word Family: **purgation** (*say* per-**gay**-sh'n), *noun.*

purify (*say* **pewri-fie**) *verb*
(**purified, purifying**)
to make pure.
Word Family: **purification,** *noun.*

purine (*say* **pew-reen**) *noun*
Biology: an organic compound whose derivatives, **adenine** and **guanine**, are important coding units in deoxyribonucleic acid (DNA).

purist (*say* **pewrist**) *noun*
1. a person who insists on purity of language, in the sense of abhorring colloquialisms, foreign words, neologisms, etc.
2. a person who insists on absolute perfection or purity in other fields.

puritan (*say* **pewri-t'n**) *noun*
a person who is excessively strict in regard to morals, religion, etc.

Word Family: **puritanical** (*say* pewri-**tanni**-k'l), *adjective*; **puritanically**, *adverb.*
[after the *Puritans*, the Dissenters (later Nonconformists) who separated from the Church of England in Cromwell's time]

purity (*say* **pewri**-tee) *noun*
Word Family: see PURE.

purl (1) *verb*
to flow or ripple with a murmuring sound, as a shallow stream over stones.
Word Family: **purl**, *noun*, the sound of this.

purl (2) *noun*
a stitch made by knitting into the back of a stitch.
Word Family: **purl**, *verb.*

purlieus (*say* **perl**-yooz) *plural noun*
the outskirts or environs.
[Old French *pourallee* beating the bounds (confused with *lieu* place)]

purlin *noun*
Building: a beam which crosses rafters and supports roofing material.

purloin *verb*
to steal.

purple *noun*
a reddish-violet colour.
purple *adjective*
of the colour purple.
Usage: '*purple* prose' (= ornate, elaborate).
[Greek *porphyra* a shellfish used in dyeing purple]

purport (*say* perport) *verb*
1. to claim: 'he *purports* to be an expert'.
2. to imply or appear to mean: 'his speech *purports* that there will be war'.
purport (*say* **perput** *or* **perport**) *noun*
the gist or meaning of something: 'what was the *purport* of his speech?'.

purpose (*say* **perpus**) *noun*
something which forms the basis or reason for some action, event, etc.: 'what is the *purpose* of your visit?'.
Usage: 'he is weak of *purpose*' (= will).
Phrases:
on purpose, deliberately.
to little purpose, with little or no result or effect.
to the purpose, 'what you say is not *to the purpose*' (= relevant).
purpose *verb*
to have as a purpose.

purposely *adverb*
1. on purpose: 'you hit her *purposely*'.
2. carefully or specifically: 'I *purposely* asked you to remember'.
Word Family: **purposeful**, *adjective*, a) having a purpose, b) determined or resolute; **purposefully**, *adverb*; **purposefulness**, *noun.*
[Latin *propositus* put forward]

purr *verb*
to make a low vibrating sound, as a cat does in pleasure or satisfaction.
Word Family: **purr**, *noun.*

purse *noun*
a small bag for carrying money, etc.
Usages:
a) 'that car is beyond my *purse*' (= finances).
b) 'the race was for a *purse* of £100' (= prize).
purse strings, power or authority to control the use of money.
purse *verb*
to draw into folds or wrinkles.
[Greek *byrsa* leather]

purser *noun*
a ship's officer in charge of accounts.

pursuance (*say* per-**sew**'nce) *noun*
in the pursuance of, in the carrying out of something, such as a plan, duty, etc.

pursuant *adjective*
pursuant to, in accordance or agreement with.

pursue (*say* pers-**yoo**) *verb*
(pursued, pursuing)
to go after in order to catch up with, capture or kill: 'the bank robbers were *pursued* by the police'.
Usages:
a) 'bad luck *pursues* her everywhere' (= follows, stays with).
b) 'I shall continue to *pursue* my enquiries' (= carry on).
c) 'he *pursued* pleasure all his life' (= sought, aimed at).
pursuit *noun*
a) the act of pursuing: 'we are in *pursuit* of the thieves'. b) an activity or profession: 'she spends her time in scientific *pursuits*'.
[Latin *persecutus* followed to the end]

purulent (*say* **pewra**-l'nt) *adjective*
containing or forming pus.
Word Family: **purulence**, *noun.*
[Latin *puris* of pus]

purvey (*say* pervay) *verb*
to supply or provide, especially food.
Word Family: **purveyor**, *noun*, a person who purveys; **purveyance**,

noun, a) the act of purveying, b) the goods and provisions purveyed.

pus *noun*
a thick, yellowish-white substance containing dead bacteria and white blood cells, produced in abscesses, pimples, boils, etc.
[Latin]

push (*say* p*u*sh) *verb*
1. to move by force: 'help me *push* the car uphill'.
Usages:
a) 'don't *push* your luck' (= rely too much on).
b) 'the shop is *pushing* a new product' (= promoting).
c) 'she *pushes* illegal drugs' (= sells).
d) 'the army *pushed* into the enemy territory' (= forced a way).
e) 'don't *push* me too hard or you'll be sorry' (= test, antagonize).
f) 'I'm *pushed* for time' (= troubled).
g) 'he's *pushing* 30' (= approaching).
2. *Sport:* to make a stiff, driving stroke at the ball in golf, cricket, etc.
Phrases:
push off, to move away or leave.
push on, to continue or proceed.
push *noun*
the act of pushing: 'give the car a *push*'.
Usages:
a) 'I'm in a bit of a *push*' (= difficulty).
b) 'she has a lot of *push*' (= energy, drive).
at a push, if absolutely necessary.
Word Family: **pushy**, *adjective*, assertive or aggressive.

pushbike *noun*
(*informal*) a bicycle.

pusher *noun*
a person or thing that pushes, such as a person who sells drugs illegally.

push-over *noun*
(*informal*) a) anything which is done very easily. b) a person, team, etc. that is easily defeated.

pushrod *noun*
a rod which is moved by the camshaft to operate the valves in an internal combustion engine.

pusillanimous (*say* pewsi-**lanni**-mus) *adjective*
cowardly or timid.
Word Family: **pusillanimously**, *adverb*; **pusillanimity** (*say* pew-silla-**nimmi**-tee), *noun*.
[Latin *pusillus* petty + *animus* spirit]

puss (1) *noun*
also called a **pussy**
a cat.

puss (2) *noun*
(*informal*) the face.

pussyfoot *verb*
to act cautiously or timidly.
Word Family: **pussyfoot**, *noun*.

pussywillow *noun*
the Goat willow or Sallow, so named for its silky catkins.

pustule (*say* **pust**-yool) *noun*
a small swelling in the skin, containing pus.

put (*say* p*u*t) *noun*
(**put, putting**)
1. to move something to a particular position: a) 'let's *put* the picture here'; b) '*put* that gun down'; c) 'she *put* money in the bank'.
2. to make someone do or experience something: a) 'he was *put* to death at dawn'; b) 'I'll *put* you to work in the garden'; c) 'you've *put* me to a lot of trouble'.
Usages:
a) '*put* your request in writing' (= express).
b) 'I *put* the crowd at 750' (= estimate).
c) 'she *put* £2 on the winner' (= bet).
d) 'I'll *put* a stop to this' (= make, force).
e) 'to what use will you *put* it?' (= apply).
f) 'she *put* the shot' (= hurled, cast).
g) 'I'd like to *put* a question' (= ask).
h) '*put* the idea to her after tea' (= suggest).
i) 'the boat *put* to sea' (= moved, went out).
Phrases:
put about, a) to circulate a rumour, etc.; b) (of a ship) to change direction.
put across, to communicate.
put aside, put by, to save or store up.
put down, a) to suppress; b) 'I *put* her actions *down* to shyness' (= attribute); c) 'the old horse was *put down*' (= destroyed); d) (*informal*) to criticize or belittle.
put in, a) 'what job have you *put in* for?' (= applied); b) 'we *put in* a good day's work' (= did).
put it past, 'I wouldn't *put it past* him' (= think it unlikely for).
put off, a) 'the meeting was *put off* until tomorrow' (= postponed); b) 'the smell *put* me *off* the meal' (= disconcerted from).
put on, a) 'he *put on* an air of humility' (= assumed); b) 'our school *puts on*

a play every year' (= stages). *Word Family*: **put-on,** ***noun,*** a pretence.
put out, a) '*put out* that fire' (= end, cause to stop burning); b) 'I hope we have not *put* you *out*' (= inconvenienced).
put up, a) 'who will *put up* the money?' (= provide); b) 'where will you *put up* for the night?' (= sleep); c) 'who *put* you *up* to this?' (= persuaded to do); d) 'the building was *put up* last year' (= erected).
put upon, 'don't let them *put upon* you' (= take advantage of).
put up with, to tolerate.
Word Family: **put,** ***noun,*** a throw or cast, especially when throwing a weight or shot.

putative (*say* **pew**ta-tiv) *adjective*
supposed or reputed: 'she is his *putative* mother'.

putrefy (*say* **pew**tri-fie) *verb*
(putrefied, putrefying)
to rot or decay.
Word Family: **putrefaction** (*say* pewtri-**fak**-sh'n), ***noun.***

putrid (*say* **pew**trid) *adjective*
rotten, decayed or foul-smelling.
[from Latin]

Putsch (*say* putch) ***noun***
a coup d'état.
[Swiss-German, a thrust, blow]

putt *verb*
Golf: to strike the ball towards the hole when on the green.
Word Family: **putt,** ***noun***; **putter,** ***noun,*** a straight, iron-headed club used for putting.

putty *noun*
1. a soft, easily moulded mixture, usually of linseed oil and ground chalk, used to secure window panes, fill holes, etc.
2. a person or thing that is easily influenced, formed, etc.

put-up job
(*informal*) a secretly planned deception.

puzzle *noun*
1. any toy or game requiring skill to solve, such as a crossword or jigsaw.
2. a person or thing that is hard to understand.
puzzle *verb*
1. to be or cause to be unable to understand: 'her strange behaviour *puzzles* me'.
2. to think deeply and work something out: 'I'll *puzzle* over the problem and give you an answer tomorrow'.

puzzlement *noun*
a) the state of being puzzled. b) something puzzling.
Word Family: **puzzler,** ***noun,*** a difficult question or problem.

Pygmy (*say* **pig**-mee) ***noun***
also spelt **Pigmy**
1. a member of a race of Negroes in equatorial Africa, only growing to about 1·5 m in height.
2. (*not capital*) any very small person or thing.
[Greek *pygmeios* dwarfish]

pyjamas (*say* pa-**jah**mas) ***plural noun***
a loose jacket and trousers for sleeping in.
[Urdu, leg clothes]

pylon (*say* **pie**-lon) ***noun***
a high tower or similar structure, especially one with a steel framework for carrying overhead cables.
[Greek, gateway]

pyorrhoea (*say* pie-a-**ree**-a) ***noun***
an infection of the gums, causing them to bleed easily and discharge pus around the base of the teeth.
[Greek *pyon* pus + *rhoia* flowing]

pyramid (*say* **pirr**a-mid) ***noun***
1. a solid or hollow body on a square base with sloping triangular faces which meet at the apex.
2. any structure, arrangement, etc. with this form.
Word Family: **pyramid, pyramidal** (*say* pirra-**midd**'l), *adjective.*
[Greek, probably from Egyptian]

pyre (*say* pire) ***noun***
a large pile of firewood, especially for burning a dead body.
[Greek *pyr* fire]

pyrethrin (*say* pie-**ree**-thren) ***noun***
a white powder used as a contact insecticide, obtained from the flower heads of a plant (called pyrethrum) related to the chrysanthemum.

pyretic (*say* pie-**rett**ik) *adjective*
of, relating to or producing fever.

Pyrex (*say* **pie**-reks) ***noun***
a heat-resistant glassware used for cooking.
[a trademark]

pyridoxine (*say* pie-ree-**dok**-seen) ***noun***
see VITAMIN B_6 under VITAMIN.

pyrimidine (*say* **pie**-rimma-deen) ***noun***
Biology: an organic compound whose derivatives, **cytosine, thymine** and

uracil, are important coding units in deoxyribonucleic acid (DNA).

pyrites, pyrite (*say* pie–**rye**–teez *and* **pie**–a–rite) *noun*
also called **fool's gold**
any natural sulphide of certain metals, such as of iron or copper, often golden in colour.
[Greek, of fire]

pyromania *noun*
a mania for setting fire to things.
[Greek *pyros* fire + MANIA]

pyrotechnics (*say* pie–ro–**tekniks**) *plural noun*
fireworks.
Word Family: **pyrotechnic,** *adjective.*

Pyrrhic victory (*say* **pirr**ik vikta–ree)
a victory gained at a great cost.
[after *Pyrrhus,* who defeated the Romans in a battle in 279 B.C. but lost many men]

python (*say* **pie**–th'n) *noun*
any of a group of large, non–poisonous snakes found mostly in Africa and western Asia, which coil around and crush their victims.
[after *Python,* a huge monster in Greek mythology]

Qq

qua (*say* kwa) *conjunction*
in the role of: 'I ask you *qua* doctor, not as my friend'.
[Latin]

quack (1) (*say* kwak) *verb*
to make the loud, harsh cry of a duck.
Word Family: **quack,** *noun.*

quack (2) (*say* kwak) *noun*
1. a person who pretends dishonestly to be competent in a skill, especially in medicine.
2. (*informal*) any medical doctor.
Word Family: **quack,** *adjective*; **quackery,** *noun.*

quad (1) (*say* kwod) *noun*
(*informal*) a quadrangle.

quad (2) (*say* kwod) *noun*
(*informal*) a quadruplet.

quadrangle (*say* **kwod**–rang'l) *noun*
1. a closed, plane figure with four straight sides, especially a square or rectangle.
2. a square, open space surrounded by buildings.
Word Family: **quadrangular** (*say* kwod–**rang**–gew–la), *adjective.*
[QUADRI + ANGLE]

quadrant (*say* **kwod**–r'nt) *noun*
1. a sector equal to a quarter of a circle, or a quarter of the circumference.
2. something with the shape of a quarter of a circle.
3. an instrument used to measure angles of altitude in astronomy, navigation, etc.
[Latin *quadrans* a fourth part]

quadraphonic (*say* kwodra–**fonn**ik) *adjective*
of or relating to sound reproduction through four distinct sound sources. Compare MONOPHONIC and STEREOPHONIC.
[QUADRI– + Greek *phoné* sound]

quadrate (*say* **kwod**–rit) *adjective*
square or rectangular.
Word Family: **quadrate,** *noun*; **quadrature** (*say* **kwodra**–cher), *noun,* the act of squaring.

quadratic (*say* kwod–**ratt**ik) *adjective*
1. square.
2. *Maths:* (of an expression) involving a variable whose power is not greater than 2.
Word Family: **quadratic,** *noun,* (Maths) a quadratic equation.

quadri–
a prefix meaning four, as in *quadrilateral.*

quadrilateral (*say* kwodri–**latt**a–r'l) *noun*
any closed, plane figure with four straight sides.
Word Family: **quadrilateral,** *adjective,* having four sides.
[QUADRI– + Latin *lateris* of a side]

quadrille (*say* kwod–**ril**) *noun*
a) a dance for four couples. b) the music for such a dance.
[French]

quadriplegic (*say* kwodri–**plee**jik) *adjective*
having the arms and legs paralysed.
Word Family: **quadriplegic,** *noun,* a person who is quadriplegic; **quadriplegia,** *noun.*
[QUADRI– + Greek *plegé* a stroke]

quadruped (*say* **kwod**roo–ped) *noun*
any animal with four feet.
Word Family: **quadruped,** *adjective,* having four feet.
[QUADRI– + Latin *pedis* of a foot]

quadruple (*say* kwod–**roo**–p'l) *adjective*
1. consisting of four parts.
2. being four times as big.
Word Family: **quadruple,** *verb*; **quadruple,** *noun.*

quadruplet (*say* kwod–**roo**plit) *noun*
any of four offspring born at one birth.

quadruplicate (*say* kwod–**roo**pli–kate) *verb*
to make four times as big.
quadruplicate (*say* kwod–**roo**pli–kit) *noun*
any of four identical things.

quaff (*say* kwof) *verb*
to drink at one go, or in large gulps.

quagmire (*say* **kwog**-mire) *noun*
an area of soft, muddy ground.

quail (1) (*say* kwale) *noun*
a small, sandy-coloured game-bird related to the partridge.

quail (2) (*say* kwale) *verb*
to feel or show fear.

quaint (*say* kwaint) *adjective*
1. old-fashioned in an attractive way: 'a *quaint* little old lady'.
2. curiously strange or unusual.
Word Family: **quaintly,** *adverb*; **quaintness,** *noun.*

quake (*say* kwake) *verb*
to shake or tremble: 'he *quaked* with fear'.
quake *noun*
1. (*informal*) an earthquake.
2. a shaking or trembling.

Quaker (*say* **kway**-ka) *noun*
a member of the Society of Friends, a Christian sect rejecting formal belief, etc. and emphasizing simple, personal experience of divine revelation.
Word Family: **Quakerish,** *adjective*; **Quakerism,** *noun.*
[from George Fox's bidding to a magistrate to '*quake* at the word of the Lord']

qualification (*say* kwolli-fikkay-sh'n) *noun*
1. a quality, accomplishment, etc. which makes a person suitable for a particular position or job.
2. a) the act of qualifying: 'her *qualification* of the statement'. b) something which qualifies or modifies.
[Latin *qualitas* quality + *facere* to make]

qualify (*say* **kwolli**-fie) *verb*
(qualified, qualifying)
1. to have the qualities or training necessary for something: a) 'he is 70 so he *qualifies* for the old age pension'; b) 'he *qualified* as a doctor after 6 years of studying'.
2. to modify or limit: a) 'adverbs *qualify* verbs'; b) 'please *qualify* your statement'.
Word Family: **qualifier,** *noun.*

quality (*say* **kwolli**-tee) *noun*
1. a characteristic.
2. character with respect to excellence: 'meat of the highest *quality* is very expensive'.
Word Family: **qualitative** (*say* **kwol**lita-tiv), *adjective,* of or concerning quality or characteristics; **qualitatively,** *adverb.*
[Latin]

qualm (*say* kwahm) *noun*
a) a sudden misgiving or apprehensive feeling. b) a pang of conscience.

quandary (*say* **kwon**da-ree) *noun*
a state of uncertainty or perplexity.

quanta (*say* **kwon**ta) *plural noun*
see QUANTUM.

quantify (*say* **kwonti**-fie) *verb*
(quantified, quantifying)
to express as a quantity.
[Latin *quantus* how much + *facere* to make]

quantity (*say* **kwonti**-tee) *noun*
1. a particular or indefinite amount of something.
2. a considerable amount: 'if you find gold in *quantity* you will soon be rich'.
Word Family: **quantitative** (*say* **kwon**-titta-tiv), *adjective,* of or concerning quantity.
[from Latin]

quantity surveyor
a person who estimates the quantities and costs of materials required for the construction of a building.

quantum (*say* **kwont**'m) *noun*
plural is **quanta**
1. quantity or amount.
2. a share or portion.
3. *Physics:* the fundamental unit of quantity for the energy of atoms or parts of atoms.
See QUANTUM THEORY.

quantum theory
Physics: the theory that the energy of electromagnetic waves (e.g. light) is emitted or absorbed not continuously but in separate packets (*quanta*) the size of which is determined by the frequency of the radiation.
See PLANCK'S CONSTANT and WAVE MECHANICS.

quarantine (*say* **kworr**'n-teen) *noun*
1. a period of isolation imposed on people, animals or plants thought to have an infectious disease.
2. a government system maintained at ports, etc. to prevent the spread of disease brought in from overseas.
Word Family: **quarantine,** *verb,* to put in or subject to quarantine.
[Italian *quarantina* 40 days (the original period of isolation)]

quark (*say* kwark) *noun*
Physics: any of three hypothetical elementary particles suggested to be the basis of all other elementary particles.

[from a phrase in James Joyce's 'Finnegans Wake', 'Three *quarks* for Muster Mark']

quarrel (1) (*say* **kworr**'l) *noun*
1. an angry argument.
2. a cause for argument or complaint: 'what is your *quarrel* with the plan?'.
Word Family: **quarrel** (**quarrelled, quarrelling**), *verb*; **quarrelsome,** *adjective*, tending to quarrel.
[Latin *querella* a complaint]

quarrel (2) (*say* **kworr**'l) *noun*
Medieval history: a short, heavy arrow used with a crossbow.

quarry (1) (*say* **kwor**ree) *noun*
a large pit, formed as a result of stone, etc. being extracted by digging and blasting.
Word Family: **quarry** (**quarried, quarrying**), *verb*, a) to obtain stone from a quarry, b) to dig a quarry.

quarry (2) (*say* **kwor**ree) *noun*
a person or animal that is hunted or pursued.

quart (*say* kwort) *noun*
Units: a) see BUSHEL. b) see GALLON.
[Latin *quartus* fourth]

quarter (*say* **kwor**ta) *noun*
1. any of four equal parts into which something is divided.
Usages:
a) 'the officers' *quarters*' (= lodgings).
b) 'he lives in the Latin *quarter* of Paris' (= district).
c) 'from what *quarter* is your information?' (= area, source).
d) 'the judge showed no *quarter* to the murderers' (= mercy).
2. *American:* a 25-cent coin.
3. a unit of mass equal to about 12·6 kg.
close quarters, a close position or contact.
quarter *verb*
1. to divide into four equal parts.
2. *Military:* to billet troops.
Word Family: **quarter,** *adjective.*

quarter day
one of the four days in the year when rents become payable and quarterly tenancies end or commence.

quarterdeck *noun*
the part of a ship's upper deck abaft (behind) the after (hindmost) superstructure.

quarterfinal *noun*
the last competitions or matches played before a semifinal.

quarterly (*say* **kwor**ta-lee) *adjective*
a) of or occurring once in three months. b) every three months.
quarterly *noun*
a magazine published four times a year.
Word Family: **quarterly,** *adverb.*

quartermaster *noun*
1. *Army:* the officer in charge of stores, rations, camp-siting, allocation of quarters, etc.
2. *Navy:* the petty officer in charge of steering, taking soundings, signalling, etc.

quarter note
Music: see CROTCHET.

Quarter Sessions
criminal courts formerly sitting at least quarterly; now superseded by the Crown Courts.

quarterstaff (*say* **kwor**ta-stahf) *noun*
plural is **quarterstaves**
Medieval history: a long, heavy pole with an iron tip, used by villagers as a weapon and in fencing contests.

quartet (*say* kwor-**tet**) *noun*
1. a) a group of four musicians. b) a musical composition for four musicians or instruments.
a **string quartet** consists of two violins, a viola and a cello.
2. any group of four people or things.

quartile (*say* **kwor**-tile) *noun*
Maths: a value which divides a distribution into four groups of equal frequency.

quarto (*say* **kwor**-toe) *noun*
a paper size achieved by folding a sheet into four.

quartz (*say* kworts) *noun*
a very common mineral, silicon dioxide (formula SiO_2), used in glass-making, abrasives, electronics, etc. See AMETHYST and CHALCEDONY.
[German]

quartz clock
an extremely precise clock deriving its accuracy from the constant frequency of the vibrations of a quartz crystal.

quasar (*say* **kway**-sar) *noun*
Astronomy: a small, very distant star-like source of intense radio energy emitted at much longer intervals than those of a pulsar.
[QUAS(i) (stell)AR (radio source)]

quash (1) (*say* kwosh) *verb*
to suppress completely.

quash (2) (*say* kwosh) *verb*
Law: to cancel a decision.

quasi (*say* **kwa**–zee *or* **kway**–zigh) *adjective*
having a resemblance only: 'a *quasi–victory*'.
Word Family: **quasi**, *adverb.*
[Latin, as if]

Quaternary (*say* kwa–**terna**–ree) *noun*
Geology: a geological period which began about 1·5 million years ago and contains the **Pleistocene** and **Holocene** (or **Recent**) epochs.
quaternary *adjective*
1. a) consisting of four. b) arranged in fours.
2. (*capital*) of or produced in the geological Quaternary.

quatrain (*say* **kwot**–rane) *noun*
Poetry: a stanza with four lines.

quattrocento (*say* kwotro **chen** toe) *noun*
the 15th century, especially in relation to Italian art of that time.
[Italian 400 (i.e. the 1400s)]

quaver (*say* **kway**–va) *verb*
to shake or tremble.
quaver *noun*
1. a sound that quavers.
2. *Music:* a note with a half of the time value of a crochet.
Word Family: **quavery,** *adjective,* trembling.

quay (*say* kee) *noun*
a wharf.

queasy (*say* **kwee**–zee) *adjective*
1. feeling nausea.
2. easily disturbed, shocked or made uncomfortable.
Word Family: **queasily**, *adverb*; **queasiness**, *noun.*

queen (*say* kween) *noun*
1. a) a female ruler of a country, usually inheriting her position and having authority throughout her lifetime. b) the wife of a king.
2. *Cards:* a playing card with a picture of a queen, usually having a value just below a king.
3. *Chess:* the most powerful piece which may move any number of squares in any direction.
4. a fertile female ant, bee, etc.
5. (*informal*) a male homosexual.
queen *verb*
queen it, to act in an imperious or overbearing manner.
Word Family: **queenly**, *adverb, adjective.*

queen mother
the widow of a king, who is also the mother of a reigning monarch.

Queen's Bench
a division of the High Court which deals with Common Law cases such as damages, debt, breach of contract, etc.

Queen's Counsel
also called a **Silk**
Law: a barrister of at least 10 years' standing, appointed as such by the Lord Chancellor and entitled to wear a silk gown in court.

Queen's English
a standard form of written and spoken English considered to be correct and desirable.

Queen's evidence
Law: any evidence given by an accomplice in a crime against others who took part.

queer *adjective*
1. strange or unusual: 'he has some *queer* ideas'.
2. suspicious: 'we could hear *queer* noises in the garden'.
Usage: 'the hot weather has made me feel *queer*' (= faint, unwell).
3. (*informal*) homosexual.
in queer street, (*informal*) in debt.
queer *noun*
(*informal*) a homosexual.
Word Family: **queerly**, *adverb*; **queerness**, *noun*; **queer**, *verb*, to spoil or ruin.

quell (*say* kwel) *verb*
to suppress or subdue.

quench (*say* kwench) *verb*
1. to put out fire, flames, etc.
2. to cool hot metal, etc. by plunging it in oil or water.
Usages:
a) 'to *quench* one's thirst' (= satisfy).
b) 'his anger was *quenched* by her mild, loving words' (= ended).

quern (*say* kwern) *noun*
a hand–operated mill for grinding corn.

querulous (*say* **kwerra**–lus) *adjective*
complaining.
Word Family: **querulously**, *adverb*; **querulousness**, *noun.*
[Latin]

query (*say* **kweer**–ee) *noun*
1. a question or enquiry.
2. *Grammar:* a question mark.
Word Family: **query** (**queried, querying**), *verb.*
[Latin *quaere* ask!]

quest (*say* kwest) *noun*
a search or pursuit: 'a *quest* for gold'.
Word Family: **quest**, *verb*, to search.
[Latin *quaesitus* searched for]

question (*say* **kwes**–ch'n) *noun*
1. a sentence which asks something.
2. a problem or subject for discussion, investigation, etc.
3. debate or dispute: 'your argument is open to *question*'.
Usage: 'it is simply a *question* of turning up on time' (= matter).
Phrases:
beyond question, without a doubt.
call in question, to challenge or cast doubt upon.
in question, under consideration.
out of the question, impossible.
Word Family: **question**, *verb*; **questionable**, *adjective*, open to question; **questionably**, *adverb*; **questioning**, *adjective*, implying a question; **questioningly**, *adverb*.
[Latin *quaestio* a seeking]

question mark
also called a **query** or **interrogation mark**
a punctuation mark (?), used when asking a question or expressing doubt.

questionnaire (*say* kwes–ch'n–**air**) *noun*
a set of questions, usually printed on a form, designed to obtain a person's opinion or gather information for a survey, statistics, etc.
[French]

queue (*say* kew) *noun*
1. a line of people, vehicles, etc. awaiting their turn.
2. a single plait or pigtail of hair worn hanging down behind.
Word Family: **queue (queued, queuing)**, *verb*, to form in a line.
[French, tail]

quibble (*say* **kwibb**'l) *verb*
to make petty distinctions or argue about unimportant details.
Word Family: **quibble**, *noun*, a petty distinction.

quick (*say* kwik) *adjective*
1. moving rapidly.
2. being done in a short time: 'a *quick* meal'.
Usage: 'he has a *quick* temper' (= impatient).
3. understanding or learning with speed: 'he is *quick* at figures'.

quick *noun*
1. the tender skin under the nails.
2. living people: 'the *quick* and the dead'.
cut to the quick, to hurt or upset deeply.
Word Family: **quick, quickly**, *adverbs*; **quickness**, *noun*.

quicken (*say* **kwikk**'n) *verb*
1. to make or become more rapid.
2. to excite or stimulate feelings, etc.

quickie (*say* **kwik**–ee) *noun*
(*informal*) something made or done very quickly.

quicklime *noun*
also called **unslaked lime**
a white substance, calcium oxide (formula CaO), formed by heating limestone and used to make mortar or cement.

quicksand *noun*
an area of wet sand which yields to pressure and tends to suck down any object resting on its surface.

quicksilver *noun*
mercury.

quickstep *noun*
a fast ballroom dance.

quid (1) (*say* kwid) *noun*
a lump of tobacco, etc. for chewing.

quid (2) (*say* kwid) *noun*
plural is **quid**
(*informal*) a one-pound note.

quid pro quo (*say* kwid pro kwo)
one thing in return for another.
[Latin]

quiescent (*say* kwee–**ess**'nt) *adjective*
inactive or at rest.
Word Family: **quiescently**, *adverb*; **quiescence**, *noun*.
[Latin]

quiet (*say* **kwy**–et) *adjective*
having little or no sound or movement.
Usages:
a) 'a *quiet* afternoon reading' (= peaceful, tranquil).
b) 'the *quiet* colours added warmth to the room' (= not bright).
on the quiet, secretly.
Word Family: **quiet**, *noun*, peace or freedom from disturbance; **quiet, quieten**, *verbs*, to make or become quiet; **quietly**, *adverb*; **quietness**, *noun*; **quietude**, *noun*, the state of being calm or still.
[Latin *quietus* at rest]

quill (*say* kwil) *noun*
1. the hard base of a feather where it is attached to the bird.

2. a feather used as a pen for writing. 3. one of the spines on a hedgehog or porcupine.

quilt (*say* kwilt) *noun*
a) a bedspread with padding which is stitched into place between two layers of fabric. b) any bedspread.
Word Family: **quilt**, *verb*, to pad and stitch fabric into a quilt or quilt-like form; **quilted**, *adjective.*

quin (*say* kwin) *noun*
(*informal*) a quintuplet.

quince (*say* kwince) *noun*
a yellow, pear-shaped fruit with an acid taste, used in jams and jellies.

quinine (*say* kwin-**een**) *noun*
a bitter, colourless drug used in medicine to treat and prevent malaria.

quinquennial (*say* kwin-**kwenniul**) *adjective*
of, for or occurring every five years.
[Latin *quinque* five + *annus* year]

quinsy (*say* **kwin**-zee) *noun*
an abscess which causes swelling of the tonsils.
[Greek *kynagkhé*]

quintessence (*say* kwin-**tess**'nce) *noun*
1. the most essential part of a thing. 2. a pure or perfect example: 'she is the *quintessence* of beauty'.
Word Family: **quintessential** (*say* kwinti-**sen**-sh'l), *adjective.*
[Medieval Latin *quinta essentia* the fifth element, of which the heavenly bodies were supposed to consist]

quintet (*say* kwin-**tet**) *noun*
1. a) a group of five musicians. b) a musical composition for five musicians or instruments.
2. any group of five people or things.
[Latin *quintus* fifth]

quintuplet (*say* kwin-**chup**-lit *or* kwin-**choop**-lit) *noun*
any of five offspring born at one birth.

quip (*say* kwip) *noun*
a witty or sarcastic remark.
Word Family: **quip** (**quipped, quipping**), *verb.*

quire (1) (*say* kwire) *noun*
a measure of paper containing 24 sheets.

quire (2) (*say* kwire) *noun*
an old word for choir.

quirk (*say* kwerk) *noun*
1. a peculiarity of manner or action.
2. a sudden twist or turn.
Word Family: **quirky**, *adjective.*

quisling (*say* **kwiz**-ling) *noun*
a person who works with an enemy occupying his country.
[after *V. Quisling*, 1887–1945, a Norwegian army major who helped the Germans in World War 2]

quit (*say* kwit) *verb*
(**quit** or **quitted, quitting**)
1. to leave or go away.
2. (*informal*) to stop: '*quit* talking and do some work'.
Word Family: **quitter**, *noun*, (informal) a person who gives up easily.

quite *adverb*
1. completely or entirely: 'he has *quite* recovered'.
2. actually or really: 'I find the job *quite* a bore'.
3. (*informal*) to some extent: 'she is *quite* pretty, but not beautiful'.

quits (*say* kwits) *adjective*
equal by paying or retaliating.
call it quits, to end or give up a contest, quarrel, etc.

quiver (1) (*say* **kwivva**) *verb*
to tremble.
Word Family: **quiver**, *noun*; **quivery**, *adjective.*

quiver (2) (*say* **kwivva**) *noun*
a container for arrows.

quixotic (*say* kwik-**sottik**) *adjective*
extravagantly romantic or idealistic.
[after *Don Quixote*, a chivalrous but impractical hero in a romantic novel by Cervantes]

quiz (*say* kwiz) *verb*
(**quizzed, quizzing**)
to question closely.
quiz *noun*
plural is **quizzes**
1. a test, especially of general knowledge.
2. a questioning.

quizzical (*say* **kwizzi**-k'l) *adjective*
1. suggesting puzzlement.
2. teasing or mocking.
Word Family: **quizzically**, *adverb.*

quizzing glass
a monocle.

quoin (*say* koyn) *noun*
also spelt **coign**
a projecting brick or stone at the corner of a building.

quoit (*say* koyt) *noun*
1. a flat ring made of rope or iron.
2. (*plural, used with singular verb*) a game in which such rings are aimed and thrown around a peg.

quondam *adjective*
an old word for former.
[Latin]

quorum *noun*
the least number of people needed to make a formal meeting valid, e.g. in parliament or a club.
Usage: 'he surrounds himself with a *quorum* of supporters' (= select group).
[Latin, of whom (from a legal phrase)]

quota (*say* **kwo**–ta) *noun*
an allotment: 'what is your *quota* of work?'.
Usage: 'what is the import *quota*?' (= maximum number allowed).
[Latin *quot*? how many?]

quotation (*say* kwo–**tay**–sh'n) *noun*
1. a) the act of quoting. b) the passage that is quoted.
2. a statement of the current price of something.

quotation marks
also called **inverted commas**
the punctuation marks ('....') used to indicate spoken words or a quotation.

quote (*say* kwote) *verb*
1. to repeat or copy exactly the writing or speech of another, usually with acknowledgement.
2. to refer to for proof: 'I could *quote* many more examples'.
3. to state a price of goods or services: 'he *quoted* £50 for the repair'.
Word Family: **quote**, *noun.*

quoth (*say* kwothe) *verb*
an old word for said.

quotidian (*say* kwot**tiddi**–an) *adjective*
daily.
[Latin]

quotient (*say* **kwo**–sh'nt) *noun*
Maths: the result of division. Compare PRODUCT.
[Latin *quotiens*? how many times?]

Rr

rabbet *noun*
a joint made by cutting a step-shaped hole at the end of one piece, into which the matching end of the other piece is fitted, usually at right angles.
[for REBATE]

rabbi (*say* **rab**-eye) *noun*
plural is **rabbis**
a Jewish teacher of the Law, especially the ordained spiritual leader of a synagogue.
Word Family: **rabbinical** (*say* rab-**inni**-k'l), *adjective*; **rabbinate** (*say* **rabbi**-nate), *noun*, a) the office of a rabbi, b) rabbis considered as a group.
[Hebrew, my master]

rabbit *noun*
1. any of various small, long-eared, grass-eating mammals, often kept and bred as pets.
2. the flesh or fur of this animal.
Word Family: **rabbit**, *verb*, to hunt for rabbits.

rabble *noun*
a disorderly crowd.

rabble-rouser *noun*
a person who tries to incite mobs by arousing prejudices and passions.

Rabelaisian (*say* rabba-**lay**-*zh*'n) *adjective*
characterized by bawdy and boisterous humour.
[after *F. Rabelais,* 1494?–1553, a French satirist]

rabid (*say* **rab**-id) *adjective*
1. extreme, e.g. in opinion, etc.: 'he is a *rabid* conservative'.
2. having rabies.

rabies (*say* **ray**-beez) *noun*
an infectious, viral disease of dogs, cats, etc. that may be transmitted to man if bitten, causing convulsions, delirium, frothing at the mouth and a terror of water.
[Latin, madness, rage]

raccoon (*say* ra-**koon**) **racoon** *noun*
a small, flesh-eating American mammal with a bushy tail ringed with black and white.

race (1) *noun*
1. a competition of speed.
2. (*plural*) a series of such competitions, especially between horses.
Usage: 'the *race* for the presidency' (= competition, contest).
3. a) a swift current of water. b) a channel carrying water.
4. *Engineering:* the groove in which ballbearings or a shuttle move.
race *verb*
1. to compete in a race.
2. to move or cause to move, operate, etc. at a high speed.
Word Family: **racer,** *noun,* a person or thing that races.

race (2) *noun*
1. a group of people having or supposed to have common ancestors and with similar physical characteristics.
2. any group which shares some distinctive features: 'the human *race*'.
3. *Biology:* see SUBSPECIES.
Word Family: **racial** (*say* **ray**-sh'l), *adjective*; **racially,** *adverb.*

racecourse *noun*
also called a **racetrack**
a place where races, especially horseraces, are held.

racily (*say* **ray**sa-lee) *adverb*
Word Family: see RACY.

racism (*say* **ray**-sizm) *noun*
also called **racialism**
a) any discrimination based on the supposed differences between races. b) any political or social system based on such discrimination.
Word Family: **racist, racialist,** *nouns, adjectives.*

rack (1) *noun*
1. a framework or shelf: 'a luggage *rack* in a train'.
2. a bar with teeth on one side, which engages with the teeth of a pinion, etc. A **rack-and-pinion** is a system for converting circular motion into

linear motion, especially in the steering assembly of a motor vehicle.
3. a device for torture which stretches the body.
on the rack, suffering severely.
rack *verb*
1. to strain: 'I *racked* my brain for a solution'.
2. to cause to suffer distress: 'she was *racked* with pain'.

rack (2) *noun*
also spelt **wrack**
rack and ruin, a state of neglect and collapse.

rack (3) *noun*
see WRACK (2).

rack (4) *verb*
to draw off wine, etc. from its sediment.

rack (5) *noun*
a cut of lamb, veal, etc. from the neck of the animal.

rack-and-pinion *noun*
see RACK (1).

racket (1) *noun*
1. a loud noise or uproar.
2. any scheme or activity to make money illegally or by exploitation.
Word Family: **racketeer** (*say* rakka-**teer**), *noun*, a person engaged in an illegal racket.

racket (2) *noun*
also spelt **racquet**
a long-handled bat with interlaced nylon or catgut for hitting the ball in tennis, squash, etc.

rackety (*say* **rakki**-tee) *adjective*
noisy.

rack rent
an extortionate rent.

raconteur (*say* rakon-**ter**) *noun*
a person skilled in telling stories or anecdotes.
[French]

racoon (*say* ra-**koon**) *noun*
a raccoon.

racquet (*say* **rakk**it) *noun*
see RACKET (2).

racy (*say* **ray**-see) *adjective*
1. spirited or vivid: 'it was a *racy* story about mountaineers'.
2. risqué: '*racy* jokes'.
Word Family: **racily**, *adverb*; **raciness**, *noun*.

rad *noun*
a unit of dosage for radiation.

radar (*say* **ray**-dar) *noun*
a device used to track or locate objects which are out of sight, by measuring the time, etc. for a microwave to return from the object.
[RA(dio) D(etection) A(nd) R(anging)]

radial (*say* **ray**-dee-al) *adjective*
1. having or arranged like rays or radii.
2. *Anatomy:* of or relating to the radius of the forearm.
radial *noun*
short form of **radial-ply tyre**
a thin-walled pneumatic tyre with a reinforced tread and fabric running across the line of the tyre.
[Latin *radius* a wheel spoke, a ray]

radian (*say* **ray**-dee-an) *noun*
the SI unit of plane angle, equal to 57·296°, which is the angle made at the centre of a circle by an arc the same length as the radius. See UNITS in grey pages.

radiant (*say* **ray**-dee-ant) *adjective*
1. emitting or consisting of heat, light or other radiation.
2. bright or lit up: 'a *radiant* smile'.
Word Family: **radiantly**, *adverb*; **radiance**, *noun*.
[Latin *radians* emitting beams]

radiate (*say* **ray**-dee-ate) *verb*
1. to spread out like rays from a centre.
2. to give off rays, waves or particles.
Usage: 'she *radiates* health' (= has an obvious air of).
Word Family: **radiation**, *noun*, a) the act of radiating, b) (Physics) any rays, energy or particles which are radiated.

radiation sickness
a disease due to exposure to large doses of radioactive matter or radiation, causing diarrhoea, anaemia and haemorrhage.

radiator (*say* **ray**-dee-ayta) *noun*
1. a person or thing that radiates.
2. any of various heating appliances, usually electric.
3. a device for cooling liquids consisting of fine tubes through which the liquid flows, being cooled by air passed over the tubes: 'a motor car *radiator*'.

radical (*say* **raddi**-k'l) *adjective*
1. fundamental: 'the plan failed because of a *radical* fault'.
2. favouring basic social or political change: 'his *radical* ideas upset his conservative parents'.
3. *Maths:* of or relating to a root.
4. *Biology:* of or arising from the root or the base of the stem of a plant.
radical *noun*
1. a person who holds political beliefs which favour fundamental reform.

2. *Maths:* a quantity expressed as a root, such as $\sqrt{3x - 1}$.
3. *Chemistry:* an atom or group of atoms, such as the methyl group, which acts as a unit in a chemical reaction and is incapable of existing independently beyond the reaction. Compare ION.
Word Family: **radically**, *adverb.*
[Latin *radicis* of a root]

radicalism *noun*
the principles or practices of political radicals.

radices (*say* **ray**di-seez) *plural noun*
see RADIX.

radicle (*say* **raddi**-k'l) *noun*
Biology: the root of an embryo of a seed plant.

radii (*say* **ray**-dee-eye) *plural noun*
the plural of **radius**.

radio (*say* **ray**-dee-o) *noun*
1. a) the use of electromagnetic waves to send sounds or pictures without wires. b) sound broadcasting.
2. a radio receiver. Also called a **wireless** or **transistor**.
radio *verb*
(radioed, radioing)
to send a message by radio.
[Latin *radius* a wheel spoke, a ray]

radioactivity
(*say* ray-dee-o-ak-**tivvi**-tee) *noun*
Physics: the property of some atomic nuclei to break down into simpler nuclei and release alpha particles, beta particles, neutrinos or gamma rays.
Word Family: **radioactive** (*say* ray-dee-o-**aktiv**), *adjective.*

radio astronomy
the use of radio telescopes to pick up stellar radiations, thus making it possible to map regions of space which are inaccessible to optical instruments because of the presence of interstellar matter, and leading to the discovery of quasars, pulsars, etc.

radiobiology
(*say* ray-dee-o-by-**olla**-jee) *noun*
the study of the effect of radiation on organisms.

radiocarbon dating
short form is **carbon dating**
a method of estimating the age of ancient animal or plant products by measuring their content of radioactive carbon.

radioelement
(*say* ray-dee-o-**elli**-m'nt) *noun*
a) a radioactive element. b) a radioactive isotope.

radiogram (*say* **ray**-dee-o-gram) *noun*
1. an instrument consisting of a radio and a record-player.
2. a wireless telegram.
3. an X-ray photograph.

radiography (*say* ray-dee-**ogra**-fee) *noun*
the production of pictures and images, especially of the interior of the body, using X-rays or other radioactive rays.
Word Family: **radiographer**, *noun.*

radioisotope
(*say* ray-dee-o-**eye**-so-tope) *noun*
a radioactive isotope, usually produced artifically.

radiological (*say* ray-dee-o-**loji**-k'l) *adjective*
1. of or relating to radioactive substances.
2. of or relating to radiology.

radiology (*say* ray-dee-**olla**-jee) *noun*
the study of X-rays and their uses in medicine.
Word Family: **radiologist**, *noun.*

radio telescope
a device for picking up and focusing radio signals from objects in space.

radiotherapy
(*say* ray-dee-o-**therra**-pee) *noun*
the treatment of disease, especially cancer, using X-rays or other radioactive substances.

radiowave *noun*
any electromagnetic wave suitable for carrying sounds or pictures through the air from a transmitter to a receiver.

radish (*say* **raddish**) *noun*
a small, red-skinned root used as a vegetable, usually eaten raw.

radium (*say* **ray**-dee-um) *noun*
element number 88, a rare, naturally occurring, radioactive metal used in the treatment of cancer. See ALKALINE EARTH METAL.
See CHEMICAL ELEMENTS in grey pages.
[Latin *radius* a ray]

radius (*say* **ray**-dee-us) *noun*
plural is **radii** (*say* **ray**-dee-eye)
1. *Maths:* a) a straight line drawn from the centre of a circle to any point on its circumference, or from the centre of a sphere to its surface. b) the length of such a line.
Usage: 'they searched within a 10 km *radius* of the city' (= range, distance).
2. *Anatomy:* the shorter of the two long bones in a forearm or foreleg.

radius vector
plural is **radius vectors**
Maths: a straight line joining a fixed point to a variable point, such as a point to the origin of a graph.

radix (*say* **ray–diks**) *noun*
plural is **radices** (*say* **rayda–seez**) or **radixes**
Maths: a number used as the base of a system of numbers, logarithms, etc.
[Latin, a root]

radon (*say* **raydon**) *noun*
element number 86, a rare, radioactive, inert gas. See CHEMICAL ELEMENTS in grey pages.

raffia *noun*
a fibre obtained from a palm and used to make baskets, hats, etc.
[Malagasy]

raffish *adjective*
disreputable.

raffle *noun*
a form of lottery where the winners receive objects as prizes, usually held to raise money for a charity, etc.
Word Family: **raffle**, *verb*, to dispose of in a raffle.

raft (*say* rahft) *noun*
a floating platform used for moving people or goods over water, or moored for use by divers, etc.

rafter (*say* **rahf**ta) *noun*
a timber support in a roof.

rag (1) *noun*
1. a scrap of fabric, especially one that is old or torn.
2. (*plural*) any old or torn clothes.
3. (*informal*) a newspaper or magazine, especially one considered to be of poor quality.
4. a piece of music in ragtime.
glad rags, (*informal*) fine clothes.

rag (2) *verb*
(ragged, ragging)
to tease or play jokes on.
Word Family: **rag**, *noun*, a prank, especially one played by students.

ragamuffin *noun*
a ragged or dirty person, especially a child.

rag–and–bone man
a man who goes round collecting old clothes, etc.

rage *noun*
1. violent anger.
Usage: 'the *rage* of the fire made it difficult to fight' (= violence, fury).
2. a craze: 'in winter skiing is the *rage*'.

rage *verb*
1. to act or speak in rage.
2. to proceed with great violence or intensity: 'the fire *raged* out of control'.

ragged (*say* **raggid**) *adjective*
1. tattered or wearing tattered clothes.
Usage: 'we were disappointed at the *ragged* performance' (= faulty).
2. having rough or sharp projections.

raglan *adjective*
(of a sleeve) continuing up to the neck and joining the garment by two diagonal seams.
[after *Lord Raglan*, 1788–1855, a British field marshal]

ragout (*say* **rag–oo**) *noun*
a well–seasoned meat and vegetable stew.
[from French]

ragtime *noun*
a style of jazz with a syncopated rhythm, first popular in America in about 1900.

rag trade
(*informal*) the clothes–manufacturing trade.

ragwort *noun*
a herbal weed with yellow daisy–like flowers.

raid *noun*
a sudden, surprise attack.
Word Family: **raid**, *verb*; **raider**, *noun*.

rail (1) *noun*
1. a horizontal bar of metal or wood used as a support, in a fence, etc.
2. either of two steel girders on which a train, tram, etc. travels. Also called a **track**.
3. the railway: 'we travelled by *rail* to Newcastle'.
Word Family: **rail**, *verb*, a) to furnish with a rail or rails, b) to send by railway.

rail (2) *verb*
to complain or abuse bitterly.

rail (3) *noun*
any of a group of short–winged wading birds, some of which are unable to fly.

railhead *noun*
the farthest point to which a railway has been laid.

railing *noun*
(*often plural*) a barrier made of rails.

raillery (*say* **rayla–ree**) *noun*
any good–natured teasing or ridicule in conversation.

railroad *noun*
American: a railway.
railroad *verb*
to send by railway.
Usage: 'he was *railroaded* out of office by his enemies' (= forced, pushed).

railway *noun*
1. a pair of parallel steel rails, or a system of such rails, designed to carry vehicles with flanged wheels.
2. a) a company or organization which owns or operates such a system. b) the whole property of such a company, including track, vehicles and buildings.

raiment (*say* **ray**–m'nt) *noun*
an old word for clothes.

rain *noun*
1. *Weather:* a) drops of water which fall to the ground from the clouds. b) a shower of such drops.
2. anything falling thickly: 'a *rain* of blows upon his head'.
right as rain, perfectly all right.
Word Family: **rain,** *verb,* to fall as or like rain.

rainbow *noun*
a) an arc of the colours of the spectrum, especially one seen in the sky, due to the reflection and refraction of light in drops of water. b) any similar arc of colours.
Word Family: **rainbow,** *adjective,* multicoloured.

rainbow trout
a large brightly coloured trout, originally from the American West Coast.

rain check
American: (*informal*) a postponement, especially of accepting an invitation. [from *rain check* a ticket for future use given to sporting spectators when an event is postponed owing to rain]

raincoat *noun*
a waterproof coat.

rainfall *noun*
1. the total amount of rain, snow, etc. which falls at a location during a given period. Also called **precipitation.**
2. a shower of rain.

rainforest *noun*
the dense, hot, evergreen forest found in equatorial areas which have heavy rainfall and no dry season.

rain shadow
an area where the rainfall is light, because nearby hills or mountains shelter it from rain-bearing winds.

rainy *adjective*
wet with or bringing rain.
a rainy day, a time of need in the future.

raise (*say* raze) *verb*
1. to move to a higher position.
2. to build: 'a monument was *raised* in his honour'.
Usages:
a) 'to *raise* from the dead' (= cause to appear or rise).
b) 'it's time you got married and *raised* a family' (= brought up).
c) 'his salary was *raised* by £5 a week' (= increased).
d) 'your helpful advice *raised* our spirits' (= cheered, improved).
e) 'we helped to *raise* money for the Red Cross' (= collect).
f) 'he *raised* several objections' (= introduced).
g) (*informal*) 'I rang all morning but could not *raise* him' (= contact).
h) 'I *raised* my eyes from the book' (= turned upwards).
i) 'he *raised* the alarm' (= made known, caused).
j) 'she *raised* a terrible cry' (= uttered).
raise hell, (*informal*) to make a great fuss.
raise *noun*
a lifting.

raisin (*say* **ray**–z'n) *noun*
a dried grape.

raison d'être (*say* rayzon **det**ra)
the chief purpose or justification for the existence of something.
[French]

raj (*say* rahj) *noun*
Indian history: rule: 'the British *raj*'.
[Hindi, reign]

rajah (*say* **rah**–jah) **raja** *noun*
a title for a ruler in India.
[Hindi]

rake (1) *noun*
1. a long-handled tool with a comb-like row of teeth for levelling earth, gathering grass, etc.
2. any similar implement.
rake *verb*
to gather or remove with, or as if with, a rake.
Usages:
a) 'his eyes *raked* the crowd' (= searched, examined).
b) 'gunfire *raked* the ship' (= struck along the length of).
rake up, a) 'I could only *rake up* £3 for the ticket' (= gather, collect); b)

'the newspaper has *raked up* another scandal' (= revealed).

rake (2) *noun*
a self-indulgent or immoral man, especially one in fashionable or sophisticated society.

rake (3) *noun*
the inclination from the vertical or horizontal, as of a ship's mast.

rake-off *noun*
(*informal*) a commission or share of profits, especially if dishonest or illegal.

rakish (*say* **ray**-kish) *adjective*
1. jaunty or smart: 'a *rakish* hat'.
2. like a sophistocated person or rake.
Word Family: **rakishly**, *adverb*; **rakishness**, *noun.*

rally (1) *verb*
(rallied, rallying)
to bring or come together for a common purpose: 'to *rally* support for a cause'.
Usage: 'she began to *rally* after weeks of fever' (= recover strength, improve).
rally round, to give support or assistance to.
rally *noun*
1. a mass meeting, especially one to promote a cause.
2. a reassembling.
3. *Commerce:* a rise in price and trading after a decline.
4. *Tennis:* an exchange of strokes between players before a point is scored.
5. a race for motor cars, etc. in which skill at following rules and schedules is more important than speed.

rally (2) *verb*
(rallied, rallying)
to tease.

ram *noun*
1. a male sheep.
2. *Astrology:* (*capital*) see ARIES.
3. any of various devices for battering, crushing or forcing.
ram *verb*
(rammed, ramming)
to strike or force with heavy blows.
Usage: 'he *rammed* his hat on' (= pushed firmly).

Ramadan (*say* ramma-**dan**) *noun*
the ninth month of the Moslem year when no food or drink may be taken during daylight.

ramble *verb*
to walk in a wandering or aimless manner.
Usage: 'the vine *rambles* over the wall' (= winds irregularly).
ramble on, to talk in a disjointed way.
Word Family: **ramble**, *noun*, a leisurely walk; **rambler**, *noun*, a person or thing that rambles, such as a climbing rose.

ramekin (*say* **ramma**-kin) *noun*
also spelt **ramequin**
a) a cheese and egg dish. b) the small, deep dish with a handle, in which it is baked or served.

ramification (*say* rammifi-**kay**-sh'n) *noun*
a) the act of branching out or dividing. b) a branch or extending part.
Usage: 'this decision will have widespread *ramifications*' (= consequences, effects).
Word Family: **ramify** (*say* **rammi**-fie), **(ramified, ramifying)**, *verb*, to divide or cause to divide into branches.
[Latin *ramus* a branch + *facere* to make]

ramjet *noun*
a jet engine in which the air entering the engine is compressed before combustion due to the speed of the aircraft.

ramp *noun*
a sloping surface connecting two different levels.
[French *ramper* to creep or crawl]

rampage (*say* ram-**page**) *verb*
to act or move about violently or furiously.
Word Family: **rampage**, *noun*, any violent or wild action or behaviour.

rampant *adjective*
1. wild or uncontrolled: 'the garden was choked by *rampant* weeds'.
2. *Heraldry:* (of an animal) rearing up on its hind legs.

rampart *noun*
1. an earth mound, usually with a wall on it, built for protection.
2. anything used for protection or defence.

ramrod *noun*
1. a) a long rod formerly used for ramming the charge down the barrel of a muzzle-loading gun. b) a long rod for cleaning the barrel of a rifle.
2. (*informal*) a stiffly formal person.
Word Family: **ramrod**, *adjective*, stiff or severe.

ramshackle *adjective*
badly made or liable to collapse: 'a *ramshackle* old house'.

ran *verb*
the past tense of the verb **run**.

ranch *noun*
American: a large farm, especially one for cattle.
Word Family: **ranch**, *verb*, to own or manage a ranch; **rancher**, *noun*, a person who owns or works on a ranch.
[Spanish *rancho* a communal mess]

rancid (*say* **ran**sid) *adjective*
unpleasantly stale.
Word Family: **rancidness**, *noun*.
[Latin *rancidus* stinking]

rancour (*say* **ran**ka) *noun*
in America spelt **rancor**
a bitter resentment or hatred.
Word Family: **rancorous**, *adjective*; **rancorously**, *adverb*.

rand *noun*
1. the basic unit of money in South Africa.
2. *South African:* a low ridge of hills.
3. (*capital*) the Witwatersrand, the main gold-mining area, near Johannesburg.
[Afrikaans, edge]

random *adjective*
having no definite order, aim or method.
random *noun*
at random, in an unmethodical way.
Word Family: **randomly**, *adverb*; **randomness**, *noun*; **randomize**, **randomise**, *verb*.
[Old French *randir* to gallop]

random sampling
Maths: a method of selecting members from a population so that each one has an equal chance of being chosen.

randy *adjective*
(*informal*) sexually aroused.

ranee (*say* **rah**-nee) *noun*
also spelt **rani**
a) the wife of a rajah, king or prince in India, etc. b) a reigning queen or princess in India.
[Hindi]

rang *verb*
the past tense of the verb **ring (2)**.

range *noun*
1. the limits between which something may exist, occur or vary: a) 'a *range* of prices'; b) 'a *range* of colours'; c) 'the *range* of a singing voice'.
2. a line or group of mountains.
3. an area on which shooting takes place: 'a rifle *range*'.
4. the distance to which something is effective or will operate: a) 'hearing *range*'; b) 'the *range* of an aircraft'.
5. *American:* a large area of open land for grazing, hunting, etc.
6. a stove having a flat surface with coils or plates for cooking, an oven, etc.

range *verb*
1. to put or arrange: 'he *ranged* the books in order of height'.
Usages:
a) '*range* the plants botanically' (= classify).
b) 'this species *ranges* across the countryside' (= is found, occurs).
c) 'our prices *range* between £10 and £15' (= vary).
2. to move or travel through or about: 'wild herds *ranged* across the land in search of food'.
Word Family: **ranger**, *noun*, a warden who patrols and guards a forest, etc.

rangefinder *noun*
any of various devices for determining the distance of an object, such as that used in focusing a camera.

rangy (*say* **rane**-jee) *adjective*
having slender, long legs.

rank (1) *noun*
1. a position in society or any group or organization: a) 'a poet of the highest *rank*'; b) 'the *rank* of general'.
2. a high position, place or status: 'he is a man of *rank* in the literary world'.
3. (*usually plural*) a row, line or series: '*ranks* of bright flowers lined the garden bed'.
Usage: 'he left the party's *ranks* to form an independent movement' (= membership, organization).
4. (*plural*) ordinary soldiers as distinct from officers, etc.
Phrases:
pull rank, to use one's high position to achieve one's aim.
rank and file, the main body of an organization, as distinct from its leaders.
Word Family: **rank**, *verb*, a) to have or hold a particular position, b) to arrange or place in a row.

rank (2) *adjective*
1. growing strongly or vigorously: 'the deserted garden was filled with *rank* weeds'.
2. having an unpleasant or offensive smell.
3. unmistakeable: 'assassinating a king is *rank* treason'.
Word Family: **rankly**, *adverb*.

rankle *verb*
to cause or continue to cause irritation, bitterness or unpleasantness: 'after a time their cruel remarks began to *rankle*'.

ransack *verb*
to search vigorously or violently, especially in order to rob or plunder: 'the burglar had *ransacked* the house for jewellery'.

ransom *noun*
the money extorted by criminals for the release of a person captured or detained.
king's ransom, a large or valuable amount of money.
Word Family: **ransom**, *verb*, a) to free by paying a ransom, b) to release after receiving a ransom.
[Latin *redemptio* redemption]

rant *verb*
to talk wildly or violently.
Word Family: **rant**, *noun*.

ranunculus (*say* ra-**nunk**-yoolus) *noun*
plural is **ranunculuses** or **ranunculi** (*say* ra-**nunk**-yoo-lie)
any of a group of widely found plants with divided leaves, such as the buttercup.
[Latin, a little frog, tadpole]

rap *verb*
(rapped, rapping)
to hit or knock sharply, quickly or lightly.
Phrases:
rap out, 'he *rapped out* an indignant curse' (= uttered sharply).
rap over the knuckles, to reprove.
rap *noun*
1. a) a sharp, quick knock or blow. b) the sound it makes.
2. (*informal*) punishment or blame: 'who will take the *rap* for the robbery?'.

rapacious (*say* ra-**pay**-shus) *adjective*
excessively or unpleasantly greedy or plundering.
Word Family: **rapacity** (*say* ra-**passi**-tee), **rapaciousness**, *nouns*; **rapaciously**, *adverb*.
[Latin *rapax* grasping]

rape (1) *noun*
1. the crime of having sexual intercourse with a woman without her consent.
2. a seizing or theft.
3. any abusive or improper treatment.
Word Family: **rape**, *verb*; **rapist**, *noun*.
[Latin *rapere* to seize or carry off]

rape (2) *noun*
a plant with yellow flowers, grown as food for livestock and for the oil of its seeds.
[Latin *rapum* turnip]

rape (3) *noun*
the pulp remaining after the juice has been extracted from grapes in wine-making.

rapid (*say* **rapp**id) *adjective*
with great speed.
rapid *noun*
(*usually plural*) the swiftly moving part of a river where it flows over or between rocks, or down a steep slope.
Word Family: **rapidly**, *adverb*; **rapidity** (*say* ra-**piddi**-tee), *noun*.
[from Latin]

rapier (*say* **ray**-pee-a) *noun*
a sword with a long, straight blade, used chiefly for thrusting.

rapine (*say* **ray**-pine) *noun*
an old word meaning plunder.

rapist (*say* **ray**-pist) *noun*
Word Family: see RAPE (1).

rapport (*say* ra-**por**) *noun*
a feeling of understanding or sympathy.
[French]

rapprochement (*say* ra-**prosh**-mon) *noun*
the re-establishing of a friendly relationship.
[French *rapprocher* to bring closer]

rapscallion (*say* rap-**skal**-y'n) *noun*
an old word meaning a rogue or rascal.

rapt *adjective*
1. deeply absorbed or fascinated: 'he was so *rapt* in his book that he did not hear the doorbell'.
2. full of emotion or delight: 'her *rapt* smile expressed her pleasure'.
[Latin *raptus* seized]

rapture (*say* **rap**cher) *noun*
extreme delight or joy.
in raptures, full of delight or enthusiasm.
Word Family: **rapturous**, *adjective*; **rapturously**, *adverb*; **rapturousness**, *noun*.

rare (1) (*rhymes with* air) *adjective*
1. not occurring often: 'a *rare* disease'.
Usage: 'she displayed a *rare* knowledge' (= remarkable, unusual).
2. of low density or pressure.
Word Family: **rareness**, *noun*; **rarely**, *adverb*; **rarity** (*say* **rairi**-tee), *noun*,

a) something which is rare, b) the state of being rare.
[Latin *rarus* thin, not dense]

rare (2) (*rhymes with* air) *adjective*
(of meat) lightly cooked.

rare earth
Chemistry: an oxide of a lanthanide, occurring in various minerals.

rare earth element
Chemistry: see LANTHANIDE.

rarefy (*say* **rair**i–fie) *verb*
(rarefied, rarefying)
1. to make or become less dense.
2. to refine.
rarefied *adjective*
very subtle: 'his *rarefied* distinctions were impossible to understand'.
Word Family: **rarefaction** (*say* rairi–**fak**–sh'n), *noun.*

raring *adjective*
(*informal*) very eager to set off or start on something: '*raring* to go'.

rarity (*say* **rair**i–tee) *noun*
Word Family: see RARE (1).

rascal (*say* **rahs**–k'l) *noun*
a roguish or mischievous person.
Word Family: **rascally**, *adjective, adverb*; **rascality** (*say* ras–**kalli**–tee), *noun.*

rase (*say* raze) *verb*
see RAZE.

rash (1) *adjective*
done hastily without caution.
Word Family: **rashly**, *adverb*; **rashness**, *noun.*
[Middle English *rasch* nimble]

rash (2) *noun*
any reddening of the skin.
Usage: 'there has been a *rash* of bombings throughout the country' (= sudden outbreak).

rasher *noun*
a thin slice of bacon.

rasp (*say* rahsp) *verb*
1. to scrape or rub roughly.
2. to make a harsh scraping sound.
Usage: 'the children's cries *rasped* on her nerves' (= irritated).
rasp *noun*
1. the act or sound of rasping.
2. a file with a coarse, pointed surface.

raspberry (*say* **rahz**–b'ree) *noun*
1. a small, juicy, edible red berry forming around a receptacle and growing on a bush.
2. a dark reddish-purple colour.
3. (*informal*) a harsh noise made with the tongue and lips to express contempt, etc.
Word Family: **raspberry**, *adjective.*

rat *noun*
1. any of various common rodents, larger than mice, with long, hairless tails.
2. (*informal*) a sneaky or contemptible person.
smell a rat, (*informal*) to be or become suspicious.
Word Family: **rat (ratted, ratting)**, *verb*, (informal) to betray or desert.

ratable (*say* **ray**ta–b'l) *adjective*
Word Family: see RATE (1).

ratafia (*say* ratta–**fee**–a) *noun*
a) a cordial or liqueur flavoured with almonds. b) an almond biscuit or cake.

ratchet *noun*
a device consisting of a toothed wheel with a catch which allows it to move in only one direction.

rate (1) *noun*
1. a measured amount in relation to a unit or fixed quantity of something else: 'at the *rate* of 60 kilometres an hour'.
Usages:
a) 'what is the interest *rate* on the loan?' (= payment).
b) 'we buy our groceries at cut *rates*' (= prices).
c) 'as a cricketer he was *first–rate*' (= highest quality).
2. (*plural*) a tax on land and buildings imposed by local governments and used for local services, such as street lighting, etc.
at any rate, 'come for a short time *at any rate*' (= anyway, anyhow).
rate *verb*
1. to estimate the value or quality of: 'how do you *rate* this painting?'.
2. to regard or consider: 'I *rate* him as a highly intelligent person'.
Usage: 'such a small matter would not *rate* a mention in the newspaper' (= deserve, obtain).
Word Family: **rateable, ratable**, *adjective*, a) able to be estimated, b) liable to payment of rates.
[Latin *ratus* reckoned]

rate (2) *verb*
to scold.

rate of exchange
also called the **exchange rate**
the ratio used, or the price quoted, in exchanging one currency for

another, as from Australian dollars to pounds sterling.

ratepayer *noun*
a person who pays rates.

rather (*rhymes with* father) *adverb*
1. preferably or more willingly: 'I would *rather* not come with you'.
2. to a certain degree: 'I *rather* like her, though I'm not sure why'.
3. with more truth or accuracy: 'it's raining, or *rather* it rained earlier'.

ratify (*say* **ratti**–fie) *verb*
(ratified, ratifying)
to approve or confirm, especially formally or officially: 'Russia has *ratified* the nuclear arms agreement'.
Word Family: **ratification,** *noun.*

rating (1) (*say* **ray**–ting) *noun*
1. a measured position relative to others: 'what is the popularity *rating* of that radio station?'.
2. *Navy:* any non–commissioned sailor.
3. *Rowing:* the number of strokes rowed in one minute. Also called the **rate (of striking).**
4. (of machines, etc.) the designed limits of performance.
5. (of yachts) classification by tonnage, etc.

rating (2) (*say* **ray**–ting) *noun*
a scolding.

ratio (*say* **ray**–she–o) *noun*
1. a comparison or proportion of the value, quantity, etc. of two things.
2. *Maths:* the relative size of two numbers or quantities. *Example*: 2:3 is the ratio of 2 to 3 and means $\frac{2}{3}$.
[Latin, a reckoning]

ratiocination (*say* ratti–o–sin–**ay**–sh'n) *noun*
the process of logical reasoning and thought.
Word Family: **ratiocinate,** *verb.*

ration (*say* **rash**'n) *noun*
a fixed amount permitted or supplied, especially of food.
Word Family: **ration,** *verb,* a) to restrict to limited amounts, b) to supply with rations; **rationing,** *noun.*

rational (*say* **rash**–n'l) *adjective*
1. using sense, reason or logic: 'a *rational* argument'.
2. able to think or reason: 'man is a *rational* animal'.
3. behaving according to reason or logic rather than emotions, etc.
4. *Maths:* relating to a number that can be expressed as a ratio of two integers. Compare IRRATIONAL.
Word Family: **rationally,** *adverb*; **rationality** (*say* rasha–**nalli**–tee), *noun.*

rationale (*say* rasha–**nahl**) *noun*
1. the basic reasons for or logic of something.
2. a statement or explanation of reasons.

rationalism (*say* **rash**'n–a–lizm) *noun*
Philosophy: the belief that reason is the only valid basis of knowledge, action or belief. Compare EMPIRICISM.
Word Family: **rationalist,** *noun*; **rationalist, rationalistic,** *adjectives.*

rationalize (*say* **rash**'n–a–lize)
rationalise *verb*
1. to make reasonable or rational.
2. to invent an acceptable explanation to justify behaviour.
3. to introduce new or efficient methods into a business, etc.
Word Family: **rationalization,** *noun.*

ratline (*say* **rat**lin) **ratlin** *noun*
any of the small ropes across the shrouds of a sailing ship used as a ladder.

rat–race *noun*
the unscrupulous, competitive struggle for success, social status, etc.

rattan (*say* ratt–**an**) *noun*
any of a group of tropical climbing palms, the branches of which are used for wickerwork.
[Malay]

rattle *verb*
1. a) to make a rapid series of short, sharp sounds. b) to move with such sounds: 'the train *rattled* over the bridge'.
Usage: 'she *rattled* on for hours about her trip' (= talked, chattered).
2. (*informal*) to fluster or confuse: 'don't let her direct questions *rattle* you'.
rattle off, (*informal*) 'he *rattled off* a list of things to buy' (= said quickly).
rattle *noun*
1. a rapid series of short, sharp sounds.
2. any of various devices designed to make such a sound, such as a child's toy.
Word Family: **rattly,** *adjective,* making or tending to make a rattling sound.

rattler *noun*
a rattlesnake.

rattlesnake *noun*
any of a group of poisonous American snakes related to the viper, but having a tail made of horny, loosely connected joints which make a rattling sound when the snake is angry.

rattletrap *noun*
a shaky or rickety object, especially an old car.

ratty *adjective*
1. of or like a rat.
2. irritable.

raucous (*say* **rawkus**) *adjective*
hoarsely or harshly loud.
Word Family: **raucously,** *adverb*; **raucousness,** *noun.*
[from Latin]

ravage (*say* **ravvij**) *verb*
to spoil, ruin or destroy.
Word Family: **ravage,** *noun,* (usually plural) extreme destruction.

rave *verb*
1. to talk wildly or incoherently.
2. (*informal*) a) to talk or write very enthusiastically. b) to talk nonsense.
Word Family: **rave,** *noun*; **rave,** *adjective,* (informal) wildly enthusiastic; **raving,** *adjective,* a) wildly excited or incoherent, b) extraordinary or remarkable.

raven (1) (*say* **ray–v'n**) *noun*
a large bird related to the crow, with shiny, black feathers.
Word Family: **raven,** *adjective,* shiny black.

raven (2) (*say* **ravv'n**) *verb*
to seize or eat greedily.
Word Family: **ravening,** *adjective,* fiercely greedy.
[Latin *rapina* plundering]

ravenous (*say* **ravven–us**) *adjective*
extremely hungry.
Usage: 'the army leader was *ravenous* for power' (= greedy).
Word Family: **ravenously,** *adverb*; **ravenousness,** *noun.*

ravine (*say* ra–**veen**) *noun*
a long, narrow and deep valley.

ravioli (*say* ravvi–**o**–lee) *plural noun*
envelopes of pasta filled with chopped meat, etc. and usually served with a tomato sauce.
[Italian]

ravish (*say* **ravvish**) *verb*
1. to seize and take by force: 'soldiers *ravished* the small town'.
2. to fill with strong emotion: '*ravished* with joy'.

ravishing *adjective*
enchanting or delightful.
Word Family: **ravishingly,** *adverb*; **ravishment,** *noun.*
[Latin *rapere* to seize]

raw *adjective*
1. not cooked.
2. not prepared, treated or refined: '*raw* sugar'.
Usages:
a) 'he is still a *raw* beginner' (= ignorant, inexperienced).
b) 'the *raw* wound looked very painful' (= open, exposed)
c) 'a *raw* description of family life' (= brutal, crude).
3. (*informal*) unfair: 'she got a *raw* deal'.
4. harsh and cold: 'a *raw* wind'.
raw *noun*
Phrases:
in the raw, a) not refined; b) naked.
on the raw, 'her remarks touched him *on the raw*' (= on a sensitive spot).
Word Family: **rawly,** *adverb*; **rawness,** *noun.*

rawhide *noun*
the untanned skin of an animal.

raw materials
the materials used in manufacture, especially in their natural state.

ray (1) *noun*
1. a narrow line: 'a *ray* of sunlight'.
Usage: 'there is not even a *ray* of hope' (= slight indication).
2. *Physics:* a straight line along which a wave travels.
Maths: an infinite straight line which starts from a given point (called the **end–point**).
3. *Biology:* a) any of the arms of a starfish. b) a bony spine supporting a fin.
ray *verb*
to send out rays.
Word Family: **rayless,** *adjective,* dark or gloomy.
[Latin *radius*]

ray (2) *noun*
any of various cartilaginous fish, with gills on the lower surface of their flattened bodies, e.g. the skate.
[Latin *raia*]

rayon *noun*
any of various synthetic fibres made from cellulose, e.g. viscous rayon.

raze, rase *verb*
to demolish or destroy completely.

razor (*say* **ray**–za) *noun*
any of various sharp cutting instruments, used especially to shave hair, etc.
Word Family: **razor**, *verb*, to cut or shape with a razor.
[Latin *rasus* scraped]

razorbill *noun*
a bird related to the auk, with a flat, hooked beak.

razz *verb*
American: (*informal*) to make fun of or mock.

razzmatazz *noun*
1. (*informal*) any noisy activity or display.
2. traditional jazz music.

re (*say* ray *or* ree) *preposition*
concerning or with reference to.
[Latin]

re– (*say* ree)
a prefix indicating: a) repetition, as in *recur*; b) return or movement backwards, as in *retreat.*
[Latin]

reach *verb*
1. to get to: 'we *reached* Sydney at midnight'.
2. to put or stretch out or towards: 'she *reached* into her bag for her cigarettes'.
Usages:
a) 'the dress *reaches* her ankles' (= touches, goes as far as).
b) 'the donations have already *reached* one million' (= mounted to, added up to).
c) 'try to *reach* him with a more friendly approach' (= communicate with).
d) 'my garden *reaches* to the river' (= extends).
3. *Sailing:* to sail across the wind.
reach *noun*
1. the act of reaching or stretching.
2. the distance which something can reach or be reached: 'what is the *reach* of his influence?'; b) 'within close *reach* of the shops'.
3. a continuous area or expanse: 'they flew low over a vast *reach* of desert'.
4. the part of a river, channel, etc. between its curves.
5. *Sailing:* the distance travelled between tacks.

react (*say* ree–**akt**) *verb*
1. to act in return or opposition to something earlier: 'the radical student *reacted* against her strict upbringing'.
Usage: 'how did he *react* to the idea?' (= respond, act in relation).
2. *Chemistry:* to take part in a reaction.
reaction (*say* ree–**ak**–sh'n) *noun*
1. an action, force or effect produced by or in response to another.
2. *Chemistry:* the interaction of two or more substances, resulting in chemical changes in them.
3. a tendency to conservatism and opposition to progress, reform, etc., especially in politics.
Word Family: **reactionary**, *adjective*, extremely conservative or opposed to progress; **reactionary, reactionist,** *nouns.*

reactive (*say* ree–**ak**tiv) *adjective*
1. tending or likely to react.
2. *Chemistry:* readily entering into a reaction.

reactor (*say* ree–**ak**tor) *noun*
1. a person or thing that reacts.
2. *Electricity:* a device used to introduce opposition to the flow of alternating electric current.
3. *Physics:* a nuclear reactor.

reactor core
Physics: the central region of a reactor where the fuel is and therefore where the highest intensity of nuclear reactions leading to the production of energy takes place.

read *verb*
(**read** (*say* red), **reading**)
to look at, understand or say aloud written words: a) 'can you *read*?'; b) '*read* me the first paragraph'.
Usages:
a) 'I *read* disbelief on her face' (= saw).
b) 'she must have *read* my mind as she said exactly what I was thinking' (= interpreted, analysed).
c) 'don't *read* the wrong meaning into her words' (= interpret, introduce).
d) 'the thermometer *reads* 7°' (= indicates, registers).
e) 'he did not express himself very clearly but I still *read* his meaning' (= understood).
f) 'he *read* us a lecture on dishonesty' (= gave).
g) 'I am *reading* law and history' (= studying).
h) 'in this poem for 'I' *read* 'the author'' (= take as the intended meaning).
i) (*informal*) 'you need your head *read* for doing such a silly thing' (= examined by a psychiatrist).

Phrases:
read between the lines, to deduce what has been intentionally left out of a letter, speech, etc.
read (someone) like a book, 'he can *read me like a book*' (= see into my mind and heart).
take as read, 'I think we can *take* these minutes *as read*' (= accept unread).
reading *noun*
any matter that is read, especially aloud: 'a poetry *reading*'.
Word Family: **read,** *noun,* the act of reading; **readable,** *adjective,* a) easy or interesting to read, b) able to be read or deciphered.

reader *noun*
1. a person who reads.
2. a book for instruction or practice in reading.
3. a university lecturer next in rank below a professor, usually one who has done special research.
Word Family: **readership,** *noun,* a) all the readers of some publication, especially a regular one, b) the position or duties of a university or other professional reader.

readily (*say* **reddi**–lee) *adverb*
Word Family: see READY.

readjust (*say* ree–a–**just**) *verb*
to adjust or arrange again.
Word Family: **readjustment,** *noun.*

readmit (*say* ree–ad**mit**) *verb*
to admit or let in again.
Word Family: **readmittance, readmission,** *nouns.*

ready (*say* **reddee**) *adjective*
equipped or arranged for action or use: 'is dinner *ready* yet?'.
Usages:
a) 'she is always *ready* to help' (= willing).
b) 'we have *ready* money for housing loans' (= available immediately).
c) 'he has a *ready* wit' (= spontaneous, quick).
ready *noun*
at the ready, ready for action.
Word Family: **readily,** *adverb*; **readiness,** *noun.*

ready-made *adjective*
1. made to a standard size or pattern rather than for a particular person or thing.
2. conventional or borrowed: 'his essay is full of *ready-made* opinions'.
3. suitable and available: 'here is a *ready-made* opportunity for making money'.

ready-mix *adjective*
already mixed for immediate use.

ready reckoner
a book of mathematical tables used in business calculations.

reafforestation
(*say* ree–a–forri–**stay**–sh'n) *noun*
the redevelopment of a forest area.
Word Family: **reafforest,** *verb.*

reagent (*say* ree–**ay**–j'nt) *noun*
any substance used in a chemical reaction.

real *adjective*
1. existing as fact, especially in nature or the universe: '*real* animals'.
2. true, as distinct from apparent or imagined: '*real* love'.
3. not artificial or false: '*real* diamonds'.
4. *Maths:* relating to a number that is representable as a finite or infinite decimal fraction. Compare IMAGINARY.
5. *Law:* (of property) not able to be moved, e.g. a house. Compare PERSONAL.
Word Family: **real,** *adverb,* (informal) very; **realness,** *noun*; **really,** *adverb,* a) truly, b) indeed.
[Latin *res* a thing]

real estate
also called **realty**
any immovable property, such as land or a house.

realism (*say* **ree**–a–lizm) *noun*
1. a tendency to be practical, sensible or see things as they really are.
2. the portrayal of accurate or realistic detail, e.g. in a painting, book, film, etc.
Word Family: **realist,** *noun, adjective.*

realistic (*say* ree–a–**listik**) *adjective*
1. having a practical or sensible attitude to life, etc.
2. representing or showing something as it is in life or fact: 'a *realistic* portrait'.
Word Family: **realistically,** *adverb.*

reality (*say* ree–**alli**–tee) *noun*
a) the state of being real. b) something which is real or exists in fact: 'his dream of success had become a *reality*'.
in reality, in truth.

realize (*say* **ree**–a–lize) **realise** *verb*
1. to understand clearly or fully: 'do you *realize* what you have done?'.
2. to make real or a fact: 'he trained hard to *realize* his ambition of playing in the orchestra'.

Usages:
a) 'the house *realized* a high price at the auction' (= obtained, brought).
b) 'she decided to *realize* her shares to help pay her debts' (= exchange for money).
Word Family: **realization,** *noun*; **realizable,** *adjective.*

really (*say* **reel**–ee) *adverb*
Word Family: see REAL.

realm (*say* relm) *noun*
a kingdom.
Usage: 'her studies are in the *realm* of biology' (= area).

real tennis
also called **royal tennis**
the earliest form of tennis, played over a sagging net in a specially constructed walled court, with racquets and a solid ball.
[Old French *real* royal]

realtor (*say* **reel**–tor) *noun*
American: an estate agent.

realty (*say* **reel**–tee) *noun*
real estate.

ream (1) *noun*
a measure of paper consisting of 500 sheets.
Usage: 'he writes *reams* of poetry' (= large amounts).

ream (2) *verb*
to finish or shape a hole or opening.
Word Family: **reamer,** *noun,* a cylindrical tool with jutting blades for reaming.

reap *verb*
to cut and harvest grain.
Usage: 'she *reaped* the benefits of hard work' (= gained, received).
reaper *noun*
1. a person who reaps.
2. any of various machines for cutting crops. A **header** cuts and gathers only the heads of the stalks.

reappear (*say* ree–a–**peer**) *verb*
to appear again.
Word Family: **reappearance,** *noun.*

reapply (*say* ree–a–**ply**) *verb*
(reapplied, reapplying)
to apply again.
Word Family: **reapplication** (*say* ree–apli–**kay**–sh'n), *noun.*

reappraisal (*say* ree–a–**pray**–z'l) *noun*
a new examination and judgement.
Word Family: **reappraise,** *verb.*

rear (1) *noun*
the back part of something: 'the entrance is at the *rear* of the shop'.

rearguard *noun*
the part of an army, etc. prepared to meet any sudden attack from the rear.
Word Family: **rear,** *adjective*; **rearward, rearwards,** *adjective, adverb,* in or towards the rear.

rear (2) *verb*
1. to care for and support a child or young animal until adulthood.
2. (of a horse) to rise on its hind legs, so that its body is nearly vertical.
Usage: 'the spectre of famine *reared* its ugly head' (= lifted up).

rear admiral
a commissioned officer in the navy next in rank below a vice-admiral.

rearm (*say* ree–**arm**) *verb*
to arm again, especially an army with new or better equipment.
Word Family: **rearmament,** *noun.*

rearrange (*say* ree–a–**range**) *verb*
to arrange in a different way.
Word Family: **rearrangement,** *noun.*

reason (*say* **ree**–z'n) *noun*
1. a motive for doing or believing something: 'what are your *reasons* for acting like this?'.
2. a) the mind or intellect. b) sanity or good sense: 'have you lost your *reason*?'.
Phrases:
it stands to reason, it is obvious.
within reason, within sensible limits.
reason *verb*
to think or draw conclusions which follow naturally and in correct sequence from the original statements or assumptions.
reason with someone, to persuade someone with arguments.
Word Family: **reasoned,** *adjective,* logically argued or thought out.
[Latin *rationis* of a calculation]

reasonable (*say* **ree**–z'n–a–b'l) *adjective*
having or showing reason or common sense: 'your plan sounds quite *reasonable*'.
Usage: 'she paid a *reasonable* price for the shoes' (= moderate).
Word Family: **reasonably,** *adverb*; **reasonableness,** *noun.*

reasoning (*say* **ree**–z'n–ing) *noun*
a) the process of thinking or drawing correct conclusions: 'her powers of *reasoning* are amazing'. b) the arguments in arriving at conclusions: 'what is your *reasoning* for this decision?'.

reassess (*say* ree–a–**sess**) *verb*
to assess again.
Word Family: **reassessment**, *noun.*

reassure (*say* ree–a–**shor**) *verb*
1. to assure again.
2. to restore the confidence of: 'he was afraid at first but I *reassured* him with my arguments'.
Word Family: **reassurance**, *noun*; **reassuringly**, *adverb.*

rebate (*say* **ree**–bate) *noun*
a sum of money which is returned, such as a discount or a tax refund.
[RE– + ABATE]

rebel (*say* **rebb**'l) *noun*
a person who resists or defies authority.
Usage: 'she is a *rebel* in her ideas' (= nonconformist).
rebel (*say* re–**bel**) *verb*
(**rebelled**, **rebelling**)
to openly resist authority.
Usage: 'her mind *rebelled* at the thought' (= felt repugnance).
[RE– + Latin *bellum* war]

rebellion (*say* re–**bel**–y'n) *noun*
the act of rebelling, especially an organized armed resistance to the established government in a country.

rebellious (*say* re–**bel**–yus) *adjective*
1. of or relating to rebels or rebellion.
2. defiant or disposed to rebel.
Word Family: **rebelliously**, *adverb*; **rebelliousness**, *noun.*

rebirth *noun*
a new or second birth.

reborn *adjective*
born again: 'after the holiday he tackled the job with *reborn* energy'.

rebound (*say* ree–**bound**) *verb*
to bounce or spring back after hitting something: 'the ball *rebounded* from the wall and broke a window'.
Usage: 'his own insults later *rebounded* on him' (= returned).
rebound (*say* **ree**–bound) *noun*
a bouncing or springing back.
on the rebound, 'she married him *on the rebound* after an unhappy affair' (= as a reaction).

rebuff (*say* re–**buff**) *verb*
to refuse or reject something coldly and abruptly: 'she *rebuffed* my offer of help'.
Usage: 'the troops were *rebuffed* in their efforts to take the town' (= repelled).
Word Family: **rebuff**, *noun*, a repulse, rejection or defeat.
[RE– + Italian *buffo* a puff]

rebuke *verb*
to criticize sharply: 'I was *rebuked* for continually being late'.
Word Family: **rebuke**, *noun.*
[Old French *rebuchier* to fell trees]

rebus (*say* **ree**bus) *noun*
a game in which words must be guessed from pictures which represent the sounds.

rebut (*say* re–**but**) *verb*
(**rebutted**, **rebutting**)
to prove something wrong by using argument and evidence.
Word Family: **rebuttal**, *noun*, a) the act of rebutting, b) the evidence used in rebutting.

recalcitrant (*say* re–**kal**si–tr'nt) *adjective*
rebellious or actively disobedient.
Word Family: **recalcitrant**, *noun*, a recalcitrant person; **recalcitrance**, *noun.*
[Latin *recalcitrare* to kick back]

recall (*say* re–**kawl**) *verb*
1. to bring back to mind: 'can you *recall* her name?'.
2. to summon back: 'the king *recalled* his foreign ambassadors'.
Usage: 'he *recalled* his earlier instructions' (= cancelled).
recall *noun*
1. the act of recalling.
2. recollection: 'the author, in his autobiography, seems to have the gift of total *recall*'.

recant (*say* re–**kant**) *verb*
to formally withdraw or give up a statement or belief.
Word Family: **recantation**, *noun.*
[RE– + Latin *cantare* to sing]

recap *verb*
(*informal*) to recapitulate.
Word Family: **recap**, *noun.*

recapitulate (*say* reeka–**pit**–yoo–late) *verb*
1. to stress again or summarize the main points at the end of a speech, etc.
2. *Music:* to repeat or restate an earlier theme.
Word Family: **recapitulation**, *noun.*
[RE– + Latin *capitulum* a small head]

recede (*say* re–**seed**) *verb*
1. to move back or to a more distant position: 'we were able to cross when the tide *receded*'.
2. to slope backwards: 'a *receding* chin'.
[Latin *recedere* to go back]

receipt (*say* re–**seet**) *noun*
1. a written statement acknowledging payment.
2. something which is received: 'the *receipts* for the play were £400'.
be in receipt of, 'I *am in receipt of* your letter' (= have received).
Word Family: **receipt,** *verb,* to give a receipt.
[Latin *receptus* recovered]

receivable *adjective*
American: requiring payment: 'accounts *receivable*'.

receive (*say* re–**seev**) *verb*
1. to get into one's hand or possession: a) 'I *received* a letter this morning'; b) 'he *received* the bad news'.
2. to undergo or experience: 'he *received* a blow on the jaw'.
Usages:
a) 'we *received* our guests in the lounge' (= greeted, welcomed).
b) 'he was *received* into the Catholic Church' (= admitted).
c) 'the *received* opinion' (= generally accepted).

receiver *noun*
1. a person who receives something, such as a person who accepts stolen goods, or the player to whom the ball is served in tennis.
2. any device, such as a radio or telephone, which receives electromagnetic waves and reproduces them as sound or pictures.
3. *Law:* a person appointed by a court to take charge of a bankrupt business or a property which is involved in a dispute.
Word Family: **receivership,** *noun,* (Law) the state of being in the hands of a receiver.

recent (*say* **ree**–s'nt) *adjective*
having appeared or happened not long ago: a) 'a *recent* illness'; b) 'a *recent* newspaper'.
Word Family: **recently,** *adverb.*
[from Latin]

receptacle (*say* re–**sept**i–k'l) *noun*
1. anything that holds or contains something.
2. *Biology:* the top of a stalk that bears the parts of the flower.

reception (*say* re–**sep**–sh'n) *noun*
1. a) the act or manner of receiving: 'my theory met with a cold *reception*'.
b) the area where someone is received.
2. *Radio:* the signals received on a radio or television receiver.
3. a formal occasion held by a person or group: 'a wedding *reception*'.

receptionist (*say* re–**sep**–sh'n–ist) *noun*
a person employed to receive guests, visitors or clients in an office or hotel.

receptive (*say* re–**sep**tiv) *adjective*
able to take in or receive.
Usage: 'she has a *receptive* mind' (= quick or ready to receive new ideas).

recess (*say* re–**sess** *or* **ree**–sess) *noun*
1. a part or space that is set back from the main wall or line.
Usage: 'she lived deep in the *recesses* of the forest' (= hidden, central parts).
2. a period of time when work stops, e.g. in parliament.
recess *verb*
1. to make or place in a recess.
2. to take a recess.

recession (*say* re–**sesh**'n) *noun*
1. the act of receding or withdrawing.
2. a decline in commercial and industrial activity, less severe than a depression.
[Latin *recessus* gone back]

recessive (*say* re–**sess**iv) *adjective*
1. tending to recede or go back.
2. *Biology:* of or relating to a hereditary character that only shows itself when two identical alleles are present in a cell. Compare DOMINANT.

recharge *verb*
to charge again.
Word Family: **recharge,** *noun.*

recherché (*say* ra–**shair**–shay) *adjective*
1. carefully selected or thought out.
2. too carefully chosen or far-fetched.
[French]

recidivism (*say* re–**siddi**–vizm) *noun*
the tendency to repeat or make a habit of crimes.
Word Family: **recidivist,** *noun.*
[Latin *recidivus* recurring]

recipe (*say* **ressi**–pee) *noun*
a list of ingredients and instructions on preparing food, etc.
Usage: 'what's your *recipe* for success?' (= formula).
[Latin, take!]

recipient (*say* re–**sippi**–ent) *noun*
a person or thing that receives.

reciprocal (*say* re–**sip**ra–k'l) *adjective*
mutual: 'the two countries have a *reciprocal* trade agreement'.

reciprocal *noun*
Maths: a number by which another must be multiplied to give one. *Example*: $\frac{4}{3}$ is the reciprocal of $\frac{3}{4}$.
Word Family: **reciprocally,** *adverb.*

reciprocate (*say* re–**sipra**–kate) *verb*
a) to give in return: 'she does not *reciprocate* my mad passion'. b) to give and receive mutually: 'the countries *reciprocate* trade concessions'.
Word Family: **reciprocation,** *noun.*
[Latin *reciprocare* to move back and forth]

reciprocity (*say* ressi–**prossi**–tee) *noun*
the practice or principle of reciprocating, especially relating to formal agreements between countries.

recital (*say* re–**sigh**–t'l) *noun*
a performance given by one or two musicians, etc.
Usage: 'he gave a *recital* of the places he'd visited' (= detailed account).

recitative (*say* ressita–**teev**) *noun*
a style of spoken music intermediate between singing and speaking.
[from Italian]

recite (*say* re–**site**) *verb*
to say from memory, e.g. a poem, etc.
Usage: 'she *recited* her adventures' (= gave an account of).
Word Family: **recitation,** *noun.*
[Latin *recitare* read aloud]

reck *verb*
an old word meaning to heed.

reckless *adjective*
unthinkingly careless or rash: 'the accident was caused by *reckless* driving'.
Word Family: **recklessly,** *adverb*; **recklessness,** *noun.*

reckon *verb*
to count or calculate.
Usages:
a) (*informal*) 'I *reckon* it will rain later' (= think, consider).
b) 'can we *reckon* on your support?' (= depend, rely).
reckon with, a) 'I'll *reckon with* the troublemakers' (= deal with); b) 'he's a person to be *reckoned with*' (= taken seriously).
reckoning *noun*
a calculation: 'by my *reckoning* we're lost'.
day of reckoning, a time when something must be atoned or accounted for.

reclaim *verb*
to make something productive or useful again: 'the swamp was *reclaimed* by draining'.
reclaim *noun*
the possibility of being reclaimed: 'beyond *reclaim*'.
Word Family: **reclamation** (*say* rekla–**may**–sh'n), *noun*, the act or process of reclaiming.

re–claim *verb*
to claim back.

recline *verb*
to lean back in a resting position.
[Latin *reclinare* to bend back]

recluse (*say* re–**kloose**) *noun*
a person who lives apart from others.
Word Family: **reclusive,** *adjective.*
[Latin *reclusus* shut up]

recognizance (*say* re–**kogni**–z'nce) **recognisance** *noun*
1. recognition.
2. *Law:* a bond or obligation.

recognize (*say* **rekk**'g–nize) **recognise** *verb*
1. to identify again: a) 'do you *recognize* this tune?'; b) 'would you *recognize* me without a beard?'.
2. to accept something as true or valid: 'some countries do not *recognize* the governments of other countries'.
recognition (*say* rekk'g–**nish**'n) *noun*
a) the act of recognizing: 'my *recognition* of him was immediate'. b) the state of being recognized: 'in *recognition* of your services, accept this gift'.
Word Family: **recognizable,** *adjective*; **recognizably,** *adverb.*
[Latin *recognoscere* to call to mind again]

recoil (*say* re–**koil**) *verb*
to jump or spring back: a) 'the gun *recoiled* after being fired'; b) 'I *recoiled* from the dead body in disgust'.
recoil (*say* **ree**–koil) *noun*
the act of recoiling, such as the backward movement of a gun when it is fired.
[RE– + Latin *culus* buttocks]

recollect (*say* rekka–**lekt**) *verb*
to remember or succeed in remembering.
recollection (*say* rekka–**lek**–sh'n) *noun*
a) the act or power of recollecting.
b) something that is recollected.

recommence (*say* reeka–**mence**) *verb*
to commence again.

Word Family: **recommencement,** *noun.*

recommend (*say* rekka–**mend**) *verb*
to present something as worthwhile or advisable: a) 'I can *recommend* this book'; b) 'I *recommend* that you see a doctor'.
Word Family: **recommendation,** *noun.*

recompense (*say* **rekk**em–pence) *verb*
to repay or make compensation: 'I will *recompense* you for all your trouble'.
Word Family: **recompense,** *noun,* repayment or compensation.

reconcile (*say* **rekk**'n–sile) *verb*
to bring or come into a state of harmony or agreement: a) 'the enemies *reconciled* their differences after the fight'; b) 'how does this statement *reconcile* with what you said yesterday?'.
Word Family: **reconciliation** (*say* rekk'n–silli–**ay**–sh'n), *noun*; **reconcilable,** *adjective,* able to be reconciled; **reconciliatory** (*say* rekk'n–**sil**lia–tree), *adjective,* tending to reconcile.
[RE– + CONCILIATE]

recondite (*say* **rekk**'n–dite) *adjective*
dealing with obscure or little known matters.
[Latin *reconditus* hidden]

recondition (*say* ree–k'n–**dish**'n) *verb*
to repair or overhaul.

reconnaissance (*say* re–**konni**–sance) *noun*
short form is **recce**
1. *Military:* any air or ground operation designed to assess the position, strength and movements of the enemy.
2. any preliminary study or survey.
[French, recognition]

reconnoitre (*say* rekka–**noy**ta) *verb*
in America spelt **reconnoiter**
to make a reconnaissance.

reconsider (*say* ree–k'n–**sidda**) *verb*
to consider again, especially with a view to changing a decision.
Word Family: **reconsideration,** *noun.*

reconstitute (*say* ree–**konsti**–tewt) *verb*
to make up or put together again.
Word Family: **reconstitution,** *noun.*

reconstruct *verb*
1. to construct again.
2. to re–create or re–enact past events: 'the detective *reconstructed* the scene of the crime'
Word Family: **reconstruction,** *noun.*

record (*say* re–**kord**) *verb*
to register or set down in writing, on tape, etc.: a) 'the concert was *recorded* for television'; b) 'this book *records* the history of cinema'.
Usage: 'the thermometer *recorded* 40 degrees' (= registered).

record (*say* **rek**–ord) *noun*
1. a written account: a) 'a *record* is kept of all court cases'; b) 'she wrote a *record* of the early history of her town'.
2. a thin, plastic plate with a continuous groove in each side for recording and reproducing sounds. Short form of **gramophone record.** Also called a **disc.**
3. facts known about the past of a person, company, etc.: 'this airline has a good safety *record*'.
Usage: 'this woman has a *record*' (= a criminal past).
4. the best rate or amount so far achieved: 'his time for the race is a new *record*'.
Phrases:
off the record, unofficial, not to be published.
on record, 'this is the fastest time *on record*' (= recorded).
[Latin *recordari* to remember]

recorder (*say* re–**kord**a) *noun*
1. a person or thing that records.
2. *Music:* any of a family of simple wind instruments without reeds.

recording *noun*
a record of sounds, music, etc., on tape or record.

recording head
Audio: see HEAD.

record–player *noun*
a machine that reproduces the sounds on a record.

recount *verb*
to relate or give an account of.

re–count *verb*
to count again.
Word Family: **re–count,** *noun.*

recoup (*say* re–**koop**) *verb*
to recover or receive compensation for.

recourse (*say* re–**korse**) *noun*
have recourse to, 'when I'm in trouble I *have recourse to* my friends' (= seek help from).
[Latin *recursus* a retreat]

recover *verb*
1. to get back again: a) 'the police *recovered* the stolen goods'; b) 'he *recovered* his wits after the accident'.
2. to return to a healthy or normal situation: 'I've *recovered* from my illness'.
recovery *noun*
the act of recovering: 'the *recovery* of stolen goods'.
[Latin *recuperare*]

re–cover *verb*
to cover again.

recreant (*say* **rekri**–ant) *adjective*
an old word meaning: a) cowardly; b) false or disloyal.
Word Family: **recreant,** *noun,* a recreant person.

re–create (*say* ree–kree–**ate**) *verb*
to create again.
Word Family: **recreation,** *noun.*

recreation (*say* rekri–**ay**–sh'n) *noun*
a) any relaxing pastime, hobby, amusement, etc. b) the relaxation and refreshment produced by such pastimes.
Word Family: **recreational,** *adjective.*

recrimination
(*say* re–krimmi–**nay**–sh'n) *noun*
a countercharge against an accuser.
Word Family: **recriminate** (*say* re–**krimmi**–nate), *verb,* to accuse in return; **recriminatory,** *adjective.*
[RE– + Latin *criminis* of an accusation]

recrudescence
(*say* ree–kroo–**dess**'nce) *noun*
a new outburst or breaking out.
Word Family: **recrudescent,** *adjective;* **recrudesce,** *verb.*
[RE– + Latin *crudescere* to become raw]

recruit (*say* re–**kroot**) *verb*
to enlist persons for service or membership in a group, society or in the armed forces.
recruit *noun*
a new or recently enlisted member, especially a newly enlisted soldier.
[French *recrue* new growth]

rectal *adjective*
Anatomy: of or relating to the rectum.

rectangle (*say* **rek**–tangle) *noun*
a quadrilateral having four right angles and usually with adjacent sides of unequal length.
Word Family: **rectangular,** *adjective.*
[Latin *rectus* straight + ANGLE]

rectify (*say* **rekti**–fie) *verb*
(rectified, rectifying)
1. to remedy or put right: 'it will take days to *rectify* the damage'.
2. *Chemistry:* to purify a liquid by distillation.
3. *Electricity:* to convert alternating current into direct current using a device which has a much higher resistance to current flowing in one direction than in the other.
Word Family: **rectification,** *noun;* **rectifier,** *noun,* a person or thing that rectifies.

rectilinear (*say* rekti–**linni**–a)
rectilineal *adjective*
Maths: relating to straight lines.
[Latin *rectus* straight + *linea* line]

rectitude (*say* **rekti**–tewd) *noun*
rightness or correctness of thought or conduct.

rector *noun*
1. *Christian:* a clergyman in charge of a parish, formerly one who received tithes (unlike a vicar).
2. the head of certain universities and colleges.
rectory (*say* **rekta**–ree) *noun*
the house of a rector.
[Latin, a controller]

rectum *noun*
Anatomy: the end portion of the colon, connected to the anus.
[Latin, straight (intestine)]

recumbent (*say* re–**kum**–b'nt)
adjective
lying down or reclining.
Word Family: **recumbently,** *adverb;* **recumbency,** *noun.*
[from Latin]

recuperate (*say* re–**koopa**–rate) *verb*
to recover, especially from ill health.
Word Family: **recuperative,** *adjective,* of or helping recovery; **recuperation,** *noun.*
[from Latin]

recur (*say* re–**ker**) *verb*
(recurred, recurring)
to repeat, return or occur again: a) 'if this behaviour *recurs* I'll be angry'; b) 'she suffers from *recurring* back trouble'.
recurring decimal, one that recurs to infinity. *Example:* a third of 10 is 3·3333 . . . .
recurrence (*say* ree–**kurr**'nce) *noun*
the act or process of recurring: 'there has been a *recurrence* of bad weather lately'.
Word Family: **recurrent,** *adjective.*
[Latin *recurrere* to run back]

recusant (*say* **rek**–yoo–z'nt) *adjective*
refusing to obey or submit to authority.
Word Family: **recusant,** *noun,* a recusant person.
[Latin *recusans* making objections]

recycle (*say* ree–**sigh**–k'l) *verb*
to put waste products through a cycle of purification and conversion to useful products.

red *noun*
1. a) a primary colour like that of fresh blood. b) the colour next to orange at the end of the spectrum.
2. (*informal*) a person with left–wing political views.
Phrases:
in the red, a) being on the debit side of an account, entered in red ink; b) being in debt. Compare IN THE BLACK under BLACK.
see red, (*informal*) to become extremely angry.
Word Family: **red,** *adjective*; **redden,** *verb,* to make or become red; **reddish,** *adjective,* slightly red.

redact (*say* re–**dakt**) *verb*
to edit or revise a piece of writing.
Word Family: **redaction,** *noun.*

red blood cell
also called an **erythrocyte**
any of the minute, disc–like cells in the blood of vertebrates, containing haemoglobin and carrying oxygen through the body.

red–blooded *adjective*
vigorous or virile.

redcoat *noun*
History: a British soldier, named after the scarlet jackets worn by the regiments.

Red Cross
the international organization which looks after the interests of the victims of war and large–scale natural disasters, such as earthquakes.
[from its flag, a *red cross* on a white ground, used to indicate neutrality in war]

red deer
a reddish–brown deer distinguished by its antlers of up to 12 points; it is stalked in Scotland and hunted with hounds in England.

redden *verb*
Word Family: see RED.

redeem (*say* re–**deem**) *verb*
1. to get back by payment, etc.: 'she *redeemed* her pawned ring'.
2. to fulfil a promise, pledge, etc.
3. to compensate or make amends for: 'to *redeem* oneself for past rudeness'.
4. *Religion:* to deliver from sin or its consequences by means of a sacrifice, etc.
Word Family: **redeemable,** *adjective,* able to be redeemed; **redeemer,** *noun,* a person who redeems; **redemptive,** *adjective,* serving to redeem.

redemption (*say* re–**demp**–sh'n) *noun*
a) the act of redeeming: 'her *redemption* of the ring only took a few minutes'. b) the state of being redeemed: 'he returned from confession assured of his *redemption*'.
[Latin *redemptus* bought back]

redeploy (*say* ree–dee–**ploy**) *verb*
to reorganize troops, etc. so as to use them more effectively.
Word Family: **redeployment,** *noun.*

redevelop (*say* re–devellup) *verb*
to develop again: 'the slum area was *redeveloped* into a modern housing estate'.
Word Family: **redeveloper,** *noun,* a person or company that redevelops; **redevelopment,** *noun.*

red–faced *adjective*
having a red face, especially due to embarrassment.

red flag
1. a symbol of socialism or revolution.
2. a red banner used as a signal of danger.

red–handed *adjective, adverb*
in the act of committing a crime or misdeed.

red herring
something irrelevant, introduced to distract attention.
[as once used in exercising hounds]

red–hot *adjective*
1. red with heat.
2. highly excited or angry.
3. (*informal*) fresh or most recent: 'a *red–hot* tip for a horse in the next race'.

red lead (*say* red led)
a heavy, orangish–red substance containing lead and used as a paint pigment and in the manufacture of glass and glazes.

red–letter day
a memorable occasion.
[so marked on Church calendars]

red–light district
an area sometimes indicated by red lights, with prostitutes, brothels, etc.

red mullet
a small round edible fish with rosy-pink skin.
[Latin *mullus*]

redolent (*say* **reddo**–l'nt) *adjective*
having a strong smell, especially one that is reminiscent of something.
Usage: 'stories *redolent* of mystery' (= suggestive).
Word Family: **redolence,** *noun*; **redolently,** *adverb.*
[from Latin]

redouble (*say* ree–**dubb**'l) *verb*
1. to double or increase greatly.
2. to repeat: 'the army *redoubled* its attack'.
Word Family: **redouble,** *noun.*

redoubt (*say* re–**dowt**) *noun*
a small fort in a system of fortifications surrounded by or joined to others by a parapet.
[Latin *reductus* retired]

redoubtable, redoubted *adjective*
1. formidable.
2. worthy of respect: '*redoubtable* acts of bravery'.
Word Family: **redoubtably,** *adverb*; **redoubtableness,** *noun.*
[RE– + Latin *dubitare* to doubt]

redound *verb*
(of an action) to react to the credit or discredit of the performer: a) 'the whole affair *redounded* greatly to his credit'; b) 'all the consequences of his actions *redounded* on his own head'.
[Latin *redundare* to surge back]

redress (*say* re–**dress**) *noun*
1. the setting right of what is wrong.
2. any relief or compensation from wrong or injury: 'after the accident he sought *redress* through the courts'.
Word Family: **redress,** *verb.*

re–dress *verb*
to dress again.

red setter
an Irish setter dog.

red shift
a phenomenon, resulting from the Doppler effect, in which the spectrum of light from a receding star is observed on earth with all lines shifted to the red end, the magnitude of the shift being a measure of the star's velocity relative to the earth.

redskin *noun*
(*informal*) a Red Indian.

red tape
excessive attention to rules and regulations.
Word Family: **red-tape,** *adjective.*
[from the *red tape* used to tie up documents]

reduce (*say* re–**dewce**) *verb*
1. to lower in degree, size, number, etc.: a) 'the car *reduced* speed'; b) 'I'd like to *reduce* my weight!'.
2. to bring into a particular state, condition, etc.: 'the fire *reduced* the house to ashes'.
Usage: 'the students had to *reduce* the fractions' (= simplify).
3. *Chemistry:* a) to remove oxygen from a substance. b) to add hydrogen to a substance. c) to add electrons to an atom or ion.
reduced circumstances, 'after the collapse of his company, Hudson had to live in *reduced circumstances*' (= comparative poverty).
reduction (*say* re–**duk**–sh'n) *noun*
1. the act of reducing.
2. the amount by which something is reduced: 'a 10 per cent *reduction* on all goods in the sale'.
Word Family: **reducible,** *adjective,* able to be reduced; **reducibly,** *adverb*; **reducer,** *noun,* a person or thing that reduces.
[Latin *reducere* to bring back]

reduction division
Biology: see MEIOSIS.

reductionism (*say* rid**duk**–sh'n–ism) *noun*
the orthodox scientific view that all phenomena of life, including consciousness and behaviour, can be explained by, and reduced to, physics and chemistry.

redundant (*say* re–**dun**–d'nt) *adjective*
unnecessary or excessive.
Usage: 'the workman was made *redundant* by the installation of a new machine' (= superfluous).
Word Family: **redundantly,** *adverb*; **redundancy,** *noun.*
[Latin *redundantia* an overflow]

redwood (*say* **red**–w*u*d) *noun*
a very tall, Californian tree (a sequoia), usually 60–100 m in height, with brownish-red wood which is used as timber.

reed *noun*
1. a) any of various tall grasses, usually growing in marshy areas. b) the stalk of such a grass.

2. *Music:* a) (in some wind instruments) a small piece of cane or metal, fixed at one end inside the mouthpiece, while the other end vibrates freely. b) any instrument, such as the clarinet, fitted with such a device.
3. a weaver's instrument for separating the warp threads and beating up the weft.
reedy *adjective*
1. full of reeds.
2. having a tone like that of a reed instrument.

reef (1) *noun*
1. *Geography:* a line or group of rocks or coral near the surface of the sea, sometimes visible at low tide.
a **barrier reef** is a coral reef which rises from deep water, with a wide, deep lagoon between it and the coast.
2. *Mining:* a vein.

reef (2) *noun*
Nautical: a part of a sail rolled and tied down to lessen the area exposed to the wind.
Word Family: **reef**, *verb*, to reduce the size of a sail.

reefer (1) *noun*
1. *Nautical:* a person who reefs.
2. (*informal*) a reefer jacket.

reefer (2) *noun*
(*informal*) a cigarette containing marijuana.

reefer jacket
a fine woollen blazer, sometimes double-breasted.

reef knot
a flat knot which does not slip, consisting of two loops passing through and over each other.

reek *verb*
1. to smell strongly and unpleasantly.
2. to give off steam, smoke, etc.
3. to be wet with sweat, blood, etc.
Word Family: **reek**, *noun.*

reel (1) *noun*
1. any of various devices on which a fishing line, cable, etc. may be wound.
2. a quantity of something wound on such a device: 'he bought two *reels* of wire'.
reel *verb*
to draw with a reel or by winding.
reel off, 'she *reeled off* the list of governors' (= recited fluently).

reel (2) *verb*
to stagger or sway under a blow, shock, etc.
Usage: 'his brain *reeled*' (= whirled).
Word Family: **reel**, *noun.*

reel (3) *noun*
a) a fast and lively Scottish dance. b) the music for such a dance.

re-elect *verb*
to elect again.

re-enact *verb*
to enact or act out again.

reeve (1) *noun*
Medieval history: a bailiff.

reeve (2) *verb*
(**reeved** or **rove**, **reeving**)
Nautical: to pass a rope through an opening.

refectory (*say* re-**fek**ta-ree) *noun*
a dining room, usually in a school or monastery.
[Latin *refectus* refreshed]

refer (*say* re-**fer**) *verb*
(**referred, referring**)
1. to direct to a source of information, help, etc.
2. to speak of: 'this matter is finished, so please do not *refer* to it again'.
Usages:
a) 'the dispute was *referred* to a court' (= submitted for a decision).
b) 'I *referred* to my notes before answering the question' (= consulted).
Word Family: **referable**, *adjective*; **referral**, *noun*, a letter, etc. referring one person to another; **referrer**, *noun.*
[RE- + Latin *ferre* to bring]

referee (*say* reffa-**ree**) *noun*
1. a person, such as an umpire, to whom disputes, etc. are referred.
2. a person who provides a reference, especially a character reference.
Word Family: **referee** (**refereed, refereeing**), *verb*, to act as a referee.

reference (*say* **ref**-r'nce) *noun*
1. a) the act of referring: 'he made *reference* to the original documents'. b) the state of being referred: 'with *reference* to those documents, I think they are fake'.
2. a written statement concerning the character, abilities, etc. of a person.
terms of reference, the scope allowed in an investigation, discussion, etc.

referendum (*say* reffa-**ren**-dum) *noun*
plural is **referenda** or **referendums**
also called a **plebiscite**

a) the making of a political decision by asking each person in a country to vote on it. b) such a vote.

refill (*say* ree–**fil**) *verb*
to fill again.
refill (*say* **ree**–fil) *noun*
a replacement for the used contents of a container.

refine (*say* re–**fine**) *verb*
1. to make something pure or clean: 'to *refine* sugar'.
2. (of petroleum) to separate the components of crude oil by fractional distillation.
3. to make more tasteful, artistic, etc.
Word Family: **refiner,** *noun,* a person who refines.

refinement *noun*
1. a) the act of refining: 'the *refinement* of sugar'. b) the state of having refined manners, etc.: 'the students lacked *refinement*'.
2. an increase in subtlety or ingenuity: 'he introduced new *refinements* in mathematical analysis'.

refinery (*say* re–**fie**–na–ree) *noun*
a place where something is refined, such as petroleum or sugar.

reflation (*say* re–**flay**–sh'n) *noun*
Economics: measures taken to increase demand for goods and services, introduced after a recession to restore the economy to a stable position.
Word Family: **reflate,** *verb.*

reflect (*say* re–**flekt**) *verb*
1. to throw or cast back light, sound, etc. from a surface.
Usage: 'the boy *reflects* the views of his dominating father' (= reproduces).
2. to rebound or return: 'your outrageous behaviour *reflects* badly upon your parents'.
3. to think carefully: 'before I can answer I must *reflect* upon what you have told me'.
Word Family: **reflection,** *noun*; **reflective,** *adjective*; **reflectively,** *adverb*; **reflector,** *noun,* a substance or device that reflects light, sound, etc.
[Latin *reflectere* to bend back]

reflex (*say* **ree**–fleks) *noun*
1. an involuntary or immediate movement, such as sneezing, in response to a stimulus.
2. an image produced by reflection.
Word Family: **reflex,** *adjective,* occurring in or as a reaction.

reflex angle
Maths: an angle between 180° and 360°.

reflex camera
a camera with a mirror which reflects the lens image into the eyepiece, so that it may be focused up to the time of exposure.

reflexive (*say* re–**fleksiv**) *adjective*
Grammar: of a pronoun or verb which refers back to the subject of the sentence. *Example*: he *cut himself* (reflexive verb); he cut *himself* (reflexive pronoun).
Word Family: **reflexively,** *adverb.*

reflux (*say* **ree**–fluks) *noun*
a flowing back.

reform (*say* re–**form**) *verb*
to improve by changing, as by giving up a bad habit, etc.
Word Family: **reform,** *noun,* an improvement or amendment; **reformative,** *adjective,* tending to reform; **reformer,** *noun.*

re–form *verb*
to form again.

reformation (*say* reffa–**may**–sh'n) *noun*
1. a) the act of reforming: 'his *reformation* from a helpless alcoholic took a long time'. b) the state of being reformed.
2. *History:* (*capital*) the religious movement which began in Europe in the 16th century to reform the Roman Catholic Church, and led to the formation of the Protestant churches.

reformatory (*say* re–**forma**–tree) *adjective*
serving or designed to reform.
reformatory *noun*
also called a **reform school**
History: an institution where children convicted of crimes were held in detention. Now replaced by Approved Schools.

refraction (*say* re–**frak**–sh'n) *noun*
Physics: the change in direction of an oblique wave when it passes from one medium to another. *Example*: a ray of light is bent as it passes from air into glass.
Word Family: **refract,** *verb,* to deflect by refraction; **refractive,** *adjective*; **refractiveness,** *noun.*
[RE– + Latin *fractus* broken]

refractory (*say* re–**frak**ta–ree) *adjective*
1. stubborn or unmanageable: 'the teacher could not cope with the *refractory* child'.
2. (of a substance) having the ability to retain its physical form and chemical properties when subjected to high temperatures, e.g. the bricks used for lining furnaces.

refrain (1) (*say* re–**frane**) *verb*
to keep oneself from doing or saying something: 'I *refrained* from shouting at the naughty child'.
[RE– + Latin *frenum* a bridle]

refrain (2) (*say* re–**frane**) *noun*
a phrase or verse recurring at intervals in a song or poem.
[RE– + Latin *fringere* to break]

refresh (*say* re–**fresh**) *verb*
to revive or make fresh, as by rest, food, etc.
Usage: 'to *refresh* one's memory' (= stimulate).
refresher course, a course of instruction to bring practising doctors, teachers, etc. up to date with recent developments in their field.
Word Family: **refresher**, *noun*, a person or thing that refreshes; **refreshing**, *adjective*, capable of refreshing.

refreshment *noun*
something which refreshes, such as food or drink for a light meal.

refrigerant (*say* re–**frij**a–r'nt) *noun*
a substance, such as ammonia, which reduces temperature.
[RE– + Latin *frigoris* of cold]

refrigerate (*say* re–**frij**a–rate) *verb*
to make or keep cool or cold.
Word Family: **refrigeration**, *noun*.

refrigerator (*say* re–**frij**a–rayta) *noun*
any of various appliances consisting of an enclosed space which can be kept at a constantly low temperature, used for storing foods, medicines, etc.

refuel *verb*
(refuelled, refuelling)
to supply again with fuel.

refuge (*say* **ref**–yooj) *noun*
shelter or protection from danger, trouble, etc.
[Latin *refugere* to run away from]

refugee (*say* ref–yoo–**jee**) *noun*
a person who has fled from his home or country because of some danger or disaster, such as a flood, war, dictatorship, etc.

refund (*say* re–**fund**) *verb*
to give back, especially money.
Word Family: **refund** (*say* **ree**–fund), *noun*.

re-fund (*say* re–**fund**) *verb*
to fund anew.

refurbish (*say* re–**fer**bish) *verb*
to renovate or make clean.

refuse (1) (*say* re–**fewz**) *verb*
to say one will not do, accept, give, allow, etc.
Word Family: **refusal**, *noun*.

refuse (2) (*say* **ref**–yooce) *noun*
anything discarded as worthless or useless.

refute (*say* re–**fewt**) *verb*
to prove a statement to be false.
Word Family: **refutable** (*say* **ref**–yoota–b'l *or* re–**few**ta–b'l), *adjective*, able to be refuted; **refutation**, *noun*.
[Latin *refutare* to check]

regain (*say* re–**gane**) *verb*
1. to get back again: 'after the illness it took a month for her to *regain* her strength'.
2. to reach again: 'we *regained* the shore after swimming for an hour'.

regal (*say* **ree**–g'l) *adjective*
1. of or relating to a monarch.
2. dignified and stately.
Word Family: **regally**, *adverb*; **regality** (*say* ree–**galli**–tee), *noun*.
[from Latin]

regale (*say* re–**gale**) *verb*
to entertain, especially with good food or drink.
Word Family: **regalement**, *noun*.
[from French]

regalia (*say* re–**gale**–ya) *plural noun*
the insignia, decorations or emblems of an office, especially of a monarch.

regard (*say* re–**gard**) *verb*
1. to think of in a particular way: a) 'she is *regarded* as the best student in the school'; b) 'I *regard* him with affection'.
2. to concern or relate to: 'a matter *regarding* the new law'.
Usage: 'she seldom *regards* her parents' (= heeds, follows).
3. to look at in some specific way: 'she *regarded* him with a hostile stare'.
regard *noun*
1. reference or relation: 'in *regard* to that money'.
2. any concern or attention: 'he carries on with no *regard* to my wishes'.

3. esteem or respect: 'I have little *regard* for him'.
4. (*plural*) sentiments of affection, esteem, etc.: 'please send my *regards* to your parents'.
Usage: 'your plan is excellent in all *regards*' (= particulars, points).
Word Family: **regardless,** *adjective,* without care, consideration or thought for; **regardlessly,** *adverb*; **regardful,** *adjective,* attentive or concerned.

regatta (*say* re-**gatta**) *noun*
a gathering of boats at which contests or races are held.
[Italian *regata* a gondola race]

regenerate (*say* ree-**jenna**-rate) *verb*
1. to construct or create anew.
2. *Biology:* to grow again a part of an organism that has been removed.
Word Family: **regenerative,** *adjective*; **regeneration,** *noun.*

regent (*say* **ree**-j'nt) *noun*
a person who carries out the duties of a monarch who is too young, ill, etc. to rule.
Word Family: **regency,** *noun,* a) the office of a regent, b) his period of regency, especially (capital) that of the future George IV, 1811–20; **regent,** *adjective.*
[Latin *regens* guiding, controlling]

regicide (*say* **reji**-side) *noun*
Law: a) the crime of killing a monarch. b) the person who does this.
[Latin *regis* of a king + *caedere* to kill]

régime (*say* ray-**zheem**) *noun*
1. a) any system of government. b) a particular government.
2. a regimen.
[French]

regimen (*say* **reji**-m'n) *noun*
Medicine: a balanced programme of careful diet and exercise intended to maintain or restore good health.
[Latin, guidance]

regiment (*say* **reji**-m'nt) *noun*
Military: a tactical army unit consisting of two or more battalions.
regiment *verb*
1. a) to form into a regiment. b) to assign to a regiment.
2. to subject to strict discipline.
Word Family: **regimentation,** *noun*; **regimental** (*say* reji-**men**-t'l), *adjective.*

region (*say* **reejun**) *noun*
1. *Geography:* an area with generally similar features which separate it from another area.
2. any area or part: 'the pain is in the upper *region* of my chest'.
regional *adjective*
a) relating to a large geographic region. b) relating to a particular region.
Word Family: **regionally,** *adverb.*
[from Latin]

register (*say* **rejis**-ter) *noun*
1. a) a formal or official list of items, names, etc. b) a book for such entries.
2. any machine which lists and indicates numbers: 'a cash *register*'.
3. the range of a voice or instrument.
4. *Linguistics:* a range of language relating to particular circumstances or contexts, e.g. legal, medical, family, etc.
register *verb*
1. to enter in a register.
2. to indicate on a scale, etc.
Usages:
a) 'she *registered* no signs of stress or worry' (= indicated).
b) 'he told me his name but it didn't *register*' (= make an impression).
3. to register the contents of a letter, etc. at a post office to ensure safe delivery.
Word Family: **registration,** *noun.*
[Latin *regestus* recorded]

registrar (*say* **reji**-strar) *noun*
1. a person who keeps registers, especially in a university.
2. a doctor, in a hospital, who is training to be a specialist.

registration plate
a numberplate.

registry (*say* **rejis**-tree) *noun*
a place where registers are kept.
registry office
an office where births, marriages and deaths are recorded and civil marriages take place.

Regius professor
the holder of a professorship founded by a monarch, especially Henry VIII.
[Latin *regius* royal]

regnant (*say* **regnent**) *adjective*
reigning: 'the Queen *regnant*'.
[from Latin]

regression (*say* re-**gresh**'n) *noun*
1. backward movement.
2. a return to an earlier or less mature level of development.
Word Family: **regress,** *verb*; **regressive,** *adjective*; **regressively,** *adverb.*
[from Latin]

regret *verb*
(regretted, regretting)

to feel sorry, dissatisfied or distressed, especially about something one has done or said.
regret *noun*
1. a feeling of loss, repentance or sorrow, as for a mishandled opportunity.
2. (*plural*) a formal expression of disappointment, as when declining an invitation.
Word Family: **regrettable,** *adjective*; **regrettably,** *adverb*; **regretful,** *adjective*, full of regret; **regretfully** *adverb*; **regretfulness,** *noun.*
[Old French *regreter* to bewail]

regular (*say* **reg**-yoola) *adjective*
1. normal, usual or customary.
2. orderly or symmetrical: 'a *regular* polygon'.
3. (of a verb) having the most common changes of form for each tense, usually by means of endings, as in *talk* (present), *talked* (past) and *talked* (past participle). Also called **weak.**
Usage: (*informal*) 'he's a *regular* villain' (= thorough).
regular *noun*
1. a) a member of the permanent armed forces. b) a member of a religious order.
2. (*informal*) a regular customer or visitor.
Word Family: **regularly,** *adverb*; **regularity** (*say* reg-yoo-**larri**-tee), *noun*; **regularize, regularise,** *verb*, to make regular.
[Latin *regula* a rule]

regulate (*say* **reg**-yoo-late) *verb*
1. to control by a rule, method, etc.
2. to adjust to a standard, e.g. for accuracy.
Word Family: **regulator,** *noun*, a person or device that regulates; **regulative, regulatory,** *adjectives.*

regulation (*say* reg-yoo-**lay**-sh'n) *noun*
1. a rule or law designed to control behaviour or actions: 'office *regulations*'.
2. a) the act of regulating: 'the *regulation* of the machine was difficult'. b) the state of being regulated.

regurgitate (*say* re-**ger**ji-tate) *verb*
a) to flow backwards, as liquids, gases and undigested food. b) to vomit or disgorge.
Word Family: **regurgitation,** *noun.*
[RE- + Latin *gurgitis* of a flood]

rehabilitate (*say* ree-ha-**billi**-tate) *verb*
to restore to a state of health, well-being or usefulness.
Word Family: **rehabilitation,** *noun.*

rehash (*say* ree-**hash**) *verb*
to work into a new or different form.
Word Family: **rehash** (*say* **ree**-hash), *noun.*

rehearsal (*say* re-**her**-s'l) *noun*
the practice or trial performance before an event, especially of a play, film, etc. before it is performed in public.
a **dress rehearsal** is the last full rehearsal of a play, etc., with costumes lights and music, before the first performance.

rehearse (*say* re-**herse**) *verb*
to practise a play, part, etc. to prepare for a public performance.

reheat *verb*
to heat again.

reify (*say* ree-iffie) *verb*
(**reified, reifying**)
to treat or imagine an abstract idea as having material existence.
Word Family: **reification,** *noun.*
[Latin *res* thing + *facere* to make]

reign (*say* rane) *noun*
1. the length of time for which a monarch rules.
2. any dominating power or influence: 'a *reign* of fear'.
Word Family: **reign,** *verb*, a) to have the power or title of a monarch, b) to be dominant or in control.
[Latin *regnum* monarchy]

reimburse (*say* ree-im-**berse**) *verb*
to repay or make a refund for money spent or lost.
Word Family: **reimbursement,** *noun.*

rein (*say* rane) *noun*
(*usually plural*) a long strip of leather on a bridle, passing from the bit to the rider's hands, used to control and guide a horse.
Phrases:
give free rein to, to allow complete freedom to.
keep a tight rein on, to control closely.
Word Family: **rein,** *verb*, a) to control with reins, b) to check, control or restrain.

reincarnation
(*say* ree-inkar-**nay**-sh'n) *noun*
1. the belief that after a person's death his soul moves into another bodily form and continues to live.
2. a) the act of being born again in a new body. Also called

metempsychosis. b) the actual form taken on by the reborn soul.
Word Family: **reincarnate** (*say* ree–inkar–**nate**), *verb*; **reincarnate** (*say* ree–in–**karnit**), *adjective.*

reindeer (*say* **rane**–deer) *noun*
a large northern European deer, with branched antlers.

reinforce (*say* ree–**inforce**) *verb*
to make stronger or more effective, especially by adding extra pieces, support, etc.
reinforcement *noun*
1. the act of reinforcing: 'the *reinforcement* of an argument with facts'.
2. (*often plural*) something used to add strength or support, such as extra troops sent to help in a battle.

reinforced concrete
ferroconcrete.

reinstate (*say* ree–**instate**) *verb*
to put back in a former position, state, etc.: 'the king was *reinstated* after the revolutionaries were overthrown'.
Word Family: **reinstatement**, *noun.*

reinsure (*say* ree–**inshoor**) *verb*
1. to insure again.
2. to provide insurance for a risk, by sharing it amongst several companies.
Word Family: **reinsurance**, *noun.*

reinvest (*say* ree–**invest**) *verb*
to invest one's capital, etc. again.
Word Family: **reinvestment**, *noun.*

reiterate (*say* ree–**itta**–rate) *verb*
to repeat.
Word Family: **reiteration**, *noun*; **reiterative**, *adjective.*

reject (*say* re–**jekt**) *verb*
1. to refuse to accept or use: 'the committee *rejected* the union's claims'.
2. to throw away.
reject (*say* **ree**–jekt) *noun*
something which is rejected, refused or discarded.
Word Family: **rejection**, *noun.*
[Latin *rejectus* thrown back]

rejoice (*say* re–**joice**) *verb*
to be glad or joyful.
Word Family: **rejoicing**, *noun.*

rejoin (1) (*say* **ree**–join) *verb*
to join or come together with again: 'let's *rejoin* the party now'.

rejoin (2) (*say* re–**join**) *verb*
to answer or reply.
Word Family: **rejoinder**, *noun*, an answer or response.

rejuvenate (*say* re–**joovi**–nate) *verb*
1. to make young or new again.
2. *Geography:* to renew the activity of a stream or river, as by uplift of the land over which it flows, so that it begins to cut into its bed once more.
Word Family: **rejuvenation**, *noun.*
[RE– + Latin *juvenis* young]

rekindle (*say* ree–**kindel**) *verb*
to kindle or stir up again.

relapse (*say* re–**laps**) *verb*
to fall or slip back to a former, usually worse, condition.
Word Family: **relapse** (*say* **ree** laps), *noun.*
[from Latin]

relate *verb*
1. to tell or describe: 'he *related* his adventures'.
2. to be or become connected, associated or relevant: a) 'my complaint *relates* to my neighbour's children'; b) 'are you *related* to the Smiths of Inverness?'.
[Latin *relatus* brought back]

relation (*say* re–**lay**–sh'n) *noun*
1. an existing connection or association, as between people or things: a) 'what is the *relation* between these two numbers?'; b) 'personal *relations* are not good between them'.
2. a relative: 'she is a distant *relation* of my mother's'.
3. the act of telling or narrating.
Word Family: **relationship**, *noun*, a connection or association.

relative (*say* **rella**–tiv) *adjective*
1. existing or considered only in comparison or connection with something else: 'they live in *relative* luxury for such a large family'.
Usage: 'you say this jalopy has passed its test. May I see the *relative* certificate?' (= pertinent).
2. *Grammar:* of a pronoun or adverb which joins two clauses, by referring to a noun in the first clause.
relative *noun*
a person who is related to another by blood or marriage.
Word Family: **relatively**, *adverb*, comparatively.

relative atomic mass
Chemistry, Physics: the mass of an atom of an element, measured on a scale in which the mass of an atom of the carbon–12 isotope is exactly 12.

relative density
see SPECIFIC GRAVITY.

relative humidity
see HUMIDITY.

relative molecular mass
Chemistry, Physics: the mass of a molecule of substance, measured on a scale in which the mass of an atom of the carbon–12 isotope is exactly 12.

relativism (*say* **rell**a–tiv–izm) *noun*
the belief that all knowledge varies according to the individual or the situation and that absolute truth is therefore unattainable.
Word Family: **relativist,** *noun.*

relativity (*say* rella–**tivvi**–tee) *noun*
1. the fact of being relative.
2. theories derived from the proposition that time and space are not absolute but relative to the observer; e.g. that the velocity of light is a constant, mass depends on velocity, mass and energy are interchangeable, and that space–time forms a curved four–dimensional continuum and differs in outer space from that observed here.

relax (*say* re–**laks**) *verb*
1. to make or become looser, less strict or firm: a) 'she escaped as his grip *relaxed*'; b) 'if you behave, we'll *relax* the rules'.
2. to make or become less formal, tense, etc.: 'please sit down and *relax*'.
[RE– + Latin *laxus* loose]

relaxation (*say* ree–lak–**say**–sh'n) *noun*
1. a loosening or relaxing: 'the *relaxation* of his grip enabled her to escape'.
2. an activity or diversion which provides relief, enjoyment or rest: 'gardening is my greatest *relaxation*'.

relay (*say* **ree**–lay) *noun*
1. a group or set of persons, etc. who take the place of or relieve others, such as a shift of workers.
2. *Sport:* a race whose distance is divided into four or more parts, each of which is run or swum by one member of a team.
3. *Electricity:* a device which is controlled by electric currents in one circuit so that it acts as a switch in another circuit.
relay (*say* **ree**–lay *or* re–**lay**) *verb*
1. to pass or carry by or as if by relay: 'please *relay* this message to her'.
2. *Electricity:* to control by means of a relay.

relay station
Radio: a station which broadcasts programmes received from a different station.

release *verb*
to set free or let go: 'he was *released* from prison a week ago'.
Usage: 'the government has *released* a public statement' (= put into circulation, issued).
release *noun*
1. a freeing or setting free: 'a *release* from pain'.
2. a) something which sets free or releases: 'she finds shouting a great *release* for tension'. b) a device which releases or unfastens something: 'press the *release* to open the box'.
3. a) the putting out of something for public exhibition, use, purchase, etc.: 'the *release* of his new play'. b) something circulated in this way: 'the group's new *release* was an instant hit'.

re–lease *verb*
to lease again: 'we have *re–leased* the house we had last summer'.

relegate (*say* **rell**a–gate) *verb*
to send to a particular place, condition, etc., especially an inferior one: 'the team was *relegated* to a lower division'.
Word Family: **relegation,** *noun.*
[Latin *relegare* to send into retirement]

relent (*say* re–**lent**) *verb*
to become less severe or unyielding: 'he finally *relented* and let us go too'.
Word Family: **relentless,** *adjective,* a) without pity, b) steady or persistent; **relentlessly,** *adverb*; **relentlessness,** *noun.*
[RE– + Latin *lentus* flexible]

relevant (*say* **rell**a–v'nt) *adjective*
connected to the matter being discussed: 'your suggestion is not *relevant* to our discussion at all'.
Word Family: **relevance, relevancy,** *noun*; **relevantly,** *adverb.*

reliable (*say* re–**lie**–a–b'l) *adjective*
able to be relied or depended on: 'I can prove that the witness is not *reliable*'.
Word Family: **reliably,** *adverb*; **reliability** (*say* re–lie–a–**billi**–tee), *noun.*

reliant (*say* re–**lie**–ant) *adjective*
having trust, confidence or dependence: 'we are *reliant* on you for a solution'.
Word Family: **reliance,** *noun.*

relic (*say* **rel**lik) *noun*
1. something which has survived from a past time and serves as a reminder. Also called a **relict**.
2. something kept as an object of religious worship, especially some part or personal reminder of a holy person.
[Latin *reliquiae* leavings]

relied *verb*
the past tense and past participle of the verb **rely**.

relief (*say* re-**leef**) *noun*
1. a lessening or removal of pain, anxiety, etc.: 'what a *relief* to see the road again!'.
2. something which provides relief, help or comfort: 'please send *relief* to the flood victims'.
Usage: 'the watchman waited for his *relief* to arrive' (= replacement).
3. a) the projecting of a part or figure from its background or a surface, such as a sculptured figure from a wall. b) a work, design, etc. done in this way.
Usage: 'the crisis showed up their different characters in strong *relief*' (= contrast).
4. *Geography:* the different heights of parts of the earth's surface. A **relief map** shows the physical features of land by contours and shading.
[RE- + Latin *levis* light (in weight)]

relief printing
see LETTERPRESS.

relieve (*say* re-**leev**) *verb*
to bring relief or ease to: 'nothing could *relieve* her distress'.
Usages:
a) 'he was *relieved* of all duties until the trial' (= set free, dismissed from).
b) 'someone must *relieve* the exhausted fire-fighters' (= take over the duties of).
Word Family: **reliever**, *noun*.

religion (*say* re-**lij**'n) *noun*
1. any of various systems of belief or worship concerned with the spiritual or inner nature of man and usually a superhuman power recognized as creator or controller.
2. any practice, matter, etc. treated with devotion or keen conscientiousness: 'collecting butterflies is a *religion* with her'.
[Latin *religio* scrupulousness or obligation]

religious (*say* re-**lij**-us) *adjective*
a) of or relating to religion. b) godly or faithful to one's religion.
Usage: 'she makes each piece of sculpture with *religious* devotion' (= faithful, conscientious).
Word Family: **religiously**, *adverb*; **religiousness**, *noun*; **religiosity** (*say* re-liji-**ossi**-tee), *noun*, the state of being religious, especially to an extreme degree.

relinquish (*say* re-**lin**-kwish) *verb*
to let go, surrender or give up.
Word Family: **relinquishment**, *noun*.
[Latin *relinquere* to leave behind]

reliquary (*say* **rel**likwa-ree) *noun*
a container for religious relics.

relish (*say* **rel**lish) *noun*
1. an appreciation, pleasure or enjoyment: 'he watched the exciting contest with *relish*'.
2. a savoury substance, such as a pickle or sauce, added to a meal.
3. a pleasing or appetizing taste: 'our soups are full of goodness and *relish*'.
relish *verb*
to take pleasure in or enjoy: 'I *relish* the thought of getting revenge'.

relive (*say* ree-**liv**) *verb*
to live or experience again.

relocate (*say* reelo-**kate**) *verb*
to establish or become established in a new place.
Word Family: **relocation**, *noun*.

reluctant (*say* re-**luk**-t'nt) *adjective*
disinclined, not eager: 'I'm *reluctant* to lend you my new car'.
Word Family: **reluctantly**, *adverb*; **reluctance, reluctancy**, *noun*.
[RE- + Latin *luctans* struggling]

rely (*say* re-**lie**) *verb*
(relied, relying)
to have trust or confidence in: 'I'll *rely* on your judgement for the decision'.

remain *verb*
1. to stay or continue: a) '*remain* in your seats'; b) 'he *remained* calm during the crisis'.
2. to be left: 'much work *remains* to be done'.
remains *plural noun*
any parts left over after destruction, use, etc.: a) 'the *remains* of a bombed city'; b) 'the *remains* of dinner'.
Usage: 'the victim's *remains* have not been identified' (= corpse, body).
remainder *noun*
the part which is left: 'if you take 6 from 10 the *remainder* is 4'.
[from Latin]

remake (*say* ree-**make**) *verb*
(**remade, remaking**)
to make or construct again.
Word Family: **remake** (*say* **ree**-make), *noun*, something which is made again, especially a film.

remand (*say* re-**mahnd**) *verb*
Law: to hold an accused person to await further trial.
Word Family: **remand**, *noun*, a) the act of remanding, b) the state of being remanded.
[RE- + Latin *mandare* to commit]

remark (*say* re-**mark**) *verb*
1. to say casually.
2. to notice: 'did you *remark* his extraordinary clothes?'.
remark *noun*
1. the act of commenting or noticing: 'the event was scarcely worthy of *remark*'.
2. a comment or casual expression.
Word Family: **remarkable**, *adjective*, unusual or worthy of remark; **remarkably**, *adverb*.

re-mark (*say* **ree**-mark) *verb*
to mark or correct again.

remarry *verb*
(**remarried, remarrying**)
to marry again after widowhood or divorce.
Word Family: **remarriage**, *noun*.

remedial (*say* re-**meed**i-ul) *adjective*
a) providing a remedy. b) intended to correct or improve, as with special extra help: '*remedial* teaching'.

remedy (*say* **remma**-dee) *noun*
anything which heals, removes or relieves pain, fault, etc.
remedy *verb*
(**remedied, remedying**)
to fix or put right.
Word Family: **remediable** (*say* re-**meedia**-b'l), *adjective*, able to be cured or fixed.
[from Latin]

remember *verb*
to keep in or recall to the mind: a) 'please *remember* to bring your coat'; b) 'I can't *remember* his name'.
Usages:
a) 'please *remember* me to your parents' (= send greetings from).
b) 'were you *remembered* in grandfather's will?' (= left something).
[RE- + Latin *memor* mindful]

remembrance (*say* re-**mem**-br'nce) *noun*
1. the act of remembering.
2. a token or souvenir, especially one given to serve as a reminder.

remind *verb*
to cause to remember: 'please *remind* me to buy the meat'.
Word Family: **reminder**, *noun*, something which causes one to remember.

reminisce (*say* remmi-**niss**) *verb*
(*informal*) to remember and enjoy or describe past experiences, events, etc.
reminiscence *noun*
1. a) the act of reminiscing. b) a memory or impression remembered and renewed.
2. (*usually plural*) a person's description of past experiences.
Word Family: **reminiscent**, *adjective*, inspiring memories of.
[from Latin]

remiss (*say* re-**miss**) *adjective*
careless or neglectful.
Word Family: **remissness**, *noun*.
[Latin *remissus* sent back, slackened]

remission (*say* re-**mish**'n) *noun*
1. the act of remitting.
2. a pardon, release or forgiveness: 'the *remission* of sins'.
3. a lessening in strength or intensity: 'a temporary *remission* of the disease enabled the patient to leave hospital'.

remit (*say* re-**mit**) *verb*
(**remitted, remitting**)
1. to send, especially money.
2. a) to forgive or pardon. b) to excuse from punishment, debt, etc.
3. to become less strong: 'the disease began to *remit*'.
Word Family: **remittance**, *noun*, a) the sending of money or credit to a person, b) money or payment sent or given.
[Latin *remittere* to let go back]

remittent *adjective*
recurring at intervals, e.g. the symptoms of a disease.

remnant *noun*
a remaining part, quantity or fragment.

remonstrate (*say* **remm**'n-strate) *verb*
to say in protest or objection.
Word Family: **remonstrant**, *adjective*; **remonstration**, **remonstrance** (*say* re-**mon**-str'nce), *nouns*.
[RE- + Latin *monstrare* to show]

remora (*say* **remmera**) *noun*
any of a group of fish having a flattened head with a sucking disc on the top,

by which it may attach itself to a larger fish or a ship.
[Latin, a hindrance]

remorse *noun*
a feeling of sincere and painful regret or sorrow for one's misdeeds.
Word Family: **remorseful**, *adjective*; **remorsefully**, *adverb*; **remorsefulness**, *noun*; **remorseless**, *adjective*, without pity or remorse; **remorselessly**, *adverb*; **remorselessness**, *noun*.
[RE– + Latin *morsus* bitten]

remote *adjective*
far away or distant: a) 'a *remote* town'; b) 'the *remote* past'.
Usages:
a) 'her *remote* manner makes people rather nervous' (= aloof, cold).
b) 'I do not have even a *remote* idea of the answer' (= slight).
Word Family: **remotely**, *adverb*; **remoteness**, *noun*.
[Latin *remotus* removed]

remote control
the control or direction of a process, machine, etc. by electrical or radio signals at a distance.

remould (*say* ree–**mold**) *verb*
to mould or shape again, as by adding new rubber walls, etc. to a used tyre.
Word Family: **remould** (*say* **ree**–mold), *noun*, a tyre which has been remoulded.

remove (*say* re–**moov**) *verb*
to take off or away: '*remove* your shoes before entering'.
Usage: 'the Prime Minister was *removed* from office' (= sacked).
remove *noun*
1. the distance by which things are separated: 'this party is a far *remove* from last year's celebrations'.
2. *Education:* an intermediate class.
Word Family: **removal** (*say* re–**moo**–v'l), *noun*, a) the act of removing, b) a change of position, location, etc.; **removable**, *adjective*.
[Latin *removere* to put away]

remunerate (*say* re–**mewna**–rate) *verb*
to pay, reward or compensate.
Word Family: **remuneration**, *noun*; **remunerative**, *adjective*, profitable.
[RE– + Latin *muneris* of a gift]

Renaissance (*say* rennay–sonce) *noun*
also spelt **Renascence**
1. the revival of Classical learning and art in Europe from the 14th to the 16th century.
2. (*not capital*) any revival or rebirth.
[French, rebirth]

renal (*say* **ree**–n'l) *adjective*
Anatomy: of or relating to the kidneys.
[Latin *ren* kidney]

rename (*say* ree–**name**) *verb*
to give a new name to.

renascent (*say* re–**nass**'nt) *adjective*
being renewed or growing again.

rend *verb*
(**rent, rending**)
to split or tear apart violently.
Usages:
a) 'a terrible cry *rent* the silent air' (= penetrated, disturbed).
b) 'his tears could *rend* her heart' (= distress painfully).

render *verb*
1. to provide, give or make available: a) 'to *render* assistance'; b) 'to *render* an account for payment'; c) '*render* up the hostages or we'll shoot'.
2. to represent or depict: 'the artist *rendered* the scene in great detail'.
Usages:
a) 'the song was *rendered* in the wrong key' (= performed).
b) '*render* this paragraph from French into English' (= translate).
c) 'she was *rendered* mad by drink' (= caused to become).
3. to extract or reduce by melting: 'to *render* bacon fat'.
4. *Building:* to coat a wall with a layer of plaster or mortar.
[Latin *reddere* to give back]

rendezvous (*say* **ron**day–voo) *noun*
a) an arranged meeting. b) a meeting place.
Word Family: **rendezvous**, *verb*.
[French *rendez-vous* present yourself]

rendition (*say* ren–**dish**'n) *noun*
a rendering, performance or interpretation.

renegade (*say* **renna**–gade) *noun*
a person who leaves or betrays a party, belief or cause.
[Spanish *renegado* renounced]

renege (*say* re–**neeg**) *verb*
1. *Cards:* to fail to follow suit when one is able to do so by the rules.
2. to fail to carry out one's word or promise.
[RE– + Latin *negare* to deny]

renegotiate (*say* reena–**go**–shee–ate) *verb*
to negotiate or revise a contract or agreement again.

renew (*say* re–**new**) *verb*
to begin again or make new: '*renew* a friendship'.

Usages:
a) 'we will *renew* the lease for another year" (= extend).
b) 'he returned from his holiday with *renewed* vigour' (= revived).
Word Family: **renewal**, *noun*; **renewable**, *adjective*, able or due to be renewed.

rennet *noun*
a substance obtained from the inner lining of a calf's stomach and used to curdle milk, e.g. in making cheese or junket.

renounce (*say* re-**nounce**) *verb*
to reject or disown: 'I *renounce* all claim to the inheritance'.
Word Family: **renunciation,** *noun.*
[RE- + Latin *nuntiare* to announce]

renovate (*say* **renn**a-vate) *verb*
to repair to the original condition: 'to *renovate* an old house'.
Word Family: **renovation**, *noun*, a) the act of renovating, b) (plural) the changes or repairs made; **renovator,** *noun.*
[RE- + Latin *novus* new]

renown (*say* ree-**noun**) *noun*
fame.
Word Family: **renowned**, *adjective.*
[RE- + Latin *nomen* a name]

rent (1) *noun*
the payment made by one person or group in return for the use or occupation of a property which belongs to another.
Word Family: **rent**, *verb*, to give or obtain use or occupation of property in exchange for payment; **rental,** *adjective.*

rent (2) *noun*
a tear or rip.
rent *verb*
the past tense and past participle of the verb **rend**.

rental *noun*
the amount received or paid as rent.

rentier (*say* **ron**-tee-ay) *noun*
a person of independent means who lives on interest from investments.
[French *rente* rent, dividend]

renunciation *noun*
Word Family: see RENOUNCE.

reoccupy (*say* ree-**ok**-yoo-pie) *verb*
(**reoccupied, reoccupying**)
to occupy or live in again.

reopen (*say* ree-**o**-pen) *verb*
to open or begin again: 'his words *reopened* an old wound'.

reorganize (*say* ree-**or**ga-nize)
reorganise *verb*
to organize again.
Word Family: **reorganization,** *noun.*

rep (1) *noun*
(*informal*) a representative.

rep (2) *noun*
(*informal*) repertory theatre.

repaid *verb*
the past tense and past participle of the verb **repay.**

repair (1) (*say* re-**pair**) *verb*
to put back into good or whole condition.
Usage: 'nothing could *repair* the damage to her heart' (= make up for).
Word Family: **repair,** *noun,* a) the work or process of repairing, b) the condition due to repairing; **repairable, reparable** (*say* **rep**ra-b'l), *adjectives.*
[RE- + Latin *parare* to make ready]

repair (2) (*say* re-**pair**) *verb*
an old word meaning to go or take oneself.
Word Family: **repair,** *noun.*
[Old French *reparer* to return to one's own country]

reparation (*say* reppa-**ray**-sh'n) *noun*
a) the act of making amends or compensating. b) something done or given as compensation.

repartee (*say* reppar-**tee**) *noun*
a) a quick or clever reply. b) the art of making such replies. c) a conversation made up of quick or witty exchanges.
[French *repartir* to reply promptly]

repast (*say* re-**pahst**) *noun*
a meal.
[RE- + Latin *pastus* fed]

repatriate (*say* ree-**patri**-ate) *verb*
to send back a person, such as a refugee or prisoner of war, to his own country.
Word Family: **repatriate** (*say* ree-**patri**-it), *noun,* a person who has been repatriated; **repatriation,** *noun.*
[RE- + Latin *patria* native land]

repay (*say* re-**pay**) *verb*
(**repaid, repaying**)
to pay back: '*repay* a loan'.
Usage: 'have you *repaid* her kindness?' (= returned).
Word Family: **repayment,** *noun.*

repeal *verb*
to cancel or withdraw: 'Parliament has *repealed* the law'.
Word Family: **repeal,** *noun.*
[Old French *rapeler* to call back]

repeat *verb*
to say or do again: '*repeat* the poem until you know it by memory'.
Usages:
a) 'please don't *repeat* what I have just told you' (= tell anybody).
b) 'I'd hate to *repeat* that terrible experience' (= go through again).
repeat *noun*
a) the act of repeating. b) something which is repeated, such as a television programme.
repeater *noun*
1. a gun capable of firing several times without reloading.
2. something which repeats, such as a watch which can be actuated to strike the last quarter-hour and the subsequent minutes (for use in the dark).
Word Family: **repeated,** *adjective,* done or said again and again; **repeatedly,** *adverb;* **repetition,** *noun,* a) the act of repeating, b) something repeated.
[RE- + Latin *petere* to seek]

repel (*say* re-**pel**) *verb*
(repelled, repelling)
to turn back or force away: 'to *repel* an invading army'.
Usages:
a) 'his lack of manners *repelled* her' (= was distasteful to).
b) 'this spray will *repel* insects' (= keep away).
c) 'oil will *repel* water' (= not mix with).
Word Family: **repellence, repellency,** *noun.*
[RE- + Latin *pellere* to drive]

repellent (*say* re-**pell**'nt) *noun*
something which repels, especially a substance or solution used to repel insects, etc.
Word Family: **repellent,** *adjective,* a) able to repel or keep off, b) distateful or revolting.

repent (*say* re-**pent**) *verb*
to feel sorry or remorseful, especially with the intention to improve or reform: 'I hope that you *repent* of your rudeness'.
Word Family: **repentance,** *noun;* **repentant,** *adjective.*
[RE- + Latin *paenitere* to regret]

repercussion (*say* reepa-**kush**'n) *noun*
1. an indirect result or effect of some action, event, etc., especially if unexpected, unpleasant and self-proliferating.
2. a rebounding, such as an echo.
[RE- + Latin *percussus* struck]

repertoire (*say* **reppa**-twa) *noun*
1. the stock or range of works, parts or pieces presented by a performer or company.
2. a range or number of skills belonging to a particular person or group.
[French]

repertory (*say* **reppa**-tree) *noun*
a theatre or company of actors which presents a number of plays for a limited time.

repetition (*say* reppa-**tish**'n) *noun*
Word Family: see REPEAT.

repetitious (*say* reppa-**tish**us) *adjective*
tending to repeat, especially in a needless way.

repetitive (*say* re-**petta**-tiv) *adjective*
of or tending to repeat.
Word Family: **repetitively,** *adverb.*

repine (*say* re-**pine**) *verb*
to complain or fret.

replace (*say* re-**place**) *verb*
1. to put back in place or position: 'please *replace* books on their correct shelves'.
2. to take the place of: 'nothing can *replace* the good old days'.
Word Family: **replacement,** *noun.*

replay (*say* ree-**play**) *verb*
to play over again: 'to *replay* a game'.
Word Family: **replay** (*say* **ree**-play), *noun.*

replenish (*say* re-**plenn**ish) *verb*
to supply or fill again: 'let the waiter *replenish* your glasses'.
Word Family: **replenishment,** *noun.*
[RE- + Latin *plenus* full]

replete (*say* re-**pleet**) *adjective*
well supplied or filled: 'the guests sat back *replete* with rich food and wine'.
Word Family: **repletion,** *noun.*
[Latin *repletus* filled]

replica (*say* **repli**-ka) *noun*
a copy or reproduction, especially of a work of art.
Word Family: **replicate,** *verb,* to make an exact copy of; **replication,** *noun.*
[Italian]

reply (*say* re-**ply**) *verb*
(replied, replying)
to say or do something in return: 'have you *replied* to his letter yet?'.
Word Family: **reply,** *noun,* a statement or action made or given in return.
[Latin *replicare* to repeat]

report *noun*
1. an account of a particular subject: a) 'a *report* on today's market prices'; b) 'a *report* on a student's progress at school'.
Usage: 'according to *report*, she is the most likely candidate' (= talk, reputation).
2. a loud bang or explosion.
report *verb*
1. to give an account, statement or description of: 'his speech was *reported* in the newspapers'.
Usage: 'he *reported* his noisy neighbours to the police' (= made a complaint or charge against).
2. to present oneself: 'you should *report* for work at noon'.
[Latin *reportare* to bring back]

reported speech
the words of one person as described or modified by another.

reporter *noun*
1. a person employed to collect and report or write about news, current events, etc.
2. a person appointed to take notes or report on official proceedings, etc.: 'a court *reporter*'.

repose (1) (*say* re-**poze**) *noun*
1. rest or relaxation.
2. a calm confidence.
Word Family: **repose**, *verb,* a) to lie on something, b) to be resting or peaceful; **reposeful**, *adjective,* calm; **reposefully**, *adverb.*
[RE- + Latin *pausa* a pause]

repose (2) (*say* re-**poze**) *verb*
to place or put, usually one's faith, trust or confidence.
[RE- + Latin *positus* placed]

repository (*say* re-**pozzi**-tree) *noun*
a place where things are deposited or stored.

repossess (*say* reepo-**zess**) *noun*
to take back possession of: 'his creditors have *repossessed* the car'.
Word Family: **repossession**, *noun.*

repp, rep *noun*
a plain-woven fabric with a prominent cross-rib, used in curtains, upholstery, etc.
[from French]

reprehensible (*say* repri-**hensi**-b'l) *adjective*
deserving blame or rebuke: 'a *reprehensible* attack on an innocent person'.
Word Family: **reprehensibly**, *adverb*; **reprehend**, *verb,* to blame or find fault with; **reprehension**, *noun.*
[RE- + Latin *prehensus* seized]

represent (*say* repri-**zent**) *verb*
1. to stand for: 'each sign on the scale *represents* a note'.
Usage: 'the young politician *represents* a large electorate' (= acts on behalf of).
2. to present, describe or give a picture of: 'father *represents* his son as a brilliant scholar'.
representative *noun*
a person who acts for or instead of another or others: a) 'who is your legal *representative*?'; b) 'I got a job as a sales *representative*'.
Word Family: **representative**, *adjective,* a) serving to represent, b) typical.

representation
(*say* repri-zen-**tay**-sh'n) *noun*
1. a) the act of representing: 'his *representation* of the facts was rather misleading'. b) the state of being represented: 'we demand equal *representation* in parliament'.
2. something which represents or depicts, such as a statue.
3. a speech or action made on behalf of a person, group, etc.: 'his spokesman will make a *representation* to the court'.

repress (*say* re-**press**) *verb*
to hold back or restrain: a) 'she could not *repress* a smile'; b) 'the new law tried to *repress* the workers'.
Word Family: **repression** (*say* re-**presh**'n), *noun*; **represser**, *noun*; **repressible**, *adjective,* able to be repressed; **repressive**, *adjective,* tending to repress.
[Latin *repressus* checked]

reprieve (*say* re-**preev**) *verb*
to postpone, suspend or cancel the punishment of.
Word Family: **reprieve**, *noun,* a) the postponement, etc. of a punishment, b) a temporary relief or release.

reprimand (*say* repri-mahnd) *verb*
to rebuke sharply, usually publicly.
Word Family: **reprimand**, *noun.*
[Latin *reprimanda* that should be repressed]

reprint (*say* ree-**print**) *verb*
to print again.
reprint (*say* **ree**-print) *noun*
anything which has been printed again, such as a new, unchanged edition of a book.

reprisal (*say* re-**pry**-z'l) *noun*
an attack, punishment, injury, etc. made in retaliation for some injury.

reproach *verb*
to express disapproval, usually about a personal matter and intending to cause a feeling of shame.
Word Family: **reproach**, *noun*; **reproachful**, *adjective*, expressing blame; **reproachfully**, *adverb*; **reproachfulness**, *noun*.

reprobate (*say* **repra**-bate) *noun*
a person without principles or morals.
reprobate *adjective*
depraved or corrupt.
Word Family: **reprobate**, *verb*, to disapprove or condemn; **reprobation**, *noun*.
[Latin *reprobatus* disapproved of]

reprocessing *noun*
Physics: the treatment of used nuclear reactor fuel elements to extract fissionable material which may be reused.

reproduce (*say* ree-pro-**dewce**) *verb*
1. to have or give birth to offspring.
2. to produce an identical or very similar form of: 'to *reproduce* a painting from the original'.
Usage: 'can you *reproduce* the scene for the jury?' (= create again).
Word Family: **reproduction**, *noun*, a) the act of reproducing, b) something which is produced again or in an identical form; **reproductive**, *adjective*, a) of or relating to reproduction, b) able to reproduce; **reproducible**, *adjective*, able to be reproduced.

reprove (*say* re-**proov**) *verb*
to scold or express disapproval.
Word Family: **reproof**, **reproval**, *nouns*, a) the act of reproving, b) an expression of disapproval, etc.; **reprovingly**, *adverb*.

reptile *noun*
1. any of a group of cold-blooded, air-breathing animals, such as the snake, turtle, etc., having a backbone and usually scales or tough, horny skin.
2. a sly or treacherous person.
Word Family: **reptilian** (*say* rep-**tillian**), *adjective*.
[Latin *reptilis* creeping]

republic (*say* re-**pub**lik) *noun*
a country without a monarch, especially one with a single, elected leader.
Word Family: **republican**, *adjective*, a) relating to a republic, b) in favour of a republic as the form of government; **republican**, *noun*, a person who favours a republic as the form of government; **republicanism**, *noun*.
[Latin *res publica* public concern]

repudiate (*say* re-**pew**di-ate) *verb*
to refuse to accept, recognize or own: a) 'scientists have *repudiated* this man's theory'; b) 'I *repudiate* any debts my husband incurs'.
Word Family: **repudiation**, *noun*.
[Latin *repudium* divorce]

repugnant *adjective*
offensive or distasteful.
Word Family: **repugnance**, *noun*, a) an extreme dislike or distaste, b) the state of being repugnant.
[Latin *repugnans* fighting against]

repulse (*say* re-**puls**) *verb*
to drive back or resist: a) 'our troops have *repulsed* the enemy'; b) 'do not *repulse* his friendly approaches'.
Word Family: **repulse**, *noun*, a rejection; **repulsion** (*say* re-**pul**-sh'n), *noun*, a) the act of repulsing or repelling, b) a feeling of disgust.
[Latin *repulsus* repelled]

repulsive *adjective*
causing extreme distaste or dislike: 'please get rid of that *repulsive* smell!'.

reputable (*say* **rep**-yoota-b'l) *adjective*
having a good reputation.
Word Family: **reputably** (*say* rep-**yoo**ta-blee), *adverb*; **reputability** (*say* rep-yoota-**billi**-tee), *noun*.

reputation (*say* rep-yoo-**tay**-sh'n) *noun*
the general opinion concerning the character or qualities of a person or thing: 'he has a *reputation* for cheating his customers'.
Usage: 'he is a man of some *reputation* in this town' (= favour, credit).
[Latin *reputare* to think over]

repute (*say* re-**pewt**) *noun*
fame or reputation, especially favourable reputation.
repute *verb*
to consider or regard as: 'she's *reputed* to be a witch'.
Word Family: **reputedly**, *adverb*.

request (*say* re-**kwest**) *verb*
to express a wish or desired favour: 'she *requested* a loan from the bank'.
Word Family: **request**, *noun*, a) the act of asking, b) something which is asked for.
[Latin *requisitus* searched for]

requiem (*say* **rek**wi-em) *noun*
1. *Roman Catholic:* a mass celebrated for the peace of the dead.
2. any ceremony, composition, etc. for the dead.
[Latin *requies* rest]

require (*say* re-**kwire**) *verb*
to need: a) 'all visitors *require* permission to enter'; b) 'I *require* you to remain silent at all times'.
Usage: 'do you *require* anything else, sir?' (= want, wish for).
Word Family: **requirement**, *noun*, something which is required or obligatory.
[Latin *requirere* to search for]

requisite (*say* **rek**wi-zit) *adjective*
necessary or required.
Word Family: **requisite**, *noun*, a requirement.

requisition (*say* rekwi-**zish**'n) *noun*
1. a formal demand or request.
2. the act of demanding or requesting.
Word Family: **requisition**, *verb*, to take over or demand for use, especially for official or military purposes.

requite (*say* re-**kwite**) *verb*
to give in return.
Usage: 'they were determined to *requite* the murder of their leader' (= revenge).
Word Family: **requital**, *noun*, repayment or retaliation.
[RE- + QUIT]

reredos (*say* **reer**-doss) *noun*
a screen or wall behind the altar in a church.
[REAR + French *dos* back]

re-run *noun*
a film or programme which is repeated, e.g. on television, etc.
Word Family: **re-run (re-ran, re-run, re-running)**, *verb.*

rescind (*say* re-**sind**) *verb*
to cancel or withdraw formally: 'to *rescind* a trade agreement'.
Word Family: **rescission** (*say* re-**si*zh***'n), *noun*, the act of rescinding.
[Latin *rescindere* to cut back]

rescue (*say* **res**kew) *verb*
to free from danger, imprisonment or unpleasantness.
Word Family: **rescue**, *noun*, the act of rescuing; **rescuer**, *noun.*

research (*say* re-**serch**) *noun*
careful or systematic work to seek facts, information, etc.
Word Family: **research**, *verb*, to investigate thoroughly.

resection (*say* ree-**sek**-sh'n) *noun*
an operation to remove part of a bone, organ, etc.
Word Family: **resect**, *verb.*
[RE- + Latin *sectus* cut]

resemble (*say* re-**zem**-b'l) *verb*
to be or appear like or similar to: 'she *resembles* her grandmother'.
resemblance *noun*
a) the fact of resembling. b) the degree or amount to which something resembles another: 'there is little *resemblance* between the two languages'.
[RE- + Latin *similis* like]

resent (*say* re-**zent**) *verb*
to feel an indignant or angry dislike for: 'I *resent* those rude comments'.
Word Family: **resentment**, *noun*; **resentful**, *adjective*; **resentfully**, *adverb*; **resentfulness**, *noun.*
[RE- + Latin *sentire* to feel]

reservation (*say* rezza-**vay**-sh'n) *noun*
1. a) the act of keeping, withholding or setting aside. b) something which is reserved.
Usage: 'you seem to have *reservations* about our agreement' (= uncertainties, possible objections).
2. a) an arrangement in advance to keep something, such as a hotel room, seat in an aeroplane, etc. b) a record of such an arrangement.
3. an area of public land set aside for a particular purpose, especially for the use of native or aboriginal peoples.

reserve (*say* re-**zerv**) *verb*
to keep back or save: a) 'the judge has *reserved* his decision; b) 'we must *reserve* some water for the horses'.
Usages:
a) 'this park is *reserved* for camping' (= set aside).
b) 'we *reserved* a seat for you on tomorrow's train' (= booked, organized).
c) 'he *reserves* the right to make the final decision' (= claims).
reserve *noun*
1. something which is kept, saved or set aside: 'a *reserve* of food'.
2. the state of being reserved: 'food kept in *reserve* for emergencies'.
3. a quality of aloofness, self-restraint or discretion.
4. *Sport:* an extra member of a team who is prepared to replace any player unable to take part in or continue a game.
5. a land reservation: 'a wildlife *reserve*'.

6. the part of the armed forces not belonging to the regular forces of the country but called to active service in time of war.
Word Family: **reservedly**, *adverb*; **reservedness**, *noun.*
[RE– + Latin *servare* to keep]

reservoir (*say* **rezza**–vwa) *noun*
1. a) a place or container for storing water. b) the water which is stored.
2. any container for a fluid.
Usage: 'he has a vast *reservoir* of knowledge' (= supply, store).
[French]

reset (*say* ree–**set**) *verb*
(reset, resetting)
to set again: '*reset* the clock to daylight-saving time'.

reside (*say* re–**zide**) *verb*
to have one's place or home for a particular time: 'she now *resides* in Italy'.
Usage: 'where does authority really *reside*, in Parliament or the trade unions?' (= rest, exist).
residence (*say* **rezzi**–d'nce) *noun*
1. a) the place in which one lives or resides. b) a large house.
2. a) the act of residing. b) the fact of being a resident, especially a medical resident.

resident (*say* **rezzi**–d'nt) *noun*
1. a person who lives or resides in a particular place.
2. *Medicine:* a doctor who lives in a hospital, often during his first year as a qualified doctor.
3. *Biology:* any animal which does not migrate.
Word Family: **resident**, *adjective*, a) living or dwelling, b) living in the place of one's work; **residency**, *noun*, the fact or time of residing, especially of a medical resident; **residential** (*say* rezzi–**den**–sh'l), *adjective*, a) of or used for residence, b) providing accommodation, as a hotel.
[RE– + Latin *sedens* sitting]

residual (*say* re–**zid**–yew'l) *adjective*
left over or remaining.
Word Family: **residual**, *noun.*

residue (*say* **rezzi**–dew) *noun*
something which remains or is left over: 'what is that *residue* in your glass?'.
[Latin *residuus* remaining]

resign (*say* re–**zine**) *verb*
to give up a position, etc.
be resigned to, 'I *am resigned to* the fact that we may not win' (= accept).
Word Family: **resignation** (*say* rezzig–**nay**–sh'n), *noun*, a) the act of resigning one's position or job, b) a statement of this, c) the state of being submissive or unresisting; **resignedly**, *adverb.*
[Latin *resignare* to unseal, cancel]

re–sign *verb*
to sign again.

resilient (*say* re–**zill**–y'nt) *adjective*
elastic or springing back.
Usage: 'her *resilient* nature helped her to get better quickly' (= quick to recover).
Word Family: **resilience, resiliency**, *noun*, the quality of being resilient; **resiliently**, *adverb.*
[RE– + Latin *salire* to jump]

resin (*say* **rezzin**) *noun*
Chemistry: any of a class of synthetic or organic, amorphous substances, such as rosin or shellac, which is insoluble in water, but soluble in organic solvents and used as polishes and lacquers.
Word Family: **resinous**, *adjective*, resembling or containing resin.
[from Latin]

resist (*say* re–**zist**) *verb*
to fight or act against: 'do not try to *resist* temptation'.
Usage: 'we could not *resist* a smile at his antics' (= hold back).
resistance *noun*
1. the act or power of resisting or opposing: 'this medicine will increase your *resistance* to infection'.
2. *Electricity:* the tendency of all substances to resist the flow of electric current and to convert it into heat.
3. (*often capital*) the secret organizations in an enemy-occupied country, which continue to work for liberation.
line of least resistance, the easiest, least troublesome way.
Word Family: **resistant, resistive**, *adjectives*, able or working to resist; **resistible**, *adjective*, able to resist; **resistless**, *adjective*, not able to resist or be resisted; **resister**, *noun.*
[RE– + Latin *sistere* to stand fast]

resistor *noun*
Electricity: a body with a high electrical resistance.

resolute (*say* **rezza**–loot) *adjective*
firmly determined.
Word Family: **resolutely**, *adverb*; **resoluteness**, *noun.*

resolution (*say* rezza–**loo**–sh'n) *noun*
1. a firm decision or determination: 'I've made a *resolution* not to swear any more'.
2. a formal statement of a decision or proposal: 'please read out the *resolution* so it may be voted on'.
3. a solution or answer: 'the *resolution* of this problem is going to be difficult'.
4. the act or process of separating into parts.

resolve (*say* re–**zolv**) *verb*
1. to fix or decide firmly: 'I *resolved* never to do it again'.
2. to deal with, solve or settle: 'we must *resolve* the issue now'.
3. to separate or break up: 'it *resolved* into tiny particles'.
resolve *noun*
a firm determination: 'she was filled with *resolve* not to fail'.
[Latin *resolvere* to untie]

resonance (*say* **rezza**–nance) *noun*
1. the prolonging, vibrating or re–echoing of sound: 'the *resonance* of the ringing bells filled the church'.
2. *Physics:* the increasing amplification of a vibration of a given frequency in a mechanical or electrical system as an external vibratory stimulus approaches the same frequency.
resonant *adjective*
of, producing or showing resonance.
Usage: 'her *resonant* voice held the audience's attention' (= deep, rich).
Word Family: **resonate**, *verb*, to resound or re–echo; **resonantly**, *adverb*.
[RE– + Latin *sonare* to sound]

resort (*say* re–**zort**) *verb*
1. to make use of for help, etc.: 'we were forced to *resort* to walking during the transport strike'.
2. to go to or visit often: 'he was known to *resort* to the local pubs'.
resort *noun*
1. a) the act of resorting: 'we must try to win without *resort* to violence'.
b) a person or thing to which one resorts.
2. a place visited or used often: 'a popular beach *resort*'.
last resort, a person or thing used when all else has failed.

resound (*say* re–**zound**) *verb*
to echo or ring again, especially loudly.
Usage: 'the news *resounded* throughout the country' (= produced a sensation).
resounding *adjective*
echoing or ringing: 'a *resounding* knock'.
Usages:
a) 'the play has been a *resounding* success' (= very great, absolute).
b) 'she received a *resounding* slap' (= strong, firm).
Word Family: **resoundingly**, *adverb*.

resource (*say* re–**sorce** *or* re–**zorce**) *noun*
1. (*usually plural*) a source or supply: 'he was at the end of his *resources*'.
2. (*plural*) reserves of potential wealth in the form of goods, raw materials, etc.: 'a nation rich in natural *resources*'.
3. skill or ability, especially in dealing with difficulties, etc.: 'a man of great *resource*'.
Word Family: **resourceful**, *adjective*, able to act, help, etc. skilfully or efficiently; **resourcefully**, *adverb*; **resourcefulness**, *noun*.
[RE– + Latin *surrectus* risen]

respect *noun*
1. an appreciation of a person's worth or qualities: a) 'we have a high *respect* for him as a leader'; b) 'please show your mother more *respect*'.
Usage: 'mother sends her *respects* to you all' (= best or polite wishes).
2. a detail or aspect: 'our opinions differ in many *respects*'.
3. reference: 'he writes with *respect* to your visit next month'.
respectable *adjective*
of an acceptable moral or social standard, reputation, etc.: 'this does not look like a *respectable* neighbourhood'.
Usages:
a) 'she inherited a *respectable* sum' (= fair, moderate).
b) 'is my shirt *respectable* enough to wear?' (= presentable, acceptable).
Word Family: **respect**, *verb*, to feel or show respect, consideration, etc. for; **respectful**, *adjective*, feeling or showing respect; **respectfully**, *adverb*; **respectfulness**, *noun*; **respectably**, *adverb*; **respectability** (*say* ree–spekta–**billi**–tee), *noun*.
[Latin *respectus* consideration, regard]

respective *adjective*
particular or individual: 'what are the *respective* merits of the two towns?'.
Word Family: **respectively**, *adverb*.

respiration (*say* respi–**ray**–sh'n) *noun*
1. breathing, a breath.
2. *Biology:* a) the process by which oxygen and carbohydrates are incorporated into an organism and carbon dioxide and water are given

off. b) the exchange of gases between an organism and its environment.
Word Family: **respire** (*say* re–**spire**), *verb*, to breathe; **respiratory** (*say* ress–**pirra**–tree), *adjective*, of or used for respiration.
[RE– + Latin *spirare* to breathe]

respirator (*say* **respi**–rayta) *noun*
1. see GASMASK.
2. a machine to induce artificial respiration.

respite (*say* **respit** *or* re–**spite**) *noun*
a brief or temporary rest, delay or relief: 'the rain provided a little *respite* from the intense heat'.
Word Family: **respite,** *verb*, to delay or relieve temporarily.

resplendent (*say* re–**splen**–d'nt) *adjective*
splendid or shining brilliantly.
Word Family: **resplendency, resplendence,** *noun.*
[RE– + Latin *splendens* shining]

respond (*say* re–**spond**) *verb*
to speak or act in return: 'she *responded* to the joke with a smile'.
[RE– + Latin *spondere* to pledge]

respondent *noun*
1. *Law:* the defendant in a court case, especially in a divorce case.
2. a person who responds.
Word Family: **respondent,** *adjective*, answering.

response *noun*
a) the act of responding. b) something said or done in return.
Word Family: **responsive,** *adjective*, readily responding or reacting; **responsively,** *adverb*; **responsiveness,** *noun.*

responsible (*say* re–**sponsi**–b'l) *adjective*
having to look after, manage, take blame on behalf of, etc.: 'parents are *responsible* for their children'.
Usages:
a) 'after the accident the police looked for the person *responsible*' (= who caused it).
b) 'she has a very *responsible* position in the company' (= involving decision, control, etc.).
c) 'she is a very *responsible* child for her age' (= reliable).
Word Family: **responsibility** (*say* re–sponsi–**billi**–tee), *noun*, a) the state of being responsible, b) a person or thing for which one is responsible; **responsibly,** *adverb*, in a responsible or reliable manner.

rest (1) *noun*
1. a stopping of or relief from activity, work, etc.: 'let's have a *rest* after one more practice'.
2. a refreshing calm, peace or relaxation: 'a night of *rest* after a troubled day'.
3. a freedom from worry, disturbance, etc.: 'please put her mind at *rest*'.
4. a pause, such as a silence between musical notes or a break in a line of poetry.
5. a device or object which supports: 'an *armrest*'.
lay, put to rest, a) to bury; b) to suppress or put down.
rest *verb*
1. to have a rest: a) 'they *rested* from the tedious work for a while'; b) '*rest* on the bed'.
2. to be supported: 'her chin *rested* on her cupped hands'.
Usages:
a) 'his eyes *rested* briefly on the window' (= were directed or fixed).
b) 'the success of the party *rests* on good music' (= depends).
c) 'I think we should let the matter *rest* here' (= remain).
rest with, to be the concern of.

rest (2) *noun*
the part or amount which remains or is left over: 'where is the *rest* of the cake?'.
Usage: 'the *rest* of us will all come except Sally' (= others).
Word Family: **rest,** *verb*, to remain or continue to be.

restate (*say* ree–**state**) *verb*
to state again or in a different way.
Word Family: **restatement,** *noun.*

restaurant (*say* **resta**–ront) *noun*
a place where meals are bought, served and eaten.
Word Family: **restaurateur** (*say* resta–ra–**ter**), *noun*, a person who owns or manages a restaurant.
[French, restoring]

restful *adjective*
a) giving rest. b) quiet or peaceful.
Word Family: **restfully,** *adverb*; **restfulness,** *noun.*

restitution (*say* resti–**tew**–sh'n) *noun*
a restoring of or compensation for loss, damage, expense, etc.
Word Family: **restitute,** *verb.*
[from Latin]

restive (*say* **res**tiv) *adjective*
impatiently discontented or irritated: 'the crowd became *restive* waiting for the game to begin'.
Word Family: **restively,** *adverb*; **restiveness,** *noun.*

restless *adjective*
not able to rest, relax or remain quiet: 'a *restless* sleeper'.
Word Family: **restlessly,** *adverb*; **restlessness,** *noun.*

restore (*say* re–**stor**) *verb*
to bring back: 'the police tried to *restore* order after the riot'.
restoration (*say* resta–**ray**–sh'n) *noun*
1. the act of restoring: a) 'the *restoration* of old houses to their original condition'; b) 'the *restoration* of peace after war'.
2. something which has been returned to its original condition.
Word Family: **restorative,** *adjective,* able to renew or restore; **restorative,** *noun.*
[from Latin]

restrain *verb*
to hold back.
restraint *noun*
1. the act of restraining.
2. an action, influence, etc. which restrains or restricts: a) 'we were forced to use physical *restraint*'; b) 'solitary confinement is a *restraint* used on prisoners'.

restrict *verb*
to keep within limits, etc.: a) 'her movements will be *restricted* by the brace on her leg'; b) '*restrict* your questions to the main topic'.
Word Family: **restriction,** *noun*; **restrictive,** *adjective,* tending or used to restrict; **restricted,** *adjective,* (of an area, etc.) for the use of authorized or chosen people only.
[Latin *restrictus* tightened]

restrictive trade practice
a trade agreement which is not in the interests of the public.

result (*say* re–**zult**) *noun*
1. something which is caused by or arises from an action, condition, etc.: 'this dreadful mess is the direct *result* of your untidiness'.
2. *Maths:* a quantity or answer obtained by calculation.
3. the outcome of a game, contest, etc.
result *verb*
to exist or occur because of: 'the crash *resulted* from careless driving'.
Word Family: **resultant,** *adjective,* following as a result; **resultant,** *noun.*
[Latin *resultare* to rebound]

resume (*say* re–**zewm**) *verb*
1. to begin or take up again: 'we will *resume* this lesson tomorrow'.
2. to occupy or take again: 'please *resume* your seats for the speech'.
Word Family: **resumption** (*say* re–**zump**–sh'n), *noun*; **resumptive,** *adjective,* repeating.
[from Latin]

résumé (*say* **rez**–yoo–may) *noun*
a summary.
[French]

resurgent (*say* re–**sir**–j'nt) *adjective*
rising or returning again: 'a *resurgent* disease'.
Word Family: **resurgence,** *noun*; **resurge,** *verb.*
[from Latin]

resurrect (*say* rezza–**rekt**) *verb*
to bring back to life.
Usage: 'they tried to *resurrect* their old friendship' (= resume).
resurrection (*say* rezza–**rek**–sh'n) *noun*
1. the act of coming back to life.
2. any revival or return.
3. *Christianity:* (*capital*) a) the rising of Christ from the tomb, on the third day after the Crucifixion. b) the rising of the dead on the Day of Judgement.

resuscitate (*say* re–**sussi**–tate) *verb*
to revive, especially from collapse or unconsciousness.
Word Family: **resuscitator,** *noun,* something which resuscitates, especially a machine for this purpose; **resuscitation,** *noun.*
[RE– + Latin *suscitare* to stir up]

retail *noun*
the selling of goods to the general public, usually in small quantities. Compare WHOLESALE.
retail *verb*
to sell or be sold directly to individuals: 'sugar *retails* at the price of 35 pence per kilogram'.
Usage: 'she will *retail* all the local gossip' (= tell or repeat in detail).
Word Family: **retail,** *adverb*; **retailer,** *noun,* a person or shop that deals in retail; **retail,** *adjective.*
[Old French *retaille* a piece cut off]

retain *verb*
1. to continue to hold, do, use, etc.: a) 'she *retained* her dignity despite the embarrassing mistake'; b) 'her memory *retains* everything she reads'.

2. to hire: 'they *retained* the services of a leading barrister'.
[from Latin]

retainer (1) *noun*
1. a servant, especially a personal one.
2. *Medieval history:* a follower or dependant of a nobleman.
3. a device for holding a part in place.

retainer (2) *noun*
a fee paid to reserve the services of a professional, such as a lawyer.

retaliate (*say* re–**talli**–ate) *verb*
to repay an injury, wrong, etc. with another: 'the bombed troops *retaliated* with a surprise attack'.
Word Family: **retaliation**, *noun*; **retaliatory, retaliative**, *adjectives.*
[RE– + Latin *talis* such]

retard (*say* re–**tard**) *verb*
to slow down or delay the progress of: a) 'frosts *retarded* the growth of the vegetables'; b) 'the slow development of a mentally *retarded* child'.
retardation (*say* re–tar–**day**–sh'n) *noun*
1. a) the state of being retarded. b) the act of retarding.
2. *Physics:* the rate of decrease of velocity. Also called **deceleration**.
Word Family: **retarder, retardant**, *nouns.*
[RE– + Latin *tardus* slow]

retch (*say* retch *or* reech) *verb*
to try to vomit.
Word Family: **retch**, *noun.*
[Old English *hraca* a clearing of the throat]

retention (*say* re–**ten**–sh'n) *noun*
a) the act or power of retaining. b) the capacity for retaining.

retentive (*say* re–**tentiv**) *adjective*
having the ability to retain.
Word Family: **retentiveness**, *noun*

rethink (*say* ree–**think**) *verb*
(rethought, rethinking)
to reconsider.

reticent (*say* **retti**–s'nt) *adjective*
not communicative.
Word Family: **reticently**, *adverb*; **reticence**, *noun.*
[Latin *reticens* keeping silent]

reticulate (*say* re–**tik**–yoo–late) *verb*
to form into a net or network.
Word Family: **reticulate** (*say* re–**tik**–yoo–lit), **reticular**, *adjectives,* of or like a net; **reticulation**, *noun.*
[Latin *reticulum* a fishing–net]

reticule (*say* **retti**–kewl) *noun*
a small purse or handbag, originally made of network.

retina (*say* **rett**ina) *noun*
plural is **retinas** or **retinae** (*say* **retti**–nee)
Anatomy: the inner lining at the back of the eye, containing the light–sensitive cells (called **rods** and **cones**).
Word Family: **retinal**, *adjective.*
[Latin *rete* a net]

retinue (*say* **retti**–new) *noun*
a group of attendants accompanying an important person.
[French, retained]

retire *verb*
1. to go away or withdraw to another place, as for rest, etc.
2. to give up work permanently.
Word Family: **retirement**, *noun.*
[from French]

retiring *adjective*
shy or reserved.

retort (1) *verb*
to reply to an argument, accusation, etc. with another, usually quickly and sharply.
Word Family: **retort**, *noun.*

retort (2) *noun*
Chemistry: a) a bulb–shaped glass vessel with a long neck sloping downwards from the top, used in distillation. b) any vessel in which chemical reactions take place in industrial processes.
[Latin *retortus* twisted back]

retouch (*say* re–**tutch**) *verb*
to improve or correct by adding new details, etc.: 'to *retouch* a photograph'.

retrace *verb*
to go back over: 'we *retraced* our steps to look for the lost keys'.

retract *verb*
to withdraw or take back: a) 'the tortoise *retracted* its head'; b) 'I insist that you *retract* your statement'.
Word Family: **retractable**, *adjective*; **retractile**, *adjective*, able to be drawn back or in, as the body of a snail into its shell; **retraction**, *noun*, a) the act or power of retracting, b) a withdrawal; **retractor**, *noun*, a person or thing that retracts.
[from Latin]

retread (*say* **ree**–tred) *noun*
a tyre which is restored or renewed by moulding a new rubber tread onto it.

Word Family: **retread** (*say* ree-**tred**), *verb*, to restore a tyre in this way.

re-tread (*say* ree-**tred**) *verb*
(**re-trod**, **re-trodden** or **re-trod**, **re-treading**)
to tread or walk on again.

retreat *noun*
1. the act of withdrawing to safety, etc., such as the forced withdrawal of a military force.
2. a place which is quiet, safe or peaceful: 'a holiday *retreat*'.
3. a period of seclusion or retirement: 'a religious *retreat*'.
Word Family: **retreat**, *verb*, to go back or withdraw.
[Latin *retrahere* to draw back]

retrench *verb*
to dismiss or cut down: 'the company is forced to *retrench* half the staff'.
Word Family: **retrenchment**, *noun*.
[Old French *retrencher* to cut back]

retrial *noun*
a second trial.

retribution (*say* retri-**bew**-sh'n) *noun*
a repayment, especially in the form of punishment.
Word Family: **retributive** (*say* ree-**trib**-yoo-tiv), *adjective*, relating to or involving retribution.
[RE- + Latin *tribuere* to assign]

retrieve (*say* re-**treev**) *verb*
to bring back or recover: 'watch the dog *retrieve* the stick'.
Usages:
a) 'it's too late to *retrieve* the situation now' (= restore).
b) 'he can never *retrieve* his honourable reputation' (= regain).
retriever *noun*
something which retrieves, such as a breed of dog trained to retrieve game.
Word Family: **retrieve**, **retrieval**, *nouns*, recovery.
[Old French *retrover* to find again]

retro-
a prefix meaning backwards, as in *retrospect*.
[Latin]

retroactive (*say* retro-**aktiv**) *adjective*
(of a law, etc.) having retrospective effect.
Word Family: **retroactively**, *adverb*; **retroaction**, *noun*, action which is opposite to the action before it; **retroactivity** (*say* retro-ak-**tivvi**-tee), *noun*, the fact of being retroactive.

retrograde *adjective*
moving backwards, especially to an earlier or less developed condition.
[RETRO- + Latin *gradus* a step]

retrogress *verb*
to move backwards, especially to an earlier or worse condition.
Word Family: **retrogressive**, *adjective*; **retrogression**, *noun*.

retro-rocket *noun*
short form of **retrograde rocket**
a rocket motor attached to a spacecraft, fired in the direction in which the spacecraft is travelling in order to slow it down.

retrospect *noun*
a survey of past events.
in retrospect, when subsequently considered.
Word Family: **retrospection**, *noun*, a survey of the past; **retrospective**, *adjective*, a) looking back or to the past, b) (of a law, etc.) having effect from a past date, c) applying to past actions.
[RETRO- + Latin *spectus* looked]

return *verb*
1. to come or go back: a) 'at last I *returned* home'; b) 'he has *returned* to his old habits'.
2. to cause something to come or go back: a) '*return* the money I lent you'; b) 'the tennis player *returned* the ball with a powerful stroke'.
Usages:
a) 'to *return* good for evil' (= pay back).
b) 'the shares *returned* a small profit' (= produced).
c) 'a new government was *returned*' (= elected).
d) 'the jury *returned* its verdict' (= gave).
return *noun*
1. the act of returning: a) 'on my *return*, I went to bed'; b) 'the tennis player hit a splendid *return*'.
2. (*often plural*) something which is returned, such as the votes counted in an election.
3. a restoration, reappearance or repetition: 'I'm still waiting for the *return* of the book I lent you'.
Usages:
a) 'what *return* did you get on your investment?' (= profit).
b) 'she filled in her tax *return*' (= official statement).
Phrases:
by return, 'please reply *by return*' (= by the next post).

many happy returns, a greeting offered to people on their birthday.
point of no return, the point at which one has gone too far to be able to turn back.
return *adjective*
of or relating to returning: a) 'buy a *return* ticket if you're coming back tonight'; b) 'she had a *return* attack of measles'.
Word Family: **returnable**, *adjective*, a) able to be returned, b) to be returned.

returning officer
the official who supervises an election and announces the result.

return match
a game played again so that the loser has a chance of challenging the winner.

reunion (*say* re-**yoon**-y'n) *noun*
the act of being reunited, especially the meeting of people after a separation.

reunite (*say* ree-yoo-**nite**) *verb*
to unite or bring together again.

rev *verb*
(**revved, revving**)
(*informal*) to increase engine speed quickly.
Word Family: **rev**, *noun*, an engine revolution.

revalue (*say* ree-**val**-yoo) *verb*
to give a new value to.
Word Family: **revaluation**, *noun*.

revamp *verb*
to renovate or repair.
[RE + VAMP (1)]

reveal *verb*
a) to display: 'this dress *reveals* your horrible knees'. b) to make known: 'don't *reveal* my secret to anyone'.
[Latin *revelare* to unveil]

reveille (*say* re-**vall**-ee) *noun*
Military: the bugle call signalling soldiers to get up in the morning. Compare LAST POST.
[French *réveillez* wake up]

revel (*say* **revv**'l) *verb*
(**revelled, revelling**)
to celebrate merrily and noisily.
revel in, to take great pleasure or delight in.
revel *noun*
(*often plural*) merrymaking.
Word Family: **revelry**, *noun*.
[French *reveler* to rebel or make a noise]

revelation (*say* revva-**lay**-sh'n) *noun*
a) the act of revealing: 'we were shocked by the *revelation* of his secret'. b) something that is revealed: 'the news was a *revelation* to us'.

revenge (*say* re-**venj**) *noun*
any repayment for a wrong or injury: 'I'll get *revenge* for that insult!'.
revenge *verb*
to take revenge: 'I *revenged* myself on the murderer'.
Word Family: **revengeful**, *adjective*; **revengefully**, *adverb*; **revengefulness**, *noun*.
[RE- + Latin *vindicare* to lay claim to]

revenue (*say* **revva**-new) *noun*
any income, especially that received by a government from taxation.
[French, returned]

reverberate (*say* re-**verba**-rate) *verb*
to sound or echo again and again: 'his screams *reverberated* in the tunnel'.
Word Family: **reverberation**, *noun*; **reverberatory**, *adjective*.
[RE- + Latin *verber* a lash]

revere (*say* re-**veer**) *verb*
to treat or regard with deep respect.
reverence (*say* **revva**-r'nce) *noun*
1. a feeling of deep respect and awe.
2. (*capital*) a title of respect for a clergyman of high rank.
Word Family: **reverent, reverential** (*say* revva-**ren**-sh'l), *adjectives*, feeling, showing or characterized by reverence; **reverently, reverentially**, *adverbs*.
[RE- + Latin *vereri* to feel awe]

reverend (*say* **revva**-r'nd) *adjective*
Christian: (*capital*) a title of respect for a clergyman: 'the *Reverend* Mr Hudson'.
Word Family: **reverend**, *noun*, (informal) a clergyman.

reverie (*say* **revva**-ree) *noun*
a) quiet, pleasant dreaminess. b) a daydream.
[French *rêver* to dream]

revers (*say* re-**veer**) *noun*
plural is **revers** (*say* re-**veerz**)
a section of a piece of clothing folded back to show the other side, such as a lapel.
[French]

reverse *adjective*
opposite in order, direction, position or character: 'what's on the *reverse* side of that record?'.

reverse *noun*
1. the opposite of something: 'the *reverse* of what he says is true'.
2. the back of a coin, medal or postage stamp. Compare OBVERSE.
3. *Mechanics:* a gear that enables a car to move backwards.
Usage: 'our plans suffered a major *reverse*' (= defeat, check).
reverse *verb*
to turn in or into an opposite direction, order, position or character: a) 'he has *reversed* his decision and given his full consent'; b) 'she *reversed* the car into the parking space'.
reversal *noun*
the act or an instance of reversing: 'the new system was a *reversal* of the usual procedure'.
[Latin *reversus* turned round]

reversible *adjective*
able to be reversed, e.g. a piece of clothing made so that it can be worn inside out.

reversion (*say* re–**ver**–*zh*'n) *noun*
1. the act of reverting: 'the court ordered the *reversion* of the house to its original owner'.
2. *Biology:* a) the appearance of ancestral characters in an organism. b) a reverse mutation.

revert *verb*
1. to return to a former state, condition, subject, etc.: a) 'he quickly *reverted* to his old ways'; b) 'I *revert* to what I said earlier'.
2. *Law:* to return to the original owner.

review (*say* re–**vew**) *noun*
1. a general survey or examination: a) 'a *review* of the year's political events'; b) 'the general conducted a *review* of the troops'.
Usage: 'his parole application comes up for *review* every third year' (= re-examination).
2. a short critical article about a new book, film, play, art exhibition, etc.
3. a magazine which contains articles examining current events, books, etc.
review *verb*
1. to make, write or publish a review.
2. to go over again: 'the court *reviewed* the earlier judgement'.
Word Family: **reviewer,** *noun,* a person who reviews books, films, etc.

revile *verb*
to insult or abuse.
[Old French *reviler* to despise]

revise (*say* re–**vize**) *verb*
1. to alter or change: 'I have *revised* my opinion'.
2. to read or study again, especially before an examination.
revision (*say* re–**vizh**'n) *noun*
a) the act or process of revising: 'a week's *revision* before the exams'. b) something which is revised, such as a new edition of a book.
[RE– + Latin *visere* scrutinize]

revisionism (*say* re–**vizh**'n–izm) *noun*
a modified form of communism based on a belief in peaceful change rather than revolution.
Word Family: **revisionist,** *noun.*

revitalize (*say* re–**vie**–ta–lize)
revitalise *verb*
to put new life or energy into: 'the new manager *revitalized* the company'.

revive *verb*
to bring back to life or existence: a) 'we *revived* her after we pulled her from the surf'; b) 'the government *revived* an old law'.
revival (*say* re–**vie**–v'l) *noun*
1. the act of reviving: 'a *revival* of an old argument'.
2. a reawakening of religious interest in a church or community.
Word Family: **revivalist,** *noun;* **revivalism,** *noun.*
[RE– + Latin *vivus* alive]

revivify (*say* re–**vivvi**–fie) *verb* (**revivified, revivifying**)
to give new life to.

revoke *verb*
1. to withdraw, cancel or repeal: 'I'll *revoke* your privileges'.
2. *Cards:* to omit to follow suit when able to do so.
[RE– + Latin *vocare* to call]

revolt *noun*
a) the act of resisting authority, especially as a protest against oppression. b) the state of a person or persons who revolt: 'to be in *revolt*'.
revolt *verb*
1. to rise in rebellion against authority.
2. to be or become disgusted or horrified: 'I was *revolted* by the terrible crime'.
Word Family: **revoltingly,** *adverb.*

revolution (*say* revva–**loo**–sh'n) *noun*
1. a) the act or process of rotating or revolving: 'the *revolution* of the earth around the sun'. b) a single turn or rotation: 'this record turns at 78 *revolutions* per minute'.

2. a complete change, such as that caused by the overthrow of a government or political system.
Word Family: **revolutionize, revolutionise,** *verb,* to bring about a revolution or radical change.

revolutionary
(*say* revva-**loo**-sh'n-ree) *noun*
a person favouring or taking part in a revolution.
revolutionary *adjective*
of, like or characterized by revolution.

revolve *verb*
to turn or cause to turn around something: 'the earth *revolves* around the sun'.
[RE- + Latin *volvere* to roll]

revolver *noun*
a pistol having a revolving cylinder with a number of chambers so that the bullets may be fired in succession.

revue (*say* re-**vew**) *noun*
a form of entertainment consisting of a series of short acts and songs which usually satirize people and events.
[French, review]

revulsion (*say* re-**vul**-sh'n) *noun*
a violent, revolted reaction against something: 'I shrank back in *revulsion*'.
[Latin *revulsio* a plucking away]

reward *noun*
something offered or given in return for service or merit: 'what *reward* will I get for my hard work?'.
Word Family: **reward,** *verb,* to give a reward to; **rewarding,** *adjective,* satisfying.

rewind (*say* ree-**wined**) *verb*
(rewound, rewinding)
a) to wind again. b) to wind back.

rewire *verb*
to provide with new wiring.

reword *verb*
to put into other words.

rhapsody (*say* **rap**sa-dee) *noun*
1. a feeling or expression of great enthusiasm or delight: 'the critics are in *rhapsodies* about my latest novel'.
2. *Music:* a short piece of romantic music.
Word Family: **rhapsodical** (*say* rap-**soddi**-k'l), *adjective,* of or like a rhapsody; **rhapsodically,** *adverb*; **rhapsodize, rhapsodise,** *verb.*
[Greek *rhapsoidos* one who strings songs together]

rhea (*say* **ree**-a) *noun*
any of various South American birds with three toes, similar to a small ostrich.

rhenium (*say* **reeni**-um) *noun*
element number 75, a hard metal, used in thermocouples and as a catalyst. See TRANSITION ELEMENT. See CHEMICAL ELEMENTS in grey pages.

rheostat (*say* **ree**-o-stat) *noun*
a variable electrical resistor, such as a dimmer for theatrical lighting.
[Greek *rheos* stream + *statos* stationary]

rhesus (*say* **ree**-sus) *noun*
a small, Indian monkey with a short tail, widely used in medical research.

rhetoric (*say* **retta**-rik) *noun*
the art of using words persuasively in speech and writing.
Usage: 'ignore his pompous *rhetoric*' (= insincere or artificial words).
rhetorical (*say* re-**torri**-k'l) *adjective*
1. of or characteristic of rhetoric: 'we were impressed by his *rhetorical* speech'.
2. artificial or exaggerated in language: 'this essay is empty and *rhetorical*'.
Word Family: **rhetorically,** *adverb*; **rhetorician** (*say* retta-**rish**'n), *noun,* a student, teacher or user of rhetoric.
[from Greek]

rhetorical question
a question that is asked for effect rather than to get an answer.

rheum (*say* room) *noun*
an old word for a cold or catarrh.

rheumatic fever (*say* roo-**mattik** fever)
also called **acute rheumatism** or **rheumatic heart disease**
the after-effects of a bacterial infection, especially in children, which causes fever, joint pains, and affects the lining of the heart.

rheumatism (*say* **rooma**-tizm) *noun*
any of various diseases linked by the presence of pain and stiffness in joints and joint-muscles, including osteoarthritis, fibrositis and gout.
rheumatic (*say* roo-**mattik**) *adjective*
also called **rheumatoid** (*say* **rooma**-toyd)
of, relating to or affected by rheumatism.
rheumatoid arthritis, a disease affecting the joints of fingers and toes which progressively stiffen.
Word Family: **rheumatic,** *noun,* a person suffering from rheumatism;

rheumatics, *plural noun*, rheumatic pains; **rheumatically**, *adverb*.
[Greek *rheumatos* of catarrh]

Rh factor
short form of **rhesus factor**
an antigen which is often present in blood. Blood containing this factor is called **Rh positive** and blood lacking it is called **Rh negative**.
[first found in the blood of *rhesus* monkeys]

rhinestone (*say* **rine**-stone) *noun*
a colourless, imitation gem, usually imitating a diamond, made out of paste or glass.
[a translation of French *caillou du Rhin*]

rhinoceros (*say* rye-**nosserus**) *noun*
short form is **rhino**
a large, thick-skinned, heavily built mammal with one or two horns on its snout, found on the plains of Africa and Asia.
[Greek *rhinos* nose + *keras* horn]

rhizome (*say* **rye**-zome) *noun*
Biology: an underground stem which is an organ of vegetative reproduction.
[from Greek]

rhodium (*say* **ro**-dee-um) *noun*
element number 45, a metal similar to and occurring with platinum and used as a catalyst and in alloys. See TRANSITION ELEMENT. See CHEMICAL ELEMENTS in grey pages.

rhododendron (*say* ro-da-**dendr**'n) *noun*
any of a group of shrubs, related to the heath, with large clusters of flowers.
[Greek *rhodon* rose + *dendron* tree]

rhomboid (*say* **rom**-boyd) *noun*
a quadrilateral having each pair of opposite sides parallel, but with adjacent sides unequal and no right angles.
Word Family: **rhomboid**, *adjective*.
[RHOMBUS + -OID]

rhombus (*say* **rom**bus) *noun*
a quadrilateral having equal, parallel sides but no right angles.
Word Family: **rhombic**, *adjective*.

rhubarb (*say* **roo**-barb) *noun*
1. the thick, long red stalks of a garden vegetable, usually eaten cooked as a dessert.
2. (*informal*) a confused noise (from stage extras repeating this word to imitate the hubbub of a crowd).
[Greek *rha* rhubarb + *barbaros* foreign]

rhyme (*say* rime) *noun*
also spelt **rime**
1. the repetition of similar or identical sounds. *Example*: *park*, *mark* and *lark*.
2. a verse or poem in which the last words of each line are rhymes.
rhyme or reason, 'she acted without *rhyme or reason*' (= sense, explanation).
rhyme *verb*
1. (of words or verses) to have identical sounds. *Example*: 'dog' *rhymes* with 'log'.
2. to make or write rhymes or verses.
[Greek *rhythmos* rhythm]

rhyming slang
a form of slang where the last word of a phrase rhymes with the word which is really meant, such as **dog's eye and dead horse** (pie and sauce).

rhythm (*say* ri*th*'m) *noun*
any regular or recurrent pattern: 'the *rhythm* of the seasons'.
rhythmical (*say* **ri*th***mi-k'l) **rhythmic** *adjective*
having a marked rhythm.
Word Family: **rhythmically**, *adverb*.
[from Greek]

rhythm and blues
a style of popular music combining modern elements with the traditional Negro blues style.

rib (1) *noun*
1. *Anatomy:* any of the slender bones forming a cage around the heart and lungs.
2. something which has the shape or function of a rib, such as the vein of a leaf or a curved timber in a ship's frame.
Word Family: **rib (ribbed, ribbing)**, *verb*, a) to supply with or mark off in ribs, b) to knit ribbing.

rib (2) *verb*
(ribbed, ribbing)
(*informal*) to tease.

ribald (*say* **ribb**uld) *adjective*
irreverent, coarsely humorous or scurrilous.
Word Family: **ribaldry**, *noun*, ribald speech or behaviour.

ribbing *noun*
1. an arrangement of ribs or rib-like parts, such as a ship's framework.
2. a raised pattern made by knitting plain and purl stitches alternately, or by knitting clearly separated ridges.

ribbon *noun*

1. a band of fabric used for tying, etc.

2. anything that is long and thin like a ribbon: 'a *ribbon* of flowerbed along the fence'.

Usage: 'my coat was torn to *ribbons*' (= shreds).

riboflavin (*say* rybo–**flay**–vin) *noun*

see VITAMIN B_2 under VITAMIN.

rice *noun*

a cereal plant with white seeds that are an important food, often grown in water in warmer climates.

[Greek *oryza*]

rice paper

1. a very thin, edible paper made from rice.

2. a paper made from the pith of a Chinese shrub.

rich *adjective*

1. having great wealth, resources or possessions.

2. strong in taste, colour, smell, sound, etc.

3. expensive or elaborate in dress, jewellery, decoration, etc.

4. (of land, soil, etc.) producing abundantly.

Usages:

a) 'we have a *rich* supply of paintings' (= abundant).

b) 'Sarah told a *rich* joke' (= very amusing).

c) 'that's a bit *rich*!' (= too much).

richly *adverb*

in a rich manner: 'he was *richly* dressed'.

Usage. 'you *richly* deserve your fate' (= fully).

Word Family: **richness,** *noun*; **riches,** *plural noun*, wealth.

rick (1) *noun*

a stack of hay or straw, usually thatched or covered for protection.

rick (2) *verb*

to strain the muscles or ligaments of the neck, back, etc.

rickets *plural noun*

a disease due to a lack of vitamin D in the diet, causing deformed bones.

rickettsia (*say* rikketsi–a) *noun*

a group of parasitic micro-organisms, usually found on lice, ticks and fleas and which may cause serious diseases, including typhus.

[after *H. T. Ricketts*, 1871–1910, an American pathologist]

rickety (*say* **rikka**–tee) *adjective*

1. shaky or tottering: 'the *rickety* table finally collapsed'.

2. of or affected by rickets.

rickshaw *noun*

a small two-wheeled vehicle with a canopy, pulled by one or more men and used in Asia to carry goods or passengers.

[Japanese *jinrikisha* man-power-vehicle]

ricochet (*say* **rikk**o–shay) *verb*

(**ricocheted** (*say* rikko–**shade**), **ricocheting** (*say* rikko–**shay**–ing))

(of a stone, bullet, etc.) to skip or rebound one or more times from the surface which it hits.

Word Family: **ricochet,** *noun*, a rebound.

[French]

ricrac, rickrack *noun*

a narrow braid made in a zigzag pattern.

rid *verb*

(**rid** or **ridded, ridding**)

to make free of: 'at last my mind was *rid* of worries'.

riddance *noun*

a removal or clearing away.

good riddance, an expression of relief that a person or thing has gone.

riddle (1) *noun*

a) a puzzle using words. b) any puzzling person or thing.

riddle (2) *verb*

to make many holes in something: 'the gangster's corpse was *riddled* with bullets'.

[Middle English *riddil* sieve]

ride *verb*

(**rode, ridden, riding**)

1. to sit on a horse, bicycle, etc. and drive it forward.

2. to be carried as a passenger, e.g. in a vehicle or on someone's back.

3. to float or move as if by riding: a) 'the ship *rode* at anchor'; b) 'the eagle *rode* the wind'.

Usages:

a) 'the crankshaft *rides* on four bearings' (= is supported in moving).

b) 'this car *rides* well' (= travels, handles).

c) (*informal*) 'it's such a small mistake you can let it *ride*' (= remain unchanged).

Phrases:

ride high, 'she is *riding high* at the moment' (= successful).

ride out, 'sit back and *ride out* the scandal' (= survive by enduring).
riding for a fall, heading for trouble.
ride *noun*
a trip on horseback, bicycle, in a car, etc.
take for a ride, 'you were foolish to be *taken for a ride*' (= deceived).

rider *noun*
1. a person who rides.
2. *Maths:* a secondary result arising from a proposition.
3. an extra provision or condition: 'a clause was added to the document as a *rider*'.

ridge (*say* rij) *noun*
1. a) a long, narrow area of raised land. b) any long, raised line where two sloping sides meet, e.g. along a roof or the backbone of an animal.
2. *Weather:* an area of high pressure extending from a high.

ridgepole (*say* **rij**-pole) *noun*
Building: the beam or board which forms the central line of a roof.

ridicule (*say* **riddi**-kewl) *verb*
to scoff at or make fun of: 'don't *ridicule* my serious suggestions'.
ridicule *noun*
words intended to provoke contempt or humorous derision for a person or thing.
[from Latin]

ridiculous (*say* riddi**k**-yoolus) *adjective*
absurd, preposterous or laughable.
Word Family: **ridiculously**, *adverb*; **ridiculousness**, *noun*.

rife *adjective*
widespread or common: 'corruption was *rife* during the dictatorship'.

riff *noun*
(*informal*) a melodic phrase played repeatedly as background or used as the main theme in jazz, etc.

riffle *verb*
1. a) to flutter and shift: 'the pages of the book *riffled* in the breeze'. b) to thumb through: 'I *riffled* quickly through the book'.
2. *Cards:* to shuffle cards by dividing the pack in two and slipping the cards alternately together.

riffraff *noun*
any low or worthless people.

rifle (1) (*say* rye-f'l) *noun*
a gun that is fired from the shoulder and has spiral grooves, called **rifling**, cut inside the barrel to make the bullet spin and so give greater accuracy.

rifle (2) (*say* **rye**-f'l) *verb*
a) to search through in order to steal something: 'the desk had been *rifled* by a thief'. b) to steal.

rift *noun*
a split or opening: 'a *rift* in the cliff face'.
Usage: 'there is a *rift* between the two friends' (= disagreement, dispute).
Word Family: **rift**, *verb*, to split or burst open.

rift valley
also called a **graben**
Geography: a valley formed by land sinking between two parallel faults.

rig *noun*
1. *Nautical:* the arrangement of masts, spars and sails on a boat.
2. the equipment for some purpose, such as the drilling apparatus, derricks, etc. for mining.
3. (*informal*) dress or costume: 'you've got a strange *rig* on today'.
rig *verb*
(rigged, rigging)
1. to fit a ship with masts, sails, etc.
2. to manipulate or control dishonestly: 'the election was *rigged*'.
Phrases:
rig out, 'she *rigged* herself *out* in a new outfit' (= dressed).
rig up, 'I'll *rig up* an aerial for the radio' (= quickly make or assemble).

rigger *noun*
1. a person who rigs ships, etc.
2. a person who assembles and repairs aeroplane parts, etc.

rigging *noun*
Nautical: the ropes, lines and stays used on or above the deck of a boat.

right *adjective*
1. of or relating to the side opposite to left.
2. in accordance with what is considered good, correct, true, honourable, etc.: 'it's not *right* to treat someone cruelly'.
3. true, correct or accurate: 'what is the *right* time?'.
Usages:
a) 'he's not in his *right* mind' (= normal, sound).
b) 'she can be relied on to say the *right* thing' (= appropriate).
c) (*informal*) 'well, you're a *right* idiot, aren't you?' (= proper, real).
d) 'the *right* honourable speaker' (= very).

right *noun*
1. that which is right: 'he can't tell the difference between *right* and wrong'.
2. a) a just claim or title: 'I have a *right* to be here'. b) that which one has a just claim to: 'I demand my *rights*'.
3. anything on or towards the right.
4. *Politics:* (*often capital*) a collective term for all individuals and groups with a conservative outlook.
Phrases:
by rights, in all fairness or justice.
in the right, having truth, justice, etc. on one's side.
put, set to rights, to put things into their correct or proper state.
right *adverb*
1. toward the right.
2. straight or directly: a) 'go *right* home'; b) 'let's get *right* to the point'.
3. completely or all the way: 'run *right* around the oval'.
4. correctly or properly: 'I can't do a thing *right* today'.
Usages:
a) 'and *right* at the crucial moment, who do you think appeared?' (= just, precisely).
b) 'I'll come *right* away' (= at once).
right *verb*
1. to set upright again: 'the driver *righted* the car after the accident'.
2. to correct: 'these mistakes must be *righted*'.
rightly *adverb*
1. in a morally right manner.
2. correctly or properly.
Usage: 'I don't *rightly* know' (= really).
Word Family: **rightness**, *noun*.

right angle
Maths: an angle of 90°, which is one quarter of a circle.

righteous (*say* **rite**–yus) *adjective*
virtuous or just: 'the *righteous* person obeyed all the laws'.
Word Family: **righteously**, *adverb*; **righteousness**, *noun*.

rightful *adjective*
proper or correct: 'who is the *rightful* owner?'.
Word Family: **rightfully**, *adverb*; **rightfulness**, *noun*.

right–hand *adjective*
on, of or relating to the direction of right: 'the *right–hand* side'.
Usage: 'he is my *right–hand* man' (= most helpful or efficient).

right–handed *adjective*
a) preferring to use the right hand.
b) being done with or adapted to the right hand.
Word Family: **right–handedly**, *adverb*; **right–handedness**, *noun*.

rightist *noun*
Politics: (*often capital*) a person who supports the views of the right wing.

rightly *adverb*
see RIGHT.

rightness *noun*
Word Family: see RIGHT.

right of way
1. a) the right of a person to pass over the land of another. b) the piece of land over which passage is made.
2. the right of a vehicle or vessel to proceed ahead of another.

right–wing *adjective*
Politics: conservative: 'Mike joined the Communist Party in rebellion against his father's *right–wing* attitudes'.
right wing
the most conservative section of a political party or group, usually meaning (in a parliamentary democracy) extremists in conservative parties and moderates in socialist parties. Compare LEFT–WING and CENTRE.
Word Family: **right–winger**, *noun*.

rigid (*say* **rij**–id) *adjective*
stiff or unbending.
Usage: 'she believes in *rigid* discipline' (= strict, severe).
Word Family: **rigidly**, *adverb*; **rigidity** (*say* rijiddi–tee), *noun*.
[from Latin]

rigmarole (*say* **rigma**–role) *noun*
any long or complicated process.

rigor mortis (*say* rigga **mor**tis)
the stiffening of a body after death.
[Latin, stiffness of death]

rigorous (*say* **rigga** rus) *adjective*
strict, exacting or demanding: 'the athlete went into *rigorous* training'.
Word Family: **rigorously**, *adverb*; **rigorousness**, *noun*.

rigour (*say* **rigga**) *noun*
in America spelt **rigor**
severity or harshness: 'the *rigour* of a long winter'.
[Latin *rigor* stiffness, coldness, strictness]

rile *verb*
to irritate or annoy.

rill *noun*
a very small stream.

rim *noun*
the outer edge or margin, especially of a curved or circular object, such as a wheel or cup.
Word Family: **rim (rimmed, rimming)**, *verb*, a) to provide with a rim or border, b) (of a ball in golf, etc.) to roll around the edge of the cup, etc. without falling in.

rime (1) *noun*
see RHYME.

rime (2) *noun*
a deposit of ice formed by water droplets of fog or drizzle as they settle and freeze.
Word Family: **rimy**, *adjective.*

rind (*rhymes with* find) *noun*
a hard, outer skin, as on fruit or cheese. [Old English, bark]

rinderpest (*say* **rin**da-pest) *noun*
an infectious and often fatal viral disease of livestock, causing high fever, diarrhoea, and skin sores. [German *Rinder* cattle + *Pest* plague]

ring (1) *noun*
1. a circular band, especially one of precious metal worn on the finger.
2. a space or area, often enclosed and circular in shape, used for a particular purpose: a) 'a circus *ring*'; b) 'a boxing *ring*'; c) 'the betting *ring*'.
3. *Biology:* one of the circular layers of wood produced by some trees as a result of growth during a season.
4. (*informal*) an exclusive group of persons acting privately or illegally: 'a smuggling *ring*'.
run rings around, (*informal*) to surpass easily or be superior to.
ring *verb*
(ringed, ringing)
1. to encircle or surround with a ring.
2. to form into a ring.
3. to ringbark.

ring (2) *verb*
(rang, rung, ringing)
1. to give forth a clear sound when vibrating, as a bell does.
2. to cause a bell to sound, especially in order to summon: 'he *rang* for his butler'.
Usages:
a) 'her story of the escape does not *ring* true' (= sound, appear to be).
b) 'his ears were *ringing* for some time after the explosion' (= filled with sound).
Phrases:
ring a bell, 'does his name *ring a bell*?' (= sound familiar).
ring in, to announce the arrival of something, e.g. the New Year.
ring off, to end a telephone conversation.
ring out, a) to make a loud ringing noise; b) to announce the departure of something.
ring up, a) to telephone; b) to record an amount on a cash register.
Word Family: **ring**, *noun.*

ringbark *verb*
to cut away a ring of bark from a branch or trunk.

ringbolt *noun*
a bolt into which a heavy ring is set.

ring finger
the third finger of the hand, on which a wedding ring is often worn.

ringleader *noun*
a person who leads others, especially in improper or illegal activities.

ringlet *noun*
a long spiral curl of hair.

ringmaster *noun*
the person in charge of the performances in the ring of a circus.

ring-road *noun*
a road linking different suburbs without passing through the city centre.

ringside *noun*
1. the seats or area closest to and surrounding a boxing or similar ring.
2. any place providing a close view.

ringworm *noun*
a fungal infection of the skin, often the scalp, causing an itchy, circular rash.

rink *noun*
a) a smooth, artificial surface of ice for ice hockey, curling, or ice-skating.
b) any flat surface for roller-skating.

rinse *verb*
1. to wash lightly.
2. to remove soap, etc. with water.
rinse *noun*
1. the act of rinsing.
2. a hair-colouring which lasts only until the hair is washed.

riot (*say* **rye**-ot) *noun*
1. a wild disturbance created by a large number of people.
2. a brilliant display of colours, etc.
3. (*informal*) a person or thing that causes great amusement, enthusiasm, etc.
Phrases:
read the riot act, (*informal*) to censure or reprimand severely.

run riot, a) to act with wild abandon; b) to grow wildly.
Word Family: **riot**, *verb*; **riotous**, *adjective*; **riotously**, *adverb*.

rip (1) *verb*
(ripped, ripping)
1. a) to cut or tear roughly. b) to be torn or cut apart.
2. (*informal*) to move along with great speed.
Word Family: **rip**, *noun*; **ripper**, *noun*.

rip (2) *noun*
a stretch of rough water at sea or in a river.

rip (3) *verb*
(ripped, ripping)
rip off, (*informal*) to exploit or take financial advantage of.
Word Family: **rip-off**, *noun*.

ripcord *noun*
a control cord which opens a parachute.

ripe *adjective*
a) mature or fully developed: 'a *ripe* apple'. b) resembling ripe fruit in colour or fullness: '*ripe* lips'.
Usages:
a) 'he lived to a *ripe* old age' (= advanced).
b) 'the time is *ripe* and we must act quickly' (= ready, right).
Word Family: **ripen**, *verb*; **ripeness**, *noun*.

riposte (*say* ree-**posst**) *noun*
1. *Fencing:* a thrust made by a fencer after he has parried an opponent's attack.
2. a quick, sharp reply or action.
Word Family: **riposte**, *verb*.
[from Italian]

ripple *noun*
1. a small wave or undulation on a surface, especially water.
2. any sound or movement like that of water flowing in ripples: 'a *ripple* of laughter'.
Word Family: **ripple**, *verb*; **ripply**, *adjective*.

rip-roaring *adjective*
(*informal*) a) wild and noisy. b) absolute or total: 'a *rip-roaring* success'.

rise (*say* rize) *verb*
(rose, risen, rising)
1. to assume a standing position; to stand up.
2. to move from a lower to a higher position, rank, amount, etc.
3. to come into existence: 'the river *rises* in the hills'.
4. to rebel or revolt: 'the army *rose* against the government and assumed control'.
5. to swell, as dough does from the action of yeast or heat.
Usages:
a) 'he is very active and *rises* early' (= gets out of bed).
b) 'the building *rises* to a height of 50 m' (= extends upwards).
c) 'his voice *rose* above the children's chatter' (= became louder).
d) 'he is said to have *risen* from the dead' (= returned).
e) 'the bill was not passed before the House *rose*' (= adjourned).
f) 'he *rose* to the occasion quite splendidly' (= was able to cope (with)).
rise *noun*
1. a) the act of rising. b) the degree of ascent: 'how steep is the *rise* here?'.
2. an elevated place, such as a small hill.
3. a) an increase in rank, amount, etc. b) the amount of such an increase.
4. the height of each step in a flight of stairs.
5. (*informal*) an emotional reaction: 'I only said it to get a *rise* out of him'.
give rise to, to cause or produce.
Word Family: **riser**, *noun*.

risible (*say* **rizzi**-b'l) *adjective*
a) inclined to laugh. b) causing laughter.
Word Family: **risibility** (*say* rizzi-**billi**-tee), *noun*.
[from Latin]

risk *noun*
1. the possibility of suffering harm, loss, etc.: 'there is a great *risk* involved in the parachute drop'.
2. *Insurance:* a) the total amount an insurer might have to pay out under a specific policy. b) any property or person insured.
run, take the risk, to expose oneself to risks.
Word Family: **risk**, *verb*, to expose to risk; **risky**, *adjective*.
[Italian *riscare* to run into danger]

risotto *noun*
a dish of rice, meat and onions.
[Italian *riso* rice]

risqué (*say* **riss**-kay) *adjective*
daringly close to indecency.
[French]

rissole *noun*
a fried patty of minced meat or vegetables, often coated in breadcrumbs.
[French]

rite *noun*
a) a formal religious or solemn ceremony. b) the particular form of such a ceremony.
[from Latin]

ritual (*say* **rit–yew'l**) *noun*
a formal or ceremonial action.
Word Family: **ritual**, *adjective*, of or relating to a rite or rites; **ritualism**, *noun*, a) adherence to ritual, b) the study of ritual; **ritualist**, *noun*; **ritualistic**, *adjective*; **ritualistically**, *adverb*.

ritzy *adjective*
(*informal*) luxurious or elegant.
[after the *Ritz*, a luxurious hotel in London]

rival (*say* **rye–v'l**) *noun*
a person who competes against another.
Usage: 'that sea–food restaurant has no *rival* in this town' (= equal).
Word Family: **rival**, *adjective*; **rival** (**rivalled**, **rivalling**), *verb*; **rivalry**, *noun*, competition.
[Latin *rivales* those living near the same stream]

riven *adjective*
split apart.
[past participle of old verb to *rive*]

river (*say* **rivva**) *noun*
1. a large permanent flow of water in a natural channel with banks, which flows into the sea, a lake, etc.
2. any flow: 'a *river* of blood'.
[Latin *riparius* of river–banks]

river basin
Geography: see BASIN.

rivet (*say* **rivvit**) *noun*
a pin with a head, used as a fastener by placing it through a hole and flattening the end opposite the head.
Word Family: **rivet**, *verb*, a) to fasten with or as if with a rivet or rivets, b) to engross or hold firmly; **riveter**, *noun*.

rivulet (*say* **riv–yoo–let**) *noun*
a very small river.

road *noun*
a prepared surface or route for the movement of motor vehicles, people, etc.
Usage: 'it was a long and difficult *road* to peace' (= way, course).
one for the road, (*informal*) a last alcoholic drink before setting out.

roadblock *noun*
a barrier placed across a road by police, soldiers, etc. to control or inspect passing traffic.

road–hog *noun*
(*informal*) a motorist who hogs the road.

roadhouse *noun*
a restaurant, etc. on the side of a main road, for travellers.

road metal
the small stones or gravel used for road surfaces.

roadstead *noun*
also called **roads**
any sheltered water near a shore, where ships may lie at anchor.

roadway *noun*
a road.

roadworthy *adjective*
(of a motor vehicle) being fit to be used on the roads.

roam (*rhymes with* home) *verb*
to move or travel without purpose or plan.
Word Family: **roam**, *noun*; **roamer**, *noun*, a person who roams.

roan *noun*
a horse of a plain colour with white hairs sprinkled throughout.

roar (*say* ror) *verb*
to make a loud, deep sound, especially in excitement, anger, etc.
Word Family: **roar**, *noun*.

roaring (*say* **ror–ing**) *adjective*
1. uttering roars.
2. brisk: 'doing a *roaring* trade'.

roaring forties
the stormy ocean areas of westerly winds between latitudes 40° and 50° South.

roast (*rhymes with* most) *verb*
1. to cook food by using dry heat, e.g. in an oven.
2. (*informal*) to criticize severely.
roast *noun*
a) a meal of roasted meat and vegetables. b) a piece of meat which may be cooked by roasting.

rob *verb*
(**robbed, robbing**)
to take something that belongs to someone else, especially by force or threat of violence.

Usage: 'he was *robbed* of an opportunity to go overseas' (= deprived).
Word Family: **robber**, *noun*, a person who robs; **robbery**, *noun.*
[Old French *robe* booty]

robe *noun*
a) a gown. b) any long, loose piece of clothing, such as a dressing-gown.
Word Family: **robe**, *verb.*

robin *noun*
short form of **robin redbreast**
a friendly little short-necked brown bird with a bright orange breast.

robot (*say* **ro**-bot) *noun*
1. a machine in the shape of a man.
2. (*informal*) a person who thinks or acts like a machine.
[from K. Capek's play *Rossum's Universal Robots*, 1920 (from Czech *robota* compulsory service)]

robust (*say* **ro**-bust) *adjective*
strong and vigorous.
Word Family: **robustly**, *adverb*; **robustness**, *noun.*
[Latin *robur* an oak]

rock (1) *noun*
1. a large mass of stone.
2. something which is very hard: 'peppermint *rock*'.
3. *Geology:* a mass of mineral matter of varying composition.
4. a firm foundation or support: 'father was a *rock* of strength during the crisis'.
5. (*informal*) any large gem, especially a diamond.
on the rocks, a) (*informal*) in a state of disaster; b) (of drinks) with ice only.

rock (2) *verb*
1. to sway back and forth or from side to side.
Usage: 'I was *rocked* by the news of his death' (= moved or affected strongly).
2. to dance to rock-and-roll music.
rock *noun*
1. the act of rocking.
2. a form of popular music which has developed from rock-and-roll music.
3. rock-and-roll.

rock-and-roll *noun*
a) a form of popular music originating during the 1950's characterized by a strong beat, repetitious melody and rhythm, and an exaggerated style of singing. b) a vigorous, improvisatory dance performed to such music.

rock bottom
the lowest level.
Word Family: **rock-bottom**, *adjective.*

rocker *noun*
1. a rocking chair.
2. one of the curved pieces on which a cradle or rocking chair rocks.
off one's rocker, (*informal*) mad or crazy.

rocker arm
a lever, usually pivoting about the middle, connected to a pushrod and operating a valve in an internal combustion engine.

rockery *noun*
also called a **rock-garden**
a garden with earth and rocks amongst which plants are set.

rocket *noun*
1. a structure, usually shaped like a cylinder, which moves by expelling burning gases.
2. a firework that rises into the air and then explodes.
3. (*informal*) a reprimand.
Word Family: **rocket**, *verb*, a) to move like a rocket, b) to increase rapidly.

rocket engine
a reaction engine used in missiles and spacecraft, which produces thrust from the hot gases created by chemically combining oxidant and fuel, both of which are carried in the rocket.

rocket range
a large area used for testing missiles and rocket engines.

rocketry *noun*
the study of rockets, their design, development and flight.

rock-garden *noun*
a rockery.

rocking chair
a chair mounted on rockers which allow it to swing back and forth.

rocking horse
a toy horse, set on rockers, for children to ride.

rock salmon
a trade name for catfish and other fish used in fish-stews and in the fish-and-chips trade.

rock-salt *noun*
common salt, sodium chloride (formula $NaCl$), occurring in large rock-like masses.

rocky (1) *adjective*
1. containing or consisting of rocks.
2. firm or hard like a rock.

rocky (2) *adjective*
shaky or inclined to rock.
Usage: 'a *rocky* road to success' (= uncertain, difficult).

Rococo *noun*
an 18th-century style of art and architecture developed from, and more exaggerated than, the Baroque, characterized by shell-motifs, scrolls and curves in general.
[French *rocaille* shell-work]

rod *noun*
1. a stick or pole made of wood, metal, etc.
2. *Units:* see PERCH (1).
3. *Anatomy:* any of the light-sensitive cells in the retina of higher animals, used for vision in very dim light. Compare CONE.
4. *Biology:* an elongated bacterium.

rode *verb*
the past tense of the verb **ride.**

rodent (*say* **ro**–d'nt) *noun*
any of a large group of gnawing animals such as beavers, squirrels, mice, etc.
[Latin *rodens* gnawing]

rodeo (*say* ro–**dayo** *or* **ro**–dee–o) *noun*
1. a series of competitions covering different aspects of a cowboy's skill, usually for entertainment.
2. a cattle muster.
[Spanish *rodear* to go round]

roe (1) *noun*
the eggs of a female fish. Compare MILT.

roe (2) *noun*
plural is **roe**
a roedeer.

roebuck *noun*
a male roedeer.

roedeer *noun*
a small agile deer, the male of which has three-pointed antlers.

rogue *noun*
1. a dishonest person.
2. a playfully mischievous person.
Word Family: **roguish,** *adjective*; **roguishly,** *adverb*; **roguery, roguishness,** *nouns.*

rogue elephant
an elephant which has left or been cast out from the herd, notorious for savagery.

roister (*say* **roy**–sta) *verb*
to act in a boisterous manner.
Word Family: **roisterous,** *adjective.*
[Latin *rusticus* a peasant]

role, rôle *noun*
1. the character represented by an actor in a play, film, etc.
2. a person's job or function: 'what is a teacher's *role*?'.

roll (*say* role) *verb*
1. to move by turning over and over: a) 'the ball *rolled* along the floor'; b) 'he *rolled* the dice'.
2. to move or be moved on wheels or castors: 'the car *rolled* backwards'.
Usages:
a) 'the waves *rolled* onto the beach' (= advanced).
b) 'the country *rolls* as far as the eye can see' (= undulates).
c) 'the thunder *rolled* across the sky' (= made a deep, long sound).
d) 'that family is obviously *rolling* in money' (= abounding).
e) 'the ship *rolled* in the rough seas' (= rocked from side to side).
f) 'the years *rolled* by' (= passed).
g) 'she manages to *roll* her r's when she speaks French' (= utter with a trill).
h) 'he *rolled* his eyes in amazement' (= rotated).
i) 'she *rolls* her own cigarettes' (= makes by forming into a cylinder).
j) '*roll* the dough very thinly' (= flatten or spread with a roller).
Phrases:
roll out, to spread out or unroll.
roll up, a) to form into a roll; b) (*informal*) to arrive or gather round.

roll *noun*
1. something rolled up in cylindrical form.
2. a list containing the names of people in a class, group, etc.
3. a very small loaf of bread that is baked into various shapes.
4. the act or an instance of rolling: a) 'he walks with a *roll*'; b) 'a *roll* of drums'.
5. a swell or undulation.
6. (*informal*) a wad of banknotes.
[Latin *rotulus* a small wheel]

rollcall (*say* **role**–cawl) *noun*
the calling of a list of names of soldiers, students, etc. to determine those present.

roller *noun*
1. a person or thing that rolls.
2. a small wheel, such as a castor.
3. an elongated cylinder upon which something is wound.
4. a cylindrical device for spreading or crushing something.

5. *Beauty:* a small roll of plastic or metal around which the hair is wrapped to set it into curls or waves. Also called a **curler**.

roller-bearing *noun*
a low-friction bearing, running on cylindrical steel rollers.

roller-coaster *noun*
also called a **scenic railway** or **big dipper**
an open-car railway with sharp turns and steep slopes, ridden for amusement at fairs, etc.

roller-skate *noun*
a form of skate running on small wheels or rollers, used on a smooth surface.
Word Family: **roller-skate**, *verb.*

rollicking *adjective*
behaving or moving in a carefree manner.
Word Family: **rollick**, *verb.*

rolling pin
a cylinder, often wooden, with a handle at each end, for flattening dough or pastry.

rolling stock
the wheeled vehicles of a railway, such as locomotives, carriages, wagons, etc.

roll-neck *adjective*
see POLO-NECK.

roll-top desk
a desk fitted with a lid which can be rolled up or down.

roly-poly *adjective*
plump.

roman (*say* **ro**-m'n) *noun*
the usual style of upright printing, such as this is. Compare ITALIC.
Roman alphabet, the alphabet used for writing western European and other languages.

Roman Catholic
a member of the Western or Roman Church, a Christian denomination with the Pope as its supreme head.
Word Family: **Roman Catholicism**, the faith, practices, etc. of Roman Catholics; **Roman Catholic**, of or relating to Roman Catholicism.

romance (*say* ro-**mance** *or* **ro**-mance) *noun*
1. a) a story about love. b) a story about unusual or exciting adventures.
2. the quality of adventure and idealized exploits found in such stories.
3. a love affair.

romance *verb*
to indulge in fanciful or extravagant ideas or stories.
Word Family: **romantic**, *adjective*, of or relating to a romance; **romantic**, *noun*, a person who enjoys romance; **romanticism**, *noun*, romantic spirit or style; **romanticist**, *noun*; **romanticize**, **romanticise**, to make romantic.
[as derived from medieval tales of chivalry written in the *Romance* languages]

Romance language
any of a group of languages, such as French, Italian, Spanish and Portuguese, which has developed from the Latin spoken by people in ancient Rome.

Roman law
a codified system of law based on that of Ancient Rome, which forms the basis of civil law in many countries.

Roman numerals
the letters used in the ancient Roman system of counting, now used in more formal contexts such as for dates on monuments. The common basic symbols are I(=1), V(=5), X(=10), L(=50), C(=100), D(=500) and M(=1000).
Examples: IX = 9; XI = 11; XLI = 41; LXI = 61.

Romanticism *noun*
a style in art, literature and music which, in contrast to Classicism, emphasized individualism, emotion, grandeur and imagination, and which attached less importance to form than to content.

Romany (*say* **ro**-ma-nee) *adjective*
of the gipsies, their language and culture.
Word Family: **Romany**, *noun*, a gipsy.
[Romany *rom* a man]

romp *verb*
to play or frolic boisterously.
romp home, (*informal*) to win a race, etc. easily.
Word Family: **romp**, *noun.*

roneo *verb*
to produce copies on a duplicating machine.
[a trademark for a duplicating machine]

rood *noun*
Christian: a) a large cross or crucifix in a church, usually set into a screen. b) an old word for the Cross on which Christ died.

roof *noun*
plural is **roofs**
1. a protective structure placed over a building and supported by the walls, usually made of tiles, iron or timber.
2. something resembling or serving as a roof, such as the top of a car, etc.
Phrases:
hit the roof, (*informal*) to become very angry.
raise the roof, a) to make a loud noise; b) to complain or protest loudly.
Word Family: **roof**, *verb*, to provide or cover with a roof.

roofing *noun*
the materials used to make a roof, such as iron, slate or tiles.

roof-rack *noun*
a metal frame placed on the roof of a motor car to carry bulky goods.

rook (1) (*rhymes with* book) *noun*
1. a black crow with a bare face-patch, which nests in colonies.
2. (*informal*) a) a swindle. b) a swindler.
Word Family: **rook**, *verb*, to cheat or swindle.

rook (2) (*rhymes with* book) *noun*
also called a **castle**
Chess: a piece that may move any number of squares horizontally or vertically.
[Persian *rukh*]

rookery *noun*
a) a group of rooks. b) a breeding place for rooks or other birds or animals, such as penguins and seals.

rookie *noun*
(*informal*) a new recruit in the army, police, etc.

room *noun*
1. any of the various areas into which a house is divided by the walls.
2. the people present in such an area: 'the whole *room* was silent'.
3. (*plural*) lodgings.
4. the space occupied by or available for something: 'the furniture took up a lot of *room*'.
Usage: 'your work leaves *room* for improvement' (= scope, opportunity).
room *verb*
room with, to share a room with.
Word Family: **room-mate**, *noun*, a person with whom one shares a room.

rooming house
a boarding house.

room service
the serving of food or drink to a guest in his room in a hotel, etc.

roomy *adjective*
spacious or large.
Word Family: **roomily**, *adverb*; **roominess**, *noun*.

roost *noun*
a) a perch upon which domestic fowl or other birds rest. b) a place containing such perches.
Word Family: **roost**, *verb*, a) to sit or rest on a roost, b) to settle or stay, especially for the night.

rooster *noun*
a male domestic fowl.

root (1) *noun*
1. *Biology:* the part of a plant which grows down into the soil, fixing it and absorbing water and minerals from the soil.
2. something which has the position or function of a root.
3. the fundamental or essential part: 'the *root* of the problem'.
Usage: 'the *root* of all evil' (= source, origin).
4. (*plural*) the condition or feeling of belonging to a place, society, etc.
5. *Maths:* a) a number which, when multiplied by itself a certain number of times, results in a given number. *Example*: 3 is the square root of $9 (3 \times 3)$, written $\sqrt{9}$, the cube root of $27 (3 \times 3 \times 3)$ written $\sqrt[3]{27}$, and the fourth root of $81 (3 \times 3 \times 3 \times 3)$, written $\sqrt[4]{81}$.
b) the values of a variable in an expression which make that expression equal to zero.
6. *Grammar:* a word, or part of a word, on which all other forms of that word are based. *Example*: *dance* is the root of *dancer* and *dancing*.
root *verb*
1. to send out roots and begin to grow.
2. to become fixed or established.

root (2) *verb*
to dig with or as if with the snout or nose.
Usage: 'the detective *rooted* up a lot of scandal' (= revealed).

root (3) *verb*
(*informal*) to shout encouragement: 'which team are you *rooting* for?'.

root beer
an American drink made from the juices of various roots, such as sarsaparilla and dandelion.

rootlet *noun*
a small root.

root nodules
the swellings on the roots of legumes containing bacteria which are important in the nitrogen cycle.

rope *noun*
1. a strong, twisted cord made from strands of hemp, flax, etc.
2. (*plural*) methods or procedures: 'to learn the *ropes*'.
rope *verb*
to catch a horse, cow, etc. with a rope.
Phrases:
rope in, (*informal*) 'I was *roped in* to wash the dishes' (= drawn in, persuaded).
rope off, 'the main arena was *roped off*' (= enclosed with a rope).

rosary (*say* **ro**–za–ree) *noun*
Roman Catholic: a string of beads used to count when reciting a certain series of prayers.

rose (1) (*say* roze) *noun*
1. any of a group of garden shrubs with prickly stems and showy, sometimes fragrant, flowers.
2. a pinkish–red colour.
3. an ornamental plate or moulding surrounding a fitting such as a door knob.
4. a nozzle, cap, etc. with many holes in it, attached to a pipe or hose to spray water.
[from Latin]

rose (2) (*say* roze) *verb*
the past tense of the verb **rise.**

rosé (*say* **ro**–zay *or* ro–**zay**) *noun*
a pink wine.
[French]

roseate (*say* **ro**–zee–it) *adjective*
rosy.

rosemary *noun*
a Mediterranean shrub with fragrant leaves that are used as a herb.

rosette (*say* ro–**zet**) *noun*
a rose–shaped arrangement of ribbons or other materials, used for decoration.

rosewater *noun*
a pleasant smelling water made from rose petals or oil extracted from roses, used on the skin, in cooking, etc.

rose window
a round window divided into sections.

rosewood *noun*
a tropical tree with soft reddish wood, used to make furniture, instruments, etc.

rosily *adverb*
Word Family: see ROSY.

rosin (*say* **rozz**in) *noun*
a yellowish, solid resin obtained from the distillation of turpentine, used in varnishes, soaps and soldering fluxes.

roster *noun*
a list of names, especially one showing periods of duty.
Word Family: **roster,** *verb,* to put on a roster.

rostrum *noun*
plural is **rostrums** or **rostra**
1. a raised platform for a conductor of an orchestra, a speaker, etc. to stand on.
2. a movable platform, such as is used for scenery in a theatre.
[Latin]

rosy (*say* **ro**–zee) *adjective*
pink or pinkish–red.
Usage: 'the future looks *rosy* for you' (= promising, hopeful).
Word Family: **rosily,** *adverb*; **rosiness,** *noun.*

rot *verb*
(rotted, rotting)
to become bad or decomposed.
rot *noun*
1. a) the process of rotting. b) the state of being rotten.
2. (*informal*) nonsense: 'he talks a lot of *rot*'.

rotary (*say* **ro**–ta–ree) *adjective*
of or involving rotation, especially on an axis.

rotary engine
an engine worked by a rotor instead of reciprocating pistons.

rotate (*say* ro–**tate**) *verb*
1. to turn or spin on an axis.
2. to alternate in sequence: 'to *rotate* crops'.
[Latin *rota* a wheel]

rotation (*say* ro–**tay**–sh'n) *noun*
1. the act of rotating: 'the *rotation* of crops'.
2. a) the spinning of a planet or star on its axis. b) one complete spin.

rote *noun*
by rote, in a mechanical way without understanding or thinking of the meaning.
Word Family: **rote,** *adjective.*

rotisserie (*say* ro–**tissa**–ree) *noun*
a) a revolving skewer on which meat, poultry, etc. is cooked over heat. b)

a restaurant where such a device is used.
[French, roasting place]

rotor *noun*
1. a rotating part of a machine.
2. a system of rotating blades used to lift and control helicopters.

rotten *adjective*
1. bad or decomposed.
2. a) corrupt. b) mean or contemptible.
Usage: (*informal*) 'what *rotten* luck!' (= bad, unfortunate).
Word Family: **rottenly,** *adverb*; **rottenness,** *noun.*

rotter *noun*
(*informal*) a thoroughly worthless or objectionable person.

rotund (*say* ro-**tund**) *adjective*
plump or rounded.
Word Family: **rotundity** (*say* ro-**tundi**-tee), **rotundness,** *nouns*; **rotundly,** *adverb.*
[Latin *rotundus* round]

rotunda (*say* ro-**tunda**) *noun*
a round building, usually with a dome.

rouble (*say* **roo**-b'l) *noun*
also spelt **ruble**
the basic unit of money in Russia.

roué (*say* **roo**-ay) *noun*
an ageing and dissolute man.
[French, (deserving to be) broken on the wheel]

rouge (*say* roo*zh*) *noun*
a red cream or powder used to colour the cheeks.
Word Family: **rouge,** *verb.*
[French, red]

rough (*say* ruf) *adjective*
1. having an uneven surface.
2. violent: 'the *rough* seas made us seasick'.
3. imperfectly finished, polished, refined, etc.: a) 'she made a *rough* draft of her speech'; b) 'the *rough* diamond doubled in value after it was cut'.
Usages:
a) 'his *rough* behaviour embarrassed his parents' (= impolite, disorderly).
b) (*informal*) 'after the car accident he had a *rough* time' (= difficult, unpleasant).
rough on, a) 'as she was so young we were not *rough on* her when she misbehaved' (= severe towards); b) 'it was *rough on* him to have both his parents die within a month' (= unfortunate for).

rough *noun*
1. something which is rough.
2. *Golf:* any uncleared part of the golf course, especially with long grass or trees.
3. *Tennis:* the side of a racket on which the loops formed by the strings are uppermost.
4. (*informal*) a rowdy or rough person.
in the rough, in a crude or unpolished state.

rough *verb*
Phrases:
rough in, rough out, to shape or sketch in a rough or incomplete form.
rough it, to live without the ordinary comforts, etc., as while camping.
rough up, 'the witness claimed the police had *roughed* him *up*' (= treated in a rough or violent way).
Word Family: **roughly,** *adverb*; **roughen,** *verb*; **roughness,** *noun.*

roughage (*say* **ruff**ij) *noun*
1. any rough or coarse material.
2. the coarser parts of fodder or food which are of little nutritive value, but aid digestion.

rough-and-ready *adjective*
crude in method or manner, but effective in action or use.

rough-and-tumble *adjective*
disorderly, haphazard or scrambling.
Word Family: **rough-and-tumble,** *noun,* a scuffle.

roughcast *noun*
a type of coarse plaster mixed with gravel or shells, used for outside surfaces.
Word Family: **roughcast,** *adjective, verb.*

rough diamond
a coarse or unrefined person with likable qualities.

roughen *verb*
Word Family: see ROUGH.

rough-house *noun*
boisterous or rough behaviour, games, fighting, etc.
Word Family: **rough-house,** *verb.*

roughly *adverb*
Word Family: see ROUGH.

roughneck *noun*
(*informal*) a rough, rowdy person.

roughrider *noun*
a person who breaks in horses.

roughshod *adjective*
ride roughshod over, to dominate or treat without consideration.

roulette (*say* roo–let) *noun*
1. a game in which one bets on where a small ball will come to rest on a horizontal, revolving wheel with numbered divisions.
2. a tool with a handle and a small notched wheel which makes dotted lines in engraving.
Russian roulette
a suicidal game of chance in which a revolver loaded with a bullet in only one of its chambers is held to one's head and the trigger pulled.
[French, little wheel]

round *adjective*
1. shaped like a ball, ring or circle.
2. curved or without angles: 'a *round* face'.
Usages:
a) 'I'll have a *round* dozen please' (= exact, complete).
b) 'I can only give you a *round* estimate' (= approximate).
c) 'what is the answer in *round* numbers?' (= whole).
d) 'I paid for a *round* trip' (= returning to the point of departure).
round *noun*
1. a complete course, succession or series: 'the *round* of Christmas parties'.
2. (*sometimes plural*) a course of usual actions, duties, etc.: 'the doctor did his *round* of the wards'.
3. a) a single shot or volley from a gun or guns. b) ammunition for a single shot.
4. *Music:* a song in which each voice copies the last, at the same pitch or in octaves.
5. a sandwich made with two slices of bread.
6. a cut of beef from the haunch of the animal.
7. the state of being carved out on all sides: 'sculpture in the *round*'.
Usages:
a) 'I bought a *round* of drinks' (= one for each person).
b) 'a *round* of applause followed his speech' (= single outburst).
round *verb*
1. to make or become round.
2. to go or pass around: 'to *round* a cape'.
round off, to complete or perfect.
round *adverb*
1. on every side of: 'they swarmed *round* us'.
2. here and there: 'his clothes were scattered *round*'.
3. throughout: 'the year *round*'.
4. in a circle: 'the wheels go *round*'.
Usage: 'come *round* tonight' (= to our house).
come round, a) 'we *came round* to your view' (= accepted); b) 'after 5 minutes he *came round*' (= regained consciousness).
round *preposition*
1. encircling: 'tie the string *round* the parcel'.
2. on every side of: 'all *round* us'.
3. near: 'we've had burglaries *round* here'.
Word Family: **roundness,** *noun*; **rounded**, *adjective*, made round.
[Latin *rotundus*]

roundabout *noun*
1. an intersection laid out so that traffic moves in one direction around a central structure.
2. a merry–go–round.
Word Family: **roundabout**, *adjective*, indirect.

rounders *plural noun*
(*used with singular verb*) a game similar to baseball, usually played by children with a small, soft ball and a bat.

roundly *adverb*
thoroughly or bluntly: 'I was told off *roundly* for misbehaving'.

round–the–clock *adjective*
continuing all day and all night: 'a *round–the–clock* guard'.

round–up *noun*
a collecting together, especially of cattle or other animals.
Word Family: **round up**, to collect or bring together.

roundworm *noun*
also called a **nematode**
any of a group of smooth, unsegmented, often parasitic, worms which are pointed at both ends.

rouse (*rhymes with* cows) *verb*
1. to stir out of a state of sleep, inactivity, apathy, etc.
2. to stir to anger, action, etc.
Word Family: **rousingly**, *adverb.*

rout (1) (*rhymes with* out) *noun*
1. *Military:* a disorderly retreat after an overwhelming defeat.
2. a disorderly crowd of people.
Word Family: **rout,** *verb,* to defeat utterly.

rout (2) (*rhymes with* out) *verb*
to search or rummage.

route (*say* root) *noun*
the way taken or planned for travel.

route–march *noun*
a long march by soldiers during training.

routine (*say* roo–**teen**) *noun*
a set or usual way of doing something.
Word Family: **routine**, *adjective*, like or according to a routine.
[French]

roux (*say* roo) *noun*
a mixture of flour and butter heated to form a binding element in sauces and soups.
[French, browned]

rove (1) *verb*
to wander freely or aimlessly.
Word Family: **rove**, *noun*.

rove (2) *verb*
a past tense and past participle of the verb **reeve (2)**.

rover *noun*
1. a person who roves or wanders.
2. a pirate or pirate vessel.

row (1) (*say* ro) *noun*
1. an arrangement of people or objects arranged beside or behind each other.
2. a line of seats facing in the same direction, e.g. in a theatre.

row (2) (*say* ro) *verb*
to propel a boat with oars supported in rowlocks.
Word Family: **row**, *noun*, a) the act of rowing, b) a trip in a rowing boat; **rower**, *noun*, a person who rows.

row (3) (*rhymes with* cow) *noun*
a) a noisy quarrel. b) a loud noise.
Word Family: **row**, *verb*.

rowan *noun*
the mountain ash.

rowdy *adjective*
rough, loud and disorderly.
Word Family: **rowdy**, *noun*, a rough, disorderly person; **rowdily**, *adverb*; **rowdiness**, *noun*.

rowel (*rhymes with* towel) *noun*
a toothed wheel, e.g. on a spur.

rowing boat
a boat propelled by oars.

rowlock (*say* **rolluk**) *noun*
a U–shaped device attached to the side of a boat to hold an oar in place.

royal *adjective*
1. of or relating to a monarch.
2. befitting a monarch: 'his mother gave us a *royal* welcome'.
Word Family: **royally**, *adverb*; **royal**, *noun*, (informal) a member of a royal family.
[Latin *regalis*]

royal blue
a deep blue colour, often with a faint reddish tinge.

royal commission
a body of people nominated by a government to inquire into and report on some matter.

royalist *noun*
(*sometimes capital*) any supporter of monarchy.

royal jelly
a substance made by bees and fed to the young larvae that are to become queen bees.

royal purple
a deep, bluish–purple colour.

royal tennis
see REAL TENNIS.

royalty *noun*
1. monarchs and their families considered as a group.
2. the power, status or dignity of a monarch.
3. a share paid to an inventor, author, etc. out of the proceeds from the sale or performance of his work.

rub *verb*
(**rubbed, rubbing**)
1. to move something over a surface with pressure or friction, especially to clean, smooth, polish, etc.
2. to become or cause to become chafed or irritated.
Phrases:
rub down, a) to rub smooth, etc.; b) to massage, dry or clean by rubbing.
rub off, a) to remove by or as if by rubbing, b) to transfer or be transferred.
rub out, a) to remove by rubbing; (*informal*) to kill.
rub *noun*
1. the act of rubbing.
2. an obstacle or difficulty: 'the *rub* is I have no money'.

rubber (1) *noun*
1. an elastic solid obtained from the sap of a tropical tree (called **indiarubber** or **natural rubber**), or man–made (called **synthetic rubber**), usually combined with other substances, such as sulphur, when made into articles. See VULCANIZE.
2. a piece of rubber or synthetic material used to remove pencil or pen marks. Also called an **eraser**.
3. (*plural*) any waterproof clothes or shoes.
[from RUB]

rubber (2) *noun*
1. *Cards:* the best of three games of bridge, etc.
2. any tournament consisting of a series of separate games.

rubber band
a thin loop of elastic rubber used for holding objects, etc. together.

rubber plant
a) a Brazilian plant with milky sap, used to make rubber. b) an Indian plant with large, shiny leaves, usually grown indoors.

rubber stamp
1. a small rubber device with raised figures for printing dates, etc.
2. (*informal*) a person or group that gives immediate or unthinking approval.
Word Family: **rubber-stamp**, *verb.*

rubbing *noun*
a reproduction or print made by rubbing, especially using a dark crayon on paper placed over a raised design, e.g. of church brass.

rubbish *noun*
any waste or worthless material.
Usage: 'you're talking utter *rubbish*' (= nonsense).
Word Family: **rubbishy**, *adjective*, worthless.

rubble *noun*
any fragments of broken rock or masonry.

rub-down *noun*
a massage.

rubella (*say* roo-bella) *noun*
German measles.
[Latin *rubellus* reddish]

rubicund (*say* roobi-kund) *adjective*
having a healthy, rosy complexion.
[Latin *rubicundus* red]

rubidium (*say* roobiddi-um) *noun*
element number 37, a soft, strongly reactive metal. See ALKALI METAL. See CHEMICAL ELEMENTS in grey pages.
[Latin *rubidus* red (referring to the spectrum)]

ruble *noun*
see ROUBLE.

rubric (*say* roo-brik) *noun*
any title or instruction inserted in a book, etc., in a different colour or lettering.
[Latin *rubrica* red earth, title of a law (written with red ochre)]

ruby (*say* roo-bee) *noun*
1. a rich deep red.
2. a red crystalline variety of corundum used as a gemstone and in watch bearings.
Word Family: **ruby**, *adjective.*
[Latin *rubeus* red]

ruck (1) *noun*
the usual run of people or things.

ruck (2) *verb*
(of cloth) to crease or wrinkle.
Word Family: **ruck**, *noun.*

rucksack *noun*
a knapsack with a supporting frame.
[German *Rücken* back + SACK]

ructions *plural noun*
(*informal*) a row or disturbance.

rudd *noun*
a freshwater fish of the carp family.

rudder *noun*
a flat structure hinged to the stern of a boat or the tail of an aeroplane and used for steering.

ruddle *noun*
a red type of ochre used for marking sheep and for colouring.

ruddy *adjective*
1. reddish in colour: 'a *ruddy* complexion'.
2. (*informal*) damned: 'you're a *ruddy* lunatic'.
Word Family: **ruddy**, *adverb*, extremely; **ruddiness**, *noun.*

rude *adjective*
1. impolite, disrespectful or discourteous.
Usage: 'that is a *rude* word' (= improper, obscene).
2. rough or crude: 'we quickly built a *rude* shelter for the night'.
3. without culture or refinement.
Word Family: **rudely**, *adverb*; **rudeness**, *noun.*
[Latin *rudis* in the natural state]

rudiment (*say* roodi-m'nt) *noun*
(*plural*) the elementary principles of a subject or skill: 'teach me the *rudiments* of algebra'.
rudimentary (*say* roodi-menta-ree) *adjective*
1. elementary: 'a *rudimentary* lesson in musical theory'.
2. undeveloped: 'flightless birds have *rudimentary* wings'.
[Latin *rudimentum* a first attempt]

rue (1) (*say* roo) *verb*
(rued, ruing)

to regret or think about bitterly: 'I *rue* the day we met'.
rueful *adjective*
1. deplorable or pitiable: 'a *rueful* situation'.
2. sorry or regretful: 'a *rueful* smile'.
Word Family: **ruefully,** *adverb*; **ruefulness,** *noun.*

rue (2) (*say* roo) *noun*
a small, evergreen shrub with bitter-tasting leaves, formerly used in medicine.

ruff (1) *noun*
1. a collar drawn into stiff, regular folds, popular in the 16th century.
2. a ring of differently marked hair or feathers around the neck of an animal.

ruff (2) *verb*
Cards: to trump when one cannot follow suit.
Word Family: **ruff,** *noun.*

ruffian *noun*
a violent or rough person.
Word Family: **ruffianism,** *noun.*
[from Italian]

ruffle *verb*
to disturb the smoothness of something: 'the bird *ruffled* its feathers while cleaning itself'.
Usage: 'their harsh words *ruffled* her' (= upset, annoyed).
ruffle *noun*
a strip of cloth drawn together to form a frill, as on a shirt.

rufous (*say* **roo**fus) *adjective*
rusty red or orange in colour.
[Latin *rufus* reddish]

rug *noun*
a) a small, thick carpet. b) a thick, warm blanket.

rugby football
a type of football played with an oval ball which may be handled.
Rugby League
a type of Rugby football played by professionals, with 13 players in a side.
Rugby Union
short form is **Rugby** or **Union**
a type of Rugby football played by amateurs, with 15 players in a side.
[invented at *Rugby* School]

rugged (*say* **rugg**id) *adjective*
rough, uneven or rocky: a) 'a *rugged* range of mountains'; b) 'a *rugged,* weather-beaten face'.
Usages:
a) 'those pioneers had a *rugged* existence' (= difficult).
b) 'she's a person of *rugged* independence' (= direct, vigorous).
Word Family: **ruggedly,** *adverb*; **ruggedness,** *noun.*

rugger *noun*
(*informal*) rugby football.

ruin (*say* **roo**-in) *noun*
a) decay, collapse or demolition: 'gambling was the *ruin* of me'. b) a state of collapse or decay: 'the old castle fell into *ruin*'. c) something that is collapsed or destroyed: 'the castle is now a *ruin*'
in ruins, in a state of ruin.
ruin *verb*
to reduce or bring to ruin: a) 'the rain *ruined* the harvest'; b) 'you'll *ruin* your shoes if you wear them in the mud'.
Usage: 'Smith was *ruined* during the depression' (= made bankrupt).
ruinous (*say* **roo**-in-us) *adjective*
a) causing ruin: 'a *ruinous* war'. b) in ruins: 'a *ruinous* castle'.
Word Family: **ruinously,** *adverb*; **ruinousness,** *noun*; **ruination,** *noun.*
[Latin *ruina* a tumbling down]

rule *noun*
1. a principle or code of behaviour or action: 'do you know the *rules* of the game?'.
Usage: 'the *rule* in this town is to eat late' (= custom, habit).
2. authority or control: 'Australia was once under British *rule*'.
3. a ruler for measuring, etc.
as a rule, usually.
rule *verb*
1. to control or direct: a) 'the king *ruled* for 40 years'; b) 'be *ruled* by my advice in this matter'.
Usages:
a) 'the court *ruled* the will invalid' (= declared).
b) 'high prices *ruled* for beef' (= were current).
2. to draw lines with a ruler.
rule out, 'we can *rule out* the possibility of murder' (= dismiss).
[Latin *regula* a straight stick]

rule of thumb
any practical method or procedure based on experience rather than theory.

ruler *noun*
1. a person who rules, especially a monarch.
2. a strip of wood, metal, plastic, etc., with a straight edge for ruling lines, measuring, etc.

ruling *noun*
an authoritative judgement or decision, such as one given by a court.

rum (1) *noun*
a strong liquor made from molasses or sugar cane.

rum (2) *adjective*
(*informal*) odd or strange: 'he's a *rum* lad'.

rumba *noun*
a) a ballroom dance from Cuba with a complex rhythm. b) the music for such a dance.
[American Spanish]

rumble *verb*
a) to make a low, continuous, heavy sound, such as distant thunder. b) to move with this sound: 'the heavy carts *rumbled* across the cobblestones'.
Usage: (*informal*) 'the police have *rumbled* our plan' (= detected, uncovered).
Word Family: **rumble**, *noun*; **rumbly**, *adverb.*

rumen (*say* **roo**–m'n) *noun*
the first stomach of a ruminant.
[Latin, throat]

ruminant (*say* **roomi**–nant) *noun*
any mammal, such as a cow or sheep, that returns partly digested food to the mouth to be re-chewed.

ruminate (*say* **roomi**–nate) *verb*
1. (of a person) to meditate or ponder: 'don't sit there *ruminating* on your problems'.
2. (of an animal) to chew the cud.
Word Family: **ruminatingly**, *adverb*; **rumination**, *noun*; **ruminative** (*say* **roomi**na–tiv), *adjective.*

rummage (*say* **rummi**j) *verb*
to look for something, especially by moving things around: 'she *rummaged* through the drawers of the desk for a pencil'.
Word Family: **rummage**, *noun*, a) odds and ends, b) the act of rummaging.
[French *arrumer* to stow cargo]

rummage sale
a sale of used articles to raise money for charity.

rummy (1) *noun*
a card game for two or more players who try to match cards into sets or sequences of at least three cards.

rummy (2) *adjective*
(*informal*) odd or strange.

rumour (*say* **room**a) *noun*
in America spelt **rumor**
a) an unconfirmed story or report in circulation: 'there is a *rumour* that you are going away'. b) general gossip: '*rumour* has it you're leaving'.
rumour *verb*
to report or circulate rumours: 'it is *rumoured* that you're going to Africa'.
[Latin *rumor* a noise]

rump *noun*
1. a) the fleshy hind-parts of most mammals, equivalent to the buttocks in man. b) a cut of beef from this area.
2. any lesser or unimportant parts or remnants.

rumple *verb*
to crush or crumple: 'my dress was *rumpled* in the crowded train'.

rumpus *noun*
(*informal*) a noisy uproar or disturbance.

run *verb*
(ran, run, running)
1. to move quickly on foot: '*run* and answer the telephone'.
2. to go or make to go: 'the ship *ran* aground'.
3. to pass or move quickly: a) 'a brilliant idea *ran* through my mind'; b) 'he *ran* his eyes over the page'.
4. to move or operate: a) 'this engine *runs* quietly'; b) 'I *run* this business myself'; c) 'trains *run* every half-hour'.
5. to continue or extend: a) 'the fence *runs* round the property'; b) 'the play *ran* for 6 weeks'; c) 'my tastes don't *run* to champagne'.
6. to pass a particular state: a) 'to *run* dry'; b) 'they *ran* riot'.
Usages:
a) 'the horse I backed *ran* last' (= finished).
b) 'he *ran* for public office' (= was a candidate).
c) 'artistic ability *runs* in our family' (= recurs).
d) 'my stockings always *run*' (= ladder).
e) 'the water *ran* from the taps' (= flowed).
f) 'the colours of my new shirt *ran*' (= spread, mingled).
g) 'my arrangements *ran* smoothly' (= proceeded).
h) 'you'll *run* into trouble' (= get).
i) 'we'll *run* over to visit Mrs Jones' (= make a short or casual trip).
j) 'who will *run* this errand for me?' (= perform).
k) 'the story *runs* like this' (= goes).

l) 'he was convicted of *running* guns' (= smuggling).
m) 'you're *running* a risk by smoking so heavily' (= incurring).
n) 'she's *running* a mild fever' (= suffering from).
Phrases:
run across, to meet unexpectedly.
run down, a) (of a clock, etc.) to slow down and stop; b) 'I *ran down* a pedestrian' (= knocked down while in a car, etc.); c) to disparage.
run in, a) (of a new motor vehicle) to operate carefully to bring it to full working condition; b) (*informal*) to arrest.
run into, a) to meet unexpectedly; b) 'the final cost *ran into* 4 figures' (= amounted to).
run off, a) to abscond; b) 'the printer *ran off* a 1000 copies of the leaflet' (= produced).
run out, a) 'time has *run out*' (= been all used up); b) (*Cricket*) to put a batsman out by hitting the wicket with the ball while he is out of his crease; c) 'we *ran* the thieves *out* of town' (= expelled from).
run out on, to desert or abandon.
run over, a) to knock down with a vehicle and injure or kill; b) 'we'll *run over* what I said last time' (= review).
run short, 'time is *running short*' (= nearly all used up).
run through, a) 'I *ran* him *through* with my sword' (= pierced); b) 'we'll *run through* that last scene again' (= do, rehearse).
run up, a) '*run up* the flag' (= hoist); b) 'you've *run up* a large bill' (= amassed); c) 'I'll *run* you *up* a new frock on the sewing machine' (= make quickly).
run up against, 'the plan *ran up against* bitter opposition' (= met with).

run *noun*
1. the act of running: a) 'go for a *run* in the park'; b) 'the play had a 6 week *run*'.
2. an excursion or journey: a) 'let's go for a *run* in the car'; b) 'it's a 2 hour *run* by bus'.
3. *Sport:* the score unit in cricket, baseball, etc.
Usages:
a) 'you've had a *run* of bad luck' (= sequence).
b) 'I'll give you the *run* of the house while I'm away' (= freedom).
c) 'lately there's been a *run* on these goods' (= heavy demand).
d) 'did you find the ski *run*?' (= track, course).
e) 'the general *run* of people' (= type).
f) 'she has a *run* in her stocking' (= ladder).
Phrases:
in the long run, ultimately.
in the short run, considering only the immediate effects.
on the run, a) 'the criminals are *on the run*' (= escaped and in hiding); b) 'now we have the enemy forces *on the run*' (= retreating).

run-around *noun*
give someone the run-around, to evade or prevaricate.

runaway *adjective*
escaped or fugitive: 'a *runaway* convict'.
Usages:
a) 'we must stop *runaway* inflation' (= uncontrolled).
b) 'he was the *runaway* winner of the race' (= easy).
Word Family: **runaway**, *noun*.

run-down *noun*
a brief review or summary.
run-down *adjective*
in a poor or dilapidated condition: 'a *run-down* old house'.

rune (*say* roon) *noun*
any of the characters of an alphabet formerly used in Scandinavian and Anglo-Saxon inscriptions.
Word Family: **runic**, *adjective*.
[Old English *run* a mystery]

rung (1) *verb*
the past participle of the verb **ring (2)**.

rung (2) *noun*
a crosspiece set in a ladder or between the legs of a chair for support.
[Old English *hrung* a pole]

runnel *noun*
a) a small stream or rivulet. b) a small channel for water.

runner *noun*
1. a person or thing that runs: 'how many *runners* in the next race?'.
2. a messenger or scout for an employer.
3. the part by which something moves or glides along, such as strips of wood on the edges of a drawer or the blade on an ice-skate.
4. a long, narrow carpet extending along a hallway.
5. *Biology:* a slender stem that grows along the ground and may produce roots.

runner bean
also called **scarlet runner**
a plant with large red flowers and red and black edible seeds in edible pods which are cooked after stringing and slicing.

runner-up *noun*
a competitor who comes second in a competition.

running *noun*
Phrases:
in the running, having a chance of success.
make the running, to set the pace.
out of the running, having no chance of success.
running *adjective*
1. of or relating to a person or thing that runs: a) '*running* water'; b) 'a *running* knot on a noose'.
2. continuous: 'during the match I'll give a *running* commentary'.
Usages:
a) 'she stayed out late for three nights *running*' (= in succession).
b) 'this machine is not in *running* order' (= operating, working).

running board
a narrow ledge beneath the doors on the side of a vehicle, to assist people getting in or out.

running mate
American: the less important candidate on an electoral ticket, such as the person running for vice-president.

running stitch
Needlework: a small, continuous stitch.

runny *adjective*
a) liquid or flowing: 'the butter has become *runny*'. b) discharging a fluid: 'a *runny* nose'.

run-of-the-mill *adjective*
ordinary or mediocre.

runt *noun*
1. an undersized animal, especially the smallest in a litter.
2. (*informal*) an undersized person.

runway *noun*
a cleared, usually concrete, strip of ground for aeroplanes to take off from and land on.

rupee (*say* roo-**pee**) *noun*
the basic unit of money in India, Pakistan and elsewhere.
[Hindi]

rupture (*say* **rup**cher) *verb*
to break or burst: 'she *ruptured* a blood vessel'.
rupture *noun*
1. a breaking or bursting.
2. *Medicine:* see HERNIA.
[Latin *ruptus* broken]

rural (*say* **roo**-r'l) *adjective*
1. of or relating to the country or countryside.
2. of or relating to agriculture.
Word Family: **rurally**, *adverb.*
[Latin *ruris* of the countryside]

ruse (*say* rooz) *noun*
a trick or deceitful scheme.

rush (1) *verb*
1. to go or move quickly and forcefully: a) 'the surging crowd *rushed* forward'; b) 'the tears *rushed* to his eyes'.
2. to do something very quickly: 'a new law was *rushed* through parliament'.
Usage: 'don't *rush* me' (= hurry).
rush *noun*
1. any rapid or forceful movement: a) 'there was a mad *rush* for seats'; b) 'the *rush* of life in a big city'.
Usages:
a) 'there's been a *rush* on lemonade this summer' (= heavy demand).
b) 'what's the *rush*?' (= hurry).
2. *Film:* (*plural*) the first proofs of a movie.
rush *adjective*
requiring speed: 'a *rush* delivery'.

rush (2) *noun*
any of various slender, leafless marsh plants used in weaving baskets, etc.

rush hour
one of the busy times of day for traffic, when people travel between home and work.

rusk *noun*
a crisp, dry biscuit, given to babies to help them when teething.

russet *noun*
a brown colour with a reddish or yellowish hue.
Word Family: **russet**, *adjective.*
[Latin *russus* red]

Russian roulette
see ROULETTE.

rust *noun*
1. *Chemistry:* a flaky, reddish-brown coating of hydrated ferric oxide, which forms on iron when it is exposed to air and moisture.
2. a reddish-brown or orange colour.
3. *Biology:* a plant disease caused by fungi, which stains leaves and stems a rust colour.

rust *verb*
to corrode or develop rust.
Word Family: **rust**, *adjective.*

rustic *adjective*
rural.
Usage: 'he has *rustic* manners' (= unsophisticated).
rustic *noun*
a country person, especially an unsophisticated one.
Word Family: **rustically**, *adverb.*
[from Latin]

rusticate *verb*
1. to make rustic.
2. to send down temporarily from a university.

rustle (*say* **russ**'l) *verb*
1. a) to make soft, quiet sounds, as of things rubbing gently together: 'the leaves *rustled* in the wind'. b) to move with such a sound: 'a deer *rustled* through the undergrowth'.
2. to steal cattle, etc.
rustle up, (*informal*) '*rustle up* a bit of courage' (= muster).
Word Family: **rustle**, *noun*, a rustling sound; **rustler**, *noun.*

rusty *adjective*
a) affected with rust. b) having the colour of rust.
Usage: 'my Spanish is a little *rusty*' (= weak through lack of practice).

rut (1) *noun*
a narrow furrow in the ground, especially one made by the wheels of a vehicle.
Usage: 'I mustn't get into a *rut*' (= fixed or established way of life).

rut (2) *noun*
a period of recurring sexual excitement in animals such as sheep and goats.
Word Family: **rut** (**rutted**, **rutting**), *verb*, to be affected by rut.
[Latin *rugitus* bellowing]

ruth (*say* rooth) *noun*
an old word for pity or sorrow.
Word Family: **ruthful**, *adjective*; **ruthfully**, *adverb*; **ruthfulness**, *noun.*

ruthenium (*say* roo–**theeni**–um) *noun*
element number 44, a rare, brittle metal used in hardening platinum alloys and as a catalyst. See TRANSITION ELEMENT.
See CHEMICAL ELEMENTS in grey pages.

ruthless (*say* rooth–less) *adjective*
pitiless or merciless: 'the ambitious prince was *ruthless* in his desire to become king'.
Word Family: **ruthlessly**, *adverb*; **ruthlessness**, *noun.*

rutile (*say* **roo**–tile) *noun*
a naturally occurring form of titanium dioxide, often occurring as sands. It is used as a source of titanium.
[Latin *rutilus* golden red]

rye *noun*
1. a cereal plant used to make flour, whisky and as food for cattle.
2. a whisky distilled from rye.

rye–bread *noun*
a dark bread made with flour from rye.

Ss

Sabbath *noun*
1. *Religion:* a) the seventh day of the week, Saturday, kept as a day of rest by Jews and certain Christian sects. b) the first day of the week, Sunday, kept by Christians as a day of rest in celebration of Christ's resurrection.
2. (*not capital*) a secret meeting of witches held at night.
[Hebrew *shabath* to rest]

sabbatical (*say* **sa-batti-k'l**) **sabbatic** *adjective*
1. of or relating to the Sabbath.
2. of or relating to a period of rest.
sabbatical *noun*
a year or other period of time when an employed person, especially a university teacher, is freed from duties for travel, study, etc.
[under Mosaic law land was left untilled (fallow) every seventh year]

sable *noun*
a) a small, ferret-like mammal of North America, Europe and Asia. b) the fur of this animal.
Word Family: **sable,** *adjective,* a) made of sable, b) black.

sabotage (*say* **sabba-tahzh**) *noun*
any deliberate destruction or obstruction, such as of machinery or installations during wartime or during an industrial dispute.
Word Family: **sabotage,** *verb*; **saboteur** (*say* **sabba-ter**), *noun,* a person who commits sabotage.
[from French]

sabre (*say* **sayba**) **saber** *noun*
1. a heavy sword with a slightly curved blade, having one cutting edge, used by cavalry.
2. a light fencing sword with a flexible, tapering, blunt-edged blade and a semicircular guard.
sabre-rattling, a provocative or warning display of military strength.
[from Hungarian]

sabre-toothed tiger
a long-extinct, large tiger with big, upper, front teeth.

sac *noun*
a small, bag-like part of an animal or plant, often containing fluid.
[French]

saccharin (*say* **sakka-rin**) **saccharine** *noun*
Chemistry: a crystalline solid which is about 400 times sweeter than cane sugar and is used as a sugar substitute in cases of diabetes or obesity.
saccharine *adjective*
cloyingly sweet: 'a *saccharine* smile'.
[Greek *sakkharon* sugar]

sacerdotal (*say* **sassa-doe-t'l** *or* **sakka-doe-t'l**) *adjective*
of or relating to priests.
[Latin *sacerdotis* of a priest]

sachet (*say* **sashay**) *noun*
a small, sealed envelope or bag used to hold perfume, shampoo, etc.
[French]

sack (1) *noun*
1. a large, strong bag, usually made of hessian, for carrying wood, potatoes, etc.
2. (*informal*) dismissal from employment.
hit the sack, (*informal*) to go to bed.
Word Family: **sack,** *verb,* a) to put into sacks, b) (informal) to dismiss.
[Greek *sakkos*]

sack (2) *verb*
to loot or plunder after capture: 'to *sack* a city'.
Word Family: **sack,** *noun.*
[French *mettre à sac* to put to the sack]

sack (3) *noun*
an old word for various strong wines, originally from Spain and the Canary Islands.
[French *vin sec* dry wine]

sackcloth *noun*
sacking.
in sackcloth and ashes, extremely repentant.

sacking *noun*
any coarse fabric used for sacks, such as hessian.

sack-race *noun*
a race in which each contestant jumps forward with his legs in a sack.

sacra *plural noun*
see SACRUM.

sacrament (*say* **sak**ra–m'nt) *noun*
1. *Christian:* any of seven rites, especially baptism and the Eucharist, believed to confer grace on believers who participate.
2. any sacred or solemn event or undertaking.
Word Family: **sacramental** (*say* sakra–**men**–t'l), *adjective.*
[Church Latin *sacramentum* a mystery]

sacred (*say* **say**–krid) *adjective*
dedicated to a god or religious purpose.
Usages:
a) 'this statue is *sacred* to her memory' (= reverently dedicated).
b) 'the *sacred* memory of the king' (= revered).
Word Family: **sacredly**, *adverb*; **sacredness**, *noun.*
[Latin *sacer* holy]

Sacred College
see CARDINAL.

sacred cow
a person or thing that escapes critical examination because of popular esteem, high repute, etc.
[from the Hindu belief that the *cow* is holy]

sacrifice (*say* **sak**ri–fice) *noun*
1. a) the giving up of something one values for the sake of something considered more important. b) something which is lost or given up in this way.
2. a) the offering of something to a deity. b) something which is offered.
Word Family: **sacrifice**, *verb*; **sacrificial** (*say* sakri–**fish**ul), *adjective*; **sacrificially**, *adverb.*
[from Latin]

sacrilege (*say* **sak**ri–lij) *noun*
any injury to or disrespectful treatment of anything regarded as sacred.
Word Family: **sacrilegious**, *adjective*; **sacrilegiously**, *adverb*; **sacrilegiousness**, *noun.*
[Latin *sacra* sacred things + *legere* to steal]

sacristan (*say* **sak**ris–t'n) *noun*
a sexton.
[Latin *sacrare* to regard as holy]

sacristy (*say* **sak**ris–tee) *noun*
a vestry.

sacrosanct (*say* **sak**ro–sankt) *adjective*
extremely sacred or inviolable.
[Latin *sacro* by a sacred rite + *sanctus* made holy]

sacrum (*say* **say**–krum) *noun*
plural is **sacra**
Anatomy: a bone in the lower back, consisting of five vertebrae fused together.
[Latin *os sacrum* sacred bone (as used in sacrifices)]

sad *adjective*
1. sorrowful or unhappy.
2. causing or expressing sorrow.
3. pitifully inadequate: 'a *sad* attempt'.
Word Family: **sadly**, *adverb*; **sadness**, *noun*; **sadden**, *verb*, to make or become sad.

saddle *noun*
1. a) a padded leather seat for a rider on the back of a horse or similar animal. b) a similar seat on a bicycle, etc.
2. something which has the shape or position of a saddle, such as a hollow ridge between two mountain peaks.
3. a cut of lamb taken from the upper back of the animal.
in the saddle, in control.
saddle *verb*
to put a saddle on a horse, etc.
Usage: 'she was *saddled* with all the responsibilities during his absence' (= loaded, left).

saddlebag *noun*
a bag buckled to, or hung over, the saddle, used for carrying things.

saddlecloth *noun*
a cloth placed between a saddle and the horse's back.

saddlery (*say* **sad**la–ree) *noun*
1. saddles, bridles and related equipment for horses.
2. a shop or business which deals in such equipment.
Word Family: **saddler**, *noun*, a person who makes or sells saddlery.

sadism (*say* **say**–dizm) *noun*
a pleasure, especially sexual pleasure, in causing suffering, pain or humiliation to another person.
Word Family: **sadist**, *noun*; **sadistic** (*say* sa–**dis**tik), *adjective*; **sadistically**, *adverb.*
[after the *Marquis de Sade*, 1740–1814, a French novelist notorious for a mixture of sex and cruelty in his books]

sadomasochism
(*say* say–doe–**massa**–kizm) *noun*

a liking for both sadism and masochism.

safari (*say* sa–**far**–ee) *noun*
a) an expedition, especially for hunting. b) the people, animals, etc. forming such an expedition.
[Arabic *safara* to travel]

safe *adjective*
1. free from danger, injury or risk: a) 'keep the jewels in a *safe* place'; b) 'we arrived *safe* and sound'.
2. unable to do any further harm: 'he's *safe* in jail now'.
Usage: 'he is a *safe* player' (= cautious).
safe *noun*
1. a strong metal box, usually with a complex lock or combination, in which money and other valuables are kept.
2. a cupboard or box, often with mesh sides, for storing and protecting food: 'a meat *safe*'.
Word Family: **safely,** *adverb*; **safety,** *noun.*
[Latin *salvus*]

safe–conduct *noun*
a) a document which ensures safe passage through an area, especially in wartime. b) the privilege of so passing.

safe–deposit *noun*
a room or building fitted with safes, etc. for storing valuable articles.

safeguard (*say* **safe**–gard) *noun*
a protective measure or device.
Word Family: **safeguard,** *verb,* to protect.

safekeeping *noun*
protection.

safety *noun*
Word Family: see SAFE.

safety belt
see SEAT BELT.

safety catch
a locking device to prevent a gun being fired accidentally.

safety glass
any of various forms of specially strengthened glass, such as two panes joined by a layer of plastic, which is designed not to shatter.

safety match
a match designed to light only on contact with special surfaces.

safety pin
1. a pin with a rounded guard in which the point is held.
2. a device which prevents a grenade, etc. exploding accidentally.

safety razor
a razor blade with a protective guard.

safflower *noun*
a thistle–like plant with large, reddish–orange flowers used as a dye, a source of oil and in medicine.

saffron *noun*
1. the dried, orange–coloured stigmas of a variety of crocus, used whole or powdered to colour or flavour food.
2. a deep, yellowish–orange colour.
Word Family: **saffron,** *adjective.*
[from Arabic]

sag *verb*
(sagged, sagging)
to sink or bend downwards, especially in the middle, due to weight or pressure.
Usage: 'her shoulders *sagged* after the busy day' (= drooped).
Word Family: **sag,** *noun.*

saga (*say* **sah**ga) *noun*
1. a medieval Icelandic epic written in prose.
2. a novel that traces a family's fortunes through several generations: 'the Forsyte *saga*'.
3. any long story or description: 'he told the *saga* of his journey across Asia'.
[Old Norse, narrative]

sagacious (*say* sa–**gay**–shus) *adjective*
showing keen judgement and common sense.
Word Family: **sagaciously,** *adverb*; **sagacity** (*say* sa–**gassi** tee), *noun.*
[Latin *sagax*]

sage (1) *noun*
an extremely wise person.
Word Family: **sage,** *adjective,* wise; **sagely,** *adverb*; **sageness,** *noun.*
[Latin *sapere* to be wise]

sage (2) *noun*
a herb with strongly flavoured greyish–green leaves.
[Latin *salvia* a healing plant]

sage–green *noun*
a greyish–green colour.
Word Family: **sage–green,** *adjective.*

Sagittarius (*say* saji–**tairius**) *noun*
also called the **Archer**
Astrology: a group of stars, the ninth sign of the zodiac.
[Latin *sagitta* an arrow]

sago (*say* **say**–go) *noun*
a starchy, rice–like substance obtained from plants, used in puddings and soups.
[Malay]

sahib (*say* sahb *or* **sa**–ib) *noun*
a form of address used by Indians to a superior.
[Arabic, friend]

said (*say* sed) *adjective*
named or mentioned already: 'the *said* witness'.
said *verb*
the past tense and past participle of the verb **say**.

sail *noun*
1. a piece of fabric, originally canvas, fastened to a mast so that it catches the wind and propels a boat.
2. something which has the shape, position or function of a sail: 'the *sails* of a windmill'.
3. a trip in a sailing boat: 'we went for a *sail* before the storm'.
set sail, to start a trip or voyage.
sail *verb*
1. to move across the surface of water by the action of wind in a sail or sails.
2. to travel by water: 'we *sailed* to Cape Town in a luxury ship'.
3. to manage a sailing boat.
Usages:
a) 'a bullet *sailed* past her ear' (= moved rapidly).
b) 'she *sailed* angrily out of the room' (= moved with dignity).
sail in, sail into, to go boldly or aggressively into action.

sailcloth *noun*
a) a strong canvas used for sails, etc.
b) a lightweight canvas used to make clothes, etc.

sailfish *noun*
any of a group of large, fast–swimming fish related to the marlin, having a high, sail–like, dorsal fin.

sailor *noun*
a member of the crew of any boat or ship.

sailplane *noun*
a glider with very long wings intended for sustained flying.

saint *noun*
1. *Christian:* any person of exceptional holiness, formally recognized and venerated by the Church.
2. any very holy or unselfish person.
Word Family: **saintly**, *adjective*; **saintliness**, *noun*; **sainthood**, *noun*.
[Latin *sanctus* holy]

Saint Bernard
any of a breed of large, heavy, wavy–haired dogs.
[originally used by monks in the monastery of *Saint Bernard* in the Swiss Alps to search for lost travellers]

Saint's day
a church feast–day in memory of a saint.

St Vitus's dance
see CHOREA.

saith (*say* seth) *verb*
the old form of the third person singular, present tense of the verb **say**.

sake *noun*
1. benefit, cause or interest: 'please do it for my *sake*'.
2. purpose, motive or end: 'for the *sake* of argument'.

salaam (*say* sa–**lahm**) *noun*
a word or bow given in greeting, especially amongst Moslems.
Word Family: **salaam**, *verb*.
[Arabic *salam* peace]

salacious (*say* sa–**lay**–shus) *adjective*
lustful or erotic.
Word Family: **salaciously**, *adverb*; **salaciousness**, **salacity** (*say* sa–**lassi**–tee), *nouns*.
[from Latin]

salad *noun*
a dish of cold, raw or cooked vegetables, meat, fruit, etc., usually served with a dressing.
[Latin *sal* salt]

salad days
days of youthful inexperience.

salamander (*say* **salla**–manda) *noun*
any of a group of amphibians whose larvae usually live in the water although the adults live on land.
[from Greek]

salami (*say* sa–**lah**–mee) *noun*
a spicy sausage, often containing garlic.
[Italian]

salary (*say* **salla**–ree) *noun*
a regular payment to an employee, usually monthly.
Word Family: **salaried**, *adjective*, earning or yielding a salary.
[Latin *salarium* money paid to Roman soldiers to buy salt]

sale *noun*
1. a) the act of selling. b) the exchange of anything, especially goods, for money.
2. a special disposal of goods at reduced prices.

saleable *adjective*
subject to or suitable for sale.
Word Family: **saleability** (*say* sale-abilli-tee), *noun.*

salesmanship *noun*
the art of persuading people to buy goods.

sales resistance
a failure by the public to respond to the sales efforts of advertisers and salesmen.

sales tax
also called **purchase tax**
a tax added to the retail price of certain articles.

salient (*say* **sayli**-ent) *adjective*
1. striking or prominent.
2. jutting out.
salient *noun*
a part of a fortification, trench, or battle line that projects towards the enemy.
Word Family: **saliently,** *adverb*; **salience, saliency,** *noun.*
[Latin *saliens* leaping]

saline (*say* **say**-line) *adjective*
of or containing salt.
Word Family: **salinity** (*say* sa-**linni**-tee), *noun.*
[Latin *sal* salt]

saliva (*say* sa-**lie**-va) *noun*
the fluid, containing ptyalin, secreted by glands in the mouth and beginning the digestion of food.
Word Family: **salivary** (*say* sa-**lie**-va-ree), *adjective*; **salivate** (*say* **salli**-vate), *verb*, to produce saliva; **salivation,** *noun.*
[from Latin]

Salk vaccine (*say* **sawlk vak**-seen)
a vaccine used against poliomyelitis.
[first introduced by *J. E. Salk*, born 1914, an American microbiologist]

sallow *adjective*
(of the complexion) yellowish or sickly.
Word Family: **sallowness,** *noun.*

sally *noun*
1. a sudden sortie by besieged troops against the enemy.
2. an excursion or a burst of activity.
3. a quick or witty remark.
Word Family: **sally (sallied, sallying),** *verb.*
[Latin *salire* to leap]

salmon (*say* **samm**'n) *noun*
plural is **salmon**
1. any of a large group of highly prized fish with pink flesh, which live in the sea but go up rivers to spawn.
2. a light, pinkish-orange colour.

salmonella (*say* salma-**nella**) *noun*
a group of bacteria, many of which may cause diseases, including typhoid and food poisoning.
[after *D. E. Salmon*, 1861-1914, an American veterinary surgeon]

salmon trout
also called **sea trout**
a variety of trout which lives at sea but comes up rivers to spawn.

salon *noun*
1. a building or room used for a particular, usually fashionable, business: 'a beauty *salon*'.
2. a private meeting between selected guests, such as artists or politicians, first held in France in the 18th century by wealthy women.
3. an exhibition of modern art.
[French, drawing-room]

saloon *noun*
1. a ship's cabin, originally one for first-class passengers.
2. the standard closed motor car.
3. *American:* a place where alcoholic drinks are sold to be drunk on the premises.
saloon bar, the most elegant bar in a pub, more expensive than the public bar.
[from Latin]

salsify (*say* **salsi**-fie) *noun*
a winter root vegetable which tastes rather like asparagus; there are white and black varieties.
[from Italian]

salt (*say* sawlt) *noun*
1. a white compound, sodium chloride (formula NaCl), widely used to flavour and preserve food.
2. *Chemistry:* a compound formed by the action of an acid on a metal or base.
3. (*plural*) a) any of a group of salts used as laxatives. b) smelling salts.
4. (*informal*) a sailor, especially an experienced one.
Phrases:
salt of the earth, the best type of people.
take with a grain of salt, to believe with reservation.
worth one's salt, deserving one's pay, reward or position.

salt *verb*
1. to add salt in order to season or preserve food.
2. to introduce rich ore into a mine, etc. to give a false impression of value.
Word Family: **salt**, **salty**, *adjectives*, containing or tasting of salt; **saltily**, *adverb*; **saltiness**, *noun*.
[Latin *sal*]

saltcellar *noun*
a small, often decorative container for sprinkling salt.

salt marsh
a) a coastal marsh which is sometimes covered by seawater. b) an inland marsh in a dry area where the water contains much salt.

saltpan *noun*
a hollow from which water has evaporated, leaving a layer of salt.

saltpetre (*say* sawlt-**peeta**) *noun*
potassium nitrate (formula KNO_3), a white crystalline solid used in medicine, for pickling meat and in gunpowder.
[Latin *sal* salt + *petra* a rock]

salty *adjective*
Word Family: see SALT.

salubrious (*say* sa-**loobri**-us) *adjective*
good for one's health.
Word Family: **salubriously**, *adverb*; **salubriousness**, **salubrity** (*say* sa-**loobri**-tee), *nouns*.
[Latin *salubris*]

saluki (*say* sa-**loo**-kee) *noun*
any of a breed of tall, slender dogs related to the greyhound and having a tawny coat.
[from Arabic]

salutary (*say* **sal**-yoo-tree) *adjective*
1. promoting some beneficial purpose.
2. good for one's health.
Word Family: **salutarily**, *adverb*; **salutariness**, *noun*.
[Latin *salutis* of health]

salutation (*say* sal-yoo-**tay**-sh'n) *noun*
a greeting.

salute (*say* sa-**loot**) *verb*
1. to greet.
2. *Military:* to make a gesture of respect or acknowledgement by raising the right hand to the cap or forehead, firing artillery, etc.
Word Family: **salute**, *noun*.
[Latin *salutare* to wish health to]

salvage (*say* **salvij**) *noun*
a) the act of saving a ship from shipwreck, goods from a fire, etc. b) the property saved.
Word Family: **salvage**, *verb*, to save from loss or destruction.

salvation (*say* sal-**vay**-sh'n) *noun*
a) preservation or deliverance from sin, evil or difficulty. b) a means or cause of such deliverance.
[Latin *salvare* to save]

Salvation Army
Christian: a religious organization founded by William Booth in 1865, with a military structure and concerned with a general revival of religion, helping the poor, etc.
Word Family: **Salvationist**, *noun*.

salve (1) (*say* salv) *noun*
something which soothes, such as an ointment.
Word Family: **salve**, *verb*, to soothe.

salve (2) (*say* salv) *verb*
to salvage.

salver *noun*
a tray, usually of silver.
[from French]

salvo *noun*
1. the firing of guns together or in succession, especially as a salute.
2. any sudden outburst, as of applause.
[Italian *salva* salutation]

sal volatile
ammonium carbonate, an aromatic solution used as smelling salts.
[Latin, volatile salt]

Samaritan (*say* sa-**marri**-tan) *noun*
a person who helps another who is in trouble.
[from the Biblical parable of the *Good Samaritan*, Luke 10.33]

samarium (*say* sa-**mairi**-um) *noun*
element number 62, a rare metal. See LANTHANIDE.
See CHEMICAL ELEMENTS in grey pages.

samba *noun*
a ballroom dance from Brazil.

same *adjective, pronoun*
corresponding or unchanged:
(as an adjective) 'he gets up at the *same* hour every morning'.
(as a pronoun) 'Tom ordered lobster and I asked for the *same*'.
all the same, just the same, despite all that.

sameness *noun*
1. the state of being the same: 'there is a marked *sameness* about your cooking, lately'.
2. lack of variety: 'the monotonous *sameness* of the desert scenery'.

samizdat *noun*
the organized publication of underground dissident literature in Russia.

samovar (*say* **samma**–var) *noun*
a metal urn for heating water, especially to make tea.
[Russian *samo* self + *varit* boil]

Samoyed (*say* **sam**–oyd) *noun*
one of a breed of white, long-haired watch-dogs, originally from Asia.
[Russian]

sampan *noun*
a small flat-bottomed boat with a small roof of mats, used in China and nearby countries.
[Chinese]

sample (*say* **sahm**–p'l *or* **sam**–p'l) *noun*
a part of something which shows the quality or character of the whole: 'taste a *sample* of this cheese before you buy it'.
sample *verb*
to test something by taking a sample: 'would you like to *sample* the cheese?'.
Word Family: **sample,** *adjective.*
[Old French *essample* example]

sampler (*say* **sahm**pla) *noun*
1. a person or thing that samples.
2. a piece of cloth with various designs embroidered on it, to demonstrate skill in needlework.

samurai (*say* **sam**–yoo–rye) *noun*
History: a member of the Japanese military class.

sanatorium (*say* sanna–**tawri**–um) *noun*
a place for people convalescing after an illness or operation, originally a place for tuberculosis patients in a favourable climate.
[Latin *sanare* to make healthy]

sanctify (*say* **sankti**–fie) *verb*
(**sanctified, sanctifying**)
to make holy or sacred.
Word Family: **sanctified,** *adjective*; **sanctification,** *noun.*
[Latin *sanctus* holy + *facere* to make]

sanctimonious
(*say* sankti–**mo**–nee–us) *adjective*
hypocritical, pretending to be holy or saintly.
Word Family: **sanctimoniously,** *adverb*; **sanctimoniousness, sanctimony,** *nouns.*
[Latin *sanctimonia* sacredness]

sanction (*say* **sank**–sh'n) *noun*
1. permission granted by authority: 'you may only travel in restricted areas with official *sanction*'.
Usage: 'this ancient ceremony has the *sanction* of centuries' (= approval).
2. any punishment or threat provided as a way of enforcing a law: 'trade *sanctions* were applied against the illegal regime'.
Word Family: **sanction,** *verb,* to approve or authorize.
[Latin *sanctio* a law dealing with penalties for contravention]

sanctity (*say* **sankti**–tee) *noun*
holiness or sacredness.

sanctuary (*say* **sank**–tew–ree) *noun*
1. an especially sacred or holy place, such as the area around the altar in a Christian church.
2. a) protection or refuge. b) any place which provides protection, such as a reserve for wildlife.
[Latin *sanctus* holy]

sanctum *noun*
a holy or private place.

sand *noun*
the fine, loose particles of decomposed and weathered rocks, finer than gravel but coarser than silt.
sand *verb*
1. to smooth or polish with sand or sandpaper.
2. to sprinkle with or add sand to.
Word Family: **sander,** *noun,* a person or thing that sands.

sandal *noun*
any of various light shoes with a leather, wooden or plastic sole and straps enclosing the foot.
[Greek *sandalion*]

sandalwood *noun*
the fragrant central wood of certain Asian trees, used for carving, as a dye and for incense.

sandbag *noun*
a bag filled with sand, used to make protective walls in wartime trenches, during a flood, etc., or as ballast.

sandbank *noun*
a ridge of sand in the sea or a river, often uncovered at low tide.

sandbar *noun*
a bar of sand formed in the sea or a river by the action of tides or currents.

sandblast *verb*
to clean metal or other hard surfaces with a blast of air containing sand or grit.

sand–dune *noun*
see DUNE.

sander *noun*
Word Family: see SAND.

sandfly *noun*
any of a group of small bloodsucking flies similar to mosquitoes, which may transmit diseases.

sandglass *noun*
an hourglass.

sandhopper *noun*
a hopping flea–like insect found on beaches.

sandman *noun*
a fairytale man who puts children to sleep by putting sand in their eyes.

sandpaper *noun*
a sheet of heavy paper coated with sand or a similar substance and used as an abrasive.
Word Family: **sandpaper,** *verb.*

sandpiper *noun*
a bird related to the snipe and plover, which lives on the seashore and makes a piping sound.

sandpit *noun*
a hollow filled with sand, set in a garden or park, in which children play.

sandshoe (*say* **sand**–shoo) *noun*
also called a **plimsoll**
a light canvas shoe with rubber or hemp sole, for beach–wear.

sandstone *noun*
a sedimentary rock formed of layers of sand laid down and held together by silica, lime, etc.

sandwich *noun*
1. two pieces of buttered bread with a filling between.
2. something which has the shape or arrangement of a sandwich.
sandwich *verb*
to squeeze something between two other things: 'the lady was *sandwiched* between two fat men in the train'.
[invented by the *Earl of Sandwich,* 1718–92, so that he could eat meals at the gaming table]

sandwich board
one of a pair of boards bearing advertisements, etc. carried on a person's back and chest.
sandwichman, a person who carries sandwich boards.

sandy *adjective*
1. having or containing sand.
2. of a yellowish–orange colour.
Word Family: **sandiness,** *noun.*

sane *adjective*
having a normal mental condition.
Usage: 'that is a very *sane* idea' (= sensible).
Word Family: **sanely,** *adverb.*
[Latin *sanus* healthy]

sang *verb*
a past tense of the verb **sing.**

sangfroid (*say* song–**frwa**) *noun*
self–control or cool–headedness.
[French *sang* blood + *froid* cold]

sanguinary (*say* **san**–gwin–ree) *adjective*
a) causing much bloodshed: 'a *sanguinary* war'. b) bloodthirsty.

sanguine (*say* **san**–gwin) *adjective*
1. hopeful or optimistic.
2. (of a complexion) red.
Word Family: **sanguinely,** *adverb;* **sanguineness,** *noun.*
[Latin *sanguinis* of blood]

sanitary (*say* **sanni**–tree) *adjective*
1. clean and healthy, especially in regard to precautions against disease.
2. of or relating to health.
[Latin *sanitatis* of health]

sanitation (*say* sanni–**tay**–sh'n) *noun*
1. the use or practice of sanitary methods.
2. a drainage or sewerage system.

sanity (*say* **sanni**–tee) *noun*
the fact or quality of being sane.

sank *verb*
a past tense of the verb **sink.**

Santa Claus (*say* **san**ta klawz)
the legendary person bringing presents to children at Christmas.
[Dutch–American, *St. Nicholas*]

sap (1) *noun*
1. the fluid in a plant.
2. (*informal*) a fool.
Word Family: **sappy,** *adjective,* a) full of sap, b) full of life and energy.

sap (2) *noun*
Military: a deep trench or tunnel dug to approach or undermine enemy fortifications.
sap *verb*
(sapped, sapping)
to undermine or weaken, as if by digging a sap.
[Italian *zappa* a spade]

sapient (*say* **say**pi–ent) *adjective*
wise.

Word Family: **sapiently,** *adverb*; **sapience,** *noun.*
[Latin *sapiens* being wise]

sapling *noun*
a young tree.

saponify (*say* sa-**ponni**-fie) *verb* **(saponified, saponifying)**
Chemistry: to convert an ester to a salt by treating it with an alkali, e.g. treating animal or vegetable fats and oils to make soaps.
Word Family: **saponification,** *noun.*
[Latin *saponis* of soap + *facere* to make]

sapper *noun*
a private soldier in the engineering or survey corps of an army.

sapphire (*say* **saff**ire) *noun*
1. *Geology:* a blue variety of corundum, used as a gem and for watch bearings. **2.** a deep blue colour.
Word Family: **sapphire,** *adjective.*
[Greek *sappheiros* lapis lazuli]

sappy *adjective*
Word Family: see SAP (1).

saprophyte (*say* **sapro**-fite) *noun*
an organism, such as certain fungi and bacteria, which lives on dead organic matter.
[Greek *sapros* putrid + *phyton* a plant]

saraband (*say* **sarra**-band) **sarabande** *noun*
Music: a slow dance from Spain, often part of a suite.
[Spanish *zarabanda*]

sarcastic *adjective*
using harsh, bitter words intended to hurt or insult, especially in an exaggerated or ironical way.
Word Family: **sarcastically,** *adverb*; **sarcasm,** *noun,* a) the quality of being sarcastic, b) a sarcastic remark.
[Greek *sarkazein* to tear flesh]

sarcophagus (*say* sar-**koffa**-gus) *noun*
a stone coffin.
[Greek *sarkos* of flesh + *phagein* to eat]

sardine (*say* sar**deen**) *noun*
any of a group of small edible fish related to the pilchard, often preserved in oil and canned.
[Greek *Sardo* Sardinia]

sardonic (*say* sar-**donnik**) *adjective*
gloomily scornful or mocking, especially of oneself.
Word Family: **sardonically,** *adverb.*
[Greek *sardanios* scornful laughter]

sari (*say* **sar**-ee) *noun*
a long Indian dress, consisting of a piece of material wound around the body with one end over the shoulder. Compare SARONG.
[Hindi]

sarong (*say* sa-**rong**) *noun*
a skirt consisting of a piece of material wound around the lower half of the body and tucked in at the waist, worn by Asian men and women. Compare SARI.
[Malay, a sheath]

sarsaparilla (*say* sarspa-**rilla**) *noun*
a) the dried root of certain tropical climbing plants of the lily family, used in medicine and to flavour food or drink. b) a soft drink flavoured with this.
[Spanish *zarza* bramble + *parilla* little vine]

sartorial (*say* sar-**tawr**iul) *adjective*
relating to men's clothing or tailoring.
[Latin *sartor* mender of old clothes]

sartorius (*say* sar-**tawri**-us) *noun*
Anatomy: the longest muscle in the body, which stretches from the upper hip across the thigh to the tibia and controls leg movement.

sash (1) *noun*
a wide strip of cloth worn around the waist or over the shoulder, for decoration or as part of a uniform.
[Arabic *shash* turban]

sash (2) *noun*
the separate frame which supports the glass in a window, often sliding or hinged.
sash-window *noun*
a window which slides up and down on a rope (the **sashcord**), which is attached to weights acting as a counterbalance.

sassafras *noun*
a deciduous American tree from which oil for perfume is obtained.
[Spanish]

Sassenach (*say* **sassa**-nak) *noun*
a Scotsman's name for an Englishman.
[Gaelic, Saxon]

sat *verb*
the past tense and past participle of the verb **sit**.

Satan (*say* **say**-t'n) *noun*
the devil.
Word Family: **Satanism,** *noun,* worship of the devil; **Satanist,** *noun.*
[Hebrew *shatan* adversary]

satanic (*say* sa–**tannik**) **satanical** *adjective*
very wicked or evil.
Word Family: **satanically**, *adverb.*

satchel *noun*
a light, leather or canvas bag with a shoulder–strap, e.g. for carrying books.
[Latin *sacellus* little sack]

sate *verb*
to satisfy fully: 'my appetite was *sated* after the huge meal'.

sateen (*say* sa–**teen**) *noun*
a cotton fabric with a satin–like shine.
Word Family: **sateen**, *adjective.*

satellite (*say* **satta**–lite) *noun*
1. any body that revolves around another of greater mass, including artificial bodies launched into orbit by man. Compare PLANET.
2. a town or country dependent on or controlled by another.
Word Family: **satellite**, *adjective.*
[Latin *satellus* a bodyguard]

satiate (*say* **sayshi**–ate) *verb*
to satisfy to excess.
Word Family: **satiation**, *noun*; **satiable**, *adjective*; **satiety** (*say* sa–**tie**–a–tee), *noun*, the state of being satiated.
[Latin *satiare* to glut]

satin (*say* **sat**–in) *noun*
a smooth, shiny fabric, usually woven from rayon or silk.
Word Family: **satin, satiny**, *adjectives*, a) of or like satin, b) smooth.
[from the Arabic name of a Chinese town]

satinet, satinette *noun*
a type of satin containing cotton.

satin stitch
an embroidery stitch consisting of very close, parallel stitches.

satinwood *noun*
the hard, light–coloured wood of an Asian tree, used for making furniture.

satire *noun*
a) the use of mocking or exaggerated humour to ridicule faults and vices. b) a piece of writing, song, etc. which does this.
satirical (*say* sa–**tirri**–k'l) **satiric** *adjective*
a) of, like or containing satire: 'a *satirical* book'. b) using or fond of satire: 'a *satirical* author'.
satirize, satirise *verb*
to attack or describe in a satire: 'this book *satirizes* the clergy'.
Word Family: **satirically**, *adverb*; **satirist** (*say* **satta**–rist), *noun*, a writer of satires.
[Latin *satura* a medley]

satisfaction (*say* sattis–**fak**–sh'n) *noun*
1. a) the act of satisfying: 'the *satisfaction* of his demands was almost impossible'. b) the state of being satisfied: 'I felt *satisfaction* after my horse won'.
2. something that satisfies: 'your daughter must be a great *satisfaction* to you'.
Usage: 'I demand *satisfaction* for that insult' (= reparation, payment).
[Latin *satis* enough + *facere* to make]

satisfactory (*say* sattis–**fakta**–ree) *adjective*
giving satisfaction, as by meeting the required standard: 'did you find your rooms *satisfactory*?'.
Word Family: **satisfactorily**, *adverb*; **satisfactoriness**, *noun.*

satisfy (*say* **sattis**–fie) *verb*
(satisfied, satisfying)
to make happy by supplying needs or demands: 'did my answer *satisfy* your curiosity?'.
Usages:
a) 'how can I *satisfy* you that I'm telling the truth?' (= convince).
b) 'I finally *satisfied* my debt' (= repaid in full).
Word Family: **satisfyingly**, *adverb.*

satrap *noun*
a subordinate ruler, e.g. of a province.
Word Family: **satrapy** (*say* **satra**–pee), *noun*, the territory ruled by a satrap.
[Persian, district chief]

saturate (*say* **satcha**–rate) *verb*
1. to wet thoroughly: 'rain *saturated* the dry earth'.
2. *Chemistry:* to cause a substance to absorb as much as possible of another substance.

saturation (*say* satcha–**ray**–sh'n) *noun*
1. a) the act of saturating. b) the state of being saturated.
2. *Weather:* the condition of the atmosphere when it can store no more water–vapour and any excess moisture will condense as droplets or crystals.
[Latin *saturare* to glut]

saturation point
the point at which a substance can absorb no more of another substance.

Saturday *noun*
the seventh day of the week.
[after the planet *Saturn*]

Saturn *noun*
1. *Roman mythology:* the god of fertility and agriculture.
2. *Astronomy:* the planet in the solar system sixth from the sun, and surrounded by three rings, one inside the other, probably from a broken-up satellite.

saturnine (*say* **satta**–nine) *adjective*
gloomy or morose.
[as if born under the influence of Saturn]

satyr (*say* **satta**) *noun*
1. *Greek mythology:* a god of the woods, with the body of a man and the ears, horns, tail and legs of a goat or horse, identified with the Roman gods called fauns.
2. a man with a very strong sexual desire.
[from Greek]

satyriasis (*say* satta–**rye**–a–sis) *noun*
an abnormally strong sexual desire in men. Compare NYMPHOMANIA.

sauce (*rhymes with* horse) *noun*
1. a sweet or savoury liquid, usually thickened, served with food to give it extra flavour.
2. (*informal*) impudence or impertinence.
Word Family: **sauce**, *verb*; **saucy**, *adjective*, impertinent; **saucily**, *adverb*; **sauciness**, *noun*.
[Latin *salsus* salted, flavoured]

saucepan *noun*
a round, deep, metal cooking-pot with a detachable lid and a handle.

saucer (*say* **saw**sa) *noun*
1. a shallow, curved dish on which a cup stands.
2. something which has the shape of a saucer, such as a wide, shallow depression in land.
[Old French *saussiere* sauce-boat]

sauerkraut (*say* **sour**–krout) *noun*
shredded cabbage fermented in salt.
[German *sauer* sour + *Kraut* cabbage]

sauna (*say* **saw**na) *noun*
a closed room filled with steam as a form of bath, originally from Finland.

saunter (*say* **saw**nta) *verb*
to stroll or wander slowly.
saunter *noun*
a) a leisurely stroll. b) a leisurely pace.

sausage (*say* **soss**ij) *noun*
minced meat, such as pork or beef, mixed with spices, etc. and packed into a skin.
[same root as SAUCE]

sausage dog
(*informal*) a dachshund.

sausage roll
a small patty of minced meat enclosed in pastry and baked.

sauté (*say* **so**–tay) *verb*
(**sautéed, sautéeing**)
to cook lightly in a small amount of fat.
Word Family: **sauté**, *noun*, a dish of lightly fried food.
[French]

sauterne *noun*
a rich, sweet, white wine.

savage (*say* **savv**ij) *adjective*
1. wild, untamed or uncivilized: 'a *savage* tribe'.
2. fierce or vicious: 'a *savage* glare'.
savage *verb*
to maul or injure viciously: 'the swimmer was *savaged* by a shark'.
savagery (*say* **savv**ij–ree) *noun*
a) the state of being savage: 'the primitive tribe lived in a condition of *savagery*'. b) savage behaviour: 'the cruel king treated his subjects with *savagery*'.
Word Family: **savage**, *noun*, a wild or uncivilized person; **savagely**, *adverb*; **savageness**, *noun*.
[Latin *silvaticus* of the woods]

savanna (*say* sa–**vanna**) **savannah** *noun*
a region, usually bordering equatorial rainforests, which has a wet and a dry season and a vegetation of grass and scattered trees.
[Old Spanish *zavana*]

savant (*say* **savv**'nt) *noun*
a person of learning.
[French, knowing]

save (1) *verb*
1. to rescue or keep safe from danger, harm or loss: 'I was *saved* from drowning'.
Usage: 'to *save* time' (= not waste).
2. to keep for future use: 'she *saved* her money for a holiday'.
Word Family: **saver**, *noun*, a person or thing that saves; **save**, *noun*, the act of saving.
[Latin *salvus* safe]

save (2) *preposition*
except: 'everyone may leave *save* you two'.

saveloy (*say* **savva**–loy) *noun*
a highly seasoned dry sausage.
[Italian *cervello* brain (as originally made of pig's brains)]

saving (*say* **say**–ving) *noun*
1. something which is saved: 'the bargain price means a *saving* of £10'.
2. (*plural*) any money which has been saved.
saving *adjective*
rescuing or redeeming.
saving grace
one good quality which makes up for all the bad ones.
Word Family: **saving,** *preposition,* except.

saviour (*say* **save**–yer) *noun*
1. a person who rescues or saves.
2. *Christian:* (*capital*) God or Christ.

savoir-faire (*say* sav–wa–**fair**) *noun*
knowledge of how to act correctly or tactfully in any situation.
[French *savoir* to know + *faire* to do]

savour (*say* **say**vor) *noun*
in America spelt **savor**
taste, smell or flavour.
savour *verb*
1. to give a savour to: 'the chillies *savoured* the whole dish'.
2. to enjoy, especially the taste or flavour of something: 'he *savoured* the spicy cheese'.
Usage: 'your behaviour *savours* of rudeness' (= suggests, smacks).
[Latin *sapor* flavour]

savoury (*say* **say**va–ree) *noun*
in America spelt **savory**
any small tasty food, such as an appetizer or, especially, a course at the beginning or end of a meal.
savoury *adjective*
1. having an appetizing taste or smell.
2. sharp or spiced, not sweet: 'a *savoury* biscuit'.
Word Family: **savouriness,** *noun.*

savoy *noun*
a winter cabbage with wrinkled leaves and a compact head.
[originally from *Savoy,* France]

savvy *verb*
(*informal*) to understand.
Word Family: **savvy,** *noun,* understanding or common sense.
[Spanish *sabe* do you know?]

saw (1) *noun*
a tool with a sharp-toothed blade for cutting, usually by pulling it back and forth across a surface.
saw *verb*
(**sawed, sawn** or **sawed, sawing**)
1. to use or cut with a saw.
2. to move as though using a saw: 'he *sawed* the air with his hands'.

saw (2) *verb*
the past tense of the verb **see (1).**

saw (3) *noun*
a saying such as a proverb or a maxim.

sawbones *noun*
(*informal*) a surgeon.

sawdust *noun*
the fine powder or shavings produced by cutting or sawing wood.

sawfish *noun*
any of a group of shark-like rays with a large, ridged snout resembling a saw.

sawmill *noun*
a place where logs are cut into boards, etc.

sawn *verb*
a past tense of the verb **saw (1).**

sawyer *noun*
a person whose occupation is sawing wood.

saxhorn *noun*
a brass musical instrument similar to a cornet.

saxifrage (*say* **saxi**–frij) *noun*
any of a very large and varied group of rock plants with tufted leaves.
[Latin *saxum* rock + *frangere* to break]

saxophone (*say* **sak**sa–fone) *noun*
Music: any of a family of wind instruments with a single reed and a metal body.
Word Family: **saxophonist** (*say* sak–**soffa**–nist), *noun.*
[after *A. Sax,* 1814–94, its Belgian inventor]

say *verb*
(**said, saying**)
to speak or express in words.
Usages:
a) 'I can't *say* who is right or wrong' (= state with certainty).
b) 'I'll meet you at, *say,* 6 o'clock' (= possibly, approximately).
Phrases:
go without saying, 'it *goes without saying* that you are absolutely correct' (= is obvious).
that is to say, 'in four days time, *that is to say* next Saturday' (= in other words).

say *noun*
1. what a person has to say: 'have you finished your *say*?'.
2. the right to take part in decisions, etc.: 'a *say* in the running of the country'.
Usage: 'be quiet, it's my *say* now' (= turn to speak).

saying *noun*
something said, usually a short, well-known phrase or sentence expressing a truth, etc.

say-so *noun*
(*informal*) command or authority: 'on whose *say-so* are you acting?'.

scab *noun*
1. the crust that forms over a wound or sore as it heals.
2. (*informal*) a blackleg.
Word Family: **scabby**, *adjective*; **scabbiness**, *noun.*

scabbard (*say* **skabbud**) *noun*
a sheath or cover for the blade of a sword, dagger, etc., usually worn on the belt.

scabies (*say* **skay-beez**) *noun*
also called **the itch**
an infectious skin disease due to mites burrowing into the skin.
[Latin *scabere* to scratch]

scaffold *noun*
1. a raised platform on which criminals are executed.
2. any raised framework, such as scaffolding.

scaffolding (*say* **skaffel-ding**) *noun*
a temporary platform of pipes, posts and boards, used especially when constructing, cleaning or repairing a building.

scalar (*say* **skaylar**) *noun*
Maths: a quantity having magnitude, but not direction. Compare VECTOR.
Word Family: **scalar**, *adjective.*

scald (*say* skawld) *verb*
1. to burn or hurt with hot liquid or steam.
2. to heat to just below boiling point.
scald *noun*
a burn caused by hot liquid, steam, etc.

scale (1) *noun*
1. *Biology:* any of the thin, flat pieces forming the skin covering of certain animals, such as fish, snakes, etc.
2. any small, flat flake or piece, e.g. on a plant.
scale *verb*
a) to remove the scales from: 'please *scale* this fish'. b) to come off in flakes or scales: 'the paint *scaled* from the wall'.
Word Family: **scaly**, *adjective*; **scaliness**, *noun.*

scale (2) *noun*
a) (*usually plural*) a balance or device for weighing. b) a pan or dish on a balance.
tip, turn the scales, 'the arrival of reinforcements *tipped the scales* in our favour' (= influenced events).

scale (3) *noun*
1. a sequence of points at regular intervals used for measuring, as on a thermometer.
2. *Music:* a succession of notes ascending or descending according to fixed intervals, especially such a series beginning on a particular note.
3. any arrangement in steps or degrees: a) 'the decimal *scale*'; b) 'a wage *scale*'.
4. the relative or proportional size or standard of something: a) 'what *scale* is this map?'; b) 'their house is on a modest *scale*'.
scale *verb*
1. to climb up or over something.
2. to vary in amount according to a fixed scale: 'we must *scale* down our expenses'.
Word Family: **scalable**, *adjective.*
[Latin *scalae* a ladder]

scalene (*say* **skay-leen**) *adjective*
(of a triangle) having three unequal sides.
[Greek *skalenos* unequal]

scallion (*say* **skal-y'n**) *noun*
an onion, such as a spring onion, which does not develop an enlarged bulb.

scallop (*say* **skollop**) *noun*
also spelt **scollop**
1. an edible shellfish consisting of twin shells with ribbed edges held by a muscle.
2. this shell or a small pan, used for cooking and serving food.
3. a wavy edge, e.g. on pastry, fabric or a garment.
Word Family: **scallop**, *verb.*

scallywag *noun*
(*informal*) a naughty or mischievous young person.

scalp *noun*
1. *Anatomy:* the skin covering the human cranium, usually hair-covered.

2. a) this covering used as a token of victory. b) any token of victory.
scalp *verb*
to cut the scalp from.
Word Family: **scalper**, *noun.*

scalpel *noun*
a small, light knife used in surgical operations and dissections.
[Latin *scalpellum* little chisel]

scaly (*say* **skay**-lee) *adjective*
Word Family: see SCALE (1).

scamp *noun*
a mischievous or idle person.

scamper *verb*
to run or move lightly and quickly.
Word Family: **scamper**, *noun.*

scampi (*say* **skam**-pee) *plural noun*
large prawns, usually fried in batter or breadcrumbs.
[Italian]

scan *verb*
(scanned, scanning)
1. to examine closely: 'he *scanned* her face for a sign of feeling'.
2. to sweep broadly across: 'the radio telescope *scanned* the skies'.
Usage: 'I only *scanned* the newspaper this morning' (= glanced at).
3. *Poetry:* to analyse the metre of lines.
Word Family: **scan**, *noun*; **scanner**, *noun*, a person or thing that scans.

scandal (*say* **skan**-d'l) *noun*
1. a shameful or disgraceful action or situation: 'it is a *scandal* that the innocent person was imprisoned'.
2. sensational or malicious gossip: 'have you heard the *scandal* about Mrs Smith and the milkman?'.
3. a person whose conduct brings disgrace: 'he is a *scandal* to the profession'.
Word Family: **scandalize, scandalise**, *verb*, to shock; **scandalmonger**, *noun*, a person who spreads scandal.
[Greek *skandalon* a stumbling-block]

scandalous *adjective*
causing or full of scandal: 'it is a *scandalous* rumour, and not based on truth'.
Usage: 'his behaviour is *scandalous*' (= shocking, disgraceful).
Word Family: **scandalously**, *adverb.*

scandium *noun*
element number 21, a rare metal. See TRANSITION ELEMENT.
See CHEMICAL ELEMENTS in grey pages.

scansion (*say* **skan**-sh'n) *noun*
Poetry: the analysis of the metre of lines.

scant *adjective*
very little or barely enough: 'she paid *scant* attention to my advice'.

scantling *noun*
a narrow board or beam.

scanty *adjective*
scant or inadequate: 'the poor rain meant only a *scanty* harvest'.
Word Family: **scantily**, *adverb*; **scantiness**, *noun.*

scapegoat *noun*
a person blamed or punished for things others have done.
[after the ancient Jewish practice of symbolically placing the people's sins onto a goat which was then driven away into the wilderness]

scapula (*say* **skap**-yoo-la) *noun*
also called a **shoulder-blade**
Anatomy: either of two large triangular bones behind the shoulder.
Word Family: **scapular**, *adjective.*
[Latin]

scar (1) *noun*
a mark left by a healed cut or wound, e.g. on the human skin or on a plant where a leaf was once attached.
Usage: 'your gossip left a *scar* on my reputation' (= blemish).
scar *verb*
(scarred, scarring)
to mark with a scar or scars: 'the bombs *scarred* the countryside with giant craters'.
[Greek *eskhara* a scab]

scar (2) *noun*
a steep rocky place or cliff.

scarab (*say* **skarr**ab) *noun*
a) a type of beetle considered sacred by the ancient Egyptians. b) an image or carving in the shape of a scarab.
[from Greek]

scarce (*say* skairce) *adjective*
in short supply: 'tomatoes were *scarce* during the floods'.
make oneself scarce, to leave or keep out of the way.
scarcely *adverb*
barely or hardly: 'there were *scarcely* 25 people at the meeting'.
scarcity (*say* **skair**si-tee) *noun*
shortness of supply: 'the *scarcity* of tomatoes was caused by the floods'.
Word Family: **scarceness**, *noun*, scarcity.
[Latin *excerptus* picked out]

scare (*rhymes with* air) *verb*
to frighten.

scare *noun*
a feeling of fear or alarm: a) 'you gave me quite a *scare*'; b) 'after the cyclone there was a *scare* of cholera'.

scarecrow *noun*
1. an object, usually a figure of a man in old clothes, set up to scare birds away from a crop.
2. a) a person or thing with a ragged or frightening appearance. b) a very thin person.

scarf (1) *noun*
plural is **scarves**
a strip or square of cloth worn around the head or neck.
Word Family: **scarf,** *verb.*

scarf (2) *noun*
plural is **scarfs**
a joint made by fitting two tapered pieces together.

scarify (*say* **skairi**–fie) *verb*
(**scarified, scarifying**)
1. to scratch or break the surface of.
2. to criticize severely.
Word Family: **scarification,** *noun.*

scarlet *noun*
a vivid reddish–orange colour.
Word Family: **scarlet,** *adjective.*

scarlet fever
also called **scarlatina**
an infectious bacterial disease causing tonsillitis and a red rash.

scarlet runner
see RUNNER BEAN.

scarp *noun*
a steep slope or ridge of rock.
[from Italian]

scarper *verb*
(*informal*) to run away, especially after having done something wrong.
[rhyming slang *Scapa Flow* = go]

scary (*say* **skairi**) *adjective*
(*informal*) frightening.

scat *interjection*
(*informal*) go away!
[for SCATTER]

scathing (*say* **skay–*th*ing**) *adjective*
severely critical or scornful: 'a *scathing* review of a bad film'.
Word Family: **scathingly,** *adverb.*

scatology (*say* ska–**tolla**–jee) *noun*
the continual use in literature of images of human waste, etc.
Word Family: **scatological,** *adjective.*
[Greek *skatos* of dung + –LOGY]

scatter *verb*
to send, move or distribute in many different directions: a) 'we *scattered* the seed on the ploughed land'; b) 'the crowd *scattered* when it heard the sirens'.
Word Family: **scattering,** *noun,* a scattered number or quantity.

scatterbrain *noun*
a person who cannot remember or concentrate on things.
Word Family: **scatterbrained,** *adjective.*

scatter diagram
Maths: a graph which compares two variables, such as the health and wealth of a population. The distribution of the resultant coordinate points shows the degree of correlation between the variables.

scatty *adjective*
scatterbrained or silly.

scavenger (*say* **skavvinja**) *noun*
any person or thing that searches for or lives on decaying or discarded material.
Word Family: **scavenge,** *verb,* to search for or amongst, especially for discarded matter which may be used, etc.

scenario (*say* sin–**ario**) *noun*
a detailed outline of the plot of a play, film, ballet or opera.
Word Family: **scenarist** (*say* **seena**–rist), *noun,* a writer of scenarios.
[Italian]

scene (*say* seen) *noun*
1. a place or area where action occurs: 'the *scene* of the crime'.
Usages:
a) 'this painting is a *scene* of Paris' (= view).
b) 'there was a terrible *scene* when I came home late' (= incident, outburst).
c) (*informal*) 'the music *scene* is always changing' (= world, sphere of influence).
2. a minor division of an act in a play, etc., usually with a fixed setting.
Phrases:
behind the scenes, privately or secretly.
on the scene, 'were you *on the scene* at the time?' (= present).
[Greek *skené* a tent, stage]

scenery (*say* **seena**–ree) *noun*
1. the natural features of a landscape: 'impressive mountain *scenery*'.
2. the structures and props used to decorate a stage during a play, film, etc.

scenic (*say* **seenik**) *adjective*
of or having fine or impressive scenery.
Word Family: **scenically**, *adverb.*

scenic railway
see ROLLER-COASTER.

scent (*say* sent) *noun*
1. a perfume.
2. a smell that is left in passing, such as one that can be followed by an animal.
3. the sense of smell: 'dogs hunt by *scent*'.
scent *verb*
1. to detect by or as if by smelling: a) 'the dogs *scented* a rabbit'; b) 'to *scent* trouble'.
2. to make fragrant with scent: 'the flowers *scented* the whole house'.
[Latin *sentire* to perceive]

sceptic (*say* **skeptik**) *noun*
in America spelt **skeptic**
a person who doubts the truth of a claim, theory or belief.
sceptical *adjective*
unwilling to believe without questioning or doubting.
Word Family: **sceptically**, *adverb*; **scepticism** (*say* **skepti**-sizm), *noun*, an attitude of doubt or disbelief.
[Greek *skeptikos* thoughtful]

sceptre (*say* **septa**) *noun*
a rod, often highly decorated, carried by a ruler as a symbol of power.
[Greek *skeptron* a staff]

schedule (*say* **shed**-yool *or* **sked**-yool) *noun*
1. a timetable of events, duties, appointments, etc.
2. a written list or table of classifications, etc.: 'a *schedule* of poisons'.
schedule *verb*
to arrange or put in a schedule: 'you are *scheduled* to give a speech after the dinner'.
[Greek *skhedé* a papyrus-strip]

schema (*say* **skeema**) *noun*
plural is **schemata** (*say* **skeema**-ta)
a diagram, plan, chart or scheme.
Word Family: **schematic** (*say* skee-**mattik**), *adjective*; **schematically**, *adverb.*

schematize (*say* **skeema**-tize)
schematise *verb*
to arrange or organize according to a plan or scheme.

scheme (*say* skeem) *noun*
any plan designed to accomplish something.
Usage: 'a colour *scheme*' (= system, arrangement).
scheme *verb*
to plan or plot, especially dishonestly.
Word Family: **schemer**, *noun*, a person who schemes.
[Greek *skhema* form]

scherzo (*say* **skert**-so *or* **skairt**-so) *noun*
a lively, very rhythmic piece of music, often the second or third movement of a sonata or symphony.
[Italian, sport or jest]

schism (*say* sizm *or* skizm) *noun*
the splitting of a group or organization into opposing parties.
Word Family: **schismatic** (*say* siz-**mattik**), *adjective*, of or guilty of schism; **schismatic**, *noun*, a person who supports schism or any breakaway group.
[Greek *skhisma* a cleft]

schist (*say* shist) *noun*
Geology: a medium-grained metamorphic rock, often with a glistening appearance, which splits unevenly into flaky sheets.
[Greek *skhistos* split]

schizo (*say* **skit**-so) *noun*
(*informal*) a schizophrenic.
Word Family: **schizo**, *adjective.*

schizoid (*say* **skit**-soyd) *adjective*
resembling or tending towards schizophrenia.
Word Family: **schizoid**, *noun*, a schizoid person.
[SCHIZ(ophrenia) + -OID]

schizophrenia (*say* skitso-**freenia**) *noun*
any of a wide group of psychoses characterized by the inability to act or think realistically, sometimes marked by delusions and the withdrawal into a private world.
Word Family: **schizophrenic**, *noun*, a person suffering from schizophrenia; **schizophrenic**, *adjective.*
[Greek *skhizein* to split + *phren* mind]

schmaltz (*say* shmolts) **schmalz** *noun*
(*informal*) excessive sentimentality, especially in art, music, etc.
Word Family: **schmaltzy**, *adjective.*
[Yiddish, lard, grease]

scholar (*say* **skolla**) *noun*
a) a person specializing in a field of study. b) a pupil or student, especially one who has won an award.

scholarly *adjective*
1. of or like a scholar.
2. showing knowledge or careful study: 'a *scholarly* text'.
Word Family: **scholarliness**, *noun.*

scholarship (*say* **skol**la–ship) *noun*
1. a sum of money given to a student so he may continue his studies.
2. knowledge or skill gained by advanced study: 'the professor was a man of great *scholarship*'.

scholastic (*say* skol–**ass**–tik) *adjective*
of schools or learning: 'what is your *scholastic* record?'.
Word Family: **scholastic**, *noun*, a scholarly or pedantic person; **scholasticism** (*say* skol–**asti**–sizm), *noun.*

school (1) (*say* skool) *noun*
1. an institution for training or instruction, especially one for children.
2. the body of people attending such an institution.
3. any regular course of lessons or meetings for instructions.
Usage: 'no *school* today' (= lessons).
4. a university or college faculty.
5. a group of people who have a common style or method: 'the Heidelberg *school* of painters'.
school *verb*
to train or instruct: 'I'll *school* you in the art of singing'.
[Greek *skholé* leisure, disputation, school]

school (2) *noun*
a large group of fish swimming together.
[same root as SHOAL]

schooner (*say* **skoo**na) *noun*
1. a ship with two or more masts, all fore–and–aft rigged.
2. a larger–than–normal glass for sherry or beer.

sciatica (*say* sigh–**attika**) *noun*
a pain in the area of the hip and thigh, sometimes due to pressure on a nerve.
Word Family: **sciatic**, *adjective.*
[Greek *iskhion* hip joint]

science (*say* **sigh**–ence) *noun*
1. a) a particular body of knowledge obtained by systematic observation and testing. b) the systematic study or methods used.
2. a branch of knowledge or study, such as chemistry or botany, concerned with the investigation of natural or physical substances, facts, laws, etc.
Word Family: **scientist**, *noun*, a person skilled or trained in science.
[Latin *sciens* knowing]

science fiction
any fiction, often set in the future, that uses scientific facts or theories in an imaginative way.

scientific (*say* sigh–en–**tiff**ik) *adjective*
1. of or relating to science: '*scientific* instruments'.
2. of or according to the principles or methods of science: 'a *scientfic* mind'.
Word Family: **scientifically**, *adverb.*

scientology (*say* sigh–en–**tolla**–jee) *noun*
a religious and psychological system which emphasizes personal development.
Word Family: **scientologist**, *noun.*

scimitar (*say* **simmi**–ta) *noun*
a sword with a curved blade and one cutting edge, formerly used by Turkish and Persian soldiers.

scintillating (*say* **sin**ti–lay–ting) *adjective*
a) sparkling or flashing. b) witty.
Word Family: **scintillate**, *verb*; **scintillation**, *noun*; **scintilla** (*say* sin–**tilla**), *noun*, a spark or trace.
[Latin *scintilla* a spark]

scion (*say* **sigh**–on) *noun*
1. a young member of a family.
2. a shoot of a plant with one or more buds, especially one used for grafting.

scissors (*say* **sizz**ers) *plural noun*
1. an instrument consisting of two sharp blades with handles, joined at the centre so that they may open and close for cutting.
2. any position or movement which resembles the opening and closing of scissors.
[Latin *scissus* cut]

sclerosis (*say* skle–**ro**–sis) *noun*
plural is **scleroses**
a hardening or thickening of a tissue.
[Greek *skleroun* to harden + –OSIS]

scoff (1) *verb*
to deride or treat with contempt: 'he *scoffed* at my fears'.
Word Family: **scoff**, *noun*, a jeer; **scoffer**, *noun*, a person who scoffs; **scoffingly**, *adverb.*

scoff (2) *verb*
to eat greedily and quickly.

scold *verb*
to criticize or find fault angrily.

Word Family: **scold**, *noun*, a person who scolds; **scoldingly**, *adverb*.

scollop *noun*
see SCALLOP.

scone (*say* skon) *noun*
a small, light round cake, usually baked in a very hot oven.

scoop *noun*
1. a utensil with a shovel or cup-like holder at one end for lifting loose substances such as sugar.
2. (*informal*) an important news item which a reporter or publisher obtains before anyone else.
scoop *verb*
1. to lift with or as though with a scoop: a) '*scoop* the coal onto the fire'; b) 'he *scooped* the papers up in his arms'.
2. (*informal*) to obtain a newspaper scoop.
scoop the pool, to win or obtain everything.

scoot *verb*
(*informal*) a) to move very quickly. b) to run away.

scooter *noun*
1. a two-wheeled vehicle, used by children, with a flat board to stand on and an upright support for a handlebar.
2. a motor scooter.
Word Family: **scooter**, *verb*, to use or go on a scooter.

scope *noun*
the space which something exists within, covers or is limited to: 'he has a wide *scope* of knowledge'.
Usage: 'there is little *scope* for promotion in that job' (= opportunity).
[Greek *skopos* a target]

scorch *verb*
to burn slightly: 'I've *scorched* my shirt with the iron'.
Usage: (*informal*) 'we *scorched* along at 200 km an hour' (= raced, sped).
Word Family: **scorch**, *noun*, a slight burn; **scorcher**, *noun*, a) a person or thing that scorches, b) (informal) a very hot day; **scorchingly**, *adverb*.

scorched earth
the process of destroying things which could be useful to an invading army, e.g. by burning crops.

score *noun*
1. the points won by a player or team.
Usage: 'settle your mind on that *score*' (= account, matter).
2. a line or scratch.
Usage: 'add up the bill and I'll pay the *score*' (= total).
3. a) any written music, especially for a group, showing the parts for each musician printed one under the other. b) the background music of a film, etc.
4. a group of twenty: '*fourscore* years and ten' (= eighty, and a total of ninety).
5. (*plural*) very many: '*scores* of lives were lost'.
6. (*informal*) the state of progress: 'what's the *score* on the new space programme?'.
score *verb*
1. a) to win points in a game. b) to keep a record of points won. c) to be worth in points: 'red aces *score* twenty'.
Usage: 'mother *scored* a great success with her poetry' (= gained).
2. to mark or cut with lines, notches or scratches: 'the lashes of the whip *scored* the slave's back'.
3. to arrange music for an orchestra or other group.
score off, 'you couldn't resist the opportunity to *score off* her' (= gain an advantage over).
Word Family: **scorer**, *noun*.

scoria (*say* **skaw**ria) *noun*
a very porous, dark rock formed from fragments of lava that have been blown out of a volcano and quickly cooled.
[Greek, refuse]

scorn *noun*
extreme lack of respect.
scorn *verb*
a) to feel or show scorn for: 'she *scorns* all politicians'. b) to reject with scorn: 'I *scorned* his offer to help'.
scornful *adjective*
full of scorn: 'I'm *scornful* of your offer to help'.
Word Family: **scornfully**, *adverb*.

Scorpio *noun*
also called **Scorpius** or the **Scorpion** a group of stars, the eighth sign of the zodiac.

scorpion *noun*
1. an arachnid, usually found in warm climates, having a long, narrow tail with a poison gland.
2. (*capital*) Scorpio.
[from Greek]

scotch (1) *verb*
a) to maim or cripple. b) to cut or gash.
Usage: 'I'll have to *scotch* that rumour' (= put an end to).

Scotch (2) *noun*
short form of **Scotch whisky**
a whisky distilled in Scotland from barley and malt.

Scotch mist
a very fine, light drizzle.

scot-free *adjective*
completely free from any penalty or harm.
[from an old word, *scot*, tax or payment]

scoundrel *noun*
a wicked or dishonourable person.

scour (1) (*rhymes with* power) *verb*
1. a) to clean or polish by hard rubbing: '*scour* the saucepans'. b) to remove dirt, grease, etc.: 'to *scour* wool'.
Usage: 'the storm *scoured* a gully in the hillside' (= cleared out).
2. (of cattle, etc.) to have diarrhoea.
Word Family: **scour**, *noun*, the act of scouring; **scourer**, *noun*, a person or thing that scours, especially a pad for cleaning saucepans, etc.

scour (2) (*rhymes with* power) *verb*
to search thoroughly and energetically: 'she *scoured* the city looking for work'.

scourge (*say* skerj) *noun*
a whip used for punishment.
Usage: 'war is a *scourge* of civilization' (= affliction, source of suffering).
Word Family: **scourge**, *verb*, a) to whip, b) to cause suffering to.

scout *noun*
1. a person sent out to gain information.
2. (*capital*) a member of the Scout Association, a youth organization which emphasizes self-reliance and proficiency in a wide range of activities.
good scout, a good fellow.
scout *verb*
to act as a scout.
Usage: '*scout* around for some coffee' (= hunt).

scowl *noun*
an angry or bad-tempered expression.
Word Family: **scowl**, *verb*, to have or make a scowl; **scowlingly**, *adverb*.

scrabble *verb*
1. to scrape or claw at.
2. to struggle to possess or obtain.
scrabble *noun*
1. a scramble or scratching.
2. (*capital*) a word game for 2 to 4 players.

scrag *noun*
1. (*informal*) a skinny person or animal.
2. the butcher's name for the thin part of the neck, especially in mutton.
Word Family: **scraggy**, *adjective*, thin and bony.

scraggy *adjective*
thin or bony.

scram *interjection*
(*informal*) go away!

scramble *verb*
1. to move, crawl or climb hurriedly.
Usage: 'children *scrambled* for the spilt sweets' (= struggled, scuffled).
2. to mix or put together confusedly.
3. *Radio:* to send a jumbled signal which can only be translated by a special receiver.
scrambled eggs, eggs beaten with milk and butter and cooked gently.
scramble *noun*
1. a confused or wild struggle, scuffle, etc.: 'there was a violent *scramble* to get the last two seats'.
2. a motorcycle race over rough ground.
Word Family: **scrambler**, *noun*, a device for scrambling radio-telephone messages.

scrap (1) *noun*
1. a small piece or fragment, especially a remnant.
2. anything useless or unwanted.
3. scrap metal.
Usage: 'she refuses to eat *scraps*' (= leftover food).
scrap *verb*
(scrapped, scrapping)
1. to discard as useless or unwanted: 'let's *scrap* that idea and start again'.
2. to make into scrap.

scrap (2) *noun*
(*informal*) a fight or argument.

scrapbook *noun*
a book with blank pages in which press-cuttings, pictures, etc. are pasted.

scrape *verb*
to rub or scratch, especially in order to remove an outer layer: 'do not peel or *scrape* the potatoes before cooking'.
Phrases:
scrape through, 'Peter *scraped through* his exams' (= only just succeeded in).
scrape together, scrape up, 'I managed to *scrape together* some money for a ticket' (= collect with difficulty).

scrape *noun*
1. a) the act of scraping. b) a sound or mark made by scraping.
2. (*informal*) a) a fight. b) a difficult or embarrassing situation.
Word Family: **scraper,** *noun,* something which scrapes, especially a device used for this purpose; **scraping,** *noun,* a) the act or sound of rubbing or scratching, b) (plural) any pieces or parts which are scraped.

scraperboard *noun*
a method of line-drawing by scraping away parts of the blackened surface of a prepared board.

scrap metal
any pieces of metal which can be used or processed again.

scrappy *adjective*
like or made up of scraps or fragments.
Usage: 'the plumber did a very *scrappy* job fixing the pipes' (= careless).
Word Family: **scrappily,** *adverb.*

scratch *verb*
1. to mark, cut or tear with something sharp or rough: 'be careful those thorns don't *scratch* you'.
2. to rub with a grating sound or effect, e.g. with the fingernails to relieve itching.
3. to erase or cross off: 'your name has been *scratched* from our records'.
Usage: 'several horses have been *scratched* from the race' (= withdrawn).
scratch *noun*
1. a) the act of scratching: 'the dog had a vigorous *scratch* at its fleas'. b) a mark left by scratching: 'the cat caused this nasty *scratch*'.
2. *Sport:* a score, time or starting position to which no handicap has been added or subtracted.
Phrases:
from scratch, 'tell me your story again *from scratch*' (= from the beginning).
scratch the surface, 'this new book on the Roman Empire only *scratches the surface* of such a big subject' (= covers superficially).
up to scratch, 'his playing has not been *up to scratch* because of his injury' (= at a good enough standard).
scratch *adjective*
1. chosen at random: 'a *scratch* search-party assembled at once'.
2. *Sport:* without a handicap in a competition or race.
Word Family: **scratcher,** *noun,* a person or thing that scratches; **scratching,** *noun,* a competitor withdrawn from a race; **scratchy,** *adjective,* a) making a scratching noise or movement, b) uneven or disorganized; **scratchily,** *adverb;* **scratchiness,** *noun.*

scrawl *verb*
to write hastily or carelessly.
Word Family: **scrawl,** *noun;* **scrawly,** *adjective.*

scrawny *adjective*
thin or bony.
Word Family: **scrawniness,** *noun.*

scream *verb*
to make a loud, sharp or violent cry or sound: 'the child *screamed* in pain'.
Usage: 'bright colours would *scream* in such a small room' (= be very conspicuous).
scream *noun*
1. a loud, piercing sound or cry.
2. (*informal*) a person or thing that is very funny.

scree *noun*
a wide expanse of small stones piled up on a mountain slope, which slide away underfoot.

screech *verb*
to make a harsh, shrill cry or sound.
Word Family: **screech,** *noun;* **screechy,** *adjective.*

screed *noun*
1. a long speech or piece of writing.
2. *Building:* a) a strip of wood or plaster used for levelling the plaster on a surface. b) a finishing layer of plaster or concrete.

screen *noun*
1. something which divides, protects or shelters, especially any of various covered frames, etc.
2. a smooth surface on which slides, films, etc. may be projected.
3. (*informal*) films or the profession of acting in films: 'Humphrey Bogart was a star of the *screen* for many years'.
4. the fluorescent end of the picture tube in a television set, where electric currents are changed into pictures.
screen *verb*
1. to hide, protect or shelter: 'clouds *screened* the sun from our sight'.
Usage: 'all applicants for the job were *screened* by the committee' (= checked closely).
2. to show on a screen: 'the society is *screening* a travel film tonight'.

screenplay *noun*
a detailed script of a film, usually including technical descriptions such as camera positions, etc.

screen printing
a method of printing by squeezing ink through a stretched fabric screen, prepared by blocking off non-printing areas with a stencil.

screw (*say* skroo) *noun*
1. a metal pin with a head and a spiral thread around its length, used to fasten wood, metal, etc. together.
2. the twisting or turning movement of or like a screw: 'give that lid another *screw*'.
3. something twisted in such a way: 'a *screw* of paper'.
4. a propeller.
5. (*informal*) a) salary or wages. b) sexual intercourse. c) a prison warder.
Phrases:
have a screw loose, to be mad or eccentric.
put the screws on, (*informal*) to use force or pressure, especially in order to persuade.
screw *verb*
1. to attach, fasten or tighten by means of a screw: '*screw* down the lid of the box'.
2. to twist into position: '*screw* the cap on the jar'.
Usages:
a) 'she *screwed* her face into a grimace of pain' (= contorted).
b) 'he *screwed* up the letter and threw it away' (= pressed and twisted into a ball).
c) 'he *screwed* up his courage and asked for a holiday' (= gathered, forced).
3. (*informal*) to have sexual intercourse.

screwball *noun*
American: (*informal*) an eccentric person.
Word Family: **screwball,** *adjective.*

screwdriver *noun*
1. a tool with a narrow, shaped end which fits into the slot in the head of a screw to drive it into or withdraw it from a surface.
2. an alcoholic drink made with vodka and orange juice.

screwy *adjective*
(*informal*) mad or peculiar.

scribble *verb*
1. to write or draw carelessly.
2. to make meaningless marks or lines.
Word Family: **scribble,** *noun,* any careless handwriting or written work.
[Latin *scribere* to write]

scribe (1) *noun*
History: a) a person employed to make copies of manuscripts, etc. b) a teacher of Jewish laws or keeper of Jewish records.
Word Family: **scribal,** *adjective.*

scribe (2) *verb*
to mark or score something with a pointed instrument.
Word Family: **scribe,** *noun,* a pointed instrument for marking things.

scrimmage (*say* **skrimm**ij) *noun*
a rough or disorganized struggle.
Word Family: **scrimmage,** *verb.*
[for SKIRMISH]

scrimp *verb*
to skimp or be frugal: 'she *scrimps* on food so that she can buy more clothes'.
Word Family: **scrimpy,** *adjective,* scarce or skimpy; **scrimpiness,** *noun.*

scrip *noun*
a provisional document entitling the holder to a share in the stock of a business company.
[abbreviation of *subscription receipt*]

script *noun*
1. handwriting: 'she has a clear, legible *script*'.
2. a manuscript.
3. a copy of the text of a play, film, etc. used by an actor or director, e.g. for rehearsing.

scripture (*say* **skrip**-cher) *noun*
(*usually capital, plural*) any sacred writing or book regarded as a religious authority, such as the Christian Bible.
Word Family: **scriptural,** *adjective,* of or according to scriptures; **scripturally,** *adverb.*
[Latin *scriptus* written]

scrivener (*say* **skriv**na) *noun*
an old word for a clerk or public writer.

scroll (*say* skrole) *noun*
1. a roll of paper, especially parchment, used for writing, etc.
2. something which has a coiled or partly rolled form, such as decoration on a column, etc.

scrooge (*say* skrooj) *noun*
a miserly or mean person.
[after *Ebenezer Scrooge,* a miserly old man in Charles Dickens' 'Christmas Carol']

scrotum (*say* **skro**-tum) *noun*
Anatomy: the sac in males which hangs between the legs and contains the testes.
[Latin]

scrounge *verb*
(*informal*) to beg, borrow or gather, especially by wheedling.
Word Family: **scrounger,** *noun,* a person who scrounges.

scrub (1) *verb*
(scrubbed, scrubbing)
1. to rub vigorously in order to clean.
2. (*informal*) to remove or cancel: 'he was *scrubbed* from the team'.
Word Family: **scrub,** *noun.*

scrub (2) *noun*
an area covered with low trees or bushes.

scrubby *adjective*
1. covered with scrub or undergrowth.
2. inferior, shabby or wretched.
Word Family: **scrubbiness,** *noun.*

scruff *noun*
the back of the neck.

scruffy *adjective*
(*informal*) untidy or dirty.
Word Family: **scruffily,** *adverb*; **scruffiness,** *noun.*
[for SCURFY]

scrum *noun*
Football: (in Rugby) a) a stage in the game at which the opposing forwards pack down and push against one another. b) the players who take part in the scrum.

scrummage (*say* **skrumm**ij) *noun*
1. *Football:* a Rugby scrum.
2. a struggle or fight.
Word Family: **scrummage,** *verb.*
[for SKIRMISH]

scrumptious (*say* **skrump**–shus) *adjective*
(*informal*) delicious or splendid.

scrumpy *noun*
a potent, dry, farm cider that is famous in south-west England.
[dialect *scrump* a small apple]

scruple (*say* skroo–p'l) *noun*
1. (*usually plural*) a hesitation or objection due to conscience or moral principles.
2. a unit of mass in the apothecaries' system, equal to about 1·3 g.
scrupulous (*say* **skroo**–pew–lus) *adjective*
1. having a conscience or moral principles.
2. precise or carefully exact: 'she copied the text with *scrupulous* care'.
Word Family: **scruple,** *verb,* to have scruples; **scrupulously,** *adverb*; **scrupulousness,** *noun.*
[Latin *scrupulus* a rough pebble, an uneasy feeling]

scrutineer (*say* skroota–**neer**) *noun*
a person who checks that votes have been correctly made and counted in an election.

scrutinize (*say* **skroo**ta–nize)
scrutinise *verb*
to examine closely or carefully.
Word Family: **scrutinizingly,** *adverb*; **scrutiny,** *noun.*

scuba (*say* **skoo**ba) *noun*
an aqualung.
[from S(elf) C(ontained) U(nderwater) B(reathing) A(pparatus)]

scud *verb*
(scudded, scudding)
to move or race along swiftly.
Word Family: **scud,** *noun.*

scuff *verb*
1. to scrape or shuffle when walking.
2. to mark or wear away by use.
scuff *noun*
1. the act or sound of scuffing.
2. (*plural*) a pair of light, flat slipper-like shoes.

scuffle *verb*
1. to struggle or fight confusedly.
2. to scamper noisily.
Word Family: **scuffle,** *noun,* a) a confused struggle, b) a scuffling noise.

scull *noun*
Rowing: a) a racing boat for one person with a pair of oars. b) either of a pair of oars used by one person.
Word Family: **scull,** *verb*; **sculler,** *noun.*

scullery (*say* **skull**a–ree) *noun*
a small room for kitchen work such as washing up.
[Latin *scutella* a salver]

scullion (*say* **skull**–y'n) *noun*
an old word for a kitchen servant.
[Old French *escouillon* a dishcloth]

sculpture (*say* **skulp**–cher) *noun*
a) the modelling, carving or constructing of three-dimensional objects. b) any object or objects created in this way.
Word Family: **sculpt, sculpture,** *verbs,* to carve or make a sculpture; **sculptor, sculptress,** *nouns,* a person who practises sculpture; **sculptural,** *adjective*; **sculpturally,** *adverb*; **sculpturesque,** *adjective,* having the qualities of a sculpture.

scum *noun*
1. a layer of impure or waste matter on a liquid.

2. something worthless or vile.
Word Family: **scum** (**scummed**, **scumming**), *verb*, a) to become covered with scum, b) to remove scum; **scummy**, *adjective*, a) covered with scum, b) worthless.

scumble *noun*
Art: a layer of opaque paint applied so that the colour underneath it is partly visible.
Word Family: **scumble**, *verb*, to apply scumble to a surface.

scupper *noun*
an opening in the side of a ship at deck level to let water drain away.
scupper *verb*
to sink a ship deliberately.

scurf *noun*
dandruff or any scaly crust formed on a surface.
Word Family: **scurfy**, *adjective*.

scurrilous *adjective*
1. outrageously abusive.
2. coarsely jocular.
Word Family: **scurrilously**, *adverb*; **scurrility** (*say* skurrilli-tee), **scurrilousness**, *nouns*.

scurry *verb*
(**scurried**, **scurrying**)
to move or rush quickly.
Word Family: **scurry**, *noun*, a rushing noise or movement.

scurvy *noun*
a disease due to a lack of vitamin C in the diet, causing swollen gums, anaemia and bruising.
scurvy *adjective*
mean or contemptible.
Word Family: **scurvily**, *adverb*, **scurviness**, *noun*.

scuttle (1) *noun*
a coalscuttle.

scuttle (2) *verb*
to run or move hurriedly.
Word Family: **scuttle**, *noun*.

scuttle (3) *noun*
a small, rectangular opening with a movable cover in a ship's deck or side.
scuttle *verb*
to sink a ship by cutting holes in its sides or bottom.

scythe (*say* si*the*) *noun*
a long-handled farm tool with a long, thin, slightly curved blade for reaping grass, etc. Compare SICKLE.
Word Family: **scythe**, *verb*, to cut with a scythe.

sea *noun*
1. a) an area of an ocean, often surrounded by land. b) the ocean.
Usage: 'a *sea* of faces was turned towards the stage' (= large expanse or mass).
2. *Astronomy:* any of the smooth, featureless areas on the moon, formerly believed to contain water.
at sea, 'I'm all *at sea* with maths' (= puzzled, bewildered).

sea-anchor *noun*
a device, usually a canvas cone held open at the wider end, trailed behind a ship to slow and steady it.

sea-anemone *noun*
a non-mobile, marine animal, having a circular body with a ring of tentacles to trap food from the water.

seabird *noun*
any bird, such as the albatross, which is usually found around the coast or sea.

seaboard *noun*
the coastline or land near the sea.

sea-cock *noun*
a valve in the hull of a ship used to admit water.

sea-cow *noun*
a dugong.

sea-dog *noun*
a sailor with many years of experience.

sea-elephant *noun*
a large seal with a trunk-like nose, found in arctic and antarctic waters.

seafarer (*say* **see**-faira) *noun*
a sailor or traveller on the sea.
Word Family: **seafaring**, *adjective*, travelling by or working at sea.

seafront *noun*
any land or road which borders the very edge of the sea.

seagoing *adjective*
built for or travelling at sea.

seagull *noun*
see GULL (1).

seahorse *noun*
any of a group of small fish with a long tail and a beaked head.

seakale *noun*
a winter vegetable, the blanched shoots of which have a delicate flavour.

seal (1) *noun*
1. a) a device, such as a stamp or ring, with a raised, engraved mark which is impressed onto wax or a similar surface. b) the impression made, especially as a token attached to a

document to indicate authenticity, consent, etc.
2. any thing or substance which closes, fixes or prevents leakage, exposure, etc.
Usage: 'this product has the company's *seal* of approval' (= pledge).
Phrases:
set one's seal to, to approve or confirm.
under seal, having an official seal.
seal *verb*
1. to fix or close with or as with a seal: '*seal* all the envelopes'.
2. to close so as to be airtight: '*seal* the jars of jam after cooling'.
Usages:
a) 'the nations *sealed* the cultural agreement' (= confirmed, approved).
b) 'the accident *sealed* her fate' (= fixed firmly).
[Latin *sigilla*]

seal (2) *noun*
any of various large fish–eating marine mammals with a sleek, furry body.

sealant *noun*
any substance, such as liquid or wax, used to seal or protect a surface.

sea–legs *plural noun*
(*informal*) the ability to walk steadily on a ship or not become seasick.

sealer (1) *noun*
1. an undercoat of paint, varnish, etc. used to seal a surface.
2. a person or device that attaches or impresses seals onto a surface.

sealer (2) *noun*
a person or boat taking part in hunting seals.

sea–level *noun*
the height of the sea, especially when it is halfway between high and low tide.

sealing wax
a resinous substance, originally of beeswax, melted and used to seal envelopes, packages and documents.

sea–lion *noun*
any of various large seals with prominent ears, found in the Pacific ocean.

seam *noun*
1. a line of sewing joining two pieces of cloth.
2. any line, ridge, etc., especially one which joins edges.
3. a comparatively thin stratum, such as a coal stratum.

seam *verb*
1. to join with a seam.
2. to become wrinkled, cracked or lined.

seaman *noun*
a member of a ship's crew other than an officer.
seamanship *noun*
the theory, practice or skill of handling a ship.

sea mile
a unit of length equal to about 1·9 km.

seamstress *noun*
a woman whose work is sewing.

seamy *adjective*
(*informal*) sordid, wretched or depressing.

seance (*say* **say–ons**) *noun*
a meeting to communicate with spirits.
[French *séance* a sitting]

seaplane *noun*
any aeroplane able to take off or land on water, such as an amphibian or a flying boat.

sear (*say* seer) *verb*
1. to burn or scorch: 'the flames *seared* her eyebrows'.
2. to cause to dry up or wither: 'the grass was *seared* by the summer sun'.
3. to brown and seal the surface of meat by briefly applying very intense heat.

search (*say* serch) *verb*
1. to look carefully or thoroughly in order to find something.
2. to frisk a person or ransack a house when looking for stolen goods, weapons, contraband, etc.
search me, (*informal*) I don't know.
Word Family: **search**, *noun*, the act of searching or examining; **searching**, *adjective*, thorough; **searchingly**, *adverb*.

searchlight *noun*
a very strong electric light with a reflector, mounted so that it can be turned in any direction.

search warrant
a written authority issued by a magistrate for the police to search premises where it is suspected that stolen goods, wanted persons, etc. may be found.

seascape *noun*
a view or picture of the sea.

seashore *noun*
the land along the sea, especially the ground covered and uncovered by the tide.

seasick *adjective*
suffering nausea caused by the movement of a ship at sea.
Word Family: **seasickness,** *noun.*

seaside *noun*
the land along the seashore, especially towns or suburbs used as resorts.

season (*say* **see**–z'n) *noun*
1. one of the natural climatic divisions of the year, of which there are four (spring, summer, autumn, winter) in temperate areas.
2. a time of year distinguished by a particular activity, crop, etc.: 'the football *season*'.
Usage: 'the London *Season*' (= the high point of social activities).
3. a season ticket.
Phrases:
in season, a) available for eating, etc.; b) at the right time; c) (of animals) on heat.
out of season, a) not available for eating, etc.; b) at the wrong time.
season *verb*
1. to improve the flavour of food by adding spices or herbs.
2. to dry, harden and treat timber.
Usages:
a) 'the discussion was *seasoned* with angry words' (= given life or interest).
b) 'he was now a *seasoned* soldier of many battles' (= experienced).
c) 'you must *season* your recklessness' (= moderate).
Word Family: **seasonal,** *adjective,* relating to or occurring in a particular season; **seasonally,** *adverb*; **seasonable,** *adjective,* at the suitable or correct time; **seasonably,** *adverb*; **seasonableness,** *noun.*
[Latin *satio* a sowing, planting]

seasoning (*say* **seez**–ning) *noun*
any spices, herbs or flavourings used to season food.

season ticket
a ticket which may be used for an unlimited number of journeys, performances, etc. over a particular period, bought at a reduced rate.

seat *noun*
1. something on which one sits, especially a chair, etc.
2. a) the buttocks. b) the part of a garment covering the buttocks: 'the *seat* of his pants'.
3. the base or bottom of anything.
Usages:
a) 'our city is the *seat* of local government' (= centre, location).
b) 'in the old days a rich man would divide his time between his town house and his country *seat*' (= house and estate).
4. a manner of sitting: 'she has a very relaxed *seat* on a horse'.
seat *verb*
to place in or on a seat: 'please *seat* yourselves for dinner'.
Usages:
a) 'this hall *seats* 700 people' (= has seats or room for).
b) 'the fears were deeply *seated* in his mind' (= fixed).

seat belt
also called a **safety belt**
a harness in a car, aircraft, etc. to keep an occupant in his seat in rough conditions, in a crash, etc.

seating *noun*
the number or arrangement of seats.

sea trout
see SALMON TROUT.

sea–urchin *noun*
any of a group of spiny, marine animals with a spherical shape and a shell made up of many calcareous discs.

seawall *noun*
a wall or embankment to prevent the sea eroding the land.

seaward *adjective*
situated or facing towards the sea: 'the house has a *seaward* aspect'.
Word Family: **seawards, seaward,** *adverb,* towards the sea from land.

seaway *noun*
a ship's route or progress at sea.

seaweed *noun*
any plant growing in salt water.

seaworthy *adjective*
(of a ship) strong enough and suitably equipped for going to sea.
Word Family: **seaworthiness,** *noun.*

sebaceous glands (*say* sib**bay**–shus glands)
Anatomy: any of numerous small glands in the skin, usually near hair, which secrete oils.
[Latin *sebum* grease]

sec (1) (*say* sek) *noun*
(*informal*) a second: 'wait a *sec*'.

sec (2) *noun*
Maths: the short form of **secant.**

secant (*say* **see**–kant) *noun*
1. *Maths:* the reciprocal of cosine. See TRIGONOMETRIC FUNCTIONS.
2. any straight line that cuts a curve.
[Latin *secans* cutting]

secateurs (*say* sekka–**terz** *or* **sekk**a–terz) *plural noun*
a small pair of shears with short curved, crossed blades for pruning trees, etc.
[French]

secede (*say* se–**seed**) *verb*
to withdraw officially from a federation, organization or group.
Word Family: **secession** (*say* se–**sesh**'n), *noun*, the act of seceding; **secessionist**, *noun*, a person who secedes or favours secession.
[from Latin]

seclude (*say* se–**klood**) *verb*
to keep apart from the company of others: 'he *secluded* himself in a mountain retreat to meditate'.
secluded *adjective*
1. living apart from others.
2. protected from view or disturbance.
Word Family: **seclusion** (*say* se–**kloo**–*zh*'n), *noun*, a) the act of secluding, b) solitude or retirement.
[from Latin]

second (1) (*say* **sek**'nd) *adjective*
1. being number two in order or a series.
Usage: 'you won't get a *second* chance' (= another).
2. *Music:* relating to the performing of a lower-pitched part and sometimes being lesser in rank: 'the *second* violin'.
second *noun*
1. the basic SI unit of time. See SI UNIT.
2. a person or thing that is second.
3. a person who aids or assists another person: 'a duellist's *second* is his representative'.
4. (*informal*, *plural*) a) a second helping. b) a second course.
5. (*usually plural*) any products which are damaged or marked, offered for sale at a reduced price.
6. a unit of plane angle equal to one 60th part of a minute.
second *verb*
1. to assist or back up.
2. to give support to a suggestion or nomination.
Word Family: **second**, *adverb*, in second place; **secondly**, *adverb*; **seconder** (*say* **sekk**onder), *noun*, a person who seconds a suggestion or nomination.
[Latin *secundus* following, next]

second (2) (*say* se–**kond**) *verb*
to transfer a person temporarily to another post, position or responsibility.
Word Family: **secondment**, *noun*.

secondary (*say* **sekk**un–dree) *adjective*
coming second in time, place, importance, etc.
Usages:
a) 'that's only a matter of *secondary* importance now' (= minor).
b) 'a historian should avoid relying too much on *secondary* sources' (= not primary or original).
Word Family: **secondary**, *noun*, a person or thing that is secondary.

secondary colour
any colour produced by mixing two primary colours, such as orange which is a mixture of red and yellow. Compare TERTIARY COLOUR.

secondary industry
see INDUSTRY.

secondary school
a school for children over the age of about 11 years old.

second childhood
feebleness of mind due to being senile.

second cousin
see COUSIN.

second edition
see EDITION.

seconder *noun*
Word Family: see SECOND (1).

second–hand *adjective*
having been previously owned or used.
Usage: 'the essay was filled with *second–hand* ideas' (= not original).
Word Family: **second–hand**, *adverb*.

second lieutenant
the lowest rank of commissioned officer in the army.

secondly *adverb*
Word Family: see SECOND (1).

second nature
a habit which a person has practised for so long that it has become a fixed part of his character.

second person
Grammar: see PERSON.

second–rate *adjective*
inferior or only of average quality.
Word Family: **second–rater**, *noun*.

second sight
clairvoyance.

second string
have a second string to one's bow, to have an alternative course of action ready.

second thoughts
see THOUGHT (1).

second wind
get one's second wind, to recover after exhaustion or great effort.

secret (*say* **see**–krit) *adjective*
1. kept from the knowledge of others: a) 'the diplomats were conducting *secret* negotiations'; b) 'a *secret* society'.
2. secretive.
secret *noun*
1. something which is secret or hidden.
2. a hidden reason or cause: 'the *secret* of his success is hard work'.
Word Family: **secretly**, *adverb*; **secrecy** (*say* **seekra**–see), *noun*, a) the state of being secret or hidden, b) lack of frankness or openness.
[Latin *secretus* put apart, separated]
Common Error: do not confuse with SECRETE.

secret agent
a spy.

secretaire (*say* **sekra–tair**) *noun*
an escritoire.

secretariat (*say* sekra–**tairi**–at) *noun*
a) the administrative officials of a government or other large organization, such as the United Nations. b) their offices.

secretary (*say* **sekra**–tree) *noun*
1. a person who writes letters, keeps records, etc. for another person or an organization.
2. an administrative assistant to a government minister, ambassador, etc.
Word Family: **secretarial** (*say* sekra–**tairiul**), *adjective*; **secretaryship**, *noun*.

secretary bird
a long-legged, African bird over 1 m long, which eats reptiles.
[from its crest, like a quill pen]

secretary-general *noun*
plural is **secretaries-general**
the head of a secretariat.

Secretary of State
a person who is in charge of a government department: 'the *Secretary of State* for Foreign Affairs'.

secrete (*say* se–**kreet**) *verb*
1. *Biology:* to produce a secretion.
2. to hide or conceal: 'to *secrete* one's cigarettes under the mattress'.
Common Error: do not confuse with SECRET.

secretion (*say* se–**kree**–sh'n) *noun*
Biology: a) the process of passing the products of a cell from inside to outside the cell membrane. b) the products so passed.
Word Family: **secretory** (*say* se–**kree**ta–ree), *adjective*.
[Latin *secretio* a separating]

secretive (*say* **seekra**–tiv) *adjective*
inclined to secrecy.
Word Family: **secretively**, *adverb*; **secretiveness**, *noun*.

secretly *adverb*
Word Family: see SECRET.

secret service
a secret government organization whose duties may include spying, counter-spying, code-breaking, subversion in enemy territory, surveillance of dissidents, psychological warfare, etc.

sect *noun*
a group of persons sharing the same religious beliefs.
sectarian (*say* sek–**tairi**–un) *adjective*
1. relating to a particular sect.
2. concerned for or relating to the interests of one's own group: '*sectarian* squabbles divided the country into hostile camps'.
Word Family: **sectarian**, *noun*, a member of a sect; **sectarianism**, *noun*.
[Latin *sectus* cut]

section (*say* **sek**–sh'n) *noun*
1. a distinct or separate part or division: a) 'this *section* of the book is boring'; b) 'a military *section* is a part of a platoon'.
2. a cross-section.
3. a very thin slice of tissue for microscopic study.
sectional *adjective*
1. made of sections.
2. concerned with or interested in one's own area or group, especially to the exclusion of others.
Word Family: **section**, *verb*, to cut into sections; **sectionally**, *adverb*; **sectionalism**, *noun*, sectional interests or bias.

sector (*say* **sekta**) *noun*
1. *Maths:* the part of a circle between two radii and the included arc.
2. any field or part of a field of activity: 'the Prime Minister antagonized the business *sector* by his statements'.

secular (*say* **sek**–yoo–la) *adjective*
1. a) worldly or material rather than spiritual or religious: 'a *secular* attitude prevails in this age'. b) not relating to or dealing with religion: '*secular* education'.
2. not living inside monasteries: 'the *secular* clergy'.

Word Family: **secularly**, *adverb*; **secularism**, *noun*, the belief that morality, public education or civil policy should not be based on religion; **secularist**, *noun*; **secularize, secularise**, *verb*, to make secular; **secularization**, *noun*.
[Latin *saeculum* a generation, the spirit of the age]

secure (*say* se-**kewer**) *adjective*
1. free from danger or anxiety: a) 'a *secure* hiding-place'; b) 'to feel *secure* about one's future'.
2. well fastened or not likely to fall, give way, fail, etc.: 'is that ladder *secure*?'.
Usage: 'our victory in the competition is *secure*' (= certain, sure).
secure *verb*
to make secure.
Usages:
a) 'I have *secured* good seats for the concert' (= obtained).
b) 'the creditor requires something to *secure* the loan' (= cover the risk of).
security *noun*
1. a) something which protects or makes safe. b) protective measures taken against theft, spying, etc.
2. something given as a pledge that a person will fulfil a promise or undertaking.
3. a certificate of ownership, e.g. a bond, stock or share.
Word Family: **securely**, *adverb*; **secureness**, *noun*.
[Latin *se-* apart + *cura* care]

sedan (*say* se-**dan**) *noun*
1. a vehicle for a person, consisting of an enclosed chair carried on poles by two men. Short form of **sedan chair**.
2. *American:* a large, closed motor car for four or more persons. Also called a **saloon**.

sedate (*say* se-**date**) *adjective*
composed or calm: 'to live a life of *sedate* retirement'.
sedate *verb*
to administer a sedative to.
Word Family: **sedation**, *noun*, a) the state of being sedated, b) the act of sedating; **sedately**, *adverb*; **sedateness**, *noun*.
[Latin *sedatus* settled]

sedative (*say* **sedda**-tiv) *noun*
also called a **depressant**
Medicine: any substance that temporarily decreases the function of part or all of the body and is used to relieve anxiety, pain, etc. Compare STIMULANT.
Word Family: **sedative**, *adjective*, having a soothing or calming effect.

sedentary (*say* **sedd**'n-tree) *adjective*
1. a) done sitting down: 'writing is a *sedentary* occupation'. b) taking or requiring little exercise: 'to lead a *sedentary* life'.
2. *Biology:* (of animals) moving little or fixed to one spot.
Word Family: **sedentariness**, *noun*.
[Latin *sedens* sitting]

sedge (*say* sej) *noun*
any of a group of grass-like plants, usually growing in swampy areas.

sediment (*say* **seddi**-m'nt) *noun*
1. the material which settles to the bottom of a liquid.
2. *Geology:* any mineral or organic matter deposited by wind, ice or water.
sedimentary (*say* seddi-**men**-tree) *adjective*
1. of or relating to sediment.
2. *Geology:* relating to rocks, such as sandstone and limestone, formed of compressed sediment of shells, rock fragments, etc.
Word Family: **sedimentation**, *noun*.
[Latin *sedere* to sit]

sedition (*say* se-**dish**'n) *noun*
the act of trying to promote rebellion or revolt against the government.
Word Family: **seditious**, *adjective*; **seditiously**, *adverb*.
[Latin *seditio* a going apart]

seduce (*say* se-**dewce**) *verb*
1. to persuade to have sexual intercourse.
2. to lead into wrongdoing: 'he has *seduced* me into bad habits'.
Word Family: **seduction**, *noun*, a) the act of seducing, b) something which seduces; **seducer**, *noun*; **seductive** (*say* se-**duk**tiv), *adjective*, a) sexually attractive, b) tending to seduce; **seductively**, *adverb*; **seductiveness**, *noun*; **seductress**, *noun*.

sedulous (*say* **sed**-yew-lus) *adjective*
diligent or persevering: 'Tim worked with *sedulous* attention to detail'.
Word Family: **sedulously**, *adverb*.
[Latin]

see (1) *verb*
(saw, seen, seeing)
to perceive through the eyes.
Usages:
a) 'he travelled the world to *see* a bit of life' (= experience).

b) 'do you *see* the error of your ways now?' (= appreciate, understand).
c) (*informal*) 'please *see* that you do the job properly' (= make sure).
d) 'I *see* some things very differently from my parents' (= consider, regard).
e) 'I just can't *see* her as vice-president of the company' (= imagine).
f) 'my secretary *sees* to that side of the business' (= attends).
g) '*see* who that is at the door' (= find out).
h) 'I went to *see* your aunt today' (= visit).
i) 'the manager will *see* you shortly' (= receive).
j) 'let me *see* you to the door' (= escort).
Phrases:
see about, a) to take care of or attend to; b) 'we'll have to *see about* that request, young man' (= consider, deliberate over).
see out, 'she's determined to *see* the job *out*' (= continue until completion).
see over, 'I'd like to *see over* the factory' (= inspect).
see through, a) 'we *saw through* his disguise' (= were not deceived by); b) 'I need something to *see* me *through* the sleepless nights' (= help, support).

see (2) *noun*
see DIOCESE.
[Latin *sedes* a seat]

seed *noun*
1. *Biology:* the mature fruit of a plant containing an embryo ready for germination.
Usage: 'the *seeds* of revolt lay in the harsh laws' (= beginnings).
2. a) semen or sperm. b) offspring: 'and the *seed* of Abraham shall be mighty in the land'.
3. *Tennis:* a player classified according to skill and distributed in a tournament so as not to meet other skilled players in the early matches.
go, run to seed, a) to come to the stage of yielding seed; b) to deteriorate.
seed *verb*
1. to plant seed in the soil.
2. to remove the seeds from fruit or plants.
3. to produce or shed seeds.
4. *Weather:* to scatter fine particles of material in a cloud to encourage large droplets or ice crystals to form and make rain.
5. *Tennis:* to classify.

seedbed *noun*
a small area of soil prepared for the growing of seeds.
Usage: 'this place is a *seedbed* of rebels and anarchists' (= source, place of origin).

seed cake
a cake flavoured with caraway seed.

seed drill
1. a machine which sows seeds in rows and covers them over.
2. a furrow in which seeds are planted.

seeder *noun*
1. a machine which plants seeds.
2. a machine which removes seeds from fruit, etc.

seed leaf
Biology: see COTYLEDON.

seedling *noun*
a young plant.

seed pearl
a very small pearl, less than $\frac{1}{4}$ grain in weight.

seedy *adjective*
1. a) full of seed. b) gone to seed.
2. (*informal*) a) shabbily disreputable. b) physically unwell.
Word Family: **seedily**, *adverb*; **seediness**, *noun.*

seeing *conjunction*
considering or in view of the fact: '*seeing* that he is two hours late, we should not expect him this evening'.

seek *verb*
(sought, seeking)
to try to find or obtain: a) 'he *sought* his fortune in the city'; b) 'I shall *seek* to persuade him by flattery'.
be sought after, to be in demand.
Word Family: **seeker**, *noun.*

seem *verb*
to appear: a) 'the old man *seemed* to hear voices'; b) 'it *seems* best to leave now'.
Word Family: **seeming**, *adjective*, apparent; **seemingly**, *adverb.*

seemly *adjective*
(of conduct, etc.) fitting or becoming: 'belching in church is not considered *seemly* behaviour'.

seen *verb*
the past participle of the verb **see (1)**.

seep *verb*
(of a liquid) to pass slowly through or out of.
Usage: 'new ideas *seep* gradually into circulation' (= pass, enter).

Word Family: **seepage** (*say* **see**–pij), *noun,* a) the act of seeping, b) the liquid that seeps or leaks out.

seer *noun*
a person reputed to be able to see into the future.

seersucker *noun*
a usually striped lightweight fabric with a regularly crinkled surface, made of various fibres.
[Persian *shir o shakkar* milk and sugar]

seesaw *noun*
1. a plank fastened in the middle so that each of the two ends, on which a child sits, moves up and down in turn.
2. a) the act of moving up and down or back and forth. b) an up–and–down or back–and–forth movement.
Word Family: **seesaw,** *verb, adjective.*

seethe (*say* see*th*) *verb*
(of a liquid) to bubble and foam as if boiling: 'the floodwaters *seethed* around lampposts and doorways'.
Usage: 'the troops *seethed* with rebellion' (= were in a state of agitation).

segment (*say* **seg**–m'nt) *noun*
1. a part into which something naturally divides: 'the *segments* of an orange'.
2. *Maths:* a) the part of a circle or sphere cut off by a line or plane. b) a finite part of a line.
Word Family: **segment** (*say* seg–**ment**), *verb,* to divide into segments; **segmental, segmentary,** *adjectives;* **segmentation,** *noun,* a) the act of dividing into segments, b) the state of being divided into segments.
[from Latin]

segregate (*say* **segra**–gate) *verb*
to separate people or groups from each other. Compare INTEGRATE.
segregation (*say* segra–**gay**–sh'n) *noun*
1. a) the act of segregating. b) the state of being segregated.
2. a policy, law or process of separating one racial, ethnic or religious group from the main body of society.
Word Family: **segregationist,** *noun,* a person who advocates segregation.
[Latin *se*– apart + *gregis* of the flock]

seigneur (*say* sane–**yer**) *noun*
Medieval history: the superior party in a feudal contract, such as a nobleman who rented out sections of his estate in exchange for military service, etc. Compare VASSAL.
Word Family: **seigneurial,** *adjective.*
[from Old French, from Latin SENIOR]

seismic (*say* **size**–mik) *adjective*
of, relating to or caused by earthquakes.
seismology (*say* size–**molla**–jee) *noun*
the science of earthquake phenomena.
seismograph (*say* **size**–ma–graf) *noun*
an instrument for measuring the vibrations caused by earthquakes.
Word Family: **seismologist,** *noun.*
[Greek *seismos* an earthquake]

seize (*say* seez) *verb*
1. to lay hold of firmly:a) 'he *seized* her by the arm'; b) 'his mind *seized* upon the idea that he was a genius'.
Usages:
a) 'the mob was *seized* by a blind urge to burn and kill' (= possessed).
b) 'never fail to *seize* an opportunity' (= take advantage of).
2. to bind or become jammed, as an engine through overheating.
Word Family: **seizure** (*say* **see**–*zh*er), *noun,* a) the act of seizing, b) a fit.

seldom *adverb*
not often.

select (*say* se–**lekt**) *verb*
to choose.
select *adjective*
specially chosen: a) 'a *select* crew of sailors'; b) 'Wilson's *select* brand of chocolates'.
selection *noun*
1. a) a choice: 'will you please make your *selection*?'. b) something which has been selected: 'take your *selections* to the nearest cash register'. c) a range of things to choose from: 'we have a very wide *selection* of shirts'.
2. *Biology:* the choosing of certain animals or plants for purposes of reproduction. This may occur naturally or may be artificially guided by man, as in the breeding of cattle, etc.
Word Family: **selective,** *adjective,* a) having the power to select, b) fastidious or exclusive; **selector,** *noun,* a person or thing that selects.
[Latin *se*– apart + *lectus* picked]

selenium (*say* se–**leeni**–um) *noun*
element number 34, a non–metal, forming allotropes and used in making glass and rubber. The grey crystalline form, called 'metallic' selenium, varies in electrical resistance with the intensity of light, and is used in photoelectric cells.

See CHEMICAL ELEMENTS in grey pages. [Greek *selené* moon]

selenography (*say* sella-**nogra**-fee) *noun*
the study of the physical features of the moon.
selenology (*say* sella-**nolla**-jee) *noun*
the branch of astronomy dealing with the moon.
[Greek *selené* moon + *graphein* to write]

self *noun*
plural is **selves**
1. one's own person.
Usages:
a) 'when he's tired his better *self* disappears' (= nature, character).
b) 'whatever she does she does for reasons of *self*' (= selfishness, personal interest).
2. the ego.
Word Family: **self**, *pronoun.*

self-
a prefix meaning: a) of or over oneself, etc., as in *self-control*; b) by or in oneself, etc., as in *self-evident*; c) to or for oneself, etc., as in *self-addressed*; d) automatic or automatically, as in *self-starter.*

self-absorbed *adjective*
preoccupied with one's own thoughts, interests, etc.
Word Family: **self-absorption**, *noun.*

self-acting *adjective*
automatic.

self-addressed *adjective*
addressed to oneself.

self-aggrandizement, self-aggrandisement *noun*
an increase in one's own power, prestige, wealth, etc., usually achieved aggressively.

self-appointed *adjective*
acting or speaking as if having authority, without having been requested or authorized to do so: 'a *self-appointed* spokesman'.

self-assertive *adjective*
insisting on one's own wishes, opinions, importance, etc.
Word Family: **self-assertion**, *noun.*

self-assured *adjective*
confident in one's own abilities, etc., especially to an extreme degree.
Word Family: **self-assurance**, *noun.*

self-aware *adjective*
aware of one's own nature, weaknesses and abilities.
Word Family: **self-awareness**, *noun.*

self-centred *adjective*
selfish or excessively concerned with oneself.
Word Family: **self-centredness**, *noun.*

self-centring *adjective*
returning automatically to a central position after being displaced.

self-composed *adjective*
calm within oneself.
Word Family: **self-composedly**, *adverb*; **self-composure**, *noun.*

self-confidence *noun*
belief in one's own abilities, worth, judgement, etc.
Word Family: **self-confident**, *adjective*; **self-confidently**, *adverb.*

self-congratulation *noun*
an uncritical or excessive approval of one's own qualities, actions, etc.
Word Family: **self-congratulatory**, *adjective.*

self conscious *adjective*
1. excessively conscious of how one appears to other people.
2. conscious of one's own self, existence, thoughts, etc.
Word Family: **self-consciously**, *adverb*; **self-consciousness**, *noun.*

self-contained *adjective*
1. a) reserved or disposed to say little.
b) self-possessed or calm.
2. independent, such as a flat or house which has its own bathroom and kitchen, so that sharing is not necessary.

self-control *noun*
control of one's self, feelings, actions, etc.
Word Family: **self-controlled**, *adjective.*

self-critical *adjective*
inclined to find fault with one's own actions, motives, etc.
Word Family: **self-critically**, *adverb*; **self-criticism**, *noun.*

self-deception *noun*
the fact or act of deceiving oneself.

self-defeating *adjective*
(of an action, plan, etc.) having inherent defects which prevent its successful achievement, conclusion, etc.

self-defence *noun*
the defence of one's person, property, etc., especially when involving the use of physical force.

self-denial *noun*
the denial of one's own desires.
Word Family: **self-denying**, *adjective.*

self-determination *noun*
any decision made by oneself without outside influence, especially the decision by the people of a country as to its political destiny.
Word Family: **self-determined,** *adjective*; **self-determining,** *adjective.*

self-discipline *noun*
the discipline or training of oneself, especially for self-improvement.

self-effacement *noun*
the act or habit of not drawing attention to oneself, especially through modesty or timidity.
Word Family: **self-effacing,** *adjective.*

self-employed *adjective*
earning one's income from one's own business, skills, etc., and not as a salary or wages from an employer.

self-esteem *noun*
a good opinion of oneself, often excessive.

self-evident *adjective*
obviously true and therefore requiring no proof or explanation.
Word Family: **self-evidently,** *adverb.*

self-explanatory *adjective*
obvious.

self-expression *noun*
the expression of one's own personality in art or in one's behaviour.

self-fertilization, self-fertilisation *noun*
Biology: the union of male and female gametes from the same animal or flower. Compare CROSS-FERTILIZATION.

self-governed *adjective*
governed by itself, such as a state or community.
Word Family: **self-governing,** *adjective*; **self-government,** *noun.*

selfhood *noun*
the state of being an individual person: 'to achieve *selfhood*'.

self-important *adjective*
having an exaggerated idea of one's own importance.
Word Family: **self-importantly,** *adverb*; **self-importance,** *noun.*

self-improvement *noun*
an improvement of one's skills, status, etc. by one's own efforts.

self-indulgent *adjective*
indulging one's own desires, passions, etc. with little regard for the welfare of others.
Word Family: **self-indulgently,** *adverb*; **self-indulgence,** *noun.*

self-interest *noun*
personal advantage or interest.
Word Family: **self-interested,** *adjective.*

selfish *adjective*
caring too much for oneself and too little for others.
Word Family: **selfishly,** *adverb*; **selfishness,** *noun.*

self-knowledge *noun*
knowledge of one's own character, abilities, etc.

selfless *adjective*
unselfish.
Word Family: **selflessness,** *noun*; **selflessly,** *adverb.*

self-loading *adjective*
(of a firearm) reloading automatically.

self-locking *adjective*
locking automatically when closed.

self-love *noun*
selfishness or egotism.

self-made *adjective*
having achieved success unaided.

self-opinionated *adjective*
1. conceited.
2. obstinate in one's opinions.

self-pity *noun*
excessive pity for oneself.
Word Family: **self-pitying,** *adjective.*

self-pollination *noun*
Biology: the process of transferring pollen from the anthers to the stigma of the same flower.

self-portrait *noun*
an artist's portrait of himself.

self-possessed *adjective*
having or showing control of one's feelings, behaviour, etc.
Word Family: **self-possession,** *noun.*

self-propelled *adjective*
propelled or driven by itself.
Word Family: **self-propelling,** *adjective.*

self-raising *adjective*
(of flour) containing a substance, such as baking powder, to make it rise.

self-realization, self-realisation *noun*
the full development of one's capabilities.

self-reliance *noun*
a reliance on one's own resources.

self-reproach *noun*
a blaming or reproaching of oneself.

self-respect *noun*
a respect or esteem for one's own character and conduct.

Word Family: **self-respecting,** *adjective.*

self-restraint *noun*
any self-control.

self-righteous *adjective*
piously sure of one's own righteousness or virtue.
Word Family: **self-righteously,** *adverb*; **self-righteousness,** *noun.*

self-sacrifice *noun*
the sacrifice of one's own interests, desires, etc. for the sake of some other person, principle, etc.
Word Family: **self-sacrificing,** *adjective.*

selfsame *adjective*
the very same: 'is that the *selfsame* John Smith I was talking about before?'.

self-satisfied *adjective*
feeling satisfied with oneself
Word Family: **self-satisfaction,** *noun.*

self-seeking *adjective*
pursuing or seeking one's own interests.
Word Family: **self-seeker,** *noun*;

self-service *adjective*
(of a restaurant, shop, lift, etc.) served, operated or performed partly or wholly by the customer, passenger, etc.

self-sown *adjective*
sown without the aid of man.

self-starter *noun*
a device, such as a starter motor, which starts an internal combustion engine without cranking by hand.

self-styled *adjective*
(of a name, etc.) applied to oneself, especially undeservedly.

self-sufficient *adjective*
able to provide or manage for oneself without aid
Word Family: **self-sufficiency,** *noun.*

self-tapping screw
a screw which cuts a thread into the sides of a hole as it is screwed in.

self-willed *adjective*
obstinate.

sell *verb*
(sold, selling)
1. to exchange for money or its equivalent.
2. to offer for sale or deal in, e.g. for one's livelihood: 'he *sells* motor cars'.
3. to attract buyers: 'the bright package *sells* this soap powder'.
Usage: 'we finally *sold* him on the idea' (= convinced, caused to accept).
Phrases:
hard sell, forceful salesmanship.
sell off, to sell at a reduced price.
sell oneself short, to underestimate or belittle one's own worth or abilities.
sell out, a) to dispose of completely by selling, b) to betray.
sell up, to sell all of one's goods or property.
Word Family: **sell,** *noun.*

seller *noun*
1. a person who sells.
2. something considered in terms of its sales potential: 'all books in this series are good *sellers*'.

Sellotape *noun*
an adhesive tape.
[a trademark]

seltzer (*say* **selt**sa) *noun*
an effervescent mineral water.
[originally from *Selters* a German spa]

selvage (*say* **sel**vij) **selvedge** *noun*
the edge of a length of fabric, wallpaper, etc. sewn or finished so that it will not pull undone.
[SELF + EDGE]

selves *plural noun*
see SELF.

semantics (*say* se-**man**tiks) *plural noun*
(*used with singular verb*) the science or study of the meanings of words, especially in relation to their historical change.
Word Family: **semantic,** *adjective.*
[Greek *semantikos* significant]

semaphore (*say* **semma**-for) *noun*
a method of signalling, using flags or a mechanical device with arms, where different positions represent the letters of the alphabet.
[Greek *sema* sign + *phoros* bearing]

semblance *noun*
an outward appearance: 'the deserted house had a *semblance* of decay'.
Usage: 'not a *semblance* of guilt showed in his face' (= trace).
[Latin *simulare* to make like]

semen (*say* **see**-m'n) *noun*
also called **seminal fluid**
Biology: the combined secretions of the male reproductive organs, including the testes and prostate gland, which forms the fluid expelled from the penis in ejaculation.
[Latin, seed]

semester (*say* se-**mes**ta) *noun*
either of the two halves into which the teaching year at a university,

college, etc. may be divided, especially in Germany or America.
Word Family: **semestral**, *adjective.*
[Latin *sex* six + *mensis* a month]

semi *noun*
(*informal*) a semi-detached house.

semi-
a prefix meaning: a) partially or partly, as in *semidetached*; b) half of, as in *semicircle*; c) occurring twice within a particular period of time, as in *semiannual.*
[Latin, half]

semiannual (*say* semmi-**an**-yew'l) *adjective*
a) occurring twice a year. b) lasting for half a year.

semiautomatic
(*say* semmi-awto-**mattik**) *adjective*
1. partly automatic.
2. (of a firearm) loading automatically but requiring a separate pull of the trigger at each shot.

semibreve (*say* **semmi**-breev) *noun*
Music: a note with a half of the time value of a breve.

semicircle (*say* **semmi**-sir-k'l) *noun*
a) a half of a circle. b) something which has this shape.
Word Family: **semicircular**, *adjective.*

semicolon (*say* semmi-**kole**-on) *noun*
Grammar: a punctuation mark (;), used in a sentence to separate clauses or introduce a pause longer than that of a comma.

semiconductor *noun*
Electronics: any of a class of crystals, such as silicon and germanium, with conductivity ranging from nil at -200°C to poor at normal temperatures and good when heated or when impurities are added (as in transistors). They are used in electronic and microelectronic circuits and photoelectric cells.

semiconscious (*say* semmi-**kon**shus) *adjective*
not fully conscious.
Word Family: **semiconsciousness**, *noun.*

semidetached *adjective*
partly detached, as a pair of houses, detached from other buildings but with a common wall.

semifinal (*say* semmi-**fie**-n'l) *noun*
the last competition or match played before a final game in a series.
Word Family: **semifinal**, *adjective*; **semifinalist**, *noun*, a person or team that competes in a semifinal.

seminal (*say* **semmi**-n'l) *adjective*
1. *Biology:* of or relating to semen.
2. of or relating to a seed.
3. having possibilities of future development.
[Latin *seminis* of seed]

seminal fluid
Biology: see SEMEN.

seminar (*say* **semmi**-nar) *noun*
a class or group discussion usually for advanced study or research.
[Latin *seminarium* a seedbed]

seminary (*say* **semmin**-ree) *noun*
1. *Christian:* a training college for priests.
2. (*formerly*) a private school, especially one for girls.
Word Family: **seminarist**, *noun*, a person who attends or teaches in a seminary.

semiofficial (*say* semmi-a-**fish**'l) *adjective*
having some official authority.

semipermanent
(*say* semmi-**perma**-nent) *adjective*
intended to last for some time but not for ever, such as a dye for hair.

semipermeable
(*say* semmi-**perm**ia-b'l) *adjective*
(of a membrane) permeable to some molecules in a solution but not to others.

semiprecious (*say* semmi-**preshus**) *adjective*
having some value as a gem but not classified as precious, e.g. amethyst.

semiquaver (*say* **semmi**-kway-va) *noun*
Music: a note with a half of the time value of a quaver.

semiskilled *adjective*
partly skilled or trained for work, but not professional.

semisolid (*say* semmi-**sollid**) *adjective*
not completely solid.

Semite (*say* **sem**-ite *or* **see**-mite) *noun*
1. any of a race of people now represented by the Jews and Arabs.
2. a Jew.
Word Family: **Semitic** (*say* se-**mittik**), *adjective*; **Semitism** (*say* **semmi**-tizm), *noun.*

semitone *noun*
Music: the smallest interval used in European music. On the piano this

represents the interval between one note and the next, whether it is white or black.

semitropical (*say* semmi–**troppi**–k'l) *adjective*
subtropical.

semolina (*say* semma–**leena**) *noun*
the hard parts of wheat grain left after making flour, used to make puddings, etc.
[Italian *semolino* little bran]

senate *noun*
1. the supreme council of state in Ancient Rome.
2. the upper house of the American Congress and some other legislatures.
3. the governing body of some universities.
Word Family: **senator**, *noun*, a member of the senate; **senatorial** (*say* senna–**tawriul**), *adjective*.
[Latin *senatus* from *senex* old man]

send *verb*
(sent, sending)
to cause to go or be carried: a) 'to *send* a letter'; b) 'the bowler *sent* down a fast ball'.
Usage: (*informal*) 'this music really *sends* me' (= excites, inspires).
Phrases:
send down, a) to expel from a university; b) 'the judge *sent* him *down* for five years' (= imprisoned).
send for, to ask or demand to appear.
send up, (*informal*) to mock or mimic.
Word Family: **sender**, *noun*.

send–off *noun*
(*informal*) a friendly gathering for a person who is leaving.

send–up *noun*
(*informal*) a mockery or satire.

senescent (*say* se–**nessent**) *adjective*
growing old.
Word Family: **senescence**, *noun*.
[from Latin]

senile (*say* **senile** *or* **seenile**) *adjective*
a) of or relating to old age. b) lacking mental or physical health due to old age.
Word Family: **senility** (*say* se–**nilli**–tee), *noun*.
[from Latin]

senior (*say* **seen**–ya) *adjective*
1. being more advanced in years, rank, standing, etc.
2. (*capital*) used by the father when father and son have the same name: 'Sammy Davis *Senior*'.

senior *noun*
1. a senior person or student.
2. *American:* a student in fourth year at college.
[Latin, an elder, older]

seniority (*say* seeni–**orri**–tee) *noun*
1. the state of being senior.
2. precedence of position, especially by reason of age or long service.

señor (*say* sen–**yor**) *noun*
the title for a Spanish man.

señora (*say* sen–**yor**–a) *noun*
the title for a married Spanish woman.

senorita (*say* sen–yor–**eeta**) *noun*
the title for an unmarried Spanish woman.

sensation (*say* sen–**say**–sh'n) *noun*
1. any perception through the senses.
Usage: 'I had the *sensation* that someone was watching me' (= impression, idea).
2. a) a state of great interest and excitement: 'the pop group caused a *sensation* when they visited Australia'. b) an event, person, etc. causing such interest and excitement.
Word Family: **sensational**, *adjective*; **sensationally**, *adverb*.

sensationalism
(*say* sen–**say**–sh'n–a–lizm) *noun*
the deliberate use of startling or thrilling methods in writing, politics, etc.
Word Family: **sensationalist**, *noun*.

sense *noun*
1. any of the faculties of sight, hearing, smell, taste and touch.
2. a feeling or perception: 'there was a *sense* of menace in his voice'.
Usage: 'old Smith has no *sense* of humour' (= appreciation).
3. a) practical judgement. b) sound mental faculties.
4. the meaning of a word, statement, etc.: 'in what *sense* are you using the word?'.
5. *Maths:* the direction of a vector.
Phrases:
in a sense, to a certain extent.
make sense, to be intelligible or acceptable.
to make sense of, to understand the meaning of.

sense *verb*
to be or become aware of: 'I *sensed* someone was looking at me'.
[from Latin]

senseless *adjective*
1. unconscious: 'he was knocked *senseless* in the fight'.

2. stupid or foolish: 'being rude to the policeman was a *senseless* thing to do'.
Usage: 'his *senseless* speech confused all of us' (= lacking meaning).
Word Family: **senselessly**, *adverb*; **senselessness**, *noun.*

sense organ
Anatomy: an organ or structure, such as a tastebud, which passes outside information to nerves inside the body.

sensibility (*say* sensa-**billi**-tee) *noun*
1. the ability to feel or perceive.
2. a keen perception or sensitivity.
3. (*plural*) emotions or feelings.

sensible (*say* **sen**sa-b'l) *adjective*
1. having or showing good sense or sound judgement.
Usage: 'he is *sensible* of the danger of his situation' (= aware).
2. able to be perceived by the senses.
3. conscious: 'I was stunned but still *sensible*'.
Word Family: **sensibly**, *adverb*; **sensibleness**, *noun.*

sensitive (*say* **sen**sa-tiv) *adjective*
1. affected by stimuli or impressions.
2. easily offended or hurt: 'she is very *sensitive* about being so tall'.
3. able to measure finely and exactly: 'a *sensitive* thermometer'.
Word Family: **sensitively**, *adverb*; **sensitivity** (*say* sensa-**tivvi**-tee), **sensitiveness**, *nouns.*

sensitize (*say* **sen**sa-tize) **sensitise** *verb*
to make sensitive, e.g. making a photographic film sensitive to light.
Word Family: **sensitization**, *noun.*

sensory (*say* **sen**sa-ree) *adjective*
of or relating to the senses or sensation.

sensual (*say* **sens**-yew'l) *adjective*
1. relating to or affecting the senses.
2. sexy or erotic.
Word Family: **sensually**, *adverb*; **sensuality** (*say* sen-sew-**alli**-tee), **sensualness**, *nouns*; **sensualist**, *noun*, a person who seeks sensual pleasure; **sensualism**, *noun*; **sensualistic**, *adjective.*

sensuous (*say* **sens**-yew-us) *adjective*
affecting or giving pleasure to the senses.
Word Family: **sensuously**, *adverb*; **sensuousness**, *noun.*

sent *verb*
the past tense and past participle of the verb **send.**

sentence *noun*
1. *Grammar:* a group of words which express a complete thought, having a subject and a predicate. *Example:* The boy bought a book.
2. *Law:* a) the decision of a court, stating the punishment a convicted person is to receive. b) the punishment itself.
Word Family: **sentence**, *verb*, to condemn to punishment.
[Latin *sententia* opinion]

sententious (*say* sen-**ten**shus) *adjective*
a) given to pompous moralizing. b) self-righteous.
Word Family: **sententiously**, *adverb*; **sententiousness**, *noun.*
[from Latin]

sentient (*say* **sen**-sh'nt) *adjective*
perceiving by the senses.
Word Family: **sentiently**, *adverb*; **sentience**, *noun.*
[Latin *sentiens* feeling]

sentiment (*say* **sen**ti-m'nt) *noun*
1. any attitudes based on tender or emotional feelings rather than reason.
2. an opinion or attitude: 'what are your *sentiments* on the subject?'.
3. the emotional meaning of something.
[Latin *sentire* to feel]

sentimental (*say* senti-**men**-t'l) *adjective*
having, causing or appealing to tender or romantic feelings: 'we all cried during the *sentimental* film'.
Word Family: **sentimentalize**, **sentimentalise**, *verb*, a) to indulge in sentiment, b) to make sentimental; **sentimentally**, *adverb*; **sentimentality** (*say* senti-men-**talli**-tee), *noun.*

sentinel *noun*
a sentry.
[from Italian]

sentry *noun*
1. a soldier placed to keep watch and warn of attacks.
2. any person who guards or watches.

sepal (*say* **see**-p'l) *noun*
Biology: one of the small, green, leaf-like, outer parts of a flower, forming the calyx and found under the petals and surrounding a bud.
[from SEP(arate) + (pet)AL]

separable (*say* **sep**pera-b'l) *adjective*
capable of being separated.
Word Family: **separably**, *adverb*; **separability** (*say* seppera-**billi**-tee), *noun.*

separate (*say* **seppa**–rate) *verb*
1. to remove parts so that they are no longer together: '*separate* the milk from the cream'.
2. to distinguish between: 'you must *separate* right and wrong in your own mind'.
3. a) to part company. b) to stop living together.
separate (*say* **seppa**–rit) *adjective*
not shared or joined: a) 'we sleep in *separate* rooms'; b) 'list each *separate* item'.
Word Family: **separately,** *adverb*; **separation,** *noun,* the act or fact of separating; **separateness,** *noun,* the fact of being separate.
[Latin *se–* apart + *parare* to make ready]

separatist (*say* **seppera**–tist) *noun*
a person who wants political or religious independence.
Word Family: **separatism,** *noun.*

separator (*say* **seppa**–rayta) *noun*
any of various machines which separates one substance from another, such as cream from milk.

sepia (*say* **seepia**) *noun*
1. a brown pigment obtained from an ink–like secretion of various cuttlefish.
2. a deep brown colour.
[Greek, cuttlefish]

sepoy (*say* **see**–poy) *noun*
History: an Indian soldier, especially one serving in the British Indian Army.
[Urdu *sipahi* a soldier]

sepsis *noun*
the presence of pathogenic organisms or their poisons in the blood or tissues.
[Greek, going rotten]

septa *plural noun*
see SEPTUM.

September *noun*
the ninth month of the year in the Gregorian calendar.
[Latin, the seventh month of the Roman calendar]

septet *noun*
any group of seven people or things.
[Latin *septem* seven]

septic *adjective*
of or causing sepsis or infection.

septicaemia (*say* septi–**seemia**) *noun*
also called **blood–poisoning**
an infection originating in a wound, in which the organisms breed in the blood.
[Greek *septikos* rotten + *haima* blood]

septic tank
a tank in which sewage is broken down by the action of bacteria.

septuagenarian
(*say* septewa–j'n–**airian**) *noun*
a person who is over 70 but less than 80 years old.
Word Family: **septuagenarian,** *adjective,* a) being 70 years old, b) being between 70 and 80 years old.
[Latin *septuageni* seventy each]

septum *noun*
plural is **septa**
Biology: a wall separating parts of a structure in an animal or plant.
[Latin, a fence]

sepulchre (*say* **seppul**–ka) *noun*
a tomb or burial vault.
Word Family: **sepulchral** (*say* se–**pul**–kr'l), *adjective,* a) of or for a tomb, b) (of a voice) deep and hollow.
[Latin *sepultus* buried]

sequel (*say* **seekwel**) *noun*
something that follows.
Usage: 'what was the *sequel* to your visit to your ex–boyfriend?' (= result, consequence).

sequence (*say* **see**–kw'nce) *noun*
a) the following of one thing after another. b) the order in which one or more things follow each other: 'we arranged the words in alphabetical *sequence*'.
Usage: 'a strange *sequence* of events led to my adventure' (= continuous or connected series).
Word Family: **sequential** (*say* see–**kwen**–sh'l), *adjective,* **sequentially,** *adverb.*
[Latin *sequens* following]

sequester (*say* se–**kwesta**) *verb*
1. to remove or withdraw into solitude or retirement.
2. *Law:* to hold or confiscate, etc. Also called to **sequestrate.**
Word Family: **sequestration,** *noun.*
[Latin, a trustee]

sequin (*say* **see**–kwin) *noun*
a small, coloured, shining disc, used to decorate clothes, etc.
[from Italian]

sequoia (*say* see–**koya**) *noun*
either of two species of very tall evergreen trees native to California, one of which is the redwood.
[named after an Amerindian chief]

seraglio (*say* ser-**rah**lio) *noun*
the part of a Moslem house in which the females live.
[Italian]

seraph (*say* **serr**af) *noun*
plural is **seraphs** or **seraphim** (*say* **serr**a-fim)
an angel of the highest rank.
seraphic *adjective*
angelic: 'a *seraphic* smile'.
[Hebrew]

sere *adjective*
dry or withered.

serenade (*say* serra-**nade**) *noun*
music of the kind originally sung or played beneath a loved one's window in the evening.
Word Family: **serenade**, *verb.*
[from Italian from Latin *serenus* cloudless + *serus* late]

serendipity (*say* serren-**dippi**-tee) *noun*
the faculty of making unexpected but desirable discoveries.
[after *The Three Princes of Serendip*, by Horace Walpole, 1754, whose heroes had this quality]

serene (*say* se-**reen**) *adjective*
calm and tranquil.
Word Family: **serenely**, *adverb*; **serenity** (*say* se-**renn**i-tee), *noun.*
[from Latin]

serf *noun*
1. *Medieval history:* a labourer forced to work on the land for a feudal lord.
2. (*informal*) a person who is treated like a slave.
Word Family: **serfdom**, *noun.*
[Latin *servus* a slave]

serge (*say* serj) *noun*
a very durable worsted or woollen fabric, used for clothing.

sergeant (*say* **sar**-j'nt) *noun*
1. a non-commissioned officer ranking above a corporal in the armed forces.
2. a police officer ranking between a constable and an inspector.
[Latin *servientis* of a servant]

serial (*say* **seer**i-ul) *noun*
1. a story which is presented in parts, e.g. week by week in a magazine or on television or radio.
2. a publication issued in successive numbered parts.
Word Family: **serial**, *adjective*, of or arranged in a series; **serially**, *adverb*; **serialize**, **serialise**, *verb*, to publish or broadcast in the form of a serial; **serialization**, *noun.*

sericulture (*say* **serr**i-kulcher) *noun*
the breeding of silkworms to produce silk.
[Latin *sericum* silk + CULTURE]

series (*say* **seer**-eez) *noun*
plural is **series**
1. any ordered arrangement of a number of related things, events, etc.
2. *Electricity:* an arrangement of conductors end to end, so that current flows through each in turn. Compare PARALLEL.
[Latin, a row, a chain]

serif *noun*
Printing: the curved or projecting ends on the main stroke of a letter, as those at the top and bottom of M.

serious (*say* **seer**i-us) *adjective*
1. thoughtful or solemn: 'her *serious* face told us something was wrong'.
2. important: 'this is a *serious* decision'.
3. critical: 'a *serious* illness'.
4. sincere or meaning what one says: 'stop teasing and be *serious* for once'.
Word Family: **seriously**, *adverb*; **seriousness**, *noun.*
[from Latin]

sermon *noun*
a speech on a religious or moral subject, especially one based on the Bible and spoken from a church pulpit.
Word Family: **sermonize**, **sermonise**, *verb*, to preach or lecture.
[Latin *sermonis* of a talk]

serpent *noun*
1. a snake.
2. *Music:* an old serpent-shaped wind instrument with a deep tone.
[Latin *serpere* to creep]

serpentine (*say* **ser**pen-tine) *adjective*
1. of or like a serpent.
2. twisting and turning like a snake: 'the *serpentine* meanderings of a river'.

serrated (*say* ser-**ay**tid) *adjective*
having a sharply notched or grooved edge, e.g. as a saw.
Word Family: **serrate**, *verb*, to make serrated; **serration**, *noun*, a) the act of serrating, b) a serrated notch or edge.
[from Latin]

serried *adjective*
an old word meaning pressed close together: 'the *serried* ranks of troops'.
[French *serré* closed]

serum (*say* **seer**um) *noun*
plural is **sera** or **serums**

1. *Biology:* the pale yellow, liquid part of blood, after the cells and the parts which cause clotting have been removed. Compare PLASMA.
2. this substance obtained from immunized animals and used for medical purposes as antiserum.
[Latin, whey]

servant *noun*
1. a person who works in the household of another, such as a maid.
2. a person employed by the government: 'a civil *servant*'.

serve *verb*
1. to perform work or duties for: a) 'I *served* the king for 40 years'; b) 'how long did you *serve* in the army?'.
Usages:
a) 'this box will *serve* as a table' (= act, suffice).
b) 'the bull *served* the cow' (= mated with).
2. to provide with or deal out goods, etc.: a) 'she *serves* in a milk bar'; b) 'may I *serve* dinner now?'.
Usage: 'I was *served* with a summons to appear in court' (= presented).
3. *Tennis:* to hit the ball into play with an overarm stroke from the back line.
Phrases:
serve right, 'your punishment *serves* you *right* for telling fibs' (= is just or deserved).
serve time, to spend time in prison.
serve *noun*
Tennis: a service.
[Latin *servus* a slave]

server *noun*
1. a) a person who serves. b) something used to serve food, etc., such as a special tray or a salad spoon.
2. *Tennis:* the player whose turn it is to serve.
3. *Christian:* see ACOLYTE.

service (*say* **servis**) *noun*
1. the act of helping or serving: a) 'I gave good *service* to the king'; b) 'does this shop give quick *service*?'.
2. the providing of some facility required by the public: 'a bus *service*'.
3. the act of checking and repairing equipment and machinery: 'my car needs a *service*'.
4. *Religion:* a) a meeting for worship. b) the form of such a meeting: 'the marriage *service*'.
5. a set of objects used for a special purpose: 'a *tea-service*'.
6. a government department or the people in it: 'the diplomatic *service*'.
7. (*plural*) a) the armed forces. b) activities in employment: 'they dispensed with his *services*'.
8. *Tennis:* the act of playing the delivery ball. Also called a **serve**.
Phrases:
at your service, 'I am always *at your service*' (= ready to help).
be of service, 'can I *be of service* to you?' (= be helpful).
service *verb*
1. to maintain or repair machinery, etc.
2. (of a male animal) to mate with.
service *adjective*
1. relating to servants or tradesmen: 'please use the *service* entrance'.
2. relating to the armed forces: '*service* uniforms'.

serviceable (*say* **servissa-b'l**) *adjective*
able to give good service, especially by being strong and durable: 'active children need *serviceable* clothes'.
Word Family: **serviceably**, *adverb*; **serviceability** (*say* servissa-**billi**-tee), **serviceableness**, *nouns*.

service charge
a percentage or a sum of money added to a bill to pay for service given.

service court
Tennis: a division of the court into which the ball must be hit by the server.

service hatch
see SERVING HATCH.

service line
see BASELINE.

serviceman *noun*
a member of the armed forces.
Word Family: **servicewoman**, *noun*.

service pipe
a pipe carrying water or gas to a building from an outside central system.

service road
a road parallel to a main road, used to provide access to buildings without interrupting the main traffic.

service station
also called a **petrol station**
a place where petrol, oil, etc. is sold, and where motor vehicles may be repaired.

serviette (*say* servi-**et**) *noun*
also called a **table napkin**
a piece of cloth or paper used at table to protect the clothes, wipe the lips, etc.
[Old French]

servile (*say* **ser**–vile) *adjective*
fawning: 'she paid no attention to his *servile* flattery'.
Word Family: **servilely,** *adverb*; **servility** (*say* ser–**villi**–tee), *noun.*

serving *noun*
a portion of food.

serving hatch
also called a **service hatch**
an opening in a wall through which food, etc. can be passed, often between a kitchen and dining room.

servitor (*say* **servi**–tor) *noun*
an old word for a servant or attendant.

servitude (*say* **servi**–tewd) *noun*
compulsory labour: 'penal *servitude* on Devil's Island'.
Usage: 'the peasants struggled for centuries under the *servitude* of greedy landowners' (= control).

servomechanism
(*say* servo–**mekka**–nizm) *noun*
short form is **servo**
a device to control speed, position, direction, voltage, etc. of a mechanism using electrical, hydraulic, etc. power governed by feedback to correct deviations. Applications include power-assisted steering, automatic pilots, etc.
Word Family: **servomechanical** (*say* servo–ma–**kanni**–k'l), *adjective*; **servomotor,** *noun,* a motor supplying power to a servomechanism.

sesame (*say* **sessa**–mee) *noun*
the seeds from a tropical plant, used in bread, sweets, cakes or as a spice. [Greek]

sessile *adjective*
Biology: a) of part of a plant without a stalk or a support. b) of animals which are permanently in one place, such as an oyster.
[Latin *sessilis* sitting down]

session (*say* **sesh**'n) *noun*
1. a) the meeting together of a court, group or organization. b) a period in the life of a parliament, from its opening to its prorogation, when it goes into recess.
2. any single meeting for a particular purpose: 'the orchestra has two practice *sessions* weekly'.
Word Family: **sessional,** *adjective.*

set *verb*
(set, setting)
1. to put: a) '*set* the eggs on the table'; b) '*set* a limit to your spending'; c) '*set* your mind at rest'.
Usages:
a) 'his behaviour *sets* a fine example' (= presents).
b) 'which books are *set* for study?' (= prescribed).
c) 'please *set* the table' (= put cutlery and crockery on).
d) '*set* the alarm before going to bed' (= adjust).
2. to become hard or firm: 'the ice-cream *set* quickly in the freezer'.
3. to give a fixed position or shape to: a) 'the gem was *set* in gold'; b) 'I washed and *set* my hair in curlers'.
4. to start: a) 'the book *set* me thinking'; b) 'his father *set* him up in business'.
5. (of the sun, moon, etc.) to sink below the horizon.
Phrases:
set in, 'the cold weather has *set in* early this year' (= begun).
set off, a) 'he *set off* for Canada' (= departed); b) 'the black jumper *sets off* your pearls' (= shows to advantage).
set on, set upon, a) 'the thugs *set on* the old man' (= suddenly attacked); b) 'he is *set on* being a doctor' (= determined on).
set out, a) 'she *set out* to become boss' (= aimed); b) '*set out* your request in writing' (= state).
set up, a) 'don't *set* yourself *up* as an expert' (= claim to be); b) (*informal*) 'the murderer *set up* his victim for the kill' (= trapped). *Word Family*: **set-up,** *noun,* an arrangement.

set *noun*
1. a number of things which together form a complete collection: 'a *set* of dinner plates'.
Usage: 'he's a member of the artistic *set*' (= group of people, clique).
2. the way in which something stands or is placed: 'the determined *set* of his jaw'.
3. an apparatus which receives radio signals, etc.: 'a television *set*'.
4. a) the scenery used to represent a particular place during a play or film. b) an area where filming takes place.
5. *Tennis:* a division of the match where one player has won at least 6 games and is 2 games ahead of his opponent.
6. *Maths:* a collection of distinct elements considered together as a single unit. A **subset** is a set of elements contained within another set which is called the **superset. Set theory** studies sets, their construction, algebra and interrelationships.

set *adjective*
fixed: a) 'a *set* smile'; b) 'meet me at a *set* time'; c) 'have you read the *set* texts?'.

setback *noun*
a reverse or check to progress: 'farming suffered a *setback* during the drought'.

set square
a flat instrument in the shape of a right-angled triangle, used for architectural drawing, etc.

settee *noun*
a sofa.

setter *noun*
any of various large, long-haired gun-dogs, which stand rigid when scenting game.

setting *noun*
1. that in which something is set: a) 'the diamond was in a gold *setting*'; b) 'the play's *setting* was ancient Rome'.
Usage: 'the lake is a wonderful *setting* for a restaurant' (= environment).
2. the arrangement of cutlery, mats, glasses, etc. on a table, especially for one person.

settle *verb*
1. to agree 'we finally *settled* on where to spend our holiday'.
Usage: 'who'll *settle* the bill?' (= pay).
2. to go and live in a new place: 'colonists *settled* on the coast of the new continent'.
3. a) to sink down or rest: 'the mud *settled* on the river bottom'. b) to cause this to happen: 'this drink will *settle* your stomach'.
Usage: 'are you *settling* into your new job quickly?' (= adapting).
4. to bestow property on someone by gift or legal deed, especially on a wife at marriage.
Word Family: **settled**, *adjective*, fixed or unchanging.

settlement *noun*
1. the act of settling: a) '*settlement* of the argument took months'; b) '*settlement* of the new continent was rapid'.
Usage: 'please find enclosed the full *settlement*' (= payment).
2. a small collection of houses, etc., especially in a new or sparsely populated area.

settler *noun*
a person who settles, especially in a new country or area.

seven *adjective*
a cardinal number, the symbol 7 in Arabic numerals, VII in Roman numerals.
Word Family: **seven**, *adjective*; **seventh**, *noun*, *adjective*.

seventeen *noun*
a cardinal number, the symbol 17 in Arabic numerals, XVII in Roman numerals.
Word Family: **seventeen**, *adjective*; **seventeenth**, *noun*, *adjective*.

seventy *noun*
1. a cardinal number, the symbol 70 in Arabic numerals, LXX in Roman numerals.
2. (*plural*) the numbers 70–79 in a series, such as the years in a century.
Word Family: **seventy**, *adjective*; **seventieth**, *noun*, *adjective*.

sever (*say* **sevva**) *verb*
to cut as though by a sharp blow.
Usage: 'he *severed* all ties with his ex-girlfriend' (= broke off).
severance *noun*
the act of severing, dividing or breaking off: 'a *severance* of diplomatic relations'.
[Latin *separare*]

several *adjective*
more than two or three, but not a great number.
Usage: 'after the conference, the speakers returned to their *several* countries' (= individual, respective).
Word Family: **several**, *pronoun*, some or a few; **severally**, *adverb*, respectively or individually.

severance pay
the money paid to an employee by his employer to compensate for the loss of his job.

severe (*say* se-**veer**) *adjective*
stern or strict: 'don't be too *severe* with the child'.
Usage: 'is the illness *severe*?' (= serious).
severity (*say* se-**verri**-tee) *noun*
sternness: 'the *severity* of the long winter'.
Word Family: **severely**, *adverb*.
[from Latin]

sew (*say* so) *verb*
(**sewed, sewn** or **sewed, sewing**)
to join, mend, decorate or make with a needle and thread, either by hand or machine.
Word Family: **sewing**, *noun*, any work being sewn.

sewage (*say* **soo**–ij) *noun*
waste matter carried in sewers.
sewage farm
a place where sewage is made harmless by absorbing it over a large area of land.

sewer (1) (*say* **soo**–a) *noun*
a pipe, usually underground, for carrying human waste, etc. from buildings.
sewerage (*say* **soo**–a–rij) *noun*
a) the removal of waste matter by sewers. b) a system of sewers.

sewer (2) (*say* **so**–a) *noun*
a person who sews.

sewer gas (*say* **soo**–a gas)
a gas, mainly methane and carbon dioxide, produced during the breakdown of sewage.

sewn (*say* sone) *verb*
a past participle of the verb **sew**.

sex *noun*
a) the character of being male or female. b) the differences between males and females.
Usage: 'the film is full of *sex*' (= sexual activity).
Word Family: **sex**, *verb*, to ascertain the sex of; **sexed**, *adjective*, having a certain degree of sexuality; **sexless**, *adjective*, a) neither male nor female, b) (informal) having no sex appeal.
[Latin *secus* a division]

sex chromosome
a chromosome which carries sex–determining factors. In humans the **X chromosome** carries female factors and the **Y chromosome** carries male factors. Males have one X and one Y chromosome, and females have two X chromosomes.

sexist *noun*
a person who discriminates against another because of his or her sex.
Word Family: **sexism**, *noun*.

sextant *noun*
an instrument for measuring the angle of altitude of planets and stars, used in determining latitude and longitude.
[Latin *sextantis* of the sixth part (as it has an arc of 60°)]

sextet *noun*
1. a) a group of six musicians. b) a musical composition for six musicians or instruments. Also called a **sestet**.
2. any group of six people or things.

sexton *noun*
Christian: an official in charge of a church building and its contents.

sextuplet (*say* seks–**choop**–lit) *noun*
any of six offspring born at one birth.

sexual (*say* **seks**–yew'l) *adjective*
1. of or relating to sex or the sexes.
2. suggesting or involving sex.
sexuality (*say* seks–yoo–**alli**–tee) *noun*
1. the fact of belonging to a particular sex.
2. the fact of being sexy.
Word Family: **sexually**, *adverb*.

sexual intercourse
the inserting of the male's erect penis into the female's vagina, followed by ejaculation.

sexy *adjective*
sexually attractive or exciting.
Word Family: **sexily**, *adverb*; **sexiness**, *noun*.

sforzando (*say* sfort–**san**do) *adjective, adverb*
Music: playing a note or chord loudly and with special emphasis.
[Italian]

shabby *adjective*
in a poor, used or worn–out condition: 'a *shabby* old coat'.
Usage: 'your treatment of her was rather *shabby*' (= mean, contemptible).

shack *noun*
also called a **shanty**
a small hut or house, usually roughly built or in poor condition.
shack *verb*
shack up, (*informal*) 'come and *shack up* at my house' (= stay, live).

shackle *noun*
an iron ring to lock around a person's wrist or ankle.
Usage: 'I am bound by the *shackles* of politeness' (= restraints).
Word Family: **shackle**, *verb*.

shaddock *noun*
the large, yellow, thick–skinned, edible fruit of a Polynesian citrus tree.

shade *noun*
1. the comparative darkness and coolness caused by cutting off the sun's rays: 'the *shade* of a tree'.
Usage: 'her brilliant wit put me in the *shade*' (= state of insignificance).
2. a hue, usually one made by mixing a colour with black to reduce its chroma. Compare TINT.
Usage: 'there is only a *shade* of difference between their ages' (= slight amount).
3. a) anything, such as a window blind, used for protection against light, heat, etc. b) a lampshade.

4. a ghost or spirit of the dead.

shade *verb*

1. to protect or cover from direct light or heat.

2. to draw or paint light and dark sections in a sketch, etc.

shading *noun*

Art: the lines, etc. in a drawing or painting which indicate the degree of darkness or light.

shadow *noun*

1. a) a dark shape or image of something, cast on a surface when the light is intercepted. b) any dark area: '*shadows* under the eyes'.

Usages:

a) 'poor countries live in the *shadow* of starvation' (= constant fear).

b) 'he is only a *shadow* of his former self' (= faintly similar image).

c) 'not a *shadow* of a doubt' (= trace).

2. (*informal*) a person who follows another closely.

shadow *verb*

1. to cast shade or shadow.

2. (*informal*) to follow a person closely.

shadow *adjective*

imitating the actions, organization, etc. of something: 'the Opposition's *shadow* Cabinet is ready to take office if the Government resigns'.

Word Family: **shadowy,** *adjective,* a) having or casting a shadow, b) faint or vague.

shadow-boxing *noun*

the act of boxing with an imaginary opponent, for practice, exercise, etc.

shady (*say* **shay**-dee) *adjective*

1. having or giving shade.

2. (*informal*) of doubtful honesty or character: 'a *shady* business deal'.

Word Family: **shadily,** *adverb*; **shadiness,** *noun.*

shaft (*say* shahft) *noun*

1. a) the long slender stem of a tool or weapon, as of an arrow or axe. b) something resembling this in shape, such as the length of a column or a ray of sunlight.

2. a well-like passage or enclosed space: a) 'a mine *shaft*'; b) 'a lift *shaft*'.

shag (1) *noun*

1. a) a mass of rough, matted hair, wool, etc. b) a fabric with long woollen pile on one side.

2. a coarse-cut tobacco.

shaggy *adjective*

roughly matted or unkempt.

Word Family: **shagginess,** *noun.*

shag (2) *noun*

see CORMORANT.

shaggy dog story

a long, complicated and amusing but pointless joke or story.

shagreen (*say* sha-**green**) *noun*

a rough, untanned leather made from the skin of a horse, shark or seal and usually dyed green.

shah *noun*

a title for the King of Iran. [Persian]

shake *verb*

(**shook, shaken, shaking**)

1. to move from side to side or to and fro with short, sharp, quick movements: a) 'take the carpet outside and *shake* it'; b) '*shake* the bottle before using'; c) 'the whole house *shook* in the gale'.

Usage: 'the bad news *shook* me' (= affected violently).

2. to waver or tremble: 'her voice *shook* with emotion'.

Phrases:

shake off, to get rid of or escape.

shake up, 'we must *shake up* things in this office' (= liven up).

shake *noun*

1. a shaking movement: 'give the bottle a good *shake*'.

2. a drink made by shaking the ingredients together: 'a milk *shake*'.

Phrases:

no great shakes, (*informal*) not very good.

two shakes, (*informal*) a moment.

shako (*say* **shay**-ko) *noun*

a cylindrical hat with a peak at the front and a plume, worn by soldiers. [Hungarian, peaked]

shaky (*say* **shay**-kee) *adjective*

unsteady or unsafe.

Word Family. **shakily,** *adverb*; **shakiness,** *noun.*

shale *noun*

Geology: a soft, slate-like rock formed of compacted layers of mud and clay.

shall *verb*

(**should**; *old forms*: **shalt, shouldst** or **shouldest**)

an auxiliary verb indicating the future tense: 'I *shall* go there tomorrow'.

shallot (*say* sha-**lot**) *noun*

a small, onion-like bulb which divides into smaller sections and is used as a vegetable, etc.

shallow (*say* **shall**o) *adjective*
of little depth: a) '*shallow* water'; b) '*shallow* arguments'.
shallow *noun*
(*usually plural*) a shallow part of a body of water.
Word Family: **shallowly**, *adverb*; **shallowness**, *noun.*

sham *noun*
a pretence: 'his illness was only a *sham*'.
Word Family: **sham** (**shammed**, **shamming**), *verb*, to pretend.

shaman (*say* **shah**man) *noun*
a medicine man and priest who works with the supernatural.
[Russian]

shamble *verb*
to shuffle or walk clumsily.
Word Family: **shamble**, *noun*, a shambling walk.

shambles *plural noun*
(*used with singular verb*) a state of confused muddle or disorder.
[originally a slaughter-house]

shame *noun*
pain or embarrassment caused by dishonourable or foolish behaviour: 'I blushed with *shame* after telling such a lie'.
Usages:
a) 'have you no *shame*?' (= modesty).
b) 'what a *shame*!' (= pity).
put to shame, 'her skill at maths *puts* me *to shame*' (= disgraces).
shame *verb*
a) to disgrace or make ashamed. b) to force or compel through shame: 'my actions *shamed* me into apologizing'.
Word Family: **shamefaced**, *adjective*, showing shame; **shamefacedly**, *adverb*; **shameful**, *adjective*, causing or bringing shame or disgrace; **shamefully**, *adverb*; **shamefulness**, *noun*; **shameless**, *adjective*, immodest or lacking in shame; **shamelessly**, *adverb*; **shamelessness**, *noun.*

shammy *noun*
see CHAMOIS.

shampoo *noun*
a) a soap or detergent, especially used for washing hair or carpets. b) a wash using such a soap.
Word Family: **shampoo** (**shampooed**, **shampooing**), *verb.*
[Hindi]

shamrock *noun*
a small clover-like plant with three leaves on each stem, the national emblem of Ireland.
[Irish, little clover]

shandy *noun*
a drink made by mixing beer with lemonade or ginger beer.

shanghai (*say* **shang**-high) *verb*
to force a person to join a ship's crew by means of alcohol, drugs or violence.
[after *Shanghai*, China]

Shangri-La (*say* shangri-**la**) *noun*
a paradise on earth.
[after a hidden paradise in 'Lost Horizon' by James Hilton]

shank *noun*
1. a) the part of the leg between the knee and the ankle. b) a cut of meat from the lower leg of an animal.
2. the main straight part of an anchor, key, spoon, etc.

shanks's pony
(*informal*) on foot.

shantung *noun*
a fabric with a rough surface, woven from coarse silk.
[after *Shantung*, a province in China]

shanty (1) *noun*
a shack.

shanty (2) *noun*
a sailor's song with a strong rhythm.
[French *chanter* to sing]

shape *noun*
an external line or outline: 'that cloud has the *shape* of a camel'.
Usage: 'the garden is in poor *shape*' (= condition).
take shape, 'our plans slowly *took shape*' (= took on definite form, developed).
shape *verb*
to make or fashion: 'he *shaped* the wood into a broom-handle'.
shape up, 'the new recruits are *shaping up* well' (= developing).
Word Family: **shapeless**, *adjective*, having no regular or definite shape; **shapelessly**, *adverb*; **shapelessness**, *noun*; **shapely**, *adjective*, having a pleasing or attractive shape; **shapeliness**, *noun.*

shard *noun*
also called a **sherd**
a fragment, especially of broken pottery.

share (1) (*rhymes with* air) *noun*
1. a part divided out: 'each will have to do his *share* of the work'.

2. *Commerce:* a part of the capital of a company, returning to the holder a proportion of the profits.
share *verb*
to give or receive a part of something: '*share* these sweets with your friends'.

share (2) (*rhymes with* air) *noun*
a ploughshare.

share farmer
in America called a **sharecropper**
a farmer who pays a share of the crop as rent.

shareholder *noun*
in America called a **stockholder**
a person who owns shares in a company.

shark *noun*
1. any of a group of large, powerful, often dangerous, cartilaginous marine fish, the most primitive jaw-bearing vertebrates.
2. a cheat or swindler.

sharp *adjective*
1. having a fine cutting or piercing edge or point: a) 'a *sharp* sword'; b) 'a *sharp* pencil'.
Usages:
a) 'that corner is too *sharp*' (= abrupt).
b) 'I now saw the *sharp* outline' (= distinct).
c) 'his retort was *sharp*' (= harsh, biting).
d) 'keep a *sharp* lookout' (= alert).
e) 'I call that *sharp* practice' (= dishonest).
2. *Music:* being raised in pitch by a semitone. Compare FLAT (1).
sharp *adverb*
suddenly: 'the horse pulled up *sharp*'.
Usage: 'come at noon *sharp*' (= punctually).
look sharp, be quick!
sharp *noun*
1. *Music:* a) a sharp note. b) the symbol indicating this.
2. (*informal*) a cheat: 'a *cardsharp*'.
Word Family: **sharply**, *adverb*; **sharpness**, *noun*.

sharpen *verb*
to make or become sharp or sharper.
Word Family: **sharpener**, *noun*, a person or thing that sharpens, such as a device for sharpening pencils.

sharper *noun*
a swindler or trickster.

sharpshooter *noun*
a person skilled at shooting.

sharp-sighted *adjective*
1. having keen eyesight.
2. mentally alert.

sharp-tongued *adjective*
speaking harshly or bitterly.

sharp-witted *adjective*
being mentally quick or alert.

shaslick (*say* **shazlik**) *noun*
see SHISH KEBAB.

shatter *verb*
to break violently into fragments: 'the bullet *shattered* the glass'.
Usage: 'I'm *shattered* to hear the terrible news' (= extremely distressed).

shave *verb*
(**shaved**, **shaved** or **shaven**, **shaving**)
1. to remove hair from the face, legs, etc. with a razor.
2. to remove in layers or thin slices: 'to *shave* wood'.
Usage: 'the car *shaved* the fence' (= scraped).
shave *noun*
the act of shaving, especially of the face.
Usage: 'that was a close *shave*' (= narrow escape).
Word Family: **shavings**, *plural noun*, thin slices of wood, etc. shaved off.

shaver *noun*
1. an electric razor.
2. (*informal*) a youngster.

shawl *noun*
a large, often thick, scarf, especially one worn around the shoulders.

she *pronoun*
plural is **they**
1. the third person singular nominative pronoun, used to indicate a female: '*she* ate the cake'.
2. (used traditionally of certain objects and institutions, such as ships and nations) 'the ship looked splendid as *she* sailed into the bay'.
3. (used as a noun) 'is the cat a *she*?'.
4. (used in combination to indicate a female) 'a *she-goat*'.
See HER, HERS and HE.

sheaf *noun*
plural is **sheaves**
1. a small bundle of cut cereal plants.
2. any small bundle: 'a *sheaf* of papers'.

shear *verb*
(**sheared**, **shorn**, **shearing**)
1. to cut the wool or hair off: 'to *shear* sheep'.
Usage: 'the king was *shorn* of his powers' (= stripped).

2. (of metals, etc.) to crack or break off through strain or fatigue.
Word Family: **shearer,** *noun,* a person who shears, especially one who shears sheep.

shears *plural noun*
a pair of large scissors with long, heavy blades.

shearwater *noun*
any of various kinds of ocean birds which skim the waves on long, narrow, stiff wings and visit land only to breed.

sheath (*say* sheeth) *noun*
1. a case for the blade of a knife, etc.
2. any closely fitting covering on part of an animal or plant.

sheathe (*say* shee*th*) *verb*
1. to replace a knife, etc. in its sheath.
2. to cover with a protective layer: 'to *sheathe* a roof with copper'.
Word Family: **sheathing,** *noun,* a protective cover or sheath.

sheath-knife *noun*
a knife having a fixed blade fitting into a sheath.

sheave *verb*
to gather or bind into a sheaf or sheaves.

sheaves *plural noun*
see SHEAF.

shed (1) *noun*
a simple building for storage, etc.

shed (2) *verb*
(**shed, shedding**)
to lose or let fall: 'the cattle had *shed* their winter coats'.
shed blood, to injure or kill.

sheen *noun*
a shining or glossy brightness.
Word Family: **sheeny,** *adjective,* shiny.

sheep *noun*
plural is **sheep**
1. any of various wild or domesticated grass-eating mammals, valued for their wool and flesh.
2. a meek or timid person.

sheep dip
a solution in which sheep are immersed to destroy bacteria, parasites, etc.

sheep-dog *noun*
any of various breeds of dog trained to guard and control sheep.

sheepish *adjective*
embarrassed or timid.
Word Family: **sheepishly,** *adverb*; **sheepishness,** *noun.*

sheepshank *noun*
a knot used to shorten a piece of rope.

sheer (1) *adjective*
1. fine and transparent: '*sheer* silk'.
2. pure or absolute: 'she laughed for *sheer* joy'.
3. steep: '*sheer* cliffs'.
Word Family: **sheer, sheerly,** *adverbs*; **sheerness,** *noun.*

sheer (2) *verb*
to swerve or turn aside.

sheet (1) *noun*
1. a large rectangle of cloth, usually cotton or linen, used in pairs on a bed, one to cover the mattress and the other to cover the person in bed.
2. any thin piece or mass: 'a *sheet* of paper'.
Usage: 'a *sheet* of flame swept across the field' (= broad expanse).
Word Family: **sheet,** *verb,* to provide or cover with a sheet or sheets; **sheeting,** *noun,* any material used to make sheets.

sheet (2) *noun*
Sailing: a rope used to adjust and control a sail.
Word Family: **sheet,** *verb,* to secure or extend by means of a sheet or sheets.

sheet anchor
1. *Nautical:* a large anchor used in an emergency.
2. a dependable person or resource.

sheet bend
a knot used to join one piece of rope to another.

sheet lightning
the diffused light from a flash within a cloud, or the reflection of a distant flash.

sheikh (*say* shake *or* sheek) **sheik** *noun*
a Moslem chief or leader.
Word Family: **sheikhdom,** *noun,* a country or state ruled by a sheikh.
[Arabic *shaikh* old man]

sheila (*say* **shee**la) *noun*
Australian: (informal) a girl or woman.

shekels *plural noun*
(*informal*) money.
[from *shekel,* an ancient Babylonian coin]

shelf *noun*
plural is **shelves**
1. a piece of wood, etc. fixed to a wall or as part of a cupboard, for supporting objects.
2. a ledge on a cliff face.
3. a continental shelf.

on the shelf, a) not in use; b) not married or likely to be married.

shell *noun*
1. the hard covering or case of some animals, such as mussels, snails, etc.
2. any outer covering, usually hard: 'an *eggshell*'.
Usages:
a) 'only the *shell* of the house remained after the fire' (= framework).
b) 'it was difficult to penetrate her *shell*' (= reserve, shyness).
3. a) any of various projectiles containing an explosive charge and designed to explode in the air or upon impact. b) a cartridge.
4. *Science:* a class of electron orbits in an atom, all of which have the same energy.
5. *Rowing:* a light, narrow racing boat with a smooth hull.
shell *verb*
1. to remove the shell of: '*shell* these peas'.
2. to fire shells or explosives at.

shellac (*say* sha-**lak**) *noun*
a yellowish resin produced by an insect of India and Thailand, used as a varnish and for electrical insulation.
Word Family: **shellac** (**shellacked, shellacking**), *verb*, to coat with shellac.

shellfire *noun*
the firing of shells or explosives.

shellfish *noun*
an aquatic animal, such as an oyster, with a shell or hard, outer covering.

shellproof *adjective*
able to survive the effects of explosive shells.

shell shock see COMBAT FATIGUE.

shelter *noun*
a place or structure which provides protection, covering or safety.
Word Family: **shelter**, *verb*, to find or provide with a shelter.

shelve (1) *verb*
a) to place on a shelf or shelves. b) to provide with a shelf or shelves.
Usage: 'the plans were *shelved* for another year' (= put aside, postponed).

shelve (2) *verb* to slope gradually.

shelves *plural noun* see SHELF.

shemozzle (*say* she-**mozz'l**) *noun*
(*informal*) a state of disturbance or confusion. [Yiddish]

shenanigan (*say* she-nanni-gan) *noun*
(*usually plural*) trickery or nonsense.

shepherd (*say* **shepperd**) *noun*
1. a person who guards or herds sheep.
2. a person who protects or cares for a group.
shepherd *verb*
to protect, guard or watch over.
Word Family: **shepherdess**, *noun*, a female shepherd.

shepherd's pie
also called **cottage pie**
a dish of minced meat covered with a layer of mashed potato and baked.

sherbet *noun*
a sweet, fizzy powder used in drinks and sweets.
[Arabic *sharab* a drink]

sherd *noun*
see SHARD.

sheriff (*say* **sherrif**) *noun*
1. *American:* an officer appointed to enforce the law in a county.
2. an honorary official appointed by the Crown to carry out judicial and electoral functions, which vary in different parts of the country.
[from SHIRE + REEVE]

sherry *noun*
a) a sweet or dry fortified Spanish wine. b) similar wine made elsewhere.
[*Xeres* (now Jerez) in Spain]

Shetland pony
any of a breed of very small, strong ponies.
[originally from the *Shetland Islands*]

shibboleth (*say* **shibba**-leth) *noun*
a catchphrase, tenet or social trick arbitrarily selected as a test of loyalty to a political party, conformity to a social group, etc.
[in the Bible the Ephraimites gave themselves away by not being able to pronounce the word *shibboleth*]

shied (*say* shide) *verb*
the past tense and past participle of the verb **shy (1)** and **shy (2)**.

shield (*say* sheeld) *noun*
1. any of various types of defensive armour carried in the hand or on the arm.
2. something used to protect, hide or defend: 'he wanted a *shield* against poverty in old age'.
Word Family: **shield**, *verb*, to protect or hide; **shielder**, *noun*.

shift *verb*
to move from one place or position to another: '*shift* the logs into the yard'.
shift *noun*
1. a movement or change to another place, position, etc.
2. a) a period of working time,

especially in a factory, etc. b) the employees who work during this time.
3. a simple dress, usually sleeveless.

shift key
a typewriter lever which adjusts the machine to type capital letters.

shiftless *adjective*
lazy, inefficient or lacking purpose.
Word Family: **shiftlessly**, *adverb*; **shiftlessness**, *noun*.

shifty *adjective*
sly or furtive.
Word Family: **shiftily**, *adverb*; **shiftiness**, *noun*.

shillelagh (*say* shillay-lee) **shillelah** *noun*
an Irish cudgel made of blackthorn or oak.
[after *Shillelagh*, County Wicklow]

shilling *noun*
see POUND (2).

shillyshally *verb*
(shillyshallied, shillyshallying)
to hesitate or remain undecided.
[from older *shill I? shall I?*]

shim *noun*
a thin strip of metal, plastic, etc., placed between two close surfaces to fill a gap.
Word Family: **shim (shimmed, shimming)**, *verb*, to insert a shim or shims.

shimmer *verb*
to shine with a faintly flickering light.
Word Family: **shimmer**, *noun*, a faint, flickering light.

shin *noun*
1. *Anatomy:* the front of the leg between the knee and the ankle.
2. a cut of beef containing the lower front leg of the animal.
Word Family: **shin (shinned, shinning)**, *verb*, to climb by gripping with the arms and legs.

shindig *noun*
(*informal*) a party, especially a noisy one.

shindy *noun*
(*informal*) a brawl or noise.

shine *verb*
(shone or **shined, shining)**
1. to give out light or brightness.
Usages:
a) 'I must *shine* my shoes' (= clean).
b) 'he *shines* in all his subjects' (= is excellent or outstanding).
2. to aim or point the light of: '*shine* that torch over here'.

shine *noun*
1. light or brightness.
2. the act of cleaning: 'give those forks a *shine*'.
Usage: 'come rain or *shine*' (= fair weather).
take a shine to, to like or fancy immediately.
Word Family: **shiny**, *adjective*, bright or glossy.

shiner *noun* (*informal*) a black eye.

shingle (1) *noun*
1. a thin oblong piece of wood used in overlapping rows to form a roof or as wall cladding.
2. a tapered haircut.
Word Family: **shingle**, *verb*.

shingle (2) *noun*
large and small rounded stones, especially on a beach.
Word Family: **shingly**, *adjective*.

shingles *plural noun*
(*used with singular verb*) a viral infection of the nerves causing severe pain and a rash of blisters, often around the waist.
[Latin *cingulum* a girdle]

shinty *noun*
Scottish Highlands: a simplified version of hockey.

shiny (*say* **shie**-nee) *adjective*
Word Family: see SHINE.

ship *noun*
1. a large sea-going vessel, other than a coastal trader.
2. a warship, other than a submarine.
3. *History:* a square-rigged sailing vessel with more than two masts.
Compare SCHOONER.
when one's ship comes in, when one has become rich.

ship *verb*
(shipped, shipping)
to send or transport by ship, rail, etc.
Usage: (*informal*) 'he was *shipped* off to school at an early age' (= sent).
Word Family: **shipping**, *noun*, a) the act or business of sending goods by sea, b) any or all ships.

-ship
a suffix of nouns indicating condition, office, skill, etc., as in *friendship*.

shipboard *noun*
on shipboard, aboard ship.

shipment *noun*
a) the shipping of goods. b) the goods shipped.

ship's articles
the conditions of employment under which seamen agree to work on a ship.

shipshape *adjective*
neatly arranged or in order.

shipwreck (*say* **ship**–rek) *noun*
a) the destruction of a ship, as by a storm, etc. b) the wrecked remains of a ship.
Usage: 'she saw the disaster as the *shipwreck* of her hopes' (= ruin, failure).
Word Family: **shipwreck**, *verb.*

shipyard *noun*
an area where ships are built or repaired.

shire *noun*
see COUNTY.

shire horse
a large and powerful draught horse. [bred in the Shires, that is the Midlands]

shirk *verb*
to avoid or put off, especially work, duty, etc.
Word Family: **shirker**, **shirk**, *nouns*, a person who shirks work, etc.
[German *Schurke* scoundrel or parasite]

shirr (*say* sher) *verb*
to gather fabric into parallel folds by stitching or elastic.
Word Family: **shirring**, **shirr**, *nouns*, an arrangement of shirred folds.

shirt (*rhymes with* hurt) *noun*
a light piece of clothing, usually reaching to the waist, having sleeves, a collar and fastened down the front.
Usage: 'he bet his *shirt* on the favourite for the race' (= total supply of money).
keep one's shirt on, to refrain from being angry or impatient.

shirty *adjective*
(*informal*) annoyed or irritated.

shish kebab (*say* **shish** ka–bab)
short form is **kebab**
also called a **shaslick**
small pieces of seasoned meat grilled on a skewer, usually with vegetables. [Turkish *sis* skewer + *kebap* roast meat]

shit *noun*
1. (*informal*) faeces.
2. (*informal*) an unprincipled person.
3 (*informal*) nonsense.
Word Family: **shit**, *verb*, to defecate; **shit!**, *interjection*; **shitty**, *adjective.*

shiver (1) (*say* **shivva**) *verb*
to shake or tremble, as from cold, fear, etc.
Word Family: **shiver**, *noun*; **shivery**, *adjective*, shaking or trembling.

shiver (2) (*say* **shivva**) *noun*
a sliver or fragment.

shoal (1) *noun*
a sandbank on the bed of the sea, a river, etc. creating an area of shallow water.
Word Family: **shoal**, *verb*, to make or become shallow.

shoal (2) *noun*
a) a group of fish. b) any large group of people or things.

shock (1) *noun*
1. a sudden, violent impact or disturbance.
2. *Medicine:* a sudden nervous collapse caused by severe physical injury or emotional disturbance.
3. something which causes a mental or physical disturbance: 'his death was a great *shock* to us all'.
shock *verb*
to strike or affect with great surprise, horror or disgust: 'the news *shocked* the world'.
Word Family: **shocking**, *adjective*, a) causing horror or disgust, b) (informal) very bad.

shock (2) *noun*
a thick, bushy mass: 'a *shock* of red hair'.

shock absorber
any of a variety of devices used to absorb impacts, especially those used on a motor vehicle to prevent excessive movement of the suspension.

shocker *noun*
(*informal*) something which is shocking, unpleasant or disagreeable.

shockproof *adjective*
able to survive damage caused by shocks.

shock treatment
also called **shock therapy**
a method of treating certain mental disorders, by giving shocks to the brain with electricity.

shock troops
any troops trained to begin an assault.

shockwave *noun*
Physics: a very narrow region of high pressure and temperature caused by an explosion or by a body moving faster than the speed of sound.

shoddy *adjective*
badly or cheaply made: 'a *shoddy* imitation gold bracelet'.
Word Family: **shoddily**, *adverb*; **shoddiness**, *noun.*

shoe (*say* shoo) *noun*
1. any of various strong coverings for the foot, usually of leather and reaching to the ankle.
2. something which has the shape, position or function of a shoe: 'a *horseshoe*'.
3. *Building:* a metal holder which supports the end of a beam or joist.
4. *Engineering:* the part of a brake that is pressed against a wheel or drum to produce the friction necessary for braking.
in someone's shoes, 'I'm glad I'm not *in your shoes*' (= in the position you are in).
Word Family: **shoe (shod, shoeing),** *verb,* a) to provide or fit with shoes, b) to cover or protect with a wooden or metal guard.

shoehorn *noun*
a spoon-shaped piece of horn or metal used to help ease on a shoe.

shoestring *noun*
on a shoestring, with a small or inadequate sum of money.
Word Family: **shoestring,** *adjective.*

shoetree *noun*
an implement inserted into shoes to help them keep their shape or stretch them.

shone (*say* shon) *verb*
a past tense and past participle of the verb **shine.**

shoo *interjection*
go away!
Word Family: **shoo (shooed, shooing),** *verb.*

shook (*rhymes with* book) *verb*
the past tense of the verb **shake.**

shoot (*rhymes with* boot) *verb*
(shot, shooting)
1. to fire or discharge a missile from a weapon.
2. to wound or kill with a bullet from a weapon: 'police *shot* the hijacker'.
Usages:
a) 'he *shot* out his leg to trip her' (= moved or sent quickly).
b) 'make sure that you *shoot* the bolt back' (= slide).
c) 'the player *shot* towards the goal area' (= aimed or sent the ball).
d) 'the model's dress was *shot* with gold' (= marked, streaked).
3. to photograph or film.
4. (of plants) to put out new growths, such as buds.
Phrases:
shoot off one's mouth, (*informal*) to talk wildly or indiscreetly.
shoot up, 'you have really *shot up* since I last saw you' (= grown quickly).
shoot *noun*
1. an act of shooting.
2. an outing or contest for shooting: 'a duck *shoot*'.
3. a new or young growth on a plant.
Word Family: **shooter,** *noun,* a thing that shoots; **shooting,** *noun,* an incident involving the firing of bullets.

shooting box
a lodge used by sportsmen during the shooting season.

shooting gallery
an enclosed or indoor area with targets, used for shooting practice, competitions, etc.

shooting star
see METEOR.

shooting stick
a walking stick with a small, folding seat at one end, used by people watching sports.

shop *noun*
1. a place where goods are sold.
2. a place where work is carried out: 'a *workshop*'.
Phrases:
set up shop, to establish a business or similar activity.
talk shop, to talk about one's business or work.
shop *verb*
(shopped, shopping)
1. to visit shops in order to inspect or buy.
2. (*informal*) a) to inform on. b) to put in prison.
Usage: 'they say he is *shopping* around for a wife' (= looking, searching).
Word Family: **shopper,** *noun,* a person who shops; **shopping,** *noun,* a) the act of buying at shops, b) the goods bought.

shop floor
1. workers, especially factory workers.
2. the part of a factory where machines, workers, etc. are situated.

shopkeeper *noun*
a person who owns or manages a shop.

shoplifter *noun*
a person who steals goods from a shop.
Word Family: **shoplift,** *verb;* **shoplifting,** *noun.*

shopsoiled *adjective*
also called **shopworn**

dirtied or damaged due to being displayed or handled in a shop.

shop steward
a trade union official appointed to represent the workers in a particular factory or place of work.

shopwalker *noun*
a person employed in a department store to direct customers, detect shoplifters, etc.

shore (1) *noun*
the area along the edge of a sea, lake, river, etc.
Word Family: **shore**, *adjective*, of or situated on land.

shore (2) *noun*
a wooden support, usually for a wall, with one end fixed to the ground and the top fixed to the wall.
Word Family: **shore**, *verb*, to prop up or support.

shoreline *noun*
the line at which the sea meets land.

shorn *verb*
the past participle of the verb **shear**.

short *adjective*
not long or tall: a) 'a *short* distance'; b) 'a *short* man'.
Usages:
a) 'rations are in *short* supply' (= scanty, low in amount).
b) 'do not be so *short* with your mother' (= rudely abrupt).
Phrases:
make short work of, to finish, etc. quickly.
nothing short of, 'the decision was *nothing short of* madness' (= real, absolute).
short back and sides, a conservative short hairstyle.
short for, 'TV is *short for* television' (= a shorter form of).
short *adverb*
1. abruptly or suddenly: 'the horse stopped *short*'.
2. before reaching: 'the bombs fell *short* of the mark'.
Phrases:
cut short, 'the chairman *cut short* the meeting' (= ended abruptly).
short of, 'I am *short of* money this month' (= lacking in).
short *noun*
1. something which is short, such as a short film shown before the feature film at a cinema.
2. (*plural*) a pair of short trousers usually reaching to somewhere between the thigh and the knee.
3. *Electricity:* a short circuit.
in short, '*in short*, this is my suggestion' (= briefly).
Word Family: **short**, *verb*, to short-circuit; **shortly**, *adverb*, a) soon, b) briefly or abruptly; **shortness**, *noun*.

shortage (*say* **short**ij) *noun*
an insufficient amount.

shortbread (*say* **short**-bred) *noun*
a thick, crumbly biscuit made with flour, sugar and butter.

short-change *verb*
(*informal*) a) to give less change than is due. b) to cheat or deceive.

short circuit
Electricity: a fault in an electric circuit, in which two points of different voltage become connected, causing the current to flow directly between them rather than through the complete circuit.
Word Family: **short-circuit**, *verb*.

shortcoming (*say* **short**-kumming) *noun*
a flaw or weakness: 'the plan has some obvious *shortcomings* which must be corrected'.

short cut
a quicker way.

shorten *verb*
to make or become shorter.

shortening *noun*
any fat, such as butter or lard, used in cakes or pastry.

shorthand *noun*
a method of rapid writing, by using symbols instead of words and phrases. Compare LONGHAND.

shorthanded *adjective*
not having enough workers, helpers, etc.

short leg
Cricket: a fielding position close to and almost level with the batsman on the on side.

short list
a list of the most likely candidates, chosen from a larger group of applicants.
Word Family: **short-list**, *verb*.

shortly *adverb*
Word Family: see SHORT.

short-range *adjective*
having a limited extent in distance or time.

short-sighted *adjective*
not able to see far.

Usage: 'the *short-sighted* plan had failed by the end of the year' (= lacking concern for the future).
Word Family: **short-sightedly,** *adverb*; **short-sightedness,** *noun.*

short-tempered *adjective*
irritable or easily made angry.

short-term *adjective*
existing or developing within a short time.

short-wave *adjective*
(of a radiowave) having a wavelength of less than 100 m, used for long-range radio broadcasts. Compare MEDIUM-WAVE and LONG-WAVE.

short-winded *adjective*
becoming out of breath easily.

shot (1) *noun*
1. the firing or discharge of a weapon, especially a gun.
Usages:
a) 'the golfer drove a brilliant *shot* down the fairway' (= hit, stroke).
b) 'have a *shot* at this puzzle' (= try, attempt).
c) 'the vet gave the dog a tetanus *shot*' (= injection).
d) 'her parting *shot* was a cynical laugh' (= reply, remark).
e) 'the colour returned to her face after a *shot* of brandy' (= drink).
2. a) a pellet, bullet, etc. discharged from a weapon. b) any or all such pellets.
3. a marksman: 'he is a very good *shot*'.
4. (*informal*) a photograph.
5. *Athletics:* the heavy iron ball thrown in the contest of putting the shot. Also called the **weight.**
Phrases:
big shot, (*informal*) an important person.
like a shot, 'she accepted the exciting invitation *like a shot*' (= at once).
shot in the arm, (*informal*) something which brings back energy, interest, etc.
shot in the dark, a wild guess.

shot (2) *adjective*
woven so that different or changing colours are visible: '*shot* silk'.
shot *verb*
the past tense and past participle of the verb **shoot.**

shotgun *noun*
a sporting gun having one or two barrels with a smooth bore, used to fire small shot or pellets.

shotgun wedding
(*informal*) a wedding occurring, or hastened, because the bride is pregnant.

should (*rhymes with* good) *verb*
1. the past tense of the auxiliary verb **shall.**
2. used to indicate: a) duty or necessity: 'you *should* apologize for your rudeness'; b) likelihood: 'they *should* get there before dark'.

shoulder (*say* **shole**-da) *noun*
1. *Anatomy:* the upper part of the trunk between the arm and the neck.
2. a) the corresponding part of an animal. b) a cut of meat from this part.
3. the part of a garment covering the shoulders: 'this coat has padded *shoulders*'.
4. something shaped like a shoulder: 'a *shoulder* of rock'.
Phrases:
give someone the cold shoulder, to snub.
rub shoulders with, to meet or associate with.
straight from the shoulder, (of a reprimand, etc.) direct and frank.
shoulder *verb*
1. to push with the shoulder or shoulders.
2. to carry or take on the shoulders.
Usage: 'the company will *shoulder* your travelling expenses' (= carry, bear).

shoulder-blade *noun*
see SCAPULA.

shout *verb*
to call or cry out loudly.
shout down, to silence by talking or shouting more loudly than.
Word Family: **shout,** *noun.*

shove (*say* shuv) *verb*
to push rudely or roughly.
shove off, (*informal*) to go away or leave.
Word Family: **shove,** *noun.*

shovel (*say* **shuvv'l**) *noun*
a long-handled tool with a broad scooped blade for moving things, such as soil, coal, etc.
Word Family: **shoveller,** *noun*; **shovel (shovelled, shovelling),** *verb,* a) to lift or move with a shovel, b) to put in or lift in large quantities or with great speed.

show (*say* sho) *verb*
(showed, shown or **showed, showing)** to cause or allow to be seen: '*show* me the book that you mentioned'.

Usages:
a) 'can you *show* the gentleman out?' (= conduct).
b) 'the clock *showed* midnight' (= registered).
c) 'I'll *show* you how to do it' (= instruct).
Phrases:
show off, 'he *showed off* his new car' (= exhibited for attention or approval).
Word Family: **show–off**, *noun*, a person who ostentatiously displays skill or wealth.
show up, a) 'the argument *showed up* her ignorance' (= made obvious, revealed); b) 'he did not *show up* at the office until lunchtime' (= arrive).

show *noun*
1. the act of showing.
2. a public performance or exhibition: a) 'a cattle *show*'; b) 'there's a new *show* on at the local theatre'.
Usages:
a) 'that company is quite a big *show* now' (= organization, undertaking).
b) 'her fright was all *show*' (= pretence).
Phrases:
give the show away, to reveal the details of some plan, etc. especially a secret one.
good show!, splendid!
show of hands, a vote taken, especially by counting raised hands.
steal the show, 'she *stole the show* with her exciting speech' (= won the most attention or popularity).
Word Family: **shower** (*say* **sho**–a), *noun*, a person or thing that shows; **showing**, *noun*, an exhibition, display or performance.

show biz
(*informal*) show business.

show business
all forms of public entertainment, such as plays, films, etc.

showcase *noun*
1. a glass cabinet for displaying objects.
2. a situation, place, etc. by or in which something is shown at its best.

showdown *noun*
a) a final revelation of intentions, hostility, etc. b) an open trial of strength.

shower (*rhymes with* flower) *noun*
1. a brief fall of rain, snow, etc.
Usages:
a) 'a *shower* of sparks shot from the soldering iron' (= fall, scattering).
b) 'he was met with a *shower* of abuse' (= stream, flow).
2. a) a bathroom fitting usually mounted above head height, consisting of a nozzle with small holes to spray the water. b) the room or area containing this. c) the act of washing oneself using such equipment.
3. a party for a prospective bride.
4. *Army:* (*informal*) an unutterably incompetent person: 'you 'orrible *shower*'.
Word Family: **shower**, *verb*, a) to fall in or as if in a shower, b) to wash under a shower; **showery**, *adjective*.

showgirl *noun*
a chorus girl, especially in a musical, nightclub, etc.

show–jumping *noun*
a horseriding competition in which a series of obstacles must be jumped in a certain order.

showman *noun*
1. a man who owns or exhibits a show.
2. a person who has a flair for doing things in a dramatic or entertaining way.
Word Family: **showmanship**, *noun*.

shown *verb*
a past participle of the verb **show**.

show–off *noun*
see SHOW OFF under SHOW.

showplace *noun*
a) a building exhibited to the public because of its beauty, interest, etc. b) any impressive building: 'the architect's home was a real *showplace*'.

showroom *noun*
a room used for displaying goods.

showy *adjective*
a) making a brilliant or impressive display: 'a plant with large, *showy* flowers'. b) ostentatious or making a vulgar display: 'a *showy* dress'.
Word Family: **showily**, *adverb*; **showiness**, *noun*.

shrank *verb*
the past tense of the verb **shrink**.

shrapnel *noun*
a) the fragments from an exploding shell. b) a type of shell designed to explode in the air and send fragments in all directions.
[invented by *H. Shrapnel*, 1761–1842, a British army officer]

shred *noun*
a small, narrow strip cut or torn off: 'the cat tore my slippers to *shreds*'.

Usage: 'there's not a *shred* of evidence to support your story' (= piece, particle).
Word Family: **shred (shredded, shredding)**, *verb*, to reduce to shreds; **shredder**, *noun.*

shrew *noun*
1. a bad-tempered, scolding woman.
2. a mouse-like insect-eating mammal with a pointed snout. Short form of **shrewmouse.**
Word Family: **shrewish**, *adjective.*

shrewd (*say* **shrood**) *adjective*
clever or showing good judgement, often in a sharp way: 'a *shrewd* businessman'.
Word Family: **shrewdly**, *adverb*; **shrewdness**, *noun.*

shriek (*say* shreek) *noun*
a loud, shrill cry: 'I heard a *shriek* from the bushes'.
Word Family: **shriek**, *verb*, a) to utter a shriek, b) to utter with or in a shriek; **shrieker**, *noun.*

shrift *noun*
the absolution granted by a priest.
short shrift, 'her request was given *short shrift* by the busy official' (= hasty or unsympathetic treatment).

shrike *noun*
any of various birds with a strong, hooked beak which impale their prey on thorns.

shrill *adjective*
high-pitched and piercing: 'a *shrill* whistle'.
Word Family: **shrill**, *verb*, a) to make a shrill sound, b) to utter in a shrill voice; **shrilly** (*say* **shril**-lee), *adverb*; **shrillness**, *noun.*

shrimp *noun*
1. any of a group of small, edible marine shellfish, considered a delicacy.
2. (*informal*) a very small or thin person, especially a child.

shrine *noun*
a) a tomb or casket containing sacred remains, such as those of a saint. b) any building or place considered sacred because of its historic or religious associations.
[Latin *scrinium* a box]

shrink *verb*
(shrank, shrunk or **shrunken, shrinking)**
1. to become or make smaller: 'some fabrics *shrink* in hot water'.
2. to draw back or recoil: 'the frightened child *shrank* back against the hedge'.
Usage: 'the authorities *shrank* from taking such extreme steps' (= held back in reluctance).
shrinkage *noun*
a) the act or fact of shrinking: 'this fabric is subject to *shrinkage*'. b) the amount or degree of shrinking: 'the *shrinkage* of this garment was excessive'.
shrink *noun*
short form of **head-shrinker** (*informal*) a psychiatrist.
Word Family: **shrinkable**, *adjective*; **shrinkingly**, *adverb.*

shrive *verb*
(shrove, shriven, shriving)
Christian: to give absolution to a person.

shrivel (*say* **shrivv**'l) *verb*
(shrivelled, shrivelling)
to shrink or become dry.

shroud (*rhymes with* loud) *noun*
1. a cloth in which a dead person is wrapped for burial.
2. *Nautical:* a wire or rope leading from the top of a mast to either side of a ship.
shroud *verb*
to clothe in a shroud.
Usage: 'the whole affair is *shrouded* in mystery' (= covered, hidden).

shrub *noun*
a woody perennial plant, smaller than a tree and lacking a main trunk.
Word Family: **shrubby**, *adjective*; **shrubbery**, *noun*, a) a place planted with shrubs, b) any or all shrubs.

shrug *verb*
(shrugged, shrugging)
to lift and lower the shoulders as an expression of disbelief, indifference, perplexity, disdain, etc.
shrug off, a) 'she *shrugged off* their insults with a laugh' (= let pass, paid no attention to); b) 'he could not *shrug off* his pursuers' (= escape, get rid of).
Word Family: **shrug**, *noun.*

shrunk *verb*
a past participle of the verb **shrink.**
shrunken *verb*
a past participle of the verb **shrink.**

shucks *interjection*
American: an exclamation of disappointment, annoyance or disgust.

shudder *verb*
to shiver violently with cold, fear, etc.

Word Family: **shudder**, *noun*; **shudderingly**, *adverb*.

shuffle *verb*

1. to walk with dragging or scraping steps.

2. *Cards:* to mix the cards in a pack so as to change their order, especially before dealing.

Usages:

a) 'he was *shuffled* from one job to another' (= moved about).

b) 'she always *shuffles* if asked a direct question' (= acts evasively).

shuffle off, to shrug off.

Word Family: **shuffle**, *noun*.

shuffleboard *noun*

a) a board or table game in which discs or coins are driven towards squares in order to score. b) a similar game on a large scale played on a ship's deck.

shun *verb*

(**shunned**, **shunning**).

to avoid consistently or deliberately: 'he *shuns* all publicity'.

shunt *verb*

1. to turn or move aside or onto another course: 'the discussion got *shunted* off into trivialities'.

Usage: 'the teacher was *shunted* from one school to another' (= shifted, transferred).

2. *Railways:* to sort and marshal trains.

shunt *noun*

1. the act of shunting.

2. *Electricity:* a low resistance alternative path for a portion of an electric current.

Word Family: **shunter**, *noun*.

shush *verb*

to ask for quiet, especially by making the sound 'shh'.

Word Family: **shush**, *interjection*, hush.

shut *verb*

(**shut**, **shutting**)

1. to move something into position so as to block an opening: a) 'please *shut* the window'; b) '*shut* the valve on the pipeline'.

2. to secure by fastening doors, windows, etc.: 'he always *shuts* the shop himself'.

3. to bring together or fold: 'I can't *shut* my umbrella'.

4. to cease normal operations: 'the cinema was *shut* for two weeks while the roof was repaired'.

Phrases:

shut down, a) to secure by lowering a lid, cover, etc.; b) to cease operating for a time, e.g. a factory, machine, etc.

shut off, a) to stop the flow of water, electricity, etc.; b) to isolate.

shut up, a) to confine or imprison; b) (*informal*) to stop talking; c) to secure by fastening windows, doors, etc.

shutdown *noun*

also called a **closedown**

the closing of a factory or other place of work.

shut-eye *noun*

(*informal*) sleep.

shutter *noun*

1. a hinged cover for a window.

2. *Photography:* a device on a camera which opens and shuts to allow light to pass through the lens onto the film.

Word Family: **shutter**, *verb*, to provide or close with shutters.

shuttle *noun*

a device on a loom, used for passing the threads of the weft to and fro between the threads of the warp.

shuttle *verb*

to move rapidly to and fro: 'the ants *shuttled* back and forth moving the breadcrumbs into their nest'.

shuttle service

a transport system, usually making frequent trips back and forth over a short distance, e.g. in an emergency.

[Old English *seytel* dart, arrow]

shuttlecock *noun*

1. a piece of cork or plastic stuck with feathers and used instead of a ball in certain games such as badminton.

2. see BATTLEDORE.

shy (1) *adjective*

1. a) lacking confidence when with others. b) easily startled or frightened.

Usage: 'I'm a bit *shy* of putting my money in banks' (= wary, cautious).

2. (*informal*) short or lacking: 'I'm a bit *shy* of funds at the moment'.

fight shy of, to avoid.

shy *verb*

(**shied**, **shying**)

1. (of a horse) to jump suddenly sideways, usually in fright.

2. to draw back, as from doubt or caution: 'never bully a client or he'll *shy* away from the deal'.

Word Family: **shy**, *noun*.

shy (2) *verb*

(**shied**, **shying**)

to throw, especially with a swift sideways motion: 'we *shied* stones across the lake'.
Word Family: **shy,** *noun,* a) a sudden swift throw, b) a coconut-shy.

shyster (*say* **shy**-ster) *noun*
(*informal*) a person who conducts business in an unscrupulous or unethical way.

sial (*say* **sigh**-ul) *noun*
Geology: the lighter portion of the earth's crust, composed mainly of granite and occurring in separate masses to form the continents.
[SI(lica) + AL(umina)]

Siamese cat (*say* sigh-a-**meez** cat)
one of several breeds of short-haired cats, having a light grey or fawn coat with darker ears, face, paws and tail.

Siamese twins (*say* sigh-a-**meez** twins)
a set of twins joined together at some part of the body.

sibilant (*say* **sibbi**-l'nt) *adjective*
hissing.
sibilant *noun*
Language: a sibilant sound, such as in *less, past,* etc.
Word Family: **sibilance, sibilancy,** *noun*; **sibilantly,** *adverb.*

sibling *noun*
a brother or sister.

sibyl (*say* **sibbil**) *noun*
Mythology: a prophetess.

sic *adverb*
so or thus. Inserted in brackets after a word or phrase, etc. to show that it appears in this form in the original.
[Latin]

sick *adjective*
1. a) ill or affected by disease. b) vomiting or feeling like vomiting: 'sea trips always make me *sick*'.
2. of or for sick people: 'a *sick* ward'.
3. a) mentally disturbed. b) morbid or macabre: 'no more *sick* jokes, please'.
Usages:
a) 'I'm *sick* of working today' (= tired, weary).
b) (*informal*) 'his constant arrogance makes me *sick*' (= disgusted).
sickness *noun*
1. a) the state of being sick. b) a particular disease. c) a feeling of being sick.
2. a sick feeling in the stomach.
Word Family: **sick,** *noun,* (informal) vomit; **sicken,** *verb,* to make or become sick; **sickening,** *adjective,* disgusting or revolting; **sickeningly,** *adverb.*

sickle *noun*
a short-handled tool with a curved blade for cutting, trimming plants, etc. Compare SCYTHE.

sickly (*say* **sik**-lee) *adjective*
1. not strong or healthy: 'a *sickly* child'.
2. of, caused by or associated with sickness: 'a *sickly* pallor'.
3. being too sweet or rich: a) '*sickly* sweet tea'; b) '*sickly* sentimentality'.
Word Family: **sickliness,** *noun.*

sickness *noun*
see SICK.

side *noun*
1. a surface of an object, especially a surface joining a top and a bottom: a) 'the *side* of a hill'; b) 'the *sides* of a crate'.
2. either of the two surfaces of a piece of paper, cloth, etc.: 'do not write on both *sides* of the page'.
Usages:
a) 'which *side* of your body is the pain on?' (= half).
b) 'the east *side* of the city is the business sector' (= part).
3. one of two or more opposing groups, sets of opinion, etc.: a) 'whose *side* are you on?'; b) 'everyone has ignored my *side* of the question'.
4. the space immediately next to a person or thing: 'I stood at his *side*'.
5. a line of descent: 'on my mother's *side* of the family everyone was tall and fair'.
6. (*informal*) a supercilious or pretentious manner: 'it's no good putting on *side* with me'.
7. *Billiards:* a spin given to a ball by striking it on one side.
8. half a carcass: 'a *side* of bacon'.
Phrases:
get on the right side of, to have or achieve the approval of.
get on the wrong side of, to incur the displeasure of.
on the side, (*informal*) a) as a sideline; b) secretly.
side *adjective*
a) at or on one side: 'a *side* door'.
b) from or to one side: 'a *side* glance'.
Usage: 'don't get confused by *side* issues' (= secondary, incidental).
side *verb*
Phrases:
side against, to set oneself against.
side with, to support or take the part of.

side-arms *plural noun*
any weapons worn at the side, such as swords, bayonets, etc.

sideboard *noun*
1. a piece of furniture with drawers and shelves, for storing tableware or serving food. Also called a **buffet.**
2. (*plural*) sideburns.

sideburns *plural noun*
also called **sideboards**
the hair growing down the side of a man's face in front of his ears.

sidecar *noun*
a one-wheeled compartment for a passenger, attached to the side of motorcycle.

side-dish *noun*
a dish served to accompany the main dish of a course.

side effect
any effect produced in addition to those intended, e.g. by a drug.

sidekick *noun*
(*informal*) a close associate or friend.

sidelight *noun*
1. a light at or coming from the side.
Usage: 'the book contains some interesting *sidelights* on Napoleon's private life' (= incidental details).
2. a window in the side of a building, at the side of a door, another window, etc.
3. a motor car's parking or subsidiary front light.

sideline *noun*
1. any activity pursued in addition to one's regular business or work.
2. a subsidiary line of merchandise.
3. *Sport:* (*plural*) a) the area beyond the boundary lines. b) the place where the spectators sit.
from the sidelines, from the point of view of a spectator or outsider.

sidelong *adjective, adverb*
directed to one side: 'a *sidelong* glance'.

sidereal (*say* sigh-**deeriul**) *adjective*
of or relative to the stars.
sidereal day
see DAY.

side-saddle *noun*
a saddle designed for women wearing long skirts, in which both of the rider's legs are on the same side, usually the left side, of the horse.
Word Family: **side-saddle,** *adverb,* seated on or as if on a side-saddle.

sideshow *noun*
a small show or exhibition associated with a fair, circus, etc.

sidesman *noun*
a churchwarden's assistant who acts as usher and takes the collection.

side-splitting *adjective*
extremely funny.

sidestep *verb*
(sidestepped, sidestepping)
to step out of the way of: 'to *sidestep* a puddle'.
Usage: 'you are always trying to *sidestep* your responsibilities' (= avoid).
Word Family: **sidestep,** *noun.*

side street
a street leading off a main street.

sidestroke *noun*
a swimming style in which the swimmer lies on his side, while each arm pulls alternately and the legs kick.

sidetrack *verb*
to distract or divert from the main issue or course.

sidewalk *noun*
American: a pedestrians' pavement.

sidewall *noun*
one of the side surfaces of a tyre.

sideways *adjective, adverb*
a) towards or from one side. b) with one side towards the front.

siding (*say* **side**-ing) *noun*
Railways: a length of track running off a main line, used for parking, loading and marshalling trains.

sidle *verb*
to move sideways, especially in a furtive manner.

siege (*say* seej) *noun*
the surrounding of a fortified place by a military force intent on capturing it.
lay siege to, to besiege.
[Latin *sedere* to sit]

sienna (*say* see-**enna**) *noun*
any of a group of colours ranging from yellowish-brown (**raw sienna**) to deep orange-brown (**burnt sienna**).
[after *Siena,* Italy]

sierra (*say* see-**erra**) *noun*
a range of hills or mountains with sharp peaks.
[Spanish, a saw]

siesta (*say* see-**esta**) *noun*
a rest or short sleep, especially one taken after the midday meal.
[Spanish, from Latin *sexta* (*hora*) sixth hour]

sieve (*say* siv) ***noun***
a round container made of wire mesh or finely perforated metal, used for straining or sifting.
Word Family: **sieve,** ***verb,*** to put or force through a sieve.

sieve tube
Biology: any of the elongated cells which form the phloem in plants.

sift *verb*
a) to separate fine particles from coarse ones using a sieve. b) to scatter with a sieve: '*sift* the sugar over the plums'.
Usages:
a) 'the snow *sifted* gently down' (= fell in fine particles).
b) 'the detective carefully *sifted* all the evidence' (= sorted through).
Word Family: **sifter,** ***noun***

sigh *verb*
to give out a deep, long, audible breath, as in weariness, sorrow, relief, etc.
Usage: 'the homesick lad *sighs* continually for home' (= yearns).
Word Family: **sigh,** ***noun.***

sight *noun*
1. a) the ability to see: 'to lose one's *sight*'. b) the act or fact of seeing. c) the range or field of one's vision: 'in *sight* of land'.
2. something which is seen: 'a beautiful *sight* lay before us'.
3. (*plural*) something worth seeing: 'to see the *sights* of New York'.
4. (*informal*) a) a lot: 'the party was a *sight* better than we expected'. b) something odd or unattractive to see: 'he looked a *sight* in the tattered old coat'.
Phrases:
at sight, on sight, a) as soon as seen; b) 'a sterling draft payable *at sight*' (= on being presented).
not by a long sight, definitely not.
sight unseen, without having seen the thing in question.
sight *verb*
1. to get a glimpse or view of: 'to *sight* a school of whales'.
2. to take a sight or observation with an instrument.
3. to take aim with a gun, etc.
Word Family: **sighted,** *adjective,* not blind; **sightless,** *adjective,* blind; **sightly,** *adjective,* pleasing to see; **sightliness,** *noun.*

sight-read *verb*
Music: to be able to read, play or sing from written music without previous practice or rehearsal.

sightseeing *noun*
the act of seeing places and things of interest, especially as a tourist.
Word Family: **sightseer,** ***noun***

sign (*say* sine) *noun*
1. something that points to the existence or likelihood of something: a) 'he gave no *sign* that suicide was on his mind'; b) 'dark clouds are a *sign* of rain'.
2. an action or gesture intended to convey an idea, information, etc.: 'he made a *sign* with his finger that warned us to keep quiet'.
3. a board or poster serving to display information or advertise.
4. a conventional symbol or figure which stands for a word, mathematical operation, division of the zodiac, etc.
Usage: 'he disappeared without a *sign*' (= indication).
sign *verb*
1. to write one's signature on.
2. to communicate by a sign: 'he *signed* to me to follow him up the stairs'.
Usage: 'the team has just *signed* a new player' (= hired by written contract).
Phrases:
sign off, to cease broadcasting, etc.
sign on, a) to be hired or employed by a contract; b) to begin broadcasting, etc.
sign up, to enlist, e.g. in the armed forces.
[Latin *signum* a mark, token]

signal (*say* sig-n'l) *noun*
1. any action, message, device, etc., used to convey a warning, order, or information: a) 'a railway *signal*'; b) 'give the *signal* to begin'.
2. *Electricity:* a wave, sound, etc. which transmits information.
signal *verb*
(signalled, signalling)
a) to make a signal to. b) to make known by signals or signs: 'her face *signalled* her distress'.
signal *adjective*
1. conspicuous or notable: 'a *signal* victory for our side'.
2. used to signal: 'a *signal* fire burning on the hilltop'.
Word Family: **signaller,** ***noun***; **signally,** *adverb,* notably.

signatory (*say* signa-tree) *noun*
a person or nation that has signed a treaty or other document.

signature (*say* signa-cher) *noun*
1. a) a person's name as signed by himself. b) the act of signing a document.

2. *Music:* a sign used to indicate key or tempo.

signature tune
a piece of music always played with a particular programme, etc. to identify it.

signboard (*say* **sine**–bord) *noun*
a board or hoarding bearing writing, advertisements, etc.

signet (*say* **signit**) *noun*
a small seal, impressed on a document to authenticate it.

signet ring
a ring in which initials or a seal are set.

significant (*say* sig–**niffi**–k'nt) *adjective*
1. notable: 'a *significant* victory'.
2. full of meaning: 'a *significant* glance'.
Word Family: **significantly**, *adverb*; **significance**, *noun.*

signify (*say* **signi**–fie) *verb*
(**signified, signifying**)
1. a) to be a sign of: 'raised eyebrows *signify* surprise'. b) to make known by signs: 'he *signified* his approval by nodding his head'.
2. to matter: 'what does it *signify* if they do not believe us?'.
Word Family: **signification,** *noun,* a) the act of signifying, b) what is signified.
[Latin *significare* show by signs]

sign language
the use of certain gestures as a method of communication with and between deaf or dumb people.

signor (*say* **seen**–yor) *noun*
plural is **signori** (*say* seen–**yor**–ee)
the title for an Italian man.

signora (*say* seen–**yor**–a) *noun*
plural is **signore** (*say* seen–**yor**–ay)
the title for a married Italian woman.

signorina (*say* sin–ya–**reena**) *noun*
plural is **signorine** (*say* sin–ya–**reenay**)
the title for an unmarried Italian woman.

signpost *noun*
a) a post bearing a sign which points out a particular place, direction, etc.
b) any indication, sign or clue.

sign–writer *noun*
a person who designs and produces signboards, notices, etc.
Word Family: **sign–writing**, *noun.*

Sikh (*say* seek) *noun*
a member of an Indian religious movement founded in the 16th century and combining elements of Hinduism and Islam.
[Hindi, disciple]

silage (*say* **sigh**–lij) *noun*
fodder for farm animals, made from green plants preserved in a silo.

silence (*say* **sigh**–l'nce) *noun*
a) the absence of sound: 'the *silence* of an underground cave'. b) the state or fact of being silent: 'he was reduced to *silence* by the teacher's anger'.
Usage: 'I shall have to swear you to *silence* about this matter' (= secrecy).
silence *verb*
to make silent or bring to silence.
Usage: 'his convincing explanation *silenced* all our doubts' (= put an end to).
[from Latin]

silencer (*say* **sigh**—l'n–sir) *noun*
a device attached to a gun, motor car exhaust system, etc. to reduce noise.

silent (*say* **sigh**–l'nt) *adjective*
making no sound or noise.
Usages:
a) 'he's one of the strong *silent* types' (= taciturn, reticent).
b) 'she was a star of the *silent* movies' (= having no soundtrack).
c) 'pneumonia has a *silent* **p**' (= not pronounced).
silent majority, those who do not agitate, demonstrate or campaign and whose views are therefore liable to be forgotten.
Word Family: **silently**, *adverb.*

silent partner
a sleeping partner.

silhouette (*say* silloo–**et**) *noun*
a) a portrait in profile, showing an outline only, usually black on white.
b) the outline of a solid figure seen against a contrasting background.
Word Family: **silhouette**, *verb.*

silica (*say* **sillika**) *noun*
silicon dioxide (formula SiO_2), a hard white mineral occurring in many forms, such as quartz.
Word Family: **siliceous** (*say* sil–**lishus**), *adjective,* containing, resembling or consisting of silica.
[Latin *silicis* a flint]

silica gel
a form of silica with a highly porous structure, capable of containing or absorbing 40 per cent of its weight

of water. It is used as a drying agent, especially for drying gases.

silicate (*say* **silli**–kate) *noun*
Chemistry: any compound containing the bivalent $(SiO_3)^{2-}$ radical.

silicon (*say* **silli**–kon) *noun*
element number 14, a very common non–metal, forming allotropes. Widely occurring as silica, it is used in glass, silicones and alloys. See CHEMICAL ELEMENTS in grey pages.

silicone (*say* **silli**–kone) *noun*
Chemistry: any of a group of complex polymers of carbon and silicon, used as lubricants, resins and lacquers.

silicosis (*say* silli–**ko**–sis) *noun*
a disease of the lungs caused by inhaling siliceous particles in stone–dust, etc.

silk *noun*
1. a) a fine, soft fibre obtained from the cocoon of a silkworm, used to make yarn or fabric. b) any substance resembling silk, such as the fibres on an ear of corn.
2. see QUEEN'S COUNSEL.
3. (*plural*) a jockey's racing clothes, usually in the horse owner's registered colours.
Word Family: **silky**, *adjective*, smooth, soft and glossy like silk; **silkily**, *adverb*; **silkiness**, *noun*; **silken**, *adjective*, a) made of silk, b) silky.
[Latin *sericum*]

silk screen
a printing process in which the ink is pressed through a stencil in the form of specially prepared fine material, originally silk.

silkworm *noun*
a caterpillar which spins a soft cocoon of fine silk threads.

sill *noun*
1. a horizontal piece of wood or stone across the bottom of a door, window, etc.
2. *Geology:* a sheet of lava, which has solidified between layers of other rock.

silly *adjective*
1. showing a lack of good sense.
Usage: 'the blow knocked me *silly*' (= stunned, dazed).
2. *Cricket:* (of a fielding position) very close to the batsman.
Word Family: **silly**, *noun*, a silly person.
[Middle English *sely* happy]

silly season
the summer holiday season when journalists short of copy traditionally fill newspapers, television news programmes, etc. with exaggerated or sensationalized accounts of trivial events.

silo (*say* **sigh**–lo) *noun*
plural is **silos**
1. a large tower–like building in which grain or fodder is stored.
2. an underground launching place for ballistic missiles.
[Greek *siros* a pit to keep grain in]

silt *noun*
an earthy deposit laid down by a river, lake, etc. which is finer than sand but coarser than clay.
silt *verb*
silt up, to fill or become filled with silt.

Silurian (*say* sil–**yoo**rian) *noun*
Geology: see PALAEOZOIC.
[Latin *Silures* a Welsh tribe]

silvan *adjective*
see SYLVAN.

silver *noun*
1. element number 47, a ductile, malleable metal, a good conductor of heat and electricity. It is used for making mirrors, coins and ornaments and its light–sensitive compounds are used in photography. See TRANSITION ELEMENT.
See CHEMICAL ELEMENTS in grey pages.
2. a lustrous white or whitish–grey colour.
3. any objects, such as coins, cutlery, etc., which are made of silver.
silver *adjective*
1. of, made of or containing silver.
2. having the colour of silver.
Usages:
a) 'the *silver* notes of a soprano voice' (= clear and ringing).
b) 'the orator had a *silver* tongue' (= eloquent, persuasive).
3. of or designating a 25th anniversary: 'a *silver* jubilee'.
silver *verb*
1. to coat or plate with silver or a silver–like substance.
2. to become the colour of silver.
Word Family: **silvery**, *adjective*, a) covered with or containing silver, b) having the colour or lustre of silver, c) having a soft, clear ringing sound; **silveriness**, *noun*.

silver birch
the common birch, which has silvery white bark that it sheds in layers.

silverfish *noun*
plural is **silverfish**
a primitive, wingless insect which feeds on paper, sugar, starch, etc.

silver foil
see ALUMINIUM FOIL.

silver plate
a thin, silver veneer applied to another metal surface.
Word Family: **silver plate**, *verb*.

silverside *noun*
the upper side of a round of beef, often eaten boiled or pressed.

silversmith *noun*
a person who makes and repairs articles of silver.

silverware *noun*
any articles, such as candlesticks, etc., which are made of silver.

silvery (*say* **silva**–ree) *adjective*
Word Family: see SILVER.

simian (*say* **simmi**–an) *adjective*
of or relating to monkeys.
[Greek *simos* snub-nosed]

similar (*say* **simmi**–la) *adjective*
1. close or related in appearance, nature, etc.
2. *Maths:* relating to figures with equal angles and proportional sides.
Word Family: **similarly**, *adverb*; **similarity** (*say* simmi–**larri**–tee), *noun*, a) the state of being similar, b) a point of likeness.

simile (*say* **simmi**–lee) *noun*
a figure of speech in which two unlike things are compared. *Example*: he chattered like a magpie. Compare METAPHOR.
[Latin *similis* like]

similitude (*say* sim–**illi**–tewd) *noun*
similarity.

simmer *verb*
1. to cook gently just below boiling point.
2. to be filled with suppressed emotion.
simmer down, (*informal*) to become calm or calmer.
Word Family: **simmer**, *noun*.

simony (*say* **sigh**–ma–nee) *noun*
the buying and selling of church offices.
[after *Simon Magus* who tried to buy apostolic powers]

simper *verb*
to smile in a silly or self-conscious way.
Word Family: **simper**, *noun*; **simperer**, *noun*, a person who simpers; **simperingly**, *adverb*.

simple *adjective*
1. easy: 'it was a *simple* test and everyone passed'.
2. having one part only: 'a *simple* leaf'.
Usages:
a) 'his *simple* style of writing is very popular' (= not elaborate, unaffected).
b) 'a *simple* cottage' (= not complicated).
c) 'a *simple* cold' (= ordinary).
d) 'what a *simple* girl to be talked into such a thing' (= ignorant, silly).
Word Family: **simplicity** (*say* sim–**plissi**–tee), **simpleness**, *nouns*; **simplify** (*say* **simpli**–fie), *verb*, to make simple or more simple; **simplification**, *noun*.
[from Latin]

simple fraction
see FRACTION.

simple harmonic motion
Physics: the movement of a body, such as a pendulum or a weighted spring, about a central point so that its acceleration towards that point is proportional to the distance from it.

simple interest
see INTEREST.

simple-minded *adjective*
1. artless or unsophisticated.
2. mentally deficient.

simpleton (*say* **sim**–p'l–t'n) *noun*
a silly or ignorant person.

simplicity *noun*
Word Family: see SIMPLE.

simplify *verb*
Word Family: see SIMPLE.

simplistic *adjective*
adopting an over-simple or unsophisticated approach to a complex problem.
Word Family: **simplistically**, *adverb*.

simply *adverb*
1. in a simple manner: 'the catering was done *simply* but quite adequately'.
2. merely or only: 'it is *simply* a question of money'.
3. absolutely: 'it is *simply* ridiculous to try such a scheme'.

simulate (*say* **sim**–yoo–late) *verb*
to imitate: 'we *simulated* real conditions for the experiment'.

Usage: 'she *simulated* enthusiasm' (= pretended).
Word Family: **simulation,** *noun*; **simulator,** *noun*, a person or thing that simulates.
[Latin *similis* like]

simultaneous (*say* simm'l-**tayni**-us) *adjective*
happening, existing or done at the same time.
Word Family: **simultaneously,** *adverb*; **simultaneousness, simultaneity** (*say* simm'l-ta-**nee**-a-tee), *nouns*.
[Latin *simul* at the same time]

simultaneous equations
1. *Maths:* a group of algebraic equations which are all satisfied by the same sets of values of the variables.
2. *Example:* $2x + y = 4$, $x + 2y = 5$ and $x^2 + y = 3$ are simultaneous equations where $x = 1$ and $y = 2$.

sin (1) *noun*
an offence or fault, especially against moral or religious laws.
live in sin, (of an unmarried couple) to live together.
original sin
Christian: mankind's natural tendency to commit sin, considered to be the inherited result of Adam's disobedience.
Word Family: **sin (sinned, sinning),** *verb*; **sinner,** *noun*; **sinful,** *adjective*, wrong or wrongful; **sinfully,** *adverb*; **sinfulness,** *noun*.

sin (2) (*say* sine) *noun*
Maths: see SINE.

since *adverb*
1. between a particular past time and the present: 'he went overseas and I have not heard from him *since*'.
2. in the past: 'I had long *since* forgotten our quarrel'.
ever since, from then until now.
since *preposition*
after or during the time after: 'we have been working *since* daybreak'.
since *conjunction*
1. in the period following the time when: 'he has not written *since* he went overseas'.
2. because: '*since* it is late I shall go home now'.

sincere (*say* sin-**seer**) *adjective*
(of feelings, behaviour, etc.) free from pretence, deceit, etc.
Word Family: **sincerely,** *adverb*; **sincerity** (*say* sin-**serri**-tee), *noun*.
[Latin *sincerus* clean, untainted]

sine *noun*
short form is **sin**
Maths: the ratio of the length of the side opposite an angle to the hypotenuse of a right-angled triangle. See TRIGONOMETRIC FUNCTIONS.
[Latin *sinus* a curve]

sinecure (*say* **sigh**-nikkewer) *noun*
a position or office which requires little or no work but yields profitable returns.
[Latin *sine cura* without a care]

sine die (*say* sinni **dee**-ay)
Law: with no date announced for reassembly or resumption: 'the court adjourned *sine die*'.
[Latin, without a day (mentioned)]

sine qua non (*say* **sinni** kwa non)
something which is essential.
[Latin, without which not]

sinew (*say* **sin**-yoo) *noun*
1. a tendon.
2. strength or vigour.
Word Family: **sinewy,** *adjective*.

sine wave
Maths: a wave-shaped graph of a function given by the formula $y = a \sin x$.

sinfonia *noun*
Music: a symphony.

sinful *adjective*
Word Family: see SIN (1).

sing *verb*
(sang or **sung, sung, singing)**
1. to make musical sounds with the voice.
2. to make a humming or buzzing sound: 'my ears are *singing*'.
3. to proclaim enthusiastically: 'to *sing* someone's praises'.
4. (*informal*) to inform against: 'the robber was worried that his accomplice might *sing* to the police'.
sing out, (*informal*) to shout.
Word Family: **singer,** *noun*.

singe (*say* sinj) *verb*
(singed, singeing)
to burn slightly, as in order to remove the ends of hair, etc.
Word Family: **singe,** *noun*.

single *adjective*
separate or being one only: a) 'not a *single* person arrived'; b) 'every *single* seat was empty'.
Usages:
a) 'a *single* man desires lodgings' (= unmarried).
b) 'the room contained two *single* beds and a divan' (= for one person).

c) 'she bought a *single* ticket for the city' (= for one trip or direction only).
single *verb*
single out, to choose or pick out from others.
single *noun*
1. a single thing, e.g. a hit for one run at cricket or a one-way rail ticket.
2. a room in a hotel, etc. for one person.
3. a record played at 45 revolutions per minute, usually 7 inches (17·46 cm) in diameter. Also called a **forty-five**. Compare EXTENDED PLAY and LONG PLAY.
4. *Sport:* (*plural*) a game of tennis, etc. between two players.
Word Family: **singly**, *adverb*, a) one by one, b) by oneself; **singleness**, *noun*.
[from Latin]

single-action *adjective*
(of a firearm) needing the hammer cocked before it can be fired.

single-breasted *adjective*
having flaps fastened with one row of buttons, as certain coats, etc. Compare DOUBLE-BREASTED.

single file
also called **Indian file**
a line of people or things arranged one behind the other.

single-handed *adjective*
1. working or done alone or unaided.
2. having or requiring the use of only one hand or person.
Word Family: **single-handedly**, *adverb*.

single-minded *adjective*
devoted exclusively to one cause, interest, etc.
Word Family: **single-mindedly**, *adverb*; **single-mindedness**, *noun*.

singlet *noun*
a short-sleeved or sleeveless garment with a round neck, worn as a shirt or vest.

singleton *noun*
something occurring singly, especially a playing card which is the only one of a suit in a hand.

singly *adverb*
Word Family: see SINGLE.

singsong *adjective*
having a regular, often monotonous, rising and falling rhythm, intonation, etc.
singsong *noun*
an informal gathering at which everyone sings.

singular (*say* **sing**-yoo-la) *adjective*
1. extraordinary, strange or remarkable: 'the Christmas party was a *singular* success'.
2. *Grammar:* (of a word) expressing only one. *Example*: *I* went to buy a *book*.
Word Family: **singularly**, *adverb*; **singularity** (*say* sing-yoo-**larri**-tee), *noun*.
[Latin *singularis* alone, unique]

sinister (*say* **sinnista**) *adjective*
suggesting or threatening evil.
[Latin, on the left, ill-omened]

sink *verb*
(**sank** or **sunk**, **sunk** or **sunken**, **sinking**)
1. to go or cause to go below the surface or to the bottom of a liquid, etc.
2. to fall slowly: 'she *sank* weakly to her knees'.
3. *Sport:* to hit the ball directly into the hole, etc.: 'to *sink* a putt'.
Usages:
a) 'to *sink* a well' (= drill, dig).
b) 'the sick man *sank* fast' (= became weaker).
c) 'prices *sank* during the depression' (= fell).
d) 'her face *sank* at the news' (= became depressed).
e) 'he *sank* his money into the worthless shares' (= invested).
sink in, to be understood.
sink *noun*
a basin, usually connected to a water supply and drain, and often set into a bench, used for washing dishes, etc.
Word Family: **sinkable**, *adjective*.

sinker *noun*
a weight attached to a fishing line or net to make it sink in the water.

sinkhole *noun*
also called a **swallow-hole**
a hole formed in soluble rock by the action of water, which conducts surface water to an underground passage.

sinking fund
a fund formed from annual income left to accumulate interest and used eventually to reduce a debt or replace equipment.

sinner *noun*
Word Family: see SIN (1).

Sino– (*say* **sigh**-no)
a prefix meaning Chinese: 'the *Sino-Soviet* border'.
[Greek *Sinai* the Chinese]

sinuous (*say* **sin**–yewus) *adjective*
having many bends or curves.
Usage: '*sinuous* arm movements' (= supple).
Word Family: **sinuously,** *adverb.*
[from Latin]

sinus (*say* **sigh**–nus) *noun*
plural is **sinuses**
Anatomy: any cavity within a bone, especially one of those within the nose and face.
[Latin, a curve, a fold]

sinusitis (*say* sigh–na–**sigh**–tis) *noun*
an inflammation, often chronic, of the sinuses.
[SINUS + –ITIS]

sip *verb*
(sipped, sipping)
to drink a little at a time.
Word Family: **sip,** *noun.*

siphon (*say* **sigh**–f'n) *noun*
also spelt **syphon**
1. a piece of tube through which a liquid may flow up over the wall of its container and down to a lower level by atmospheric pressure.
2. a soda siphon.
Word Family: **siphon,** *verb,* a) to pass through a siphon, b) to draw off or remove from a larger source.
[Greek, a pipe]

sippet *noun*
a small bit, especially a small piece of toasted or fried bread dipped in soup, etc.

sir *noun*
1. a respectful form of address used to a man.
2. (*capital*) a title for a knight, etc.

sire (*rhymes with* fire) *noun*
1. the male parent, especially of horses and dogs.
2. a form of address formerly used to a monarch.
sire *verb*
(of a male) to produce offspring.

siren (*say* **sigh**–r'n) *noun*
1. any of various devices, e.g. on an ambulance, which produces a loud, wailing sound.
2. any alluring or seductive woman.
[from the *Sirens,* a group of sea nymphs in Greek mythology who lured sailors to shipwreck by their sweet singing]

sirloin *noun*
a choice cut of beef from the upper part of the loin.
[French *sur* over + LOIN]

sirocco *noun*
a dry, dusty wind from the Sahara which picks up humidity over the Mediterranean and brings hot, enervating, rainy weather to southern Europe.
[Italian *scirocco*]

sisal (*say* **sigh**–z'l) *noun*
a fibre made from the stems of a cactus–like plant and used for ropes.
[from *Sisal* a port of Yucatan, Mexico]

sissy *noun*
see CISSY.

sister *noun*
1. a daughter of the same parents as another child (a **full sister**), or having only one parent the same as another child (a **half–sister**).
2. any female who has a close bond with another.
3. a woman belonging to a religious order.
4. a senior nurse.
Word Family: **sisterly,** *adjective;* **sisterhood,** *noun.*

sister–in–law *noun*
plural is **sisters–in–law**
1. the sister of one's husband or wife.
2. the wife of one's brother.
3. the wife of a husband's or wife's brother.

sit *verb*
(sat, sitting)
1. a) to rest with the body supported upon the buttocks. b) to cause to sit: 'I *sat* the child in the chair'.
2. to be in session: 'parliament *sat* every day last week'.
3. to baby–sit.
Usages:
a) 'when the artist's model was sick I *sat* for him' (= posed).
b) 'the bird was *sitting* on a branch' (= perching).
c) 'this skirt does not *sit* properly' (= fit, hang).
d) 'did you *sit* for the exam?' (= enter as a candidate).
Phrases:
be sitting pretty, (*informal*) to be established in comfort or at an advantage.
sit back, to take no action.
sit down, to sit after standing.
sit for, to be the member of parliament for.
sit in on, to take part as an observer or visitor.
sit on, a) to snub; b) to delay (a project).

sit out, a) to stay until the end; b) 'I *sat out* while they danced' (= took no part).
sit tight, to bide one's time.
sit up, a) to raise oneself from a lying position; b) to remain awake or out of bed; c) to become interested and alert.

sitar (*say* see–**tar**) *noun*
a guitar-like, Indian musical instrument with a main set of strings and a second group which provides resonance.

sit-down strike
a strike in which those taking part refuse either to work or leave their place of employment, etc. until their demands are satisfied.

site *noun*
the physical position of something, such as a town.
Word Family: **site**, *verb*, to locate or place.
[Latin *situs* situated]

sit-in *noun*
an organized passive protest in which workers or demonstrators sit down in a place normally prohibited to them and refuse to move.

sitter *noun*
1. a person who sits: 'a *baby-sitter*'.
2. (*informal*) something which is easily accomplished.

sitting *noun*
1. a period of remaining seated, such as when posing for a portrait.
2. a session of a parliament, court, etc.

sitting duck
(*informal*) a person who is an easy target or victim.

sitting room
a living room.

sitting tenant
a tenant in occupation of premises when their ownership changes.

situate (*say* **sit**–yoo–ate) *verb*
1. to give a particular place to.
2. to place in a particular condition or circumstances: 'how are you *situated* financially?'.

situation (*say* sit–yoo–**ay**–sh'n) *noun*
1. a location: 'the *situation* of the new house is very beautiful'.
2. a state of affairs: 'the present *situation* could easily lead to war'.
3. a job: 'I am applying for a *situation* with the bank'.

SI unit
a unit of the International System of units, in which the units for all quantities are interrelated and derived from seven base units, namely: metre, kilogram, second, ampere, kelvin, mole and candela.
Unlike most words in our language, the definitions of the SI units have been chosen by an international committee. The object of the choice is to relate each unit to a phenomenon which can be reproduced in a standards laboratory anywhere in the world. No such definition has yet been agreed on for the **kilogram**, which is therefore still defined as a mass equal to that of the International Prototype Kilogram held in France. The others, however, are all now defined independently of a prototype:
the **metre**, the **second** and the **candela** are defined in terms of the wavelength, period and luminous intensity of radiation produced under specified circumstances.
the **ampere** is defined in terms of the force produced by the passage of a current through two parallel conductors under specified circumstances.
the **mole** is defined as an amount of substance containing the same number of atoms or molecules as 12 g of the carbon 12 isotope.
the **kelvin** is defined, like the degree Celsius, in terms of the properties of water, but the kelvin scale starts at absolute zero.
[French S(ystème) I(nternational d') UNIT(és)]

six *noun*
1. a cardinal number, the symbol 6 in Arabic numerals, VI in Roman numerals.
2. *Cricket:* a score of six runs, obtained by a batsman hitting the ball over the boundary of the field without it bouncing.
at sixes and sevens, in disorder or confusion.
Word Family: **six**, *adjective*; **sixth**, *noun*, *adjective*.

sixpence *noun*
a) six pennies. b) a coin of this value.

six-shooter *noun*
a revolver with 6 chambers.

sixteen *noun*
a cardinal number, the symbol 16 in Arabic numerals, XVI in Roman numerals.

Word Family: **sixteen**, *adjective*; **sixteenth**, *adjective, noun.*

sixth form
the top form of a secondary school.

sixth sense
intuition or perception beyond the five senses.

sixty *noun*
plural is **sixties**
1. a cardinal number, the symbol 60 in Arabic numerals, LX in Roman numerals.
2. (*plural*) the numbers 60 to 69 in a series, such as the years within a century.
the 64 000 dollar question, the crucial or most difficult question, originally in a quiz programme.
Word Family: **sixty**, *adjective*; **sixtieth**, *adjective, noun.*

size (1) *noun*
1. the amount of space taken up by something: 'what *size* is the land?'.
2. any of the measured categories into which manufactured articles are divided: 'what *size* are your shoes?'.
Usages:
a) 'he is more concerned with *size* than quality' (= largeness).
b) 'that is about the *size* of the matter' (= actual condition).
size *verb*
to make or sort according to size.
size up, to form a judgement or opinion about.

size (2) *noun*
any of various glues or starches used for mixing paints, sealing surfaces, etc.
Word Family: **size**, *verb*, to coat or treat with size.

sizeable (*say* **size**–a–b'l) *adjective*
of considerable size: 'he has a *sizeable* fortune'.
Word Family: **sizeably**, *adverb.*

sizzle *verb*
1. to make a hissing sound, as in frying or burning.
2. (*informal*) to be very hot.
Word Family: **sizzle**, *noun*, the sound of sizzling; **sizzler**, *noun.*

sjambok (*say* **sham**–bok) *noun*
a rhinoceros–hide whip.
[Afrikaans]

skate (1) *noun*
a device consisting of a two–edged blade, wheels, etc., attached to the underside of a shoe or boot for moving over a smooth surface: 'an *ice–skate*'.
skate *verb*
to glide over ice or other smooth surfaces wearing a pair of skates.
skate over, skate round, to avoid in conversation, etc.
Word Family: **skater**, *noun.*

skate (2) *noun*
any of a group of flat, edible rays, with a blunt tail and a pointed snout.

skateboard *noun*
a flat board with flexible wheels for skating, particularly on sloping surfaces.
[SKATE + BOARD]

skedaddle (*say* ske–**dadd**'l) *verb*
(*informal*) to run away.

skein (*say* skane) *noun*
a length of thread or yarn wound into a coil.

skeleton (*say* **skell**a–t'n) *noun*
1. *Anatomy:* the framework of bones of the body.
2. any supporting framework.
3. (*informal*) a very thin or bony person or animal.
Usage: 'the author prepared a rough *skeleton* of his next book' (= outline).
skeleton in the cupboard, a fact which is kept secret because it may cause shame or embarrassment.
skeleton *adjective*
forming a nucleus: 'a *skeleton* staff'.
Word Family: **skeletal** (*say* **skelli**–t'l), *adjective.*
[Greek *skeletos* dried up]

skeleton key
also called a **master key**
a key which fits various locks which usually require separate keys.

skeptic *noun*
see SCEPTIC.

sketch *noun*
1. a hastily or roughly drawn picture, etc., especially a preliminary one giving an outline but no details.
2. any rough or brief outline, e.g. of a story, incident or plan.
3. a short, comic play, etc.
Word Family: **sketch**, *verb*; **sketchy**, *adjective*, a) giving only outlines, b) incomplete or superficial; **sketchily**, *adverb*; **sketchiness**, *noun.*
[Greek *skhedios* impromptu]

skew *adjective*
having an oblique direction or position.
Word Family: **skew**, *verb*, to move or cause to move at an angle.

skewbald (*say* **skew**-bawld) *adjective*
having patches of different colours, especially brown and white. Compare PIEBALD.
Word Family: **skewbald,** *noun,* a skewbald animal, especially a horse.

skewer *noun*
a long pin of wood or metal, especially one put through meat during cooking to hold it in shape, etc.
Word Family: **skewer,** *verb.*

ski (*say* skee) *noun*
a long narrow strip of wood, metal or plastic turned up at the front and attached to a boot, etc. for travelling over snow or water.
Word Family: **ski (skied, skiing),** *verb,* to travel on or use skis; **skier,** *noun.*
[Norwegian]

skid *verb*
(skidded, skidding)
to slide or slip sideways due to loss of traction, e.g. when a vehicle turns a corner.
skid *noun*
1. the act of skidding over a surface.
2. a runner on the underpart of some aircraft.
on the skids, (*informal*) on the way to ruin or disaster.

skid-pan *noun*
a prepared slippery surface on which motorists are taught to control skids.

skiff *noun*
a light racing boat for one sculler.

skiffle *noun*
a style of music based on American folk songs and played on a variety of instruments.

ski-lift *noun*
any form of rope, tow or lift to take skiers up a mountain, such as a **T-bar** which supports a skier while his skis run over the snow.

skill *noun*
an ability to do something well, due to knowledge, practice, training, etc.
Word Family: **skilful,** *adjective,* having or showing skill; **skilfully,** *adverb*; **skilfulness,** *noun*; **skilled,** *adjective,* trained or experienced.

skillet *noun*
1. a long-handled saucepan on legs.
2. *American:* a frying pan.

skilly *noun*
a thin oatmeal broth flavoured with meat: 'officers' wives have puddings and pies, but soldiers' wives have *skilly*'.

skim *verb*
(skimmed, skimming)
1. to move or glide lightly over or along a surface.
Usage: 'she *skimmed* over her essay before handing it to the teacher' (= read superficially).
2. to remove any floating matter from a liquid with a spoon, etc.
Word Family: **skimmer,** *noun,* a person or thing that skims, such as a ladle-like utensil with holes, used to skim fat, etc. from liquids.

skim milk
short form of **skimmed milk**
the milk from which the cream has been removed.

skimp *verb*
1. to use sparingly or be frugal.
2. to do hastily or inattentively.
Word Family: **skimpy,** *adjective,* a) not big enough, b) mean; **skimpily,** *adverb*; **skimpiness,** *noun.*

skin *noun*
1. the external covering of an animal body, fruit, etc.
2. any layer or coating on a surface: 'a *skin* formed on the boiling milk'.
Phrases:
get under one's skin, to have an irresistible or infuriating effect on.
jump out of one's skin, to be very frightened or surprised.
save one's skin, to escape harm.
skin and bones, emaciated.
skin *verb*
(skinned, skinning)
1. a) to remove skin from: 'to *skin* a rabbit'. b) to cut or injure the skin or surface of: 'to fall and *skin* one's knee'.
2. (*informal*) to strip of money or belongings.

skin-deep *adjective*
slight or superficial.

skin-diver *noun*
a person equipped with an aqualung, etc. for swimming under water.
Word Family: **skin-dive,** *verb.*

skinflint *noun*
a mean, extremely frugal person.

skinny *adjective*
very thin.

skint *adjective*
(*informal*) with no money at all.
[for SKINNED]

skin-tight *adjective*
fitting as tightly as skin.

skip (1) *verb*
(skipped, skipping)
to jump lightly, as over a skipping-rope.
Usages:
a) 'please don't *skip* the interesting parts' (= leave out).
b) 'the robbers had *skipped* the country' (= left hastily).
c) 'he *skipped* through the first pages' (= passed without attention to details).
Word Family: **skip**, *noun*; **skipper**, *noun*, a person or thing that skips.

skip (2) *noun*
a container attached to a crane, etc. for transporting materials in building or mining operations.

ski-plane *noun*
an aeroplane fitted with skis to enable it to land on snow or ice.

skipper (1) *noun*
a captain or leader.

skipper (2) *noun*
Word Family: see SKIP (1).

skipping-rope *noun*
a rope which one or more people hold, swinging it in a loop and jumping over it.

skirmish (*say* **skermish**) *noun*
a minor, especially an unexpected, encounter with enemy forces.

skirt *noun*
1. a piece of clothing which wraps around the lower half of the body.
2. a cut of meat taken from below the fillet, used in steak pies, etc.
3. (*informal*) a girl or woman.
skirt *verb*
1. to lie on or along the border of: 'our land *skirts* the river'.
2. to pass or go around: 'we *skirted* the city to avoid the traffic'.

skirting board
a protective strip of wood set around the base of a wall where it joins the floor.

skit *noun*
a short play or piece of writing which makes fun of a person or event.

skittish *adjective*
1. (of a horse) nervous.
2. (of a female) flirtatious or frivolous.
Word Family: **skittishness**, *noun*; **skittishly**, *adverb*.

skittle *verb*
to knock over or send flying.
skittle *noun*
1. a wooden pin, as used in tenpin bowling.
2. (*plural*) a bowling game in which such pins are used.

skivvy *noun*
(*use is derogatory*) a female servant, especially one doing heavy work.

skua *noun*
any of various hawk-like sea-birds which chase other birds until they disgorge their catch of fish.

skulduggery *noun*
any mean dishonesty or trickery.

skulk *verb*
to move about stealthily, sneak away, lurk or shirk.

skull *noun*
1. *Anatomy:* the framework of fused bones forming the head of animals.
2. (*informal*) the head considered as the source of intelligence, etc.

skull and crossbones
a representation of the human skull above two crossed bones, formerly used by pirates as a symbol of death.

skullcap *noun*
a small, closely fitting cap.

skunk *noun*
1. a) a small, black, North American mammal with a white stripe down its back, noted for the strong-smelling liquid it ejects when in danger. b) the fur of this animal.
2. (*informal*) a thoroughly contemptible person.

sky *noun*
the upper air, seen as blue where there are no clouds.
Phrases:
the sky's the limit, there is no limit.
to the skies, 'the critics praised his new play *to the skies*' (= highly, extravagantly).
sky *verb*
(skyed, skying)
(*informal*) to strike or raise high into the air.

sky-diving *noun*
the sport of jumping from an aircraft, and only opening the parachute late in descent.
Word Family: **sky-diver**, *noun*; **sky-dive**, *verb*.

sky-high *adjective, adverb*
very high.

skyjack *verb*
to hijack an aircraft.
Word Family: **skyjacker**, *noun*.

skylark (1) *noun*
a lark which sings a sustained high-pitched song in flight.

skylark (2) *verb*
to frolic boisterously or in high spirits.

skylight *noun*
an opening in a roof, often with glass set into it, to let in light.

skyline *noun*
1. the boundary line between earth and sky; the apparent horizon.
2. the outline of something seen against the sky.

skyrocket *noun*
a firework in the shape of a rocket.
skyrocket *verb*
(*informal*) to rise quickly and suddenly: 'prices *skyrocketed*'.

skyscraper *noun*
a tall multistorey building.

skyward *adjective*
directed or tending towards the sky.
Word Family: **skywards, skyward,** *adverb.*

skywriting *noun*
any writing made in the sky by smoke released from an aeroplane.

slab *noun*
a broad, flat piece of stone, wood, etc.
Usage: 'for lunch we had *slabs* of bread with jam' (= thick slices).

slack (1) *adjective*
1. not tense or taut, as of rope.
2. sluggish, as of tide, wind, etc.
Usages:
a) 'she was scolded for producing such *slack* work' (= careless, lazy).
b) 'trade was *slack* after the Christmas rush' (= dull, inactive).
slack *noun*
1. a loose or slack part or portion of something, such as a rope, sail, etc.
2. a period of little activity.
slack *verb*
1. to shirk a duty, etc.
2. to slacken or relax.
Word Family: **slackly,** *adverb;* **slackness,** *noun.*

slack (2) *noun*
the fine refuse of coal.

slacken *verb*
1. to loosen: '*slacken* the rope or it will break'.
2. to make or become less active, intense, etc.: '*slacken* speed so that I can catch up'.

slacker *noun*
(*informal*) a lazy person.

slacks *plural noun*
trousers.

slag *noun*
1. any non-metallic residue obtained during the smelting of metal ores.
2. *Geology:* the scoria from a volcano.
slagheap *noun*
a mound of waste matter from mining or a similar process.

slain *verb*
the past participle of the verb **slay.**

slake *verb*
1. to satisfy or partly satisfy a desire, thirst, etc.
2. to add water to lime to form calcium hydroxide (called **slaked lime**).

slalom (*say* **slay**–l'm) *noun*
the art of racing in and out of a line of posts or other obstacles, as in skiing. [Norwegian, sloping track]

slam (1) *verb*
(slammed, slamming)
1. to shut violently and noisily: 'she *slammed* the door'.
2. to put or knock down violently and noisily: 'she *slammed* the books onto the table'.
Usage: 'the critics *slammed* my new book' (= criticized severely).
slam *noun*
a violent and noisy closing or impact.

slam (2) *noun*
Cards: the winning of all the tricks (called a **grand slam**) or all but one (called a **small slam**) at whist, bridge, etc.

slander *noun*
Law: a false spoken statement against another person. Compare LIBEL.
Word Family: **slander,** *verb;* **slanderer,** *noun,* a person who slanders; **slanderous,** *adjective;* **slanderously,** *adverb.*

slang *noun*
the form of a language consisting of words in popular, current, informal use, as distinct from the formal, established language. Compare COLLOQUIAL.
Word Family: **slangy,** *adjective.*

slanging match
an exchange of insults or abuse.

slant (*say* slahnt) *verb*
to slope or lean at an angle: 'my writing *slants* forwards'.
Usage: 'the story was *slanted* to make him appear guilty' (= distorted).

slant *noun*
a lean or slope: 'the *slant* of a roof'.
Usage: 'the news gave a new *slant* to the situation' (= point of view, aspect).

slap *verb*
(slapped, slapping)
1. to strike or smack, especially with the open hand: 'he *slapped* my face'.
2. to put down loudly and forcefully: 'he *slapped* his wallet onto the counter'.
slap *noun*
a) a smart blow or smack. b) the sound of such a blow.
Phrases:
slap in the face, a rebuff or disappointment.
slap on the back, congratulations.
slap *adverb*
1. exactly: '*slap* in the middle of the road'.
2. straight: 'it hit me *slap* on the head'.

slap-bang *adverb*
(*informal*) suddenly or violently.

slapdash *adjective, adverb*
in a careless or hasty manner.

slaphappy *adjective*
(*informal*) cheerfully carefree or irresponsible.

slapstick *noun*
any form of entertainment based on practical jokes or loud and boisterous play-acting, e.g. between two circus clowns.

slap-up *adjective*
(*informal*) first-class.

slash *verb*
to cut with long, sweeping strokes: a) 'he *slashed* at the horse with a whip'; b) 'the chair has been *slashed* with a knife'.
Usage: 'the new government *slashed* taxes' (= greatly reduced).
slash *noun*
a) a sweeping stroke or cut. b) a gash made by such a stroke.

slat *noun*
a long, thin, narrow piece of wood, metal, etc., such as is used in venetian blinds.

slate *noun*
1. *Geology:* a hard, grey fine-grained rock, formed from compressed mudstone which splits easily into sheets.
2. a thin sheet of slate used in overlapping rows to form a roof, to put in a frame to write on, etc.
3. a dark, bluish-grey colour.
Phrases:
a clean slate, a good record.
put on the slate, to record an amount for future payment.
slate *verb*
to cover with slates.
Usage: 'why do the critics always *slate* my novels?' (= criticize severely).

slate club
a mutual benefit club collecting weekly contributions, usually at a pub.
[so called as accounts were originally chalked on a *slate*]

slattern *noun*
a dirty or untidy girl or woman.
Word Family: **slatternly**, *adjective, adverb.*

slaughter (*say* **slaw**ta) *noun*
the killing of animals, especially for food.
Usage: 'the *slaughter* of civilians in a war is tragic' (= brutal killing).
slaughter *verb*
1. to kill and cut up animals for food.
2. to massacre.
Usage: 'we *slaughtered* our opponents in the game' (= thoroughly defeated).
Word Family: **slaughterous**, *adjective*, brutal or destructive.

slaughterhouse *noun*
an abattoir.

slave *noun*
1. a person who is owned by another for whom he works without pay, rights, etc.
2. a person who is completely dominated by or in the power of another person, influence, etc.: 'a *slave* to fashion'.
slave *verb*
to work very hard: 'he *slaved* all night on his essay'.
Word Family: **slaver**, *noun*, a) a person who owns or deals in slaves, b) a ship used to transport slaves; **slavery**, *noun*, a) the condition of being a slave, b) the practice of keeping slaves.

slavedriver *noun*
1. a person who makes people work very hard.
2. an overseer of slaves.

slaver (*say* **slav**va) *verb*
to slobber or dribble.
Word Family: **slaver**, *noun*, saliva.

slavish (*say* **slay**-vish) *adjective*
of or like a slave: '*slavish* obedience to his every command'.
Word Family: **slavishly**, *adverb*; **slavishness**, *noun*.

slay *verb*
(slew, slain, slaying)
an old word meaning to kill or destroy.

sleazy *adjective*
shabby or dirty.

sled *noun*
a sledge, often used for transporting loads.

sledge *noun*
a) a vehicle mounted on runners, used over snow and ice and drawn by huskies, etc. b) a smaller version of this to take one or two persons, used in the pastime of sliding down snowy slopes. Also called a **toboggan**.
Word Family: **sledge**, *verb.*

sledge-hammer *noun*
a large, heavy hammer.

sleek *adjective*
1. soft, smooth and glossy.
2. (of a person) well-fed or well-groomed.
Usage: 'the new boss is a little too *sleek* in his manners' (= suave).
Word Family: **sleek**, *verb*, to smooth or make sleek; **sleekly**, *adverb*; **sleekness**, *noun.*

sleep *noun*
the condition or period during which the mind and body rest, and voluntary movements and full consciousness are suspended.
sleep *verb*
(slept, sleeping)
to rest or repose in sleep.
Usages:
a) 'this hotel *sleeps* 60 persons' (= has beds for).
b) 'I shall *sleep* in the open tonight' (= pass the night).
Phrases:
let sleeping dogs lie, to leave a situation as it is and not create trouble unnecessarily.
sleep on, 'I'll *sleep on* the problem' (= think about for a while).
sleep with, to have sexual intercourse with.
Word Family: **sleepless**, *adjective*; **sleeplessly**, *adverb*; **sleeplessness**, *noun.*

sleeper *noun*
1. a person or animal that sleeps.
2. a railway carriage with sleeping accommodation.
3. a beam or slab forming part of the foundation for railway tracks.
4. a ring worn in the ear after it has been pierced, to prevent the hole closing.

sleepily *adverb*
Word Family: see SLEEPY.

sleeping-bag *noun*
a long bag, often waterproof, for sleeping outdoors, etc.

sleeping partner
also called a **silent partner**
a person who puts money into a business but takes no active part in it.

sleeping-pill *noun*
any tablet taken to induce sleep.

sleeping sickness
a tropical African disease transmitted to man by the tsetse fly and causing increasing lethargy and, if untreated, death.

sleepwalker *noun*
a person who walks or performs other activities while asleep.
Word Family: **sleepwalk**, *verb.*

sleepy *adjective*
ready or wishing to sleep.
Usage: 'this is a *sleepy* little town' (= quiet).
Word Family: **sleepily**, *adverb*; **sleepiness**, *noun.*

sleepyhead *noun*
(*informal*) a sleepy or inattentive person.

sleepy sickness
a viral, sometimes epidemic, form of encephalitis marked by extreme lethargy, which may be followed by partial or complete recovery or may lead on to Parkinson's disease. Not to be confused with sleeping sickness.

sleet *noun*
a mixture of falling rain and snow.
Word Family: **sleet**, *verb.*

sleeve *noun*
1. the part of a garment which encloses all or part of the arm.
2. something, such as the protective cover for a gramophone record, which fits over or encloses another thing.
Word Family: **sleeveless**, *adjective.*

sleigh (*say* slay) *noun*
1. a light sledge drawn by one or more horses.
2. any of the various light sledges used in winter sports, e.g. the bobsleigh.
Word Family: **sleigh**, *verb.*

sleight of hand (*say* slite of hand)
also called **legerdemain**
any conjuring trick, such as making cards disappear, pulling rabbits out of hats, etc.
[*sleight* = slyness]

slender *adjective*
attractively thin: 'the *slender* stem of a wineglass'.
Usage: 'I only had a *slender* chance of winning' (= small).
Word Family: **slenderly,** *adverb*; **slenderness,** *noun.*

slept *verb*
the past tense and past participle of the verb **sleep.**

sleuth (*say* slooth) *noun*
(*informal*) a detective or investigator. [Icelandic *slodh* track]

slew (1) (*say* sloo) *verb*
the past tense of the verb **slay.**

slew (2) (*say* sloo) *verb*
to twist or swerve around, especially without moving from one place.

slice *noun*
1. a thin, flat and wide piece cut off from something: 'a *slice* of bread'.
2. any piece or portion: 'a *slice* of good luck'.
3. any tool or utensil with a broad, flat blade: 'an *eggslice*'.
4. *Sport:* a stroke which causes the ball to spin away from the desired direction, e.g. to the right of a right-handed player. Compare **HOOK.**
slice *verb*
1. to cut up into slices.
Usage: 'the boat *sliced* through the waves' (= cut).
2. *Sport:* to hit a slice.

slick (1) *adjective*
suave: 'the *slick* talk of a salesman'.
Usages:
a) (*informal*) 'that new suit looks *slick*' (= smart).
b) 'a *slick* business deal' (= shrewd, clever).
slick *noun*
a smooth or slippery area, such as a film of oil on water.
Word Family: **slick, slickly,** *adverbs*; **slickness,** *noun.*

slick (2) *verb*
to make sleek or smooth: 'to *slick* one's hair with oil'.

slicker *noun*
1. (*informal*) a slick person.
2. a person rather too smartly dressed.
city slicker, a smartly dressed businessman who arouses suspicions of sharp practice.

slide *verb*
(slid, sliding)
to move smoothly over a polished or slippery surface: 'the car *slid* on the icy road'.
Usages:
a) 'she *slid* out of the back door' (= went quickly or quietly, without fuss).
b) 'he *slid* into bad habits' (= passed gradually).
c) 'he had let things *slide*' (= deteriorate, fall into neglect).
slide *noun*
1. a sliding movement.
2. a structure with a smooth, sloping surface down which children may slide.
3. *Photography:* a positive image on film, usually in colour and projected on to a screen. Also called a **transparency.**
4. a small oblong piece of glass on which objects are placed for study under a microscope.
5. something which slides, such as a clasp worn in the hair, a movable part in a musical instrument, etc.

slide rule
a device for calculations, consisting of two or more logarithmic scales which slide past each other on a rule.

sliding scale
a scale of prices, wages, etc. which may be varied in relation to other factors such as taxes or cost of living.

slight *adjective*
1. small in amount, importance, etc.: 'a *slight* increase in salary'.
2. slender or frail-looking: 'a young girl of *slight* build'.
in the slightest, 'I'm not *in the slightest* worried' (= at all).
slight *verb*
to snub or ignore: 'he felt *slighted* because I had no time for a chat'.
Word Family: **slight,** *noun,* a snub or rebuff; **slightly,** *adverb,* a) to a small degree, b) slenderly; **slightness,** *noun*; **slighting,** *adjective,* insulting; **slightingly,** *adverb.*

slim *adjective*
(of a person) not stout or heavy.
Usages:
a) 'your *slim* excuse isn't convincing' (= poor, insufficient).
b) 'a *slim* chance' (= small).
slim *verb*
(slimmed, slimming)
to lose weight by dieting, etc.
Word Family: **slimly,** *adverb*; **slimness,** *noun.*

slime *noun*
a) soft, sticky, oozing mud. b) any thick, sticky fluid.

slime mould
Biology: a group of simple organisms having characteristics of both animals and plants.

slimy (*say* **slime**–ee) *adjective*
of, like or covered in slime.
Usage: 'he's only a *slimy* flatterer' (= unpleasantly servile).
Word Family: **slimily,** *adverb*; **sliminess,** *noun.*

sling *noun*
1. a loop or band by which something is suspended, such as the bandage supporting a broken arm.
2. a strap with a string attached to each end from which a stone is hurled by whirling it around the head and releasing one of the strings.
sling *verb*
(slung, slinging)
1. to hurl or fling: 'stop *slinging* stones'.
2. to arrange or support something so that it swings loosely: 'he *slung* the bag over his shoulder'.

slink *verb*
(slunk, slinking)
to move in a secret, guilty or ashamed manner.
Word Family: **slinkingly,** *adverb.*

slinky *adjective*
(*informal*) slender and flowing.

slip (1) *verb*
(slipped, slipping)
1. to lose one's balance or foothold: 'I *slipped* and fell from the tree'.
2. to fall or escape by not being held firmly: a) 'the glass *slipped* from my hand'; b) 'the dog *slipped* its leash'.
3. to move smoothly and gently: 'the boat *slipped* through the water'.
Usages:
a) 'let's *slip* away from the party' (= go quickly or quietly, without fuss).
b) 'she *slipped* a note into my hand' (= put quietly).
c) 'the stock market *slipped*' (= declined).
Phrases:
let slip, 'now you've *let slip* the secret' (= revealed unintentionally).
slip up, to be careless or make a mistake. *Word Family*: **slip–up,** *noun,* a mistake.
slip *noun*
1. the act of slipping.
2. a mistake, especially a careless one.
3. something which is easily slipped on or off: 'a *pillowslip*'.
4. a petticoat.
5. *Cricket:* a fielding position on the off–side close to and behind the wicket.
give someone the slip, to escape from someone.

slip (2) *noun*
1. a strip or narrow piece of wood, paper, etc.: 'a bank deposit *slip*'.
2. a part of a plant suitable for grafting or planting.
slip of a, 'he's only a *slip of a* boy' (= slim or young).

slipknot (*say* **slip**–not) *noun*
a knot which can slide along the piece of rope around which it is tied.

slipped disc
a painful condition caused by a disc between the spinal vertebrae becoming displaced and pressing on adjacent nerves, with sciatica as a common symptom.

slipper *noun*
a loose, light shoe for wearing in the house.

slippery (*say* **slippa**–ree) *adjective*
smooth and wet so as to cause slipping or sliding: 'I could not hold the *slippery* fish'.
Usage: 'he's a *slippery* rascal' (= untrustworthy).
Word Family: **slipperiness,** *noun.*

slipshod (*say* **slip**–shod) *adjective*
careless or untidy.

slip–up *noun*
Word Family: see SLIP UP under SLIP (1).

slipway *noun*
a ramp, from the shore into the water, from which boats may be launched or repaired.

slit *noun*
a long, narrow cut or opening.
slit *verb*
(slit, slitting)
to make a long cut or opening: 'she *slit* open the letter with a paperknife'.

slither (*say* **sli*th*a**) *verb*
to slide or slip unsteadily or awkwardly.
Word Family: **slither,** *noun.*

sliver (*say* **slivva**) *noun*
a small thin piece broken or split off from a larger piece.
Word Family: **sliver,** *verb,* to cut or break off in slivers.

slob *noun*
(*informal*) a clumsy, uncouth or untidy person.

slobber *verb*
to let saliva, etc. run from the mouth.
Word Family: **slobber**, *noun*, saliva; **slobbery**, *adjective*, a) unpleasantly wet, b) slobbering.

sloe *noun*
the small, astringent black plum of the blackthorn.
sloe gin, a liqueur made by steeping sloes in gin.

sloe-eyed *adjective*
having attractively dark, oval-shaped eyes.

slog *verb*
(**slogged, slogging**)
(*informal*) a) to hit hard. b) to work hard and steadily. c) to trudge or walk heavily.
Word Family: **slog**, *noun*, a) a strong heavy blow, b) hard work; **slogger**, *noun*.

slogan (*say* **slo**-gun) *noun*
a distinctive, easily remembered phrase, used to advertise a product, political party, etc.
[Gaelic *sluagh* army + *gairm* cry]

sloop *noun*
a yacht with one mast, a mainsail and one foresail.
[from Dutch]

slop *verb*
(**slopped, slopping**)
to spill or splash.
slop *noun*
(*often plural*) any dirty water or other liquid waste from a kitchen, etc.

slope *verb*
to lean or be at an angle: 'the roof *slopes* downwards'.
slope arms, to move a rifle from ground to shoulder in military drill.
slope *noun*
1. a) a sloping line. b) the degree of deviation of a line from the horizontal.
2. (*often plural*) an area of rising or falling ground: 'mountain *slopes*'.
Word Family: **slopingly**, *adverb*.

sloppy *adjective*
1. wet, muddy or slushy.
2. (*informal*) a) careless or untidy. b) foolishly sentimental.
Word Family: **sloppily**, *adverb*; **sloppiness**, *noun*.

sloppy joe
a loose, thick jumper.

slosh *verb*
1. to splash about in mud or slush.
2. (*informal*) to hit heavily.
Word Family: **slosh**, *noun*, a) slush, b) a heavy blow.

slot *noun*
a narrow groove or opening into which something is put or fitted.
Usage: 'the programme is scheduled for the midday time *slot*' (= particular position).
Word Family: **slot (slotted, slotting)**, *verb*, to make a slot or slots in or for.

sloth *noun*
1. laziness.
2. a slow-moving South American mammal, noted for hanging upside down from tree branches.
Word Family: **slothful**, *adjective*; **slothfully**, *adverb*; **slothfulness**, *noun*.
[from SLOW]

slot-machine *noun*
any coin-operated machine.

slouch (*rhymes with* ouch) *verb*
to sit, stand or move with a lazy, drooping posture.
Word Family: **slouch**, *noun*, a) a slouching posture, b) (informal) a slovenly performer.

slough (1) (*rhymes with* cow) *noun*
a swamp or a marshy area.

slough (2) (*say* sluf) *verb*
to shed or cast off: 'snakes *slough* their outer layer of skin'.
Word Family: **slough**, *noun*, a layer of dead skin or tissue.

slovenly (*say* **sluvv**'n-lee) *adjective*
dirty, careless or untidy in dress, habits, etc.
Word Family: **sloven**, *noun*, a slovenly person; **slovenliness**, *noun*.
[Dutch *slof* careless]

slow (*say* slo) *adjective*
1. taking a comparatively long time: a) 'a *slow* train'; b) 'I'm a *slow* reader'.
Usages:
a) 'the clock is *slow*' (= behind the correct time).
b) 'the *slow* child had trouble reading' (= not quick to learn).
c) 'we left the party early as it was so *slow*' (= dull, uninteresting).
d) 'put the meat in a *slow* oven' (= only warm).
2. *Sport:* (of a field, court, etc.) tending to make movement slow because the surface is wet.

slow *verb*
to make or become slow or slower.
Word Family: **slow**, **slowly**, *adverbs*; **slowness**, *noun.*

slowcoach *noun*
(*informal*) a person who is slow.

slow-motion *adjective*
relating to films in which the images move slowly, having been photographed at a greater number of frames per second than normal or being projected more slowly than normal.

slow-worm *noun*
also called a **blindworm**
a snake-like lizard without legs.

sloyd *noun*
a system of training in the use of the hands, based on woodworking and similar skills.
[Swedish *slojd* craft]

sludge (*say* sluj) *noun*
a) thick oozing mud or mire. b) any mud-like substance or deposit.

slug (1) *noun*
1. a slimy snail-like animal without a shell.
2. a small metal bullet.
3. (*informal*) a serving of alcohol.
Word Family: **slug** (**slugged, slugging**), *verb,* (informal) to fire bullets into.

slug (2) *verb*
(slugged, slugging)
(*informal*) to hit very hard, especially with the fist.
Word Family: **slug**, *noun,* a heavy blow with the fist.

sluggard *noun*
a lazy or slow-moving person.

sluggish *adjective*
moving or acting slowly and without energy.
Word Family: **sluggishly**, *adverb*, **sluggishness**, *noun.*

sluice (*say* sloose) *noun*
1. a channel which carries or controls a flow of water. Short form of **sluiceway**.
2. a gate or valve used to control such a flow.
sluice *verb*
to send a stream of water out, over or through.

slum *noun*
a) (*often plural*) a dirty, poor and overcrowded section of a city. b) a squalid building, house, etc.

slum *verb*
(slummed, slumming)
1. to go visiting in a slum area.
2. (*informal*) to live at a low or degraded level.
Word Family: **slummy**, *adjective.*

slumber *verb*
to sleep.
slumber *noun*
(*often plural*) sleep, especially deep sleep.
Word Family: **slumberous**, **slumbrous**, *adjective,* a) sleepy, b) causing sleep.

slump *verb*
1. to fall or drop heavily: a) 'he *slumped* exhausted into a chair'; b) 'prices *slumped*'.
2. to droop limply: '*slumped* over a book'.
Word Family: **slump**, *noun,* a heavy or sudden fall.

slung *verb*
the past tense and past participle of the verb **sling**.

slunk *verb*
the past tense and past participle of the verb **slink**.

slur *verb*
(slurred, slurring)
to pronounce words indistinctly by running them together.
slur *noun*
1. the act of slurring: 'he speaks with a *slur*'.
2. a suggestion of disgrace; a stain: 'it's a *slur* on my good name'.
3. *Music:* a curved line over two or more notes, indicating that they should be played together smoothly.

slurry *noun*
a thin watery mixture, especially of cement.

slush *noun*
1. a) a mixture of melting snow, ice and mud. b) any soft or watery substance.
2. (*informal*) silly or sentimental talk, writing, etc.
Word Family: **slushy**, *adjective*; **slushiness**, *noun.*

slush fund
a secret fund of money used to bribe officials, especially so as to gain orders and favours for an organization.

slut *noun*
a slovenly or immoral woman.
Word Family: **sluttish**, *adjective.*

sly *adjective*
1. secretive and cunning: 'a *sly* pickpocket'.
2. playful or mischievous: '*sly* humour'.
on the sly, secretly.
Word Family: **slyly**, *adverb*; **slyness**, *noun*.

smack (1) *verb*
to strike sharply, especially with the palm of the hand.
smack one's lips, to make a loud, sharp sound with the lips, e.g. in enjoyment or anticipation.
smack *noun*
1. a sharp, quick stroke or blow.
2. a smacking of the lips.
3. (*informal*) a loud kiss.
smack in the eye, a rebuff.
smack *adverb*
suddenly or sharply: 'the car ran *smack* into a tree'.
Word Family: **smacking**, *adjective*, a) strong or brisk, b) very big.

smack (2) *verb*
to have a trace or suggestion: 'your behaviour *smacks* of insolence'.
Word Family: **smack**, *noun*, a slight flavour or trace.

smack (3) *noun*
a small sailing boat, especially one used for fishing.

smacker *noun*
(*informal*) a dollar or pound.

small (*rhymes with* ball) *adjective*
1. not large or great in size, amount, etc.: a) 'a *small* house'; b) 'there's still one *small* problem'.
2. doing things on a limited scale: a) 'a *small* shopkeeper'; b) 'he's only a *small* eater'.
Usages:
a) 'you have a *small* mind' (= mean, petty).
b) 'caught in the act of stealing, she felt really *small*' (= ashamed, humble).
small change, coins of low value.
small *noun*
(*plural*) underwear.
the small of the back, (of the body) the lower middle part of the back.
Word Family: **small**, *adverb*, into small pieces; **smallness**, *noun*; **smallish**, *adjective*, rather small.

small arms
any firearms which can be carried, such as rifles, machine-guns, pistols, etc.

small fry
young or insignificant people or things.

smallholding *noun*
a small farm.
Word Family: **smallholder**, *noun*.

small hours
the early hours of the morning.

small intestine
Anatomy: the long thin tube connecting the stomach and the caecum, divided into three parts, the duodenum, the jejunum, and the ileum.

small-minded *adjective*
selfish or petty.

smallpox *noun*
an infectious, viral disease causing blisters which often form permanent pockmarks.

small print
(*informal*) the numerous restrictive and exclusive clauses printed on a contract, e.g. of insurance, often in small close-set type so that they do not get read.

smalls *plural noun*
see SMALL.

small-scale *adjective*
of small size or scope: a) 'a *small-scale* model of the solar system'; b) 'a *small-scale* business venture'.

small slam
Cards: see SLAM (2).

small talk
any unimportant chatter.

small-time *adjective*
(*informal*) petty or unimportant: 'a *small-time* hoodlum'.

smalt (*say* smawlt) *noun*
a form of blue glass made by blending silica with cobalt oxide.

smarmy *adjective*
(*informal*) unpleasantly flattering.
Word Family: **smarminess**, *noun*.

smart *adjective*
1. clever or bright: 'that's a *smart* little lad'.
Usages:
a) 'a *smart* remark' (= cleverly rude).
b) 'a *smart* businessman' (= shrewd).
2. brisk, vigorous or lively: 'we set off at a *smart* pace'.
3. elegantly neat or fashionable: a) 'a *smart* outfit'; b) she belongs to a very *smart* set'.
4. stinging or severe: 'a *smart* slap'.

smart aleck, (*informal*) a conceited know–all.
smart *verb*
to cause or feel a stinging pain: 'this cut *smarts*'.
Usage: 'he *smarted* under the stinging rebuke' (= felt hurt and distressed).
smarten *verb*
smarten up, a) to make or become more trim and neat in appearance; b) to make brisker or more vigorous.
smart *noun*
a) a sharp, stinging pain. b) acute mental distress.
Word Family: **smartly**, *adverb*; **smartness**, *noun*.

smarty–pants, smarty–boots *noun*
(*informal*) a person who tries to be too smart.

smash *verb*
1. to break violently, especially into pieces: 'the windscreen was *smashed* in the accident'.
2. to rush violently or crash: 'the car *smashed* into the wall'.
Usage: 'all my illusions about work were *smashed*' (= destroyed, shattered).
3. *Sport:* to hit the ball with a hard, fast overarm stroke.
smash *noun*
1. the act or sound of smashing: 'the tea–tray fell with an awful *smash*'.
Usage: 'many banks failed in the *smash*' (= financial collapse).
2. (*informal*) a smash–hit.
smash *adverb*
with a smashing movement or sound: 'he ran *smash* into the brick wall'.
smasher *noun*
(*informal*) a) a smashing blow or crash. b) a strikingly good–looking person. c) a smash–hit.
Word Family: **smashing**, *adjective*, (informal) very good; **smashingly**, *adverb*.

smash–and–grab *noun*
a very swift robbery performed by breaking a shop window, grabbing the goods and running off.

smash–hit *noun*
(*informal*) something which is an immediate and great success.

smash–up *noun*
a violent collision or accident.

smattering, smatter *noun*
a superficial or incomplete knowledge of something.
Word Family: **smatter**, *verb*, to do superficially.

smear *verb*
to spread with a sticky or greasy substance.
Usages:
a) 'do not *smear* the drawing' (= smudge).
b) 'the scandal *smeared* his reputation' (= damaged).
smear *noun*
1. a mark made by or as if by smearing.
2. slander or libel: 'a *smear* campaign'.
3. something which is smeared, such as a small amount of substance examined on a microscopic slide
Word Family: **smeary**, *adjective*, a) tending to smear or dirty, b) covered with smears.

smell *verb*
(**smelt** or **smelled, smelling**)
1. to perceive by means of the nose.
Usage: 'I *smell* trouble' (= anticipate).
2. a) to be perceived by the nose as: 'the roses *smell* sweet'. b) to be perceived by the nose as offensive: 'you *smell*!'.
Phrases:
smell of, 'the plan *smells of* crime' (= suggests).
smell out, 'a good reporter can *smell out* stories' (= find, search out).
smell *noun*
1. a) the sense of smelling. b) the quality of something which may be smelt: 'certain flowers have no *smell*'.
2. the act of smelling: 'may I have a *smell* of that perfume?'.
Usage: 'it all had the *smell* of a trick' (= suggestion).
Word Family: **smelly**, *adjective*, having an offensive smell; **smelliness**, *noun*.

smelling salts
any substance, consisting mainly of ammonium carbonate, which is sniffed to cure faintness, headache, etc.

smelt (1) *verb*
to extract a metal from its ores by heating, melting, etc.

smelt (2) *noun*
a small round fish of the salmon family with a delicate flavour.

smile *verb*
to express pleasure, amusement, kindliness, scorn, etc. by curving the corners of the mouth upwards.
Usage: 'the gods *smile* upon the brave' (= look with approval or kindness).
Word Family: **smile**, *noun*; **smilingly**, *adverb*.

smirch *verb*
to soil, stain or dirty.
Usage: 'the violent attacks *smirched* the city's reputation' (= disgraced).
Word Family: **smirch**, *noun.*

smirk *verb*
to smile in an affected, silly or self-satisfied way.
Word Family: **smirk**, *noun.*

smite *verb*
(smote, smitten, smiting)
an old word meaning to stroke or hit hard: 'he *smote* the ball as far as he could'.
Usages:
a) 'the town was *smitten* with plague' (= affected severely).
b) 'I think he is rather *smitten* by her' (= in love (with)).

smith *noun*
a person who works with metals, especially a blacksmith.

smithereens (*say* smi*tha*-**reenz**) *plural noun*
(*informal*) small bits and pieces: 'smashed to *smithereens*'.

smithy (*say* smi*th*-ee) *noun*
a forge.

smitten *verb*
the past participle of the verb **smite**.

smock *noun*
also called a **pinafore**
a loose dress or apron, sometimes worn to protect clothes.
smocking *noun*
a style of needlework in which the fabric is gathered with small stitches to form a decorative pattern of folds.
Word Family: **smock**, *verb.*

smog *noun*
fog contaminated by pollution.
Word Family: **smoggy**, *adjective.*
[SM(oke) + (f)OG]

smoke *noun*
1. the suspension of fine, solid particles in a gas, given off by burning substances.
2. (*informal*) a) the act of taking in and breathing out the smoke from a cigarette, etc. b) a cigarette, etc.
go up in smoke, a) to be burnt up completely; b) to end in failure.
smoke *verb*
1. to give off smoke.
2. to inhale and exhale the smoke of a cigarette, etc.
3. to preserve and flavour food by drying it in smoke.
smoke out, a) to drive out from concealment with smoke; b) to bring to public view or awareness.
smoker *noun*
1. a person or thing that smokes.
2. *Railways:* a railway compartment or carriage in which smoking is allowed.
Word Family: **smoky**, *adjective*, a) full of or giving off much smoke, b) having the taste or colour of smoke; **smokily**, *adverb*; **smokiness**, *noun*; **smokeless**, *adjective.*

smokebomb (*say* **smoke-bom**) *noun*
a bomb which sends out clouds of smoke, used for concealment or in theatrical productions.

smokeless zone
an area where it is illegal to burn fuels which produce smoke.

smokescreen *noun*
1. a dense smoke made to conceal military operations from enemy observation.
2. anything used to conceal the truth: 'he threw up a *smokescreen* of excuses'.

smokestack *noun*
a chimney or funnel, e.g. on a factory or steamboat, through which smoke, gases, etc. are discharged.

smokiness *noun*
Word Family: see SMOKE.

smoking-jacket *noun*
a man's loose, soft jacket, often made of silk or velvet, worn in the house.

smoky *adjective*
Word Family: see SMOKE.

smolder *verb*
American: to smoulder.

smooch *verb*
(*informal*) to kiss and cuddle.
Word Family: **smooch**, *noun.*

smooth (*say* smoo*th*) *adjective*
having a surface without irregularities: a) 'a *smooth* tabletop'; b) '*smooth* seas'.
Usages:
a) 'a *smooth* ride' (= free from bumps and jolts).
b) 'I don't like his *smooth* manners' (= suave).
c) 'this old whisky is very *smooth*' (= free from sharpness or harshness of taste).
d) 'add the milk to the flour and stir to a *smooth* paste' (= without lumps).
e) 'the skater traced out a *smooth* curve' (= easy and uninterrupted).

smooth *verb*
to make or become smooth: 'he *smoothed* out the crumpled paper'.
Usages:
a) 'to *smooth* the way' (= remove difficulties or hindrances from).
b) 'she tried to *smooth* my ruffled feelings' (= calm down).
smooth over, 'he's always trying to *smooth over* the difficulties' (= cover up, gloss over).
smooth *noun*
something which is smooth, such as the side of a tennis racket on which the strings form a flat surface.
Word Family: **smoothly**, *adverb*; **smoothness**, *noun.*

smoothbore *adjective*
(of a gun) with no spiral grooves inside the barrel.

smoothie (*say* **smoo–*th*ee**) *noun*
(*informal*) a glib, soft-spoken plausible rogue.

smooth-spoken *adjective*
smooth-tongued.

smooth-tongued *adjective*
glib and plausible: 'a *smooth-tongued* rascal'.

smorgasbord (*say* **smorguz**–bord) *noun*
a meal with many different dishes, usually cold meats and salads, to which diners help themselves.
[Swedish *smorgas* sandwich + *bord* table]

smote *verb*
the past tense of the verb **smite**.

smother (*rhymes with* mother) *verb*
to stifle or suffocate: 'the baby was *smothered* by his pillow'.
Usages:
a) 'he *smothered* his anger' (= suppressed).
b) 'he *smothered* himself up in a coat and scarf' (= thickly covered or wrapped).

smoulder (*say* **smole**–da) *verb*
to burn and smoke without flame: 'the embers *smouldered* in the grate'.
Usages:
a) 'her eyes *smouldered* with rage' (= showed suppressed feelings).
b) 'rebellion *smouldered* in the hearts of the soldiers' (= existed inwardly).
Word Family: **smoulder**, *noun.*

smudge (*say* smuj) *noun*
a dirty, blotted or blurred mark: a) 'there's a *smudge* on your forehead'; b) 'the castle was just a *smudge* on the horizon'.
Word Family: **smudge**, *verb*, a) to make a smudge or smudges on, b) to become blurred or blotted; **smudgy**, *adjective*; **smudgily**, *adverb*; **smudginess**, *noun.*

smug *adjective*
self-satisfied.
Word Family: **smugly**, *adverb*; **smugness**, *noun.*

smuggle *verb*
to bring goods into a country without paying customs duty on them.
Usage: 'she *smuggled* a file into the prison' (= got secretly).
Word Family: **smuggler**, *noun.*

smut *noun*
1. a) a piece of soot or dirt. b) a black dirty mark.
2. any indecent language or writing.
3. a fungal disease of plants, especially cereals, causing a black, powdery surface.
Word Family: **smutty**, *adjective*, a) grimy or dirty, b) indecent or obscene; **smuttily**, *adverb*; **smuttiness**, *noun.*

snack *noun*
a small meal or refreshment.

snaffle *noun*
a jointed bit for a horse.
ride on a snaffle, to coax gently and tactfully.
snaffle *verb*
1. a) to put a snaffle on a horse. b) to control by or as if by a snaffle.
2. (*informal*) to steal or appropriate.

snag *noun*
1. a sharp or jagged projection, especially one below the surface of water.
Usage: 'there's been a *snag* in our plans' (= unexpected or hidden difficulty).
2. a small hole or ladder in a garment, caused by catching it on a sharp object.
snag *verb*
(**snagged**, **snagging**)
to get caught by or as if by a snag: a) 'I've *snagged* my stocking'; b) 'the boat was *snagged* fast'.

snail *noun*
1. a slimy, air-breathing gastropod with a single, often spirally coiled, external shell.
2. a slow or lazy person.
at a snail's pace, very slowly.

snake *noun*
1. any of various slender, scaly, legless reptiles without eardrums or movable

eyelids, and having the two halves of the lower jaw connected by elastic fibres.
2. a treacherous person.
snake in the grass, an insidious or hidden enemy.
Word Family: **snake,** *verb,* to move, wind or curve like a snake; **snaky,** *adjective,* a) of or like a snake, b) (informal) ungrateful or treacherous.

snake–charmer
a person who controls a snake by means of rhythmic music and bodily movements.

snakes and ladders
any of a variety of children's board games in which dice are thrown to determine progress up or down the ladder of success.

snap *verb*
(snapped, snapping)
1. to make or cause to make a sudden, sharp sound: 'he *snapped* his fingers to attract the waiter's attention'.
2. to break suddenly with a sharp sound: 'a twig *snapped* under her foot'.
3. to make a sudden, quick bite or snatch: 'the dog *snapped* at my ankles'.
Usages:
a) 'he *snapped* the lid shut crossly' (= closed with a snap).
b) 'he *snapped* to attention as the general passed him' (= moved quickly).
c) 'his self–control finally *snapped* under the continual taunting' (= gave way).
d) 'he *snapped* angrily in reply' (= spoke sharply).
4. to take a photograph of.
Phrases:
snap one's fingers at, to scorn or be unintimidated by.
snap out of it, to recover from a mood quickly.
snap someone's head off, to speak very sharply or rudely to.
snap up, 'you should *snap up* this bargain' (= seize quickly).
snap *noun*
1. a) a sudden, sharp sound: 'the rope broke with a *snap*'. b) a sudden, sharp breaking.
2. a) a quick, sudden bite or snatch. b) a quick, sharp speech.
3. a catch or clasp: 'we had to break the *snap* to get the box open'.
4. a thin, crisp biscuit: 'a *gingersnap*'.
5. a short spell of weather: 'we're in for a cold *snap*'.
6. *Cards:* a simple game in which each player throws cards onto a pile aiming to win by being first to notice two consecutive cards of equal value.
7. a snapshot.
not a snap, not at all.
snap *adjective*
made or done hastily or without considering: 'a *snap* decision'.
snappy *adjective*
1. impatient or irritable: 'don't get *snappy* with me'.
2. quick or lively in action: 'she walks along at a very *snappy* pace'.
3. (*informal*) neat and smart: 'air–hostesses wear *snappy* uniforms'.
make it snappy, (*informal*) to hurry up.
Word Family: **snappily,** *adverb*; **snappiness,** *noun*; **snappish,** *adjective,* a) apt to snap, b) impatient or irritable; **snappishly,** *adverb*; **snappishness,** *noun.*

snapdragon *noun*
a plant with showy, brightly coloured spikes of flowers.

snapshot *noun*
a quickly taken or informal photograph.

snare (1) (*rhymes with* air) *noun*
1. a device, usually a noose, for trapping animals.
2. anything which catches or traps unexpectedly.
Word Family: **snare,** *verb,* to catch in a snare.

snare (2) (*rhymes with* air) *noun*
any of the strings or wires stretched across the skin of a small double–headed drum to increase reverberation.

snark *noun*
any of a variety of imaginary creatures, some of which have feathers and bite and others have whiskers and scratch. [invented by Lewis Carroll in a narrative poem, 1876]

snarl (1) *verb*
1. to make a harsh, angry growl: 'the dog *snarled* at the strangers'.
2. to speak in an angry, resentful or quarrelsome manner: 'he just *snarled* at her from behind his paper'.
Word Family: **snarl,** *noun*; **snarly,** *adjective.*

snarl (2) *noun*
a tangle: a) 'a traffic *snarl*'; b) 'try and pull a comb through these *snarls*!'.

Usage: 'he tried to sort out a *snarl* which had arisen at work' (= complication).
Word Family: **snarl**, *verb.*

snarl-up *noun*
a confusion or mix-up.

snatch *verb*
to seize suddenly: 'he *snatched* up his hat and ran'.
Usages:
a) 'he *snatched* off his hat and bent his knee to the king' (= took hastily).
b) 'they *snatched* victory at the last minute' (= rescued by prompt action).
snatch at, a) to try to seize; b) to take eagerly.
snatch *noun*
1. the act of snatching: 'he made a *snatch* at my sandwich'.
2. a) a small fragment: 'I can only remember *snatches* of the melody'. b) a brief period of time: 'to sleep in *snatches*'.
Word Family: **snatchy**, *adjective,* done or occurring in snatches; **snatcher,** *noun.*

snazzy *adjective*
(*informal*) very smart or well-dressed.

sneak *verb*
1. to move or act in a furtive way: 'he *sneaked* down the hall to the fridge'.
2. to do or act secretly or stealthily: '*sneak* a look through the keyhole'.
3. (*informal*) to tell tales: 'it's just like him to *sneak* on us to teacher'.
sneak *noun*
(*informal*) a telltale.
sneaking *adjective*
a) acting in an underhand way. b) secret or unavowed: 'I think she feels a *sneaking* sympathy for him'. c) growing insidiously: 'a *sneaking* suspicion'.
Word Family: **sneaky,** *adjective,* mean, tricky, cowardly or contemptible; **sneakily,** *adverb*; **sneakiness,** *noun.*

sneaker *noun*
1. a light, canvas shoe with a rope or rubber sole.
2. a person who sneaks about.

sneer *verb*
to show contempt by a curl of the lips, scornful words, etc.
Word Family: **sneer,** *noun,* a sneering remark or expression; **sneerer,** *noun,* a person who sneers; **sneering,** *adjective*; **sneeringly,** *adverb.*

sneeze *verb*
to expel air through the nose and mouth in a sudden, explosive action.
not to be sneezed at, (*informal*) not to be dismissed lightly.
Word Family: **sneeze,** *noun,* the act or sound of sneezing; **sneezer,** *noun.*

snick *noun*
1. a small cut: 'he made a *snick* in the wood with his penknife'.
2. a click: 'the door closed behind him with a *snick*'.
3. *Sport:* a hit which deflects the ball sideways.
Word Family: **snick,** *verb.*

snicker *noun*
1. a long soft snorting neigh.
2. a snigger.
Word Family: **snicker,** *verb.*

snide *adjective*
slyly nasty or derogatory: '*snide* remarks'.
Word Family: **snidely,** *adverb.*

sniff *verb*
to draw into the nose in short, audible breaths: 'to *sniff* snuff'.
Usages:
a) 'he *sniffed* the wine before he tasted it' (= smelt by sniffing).
b) 'they *sniffed* at her modern ideas' (= expressed contempt).
c) 'the police have been *sniffing* around' (= looking, investigating).
sniff out, 'he could *sniff out* trouble like nobody else I knew' (= detect).
Word Family: **sniff,** *noun,* a) the act or sound of sniffing, b) something which is inhaled by sniffing; **sniffer,** *noun*; **sniffy,** *adjective,* (informal) scornful or disdainful.

sniffle *verb*
to sniff repeatedly.
Word Family: **sniffle,** *noun.*

snigger *noun*
a half-suppressed or smothered laugh, usually expressing derision, disrespect, etc.
Word Family: **snigger,** *verb.*

snip *verb*
(snipped, snipping)
to cut with a small, quick stroke or strokes: 'to *snip* a person's fringe'.
snip *noun*
1. the act or sound of snipping: 'with a few quick *snips* she pruned the bush'.
2. a) a small cut: 'make a *snip* here for the buttonhole'. b) a small piece snipped off.
3. a bargain.

4. (*plural*) small shears for cutting metal: 'a pair of *tinsnips*'.

snipe *noun*
1. a long-billed marshbird, often shot as game.
2. a shot, etc. fired from a concealed position.
snipe *verb*
1. to fire shots from a concealed position.
2. to make nasty or critical remarks.
Word Family: **sniper**, *noun*.

snippet *noun*
a small piece or amount.

snitch (1) *verb*
(*informal*) to steal.

snitch (2) *verb*
(*informal*) to turn informer.
Word Family: **snitcher**, *noun*.

snivel (*say* **snivv'l**) *verb*
(snivelled, snivelling)
1. to weep and sniff.
2. to complain in a tearful or whining way.
3. to have mucus running from the nose.
Word Family: **snivel**, *noun*, the act of snivelling; **sniveller**, *noun*.
[Old English *snofl* mucus]

snob *noun*
a person who sets too high a value on social standing and wealth, seeking to imitate or associate with those he believes to be his superiors and despising those he regards as his inferiors.
Word Family: **snobbery**, **snobbishness**, *nouns*, the state or quality of being a snob; **snobbish**, *adjective*, of or like a snob; **snobbishly**, *adverb*.

snog *verb*
(*informal*) to kiss and cuddle.

snood (*rhymes with* food) *noun*
an old-fashioned, net-like hat holding the hair at the back of the head.
Word Family: **snood**, *verb*.

snook *noun*
a gesture of contempt made with thumb to nose and outstretched fingers: 'he cocked a *snook* at me'.

snooker *noun*
a game similar to billiards, using 22 balls of different colours which are hit into the pockets in various orders.
Compare POOL (2).
snooker *verb*
(*informal*) to prevent a person from achieving some aim, etc.

snoop *verb*
(*informal*) to prowl or pry.
Word Family: **snooper**, **snoop**, *nouns*, a person who snoops; **snoopy**, *adjective*.

snoot *noun*
(*informal*) the nose.

snooty (*say* **snoo**-tee) *adjective*
(*informal*) haughty or snobbish.

snooze *verb*
(*informal*) to doze.
Word Family: **snooze**, *noun*.

snore *verb*
to breathe during sleep with a harsh, rough sound.
Word Family: **snore**, *noun*; **snorer**, *noun*, a person who snores.

snorkel *noun*
a breathing tube held in the mouth and projecting upwards, so that a swimmer may breathe when just under water.
Word Family: **snorkel**, *verb*, to swim under water with a snorkel.
[German *Schnorkel*]

snort *verb*
1. to force breath through the nostrils with a loud, harsh sound.
2. to let out a loud burst of laughter.
3. to express contempt, indignation, etc. with a snort.
Word Family: **snort**, *noun*, a) the act or sound of snorting, b) (informal) a small drink of alcohol.

snot *noun*
(*informal*) a) mucus from the nose. b) a contemptible person.
Word Family: **snotty**, *adjective*, a) dirty, b) (informal) conceited or arrogant.

snout (*rhymes with* out) *noun*
1. the nose of an animal, often including the jaws.
2. something which has the shape, position or function of a snout.

snow (*say* sno) *noun*
1. the delicate ice crystals formed in clouds from water-vapour below freezing point, which join together and fall to the ground as flakes.
2. any white spots on a television screen, caused by interference or weak signals.
snow *verb*
to fall as snow: 'it has been *snowing*'.
Usage: 'letters and telegrams *snowed* in all day for her birthday' (= poured).

Phrases:
be snowed in, be snowed up, to be shut in by snow.
snowed under, a) covered with snow; b) 'we are *snowed under* with work' (= overwhelmed).
Word Family: **snowy,** *adjective,* a) white as snow, b) covered with snow.

snowball *noun*
a ball of snow pressed together to be thrown.
Word Family: **snowball,** *verb,* a) to throw snowballs at, b) to grow larger in continual stages.

snowdrop *noun*
a small, early spring plant with white flowers, growing from a bulb.

snowfall *noun*
a) a fall of snow. b) the amount of snow which has fallen at a particular time or place.

snowfield *noun*
an area of permanent snow.

snow goose
a pure white goose with black wing-tips.

snow leopard
see OUNCE (2).

snowline *noun*
the height on a mountain above which there is always snow.

snowman *noun*
the shape of a man, made in snow.
Abominable Snowman, see YETI.

snowplough *noun*
a device attached to the front of a vehicle and used to push snow aside.

snowshoe *noun*
a device, similar to a tennis racket, consisting of a network of thongs in a wooden frame and attached to boots for walking over soft snow.

snowy *adjective*
Word Family: see SNOW.

snub *verb*
(snubbed, snubbing)
to treat a person with contempt or coolness, especially by ignoring him.
Word Family: **snub,** *noun,* contemptuous words or behaviour.

snub-nosed *adjective*
having a short, turned-up nose.

snuff (1) *noun*
1. a form of powdered tobacco taken into the nose by sniffing.
2. a sniff or snort.
snuff *verb*
to inhale through the nose: '*snuff* this medicine'.
Usages:
a) 'the dog *snuffed* at the tree' (= sniffed).
b) 'he *snuffed* and coughed' (= snorted).

snuff (2) *verb*
to extinguish a candle.
snuff it, (*informal*) to die.
Word Family: **snuff,** *noun,* the burnt part of a candlewick; **snuffer,** *noun,* an instrument for snuffing candles.

snuffle *verb*
1. to breathe or sniff noisily, as with a cold.
2. to speak through the nose or with a nasal tone.
Word Family: **snuffle,** *noun*; **snuffly,** *adjective.*

snuffy *adjective*
easily displeased or huffy.
Word Family: **snuffily,** *adverb*; **snuffiness,** *noun.*

snug *adjective*
1. cosy: 'a *snug* corner beside the fire'.
2. close-fitting: 'a *snug* waistcoat'.
Word Family: **snugly,** *adverb*; **snugness,** *noun.*

snuggle *verb*
to cuddle up or more closely, for warmth, comfort, affection, etc.

so *adverb*
1. just as said, directed, suggested or implied: a) 'hold your arm out *so*'; b) 'he said he would succeed, and he did *so*'.
2. in the same way: 'Keith says we should go, and I think *so* too'.
3. then: 'home we went, and *so* to bed'.
4. to an indicated or suggested degree or extent: 'I didn't realize the plains stretched *so* far'.
5. very or extremely: 'you are *so* helpful'.
6. to a definite but unspecified extent or degree: 'I can only stay for a day or *so*'.
7. most certainly or indeed: 'midnight? *So* it is!'.
8. therefore: 'the camel was thirsty, *so* we gave it a drink'.
9. true: 'that is just not *so*'.
10. according to the truth of what has been sworn or asserted: '*so* help me God'.
11. apparently: '*so* you don't have an alibi'.

Phrases:
and so on, and so forth, et cetera.
just so, 'he always wants to have everything *just so*' (= in perfect order).
so as, 'I'll work late tonight *so as* to catch up' (= with the purpose of).
so much for, '*so much for* your hopes of wealth and power' (= that's the end of).
so that, a) 'he shunned society, *so that* people thought he was dead' (= with the result that); b) 'write to me *so that* I know how you are' (= in order that).
so what!, (*informal*) what does that matter.
so *conjunction*
1. in order that: 'be quiet *so* that he won't wake'.
2. therefore: 'they were expensive, *so* use them sparingly'.
so *interjection*
used to indicate realization of fact, situation, etc.: '*So*! You've been lying to me again'.

soak *verb*
to remain or allow to remain in a liquid until saturated.
Usages:
a) 'water was *soaking* through the roof of the tent' (= seeping).
b) 'the news has not *soaked* in yet' (= been taken in).
c) 'blotting paper *soaks* up ink' (= draws, dries).
d) 'she *soaks* herself in romantic novels' (= involves eagerly).
soak *noun*
1. the act of soaking: 'give the sheets a good *soak*'.
2. (*informal*) a drunkard.

so-and-so *noun*
1. a person or thing that is not definitely named.
2. (*informal*) a mean or nasty person.

soap *noun*
a substance made from a mixture of natural oils and fats with an alkali, used for washing.
Word Family: **soap**, *verb*, to rub or cover with soap; **soapy**, *adjective*; **soapily**, *adverb*; **soapiness**, *noun*.

soapbox *noun*
a place or means, originally an improvised platform, used to make a speech, express one's opinions, etc.

soap opera
any radio or television serial using extreme sentiment to describe domestic scenes.
[of the type sponsored by advertisers of soap, detergents, etc.]

soapstone *noun*
Geology: any soft stone with a greasy feeling, usually a variety of talc and used for tabletops, hearths, etc.

soar (*rhymes with* roar) *verb*
a) to rise or fly upwards, like a bird.
b) to glide at a great height.
Usages:
a) 'the mountain *soars* into the clouds' (= ascends).
b) 'her heart *soared* with delight' (= was inspired).
Word Family: **soarer**, *noun*.

sob *verb*
(sobbed, sobbing)
1. to weep with loud or shaking catches of the breath.
2. to make a similar sound: 'the wind *sobbed* in the trees'.
Word Family: **sob**, *noun*, a sobbing sound.

sober (*say* **so**–ba) *adjective*
1. not drunk.
2. serious: 'a *sober* young student'.
Usages:
a) 'all employees should wear *sober* clothes' (= plain, not elaborate).
b) 'he made a *sober* decision concerning his career' (= rational, sensible).
Word Family: **sober**, *verb*, to make or become sober; **soberly**, *adverb*; **soberness**, *noun*.
[from Latin]

sobriety (*say* so–**brie**–a–tee) *noun*
1. the state of being sober.
2. seriousness.

sobriquet (*say* **sob**–ree–kay) *noun*
also spelt **soubriquet**
a nickname.
[French]

sob-story *noun*
a story intended to inspire sentiment or pity, especially one used as an excuse.

so-called *adjective*
known by this term, often incorrectly: 'he was deserted by all his *so-called* friends'.

soccer (*say* **sokk**a) *noun*
a type of football played with a spherical ball which must not be handled except by the goalkeeper, and having 11 players in a side.
[for *Association* football]

sociable (*say* **so**–sha–b'l) *adjective*
friendly or enjoying the company of others.
Word Family: **sociably**, *adverb*; **sociability**, *noun.*

social (*say* **so**–sh'l) *adjective*
1. living or tending to live in a community rather than alone: 'bees are *social* insects'.
2. of or relating to life within a society: 'democracy is a *social* and political theory'.
Usages:
a) 'she is part of a *social* clique' (= wealthy and worldly).
b) 'the politician attended several *social* functions in the district' (= organized for friendly gathering).
Word Family: **social**, *noun*, a party or friendly gathering; **socially**, *adverb*; **sociality** (*say* so–shee–**alli**–tee), *noun*, the state of being social or sociable, especially as the tendency to form communities.
[Latin *socius* a partner or acting jointly]

social class
short form is **class**
a group of people in a society, classified by their sharing of similar occupations, incomes and social and political attitudes and forming part of a hierarchy.

social climber
a person who tries to move into a higher social class.

social credit
an economic theory that universal prosperity could be based on the payment to all of an annual national dividend varying with a country's wealth.

socialism (*say* **so**–sha–lizm) *noun*
a social theory or system based on public control and ownership of the means of production and distribution of goods.
Word Family: **socialist**, *noun*; **socialist, socialistic**, *adjective.*

socialite (*say* **so**–sha–lite) *noun*
a person who moves in rich or fashionable circles.

socialize (*say* **so**–sha–lize) **socialise** *verb*
1. to make an individual ready for life in a community, e.g. by acquiring accepted behaviour patterns.
2. to establish or organize according to socialism: '*socialized* medicine'.
3. (*informal*) to take part in social activities.
Word Family: **socialization**, *noun.*

social science
also called **social studies**
the study of subjects such as economics, sociology, politics, etc. which relate to man within a society.

social security
the financial care provided by a government for the elderly, the sick and the unemployed.

social service
1. the organized work of people trained to improve social conditions.
2. (*plural*) social welfare.

social studies
see SOCIAL SCIENCE.

social welfare
the services and aid established by a government for the welfare of its people.

social worker
a person trained to take part in social welfare, giving advice to individuals in need and working to improve conditions for poor people, etc.

society (*say* so–**sigh**–a–tee) *noun*
1. a) mankind, considered as a group or community: '20th–century *society*'.
b) a relatively settled group of people or animals who have some degree of organization and cooperation.
2. the structure, institutions, culture, way of life, etc. of such a group: 'Western *society* has reached a turning point'.
3. the wealthy and privileged people and their interrelationships.
4. a group of people associated by their calling or interests: 'a *society* of engineers'.
Usage: 'he enjoyed their *society* immensely' (= companionship, company).

Society of Friends
Christian: see QUAKER.

sociology (*say* so–see–**olla**–jee) *noun*
the study of social behaviour, especially in relation to the development or changing of societies and social institutions.
Word Family: **sociologist**, *noun*; **sociological** (*say* so–see–a–**loji**–k'l), *adjective.*

sock (1) *noun*
a short stocking, usually of nylon or wool and reaching to the ankle or knee.

pull one's socks up, (*informal*) to try to improve.

sock (2) *verb*
(*informal*) to hit.
Word Family: **sock,** *noun.*

socket *noun*
a hollow part or opening, especially one into which something fits: 'the eye *socket*'.

sod (1) *noun*
1. a piece of grassy soil or turf.
2. the ground, especially grass-covered earth.

sod (2) *noun*
(*informal*) a disagreeable person.
[short form of *sodomite*]

soda (*say* **so**-da) *noun*
1. soda-water.
2. a drink made with soda-water flavoured with syrup, ice-cream, etc.
3. any simple sodium compound.
[from Arabic]

soda fountain
American: a counter at which ice-creams, milk shakes, etc. are sold.

soda siphon
a bottle containing soda-water under pressure which can be dispensed by opening a valve.

soda-water *noun*
short form is **soda**
carbonated water.

sodden *adjective*
completely soaked or wet.
Usage: 'we couldn't digest the *sodden* cake' (= heavy, dough-like).

sodium (*say* **so**-dee-um) *noun*
element number 11, a strongly reactive metal. Its compounds are very abundant, especially **sodium chloride** (common salt). See ALKALI METAL. See CHEMICAL ELEMENTS in grey pages.

sodium hydroxide
see CAUSTIC SODA.

sodium pentothal (*say* so-dee-um **penta**-thal)
a drug used in medicine as a general anaesthetic.

sodomy (*say* **sodda**-mee) *noun*
sexual intercourse using the anal opening, especially when performed between males.
Word Family: **sodomite,** *noun.*
[after *Sodom*, a Biblical town]

-soever (*say* so-**evva**)
a suffix meaning at all, to whatever extent, etc., as in *whatsoever.*

sofa *noun*
also called a **couch** or a **settee**
a long upholstered seat, with a back and armrests.

soft *adjective*
1. not firm, hard or stiff: 'the *soft* skin of a baby'.
Usages:
a) 'her *soft* voice lulled us to sleep' (= pleasant, smooth).
b) 'his *soft* glance was sympathetic' (= tender).
c) 'you must not be *soft* with the students' (= weak).
d) 'the *soft* lights gave the room an intimate atmosphere' (= not bright or harsh).
e) (*informal*) 'his father got a *soft* job for him' (= easy).
f) (*informal*) 'I think he's a bit *soft* in the head' (= simple, foolish).
2. *Physics:* (of radiation) having low penetrating power.
3. (of water) relatively free of mineral salts that prevent the lathering of soap.
4. (of the sounds *c* and *g*) pronounced softly as in *cent* and *gem.*
have a soft spot for, to like or be fond of.
Word Family: **softly,** *adverb*; **softness,** *noun*; **soften,** *verb*, to make or become soft or softer; **softener,** *noun.*

soft drink
any non-alcoholic drink.

soft drug
any drug which is considered to be non-addictive.

soft-focus *adjective*
Photography: slightly and intentionally out of focus, to achieve a romantic effect.

soft furnishings
the fabrics used for decorating rooms in a house, such as curtains, covers and carpets.

soft goods
products such as fabrics, etc.

soft-headed *adjective*
foolish.
Word Family: **soft-headedly,** *adverb*; **soft-headedness,** *noun.*

soft-hearted *adjective*
ready to feel or show sympathy, pity, etc.
Word Family: **soft-heartedly,** *adverb*; **soft-heartedness,** *noun.*

softly *adverb*
Word Family: see SOFT.

soft-pedal *verb*
(soft-pedalled, soft-pedalling)
to put little emphasis on.
soft pedal
a pedal, especially on a piano, which is used to lessen the volume of the sound.

soft sell
gentle, persuasive salesmanship. Compare HARD SELL.

soft soap
(*informal*) flattery, especially to gain something.
Word Family: **soft-soap**, *verb*, to flatter.

software *noun*
computer programs, etc. Compare HARDWARE.

softwood *noun*
the wood from coniferous trees, such as pine. Compare HARDWOOD.

softy *noun*
(*informal*) a person who is weak or easily upset.

soggy *adjective*
wet through.
Word Family: **sogginess**, *noun*.

soh *noun*
Music: see DOH.

soi-disant (*say* swa-**dee**zon) *adjective*
self-styled, would-be or professed.
[French, oneself saying]

soigné (*say* **swan**-yay) *adjective*
feminine form is **soignée**
very well groomed.
[French, taken care of]

soil (1) *noun*
a) the top layer of the earth's surface, in which plants will grow. It contains organic matter, inorganic matter and living organisms. b) a particular type of this earth: 'sandy *soil*'.
Usages:
a) 'he has worked on the *soil* all his life' (= land).
b) 'they returned to their native *soil*' (= country).

soil (2) *verb*
to make dirty: a) 'try not to *soil* your new shirt'; b) 'his reputation was *soiled* by the rumours'.

soil mechanics
Engineering: the study of the properties and suitability of soils as foundations for airfields, roads, high-rise buildings, etc.

soirée (*say* **swa**-ray) *noun*
a small evening party.
[French *soir* evening]

sojourn (*say* **soj**-ern *or* **so**-jern) *verb*
to stay temporarily.
Word Family: **sojourn**, *noun*, a stay.

solace (*say* **sol**lis) *noun*
a) the giving of comfort in sorrow or trouble. b) something which gives comfort, relief, etc.: 'drink was her only *solace*'.
Word Family: **solace**, *verb*.

solar (*say* **sole**-a) *adjective*
1. of or relating to the sun.
2. using or operated by energy from the sun.
[Latin *sol* sun]

solar day
see DAY.

solar energy
energy from the sun's rays which may be used to heat water.

solar flare
Astronomy: a brief, high-temperature outburst seen as a bright area in the sun's atmosphere, apparently occurring with sunspots.

solar furnace
a parabolic reflector which focuses sunlight at a point, used to obtain temperatures as high as 4000° C.

solarium (*say* so-**lair**ium) *noun*
a room or area exposed to the sun's rays, as in a hospital, etc.

solar plexus
1. an important centre of the autonomous nervous system situated behind the stomach.
2. (*informal*) the vulnerable front of the stomach just below the ribs.

solar system
Astronomy: a) the nine planets, the periodic comets and the asteroids moving in elliptical orbits around the sun. b) any group of planets orbiting around a star.

solar wind
Astronomy: the streams of electrons and protons given off by the sun, chiefly from solar flares.

sola topi, sola topee
a thick pith helmet, formerly worn by Europeans in the tropics as protection against sunstroke.
[Hindi]

sold *verb*
the past tense and past participle of the verb **sell**.

solder (*say* **sol**–da) *noun*
any of various alloys used, when molten, for joining metals.
solder *verb*
to join with or as if with a solder.
[Latin *solidare* to make firm]

soldering–iron *noun*
a tool used for applying solder.

soldier (*say* **sole**–jer) *noun*
a person serving in an army.
Word Family: **soldier**, *verb*, to act or serve as or like a soldier; **soldierly**, *adjective*, of or characteristic of a soldier; **soldiery**, *noun*, a) soldiers considered as a group, b) the profession of being a soldier.

soldier of fortune
a person who will serve in an army wherever there is adventure or personal gain.

sole (1) *adjective*
being the only one: 'I am the *sole* owner of this house'.
Word Family: **solely**, *adverb*.

sole (2) *noun*
1. *Anatomy:* the under surface of the foot.
2. the bottom surface of a shoe, boot, etc., excluding the heel.
3. anything which has the position or function of a sole: 'she rested the *sole* of her golf club on the grass'.
Word Family: **sole**, *verb*, to fit a shoe, etc. with a sole.

sole (3) *noun*
any of a group of small edible flatfish with a hooked snout.

solecism (*say* **soll**a–sizm) *noun*
1. the ungrammatical use of language.
2. a social gaffe.
[Greek *soloikos* speaking incorrectly]

solely *adverb*
Word Family: see SOLE (1).

solemn (*say* **soll**em) *adjective*
1. very grave: 'a *solemn* warning'.
2. full of dignity or ceremony: 'this is a *solemn* occasion'.
Usage: 'a *solemn* vow of chastity' (= religious, sacred).
Word Family: **solemnly**, *adverb*; **solemnness**, *noun*; **solemnity** (*say* so–**lemni**–tee), *noun*, a) the state of being solemn, b) (often plural) a formal or solemn ceremony, procedure, etc.
[Latin *sollemnis* annual, customary]

solemnize (*say* **sollem**–nize)
solemnise *verb*
to perform or celebrate, especially with a formal ceremony: 'to *solemnize* a marriage'.
Word Family: **solemnization**, *noun*.

solenoid (*say* **solli**–noyd) *noun*
an electrical conductor consisting of tightly wound coils, through which an electric current is passed to produce a magnetic field.
[Greek *solen* a tube + –OID]

solicit (*say* so–**lissit**) *verb*
1. to seek or request, especially in a formal or persistent manner.
2. (of a prostitute, etc.) to approach and offer sexual services to.
Word Family: **solicitation**, *noun*.

solicitor (*say* so–**lissita**) *noun*
Law: a lawyer who advises clients and gives facts and opinions to barristers on cases to be tried in the higher courts. Compare BARRISTER.
[Latin *sollicitus* worrying]

solicitous (*say* so–**lissitus**) *adjective*
full of anxiety or concern: 'a *solicitous* care for the sick child'.
Word Family: **solicitude**, *noun*; **solicitously**, *adverb*.

solid *adjective*
1. having a definite shape and volume: 'ice is water in its *solid* state'.
2. having the inside filled, especially with the same substance throughout: 'a *solid* gold ring'.
Usages:
a) 'they built a *solid* wall of stones' (= closely packed).
b) 'an athlete's *solid* muscles' (= strong).
c) 'this job will take a *solid* day's work' (= full, entire).
d) 'we were swayed by her *solid* argument' (= convincing).
e) 'a *solid* and respected leader' (= responsible, reliable).
f) 'it was a *solid* vote in favour of the idea' (= united).
3. three–dimensional: 'a *solid* figure'.
solid *noun*
something which is solid, especially that which maintains its shape unless forcefully changed. Compare GAS and LIQUID.
Word Family: **solidly**, *adverb*; **solidness**, **solidity** (*say* so–**liddi**–tee), *nouns*.
[Latin *solidus* compact]

solidarity (*say* solli–**darri**–tee) *noun*
a unity or agreement in interests, opinions, relationships, etc.

solid geometry
the geometry of three-dimensional figures.

solidify (*say* so–liddi–fie) *verb*
(solidified, solidifying)
to make solid, hard or compact.
Usage: 'we must *solidify* our position' (= make strong).
Word Family: **solidification,** *noun.*

solid-state *adjective*
(of electronic devices) consisting of solid components such as semiconductors, transistors, etc.
solid-state physics
the study of the physical properties of solids.

soliloquy (*say* so–lilla–kwee) *noun*
1. talking to oneself.
2. a speech made by a character in a play when alone on the stage.
Word Family: **soliloquize** (*say* so–lilla–kwize), **soliloquise,** *verb,* to talk to oneself.
[Latin *solus* alone + *loqui* to speak]

solipsism (*say* sollip–sizm) *noun*
Philosophy: the belief that only the self or ego exists or can be known.
Word Family: **solipsist,** *noun.*

solitaire (*say* **solli**–tair) *noun*
1. a board game for one played with marbles or pegs, the object being to end with one peg remaining, preferably in the centre.
2. a ring or earring containing a single gem.
[French]

solitary (*say* **solli**–tree) *adjective*
single: 'a *solitary* lighthouse to guide the ships'.
Usage: 'he felt afraid in such a *solitary* area' (= lonely, secluded).
Word Family: **solitary,** *noun,* a) a person who lives alone, b) solitary confinement; **solitariness,** *noun.*
[Latin *solitarius* alone]

solitary confinement
the keeping of a prisoner in a cell by himself.

solitude (*say* **solli**–tewd) *noun*
1. the state of being alone.
2. a lonely life or place.

solo *noun*
1. something designed for or performed by one person, such as a song or piece of music for one person.
2. a flight in which the pilot, usually a learner pilot, is not accompanied by an instructor.
3. *Cards:* a game based on whist, in which one player plays against the rest.
Word Family: **solo,** *adjective,* performed or performing alone; **soloist** (*say* **so**–lo–ist), *noun,* a person, especially a musician, who performs a solo; **solo,** *adverb.*
[Latin *solus* alone]

solstice (*say* **sol**stis) *noun*
either of two times, about June 21st or December 22nd, when the sun is the greatest distance from the equator and the longest or shortest day occurs.
Word Family: **solstitial** (*say* sol–**stish**'l), *adjective.*
[Latin *sol* sun + *sistere* to stand still]

soluble *adjective*
1. capable of being dissolved, especially in water.
2. able to be solved or explained: 'this puzzle is easily *soluble*'. Also called **solvable.**
solubility (*say* sol–yoo–**billi**–tee) *noun*
1. the ability to be dissolved.
2. *Chemistry:* the extent to which one substance will dissolve in another at a given temperature.

solute (*say* **sol**–yoot) *noun*
Chemistry: the substance which dissolves in another to form a solution.
Example: in a solution of salt in water, salt is the solute and water is the solvent.
Word Family: **solute,** *adjective,* dissolved.

solution (*say* so–**loo**–sh'n) *noun*
1. an explanation: 'we cannot find a *solution* to this problem'.
2. the method or process of solving or explaining a problem.
3. *Chemistry:* a homogeneous mixture of the molecules of two or more substances with different molecular structures. This usually refers to solids in liquids, but includes gases in liquids, liquids in liquids, gases in solids and solids in solids.
[Latin *solutus* untied, loosened]

solvable (*say* **solva**–b'l) *adjective*
see SOLUBLE.
Word Family: **solvability** (*say* solva–**billi**–tee), *noun.*

solve *verb*
to find an answer or explanation for.
[Latin *solvere* to untie]

solvent *adjective*
1. having money, especially enough to pay one's debts.
2. able to dissolve other substances.

solvent *noun*
Chemistry: a substance, usually liquid, able to dissolve other substances in it. See SOLUTE.
Word Family: **solvency,** *noun,* the ability to pay one's debts.

sombre (*say* **som**ba) *adjective*
in America spelt **somber**
dark, especially in a gloomy or dull way.
Usage: 'her *sombre* expression made us stop laughing' (= serious, gloomy).
Word Family: **sombrely,** *adverb*; **sombreness,** *noun.*
[SUB– + Latin *umbra* shade]

sombrero (*say* som–**brair**–o) *noun*
a pointed hat with a very wide, upturned brim, as is worn in Mexico and south-west America.
[from Spanish, *sombra,* shade]

some (*say* sum) *adjective*
not indicating a particular one, type, number, etc.: a) '*some* day you will understand'; b) '*some* of us were late'.
Usages:
a) 'he remained silent for *some* time' (= a fairly long).
b) 'that was certainly *some* feat' (= a remarkable).
some *pronoun*
an indefinite number of people or things: '*some* were seen to leave early'.

somebody (*say* **sum**–bod–ee) *pronoun*
some person: 'I saw *somebody* who looks like you'.
Word Family: **somebody,** *noun,* a person of importance.

somehow *adverb*
in a way which is not known or understood: '*somehow* I'll get my revenge'.
Usage: 'I think *somehow* that he won't try it' (= for no definite reason).

someone *pronoun*
somebody.

somersault (*say* **summa**–solt) *noun*
a complete circular roll of the body head over heels, either forwards or backwards.
Usage: 'her first feelings had undergone a *somersault*' (= complete reversal).
Word Family: **somersault,** *verb.*
[Old French *sombre saut* leap over]

something *pronoun*
a thing which is not specified: 'I've got *something* to show you'.

sometime *adverb*
at a time not stated, especially in the future: 'we will arrive *sometime* after lunch'.
sometime *adjective*
former: 'a *sometime* director of our company'.

sometimes *adverb*
at times.

somewhat *adverb*
to a certain degree: 'she is *somewhat* foolish'.

somewhere *adverb*
in, at or to a place not stated or known: 'I know that she is *somewhere* in the garden'.
Usage: 'the train arrives *somewhere* between six and seven o'clock' (= sometime).

somnambulism
(*say* som–**nam**–bew–lizm) *noun*
the habit or practice of sleepwalking.
Word Family: **somnambulist,** *noun,* a sleepwalker.
[Latin *somnus* sleep + *ambulare* to walk]

somnolent (*say* **som**na–l'nt) *adjective*
sleepy.
Word Family: **somnolence,** *noun*; **somnolently,** *adverb.*
[Latin *somnus* sleep]

son (*say* sun) *noun*
1. a male child in relation to his parents.
2. any male descendant.
3. a male person strongly influenced by or involved with something: '*sons* of the soil'.
4. a familiar term of address to a younger man from an older person.

sonar (*say* **so**–nar) *noun*
an electronic device or system using echoes from underwater soundwaves for directing submarines, mines, shoals of fish, etc.
[SO(und) N(avigation) A(nd) R(anging)]

sonata (*say* son–**ah**ta) *noun*
Music: an instrumental composition in three or four distinct and often contrasting movements. A **sonatina** (*say* sonna–**tee**na) is a short or simplified sonata.
[Italian, sounded]

song *noun*
1. a musical composition with words.
2. any musical or melodious sound: 'the *song* of a bird'.

for a song, 'I bought these old chairs *for a song* because they are damaged' (= very cheaply).
Word Family: **songster**, *noun*, a) a singer, b) a bird which sings; **songful**, *adjective*, tuneful or full of melody.

songbird *noun*
a bird which sings.

sonic (*say* **sonn**ik) *adjective*
relating to sound: 'a *sonic* boom'.
[Latin *sonus* sound]

sonic barrier
see SOUND BARRIER.

sonic boom
a loud, explosive sound caused by an aircraft or missile moving faster than the speed of sound.

son-in-law *noun*
plural is **sons-in-law**
the husband of one's daughter.

sonnet *noun*
a poem of 14 lines, normally with ten syllables per line and a formal rhyme scheme.

sonny (*say* **sunn**-ee) *noun*
a familiar or affectionate term of address to a little boy.

sonorous (*say* **sonn**a-rus *or* sa-**naw**rus) *adjective*
having a deep, full sound: 'her *sonorous* snores woke me'.
Word Family: **sonorously**, *adverb*; **sonorousness**, **sonority** (*say* so-**norr**i-tee), *nouns*.
[Latin *sonor* sound]

soon *adverb*
in the near future: 'write to me *soon*'.
Usage: 'the rainy season came too *soon* this year' (= early).
Phrases:
as soon, 'I would *as soon* not come' (= willingly, in preference).
as soon as, '*as soon as* she spoke, the crowd cheered' (= immediately).

soot (*rhymes with* foot) *noun*
a black, usually powdery, substance formed by the incomplete burning of carbon fuels. It contains carbon plus many other substances, including sulphur and hydrocarbons.
Word Family: **sooty**, *adjective*, a) covered with soot, b) black or dark; **sootiness**, *noun*.

sooth (*rhymes with* tooth) *noun*
an old word meaning truth or fact.

soothe *verb*
to bring ease or comfort to.
Word Family: **soothingly**, *adverb*.

soothsayer *noun*
a prophet or fortune-teller.

sop *noun*
1. something, such as a piece of bread, which is soaked or dipped in a liquid.
2. (*informal*) something given to appease or pacify another.
Word Family: **sop** (**sopped**, **sopping**), *verb*, to absorb, soak or become soaked.

sophism (*say* **sof**-izm) *noun*
sophistry.

sophisticated (*say* so-**fis**ti-kaytid) *adjective*
1. fine, refined or cultured: 'she has a *sophisticated* taste in music'.
2. worldly or having lost natural innocence or simplicity through education, experience, etc.
Usage: 'this is a very *sophisticated* device' (= technologically advanced, complex).
Word Family: **sophistication**, *noun*.

sophistry (*say* **soff**is-tree) *noun*
a) a false, tricky or deceptive argument. b) the use of such arguments.
Word Family: **sophist**, *noun*.
[Greek *sophizein* to make wise]

sophomore (*say* **soff**a-mor) *noun*
American: a student in second year at college.

soporific (*say* soppa-**riff**ik) *adjective*
of or producing sleep.
[Latin *sopor* deep sleep + *facere* to make]

sopping *adjective*
soaked or drenched.

soppy *adjective*
1. very wet.
2. (*informal*) sloppily sentimental.

soprano (*say* so-**prah**no) *noun*
a) the highest singing voice in women and boys. b) any instrument having this range.
[Italian *sopra* above]

sorcerer (*say* **sor**sa-ra) *noun*
a person who practises magic, especially witchcraft.
Word Family: **sorceress**, *noun*, a female sorcerer; **sorcery**, *noun*, magic, especially witchcraft.

sordid *adjective*
1. wretched, filthy and shabby: 'a *sordid* slum'.
2. mean, selfish and ignoble: '*sordid* deeds of cheats and swindlers'.
Word Family: **sordidly**, *adverb*; **sordidness**, *noun*.
[Latin *sordidus* dirty]

sore *adjective*
physically tender or painful.
Usages:
a) 'that subject is a *sore* point with her' (= annoying, irritating).
b) 'don't get *sore* at me' (= annoyed, irritated).
c) 'I'm in *sore* need of money' (= great).
sore *noun*
1. a place on the body which is sore, inflamed or injured.
2. a cause of distress, irritation, etc.
Word Family: **sorely,** *adverb*; **soreness,** *noun.*

sorghum (*say* **sor**gum) *noun*
a cereal grass in warm climates used as a grain and a source of syrup or treacle.

sorority (*say* so-**rorri**-tee) *noun*
American: a society of female students. Compare FRATERNITY.
[Latin *soror* sister]

sorrel (1) *noun*
1. a reddish-brown colour.
2. a horse of this colour.

sorrel (2) *noun*
a plant similar to spinach, having smaller, sour-tasting leaves.

sorrow *noun*
1. unhappiness or regret due to loss, etc.
2. something which causes such feelings: 'his death was a great *sorrow* to us'.
Word Family: **sorrow,** *verb,* to feel unhappiness or regret; **sorrowful,** *adjective,* feeling or causing sorrow; **sorrowfully,** *adverb.*

sorry *adjective*
1. feeling regret, sympathy, etc.: a) 'I'm *sorry* for my rudeness'; b) 'I'm *sorry* to hear you've been ill'.
2. miserable or pitiful: 'the old camel was in a *sorry* condition'.

sort *noun*
a particular kind or type: a) 'what *sort* of music do you like?; b) 'I said nothing of the *sort*'.
Usage: (*informal*) 'she's a decent *sort*' (= person).
Phrases:
of sorts, of a sort, 'food *of sorts* was provided' (= of a mediocre or poor kind).
out of sorts, not in one's normal or best health or condition.
sort of, (*informal*) to some extent.

sort *verb*
to arrange or separate into groups or sorts: '*sort* these eggs into their sizes'.
Word Family: **sorter,** *noun,* a person or thing that sorts, such as a post-office employee who sorts letters.

sortie (*say* **sor**-tee) *noun*
a raid or attack made against a besieging enemy.
[French *sortir* to go out]

SOS (*say* ess-o-**ess**) *noun*
a distress signal or call for help.
[s(ave) o(ur) s(ouls)]

so-so *adjective*
(*informal*) neither good nor bad.
Word Family: **so-so,** *adverb.*

sot *noun*
a drunkard.
[French]

sotto voce (*say* sotto **vo**-chay)
in a low voice.
[Italian, under the voice]

sou (*say* soo) *noun*
a very small sum of money.
[an old French coin of little value]

soubrette (*say* soo-**bret**) *noun*
a pert or coquettish young woman, especially such a character in an opera or play.
[French]

soufflé (*say* **soo**-flay) *noun*
a light, fluffy, baked dish made of savoury or sweet ingredients with beaten eggwhites.
[French, puffed]

sough (*rhymes with* cow) *verb*
to make a sighing or murmuring sound.
Word Family: **sough,** *noun,* a soughing sound.

sought (*say* sawt) *verb*
the past tense and past participle of the verb **seek.**

soul (*say* sole) *noun*
1. a) the non-physical, spiritual or emotional centre of a person. b) this as the element which survives death.
2. the nobler feelings or instincts: 'he has no *soul*'.
Usages:
a) 'there wasn't a *soul* in sight' (= person).
b) 'she's the *soul* of wit' (= embodiment).
c) 'she was the life and *soul* of the party' (= enlivening element).
sell one's soul for, 'I'd *sell my soul for* a cup of tea' (= go to any lengths to get).

soul–destroying *adjective*
unendurably monotonous or tedious; demoralizing.

soulful *adjective*
having or showing deep feeling: '*soulful* eyes'.
Word Family: **soulfully,** *adverb*; **soulfulness,** *noun.*

soulless (*say* **sole**–less) *adjective*
heartless or unfeeling.

soul mate
a perfect companion and partner in life.

sound (1) *noun*
any vibrations in the air which are detectable by the ear: 'the *sound* of music'.
Usage: 'I don't like the *sound* of the news' (= implications).
sound *verb*
1. a) to make or give out a sound: 'the trumpets *sounded*'. b) to cause to make a sound: '*sound* the bells'.
2. to give a certain impression: 'your story *sounds* odd'.
sound off, (*informal*) a) to speak angrily or dogmatically; b) to boast.
Word Family: **soundless,** *adjective*; **soundlessly,** *adverb.*
[Latin *sonare* to make a noise]

sound (2) *adjective*
1. in good or healthy condition: '*sound* teeth'.
2. reasonable or reliable: '*sound* advice'.
Usage: 'I gave him a *sound* thrashing' (= thorough).
Word Family: **soundly,** *adverb*; **soundness,** *noun.*

sound (3) *verb*
to test or measure the depth of water, etc. e.g. by dropping a weighted line.
sound someone out, to discover or try to discover someone's views by means of indirect questions, etc.
sound *noun*
something used for sounding, such as a slender instrument used to probe tubes or cavities in the body.
[SUB– + Latin *unda* a wave]

sound (4) *noun*
Geography: a) a narrow channel of water, such as a strait. b) an inlet of the sea.

sound barrier
also called the **sonic barrier**
the rapid increase in drag as an aeroplane reaches the speed of sound.

soundbox *noun*
the hollow part of a stringed instrument which increases the resonance.

sound effects
any sounds other than speech or music, used on radio or film, such as the noise of trains, traffic, etc.

sounding–board, soundboard *noun*
1. a wooden board on a stringed instrument which increases and improves the sound by vibrating when the strings are struck.
2. a person or thing used to give wider publicity to plans, theories, etc.: 'he is acting as the minister's *sounding–board*'.

soundproof *adjective*
not able to be penetrated by sound.
Word Family: **soundproof,** *verb,* to make soundproof.

soundtrack *noun*
a magnetic or other strip attached to a cine–film, etc. on which sounds are recorded to be played through a loudspeaker.

soundwave *noun*
Physics: a wave by which sound is transmitted.

soup (*say* soop) *noun*
a liquid food made from meat, fish or vegetables and usually served hot.
in the soup, (*informal*) in trouble.
soup *verb*
soup up, (*informal*) to modify a car engine to make it more powerful, especially by fitting a supercharger.

soupçon (*say* **soop**–son) *noun*
a very small trace or amount.
[French, suspicion]

soup kitchen
a place where soup or other food is served to poor people.

sour *adjective*
having a sharp, acid taste, as of vinegar or unripe fruit.
Usage: 'she had a *sour* expression' (= bad–tempered, surly).
Word Family: **sour,** *verb,* to make or become sour; **sourly,** *adverb*; **sourness,** *noun.*

source (*rhymes with* horse) *noun*
any place or thing from which something comes or starts: a) 'where is the *source* of the river?'; b) 'my news is from a reliable *source*'.
[from Latin]

sour grapes
the act of criticizing or pretending to despise something which one cannot have for oneself.
[from a fable by Aesop in which the fox pretended that the grapes he couldn't reach were sour]

souse (*rhymes with* house) *verb*
1. to throw into or drench with water.
2. to pickle, usually fish.
Usage: (*informal*) 'I feel slightly *soused*' (= drunk).

soutane (*say* soo–**tahn**) *noun*
Roman Catholic: a priest's cassock.
[Italian *sotto* under]

south *noun*
1. the direction along a meridian to the right of the position where the sun rises.
2. the cardinal point of the compass at 90° to the right of east and opposite north.
Word Family: **south**, *adjective, adverb.*

south–east *noun*
a) the point or direction midway between south and east. b) a region in this direction.
Word Family: **south–east**, *adjective, adverb*, a) in or towards the south–east, b) coming from the south–east; **south–easterly**, **south–eastern**, *adjectives*, from or towards the south–east; **south–easterly**, **south–easter**, *nouns*, a wind coming from the south–east; **south–easterly**, *adverb.*

southerly (*say* **su***th***a**–lee) *noun*
a wind coming from the south.
southerly *adjective*
(of a direction, course, etc.) from or towards the south.

southern (*say* **su***th*ern) *adjective*
(of a place) situated in the south.

southward *adjective*
towards the south.
Word Family: **southwards**, **southward**, *adverb.*

south–west *noun*
a) the point or direction midway between south and west. b) a region in this direction.
Word Family: **south–west**, *adjective, adverb*, a) in or towards the south–west, b) coming from the south–west; **south–westerly**, **south–western**, *adjectives*, from or towards the south–west; **south–westerly**; **south–wester**, *nouns*, a wind coming from the south–west; **south–westerly**, *adverb.*

souvenir (*say* **soova**–neer) *noun*
an object given or kept as a memento.
[French *se souvenir* to remember]

sou'wester (*say* sow–**west**a) *noun*
a waterproof hat with a downturned brim long enough to cover a collar at the back.

sovereign (*say* **sov**–rin) *noun*
a monarch.
sovereign *adjective*
having supreme rank, power or authority.
Usage: 'the colony fought to become a *sovereign* state' (= independent).
sovereignty *noun*
the status or power of a sovereign or sovereign state.

sow (1) (*say* so) *verb*
(**sowed, sown, sowing**)
to plant or scatter seed, etc. so that it will grow.
Usage: 'you are *sowing* discontent among the people' (= introducing, spreading).
Word Family: **sower**, *noun*, a person or thing that sows.

sow (2) (*rhymes with* cow) *noun*
an adult female pig.

soya bean, soy bean
the nutritious seed of an Asian plant, used as food and as a source of oil.
[from Chinese, salted–beans–oil]

sozzled *adjective*
(*informal*) drunk.

spa *noun*
a) a mineral spring. b) a health resort where there is a mineral spring.
[after *Spa*, a resort town in Belgium]

space *noun*
1. a) that in which all objects exist and move. b) a portion of this: 'how much *space* will this table take up?'.
2. the part of the universe beyond the earth's atmosphere. Also called **outer space.**
3. a) an area or extent of a surface: 'fill in the blank *spaces* on the form'. b) an extent of time: 'a *space* of half an hour'.
space *verb*
to fix, divide or separate into spaces or intervals: '*space* your words further apart'.
[from Latin]

space capsule
a container for instruments or astronauts, which may be sent into space and recovered on its return.

spacecraft *noun*
a vehicle designed to travel outside the earth's atmosphere.
a **spaceship** is a manned spacecraft.
a **space station** is a manned spacecraft or satellite in semi-permanent orbit.

space heater
a heater designed to heat the whole of an enclosed area, such as a single room.

spaceman *noun*
a) an astronaut. b) a being who lives in outer space.

space probe
a spacecraft which sends information back to earth on conditions in space.

spaceship *noun*
see SPACECRAFT.

space station
see SPACECRAFT.

spacesuit *noun*
a protective garment worn by astronauts, which can withstand high or low temperatures, radiation, etc. and carries its own oxygen supply.

spacious (*say* **spay**-shus) *adjective*
occupying or providing much space: 'a comfortable, *spacious* house'.
Word Family: **spaciously**, *adverb*; **spaciousness**, *noun*.

spade (1) *noun*
a long-handled tool with a broad, flat blade for digging.
call a spade a spade, to speak plainly.

spade (2) *noun*
Cards: a) a black figure like an inverted heart on a playing card. b) a playing card with this figure. c) (*plural*) the suit with this figure.

spadework *noun*
any hard work needed at the start of something.

spaghetti (*say* spa-**getti**) *noun*
a pasta made into long, thin tubes or threads.
[Italian, little cords]

spake *verb*
the old past tense of the verb **speak**.

spam *noun*
a tinned pressed meat mixture, mainly ham.
[a trade name from SP(iced) (h)AM]

span *noun*
1. the distance between two edges or extremes of something, such as the tips of a pair of wings or two supports of a bridge.
2. the full reach or extent of anything: 'a life *span* of 60 years'.
span *verb*
(**spanned, spanning**)
to extend over or across: 'a bridge *spanned* the river'.

spangle *noun*
1. a small thin disc of shining metal, used to decorate dresses, etc.
2. any bright or glittering part, piece, etc.
Word Family: **spangle**, *verb*, to decorate or glitter with spangles.

spaniel (*say* **span**-y'l) *noun*
any of various small, long-haired gun-dogs.
[Latin *Hispania* Spain]

spank *verb*
to slap the buttocks with the open hand, etc.
spanking *noun*
a slapping on the buttocks, especially as a punishment.
spanking *adjective*
1. brisk or rapid: 'a *spanking* pace'.
2. (*informal*) very fine or excellent: 'in *spanking* health'.
Word Family: **spank**, *noun*, a smart or resounding slap; **spanking**, *adverb*, (informal) very.

spanner *noun*
a metal bar with jaws or a hole at its end for turning a bolt, nut, pipe, etc.
spanner in the works, (*informal*) something which disrupts, confuses or obstructs.
[German *spannen* to tighten up]

spar (1) *noun*
any strong pole, such as a mast or a boom supporting a ship's sails.

spar (2) *verb*
(**sparred, sparring**)
1. to strike or box with light punches, e.g. for exercise or practice.
2. (*informal*) to argue or dispute.
Word Family: **spar**, *noun*.

spar (3) *noun*
Geology: any of various lustrous and easily cleavable crystalline minerals.

spare (*rhymes with* air) *adjective*
1. extra: a) 'I've no *spare* time'; b) 'a *spare* tyre'.
2. small or meagre: 'a *spare* diet'.
spare *verb*
1. to refrain from hurting, damaging, destroying, etc.: 'the judge *spared* the man's life'.
2. to dispense or part with from a supply: 'can you *spare* me a dollar?'.

3. to use economically: '*spare* the butter as there's not much left'.
Usage: 'no expense was *spared*' (= denied).

spare *noun*
1. something extra or in reserve: 'this tyre is a *spare*'.
2. *Tenpin Bowling:* a score obtained by knocking over all the tenpins in two successive shots. Compare STRIKE.
Word Family: **sparely**, *adverb*; **spareness**, *noun*.

sparerib *noun*
a cut of meat, especially pork, containing a front rib with little fat on it.

sparing (say **spairing**) *adjective*
careful or economical: 'she's *sparing* in her use of money'.
Word Family: **sparingly**, *adverb*.

spark *noun*
1. a tiny glowing particle, especially one thrown out by a fire or produced by striking flint and metal.
2. a brief electrical discharge usually with a visible flash, and some sound.
Usages:
a) 'Bill didn't show much *spark* at the party' (= liveliness).
b) 'he hasn't a *spark* of kindness in him' (= slight bit).

spark *verb*
1. to produce or throw out sparks.
2. (of an ignition system) to start functioning correctly.
Usage: 'he tried to *spark* some interest' (= stimulate).
spark off, 'the speech *sparked off* a riot' (= started).

sparkle *verb*
to send out or shine with sparks or little gleams of light.
Usage: 'the hostess *sparkled* with wit' (= was brilliant).

sparkle *noun*
a small spark or gleam.
Usage: 'she was full of *sparkle*' (= liveliness, brilliance).

sparkler *noun*
1. a taper-like firework that gives off small sparks and is held in the hand.
2. (*informal*) a diamond.

spark plug
also called a **sparking plug**
a device screwed into the combustion chamber of an internal combustion engine, used to ignite the fuel by an electric spark.

sparrow *noun*
a small, brown bird related to the finch.

sparrowhawk *noun*
a long-legged, short-winged bird related to the falcon and preying on other birds.

sparse *adjective*
thin or thinly scattered: a) 'a *sparse* beard'; b) 'the *sparse* population in a desert'.
Word Family: **sparsely**, *adverb*; **sparseness**, **sparsity**, *nouns*.
[Latin *sparsus* scattered]

Spartan *adjective*
sternly and rigorously austere or disciplined.
Word Family: **Spartan**, *noun*.
[after *Sparta*, an ancient Greek city famous for strict discipline]

spasm *noun*
a sudden, involuntary movement of the muscles.
Usage: 'he only works in *spasms*' (= short, sudden bursts).

spasmodic (*say* spaz-**moddik**) *adjective*
done or occurring in short, irregular bursts.
Word Family: **spasmodically**, *adverb*.
[from Greek]

spastic *adjective*
suffering from continuous or uncontrollable muscle spasms, as in cerebral palsy.
Word Family: **spastic**, *noun*, a person who is spastic; **spastically**, *adverb*.

spat *verb*
a past tense and past participle of the verb **spit (1)**.

spatchcock *noun*
a very small chicken which is split open, skewered flat and grilled.

spate *noun*
a sudden flood or rush: 'a *spate* of business activity before Christmas'.

spatial (*say* **spay**-sh'l) *adjective*
1. of or relating to space or spaces: 'the painting's *spatial* qualities'.
2. existing or occurring in space.
Word Family: **spatially**, *adverb*; **spatiality** (*say* spay-shee-**alli** tee), *noun*.

spats *plural noun*
a pair of stiff, cloth covers enclosing the ankle and the top part of a shoe.

spatter *verb*
to splash or sprinkle in many directions: 'the bus *spattered* mud all over my new trousers'.

Word Family: **spatter**, *noun*, a) a shower or sprinkling, b) a splash or spot of something spattered.

spatula (*say* **spat**–yoo–la) *noun*
a tool with a flat blade for lifting, mixing or spreading food, etc.
[Latin]

spavin (*say* **spav**vin) *noun*
any of a group of diseases of horses causing enlargement of the hock joint.

spawn *noun*
Biology: a) the mass of egg cells emitted by fish and other aquatic organisms. b) the thread–like matter from which mushrooms, etc. grow.
spawn *verb*
to produce or shed spawn.
Usage: 'high prices *spawned* discontent and riots' (= caused).

spay *verb*
to remove the ovaries of a female animal to prevent it having offspring. Compare CASTRATE.
[Old French *espeer* to cut with a sword]

speak *verb*
(**spoke, spoken, speaking**; *old forms*: **spake, spoke**)
to utter or pronounce words in an ordinary voice: 'can your baby *speak* yet?'.
Usages:
a) 'she wants to *speak* to you' (= converse).
b) 'he's *speaking* the truth' (= expressing).
c) 'she *spoke* for 4 hours to a packed hall' (= lectured).
d) 'do you *speak* Spanish?' (= know and are able to use).
Phrases:
so to speak, as one might say.
speak for, a) 'this *speaks* well *for* his ability' (= is evidence of); b) 'I shall *speak for* you in court' (= act on behalf of); c) 'this chair is *spoken for*' (= reserved).
speaking likeness, a real or lifelike resemblance.
speak out, to express one's views boldly.
to speak of, 'nothing exciting happened *to speak of*' (= worth mentioning).

speak–easy *noun*
American: a place where alcoholic drinks were sold illegally, especially during prohibition.

speaker *noun*
1. a person who speaks, especially one who addresses a meeting, etc.
2. *Audio:* a loudspeaker.
3. *Parliament:* (*capital*) a member of the House of Commons elected to control its meeting.

speaking clock
a telephone service which gives the time to the nearest second, announced by recorded tape.

spear *noun*
a weapon with a sharp, pointed blade mounted on a long pole.
spear *verb*
to pierce or wound with or as with a spear.

spear–grass *noun*
a tall grass with upright, stiff, sharp leaves.

spear gun
an underwater gun that fires a barbed spear, powered by springs or compressed air.

spearhead *noun*
1. the sharply pointed head of a spear.
2. a person or thing that leads an attack, etc.
Word Family: **spearhead**, *verb*.

spearmint *noun*
a variety of mint with small purplish flowers, yielding an aromatic oil used as a flavouring.

spec *noun*
on spec, as a risk or gamble.
[short form of *speculation*]

special (*say* **spesh**'l) *adjective*
1. of a distinct kind: a) 'this is a *special* holiday train'; b) 'did you come here for any *special* purpose?'.
2. belonging exclusively to a particular person or thing: 'the *special* features of our leasing arrangements'.
Usages:
a) 'dining out on a *special* occasion' (= not ordinary or usual).
b) 'he is a very *special* friend' (= to an exceptional degree).
special offer, an article offered at, or as if at, a reduced price.
special *noun*
something which is special, such as a special edition of a newspaper.
Word Family: **specially**, *adverb*, particularly.
[Latin *specialis* individual]

special constable
a part–time auxiliary policeman.

special correspondent
a journalist commissioned to report on a particular field of interest or a specific event.

specialist *noun*
a person who studies or is skilled in one particular subject or branch of a subject: 'a skin *specialist*'.
Word Family: **specialism**, *noun.*

speciality (*say* speshi-alli-tee) *noun*
also spelt **specialty** (*say* **spesh**ul-tee)
1. something which is special or distinct.
2. an activity or product particularly dealt with by a person or business: 'the chef's *speciality* is curried beef'.

specialize (*say* **spesha**-lize) **specialise** *verb*
1. to follow a special line of study or activity: 'she *specializes* in foreign languages'.
2. *Biology:* to adapt for a particular purpose: 'a fish's gills are *specialized* to allow it to breathe in water'.
Word Family: **specialization**, *noun.*

special licence
a licence to marry without following all the normal legal procedure.

special pleading
(*informal*) making out a plausible case without real justification.

special school
a school for physically or mentally disabled children.

specie (*say* **spee**-shee) *noun*
plural is **specie**
coin or coined money.

species (*say* **spee**-seez *or* **spee**-sheez) *noun*
plural is **species**
1. *Biology:* the group below genus, used in the classification of animals or plants. It indicates a group of individuals able to breed among themselves but not with members of another such group.
2. a distinct group or sort.
[Latin, outward appearance]

specific (*say* spe-**siffi**k) *adjective*
precise or particular: 'try to give a *specific* description'.
Word Family: **specific**, *noun*, something that is specific, such as a remedy for a particular disease; **specifically**, *adverb.*

specification (*say* spessifi-**kay**-sh'n) *noun*
1. the act of specifying.
2. a statement of details and instructions, such as the dimensions and materials to be used for a building.

specific gravity
also called **relative density**
Physics: the ratio of the density of a substance to the density of water at a given temperature, commonly 15°C.

specific heat
Physics: the amount of heat required to raise the temperature of a unit of mass of a substance by one degree.

specific volume
Physics: the volume occupied by one gram of a substance at a given temperature and pressure.

specify (*say* **spessi**-fie) *verb*
to mention specifically or definitely: 'please *specify* your time of arrival'.

specimen (*say* **spessi**-m'n) *noun*
a single part or thing taken as typical or representative: 'this painting is a *specimen* of the work I do'.
Usage: 'he's a very strange *specimen*' (= person).
[Latin, visible evidence]

specious (*say* **spee**-shus) *adjective*
deceptively good, correct or pleasing: 'a *specious* argument'.
Word Family: **speciously**, *adverb*; **speciousness**, *noun.*
[Latin *speciosus* showy]

speck *noun*
a very small spot or particle.
Word Family: **specked**, *adjective*, marked with specks.

speckle *noun*
a small mark or spot.
Word Family: **speckle**, *verb*, to mark with speckles.

specs *plural noun*
(*informal*) spectacles.

spectacle (*say* **spek**ti-k'l) *noun*
1. anything viewed or seen: 'the sunset was a fine *spectacle*'.
2. an impressive or large-scale public show or display.
3. (*plural*) a pair of glass lenses in a frame which rests on the nose and ears, worn to aid or improve eyesight. Also called **glasses**.
make a spectacle of oneself, to draw attention to oneself by unseemly dress or behaviour.
[from Latin]

spectacular (*say* spek-**tak**-yoola) *adjective*
making an impressive sight: 'a *spectacular* display of fireworks'.
spectacular *noun*
a film, etc. which is lavishly produced, relying on crowd scenes, elaborate

scenic effects, etc. rather than subtlety of plot or characters.
Word Family: **spectacularly**, *adverb.*

spectator (*say* spek–**tay**ta) *noun*
a person who watches or looks on.

spectral *adjective*
1. of or like a spectre.
2. of or relating to a spectrum.

spectre (*say* **spek**ta) *noun*
in America spelt **specter**
a ghost or apparition.
[from Latin]

spectrometer (*say* spek–**tromm**ita) *noun*
an instrument used in measuring refractions of a spectrum.

spectroscope (*say* **spek**tra–skope) *noun*
an optical instrument which separates light into its component colours.
Word Family: **spectroscopic** (*say* spektra–**skop**pik), *adjective.*
[SPECTRUM + Greek *skopein* to look at]

spectrum *noun*
plural is **spectra**
1. *Physics:* the series of bands produced when a wave is split up into its component frequencies. White light forms bands of red, orange, yellow, green, blue, indigo and violet.
2. a range of ideas, beliefs, etc.
[Latin, image]

spectrum analysis
Physics: the determination of the chemical composition of substances by means of the spectra they produce.

speculate (*say* **spek**–yoo–late) *verb*
1. to meditate or reflect on a given subject.
2. to form hypotheses or opinions on the basis of little or no evidence.
3. to undertake risky business or investments in the hope of making a large profit.
Word Family: **speculator**, *noun*, a person who speculates; **speculative**, *adjective*; **speculation**, *noun.*
[Latin *specula* a look–out, watch–tower]

speculum (*say* **spek**–yoo–lum) *noun*
plural is **specula**
1. a mirror or reflector, especially one of polished metal.
2. *Medicine:* any instrument used to inspect an inaccessible part of the body.
3. *Biology:* a brightly coloured area on the wing of certain birds.
[Latin]

speech *noun*
1. the power or act of speaking.
2. a spoken address, usually formal.
3. a person's manner of speaking: 'her *speech* is slow and difficult to hear'.
4. the language or dialect of a region, country, etc.
Word Family: **speechless**, *adjective*, characterized by absence or loss of speech; **speechlessly**, *adverb*; **speechlessness**, *noun.*

speed *noun*
1. a swiftness in moving, travelling, etc.
2. *Physics:* the rate of change of linear displacement, regardless of direction. Compare VELOCITY.
3. (*informal*) any of various strong amphetamines.
4. *Photography:* a measure of the exposure required by an emulsion.
at full speed, as fast as possible.
speed *verb*
(**sped** or **speeded**, **speeding**)
1. to move or cause to move swiftly: 'he *sped* past'.
2. to increase the rate of progress: 'we must *speed* up production'.
3. to drive a motor vehicle faster than the speed–limit.
Word Family: **speedy**, *adjective*; **speedily**, *adverb*; **speediness**, *noun*; **speeder**, *noun.*

speedboat *noun*
a small, fast motor boat.

speed–limit *noun*
a) the maximum legal speed at which a vehicle may travel in a particular area. b) the regulation which orders this.

speedometer (*say* spee–**domm**ita) *noun*
an instrument for measuring the speed of, and distance travelled in, a vehicle.

speed–trap *noun*
any of various devices, such as radar, etc., used by police to verify the speed of motor vehicles.

speedway *noun*
a racetrack for motorcycles.

speedy *adjective*
Word Family: see SPEED.

speleology (*say* speeli–**olla**–jee) *noun*
the study and exploration of caves.
Word Family: **speleologist**, *noun*; **speleological** (*say* speelia–**loj**i–k'l), *adjective.*
[Greek *spelaion* cave + –LOGY]

spell (1) *verb*
(**spelt** or **spelled, spelling**)
1. to name or write the letters of a word, etc. correctly.
2. (of letters) to form: 'c–a–t *spells* cat'.
3. to signify: 'the storm *spelt* disaster for the rowing boat'.
spell out, a) to read slowly or laboriously; b) to explain in detail.
Word Family: **speller,** *noun,* a) a person who spells, b) a spelling textbook.

spell (2) *noun*
1. a word or words believed to have magic power.
2. any strong influence.

spell (3) *noun*
1. a) a short period of time: 'she went away for a *spell*'. b) a period of weather: 'a hot *spell*'.
2. a short turn of work: 'I took a *spell* at the wheel so that the driver could rest'.
Usage: 'a coughing *spell*' (= fit).
Word Family: **spell,** *verb* to give a period of rest to.

spellbound *adjective*
entranced.

spelt *verb*
a past tense and past participle of the verb **spell (1)**.

spencer (*say* **spen**sa) *noun*
a knitted woollen jacket.

spend *verb*
(**spent, spending**)
1. to pay out money, etc.: 'I *spent* £20 at the supermarket'.
Usage: 'the storm had *spent* its fury' (= used up, exhausted).
2. to make use of time, etc.: 'we *spent* the weekend in the country'.
Word Family: **spender,** *noun.*
[Latin *dispendere* to weigh out]

spendthrift *noun*
a person who is extravagant or wasteful with money or possessions.

sperm *noun*
plural is **sperm**
a) a spermatozoon. b) semen.
Word Family: **spermatic** (*say* sper–**mat**tik), *adjective.*
[Greek *sperma* seed]

spermaceti (*say* sperma–**seeti** *or* sperma–**setti**) *noun*
a waxy substance obtained from the oil of certain whales and used in ointments and cosmetics.
[SPERM + Greek *ketos* whale]

spermatozoon (*say* spermita–**zo**–on) *noun*
plural is **spermatozoa**
Biology: a male reproductive cell.
[Greek *spermatos* of seed + *zoion* animal]

spew *verb*
(*informal*) to vomit.
Usage: 'the factory *spews* all its waste into the river' (= discharges).

sphagnum (*say* **sfag**–num) *noun*
any of a group of mosses growing in damp areas and building up into layers of peat.
[from Greek]

sphere (*say* sfeer) *noun*
1. a three–dimensional circular figure with all points on its surface equidistant from its centre, e.g. the moon, a tennis–ball.
2. an environment or field of activity, etc.: 'my social *sphere* is rather limited'.
Word Family: **spherical** (*say* **sferri**–k'l), *adjective,* having the rounded shape of a sphere.
[Greek *sphaira* a ball]

spherical aberration
Physics: see ABERRATION.

sphincter (*say* **sfink**ta) *noun*
Anatomy: a ring of muscle, such as the anus, surrounding an opening or tube within the body and able to close it.
[Greek *sphingein* to throttle]

Sphinx *noun*
1. *Egyptian mythology:* a wingless monster with the head of a man and the body of a lion.
2. *Greek mythology:* a winged monster with the head and breasts of a woman, and the body of a lion, who killed those that could not solve her riddles.
3. (*not capital*) an enigmatic person.
[Greek *sphingein* to throttle]

spice *noun*
1. a substance from a plant, such as pepper, etc., which is used to add flavour to food.
2. something that is interesting or adds flavour: 'variety is the *spice* of life'.
Word Family: **spice,** *verb*; **spicy,** *adjective,* a) of, like or containing spice, b) scandalous or sensational; **spicily,** *adverb*; **spiciness,** *noun.*
[Late Latin *species* merchandise]

spick and span
very neat and clean.
Word Family: **spick–and–span**, *adjective.*

spider *noun*
Biology: any of various wingless, eight-legged arthropods, which usually spin webs and with head and thorax fused together but separated from the abdomen.
Word Family: **spidery**, *adjective*, long and thin.

spiel (*say* shpeel *or* speel) *noun*
(*informal*) any glib or plausible talk, such as a salesman's prepared speech.
[German, play]

spier (*say* **spy**-er) *noun*
Word Family: see SPY.

spigot (*say* **spigg**et) *noun*
a device for stopping the hole in a barrel, etc.

spike (1) *noun*
1. a strong, pointed piece of metal, etc.
2. a sharp metal projection on the sole of a running-shoe.
3. (*plural*) a pair of shoes with such projections, worn by athletes, etc.
spike *verb*
1. to impale or injure with a spike.
2. to put an end to: 'his reappearance *spiked* all rumours about his death'.
3. (*informal*) to add alcohol to.
Word Family: **spiky** (*say* **spy**-kee), *adjective*, a) like or having a spike or spikes, b) easily irritated.

spike (2) *noun*
1. an ear of grain.
2. a long cluster of stalkless or nearly stalkless flowers.
[from Latin]

spill (1) *verb*
(spilt or **spilled, spilling)**
1. to run or fall out, as from a container.
Usages:
a) (*informal*) 'who *spilt* the story to the newspapers?' (= told, disclosed).
b) 'much blood was *spilt* in the battle' (= shed).
c) 'he was *spilt* from his horse at the first jump' (= caused to fall).
2. *Nautical:* to let the wind out of the sails.
Word Family: **spill**, *noun*, the act of spilling.

spill (2) *noun*
a piece of wood or paper used to light candles, etc.

spillway *noun*
an overflow channel on a dam, reservoir, etc.

spin *verb*
(spun or **span, spun, spinning)**
1. to make yarn by twisting and winding fibres into a long thread.
2. (of spiders, etc.) to form a thread, web, etc. by giving out a sticky substance.
3. to rotate rapidly: 'she *spun* the coin on the table'.
Usage: 'to *spin* a story' (= tell).
spin out, to draw out or make last.
spin *noun*
a rapid rotating movement.
Usages:
a) 'her head was in a *spin* due to all the excitement' (= confused state).
b) 'let's take the car for a *spin*' (= short journey).
c) 'the plane went into a *spin*' (= continuously spinning descent).
Word Family: **spinner**, *noun*, a person or thing that spins, such as a fishing lure which rotates rapidly in the water.

spina bifida (*say* spine-a **biffi**-da)
a disabling, congenital condition in which the spinal meninges protrude through their bony coverings.
[Latin *spina* spine + *bifidus* split in two]

spinach (*say* **spin**itch) *noun*
a green, leafy vegetable.
[from Persian]

spinal (*say* **spy**-n'l) *adjective*
Word Family: see SPINE.

spinal column
see VERTEBRAL COLUMN.

spinal cord
Anatomy: a cylinder of nerve tissue extending from the base of the brain down the inside of the vertebral column.

spindle *noun*
1. a rod onto which thread or yarn is wound for spinning or sewing.
2. any of various rods or thin shafts which revolve or serve as an axis for larger revolving parts, e.g. in a lathe.

spindly *adjective*
long and thin.

spin-dry *verb*
(spin-dried, spin-drying)
to extract most of the water from wet clothes by spinning them rapidly in a machine.
Word Family: **spin-drier, spin-dryer,** *noun*, a machine for spin-drying clothes.

spine *noun*
1. *Anatomy:* the vertebral column.

2. a ridge, e.g. of ground, rock, etc.
3. a pointed projection on an animal or plant, such as a quill or thorn.
4. the part of a cover of a book which holds the pages together.
Word Family: **spinal**, *adjective*, of or relating to a spine, especially the vertebral column; **spiny**, *adverb*, (of animals and plants) having or resembling spines.
[from Latin]

spine-chilling *adjective*
(*informal*) making one fearfully apprehensive.
Word Family: **spine-chiller**, *noun*, a book, play or film designed to make one fearful.

spineless *adjective*
1. lacking moral courage or resolution.
2. lacking a spine or spines.
Word Family: **spinelessly**, *adverb*; **spinelessness**, *noun*.

spinet (*say* **spinnet**) *noun*
Music: a small, wing-shaped type of harpsichord, now seldom played.
[Latin *spina* spine (as the strings were plucked by quills)]

spinnaker (*say* **spinna**-ka) *noun*
Nautical: a very large ballooning jib-sail hoisted when racing before the wind.
[from *Sphinx*, the first yacht to use one]

spinner *noun*
Word Family: see SPIN.

spinneret (*say* **spinna**-ret) *noun*
an organ in an insect or spider which produces the thread for a cocoon or web.

spinney (*say* **spin**-ee) *noun*
a small, dense group of trees or shrubs.
[from Latin]

spinning jenny
an early spinning machine which had several spindles, so that more than one yarn could be spun at one time.

spinning wheel
any of various machines for spinning flax or wool, consisting of a spindle driven by a wheel which is worked by a foot treadle.

spin-off *noun*
any incidental benefits in other fields resulting from research and development in a particular field: 'pocket calculators are a *spin-off* from space research'.

spinster *noun*
an unmarried woman.
Word Family: **spinsterhood**, *noun*.
[Middle English, one who spins]

spiny *adjective*
Word Family: see SPINE.

spiracle (*say* **spirra**-k'l) *noun*
Biology: a small hole for exchange of gases during respiration, found in insects, fish and some other animals.
[from Latin]

spiral (*say* **spy**-r'l) *noun*
1. a continuous curve moving around a fixed point at a steadily increasing or decreasing distance, as a watch-spring.
2. a continuous curve winding round a central axis but continually changing plane, as in a spiral staircase or the thread of a screw.
3. a continuously quickening increase or decrease: 'a wage *spiral*'.
Word Family: **spiral**, *adjective*; **spiral** (**spiralled**, **spiralling**), *verb*, to have a spiral shape or movement; **spirally**, *adverb*.

spire *noun*
1. an upright, tapering structure on top of a church tower or other building.
2. the top part or point of something which tapers upwards.
[Greek *speira* a coil]

spirit *noun*
1. the soul.
2. any supernatural or divine being, such as a ghost, fairy, etc.
3. the essential part of a person's feelings, emotions, character, etc.: 'the hard life had broken her *spirit*'.
4. (*plural*) the state of one's mind, feelings, etc.: 'to be in high *spirits*'.
Usages:
a) 'the university was filled with the *spirit* of revolution' (= inspiring force).
b) 'he is well liked for his intelligence and *spirit*' (= liveliness, courage).
c) 'try to join in the *spirit* of Christmas' (= dominant mood).
d) 'I could only grasp the *spirit* of her letter' (= general meaning).
e) 'all players have a strong team *spirit*' (= loyalty).
5. (*usually plural*) any strong distilled alcoholic liquor.
6. *Medicine:* a solution of a substance in alcohol.

spirit *verb*
to carry off secretly or mysteriously.

spirited *adjective*
1. having liveliness or courage.
2. relating to a person's mood or emotional state: 'a *high-spirited* young man'.
Word Family: **spiritedly,** *adverb*; **spiritedness,** *noun.*
[Latin *spiritus* breathing]

spirit level
an instrument for finding a true horizontal level, by means of a bubble of air which floats in a tube of alcohol set in a frame.

spirits of salt
a solution of hydrochloric acid in water.

spiritual (*say* **spirri-tew'l**) *adjective*
1. of or relating to the soul rather than the physical body.
2. of or relating to supernatural beings.
3. of or relating to religious or sacred things.
spiritual *noun*
a religious folk song which originated among the American Negroes.
Word Family: **spiritually,** *adverb*; **spirituality** (*say* spirri-tew-**alli**-tee), *noun.*

spiritualism (*say* **spirri**-tew-lizm) *noun*
a) the belief that spirits of the dead can be contacted by the living. b) the practices, such as seances, associated with such a belief.
Word Family: **spiritualist,** *noun.*

spirochaete (*say* **spy**-ro-keet) *noun*
a bacterium with an elongated and spirally twisted cell, many types of which cause diseases.
[Greek *speira* a coil + *khaitē* hair]

spit (1) *verb*
(**spat** or **spit, spitting**)
1. to eject from the mouth, especially saliva: 'I *spat* out the tablet'.
Usage: 'he *spat* out his words' (= uttered violently).
2. (of rain or snow) to fall in light, scattered drops.
3. to make a noise as if spitting: 'the wood fire hissed and *spat*'.
spit it out, (*informal*) to speak.
spit *noun*
1. saliva.
2. the act of spitting.
3. (*informal*) a spitting image.
spit and polish, a careful cleaning, as of military equipment, etc.

spit (2) *noun*
1. a pointed, revolving rod for roasting food over a grill or fire.
2. a narrow ridge of land projecting into the sea.
Word Family: **spit (spitted, spitting),** *verb,* to pierce or stab with or as if with a spit.

spite *noun*
a malicious urge or desire to hurt, humilitate or annoy.
in spite of, 'I will do it *in spite of* your advice' (= regardless of).
spite *verb*
to annoy or thwart because of spite.
Word Family: **spiteful,** *adjective,* full of spite; **spitefully,** *adverb*; **spitefulness,** *noun.*
[from DESPITE]

spitfire *noun*
a person who has a fiery temper.

spitting image
(*informal*) the close likeness or counterpart of a person, etc.

spittle *noun*
saliva.

spittoon *noun*
a vessel or bowl for spitting into.

spiv *noun*
(*informal*) a black-market dealer or petty criminal, especially one who dresses in a vulgar or flashy way and does no regular work.

splash *verb*
1. to wet or soil with drops of water, mud, etc.
2. (of a liquid) to fly about and fall in drops.
3. to make a noise similar to that made by splashing.
Usage: 'the news was *splashed* across the front page of the newspaper' (= displayed very prominently).
splash out, (*informal*) to spend money lavishly.
splash *noun*
1. the act or sound of splashing.
2. a) a quantity of liquid splashed around or on something. b) a mark or spot caused by something splashed.
Usages:
a) 'a *splash* of colour' (= patch, small area).
b) 'the extravagant party made a big *splash*' (= sensation).
Word Family: **splashy,** *adjective.*
[for PLASH]

splash-down *noun*
the landing of a spacecraft in the sea following its flight.

splatter *verb*
to splash.

splay *verb*
to spread out or extend.
splay *adjective*
spread out.
[for DISPLAY]

splay-footed *adjective*
having broad flat feet which turn outwards.

spleen *noun*
1. *Anatomy:* the large, red organ which lies between the stomach and the left kidney and produces lymph cells and stores red blood cells.
2. a bad temper or spite: 'he always vents his *spleen* on his poor wife'.
Word Family: **splenetic** (*say* splee-**nettik**), *adjective.*
[from Greek]

splendid *adjective*
1. superb or brilliant: 'a *splendid* sunset'.
2. (*informal*) very satisfactory: 'what a *splendid* end to the story'.
Word Family: **splendidly,** *adverb*; **splendidness,** *noun*; **splendiferous** (*say* splen-**diff**'rus), *adjective,* (informal) splendid.
[Latin *splendidus* shining]

splendour (*say* **splender**) *noun*
1. a superb or brilliant appearance, colouring, etc.: 'the *splendour* and display of the royal visit'.
2. glory or distinction: 'the *splendour* of ancient Rome'.

splice *verb*
1. to join two parts or pieces by interweaving e.g. ropes, overlapping e.g. wood, etc.
2. (*informal*) to join in marriage.
Word Family: **splice,** *noun,* a joint made by splicing.

spline *noun*
a) a strip of metal which fits into and locks with matching slots, e.g. in a shaft and wheel. b) one of the slots.

splint *noun*
a thin piece of wood, metal or leather used to keep an injured or diseased bone or joint fixed in a desirable position.
Word Family: **splint,** *verb,* to secure in position by means of a splint or splints.

splinter *noun*
a sharp, slender piece of wood, metal, glass, etc. split or broken off from a main body.
Word Family: **splinter,** *verb,* to split or break into splinters; **splintery,** *adjective.*

splinter group
a group of members of an organization who separate from the others, especially after a disagreement.

split *verb*
(split, splitting)
1. to break or divide, especially from one end to the other.
2. to divide or separate in any way: a) 'the substance was *split* into its elements'; b) 'opinions were *split* over the matter'.
Usage: 'he *split* his trousers as he sat down' (= burst, ripped).
3. (*informal*) to leave.
Phrases:
split on, (*informal*) 'the criminal *split on* his mates' (= betrayed, divulged secrets about).
split one's sides, to laugh heartily.
split the difference, to reach agreement by both sides compromising an equal amount.
split up, (*informal*) a) to share or divide up; b) to part or become separated.
split *noun*
1. a crack caused by splitting.
Usage: 'a *split* within the committee' (= sharp division of opinion).
2. (*informal*) a share: 'here's your *split* of the loot'.
3. (*plural*) the spreading of one's legs along the floor so that they form a straight line at right angles to, or in the plane of, the body.
4. a dish made from sliced fruit and ice-cream covered with nuts and syrup.

split infinitive
a simple infinitive, such as *to leave,* with a word dividing it. *Example: to* hurriedly *leave.*

split-level *adjective*
(of a building, etc.) having certain floors slightly above or below the main storey level.

split pea
a dried pea, cut in half, used in soups and as a vegetable.

split personality
1. a tendency to behave in conflicting ways.
2. (*informal*) schizophrenia.

split pin
a fastener which is made from a strip of metal folded in half so that it may be passed through a hole and the ends bent apart to hold it in place.

split ring
a ring, such as a key ring, with a movable opening through which objects may be inserted.

split-second *adjective*
1. performed with great precision.
2. achieved immediately: '*a split-second* decision'.
Word Family: **split second,** a very short time.

splotch *noun*
also called a **splodge**
a large, messy spot, stain, etc.
Word Family: **splotch,** *verb*; **splotchy,** *adjective.*

splurge (*say* splerj) *noun*
(*informal*) an extravagant display or indulgence: 'we had a *splurge* and went to an expensive restaurant'.
Word Family: **splurge,** *verb.*

splutter *verb*
1. to speak confusedly or with a spitting sound, e.g. from excitement or embarrassment.
2. to spit drops of liquid noisily.
Word Family: **splutter,** *noun*; **splutterer,** *noun,* a person who splutters.

spoil *verb*
(**spoilt** or **spoiled, spoiling**)
1. to damage the quality, value or usefulness of: a) 'the rain *spoilt* our holiday'; b) 'rust will *spoil* those scissors'.
2. to harm or damage the character or nature of by excessive indulgence: 'that child is *spoilt* by its grandparents'.
3. (of food, etc.) to go bad.
be spoiling for, 'you could see the gang *was spoiling for* a fight' (= eager for).
spoil *noun*
(*usually plural*) the booty or plunder taken in war, robbery, etc.
Usage: 'the *spoils* of public office' (= profits, advantages).
Word Family: **spoilage,** *noun,* a) the act of spoiling, b) something which is spoilt; **spoiler,** *noun.*
[Latin *spolium* plunder]

spoilsport *noun*
a person who ruins the enjoyment of others.

spoke (1) *verb*
the past tense and old past participle of the verb **speak.**

spoke (2) *noun*
1. any of the rods which connect the hub of a wheel to the rim.
2. any similar rod, e.g. on an umbrella.
3. a rung of a ladder.
put a spoke in someone's wheel, to interfere with someone's plans.

spoken *verb*
the past participle of the verb **speak.**

spokesman *noun*
a person who speaks on behalf of another or others.

spoliation (*say* spo-lee-**ay**-sh'n) *noun*
the act of plundering or spoiling.
Word Family: **spoliate** (*say* spo-lee-ate), *verb.*

spondee *noun*
Poetry: see FOOT.
Word Family: **spondaic** (*say* spon-**day**-ik), *adjective.*
[from Greek]

sponge (*say* spunj) *noun*
1. a) a non-mobile, aquatic animal consisting of many cells arranged in a porous structure. b) the light, absorbent skeleton of this animal, used for washing, bathing, etc.
2. something which has the texture of or qualities of a sponge, such as a light, fluffy cake.
throw up the sponge, (*informal*) to admit defeat or failure.
sponge *verb*
1. to wash, wipe, clean or absorb with a sponge.
2. (*informal*) to live at the expense of others.
Word Family: **sponger,** *noun*; **spongy,** *adjective,* soft or absorbent like a sponge.
[from Greek]

sponsor *noun*
1. a person, such as a godfather, who takes responsibility for another.
2. a person who proposes or supports something: 'who was the *sponsor* for the divorce reform Bill?'.
3. a person, business, etc. that finances or helps to finance a sport, cultural event, broadcast, etc., usually in return for advertising facilities.
[Latin]

spontaneous (*say* spon-**tay**-nee-us) *adjective*
occurring or produced naturally and not caused by external forces: '*spontaneous* combustion'.
Usage: 'a *spontaneous* laugh' (= not rehearsed, impulsive).
Word Family: **spontaneously,** *adverb*; **spontaneousness, spontaneity** (*say* sponta-**naya**-tee), *nouns,* the state of being spontaneous.
[Latin *sponte* voluntarily]

spontaneous generation
also called **abiogenesis**
Biology: the incorrect theory that living things can be produced from non-living matter. Compare BIOGENESIS.

spoof *noun*
(*informal*) a parody or hoax.

spook *noun*
(*informal*) a ghost.
Word Family: **spooky**, *adjective*, eerie or suggestive of spooks.

spool *noun*
a cylindrical device onto which tape, thread, etc. is wound for use.

spoon *noun*
1. any kitchen utensil with a handle and small bowl-shaped end used for eating, measuring, serving, etc.
2. something which has the shape or function of a spoon.
the wooden spoon, the booby prize.
spoon *verb*
1. to lift or carry with or as if with a spoon.
2. *Sport:* to hit a ball high into the air.
3. (*informal*) to act in a playfully amorous way.

spoonbill *noun*
a wading bird related to the ibis, having a long, flat beak with a spoon-like end.

spoonerism (*say* **spoona-rizm**) *noun*
an unintentional changing of the order of sounds in words. *Example*: the teacher accused him of ***tasting two worms*** (= wasting two terms).
[after *W. A. Spooner*, 1844–1930, a British clergyman noted for such slips]

spoon-fed *adjective*
1. fed food with a spoon.
2. looked after too carefully.

spoor (*say* spore) *noun*
the tracks left by wild animals.

sporadic (*say* spor-raddik) *adjective*
occurring or appearing at only occasional intervals in time or space: a) 'we heard *sporadic* firing all afternoon'; b) '*sporadic* outcrops of granite'.
Word Family: **sporadically**, *adverb*.
[Greek *sporas* scattered (seed)]

spore *noun*
Biology: a reproductive cell, or group of cells, which separates from the parent before it begins to develop.
[Greek *spora* a sowing]

sporran *noun*
a fur or leather pouch hung at the front of a belt as part of Scottish Highland costume.
[Gaelic]

sport *noun*
1. any activity for exercise or enjoyment, especially one involving physical skill and organized with a set form, rules, etc.
2. (*plural*) an athletic competition between several teams.
Usages:
a) 'we made great *sport* of her shyness' (= fun, mockery).
b) 'we had quite good *sport*' (= shooting, hunting, etc.).
3. a person considered in relation to his attitudes or fairness in competition, difficult situations, etc.: 'she's a good *sport* and doesn't mind a bit of teasing'.
sport *verb*
1. to play or frolic: 'lambs *sported* in the fields'.
2. to display, wear or carry ostentatiously: 'he was *sporting* a bright red scarf'.
Word Family: **sporting**, *adjective*, a) used for or connected with sport, b) fair or honourable, especially in competition; **sportingly**, *adverb*; **sportive**, *adjective*; **sportively**, *adverb*; **sportiveness**, *noun*; **sportsman**, **sportswoman**, *nouns*, a person who takes part in sport, b) a person who is fair or honourable in competition, etc.
[for DISPORT]

sporting chance
a reasonable chance, given luck.

sports car
a high-powered, low-built car, usually with two seats and a removable, or soft folding, roof.

sports coat
also called a **sports jacket**
a man's casual jacket made of tweed or checked fabric.

sportsmanship *noun*
the behaviour or qualities considered appropriate to a competitor or person taking part in sport.

sportswear *noun*
any casual clothes.

sporty *adjective*
1. stylish in a vulgar or flashy way.
2. interested or showing talent in sports.

spot *noun*
1. a round, usually small, mark on a surface, having a different colour from its surroundings.
2. any mark on a surface, such as a stain, pimple, etc.
Usages:
a) 'this seems like a good *spot* to fish' (= place).
b) 'I'm in rather a difficult *spot* at the moment' (= predicament).
c) 'just a *spot* of milk in my tea, please' (= little bit).
3. a spotlight.
Phrases:
hit the spot, (*informal*) to provide what is necessary or satisfying.
knock spots off, (*informal*) to outdo or defeat easily.
on the spot, a) 'we will mend shoes *on the spot*' (= here, at once); b) 'that tricky question put her *on the spot*' (= in a difficult or embarrassing situation).
spot *verb*
(**spotted, spotting**)
1. to mark or stain with spots: 'her hands were *spotted* with paint'.
2. to find or discover: 'can you *spot* any mistakes on this page?'.
3. *Billiards:* to place the ball on any of the various spots marked on the table.
Word Family: **spot**, *adjective*, done or delivered immediately; **spotless**, *adjective*, very clean; **spotlessly**, *adverb*; **spotlessness**, *noun*; **spotty**, *adjective*, a) marked with spots, b) uneven or irregular.

spot check
an unannounced and random examination: 'police are conducting *spot checks* on cars in the area'.

spotlight *noun*
a light with a strong, narrow beam, as used in a theatre.
Usage: 'shy people dislike being in the *spotlight*' (= public attention or notice).
Word Family: **spotlight** (**spotlit** or **spotlighted, spotlighting**), *verb*.

spot-on *adjective*
(*informal*) absolutely correct or accurate.

spotter *noun*
a person or thing that spots, especially one that looks for and reports something: 'a talent *spotter*'.

spotty *adjective*
Word Family: see SPOT.

spot-weld *verb*
to weld in one place by pressing electrical conductors to either side of two pieces of metal and briefly applying a high electric current.

spouse (*rhymes with* cows) *noun*
one's husband or wife.
[Latin *sponsus* betrothed]

spout *noun*
1. a pipe or tube, usually with a lip-like end, for pouring.
2. a stream or gush of liquid discharged under pressure.
up the spout, (*informal*) a) 'his small business is completely *up the spout* because of wage increases' (= ruined); b) 'my diamond ring is *up the spout*' (= at the pawnbrokers).
spout *noun*
to pour out in gushes.
Usage: (*informal*) 'he loves *spouting* pieces of Greek verse' (= uttering pompously).

sprain *verb*
to twist or strain a part of the body without breaking it.
Word Family: **sprain**, *noun*, a twisting or straining without actual breakage.

sprang *verb*
the past tense of the verb **spring**.

sprat *noun*
a small, edible, marine fish, related to the herring.
sprat to catch a mackerel, a small favour or concession made in hopes of a far larger one in return.

sprawl *verb*
to stretch out in a careless or ungraceful manner: 'stop *sprawling* in your chair'.
Usage: 'the suburbs *sprawled* across the countryside' (= spread out, straggled).
Word Family: **sprawl**, *noun*, an ungraceful or irregular stretch or extent.

spray (1) *noun*
1. a liquid blown or forced through the air as fine drops.
Usage: 'Bonnie and Clyde were met with a *spray* of bullets' (= fine shower, scattering).
2. any of various devices which force out a shower of fine particles or drops: 'a perfume *spray*'.
Word Family: **spray**, *verb*, a) to apply a liquid as a spray, b) to move or fall as a spray.

spray (2) *noun*
a) a small, fine branch with leaves, flowers, berries, etc., often used for decoration. b) a design or ornament with this form.

spray–gun *noun*
a gun–shaped device using compressed air to spray liquids, such as paint, insecticides, etc. evenly over an area.

spread (*say* spred) *verb*
(**spread, spreading**)
1. to make or become larger, wider or more full: a) 'the eagle *spread* his wings'; b) '*spread* the map out on the table'.
2. to distribute or extend over an area, especially evenly: a) '*spread* the butter on the bread'; b) 'the payments are *spread* over 12 months'; c) 'the disease *spread* throughout the country'.
Usages:
a) 'the news *spread* rapidly' (= was made widely known).
b) 'he *spread* the hair on either side of the cut' (= forced apart, separated).
c) '*spread* your clothes out to dry by the fire' (= lay).
d) 'who will *spread* the table for dinner?' (= set, arrange).
spread *noun*
1. the act of spreading: 'he watched the slow *spread* of the eagle's wings'.
2. the amount by which something spreads: 'the aircraft's wings had a *spread* of 30 m'.
3. something which spreads, covers or is spread: a) 'a *bedspread*'; b) 'cheese *spread*'.
4. something which extends or stretches: 'we could see a wide *spread* of forest ahead'.
5. a) two pages which face each other in a book, magazine, etc. b) a story, advertisement, etc. which extends across all or part of two such pages.
Usages:
a) (*informal*) 'the dinner they provided was a real *spread*' (= feast).
b) 'mother has developed a middle–age *spread*' (= fatness, wideness).
Word Family: **spreader,** *noun,* a person or thing that spreads.

spread–eagled, spread–eagle *adjective*
with the arms and legs stretched out.
Word Family: **spread–eagle,** *verb.*

spree *noun*
a period of indulgence or excess in some activity: 'a shopping *spree*'.

sprig *noun*
a twig or small branch, often used for decoration: 'a *sprig* of holly'.

sprightly (*say* **sprite**–lee) *adjective*
full of life or nimble energy.
Word Family: **sprightliness,** *noun.*

spring *verb*
(**sprang, sprung, springing**)
1. to rise or move lightly and suddenly.
2. to make or become bent: 'these old floorboards have *sprung*'.
Usages:
a) 'angry words *sprang* to her lips' (= rushed, came quickly).
b) 'the trap *sprang* closed' (= flew, snapped).
c) 'we *sprang* the dinner party as a surprise' (= produced unexpectedly).
d) 'the boat has *sprung* another leak' (= developed).
e) 'the feud *sprang* from a misunderstanding' (= arose, originated).
f) (*informal*) 'his friends intend to *spring* him from prison' (= cause to escape).
spring *noun*
1. the act of springing: 'a tiger's *spring* at its prey'.
2. any of various devices made from twisted, bent or layered metal which regains its shape after force has been applied, such as a spiral spring in a sofa.
3. a springing quality, force or movement: 'her walk has no *spring* or liveliness in it'.
4. the season of the year between winter and summer.
5. a natural flow or stream of water: 'this river starts at a mountain *spring*'.
6. the source of something.
Word Family: **springer,** *noun,* a) a person or thing that springs, b) any of various breeds of short–haired spaniels.

springbok *noun*
a small, South African antelope.
[Afrikaans, SPRING + BUCK]

spring chicken
(*informal*) a young or inexperienced person.

spring–clean *verb*
to clean or tidy thoroughly, especially as an annual clean–up of the whole house in spring.
Word Family: **spring–cleaning,** *noun.*

spring fever
a feeling of listlessness or restless desire, often experienced at the beginning of spring.

spring onion
an onion with a small bulb and long, green shoots, usually eaten raw.

springy *adjective*
tending to spring, bounce or rebound.
Word Family: **springiness,** *noun.*

sprinkle *verb*
to scatter or fall in drops or small particles.
Usage: 'her conversation was *sprinkled* with little laughs' (= interrupted at intervals).
Word Family: **sprinkle,** *noun,* a) a light fall of drops, b) a small quantity; **sprinkler,** *noun,* something which sprinkles, especially a device with a nozzle which scatters drops of water over a garden, etc.; **sprinkling,** *noun,* a light, small shower or scattering.

sprint *verb*
to run or race at full speed, especially over a short distance.
Word Family: **sprint,** *noun,* a short race at top speed; **sprinter,** *noun,* a person who sprints.

sprite *noun*
Folklore: a fairy.

sprocket *noun*
any of the pointed teeth on a wheel, which fit into the links of a chain, as on a bicycle.

sprout *verb*
to begin to grow or develop.
Word Family: **sprout,** *noun,* a) a young growth or shoot, b) (informal) a brussels sprout.

spruce (1) *noun*
any of a group of evergreen fir trees with cones and short, angular, needle-like leaves arranged densely around a twig.
[Old English *Pruce* Prussia]

spruce (2) *adjective*
neat and smart, especially in one's dress.
spruce oneself up, to make oneself neat and smart.

sprung *verb*
the past participle of the verb **spring.**

spry *adjective*
nimble or sprightly.
Word Family: **spryly,** *adverb*; **spryness,** *noun.*

spud *noun*
1. (*informal*) a potato.
2. a small spade with a narrow blade or prongs, for digging up weeds, etc.

spume (*say* **spewm**) *noun*
foam or froth.
Word Family: **spume,** *verb*; **spumy,** *adjective,* frothy.
[from Latin]

spun *verb*
the past tense and past participle of the verb **spin.**

spunk *noun*
(*informal*) courage.
Word Family: **spunky,** *adjective.*

spur *noun*
1. a sharp metal projection strapped to the heel of a rider's boot to urge the horse on.
Usage: 'the prize was a *spur* to the competitors' (= stimulus, inspiration).
2. a projecting part, such as a ridge on the side of a hill or a horny growth on the leg of certain birds or animals.
3. a short or undeveloped branch on a tree.
on the spur of the moment, suddenly or spontaneously.
spur *verb*
(spurred, spurring)
to prick or strike with a spur: 'the huntsman *spurred* his horse'.
Usage: 'fear *spurred* her to greater efforts' (= inspired).

spurious (*say* **spewri-us**) *adjective*
false or counterfeit.
Word Family: **spuriously,** *adverb*; **spuriousness,** *noun.*
[from Latin]

spurn *verb*
to treat or reject with scorn or contempt.

spurt *noun*
a sudden flow or outpouring: 'a *spurt* of water from the burst pipe'.
Usages:
a) 'his last *spurt* to the line won him the race' (= burst of energy).
b) 'in a *spurt* of jealousy he killed his lover' (= outburst).
Word Family: **spurt,** *verb.*

sputnik *noun*
any of the early man-made satellites used by Russia for space research.
[Russian, travelling companion]

sputter *verb*
to spit or splash in an explosive manner.
Usage: 'she *sputtered* with rage at their rudeness' (= stammered, spluttered).
Word Family: **sputter,** *noun.*

sputum (*say* **spew**–t'm) *noun*
spittle or phlegm.
[Latin]

spy *noun*
1. a person sent to gather information secretly in enemy or potentially enemy territory.
2. a person employed to watch and report secretly on the activities of others.
Word Family: **spy** (**spied**, **spying**), *verb*, a) to act as a spy, b) to catch sight of or see; **spier**, *noun*.

squab (*say* skwob) *noun*
1. a young pigeon.
2. a soft cushion.

squabble (*say* **skwobb**'l) *noun*
a trivial argument.
Word Family: **squabble**, *verb*.

squad (*say* skwod) *noun*
any small group selected for a particular purpose, such as a group of soldiers.
[Old French *esquadre* a square]

squad–car *noun*
a police patrol–car.

squadron (*say* **skwod**–r'n) *noun*
a) a group of warships on a particular mission. b) a unit of the airforce, cavalry or tank regiments.
[Italian *squadra* square]

squadron leader
a commissioned officer in the airforce, ranking between a flight lieutenant and a wing–commander.

squalid (*say* **skwollid**) *adjective*
1. depressingly or miserably dirty.
2. degraded.
Word Family: **squalidly**, *adverb*; **squalidness**, *noun*.
[Latin *squalidus* rough, unkempt]

squall (1) (*say* skwawl) *noun*
1. a sudden gust of strong wind.
2. a noisy disturbance or fight.
Word Family: **squally**, *adjective*,

squall (2) (*say* skwawl) *verb*
to scream or cry out harshly.
Word Family: **squall**, *noun*.

squalor (*say* **skwolla**) *noun*
depressing or wretched conditions.

squamous (*say* **skway**–mus) *adjective*
Biology: covered with or consisting of scales.
[Latin]

squander (*say* **skwonda**) *verb*
to spend or use wastefully: 'do not *squander* your spare hours'.
Word Family: **squanderer**, *noun*.

square (*say* skwair) *noun*
1. a quadrilateral having equal sides and four right angles.
2. something which has this shape, such as the divisions on a chessboard, etc.
3. *Maths:* the second power of a number. *Example*: the square of 2, written 2^2, is $2 \times 2 = 4$.
4. an open area in a town or city, usually bordered by buildings or streets, and planted with trees, etc.
5. (*informal*) a person considered to be dully conservative or old–fashioned.
6. a unit of area in buildings equal to 100 sq. ft. or $9{\cdot}3$ m^2.
Phrases:
back to square one, back to where one started, so one has to begin again.
square bashing, army drill on the barrack square.

square *verb*
1. to make into a square or similar shape.
Usages:
a) 'his story does not *square* with yours' (= agree).
b) 'he *squared* his shoulders and stood to attention' (= straightened, made level).
c) 'you must *square* your debts first' (= pay, settle).
2. *Maths:* to multiply a number by itself.
Phrases:
square up, 'the company has *squared up* all its overdue accounts' (= settled).
square up to, 'she must *square up to* these responsibilities' (= face bravely).

square *adjective*
1. having four sides and four right angles: 'a *square* box'.
2. being in the form of a right angle: 'a *square* corner'.
3. presenting a measured unit of area in the form of a square: 'a *square* metre'.
Usages:
a) 'our accounts are *square* now' (= settled).
b) 'we must have a *square* answer' (= honest, straightforward).
c) (*informal*) 'this is the first *square* meal I've had for a week' (= good, substantial).
d) 'the players finished with their scores *square*' (= equal).
4. (*informal*) dull, conservative or old–fashioned.
Word Family: **square**, *adverb*, a) in a square form or at right angles, b)

(informal) honestly or directly; **squarely**, *adverb.* [from Latin]

square dance
a dance by couples arranged in a square or other set pattern, and who follow instructions by a caller in order to make a pattern.
Word Family: **square-dance**, *verb.*

square number
Maths: any number that is the square of another number. *Examples*: 1 (= 1×1), 4 (= 2×2), and 9 (= 3×3), are **square numbers.**

square-rigged *adjective*
Nautical: having square sails set on horizontal yards across the length of the ship. Compare FORE-AND-AFT RIGGED.

square root
Maths: the number which, when multiplied by itself, equals the given number: '4 is the *square root* of 16'.

squash (1) (*say* skwosh) *verb*
to press or beat, especially into a flat mass.
Usage: 'the rebellion was *squashed* by government troops' (= stopped, put down).
squash *noun*
1. the act or sound of squashing: 'the plums made a soft *squash* as they fell'.
2. something which is squashed or pressed.
3. a game played by two or four players in a walled court, with rackets and a small rubber ball. Also called **squash rackets.**
4. a drink made with fruit juice or cordial as a base.
5. a crowd or crowded gathering.
Word Family: **squashy**, *adjective,* soft and easily squashed. [for QUASH]

squash (2) (*say* skwosh) *noun*
an edible vegetable similar to a marrow.

squat (*say* skwot) *verb*
(squatted or **squat, squatting)**
1. to sit on one's heels or in a crouching position.
2. to settle on an area of public land before acquiring a legal right to it.
3. to enter an unoccupied house and live there without paying rent.
squatter *noun*
a person who squats.
Word Family: **squat**, *noun,* a) the act of squatting, b) the position when squatting; **squat**, *adjective,* short and thick.

squaw (*say* skwaw) *noun*
a North American Indian woman.

squawk (*say* skwawk) *verb*
to utter a harsh cry, as poultry, etc. when frightened.
Usage: (*informal*) 'buyers are *squawking* about increased prices' (= protesting angrily or noisily).
Word Family: **squawk**, *noun.*

squeak (*say* skweek) *verb*
to make a short, high-pitched sound.
Usage: 'he just *squeaked* through the entrance exam' (= got by a small margin).
squeak *noun*
1. the act or sound of squeaking.
2. (*informal*) an escape: 'that was a narrow *squeak*!'.
Word Family: **squeaky**, *adjective,* making squeaks; **squeakily**, *adverb;* **squeakiness**, *noun.*

squeal (*say* skweel) *verb*
to make a long, loud, high-pitched cry or sound.
Usage: (*informal*) 'the traitor has *squealed* to the police' (= turned informer).
Word Family: **squeal**, *noun,* a squealing sound; **squealer**, *noun.*

squeamish (*say* **skwee**-mish) *adjective*
easily sickened or shocked.
Word Family: **squeamishly**, *adverb;* **squeamishness**, *noun.*

squeegee (*say* **skwee**-jee) *noun*
a device with a flexible sponge or rubber edge for cleaning.

squeeze (*say* skweez) *verb*
1. to press firmly: 'he *squeezed* her hand in sympathy'.
2. to extract by pressing: a) '*squeeze* the juice from three lemons'; b) 'he tried to *squeeze* a confession out of me'.
Usages:
a) 'can we all *squeeze* into the back seat?' (= fit or force by pressure).
b) 'the bank is *squeezing* us to repay the loan' (= urging, putting pressure on).
squeeze *noun*
the act of squeezing: 'a *squeeze* of the hand'.
Usages:
a) 'we managed to get into the bus, but it was a tight *squeeze*' (= crush, squash).
b) 'add a *squeeze* of lemon' (= small amount).
c) 'a financial *squeeze*' (= time of restriction or difficulty).
Word Family: **squeezer**, *noun,* something which squeezes, especially

a device for extracting juice from fruits.

squelch (*say* skwelsh) *verb*
to make a splashing, sucking sound.
Usage: 'his sharp retort *squelched* her' (= made quiet or subdued).
Word Family: **squelch,** *noun.*

squib (*say* skwib) *noun*
a small firework which sparkles and then explodes.
damp squib, an effort which fails miserably.

squid (*say* skwid) *noun*
any of a group of edible cephalopods with ten arms, some spanning 15 m.

squiggle (*say* **skwigg**'l) *noun*
a wiggly or careless mark in drawing or writing.
Word Family: **squiggle,** *verb.*

squint (*say* skwint) *verb*
1. to look with the eyes partly closed or screwed up: 'to *squint* against the sun's glare'.
2. to be cross-eyed.
Word Family: **squint,** *noun.*

squire (*say* skwire) *noun*
1. a country gentleman, used as an unofficial title for the owner of a manor house, etc.
2. *Medieval history:* a young nobleman serving as attendant to a knight, as training for his own knighthood. Also called an **esquire.**
Word Family: **squire,** *verb,* (of a man) to escort or accompany women.

squirm (*say* skwerm) *verb*
to wriggle or twist the body about.
Usage: 'we *squirmed* under his angry scrutiny' (= felt embarrassed or uncomfortable).
Word Family: **squirm,** *noun;* **squirmy,** *adjective.*

squirrel (*say* **skwirr**'l) *noun*
a) any of various small rodents with reddish-brown or grey fur and a bushy tail, usually living in trees. b) the fur of such an animal, used to make or line coats, etc.
[Greek *skiouros* from *skia* shade + *oura* tail]

squirt (*say* skwert) *verb*
to discharge liquid in a quick stream: '*squirt* water on a fire'.
squirt *noun*
1. a) the act of squirting. b) a thin, fast stream of liquid.
2. (*informal*) a small or insignificant person, especially if impudent or presumptuous.

squish *noun*
a squashing sound.
Word Family: **squish,** *verb,* to squash.

squit *noun*
(*informal*) a contemptible person, usually small.
Word Family: **squitters,** *noun* (*informal*), diarrhoea.

stab *verb*
(stabbed, stabbing)
to pierce or wound with or as if with a knife: '*stabbed* by a robber'.
Usage: 'she was *stabbed* by feelings of guilt' (= affected sharply).
stab *noun*
1. a) the act of stabbing. b) a thrust made with or as if with a pointed weapon.
2. a wound caused by stabbing.
Usages:
a) 'he felt a *stab* of remorse' (= painful feeling).
b) (*informal*) 'at least have a *stab* at the answer!' (= attempt, guess).
a stab in the back, a betrayal or unfair attack.

stabilize (*say* **stay**bi-lize) **stabilise** *verb*
to make stable or level: 'the government is trying to *stabilize* prices'.
stabilizer *noun*
1. something which stabilizes, such as a substance used to control or limit chemical changes in other substances, etc.
2. any of various systems which stabilize a ship in rough seas.
Word Family: **stabilization,** *noun.*

stable (1) *noun*
a) a building in which horses are kept.
b) all the horses owned by one person or establishment: 'a racing *stable*'.
Usage: 'the speakers obviously belong to the same political *stable*' (= group, organization).
Word Family: **stable,** *verb,* to put or keep in a stable; **stabling,** *noun,* a) any or all stables, b) accommodation for horses in a stable. [from Latin]

stable (2) *adjective*
1. steady and not likely to fall or collapse: 'that bridge does not look very *stable*'.
Usages:
a) 'we need a reliable, *stable* character for this position' (= well-balanced, dependable).

b) 'they have built up a *stable* relationship' (= lasting).
2. *Chemistry:* not easily decomposed.
Word Family: **stability** (*say* sta-**billi**-tee), *noun*; **stably** (*say* **stay**-blee), *adverb.*

staccato (*say* sta-**kah**-toe) *adjective*
Music: short and abrupt.
Word Family: **staccato**, *adverb.*
[Italian, detached]

stack *noun*
1. a large pile, often arranged in layers: 'a *haystack*'.
2. a number of things grouped together.
Usage: (*informal*) 'I have a *stack* of things to do today' (= great number).
3. a) a single chimney or flue. b) a group of chimneys.
stack *verb*
1. to place or arrange in a stack: '*stack* those chairs in the corner'.
2. to arrange so as to give oneself an advantage: 'he *stacked* the rally with his own supporters'.

stadium (*say* **stay**-dee-um) *noun*
plural is **stadiums** or **stadia**
a sports ground surrounded by raised banks of seats for spectators.
[from Greek]

staff (*say* stahf) *noun*
1. a group of people working together under a manager or other authority in an organization, business, etc.: 'the *staff* of a hospital'.
2. a rod, pole or stick used as a weapon, flagpole, etc.
Usage: 'food is the *staff* of life' (= sustainer, supporter).
3. *Music:* the framework of lines and spaces on which music is written. Plural is **staves**. Also called a **stave**.
Word Family: **staff**, *verb*, to provide an office, etc. with a staff.

staff college
1. a college where staff officers are given special training.
2. a college which gives training in business management and administration.

staff officer
Military: a commissioned officer directly responsible to, and issuing the orders of, a commander.

stag *noun*
1. a male deer, especially a red deer.
2. (*informal*) a male, especially one at a party, etc. without a female.
Word Family: **stag**, *adjective*, (of a party, etc.) excluding females.

stage *noun*
1. a) the platform or area, usually raised, on which actors perform, especially in a theatre. b) any raised floor or platform, such as a scaffolding.
2. a) the profession of acting: 'he is training to go on the *stage*'. b) the theatre: 'a work written for the *stage*'.
3. a single step in a progress, development, series, etc.: a) 'the first *stage* of our research is complete'; b) 'the larval *stage* of an insect'.
4. a) a main bus-stop. b) a section of a bus route.
5. a powered section of a rocket vehicle, which is ejected after firing.
Usage: 'the *stage* was set for war' (= scene, atmosphere).
hold the stage, to be the centre of attention.
stage *verb*
to put or exhibit on or as if on a stage.
Usage: 'the workers have *staged* a massive strike' (= arranged and carried out).
Word Family: **staging**, *noun*, a) the act of putting on a play, b) a temporary platform or structure, usually raised.

stagecoach *noun*
an enclosed carriage with the driver's seat outside at the front, once used to carry passengers, mail, etc. over a set route.

stage door
an outside door for performers, etc. to enter the backstage area of a theatre.

stage fright
any nervousness caused by being in front of an audience, especially for the first time.

stage-manager *noun*
Theatre: a person appointed to organize and control the rehearsals and performance of a play.

stager (*say* **stay**-ja) *noun*
old stager, a person with long experience in some activity, occupation, etc.

stagestruck *adjective*
fascinated by or eager to have a career in acting or the theatre.

stage whisper
a loud or exaggerated whisper, such as one from an actor intended to be heard by the audience.

stagger *verb*
1. to walk or move unsteadily: 'she *staggered* with exhaustion'.

Usage: 'we were *staggered* by the brilliant results' (= amazed, overwhelmed).
2. to arrange in alternating or overlapping periods or intervals: 'employees should *stagger* their lunchtimes so that the office is never empty'.
stagger *noun*
1. the act of staggering.
2. (*plural, used with singular verb*) any of various diseases affecting horses, cattle, etc., causing blindness and staggering movements.
Word Family: **staggeringly**, *adverb.*

staging (*say* **stay**–jing) *noun*
Word Family: see STAGE.

stagnant *adjective*
a) not flowing. b) stale or foul due to lack of movement: 'a *stagnant* pool'.
Usage: 'they found the local art scene quite *stagnant*' (= lifeless, inactive).
Word Family: **stagnantly**, *adverb*; **stagnation**, *noun*; **stagnate**, *verb.*
[Latin *stagnum* a pool]

stagy (*say* **stay**–jee) *adjective*
theatrical, especially in an artificial way.
Word Family: **staginess**, *noun.*

staid (*say* stade) *adjective*
serious and sedate, especially in a tedious way.
Word Family: **staidly**, *adverb*; **staidness**, *noun.*
[for STAYED]

stain (*say* stane) *noun*
1. a discoloured area or mark produced or left by a substance: 'coffee *stains* are difficult to get rid of'.
Usage: 'the crime left a serious *stain* on his reputation' (= bad mark).
2. a liquid dye, consisting of colour dissolved in water or spirit, which soaks into and colours a surface.
Word Family: **stain**, *verb*, a) to make a stain upon, b) to colour with a liquid dye, c) to corrupt or bring blame upon; **stainer**, *noun*; **stainless**, *adjective.*

stained glass
a decorative form of glass, usually coloured with metallic oxides, used in church windows, etc.

stainless steel
any of a group of alloys of iron and chromium, which is very resistant to corrosion and is used for making utensils, etc.

stair *noun*
1. any of a series of steps leading from one level of a building to another.
2. (*plural*) a series of such steps.
below stairs, the servants' quarters, in the basement.

staircase, stairway *noun*
a series of fixed steps and its framework, etc., between two levels in a building.

stairwell *noun*
the opening around which a staircase is built.

stake (1) *noun*
a pointed stick or post, usually of wood or metal, driven into the ground as a support, marker, etc.
stake *verb*
1. to mark a position or boundary with a stake or stakes: 'to *stake* off the garden'.
2. to support or secure with or to a stake: 'you should *stake* those tomato plants'.

stake (2) *noun*
(*plural*) a) the money or any other thing promised as payment for a bet. b) the prize for a competition: 'the *stakes* for the race were £1000'.
Usage: 'he has a personal *stake* in this matter' (= interest, involvement).
at stake, 'there is too much *at stake* for us to fail' (= being risked, involved).
stake *verb*
to offer money or any other thing as part of a bet.

stalactite (*say* **stal**lak–tite) *noun*
Geology: any tapering mass of calcium carbonate, formed by dripping water, hanging from the roof of a cave, etc. Compare STALAGMITE.
[Greek *stalaktos* dripping]

stalagmite (*say* **stal**lag–mite) *noun*
Geology: any mass of calcium carbonate rock deposited on the floor of a cave, usually projecting upwards. Compare STALACTITE.
[Greek *stalagma* a dripping]

stale *adjective*
not fresh: a) '*stale* bread'; b) 'a *stale* old joke'.
Word Family: **stale**, *verb*, to make or become stale; **staleness**, *noun*; **stalely**, *adverb.*

stalemate *noun*
1. *Chess:* a position where neither player can move without putting his king in check, resulting in a draw.
2. any deadlock.
Word Family: **stalemate**, *verb*, to bring into a stalemate.

stalk (1) (*say* stawk) ***noun***
the stem of a plant, flower, leaf, fruit, etc.

stalk (2) (*say* stawk) ***verb***
1. to approach stealthily: 'the cat *stalked* the mouse'.
2. to walk slowly and stiffly: 'he *stalked* off in a huff'.
Word Family: **stalk,** *noun*; **stalker,** *noun*, a person or thing that stalks.

stalking-horse ***noun***
1. a horse or dummy-horse behind which a hunter hides.
2. something used to hide one's real intentions.

stall (1) (*rhymes with* ball) ***noun***
1. a compartment of a cowshed or stable for one animal.
2. a) a bench or table used to display goods for sale, e.g. in a market. b) a small, open-fronted shop: 'a newspaper *stall*'.
3. (*plural*) the seats on the ground floor of a theatre.
4. any of the fixed seats used by the choir or clergy in a church.
stall *verb*
1. to put or keep animals in a stall.
2. (of a motor) to stop running owing to insufficient power, speed, etc.
3. (of an aircraft) to lose flying speed and plummet out of control.

stall (2) (*rhymes with* ball) ***verb***
to act evasively or deceptively: 'stop *stalling* and answer the question'.
Word Family: **stall,** *noun.*

stallion (*say* **stal**-y'n) ***noun***
a male horse, especially one used for breeding.

stalwart (*say* **stawl**-wort) ***adjective***
1. strongly and stoutly built.
2. firm and steadfast: 'my *stalwart* supporters will never desert me'.
Word Family: **stalwart,** *noun*, a stalwart person.

stamen (*say* **stay**-m'n) ***noun***
Biology: the organ of a flower which produces pollen, consisting of the filament, and the anther.
[Latin, the warp]

stamina (*say* **stammina**) ***noun***
strength and the power to endure.

stammer ***noun***
a) a stutter. b) any hesitation in speech.
Word Family: **stammer,** *verb*; **stammerer,** *noun*; **stammeringly,** *adverb.*

stamp ***noun***
1. the act of bringing the foot down forcefully: 'he gave a *stamp* of impatience'.
2. a postage stamp.
Usage: 'the story has the *stamp* of truth' (= distinctive mark).
3. a) any device used to impress a shape, design or mark. b) the design, etc. made. c) a device used to cut or crush.
stamp *verb*
1. a) to put one's foot down forcefully. b) to walk with heavy or violent steps: 'he *stamped* across the room'.
2. to mark with a design, shape, etc. by means of pressure.
Usages:
a) '*stamp* this on your memory' (= mark firmly).
b) 'your actions *stamp* you as a coward' (= mark, distinguish).
3. to stick a stamp on a letter, etc.
stamp out, to end or destroy something by force.

stamp duty
a tax charged by the government on certain legal documents, payment being shown by sticking a stamp on the document.

stampede (*say* stam-**peed**) ***noun***
a sudden, uncontrolled rush by a large group of horses, cattle or people.
Word Family: **stampede,** *verb*, to rush or cause to rush in a stampede.

stamping ground
(*informal*) a place habitually frequented by a person or animal.

stance ***noun***
Sport: the positioning of the body when making a stroke at golf, cricket, fencing, etc.
Usage: 'she has adopted a firm *stance* on Women's Lib.' (= attitude, standpoint).
[Italian *stanza* a standing-place]

stanch ***verb***
to staunch.

stanchion (*say* **stan**-sh'n) ***noun***
any upright post or support, e.g. in the steel framework of a building.

stand ***verb***
(stood, standing)
1. a) to take or keep an upright position on the feet: 'everyone *stood* when the heiress entered'. b) to be or put in an upright position: '*stand* the bottle on the table'.
2. to be or remain in a certain condition, situation or position: a) 'the

shop *stood* on the corner for 60 years'; b) 'you *stand* convicted of treason'; c) 'how much money do you *stand* to win?'; d) 'she *stood* firm in her beliefs'.
3. to undergo: 'you must *stand* trial'.
Usages:
a) 'I can't *stand* the noise' (= tolerate).
b) 'she *stood* for parliament' (= was a candidate).
c) (*informal*) 'she *stood* us a meal in a restaurant' (= paid for).
d) '*stand* and deliver' (= halt, stop).
e) 'the pony *stands* 14 hands high' (= measures).
Phrases:
as it stands, 'I shall buy the car *as it stands*' (= in its present state).
stand alone, 'as a boxer he *stands alone*' (= has no equal).
stand by, a) '*stand by* for further orders' (= wait and be ready); b) 'she *stood by* me when I was in trouble' (= supported); c) 'you'll have to *stand by* our agreement' (= stick to). *Word Family:* **stand-by,** *noun,* a) something kept for emergency use, b) last-minute allocation of unclaimed airline seats; **stand-by,** *adjective.*
stand down, a) 'the candidate *stood down* from the contest' (= withdrew); b) 'the factory *stood down* 50 workers' (= suspended).
stand for, a) 'I won't *stand for* your nonsense' (= tolerate); b) 'what does this hieroglyph *stand for*?' (= serve to designate or express).
stand in, 'we need someone to *stand in* for Andrew while he's away' (= be a substitute). *Word Family*: **stand-in,** *noun,* a substitute.
stand off, a) to keep at a distance; b) to suspend from work.
stand on, 'I *stand on* my rights' (= insist on).
stand one's ground, to remain firm.
stand out, a) 'she *stands out* from her friends' (= is noticeably different); b) 'they are still *standing out* for more money' (= insisting on).
stand over, a) to remain near and watch; b) (*informal*) 'I refuse to let them *stand over* me like that' (= intimidate).
stand someone up, (*informal*) to fail to keep an appointment with.
stand up, to stand, especially after sitting.
stand up for, to defend or support.
stand up to, a) 'the table won't *stand up to* rough treatment' (= remain in good condition during); b) '*stand up to* him and his insults' (= oppose, resist).
stand *noun*
1. a position taken: a) 'she took a *stand* by the door'; b) 'what's your *stand* on censorship?'.
2. a halt or stop: 'the battle came to a *stand*'.
3. a platform or other structure for people to watch sports, etc.
4. a piece of furniture or other support on or in which something is placed: 'an umbrella *stand*'.
5. a) a small stall or shop: 'a *news-stand*'. b) an area or building at a trade fair, etc.: 'the Australian *stand* at the World Fair'.
6. a place where vehicles wait to be hired: 'a taxi *stand*'.
Usages:
a) 'we made a *stand* against the enemy' (= defence, resistance).
b) 'the theatrical company had a three-week *stand* in Newcastle' (= season).

standard *noun*
1. a level, especially of achievement or excellence: a) 'what *standard* have you reached in school?'; b) 'we expect high *standards* of behaviour'.
2. *Commerce:* a monetary system based on a certain commodity: 'the gold *standard*'.
3. an established measure of extent, quantity, value, etc.: 'there are no *standards* of comparison'.
4. an image or a symbol on a flag used as an emblem for a nation or an army.
Usage: 'this song is an old *standard*' (= popular piece).
standard *adjective*
1. of recognized or established authority: a) 'a *standard* text'; b) 'speak in *standard* English'.
2. accepted or normal: a) 'a *standard* shoe size'; b) 'follow the *standard* procedure'.

standard deviation
Maths: see DEVIATION.

standardize, standardise *verb*
to make of a standard size, shape, quality, etc.
Word Family: **standardization,** *noun.*

standard-lamp *noun*
a tall lamp set on an upright support whose base rests on the floor.

standard of living
Economics: the level of incomes, possessions, consumption, etc. of a nation, group, family, etc.: 'most

people expect their *standard of living* to improve year by year'.

standard time

the time officially adopted for the whole or part of a country, usually the time of some nearby meridian.

standing *noun*

1. reputation or status: 'a family of good *standing*'.
2. existence or duration: 'a dispute of long *standing*'.
standing *adjective*
1. continuing or permanent: a) 'a *standing* dispute'; b) 'a *standing* order for the morning newspaper'.
2. done in or from an upright position: 'a *standing* jump'.
3. stagnant: '*standing* water'.

standing army

a permanent armed force that is kept ready for action.

standing order

1. any of various rules for the procedures during a meeting, especially in a parliament.
2. an order to a bank to make periodic payments to a specified person until further notice.

standing wave

Physics: a wave which does not move along but which oscillates in the one plane, produced by two identical waves travelling in opposite directions in a medium.

stand-offish *adjective*

aloof or reserved.

Word Family: **stand-offishly**, *adverb*; **stand-offishness**, *noun*.

standpipe *noun*

a vertical pipe directly tapping a water-main, used as a hydrant or for communal water-supply when domestic supplies are cut off in a drought, etc.

standpoint *noun*

an attitude or point of view.

standstill *noun*

a halt or stop: 'the strike brought public transport to a *standstill*'.

stank *verb*

a past tense of the verb **stink**.

stannic *adjective*

Chemistry: of or relating to compounds of tin in which tin has a valency of four.

[Latin *stannum* tin]

stannous *adjective*

Chemistry: of or relating to compounds of tin in which tin has a valency of two.

stanza *noun*

also called a **verse**

one of a series of generally uniform groups of lines into which a poem may be divided.

[Italian]

staphylococcus (*say* staffi-lo-**kokk**us) *noun*

plural is **staphylococci**

any of a group of round bacteria occurring in clusters and which may cause infections such as boils.

[Greek *staphylé* bunch of grapes + *kokkos* a berry]

staple (1) *noun*

a U-shaped piece of wire or metal pressed into a surface to hold something in position, e.g. electric cables, or to fasten together, e.g. sheets of paper.

Word Family: **staple**, *verb*, to secure or fasten with a staple; **stapler**, *noun*, any of various machines for driving staples into a surface.

staple (2) *noun*

1. the chief commodity produced or used in a country or a region.
2. the main constituent of something.
3. a particular length and degree of fineness of fibre in wool, etc.

Word Family: **staple**, *adjective*, chief or most important.

star *noun*

1. *Astronomy:* any large body like the sun, intensely hot and producing its own energy by nuclear reactions.
2. a figure, shape or design with points around it, suggesting a star in shape.
3. (*informal*) a) a heavenly body regarded as influencing a person's life, etc. b) (*plural*) a horoscope.
4. a famous or very talented person, such as a leading actor or sportsman.
star *verb*
(**starred, starring**)
1. to mark with or as with a star or stars.
2. a) to have or present in the lead role: 'who *stars* in the film?'. b) to be in the lead role: 'the captain *starred* in the match'.

Word Family: **star**, *adjective*, a) brilliant or distinguished, b) chief.

starboard *noun*
the right side of a boat or aeroplane when looking towards the front. Compare PORT (2).

starch *noun*
1. the common carbohydrate formed by green plants and stored in seeds, tubers, etc.
2. a preparation of this substance, used to stiffen linen, etc.
3. a food rich in starch.
Usage: 'his manner was full of *starch*' (= stiffness, formality).
Word Family: **starch,** *verb,* to stiffen with starch; **starchy,** *adjective;* **starchily,** *adverb;* **starchiness,** *noun.*

starch–reduced *adjective*
(of food) prepared so as to contain less starch than usual, for use in diets, etc.

star–crossed *adjective*
having consistent bad luck, as if due to the influence of the stars.

stardom *noun*
the status of a star or famous person.

stardust *noun*
a dreamy romantic quality.

stare (*rhymes with* air) *verb*
to look fixedly.
stare down, stare out, to look fixedly at someone until he looks away.
Word Family: **stare,** *noun,* a fixed look.

starfish *noun*
a marine animal with its body in the shape of a star.

stark *adjective*
1. complete or utter: 'your idea is *stark* madness'.
2. harsh or severely desolate: 'a *stark* landscape'.
stark *adverb*
utterly or absolutely: '*stark* naked'.

starkers *adjective*
(*informal*) completely naked.

starlet *noun*
a young actress who is publicized as a future star.

starling *noun*
a black, brown–spotted bird with a purple or green sheen, which mimics sounds and makes a chattering noise.

starry (*say* **star**–ee) *adjective*
a) of, like or relating to stars. b) lit by or shining like stars.
starry–eyed *adjective*
1. having brightly shining eyes, due to joy, excitement, etc.
2. fanciful or romantically impractical.

start *verb*
1. to come or bring into being, activity or operation: a) '*start* work immediately'; b) 'I can't *start* the car on cold mornings'; c) 'it is *starting* to rain'.
Usages:
a) 'we *started* for Egypt' (= left).
b) 'my horse *started* in the third race' (= took part).
2. to make a sudden involuntary movement, as from surprise, fright, pain, etc.
start *noun*
1. the act of starting: a) 'make a *start* on your work'; b) 'she gave a *start* at the loud bang'.
2. the place where something starts: 'competitors should assemble at the *start*'.
Usage: 'the *start* of the film was boring' (= first part).
3. a lead or advantage, such as given to weaker competitors at the beginning of a race.
for a start, as a first step.

starter *noun*
1. a person or thing that starts, such as the first course of a meal.
2. a) any competitor in a race or contest. b) a person who gives the signal for a race to start.
3. a small motor used to start an internal combustion engine. Short form of **starter motor.**
under starter's orders, (of racehorses) all ready and waiting for the signal to start.

starting block
Athletics: either of a pair of angled blocks fixed to the track to give a sprinter a foothold when making a crouching start.

starting gate
a set of stalls which open simultaneously at the start of a horserace, etc.

starting price
the betting odds on a horse, etc., at the time when a race starts.

startle *verb*
to alarm or surprise suddenly.
Word Family: **startle,** *noun;* **startlingly,** *adverb.*

starve *verb*
a) to suffer or die from hunger. b) to cause suffering or death from hunger: 'the army *starved* the rebels by cutting off their supplies'.

Word Family: **starvation,** *noun;* **starveling,** *noun,* a starving person or animal.

stash *verb*
(*informal*) to hide or store away.

stasis (*say* **stay–sis**) *noun*
a state or condition in which there is no progress or movement.
[Greek]

state *noun*
1. the circumstances of a person or thing: a) 'the house was in a filthy *state*'; b) 'how's your *state* of health?'.
Usage: 'the sick man was in quite a *state*' (= tense, nervous or excited frame of mind).
2. the form of something: 'the ice was melting to a liquid *state*'.
3. a) a country. b) (*usually capital*) a division of a country for the purposes of local government: 'the 6 *States* of Australia'.
4. (*usually capital*) a country's civil government or administration: 'the police force is controlled by the *State*'.
in state, with great dignity and honour.
state *verb*
to set forth clearly and specifically: 'the barrister *stated* his client's case'.
Word Family: **statehood,** *noun,* the fact or status of being a state; **statecraft,** *noun,* the art of government and diplomacy.
[from ESTATE and STATUS]

stateless *adjective*
having lost the citizenship of one country without acquiring that of another.

stately *adjective*
majestic or dignified.
Word Family: **stateliness,** *noun.*

statement *noun*
1. a declaration.
2. a report showing the amount of money owed or in credit in an account.

stateroom *noun*
1. a first-class cabin on a passenger ship.
2. a large room in a palace or public building, for formal occasions.

state school
a school organized and financed by local authorities and government.

statesman *noun*
a person respected for his skill in important government affairs, especially diplomacy.
Word Family: **statesmanlike,** *adjective,* wise or diplomatic; **statesmanship,** *noun,* skill or wisdom in managing government affairs.

static (*say* **stattik**) *adjective*
not active, moving or changing.
static *noun*
1. a discharge of electricity in the atmosphere which causes a radio or television receiver to crackle.
2. any stationary electric charges, such as may be produced when brushing one's hair.
Word Family: **statically,** *adverb.*
[Greek *statikos* standing]

statics *plural noun*
Physics: (*used with singular verb*) the branch of mechanics which deals with bodies at rest and forces that produce equilibrium. Compare DYNAMICS.

station (*say* **stay–sh'n**) *noun*
1. a place or position occupied or equipped for a particular job: a) 'take your action *stations*'; b) 'a police *station*'.
Usage: 'he had ideas above his *station*' (= social rank).
2. a) a stopping place on a railway, bus route, etc. b) the buildings etc. at a stopping place.
3. *Australian, New Zealand:* a very large farm for raising cattle or sheep, usually in the outback.
station *verb*
to put at or in a certain place: 'sentries were *stationed* at each gate'.
[Latin *statio* a standing still]

stationary (*say* **stay–sh'n–ree**) *adjective*
a) not moving: 'a *stationary* tram'. b) not movable: 'a *stationary* crane'.
Common Error: do not confuse with STATIONERY.

stationery (*say* **stay–sh'n–ree**) *noun*
writing paper and related materials such as pens, pencils, etc.
Word Family: **stationer,** *noun,* a person who sells stationery.
[Medieval English *stationer* bookseller]
Common Error: do not confuse with STATIONARY.

stationmaster *noun*
a person in charge of a railway station.

statistics (*say* sta–**tistiks**) *plural noun*
a) (*used with singular verb*) the collection and analysis of facts and data in the form of numbers. b) the facts and data themselves.
vital statistics
(*informal*) a woman's measurements at the bust, waist and hips.

statistician, statist (*say* stattis-**tish**'n *and* stattist) *noun*
an expert in, or compiler of, statistics.
Word Family: **statistical**, *adjective*; **statistically**, *adverb.*

statue (*say* **stat**-yoo) *noun*
a free-standing sculpture of a human or animal figure.
statuary *noun*
any or all statues.
Word Family: **statuary** (*say* **stat**-yewa-ree), *adjective,* of or for statues; **statuette** (*say* stat-yoo-**et**), *noun,* a small statue.
[from Latin]

statuesque (*say* stat-yoo-**esk**) *adjective*
like a statue in stillness, dignity, beauty, etc.

stature (*say* **stat**-yoor) *noun*
the height of something, especially of a person.
Usage: 'he's a person of great *stature* in the music world' (= achievement, importance).
[from Latin]

status (*say* **stay**-tus) *noun*
a person's or group's social, professional or legal position in relation to others.
[Latin, posture, position]

status quo (*say* staytus **kwo**)
the existing condition or state of things.
[Latin, state in which]

status symbol
a possession, such as an expensive car, which is considered to indicate the owner's wealth, social position, etc.

statute (*say* **stat**-yoot) *noun*
a law made by Act of Parliament.
statutory (*say* **stat**-yoo-tree) *adjective*
a) of or like a statute. b) fixed, done or required by statute: 'is death the *statutory* penalty for murder?'.
[Latin *statutus* set up]

statutory declaration
a written declaration in a form required by statute.

staunch (*say* stawnch) *adjective*
firmly loyal or steadfast: 'she's a *staunch* supporter of law reform'.
staunch *verb*
also called to **stanch**
1. to stop the flow of a liquid, especially of blood from a wound.
2. (*formerly*) to quell.
Word Family: **staunchly**, *adverb*; **staunchness**, *noun.*
[Old French *estanche* watertight, reliable]

stave *noun*
1. any of the thin curved pieces of wood forming the sides of a barrel.
2. a) a rung of a chair, ladder, etc. b) a rod or pole.
3. *Music:* see STAFF.
stave *verb*
(**staved** or **stove**, **staving**)
to crush inwards or make a hole in.
stave off, 'it was impossible to *stave off* disaster' (= delay, ward off).
[from STAFF]

staves *plural noun*
1. a plural of **staff**.
2. the plural of **stave**.

stay (1) *verb*
1. to continue to be in a place or condition: '*stay* in bed for a few days'.
2. to stop, check or delay: 'this snack will *stay* your hunger'.
3. to reside on a temporary basis: 'where are you *staying* while you're in town?'.
Usage: 'I will *stay* the night' (= reside for the duration of).
4. to be able to endure or continue: 'he will not *stay* the course'.
Phrases:
come to stay, 'frozen foods have *come to stay*' (= to be accepted as a permanent feature).
stay up, not to go to bed until later than usual.
stay *noun*
1. a halt, stop or period of staying: 'he had a short *stay* in Mexico'.
2. a postponement: 'a *stay* of execution was granted to the condemned prisoner'.

stay (2) *noun*
a brace or other structure to prevent movement, such as a corset, or a rope supporting a ship's mast.

stead (*say* sted) *noun*
place: 'I couldn't go, but sent another in my *stead*'.
stand in good stead, 'this money will *stand* you *in good stead*' (= be useful to).

steadfast (*say* **sted**-fahst) *adjective*
firm, steady or unwavering: a) '*steadfast* loyalty'; b) 'a *steadfast* gaze'.
Word Family: **steadfastly**, *adverb*; **steadfastness**, *noun.*

steady (*say* **steddee**) *adjective*
1. not likely to fall over, topple, etc.: 'is this ladder *steady*?'.

Usage: 'you need *steady* nerves for this job' (= not easily disturbed or upset).
2. constant or regular: a) 'a *steady* breeze'; b) 'he's a good *steady* worker'.
steady *adverb*
in a steady manner.
go steady, (*informal*) to go out regularly with one girlfriend or boyfriend.
Word Family: **steady,** (**steadied, steadying**), *verb,* to make or become steady; **steadily,** *adverb*; **steadiness,** *noun*; **steadier,** *noun,* a person or thing that makes something steady.

steak (*say* stake) *noun*
a thick slice of meat, usually beef, which is grilled, fried, etc.

steal (*say* steel) *verb*
(**stole, stolen, stealing**)
1. to take something that belongs to someone else without their knowledge or permission.
2. to move quietly or secretly: 'I *stole* into the house at midnight'.
Usages:
a) 'the kitten *stole* his heart' (= won).
b) 'I *stole* a sleep at work' (= took secretly).

stealth (*say* stelth) *noun*
quiet secrecy or cunning.
Word Family: **stealthy,** *adjective*; **stealthily,** *adverb*; **stealthiness,** *noun.*

steam *noun*
1. water in the form of gas or vapour, caused by boiling.
2. (*informal*) energy or power.
let, blow off steam, (*informal*) to release suppressed energy or feeling.
steam *verb*
1. to give off steam: 'the kettle is *steaming*'.
2. to become covered with water-vapour: 'the kitchen windows are all *steamed* up'.
3. to move, work, etc. under the power of steam: 'the ship *steamed* into port'.
4. to cook, soften, clean, etc. using steam.
steam radio, radio broadcasting, viewed as old-fashioned in a television age.
Word Family: **steamy,** *adjective,* of, covered with or full of steam.

steamboat *noun*
a steamship.

steamed-up *adjective*
(*informal*) angry or excited.

steam-engine *noun*
any engine worked by the force of steam.

steamer *noun*
1. a steamship.
2. a container in which things are steamed, especially food.

steam iron
an iron which releases steam onto clothes, etc. to make them easier to iron.

steamroller *noun*
a heavy vehicle with large rollers for levelling roads, etc., formerly powered by a steam-engine.

steamship *noun*
also called a **steamboat** or a **steamer**
a ship driven by a steam-engine.

steam-shovel *noun*
a digging or earth-moving machine formerly powered by a steam-engine but now powered by a diesel engine.

steamy *adjective*
Word Family: see STEAM.

steed *noun*
an old word for a horse.
[Old English *steda* a stud horse]

steel *noun*
1. any of a large group of hard alloys of iron, carbon and various other elements.
2. something made of steel, such as a sword or a rod for sharpening knives.
3. a steel-like quality or nature: 'there was *steel* in his voice'.
steel *verb*
to make hard, determined, etc.: '*steel* yourself against fear'.
steel *adjective*
of, containing or like steel.
Word Family: **steely,** *adjective,* of or like steel in colour, hardness or strength.

steel band
a West Indian band playing percussion instruments made from steel oil-drums, etc.

steel wool
a pad made of steel shavings and used for scraping or cleaning.

steelyard *noun*
a weighing device consisting of an arm with a movable counterpoise at one end and a hook at the other to hold the object being weighed.

steep (1) *adjective*
1. (of a slope) rising or falling sharply: 'a *steep* flight of stairs'.
2. (*informal*) unreasonable or excessive: 'the price is too *steep*'.
Word Family: **steep,** *noun,* a steep slope or place; **steepen,** *verb,* to make

or become steep or steeper; **steeply,** *adverb*; **steepness,** *noun.*

steep (2) *verb*
to soak thoroughly: '*steep* the meat in claret before cooking'.
steeped in, 'he sat there, *steeped in* misery' (= saturated with).

steeple *noun*
the tower and spire on top of a church.

steeplechase *noun*
a horserace over ditches, hedges, etc. on a racetrack or across country.
Word Family: **steeplechaser,** *noun,* a participant in a steeplechase.
[so called because the goal of the race was originally a distant church steeple]

steeplejack *noun*
a person who climbs steeples, tall chimneys, etc. to do repairs.

steer (1) *verb*
to guide or direct the course of something, such as a vehicle.
Usage: 'she *steers* a path between conservatism and reform' (= takes).
steer clear of, to avoid.

steer (2) *noun*
a bullock.

steerage (*say* **steer**ij) *noun*
(in a passenger ship) the accommodation allotted to the passengers who travel at the cheapest rate.
[originally the part of the ship containing the steering gear]

steersman *noun*
a person who steers a ship.

stein (*say* stine) *noun*
an earthenware mug, especially one for drinking beer.
[German, stone]

stele *noun*
1. *Archaeology:* (*say* **stee**-lee) a stone column or upright slab, inscribed or carved with decoration.
2. *Biology:* (*say* steel) the central core of vascular tissue in the stem or root of a plant.
[Greek]

stellar *adjective*
of or relating to a star.
[from Latin]

stellate *adjective*
having the shape of a star.

stem (1) *noun*
1. *Biology:* the part of a plant which is normally above ground and carries the leaves and buds.
2. something resembling the stem of a plant: a) 'the *stem* of a pipe'; b) 'the *stem* of a wineglass'.
3. *Grammar:* the main part of a word to which affixes are attached.
4. the forward part of a ship: 'from *stem* to stern'.
stem *verb*
(stemmed, stemming)
to originate or develop: 'his fear of dogs *stems* from his childhood'.

stem (2) *verb*
(stemmed, stemming)
to stop or hold back a flow, movement, etc.

stench *noun*
an offensive smell.

stencil (*say* **sten**sil) *noun*
a sheet of paper or other material with a pattern cut into it which may be reproduced on a surface on which the stencil is placed, by applying ink or paint to the areas left uncovered by the stencil.
Word Family: **stencil (stencilled, stencilling),** *verb.*

sten gun
a submachine gun.
[named from the British inventors' initials]

stenographer (*say* ste-**nogra**-fa) *noun*
a person who specializes in taking dictation in shorthand.
Word Family: **stenography,** *noun,* the art of writing in shorthand; **stenographic** (*say* stenno-**graffik**), *adjective.*
[Greek *stenos* narrow + *graphein* to write]

stentorian (*say* sten-**tawrian**) *adjective*
very loud or powerful in sound: 'his *stentorian* voice could be heard everywhere in the large hall'.
[after *Stentor,* a herald in Greek mythology who had a very loud voice]

step *noun*
1. a) a movement made by lifting the foot and setting it down in another place, such as in walking, running or dancing. b) the distance covered by such a movement: 'he moved back a *step* when I shouted at him'. c) the sound of such a movement: 'I heard a *step* on the gravel'.
2. a ledge-like support for the foot in ascending or descending: 'I had to climb many *steps* to reach the observation platform'.
3. (*plural*) course: 'I retraced my *steps* to look for my lost ring'.

Usage: 'the first *steps* towards peace' (= moves).
Phrases:
in step, a) at the same pace, and usually with the same foot movements, as others; b) in harmony or conformity.
out of step, a) at a different pace or with different foot movements from others; b) not in harmony or conformity.
take steps, to start a course of action.
watch one's step, to take care.
step *verb*
(stepped, stepping)
1. to move by taking steps.
2. to put or press the foot down: 'I *stepped* on a piece of glass'.
3. to measure by pacing: 'he *stepped* out the 100 m length'.
Usages:
a) 'he *stepped* back when I shouted' (= took a step).
b) 'please *step* this way' (= come, walk).
c) 'the steep slope had been *stepped* to make climbing easier' (= cut in steps).
Phrases:
step down, a) 'when sales increased the advertising campaign was *stepped down*' (= decreased); b) 'after the scandal the mayor decided to *step down*' (= resign); c) (of a transformer) to decrease voltage.
step in, to intervene or become involved.
step on it, (*informal*) to hurry.
step up, a) 'because the goods were not selling the advertising campaign was *stepped up*' (= increased); b) (of a transformer) to increase voltage.

step–
a prefix indicating a relationship which is not due to blood but to the remarriage of a parent, as in *stepmother.*

stepchild *noun*
a husband's or wife's child from a previous marriage.
Word Family: **stepdaughter, stepson,** *nouns.*

stepladder *noun*
a ladder with a hinged support to keep it upright.

step–parent *noun*
a person who marries one's father or mother.
Word Family: **stepmother, stepfather,** *nouns.*

steppe (*say* step) *noun*
in America called a **prairie**
in South Africa called a **veld**
in South America called the **pampas**
a wide plain, the climate of which generally allows grass but not trees to grow.
[Russian]

stepping–stone *noun*
1. a stone which provides a place to step, e.g. over a stream.
2. a means of advancing or rising.

steradian (*say* ster–**ray**–dee–an) *noun*
a unit of solid angle, equal to the angle at the centre of a sphere which encloses an area on its surface equal to the square of its radius.
[Greek *stereos* solid + RADIAN]

stereo (*say* **ster**rio *or* **steer**io) *noun*
an instrument for stereophonic sound reproduction.
stereo *adjective*
(*informal*) stereophonic.

stereochemistry
(*say* sterrio–**kemmis**–tree) *noun*
a branch of chemistry studying the arrangement in space of atoms within a molecule.
[Greek *stereos* solid + CHEMISTRY]

stereogram *noun*
a stereophonic record–player.

stereometry (*say* sterri–**omma**–tree) *noun*
the measurement of volumes.
Word Family: **stereometric** (*say* sterrio–**met**rik), *adjective.*

stereophonic (*say* sterrio–**fonn**ik) *adjective*
of or relating to sound reproduction through two distinct sound sources. Compare MONOPHONIC and QUADRAPHONIC.
[Greek *stereos* solid + *phoné* a sound]

stereoscope (*say* **sterr**io–skope) *noun*
a device which blends two pictures taken from slightly different points of view into one image which has an impression of relief and solidity.
Word Family: **stereoscopy** (*say* sterri–**osk**a–pee), *noun*; **stereoscopic** (*say* sterria–**skopp**ik), *adjective.*
[Greek *stereos* solid + *skopein* to look at]

stereotype (*say* **ster**rio–tipe) *noun*
a person or thing considered to represent a set or conventional type.
Word Family: **stereotype,** *verb.*
[Greek *stereos* solid + *typos* impression]

sterile (*say* **sterrile**) *adjective*
Biology: a) being unable to reproduce. b) being free from living micro-organisms.
Word Family: **sterility** (*say* ste-rilli-tee), *noun.*
[from Latin]

sterilize (*say* **sterri-lize**) **sterilise** *verb*
1. to make infertile, usually by an operation on the Fallopian tubes in females, or on the vas deferens in males.
2. to destroy the micro-organisms in something, usually by bringing it to a high temperature.
Word Family: **sterilization,** *noun*; **sterilizer,** *noun,* a person or thing that sterilizes.

sterling *noun*
1. the British currency with the pound as its basic unit.
2. sterling silver.
sterling *adjective*
1. of or relating to sterling: 'a *sterling* draft'.
2. excellent: 'a man of *sterling* character'.
[probably from Old English *steorling* a coin with a star on it]

sterling silver
an alloy of 92·5 per cent silver and 7·5 per cent copper, used as a standard for silver in jewellery, cutlery, etc.

stern (1) *adjective*
1. grave or harsh: 'we received a *stern* reprimand for breaking the rules'.
2. demanding and enforcing obedience: 'a *stern* schoolteacher'.
Word Family: **sternly,** *adverb*; **sternness,** *noun.*

stern (2) *noun*
1. *Nautical:* the back end of a boat. Compare BOW (3).
2. the back of anything.
stern sheets, the space at the stern of an open boat.

sternum *noun*
plural is **sterna** or **sternums**
also called the **breastbone**
Anatomy: a flat bone in the front of the chest, joined to the ribs.
[Greek *sternon* chest, breast]

steroid (*say* **sterroyd** *or* **steer-oyd**) *noun*
any of a large group of fat-soluble organic compounds widely distributed in nature and including the sterols and sex hormones.
[Greek *stereos* stiff + -OID]

sterol (*say* **sterrol** *or* **steerol**) *noun*
any of a group of fatty alcohols, such as cholesterol, made by animals and plants.

stertorous (*say* **sterta-rus**) *adjective*
characterized or accompanied by a snoring sound.
Word Family: **stertorously,** *adverb*; **stertorousness,** *noun.*
[Latin *stertere* to snore]

stet *noun*
a word used by a printer to indicate that a word or words marked for alteration, etc. should remain.
[Latin, let it stand]

stethoscope (*say* **stetha-skope**) *noun*
Medicine: an instrument used for listening to the sounds of the heart and lungs.
[Greek *stethos* breast + *skopein* to look at]

stetson *noun*
a man's hat with a wide crown and brim.
[invented by *J. B. Stetson,* 1830–1906, an American hatmaker]

stevedore (*say* **steeva-dor**) *noun*
a person who supervises the loading or unloading of ships.
Word Family: **stevedore,** *verb.*
[Spanish *estivador* from Latin *stipare* to pack tight]

stew *verb*
1. to cook slowly by simmering in liquid.
2. (*informal*) to fret or worry.
stew *noun*
1. a combination of meat and vegetables, or fish, cooked slowly in liquid.
2. (*informal*) a state of agitation or uneasiness.

steward *noun*
1. a man who waits on passengers in a ship, aeroplane, train, etc.
2. a man who organizes, arranges or manages, e.g. the details of a race meeting, etc.
Word Family: **stewardess,** *noun,* a female steward.

stick (1) *noun*
1. a) a long slender piece of wood, especially a branch or stem from a tree, etc. b) something resembling this: a) 'a walking *stick*'; b) 'a hockey *stick*'.
Usage: 'I only possess a few *sticks* of furniture' (= pieces).
2. a joystick.
3. (*informal, plural*) an area far from a city or town.

the wrong end of the stick, a complete misunderstanding of facts, etc.

stick (2) *verb*
(stuck, sticking)
1. to pierce, puncture or penetrate with a pointed instrument: 'to *stick* a skewer into meat'.
2. to attach or fasten with or as if with adhesive: 'to *stick* a stamp on an envelope'.
3. (*informal*) to put or place in a particular position: a) 'he *stuck* his hands in his pocket'; b) 'please *stick* the kettle on the stove'.
4. to be at or come to a standstill: 'we got *stuck* in the peak-hour traffic'.
Usages:
a) 'I am completely *stuck* by this question' (= puzzled, confused).
b) 'the thought of their suffering *stuck* in my mind' (= stayed, remained fixed).
c) 'I *stuck* to my promise despite the difficulties' (= held faithfully).
Phrases:
stick at it, to persevere.
stick in one's throat, to be hard to accept.
stick it out, to persevere to the end.
stick out, a) to protrude; b) to be very obvious.
stick out for, 'we shall *stick out for* better working conditions' (= continue to demand).
stick up, a) to protrude vertically; b) (*informal*) to rob, especially at gunpoint.
stick up for, to speak or act in defence of.
stuck with, 'well I asked for the job and now I'm *stuck with* it' (= unable to get out of it).

sticker *noun*
1. a person or thing that sticks.
2. an adhesive label.

sticking plaster
short form is **plaster**
an adhesive dressing for covering and protecting minor wounds.

stick insect
any of a group of insects with long, slender, twig-like bodies.

stick-in-the-mud *noun*
an unadventurous person who is opposed to new ideas, novelty, etc.

stickleback *noun*
any of a group of small, freshwater fish with one or more spines on their backs.

stickler *noun*
a person who insists on something unyieldingly: 'he is a *stickler* for accuracy'.

stick-up *noun*
(*informal*) a robbery, especially at gunpoint.

sticky *adjective*
1. tending to stick or adhere.
Usage: 'I don't like this *sticky* weather' (= humid).
2. (*informal*) difficult or awkward: 'a *sticky* problem'.

stiff *adjective*
1. not easily bent or changed in shape: 'a *stiff* piece of cardboard'.
2. hard to stir, move, work, etc.: a) 'the new car had *stiff* gears'; b) 'I had *stiff* muscles after the long walk'.
Usages:
a) 'the teacher set a *stiff* examination and most students failed' (= difficult).
b) 'the prince gave a *stiff* bow' (= ceremonious).
c) 'after the accident I needed a *stiff* drink' (= strong).
d) 'the judge gave him a *stiff* sentence' (= severe).
stiff *adverb*
1. in or to a rigid state: 'the animal was frozen *stiff*'.
2. extremely or completely: 'I was bored *stiff* by the dull lecture'.
stiff *noun*
(*informal*) a dead body.
Word Family: **stiffly**, *adverb*; **stiffness**, *noun*; **stiffen**, *verb*, to make or become stiff; **stiffener**, *noun*.

stiff-necked *adjective*
perversely obstinate.

stifle (*say* **sty-f'l**) *verb*
1. to suffocate.
2. to suppress: 'she *stifled* a yawn'.
Usage: 'he *stifled* his children by excessive discipline' (= repressed).
Word Family: **stifling**, *adjective*, suffocating; **stiflingly**, *adverb*.

stigma *noun*
1. a mark of disgrace or reproach: 'the *stigma* of divorce is disappearing in many countries'.
2. *Biology:* the end of the style of a flower, which receives the pollen.
Word Family: **stigmatic** (*say* **stig-mattik**), *adjective*; **stigmatize**, **stigmatise**, *verb*, to characterize as disgraceful.
[Greek, a mark, a spot]

stigmata (*say* stig–**mah**ta) *plural noun*
the marks upon certain people, believed to be a supernatural replica of the wounds received by Christ on the cross.

stile *noun*
1. a group of steps on both sides of a fence allowing people to climb over.
2. a turnstile.

stiletto (*say* stil**lett**o) *noun*
a dagger with a slender, tapering blade.
[Latin *stilus* pointed instrument]

stiletto heel
a high heel on a woman's shoe which tapers to an extremely small base.

still (1) *adjective*
1. free from movement.
2. free from disturbance or commotion: 'a *still* night'.
3. silent.
4. relating to a single or static photograph.
Usages:
a) 'the *still*, small voice of conscience' (= hushed, subdued).
b) 'we ordered a *still* wine' (= not effervescent).
still *noun*
1. a single photograph, especially one showing a scene from a film.
2. silence or calm.
still *adverb*
1. free from movement.
2. a) now as before: 'she is *still* away'.
b) in the future as in the past: 'now and then questions will *still* be asked about the murder'.
3. in increasing amount or degree: '*still* warmer weather is forecast'.
4. nevertheless: 'she has many clothes and *still* wants more'.
Word Family: **still**, *verb*, a) to make or become still, b) to calm; **stillness**, *noun.*

still (2) *noun*
a machine used for distilling a liquid, especially alcohol.

still–born *adjective*
born dead.
Word Family: **still–birth**, *noun.*

still life
a painting or drawing of a collection of inanimate objects, such as fruit, bottles, etc.
Word Family: **still–life**, *adjective.*

stilt *noun*
1. a heavy pole used with others to support a house, etc. above the ground, especially near water.
2. either of two long poles with supports for the feet, used for walking high above the ground.

stilted *adjective*
stiffly or unnaturally formal.
Word Family: **stiltedly**, *adverb*; **stiltedness**, *noun.*

stimulant (*say* **stim**–yoo–l'nt) *noun*
Medicine: any substance, such as caffeine, which temporarily quickens the functioning of some processes. Compare SEDATIVE.

stimulate (*say* **stim**–yoo–late) *verb*
to rouse to action or increased activity.
Word Family: **stimulation**, *noun.*

stimulus *noun*
plural is **stimuli** (*say* **stim**–yoo–lie)
1. something which causes a response.
2. an incentive.
[Latin, a goad]

sting *verb*
(stung, stinging)
1. to pierce with or as if with a sharply pointed structure or organ: 'I was *stung* by a bee'.
2. to cause a sharp pain.
3. (*informal*) to obtain money from: 'he *stung* me for £10'.
Usages:
a) 'she was *stung* by his cruel remarks' (= caused to suffer acutely).
b) 'that *stung* him into action' (= stimulated).
sting *noun*
1. the act of stinging.
2. a wound or pain caused by or as if by stinging.
3. a keen stimulus or spur.
4. *Biology:* any sharp organ for piercing or injecting poison, used in attack or defence by an organism.
sting in the tail, 'he offered me a new job but–and this was the *sting in the tail*–at lower pay' (= unpleasant aspect mentioned last).
Word Family: **stinger**, *noun*, a person or thing that stings.

stingray *noun*
any of a group of rays, having a flat disc–like body with a long, narrow tail, usually ending in three poisonous spines.

stingy (*say* **stin**–jee) *adjective*
1. reluctant to give or spend money.
2. scanty or meagre: 'we paid a lot of money but only got a *stingy* meal'.
Word Family: **stinginess**, *noun.*

stink *verb*
(stank or **stunk, stunk, stinking)**
1. to emit a strong offensive smell.

2. to be highly offensive.
Usage: 'he *stinks* of money' (= has a large amount).
stink *noun*
1. a strong offensive smell.
2. (*informal*) a scandal or fuss.

stinker *noun*
1. a person or thing that stinks.
2. (*informal*) a) a disgusting or objectionable person. b) something which is difficult or unpleasant.

stint *noun*
an amount or period of work to be done: 'we all did a *stint* in the garden'.
without stint, 'he gave to charity *without stint*' (= without limit).
stint *verb*
1. to limit or restrict.
2. to be sparing or frugal: 'don't *stint* yourself with the butter'.

stipe *noun*
Biology: a stalk or similar support.
[Latin *stipes* a tree trunk]

stipend (*say* **sty**–pend) *noun*
a fixed or regular payment, especially a clergyman's salary.
Word Family: **stipendiary** (*say* sty–**penda**–ree), *adjective,* a) receiving a stipend, b) relating to a stipend.
[Latin *stipendium* tax, pay]

stipendiary magistrate
a magistrate who, unlike a justice of the peace, is salaried, serving in certain city police courts.

stipple *verb*
to engrave, paint or draw with dots.
[Dutch *stippen* to prick]

stipulate (*say* **stip**–yoo–late) *verb*
to specify or promise in an agreement: 'I *stipulate* that I will only come to Australia if you pay my fares'.
Word Family: **stipulation,** *noun.*
[from Latin]

stir *verb*
(stirred, stirring)
1. to mix by circular movements.
2. to move or cause to move, especially slightly: a) 'the breeze *stirred* the leaves'; b) 'she did not *stir* a finger to help us'.
3. to rouse or be roused: a) 'the story *stirred* my imagination'; b) 'pity *stirred* in his heart when he heard our story'.
Usage: (*informal*) 'don't listen to him, he's only *stirring*' (= being provocative).
stir *noun*
1. the act of stirring: 'give the paint a *stir*'.
2. a commotion.
Word Family: **stirring,** *adjective,* rousing or exciting; **stirringly,** *adverb;* **stirrer,** *noun,* a person or thing that stirs, especially a person who stirs up trouble or difficulty.

stirrup *noun*
1. either of two loops, usually made of metal, hanging from the saddle on straps and into which the rider places his foot for support and balance.
2. any of various similar supports.
[Old English *stigan* to climb + ROPE]

stirrup cup
a parting drink.
[originally given to a guest mounted and ready to depart]

stitch *noun*
1. a) one complete movement of the needle in knitting, sewing, crocheting, etc. b) the loop of cotton, wool, etc. left by the movement of a needle. c) a particular method used in sewing, etc.
2. a sudden sharp pain in the side, e.g. after strenuous exercise.
Usages:
a) (*informal*) 'she went swimming without a *stitch* on' (= piece of clothing).
b) (*informal*) 'I did not do a *stitch* of work all afternoon' (= bit).
in stitches, 'he had us *in stitches* with his stories' (= laughing uproariously).
Word Family: **stitch,** *verb,* to fasten, join or ornament with stitches.

stoat (*say* stote) *noun*
see ERMINE.

stock *noun*
1. the complete supply of goods kept by a merchant, etc.
2. a supply accumulated for future use.
3. livestock.
4. *Commerce:* (*usually plural*) a) government gilt-edged securities, that is, money lent to government at a fixed rate of interest. b) a company's fully paid-up capital not divided into shares.
5. a line of ancestry: 'a girl who comes from Scottish *stock*'.
6. a plant from which cuttings are obtained, or onto which a graft is made.
7. the clear liquid obtained by boiling bones, meat or vegetables, used as a base for soups or sauces.
8. (*plural*) a) a heavy wooden frame locking a person by the ankles, formerly used as a public punishment. b) the frame on which a ship rests during construction.
9. a stiff, wide cravat.

10. a supporting structure or handle of a gun, plough, whip, etc.
11. a plant with brightly coloured, fragrant flowers.
Phrases:
in stock, (of manufactured goods) available.
out of stock, (of manufactured goods) temporarily unavailable.
take stock, a) to make a list of stock in hand; b) to make an estimate, such as of prospects, resources, etc.
stock *adjective*
1. kept readily available for sale or use.
2. commonplace: 'a *stock* reply to that question'.
3. of or relating to stock: 'a *stock* clerk'.
Word Family: **stock**, *verb*, a) to provide with stock, b) to have as a supply or stock; **stockist**, *noun*.

stockade (*say* stok-ade) *noun*
a fortification or enclosure consisting of a wall of posts set in the ground.

stockbroker *noun*
a member of a stock exchange, who buys and sells stocks and shares on behalf of his clients for a commission.
Word Family: **stockbrokerage**, **stockbroking**, *nouns*.

stock car
an old car used in special races where competitors aim to collide with, and knock aside, the other cars.

stock exchange
1. a place where stocks or shares may be bought and sold.
2. an association of dealers in stocks and shares.

stockholder *noun*
American: a shareholder.

stocking *noun*
a) a light, closely fitting piece of clothing worn on the foot and leg.
b) something that has the shape of a stocking.
Word Family: **stockinged**, *adjective*.

stock-in-trade *noun*
1. the stock of a merchant, store, etc.
2. the resources, ability or speciality of a company, person, etc.

stockman *noun*
a man who works on a sheep or cattle station.

stock market
1. a stock exchange.
2. the business transactions in a stock exchange.

stockpile *verb*
to accumulate raw materials, arms, etc. for future use.
Word Family: **stockpile**, *noun*, a supply of goods or materials.

stock-still *adverb*
absolutely motionless.

stocktaking *noun*
1. the examining, valuing and listing of all stock held in a warehouse, shop, etc., usually done once a year.
2. a reappraisal or reassessment of one's position, progress, etc.

stockwhip *noun*
a long leather whip with a heavy handle, used for rounding up cattle, etc.

stocky *adjective*
solidly built.
Word Family: **stockily**, *adverb*; **stockiness**, *noun*.

stockyard *noun*
an enclosed area for keeping cattle, etc. for a short time, before marketing, slaughtering or shipment.

stodgy (*say* **stoj**-ee) *adjective*
1. dull or uninteresting.
2. (of food) heavy and solid.
Word Family: **stodgily**, *adverb*; **stodge**, **stodginess**, *nouns*.

stoep (*say* stoop) *noun*
South African: a raised verandah in front of a house.
[Afrikaans, step]

stoical (*say* **sto**-ik'l) **stoic** *adjective*
1. showing fortitude, self-control or imperturbability in adversity.
2. indifferent to or unaffected by pleasure, pain, etc.
stoicism (*say* **sto**-a-sizm) *noun*
the belief or practice of being stoical.
Word Family: **stoic**, *noun*.
[Greek *stoa* the porch in Athens where Zeno taught this philosophy of life]

stoichiometry (*say* **stoy**ki-omma-tree) *noun*
the branch of chemistry studying the quantities of chemical elements or compounds involved in chemical reactions.
Word Family: **stoichiometric** (*say* stoyki-a-**met**rik), *adjective*.
[Greek *stoikheion* a component part + *metron* a measure]

stoke *verb*
to stir or feed a fire.
Word Family: **stoker**, *noun*.

stole (1) *verb*
the past tense of the verb **steal**.

stole (2) *noun*
1. a long strip of silk, etc. hung over the shoulders and reaching beneath the knees, worn by Christian priests while administering the sacraments.
2. a wide strip, especially of fur, worn by women round the shoulders.
[Greek *stolé* clothing]

stolen *verb*
the past participle of the verb **steal**.

stolid (*say* **stol**lid) *adjective*
having or showing little emotion or perception.
Word Family: **stolidity** (*say* sto–**liddi**–tee), *noun*; **stolidly**, *adverb*.
[Latin *stolidus* dull]

stoma (*say* **sto**–ma) *noun*
plural is **stomata** (*say* **sto**–ma–ta)
Biology: a pore on the surface of a plant, usually on the lower surface of a leaf, allowing the movement of gases in and out of the plant.
[Greek, mouth]

stomach (*say* **stumm**'k) *noun*
1. *Anatomy:* a thick–walled bag between the oesophagus and the duodenum, where food is mixed with gastric juices and digestion begins.
2. (*informal*) the abdomen.
3. an appetite for food.
Usage: 'I had no *stomach* for their jokes' (= liking).
stomach *verb*
to endure or tolerate.
[Greek *stomakhos* gullet]

stomach pump
a small pump used to withdraw the contents of the stomach through a long tube passed down the oesophagus.

stomp *verb*
(*informal*) to stamp.
stomp *noun*
1. the act or sound of stamping.
2. a dance, including stamping of the feet, performed to jazz–type music.
[for STAMP]

stone *noun*
1. a) the hard non–metallic substance of which rock is composed. b) a small piece of rock. c) a particular type of rock: '*sandstone*'.
2. something which resembles a stone: 'a *hailstone*'.
3. a stone designed for a particular purpose: 'a *tombstone*'.
4. a gem.
5. a unit of mass in the avoirdupois system, equal to about 6·35 kg. See UNITS in grey pages.
6. the hard, central seed of many fruits, such as peaches, apricots, etc.
7. *Medicine:* a solid body formed in an organ, such as the kidney, gall bladder, etc. Also called a **calculus**.
8. a light grey colour.
leave no stone unturned, to try every means.
stone *verb*
1. to remove the stones from fruit, etc.
2. to throw stones at.
Word Family: **stone**, *adjective*.

Stone Age
the long period in the development of man when weapons and tools were first made from stone, before the use of metals was discovered. The earliest part was called the **Palaeolithic**, the middle period was called the **Mesolithic**, and the later part was called the **Neolithic**.

stoned *adjective*
(*informal*) very drunk or under the influence of a drug, such as marijuana.

stone–dead *adjective*
completely dead.

stone–deaf *adjective*
completely deaf.

stone fruit
see DRUPE.

stonemason *noun*
a) a dresser of stone. b) a builder in stone. c) a person who carves inscriptions on stone.

stone's–throw *noun*
a short distance.

stonewall *verb*
1. *Cricket:* to bat defensively, aiming to stay in rather than score.
2. to obstruct, e.g. the passage of a parliamentary bill.

stoneware *noun*
a type of pottery fired to extremely high temperatures, so that the clay becomes hard and glassy. Compare PORCELAIN and EARTHENWARE.

stony (*say* **sto**–nee) *adjective*
a) full of stones. b) hard like stone.
Usage: 'he met my request with a *stony* silence' (= hard–hearted, unmoved).

stony–broke *adjective*
(*informal*) having no money at all.

stood *verb*
the past tense and past participle of the verb **stand**.

stooge (*say* stooj) *noun*
1. (*informal*) a) the partner in a comedy duo who is the butt of the comedian's

jokes. b) a person who acts as or is the tool or dupe of another.
2. (*informal*) a person placed or stationed for the purposes of spying or informing on others: 'a police *stooge*'.
Word Family: **stooge,** *verb,* to act as a stooge.

stool *noun*
1. a) a movable seat without armrests or a back, usually for one person. b) a portable support for the feet or knees: 'a prayer *stool*'.
2. faeces.
fall between two stools, to fail to choose between two alternatives due to hesitation or indecision.

stool pigeon
(*informal*) a decoy or informer.

stoop (1) *verb*
1. to bend the head and shoulders forward.
Usages:
a) 'I would never *stoop* so low as to beg' (= descend).
b) 'he would never *stoop* to listen to a mere buying clerk' (= condescend).
2. (of a hawk) to swoop on prey.
stoop to conquer, to swallow indignities in order to gain one's ends.
Word Family: **stoop,** *noun.*

stoop (2) *noun*
American: a small porch or platform at the entrance to a house.

stop *verb*
(stopped, stopping)
1. to come or put to an end the motion or progress of: a) 'please *stop* the car here'; b) 'you can't *stop* me coming if I want to'; c) 'the bank *stopped* payment on the forged cheque'; d) 'I shall *stop* at nothing to get my way'.
2. to fill or cover an opening, hole, etc.: '*stop* that leak with a bung'.
Usage: (*informal*) 'I'll *stop* at home, if it's all the same to you' (= stay).
3. *Music:* a) to place a finger on a string so that only part of it may vibrate. b) to alter pitch in a wind instrument by opening or closing a device (a stop).
4. to fill a tooth cavity.
stop by, stop off, stop over, to visit briefly, especially on the way to somewhere else.
stop *noun*
1. a) the act of stopping: 'we drove all the way without one *stop*'. b) the state of being stopped: 'we must bring this business to a *stop*'.
2. the place where something stops: 'a *bus-stop*'.
3. something which stops: a) 'a *doorstop*'; b) 'plug the bottle with a *stop*'; c) 'the finger-holes in a penny whistle are *stops*'; d) 'an organ *stop* allows the sounding of particular sets of pipes'.
4. *Grammar:* any punctuation mark, especially a full stop.
Word Family: **stoppage,** *noun,* a) the act of stopping, b) an obstruction.

stopcock *noun*
a valve in a pipe to control the flow of liquids.

stope *noun*
Mining: an underground opening with access from the shaft, etc., especially used for extracting ore from a vertical or steeply inclined vein.

stopgap *noun*
a temporary substitute.

stoplight *noun*
1. a red light at an intersection etc., indicating that a vehicle facing it must stop.
2. a red light on a vehicle indicating that it is stopping or slowing down.

stopover *noun*
a temporary stay in the course of a journey, etc.

stoppage (*say* **stoppij**) *noun*
Word Family: see STOP.

stopper *noun*
any plug or cork used to block a hole.
Word Family: **stopper,** *verb.*

stop press
a column for news inserted in a newspaper just before it is printed.

stopwatch *noun*
an accurate watch with a hand or hands which may be started at any instant and is used for timing races, etc. to a fraction of a second.

storage heater
a domestic room heater filled with bricks warmed by electricity at off-peak periods and at cheaper rates.

store *noun*
1. a quantity or supply of something which has been kept or saved: 'I've got a *store* of cold beer in the fridge'.
2. (*plural*) goods kept or supplied for a purpose: 'military *stores*'.
3. a place where goods are kept.
4. a shop, often large.
Phrases:
in store, a) 'there's a surprise *in store* for you tonight' (= coming); b) kept in a warehouse until required.

set store by, 'I usually don't *set* much *store by* astrologers' predictions' (= value, have regard for).

store *verb*

1. to collect and keep for future use: 'to *store* coal for the winter'.

2. to put away or deposit for keeping.

Usage: 'his mind is well *stored* with all kinds of facts' (= stocked).

Word Family: **storage**, *noun*, a) the act of storing, b) the space for storing goods, c) a charge for storing; **storekeeper**, *noun*.

storehouse *noun*

a building in which things are stored.

Usage: 'his mind is a *storehouse* of information' (= source of supply).

storey (*say* **stor-ee**) *noun*

any of the levels of a building above the ground floor.

stork *noun*

a large, black and white wading bird with long legs, neck and bill.

storm *noun*

1. a) a disturbance of the atmosphere by very strong winds, with rain, snow etc. b) a heavy fall of rain, hail, or snow.

2. a heavy or violent fall or outburst: a) 'a *storm* of arrows'; b) 'a *storm* of tears'.

Phrases:

storm in a teacup, a great fuss over a minor matter.

take by storm, a) to capture by a sudden and violent military assault; b) 'the new singer *took* the town *by storm*' (= completely captivated).

storm *verb*

1. to rain, hail, snow or blow hard: 'it *stormed* all night'.

Usages:

a) 'he *stormed* out of the room' (= went angrily and violently).

b) 'she *stormed* at them to leave her alone' (= said angrily).

2. *Military:* to capture a place by a sudden and violent attack.

Word Family: **stormy**, *adjective*, a) affected by storms, b) violent; **stormily**, *adverb*; **storminess**, *noun*.

storm centre

1. the area at the centre of a cyclone, where the air pressure is lowest and relative calm prevails.

2. any centre of trouble, chaos, disturbance, etc.

storm cone

a cone-shaped signal hoisted by coastguards, etc. to warn of an approaching storm.

storm-lantern *noun*

see LANTERN.

storm-trooper *noun*

a member of troops trained for violent attacks.

stormy petrel

1. a very small black seabird with a white rump, which follows ships and whose appearance was thought to announce a coming storm.

2. a person who foreshadows or seems to attract trouble, e.g. by rebelling against accepted ideas, practices, etc.

story (1) *noun*

1. a) a narrative, usually fictitious, intended to entertain a reader or hearer. b) the main narrative or events of a novel, poem, etc.

2. a) a journalist's account of an event: 'he expects us to print his *story* on a flower show!'. b) the subject matter of such an account.

3. (*informal*) a) a lie: 'that's all a *story* about Santa Claus'. b) an excuse: 'so that's your *story*, young man!'.

[Greek *historia* a finding out, a narrative]

story (2) *noun*

American: a storey.

storybook *adjective*

romantic or like a childish story: 'she lives in a *storybook* world of knights and princesses'.

stout *adjective*

1. rather fat or bulky in figure: 'he's grown rather *stout*'.

Usage: 'a castle must be built with *stout* walls' (= strongly made).

2. brave, bold or stubborn: 'they made a *stout* defence of their lands'.

stout *noun*

a dark beer flavoured with roasted malt.

Word Family: **stoutly**, *adverb*; **stoutness**, *noun*.

stout-hearted *adjective*

courageous or resolute.

Word Family: **stout-heartedly**, *adverb*; **stout-heartedness**, *noun*.

stove (1) *noun*

a closed apparatus for cooking or heating, in which coke, wood, etc. is burnt.

stove (2) *verb*

a past tense and past participle of the verb **stave**.

stovepipe *noun*
a pipe carrying smoke from a stove to a chimney.

stow (*say* sto) *verb*
to pack or place: 'the goods were *stowed* below deck'.
Phrases:
stow away, to hide oneself on a ship, aeroplane, etc. to get a free trip. *Word Family*: **stowaway,** *noun.*
stow it, (*informal*) 'you can *stow it*' (= be quiet).
stowage (*say* **sto–**ij) *noun*
1. a) the act or manner of stowing. b) the state of being stowed.
2. a) the space for stowing goods. b) the goods stowed. c) the charge for stowing goods.
[for BESTOW]

straddle *verb*
1. to stand or sit with one leg or part on either side of something: a) 'to *straddle* a horse'; b) 'the bridge *straddles* the river'.
2. to have the legs wide apart: 'he sat with his legs *straddled*'.

strafe *verb*
1. *Military:* to fire upon ground troops, etc. from the air with machine-guns.
2. (*informal*) to reprimand or berate. *Word Family:* **strafe,** *noun.*
[German *strafen* to punish]

straggle *verb*
1. to stray or lag behind the main body.
2. to grow, spread, etc. in an irregular or rambling manner: 'tendrils of ivy *straggling* all over the place'.

straight (*say* strate) *adjective*
1. extending uniformly in one direction without a bend or curve: 'a *straight* line'.
2. level or symmetrical: 'are the pictures *straight*?'.
3. tidy or in proper order: 'I have to get my business affairs *straight* before my holiday'.
4. honest or open: a) 'he isn't *straight* in his business dealings'; b) 'please give us a *straight* answer'.
Usages:
a) 'she has *straight*, black hair' (= without waves or curls).
b) 'he isn't *straight* in his business dealings' (= honest, upright).
c) 'you must get your facts *straight*' (= correct).
5. (of an alcoholic drink) neat: 'a *straight* whisky'.
6. *Theatre:* of or relating to a serious play or film, as distinct from a comedy or musical.
Phrases:
keep a straight face, to show no emotion or amusement.
the straight and narrow, 'after a dissolute youth Gordon kept to the *straight and narrow* for the rest of his life' (= religious or moral rectitude).
straight *adverb*
in a straight line or way.
Usages:
a) 'come *straight* home' (= directly).
b) 'she put him *straight* about who was in charge' (= right, clear).
Phrases:
go straight, to lead an honest life, especially after having been a criminal.
straight away, straight off, immediately.
straight out, 'I told him *straight out* what I thought of him' (= directly).
straight *noun*
1. the condition of being straight.
2. a straight part, especially of a racecourse.
3. *Cards:* a hand having all consecutive cards.
straighten *verb*
to make or become straight.
Phrases:
straighten out, to set right or restore order to.
straighten up, to make tidy.
Word Family: **straightly,** *adverb*; **straightness,** *noun*; **straightener,** *noun,* a person or thing that straightens.

straightedge *noun*
a length of wood or metal with straight sides, used to check accuracy in carpentry, etc.

straightforward *adjective*
a) open, honest or without evasion: 'a *straightforward* explanation'. b) easy or simple: 'a dictionary written in *straightforward* language'.
Word Family: **straightforwardly,** *adverb*; **straightforwardness,** *noun.*

straight–out *adjective*
(*informal*) direct or uncompromising: 'I gave him a *straight–out* refusal'.

strain (1) *verb*
1. a) to draw tight or stretch: 'the rope was *strained* by the weight'. b) to pull hard: 'the dog *strained* at his lead'.
2. to make extreme or excessive demands on: a) 'he *strained* his ears to try and hear'; b) 'the hurdler *strained* and damaged a muscle'.
3. to pour through a filter, etc. to separate liquid from solid matter.

strain *noun*
1. a) a straining force, weight or effort. b) an injury caused by too great an effort.
2. *Science:* the change in shape of a body as a result of some external force. Compare STRESS.
3. (*usually plural*) musical sounds or a tune: 'the distant *strains* of a street organ'.
Word Family: **strained**, *adjective*, a) tense, b) forced; **strainer**, *noun*, a) a device which strains, b) a main post in a wire fence.
[Latin *stringere* to draw tight]

strain (2) *noun*
1. a) a race or stock: 'he comes from a hardy peasant *strain*'. b) inherited quality or character: 'it's the peasant *strain* in him that gives him his stubbornness'.
2. *Biology:* a group of animals or plants bred from a certain species or variety.

strait *noun*
1. a narrow strip of water between two pieces of land.
2. (*plural*) a situation of great difficulty, need or distress: 'when the father died the family was left in financial *straits*'.
straitened *adjective*
in straitened circumstances, short of money.
[Latin *strictus* tightened]

straitjacket *noun*
a tight canvas jacket for restraining the arms of violent patients or prisoners.

straitlaced *adjective*
very strict or prudish in behaviour, etc.

strand (1) *noun*
a single fibre, thread, hair, string of yarn, etc.

strand (2) *noun*
(*formerly*) the shore of a lake or sea.
strand *verb*
1. (of a ship) to drive aground.
2. (of a person) to leave helpless or in difficulties.

strange *adjective*
1. odd or unusual: 'what a *strange* thing to do'.
2. not previously known: a) 'we moved to a *strange* area'; b) 'that particular moth is *strange* to me'.
Word Family: **strangely**, *adverb*; **strangeness**, *noun*.
[Latin *extraneus* foreign]

stranger (*say* **strane**–jer) *noun*
1. a person one has not known, seen or heard of before.
2. a person who is new to a place: 'I am a *stranger* to your city'.
Usage: 'he is no *stranger* to suffering' (= person unacquainted with).

strangle *verb*
to choke to death: 'he *strangled* the old lady with his bare hands'.
Usages:
a) 'he tried to *strangle* a sob' (= stifle, suppress).
b) 'the flowers had been *strangled* by the lush growth' (= choked).
strangles *plural noun*
(*used with singular verb*) an infectious disease of horses causing blockages in the air passages.
Word Family: **strangler**, *noun*, a person who murders by strangling his victims.
[Greek *strangalé* a halter]

stranglehold *noun*
1. a wrestling hold by which one chokes one's opponent.
2. anything that prevents or restricts free movement, development, etc.

strangulate (*say* **strang**–yoo–late) *verb*
a) to strangle. b) to interfere with the blood supply to some part of the body.
Word Family: **strangulation**, *noun*.

strap *noun*
1. a strip of leather or other flexible material for supporting, fastening or holding things together: 'fasten the *straps* on your pack'.
2. something which has the shape or function of a strap, such as a metal or leather loop in a train for a standing passenger to grip.
strap *verb*
(strapped, strapping)
a) to fasten with a strap. b) to beat with a strap.
Word Family: **strapless**, *adjective*.
[from STROP]

straphanger *noun*
(*informal*) a standing passenger in a bus, train, tram, etc., who holds a strap for support.

strapping *adjective*
tall, strong and healthy.

strata (*say* **strar**ta) *plural noun*
the plural of **stratum**.

stratagem (*say* **stratta**–jem) *noun*
a plan or trick, especially one for deceiving the enemy.
[Greek *stratagema* generalship]

Common Error: do not confuse with STRATEGY.

strategy (*say* **stratta**–jee) *noun*
planning or management on a large scale, e.g. a military campaign.
strategic (*say* stra–**tee**–jik) *adjective*
1. of or relating to strategy.
2. (of weapons, bombing, etc.) intended or used to injure the whole economy or offensive power of an enemy. Compare TACTICAL.
Word Family: **strategically**, *adverb*; **strategist** (*say* **stratta**–jist), *noun*, a person who is expert in strategy.
[Greek *strategos* a general]
Common Error: do not confuse with STRATAGEM.

stratify (*say* **strah**ti–fie *or* **stratti**–fie) *verb*
(**stratified, stratifying**)
1. to form in layers.
2. to form social groups at different levels as determined by class, status, etc.
Word Family: **stratification**, *noun.*

stratosphere (*say* **strah**ta–sfeer *or* **stratta**–sfeer) *noun*
the upper layers of the atmosphere above the troposphere, beginning about 20 km from the earth's surface.
[STRATUM + SPHERE]

stratum (*say* **strah**tum) *noun*
plural is **strata**
1. a horizontal layer of any material, especially a layer of sedimentary rock, usually one of several parallel layers.
2. any level or grade.
[Latin, strewn]

stratus (*say* **strah**–tus) *noun*
plural is **strati**
a low, smooth layer of cloud resembling fog.

straw *noun*
1. a) a collection of coarse stems and leaves of cereal plants, usually dried, cut and used for bedding. Compare HAY. b) a natural or artificial fibre resembling straw, used for making hats, etc.
2. a hollow tube for sucking up liquids.
3. a trifle: 'I don't care a *straw* for him'.
Phrases:
catch, clutch, seize at a straw, to try anything in a desperate situation.
last straw, an added burden, task, etc. which makes a situation intolerable.
straws in the wind, a hint or sign of things to come, showing which way the wind is blowing.
Word Family: **straw**, *adjective*, a) made of straw, b) yellowish.

strawberry *noun*
a red, fleshy edible berry with a sweet taste.
Word Family: **strawberry**, *adjective*, reddish.

straw vote
an unofficial vote to give an indication of the general trend of opinion.

stray *verb*
to wander or lose one's way.
stray *noun*
a domestic animal that has strayed.
Word Family: **stray**, *adjective*, a) lost or out of place, b) scattered or occasional.
[from ASTRAY]

streak *noun*
1. a long, thin line or mark: 'there's a *streak* of dirt on your forehead'.
Usages:
a) 'there's a *streak* of cruelty in you' (= trace).
b) 'let's hope for a *streak* of good luck now' (= spell, period).
2. *Geology:* the colour of a finely powdered mineral.
streak of lightning, 'he disappeared like a *streak of lightning*' (= very fast indeed).
streak *verb*
1. to mark with a streak or streaks.
2. to move at great speed: 'the runner *streaked* past the finishing line'.
3. (*informal*) to appear naked in a public place.
Word Family: **streaky**, *adjective*; **streakily**, *adverb*; **streakiness**, *noun*, **streaker** (informal), *noun.*

stream *noun*
1. a) a small river. b) a steady flow of water or other liquid: 'the Gulf *Stream*'.
2. a steady flow or emission: a) 'the spotlight sent a *stream* of light onto the stage'; b) 'a *stream* of abuse fell from his lips'.
Usage: 'the *stream* of opinion is against you' (= drift, run).
stream *verb*
1. to flow in or as if in a stream: a) 'water *streamed* down the window'; b) 'the crowd *streamed* through the stadium gates'.
2. to divide students into classes according to their ability, or the subjects they are studying.

streamer *noun*
1. a long narrow strip of material: 'her bonnet was decorated with *streamers*'.
2. *Newspapers:* a headline that runs across a full page.

streamlined *adjective*
1. having a shape designed to offer the least possible resistance to air or water.
2. made more efficient, modern, etc.
Word Family: **streamline,** *verb.*

street *noun*
1. a road in an urban area, usually lined with houses, shops, etc.
2. (*informal*) the people living in a street: 'the whole *street* protested about the increased rates'.
Phrases:
not in the same street, not to be classed with.
streets ahead, far ahead.
up one's street, within one's field of skill, interest, etc.
[Latin (*via*) *strata* a paved (way)]

streetcar *noun*
American: a tram.

streetwalker *noun*
a prostitute who seeks her customers in the street.

strength *noun*
1. bodily or muscular power: 'Samson was a man of great *strength*'.
2. the capacity to resist or sustain stress: a) 'the *strength* of the steel in the main girders is crucial'; b) '*strength* of character'.
Usages:
a) '*strength* of numbers favours our side' (= superiority).
b) 'the normal *strength* of the regiment is 3000 men' (= number).
c) 'what's the *strength* of this rumour I heard?' (= reliability).
3. degree of intensity: a) 'what *strength* do you like your coffee?'; b) 'what *strength* of colour there is in that painting!'.
Phrases:
from strength, 'I am negotiating *from strength*' (= from a strong bargaining position).
on the strength, (*Military*) on the muster roll.
on the strength of, 'I went to visit the art gallery *on the strength of* your recommendation' (= on the basis of).
Word Family: **strengthen,** *verb,* to make or become strong or stronger; **strengthener,** *noun.*

strenuous (*say* **stren**-yewus) *adjective*
requiring great effort or exertion: a) 'a *strenuous* hike through the hills'; b) 'a *strenuous* appeal for funds'.
Word Family: **strenuously,** *noun*; **strenuousness,** *noun.*
[Latin *strenuus* vigorous]

streptococcus (*say* strepto-**kokkus**) *noun*
plural is **streptococci**
a group of round bacteria which occur in pairs or chains and may cause disease, such as throat infections, in man.
[Greek *streptos* twisted + *kokkos* a berry]

streptomycin (*say* strepto-**my**-sin) *noun*
an antibiotic used mainly in the treatment of tuberculosis.
[Greek *streptos* twisted + *mykes* fungus]

stress *noun*
1. special weight or significance: 'the school lays great *stress* on discipline'.
2. the extra force placed on a word or syllable. *Example*: in the word '*window*' the *stress* is on the first syllable.
3. *Science:* the force per unit of area applied to a body. Compare STRAIN (1).
4. emotional or intellectual pressure or tension: 'the court case placed him under a great deal of *stress*'.
Word Family: **stress,** *verb,* a) to lay stress on, b) to subject to mechanical stress.
[Latin *strictus* tightened]

stress disease
any of numerous conditions which arise, or may arise, from emotional troubles and tension, e.g. gastric ulcers, coronaries, allergic diseases, migraine, etc.

stretch *verb*
to make or become longer, wider, larger, tighter, etc. by pulling: a) 'he *stretched* the new shoes to make them pinch less'; b) 'he *stretched* the skin of the drum'.
Usages:
a) 'the blow *stretched* him out on the floor' (= laid at full length).
b) 'he *stretches* the truth a bit' (= distorts, exaggerates).
c) 'her continual chatter *stretched* my patience to the limit' (= strained).
d) 'the hills *stretch* for miles' (= continue).
e) 'he *stretched* out a hand' (= reached).

f) 'he got up from a cramped position and *stretched*' (= extended his body and limbs)..
stretch a point, to make concessions.
stretch *noun*
1. the act of stretching: a) 'he gave a *stretch* and got up'; b) 'it takes quite a *stretch* of the imagination to believe that'.
2. a continuous length, distance, period, etc.: a) 'a *stretch* of shallow water'; b) 'there was a considerable *stretch* when I couldn't get work'.
3. (*informal*) a term in prison.
4. *Horseracing:* either of the two straight parts of a racecourse, especially the part between the last turn and the finishing post.
at full stretch, to the utmost of one's powers.
Word Family: **stretchy**, *adjective.*

stretcher *noun*
1. a piece of material supported by two long poles, used to carry sick or injured people.
2. a wooden frame over which canvas or other fabric may be held taut.

strew (*say* stroo) *verb*
(**strewed, strewn** or **strewed, strewing**)
to spread about loosely or randomly: a) 'the untidy children *strewed* the streets with litter'; b) 'papers were *strewn* about all over the floor'.

striated (*say* stry–ay–tid) *adjective*
marked with fine grooves or furrows: 'a glacier will often leave a mass of *striated* rocks behind it'.
Word Family: **striation**, *noun.*
[from Latin]

stricken *adjective*
1. afflicted or affected by: 'the *fever–stricken* town'.
2. deeply affected by emotion, especially fear, despair, etc.
stricken *verb*
a past participle of the verb **strike**.

strict (*say* strikt) *adjective*
1. a) demanding obedience: 'a *strict* teacher'. b) harsh: '*strict* discipline'.
2. exact: 'my watch doesn't keep very *strict* time'.
Usages:
a) 'I am telling you this in *strict* confidence' (= absolute, complete).
b) 'he's a very *strict* Catholic' (= devout, closely conforming).
c) 'keep a *strict* eye on the children while I'm away' (= close, careful).
Word Family: **strictly**, *adverb*; **strictness**, *noun.*
[Latin *strictus* tightened]

stricture (*say* **strik**–cher) *noun*
1. severe criticism: 'to pass *strictures* on the quality of my work'.
2. *Medicine:* a narrowing in a duct or vessel, causing an obstruction.

stride *verb*
(**strode, stridden, striding**)
1. to walk with long steps.
2. to sit or stand with one leg on each side of: 'to *stride* a stile'.
stride *noun*
a) a long step. b) the space covered in such a step.
Phrases:
make rapid strides, to make quick progress.
to take in one's stride, to do or respond without difficulty or extra effort.
Word Family: **strider**, *noun.*

strident (*say* **stry**–d'nt) *adjective*
(of a sound) shrill and harsh.
Word Family: **stridently**, *adverb*; **stridency**, *noun.*
[Latin *stridens* grating, hissing]

strife *noun*
angry fighting or quarrelling.

strike *verb*
(**struck, struck** or **stricken, striking**)
a) to give a blow to or with: 'I *struck* him on the chin'. b) to come or cause to come into violent contact with: 'the ship *struck* a reef'.
Usages:
a) 'the cattle raiders *struck* at dusk' (= attacked).
b) '*strike* that remark from the record' (= remove).
c) 'he tried to *strike* a match in the wind' (= ignite).
d) 'new coins were *struck* for decimal currency' (= minted).
e) 'the clock *struck* four' (= announced by chiming).
f) 'at midday a shaft of light *strikes* the unknown soldier's tomb' (= falls upon).
g) 'we walked for hours without *striking* another track' (= coming upon, discovering).
h) 'the news *struck* me speechless' (= rendered).
i) 'an idea suddenly *struck* him' (= occurred to).
j) 'does he *strike* you as an honest man?' (= impress).
k) 'the ham actor *struck* a pose' (= assumed).
l) 'the ship *struck* its sails and put down its anchor' (= lowered, took down).

m) 'the workers *struck* for better conditions' (= stopped work in order to gain).
n) 'we managed to *strike* some kind of an agreement' (= make).
o) 'I planted the cutting but I don't think it will *strike* in this cold weather' (= take root).
Phrases:
strike home, to deal an effective or telling blow.
strike out, 'the shipwrecked sailor *struck out* for the distant shore' (= set out).
strike up, 'we immediately *struck up* a conversation' (= began, formed).
struck on, to be infatuated with.
strike *noun*
1. the act of striking: 'a bombing *strike* by enemy aircraft'.
2. the stopping of work as a threat or protest.
3. *Baseball:* an unsuccessful attempt to hit a pitched ball.
4. *Tenpin bowling:* a score obtained by knocking over all the tenpins in one shot. Compare SPARE.
5. a discovery of oil, ore, etc. in an oilwell or mine.
Word Family: **striker**, *noun*, a) a worker who is on strike, b) something which strikes, such as the hammer of a bell, etc., c) (Tennis) the player who faces the server; **striking**, *adjective*, a) attractive or impressive, b) on strike; **strikingly**, *adverb.*

strikebreaker *noun*
a person who helps to break up a strike by taking a striker's job or supplying workers who will do so.

strike pay
the money paid by a trade union to members who are on strike.

strine *noun*
(*informal*) Australian English.
[the supposed Australian pronunciation of the word Australian]

string *noun*
1. a) a long slender flexible material, usually made of fibres twisted together and used for tying. b) something which has the shape or function of a string: 'the *string* of a bean'.
2. a set of objects threaded together: 'a *string* of pearls'.
3. *Music:* a) a tightly stretched length of catgut or wire which produces a note when made to vibrate. b) (*plural*) any instruments having such strings, especially those of the violin family.
Usages:
a) 'the speaker had to answer a *string* of questions' (= series, collection).
b) 'he was seeking a relationship with no *strings* attached' (= conditions, limitations).
Phrases:
keep on a string, to have under one's control.
pull strings, to use influence and social contacts to gain something.
string *verb*
(strung, stringing)
to furnish with or as if with a string or strings.
Usages:
a) 'I *strung* the beans' (= removed the strings of).
b) '*stringing* the beads on the thread was tedious work' (= threading).
c) 'the streets were *strung* with lanterns' (= adorned, hung).
Phrases:
string along, string on, to lead on.
string along with, (*informal*) to cooperate with.
string out, a) 'the horses were *strung out* all over the field' (= spread out); b) 'he *strung* the discussion *out* because he had time to waste' (= prolonged).
string up, (*informal*) to hang.
Word Family: **stringer**, *noun*, a) a device which removes bean strings, b) a horizontal timber beam, used as a support, etc; **stringy**, *adjective*, a) containing tough fibre, b) wiry or sinewy; **stringiness**, *noun.*

stringent (*say* **strin–j'nt**) *adjective*
imposing rigorous standards of performance or obedience: a) '*stringent* laws'; b) '*stringent* discipline'.
Usage: 'he presented a very *stringent* argument for his proposal' (= convincing, forcible).
Word Family: **stringently**, *adverb*; **stringency**, *noun.*
[Latin *stringens* drawing tight]

strip *verb*
(stripped, stripping)
1. to take the covering from: 'they *stripped* the bark from the trees'.
Usages:
a) 'the suspects were *stripped* and searched' (= undressed).
b) 'the wind *stripped* all the leaves from the boughs' (= removed, took off).
2. to tear the thread or teeth from a screw or gear.

strip *noun*
1. a long narrow piece: a) 'a *strip* of cloth'; b) 'a *strip* of land'.
2. (*informal*) a striptease.

strip cartoon
a story told, or information conveyed, in a series of small drawings, often with the dialogue encased in balloons emerging from the mouths of the characters depicted.

stripe *noun*
1. a long, narrow piece or section, different in colour, texture, etc. from the rest of a surface or thing.
2. *Military:* a piece of cloth worn on a uniform to indicate rank, etc.
3. a blow struck with a whip or rod, as in punishment: 'he was sentenced to 100 *stripes*'.
Word Family: **stripe**, *verb*, to mark with a stripe or stripes; **stripy**, *adjective*.

strip lighting
a form of lighting consisting of long fluorescent tubes or glass strips containing a filament.

stripling *noun*
a young man who is not yet fully grown.

stripper *noun*
1. an entertainer who performs the striptease.
2. a machine or solvent which strips.

striptease *noun*
a form of entertainment performed to music, in which a person gradually undresses.
Word Family: **stripteaser**, *noun*.

strive *verb*
(**strove, striven, striving**)
to try hard: 'he *strove* for success'.
Usage: 'the swimmer *strove* against the current' (= fought).

stroboscope (*say* **stro**-ba-skope) *noun*
1. a device used to make moving objects appear stationary, as by regularly interrupting vision, using intermittent lighting, etc.
2. a lamp which flashes coloured lights intermittently on stage or dance-floor.
Word Family: **stroboscopic** (*say* stro-ba-**skop**pic), *adjective*; **strobe**, *noun*, a) a stroboscope, b) stroboscopic light.
[Greek *strobos* whirling + *skopein* to look at]

strode *verb*
the past tense of the verb **stride**.

stroke *noun*
1. a blow or act of striking, e.g. of an axe, lightning, a clock, etc.
2. a) a single movement of the hand, arm, etc. by which something is made or done. b) a mark made by one movement of a pen, pencil, brush, etc.
Usages:
a) 'that was a *stroke* of luck' (= piece).
b) 'you be home on the *stroke* of eleven' (= exact moment).
c) 'it was a *stroke* of genius to solve that problem' (= brilliant or sudden act).
3. *Medicine:* a sudden loss of consciousness and paralysis due to a blockage in a blood vessel that supplies blood to part of the brain.
4. any of a series of alternating movements between two extreme positions, as one made by the pistons of a car engine.
5. *Rowing:* the oarsman, nearest the stern of the boat, who sets the pace for the crew.
6. *Sport:* a way of hitting a ball: 'the tennis player replied with a powerful backhand *stroke*'.

stroke *verb*
1. to pass the hand over gently or caressingly.
2. *Rowing:* to act as stroke.

stroll (*say* strole) *verb*
to walk in a leisurely or casual manner.
Word Family: **stroll**, *noun*; **stroller**, *noun*.

strong *adjective*
1. powerful: a) 'Hercules was a very *strong* man'; b) 'have a cup of *strong* coffee'.
2. distinct or marked: 'a *strong* contrast in their attitudes'.
Usages:
a) 'he proved *strong* against temptation' (= firm).
b) 'he's *strong* in languages' (= very competent).
c) 'school clothes have to be made of *strong* cloth' (= lasting, durable).
d) 'the battalion dug itself into a *strong* position' (= easy to defend).
e) 'the government used *strong* measures to stop the riots' (= harsh, extreme).
f) 'he used *strong* language' (= forceful, bad).

strong *adverb*
1. in a strong manner: 'he's still going *strong* at 90'.

2. in numbers: 'their army is 200 000 *strong*'.
Word Family: **strongly**, *adverb.*

strongarm *adjective*
(*informal*) depending on physical force: 'the police had to use *strongarm* tactics to disperse the demonstrators'.

strongbox *noun*
a metal box for keeping money or valuables.

stronghold *noun*
1. a fortress.
2. a place where an attitude, belief, etc. is strong.

strong man
an entertainer who performs feats of strength.

strong-minded *adjective*
having a vigorous, determined will or mind: 'she's being very *strong-minded* about her diet'.

strong point
a special aptitude or quality: 'writing is not my *strong point*'.

strongroom *noun*
a room in a bank for valuable articles, etc., built to resist fire and theft.

strontium *noun*
element number 38, a reactive metal similar to calcium and whose compounds are used in fireworks. Radioactive strontium-90 is produced in atomic explosions. See ALKALINE EARTH METAL.
See CHEMICAL ELEMENTS in grey pages.
[after *Strontian* in Scotland]

strop *noun*
a device, usually leather, with an abrasive surface for sharpening implements, such as razors.
Word Family: **strop (stropped, stropping)**, *verb*, to sharpen on a strop.

strophe (*say* **stro**-fee) *noun*
Poetry: a stanza, especially the first of a pair of alternating form.
[Greek, turning]

stroppy *adjective*
(*informal*) angry or complaining.

strove *verb*
the past tense of the verb **strive**.

struck *verb*
the past tense and a past participle of the verb **strike**.

structural formula
Chemistry: see FORMULA.

structure (*say* **struk**-cher) *noun*
a) the way something is put together: 'to study the *structure* of a single cell'. b) something which is constructed, such as a bridge, building, etc.
Word Family: **structural**, *adjective*, of or essential to a structure; **structurally**, *adverb.*
[from Latin]

strudel (*say* **stroo**-d'l) *noun*
a cake with a very thin, flaky pastry filled with fruit or cheese.
[German]

struggle *verb*
1. to make violent physical efforts: 'the policeman *struggled* with the drunken spectator'.
2. to work very hard at a task or problem: 'they *struggled* for a living'.
3. to proceed with great effort: 'they *struggled* through the dense undergrowth'.
struggle *noun*
a) the act of struggling: 'the policeman could not restrain the spectator without a *struggle*'. b) a great effort: 'the *struggle* for liberty'.
Word Family: **struggler**, *noun*; **strugglingly**, *adverb.*

strum *verb*
(strummed, strumming)
a) to sound the strings of a guitar, etc. by a downward finger movement. b) to idly or casually play a stringed musical instrument.
Word Family: **strum**, *noun.*

strumpet *noun*
an old word for a prostitute.

strung *verb*
the past tense and past participle of the verb **string**.

strut (1) *verb*
(strutted, strutting)
to walk in a stiff-legged, pompous manner.
Word Family: **strut**, *noun*, a strutting way of walking.

strut (2) *noun*
a supporting part of a structure which takes the pressure or weight along its length.

strychnine (*say* **strik**-neen) *noun*
a white, crystalline poison which may be used in small quantities to stimulate the nervous system.
[Greek *strykhnos* nightshade]

stub *noun*
1. the short blunt end of something which has been worn down, used up, cut, etc.: 'the *stub* of a cigar'.
2. *Commerce:* the portion of a cheque remaining in a chequebook, on which

the details are recorded. Also called a **counterfoil.**
stub *verb*
(**stubbed, stubbing**)
to strike against something: 'to *stub* one's toe on the leg of the bed'.
stub out, to extinguish a cigarette, etc. by crushing the lighted end against a surface.

stub axle
either of the two short axles carrying the front wheels of a motor vehicle, which pivot about the kingpin to allow the car to be steered.

stubble *noun*
a) the cut stalks of cereal plants left in the ground after a harvest. b) anything resembling stubble, such as the unshaven growth of beard on a face.
Word Family: **stubbled, stubbly,** *adjectives.*
[Latin *stipula* straw]

stubborn (*say* **stubb**'n) *adjective*
1. inflexible in intention or opinion: 'her *stubborn* refusal'.
2. difficult to manage, control, etc.: 'a *stubborn* horse'.
Word Family: **stubbornly,** *adverb*; **stubbornness,** *noun.*

stubby *adjective*
short and thick: '*stubby* fingers'.
Word Family: **stubbily,** *adverb*; **stubbiness,** *noun.*

stucco (*say* **stuk**–o) *noun*
a type of plaster used on walls or other surfaces to form a rough, knobbled surface.
Word Family: **stucco** (**stuccoed, stuccoing**), *verb*, to cover with stucco.
[Italian]

stuck *verb*
the past tense and past participle of the verb **stick** (2).

stuck–up *adjective*
(*informal*) conceited or superior.

stud (1) *noun*
1. a) a small metal button for fastening shirt collars, etc. b) a large–headed nail or knob projecting from a surface, especially as a decoration.
2. a threaded rod or bolt without a head.
3. an upright post or support, e.g. in the framework of a wall or house.
stud *verb*
(**studded, studding**)
to set or decorate with or as if with studs: 'a shield *studded* with jewels'.

stud (2) *noun*
1. a) a collection of horses for racing, hunting, breeding, etc. b) a stallion or other male animal kept for breeding.
2. (*informal*) an attractive, virile man.
at stud, (of a male animal) used or available for breeding purposes.
Word Family: **studbook,** *noun*, a register of horses' pedigrees.

stud (3) *noun*
stud poker.

student (*say* **stew**–d'nt) *noun*
1. a person who studies at a school or other institution.
2. any person who studies: 'a *student* of Hebrew'.
studentship *noun*
a) the state or condition of being a student. b) a scholarship for a student.
[Latin *studens* being zealous]

studied (*say* **stud**–id) *adjective*
a) not spontaneous or natural: 'a *studied* smile'. b) deliberate: 'a *studied* insult'.

studio (*say* **stew**–dee–o) *noun*
1. the workroom of an artist, photographer, etc.
2. a room or building with equipment for broadcasting, making films, etc.
[Italian]

studious (*say* **stew**–dee–us) *adjective*
a) devoted to study: 'a *studious* pupil'. b) painstaking: 'definitions written with *studious* care'.

stud poker
Cards: a form of poker in which some rounds of cards are dealt face up.

study (*say* **stud**–ee) *noun*
1. a) the process of acquiring knowledge through reading, investigation or thinking. b) a branch of knowledge or something that is to be studied: 'he is engaged on several archaeological *studies* now'.
Usages:
a) 'she sank into a deep *study*' (= reverie, state of thought).
b) 'he has several distinguished *studies* to his credit' (= publications, reports).
c) 'his face was a real *study*' (= something worth seeing).
2. a room for studying, reading or writing.
3. a work, such as a musical composition for one instrument, which is produced as a technical or preliminary exercise.

study *verb*
(studied, studying)
to engage in or conduct a study or studies.
Usage: 'we're *studying* your suggestions carefully' (= examining).

stuff *verb*
1. to cram or fill tightly: 'we *stuffed* the cushion with down'.
2. to fill meat, poultry, vegetables, etc. with a highly seasoned mixture.
3. to fill the empty carcass of an animal, etc. with material in order to make it appear lifelike for display purposes.
Usages:
a) 'my nose is all *stuffed* up' (= blocked).
b) 'she *stuffed* herself at the feast' (= ate too much).
stuff *noun*
1. the material out of which something is made: 'he's just not the *stuff* a leader is made of'.
2. material or substance of any indefinite kind: 'just give me some *stuff* to rub on it when it aches'.
Usages:
a) (*informal*) 'you can just pack up your *stuff* and go' (= belongings).
b) (*informal*) 'you can cut out the rough *stuff*' (= actions, language).
c) (*informal*) 'we've hired a man there who really knows his *stuff*' (= trade, profession).
Phrases:
do one's stuff, (*informal*) to do what is expected of one or show what one can do.
get stuffed! (*informal*) go away! shut up!
stuff and nonsense, foolish talk, ideas, writing, etc.
stuffing *noun*
any material used to fill or pack something, such as a mixture of seasoned breadcrumbs, etc. used to stuff poultry, etc. before cooking.
knock the stuffing out of, (*informal*) to weaken or defeat.
[Greek *styphein* to draw together]

stuffed shirt
(*informal*) a pompous or pretentious person.

stuffy *adjective*
1. (of a room, etc.) poorly ventilated.
Usage: '*stuffy* old textbooks' (= dull, lacking interest).
2. blocked: 'a *stuffy* nose'.
3. prim or easily shocked: 'my *stuffy* old relations'.
Word Family: **stuffily,** *adverb*; **stuffiness,** *noun.*

stultify (*say* **stulti**–fie) *verb*
(stultified, stultifying)
to make useless or futile.
Word Family: **stultification** (*say* stultifi–**kay**–sh'n), *noun.*
[Latin *stultus* foolish + *facere* to make]

stumble *verb*
a) to trip and almost fall. b) to walk or proceed in an unsteady or blundering way.
Usages:
a) 'he *stumbled* badly in his estimate of the cost of the project' (= blundered, made a mistake).
b) 'he *stumbled* upon the new drug in the course of other research' (= came accidentally or unexpectedly).
Word Family: **stumble,** *noun*; **stumblingly,** *adverb*; **stumbler,** *noun.*

stumbling block
an obstacle or hindrance.

stump *noun*
1. the part of a tree remaining after the tree has fallen or been cut down.
2. anything remaining after the main part has been cut off, worn down, etc.: 'the *stump* of a leg'.
3. *Cricket:* any of the three upright wooden pegs (called the leg, middle and off stumps) set at either end of the pitch.
stump *verb*
1. to walk heavily or clumsily: 'he *stumped* up the stairs in a huff'.
2. to baffle or leave at a loss: 'the last question *stumped* all the candidates'.
3. *American:* to travel through a district making political speeches.
4. *Cricket:* to dismiss the batsman by knocking the bails off with the ball while he is out of his crease attempting a stroke.
stump up, (*informal*) to pay up.
Word Family: **stumper,** *noun,* a puzzling question; **stumpy,** *adjective,* short and thick; **stumpily,** *adverb*; **stumpiness,** *noun.*

stun *verb*
(stunned, stunning)
to knock unconscious or nearly unconscious by a blow, shock, etc.
Word Family: **stunning,** *adjective,* (informal) strikingly attractive; **stunningly,** *adverb*; **stunner,** *noun,* a) (informal) a strikingly attractive person or thing, b) a person or thing that stuns.

stung *verb*
the past tense and past participle of the verb **sting.**

stunk *verb*
a past tense and the past participle of the verb **stink.**

stunt (1) *verb*
to hinder the growth or development of: 'the cold winters have *stunted* the trees'.
Word Family: **stunted,** *adjective*; **stuntedness,** *noun.*

stunt (2) *noun*
1. a bold, daring or unusual feat.
2. an action meant to attract attention, etc.: 'it was an advertising *stunt*'.
stunt man
a person paid to perform stunts, especially as a substitute for an actor in dangerous scenes.

stupefy (*say* **stew**pi-fie) *verb*
(stupefied, stupefying)
to make stupid or senseless: 'he was completely *stupefied* with drink'.

stupendous (*say* stew-**pen**dus) *adjective*
1. amazing or astounding: 'the Grand Canyon is a *stupendous* sight'.
2. immense: 'I have a *stupendous* amount of work to get through'.
Word Family: **stupendously,** *adverb*; **stupendousness,** *noun.*

stupid (*say* **stew**-pid) *adjective*
slow to apprehend or understand: 'speak slowly to him, he's a bit *stupid*'.
Usages:
a) 'that was a *stupid* thing to say' (= unthinking, silly).
b) 'I really hate this *stupid* job' (= boring, uninteresting).
Word Family: **stupidity** (*say* stew-**piddi**-tee), *noun,* dullness or lack of intelligence; **stupidly,** *adverb.*
[Latin *stupidus* struck senseless]

stupor (*say* **stew**-pa) *noun*
a state of apathy and drowsiness.
Word Family: **stuporous,** *adjective.*
[Latin, numbness]

sturdy (*say* **ster**-dee) *adjective*
strong or robust: a) 'children's *sturdy* little legs'; b) '*sturdy* common sense'.
Word Family: **sturdily,** *adverb*; **sturdiness,** *noun.*

sturgeon (*say* **ster**-j'n) *noun*
any of a group of large, edible fish found in the Northern Hemisphere, used as a source of caviar.

stutter *noun*
a speech defect in which sounds are repeated, or found difficult to say, often accompanied by facial contortions and uncontrollable pauses.
Word Family: **stutter,** *verb*; **stutterer,** *noun*; **stutteringly,** *adverb.*

sty (1) *noun*
a) a pigsty. b) any filthy place.

sty (2) *noun*
also spelt **stye**
a small swelling, like a boil, on the edge of an eyelid.

style (*say* stile) *noun*
1. the particular manner in which something appears, is done, etc.: a) 'a *hairstyle*'; b) 'he won in fine *style*'; c) 'the author writes in a natural *style*'.
2. the combination of characteristics that distinguish a period of art, etc.: 'the Gothic *style*'.
Usage: 'live in *style* while the money lasts' (= an elegant manner).
3. *Biology:* the slender, upper part of the carpel of a flower.
New Style, by the Gregorian calendar.
Old Style, by the Julian calendar, abandoned in Britain and America in 1752.
style *verb*
1. to give a title or name to: 'he *styled* himself Emperor of the World'.
2. to design or give a style to: 'she cut and *styled* his hair'.
stylize, stylise *verb*
to represent or treat in accordance with a principle of design or style rather than as it is in nature: 'most Egyptian sculpture is highly *stylized*'.
Word Family: **stylish,** *adjective,* elegant or fashionable; **stylishly,** *adverb*; **stylishness,** *noun*; **stylistic,** *adjective,* of or relating to style; **stylistically,** *adverb*; **stylization,** *noun.*
[Latin *stilus* a writing instrument, a way of writing]

stylist (*say* **stile**-ist) *noun*
1. a person, especially a writer, who cultivates a good style.
2. a person who designs or creates styles in hairdressing, etc.

stylus (*say* **sty**-lus) *noun*
1. a pointed implement for writing or engraving.
2. a very fine sapphire or diamond which follows the groove in a gramophone record and transmits the resulting vibrations to the cartridge. Also called a **needle.**

stymie (*say* **sty**–mee) *verb*
1. *Golf:* to play a ball to a position between the opponent's ball and the tin, thus preventing him, under the old rules, from making a direct putt.
2. to block or thwart: 'her ambition was *stymied* by opposition from the family'.

suave (*say* swahv) *adjective*
graciously pleasant in manner, often to an excessive degree.
Word Family: **suavely,** *adverb*; **suavity** (*say* **swahvi**–tee), **suaveness,** *nouns.*
[Latin *suavis* pleasant]

sub–
a prefix meaning: a) near, as in *subtropical*; b) under, as in *submarine*; c) further, as in *subdivide.*
[Latin]

subaltern (*say* **subb**'l–tern *or* sub–**awl**–tern) *noun*
Military: an army officer below the rank of captain.

subatomic (*say* subba–**tommik**) *adjective*
consisting of particles smaller than, or forming part of, an atom.

subcommittee *noun*
a committee appointed from a larger committee.

subconscious (*say* sub–**kon**–shus) *adjective*
(of mental processes) outside the immediate field of consciousness, but able to be recalled to conscious awareness under hypnosis, etc.
Word Family: **subconscious,** *noun*; **subconsciously,** *adverb.*

subcontinent *noun*
a land mass which is part of a continent, e.g. the Indian subcontinent (of Asia).

subcontract *noun*
an arrangement by which a person who has agreed to do a job makes a contract with some other person to do part or all of the job for him.
Word Family: **subcontract,** *verb*; **subcontractor,** *noun.*

subculture *noun*
1. a separate system of behaviour or beliefs existing within a larger culture or society.
2. *Biology:* see CULTURE.

subcutaneous (*say* sub–kew–**tayni**–us) *adjective*
under the skin.
[SUB– + Latin *cutis* skin]

subdivide *verb*
to divide again or into smaller parts: 'to *subdivide* land for a housing estate'.
subdivision *noun*
1. another or further division.
2. a) a part, such as a piece of land, resulting from subdividing. b) an area of land, etc. composed of subdivided lots.

subdue (*say* sub–**dew**) *verb*
1. to conquer or overcome: 'I *subdued* my fears and stepped out into the dark'.
2. to soften or tone down: 'curtains will *subdue* the harshness of the light in this room'.

subheading *noun*
a) a heading given to a section of an article, etc. b) a second or lesser part of a main title. Also called a **subhead.**

subjacent (*say* sub–**jay**–s'nt) *adjective*
located beneath or at a lower level.

subject (*say* **sub**–jekt) *noun*
1. a topic or main theme: a) 'the *subject* of my talk will be collecting antiques'; b) 'orchestral variations on a musical *subject*'.
2. a person or thing that is the object of experiment, testing, etc.: 'we need 100 *subjects* for a psychological test'.
3. the thing represented in or the model for a painting, sculpture, etc.
4. a person who owes allegiance to a sovereign or a government: 'a British *subject*'.
5. any area of knowledge which may be studied.
6. *Grammar:* the word or words in a sentence which represent the person or thing about which something is said. *Example: the girl* ran across the road. Compare OBJECT.
subject (*say* sub–**jekt**) *verb*
1. to bring under some power or influence: 'the Moors *subjected* all Spain to their rule'.
2. to cause to undergo or experience: 'to *subject* a patient to massive doses of radiation'.
subject (*say* **sub**–jekt) *adjective*
1. under the power of another: 'a *subject* nation'.
2. open or exposed to: 'the decision is *subject* to appeal'.
3. dependent upon: '*subject* to the council's approval, the tree-planting ceremony will go on'.
Word Family: **subjection** (*say* sub–**jek**–sh'n), *noun.*
[SUB– + Latin *jactus* thrown]

subjective (*say* sub–**jek**–tiv) *adjective*
1. taking place solely within the mind.

2. influenced by one's personal interests, emotions or prejudices: 'to take a *subjective* view of things'.

subjectivism (*say* sub-**jektiv**-izm) *noun*
Philosophy: the belief that the mind can know only things related to itself and that there can be no objective test of truth. Compare OBJECTIVISM.

sub judice (*say* sub **jooda**-see)
Law: before, or about to come before, a court.
[Latin, under the judge]

subjugate (*say* **sub**-joo-gate) *verb*
to conquer or bring under control: a) 'to *subjugate* a nation'; b) 'to *subjugate* one's passions'.
Word Family: **subjugation,** *noun.*
[SUB- + Latin *jugum* a yoke]

subjunctive (*say* sub-**junk**-tiv) *adjective*
Grammar: see MOOD (2).
Word Family: **subjunctive,** *noun,* a) the subjunctive mood, b) a verb in the subjunctive mood.
[SUB- + Latin *junctus* joined]

sublet (*say* sub-**let**) *verb*
(sublet, subletting)
also called to **sublease**
to rent out to another, property that one is already renting.

sublimate (*say* **subli**-mate) *verb*
1. *Psychology:* to redirect a socially unacceptable impulse into some other, more acceptable activity.
2. *Chemistry, Physics:* to sublime.
Word Family: **sublimate** (*say* **subli**-mit), *noun,* the material obtained when a substance is sublimed, especially when regarded as purified by the process; **sublimation,** *noun.*
[Latin *sublimare* to lift up]

sublime (*say* sa-**blime**) *adjective*
lofty or noble: a) '*sublime* music'; b) '*sublime* mountain scenery'.
Usage: 'we tried to regain that *sublime* moment of happiness' (= perfect, complete).
sublime *verb*
Chemistry, Physics: to cause a solid substance to convert to a gas, and then to solidify again without passing through a liquid phase, by the application of heat or pressure.
Word Family: **sublimely,** *adverb;* **sublimity** (*say* sa-**blimmi**-tee), **sublimeness,** *nouns.*
[Latin *sublimis* uplifted]

subliminal (*say* sub-**limmi**-n'l) *adjective*
Psychology: perceived below the threshold of consciousness, such as an image or stimulus of too low an intensity for one to become clearly conscious of it.
[SUB- + Latin *liminis* of a threshold]

submachine gun
a light, automatic weapon fired from the shoulder or the hip.

submarine (*say* subma-**reen**) *noun*
a ship designed and equipped to travel and operate both on and below water.
submarine *adjective*
beneath the surface of the sea: '*submarine* plants'.
[SUB- + Latin *marinus* of the sea]

submerge (*say* sub-**merj**) **submerse** *verb*
to plunge under water or some other liquid: a) 'the sandbank is *submerged* at high tide'; b) 'the submarine *submerged*'.
Word Family: **submergence, submersion** (*say* sub-**mer***zh*'n), *nouns;* **submerged,** *adjective,* (Biology) growing under water.
[SUB- + Latin *mergere* to dip]

submit (*say* sub-**mit**) *verb*
(submitted, submitting)
1. to surrender to the will or authority of another: 'the defeated troops agreed to *submit* to the enemy's terms'.
2. to present for the consideration, judgement, approval, etc. of another: 'to *submit* a manuscript to a publisher'.
Usage: 'I *submit* that the punishment is unfair' (= suggest).
submission (*say* sub-**mish**'n) *noun*
1. a) the act of submitting: 'a willing *submission* to punishment'. b) the state of having submitted: '*submission* was written all over his face'.
2. something which is submitted: 'a written *submission* from each applicant'.
submissive (*say* sub-**missiv**) *adjective*
a) willing or inclined to submit: 'a *submissive* child'. b) marked by or indicating submission: 'a *submissive* answer'.
Word Family: **submissively,** *adverb;* **submissiveness,** *noun.*
[SUB- + Latin *mittere* to send]

subnormal *adjective*
1. below the average: '*subnormal* temperatures for this time of year'.
2. *Psychology:* having some mental deficiency.
Word Family: **subnormally,** *adverb;* **subnormality** (*say* sub-nor-**malli**-tee), *noun.*

subordinate (*say* subordi–nit)
adjective
1. belonging to a lower rank or status.
2. secondary: 'that's only of *subordinate* importance'.
3. *Grammar:* a) of a clause or phrase which adds to the meaning of another, but makes no sense by itself. *Example*: he visited his sister, *who was in hospital.* b) of a conjunction which introduces a subordinate clause or phrase. *Example*: *because, since, if, as* and *whether* are subordinate conjunctions.
subordinate (*say* subordi–nate) *verb*
to make subordinate: 'you must learn to *subordinate* your unruly temper'.
subordinate (*say* subordi–nit) *noun*
a subordinate person or thing.
Word Family: **subordinately,** *adverb*; **subordination,** *noun.*
[SUB– + Latin *ordinare* to set in order]

suborn (*say* sub–orn) *verb*
to persuade a person to commit an illegal act, especially perjury.
Word Family: **subornation** (*say* subba–nay–sh'n), *noun.*
[Latin *subornare* to supply secretly]

subpoena (*say* sa–peena) *noun*
plural is **subpoenas**
Law: a court document which summons a person to appear in court as a witness.
subpoena *verb*
(subpoenaed, subpoenaing)
to serve or summon with a subpoena.
[Latin, under penalty (first words of the document)]

subpolar *adjective*
between the polar and the cool temperate regions, having long, cold winters, low rainfall and coniferous forests.

sub rosa (*say* sub ro–za)
confidentially or in secret.
[Latin, under the rose, which was the symbol of Horus, the Egyptian god of silence]

subscribe *verb*
1. to undertake to receive and pay for a certain number of issues of a periodical, tickets to concerts, etc.
2. to express agreement or approval: 'I heartily *subscribe* to that theory'.
3. to promise or contribute a sum of money: 'will you *subscribe* to the new government loan?'.
4. to sign one's name at the end of a document, especially as a sign of agreement, approval, acceptance, etc.

subscription (*say* sub–skrip–sh'n)
noun
a) the act of subscribing. b) something which is subscribed, such as a collection of money.
Word Family: **subscriber,** *noun,* a) a person who subscribes to a periodical, etc., b) a person who rents a telephone.
[SUB– + Latin *scribere* to write]

subscriber trunk dialling
short form is **STD**
a direct system for making long–distance telephone calls, in which the subscriber dials the number himself.

subscript *noun*
a letter or number placed below the line, such as the 2 in CO_2.
[SUB– + Latin *scriptus* written]

subsequent (*say* subsa–kwent)
adjective
following or coming after or later: '*subsequent* developments changed our first opinion of the case'.
[SUB– + Latin *sequens* following]

subsequently *adverb*
later or afterwards: 'she *subsequently* changed her mind'.
Common Error: see CONSEQUENTLY.

subserve (*say* sub–serv) *verb*
to be useful in forwarding or promoting: 'the secondary plot *subserves* the main plot'.

subservient (*say* sub–servi–ent)
adjective
servile or tamely submissive.
Word Family: **subserviently,** *adverb*; **subservience,** *noun.*

subset *noun*
Maths: see SET.

subside (*say* sub–side) *verb*
to sink to a lower level or the bottom: 'the side of the hill *subsided*'.
Usage: 'the storm of applause *subsided*' (= abated, quietened down).
Word Family: **subsidence** (*say* sub–sigh–d'nce *or* subsi–d'nce), *noun.*
[SUB– + Latin *sidere* to settle]

subsidiary (*say* sub–sid–ya–ree)
adjective
of secondary or subordinate importance.
subsidiary *noun*
1. a subsidiary person or thing.
2. *Commerce:* a company which has more than half its shares owned by another company.
[Latin *subsidium* aid]

subsidy (*say* **subsi**–dee) *noun*
1. any financial assistance given by one government or individual to another.
2. government funds used to keep down the price of food, rent, etc.
Word Family: **subsidize, subsidise,** *verb,* to give a subsidy to; **subsidization** (*say* subsi–die–**zay**–sh'n), *noun*; **subsidizer,** *noun,* a person or group that subsidizes.

subsist (*say* sub–**sist**) *verb*
to continue in existence or keep alive: a) 'man cannot *subsist* without water'; b) 'superstition still *subsists* in our scientific age'.
subsistence *noun*
a) the act or fact of keeping alive: 'what is your means of *subsistence*?'. b) a means of keeping alive: 'selling matches is her *subsistence*'.
subsistence farming
farming which provides only enough food for the farmer and his family to live on.
subsistence level
a standard of living only just sufficient to sustain life.
[SUB– + Latin *sistere* to stand]

subsoil *noun*
the layer between the soil and bedrock, which has less organic material and is less fertile than soil.

subsonic (*say* sub–**sonnik**) *adjective*
1. moving slower than the speed of sound.
2. below the limits of human hearing.
[SUB– + Latin *sonus* sound]

subspecies (*say* **sub**–spee–seez *or* **sub**–spee–sheez) *noun*
also called a **race**
Biology: a subdivision of a species, sometimes used in the classification of animals and plants.

substance *noun*
1. a) what a thing consists of: 'ice, water and steam are the same *substance* in different states'. b) a particular kind of this: 'oil is a greasy *substance*'.
2. an object itself, as distinct from its properties.
Usages:
a) 'skip the details, and give me the *substance* of what he said' (= main or essential part).
b) 'broth has almost no *substance* to it' (= body).
c) 'her mother is a woman of *substance*' (= wealth).
[from Latin]

substandard *adjective*
inadequate or not meeting an established standard: '*substandard* housing'.

substantial (*say* sub–**stan**–sh'l) *adjective*
1. of or consisting of substance.
2. of considerable size, importance, value or amount: a) 'a *substantial* rise in salary'; b) 'we need a more *substantial* reason'.
3. *Philosophy:* of or relating to objects rather than events.
Word Family: **substantially,** *adverb*; **substantialness, substantiality** (*say* sub–stanchi–**alli**–tee), *nouns.*

substantiate (*say* sub–**stan**shi–ate) *verb*
to provide proof for: 'can you *substantiate* your claims?'.
Word Family: **substantiation,** *noun.*

substantive (*say* sub–**stan**tiv) *adjective*
1. having an independent existence.
2. essential or basic.
3. (of military rank) permanent.
Word Family: **substantive,** *noun,* (Grammar) a noun; **substantively,** *adverb.*

substation (*say* **sub**–stay–sh'n) *noun*
an auxiliary station, etc., especially one for transforming, distributing or converting electric current in a system.

substitute (*say* **substi**–tewt) *noun*
a person or thing that acts or stands in place of another.
substitute *verb*
to put a person or thing in the place of another: 'if you *substituted* red for green curtains the room would look better'.
Word Family: **substitution,** *noun.*
[SUB– + Latin *statuere* to set]

substrate *noun*
Biology: a) the solid substance to which an animal may be attached, or on which a micro-organism grows. b) the substance on which an enzyme acts.

substratum (*say* sub–**strah**tum) *noun*
plural is **substrata**
a layer beneath another, such as an underlayer of earth, rock or subsoil.
Usage: 'there is a *substratum* of truth in what you say' (= an underlying basis).

substructure *noun*
the foundations, especially of a structure such as a building or bridge.
Word Family: **substructural,** *adjective.*

subsume *verb*
to place in a larger group or category.
[SUB- + Latin *sumere* to take]

subtenant (*say* sub-**tenn**ent) *noun*
a person who rents a house, land, etc. from a tenant.
Word Family: **subtenancy**, *noun.*

subtend *verb*
Maths: to be opposite to: 'the chord *subtends* an arc'.
[SUB- + Latin *tendere* to stretch]

subterfuge (*say* **sub**ta-fewj) *noun*
an underhand method used to escape or avoid an awkward situation, etc.
[Latin *subter* underneath + *fugere* to flee]

subterranean (*say* subta-**rayni**-un) *adjective*
underground.
[SUB- + Latin *terra* earth]

subtitle *noun*
1. a second or alternative title of a book, poem, etc., often serving as an explanation of the first.
2. any of the short sentences shown on the screen during a foreign film to translate the soundtrack.
Word Family: **subtitle**, *verb*, to give a subtitle or subtitles to.

subtle (*say* **sutt**'l) *adjective*
fine, slight or delicate, so as to be difficult to detect, etc.: a) '*subtle* perfume'; b) 'a *subtle* distinction'.
Usages:
a) 'she has a *subtle* understanding of the problem' (= penetrating, acute).
b) 'a *subtle* smile' (= faint).
subtlety (*say* **sutt**'l-tee) *noun*
1. the state of being subtle.
2. something which is subtle, such as a fine distinction or shade of meaning.
Word Family: **subtleness**, *noun*; **subtly**, *adverb.*
[Latin *subtilis* fine-woven]

subtopia *noun*
the sprawl of suburbs that surrounds the modern city.
[SUB(urb) + (u)TOPIA]

subtract *verb*
to take away, especially one quantity from another.
subtraction (*say* sub-**trak**-sh'n) *noun*
the act of subtracting, especially as a problem in arithmetic.
[SUB- + Latin *tractus* dragged]

subtropical *adjective*
also called **semitropical**
of or occurring in the regions near the tropics.

suburb (*say* **sub**-erb) *noun*
a) an area of a city with its own shops and services, but not always a local government division. b) (*plural*) the residential areas near or outside the edge of a city.
suburbia (*say* sub-**erbia**) *noun*
a) the suburbs. b) the style of life in the suburbs.
Word Family: **suburban**, *adjective*, a) relating to a suburb or suburbs, b) conventional or narrow-minded; **suburbanite**, *noun.*
[SUB- + Latin *urbs* city]

subvention (*say* sub-**ven**-sh'n) *noun*
an official gift of money to an institution, etc., e.g. by a government.
[SUB- + Latin *venire* to come]

subversive (*say* sub-**versiv**) *adjective*
tending or intending to weaken, destroy or overthrow: 'a *subversive* revolutionary'.
Word Family: **subversion** (*say* sub-**ver**-*zh*'n), *noun*; **subvert**, *verb*, to overthrow or destroy.
[SUB- + Latin *versus* turned]

subway *noun*
1. a passage or tunnel under a road, for use by pedestrians.
2. *American:* an underground railway.

succeed (*say* suk-**seed**) *verb*
1. to achieve the desired or intended result.
2. to come after in time, position, etc.: 'who will *succeed* the king when he dies?'.
success (*say* suk-**sess**) *noun*
1. the achievement of what is attempted, intended or desired: 'did you have *success* with your plan?'.
Usage: 'she has achieved worldwide *success* as an author' (= fame, prosperity).
2. a person or thing that succeeds: 'his birthday party was a great *success*'.
Word Family: **successful**, *adjective*, a) having or achieving the desired or intended result, b) having gained wealth, fame or prosperity; **successfully**, *adverb.*
[Latin *succedere* to go upwards]

succession (*say* suk-**sesh**'n) *noun*
1. the act of following in order or a series: 'her *succession* to the throne was at a late age'.
2. a line or series of people or things: 'a *succession* of hereditary kings'.

3. *Biology:* the slow, progressive change in the composition of animals and plants in an area, from the first stages of colonization towards a stable, climax community.
Word Family: **successor,** *noun,* a person or thing that follows another, especially in a position, office, etc.

successive (*say* suk–**sess**iv) *adjective*
following, especially in an uninterrupted order: 'it rained for four *successive* days'.
Word Family: **successively,** *adverb.*
Common Error: see CONSECUTIVE.

succinct (*say* suk–**sinkt**) *adjective*
clearly expressed in a few words.
Word Family: **succinctly,** *adverb;* **succinctness,** *noun.*
[Latin *succinctus* girded up]

succour (*say* **suk**ka) *noun*
in America spelt **succor**
help or relief.
Word Family: **succour,** *verb.*
[Latin *succurrere* to run to the aid of]

succulent (*say* **suk**–yoo–l'nt) *adjective*
fleshy and full of juice: 'a cactus has *succulent* stems'.
Usage: 'a *succulent* roast' (= rich, delicious).
[Latin *succus* juice]

succumb (*say* suk**kum**) *verb*
to give in or give up: 'do not *succumb* to temptation!'.
[Latin *succumbere* to fall under]

such *adjective*
1. of this or that kind: 'I haven't read *such* an interesting novel for years'.
Usages:
a) 'nuts, dried fruits and all *such* foods' (= similar).
b) 'she really is *such* a telltale' (= so great or extreme).
2. being as indicated or mentioned already: '*such* are the facts of the matter'.
Phrases:
as such, 'fame, *as such,* no longer appeals to him' (= in itself).
such and such, 'it was at *such and such* a time' (= particular but not indicated).
such as, a) 'I love all old houses *such as* this one' (= similar to); b) 'do you need anything, *such as* fruit or vegetables?' (= for example).
Word Family: **suchlike,** *adjective,* of a similar kind.
Common Error: SUCH AS should introduce a noun. *Example:* 'treatment *such as* vaccination' but 'treatment *such as* by vaccination' is undesirable.

suck *verb*
1. to draw up or in: 'the vacuum cleaner *sucks* up dirt'.
2. to hold and moisten or absorb in the mouth: 'to *suck* sweets'.
Phrases:
suck in, (*informal*) 'don't be *sucked in* by her innocent smile' (= deceived).
suck up to, (*informal*) 'he's always *sucking up to* the teacher' (= flattering).
Word Family: **suck,** *noun,* the act or sound of sucking.

sucker *noun*
1. a person or device that sucks.
2. a sweet for sucking.
3. (*informal*) a person who is easily tricked or deceived.
4. a shoot arising from an underground stem or root.

sucking-pig *noun*
a very young pig, especially one used for roasting.

suckle *verb*
to cause or allow to take milk at the breast.
Word Family: **suckling,** *noun,* a young mammal which has not been weaned.

sucrose (*say* **soo**–kroze) *noun*
also called **cane sugar**
a crystalline carbohydrate found in sugar cane, sugar beet, etc. and used as a sweetener, preservative, etc.
[French *sucre* sugar]

suction (*say* **suk**–sh'n) *noun*
1. the act or force of sucking.
2. *Physics:* the process of removing, or attempting to remove, gas from an enclosed space.
[Latin *suctus* sucked]

suction pump
a pump for raising water, etc. by suction, consisting of a piston working in a cylinder with valves to control the pressure.

sudden *adjective*
done or occurring quickly and usually unexpectedly: 'a *sudden* storm'.
Word Family: **suddenly,** *adverb;* **suddenness,** *noun.*

suds (*say* sudz) *plural noun*
soapy water.
Word Family: **sudsy,** *adjective.*

sue (*say* soo) *verb*
to bring legal action against.

suede (*say* swade) *noun*
a leather with a soft surface, made from skins with the flesh side napped.
[French *Suède* Sweden]

suet (*say* **soo**–it) *noun*
the fat from the kidneys and loin of sheep and cattle, often used in boiled or baked puddings.

suffer *verb*
to feel bad or unpleasant effects: a) 'he's *suffering* from a cold'; b) 'the country *suffered* from bad government'.
Usages:
a) 'the family has *suffered* great hardship' (= experienced).
b) 'I will not *suffer* such foolishness' (= tolerate, put up with).
Word Family: **sufferer**, *noun*, a person who suffers; **sufferable**, *adjective*; **sufferably**, *adverb*; **suffering**, *noun*.
[Latin *suffere* to bear up under]

sufferance *noun*
the ability to bear pain, distress, etc.
under, on sufferance, 'he is only here *under sufferance*' (= reluctantly tolerated).

suffice *verb*
to be enough or adequate for: 'this meat won't *suffice* for six of us'.

sufficient (*say* suf**fish**'nt) *adjective*
as much as is needed: 'do you have *sufficient* time to catch the train?'.
Word Family: **sufficiently**, *adverb*; **sufficiency**, *noun*, a sufficient supply or amount.
[from Latin]

suffix *noun*
Grammar: see AFFIX.

suffocate (*say* **suffa**–kate) *verb*
1. to die or cause to die due to insufficient oxygen.
2. to cause discomfort or difficulty in breathing due to lack of fresh air.
Word Family: **suffocation**, *noun*; **suffocatingly**, *adverb*.
[Latin *suffocare* to choke]

suffragan (*say* **suffra**–g'n) *noun*
an assistant bishop.

suffrage (*say* **suffrij**) *noun*
a) a vote. b) the right to vote in political elections.
suffragette (*say* suffra–**jet**) *noun*
a woman who fought for suffrage for women, especially in the first part of the 20th century.
Word Family: **suffragist**, *noun*, a person in favour of extending the right to vote.
[from Latin]

suffuse (*say* suff–**yooz**) *verb*
to spread over the surface of: 'a blush *suffused* her cheeks'.
Word Family: **suffusion**, *noun*.
[Latin *suffusus* poured over]

sugar (*say* **shugga**) *noun*
a granular substance obtained from sugar cane or sugar beet.
Word Family: **sugar**, *verb*, to add, coat or mix with sugar; **sugary**, *adjective*, a) containing or resembling sugar, b) pleasant to an excessive degree.
[Arabic *sukkar*]

sugar beet
a variety of beet with white roots.

sugar cane
a tall tropical grass with thick, segmented stems.

sugar daddy
(*informal*) a wealthy, older man who gives money or gifts to a young woman.

suggest (*say* su**jjest**) *verb*
to offer or put forward to be considered or acted upon: 'let me *suggest* a better method'.
Usages:
a) 'this painting *suggests* many things to me' (= calls to mind).
b) 'are you *suggesting* I'm a liar?' (= saying).
suggestion (*say* suj–**es**–ch'n) *noun*
1. a) the act of suggesting. b) something which is suggested: 'that's a stupid *suggestion*!'.
Usage: 'there was just a *suggestion* of mockery in her laugh' (= slight trace).
2. the process by which one thought, action, etc. leads to or is associated with another.
3. *Psychology:* the process of getting others to accept one's belief or ideas without using force.
Word Family: **suggestive**, *adjective*, tending to suggest, especially something indecent; **suggestively**, *adverb*; **suggestiveness**, *noun*; **suggestible**, *adjective*, easily influenced by suggestion.
[Latin *suggestus* supplied]

suicide (*say* **soo**–isside) *noun*
1. the act of deliberately killing oneself: 'to commit *suicide*'.
Usage: 'it's *suicide* to invest all your money in that company' (= ruin inflicted on oneself).

2. a person who deliberately kills himself.
Word Family: **suicidal,** *adjective,* a) of or likely to commit or lead to suicide, b) dangerously foolish; **suicidally,** *adverb.*
[Latin *sui* of oneself + *caedere* to kill]

suit (*rhymes with* boot) *noun*
1. a) a set of clothes worn together, such as a skirt or trousers with a matching jacket, usually of the same colour or material. b) an outfit for a particular purpose: 'a bathing *suit*'.
2. *Cards:* any of the four sets (clubs, diamonds, hearts or spades) of 13 cards which make up a pack.
3. any legal action taken by one person against another in a court.
4. the act of wooing.
follow suit, a) (*Cards*) to play a card of the same suit as one led; b) to follow an example.
suit *verb*
to be acceptable, appropriate or adequate to: 'I hope this room will *suit* you'.
Usage: 'you must *suit* your clothes to the occasion' (= make suitable).
suit oneself, 'he *suits himself* about what food he eats' (= does as he chooses).

suitable (*say* soota-b'l) *adjective*
correct, adequate or pleasing for a particular event, situation, etc.: a) 'I'm afraid your qualifications are not *suitable* for the job'; b) 'those jeans are not *suitable* for work'.
Word Family: **suitably,** *adverb;* **suitability** (*say* soota-billi-tee), **suitableness,** *nouns.*

suitcase *noun*
a bag with a stiffened frame, or of rigid material such as leather, for carrying clothes, etc. when travelling.

suite (*say* sweet) *noun*
1. a group of connected or related things forming a set or series: a) 'an opera *suite*'; b) 'a *suite* of hotel rooms'; c) 'a furniture *suite*'.
2. a group of attendants or followers.

suitor (*say* soota) *noun*
a person wooing a woman.

sulfur *noun*
American: sulphur.

sulk *verb*
to be silent in a gloomy or resentful manner.
Word Family: **sulk,** *noun,* a) (usually plural) a fit of sulking, b) a person who sulks.

sulky *adjective*
resentfully silent or angry.
sulky, sulkie *noun*
a) a two-wheeled carriage for one person and pulled by one horse, as in trotting races. b) a gig.

sullen *adjective*
sulky, especially in a persistent or unpleasant manner.
Word Family: **sullenly,** *adverb;* **sullenness,** *noun.*

sully *verb*
to stain, spoil or make dirty.

sulpha drugs (*say* sulfa drugs)
a group of drugs used against bacterial diseases, infections, etc.

sulphate (*say* sul-fate) *noun*
Chemistry: any compound containing the bivalent $(SO_4)^{2-}$ ion.

sulphide (*say* sul-fide) *noun*
Chemistry: any compound containing the bivalent S^{2-} ion.

sulphur (*say* sulfa) *noun*
element number 16, a yellow non-metal forming allotropes. It is essential for living tissue and is used in making gunpowder, matches, sulphuric acid and for vulcanizing rubber.
See CHEMICAL ELEMENTS in grey pages.
Word Family: **sulphurize, sulphurise,** *verb,* to treat or combine with sulphur; **sulphurous,** *adjective,* a) of or containing sulphur, b) fiery; **sulphuric** (*say* sul-fewrik), *adjective,* of or containing sulphur.
[from Latin]

sulphur dioxide
a colourless, suffocating gas (formula SO_2), used in various industrial processes.

sulphuric acid
Chemistry: a colourless, oily liquid (formula H_2SO_4), which is an acid of sulphur and is used in many industrial processes.

sultan *noun*
the ruler of a Moslem city or country.
Word Family: **sultanate,** *noun,* a country or state ruled by a sultan.
[Arabic]

sultana (*say* sul-tahna) *noun*
1. a small, sweet, seedless grape.
2. the wife, concubine or close female relative of a sultan.

sultry *adjective*
hot, moist and oppressive: 'a *sultry* tropical climate'.

Usage: 'a *sultry* Spanish dancer' (= sensual).
Word Family: **sultriness,** *noun*; **sultrily,** *adverb.*

sum *noun*
1. the amount obtained by adding: 'what is the *sum* of 7 and 13?'.
Usages:
a) 'she inherited a huge *sum* from her father' (= amount of money).
b) 'and is that the *sum* of your complaints?' (= whole amount or number).
c) 'give the court a *sum* of the charges' (= summary).
2. a simple arithmetical problem of addition, division, multiplication, etc.
sum *verb*
(summed, summing)
to add together.
sum up, a) to make or give a summary of; b) 'it is difficult to *sum up* such a temperamental person' (= assess, describe).
[Latin *summa* the main thing]

sumac (*say* **soo**–mak) **sumach** *noun*
a mixture of the dried and powdered leaves of certain plants used as dyes, for tanning, etc.
[from Arabic]

summary (*say* **summa**–ree) *noun*
a short statement of important points or details.
Word Family: **summary,** *adjective,* a) concise or brief, b) quick; **summarily,** *adverb*; **summarize, summarise,** *verb,* to be or make a summary of; **summariness,** *noun.*

summation (*say* summay–sh'n) *noun*
1. a summary, especially as a concluding statement.
2. the act of adding.

summer *noun*
the warmest season of the year, between spring and autumn.
Usage: 'a young girl of 20 *summers*' (= years).
Word Family: **summery,** *adjective,* like or suitable for summer; **summer,** *verb,* to spend the summer.

summerhouse *noun*
a simple building providing shade in a garden or park.

summer school
a course of teaching or lectures held at a university or school during the summer holidays.

summer time
a system of putting the clock forward one or more hours, usually in summer, to increase the number of hours of daylight in the working day.

summit *noun*
1. the highest point or top: 'the *summit* of a hill'.
2. (*informal*) a meeting between leaders, especially from powerful countries.
[Latin *summus* highest]

summon *verb*
to send for or ask to appear: 'Sir Richard *summoned* the cook'.
Usages:
a) 'you must *summon* all your courage' (= gather together).
b) 'the garrison was *summoned* to surrender' (= called upon).
[Latin *summonere* to give a hint to]

summons *noun*
plural is **summonses**
1. *Law:* an order or notice to appear in court.
2. any call or command.
Word Family: **summons,** *verb,* to issue or present with a summons.

sump *noun*
1. a metal pan fastened to the underside of an engine crankcase, usually forming a reservoir for lubricating oil.
2. a pit or well in which water collects, especially at the bottom of a mine shaft.

sumptuary (*say* **sump**–tewa–ree) *adjective*
relating to expense or spending.

sumptuous (*say* **sump**–tewus) *adjective*
suggesting or involving great expense: 'a *sumptuous* meal at the best restaurant'.
Word Family: **sumptuously,** *adverb*; **sumptuousness,** *noun.*
[from Latin]

sun *noun*
1. *Astronomy:* the star around which the earth and the other eight planets of the solar system revolve.
2. the energy, especially heat and light, radiated by the sun: 'go out and play in the *sun*'.
under the sun, 'the richest person *under the sun*' (= anywhere).
Word Family: **sun (sunned, sunning),** *verb,* to expose to the sun, especially in order to warm, dry or colour; **sunny,** *adjective,* a) full of sunlight, b) cheerful; **sunnily,** *adverb*; **sunniness,** *noun.*

sunbathe *verb*
to expose the body to the sun's rays, especially in order to acquire a suntan.
Word Family: **sunbather**, *noun.*

sunbeam *noun*
a ray of sunlight.

sunburn *noun*
a reddening or blistering of the skin due to too much exposure to the sun's rays.
Word Family: **sunburnt**, *adjective.*

sundae (*say* **sun**day) *noun*
a serving of ice-cream with fruit and sauce, often topped with chopped nuts and whipped cream.

Sunday *noun*
the first day of the week, the Christian Sabbath.
a month of Sundays, 'I have not seen her in *a month of Sundays*' (= a very long time).
Sunday school
Christian: a class for religious instruction held on a Sunday.

Sunday best
(*informal*) a person's best clothes.

sundeck *noun*
a passenger ship's top deck.

sunder *verb*
to part or separate.

sundial (*say* **sun**-dile) *noun*
an instrument with a flat base and upright rod which indicates the time by the position of the shadow cast by the rod upon the base.

sundown *noun*
sunset.

sundowner *noun*
Australian: a swagman who arrives at a place at sunset so that he can, by long-established tradition, ask for food and shelter but will not have to work in exchange.

sundry (*say* **sun**-dree) *adjective*
various or miscellaneous.
all and sundry, everybody.
sundry *noun*
(*plural*) various small items.

sunflower *noun*
a tall garden plant having large, yellow daisy-like flowers with blackish-brown centres. The seeds are used as a source of oil.

sung *verb*
a past tense and the past participle of the verb **sing**.

sunglasses *plural noun*
a pair of spectacles with tinted lenses, worn to protect the eyes from the glare and invisible rays of the sun.

sunk *verb*
a past tense and past participle of the verb **sink**.

sunken *adjective*
lying below the surface of the ground, etc.: 'a *sunken* bath'.
Usage: 'her *sunken* cheeks told of the weeks of starvation' (= deeply recessed).
sunken *verb*
a past participle of the verb **sink**.

sunlamp *noun*
1. an appliance which gives off ultraviolet rays to produce an artificial suntan or for skin treatment.
2. a very bright light with parabolic mirrors, used in making films.

sunny *adjective*
Word Family: see SUN.

sunray *noun*
(*plural*) ultraviolet rays, as produced by a sunlamp.

sunrise *noun*
a) the rising of the sun above the horizon in the morning. b) the time at which this occurs.

sunroof *noun*
see SUNSHINE ROOF.

sunset *noun*
a) the passing of the sun below the horizon in the evening. b) the time at which this occurs.

sunshade *noun*
something used as protection from the sun's rays, such as a parasol, blind, etc.

sun shield
also called a **sun visor**
a metal sheet mounted on the outside of a motor vehicle above the windscreen to protect the driver from the sun.

sunshine *noun*
the direct light or brightness of the sun.

sunshine roof
also called a **sunroof**
a section in the roof of a motor vehicle, which may be opened to allow the sun and fresh air to enter.

sunspot *noun*
Astronomy: any dark patch on the surface of the sun, usually associated

with turbulent motion such as magnetic storms.

sunstroke *noun*
heatstroke.

sunsuit *noun*
a light piece of clothing, such as shorts or a skirt with a top, often in one piece.

suntan *noun*
a brownness of the skin achieved by exposure to the sun's rays.

sun–up *noun*
sunrise.

sun visor
see SUN SHIELD.

sup (1) *verb*
(supped, supping)
an old word meaning to entertain with, or eat, supper.

sup (2) *verb*
(supped, supping)
to eat or drink in sips or small mouthfuls.

super (*say* **soo**per) *adjective*
(*informal*) extremely pleasing or excellent.
super *noun*
(*informal*) a) a superintendent. b) supernumerary.

super–
a prefix indicating: a) position above or outside, as in *superstructure*; b) superiority in size or quality, as in *superman*; c) an extreme or greater than usual degree, as in *supercharge*.
[Latin]

superable (*say* **soo**pra–b'l) *adjective*
able to be overcome: 'a *superable* risk'.

superabundance
(*say* sooper–a–**bun**–d'nce) *noun*
an amount which is more than enough or too great.
Word Family: **superabundant,** *adjective*; **superabound,** *verb.*

superannuation
(*say* sooper–an–yoo–**ay**–sh'n) *noun*
a pension or allowance paid to an employee after retirement, usually one towards which he has contributed.
Word Family: **superannuate** (*say* sooper–**an**–yoo–ate), *verb*, to allow an employee to retire and receive superannuation.
[SUPER– + Latin *annus* a year]

superb (*say* soo–**perb**) *adjective*
magnificent.
Word Family: **superbly,** *adverb*; **superbness,** *noun.*
[Latin *superbus* haughty, splendid]

supercargo *noun*
an agent in a merchant ship, in charge of her cargo and of all commercial transactions.

supercharge *verb*
to fill or supply with a large amount of something.

supercharger *noun*
a device which supplies air at high pressure to an internal combustion engine in order to increase its performance.

supercilious (*say* sooper–**silli**–us) *adjective*
disdainful or contemptuous: 'the *supercilious* snob'.
Word Family: **superciliously,** *adverb*; **superciliousness,** *noun.*
[SUPER– + Latin *cilium* eyelid]

superconductivity *noun*
1. the property of zero electrical resistance which appears abruptly in some metals at specific temperatures near absolute zero, put to use in computer memory storage, particle accelerators, etc.
2. *Physics:* a phenomenon observed at temperatures near absolute zero, at which electric current appears to flow without resistance.

supercool *verb*
Physics: to cool a liquid, by careful control of pressure, etc., below its freezing point without it becoming solid. Compare SUPERHEAT.

super–duper *adjective*
(*informal*) very good, fine, pleasing, etc.

superego (*say* sooper–**ee**go) *noun*
Psychology: that part of the personality which absorbs the moral codes of society, similar to the conscience.

supererogation
(*say* sooper–erra–**gay**–sh'n) *noun*
Christian: the doing of more than is required by duty or obligation: 'works of *supererogation*'.
[SUPER– + Latin *erogare* to pay out]

superficial (*say* sooper–**fish**'l) *adjective*
of or on the surface: 'the cut was only *superficial*'.
Usage: 'my understanding of physics is very *superficial*' (= not deep or thorough).

Word Family: **superficiality** (*say* sooper-fishi-**alli**-tee), *noun*; **superficially**, *adverb.*
[Latin *superficies* the upper side]

superfine *adjective*
exceptionally fine: '*superfine* sugar'.

superfluid (*say* sooper-**floo**-id) *noun*
Physics: a fluid which flows without friction and has a very high thermal conductivity.
Word Family: **superfluidity** (*say* sooper-floo-**iddi**-tee), *noun.*

superfluous (soo-**per**floo-us) *adjective*
more than is needed: 'as I have one car another would be *superfluous*'.
Word Family: **superfluously**, *adverb*; **superfluousness**, *noun*; **superfluity** (*say* sooper-**floo**-a-tee), *noun*, a) the fact of being superfluous, b) the amount by which something is superfluous.
[Latin *superfluus* overflowing]

superheat *verb*
Physics: to heat to a temperature higher than normal. *Example:* steam is produced by boiling water at 100°C, but it can be superheated to any desired temperature above this.

superhuman *adjective*
exceeding ordinary human power, achievement, etc.: 'we needed a *superhuman* effort to finish the job in time'.

superimpose (*say* sooper-**impoze**) *verb*
to put on top of something else: 'a map of Tasmania was *superimposed* on the map of Queensland to show their relative sizes'.
Word Family: **superimposition** (*say* sooper-impa-**zish**'n), *noun.*

superintend (*say* sooper-**intend**) *verb*
to supervise.
superintendent *noun*
1. a supervisor.
2. a police officer above the rank of inspector.
Word Family: **superintendence**, *noun.*

superior (*say* soo-**peer**ia) *adjective*
1. high or higher in order, degree, rank, etc.: 'he is my *superior* officer'.
Usages:
a) 'the enemy defeated us with *superior* numbers' (= greater).
b) 'he gave a *superior* smile' (= supercilious).
2. of a high quality: 'a *superior* product'.
3. situated above or on top: 'the 2 in 10^2 is a *superior* number'.
4. *Astronomy:* of or relating to planets in our solar system which are further from the sun than the earth.
Word Family: **superior**, *noun*, a person or thing that is superior; **superiority** (*say* soo-peeri-**orri**-tee), *noun.*
[Latin]

superiority complex
(*informal*) an exaggerated idea of one's own worth.

superlative (*say* soo-**per**la-tiv) *adjective*
1. of the highest degree or quality: 'Geoffrey's job called for *superlative* skill'.
2. *Grammar:* see DEGREE.
superlative *noun*
a word in the superlative degree.
Usage: 'the critics greeted the film with a fanfare of *superlatives*' (= extreme or exaggerated expressions).
[SUPER- + Latin *latus* carried]

superman *noun*
a man of more than ordinary human powers.

supermarket *noun*
a large, self-service shop selling food and other domestic goods.

supernatural (*say* sooper-**natcha**-r'l) *adjective*
1. not belonging to the natural world: 'ghosts are *supernatural* beings'.
2. greater than what is normal or usual: 'she has a *supernatural* ability to remember things'.
Word Family: **supernaturally**, *adverb*; **supernatural**, *noun*, supernatural beings, forces, etc.

supernova *noun*
an exploding star which, at maximum, may emit light equivalent to that of 300 million suns.
[a misleading term, as it has no relation to a *nova*]

supernumerary
(*say* sooper-**new**mera-ree) *adjective*
in excess of or additional to the usual number.
Word Family: **supernumerary**, *noun*, an extra person or thing.

superphosphate (*say* sooper-**fos**fate) *noun*
a widely used artificial fertilizer prepared by treating rock phosphate or guano with sulphuric acid.

superpower *noun*
an extremely powerful and influential country.

supersaturated
(*say* sooper–**satcha**–raytid) *adjective*
(of a solution) abnormally saturated.

supersede (*say* sooper–**seed**) *verb*
to replace with something more powerful, modern, effective, etc.: 'the new car *supersedes* all previous models'.
[Latin *supersedere* sit above]

superset *noun*
Maths: see SET.

supersonic (*say* sooper–**sonnik**) *adjective*
relating to bodies moving faster than the speed of sound.
[SUPER– + Latin *sonus* sound]

superstition (*say* sooper–**stish**'n) *noun*
1. an irrational fear of mysterious or unknown things.
2. a belief or practice based on faith in magic or chance.
superstitious *adjective*
1. of, like or resulting from superstition.
2. believing in superstition.
Word Family: **superstitiously**, *adverb*; **superstitiousness**, *noun.*
[Latin *superstitio* an unreasonable belief or fear]

superstructure (*say* **sooper**–strukcher) *noun*
1. the parts of a structure which rest on the foundations, especially if above ground level.
2. any structure built on something else, such as the parts of a ship above the deck.

supertanker *noun*
a modern, very large ship built with tanks for transporting liquid goods such as oil.

supervene (*say* sooper–veen) *verb*
to come or follow as a change or interruption: 'rain *supervened* and the picnic was postponed'.
Word Family: **supervention** (*say* sooper–**ven**–sh'n), *noun.*
[SUPER– + Latin *venire* to come]

supervise (*say* **sooper**–vize) *verb*
to direct or manage work, workers, etc.
Word Family: **supervisor**, *noun*, a person who supervises; **supervisory**, *adjective*; **supervision** (*say* sooper–**vizh**'n), *noun.*
[SUPER– + Latin *visus* seen]

supine (*say* **syoo**–pine *or* **soo**–pine) *adjective*
1. lying flat on the back.
2. lazy or inactive.
Word Family: **supinely**, *adverb.*
[Latin *supinus* face upwards]

supper *noun*
a) a late–night snack. b) the main evening meal.

supplant (*say* sup–**lahnt**) *verb*
to replace, especially by strategy, etc.: 'the dictator was *supplanted* by an elected government'.
[Latin *supplantare* to trip up]

supple *adjective*
easily bent or bending: 'the gymnast had *supple* limbs'.
Usage: 'she has a *supple* mind' (= adaptable, quick).
[Latin *supplex* kneeling in supplication]

supplement (*say* **suppli**–m'nt) *noun*
1. something added to improve or complete: 'a *supplement* of technical terms at the back of the book'.
2. an extra part of a newspaper, etc.: 'a literary *supplement*'.
supplement *verb*
to complete or add to: 'she must *supplement* her income by working on Saturdays'.
Word Family: **supplementary**, *adjective*; **supplementation**, *noun.*
[from Latin]

suppliant (*say* **suppli**–ant) *noun*
a person who asks for something humbly.
suppliant *adjective*
asking humbly.

supplicate (*say* **suppli**–kate) *verb*
to ask or entreat humbly and earnestly.
Word Family: **supplicant**, *noun*, a person who supplicates; **supplicatory** (*say* suppli–**kayta**–ree), *adjective*; **supplication**, *noun.*
[Latin *supplicare* to bend, kneel]

supply (*say* sup–**lie**) *verb*
(supplied, supplying)
to give or make available: 'the chickens *supply* us with all the eggs we need'.
Usage: 'we still want you to *supply* our need for meat' (= satisfy).
supply *noun*
1. a) the act of supplying. b) an amount that is supplied: 'we'll have a fresh *supply* of caviar tomorrow'.
2. (*plural*) any stores, such as materials used by the armed forces.
3. *Commerce:* the quantity of goods and services available to consumers.
4. a grant made by parliament for government expenses.

Word Family: **supplier,** *noun,* a person or thing that supplies.

support *verb*
1. to hold up or add strength to: a) 'tall columns *supported* the roof'; b) '*support* your theory with evidence'.
Usages:
a) 'he *supports* the socialist party' (= gives loyalty, belief or aid to).
b) 'she *supports* 12 children' (= provides for).
c) 'I can't *support* bad language' (= tolerate).
2. to have a secondary role to: 'the film was *supported* by some cartoons'.
support *noun*
1. a) the act of supporting: 'can I rely on your *support*?'. b) the state of being supported.
2. a person or thing that supports: a) 'she's the main *support* of her family'; b) 'the *supports* of the bridge collapsed'.
supporter *noun*
a person or thing that supports, such as a person who favours and encourages a football team, etc.
Word Family: **supportable,** *adjective.*
[Latin *supportare* to carry up to]

suppose (*say* sup-**oze**) *verb*
to take as a fact or likelihood: 'I *suppose* his advice is sensible'.
Usages:
a) 'am I *supposed* to clean up?' (= meant).
b) 'a belief in flying saucers *supposes* the existence of life on other planets' (= implies).
supposed *adjective*
accepted as probable: 'this is the *supposed* site of an ancient city'.
supposition (*say* suppa-**zish**'n) *noun*
a) the act of supposing. b) something guessed or supposed.
Word Family: **supposing,** *conjunction,* in the case that; **supposedly,** *adverb.*
[Latin *suppositus* placed under]

suppository (*say* sup-**ozzi**-tree) *noun*
a solid mass of medicine inserted into the rectum or vagina where it dissolves.

suppress *verb*
1. to end or abolish: a) 'the army *suppressed* the rebellion'; b) 'the slave trade was *suppressed* by parliament'.
2. to prevent something being seen, known, etc.: 'the government *suppressed* news of the scandal'.
Word Family: **suppressive,** *adjective;* **suppression** (*say* sup-**presh**'n), *noun;* **suppressor,** *noun,* a person or thing that suppresses.
[Latin *suppressus* pressed down]

suppurate (*say* **sup**-yoo-rate) *verb*
to form or discharge pus.
Word Family: **suppuration,** *noun.*
[from Latin]

supremacist (*say* soo-**premma**-sist) **suprematist** *noun*
a person who believes that his own race or group is superior or supreme.
Word Family: **suprematism,** *noun.*

supreme (*say* soo-**preem**) *adjective*
1. of highest rank or authority: 'the dictator had *supreme* power'.
2. utmost or greatest: 'I have *supreme* confidence in you'.
supremacy (*say* soo-**premma**-see) *noun*
supreme power or authority.
[Latin *supremus* topmost]

Supreme Court
the highest court of justice.

supremo (*say* soo-**preemo**) *noun*
a person with supreme power.
[Spanish]

surcharge *noun*
1. an extra charge.
2. a mark overprinted on a postage stamp showing a new value.
Word Family: **surcharge,** *verb.*

surd *noun*
a quantity not capable of being expressed as a rational number, such as $\sqrt{3}$.
[from Latin]

sure (*say* shore) *adjective*
1. convinced or free from doubt: 'are you *sure* of your facts?'.
Usages:
a) 'she is *sure* to be late' (= bound).
b) 'be *sure* to lock the door' (= careful).
2. solid, tested or reliable: a) '*sure* ground'; b) 'is there a *sure* cure for a hangover?'.
sure *adverb*
(*informal*) really or undoubtedly: 'you *sure* were lucky'.
Phrases:
make sure, to guarantee or make certain.
sure enough, 'I said you'd win, and *sure enough* you did' (= in fact).
surely *adverb*
almost without doubt: 'it will *surely* rain tomorrow'.
Usage: 'he worked slowly but *surely*' (= steadily).
b) '*surely* you wouldn't do that!' (= I fervently hope or believe).

Word Family: **sureness**, *noun.*
[Latin *securus* carefree]

sure-footed *adjective*
not likely to slip or stumble.

surety (*say* **shoora**-tee) *noun*
a person who agrees to be responsible for someone else's debts or behaviour.

surf *noun*
the waves, especially large ones, which break on the shore into foamy water.
Word Family: **surf**, *verb*, to bathe in or ride on surf; **surfer**, *noun.*

surface (*say* **sir**-fis) *noun*
1. the outside or outer boundary of something: a) 'most glass has a smooth *surface*'; b) 'a cube has six *surfaces*'.
2. the top level: 'the ship sank beneath the sea's *surface*'.
Usage: 'beneath the *surface* he's a nice chap' (= outward appearance).
surface *verb*
1. to rise to the surface.
2. to give a surface to: 'the road was *surfaced* with tar'.
[French]

surface mail
the carrying of post by land or sea. Compare AIR MAIL.

surface tension
Physics: the tendency of a liquid surface to contract due to unbalanced molecular forces at or near the surface.

surfboard *noun*
a narrow board on which a person balances to ride to shore on the crest of a wave.

surfboat *noun*
a rowing boat with high ends, suitable for use in surf.

surfeit (*say* **sir**-fit) *noun*
a) too much of something. b) nausea or disgust due to having had too much.
Word Family: **surfeit**, *verb.*

surfing *noun*
the sport of swimming in or riding a surfboard on surf.

surge (*say* sirj) *verb*
to rush or swell strongly like rolling waves.
surge *noun*
an onrush or strong forward or upward movement.
[Latin *surgere* to rise]

surgeon (*say* **sir**-j'n) *noun*
a doctor who performs operations.

surgery (*say* **sir**ja-ree) *noun*
1. a) the art of treating diseases, injuries, etc. by operations, appliances, etc. b) the branch of medicine using this treatment. c) any operation done by a surgeon.
2. the room or building in which a doctor, dentist, etc. treats patients.
Word Family: **surgical**, *adjective*; **surgically**, *adverb.*
[Greek *kheirourgia* handiwork]

surgical spirit
methylated spirits, used in surgery for disinfecting and cleansing.

surly *adjective*
rude, bad-tempered or unfriendly.
Word Family: **surlily**, *adverb*; **surliness**, *noun.*

surmise (*say* sir-**mize**) *verb*
to guess.
Word Family: **surmise**, *noun.*

surmount (*say* sir-**mount**) *verb*
1. to get over, across or on top of: 'it was difficult to *surmount* the obstacle'.
2. to be or have on top: 'a steeple *surmounted* the tower'.
Word Family: **surmountable**, *noun.*

surname *noun*
the name of one's family.

surpass *verb*
to be better or greater than: 'your new book *surpasses* all your earlier ones'.

surplice (*say* **sir**-plis) *noun*
a loose white linen robe with wide sleeves, as is worn by clergymen during religious services.

surplus (*say* **sir**-plus) *noun*
that which is left above what is used or needed: 'the good harvest resulted in a *surplus* of grain'.

surprise (*say* sir-**prize**) *noun*
a) something sudden or unexpected: 'what a pleasant *surprise* to see you again'. b) the feeling of shock or wonder caused by this: 'he almost fainted with *surprise*'.
take by surprise, 'your early arrival *took* us *by surprise*' (= caught unprepared).
surprise *verb*
1. to give a feeling of surprise to: 'her unkind remark *surprised* me'.
2. to face or come upon suddenly and without warning: 'I *surprised* him in the act of stealing fruit'.
Word Family: **surprisingly**, *adverb.*

surrealism (*say* sir-**reel**-izm) *noun*
a 20th-century movement in art and literature seeking to reveal the inner world of fantasy and dreams by using distorted images.

Word Family: **surrealist, surreal,** *adjectives*; **surrealist,** *noun*; **surrealistically,** *adverb.*

surrender (*say* sir–**ren**da) *verb*
to deliver up to the control or power of someone or something else: a) 'the criminals refused to *surrender* themselves to the police'; b) 'don't *surrender* to despair'.
Word Family: **surrender,** *noun.*

surreptitious (*say* surrep–**tish**us) *adjective*
secret or stealthy: 'she stole a *surreptitious* glance at him'.
Word Family: **surreptitiously,** *adverb*; **surreptitiousness,** *noun.*
[Latin *surreptitius* snatched away secretly]

surrogate (*say* **surra**–git) *noun*
a) a substitute. b) a deputy.
[Latin *surrogare* to propose as substitute]

surround *verb*
to enclose or extend completely around: a) 'the house is *surrounded* by trees'; b) 'we *surrounded* the enemy so that he was trapped'.
surroundings *plural noun*
everything around and about a person, thing or place: 'where can I see lions in their natural *surroundings*?'.
surround *noun*
1. a border that surrounds.
2. (*plural*) surroundings.

surtax *noun*
an additional tax, especially one on any personal income which exceeds a specified amount.

surveillance (*say* sir–**vay**–l'nce) *noun*
a close watch or guard.
[French]

survey (*say* sir–**vay**) *verb*
1. to take an overall view: 'you can *survey* the whole town from this lookout'.
2. to collect sample opinions, etc. in order to estimate the general situation.
3. to plot or measure boundaries, positions, etc. on land.
survey (*say* **sir**–vay) *noun*
1. a) a general view or examination: 'a *survey* of public opinion'. b) a record or report of this.
2. a) the act of surveying land. b) a map or record of this.
Word Family: **surveyor** (*say* sir–**vay**a), *noun*, a person who examines or surveys.

survive (*say* sir–**vive**) *verb*
to continue to live or exist after something: 'everyone *survived* the earthquake'.
Word Family: **survivor,** *noun*, a person or thing that survives; **survival,** *noun*, the act of surviving.

susceptible (*say* sus**sep**ti–b'l) *adjective*
likely to experience or be affected by: 'the old lady was highly *susceptible* to rheumatism'.
susceptibility (*say* sussepti–**billi**–tee) *noun*
1. the capacity or tendency to be affected by: 'his *susceptibility* to flattery is obvious'.
2. (*plural*) a person's sensitive feelings.
Word Family: **susceptibly,** *adverb.*
[Latin *suscipere* to catch]

suspect (*say* sus–**pekt**) *verb*
1. to think something likely or possible: 'I *suspect* it will rain soon'.
2. to consider guilty without actual or adequate proof: 'I *suspect* her of arson'.
Usage: 'I *suspect* his motives' (= doubt, distrust).
suspect (*say* **sus**–pekt) *noun*
a person suspected of being guilty.
Word Family: **suspect** (*say* **sus**–pekt), *adjective*, open to suspicion.
[Latin *suspectus* looked up at]

suspend *verb*
to attach from above: 'the light bulb was *suspended* from the ceiling'.
Usages:
a) 'dust was *suspended* in the hot, still air' (= held stationary).
b) 'you may *suspend* payment for a month' (= defer, postpone).
c) 'the football player was *suspended* for 3 matches' (= debarred).

suspended sentence
a sentence of imprisonment not implemented provided the offender is of good behaviour over a specified period.

suspender *noun*
something that suspends, such as a strip of elastic with a fastener for holding up stockings.

suspense *noun*
a state of anxious uncertainty: 'the film kept us in *suspense* about the murderer's identity'.
Word Family: **suspenseful,** *adjective.*
[Latin *suspensus* hung up]

suspension (*say* sus-**pen**-sh'n) *noun*
1. a) the act of suspending: 'the tribunal's *suspension* of our best player is disastrous'. b) the state of being suspended: 'he is under *suspension* from school'.
2. the springs, shock absorbers, etc., connecting the wheels or axles of a vehicle to the chassis or body.

suspension bridge
a bridge hung from steel cables, supported by towers and anchored at either side.

suspicion (*say* sus-**pish**'n) *noun*
a feeling that something is likely or possible: 'I had a *suspicion* you'd be late'.
Usages:
a) 'she was arrested on *suspicion*' (= suspected guilt).
b) 'I have *suspicions* about your motives' (= doubts, distrusts).
c) 'there was a *suspicion* of garlic in the soup' (= suggestion or slight taste).
Word Family: **suspicious**, *adjective*, feeling or causing suspicion; **suspiciously**, *adverb*; **suspiciousness**, *noun*.
[from Latin]

sustain *verb*
1. to support or bear the weight of: 'will this chair *sustain* my weight?'.
Usages:
a) 'it's hard to *sustain* a conversation with her' (= maintain).
b) 'the court *sustained* my claim' (= upheld).
2. to suffer or undergo: 'the victim *sustained* a broken arm'.
[from Latin]

sustenance (*say* **sus**ta-nence) *noun*
a) a means of sustaining life, especially food. b) the act of sustaining.

sutra (*say* **soo**-tra) *noun*
any of various writings on ritual, spiritual, philosophical or scientific subjects in various Eastern religions, such as Buddhism.
[Sanskrit, thread, rule]

suture (*say* **soo**-cher) *noun*
Medicine: a) the joining of the edges of a cut or wound by stitching. b) the thread, wire or material used to do this.
[from Latin]

svelte (*say* svelt) *adjective*
slender and graceful.
[French]

swab (*say* swob) **swob** *noun*
1. *Medicine:* a) a small piece of fabric used to wipe away fluids, apply medication or take samples of bodily secretions for analysis. b) the sample taken.
2. a large mop used to clean floors, etc.
swab *verb*
(swabbed, swabbing)
1. to clean with or as if with a swab.
2. to take specimens with a swab.

swaddle (*say* **swodd**'l) *verb*
to wrap or bind with long strips of cloth.

swag *noun*
1. *Australian:* a roll or bundle containing the possessions of a bush traveller, miner, etc.
2. (*informal*) stolen goods.
Word Family: **swagman**, *noun*, a) a tramp, b) a person who carries a swag.

swagger *verb*
to walk or strut proudly or smugly.
Word Family: **swagger**, *noun*; **swaggeringly**, *adverb*.

swain *noun*
an old word for a young, rustic lover.
[Old English, swineherd]

swallow (1) (*say* **swollo**) *verb*
a) to take food, etc. into the stomach through the throat. b) to move the throat muscles to do, or as if doing, this.
Usages:
a) 'the clouds *swallowed* the mountain completely' (= enveloped, made disappear).
b) 'it was an insult I could not *swallow*' (= accept).
c) '*swallow* your fears and follow us' (= suppress).
Word Family: **swallow**, *noun*, a) the act of swallowing, b) the amount swallowed at one time.

swallow (2) (*say* **swollo**) *noun*
any of various long-winged, graceful, migrating birds which catch insects while flying.

swallow dive
a dive performed with the arms extended until near the water.

swallow-hole *noun*
see SINKHOLE.

swam *verb*
the past tense of the verb **swim**.

swami (*say* **swah**-mee) *noun*
Hinduism: a title for a religious teacher.
[Hindi, master]

swamp (*say* swomp) *noun*
also called a **marsh**
an area of soft, permanently wet ground, often with coarse grasses.
swamp *verb*
to flood or soak with water.
Usage: 'the firm was *swamped* with orders' (= overwhelmed).
Word Family: **swampy**, *adjective.*

swan (*say* swon) *noun*
a large, graceful bird of the duck family with a long, slender neck.

swank, swanky *adjective*
(*informal*) smart or stylish.

swan song
the last work or creation of an artist, etc. before his death.
[from the legend that a dying swan sings sweetly]

swap (*say* swop) **swop** *verb*
(swapped, swapping)
to exchange one thing for another.
Word Family: **swap,** *noun.*

sward *noun*
short form of **greensward**
an old word for a lawn.

swarm (1) *noun*
a) a large group of bees or other insects moving together. b) any large group of people or things in motion.
swarm *verb*
to move in large numbers: 'crowds *swarmed* to the beach in the hot weather'.
Usage: 'the beaches were *swarming* with swimmers' (= abounding).

swarm (2) *verb*
to climb a rope, etc. by clasping it with the hands and legs and pulling oneself up.

swarthy (*say* **swor**-*thee*) *adjective*
having a dark complexion.
Word Family: **swarthiness,** *noun.*

swashbuckler (*say* **swosh**-bukla) *noun*
a daring or showy swordsman.

swastika (*say* **swos**tikka) *noun*
an ancient symbol comprising a regular cross with its arms extended and bent at right angles in a clockwise direction, and adopted by the Nazi Party as its symbol.
[Sanskrit *svasti* well-being]

swat (*say* swot) *verb*
(swatted, swatting)
to hit, e.g. flies, with a sharp blow.
Word Family: **swat,** *noun,* a sharp blow; **swatter,** *noun.*

swatch (*say* swotch) *noun*
a small sample of a fabric.

swath *noun*
also called a **swathe**
a row of grass or grain cut by a scythe or machine.
Usage: 'the police charge cut a *swath* through the crowd' (= path, broad strip).

swathe (*say* sway*th*) *verb*
to wrap or bind in or as if in bandages: 'the baby was absolutely *swathed* in clothes'.
swathe *noun*
a swath.

sway *verb*
1. to swing or cause to swing from side to side: a) 'she was *swaying* from exhaustion'; b) 'a breath of wind *swayed* the trees'.
2. to influence or exert control over: 'the passionate speech *swayed* the voters'.
Word Family: **sway,** *noun,* a) a swaying motion, b) any rule, control or influence; **swayingly,** *adverb.*

sway-back *noun*
a sagging back, especially in horses, caused by an excessive bend in the spinal column.
Word Family: **sway-backed,** *adjective.*

swear (*say* swair) *verb*
(swore, sworn, swearing)
1. to promise or declare solemnly: 'he *swore* he'd be on time'.
2. *Law:* to take or cause to take an oath to tell the truth.
3. to curse or utter blasphemous or obscene oaths.
Phrases:
swear by, (*informal*) 'he *swears by* that remedy' (= has complete confidence in).
swear in, 'the President was *sworn in* at an official ceremony' (= admitted to office by taking an oath).
swear off, (*informal*) 'he's *sworn off* alcohol for life' (= promised to give up).
sworn enemies, irreconcilable enemies.
sworn friends, devout friends.
Word Family: **swearer,** *noun*; **swearword,** *noun,* a word used as a curse or obscene oath.

sweat (*say* swet) *verb*
1. to excrete a watery substance through the pores in an attempt to

reduce body temperature. Also called to **perspire**.

Usage: 'the damp concrete wall was *sweating* moisture' (= giving off in droplets).

2. (*informal*) a) to work very hard: 'I really *sweated* over that assignment'. b) to worry or suffer: 'he made me *sweat* for three weeks before he told me the job was mine'.

Phrases:

sweat blood, to work very hard.

sweat it out, (*informal*) to wait anxiously or helplessly.

sweat *noun*

1. the salty fluid secreted through the sweat glands.

2. the act or state of sweating: 'he brought the horse back in a *sweat*'.

3. (*informal*) a state of impatience or worry: 'there's no need to get into a *sweat*'.

no sweat, (*informal*) no difficulty at all.

sweated *adjective*

employed in hard work for low wages: '*sweated* labour was rife in 19th-century Britain'.

Word Family: **sweaty**, *adjective*; **sweatily**, *adverb*; **sweatiness**, *noun*.

sweater (*say* swetta) *noun*

a knitted jumper.

sweat gland

Anatomy: any of numerous small glands which secrete moisture and help to maintain a constant body temperature. They are most abundant on the palms of the hands, soles of the feet, and in the armpits.

sweatshirt *noun*

a loose, collarless jumper worn by athletes, etc.

sweatshop (*say* swet-shop) *noun*

a factory or workshop where employees work very long hours, often in unpleasant conditions and for low wages.

sweaty *adjective*

Word Family: see SWEAT.

swede *noun*

a white root related to the turnip and used as a vegetable.

sweep *verb*

(swept, sweeping)

to clean or clear with or as if with a broom: a) 'he *swept* the floor'; b) 'the king promised to *sweep* the seas of pirates'.

Usages:

a) 'her dress *swept* the floor as she walked' (= touched lightly).

b) 'his eyes *swept* over the page' (= passed quickly).

c) 'the floods *swept* away houses and trees' (= carried).

d) 'the road *sweeps* along the coast' (= extends, follows).

Phrases:

be swept off one's feet, to be overwhelmed by emotion or enthusiasm.

sweep under the carpet, to conceal or cover up a problem, incident, etc.

sweep *noun*

1. the act of sweeping: 'give the room a *sweep*'.

Usages:

a) 'with a *sweep* of his arm he cleared his desk' (= long stroke or movement).

b) 'we surveyed the long *sweep* of coastline' (= unbroken stretch).

c) 'listen to the *sweep* of the wind over the plains' (= uninterrupted movement).

2. a person who cleans soot, etc. from chimneys.

3. a form of gambling, usually on the result of a horserace, where tickets representing all the horses are sold and the money paid in becomes the prize money for the winners. Short form of **sweepstake**.

make a clean sweep of, to get rid of or reorganize completely.

sweeping *adjective*

of wide range: 'a *sweeping* generalization'.

Usage: 'a *sweeping* victory' (= decisive).

Word Family: **sweeper**, *noun*, a person or thing that sweeps; **sweepingly**, *adverb*.

sweepback *noun*

the angle formed by aeroplane wings which slant backwards.

sweet *adjective*

1. having the pleasant taste of sugar: 'I don't like my coffee too *sweet*'.

2. pleasant to the senses, feelings or mind: 'the *sweet* sounds of birds singing'.

3. having or showing a pleasant disposition: 'she is a *sweet* girl'.

Phrases:

keep someone sweet, to stay on the right side of someone.

sweet on, (*informal*) fond of.

sweet *noun*
1. a small piece of food which contains a large amount of sugar, such as a chocolate, toffee, etc.
2. (*often plural*) dessert.
Word Family: **sweet, sweetly,** *adverbs*; **sweetness,** *noun*; **sweeten,** *verb,* to make sweet; **sweetening, sweetener,** *nouns,* something that sweetens.

sweetbread *noun*
the pancreas of an animal, usually calf or lamb.

sweet corn
the small, yellow kernels of maize, especially when removed from the cob and eaten as a vegetable.

sweeten *verb*
Word Family: see SWEET.

sweetheart (*say* **sweet**-hart) *noun*
a lover.

sweetmeat *noun*
an old word for any sweet food.

sweetness *noun*
Word Family: see SWEET.

sweet pea
a climbing garden plant with fragrant, brightly coloured, pea-shaped flowers.

sweet potato
the edible root of a vine.

sweet tooth
(*informal*) a great liking for sweet foods.

sweet william
a garden plant with coloured flowers which form in dense, rounded clusters.

swell *verb*
(**swelled, swelled** or **swollen, swelling**)
1. to become or cause to become greater in size, force, intensity, etc.: a) 'the wood *swelled* after being saturated in the rain'; b) 'the noise *swelled* until it was unbearable'.
2. to cause to protrude: 'the wind *swelled* the sails'.
swell *noun*
1. a) the act of swelling: 'there was a *swell* in the music'. b) the condition of being enlarged in size, force, etc.
2. a regular, undulating movement of the surface of the sea.
3. (*informal*) a distinguished person, or one very fashionably dressed: 'he was all dressed up and looking like a *swell*'.
swell *adjective*
(*informal*) a) fashionable or stylish: 'a *swell* hotel'. b) excellent or first-rate: 'what a *swell* idea'.

swelling *noun*
1. a swollen part: 'I'm worried about this *swelling* on my knee'.
2. an increase in size.

swelled head
(*informal*) an excessively high opinion of oneself.
Word Family: **swollen-headed,** *adjective.*

swelter *verb*
to suffer from oppressive heat: 'I always *swelter* during summer'.
Word Family: **sweltering,** *adjective,* a) suffering from oppressive heat, b) oppressively hot and humid; **swelteringly,** *adverb.*

swept *verb*
the past tense and past participle of the verb **sweep.**

swerve *verb*
to turn aside suddenly or sharply from a course or purpose.
Word Family: **swerve,** *noun.*

swift *adjective*
1. moving or performing movements in a brief time: a) 'we caught a *swift* train'; b) 'her *swift* fingers moved across the loom'.
2. prompt or ready: 'he's always been very *swift* to anger'.
swift *noun*
any of various small, fast-flying birds similar to the swallow.
Word Family: **swiftly,** *adverb*; **swiftness,** *noun.*

swig *verb*
(**swigged, swigging**)
(*informal*) to take a deep drink: 'he was *swigging* from the bottle'.
Word Family: **swig,** *noun.*

swill *noun*
1. a rinse: 'give the barrel a good *swill* out with water'.
2. a mixture of liquid and solid food, especially as a food for pigs.
Word Family: **swill,** *verb,* a) to drink greedily or excessively, b) to rinse.

swim *verb*
(**swam, swum, swimming**)
1. to move or cause to move through water by movements of the arms, legs, fins, etc.: a) 'everyone should learn to *swim*'; b) 'he *swam* across the flooded river'.
2. to seem to whirl: a) 'the room *swam* before his eyes'; b) 'my head is *swimming* and I feel sick'.
Usages:
a) 'I don't like my meat to be *swimming* in gravy' (= immersed, floating).

b) 'his eyes were *swimming* with tears' (= overflowing).
swim with the stream, tide, etc., to follow the fashion or majority.
swim *noun*
the act of swimming.
in the swim, (*informal*) actively taking part in social activities, current affairs, etc.
Word Family: **swimmer**, *noun*, a person who swims; **swimmingly**, *adverb*, easily or with great success.

swim bladder
a bladder containing gas, present in the abdomen of fish.

swimsuit *noun*
a garment worn when bathing.

swindle *verb*
to cheat someone out of money or property.
Word Family: **swindle**, *noun*; **swindler**, *noun*, a person who swindles. [from German]

swine *noun*
1. an old word for pigs.
2. (*informal*) a brutish, stupid, vicious or greedy person.
Word Family: **swinish**, *adjective*; **swinishly**, *adverb*.

swing *verb*
(swung, swinging)
1. to move or cause to move back and forth in a regular motion, such as something suspended from above: a) 'the pendulum *swung* evenly'; b) 'he *swung* his arms as he walked'.
2. to pivot: 'a gate *swings* on its hinges'.
3. to move or cause to move in a circular or sweeping motion: a) 'he *swung* his sword above his head'; b) 'the car *swung* round the corner'.
Usages:
a) 'he *swings* from one opinion to another' (= fluctuates).
b) (*informal*) 'I'm trying to *swing* a big deal with the oil company' (= complete successfully).
c) (*informal*) 'I want to go somewhere that really *swings*' (= is lively and modern).
swing the lead, to malinger.
swing *noun*
1. a swinging movement: 'a golfer's *swing*'.
2. a) a seat suspended from above, on which children swing to and fro. b) a ride on such a swing.
3. a swinging gait or movement: 'a rollicking old song that goes with a *swing*'.
4. *Music:* a form of dance music popular after 1935, based on jazz rhythms.
Phrases:
get into the swing of, to become familiar with or active in something.
go with a swing, to be lively.
in full swing, 'production will be *in full swing* by April' (= in full operation).
Word Family: **swinger**, *noun*, a) a person or thing that swings, b) (informal) a lively, modern person; **swinging** *adjective*, (informal) lively or modern.

swing bridge
a bridge, part of which is pivoted in the centre and may be turned horizontally, to allow boats, etc. to pass.

swing-wing *adjective*
(of an aeroplane) having the wings pivoted at the fuselage so that they may be swept back to varying degrees to suit the aeroplane's speed.

swinish (*say* **swine**-ish) *adjective*
Word Family: see SWINE.

swipe *noun*
a long, sweeping blow or stroke: 'the batsman made a *swipe* at the ball'.
swipe *verb*
1. to hit with a sweeping blow.
2. (*informal*) to steal.

swirl *verb*
to move or cause to move in a twisting or whirling motion: 'the leaves *swirled* around the foot of the tree'.
Word Family: **swirl**, *noun*; **swirly**, *adjective*.

swish *verb*
1. to move through the air with a hissing or whistling sound: 'the horse *swished* its tail'.
2. (of clothes) to rustle.
Word Family: **swish**, *noun*, a swishing sound or movement; **swish**, *adjective*, (informal) smart or fashionable.

switch *noun*
1. any device for opening, closing or directing an electric circuit.
2. *Railways:* see POINT.
3. a turning, shifting or changing: 'a *switch* of voters' preferences'.
4. a long, separate lock of hair fastened together at one end and used to add to a hairstyle.
5. a flexible rod or cane, used for whipping.
6. (*informal*) a switchboard.

switch *verb*
1. to connect or disconnect by a switch: '*switch* off that fan'.
2. to shift, change or divert: a) 'let's *switch* the conversation to something else'; b) 'the train was *switched* to another track'.
3. to exchange: 'let's *switch* rooms for a week'.
4. to swing or lash: 'the cow *switched* her tail'.
Word Family: **switcher,** *noun.*

switchback *noun*
1. an undulating road.
2. a roller–coaster.
3. a zigzag railway or road climbing a steep incline.

switchblade *noun*
see FLICK–KNIFE.

switchboard *noun*
Electricity: a panel containing switches for connecting and disconnecting electrical circuits, e.g. in a telephone exchange.

swivel (*say* **swivv**'l) *noun*
a link, pivot or other fitting which allows one section of two attached parts to turn independently of the other, e.g. in a **swivel chair,** where the seat revolves without revolving the base.
Word Family: **swivel (swivelled, swivelling),** *verb,* to turn on or as if on a swivel.

swizz, swiz *noun*
(*informal*) a) a disappointment. b) deception or fraud.

swizzle stick
a small stick used to make fizzy drinks less or more fizzy.

swob *noun*
see SWAB.

swollen (*say* **swole**–en) *verb*
a past participle of the verb **swell.**

swollen–headed *adjective*
Word Family: see SWELLED HEAD.

swoon *verb*
to faint.
Word Family: **swoon,** *noun.*

swoop *verb*
1. to descend upon suddenly: 'the eagle *swooped* down on the rabbit'.
2. to take or seize suddenly: 'he *swooped* up his trophy and marched out of the room'.
swoop *noun*
a swooping movement.
at one fell swoop, all at once.

swop *verb*
see SWAP.

sword (*say* sord) *noun*
a weapon with a long, sharp blade and a handle.
Phrases:
cross swords, to disagree violently.
put to the sword, to massacre.
Word Family: **swordsman,** *noun,* a person who is trained or skilled in the use of a sword; **swordsmanship,** *noun.*

swordfish *noun*
any of a group of large, edible, marine fish with the upper jaw elongated into a sword–like weapon.

swore *verb*
the past tense of the verb **swear.**
sworn *verb*
the past participle of the verb **swear.**

swot *verb*
(swotted, swotting)
(*informal*) to study hard, especially for examinations.
swot up, (*informal*) to learn or memorize.
Word Family: **swot,** *noun,* a) a person who studies hard, b) hard work or study.
[for SWEAT]

swum *verb*
the past participle of the verb **swim.**

swung *verb*
the past tense and past participle of the verb **swing.**

sybarite (*say* **sibba**–rite) *noun*
a person who is fond of luxury and pleasure.
[after *Sybaris* in southern Italy, noted in ancient times for luxury]

sycamore (*say* **sikka**–mor) *noun*
a variety of European maple.
[Greek *sykon* fig + *moron* mulberry]

sycophant (*say* **sikka**–fant) *noun*
a servile flatterer.
Word Family: **sycophantic** (*say* sikka–**fan**tik), *adjective*; **sycophancy** (*say* **sikka**–fan–see), *noun.*
[Greek *sykophantes* an informer]

syllable (*say* **silla**–b'l) *noun*
Language: the smallest unit of speech, consisting of a vowel sound with or without one or more consonant sounds. *Example:* asleep (*say* a–sleep) contains two syllables.
Word Family: **syllabic** (*say* sil–**labbik**), *adjective,* of, relating to or consisting of a syllable or syllables.

[Greek *syllabé* something held together]

syllabus (*say* **sill**a-bus) *noun*
plural is **syllabuses** or **syllabi**
the set programme of a course of study.
[Greek *sittyba* a label]

syllogism (*say* **sill**a-jizm) *noun*
Logic: an argument with two premises from which a conclusion is drawn. *Example*: all birds can fly; seagulls are birds; therefore seagulls can fly.
Word Family: **syllogistic** (*say* silla-**jis**tik), *adjective*; **syllogistically,** *adverb.*
[Greek *syn-* together + *logizesthai* to reason]

sylph (*say* silf) *noun*
1. a spirit of the air.
2. a slender, graceful young woman.
Word Family: **sylphid** (*say* **sil**-fid), *noun*, a young or small sylph.
[from Greek]

sylvan (*say* **sil**-v'n) *adjective*
also spelt **silvan**
of or relating to woods or forests.

symbiosis (*say* simbi-**o**-sis) *noun*
Biology: the living together of two types of organisms for their mutual benefit.
Word Family: **symbiotic** (*say* simbi-**ott**ik), *adjective*; **symbiotically,** *adverb.*
[Greek]

symbol (*say* **sim**-b'l) *noun*
something which is used to suggest or represent something else: 'a dove is a *symbol* of peace'.
Word Family: **symbolic** (*say* sim-**boll**ik), *adjective*; **symbolically,** *adverb*; **symbolize** (*say* **sim**ba-lize), **symbolise,** *verb*, a) to be a symbol of, b) to represent by a symbol or symbols.
[Greek *symbolon* a token]

symbolism (*say* **sim**ba-lizm) *noun*
1. the use of symbols to denote relationships, objects, emotions, etc. as in art and literature.
2. the symbolic meaning or significance of something.

symmetry (*say* **sim**ma-tree) *noun*
1. an exact correspondence between the opposite halves of a figure, form, line, pattern, etc., on either side of an axis or centre.
2. a balance or proportion between parts of a whole, etc., e.g. in a painting or sculpture.
Word Family: **symmetrical** (*say* sim**met**ri-k'l), *adjective*; **symmetrically,** *adverb.*
[Greek *sym-* together + *metron* a measure]

sympathetic string
Music: (in stringed instruments) a string which is not played but which vibrates in resonance with another string.

sympathy (*say* **simp**a-thee) *noun*
1. the capacity for sharing the feelings of others.
2. a feeling or expression of pity, etc. for another person's distress or suffering.
Usage: 'we are in *sympathy* on many of the issues' (= agreement).
Word Family: **sympathetic** (*say* simpa-**thett**ik), *adjective*; **sympathetically,** *adverb*; **sympathize, sympathise,** *verb*, to feel or express sympathy for; **sympathizer,** *noun.*
[Greek *sym-* together + *pathos* feeling]

symphonic poem
see TONE POEM.

symphony (*say* **sim**fa-nee) *noun*
1. *Music:* a long, serious, orchestral composition, usually having four movements.
2. (*informal*) a symphony orchestra.
Word Family: **symphonic** (*say* sim-**fonn**ik), *adjective*, of or having the character of a symphony.
[Greek *sym-* together + *phoné* sound]

symphony orchestra
a large orchestra designed to play symphonies.

symposium (*say* sim-**po**-zee-um) *noun*
plural is **symposia**
a) a meeting to discuss a particular topic. b) a collection of writings by different authors on the same subject.
[Greek *symposion* a drinks party]

symptom (*say* **simp**-t'm) *noun*
1. *Medicine:* an observable change in bodily or mental condition that indicates the presence of disease.
2. a sign of the existence of something: 'the riots were the most obvious *symptoms* of social unrest'.
Word Family: **symptomatic** (*say* simpta-**matt**ik), *adjective*, serving as a symptom of; **symptomatically,** *adverb.*
[from Greek]

synagogue (*say* **sinn**a-gog) *noun*
a) a regular assembly of Jews for worship and religious instruction. b)

a building where such an assembly is held.
[Greek *synagogé* a meeting]

synapse (*say* **sigh**–naps) *noun*
Biology: the region where two or more nerve cells meet and across which an impulse passes.
[Greek *syn–* together + *hapsis* a join]

synchromesh (*say* **sinkro**–mesh) *noun*
a system used in the gearbox of a motor vehicle, in which the gears are made to spin at the same speed before being engaged.
[for SYNCHRO(nized) MESH]

synchronize (*say* **sinkra**–nize)
synchronise *verb*
1. a) to occur at the same time: 'his arrival *synchronized* with my departure'. b) to make agree in time: 'they *synchronized* their watches'.
2. to move or take place at the same rate or exactly together: 'the soundtrack was not *synchronized* with the picture'.
Word Family: **synchronization**, *noun.*

synchronous (*say* **sinkra**–nus)
adjective
occurring at the same time or in the same phase as.
synchronous orbit
the orbit of a satellite which causes the satellite to stay over one spot on the earth.
Word Family: **synchronously**, *adverb.*
[Greek *syn–* together + *khronos* time]

syncline (*say* **sin**–kline) *noun*
Geology: a downward curve in layers of folded rock. Compare ANTICLINE.
Word Family: **synclinal** (*say* sin–**klie**–n'l), *adjective.*
[Greek *syn–* together + *klinein* to slope]

syncopate (*say* **sinko**–pate) *verb*
1. *Music:* to place the stress on beats that are normally unstressed.
2. *Grammar:* to shorten a word by omitting certain syllables. *Example: synchromesh* for *synchronized mesh.*
Word Family: **syncopation**, *noun.*
[Latin *syn–* together + *koptein* to cut off]

syndicate (*say* **sindi**–kit) *noun*
a combination of individuals or companies to carry out a project, usually commercial, such as a newspaper organization which sells news or an article to several publications at once.
Word Family: **syndicate** (*say* **sindi**–kate), *verb*; **syndication**, *noun.*
[Greek *syn–* together + *diké* justice]

syndrome (*say* **sin**–drome) *noun*
1. a set of symptoms and signs typically found together and associated with a particular disease or psychological disorder.
2. a distinctive pattern of behaviour.
[Greek *syndromé* a running together]

synergism, synergy (*say* **sinna**–jizm *and* **sinna**–jee) *noun*
the joint action of two substances, organs or organisms to achieve an effect of which each is incapable alone.
[Greek *synergos* working together]

synod (*say* **sinnod**) *noun*
a council, especially of clergymen to conduct church business.
[Greek *synodos* an assembly]

synonym (*say* **sinna**–nim) *noun*
a word with the same or a similar meaning to another: 'happy is a *synonym* of glad'. Compare ANTONYM.
[Greek *syn–* together + *onyma* name]

synonymous (*say* se–**nonni**–mus)
adjective
expressing or suggesting the same idea: a) 'these two words are *synonymous*'; b) 'our company's name is *synonymous* with good value'.
Word Family: **synonymously**, *adverb.*

synopsis (*say* se–**nopsis**) *noun*
a summary, especially of the plot of a novel, play, etc.
[Greek, a general view]

synoptic chart
see WEATHER MAP.

syntax (*say* **sin**–taks) *noun*
Grammar: the arrangement and interrelationships of words in phrases and sentences.
Word Family: **syntactic** (*say* sin–**taktik**), **syntactical**, *adjective.*
[Greek *syn–* together + *tassein* to arrange]

synthesis (*say* **sintha**–sis) *noun*
the combination of parts or elements into a complex whole. Compare ANALYSIS.
Word Family: **synthesize**, **synthesise**, *verb*, to make up by combining parts or elements.
[Greek]

synthesizer (*say* **sintha**–size–a)
synthesiser *noun*
an electronic device consisting of a keyboard which is programmed by a computer to make music.

synthetic (*say* sin–**thet**tik) *adjective*
1. artificially made: '*synthetic* rubber'.
2. produced by synthesis.
Word Family: **synthetically**, *adverb.*

syphilis (*say* **siffi**–lis) *noun*
a venereal disease which develops in stages and, if untreated, can eventually affect many parts of the body.
Word Family: **syphilitic** (*say* siffi–**lit**tik), *adjective*, relating to or affected with syphilis; **syphilitic**, *noun*, a person suffering from syphilis.
[the name of a character in a Latin poem, 1530, who was a victim of it]

syphon *noun*
see SIPHON.

syringe (*say* se–**rinj**) *noun*
Medicine: a hollow tube with a piston which can be fitted on to a hypodermic needle and used to inject fluids into, or withdraw them from, the body.
Word Family: **syringe**, *verb*, to cleanse or inject by means of a syringe.
[Greek *syringos* a (musical) pipe]

syrup (*say* **sir**rup) *noun*
a thick, sweet liquid made by boiling sugar, water and often flavouring.
Word Family: **syrupy** (*say* **sirra**–pee), *adjective.*
[Arabic *sharab* a drink]

system (*say* **sis**–t'm) *noun*
1. a group of things or parts forming a whole: a) 'a railway *system*'; b) 'the digestive *system*'.
2. an organized group of ideas, principles, beliefs, etc.: a) 'a *system* of philosophy'; b) 'a *system* of government'.
Usages:
a) 'there's no *system* in the way he works' (= organized basis).
b) 'a new *system* of marking exams' (= procedure).
c) 'your whole *system* is run–down and you need a holiday' (= body).
the System
(*informal*) the network of established institutions which controls a country, regarded as suppressing any attempt to change it.
systematic (*say* sista–**mat**tik) *adjective*
1. according to a system: 'a *systematic* search'.
2. arranged in a system.
Word Family: **systematically**, *adverb*; **systematize** (*say* **sist**'ma–tize), **systematise**, *verb*, to arrange in or according to a system; **systemization**, *noun.*
[Greek *systema* a setting together]

systemic (*say* sis–**tee**mik) *adjective*
of or relating to a system as a whole.

systems analysis
the use of maths to predict future behaviour in various circumstances of complex groups of related objects or persons, of value in planning or designing automation, transport systems, ballistic missiles, etc.

systole (*say* **sis**ta–lee) *noun*
Biology: the rhythmical contraction phase of the heartbeat. Compare DIASTOLE.
Word Family: **systolic** (*say* sis–**tol**lik), *adjective.*
[Greek]

Tt

ta *interjection*
(*informal*) thank you.

tab *noun*
1. a small flap or loop on a garment, etc.
2. (*informal*) a bill, e.g. in a restaurant.
keep tabs on, (*informal*) to keep a check on.

tabard (*say* **tabbud**) *noun*
a loose outer garment worn in medieval times.

tabasco *noun*
a very hot sauce made from capsicums.
[name of a Mexican state]

tabby cat
a cat with a striped or brindled coat.

tabernacle (*say* **tabba**–nak'l) *noun*
Religion: a) a place of worship. b) an ornamental recess or cabinet for consecrated bread and wine at the Eucharist.
[Latin *tabernaculum* tent, booth]

table *noun*
1. a piece of furniture which has a flat top and is supported by legs.
2. the food placed on a table to be eaten.
3. a) an orderly arrangement of data, usually shown in rows and columns. b) a sequential listing of the multiples of any number: 'Tony did not know his seven times *table*'.
turn the tables, to cause a complete reversal of circumstances.
table *verb*
1. to place on a table: 'to *table* one's cards'.
2. *Parliament:* to place a resolution, proposal, etc. on the table for discussion.
[Latin *tabula* a plank]

tableau (*say* **tab**–lo) *noun*
plural is **tableaux** (*say* **tab**–lo)
a colourful scene, e.g. one represented by a group of actors in period costume.
[French]

table d'hôte (*say* **tahbla** dote)
a meal at a fixed price and offering no or limited choice of dishes. Compare À LA CARTE.
[French, the host's (choice of) food]

tableland *noun*
see PLATEAU.

table linen
the cloth, serviettes, etc. used at meals.

table napkin
a serviette.

tablespoon *noun*
a large oval spoon used to serve or measure food.

tablet (*say* **tab**–l't) *noun*
1. a) any small, round, solid preparation containing a medicine, etc. b) a piece of some prepared substance, such as soap.
2. a slab of stone, etc. bearing an inscription.
3. a pad of paper, especially writing paper.

table tennis
also called **ping-pong**
a miniature game of tennis, played on a table using small cork or wooden bats and a light plastic ball.

tableware *noun*
the crockery and cutlery used at meals.

tabloid (*say* **tab**–loyd) *noun*
1. a small newspaper, about 40 cm long and 30 cm wide, which usually emphasizes pictures and popular features.
2. something compressed or condensed.

taboo (*say* ta–**boo**) *adjective*
also spelt **tabu**
1. being banned by social custom: 'sex is a *taboo* topic in some homes'.
2. excluded from use, approach or mention because of the sacred quality of an object, etc.
Word Family: **taboo,** *noun.*
[Polynesian]

tabor (*say* **tay**–ba) *noun*
Music: a small drum struck with the fingers.
[Persian *tabira* a drum]

tabular (*say* **tab**–yoo–la) *adjective*
1. arranged as a table or list.
2. having the form of a table or tablet.

tabulate (*say* **tab**–yoo–late) *verb*
1. to arrange information in a table.
2. to operate or set the tabulator on a typewriter.
Word Family: **tabulation,** *noun.*

tabulator *noun*
1. a person or thing that tabulates.
2. a device on a typewriter which moves the carriage a set number of spaces each time it is pressed.

tachometer (*say* ta–**kommita**) *noun*
an instrument used to measure the rate at which something, such as an engine, is turning.
[Greek *takhos* speed + –METER]

tacit (*say* **tassit**) *adjective*
implied but not spoken.
Word Family: **tacitly,** *adverb*; **tacitness,** *noun.*
[Latin *tacitus* silent]

taciturn (*say* **tassi**–tern) *adjective*
saying very little.
Word Family: **taciturnly,** *adverb*; **taciturnity** (*say* tassi–**terni**–tee), *noun.*

tack *noun*
1. a short sharp nail with a large flat head.
2. a long loose stitch used to fasten seams in preparation for more thorough sewing.
3. *Sailing:* the direction in which a boat is moving.
Usage: 'this has not worked so let's try a different *tack*' (= course, approach).
4. all the equipment, such as saddles, bridles, etc. used for horseriding.
tack *verb*
1. to fasten or attach with a tack.
2. to sew with long, loose stitches. Also called to **baste.**
3. to sail a boat in a series of zigzags.
tack on, to add.

tackle *noun*
1. any equipment, especially the rods, reels, etc. used in fishing.
2. see BLOCK AND TACKLE.
3. the act of tackling, e.g. in football.
tackle *verb*
to try to seize and pull down by force.
Usage: 'let's *tackle* the problem together' (= try to deal with).

tacky *adjective*
sticky or slightly adhesive to the touch.
Word Family: **tackiness,** *noun.*

tact *noun*
the ability to appreciate the delicate or difficult nature of a situation and handle it without giving offence.
Word Family: **tactful,** *adjective,* showing tact; **tactfully,** *adverb*; **tactless,** *adjective,* lacking tact; **tactlessly,** *adverb*; **tactlessness,** *noun.*
[Latin *tactus* sense of touch]

tactic (*say* **tak**–tik) *noun*
(*usually plural*) a plan or procedure for achieving a desired end, especially for limited objectives, e.g. on a sector of a battle front.
tactical *adjective*
(of weapons, bombing, etc.) intended or used to achieve small-scale local objectives. Compare STRATEGIC.
Word Family: **tactically,** *adverb*; **tactician** (*say* tak–**tish**'n), *noun,* a person experienced in using tactics in the army, etc.
[Greek *taktos* arranged]

tactile (*say* **tak**–tile) *adjective*
a) of or relating to the sense of touch.
b) able to be felt through touch.
[Latin *tactus* touched]

tadpole *noun*
the stage after the egg in the development of a frog before the growth of forelimbs and when it still has a tail.
[Middle English *tadde* toad + *poll* head]

taffeta (*say* **taffi**–ta) *noun*
a thin, smooth, rather stiff fabric of shot silk, nylon, etc.
[from Persian]

tag (1) *noun*
1. a strip of paper, metal, etc. attached to something as a label.
2. a) a word applied as characteristic of a person. b) an often quoted phrase, especially one from another language.
3. the hard substance at the end of a cord, shoelace, etc.
tag *verb*
(tagged, tagging)
1. to attach a tag to.
2. to follow closely.

tag (2) *noun*
1. *Wrestling:* a match between two teams of two, in which only one of a team is allowed in the ring at a time.
2. a children's game in which one person chases the other players until he touches someone who then becomes the chaser.
Word Family: **tag (tagged, tagging),** *verb.*

tail *noun*
1. a) the hind part of an animal, especially when elongated and extending beyond the main part of the body. b) something which has the shape or position of a tail: 'the *tail* of a comet'.
2. the bottom or concluding part of anything: 'the story had a sting in its *tail*'.
3. *Dress:* (*plural*) a coat with a short front and two long tapering flaps at the back, worn on formal occasions. Short form of **tail coat**.
4. (*informal*) a) the buttocks. b) a person who follows another.
5. (*usually plural*) the side of a coin which does not bear the image of a head.
tail *verb*
(*informal*) to follow and watch someone.
tail off, to decrease gradually.
Word Family: **tail**, *adjective*, being or coming from behind; **tail-less**, *adjective*, having no tail.

tailgate *noun*
also called a **tailboard**
a door or gate at the rear of an estate car, etc., which may be folded open for loading or unloading the vehicle.

tailings *plural noun*
the waste material removed during the processing of mineral ores.

tail-light *noun*
a red light at the back of a motor vehicle.

tailor *noun*
a person who makes clothes, especially for men.
Word Family: **tailor**, *verb*, a) to make, adapt or fit clothes, b) to adjust, adapt or make for a specific purpose.
[French *tailler* to cut]

tailor-made *adjective*
1. made by a tailor.
2. designed for a particular need.

tailshaft *noun*
also called a **driveshaft**
a spinning shaft which transmits power from the gearbox to the differential of a motor vehicle.

tail spin
the steep, spinning descent of a stalled aircraft.

tailwind *noun*
a wind blowing in the same direction as a vehicle is travelling, thus increasing its speed. Compare HEADWIND.

taint *verb*
1. to affect slightly with something undesirable.
2. to infect or spoil.
Word Family: **taint**, *noun*.

take *verb*
(**took, taken, taking**)
1. to get into one's hands, possession or control: a) '*take* this hammer'; b) 'the army *took* the city'.
2. to catch: a) 'you *took* me by surprise'; b) 'she was *taken* ill last week'.
3. to bring or receive into some relation with oneself: a) 'she was forced to *take* lodgers'; b) 'it's time he *took* a wife'.
4. to adopt: a) 'the god *took* the shape of a bull'; b) 'the nun *took* a vow of silence'.
5. to have recourse to: a) 'he *took* an axe to the tree'; b) 'we *took* shelter under a tree'.
6. to admit or let in: a) 'the boat was *taking* water fast'; b) 'the car *takes* six passengers'.
7. to feel: 'she seems to *take* pleasure in being nasty'.
8. to lead, carry or cause to go to another place: a) 'the bus will *take* you to the city'; b) 'who *took* you to the ball?'.
9. (of an action) to perform, do, etc.: a) 'we *took* a walk'; b) '*take* careful aim'; c) 'he *took* revenge'.
Usages:
a) 'don't *take* his words the wrong way' (= understand, interpret).
b) 'she *took* first prize in both events' (= won).
c) 'it *takes* courage to do what he did' (= requires).
d) 'the seedlings *took*' (= began to grow).
e) 'would you ever *take* a bribe?' (= accept).
f) 'he *took* a nasty beating at the last election' (= underwent).
g) 'if you *take* 3 from 6 you leave 3' (= subtract).
h) 'this fabric will not *take* dye' (= absorb).
i) 'I *took* him to be an honest man' (= considered).
j) (*informal*) 'he was *taken* in the oil deal' (= cheated, swindled).
Phrases:
have what it takes, to have the qualities required for success, etc.
take aback, see ABACK.
take after, to inherit from or resemble in appearance, etc.

take against, 'he's *taken against* her' (= begun to dislike).
take care of, to look after or protect.
take down, to write down.
take in, a) to provide lodging for; b) to make a garment smaller; c) to include; d) to understand; e) to trick or deceive.
take it, 'you're coming too, I *take it*?' (= assume).
take it or leave it, you can accept it or not, it is immaterial to me.
take off, a) 'why don't you *take* an hour *off*?' (= stop working, etc. for); b) to leave the ground; c) (*informal*) to imitate or mimic.
take on, a) to hire; b) to undertake to do something; c) to start a fight with.
take out, a) to remove or extract; b) 'he *took out* a patent on his invention' (= obtained); c) to accompany or escort; d) to vent one's anger, etc.
take over, to assume or acquire control.
take place, to happen or occur.
take to, 'they *took to* each other right away' (= became attracted to).
take up, a) to raise or lift; b) to make a garment shorter or smaller; c) to begin or begin again; d) 'the fridge *takes up* a lot of space' (= uses); e) 'to *take up* a cause' (= espouse); f) 'to *take up* an option' (= accept).
take up with, to begin an association, etc. with.

take *noun*
1. the amount of something taken: 'today's *take* in the shop was £500'.
2. a scene filmed without stopping the camera.
Word Family: **taker**, *noun*, a person who takes, especially one who accepts a bet.

takeaway *noun*
any quick-service food which is eaten off the premises.

take-home pay
the actual money received by an employee, after tax and other payments have been taken out.

take-off *noun*
1. the act of leaving the ground, especially by an aircraft.
2. (*informal*) a satirical imitation.

take-over *noun*
an assuming of control, ownership, etc.

taking *noun*
(*plural*) any receipts, especially of money.

taking *adjective*
pleasing or captivating.

talc *noun*
1. *Geology:* a soft, pale, greenish-grey mineral (hydrous magnesium silicate), used as a lubricant or in talcum powder.
2. talcum powder.
[from Persian]

talcum powder
short form is **talc**
a purified, whitened and perfumed form of talc used on the skin to dry and soothe it.

tale *noun*
1. a story.
2. a) a malicious story. b) a deliberate lie.

talent *noun*
a natural or acquired ability, especially an outstanding one.
Word Family: **talented**, *adjective*, having talent.
[Greek *talanton* a sum of money (through the Biblical phrase 'hiding one's talents')]

talent scout
a person appointed to find and employ people who appear to have talent.

tale-teller, tale-bearer *noun*
a person who spreads malicious stories or gossip.

talisman (*say* **tal**liz-man) *noun*
any object worn because it is supposed to work wonders due to its possessing and transmitting magic powers.
[Greek *telesma* a consecrated object]

talk (*say* tawk) *verb*
to say things or communicate by words: 'we *talked* about her trip'.
Usages:
a) 'people will *talk* if we are seen together' (= gossip).
b) 'the spy was made to *talk*' (= reveal information).
c) 'we must *talk* business' (= discuss).
d) 'I was *talked* into buying a new car by the salesman' (= persuaded).
e) 'now you're *talking*' (= beginning to talk sense).
f) 'you can't *talk* after what you've done' (= criticize).
Phrases:
talk back, to answer impudently.
talk big, (*informal*) to boast.
talk down to, to speak condescendingly to.
talk over, to discuss.

talk *noun*
1. a conversation: 'there was a lot of *talk* about the space launching'.
2. an informal speech: 'he gave a *talk* on wild flowers'.
Usages:
a) 'the scandal has made her the *talk* of the town' (= subject of conversation).
b) 'it will all end in *talk*' (= nothing being done).
Word Family: **talker**, *noun*; **talkative**, *adjective*, inclined to talk a great deal; **talkatively**, *adverb*; **talkativeness**, *noun*.

talkie *noun*
an old word for a film with a soundtrack.

talking-to *noun*
(*informal*) a scolding.

tall *adjective*
1. of more than average height.
2. having a height as specified: 'he's 6 foot *tall*'.
Usages:
a) (*informal*) '*tall* stories' (= unlikely, exaggerated).
b) 'that's a *tall* order for one person to carry out' (= very difficult).
Word Family: **tall** (informal), *adverb*; **tallness**, *noun*.

tallboy *noun*
a chest of drawers mounted on short legs.

tallow (*say* **tal**-o) *noun*
the melted fat of animals, especially cattle and sheep, used to make candles, soap, etc.

tally *noun*
1. a score or account.
2. a stick on which notches were made to keep a count or score.
tally *verb*
(tallied, tallying)
1. to reckon or count.
2. to agree or correspond: 'do their answers *tally*?'.

tally-ho *interjection*
a hunting cry signalling to hounds that a fox has been sighted.
[from French]

Talmud (*say* **tal**-m*u*d) *noun*
the books of traditional Jewish ceremonial and civil laws.
[Hebrew *talmudh* instruction]

talon (*say* **tal**-on) *noun*
a claw, especially of a bird of prey.
[Latin *talus* ankle]

tamable *adjective*
Word Family: see TAME.

tamarind *noun*
a) a tropical tree used for timber. b) the large, edible fruit of this tree, consisting of a long pod with seeds and acid-tasting flesh.
[Arabic *tamr-hindi* Indian date]

tambour *noun*
1. a drum.
2. a frame consisting of two hoops to keep a section of material firm while embroidery is being worked.
[same root as TABOR]

tambourine (*say* tamba-**reen**) *noun*
Music: a small, flat, one-sided drum with small metal plates set in the side, which is hit or shaken to produce sound.

tame *adjective*
changed from the wild or savage state and used to living with human beings.
Usages:
a) 'he has a very *tame* wife who asks no questions' (= docile).
b) 'this story has a *tame* ending' (= dull).
Word Family: **tame**, *verb*; **tamer**, *noun*, a person who tames animals; **tamely**, *adverb*; **tameness**, *noun*; **tamable**, *adjective*, able to be tamed.

tam-o'-shanter (*say* tamma-**shanta**) *noun*
a soft, round cap similar to a beret, first worn in Scotland.

tamp *verb*
to press down or pack closer by firm, repeated blows: '*tamp* down the earth around the base of the seedlings'.

tamper *verb*
to interfere or meddle.
[for TEMPER]

tampon *noun*
Medicine: a) a plug of absorbent material used to stop haemorrhage. b) a similar plug placed in the vagina to absorb blood during menstruation.
[French]

tan (1) *verb*
(tanned, tanning)
1. to make a hide into leather, usually by soaking in any of a variety of substances, such as oak bark.
2. to brown the skin in the sun or with a sunlamp.
3. (*informal*) to beat or thrash.

tan *noun*
1. a light, reddish-brown colour.
2. the brown colour imparted to the skin by the sun's rays.
Word Family: **tan,** *adjective.*

tan (2) *noun*
Maths: see TANGENT.

tandem *adjective, adverb*
one behind the other.
tandem *noun*
see BICYCLE.
[Latin, at length]

tang *noun*
a sharp, distinctive taste, flavour or smell of something.
Word Family: **tangy,** *adjective.*

tangent (*say* **tan**–j'nt) *noun*
1. *Maths:* a) any straight line touching a curve. b) a ratio of the length of the side opposite an angle to the adjacent side of a right-angled triangle. Short form is **tan.** See TRIGONOMETRIC FUNCTIONS.
2. a sudden change of course.
Word Family: **tangential** (*say* tan–**jen**–sh'l), **tangental** (*say* tan–**jen**–t'l), *adjectives,* a) relating to a tangent, b) only partially relevant.
[Latin *tangens* touching]

tangerine (*say* tanja–**reen**) *noun*
1. a type of mandarin.
2. a reddish-orange colour.
Word Family: **tangerine,** *adjective.*
[after *Tangiers,* Morocco]

tangible (*say* **tan**ji–b'l) *adjective*
1. real or definite: 'we need *tangible* evidence, not just theories'.
2. capable of being touched.
Word Family: **tangibly,** *adverb;* **tangibility** (*say* tanji–**billi**–tee), **tangibleness,** *nouns.*

tangible asset
an asset of a business, such as property or chattels. Compare INTANGIBLE ASSET.

tangle *verb*
to intertwine in a confused mass: 'the wool became *tangled* as the cat played with it'.
Usage: 'we became *tangled* in the family quarrel' (= mixed up, involved).
Word Family: **tangle,** *noun.*

tango *noun*
a) a ballroom dance of Spanish-American origin with varied steps and turns. b) the music for such a dance.

tangy *adjective*
Word Family: see TANG.

tank *noun*
1. a large container for holding a liquid or gas.
2. a heavily armoured military vehicle with tracks and a powerful gun.

tankard (*say* **tank**kud) *noun*
a large glass or pewter drinking vessel with a handle and often a hinged lid.

tanked-up *adjective*
(*informal*) intoxicated with alcohol.

tanker *noun*
a ship, aircraft or road vehicle designed to carry liquid, such as oil, in bulk.

tanner (1) *noun*
a person who tans hides.

tanner (2) *noun*
(*informal*) a sixpenny coin.

tannery *noun*
a place where hides and skins are made into leather.

tannin *noun*
any of a group of complex substances found in plants and used in the making of ink and leather.

tanning *noun*
1. the process of converting hides and skins into leather.
2. the process of becoming brown, e.g. by exposure to the sun's rays.
3. (*informal*) a thrashing.

tantalize (*say* **tanta**–lize) **tantalise** *verb*
to tease or torment with, or as if with, something which is desired but out of reach.
Word Family: **tantalizingly,** *adverb;* **tantalization,** *noun;* **tantalizer,** *noun;* **tantalus,** *noun,* a lockable stand for decanters.
[after *Tantulus* in Greek mythology, who was punished by being made to stand in water which receded when he tried to drink, and under fruit-laden boughs which he could not reach]

tantalum (*say* **tanta**–l'm) *noun*
element number 73, a ductile, malleable metal used in alloys, filaments for electric lights and in cemented carbides for very hard tools. See TRANSITION ELEMENT.
See CHEMICAL ELEMENTS in grey pages.

tantamount *adjective*
equivalent in effect, value, force, etc.: 'his manner was *tantamount* to rudeness'.
[Italian *tanto montare* to amount to so much]

tantrum *noun*
a sudden, violent fit of bad temper.

tap (1) *verb*
(tapped, tapping)
to strike gently.
tap *noun*
1. a) a gentle blow. b) the sound this makes.
2. *American Military:* (*plural*) see LAST POST.

tap (2) *noun*
1. any device for controlling the flow of a liquid or gas from a pipe, etc.
2. a plug for a cask, etc.
3. a tool for cutting an internal screw thread.
on tap, a) ready to be drawn off and served, such as beer in a cask; b) ready for immediate use.
tap *verb*
(tapped, tapping)
1. to draw a liquid or gas from a container, etc.
2. a) to open the outlets of: 'to *tap* a water main'. b) to provide with a plug, etc.
Usages:
a) 'the reporter *tapped* all his usual news sources' (= used, drew upon).
b) 'my phone conversation was *tapped*' (= listened to secretly).
3. to make an internal screw thread.

tap dance
a style of dancing in which metal heel and toe plates are attached to the shoes to enable the steps and rhythms to be beaten loudly.
Word Family: **tap-dance**, *verb*, **tap-dancer**, *noun.*

tape *noun*
1. a narrow strip of fabric, paper, etc.
2. *Audio:* a plastic ribbon coated with a magnetic substance and used to record sounds. Short form of **magnetic tape.**
3. a string, etc. stretched across the finishing line in a race and broken by the winning contestant.
tape *verb*
1. to tie up or bind with tape.
2. to tape-record or video-tape.

tape deck
short form is **deck**
the part of a tape-recorder containing the motors, spindles and all the circuitry except the amplifiers and speakers.

tape machine
a telegraphic instrument that prints share prices, etc., directly onto a tape.

taper *verb*
to make or become gradually narrower at one end: 'the blade *tapered* to a sharp point'.
taper *noun*
1. a) a long wick covered with wax, used to light candles or gas. b) a slender candle.
2. a gradual lessening of thickness, size, etc.
Word Family: **taperingly**, *adverb.*

tape-recorder *noun*
a device, using magnetic tape wound from one spool to another, to record and reproduce sound.
Word Family: **tape-recording**, *noun*, a magnetic tape on which sound has been recorded; **tape-record**, *verb.*

tapestry (*say* **tappa-stree**) *noun*
a fabric on which coloured threads are woven or stitched by hand to make a design, used as wall-hangings, etc. [French *tapis* carpet]

tapeworm *noun*
any of a group of long, flat worms living as parasites in the intestine of some mammals, including man.

tapioca (*say* tappi-o-ka) *noun*
a granular substance made by drying cassava starch, used in puddings and soups.

tapir (*say* **tay-pa**) *noun*
a large, pig-like mammal, with short legs and a long fleshy nose, found in South America and south-eastern Asia.

tappet *noun*
a projecting part in a machine or engine which regularly comes into contact with another part, from or to which movement is passed.

taproot *noun*
Biology: the main root of a plant, which gives off lateral roots: 'a carrot is a *taproot*'.

tar (1) *noun*
any of various dark, viscid substances obtained from the distillation of coal, wood, etc.
tar *verb*
(tarred, tarring)
to smear or cover with tar.
Phrases:
tar and feather, to smear a person with tar and feathers as a form of punishment or ridicule.
tarred with the same brush, having the same faults.

tar (2) ***noun***
(*informal*) a sailor.
[short form of *tarpaulin*]

tarantella (*say* tarren–**tella**) ***noun***
a) a fast Italian dance usually for two people. b) the music for such a dance.
[the dance was formerly believed to be a remedy for the bite of a *tarantula*]

tarantula (*say* ta–**rant**–yoola) ***noun***
a large, hairy, poisonous spider found in southern Europe and America.
[after *Taranto*, Italy]

tardy *adjective*
late or slow.
Word Family: **tardily**, *adverb*; **tardiness**, *noun*.
[from Latin]

tare (1) (*say* tair) ***noun***
the weight of a container, motor vehicle, etc. without its load or contents. Compare GROSS.

tare (2) (*say* tair) ***noun***
a weed.

target ***noun***
something which is aimed at, such as the object marked with circles or numbers in archery, a particular output of manufactured goods, etc.

tariff ***noun***
1. a) a list of customs duties imposed by a government, especially on imported goods. b) a customs duty.
2. any list of prices or charges: 'a hotel *tariff*'.
Word Family: **tariff**, *verb*, to fix a duty or price on.
[Arabic *tarif* notification]

tarmac (*say* **tar**–mak) ***noun***
short form of **tarmacadam**
1. asphalt.
2. a road, airport runway etc. made of asphalt.
[TAR + MAC(adam)]

tarn ***noun***
a small mountain lake.

tarnish *verb*
to dull or discolour, especially a metal surface by oxidation.
Usage: 'the crime *tarnished* the school's reputation' (= spoilt).
Word Family: **tarnish**, *noun*.

tarot (*rhymes with* barrow) ***noun***
any of a pack of 78 cards used to predict future events.
[French]

tarpaulin (*say* tar–**pawlin**) ***noun***
a large piece of tarred canvas or other waterproof fabric used as a protective covering.

tarpon ***noun***
a huge game-fish, weighing up to 130 kg, found in warm Atlantic and Pacific waters.
[from Dutch]

tarradiddle ***noun***
1. a fib.
2. nonsense.

tarragon (*say* **tarra**–gon) ***noun***
also called **estragon**
a herb with narrow green leaves used in cooking.

tarry (1) (*rhymes with* marry) ***verb***
(**tarried, tarrying**)
to wait or linger.

tarry (2) (*say* **tah**–ree) *adjective*
like or smeared with tar.

tarsal bone
see ANKLE.

tarsier ***noun***
a very small, monkey-like primate with large round eyes, found in Indonesia, etc.

tarsus ***noun***
the group of bones which join the leg to the foot.

tart (1) *adjective*
sharp or sour in taste.
Usage: 'her *tart* reply brought tears to my eyes' (= bitter, cutting).
Word Family: **tartly**, *adverb*; **tartness**, *noun*.

tart (2) ***noun***
1. a sweet pie, especially one without a top crust.
2. (*informal*) a vulgar or immoral woman.
tart *verb*
tart up, (*informal*) to decorate or make attractive, especially cheaply.

tartan ***noun***
a worsted or woollen, woven fabric with checks of different colours and sizes, associated with different Scottish clans and localities.

tartar (1) (*say* **tarta**) ***noun***
1. a hard substance such as calcium phosphate, mucus, etc., deposited on the teeth from the saliva.
2. a deposit, potassium bicarbonate, from wines.
Word Family: **tartaric** (*say* tar–**tarrik**), *adjective*.

tartar (2) (*say* **tarta**) ***noun***
(*sometimes capital*) a savage or cruel person.
[after the *Tartars*, the Mongolian tribesmen who conquered Asia and

eastern Europe under Genghis Khan in the Middle Ages]

task (*say* tahsk) ***noun***
any piece of work, especially a difficult one.
take to task, to blame or reprimand.
Word Family: **task**, ***verb***, to strain or overburden.

task force
1. *Military:* a temporary joining of battalions or units under one commander for a particular operation.
2. any team or group formed for a particular task.

taskmaster ***noun***
a person who assigns work, especially hard or heavy work, to others.

tassel ***noun***
a knot of threads or cords with the ends left hanging, used for decoration.

taste ***noun***
1. a) the sensation produced when food, etc. is put in the mouth or on the tongue. b) the sense by which this is perceived.
2. a discernment or understanding of what is excellent or appropriate, as in art, dress, manners, etc.
Usages:
a) 'do have a *taste* of this delicious soup' (= small amount, mouthful).
b) 'she developed quite a *taste* for garlic while in France' (= liking, preference).
c) 'these warm spring days are just a *taste* of our summer weather' (= sample).
taste ***verb***
to experience a taste: 'can you *taste* caraway in the biscuits?'.
Usages:
a) '*taste* the wine and see if you like it' (= try, have some of).
b) 'she *tasted* success with her first novel' (= experienced).
Word Family: **tasty**, *adjective*, having a pleasing or full taste; **tastiness**, *noun*; **tasteful**, *adjective*, showing good taste, judgement or discernment; **tastefully**, *adverb*; **tastefulness**, *noun*; **tasteless**, *adjective*, a) having little or no taste, b) showing a lack of good taste; **tastelessly**, *adverb*; **tastelessness**, *noun*; **taster**, *noun*, a person who tastes, especially one who samples wine, etc. for quality.

tastebud ***noun***
Anatomy: any of numerous small structures inside the mouth, particularly on the tongue, which together form the organ of taste.

tatter ***noun***
1. a torn piece hanging loose.
2. (*plural*) any torn clothes.
Word Family: **tattered**, *adjective*, torn or made up of tatters.

tatting ***noun***
handmade lace made by knotting cotton or linen thread with a shuttle.
Word Family: **tat** (**tatted**, **tatting**), *verb*.

tattle ***verb***
to gossip or reveal secrets.
Word Family: **tattle**, *noun*; **tattler**, **tattletale**, *nouns*, a telltale.

tattoo (1) ***noun***
a permanent design put on the body by pricking the skin and marking it with dyes.
Word Family: **tattoo**, *verb*; **tattooist**, **tattooer**, *nouns*.
[Polynesian]

tattoo (2) ***noun***
1. a rhythmic beating, tapping, etc., such as drum taps signalling troops to retire to their quarters in the evening.
2. a public military display, usually outdoors.
Word Family: **tattoo** (**tattooed**, **tattooing**), *verb*.
[Dutch *taptoe* close the tap (of beer casks)]

tatty ***noun***
shabby or tattered: 'please don't wear that *tatty* old coat'.
Word Family: **tattiness**, *noun*.

taught (*say* tawt) ***verb***
the past tense and past participle of the verb **teach**.

taunt (*say* tawnt) ***verb***
to provoke or try to anger by insult, mockery, etc.
Word Family: **taunt**, *noun*, a taunting remark or action.
[French *tant pour tant* tit for tat]

Taurus (*say* taw-rus) ***noun***
also called the **Bull**
Astrology: a group of stars, the second sign of the zodiac.
[Latin]

taut (*say* tawt) ***adjective***
tightly pulled or strained: 'the rope was so *taut* that it almost snapped'.
Usage: 'he was *taut* with anxiety' (= on edge).

Word Family: **tautly,** *adverb*; **tautness,** *noun*; **tauten,** *verb*, to make or become tightly stretched.

tautology (*say* taw-**tolla**-jee) *noun*
the needless use or repetition of a word or idea in a sentence, which does not make the meaning any clearer.
Word Family: **tautological** (*say* tawta-**loji**-k'l), *adjective*.
[Greek *tautos* the same + *logos* word]

tavern *noun*
1. a place where alcohol is served to be drunk on the premises.
2. (*formerly*) a public inn providing accommodation, etc. for travellers.
[from Latin]

taw *noun*
1. a marker used in hopscotch.
2. a) a large marble. b) a game of marbles.

tawdry (*say* **taw**-dree) *adjective*
cheap and gaudy.
Word Family: **tawdrily,** *adverb*; **tawdriness,** *noun*.
[(Sain)T AUDREY ('s Fair) at Ely, where cheap lace was sold]

tawny *noun*
a yellowish-brown colour.
Word Family: **tawny,** *adjective*.

tax *noun*
1. a sum of money claimed by a government for its support and paid by citizens on income and property (called **direct tax**), or on purchases (called **indirect tax**).
2. a burden or oppressive strain: 'the heating bills were a *tax* on the family's resources'.
tax *verb*
to claim tax from.
Usages:
a) 'the race *taxed* his strength' (= made great demands on).
b) 'he *taxed* the team for its laziness' (= reprimanded, accused).
taxation (*say* tak-**say**-sh'n) *noun*
a) a system of taxes. b) the amount of tax paid or received.
Word Family: **taxable,** *adjective*, subject to tax.
[Latin *taxare* to estimate]

taxi (*say* **tak**-see) *noun*
short form of **taxicab**
also called a **cab**
a car which may be hired with its driver, usually fitted with a device (called a **taximeter**) which calculates and indicates the fare due.
taxi *verb*
(**taxied, taxiing**)
(of an aeroplane) to move slowly along the ground, as before take-off or after landing.
[French *taxe* a tariff]

taxidermy (*say* **tak**si-dermi) *noun*
the art of preserving and stuffing animal skins.
Word Family: **taxidermist,** *noun*.
[Greek *taxis* arrangement + *derma* skin]

taxonomy (*say* tak-**sonna**-mee) *noun*
a process or system of classification.
Word Family: **taxonomic** (*say* takso-**nommik**), *adjective*.
[Greek *taxis* arrangement + *nomos* law]

T-bar *noun*
see SKI-LIFT.

T-bone *noun*
a cut of beef from the loin of the animal, containing a T-shaped bone.

te (*say* tee) *noun*
Music: see DOH.

tea *noun*
1. a) the dried leaves of an Asian shrub. b) a drink made from these leaves brewed in water.
2. any similar drink made by brewing: a) 'herbal *tea*'; b) 'beef *tea*'.
3. a meal taken in the late afternoon or early evening.
[Chinese *ch'a*]

tea bag
a small paper or cloth packet containing tea-leaves, placed in boiling water to make tea.

tea-break *noun*
a rest from work to have tea, coffee, etc, usually in the middle of the morning or afternoon.

teacake *noun*
a round currant bun, often toasted, sliced in half and buttered.

teach *verb*
(**taught, teaching**)
1. a) to impart knowledge by lessons: 'he *teaches* a class of 50 pupils'. b) to communicate the knowledge of: 'he *teaches* maths'.
2. to train by practice or exercise: 'to *teach* a horse to jump hurdles'.
Usage: 'that will *teach* you not to be so reckless again!' (= cause to learn by experience).
Word Family: **teacher,** *noun*, a person who teaches or instructs, especially one trained to do so in a school, etc.;

teaching, *noun*, a) the work or profession of a teacher, b) something which is taught.

tea-chest *noun*
a large, wooden box in which tea is stored or carried.

teach-in *noun*
a long public debate or discussion at which different points of view are given on current topics.

teaching hospital
a hospital in which medical students and nurses are trained, usually associated with the medical school of a university.

teacloth *noun*
a tea-towel.

teacup *noun*
a small cup for drinking tea or used for measuring quantities.

teak *noun*
a large, Asian tree with hard, durable wood which is used for shipbuilding and making furniture.

teal *noun*
any of various small, freshwater ducks.
Word Family: **teal**, *adjective.*

team *noun*
1. an organized group of people doing something together, especially playing sport against another such group: 'a football *team*'.
2. two or more animals harnessed together to pull a plough, etc.
team *verb*
team up, to work together.
Word Family: **team-mate**, *noun*, a person belonging to the same team as another.

teamster *noun*
American: a truckdriver.

teamwork *noun*
any combined effort or organized cooperation between a group of people.

teapot *noun*
a round pot, usually porcelain or enamel, with a spout, lid and handle, and in which tea is made or served.

tear (1) (*say* teer) *noun*
a drop of salty fluid produced in the lachrymal glands, moistening the eye and usually released as a result of emotion. Short form of **teardrop**.
in tears, weeping.
Word Family: **tearful**, *adjective*, a) weeping or shedding tears, b) causing tears; **tearfully**, *adverb*; **tearfulness**, *noun.*

tear (2) (*say* tair) *verb*
(tore, torn, tearing)
1. to pull apart with force or violence: 'he *tore* the page in two'.
2. to make an opening in by catching or pulling at violently: 'the branch *tore* her shirt'.
Usages:
a) 'he *tore* the book angrily from his father's hands' (= pulled violently).
b) 'the state has been *torn* for years by civil violence' (= disturbed).
c) 'we could not *tear* ourselves away' (= remove, drag).
d) (*informal*) 'they *tore* across the road to the bus-stop' (= raced, rushed).
Phrases:
tear down, to destroy or demolish.
tear into, (*informal*) to attack without restraint.
tear strips off, (*informal*) to criticize harshly.
tear up, to pull into pieces.
torn between, unable to choose between.
Word Family: **tear**, *noun*, a) the act of tearing, b) an opening caused by pulling apart.

tearaway (*say* **taira**-way) *noun*
(*informal*) a person or thing that is wildly uncontrollable.

tear gas (*say* **teer** gas)
any substance that strongly irritates and brings tears to the eyes, usually distributed as vapour or smoke.

tearing (*say* **tair**-ing) *adjective*
(*informal*) violent or headlong: 'a *tearing* hurry'.

tear-jerker (*say* **teer**-jerker) *noun*
(*informal*) a film, play, story, etc. which is very sentimental.

tearoom *noun*
a shop or restaurant where tea, etc. is served.

tease (*say* teez) *verb*
1. to annoy, make fun of or raise the hopes of in a playful manner.
2. to raise the nap of fabrics.
3. *Beauty:* to fluff up hair by combing it towards the roots. Also called to **backcomb**.
4. to separate fibres, e.g. in tissues for examination or in combing wool, flax, etc.
tease *noun*
1. a person or thing that teases, puzzles or annoys. Also called a **teaser**.
2. the act of teasing.
Word Family: **teasingly**, *adverb.*

teasel (*say* **tee**–z'l) *noun*
also spelt **teazel**
a plant with prickly leaves, stems and seed–pods formerly used to raise the nap of fabrics.

tea–set *noun*
the cups, saucers, plates, etc., usually with a matching pattern, used for serving tea.

teaspoon *noun*
a small oval–shaped spoon used for stirring tea, coffee, etc. and measuring quantities.

teat *noun*
1. *Anatomy:* a nipple.
2. the nipple–shaped mouthpiece of a baby's bottle.

tea–towel *noun*
also called a **teacloth**
a piece of cloth for drying dishes.

tea–trolley *noun*
also called a **tea–wagon**
a small table on wheels used for serving tea, etc.

tech (*say* tek) *noun*
(*informal*) a technical college or technical school.

technetium (*say* tek–**nee**shium) *noun*
element number 43, a radioactive metal, the first element to be made by man, formed as a fission product of uranium. See TRANSITION ELEMENT. See CHEMICAL ELEMENTS in grey pages.
[Greek *tekhnetos* artificial]

technical (*say* **tekni**–k'l) *adjective*
relating or belonging to technology or a particular trade, science, etc.: 'building is a *technical* skill'.
Usages:
a) 'our company provides *technical* advisers for all your queries' (= having specialized skill or knowledge, especially scientific or mechanical).
b) 'your argument is based on a purely *technical* distinction' (= formal, theoretical).
Word Family: **technically**, *adverb*.
[Greek *tekhnikos* skilful, workmanlike]

technical college
a college which provides courses in technology, commerce, art, etc.

technicality (*say* tekni–**kalli**–tee) *noun*
1. the fact of being technical.
2. a petty distinction, especially one based only on theory.

technical knockout
Boxing: a victory based on the referee's decision to stop the fight because one boxer is considered unable to continue.

technical school
a secondary school which provides courses in technology, trades, etc.

technician (*say* tek–**nish**'n) *noun*
a person skilled in a particular process or method, especially one requiring special mechanical or scientific training.

Technicolor (*say* **tekni**–kulla) *noun*
a process of making colour films by superimposing the three primary colours to produce a final colour print.
[a trademark]

technique (*say* tek–**neek**) *noun*
the particular method or procedure for doing something: 'the champion has an unusual swimming *technique*'.
Usage: 'the young pianist's *technique* was perfect' (= skill).

technocracy (*say* tek–**nokra**–see) *noun*
a government or social system based on the organization of industry, etc. by technical experts.
Word Family: **technocrat** (*say* **tekna**–krat), *noun*, a) a member or supporter of a technocracy, b) a person who believes that problems, etc. should be solved scientifically.
[Greek *tekhné* art + *kratia* rule]

technology (*say* tek–**nolla**–jee) *noun*
the study of the application of science and scientific knowledge, especially to industry.
Word Family: **technological** (*say* tekna–**loji**–k'l), *adjective*, relating to or resulting from science or technology; **technologist**, *noun*.
[Greek *tekhné* art + –LOGY]

tectonic (*say* tek–**tonnik**) *adjective*
Geology: of or relating to the structures of the earth's crust and the forces which cause it to move.
[Greek *tekton* carpenter]

teddy bear
a stuffed toy bear.
[from *Teddy*, a nickname for Theodore Roosevelt, 1858–1919, a President of the United States of America]

tedious (*say* **teedi**–us) *adjective*
tiresome or uninteresting, especially if long: 'a *tedious* speech'.
Word Family: **tediously**, *adverb*; **tediousness**, **tedium** (*say* **teedi**–um), *nouns*.
[Latin *taedium* weariness]

tee *noun*
Golf: a) a level area of ground from which the player first hits the ball for each hole. b) a wooden or plastic peg

on which the ball is placed for the first stroke.
tee *verb*
(**teed, teeing**)
to place the ball on a tee.
Phrases:
tee off, a) to hit a golfball from the tee; b) to start.
tee up, to place a golfball on the tee.

teem *verb*
1. to rain heavily.
2. to swarm or be full: 'the playground *teemed* with shouting children'.

teenager *noun*
a person who is over 12 but less than 20 years old.
Word Family: **teenage**, *adjective*; **teens**, *plural noun*, the years of being a teenager.

teeny *adjective*
(*informal*) tiny.

teenybopper *noun*
(*informal*) a young teenager who is wildly enthusiastic about pop music and its musicians.

teepee *noun*
a tepee.

tee-shirt *noun*
a T-shirt.

teeter *verb*
to totter or wobble: 'the glass *teetered* on the very edge of the table'.
Word Family: **teeter**, *noun*.

teeth *plural noun*
see TOOTH.

teething (*say* **tee***th*ing) *noun*
the process of teeth emerging from the gums.
teething problems, problems in the initial stages of a project, etc.
Word Family: **teethe** (*say* tee*th*), *verb*, to develop teeth.

teething ring
a hard, circular disc on which babies may bite to comfort their gums, etc. during teething.

teetotaller (*say* tee-**toe**-t'la) *noun*
a person who abstains completely from alcoholic drinks.
Word Family: **teetotal**, *adjective*.
[*t-total* (emphatic repetition of *t*)]

Teflon *noun*
Chemistry: a tough, waxy plastic, used in bearings and in articles requiring a non-adhesive chemically resistant surface, such as 'non-stick' frying pans.
[a trademark]

tektite *noun*
a variety of small, glassy meteorite.
[Greek *tektos* molten]

telecast (*say* **telli**-kast) *noun*
any television broadcast.
Word Family: **telecast**, *verb*.

telecommunication
(*say* telli-ko-mewni-**kay**-sh'n) *noun*
(*often plural*) the science or technology of communicating sounds, signals or pictures by wire or radio.
[Greek *telé* afar + COMMUNICATION]

telegram (*say* **telli**-gram) *noun*
also called a **cable** or a **wire**
a message sent by telegraph.

telegraph (*say* **telli**-grahf) *noun*
a method, device or system for sending messages from a transmitter to a receiver, usually along electrical wires.
Word Family: **telegraph**, *verb*, to send a message by telegraph; **telegraphy** (*say* tel-**egra**-fee), *noun*, the process of communicating by telegraph; **telegraphist**, **telegrapher**, *nouns*; **telegraphic** (*say* telli-**graff**ik), *adjective*; **telegraphically**, *adverb*.
[Greek *telé* afar + *graphein* to write]

telekinesis (*say* telli-kie-**neesis**) *noun*
the apparent movement of objects without physical means, as in levitation.
[Greek *telé* afar + *kinesis* movement]

telemeter (*say* tee-**lemmita**) *noun*
any device for recording information about something distant, such as the instruments on a space capsule which transmit measurements by radio from space back to earth.

teleology (*say* telli-**olla**-jee) *noun*
the belief that events occur because they have a particular purpose.
Word Family: **teleological** (*say* tellio-**loji**-k'l), *adjective*.
[Greek *teleos* end + -LOGY]

telepathy (*say* te-**leppa**-thee) *noun*
short form of **mental telepathy**
also called **mind-reading**
the communication of one person's thoughts to another, without using normal methods of communication.
[Greek *telé* afar + *pathos* feeling]

telephone (*say* **telli**-fone) *noun*
a) an apparatus for sending or receiving voice messages, usually along electrical wires. b) the method or system of doing this.

telephone *verb*
a) to speak to or contact by telephone. b) to send by telephone.
[Greek *telé* afar + *phoné* a sound]

telephone box
also called a **callbox**
an upright structure containing a public telephone.

telephonist (*say* te-leffa-nist) *noun*
a person who operates a telephone switchboard.

telephoto lens (*say* telli-foto lenz)
Photography: a lens with a narrow viewing angle like a telescope, used for photographing distant objects.

teleprinter (*say* telli-printa) *noun*
a device similar to a typewriter, which sends or receives messages by telegraph.

teleprompter *noun*
a screen, for television broadcasters, which displays their scripts in large letters, from which they can read without appearing to do so.

telescope (*say* telli-skope) *noun*
an instrument making distant objects appear nearer and larger.
telescope *verb*
1. to slide together so that one part fits inside another, as in a small telescope.
2. to condense or shorten: 'the survey *telescopes* her life's work into a few pages'.
Word Family: **telescopic** (*say* telli-skoppik), *adjective.*
[Greek *telé* afar + *skopein* to look at]

televise (*say* telli-vize) *verb*
to make, send or receive pictures by television.
[Greek *telé* afar + Latin *visus* seen]

television (*say* telli-vi*zh*'n) *noun*
a) the use of cables or radio to send pictures to a place where they are reproduced by a receiver. b) an apparatus for receiving these pictures.

telex (*say* tel-eks) *noun*
a) a teleprinter. b) a message received by a teleprinter.
[TEL(eprinter) + EX(change)]

tell *verb*
(told, telling)
1. to make known or give information, especially by speaking: a) '*tell* me your name'; b) 'she *told* me the news'.
2. to utter: 'don't *tell* lies'.
3. an old word meaning to count: 'to *tell* one's rosary beads'.
Usages:
a) 'can you *tell* the twins apart?' (= distinguish).
b) 'how can you *tell* for certain?' (= know).
c) 'I *told* you to be quiet' (= ordered).
d) 'the effort was *telling* on his health' (= having a bad effect).
Phrases:
all told, in all, in total.
tell off, (*informal*) to scold severely.
tell on, 'I'm going to *tell on* you' (= inform against).

teller *noun*
1. a person who tells: 'the *teller* of a tale'.
2. a person who receives or pays out money at a bank, etc.

telling *adjective*
impressive or effective: 'a *telling* argument'.
Word Family: **tellingly**, *adverb.*

telltale *noun*
a person who reveals secrets or informs on others.
telltale *adjective*
unconsciously revealing.

tellurium (*say* tel-yoorium) *noun*
element number 52, a non-metal forming allotropes. It is used in alloys and to colour glass.
See CHEMICAL ELEMENTS in grey pages.

telly *noun*
(*informal*) television.

temerity (*say* te-merri-tee) *noun*
reckless boldness.
[from Latin]

temper *noun*
1. a) a particular state of mind: 'a good *temper*'. b) composure of mind: 'he lost his *temper*'.
Usage: 'she's always in a *temper*' (= angry mood).
2. a degree of hardness or elasticity of steel.
temper *verb*
1. to soften or modify: '*temper* your rashness with common sense'.
2. *Metallurgy:* to heat and then cool steel quickly to bring it to the proper degree of hardness.
tempered *adjective*
1. having a certain kind of temper: 'an *even-tempered* child'.
2. (of steel) having undergone tempering.

tempera (*say* tempera) *noun*
a) a fast-drying paint, originally mixed with egg yolk, but now mixed with

other, similar substances. b) a painting done in tempera.
[Italian]

temperament (*say* **tem**pra–m'nt) *noun*
the emotional nature of a person: 'the shy boy had a nervous *temperament*'.
Usage: 'that actress is a woman of *temperament*' (= unrestrained or passionate behaviour).
temperamental (*say* tempra–**men**–t'l) *adjective*
a) having quickly changing moods, ideas, etc. b) easily upset.
Word Family: **temperamentally,** *adverb.*
[Latin *temperamentum* moderation]

temperance *noun*
1. a moderation or self-control in speech and behaviour.
2. a total abstinence from alcoholic drink.

temperate (*say* **temp**–rit) *adjective*
moderate: 'the *temperate* climate had no extremes of hot or cold'.
Word Family: **temperately,** *adverb*; **temperateness,** *noun.*
[Latin *temperatus* kept within due measure]

temperate zone
any area of the earth between the tropics and the Arctic and Antarctic Circles, having a clearly defined winter and summer.

temperature (*say* **tem**pri–cher) *noun*
1. a measure of the degree of hotness or coldness.
2. an excessive degree of heat in the body: 'she's in bed with a *temperature*'.
3. *Physics:* the fundamental quantity describing the average velocity of particles in a body of matter, expressed in kelvin.

tempered *adjective*
see TEMPER.

tempest (*say* **tem**pest) *noun*
a violent storm.
tempestuous (*say* tem–**pess**tew–us) *adjective*
violent, stormy or turbulent: a) '*tempestuous* weather'; b) 'a *tempestuous* period of history'.
Word Family: **tempestuously,** *adverb*; **tempestuousness,** *noun.*
[Latin *tempestas* a season, (stormy) weather]

template (*say* **tem**plet) *noun*
also spelt **templet**
a thin plate of metal, etc. used as a guide or gauge in mechanical work.

temple (1) *noun*
a) a building used for worship. b) a building in which it is believed a god or divine presence resides.
[Latin *templum* a place set apart]

temple (2) *noun*
Anatomy: the area on the side of the head, just next to the eye.
[Latin *tempus*]

tempo *noun*
plural is **tempos** or **tempi**
speed or pace: 'play the music at a brisk *tempo*'.
[Latin *tempus* time]

temporal (*say* **tem**pa–r'l) *adjective*
1. of or relating to the present, physical world as distinct from eternal or spiritual things.
2. of or relating to time.
Word Family: **temporally,** *adverb.*
[Latin *temporis* of time]

temporal bone
Anatomy: either of two bones just above the ears, forming the side of the skull.
[Latin *temporis* of the temple]

temporary (*say* **temp**'ra–ree) *adjective*
intended or lasting for a short time only: 'she sought a *temporary* job for the summer'.
Word Family: **temporarily,** *adverb*; **temporariness,** *noun*; **temporary,** *noun,* (informal) a person in a temporary job.

temporize, temporise *verb*
to be indecisive or evasive in order to delay and gain time.

tempt *verb*
to persuade or try to persuade someone to do something regarded as against one's right or proper judgement.
Usage: 'don't *tempt* your luck' (= test, provoke).
temptation (*say* tem–**tay**–sh'n) *noun*
a) the act of tempting. b) the state of being tempted: 'I yielded to *temptation*'. c) something which tempts or attracts: 'the money was too great a *temptation* to resist'.
Word Family: **tempter,** *noun,* a person who tempts, especially to do wrong; **temptress,** *noun,* a female tempter.
[Latin *temptare* to test by probing]

ten *noun*
a cardinal number, the symbol 10 in Arabic numerals, X in Roman numerals.
Word Family: **ten,** *adjective*; **tenth,** *noun, adjective.*

tenable (*say* **tenna**-b'l) *adjective*
able to be held or maintained: a) 'the job is *tenable* for 12 months'; b) 'new evidence makes your theory less *tenable*'.
Word Family: **tenably**, *adverb*; **tenability** (*say* tenna-**billi**-tee), *noun*.
[French *tenir* to hold]

tenacious (*say* te-**nay**-shus) *adjective*
sticking or holding on firmly and persistently: 'he's so *tenacious* in his beliefs that he refuses to listen to anyone else'.
Word Family: **tenaciously**, *adverb*; **tenacity** (*say* te-**nassi**-tee), **tenaciousness**, *nouns*.
[Latin *tenax* holding fast]

tenant (*say* **tennunt**) *noun*
a person who rents a house, land, etc. from the owner.
tenancy (*say* **tennen**-see) *noun*
a) the holding or use of property as a tenant. b) the period of a tenant's occupancy.
[Latin *tenens* holding]

tench *noun*
a freshwater fish, resembling the carp.

tend (1) *verb*
to have a favourable attitude or bias towards: a) 'I *tend* to agree with you'; b) 'she *tends* to swear when angry'; c) 'the government *tended* towards socialism'.
Usage: 'quietness *tends* towards peace of mind' (= helps produce).
[Latin *tendere* to stretch]

tend (2) *verb*
to mind or attend to.
[from ATTEND]

tendency (*say* **ten**-d'n-see) *noun*
a movement, leaning or bias towards: 'she has a *tendency* to swear when angry'.

tendentious (*say* ten-**denshus**) *adjective*
a) having a definite bias or underlying purpose. b) not impartial.
Word Family: **tendentiously**, *adverb*; **tendentiousness**, *noun*.

tender (1) *adjective*
not hard or tough: '*tender* meat'.
Usages:
a) 'the injury is still quite *tender*' (= painful, sensitive).
b) 'a child of *tender* years' (= young).
c) 'she gave him a *tender* smile' (= gentle, affectionate).
Word Family: **tenderly**, *adverb*; **tenderness**, *noun*.
[Latin *tener*]

tender (2) *verb*
to offer or present: 'I *tendered* my resignation'.
tender *noun*
an offer, especially one to provide goods or services, which includes detailed estimates of the total cost: 'we called for *tenders* to build the bridge'.
legal tender, banknotes and coins which may legally be offered as payment for a debt and must be accepted.
[Old French *tendre* to stretch]

tender (3) *noun*
1. a person who looks after or tends: 'a *bartender*'.
2. something which attends or supplies, such as a small wagon carrying fuel and water for a locomotive.
[for ATTENDER]

tenderfoot *noun*
(*informal*) an inexperienced person.

tender-hearted *adjective*
easily moved to pity or sympathy.
Word Family: **tender-heartedness**, *noun*.

tenderize (*say* **tenda**-rize) **tenderise** *verb*
to beat or add chemicals to meat to make it tender.

tenderness *noun*
Word Family: see TENDER (1).

tendon *noun*
also called a **sinew**
Anatomy: a dense cord of tissue joining a muscle to a bone.
[Greek *tenon*]

tendril *noun*
Biology: a slender specialized leaf or stem used by climbing plants to attach themselves to a support.
[Latin *tener* tender]

tenement (*say* **tenna**-m'nt) *noun*
a) a large house or building divided into flats. b) any house or building.
[Latin *tenere* to hold]

tenet (*say* **tennet**) *noun*
a belief, principle or doctrine.
[Latin, he holds]

tenner *noun*
(*informal*) a ten-pound note.

tennis *noun*
a ball game for two or four people played on a court divided by a central net over which the ball is hit with rackets.

See LAWN TENNIS and REAL TENNIS.
[Old French *tenez!* receive!]

tennis elbow
a pain in the elbow joint due to excessive or unaccustomed movement of the arm or wrist, as in playing tennis.

tenon *noun*
see MORTISE.

tenon saw
a short saw used for cutting accurate angles for joints, etc.

tenor (*say* **tenna**) *noun*
1. the general sense or meaning: 'don't report the whole speech – just give us the *tenor* of it'.
2. *Music:* a) the adult male singing voice between countertenor and baritone. b) any instrument having this range.

tenpin bowling
a game in which a ball is rolled along a long alleyway in an attempt to knock over the bottle-shaped objects, called **tenpins** or **pins**, arranged in a triangle at the other end.

tense (1) *adjective*
tightly stretched or strained.
Usage: 'she was *tense* for days before the job interview' (= in a state of nervous strain).
Word Family: **tense**, *verb*, to make or become stiff or tense; **tensely**, *adverb*; **tenseness**, *noun*.
[Latin *tensus* stretched]

tense (2) *noun*
Grammar: the change of form in a verb, expressing the time during which the action takes place. In English there are three simple tenses: a) **present**, as in *I go*; b) **past**, as in *I went*; c) **future**, as in *I shall go*.
[Latin *tempus* time]

tensile *adjective*
1. of or relating to tension.
2. capable of being stretched.

tensile strength
the force needed to stretch a body along its length until it breaks.

tension (*say* **ten**-sh'n) *noun*
1. the state or degree of being tense: 'the *tension* of a guitar string'.
Usage: 'the *tensions* between us led to angry words' (= strained relations).
2. *Physics:* a force which tends to stretch a body.

tent *noun*
a shelter, usually made of waterproof canvas or plastic, held up by poles and with the sides pinned to the ground with ropes and pegs.
[Latin *tensus* stretched]

tentacle (*say* **tenti**-k'l) *noun*
a long, flexible outgrowth on an organism, such as on an octopus, used as an organ of touch or attachment.

tentative (*say* **tenta**-tiv) *adjective*
provisional or experimental: 'the agreement is only *tentative* since he may change his mind'.
Usage: 'the baby took a few *tentative* steps' (= hesitant).
Word Family: **tentatively**, *adverb*; **tentativeness**, *noun*.

tenterhooks *plural noun*
on tenterhooks, in a state of anxious suspense.
[from *tenter*, a frame on which fabric is stretched on hooks to dry]

tenuous (*say* **ten**-yewus) *adjective*
weak or flimsy: 'the old man only had a *tenuous* hold on life'.
Usage: 'the spider spun a *tenuous* web' (= delicate).
Word Family: **tenuously**, *adverb*; **tenuity** (*say* ten-**yoo**-a-tee), *noun*.
[Latin *tenuis* thin]

tenure (*say* **ten**-yoor) *noun*
the holding or possession of something: a) 'the *tenure* of office of chairman is 12 months'; b) 'she signed the lease and now has *tenure* of the house'.
[Latin *tenere* to hold]

tepee (*say* **teepee**) *noun*
also spelt **teepee**
a tent of animal hides or bark used by American Indians.

tepid (*say* **teppid**) *adjective*
moderately warm.
Word Family: **tepidly**, *adverb*; **tepidity** (*say* **tepiddi**-tee), **tepidness**, *nouns*.
[from Latin]

tequila (*say* te-**keela**) *noun*
a Mexican alcoholic drink made from a cactus-like plant.

tera-
a prefix used for SI units meaning one million million (10^{12}). See UNITS in grey pages.
[Greek *teras* monster]

terbium *noun*
element number 65, a rare metal. See LANTHANIDE.
See CHEMICAL ELEMENTS in grey pages.

tercentenary (*say* ter-sen-**teena**-ree) *noun*

a) a period of 300 years. b) a 300th anniversary.
Word Family: **tercentennial,** *adjective.*
[Latin *ter* thrice + CENTENARY]

term *noun*
1. any fixed or definite period of time: a) 'he's serving a *term* of imprisonment'; b) 'the school year is divided into 3 *terms*'.
2. a condition: 'the treaty was signed when its *terms* were finally agreed on'.
Usage: 'she's on excellent *terms* with her neighbours' (= relations, standing).
3. a word or phrase: a) 'legal *terms* are sometimes hard to understand'; b) 'she speaks of you in warm *terms*'.
Phrases:
come to terms, a) to reach agreement; b) to become accustomed.
in terms of, as expressed by, in the language of.
terms of trade, the purchasing power of exports in terms of imports; if raw materials are relatively cheap, for example, the terms of trade tend to be good for a manufacturing country.
term *verb*
to name or call: 'I'd *term* your behaviour sheer vandalism'.
[Latin *terminus* a boundary]

termagant (*say* **terma**–gant) *noun*
a noisy, quarrelsome woman.

terminable (*say* **termina**–b'l) *adjective*
able to be terminated.

terminal *noun*
1. a building at a bus terminus, airport, etc.
2. *Electricity:* either of the points at which electric current enters or leaves an electrical device.
terminal *adjective*
of, situated or occurring at the end: 'the twig had small *terminal* buds'.
Usage: 'the patient had a *terminal* disease' (= fatal).

terminal velocity
the maximum speed reached by a falling object.

terminate *verb*
to end.
termination (*say* termi–**nay**–sh'n) *noun*
a) the act of ending: 'your *termination* of my contract is unfair'. b) the state of being ended: 'the meeting was brought to a *termination*'. c) the place where something ends: 'we followed the road to its *termination*'.
[Latin *terminare* to set bounds to]

terminology (*say* termi–**nolla**–jee) *noun*
the special words used in a particular field or study.

terminus *noun*
plural is **termini** or **terminuses**
the end of anything, especially either of the ends of a railway line, bus or air route, etc.
[Latin]

termite *noun*
also called a **white ant**
any of a group of soft-bodied tropical insects, not related to ants, which cause damage to wooden buildings, furniture, etc.
[Latin *tarmes* a woodworm]

tern *noun*
a seabird related to the gull, having a slender body, long wings, and graceful flight.

ternary (*say* **terna**–ree) *adjective*
formed from or consisting of three.
[Latin *terni* three each]

terrace (*say* **terrus**) *noun*
1. one of a series of raised strips of land with vertical or sloping banks which rise one above the other.
2. an open, outdoor living area, usually paved, connected to a house.
3. a row of joined houses.
Word Family: **terrace,** *verb,* to form or provide with a terrace or terraces.
[Italian *terrazza*]

terracotta (*say* terra–**kotta**) *noun*
1. a) a type of pottery, usually reddish in colour and unglazed, fired to low temperatures. b) a small sculpture in this material.
2. a strong, reddish-brown colour.
Word Family: **terracotta,** *adjective.*
[Italian, baked earth]

terra firma (*say* terra **firma**)
the dry land.
[Latin, solid earth]

terrain (*say* te–**rane**) *noun*
the shape or features of the land surface, especially with regard to its suitability for military purposes.

terrapin (*say* **terra**–pin) *noun*
any of a group of freshwater, edible, North American turtles, often kept as pets.
[Amerindian]

terrazzo (*say* te–**rahtso**) *noun*
a floor covering made of small pieces of polished stone set into concrete.
[Italian]

terrestrial (*say* te–**re**striul) *adjective*
of or relating to the earth or land.
[from Latin]

terrestrial magnetism
Physics: the magnetic field of the earth, pointing approximately north–south and having the same effect as a powerful magnet at the centre of the earth.

terrible *adjective*
causing great fear, shock, distress, discomfort, etc.: 'he died in *terrible* agony'.
Usage: 'my finances are in a *terrible* state' (= very bad).
Word Family: **terribly**, *adverb*, a) in a terrible manner, b) (informal) very.

terrier *noun*
one of various breeds of small dog, originally bred to pursue game into its hole or burrow: 'a *fox–terrier*'.
[Latin *terra* earth]

terrific (*say* te–**riff**ik) *adjective*
1. terrible or terrifying: 'the *terrific* cyclone lasted 3 days'.
2. (*informal*) a) very great: 'she drove at a *terrific* speed'. b) very good: 'the book was really *terrific*'.
Word Family: **terrifically**, *adverb.*

terrify (*say* **terri**–fie) *verb*
(**terrified, terrifying**)
to fill with terror or make extremely afraid: 'the sound of guns *terrified* the timid lad'.

territorial (*say* terri–**taw**riul) *adjective*
relating to land or territory: 'the peasants demanded their *territorial* rights'.

territorial waters
the area of sea around the coast of a country and controlled by it.

territory (*say* **terri**–tree) *noun*
1. a) any land, region or district. b) the land under the control of a state or ruler.
2. (*often capital*) a region administered by the central government of its own or another country, but having some degree of autonomy.
3. the area which an animal claims as its own and will defend against intruders.
[from Latin]

terror *noun*
intense or extreme fear: 'the trapped animal bristled with *terror*'.
Usage: 'that boy is a real *terror*' (= great nuisance).
[Latin]

terrorism (*say* **terra**–rizm) *noun*
the use of violence or threats to generate fear, especially for political purposes.
Word Family: **terrorist**, *noun*, a person who uses or favours the use of terrorism.

terrorize (*say* **terra**–rize) **terrorise** *verb*
a) to fill with terror. b) to coerce or intimidate by threats, etc.: 'the bandits *terrorized* the town to obtain supplies'.
Word Family: **terrorization**, *noun.*

terror–stricken, terror–struck *adjective*
filled with terror.

terry *noun*
an uncut loop in the pile of a fabric, e.g. as in towelling.

terse *adjective*
short and to the point.
Word Family: **tersely**, *adverb*; **terseness**, *noun.*
[Latin *tersus* polished]

tertiary (*say* **ter**sha–ree) *adjective*
third.
Tertiary *noun*
a geological period which extended from about 65 million years ago to about 1·5 million years ago and contains the **Pliocene, Miocene, Oligocene, Eocene** and **Palaeocene** epochs.
[Latin *tertius* third]

tertiary colour
any colour produced by mixing secondary colours, such as brown which may be a mixture of orange and purple. Compare PRIMARY COLOUR.

tertiary education
any education more advanced than that undertaken at school, such as college or university studies.

Terylene (*say* terra–**leen**) *noun*
a synthetic polyester fibre used in clothing, etc.
[a trademark]

tessellated (*say* **tess**a–lay–tid) *adjective*
formed from small squares or pieces, as in a mosaic.
[from Latin]

test *noun*
1. a trial or procedure to determine quality, ability, composition, etc.: a) 'an intelligence *test*'; b) 'a blood *test* for disease'.
2. *Sport:* a test match.
Word Family: **test**, *verb.*

[Latin *testa* a pot in which metals were tested]

testament *noun*
1. *Law:* a will.
2. (*capital*) either of the collections of books which form the Bible, the **Old Testament** and the **New Testament.**
[from Latin]

testate (*say* **tess**–tate) *adjective*
Law: leaving a valid will. Compare INTESTATE.
testator (*say* tess–**taytor**) *noun*
any person who makes a will.

test ban
an agreement between countries to control or forbid the testing of nuclear weapons.

test case
a case which establishes a precedent which can be referred to later in similar cases.

tester *noun*
a person or thing that tests.

testicle (*say* **testi**–k'l) *noun*
also called a **testis**
Anatomy: either of two rounded organs in the male, suspended below the trunk in the scrotum, producing spermatozoa.

testify (*say* **testi**–fie) *verb*
(testified, testifying)
a) to give evidence: 'the witness *testified* that he saw the crime'. b) to serve as evidence: 'the murder weapon *testifies* to your guilt'.
[Latin *testis* a witness + *facere* to make]

testimonial (*say* testi–**mo**–nee–ul) *noun*
1. a written statement testifying to the quality of someone or something.
2. something done or given as a mark of esteem, appreciation, etc.
[Latin *testimonium* evidence]

testimony (*say* **testi**–mo–nee) *noun*
any statement or evidence, such as that given in a court of law.

testis *noun*
plural is **testes** (*say* **tess**–teez)
a testicle.
[Latin]

test match
Sport: a match between teams representing two countries, especially in cricket.

testosterone (*say* tess–**tosta**–rone) *noun*
the hormone made in the testes of animals, producing male characteristics.

test–pilot *noun*
a pilot who flies newly designed aircraft in order to test their qualities, performance, etc.

test–tube *noun*
a hollow cylinder of thin glass, closed at one end and used in chemical tests.

test–tube baby
a baby whose conception or part of its development is produced scientifically outside the mother's body.

testy *adjective*
irritable or impatient.
Word Family: **testily,** *adverb*; **testiness,** *noun.*

tetanus (*say* **tet**–nus) *noun*
also called **lockjaw**
an infectious, bacterial disease, sometimes fatal, which affects the nervous system, causing severe muscle spasms.
[Greek *tetanos* a spasm]

tetchy *adjective*
irritable.
Word Family: **tetchily,** *adverb*; **tetchiness,** *noun.*

tête–à–tête (*say* tate–ah–**tate**) *noun*
a private conversation, usually between two people.
[French, head to head]

tether (*say* te*tha*) *noun*
a rope or chain by which an animal is tied to a tree, fence, etc. to limit its movements.
at the end of one's tether, at the end of one's patience or endurance.
Word Family: **tether,** *verb.*

tetra–
a prefix meaning four, as in *tetrahedron.*
[Greek *tettares*]

tetracycline (*say* tetra–**sigh**–kleen) *noun*
any of a group of drugs used as antibiotics to overcome bacterial infections.

tetrahedron (*say* tetra–**heedron**) *noun*
a solid or hollow body with four triangular faces; a triangular pyramid.
Word Family: **tetrahedral,** *adjective.*
[TETRA– + Greek *hedra* a base]

tetralogy (*say* tet–**ralla**–jee) *noun*
a series of four related plays, operas, literary compositions, etc.
[TETRA– + –LOGY]

Teutonic (*say* tew–**tonnik**) *adjective*
see GERMANIC.

text *noun*
1. the actual words of something written or printed.
2. the main body of words in a book, or newspaper, excluding footnotes, index, etc.
3. a short extract or quotation used as the subject of a lecture, etc.
Word Family: **textual** (*say* **teks**–tew'l), *adjective*.
[Latin *textus* literary style]

textbook *noun*
a book giving instruction and information in a subject.

textile *noun*
1. any woven fabric.
2. any substance which is suitable for weaving.

texture (*say* **teks**–cher) *noun*
the composition or structure of a substance, especially as conveyed to the touch.
Word Family: **textural**, *adjective*; **texturally**, *adverb*.
[Latin *textus* woven]

-th
a suffix used to form ordinal numbers, as in *sixth*.

thalidomide (*say* tha–**lidda**–mide) *noun*
a drug used as a sedative until it was found to damage a foetus if taken during pregnancy.

thallium *noun*
element number 81, a malleable metal, used in alloys. Its compounds are used in rat poisons and insecticides.
See CHEMICAL ELEMENTS in grey pages.

thallus *noun*
plural is **thalli** (*say* **thall**–eye)
Biology: a simple vegetative plant body which is not divided into root, stem and leaf.
[Greek *thallos* young shoot, twig]

than *preposition, conjunction*
(introducing the second part of a comparison) 'I am older *than* you'.

thane *noun*
History: a person who held land in exchange for military service.

thank *verb*
to express thanks.

thankless *adjective*
1. not feeling or showing gratitude.
2. not appreciated: 'housework is a *thankless* task'.
Word Family: **thanklessly**, *adverb*; **thanklessness**, *noun*.

thanks *plural noun*
a grateful acknowledgement of a favour, gift, etc.
thanks to, as a result or consequence of.
Word Family: **thankful**, *adjective*; **thankfully**, *adverb*; **thankfulness**, *noun*.

thanksgiving *noun*
any grateful acknowledgement of favours or benefits, especially to God.

thank you
an expression of gratitude.
Word Family: **thankyou**, *noun*.

that *pronoun*
plural is **those**
1. a demonstrative pronoun used to indicate the following:
a) the person, place, thing, etc. present or just mentioned.
b) the person, place, thing, etc. further removed or less obvious: '*that* red chair over there!'.
2. a relative pronoun used to introduce a clause: a) 'there is the man *that* I saw'; b) 'fool *that* I am'.
3. something: 'there is *that* about the man which intrigues me'.
Phrases:
at that, 'she won, and won easily *at that*' (= as well).
that is, in clarification or example.
that's that, that is the finish of the matter.
with that, 'and *with that* she burst into tears' (= immediately afterwards).
that *conjunction*
1. used to introduce a clause stating a fact, wish, reason, etc.: 'I thought *that* I was late'.
2. used to introduce a sentence or clause expressing desire, surprise, etc.: '*that* is so rude!'.
Word Family: **that**, *adjective*.

thatch *noun*
a roof covering made from straw, reeds, etc.
Word Family: **thatch**, *verb*, to cover a roof with thatch; **thatching**, *noun*, any material used as thatch.

thaw *verb*
1. to melt.
2. (of weather) to become warm enough to melt ice and snow.
Usage: 'her manner *thawed* in the friendly atmosphere' (= relaxed).

Word Family: **thaw**, *noun*, a) the process of thawing, b) a period during which ice and snow melt.

the (1) *article*
Grammar: the definite article. See ARTICLE.

the (2) *adverb*
(used to modify an adjective or adverb in the comparative degree) to that extent: '*the* sooner *the* better'.

theatre (*say* **thee**–atta) *noun*
in America spelt **theater**
1. a building where plays, ballet or opera are performed on a stage.
2. any similar room or place where particular actions are performed: a) 'a lecture *theatre*'; b) 'an operating *theatre*'.
3. the world or profession of actors, playwrights, etc.
4. any dramatic writing or performance.
5. a cinema.
Usage: 'the *theatre* of war' (= place of action).
[Greek *theatron* seeing place]

theatre-in-the-round *noun*
a form of theatre where the acting area is surrounded by the audience.

theatrical (*say* thee–atri–k'l) *adjective*
1. of or relating to the theatre.
2. exaggerated or artificial.
theatrical *noun*
(*plural*) a dramatic performance, especially as given by amateurs.
Word Family: **theatrically**, *adverb.*

thee (*say* *th*ee) *pronoun*
an old word meaning you.

theft *noun*
the act of stealing.

their *possessive adjective*
singular is **his**, **her** or **its**
belonging to them: 'it is *their* cake'.

theirs *possessive pronoun*
singular is **his**, **hers** or **its**
belonging to them: 'the cake is *theirs*'.

theism (*say* **thee**–izm) *noun*
a belief in a supernaturally revealed God, especially one with whom a personal relationship is possible, and in Providence. Compare DEISM.
Word Family: **theist**, *noun, adjective*; **theistic** (*say* thee–ist–ik), **theistical**, *adjective*; **theistically**, *adverb.*
[Greek *theos* a god]

them *pronoun*
singular is **him**, **her**, or **it**
the objective form of the pronoun **they**: a) 'we hit *them*; b) 'give the cake to *them*'.

theme *noun*
a central topic, basis or idea which is expressed, expanded, etc., as in a speech, essay or musical composition.
Word Family: **thematic** (*say* thee–**mattik**), *adjective.*
[from Greek]

theme song
a song or tune heard often throughout a play or film.

themselves *pronoun*
1. the reflexive form of **they**: 'they washed *themselves*'.
2. the emphatic form of **they**: 'they did it *themselves*'.
3. their normal or usual selves: 'for many weeks after the accident they were not *themselves*'.

then *adverb*
1. at another time in the past or future: 'I was happier *then*'.
2. next in time, space or order: 'I stayed in Hong Kong first and *then* went to Singapore'.
3. in that case; accordingly.
4. in addition: 'and *then* you must remember to buy some vegetables'.
Phrases:
but then, but on the other hand.
then and there, there and then, at once, on the spot.
then *adjective*
being so at that time: 'the *then* President'.
then *noun*
that time: 'since *then* he has not looked back'.

thence (*say* *th*ence) *adverb*
1. from that time or place.
2. for that reason.
Word Family: **thenceforth**, **thenceforward**, **thenceforwards**, *adverbs*, from that time or place onwards.

theocracy (*say* thee–**okra**–see) *noun*
1. a system of government in which the established Church has political power.
2. a government by a god, either directly or through a class of priests.
Word Family: **theocratic** (*say* thee–o–**krattik**), **theocratical**, *adjective.*
[Greek *theos* a god + *kratia* rule]

theodolite (*say* thee–**odda**–lite) *noun*
a surveyor's instrument resembling a small telescope, used for measuring horizontal and vertical angles.

theology (*say* thee–**olla**–jee) *noun*
the study of divinity or religious doctrines, such as the characteristics of a god or gods in relation to man and the universe.
Word Family: **theological** (*say* thee–a–**loji**–k'l), *adjective*; **theologically**, *adverb*; **theologian** (*say* thee–a–**lo**–j'n), *noun*, a person teaching or having knowledge of theology.
[Greek *theos* a god + -LOGY]

theorem (*say* **theer**–um) *noun*
1. a general proposition the truth of which is demonstrable by argument.
2. *Maths:* a general law in the form of an equation or formula, e.g. in algebra, used as a basis for further operations.
[Greek *theorema* speculation]

theory (*say* **theer**–ee) *noun*
1. a systematically organized group of general propositions used to analyse, predict or explain facts or events.
2. the whole collection of ideas, methods and theorems associated with some study: 'the number *theory*'.
3. an explanation of the principles of a subject, such as art, as distinct from the practice of it.
4. a conjecture or opinion: 'that's your *theory*, but I disagree'.
theoretical (*say* thee–a–**retti**–k'l)
theoretic *adjective*
1. not proved to exist, be practical or true.
2. forming or dealing with theories: 'a *theoretical* study'.
Word Family: **theoretically**, *adverb*; **theorize, theorise**, *verb*, a) to form a theory or theories, b) to speculate; **theorist**, *noun*, a) a person who theorizes, b) a person who deals with the theoretical side of a subject; **theoretician** (*say* thee–ora–**tish**'n), *noun*, a person who deals with the theoretical side of a subject.
[Greek *theoros* a spectator]

theosophy (*say* thee–**ossa**–fee) *noun*
1. any religious or philosophical system of thought claiming direct knowledge of divine or supernatural things.
2. (*capital*) a religious movement making such claims, founded in 1875 and based on Eastern teachings, such as Buddhism and Hinduism.
Word Family: **theosophist**, *noun*; **theosophical** (*say* thee–o–**soffi**–k'l), *adjective*.
[Greek *theos* a god + *sophia* wisdom]

therapy (*say* **therra**–pee) *noun*
1. the treatment of disease or disorders.
2. the power or quality of curing.
therapeutic (*say* therra–**pewtik**) *adjective*
1. having the power to heal or cure.
2. relating to the treatment or curing of disease, etc.
Word Family: **therapist**, *noun*, a person trained to treat disease, etc.
[from Greek]

there *adverb*
1. in or at that place: 'the book is *there*, where I left it'.
2. to, into or towards that place: 'let's go *there* now'.
3. at a particular point of time, action, etc.: 'she paused *there* and asked if we understood'.
been there before, 'I seem to have *been there before*' (= heard all that earlier).
there *interjection*
an exclamation of satisfaction, encouragement, etc.: '*there*! I've finished!'.
thereabouts, thereabout *adverb*
near that place, time, number, etc.: 'at 7 o'clock or *thereabouts*'.
thereafter *adverb*
from a particular time onwards.
thereby *adverb*
1. by that means: 'she fell and *thereby* lost the race'.
2. related to that: '*thereby* hangs a tale'.
therefore *adverb*
as a result.
therein *adverb*
in that place, matter, etc.
thereof *adverb*
of, from or relating to that.
thereon *adverb*
on or upon that.
thereto *adverb*
to that place, subject, etc.
thereunder *adverb*
under that.
thereupon *adverb*
immediately after, especially as a result.

therm *noun*
a unit of energy, equal to about 106 megajoule.
[Greek *thermé* heat]

thermal, thermic *adjective*
of or relating to heat or temperature.
thermal *noun*
a rising current of warm air.
Word Family: **thermally**, *adverb*.

thermion (*say* **thermi**–on) *noun*
Physics: an ion given out by a very hot object.
Word Family: **thermionic** (*say* thermi–**onnik**), *adjective*; **thermionics**, *noun*, the study of thermions and related phenomena.

thermionic valve
a radio valve which contains a heated cathode.

thermistor (*say* ther–**mista**) *noun*
Electricity: a small device whose electrical resistance varies with temperature.
[THERM(al) (res)ISTOR]

thermochemistry
(*say* thermo–**kemmi**–stree) *noun*
the branch of chemistry studying the quantities of heat absorbed or produced by chemical reactions.
Word Family: **thermochemical**, *adjective*.

thermocouple (*say* **thermo**–kupp'l) *noun*
Electronics: a device consisting of two different conductors joined at each end, used for measuring temperature. An electric current is generated if the temperature of one junction changes with respect to the other.

thermodynamics
(*say* thermo–die–**nammiks**) *plural noun*
(*used with singular verb*) the branch of physics studying the relationships between heat and work and the conversion of one to another.
Word Family: **thermodynamic**, **thermodynamical**, *adjective*; **thermodynamically**, *adverb*.

thermoelectricity
(*say* thermo–illek–**trissi**–tee) *noun*
Electricity: any electric current produced by direct conversion of heat into electricity.

thermometer (*say* ther–**mommita**) *noun*
an instrument used to measure temperature.

thermonuclear reaction
(*say* thermo–**newklia** ree–**ak**–sh'n)
Physics: a nuclear reaction which occurs only at high temperature, such as nuclear fusion.

thermos flask
short form is **thermos**
also called a **Dewar flask**
a double-walled container with a vacuum between, usually of silvered glass or stainless steel, used to keep substances at a constant temperature.
[a trademark]

thermosphere (*say* **thermo**–sfeer) *noun*
the outer regions of the earth's atmosphere where the temperature continues to increase towards the sun.

thermostat *noun*
any of various devices used to control temperature.
Word Family: **thermostatic** (*say* thermo–**stattik**), *adjective*; **thermostatically**, *adverb*.
[Greek *thermé* heat + *statos* stationary]

thesaurus (*say* tha–**sawrus**) *noun*
a store of things, especially a book of words and phrases grouped according to meaning.
[Greek *thesauros* treasure]

these (*say* theez) *pronoun*
see THIS.

thesis (*say* **thee**–sis) *noun*
plural is **theses** (*say* **thee**–seez)
a statement or theory, especially a long original work presented by a student for a postgraduate degree.
[Greek, putting]

Thespian (*say* **thes**pian) *adjective*
of or relating to drama, especially tragedy.
Word Family: **Thespian**, *noun*, an actor.
[after *Thespis*, a Greek poet in the 6th century B.C.]

thew *noun*
(*plural*) a) muscle or sinew. b) physical strength.

they (*say* thay) *pronoun*
singular is **he**, **she**, or **it**
1. the third person plural nominative pronoun, used to indicate persons or things: '*they* ate the cake'.
2. used to indicate people in general: '*they* say he is guilty'.
see THEM, THEIR and THEIRS.

thiamine (*say* **thya**–min) *noun*
see VITAMIN B_1 under VITAMIN.

thick *adjective*
1. having relatively great extent from one surface or side to its opposite: 'a *thick* wall in a castle'.
2. measuring in this dimension: 'a wall 1 m *thick*'.
Usages:
a) 'we had to crawl through the *thick* undergrowth' (= closely packed).
b) 'the room was *thick* with smoke' (= filled, abounding).

c) 'we spilt the *thick*, sticky syrup all over the floor' (= viscous).
d) 'there was no way of covering his *thick* accent' (= very pronounced).
e) (*informal*) 'everyone thinks he is rather *thick*, but in fact he is quite smart' (= stupid, dull).
f) (*informal*) 'the boys are as *thick* as thieves' (= friendly, intimate).
g) (*informal*) 'everyone felt the new law was a bit *thick*' (= excessive, beyond what was reasonable).
thick *noun*
1. the most active or intense part: 'I was caught in the *thick* of the crowd'.
2. something which is thick.
through thick and thin, under all circumstances.
Word Family: **thickly**, *adverb*; **thickness**, *noun*; **thicken**, *verb*, a) to make or become thick or thicker, b) to make or grow more intense or complex; **thickening**, *noun*, a) a thickened part or place, b) something used to thicken.

thicket *noun*
a small group of shrubs or trees growing very close together.

thickset *adjective*
1. having a short, stocky body.
2. placed or planted close together.

thick-skinned *adjective*
1. having a thick skin.
2. not sensitive to insult, criticism, etc.

thief (*say* theef) *noun*
plural is **thieves** (*say* theevz)
a person who steals, especially secretly and without force.
thieve (*say* theev) *verb*
to take by theft.
Word Family: **thievery**, (*say* **theeva-ree**), *noun.*

thigh *noun*
Anatomy: the upper part of the leg or hind limb.

thighbone *noun*
the femur.

thimble *noun*
a small metal or plastic cap used to protect the end of the finger when sewing.
Word Family: **thimbleful**, *noun*, a very small quantity.

thin *adjective*
(**thinner, thinnest**)
1. having relatively little extent from one surface or side to its opposite: 'the *thin* ice cracked under her weight'.
2. not great in diameter or cross-section: 'a *thin* wire'.
Usages:
a) '*thin* legs' (= lean).
b) '*thin* vegetation' (= not dense).
c) '*thin* cream' (= fluid).
d) 'her *thin* excuse fooled no-one' (= feeble, inadequate).
e) 'the sound on old recordings is a bit *thin*' (= lacking fullness or volume).
Phrases:
thin on the ground, not many about.
thin on top, going bald.
vanish into thin air, to vanish completely.
Word Family: **thinly**, *adverb*; **thinness**, *noun*; **thin** (**thinned, thinning**), *verb*, to make or become thin or thinner.

thine (*say* *th*ine) *pronoun*
an old word meaning yours.

thing *noun*
1. any material object lacking life or consciousness: 'a chair is a *thing*, a cat is not'.
2. something which cannot be described or named exactly: 'it had a *thing* on the end like a tassle'.
3. (*plural*) a) possessions or belongings: 'I packed a few *things* and left'. b) the general state of affairs: 'how are *things?*'.
4. (*informal*) an unaccountable attitude or feeling, such as aversion: 'I've developed a *thing* about pink cars'.
Usages:
a) 'he did great *things* during the war' (= deeds).
b) 'you poor *thing*!' (= person).
c) 'he said the right *thing*' (= words).
d) 'one *thing* about the situation was not considered' (= aspect, area).
e) 'I read a few *things* by him, but I didn't like them' (= works).
f) 'it doesn't mean a *thing* to me' (= anything).
Phrases:
do one's thing, do one's own thing, (*informal*) to do what one likes or does best.
make a thing of, (*informal*) to turn into a major issue.
one of those things, an event which was unavoidable.

think *verb*
(**thought, thinking**)
to use the mind to form ideas, judgement, etc.

Usages:
a) 'I can't *think* of his name' (= bring to mind).
b) 'he *thought* you were joking' (= believed).
c) 'I never *thought* to find you here' (= expected).
d) 'did you *think* to bring in the milk?' (= remember).
Phrases:
think big, to have great ambitions.
think twice, to consider with great care.
Word Family: **thinker**, *noun*; **think**, *noun*, (informal) an act or process of thinking; **thinking**, *noun*, opinion, conclusions.

think-tank *noun*
(*informal*) a government organization or private company which tries to forecast economic or other trends and give advice on long-term policies.

thinly *adverb*
Word Family: see THIN.

thinner *noun*
a liquid added to a substance to dilute it, such as turpentine added to paint.

thinness *noun*
Word Family: see THIN.

thin-skinned *adjective*
1. having a thin skin.
2. sensitive to insult, criticism, etc.

third *adjective*
1. being number three in a series.
2. being one out of every three: 'we get paid every *third* week'.
third *noun*
1. any of three equal parts into which something is divided.
2. a person or thing that is number three in a series.
Word Family: **thirdly**, *adverb*.

third degree
any prolonged or intense questioning or use of violence to obtain information, etc.

third-party *adjective*
relating to a policy which insures against liability or damage to another person or his property in a motor accident.
Word Family: **third party**, any person other than the principals involved in an agreement, etc.

third person
Grammar: see PERSON.

third-rate *adjective*
distinctly inferior.

Third World
the underdeveloped countries of the world.

thirst *noun*
a dryness of the mouth and throat leading to a desire to drink liquid.
Usage: 'a *thirst* for adventure' (= strong or eager desire).
thirsty *adjective*
needing or craving liquid or moisture.
Usage: '*thirsty* for details the crowd pressed round the courtroom' (= eager).
Word Family: **thirst**, *verb*; **thirstily**, *adverb*; **thirstiness**, *noun*.

thirteen *noun*
a cardinal number, the symbol 13 in Arabic numerals, XIII in Roman numerals.
Word Family: **thirteen**, *adjective*; **thirteenth**, *adjective*, *noun*.

thirty *noun*
1. a cardinal number, the symbol 30 in Arabic numberals, XXX in Roman numerals.
2. (*plural*) the numbers 30 to 39 in a series, such as the years within a century.
Word Family: **thirty**, *adjective*; **thirtieth**, *adjective*, *noun*.

this (*say this*) *pronoun*
plural is **these**
a demonstrative pronoun used to indicate the following:
a) the person, place, thing, etc. present, nearby or just mentioned.
b) the person, place, thing, etc. nearer or more obvious: '*this* chair is nicer than that one over there'.
Word Family: **this**, *adjective*, *adverb*

thistle (*say* **thiss**'l) *noun*
any of a group of wild plants with prickly leaves and fluffy flowers.

thistledown *noun*
the fluff of a thistle flower, which carries the seeds.

thither (*say thither*) *adverb*
to or towards that place or point.

thong *noun*
a narrow strip of leather used for fastening things, etc.

thorax (*say* **thor**-aks) *noun*
a) (in man and other higher vertebrates) the upper part of the trunk between the neck and abdomen. b) a corresponding part in insects, etc.
Word Family: **thoracic** (*say* tho-**rassik**), *adjective*.
[Greek]

thorium *noun*
element number 90, a radioactive metal used in alloys and filaments. See ACTINIDE.
See CHEMICAL ELEMENTS in grey pages. [after *Thor*, the Scandinavian god of thunder]

thorn *noun*
a small, sharp outgrowth on a plant.
thorn in one's side, a source of annoyance or discomfort.
Word Family: **thorny**, *adjective*, a) having many thorns, b) difficult or complex.

thorough (*say* **thurra**) *adjective*
1. full, perfect or complete: 'give the back of your ears a *thorough* scrubbing'.
2. working methodically and leaving nothing incomplete.
thoroughgoing *adjective*
1. complete.
2. methodical or detailed.
Word Family: **thoroughly**, *adverb*; **thoroughness**, *noun.*

thoroughbred *noun*
(*sometimes capital*) any of a breed of racehorses bred from English and Arabian stock.
thoroughbred *adjective*
of pure stock or breed.

thoroughfare *noun*
a road or route.

those (*say* *th*oze) *pronoun*
see THAT.

thou (*say* *th*ou) *pronoun*
an old word meaning you (singular).

though (*say* *th*o) *conjunction*
1. in spite of the fact that: 'I disagree, *though* I see your point'.
2. if: 'act as *though* you didn't hear'.
Word Family: **though**, *adverb*, however.

thought (1) (*say* thawt) *noun*
1. the act or process of thinking: 'she sat in *thought*'.
2. the result of thinking: 'a clever *thought*'.
3. a) intention: 'I had some *thought* of going'. b) expectation: 'I had no *thought* of meeting you here'.
Usage: 'without *thought* for the consequences' (= care, concern).
4. the ideas or way of thinking of a particular time, place, group, etc.: 'Greek *thought*'.
second thoughts, reconsideration.

thought (2) (*say* thawt) *verb*
the past tense and past participle of the verb **think**.

thoughtful *adjective*
1. showing or full of thought: 'a sensible, *thoughtful* suggestion'.
2. attentive or careful, especially towards others.
Word Family: **thoughtfully**, *adverb*; **thoughtfulness**, *noun.*

thoughtless *adjective*
1. showing little or no thought: 'a careless and *thoughtless* answer'.
2. selfish or inconsiderate.
Word Family: **thoughtlessly**, *adverb*; **thoughtlessness**, *noun.*

thousand *noun*
a cardinal number, the symbol 1000 in Arabic numerals, M in Roman numerals.
Phrases:
one in a thousand, exceptional.
thousand and one, far too many.
Word Family: **thousand**, *adjective*; **thousandth**, *adjective*, *noun.*

thrall (*say* thrawl) *noun*
a) a slave. b) slavery: 'he's in *thrall* to alcohol'.
Word Family: **thraldom**, *noun*, slavery.

thrash *verb*
to beat soundly, especially as punishment.
Usages:
a) 'we *thrashed* them by six goals' (= defeated easily).
b) 'he *thrashed* about in the water' (= struck or plunged violently).
thrash out, to solve or decide by discussion.

thread (*say* thred) *noun*
1. a long, fine piece of a spun substance.
2. something with the shape of a thread, such as a thin line of colour, etc.
Usage: 'I lost the *thread* of the story' (= connecting link or sequence).
3. a spiral ridge cut around the length of a bolt or screw.
hang by a thread, to be in a dangerous or uncertain position.
thread *verb*
1. to pass a thread through.
2. to move in a twisting or winding way: 'she *threaded* her way through the crowd'.
3. to cut a thread on or in a bolt, hole, etc.

threadbare *adjective*
1. (of cloth or clothing) very worn or thin.
2. *Usage:* 'it was a humble *threadbare* house' (= poor, shabby).

threadworm *noun*
a thread-like worm found in the human intestine, usually in children.

threat (*say* thret) *noun*
a statement of intention to hurt or punish, especially in order to force someone to do something: 'she only paid the money under *threat* of violence'.
Usage: 'there's a *threat* of rain in the dark clouds' (= warning, sign).
threaten *verb*
to utter a threat against: 'she *threatened* me with dismissal unless I behaved'.
Usage: 'rain *threatened* the chance of a picnic' (= endangered).

three *noun*
a cardinal number, the symbol 3 in Arabic numerals, III in Roman numerals.

three-dimensional
(*say* three-de-**men**-sh'n-al) *adjective*
having or appearing to have the dimension of depth.
Usage: 'the book's main character is not *three-dimensional* enough' (= realistic).

three-legged race
a running-race in which pairs of competitors have their adjacent legs bandaged together.

three-ply *adjective*
consisting of three layers or thicknesses, such as plywood.

three-point landing
a landing in which all three sets of wheels of an aeroplane touch the ground at the same time, considered a perfect landing.

three-point turn
a turning of a car in a narrow road in three moves.

threnody (*say* **threnna**-dee) *noun*
a funeral dirge.
[Greek *threnos* wailing + *oidé* an ode]

thresh *verb*
to beat or thrash, e.g. to separate the seeds of a cereal plant from the chaff.
thresher *noun*
a person or thing that threshes, especially a flail or machine.
[for THRASH]

threshold (*say* **thresh**-hold) *noun*
1. the entrance to a building, especially the stone, etc. laid in front of a door.
Usage: 'she was at the *threshold* of a new career' (= beginning).
2. the lowest level at which a stimulus will produce an effect: 'the *threshold* of consciousness'.

threw (*say* throo) *verb*
the past tense of the verb **throw**.

thrice *adverb*
three times.

thrift *noun*
any careful or economical use, especially of money.
Word Family: **thrifty**, *adjective*, using thrift; **thriftily**, *adverb*; **thriftiness**, *noun*.

thrill *noun*
a) a nervous tremor or tingle of great excitement: 'it gave him a *thrill* to ride the camel'. b) an experience causing this: 'it's a *thrill* to meet you'.
thrill *verb*
to feel or cause a thrill in: 'winning the race *thrilled* me'.

thriller *noun*
a book, play or film dealing with exciting or mysterious events.

thrips *noun*
any of a group of very small, sap-sucking insects which may be destructive to cereals and fruit trees.
[Greek, woodworm]

thrive *verb*
(**thrived** or **throve, thrived** or **thriven, thriving**)
to grow strong and healthy: 'the garden cannot *thrive* in this drought'.
Usage: 'I hope your plan *thrives*' (= succeeds).

throat *noun*
a) the oesophagus. b) the front part of the neck.
Phrases:
jump down someone's throat, (*informal*) to criticize severely.
lump in one's throat, an unpleasant sensation in the throat, caused by emotion.
throaty *adjective*
a) hoarse. b) produced deep in the throat.
Word Family: **throatily**, *adverb*; **throatiness**, *noun*.

throb *verb*
(**throbbed, throbbing**)
to beat with a strong or rapid rhythm.

Word Family: **throb,** *noun,* a strong beat or rhythm.

throe *noun*
(*usually plural*) violent pains or convulsions: 'the wounded person was in his death *throes*'.
in the throes of, a) in violent struggle with; b) in the process of.

thrombosis (*say* throm–**bo**–sis) *noun*
the formation of a stationary clot which develops inside a blood vessel and blocks the flow of blood. Compare EMBOLUS.
[Greek *thrombos* a lump + –OSIS]

throne *noun*
1. a raised, ornamental chair used on important occasions, e.g. by a monarch.
2. sovereign power or authority: 'the republicans sought abolition of the *throne*'.
[Greek *thronos* a high seat]

throng *noun*
a crowd: '*throngs* of people watched the procession'.
throng *verb*
to crowd: 'thousands *thronged* to the beaches last summer'.

throttle *verb*
1. to choke or strangle.
2. to reduce the speed of an engine.
throttle *noun*
a device in the carburettor of an internal combustion engine, connected to the accelerator pedal, which controls engine speed.

through (*say* throo) *preposition*
1. in one side and out the other: a) 'climb *through* the window'; b) 'the road goes *through* the jungle'.
2. between: 'Tarzan swinging *through* the trees'.
3. from beginning to end: a) 'you talked *through* the whole speech'; b) 'look *through* the book for the answer'.
4. at the end of: 'will you be *through* your work by 5?'.
5. due to or because of: 'she succeeded *through* hard work'.
get through, 'did you *get through* your exams?' (= pass).
through *adverb*
1. from side to side or beginning to end: a) 'let us pass *through*'; b) 'she slept the night *through*'.
2. at or to the end or all the way: a) 'are you *through* with this book?'; b) 'the train goes *through* to Perth'.
Usage: 'put me *through* to the manager's private telephone' (= in connection).
Word Family: **through,** *adjective.*

throughout (*say* throo–**out**) *preposition*
1. in or to every part: 'search *throughout* the countryside'.
2. from the beginning to end of: 'she slept *throughout* the film'.
throughout *adverb*
1. in every part: 'the house has carpet *throughout*'.
2. at all times: 'the baby cried *throughout*'.

throve *verb*
a past tense of the verb **thrive.**

throw *verb*
(**threw, thrown, throwing**)
1. to send forcibly through the air, especially by a movement of the arm: 'don't *throw* stones at the dog'.
2. to put as if by throwing: a) '*throw* him into prison'; b) 'we were *thrown* into confusion'.
Usages:
a) 'the building *threw* a long shadow' (= made).
b) 'she *threw* a punch at him' (= aimed).
c) 'the mare *threw* a fine foal' (= gave birth to).
d) 'she *threw* a tantrum' (= performed).
e) 'the electrician *threw* the switch' (= operated).
f) (*informal*) 'the refusal really *threw* me' (= disconcerted).
Phrases:
throw away, 'you've *thrown away* the wonderful opportunity' (= wasted).
thrown in, 'we paid for the coach tour and the meals were *thrown in*' (= included free of charge).
throw off, to free oneself from.
throw out, a) 'they *threw out* the proposal' (= did not accept or keep); b) 'he *threw out* a hint' (= uttered casually); c) 'the noise *threw* me *out* in my counting' (= caused to make a mistake).
throw up, a) (*informal*) to vomit; b) to abandon.
throw *noun*
the act of throwing: a) 'she returned the ball with a fine *throw*'; b) 'a *throw* of the dice'.

throwaway *adjective*
(of a remark, etc.) uttered casually with apparent disregard for effect.

throwback *noun*
a) a reversion to an ancestral type or character. b) an example of this.

thrush (1) *noun*
any of a family of songbirds, often brown.

thrush (2) *noun*
1. a fungal disease of mucous membranes, especially in the mouth of a child.
2. an infection in the hoof of a horse.

thrust *verb*
(thrust, thrusting)
to push suddenly or forcibly: a) 'he *thrust* the sword into his opponent's heart'; b) 'the girl *thrust* her way through the crowd'.
thrust *noun*
the act of thrusting: a) 'a sword *thrust*'; b) 'the forward *thrust* of a jet engine'.

thud *noun*
a dull sound, as of a heavy blow or fall.
Word Family: **thud (thudded, thudding),** *verb,* to strike or fall with a thud.

thug *noun*
a brutal, violent ruffian or criminal.
Word Family: **thuggish,** *adjective*; **thuggery,** *noun.*
[Hindi *thag* a cheat or murderer]

thulium (*say* **thew**lium) *noun*
element number 69, a rare metal. See LANTHANIDE.
See CHEMICAL ELEMENTS in grey pages.

thumb (*say* thum) *noun*
1. *Anatomy:* the short thick digit set apart from the fingers.
2. the part of a glove, etc. covering the thumb.
Phrases:
all thumbs, clumsy or awkward.
thumbs down, an expression of disapproval.
thumbs up, an expression of approval or triumph.
under someone's thumb, under someone's power or influence.
thumb *verb*
1. to turn pages, etc. over quickly: '*thumb* through the book to chapter 6'.
2. (of a hitchhiker) to solicit a free ride.
thumb one's nose, to express defiance or contempt.

thumbnail sketch
a brief, concise description.

thumbscrew *noun*
1. an instrument of torture designed to crush one or both thumbs.
2. a screw which can be twisted into a surface by the thumb and finger.

thump *verb*
to beat heavily, especially with a thick, dull sound.
thump *noun*
a) a heavy strike or blow. b) the dull sound of this.

thumping *adjective*
(*informal*) very: 'a *thumping* good book'.

thunder *noun*
1. the loud noise produced when the heat from lightning causes the air to expand suddenly.
2. any loud noise: 'a *thunder* of applause'.
steal someone's thunder, to steal the credit of another's ideas, inventions, policy, etc. before he has been able to act on them himself.
thunder *verb*
1. to make thunder.
2. to speak or act loudly or violently: 'she *thundered* on the door with her fists'.
Word Family: **thunderous, thundery,** *adjectives*; **thunderously,** *adverb.*

thunderbolt *noun*
1. a flash of lightning accompanied by thunder.
2. an unexpected disaster or unpleasant surprise: 'the news came as a *thunderbolt*'.

thunderclap *noun*
a crash of thunder.

thundering *adjective*
(*informal*) very: 'she's in a *thundering* bad mood'.

thunderstorm *noun*
a storm in which strong upward air currents generate static electricity, producing thunder and lightning.

thunderstruck *adjective*
amazed or astounded.

Thursday *noun*
the fifth day of the week.
[after *Thor,* the ancient Scandinavian god of thunder]

thus (*say th*us) *adverb*
1. in this way: 'watch me and do it *thus*'.
2. consequently: '*thus,* after all the evidence, I must be right'.
thus far, up to this point.

thwack *verb*
to whack.
Word Family: **thwack,** *noun.*

thwart (*say* thwort) *verb*
to prevent something being done successfully: 'the police *thwarted* the attempted bank robbery'.
thwart *noun*
a seat across a small boat.

thy (*say thy*) *pronoun*
an old word meaning your (singular).

thyme (*say* time) *noun*
a low shrub with fragrant leaves used in cooking.
[from Greek]

thymine (*say* **thy**-meen) *noun*
Biology: see PYRIMIDINE.

thymus (*say* **thy**mus) *noun*
Anatomy: a gland, large in children but very small in adults, situated near the base of the neck.
[Greek *thymos* the soul]

thyroid gland
Anatomy: a gland in the lower neck, secreting hormones which control the metabolic rate of the body.
[Greek *thyreoeides* shield-shaped, oblong]

thyself *pronoun*
an old word meaning yourself.

tiara (*say* tee-**ar**-a) *noun*
a semicircular band of jewels, etc. worn as a head ornament.
[Greek]

tibia (*say* **tib**bi-a) *noun*
Anatomy: the thicker of the two long bones of the lower leg.
[Latin]

tic *noun*
a twitch, especially of the facial muscles.
[French]

tick (1) *noun*
1. a light recurring click or beat, as of a clock or watch.
Usage: 'wait here, I'll only be a *tick*' (= moment).
2. a small written mark to show that something is correct, noted, etc.
on the tick, punctually.
tick *verb*
to make a tick or ticks: a) 'the time bomb *ticked* away quietly'; b) 'the customer *ticked* her list'
Usage: 'what makes him *tick*?' (= behave as he does).
Phrases:
tick off, (*informal*) to scold.
tick over, a) (of an engine) to run slowly and quietly in neutral; b) 'his mind was *ticking over*' (= working).

tick (2) *noun*
any of a group of blood-sucking arachnids, often parasitic on mammals.

tick (3) *noun*
(*informal*) credit: 'all their furniture was bought on *tick*'.
[short form of *ticket*]

ticker *noun*
(*informal*) a) the heart. b) a watch.

ticker tape
the long strips of paper on which a tape machine prints information.
ticker tape parade
American: a parade in which ticker tape, streamers, etc. are thrown from windows onto the celebrity.

ticket *noun*
1. a small piece of cardboard or paper indicating that its owner is entitled to something: a) 'a train *ticket*'; b) 'a theatre *ticket*'.
2. a tag or label showing price, etc.
3. a fine or summons for a traffic offence: 'a parking *ticket*'.
4. *American politics:* the list of candidates from any one party.
that's the ticket, that's the correct thing to do.
Word Family: **ticket**, *verb*.

ticket of leave
History: a conditional freedom granted to convicts who had served part of their sentences.

ticking *noun*
a strong, cotton fabric used for covering mattresses, pillows, etc.

tickle *verb*
1. to excite the nerves by lightly touching sensitive parts of the skin.
2. to amuse or please: a) 'the children were *tickled* by the antics of the clowns'; b) 'the flattery *tickled* his pride'.
tickled pink, greatly amused or pleased.
Word Family: **tickle**, *noun*; **tickler**, *noun*, (informal) a difficult problem or situation.

ticklish *adjective*
1. sensitive to tickling.
2. needing delicate care or handling: 'are you able to handle such a *ticklish* situation?'.

tidal (*say* **tide**-al) *adjective*
of or relating to the tide.

tidal basin
Geography: see BASIN.

tidal current
the movement of seawater into a restricted area such as a bay or river.

tidal river
a river up which the tide travels a considerable distance.

tidal wave
a large destructive wave produced by an earthquake at sea.

tiddly *adjective*
(*informal*) tipsy.

tiddlywinks *noun*
a game in which small discs must be flicked into a cup.

tide *noun*
the rise and fall of the surface of the sea, caused by the gravitational pull of the sun and moon; the sea **floods** in to high tide and **ebbs** out to low tide twice a day; the maximum and minimum range between the two occur twice a month, at **spring** and **neap** tide respectively.
Usage: 'the *tide* of public opinion changes quickly' (= stream, current).
tide *verb*
tide over, 'lend me some money to *tide* me *over* until payday' (= support).

tidemark *noun*
a) the line of wrack and flotsam which marks the highest point of recent tides.
b) a similar mark in a dirty bath or on a child's unwashed neck.

tidings (*say* **tide–ings**) *plural noun*
news or information.

tidy *adjective*
1. a) having everything in its right place. b) (of a person) in the habit of arranging things in their right place.
2. (*informal*) large: 'a *tidy* sum of money'.
tidy *noun*
a box or container for keeping things in, etc.
Word Family: **tidy (tidied, tidying),** *verb.*

tie *verb*
(tied, tying)
1. to fasten or attach by string, rope, etc.: a) '*tie* the prisoner's hands'; b) '*tie* this label to his coat'.
2. to form by interlacing, etc.: 'please *tie* this knot for me'.
Usages:
a) 'why should I be always *tied* to the kitchen?' (= confined).
b) 'how can we *tie* the suspect to the crime?' (= connect).
3. to score equally in a contest.
Phrases:
tie in with, to connect or agree with.
tie up, a) 'she's *tied up* every night this week' (= occupied, busy); b) 'the agreement was finally *tied up*' (= concluded, settled); c) 'the strike *tied up* shipping for a month' (= hindered). d) 'he was *tied up* with the scandal' (= connected).
tie *noun*
1. something which ties or connects: 'a *tie* of friendship'.
2. a strip of cloth, usually of cotton, silk or wool, worn around the neck under a collar and knotted at the front.
3. an equality of votes, points, etc. between contestants.

tied cottage
a cottage which goes with a farming job and must be vacated on leaving the job.

tied house
a pub owned by a brewery, whose brands it sells in preference to others. Compare FREE HOUSE.

tie–dye *verb*
(tie–dyed, tie–dyeing)
to dye fabric or clothes by tying them in patterns of knots before applying the dye, so that the knotted areas are not coloured.

tier (*say* teer) *noun*
a row or level, especially one of a series rising one above or behind the other, as of seats in a theatre.

tie–up *noun*
an association or connection.

tiff *noun*
a slight quarrel.

tiger (*say* **tie–ga**) *noun*
a large flesh–eating, Asian mammal of the cat family, having a tawny coat with black stripes.
[from Greek]

tiger cat
the ocelot.

tight *adjective*
1. fastened, fixed or fitting firmly or closely: 'these shoes are too *tight*'.
Usages:
a) 'the race ended in a *tight* finish' (= close).
b) 'she's *tight* with her money' (= stingy).
c) 'money seems to be *tight* this month' (= in short supply).
2. difficult, demanding: a) 'I'm in a *tight* spot'; b) 'I have a *tight* schedule'.

3. impervious to water, air, etc.: 'is the boat *watertight*?'.
4. (*informal*) tipsy.
Word Family: **tight, tightly,** *adverbs*; **tightness,** *noun*; **tighten,** *verb*, to make or become tight.

tight-fisted *adjective*
miserly or stingy.

tight-lipped *adjective*
saying little or nothing.

tightrope *noun*
a rope or wire stretched high above the ground, on which an acrobat walks or performs tricks.

tights *plural noun*
1. a close-fitting garment covering the lower part of the body and the legs, as worn by ballet-dancers, acrobats, etc.
2. an item of female underwear consisting of stockings and underpants in one piece. Also called **pantihose.**

tightwad (*say* **tite-wod**) *noun*
(*informal*) a mean or miserly person.

tigress (*say* **tie-gress**) *noun*
a female tiger.

tilde (*say* **tilda**) *noun*
Language: see ACCENT.
[Spanish]

tile *noun*
a sheet, usually of baked clay, used in overlapping rows to form a roof, or glazed on one side and used to cover floors, walls, etc.
Phrases:
a tile loose, a little crazy.
on the tiles, on a spree (like a cat in season).
Word Family: **tile,** *verb*, to cover with tiles; **tiler,** *noun*, a person who lays tiles.

till (1) *preposition, conjunction*
until.

till (2) *verb*
to plough or cultivate the soil.
Word Family: **tillage,** *noun*, a) the practice of tilling, b) land which has been tilled.

till (3) *noun*
a special drawer-like container with compartments for money, e.g. in a cash register.

tiller (1) *noun*
a person who tills soil, etc.

tiller (2) *noun*
Nautical: the handle attached to the top of a rudder for steering.

tilt *verb*
1. to put or be put in a sloping position: 'if you *tilt* the table the plates will fall off'.
2. to joust.
tilt *noun*
a) the act of tilting. b) a tilting position: 'the table was at a *tilt*'.

timber *noun*
also called **lumber**
a) wood which has been cut and treated, used in building, making furniture, etc. b) the trees used for this.
Word Family: **timber,** *verb*, to provide with timber.

timber line
the height on a mountain above which trees will not grow.

timbre (*say* **tambra**) *noun*
the characteristic quality of a sound produced by a particular voice or instrument.
[French]

time *noun*
1. a) the fact or concept of continuous existence. b) a system of measuring or dividing this: 'Greenwich Mean *Time*'.
2. a portion or measure of this, especially as a definite moment or period: a) 'the *time* is 12 midday'; b) 'do you have *time* to help?'; c) 'in the *time* of the ancient Greeks'.
Usages:
a) '*times* were hard in the war' (= conditions).
b) 'did you have a good *time*?' (= experience).
c) 'the train is running behind *time*' (= the appointed instant of arrival, etc.).
d) '*time*, gentlemen' (= closing time at this pub).
3. an instance: 'how many *times* do I have to tell you?'.
4. (*plural*) used to indicate multiplication: 'five *times* five equals twenty-five'.
5. *Physics:* the fundamental quantity describing the period over which a physical change takes place, expressed in seconds.
6. *Music:* a) the basic rhythmical patterns. b) the length of a particular note.
Phrases:
at the same time, 'I'll give you my permission, but *at the same time* I think you're being foolish' (= nevertheless).

at times, from time to time, occasionally.
behind the times, old-fashioned.
do time, (*informal*) to undergo imprisonment.
have no time for, to be unable to tolerate.
in good time, a) 'the pain will go away *in good time*' (= eventually); b) 'we arrived *in good time* and got the best seats' (= early).
in no time, very quickly.
in time, a) 'we arrived *in time* for the first film' (= early enough); b) 'all will be well *in time*' (= eventually); c) 'play your tuba *in time* with the piccolo' (= in the same rhythm).
on time, punctually.
pass the time of day, to exchange brief greetings.
play for time, to manoeuvre to gain extra time.
race against time, to try hard to finish in time.
take one's time, to act in a leisurely way.
time of day, a) 'we can't change our plans at this *time of day*' (= late stage); b) 'he knows the *time of day*' (= what's going on around him).
time off, 'he was going to ask me to work in my *time off*' (= rest period).
time *verb*
1. to record or measure the time of something: 'the race was *timed* on a stopwatch'.
2. to arrange or choose the moment for: 'we *timed* our holidays to coincide with the good weather'.

time and a half
the payment of 50 per cent more than usual wages, especially for overtime.

time and motion study
the analysis of work methods, to improve efficiency or increase production in a business.

time bomb
a bomb containing a mechanism that will cause it to explode at a set time.

timecard *noun*
see TIMESHEET.

time clock
a clock with a device attached, to record the times of arrival and departure of employees.

time exposure
Photography: the process of keeping the shutter open for a long time, usually at least one second.

time-honoured *adjective*
respected because of tradition or long use: 'a *time-honoured* custom'.

timekeeper *noun*
a person or thing that keeps time, such as an official who times races in a sporting contest.

time-lag *noun*
the period of time between two events, etc.

time-lapse photography
the process of taking a series of pictures over a long period of time to record a particular event, such as the gradual opening of a flower bud.

timeless *adjective*
1. relating to no particular time: 'a *timeless* fairy story'.
2. having no end.

timely *adjective*
occurring at the right or favourable time: 'a *timely* rescue'.

timepiece *noun*
any instrument used to measure and show time.

time-server *noun*
a person who seeks advancement by pretending to hold the views of his employer or of the circle in which he moves.

time sheet
also called a **timecard**
a card or sheet of paper on which an employee's time of arrival and departure, or the actual hours worked, is recorded.

time signature
Music: the sign at the beginning of a work to indicate the type and number of beats in each bar.

timetable *noun*
1. a list or table showing the times of particular events: a) 'a train *timetable*'; b) 'a lecture *timetable*'.
2. any plan or list of the order of events.
Word Family: **timetable,** *verb,* to s a timetable for any activity.

timeworn *adjective*
showing the effects or deterioration of age, long use, etc.

time zone
a geographical region within which the same standard time is used.

timid *adjective*
easily frightened or made nervous.

Word Family: **timidly**, *adverb*; **timidity** (*say* tim–**iddi**–tee), **timidness**, *nouns*.
[from Latin]

timing (*say* **time**–ing) *noun*
the art or process of establishing or maintaining the correct and most effective time, speed, sequence, etc.: a) 'the *timing* of her jokes is always perfect'; b) 'the *timing* in this engine is not quite right'.

timorous (*say* **timma**–rus) *adjective*
timid or full of fear.
Word Family: **timorously**, *adverb*; **timorousness**, *noun*.
[Latin *timor* fear]

timpani (*say* **timpa**–nee) *plural noun*
singular is **timpano**
kettledrums.
Word Family: **timpanist**, *noun*, a person who plays the timpani.
[Italian]

tin *noun*
1. element number 50, a malleable, ductile metal used in protective coating and alloys.
See CHEMICAL ELEMENTS in grey pages.
2. a container made from tin or tin plate, especially one which is sealed: 'a *tin* of soup'.
3. an unsealed metal container, used for storing, baking, etc.
Word Family: **tin** (**tinned, tinning**), *verb*, to cover with or pack in tins; **tin**, *adjective*, a) made of tin, b) worthless or unworthy.

tincture (*say* **tink**–cher) *noun*
1. a solution of a medicine in alcohol.
2. a slight trace.
3. *Heraldry:* any of the colours, metals or furs used in coats of arms.
Word Family: **tincture**, *verb*, to stain or dye.
[Latin *tinctura* dyeing]

tinder *noun*
dry twigs, etc. used to start a fire.

tine *noun*
a prong or other projecting point.

tinea (*say* **tinnia**) *noun*
any skin condition caused by fungus, especially ringworm.
[Latin, gnawing worm]

tinfoil *noun*
see ALUMINIUM FOIL.

tinge (*say* tinj) *verb*
to give a slight colour, taste or smell to: a) 'black hair *tinged* with grey'; b) 'air *tinged* with smoke'.
Word Family: **tinge**, *noun*.
[Latin *tingere* to dye]

tingle *verb*
to feel a slight pricking or prickling: 'her face *tingled* with cold'.
Word Family: **tingle**, *noun*.

tin god
a person whom someone admires greatly but ill–advisedly.

tinker *noun*
1. a person who travels about mending pots and pans, etc.
2. any person who enjoys doing repairs, etc. to mechanical things.
Word Family: **tinker**, *verb*, a) to fiddle or experiment with, b) to work as a tinker.

tinkle *noun*
1. a light, high–pitched ringing sound.
2. (*informal*) a telephone call: 'give me a *tinkle* this afternoon'.
Word Family: **tinkle**, *verb*.

tin lizzie
(*informal*) an old motor car.

tinman's solder
a solder with a low melting point, containing up to 65 per cent tin with lead.

tinnitus (*say* tin–**eye**–tus) *noun*
ringing in the ears.
[Latin *tinnire* to ring]

tinny *adjective*
1. of or characteristic of tin.
2. cheaply or badly made and unlikely to last.
Word Family: **tinnily**, *adverb*; **tinniness**, *noun*.

tin–pan alley
(*informal*) a) the publishers and composers of pop music. b) the part of a city where they work.
[originally applied to an area of New York City (14th Street)]

tin plate
a sheet of metal coated with a layer of tin.

tin–pot *adjective*
cheap or worthless.

tinsel *noun*
1. a glittering, metallic substance used in thin strips, threads or sheets for decoration, e.g. on a Christmas tree.
2. something which is gaudy but worthless.

tinsmith *noun*
a person who makes or repairs tin or metal goods.

tinsnips *plural noun*
a pair of metal shears used for cutting wire, tin, etc.

tint *noun*
1. a variety of a particular colour, especially one mixed with white to reduce its chroma. Compare SHADE.
2. any slight or pale colour, such as a temporary hair dye.
Word Family: **tint,** *verb.*
[Latin *tinctus* dyed]

tiny (*say* **tie**-nee) *adjective*
very small.

tip (1) *noun*
a) a tapered end or top: 'a *fingertip*'. b) a piece or part at the end of something: 'a filter *tip* on a cigarette'.
Word Family: **tip** (**tipped, tipping**), *verb,* a) to provide with a tip, b) to decorate or mark the tip of.

tip (2) *verb*
(**tipped, tipping**)
to move or cause to move to a slanting position: 'the bucket *tipped* dangerously but stayed upright'.
Usage: 'he *tipped* his hat in greeting' (= lifted, took off).
tip over, 'the car *tipped over* after the collision' (= turned over).
tip *noun*
1. the act of tipping.
2. a rubbish dump.

tip (3) *noun*
1. a small gift of money to a waiter, porter, servant, etc. to show appreciation for service.
2. a private hint or piece of information given as a guide: 'a betting *tip*'
tip *verb*
(**tipped, tipping**)
to give a tip to.
tip off, (*informal*) 'he *tipped off* the police about the robbery' (= warned or informed in advance). *Word Family:* **tip-off,** *noun.*
Word Family: **tipster,** *noun,* a person who provides tips, especially as an occupation or business.

tip (4) *verb*
(**tipped, tipping**)
to strike with a light, glancing blow: 'the ball just *tipped* his bat and flew into the keeper's hands'.
Word Family: **tip,** *noun.*

tipple *verb*
to drink alcohol, especially often or excessively.
Word Family: **tipple,** *noun,* alcohol; **tippler,** *noun,* a person who tipples.

tipsy *adjective*
1. (*informal*) slightly drunk.
2. unsteady.
Word Family: **tipsily,** *adverb*; **tipsiness,** *noun.*

tiptoe *verb*
(**tiptoed, tiptoeing**)
to walk very quietly on or as if on the tips of the toes.
Word Family: **tiptoe,** *adverb*; **tiptoe,** *noun.*

tiptop *adjective*
(*informal*) excellent or best.

tirade (*say* tie-**rade**) *noun*
a long speech, especially a violently angry or critical one.
[Italian *tirata* a volley]

tire (1) *verb*
1. to use up or lessen the energy or strength of: 'don't *tire* yourself playing'.
2. to lose patience or interest: 'we soon *tired* of the boring game'.
tired *adjective*
1. having lost one's energy, strength, interest, etc., often owing to a need for sleep.
2. trite or lacking originality: 'no more *tired* old jokes please!'.
tired of, 'I'm *tired of* that restaurant' (= had enough of).
Word Family: **tiredly,** *adverb*; **tiredness,** *noun*; **tireless,** *adjective,* never becoming tired; **tiresome,** *adjective,* irritating or annoying.

tire (2) *noun*
American: a tyre.

tiro (*say* **tie**-ro) **tyro** *noun*
plural is **tiros**
a beginner or learner.
[Latin, recruit]

'tis (*say* tiz)
an old poetic word for it is.

tisane (*say* tiz-**an**) *noun*
a herbal tea.
[French]

tissue (*say* **tish**-oo) *noun*
1. *Biology:* an organized group of similar cells in an organism, such as bone, cartilage, etc.
Usage: 'the criminal's evidence was a *tissue* of lies' (= carefully connected or constructed mass).
2. a thin, soft, paper handkerchief.
3. a light, transparent paper used for wrapping, protecting, etc. Short form of **tissue paper.**

tissue culture
Biology: see CULTURE.

tit (1) *noun*
any of a group of small birds, such as the **tomtit**.

tit (2) *noun*
(*informal*) a) a nipple. b) a breast.

titan (*say* **tie**–t'n) *noun*
a person of great strength, size or importance.
Word Family: **titanic** (*say* tie–**tannik**), *adjective*, very large or strong.
[after the *Titans*, a family of twelve gods and goddesses of Greek mythology who ruled Olympus until overthrown by Zeus]

titanium (*say* tie–**tay**–nee–um) *noun*
element number 22, a malleable, ductile metal, used in alloys and to toughen steel. See TRANSITION ELEMENT.
See CHEMICAL ELEMENTS in grey pages.
Word Family: **titanic** (*say* tie–**tannik**), *adjective*.

titbit *noun*
a small choice piece, e.g. of food.

tit for tat
repayment, especially retaliation.

tithe (*say* ti*the*) *noun*
one tenth, especially one tenth of one's farm produce, taken as a tax to support the clergy, etc.
Word Family: **tithe**, *verb*, to demand a tithe.

titian (*say* **tish**'n) *noun*
a reddish-brown colour.
[after *Titian*, died 1576, an Italian painter who often used this colour to paint hair]

titillate (*say* **titti**–late) *verb*
to excite or tease pleasantly.
Word Family: **titillation**, *noun*.

titivate (*say* **titti**–vate) *verb*
(*informal*) to decorate or make smart.
Word Family: **titivation**, *noun*.

title (*say* **tie**–t'l) *noun*
1. a word or words giving the distinctive name of a book, play, painting, etc.
2. a form of address which indicates a person's occupation, rank, social position, etc.
Usage: 'the young boxer won the world *title*' (= championship).
3. a right: 'his friendship with the old man did not give him *title* to an inheritance'.
4. *Law:* a deed or document which proves a person's right of possession, control, etc., especially of land or property. Short form of **title-deed**.
Word Family: **title**, *verb*.

titration (*say* tie–**tray**–sh'n) *noun*
Chemistry: the estimation of the quantity of a substance in a solution, by adding a second solution of known composition and concentration (called the **titre**), until the end point of a reaction is reached.
Word Family: **titrate**, *verb*.
[French *titrer* to give a name to]

titter *verb*
to laugh or giggle in a nervous or half-restrained way.
Word Family: **titter**, *noun*.

tittle *noun*
a dot or mark, such as an accent.
Usage: 'I don't care a jot or *tittle* for your complaints' (= tiniest bit).

tittle-tattle *noun*
gossip or foolish chatter.
Word Family: **tittle-tattle**, *verb*.

titular (*say* **tit**–yoo–la) *adjective*
of, being or having a title.
Usage: 'she is the *titular* head of the government' (= in name but not in fact).
Word Family: **titular, titulary**, *nouns*, a person who has a title.

tizzy, tiz *noun*
(*informal*) a state of nervous confusion or excitement.

to *preposition*
a word used to indicate the following:
1. movement in the direction of: 'from Sydney *to* Singapore'.
2. limit: a) 'prizes *to* the value of £100'; b) 'open from 1 o'clock *to* 6 o'clock'.
3. aim or intention: 'let's go *to* see a film'.
4. attachment or contact: a) 'stick *to* your view'; b) 'apply paint *to* the wall'.
5. addition or accompaniment: 'garlic gives flavour *to* this soup'.
6. comparison or contrast: 'at right angles *to* the wall'.
7. result: 'he tore it *to* pieces'.
8. relation or reference: 'she claims her right *to* the pension'.
Usages:
a) 'it is 10 *to* 5' (= before).
b) 'how many metres *to* one kilometre?' (= in).
c) 'the score was 4 *to* 6' (= versus, against).
d) 'is this *to* your liking?' (= in agreement with).
9. special use before a verb in its infinitive form: '*to* see'.

to *adverb*
1. into a particular position, especially closed: 'pull that door *to* behind you'. **2.** into consciousness: 'he came *to* as they splashed water on his face'.
to and fro, backwards and forwards.

toad *noun*
any of a group of amphibians, resembling the frog but with drier and more warty skins.

toad-in-the-hole *noun*
a batter pudding containing sausages.

toadstool *noun*
any of various fleshy fungi, other than mushrooms, with a stalk and umbrella-like cap, some of which are poisonous.

toady *verb*
(toadied, toadying)
to flatter or pander in a servile fashion.
Word Family: **toady**, *noun.*

toast (1) *noun*
a slice of bread heated so that it becomes crisp and brown.
toast *verb*
to heat in order to make into toast.
Usage: 'come and *toast* yourself by the fire' (= warm).
Word Family: **toaster**, *noun*, a person or thing that toasts, such as an electrical device into which slices of bread are put to be toasted.
[Latin *tostus* parched]

toast (2) *verb*
to drink in honour of: 'let's *toast* the happy couple!'.
toast *noun*
a) the act of toasting. b) the words spoken before such an act.
Usage: 'the young writer was the *toast* of the local literary world' (= person most praised or celebrated).
Word Family: **toastmaster**, *noun*, a person who proposes toasts, introduces speakers, etc. at formal dinners.

tobacco (*say* to-**bakko**) *noun*
a) the dried leaves of a tropical plant which are prepared for smoking, chewing or as snuff. b) the plant itself.
Word Family: **tobacconist** *noun*, a person who sells tobacco, cigarettes, etc.
[from Spanish]

toboggan (*say* te-**bogg**'n) *noun*
see SLEDGE.
Word Family: **toboggan**, *verb*, to use or ride on a toboggan.
[Canadian French]

toby jug
a large drinking mug in the shape of a stout old man wearing a three-cornered hat.
[after *Toby Philpot*, a legendary drinker of fabulous capacity]

toccata (*say* tok-**ahta**) *noun*
Music: a brilliant piece of instrumental music designed to display the soloist's technique.
[Italian, touched]

tocsin (*say* **tok**-sin) *noun*
a bell rung, especially as a signal of alarm.
[French]

today *adverb*
on this or the present day.
Word Family: **today**, *noun.*

toddle *verb*
to walk with short unsteady steps.
Word Family: **toddle**, *noun*; **toddler**, *noun*, a very young child.

toddy *noun*
a hot, alcoholic drink made from spirits, hot water and spices.

to-do *noun*
(*informal*) a fuss.

toe *noun*
1. any of the 10 end parts of the feet. **2.** the part of a garment covering a toe or toes.
Phrases:
on one's toes, ready and alert.
turn one's toes up, (*informal*) to die.
toe *verb*
(toed, toeing)
to touch or kick with the toes.
toe the line, to obey or conform.

toehold *noun*
a small ledge, etc. which may support the toe in climbing.
Usage: 'the promotion gave him a *toehold* in the running of the company' (= opportunity to participate).

toe-in *noun*
the slight degree to which the front wheels of a motor vehicle are turned inwards to improve steering and handling.

toff *noun*
(*informal*) a rich gentleman.

toffee *noun*
a sweet, often hard and brittle, made by boiling sugar or treacle with butter and other ingredients.
toffee apple, a toffee-coated apple on a stick.
Word Family: **toffee-nosed**, *adjective*, snobbish, supercilious.

toga (*say* **toe–ga**) *noun*
a long, loose robe worn in ancient Rome.

together *adverb*
1. in or as one group, etc.: a) 'let's go there *together*'; b) 'he weighs more than all of us *together*'.
2. so as to be joined, near or in contact: 'stick the two parts *together*'.
Usages:
a) 'the shared danger brought them *together*' (= to a closer relationship).
b) 'we will all work *together*' (= in harmony or cooperation).
c) 'they are always fighting *together*' (= with each other).
d) 'multiply these two numbers *together*' (= by each other).
Word Family: **togetherness,** *noun,* a feeling of harmony, closeness or friendship.

toggle *noun*
a fastener consisting of a rod or pin mounted at its centre and passed through a loop or eye of rope, cable, etc., e.g. on a duffel coat.

toggle switch
an electrical switch in which a jointed arm, when moved through a small arc, causes the contacts to open or close suddenly.

togs *plural noun*
(*informal*) clothes: 'get your bathing *togs*'.

toil (1) *verb*
to work hard or continuously.
Usage: 'the hikers *toiled* up the last steep slope' (= proceeded with difficulty).
Word Family: **toil,** *noun.*

toil (2) *noun*
in the toils of, 'she was *in the toils of* despair' (= in the power of, ensnared by).

toile (*say* twahl) *noun*
a fine, stiff, linen fabric.

toilet (*say* **toy**–let) *noun*
also called a **lavatory** or **w.c.**
1. a bowl-like receptacle for urination and defecation, fitted with a device to flush it clean with water and connected by a pipe to the drains.
2. a room or similar structure containing such an apparatus.
3. the process of washing, dressing or grooming oneself.
4. an old word for a costume or outfit.
[French *toilette* a cloth]

toiletry *noun*
any article or cosmetic used in washing, dressing or grooming oneself.

toilet water
see EAU DE COLOGNE.

toilworn *adjective*
showing the effects of hard work.

token (*say* **toe**–k'n) *noun*
1. something which represents or indicates a feeling, fact, etc.: 'a *token* of affection'.
2. a symbol or sign.
Usage: 'the Queen possesses only the *tokens* of power' (= outward signs but not real bases).
3. a voucher exchangeable in shops for goods, especially books, records, etc.
4. a stamped piece of metal or plastic used in place of coins in some machines.
by the same token, similarly, moreover or incidentally.
token *adjective*
done as a minimal gesture only: 'you only have to make a *token* payment to become a member'.

told *verb*
the past tense and past participle of the verb **tell.**
all told, 'there were 10 of us *all told*' (= in total).

tolerance (*say* **tolla**–r'nce) *noun*
1. the ability to endure or put up with difficulties, etc.
Usage: 'the patient developed a *tolerance* to the antibiotics' (= resistance).
2. the quality or practice of accepting or being fair towards beliefs, customs, etc. which are different from one's own: 'religious *tolerance*'.
3. a permitted variation from a standard quality, dimension, etc.
Word Family: **tolerant,** *adjective,* showing or feeling tolerance; **tolerantly,** *adverb.*

tolerate (*say* **tolla**–rate) *verb*
to allow or bear the existence or practice of without opposition: 'I will not *tolerate* such rudeness'.
Usage: 'the government *tolerates* all sectarian religions' (= accepts and recognizes).
Word Family: **toleration,** *noun;* **tolerable,** *adjective,* a) able to be tolerated or endured, b) (informal) reasonable; **tolerably,** *adverb;*

tolerability (*say* tollera-**billi**-tee), *noun.*
[Latin *tolerare* to endure]

toll (1) (*rhymes with* roll) *verb*
1. (of a bell) to sound or cause to sound with slow, regular rings.
2. to announce by ringing a bell in such a way: 'to *toll* an alarm'.
Word Family: **toll,** *noun.*

toll (2) (*rhymes with* roll) *noun*
a charge made for the use of a road, bridge, etc.
Usage: 'the flood took a heavy *toll* in crops' (= loss).
Word Family: **tollgate,** *noun,* a gate or other barrier at which a toll is collected.

toluene (*say* **tol**-yoo-een) *noun*
also called **toluol**
Chemistry: a colourless, liquid, aromatic hydrocarbon used in petrol, dyes, drugs, saccharine and trinitrotoluene (TNT).

tom *noun*
a male animal: 'a *tomcat*'.

tomahawk (*say* **tomma**-hawk) *noun*
also called a **hatchet**
a small axe, such as that used as a weapon by North American Indians.
Word Family: **tomahawk,** *verb,* to cut or injure with a tomahawk.

tomato *noun*
plural is **tomatoes**
a medium-sized, fleshy, red fruit with many pips, used as a vegetable.
[Mexican]

tomb (*say* toom) *noun*
a grave or vault for the dead.
Word Family: **tombstone,** *noun,* an inscribed stone set above a grave.
[from Greek]

tomboy *noun*
a rough or boisterous young girl.

tome *noun*
a large book.
[from Greek]

tomfoolery (*say* tom-**foola**-ree) *noun*
foolish behaviour.
Word Family: **tomfool,** *adjective,* very foolish; **tomfool,** *noun, verb.*

tommy *noun*
(*informal, often capital*) a British soldier.
[after *Tommy Atkins,* a fictitious name used in sample forms for army privates]

tommy-gun *noun*
a type of submachine gun used in World War 2.
[after *J. T. Thompson,* 1860–1940, an American army officer]

tommyrot *noun*
nonsense.

tomorrow (*say* to-**morro**) *noun*
the day after today.

tomtit *noun*
see TIT (1).

tom-tom *noun*
a small drum, especially one used by Africans, etc. and beaten with the hands.

ton (1) (*say* tun) *noun*
1. a) a unit of mass of the avoirdupois system, equal to about 1020 kg. Also called a **long ton.** See UNITS in grey pages. b) (in America) a unit of mass equal to about 907 kg. Also called a **short ton** or a **net ton.**
2. (*informal*) a large amount.

ton (2) (*say* tun) *noun*
(*informal*) a speed of 100 miles (160 km) per hour, especially on a motorcycle.

tonality (*say* toe-**nalli**-tee) *noun*
a balance or harmony in a system, e.g. of the colours of a painting, or the keys used in a musical composition.

tone *noun*
1. a sound, especially one with a particular quality, length, etc.: 'the clear *tones* of a church bell'.
Usages:
a) 'the furious *tone* of her voice made me apologize nervously' (= quality, expression).
b) 'there was a light-hearted *tone* to the meeting' (= feeling, mood).
2. *Music:* the interval which equals two semitones.
3. a shade or hue, or any slight variation in a colour: 'the wall was painted in a bluish *tone*'.
4. *Medicine:* the usual firmness in the muscles of a healthy body.
5. elegance or style: 'she dresses with distinctive *tone*'.
tone *verb*
to give a particular tone or quality to.
Phrases:
tone down, 'please try to *tone down* your language' (= soften, moderate).
tone in with, tone with, 'that furniture *tones in with* the modern house' (= harmonizes).
tone up, 'exercises will *tone up* your muscles' (= make firm or strong).

Word Family: **tonal**, *adjective*, relating to tone or tonality, especially in music. [Greek *tonos* tension]

tone-deaf (*say* tone-**def**) *adjective*
not able to hear the difference in pitch in musical notes.

tone poem
also called a **symphonic poem**
a piece of programme music which may try to represent the mood of a particular poem or the sounds of nature in a particular setting.

tongs *plural noun*
a device with two hinged or sprung arms, for picking up or holding something.

tongue (*say* tung) *noun*
1. *Anatomy:* the mobile muscular organ in the mouth of vertebrate animals. In mammals it is the organ of taste, and in man it is also the main organ of speech.
Usages:
a) 'answer me, or have you lost your *tongue*?' (= ability to speak).
b) 'he speaks fluent French but English is his native *tongue*' (= language).
c) 'don't be upset by her cruel *tongue*' (= manner of speaking).
2. the tongue of an animal, especially the lamb or ox, used as food.
3. something which has the shape, position or function of a tongue, such as the hanging piece inside a bell, or the flap of material under the laces or fastening of a shoe.
Phrases:
hold one's tongue, to be quiet.
on the tip of one's tongue, about to be remembered or spoken.
slip of the tongue, something said or mentioned accidentally.
tongue in cheek, with one's tongue in one's cheek, mockingly or ironically.
with one's tongue hanging out, thirsty (like a dog) or greedily waiting for something.
Word Family: **tongue**, *verb*, a) to sound a wind instrument with the tongue, b) to touch with the tongue.

tongue-and-groove *noun*
a joint made by cutting a narrow groove along the edge of one piece, into which the matching tapered edge (called the **tongue**) of another piece is fitted, especially in floorboards, etc.

tongue-lashing *noun*
a scolding.

tongue-tied *adjective*
unable to speak, especially due to shyness or embarrassment.

tongue twister
a word or words difficult to say quickly, especially because similar but slightly different sounds are continually repeated.

tonic *noun*
1. any substance, often a medicine, which invigorates.
2. *Music:* the first note of a scale.
3. (*informal*) tonic water.
tonic *adjective*
1. producing or restoring tone or vigour.
2. *Music:* of or based on the tonic.
[Greek *tonos* tension, musical pitch]

tonic water
a non-alcoholic, carbonated water containing quinine, often mixed with spirits.

tonight *noun*
this present or coming night.
Word Family: **tonight**, *adverb*.

tonnage (*say* **tunnij**) *noun*
the amount of space in which a ship can carry goods.

tonne (*say* ton) *noun*
a metric unit of mass, equal to 1000 kg.

tonsil *noun*
Anatomy: either of two masses of connected lymph nodes, forming a ring where the mouth and nose open into the throat.
[from Latin]

tonsillectomy (*say* tonsi-**lekta**-mee) *noun*
an operation to remove the tonsils.
[TONSIL + Greek *ektomé* a cutting out]

tonsillitis (*say* tonsi-**lie**-tus) *noun*
an inflammation of the tonsils, common in children, which may require removal of the tonsils.
[TONSIL + -ITIS]

tonsorial (*say* ton-**sawriul**) *adjective*
relating to a barber or his work.

tonsure (*say* **ton**-sher) *noun*
a) the shaving of the head, or part of the head, especially that of a monk.
b) the part of the head which is shaved.
Word Family: **tonsure**, *verb*.
[Latin *tonsura* shearing]

tontine (*say* ton-**teen**) *noun*
a scheme under which several friends buy a joint annuity, the share of each one who dies being divided among the rest until the last survivor inherits all.

[after the name of the 17th–century Italian originator]

too *adverb*
1. also: 'are you coming *too*?'.
2. used to indicate excess: 'the box is *too* heavy to lift'.
only too, 'I'm *only too* glad to help' (= extremely).

took (*rhymes with* book) *verb*
the past tense of the verb **take.**

tool *noun*
any of various hand–held objects or instruments which help in performing work.
Usage: 'the petty thief was a *tool* in the hands of the ringleader' (= person used or controlled by another).
Word Family: **tool,** *verb,* to shape or decorate with a tool.

toot *verb*
1. to blow a horn, whistle, trumpet, etc.
2. (of a horn, whistle, etc.) to sound.
Word Family: **toot,** *noun.*

tooth *noun*
plural is **teeth**
1. *Anatomy:* any of the hard enamel–covered objects attached in rows to the jaws, used for chewing and biting.
2. any tooth–like part or projection, as on a comb, saw, rake, etc.
Phrases:
by the skin of one's teeth, narrowly.
get one's teeth into, to tackle something vigorously.
in the teeth of, despite, in direct opposition to.
long in the tooth, old.
tooth and nail, fiercely.
Word Family: **toothless,** *adjective*; **toothy,** *adjective,* having or showing prominent teeth; **toothsome,** *adjective,* pleasant–tasting.

toothcomb *noun*
a comb with very fine teeth set closely together.

toothpaste *noun*
a flavoured paste used for cleaning the teeth.

toothpick *noun*
a small stick used to remove food, etc. from between the teeth.

top (1) *noun*
1. the highest or uppermost place, surface or position: a) 'climb to the *top* of the hill'; b) 'start at the *top* of the page'.
2. a person or thing that has the highest place or position: a) 'she is *top* of the class'; b) 'my new suit has green trousers with matching *top*'.
3. the highest point, pitch or degree: a) 'she screamed at the *top* of her voice'; b) 'a car in *top* is in the highest gear'.
4. a lid or covering: 'put the *top* back on the bottle'.
Phrases:
blow one's top, (*informal*) to lose one's temper.
on top of, 'I can't handle any more problems *on top of* all my others' (= as well as).
top *verb*
(topped, topping)
1. to be or provide a top for: 'the building was *topped* by a tower'.
2. to reach the top or above the top of: 'the sun *topped* the horizon'.
3. to cut the top or tops from: '*top* the strawberries before serving'.
4. *Sport:* to hit the ball above its centre so that it moves only a short distance.
Usages:
a) 'she *topped* my story with an even funnier one' (= surpassed).
b) 'the cake was *topped* off with a cherry' (= finished).
top up, to fill up a partly filled container.

top (2) *noun*
a toy which spins when set in motion.
sleep like a top, to sleep soundly.

topaz (*say* toe–paz) *noun*
Geology: a mineral of varying transparent shades, such as pale blue or golden brown, used as a gem.
[from Greek]

topcoat *noun*
an overcoat.

top dog
(*informal*) the person in the highest or strongest position.

top drawer
(*informal*) the best or highest level of society.
Word Family: **top–drawer,** *adjective.*

tope *verb*
to drink alcohol habitually or to excess.
Word Family: **toper,** *noun.*

topee (*say* toe–pee) **topi** *noun*
a pith helmet.

top–flight *adjective*
(*informal*) first–rate or superior.

top-hat *noun*
a man's tall, silk hat worn on ceremonial occasions.

topic *noun*
something forming the matter for discussion, conversation, etc.
[Greek *topos* a commonplace]

topical (*say* **toppi**-k'l) *adjective*
of current or local interest.
Word Family: **topically,** *adverb*; **topicality** (*say* toppi-**kalli**-tee), *noun.*

topknot (*say* **top**-not) *noun*
a knot or tuft of hair on the top of the head.

topless *adjective*
without a top, especially of a garment which leaves the breasts bare.

topnotch *adjective*
(*informal*) first-rate.

topography (*say* top-**ogra**-fee) *noun*
Geography: a detailed description or representation of the natural and man-made features of an area.
Word Family: **topographical** (*say* toppa-**graffi**-k'l), *adjective*; **topographically,** *adverb.*
[Greek *topos* place + *graphein* to write]

topology *noun*
Maths: the study of those properties of shapes which remain the same when changed by bending, stretching, etc. *Example:* a circle and a square are topologically identical as they each have one inside and one outside.
[Greek *topos* a place + -LOGY]

topping *noun*
something added on top, such as syrup served with ice-cream.

topple *verb*
to waver unsteadily and tumble down.

top-secret *adjective*
extremely secret.

topside *noun*
a boneless cut of beef from the thigh of the animal.

topsy-turvy *adjective, adverb*
1. upside-down.
2. in confusion.

top weight
Cards: (in bridge) the situation where a partnership must make all the remaining tricks to get their contract.

toque (*say* toke) *noun*
a small close-fitting, usually brimless hat.
[French]

tor *noun*
a small rocky hill or peak.

Torah (*say* **tawra**) *noun*
Jewish: a) the Law. b) the actual scrolls on which the Law is written.
[Hebrew, instruction]

torch *noun*
1. a small electric lamp powered by batteries.
2. a hand-held light of any burning substance.
carry a torch for, to suffer unrequited love for.

tore *verb*
the past tense of the verb **tear (2).**

toreador (*say* **torria**-dor) *noun*
a bullfighter.
[Spanish *toro* bull]

torment (*say* **tor**ment) *noun*
a) great suffering, worry, etc.: 'the *torments* of toothache'. b) a cause of such suffering: 'that child is a *torment* to his parents'.
torment (*say* tor-**ment**) *verb*
to cause torment to, especially in a persistent manner: 'stop *tormenting* her with your silly questions'.
Word Family: **tormentor, tormenter,** *noun.*
[Latin *tormentum* a torture rack]

torn *verb*
the past participle of the verb **tear (2).**

tornado (*say* tor-**nay**-doe) *noun*
an extremely intense tropical cyclone with a strong upward spiral force, which follows a narrow track and is caused by the meeting of two air masses of different temperatures.
[Spanish]

torpedo (*say* tor-**pee**-doe) *noun*
a self-propelled, underwater missile, used to destroy ships and fired from a submarine or low-flying aircraft.
Word Family: **torpedo,** *verb,* to attack or destroy with a torpedo.
[Latin, the electric ray-fish]

torpid *adjective*
inactive, dull and uninterested.
Word Family: **torpidly,** *adverb*; **torpidity** (*say* tor-**piddi**-tee), **torpidness,** *nouns.*
[Latin *torpidus* numb]

torpor (*say* **tor**pa) *noun*
1. a state of physical or mental inactivity.
2. the state of dormancy.
[Latin]

torque (*say* tork) *noun*
Physics: the force which tends to cause rotation. Compare COUPLE.
[Latin *torquere* to twist]

torrent *noun*
a violent, rushing stream.
Word Family: **torrential** (*say* tor–**ren**–sh'l), *adjective*, of or like a torrent.
[from Latin]

torrid *adjective*
extremely hot or scorching, e.g. the sun's heat.
Usage: 'he wrote a *torrid* love letter' (= passionate).
Word Family: **torridly**, *adverb*; **torridity** (*say* tor–**riddi**–tee), **torridness**, *nouns.*
[Latin *torridus* parched]

torsion (*say* **tor**–sh'n) *noun*
a twisting force along the axis of a body.
Word Family: **torsional**, *adjective*; **torsionally**, *adverb.*
[Latin *tortus* twisted]

torso *noun*
plural is **torsos**
a) the human figure without the head, arms and legs. b) a sculpture of this.
[Italian]

tort *noun*
Law: a careless act causing harm to another person which may lead to a claim for damages.
[French, wrong]

tortilla (*say* tor–**tee**–ya) *noun*
a thin pancake made of maize flour, used as a form of bread in Mexico, etc.
[Spanish, little cake]

tortoise (*say* **tor**tus) *noun*
any of a group of reptiles, usually living on land, with its body enclosed in a thick shell into which the legs and head can be withdrawn. Compare TURTLE.
tortoiseshell *noun*
1. the horny outer shell of a turtle, usually yellow and brown, and used in the making of decorative combs, etc.
2. a long-haired domestic cat, usually a female, with a yellowish and black coat.

tortuous (*say* **tor**–tewus) *adjective*
twisting, winding or crooked: 'a *tortuous* path down the sides of a canyon'.
Usage: 'Andrew thinks all politicians use *tortuous* logic' (= deceitfully indirect).
Word Family: **tortuously**, *adverb*; **tortuousness**, *noun.*
[Latin *tortuosus* full of turns and twists]

torture (*say* **tor**cher) *noun*
a) the inflicting of extreme pain: 'the prisoner was put to the *torture*'. b) the pain and suffering so inflicted: 'he underwent the *tortures* of hell'.
torture *verb*
to subject to torture.
Usage: 'my French teacher said I *tortured* the language' (= twisted, distorted).
Word Family: **torturer**, *noun*; **torturous**, *adjective.*
[Latin *tortus* twisted]

Tory (*say* **tor**–ee) *noun*
1. *History:* a member of the British political party which supported the monarchy and the established order of the Church and State. Compare WHIG.
2. a member or supporter of the modern Conservative Party.
Word Family: **Tory**, *adjective*; **Toryism**, *noun.*
[originally used of Irish outlaws]

toss *verb*
to throw into or through the air: a) '*toss* me the newspaper'; b) 'the horse *tossed* its head in fear'.
Usages:
a) 'the man *tossed* in his sleep' (= rocked, rolled over).
b) 'we'll *toss* for who gets the top bunk' (= decide by the toss of a coin).
Phrases:
toss down, to drink quickly.
toss up, to decide something by the toss of a coin. *Word Family:* **toss-up**, *noun*, a) the tossing of a coin, b) (informal) an even chance.
Word Family: **toss**, *noun.*

tot (1) *noun*
1. a small child.
2. a small portion of alcoholic drink.

tot (2) *verb*
(**totted**, **totting**)
tot up, to add up.
[for TOTAL]

total (*say* **toe**–t'l) *noun*
the sum or whole of something.
total *adjective*
1. full or whole.
2. complete or absolute: 'it was a *total* failure'.
total *verb*
(**totalled**, **totalling**)
to add up: a) '*total* the bill, please'; b) 'the bill *totals* £10'.

Word Family: **totally,** *adverb*; **totality** (*say* toe–**talli**–tee), *noun,* a) the state of being total, b) the total.
[Latin *totus* the whole]

totalitarianism
(*say* toe–talli–**tairian**–izm) *noun*
a political system based on the absolute power of a single party or dictator.
Word Family: **totalitarian,** *adjective, noun.*

totalizator (*say* tote–a–lie–**zay**ta)
totalisator *noun*
an organized system of betting in which winners share the total amount bet on the race, less a percentage for costs and taxes.

tote (1) *verb*
(*informal*) to carry.

tote (2) *noun*
(*informal*) a totalizator.

totem (*say* **toe**–t'm) *noun*
a) an animal, plant or object used by a tribe or clan as an emblem. b) a statue or picture of such an object.
Word Family: **totemic** (*say* toe–**tem**mik), *adjective*; **totemism,** *noun.*
[Amerindian]

totter *verb*
to move or sway unsteadily.
Word Family: **totter,** *noun*; **tottery,** *adjective.*

toucan (*say* **too**kan) *noun*
any of various large tropical American fruit–eating birds with a huge beak.

touch (*say* tutch) *verb*
1. to bring the hand, finger, etc. lightly into contact with: '*touch* the paint and see if it's still wet'.
2. to come into contact with: 'the car just *touched* me as I crossed the road'.
Usages:
a) 'no–one can *touch* him for genius' (= compare with).
b) 'divorce reform is a matter that *touches* me very closely' (= concerns).
c) 'the sad story *touched* his heart' (= affected with pity).
d) 'she only *touched* on the subject in her talk' (= mentioned briefly).
e) 'he won't *touch* stocks or shares because he's a socialist' (= have anything to do with).
f) (*informal*) 'can I *touch* you for £10?' (= persuade to lend).
Phrases:
touch down, a) (*Rugby*) to score a try; b) (of an aircraft) to land. *Word Family*: **touchdown,** *noun.*
touch off, 'the rumour *touched off* widespread panic' (= caused, started).
touch up, to add the final details to.
touch wood, a superstitious action or interjection after expressing a hope.
touch *noun*
1. a) the act of touching. b) the state of being in communication, etc.: 'we keep in *touch* by letter'.
Usages:
a) 'her voice had a *touch* of bitterness' (= trace).
b) 'he put the final *touches* to the sculpture' (= strokes, details).
2. a) the feeling caused by touching: 'the marble had a smooth *touch*'. b) the sense giving such feeling: 'it was cold to the *touch*'.
3. a style or manner of touching: 'the pianist had a delicate *touch*'.
Phrases:
personal touch, 'what he lacks is the *personal touch*' (= gift for sympathetic handling of the individual).
soft touch, a person who is easy to borrow from.
touch and go, an uncertain or risky situation. *Word Family:* **touch–and–go,** *adjective.*
Word Family: **touchable,** *adjective.*

touché (*say* **too**–shay) *interjection*
(of a perceptive or telling remark) point taken or good point!
[French, touched, a call made by a fencer to acknowledge that he has been hit by his opponent]

touchily *adverb*
Word Family: see TOUCHY.

touching (*say* **tutch**ing) *adjective*
arousing pity or sympathy.
Word Family: **touchingly,** *adverb.*

touchpaper (*say* **tutch**–paypa) *noun*
a strip of paper containing potassium nitrate, which makes it smoulder slowly. It is used as a fuse for fireworks and explosives.

touchstone (*say* **tutch**–stone) *noun*
1. a black stone on which gold and silver is rubbed to test its purity.
2. any test of quality.

touch–type (*say* **tutch**–tipe) *verb*
to use a typewriter without looking at the keys.

touchy (*say* **tutch**–ee) *adjective*
easily provoked or offended.
Word Family: **touchily,** *adverb*; **touchiness,** *noun.*

tough (*say* tuf) *adjective*
1. not easily cut, broken or worn out: 'the steak is too *tough* to chew'.

Usage: 'the prisoner was a *tough* character' (= hardened).
2. difficult, trying or severe: 'I couldn't answer her *tough* questions'.
Word Family: **toughen,** *verb,* to make or become tough or tougher; **toughly,** *adverb*; **toughness,** *noun*; **tough,** *noun,* (informal) a ruffian.

toupee (*say* **too**pay) *noun*
a small wig or hairpiece worn to cover a bald patch.
[French *toupet*]

tour (*say* toor) *noun*
1. a journey in which a number of places are visited.
2. *Military:* a period of duty in a place.
Word Family: **tour,** *verb.*
[Greek *tornos* a circle]

tour de force (*say* **toor** de force)
a feat of skill or sustained effort.
[French]

touring car
also called a **tourer**
an open motor car designed to take several passengers and much luggage.

tourist *noun*
a person who travels for sightseeing and pleasure.
tourist class, (of transport) the cheapest class.
Word Family: **tourism,** *noun.*

tournament (*say* **tor**na-m'nt) *noun*
1. a competition or series of contests, such as for sport, chess, etc.
2. *History:* a contest between knights on horseback armed with blunted weapons. Also called a **tourney.**

tournedos (*say* **toor**na-doe) *noun*
plural is **tournedos**
a cut of meat from the middle of the fillet.
[French *tourner* to turn + *dos* back]

tourniquet (*say* **toor**ni-kay) *noun*
any device used to prevent bleeding by compressing the blood vessels.
[French]

tousled *adjective*
(of hair) unkempt or disordered.
Word Family: **tousle,** *verb.*

tout *verb*
1. to pester possible customers with one's goods or services: 'the ticket *touts* were busy at the Cup Final'.
2. to obtain and sell information, especially regarding horseraces.
3. to try to gain something in a persistent manner: '*touting* for favour'. Short form of to **tout round.**
Word Family: **tout,** *noun,* a person who touts, a tipster.

tow (1) (*say* toe) *verb*
to drag or pull by a rope or chain.
tow *noun*
a) the act of towing. b) the state of being towed.
in tow, a) 'she arrived with the whole family *in tow*' (= following); b) 'keep your young brother *in tow* for his first day at school' (= under guidance).
Word Family: **towage,** *noun,* a charge made for towing.

tow (2) (*say* toe) *noun*
1. the fibre of flax, hemp, etc., prepared for spinning.
2. a pale yellow colour.

towards, toward *preposition*
1. in the direction of: 'she turned *towards* the door'.
Usagos:
a) 'it was *towards* midnight when he left' (= near).
b) 'here is some money *towards* a new suit' (= as a contribution to).
2. concerning or in relation to: 'what is your attitude *towards* compulsory sport?'.

towel *noun*
a thick cotton cloth for drying things.
throw in the towel, to give up or admit defeat.
Word Family: **towel (towelled, towelling),** *verb,* to dry with a towel; **towelling,** *noun,* an absorbent fabric used for towels, beach clothes, etc.

tower (*rhymes with* flower) *noun*
a tall, narrow building or structure, sometimes forming part of another building.
tower of strength, a source of comfort or support.
tower *verb*
to rise to a great height.
tower over, to rise above or surpass.

towering *adjective*
1. tall or lofty: 'a *towering* skyscraper'.
2. extremely violent or intense: 'a *towering* rage'.

towheaded (*say* **toe**-heddid) *adjective*
having pale yellow hair.

town *noun*
1. a) a distinct, densely populated area, with some degree of self-government. b) its inhabitants.
2. the business or commercial centre of such an area, in contrast to the suburbs.

Phrases:
go to town, to act with wild enthusiasm.
on the town, seeking entertainment in a town.

townee *noun*
(*informal*) a town-bred person, as distinct from a countryman.

town hall
a building consisting of local government offices and often a large hall for public meetings, etc.

town house
a small house in a city, often with little or no garden.

town planning
the planning of buildings, services, roads, etc. for a new town or for the extension or improvement of an existing town.

township *noun*
1. a small town.
2. *South African:* an area outside a large town set aside for the non-white population.

toxic (*say* **tok**-sik) *adjective*
a) poisonous. b) relating to or caused by poison.
Word Family: **toxically,** *adverb*; **toxicity** (*say* tok-**sissi**-tee), *noun*; **toxicology** (*say* tok-see-**kolla**-jee), *noun*, the study of poisons.
[Greek *toxikon pharmakon* arrow poison, from *toxa* arrows]

toxin (*say* **toksin**) *noun*
any poison, especially one produced by living things, such as bacteria.

toxophily (*say* toks-**offi**-lee) *noun*
archery.
[Greek *toxon* a bow + *philein* to love]

toy *noun*
1. any object made to play with.
2. a toy dog.
toy *verb*
1. to amuse oneself: 'she *toyed* with the idea of going to London'.
2. to treat or handle lightly or idly: 'she *toyed* with a pencil as she spoke'.

toy dog
short form is **toy**
any breed of dog which is very small, e.g. a Pekingese.

trace (1) *noun*
1. any sign or evidence of something having existed, happened or been present: 'the wanted man has disappeared without a *trace*'.
2. a very small amount: 'you have a *trace* of grey in your hair'.
trace *verb*
1. to follow the course of: 'we *traced* the river to its source'.
2. to draw by reproducing outlines on a transparent sheet placed on top of the original.
Usages:
a) 'the agency *traces* missing persons' (= finds, locates).
b) '*trace* the plan for me' (= outline, sketch).
[Latin *tractus* a dragging, drawing]

trace (2) *noun*
(*plural*) the two straps or chains running from each side of a horse's collar to the load or carriage being pulled.
kick over the traces, to rebel.

trace element
any chemical element which is essential for normal animal and plant growth but is only needed in very small amounts.

tracer *noun*
1. a person or thing that traces.
2. any ammunition containing a chemical which leaves a trail of smoke or fire, used to check the aim of an automatic weapon.

tracery (*say* **trace**-a-ree) *noun*
a) a decorative pattern of branch-like bars, e.g. on a window. b) any similar pattern or network.

trachea (*say* **trakk**ia) *noun*
also called the **windpipe**
the tube of joined cartilage rings forming the air passage from the larynx to the lungs.
Word Family: **tracheal** (*say* tra-**kee**-ul), *adjective*.
[Greek *trakheia* (*arteria*) rough (artery)]

tracing (*say* **trace**-ing) *noun*
a traced copy of something.

track *noun*
1. a rough road made by frequent use.
2. a) a mark or series of marks left by something that has passed. b) any line or course of movement, such as the flight path of an aircraft.
3. a course laid out for a particular purpose.
4. an endless, ribbed band of metal passing around the wheels of a vehicle such as a tank, caterpillar, etc.
5. *Audio:* a) any of the bands on a record containing a single piece of music, etc. b) one of the bands on the width of a magnetic tape.

Phrases:
cover (up) one's tracks, to conceal what one has done, where one has been, etc.
in one's tracks, where one is standing.
keep track of, to follow the course or progress of.
lose track of, to fail to stay in touch with.
make tracks, (*informal*) to depart.
off the beaten track, a) secluded; b) unusual.
off the track, away from the subject.
on the wrong track, pursuing the wrong course in investigation, reasoning, etc.
track *verb*
1. to follow the tracks of: 'we *tracked* the animal to its den'.
2. *Film:* (of a camera) to move in any direction while filming.
track down, to search for and find.
Word Family: **tracker**, *noun*, a person or thing that tracks.

track events
Athletics: running-races.

tracking station
Astronomy: an installation with instruments for following the path of a spacecraft, usually by radar.

track shoes
a pair of running shoes with a light sole in which spikes are set.

tracksuit *noun*
a warm outfit worn by athletes when training, between events, etc.

tract (1) *noun*
1. any large area of land, water, etc.
2. *Anatomy:* a group or system of parts, organs, etc. with a related function: 'the digestive *tract*'.

tract (2) *noun*
a pamphlet containing information, as those distributed by a religious group.

tractable (*say* **trak**ta-b'l) *adjective*
easily managed or dealt with: 'he has a weak and *tractable* nature'.
Word Family: **tractably**, *adverb*; **tractability** (*say* trakta-**billi**-tee), *noun*.
[from Latin]

traction (*say* **trak**-sh'n) *noun*
the act or power of drawing or pulling, e.g. by a railway engine.
in traction, (*Medicine*) being raised and supported, usually with a straining pressure applied by a pulley-like device, e.g. for a broken leg.
[Latin *tractus* drawn]

traction engine
an early form of tractor, very large and usually steam powered, for hauling very heavy loads.

tractor *noun*
a motor vehicle, especially one with heavy tyres, used for pulling machinery or heavy loads.

trad *adjective*
(*informal*) traditional.

trade *noun*
1. the business or process of buying, selling or exchanging goods.
2. the people involved in a particular business: 'discounts are available only to the *trade*'.
Usages:
a) 'I got these stamps as a *trade*' (= swap, exchange).
b) 'we do a great *trade* in cookery books' (= amount of dealing).
3. an occupation, especially one which involves skilled mechanical or manual work as distinct from a profession.
4. (*plural*) the trade winds.
trade *verb*
to engage in the business of buying, selling or exchanging goods.
Usage: 'let's *trade* ideas on the subject' (= exchange).
Phrases:
trade in, to give as part payment for something being bought, exchanged, etc. *Word Family*: **trade-in**, *noun*, anything which is traded in.
trade on, 'he will try to *trade on* your weaknesses' (= take advantage of, make use of).
Word Family: **trader**, *noun*, a) a person who buys, sells or exchanges, b) a ship used for trade.

trademark *noun*
any registered name or mark officially used by a manufacturer to identify his own product and distinguish it from others.

trade name
1. the name for an article, business process, etc. used in a trade, but not an official trademark.
2. the name under which a business operates or an article is sold.

trade price
the price paid for goods by a retailer to a wholesaler, or by members of the same trade.

trader *noun*
Word Family: see TRADE.

tradesman *noun*
a person involved in a trade, especially one who sells or delivers goods.

trade union
short form is **union**
an organized group of workers providing aid and protection, especially in relation to wages and conditions of work, for all the workers in an industry.
Word Family: **trade unionist,** a member or supporter of a trade union; **trade unionism,** a) the methods of trade unions, b) all trade unions.

trade winds
the north-east and south-east winds which blow fairly regularly from the subtropics towards the equator.

trading post
American: a general store in a sparsely populated region.

trading stamp
a stamp, given by a retailer to a customer to encourage purchases, which can be exchanged for goods.

tradition (*say* tra-**dish**'n) *noun*
a) the passing down of customs, culture, beliefs, etc. from generation to generation. b) something which is passed on in this way.
traditional *adjective*
1. based on or existing due to tradition: 'Christmas is a *traditional* celebration'.
2. (of jazz) based on the style of music developed from about 1900–20, consisting of improvised instrumental music. Short form is **trad.**
Word Family: **traditionally,** *adverb*; **traditionalist,** *noun,* a person who believes in the authority of tradition; **traditionalist, traditionalistic,** *adjectives*; **traditionalism,** *noun.*
[Latin *traditio* a handing on]

traduce (*say* tra-**dewce**) *verb*
to slander or speak maliciously of.
[Latin *traducere* to disgrace publicly]

traffic *noun*
1. a) the passing or movement of vehicles or persons along a route. b) the vehicles or persons moving.
2. the transporting of people or goods for sale, etc. by land, sea or air.
Usages:
a) 'he is involved in the *traffic* of drugs' (= shady, illegal trade).
b) 'we have little *traffic* with our local neighbours' (= communication).
Word Family: **traffic (trafficked, trafficking),** *verb,* a) to deal or trade, b) to take part in illegal business.
[from Italian]

tragedy (*say* **traj**-a-dee) *noun*
1. a story or play, with a serious theme, which usually ends with death or defeat.
2. any event which is disastrous, fatal or dreadful.
Word Family: **tragedian** (*say* tra-**jee**dian), *noun,* a man who writes or acts in tragedies; **tragedienne** (*say* tra-jeedi-**en**), *noun,* a female tragedian.
[from Greek]

tragic (*say* **traj**-ik) *adjective*
characteristic of or relating to tragedy: 'a *tragic* ending'.
Usages:
a) 'do get rid of that *tragic* expression and cheer up' (= mournful).
b) 'the *tragic* death of a young boxer' (= dreadful).
Word Family: **tragically,** *adverb.*

tragicomedy (*say* traji-**komma**-dee) *noun*
1. any form of entertainment based on a combination of tragedy and comedy.
2. an event or situation which is both serious and funny.
Word Family: **tragicomic,** *adjective.*

trail *verb*
1. to drag or allow to drag along the ground, etc.
2. to follow slowly: 'he *trailed* behind them with his sore leg'.
Usages:
a) 'the vine *trails* over the verandah posts' (= hangs, grows).
b) 'the motorcycles roared into town *trailing* clouds of dust behind them' (= floating).
c) 'a small group *trailed* along the sand by the water' (= moved in a straggling way).
d) 'his voice *trailed* away in embarrassment' (= passed gradually, lessened).
e) 'police had *trailed* the suspect for days' (= followed the path or movements of).
trail *noun*
1. a track, mark or series of marks left behind by something which has passed: a) 'a *trail* of blood led to the door'. b) 'the invaders left a *trail* of destruction'.
Usage: 'the hounds quickly found the deer's *trail*' (= track or scent left).

2. a path or track made through a remote area, etc.
[Latin *tragula* drag-net]

trail bike
a motorcycle designed for use on rough terrain.

trailer *noun*
1. a short film containing scenes from a feature film, used as an advertisement.
2. a person or thing that trails, especially a small vehicle drawn by another.
3. a caravan.

train *noun*
1. a set of railway vehicles connected to a locomotive engine.
2. a line or series of vehicles, people, etc.: a) 'the President was followed by a *train* of bodyguards'; b) 'a strange *train* of events'.
3. something which is drawn behind or follows, such as part of a skirt, etc.
train *verb*
to instruct or educate for a particular skill, occupation, etc.
Usages:
a) 'the players *trained* every night' (= practised, exercised to keep fit).
b) 'try to *train* the ivy up the wall' (= cause to grow).
c) 'he *trained* the gun at the bank clerk's head' (= aimed, pointed).
training *noun*
the process or routine of developing a particular ability, skill, etc.
out of training, physically unfit.
Word Family: **trainer**, *noun*, a person who trains others; **trainee** (*say* tray-**nee**), *noun*, a person being trained.
[Latin *trahere* to drag]

traipse *verb*
(*informal*) to walk or travel about, especially in an aimless manner.

trait (*say* tray *or* trate) *noun*
a feature or quality which distinguishes or sets apart.
[French]

traitor (*say* **tray**-ta) *noun*
a person who betrays his country, another person or a belief.
Word Family: **traitorous** (*say* **trayta**-rus), *adjective*, disloyal or treacherous; **traitorously**, *adverb*; **traitorousness**, *noun*.
[from Latin]

trajectory (*say* tra-**jekta**-ree) *noun*
the path, especially a curve, traced by a moving object, etc.
[TRANS- + Latin *jacere* to throw]

tram *noun*
1. a passenger vehicle running on rails in the street and usually powered by electricity from an overhead wire. In America called a **streetcar**.
2. *Mining:* a truck for carrying coal.

trammel *verb*
(**trammelled**, **trammelling**)
to hinder or restrict.
Word Family: **trammel**, *noun*, (usually plural) something which hinders or restricts.

tramp *verb*
to walk with steady or heavy steps.
Usage: 'they *tramped* over the hills during the summer' (= hiked).
tramp *noun*
1. a person, with no fixed home and usually little or no money, who travels about on foot.
2. a heavy, firm step or tread.
3. a long walk or hike.
4. (*informal*) a promiscuous woman.
5. a cargo boat with no fixed schedule or route. Short form of **tramp steamer**.

trample *verb*
to tread on heavily or crushingly.
Usage: 'he *trampled* on her feelings with cruel taunts' (= treated harshly).
Word Family: **trample**, *noun*, the act or sound of trampling.

trampoline (*say* **trampa**-leen) *noun*
a canvas sheet held taut by springs in a frame above the floor, used for bouncing and other acrobatic tricks.
Word Family: **trampoline**, *verb*.
[Italian *trampoli* stilts]

tramway *noun*
a) the system of tracks or cables for a tram. b) the company which owns or operates a transport system of trams.

trance *noun*
1. a half-conscious or hypnotized state.
2. a dazed or mentally absorbed state.
[Latin *transire* to pass over]

tranquil (*say* **tran**-kwil) *adjective*
free from agitation or disturbance: 'a *tranquil* sleep'.
tranquillizer, tranquilliser *noun*
any drug which has a calming effect without inducing sleep.
Word Family: **tranquillity** (*say* tran-**kwilli**-tee), *noun*, calmness or peace; **tranquilly**, *adverb*; **tranquillize**, *verb*, to make or become calm and

tranquil, especially by the use of a tranquillizer.
[from Latin]

trans–
a prefix meaning: a) across, as in *transit*; b) beyond, as in *transcend.*

transaction (*say* tran–**zak**–sh'n) *noun*
1. a piece of business, such as the sale of some object.
2. (*plural*) the written records of a society, etc.
Word Family: **transact,** *verb,* to carry out or conduct business.
[Latin *transactus* settled]

transceiver (*say* tran–**seeva**) *noun*
a radio set able to transmit and receive radiowaves.
[TRANS(mitter) + (re)CEIVER]

transcend (*say* tran–**send**) *verb*
1. to be or go beyond or above: 'the result *transcended* our wildest hopes'.
2. to be or do better than.
transcendent *adjective*
going beyond ordinary limits.
Usage: 'her *transcendent* wit made her a unique writer of comedies' (= superior, first–rate).
Word Family: **transcendence,** *noun*; **transcendently,** *adverb.*
[Latin *transcendere* to climb over or beyond]

transcendental (*say* transen–**den**–t'l) *adjective*
1. being or going completely beyond normal human experience, belief or knowledge.
2. (*informal*) very abstract, obscure or visionary.
Word Family: **transcendentally,** *adverb.*

transcendentalism
(*say* transen–**denta**–lizm) *noun*
a branch of philosophy concerned with abstract ideas or intuition rather than physical experience.
Word Family: **transcendentalist,** *noun, adjective.*

transcendental meditation
the attempted achievement of peace of mind by oriental methods of meditation taught by gurus.

transcribe *verb*
1. to express, record or make a copy of in writing.
2. *Music:* to rewrite a composition for an instrument other than the one for which it was originally written.
Word Family: **transcript,** *noun,* a written copy or record, especially an official record of a court case; **transcription,** *noun,* a) the act of transcribing, b) a written copy or reproduction, c) a musical composition which has been transcribed.
[Latin *transcribere* to copy]

transect *verb*
to cut across.
[from Latin]

transept *noun*
the side parts in a cross–shaped church.
[TRANS– + Latin *saeptum* enclosure]

transfer (*say* trans–**fer**) *verb*
(**transferred, transferring**)
to take or move from one place, person, etc. to another: 'he *transferred* his savings to another bank'.
transfer (*say* **trans**–fer) *noun*
1. the act of transferring: 'the *transfer* of the money was handled by a teller'.
2. something which is transferred, such as a design which is removed from paper and pressed onto a surface.
Word Family: **transferrer,** *noun,* a person or thing that transfers; **transference** (*say* **transfa**–r'nce), *noun,* the act of transferring.
[TRANS– + Latin *ferre* to carry]

transferable vote
a system in which the voter specifies a second choice who will get his vote if the first fails to get elected.

transfiguration
(*say* tranz–figga–**ray**–sh'n) *noun*
a change in appearance.
Word Family: **transfigure,** *verb,* to change in form or appearance.

transfix *verb*
to pierce through and fix: 'he *transfixed* the king with his sword'.
Usage: 'she was *transfixed* by the dreadful sight' (= made unable to move).

transform *verb*
1. to change in form, nature or character: 'experience had *transformed* her into a wiser person'.
2. *Electricity:* to change the magnitude of an alternating current.
transformer *noun*
a person or thing that transforms, especially a device which changes the magnitude of an alternating current.
Word Family: **transformation,** *noun,* a change in form, condition, etc.

transfusion (*say* tranz–**few**–zh'n) *noun*
the transferring of a liquid from one container to another, especially transferring blood from the veins or

arteries of one person or animal to another.
Word Family: **transfuse**, *verb.*

transgress *verb*
to go beyond a limit, etc., especially a limit set by law.
Word Family: **transgression** (*say* tranz-**gresh**'n), *noun,* a crime or sin.
[TRANS- + Latin *gressus* gone]

tranship, trans-ship *verb*
(**transhipped, transhipping**)
to transfer goods from one boat to another.
Word Family: **transhipment**, *noun.*

transhumance (*say* tranz-**yoo**-m'nce) *noun*
the seasonal movement of cattle, especially from the Alps in summer to the valleys in winter.
[French from TRANS- + Latin *humus* ground]

transient (*say* **tranzi**-ent) *adjective*
not lasting or remaining: 'he only left a *transient* impression'.
Word Family: **transience**, *noun,* **transiently**, *adverb*; **transient**, *noun,* a person who remains for only a short time, such as a guest in a hotel.
[Latin *transiens* going across]

transistor (*say* tran-**zizta**) *noun*
1. *Electronics:* a semiconductor device capable of amplification and having three or more electrodes performing the functions of a multi-electrode valve.
2. a small radio using such devices.
Word Family: **transistorize, transistorise**, *verb.*
[TRANS(fer) + (res)ISTOR]

transit (*say* **tranzit**) *noun*
1. the act of passing across or through, as the movement of people or goods from one place to another.
2. *Astronomy:* a) the passage of a planet or star across the meridian of a particular place. b) the passage of a satellite in front of its primary, such as Venus in front of the sun.
[from Latin]

transit camp
a camp temporarily accommodating troops or refugees awaiting transfer elsewhere.

transition (*say* tran-**zish**'n) *noun*
a passing or changing from one position or condition to another.
Word Family: **transitional, transitionary**, *adjectives,* of or during a transition; **transitionally**, *adverb.*

transition element
Chemistry: any of the metal elements which has multiple valencies and occurs between group II and group III of the periodic table.

transitive (*say* **tranza**-tiv) *adjective*
Grammar: (of a verb) needing a direct object to complete its meaning. *Example:* the boy *bought* (a book). Compare INTRANSITIVE.
Word Family: **transitive**, *noun*; **transitively**, *adverb.*

transitory (*say* **tranza**-tree) *adjective*
not lasting or permanent: 'a *transitory* illness'.

translate (*say* tranz-**late**) *verb*
to express the sense or meaning of something in another language.
Usages:
a) 'his energy was *translated* into a violent outburst' (= changed, transformed).
b) 'the saint's remains were *translated* to the new chapel' (= moved).

translation (*say* tranz-**lay**-sh'n) *noun*
1. the putting of words into another language.
2. a version, passage, etc. which has been or is to be translated.
3. the act of translating.
Word Family: **translator**, *noun.*
[TRANS- + Latin *latus* carried]

transliterate (*say* tranz-**litta**-rate) *verb*
to change letters or words into corresponding characters of another alphabet or language. *Example:* Greek π transliterates as English *pi.*
Word Family: **transliteration**, *noun.*
[TRANS- + Latin *littera* a letter]

translucent (*say* tranz-**loo**-s'nt) *adjective*
allowing light to pass through imperfectly so that objects cannot be seen distinctly. Compare TRANSPARENT.
Word Family: **translucently**, *adverb*; **translucence, translucency**, *noun.*
[Latin *translucens* shining through]

transmigrate (*say* tranz-my-**grate**) *verb*
1. to migrate, usually through a country en route to another.
2. (of the soul) to be reborn in another body.
Word Family: **transmigration**, *noun*; **transmigratory**, *adjective.*

transmission (*say* tranz-**mish**'n) *noun*
1. the act or process of transmitting, such as the sending of electromagnetic waves from a transmitter to a receiver.

2. a) the transfer of motion from one part of a machine to another. b) any device for doing this, such as the gearbox, differential, etc. of a motor car.

transmit (*say* tranz–**mit**) *verb*
(**transmitted, transmitting**)
to pass on: a) 'to *transmit* radio messages'; b) 'metal *transmits* heat'.
Usage: 'the disease is *transmitted* by fleas' (= spread, communicated).
transmitter *noun*
a person or thing that transmits, such as a radio apparatus which creates, modulates and sends out electromagnetic waves to be picked up by a receiver.
Word Family: **transmittance, transmittal,** *nouns.*
[TRANS– + Latin *mittere* to send]

transmogrify (*say* tranz–**mogri**–fie) *verb*
(**transmogrified, transmogrifying**)
(*informal*) to change into a different form as if by magic.
[an old word, coined as a joke]

transmutation
(*say* tranz–mew–**tay**–sh'n) *noun*
1. the act of changing from one form, substance or state to another, especially the theoretical changing of one biological species into another.
2. the conversion of base metals into silver or gold attempted by alchemists.
Word Family: **transmute,** *verb,* to change from one form or state into another; **transmutable,** *adjective.*

transom *noun*
1. a horizontal strip, often of wood or stone, which divides a window, etc.
2. a) a horizontal crossbar separating a door, etc. from a window above it. b) a small window set above a door.
3. a flat beam forming part of the stern of a boat.

transparent (*say* trans–**pairent**) *adjective*
allowing light to pass through so that objects on the other side may be seen clearly. Compare TRANSLUCENT.
Usage: 'her fear was *transparent* despite her efforts to hide it' (= obvious, easily seen).
transparency *noun*
1. the quality of being transparent. Also spelt **transparence.**
2. *Photography:* a slide.
Word Family: **transparently,** *adverb.*
[TRANS– + Latin *parere* to appear]

transpire (*say* tran–**spire**) *verb*
1. to become known: 'it *transpired* that the witness had not told the truth'.
Usage: (*informal*) 'what *transpired* after I left the party?' (= happened).
2. to give off waste matter, etc., as a plant gives off water–vapour through its leaves.
Word Family: **transpiration;** *noun;* **transpiratory** (*say* tran–**spyra**–tree), *adjective.*
[TRANS– + Latin *spirare* to breathe]

transplant (*say* tranz–**plahnt**) *verb*
to remove something, such as a tree, etc. from one place and put it in another.
transplant (*say* **tranz**–plahnt) *noun*
a) the process of transplanting. b) something which is transplanted.
Word Family: **transplantable,** *adjective.*

transport (*say* tran–**sport**) *verb*
to carry from one place to another.
Usages:
a) 'she was *transported* by the beauty of the opera' (= strongly moved or affected).
b) 'the thief was *transported* to a prison colony for 7 years' (= sent, banished).
transport (*say* **tran**–sport) *noun*
1. a) any system for carrying passengers or goods. b) any vehicle used for this.
2. (*often plural*) a state of rapture or intense excitement.
transportation
(*say* tran–spor–**tay**–sh'n) *noun*
1. a) the act of transporting. b) a vehicle used for or as a means of transport.
2. *American:* the cost of transport or travel.
[TRANS– + Latin *portare* to carry]

transpose (*say* tran–**spoze**) *verb*
1. to change or reverse the order or position of.
2. *Maths:* to move a term from one side of an equation to the other, involving a change of sign.
3. *Music:* to write or play a melody in a key other than the original one.
Word Family: **transposition** (*say* transpa–**zish**'n), **transposal,** *nouns.*
[TRANS– + Latin *positus* placed]

trans–ship *verb*
see TRANSHIP.

transubstantiation
(*say* tran–sub–stanshi–ay–sh'n) *noun*
the changing of one substance into another.
Word Family: **transubstantiate,** *verb.*

transuranic element
(*say* tranz-yoo-rannik ella-m'nt)
Chemistry: any of the elements beyond uranium in the periodic table. All are man-made, have atomic numbers greater than 92 and most are radioactive with very long half-lives.

transversal (*say* tranz-versal) *noun*
Maths: a line intersecting two or more lines.
Word Family: **transversal,** *adjective,* transverse.

transverse (*say* tranz-verse) *adjective*
lying across.
Word Family: **transversely,** *adverb.*
[TRANS- + Latin *versus* turned]

transvestite (*say* tranz-vestite) *noun*
a person who dresses in the clothing of the opposite sex.
Word Family: **transvestism,** *noun.*

trap *noun*
1. a device for catching animals, such as a cage with a door that snaps shut when the animal enters it.
2. anything used to catch or trick, especially unexpectedly.
3. a device which collects or prevents the passage of fluids, liquids, etc.
4. a light, two-wheeled passenger vehicle, pulled by a pony.
5. (*informal*) the mouth.
6. a device which flings objects, such as clay pigeons, into the air to be shot at.
7. (*informal, plural*) luggage or personal belongings.
trap *verb*
(trapped, trapping)
1. to catch in or as if in a trap.
2. to seal off or confine.

trapdoor *noun*
a hinged or sliding door in a floor, roof, etc.

trapeze (*say* tra-**peez**) *noun*
1. a short bar, with a long rope attached to each end, which is hung above the ground and used by acrobats and gymnasts.
2. *Sailing:* a harness attached to the boat by a wire and worn by a member of the crew, enabling him to lean out from the boat.

trapezium (*say* tra-peezium) *noun*
plural is **trapezia** or **trapeziums**
a quadrilateral having two sides parallel.

trapper *noun*
a person who traps, especially one who traps animals for their flesh or fur.

trappings *plural noun*
clothes or equipment, especially if ornamental or ceremonial: 'he was photographed in all the *trappings* of his office, including a plumed helmet'.

trapshooting *noun*
the sport of shooting at birds or clay pigeons, hurled into the air by a trap.

trash *noun*
1. rubbish.
2. a person or thing considered worthless or contemptible.
Word Family: **trashy,** *adjective,* worthless; **trashily,** *adverb;* **trashiness,** *noun.*

trattoria (*say* tratta-**ree**-a) *noun*
an Italian restaurant.

trauma (*say* **trawma**) *noun*
plural is **traumata** or **traumas**
1. *Medicine:* an injury.
2. an emotional shock.
Word Family: **traumatic** (*say* traw-**mattik**), *adjective,* a) relating to or produced by a trauma, b) like a trauma; **traumatically,** *adverb;* **traumatize, traumatise,** *verb.*
[Greek, wound]

travail (*say* tra-**vale**) *noun*
an old word meaning work or effort, especially if difficult or strenuous.
Word Family: **travail,** *verb.*
[Old French]

travel (*say* **travv'l**) *verb*
(travelled, travelling)
to go from one place to another, especially over a considerable distance.
Usages:
a) 'light *travels* more quickly than sound' (= moves, is transmitted).
b) (*informal*) 'that car must really be *travelling*' (= moving fast).
travel *noun*
1. the act of travelling: 'a book about *travel*'.
2. the distance moved by a part in a machine.
traveller *noun*
in America spelt **traveler**
1. a person who travels, especially to distant or foreign parts.
2. (*informal*) a commercial traveller.
Word Family: **travelled,** *adjective,* experienced in travel.

travel agency, travel bureau
an agency which books flights, passages, hotels, package tours, etc. for travellers.

traveller's cheque
a cheque issued by a bank, etc., and signed by the bearer, which can be

cashed anywhere if signed again in the presence of the payer.

travelling salesman
also called a **commercial traveller**
a salesman who travels from place to place to sell goods or obtain orders for them.

travelogue (*say* **travva**-log) *noun*
a film or book which describes travel, foreign countries, etc.
[TRAVEL + Greek *logos* speech]

traverse (*say* tra-**verse**) *verb*
1. to go across, along or through: 'to *traverse* a paddock'.
Usage: 'as to the legal position, we have *traversed* the whole ground' (= examined and discussed thoroughly).
2. *Law:* to deny formally.
3. *Mountaineering:* to climb in a horizontal or diagonal direction.
Word Family: **traverse,** *noun,* a) the act of traversing, b) something which crosses, such as an intersecting line; **traversable,** *adjective.*
[TRANS- + Latin *versus* turned]

travesty (*say* **travva**-stee) *noun*
an exaggerated, ridiculous imitation, often as a form of comedy.
Word Family: **travesty** (**travestied, travestying**), *verb,* to ridicule or make a travesty of.
[French *travesti* having changed clothes, disguised]

trawl *verb*
to fish by dragging a net along the seabed.
trawler *noun*
a person or thing that trawls, especially a fishing boat used for this purpose.
Word Family: **trawl,** *noun,* a strong net used for trawling.

tray *noun*
a flat object of metal, wood or plastic, often with a raised rim, for holding or carrying articles.

treacherous (*say* **tretcha**-rus) *adjective*
1. betraying trust or faith.
2. not to be trusted or relied on: 'a *treacherous* smile'.
Word Family: **treacherously,** *adverb*; **treacherousness, treachery,** *nouns.*

treacle (*say* **tree**-k'l) *noun*
a dark syrup obtained while refining sugar.
Word Family: **treacly,** *adjective.*
[from Greek]

tread (*say* tred) *verb*
(**trod, trodden** or **trod, treading**)
1. to walk or walk on.
Usage: 'the cattle *trod* a path to the water-hole' (= made by treading).
2. *Biology:* (of birds) to copulate.
Phrases:
tread on someone's toes, to offend someone.
tread the boards, to be an actor.
tread water, to float in a vertical position by moving the arms and legs in the water.
tread *noun*
1. the act, manner or sound of treading.
2. the part of a tyre that touches the road, usually patterned to improve its grip.
3. the part of a step or stair on which the foot is placed.

treadle (*say* **tredd**'l) *noun*
a lever worked by foot, as on a sewing machine.

treadmill (*say* **tred**-mill) *noun*
1. a machine worked by the weight of people or animals moving a wheel.
2. any job or way of life which is boring or repetitive.

treason (*say* **tree**-z'n) *noun*
Law: an act of disloyalty to or betrayal of one's country or monarch.
Word Family: **treasonable,** *adjective,* of or involving treason; **treasonably,** *adverb*; **treasonableness,** *noun.*

treasure (*say* **trezha**) *noun*
any accumulated wealth, especially in the form of gems, precious metals, etc.
Usage: 'our last gardener was a real *treasure*' (= highly valued person).
treasure *verb*
to retain carefully or cherish: 'I shall *treasure* the memory of this day'.
[Greek *thesauros*]

treasurer (*say* **trezha**-ra) *noun*
a person who is in charge of the money of a society, company, city or government.

treasure-trove *noun*
any treasure, of unknown ownership, found hidden in the earth.
Usage: 'this book is a *treasure-trove* of fascinating information' (= valuable source).
[Old French *tresor* treasure + *trové* found]

treasury (*say* **trezha**-ree) *noun*
1. a place where private or public funds are received, kept, and paid out.
2. (*capital*) the department of a government that controls such functions.

Usage: 'the Golden *Treasury* of English Poets' (= collection).

treasury bill

a bill of exchange issued by government to get short-term finance.

treat (*say* treet) *verb*

to act or behave in a specific way towards: 'he *treated* her with consideration'.

Usages:

a) 'they *treated* the idea as a laughing matter' (= regarded).

b) 'the fabric has been *treated* to resist shrinkage' (= subjected to chemical or physical processes).

c) 'the doctor is *treating* me for nervous exhaustion' (= giving medical care).

d) 'the playwright *treats* the theme of mental illness very delicately' (= handles, deals with).

e) 'they *treated* him to a birthday lunch' (= entertained).

treat *noun*

something which gives unusual pleasure, especially if unexpected: 'it was a *treat* for the orphans to go to the zoo'.

Usage: 'this is going to be my *treat*' (= turn to pay).

treatment *noun*

a) the act or process of treating: 'her skin condition improved after *treatment*'. b) the manner of treating: 'that camel has suffered from cruel *treatment*'.

[Latin *tractare* to handle]

treatise (*say* **tree**-tis) *noun*

a long, detailed, systematic book or essay on a subject.

treaty (*say* **tree**-tee) *noun*

a) a formal agreement between two or more nations. b) the document containing such an agreement.

treble (*say* **trebb**'l) *adjective*

1. being three times as big or having three parts.

2. *Music:* soprano.

treble *noun*

Music: a) a soprano singing voice, especially a child's. b) an instrument having this range.

treble *verb*

to multiply by three.

[Latin *triplus* triple]

treble chance

a football pool competition with prizes for selecting eight drawn, but not scoreless, matches.

[the name refers to the (originally three, now four) possible scores for each selection]

treble clef

Music: see CLEF.

tree *noun*

1. a perennial plant having a single, self-supporting woody trunk, often of considerable height, with branches and foliage developing at some distance from the ground.

2. something having the shape of a tree: 'a family *tree*'.

tree *verb*

(treed, treeing)

to force to seek refuge in a tree: 'the dog had the cat thoroughly *treed*'.

Usage: 'he's likely to turn vicious once he's *treed*' (= cornered).

treen *noun*

small wooden articles of domestic use made by craftsmen of earlier generations.

[an old word for *wooden*, from TREE]

trefoil (*say* **tre**-foil) *noun*

1. a plant, similar to clover, with yellow flowers.

2. an architectural ornament resembling a three-leafed clover in shape.

[TRI- + Latin *folium* leaf]

trek *verb*

(trekked, trekking)

to travel, especially arduously or in the bush.

Word Family: **trek**, *noun*.

[Afrikaans]

trellis *noun*

a light frame of crossed wooden or metal strips, used for supporting climbing plants, etc.

Word Family: **trellis**, *verb*, to furnish with or train to grow on a trellis.

trematode (*say* **tremma**-tode) *noun*

see FLUKE (3).

[Greek *trematodes* perforated]

tremble *verb*

(of a person) to shake involuntarily, e.g. from fear, cold, etc.

Usages:

a) 'the bridge *trembled* as the train roared across' (= vibrated).

b) 'I *tremble* to think what your father will do when he hears the news' (= feel anxiety).

Word Family: **tremble**, *noun*; **tremblingly**, *adverb*.

[Latin *tremulus* trembling]

tremendous (*say* tre-**men**dus) *adjective*
1. enormous or very great: 'a boulder of *tremendous* size blocked our path'.
2. (*informal*) wonderful: 'what a *tremendous* concert that was!'.
Word Family: **tremendously,** *adverb*; **tremendousness,** *noun.*
[Latin *tremendus* dreadful or fearful]

tremolo (*say* **tremma**-lo) *noun*
Music: a) the rapid reiteration of the same note. b) vibrato.
[Italian]

tremor (*say* **tremma**) *noun*
a shaking: a) 'there was a nervous *tremor* in her voice'; b) 'an earth *tremor*'.
[Latin]

tremulous (*say* **trem**-yoo-lus) *adjective*
1. trembling.
2. timid or fearful.
Word Family: **tremulously,** *adverb*; **tremulousness,** *noun.*
[from Latin]

trench *noun*
1. a long, narrow hole dug in the ground, especially one used to protect soldiers from gunfire, etc.
2. (*plural*) the front line of battle in Europe in World War I: 'to be sent to the *trenches* meant almost certain death'.
Word Family: **trench,** *verb,* a) to surround or fortify with a trench or trenches, b) to dig trenches in; **trench upon,** to encroach upon or come close to.

trenchant (*say* **tren**-ch'nt) *adjective*
incisive or keen: 'he has a *trenchant* wit'.
Word Family: **trenchantly,** *adverb*; **trenchancy,** *noun.*
[Old French *tranchier* to cut]

trench coat
a thick raincoat tied with a belt, as worn in the trenches.

trencher *noun*
a wooden board on which food was formerly served and carved.
Word Family: **trencherman,** *noun,* a person with a healthy appetite.

trend *noun*
a general movement or tendency: 'the modern *trend* is towards greater automation'.
Word Family: **trend,** *verb,* to have a general direction; **trendy,** *adjective,* (informal) keeping up with or influenced by the latest trends; **trendy,** (informal), *noun.*

trephine (*say* tree-**feen**) *noun*
also called a **trepan** (*say* tree-**pan**)
Medicine: a) a small saw for removing a disc of bone from the skull or for operating on the cornea. b) an operation to remove a small section of bone marrow, as an aid in diagnosis.
Word Family: **trephine,** *verb.*
[Greek *trypan* to bore a hole]

trepidation (*say* treppi-**day**-sh'n) *noun*
a state of alarm or agitation.
[from Latin]

trespass *verb*
1. *Law:* to enter or go on to a person's property without permission.
Usage: 'I feel I no longer have the right to *trespass* on your hospitality' (= encroach).
2. an old word meaning to do wrong: 'as we forgive them that *trespass* against us'.
Word Family: **trespass,** *noun*; **trespasser,** *noun,* a person who trespasses on another's property.
[Old French *trespasser* to pass over]

tress *noun*
a long lock or curl of hair.

-tress
a suffix used to form feminine nouns, as in *actress.*

trestle (*say* **tress**'l) *noun*
a supporting structure, usually a beam with a pair of slanted legs at each end.
trestle table
a table made of a board or boards laid across trestles.

tri-
a prefix meaning three, as in *triangle.*
[Latin *tres,* Greek *treis* three]

triad (*say* **try**-ad) *noun*
1. a group of three persons or things.
2. *Music:* any three notes played together.

trial (*say* trile) *noun*
1. *Law:* the examination of evidence, followed by a decision on the guilt or innocence of a person, made by a judge or jury.
2. a) the process of trying: 'he gave the engine one last *trial* to see if it would fire'. b) the condition of being tried: 'I have this car on *trial* for a week'.
Usage: 'that's just one of life's little *trials*' (= hardships, causes of trouble).

3. *Car racing:* a test of skill and endurance over a difficult course.
trial and error, a process of investigation, experimentation, etc. in which various theories, methods, etc. are tried, until a successful one is found.

triangle (*say* **try**–ang'l) *noun*
1. a closed, plane figure with three straight sides.
2. *Music:* an instrument consisting of a thin steel bar bent into a triangle and hit with a small steel rod.
Word Family: **triangular** (*say* try–**an**–gewla), *adjective*, of, shaped like or bounded by a triangle.
[TRI- + Latin *angulus* corner]

triangulation
(*say* try–an–gew–**lay**–sh'n) *noun*
1. the measurement of a large area of land, by dividing it into a network of triangles and adding their areas.
2. *Maths:* the determining of a position by taking bearings from two fixed points a known distance apart and calculating the position on the resultant triangle by trigonometry.
Word Family: **triangulate,** *verb.*

Triassic (*say* try–**assik**) *noun*
Geology: see MESOZOIC.
Word Family: **Triassic,** *adjective.*

tribe *noun*
1. an independent social group, especially of primitive or nomadic people, claiming or occupying a particular territory, and sharing a common ancestry, leadership or customs.
Usage: 'the winner was pestered by a *tribe* of reporters' (= group).
2. *Biology:* the group between family and genus, sometimes used in the classification of animals and plants.
Word Family: **tribal,** *adjective*; **tribesman,** *noun.*
[from Latin]

tribulation (*say* trib–yoo–**lay**–sh'n) *noun*
severe trouble or grief.
[Latin *tribulare* to oppress]

tribunal (*say* try–**bew**–n'l) *noun*
a person or group appointed to hear and settle disputes.

tribune (*say* **trib**–yoon) *noun*
1. *Ancient history:* a) an elected Roman magistrate whose duties included protection of the lower classes. b) any of six officers of a legion, each in command for two months of the year.
2. a demagogue or popular leader.
3. a raised platform from which speakers address an assembly.
Word Family: **tribuneship,** *noun*, the office of a tribune.

tributary (*say* **trib**–yoo–tree) *noun*
1. *Geography:* a river or stream which flows into a larger one.
2. a person or country that pays tribute.
tributary *adjective*
1. subsidiary: 'a *tributary* stream'.
2. offered as tribute: 'a *tributary* payment'.

tribute (*say* **trib**–yoot) *noun*
1. an acknowledgement of respect, gratitude, admiration, etc.
2. any payment that one nation or ruler demands from another for peace, protection, etc.
[Latin *tributus* assigned]

trice *noun*
a very short period of time.

tricentenary (*say* try–sen–**teena**–ree) *noun*
a) a period of 300 years. b) a 300th anniversary.
Word Family: **tricentennial** (*say* try–sen–**tennial**), *adjective.*

triceps (*say* **try**–seps) *noun*
Anatomy: the large muscle at the back of the upper arm which branches into three parts and controls movement of the forearm.
[Latin, three-headed]

trick *noun*
1. an action or device designed to deceive, outwit or gain an advantage: 'the phone call was a *trick* to lure her out of the house'.
Usages:
a) 'I don't think I'll ever get the *trick* of cooking omelettes' (= knack).
b) 'the performing dog went through its repertoire of *tricks*' (= skilful feats).
c) 'he has an odd *trick* of stroking the side of his nose when he's thoughtful' (= mannerism).
2. a spell of duty: 'the sailor came up to take his *trick* at the wheel'.
3. *Cards:* all the cards which are involved and may be won in one round.
do the trick, 'that should *do the trick*' (= achieve the desired result).
trick *verb*
to deceive or cheat by a trick or tricks.
Word Family: **trickery,** *noun*, the practice of tricks; **trickster,** *noun*, a person who habitually tricks people; **tricky,** *adjective*, a) given to or characterized by trickery, b) requiring

skill or difficult to handle; **trickily**, *adverb*; **trickiness**, *noun*.

trickle *verb*
(of a liquid) to flow or cause to flow in a thin stream or in drops.
Usage: 'at peak hour the cars just *trickle* through the city' (= move slowly).
Word Family: **trickle**, *noun*.

tricolour (*say* **try**-kulla) **tricolor** *noun*
a flag having three colours, especially the French flag.
Word Family: **tricolour, tricoloured**, *adjectives*, having three colours.

tricycle (*say* **try**-sikk'l) *noun*
see BICYCLE.

trident (*say* **try**-d'nt) *noun*
a three-pronged fork, especially as the emblem of Neptune, the sea-god.
[TRI- + Latin *dentis* of a tooth]

tried *verb*
the past tense and past participle of the verb **try**.

triennial (*say* try-**enniul**) *adjective*
of, relating to or occurring every three years.
Word Family: **triennial, triennium** (*say* try-**ennium**), *nouns*, a period of three years; **triennially**, *adverb*.
[TRI- + Latin *annus* year]

trifle (*say* **try**-f'l) *verb*
to treat something as if it had no value or importance: 'he *trifled* with the girl's affections'.
Usages:
a) 'he *trifled* with a letter opener as he spoke to me' (= played).
b) 'I seem to have *trifled* the whole day away' (= wasted, passed idly).

trifle *noun*
1. a) a thing or event of little value or importance: 'don't get upset over *trifles*'. b) a small amount of money: 'I bought it for a *trifle*'.
Usage: 'this jacket is a *trifle* too short' (= little).
2. a dessert made from sponge cake, fruit, cream and occasionally sherry or brandy.
Word Family: **trifler**, *noun*; **trifling**, *adjective*, small or unimportant; **triflingly**, *adverb*.

trigger *noun*
1. any of various mechanisms which release a spring: 'the *trigger* of a gun'.
2. *Electricity:* any circuit used to set another circuit in operation by a single pulse.

trigger *verb*
to start or set off: 'the explosion *triggered* off a series of secondary explosions'.

trigger-happy *adjective*
(*informal*) inclined to shoot at the slightest provocation.

trigonometric functions
Maths: the functions of angles used extensively in geometry and analysis and widely applied in engineering, surveying, etc. The functions are **sine, cosine, tangent, cosecant, secant** and **cotangent**.

trigonometry
(*say* trigga-**nomma**-tree) *noun*
a branch of maths studying the relationships between angles and sides of triangles and other figures.
Word Family: **trigonometric** (*say* triggona-**metrik**), **trigonometrical**, *adjective*.
[Greek *trigonos* three-cornered + *metron* a measure]

trilateral (*say* try-**latta**-r'l) *adjective*
having three sides.
Word Family: **trilaterally**, *adverb*.
[TRI- + Latin *lateris* of a side]

trilby *noun*
a soft, felt hat with a dent in the crown.
[the name of a character in a novel]

trilinear (*say* try-**linnia**) *adjective*
of, relating to or bounded by three lines.

trilingual (*say* try-**ling**-w'l) *adjective*
using or involving three languages.

trill *noun*
1. a quavering or tremulous sound, such as is made by certain birds.
2. *Music:* a very fast alternation of two notes either a tone or a semitone apart.
Word Family: **trill**, *verb*.

trillion (*say* **tril**-y'n) *noun*
a cardinal number, the symbol 1 000 000 000 000 000 000 or 10^{18} (a million billion) in most countries as distinct from 1 000 000 000 000 or 10^{12} in America and France. Compare BILLION.

trilogy (*say* **trilla**-jee) *noun*
a series of three related novels or plays, each complete by itself, but having the same general subject or characters.
[TRI- + -LOGY]

trim *verb*
(**trimmed, trimming**)
1. to make neat or tidy by clipping or pruning: 'he *trimmed* his beard'.

2. to remove by cutting: 'to *trim* away the loose threads'.
3. to ornament or decorate: 'the hat was *trimmed* with feathers'.
4. *Nautical:* a) to adjust the sails to suit the wind. b) to distribute cargo or ballast so that a ship is well-balanced.
5. (of an aircraft in flight) to level off.
trim *noun*
1. a state of good order or fitness: a) 'everything was in good *trim*', b) 'the boxer was in fighting *trim*'.
2. ornamentation or material used for decorating, such as the upholstery and other fittings of a car.
3. a haircut which neatens the appearance of the hair without altering the style.
Word Family: **trim**, *adjective*, in good or neat order; **trimmer**, *noun*, a person or thing that trims; **trimly**, *adverb*; **trimness**, *noun*.

trimaran (*say* **try**-ma-ran) *noun*
a boat or raft with three hulls which are parallel and joined above the water. Compare CATAMARAN.
[TRI- + (cata)MARAN]

trimester (*say* **try**-mesta) *noun*
a period or term of three months.
[TRI- + Latin *mensis* month]

trimming *noun*
1. something that is added for ornament or to give a finished effect.
2. a piece that is cut off or removed by trimming.
3. (*plural*) any extras or accessories: 'I bought a new bicycle with all the *trimmings*'.

trimness *noun*
Word Family: see TRIM.

trinitrotoluene
(*say* try-nite-ro-**tol**-yoo-een) *noun*
short form is **TNT**
a pale yellow crystalline solid which is a powerful explosive. It is safe to handle as it requires a detonator and is used in bombs and other weapons.

Trinity (*say* **trinni**-tee) *noun*
1. *Christian:* the three persons of the Godhead: the Father, the Son and the Holy Spirit, being one God.
2. (*not capital*) a) any group of three. b) the state of being threefold.
[Latin *trinitas* a triad]

trinket *noun*
also called a **gew-gaw**
a small ornamental article, such as a gem, usually of little value.

trio (*say* **tree**-o) *noun*
1. any group of three people or things.
2. a) a group of three musicians. b) a musical composition for three musicians or instruments. c) a middle section of a minuet, march, etc.
[Italian]

triode (*say* **try**-ode) *noun*
Electricity: a valve with three electrodes, an anode, a cathode and a grid.
[TRI- + (electr)ODE]

trioxide (*say* try-**ok**side) *noun*
Chemistry: an oxide containing three atoms of oxygen.

trip *verb*
(**tripped**, **tripping**)
1. a) to catch one's foot and almost fall: 'I *tripped* over the step'. b) to cause to almost fall: 'I put out my foot and *tripped* him'.
2. to move quickly or with short, light steps.
3. (*informal*) to take or experience the effects of a hallucinogenic substance, such as lysergic acid diethylamide (LSD).
4. to release or be released: 'this lever *trips* the catch and the door swings open'.
trip up, a) to make or cause to make a mistake; b) to catch in a mistake.
trip *noun*
1. a journey, especially one for pleasure.
2. (*informal*) the effects of a hallucinogenic drug.
Word Family: **tripper**, *noun*, a person who goes on pleasure excursions; **tripping**, *noun*, the act of a person who trips; **tripping**, *adjective*, light and nimble; **trippingly**, *adverb*.

tripartite (*say* try-**par**tite) *adjective*
being divided into, or composed of, three parts.

tripe *noun*
the flat, white, stomach-lining of cattle, often cooked.
Usage: (*informal*) 'I refuse to listen to *tripe* like that' (= nonsense).

triplane (*say* **try**-plane) *noun*
an aeroplane with three pairs of wings, one above the other.

triple (*say* **tripp**'l) *adjective*
being three times as big or having three parts.
Word Family: **triple**, *verb*, to make or become three times as many or as

large; **triple,** *noun,* a group or set of three.
[from Latin]

triple jump
see HOP, SKIP AND JUMP.

triple point
Physics: the temperature and pressure at which three phases of a material (solid, liquid and gas) can exist simultaneously.

triplet *noun*
1. a group of three of a kind.
2. any of three offspring born at one birth.
3. *Poetry:* a group of three rhyming lines.
4. *Music:* a group of three equal notes performed in the time of two.

triplicate (*say* **tripli**–kit) *adjective*
made with three copies.
triplicate *noun*
any of three identical things.
Word Family: **triplicate** (*say* tripli–kate), *verb*; **triplication,** *noun.*
[TRI– + Latin *plicare* to fold]

tripod (*say* **try**–pod) *noun*
a stool or stand with three legs, as is used to support a camera.
[TRI– + Greek *podos* of a foot]

tripping *noun, adjective*
Word Family: see TRIP.

triptych (*say* **trip**–tik) *noun*
a series of altar paintings on three panels side by side. Compare DIPTYCH.
[Greek *triptykhos* three–folded]

trireme (*say* **try**–reem) *noun*
Ancient history: a war galley with three banks of oarsmen, one above the other.
[TRI– + Latin *remus* an oar]

trisect (*say* try–**sekt**) *verb*
to divide into three, usually equal, parts.

trite *adjective*
commonplace or lacking originality.
Word Family: **tritely,** *adverb*; **triteness,** *noun.*
[Latin *tritus* worn with use]

tritium (*say* **trittium**) *noun*
Chemistry: a radioactive isotope of hydrogen, widely used in research.

triumph (*say* **try**–umf) *noun*
a) a victory or success. b) a feeling of joy because of a victory.
triumphant (*say* try–**um**–f'nt) *adjective*
1. victorious.
2. exultant because of a victory or success.
Word Family: **triumph,** *verb*; **triumphal** (*say* try–**um**–f'l), *adjective,* of, relating to or in the nature of a triumph; **triumphantly,** *adverb.*
[Latin *triumphus* a victory parade]

triumvir (*say* try–**um**ver) *noun*
Ancient history: any of three men who shared joint administrative authority in Rome.
triumvirate (*say* try–**um**va–rit) *noun*
1. the position or term of office of a triumvir.
2. any group of three people who together exercise authority or control.
[Latin *trium virorum* of three men]

trivalent (*say* tri–**vay**–l'nt) *adjective*
Chemistry: having a valency or combining power of three.

trivet *noun*
a low, metal stand on legs, used to support hot dishes, food in a pressure cooker, etc.
[Latin *tripes* three–footed]

trivial (*say* **trivvi**–al) *adjective*
insignificant or of trifling value: 'the parliamentary bill was held up by *trivial* objections'.
Word Family: **trivially,** *adverb*; **triviality** (*say* trivvi–**alli**–tee), *noun,* a) the state or quality of being trivial, b) a trivial matter, event, idea, etc.; **trivia** (*say* **trivvi**–a), *plural noun,* any insignificant or unimportant matters.
[Latin *trivialis* commonplace]

trochee (*say* **tro**–kee) *noun*
Poetry: see FOOT.
Word Family: **trochaic** (*say* tro–**kay**–ik), *adjective,* relating to or composed of trochees.
[Greek *trokheios* running]

trod *verb*
the past tense and a past participle of the verb **tread.**

trodden *verb*
a past participle of the verb **tread.**

troglodyte (*say* **trogla**–dite) *noun*
a) a cave–dweller. b) a hermit or recluse.
[Greek *troglodytes*]

troika (*say* **troyka**) *noun*
a Russian vehicle drawn by a team of three horses running abreast.
[Russian *troie* three]

Trojan *noun*
a person of great courage or determination.
[after the people of the ancient city of *Troy* who fought a ten–year war]

troll *noun*
Scandinavian mythology: a supernatural being, sometimes believed to be a giant and sometimes a mischievous dwarf.

trolley *noun*
1. a) a small table on wheels, for carrying dishes, food, etc. b) a small truck running on rails, e.g. in a coalmine.
2. a trolleybus.

trolleybus *noun*
a bus powered by electricity from two overhead wires.

trolley car
American: a tram.

trollop (*say* **trollup**) *noun*
a slovenly or immoral woman.

trombone *noun*
Music: a brass, wind instrument in which a slide is moved to lengthen or shorten the tube.
Word Family: **trombonist,** *noun.*
[Italian *tromba* trumpet]

troop *noun*
1. an assembled company: 'a *troop* of admirers followed him everywhere'.
2. *Military:* a) (*usually plural*) soldiers. b) a tactical unit of cavalry.
troop *verb*
to come, go or gather as a troop: 'the children *trooped* out of school'.
troop the colour, to carry the colour or flag of a regiment ceremoniously before the troops on parade.

trooper *noun*
1. a soldier in the cavalry or armoured corps.
2. *American:* a policeman.
swear like a trooper, to use very bad language.

trophy (*say* **tro-fee**) *noun*
1. something kept in memory of a victory: 'he took his enemy's sword for a *trophy*'.
2. a prize, especially for the winner of a sporting competition.

tropic *noun*
(*plural*) the area of the earth lying in the region of the equator. Also called the **torrid zones.**
the **tropic of Cancer** is the line of latitude at about 23° 30′ North, indicating the northernmost point at which the sun can be overhead at noon.
the **tropic of Capricorn** is the line of latitude at about 23° 30′ South, indicating the southernmost point at which the sun can be overhead at noon.
Word Family: **tropical,** *adjective,* of, relating to or occurring in the tropics.
[Greek *tropé* a turning (as the sun appears to turn back after reaching these points)]

tropical cyclone
also called a **cyclone,** a **typhoon** or a **hurricane**
an area of low pressure, with heavy rain and circular winds, up to 350 km per hour, around a central area of about 30 km in which the air is relatively calm.

tropism (*say* **tro-pizm**) *noun*
Biology: the involuntary response of an organism to an external stimulus.
Example: the orientation of the leaves of certain plants towards the sun is a tropism.
[Greek *tropé* turning]

troposphere (*say* **troppa-sfeer**) *noun*
the lower layers of the atmosphere below the stratosphere, up to about 20 km from the earth's surface.
[Greek *tropos* turning + SPHERE]

trot *noun*
1. a gait of a horse between a walk and canter, in which groups of two distinct hoof-beats may be heard as the legs move in diagonal pairs.
2. a running or jogging gait using quick, short steps.
trot *verb*
(trotted, trotting)
to move or run at a trot.
Phrases:
trot out, to produce or bring out.
trotting race, a race between horses at the trot and harnessed to sulkies.

troth *noun*
an old word meaning: a) faithfulness or loyalty; b) truth.

Trotskyite, Trotskyist *noun*
short form is **Trot**
an anti-Soviet Marxist who advocates world revolution, in contrast to Lenin's policy of 'socialism in one country' (that is, in Russia).
[the policy of *Leon Trotsky,* who was expelled from Russia in 1924]

trotter *noun*
1. the foot of an animal, especially the pig or sheep.
2. a horse bred or trained for trotting races.

troubadour (*say* **trooba-dor**) *noun*
a travelling musician and singer, especially in medieval France.
[Old French, finder, inventor, composer]

trouble (*say* **trubb**'l) *verb*
to cause worry or anxiety, etc.: 'my son's violent behaviour *troubles* me'.
Usages:
a) 'the pebble *troubled* the still water' (= agitated).
b) 'don't *trouble* to meet me at the station' (= concern yourself).
c) 'I'm sorry to *trouble* you' (= disturb).
trouble *noun*
a) worry, anxiety or misfortune: 'you do nothing but cause *trouble* for your parents'. b) a person or thing causing this: 'these beds are a *trouble* to make'.
Usage: 'strikes are a sign of industrial *trouble*' (= unrest).
in trouble, in a position likely to bring hardship or punishment.
Word Family: **troublesome**, *adjective*, causing trouble.
[Latin *turbidus* crowded, disturbed]

troubled waters
a state of unrest or confusion.

trouble-shooter *noun*
a person who finds and eliminates causes of trouble.

trough (*say* trof) *noun*
1. an open box-like container used for feeding or watering animals, washing ore, etc.
2. *Weather:* an area of low pressure extending from a low.
3. a long, narrow channel, as the low point between successive ocean waves.

trounce *verb*
1. to beat or defeat severely.
2. to punish or reprimand.
Word Family: **trouncing**, *noun.*

troupe (*say* troop) *noun*
a group of actors or performers, especially ones who travel about.
trouper *noun*
1. a member of a troupe.
2. (*informal*) a loyal and hard-working person.
[French, troop]

trousers *plural noun*
also called **slacks**
a piece of clothing covering the lower half of the body, enclosing each leg separately.
Word Family: **trouser**, *adjective.*

trousseau (*say* **troo**-so) *noun*
the clothes and household items which a bride brings with her on marriage.
[French *trousse* bundle]

trout *noun*
plural is **trout**
any of a group of freshwater fish related to the salmon and highly esteemed as sport and food.

trow (*say* tro) *verb*
an old word meaning to think or believe.

trowel *noun*
any of various short-handled tools with a flat blade for spreading mortar or a curved blade for gardening.

troy weight
a system of units of mass for precious metals and gems. The units are **grain, pennyweight, ounce**, and **pound.**

truant (*say* **troo**-ant) *noun*
a pupil who stays away from school without permission.
play truant, to be a truant
Word Family: **truant**, *adjective*, idle or wandering; **truancy** (*say* **troo**-an-see), *noun*; **truant**, *noun.*

truce *noun*
an agreement to stop fighting for a period of time.

truck (1) *noun*
1. a motor vehicle for carrying heavy loads.
2. any wheeled structure for moving heavy goods, such as a railway wagon or a railway porter's handcart.
truck *verb*
to transport goods by truck.

truck (2) *noun*
1. dealings: 'I want no *truck* with you and your mad ideas'.
2. *American:* garden produce grown for the market: '*truck* farming'.

truculent (*say* **truk**-yoo-l'nt) *adjective*
aggressive or belligerent.
Word Family: **truculence**, *noun*; **truculently**, *adverb.*
[Latin *trux* fierce]

trudge *verb*
to walk heavily or wearily.
Word Family: **trudge**, *noun.*

true (*say* troo) *adjective*
1. corresponding to the actual state of things: 'it was an unlikely story but he insisted it was *true*'.
2. not artificial or counterfeit: '*true* gold'.
Usage: 'does the instrument give *true* readings?' (= accurate).
3. loyal or faithful: 'a *true* and trusted follower'.
4. (of a compass direction) related to the earth's axis rather than the magnetic poles: '*true* north'.

true *adverb*
in a true or truthful manner.
come true, to happen in reality.

true–blue *adjective*
(of Conservatives) of firm orthodoxy or loyalty.

truffle *noun*
1. an underground fungus, considered a delicacy.
2. a round chocolate and cocoa sweet.
[Latin *tubera*]

trug *noun*
a shallow wooden basket used in gardening to collect produce, weeds, etc.

truism (*say* **troo**–izm) *noun*
an obvious or self–evident truth.

truly (*say* **troo**–lee) *adverb*
1. truthfully: 'she speaks *truly*'.
2. with accuracy: 'this sewing machine won't hem *truly*'.
3. undeniably: 'a *truly* superb meal'.

trump (1) *noun*
1. *Cards:* a) (*plural*) the chosen suit, all of whose cards outrank any others during a particular hand. b) a card of this suit.
2. a powerful or decisive stroke, resource, etc.
3. (*informal*) an admirable person.
turn, come up trumps, to turn out better or more helpful than one expected.
trump *verb*
Cards: a) to play a trump. b) to win a trick by playing a trump.
trump up, 'the police *trumped up* charges against the innocent man' (= invented dishonestly). *Word Family*: **trumped–up**, *adjective.*
[from TRIUMPH]

trump (2) *noun*
a poetic word for: a) a trumpet; b) the sound of a trumpet.
Last Trump, the trumpet call which will awaken the dead on the Day of Judgement, according to the Bible, 1 Corinthians, 15.52.

trumpery (*say* **trumpa**–ree) *noun*
worthless finery or display.
[French *tromper* to deceive]

trumpet *noun*
1. *Music:* a high–pitched, brass, wind instrument with a flared bell–shaped end.
2. something which has the shape of a trumpet.
3. a trumpet–like sound, such as the cry of an elephant.
blow one's own trumpet, to praise oneself.
trumpet *verb*
a) to blow a trumpet. b) to make a trumpet–like sound.
Usage: 'she *trumpeted* the news all over town' (= proclaimed).
Word Family: **trumpeter**, *noun*, a person who plays the trumpet.

truncated (*say* trun–**kay**–tid) *adjective*
shortened by having a part or end cut off.
Word Family: **truncate**, *verb.*
[Latin *truncare* to mutilate, lop off]

truncheon (*say* **trun**–ch'n) *noun*
a policeman's short club or baton.
[Latin *truncus* a tree–trunk]

trundle *verb*
to move or roll along, especially something which is heavy or awkward.

trunk *noun*
1. the main stem of a tree excluding the roots and branches.
2. *Anatomy:* the main part of the body excluding the head, neck, arms and legs.
3. a large box with a hinged lid, for carrying or storing clothes, etc.
4. a long, flexible snout, such as an elephant's.
5. (*plural*) any shorts or underpants, as a man's bathing shorts.
6. *American:* the boot of a car.
trunk *adjective*
1. relating to a telephone line connecting two distant exchanges.
2. relating to a main line or artery: 'the capital cities were connected by the main *trunk* railway line'.
[from Latin]

truss *noun*
1. a padded belt worn to support a hernia.
2. a framework constructed so that all the forces on its parts are either tensions or compressions, used to support bridges, roofs, etc.
3. a bundle, e.g. of hay, etc.
truss *verb*
1. to tie up or bind.
2. to support with a truss or trusses.

trust *noun*
1. a firm belief in something: 'I have full *trust* in your ability to succeed'.
Usage: 'to be treasurer of the club is a position of *trust*' (= responsibility).
2. a) something or someone committed to one's custody: 'I let him look after my finances but he betrayed the *trust*'.
b) the obligations resulting from this:

'he regarded the tending of his late wife's garden almost as a sacred *trust*'.
3. *Law:* a relationship between two people whereby property is held by one person for the benefit of the other.
4. *Commerce:* a group of firms formed to control prices, production, etc. but otherwise independent of each other.
on trust, a) 'you'll have to take my word *on trust*' (= without proof); b) 'may I buy these goods *on trust*?' (= on credit).
trust *verb*
to have or place trust in: a) 'I don't *trust* his promises'; b) 'can I *trust* you not to reveal the secret?'.
Usage: 'I *trust* you'll have a pleasant journey' (= hope).
Word Family: **trusting**, **trustful**, *adjectives*, having ready trust or confidence; **trustingly**, *adverb*; **trustingness**, *noun*; **trustworthy**, **trusty**, *adjectives*, able or worthy to be trusted; **trustworthily**, *adverb*; **trustworthiness**, *noun*; **trusty**, *noun*, a trusted person or thing.

trustee *noun*
Law: a) a person appointed to take care of the business affairs of an institution, company, etc. b) a person who holds property for the benefit of another.
Word Family: **trusteeship**, *noun*.

truth (*say* trooth) *noun*
1. a) that which is true: 'are you telling the *truth*?'. b) the quality or state of being true: 'there is no *truth* to the rumour'.
2. something which has been verified or cannot be disputed: 'a scientific *truth*'.
in truth, in fact or reality.
Word Family: **truthful**, *adjective*, a) telling the truth, b) true; **truthfully**, *adverb*; **truthfulness**, *noun*.

truth drug
a drug which, administered to a person under investigation, is said to render him more likely to blurt out the truth.

try *verb*
(tried, trying)
1. to attempt: '*try* to speak quietly'.
2. to test: '*try* the soup and see whether you like it'.
Usages:
a) 'this one won't write; *try* a new pen' (= use).
b) 'you're *trying* my patience' (= straining).
3. *Law:* to determine the guilt or innocence of a person during a trial.
Phrases:
try on, to put on clothes, etc. to see if they fit or look good.
try one's hand at, to attempt to do something, especially something which one has not done before.
try out, to test or experiment with.
Word Family: **tryout**, *noun*.
try *noun*
1. an attempt, endeavour or effort.
2. *Football:* (in Rugby) the act of carrying the ball over the opposing team's goal line and touching the ground with it. The scoring side then tries to score a goal from a place kick. Also called a **touchdown**.
Word Family: **trier**, *noun*, a person who tries hard.

trying *adjective*
annoying or irritating: 'nothing went right during the *trying* day at the office'.

try square
an implement consisting of two straight edges fastened at right angles, used to test squareness.

tryst (*say* trist) *noun*
an appointment or meeting, especially between lovers.
[Old French *triste* a waiting-place (a hunting term)]

tsar (*say* zar) *noun*
also spelt **czar** or **tzar**
History: an emperor or king, especially in Russia from 1547 to 1917.
Word Family: **tsarina** (*say* za-**reena**), *noun*, a) a female tsar, b) the wife of a tsar; **tsarevitch** (*say* **zara**-vitch), *noun*, the son or eldest son of a tsar; **tsarist**, *noun*, a supporter of a tsar or government by tsars.
[Russian, from Latin *Caesar*]

tsetse fly (*say* **tset**-tsee fly)
an African, blood-sucking fly which may transmit sleeping sickness to man and various serious diseases to cattle.

T-shirt *noun*
also spelt **tee-shirt**
a light, cotton shirt with short sleeves and no collar.
[from its shape when spread out]

T-square *noun*
a T-shaped ruler used for drawing parallel lines, etc.

tub *noun*
1. any large, open vessel made of metal, wood, etc., used for washing, growing plants, etc.
2. (*informal*) an old or slow boat.

tuba (*say* **tew**ba) *noun*
Music: a low-pitched, brass, wind instrument.
[Latin]

tubal ligation
an operation to cut and tie the Fallopian tubes to produce sterility.

tubby *adjective*
short, round and fat.
Word Family: **tubbiness**, *noun.*

tube *noun*
1. any extended hollow cylinder made from glass, metal, rubber, etc.
2. something which has the shape of this, such as some organs of the human body: 'the bronchial *tubes*'.
3. a soft metal container with a screw cap at one end: 'a *tube* of toothpaste'.
4. a) a cylindrical tunnel for an underground railway. b) an underground train or railway.
5. an electrical valve: 'a television *tube*'.
Word Family: **tubing** (*say* **tube**-ing), *noun,* any material in the form of a tube; **tubular** (*say* **tube**-yoo-la), *adjective,* having, consisting of or shaped like a tube.
[from Latin]

tuber (*say* **tew**ba) *noun*
Biology: the swollen end of an underground stem, such as a potato, containing a store of food and acting as an organ of vegetative reproduction.
Word Family: **tuberous**, *adjective,* of, like or producing tubers.
[Latin, bump or swelling]

tuberculin tested *adjective*
(of milk) from cows guaranteed to be free of tuberculosis.

tuberculosis (*say* tew-berkew-**lo**-sis) *noun*
a bacterial disease often affecting the lungs, causing a swelling (called a **tubercle**) in the affected tissue.
Word Family: **tubercular** (*say* tew-**berk**ew-la), **tuberculous**, *adjectives.*
[Latin *tuberculum* a small swelling + -OSIS]

tuberose (*say* **tew**ba-rose) *noun*
a Mexican garden plant with spikes of fragrant, cream, lily-like flowers growing from a bulb.
[Latin *tuberosus* swollen]

tubing *noun*
Word Family: see TUBE.

tubular *adjective*
Word Family: see TUBE.

tuck *noun*
Needlework: a fold made by doubling cloth on itself, and stitching parallel to the fold.
tuck *verb*
1. to fold under or press in the loose edge or end of: a) '*tuck* the blankets under the mattress'; b) '*tuck* in your shirt'.
2. to make tucks in, by folding and stitching.
Usages:
a) 'a little cottage *tucked* away in the forest' (= snugly hidden, concealed).
b) 'he *tucked* his legs under the bench' (= drew up).
c) (*informal*) 'she *tucked* into the lobster salad' (= ate heartily).

tucker, tuck *noun*
(*informal*) food.

tuckshop *noun*
(*informal*) a shop in or near a school selling food and drinks to pupils.

Tuesday *noun*
the third day of the week.
[named after the ancient German god *Tiw,* identified with Mars]

tuff *noun*
Geology: a rock formed by compacted layers of ash from a volcano.
[from Latin]

tuft *noun*
a bunch of feathers, hair, grass, etc. growing or held together at the base.
Word Family: **tufted, tufty**, *adjectives,* containing tufts.

tug *verb*
(**tugged, tugging**)
to pull or pull at forcefully: 'stop *tugging* my hair'.
tug *noun*
1. the act of tugging: 'give the rope a hard *tug*'.
2. a small boat with a powerful engine used to tow and manoeuvre other ships. Short form of **tugboat**.

tug of war
a competition between two teams, in which each holds an end of a rope, the aim being for one team to pull the other across a central line.

tuition (*say* tew-**ish**'n) *noun*
the teaching or instruction of students.
[Latin *tuitio* a looking after]

tulip (*say* **tew**lip) *noun*
a garden plant with single, showy, cup-shaped flowers growing from a bulb.
[Turkish *tulbend* turban]

tulle (*say* tewl) *noun*
a thin, net-like fabric used in millinery, veils, dressmaking, etc.
[originally made in *Tulle*, France]

tumble *verb*
a) to roll or fall over or down: 'the clumsy boy *tumbled* off the chair'. b) to cause to roll or fall: 'the bump *tumbled* me out of the seat'.
tumble to, (*informal*) 'at last she *tumbled to* his real meaning' (=understood).
Word Family: **tumble**, *noun*, a) a fall, b) a confused state or heap.

tumbledown *adjective*
dilapidated.

tumbler *noun*
1. a flat-bottomed drinking glass.
2. a person who performs somersaults and other tricks.
3. any of the parts of a lock which move when the key is turned.
4. a rotating cylindrical tank, used for polishing precious stones, drying clothes, etc.

tumbrel, tumbril *noun*
a cart which may be tilted backwards to empty its load.
[French *tomber* to fall]

tumescent (*say* tew-**mess**'nt) *adjective*
a) swelling slightly. b) swollen.
Word Family: **tumescence**, *noun*.
[from Latin]

tumid (*say* **tew**mid) *adjective*
swollen, e.g. of a part of the body.
Word Family: **tumidity** (*say* tew-**middi**-tee), *noun*.
[from Latin]

tummy *noun*
(*informal*) the stomach.

tumour (*say* **tew**ma) *noun*
in America spelt **tumor**
also called a **neoplasm**
an abnormal swelling in the body, which may be benign or malignant.
[from Latin]

tumult (*say* **tew**mult) *noun*
any commotion or disturbance made by a crowd.
Usage: 'her mind was in a *tumult*' (= confused and excited state).
Word Family: **tumultuous** (*say* tew-**mul**tew-us), *adjective*, a) noisy, b) disturbed; **tumultuously**, *adverb*.
[from Latin]

tumulus (*say* **tew**-mew-lus) *noun*
a prehistoric barrow.
[Latin, a mound]

tun *noun*
a large cask for wine or beer.

tuna (*say* **tew**na) *noun*
also called a **tunny**
any of a group of large, warm-blooded, edible, marine fish, in which the extra blood supply results in a distinctive pink flesh.
[Greek *thynnos*]

tundra *noun*
the treeless plains in the extreme north of Europe and America, where there are long, severe winters and permanently frozen subsoil.
[Russian]

tune *noun*
a rhythmic series or arrangement of musical sounds, e.g. of a song.
Phrases:
call the tune, to control or give orders.
change one's tune, to change one's ideas or behaviour.
in tune, 'can you sing *in tune*?' (= in harmony or correct pitch).
out of tune, 'this old piano is *out of tune*' (= not in harmony or correct pitch).
to the tune of, to the amount of.
tune *verb*
to adjust a musical instrument, radio, car engine, etc. to get the correct pitch, resonance or performance.
Phrases:
tune in, to locate a particular station or programme by adjusting the controls of a radio.
tune up, 'the orchestra were already *tuning up* as we took our seats' (= getting in tune).
tuner *noun*
1. a person or thing that tunes: 'a piano *tuner*'.
2. *Radio:* the part of a receiver which selects signals for amplifying, thus determining performance.
Word Family: **tuneful**, *adjective*, having or full of tune; **tunefully**, *adverb*; **tunefulness**, *noun*.
[for TONE]

tune-up *noun*
a check and adjustment of a motor vehicle's engine to obtain maximum power or efficiency.

tungsten *noun*
also called **wolfram**
element number 74, a malleable, ductile metal used for electric light filaments and cutting tools. See TRANSITION ELEMENT.
See CHEMICAL ELEMENTS in grey pages.
[Swedish *tung* heavy + *sten* stone]

tunic (*say* **tew–nik**) *noun*
1. a) a short, loose, sleeveless dress, often with a belt. b) a similar garment worn by the ancient Greeks and Romans.
2. a coat or jacket worn as part of a police or military uniform.
[from Latin]

tuning fork
a two–pronged metal object which vibrates at a set pitch when struck, and by which the pitch of musical instruments and voices may be checked.

tunnel *noun*
an underground passage, especially a man–made one.
Word Family: **tunnel** (**tunnelled, tunnelling**), *verb*, to make a tunnel.

tunny *noun* see TUNA.

tuppence *noun* twopence.

turban *noun*
a head covering consisting of a long strip of cloth wound around the head, first worn by Moslem men in Asia and Africa. [Turkish *tulbend*]

turbid (*say* **terbid**) *adjective*
not clear or transparent: 'the *turbid* river was full of silt'.
Usage: 'she had wild, *turbid* thoughts' (= confused).
Word Family: **turbidly**, *adverb*; **turbidity** (*say* ter–biddi–tee), *noun*.
[Latin *turbidus* crowded, disturbed]

turbine (*say* **terbine**) *noun*
any motor in which the shaft is turned by the action of a fluid, such as gas, steam or water, passing over blades set in a wheel.
[Latin *turbinis* of a spinning–top]

turbo–charger *noun*
see TURBO–SUPERCHARGER.

turbogenerator
(*say* terbo–**jenna**–rayta) *noun*
a generator powered by a turbine.

turbojet *noun*
a jet–engine or aircraft with a turbine–driven compressor.

turboprop *noun*
also called a **propjet**
a) a jet engine which produces thrust by a propeller connected to the turbine shaft. b) an aircraft driven by one or more such engines.

turbo–supercharger *noun*
short form is **turbo–charger**
a supercharger driven by a turbine in the exhaust pipe of an internal combustion engine.

turbot *noun*
a very large, round, marine flatfish, highly valued as food and having similarities to brill and halibut.
[French]

turbulent (*say* **terbew**–l'nt) *adjective*
violent, unruly or uncontrolled: 'the diver drowned in the *turbulent* waters of the whirlpool'.
turbulence *noun*
1. a turbulent state.
2. *Weather:* the irregular movements of air near the ground and in air currents.
Word Family: **turbulently**, *adverb*.
[from Latin]

turd *noun*
1. (*informal*) a lump of faeces.
2. (*informal*) a contemptible person.

tureen (*say* too–**reen**) *noun*
a deep, round dish with a lid, for serving soup, etc.
[French *terrine*]

turf *noun*
plural is **turfs**
the layer of earth containing grass and its matted roots.
the turf
horseracing.
turf *verb*
turf out, (*informal*) to throw out.

turf accountant
a bookmaker.

turgid (*say* **terjid**) *adjective*
1. (of language) pretentious or pompous.
2. swollen.
Word Family: **turgidly**, *adverb*; **turgidness**, *noun*.
[Latin *turgidus* swollen]

turkey (*say* **terkee**) *noun*
a large edible fowl, both wild and domesticated, originally from North America.
Phrases:
cold turkey, (*informal*) the effects of sudden withdrawal from an addictive drug, such as heroin.
talk turkey, (*informal*) to talk seriously.
[name originally given to guinea–fowl imported through *Turkey*]

Turkish bath
a) a steam bath followed by a wash and massage. b) a building where this is available.

turmeric (*say* **terma-rik**) *noun*
the yellow, powdered root of an Indian plant, used as a spice, a dye and in medicine.

turmoil *noun*
a state of great commotion or agitation: 'the government was in a *turmoil* over the scandal'.

turn *verb*
1. to move or cause to move around an axis or centre: a) 'the wheels *turned* as the car rolled forward'; b) 'the matter *turns* on the availability of finance'.
2. to change or cause to change direction, position, etc. by moving through a part of a circle: a) '*turn* the corner'; b) 'he *turned* his head to see'.
3. to change so that the upper side becomes the lower: a) '*turn* the pancakes before they burn'; b) '*turn* the page carefully'.
4. to move or orientate to a particular or new position: a) '*turn* to page 63'; b) '*turn* your thoughts to the future'.
5. to become or cause to become: a) 'she *turned* red with rage'; b) 'the twins *turn* three tomorrow'; c) 'the witch *turned* the prince into a frog'.
6. to shape or form, as in a lathe.
Usages:
a) 'the leaves *turn* in autumn' (= change colour).
b) 'the milk has *turned*' (= gone bad).
c) 'my head is *turning*' (= spinning).
d) 'the horrible sight *turned* his stomach' (= sickened).
e) 'he *turned* the bible salesman from his door' (= repelled).
f) 'I *turned* to you for help' (= resorted).
g) 'he *turns* over the tops of the pages to mark his place' (= folds).
h) 'I hope to *turn* the time to good account' (= use).
i) 'the acrobat *turned* somersaults' (= performed by turning).
j) 'too much praise can *turn* a person's head' (= unsettle, put out of order).
Phrases:
turn against, to become or cause to become hostile towards.
turn away, to refuse help or admittance to.
turn down, a) to lessen in volume, flow, etc.; b) to refuse or reject.
turn in, (*informal*) a) to go to bed; b) 'the escaped prisoner *turned* himself *in*' (= surrendered).
turn off, a) to diverge or divert; b) (*informal*) to repulse.
turn on, a) to attack suddenly; b) (*informal*) to excite.
turn out, a) '*turn out* the lights' (= turn off); b) to make or manufacture; c) '*turn out* your pockets' (= empty); d) 'the troops *turned out* at reveille' (= assembled, mustered); e) to equip or outfit.
turn over, a) to ponder or meditate; b) (of an engine) to start; c) to hand over.
turn tail, to run away.
turn to, to set to work.
turn up, a) to happen; b) to arrive; c) to find or be found.
turn *noun*
1. a turning movement: 'give the key a hard *turn*'.
2. a change in direction, condition, etc.: a) 'there were many *turns* in the road'; b) 'his health took a *turn* for the worse'.
3. the place at which something turns: 'take the second *turn* left'.
4. the time at or during which something occurs in rotation: 'wait for your *turn*'.
5. an action which affects someone: 'she did me a good *turn*'.
6. *Theatre:* an act.
Usages:
a) 'he uses a strange *turn* of phrase' (= style, form).
b) 'the bad news gave me quite a *turn*' (= shock).
c) 'she has a scientific *turn* of mind' (= tendency, aptitude).
Phrases:
at every turn, constantly.
on the turn, turning or about to turn or change.
take turns, to alternate.
to a turn, to just the right degree.
turn and turn about, alternately.
[Greek *tornos* a lathe]

turnabout *noun*
a complete change of opinion, loyalty, etc.

turncoat *noun*
a renegade.

turner *noun*
a person who fashions objects on a lathe.

turning *noun*
the place where a road turns, especially at a fork or junction.

turning point
a point at which a critical or decisive change takes place.

turnip *noun*
a white, round root used as a vegetable.

turnkey (*say* **tern**–kee) *noun*
an old word for a gaoler.

turn–off *noun*
a road, path, etc. branching off a main road.

turnout *noun*
1. a gathering of people.
2. a quantity which is produced or manufactured.

turnover *noun*
1. a) the total amount of money received from the sale of goods in a certain period of time. b) the rate at which goods, money, employees etc. are replaced.
2. a semicircular pie made by folding one half of the crust over the other.

turnpike *noun*
History, American: a road on which a toll must be paid.

turnstile *noun*
a revolving gateway admitting one person at a time, used for counting and controlling the people entering a sports ground, etc.

turntable *noun*
1. the part of a record–player on which the record sits and revolves.
2. *Railways:* a section of a railway line set on a disc, which may be rotated to transfer railway vehicles onto other lines.

turn–up *noun*
an unexpected or lucky result or event.

turpentine (*say* **terp**'n–tine) *noun*
a) a natural mixture of oil and resin produced by coniferous trees. b) an inflammable oil distilled from this, used for mixing or thinning oil paints, etc.
[Greek *terebinthos* a tree yielding it]

turpitude (*say* **ter**pi–tewd) *noun*
wickedness or depravity.
[Latin *turpis* ugly, filthy]

turps *noun*
(*informal*) turpentine.

turquoise (*say* **ter**–kwoyz *or* **ter**–kwahz) *noun*
1. *Geology:* a hard blue or blue–green mineral used as a gem.
2. a bright greenish–blue colour.
[for Turkish]

turret *noun*
1. a small tower, often decorative.
2. a revolving, heavily armoured structure containing large guns, e.g. in a warship or on a tank.
[Latin *turris* a tower]

turtle *noun*
any of a group of aquatic reptiles living in the sea or fresh water and having legs modified for swimming. Compare TORTOISE.
turn turtle, to capsize.

turtledove *noun*
a type of small, long–tailed dove noted for its gentle coo.
[Latin *turtur*]

turtle–neck *adjective*
polo–neck.
Word Family: **turtle–neck**, *noun.*

tusk *noun*
a long, protruding tooth found in some mammals, such as the elephant and walrus.
Word Family: **tusker**, *noun*, an animal with tusks.

tussle *verb*
to fight or struggle roughly.
Word Family: **tussle**, *noun.*

tussock *noun*
a thick clump of grass.

tut, tut–tut *interjection*
an exclamation expressing rebuke or disapproval.

tutelage (*say* **tew**ta–lij) *noun*
guardianship.

tutelary (*say* **tew**tela–ree) *adjective*
of or serving as a guardian or protector.

tutor (*say* **tew**ta) *noun*
1. a private teacher, especially of a single pupil or very small class.
2. a college don who supervises the work and welfare of undergraduates taking a particular degree course.
Word Family: **tutor**, *verb*; **tutorship**, *noun*, the position of a tutor.
[Latin, guardian]

tutorial (*say* tew–**taw**riul) *noun*
a period of instruction with a university tutor.

tutu (*say* too–too) *noun*
a short, frilly, flared skirt made of tulle, worn by female ballet–dancers.
[French]

tuxedo (*say* tuk–**see**do) *noun*
short form is **tux**
American: a dinner jacket.
[after a New York club]

twaddle (*say* **twodd**'l) *noun*
meaningless or foolish talk or writing.
Word Family: **twaddle**, *verb.*

twain *noun*
an old word meaning two.

twang *verb*
to make a sharp vibrating sound, as by plucking the string of a musical instrument.
twang *noun*
1. a twanging sound.
2. a sharp nasal sound in the human voice.

tweak *verb*
to pinch or twist: 'he *tweaked* the child's nose'.
Word Family: **tweak**, *noun.*

twee *adjective*
(*informal*) affectedly dainty.

tweed *noun*
1. a coarse, rough-surfaced, heavy woollen fabric in a variety of weaves and colours.
2. (*plural*) any clothes made of this fabric.
[for TWILL (confused with the River *Tweed*)]

tweeter *noun*
a loudspeaker designed for frequencies above about 3000 cycles per second. Compare WOOFER.

tweezers *plural noun*
a small implement with two arms, used for plucking or picking up small objects, etc.

twelve *noun*
a cardinal number, the symbol 12 in Arabic numerals, XII in Roman numerals.
Word Family: **twelve,** *adjective*; **twelfth**, *noun, adjective.*

twenty *noun*
1. a cardinal number, the symbol 20 in Arabic numerals, XX in Roman numerals.
2. (*plural*) the numbers 20–29 in a series, such as the years within a century.
Word Family: **twenty,** *adjective*; **twentieth**, *noun, adjective.*

twerp *noun*
(*informal*) a stupid or dislikable person.

twice *adverb*
two times.

twiddle *verb*
to twist or turn idly or aimlessly: 'to *twiddle* the knobs on a radio'.

twig (1) *noun*
a small shoot at the end of a branch or stem.

twig (2) *verb*
(twigged, twigging)
(*informal*) a) to see or observe. b) to understand.

twilight (*say* **twy**–lite) *noun*
1. the period of reduced light either after sunset or before sunrise.
2. a period or condition after full development, glory, etc.: 'the old man enjoyed the *twilight* of his life'.

twill *noun*
a woven fabric with the threads forming parallel, diagonal lines.

twin *noun*
1. either of two offspring born at one birth. **Identical twins** develop from a single fertilized ovum which splits into two, so each twin has identical hereditary characteristics. **Fraternal twins** develop from two fertilized ova, so each twin has distinct hereditary characteristics.
2. either of a pair of identical or similar things.
3. *Astrology:* (*capital, plural*) see GEMINI.
twin towns
towns in different countries, e.g. England and France, which have agreed to exchange visits by groups of representative citizens.

twine *noun*
a strong thread made by twisting two or more strands together.
twine *verb*
to twist or wind together or around.

twinge (*say* twinj) *noun*
a sudden, sharp pain.
Word Family: **twinge,** *verb.*

twinkle *verb*
to sparkle with a flickering light.
twinkle, twinkling *noun*
sparkle or brightness.
Usage: 'I'll be back in a *twinkle*' (= instant).
the twinkling of an eye, the time taken to wink an eye.

twin-set *noun*
a cardigan and jumper of the same material and colour, worn as a matching pair.

twirl *verb*
to turn round and round, especially quickly.
Word Family: **twirl,** *noun.*
[TW(ist) + (wh)IRL]

twist *verb*
1. to turn or wind strands or threads together.

2. to turn the two ends of something in opposite directions.
Usages:
a) 'she fell and *twisted* her ankle' (= turned sharply).
b) 'the stream *twisted* through the valley' (= wound).
c) 'the newspapers *twisted* his words' (= gave a different meaning to).
d) 'he *twisted* his face into a sickly grin' (= contorted).
e) 'he has a *twisted* mind' (= perverted, warped).
twist someone's arm, to put pressure on someone to do what one wishes.
twist *noun*
1. a) a twisting action or motion. b) a bend or curve.
2. something that has been twisted: 'a *twist* of tobacco'.
Usage: 'the mystery film has a *twist* at the end' (= unexpected development).
3. a dance consisting of twisting movements of the body.

twister *noun*
an unreliable, tricky person.

twit *noun*
(*informal*) a) a fool. b) a nervous or edgy state.
Word Family: **twit** (**twitted, twitting**), *verb*, to tease by reminding of a fault, mistake, etc.

twitch *noun*
1. a short jerky movement of a muscle or part of the body.
2. a short, sudden pull.
Word Family: **twitch**, *verb*.

twitter *verb*
1. a) to make light chirping sounds. b) to titter.
2. to tremble with nervous excitement.
twitter *noun*
1. the act or sound of twittering.
2. a state of nervous excitement.
Word Family: **twittery**, *adjective*.

two (*say* too) *noun*
a cardinal number, the symbol 2 in Arabic numerals, II in Roman numerals.
put two and two together, to draw an obvious conclusion.
Word Family: **two**, *adjective*.

two-bit *adjective*
(*informal*) small-time: 'a *two-bit* hoodlum'.

two-dimensional *adjective*
having two dimensions, as height and width.

two-faced *adjective*
deceitful or hypocritical.

two-handed *adjective*
1. needing two hands to use: 'a *two-handed* sword'.
2. needing or involving two people: 'a *two-handed* saw'.
3. ambidextrous.

twopence (*say* **tuppence**) *noun*
also spelt **tuppence**
a sum of money to the value of two pennies.
Usage: 'she doesn't care *twopence* about him' (= a bit).

twosome (*say* **too**-sum) *noun*
1. two persons or things together.
2. *Sport:* a competition between two people.

twostep *noun*
a) a ballroom dance of sliding steps. b) the music for such a dance.

two-stroke *adjective*
of or relating to an internal combustion engine in which the fuel is taken into the cylinder, compressed, burnt and released into the exhaust in two successive strokes of the piston. Compare FOUR-STROKE.

two-time *verb*
(*informal*) to deceive or double-cross.
Word Family: **two-timer**, *noun*.

tycoon (*say* tie-**koon**) *noun*
a very wealthy or powerful businessman.
[Japanese *taikun* great prince]

tympanum (*say* **timpa**-num) *noun*
plural is **tympana**
1. *Architecture:* the recessed space of a pediment or arch above a doorway, etc.
2. *Anatomy:* a) the middle part of the ear. b) the eardrum.
Word Family: **tympanic** (Anatomy), *adjective*.
[Greek *tympanon* a drum]

type *noun*
1. a) a group or grouping with common characteristics: 'hers is the classical *type* of beauty'. b) a variety of such a group: 'what *type* of cheese is this?'.
Usage: 'she's a generous *type*' (= person).
2. a) a piece or pieces of metal cast with the imprint of a letter, figure, etc. b) printed characters: 'a headline in huge *type*'.
type *verb*
1. to assign a type to: 'your actions *type* you as a gentleman'.

2. to identify the type of: 'to *type* a blood sample'.
3. to produce words in print using a typewriter.
[Greek *typos* something impressed]

typecast *verb*
(typecast, typecasting)
to persist in giving a person the same kind of role.

typeface *noun*
Printing: the design of a certain piece of type.

typescript *noun*
any typewritten material.

typeset *verb*
(typeset, typesetting)
to arrange metal type for printing.
Word Family: **typesetter,** *noun.*

typewriter (*say* **tipe**–rite–a) *noun*
a machine with a keyboard, which produces printed characters by pressing each letter or symbol separately onto paper through an inked ribbon.

typhoid fever (*say* **tie**–foyd feeva)
short form is **typhoid**
an infectious, bacterial disease spread by contaminated food and water, causing severe intestinal disorders.
[TYPHUS + –OID FEVER]

typhoon (*say* tie–**foon**) *noun*
Weather: see TROPICAL CYCLONE.
[Chinese *tai* big + *feng* wind]

typhus (*say* **tie**–fus) *noun*
an infectious, viral disease transmitted by lice or mites, causing fever, weakness and a rash.
[Greek *typhos* a vapour]

typical (*say* **tippi**–k'l) *adjective*
conforming to a particular type or character: 'it is *typical* of you to be late'.
Word Family: **typically,** *adverb.*

typify (*say* **tippi**–fie) *verb*
(typified, typifying)
1. to be a typical example of: 'his swearing *typifies* his bad manners'.
2. to represent by a type.

typing (*say* **tie**–ping) *noun*
a) the skill of using a typewriter. b) any work produced on a typewriter.

typist (*say* **tie**–pist) *noun*
a person who uses a typewriter.

typography (*say* tie–**pogra**–fee) *noun*
the art or process of designing the printed layout of a book, magazine, etc.
Word Family: **typographic** (*say* tie–po–**graffik**), **typographical,** *adjective.*

typology (*say* tie–**polla**–jee) *noun*
the study of types, e.g. in a system of classification.

tyrannosaurus (*say* tee–ranna–**sawrus**) *noun*
a very large carnivorous dinosaur which walked erect on its hind limbs.

tyrant (*say* **tie**–r'nt) *noun*
a ruler who exercises absolute power cruelly and oppressively.
tyranny (*say* **tirra**–nee) *noun*
a) the rule of a tyrant. b) any cruel or unjust use of power: 'the *tyranny* of a harsh father's discipline'.
Word Family: **tyrannical** (*say* tie–**ranni**–k'l), **tyrannous** (*say* **tirra**–nus), *adjectives*; **tyrannically,** *adverb*; **tyrannize, tyrannise,** *verb.*
[from Greek]

tyre *noun*
a band of hollow, inflated rubber around the rim of a wheel to grip the road and cushion vibration.

tyro (*say* **tie**–ro) *noun*
see TIRO.

tzar (*say* zar) *noun*
see TSAR.

Uu

ubiquitous (*say* yoo–**bikwi**–tus) *adjective*
being everywhere at the same time.
Word Family: **ubiquitously**, *adverb*; **ubiquity** (*say* yoo–**bikwi**–tee), *noun*.
[Latin *ubique* everywhere]

U–boat *noun*
a German submarine.
[German *untersee* undersea + BOAT]

udder *noun*
a mammary gland, especially when having more than one teat, as on a cow.

ugly (*say* **ug**–lee) *adjective*
unpleasant in appearance.
Usage: 'an *ugly* temper' (= unpleasant, bad).
Word Family: **ugliness**, *noun*.

ugly duckling
an apparent dunce or unprepossessing child who grows up to be clever or handsome.
[from a Hans Andersen fairytale]

ukase (*say* yoo–**kaze**) *noun*
a dictatorial command from on high.
[Russian, edict]

ukulele (*say* yooka–**lay**–lee) *noun*
also spelt **ukelele**
Music: a small, guitar–like instrument with four strings.
[Hawaiian]

ulcer (*say* **ulsa**) *noun*
an open sore, usually occurring on the skin or on the inner surface of an organ, such as the stomach.
Word Family: **ulcerous**, *adjective*, a) like an ulcer, b) affected with ulcers; **ulcerate**, *verb*, to make or become ulcerous; **ulceration**, *noun*, a) the forming of an ulcer, b) an ulcer.

ullage *noun*
the part of an opened cask, bottle or other container which has not been or is no longer filled.

ulna *noun*
plural is **ulnae** (*say* **ul**–nee)
Anatomy: the longer of the two bones of the forearm or forelimb.
[Latin]

ulster *noun*
a long, loose overcoat.

ulterior (*say* ul–**teeria**) *adjective*
concealed by what is evident or expressed: 'an *ulterior* motive'.
[Latin]

ultimate (*say* **ulti**–mit) *adjective*
1. final or fundamental: 'death is man's *ultimate* fate'.
2. the maximum or greatest possible: 'the *ultimate* folly is driving with one's eyes closed'.
Word Family: **ultimately**, *adverb*, finally or at last.
[Latin *ultimus* last]

ultimatum (*say* ulti–**may**–t'm *or* ulti–**mah**–t'm) *noun*
a final proposal in a discussion, refusal of which causes negotiation to end and other action to be taken.

ultimo *adverb*
short form is **ult**
in or of the preceding month.

ultra–
a prefix meaning: a) beyond, as in *ultrasonic*; b) extremely, as in *ultraconservative*.
[Latin, beyond]

ultra high frequency
short form is **UHF**
Radio: a high frequency used for television, and some kinds of radar.

ultramarine (*say* ultra–ma–**reen**) *noun*
a brilliant, pure blue colour or pigment.
Word Family: **ultramarine**, *adjective*.
[ULTRA– + Latin *marinus* of the sea (as originally obtained from the lapis lazuli which came from 'beyond the sea')]

ultrasonic (*say* ultra–**sonnik**) *adjective*
Physics: (of waves) having such a high frequency that they are not within the range of normal human hearing.
ultrasonics *plural noun*
(*used with singular verb*) the study of ultrasonic phenomena and their varied

applications, e.g. in detecting flaws in metal, killing bacteria, sonar, etc.
[ULTRA- + Latin *sonus* a sound]

ultraviolet *noun*
Physics: see LIGHT (1).

ultra vires (*say* ultra **vie**-raze)
Law: exceeding the legal powers of a court, etc.
[Latin, beyond the powers]

umbel *noun*
a flower cluster in which the individual flower stalks rise from a common point.
[Latin *umbella* a sunshade]

umber *noun*
any of a group of brown colours ranging from light brown (**raw umber**), to deep brown (**burnt umber**).
Word Family: **umber**, *adjective.*
[Latin *umbra* shade]

umbilical cord (*say* um-**billi**-k'l kord)
Anatomy: a cord-like structure containing a network of blood vessels connecting the bloodstream of the unborn child to the bloodstream of the mother through the placenta.

umbilicus (*say* um-**billi**-kus) *noun*
Anatomy: the navel.
[Latin]

umbra *noun*
plural is **umbrae** (*say* **um**-bree)
Physics: the darker part at the centre of a shadow. Compare PENUMBRA.
[Latin, shade]

umbrage (*say* **um**-brij) *noun*
offence: 'he took *umbrage* at my suggestions'.

umbrageous (*say* um-**bray**jus) *adjective*
an old word meaning shady.

umbrella *noun*
1. a folding, circular frame with a stick and handle, covered in a waterproof material and used for protection from the rain.
2. something which has the shape or function of an umbrella, such as a protective air-cover for ground troops.
[Italian *ombrella* a little shade]

umlaut (*say* **um**-lout) *noun*
see ACCENT.
[German *um* about + *Laut* sound]

umpire *noun*
a person appointed to judge or make decisions on rules during a competition or game.
Word Family: **umpire**, *verb.*

umpteen *adjective*
(*informal*) of an indefinite, but usually large, number.
Word Family: **umpteenth**, *adjective.*

un-
a prefix meaning: a) (with adjectives) not, as in *unable* or *unsure*; b) (with nouns) the opposite or absence of something, as in *undesirability* or *untruth*; c) (with verbs) the reversal of an action or state, as in *undo* or *unseat.* In general, the negative *un-* can be added to most adjectives, but *in-* (or *il-*, *im-*, *ir-*) is more usual with words of obvious Latin derivation, such as *infidelity.* There are exceptions, and some adjectives are found with both *un-* and *in-*, e.g. *unessential, inessential.*

'un *pronoun*
(*informal*) one: 'the big *'un* that got away'.

unable *adjective*
not able to do something.

unaccompanied *adjective*
not accompanied: '*unaccompanied* singing'.

unaccountable *adjective*
1. a) impossible to find an explanation for. b) very odd.
2. not responsible: 'he is *unaccountable* for his actions'.
Word Family: **unaccountably**, *adverb.*

unaccounted-for *adjective*
not explained or taken into account.

unaccustomed *adjective*
not accustomed: '*unaccustomed* to public speaking'.

unadopted *adjective*
(of a road) not taken over by the local authority and therefore maintained, if at all, by residents.

unadvisedly *adverb*
unwisely or rashly.

unaesthetic *adjective*
not pleasing to the aesthetic sense.

unaffected (1) *adjective*
not affected or influenced.

unaffected (2) *adjective*
genuine or free from affectedness.
Word Family: **unaffectedly**, *adverb*; **unaffectedness**, *noun.*

unalloyed *adjective*
pure or unmixed: 'she welcomed him with *unalloyed* delight'.

unanimous (*say* yoo-**nanni**mus) *adjective*

in or demonstrating complete agreement.
Word Family: **unanimously**, *adverb*; **unanimity** (*say* yoona-**nimmi**-tee), **unanimousness**, *nouns*.
[Latin *unus* one + *animus* mind]

unanswerable *adjective*
1. not able to be refuted or disproved.
2. having no answer.
Word Family: **unanswerably**, *adverb*.

unapproachable *adjective*
a) not able to be approached or reached. b) haughty or not encouraging friendliness.
Word Family: **unapproachably**, *adverb*; **unapproachableness**, *noun*.

unarmed *adjective*
1. not carrying weapons.
2. defenceless.

unashamed *adjective*
1. not sorry or contrite.
2. not concealed: '*unashamed* malingering'.
Word Family: **unashamedly**, *adverb*.

unassuming *adjective*
modest.
Word Family: **unassumingly**, *adverb*; **unassumingness**, *noun*.

unattached *adjective*
a) not attached. b) not engaged or married.

unattended *adjective*
1. not accompanied: 'I am allowed to go out *unattended*'.
2. not taken care of: 'his wounds were left *unattended*'.

unauthorized *adjective*
not having authority or permission.

unavailing *adjective*
producing no effect; unsuccessful.

unaware *adjective*
not conscious or aware of.
unawares *adverb*
unexpectedly: 'we crept up on him *unawares*'.

unbalanced *adjective*
1. not balanced.
2. mentally disturbed or lacking soundness of judgement.
Word Family: **unbalance**, *verb*.

unbearable *adjective*
not able to be tolerated or endured.
Word Family: **unbearably**, *adverb*; **unbearableness**, *noun*.

unbeatable *adjective*
not able to be surpassed or beaten.

unbecoming (*say* un-be-**kumming**) *adjective*
1. improper or unsuitable.
2. not attractive.
Word Family: **unbecomingly**, *adverb*; **unbecomingness**, *noun*.

unbeknown, unbeknownst
(*say* un-be-**nohn** *and* un-be-**nohn**st) *adjective*
(*informal*) unknown: '*unbeknown* to her, he was already married'.

unbeliever *noun*
a person who does not believe, especially in some religious doctrine.

unbend *verb*
1. to relax or become less formal.
2. to straighten or release from a bent position or form.

unbidden *adjective*
not invited: 'strange thoughts came *unbidden* to his mind'.

unblushing *adjective*
shameless.

unbosom (*say* un-**buz**'m) *verb*
to tell or reveal, especially one's thoughts, secrets, feelings, etc.

unbridled *adjective*
without restraint: 'she was a victim of his *unbridled* lust'.

unbroken *adjective*
1. not broken: 'his record for the high jump remains *unbroken*'.
2. continuous, without interruption.
3. (of a horse) not yet broken in.

unburden *verb*
a) to free from or get rid of a burden.
b) to relieve by confession: 'he *unburdened* his soul to me'.

unbuttoned *adjective*
1. having the buttons undone.
2. relaxed or informal: 'he told me this story in an *unbuttoned* moment'.
Word Family: **unbutton**, *verb*.

uncalled-for *adjective*
not justified; impertinent: 'that rebuke was quite *uncalled-for*'.

uncanny *adjective*
strange or unnatural.
Word Family: **uncannily**, *adverb*; **uncanniness**, *noun*.

unceremonious
(*say* un-serri-**mo**-nee-us) *adjective*
abrupt and brusque: 'he made an *unceremonious* exit through the window'.
Word Family: **unceremoniously**, *adverb*.

uncertain *adjective*
1. doubtful or not certainly known.

2. changing unpredictably: 'he has an *uncertain* temper'.
uncertainty *noun*
uncertainty principle, that the more accurately the position of an elementary particle is determined the less accurately can its momentum be determined, and vice versa.

uncharitable *adjective*
1. unforgiving.
2. miserly.
Word Family: **uncharitably,** *adverb.*

uncivil (*say* un-**sivv**'l) *adjective*
rude or discourteous.
Word Family: **uncivilly,** *adverb.*

uncle *noun*
1. a brother of a parent.
2. the husband of an aunt.
[Latin *avunculus* maternal uncle]

Uncle Sam
(*informal*) America or its government.

uncomfortable (*say* un-**kum**fta-b'l) *adjective*
a) causing discomfort: 'that's one of the *uncomfortable* facts of life'. b) in a state of discomfort: 'he made me feel *uncomfortable*'.
Word Family: **uncomfortably,** *adverb*; **uncomfortableness,** *noun.*

uncommitted *adjective*
1. not committed one way or the other.
2. (*informal*) not actively supporting some cause espoused by the speaker or writer.

uncommon *adjective*
not usual: 'she spoke with *uncommon* anger'.
uncommonly *adverb*
1. remarkably: '*uncommonly* beautiful'.
2. rarely.

uncompromising
(*say* un-**kom**pra-my-zing) *adjective*
not allowing any compromise: 'he took an *uncompromising* stand on the issue'.
Word Family: **uncompromisingly,** *adverb.*

unconcerned (*say* un-k'n-**sirnd**) *adjective*
1. having or showing no concern: 'he seemed *unconcerned* about his future'.
2. not involved or taking part: 'I don't believe that he was completely *unconcerned* in the plot'.
Word Family: **unconcernedly,** *adverb.*

unconditional (*say* un-k'n-**dish**'n-al) *adjective*
without any conditions attached: 'an *unconditional* surrender'.
Word Family: **unconditionally,** *adverb.*

unconscionable
(*say* un-**kon**shena-b'l) *adjective*
not in accordance with what is right or reasonable.
Word Family: **unconscionably,** *adverb.*

unconscious (*say* un-**kon**-shus) *adjective*
1. not conscious: 'the *unconscious* boxer was carried off'.
2. *Psychology:* of or relating to mental processes that take place below consciousness.
unconscious *noun*
Psychology: the system of mental processes of which a person cannot become directly conscious, but which is capable of influencing conscious processes and behaviour.
Word Family: **unconsciously,** *adverb.*

unconsidered *adjective*
1. not given due thought: 'he gave us what was obviously an *unconsidered* opinion'.
2. disregarded: '*unconsidered* trifles'.

unconstitutional
(*say* un-konsti-**tew**-sh'nal) *adjective*
not in accordance with the political constitution of a country.
Word Family: **unconstitutionally,** *adverb.*

unconventional *adjective*
flouting accepted or traditional views or standards.

uncouth (*say* un-**kooth**) *adjective*
uncultured, awkward or ungraceful.
Word Family: **uncouthly,** *adverb*; **uncouthness,** *noun.*
[UN- + Old English *cuth* known]

uncover (*say* un-**kuvva**) *verb*
a) to remove the cover from. b) to reveal or disclose.

uncritical *adjective*
a) not inclined to make a critical analysis: 'an ordinary, *uncritical* response'. b) not discriminating or critically perceptive.

unction (*say* **unk**-sh'n) *noun*
1. *Religion:* the act of anointing with oil. **Extreme unction** is the sacrament of anointing a dying person with oil.
2. gusto: 'he described her downfall with *unction*'.
3. insincere emotion: 'for my taste, there was too much *unction* in his sympathy'.
[from Latin]

unctuous (*say* **unk**–chew–us) *adjective*
earnest in an exaggerated or insincere way.
Word Family: **unctuously,** *adverb*; **unctuousness,** *noun.*
[Latin *unctus* greasy]

undaunted (*say* un–**dawn**–tid) *adjective*
not discouraged or dismayed.

undecided (*say* un–de–**side**–id) *adjective*
1. not having been decided.
2. not having made up one's mind.

undemonstrative *adjective*
impassive or not given to showing emotion.

under *preposition*
below: 'we sat *under* the trees'.
Usages:
a) 'the matter is *under* consideration' (= in the process of).
b) 'the driver was *under* the influence of alcohol' (= subject to, experiencing).
c) 'the farmer had fifty hectares *under* barley' (= planted with, bearing).
d) 'you'll find it *under* Botany' (= within the classification or group of).
e) 'he travelled *under* an assumed name' (= using).
f) 'children *under* 18 will not be admitted to this film' (= less than).
g) 'a captain is *under* a major' (= lower in rank than).
h) '*under* the existing provisions of the law, I must sentence you' (= in accordance with).
Word Family: **under,** *adverb, adjective.*

under–
a prefix meaning: a) situated below or beneath, as in *underbrush*; b) inferior in rank or subordinate to, as in *understudy*; c) lower than, as in *underprice*; d) not sufficiently, as in *underexposed*; e) worn or being beneath, as in *underwear.*

underachieve *verb*
to perform below the accepted standard, especially of one's own ability.

underarm *adjective*
1. under the arm: 'an *underarm* odour'.
2. *Sport:* (of a stroke or throw) made with the arm moving forward and up. Compare OVERARM.

underbelly *noun*
a) the lower part of the belly. b) any similarly unprotected part.

underbidder *noun*
the person at an auction who makes the second highest bid for a particular lot.

underbrush *noun*
small trees and shrubs growing beneath forest trees.

undercarriage *noun*
landing gear.

underclothes *plural noun*
underwear.

undercoat *noun*
the paint applied to a surface as a base before the main colour or layer is put on.
Word Family: **undercoat,** *verb,* to apply an undercoat to.

undercover *adjective*
secret: 'an *undercover* agent'.

undercurrent *noun*
1. a current below another current or a surface.
2. a hidden tendency: 'there's an *undercurrent* of bitterness in his jokes about women'.

undercut *verb*
(**undercut, undercutting**)
1. to offer goods or services at a lower price than one's competitors.
2. *Sport:* to hit a ball from underneath, causing a backspin.
Word Family: **undercut,** *noun.*

underdeveloped
(*say* under–de–**vellupt**) *adjective*
1. (of a country) not highly industrialized.
2. *Photography:* not sufficiently developed, so that there is a lack of contrast.
3. not adequately or normally developed: 'an *underdeveloped* body'.
Word Family: **underdevelop,** *verb.*

underdog *noun*
a person or team that loses or is expected to lose a struggle, contest, etc.

underdone (*say* under–**dun**) *adjective*
(of meat, vegetables, etc.) lightly or too lightly cooked.

underestimate *verb*
to form too low an estimate of: a) 'they *underestimated* the cost of the project'; b) 'I *underestimated* his tenacity'.

underexpose *verb*
Photography: to expose a film to light for too short a time.
Word Family: **underexposure,** *noun,* a) insufficient exposure to light, b)

a photographic negative or print that has been underexposed.

underfelt *noun*
a thick layer of fabric laid beneath a carpet to make it more comfortable or for insulation.

underfoot *adverb*
beneath the feet.
Usage: 'I'm sick of the children being *underfoot* all day' (= in the way).

undergo *verb*
(**underwent, undergone, undergoing**)
to experience or be subjected to: 'to *undergo* surgery'.

undergraduate
(*say* under-**grad**-yewit) *noun*
a university student who is studying for his first degree.
Word Family: **undergraduate**, *adjective.*

underground *adjective*
1. below the surface of the earth.
2. secret, subversive or not generally known: a) 'an *underground* movement'; b) '*underground* movies'.
underground *adverb*
1. below the surface of the earth.
2. in secret.
underground *noun*
1. a movement or organization which is secret or outside the established or accepted society, etc., such as nationalist groups during World War 2 who worked to overthrow enemy forces occupying their country.
2. a railway system running through underground tunnels.

undergrowth *noun*
the small trees and plants which grow below and among larger trees.

underhand *adjective*
devious or sly: 'he won the election by *underhand* tactics'.

underhung *adjective*
having the lower jaw projecting beyond the upper jaw.

underline *verb*
to draw a line under.
Usage: 'he hit the desk to *underline* his point' (= emphasize).

underling *noun*
a subordinate.

underlying *adjective*
1. basic or fundamental: 'the *underlying* aim of a society'.
2. hidden or implicit: 'an *underlying* note of sarcasm'.

undermine *verb*
to make an excavation beneath, especially as a means of weakening a foundation.
Usage: 'alcohol *undermined* his constitution' (= weakened or destroyed gradually).

underneath *adverb, preposition*
beneath or below.
Word Family: **underneath,** *adjective,* lower; **underneath,** *noun,* a lower part or surface.

underpants *plural noun*
a pair of light short trousers worn next to the skin.

underpass *noun*
a passage under a roadway, usually for pedestrians and sometimes for traffic.

underpin *verb*
(**underpinned, underpinning**)
1. *Building:* to support a wall, etc. with props. Also called to **pin**.
2. to support: 'careful research *underpinned* her theory'.
Word Family: **underpinning,** *noun,* the supports placed under a completed wall.

underplay *noun*
to act subtly or with restraint.

underprice *verb*
to give a price below the normal price or value.

underprivileged *adjective*
with less than the usual rights and opportunities provided by society, because of poverty, etc.

underproof *adjective*
containing less alcohol than proof spirit does.

underquote *verb*
to quote a lower price than.

underrate (*say* under-**rate**) *verb*
to underestimate: 'to *underrate* an opponent'.

underscore *verb*
to underline.

undersea *adjective*
existing, carried on or adapted for use beneath the surface of the sea.
Word Family: **undersea,** *adverb,* beneath the surface of the sea.

undersecretary *noun*
a secretary subordinate to a principal secretary, especially in a government department.

undersell *verb*
(**undersold, underselling**)

to sell something at a lower price than one's competitors.

undersexed *adjective*
having less than normal sexual drives or interest in sex.

undershoot *verb*
(**undershot, undershooting**)
(of an aeroplane, missile, etc.) to land short of the runway, target, etc.

undershot *adjective*
underhung.

undersized *adjective*
being less than the normal size.

understand *verb*
(**understood, understanding**)
to apprehend the meaning, significance, nature or explanation of: a) 'the student could not *understand* the physics problem'; b) 'you can *understand* why he was upset'; c) 'I just don't *understand* kids'.
Usages:
a) 'do you *understand* French?' (= have a mastery of).
b) 'you *understand* that you may lose?' (= accept).
c) 'I *understand* that the funeral took place yesterday' (= have been told).
d) 'and what am I to *understand* from that remark?' (= infer).
understanding *noun*
1. the ability or power to understand: 'he has a clear *understanding* of the problem'.
2. sympathy: 'all he was asking for was a little *understanding*'.
3. an agreement: 'we came to a friendly *understanding*'.
on the understanding that, on the condition that.
Word Family: **understandable**, *adjective*, capable of being understood; **understandably**, *adverb*.

understate *verb*
1. to state less forcefully than is necessary or desirable.
2. to declare to be less than is actually so: 'to *understate* one's income'.
Word Family: **understatement**, *noun*.

understeer *noun*
the tendency of a motor vehicle to turn in a wider circle than is indicated by the amount the front wheels have been turned.

understood *verb*
the past tense and past participle of the verb **understand**.

understudy *noun*
a person prepared to take over an important role in a play, ballet, etc. if the actor is unable to appear.
Word Family: **understudy** (**understudied, understudying**), *verb*.

undertake *verb*
(**undertook, undertaken, undertaking**)
1. to take upon oneself or attempt: 'he *undertook* the flight despite the stormy weather'.
2. to decide or agree to do: 'he *undertook* to finish the job by Tuesday'.
3. to promise or pledge: 'I can't *undertake* to be there on time'.
undertaking *noun*
1. a task or enterprise, especially one which one has undertaken to do.
2. a promise or guarantee: 'he gave me a solemn *undertaking* that he would give up drink'.

undertaker *noun*
a person whose business it is to arrange for the burial of the dead.

under-the-counter *adjective*
(of goods) kept hidden to be disposed of in some illegal way, such as on the black market.

undertone *noun*
a low, quiet voice: 'they conversed in *undertones*'.
Usage: 'there's an *undertone* of sadness in his humour' (= underlying quality).

undertook *verb*
the past tense of the verb **undertake**.

undertow *noun*
a backward flow under the water, from a wave or waves breaking on the shore.

undervalue *verb*
a) to put too low a value on something.
b) to underestimate something or someone.

underwater *adjective*
being, occurring or used below the surface of a body of water.
Word Family: **underwater**, *adverb*.

under way
1. *Nautical:* (of a ship) having raised anchor or slipped moorings and started on her way.
2. in progress: 'the meeting had been *under way* for only a few minutes when the lights failed'.

underwear *noun*
also called **underclothes**
any clothing, e.g. underpants, etc., worn near to the skin under trousers, dresses, etc.

underweight (*say* under–**wate**)
adjective
having less than normal or accepted weight.

underwent *verb*
the past tense of the verb **undergo**.

underworld *noun*
1. the criminal world of a society.
2. Hades.

underwrite *verb*
(**underwrote, underwritten, underwriting**)
1. to agree to buy all the stock of a newly formed company that is not bought by the public.
2. to guarantee or assume responsibility for, e.g. by signing an insurance policy.
Word Family: **underwriter,** *noun.*

undesirable *adjective*
unpleasant or objectionable.
Word Family: **undesirable,** *noun,* an objectionable person.

undetermined *adjective*
not established or certain: 'a word of *undetermined* meaning'.

undeveloped (*say* un–de–**vellupt**)
adjective
1. a) not fully grown: 'a child is an *undeveloped* adult'. b) not developed: 'an *undeveloped* roll of film'.
2. (of land) a) not built on. b) not made to yield a profit.

undies (*say* **un**–deez) *plural noun*
(*informal*) underwear.

undigested *adjective*
1. not or incompletely digested.
2. (of facts, etc.) not properly understood or assimilated.

undiscriminating *adjective*
not knowing good from bad or not bothering to distinguish between them; uncritical.

undisguisedly *adverb*
frankly or without an attempt to conceal feelings: 'she was *undisguisedly* glad when he left'.

undistinguished
(*say* un–dis–**ting**–wisht) *adjective*
not outstanding or distinctive.

undivided *adjective*
complete: 'this job requires my *undivided* attention'.

undo (*say* un–**doo**) *verb*
(**undid, undone, undoing**)
to unfasten and open: '*undo* your parcels'.
Usages:
a) 'you have *undone* all my good work' (= reversed the effects of).
b) 'gambling *undid* him' (= ruined).
undoing *noun*
a) ruin. b) the cause of ruin: 'drink was her *undoing*'.

undoubted (*say* un–**dow**–tid) *adjective*
accepted as beyond question.
Word Family: **undoubtedly,** *adverb.*

undress *verb*
to remove clothing.
Usage: 'the nurse *undressed* the wound' (= removed the bandages from).
Word Family: **undress,** *noun,* a state of having little or no clothes on; **undressed,** *adjective,* a) not clothed, b) (of leather, etc.) not treated or prepared.

undue *adjective*
excessive or extreme.
Word Family: **unduly,** *adverb.*

undulate (*say* **un**–dew–late) *verb*
1. to move or cause to move like a wave or waves.
2. to have a wavy surface or outline: '*undulating* hills'.
Word Family: **undulation,** *noun,* a wave–like part, motion, form, outline, etc.; **undulatory** (*say* undew–**layta**–ree), *adjective.*
[Latin *unda* a wave]

undying *adjective*
everlasting.
Word Family: **undyingly,** *adverb.*

unearned income
any income received from interest on investments, etc. rather than from employment. Compare EARNED INCOME.

unearth *verb*
to dig up or uncover: 'the detective *unearthed* new evidence'.

unearthly *adjective*
supernatural or ghostly: 'an *unearthly* scream'.
Usage: (*informal*) 'why wake me at this *unearthly* hour?' (= unreasonable, absurd).

uneasy *adjective*
uncomfortable or anxiously restless: 'she felt *uneasy* having to recite to a strange audience'.
Word Family: **uneasily,** *adverb*; **uneasiness, unease,** *nouns.*

uneconomical, uneconomic *adjective*
wasteful or unprofitable.

unemotional *adjective*
calm, rational and unexcitable.

unemployment *noun*
a) the lack of a job or jobs. b) the number of people who cannot get a job: 'the level of *unemployment* rose at the end of the year'.
Word Family: **unemployed,** *adjective*; **unemployable,** *adjective.*

unending *adjective*
a) everlasting. b) continual.
Word Family: **unendingly,** *adverb.*

unenlightened *adjective*
1. not informed or instructed.
2. ignorant, superstitious or prejudiced.

unenviable *adjective*
difficult or unpleasant: 'the *unenviable* job involved long hours for little pay'.

unequal *adjective*
not equal: 'coins of *unequal* value'.
Usages:
a) 'your book is of *unequal* quality' (= uneven).
b) 'he felt *unequal* to the task' (= inadequate).
Word Family: **unequalled,** *adjective.*

unequivocal (*say* un-ikwivvi-k'l) *adjective*
plain, clear or without ambiguity.
Word Family: **unequivocally,** *adverb.*

unerring *adjective*
without error or well-aimed.
Word Family: **unerringly,** *adverb.*

unethical *adjective*
1. immoral.
2. contrary to a code of professional conduct.
Word Family: **unethically,** *adverb.*

uneven *adjective*
1. not level or flat: '*uneven* terrain'.
2. not equal or balanced: 'an *uneven* contest'.
3. irregular: 'a book of *uneven* quality'.
4. (of a number) odd.
Word Family: **unevenly,** *adverb*; **unevenness,** *noun.*

unexampled *adjective*
exceptional or without parallel.

unexceptionable
(*say* un-ek-sepsh'na-b'l) *adjective*
not able to be criticized or objected to.

unexceptional
(*say* un-ek-sep-sh'n-al) *adjective*
usual or ordinary.

unexpected *adjective*
coming without warning.
Word Family: **unexpectedly,** *adverb*; **unexpectedness,** *noun.*

unexposed *adjective*
(of photographic film) unused.

unfailing *adjective*
continuous or dependable: 'an *unfailing* supply of jokes'.
Word Family: **unfailingly,** *adverb.*

unfair *adjective*
not fair or just.
Word Family: **unfairly,** *adverb*; **unfairness,** *noun.*

unfaithful *adjective*
not loyal or true to a promise, duty, or other person.
Word Family: **unfaithfully,** *adverb*; **unfaithfulness,** *noun.*

unfamiliar *adjective*
1. not previously or familiarly known: 'an *unfamiliar* country'.
2. not acquainted: 'he's *unfamiliar* with classical Greek'.

unfathomable *adjective*
not able to be fathomed or comprehended.

unfeeling *adjective*
not sensitive or sympathetic.

unfettered *adjective*
not restrained or restricted.

unfit *adjective*
a) not physically fit. b) not fit, suited or suitable.
Word Family: **unfitness,** *noun*; **unfitted,** *adjective.*

unflappable *adjective*
not easily upset.

unfold *verb*
1. to open or spread out: '*unfold* the newspaper'.
2. to make or become known or visible: 'the landscape *unfolded* before us'.

unforeseen *adjective*
not expected or predicted.
Word Family: **unforeseeable,** *adjective.*

unforgettable *adjective*
never to be forgotten, memorable.
Word Family: **unforgettably,** *adverb.*

unfortunate *adjective*
not lucky: 'the *unfortunate* driver has had 3 accidents this week'.
Usage: 'he made an *unfortunate* decision to resign' (= regrettable).
Word Family: **unfortunately,** *adverb.*

unfounded *adjective*
without foundation: '*unfounded* accusations against an innocent person'.

unfreeze *verb*
1. to thaw or thaw out.
2. to lift restrictions or controls from.

unfrequented (*say* un-fre-**kwentid**) *adjective*
not often visited.

unfrock *verb*
to defrock.

unfulfilled *adjective*
not satisfied: 'her ambitions are still *unfulfilled*'.

unfurl *verb*
to open or spread out, e.g. a flag.

ungainly *adjective*
clumsy or awkward.
Word Family: **ungainliness**, *noun.*

ungetatable (*say* un-get-**at**-a-b'l) *adjective*
(*informal*) not accessible.

ungodly *adjective*
1. sinful or irreligious.
2. (*informal*) outrageous: 'an *ungodly* hour of the morning to get up'.
Word Family: **ungodliness**, *noun.*

ungovernable *adjective*
uncontrollable: 'he has an *ungovernable* temper'.

ungraceful *adjective*
clumsy or awkward.
Word Family: **ungracefully**, *adverb.*

ungracious (*say* un-**gray**-shus) *adjective*
not gracious or courteous.
Word Family: **ungraciously**, *adverb*; **ungraciousness**, *noun.*

unguarded *adjective*
1. not guarded.
2. incautious, thoughtless or not discreet: 'he gave himself away in an *unguarded* moment'.

unguent (*say* **un**-gw'nt) *noun*
any soft, creamy paste, such as an ointment, used on sores, etc.
[from Latin]

ungulate *noun*
any hoofed, grass-eating mammal.

unhand *verb*
an old word meaning to release or let go.

unhappy *adjective*
1. not happy.
2. not lucky: 'an *unhappy* accident'.
Word Family: **unhappily**, *adverb*; **unhappiness**, *noun.*

unhealthy *adjective*
1. not healthy.
2. dangerous to health: 'an *unhealthy* drain'.
3. indicating poor health: 'an *unhealthy* complexion'.
4. (*informal*) dangerous or difficult: 'an *unhealthy* situation'.
Word Family: **unhealthily**, *adverb*; **unhealthiness**, *noun.*

unheard-of *adjective*
1. never known or heard of before.
2. (*informal*) outrageous.

unheralded *adjective*
a) not announced in advance. b) not expected.

unhinge (*say* un-**hinj**) *verb*
1. to remove from the hinges.
2. to upset or unbalance: 'his mind is *unhinged*'.

unhistorical (*say* un-hiss-**torri**-k'l) *adjective*
1. not in accordance with the methods or principles of historians.
2. not having occurred or existed in history.

unholy *adjective*
1. wicked or sinful.
2. (*informal*) outrageous.

unhoped-for *adjective*
not expected.

uni- (*say* **yoo**ni)
a prefix meaning one or single, as in *unicorn.*
[Latin *unus* one]

unicameral (*say* yooni-**kamma**-r'l) *adjective*
Parliament: having one chamber or house only, such as the New Zealand parliament. Compare BICAMERAL.

unicellular (*say* yooni-**sel**-yoola) *adjective*
consisting of one cell.

unicorn (*say* **yoo**ni-korn) *noun*
Mythology: a creature similar to a horse, with one long horn in the centre of its forehead.
[UNI- + Latin *cornu* a horn]

unicycle (*say* **yoo**ni-sigh-k'l) *noun*
a vehicle with a single wheel and propelled by pedals, as is used by acrobats.

unidentified flying object
short form is **UFO**
any object which is detected in the sky but which cannot be identified.

uniform (*say* **yoo**ni-form) *noun*
the clothes worn by members of a particular group or institution, used to distinguish or identify them.

uniform *adjective*
not varying in form, quality, character, etc.: 'mix the ingredients to a *uniform* thickness'.
Word Family: **uniformly**, *adverb*; **uniformity** (*say* yooni-**formi**-tee), *noun*, sameness.
[UNI- + Latin *forma* form]

unify (*say* **yooni**-fie) *verb*
(**unified, unifying**)
to make into one.
Word Family: **unification**, *noun*.
[UNI- + Latin *facere* to make]

unilateral (*say* yooni-**latta**-r'l) *adjective*
of, on or by one side only: 'the rebel colony made a *unilateral* declaration of independence'.
Word Family: **unilaterally**, *adverb*.
[UNI- + Latin *lateris* of a side]

unilingual (*say* yooni-**ling**-w'l) *adjective*
of or knowing one language only.
[UNI- + Latin *lingua* a tongue]

unimaginable (*say* un-im**maj**-inna-b'l) *adjective*
not able to be imagined or comprehended.
Word Family: **unimaginably**, *adverb*.

unimpeachable *adjective*
1. that cannot be questioned or doubted: '*unimpeachable* evidence'.
2. blameless: '*unimpeachable* conduct'.

uninhibited *adjective*
free from restraints or inhibitions.

uninspiring, uninspired *adjective*
dull or dreary.

unintelligent *adjective*
a) having no intelligence. b) deficient in intelligence.
Word Family: **unintelligently**, *adverb*.

unintelligible *adjective*
not able to be understood.
Word Family: **unintelligibly**, *adverb*.

uninterested *adjective*
having or showing no interest or concern.
Common Error: see DISINTERESTED.

uninteresting *adjective*
not interesting.

union (*say* **yooni**-un) *noun*
1. a) the act of uniting into one: 'the *union* of colonies into a single state'. b) a combination formed by uniting: 'their marriage is a happy *union*'.
2. a trade union.
3. a social organization for students in a college or university.
4. *Maths:* the set of elements containing the elements of two given sets.
[Latin *unio* unity]

unionist (*say* **yooni**-un-ist) *noun*
a) a person who supports union. b) a member of a trade union.

unique (*say* yoo-**neek**) *adjective*
being the only one of its kind.
Usage: 'she sings with *unique* grace' (= unequalled).
Word Family: **uniquely**, *adverb*; **uniqueness**, *noun*.
[from Latin]

unisex *adjective*
of, for or not distinguishing between both sexes.

unison (*say* **yooni**-sun) *noun*
a speaking or sounding together or simultaneously: 'the class recited the poem in *unison*'.
Usage: 'we are in *unison* about the proposal' (= agreement).
[UNI- + Latin *sonus* a sound]

unit (*say* **yoonit**) *noun*
1. any person, thing or group considered as a single thing but forming part of a larger group or whole: a) 'the block of flats contained 10 individual *units*'; b) 'a *unit* of soldiers'; c) 'the stereogram contained a radio *unit*'.
2. a quantity or amount used as a standard of measurement: 'the litre is a *unit* of volume'.
3. the smallest whole number (1).
[Latin *unus* one]

Unitarian (*say* yooni-**tair**iun) *noun*
Religion: a member of the denomination that rejects the Trinity, original sin, atonement, eternal punishment, etc.

unitary (*say* **yooni**-tree) *adjective*
1. of or like a unit or units.
2. of or characterized by unity.

unite (*say* yoo-**nite**) *verb*
to combine together: 'the states *united* to form a single country'.
Word Family: **unity** (*say* **yooni**-tee), *noun*, the state of being united, especially into a complete or harmonious whole; **unitedly**, *adverb*.
[from Latin]

unit trust
a company which spreads subscribers' funds over a wide range of shares and distributes the proceeds to each subscriber in proportion to the number of units he has bought.

univalent (*say* yooni-vay-l'nt) *adjective*
also called **monovalent**
Chemistry: having a valency or combining power of one.
[UNI- + Latin *valens* strong]

univalve (*say* yooni-valv) *noun*
a mollusc with only one part to its shell. Compare BIVALVE.

universal (*say* yooni-**ver**-s'l) *adjective*
of, by, including or affecting all: '*universal* peace'.
universal *noun*
something which is universal, such as an unchanging quality, a common pattern of behaviour, etc.
Word Family: **universally**, *adverb*; **universality** (*say* yooni-ver-**salli**-tee), *noun*.

universal joint
also called a **universal coupling**
a joint between two rotating shafts which allows a limited amount of movement in any direction.

universal set
Maths: the set composed of all possible elements in the field of discussion.

universal time
a system of time measurement based on Greenwich Mean Time, used by astronomers.

universe (*say* yooni-vers) *noun*
1. all the space, matter, and energy which is thought to exist.
2. the world and all mankind.
[Latin *universus* all together]

university (*say* yooni-versi-tee) *noun*
1. an institution for teaching at a more advanced level than a school, and which awards degrees to its students and also offers facilities for post-graduate research.
2. the members of a university considered as a group.

unjust *adjective*
not fair or just.
Word Family: **unjustly**, *adverb*.

unjustified *adjective*
not justified.
Word Family: **unjustifiable**, *adjective*; **unjustifiably**, *adverb*.

unkempt *adjective*
untidy or neglected.
[UN- + Medieval English *kempt* combed]

unkind *adjective*
not kind; harsh.
Word Family: **unkindly**, *adverb*; **unkindness**, *noun*.

unknown *adjective*
not known.
the unknown, anything mysterious or beyond normal experience.

unlawful *adjective*
relating to an act or relationship which the law forbids.

unlearned *adjective*
1. (*say* un-**lern**-id) ignorant or not learned.
2. (*say* un-**lernd**) not learnt.

unleash *verb*
to release or let loose.

unleavened (*say* un-**levv**'nd) *adjective*
(of bread) made without yeast.

unless *conjunction*
except on the condition that: 'you'll catch cold *unless* you dress warmly'.

unlettered *adjective*
illiterate or not educated.

unlike *adjective*
not like or alike.
unlike *preposition*
not typical of: 'it is *unlike* you to be so angry'.

unlikely *adjective*
a) not likely or probable. b) not likely to succeed.
Word Family: **unlikelihood**, **unlikeliness**, *nouns*.

unlimited *adjective*
having no limits or restrictions.

unload *verb*
1. to remove the load or charge from: a) 'the ship was quickly *unloaded*'; b) '*unload* that rifle at once'.
2. to get rid of: 'farmers *unloaded* their bumper crop at give-away prices'.

unlooked-for *adjective*
not expected or foreseen.

unloose *verb*
to let loose or free.

unmake *verb*
(**unmade, unmaking**)
to undo or take to pieces: 'the plans we had made had to be *unmade* the following day'.

unmanageable (*say* un-**manni**ja-b'l) *adjective*
impossible to handle or control properly.

unmanly *adjective*
cowardly or not manly.

unmask *verb*
to take off a mask or disguise.
Usage: 'the traitor was *unmasked* and punished' (= revealed).

unmatched *adjective*
not matched or equalled.

unmentionable
(*say* un-**men**-sh'na-b'l) *adjective*
not fit or worthy to be mentioned.

unmindful *adjective*
paying no heed or regard.
Word Family: **unmindfully**, *adverb.*

unmistakeable, unmistakable
adjective
about which no mistake is possible.
Word Family: **unmistakeably**, *adverb.*

unmitigated *adjective*
1. not softened or lessened: 'the *unmitigated* fury of the storm'.
2. complete or absolute: 'Simon is an *unmitigated* ass'.

unmoved (*say* un-**moovd**) *adjective*
not moved or affected: 'he was *unmoved* by their pleas'.

unnatural *adjective*
not natural or normal.
Word Family: **unnaturally**, *adverb*; **unnaturalness**, *noun.*

unnecessary (*say* un-**nessis**-ree *or* un-**nessa**-serri) *adjective*
a) not necessary. b) more than is necessary: 'he acted with *unnecessary* caution'.
Word Family: **unnecessarily**, *adverb.*

unnerve *verb*
to deprive of nerve, courage or self-control.

unnumbered *adjective*
1. not counted: 'an *unnumbered* quantity of old cups and saucers'.
2. not marked with a number: '*unnumbered* pages'.
Usage: '*unnumbered* thousands flocked to the opera' (= countless).

unobtrusive (*say* unnob-**troosiv**)
adjective
a) not obtrusive. b) quiet or discreet.
Word Family: **unobtrusively**, *adverb.*

unofficial *adjective*
not official.
unofficial strike
a strike not supported by the strikers' trade union.
Word Family: **unofficially**, *adverb.*

unorthodox *adjective*
not orthodox, conventional or approved.
Word Family: **unorthodoxy**, *noun.*

unpack *verb*
to take out of a suitcase, etc.

unpalatable (*say* un-**pallita**-b'l)
adjective
distasteful.

unparalleled *adjective*
having no parallel or equal.

unparliamentary *adjective*
not in accordance with parliamentary procedure.
Usage: 'he used *unparliamentary* language' (= bad).

unpeg *verb*
(**unpegged, unpegging**)
1. to remove the peg or pegs from, e.g. to open.
2. to permit an increase in, e.g. wages or prices.

unpick *verb*
to undo the stitches of.

unpleasant (*say* un-**plezz**'nt) *adjective*
not pleasant.
Word Family: **unpleasantly**, *adverb*; **unpleasantness**, *noun.*

unplug *verb*
(**unplugged, unplugging**)
to remove the plug from, e.g. to disconnect an electrical appliance.

unplumbed (*say* un-**plumd**) *adjective*
unfathomed or of unknown depth: 'we shall never know to what *unplumbed* depths of misery he sank'.

unpopular (*say* un-**pop**-yoola)
adjective
not popular.
Word Family: **unpopularity** (*say* un-pop-yoo-**larri**-tee), *noun*; **unpopularly**, *adverb.*

unprecedented
(*say* un-**preesa**-dentid) *adjective*
without precedent.

unpredictable *adjective*
not able to be predicted: 'an *unpredictable* temper'.
Word Family: **unpredictably**, *adverb.*

unpremeditated *adjective*
not planned or decided on in advance.

unpresentable (*say* un-pre-**zenta**-b'l)
adjective
not fit to be seen.

unprincipled (*say* un-**prin**-sip'ld)
adjective
without moral principles or scruples.

unprintable *adjective*
not considered fit to be printed.

unprofessional *adjective*
not in accordance with the standards of a particular profession.

unprofitable *adjective*
showing no profit or advantage.
Word Family: **unprofitably,** *adverb.*

unproved, unproven *adjective*
not proved.
Word Family: **unprovable,** *adjective.*

unprovoked *adjective*
without provocation.

unqualified *adjective*
1. having insufficient qualifications.
2. total or absolute: 'an *unqualified* success'.

unquestionable
(*say* un-**kwes**-ch'na-b'l) *adjective*
beyond doubt.
Word Family: **unquestionably,** *adverb.*

unquestioned *adjective*
without challenge or dispute: 'I can't accept that statement *unquestioned*'.

unquestioning
(*say* un-**kwes**-ch'n-ing) *adjective*
without question or protest: 'an *unquestioning* obedience'.
Word Family: **unquestioningly,** *adverb.*

unquiet *adjective*
restless or uneasy.

unravel *verb*
(**unravelled, unravelling**)
to pull apart or separate the threads of.
Usage: 'at last the mystery was *unravelled*' (= solved).

unread (*say* un-**red**) *adjective*
not read.
Word Family: **unreadable** (*say* un-**reed**-a-b'l), *adjective,* a) not worth reading as it is too badly written to be read with pleasure, b) illegible.

unready *adjective*
1. not ready or prepared.
2. reluctant.

unreal *adjective*
1. imaginary or visionary: '*unreal* fears'.
2. not true to life: 'an *unreal* portrayal of characters in a book'.
3. (*informal*) unbelievable.
Word Family: **unreality,** *noun.*

unrealized, unrealised *adjective*
not fulfilled or developed.

unreasonable *adjective*
not reasonable; excessive.
Word Family: **unreasonably,** *adverb.*

unreasoned *adjective*
1. irrational: 'an *unreasoned* fear of air travel'.
2. not well reasoned or thought out: 'an *unreasoned* argument'.
Word Family: **unreasoning,** *adjective,* not using or guided by reason.

unrefined *adjective*
not refined or purified: '*unrefined* sugar'.
Usage: 'she uses *unrefined* language' (= coarse, vulgar).

unregenerate *adjective*
not having repented or reformed.

unrelated *adjective*
1. having no connection or relationship.
2. untold, e.g. of a story.

unrelenting *adjective*
1. remaining harsh or severe.
2. maintaining a constant rate or speed.
Word Family: **unrelentingly,** *adjective.*

unreliable (*say* un-re-**lie**-ab'l) *adjective*
not to be relied or depended upon.
Word Family: **unreliably,** *adverb*; **unreliability,** *noun.*

unrelieved *adjective*
not varied or made less monotonous.

unremarkable *adjective*
ordinary.
Word Family: **unremarkably,** *adverb.*

unremitting *adjective*
not stopping or relaxing.
Word Family: **unremittingly,** *adverb.*

unrepentant *adjective*
not repentant.
Word Family: **unrepentantly,** *adverb.*

unrequited (*say* un-re-**kwy**-tid) *adjective*
not returned or reciprocated.

unreserved *adjective*
1. full or complete: '*unreserved* support'.
2. frank: 'an *unreserved* statement of his real feelings'.
3. not booked or reserved in advance.
Word Family: **unreservedly,** *adverb.*

unresolved *adjective*
1. (of a problem, etc.) not decided or solved.
2. (of a person) uncertain what to do or think.

unresponsive *adjective*
showing no, or no favourable, reaction or response.
Word Family: **unresponsively,** *adverb*; **unresponsiveness,** *noun.*

unrest *noun*
strong restlessness or dissatisfaction.

unrivalled *adjective*
1. having no rival.
2. having no equal.

unroll *verb*
to open or spread out.

unruffled *adjective*
calm and undisturbed.

unruly (*say* un–**roo**–lee) *adjective*
uncontrollable and noisy.

unsaddle *verb*
1. to take the saddle from.
2. to throw out of the saddle: 'the colt *unsaddled* its rider'.

unsaid (*say* un–**sed**) *verb*
not said or expressed.

unsatisfactory *adjective*
not satisfactory: 'your work is of an *unsatisfactory* standard'.

unsaturated *adjective*
1. not saturated.
2. *Chemistry:* able to combine with another atom without liberating any part of the existing compound.

unsavoury *adjective*
in America spelt **unsavory**
unpleasant or distasteful.
Word Family: **unsavouriness,** *noun.*

unscathed (*say* un–**skay*th*d**) *adjective*
unhurt or unharmed.

unschooled *adjective*
not trained or educated.
Usage: '*unschooled* passions' (= uncontrolled).

unscramble *verb*
to restore to an ordered or proper state.

unscrew *verb*
1. to draw the screw or screws from.
2. to remove a screw–top by turning.

unscrupulous
(*say* un–**skroo**–pew–lus) *adjective*
having no conscience or scruples.
Word Family: **unscrupulously,** *adverb*; **unscrupulousness,** *noun.*

unseal *verb*
a) to break or remove the seal of. b) to open something sealed.
Word Family: **unsealed,** *adjective,* not sealed or closed.

unseasonable *adjective*
1. not in or characteristic of the proper season.
2. ill–timed.
Word Family: **unseasonably,** *adverb.*

unseasoned *adjective*
not seasoned.

unseat *verb*
1. to throw or remove from a seat or saddle.
2. to depose from an official position.

unsecured *adjective*
1. not made secure or fastened.
2. (of a mortgage, bond, etc.) not covered by assets.

unseemly *adjective*
not seemly or becoming.
Word Family: **unseemliness,** *noun.*

unseen *adjective*
a) not seen or evident. b) invisible.
Word Family: **unseen,** *noun,* a passage not previously seen, set for translation in examinations, etc.

unserviceable (*say* un–**servissa**–b'l) *adjective*
no longer able to be used, e.g. because of wear, damage, etc.

unsettle *verb*
1. to change or move from a settled condition.
2. to make troubled, anxious or uncertain.
Word Family: **unsettled,** *adjective.*

unshackle *verb*
to free from or as if from shackles.

unshakeable, unshakable *adjective*
(of opinions, beliefs, etc.) not easily changed or shaken.
Word Family: **unshakeably,** *adverb*; **unshaken,** *adjective.*

unsheathe *verb*
to remove a sword, etc. from a sheath or scabbard.

unshriven *adjective*
Roman Catholic: not having confessed or received the last sacrament.

unsightly *adjective*
not pleasant to look at: 'her room was an *unsightly* mess'.
Word Family: **unsightliness,** *noun.*

unskilled *adjective*
(of a worker) having or needing no special training for his job.
Word Family: **unskilful,** *adjective.*

unslaked lime
quicklime.

unsling *verb*
to remove a rifle, pack, etc. from a slung position.

unsociable (*say* un–**so**–sha–b'l) *adjective*
not inclined to seek the company of others.
Word Family: **unsociably,** *adverb*; **unsociability,** *noun.*

unsolicited *adjective*
not requested: 'her *unsolicited* advice was not welcome'.

unsophisticated
(*say* un–sof–isti–kaytid) *adjective*
naïve or ingenuous.

unsound *adjective*
not sound: 'he was declared to be of *unsound* mind'.
Word Family: **unsoundly**, *adverb*; **unsoundness**, *noun.*

unsparing *adjective*
holding nothing back: '*unsparing* criticism'.
Word Family: **unsparingly**, *adverb*; **unsparingness**, *noun.*

unspeakable *adjective*
1. extremely bad: 'an *unspeakable* crime'.
2. not capable of expression in words: 'she was filled with an *unspeakable* joy'.
Word Family: **unspeakably**, *adverb.*

unstable *adjective*
1. not stable: a) 'an *unstable* structure'; b) 'his character is *unstable*'.
2. *Chemistry:* (of certain compounds) readily decomposing into other compounds.

unsteady *adjective*
1. not stable: 'you look a bit *unsteady* on top of that ladder'.
2. uneven or wavering: 'the drunk steered an *unsteady* course'.
Word Family: **unsteadily**, *adverb*; **unsteadiness**, *noun.*

unstick *verb*
(**unstuck, unsticking**)
to free, e.g. one thing which is stuck to another.
come unstuck, (*informal*) to end in disaster or defeat.

unstressed *adjective*
a) not under stress or strain. b) not stressed or accented.

unstudied *adjective*
a) not planned or premeditated: 'an *unstudied* action'. b) natural or not affected: 'an *unstudied* grace'.

unsuited (*say* un–soo–tid) *adjective*
1. not suited: '*unsuited* for that purpose'.
2. incompatible.

unsung *adjective*
not celebrated in, or as if in, song: 'an *unsung* hero'.

unsure (*say* un–**shor**) *adjective*
1. lacking confidence or assurance.
2. not certain: 'the outcome is still *unsure*'.

unswerving *adjective*
not altering direction, constant.

untangle *verb*
a) to free from tangles. b) to clear up or straighten out: '*untangle* a problem'.

untapped *adjective*
not drawn from: 'the *untapped* resources of the human brain'.

untenable *adjective*
not able to be defended or maintained: 'his theories are quite *untenable*'.

unthinkable *adjective*
1. not imaginable.
2. outrageous or out of the question: 'that's *unthinkable*!'.

unthinking *adjective*
lacking thoughtfulness, care or attention.
Word Family: **unthinkingly**, *adverb.*

untidy *adjective*
not tidy or neat.
Word Family: **untidy** (**untidied, untidying**), *verb*; **untidily**, *adverb*; **untidiness**, *noun.*

untie *verb*
a) to loosen or unknot. b) to free from something that binds or restrains.

until *preposition*
1. up to the time of: 'we will wait *until* midday'.
2. before: 'the dance doesn't warm up *until* ten'.
until *conjunction*
1. to the time when: 'I'll stay here *until* I die'.
2. before: 'I couldn't leave *until* the boss left'.
3. to the place or degree that: 'travel straight on *until* you reach the motorway'.

untimely *adjective*
1. premature: 'his *untimely* death'.
2. badly timed.

untinged (*say* un–**tinjd**) *adjective*
not marked or modified.

unto *preposition*
an old word meaning to.

untold *adjective*
1. not told or revealed: 'an *untold* secret'.
2. incapable of being counted or numbered: '*untold* thousands perished'.

untouchable (*say* un–**tutch**–a–b'l)
adjective

1. not, or not able, to be touched.
2. (*capital*) a Hindu who belongs to none of the main Hindu castes and whose very shadow is held by high-caste Hindus to pollute them.

untoward *adjective*
unseemly or uncouth: 'an *untoward* remark'.
Word Family: **untowardness,** *noun.*

untried *adjective*
1. not tested: 'the raw, *untried* recruits'.
2. not tried in a court of law.

untrue *adjective*
1. contrary to fact: 'an *untrue* assertion'.
2. unfaithful or disloyal: 'he was *untrue* to her'.
untruth *noun*
1. a lie.
2. falseness.
Word Family: **untruthful,** *adjective;* **untruthfully,** *adverb;* **untruthfulness,** *noun.*

untutored (*say* un-tewterd) *adjective*
not taught or instructed.

unused *adjective*
1. (*say* un-**yoozd**) a) not yet used. b) not made use of.
2. (*say* un-**yoost**) not accustomed: 'I am *unused* to such rudeness'.

unusual *adjective*
not usual, common or ordinary.
Word Family: **unusually,** *adverb;* **unusualness,** *noun.*

unutterable *adjective*
1. not able to be expressed: '*unutterable* bliss'.
2. not able to be pronounced.
Word Family: **unutterably,** *adverb.*

unvarnished *adjective*
straightforward, plain or simple: 'the *unvarnished* truth'.

unveil (*say* un-**vale**) *verb*
1. to remove a veil from.
2. to reveal: 'the clouds parted to *unveil* the sun'.

unvoiced *adjective*
Language: uttered without vibration of the vocal cords. See VOICE.

unwarranted *adjective*
1. not justified: 'an *unwarranted* hypothesis'.
2. not authorized.
Word Family: **unwarrantedly,** *adverb.*

unwell *adjective*
not well or healthy.

unwept *adjective*
for whom no tears are shed: '*unwept*, unhonour'd and unsung'.

unwholesome (*say* un-**hole**-sum) *adjective*
1. harmful to health or morals.
2. unhealthy.
3. morbid or liable to incite to immorality.

unwieldy (*say* un-**weel**-dee) *adjective*
difficult to move or manage, because of great size, awkward shape, etc.
Word Family: **unwieldiness,** *noun.*

unwilling *adjective*
reluctant.
Word Family: **unwillingly,** *adverb;* **unwillingness,** *noun.*

unwind *verb*
(**unwound, unwinding**)
1. to wind off: 'she *unwound* a length of cotton from the spool'.
2. to remove the tension from: 'to *unwind* a spring'.
Usage: 'it takes me a couple of hours to *unwind* after work' (= relax, become free of strain).

unwitting *adjective*
not intended: 'an *unwitting* insult'.
Word Family: **unwittingly,** *adverb.*

unwonted *adjective*
not usual, habitual or regular: 'what brings you here at this *unwonted* hour?'.

unworkable *adjective*
a) not capable of being put into operation: 'his plan is completely *unworkable*'. b) not able to be worked.

unworldly *adverb*
1. not motivated by materialistic values or interests.
2. spiritual or not belonging to this world.
Word Family: **unworldliness,** *noun.*

unworthy *adjective*
not worthy: '*unworthy* of high office'.
unworthy of, a) 'that remark was quite *unworthy of* you' (= unbecoming); b) not deserving respect, reward, etc.

unwound *verb*
the past tense and past participle of the verb **unwind.**

unwritten law
a law, custom or rule which is generally assumed or agreed upon rather than officially recorded.

up *adverb, preposition, adjective*
1. from a lower to a higher level, position, etc.

2. in or into existence or a particular situation, condition, etc.: a) 'the money will turn *up*'; b) 'who is *up* for election?'.
Usages:
a) 'he stood *up* to greet his guests' (= in an erect position).
b) 'I got *up* late on Saturday' (= out of bed).
c) 'your time is *up*' (= over).
d) 'we walked *up* the road' (= along).
e) 'what is *up*?' (= occurring, the matter).
f) 'he is *up* on a charge of murder' (= before a court).
Phrases:
all up, (*informal*) 'it's *all up*, the police are here' (= at an end).
up against, (*informal*) 'he sensed he was *up against* a lot of opposition' (= faced with).
up to, a) 'what are you *up to* now?' (= doing); b) 'it's *up to* you to make a success of this job' (= incumbent upon); c) 'this bus holds *up to* 45 people' (= no more than); d) 'he was *up to* his neck in mud' (= as far as); e) (*informal*) 'he's not *up to* travelling yet' (= capable of, fit for).
up *verb*
(**upped, upping**)
1. to raise: 'I *upped* his bet £5'.
2. (*informal*) to get or start up: 'he'd *upped* and fled before the wedding had begun'.
up *noun*
a rise or an ascent: 'the *ups* and downs of life'.
on the up and up, achieving success.

up–
a prefix meaning up, as in *upheaval*.

up–and–coming *adjective*
promising or becoming successful: 'an *up–and–coming* young businessman'.

up–and–down *adjective*
alternately rising and falling.

upbeat *adjective*
(*informal*) cheerful or hopeful.

upbraid *verb*
to reprove severely.

upbringing *noun*
the rearing and training received during childhood.

up–country *adjective*
remote from the coast, the lowlands or the border: 'an *up–country* settlement'.
Word Family: **up–country**, *adverb*; **up–country**, *noun*.

update *verb*
to make up–to–date.

up–end *verb*
a) to stand or place on its end. b) to upset or alter drastically.

upgrade *verb*
to raise to a higher position, rank or standard.
upgrade *noun*
an uphill slope or incline.
on the upgrade, improving.

upheaval *noun*
a violent disturbance or change.

uphill *adjective*
going up a hill or slope: 'an *uphill* climb'.
Usage: 'you'll have an *uphill* job to convince him' (= difficult).
Word Family: **uphill**, *adverb*.

uphold *verb*
(**upheld, upholding**).
to maintain or give support to: 'the court *upheld* the judge's decision'.

upholster *verb*
to provide chairs, etc. with stuffing, springs, cushions and coverings.
Word Family: **upholsterer**, *noun*; **upholstery**, *noun*, the fabrics, etc., used in upholstering.
[Medieval English *uphold* to keep in repair]

upkeep *noun*
a) the maintenance of an establishment, machine, etc. b) the cost of such maintenance.

upland *noun*
an area of high land.

uplift *verb*
a) to raise up or aloft. b) to raise spiritually or mentally: 'his spirits were *uplifted* by the hymn'.
Word Family: **uplift**, *noun*.

upon *preposition*
on.

upper *adjective*
1. higher than something else: 'he's in the *upper* income bracket'.
2. (of a surface) facing upwards.

upper case
Printing: capital letters, as this WORD has. Compare LOWER CASE.

upper circle
the section of seats above the dress circle in a theatre.

upper crust
(*informal*) the aristocracy or very wealthy class.

uppercut *noun*
Boxing: a heavy punch to the head, made by swinging the arm upwards with the elbow bent.

Upper House
a) the House of Lords. b) a Senate.

uppermost *adjective*
highest in place, rank, authority, etc.
Word Family: **uppermost**, *adverb*.

uppish, uppity *adjective*
(*informal*) inclined to be snobbish or arrogant.
Word Family: **uppishly**, *adverb*; **uppishness**, *noun*.

upright *adjective*
being in a vertical position.
Usage: 'an *upright* and decent man' (= honest and just).
upright *noun*
an object standing vertical, such as a piece of timber used as a support.
Word Family: **upright**, *adverb*, in a vertical position or direction.

upright piano
see PIANO (1).

uprising *noun*
an act of popular resistance or protest: 'the new corn tax led to *uprisings* in the provinces'.

uproar *noun*
a state of noisy excitement and confusion: 'the meeting ended in an *uproar*'.
uproarious *adjective*
1. loud, noisy and boisterous: '*uproarious* laughter greeted us'.
2. very funny: 'it was an *uproarious* sight'.
Word Family: **uproariously**, *adverb*.

uproot *verb*
to tear or pull up by the roots: 'the high winds *uprooted* an ancient oak tree'.
Usage: 'the war *uprooted* millions of citizens' (= displaced).

uprush *noun*
a sudden or violent upward movement, flow, etc.: 'he felt an *uprush* of hatred possess him'.

upset (*say* up-**set**) *verb*
(**upset, upsetting**)
1. to knock or tip over: 'he *upset* the cup of tea in his lap'.
2. to disturb, disorder or defeat: a) 'the bad news *upset* me considerably'; b) 'the hail *upset* our plans for a picnic'.
upset (*say* **up**-set) *noun*
a disturbance or disorder, especially an unexpected one: a) 'a stomach *upset*'; b) 'the news was a terrible *upset*'.
Word Family: **upset**, *adjective*.

upset price
(at auctions) the reserve price, below which the owner will not sell.

upshot *noun*
the final outcome.

upside-down *adjective*
1. with the upper side down.
2. in disorder.
Word Family: **upside down**, in or to an upside-down position.

upstage *verb*
1. *Theatre:* to distract the attention of the audience from another actor by manoeuvring him to the back of the stage.
2. to distract attention or interest from another person to oneself.
upstage *noun*
the back or furthest part of the stage in a theatre.
Word Family: **upstage**, *adverb*, *adjective*.

upstairs *adjective*
of or relating to an upper floor or floors.
upstairs *adverb*
1. a) up the stairs: 'she walked *upstairs*'. b) in, to or on an upper floor.
2. to or in a higher rank or office.
kick upstairs, (*informal*) to remove someone by promoting him, especially to a position where he can exercise less power.
Word Family: **upstairs**, *noun*, an upper storey.

upstanding *adjective*
1. an old ceremonial word meaning standing erect: 'let us be *upstanding* to drink the toast'.
2. honest or upright: 'an *upstanding* citizen'.

upstart *noun*
a person who has an arrogant or presumptuous self-confidence, often due to achieving wealth or importance very quickly.
Word Family: **upstart**, *adjective*.

upstate *noun*
American: the section of a State lying north of the principal city or away from the coast.
Word Family: **upstate**, *adverb*.

upstream *adverb*
to or at the upper part of a stream, against the direction of the current.

upsurge (*say* **up**-sirj) *noun*
a surge upwards.

upswing *noun*
a swinging or movement upwards.
Usage: 'the economy is on the *upswing* now' (= improvement).

uptake *noun*
the act of understanding or comprehending: 'he's a bit slow on the *uptake*'.

upthrust *noun*
an upward thrust.

uptight *adjective*
(*informal*) tense, annoyed or anxious.

up-to-date *adjective*
a) modern or fashionable: 'she's got very *up-to-date* clothes'. b) containing the latest information, improvements, etc.: 'an *up-to-date* atlas'.

up-to-the-minute *adjective*
incorporating the latest news, information, etc.: 'an *up-to-the-minute* sports report'.

upturn *verb*
to turn up or over.
Word Family: **upturn**, *noun*, an upward turn, e.g. in prices, business, etc.

upward *adjective*
moving or directed up: 'the hill has an *upward* slope'.
upwards, upward *adverb*
towards a higher place or level: 'the hikers climbed *upwards* for what seemed like an age'.
upwards of, more than, in excess of.

upwind *adverb*
in the direction from which the wind is blowing: 'the ship was sailing *upwind*'.
Word Family: **upwind**, *adjective*, facing or moving towards the direction from which the wind is blowing.

uracil (*say* **yoora**-sil) *noun*
Biology: see PYRIMIDINE.

uranium (*say* yoo-**raynium**) *noun*
element number 92, a radioactive metal occurring in two isotopes $^{238}_{92}U$ and $^{235}_{92}U$, the latter of which is used in nuclear reactors and formed the basis of the first atomic bombs. See ACTINIDE.
See CHEMICAL ELEMENTS in grey pages.
[after URANUS]

Uranus (*say* yoo-**raynus**) *noun*
Astronomy: the planet in the solar system seventh from the sun.
[after *Uranus*, god of the sky in Greek mythology]

urban *adjective*
of or relating to cities and large towns.
Word Family: **urbanize, urbanise,** *verb*, to cause or to become urban in character or nature; **urbanization,** *noun*; **urbanism**, *noun*.
[Latin *urbis* of a city]

urbane (*say* **erbane**) *adjective*
sophisticated, refined or smoothly polite.
Word Family: **urbanely,** *adverb*; **urbanity** (*say* er-**banni**-tee), *noun*, the quality of being urbane.
[Latin *urbanus* a city-dweller, courteous]

urban guerrilla
a terrorist who specializes in sporadic acts of bombing, kidnapping or assassination in cities.

urban renewal
the rebuilding of slum areas in a city, based on extensive planning for social and physical needs.

urchin (*say* **erchin**) *noun*
1. a small, mischievous, shabbily dressed child: 'a street *urchin*'.
2. *Biology:* a sea-urchin.
[Latin *hericius* hedgehog]

urea (*say* yoo-**ree**-a) *noun*
Biology: the main nitrogenous product excreted by mammals, some fish, etc.
[Greek *ouron* urine]

ureter (*say* yoo-**reeta**) *noun*
Anatomy: either of two tubes through which the urine, collected in the kidneys, passes to be stored in the bladder.
[from Greek]

urethra (*say* yoo-**reethra**) *noun*
Anatomy: the tube through which urine is emptied from the bladder.
[from Greek]

urge (*say* **erj**) *verb*
to push or drive forward with force, threats, etc.: 'with whip and spur he *urged* his filly on'.
Usage: 'he *urged* me to buy some insurance' (= tried to persuade).
urge *noun*
a strong desire: 'the sexual *urge*'.

urgent (*say* **er**-j'nt) *adjective*
1. requiring immediate attention or action: 'an *urgent* telegram'.
2. insistent: 'she made her request in an *urgent* whisper'.
Word Family: **urgently,** *adverb*; **urgency**, *noun*.
[Latin *urgens* pressing onwards]

uric acid (*say* **yoor**ik assid)
Biology: the main nitrogenous product excreted by birds and most reptiles.

urinal (*say* **yoori**–n'l *or* yoo–**rye**–n'l) *noun*
a fixture, room or building for urinating.

urinary bladder
short form is **bladder**
Anatomy: a hollow muscular bag in the pelvic cavity, which receives urine from the kidneys and discharges it through the urethra.

urinate (*say* **yoori**–nate) *verb*
to pass urine.
Word Family: **urination**, *noun*.

urine (*say* **yoo**–rin) *noun*
a fluid secreted by the kidneys and excreted from the body as a waste.
Word Family: **urinary**, *adjective*, of, relating to or involved in the production and excretion of urine.
[from Latin]

urn (*say* ern) *noun*
1. a vase, usually with a base or stem, used for storing the ashes of the dead.
2. a large metal container in which heated drinks may be made or kept hot.
[from Latin]

urogenital (*say* yoor–o–**jenni**–t'l) *adjective*
of or relating to the urinary and genital organs and their functions.

urology (*say* yoo–**rolla**–jee) *noun*
the branch of medicine dealing with urine and the urogenital tissues.
Word Family: **urologist**, *noun*.

ursine *adjective*
of or relating to bears.
[Latin *ursus* bear]

us *pronoun*
singular is **me**
the objective form of the pronoun **we**: a) 'he hit *us*'; b) 'give the books to *us*'.

use (*say* yooz) *verb*
to bring or put into action or service: a) 'we could *use* a man with your talents'; b) 'we *use* the front room as a study'.
Usages:
a) 'she had been badly *used* by her husband' (= treated).
b) 'he *used* us selfishly' (= exploited).
Phrases:
used to (*say* yoost too), a) 'I got *used to* having you around' (= accustomed to); b) 'you *used* not *to* behave like that' (= did formerly).
use up, to consume something entirely.

use (*say* yooce) *noun*
1. a) the act of using: 'make good *use* of your youth'. b) the condition of being used: 'is that custom still in *use* here?'.
2. the purpose for which something is used: 'a dictionary has many *uses*'.
3. a) the right or ability to use something: 'I've lost the *use* of one eye'. b) the way or manner of using: 'the correct *use* of a telescope'.
4. the need or occasion to use: 'do you have any further *use* for this book?'.
Usage: 'it's a custom that has become established with *use*' (= continued practice or using).
usage (*say* **yoo**sij) *noun*
1. the way of treating or using a person or thing: 'books deteriorate with rough *usage*'.
2. customary or habitual practice: 'that word has become accepted due to long *usage*'.
3. a) the actual way in which words, etc. are used in a language. b) a particular written or verbal expression: 'a contemptuous *usage*'.
have no use for, to dislike heartily or find irritating.
Word Family: **useable** (*say* **yooza**–b'l), *adjective*, a) available for use, b) in a condition to be used; **useful** (*say* yooce–ful), *adjective*, serving a use or purpose, especially a beneficial one; **usefully**, *adverb*; **usefulness**, *noun*; **useless** (*say* **yooce**–less), *adjective*, a) not serving any beneficial purpose, b) futile.
[from Latin]

usher *noun*
a) a person who escorts others to their seats in a cinema, church, etc. b) an official in a law court who maintains order.
usher *verb*
to escort or conduct.
Word Family: **usherette** (*say* usha–**ret**), *noun*, a female usher, especially in a cinema.
[Latin *ostiārius* doorman]

usual (*say* **yoo**–*zh*ew'l) *adjective*
expected because of past experience or occurrence: 'this is the *usual* weather for March'.
Usage: 'he arrived earlier than *usual*' (= habitual).
Word Family: **usually**, *adverb*.

usurp (*say* yoo–**zerp** *or* yoo–**serp**) *verb*
to seize wrongfully or by force something belonging to another, such as power or property.
Word Family: **usurper**, *noun*; **usurpation** (*say* yoozer–**pay**–sh'n), *noun*.
[from Latin]

usury (*say* yoo*zh*a–ree) *noun*
a) the business of lending money, especially at a rate of interest which is high or above the legal rate. b) this rate of interest.
Word Family: **usurer**, *noun*; **usurious** (*say* yoo–*zh*oori–us), *adjective*; **usuriously**, *adverb*.
[from Latin]

utensil (*say* yoo–**ten**sil) *noun*
any instrument, container or tool serving some useful purpose: a) 'kitchen *utensils*'; b) 'writing *utensils*'.
[Latin *utensilis* fit for use]

uterus (*say* **yoo**ta–rus) *noun*
also called the **womb**
Anatomy: the thick–walled organ lying in the pelvic cavity in females, in which the young grow between fertilization and birth.
uterine tube
see FALLOPIAN TUBE.
[Latin]

utilitarian (*say* yoo–tilli–**tai**rian) *adjective*
believing that all actions should be aimed at the greatest happiness for the greatest number of people.
Word Family: **utilitarian**, *noun*, a utilitarian person, especially one concerned with only practical matters or material interests and aims; **utilitarianism**, *noun*.

utility (*say* yoo–**tilli**–tee) *noun*
1. a) the quality of being useful: 'science has more *utility* than poetry'. b) something which is useful.
2. a government–owned organization which supplies basic needs, such as water, electricity, gas, etc.
3. a motor vehicle with a tray at the back used for carrying medium–sized loads.
[Latin *utilis* useful]

utilize (*say* **yoo**ti–lize) **utilise** *verb*
to make use of.
Word Family: **utilizer**, *noun*; **utilization**, *noun*.

utmost, uttermost *adjective*
1. greatest: 'he's in the *utmost* peril'.
2. furthest: 'he travelled to the *utmost* corners of the globe'.
Word Family: **utmost**, *noun*, the most possible.

utopia (*say* yoo–**toe**–pee–a) *noun*
any perfect place or situation.
Word Family: **utopian**, *adjective*, excellent but impractical; **utopian**, *noun*, an idealistic but impractical reformer; **utopianism**, *noun*.
[after *Utopia*, a book by Sir Thomas More, 1478–1535, describing an island of political and social perfection]

utter (1) *verb*
1. to express audibly: 'the mouse *uttered* a squeak'.
2. to put counterfeit or forged money, etc. into circulation.
utterance *noun*
a) the act or manner of uttering. b) something which is uttered or expressed.

utter (2) *adjective*
total: 'they lived in *utter* misery for years'.
Word Family: **utterly**, *adverb*.

uttermost *adjective*
see UTMOST.

U–turn *noun*
a turn to completely reverse the direction of travel of a vehicle.

uvula (*say* **yoo**–vew–la) *noun*
the small, conical mass of tissue hanging above the back of the tongue.
Word Family: **uvular**, *adjective*.
[Latin, a small grape]

uxorious (*say* uk–**saw**rius) *adjective*
excessively or foolishly fond of one's wife.
[Latin *uxor* wife]

Vv

vac *noun*
(*informal*) a vacation.

vacant (*say* **vay**–k'nt) *adjective*
not occupied: 'are these seats *vacant*?'.
Usage: 'he gave a *vacant* stare into space' (= vague).
vacancy *noun*
1. the state or condition of being vacant.
2. a space, position or place which is vacant: a) 'a motel *vacancy*'; b) 'an office *vacancy* for a typist'.
vacate (*say* vay–**kate** *or* va–**kate**) *verb*
to leave or give up: 'the landlord insisted we *vacate* the house'.
Word Family: **vacantly**, *adverb*.
[Latin *vacans* being empty]

vacant possession
freehold possession of a house, etc. with no sitting tenant in it.

vacation (*say* vay–**kay**–sh'n *or* va–**kay**–sh'n) *noun*
1. a) a holiday. b) the period between terms at universities and law–courts.
2. the act of vacating: 'his *vacation* of the position gave me a chance for promotion'.
[Latin *vacatio* freedom]

vaccine (*say* **vak**seen) *noun*
a modified infective agent such as a virus, which gives immunity to a disease, often by introducing a mild form of the disease.
vaccinate (*say* **vak**si–nate) *verb*
to administer a vaccine. Compare INOCULATE.
Word Family: **vaccination**, *noun*.
[Latin *vacca* a cow]

vacillate (*say* **vassi**–late) *verb*
to waver.
Word Family: **vacillation**, *noun*.
[from Latin]

vacuole (*say* **vak**–yoo–ole) *noun*
Biology: a space in cell protoplasm containing air, fluid or partially digested food.

vacuous (*say* **vak**–yewus) *adjective*
empty or blank: 'a dull, *vacuous* stare into space'.
vacuity (*say* va–**kewi**–tee) *noun*
a) the state of being vacuous. b) something which is vacuous.
Word Family: **vacuously**, *adverb*.
[Latin *vacuus* empty]

vacuum (*say* **vak**–yoom) *noun*
1. a space entirely void of matter.
2. *Physics:* an enclosed space from which air and all other gases have been removed.
3. (*informal*) a vacuum cleaner.
vacuum *adjective*
relating to an apparatus or process using gas pressures below atmospheric pressure.
Word Family: **vacuum**, *verb*, to clean with a vacuum cleaner.
[Latin]

vacuum cleaner
an electrical appliance which sucks up dirt and dust.

vacuum flask
a thermos flask.

vacuum tube
a sealed glass tube with an almost perfect vacuum, used to observe the passage of an electric charge.

vade–mecum (*say* vay–dee–**mee**–k'm) *noun*
plural is **vade–mecums**
a pocket handbook or guide.
[Latin, go with me]

vagabond (*say* **vagga**–bond) *noun*
1. a person, especially one with no fixed abode, who wanders from place to place.
2. an idle or worthless person.
Word Family: **vagabond**, *adjective*, a) nomadic, b) idle.
[Latin *vagari* to wander]

vagary (*say* **vay**–ga–ree) *noun*
an extravagant whim or fancy.

vagina (*say* va–**jie**–na) *noun*
Anatomy: the tube which connects the uterus to the vulva in female mammals.
Word Family: **vaginal**, *adjective*.
[Latin, a sheath]

vagrant (*say* **vay**–gr'nt) *noun*
a tramp.

Word Family: **vagrant**, *adjective*, wandering or with no fixed abode; **vagrantly**, *adverb*; **vagrancy**, *noun*.

vague (*say* vaig) *adjective*
1. not clear or distinct: a) 'a *vague*, shadowy figure in the fog'; b) 'a *vague* memory'.
2. vacant or without a clear expression: 'a *vague* stare'.
Word Family: **vaguely**, *adverb*; **vagueness**, *noun*.
[Latin *vagus* wandering]

vain *adjective*
1. too proud of one's looks, abilities, etc.
2. futile or useless: 'it was a *vain* attempt to try and stop the flood'.
Usage: 'ignore her *vain* boasts' (= without value).
Phrases:
in vain, to no use or effect.
take someone's name in vain, to use someone's name disrespectfully, especially God's name.
vanity (*say* **vanni**-tee) *noun*
1. excessive pride or desire for praise.
2. the quality of being worthless or futile: 'she tired of the *vanity* of her aimless life'.
Word Family: **vainly**, *adverb*.
[Latin *vanus* empty]

vainglory *noun*
1. extreme or boastful vanity.
2. vain pomp or show.
Word Family: **vainglorious**, *adjective*.

vale *noun*
an old word for a valley.

valediction (*say* valla-**dik**-sh'n) *noun*
a farewell, especially as expressed in speech or writing.
Word Family: **valedictory**, *adjective*; **valedictory**, *noun*, a farewell speech.
[Latin *vale* goodbye + *dicere* to say]

valency (*say* **vayl**'n-see) **valence** *noun*
short form of **electrovalency**
Chemistry: the combining power of an atom, equal to the number of hydrogen atoms which an atom will combine with or replace. *Example*: the valency of oxygen is two, so it combines with two atoms of hydrogen to form water, H_2O.
[Latin *valens* being strong]

valentine (*say* **vallen**-tine) *noun*
a) a token of love or friendship sent to a person on February 14th (St. Valentine's Day), which is set aside for this tradition. b) the person to whom the token is sent.

valet (*say* **vallay** *or* **vallet**) *noun*
1. a male servant who attends his employer personally.
2. a hotel employee who cleans the guests' clothes, etc.
[French]

valetudinarian
(*say* valla-tewdi-**nair**ian) *noun*
a) a person in poor health. b) a person obsessed with the state of his health.
[Latin *valetudo* state of health]

Valhalla *noun*
Norse mythology: the hall where heroes slain in battle were feasted.
[Old Norse, hall of the slain]

valiant (*say* **valli**-unt) *adjective*
brave.
Word Family: **valiantly**, *adverb*; **valiance**, **valiancy**, *nouns*.

valid *adjective*
having full or official force or effect: 'the ticket is only *valid* for one person'.
Usage: 'do you have a *valid* excuse?' (= sound, reasonable).
Word Family: **validly**, *adverb*; **validity** (*say* va-**liddi**-tee), *noun*; **validate**, *verb*, to make valid.
[Latin *validus* strong]

valise (*say* va-**leez**) *noun*
1. a small travelling bag or case, carried in the hand.
2. *Military:* a kitbag.
[French]

valium (*say* **vayli**-um) *noun*
Medicine: a drug used as a sedative.

Valkyrie *noun*
Norse mythology: any of the war god's daughters who roamed the battlefield selecting those who were to be slain, and then conducted them to Valhalla.
[Old Norse, choosers of the slain]

valley *noun*
any low stretch of land between hills or higher land, often with a river flowing through it.
[from Latin]

valour (*say* **valla**) *noun*
in America spelt **valor**
heroic courage.
Word Family: **valorous**, *adjective*.
[Latin *valere* to be strong]

value (*say* **val**-yoo) *noun*
1. the fact of being useful or desirable: 'what is the *value* of 10 years at school?'.
2. equivalence in money: 'the property's *value* increased last year'.
3. weight or emphasis: 'give the notes full *value* in this passage of music'.

4. (*plural*) any ideals, goals or standards upon which actions or beliefs are based.

value *verb*
1. to estimate the value of.
2. to regard highly: 'I *value* your friendship'.

valuable (*say* **val**–yoo–b'l) *adjective*
of great value: a) 'a *valuable* antique'; b) '*valuable* friends'.

valuable *noun*
(*usually plural*) any object, such as jewellery, etc., which has financial value.
Word Family: **valuer**, *noun*, a person who estimates values; **valuation**, *noun*, a) the process of deciding the value of something, b) an estimated value.
[Latin *valere* to be worth]

value added tax
short form is **VAT**
a tax on the amount by which total sales, other than exports, exceed total purchases, in theory a tax on the value added to an article at each stage of manufacture.

value–judgement *noun*
a personal assessment of quality, merit, etc. as contrasted with an objective assessment or statement of facts.

valve *noun*
1. any of various devices controlling or regulating the flow of fluids or gases in a pipe or tube.
2. *Electronics:* a device in which electrons operate in a gas or vacuum inside a closed container.
3. *Biology:* one of the parts of a shell.
Word Family: **valvular** (*say* valvew–la), *adjective*.
[Latin *valva* a door]

vamoose *verb*
(*informal*) to decamp or disappear.
[Spanish *vamos* let us go]

vamp (1) *noun*
the upper front part of a boot or shoe.

vamp *verb*
1. to repair or add a new vamp to.
2. a) to patch up or repair. b) to improvise a musical accompaniment, etc.
[French *avant–pied* front of foot]

vamp (2) *noun*
a seductive woman who uses her physical charms to exploit men.
Word Family: **vamp**, *verb*.
[short form of *vampire*]

vampire *noun*
1. *Folklore:* an unnatural evil being or revived corpse, believed to leave its grave at night and suck the blood of sleeping people.
2. a vampire bat.
[Hungarian]

vampire bat
a tropical American bat which feeds on the blood of animals.

van (1) *noun*
the vanguard.

van (2) *noun*
a covered vehicle, often large, for carrying goods, etc.: 'a removal *van*'.
guard's van, the end carriage of a train in which the guard travels.
luggage van, a railway carriage for luggage and parcels.
[short form of *caravan*]

vanadium (*say* va–**nay**–dee–um) *noun*
element number 23, a metal used to toughen steel.
See CHEMICAL ELEMENTS in grey pages.

Van Allen belt
Astronomy: either of two belts of charged particles trapped by the earth's magnetic field.
[after *J. A. Van Allen*, born 1914, an American physicist]

vandal *noun*
a person who destroys or defaces things on purpose.
Word Family: **vandalism**, *noun*; **vandalize, vandalise**, *verb*.
[after the *Vandals*, a Germanic tribe which sacked Rome in A.D. 455]

vane *noun*
a blade or flat surface fixed to a rotating axis, as in a windmill.

vanguard (*say* **van**–gard) *noun*
1. the leading part of a military force, providing warning and protection.
2. a) the forefront of a trend or movement. b) those in this position.
[French *avant* before + *garde* guard]

vanilla *noun*
an extract from a pod–like fruit, widely used as a flavouring in cooking.
[Spanish *vainilla* pod]

vanish *verb*
1. to disappear completely, especially quickly.
2. *Maths:* to become zero.
[Latin *evanescere* to evanesce]

vanishing cream
a white cream which is absorbed when put on the face, used as a base for powder, etc.

vanity *noun*
Word Family: see VAIN.
[Latin *vanitas* emptiness]

vanity case
a fitted travelling-case for cosmetics, hairbrushes, etc.

vanquish (*say* **van**-kwish) *verb*
to conquer or defeat.
[from Latin]

vantage (*say* **van**-tij) *noun*
1. advantage or superiority.
2. *Tennis:* see ADVANTAGE.

vantage point
a position giving a wide or clear view.

vapid (*say* **vap**pid) *adjective*
flat, dull or tasteless.
Word Family: **vapidly**, *adverb*; **vapidity** (*say* va-**piddi**-tee), **vapidness**, *nouns.*
[from Latin]

vaporize (*say* **vay**pa-rize) **vaporise** *verb*
to change into vapour.
Word Family: **vaporizer**, *noun*, a thing which vaporizes, such as a perfume spray; **vaporization**, *noun.*

vapour (*say* **vay**-pa) *noun*
in America spelt **vapor**
1. a gaseous substance, such as mist, to which some substances may be reduced by heat.
2. (*plural*) an old word for low spirits.
vapour trail, the condensation trail left by a high-flying aeroplane.
Word Family: **vaporous**, *adjective*, of, like or covered with vapour.
[from Latin]

vapour pressure
Physics: the pressure exerted by molecules which escape from liquid as vapour.

variable (*say* **vair**ia-b'l) *adjective*
changing or changeable: 'our *variable* weather is impossible to predict'.
variable *noun*
1. something liable to change.
2. *Maths:* a symbol for any member of a set of numbers.
Word Family: **variably**, *adverb*; **variability** (*say* vairia-**billi**-tee), **variableness**, *nouns.*
[from Latin]

variable-geometry *noun*
short form is **VG**
(of an aeroplane) swing-wing.

variable star
any of numerous kinds of remote stars whose brilliancy varies, usually over short periods.

variance (*say* **vair**i-ence) *noun*
1. difference or disagreement: 'explain the *variance* between your two statements'.
2. *Maths:* the square of the standard deviation.
Word Family: **variant**, *adjective*, alternative or different; **variant**, *noun*, something variant, such as a different spelling of the same word.

variation (*say* vairi-**ay**-sh'n) *noun*
1. a change from the normal or a standard: 'the *variations* in temperature gave her a cold'.
2. *Music:* one of a set of versions of a given theme, differing in key, tempo, orchestration, etc.

varicose (*say* **varr**i-kose) *adjective*
(of veins) enlarged or swollen.
[Latin *varicis* of a dilated vein]

variegate (*say* **vair**ia-gate) *verb*
to mark with different colours or patches.
Word Family: **variegation**, *noun.*

variety (*say* va-**rye**-a-tee) *noun*
1. the quality of being different or varied: 'I want a job with *variety* not dull routine'.
2. a different kind, sort or form: 'we have 37 *varieties* of ice-cream'.
3. a number or collection of different things: 'she supported her argument with a *variety* of reasons'.

variety show
a form of entertainment consisting of songs, dances and comedy acts.

various (*say* **vair**i-us) *adjective*
1. different: 'we have it in *various* colours'.
2. several: 'he spoke to *various* guests before leaving'.
Word Family: **variously**, *adverb.*
[from Latin]

varlet *noun*
an old word for a scoundrel.

varmint *noun*
(*informal*) an annoying person or animal.

varnish *noun*
a) a preparation consisting of a resin dissolved in a solvent, which dries and leaves a glossy, transparent finish when applied to a surface. b) the result of applying this.
Usage: 'his good manners are only a *varnish*' (= deceptive veneer).
Word Family: **varnish**, *verb*, to apply varnish to.
[French *vernis*]

varsity (*say* varsi–tee) *noun*
(*informal*) a university.

vary (*say* **vair**–ee) *verb*
(**varied, varying**)
1. to change or alter: 'the quality of our product never *varies*'.
2. to introduce new or different forms to: 'you should *vary* your diet'.

vascular (*say* **vass**–kewla) *adjective*
Biology: relating to or consisting of vessels which conduct fluids.
[Latin *vasculum* a small vessel]

vas deferens (*say* vass **deffa**–renz)
Anatomy: the tube in the testicle which transports semen to the penis.
[Latin, a vessel carrying downwards]

vase (*say* vahz) *noun*
an ornamental container for flowers.
[Latin *vasum* a vessel]

vasectomy (*say* va–**sekta**–mee) *noun*
an operation to cut or remove part of the vas deferens.
[Latin *vas* a vessel + Greek *ektomé* a cutting out]

Vaseline (*say* **vassa**–leen) *noun*
a yellow or whitish form of petroleum jelly, used as an ointment, etc.
[a trademark]

vassal *noun*
1. *Medieval history:* a person subject to a feudal contract, such as a peasant given a piece of land from a nobleman's estate in exchange for military service, etc. Compare SEIGNEUR.
2. any person who is subservient to or dependent on another.
Word Family: **vassalage**, *noun*.

vast (*say* vahst) *adjective*
of very great size or extent: a) 'a *vast* desert'; b) '*vast* sums of money'.
Word Family: **vastly**, *adverb*; **vastness**, *noun*.
[Latin *vastus* empty, desert]

vat *noun*
a large container for liquids.

vaudeville (*say* **vawda**–vil) *noun*
American: music-hall or variety entertainment.
[after *Vau de Vire*, a Normandy valley where satirical songs were popular]

vault (1) (*say* volt) *noun*
1. an underground room or chamber, such as a burial place under a church, or a room for storing valuable objects in a bank.
2. an arched roof.
[Latin *volutus* turned over]

vault (2) (*say* volt) *verb*
to spring or leap over something, using the hands or a pole as support.
Word Family: **vault**, *noun*; **vaulter**, *noun*.

vaunt (*say* vawnt) *verb*
to boast about.
Word Family: **vauntingly**, *adverb*.
[Latin *vanitas* vanity]

veal *noun*
the flesh of a calf.
[Latin *vitellus* calf]

vector *noun*
1. *Maths:* a quantity with both magnitude and direction. Compare SCALAR.
2. *Biology:* any organism transmitting parasites from one host to the next, such as a malaria-carrying mosquito.
[Latin, a carrier]

veer *verb*
to change course or direction.
[Dutch]

vegan (*say* **vee**–g'n) *noun*
a strict vegetarian who eats no animals or animal products.

vegetable (*say* **vej**ta–b'l) *noun*
1. a plant or part of a plant that is used as food.
2. *Biology:* any plant.
3. (*informal*) a person who leads an inactive or monotonous existence. Also called a **cabbage**.
[Latin *vegetare* to animate]

vegetable oil
any of various oils obtained from the fruit or seeds of plants.

vegetarian (*say* veja–**tair**iun) *noun*
a person who eats vegetable foods only, except, usually, for eggs and dairy produce.
Word Family: **vegetarianism**, *noun*.

vegetate (*say* **veja**–tate) *verb*
to live in an unthinking or inactive way.

vegetation (*say* veja–**tay**–sh'n) *noun*
any or all the plants in a certain area.

vegetative (*say* **vejita**–tiv) **vegetive** *adjective*
1. of vegetation or vegetable growth.
2. existing or growing as or like a plant.
3. (of reproduction) asexual.

vehement (*say* **vee**–a–m'nt) *adjective*
having or showing strong or passionate feeling: 'a bitter and *vehement* election campaign'.
Usage: 'she worked with *vehement* keenness' (= eager, energetic).

Word Family: **vehemently,** *adverb*; **vehemence,** *noun.*
[from Latin]

vehicle (*say* vee–ik'l) *noun*
1. any device for moving or carrying, especially one on wheels.
2. any medium for carrying or communicating: 'the director used the film as a *vehicle* for his political ideas'.
Word Family: **vehicular** (*say* vee–**hik**–yoola), *adjective.*
[Latin *vehere* to carry]

veil (*say* vale) *noun*
1. a fine piece of cloth, often transparent, worn on the head and hanging over the face or shoulders.
2. anything that hides or disguises: 'the guilty person tried to hide under the *veil* of ignorance'.
take the veil, to become a nun.
Word Family: **veil,** *verb,* to cover or conceal with or as with a veil.
[Latin *velum* a curtain]

vein (*say* vane) *noun*
1. *Anatomy:* any of the thin–walled tubes carrying blood back from the tissues of the body to the heart. Compare ARTERY and CAPILLARY.
2. a vein–like part or support, as in a leaf or an insect's wing.
3. *Geology:* a strip of minerals along a joint or fault line in rocks. Also called a **lode,** a **lead** or a **reef.**
4. any streak or marking: 'wood with a dark *vein* running through it'.
Usages:
a) 'he'll sing operatic arias when in the right *vein*' (= mood).
b) 'the dog has a *vein* of viciousness in him' (= streak).
[from Latin]

veld (*say* velt) **veldt** *noun*
South African: a steppe.
[Afrikaans, field]

vellum *noun*
a smooth parchment, usually made from calfskin.
[Latin *vitulus* a calf]

velocipede (*say* ve–**lossi**–peed) *noun*
an early form of bicycle.
[Latin *velox* swift + *pedis* of a foot]

velocity (*say* ve–**lossi**–tee) *noun*
1. *Physics:* the vector quantity describing the rate of change in the displacement of an object in both magnitude and direction, including linear velocity, expressed in metres per second and angular velocity, expressed in radians per second. Compare SPEED.
2. (*informal*) speed.
[Latin *velox* swift]

velour (*say* vel–**oor**) **velours** *noun*
a fabric with a velvet–like pile.
[French, velvet]

velvet *noun*
1. a silk, cotton or fibre fabric with a soft, short, thick pile.
2. something which is soft or smooth like this fabric.
3. the covering, which is rich in blood vessels, on developing antler in deer.
Word Family: **velvety,** *adjective.*
[Latin *villus* shaggy hair]

velveteen (*say* velva–**teen**) *noun*
an imitation velvet made from cotton.

vena cava (*say* veena **kay**–va)
plural is **venae cavae** (*say* vee–nigh **kay**–vigh)
Anatomy: either of the two large veins which carry blood from all the other veins to the heart.
[Latin, hollow vein]

venal (*say* **vee**–n'l) *adjective*
corrupt or easily corruptible.
Word Family: **venally,** *adverb*; **venality** (*say* vee–**nalli**–tee), *noun.*
[Latin *venalis* for sale]

vendetta *noun*
1. a sustained campaign of relentless hostility.
2. a feud in which the family of a murdered person takes revenge on the murderer or his family.
[Italian, vengeance]

vending machine
a coin–operated machine dispensing small articles for sale, such as cigarettes, soft drinks, etc.

vendor *noun*
a person who sells something.
Word Family: **vend,** *verb.*
[from Latin]

veneer (*say* ve–**neer**) *noun*
a thin layer of wood, plastic, etc. used to cover a surface.
Usage: 'under his *veneer* of meekness he's a vicious person' (= appearance).
Word Family: **veneer,** *verb,* to apply a veneer to.
[Old French *fournir* to furnish]

venerate (*say* **venna**–rate) *verb*
to treat with great respect or reverence.
Word Family: **veneration,** *noun,* a) the act of venerating, b) a feeling of deep respect; **venerable** (*say* **ven**'ra–b'l), *adjective,* worthy of being

venerated; **venerability** (*say* ven'ra-**billi**-tee), *noun.*
[from Latin]

venereal disease (*say* ve-**neerial** diz-eez)
any disease transmitted by sexual intercourse.
[Latin *veneris* of sexual love, from Venus, see APHRODITE]

venetian blind
a window blind with overlapping slats which may be opened, closed, or raised by pulling a cord.
[from *Venice*]

vengeance (*say* **ven**-j'nce) *noun*
revenge or retribution.
with a vengeance, 'this is democracy, *with a vengeance*' (= carried too far).
[Latin *vindicare* to claim]

vengeful *adjective*
having or showing a desire for revenge.
Word Family: **vengefully**, *adverb*; **vengefulness**, *noun.*

venial (*say* **vee**niul) *adjective*
(of a fault or sin) forgivable or excusable.
Word Family: **veniality** (*say* veeni-**alli**-tee), *noun.*
[from Latin]

venison *noun*
the flesh of a deer.
[Latin *venatio* hunting]

Venn diagram
Maths: a drawing using circles to represent the relationships of sets to one another.
[after *J. Venn*, died 1923, an English logician]

venom *noun*
a poison made by certain animals, such as snakes, and transmitted to victims by a bite or sting.
Usage: 'the critic's attack was full of *venom*' (= spite, malice).
venomous (*say* **venna**-mus) *adjective*
1. having the ability to make venom.
2. full of venom.
Word Family: **venomously**, *adverb*; **venomousness**, *noun.*
[from Latin]

venous (*say* **vee**nus) *adjective*
of or relating to veins or the blood carried in them.

vent *noun*
1. any opening serving as an outlet, such as one allowing air or smoke to escape from a room, or lava from a volcano.
2. a slit in the back or sides of a coat or skirt.
give vent to, to express or utter.
vent *verb*
to find or provide an outlet for: 'she *vented* her anger on the unfortunate bystanders'.
[Old French *fente* a slit]

ventilate (*say* **venti**-late) *verb*
to provide with or circulate fresh air.
Usage: 'you'll be able to *ventilate* your complaints at the meeting' (= make known).
Word Family: **ventilator**, *noun*, something which ventilates, such as a device in the wall of a building; **ventilation**, *noun*, a) the act of ventilating, b) a device or means for ventilating.
[Latin *ventilare* to fan]

ventral *adjective*
a) of or relating to the abdomen. b) of or relating to the front of the human body or the lower surface of an animal.
[from Latin]

ventricle (*say* **ventri**-k'l) *noun*
Anatomy: a) either of the two pumping chambers of the heart. b) any of various cavities in the body, e.g. in the brain.
[Latin *ventriculus* little belly]

ventriloquist (*say* ven-**trilla**-kwist) *noun*
a person producing sounds or voices which seem to come from another source.
Word Family: **ventriloquism**, **ventriloquy** (*say* ven-**trilla**-kwee), *nouns.*
[Latin *ventris* of the belly + *loqui* to speak]

venture *noun*
any undertaking involving some risk.
venture *verb*
to risk.
Usage: 'might I *venture* a suggestion?' (= dare to offer).
Word Family: **venturous**, **venturesome**, *adjective*, a) willing to take risks, b) risky; **venturously**, *adverb*; **venturousness**, *noun*; **venturer**, *noun.*
[for ADVENTURE]

venue (*say* **ven**-yoo) *noun*
the place where an event, action, etc. takes place.
[French]

venule *noun*
a small vein or branch of a vein.

Venus (*say* **vee**nus) *noun*
Astronomy: the planet in the solar system next to the earth and second from the sun. Also called the **morning star** or the **evening star**.
[after *Venus*, the goddess of love, beauty, fertility, etc. in Roman mythology]

veracity (*say* ve–**rassi**–tee) *noun*
a) truth. b) truthfulness or accuracy.
Word Family: **veracious** (*say* ve–**ray**–shus), *adjective*; **veraciously**, *adverb*.
[from Latin]

verandah (*say* ve–**randa**) **veranda** *noun*
an open area with a floor and roof, attached to the outside of a building.
[Hindi]

verb *noun*
Grammar: a word which expresses an action or state of being. *Example*: the boy *sang* because he *was* happy. Compare INTRANSITIVE, TRANSITIVE and VOICE.
[Latin *verbum* word]

verbal *adjective*
1. of, relating to or expressed in words.
2. *Grammar:* of or relating to verbs.
3. (*informal*) oral: 'a *verbal* agreement'.
4. (of translations) word for word; literal.
verbal *noun*
(*informal*) a verbal statement made by the accused, according to police evidence.
Word Family: **verbally**, *adverb*.

verbatim (*say* ver–**bay**tim) *adjective, adverb*
using exactly the same words.

verbena (*say* ver–**bee**na) *noun*
a garden plant having thick spikes of flowers.
[Latin *verbenae* sacred herbs]

verbiage (*say* **ver**bi–ij) *noun*
too many useless words.

verbose (*say* ver–**bose**) *adjective*
using or having too many unnecessary words.
Word Family: **verbosely**, *adverb*; **verbosity** (*say* ver–**bossi**–tee), **verboseness**, *nouns*.

verdant *adjective*
fresh or green with vegetation.
[Latin *viridans* green]

verdict *noun*
a judgement or decision, especially that of a jury in a court case.
[Latin *vere* true + *dictus* said]

verdigris *noun*
a greenish–blue pigment formed on copper by the action of acetic acid.
[Old French *vert de Grèce* Greek green]

verdure (*say* **verd**–ya) *noun*
a) the fresh greenness of vegetation.
b) the vegetation itself.
[Old French *verd* green]

verge (1) (*say* verj) *noun*
an edge, margin or border, such as a strip of grass beside a road.
on, to the verge of, very close or just about to.
[Latin *virga* a rod]

verge (2) (*say* verj) *verb*
to tend towards: 'he must be *verging* on 60'.
[Latin *vergere* to bend]

verger (*say* **ver**ja) *noun*
Christian: a person who takes care of the interior of a church.
[Latin *virga* a rod (of office)]

verify (*say* **verri**–fie) *verb*
(**verified, verifying**)
to confirm the truth or accuracy of: 'we can *verify* your alibi by asking your witnesses'.
Word Family: **verifier**, *noun*, a person or thing that verifies; **verification**, *noun*, a) the act of verifying, b) proof or confirmation; **verifiable**, *adjective*.
[Latin *verus* true + *facere* to make]

verily *adverb*
an old word meaning truly or indeed.

verisimilitude (*say* verri–**simil**li–tewd) *noun*
a) an appearance or semblance of truth.
b) a resemblance or trueness to life.

veritable (*say* **verr**ita–b'l) *adverb*
real or unquestionable: 'he's a *veritable* lunatic'.
Word Family: **veritably**, *adverb*.

verity (*say* **verri**–tee) *noun*
1. the quality of being true: 'I doubt the *verity* of your statement'.
2. a true statement, belief, etc.
[from Latin]

vermicelli (*say* vermi–**chellee**) *noun*
pasta in long, thin threads.
[Italian, little worms]

vermilion (*say* ver–**mil**–y'n) *noun*
a vivid red to reddish–orange colour or pigment.
[Latin *vermiculus* a small worm]

vermin *noun*
plural is **vermin**
1. any harmful or objectionable small animals or parasitic insects, such as rats, lice, etc.
2. any obnoxious person or persons.
Word Family: **verminous**, *adjective.*
[Latin *vermis* worm]

vermouth (*say* **ver**–muth) *noun*
a fortified wine flavoured with herbs and having a sweet or dry taste.
[German *Wermuth* wormwood]

vernacular (*say* ver–**nak**–yoola) *noun*
the native language of a country or nation, especially its colloquial form.
Word Family: **vernacular**, *adjective,* a) relating to the native language, b) popular or informal.

vernal *adjective*
of, occurring in or appropriate to spring.
[Latin *ver* spring]

vernier *noun*
an auxiliary movable scale making possible minutely precise readings on a conventional scale, e.g. on a theodolite.
[after *P. Vernier*, 1580–1637, a French mathematician]

versatile (*say* **versa**–tile) *adjective*
having many abilities or interests.
Word Family: **versatility** (*say* versa–**tilli**–tee), *noun*; **versatilely**, *adverb.*
[Latin *versatilis* capable of turning]

verse *noun*
1. a) a division of a poem, similar to a paragraph in prose. b) a single line of a poem.
2. a poem or poems.
blank verse does not rhyme, but has a regular rhythm.
free verse has neither rhyme nor regular rhythm.
3. a short division of a chapter in the Bible.
[Latin *versus* a line (of writing)]

versed *adjective*
skilled or experienced.
[Latin *versatus* engaged in]

versify (*say* **versi**–fie) *verb*
(**versified, versifying**)
a) to put into verse. b) to write verses.
Word Family: **versification**, *noun*; **versifier**, *noun.*
[Latin *versus* a line + *facere* to make]

version (*say* **ver**–*zh*'n) *noun*
1. an account or description from a single point of view: 'don't believe his *version* of the accident'.
2. an adaptation or variation: 'the film *version* of a novel'.
[Latin *versus* turned]

vers–libre (*say* vair–**leebra**) *noun*
free verse. See VERSE.
[French]

versus *preposition*
against.
[Latin]

vertebra (*say* **verta**–bra) *noun*
plural is **vertebrae** (*say* **verta**–bray)
any of the chain of bones that form the vertebral column.
Word Family: **vertebral**, *adjective.*
[Latin]

vertebral column
also called the **backbone**, the **spine** or the **spinal column**
Anatomy: a series of bones enclosing and protecting the spinal cord, and supporting the other bones of the skeleton.

vertebrate (*say* **verta**–brit) *noun*
any animal with a vertebral column, a member of one of the two main animal phyla. Compare INVERTEBRATE.

vertex *noun*
plural is **vertices** (*say* **verti**–seez) or **vertexes**
Maths: a) the highest point, such as the apex of a pyramid. b) a point where two or more lines or three or more planes intersect.
[Latin, top of the head]

vertical *adjective*
at right angles to the plane of the horizon.
Word Family: **vertical**, *noun*, a vertical line, plane or position; **vertically**, *adverb*; **verticality** (*say* verti–**kalli**–tee), *noun.*

vertigo *noun*
dizziness and loss of balance, especially when at a height.
[Latin, whirling]

verve *noun*
enthusiasm, energy or vigour.

very *adverb*
1. to a high degree: 'you speak French *very* well'.
2. used to intensify or emphasize: a) 'the *very* best quality'; b) 'the *very* next day'.

very *adjective*
1. actual or exact: 'caught in the *very* act'.
2. mere: 'the *very* thought frightens me'.
[Latin *verus* true]

very high frequency
short form is **VHF**
Radio: the frequency used in short-range radio, which is relatively free from interference.

Very light (*say* veeri light)
a coloured flare used as a signal.
[invented by *E. M. Very*, 1847–1910, an American naval officer]

very low frequency
Radio: the frequency used for maritime radio navigation, etc.

vesicle (*say* **vessi**-k'l) *noun*
any small bladder-like cavity, such as a blister on the skin, an air bubble in volcanic rock, etc.
Word Family: **vesicular** (*say* ve-**sik**-yoola), *adjective*.
[from Latin]

vespers *plural noun*
Christian: (used with singular verb) a service held in the evening.
[Latin *vespera* evening]

vessel *noun*
1. a ship or large boat.
2. any container for liquids, etc.
3. *Anatomy:* a tube or duct in the body, which carries some fluid, especially blood.
4. *Biology:* a tube-like series of cells arranged end to end, found in the xylem of a plant.
[Latin *vascellum* small vase]

vest *noun*
a) a light collarless shirt without sleeves, worn as underwear. b) a waistcoat.
vest *verb*
to invest with or confer upon: 'I *vest* you with full authority'.
[Latin *vestis* garment]

vestal *adjective*
chaste or pure.
[after *Vesta*, the Roman goddess of hearth and home]

vested interest
1. a personal, usually financial, interest in opposing change in a political or other system.
2. *Law:* an absolute possession or right.

vestibule (*say* **vesti**-bewl) *noun*
an entrance hall or lobby.

vestige (*say* **vestij**) *noun*
a mark or trace of something that once existed: 'not a *vestige* of the castle remained'.
Word Family: **vestigial** (*say* vess-**tij**'l), *adjective*.
[Latin *vestigium* footprint]

vestment *noun*
a ceremonial robe, especially one worn by the clergy during religious services.

vestry *noun*
1. *Christian:* the part of a church where the sacred vessels, robes, etc. are kept. Also called a **sacristy**.
2. a name for a meeting of the parish council, in some Anglican parishes.

vet *verb*
(**vetted, vetting**)
to check carefully.
vet *noun*
(*informal*) a veterinary surgeon.

vetch *noun*
any of various plants of the bean family, often used as cattle fodder.
[from Latin]

veteran (*say* **vetta**-run) *noun*
a person who has had long service or experience: 'a war *veteran*'.
veteran *adjective*
(of a motor vehicle) built before 1918. Compare VINTAGE.
[Latin *vetus* old]

veterinarian (*say* vettera-**nair**ian) *noun*
American: a veterinary surgeon.

veterinary (*say* **vett**'rin-ree) *adjective*
relating to medical or surgical treatment of animals. A **veterinary surgeon** is a person qualified to perform such treatment.
[Latin *veterina* draught cattle]

veto (*say* **vee**-toe) *noun*
plural is **vetoes**
a) the right or power to prevent or reject something, often by a vote. b) the exercise of this.
Word Family: **veto** (**vetoed, vetoing**), *verb*.
[Latin, I forbid]

vex *verb*
to trouble, worry or annoy.
vexed question, a difficult, often-debated problem.
Word Family: **vexatious** (*say* vek-**say**shus), *adjective*; **vexation**, *noun*, a) the act of vexing, b) the state of being vexed, c) a person or thing that vexes.
[Latin *vexare* to jostle]

via (*say* **vie**–a) *preposition*
by way or means of.
[Latin, way]

viable (*say* **vie**–a–b'l) *adjective*
1. practicable or workable; 'that plan does not seem *viable*'.
2. *Biology:* being able to live and grow independently.
Word Family: **viably**, *adverb*; **viability** (*say* vie–a–**billi**–tee), *noun.*
[French from Latin *vita* life]

viaduct (*say* **vie**–a–dukt) *noun*
a long bridge, especially one of arched masonry spanning a valley.
[Latin *via* way + *ductus* brought]

vial (*say* vile) *noun*
a phial.

vibrant (*say* **vie**–br'nt) *adjective*
vibrating.
Usages:
a) she has a *vibrant* personality' (= lively and energetic).
b) 'the painting was in *vibrant* colours' (= rich).
Word Family: **vibrantly**, *adverb*; **vibrancy**, *noun.*
[Latin *vibrare* to tremble]

vibraphone (*say* **vie**–bra–fone) *noun*
Music: a percussion instrument consisting of tuned metal bars which are struck with small, mechanical hammers.

vibrate (*say* vie–**brate**) *verb*
1. to throb or shake.
2. (of sounds) to sound or resound.
vibration (*say* vie–**bray**–sh'n) *noun*
a) the act of vibrating. b) a vibrating movement.
Word Family: **vibratory**, **vibrational**, *adjectives*; **vibrator**, *noun*, something which vibrates or causes vibration.

vibrato (*say* vi–**brah**–toe) *noun*
Music: the rapid alternation of two notes close in pitch. Compare TREMOLO.
[Italian]

vicar (*say* **vikka**) *noun*
1. *Christian:* an Anglican clergyman in charge of a parish. Compare RECTOR.
2. *Roman Catholic:* a representative: 'the Pope is considered the *vicar* of Christ'.
Word Family: **vicarage**, *noun*, the home of a vicar.
[Latin *vicarius* taking another's place]

vicarious (*say* vik–**airi**–us) *adjective*
1. done, received or undergone on behalf of someone else.
2. (*informal*) imagined through the experience of another: '*vicarious* pleasure'.
Word Family: **vicariously**, *adverb*; **vicariousness**, *noun.*
[Latin *vicarius* substituted]

vice (1) *noun*
1. a bad habit: 'smoking isn't one of my *vices*'.
2. immoral conduct.
[Latin *vitium* a blemish]

vice (2) *noun*
any of various instruments with two jaws which may be tightened to hold an object.
[Italian *vite* a screw]

vice–
a prefix meaning: a) deputy, as in *vice–admiral*; b) substitute, as in *viceroy.*
[Latin, in place of]

vice–admiral *noun*
a commissioned officer in the navy next in rank below an admiral.

vice–chancellor *noun*
the chief administrative officer of a university.

viceroy (*say* **vice**–roy) *noun*
a person, such as a governor, appointed to rule as a representative of a monarch.
Word Family: **viceregal** (*say* vice–**ree**–g'l), *adjective.*
[VICE– + French *roi* king]

vice versa
the other way around also.
[Latin]

vichy water (*say* **veeshi** wawta)
(*sometimes capital*) a mineral water.
[first obtained from springs at *Vichy*, France]

vicinity (*say* viss–**inni**–tee) *noun*
1. the area near or around a place.
2. closeness or proximity.
[Latin *vicus* a row of houses]

vicious (*say* **vishus**) *adjective*
1. fierce: 'a *vicious* animal'.
2. evil, spiteful or malicious: 'a *vicious* lie'.
Word Family: **viciously**, *adverb*; **viciousness**, *noun.*
[Latin *vitiosus* bad]

vicious circle
a situation in which a difficulty only leads to further problems or difficulties and eventually back to the first: 'if higher wages produce inflation and inflation produces higher wage claims, we are indeed in a *vicious circle*'.

vicissitude (*say* viss-**issi**-tewd) ***noun***
a change or variation, especially in fortune: 'he could not cope with life's little *vicissitudes*'.

victim ***noun***
a person or thing that suffers any harm or injury: a) 'a cemetery for war *victims*'; b) 'he's the *victim* of a confidence man'.
[Latin *victima* beast for sacrifice]

victimize, victimise ***verb***
1. to make a victim of.
2. to punish selectively or unfairly.
Word Family: **victimization,** ***noun.***

victory (*say* **vikta**-ree) ***noun***
a) success against an opponent, etc. b) an instance of this.
Word Family: **victor,** ***noun,*** a person or thing that achieves victory; **victorious** (*say* vik-**torius**), *adjective*; **victoriously,** *adverb.*
[from Latin]

victual (*say* **vitt'l**) ***noun***
(*plural*) any food prepared for eating.
victual *verb*
(victualled, victualling)
to supply with food or provisions.
Word Family: **victualler,** ***noun.***
[Latin *victus* food]

vicuña (*say* vik-**yoon**-ya) ***noun***
a) a South American animal related to the llama. b) the fine, silky fleece of this animal.
[Spanish]

vide (*say* **vee**-day) ***verb***
see.
[Latin]

video (*say* **vid**-ee-o) *adjective*
of or relating to television.
Word Family: **video,** ***noun,*** a) a kind of magnetic tape used for recording television programmes, b) a television set on which videotapes can be shown.
[Latin, I see]

video-tape ***noun***
a magnetic tape for recording film.
Word Family: **video-tape,** ***verb.***

vie *verb*
(vied, vying)
to compete or contend against.

view ***noun***
1. a) sight or vision. b) the range of this: 'the car sped into *view*'.
2. a particular way of looking at something: 'a general *view* of a topic'.
3. a) a sight of land, countryside, etc. b) a picture of this.
Usage: 'what are your *views* on marriage?' (= opinions, ideas).
Phrases:
a dim view, an unfavourable opinion.
in view of, '*in view of* the bad weather we'll stay home' (= considering).
on view, in a place for public inspection.
with a view to, 'she bought the car *with a view to* selling it at a profit' (= with the intention of).
view *verb*
1. to see or look at.
2. to regard or consider.
Word Family: **viewable,** *adjective.*
[French *vu* seen]

viewer ***noun***
1. a person or thing that views: 'a television *viewer*'.
2. a small device for lighting or magnifying photographic slides.

viewfinder ***noun***
Photography: a small window in a camera, through which the subject can be viewed.

viewpoint ***noun***
a point of view.

vigil (*say* **vijil**) ***noun***
a) the act of staying awake at night, especially to keep watch. b) a watch kept in this way.
[Latin *vigilia* wakefulness]

vigilant (*say* **viji**-l'nt) *adjective*
keenly attentive or watchful.
Word Family: **vigilantly,** *adverb*; **vigilance,** ***noun.***
[Latin *vigilans* keeping awake]

vigilante (*say* viji-**lan**-tee) ***noun***
a member of an unauthorized and usually extreme group who seek justice by their own means.
[Spanish, vigilant]

vignette (*say* vin-**yet**) ***noun***
1. a decorative design or small illustration without a clear-cut border.
2. a short, graceful literary description.
[French]

vigour (*say* **vigga**) ***noun***
in America spelt **vigor**
energetic strength or force.
Word Family: **vigorous,** *adjective*; **vigorously,** *adverb.*
[from Latin]

vile *adjective*
repulsive or disgusting: 'I'm shocked at your *vile* language'.
Usage: 'they lived in *vile* poverty' (= wretched).
Word Family: **vilely,** *adverb*; **vileness,** ***noun.***
[Latin *vilis* cheap]

vilify (*say* **villi**–fie) *verb*
(**vilified**, **vilifying**)
to speak maliciously of.
Word Family: **vilification**, *noun.*
[Latin *vilis* cheap + *facere* to make]

villa *noun*
any house, especially one in the suburbs or at a seaside resort.
[Latin]

village (*say* **villij**) *noun*
a) a populated area in the country, which is smaller than a town. b) its inhabitants.
Word Family: **villager**, *noun*, an inhabitant of a village.
[Latin *villa*, a country-house or farm]

villain (*say* **villun**) *noun*
1. an evil or wicked person
2. (*informal*) a rascal.
Word Family: **villainous**, *adjective*, wicked or evil; **villainy**, *noun*, a) evil conduct, b) an evil act.

villein (*say* villun) *noun*
Medieval history: a serf.
[Latin *villanus* a farmer]

villus *noun*
plural is **villi**
Biology: a small, finger-like projection, many of which line the small intestine and absorb digested food.
[Latin, shaggy hair]

vim *noun*
(*informal*) energy.
[from Latin]

vinaigrette (*say* **vinni**–gret) *noun*
1. a small ornamental container holding a sponge soaked in sal volatile. Also called a **smelling-bottle**.
2. a dressing for salads, etc. made of oil, vinegar and seasoning.
[French]

vinculum (*say* **ving**-kew-lum) *noun*
plural is **vincula**
Maths: the horizontal line separating the numerator and denominator of a fraction.

vindicate (*say* **vindi**-kate) *verb*
to clear from suspicion, blame, criticism, etc.
Word Family: **vindication**, *noun*, a) the act of vindicating, b) the state of being vindicated, c) defence or justification; **vindicatory**, *adjective.*
[Latin *vindicare* to lay claim]

vindictive (*say* vin-**diktiv**) *adjective*
vengeful or spiteful.
Word Family: **vindictively**, *adverb*; **vindictiveness**, *noun.*
[Latin *vindicta* vengeance]

vine *noun*
a) any plant that trails or climbs by winding its slender stem around or over a support. b) a grapevine.
[from Latin]

vinegar (*say* **vinni**–ga) *noun*
a sour liquid of diluted acetic acid, obtained by fermenting wine, beer, etc. and used for flavouring, pickling, etc.
Word Family: **vinegary**, *adjective.*
[French *vin* wine + *aigre* sour]

vineyard (*say* **vinyud**) *noun*
a plantation of grapevines.

vingt–et–un (*say* vant–ay–**un**) *noun*
also called **vingt–et** or **vingt–un**
Cards: pontoon.
[French, twenty–one]

viniculture (*say* **vinni**–kulcher) *noun*
1. the cultivation of grapevines.
2. the science or study of wine–making.

vin ordinaire (*say* van ordi–**nair**)
undistinguished, run–of–the–mill wine; plonk.
[French]

vintage (*say* **vintij**) *noun*
1. the grape harvest, especially that obtained in one year from a particular area.
2. any especially good wine.
Usage: (*informal*) 'his coat is of last year's *vintage*' (= production).
vintage *adjective*
1. (of wine) made or harvested during a particularly good year.
Usage: 'this has been a *vintage* year for travel books' (= especially good).
2. (of a motor vehicle) built between 1918 and 1930. Compare VETERAN.

vintner *noun*
a person who deals in or sells wines.
[Latin *vinetum* a vineyard]

vinyl (*say* **vie**–nil) *noun*
a substance derived from ethylene, compounds of which form plastics and resins.

vinyl chloride
Chemistry: a compound of vinyl and chlorine (formula CH_2CHCl), widely used in the plastics industry.

viol (*say* vile) *noun*
a medieval stringed instrument from which the violin, etc. developed.

viola (*say* vee–**ole**–a) *noun*
Music: a stringed instrument played with a bow, slightly larger and having a lower pitch than a violin.

violate (*say* **vie**–a–late) *verb*
to break a law, promise, agreement, etc.
Usages:
a) 'the temple was *violated* by obscene writings on the walls' (= desecrated, profaned).
b) 'the soldiers had *violated* the young women before shooting them' (= raped).
c) 'shouts from the street *violated* her peace and quiet' (= disturbed, broke in upon).
Word Family: **violator**, *noun*; **violation**, *noun*.
[Latin *violare* to do violent harm to]

violent (*say* **vie**–a–l'nt) *adjective*
having or showing great strength or power: a) 'a *violent* storm'; b) '*violent* abuse'.
Usages:
a) 'a *violent* temper' (= furious).
b) 'a *violent* headache' (= severe, extreme).
violence (*say* **vie**–a–l'nce) *noun*
a) the state of being violent. b) violent behaviour.
Usage: 'the *violence* of his feelings astonished her' (= strength, intensity).
do violence to, a) to injure or damage by rough treatment; b) to distort the meaning of.
Word Family: **violently**, *adverb*.

violet (*say* **vie**–a–let) *noun*
1. a small plant with fragrant, dark purple flowers and bright green leaves.
2. a) a deep bluish-red colour. b) the colour next to indigo at the end of the spectrum.
shrinking violet, (*informal*) a timid or retiring person.
Word Family: **violet**, *adjective*.
[from Latin]

violin (*say* vie–a–**lin**) *noun*
Music: a stringed, high-pitched instrument held horizontally between the chin and the neck and played with a bow.
Word Family: **violinist**, *noun*.
[Italian from Latin *vitulari* to make merry]

violoncello (*say* vie–a–lin–**chello**) *noun*
see CELLO.

viper *noun*
1. any of a group of thick-bodied, poisonous snakes, with erectile fangs, found in Europe, Africa and Asia, especially the adder.
2. a treacherous or malicious person.
Word Family: **viperish**, **viperous**, *adjectives*.
[from Latin]

virago (*say* vir**rah**–go) *noun*
a sharp-tongued, bad-tempered woman.
[Latin, a woman soldier]

viral (*say* **vie**–rul) *adjective*
Word Family: see VIRUS.

virgin (*say* **ver**–jin) *noun*
1. a person who has not had sexual intercourse.
2. *Astrology:* (*capital*) see VIRGO.
the Virgin, Mary, the mother of Christ.
virgin *adjective*
being a virgin.
Usages:
a) 'the *virgin* snow lay all about' (= pure, untouched).
b) '*virgin* soil' (= uncultivated).
Word Family: **virginal**, *adjective*, of, like or as pure as a virgin; **virginity** (*say* ver–**jinni**–tee), *noun*, the state or condition of being a virgin.
[from Latin]

virginal *noun*
also called **virginals**
Music: a small oblong type of harpsichord.

Virgo (*say* **ver**–go) *noun*
also called the **Virgin**
Astrology: a group of stars, the sixth sign of the zodiac.
[Latin]

virile (*say* **virr**ile) *adjective*
having or showing vigorous strength or forcefulness.
Word Family: **virility** (*say* vir**rilli**–tee), *noun*, the state or quality of being virile.
[Latin *virilis* like a man]

virology (*say* vie–**rolla**–jee) *noun*
the study of viruses and the diseases they cause.
Word Family: **virologist**, *noun*.

virtual (*say* **ver**–tew–ul) *adjective*
being something in effect but not in actual name or form: 'the accountant had so much power he was the *virtual* head of the company'.
Word Family: **virtually**, *adverb*, essentially.

virtue (*say* **ver**–tew) *noun*
a) the quality of moral goodness or excellence. b) a particular kind of moral excellence: 'patience is a *virtue*'.
Usages:
a) 'the villain forced the maiden to surrender her *virtue*' (= chastity).

b) 'the *virtue* of his plan lies in its simplicity' (= advantage, merit).
c) 'do you have faith in the *virtue* of mineral waters to produce cures?' (= power, effectiveness).
Phrases:
by virtue of, because of.
make a virtue of necessity, to do what one is forced to do with a good grace, or pretend to do it from a sense of duty.
Word Family: **virtuous**, *adjective*; **virtuously**, *adverb*; **virtuousness**, *noun*.
[Latin *virtus* courage, moral excellence]

virtuoso (*say* vertew–**o**–so) *noun*
plural is **virtuosi**
a person who displays masterly or dazzling skill in the arts, especially in music.
Word Family: **virtuosity** (*say* vertew–**ossi**–tee), *noun*, the skill of a virtuoso.
[Italian, skilful]

virulent (*say* **virr**a–l'nt) *adjective*
Medicine: causing severe effects on the patient.
Usage: 'he heaped *virulent* abuse upon my head' (= bitter).
Word Family: **virulently**, *adverb*; **virulence**, *noun*, the quality of being virulent.
[Latin *virulentus* poisonous (wound)]

virus (*say* **vie**–rus) *noun*
1. a tiny agent, too small to be seen with the light microscope, which can only multiply within a living cell and which may cause disease.
2. (*informal*) an illness caused by a virus.
Word Family: **viral** (*say* **vie**–rul), *adjective*, of, like or caused by a virus.
[Latin, poison]

visa (*say* **vee**za) *noun*
an official permit from a foreign country allowing a person to visit. Compare PASSPORT.
[Latin, seen]

visage (*say* **vizz**ij) *noun*
a person's face or facial expression.
[Latin *visus* seen]

vis–à–vis (*say* veez–a–**vee**) *preposition*
face to face with or in relation to: 'his position *vis–à–vis* the coming election was ambiguous'.
vis–à–vis *noun*
one's opposite number.
[French]

viscera (*say* **viss**era) *plural noun*
singular is **viscus** (*say* **vis**kus)
all the soft, inner organs in the cavities of the body, such as the lungs, stomach, heart, etc.
Word Family: **visceral**, *adjective*, a) of, relating to or affecting the viscera, b) arising from deep emotion, intuition, etc.
[Latin]

viscid (*say* **viss**id) *adjective*
sticky and thick, like heavy syrup or glue.
Word Family: **viscidly**, *adverb*; **viscidness**, **viscidity** (*say* vis–**siddi**–tee), *nouns*; **viscoid** (*say* **vis**–koyd), *adjective*, slightly viscid.
[Latin *viscum* birdlime]

viscose (*say* **vis**–kose) *noun*
1. *Chemistry:* a thick, brown, treacly liquid prepared from cellulose, used for making rayon, cellulose film for transparent wrappings, etc.
2. rayon made with viscose (formerly **viscose rayon**).

viscount (*say* **vie**–kount) *noun*
a nobleman ranking between an earl and a baron.
Word Family: **viscountess**, *noun*, a) a female viscount, b) the wife of a viscount; **viscountcy**, **viscounty**, *noun*.
[Latin *vice* in place of + COUNT]

viscous (*say* **vis**kus) *adjective*
sticky and having the consistency of heavy syrup or glue.
Word Family: **viscously**, *adverb*; **viscousness**, **viscosity** (*say* vis–**kossi**–tee), *nouns*.

vise *noun*
American: a vice.

visible (*say* **vizz**i–b'l) *adjective*
able to be seen: 'the road was scarcely *visible* through the fog'.
Usage: 'there's a *visible* discrepancy in the witnesses' accounts of the accident' (= marked, evident).
visibility (*say* vizzi–**billi**–tee) *noun*
1. the capability or degree to which sight is possible.
2. the distance at which things are visible: '*visibility* was down to 45 m the day the plane crashed'.
Word Family: **visibly**, *adverb*.
[Latin *visus* seen]

visible horizon
see HORIZON.

vision (*say* **vizh**'n) *noun*
1. the power of seeing: 'my *vision* is rather poor'.
2. something seen, actually or in the imagination: 'I switched on the T.V but got no *vision*, only sound'.

3. an apparition or prophetic dream.
Usages:
a) 'she was a *vision* in that blue dress' (= thing of beauty).
b) 'our leaders lack political *vision*' (= imaginative foresight).
visionary (*say* **vizh**'n-ree) *adjective*
a) imaginary: 'the *visionary* scene dissolved and I awoke'. b) impractical or dreamy: 'such *visionary* schemes will not help our nation'.
visionary *noun*
a) a person who has visions. b) an impractical or idealistic dreamer.

visit (*say* **vizzit**) *verb*
to go or come to see: 'have you *visited* the exhibition yet?'.
Usages:
a) 'we spent last month *visiting* relations' (= staying with).
b) 'her family was *visited* with great misfortune' (= afflicted).
Word Family: **visit,** *noun*; **visitor,** *noun*, a person or thing that visits.
[from Latin]

visitant (*say* **vizzi**-tant) *noun*
a visitor, especially a strange or supernatural being.

visitation (*say* vizzi-**tay**-sh'n) *noun*
a visit, especially one of official inspection.

visor (*say* **vie**-zor) **vizor** *noun*
1. the movable part of a helmet which protects the face.
2. a small movable shield set above the windscreen of a motor vehicle to protect the driver's eyes from the sun. Short form of **sun visor.** Also called a **sun shield.**

vista *noun*
a view, especially one seen through an opening or along a passage.
Usage: 'education should open up new *vistas*' (= mental possibilities).
[Italian, sight]

visual (*say* **viz**-yew'l) *adjective*
of or involving the sense of sight: '*visual* aids for teaching include maps, films, etc.'.
visualize, visualise *verb*
to form a mental image of: 'try to *visualize* the scene of the accident'.
Word Family: **visualization,** *noun*; **visually,** *adverb.*

vital (*say* **vie**-t'l) *adjective*
of, relating to or necessary for life: a) 'eating is a *vital* function'; b) 'the heart is a *vital* organ'.
Usages:
a) 'control of pollution is *vital* for the survival of our environment' (= essential, very important).
b) 'she was a *vital*, happy girl before the accident' (= full of life, vigorous).
c) 'industrialization dealt a *vital* blow to the cottage industries' (= causing ruin or death).
vital statistics, see STATISTICS.
vitals *plural noun*
the vital parts of the body, especially the lungs, heart and brain.
Word Family: **vitally,** *adverb.*
[Latin *vita* life]

vitality (*say* vie-**talli**-tee) *noun*
1. vigorousness of mind or body: 'her *vitality* decreased with the years'.
2. the power to endure or continue in activity.
Word Family: **vitalize, vitalise,** *verb,* to give vitality to.

vitamin (*say* **vie**-ta-min *or* **vitta**-min) *noun*
Biology: an organic dietary compound essential for the life and growth of organisms, but which does not supply energy and is only needed in very small amounts.
vitamin A
a vitamin found in fruit and vegetables which is essential for growth. Deficiency may cause night blindness and dry skin.
vitamin A_2
a compound very similar to vitamin A, found in the liver of freshwater fish.
vitamin B complex
an important group of water-soluble vitamins, including vitamin B_1, vitamin B_2, etc.
vitamin B_1
also called **thiamine**
a vitamin found in liver and cereal grains. Deficiency may cause beri-beri and neuritis.
vitamin B_2
also called **riboflavin**
a vitamin found in liver and milk. Deficiency may cause inflammation of the lips and tongue.
vitamin B_6
also called **pyridoxine**
a vitamin found in yeast, wheat, corn, liver, etc. Deficiency may cause convulsions and irritability.

vitamin C
also called **ascorbic acid**
a vitamin found in citrus fruits, vegetables, etc. Deficiency may cause scurvy.
vitamin D
a group of fat-soluble vitamins found in milk and the liver of fish. Deficiency may cause rickets.
vitamin E
a vitamin found in wheat-germ oil that promotes fertility in mammals and helps prevent miscarriages.
vitamin K_1
a vitamin found in vegetables, rice, etc., which promotes clotting of the blood.
vitamin P
a water-soluble vitamin found in citrus fruits and paprika. It is essential for growth of cell walls and capillaries.
[Latin *vita* life + AMINO]

vitiate (*say* **vishi**-ate) *verb*
to weaken or spoil the quality or force of.
Word Family: **vitiation**, *noun.*
[Latin *vitium* vice]

viticulture (*say* **vitti**-kulcher) *noun*
the planting and maintaining of grapevines.
[Latin *vitis* a vine + CULTURE]

vitreous (*say* **vit**-ree-us) *adjective*
glassy or resembling glass.
vitreous humour
Anatomy: the transparent jelly-like substance which fills the eyeball behind the lens. Compare AQUEOUS HUMOUR under AQUEOUS.
[Latin *vitrum* glass]

vitrify (*say* **vitri**-fie) *verb*
(**vitrified**, **vitrifying**)
to turn into glass: 'during the firing of pottery the glaze will *vitrify*'.
Word Family: **vitrification**, *noun.*
[Latin *vitrum* glass + *facere* to make]

vitriol (*say* **vit**-ree-ol) *noun*
Chemistry: any of various compounds of sulphuric acid, such as **blue vitriol** (copper sulphate) or **oil of vitriol** (concentrated sulphuric acid).
Usage: 'there's real *vitriol* in his pen portraits of our political leaders' (= biting criticism, malice).
Word Family: **vitriolic** (*say* vitri-**ollik**), *adjective.*
[Latin *vitrum* glass]

vituperation (*say* vit-yoopa-**ray**-sh'n) *noun*
bitter abuse or censure.
Word Family: **vituperative**, *adjective*, abusive; **vituperate**, *verb.*
[from Latin]

viva *noun*
short form of **viva voce** (*say* vie-va **vo**-chee)
an oral exam.
[Latin, with the living voice]

vivace (*say* viv-**ah**-chay) *adjective*
Music: lively.
[Italian]

vivacious (*say* viv-**ay**-shus) *adjective*
full of life and spirits.
Word Family: **vivaciously**, *adverb*; **vivaciousness**, **vivacity** (*say* viv-**assi**-tee), *nouns.*
[Latin *vivax* long-lived, brisk]

vivid *adjective*
intense: a) '*vivid* blue'; b) '*vivid* sunlight'.
Usages:
a) 'you certainly have a *vivid* imagination' (= lively, active).
b) 'I have a *vivid* recollection of that day' (= clear and distinct).
Word Family: **vividly**, *adverb*; **vividness**, *noun.*
[Latin *vividus* full of life]

viviparous (*say* viv-**ippa**-rus) *adjective*
of or relating to animals of which the young are born live and fully formed.
[Latin *vivus* alive + *parus* bringing forth]

vivisection (*say* vivvi-**sek**-sh'n) *noun*
the act of dissecting a living body, such as a cat, dog, etc., for medical research.
Word Family: **vivisectionist**, *noun*; **vivisect**, *verb.*
[Latin *vivus* alive + *sectus* cut]

vixen (*say* **vik**sen) *noun*
1. a female fox.
2. a vicious or bad-tempered woman.

Viyella (*say* vie-**ella**) *noun*
a soft fabric made of cotton and wool.
[a trademark]

viz *adverb*
namely.
[old abbreviation of Latin *videlicet* from Latin *videre* to see + *licet* it is permissible]

vizier (*say* **vizzi**-er) *noun*
also spelt **vizir**
a high Moslem official.
[Arabic *wazir*]

vizor *noun*
see VISOR.

vocabulary (*say* vo–**kab**–yoola–ree) *noun*
a) the whole range of words known and used by a person or group. b) a list of common words in a foreign language or book, with translations.
[Latin *vocabulum* a name]

vocal (*say* vo–k'l) *adjective*
1. of or spoken by the voice.
2. a piece of music with an accompanying song.
Usage: 'a *vocal* opponent of war' (= outspoken).
vocal cords
Anatomy: the two folds of membrane in the larynx which vibrate and produce sound when air is passed over them.
Word Family: **vocally**, *adverb*; **vocalness**, *noun*; **vocalist**, *noun*, a singer; **vocalize, vocalise**, *verb*, a) to speak, sing, shout, etc., b) to utter or make vocal.
[Latin *vocis* of a voice]

vocation (*say* vo–**kay**–sh'n) *noun*
a profession or occupation, especially one to which a person is particularly drawn or suited: 'she had a *vocation* for nursing'.
vocational *adjective*
of or relating to a vocation. **Vocational guidance** is professional help offered to students, etc. to help them choose a career.
[Latin *vocare* to call]

vociferous (*say* vo–**sifferus**) *adjective*
vehement or making a loud outcry: 'he was *vociferous* in his denials of all guilt'.
Word Family: **vociferously**, *adverb*; **vociferousness**, *noun*; **vociferate**, *verb*.
[Latin *vocis* of a voice + *ferre* to carry]

vodka *noun*
a strong liquor made from rye, corn or potatoes and originally made in Russia from wheat.
[Russian *voda* water]

vogue *noun*
the current fashion, style, etc.
Usage: 'that book was in *vogue* some years ago' (= popular).
[from Italian]

voice *noun*
1. a) the sounds made by a human being in speaking or singing. b) any similar sounds: 'the murmuring *voice* of the river'.
Usages:
a) 'he's lost his *voice*' (= the power of speaking or singing).
b) 'she demands that she have a *voice* in this matter' (= opinion, say).
2. *Grammar:* the change in the form of a verb to show whether a person or thing performs the action (**active voice**), or is acted upon (**passive voice**). *Examples*: a) the shop sells books (active). b) books are sold by the shop (passive).
give voice, to express or utter.
voice *verb*
1. to express: 'he *voiced* his opinion'.
2. *Language:* to utter with vibration of the vocal cords. *Example*: when saying the **th** in *this* and *thin* the lips and tongue are in the same position, but in *this* the **th** is voiced and in *thin* it is unvoiced.
voiceless *adjective*
1. having no voice.
2. *Language:* (of sounds) made without using the vocal cords, as in the letters **s** or **f**.
[from Latin]

voice box
see LARYNX.

voice–over *noun*
the commentary of an unseen speaker recorded on a film's soundtrack.

voice–print *noun*
the oral equivalent of a fingerprint, used in identifying anonymous telephone callers, etc. and consisting of a visual analysis of the characteristics of a voice.

void *noun*
empty space: 'the spaceship was swallowed up in the *void*'.
Usage: 'an aching *void* in one's heart' (= feeling of emptiness or loneliness).
void *adjective*
1. containing no matter: 'the *void* regions of outer space'.
Usage: 'the room was *void* of all furniture' (= empty, destitute).
2. having no legal effect: 'the court declared the contract *void*'.
Word Family: **void**, *verb*, to make void; **voidable**, *adjective*, (of a contract, etc.) having legal force but able to be cancelled.

voile *noun*
a soft, semi–transparent fabric used for dresses, etc.
[French, a veil]

volatile (*say* **volla**–tile) *adjective*
1. changing rapidly or readily from one mood, idea or state to another.

2. *Chemistry:* having a low boiling point, and so easily changing from a liquid into a vapour.
[Latin *volatilis* flying, fleeting]

vol-au-vent (*say* **vol**-o-von) *noun*
puff pastry filled with chicken, fish, etc. and a sauce.
[French, a puff of wind]

volcano (*say* vol-**kay**-no) *noun*
plural is **volcanoes**
a) a hole or fissure in the earth's crust, through which lava, hot gases and other fluids escape. b) the mountain, hill, etc. having such a hole or fissure and formed partly or wholly by material ejected in this way.
volcanic (*say* vol-**kan**nik) *adjective*
1. of, relating to or characteristic of a volcano: 'a *volcanic* eruption'.
2. *Geology:* of or relating to igneous rocks, such as tuff, formed at or above the earth's surface.
Word Family: **vulcanology** (*say* vulka-**nolla**-jee), *noun*, the study of volcanoes; **vulcanologist**, *noun.*
[after *Vulcan*, the ancient Roman god of fire]

vole *noun*
any of various small rodents resembling rats and mice, but having a heavier body and shorter tail.
[Scandinavian, a field]

volition (*say* vo-**lish**'n) *noun*
the act or power of using one's own will: 'I did it of my own *volition*'.
Word Family: **volitional**, *adjective*; **volitionally**, *adverb.*
[Latin *volo* I wish]

volley (*say* **vol**-ee) *noun*
1. the simultaneous firing of a number of weapons.
Usage: 'a *volley* of oaths' (= string).
2. *Tennis:* a return of the ball before it has hit the ground.
Word Family: **volley** *verb.*
[French *volée* flight]

volleyball *noun*
a) a game played on a court with a high net, usually between two teams of six players, the aim being to stop the ball touching the ground by hitting it over the net by hand. b) the ball used in this game.

volt (*rhymes with* bolt) *noun*
the SI unit of electric potential.
[after *Alessandro Volta*, 1745-1827, an Italian physicist]

voltage (*say* **vole**-tij *or* **vol**tij) *noun*
Electricity: the potential difference expressed in volts.

voltaic cell (*say* vol-**tay**-ik sel)
Electricity: see GALVANIC CELL.

voltameter (*say* vol-**tam**mita) *noun*
Electricity: an instrument for measuring an electric current by means of the amount of metal deposited or gas liberated from an electrolyte in a given time by the passage of the current.

volte-face (*say* volt-**fahce**) *noun*
an about-face.
[Italian *voltare* to turn + *faccia* the face]

voltmeter *noun*
an instrument used to measure potential difference in volts.

voluble (*say* **vol**-yoo-b'l) *adjective*
talking or able to talk easily or readily.
Word Family: **volubly**, *adverb*; **volubility** (*say* vol-yoo-**billi**-tee), *noun.*
[Latin *volubilis* revolving]

volume (*say* **vol**-yoom) *noun*
1. the amount of space a body takes up.
2. a quantity or amount, especially a large quantity: a) 'the *volume* of business we do is steadily increasing'; b) '*volumes* of smoke billowed from the tyre factory'.
3. a book, especially one of a set of books.
4. (of sounds) the loudness.
speak volumes, 'his guilty start *spoke volumes*' (= expressed a great deal).
[Latin *volumen* a roll of manuscript]

volumetric (*say* vol-yoo-**met**rik) *adjective*
of or relating to volume.
volumetric analysis
Chemistry: any of various methods of quantitative chemical analysis involving measuring the volumes of reacting substances.

voluminous (*say* vol-**yoomin**-us) *adjective*
of great size, extent, etc.: a) '*voluminous* skirts'; b) 'Napoleon's *voluminous* correspondence'.
Word Family: **voluminously**, *adverb*; **voluminousness**, *noun.*

voluntary (*say* **vol**lun-tree) *adjective*
1. done or acting of one's own free choice, without being compelled or motivated by hopes of reward: 'I made a *voluntary* statement to the police'.
2. supported by voluntary contributions: 'the Red Cross is a *voluntary* organization'.

3. occurring through conscious control: 'speech is a *voluntary* activity, the beating of the heart is not'.
voluntary *noun*
Music: an organ solo played as the congregation enters or leaves the church.
Word Family: **voluntarily** (*say* vollun-**tairi**-lee), *adverb.*
[Latin *voluntas* a wish]

volunteer (*say* vollun-**teer**) *noun*
a person who offers to do something of his own free will, such as a soldier who is not conscripted.
Word Family: **volunteer,** *verb,* a) to offer voluntarily, b) to come forward as a volunteer.

voluptuous (*say* vol-**up**-tewus) *adjective*
luxuriously sensuous or sensual.
Word Family: **voluptuously,** *adverb;* **voluptuousness,** *noun;* **voluptuary,** *noun,* a person who devotes himself to voluptuous pleasures.
[Latin *voluptas* pleasure]

volute (*say* va-**loot**) *noun*
1. *Biology:* any of the whorls of a spiral shell.
2. any spiral or twisted shape.
[Latin *volutus* rolled]

vomit *verb*
to bring up the contents of the stomach through the mouth; to be sick.
Usage: 'the volcano *vomited* lava high into the air' (= ejected forcibly).
Word Family: **vomit,** *noun,* the matter ejected when vomiting.
[from Latin]

voodoo *noun*
also called **hoodoo**
a) the practices of some people of the West Indies, especially Haiti, involving sorcery and witchcraft. b) a charm or fetish used in such practices.
Word Family: **voodoo,** *verb,* to affect by voodoo or sorcery; **voodooism,** *noun.*
[Creole]

voracious (*say* vo-**ray**-shus) *adjective*
very greedy: 'a *voracious* appetite'.
Usage: 'she is a *voracious* reader of sentimental novels' (= eager and untiring).
Word Family: **voraciously,** *adverb;* **voraciousness, voracity** (*say* vo-**rassi**-tee), *nouns.*
[Latin *vorax* devouring]

vortex (*say* **vor**-teks) *noun*
plural is **vortices** (*say* **vorti**-seez) or **vortexes**
a whirling mass of water, air, etc., such as a whirlpool or whirlwind.
Usage: 'the *vortex* of war' (= violent movement, irresistible force).
[Latin]

votary (**vo**-ta-ree) *noun*
a) a person who has bound himself by a vow, such as a monk or nun. b) any devoted follower.
Word Family: **votaress,** *noun,* a female votary.
[Latin *votus* vowed]

vote *noun*
an expression of preference for a candidate, proposal, etc.
Usages:
a) 'the suffragettes demanded the *vote* for women' (= the right to vote).
b) 'the *vote* was for delaying the church picnic until after the vicar's funeral' (= majority decision).
c) 'the Independent *vote* was lower than last year's' (= total number of votes).
d) 'a *vote* of thanks' (= expression).
vote *verb*
to cast a vote: 'I *voted* for Hislop'.
Usages:
a) 'the children *voted* the trip a great success' (= declared by general consent).
b) 'I *vote* we ask him to do the dishes' (= suggest, propose).
Word Family: **voter,** *noun,* a person who votes or has the right to vote.
[Latin *votum* a vow]

votive (*say* **vo**-tiv) *adjective*
1. given in fulfilment of a vow.
2. expressing a wish or prayer: 'the old woman lit a *votive* candle for her missing son'.

vouch *verb*
to guarantee: 'I can *vouch* for the truth of his story'.

voucher (*say* **vow**-cha) *noun*
a) a document, receipt, etc. which proves that a certain sum of money has been spent. b) a document or form which may be used in place of cash to buy certain items. c) any similar document.

vouchsafe *verb*
to grant graciously or condescendingly.

vow *noun*
a solemn promise or declaration: 'marriage *vows*'.
Word Family: **vow,** *verb,* to make a vow.

vowel *noun*
Language: a) a sound made without blockage of the breath. b) the letters which express these sounds, being **a**, **e**, **i**, **o** and **u**. Compare CONSONANT.

voyage (*say* **voy**–ij) *noun*
a journey, especially one in a ship.
Word Family: **voyage**, *verb*, to go on a voyage; **voyager**, *noun*.

voyeur (*say* voy–**er**) *noun*
a person who gains sexual pleasure by looking at pictures, watching others undressing, etc.
Word Family: **voyeurism**, *noun*.
[French, looker]

vulcanite (*say* **vulka**–nite) *noun*
a hard, black substance made by heating rubber with an excess of sulphur. It is used for making buttons, combs, etc. and for electrical insulation.

vulcanize (*say* **vulka**–nize) **vulcanise** *verb*
Chemistry: to heat rubber with sulphur to increase its elasticity and durability, e.g. for car tyres. The hardness of the rubber depends on the amount of sulphur used.
Word Family: **vulcanization**, *noun*.
[after *Vulcan*, the ancient Roman god of fire]

vulcanology *noun*
Word Family: see VOLCANO.

vulgar *adjective*
1. showing a lack of good taste, manners or breeding: 'he told a *vulgar* story at dinner'.
2. unrefined or of the common people: 'a century ago ordinary people were known as the *vulgar* herd'.

vulgarity (*say* vul–**garri**–tee) *noun*
1. the quality or character of being vulgar.
2. a vulgar word, gesture, etc.

vulgarize, vulgarise *verb*
1. to make vulgar.
2. to popularize.
Word Family: **vulgarly**, *adverb*; **vulgarian** (*say* vul–**gairian**), *noun*, a vulgar person; **vulgarizer**, *noun*; **vulgarization**, *noun*; **vulgate**, *noun*, the popular or common language.
[Latin *vulgus* the masses, the people, the public]

vulnerable (*say* **vul**–n'ra–b'l) *adjective*
capable of being hurt, damaged or attacked: a) 'she is very *vulnerable* to criticism'; b) 'the troops were in a *vulnerable* position'.
Word Family: **vulnerably**, *adverb*; **vulnerability** (*say* vulnera–**billi**–tee), *noun*.
[Latin *vulneris* of a wound]

vulpine (*say* **vul**–pine) *adjective*
of or like foxes.
[Latin *vulpes* fox]

vulture (*say* **vul**–cher) *noun*
1. a large scavenging bird of prey.
2. a greedy, ruthless person who preys on the misfortunes of others.
[from Latin]

vulva *noun*
plural is **vulvae** (*say* **vul**–vee) or **vulvas**
Anatomy: the area immediately around the clitoris and the openings of the urethra and vagina in females.
[Latin]

vying *verb*
the present participle of the verb **vie**.

Ww

wacky *adjective*
see WHACKY.

wad (*say* wod) *noun*
1. any soft mass, e.g. of fabric.
2. any paper, banknotes, etc. folded or rolled together.
wadding *noun*
any soft substance used for padding or packing.
Word Family: **wad** (**wadded, wadding**), *verb*, a) to make into a wad, b) to fill out with a wad or wadding.

waddle (*say* **wodd'l**) *verb*
to walk with short swaying steps.
Word Family: **waddle**, *noun*.

wade *verb*
to walk through any substance, such as water, mud, etc., which makes progress difficult.
Usage: 'I *waded* through the boring book' (= proceeded with difficulty).
wader (*say* **way-der**) *noun*
1. a person or thing that wades, such as a long-legged bird which wades in water looking for food.
2. (*plural*) waterproof boots reaching to the top of the legs.
Word Family: **wade**, *noun*.

wadi (*say* **woddi**) **wady** *noun*
a desert watercourse which carries water only after heavy rain.
[Arabic]

wafer *noun*
1. any thin flat sheet or slice.
2. a sweet, thin biscuit.
3. *Christian:* a thin disc of unleavened bread used in the Eucharist.

waffle (1) (*say* **woff'l**) *noun*
a flat cake made from batter cooked in a special mould.

waffle (2) (*say* **woff'l**) *noun*
(*informal*) any vague or nonsensical speech or writing.
Word Family: **waffle**, *verb*.

waft (*say* woft) *verb*
to carry or float gently, especially through the air: 'the voices *wafted* up from the street below'.
Word Family: **waft**, *noun*, a) a wafting movement, b) a sound or smell carried through the air.

wag *verb*
(**wagged, wagging**)
to move from side to side or up and down, especially quickly.
wag *noun*
1. a wagging movement.
2. a person who teases or plays jokes.
Word Family: **waggish**, *adjective*, full of jokes or mischief.

wage *noun*
1. a payment to an employee, usually on an hourly or weekly rate. Compare SALARY.
2. (*plural, used with singular verb*) an old word meaning reward: 'the *wages* of sin is death'.
wage *verb*
to engage in: 'to *wage* war'.

wager *noun*
a bet.
Word Family: **wager**, *verb*.

waggle *verb*
to wag with quick, short movements.

wagon, waggon *noun*
any of various four-wheeled vehicles, usually for carrying heavy loads.
on the wagon, (*informal*) abstaining from alcoholic drink.

wagtail *noun*
any of a large group of small birds with a slender body and long, narrow tail which is habitually wagged up and down.

waif *noun*
a homeless neglected person, especially a child.

wail *verb*
to make a long, high, mournful cry.
Usage: 'stop *wailing* about your bad luck' (= complaining).
Word Family: **wail**, *noun*.

wain *noun*
a poetic word for a cart or wagon.

wainscot *noun*
any wooden panelling at the foot of the walls of a room.

wainwright *noun*
a person who makes wagons.

waist *noun*
1. *Anatomy:* the slender part of the human body between the ribs and hips.
2. the part of a garment covering the waist.

waistcoat *noun*
a closely fitting, sleeveless jacket reaching to the waist, sometimes worn under a jacket.

wait *verb*
1. to stay or rest in expectation: a) '*wait* here till I return'; b) 'you'll have to *wait* your turn'.
2. to remain neglected for a time: 'is this urgent or can it *wait*?'.
Phrases:
wait on, wait upon, to serve or attend personally, e.g. at table or in a shop.
wait up, to stay awake at night in expectation.
wait *noun*
the act or time of waiting: 'a long *wait* for the bus'.
lie in wait, to wait in ambush.

waiter *noun*
a man who waits at table, e.g. as in a restaurant.
Word Family: **waitress,** *noun,* a female waiter.

waive (*say* wave) *verb*
to give up or not insist on: 'the eldest son *waived* his right to inherit his father's title'.
Word Family: **waiver,** *noun,* the intentional relinquishing of a right, etc.

wake (1) *verb*
(woke, woken or **waked, waking)**
1. to rouse from sleep: a) 'I *woke* late'; b) 'don't *wake* the baby'.
2. to rouse into full alertness or awareness: 'she finally *woke* to what I meant'.
wake up, to stop sleeping.
wake *noun*
1. a watch, especially one at night before or after a funeral.
2. (*usually plural*) name in northern England for workers' holidays.
Word Family: **waking,** *adjective,* being awake.

wake (2) *noun*
the pattern of disturbed water left behind a moving ship.
in the wake of, following or as a result of.

wakeful *adjective*
1. unable to sleep.
2. with little sleep: 'she passed a restless, *wakeful* night'.
Usage: 'he deluded himself that he was surrounded by *ever–wakeful* enemies' (= vigilant).
Word Family: **wakefully,** *adverb*; **wakefulness,** *noun.*

waken *verb*
to rouse from sleep.
Usage: 'how can I *waken* your interest?' (= excite).

wale *noun*
1. a weal.
2. a ridge or raised line in a fabric, especially in knitting.

walk (*say* wawk) *verb*
to go or proceed on foot at a moderate pace.
Phrases:
walk off with, a) to steal; b) to win easily.
walk out, to go on strike.
walk out on, to abandon or desert.
walk out with, to go courting.
walk *noun*
a) the act of walking. b) a place, distance or time of walking. c) a manner of walking: 'what an odd *walk* he has'.
Phrases:
walk of life, 'she met people from all *walks of life*' (= occupations, activities).
walk–on part, a part in a play in which one comes on stage but has no lines to speak.

walkabout *noun*
1. *Aboriginal:* a period of wandering.
2. (of monarchs, heads of state, etc.) an informal stroll through the crowd: 'the Queen went *walkabout* in Sydney'.

walkie–talkie *noun*
a light radio device which combines a transmitter and receiver and which can be carried and operated while moving.

walking stick
a narrow stick, carried or used as a support when walking.

walkout *noun*
a walking out or leaving as an act of protest, such as a strike.

walkover *noun*
(*informal*) an unopposed or easy victory.

wall (*rhymes with* ball) *noun*
1. a solid upright structure used for supporting, surrounding or dividing: a) 'the brick *walls* of a house'; b) 'a defensive *wall* surrounding the city'.

2. something resembling a wall in shape or solidity: a) 'a *wall* of fire'; b) 'a *wall* of prejudice'.
3. *Biology:* the outside layer surrounding an organ or cell.
Phrases:
walls have ears, beware of eavesdroppers.
wall-to-wall, (of carpeting) covering the whole floor.
with one's back to the wall, in a very difficult situation.
wall *verb*
to enclose, shut off or divide with or as with a wall.
[Latin *vallum* a rampart]

wallaby (*say* **wolla**-bee) *noun*
any of a large group of Australian marsupials, similar to kangaroos but smaller and furrier. [Aboriginal]

wallet (*say* **woll**it) *noun*
a small folding holder for paper money, stamps, etc. carried in the pocket.

wall-eyed *adjective*
having eyes with an abnormal amount of white, often associated with blindness.

wallflower *noun*
1. a perennial plant with sweet-scented flowers.
2. (*informal*) a girl left partnerless at a dance.

wallop (*say* **woll**up) *verb*
(*informal*) a) to strike heavily. b) to defeat soundly.
Word Family: **wallop,** *noun,* a forceful blow or impact; **walloping,** *noun,* a thrashing.

wallow (*say* **woll**o) *verb*
to roll about: 'the children *wallowed* happily in the snow'.
Usage: 'the rich man *wallowed* in luxury' (= indulged fully).

wallpaper *noun*
any paper, usually with a decorative pattern, for covering interior walls.
Word Family: **wallpaper,** *verb.*

walnut (*say* **wawl**-nut) *noun*
1. a) the edible wrinkled kernel of a large and handsome deciduous tree. b) the wood of this tree, used to make furniture.
2. a very dark brown colour.
[for *Welsh* (that is, foreign) *nut*]

walrus (*say* **wawl**-russ) *noun*
an arctic marine mammal, related to the seal, having two long tusks.

waltz (*rhymes with* false) *noun*
a) a ballroom dance in which partners revolve in a one-two-three rhythm. b) the music for such a dance in triple time.
waltz *verb*
1. to dance a waltz.
2. to move lightly and quickly.
Usage: 'he *waltzed* off with first prize' (= took easily).
[German *walzen* to revolve]

wan (*rhymes with* on) *adjective*
pale or sickly.
Word Family: **wanly,** *adverb.*

wand (*say* wond) *noun*
1. a stick, such as one used by a conjurer performing magic tricks.
2. a rod or staff used as a symbol of authority on ceremonial occasions.

wander (*say* **won**da) *verb*
1. to move or roam aimlessly or casually.
2. to leave the right path or direction.
Word Family: **wander,** *noun,* a casual walk or stroll; **wanderer,** *noun.*

wanderlust (*say* **won**da-lust) *noun*
a strong urge to travel or roam about. [German]

wane *verb*
1. *Astronomy:* to decrease in size, as the moon's face does in changing from full moon to new moon. Compare WAX
2. to decrease in power or intensity.
wane *noun*
the act or process of waning.
on the wane, decreasing.

wangle *verb*
(*informal*) to accomplish, especially by scheming or indirect methods.
Word Family: **wangle,** *noun.*

wank *verb*
(*informal*) to masturbate.
Word Family: **wanker,** *noun* a weak person.

Wankel engine
a rotary engine which instead of pistons has rotors shaped like triangles with curved sides, and dispenses with clutch, crankshaft and valves.
[after *F. Wankel,* born 1902, a German engineer]

want (*say* wont) *verb*
to desire: 'I *want* a bicycle for Christmas'.
Usages:
a) 'your hair *wants* a cut' (= should have).
b) 'he is *wanted* by the police' (= being sought).
c) 'I *want* Leonie please' (= require to see, speak to, etc.).
want for, 'she never *wants for* money' (= is short of).

want *noun*
1. a) the state of wanting: 'the garden is in *want* of water'. b) something wanted: 'money is not his most important *want*'.
2. lack: 'I took this job for *want* of anything better'.

wanting *adjective*
1. lacking or deficient: 'you are *wanting* in manners, young lady'.
2. simple-minded: 'I think he's a bit *wanting*'.

wanton (*say* **won**-t'n) *adjective*
1. pointless or unprovoked: '*wanton* cruelty'.
2. unrestrained or wild: '*wanton* profusion'.
Word Family: **wanton,** *noun,* an old word for an immoral woman; **wantonly,** *adverb*; **wantonness,** *noun.*

wapiti *noun*
see ELK.

war (*say* wor) *noun*
1. the use of armed forces in a conflict, especially between countries.
2. any conflict: 'a propaganda *war*'.
Word Family: **war (warred, warring),** *verb,* to engage in war or conflict; **warfare,** *noun,* war; **warlike,** *adjective,* a) of, like, ready for or fond of war, b) hostile.

warble (*say* **wor**-b'l) *verb*
to sing with trills or vibrations.
warbler *noun*
a person or thing that warbles, especially any of various types of birds.

ward (*rhymes with* ford) *noun*
1. a district, especially an electoral district, of a town or city.
2. *Law:* any person under the care of a guardian.
3. any of the separate divisions of a large building, e.g. in a hospital, gaol, castle, etc.
ward *verb*
ward off, to avert or repel.
Word Family: **wardship,** *noun,* care or custody.

-ward, -wards
a suffix indicating direction, as in *onward.*

warden (*say* **wor**-d'n) *noun*
a person having control or superintendence over: 'a hostel *warden*'.

warder (*say* **wor**-da) *noun*
a guard or officer in a gaol.

wardrobe (*say* **wor**-drobe) *noun*
1. a large cupboard for storing and hanging clothes, etc.
2. any collection of clothes.

wardroom *noun*
Nautical: the room where officers eat.

ware (1) (*rhymes with* care) *noun*
1. manufactured goods of a specified type: a) '*silverware*'; b) '*hardware*'.
2. (*plural*) any articles for sale.

ware (2) (*rhymes with* care) *verb*
an old word meaning to beware of.

warehouse *noun*
a large building where goods are stored, such as one in which a wholesaler keeps his stock.

warfare (*say* **wor**-fare) *noun*
Word Family: see WAR.

war games
also called **scenario analysis**
the application of game theory to warfare or potential warfare in an effort to select the most effective strategy whatever the other side may do, and especially to forecast likely stages in the controlled escalation of nuclear warfare.

warhead (*say* **wor**-hed) *noun*
the front part of a self-propelled missile, containing the explosive charge.

warily (*say* **wair**-illee) *adverb*
Word Family: see WARY.

warlike *adjective*
Word Family: see WAR.

warlock (*say* **wor**-lok) *noun*
a male witch.

war lord
the military leader of a warlike nation, tribe, etc.

warm (*rhymes with* form) *adjective*
1. moderately hot.
2. involving lively or enthusiastic feeling: 'a *warm* welcome'.
3. (of colour) towards the reddish tones.
warm *verb*
to make or become warm or warmer.
warm up, to practise or do exercises before a game, performance, etc.
Word Family: **warmly,** *adverb*; **warmth,** *noun,* a) moderate heat, b) affection or enthusiasm; **warmer,** *noun,* anything which makes or keeps things warm.

warm-blooded *adjective*
also called **homoiothermic**

Biology: having a constant body temperature, e.g. birds and mammals. Compare COLD-BLOODED.

warm front
Weather: see FRONT.

warm-hearted *adjective*
cordial or sympathetic.
Word Family: **warm-heartedly,** *adverb.*

warming pan
a long-handled, metal vessel filled with hot coals, etc. formerly used to warm a bed.

warmly *adverb*
Word Family: see WARM.

warmonger (*say* **wor**-munga) *noun*
a person eager for or provoking war.

warmth *noun*
Word Family: see WARM.

warm-up *noun*
the act of warming up.

warn (*say* worn) *verb*
to inform in advance, especially of possible unpleasant consequences: 'I *warn* you not to be late or I'll be angry'.
Word Family: **warning,** *noun*; **warningly,** *adverb.*

warp (*say* worp) *verb*
to twist or bend out of shape.
Usage: 'don't listen to his *warped* ideas' (= distorted, biased).
warp *noun*
1. a bend, twist or distortion.
2. the yarn placed lengthwise in a loom to form the basis of a fabric. Compare WEFT.

warpath *noun*
on the warpath, very angry.

warrant (*say* **worrunt**) *noun*
1. a justification or authorization: 'you've got no *warrant* for such an accusation'.
Usage: 'what *warrant* of success is there?' (= guarantee).
2. *Law:* a document giving authority: a) 'a *warrant* of arrest'; b) 'a death *warrant*'.
Word Family: **warrant,** *verb,* a) to authorize, b) to justify, c) to guarantee.

warrant officer
an army officer who ranks between commissioned and non-commissioned officers.
[appointed by Secretary of State's *warrant*]

warranty (*say* **worrun**-tee) *noun*
an assurance.

warren (*say* **worrun**) *noun*
an area where rabbits breed and abound.

warrior (*say* **worri**-a) *noun*
a soldier or fighter.

wart (*say* wort) *noun*
a small hard swelling on the skin, caused by a viral infection.
warts and all, (of portraits, etc.) not omitting defects and blemishes.

wart-hog *noun*
a large African pig with two large tusks and wart-like growths on the face.

wary (*say* **wair**-ee) *adjective*
careful or guarded.
Word Family: **warily,** *adverb*; **wariness,** *noun.*

was (*say* woz) *verb*
the first and third person singular, past tense of the verb **be**.

wash (*rhymes with* posh) *verb*
1. a) to clean with water or other liquid. b) to cover or wet with a liquid, e.g. in order to separate gold from gravel.
Usage: 'your excuse won't *wash*' (= convince).
2. a) to flow: 'the waves *washed* against the cliff'. b) to carry with a flow: 'the river *washed* away the hillside'.
Phrases:
wash down, a) to wash thoroughly; b) to swallow food with the aid of liquid.
washed out, 'the sports meeting was *washed out*' (= abandoned owing to rain).
wash up, to wash dishes, cutlery, etc. after a meal.
wash *noun*
1. an act or instance of washing: 'give your hair a good *wash*'.
2. any clothes, etc. washed or to be washed.
3. any liquid with which something is washed: '*whitewash*'.
4. the pattern of disturbed water made by a moving boat.
5. *Geography:* a formation of alluvial deposits.
6. *Art:* a thin watery pigment spread over a surface.
come out in the wash, to come out all right in the end.
Word Family: **washable,** *adjective.*

washboard *noun*
1. a board or frame with a ridged surface on which clothes may be rubbed while washing them.

2. such a device scratched or scraped as a musical accompaniment in jazz, etc.

washed–out *adjective*
(*informal*) a) pale or faded. b) exhausted.

washed–up *adjective*
(*informal*) ruined or finished.

washer (*say* **wosha**) *noun*
1. a person or thing that washes.
2. any flat circular piece of metal, rubber or leather with a hole in the centre, used with a nut and bolt to give tension or to seal a joint.

washing *noun*
1. the act of washing.
2. any clothes, etc. washed or to be washed.

washing soda
crystalline sodium carbonate used to soften water.

wash–out *noun*
a failure or fiasco.

washroom *noun*
American: a room with toilets, basins, etc., especially one in a large building.

washstand *noun*
a support for a bowl and jug for washing.

wasp (*say* wosp) *noun*
any of a very varied group of insects, of which the best-known are yellow and black, have a painful sting and live in colonies.
WASP, (*American*) an acronym for White Anglo-Saxon Protestant.

waspish (*say* **wospish**) *adjective*
irritable or given to spiteful, stinging remarks.
Word Family: **waspishly,** *adverb.*

waste *verb*
a) to use unnecessarily or without purpose: 'she *wastes* money'. b) to fail to use: 'he *wasted* the perfect opportunity'.
Usages:
a) 'his body was *wasted* with disease' (= emaciated).
b) 'the country was *wasted* with war' (= ruined, devastated).
waste *noun*
1. the act of wasting: 'a *waste* of time'.
2. something which is not or cannot be used, e.g. refuse, desert, unproductive land, etc.
lay waste, to destroy or devastate.
waste *adjective*
1. desolate: 'the *waste* spaces of the world'.
2. no longer wanted or useful: '*waste* paper'.
Word Family: **wastage,** *noun,* loss due to waste, etc.; **wasteful,** *adjective*; **wastefully,** *adverb*; **wastefulness,** *noun.*
[Latin *vastus* empty]

watch (*say* wotch) *verb*
to look at or look out attentively.
Usage: 'who's *watching* the shop while you're away?' (= minding, guarding).
Phrases:
watching brief, a brief to attend a court case on behalf of someone not, or not yet, involved.
watch over, to guard or protect.
watched pot never boils, impatience only makes the waiting period seem longer.
watch *noun*
1. a) the act of watching: 'keep a *watch* on my clothes'. b) a period of time for watching or keeping guard, especially on a ship.
2. any small clock designed to be worn or carried.
Word Family: **watchful,** *adjective,* alert; **watchfully,** *adverb*; **watchfulness,** *noun.*

watch–dog *noun*
1. a dog kept to guard property.
2. (*informal*) any watchful guardian.

watchmaker *noun*
a person who makes and repairs watches.

watchman *noun*
a person who keeps watch, e.g. at night in an empty factory.

watchword *noun*
1. a short phrase summarizing a guiding principle: 'let "safety first" be our *watchword*'.
2. a slogan, especially of a political party.
[originally a password]

water (*say* wawta) *noun*
1. *Chemistry:* hydrogen oxide (formula H_2O), a colourless, odourless, tasteless, liquid.
2. (*sometimes plural*) the water or liquid of a river, sea, mineral spring, tide, etc.
3. any liquid secretion, especially urine.
4. a solution of a substance in water: '*rosewater*'.
5. a wavy pattern, e.g. on a fabric.
6. the degree of transparency or brilliance of a diamond or other gem.
Phrases:
hold water, to prove sound or valid.

in deep water, in trouble.
like water, 'he spends money *like water*' (= very freely).
throw cold water on, to discourage.
water under the bridge, 'all that is *water under the bridge*' (= in the past and cannot be remedied).
water *verb*
1. to wet with water.
2. to supply with water.
3. to dilute with water.
4. (of the eyes or mouth) to secrete, or fill with, water: 'the smoke made his eyes *water*'.
watered down, less vivid or weakened.

Water-bearer *noun*
Astrology: see AQUARIUS.

waterbed *noun*
a bed consisting of a plastie or rubber mattress filled with water and set into a wooden frame.

water-boatman *noun*
a long-legged insect which skims over the surface of fresh water.

water-buffalo *noun*
the large buffalo of tropical Asia, often domesticated as a work animal.

water-cannon *noun*
a device for projecting powerful jets of water, used in quelling riots, etc.

water-chestnut *noun*
the edible nut-like fruit of an aquatic plant, much used in Chinese cooking.

water-closet *noun*
short form is **w.c.**
a toilet.

watercolour *noun*
a) a pigment mixed with water. b) a painting done with such pigment. c) the art or method of using such pigments.

watercourse *noun*
a) a stream or river. b) the bed of a stream or river.

watercress *noun*
a herb, the pungent leaves of which are used in salads and soups.

water diviner
a person who tries to find water or minerals under the earth, often using a Y-shaped stick called a **divining rod**.

water equivalent
Physics: see HEAT CAPACITY.

waterfall *noun*
a steep fall or flow of water from a height.

water-gas *noun*
Chemistry: a gas made by passing steam over red-hot coke, used as a fuel.

water-hammer *noun*
a pressure wave, created e.g. by suddenly turning off a tap in a domestic water system, and causing a pipe to vibrate with a thump against a wall, floorboard, etc.

waterhen *noun*
see MOORHEN.

water-hole *noun*
a well, spring or hollow where water collects naturally.

waterlily *noun*
a plant which grows from rhizomes in the mud at the bottom of ponds, etc., having large, flat leaves and big flowers which float on the surface of the water.

waterline *noun*
the level reached by the water on the side of a boat.

waterlogged *adjective*
excessively filled or saturated with water.
Word Family: **waterlog** (**waterlogged, waterlogging**), *verb.*

watermark *noun*
1. a mark showing the extent to which water rises, as in a river or on a beach.
2. a mark or design in paper, visible when held to the light, indicating its quality, authenticity, etc.

watermelon *noun*
a very large, green fruit with a hard skin and juicy red flesh with many pips.

water-pipe *noun*
see HOOKAH.

water-pistol *noun*
a toy gun which sprays water.

water-polo *noun*
a game played in a swimming-pool in which each team tries to throw the ball into the opponent's goal.

waterproof *adjective*
permitting no water to enter or pass through.
Word Family: **waterproof**, *verb*; **waterproofing**, *noun*, material used to make something waterproof.

watershed *noun*
Geography: a boundary between areas drained by different river systems.
Usage: 'the event is a historical *watershed*' (= dividing point).

[a translation of German *Wasserscheide* water-boundary]

water-skiing *noun*
the sport of skimming over water on skis when towed by a motor boat.

water-softener *noun*
any substance added to hard water to counteract the effect of its mineral content.

water-soluble *adjective*
able to dissolve in water.

waterspout *noun*
1. a downpipe.
2. *Weather:* a whirling, funnel-shaped mass of cloud and water, formed at sea.

water-table *noun*
the level below which porous rocks are saturated with water.

watertight *adjective*
made so that water cannot enter or leak through.
Usage: 'she had a *watertight* excuse' (= foolproof).

water-tower *noun*
a large tank raised above the ground to regulate the flow and give pressure to a town's water system.

water-vapour *noun*
gaseous water, below the critical temperature for water, the presence of which governs the humidity of the atmosphere.

waterway *noun*
a navigable canal or river.

waterwheel *noun*
a wheel which is turned by the force of water striking the blades or buckets attached to it.

water-wings *plural noun*
an inflatable device worn under the arms by people learning to swim.

waterworks *plural noun*
1. the system of buildings and structures by which water is provided for a town, etc.
2. (*informal*) a) the urinary system. b) tears.

watery *adjective*
1. of or like water.
2. containing much or too much water.
3. (of colour, etc.) pale or weak.
Word Family: **wateriness**, *noun.*

watt (*say* wot) *noun*
the SI unit of power.
Word Family: **wattage**, *noun*, the amount of electrical power expressed in watts.
[after *James Watt*, 1736–1819, a Scottish inventor]

wattle (*say* **wott'l**) *noun*
1. any of the Australian acacias.
2. the branches of trees intertwined with twigs to make fencing.
3. a fold of skin, often brightly coloured, hanging from the throat, especially in birds.

waul (*say* wawl) *verb*
to give a long piercing cry.

wave *noun*
1. a ridge or swell moving on the surface of a body of water, e.g. on the sea.
2. a surging or swelling movement: 'a *wave* of relief passed over him'.
Usage: 'a fresh *wave* of infantry came into the attack' (= surging mass).
3. a change in temperature passing over a large area: 'a *heatwave*'.
4. an up-and-down or to-and-fro movement: 'a *wave* of the hand'.
5. a rising curve or series of curves.
6. *Physics:* a regular, progressive vibration by which energy is transmitted through a medium without any net movement of the medium itself.

wave *verb*
to move in a wave or waves.
Usage: 'she *waved* me to a seat' (= indicated with a wave of the hand).
Word Family: **wavy**, *adjective*; **wavily**, *adverb*; **waviness**, *noun.*

waveband *noun*
short form is **band**
the range of frequencies allocated for particular purposes or to broadcasting or other telecommunication stations.

wavelength *noun*
Physics: the distance in a wave between two points of equal phase. *Example*: in waves at sea, the wavelength is the distance between two successive crests. In electromagnetic radiation the wavelength is in inverse proportion to the frequency.

wave mechanics
Physics: the mathematical analysis of the behaviour of elementary particles, which has shown that it has wave-like characteristics.

waver *verb*
to sway to and fro.
Usage: 'not sure what to think, he *wavered* between the two opinions' (= was undecided or uncertain).
Word Family: **waveringly**, *adverb.*

wax (1) *noun*
any of a variety of solid, non-greasy, organic substances with a low melting point.
Word Family: **wax,** *verb,* to rub, cover or polish with wax; **waxy, waxen,** *adjectives,* a) of, like or covered with wax, b) pale white or yellow in colour; **waxiness,** *noun.*

wax (2) *verb*
Astronomy: to increase in size, as the moon's face does in changing from new moon to full moon. Compare WANE.
Usage: 'she *waxed* eloquent with the wine' (= became, grew).

wax-paper *noun*
any paper made waterproof by a coating of wax.

waxwork *noun*
a) a model of the human figure in wax. b) (*plural*) an exhibition of such models.

way *noun*
1. a course: a) 'which is the *way* home?'; b) 'a *railway*'.
Usages:
a) 'get out of the *way*' (= line of passage, sight, etc.).
b) 'it's a long *way* to Tipperary' (= distance).
c) 'which *way* did they go?' (= direction).
d) 'make *way* for the lady with the pram' (= room, space).
e) 'she insists on paying her own *way*' (= expenses).
2. a course of action or proceeding: a) 'do it the *way* I told you'; b) 'there are many *ways* of looking at this problem'.
Usages:
a) 'he's a good man in many *ways*' (= respects).
b) 'he dislikes the *ways* of the city' (= habits, customs).
c) 'since the accident John has been in a bad *way*' (= state of health, condition).
d) 'we shall find a *way*' (= solution).
Phrases:
by the way, see BY.
by way of, '*by way of* a change, let's have some peace and quiet' (= as).
give way, a) to yield; b) to collapse.
go out of one's way, to make a special effort.
have a way with, to be skilful in dealing with.
in a way, to a certain extent.
in the family way, (*informal*) pregnant.
look the other way, to connive at or pretend not to have seen.
nothing out of the way, nothing extraordinary or uncommon.
no way!, (*informal*) it is absolutely impossible.

wayfarer *noun*
a traveller, especially one on foot.
Word Family: **wayfaring,** *noun.*

waylay *verb*
(waylaid, waylaying)
to lie in ambush for and attack suddenly.

way-out *adjective*
(*informal*) very unusual, eccentric or excellent.

wayward (*say* **way-wud**) *adjective*
1. wanting one's own way: 'a *wayward* child'.
2. irregular or unsteady: 'a *wayward* breeze'.
Word Family: **waywardness,** *noun.*

we *pronoun*
singular is **I**
1. the first person plural nominative pronoun, used to represent the speaker and one or more others: '*we* bought the books'.
2. (used by a monarch or by an editor when referring to himself or herself in formal speech or writing) '*we* are not amused'.
see US, OUR and OURS.

weak *adjective*
1. not strong: a) 'a *weak* cup of tea'; b) 'a *weak* leader'.
2. *Grammar:* see REGULAR.
weakness *noun*
the state or quality of being weak.
Usages:
a) 'even strong characters have a few *weaknesses* in them' (= weak points, slight faults).
b) 'I have a *weakness* for pretty girls' (= fondness, liking).
Word Family: **weaken,** *verb,* to make or become weak or weaker; **weakly,** *adverb.*

weak-kneed (*say* week-need) *adjective*
easily frightened or intimidated.

weakling *noun*
a feeble person or animal.

weal (1) *noun*
also called a **wale**
a raised mark on the skin caused by a whip or cane.

weal (2) *noun*
an old word for happiness or well-being.

weald (*say* weeld) *noun*
an old word for the formerly thickly wooded country of parts of south-east England.

wealth (*say* welth) *noun*
any goods, assets, currency or property which have value.
Usage: 'the painter uses a *wealth* of bright colours' (= abundance).
Word Family: **wealthy**, *adjective*; **wealthily**, *adverb.*

wean *verb*
1. to introduce a child or other mammal to food other than its mother's milk.
2. to gradually turn away from: 'try and *wean* her off cigarettes'.

weapon (*say* wepp'n) *noun*
any instrument used for fighting.
Word Family: **weaponry**, *noun*, any or all weapons.

wear (*say* wair) *verb*
(wore, worn, wearing)
1. to have or carry on the body, face, etc.: a) 'he *wears* a beard and spectacles'; b) 'he *wears* a constant frown'.
2. to impair or be impaired by use, exposure to the elements, etc.: 'some rocks *wear* more quickly than others'.
3. to make or become by constant use, exposure, etc.: a) 'he *wore* a hole in his sock'; b) 'my patience is *wearing* thin'.
Usages:
a) 'your arguments are *wearing* my nerves' (= exhausting).
b) 'he *wears* his age well' (= bears, carries).
c) 'the day *wore* on' (= passed gradually or tediously).
Phrases:
wear out, a) to make or become unuseable through constant use; b) to exhaust.
wear the trousers, 'she *wears the trousers* in that household' (= dominates her husband).
wear *noun*
1. a) the act of wearing: 'my shoes are a bit the worse for *wear*'. b) damage or loss of quality from use: 'there's quite a bit of *wear* on that front tyre'.
2. things to wear: 'beach *wear*'.
Phrases:
fair wear and tear, no more than the normal damage from usage.
the worse for wear, a) damaged by use; b) not looking one's (or its) best.
Word Family: **wearer**, *noun*; **wearable**, *adjective.*

weary (*say* **weer-ee**) *adjective*
very tired.
Word Family: **weary (wearied, wearying)**, *verb*; **wearily**, *adverb*; **weariness**, *noun*; **wearisome**, *adjective*, causing fatigue.

weasel (*say* **wee-z'l**) *noun*
1. a) a small, flesh-eating, ferret-like mammal with reddish-brown fur. b) any of a group of similar animals.
2. (*informal*) a cunning, sneaky person.
weasel *verb*
weasel out, (*informal*) to evade a commitment, obligation, etc.

weather (*say* **we*th*-a**) *noun*
the state of the atmosphere at a given place and time, described by temperature, rainfall, wind, etc.
Phrases:
make heavy weather of, to make difficulties for oneself in doing something.
under the weather, (*informal*) not feeling very well.
weather *verb*
1. to go or come through safely: a) 'the ship *weathered* the storm'; b) 'the young man *weathered* the crisis'.
2. a) to expose to the weather. b) to show the effects of exposure to the weather: 'granite *weathers* slowly'.

weather-beaten *adjective*
1. seasoned or hardened by exposure to the weather.
2. damaged or showing the ill effects of exposure to the weather.

weatherboard *noun*
a thin plank of wood used in overlapping rows to cover the outside walls of a house.

weather map
also called a **synoptic chart**
a map of collected weather information such as pressure given in isobars, for a region at a certain time and used in forecasting.

weather strip, weather-stripping
a protective strip covering a space, e.g. where a door meets its frame, to keep out draughts and rain.

weathervane *noun*
also called a **weathercock**
a device consisting of a pole with a piece of metal, often in the shape of a rooster, which spins in the wind and indicates its direction.

weave (*say* weev) *verb*
(**wove** or **weaved, woven, weaving**)
1. to intertwine threads, etc. to make a fabric: 'to *weave* a rug'.
Usage: 'she *wove* the flowers through her hair' (= intertwined).
2. to move in a twisting and turning path: 'the drunk *weaved* across the road'.
Word Family: **weave,** *noun,* the style of weaving; **weaver,** *noun.*

web *noun*
1. anything made of interlaced threads: 'a spider's *web*'.
2. any complex network: 'a *web* of roads across the country'.
3. *Biology:* a piece of skin joining two digits on the foot of some animals and birds that swim, such as ducks.
Word Family: **webbed,** *adjective.*

webbing *noun*
a strong, woven fabric made from hemp, cotton, etc. and used in upholstery.

weber *noun*
the derived SI unit of magnetic flux.

wedding *noun*
a marriage ceremony.
Word Family: **wed** (**wedded** or **wed, wedding**), *verb.*
[Old English *weddian* to pledge]

wedge (*say* wej) *noun*
1. a) any solid triangular or tapered implement or piece used to split a piece of wood or to fix something firmly. b) something which has the shape or function of a wedge: a) 'a *wedge* of pie'; b) 'a flying *wedge* of Rugby players'.
2. *Golf:* a club with a wedge-shaped base, used to lift the ball out of sand, etc.
thin end of the wedge, a small change or demand that is likely to lead to big changes or demands.
wedge *verb*
1. to fix in place with a wedge: '*wedge* the wheels or the car will roll'.
2. to split with a wedge.
3. to crowd or force into a narrow space: 'we were tightly *wedged* into the lift'.

wedlock *noun*
the state, relationship or bondage of marriage.

Wednesday (*say* **wenz**-day) *noun*
the fourth day of the week.
[named after the ancient German god *Woden*]

wee *adjective*
tiny: 'he's only a *wee* lad'.

weed *noun*
1. a troublesome or useless plant, especially one growing where it is not wanted.
2. (*informal*) a thin, unhealthy-looking person.
weed *verb*
to remove weeds.
weed out, to remove, especially something which is undesirable or unwanted.
Word Family: **weedy,** *adjective,* a) full of weeds, b) (of a plant) of poor, straggling growth, c) (of a person) thin and unhealthy.

weeds *plural noun*
the clothes, usually black, worn by a widow in mourning.

week *noun*
1. a period of seven days.
2. the period of time devoted to work during a week: 'the unions are asking for a 35-hour *week*'.
weekly *adjective*
of, done or occurring once a week or every week.
weekly *noun*
a newspaper or periodical published once a week.
Word Family: **weekly,** *adverb,* once a week.

weekday *noun*
any day of the week except Sunday.

weekend *noun*
Saturday and Sunday.

weeny *adjective*
(*informal*) very small.

weep *verb*
(**wept, weeping**)
to shed tears.
Usage: 'the tree was *weeping* sap where the branch had been torn off' (= dripping).
Word Family: **weepy,** *adjective,* (informal) inclined to weep; **weepie,** *noun* (informal) a sentimental film or novel.

weevil *noun*
any of a group of beetles with elongated heads which eat grain, nuts, etc.
Word Family: **weevilly,** *adjective,* infested with weevils.

weft *noun*
also called a **woof**
the yarn that is interlaced horizontally between the warp on a loom.

weigh (*say* way) *verb*
a) to find the weight of. b) to have weight: 'I *weigh* more than my sister'.
Usages:
a) 'I advise you to *weigh* your decision carefully' (= consider).
b) 'she was *weighed* down by sorrow and guilt' (= burdened).
c) 'her testimony *weighed* heavily against the accused' (= counted).
Phrases:
weigh anchor, to raise or hoist the anchor.
weigh in, (*Sport*) to be weighed before or after a competition in which qualifications are based on weight, as in boxing or horseracing. *Word Family:* **weigh-in**, *noun.*

weighbridge *noun*
a platform onto which a motor vehicle may be driven to measure its weight when loaded up.

weight (*say* wate) *noun*
1. the amount or degree of heaviness.
2. *Physics:* the force of gravitational attraction between two bodies, especially that between any massive body and the earth. Compare GRAVITY and MASS (1).
3. a) a solid object used as a standard in weighing. b) an object used to hold something in place or down: 'a *paperweight*'. c) (*often plural*) an object used in weight-lifting such as a dumbbell. d) see SHOT.
Usages:
a) 'I am bowed down by a *weight* of care' (= burden).
b) 'I called you here to discuss a matter of some *weight*' (= importance).
Phrases:
carry weight, to have influence or importance.
pull one's weight, to do one's full share.
throw one's weight around, to exercise one's authority more than is necessary.

weight *verb*
1. to add weight to: 'they *weight* a diver's suit to help him sink'.
2. to burden or oppress: 'he is *weighted* with care'.
Word Family: **weightless**, *adjective,* a) having little or no weight, b) experiencing little or no gravitational pull; **weightlessness**, *noun*; **weighty**, *adjective,* having great weight; **weightily**, *adverb*; **weightiness**, *noun.*

weighting *noun*
1. *Maths:* multiplying some items of a group of statistics by factors which reflect their relative importance.
2. an extra allowance to reflect the higher cost of living in certain areas.

weight-lifting *noun*
the sport of lifting barbells, etc.
Word Family: **weight-lifter**, *noun.*

weir (*say* weer) *noun*
a dam across a watercourse, over which the water may flow.

weird (*say* weerd) *adjective*
1. supernatural: 'a *weird* light surrounded the headless horseman'.
2. (*informal*) odd or strange: 'the *weird* hairstyles kids wear these days'.
Word Family: **weirdly**, *adverb*; **weirdness**, *noun*; **weirdie**, **weirdo**, *nouns,* (informal) a bizarre or freakish person.

welch *verb*
see WELSH.

welcome (*say* welkum) *adjective*
gladly received or admitted: a) 'a *welcome* guest'; b) 'a *welcome* letter'.
Usage: 'you're *welcome* to whatever money I have' (= free to use, take, etc.).
you're welcome, a conventional response to 'thank you'.
Word Family: **welcome**, *noun*; **welcome**, *verb,* to give a welcome to; **welcome!**, *interjection.*

weld *verb*
1. to join metals, plastics, etc. by applying heat and melting them together.
2. to unite closely or intimately.
Word Family: **weld**, *noun*; **welder**, *noun.*

welfare (*say* wel-fair) *noun*
1. a state of well-being, either physical or mental.
2. any aid given to those in need.
welfare state
a state in which the government assumes primary responsibility for the social welfare of its members, e.g. through unemployment benefits, health insurance, etc.

welkin *noun*
an old word for the sky.
[Old English *wolcen* a cloud]

well (1) *adverb*
(better, best)
satisfactorily, commendably or favourably: 'if you do *well* the boss will give you a bonus'.

Usages:
a) 'they have the money to live *well*' (= comfortably, in an affluent manner).
b) 'you would do *well* to say nothing at this stage' (= prudently).
c) 'I don't know him *well*' (= intimately).
d) 'the whole business will have to be *well* looked into' (= thoroughly).
e) 'we are *well* behind America in space research' (= far).
Phrases:
as well, a) 'he's trimmed his beard, and cut his hair *as well*' (= in addition, besides); b) 'he might *as well* have given it away' (= with equal effect).
as well as, 'he's surly *as well as* ignorant' (= in addition to being).
just as well, a) preferable; b) 'it was *just as well* you came in time' (= lucky).
very well, a) 'I can't *very well* refuse him a favour' (= with reason or propriety); b) 'you know *very well* you can't do that' (= undeniably); c) '*very well*, leave me alone to shiver in the cold' (= all right, certainly).
well *adjective*
1. in a satisfactory state: 'four bells, and all's *well*'.
2. a) in good health: 'I feel *well*'. b) cured or healed: 'make me *well*, doctor'.
3. advisable or prudent: 'it is *well* not to swim immediately after eating'.
leave well alone, to leave things as they are for fear of making them worse.
Word Family: **well**, *interjection*, a) an exclamation expressing surprise, indignation, etc., b) an exclamation used to cover a pause, begin a speech, etc.

well (2) *noun*
1. a hole drilled in the earth, to obtain water, oil, sulphur, etc.
2. something which has the shape or function of a well: a) 'a *stairwell*'; b) 'an *inkwell*'.
well *verb*
to rise or flow up like water in a spring: a) 'blood *welled* up out of the wound'; b) 'her eyes *welled* with tears'.

well-appointed *adjective*
properly equipped, furnished, etc.

well-balanced *adjective*
1. properly balanced, adjusted or regulated.
2. sensible or sane.

well-being *noun*
the state of being healthy, happy or prosperous.

well-connected *adjective*
having useful connections with important or influential people.

well-earned *adjective*
thoroughly deserved.

well-established *adjective*
1. having a reliable reputation and an apparently stable and successful future: 'a *well-established* firm'.
2. unlikely to change or give way: a *well-established* usage'.

well-heeled *adjective*
(*informal*) wealthy.

wellingtons *plural noun*
also called **wellies**
see GUMBOOT.
[after the *Duke of Wellington*]

well-lined *adjective*
(*informal*) (of a purse, pocket, etc.) full of money.

wellnigh *adverb*
almost: 'I *wellnigh* died of fright'.

well-off *adjective*
1. in fortunate circumstances.
2. (*informal*) wealthy.

wellspring *noun*
an origin or source, as of a stream or spring.

well-to-do *adjective*
wealthy.

well-turned *adjective*
1. nicely formed: 'a *well-turned* ankle'.
2. pleasingly expressed: 'a *well-turned* compliment'.

well-worn *adjective*
worn through use: a) '*well-worn* carpets'; b) 'a *well-worn* saying'.

welsh, welch *verb*
(*informal*) to evade paying: 'to *welsh* on a bet'.
Word Family: **welshĕr**, *noun*.

Welsh corgi
see CORGI.

Welsh rabbit
toasted, seasoned cheese on toast.
[the name is a joke; there is no justification for the genteel variation *Welsh rarebit*]

welt *noun*
1. a stripe raised on the skin by a blow.
2. a strip of cloth or covered cord sewn into a seam to strengthen it.
3. the strip of leather attaching the upper and sole of a shoe.
Word Family: **welt**, *verb*, to furnish with a welt or welts.

welter *noun*
1. a rolling movement, as of waves.
2. a confusion or medley, e.g. of thoughts.
3. *Horseracing:* a race in which all horses carry more weight than normally.
Word Family: **welter**, *verb*, to lie or wallow in a liquid.

welterweight (*say* **welta–wate**) *noun*
a weight division in boxing, not more than 67 kg for amateurs and professionals.

wench *noun*
an old or jocular word for a girl or young woman, often a farm girl or servant.
Word Family: **wench**, *verb*, to keep company with wenches.

wend *verb*
an old word for to go: 'to *wend* one's way home'.

went *verb*
the past tense of the verb **go**.

wept *verb*
the past tense and past participle of the verb **weep**.

were (*say* wer) *verb*
the plural and second person singular past indicative of the verb **be**.

werewolf (*say* **weer–wulf**) **werwolf** *noun*
plural is **werewolves**
Folklore: a person who is able to turn into a wolf.
[Old English *wer* man + WOLF]

Wesleyan *noun*
see METHODIST.

west *noun*
a) the direction of the sun at sunset. b) the cardinal point of the compass at 90° to the left of north and opposite east.
the West
1. *Geography:* a) Western Europe. b) western America.
2. *Politics:* a) the non-Communist countries of Europe, North America and associated countries, e.g. Australia, New Zealand and South Africa. b) European civilization, as distinct from the East, etc.
Word Family: **west**, *adjective*, *adverb*.

West End
the City of Westminster and adjacent areas, in which are situated the palaces, government buildings and the main hotel, theatre and shopping districts of London.

westerly (*say* **westa–lee**) *adjective*
(of a direction, course, etc.) from or towards the west.
westerly *noun*
a wind coming from the west.
Word Family: **westerly**, *adverb*.

western *adjective*
(of a place) situated in the west.
Word Family: **western**, *noun*, (informal) a film or book about frontier America, cowboys, etc.

Weston cell
Electricity: a cadmium–mercury cell used as a standard of electromotive force.

westward (*say* **west–wud**) *adjective*
toward the west.
Word Family: **westwards**, *adverb*, towards the west.

wet *adjective*
1. a) covered or soaked with water or some other liquid. b) still in a liquid state: '*wet* paint'.
2. having a rainy climate.
3. allowing the consumption of alcohol: 'a *wet* State'.
4. (*informal*) stupid or senseless: 'how *wet* can you get?'.
wet behind the ears, see EAR.
wet *verb*
(**wet** or **wetted**, **wetting**)
to make wet.
wet one's whistle, (*informal*) to have a drink.
Word Family: **wet**, *noun*, a) moisture, b) rainy weather, c) (informal) a stupid person.

wet and dry
see EMERY.

wet blanket
(*informal*) a person or thing that has a discouraging or depressing effect.

wet cell
Electricity: see CELL.

wet dream
(of males) a sexually exciting dream which is accompanied by an ejaculation of semen during sleep.

wether (*say* **wetha**) *noun*
a castrated male sheep or goat.

wet nurse
a woman hired to breastfeed another woman's child.
Word Family: **wet–nurse**, *verb*.

wet suit
a garment, usually made of neoprene, worn by divers, etc. It does not prevent water getting in, but restricts the flow,

maintaining a warm layer of water around the wearer.

wetting agent
Chemistry: a substance which lowers the surface tension of a liquid, increasing its spreading, penetrating and wetting properties.

whack *noun*
(*informal*) a) a sharp, resounding stroke or blow. b) the noise made by such a blow.
Usages:
a) 'have a *whack* at the job' (= attempt, go).
b) 'a large *whack* of the money went in taxes' (= part).
Word Family: **whack,** *verb,* (informal) to strike sharply.

whacking *adjective*
(*informal*) very big.

whacky, wacky *adjective*
(*informal*) crazy.

whale (*say* wale) *noun*
1. any of a group of very large, marine mammals found in all oceans and hunted for their oil, bone and flesh.
2. (*informal*) something which is extremely good or large: 'we had a *whale* of a time'.
Word Family: **whale,** *verb,* to hunt whales.

whaleboat *noun*
also called a **whaler**
a long boat pointed at both ends, formerly used for hunting whales.

whalebone *noun*
the horny plates hanging from the upper jaw of toothless whales.

wham (*say* wam) *verb*
(**whammed, whamming**)
to hit or strike with a loud sound.
Word Family: **wham,** *noun,* a) a solid blow or impact, b) the noise made by such a blow.

wharf (*say* worf) *noun*
plural is **wharves** (*say* worvz)
a permanent landing place where ships are loaded and unloaded.
wharfage *noun*
a) the storage of goods on a wharf. b) the charge for the use of a wharf.
Word Family: **wharfie,** *noun,* (informal) a waterside worker.

what (*say* wot) *pronoun*
1. a) which particular thing?: '*what* shall we order to eat?'. b) of which kind or character?: '*what* is this plant?'. c) of how much value, significance, etc.?: '*what* is money to a dying man?'.
2. that which or the thing that: 'this is *what* I think'.
Phrases:
and what have you, and what not, and anything else that there may be.
what about?, '*what about* going to the theatre?' (= what do you say to the idea of).
what (ever) next!, (*informal*) is there anything that could be more outrageous, ridiculous, etc.
what for, (*informal*) severe treatment or punishment.
what for?, why?
what it takes, the necessary ability, personality, etc.
what of it?, what does it matter?
what's what, the true position.
what *adjective*
which one or ones of a number?: '*what* dress shall I wear?'.
Usage: 'her bad temper spoilt *what* fun we could have had' (= any possible).
what *adverb*
how?: '*what* does it matter?'.
whatever, whatsoever *pronoun*
1. everything or anything that: 'do *whatever* you like'.
2. no matter what: 'go *whatever* happens'.
Word Family: **whatever,** *adjective.*

wheat (*say* weet) *noun*
a cereal plant used to make flour.
Word Family: **wheaten,** *adjective.*

Wheatstone bridge (*say* **wetstun brij**)
Electricity: an electrical instrument used to measure resistance accurately. [invented by *C. Wheatstone,* 1802–75, an English physicist]

wheedle (*say* **wee-d'l**) *verb*
to persuade or obtain by flattery, etc.
Word Family: **wheedler,** *noun.*

wheel (*say* weel) *noun*
1. a) any circular construction which turns on a central axis. b) something resembling a wheel in construction or movement, such as the steering device on a vehicle.
2. an old instrument of torture, consisting of a circular frame on which a person was stretched, while his limbs were broken by beating.
Phrases:
at the wheel, a) at the wheel of a vehicle; b) in control or command.
put one's shoulder to the wheel, to exert oneself greatly.
wheels within wheels, complicated motives and influences.

Word Family: **wheel**, *verb*, a) to revolve or rotate, b) to turn or whirl around.

wheelbarrow *noun*
a vehicle, usually with a single wheel at one end and handles at the other, used in gardening, etc.

wheelbase *noun*
the distance between the front and rear axles of a vehicle.

wheelchair *noun*
a chair with wheels which may be operated by hand or mechanically, used by invalids, etc.

wheeler-dealer *noun*
(*informal*) a shrewd or cunning schemer or trader.
Word Family: **wheeler-dealing**, *noun*.

wheelwright (*say* weel-rite) *noun*
a person who makes or repairs wheels, wheeled carriages, etc.

wheeze (*say* weez) *verb*
to breathe with difficulty, producing a whistling sound.
Word Family: **wheeze**, *noun*; **wheezy**, *adjective*; **wheezily**, *adverb*; **wheeziness**, *noun*.

whelk (*say* welk) *noun*
any of a group of large, spiral gastropods, used as food.

whelp (*say* welp) *noun*
the young of a dog, wolf, or similar mammal.
Usage: (*informal*) 'what a useless *whelp* he is' (= youth).

when (*say* wen) *adverb*
at what time?: '*when* will breakfast be ready?'.
when *conjunction*
1. then at that time: 'we were about to leave *when* there was a knock on the door'.
2. at what time: 'learning *when* to be quiet'.
3. at any time: 'I get annoyed *when* I am kept waiting'.
4. while or whereas: 'she sat down *when* she should have remained standing'.
when *pronoun*
what or which time?: 'since *when* have you been in charge?'.
whenever, whensoever *conjunction*
at any time that: 'leave *whenever* you like'.

whence (*say* wence) *adverb, conjunction*
an old word meaning from what place, source, origin, etc.: 'he asked me *whence* I came'.

where (*say* wair) *adverb*
1. at or in what place?: a) '*where* could they be?'; b) '*where* did you hear that?'.
2. to what place?: '*where* are you going now?'.
where *conjunction*
1. in or at what place, position, etc.: 'find *where* the leak is'.
2. in or at the place, position, etc. in which: 'my purse is not *where* I left it'.
3. to which or any place that: 'you may wander *where* you wish'.
where *pronoun*
1. the place in which: 'this is *where* I lost it'.
2. what place?: 'from *where*?'.
whereabouts *adverb*
in, at or near what location? *Word Family*: **whereabouts**, *noun*.
whereas *conjunction*
1. while on the contrary: 'he was late, *whereas* I was early'.
2. it being the case that.
whereby *adverb, conjunction*
by what or by which: 'she blushed, *whereby* I guessed she was lying'.
wherefore *adverb, conjunction*
for what purpose or reason? *Word Family*: **wherefore**, *noun*, a purpose or reason.
whereupon *adverb, conjunction*
at, after or upon which.
wherever, wheresoever *adverb, conjunction*
in, at or to whatever place.
wherewithal *noun*
the necessary means.

whet (*say* wet) *verb*
(**whetted, whetting**)
to sharpen a knife, etc. by grinding.
Usage: 'to *whet* one's appetite with savouries' (= stimulate, heighten).

whether (*say* we*th*a) *conjunction*
1. if it is so that: 'tell me *whether* you are considering my proposal'.
2. either: '*whether* by luck or skill, she got the right answer'.

whetstone (*say* wet-stone) *noun*
a fine, abrasive stone used for sharpening tools, etc.

whew (*say* few) *interjection*
an exclamation of relief, amazement, etc.

whey (*say* way) *noun*
the milk serum which separates as a watery liquid from curd when it coagulates, as in cheese-making.

which (*say* witch) *adjective*
1. a particular one or ones?: '*which* kitten do you like best?'.
2. being previously mentioned: 'four hours, during *which* time we slept'.
which *pronoun*
1. a thing, person, event, etc. previously mentioned or implied: 'the book, *which* has a red cover, is mine'.
2. any one: 'choose *which* you'd like'.
3. a thing or circumstance that: 'and, *which* is worse, he lost his passport'.
whichever, whichsoever *pronoun*
1. any one or ones: 'take *whichever* you want'.
2. no matter which: '*whichever* you choose, people will criticize your choice'.

whiff (*say* wif) *noun*
1. a faint odour carried in the air.
2. a slight, gentle gust of air.
3. an inhalation or exhalation of air, smoke, etc.
Word Family: **whiff**, *verb.*

Whig (*say* wig) *noun*
History: a member of the British political party which supported the superiority of Parliament over the monarchy. Compare TORY.
[*whiggamore* a nickname for a Scottish presbyterian who supported the Roundheads, from *whig* to drive + MARE]

while (*say* wile) *noun*
a period of time: 'a *while* ago'.
Phrases:
once in a while, occasionally.
the while, 'we have been searching the woods and all *the while* you were sitting here' (= during this time).
worth one's while, worth one's time, effort, etc.
while, whilst *conjunction*
1. during or in the time that: '*while* you are here I shall bake a cake'.
2. although: '*while* I am flattered by the offer, I can't marry you'.
while *verb*
to spend time pleasantly or idly: 'to *while* away the day'.

whim (*say* wim) *noun*
a sudden fancy or desire.

whimper (*say* wimpa) *verb*
to cry with low, broken sounds.
Word Family: **whimper**, *noun*; **whimperer**, *noun*, a person who whimpers.

whimsical (*say* wimzi-k'l) *adjective*
1. having fanciful or odd ideas.
2. quaint or quaintly funny.
Word Family: **whimsically**, *adverb*; **whimsy, whimsey**, *noun.*

whine (*say* wine) *verb*
1. to make a low complaining cry or sound.
2. to complain in an annoying way.
Word Family: **whine**, *noun*; **whiny**, *adjective*; **whiner**, *noun.*

whinge (*say* winj) *verb*
to complain in an annoying way.

whinny (*say* winnee) *verb*
(of a horse) to neigh.
Word Family: **whinny**, *noun.*

whip (*say* wip) *verb*
(**whipped, whipping**)
1. to strike or beat with quick repeated strokes.
2. a) to flog as punishment. b) to reprove severely.
3. to wind string or cord around the end of a rope, etc. to prevent fraying.
Usages:
a) 'he *whipped* around as the door opened' (= moved or turned quickly).
b) 'I must *whip* this class into shape' (= bring).
c) (*informal*) 'our team was *whipped* last week' (= beaten).
whip up, a) 'I *whipped up* a cake for the unexpected visitors' (= created quickly); b) 'his actions were intended to *whip up* the audience' (= arouse to fury, etc.).
whip *noun*
1. a flexible cord or leather lash with a rigid handle for striking or beating.
2. *Parliament:* a) an elected officer from a political party, who organizes members to attend debates, etc. b) his instruction to attend a debate.
Word Family: **whipper**, *noun*, a person who whips; **whipping**, *noun.*

whipcord *noun*
a closely woven, ribbed, worsted fabric used for dresses, riding breeches, etc.

whip hand
the position of control or advantage.

whiplash *noun*
1. the lash of a whip.
2. a sudden, jerking movement, as of the head thrown either backwards or forwards in a car collision.

whippersnapper (*say* **wippa**-snappa) ***noun***
an insignificant person who tries to appear important.

whippet (*say* **wippet**) ***noun***
any of a breed of racing dogs like a small greyhound.

whipping boy
a person who is made to suffer or take the blame for another.

whippoorwill (*say* **wippa**-will) ***noun***
a small brownish North American nightjar
[imitating its cry]

whip-round ***noun***
an appeal among a group for subscriptions to a presentation, charitable purpose, etc.

whirl (*say* werl) ***verb***
1. to spin or cause to spin rapidly.
2. to have the sensation of turning around rapidly: 'the room ***whirled*** before her'.
3. to move or drive, especially in a curving course at high speed.
whirl ***noun***
1. a) the act of whirling. b) a whirling movement.
2. a state of confusion.

whirligig ***noun***
something which whirls, such as a toy top.

whirlpool ***noun***
a circular eddy in water, produced by two currents meeting, etc.

whirlwind ***noun***
a small nearly vertical column of air rotating rapidly about a central area of low pressure.
Usage: 'the house was a ***whirlwind*** before the party' (= place of frenzied activity).

whirr (*say* wer) ***verb***
to move quickly with a vibrating or buzzing sound.
Word Family: **whirr**, ***noun.***

whisk (1) (*say* wisk) ***verb***
to move quickly and lightly: 'she ***whisked*** into the office without knocking'.
Word Family: **whisk**, ***noun.***

whisk (2) (*say* wisk) ***noun***
a light, wire utensil for beating or mixing eggs, cream, etc.
Word Family: **whisk**, ***verb***, to mix or beat with a whisk.

whisker ***noun***
1. (***usually plural***) any hair growing on the cheek, e.g. sideburns.
2. any of the long, stiff, bristly hairs growing around the mouth of cats, rats, etc.

whisky (*say* **wiss**-kee) **whiskey** ***noun***
a strong liquor made from grain.
[Gaelic ***usquebaugh*** water of life]

whisper (*say* **wisper**) ***verb***
1. to speak very softly.
2. to talk secretly or privately.
Usage: 'the leaves ***whispered*** in the breeze' (= rustled).
Word Family: **whisper**, ***noun***; **whisperer**, ***noun***, a person who whispers.

whist (*say* wist) ***noun***
Cards: a game for four people playing in pairs, each pair trying to win more tricks than the other.
whist-drive ***noun***
a whist tournament.
[***whist!*** be silent (during the game)]

whistle (*say* **wiss**'l) ***verb***
a) to produce a clear musical sound by forcing air through the teeth or lips. b) to produce a similar sound.
whistle in the dark, to try to keep up one's courage.
whistle ***noun***
1. a sound produced by or as if by whistling.
2. any instrument which produces whistling sounds.
Word Family: **whistler**, ***noun.***

whit (*say* wit) ***noun***
a bit: 'I'm not a ***whit*** better off than I was before'.

white (*say* wite) ***noun***
1. the lightest achromatic colour, the opposite of black.
2. something which has this colour, such as the part of an egg surrounding the yolk or the part of an eye surrounding the pupil.
3. a member of one of the white (that is, light-skinned) races of Europe or European origin.
4. a) white clothes: 'dressed in ***white***'; b) (***plural***) cricket or tennis clothes.
white ***adjective***
of the colour white: a) '***white*** snow'; b) 'a ***white*** citizen'.
Usages:
a) '***white*** wine' (= light and clear in colour).
b) 'her face was ***white*** with pain' (= pale).
c) 'we all hoped for a ***white*** Christmas in Canada' (= accompanied by snow).
d) 'may I have ***white*** coffee please?' (= with milk or cream).

bleed white, to extract out of someone all the money, etc. he has.
Word Family: **whiteness**, *noun*; **whiten**, *verb*, to make or become white or whiter.

whitebait *noun*
the fry of herring, sprat or pilchard, cooked and eaten whole.

white blood cell
also called a **leucocyte**
any of the cells in the blood of vertebrates which cannot carry oxygen, including those that fight disease, etc.

white-collar worker
any person employed in professional or office work, and receiving a salary.

white elephant
something which is annoyingly useless or expensive to keep.

white feather
a symbol of cowardice.

white flag
any symbol or sign of surrender, usually a white flag.

white gold
any of a group of white alloys, containing gold and various other metals, such as platinum, used in jewellery.

white horses
the small white-crested waves whipped up by a moderate breeze at sea.

white-hot *adjective*
extremely hot, so that a bright white light is given off.
Word Family: **white heat**, a) the temperature of a substance which is white-hot, b) a state of intense excitement, activity, etc.

white lead (*say* white led)
a white powder, basic lead carbonate, used in putty, paint pigments and ointments.

white lie
a harmless or excusable lie, usually told with good intentions.

white light
Physics: the light which contains all the wavelengths of the visible spectrum.

white matter
Anatomy: the parts of the central nervous system, especially the brain, made up of nerve fibres. Compare GREY MATTER.

white metal
any of a group of alloys containing tin or lead, used for bearings, etc.

whiten *verb*
Word Family: see WHITE.

white paper
an official report produced by a government on a particular subject.

white tie
see BOW TIE.

whitewash *noun*
1. any of several preparations, such as lime and water, used to paint surfaces white.
2. anything used to disguise or cover faults, etc.
Word Family: **whitewash**, *verb*.

whither *adverb, conjunction*
an old word meaning where.

whiting (1) (*say* **wye-ting**) *noun*
any of a group of small, scaly, white-fleshed, edible fish related to the cod.

whiting (2) (*say* **wye-ting**) *noun*
a prepared form of pure white chalk, used to make white putty, etc.

whitish *adjective*
close to white in colour.

whitlow (*say* **witlo**) *noun*
a deep, bacterial infection in the tip of a finger causing an abscess, sometimes due to a thorn, splinter, etc.
[WHITE + FLAW]

Whitsun, Whitsuntide *noun*
also called **Pentecost**
Christian: the festival, held seven weeks after Easter, commemorating the descent of the Holy Ghost on the Disciples.
[*Whit* for *white*, from the white dresses worn by converts at this festival in the early days of the Church]

whittle (*say* **witt'l**) *verb*
to trim or shape by cutting off small pieces with a knife.
Usage: 'how can we *whittle* down the cost of the trip?' (= cut, reduce).

whiz (*say* wiz) **whizz** *verb*
(**whizzed, whizzing**)
1. to make a hissing or whirring sound, as of something moving quickly through the air.
2. to move with such a sound: 'a stray bullet *whizzed* past her ear'.
whiz *noun*
1. a whizzing sound or movement.
2. (*informal*) a person who is extremely skilled or clever: 'a *whiz* at maths'.

who (*say* hoo) *pronoun*
1. which person or persons?: '*who* told you that?'.

2. used as a relative pronoun referring to a person already mentioned: 'is that the teacher *who* makes films?'.
know who's who, to know which are the people who have power, influence and importance.
whoever, whosoever *pronoun*
any person who: '*whoever* wins this race will be the champion'.

whoa (*say* wo *or* woo) *interjection*
(usually used to a horse or other animal) stop!

whodunit (*say* hoo-**dunnit**) *noun*
(*informal*) a detective story.

whole (*say* hole) *adjective*
1. containing all its parts: 'a *whole* set of records'.
2. being in one piece: 'the saucer is *whole* but the cup has a broken handle'.
Usage: 'he cried the *whole* night' (= during the full extent of).
whole *noun*
a whole thing or amount.
Phrases:
as a whole, considering all things together.
on the whole, generally.
Word Family: **wholeness**, *noun*.

wholehearted (*say* hole-**hart**id) *adjective*
sincere or unqualified.
Word Family: **wholeheartedly**, *adverb*; **wholeheartedness**, *noun*.

wholemeal *adjective*
also called **wholewheat**
(of bread, flour, etc.) being made with complete wheat grains.

whole milk
milk without any of its constituents being separated or removed.

whole note
American: a semibreve.

whole number
a positive integer, such as 1, 2, 3, 4, etc.

wholesale *noun*
the selling of goods, usually in large quantities, to retailers, etc. as distinct from the general public. Compare RETAIL.
wholesale *adjective*
relating to or engaged in wholesale.
Usage: 'the strike led to the *wholesale* dismissal of employees' (= massive, indiscriminate).
Word Family: **wholesaler**, *noun*; **wholesale**, *verb*, to sell by wholesale.

wholesome (*say* **hole**-sum) *adjective*
good for one's health: 'a *wholesome* breakfast'.
Usages:
a) 'her *wholesome* good looks pleased the family' (= healthy-looking).
b) 'a *wholesome* film' (= morally pleasing or acceptable).
Word Family: **wholesomely**, *adverb*; **wholesomeness**, *noun*.

whole tone
Music: an interval of two semitones.

wholly (*say* **hole**-ee) *adverb*
to the fullest or whole amount, etc.: 'I *wholly* agree with you'.

whom (*say* hoom) *pronoun*
the objective case of the pronoun **who**: 'with *whom* do you wish to speak?'.
whomever *pronoun*
the objective case of the pronoun **whoever**.
whomsoever *pronoun*
the objective case of the pronoun **whosoever**.

whoop (*say* hoop *or* woop) *noun*
a hooting shout or cry: 'a *whoop* of laughter'.
whoop *verb*
1. to make a hooting sound.
2. to make the harsh, gasping sound characteristic of whooping cough.
whoop it up, (*informal*) to have a lively or boisterous time.

whoopee (*say* **woop**-ee) *interjection*
(*informal*) a shout of excitement or enthusiasm.
make whoopee, to celebrate noisily.

whooping cough (*say* **hoo**ping kof)
an infectious, bacterial disease, usually in children, causing severe fits of coughing.

whoops (*say* woops) *interjection*
an exclamation of dismay, surprise, etc.

whoosh (*say* woosh) *noun*
a loud rushing or swishing sound, as of water or air.
Word Family: **whoosh**, *verb*.

whop (*say* wop) *verb*
(**whopped, whopping**)
(*informal*) a) to hit. b) to defeat easily.

whopper (*say* **woppa**) *noun*
(*informal*) a) a very big person or thing. b) an outrageous lie.

whopping (*say* **wopping**) *adjective*
(*informal*) very big.

whore (*say* hor) *noun*
a prostitute or promiscuous woman.

Word Family: **whore,** *verb,* to act as or associate with a whore or whores.

whorl (*say* worl *or* werl) *noun*
1. a circular arrangement of like parts, as leaves, lines on a fingerprint, etc.
2. anything with the shape of a spiral or coil.
Word Family: **whorled,** *adjective,* having or consisting of whorls.

whortleberry (*say* **wert**'l-berree) *noun*
see BILBERRY.

whose (*say* hooz) *possessive pronoun*
the possessive case of the pronoun **who**: 'he is the one *whose* car was stolen'.

whosoever *pronoun*
see WHO.

why (*say* wye) *adverb*
1. for what reason or purpose?: '*why* did you do that?'.
2. the reason for which: 'that is *why* I don't want to go'.
why *interjection*
an exclamation of surprise, pleasure, etc.
Word Family: **why,** *noun,* a cause or reason.

wick *noun*
a piece of cord, cotton or other material in a candle or lamp through which the fuel soaks up to the flame.
get on one's wick, to annoy one intensely.

wicked (*say* **wik**kid) *adjective*
evil or sinful.
Usages:
a) 'a *wicked* smile' (= mischievous).
b) (*informal*) 'you sound as if you have a *wicked* cold' (= extremely bad or unpleasant).
Word Family: **wickedly,** *adverb*; **wickedness,** *noun.*

wicker *noun*
1. any thin, pliable twig.
2. wickerwork.
Word Family: **wicker,** *adjective.*

wickerwork *noun*
any article made by plaiting or weaving twigs.

wicket *noun*
1. *Cricket:* a) either of the two sets of three stumps joined across the top by the bails, at which the bowler aims the ball. b) see CREASE. c) the pitch or playing area: 'the ball bounced little because the *wicket* was wet'. d) the dismissing of a batsman.
2. a small door or gate, especially one next to or part of a larger one.
a sticky wicket, (*informal*) a difficult situation.

wicket-keeper *noun*
Cricket: the fielder who stands directly behind the stumps at the batsman's end, to stop all the bowled balls that pass the batsman.

wide *adjective*
1. being large from side to side: 'a *wide* river'.
Usages:
a) 'I have had a *wide* range of jobs' (= very varied).
b) 'her eyes were *wide* with horror' (= fully open).
c) 'the batsman ignored the *wide* ball' (= too far to one side).
2. having a particular measurement from one side to the other: '16 cm *wide*'.
wide of the mark, quite wrong.
wide *adverb*
1. to a wide extent: 'open your mouth *wide*'.
2. aside: 'his first shot went *wide*'.
3. over a great distance: 'travel far and *wide*'.
wide *noun*
Cricket: a ball bowled outside the batsman's reach. See EXTRA.
Word Family: **widely,** *adverb*; **wideness,** *noun*; **widen,** *verb,* to make or become wide or wider.

wide-angle lens
Photography: a lens which allows a wider angle of view than an ordinary lens, used in taking close-ups of buildings, etc.

wide-awake *adjective*
completely awake.

wide-eyed *adjective*
with the eyes wide open, especially due to innocence, amazement, etc.

widespread (*say* **wide**-spred) *adjective*
existing or scattered over a wide area or in many places, people, etc.

widow *noun*
1. a woman who has not remarried after her husband has died.
2. (*informal*) a woman whose husband neglects her in favour of a sport or other activity: 'a golf *widow*'.
Word Family: **widow,** *verb,* to make into a widow; **widowhood,** *noun,* the state or time of being a widow.

widower *noun*
a man who has not remarried after his wife has died.

widow's cruse
a supply which never runs out.

widow's mite
a small gift of money from a person who cannot really afford to give it.

widow's peak
a hairline forming a V-shaped point in the middle of the forehead.

width *noun*
1. the distance from side to side. Also called **breadth**.
2. something with a particular measurement from side to side: 'a metre *width* of gingham, please'.

wield (*say* weeld) *verb*
to handle or manage the action of: 'to *wield* a sword'.
Usage: 'political parties *wield* great power' (= have, exercise).

wife *noun*
plural is **wives**
the female partner in a marriage.
old wives' tale, an ignorant superstition or travesty of scientific fact.
Word Family: **wifely**, *adjective*, of or considered appropriate to a wife.

wig *noun*
a covering for the head, made of real or artificial hair.
wiglet *noun*
a small wig added to a woman's hair. [short form of *periwig*]

wigeon (*say* wij'n) **widgeon** *noun*
any of various freshwater ducks.

wiggle *verb*
to move or cause to move with quick movements from side to side: 'to *wiggle* one's hips when walking'.
Word Family: **wiggle**, *noun*, a wiggling movement, line, etc; **wiggly**, *adjective*, wiggling or waving.

wight (*say* wite) *noun*
an old word for a living being.

wigwag *noun*
1. the act of moving back and forth.
2. something which moves back and forth.
Word Family: **wigwag** (**wigwagged**, **wigwagging**), *verb*, to move or wave back and forth, especially in order to signal.

wigwam *noun*
a tent used by American Indians, made of bark or animal hides stretched over a round frame of poles.

wild (*rhymes with* child) *adjective*
1. living, growing or existing in a natural or uncultivated state: a) '*wild* animals'; b) 'a *wild* herb'.
Usages:
a) '*wild* fighting broke out amongst the frustrated spectators' (= uncontrolled, violent).
b) 'she was *wild* with rage' (= mad, frantic).
c) 'a *wild* guess' (= unlikely or unconsidered).
d) 'his *wild* curly hair blew about his face' (= disordered).
e) (*informal*) 'I'm *wild* about purple' (= very enthusiastic).
2. *Cards:* (of a card) having its value chosen by the player who holds it.
wild and woolly, (of an idea, etc.) incoherent or mad.
Word Family: **wild**, *noun*, (usually plural) an uncultivated or uninhabited area; **wildly**, *adverb*; **wildness**, *noun*.

wildcat *noun*
1. any of various wild, cat-like mammals, especially the lynx.
2. a violent or savage person.
3. *American:* a financially risky venture.

wildcat strike
an unofficial strike.

wildebeest *noun*
a gnu.

wilderness *noun*
1. any land or area which is uncultivated or uninhabited.
2. any uncontrolled or confused mass of things.
3. *Politics:* the state of being out of office.

wildfire *noun*
like wildfire, 'the exciting news spread *like wildfire*' (= with great or uncontrollable speed).

wild-goose chase
a hopeless or useless chase or undertaking.

wildlife *noun*
wild animals, especially those living in uncultivated areas.

Wild West
western America during the pioneering period, especially as a lawless or violent region.

wile *noun*
a trick or deceitful method.
Word Family: **wile**, *verb*, to entice.

wilful *adjective*
1. deliberate or intentional: 'he was charged with *wilful* murder'.
2. stubbornly persistent: '*wilful* disobedience must be punished'.
Word Family: **wilfully,** *adverb*; **wilfulness,** *noun.*

will (1) *verb*
(will, would)
an auxiliary verb indicating:
a) future tense: 'he *will* come afterwards'.
b) command: 'you *will* go home at once'.
c) willingness: '*will* you do some shopping for me?'.
d) habit: 'she *would* work late every night'.
e) anticipation: 'you *will* remember to buy petrol'.
f) desire: 'do what you *will*'.

will (2) *noun*
1. the power or ability to deliberately decide or choose to act: 'a weak *will*'.
Usages:
a) 'he went to the party against his *will*' (= wish).
b) 'she has a strong *will* to succeed' (= determination).
2. *Law:* a document providing for the distribution of a person's property after his death.
3. an attitude or feeling towards others: 'he is full of ill *will* towards his rival'.
Phrases:
at will, 'the tourists could wander *at will* about the friendly city' (= at their pleasure).
a will of one's own, a strong independence of mind.
with a will, 'they started the new work *with a will*' (= eagerly, willingly).
Word Family: **will,** *verb,* a) to bequeath in a will, b) to decide or influence by using the will, c) to order or command.

willies *plural noun*
(*informal*) a feeling of uneasiness, fear or dislike.

willing *adjective*
feeling or expressing consent, etc.: 'are you *willing* to agree?'.
Usage: 'a helpful and *willing* worker' (= eager).
Word Family: **willingly,** *adverb*; **willingness,** *noun.*

will-o'-the-wisp *noun*
1. a small flickering light often seen in swamp areas, once believed to lead travellers off their path.
2. something which is misleading or elusive.
[for *Will of the Wisp* (of lighted hay)]

willow *noun*
1. any of a group of trees or shrubs, often with slender drooping branches and strong, light wood used for weaving and making cricket bats.
2. a factory machine for cleaning cotton, flax or wool, consisting of a revolving cylinder with long spikes.
Word Family: **willowy** (*say* **willo-ee**), *adjective,* gracefully slender.

willpower *noun*
mental strength or control over one's wishes, actions, etc.: 'you need great *willpower* to remain on a diet'.

willy-nilly *adverb*
1. whether it is desired or not.
2. in a haphazard or disorganized way.
[for *will I, nill I* (*nill* = won't)]

willy-willy *noun*
Australian: a whirlwind caused by a tropical cyclone.
[Aboriginal]

wilt *verb*
to become or cause to become limp and drooping: 'the flowers *wilted* in the hot sun'.
wilt *noun*
any of various diseases which cause limpness or collapse in plants.

wily (*say* **wye-lee**) *adjective*
cunning or full of deceitful tricks.
Word Family: **wilily,** *adverb*; **wiliness,** *noun.*

wimple *noun*
a cloth wound around the head to frame the face and wrapped in folds around the neck under the chin, as worn by nuns.
Word Family: **wimple,** *verb,* to cover or wrap in a wimple.

win *verb*
(won, winning)
1. a) to earn or achieve success, especially when in competition against others: 'to *win* a race'. b) to be victorious in a battle, war, etc.
2. to receive as a reward for achievement or success: 'to *win* first prize'.
Usages:
a) 'her moving songs soon *won* the audience' (= gained the favour or approval of).
b) 'the guerrillas *won* several small villages' (= captured).

c) 'he *won* the river bank after fighting through the current' (= reached with effort).
Word Family: **win**, *noun*, the act of winning; **winner**, *noun*.

wince *verb*
to flinch in pain, etc.
Word Family: **wince**, *noun*.

winceyette (*say* win-see-**et**) *noun*
a soft, cotton fabric used for pyjamas, etc.

winch *noun*
a) a lifting or pulling device, often having several gearwheels attached to it. b) the crank handle used on such a device.
Word Family: **winch**, *verb*, to hoist or pull by means of a winch.

wind (1) *noun*
1. a movement of air, especially along the earth's surface.
Usages:
a) 'she ran out of *wind* after three laps of the oval' (= breath).
b) 'his claims to success are all *wind*' (= empty or meaningless words).
c) 'the *wind* of change' (= trend towards).
2. the scent of an animal carried in the air.
3. a build-up of gases produced in the stomach.
4. *Music:* (*usually plural*) a) wind instruments. b) the players of such instruments.
Phrases:
get wind of, 'the newspapers soon *got wind of* the scandal' (= became aware of, sensed).
in the wind, 'police fear that a riot is *in the wind*' (= likely to take place).
sail close to the wind, a) to sail as directly against the wind as possible; b) to get close to the limits of decency or honesty.
see how the wind blows, to test public or others' opinion.
take the wind out of one's sails, to outmanoeuvre, especially by anticipating and frustrating one's plans.
wind *verb*
a) to cause to lose one's breath, as by a knock or blow. b) to get the scent of.
Word Family: **winded** (*say* **win**-did), *adjective*, temporarily out of breath.

wind (2) (*rhymes with* find) *verb*
(wound, winding)
1. to follow a course of turns and bends: 'a lazy, *winding* river'.
2. to wrap around in rolls or coils: '*wind* the reins around that branch'.
3. to adjust a mechanical device by turning a key, etc.
4. to haul or hoist by turning a handle, etc.: '*wind* that fish in carefully'.
wind up, a) to make excited; b) to bring to an end, e.g. a speech, a firm's activities, etc. c) to end up, e.g. in gaol.
Word Family: **wind**, *noun*, a winding movement or course; **winder**, *noun*, a person or thing that winds.

windbag *noun*
(*informal*) a person who talks continually, usually about uninteresting or unimportant matters.

windblown *adjective*
windswept.

windborne *adjective*
carried by the wind.

windbreak *noun*
a line of trees, etc. giving shelter from the wind.

windcheater *noun*
a short jacket of windproof and rainproof material, gathered in at wrist and waist.

winded *adjective*
Word Family: see WIND (1).

windfall *noun*
1. an unexpected piece of good luck.
2. something blown down by the wind, especially ripe fruit.

wind-gap *noun*
Geography: a gorge through which water once flowed.

windhover (*say* **wind**-hovva) *noun*
the kestrel.

wind instrument
Music: an instrument, such as a flute, in which sound is produced by the vibration of air in a tube.

windjammer *noun*
a large sailing ship.

windlass *noun*
any of various devices for lifting objects, usually consisting of a rope or chain wound around a drum which is fitted with a crank handle.

windmill *noun*
any of various wind-driven machines with large vanes fixed on to an axle, used to grind grain, pump water, etc.

window *noun*
1. a) an opening in a wall to let in light, etc., usually consisting of a movable frame, into which glass is

set. b) the framework, glass or fittings in such an opening.
2. something which has the appearance or function of a window, as the transparent part of an envelope through which an address may be read.

window box
a container for growing plants, placed on or outside the sill of a window.

window-dressing *noun*
1. the art of arranging goods in a shop window to attract customers.
2. the presenting of something in its most attractive or appealing form, usually to disguise its less favourable qualities.
Word Family: **window-dresser**, *noun*.

window pane
see PANE.

window seat
a seat set beneath the sill of a window in an alcove, etc.

window-shop *verb*
(window-shopped, window-shopping)
to look at goods in the windows of shops, rather than buying anything.
Word Family: **window-shopper**, *noun*.

windpipe *noun*
see TRACHEA.

windrow (*say* **wind**-ro) *noun*
a row of cut hay, grain, etc. left in heaps to dry in the wind.

windscreen *noun*
in America called a **windshield**
a window of safety-glass at the front of a motor vehicle.

windscreen-wiper *noun*
a device with rubber blades for removing rain, snow, etc. from the windscreen of a vehicle.

windsock *noun*
a device for indicating wind direction at airports, etc., consisting of an open sleeve flown from a pole.

windswept *adjective*
exposed to or blown by the wind.

wind-tunnel *noun*
a machine for testing aeroplane parts or models by generating a strong airstream in a tunnel.

wind-up *noun*
an ending.

windvane *noun*
a weathervane.

windward (*say* **wind**-wud) *adjective*
of or relating to the direction from which the wind is blowing. Compare LEEWARD.
windwards, windward *adverb*
towards the wind or the direction from which it is blowing.
Word Family: **windward**, *noun*, the direction from which the wind is blowing.

windy *adjective*
1. accompanied by wind.
2. of, like or exposed to wind.
3. suffering from flatulence.

wine *noun*
1. the red or white alcoholic beverage made from grape skins and the fermented juice of grapes.
2. a similar drink made from the juice of other fruits, such as berries.
3. a dark red colour.
Word Family: **wine**, *verb*, to supply or entertain with wine.

winepress *noun*
a machine in which the juice is pressed from grapes for wine.

winery *noun*
a place where wine is made.

wineskin *noun*
a container for wine, made from the skin of an animal.

wing *noun*
1. an organ of flight, consisting of a modified forelimb in animals, a flat, movable structure in insects, etc.
2. something which has the shape or function of a wing, such as the long, flat, horizontal parts on either side of an aeroplane.
3. something which has the position of a wing, such as a section of a building which projects from the main part or the backstage areas on either side of the stage in a theatre.
4. a folding or hinged part: 'the *wing* of a folding screen'.
5. something considered to be a means of flight, progress, etc.: 'escape on the *wings* of poetry'.
6. a distinct section or group within a political party, organization, etc.: 'the right *wing*'.
7. the mudguard of a motor vehicle.
8. *Sport:* (in football, hockey, etc.) the area along the edges of the field.
9. *Military:* a) a part of an army protecting the main force from attack on the flank. b) a tactical unit in the airforce, consisting of several squadrons.

10. (*plural*) the emblem worn by a qualified pilot.
Phrases:
clip one's wings, to limit the freedom of.
in the wings, waiting in readiness in the background.
on the wing, a) flying; b) moving or active.
take wing, a) to fly away; b) to flee.
under one's wing, in one's care.
wing *verb*
1. a) to provide with wings. b) to travel on wings.
2. to wound in a wing, limb or other minor part.

wing-commander *noun*
a commissioned officer in the airforce, ranking between a squadron leader and a group captain.

winger *noun*
any player positioned on the wing in football, hockey, etc.

wing nut
a nut with two wing-like projections which enable it to be turned by the thumb and forefinger.

wingspan *noun*
the distance between the tips of the wings of an aeroplane, bird, etc.

wink *verb*
to open and close one eye quickly, often as a signal.
Usage: 'the city lights *winked* in the fog' (= flashed).
wink at, 'the police will *wink at* minor offences' (= pretend not to see).
wink *noun*
a winking movement or action, especially of an eye.
Phrases:
forty winks, (*informal*) a short sleep.
not sleep a wink, to not sleep at all.
tip someone the wink, (*informal*) to give important information to.
Word Family: **winker**, *noun*, a person or thing that winks, as an indicator on a motor vehicle.

winkle *noun*
Biology: a periwinkle.

winner *noun*
Word Family: see WIN.

winning *adjective*
1. successful: 'the *winning* team'.
2. charming or disarming: 'a *winning* smile'.
winning *noun*
(*usually plural*) anything won, especially money.

winnow *verb*
1. to separate grain from chaff, etc. using a current of air.
2. to blow away or scatter, as by a current of air.
Usage: 'the jury must *winnow* the truth from all the evidence' (= sort, separate).

wino (*say* **wine-o**) *noun*
an alcoholic.
[from WINE]

winsome (*say* **winsum**) *adjective*
charming or attractive.
[Old English *wyn* joy + -SOME]

winter *noun*
the coldest season of the year, between autumn and spring.
Usage: 'an old man of 87 *winters*' (= years).
Word Family: **winter**, *verb*, to spend the winter; **wintry**, **wintery**, *adjectives*, like or characteristic of winter.

wintergreen *noun*
a plant from which a pleasant-smelling oil is derived for use in perfumes and as a flavouring in toothpaste.

wipe *verb*
to rub or pass over lightly with a cloth, etc., in order to clean or dry: '*wipe* those sticky hands!'.
Usage: 'please *wipe* that sarcastic smile off your face' (= remove).
wipe out, a) to destroy completely; b) (of a surfer) to lose balance and fall or jump off the surfboard.
Word Family: **wipe**, *noun*, the act of wiping; **wiper**, *noun*, something used for wiping or cleaning, such as a cloth or pad, a windscreen-wiper, etc.

wire *noun*
1. a long, thin piece of metal, usually round in cross-section and having many uses, e.g. for conducting electricity, as fencing material, etc.
2. a) a telegram. b) the telegraphic system.
get one's wires crossed, to talk at cross-purposes.
wire *verb*
1. to provide or fasten with a wire or wires: 'a champagne cork is *wired* in place'.
2. to fit with a system of wires to provide electricity.
3. to send a telegram, etc.
Word Family: **wiring**, *noun*, a system of wires providing electricity, e.g. for lighting, etc.

wired glass
a sheet of glass with wire netting set into it to make it stronger.

wire-haired *adjective*
having stiff, usually curly, hair.

wireless *noun*
1. a) a radio set. b) radio programmes.
2. a) radio telegraphy. b) a message sent by this.

wire-tapper *noun*
a person who listens to or records telephone conversations, etc.
Word Family: **wire-tap (wire-tapped, wire-tapping)**, *verb.*

wire wheel
a motor vehicle wheel with wire spokes.

wiring *noun*
Word Family: see WIRE.

wiry (*say* **wire-ee**) *adjective*
resembling wire in shape, stiffness, etc.
Usage: 'a *wiry* build is usually a sign of fitness' (= slender but strong).

wisdom (*say* **wiz-d'm**) *noun*
1. a good judgement or understanding of what is right, true, etc.
2. learning or knowledge acquired by study, experience, etc.

wisdom tooth
the last molar at either end of the upper and lower jaws.

wise (1) (*say* wize) *adjective*
having or showing wisdom: 'a *wise* old professor'.
Usages:
a) 'is it *wise* to go out in the storm?' (= sensible).
b) (*informal*) 'I think the police are *wise* to our hide-out' (= alert, aware).
Phrases:
be wise after the event, to realize something too late, with the benefit of hindsight.
get wise, (*informal*) a) 'don't *get wise* with your father or you will be sorry' (= be rude or insolent); b) to face or become aware of the facts.
wise up, (*informal*) to make or become aware, informed, etc.
Word Family: **wisely**, *adverb.*

wise (2) (*say* wize) *noun*
a way or respect: 'they are in no *wise* alike'.

-wise (*say* wize)
a suffix used to form adverbs from nouns or adjectives, indicating: a) direction or position, as in *lengthwise*; b) reference or relation to, as in *weatherwise.*

wiseacre (*say* **wize**-ay-ka) *noun*
(*informal*) a know-all.

wisecrack *noun*
a smart or flippant remark.
Word Family: **wisecrack**, *verb.*

wish *verb*
1. to want or long for: 'I *wish* it would stop raining'.
Usages:
a) '*wish* your grandmother goodnight' (= say to).
b) 'I *wish* to see all the culprits in my room' (= command).
c) 'I would not *wish* such an experience on you' (= impose, bring upon).
2. to express a desire, as for magical results: 'what did you *wish* for as you blew out the candles?'.
wish *noun*
1. a) a desire or longing: 'a *wish* for peace'. b) something which is wanted: 'what is your *wish*?'.
2. a word or words which express a wish, especially as a polite greeting, etc.: 'give my best *wishes* to your parents'.

wishbone *noun*
a forked bone in front of the breast of some birds.

wishful *adjective*
hoping or longing.
wishful thinking, a hopeful confidence that what one wishes for will occur or is the case.
Word Family: **wishfully**, *adverb.*

wishy-washy (*say* **wishi**-woshee) *adjective*
lacking strength or substance.

wisp *noun*
1. a small, fine bunch of strands, etc.: 'a *wisp* of hair'.
2. a person or thing that is small, frail or thin.
Usage: 'there was a *wisp* of a smile in her eyes' (= trace, sign).
Word Family: **wispy, wispish**, *adjectives*, in wisps or resembling a wisp.

wist *verb*
the past tense and past participle of the verb **wit (2)**.

wisteria, wistaria (*say* wis-**teeria** *and* wis-**tairia**) *noun*
any of various climbing plants with compound leaves and blue, purple or white flowers.

[after *C. Wistar*, 1761–1818, an American anatomist]

wistful *adjective*
expressing sadness, regret or disappointed hope.
Word Family: **wistfully**, *adverb*; **wistfulness**, *noun.*

wit (1) *noun*
1. a clever ability to perceive, connect or express ideas, etc. especially in a fresh, unexpected and amusing way.
2. a) an example of such an ability in speech or writing. b) a person with such a talent.
3. (*plural*) acute mental powers, especially sanity or good sense.
Phrases:
at one's wits' end, thwarted and not knowing what to do next.
have one's wits about one, to be alert to what is happening.
live by one's wits, to make a living by haphazard exploitation and sharp practice.
out of one's wits, 'the explosion scared them *out of their wits*' (= to an extreme degree).
Word Family: **witty**, *adjective*, possessing or showing wit; **wittily**, *adverb*; **wittiness**, *noun*; **witticism** (*say* witti-sizm), *noun*, a would-be witty remark.

wit (2) *verb*
(**I wot**; thou **wottest**; he, she, it **wot**; **wist, witting**)
an old word meaning to know: 'a garden is a lovesome thing, God *wot*'.
to wit, that is to say.

witch *noun*
1. a woman who practises magic, especially one who uses black magic and is believed to be in league with the devil.
2. any ugly or evil old woman.
3. a fascinating or bewitching woman.
Word Family: **witchcraft, witchery**, *nouns*, a) the art or influence of magic, especially for evil purposes, b) a fascinating power.

witchdoctor *noun*
a medicine man.

witch-hazel *noun*
also spelt **wych-hazel**
1. one of the finest winter-flowering garden shrubs.
2. an astringent liquid prepared from this shrub, used on bruises, inflammations, etc.

witch-hunt *noun*
an emotional campaign, usually political, to find or investigate people considered to be unorthodox or disloyal.

witching *adjective*
enchanting or fascinating.
the witching hour, midnight.

with (*say* wi*th*) *preposition*
1. a word used to indicate the following:
a) (company) 'come *with* me'.
b) (connection) 'stir the flour *with* the butter'.
c) (manner, means) 'cut it *with* this knife'.
d) (opposition) 'don't argue *with* your father'.
e) (result, effect) 'he mellowed *with* age'.
f) (agreement) 'I'm *with* you on that matter'.
g) (understanding) 'I'm not *with* you, so could you explain?'.
h) (separation) 'I could never part *with* my dog'.
2. in the same direction as: 'swim *with* the current'.
3. having or possessing: 'the girl *with* green eyes'.
4. at the same time as: 'she gets up *with* the dawn'.
5. in the possession of: 'leave your coat *with* me'.
6. concerning: 'I am furious *with* her'.
7. in proportion to: 'prices rose *with* the increasing shortage of goods'.

withal (*say* wi*th*-awl) *adverb*
an old word meaning moreover.

withdraw *verb*
(**withdrew, withdrawn, withdrawing**)
to take out: a) 'to *withdraw* money from a bank'; b) 'he *withdrew* the poker from the fire'.
Usages:
a) 'please *withdraw* that remark' (= take back).
b) 'he *withdrew* from society' (= went away).
withdrawal *noun*
1. the act of withdrawing, such as the removal of a drug or other habit-forming substance from a person's experience.
2. an amount of money, etc. which is withdrawn.

withdrawal symptoms
the distressing or painful effects occurring in a person denied a drug, etc. to which he is addicted.

withdrawn *adjective*
reserved or lost in one's own thoughts.
withdrawn *verb*
the past participle of the verb **withdraw**.

wither (*say* wi*th*er) *verb*
to make or become faded, dry and shrunken: 'the leaves *withered* and fell from the tree'.
Usage: 'the cruel remark *withered* her' (= abashed).

withers (*say* wi*th*ers) *plural noun*
the highest part of the back behind the shoulders of a horse, donkey, etc.

withhold *verb*
(**withheld, withholding**)
to hold back or refuse to give: 'police *withheld* the victim's name for several days'.

within *preposition*
in or into: '*within* the house'.
Usages:
a) 'you must try to live *within* your means' (= according to the limits of).
b) 'their house is *within* shouting distance of ours' (= not further than).
Word Family: **within**, *adverb*.

with-it *adjective*
fashionably up-to-date.

without *preposition*
1. not having: 'the strike left us *without* transport'.
Usages:
a) '*without* doubt you are right' (= no).
b) 'it's unusual to see Bill *without* his mother' (= not accompanied by).
2. an old usage meaning outside.
Word Family: **without**, *adverb*.

withstand *verb*
(**withstood, withstanding**)
to resist or oppose successfully: 'the reinforced windows will *withstand* great pressure'.

witless *adjective*
foolish.
Word Family: **witlessly**, *adverb*; **witlessness**, *noun*.

witness *noun*
1. a person who is present at, sees or hears something: 'this man was a *witness* to the attack'.
2. *Law:* a) a person who makes a statement or gives evidence, especially in a court case. b) a person who signs a document as a declaration of or agreement to its validity.
bear witness, to be or give evidence.
Word Family: **witness**, *verb*, to be or perform the duties of a witness.

witness box
the enclosed area in a courtroom, where a witness stands to give evidence.

witticism (*say* **witti-sizm**) *noun*
Word Family: see WIT (1).

wittingly *adverb*
knowingly or deliberately.

witty *adjective*
Word Family: see WIT (1).

wives *plural noun*
the plural of **wife**.

wizard (*say* **wizzud**) *noun*
1. a magician or sorcerer.
2. a very clever or skilled person: 'a *wizard* at chess'.
wizard *adjective*
(*informal*) marvellous.
Word Family: **wizardry** (*say* **wizzud-ree**), *noun*, magic or witchcraft.
[Middle English, wise one]

wizened (*say* **wizzund**) *adjective*
withered or dried-up.

woad *noun*
a blue dye extracted from the leaves of a plant and daubed on their bodies by Ancient Britons.

wobble *verb*
to move or cause to move unsteadily from side to side: 'the loose tooth *wobbled* and fell out'.
Usage: 'her voice *wobbled* with emotion' (= trembled, quivered).
Word Family: **wobble**, *noun*; **wobbly**, *adjective*, unsteady; **wobbliness**, *noun*.

woe *noun*
1. an old word meaning sorrow or misery.
2. trouble or misfortune: '*woe* to the enemy'.
woeful *adjective*
1. unhappy: 'what a *woeful* experience'.
2. (*informal*) deplorable or worthy of pity: 'she shows a *woeful* lack of intelligence'.
woebegone (*say* **wo-bee-gon**) *adjective*
looking unhappy or miserable.
Word Family: **woefully**, *adverb*; **woefulness**, *noun*.

woke *verb*
the past tense of the verb **wake (1)**.

woken *verb*
a past participle of the verb **wake (1)**.

wolf (*say* wulf) *noun*
plural is **wolves** (*say* wulvz)
1. a mammal like a large dog, which hunts in packs and is found in the northern parts of Europe, Asia and America.
2. (*informal*) a man who pursues or flirts with many women.
Phrases:
cry wolf, to give false alarms.
keep the wolf from the door, to keep away poverty or hunger.
lone wolf, a person or animal that prefers to be or act alone.
wolf in sheep's clothing, a person who appears harmless but in fact has hostile or malicious intentions.
wolf *verb*
(*informal*) to eat ravenously: 'he *wolfed* his dinner and left'.
Word Family: **wolfish**, *adjective*; **wolfishly**, *adverb*.

wolfhound *noun*
any of various very large breeds of dog, originally bred to hunt wolves.

wolfram (*say* wulf-r'm) *noun*
see TUNGSTEN.
[German]

wolf-whistle *noun*
a loud whistle in appreciation of a woman.
Word Family: **wolf-whistle**, *verb*.

wolverine (*say* wulva-reen) *noun*
a common, American, burrowing rodent with a thick body and short legs.

wolves (*say* wulvz) *plural noun*
see WOLF.

woman (*say* wum'n) *noun*
plural is **women** (*say* **wimmin**)
an adult female human being.
Usage: 'I have a *woman* who cleans my house' (= charwoman, daily help)
old woman, a person who is pedantic and tends to fuss, etc.
Word Family: **womanly**, *adjective*, having the qualities considered to be appropriate to a woman; **womanliness**, *noun*; **womanhood**, *noun*, the state of being a woman; **womanish**, *adjective*, a) feminine, b) effeminate.
[Old English WIFE-MAN]

womanize, womanise *verb*
(of a man) to have numerous casual affairs with women.
Word Family: **womanizer**, *noun*.

womb (*rhymes with* room) *noun*
see UTERUS.

wombat *noun*
any of a group of heavily built, burrowing and grazing marsupials of south-eastern Australia, up to 120 cm long and ranging in colour from brown through grey to black.
[Aboriginal]

women (*say* **wimm**in) *plural noun*
see WOMAN.

womenfolk (*say* **wimm**in-foke) *plural noun*
a) all women. b) all the women of one's family.

won (*say* wun) *verb*
the past tense and past participle of the verb **win**.

wonder (*say* **wun**da) *verb*
1. to feel curiosity or doubt; 'I *wonder* if he is as rich as people say he is'.
2. to have a feeling of awe or admiration: 'I *wonder* at his bravery'.
wonder *noun*
1. a) something which causes awe or admiration: 'space travel is one of the *wonders* of the 20th century'. b) the emotion excited by such a thing: 'I was filled with *wonder* when they landed on the moon'.
2. a strange or suprising person, thing or event: 'it's a *wonder* she survived the accident'.
Word Family: **wonderingly**, *adverb*; **wonderment**, *noun*, awe.

wonderful (*say* **wun**da-f'l) *adjective*
1. extremely good or fine.
2. exciting wonder.
Word Family: **wonderfully**, *adverb*.

wonderland (*say* **wun**da-land) *noun*
1. a marvellous imaginary place.
2. a marvellous real place: 'Austria is a winter *wonderland* for skiers'.

wondrous (*say* **wun**drus) *adjective*
an old word for wonderful.

wonky *adjective*
(*informal*) a) shaky or feeble: 'I felt *wonky* after the operation'. b) loose or wobbly: 'this door-handle is *wonky*'.

wont *adjective*
an old word meaning accustomed: 'he is *wont* to smoke after a meal'.
Word Family: **wont**, *noun*, a habit; **wonted**, *adjective*, habitual.

woo *verb*
(**wooed, wooing**)
1. to seek the affection of, especially with intent to marry.
2. to seek to achieve: 'to *woo* fame'.
3. to invite by one's own actions: 'to *woo* disaster by dangerous living'.

Word Family: **wooer**, *noun*, a person who woos.

wood (*say* wʊd) *noun*
1. a) the hard fibrous substance of tree trunks or branches. b) this substance cut down for use in carpentry, building, etc.
2. *Biology:* the xylem tissue of a plant.
3. (*often plural*) an area of land covered with trees, usually less dense than a forest.
4. *Music:* woodwind.
5. *Golf:* any wooden-headed club, mainly used over long distances and each numbered according to the angle of the head to the handle. Compare IRON.
Phrases:
can't see the wood for the trees, being unable to distinguish the important points of a problem, etc. from the mass of detail.
out of the wood or **woods**, having overcome the most difficult or dangerous part of something.
Word Family: **wood**, *adjective*, a) made of or using wood, b) living in the woods; **wooded**, *adjective*, having trees or woods; **woody**, *adjective*, a) wooded, b) of or like wood.

woodcock *noun*
a plump game-bird related to the snipe.

woodcut *noun*
a print made from an engraved, wooden block.

wooden *adjective*
made or consisting of wood.
Usages:
a) 'a *wooden* stare' (= lifeless).
b) 'he worked slowly with *wooden* movements' (= stiff, clumsy).
Word Family: **woodenly**, *adverb*.

woodland *noun*
an area of land covered in trees.

woodlouse *noun*
any of various species of land crustacean, living in damp, shady places, as under stones, etc.

woodpecker *noun*
any of various birds which use their beaks to drill holes in tree trunks and extract insects with their long tongues.

woodwind *noun*
Music: a) the wind instruments, such as the flutes, clarinets, etc. b) the section of an orchestra having these instruments. Compare BRASS.

woodwork *noun*
1. any work done with wood.
2. any of the wooden fittings in a building.

woodworm *noun*
the larva of a species of furniture beetle, which bores its way through cracks in furniture and leaves a circular exit hole, powder and untold damage when it comes out again.

wooer *noun*
Word Family: see WOO.

woof (1) *noun*
see WEFT.

woof (2) *noun*
a dog's bark.
Word Family: **woof**, *verb*.

woofer *noun*
a loudspeaker designed for frequencies below about 3000 cycles per second. Compare TWEETER.

wool (*say* wʊl) *noun*
a) the soft, curly hair of sheep, used to make yarn or fibre. b) the yarn, used for knitting, weaving, etc., or fabric produced from this hair. c) any similar material: '*cottonwool*'.
Phrases:
dyed in the wool, see DYE.
pull the wool over someone's eyes, to deceive or delude someone.

wool-gathering *noun*
an indulgence in fanciful daydreams.

woollen *adjective*
of, relating to or consisting of wool.
woollen *noun*
(*plural*) any knitted clothing made of wool.

woolly *adjective*
1. consisting of, covered with or resembling wool.
2. confused or indistinct: 'I only have a *woolly* idea of what she was trying to say'.

woozy (*say* woo-zee) *adjective*
(*informal*) a) slightly sick. b) dazed or slightly drunk.

word (*rhymes with* bird) *noun*
1. the basic unit of language, a combination of sounds having a complete meaning.
2. an utterance, remark or expression: 'a *word* of warning before you begin'.
Usage: 'give the *word* and a hundred men will be at your side' (= command, signal).
3. speech or talk: 'may I have a *word* with you?'.
4. (*plural*) the sounds spoken or sung in a song, etc.
5. (*informal, plural*) a quarrel.

6. a promise or assurance: 'I'll keep your secret, I give you my *word*'.
7. *Christian:* (*capital*) the Scriptures.
Phrases:
in so many words, explicitly.
play on words, a pun.
take one at one's word, to act on the assumption that someone means what he says literally.
take the words out of one's mouth, to say exactly what someone else was about to say.
the last word, a) the closing remark in an argument, etc.; b) the very latest or most fashionable.
Word Family: **word**, *verb*, to express in words; **wording**, *noun*, a) the act of expressing in words, b) the words in which something is expressed.

word perfect
being able to recite word for word.

wordy (*say* **werdee**) *adjective*
expressed in or using more words than are necessary.
Word Family: **wordily**, *adverb*; **wordiness**, *noun*.

wore *verb*
the past tense of the verb **wear**.

work (*say* werk) *noun*
1. a) any effort directed towards making or doing something: '6 hours *work* in the garden'. b) something produced by effort: 'a *work* of art'.
2. an undertaking: 'you must finish this *work* today'.
3. what a person does to earn a living.
4. (*plural*) a factory, building, etc. where something is manufactured: 'the steel *works*'.
5. *Physics:* a scalar quantity equal to the force on a body multiplied by the distance it moves in the direction of the force.
6. (*plural*) the main parts of any machine, etc.
Phrases:
have one's work cut out, to have a difficult task.
set to work, to begin.
the works, the whole lot.
work *verb*
1. to engage in work.
2. to operate: a) 'to *work* a machine'; b) 'this machine won't *work*'.
Usages:
a) 'did your plan *work* or was it a failure?' (= prove successful).
b) 'we *worked* our way through the crowd' (= forced gradually).
c) 'he *worked* the clay into a pot' (= moulded).
d) 'he *works* his father's land' (= cultivates).
e) 'to *work* a miracle' (= cause, bring about).
f) 'he nervously *worked* his jaws' (= moved).
Phrases:
work out, a) to solve a problem; b) to train or practise, especially as an athlete.
work up, a) to excite or arouse; b) to increase in intensity, etc.
Word Family: **workable**, *adjective*, a) practicable or feasible, b) suitable for being worked; **worked**, *adjective*, ornamented.

worker (*say* **werka**) *noun*
1. a person who works, especially one doing manual labour.
2. *Biology:* a sterile female which, among social insects, does the work of the colony.

workhouse *noun*
History: the parish institution to which paupers were sent to work under harsh conditions.

working (*say* **werking**) *adjective*
1. employed.
2. capable of being used: 'a *working* model'.

working class
those who work in skilled trades or as manual labourers.
Word Family: **working-class**, *adjective*.

working drawing
a detailed drawing from which a house, machine, etc. is built.

workman *noun*
a worker, especially a manual or industrial worker.
Word Family: **workmanship**, *noun*, a) the art, skill or technique of a worker, b) the quality of a worker's skill or art; **workmanlike**, *adjective*, efficient or skilled.

work-out *noun*
a practice or period of training.

work party
a group appointed to carry out a particular task.

workshop (*say* **werk-shop**) *noun*
1. a room or building where work, especially mechanical work, is done.
2. an organized meeting of people with the same interests or skills, to practise together or exchange ideas: 'a theatre *workshop*'.

work–to–rule *noun*
see GO–SLOW.

world (*say* werld) *noun*
1. the earth or globe.
2. a) a particular section of the earth: 'the Western *World*'. b) a particular section of the earth's inhabitants: 'the animal *world*'.
Usages:
a) 'the *world* mourned the king's death' (= public as a whole).
b) 'the *world* of dreams' (= sphere, realm).
c) (*informal*) 'he means the *world* to me' (= everything).
d) (*informal*) 'he got into a *world* of trouble' (= lot).
Phrases:
bring into the world, to bear or deliver a child.
come into the world, to be born.
in the world, 'what *in the world* made you say that?' (= conceivable thing).
of the world, worldly.
on top of the world, extremely delighted or elated.
out of this world, marvellous or fabulous.
Word Family: **worldwide,** *adjective,* extending throughout the world.

world–beater *noun*
an exceptionally good person or thing.

world–class *adjective*
of highest or international quality.

worldly (*say* **werld**–lee) *adjective*
1. not religious or spiritual.
2. sophisticated or experienced in the ways of the world. Short form of **worldly–wise.**
Word Family: **worldliness,** *noun;* **worldling,** *noun,* a worldly person.

world war
a war involving much of the world.
First World War, that of 1914–18.
Second World War, that of 1939–45.

worm (*say* werm) *noun*
1. any of various boneless, limbless, creeping animals often living in the ground or as parasites.
2. (*informal*) a contemptible person.
3. (*plural*) any disease due to the presence of parasitic worms in the intestines.
4. *Engineering:* a coarse thread cut on a shaft, e.g. on the gear of a motor vehicle.
worm *verb*
1. to move like a worm.
Usage: 'he managed to *worm* out my secret' (= get by devious means).
2. to free from intestinal worms.
Word Family: **wormy,** *adjective.*

wormwood (*say* **werm**–w*u*d) *noun*
a bitter–tasting plant used to make vermouth, etc.

worn *adjective*
1. impaired by wear or use.
2. very tired or weary.
worn *verb*
the past participle of the verb **wear.**

worn–out *adjective*
1. used until no longer effective or valuable.
2. utterly exhausted.

worry (*say* wurree) *verb*
(worried, worrying)
1. to feel or cause to feel uneasy or slightly fearful.
2. to pull, bite or tear at repeatedly.
Phrases:
I should worry!, it's not going to worry me! (a Yiddish turn of phrase).
not to worry!, keep calm, never mind!
worry *noun*
1. the state of being worried: 'he is showing signs of *worry*'.
2. a person or thing that causes one to be worried.
Word Family: **worrisome,** *adjective,* troublesome; **worrier,** *noun.*

worry beads
a string of beads played with for relaxation or distraction, originally used in Greece and the Middle East.

worse (*say* werse) *adjective*
the comparative form of **bad.**
worse luck, 'I shan't be there, *worse luck!*' (= unfortunately).
Word Family: **worse,** *adverb;* **worsen,** *verb,* to make or become worse.

worship (*say* **wer**–ship) *noun*
1. the act of revering or honouring a god, etc., especially by ceremonies, rites or services.
2. a high regard or love for a person or thing.
3. (*capital*) a form of address, as in your Worship, used to a magistrate or mayor.
Word Family: **worship (worshipped, worshipping),** *verb;* **worshipper,** *noun;* **worshipful,** *adjective,* feeling or showing worship, adoration, etc.

worst (*say* werst) *adjective*
the superlative form of **bad.**
if the worst comes to the worst, if events turn out in the worst possible way.
Word Family: **worst,** *adverb;* **worst,** *verb,* to defeat.

worsted (*say* w*u*s–tid) *noun*
a) a firmly twisted yarn used for weaving, etc. b) a woollen fabric made from this yarn and having a firm, smooth surface.
[after *Worstead* in Norfolk, where once made]

worth (*say* werth) *noun*
1. the quality of something which makes it valuable, desirable, deserving of respect, etc.
2. the value of something.
worth *adjective*
1. deserving of: 'a place *worth* a visit'.
2. having a value of: 'he's *worth* a million dollars at least'.
for all one is worth, with all one's might.
Word Family: **worthless**, *adjective*, having no use, value, importance, etc.

worthwhile (*say* werth–**wile**) *adjective*
sufficiently rewarding to justify one's time, attention, work, trouble, etc.

worthy (*say* **wer**–*th*ee) *adjective*
having worth, merit or value: 'a *worthy* cause'.
worthy of, 'a person *worthy of* respect' (= who should be given).
Word Family: **worthily**, *adverb*; **worthiness**, *noun*; **worthy**, *noun*, an eminent person.

-worthy
a suffix meaning worth, as in *trustworthy*.

wot *verb*
the first and third persons singular present tense of the verb **wit (2)**.

would (*say* w*u*d) *verb*
the past and conditional tense of the verb **will (1)**.

would-be *adjective*
intending or hoping to be.

wound (1) (*say* woond) *noun*
any injury, usually one caused by external violence rather than due to a disease.
Usage: 'his manner caused a *wound* to her pride' (= hurt).
Word Family: **wound**, *verb*, to inflict a wound or wounds.

wound (2) (*rhymes with* round) *verb*
the past tense and past participle of the verb **wind (2)**.

wove *verb*
a past tense of the verb **weave**.

woven *verb*
a past tense and past participle of the verb **weave**.

wow *noun*
1. (*informal*) something which proves to be a great success.
2. *Audio:* any unwanted, low-frequency sound, resulting from a variation in the speed of a turntable or tape.
Word Family: **wow!**, *interjection*.

wrack (1) (*say* rak) *noun*
see RACK (2).

wrack (2) (*say* rak) *noun*
also spelt **rack**
1. any broken clouds driven by the wind.
2. seaweed washed up on the shore.

wraith (*say* raith) *noun*
an apparition, especially one of a living person supposed, in old Scottish superstition, to indicate his death.

wrangle (*say* **rangg**'l) *verb*
to quarrel.
Word Family: **wrangle**, *noun*.

wrap (*say* rap) *verb*
(**wrapped** or **wrapt**, **wrapping**)
1. to cover or enclose, e.g. with paper, etc.
2. to clasp, fold or coil about something.
Usage: 'she was *wrapped* in thought' (= immersed).
wrap up, (*informal*) to finish or settle.
wrap *noun*
(*sometimes plural*) a shawl, rug, etc. to keep one warm.
Word Family: **wrapper**, *noun*, something in which an object is wrapped or covered.

wrath (*say* roth) *noun*
any violent or resentful anger.
Word Family: **wrathful**, *adjective*; **wrathfully**, *adverb*; **wrathfulness**, *noun*.

wreak (*say* reek) *verb*
1. an old word meaning to avenge.
2. (of vengeance, rage, damage, etc.) to cause or put into operation.

wreath (*say* reeth) *noun*
a circular band of flowers, leaves, etc. sent to a funeral, put on a grave, etc.
wreathe (*say* ree*th*) *verb*
to encircle or adorn with or as if with a wreath.
Usage: 'her face was *wreathed* in smiles' (= enveloped).

wreck (*say* rek) *verb*
1. to destroy, especially accidentally: 'the ship was *wrecked* when it hit the rocks'.

2. to pull down or apart, e.g. an old house or car.
wreck *noun*
1. the remains of something that has been wrecked: 'the *wreck* was towed to the nearest port'.
2. a person in a poor mental or physical state.
Word Family: **wreckage** (*say* **rek**–ij), *noun*, the remains of something which has been wrecked; **wrecker,** *noun.*

wren (*say* ren) *noun*
a tiny skulking bird with an erect tail.

wrench (*say* rench) *verb*
a) to twist suddenly and forcibly. b) to twist and sprain.
wrench *noun*
1. a sudden, violent twist.
2. a) a spanner. b) a monkey-wrench.

wrest (*say* rest) *verb*
1. to twist or turn violently.
2. to take away by force.
Usage: 'they strove to *wrest* a living from the stony plains' (= extract).

wrestle (*say* **ress**'l) *verb*
to struggle with and try to throw an opponent to the ground.
Usage: 'he *wrestled* with the problem all night' (= struggled, tried to deal).
wrestling *noun*
a contest between two opponents who wrestle as a sport.
Word Family: **wrestler,** *noun.*

wretch (*say* retch) *noun*
1. an unfortunate or unhappy person.
2. a despicable person.

wretched (*say* **retchid**) *adjective*
1. causing or suffering misery.
2. inferior or worthless in quality.
3. contemptible or despicable: 'what a *wretched* thing to do'.
Word Family: **wretchedly,** *adverb*; **wretchedness,** *noun.*

wriggle (*say* **rigg**'l) *verb*
a) to twist or turn the body with winding motions. b) to move by such motions.
Usage: 'how did she *wriggle* out of the blame?' (= get cunningly).
Word Family: **wriggle,** *noun*; **wriggly,** *adjective*; **wriggler,** *noun.*

wright (*say* rite) *noun*
an old word for a workman or maker, now only used in compound words: 'a *playwright*'.

wring (*say* ring) *verb*
(wrung, wringing)
1. to twist and squeeze.
2. to remove liquid, etc. by twisting and squeezing: 'he *wrung* out the towels'.
3. to cause pain or distress to: 'to *wring* one's heart'.
Phrases:
wringing wet, very wet indeed.
wring one's hands, to clasp or squeeze one's hands together in despair, grief, etc.
Word Family: **wring,** *noun.*

wringer *noun*
1. a person or thing that wrings.
2. a mangle.

wrinkle (*say* **rink**'l) *noun*
a small furrow or ridge on a normally smooth surface.
Word Family: **wrinkle,** *verb*; **wrinkly,** *adjective.*

wrist (*say* rist) *noun*
1. *Anatomy:* the movable part between the forearm and the hand, made up of eight small bones, called **carpal bones.**
2. something covering the wrist.

wristlet *noun*
a band worn around the wrist for decoration, etc.

wristpin *noun*
a pin joining the piston to the connecting rod of an internal combustion engine.

writ (*say* rit) *noun*
1. *Law:* a court order, for a person to do, or refrain from doing, some act: 'a *writ* of habeas corpus'.
2. writings: 'Sacred *Writ*'.

write (*say* rite) *verb*
(wrote, written, writing)
1. to form letters, words, etc. on a surface using a pen, pencil or similar instrument.
2. to compose or produce a poem, book, letter, piece of music, etc.
Usages:
a) 'he *wrote* a cheque' (= filled in the blank spaces of).
b) 'distress was *written* on his face' (= marked, visible).
Phrases:
the writing on the wall, signs of trouble coming (a Biblical reference).
write off, to consider as a complete loss. *Word Family:* **write-off,** *noun.*
write up, to review or write about something in a newspaper, etc. *Word Family:* **write-up,** *noun.*
Word Family: **writer,** *noun,* a person who writes, especially for a living; **writing,** *noun,* a) the act of a person

who writes, b) anything which is written.

writhe (*say* ri*the*) *verb*
to twist or squirm, as in pain, etc.

wrong (*say* rong) *adjective*
1. not correct in action, opinion, method, etc.: a) 'she gave the *wrong* answer'; b) 'we took the *wrong* turn and arrived late'.
2. not in accordance with what is considered good, correct, true, etc.: 'it is *wrong* to steal'.
Usages:
a) 'this machine doesn't work, something must be *wrong* with it' (= out of order).
b) 'I always manage to say the *wrong* thing' (= inappropriate, unsuitable).
go down the wrong way, (of food) to get into the windpipe and cause a choking sensation.
wrong *noun*
something which is wrong, such as an injury or unjust act.
in the wrong, guilty or in error.
wrong *verb*
to treat unfairly or unjustly.
Word Family: **wrongly, wrong,** *adverbs*; **wrongdoer,** *noun*, a person who does wrong; **wrongdoing,** *noun*, wrong behaviour or action, such as a crime; **wrongful,** *adjective*, a) full of wrong, b) unlawful; **wrongfully,** *adverb*; **wrongfulness,** *noun*.

wrong–headed *adjective*
misguided and stubborn.

wrote (*say* rote) *verb*
the past tense of the verb **write**.

wroth (*say* roth) *adjective*
an old word meaning angry or wrathful.

wrought (*say* rawt) *adjective*
shaped by hammering, etc.
wrought–up, excited or perturbed.
[from *wrought*, the old past tense and past participle of the verb WORK]

wrought iron
the purest commercial form of iron containing very little carbon and easily worked and welded.

wrung (*say* rung) *verb*
the past tense and past participle of the verb **wring**.

wry (*say* rye) *adjective*
1. bitterly or ironically humorous.
2. slightly twisted.
Word Family: **wryly,** *adverb*; **wryness,** *noun*.

wych–hazel *noun*
see WITCH–HAZEL.

Xx

xanthous (*say* **zan**thus) *adjective*
yellow or yellowish, especially in skin colour.
[Greek *xanthos* yellow]

X chromosome
Biology: see SEX CHROMOSOME.

xeno– (*say* **zen**no)
a prefix meaning strange or foreign, as in *xenophobia.*
[Greek *xenos* stranger, foreign]

xenomorphic (*say* zenna–**mor**fik) *adjective*
Geology: of or relating to a crystalline form of a rock which does not have the form characteristic of that rock.
Word Family: **xenomorphically,** *adverb.*
[Greek *xenos* stranger + *morphé* shape]

xenon (*say* **zen**–on) *noun*
element number 54, a rare, colourless, inert gas found in the earth's atmosphere and used in some electric lights and radio valves. See CHEMICAL ELEMENTS in grey pages.

xenophobia (*say* zenna–**fo**–bee–a) *noun*
a marked dislike of foreigners.
Word Family: **xenophobic,** *adjective;* **xenophobe,** *noun.*
[Greek *xenos* foreign + PHOBIA]

xero– (*say* **zer**ro)
a prefix meaning dry, as in *xerophyte.*
[Greek]

xerography (*say* zeer–**og**ra–fee) *noun*
a method of dry copying on ordinary paper, in which carbon powder sticks to those parts of the paper that are made sensitive by a photoelectric beam.
Word Family: **xerograph,** *noun;* **xerographic** (*say* zeero–**graff**ik), *adjective.*
[XERO– + Greek *graphein* to write]

xerophyte (*say* **zer**ra–fite) *noun*
a plant which is adapted for growth under extremely dry conditions.
Word Family: **xerophytic** (*say* zerra–**fit**tik), *adjective.*
[XERO– + Greek *phyton* a plant]

Xerox (*say* **zeer**–roks) *noun*
a system of printing by xerography.
Word Family: **xerox,** *verb,* to make xerographic copies.
[a trademark]

Xmas *noun*
(*informal*) Christmas.

X–ray *noun*
also called a **Röntgen ray**
1. a form of electromagnetic radiation of wavelength shorter than ultraviolet rays, able to penetrate wood, flesh and, in varying degrees, metal.
2. a photograph of the interior of a solid substance, especially a part of the body, by a machine using X–rays which can show up fractures, tumours, barium meal in the intestines, etc.
X–ray therapy, the destruction of cancer cells, etc. by X–rays.
Word Family: **X–ray,** *verb,* to examine by means of an X–ray.

xylem (*say* **zye**–l'm) *noun*
Biology: the cells which conduct water and minerals in a plant and give it structural support.
[Greek *xylon* wood]

xylophone (*say* **zye**–la–fone) *noun*
Music: a percussion instrument consisting of tuned, wooden bars struck with small, hand–held hammers.
Word Family: **xylophonic** (*say* zye–la–**fon**nik), *adjective;* **xylophonist** (*say* zye–**loff**a–nist), *noun.*
[Greek *xylon* wood + *phoné* sound]

Yy

yacht (*say* yot) *noun*
any boat used for cruising or racing and propelled by sails or an engine.
Word Family: **yacht**, *verb*; **yachtsman**, *noun.*
[from Dutch]

yackety-yak *noun*
(*informal*) any prolonged empty or pointless talk.
Word Family: **yackety-yak (yackety-yakked, yackety-yakking)**, *verb.*

yahoo (*say* ya-hoo) *noun*
an uncouth person.
[after a tribe of vulgar brutes in 'Gulliver's Travels' by Jonathan Swift]

yak (1) *noun*
a large ox-like humped mammal with long hair, found in the mountains of Tibet, and often kept as a work animal.
[Tibetan]

yak (2) *verb*
(yakked, yakking)
(*informal*) to chatter constantly.
Word Family: **yak**, *noun.*

Yale lock
a lock with a cylinder mechanism into which a specially grooved key is placed to release the barrel and open the lock.
[a trademark, after *Linus Yale*, 1821–68, an American locksmith]

yam *noun*
a tropical, edible, starchy root.

yank (1) *verb*
to pull with a sudden jerking motion.
Word Family: **yank**, *noun.*

Yank (2) *noun*
also called a **Yankee**
(*informal*) an American, strictly one from New England or a northern State.
[either Dutch *Janke* little John or Amerindian pronunciation of *English*]

yap *verb*
(yapped, yapping)
to bark sharply.
Usage: 'no one listened as the children *yapped*' (= talked noisily or foolishly).
Word Family: **yap**, *noun.*

yarborough *noun*
Cards: (in bridge and whist) a hand which contains no card higher than a nine.
[after an *Earl of Yarborough* who bet against its happening]

yard (1) *noun*
a unit of length equal to about 0·914 m.

yard (2) *noun*
1. an enclosed area adjoining a building or surrounded by buildings.
2. an enclosed area used for a specific purpose: 'a *shipyard*'.

yardarm *noun*
either end of a long cylindrical spar which is attached crosswise to a mast.

yardstick *noun*
any standard of measurement.

yarmulka (*say* **yamm**'l-ka) *noun*
a skullcap worn by Jewish males.

yarn *noun*
1. a thread made by twisting fibres together, used for weaving, knitting, etc.
2. (*informal*) a) a chat or conversation. b) a long story, especially about unlikely events.
Word Family: **yarn**, *verb*, to chat or tell a story.

yashmak *noun*
a veil worn in public by Moslem women.
[Arabic]

yaw *verb*
Nautical: to deviate temporarily from a straight course.

yawl *noun*
Nautical: a yacht with a large mainmast and a mizzen mast whose sail extends beyond the stern. Compare KETCH.

yawn *verb*
to open the mouth involuntarily with a deep intake of breath, as from drowsiness or boredom.
Usage: 'the hole *yawned* before us' (= opened wide).
Word Family: **yawn**, *noun.*

yaws *plural noun*
an infectious, tropical, skin disease, resembling syphilis.

Y chromosome
Biology: see SEX CHROMOSOME.

ye (1) (*say* yee) *pronoun*
an old word for you (singular or plural).

ye (2) (*say* yee) *definite article*
an old word for the.
[*the* was first written with a *thorn* (*þ*), subsequently replaced by *y* and then by *th*]

yea *adverb*
an old word for yes.

year *noun*
1. a period of 365¼ days, the period during which the earth makes one revolution around the sun. See UNITS in grey pages.
2. a) a period of 12 months on the Gregorian calendar. The **calendar year** has 365 days starting on January 1st and ending on December 31st. A **leap year** has 366 days. b) any period of 12 months, such as from March to March.
3. *Astronomy:* the period during which any planet makes one revolution around the sun.
4. all or part of a 12-month period devoted to a specific purpose: 'the academic *year*'.
5. (*plural*) a) age, especially old age. b) a long time.
year in, year out, occurring continuously.
yearly *adjective, adverb*
of or occurring once a year or every year.
Usage: 'I travel on a *yearly* ticket' (= valid for a year).

yearbook *noun*
a book issued once a year giving information about that year, especially statistics and reports of business and trade.

yearling *noun*
a horse, cow, etc. that is one year old.

yearn (*say* yern) *verb*
to have a strong desire.
Word Family: **yearningly,** *adverb.*

yeast *noun*
1. a fungus with one cell which usually multiplies by budding. Some varieties are used to produce fermentation when making beer, etc.
2. a preparation consisting of living yeast cells, compressed or powdered, used as a raising agent in baking.

yell *verb*
to scream with fright, surprise, etc.
Word Family: **yell,** *noun.*

yellow *noun*
a) a primary colour like that of butter. b) the colour between orange and green in the spectrum.
yellow *adjective*
1. of or relating to the colour yellow.
2. (*informal*) cowardly.
Word Family: **yellowish,** *adjective,* somewhat yellow.

yellowcake *noun*
the uranium oxide U_3O_8 concentrate produced by a uranium treatment plant.

yellow fever
an infectious, viral disease transmitted by mosquitoes, causing fever, aching limbs and jaundice.

yellow pages
the section of a telephone directory which classifies business subscribers according to trade, etc.

yellow streak
cowardice.

yelp *verb*
to give a quick, sharp cry or bark.
Word Family: **yelp,** *noun.*

yen (1) *noun*
plural is **yen**
the basic unit of money in Japan.

yen (2) *noun*
a desire or longing: 'I have a *yen* to visit Mexico'.

yeoman (*say* **yo**-man) *noun*
1. a farmer who cultivates his own land.
2. *History:* an attendant, especially one in a royal household.
3. a petty officer in the navy who supervises signalling by flag, semaphore, etc.
yeoman service, honest hard work just when it was needed.
[probably for YOUNG MAN]

Yeoman of the Guard
also called a **beefeater**
a member of the dismounted bodyguard of the royal household.

yes *adverb*
1. used to express assent or affirmation: '*Yes,* you may go now'.
2. used to emphasize a previous statement: 'I went, *yes,* I really went'.

yes *noun*
plural is **yeses**
1. an affirmative reply: 'we were pleased that his answer was a firm *yes*'.
2. a positive vote or voter: 'less than 50 per cent of the referendum votes were *yeses*'.

yes-man *noun*
(*informal*) a person who always agrees.

yesterday *noun*
1. the day before this present day.
2. the time recently past.
Word Family: **yesterday**, *adjective, adverb.*

yet *adverb*
1. at this time; now: 'don't leave *yet*, wait a few more minutes'.
2. thus far: 'he has not *yet* left'.
3. in the time remaining; still: 'there is *yet* time'.
4. in addition: 'let us try *yet* again'.
as yet, up to the present time.
Word Family: **yet**, *conjunction*, nevertheless.

yeti *noun*
also called the **Abominable Snowman** a large hairy creature alleged to have been sighted on rare occasions high above the Himalayan snowline.
[Tibetan]

yew *noun*
an exceptionally long-lived evergreen tree, associated with churchyards, the long-bow and still used in cabinet-making.

Yiddish *noun*
a language based mainly on German, spoken by Jews and written in Hebrew characters.
Word Family: **Yiddish**, *adjective*, Jewish.
[German *jüdisch* Jewish]

yield (*say* yeeld) *verb*
1. to produce or give forth: a) 'the farm *yielded* a good wheat crop'; b) 'the bonds *yield* ten per cent interest'.
2. to submit: a) 'they *yielded* to the enemy and lost the battle'; b) 'I *yielded* to their persuasion'.
Word Family: **yield**, *noun*, a) the act of yielding, b) the amount yielded, c) something which is yielded, such as a crop.

yippee *interjection*
an exclamation of joy, pleasure, etc.

yobbo *noun*
(*informal*) a young hooligan.
[derived from *boy* spelt backwards]

yodel (*say* yo-d'l) *noun*
a) a style of singing, partly falsetto, popular in the Austrian and Swiss mountains. b) a song sung in this style.
Word Family: **yodel** (**yodelled**, **yodelling**), *verb*; **yodeller**, *noun.*
[from German]

Yoga *noun*
any of the forms of mental, physical or moral discipline practised in Indian religion to achieve spiritual union with the Absolute.
Hathi Yoga is the form of Yoga taught in the West and primarily concerned with physical well-being and peace of mind.
[Sanskrit, union]

yoghurt (*say* yo-gert *or* yoggert) *noun*
a thick liquid made from curdled milk.
[Turkish]

yogi (*say* yo-gee) *noun*
a person practising or teaching yoga.

yoke *noun*
1. a) a crossbar with two U-shaped pieces which are placed around the necks of a pair of draught animals. b) a pair of animals joined by such a device.
2. something resembling a yoke, such as a frame worn over the shoulders to carry buckets, etc.
Usage: 'the slaves finally threw off their *yoke* of bondage' (= burden).
3. a shaped part of a garment, usually below the neck, from which the rest of the garment hangs.
Word Family: **yoke**, *verb.*

yokel (*say* yo-k'l) *noun*
a country bumpkin.

yolk (*say* yoke) *noun*
the yellow centre of an egg.
[same root as YELLOW]

yon *adjective, adverb*
an old word for yonder.

yonder *adjective*
being at an indicated distance, usually within sight: '*yonder* fields'.
yonder *adverb*
over there.

yore *adverb, adjective*
of yore, 'in days *of yore*' (= long ago, of old).

yorker *noun*
Cricket: a bowled ball which pitches underneath the batsman's bat.
[introduced by *Yorkshire* bowlers]

you (*say* yoo) *pronoun*
1. a) the second person singular or plural nominative pronoun, used to

indicate the person or persons addressed by the speaker: '*you* have a book'.
b) the second person singular or plural objective pronoun: a) 'I gave *you* the book'; b) 'I gave the book to *you*'.
see YOUR and YOURS.
2. one: '*you* would think they could do better than that'.
Usage: 'that dress simply isn't *you*' (= suitable for or typical of).

young (*say* yung) *adjective*
1. being in the early stage of life or development.
2. vigorous and fresh.
young *noun*
1. young people: 'the *young* have all before them'.
2. (of animals) offspring: 'a bird and its *young*'.
with young, (of animals) pregnant.

youngster (*say* **yung**sta) *noun*
a child or young person.

your (*say* yor) *possessive adjective*
1. belonging to you: 'it is *your* book'.
2. (*informal*) used to indicate all members of a group: '*your* typical clerk does not earn much'.

yours *possessive pronoun*
belonging to you: 'the book is *yours*'.

yourself *pronoun*
plural is **yourselves**
1. the reflexive form of **you**: 'you washed *yourself*'.
2. the emphatic form of **you**: 'you did it *yourself*'.
3. your normal or usual self: 'for many weeks after the accident you were not *yourself*'.

youth (*say* yooth) *noun*
plural is **youths** (*say* yoo*thz*)
1. the condition or quality of being young.
2. an early stage of development or existence.
3. young people considered as a group: 'the *youth* of today'.
4. a young person, especially a male.
Word Family: **youthful,** *adjective*; **youthfully,** *adverb*; **youthfulness,** *noun.*

youth hostel
a hostel for young people.

yowl *verb*
to howl or wail.
Word Family: **yowl,** *noun.*

yoyo (*say* **yo**–yo) *noun*
plural is **yoyos**
a round toy containing string around its grooved centre, so that it spins up and down as the string winds and unwinds.

ytterbium (itterbi–um) *noun*
element number 70, a rare metal. See LANTHANIDE.
See CHEMICAL ELEMENTS in grey pages.
[after *Ytterby* Sweden]

yttrium (*say* **it**–ree–um) *noun*
element number 39, a rare metal. See TRANSITION ELEMENT. See CHEMICAL ELEMENTS in grey pages.

yule, yuletide *noun*
the festival of Christmas.

yummy *adjective*
(*informal*) delicious or delightful.

Zz

zany (*say* **zay–nee**) *adjective*
clownish or comical.
[Italian *Gianni* John]

zap *verb*
(zapped, zapping)
(*informal*) a) to hit or shoot. b) to do or make quickly.
Word Family: **zap,** *noun.*

zeal *noun*
eagerness or enthusiasm.
zealot (*say* **zell**ot) *noun*
1. an eager or enthusiastic person.
2. a fanatic.
zealous (*say* **zell**us) *adjective*
eager or enthusiastic.
Word Family: **zealously,** *adverb*; **zealousness,** *noun.*
[from Greek]

zebra *noun*
an African mammal resembling a donkey and having brown or black stripes.
[Congolese]

zebra crossing
a pedestrian crossing marked by broad white or yellow stripes.

zebu (*say* **zee**boo) *noun*
an ox-like Asian or African mammal with a hump on its shoulders, sometimes kept as a work animal.
[French]

Zen *noun*
a form of Buddhism based on exclusive reliance on individual intuition as a means to sudden enlightenment, rejecting metaphysical speculation.
[Japanese]

zenith *noun*
Astronomy: the highest point on the celestial sphere, being vertically above the observer and opposite the nadir.
Usage: 'becoming manager was the *zenith* of her career' (= culmination, highest point).
[Arabic]

zephyr (*say* **zeff**a) *noun*
an old word for a gentle breeze.
[Greek *zephyros* the west wind]

zeppelin *noun*
an airship.

zero (*say* **zeer**–o) *noun*
plural is **zeros**
1. a cardinal number, the symbol 0 in the Arabic system, but not represented in the Roman system.
2. the point on an instrument, such as a thermometer, between the positive and the negative values.
Usage: 'after Christmas, my bank balance was *zero*' (= nil).
zero *verb*
zero in, to approach a target, etc. accurately.
[Arabic]

zero hour
the time set for any planned move or activity to begin.

zest *noun*
1. any great enjoyment or gusto: 'she partook of the feast with *zest*'.
2. something which adds extra taste or enjoyment: 'the wine gave *zest* to the meal'.
3. a piece of citrus rind used as a flavouring.
Word Family: **zestful,** *adjective*; **zestfully,** *adverb*; **zestfulness,** *noun*; **zesty,** *adjective.*
[French *zeste* orange-peel]

Zeus (*say* zewce) *noun*
Greek Mythology: the chief god, identified with the Roman god Jupiter.

zigzag *noun*
a line or path which turns sharply right and left.
Word Family: **zigzag** (**zigzagged, zigzagging**), *verb*, to move in a zigzag; **zigzag,** *adjective, adverb.*

zinc (*say* zink) *noun*
element number 30, a metal used in alloys, especially brass, and as a protective coating. See TRANSITION ELEMENT.
See CHEMICAL ELEMENTS in grey pages.
[from German]

zing *noun*
(*informal*) vitality or enthusiasm.

zinnia *noun*
any of a group of annual garden plants with brightly coloured flowers.
[after *J. Zinn*, 1727–59, a German botanist]

Zionist (*say* **zie**–on–ist) *noun*
a member of a movement originally aimed at re-establishing a Jewish state in Palestine (then Turkish) and now concerned with the development of Israel.
Word Family: **Zionism**, *noun*.
[after *Zion*, a hill in Jerusalem on which Solomon's Temple was built]

zip *noun*
1. a long, narrow fastener consisting of two rows of interlocking teeth which can be joined or separated by a small bar pulled between them.
2. (*informal*) energy or liveliness.
Word Family: **zip (zipped, zipping)**, *verb*, a) to fasten with a zip, b) to move quickly or energetically; **zippy**, *adjective*, lively or energetic.

zip code
American: a postcode.

zipper *noun*
a zip.

zircon *noun*
a silicate mineral of zirconium, used in industry and as a gem.
[Greek]

zirconium (*say* zer–**ko**–nee–um) *noun*
element number 40, a rare metal used in alloys, abrasives, etc. See TRANSITION ELEMENT.
See CHEMICAL ELEMENTS in grey pages.

zither (*say* zi*tha*) *noun*
a flat musical instrument with many strings, usually placed on a horizontal surface to be played.
[from Greek]

zodiac (*say* **zo**–di–ak) *noun*
Astrology: a) a part of the heavens forming an imaginary band, extending about 8° on either side of the sun's apparent path and containing the path of the main planets. It is divided into 12 parts (each called a **house**) and each is given the name of a particular group of stars. b) a circular diagram of this.
[Greek *zoidion* a sculpture of an animal]

zombie *noun*
1. a dead body supposed to be brought to life by witchcraft.
2. (*informal*) a person who lacks intelligence, independent ideas, etc.
[after *Zombi* a West African snake god]

zone *noun*
any area distinguished in some way from other areas: a) 'a military *zone*'; b) 'a residential *zone*'; c) 'the geographical *zones* of the earth'.
Word Family: **zonation**, *noun*, an arrangement in zones; **zonal**, *adjective*.
[Greek *zoné* a girdle]

zoo *noun*
an area in which many types of live animals are kept and exhibited to the public.
[short form of *zoological gardens*]

zoology (*say* zo–**olla**–jee) *noun*
the study of animals.
Word Family: **zoologist**, *noun*; **zoological** (*say* zo–a–**loji**–k'l), *adjective*; **zoologically**, *adverb*.
[Greek *zoion* an animal + –LOGY]

zoom *verb*
1. to move quickly and sharply: 'the aircraft *zoomed* into the clouds'.
2. *Film:* to make the subject being filmed appear to come closer or move away by using a zoom lens.
Word Family: **zoom**, *noun*.

zoom lens
a camera lens which may continuously change the size of an image and still remain in focus.

zoomorphic (*say* zo–a–**morfik**) *adjective*
using animal forms or shapes, e.g. in a design.
Word Family: **zoomorphism**, *noun*.

zoophyte (*say* **zo**–a–fite) *noun*
Biology: any animal resembling a plant, e.g. a coral or sponge.
Word Family: **zoophytic** (*say* zo–a–**fittik**), *adjective*.

zounds *interjection*
an old word used as an exclamation of surprise, anger, etc.
[for (God')s WOUNDS]

zucchini (*say* zoo–**kee**–nee) *noun*
plural is **zucchini**
a courgette.
[Italian, little gourds]

zygote (*say* **zye**–gote) *noun*
Biology: a fertilized egg cell, formed by the fusion of two gametes.
Word Family: **zygotic** (*say* zye–**gottik**), *adjective*.
[Greek *zygotos* yoked]

'Grey Pages' Reference Section

CONTENTS

LIST OF COMMON ABBREVIATIONS

A, (SI unit of electric current) ampere
a, (SI symbol) acceleration
A.A., Automobile Association; anti-aircraft; Alcoholics Anonymous
A.A.A., Amateur Athletic Association
A. & M., (Hymns) Ancient and Modern
A.B., able-bodied seaman
A.B.M., anti-ballistic missile
Abp, Archbishop
a.c., (Electricity) alternating current
A/C, aircraftman
a/c, account
A.D., [Latin *Anno Domini*] in the year of (Our) Lord (dating from the birth of Christ)
ad, advertisement
A.D.C., aide-de-camp; (telephone) advise duration and charge
adj., adjective
ad lib., [Latin *ad libitum*] as one pleases
Adm., Admiral; Admiralty
admin., (informal) administration
ADP., (Computers) automatic data processing
adv., adverb
advt., advertisement
a.f., (auction lots) *avec fautes* (French, with faults); as found
A.F.C., Air Force Cross; Association Football Club
A.F.M., Air Force Medal
A.G., [German *Aktiengesellschaft*] joint-stock company; Attorney-General
Ag, (Chemistry) [Latin *argentum*] silver
AGM, annual general meeting
A.H., [Latin *Anno Hegirae*] in the year of the Hegira (used before dates in Moslem history)
A.I.(D.), artificial insemination (by a donor)
Ala., (America) Alabama
Alas., (America) Alaska
Ald., Alderman
A-level, Advanced level (G.C.E.)
alt., altitude; alternative; alternate
AM, (Radio) amplitude modulation
A.M., Associate Member
a.m., [Latin *ante meridiem*] before noon
A.M.D.G., [Latin *ad majorem Dei gloriam*] to the greater glory of God
amp, ampere (SI symbol is A); amperage
anon., anonymous
Anzac, (a member of the) Australian and New Zealand Army Corps
A 1, (in Lloyd's Registers) first-class (ship); first-class
A.P., Associated Press
Apr., April
Ariz., (America) Arizona
Ark., (America) Arkansas
arr., arrives; arrival
Aslef, Associated Society of Locomotive Engineers and Firemen
assoc., association; associate
asst., assistant
ATV, Associated Television
AU, astronomical unit
Au, (Chemistry) [Latin *aurum*] gold
Aug., August
aux., auxiliary
A.V., Authorized Version (of the Bible); audio-visual
av., average
Ave., avenue
AWOL, absent without leave

b., born; (Cricket) bowled
B.A., Bachelor of Arts; British Airways
B.A.C., British Aircraft Corporation Ltd
B & B, bed and breakfast
B.A.O.R., British Army of the Rhine
Bart., Baronet
BBC, British Broadcasting Corporation
B.C., before Christ
B.Ch., **B.Chir.**, see Ch. B.
B.Com., Bachelor of Commerce
B.D., Bachelor of Divinity
B.D.S., Bachelor of Dental Surgery
B.E., **B.Eng.**, Bachelor of Engineering
B.Ed., Bachelor of Education
Beds., Bedfordshire
Benelux, Belgium, the Netherlands and Luxemburg
Berks., Berkshire
b/f, (Accounts) brought forward
b.h.p., brake horse power
bk., bank; book
B.L., Bachelor of Law
bldg, building
B. Lit., Bachelor of Literature
B. Litt., Bachelor of Letters
Blvd., boulevard
B.M., Bachelor of Medicine; British Museum
B.M.A., British Medical Association
B. Mus., Bachelor of Music
B.O., (informal) body odour
B.P., British Pharmacopoeia; British Petroleum
b.p., boiling point
Bp., Bishop
B.Phil., Bachelor of Philosophy
BR, British Rail

BRM, British Racing Motors
Bro(s)., Brother(s)
B.R.S., British Road Services
B.S., Bachelor of Surgery; British Standard
B.Sc., Bachelor of Science
B.S.T., British Summer Time
Bt., Baronet
B.T.U., B.Th.U., British Thermal Unit
bu., bushel(s)
Bucks., Buckinghamshire
B.V.M., Blessed Virgin Mary

C, Celsius; Centigrade; coulomb; (Roman numerals) 100
C., Conservative
c., cubic; century; (Cricket) caught; cent(s); copyright; chapter
c., [Latin *circa*] about
C.A., chartered accountant
C.A.B., Citizens' Advice Bureau
cal, calorie
Calif., (America) California
Cambs., Cambridgeshire
Cantab., [Latin *Cantabrigiensis*] of Cambridge University
C.A.P., (Common Market) Common Agricultural Policy
cap., capital letter
Capt., Captain
car., carat
Card., Cardinal
CAT, College of Advanced Technology
Cath., (Roman) Catholic
C.B., Companion of the Bath; (Military) confined to barracks
C.B.E., Commander of (the Order of) the British Empire
C.B.I., Confederation of British Industry
CBS, (American) Columbia Broadcasting System
C.C., County Council
cc, cubic centimetre(s); carbon copy
C.C.F., Combined Cadet Force
C.D., [French *corps diplomatique*] Diplomatic Service; Civil Defence
cd, (SI unit of luminous intensity) candela
Cdr., Commander
C.E.G.B., Central Electricity Generating Board
cent., century; [Latin *centum*] in per cent
CERN, [French *Conseil européen pour la recherche nucléaire*] European Organization for Nuclear Research
cert., certificate; certified; (informal) a certainty
cf., [Latin *confer*] compare
c/f, (Accounts) carried forward
C.G.S., Chief of the General Staff
c.g.s., centimetre-gram-second system
C.H., Companion of Honour
ch., chapter; (Chess) check
chap., chapter
Ch.B., Chir.B., B.Chir., [Latin *Chirurgiae Baccalaureus*] Bachelor of Surgery
Ches., Cheshire
C.I., Channel Islands
CIA, (America) Central Intelligence Agency
C.I.D., Criminal Investigation Department
c.i.f., cost, insurance, freight
C.-in-C., Commander-in-Chief
circ., [Latin *circa*] about
C.J., Chief Justice
cl, centilitre
Cla., Clackmannan
cm, centimetre
C.M.B., Central Midwives Board
C.M.G., Companion of (the Order of) St Michael and St George
C.N.D., Campaign for Nuclear Disarmament
CNS, central nervous system
C.O., Commanding Officer; conscientious objector
Co., County; Company
c/o, (in addressing letters) care of
C.O.D., cash on delivery
C.O.D., *Concise Oxford Dictionary*
C. of E., Church of England
C.O.I., Central Office of Information
Col., Colonel
col., column
Coll., college
colloq., colloquial
Colo., (America) Colorado
comp., comparative; compare; composition; compositor; compound
conj., conjunction
Conn., (America) Connecticut
Cons., Conservative
cont., continued; containing; contents
contd., continued
co-op, co-operative shop or society
Corn., Cornwall
Corp., Corporation; Corporal
Coy, Company
cp., compare with
C.P., Communist Party
Cpl., Corporal
C.P.R., Canadian Pacific Railway
CQMS, Company Quartermaster Sergeant
cr., credit; creditor
C.S.E., Certificate of Secondary Education
CSIRO, Commonwealth Scientific and Industrial Research Organization
CSM, Company Sergeant-Major

Cu, (Chemistry) [Latin *cuprum*] copper
cu., cubic
C.V.O., Commander of the Royal Victorian Order
C.W.S., Co-operative Wholesale Society
cwt, hundredweight

D, (Roman numerals) 500
d., died; [Latin *denarius*] (old) penny; daughter; date
D.A., (America) District Attorney
dB, decibel
D.B.E., Dame Commander of (the Order of) the British Empire
D.C., (America) District of Columbia (Washington)
d.c., (Electricity) direct current
D.C.L., Doctor of Civil Law
D.C.M., Distinguished Conduct Medal
D.D., Doctor of Divinity
D-day, 6 June 1944 (invasion of Europe)
DDT, the insecticide dichloro-diphenyl-trichloro-ethane
Dec., December
dec., deceased
deg., degree
Del., (America) Delaware
D.E.P., Department of Employment and Productivity
dep., departs; departure
dept., department
derv, diesel-engined road vehicle (fuel)
D.E.S., Department of Education and Science
D.F.C., Distinguished Flying Cross
D.F.M., Distinguished Flying Medal
D.G., [Latin *Dei gratia*] by the grace of God
diag., diagram
DIN, [German *Deutsche Industrie Normal*] German Standard
Dip. Ed., Diploma of Education
D.I.Y., do it yourself
DJ, disc jockey
D.Litt., Doctor of Letters
DM, [German *Deutsche Mark*] German currency
D. Mus., Doctor of Music
DMZ, Demilitarized Zone
DNA, (Biology) deoxyribonucleic acid
do., ditto, the same
d.o.a., dead on arrival (at hospital)
D.P.H., Diploma in Public Health
D. Phil., Doctor of Philosophy
D.P.P., Director of Public Prosecutions
Dr, doctor; debtor
dr, dram
D.Sc., Doctor of Science
D.S.C., Distinguished Service Cross
D.S.M., Distinguished Service Medal
D.S.O., Distinguished Service Order
d.t's, delirium tremens
Dur., Durham
D.V., [Latin *Deo volente*] God willing
dwt, pennyweight

E, east; eastern
ea., each
E. & O.E., errors and omissions excepted
ECG, electrocardiogram
ECM, Electronic Counter-measures
ECT, electroconvulsive therapy
ed., edited by; editor; edition; education
EDP, electronic data processing
EEC, European Economic Community (the Common Market)
EEG, electroencephalogram
e.g., [Latin *exempli gratia*] for example
e.m.f., electromotive force
EMI, Electrical & Musical Industries Ltd
encl., enclosed
ENE, east-north-east
Eng., engineer(ing); England; English
Eng. Lit., English Literature
EP, extended play (gramophone record)
EPNS, electro-plated nickel silver
E.R., [Latin *Elizabetha Regina*] Queen Elizabeth
Ernie, electronic random number indicator equipment (used in selecting Premium Bonds)
ESE, east-south-east
ESP, extra-sensory perception
esp., especially
Esq., Esquire
E.S.R.O., European Space Research Organization
EST, (America) Eastern Standard Time
est., estimated; established
ETA, estimated time of arrival
et al., [Latin *et alii*] and other people; [*et alia*] and other things
etc., [Latin *et cetera*] and the rest; and so on
ETD, estimated time of departure
et seq., [Latin *et sequens*] and the following
eV, electron-volt
exch., exchange; exchequer
excl., excluding
ext., extension; external

F, Fahrenheit; (Physics) farad
***F*,** (SI symbol) force
***f*,** (SI symbol) frequency; (Music) [Italian *forte*] loud
f., following; focal length; female; feminine; franc (French currency); folio
F.A., Football Association
F.A.O., Food and Agricultural Organization (of the United Nations)

FBI, (America) Federal Bureau of Investigation
F.E., Further Education
Fe, (Chemistry) [Latin *ferrum*] iron
Feb., February
Fed., Federal; Federation
fem., female; feminine
Ferm., Fermanagh
***ff*,** (Music) [Italian *fortissimo*] very loud
ff., and the following (pages etc.); folios
F.H., fire-hydrant
FIFA, Fédération Internationale de Football Association (governing body of international soccer)
fig., figure; figurative(ly)
fl., fluid; florin
***fl.*,** [Latin *floruit*] flourished
Fla., (America) Florida
FM, (Radio) frequency modulation
F.M., Field-Marshal
fm., fathom
F.O., Foreign Office
f.o.b., free on board
fol., following; folio
f.o.r., free on rail
f.p., freezing point
F.P.A., Family Planning Association
Fr., Father; French; France
F.R.C.P., F.R.C.S., Fellow of the Royal College of Physicians (Surgeons)
F.R.G.S., Fellow of the Royal Geographical Society
Fri., Friday
F.R.S., Fellow of the Royal Society
ft, foot; feet
F.T. Index, *Financial Times* Index (of share prices)
fur., furlong
fwd., forward

G, (America; informal) grand (1000 dollars)
***G*,** (Physics) the constant of gravitation
g, gram
***g*,** (Physics) acceleration due to gravity
Ga., (America) Georgia
gal., gallon(s)
Gatt, G.A.T.T., General Agreement on Tariffs and Trade
G.B., Great Britain
G.B.E., Knight (Dame) Grand Cross of (the Order of) the British Empire
G.C., George Cross
G.C.B., Knight (Dame) Grand Cross of the (Order of the) Bath
G.C.E., General Certificate of Education
G.C.M.G., Knight (Dame) Grand Cross of (the Order of) St Michael and St George
Gdn(s), gardens
Gen., General
gen., (informal) general information
GHQ, General Headquarters
GI, (America) government issue; private soldier
Gk., Greek
G.L.C., Greater London Council
Glos., Gloucestershire
G.M., George Medal; General Manager
gm, gram (SI symbol is g)
G-man, (America; informal) Government man (Federal criminal investigation officer)
GMT, Greenwich Mean Time
GNP, gross national product
G.O.C., General Officer Commanding
Gov., Governor
govt., government
G.P., general practitioner (medical doctor)
GPO, General Post Office
gr., grain
G.S.O., General Staff Officer
GT, [Italian *gran turismo*] touring (car)
gt., great

H, (SI unit) henry; (of pencils) hard
h, (Physics) hour(s)
***h*,** (Physics) Planck's constant
H.A., hardy annual (plant)
ha, hectare
h. and c., hot and cold (water)
Hants., Hampshire
Hb, (Biology) haemoglobin
H.E., His (Her) Excellency; high explosive
Herts., Hertfordshire
h.f., (Radio) high frequency
Hg, (Chemistry) [Latin *hydrargyrum*] mercury
H.H.A., half-hardy annual (plant)
H.M., Her (His) Majesty
HMS, Her (His) Majesty's ship
H.M.S.O., Her (His) Majesty's Stationery Office
HMV, His Master's Voice
Hon., Honourable; honorary
H.P., hire purchase
hp, horsepower
HQ, headquarters
hr., hour(s)
H.R.H., Her (His) Royal Highness
h.t., high tension
HTV, Harlech Television (Wales)
Hunts., Huntingdonshire
H.W.M., high-water mark
Hz, (SI unit of frequency) hertz

I, (Roman numerals) one
***I*,** (SI symbol) electric current
I., Island(s)
i., intransitive

IATA, International Air Transport Association
ib., ibid., [Latin *ibidem*] in the same place
I.B.A., Independent Broadcasting Authority
i c, in charge
ICBM, intercontinental ballistic missile
I.C.E., Institution of Civil Engineers
ICI, Imperial Chemical Industries
i.e. [Latin *id est*] that is
IHS, [from Greek] Jesus
ILEA, Inner London Education Authority
Ill., (America) Illinois
ill., illustrated; illustration
I.L.O., International Labour Organization
IMF, International Monetary Fund
in., inch(es)
Inc., (America) incorporated
incl., including; inclusive
Ind., (America) Indiana
inf., infantry; infinitive
info., (informal) information
infra dig., [Latin *infra dignitatem*] beneath one's dignity, undignified
I.N.R.I., [Latin *Iesus Nazarenus Rex Iudaeorum*] Jesus of Nazareth, King of the Jews
Inst., Institute; Institution
inst., instant
int., internal; international; interior
interj., interjection
intro., (informal) introduction (to a person)
introd., introduction
I.o.M., I.O.M., Isle of Man
IOU, I owe you
I.O.W., Isle of Wight
I.P.A., International Phonetic Alphabet
IQ, intelligence quotient
I.R.A., Irish Republican Army
Ire., Ireland
ISBN, International Standard Book Number
I.T., income tax
It., Italian; Italy
ITN, Independent Television News
ITT, (America) International Telephones & Telegraph
ITV, Independent Television
IUD, intra-uterine device

J, (SI unit of work) joule
Jan., January
J.C., Jesus Christ
J.P., Justice of the Peace
jr, jun., junior

K, (SI unit of thermodynamic temperature) kelvin; (Chess) King; (Chemistry) [Latin *kalium*] potassium
k-, kilo-
Kan., (America) Kansas
K.B., Knight of the (Order of the) Bath
K.B.E., Knight Commander of the (Order of the) British Empire
K.C.B., Knight Commander of (the Order of) the Bath
K.C.M.G., Knight Commander of (the Order of) St Michael and St George
kc s, kilocycles per second
K.G., Knight of the (Order of the) Garter
kg, (SI unit of mass) kilogram(s)
K.G.B., [Russian] State Security Committee (secret police)
kHz, kilohertz
Kinc., Kincardin(shire)
Kirkc., Kirkcudbright
km, kilometre(s)
km h, kilometres per hour
kn., (Nautical) knot
K.O., k.o., (Boxing) knock-out
K.T., Knight of the (Order of the) Thistle
Kt, (Chess) Knight
Kt., Knight (Bachelor)
kW, kilowatt(s)
kWh, kilowatts per hour
Ky., (America) Kentucky

L, (Roman numerals) 50; learner (driver)
L., lake; Latin; law; Liberal; Licentiate
l, litre; left
l, (SI symbol) length
l., line; length; lira(s) (Italian currency)
L.A., (America) Los Angeles
La., (America) Louisiana
Lab., Labour
lab, laboratory
Lancs., Lancashire
lang., language
Lat., Latin
lat., latitude
lb (plural is **lb** or **lbs**), [Latin *libra*] pound (weight)
l.b.w., (Cricket) leg before wicket
l.c., [Latin *loco citato*] in the place cited; (Printing) lower case
L.C.J., Lord Chief Justice
L Cpl, Lance-Corporal
L.E.A., Local Education Authority
Leics., Leicestershire
l.f., (Radio) low frequency
l.h., left hand
L.I., (America) Long Island
Lib., Liberal, liberation
Lieut., Lieutenant
Lincs., Lincolnshire

lit., literal(ly); literature; literary
Litt.D., Lit.D., [Latin *Litterarum Doctor*] Doctor of Letters
ll., lines
LL.B. (D., M.), Bachelor (Doctor, Master) of Laws
loc. cit., [Latin *loco citato*] in the place cited
log, logarithm
long., longitude
LP, long-playing (gramophone record)
LSD, the drug lysergic acid diethylamide
l.s.d., £.s.d., [Latin *librae, solidi, denarii*] pounds, shillings and pence
L.S.E., London School of Economics
Lt., Lieutenant
l.t., low tension
L.T.A., Lawn Tennis Association
Ltd, limited (liability company)
LV, luncheon voucher
L.W.M., low-water mark

M, motorway; Monsieur; (Roman numerals) 1000; mega-
m, (SI basic unit of length) metre
m, (SI symbol) mass
m., mile; million; milli-; minute; male; married; month
M.A., Master of Arts
Maj., Major
Mar., March
masc., masculine
Mass., (America) Massachusetts
max., maximum
M.B., Bachelor of Medicine
M.B.E., Member of the (Order of the) British Empire
M.C., Military Cross; Master of Ceremonies; (America) Member of Congress
M.C.C., Marylebone Cricket Club
M.D., Doctor of Medicine
Md., (America) Maryland
M.E., Middle East; Middle English
Me., (America) Maine
mech., mechanic(al)
M.Ed., Master of Education
Med., Mediterranean
Messrs, [French *Messieurs*] plural of Mr
Meth., Methodist
mfg., manufacturing
M.F.H., Master of Foxhounds
mfr(s), manufacturer(s)
mg, milligram(s)
MGM, Metro-Goldwyn-Mayer
Mgr, Monsignor; Manager
Mich., (America) Michigan
M.I.5, counterespionage and internal security branch of Military Intelligence
min., minimum; minute
Minn., (America) Minnesota
MIRV, (ballistic missiles) multiple independently-targetable re-entry vehicle
misc., miscellaneous
M.I.6, Secret Intelligence Service (also called S.I.S.)
Miss., (America) Mississippi
M.I.T., (America) Massachusetts Institute of Technology
mkt., market
ml, millilitre(s)
M.Litt., Master of Letters
Mlle, Mademoiselle
M.M., Military Medal
mm, millimetre(s)
Mme, Madame
M.N., Merchant Navy
M.O., Medical Officer; money order
Mo., (America) Missouri
M.o.D., Ministry of Defence
mod., moderate; modern
mod cons, (informal) modern conveniences
M.O.H., Medical Officer of Health
mol, (SI basic unit of amount of substance) mole
Mont., (America) Montana
M.P., Member of Parliament; Military Police
m.p., melting point
m.p.g., miles per gallon
m.p.h., miles per hour
m.p.s., miles per second
Mr, Mister
MRA, Moral Rearmament
M.R.C.P., M.R.C.S., Member of the Royal College of Physicians (Surgeons)
Mrs, (abbreviation of *mistress*) title used before the name of a married woman
MS., manuscript
Ms, title used instead of *Miss* or *Mrs*
M.Sc., Master of Science
MSS., manuscripts
Mt., Mount
Mts, mountains
m.v., M.V., motor vessel

N, (SI derived unit of force) newton; north; northern
n, (SI symbol) mole
n., noun; neuter; nominative
n/a, not applicable; not available
Na, (Chemistry) [Latin *natrium*] sodium
NAAFI, Naafi, Naffy, Navy, Army and Air Force Institutes
Nalgo, National Association of Local Government Officers
NASA, (America) National Aeronautics and Space Administration
nat., national; natural
Nato, NATO, North Atlantic Treaty Organization

N.B., n.b., [Latin *nota bene*] take special note of
NBC, (America) National Broadcasting Company
N.C., (America) North Carolina
N.C.B., National Coal Board
N.C.O., Non-commissioned Officer
N. Dak., (America) North Dakota
NE, north-east
NEB, New English Bible
Nebr., (America) Nebraska
Neddy, N.E.D.C., National Economic Development Council
neg., negative
nem. con., [Latin *nemine contradicente*] unanimously
Nev., (America) Nevada
N.F.U., National Farmers' Union
N.H., (America) New Hampshire
N.H.S., National Health Service
N.J., (America) New Jersey
N. Mex., (America) New Mexico
NNE, north-north-east
NNW, north-north-west
n.o., (cricket) not out
no. (plural is **nos.**), [Italian *numero*] number
non-U, (informal) not upper-class usage
Northants., Northamptonshire
Notts., Nottinghamshire
Nov., November
n.p., not placed; new paragraph
nr, near
N.S.P.C.C., National Society for the Prevention of Cruelty to Children
N.S.W., (Australia) New South Wales
N.T., New Testament; (Australia) Northern Territory
NUGMW, National Union of General and Municipal Workers
NUJ, National Union of Journalists
NUM, National Union of Mineworkers
NUPE, National Union of Public Employees
NUR, National Union of Railwaymen
NUT, National Union of Teachers
NW, north-west
N.Y., (America) New York (State)
N.Y.C., (America) New York City
N.Z., New Zealand

O.A.P., Old Age Pension(er)
O.A.U., Organization for African Unity
ob., [Latin *obiit*] died
O.B.E., Officer of (the Order of) the British Empire
obs., obsolete
O.C., Officer Commanding
Oct., October
Octu, Officer Cadets Training Unit
o d, overdrawn
O.E., Old English
O.E.C.D., Organization for Economic Co-operation and Development
O.E.D., *Oxford English Dictionary*
O.H.M.S., On Her (His) Majesty's Service
OK, agreed; all right
Okla., (America) Oklahoma
O-level, Ordinary level (G.C.E.)
O.M., Order of Merit
o.n.o., or near offer
o.p., (Theatre) opposite the prompter's side (left side of stage viewed from auditorium)
op., (Surgery or Military) operation
op., *opus* (work)
o p, out of print
op. cit., [Latin *opere citato*] in the work cited
O.P.E.C., Organization of Petroleum Exporting Countries
opp., opposite
O.R., Operational Research; other ranks
orch., orchestra(l)
Oreg., (America) Oregon
orig., origin; original(ly)
O.S., (clothing) outsize
o s, out of stock
Oscar, annual award for film production
O.T., Old Testament
Oxfam, Oxford Committee for Famine Relief
Oxon., Oxfordshire; of Oxford University
oz, ounce(s)

P, (Chess) pawn
p, [Italian *piano*] (Music) soft
p., penny; pence; page; per; past; participle
P.A., Press Association; personal assistant
p.a., [Latin *per annum*] per year
Pa., (America) Pennsylvania
par., paragraph; parallel; parish
para., paragraph
Parl., parliament(ary)
P.A.Y.E., Pay As You Earn (income tax)
Pb, (Chemistry) [Latin *plumbum*] lead
P.C., police constable; Privy Council(lor)
p.c., postcard; per cent
p.d., [Latin *per diem*] per day; (Electricity) potential difference
pd., paid
P.D.S.A., People's Dispensary for Sick Animals
P.E., physical education
PEN Club, an international association of Poets, Playwrights, Essayists, Editors, Novelists
P.G., paying guest

P.G.A., Professional Golfers' Association
pH, a scale of acidity alkalinity
pharm., pharmaceutical; pharmacy
Ph. D., Doctor of Philosophy
Pk., park
pkt., packet
Pl., place
pl., plural
P.M., Prime Minister; post-mortem
p.m., [Latin *post meridiem*] after noon; per month
P.O., Post Office; Petty Officer; Pilot Officer; postal order
P.O.D., pay on delivery
P.O.P., Post Office preferred (size of envelope)
pop., population; popular
pos., positive
P.O.S.B., Post Office Savings Bank
poss., possible; possibly; possessive (case)
P.O.W., prisoner of war
P.P., Parish Priest
p.p., [Latin *per procurationem*] by proxy; past participle
pp., pages
***pp*,** [Italian *pianissimo*] (Music) very soft
p.p.m., (Chemistry) parts per million
P.P.S., Parliamentary Private Secretary; Principal Private Secretary
P.P.S., [Latin *post post scriptum*] a second postscript
P. Q., (Canada) Province of Quebec
P.R., public relations; proportional representation; (America) Puerto Rico
pr., pair; price
P.R.A., President of the Royal Academy
prep., preparatory; preparation; preposition
Pres., president
pro., professional
Prof., Professor
pron., pronoun; pronounced; pronunciation
Prot., Protestant
***pro tem.*,** [Latin *pro tempore*] for the time being
P.S., [Latin *post scriptum*] postscript
Ps., psalm
P.T., physical training
Pt., port
pt., pint(s); part; point; payment
P.T.A., Parent-Teacher Association
Pte., Private (soldier)
P.T.O., please turn over
Pty, proprietary (company)
PVA, (Chemistry) polyvinyl acetate
PVC, (Chemistry) polyvinyl chloride
PX, (America, military) Post Exchange (a shop at an Army 'post')

Q, (Chess) Queen
q., query
QANTAS, (Australia) Queensland and Northern Territory Aerial Service
Q.B. (D.), Queen's Bench (Division)
Q.C., Queen's Counsel
QED, [Latin *quod erat demonstrandum*] which had to be proved
Qld., (Australia) Queensland
q.t., (informal) (on the) quiet
qt, quart
q.v., [Latin *quod vide*) which see

R, (Chess) Rook
***R*,** (Physics) resistance
R., [Latin *rex, regina*] King, Queen; river; rabbi
r., radius
R.A., Royal Academy; Rear-Admiral
R.A.C., Royal Automobile Club; Royal Armoured Corps
rad, (SI unit of plane angle) radian
RADA, Royal Academy of Dramatic Art
R.A.F., Royal Air Force
R. and D., research and development (costs)
R. & R, (Military) rest and recreation
R.C., Roman Catholic
R.C.A., Radio Corporation of America
Rd, road
R D, refer to drawer (of cheque)
R.E., Royal Engineers
rec(d), received
ref., reference; refer; referee
Regt., regiment
Reme, R.E.M.E., Royal Electrical and Mechanical Engineers
Rep., repertory
rep., representative
res., resigned; reserve
ret., retired
retd., returned
Rev., Reverend
rev., revolution; revenue; reverse
r.f., radio frequency
RFC, Rugby Football Club
r.h., right hand
Rh, Rhesus factor
R.I., religious instruction; (America) Rhode Island
R.I.P., [Latin *requiescat requiescant in pace*] may he (she, they) rest in peace
rly., railway
rm., ream; room
R.M.A., Royal Military Academy
R.N., Royal Navy
RNA, (Biology) ribonucleic acid
R.N.L.I., Royal National Lifeboat Institution
RoSPA, Royal Society for the Prevention of Accidents

r.p.m., rev min revolutions per minute
R.S., Royal Society
RSM, Regimental Sergeant-Major
RSPCA, Royal Society for the Prevention of Cruelty to Animals
R.S.V.P., [French *répondez s'il vous plait*] please reply
R T, radio telegraphy; radio telephony
Rt. Hon., Right Honourable
Rt. Rev., Right Reverend
R.U.C., Royal Ulster Constabulary
R.U.F.C., Rugby Union Football Club
R.V., Revised Version (of the Bible)

S, south; southern
s, (SI unit of time) second
s., (Grammar) substantive; [Latin *solidua*] shilling
S.A., South Africa; South Australia; [French *Societé Anonyme*] Limited Company
SACEUR,, Supreme Allied Commander Europe (Nato)
s.a.e., stamped addressed envelope
SALT, Strategic Arms Limitation Talks
SAM, surface-to-air missile
S.A.S., Special Air Service; Scandinavian Airlines System
Sat., Saturday
s.a.v., stock at valuation
S.A.Y.E., Save As You Earn
S.C., (America) South Carolina
Sc., science; Scottish
sc., [Latin *scilicet*] namely
S.Dak., (America) South Dakota
SE, south-east
S E, Stock Exchange
sec., second (SI symbol is s); secretary
S.E.N., State Enrolled Nurse
Sen., Senator; Senate; Senior
Sept., September
SF, science fiction
Sgt., Sergeant
Shape, SHAPE, Supreme Headquarters, Allied Powers in Europe (Nato)
SI, [French *Système International*] International System (of units)
sic, [Latin thus] so written
sing., singular
S.I.S., Secret Intelligence Service (M.I.6)
S.J., Society of Jesus (the Jesuits)
SLBM, Submarine-Launched Ballistic Missile
Sn, (Chemistry) [Latin *stannum*] tin
S.O., Symphony Orchestra
Soc., society
S.O.E., Special Operations Executive
SOS, (said to stand for *Save Our Souls*) radio signal for help—now *Mayday*
Sp., Spanish
sp (plural is **spp**), species
S.P.Q.R., [Latin *Senatus Populusque Romanus*] the Senate and people of Rome; (informal) small profits, quick returns
sq., square
Sqn., squadron
sr, (SI unit of solid angle) steradian
S.R.C., Students' Representative Council
S.R.N., State Registered Nurse
SS., Saints
s.s., S.S., steamship
S.S.A.F.A., Soldiers', Sailors' and Airmen's Families Association
SSE, south-south-east
SSW, south-south-west
St., Saint; street; station; strait
st., stone (weight); (Cricket) stumped
Staffs., Staffordshire
STD, subscriber trunk dialling (telephone)
stet, [Latin, let it stand] cancel alteration
stg., sterling
s.t.p., standard temperature and pressure
sub., subscription; submarine; substitute
Sun., Sunday
Supt., superintendent
surg., surgeon; surgery; surgical
Sx, Sussex
Sy, Surrey

T, (SI symbol) thermodynamic temperature
t, tonne
***t*,** (SI symbol) time
t., ton; time; transitive
T.A.A.V.R., Territorial, Auxiliary, and Volunteer Reserve
TAM, Television Audience Measurement
TB, tuberculosis
tbs., tbsp., tablespoon
T.D., Territorial Decoration
Tech., (informal) technical college
tech., technology; technical
tel., telephone
temp., temperature; temporary
Tenn., (America) Tennessee
Ter., terrace
Tex., (America) Texas
TGWU, Transport and General Workers' Union
Th., Thursday
TKO, (Boxing) technical knock-out
TNT, the explosive trinitrotoluene
trans., transfer(red); translated; translator; transitive
Treas., treasurer; treasury

trig., trigonometry
tsp., teaspoon
TT, teetotal; tuberculin-tested; Tourist Trophy
TUC, Trades Union Congress
Tue., Tuesday
TV, television

U., union; university; united; upper-class usage (opposed to non-U)
U.C.C.A., University Central Clearing Agency
UDI, unilateral declaration of independence
Ufo, UFO, unidentified flying object
U.G.C., University Grants Committee
UHF, ultra-high frequency
U.K., United Kingdom
U.N., United Nations
Unesco, United Nations Educational, Scientific and Cultural Organization
Unicef, United Nations International Children's Emergency Fund
Univ., University
U.P., United Press
U.S., United States
u s, unserviceable
U.S.A., United States of America
U.S.S., United States Ship
U.S.S.R., Union of Soviet Socialist Republics
usu., usually
u-v, ultra-violet

V, (Physics) volt; (Roman numerals) 5
v, (Physics) velocity
v., versus; [Latin *vide*] refer to; verb; verse
Va., (America) Virginia
vac., vacation
VAT, Value Added Tax
vb., verb
V.C., Victoria Cross; vice-chancellor; vice-chairman
V.D., venereal disease
VE-day, Victory in Europe Day (8 May 1945)
Ven., Venerable
verb. sap., [Latin *verbum* (*satis*) *sapienti*] a word to the wise suffices
vet, veterinary surgeon
VG, variable geometry (swept-wing aircraft)
VHF, (Radio) very high frequency
v.i., intransitive verb
V.I.P., very important person
viz., [Latin *videlicet*] namely
VJ-day, Victory over Japan Day (15 August 1945)
vocab., vocabulary
vol., volume
V.S., veterinary surgeon
vs., verse; versus
V.S.O., Voluntary Services Overseas
VSOP, Very Special Old Pale (brandy)
V STOL, vertical or short take-off and landing (aircraft)
Vt., (America) Vermont
v.t., transitive verb
VTOL, vertical take-off and landing (aircraft)

W, (Physics) watt(s); west; western
W, (SI symbol) work
w., week, wife
War., Warks., Warwickshire
Wash., (America) Washington (State)
WASP, (America) White Anglo-Saxon Protestant
WC, w.c., water closet
W.E.A., Workers' Educational Association
Wed., Wednesday
W.H.O., World Health Organization
W.I., Women's Institute; West Indies
Wis., (America) Wisconsin
wk., week, work
WNW, west-north-west
W.O., warrant officer; War Office
Worcs., Worcestershire
w.p.m., words per minute
Wracs, Women's Royal Army Corps
Wrafs, Women's Royal Air Force
Wrens, Women's Royal Naval Service
W.R.V.S., Women's Royal Voluntary Services
WSW, west-south-west
wt., weight
W T, wireless telegraphy; wireless telephony
W.Va., (America) West Virginia
Wyo., (America) Wyoming

X, (Roman numerals) 10

y., year(s)
yd, yard(s)
Y.H.A., Youth Hostels Association
YMCA, Young Men's Christian Association
Yorks., Yorkshire
yr., your; year
YWCA, Young Women's Christian Association

WORD PARTS AND CLASSICAL ROOTS

Many English words are made up of parts which are words in their own right. For example:

harmless
downpour
thunderbolt
pitchfork
breakfast

Most English word parts, however, cannot stand alone as individual words. Word parts of this kind can be divided into two basic groups: English word parts and foreign word parts. The simplest example of an English word part is the final 's' added to nouns to form the plural: camel, camels.

In the past, formation of new words has often involved a modification of affixes and stems; habits of pronunciation and spelling frequently won out over strict rules for joining word parts. Thus:

actor + ess = actress (not actoress)
in + plant = implant (not inplant)

Foreign word parts have come to us mainly from ancient Greek and Latin. In many cases foreign word parts were combined in their language of origin and passed into English in only a slightly modified form:

(Greek) *demokratia*, popular government [from *demos*, people + *kratos*, rule] → (English) democracy

The following lists and tables are divided into four sections:

A: Word parts commonly used in English
B: Table of classical roots and word parts
C: Table of numbers
D: Latin verbs and prefixes

A: WORD PARTS COMMONLY USED IN ENGLISH

1 NOUN ENDINGS

A. People

(i) Indicating a person in a specific occupation, activity or situation:

-er	employ, employ*er*; drive, driv*er*
-ee	employ, employ*ee* (An *employer* is a person who employs people; an *employee* is a person who is employed.)
-eer	mountain, mountain*eer*; engine, engin*eer*
-ian	mathematics, mathematic*ian*; library, librar*ian*
-ist	violin, violin*ist*
-ant	contest, contest*ant*
-ent	depend, depend*ent*; preside, presid*ent*

(ii) Indicating a person with a specific belief or attitude:

-ist	secession, secession*ist*
-ian	Christ, Christ*ian*; vegetables, vegetar*ian*
-ite	Trotsky, Trotsky*ite*

(iii) Indicating a person from a specific place:

-n,-ian	America, America*n*; Alsace, Alsat*ian*
-er	New Zealand, New Zealand*er*

(iv) Indicating a female:

-ess	actor, actr*ess*; manager, manager*ess*
-e	fiancé, fiancé*e*

B. Places

Indicating a place for a specific activity:

-ary	dispense, dispens*ary*
-ery	hatch, hatch*ery*
-ory	reform, reformat*ory*
-arium	herb, herb*arium*
-orium	cremate, cremat*orium*

C. Objects

(i) Indicating an object for a specific purpose:

-er	harvest, harvest*er*; teleprint, teleprint*er*
-or	percolate, percolat*or*

(ii) Indicating an object originally from or associated with a specific place

-ian	Hesse, hess*ian*
-er	Frankfurt, frankfurt*er*

D. Abstract nouns

(i) Indicating a condition, achievement or status:

-cy	captain, captain*cy*; tenant, tenan*cy*
-dom	martyr, martyr*dom*; free, free*dom*

D. Abstract nouns–continued

-hood	child, child*hood*; live, liveli*hood*
-ty, -ity	certain, certain*ty*; timid, timid*ity*
-ness	busy, busi*ness*
-ics	genes, genet*ics*
-ship	friend, friend*ship*
-ing	build, build*ing*

(ii) Indicating a belief or attitude:

-ism	Chauvin, chauvin*ism*
-ity	Christian, Christian*ity*

(iii) Indicating a process or result:

-ment	derail, derail*ment*
-tion	attend, atten*tion*; examine, examina*tion*
-sion	convert, conver*sion*
-ism	critic, critic*ism*

(iv) Indicating quantity:

-age	bag, bagg*age*
-ful	spoon, spoon*ful*

(v) Indicating small size:

-let	book, book*let*
-ette	cigar, cigar*ette*

(vi) Indicating plural:

-s	fork, fork*s*
-es	bus, bus*es*

(Note also the following non-English plural forms which survive in a few words.)

from *Latin:*

-a	bacterium, bacteri*a*
-ae	larva, larv*ae*
-i	radius, radi*i*

from *Hebrew:*

-im	cherub, cherub*im*

from *Italian*

-i	gelato, gelat*i*

from *French:*

-x	tableau, tableaux

2 ADJECTIVE ENDINGS

(i) Indicating characteristics:

-ous	lustre, lustr*ous*
-eous	gas, gas*eous*
-al, -ial	nature, natur*al*; adverb, adverb*ial*
-ic, -ical	acid, acid*ic*; alphabet, alphabet*ical*

-ent	differ, differ*ent*
-ious	luxury, luxur*ious*
-ant	please, pleas*ant*
-ful	waste, waste*ful*
-en	wood, wood*en*
-ly	friend, friend*ly*
-y	air, air*y*
-ern	south, south*ern*
-erly	south, south*erly*

(ii) Indicating similarity to something specific:

-like	lady, lady*like*
-ish	green, green*ish*
-esque	picture, pictur*esque*

(iii) Indicating a possible characteristic or effect:

-some	trouble, trouble*some*
-able	avoid, avoid*able*
-ible	reverse, revers*ible*
-uble	solve, sol*uble*

(iv) Indicating lack or absence of a specific characteristic:

-less	hope, hope*less*
-free	care, care*free*

(v) Indicating purpose:

-ory	advise, advis*ory*

(vi) Indicating degree:

-er	cold, cold*er*
-est	cold, cold*est*

Note:

a) In the case of some long and complicated adjectives, these indicators are not used:

acceptable, *more* acceptable, *most* acceptable

b) Some common adjectives have special forms to indicate degree:

good, *better, best*
bad, *worse, worst*

c) Some people believe that certain adjectives cannot be qualified in this way:

unique (= the only one of its kind)
perfect (= faultless)

3 ADVERB ENDINGS

(i) The basic adverb indicator:

-ly	bad, bad*ly*; probable, probab*ly*

(ii) Indicating direction:

-wards, -ward home, home*wards*
-ways side, side*ways*
-wise length, length*wise*

(iii) Indicating manner:

-wise like, like*wise*

4 VERB FORMS

(i) Common ways of forming verbs:

a) Using a noun:
Xerox, to *xerox*

b) Adding **-ize** or **-ise** to a noun:
container, to container*ize*

c) Adding **-en** at the end of a noun:
length, length*en*

d) Adding **en-** to the beginning of a noun:
circle, *en*circle

e) Adding **be-** to the beginning of a noun:
calm, *be*calm

(ii) Indicating time present:

-ing talk, talk*ing*; move, mov*ing*; build, build*ing*

This form can be used in a number of different patterns:

a) As a *participle* in verb patterns:
I am *moving* (= I move)
I am *talking* (= I talk)
I am *building* (= I build)

b) As a *verb-noun:*
Talking is prohibited in this library (= the act of talking)
Moving house took several days (= the process of moving)
I want to learn *building* (= the skill or trade of building)
These verb-nouns can also appear in adjective patterns:
Keep off the *building* site (= the site where a building is being constructed)
That is a good *talking* point (= a point to talk about)

c) As a *verb-adjective:*
Do not jump off *moving* trains (= which are moving)
He makes *talking* dolls (= which talk)
The play was very *moving* (= impressive)

(iii) Indicating time past:

-ed lock, lock*ed*; pickle, pickl*ed*
vowel change: hang, ***hung***
vowel and consonant change: buy, ***bought***

These are known as irregular or 'strong' forms, and exist in many very common verbs.

(iv) These past-tense forms can be used in a number of patterns:

a) As *verbs* in their own right:
I *locked* the door
I *pickled* the cucumbers
I *hung* my coat on the peg
I *bought* the cake

b) As *participles* in verb patterns:
I *have locked* the door
I *have pickled* the cucumbers
I *have hung* my coat on the peg
I *have bought* the cake

c) As *verb-adjectives:*
I opened the *locked* door
I ate the *pickled* cucumber
I prefer a *bought* cake

B: TABLE OF CLASSICAL ROOTS AND WORD PARTS

In this table, the classical forms of the words have been in some cases modified (e.g. *archaeos* rather than *arkhaios*) so as to match the transliteration most often encountered in the English derivatives.

Word part or rootword	*English example*	*Literal meaning*	*Further reference*
a-, Greek, = not, without	*a*morphous	*without* shape	Becomes *an-* before a vowel or h
ab, Latin = away from	*ab*duct	to carry *off*	
acouo, Greek = I hear	*acous*tics	the science of *hearing*	
acron, Greek = a summit	*acro*phobia	a fear of *heights*	*acro*bat, *acro*polis
ad, Latin = to, towards, against	*ad*here, *ad*verse	to stick *to*; *opposed* to or *against*	
aequus, Latin = equal	*equi*lateral	*equal*-sided	*equat*or (where there is *equal* night and day); compare *isos*
aer, Greek = air	*aero*plane	wandering in the *air*	
allelos, Greek = other, another	*allelo*morphic	of *another* shape	para*llel*
alter, Latin = other	*alter* ego	the *other* me	*alter*ation, *alter*native
altus, Latin = high	*alt*itude	*high*-ness (height)	
ambi-, Latin = both-	*ambi*dextrous	*both*-handed	
amphi, Greek = both	*amphi*bious	living in *both* media	
an-, Greek = not, without	*an*archy	*without* government	*an*hydrous
ana, Greek = up	*ana*lysis	a breaking *up*	*an*ode; compare *cata*
ante, Latin = before	*ante*natal	*before* birth	Compare *post*; do not confuse with *anti*
anthropos, Greek = man	*anthropo*morphic	shaped like a *man*	
anti, Greek = against	*anti*septic	*against* infection	Compare *pro*; do not confuse with *ante*
apo, Greek = away from	*apo*gee	the end *away from* the earth	
arbor, Latin = tree	*arbor*eal	*tree*-like	Null*arbor*
archaeos, Greek = old	*archaeo*logy	the study of *ancient* things	
archos, Greek = chief	*archi*tect	the *chief* builder	mon*arch*, an*archy*
aqua, Latin = water	*aque*duct	a *water*-carrier	Compare *hydor, hydros*
astron, Greek = star	*astro*nomy	the study of *stars*	Compare *stella*
audio, Latin = I hear	*audi*torium	a place for *listening*	
auris, Latin = ear	*auri*cular	related to the *ears*	

B: Table—*continued*

Word part or rootword	*English example*	*Literal meaning*	*Further reference*
aurum, Latin = gold	*auri*ferous	*gold*-bearing	
autos, Greek = self	*auto*biography	a *self*-written life story	*auto*mobile (moves by *itself*)
bene, Latin = well	*bene*volent	*well*-wishing	Compare *male*, *eu-*
bi-, **bin-**, Latin = two	*bi*cycle	*two* wheel	*bin*oculars
biblios, Greek = a book	*biblio*graphy	a *book*-list	Compare *liber*, *libri*
bios, Greek = life	*bio*logy	the study of *life*	*bio*graphy, aero*bic*
calor, Latin = heat	*calor*imeter	*heat*-measurer	calorie; compare *thermos*
capio, **captum**, Latin = I take, taken	*capt*ive	a person who is *taken*	See section D
cata, Greek = down	*cata*strophe	a *down*-turn	*cat*hode; compare *ana*
cedo, **cessum**, Latin = I go, I yield	*cede*	to *yield*	pro*cession*; see section D
centum, Latin = a hundred	*centi*pede	a *hundred* feet	
cheir, Greek = hand	*chiro*podist	a *hand*-foot person	Compare *manus*
chroma, **chromatos**, Greek = colour	*chromatic*	*coloured*	mono*chrome*, pan*chromatic*
chronos, Greek = time	*chrono*meter	*time*-measurer	syn*chronize*
circum, Latin = around	*circum*locution	a talking-*around*	Compare *peri*
civis, Latin = a citizen	*civics*	the business of being a *citizen*	
con-, **co-**, Latin = together	*con*vene	to come *together*	*co*operate
contra, Latin = against	*contra*dict	to speak *against*	
cosmo, Greek = I arrange tidily	*cosmetic*	related to *tidy arrangement*	micro*cosm* (a small arrangement)
crypto, Greek = I hide	*crypto*gram	*hidden* writing	apo*crypha*
curro, **cursum**, Latin = I run	*curr*ent	*running*	See section D
cyclos, Greek = a wheel	bi*cycle*	two-*wheeler*	
cytos, Greek = a cell	*cyto*logy	the study of *cells*	phago*cyte*
de, Latin = down from, out of	*de*scend	to climb *down*	
deca, Greek = ten	*deca*de	a group of *ten* (years)	

B: Table—*continued*

Word part or rootword	*English example*	*Literal meaning*	*Further reference*
decem, decimus, Latin = ten, tenth	*dec*imate	to kill every *tenth* person	*Decem*ber
demos, Greek = the people	*demo*cracy	rule by *the people*	epi*dem*ic
dens, dentis, Latin = a tooth	*dent*ist	*tooth*-person	in*dent*ed; compare *odous, odontos*
derma, dermatos, Greek = skin	*dermato*logy	the study of the *skin*	ecto*derm*; hypo*derm*ic
deuteros, Greek = second	*Deutero*nomy	the second book of laws (in the Bible)	
dexter, Latin = right	*dexter*ous	as with the *right* hand	
di-, Greek = double	*di*ode	*two*-way	*di*oxide
dis-, Latin = apart aside; un-	*dis*tract, *dis*infect	to draw *aside*; to *un*-infect	
dia, Greek = through, across	*dia*meter	the measurement *across*	
dico, dictum, Latin = I speak	*dict*ionary	a collection of *spoken* things	
dies, Latin = day	*di*urnal	by *day*	
doxa, Greek = opinion	ortho*dox*	having the (right) *opinion*	*dogma*, *dogmatic* are from the same root
duo, Latin = two	*du*plicated	folded in *two*	
dys-, Greek = bad, badly	*dys*entery	*bad* guts	Compare *eu-*, *male*
ec, ecto-, Greek = out, outside	*ecto*derm	*outside* skin	gastr*ec*tomy; compare *exo-*, *endo-*
en, endo-, Greek = in, inside	*endo*thermic	taking heat *in*	Compare *ecto-*, *exo-*
enteron, Greek = insides, guts	*enter*itis	inflammation of the *guts*	dys*entery*
epi, Greek = to, on, against	*epi*taph	something *on* a grave	*epi*demic (something which comes to a community)
equus, Latin = a horse	*eques*trian	related to *horses*	See *aequus* for other words beginning with *equi-*
ethnos, Greek = a tribe	*ethno*logy	the study of *groups of people*	*ethnic*
ethos, Greek = behaviour	*eth*ics	the study of *behaviour*	
eu-, Greek = well	*eu*logy	a speaking *well* of someone	Compare *dys-*, *bene*
ex, Greek, Latin = out of	*ex*tract	to draw *out*	
exo-, Greek = outside	*exo*thermic	giving heat *out*	Compare *endo-*, *ecto-*
extra, Latin = outside	*extra*ordinary	*outside* the ordinary	

B: Table—*continued*

Word part or rootword	*English example*	*Literal meaning*	*Further reference*
facio, factum, Latin = I make, I do	*fact*ory	a *making* place	See section D
fero, ferens, Latin = I bring, I carry	aqui*fer*	a water-*carrier*	auri*fer*ous; see section D
ferrum, Latin = iron	*ferro*magnetic	magnetic like *iron*	
fugio, fugitum, Latin = I flee	*fugit*ive	one who has *fled*	re*fuge*, centri*fugal*
fundo, fusum, Latin = I pour	con*fuse*	to *pour* together	con*found*
gala, galactos, Greek = milk	*galax*y	The *Milky* Way	extra*galactic*
gaster, gastros, Greek = belly	*gastro*nomy	the looking-after of the *belly*	*gastro*-enteritis
ge, Greek = the earth	*geo*graphy	the study of the *earth*	apo*gee*
genero, generatum, Latin = I produce	*generate*	to *produce*	See Note A at end of table
genos, Greek = a family	*gene*tic	pertaining to *birth*	See Note A at end of table
genus, generis, Latin = a family	*gener*al	related to the *family* as a whole	
gonia, Greek = an angle, corner	penta*gon*	five-*angled*	tri*gono*metry (measurement of triangles)
gradior, gressum, Latin = I step	retro*grade*	*stepping* backwards	pro*gress*; see section D
gramma, grammatos, Greek = writing	*gramma*r	*writing*	*gram*ophone, tele*gram*
grapho, Greek = I write	*graph*ic	*written*	*-graphy*: see Note B at end of table
gyne, gynaecos, Greek = a woman	*gynaeco*logy	the study of *women*	miso*gyn*ist
haema, haematos, Greek = blood	*haemato*logy	the study of *blood*	*haem*ophilia, an*aem*ic
hecton, Greek = a hundred	*hect*are	a *hundred* ares	
helios, Greek = the sun	*helio*graph	a *sun*-writer	
hemi-, Greek = half	*hemi*sphere	*half*-sphere	
hepta, Greek = seven	*hept*ane	(a chemical compound) with *seven* radicals	
heteros, Greek = other	*hetero*dox	having *another* opinion	*hetero*sexual; compare *orthos*, *homoeos*
hexa-, Greek = six-	*hexa*meter	(a line) with *six* metrical feet	

B: Table:—*continued*

Word part or rootword	*English example*	*Literal meaning*	*Further reference*
hieros, Greek = holy	*hier*archy	rule by *holy* people	*hiero*glyphics (holy writings); compare *sacer*
hippos, Greek = a horse	*hippo*potamus	river *horse*	*hippo*drome; compare *equus*
homoeos, Greek = same	*homo*genous	all made the *same*	*homoeo*path; compare *isos, heteros*
hydor, hydros, Greek = water	*hydro*gen	*water*-producing ($H_2 + O \rightarrow H_2O$)	an*hydr*ous; compare *aqua*
hyper, Greek = over, beyond	*hyper*critical	*over*-critical	Compare *hypo*
hypnos, Greek = sleep	*hypno*tic	causing *sleep*	
hypo, Greek = under	*hypo*dermic	under the *skin*	Compare *hyper*
iatros, Greek = healing	psych*iatry*	mind-*healing*	
idem, Latin = same	*iden*tity	*same*ness	
in, Latin = in, into, on	*in*jection	something thrown *in*	
in-, Latin = not, un-	*in*effective	*not* effective	other forms: *il*legal, *im*proper, *irre*deemable
infra, Latin = below, underneath	*infra*structure	the thing built *underneath*	*infra*-red
inter, Latin = between	*inter*vene	to come *between*	
intra, Latin = inside	*intra*venous	*inside* the vein	*intro*verted
isos, Greek = same, equal	*iso*tope	the *same* place (in the Periodic Table)	Compare *homoeos, aequus*
-itis, Greek = inflammation	enter*itis*	*inflammation* of the guts	
jacio, jactum, Latin = I throw	pro*ject*ile	*thrown* forward	in*ject*ion, con*ject*ure; see section D
kilo- (*properly* ***khillioi***), Greek = one thousand-	*kilo*gram	a *thousand* grams	
latum, Latin = carried	e*lat*ed	*carried* off	See *fero* in section D
latus, lateris, Latin = a side	*later*al	*sideways*	equi*later*al, multi*later*al
lego, lectum, Latin = I read or I choose	*lect*ure	the thing *read out*	e*lect* (choose out)
leucos, Greek = white	*leuco*cyte	*white* cell	*leuk*emia (old dictionaries spell it *leuchaemia*)

B: Table—*continued*

Word part or rootword	*English example*	*Literal meaning*	*Further reference*
liber, liberi, Latin = free	*liber*ated	*freed*	
liber, libri, Latin = a book	*libr*ary	a *book*-place	Compare *biblios*
lithos, Greek = a stone	*litho*graphy	writing on *stone*	neo*lith*ic, mega*lith*
logos, Greek = a word	*logic*	the science of *words*	cata*logue*, ana*logy*
-logy			See Note B at end of table
ludo, lusum, Latin = I play	pre*lude*	*played* before	il*lus*ion, al*lus*ive; see section D
lyo, Greek = I release	cata*lyst*	a thing which *releases*	ana*lysis*, para*lytic*
macros, Greek = large, long	*macro*cosm	a *large* system	Compare *mega, magnus, micros*
magnus, Latin = large	*magnify*	to make *large*	Compare *macros*
male, Latin = bad, badly	*male*factor	a *bad*-doer	*mal*function
mania, Greek = madness	*maniac*	a *mad*man	pyro*maniac*
manus, Latin = hand	*manu*script	*hand*-written	*manu*facture; compare *cheir*
mater, matris, Latin = a mother	*matri*arch	*mother*-ruler	
medius, Latin = middle	*medi*an	in the *middle*	*Medi*terranean
mega, megalos, Greek = large	*mega*phone	a voice en*larger*	*megalo*maniac; compare *macros*
mesos, Greek = middle	*Meso*potamia	in the *middle* of the rivers	*meson*
meta, Greek = after; change of	*meta*morphic	of *changed* shape	*met*hod (*meta* + (*h*)*odos*)
meter, metros, Greek = a mother	*metro*polis	*mother* city	
metron, Greek = a measure	*meter*	a *measuring* instrument	See Note B at end of table
micros, Greek = small	*micro*be	a *small* form of life	Compare *macros*
mille, Latin = one thousand	*milli*pede	a *thousand* feet	
minimus, Latin = smallest	*minim*al	*smallest*	*mini*-skirt
misceo, mixtum, Latin = I mix	*misce*genation	*mixed* parentage	*mixture*
misos, Greek = hatred	*miso*gynist	woman-*hater*	*mis*anthropic; compare *philo*
mitto, missum, Latin = I send	*missile*	something *sent*	See section D
monos, Greek = one, only	*mono*cycle	*one*-wheeler	*mon*arch

Word part or rootword	*English example*	*Literal meaning*	*Further reference*
morphe, Greek = form	*morpho*logy	the study of *form*	meta*morph*ic, allelo*morph*
multus, Latin = many	*multi*lateral	*many*-sided	
nascor, natum, Latin = I am born	*nat*ive	a person *born* somewhere	ren*aiss*ance, *nat*ional
neos, Greek = new	*neo*lithic	*New* Stone Age	Compare *novus, palaeos*
neuron, Greek = a nerve	*neur*otic	*nerv*ous	*neur*ology
nomen, nominis, Latin = a name	*nomin*ate	to *name*	*nomin*al
nomos, Greek = an arrangement	astro*nomy*	the *arrangement* of the stars	eco*nomi*cal; see Note B at end of table
-nomy			See Note B at end of table
novem, Latin = nine	*Novem*ber	the *ninth* month (in the Roman calendar)	
novus, Latin = new	*nov*elty	a *new* thing	Compare *neos*
nox, noctis, Latin = night	*noct*urnal	by *night*	equi*nox* (equal night and day)
nullus, Latin = nothing, none	*null*ify	to make *nothing*	*Null*arbor (no trees)
nuncio, nunciatum, Latin = I speak out	an*nounc*ement	something *spoken out*	de*nounc*e, pro*nunci*ation
ob, Latin = in the way	*ob*struction	something built *in the way*	
octo, Greek, Latin = eight	*octo*pus	*eight*-footed	October (eighth month of the Roman year)
oculus, Latin = eye	*ocul*ist	*eye*-man	in*ocula*tion; compare *ophthalmos, opticos*
(h)odos, Greek = path, way	peri*od*	a *way* around	meth*od*, *od*ometer, cat*hode*, an*ode*
odous, odontis, Greek = a tooth	orth*odont*ist	a straight-*tooth* man	
oecos, Greek = house, environment	*eco*logy	the study of the *environment*	*econom*ics (housekeeping, old dictionaries spell it *oeconomics*)
omnis, Latin = all	*omni*bus	for *all*	
ophthalmos, Greek = an eye	*ophthalmos*cope	an *eye*-looker	Compare *oculus, opticos*
opticos, Greek = of sight	*opt*ics	the study of *sight*	Compare *ophthalmos, oculus*
orthos, Greek = straight, normal, correct	*ortho*dox	having the *normal* opinion	Compare *heteros*

B: Table—*continued*

Word part or rootword	*English example*	*Literal meaning*	*Further reference*
palaeos, Greek = old	*palaeo*lithic	*Old* Stone Age	Compare *neos*
pan, pantos, Greek = all	*pan*chromatic	(sensitive to) *all* colours	
par, Latin = equal	*parity*	*equality*	com*pare*, com*par*ison
para, Greek = alongside, against	*para*llel	*alongside* one another	*para*sol (against the sun); *para*medical
pareo, parens, paritum, Latin = I seem	ap*parent*	*seeming*	ap*pear*, ap*par*ition
pario, parens, partum, Latin = I give birth	*parent*	one who *gives birth*	vivi*par*ous
paro, parans, paratum, Latin = I prepare	ap*parat*us	something *prepared*	re*pairs*, re*par*ation, se*par*ate
pars, partis, Latin = a part	*part*icipate	to take *part*	com*part*ment, *part*ition, de*part*
pathos, Greek = suffering	*patho*logy	the study of *suffering*	sym*pathy*, psycho*path*
patior, patiens, passum, Latin = I suffer	*pati*ent	a *suffering* person	com*passi*onate, *passion*
pello, pellens, pulsum, = I push	re*pel*	to *push* back	
penta-, Greek = five-	*penta*gon	*five*-angled	
per, Latin = through, thorough	*per*mit	to let *through*	*per*fect (thoroughly made)
peri, Greek = around	*peri*meter	the measurement *around* (a circle)	Compare *circum*
pes, pedis, Latin = a foot	*ped*al	related to a *foot*	*ped*estrian, centi*pede*, im*pede*; compare *pous*
-phago, Greek = I eat	*phago*cyte	a cell-*eater*	
-pheno, Greek = I appear	*pheno*menon	an *apparition*	*pheno*type (types *appearing* the same)
philo, Greek = I love	*philo*sopher	a *lover* of wisdom	anglo*phile*; compare *phobos, misos*
phobos, Greek = fear	acro*phobia*	*fear* of heights	anglo*phobe, phobia*
phono, Greek = to produce a sound	*phono*logy	the study of voice-*sounds*	*phone*tics, tele*phone*, sym*phony*

B: Table—*continued*

Word part or rootword	*English example*	*Literal meaning*	*Further reference*
phoro, Greek = to bring	phos*pho*rus	light-*bringing* (substance)	sema*phor*; meta*phor*; compare *fero*
phos, photos, Greek = light	*phos*phorus	*light*-bringing (substance)	*photo*graph, *photo*synthesis
plico, plicans, plicatum, Latin = I fold	com*plic*ated	*folded* together	
plus, plurimus, Latin = more	*plur*al	*more* than one	
pneuma, pneumatos, Greek = air	*pneumat*ic	related to *air*	*pneum*onia (disease of breath)
polis, Greek = a city	metro*polis*	a mother *city*	Nea*polit*an (*neos* + *polis*)
polites, Greek = a citizen	*polit*ical	relating to *citizens*' affairs	
polys, Greek = many	*poly*gon	*many*-angled	*poly*mer
pono, ponens, positum, Latin = I place	*posit*ion	*place*	See section D
post, Latin = after	*post*script	written *after*	Compare *ante*
potamos, Greek = river	hippo*potamus*	*river*-horse	Meso*potamia*
pous, podos, Greek = a foot	anti*podes*	against the *feet*	gastro*pod*; compare *pes, pedis*
pre-, Latin = before	*pre*cede	to go *before*	
prehendo, prehensum, Latin = I grasp	*prehens*ile	able to *grasp*	com*prehend*, ap*prehens*ive
primus, Latin = first	*prim*ary	*first*	
pro, *Latin* = forwards; in front of	*pro*jectile	thrown *forward*	Compare *anti*
protos, Greek = first	*proto*zoa	the *first* living things	
psyche, Greek = the mind	*psycho*logy	the study of the *mind*	*psych*iatry (*psyche* + *iatros*)
pyr, Greek = fire	*pyro*mania	*fire*-mania	*pyr*exia (fever)
qualis, Latin = of what type?	*quality*	the *type* of a substance	*quali*tative, *quali*fy
quantus, Latin = of what amount?	*quantity*	the *amount* of a substance	*quant*itative, *quant*ify
quattuor, Latin = four	*quadr*uped	*four*-footed	
quinque, Latin = five	*quinqu*ennial	*five*-yearly	
quintus, Latin = fifth	*quint*et	a group of *five*	

B: Table—*continued*

Word part or rootword	*English example*	*Literal meaning*	*Further reference*
radius, Latin = a spoke	*radi*al	like the *spoke* of a wheel	*radi*ate, *radius*
re-, Latin = back, again	*re*vert	to turn *back*	
retro, Latin = back	*retro*grade	stepping *back*	
rogo, rogans, rogatum, Latin = I ask	inter*rogate*	to *ask* questions	
sacer, sacrum, Latin = holy	*sacr*ifice	to make *holy*	
sema, Greek = signal, sign	*sema*phore	*signal*-bearing	*sema*ntics
semi-, Latin = half-	*semi*circle	*half*-circle	
septem, Latin = seven	*Septem*ber	the *seventh* month (in the Roman calendar)	
servo, servans, servatum, Latin = I keep	con*serve*	to *keep* together	
sex, Latin = six	*sex*tuplets	*six* of a kind	
sol, Latin = the sun	*sol*ar	related to the *Sun*	para*sol*
solvo, solvens, solutum, Latin = I solve	*solve*; *solu*tion	*solve*; *solution*	*solvent*
sono, sonans, Latin = I make a noise	*son*ic	related to *noise*	res*onan*ce, con*sonan*t
sophia, Greek = wisdom	*soph*ist	a *clever* person	*soph*isticated, philo*sophy*
specio, speciens, spectum, Latin = I look	*spect*ator	a *looker*	See section D
spiro, spirans, spiratum, Latin	*spir*acle	a *breathing*-hole	See section D
stella, Latin = a star	*stellar*	*starry*	con*stella*tion; compare *astron*
stereos, Greek = solid	*stereo*scopic	looking *solid*	*stereo*phonic
stratus, Latin = spread out	*stratum*	something *spread out*	*strato*sphere, *strat*ify
strophe, Greek = a turning	cata*strophe*	a *turning* down	apo*strophe* (*apo* + *strophe*)

B: Table—*continued*

Word part or rootword	*English example*	*Literal meaning*	*Further reference*
struo, structum, Latin = I build	*struct*ure	something *built*	
sub, Latin = under, less than	*sub*sonic	*less than* the speed of sound	
sumo, sumptum, Latin = I take	con*sume*	to *take* together	con*sump*tion
super, Latin = over, more than	*super*sonic	*more than* the speed of sound	
supra, Latin = above, beyond	*supra*national	*beyond* national (boundaries, etc.)	
syn, Greek = together	*syn*optic	seen *together*	*syn*chronize, *sym*pathy, *syl*logism
tango, tactum, Latin = I touch	*tang*ent	*touching*	*tact*ile, in*tact*
tauto, Greek = the same	*tauto*logous	saying the *same* thing	
taxis, Greek = an arrangement	*taxo*nomy	a system of *arrangements*	*taxi*dermist (a skin-*arranger*); *taxi*
techne, Greek = art, skill	*techn*ical	*skil*ful	pyro*technics*
tecton, Greek = a builder	*tecton*ic	related to *building*	archi*tect*
tele, Greek = far off	*tele*scope	a device for seeing things *far off*	*tele*phone
tendo, tensum, Latin = I stretch	*tens*ile	capable of being *stretched out*	See section D
terra, Latin = the earth	*terre*strial	*earthly*	Medi*terra*nean; compare *ge*
tertius, Latin = third	*tertiary*	*third*ly	
tetra, Greek = four	*tetra*hedron	with *four* sides	
theos, Greek = God	*theo*logy	the study of *God*	
therapeia, Greek = healing	*therapeu*tic	related to *healing*	psycho*therapy*
thermos, Greek = hot	*thermo*meter	a *heat*-measurer	iso*therm*; compare *calor*
tome, Greek = a cut	a*tom*	un*cut*table	leuco*tomy*, gastrec*tomy*
topos, Greek = a position, place	*topo*graphy	the describing of a *place*	iso*tope*
totus, Latin = entire	*tot*al	the *entire* amount	
traho, tractum, Latin = I drag	*tract*or	*dragger*	ex*tract*, abs*tract*
trans, Latin = across	*trans*fer	to carry *across*	
tri-, Greek, Latin = three	*tri*pod	*three*-footed	
trope, Greek = a turning, disturbance	*tropo*sphere	the sphere of *turbulence*	geo*trop*ism, *tropics*

B: Table—*continued*

Word part or rootword	*English example*	*Literal meaning*	*Further reference*
ultra, Latin = beyond	*ultra*violet	*beyond* the violet (in the spectrum)	*ultra* high frequency (UHF)
unus, Latin = one	*un*ify	to make *one*	Compare *monos*
venio, veniens, ventum, Latin =I come	con*vene*	to *come* together	con*vent*; see section D
video, videns, visum, Latin = I see	pro*vide*	to *see* (a need) in advance	*vis*ions, pro*vident*
vivo, victum, Latin = I live	re*vive*	to make *live* again	*vivi*parous, con*vivi*al, *vict*uals
vinco, vincens, victum, Latin = I conquer	*vict*ory	a *conquer*ing	con*vince*
voco, vocatum, Latin = I call	*voc*ation	a *call*ing	pro*vok*e, pro*vocat*ive; see section D
zoon, (plural **zoa**), Greek = a living thing	*zoo*logy	the study of *living things*	proto*zoa*

NOTE A: THE WORD PART *GEN*

Gen is an example of a very old root from which many English words have been formed. Basically, it indicates creation or production: *gen*esis, *gen*erate, en*gen*der, hydro*gen*. It indicates:

1 the production of living things: *gene*, *gen*etic, *gen*ital

2 the concept of family: *gen*ealogy, pro*geny*, *gen*us. (Just as in biology, a *genus* is a larger group than a *species*, so our everyday language distinguishes *general* and *special* or *specific*).

3 the good characteristics of a family: *gen*ius, in*gen*ious, *gen*tleman (*gentle* originally meant 'of good family').

Other *gen* words have changed their form and are less easy to recognise. In Latin we find:

bene + *gen*us = benigenus → benignus → (English) benign
gen + atus = genatus → gnatus → natus → (English) native

In Germanic languages we find:

gen → ken → kin → (English) kind

The modern German word *kinder* is derived from *gen* in the same way and provides us with the word *kin*dergarten (= children's garden).

NOTE B: THE WORD PART *-LOGY*

The word ending *-logy*, is one of four commonly used to indicate areas of study; *-logy*, *-nomy*, *-graphy*, *-metry*. Originally, these four had quite distinct meanings:

-logy = words (or talking) about
-graphy = writing about
-metry = measurements of
-nomy = arrangement of, counting of

However, the following list of words shows that these endings no longer have such distinct meanings:

geology, geography, geometry
biology, biography, biometry
ecology, economy
astrology, astronomy
radiography, radiology

C: TABLE OF NUMBERS

English	Latin	Greek
one	*unus, singulus* (*unit, single*)	*monos* (*mon*arch)
first	*primus* (*prime, primary*)	*protos* (*proton, proto*zoa)
two	*duo, bi-, bin-* (*duet, bin*oculars)	*duo* (*duo*logue) *di-* (*di*ode)
second	*secundus* (*second*ary)	*deuteros* (*deuter*ium, *Deuter*onomy)
three	*tria, tri-* (*tri*angle)	*tria, tri-* (*tri*gonometry)
third	*tertius* (*terti*ary)	
four	*quattuor, quaternus* (*quad*rant)	*tetra* (*tetra*hedron)
fourth	*quartus* (*quarter*)	
five	*quinque* (*quinque*nnial)	*pente, penta-* (*penta*meter, *penta*gon)
fifth	*quintus* (*quintu*plets)	
six	*sex* (*sex*ennial)	*hex, hexa-* (*hexa*meter)
sixth	*sextus* (*sext*uplets)	
seven	*septem* (*Septem*ber)	*hepta* (*hep*tane)
seventh	*septimus*	
eight	*octo* (*Octo*ber)	*octo, octa-* (*octa*gon)
eighth	*octavus* (*octave*)	
nine	*novem* (*Novem*ber)	*ennea*
ninth	*nonus*	(Latin form used in *nona*gon, etc.)
ten	*decem* (*Decem*ber)	*deca* (*deca*de)
tenth	*decimus* (*decim*ate, *decim*al) *SI usage:* a tenth part (*deci*metre)	*SI usage:* times ten (*deca*metre)
hundred	*centum* (*cent, centi*pede) *SI usage:* one hundredth (*centi*metre)	*hecaton, hecto-* (*heca*tomb) *SI usage:* times one hundred (*hect*are = 100 ares)
thousand	*mille* (*milli*pede) *SI usage:* one thousandth (*milli*metre)	(*khillioi*), *kilo-* *SI usage:* times one thousand (*kilo*metre).

D: LATIN VERBS AND PREFIXES

Thousands of English words have come to us from a relatively small number of Latin verbs and prefixes. By analysing some of them it is possible to see the derivation of many English words in a fresh way. The words receive, reception, recipient, recipe and receipt, for example, all have one thing in common: their original stem is the Latin verb *capio*, I take. The following examples show how *capio*, in conjunction with basic prefixes, is a building block in a variety of English words.

Capio:

1 Basic Latin verb: *capio* (= I take)
Inflected forms: *capiens* (= taking)
captum (= taken)
English derivatives: **capture, captive, caption**

2 With prefixes, *capio* becomes *-cipio,* e.g. *recipio*
capiens becomes *-cipiens*, e.g. *recipiens*
captum becomes *-ceptum*, e.g. *receptum*
English derivatives: **recipe, recipient, reception**

3 Sometimes the Latin form is modified by the French form:
(Latin) *recipio* → (French) *recevoir* → (English) **receive, receipt**

Prefixes with capio:

ad (= to) + *capio* = *accipio*
acceptum gives us **accept, acceptable,** etc.

con (= with) + *capio* = *concipio*, which (through French) gives us **conceive**
conceptum gives us **concept, conception,** and (through French) **conceit**

contra (= *against*) + *capio* = *contracipio*
contraceptum gives us **contraceptive**

de (= down) + *capio* = *decipio*, which (through French) gives us **deceive**
deceptum gives us **deception, deceptive,** and (through French) **deceit**

ex (= out) + *capio* = *excipio*
exceptum gives us **except, exception,** etc.

in (= in) + *capio* = *incipio*
incipiens gives us **incipient**
inceptum gives us **inception**

inter (= between) + *capio* = *intercipio*
interceptum gives us **intercept, interception,** etc.

per (= through) + *capio* = *percipio*, which (through French) gives us **perceive**
percipiens gives us **percipient**
perceptum gives us **perception, perceptive,** etc.

pre (= before) + *capio* = *precipio*
preceptum gives us **precept**

re (= back) + *capio* = *recipio*, which gives us **recipe** and (through French) **receive**
recipiens gives us **recipient**
receptum gives us **receptive, reception,** etc. and (through French) **receipt**

sub (= under) + *capio* = *suscipio*
susceptum gives us **susceptible**

In the following lists, the *prefix* and the *English combining form* of the Latin verb are printed in bold type. By joining the word parts printed in bold, hundreds of existing English words can be 'regenerated'.

PREFIXES
in descending order of frequency

con- (= with, together)
Variants:
col- as in collusion
com- as in compel
cor- as in correct

ad- (= to, towards, against)
Variants:
a- as in aspect
ac- as in accept
af- as in affect
ag- as in aggression
al- as in allusive
an- as in announce
ap- as in apply
ar- as in arrogant
as- as in assume
at- as in attend

re- (= back, again)

ex- (= out of, from)
Variants:
e- as in elate
ef- as in effect

in- (= in, on *or* not)
Variants:
il- as in illusion
im- as in impatient
ir- as in irregular

pro- (= in front, forwards)

sub- (= under)
Variants:
su- as in suspect
suc- as in succeed
suf- as in sufficient
sup- as in suppose
sur- as in surrogate
sus- as in susceptible

pre- (= before)

de- (= down, away from)

VERB PARTS
in descending order of frequency

jacio (= I throw)
Latin inflected form in compounds: *-jectum*
English combining forms: **-ject, -jection, -jective, -jector, -jecture**

pono (= I put, I place)
Latin inflected forms: *ponens, positum*
English combining forms: **-pone, -ponent, -pose, -posite, -position, -positive, -positor**

fero (= I bring, I carry)
Latin inflected forms: *ferens, latum*
English combining forms: **-fer, -fere, -ferent, -ferency, -late, -lation, -lative, -lator**

verto (= I turn)
Latin inflected form: *versum*
English combining forms: **-vert, -verse, -version, -versive, -versor, -versal**

cedo (= I go, I yield)
Latin inflected forms: *cedens, cessum*
English combining forms: **-ceed, -cede, -cedent; -cess, -cession, -cessive, -cessor, -cessible**

facio (= I make, I do)
Latin inflected forms in compounds: *-ficio, -ficiens, fectum*
English combining forms: **-fice; -ficient, -ficiency, -fect, -fection, -fective, -fector**

duco (= I lead)
Latin inflected forms: *ducens, ductum* or *-ducatum*
English combining forms: **-duce; -ducent; -duct, -duction, -ductive, -ductor; -ducate; -ducation, -ducative, -ducator**

scribo (= I write)
Latin inflected form: *scriptum*
English combining forms: **-scribe; -script, -scriptive, -scription**

PREFIXES	VERB PARTS
dis (= apart, aside, not) Variant: **di-** as in digression **inter-** (= between)	*specio* (= I look), *-spicio* Latin inflected form: ***spectum*** English combining forms: **-spicious, -spicuous; -spect, -spection, -spective, -spectus**
trans (= across) Variant: **tra-** as in traduce	*curro* (= I run) Latin inflected forms: ***currens, cursum*** English combining forms: **-cur, -cour; -current, -currence; -course, -cursion, -cursive, -cursor**
ob- (= in the way, to) Variants: **oc-** as in occur **of-** as in offer **op-** as in oppose **o-** as in omit	*gradior* (= I march, I go) Latin inflected forms in compounds: ***-grediens, -gressum*** English combining forms: **-gredient; -gress, -gressive, -gression, -gressor**
ab- (= away, out of) Variant: **abs-** as in abstract	*ludo* (= I play) Latin inflected form: ***lusum*** English combining forms: **-lude; -lusion, -lusive**
per- (= through, thorough)	*mitto* (= I send) Latin inflected forms: ***mittens, missum*** English combining forms: **-mit, -mitter; -mittence; -miss, -mission, -missive**
Some less common examples: **super-** (= over) **contra, contro-** (= against) **extra-, extro-** (= outside)	 **-spire, -spirant, -spirat-** (from *spiro* = I breathe) **-vene, -venient, -vent-** (from *venio* = I come) **-pel, -pellent, -puls-** (from *pello* = I push, drive)
post- (= after) **intro-, intra-** (= inside)	**-tend, -tens, -tent-** (from *tendo* = I stretch) **-voke, -vocant, -vocat-** (from *voco* = I call) **-ply, -plicant, -plicat-** (from *plico* = I fold)

FOREIGN WORDS IN ENGLISH

Perhaps more than any other language, English was the meeting-point of the two major language groups which existed in Europe at the end of the Roman Empire: *Germanic*-based languages and *Latin*-based languages. In 1066, the Norman Conquest brought French (a Latin-based language) and Old English (a Germanic-based language) into direct contact.

For nearly two hundred years after the Conquest, English and French existed side by side. French was the language of the ruling nobility, of law, administration and government. With few exceptions it was also the language of literature. English remained the language of the mass of the people, and although it was considered socially inferior it continued to be vigorous in everyday life, in trade and commerce. By 1400, however, as England became increasingly independent of France, English had reasserted itself. It was used in Parliament, and men like Geoffrey Chaucer and William Caxton (the first English printer) helped to establish English in a recognizably modern form.

After 1400, the influence of French on English lessened considerably. English scholars and other writers turned to the past to seek new terms in philosophy, theology and the sciences. Their main sources were ancient Greek and Latin. The growth of English sea-power and trade brought contact with the Americas, Africa, India and the East, as well as closer ties with other countries in Europe. The Renaissance, too, increased cultural exchange between European nations. New ideas, inventions, theories and fashions all introduced new words into English.

English vocabulary grew in an increasingly diverse and complex way. The following lists give examples of some foreign words which have become permanent additions to our vocabulary. They have been grouped under four main headings:

A: Words from classical languages, 1500-1700
B: Words from non-European languages, 1300-1900
C: Words from European languages, 1500-1900
D: Some foreign words since 1900

Where possible, the date at which the word was first recorded in English follows after the entry. Brief etymologies have been supplied where they are interesting or significant, and in some cases the form of the word in its language of origin has been given in order to emphasize its 'foreignness.'

A: WORDS FROM CLASSICAL LANGUAGES, 1500-1700

1 LATIN

integer 1509 [= intact]
cornea 1527 [= horny]
fungus 1527 [= mushroom]
acumen 1531
alias 1535 [at another time or place]
exit 1538 [= he goes out]
peninsula 1538 [*paene* almost + *insula* island]
area 1538 [= level ground]
abdomen 1541
appendix 1542 [= something added on]
axis, axes 1549 [= axle]
vacuum 1550 [= empty]
genus, genera 1551 [= stock, category]
medium, media 1551 [= middle]
species 1551 [= outward appearance]
terminus 1555 [= boundary, end]
cerebellum, cerebella 1565 [= *brain*]
radius, radii 1599 [= wheel-spoke]
equilibrium 1608 [*equi* equal + *libra* balance]
specimen 1610
spectrum, spectra 1611 [= image]
series 1611
census 1613
affidavit 1622 [= he has sworn]
apparatus 1628 [= something prepared]
curriculum, curricula 1633 [= course, race]
forceps 1634
formula, formulae 1638
focus, foci 1644 [= hearth, fireplace]
datum, data 1646 [= the given thing(s)]
pendulum 1660 [= something hanging]
minimum 1663
serum 1672 [=whey]
fulcrum 1674 [= bedpost]
calculus 1684 [= pebble used in reckoning]
lens 1693 [= lentil; shaped like a convex lens]
antenna, antennae 1698 [= spar for sails]
momentum, momenta 1699 [= movement]

2 GREEK (mostly through Latin and French)

irony 1502 [= understatement]
alphabet 1513 [*alpha* A + *beta* B]
elegy 1514 [*elegos* lament]
drama 1515 [= deed, play]
dilemma 1523 [= double proposition]
enigma 1539 [*ainigma* riddle]
crisis, crises 1543 [*crisis* decision]
tragic 1545
cynic 1547 [*cynikos* dog-like, sullen]
scheme 1550 [*schema* form]
isthmus 1555 [*isthmos* narrow passage]
rhythm 1557
chorus 1561 [= dance, dancers]
despot 1562 [*despotes* master]
cylinder 1570 [*cylindros* roller]
prism 1570 [*prisma* something sawn]
skeleton 1578 [*skeletos* dried up]
pathos 1579 [= suffering, feeling]
amnesty 1580 [*amnestia* forgetting a wrong]
climax 1581 [*climax* ladder, staircase]
critic 1588 [*criticos* skilled in judging]
ode 1588 [*oide* song]
epic 1589 [*epos* word, story]
patriot 1596 [*patriotes* countryman]
theory 1597
energy 1599 [*energeia* force]
enthusiasm 1603
acoustic 1605
orchestra 1606 [= space where chorus danced]
museum 1615 [*mouseion* abode of the Muses]
system 1619 [*systema* a setting together]
clinic 1626 [*clinicos* of a bed]
dogma 1638 [= a philosophical opinion]
typhus 1643 [*typhos* vapour]
coma 1646 [*coma* deep sleep]
electric 1646 [*electron* amber, which produces electricity by friction]
aeon 1647 [*aion* an age]
cosmos 1650 [*cosmos* ordered whole]

B: WORDS FROM NON-EUROPEAN LANGUAGES

1 THE AMERICAS

1 The Caribbean

cannibal 1553 [*Caribe* brave, daring]
canoe 1555 [*kanoa*]
hammock 1555 [*hamaca*]
hurricane 1555 [*huracan*]
iguana 1555
savanna 1555
maize 1565 [*mahiz*]

potato 1577 [*batata*]
tobacco 1577
pawpaw 1577 [*papayo*]
buccaneer 1577 [*boucan* a frame for roasting meat]
barbecue 1697 [*barboka*]
curare 1777

2 Mexico
chocolate 1604 [*chocolatl* bitter water]
tomato 1604 [*tomatl*]
chilli 1662
cocoa 1707
mescaline 1828
coyote 1850 [*koyotl*]

3 Brazil
petunia 1577
jaguar 1604
jacaranda 1753
cayenne 1756
cougar 1796 [*cuacu ara*]

4 Peru
llama 1600
condor 1604
vicuña 1622
pampas 1704
puma 1777
alpaca 1792
quinine 1826 [*kina* bark]
cocaine 1874 [*cuca*]

5 North America
raccoon 1608
opossum 1610
persimmon 1612
moccasin 1612
moose 1613
wigwam 1628
squaw 1634
tomahawk 1634
papoose 1634
hickory 1676
kayak 1757
totem 1760
toboggan 1829
chipmunk 1842
igloo 1856

II THE EAST
1 Arabia
lute 1360 [*al-'ud*]
alchemy 1362 [*al kimiya*]
cotton 1380 [*qutn*]
alkali 1386 [*al qili*]
zenith 1387 [*semt ar-ras* path over the head]
nadir 1391 [*nazir* opposite the zenith]
almanac 1391
amber 1398
syrup 1398
cipher 1399 [*sifr* empty]
mosque 1400
lemon 1400 [*lima*]
assassin 1531 [*hashshashin* hashish eaters]
carat 1531 [*qirat* light weight]
algebra 1541 [*al jebr* bone setting]
alcohol 1543 [*al kuhl*]
apricot 1551 [*al barquq*]
sultan 1555
calibre 1567 [*kalib* mould]
arsenal 1579 [*dar sina'a* workshop]
magazine 1583 [*makhzan* storehouse]
monsoon 1584 [*mawsin* fixed season]
tariff 1591 [*tarif* notification]
giraffe 1594
hashish 1598
zero 1604 [*sifr* empty]
sequin 1617 [*sikka* a die for coins]
alcove 1623 [*al qubba* the vaulted space]
sofa 1625
harem 1634 [*harim* forbidden]
candy 1769 [*kand* sugar]
carafe 1786 [*gharraf* drinking vessel]
ghoul 1786
alfalfa 1845
safari 1892

2 Persia
checkmate 1400 (chess) [*shah mat* the king is dead]
rook 1400 (chess) [*rukh*]
mummy 1400 [*mum* embalming wax]
spinach 1530
jasmine 1548
tiara 1555
jackal 1564
divan 1586
caravan 1599
bazaar 1599
lilac 1625 [*nilak* bluish]
shawl 1662 [*shal*]
seersucker 1757 [*shir o shakkar* milk and sugar]

3 Turkey
turban 1561

caftan 1591
caviar 1591
coffee 1598
kiosk 1625 [*kiusk* pavilion]
yoghurt 1625
fez 1802

4 India
calico 1540
mango 1584
copra 1584
mandarin 1589 [*mantrin* counsellor]
curry 1598 [*kari* sauce]
coolie 1598 [*kuli* hire, wages]
guru 1613
pariah 1613
chintz 1614
pagoda 1618
cot 1634 [*khat* couch]
juggernaut 1638 [*Jagannath* lord of the world]
pundit 1672 [*pandit* learned]
bungalow 1676
catamaran 1697 [*katta-maram* tied tree]
teak 1698
mongoose 1698
verandah 1711
corundum 1728 [*kurundam* ruby]
jute 1746
shampoo 1762 [*champna* to press or squeeze]
anaconda 1768
jungle 1776 [*jangal* desert, forest]
bandicoot 1780
bangle 1787
thug 1810 [*thag* cheat, murderer]
dinghy 1810
chutney 1813
yoga 1820
cashmere 1822
karma 1828
nirvana 1836
khaki 1848 [*khak* dust]
gymkhana 1861
swastika 1871 [*svasti* well-being]
pyjamas 1886

5 Malaya
bamboo 1598
gong 1600
emu 1613
junk 1613 (ship)
cockatoo 1634
amok 1663 [*amuk* murderous frenzy]
launch 1697 (boat) [*lancha* swift]
orang-outang 1699
bantam 1749
kapok 1750

6 China and Tibet
typhoon 1588 [*tai* great + *feng* wind]
tea 1601 [*ch'a*]
sampan 1620 [*san-pan* three boards]
lama 1654 (priest)
ketchup 1711 [*ke-tsiap* brine of pickled fish]
kaolin 1727
yak 1799
kowtow 1804 [*k'o-t'ou* knock the head]
loquat 1814
polo 1872 [*pulu* ball]

7 Japan
harakiri 1856 [= belly cut]
tycoon 1863 [*tai* great + *kiun* prince]
samurai 1874
kimono 1874
geisha 1891
judo 1892
jujitsu [= the soft art]
karate [= empty hand]

III AFRICA
1 West Africa
yam 1588
banana 1597
guinea 1598
zebra 1600
tote (carry) 1676
chimpanzee 1738
gnu 1777
gorilla 1853
voodoo 1880
raffia 1882

2 South Africa (Afrikaans)
veldt 1801
spoor 1823
aardvark 1833
commando 1834
trek 1849

IV THE PACIFIC
1 Polynesia
atoll 1625
taboo 1775
tattoo 1775 (decorative marks in the skin)

2 Australian Aboriginal

kangaroo 1770
dingo 1789
corroboree 1793
waratah 1793
wombat 1798
koala 1808
boomerang 1827
wallaby 1828
budgerigar 1847
mallee 1848
didgeridoo
billabong
gunyah
billy [Aboriginal *billa* water]
barrack 1850 [Aboriginal *borak* to mock]

3 New Zealand Maori

kauri 1817 (evergreen tree)
kiwi 1835
moa 1820 (extinct bird)
paua 1820 (a shell)
poi (ball used in Maori dancing)
tiki

C: WORDS FROM EUROPEAN LANGUAGES, 1500-1700

1 DUTCH

hawker 1510 [*heuker* dealer]
splice 1524 [*splissen* split]
uproar 1526 [*oproer* tumult]
dollar 1553 [*daler*]
yacht 1557 [*jaght* ship for chasing]
burgher 1568
freebooter 1570 [*vrij* free + *buit* booty]
beleaguer 1589 [*be* about + *leger* camp]
landscape 1598 [*landschap*]
knapsack 1603 [*knappen* bite + SACK]
smack 1611 (ship)
brandy 1622 [*brandewijn* burnt wine]
furlough 1625 [*verlof* leave]
keelhaul 1626
sloop 1629
duck 1640 (cloth) [*doek* cloth]
tattoo 1644 (drum signal)
cruise 1651 [*kruisen* to cross]
easel 1654
yawl 1670
stipple 1699 [*stippen* to prick]
gin 1714
roster 1727 [*rooster* list]
boss 1822 [*baas* master]

2 FRENCH

pioneer 1523 [Old French *Peon* foot soldier]
grotesque 1561
volley 1573 [*volée* flight]
rendezvous 1591 [= present yourself]
carbine 1605 [*caribine* small gun]
role 1606 [*rôle* roll of paper of an actor's part]
coiffure 1631
platoon 1637 [*peloton* little group]
reveille 1644 [*réveillez* wake up]
repartee 1645
liaison 1648
naive 1654
decor 1656 [*décorer* to decorate]
parade 1656 [= a show]
memoir 1659
rapport 1661
contour 1662
penchant 1672 [*pencher* to incline or lean]
métier 1674
nonchalance 1678
commandant 1687
reservoir 1690 [*reserver* to keep]
verve 1697
bivouac 1706
casserole 1706 [*casse* pan]
meringue 1706
envelope 1707
debris 1708
corps 1711
brunette 1712
bouquet 1716 [*bosquet* little wood]
terrain 1727
police 1730 (to keep civil order)
roulette 1734 [= little wheel]
liqueur 1742
glacier 1744
hors d'oeuvre 1745 [= apart from the main work]
etiquette 1750
debut 1751
gauche 1751 [= left, left hand]
denouement 1752 [*dénouer* to untie]
confrère 1753
ennui 1758
ricochet 1769
boulevard 1772
souvenir 1775 [= to remember]
martinet 1779 [after *Jean Martinet*, a 17th-century army officer]
avalanche 1789
regime 1789

coup 1791
emigre 1792
echelon 1793 [= rung of a ladder]
espionage 1793
guillotine 1793
depot 1794
sortie 1795 [*sortir* to go out]
gram 1797
metre 1797
silhouette 1798
surveillance 1802
rapprochement 1809
hectare 1810
litre 1810
secretariat 1811
mirage 1812
cafe 1816
genre 1816
cul-de-sac 1819
soiree 1820
gourmet 1820
elite 1823
laissez-faire 1825
restaurant 1827
prestige 1829
morale 1831 (of troops)
lingerie 1835
negligee 1835
menu 1837
abattoir 1840
mayonnaise 1841
chef 1842
communism 1843
clairvoyance 1847
repertoire 1847
debacle 1848
beret 1850
impasse 1851
communique 1852
fiance, fiancee 1853
chic 1856
barrage 1859
foyer 1859
clientele 1860
coupon 1864
chauvinism 1870 [after *Nicolas Chauvin*, an extreme admirer of Napoleon I]
milieu 1877
entente 1877
dossier 1880
matinee 1880
cliche 1892
premiere 1895
chauffeur 1899

3 SPANISH

galleon 1529
grenade 1532 [*grenada* pomegranate]
armada 1533
peso 1555
tornado 1556 [*tornar* to turn]
alligator 1568 [*el lagarto* the lizard]
armadillo 1577
corral 1582 [*corro* a ring]
renegade 1583 [*renegado* renounced]
mosquito 1583 [= little fly]
peccadillo 1591 [= little sin]
comrade 1591 [*camarada* group living in one room]
sherry 1597 [after Xeres (now Jerez) in Spain]
sombrero 1598 [*sombra* shade]
bravado 1599
embargo 1602
garrotte 1622
doubloon 1622
junta 1623 [= meeting, council]
cockroach 1624 [*cucuracha*]
guitar 1629
castanet 1647 [*castañetas* little chestnuts]
siesta 1655
cargo 1657 [*cargar* to load]
esplanade 1681
plaza 1683
flotilla 1711 [*flota* fleet]
mantilla 1717
hacienda 1760
bolero 1787
stevedore 1788
mustang 1808
lasso 1808
guerilla 1809 [= little war]
patio 1828
adobe 1834
stampede 1834
rodeo 1834
bonanza 1878

4 ITALIAN

gambol 1503 [*gambata* a kick]
porcelaine 1519 [*porcellana* a kind of shell]
buffoon 1549 [*buffone* jester]
carnival 1549
majolica 1555
sonnet 1557
cameo 1561
squadron 1562 [*squadra* square]
piazza 1563

Machiavellian 1568 [after *Niccolo Machiavelli*, 1469-1527, Italian writer on political theory]
pastel 1578
violin 1579
miniature 1586
madrigal 1588
stanza 1588
motto 1589
canto 1590
salvo 1591
bandit 1593
stucco 1598
fresco 1598 [= cool, fresh]
relief 1606 (projection of sculpture, etc.)
umbrella 1609 [*ombrella* a little shade]
volcano 1613
balcony 1618 [*balco* scaffold]
corridor 1620 [*corridore* covered way]
gusto 1629 [= taste, relish]
allegro 1632
intaglio 1644
manifesto 1644
opera 1644
serenade 1649
regatta 1652 [*regata* a gondola race]
bust 1653 [*busto* trunk of body]
vista 1657
cartoon 1671 [*cartone* drawing; in comic sense, 1863]
piano [softly, 1683; keyboard instrument, 1803]
chiaroscuro 1686 [*chiaro* bright + *oscuro* dark]
sonata 1694
solo 1695
mezzanine 1711
bronze 1721
terracotta 1722 [= baked earth]
portfolio 1722
tempo 1724
cantata 1724
trombone 1724 [*tromba* trumpet]
concerto 1730
soprano 1730
dilettante 1733
duet 1740
malaria 1740 [*mala aria* bad air]
aria 1742
libretto 1742
influenza 1743
lava 1750 [= stream]
crescendo 1776
extravaganza 1789
torso 1797
gelatine 1800 [*gelata* jelly]
tirade 1801 [*tirata* volley]
marsala 1806
studio 1819
replica 1824
tempera 1832
chianti 1833
inferno 1834
cadenza 1836
salami 1852
vendetta 1855
fiasco 1855
magenta 1860
scherzo 1862
mafia 1875
scenario 1880
gouache 1882
spaghetti 1882

5 GERMAN

plunder 1632 [*plundern* to pillage]
zinc 1651
bismuth 1668
cobalt 1728
Fahrenheit 1753 [after *Gabriel Fahrenheit*, 1686-1736, a German physicist]
quartz 1756
feldspar 1757
nickel 1775
waltz 1781
meerschaum 1784 [*Meer* sea + *Schaum* foam]
mesmerize 1802 [after *F.A. Mesmer*, 1734-1815, an Austrian doctor]
vermouth 1806
poodle 1825 [*Pudelhund* splash-dog]
paraffin 1835
kindergarten 1852 [= children's garden]
lager 1853
ohm 1870 [after *G.S. Ohm*, 1787-1854, a German physicist]
dashchund 1881 [*Dachs* badger + *Hund* dog]
delicatessen 1889
marzipan 1891

6 SCANDINAVIAN

fiord 1674
cosy 1709
saga 1709
lemming 1713

tungsten 1770
floe 1817
ski 1885

D: SOME FOREIGN WORDS SINCE 1900

avant garde 1900 [French]
limousine 1902 [French]
hangar 1902 [French]
garage 1902 [French]
chassis 1903 (of motor car) [French]
bloc 1905 [French]
detente 1908 [French]
fuselage 1909 [French]
peyote 1909 [Mexican]
brassière 1912 [French]
tango 1913 [Spanish]
ersatz 1914 [German]
camouflage 1917 [French]
jazz 1918 [American Negro]
ukelele 1921 [Hawaiian]
fascism 1921 [Italian]
slalom 1921 [Norwegian]
robot 1923 [Czech]
marijuana 1923 [Spanish, Mexican]
anorak 1924 [Eskimo]
au pair 1928 (girl) [French]
compere 1928 [French]
blitz(krieg) 1939 [German]
snorkel 1939 [German]
strafe 1940 [German]
partisan 1940 [Italian]
flak 1940 [German]
kibbutz [Hebrew]
apartheid 1949 [Afrikaans]
juke (box) [American Negro]
cappuccino [Italian]
espresso [Italian]
minestrone [Italian]
sputnik 1957 [Russian]
bikini 1957 [French, after *Bikini* atoll in the Pacific, site of atomic tests]
ombudsman 1959 [Swedish]
aubergine 1960 [French]
boutique 1960 [French]
discotheque 1965 [French]

TABLE OF COMMON SPELLINGS

Common spelling	*Other spelling*
1 Vowel sounds	
hat	plait, meringue
ate	train, gaol, gauge, hay, break, weight, convey, vein
past	calm, hard, heart, draught, clerk
ten	many heavy, says, said, heifer, friend, guest, burial, leopard
pair	care, mayor, prayer, wear, there, their
see	gleam, encyclopaedia, quay, conceive, thief, even, magazine, key, amoeba, trio, people
hill	physics, women, business, building, England, sieve
ear	peer, pier, weird, mere, serious
bite	light, sky, lie, guy, height, eye, aisle
not	yacht, trough, wand, knowledge, cauliflower
so	bureau, sew, boat, yeoman, brooch, slow, although, owe, hoe
or	wall, saw, caught, moor, board, sought, court
shoot	drew, move, crude, suit, true, shoe, through, manoeuvre, you, ewe, queue, feud
oil	boy, buoy
crowd	loud, bough, Macleod
cup	love, does, trouble, blood
put	book, wolf, worsted, could
fern	burn, err, were, first, myrtle, learn, masseur, journey, worm
away, father, motor	soldier, probable, several, colour, metre, glorious,
2 Consonant sounds	
ball	rabbit
chair	hatch, righteous, institution, digestion
done	ladder, filled
find	philosophy, rough, cuff
give	ghost, guard, exist
help	who
jug	ridge, tragic, exaggerate, procedure, grandeur
cat	acclaim, question, ache, sack, kite, barque, biscuit, scholarship, box
let, ill	
man	summer, comb, solemn, paradigm
nose	knife, gnu, planning, pneumonia, mnemonic
sing	sink, meringue
paint, stopped	
rain	rhythm, write, carry
sound	ceiling, ice, promise, scent, boss, psalm
shout	sugar, schedule, ocean, machine, special, conscience, execution, passion, expansion
table	thyme, ptomaine, lottery
thin	
there, lathe	
vent	of, Stephen
weather	question, choir, whether
yellow	unite, euphemism, ewe
zero	was, scissors, xenophobia
mirage	treasure, decision

TABLE OF CHEMICAL ELEMENTS

Number of protons in nucleus	*Element*	*Symbol*
1	hydrogen	H
2	helium	He
3	lithium	Li
4	beryllium	Be
5	boron	B
6	carbon	C
7	nitrogen	N
8	oxygen	O
9	fluorine	F
10	neon	Ne
11	sodium	Na
12	magnesium	Mg
13	aluminium	Al
14	silicon	Si
15	phosphorus	P
16	sulphur	S
17	chlorine	Cl
18	argon	Ar
19	potassium	K
20	calcium	Ca
21	scandium	Sc
22	titanium	Ti
23	vanadium	V
24	chromium	Cr
25	manganese	Mn
26	iron	Fe
27	cobalt	Co
28	nickel	Ni
29	copper	Cu
30	zinc	Zn
31	gallium	Ga
32	germanium	Ge
33	arsenic	As
34	selenium	Se
35	bromine	Br
36	krypton	Kr
37	rubidium	Rb
38	strontium	Sr
39	yttrium	Y
40	zirconium	Zr
41	niobium	Nb
42	molybdenum	Mo
43	technetium	Tc
44	ruthenium	Ru
45	rhodium	Rh
46	palladium	Pd
47	silver	Ag
48	cadmium	Cd
49	indium	In
50	tin	Sn
51	antimony	Sb
52	tellurium	Te
53	iodine	I
54	xenon	Xe
55	caesium	Cs
56	barium	Ba
57	lanthanum	La
58	cerium	Ce
59	praseodymium	Pr
60	neodymium	Nd
61	promethium	Pm
62	samarium	Sm
63	europium	Eu
64	gadolinium	Gd
65	terbium	Tb
66	dysprosium	Dy
67	holmium	Ho
68	erbium	Er
69	thulium	Tm
70	ytterbium	Yb
71	lutetium	Lu
72	hafnium	Hf
73	tantalum	Ta
74	tungsten	W
75	rhenium	Re
76	osmium	Os
77	iridium	Ir
78	platinum	Pt
79	gold	Au
80	mercury	Hg
81	thallium	Tl
82	lead	Pb
83	bismuth	Bi
84	polonium	Po
85	astatine	At
86	radon	Rn
87	francium	Fr
88	radium	Ra
89	actinium	Ac
90	thorium	Th
91	protoactinium	Pa
92	uranium	U
93	neptunium	Np
94	plutonium	Pu
95	americium	Am
96	curium	Cm
97	berkelium	Bk
98	californium	Cf
99	einsteinium	Es
100	fermium	Fm
101	mendelevium	Md
102	nobelium	No
103	lawrencium	Lw

The horizontal lines separate the *periods*. The first element in each period (apart from hydrogen) is an *active metal*. The last element in each period is an *inert gas*.

TABLE OF SI UNITS AND SYMBOLS

Physical quantity	*Symbol*	*Unit*	*Symbol*
BASIC UNITS			
length	*l* or *s*	metre	m
mass	*m*	kilogram	kg
time	*t*	second	s
electric current	*I*	ampere	A
thermodynamic temperature	*T*	kelvin	K
luminous intensity	*I* or I_v	candela	cd
amount of a substance	*n*	mole	mol
SUPPLEMENTARY UNITS			
plane angle		radian	rad
solid angle		steradian	sr
DERIVED UNITS			
velocity	*v*	metre per second	ms^{-1}
acceleration	*a*	metre per second squared	ms^{-2}
force	*F*	newton	N
work	*W*	joule	J
power	*P*	watt	W
pressure	*p*	pascal	Pa
frequency	*f*	hertz	Hz
electric charge	*Q*	coulomb	C
potential	*V*	volt	V
resistance	*R*	ohm	Ω
capacitance	*C*	farad	F
inductance	*L*	henry	H
illuminance	*E*	lux	lx
luminous flux		lumen	lm
magnetic flux density	*B*	tesla	T
magnetic flux	Φ	weber	Wb

TABLE OF SI AND METRIC PREFIXES

Prefix	*Symbol*	*Value*		
tera	T	10^{12}	=	1 000 000 000 000
giga	G	10^{9}	=	1 000 000 000
mega	M	10^{6}	=	1 000 000
kilo	k	10^{3}	=	1 000
*hecto	h	10^{2}	=	100
*deka	da	10^{1}	=	10
*deci	d	10^{-1}	=	0.1
*centi	c	10^{-2}	=	0.01
milli	m	10^{-3}	=	0.001
micro	μ	10^{-6}	=	0.000 001
nano	n	10^{-9}	=	0.000 000 001
pico	p	10^{-12}	=	0.000 000 000 001
femto	f	10^{-15}	=	0.000 000 000 000 001
atto	a	10^{-18}	=	0.000 000 000 000 000 001

* Generally avoided in SI usage.

TABLE OF CONVERSION FACTORS TO METRIC UNITS

To change	*into*	*multiply by & move decimal point*	
Length			
inch (in)	millimetre (mm)	2.54	one place to right
foot (ft)	metre (m)	3.05	one place to left
yard (yd)	metre	9.14	one place to left
mile	kilometre (km)	1.61	(no change)
Area			
square inch (in^2)	square centimetre (cm^2)	6.45	(no change)
square foot (ft^2)	square metre (m^2)	9.29	two places to left
square yard (yd^2)	square metre	8.36	one place to left
acre (ac)	hectare (ha)	4.05	one place to left
square mile	square kilometre (km^2)	2.59	(no change)
Volume			
cubic inch (in^3)	cubic centimetre (cm^3)	1.64	one place to right
cubic foot (ft^3)	cubic metre (m^3)	2.83	two places to left
cubic yard (yd^3)	cubic metre	7.65	one place to left
bushel, Imperial (bus)	cubic metre	3.64	two places to left
bushel, US (bus US)	cubic metre	3.53	two places to the left
Volume (fluids)			
fluid ounce, Imperial (fl oz)	millilitre (ml)	2.84	one place to right
fluid ounce, US (fl oz US)	millilitre	2.96	one place to right
pint (pt)	litre (ℓ)	5.68	one place to left
gallon, Imperial (gal)	litre	4.55	(no change)
gallon, US (gal US)	litre	3.79	(no change)
Mass			
ounce (oz)	gram (g)	2.83	one place to right
	kilogram (kg)	2.83	two places to left
pound (lb)	kilogram	4.54	one place to left
stone	kilogram	6.35	(no change)
ton	tonne (t)	1.02	(no change)
Energy			
Calorie (Cal)	kilojoule (kJ)	4.19	(no change)
Power			
horsepower (hp)	watt (W)	7.46	two places to right
Speed			
mile per hour (mph)	kilometre per hour (km/h)	1.61	(no change)
knot (n)	kilometre per hour	1.85	(no change)
Pressure			
pound per square inch (psi)	kilopascal (kPa)	6.89	(no change)

EXAMPLES

1. To change 2 inches into millimetres:
   2 x 2.54 = 5.08
   move decimal point one place to the right
   = 50.8 mm
2. To change 20 feet to metres:
   20 x 3.05 = 61
   move decimal point one place to the left
   = 6.1 m
3. To change 2 ounces to kilograms:
   2 x 2.83 = 5.66
   move decimal point two places to the left
   = 0.0566 kg
4. To change 100 horsepower to watts:
   100 x 7.46 = 746
   move decimal point two places to the right
   = 74600W

edited by Antony Flew

A Dictionary of Philosophy £1.95

This important new reference work serves as a history of ideas, a handbook for the student of philosophy, and as a source of clarification and definition for the general reader. From the classic thinkers, through Aquinas, Descartes, Spinoza, Kant and Wittgenstein, this comprehensive dictionary spans the personalities, terminology and vocabulary of thousands of years of philosophical thought, and includes the more recent development of social and psychological sciences.

edited by John Daintith

A Dictionary of Physical Sciences £1.50

Concise, yet comprehensive, this invaluable reference book covers the main branches of physics, chemistry and astronomy. It includes a selection of the relevant terms from the related fields of electronics, mathematics and computer science, plus full accounts of the properties and uses of chemical elements.

edited by E. A. Martin

A Dictionary of Life Sciences £1.50

Brings together all the main branches of zoology and botany, including taxonomy, anatomy, physiology, cytology, genetics, ecology and the related fields of biochemistry, endocrinology, animal behaviour and palaeontology. All major plant and animal classes and some of the more important orders are fully described. Common names of plants and animals are cross-referenced to their appropriate taxonomic groups.

Isaac Asimov
Asimov's Biographical Encyclopedia of Science and Technology £2.50

A lively and wholly absorbing reference book which traces the history of science, from ancient Egypt to modern space flight, through 1,195 biographical sketches. Arranged in chronological order of birth, a wealth of facts and anecdotes illuminate the contribution made by each individual to the world of science. The index lists hundred of scientific topics plus the names of individuals, other than the subjects of the biographies, and completes a book that is unique in its content, width and range.

A Multilingual Commercial Dictionary £1.95

Some 3,000 words and phrases in common commercial use are listed in English, French, German, Spanish and Portuguese followed by their translation in the other languages. The equivalent American expression is also included where relevant. Simple to use and invaluable for everyday reference, the dictionary covers terms used throughout banking, accounting, insurance, shipping, export and import and international trade.

You can buy these and other Pan books from booksellers and newsagents; or direct from the following address.
Pan Books, Sales Office, Cavaye Place, London SW10 9PG
Send purchase price plus 20p for the first book and 10p for each additional book, to allow for postage and packing
Prices quoted are applicable in the UK

While every effort is made to keep prices low, it is sometimes necessary to increase prices at short notice. Pan Books reserve the right to show on covers and charge new retail prices which may differ from those advertised in the text or elsewhere